Y0-CAV-109

a MOTOR HOME *is a* MOTOR HOME *is a* MOTOR HOME. OR IS IT?

At first glance, they all look pretty much the same. Shiny exteriors. Fancy graphics. Tires. But if you look closer, you'll discover why a motor home built by Winnebago Industries is distinctly superior. First and foremost, our motor homes are built from start to finish at our self-contained manufacturing complex. (The only one in the industry, come to think of it.) So while other companies are forced to design their motor homes around off-the-shelf parts they buy, we have the luxury of building parts specifically to fit our motor homes. We also have a unique construction philosophy based on "fit and finish." Simply put, it means every motor home is crafted with amazing attention to detail. Fit and finish covers all things you can see, like the panel and rail construction of our cabinetry, and the things you can't, like how our designers make proper weight distribution a priority. And not only do our motor homes meet government and required RVIA certification standards, we also set our own safety and quality standards. From our interlocking joint design to our famous motor home drop test, we take extra steps to build motor homes that last. Of course, the most well-built motor home on the planet still needs a good set of support services. Thanks to our vast dealer network and perks like our roadside assistance program, it's easy to see why there's no better value than a Winnebago Industries motor home.

Our motor homes are built under one roof at our manufacturing facility.

We make fit and finish a priority.

Our construction methods, like our innovative joint design, are respected in the industry.

Our shake test is just one example of how we make sure our motor homes meet or exceed quality and safety standards.

From our Preferred Care Program to our Trip Saver plan, our support services are top-notch.

But don't take our word for it. See for yourself at your local dealer, or for a free brochure call **1-800-643-4892, ext. Z108C.**

© 1997 Winnebago Industries, Inc.

www.winnebagoind.com

How to Use the Exit Authority... in three easy steps...

1 Turn to the Interstate.
(Interstates are listed in numerical order)

2 Find the State.
(Organized North to South or East to West)

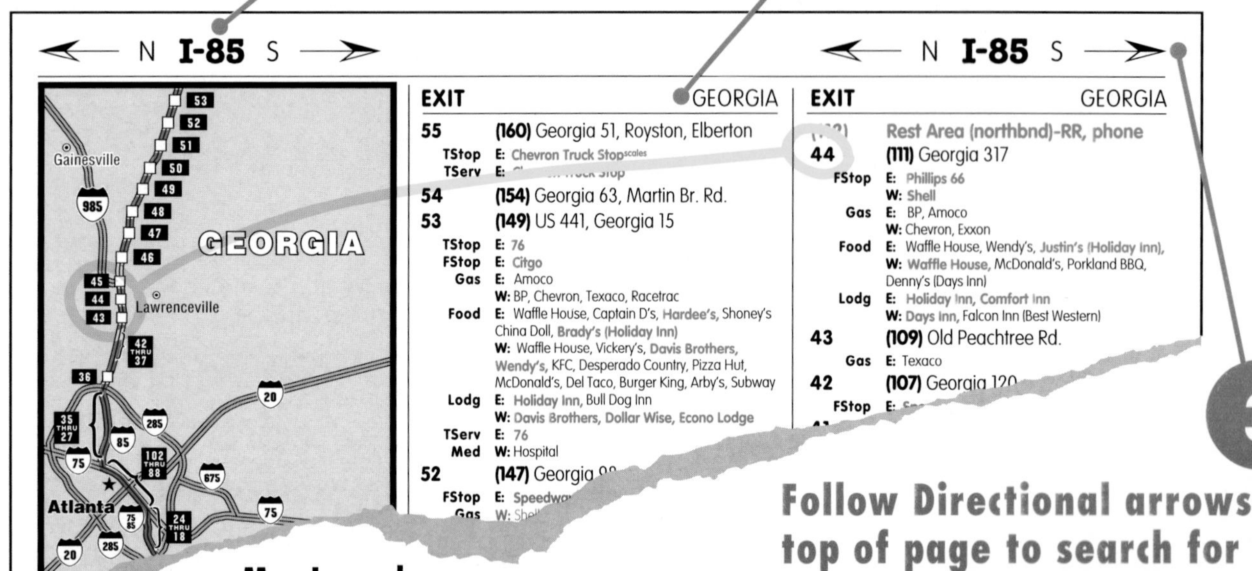

← N **I-85** S →

EXIT GEORGIA

55 **(160)** Georgia 51, Royston, Elberton
TStop E: Chevron Truck Stop(scales)
TServ E: ...

54 **(154)** Georgia 63, Martin Br. Rd.

53 **(149)** US 441, Georgia 15
TStop E: 76
FStop E: Citgo
Gas E: Amoco
W: BP, Chevron, Texaco, Racetrac
Food E: Waffle House, Captain D's, Hardee's, Shoney's China Doll, Brady's (Holiday Inn)
W: Waffle House, Vickery's, Davis Brothers, Wendy's, KFC, Desperado Country, Pizza Hut, McDonald's, Del Taco, Burger King, Arby's, Subway
Lodg E: Holiday Inn, Bull Dog Inn
W: Davis Brothers, Dollar Wise, Econo Lodge
TServ E: 76
Med W: Hospital

52 **(147)** Georgia ...
FStop E: Speedw...
Gas W: Shell...

← N **I-85** S →

EXIT GEORGIA

Rest Area (northbnd)-RR, phone

44 **(111)** Georgia 317
FStop E: Phillips 66
W: Shell
Gas E: BP, Amoco
W: Chevron, Exxon
Food E: Waffle House, Wendy's, Justin's (Holiday Inn),
W: Waffle House, McDonald's, Porkland BBQ, Denny's (Days Inn)
Lodg E: Holiday Inn, Comfort Inn
W: Days Inn, Falcon Inn (Best Western)

43 **(109)** Old Peachtree Rd.
Gas E: Texaco

42 **(107)** Georgia 120...
FStop E: ...

3 Follow Directional arrows at top of page to search for Exits in the desired direction.

Map Legend

29 Exit Number • (S) Scales • (S.A.) Service Area/Plaza

Legend For Abbreviations & Symbols:

TStop	24-Hour diesel fuel location w/restaurant (large multi-service facility)
FStop	Diesel fuel location with large vehicle clearance (small to medium facility)
Food	Food Outlets (fast food, restaurants, cafeterias, etc.)
Lodg	Hotel/Motel Accommodations
Gas	Automobile fueling locations
AServ	Facilities with Automotive Service
TServ	Diesel engine service facilities (not always available for RV's)
TWash	Commercial vehicle wash facilites
RVCamp	Camping or RV resort sites, RV service or supply facilities
Parks	National, state or local forest, parks, preserves & lakes
ATM	Banks or other services services with cash machine
Med	Hospital, emergency treatment or other medical facility
Other	Useful services, sites or attractions near interstate
(MM)	Numbers in ( ) indicate mile markers when not same as exit #.
N-S-E-W	Indicates side of the highway that services are located
I-O	Three-digit perimeter hwys – (I) inside or (O) outside perimeter

Rest Area & Welcome Center Facilities: (P) Overnight parking allowed at rest area

RR – Rest rooms
Vending – Snack & Drink Machine
Phones – Public Pay Phones
Grills – Outdoor Cooking Grills
Picnic – Picnic Tables
RV Dump – Sanitary Waste Dump
RV Water – RV Water Hookup
HF – Facilities with wheelchair access
Pet Walk – Designated Area for Pets

Superscripts: (*) Convenience store; (cw) Automatic car wash; (D) Diesel fuel available; (LP) Liquid propane gas; (24) Open 24 Hrs; (K) Kerosene; (PLAY) Play area

- Every Business at every exit for every major Interstate in the Continental U.S. & Canada's TCH within one quarter mile.
- Areas with adequate RV & Bus Parking are highlighted in Bold Red print (Parking may be nearby, but provides easy access).
- Services grouped by category (see legend) and direction from exit (N-S-E-W).
- RV Dump Stations highlighted in Red.
- Additional notations for Convenience Stores, Diesel Fuel, Propane, and Automatic Car Washes (see legend at left).
- Exit numbers are not always available, especially in California where exits are not numbered (CA numbering indicates mileage from point of interstate's origin).
- The TServ category includes services where RV owners may be able to acquire diesel service.
- Please drive safely . . . it is not recommended that you use Exit Authority while driving.
- Your suggestions are always welcome. Changes or additions? Just call us: 1-800-494-5566

don't sleep just anywhere

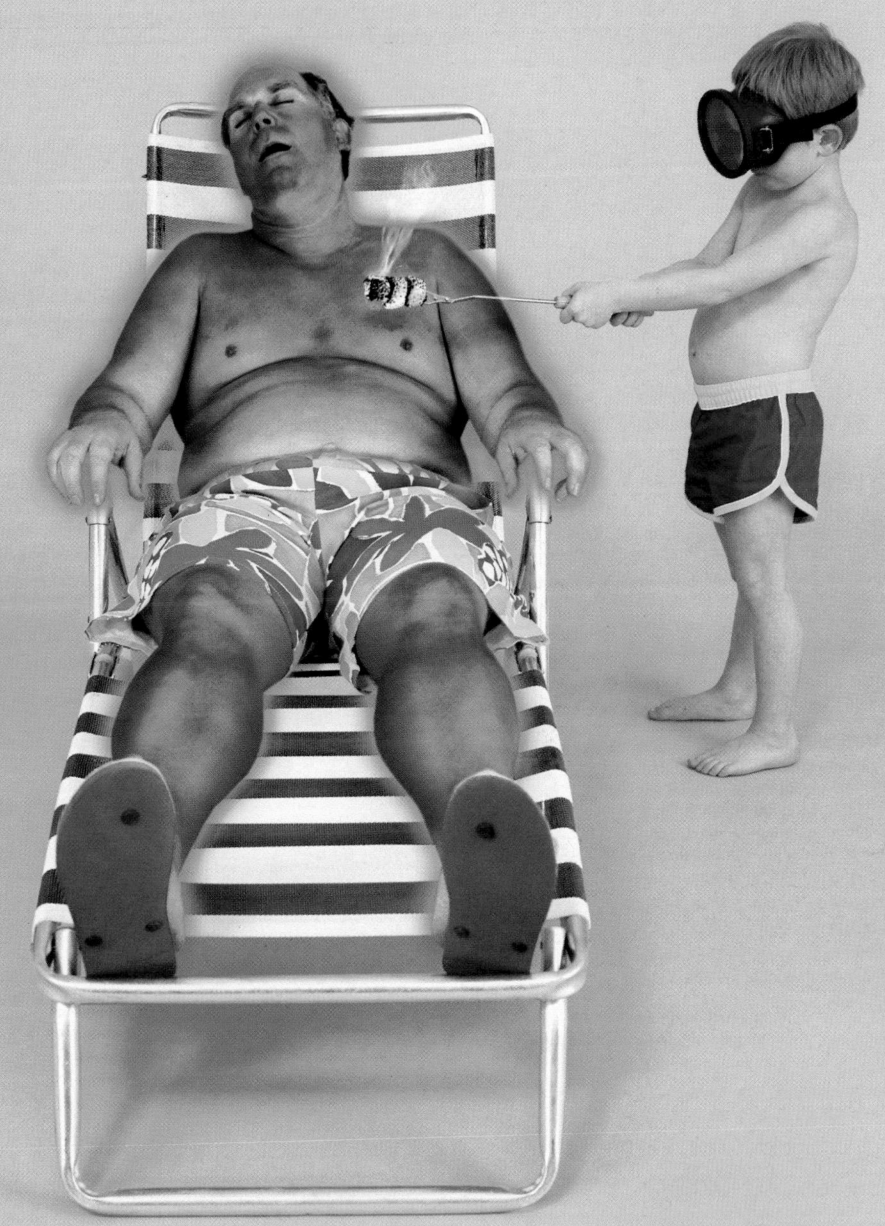

Stay at a place you know you can count on. At Fairfield Inn® by Marriott®, you always get a clean, comfortable room, free continental breakfast, a pool and smart, friendly service. All for

You can expect more℠

around $45-$65 a night*. And since it's by Marriott, Marriott Rewards® members earn points toward a free vacation. Call your travel agent or 800-228-2800. Or visit us at www.fairfieldinn.com.

*Rates vary by hotel and may be higher or lower depending on location, room type or day of week.

©1998 Fairfield Inn by Marriott

HAS DOWNED 7 SODAS FROM THE COOLER AND IS PRAYING FOR THE NEXT REST STOP. (UNFORTUNATELY IT'S GOING TO BE HUNDREDS OF MILES BEFORE THEY NEED TO STOP FOR GAS AGAIN.)

Has listened to 6 CDs including thrash metal, industrial punk and techno pop. (Lucky for Dad he has headphones.)

Has gone 528 miles without arguing with her sister even once. (This could be a new world's record.)

Has just pulled off an Indy Nosebone playing "1080° Snowboarding™."

www.chevrolet.com. Shown with conversion package from an independent supplier. See the owner's manual for information on alterations and warranties. Always use safety belts and proper child restraints, even wit

Has driven 1045 miles
and looked at 5 maps. (Still lost.)

Called **1-800-950-2438** for a free *Travel By Numbers Guide* that told her all about the Chevy Express® Conversion Van. (And the whole family has been thanking her ever since.)

Chevy Express Conversion Van from Chevy™ Trucks – the most dependable, longest-lasting trucks on the road.*

air bags. See owner's manual for more safety information. *Dependability based on longevity: 1981-1997 full-line light-duty truck company registrations. Excludes other GM divisions. ©1998 GM Corp. Buckle up, America!

Interstate America

Letter from the Publisher

Dear Fellow Traveler,

The 1999 Exit Authority is our best directory ever! Inside you'll find the most extensive and complete guide to travel related Businesses and Services at *Every Exit* on *Every major U.S. Interstate* plus . . . the TCH in Canada!*

You can travel with complete peace of mind — just use Exit Authority to plan all of your interstate travel stops well in advance, and:

- Find your favorite restaurants, shopping outlets, attractions and hotels along the way.
- Locate special RV services . . . like RV Dump Stations, RV Camps & Resorts, Truck Stops or Rest Areas with Overnight Parking.
- Easily identify stops with easy RV and bus access and parking by looking for businesses highlighted in bold red print!
- Find fuel stops by brand or type (diesel) or with repair, car wash or convenience store facilities.
- Choose the safest, busiest exits in unfamiliar areas.
- Find medical services, including pharmacies, hospitals, and minor emergency centers.
- . . . **And much more!**

Just as we did for our previous editions, we traveled every interstate and stopped at every exit to record business names and services, additional facilities, and even the size of the parking lot.

In the 1999 Exit Authority, you'll find we've added thousands of new businesses, updated name changes and new services, and listed new exits and facilities. This year you'll find more listings for major beltways and connectors, in addition to the listing of the TransCanadian Highway.

Thank you for purchasing the 1999 Exit Authority, and we wish you safe and pleasant travels in 1999.

Happy Motoring!

Dennis Robbins
Publisher

*Excludes Alaska

Interstate America • 5695 Oakbrook Pkwy. • Suite G • Norcross, GA 30093
Questions or comments? Call 1-800-494-5566

Printed in U.S.A. Entire Contents ©1999 by Interstate America • All Rights Reserved ISBN 1-880477-18-1

PRESIDENT: **Ron Peterson**
V.P./PUBLISHER: **Dennis Robbins**
MARKETING DIRECTOR: **Amy Graff**
PROMOTIONS MANAGER: **Susan Conner**
ART DIRECTOR: **Yvonne Gulley**
DATA DEVELOPMENT: **Mark Patton**
CUSTOMER SERVICE MANAGER: **Denise Makita**
DATA SALES: **Les Helms**
ADVERTISING SALES:
Jeff Mitchell - Audrey Rawls - Cory Davis
Gina Sinnett - Hesta Baker - Jennifer Jones
Michael P. Pesaturo - Dirk J. Vanden Bos

A Zenrin Company, ZENRIN CO., LTD.
San Franciso Office:
Navigation Software Planning & Development
General Manager: **Tatsuhiko Shimizu**
Manager of Business Development: **Loyd L. Love**

Interstate America exercises absolute editorial discretion over this publication and reserves the right to exclude any business the inclusion of which Interstate America deems, in its sole discretion, to be inconsistent with the purposes of this publication. Interstate America and its officers and employees shall not be responsible for general, special, consequential, or other damage alleged to result from Interstate America's editorial decisions, errors or omissions in listings.

No part of this publication may be reproduced, transmitted, or stored in a retrieval system, in any form or by any means, mechanical, magnetic, photo static, electronic, or otherwise, without the prior written permission of Interstate America. Mention of and/or acceptance of advertising is for information purposes only and constitutes neither an endorsement nor recommendation.

"Bridge A Lifetime Of Travel With Camping World."

For some folks, it's just a matter of getting from

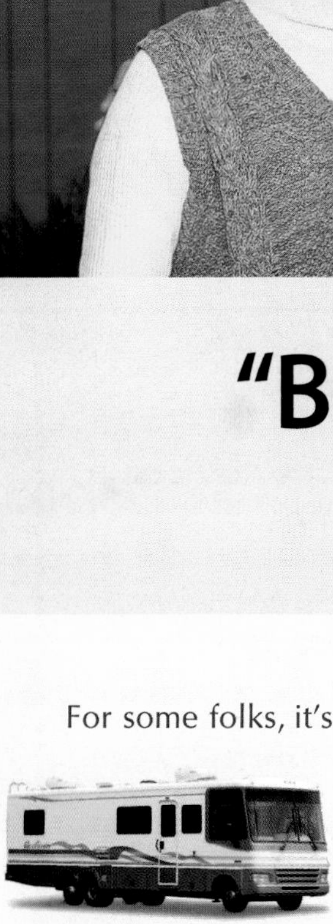

point A to point B. For us, it's a chance to span new worlds. That's why we connect with Camping World's 29 stores nationwide and 24-hour catalog ordering. Camping World has a history of quality that goes all the way back to 1966. Plus, they back every product and service with a 100% Satisfaction Guarantee and offer No Hassle Refunds & Exchanges. So visit the nearest Camping World or browse through their latest catalog . . . and cross over to new adventure.

Call toll-free 1-800-845-7875 24 hours a day for a FREE catalog and mention code EY.
Visit our Internet site: www.campingworld.com

FREE! 4-Roll Pack of THETFORD TISSUE on any purchase of $25 or more. Reg. $2.29 #15600

Present coupon at start of transaction. One coupon per customer. May not be used in combination with other offer except President's Club 10% discount. Valid through 11/30/99.

Cashier: Ring as discount: 9814

Designed to serve interstate traffic, Flying J's easy access Travel Plazas and Fuel Stops offer every amenity a traveler could imagine:

- Free RV dump stations
- Special RV fueling islands
- RV RealValue Rewards membership club
- Highest quality fuel
- Restaurants & fast food operations
- Well-stocked convenience stores
- Open 24-hours
- ATM's
- Daily U.S. Postal pickup
- UPS/FedEX boxes
- Laundry facilities
- Barber/hair salons

And more . . .

J Care Service Centers provide:
(at select locations)

- RV wash
- Oil change and lube
- Tire repair
- Roadside services

FLYING J · PO Box 678
Brigham City, UT 84302
435-734-6400

Join the FLYING J R.V. RealValue REWARDS CLUB and receive:

R.V. RealValue CLUB
0123 4567 8900
YOUR NAME HERE
RoadLink
Prepaid Calling Card Privileges
FLYING J

- 1¢ per Gallon Fuel Discount* (gas or diesel)
- 5¢ per Gallon Propane Discount*
- Plus Higher Fuel Discounts with Monthly Non-Fuel Purchases
- Discounts on Selected Products & Services
- 5% RV Insurance Discounts
- Prepaid Calling Card Privileges (5 minutes free included)
- Lifetime Membership to Audio Adventures Book on Tape Rental Program

Fill out the attached application and mail. You'll then receive your personal membership card and benefits information. It's that simple!

*Discounts will be granted unless prohibited by law.

"Bridge A Lifetime Of Travel With Camping World."

For some folks, it's just a matter of getting from

point A to point B. For us, it's a chance to span new worlds. That's why we connect with Camping World's 29 stores nationwide and 24-hour catalog ordering. Camping World has a history of quality that goes all the way back to 1966. Plus, they back every product and service with a 100% Satisfaction Guarantee and offer No Hassle Refunds & Exchanges. So visit the nearest Camping World or browse through their latest catalog . . . and cross over to new adventure.

Call toll-free 1-800-845-7875 24 hours a day for a FREE catalog and mention code EY.
Visit our Internet site: www.campingworld.com

FREE! 4-Roll Pack of THETFORD TISSUE on any purchase of $25 or more. Reg. $2.29 #15600

Present coupon at start of transaction. One coupon per customer. May not be used in combination with other offer except President's Club 10% discount. Valid through 11/30/99.

Cashier: Ring as discount: 9814

FLYING J is RV Ready

...a Highway Haven for Travelers

Designed to serve interstate traffic, Flying J's easy access Travel Plazas and Fuel Stops offer every amenity a traveler could imagine:

- Free RV dump stations
- Special RV fueling islands
- RV Real Value Rewards membership club
- Highest quality fuel
- Restaurants & fast food operations
- Well-stocked convenience stores
- Open 24-hours
- ATM's
- Daily U.S. Postal pickup
- UPS/FedEX boxes
- Laundry facilities
- Barber/hair salons

And more . . .

J Care Service Centers provide:
(at select locations)

- RV wash
- Oil change and lube
- Tire repair
- Roadside services

FLYING J · PO Box 678
Brigham City, UT 84302
435-734-6400

Join the FLYING J R.V. Real Value REWARDS CLUB and receive:

- 1¢ per Gallon Fuel Discount* (gas or diesel)
- 5¢ per Gallon Propane Discount*
- Plus Higher Fuel Discounts with Monthly Non-Fuel Purchases
- Discounts on Selected Products & Services
- 5% RV Insurance Discounts
- Prepaid Calling Card Privileges (5 minutes free included)
- Lifetime Membership to Audio Adventures Book on Tape Rental Program

Fill out the attached application and mail. You'll then receive your personal membership card and benefits information. It's that simple!

*Discounts will be granted unless prohibited by law.

FLYING J is RV Ready

Flying J RealValue Membership Application
(Please print clearly)

FOR OFFICE USE ONLY
Card No.______________
Branch No.______________ Emp. No.______________

Membership Information

Customer Name:______________________________

Customer Address:______________________________

City______________________ State __________ Zip________

Home Phone (   )______________ Work Phone (   )______________

Your date of birth Your marital status: ☐ Married ☐ Single

What is the make of your RV?__________ Value of your RV today: $________ Model year:______

How many miles do you travel annually?__________ What is your resident state?__________

Who is your current insurance carrier?__________ Policy renewal date:__________

EXA99

FLYING J is RV Ready

Flying J RealValue Membership Application
(Please print clearly)

FOR OFFICE USE ONLY
Card No.______________
Branch No.______________ Emp. No.______________

Membership Information

Customer Name:______________________________

Customer Address:______________________________

City______________________ State __________ Zip________

Home Phone (   )______________ Work Phone (   )______________

Your date of birth Your marital status: ☐ Married ☐ Single

What is the make of your RV?__________ Value of your RV today: $________ Model year:______

How many miles do you travel annually?__________ What is your resident state?__________

Who is your current insurance carrier?__________ Policy renewal date:__________

EXA99

NO POSTAGE
NECESSARY
IF MAILED
IN THE
UNITED STATES

BUSINESS REPLY MAIL

FIRST CLASS PERMIT NO. 60 BRIGHAM CITY, UTAH

POSTAGE WILL BE PAID BY

FLYING J INC.
P.O. BOX 678
BRIGHAM CITY, UTAH 84302-0678

NO POSTAGE
NECESSARY
IF MAILED
IN THE
UNITED STATES

BUSINESS REPLY MAIL

FIRST CLASS PERMIT NO. 60 BRIGHAM CITY, UTAH

POSTAGE WILL BE PAID BY

FLYING J INC.
P.O. BOX 678
BRIGHAM CITY, UTAH 84302-0678

You're in Flying J Country

★ Travel Plazas
✩ Travel Plazas with J Care Facilities
▲ Fuel Stops
● Sites Under Construction
■ Properties in Permitting Process

★ U.S. TRAVEL PLAZAS:

AL	Bessemer	I-20 & I-59, Exit 104
AR	Russellville	I-40 Exit 84
AR	Texarkana	I-30 Exit 7
AR	West Memphis	I-40 Exit 280 & I-55 Exit 4
AZ	Ehrenberg	I-10 Exit 1
AZ	Eloy	I-10 Exit 208A
AZ	Kingman	I-40 Exit 53
AZ	Winslow	I-40 Exit 255
CA	Bakersfield	Hwy 99 Exit Merced Ave.
CA	Frazier Park	I-5 Frazier Park Exit
CA	Ripon (S.E. Stockton)	Hwy 99 Exit Jacktone Rd
CO	Aurora (Denver)	I-70 Airport Blvd. So. Exit 285
FL	Dade City	I-75 Exit 59
FL	Quincy (Tallahassee)	I-10 Exit 27
FL	St. Lucie	I-95 Hwy 68 Exit 66 **(Opens 9/98)**
GA	Brunswick	I-95 Exit 6
GA	Jackson	I-75 Exit 66
GA	Lake Park (Valdosta)	I-75 Exit 1
GA	Resaca	I-75 Exit 133
IA	Clive (W. Des Moines)	I-80 & I-35 Exit 125
IA	Davenport	I-80 Exit 292
IA	Evansdale (Waterloo)	I-380 & Evansdale Rd. **(Opens 10/98)**
ID	Caldwell (Boise)	I-84 Exit 29 **(Opens 9/98)**
ID	McCammon	I-15 & Hwy 30 Exit 47
ID	Post Falls	I-90 Exit 2
IN	Gary	I-94 & I-80 Exit 9A
IN	Indianapolis	I-465 Exit 4
KS	Emporia (Opens 9/98)	Kansas Turnpike 35 & Hwy 50/57
KS	Salina	I-70 Exit 253
KY	Franklin	I-65 at 31 West Exit 2
KY	Oak Grove	I-24 Exit 86 & US Hwy 41A
KY	Walton	I-75 Exit 171
LA	Greenwood (Shreveport)	I-20 Exit 3
MD	✈North East (Elkton)	I-95 Exit 100
MO	Joplin	I-44 U.S. 71 Exit 11A
MO	Matthews (Sikeston)	I-55 Exit 58
MO	Peculiar	US Hwy 71 Exit J
MO	Sullivan	1-44 & Hwy 185 Exit 226
MO	Warrenton	I-70 Exit 188
MS	Gulfport	I-10 Exit 31
MS	Pearl (Jackson)	I-20/I-55 Exit 47
MT	✈Belgrade (Bair's)	I-90 Exit 298
MT	Billings	I-90 Exit 455
MT	Butte	I-90 Exit 122
NC	Haw River (Graham)	I-85 & I-40 Exit 150
ND	Beach	I-94 & Hwy 16 Exit 1
ND	Fargo	I-29 & I-94 Exit 62
NE	Gretna (Omaha)	I-80 Exit 432
NE	North Platte	I-80 Exit 179
NM	Albuquerque	I-40 & 98th Street Exit 153
NV	✈Battle Mountain	I-80 Exit 229
NV	✈Las Vegas	I-15 Cheyenne Exit
NV	Wells	I-80 & Hwy 93 Exit 352
NY	Pembroke (Buffalo)	I-90 Exit 48A
OH	Beaverdam	I-75 Exit 135
OH	Berkshire (N. Columbus)	I-71 Sunbury Exit 131
OH	Kirkersville	I-70 State Rd. 158 Exit 122
OH	Lake Township (Toledo)	I-280 Exit 1B
OK	Checotah	I-40 Exit 264B & Jct. Hwy 69 & Hwy 266
OK	Oklahoma City	I-40 Exit 140, Morgan Rd.
OK	Oklahoma City (North)	I-35 & N.E. 122nd St.
OR	✈LaGrande	I-84 Exit 265
PA	Carlisle	I-81 Exit 17/17A
SC	Blacksburg	I-85 Exit 102
SC	Columbia	I-20 Exit 70
SC	Latta (Dillon)	I-95 Exit 181
SD	✈Rapid City	I-90 Exit 61
TN	Fairview	I-40 & Hwy 96 Exit 182
TN	Knoxville	I-40 & I-75 Exit 369
TX	Amarillo	I-40 Exit 76
TX	Anthony (El Paso)	I-10 Exit 0
TX	Dallas	I-20 & Exit 472
TX	Orange (Beaumont)	I-10 Exit 873
TX	Pecos	I-20 Exit 42
TX	San Antonio	I-10 Exit 583
TX	Tye (Abilene)	I-20 & FM 707 Exit 277
UT	Nephi	I-15 Exit 222
UT	Ogden	I-15 Exit 346
UT	Payson	I-15 Exit 254
UT	Salt Lake City	I-15 Exit 21st So. Wstbnd
UT	Springville	I-15 Exit 265
UT	Willard Bay	I-15 Exit 360
VA	Carmel Church	I-95 Exit 104
VA	Winchester	I-81 Exit 323
VA	Wytheville	I-77 & I-81 Exit 77
WA	✈Ellensburg	I-90 Canyon Rd. Exit
WA	✈Spokane	I-90 Exit 286
WA	Tacoma	I-5 Exit 136
WY	Casper	I-25 Exit 185
WY	Cheyenne	I-25 Exit 7
WY	✈Evanston	I-80 Exit 3
WY	Gillette	I-90 & Hwy 59
WY	Rawlins	I-80 Exit 209
WY	Rock Springs	I-80 Exit 104

★ CANADA TRAVEL PLAZAS

QC	Vaudreuil (Montreal)	Hwy 540 Exit 3

▲ FUEL STOPS PROVIDE:

CA	Thousand Palms	I-10 Ramon Exit
CO	Julesburg	I-76 Hwy 385
CO	Limon	I-70 Exit 361 Main Intrchng
ID	Blackfoot	I-15 Exit 93
ID	Boise	I-84 Exit 54 (Federal Way)
ID	Lewiston	Jct Hwy 12 & 95
MO	Kansas City	I-435 Exit 57 Front Street
MT	Great Falls	I-15 Exit 280
MT	✈Hardin (Bair's)	I-90 Exit 495
MT	Miles City	I-94 & Baker Exit
NV	Winnemucca	I-80 Exit 176
OR	Troutdale	I-84 Exit 17
SD	✈Ellsworth	I-90 Exit 66 (Ellsworth Rd.)
UT	Richfield	I-70 Exit 40
UT	Snowville	I-84 Exit 7
UT	West Brigham	I-15 Exit 364
WA	✈Federal Way	I-5 Exit 142B
WA	✈Pasco	U.S. Hwy 395
WA	✈West Spokane	I-90 Exit 276

● Sites Under Construction

AZ, Phoenix I-10 & 67th Ave. SW (Opens 4/99)
CA, Redding I-5 Exit 672 (Knighton Rd) (Opening TBA)
CA, Barstow I-15 Lenwood Exit (Opening TBA)
FL, Plant City (Tampa) I-4 Thonotosassa Rd (Opening TBA)
GA, Temple (W. Atlanta) I-20 & State Hwy 113 (Opening TBA)
IN, Lebanon I-65 Exit 139 (Opens 2/99)
KY, Shelbyville I-64 & Hwy 395 Exit 43 (Opens 12/98)
MS, Olive Branch U.S. 78 & Hacks Cross Rd (Opening TBA)
NJ, Carney's Point I-295 NJ Turnpike Exit Slapmill Rd (Opens 3/99)
OH, Saybrook (Austinburg) I-90 & State Rd. 45 Exit 223 (Opens 5/99)
OK, Tulsa I-44 & I-244 (Opens 4/99)
PA, Brookville I-80 Exit 13 (Opening TBA)
UT, Lake Point I-80 Exit 98/99 (Opening TBA)
WY, Cokeville U.S. Hwy 30/State Hwy 232 (Opening TBA)

■ U.S. Properties in Permitting

CA, Dixon
CA, Lodi (No. Stockton)
CA, Mojave
CT, Ashford
ID, Bonners Ferry
IN, Lake Station
MI, Grasslake (Jackson)
MN, Woodbury (Minneapolis)
NJ, Phillipsburg
SD, Sioux Falls
TX, Denton
TX, Houston
WI, Pleasant Prairie (Kenosha)
WI, Vienna (Madison)

■ Canadian Properties in Permitting

ON, London

Plus Many More . . .

WALMART INTERSTATE LOCATIONS

State	Interstate	Exit
Alabama		
	I-10	15AB
	I-20	133
	I-20	185
	I-59	108
	I-59	218
	I-65	3AB
	I-65	130
	I-65	255
	I-65	271
	I-85	79
Arkansas		
	I-30	73
	I-30	118
	I-40	13
	I-40	58
	I-40	84
	I-40	125
	I-40	216
	I-40	241A
	I-40	276
	I-55	67
Arizona		
	I-19	4
	I-19	69
	I-40	51
	I-40	253
California		
	I-10	75
	I-15	8
	I-15	73
	I-15	112
	I-40	1
	I-5	111B
	I-5	603
	I-5	647A
	I-5	775
	I-8	24A
	I-99	21
	I-99	120
	I-99	160
	I-99	227
	I-99	243
	I-99	271
	I-99	302
Colorado		
	I-25	15
	I-25	150A
	I-70	167
	I-70	203
	I-70	264
Connecticut		
	I-395	80
	I-395	97
	I-95	81
Florida		
	I-10	12
	I-10	14
	I-10	18
	I-10	30
	I-10	48
	I-275	23AB
	I-295	2
	I-295	13
	I-75	46
	I-75	82
	I-95	35AB
	I-95	88
	I-95	91C
Georgia		
	I-20	3
	I-20	10
	I-20	36
	I-75	5
	I-75	18
	I-75	33
	I-75	62
	I-75	118
	I-85	9
	I-85	13
	I-85	40
Iowa		
	I-35	92
Idaho		
	I-15	93
	I-84	208
	I-86	61
Illinois		
	I-255	13
	I-280	2
	I-55	52
	I-55	197
	I-57	54AB
	I-57	71
	I-57	95
	I-57	116
	I-57	160
	I-57	190AB
	I-57	315
	I-64	14
	I-70	61
	I-72	141AB
	I-74	95A
	I-74	181
	I-80	19
	I-80	56
	I-80	75
	I-80	90
	I-80	112AB
	I-80	130AB
	I-88	41
	NWTL	63
	TSTL	74
Indiana		
	I-465	27
	I-64	105
	I-65	4
	I-65	29
	I-65	172
	I-69	3
	I-69	112AB
	I-69	129
	I-70	104
	I-74	116
	I-74	134AB
	I-94	34AB
Kansas		
	I-135	60
	I-135	89
	I-35	71
	I-35	128
	I-35	183AB
	I-70	53
	I-70	159
	I-70	298
Kentucky		
	I-24	4
	I-64	53AB
	I-64	137
	I-71	22
	I-75	38
Louisiana		
	I-10	64
	I-10	82
	I-10	109
	I-10	151
	I-10	157B
	I-10	163
	I-10	266
	I-12	7
	I-12	63B
	I-20	10
	I-20	114
	I-20	138
	I-49	18
	I-55	31
Massachusetts		
	I-195	1
	I-195	18
	I-495	18
	I-495	38
	I-95	9
Maryland		
	I-68	40
	I-70	54
	I-81	5
Maine		
	I-95	33
	I-95	39
	I-95	49
	I-95	62
	METNPK	4
Michigan		
	I-196	20
	I-69	13
	I-69	61
	I-69	141
	I-75	282
	I-75	392
	I-94	29
	I-94	98AB
	I-94	181AB
	I-96	30AB
Minnesota		
	I-35	42B
	I-35	56
	I-35	131
	I-35E	97AB
	I-35E	115
	I-90	119
	I-94	54
	I-94	103
Missouri		
	I-255	2
	I-270	29
	I-35	16
	I-35	54
	I-44	77
	I-44	80AB
	I-44	100
	I-44	129
	I-44	208
	I-44	226
	I-44	261
	I-55	96
	I-55	129
	I-55	191
	I-57	10
	I-70	15AB
	I-70	124
	I-70	193
	I-70	208
	I-70	227
Mississippi		
	I-10	34AB
	I-20	42AB
	I-55	18
	I-55	40
	I-55	61
	I-55	206
	I-55	243AB
	I-55	291
	I-59	4
	I-59	154AB
Montana		
	I-15	192AB
	I-90	306
North Carolina		
	I-26	18AB
	I-40	103
	I-40	151
	I-40	214
	I-85	21
	I-85	45AB
	I-85	75
	I-85	91
	I-85	141
	I-85	164
	I-85	204
	I-85	213
	I-95	173
North Dakota		
	I-29	64
	I-94	61
	I-94	258
Nebraska		
	I-80	177
New Hampshire		
	I-93	20
New Jersey		
	I-295	47AB
New Mexico		
	I-25	3
	I-40	160
Nevada		
	I-80	301
New York		
	I-81	45
	I-87	6
	I-88	15
	NYTH	59
Ohio		
	I-270	15
	I-270	32
	I-275	33
	I-275	63
	I-70	36
	I-70	91AB
	I-70	218
	I-71	8
	I-71	234
	I-75	22
	I-75	74AB
	I-75	92
	I-77	1
	I-77	81
	I-77	120
	OHTNPK	8
Oklahoma		
	I-35	109
	I-35	116
	I-40	82
	I-40	123
	I-40	136
	I-40	185
	I-40	311
	I-44	80
	I-44	108
	I-44	196
Oregon		
	I-5	21
	I-5	55
	I-5	174
	I-84	62
	I-84	376AB
Pennsylvania		
	I-70	7AB
	I-76	3
	I-79	25
	I-80	19
	I-90	6
Rhode Island		
	I-295	4
South Carolina		
	I-26	21AB
	I-26	103
	I-26	111AB
	I-26	199AB
	I-85	92
South Dakota		
	I-29	77
	I-29	132
	I-90	12
	I-90	59
Tennessee		
	I-24	4
	I-24	114
	I-24	152
	I-40	12
	I-40	80AB
	I-40	82AB
	I-40	287
	I-40	379
	I-40	435
Texas		
	I-10	11
	I-10	28B
	I-10	696
	I-10	720
	I-10	747
	I-10	780
	I-20	42
Texas (continued)		
	I-20	343
	I-20	408
	I-27	49
	I-30	7A
	I-30	68
	I-30	93AB
	I-30	124
	I-30	201
	I-30	220A
	I-30	223AB
	I-35	3B
	I-35	186
	I-35	205
	I-35	241
	I-35	250
	I-35	251
	I-35	261
	I-35	339
	I-35	368A
	I-35E	414
	I-35E	415
	I-35E	452
	I-35E	463
	I-40	72B
	I-410	13B
	I-410	21A
	I-45	25
	I-45	59
	I-45	88
	I-45	116
	I-45	251
	I-635	2
	I-635	23
	I-820	10AB
	I-820	20B
	I-820	27
Utah		
	I-15	272
	I-15	297
	I-15	334
	I-15	342
	I-80	145
Virginia		
	I-64	55
	I-64	255AB
	I-64	263AB
	I-64	290AB
	I-66	47
	I-81	7
	I-85	12
	I-95	53
	I-95	143AB
Washington		
	I-5	79
Wisconsin		
	I-43	43
	I-43	96
	I-43	149
	I-90	4
	I-90	25
	I-90	171C
	I-94	2
	I-94	41
	I-94	70
	I-94	116
	I-94	143
	I-94	287
West Virginia		
	I-64	15
	I-64	169
	I-77	138
	I-79	99
	I-79	119
	I-79	132
	I-81	12
	I-81	13
Wyoming		
	I-80	5
	I-80	102
	I-90	25
	I-90	126

Two Great Coaches – One Unbeatable Team!

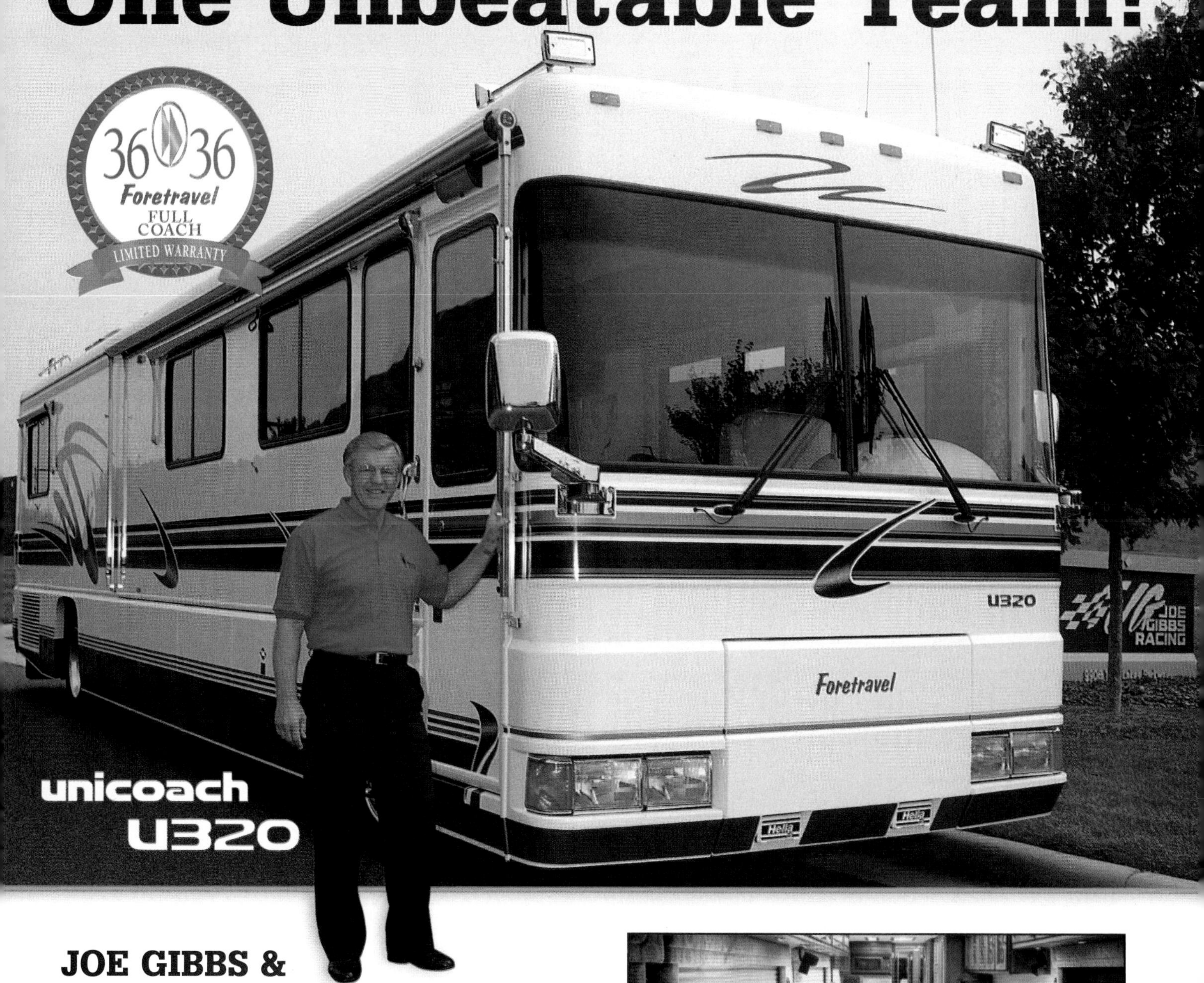

36/36 Foretravel FULL COACH LIMITED WARRANTY

unicoach U320

JOE GIBBS & The Foretravel Unicoach U320...

A winning combination!

When a second-string substitute is not an option, do what three-time Superbowl winning ***coach*** and Daytona 500 winning-team owner Joe Gibbs did... Go with a Foretravel Motorhome!

Why settle for second place when it comes to performance, safety and dependability? From our exclusive monocoque chassis to our "best-in-the-industry" 36/36 Full Coach Warranty, you'll experience that "winning" feeling every time you get behind the wheel.

Foretravel... America's winningest "coach."

Foretravel, inc.

1221 NW Stallings Drive • Nacogdoches, Texas 75964
(409) 564-8367 • (800) 955-6226 • Fax (409) 564-0391
www.foretravel.com

WANDERLODGE LXi

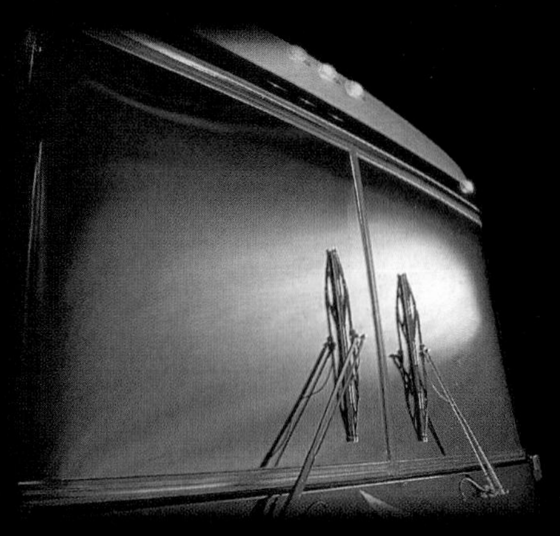

Many dream of greatness. Only a select few will drive it.

The new Wanderlodge 41' and 43' motorcoaches. We've taken the most luxurious motorhome in the world and completely redesigned it—from top to bottom, from bow to stern. The result is the new LXi series—the most extraordinary motorcoaches ever built.

Once you enter the LXi, your concept of travel will change forever. The interior is reminiscent of a five-star suite. Eight custom floor plans. Natural wood cabinetry. Cultured marble vanity and shower. Designer original fabrics, carpets, hardwoods and tiles. An unparalleled sound system with a 10-disk player in the dashboard. And thanks to the lowered engine design, you can even opt for a roomy walk-in closet—complete with drawer cabinet and shelving.

The new, sleeker exterior styling of the LXi includes an optional stainless steel package, large panoramic windshield, and a more aerodynamic front and rear.

Unlike converted buses, the LXi is designed and engineered to be a motorhome from the ground up. Everything is designed to be where it is, not merely placed where it will fit.

And the rigid steel construction of the chassis and body make it one of the safest motorhomes on the road today. Powered by a state-of-the-art 500-hp diesel engine, this masterpiece of engineering negotiates grades and quietly pushes

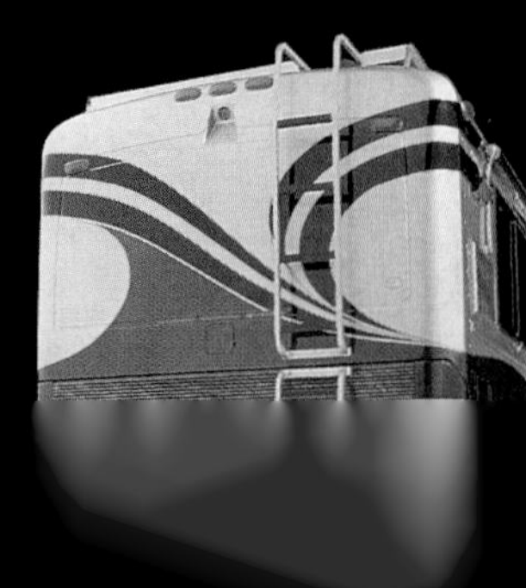

THE MOTORCOACH THAT TRANSPORTS YOU TO A NEW LEVEL OF LUXURY.

If you're ready to experience a new level of luxury, experience the new Wanderlodge LXi. For a color brochure, see your nearest Blue Bird dealer. *Or contact:* Blue Bird Corporation, One Wanderlodge Way, Fort Valley, GA 31030, 1-800-486-7122, Mon–Thurs, 8 AM to 5 PM ET.

BLUE BIRD®

Visit our web site at www.blue-bird.com

Ask about our newest member of the Blue Bird luxury motorcoach family, the 40' Wanderlodge LX.

Cracker Barrel Old Country Store

Convenient Locations in 36 States

ALABAMA
Athens*
Bessemer*
Cullman*
Dothan*
Gardendale*
Greenville*
Madison*
Mobile*
Montgomery
Moody*
Opelika*
Oxford*
Pelham
Prattville*
Trussville*
Tuscaloosa*

ARIZONA
Casa Grande*
Flagstaff*
Goodyear*
Marana*
Peoria*
Phoenix* (2)
Yuma*

ARKANSAS
Alma*
Bryant*
Conway*
Russellville*
W. Memphis*

COLORADO
Colorado Springs*
Loveland*
Northglenn*
Pueblo*

CONNECTICUT
Milford*

FLORIDA
Boynton Beach*
Bradenton*
Brooksville*
Crestview*
Daytona Beach*
Deerfield Beach*
Ft. Myers*
Ft. Pierce*
Gainesville*
Jacksonville*
Kissimmee*
Lake City*
Lakeland*
Melbourne*
Naples*
Ocala*
Orange Park*
Orlando*
Ormond Beach*
Palm Coast*
Pembrook Pines*
Pensacola*
Port Charlotte*
Sanford*
Seffner*
St. Augustine*
Stuart*
Tallahassee
Titusville*
Venice*
Vero Beach*
Wesley Chapel*
West Palm Beach*

GEORGIA
Augusta*
Brunswick*
Cartersville*
Commerce*
Conyers*
Dalton*
Douglasville*
Kennesaw
Kingsland*
Lake Park*
Macon (2)
Marietta
Morrow*
Newnan*
Norcross
Perry*
Pooler*
Savannah*
Suwanee*
Tifton*
Union City
Valdosta

IDAHO
Boise*

ILLINOIS
Bloomington*
Bradley
Caseyville*
Decatur*
Effingham*
Elgin*
Gurnee*
Joliet*
Lincoln*
Marion*
Matteson*
Morton*
Mt. Vernon*
Naperville*
Rockford*
Romeoville*
Springfield*
Tinley Park*
Troy*
Urbana*

INDIANA
Anderson
Edinburgh*
Elkhart*
Evansville*
Fishers*
Ft. Wayne*
Gas City*
Hammond*
Indianapolis (3)
Lafayette*
Merrillville*
Plainfield*
Richmond*
Sellersburg*
Seymour*
Terre Haute*

IOWA
Clive*
Council Bluffs*
Davenport*

KANSAS
Emporia*
Junction City*
Kansas City*
Olathe*
Park City*
Topeka*

KENTUCKY
Bowling Green*
Cadiz*
Corbin*
Elizabethtown
Florence*
Franklin*
Georgetown*
Jeffersontown*
LaGrange
Lexington* (2)
Mt. Sterling*
Paducah
Richmond
Shepherdsville*

LOUISIANA
Baton Rouge*
Gonzales*
Hammond*
Lafayette*
Shreveport*
Slidell*
Sulphur*
West Monroe*

MARYLAND
Frederick*
Riverside*

MASSACHUSETTS
Holyoke*

MICHIGAN
Battle Creek*
Belleville*
Brighton*
Flint*
Grand Rapids*
Grandville*
Jackson*
Kalamazoo*
Lansing*
Monroe*
Port Huron*
Roseville*
Saginaw*
Stevensville*

MINNESOTA
Brooklyn Center*
Lakeville*
Woodbury*

MISSISSIPPI
Batesville*
Brookhaven*
Hattiesburg*
Horn Lake*
Jackson*
Meridian*
Moss Point*
Pearl*
Vicksburg*

MISSOURI
Branson*
Cape Girardeau*
Columbia*
Fenton*
Independence*
Joplin*
Kansas City*
Liberty*
Springfield*
St. Charles
St. Joseph*
St. Louis*
St. Robert*

MONTANA
Billings*

NEBRASKA
Lincoln*
W. Omaha*

NEW JERSEY
Pennsville*
Clinton*

NEW MEXICO
Albuquerque*
Gallup*
Las Cruces*

NEW YORK
Blasdell*
Cicero*
Dunkirk*
E. Greenbush*
Halfmoon*
Lancaster*
Watertown*

NORTH CAROLINA
Asheville*
Burlington*
Charlotte
Clemmons*
Concord*
Durham*
Fayetteville
Garner*
Gastonia
Greensboro*
Henderson*
Hendersonville
Hickory*
Jonesville*
Lexington*
Lumberton*
Mooresville*
Roanoke Rapids*
Smithfield*
Statesville*
Wilson*

OHIO
Akron*
Austintown*
Cambridge*
Cincinnati*
Columbus*
Dayton*
Findlay*
Forest Park
Grove City*
Harrison*
Lima*
Mansfield*
Medina*
Middletown*
N. Canton*
Perrysburg*
Pickerington*
Piqua*
Sheffield*
Springfield*
Twinsburg*
Zanesville*

OKLAHOMA
Edmond*
Lawton*
Midwest City*
Norman*
Oklahoma City*
Tulsa*

PENNSYLVANIA
Chambersburg*
Erie*
Fogelsville
Frackville*
Hamburg*
Harrisburg*
Meadville*
New Stanton*
York*

SOUTH CAROLINA
Anderson*
Columbia
Florence*
Gaffney
Greenville
Hilton Head
Murrells Inlet*
N. Charleston*
N. Myrtle Beach*
Rock Hill*
Santee*
Spartanburg

TENNESSEE
Chattanooga* (3)
Clarksville
Cleveland
Cookeville*
Crossville*
Dickson*
Farragut*
Franklin*
Harriman
Jackson*
Johnson City*
Kingsport*
Knoxville (3)
Lake City*
Lebanon*
Manchester*
Memphis
Mt. Juliet*
Murfreesboro (2)
Nashville (6)
Newport
Pigeon Forge* (2)
Sweetwater*

TEXAS
Amarillo*
Arlington* (2)
Baytown*
Benbrook*
Burleson*
Conroe*
Corpus Christi*
Denton*
DeSoto*
El Paso*
Ft. Worth*
Greenville*
Houston*
League City*
Lewisville*
Mesquite*
Round Rock*
San Antonio* (2)
Texarkana*
Waco*
W. Houston*

UTAH
Layton*
Springville*
West Valley*

VIRGINIA
Abingdon*
Ashland*
Chester*
Christiansburg*
Dumfries*
Fredericksburg*
Harrisonburg*
Manassas*
Mechanicsville*
Newport News*
Staunton*
Troutville*
Williamsburg*
Winchester*

WEST VIRGINIA
Barboursville*
Beckley*
Cross Lanes*
Fairmont*
Martinsburg*
Mineralwells*
Princeton

WISCONSIN
Germantown*
Janesville*
Kenosha*
Madison*

*Designated RV and bus parking

We hope you'll visit your nearest Cracker Barrel for a detailed map of our store locations.

Step back into a time when every meal was special. Return to a place where the front porch held a cozy rocking chair to welcome weary travelers. Pass through wooden doors and enter a real country store built with hardwood floors and rough hewn walls filled with wonderful aromas, flavors, gifts and antiques from days long past. Come to the Cracker Barrel Old Country Store, where breakfast, lunch and dinner are prepared according to time-proven country recipes with a fondness for real food, good taste and honest value.

Cracker Barrel
Old Country Store®

HOURS: SUNDAY - THURSDAY 6AM - 10PM; FRIDAY & SATURDAY 6AM - 11PM

New for 1999

The One-of-A-Kind RVers Guide To Services & Amenities At Over 5,000 Travel Centers and Truck Stops In The United States & Canada.

A GREAT COMPANION TO YOUR 1999 EXIT AUTHORITY ...

Your Best Road Stop Could Be A Truck Stop!

Service Listings Include:

- Travel Centers & Truck Stops On-and-Off the Interstates
- On-Site Restaurants
- Security Patrolled Sites
- Check Cashing & Money Services
- Convenience Stores & Propane Fuel Availability
- ATM Machines
- U.S. Postal, UPS, & FedEx Locations
- Laudromat Facilities

Plus . . . New RV Specific Information:

- RV Dump Stations
- Designated RV Parking
- Internet Access
- Overnight RV Parking
- RV Wash Facilities
- RV Repair & Maintenance

ONLY $14.95

- *Call 1-800-494-5566 Ext. 16 with your credit card number ($14.95, includes standard S&H -- for Priority, add $5).*
- *Or . . . mail check or money order payable to Interstate America ($14.95, includes standard S&H -- for Priority, add $5).*

Interstate America • 5695-G Oakbrook Pkwy • Dept. 16 • Norcross, Georgia 30093

THE ONLY GUIDE CREATED ESPECIALLY FOR RVers!

INTERSTATE RV DUMP STATIONS

Hwy/Exit	Facility
Alabama	
I-10 (1)	Welcome Center
I-10 (66)	Welcome Center
I-20 (214)	AL Welcome Center
I-59 (1)	Rest Area
I-59 (38)	Rest Area
I-59 (39)	Rest Area
I-59 77	TravelCenters of America
I-59 (85)	Rest Area
I-59 104	Flying J
I-59 (165)	Rest Area
I-59 (167)	Rest Area
I-59 (241)	AL Welcome Center
I-65 (85)	Rest Area
I-65 (89)	Rest Area
I-65 (134)	Rest Area
I-65 (134)	Rest Area
I-65 (214)	Rest Area
I-65 (214)	Rest Area
I-65 (302)	Rest Area
I-65 (302)	Rest Area
I-65 (364)	Rest Area
I-85 (44)	Rest Area
I-85 (44)	Rest Area
I-85 (78)	Rest Area, Welcome Center
Arkansas	
I-30 7	Flying J
I-40 84	Flying J
I-40 280	Flying J
I-55 4	Flying J
I-55 63	Citgo Travel Center
Arizona	
I-10 103	Rip Griffin Travel Center
I-10 208	Flying J
I-10 268	Triple T Truck Stop
I-10 340	Rip Griffin Travel Center
I-10 378	4-K
I-17 (252)	Rest Area
I-17 (252)	Rest Area
I-40 48	Exxon
I-40 53	Flying J
I-40 144	Hillside RV Park
I-40 198	Little America
I-40 253	Pilot Travel Center
I-40 255	Flying J
I-40 292	Holbrook Truck Plaza
I-8 67	Dateland Cafe
I-8 119	Texaco
California	
CA99 291	Galt
I-10 (143)	Rest Area
I-10 (144)	Rest Area
I-10 (216)	Rest Area
I-15 176	Arco
I-5	Arco
I-5	Exxon
I-5	Shell
I-5 (208)	Rest Area
I-5 (208)	Rest Area
I-5 (447)	Rest Area
I-5 (447)	Rest Area
I-5 (608)	Rest Area
I-5 (608)	Rest Area
I-8	Shell
I-8 (51)	Rest Area
I-8 (109)	Rest Area
I-80 (149)	Rest Area
Colorado	
I-25 (37)	Rest Area
I-25 (37)	Rest Area
I-25 (112)	Rest Area
I-25 (115)	Rest Area
I-70 (19)	Colorado Welcome Center
I-70 90	Rest Area
I-70 310	KAO Campground
I-70 438	U.S. 24, Rose Ave.
I-76 (108)	Rest Area
I-76 (108)	Rest Area
I-76 (151)	Welcome Center
I-76 (151)	Welcome Center
Connecticut	
I-84 (2)	Rest Area
I-84 (42)	Rest Area
I-84 (84)	Rest Area
I-91 (22)	Weigh Station
I-91 (23)	Rest Area
Florida	
I-10 27	Flying J
I-4 (94)	Rest Area
I-75 24	Pilot Travel Center
I-75 59	Flying J
I-75 72	Petro Truck Plaza
Georgia	
I-16 (44)	Rest Area
I-16 (46)	Rest Area
I-20 (1)	GA Welcome Center
I-20 (103)	Rest Area
I-20 (108)	Rest Area
I-20 (182)	Rest Area
I-20 (182)	Rest Area
I-20 (201)	GA Welcome Center
I-75 1	Flying J
I-75 (3)	GA Welcome Center
I-75 16	Tifton Travel Center
I-75 43A	Happy Stores
I-75 (76)	Rest Area
I-75 (85)	Rest Area
I-75 (108)	Rest Area
I-75 (118)	Rest Area
I-75 133	Flying J
I-75 (179)	Rest Area
I-75 (308)	Rest Area
I-75 (319)	Rest Area
I-75 (352)	GA Welcome Center
I-85 (1)	GA Welcome Center
I-85 55	Petro
I-85 55	Shell
I-85 (113)	Rest Area
I-85 (160)	Rest Area
I-85 (176)	GA Welcome Center
I-95 (1)	GA Welcome Center
I-95 6	Flying J
I-95 14	Speedway
I-95 (40)	Rest Area
I-95 (111)	GA Welcome Center
Iowa	
I-29 (37)	Rest Area
I-29 (37)	Rest Area
I-29 (79)	Rest Area
I-29 (80)	Rest Area
I-29 (109)	Rest Area
I-29 (109)	Rest Area
I-29 (139)	Rest Area
I-29 (139)	Rest Area
I-35 (7)	Rest Area
I-35 (33)	Rest Area
I-35 (119)	Rest Area
I-35 (120)	Rest Area
I-35 144	Phillips 66
I-35 194	Coastal
I-35 (196)	Rest Area
I-380 (12)	Rest Area
I-80 (20)	Rest Area
I-80 (80)	Rest Area
I-80 (119)	Rest Area
I-80 (148)	Rest Area
I-80 (181)	Rest Area
I-80 (237)	Rest Area
I-80 259	Amoco
I-80 (270)	Rest Area
I-80 292	Flying J
I-80 (300)	Rest Area
Idaho	
I-15 31	Flags West
I-15 119	Texaco
I-84 165	ID 25, Jerome
I-90 6	Exxon
Illinois	
I-39 (86)	Rest Area
I-39 (86)	Rest Area
I-55 289	Speedway
I-57 159	Speedway
I-57 160	Bobbers Truck Plaza
I-57 (166)	Rest Area
I-57 (167)	Rest Area
I-57 (268)	Rest Area
I-57 (269)	Rest Area
I-57 (332)	Rest Area
I-70 (87)	Rest Area
I-74 (28)	Rest Area
I-74 (30)	Rest Area
I-74 (115)	Rest Area
I-80 (51)	Rest Area
I-80 (51)	Rest Area
I-80 75	Tiki Truck Stop
I-90 (1)	IL Welcome Center
Indiana	
I-70 (2)	Welcome Center
Kansas	
I-135 (23)	Rest Area
I-135 31	Texaco
I-135 40	Phillips 66
I-135 (68)	Rest Area
I-35 (175)	Rest Area
I-35 (175)	Rest Area
I-70 (7)	KS Welcome Center
I-70 (48)	Rest Area
I-70 (48)	Rest Area
I-70 (72)	Rest Area
I-70 (97)	Rest Area
I-70 (97)	Rest Area
I-70 127	KOA Campgrounds
I-70 (131)	Rest Area
I-70 (133)	Rest Area
I-70 184	Phillips 66
I-70 (187)	Rest Area
I-70 (187)	Rest Area
I-70 (223)	Rest Area
I-70 (224)	Rest Area
I-70 (265)	Rest Area
I-70 (265)	Rest Area
I-70 (294)	Rest Area
I-70 (294)	Rest Area
I-70 (309)	Rest Area
I-70 (336)	Rest Area
Kentucky	
I-75 11	Mapco Express
I-75 171	Flying J
Louisiana	
I-10 (1)	Rest Area
I-10 4	The Lucky Longhorn
I-10 (15)	Rest Area
I-10 (67)	Rest Area
I-10 (67)	Rest Area
I-10 (104)	Rest Area
I-10 (106)	Rest Area
I-10 (121)	Welcome Center
I-10 (121)	Rest Area
I-10 (137)	Rest Area
I-10 (137)	Rest Area
I-10 177	USA Auto Truck Plaza
I-10 (180)	Rest Area
I-10 (180)	Rest Area
I-10 266	76 Auto/Truck Plaza
I-10 (269)	Rest Area
I-12 (27)	Rest Area
I-12 (28)	Rest Area
I-12 (60)	Rest Area
I-12 (60)	Rest Area
I-20 (2)	LA Welcome Center
I-20 3	Flying J
I-20 (36)	Rest Area
I-20 (36)	Rest Area
I-20 (58)	Rest Area
I-20 (58)	Rest Area
I-20 (95)	Rest Area
I-20 (97)	Rest Area
I-20 (150)	Rest Area
I-20 (150)	Rest Area
I-20 (184)	Rest Area
I-20 (184)	Rest Area
I-49 (34)	Rest Area
I-55 (33)	Rest Area
I-55 (65)	Rest Area
I-59 (1)	Rest Area
Maryland	
I-70 (39)	Welcome Center
I-95 (36)	MD Welcome Center
I-95 (37)	MD Welcome Center
I-95 100	Flying J
I-95 109	TravelCenters of America
Michigan	
I-75144AB	76 Auto/Truck Plaza
Minnesota	
I-35 (1)	Welcome Center
I-90 233	Texaco
I-94 50	Texaco
I-94 147	Holiday
I-94 171	Holiday
I-94 207	76 Auto/Truck Plaza
Missouri	
I-29 79	Phillips 66
I-35 93	Hadden Camping
I-35 114	Conoco
I-44 11AB	Flying J
I-55 58	Flying J
I-70 24	Phillips 66
I-70 103	Shell
I-70 121	Midway Travel Center
I-70 148	Petro
I-70 188	Flying J
Mississippi	
I-10 (2)	MS Welcome Center
I-10 31	Flying J
I-10 44	Shell
I-10 (64)	Rest Area
I-10 (64)	Rest Area
I-10 (75)	Welcome Center
I-20 11	Texaco
I-20 47	Flying J
I-20 68	Conoco
I-20 (75)	Rest Area
I-20 (91)	Rest Area
I-55 (54)	Rest Area
I-55 (54)	Rest Area
I-55 119	Chevron
I-55 (163)	Rest Area
I-55 (173)	Rest Area
I-55 (202)	Parking Area
I-55 (239)	Rest Area
I-55 (276)	Rest Area
I-55 (279)	MS Welcome Center
I-59 (2)	MS Welcome Center
I-59 113	J.R.'s Truckstop
I-59 153	Conoco
I-59 (164)	Welcome Center
Montana	
I-15 (367)	Weigh Station
I-90 96	Travel Center
I-90 101	Cenex
I-90 138	Chalet Bearmouth
I-90 184	Conoco
I-90 408	Exxon
I-90 437	Sinclair
I-90 455	Flying J
I-90 495	Sinclair
I-94 (113)	Rest Area
I-94 (114)	Rest Area
I-94 138	Cenex
I-94 213	Sinclair
I-94 (240)	Weigh Station
I-94 (240)	Weigh Station
North Carolina	
I-40 (82)	Rest Area
I-40 (136)	Rest Area
I-40 (136)	Rest Area
I-95 154	KOA Campgrounds
North Dakota	
I-29 (3)	Rest Area
I-29 (40)	Rest Area
I-29 (40)	Rest Area
I-29 (74)	Rest Area
I-29 (74)	Rest Area
I-29 (99)	Rest Area
I-29 (99)	Rest Area
I-29 138	Conoco
I-29 141	StaMart
I-29 (179)	Rest Area
I-29 215	Gastrak
I-94 (69)	Rest Area
I-94 (69)	Rest Area
I-94 (94)	Rest Area
I-94 (94)	Rest Area
I-94 (119)	Rest Area
I-94 (119)	Rest Area
I-94 157	Cenex
I-94 161	Cenex
I-94 (169)	Rest Area
I-94 (169)	Rest Area
I-94 182	Cenex
I-94 (221)	Rest Area
I-94 (224)	Rest Area
I-94 (254)	Rest Area
I-94 (254)	Rest Area
Nebraska	
I-80 126	76 Auto/Truck Plaza
I-80 164	Texaco
I-80 432	Flying J
New Jersey	
I-295 (3)	Rest Area
I-295 (35)	Rest Area
I-295 (50)	Rest Area
New Mexico	
I-10 20A	Rest Area
I-10 (53)	Rest Area
I-10 (61)	Rest Area
I-10 (164)	NM Welcome Center
I-25 115	Santa Fe RV Park
I-25 (268)	Rest Area
I-25 (374)	Rest Area
I-25 (375)	Rest Area
I-25 (434)	Rest Area
I-25 (434)	Rest Area
I-40 (3)	Rest Area
I-40 (22)	NM Welcome Center
I-40 (39)	Rest Area
I-40 39	Giant
I-40 (93)	Rest Area
I-40 153	Flying J
I-40 (207)	Rest Area
I-40 (251)	Rest Area
I-40 (251)	Rest Area
I-40 (301)	Rest Area
I-40 (373)	NM Welcome Center
Nevada	
I-15 46	Flying J
I-80 4	Boomtown Truckstop
I-80 19	76 Auto/Truck Plaza
I-80 (41)	Rest Area
I-80 48	Truck Inn
I-80 (158)	Rest Area
I-80 176	Flying J
I-80 (216)	Rest Area
I-80 (258)	Rest Area
I-80 (258)	Rest Area
I-80 280	Pilot Travel Center
New York	
I-390 5	Travelport
Ohio	
I-71 131	Flying J
I-75 (81)	Rest Area
I-75 (81)	Rest Area
I-75 135	Flying J
I-80223AB	76 Auto/Truck Plaza
Oklahoma	
I-35 (3)	Rest Area
I-35 40	Total
I-35 (57)	Rest Area
I-35 (58)	Rest Area
I-35 122B	Total
I-35 (226)	Rest Area
I-35 (226)	Rest Area
I-40 (9)	OK Welcome Center
I-40 (9)	Rest Area
I-40 108	Cherokee Texaco
I-40 140	Flying J
I-40 142	TravelCenters of America
I-40 (197)	Rest Area
I-40 (197)	Rest Area
I-40 200	Phillips 66
I-40 (313)	OK Welcome Center
I-40 (316)	Rest Area
Oregon	
I-5 (63)	Rest Area
I-5 (63)	Rest Area
I-5 99	Fat Harvey's Travel Center
I-5 199	TravelCenters of America
I-5 (241)	Rest Area
I-5 (241)	Rest Area
I-5 278	Tesoro Alaska
I-5 (282)	Rest Area
I-5 (282)	Rest Area
I-84 17	Flying J
I-84 (73)	Rest Area
I-84 (269)	Rest Area
I-84 335	Rest Area
Pennsylvania	
I-70 31	Town Hill Truckstop
I-76 (172)	Sideling Hill Service Area
I-76 (325)	Rest Area
I-76 (352)	Service Plaza
I-80 13	TravelCenters of America
I-80 32	Milton 32 Truck Plaza
I-81 3	Travel Port
I-81 17	Flying J
I-90 10	Travel Port
South Carolina	
I-20 70	Flying J
I-85 102	Flying J
I-95 68	Texaco
I-95 82	Wilco Travel Center
I-95 169	Petro
I-95 181	Flying J
South Dakota	
I-29 (121)	Rest Area
I-29 (121)	Rest Area
I-29 121	Nunda, Ward
I-29 (160)	Rest Area
I-29 (160)	Rest Area
I-29 (213)	Rest Area
I-29 (235)	Weigh Station
I-29 (251)	Rest Area
I-90 (1)	Rest Area
I-90 (42)	Rest Area
I-90 (42)	Rest Area
I-90 55	Sinclair
I-90 61	Conoco
I-90 (99)	Rest Area
I-90 (99)	Rest Area
I-90 (165)	Rest Area
I-90 (166)	Rest Area
I-90 (218)	Rest Area
I-90 (221)	Rest Area
I-90 (264)	Rest Area
I-90 (301)	Rest Area
I-90 (301)	Rest Area
I-90 332	Texaco
I-90 (362)	Rest Area
I-90 (362)	Rest Area
I-90 (412)	Rest Area
I-90 (412)	Rest Area
Tennessee	
I-24 64	Speedway
I-40 (267)	Rest Area
I-40 288	Mid Tenn. A/T Plaza
I-40 (327)	Rest Area
I-40 (419)	Rest Area
I-40 (446)	TN Welcome Center
I-65 (3)	TN Welcome Center
I-65 85	TravelCenters of America
I-75 1AB	Yogi Bear Camp
Texas	
I-10 2	Petro: 2
I-10 (394)	Rest Area
I-10 (394)	Rest Area
I-10 (514)	Rest Area
I-10 (514)	Rest Area
I-10 583	Flying J
I-10 (590)	Rest Area
I-10 (590)	Rest Area
I-10 (621)	Rest Area
I-10 (621)	Rest Area
I-10 731	KOA Kampground
I-10 873	Flying J
I-20 42	Flying J
I-20 (141)	Rest Area
I-20 (142)	Rest Area
I-20 406	Conoco
I-20 470	Pilot Travel Center
I-20 482	Countryside RV
I-20 503	Rip Griffin
I-20 (537)	Rest Area
I-20 (537)	Rest Area
I-20 544	Willow Branch RV Park
I-20 591	Pine Meadows Campground
I-20 (636)	TX Welcome Center
I-35 (129)	Rest Area
I-35 (129)	Rest Area
I-35 (179)	Rest Area
I-35 (179)	Rest Area
I-35 306	Love's
I-35 (492)	Rest Area
I-37 130	Diamond Shamrock
I-40 76	Flying J
I-40 (149)	Rest Area
I-45 70A	Campground
I-45 92	Camping
I-45 98	Fish Pond RV Park
I-45 109	Huntsville State Park
I-45 (126)	Rest Area
I-45 (217)	Rest Area
I-610 2	Camping
Utah	
I-15 109	76
I-15 222	Flying J
I-70 40	Flying J
VA	
I-81 77	Flying J
I-95 11AB	Citgo
I-95 17	Jellystone Park
I-95 33	Davis Truck Plaza
I-95 89	Speed & Briscoe 76
I-95 98	Travel Plaza
Washington	
I-5 (11)	Rest Area
I-5 (13)	Rest Area
I-5 (141)	Rest Area
I-5 (188)	Weigh Station
I-5 (207)	Rest Area
I-5 (207)	Rest Area
I-5 258	Exxon
I-82 (23)	Rest Area
I-82 (25)	Rest Area
I-90 (89)	Rest Area
I-90 (162)	Rest Area
I-90 (180)	Rest Area
I-90 (242)	Rest Area
Wisconsin	
I-39 (117)	Rest Area
I-43 (33)	Rest Area
I-43 (33)	Rest Area
I-43 (168)	Rest Area
I-43 (168)	Rest Area
I-90 (1)	WI Welcome Center
I-90 (76)	Rest Area
I-90 (76)	Rest Area
I-90 87	Amoco
I-90 (114)	Rest Area
I-90 (114)	Rest Area
I-90 132	76 Auto/Truck Plaza
I-94 88	Holiday
West Virginia	
I-64 (179)	WV Welcome Center
I-70 (13)	WV Welcome Center
I-77 (17)	Travel Plaza
I-77 (18)	Rest Area
I-77 (45)	Exxon
I-77 (72)	Travel Plaza
I-77 (72)	Exxon
I-77 (166)	Rest Area
I-77 (166)	Rest Area
I-79 (49)	Rest Area
I-79 (85)	Rest Area
I-79 (85)	Rest Area
I-79 105	I-79 Truck Stop
I-79 (123)	Rest Area
I-79 (123)	Rest Area
I-79 (159)	WV Welcome Center
Wyoming	
I-25 (7)	WY Welcome Center
I-25 7	WY Welcome Center
I-25 (91)	Rest Area
I-25 (126)	Rest Area
I-25 126	Rest Area
I-25 (254)	Rest Area
I-25 254	Rest Area
I-80 (6)	Rest Area
I-80 6	WY Welcome Center
I-80 (144)	Rest Area
I-80 (228)	Rest Area
I-80 228	Rest Area
I-80 (323)	Rest Area
I-80 323	Rest Area
I-80 (401)	Rest Area
I-80 401	Rest Area
I-90 (23)	WY Welcome Center
I-90 (189)	Rest Area

Our new state-of-the-art Travel Centers have amenities such as private showers, laundry facilities, drivers' lounge, truck parking, FAX, permit services, load matching and much much more.

★ =Opening Soon ● =Travel Center

Location	Load Matching	ATM	FAX Service	Copy Service	Scales	Parking Space	Showers	Deli	Restaurant	Lounge	Laundry	Trendar
Alabama												
Birmingham - I-65, Exit 262 (205) 323-8556 Fax (205) 323-8610	*	*	*	*	*	12	*	*				*
Oxford - I-20, Exit 165 (205) 831-7334 Fax (205) 831-6342		*	*	*	*	12						*
★ ● Priceville - I-65, Exit 334 at Hwy 67 (205) 353-5252	*	*	*	*	*	70	*	*	*	*	*	*
Arkansas												
Conway - I-40, Exit 129 (501) 329-3810 Fax (501) 329-1179		*	*	*		8	*	*				*
Heth - I-40, Exit 256 (870) 657-2166 Fax (870) 657-2543		*	*	*		18	*	*				*
Marion - I-56, Exit 10 (870) 739-3007 Fax (870) 739-1641		*	*	*		9	*	*				*
● Russellville - I-40, Exit 84 (501) 967-7414 Fax (501)964-0112	*	*	*	*	*	70	*	*	*	*	*	*
● W. Memphis - (W) I-40, Exit 280 (So) I-55, Exit 4 (870) 732-1202 Fax (870) 732-1340	*	*	*	*	*	150	*	*	*	*	*	*
Wheatley - I-40, Exit 221 (870) 457-2322 Fax (870) 457-2037		*	*	*		18	*	*	*			*
Florida												
Pensacola - I-10, Exit 3A (850) 474-0329 Fax (850) 474-0355		*	*	*	*	25	*	*				*
Georgia												
Atlanta - I-20, Exit 14 (404) 696-8050 Fax (404) 696-6544		*	*	*		4	*	*				*
● Cordele - I-75, Exit 33	*	*	*	*	*	58	*	*	*	*	*	*
★ ● Kingsland - I-95, Exit 2	*	*	*	*	*	70	*	*	*	*	*	*
McDonough - I-75, Exit 71 (770) 957-5154 Fax (770) 957-6274		*	*	*		40	*					*
● Rising Fawn - I-59, Exit 1 (706) 482-2455 Fax (706) 462-2702	*	*	*	*	*	100	*	*	*	*	*	*
★ ● Temple - I-20, Exit 4	*	*	*	*	*	70	*	*	*	*	*	*
Indiana												
★ ● Brazil - I-70, Exit 23	*	*	*	*	*	70	*	*	*	*	*	*
Kentucky												
● Franklin - I-65, Exit 6 (502) 586-9544 Fax (502) 586-9687	*	*	*	*	*	64	*		*	*	*	*
● Williamsburg - I-75, Exit 11 (606) 549-0162 Fax (606) 549-0166		*	*	*	*	38	*		*	*	*	*
Louisiana												
Port Allen - I-10, Exit 151, (504) 388-9913 Fax (504) 388-0005	*	*	*	*	*	30	*	*				*
Breaux Bridge - I-10, Exit 115 (318) 332-6608 Fax (318) 332-6737		*	*	*		12		*				*
Missouri												
★ ● Hayti - I-55, Exit 19		*	*	*	*	70	*	*	*	*	*	*
Tennessee												
Cornersville - I-65, Exit 22 (931) 363-3290 Fax (931) 363-8246		*	*	*		16		*				*
Cross Plains - I-65 & Hwy 25 (615) 654-2599 Fax (615) 654-2108		*	*	*		16	*	*				*
● Dickson - I-40, Exit 172 (615)446-4600 Fax (615) 446-0763	*	*	*	*	*	72	*		*		*	*
Heiskel - I-75, Exit 117 (423) 938-1439 Fax (423) 938-1146		*	*	*		12	*	*				*
● Lebanon - I-40/Hwy 231, Exit 238 (615) 453-8866 Fax (615) 453-8860	*	*	*	*	*	97	*	*	*	*	*	*
Memphis - Hwy 78 & Shelby (901) 795-3826 Fax (901) 363-1221	*	*	*	*	*	50	*	*				*
Pleasant View - I-24, Exit 24 (615) 746-6325 Fax (615) 746-4537		*	*	*		16	*	*				*
Texas												
Baytown - I-10, Exit 789 (281) 426-5493 Fax (281) 426-5413		*	*	*	*	52	*	*			*	*
Orange - I-10, Exit 873 (409) 745-1124 Fax (409) 745-3336		*	*	*	*	18		*				*

One Stop. Lotsa Stuff.

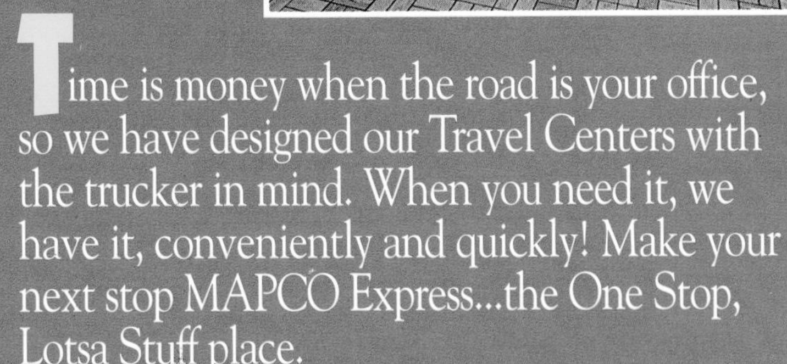

Time is money when the road is your office, so we have designed our Travel Centers with the trucker in mind. When you need it, we have it, conveniently and quickly! Make your next stop MAPCO Express...the One Stop, Lotsa Stuff place.

Visit our website: www.mapcoexpress.com

We're on your way!

SHONEY'S®

COME BACK TO WHAT'S GOOD™

www.shoneysrestaurants.com • 1-877-835-5746

SHONEY'S®
is Better Than Ever . . .

Shoney's is a family restaurant that serves breakfast, lunch, and dinner 7 days a week. Shoney's menu includes burgers, sandwiches, chicken, steaks, seafood, pasta, and a variety of "homestyle" lunches and dinners. Shoney's Restaurants also feature the following . . .

- All-You-Care-To-Eat Breakfast Bar
- All-You-Care-To-Eat Soup, Salad and Fruit Bar
- Facilities for Groups and Large Parties
- Major Credit Cards Accepted

. . . and On Your Way!

Great Outlet! Shopping

TOMMY HILFIGER

DONNA KARAN
COMPANY STORE

SONY

Calvin Klein
outlet store

LIZ claiborne
OUTLET

JONES NEW YORK

Some of the great brand names you'll find at 51 Prime Outlet Centers coast to coast.

Store selection varies by center.

Arizona

Prime Outlets – New River
I-17, Exit 229
(602) 465-9500 • 1-888-4VALUE4U

Prime Outlets – Sedona
I-17N, Exit 298
(520) 284-2150 • 1-888-545-7227

California

Prime Outlets – Anderson
I-5 at Factory Outlets Drive
(530) 378-1000 • 1-800-0490

Prime Outlets – Gilroy
Hwy. 101 at Leavesley Rd. Exit
(408) 842-3729

Prime Outlets – Lake Elsinore
I-15 to Nichols Rd. exit
(909) 245-4989

Prime Outlets – Oxnard
Ventura 101 Freeway, Rice Ave. Exit
(805) 485-2244 • 1-888-545-7228

Prime Outlets – Pismo Beach
Hwy. 101, Five Cities Drive exit
(805) 773-4661

Prime Outlets – Tracy
I-205, Exit MacArthur Dr.
(209) 833-1892 • (209) 833-1895

Colorado

Prime Outlets – Castle Rock
I-25, Exit 184
1-800-245-8351

Prime Outlets – Loveland
I-25 at US 34, Exit 257B
1-888-255-1273

Prime Outlets – Silverthorne
I-70, Exit 205
(970) 468-9440

Florida

Prime Outlets – Ellenton
I-75, Exit 43
1-888-260-7608

Prime Outlets – Florida City
Intersection of US1 and FL Tpk.
1-888-545-7198

Prime Outlets – Naples
I-75, Exit 15
(914) 775-8083 • 1-888-545-7196

Prime Outlets – Vero Beach
I-95, Exit 68
(561) 770-6171

Georgia

Prime Outlets – Calhoun
I-75, Exit 129
(706) 602-1305 • (706) 602-1300

Prime Outlets – Darien
I-95, Exit 10
(912) 437-2700 • 1-888-545-7224

Idaho

Prime Outlets – Post Falls
I-90, Exit 2
(208) 773-4555 • 1-888-678-9847

Illinois

Prime Outlets – Huntley
I-90 at Rt. 47
1-888-545-7222 • (847) 669-9100

Indiana

Prime Outlets – Edinburgh
I-65 and US 31
(812) 526-9764

Prime Outlets – Fremont
I-69 at the Indiana Toll Rd. I-80/90
(219) 833-1684

Prime Outlets – Michigan City
I-80/90, Exit 39, Downtown Mich. City
(920) 231-8911

Maine

Prime Outlets – Kittery
I-95, Exit 3N/Exit 4S
1-888-KITTERY

Maryland

Prime Outlets – Hagerstown
I-70, Exit 29
1-888-883-6288

Prime Outlets – Perryville
I-95, Exit 93
(410) 378-9399

Prime Outlets – Queenstown
Rts. 50E/301N split
(410) 827-8699

Massachusetts

Prime Outlets – Lee
I-90, Exit 2
413-243-8186

Michigan

Prime Outlets – Birch Run
I-75, Exit 136
1-888-901-SHOP

Minnesota

Prime Outlets – Woodbury
I-94, Exit 251
(651) 735-9060

Mississippi

Prime Outlets – Gulfport
Hwy. 49, Exit 34A
1-888-260-7609

Missouri

Prime Outlets – Odessa
I-70, Exit 37
1-888-394-7584

New York

Prime Outlets – Latham
I-87, Exit 7
(518) 782-0085

Prime Outlets – Niagara Falls USA
I-190, Exit 22
1-800-414-0475

Prime Outlets – Waterloo
Rt. 318, Exit 41 & 42
(315) 539-1100

North Carolina

Prime Outlets – Morrisville
I-40, Exit 284
(919) 380-8700 • 1-888-260-7610

Ohio

Prime Outlets – Lodi
I-71 & Route 83, Exit 204
1-888-746-7563 • 1-888-SHOP-LODI

Prime Outlets – Jeffersonville I&II
I-71, Exits 65 & 69
1-888-746-7644 • 1-888-SHOP-OHIO

Oregon

Prime Outlets – Bend
Hwy. 97 & Powers Rd.
(541) 382-4512 • 1-888-245-0842

Pennsylvania

Prime Outlets – Grove City
I-79, Exit 31
1-888-545-7221

South Carolina

Prime Outlets – Gaffney
I-85, Exit 90
1-888-545-7194

Tennessee

Prime Outlets – Lebanon
I-40, Exit 238
1-800-617-2588

Prime Outlets –
Warehouse Row (Chattanooga)
I-24, Exit 178
1-888-260-7620

Texas

Prime Outlets – Conroe
I-45, Exit 91
(409) 441-6003

Prime Outlets – Gainesville
IH-35, Exit 501
1-888-545-7220

Prime Outlets – Hillsboro
I-35, Exit 368A
(245) 582-9205

Prime Outlets – San Marcos
I-35, Exit 200
1-800-628-9465 • (512) 396-7183

Virginia

Prime Outlets – Williamsburg
I-64, Exit 234
(757) 565-0702

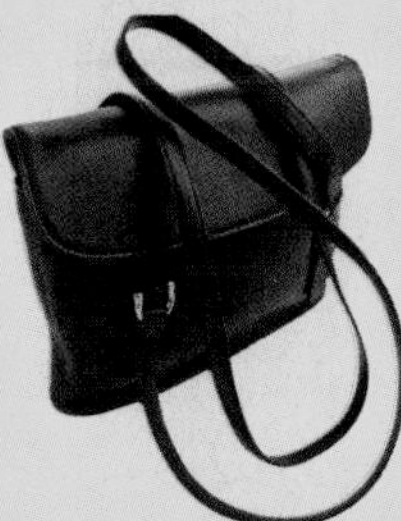

Washington

Prime Outlets – Burlington
I-5, Exit 229
(360) 757-3549

Wisconsin

Prime Outlets – Kenosha
I-94, Exit 347
(414) 857-2101

Prime Outlets – Oshkosh
US 41 & Hwy 44
(920) 231-8911

PRIME OUTLETS

This is shopping.™

Prime Tourism & Group Sales Office
Phone (410) 234-8336 • Fax (410) 234-1762
e-mail: shopusa@primeretail.com • www.primeretail.com

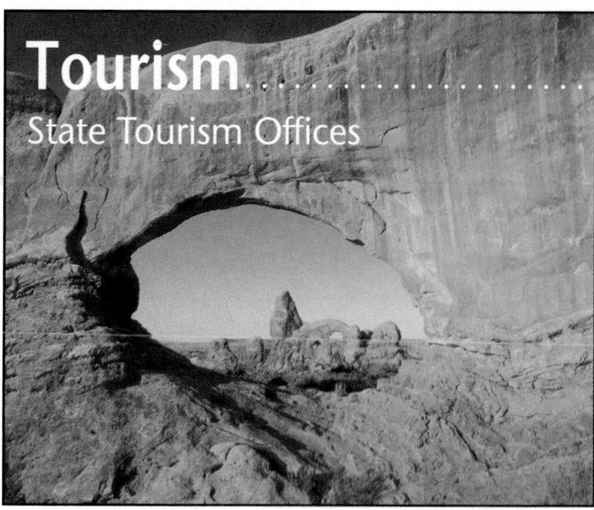

Tourism

State Tourism Offices

Alabama Bureau Of Tourism & Travel
Post Office Box 4927
Montgomery, AL 36103-4927
Web Site: http://alaweb.asc.edu/ala tours/tours.html
1-800-252-2262

Alaska Division of Tourism
Post Office Box 110801
Juneau, AK 99811
Web site: http://www.state.ak.us
1-907-465-2010

Arizona Office of Tourism
2702 North 3rd Street
Phoenix, AZ 85007
Web Site: http://www.arizonaguide. com
1-888-520-3433

Arkansas Department of Tourism
1 Capital Mall
Little Rock, AR 72201
Web site: http://www.state.ar.us/html/ark
1-800-628-8725 or 1-800-828-8974

California Office of Tourism
801 K St., Ste 1600
Sacramento, CA. 95814
Web site: http://www.gocalif.ca.gov
1-800-462-2543

Colorado Travel & Tourism Authority
3554 N. Academy Blvd.
Colorado Springs, CO 80917
Web site: http://www.colorado.com
1-800-265-6723

Connecticut Vacation Center
505 Hudson St.
Hartford, CT 06106
Web site: http://www.state.ct.us/tourism/
1-800-282-6863

Delaware Tourism Office
99 Kings Highway, Box 1401
Dover, DE 19903
Web site: http://www.state.de.us
1-800-441-8846

Washington Convention & Visitors Assoc.
1212 New York Ave NW
Washington, DC 20005
Web site: http://www.washington.org
1-800-422-8644

Florida Division of Tourism
2129 Ringland Blvd
Sarasota, FL 34230
Web site: http://www.flausa.com/
1-888-735-2872

Georgia Department of Industry & Trade
Post Office Box 1776 Dept TIA
Atlanta, GA. 30301-1776
Web site: http://www.gomm.com.
1-800-847-4842

Hawaii Visitors Bureau
Waikiki Business Plaza
2270 Kalakaua Ave #801
Honolulu, HI 96815
Web site: http://www.visit.hawaii.org
1-808-923-1811

Idaho Department of Commerce
700 West State St.
Boise, ID 83720
Web site: http://www.idoc.state.id.us
1-800-635-7820

Illinois Bureau of Tourism
100 West Randolph #3-400
Chicago, IL 60601
Web site: http://www.enjoyillinois.com
1-800-223-0120

Indiana Tourism Division
1 North Capitol Ave #700
Indianapolis, IN 46204
Web site: http://www.ai.org/tourism
1-800-289-6646

Iowa Department of Tourism
200 East Grand Ave.
Des Moines, IA 50309
Web site: http://www.state.ia.us/tourism/
1-800-345-4692

Kansas Travel & Tourism Division
700 SW Harrison St. Ste. 1300
Topeka, KS 66603
Website: http://www.kansascommerce.com
1-800-252-6727

Kentucky Dept. of Travel Development
500 Mero St.
Frankfort, KY 40601
Web site:
http:/www.state.ky.us/tour/tour.htm
1-800-225-8747

Louisiana Office of Tourism
Post Office Box 94291
Baton Rouge, LA 70804
Web site: http:/www.louisianatravel.com
1-800-334-8626

Maine Publicity Bureau
P.O. Box 2300
Hallowell, ME 04347
Web site: http:/www.visitmaine.com/
1-800-533-9595

Maryland Office of Tourism Development
217 East Redwood St. 9th Floor
Baltimore, MD 21202
Web site: http://www.mdisfun.org
1-800-543-1036

Massachusetts Office of Travel & Tourism
100 Cambridge St. 13th Floor
Boston, MA. 02202
Web site: http://www.mass-vacation.com/
1-800-447-6277

Michigan Travel Bureau
Post Office Box 3393
Livonia, MI 48151
Web site: http://www.michigan.org
1-800-543-2937

Minnesota Office of Tourism
121 7th Place East
122 St. Paul, MN 55101
Web: http://www.exploreminnesota.com
1-800-657-3700

Mississippi Division of Tourism Development
Post Office Box 1705
Ocean Springs, MS 39566
Web site: http://www.mississippi.org
1-800-927-6378

Missouri Division of Tourism
Post Office Box 1055
Jefferson City, MO 65102
Web site: http://www.missouritourism.org
1-800-877-1234

Travel Montana
Post Office Box 200533
Helena, MT 59620
Web site: http://travel.mt.gow
1-800-847-4868

Nebraska Travel & Tourism Department
Post Office Box 98913
Lincoln, NE 68509
Web site:
http://www.ded.state.ne.us/tourism/
1-800-228-4307

Nevada State Board on Tourism
Capital Complex
Carson City, NV 89710
Web site: http://www.travelnevada.com
1-800-638-2328

New Hampshire Office of Travel & Tourism
P.O. Box 1856
Concord, NH 03302-1856
Web site: http://www.visitnh.gov/
1-800-FUN-IN-NH, Ext 162

New Jersey Division of Travel & Tourism
20 West State St. CN 826
Trenton, N.J. 08628
Web: http://www.state.nj.us/travel
1-800-537-7397

New Mexico Department of Tourism
491 Old Santa Fe Trail
Santa Fe, NM 87503
Web site: http://www.newmexico.org/
1-800-545-2040

New York State Travel Info Center
1 Commerce Plaza
Albany, NY 12245
Web: http://www.iloveny.state.ny.us
1-800-225-5697

North Carolina State Board of Tourism
430 North Salisbury St.
Raleigh, NC 27603
Web site: http://www.visitnc.com
1-800-VISIT NC

North Dakota Tourism
604 East Blvd
Bismarck, ND 58505
Web site: http://www.ndtourism.com
1-800-435-5663

Ohio Division of Travel & Tourism
Post Office Box 1001
Columbus, OH 43216
Web site: http://www.ohiotourism.com
1-800-282-5393

Oklahoma Tourism & Recreation Dept.
500 Will Rogers Building
Oklahoma City, OK 73105
Web site: http://www.otrd.state.ok.us/
1-800-652-6552

Oregon Tourism Commission
775 Summer St. NE
Salem OR 97310
Web site: http://www.traveloregon.com
1-800-547-7842

Pennsylvania Office of Travel Marketing
453 Forum Bldg
Harrisburg, PA 17120
Web site: http://www.state.pa.us
1-800-847-4872

Rhode Island Tourism Division
7 Jackson Walkway
Providence, RI 02903
1-800-250-7384

South Carolina Dept. Tourism
Post Office Box 71
Columbia, SC 29202
Web site: http://www.prt.state.sc.us/sc
1-800-346-3634

South Dakota Department of Tourism
711 East Wells Ave
Pierre, SD 57501
Web site: http://www.state.sd.us
1-800-732-5682

Tennessee Tourism Division
Post Office Box 23170
Nashville, TN 37202
Web site: http://www.tennessee.net
1-800-836-6200

Texas Department of Tourism
Post Office Box 12728
Austin, Texas 78711
Web : http://www.traveltex.com
1-800-888-8839

Utah Travel Council
Capitol Hill, Dept TIA
Salt Lake City, UT 84114
Web site: http://www.utah.com
1-800-200-1160

Vermont Department of Travel & Tourism
134 State St.
Montpelier, VT 05602
Web: http://www.travel-vermont.com
1-800-837-6668

Virginia Division of Tourism
1021 E. Cary Street
Richmond, VA 23219
Web:http://www.virginia.org/
Cgi-shl/VISITVA/Tourism/Welcome
1-800-432-8747

Wyoming Division of Tourism
1-25 at College Drive
Cheyenne, WY 82002
Web Site:
http://www.state.wy.us/state/welcome.html
1-800225-5996

FREE CONTINENTAL BREAKFAST

East Hartford, CT (860) 289-4950
Coral Springs, FL (954) 344-2200
Deerfield Beach, FL (954) 428-0661
Fort Lauderdale, FL (954) 484-6909
Fort Myers, FL (941) 278-3949
Jupiter, FL (561) 575-7201
Lakeland, FL (941) 859-3399
Miami Airport, FL (305) 592-4799
Miami (Kendall), FL (305) 270-0359

FREE LOCAL PHONE CALLS

Miami Lakes, FL (305) 821-8274
Naples, FL (941) 793-4646
Orlando, FL (407) 345-0026
Plantation, FL (954) 473-8257
Sarasota, FL (941) 366-5128
Sunrise, FL (954) 845-9929
West Palm Beach, FL (561) 689-8540
Edison, NJ (908) 287-0171
Hazlet, NJ (908) 888-2800

FREE IN-ROOM COFFEE

Penns Grove, NJ (609) 299-3800
Ramsey, NJ (201) 934-9250
Buffalo, NY (716) 631-8966
Fishkill, NY (914) 896-4995
Rochester (North) (716) 621-2060
Rochester (South) (716) 427-0130
Suffern, NY (914) 368-1900
Reading, PA (610) 374-1500
Chesapeake, VA (757) 366-0100
Fairfax, VA (703) 359-2888

FREE IN-ROOM MOVIES

© 1998 Prime Hospitality Corp.

Value Never Looked This Good®

Every traveler staying at a Wellesley Inns will enjoy *free* continental breakfast, *free* local phone calls, *free* in-room coffee and *free* in-room movies. With all those *free* amenities included in our **low rates**...only Wellesley Inns has made value look this good! From Boston to Miami, business and leisure travelers have discovered our extraordinary inns. Beautifully landscaped grounds ...bright, welcoming lobbies...clean, oversized guest rooms... all freshly appointed to insure the utmost in comfort. For even greater value...travelers may join Wellesley Club®* and earn free nights fast!

Reserve your next stay at an extraordinary inn ...at an affordable price®. Call **800-444-8888**.

*Applications available at any Wellesley Inn

1-800-444-8888

Airline Access Chain Code: WL www.wellesleyinns.com

Parks

National Park Offices

Acadia National Park
P.O. Box 177
Bar Harbor, ME 04609-0177
Headquarter Phone: 207-288-9561
Fax Number: 207-288-5507

Arches National Park
P.O. Box 907
Moab, UT 84532
Headquarter Phone: 801-259-8161
Fax Number: 801-259-3411

Badlands National Park
P.O. Box 6
Interior, SD 57750
Headquarter Phone: 605-433-5361
Fax Number: 605-433-5404

Big Bend National Park
P.O Box 129
Big Bend National Park, TX 79834
Headquarter Phone: 915-477-2251
Fax Number: 915-477-2357

Biscayne National Park
P.O. Box 1369
Homestead, FL 33030
Headquarter Phone: 305-230-1144
Fax Number: 305-230-1190

Bryce Canyon National Park
P.O. Box 170001
Bryce Canyon, UT 84717-0001
Headquarter Phone: 801-834-5322
Fax Number: 801-834-4102

Canyonlands National Park
2282 S. West Resource Blvd.
Moab, UT 84532-3298
Headquarter Phone: 801-259-3911
Fax Number: 801-259-8628

Capitol Reef National Park
HC 70 Box 15
Torrey, UT 84775-9602
Headquarter Phone: 801-425-3791
Fax Number: 801-425-3026

Carlsbad Caverns National Park
3225 National Parks Highway
Carlsbad, NM 88220
Headquarter Phone: 505-785-2232
Fax Number: 505-785-2133

Channel Islands National Park
1901 Spinnaker Drive
Ventura, CA 93001
Headquarter Phone: 805-658-5700
Fax Number: 805-658-5799

Crater Lake National Park
P.O. Box 7
Crater Lake, OR 97604
Headquarter Phone: 541-594-2211
Fax Number: 541-584-2299

Death Valley National Park
Death Valley, CA 92328
Headquarter Phone: 619-786-2331
Fax Number: 619-786-3283

Denali National Park
Denali Park, AK 99755
Headquarter Phone: 907-683-2294
Fax Number: 907-683-9612

Dry Tortugas National Park
40001 State Road 9336
Homestead, FL 33034-6733
Headquarter Phone: 305-242-7700
Fax Number: 305-242-7711

Everglades National Park
40001 State Road 9336
Homestead, FL 33030
Headquarter Phone: 305-242-7700
Fax Number: 305-242-7728

Gates of the Arctic National Park
201 First Avenue
P.O. Box 74680
Fairbanks, AK 99707
Headquarter Phone: 907-456-0281
Fax Number: 907-456-0452

Glacier Bay National Park & PRES
P.O. Box 140
Gustavus, AK 99826-0140
Headquarter Phone: 907-697-2230
Fax Number: 907-697-2654

Glacier National Park
P.O. Box 128
West Glacier, MT 59936-0128
Headquarter Phone: 406-888-7800
Fax Number: 406-888-7808

Grand Canyon National Park
P.O. Box 129
Grand Canyon, AZ 86023
Headquarter Phone: 520-638-7888
Fax Number: 520-638-7797

Grand Teton National Park
P.O. Box 170
Moose, WY 83012-0170
Headquarter Phone: 307-739-3300
Fax Number: 307-739-3438

Great Basin National Park
Baker, NV 89311
Headquarter Phone: 702-234-7331
Fax Number: 702-234-7269

Great Smoky Mountains National Park
107 Park Headquarters Road
Gatlinburg, TN 37738
Headquarter Phone: 423-436-1200
Fax Number: 423-436-1220

Guadalupe Mountains National Park
HC 60, Box 400
Salt Flat, TX 79847-9400
Headquarter Phone: 915-828-3251
Fax Number: 915-828-3269

Hot Springs National Park
P.O. Box 1860
Hot Springs, AR 71902
Headquarter Phone: 501-624-3383
Fax Number: 501-624-1536

Isle Royale National Park
800 E. Lakeshore Drive
Houghton, MI 49931-1895
Headquarter Phone: 906-482-0986
Fax Number: 906-482-8753

Joshua Tree National Park
74485 National Park Drive
Twentynine Palms, CA 92277
Headquarter Phone: 619-367-6376
Fax Number: 619-367-6392

Katmai National Park
202 Center Ave. Suite 201
Kodiak, AK 99615
Headquarter Phone: 907-486-6730
Fax Number: 907-486-3331

Kenai Fjords National Park
P.O. Box 1727
Seward, AK 99664
Headquarter Phone: 907-224-3175
Fax Number: 907-224-2144

Kings Canyon National Park
Three Rivers, CA 93271
Headquarter Phone: 209-565-3341
Fax Number: 209-565-3730

Kobuk Valley National Park
P.O. Box 1029
Kotzebue, AK 99752
Headquarter Phone: 907-442-3890
Fax Number: 907-442-8316

Lake Clark National Park
4230 University Drive, Suite 311
Anchorage, AK 99508
Headquarter Phone: 907-271-3751
Fax Number: 907-271-3707

Lassen Volcanic National Park
P.O. Box 100
Mineral, CA 96063
Headquarter Phone: 916-595-4444
Fax Number: 916-595-3262

Mammoth Cave National Park
Mammoth Cave, KY 42259
Headquarter Phone: 502-758-2251
Fax Number: 502-758-2349

Mesa Verde National Park
P.O. Box 8
Mesa Verde National Park, CO 81330
Headquarter Phone: 970-529-4465
Fax Number: 970-529-4498

Mount Rainier National Park
Tahoma Woods, Star Route
Ashford, WA 98304-9751
Headquarter Phone: 360-569-2211
Fax Number: 360-569-2170

North Cascades National Park
2105 State Route 20
Sedro Woolley, WA 98284-9314
Headquarter Phone: 360-856-5700
Fax Number: 360-856-1934

Olympic National Park
600 East Park Avenue
Port Angeles, WA 98362-6798
Headquarter Phone: 360-452-4501
Fax Number: 360-452-0335

Petrified Forest National Park
Box 2217
Petrified Forest, AZ 86028
Headquarter Phone: 520-524-6228
Fax Number: 520-524-3567

Redwood National Park
1111 Second Street
Crescent City, CA 95531
Headquarter Phone: 707-464-6101
Fax Number: 707-464-1812

Rocky Mountain National Park
Estes Park, CO 80517-8397
Headquarter Phone: 970-586-1399
Fax Number: 970-586-1310

Saguaro National Park
3693 South Old Spanish Trail
Tucson, AZ 85730-5601
Headquarter Phone: 520-733-5153
Fax Number: 520-733-6681

Sequoia National Park
Three Rivers, CA 93271
Headquarter Phone: 209-565-3341
Fax Number: 209-565-3730

Shenandoah National Park
Route 4 Box 348
Luray, VA 22835
Headquarter Phone: 540-999-3500
Fax Number: 540-999-3601

Theodore Roosevelt National Park
315 Second Avenue
P.O. Box 7
Medora, ND 58645-0007
Headquarter Phone: 701-623-4466
Fax Number: 701-623-4840

Voyageurs National Park
3131 Highway 53
International Falls, MN 56649-8904
Headquarter Phone: 218-283-9821
Fax Number: 218-285-7407

Wind Cave National Park
RR #1, Box 190
Hot Springs, SD 57747-9430
Headquarter Phone: 605-745-4600
Fax Number: 605-745-4207

Wrangell-St Elias National Park
P.O. Box 439
Mile 105.5 Old Richardson Hwy.
Copper Center, AK 99573
Headquarter Phone: 907-822-5234
Fax Number: 907-822-7216

Yellowstone National Park
P.O. Box 168
Yellowstone, WY 82190
Headquarter Phone: 307-344-7381
Fax Number: 307-344-2005

Yosemite National Park
P.O. Box 577
Yosemite, CA 95389
Headquarter Phone: 209-372-0201
Fax Number: 209-372-0220

Zion National Park
Springdale, UT 84767-1099
Headquarter Phone: 801-772-3256
Fax Number: 801-772-3426

Working Room

For The Business Traveler

Our Taking Care of Business Suites® give you plenty of *room* to work in one place, then stretch out and get away from it, in another.

Your TCB Suite® is furnished with everything you need to work comfortably ... from oversized executive desk, ergonomic chair, two-line dataport speaker phones ... right down to basic office supplies. You'll even find refreshments in your fully equipped kitchen. And, it all comes in a very spacious suite, because you deserve a lot more than just a space to work in.

Great value, spacious TCB Suites, a free bountiful breakfast buffet and room for recreation are just four reasons why AmeriSuites is preferred so often by business travelers.

AMERISUITES®

AMERICA'S AFFORDABLE ALL-SUITE HOTELS

1-800-833-1516

Airline Access Code: AJ www.amerisuites.com

© 1998 Prime Hospitality Corp.

At Ramada, You Can Expect

A UNIFIED COMMITMENT TO

Locations throughout OHIO.

Whether it's business or pleasure, Ramada will make your stay in "The Buckeye" state more comfortable. At Ramada, you can always expect a clean comfortable room, friendly service and great rates. And when it comes to convenient Ohio locations, Ramada is right on the money, too. So on your next visit to Ohio, put yourself in a more comfortable state, at Ramada.

expect my personal best RAMADA

LIMITEDS • INNS • PLAZA HOTELS

FOR RESERVATIONS, CALL
1.800.2.RAMADA
OR YOUR TRAVEL AGENT
LPCT
www.ramada.com

PARTICIPATING OHIO LOCATIONS

Ramada Limited (Mansfield area)
Bellville

Ramada Inn - Airport
Cleveland

Ramada Inn - University
Columbus

Ramada Inn - West
Columbus

Ramada Inn
Middletown

Ramada Inn - Hocking Valley
Nelsonville

Ramada Inn
Portsmouth

Ramada Limited
Springfield

Ramada Limited (Dover area)
Strasburg

Ramada Limited (Akron area)
Wadsworth

Ramada Inn
Youngstown

Our Personal Best Hospitality...

PROVIDE OUR BEST SERVICE!

Locations throughout TENNESSEE & KENTUCKY.

All the warmth of real Southern hospitality is waiting for you at our many convenient Ramada locations in Kentucky and Tennessee. Drive through "The Blue Grass State's" sprawling horse farms or hike an Appalachian Mountain trail in "The Volunteer State". Then spend the night in comfort at Ramada, where clean comfortable rooms, friendly service and affordable rates are always the order of the day.

expect my personal best RAMADA

LIMITEDS • INNS • PLAZA HOTELS

FOR RESERVATIONS, CALL
1.800.2.RAMADA
OR YOUR TRAVEL AGENT
LPCT
www.ramada.com

PARTICIPATING LOCATIONS

TENNESSEE

Ramada Inn - Airport (Knoxville area) Alcoa

Ramada Limited Athens

Ramada Limited Chattanooga (Airport)

Ramada Inn Chattanooga (Downtown)

Ramada Inn - Riverview Clarksville

Ramada Limited Suites Cookeville

Ramada Inn Crossville

Ramada Limited Franklin

Ramada Inn Gatlinburg

Ramada Limited - Downtown Gatlinburg

Ramada Limited - Airport East (Nashville area) Hermitage

Ramada Inn Kingsport

Ramada Limited Suites Knoxville

Ramada Limited (Knoxville area) Lenoir City

Ramada Inn - Airport Memphis

Ramada Inn & Conference Center Morristown

Ramada Inn - Airport (Spence Lane) Nashville

Ramada Inn & Suites (Opryland/Airport) Nashville

Ramada Inn - Governors House Nashville

Ramada Limited - Downtown Nashville

Ramada Inn - Southeast Nashville

Ramada Inn & Suites Oakridge

KENTUCKY

Ramada Limited Bardstown

Ramada Inn Bowling Green

Ramada Limited Elizabethtown

Ramada Inn Fort Wright (Cincinatti area)

Ramada Limited Franklin

Ramada Inn (Calvert City area) Gilbertsville

Ramada Plaza Louisville

Ramada Inn Maysville

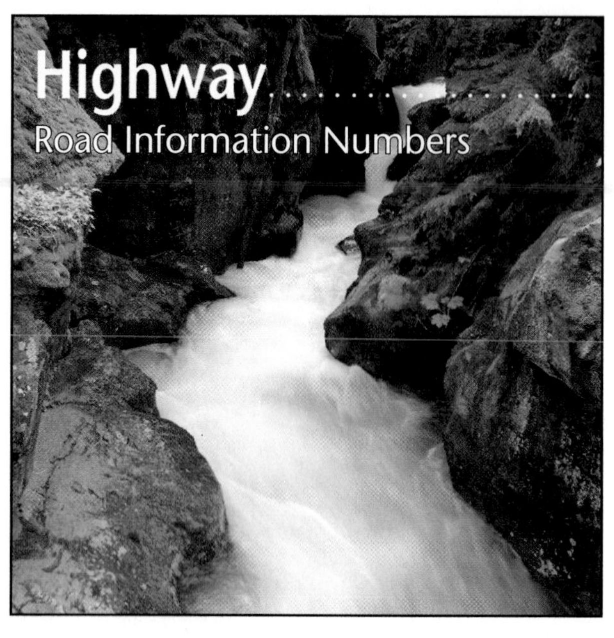

State	Number	Notes
AL	334-242-4378	State Trooper
AK	907-465-1779	
AZ	602-255-7011	
AR	501-569-2374	
CA	213-628-7623	Southern
	916-445-7623	Northern
CO	303-639-1234	
CT	860-594-2650	
DE	302-739-4313	
FL	941-338-2341	Southwest
	904-752-3300	Northeast
	904-638-0250	Panhandle
	954-777-4090	Central
	305-470-5349	Dade & Monroe
	727-975-6000	Tampa Bay
	954-583-3111	Turnpikes
GA	404-656-5276	
ID	208-336-6600	
IL	847-705-4650	
	800-452-IDOT	
IN	317-232-8300	
IA	515-288-1047	
KS	785-291-3000	
KY	502-564-5358	Weather
	800-459-7623	
LA	504-942-8356	
ME	207-287-3427	
MD	410-275-2263	In-state calls
MA	800-828-9104	Turnpike
	617-374-1234	
MI	800-337-1334	
MN	800-542-0220	
MS	601-987-1212	
MO	573-751-1000	Central
	314-340-4000	Eastern
	816-524-1407	Western
MT	800-332-6171	
NE	402-471-4533	
NV	702-793-1313	Northern
	702-486-3116	Southern
NH	603-271-6900	
NJ	609-292-2121	D.O.T.
	609-866-4940	Southern
	973-770-5025	Northern
	732-308-4074	Central
NM	505-827-9126	State Trooper
	800-432-4269	
NY	800-THRUWAY	
NC	919-549-5100	Category 7623 (recording)
ND	701-328-7623	
OH	614-466-2660	Highway Patrol
OK	405-425-2385	Construction & weather
OR	541-889-3999	
PA	717-939-9871	Turnpike
RI	401-444-1000	State Trooper
SC	803-737-1030	Highway Patrol
SD	605-773-3536	
	605-367-5707	Recording
TN	800-858-6349	Statewide
	423-594-9136	Knoxville
	615-741-2060	Nashville
	901-543-6256	Memphis
TX	800-452-9292	
UT	801-964-6000	
VT	802-828-2648	
	800-ICY-ROAD	Winter (in-state)
VA	800-367-ROAD	
WA	206-368-4499	
WI	800-ROAD-WIS	In-state
	800-762-3947	Madison
WV	304-558-2889	Winter
WY	307-772-0824	

Inns • Suites

It's more than a room. It's Comfort℠

You always enjoy extra amenities when you stay at Comfort Inn & Comfort Suites. Like our free breakfast to help you start the day off right.

1-800-228-5150

In a class by itself.℠

With low rates, a 100% satisfaction guarantee and state-of-the-art rooms, it's no wonder Sleep Inn is rated among the best hotels for satisfaction, service and value.*

1-800-SLEEP-INN

Our rates are low, not our standards.℠

An affordable hotel room is great, but only if it's clean. At Econo Lodge, our rooms are inexpensive, but we never cut corners.

1-800-55-ECONO

Save your money. Stay at Rodeway℠

You've worked hard to get where you are, so pull over and stay in a hotel that won't charge you a lot: Rodeway Inn.

1-800-228-2000

Inns • Hotels • Suites

How to run a hotel.℠

Free local calls and in-room coffee make Quality the perfect place for today's traveler. For over 50 years, Quality has been making everything just right for their guests.

1-800-228-5151

Inns • Hotels • Resorts

Upgrade your room, not your rate.℠

At Clarion, you'll find everything you expect at an upscale hotel. Well, everything except the high rates.

1-800-CLARION

MainStay Suites

Stay longer for less.℠

The reasonably-priced option for travelers who are looking for a comfortable extended-stay hotel. A great place for visits that last a night, a week, or more.

1-800-660-MAIN

If you're looking for great lodging throughout the U.S., all signs point to our hotels. For reservations, call the toll-free number or contact your travel agent.

**Source: D.K. Shifflet & Associates Ltd. Performance/Index, March 1995 - March 1997 transactions, among major mid and economy hotel chains.*

Ramada®—wherever you go.

Ramada Limited Metairie, LA

RAMADA LIMITED

Ramada Limited locations offer the best of Ramada for guests who don't need a restaurant or lounge in their hotel. They can count on the outstanding service of Ramada at a great value, which includes:

- Executive Continental breakfast buffet
- attractive accommodations
- meeting space at several locations
- often a swimming pool

Ramada Inn Safford, AZ

RAMADA INN

Ramada Inn locations are an American favorite, providing travelers with the high-quality, full-service accommodations that they need. Your clients can expect:

- full-service restaurants
- lounges
- swimming pools
- comfortable guest rooms
- a friendly staff

Ramada Plaza Hotel Fargo, ND

RAMADA PLAZA HOTEL

Ramada Plaza Hotel locations are our premier locations, designed for the traveler who expects a little more, including:

- elegant contemporary decor
- fine restaurants and room service
- swimming pools
- fitness facilities
- complete business centers at most locations

Ramada has over 950 hotels nationwide. So wherever your travel plans take you, chances are there's a Ramada location nearby with everything you need. Book Ramada today.

RAMADA LIMITEDS • INNS • PLAZA HOTELS

FOR RESERVATIONS, CALL
1.800.2.RAMADA
OR YOUR TRAVEL AGENT
www.ramada.com

DAYS INN®

No matter where life's road takes you, chances are there's a Days Inn hotel nearby. In fact, with 1,800 locations you're sure to find a clean, comfortable room at a great value. Days Inns offer special travel programs like September Days Club® for seniors and the Inn-Credible Card Plus® club for business travelers. And try one of our Days Business Place℠ hotels featuring Days Work Zone℠ rooms which include a large work desk, in-room coffee, data ports and even a snack pack for every night you stay. So plan your next trip with Days Inn. For reservations, call your travel agent or **1-800-DAYS INN.**

©1998, Days Inns of America, Inc.

www.daysinn.com

Clean and Friendly!

With more than 1,700 Super 8 Motel locations throughout North America, you're sure to find one offering affordable, clean *and* friendly lodging accommodations near wherever your travels take you. **Don't forget to ask about our V.I.P. Club – you can start saving 10% on all your visits!**

*Life's great at Super 8.*SM

For reservations, call toll-free **1-800-800-8000**

www.super8.com

Each Super 8 Motel is independently owned and operated.

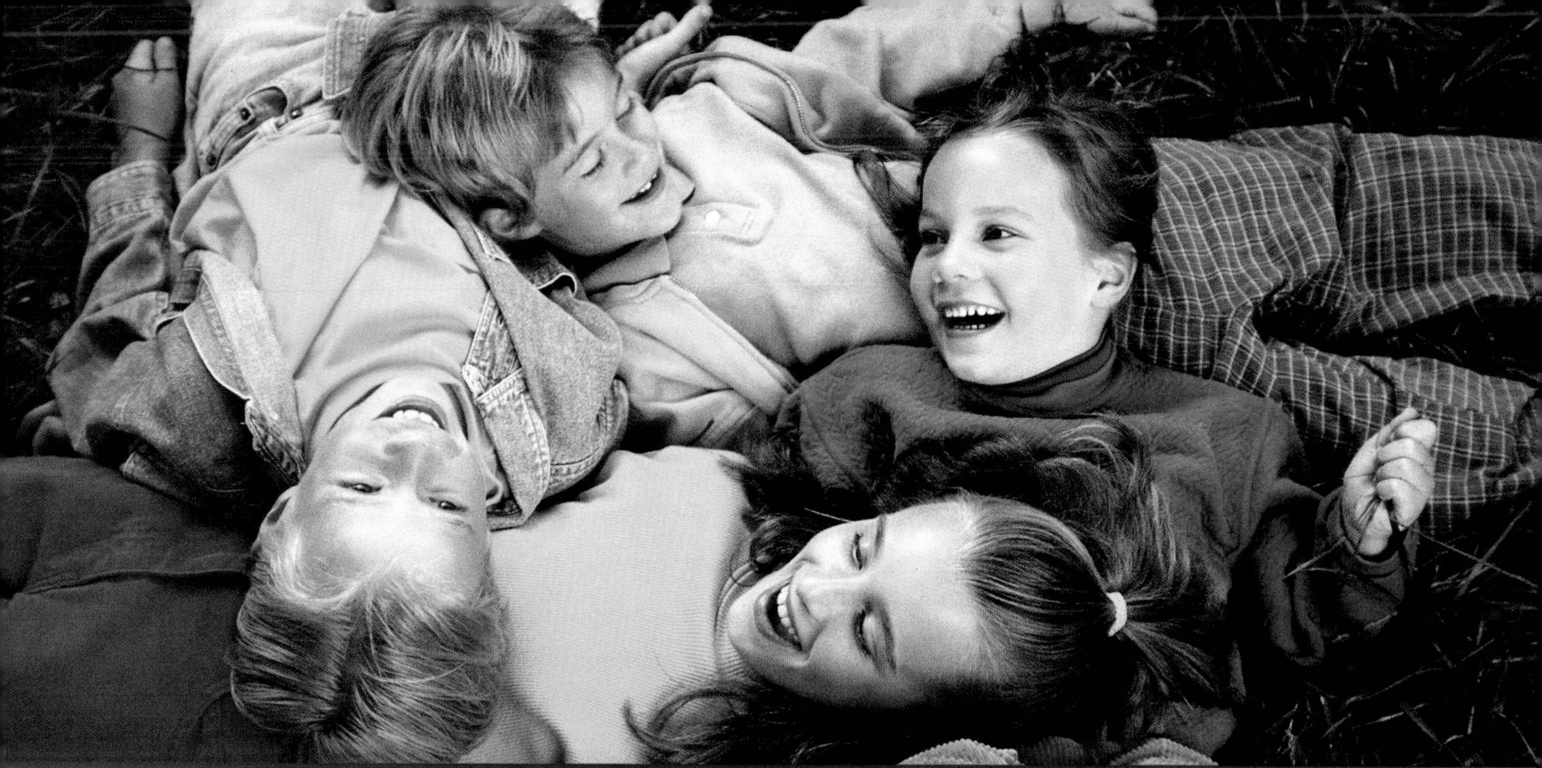

It's easy to feel at home when your kids stay free.

Discover a new world of comfort at today's Howard Johnson.® You'll have a clean, comfy room at a very friendly price. And you'll enjoy the good feeling that comes with staying with a trusted friend. Plus, seniors get discounts and kids stay free.*

1-800-I-GO-HOJO® or your travel agent or **www.hojo.com**

*Children 17 and under stay free in their parent's room with existing bedding.
©1998 Howard Johnson International, Inc. All rights reserved. Hotels are independently owned and operated.

PLAZA

HOTEL

INN

EXPRESS INN

Every amenity. *Absolutely* free. *Everywhere* we are.

That's Wingate Inn®.

Finally, a hotel chain that offers all the essential amenities necessary to wash away the stress of life on the road. All Wingate Inn® hotels are newly constructed and offer all-inclusive amenities, like a fitness room with whirlpool, in-room cordless phones and an expanded continental breakfast—at rates lower than you might expect.

At every Wingate Inn hotel you'll find:

Complimentary:

- expanded continental breakfast
- local calls and long-distance access
- fitness room with whirlpool
- 24-hour business center with fax, copier and printer

Plus Standard In-Room Amenities Like:

- two-line speakerphone with data port, conference call and voice mail capabilities
- coffee maker, iron, ironing board and safe
- 900 megahertz cordless phone
- comfortable, well-lighted work space

And:

- boardroom and meeting rooms
- automated check-in and check-out

Satisfaction *guaranteed!*

So get off the road and check in to a Wingate Inn hotel. You'll see why we're built for the road-weary traveler.

BUILT FOR BUSINESS®

For Reservations, Contact Your Travel Professional Or Call

1.800.228.1000

www.wingateinns.com

©1998 Wingate Inns International, Inc.

Travelodge® Makes Life On The Road Easier To Bear.

When you're on the road and need a comfortable place to rest your heels (and wheels) for the night, follow Sleepy Bear® into the nearest Travelodge® location. We start with a great room at an affordable rate, then add special extras* like: **Free fresh-brewed in-room coffee**, a **free weekday lobby newspaper**, **no long distance access charges**, and **free cable TV channels** including **movies, news and sports**. Plus, with our Travelodge Miles℠ Program** you can earn free night stays,† airline frequent flyer miles, or your choice of dozens of other guest rewards like watches, cameras, luggage and more. With all that, it's easy to see why so many travelers like to turn in with us. Call for reservations today.

TRAVELODGE MILES

The Guest Rewards Program

For reservations at our more than 500 locations throughout North America call:

1-800-578-7878

www.travelodge.com

*Special amenities available only at Travelodge® locations; not available at Thriftlodge® locations. Weekday newspaper available while supplies last. **To earn Travelodge Miles℠ you must pay Regular Rate, Travelodge Miles Gold Member Rate or higher. One Travelodge Mile will be awarded for each lodging dollar spent, not for dollars spent on incidentals or taxes. The Travelodge Miles program is subject to change or discontinuation without notice. Rewards vary by country of residence; see Official Brochure for details. †Free Night Certificate valid at any participating Travelodge or Thriftlodge location throughout North America. Sleepy Bear® is a registered trade-mark in Canada of Travelodge Hotels, Inc. Sleepy Bear is a registered service mark in the United States of TM Acquisition Corp., an affiliate of Travelodge Hotels, Inc. ©1998 Travelodge Hotels, Inc.

AT KNIGHTS INN

YOU'RE THE EXIT AUTHORITY.

COAST-TO-COAST, OVER 6400 KNIGHTS INN EMPLOYEES LET YOU BE THE AUTHORITY ON WHAT IT MEANS TO BE ***JUST RIGHT.*** FROM THE MINUTE WE ***WELCOME*** YOU INTO OUR DOORS, TO WHEN YOU CHECK OUT WITH OUR ***TRUE BUDGET RATES,*** KNIGHTS DELIVERS THE RESPONSIVE SERVICE THAT MAKES EVERY STAY COMFORTABLE, CONVIENENT...***JUST RIGHT.***

EVERY KNIGHT. JUST RIGHT.℠

1-800-THE KNIGHTS
(800-843-5644)
www.knightsinn.com

EVERY KNIGHT. JUST RIGHT.℠

OVER 250 LOCATIONS!

Villager® Value

There's more in it for you

At Villager Lodge our guests find all the comforts of a "Home on the Road." Villager Lodge rooms feature mini-kitchenettes and cable TV with a premium movie channel. With free hot coffee waiting in the lobby, there really is more in it for you! And we know how to take care of guests who stay a day, a week or longer by offering a choice of a convienent daily rate or an economical extended stay rate. So on your next trip, stay with us and see the value of Villager Lodge!

For accommodations, call 1-800-328-STAY or your travel professional.

Protect Your Good Times.

Flying J and Progressive Insurance Company have teamed up to offer the highway hospitality you deserve with the top-quality insurance coverage you need. Combining Flying J's state-of-the-art travel facilities and the affordable, innovative products of Progressive Insurance, we have your recreational and travel needs covered. With products for automobiles, recreational vehicles, motorcycles and personal watercraft, we have what you need to protect your good times.

Start saving today by calling 1-800-779-4760 for a no-hassle, no-obligation insurance quote.

For immediate savings on gasoline and many other worthwhile benefits, please pick-up an application for the Real Value Club Card or Rewards Program Card. Get details while visiting any Flying J facility, calling (435) 734-6427

AREA CODES U.S. & CANADA

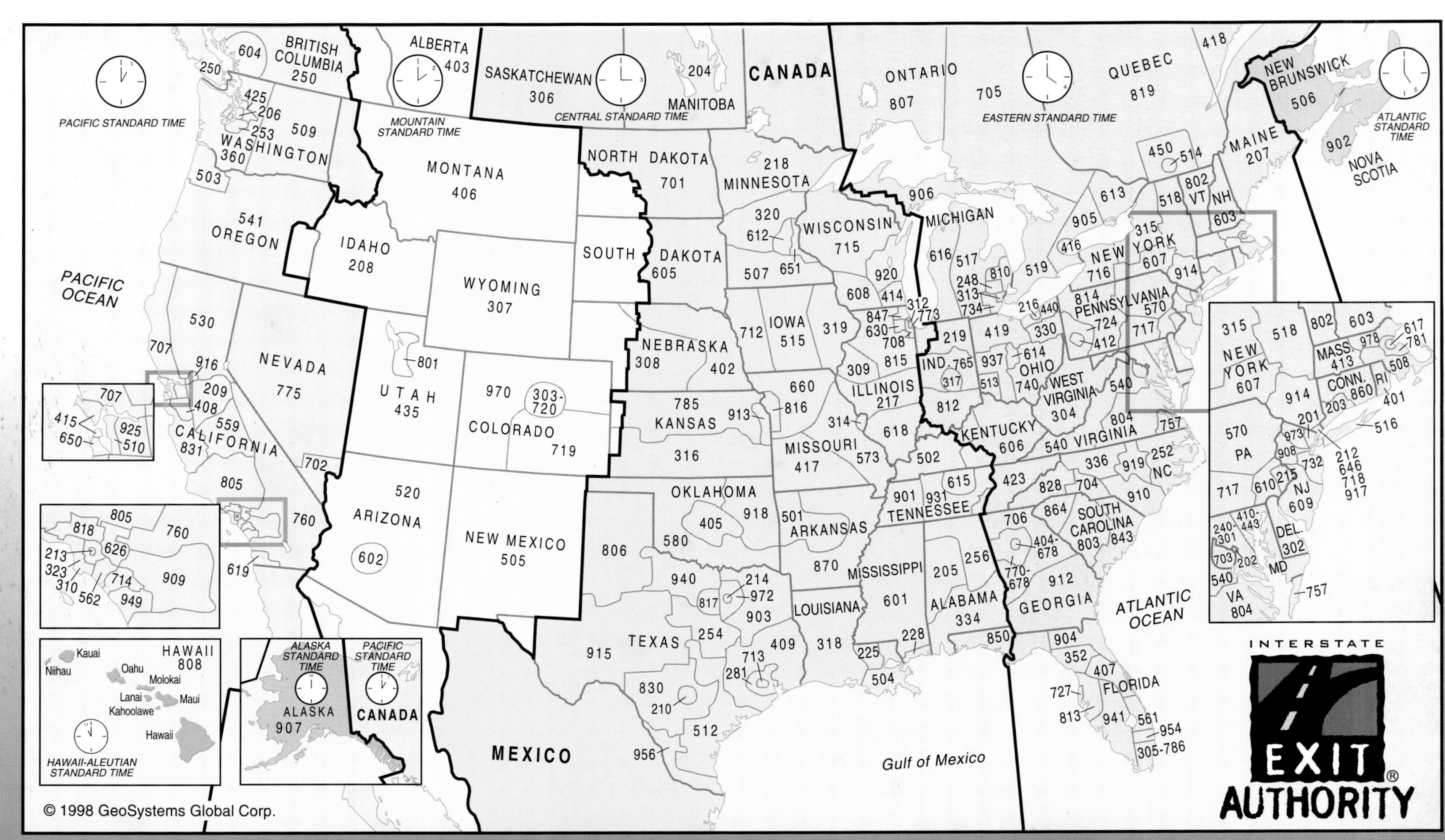

© 1998 GeoSystems Global Corp.

UNITED STATES

UNITED STATES

The Perfect Gift for your Special Traveler!

Three ways to give someone a unique gift which saves time and money all year long!

1. Pick up a copy at bookstores, AAA locations or RV Dealerships for only $21.95 or let us deliver one for you!
2. Call 1-800-494-5566 ext. 17 with your credit card number.
3. Clip or photocopy this order form and mail with payment to Interstate America.

Bill To:
Name ______
Address ______
City ______ State ______ Zip ______
Phone ______
Shipping: ☐ Regular ☐ Priority
☐ Enclosed is my check for $21.95 ($23.95 for priority shipping) payable to Interstate America.
☐ Bill my credit card ☐ MC ☐ VISA
Card # ______ Exp. date: ______
Signature ______

Deliver to: ☐ Same Address ☐ Address Below
Name ______
Address ______
City ______ State ______ Zip ______
Phone ______
Gift Message: ______

Mail to: Interstate America • Dept. 17 • 5695G Oakbrook Parkway • Norcross, GA 30093

EXIT		FLORIDA
		Begin I-4

↓FLORIDA

1 FL 585, 22nd Street, 21st Street
- **Gas** N: BP[*]
  - S: Amoco[*, 24]
- **Food** S: Burger King, Hardee's
- **ATM** N: BP
  - S: Amoco
- **Other** S: **Aquarium**, Tourist Info., **Ybor City Historic District Museum**

2 **(1)** FL 569, 40th Street
- **FStop** N: **Citgo**[*, D], **Texaco**[*]
- **Food** N: Budget Inn
- **Lodg** N: Budget Inn
- **ATM** N: **Citgo, Texaco**

3 **(2)** U.S. 41, 50th Street, Columbus Dr.
- **FStop** S: **Speedway**[*, LP], **United 500**[*]
- **Gas** N: Texaco[*, D]
  - S: Exxon[*, D, CW]
- **Food** N: Subway (Texaco), Texaco
  - S: Brocato's Sandwich Shop, Burger King[PLAY], Checker's, Church's Chicken, Days Inn (Tourist Info), Eggroll King Chinese, KFC, McDonald's, Pizza Hut, Taco Bell, Wendy's
- **Lodg** N: **EconoLodge**, La Quinta Inn, Milner Hotel, Tampa 8 Inn, Tropicana Inn
  - S: Days Inn (Tourist Info)
- **ATM** N: Texaco
  - S: **Speedway**
- **Other** S: **Cash & Karry, Eckerd Drugs**[RX], Laundromat

4 **(5)** FL 574, Martin Luther King Jr. Blvd
- **Food** N: McDonald's
  - S: Wendy's
- **Lodg** S: **Economy Inns of America**
- **TServ** S: **Fox Craft Trailers, Great Dane Trailers, Kenworth**

5 **(6)** Orient Road (Eastbound, Reaccess Westbound Only)
- **Gas** N: Citgo[*, CW]
- **Food** N: My's Chinese Vietnamese Restaurant
- **Lodg** N: Four Points Hotel Sheraton
- **Other** N: Seminole Indian Casino[24]
  - S: Florida State Fair

6AB **(7)** U.S. 92 E, to U.S. 301 N, Zephyrhills -6B, Riverview

6C **(8)** U.S. 92 West, Hillsborough Ave, Vandenberg Airport (Westbound, Reaccess Eastbound Only)
- **Food** N: Sky Box Sports Cafe
- **Lodg** N: Cypress Landing Motel, Four Points Hotel Sheraton
- **TServ** N: **United 500 (Cummings)**
- **RVCamp** N: **Beaudry's RV & Travel Trailer Service**
  - S: **Holiday RV (see our ad this page)**

7 **(9)** Junction I-75, Ocala, Naples

8 **(10)** CR 579, Mango, Thonotosassa
- **FStop** S: **Texaco**[*, D]
- **Food** N: **Cracker Barrel**
  - S: Denny's (Master's Inn), Hardee's, **Master's Inn**, Wendy's
- **Lodg** S: **Master's Inn**
- **AServ** S: Consolidated Auto
- **RVCamp** N: **Camping World (see our ad this page) LazyDays RV Resort, LazyDays RV Supercenter Sales & Service**
- **ATM** S: **Texaco**

9 **(14)** McIntosh Road, Dover
- **Gas** N: Amoco
  - S: Racetrac[*]
- **Food** S: Burger King[PLAY], McDonald's
- **AServ** N: Amoco
- **RVCamp** S: **KOA-Tampa East (.35 Miles), Tampa East Green Acres Campground (.5 Miles), Tampa East Green Acres RV Travel Park (.1 Miles)**
- **ATM** S: Racetrac
- **Other** S: **Bates RV Exchange**

10 **(17)** Branch Forbes Road
- **FStop** N: **Spur**[*]
- **Gas** N: Shell[*] (see our ad this page)
- **ATM** N: Shell

(18) **Weigh Station (Eastbound)**

(18) **Weigh Station (Westbound)**

11 **(19)** Thonotosassa Road, Plant City
- **Gas** N: Amoco[*]
  - S: Racetrac[*]
- **Food** S: Buddy Freddy's Southern Family Dining, McDonald's[PLAY], Sonny's BBQ

13 **(21)** FL. 39, Zephyrhills, Plant City
- **FStop** N: **Texaco**[*]
- **Gas** S: Amoco[*, D], Shell[*] (see our ad this page)
- **Food** N: **Texaco**
  - S: 1776 Restaurant (Ramada Inn), **Days Inn, Ramada Inn**
- **Lodg** S: **Days Inn (see our ad this page)**,

1-800-RV-FOR-FUN
Tampa, FL ¥ I-4 ¥ Exit 6C

CAMPING WORLD
Exit 8
6102 Lazy Days Blvd. • Seffner, FL
1-800-331-3638
1438

The universal sign for the world's best-selling gasoline.
1651
ATM
Easy Access
Shell
Open 24 Hours
Clean Restrooms
Fast, Courteous Service
Air & Water
Convenience Store
Fresh Hot Coffee
All Major Credit Cards
813-759-6810
FLORIDA ▪ I-4 ▪ EXIT 10

The universal sign for the world's best-selling gasoline.
1652
Fresh Hot Coffee
Easy Access

Shell
Gasoline Only
Clean Restrooms
Fast, Courteous Service
Convenience Store
All Major Credit Cards
813-759-1983
FLORIDA ▪ I-4 ▪ EXIT 13

Restaurant on Premises
Outdoor Pool
Pets Allowed
Handicapped Accessible Available
Golf within 10 Minutes
Truck/RV/Bus Parking
Coin Laundry on Premises
301 S. FRONTAGE RD
1163
813-752-0570• Plant City, FL
FLORIDA ▪ I-4 ▪ EXIT 13

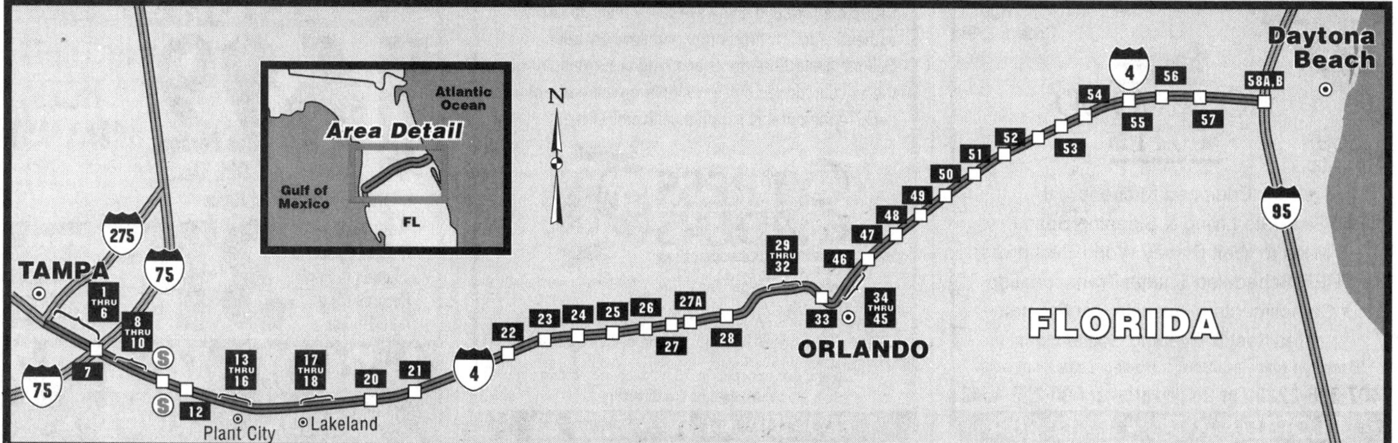

Bold red print shows RV & Bus parking available or nearby

EXIT FLORIDA

RAMADA INN®
2011 N. Wheeler St.
Plant City, FL
Restaurant & Lounge
(on Premises)
Pool • Room Service
Bus & RV Parking
Discount Tickets
(to Major Attractions)
Convention Center
(up to 600)
813-752-3141
1577
FLORIDA • I-4 • EXIT 13

Ramada Inn
(see our ad this page)

13B **(21)** Alexander Street (Westbound, Reaccess Eastbound Only)
- Med S: + Hospital

14 **(23)** Plant City, Park Road
- Gas S: Shell(*), Texaco(*, D)
- Food N: Chancy's Catfish Shack
  S: Arby's, Blimpie Sub & Salads (Texaco), Burger King, Denny's, Popeye's Chicken, Shell, Subway (Shell), Taco Bell Express (Shell), Texaco
- Lodg S: Comfort Inn
- RVCamp S: Strawberry RV Parts, Sales, & Service(LP)
- ATM S: Shell, Texaco

15 **(26)** County Line Road
- Gas S: Shell(*)
- Other S: Sun N Fun Aviation Center

16 **(28)** U.S. 92, Lakeland, Memorial Blvd. (Eastbound, Reaccess Westbound Only)

17 **(31)** FL. 539, Kathleen, Lakeland
- Other S: Munn Park Historic District

18 **(32)** U.S. 98, Lakeland
- FStop S: Citgo(*)
- Gas N: Chevron(*, D, CW), Texaco(*)
  S: Amoco(CW, 24), Coastal(*, D), Racetrac(*, 24)
- Food N: Bennigan's, Blimpie's Subs (Texaco), Chuck E Cheese's Pizza, Don Pablo's Mexican, Hooters (Lakeland Motor Lodge), IHOP (Royalty Inn), KFC, Lakeland Motor Lodge, Lone Star Steakhouse, McDonald's(PLAY), Red Lobster, Royalty Inn, SHONEY'S Shoney's, Steak & Shake(24), Texaco
  S: Bob Evan's Restaurant, Burger King(PLAY), Citgo, Denny's, Long John Silver, Ramada, Roadhouse Grill, Swan Terrace Restaurant (Ramada), Wendy's

Kissimmee, FLORIDA
1646
Code: S/EAP

HOMEWOOD SUITES®
$69* plus tax
• Fully Equipped Kitchens with Separate Living & Sleeping Space
• 1.5 Miles to Walt Disney World Resort with FREE Scheduled Shuttle Transportation
• Complimentary Upscale Continental Breakfast & Evening Social Hour
*Based on space availability. Black-out dates may apply
407-396-2229 For Reservations: 800-255-4543
FLORIDA • I-4 • EXIT 25A

EXIT FLORIDA

- Lodg N: La Quinta Inn, Lakeland Motor Lodge, Royalty Inn, Wellesley Inn & Suites
  S: Best Western, Crossroads Motor Lodge, Motel 6, Ramada
- AServ N: Montgomery Ward Auto Express
  S: Amoco(24)
- RVCamp N: Buddy Gregg Motor Homes, Inc. (.2 Miles), Tiki Village Resort (.25 Miles)
- ATM N: Texaco
  S: Coastal, National Cash Advance
- Other N: Lakeland Square Mall, Lens Crafters, Toys R Us, Wal-Mart(RX)
  S: Winn Dixie Supermarket(RX)

19 **(34)** FL. 33, to Lakeland.
- FStop S: Amoco(*, LP, K)
- Gas N: Exxon(*, CW)
- Food N: Cracker Barrel
  S: Amoco, Waffle House
- Lodg N: Budgetel Inn, Quality Inn
- RVCamp N: Lakeland RV Resorts (1.25 Miles)
- Med S: + Hospital
- ATM N: Exxon
  S: First Federal Florida

(34) Rest Area (Eastbound)

35 Rest Area (Westbound)

20 **(38)** FL. 33, USA International Speedway

21 **(44)** FL. 559, Auburndale, Polk City
- TStop S: Dixie Boy Fuel Center(*, SCALES)
- Gas S: Amoco(*)
- Food S: Dixie Boy Fuel Center
- RVCamp N: LeLynn RV Resort
- ATM S: Dixie Boy Fuel Center

(46) Rest Area (RR, HF, Phones, Picnic; Eastbound)

1811
KIDS FREE

FAMILY OF FOUR SAVES $49.40*
Each single day adult ticket purchaser may bring in one youth (ages 6-17) FREE. Kids five and under always FREE.
World Famous Botanical Garden
Ski Xtreme - Thrilling Water Ski Show
Wings of Wonder, ®The Butterfly Conservatory
New Animal Habits In Nature's Way
Exciting Live Shows
NEW AT CYPRESS GARDENS!
Cruise our lake and enjoy a leisurely meal aboard our authentic turn of the century paddlewheel boat. Delight in exquisite decor and natural surroundings in the air conditioned dining room or on the outdoor deck. A memorable experience. Nominal fee.

www.cypressgardens.com
Located off U.S.27, just 22 miles south of I-4 between Tampa & Orlando. For information call 941-324-2111
*Clip and use our coupon from the coupon section in back pages of this directory
FLORIDA • I-4W • EXIT 23

EXIT FLORIDA

(47) Rest Area (RR, HF, Phones, Picnic; Westbound)

22 **(48)** CR. 557, Lake Alfred, Winter Haven
- Gas S: BP(*, D)
- ATM S: BP

CAMPING WORLD®
Exit 25A
5175 W. Irlo Bronson Mem. Pkwy. • Kissimmee, FL
1-800-327-9153
1426

HAMPTON INN MAINGATE
$49 Rates from

Complimentary Deluxe Continental Breakfast
Outdoor Pool • Guest Laundry
Free Local Calls • Cable TV with Free HBO
1645
Code:S/EAP
407-396-8484
Based on Space Availability • Advance Reservation Required
Must Be Booked Through Hotel Directly
192 to Parkway Blvd. Turn left at the end of Parkway.
FLORIDA • I-4 • EXIT 25A

RAMADA®
1778
4559 W. HWY. 192
5 MILES TO WALT DISNEY WORLD® RESORT
15-20 Miles to Sea World, Universal Studios, Island of Adventure, Wet 'n Wild
• Large Pool & Sundeck
• Electronic Door Locks
• Guest Laundry
• Free Cable, HBO 1, 2 & 3 and Disney Channel
• Playground, BBQ Pits, Picnic Tables
Newly Renovated
BED & BREAKFAST
16.99* *Per Person, Dbl. Occ.
INCLUDES HOT BREAKFAST BUFFET
Beverage Purchase Required, Plus Tax
*Low Season Limited Space Weekends & Peak Periods May Be Higher
31.95* 1-4 People
Room Only No Breakfast
1-800-544-5712
FLORIDA • I-4 • EXIT 25A

EXIT FLORIDA

MAIN GATE HAWAIIAN

Econo Lodge
Main Gate Hawaiian

I-4 • Exit 25-B
Kissimee, FL
1-800-365-6935

• Free Scheduled Shuttle to Disney Theme Parks
• Kids Eat Free • Oasis Pool Bar & Grill
• Lounge • Free Parking
• 1 Mile from Wild World of Sports Complex
• Game Room/Arcade
• Tropical Outdoor Pool

1104

FLORIDA ▪ I-4 ▪ EXIT 25-B

RAMADA RESORT MAIN GATE

1103

RAMADA RESORT

• Disney Good Neighbor Hotel
• Free Scheduled Shuttle to Disney Theme Parks
• Sports Bar & Grill
• Kids Eat Free • Lobby Deli
• Two Heated Swimming Pools
• Exercise Room • Game Room

800-365-6935

FLORIDA ▪ I-4 ▪ EXIT 25-B

Eastgate Fountain Park

1722

407-396-1111
800-327-9179

Restaurant/Lounge on Premises
Kids Under 12 Stay & Eat Free
Outdoor Pool • Kids Pool
Lighted Tennis Courts on Premises
Jacuzzi, Basketball, Playground
Meeting/Banquet Facilities
Handicap Accessible
Interior Corridors
Coin Laundry
All Rooms Include:
Coffee Makers, Iron/Board,
Hair Dryer, Nintendo Games

TRUCK/LARGE VEHICLE PARKING

5150 West U.S. 192
Kissimmee, FL 34746

FLORIDA ▪ I-4 ▪ EXIT 25A

EXIT FLORIDA

23 **(55)** U.S. 27, Haines City, Clermont

FStop **N:** Speedway[*, D]

Gas **N:** Chevron[*, 24], Citgo[*]
S: Amoco[*, D], Citgo[*], Exxon[*], Shell[*], Texaco[*, D]

Food **N:** Burger King, McDonald's, New York Pizza World, SHONEY'S, Shoney's, Waffle House, Wendy's
S: Bob Evan's Restaurant, Denny's, Hardee's, Key West Seafood Restaurant & Family Dining, Perkins Family Restaurant[24]

Lodg **N:** Comfort Inn, Florida Southgate Inn, Super 8
S: DAYS INN Days Inn, Holiday Inn, Tropicana Resort Hotel

AServ **S:** Texaco

RVCamp **S:** Deer Creek Golf 7 RV Resort, Fort Summit Camping Resort (.1 Miles), Theme World Campground[LP]

Med **S:** + Hospital

Near Disney World

800-365-6935

Holiday Inn®
Main Gate West

• Disney Good Neighbor Hotel
• Free Scheduled Shuttle to Walt Disney
• Outdoor Heated Swimming Pool
• Kiddies Pool • Video Arcade
• Full Service Restaurant
• Kids Eat Free
• Kids Suites

1105

FLORIDA ▪ I-4 ▪ EXIT 25B

Medieval Times
DINNER & TOURNAMENT

Feast on a four course medievel banquet while watching daring knights on beautiful Andalusian horses competing in medievel tournament games& jousting matches.

Call for show times & reservations:
US & Canada: 1-800-229-8300
Kissimmee: 1-407-396-1518
Orlando: 1-407-239-0214

FREE VISIT TO MEDIEVAL LIFE
with Medieval Times
Ticket Purchase

Located on Hwy 192 in Kissimmee just 4 miles east of I-4 between guide markers 14 and 15

1201

EXIT FLORIDA

ATM **N:** Chevron, Citgo, Speedway
S: Amoco, Citgo

Other **N:** 7-11 Convenience Store (Citgo)
S: 7-11 Convenience Store (Citgo), Cypress Gardens (see our ad opposite page)

24 **(58)** CR. 532, Kissimmee (Eastbound)

24CD Disney World, Kennedy Space Center, Cape Canaveral -24C, TO U.S. 192, Disney World - 24D (24 C goes South, 24D goes North)

24E FL 417N Toll, International Airport, Sanford

25AB **(64)** U.S. 192E,Celebration, Kissimmee-25A, US 192W, Disney World - 25B (North) (Access To Theme Parks)

Food **S:** Atlantic Bay Seafood, Charly's Steakhouse, Goody's Supermarket[RX], Kobe Japanese Steakhouse, Parkway Grill Restaurant, Pizza Hut (Radisson), Pizza Lover Italian, Radisson

Lodg **N:** Parkway International Vacation Adventure, Econo Lodge (see our ad this page), Ramada (see our ad this page)
S: Hampton Inn (see our ad opposite page) , Homewood Suites (see our ad opposite page) , Hyatt Hotel, Radisson, Ramda (see our ad opposite page), Holiday Inn (see our ad this page), Days Inn (see our ad this page)

RVCamp **N:** Fort Wilderness Campground Resort (Inside Walt Disney World; 1 Miles)
S: Camping World (see our ad opposite page) Tropical Palms Resort & Campground (2 Miles)

Med **S:** + Medi Clinic

Other **N:** Animal Kingdom, Disney-MGM Studios Theme Park, Epcot, Magic Kingdom, Walt Disney World Resort
S: Goody's Supermarket[RX] Medieval Times (see our ad this page)

26AB **(68)** 26A- FL 516E to South International Drive, 26B- Disney World, Epcot, Animal Kingdom (to the North)

Lodg **S:** Marriot

Other **N:** Walt Disney World Resort

27 **(70)** FL. 535, Lake Buena Vista (Continued commerce on the west side)

Gas **N:** Chevron[*, CW, 24]
S: Citgo[*], Shell[*, CW]

Food **N:** Barnie's Coffee, Burger King, Chevy's Mexican, Goodings Seafood & Bakery, Jungle Jim's Restaurant, McDonald's, Paesano's Italian Restaurant, Pebbles Restaurant, Perkins Family

Free Disney Shuttle

1130

Days Inn
Maingate West of Walt Disney World
Kissimmee, FL

407-396-1000

• Restaurant on Premises
• Kids 12 & Under Eat & Stay Free
• Outdoor Pool • Exercise Room
• Meeting/Banquet Facilities Available
• Refrigerators in Rooms
• Truck or Large Vehicle Parking
• Coin Laundry • Exterior Corridors

2.5 Miles W of Disney's Main Gate - Past mile marker 4

FLORIDA ▪ I-4 ▪ EXIT 25B

Bold red print shows RV & Bus parking available or nearby

EXIT FLORIDA

Restaurant, Red Lobster, T.G.I. Friday's, Taco Bell, Uno Pizzaria, Waffle House
S: Chick-Fil-A, Haagen Dazs Ice Cream (Vistana Resort), Jenny's Casual Eatery (Vistana Resort), Landry's Seafood[PLAY], Lone Star Steakhouse, Pizza Hut (Vistana Resort), Shell, Vistana Resort[*], Wendy's (Shell)

Lodg **N:** Days Inn, Days Inn (see our ad this page)
S: Holiday Inn, Residence Inn, Vista Way, Vistana Resort

AServ **S:** Firestone

Med **N:** ✚ **Buena Vista Walk-In Clinic**, ✚ **Centra Care (Walk-In Clinic)**

ATM **N:** **Gooding's Supermarket**[24, RX]
S: Citgo

Other **N:** **Gooding's Supermarket**[RX], Pirates Cove Miniature Golf, **Walt Disney World Resort (Access to Theme Parks)**
S: 7-11 Convenience Store (Citgo), **WalGreens Pharmacy**[24, RX]

(70) **Rest Area (RR, Phones, Picnic, Vending; Eastbound)**

(70) **Rest Area (RR, Phones, Picnic, Vending; Westbound)**

27A **(71)** Sea World , Central Florida Parkway (Eastbound, Reaccess Westbound Only)

Med **N:** ✚ **Sandlake Hospital**

Other **S:** **Sea World of Florida Marine Park**

28 **(72)** FL. 528 East Toll Rd., Cape Canaveral

Lodg **N:** AmeriSuites (see our ad this page)

29 **(528)** FL 482, Sand Lake Road

Gas **N:** Chevron[*, CW, 24]
S: Exxon[*, D], Shell[*, CW, 24] (Tourist Info), Texaco[*, D, CW]

Food **N:** Carrino's, Days Inn, **K-Mart**[RX], Lagniappe Cafe, Lakeside Restaurant & Cafeteria (Days Inn), Taste of Japan, Wendy's
S: Austin's America's Biggest Steaks, Burger King, Cafe Tu Tu Tango, Cattlemen's Restaurant, Charlie's Steakhouse, Checkers Burgers, Chili's, China Jade Buffet, Chuck E Cheese's Pizza, Clarion Hotel (Jack's Place), Days Inn, Denny's, Dunkin Donuts, East Side Mario's, Fish Bones Restaurant, Friendly's Ice Cream, Golden Corral Family Steakhouse, Haagen Dazs Ice Cream, Holiday Inn, Howard Johnson, IHOP (Days Inn), IHOP, Italianni's, King Henry's Feast, McDonald's[PLAY], Morrisons Cafeteria, Olive Garden, Omni Hotel (Everglades Restaurant), Orlando Marriot, Perkins Family Restaurant, Pizza Hut, Pizza Hut, Popeye's Chicken, Quality Inn, Ran Getsu of Tokyo, Rodeway Inn, Shogun Japanese Steak & Seafood (Rodeway Inn), SHONEY'S Shoney's, Sizzler, T.G.I. Friday's, Tony Roma's, Wild Jack's Steak & BBQ

Lodg **N:** Days Inn
S: Best Western, Clarion Hotel (Jack's Place), Country Heart Inn, Courtyard by Marriott, Days Inn, Days Inn,, Embassy Suites, Embassy Suites, Fairfield Inn, Holiday Inn, Holiday Inn Express, Howard Johnson, Howard Johnson, Inns Of America, La Quinta Inn, Los Palmas Hotel, Omni Hotel (Everglades Restaurant), Orlando Marriot, Peabody Hotel, Quality Inn, Quality Inn, Radisson, Ramada (see our ad this page), Red Roof Inn, Residence Inn, Rodeway Inn, Summer Field Suites Hotel

RVCamp **N:** **Holiday RV Superstore-Orlando**[LP] **(1 Mile) (see our ad this page)**

Med **N:** ✚ **Hospital**

ATM **N:** Chevron, First Union, NationsBank
S: Shell (Tourist Info), Texaco

Other **N:** **K-Mart**[RX], **Publix Supermarket**[RX], **Universal Studios Florida**
S: Amazing Animals, Eckerd Drugs[RX], Pirates Cove Miniature Golf, **Ripley's Believe-it-or-Not**, Tourist Info., **WalGreens Pharmacy**[RX], Wet N' Wild Water Park

30AB **(75)** FL 435 S, International Drive, FL 435N, Kirkman Rd.- 30B

Food **N:** **Cracker Barrel**, Days Inn, Denny's (Days Inn), Holiday Inn, Kenny Wallace's Motor Sports Grill, Radisson, Wendy's
S: Bill Wong's, Burger King, Denny's, Dunkin Donuts, IHOP, Indian Cuisine (), KFC, Maingate Pizza, Mobil, Passage to India, Perkins Family Restaurant, Pizza Hut, Red Lobster, Sizzler, Subway, Trey Yuen, Western Steer Family Steakhouse

Lodg **N:** Days Inn, Delta Orlando Resort, Holiday Inn (see our ad opposite page) , Orlando Studio Plus, Radisson, Ramada Limited
S: Floridian of Orlando, Gateway Inn, Hampton Inn, Holiday Inn Express (see our ad opposite page) La Suite Suites, Las Palmas, Universal Inn

ATM **S:** Shell

Other **N:** **Universal Studios Florida**
S: 7-11 Convenience Store, **Quality Outlet Center 2**, **Quality Outlet Center 1**, Skull Kingdom A Haunted Family Attraction, **WalGreens Pharmacy**[24, RX], Wet N' Wild Water Park

31 **(76)** Junction Florida Turnpike, to Miami , Wildwood (Toll)

32 **(80)** John Young Pkwy, FL 423

Gas **S:** Citgo[*], Racetrac[*], Texaco[*, D]

Food **N:** McDonald's, Sub Station
S: Citgo, IHOP

Lodg **N:** Catalina Inn
S: **Days Inn**

AServ **S:** Texaco

ATM **S:** Citgo

Other **S:** 7-11 Convenience Store (Citgo)

33AB **(80)** U.S. 441, U.S. 17, U.S. 92 (Difficult Reaccess, A goes to the south, B goes to the north)

Gas **S:** Racetrac[*]

Food **N:** China Palace
S: Checkers, **Days Inn**, Denny's, Gary's Restaurant, Ryan's Steakhouse, Wendy's

Lodg **N:** Economy Inn
S: **Days Inn**, Melody Motel

AServ **N:** B & E, Cruz Muffler Shop, F.L.M. Automotive Inc., General Tires, Mitchell's Automotive

TServ **N:** **Florida Fleet Inc.**

Other **S:** Orlando International Airport

1606
DAYS INN
12799 Apopka-Vineland Rd.
1 Mile from Downtown Disney
Restaurant & Lounge
Outdoor Pool
Free Tickets to Water Mania Park
Free Transportation to Disney Parks
In the Heart of All Major Attractions
800-224-5058
E-mail: daylbvhtl@aol.com
FLORIDA ▪ I-4 ▪ EXIT 27

34 **(81)** Michigan Street (Westbound, Reaccess Eastbound Only)

Gas **N:** Citgo[*, D, CW]

AServ **N:** Prater Radiator & Air Conditioning
S: Auto Electric & Air Condition Shop Inc.

Other **N:** Animal Hospital

35AB **(81)** Kaley Avenue

FStop **S:** **Texaco**[*, D]

Gas **S:** Mobil[*, D]

AServ **S:** Top Auto Repair

TServ **S:** **Mauldin International Truck Sales Inc. (Bobinger)**

Med **S:** ✚ **Hospital**

Other **S:** **Coin Laundry**

36 **(82)** Junction East - West Expressway Fl. 408 (Toll)

37 **(82)** Gore Street (Difficult Reaccess)

Gas **N:** Onmark[*]

TServ **S:** **Yale International Trucks**

38 **(83)** Anderson Street,Church Street Station

ATM **S:** Alliance Bank

Other **S:** City Hall

39 **(84)** South Street

40 **(84)** FL. 526, Robinson Street (Eastbound, Difficult Reaccess)

AServ **S:** Goodyear Tire & Auto, Robinson Tire & Auto Repair

ATM **S:** NationsBank

41 **(84)** U.S. 17, U.S. 92, FL 50, Colonial Dr., Emilia Street, Naval Training Center

Food **N:** Steak & Ale

Florida • Exit 28 • 407-240-3939

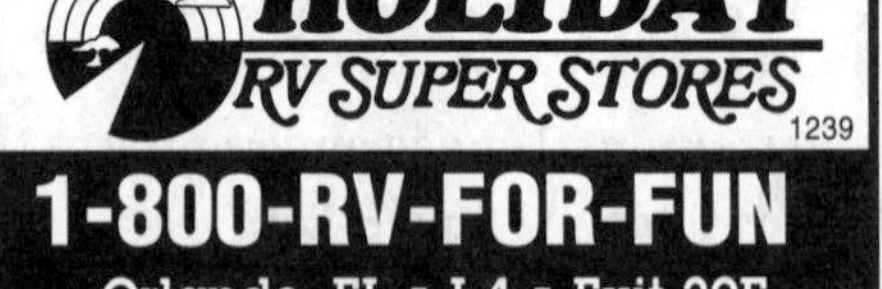

1-800-RV-FOR-FUN
Orlando, FL ▪ I-4 ▪ Exit 29E

RAMADA RESORT
1793 7400 International Dr. • Orlanda, FL
2 Outdoor Pools • Exercise Room
Restaurant/Lounge (Live Music) on Premises
Meeting/Banquet Facilities
Cable TV/HBO & Disney Channel
Free Schedule Shuttle to Disney, Universal & SeaWorld
Hair Salon on Premises
Golf/Tennis Nearby
Refrigerators in All Rooms
407-351-4600 • Toll Free Reservations: 1-800-2-RAMADA
FLORIDA ▪ I-4 ▪ EXIT 29

Bold red print shows RV & Bus parking available or nearby

EXIT FLORIDA

S: Mama B's Giant Subs, New York Deli Subs & Gyros
Lodg N: Holiday Inn, Howard Vernon Motel
S: Radisson Hotel
AServ S: BMW & Mercedes Service
ATM S: Colonial Bank

42 **(85)** Ivanhoe Blvd
Lodg S: Radisson Hotel

43 **(85)** Princeton Street, Orlando
Gas S: Shell(*), Spur(*)
Food S: Chester Fried Chicken (Spur), Spur
AServ S: Booth Auto Service, L & M Auto Repair, Rick's Import Performance, Shell
Med S: **+ Hospital**
ATM S: 7-11 Convenience Store, Spur
Parks S: **Lockhaven Park**
Other S: 7-11 Convenience Store, Lou Gardens

44 **(86)** Par Ave. (Eastbound, Reaccess Westbound Only)
Gas S: Texaco(*)
AServ N: Link's Auto Repair & Towing
ATM S: Texaco

45 **(87)** Fairbanks Ave.
Gas S: Amoco(*, 24)
Food S: Sam's Subs
AServ S: Auto Service American & Import, Firelli Tires, Auto Car
Other S: Fairbank's Foodmart & Convenient Store, **Medicine Shop Pharmacy(RX)**

46 **(88)** FL. 423, Lee Road , Winter Park
Gas N: Shell(*), Texaco(*, D)
S: Chevron(*, 24), Mobil(*, D, CW)
Food N: China Buffet, Del Frisco's Steak & Lobster, Waffle House
S: Coffee Shoppe(24), Denny's
Lodg N: Holiday Inn, InTown Suites, Intrastate Economy

EXIT FLORIDA

Inn & Suites
S: Fairfield Inn
AServ N: AAMCO Transmission, Shell
S: Foriegn Car Clinic, Phil's BMW
ATM S: Mobil
Other N: **Eckerd Drugs(RX)**

47AB **(89)** FL 414, Maitland Blvd. (47A goes south, 47B goes north)
Gas N: Citgo(*)
Food N: Pizza Hut (Sheraton), Sheraton
Lodg N: Sheraton
RVCamp N: **Green Acres RV Park of Orlando (1.6 Miles)**
ATM N: SunTrust
Other S: Maitland Arts Center

48 **(92)** FL. 436, Altamonte Springs, Apopka, Castleberry
Gas N: Citgo(*), Exxon(*, D), Mobil(*, CW), Shell(*), Texaco(*, D, CW)
S: Amoco(*, CW), Chevron(*), Texaco(*)
Food N: Amigo's Original TexMex Restaurant, Bangkok Thai & Oriental, Bennigan's, Bobby G's, Cooker's Bar & Grill, Crickets, First Watch, Holiday Inn, Kohinoor Fine Indian Cuisine, La Scala, LongHorn Steakhouse, Mak's Pastry Shop, McDonald's(PLAY), Perkins Family Restaurant, Rio Bravo, Serano's, Steak & Ale, T.G.I. Friday's, Waffle House
S: Denny's, Fuddruckers, Presto Pizza, Steak & Shake
Lodg N: Altamonte Springs Best Western, Days Inn, Hampton Inn, Holiday Inn, La Quinta Inn, Residence Inn, TraveLodge
S: Embassy Suites, Hilton, Homestead Village
AServ N: Exxon, Shell
S: Xpress Lube
Med S: **+ Hospital**
ATM N: 7-11 Convenience Store (Citgo), Citgo, Exxon, Texaco
S: Nation's Bank
Other N: 7-11 Convenience Store (Citgo), Alta Monte Lanes
S: Cat Hospital of Orlando, Interstate AMC 6 Theaters, Northlake Plaza, One Hour Photo, Renaissance Centre, Vision Works

49 **(93)** FL. 434, Longwood, Winter Springs
Gas N: Chevron(*, D), Exxon(*, D, CW), Mobil(*, D, CW), Ramada Inn
S: Mobil(*, D, CW), Shell(*, CW)
Food N: Denny's, Kalimara Italian Cuisine, Kyoto Japanese Steakhouse, Miami Subs, Wild Jack's Steak & BBQ
S: Baskin Robbins, Black Eyed Pea, Boston Market Restaurant, Bruegger's Bagel & Bakery, Figarro Italian Restaurant, Royal Dutch Cafe & Bakery

EXIT FLORIDA

Lodg N: Ramada Inn
Med S: **+ Hospital**
ATM N: First Union, Sun Trust
Parks N: **Wekiwa Springs State Park**
Other S: 7-11 Convenience Store

(94) **Rest Area (RR, HF, Phones, Picnic, RV Dump; Westbound)**

(96) **Rest Area (RR, Phones, Picnic, Vending; Eastbound)**

50 **(98)** Lake Mary, Heathrow
Gas N: Exxon(*, LP)
S: Amoco(*, CW, 24), Citgo(*)
Food N: Liguino's Pasta & Steaks
S: America's Subs, Arby's, Burger King, Carvel Ice Cream Bakery, Chick-Fil-A, Chili's, Dunkin Donuts, Einstein Bros Bagels, Eye've Had It, Fanny Mae Candy, Galleria Restaurant, KFC, Keller's Barbecue Food, Krystal, Kumquat Tree, Little Caesars Pizza, Longhorn Steakhouse, Papa John's Pizza, Rio Bravo Cantina, Uno Pizzeria, Wendy's
Lodg N: Marriot Courtyard
S: Hilton, Homewood Suites Hotel
AServ N: Exxon
S: Amoco(24), Don Olson Tire & Auto Center
ATM S: Colonial Bank, NationsBank
Other N: **Eckerd Drugs**, **Gooding's Supermarket(24)**, Visitor Information
S: **Albertson's Grocery(RX)**, **Book Rack Bookstore**, **General Cinemas**, Home Depot, **K-Mart(RX)**, **Lake Emma Animal Hospital**, Lake Mary Car Wash, **Old Time Pottery**, Quality Images One-Hour Photo

51 **(102)** FL 46, Sanford, Mount Dora
FStop N: **Amoco(*, 24)**
Gas S: Chevron, Mobil(*), Speedway(*)
Food N: **Amoco**, Pizza Hut (Amoco)
S: **Cracker Barrel**, Denny's, Don Pablo's Mexican, Hop's Restaurant & Bar, Joe's Crab Shack, McDonald's(PLAY), Outback Steakhouse, Red Lobster, Steak 'N Shake, Waffle House
Lodg S: Days Inn (see our ad this page), Super 8
AServ N: Auto Nation USA
S: Chevron, Mobil, **Sears**
RVCamp N: **12 Oaks RV Resort (2 Miles)**
Med S: **+ Hospital**
ATM S: Chevron
Other N: Sanford Historic District
S: Amtrak Terminal, **Homeplace**, **Sears**, **Seminole Town Center Mall**, Toys R Us, **United Artist Theaters**

52 **(104)** U.S. 17, U.S. 92, Sanford (Difficult Reaccess)
Gas S: Citgo(*)
Food N: Otter's
S: Citgo, Subway (Citgo)
AServ S: Fred Tire Service (U- Haul)
RVCamp N: **Lake Monroe Park (.5 Miles)**
Med S: **+ Hospital**
ATM S: Citgo
Other N: Barber Marine
S: **Central Florida Zoological Park**

53 **(108)** De Bary, Deltona
Gas N: Lil' Champ(*)
Food N: Burger King, SHONEY'S, Shoney's
S: Carol's Restaurant, Chattz Pub & Grill, Deltona Best Western Inn, Harry's Restaurant (Best Western), McDonald's(PLAY), Plaza Del Caribe
Lodg N: Hampton Inn
S: Deltona Best Western Inn
Parks N: **Gemini Springs Park**

53CA **(109)** Deltona
Gas S: Chevron(*)

EXIT FLORIDA

Food **N:** Perkin's Family Restaurant
AServ **S:** Chevron
Med **N:** ✚ **Hospital**
ATM **S: Albertson's Food Market**[RX]
Other **N:** Saxson Pharmacy[RX]
S: Albertson's Food Market[RX]

53CB **(110)** Orange City (Services Accessible To 53CA)

54 **(114)** FL. 472, Orange City, DeLand
RVCamp **N: KOA-Deland/Orange City (1.83 Miles), Village Park Luxury RV Park (.75 Miles)**
Parks **N: Blue Springs State Park**

55 **(116)** Lake Helen, DeLand
Other **S:** Shoestring Theater

56 **(118)** FL. 44, DeLand, New Smyrna Beach
Gas **N:** Texaco[*, D] (U-Haul)
S: Shell[*]
Food **N:** Quality Inn
Lodg **N:** Quality Inn
Med **N:** ✚ **Hospital**
Other **S:** Fairgrounds

(127) **Parking Area (Eastbound)**

57 **(129)** U.S. 92 East

58AB **(132)** Junction I-95, Jacksonville, Miami, Daytona

↑ FLORIDA

Begin I-4

Begin I-5

↓ WASHINGTON

EXIT WASHINGTON

(277) Canadian Border

276 WA 548S., Blaine City Center, Peace Arch Park
Gas **E:** 76[*, 24], Annex[*] (Duty Free Store), Blaine Gas[*], Border Gas, Exxon[*, D], MP[*], USA Gas[*, 24]
W: Chevron[*], Exxon[*, CW], Shell[*]
Food **E:** Denny's, Paso Del Norte
W: Annie's Place Deli, Bradley's Bordertown Tavern, Costa Azul Family Mexican, Espresso Cafe, Pastime Tavern & Casino, Subway
Lodg **E:** Northwoods Motel
AServ **W:** Chevron
ATM **W:** Exxon, Seafirst Bank
Parks **E: Peace Arch State Park**
Other **E:** Pac Can Duty Free Store
W: Punjabi Market, Used Books Buy, Sale, or Trade, **Visitor Information**

275 WA 543 North, Truck Customs (Northbound, Reaccess Southbound Only)
FStop **E: Exxon**[*] **(C F N Commercial Fueling Network)**
Gas **E:** BP[*], Texaco[*, D, CW]
Food **E: Burger King**
AServ **E:** NAPA Auto Parts
TServ **E: TC Trans Inc.**[24]
TWash **E: A & A Pressure Washing**
ATM **E: Cost Cutter Supermarket**, Texaco
Other **E: Cost Cutter Supermarket**, Rite Aid Pharmacy[RX]

274 Peace Portal Dr., Semiahmoo (Northbound, Reaccess Southbound Only)
Gas **W:** Chevron[*]
Parks **W: Birch Bay Semiahmoo Resort**
Other **W:** Semiahmoo Museum, **Visitor Information**

EXIT WASHINGTON

270 Lynden, Birch Bay
Gas **W:** Texaco[*, D]
Food **W:** Taco Bell Express (Texaco)
ATM **W:** Texaco
Other **W: Peace Arch Factory Outlets**

(269) **Rest Area (P; Southbound)**

(268) **Rest Area (RR, Picnic, Vending, P; Northbound)**

266 WA 548, Custer, Grandview Road
Gas **W:** Arco[*]
Parks **W: Birch Bay State Park (8 Miles)**

263 Portal Way
FStop **E: Pacific Pride Commercial Fueling**[*]
Gas **E:** Texaco[*, D]
RVCamp **E: Cedar's RV Resort Camping (1 Mile), Mountain View Mobile Home Park & RV**
ATM **E:** Texaco

262 Ferndale, Axton Road, Main St., City Center
FStop **E: BP**[*, LP], **Chevron**[*, SCALES]
Gas **W:** Exxon[*], Texaco[*, D]
Food **E: Chevron**, Denny's, McDonald's[PLAY]
W: Bob's Burgers & Brew, Dairy Queen, Grant's Drive-In, Great Wall Restaurant, **Market Street Cafe (Haggen Food Store)**, Mt. Baker Lanes Restaurant
Lodg **E:** Best Western, Super 8
W: Scottish Lodge
AServ **E:** Whatcom Tire Center
W: Martin's Auto Radiator & Exhaust, NAPA Auto Parts
RVCamp **E: El Monte RV**
ATM **E: Chevron**
W: Cost Cutters Grocery Store, Exxon, **Haggen Food Stores**[24, RX], Texaco
Other **E: Whatcom Veterinary Hospital**
W: Cost Cutters Grocery Store, Glacier View Animal Hospital, Haggen Food Stores[RX], Historic District, Visitor Information

260 Lummi Island, Slater Road
Gas **E:** Arco[*, LP]
TServ **E: International Trucks**
RVCamp **E: El Monty RV Service, RV Outlet Sales & Service, Unity RV Service**
ATM **E:** Arco

258 Bakerview Road, Bellingham International Airport
FStop **W: Exxon**[*, RV DUMP] **(C F N Commercial Fueling Network)**
Gas **W:** Arco[*, 24], BP[*]
Lodg **W: Hampton Inn, Shamrock Motel**
RVCamp **W: Bellingham RV Park**
Other **W:** State Police

257 Northwest Ave
AServ **E:** Jerry Chamber's Chevrolet

256AB WA 539 North, Meridian St, Lynden, Bellis Fair Mall Pkwy.
Gas **E:** Texaco[*, D, CW]
Food **E:** Burger King, Cafe Caffe, Denny's, Godfather's Pizza, Maharaja Cuisine of India, McDonald's[PLAY], Mi Mexico Mexican Restaurant, Mitzel's American Kitchen, Red Robin, Shari's Restaurant, Sizzler, Thai House
W: Eleni's Restaurant
Lodg **E:** Best Western
W: Rodeway Inn, Travelers Inn
AServ **E:** Les Schwab Tires, Riteway Service Center
Med **W:** ✚ **Hospital**
ATM **E:** Key Bank, Texaco
Other **E: Bellis Fair Mall, Rite Aid Pharmacy**[RX]
W: Family Bookstores

EXIT WASHINGTON

255 WA 542 East, Sunset Drive, Mt. Baker
Gas **E:** Chevron[*, LP, CW, 24]
Food **E: Asian Food (The Fair Food & Pharmacy), China Market Express (The Fair Food & Pharmacy)**, Jack-In-The-Box, La Pinata Mexican, Panda Palace, Port Of Subs, Round Table Pizza, Scotty B's Bagel & Cafe Co., Slo Pitch Pub & Eatery, Starbucks Coffee, Stop-n-Go Espresso, TCBY, Taco Bell
AServ **E: K-Mart**[RX], Prime Tune & Brakes
Med **W:** ✚ **Hospital**
ATM **E:** Chevron, **K-Mart**, Lucky Foods, **The Fair Food & Pharmacy**[24, RX]
Other **E: K-Mart**[RX], Lucky Foods, **Maytag Laundry Coin**, Pets, Rite Aid Pharmacy, Sunset Car Wash, **The Fair Food & Pharmacy**[RX], **US Post Office**

254 State St., Iowa St.
Gas **E:** BP[*], Texaco[*, LP]
W: 76[*, LP], Chevron[*, LP]
Food **W:** Dairy Queen, McDonald's[PLAY]
AServ **E:** Bellingham Collision Repair, Dr. John's Auto Clinic, Jerry Chambers
W: 76 Car Care Center, Diehl Ford, Lyndale Glass Auto, Commercial, & Residential, Schuck's Auto Supply, United Auto Parts
RVCamp **E: Al's RV Center Parts & Service, Vacationland RV Sales & Service**
ATM **W:** Chevron
Other **W:** Jalopy Jakoozee Car Wash[CW]

253 Lakeway Dr.
Gas **E:** USA Gasoline[24]
Food **E:** Bergsna Restaurant, Little Caesars Pizza, Pizza Hut, Port of Subs, Refreshes Beverage & Treat Bar, Rhodes Cafe, Sadighi's Restaurant, Wok 'n' Roll
Lodg **E:** Val-U-Inn Motel
AServ **E:** USA Gasoline[24]
ATM **E: Ennens Foods, Fred Meyer Grocery**[24, RX], Key Bank, US Bank
Other **E:** Bellingham Cleaning Center & Coin Laundry, **Ennens Foods, Fred Meyer Grocery**[RX], Sunshine Cleaners Coin-Op Laundry, **Visitor Information**

252 Samish Way, West Washington University (Difficult Reaccess)
Gas **W:** 76, Arco[*], Chevron[*], Texaco[*, D]
Food **W:** A & W Restaurant, Arby's, Bamboo Inn Chinese Restaurant, Black Angus Steakhouse, Boomers Drive In, Burger King, Christos' Restaurant & Lounge, Denny's, Diego's Authentic Mexican, Fryday's Food & Spirits, Godfather's Pizza, IHOP, McDonald's[PLAY], Rib'n Reef Pasta & Greek Entrees, **Starbucks Coffee (Haggen's Market)**, Subway
Lodg **E:** Evergreen Motel
W: Aloha Motel, Bay City Motor Inn, Cascade Inn, Coachman Inn, Macs Motel, Motel 6, Ramada Inn, TraveLodge, Villa Inn
AServ **W:** 76, Earl's Auto Service, Roger Job's Motors Volks, Audi, Chrysler
ATM **W:** Chevron, **Haggen's Market**[24], Texaco
Other **W:** Car Wash[CW], **Haggen's Market**, Rite Aid Pharmacy[RX]

250 WA 11 South, Chuckanut Drive, Old Fairhaven Parkway
Gas **W:** Chevron
AServ **W:** Chevron
ATM **W: Albertson's Food Market**[RX]
Other **W: Albertson's Food Market**[RX], **Old Fairhaven Historic District**

246 North Lake Samish
Gas **W: Texaco**[*, D]
Food **W: Betties Deli (Texaco)**
RVCamp **W: Camping**

Bold red print shows RV & Bus parking available or nearby

EXIT	WASHINGTON
ATM	**W:** Texaco
Parks	**W:** Lake Padden & Recreation
242	Nulle Rd., S. Lake Samish
240	Alger
Gas	**E:** Texaco[*]
RVCamp	**E:** Sudden Valley RV Park
(238)	**Rest Area (RR, Phones, Picnic, P; Southbound)**
(238)	**Rest Area (RR, Phones, Picnic, P; Northbound)**
236	Bow Hill Road
Food	**E:** Harrahs Skagit Casino & Resort
RVCamp	**E:** Thousand Trails & NACO RV Resort (1 Mile)
(235)	**Weigh Station (Southbound)**
232	Cook Road, Sedro-Woolley
FStop	**E:** Delta Western[*], Texaco[*, LP, CW]
Gas	**E:** Shell[*]
Food	**E:** Blimpie Subs & Salads (Shell)
RVCamp	**E:** KOA Campgrounds
Med	**E:** ✚ Hospital (3 Miles)
ATM	**E:** Texaco
231	WA 11 North, Chuckanut Dr., Bow-Edison
RVCamp	**E:** Foley Travel Trailers 5th Wheel
Parks	**W:** Larabee State Park
Other	**E:** Chuckanut Valley Veterinarian Clinic, Puget Propane[LP] **W:** Washington State Patrol
230	WA 20, Burlington, Anacortes, Sedro Woolley N. Cascades Hwy.
Gas	**E:** Chevron[*, LP], Exxon[*], Texaco[*, D], Thunderbird Lubrications **W:** Arco, Chevron[*, D]
Food	**E:** Bothby Best & Co. Galley Restaurant, Caffe Moka Expresso & Deli[24], China Wok, Coffee Garden Cafe, El Cazador Mexican, Hooligan's Pub & Bistro, Jack-In-The-Box, La Hacienda Taqueria Mexican, Pizza Factory, Sunny Teriyaki (Japanese, Korean) **W:** McDonald's[PLAY]
Lodg	**E:** Cocusa Motel, Sterling Motor Inn **W:** Mark 2 Motel
AServ	**E:** Les Schwab Tires, Oil Well Fast Lube, Skagit Valley Towing
RVCamp	**E:** RV Service & RV Dealer
ATM	**E:** Chevron **W:** Arco, Chevron, Holiday Market
Other	**E:** 7-11 Convenience Store, Burlington Eye Care Center, Horen's Drug[RX], Kwik-n-Kleen 1 Car Wash, Thrifty Foods **W:** Holiday Market
229	George Hopper Rd
Gas	**E:** Arco[*, 24], USA Mini-Mart[*, D, 24]
Food	**E:** The Sports Keg, V F W, Wendy's **W:** Sports Deli
AServ	**E:** Auto Beauty by Wayne, Mid-City Auto Body, Thrift-E-Lube **W:** Dents Undone, Foothill's GMC, Frontier Chrysler, Nissan, Pure Reflections Auto Salon, Sims Honda, Skagit Ford & Subaru, Toyota
RVCamp	**E:** Cascade Canopy & RV Service, V F W RV Park
ATM	**E:** Arco, Food Pavilion[24, RX], K-Mart[24, RX], Skagit State Bank, USA Mini-Mart, Whidbey Island Bank
Other	**E:** Food Pavilion[RX], K-Mart[RX], Pets-R-Us, Skagit Animal Clinic **W:** Tourist Info.
227	WA 538, East College Way, Clear Lake
Gas	**E:** 76[*, LP, 24] **W:** Shell[*, D], Texaco[*, D, CW]

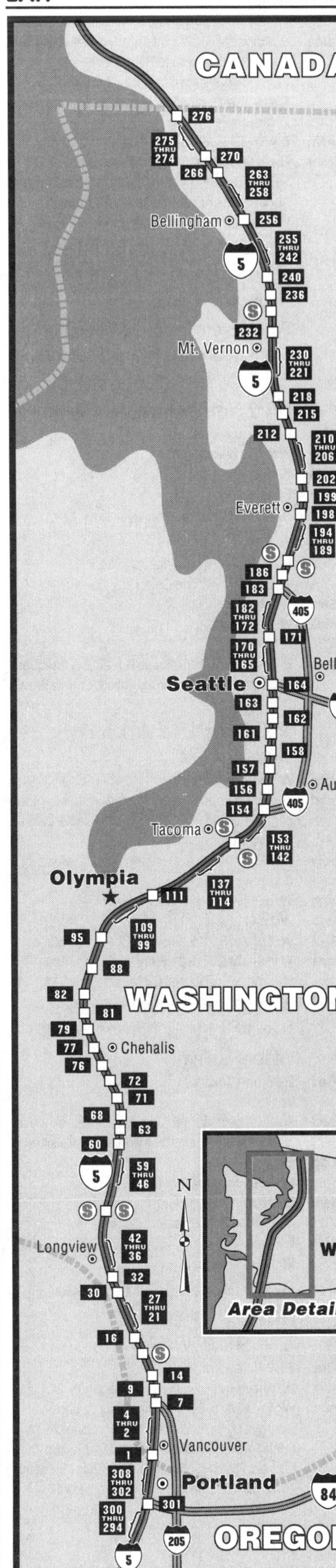

EXIT	WASHINGTON
Food	**E:** Big Scoop Sundae Palace, Cascade Pizza Inn, Days Inn, Denny's, El Gitano Mexican, Godfather's Pizza, Hong Kong Restaurant, Jack-In-The-Box, Max Dale's Restaurant, McDonald's, Port Of Subs, Round Table Pizza, Skipper's Seafood & Chowder House, Starbucks Coffee, Subway, Taco Bell, Winchells Donuts **W:** Arby's, Burger King[PLAY], Cranberry Tree Restaurant, Dairy Queen, Drumman's Restaurant, Fortune Mandarin Restaurant, Mitzel's American Kitchen, Sub Shop (Shell)
Lodg	**E:** Days Inn, West Winds Motel **W:** Best Western, Comfort Inn, Tulip Inn
AServ	**E:** 76[24], Al's Auto Supply, Dally's, Funston's Auto Service, J J & K, Midas Muffler, Schuck's Auto Supply, ShortStop Tune Up & Brake Center, Teixmen & Williams Datsun Repair, Transmission Factory, Wal-Mart[24, RX] **W:** Quaker State Oil & Lube, Walt's Radiator & Muffler
RVCamp	**E:** Country Motors Motor Home **W:** Riverbend RV Park (.5 Miles), Valley RV Service
ATM	**E:** Albertson's Market[RX], Horizon Bank, Inter West Bank, People's Bank, Safeway Grocery[24, RX], Skagit State Bank, Subway, US Bank **W:** Texaco
Other	**E:** Albertson's Market[RX], Grocery Outlet, Petco Supplies & Grooming, Plaza Cleaning Center Coin Laundry, Rite Aid Pharmacy[RX], Safeway Grocery[RX], Vision Center (Wal-Mart), Wal-Mart[RX]
226	WA 536 West, Kincaid St, City Center
FStop	**W:** Pacific Pride Commercial Fueling
Food	**W:** City Bakery, Coffee Corner, Courtyard Cafe, Draft Pics Tavern, Knotty Pine Cafe, Seane's Coffee Corner, Skagit River Brewing Co., Tacos La Vila, Thai House
AServ	**W:** Auto Parts Plus Auto Service, Car Quest Auto Parts, NAPA Auto Parts
RVCamp	**W:** Mount Vernon RV Park (1 Mile)
Med	**E:** ✚ Hospital
ATM	**W:** Seafirst Bank, Skagit State Bank, US Bank, Washington Mutual Bank
Other	**E:** Lincoln Grocery **W:** Bible Book Shop, Christian Science Reading Room, La Tiendita Cruz Mexican Grocery, Mt. Vernon Police Dept., Robert's Red Apple Market, Visitor Information
225	Anderson Rd
TStop	**W:** Truck City[*]
FStop	**E:** C F N Commercial Fueling Network[*]
Gas	**E:** BP[*]
Food	**E:** BP **W:** Crane's Restaurant (Truck City TS)
AServ	**W:** Budget Towing, Muffler, Brakes, & Hitches, Iversen Auto Body, Les Schwab Tires, Renegade Automotive, S & R Automotive
TServ	**E:** Mt. Vernon Towing & Truck Repair **W:** Motor Trucks Inc. International Cat, Detroit Diesel, Cummins, Truck City
ATM	**E:** BP
224	South Mt. Vernon (Northbound, Reaccess Southbound Only)
221	WA 534 East, Lake McMurray, Conway, LaConner
Gas	**E:** Texaco[*, D, LP]
Food	**W:** Conway Country Corner, Conway Tavern Eatery
RVCamp	**W:** Blakes RV Park
ATM	**E:** Texaco **W:** Conway Food Market
Parks	**W:** Camano State Park
Other	**W:** Conway Food Market

EXIT		WASHINGTON
218		Starbird Road
	Lodg	W: Hillside Motel
215		300th St N.W.
	Gas	W: MiniMart[*, LP]
	AServ	W: MiniMart
212		WA 532 West, Stanwood, Camano Island
	Gas	W: Shell[*, D, LP], Texaco[*, LP, 24]
	RVCamp	W: Camping
	ATM	W: Shell, Texaco
	Parks	W: Camano Island State Park (19 Miles)
	Other	W: C B Service (Texaco)
210		236th St N.E.
208		WA 530, Silvana, Arlington, Darrington
	FStop	E: Texaco[*] W: Exxon[*]
	Gas	E: Arco[*, 24], BP[*, LP], Chevron[*, LP]
	Food	E: Denny's, O'Brien Turkey House, Weller's Family Restaurant
	Lodg	E: Arlington Motor Inn
	Med	E: ✚ Hospital
	ATM	E: BP, Chevron W: Exxon
(207)		Rest Area (RR, Phones, Picnic, RV Dump, P; Southbound)
(207)		Rest Area (RR, Phones, Picnic, RV Dump, P; Northbound)
206		WA 531, Lakewood, Smokey Pt.
	Gas	E: Arco[*], Chevron[*, D, LP, CW], Citgo[*], Texaco[*, LP] W: Chevron[*, 24]
	Food	E: Alfy's Pizza, Baskin Robbins, Buzz Inn Steakhouse, Gimme A Break Coffeehouse, Jack-In-The-Box, KFC, Las Corona's Mexican, Linda's Restaurant, McDonald's[PLAY], Olympia Pizza & Pasta, Papa Murphy's Pizza, Paradise Burgers, Pizza & Teriyaki, Taco Time, Tokyo House, Wayne's Family Restaurant, Wendy's W: Nick's Place Coffeeshop Dining Room Lounge
	Lodg	E: Smokey Point Motor Inn
	AServ	E: Al's Auto Supply, Express Lube & Auto Repair, Q-Lube
	RVCamp	W: Smokey Point RV Park
	ATM	E: Arco, Cascade Bank, Chevron, Everett Mutual Bank, Key Bank, Seafirst Bank, Texaco, U.S. Bank, Washington Mutual W: Chevron
	Parks	W: State Park (7 Miles)
	Other	E: Food Pavilion[24, RX], Pro Horseman Supply & Pets, Reader's Club Books, Rite Aid Pharmacy[RX], Safeway Grocery[24, RX], Smokey Point Animal Hospital, Suds & Duds Laundry Center
202		116th St N.E.
	TStop	W: Donna's[*, SCALES]
	Gas	E: Texaco[*, D, LP]
	Other	W: State Police, Visitor Information (Donna's TS)
200		88th St. NE., Quil Ceda Way
199		WA 528 East, Marysville, Tulalip
	Gas	E: Arco[*, 24], BP[*], Chevron[24], Texaco[*, D]
	Food	E: Burger King, Conto's Pizza & Pasta, Dairy Queen, Don's Restaurant, Jack-In-The-Box[24], Las Margaritas Mexican Restaurant, Maxwell's Restaurant, Royal Fork Buffet, Subway (Texaco), Village Restaurant W: Arby's, Best Western, McDonald's, Taco Time, Tulalip Food & Cafe, Wendy's
	Lodg	E: Village Motor Inn W: Best Western, Holiday Inn Express
	AServ	E: BP, Oil Well Fast Lube W: Roy Robinson Chev. & RV Service
	RVCamp	E: Marysville Trailer RV Supply[LP], RV & Marine Supply By Cascade (1 Mile), RV Dump W: RV Outlet Supermall, Roy Robinson (.3 Miles), Roy Robinson Chev. & RV Service, Roy Robinson RV Service
	ATM	E: Arco, Chevron, Seafirst Bank
	Other	E: 4th St. Market & Deli, Albertson's Supermarket[RX], Amen Christian Bookstore, It's About Time Car Wash, Rite Aid Pharmacy[RX] W: Tulalip Indian Reservation
198		WA 529 South, North Broadway, Port of Everett (Southbound, Reaccess Northbound Only)
195		Port of Everett, Marine View Drive (Northbound, Reaccess Southbound Only)
194		U.S. 2 East, Snohomish, Wenatchee
	Gas	W: Texaco[*, D, CW]
	AServ	W: Les Schwab Tires
	ATM	W: Texaco
	Other	E: Pet Supply & Food
193		Pacific Ave, City Center, WA 529
	Gas	W: BP[*]
	Food	E: McCabe's Great American Food W: Buck's American Cafe, Kozy Cavern
	TServ	E: Peterbilt
	Med	W: ✚ Hospital
	ATM	W: BP
	Other	E: Designer's Wharehouse Furniture & Antiques W: Animal Surgery & Vaccinating, Charlie Brown Detail[CW]
192		Broadway, Navel Station, Port of Everett (Left Exit)
	Gas	W: Chevron[*, 24], Texaco[*]
	Food	W: Baskin Robbins, Colby Teriyaki, Ivar's Seafood Bar, McDonald's[PLAY], O'Donnell's Food & Drinki, Quizno's Subs
	AServ	W: Pacific Power Batteries[LP], Ron's Service Center
	RVCamp	W: Morgan-Johnson RV Service
	Med	W: ✚ Hospital
	ATM	W: Capital S 'N' S Grocery, Chevron, Texaco
	Other	W: Capital S 'N' S Grocery, Medicine Man Pharmacy, The Everett Clinic Pediatrics & Optical
189		WA 527 N., To WA 99, Broadway, Everett Mall Way, WA 526, Mukiltio, Widbey Is. Ferry
	Gas	E: Exxon[*], Texaco[*, LP] W: Shell[*]
	Food	E: Alfy's Pizza, Burger King, Buzz Inn Steakhouse, McDonald's[PLAY], Orchid Italian & Thai Cuisine
	Lodg	E: TraveLodge W: Extended Stay America Hotel
	AServ	E: Texaco
	Med	E: ✚ Silver Lake Medical Center
	ATM	E: Exxon W: Shell
(188)		Weigh Station (RR, HF, Phones, Picnic, RV Dump, P)
186		128th St S.W., WA 96
	Gas	E: BP[LP], Texaco[*, D] W: Chevron[*, CW, 24], Citgo[*], Texaco[*, CW]
	Food	W: Alfy's Pizza, Burger King, Dairy Queen[PLAY], Denny's, Fly By Java Cafe, KFC, McDonald's, Mi Casa Su Casa (Mexican), Mitzel's American Kitchen, Pizza Hut, Seattle Fish & Chips, Subway, Taco Bell, Taco Time, Teriyaki Plus, Yummy Teriyaki
	Lodg	E: Holiday Inn Express W: Everitt Inn, Motel 6
	AServ	W: Big Wheel Auto Parts, Puget Park Transmission, Q Lube, South Everett Tire & Service
	RVCamp	E: Great American RV Centers (2 Miles) W: Harbour Pointe RV Park (1.75 Miles), Lake Side RV Park (1.75 Miles)
	ATM	E: BP, Texaco W: Albertson's Market[24, RX], Cascade Federal Credit Union, Chevron, Citgo, U.S. Bank
	Other	E: 24 Hr. Deli/Market[24], Visitor Information W: Albertson's Market[RX], Maxi-Clean Car Wash[CW]
183		164th St S.W., Mill Creek
	Gas	E: Arco[*], Chevron[*], Texaco[*, D, CW]
	Food	E: 13th Ave. Pub & Eatery, Cafe Majestic Restaurant & Lounge, Happy Burger, Ishiya Teriyaki, Jack-In-The-Box, Subway, Taco Time, Thai Cuisine
	AServ	E: Premium Tune & Lube Mufflers & Brakes
	RVCamp	W: Glenn's Trailor Supplies & RV Accessories, Twin Cedars RV Park
	ATM	E: Arco, Texaco, Wells Fargo
	Other	E: Mill Creek Ankle & Foot Clinic
182		WA 525 North to WA 99, I-405 South, Bellevue, Renton, Mukilteo
181B		WA 524, 196th St. SW, Alderwood Mall Pkwy. (Northbound, Continuous commerce on west side)
	Gas	E: BP[*, D, CW], Texaco[*, LP]
	Food	E: BP, Goldie's Lynnwood Restaurant, Mountain Burgers (BP), Pizza Hut (BP), Taco Bell (BP) W: A.A.P. Barbar's Family Dining, Baskin Robbins, Burger King[PLAY], Chuck E Cheese's Pizza, Cucina Presto Pasta Pizza & Salad, Denny's, KFC, Kings Palace Restaurant, McDonald's[PLAY], Taki Japanese, The Yankee Diner, Tony Roma's, Toshi's Teriyaki
	Lodg	E: Extended Stay America W: Holiday Inn Express, Silver Cloud Inn
	AServ	E: Aldercrest Auto Rebuild Inc., BP W: Alderwood Olds, Cad, GM, Bucky's Mufflers Brakes & Radiator, Econo Lube & Tune, Speedy Auto Glass
	Med	W: ✚ Chec Medical Center
	ATM	E: BP, Evergreen Bank, Texaco
	Other	E: Barnes & Noble Bookstore (Starbucks Coffee), Eagle Hardware & Garden W: Alderwood Veterinarian Clinic, Cinema 12 Theaters, Drug Emporium[RX], Kinko's, Rocky Grocery & Deli
181A		To Lynnwood, To WA. 524, (Difficult Reaccess, Continuous commerce on the west side)
	Gas	E: Arco[*, 24] W: BP[*, D, CW], Chevron[*, LP, 24], Texaco[*, D, LP]
	Food	E: 44th Market, Darn Good Pizza (Arco), Granita Espresso W: Black Angus Steakhouse, Buca di Beppo Italian Dinners, Cafe Taka (Japanese), Chevy's Fresh Mex, Evergreen Donuts, Harvest House Teriyaki Oriental BBQ, Hawaii BBQ, Hooters, India Cuisine, Jack-in-the-Box, Kenny Roger's Roasters, McDonald's, New Great China Restaurant, Old Country Buffet, Oriental Buffet, Out A Bounz, Skipper's, Starbucks Coffee, Subway, Talay Thai Cuisine.
	Lodg	E: Embassy Suites W: Best Western
	AServ	W: Centers 3 Collision Center, Chevron[24], Dan Gilfeather's III Collision Center, Goodyear Tire & Auto, Precision Tune & Lube, Texaco
	Med	W: ✚ Health South Medical Clinic
	ATM	E: 44th Market, Arco, US Bank (Albertson's) W: 7-11 Convenience Store, BP, Key Bank, Wells Fargo

EXIT	WASHINGTON
Other	**E:** 44th Market, **Albertson's Grocery Store**(RX) **W:** 7-11 Convenience Store, **Eyes Rite Optical**
179	220th St. Southwest
Gas	**W:** Shell(*), Texaco(*, D)
Food	**W:** Azteca Mexican, Bento Teriyaki, Casanova's Pizza & Pasta, China Passage Restaurant, Countryside Donut, O'Houlies Pub, Port of Subs, Subway, Thai Terrace
Med	**W:** ✚ **Hospital**, ✚ **Mountlake Medical Immediate Care Center**
ATM	**W:** Texaco
Other	**W:** A Plus Learning Materials, **Animal Care Vet. Hosp.**, Maytag Laundry, **Mt. Baker Snoqualmie National Forest Headquarters**, Plaid Pantry (Shell), **Super Deli & Mart**, **Treasure Thoughts Bookstore**
178	236th ST. W., Mt. Lake Terrace
177	WA 104, NE 205th St, Edmonds, Lake Forest Park; 244th St. SW, Kingston Ferry follow WA 104W (Contiuous commerce on the east side)
Gas	**E:** Chevron(*, 24), Chevron(*, CW), Texaco(*, D)
Food	**E:** Buzz Inn Steakhouse, Canyon's Restaurant, Kings III Chinese Restaurant, McDonald's(PLAY), Subway, Taco Bell Express (Texaco), Teriyaki Plus, Texaco, Todo Mexico, Toshi's Teriyaki, Western Co Donut
AServ	**E:** Auto Man Datsun Repair, Ballinger Auto Clinic, Chevron(24), Q-Lube, Shucks, Super Tune & Brake
Med	**E:** ✚ **Ballinger Clinic**
ATM	**E:** Chevron, City Bank, Texaco
Other	**E:** Axe III Cinemas, **Terrace Pharmacy**, **Thriftway**, **Village Market Thriftway**
176	NE 175th St, Shoreline
175	WA 523, NE 145th St, 5th Ave
174	NE 130th St, Roosevelt Way (Northbound)
173	Northgate Way, 1st Ave NE
Gas	**W:** BP(*, LP), Chevron(*), Texaco(*, D)
Food	**E:** Heartland's Pot Pies, Krazy Bird, Marie Callender's Restaurant, Orweat Bakery Outlet, Round Table Pizza, Starbucks Coffee, Sub Shop, Subway, Taco Time, Tony Roma's **W:** Arby's, Barnaby's, Denny's, Family Donut, McDonald's, Teriyaki Plus, The Pickle Barrel Sandwich Shop
Lodg	**W:** Ramada Inn
AServ	**W:** BP, Chevron, Texaco
Med	**E:** ✚ **North Gate Medical Hospital**, ✚ **Seattle Chinese Med Center** **W:** ✚ **Northwest Hospital**
ATM	**E:** Key Bank, Seafirst Bank, Washington Mutual **W:** **7-11 Convenience Store**, BP, Texaco
Other	**E:** Mail Boxes Etc, Northgate Cinema, **Northgate Mall** **W:** **7-11 Convenience Store**
172	N. 85th St, Aurora Ave. North
171	WA 522, Bothell, Lake City Way
170	Ravenna Blvd, NE 65th St (Northbound)
Gas	**E:** ARCO(*, 24), Texaco(*, D, CW)
Food	**E:** The Bus Stop Espresso
ATM	**E:** ARCO, Texaco
169	NE 45th St, NE 50th St
Gas	**E:** 76(*), BP(*), Chevron(*), Texaco(*, CW) **W:** Texaco(*, D)
Food	**E:** Baskin Robbins, Burger King, Cedars Restaurant, China First on 45th St., City Saloon, Club Moon, Eddie's News Cafe, Espresso Bar, India House, Kyoto Teryaki, Little Saigon Food & Deli, Mama Malina's, Pagliacci Pizza, Plaid Pantry, Seven Gables, Stella's Saloon, Subway, Teryaki Plus, Westernco Donuts **W:** Bagel Factory, Boston Market Restaurant, Dick's Hamburgers, Excalibur's, Fudge Bros. Pizza, Juli's Restaurant, Kabul Afghan Cuisine, Market & Deli, Moon Temple Restaurant, Nikolas Cafe, Pizza, Sea-Thia Restaurant, Taco Time, Tatto Pizza, Winchells Donuts
Lodg	**E:** University Inn, University Motel **W:** University Plaza Motel
AServ	**E:** 76, Affordable Tire & Brakes, University Audi & Suburu, University Ford, University Mazda **W:** Quaker State Oil & Lube, Walt's Radiator & Brakes
Med	**E:** ✚ **U. of WA Medical Center**
ATM	**E:** BP, Chevron, Key Bank, Texaco **W:** Texaco
Other	**E:** **Art Gallery**, **Burke Museum**, Half Price Books, **Kinko's Copies**(24), Rite Aid(RX), **Safeway Grocery** **W:** **Bartell Drugs**(RX), **Heathway Natural Foods**, **Payless Drugs**(RX), **Zoo**
168B	WA 520, Bellevue, Kirkland
168A	Lakeview Blvd, Roanoke St (Reaccess Southbound Only)
167	Mercer St., Seattle Center (Left Exit, No Reaccess)
Food	**W:** Benjamin's Fish & Chips, Burger King, Chandler's, Cucina Cucina, Denny's(24), Home Deli, Hooter's, T.G.I. Friday's
Lodg	**W:** Residence Inn
AServ	**W:** East Lake Auto Center, Lincoln Towing, Pacific Nissan, People's Auto Service
Other	**W:** Maritime Heritage Center, Seattle Space Needle
166	Olive Way
165	Seneca St. (Left Exit Northbound)
164B	4th Ave South
164A	Junction I-90 East, Spokane
163	Columbian Way, West Seattle Br
Other	**W:** **King Dome**
162	Corson Ave, Michigan St (Left Exit Northbound)
Gas	**W:** Texaco(*, D), Texaco(*, D, CW)
Food	**W:** Aerie #1, Arby's, CP Thai, Daimonji, Herfy's Hamburgers, Original Deli, Taco Del Mar
Lodg	**W:** Georgetown Inn
AServ	**W:** Alki Auto Body
ATM	**W:** Texaco, Texaco
161	Albro Place, Swift Ave
158	East Marginal Way
157	ML King Way
156	WA 599 Tukwila, West Marginal Way (Reaccess Southbound Only)
Gas	**E:** 76(LP), BP(*), Texaco(*, D, LP)
Food	**E:** BP, Deli, Denny's, Jack-In-The-Box
Lodg	**E:** Silver Cloud Motel
AServ	**E:** 76, 76, BP(*), BP
TServ	**E:** **Husky International**
ATM	**E:** Texaco, Texaco
154B	WA 518 West, Burien
154A	I-405 North, Renton
153	Southcenter Parkway & Mall (Northbound)
Gas	**E:** Chevron(*, D)
Food	**E:** Cee's Candy, China Coin Restaurant, Houlihan's, McDonald's, Miyabi Japanese Restaurant, Outback Steakhouse, Quizno's Subs, Sizzler Steak House, StarBucks Coffee, Zi Pani Breads Cafe, Zoopa
Lodg	**E:** Doubletree Inn (Restaurant)
AServ	**E:** Acura of Seattle, Chevron, Chevron, Firestone Tire & Auto
ATM	**E:** Key Bank, Washington Mutual, Washington Mutual
Other	**E:** Half Price Books, **South Center Mall**, **Target**, **United States Post Office**, Western Optical
152	South 188th St., Orillia Road South
Gas	**W:** BP(*)
Food	**W:** BP, Cindy's Deli (BP)
Lodg	**W:** Motel 6
RVCamp	**E:** **KOA Campgrounds (2 Miles)**
151	South 200th St, Military Road
Gas	**W:** BP(*), Chevron(*), Citgo(*)
Food	**W:** Bullpin, Gikan 5 Teriyaki
Lodg	**E:** **Motel 6** **W:** Comfort Inn, Hampton Inn, Holiday Inn Express, Howard Johnson, Super 8
TServ	**W:** **Kenworth Northwest**
149AB	WA 516 East, Kent - 149A, WA 516 West, Des Moines - 149 B
Gas	**W:** Texaco(*, D, CW), Texaco(*, CW)
Food	**W:** Baskin Robbins, Big Apple Bagels, **Blockhouse Restaurant**, Burger King(PLAY), Circo Circo, Dunkin Donuts, Konich's Teriyaki, McDonald's(PLAY), Meal Time Drive In, Pizza Hut, Skipper's, Starbucks Coffee, Subway, Taco Bell, Taco Del Mar
Lodg	**E:** Century Motel **W:** King's Arms Motor Inn, New Best Inn
AServ	**E:** Lloyd's Automotive Repair, Timlick's Auto Repair **W:** A to B Auto, Automotive Service Specialist, General Transmissions, Midas Muffler & Brake, Q Lube, Schuck's Auto Supply, Used Tire World
RVCamp	**E:** **Valley I-5 RV Center**
ATM	**W:** 7-11 Convenience Store, Key Bank, Texaco
Other	**W:** 7-11 Convenience Store, **Book World**, **EZ-Clean Car Wash**, Key Discount Drugs, **Kinko's**(24), QFC, **United States Post Office**
147	South 272nd St
Gas	**E:** BP(*)
ATM	**E:** BP
Parks	**W:** **Saltwater State Park**
143	Federal Way, South 320th St (Continuous commerce on the west side)
Gas	**W:** Arco, BP(*, CW)
Food	**W:** Applebee's, Azteca Mexican Restaurant, Egg Roll King, Gateway Espresso, Great Harvest Bread Co., Marlene's, McDonald's, Outback Steakhouse, Pho Hoang, Red Robin, Stewart Anderson's Black Angus, Tony Roma's, Wendy's
Med	**W:** ✚ **Hospital**
ATM	**W:** BP, Key Bank, Washington Federal Savings & Loans
Parks	**W:** **Dash Point State Park**
Other	**W:** Family Bookstores, Gateway Center Cinemas, **Kinko's**, **Seattle Tacoma Mall**
142AB	WA 18 East, Federal Way, Auburn (142 A is a junction, 142B is where the west side services are)
TStop	**W:** **Flying J Travel Plaza**(*, LP, SCALES) **(Truck wash)**
Gas	**W:** Chevron(*, 24) (Sub Shop), Texaco(*, D, CW)
Food	**W:** Burger King, Chevron (Sub Shop), Dairy Queen, Denny's, Dillano's Coffee, McDonald's(PLAY), Olive Garden, Pacific Highway Diner, Popeye's Chicken, Shari's Restaurant, Subway, Taco Bell
Lodg	**W:** **Flying J Travel Plaza (Truck wash)**, Holiday Inn Express, **Roadrunner Motel**, **Super 8**
AServ	**W:** Complete Collision Center, Cooper's Tire

Service, Eagle Tire and Automotive, Greg's Japanese Auto, Les Schwab Tires, Performance Prep, Safe Lite Auto Glass

TServ W: Bay Engine & Transmission, Federal Way Radiator and Muffler[LP], Flying J Travel Plaza[SCALES] (Truck wash)

Med W: + Hospital

ATM W: Flying J Travel Plaza (Truck wash), Texaco

Other W: Animal Hospital, Costco, Home Depot

(141) Weigh Station, Rest Area (RR, Phones, Picnic, RV Dump, P; Northbound)

(141) Weigh Station, Rest Area (RR, Phones, Picnic, RV Dump, P; Southbound)

137 WA 99, Junction, Fife, Milton

Gas E: Arco[*], BP[*, LP, 24], Chevron[*, 24], Texaco[*, CW]
W: BP[*, CW]

Food E: Dairy Queen, Johnny's, Texaco
W: Alpine German Deli & Restaurant, Baskin Robbins, Burger King[PLAY], Denny's, KFC, King's Palace Restaurant, McDonald's, Mitzel's American Kitchen, Mountain High Espresso, Poodle Dog, Skipper's, Taco Bell, Wendy's

Lodg E: Motel 6
W: Best Western, Comfort Inn, Kings Motor Inn, Royal Coachman

AServ E: Topping Nissan & Volvo
W: Big Wheel Auto Parts, Fife National Auto Parts, Les Schwab Tire Center

TServ W: Great American Truck & RV Wash

RVCamp W: Camping World (see our ad this page) Great American RV Superstores

ATM E: BP, Chevron, Johnny's, Texaco
W: Key Bank, Seafirst Bank, US Bank

Other E: Sam's
W: Coin Laundry, Fife Post Office (United Drugs), Shop-Rite Pharmacy, United Drugs

136AB Port of Tacoma, 20th St

TStop W: Flying J Travel Plaza[*, LP, SCALES]

FStop E: CFN Fuel Stop[SCALES]

Gas W: Chevron[*], Texaco[*, D, CW]

Food E: Deli & Grocery, Joe's Deli
W: DAYS INN Days Inn, Fife City Bar & Grill (Days Inn), Flying J Travel Plaza, Jack-In-The-Box, La Casa Real, Thads Restaurant[SCALES] (Flying J Travel Plaza)

Lodg W: DAYS INN Days Inn, Econolodge, Extended Stay America, Glacier Motel, Hometel Inn, Ramada Limited, Travelers Inn

AServ W: Walt's Radiator & Muffler

TServ E: Peterbilt
W: CBC Commercial Break & Clutch, Goodyear Tire & Auto (Fueling), Walt's Radiator & Muffler

RVCamp E: Wescraft RV & Marine Services

ATM E: Deli & Grocery, Viking Community Bank
W: Chevron, Texaco

135 WA 167 Junction, Puyallup, Portland Ave.

134 Portland Ave. (Northbound)

FStop W: BP[*, D, 24]

Gas W: Arco[*, 24]

Food W: BP, Dairy Queen, Pegasus Restaurant, Western Cafe

Lodg W: La Quinta Inn, The Bay Motel[24]

AServ W: Phelp's Tire Co., Phil's Auto Care

TServ W: Courtwright

ATM W: Arco, BP

Other W: D & L Liquidation

133 I-705 North, South WA 7, City Center

132 WA 16 West, South 38th St, Gig Harbor Bremerton (Continuous commerce on the east and west sides)

Food W: Arby's, Blimpie's Subs, Chevy's Mexican, Curtina Curtina, Happy Teriyaki, Houlihan's, Le Donut, Little Tokyo Teriyaki, Red Robbin, Starbucks Coffee, T.G.I. Friday's, Wendy's

AServ W: Tacoma Mall (Sears & JC Penney Auto Service)

Med E: + Hospital

ATM W: Seafirst Bank, Wells Fargo

Other W: Borders Books & Music, Costco, Crown Books Superstore, Kinko's[24], Mail Boxes Etc, Pearl Vision Center, Tacoma Mall (Sears & JC Penney Auto Service), Western Optical

130 South 56th St, Tacoma Mall Blvd

Gas W: Texaco[*, D, CW]

Food W: Azteca Mexican, Chuck E Cheese's Pizza, Pizza Hut (Texaco), Saigon Cafe, Subway, Texaco, Tony Roma's, Wendy's II Vietnamese Restaurant

Lodg W: Extended Stay America

ATM W: Texaco

Other W: Sterling Savings Bank, Tacoma Cat Hospital

129 South 72nd St, South 84th St

Gas E: Arco[*], Exxon[*]

Food E: Angel's Candy (Mega Foods), Applebee's, Burger King[PLAY], Chinese Kitchen (Mega Foods), Dairy Queen[PLAY], Elmer's, IHOP, Jack-in-the-Box, Little Tokyo, Mega Foods (Chinese Kitchen, Planet Burrito, Angel's Candy), Mitzel's, Mongolian Grill, Olive Garden, Planet Burrito (Mega Foods), Red Lobster, Round Table Pizza, Shari's Restaurant, StarBucks Coffee, Taco Bell, The Yankee Diner, Zoopa

Lodg E: DAYS INN Days Inn, Motel 6, Shilo Inn

AServ E: Precision Tune

ATM E: Exxon, Harbor Stone Credit Union, Mega Foods (Chinese Kitchen, Planet Burrito, Angel's Candy)

Other E: America's Best Contacts & Eyeglasses, Drug Emporium, Home Base, Home Depot, Mega Foods (Chinese Kitchen, Planet Burrito, Angel's Candy), Optical Eyes Rite, Snappy Car Rental, Tacoma South Cinemas

128 South 84th St

Gas E: BP[*], Chevron[*, 24], Texaco[*, D, CW]
W: Arco[*]

Food E: Alligater Pub and Grill, Best Western, Copperfield's Restaurant, Denny's, Ichiban Teriyaki, Subway

Lodg E: Best Western, Holiday Inn Express, Howard Johnson, King Oscar Motel, Rothem Inn, Sherwood Travelodge

AServ E: BP
W: Discount Tire Company

Other E: Handy Deli & Grocery, Laundry

127 East WA 512, Puyallup, Mt Rainier (From the north side, difficult access to the west services)

Gas W: Arco[*, D], BP[*], Chevron[*], Texaco[*, D, CW]

Food W: Billy McHale's Restaurant, Brooklyn's, Burger King[PLAY], Dairy Queen[PLAY], Ivar's Seafood, Jim Moore's Restaurant (Quality Inn), Kajika's Teriyummie's, Lessie's Southern Quisine, Mazatlan Mexican Restaurant, McDonald's[PLAY], N & Z BBQ, Quality Inn, Sizzler Steak House, Subway, Taco Time, Tita Perl's, Wendy's

Lodg W: Budget Inn, Quality Inn, Vagabond Motel

AServ W: BP, Nationwide Transmission & Parts

RVCamp W: Baydo's RV Sales, Oaknoll RV & Trailer Park

ATM W: Arco, Texaco

125 McChord A.F.B., Bridgeport Way

Gas E: Exxon[*]
W: 76[*, D]

Food E: Exxon
W: ABC Deli & Grocery, Denny's, Doughnut House, Happy Day's Diner[24], KFC, Mory's Family Dining[24]

Lodg W: Colonial Motel, Home Motel, Lakewood Lodge, Rose Garden Motel, The Madigan Hotel

AServ W: AAMCO Transmission, Ace's Auto Repair, Japanese Auto Repair, Lakewood Auto Body, Lakewood Foriegn Cars Inc., Lakewood Transmission, Precision Honda, Rich's Auto Service, Tacoma BMW, Ty's Auto Repair, Walt's

Med W: + Hospital

ATM E: Exxon
W: 76, Happy Day's Diner

Other W: Lakewood Car Wash

124 Gravelly Lake Drive

Gas W: Arco, BP[*]

AServ W: BP, BP

ATM W: Arco

123 Thorne Lane

AServ E: A-1 Transmission

122 Madigan Hospital, Camp Murray

Gas W: Chevron[*, 24]

Food W: Baskin Robbins, Burger & Steak Shop, Gertie's Grill, House Of Teriyaki, KFC, Kwang's Palace, McDonald's, Pizza Hut, Subway, Taco Bell[24], The First Deli & Mart, The Wok Inn

AServ W: Chevron, Chevron[24], Mobile Auto 1

ATM W: 7-11 Convenience Store, Chevron

Other E: Fort Lewis Military Reservation
W: 7-11 Convenience Store, Coin Car Wash, Plaza Laundry & Dry Cleaners, Young's Barber & Styling Center

120 Fort Lewis, North Fort Lewis

Other W: Fort Lewis Military Museum (3 Miles)

119 Dupont, Steilacoom

118 Center Drive

(117) Weigh Station (Northbound)

116 Mounts Road

114 Old Nisqually , Nisqually

Gas E: Chevron[*, LP], Texaco[*]

Food E: Tiny's Burger House

AServ E: Chevron, Chevron

RVCamp E: Happy Days RV Super Store, Nisqually

ATM E: Texaco

Other E: All Marine

111 WA 510, Yelm, Marvin Road

TStop E: BP[*]

FStop W: Pacific Pride Commercial Fueling

Gas E: BP[*, CW], Chevron[*], Shell[*, D], Texaco[*, D, CW]

Food E: BP, Blimpie's Subs, Burger King, Dairy Queen[PLAY], Godfather's Pizza, Hawk's Prairie, McDonald's[PLAY], Mocha Magic, Pizza Hut (Texaco), Seasons Teriyaki, Shell, Taco Bell (Shell), Taco Time, Texaco
W: Country Junction Family Restaurant

Lodg E: King Oscar Motel

AServ E: Q Lube

ATM E: BP, Safeway Grocery[24, RX], Texaco, Timberland Savings Bank

Other E: Package Express Postal & Copy Center, Rite Aid Pharmacy, Safeway Grocery[RX]

109 Martin Way, Sleater - Kinney Road

CAMPING WORLD®
Exit 137
4650 16th St. East • Tacoma, WA
1-800-526-4165
1437

EXIT		WASHINGTON
	Gas	**W:** BP[*], Texaco[*, D, CW]
	Food	**E:** Taco Bell **W:** Casa Mia, City Pizza, Denny's, Espresso Bar, Red Lobster, Shari's Restaurant
	Lodg	**W:** Comfort Inn, Days Inn, Holiday Inn Express, Super 8
	AServ	**E:** Discount Tire Company **W:** Gary's Tire Factory
	ATM	**E:** US Bank **W:** BP
	Other	**E:** Home Base, Shopko[RX], **Top Food Supermarket[24]** **W:** Car Wash, Lacy's Cinemas
108		Sleater - Kinney Road, South College St. (Difficult Reaccess)
	Gas	**E:** Texaco[*, D], Texaco[*] **W:** 76, Arco[*], Shell[*]
	Food	**E:** Arby's, Bagel Brothers, Baskin Robbins, Blimpie Subs & Salads, Crazy Espresso, Godfather's Pizza, Golden Dragon Chinese Restaurant, Lucky's Tavern & Eatery, McDonald's[PLAY], Mongolian Grill & Lounge, Oscar's German Deli, Pizza Hut, Red Corral, Saripa's Mexican Restaurant, Skipper's Seafood, Wendy's, Winchells Donuts **W:** Burger King, Dirty Dave's Pizza and Spaghetti Parlor, El Sarape Mexican, Jack-In-The-Box, Mandarin House, Shell, Subway
	AServ	**E:** Al's Auto Supply, Firestone Tire & Auto, Midas Muffler Shop, Q Lube, Qual-A-Ty Auto Care, Schuck's Auto Supply, Tire Dogs **W:** 76, 76, Advanced Glass Repair, **K-Mart[RX]**, K-Mart
	Med	**W:** ✚ **Hospital**
	ATM	**E:** Sea First Bank, Sterling Savings Bank, Texaco, Washington Mutual
	Other	**E:** Expressit, **Fred Meyer Grocery**, **Mall**, Pet Smart

CENTRALIA

1737

London Fog, Corning-Revere, Bass
Levi's, Quiksilver, Pfaltzgraff

Both Sides Exit 82

50 Factory Outlets

1/2 OFF YOUR FAVORITE BRANDS EVERY DAY

VF Factory Outlet

Lea-Vanity Fair-Healthtex-Jantzen-Wrangler
Buses Welcome-East Side Exit 82 next to Wendy's

350 Antique Dealers
downtown Centralia

Centralia Square & Annex

39,000 sq. ft.
• Collectables
• Furniture
• Antiques
• Cafe

"SW Washington's Original Antique Mall"
201 S. Pearl (across from city park) 360-736-3327

CENTER of the NW
halfway between Seattle & Portland

EXIT		WASHINGTON
		W: **K-Mart[RX]**, Wsahington State Patrol
107		Pacific Ave
	Gas	**E:** Texaco[*]
	Food	**E:** Figaro's Pizza, Izzy's Pizza, Schlotzsky's Deli, Shari's Restaurant, Sizzler Steak House, Taco Time, Yukio's Teriyaki **W:** Olympia Food Co-op
	AServ	**E:** Rick's Automotives **W:** Auto Glass Pro, Boone Ford and Suzuki Dealership, Foriegn Auto Work, Olympia Collision Center
	RVCamp	**W:** **Coumbs RV Service**
	Med	**E:** ✚ **Hospital**
	ATM	**E:** **Albertson's Grocery[24, RX]**, Texaco
	Other	**E:** **Albertson's Grocery[RX]**, Books Aloud, **Cash & Carry United Grocery**, Family Bookstores, **Kinko's**, Maytag Laundry, United Postal
105		State Capitol, City Center, Port of Olympia (Difficult Reaccess)
	Gas	**W:** Chevron[*]
	Food	**W:** Carriage Inn Motel, Carriage Inn Restaurant, Chevron
	Lodg	**W:** Carriage Inn Motel
	AServ	**W:** Chevron[*], Chevron, Hulbert Auto Park (Pontiac, Cadillac, Saturn)
104		U.S. 101 North, Aberdeen, Port Angeles
103		Deschutes Way (Reaccess Northbound Only)
	Food	**E:** Falls Terrace Restaurant
102		Trosper Road, Black Lake
	Gas	**E:** Citgo[*], Texaco[*, D, 24] **W:** BP[*], Chevron[*, 24], Shell[*]
	Food	**E:** Arby's, Brewery City Pizza, Burger King, Cattin's Family Restaurant, Domino's Pizza, El Sarape, Happy Teriyaki V, Jack-In-The-Box, KFC, McDonald's[PLAY], Pizza Hut, Subway, Taco Bell[24] (24 hour drive-thru) **W:** Bagel Brothers, Blimpie's Subs, Iron Skillet, Mountain Shoots Espresso Bar, Nickelby's Restaurant, Seasons Teriyaki II
	Lodg	**E:** Best Western **W:** Tyee Hotel
	AServ	**E:** Al's, Goodyear Tire & Auto, Poages Auto Repair, Tumwater Auto Parts **W:** Cut Rate Auto Parts
	ATM	**E:** Citgo, First Community Bank, Heritage Bank, Key Bank, Texaco **W:** BP, Chevron, **Megafoods Supermarket[24, RX]**, Shell
	Other	**E:** 7-11 Convenience Store (Citgo), Laundromat, **Martin's Southgate Drug** **W:** **Albertson's Grocery[RX]**, Mail Boxes Etc, **Megafoods Supermarket[RX]**, Tumwater Veterinary Hospital
101		Airdustrial Way
	RVCamp	**E:** **Olympia Campground (.25 Miles)**
99		93rd Ave, Scott Lake
	TStop	**W:** **Shell[LP, SCALES]**
	Food	**W:** **Hannah's Restaurant (Shell)**, **Shell**
	TServ	**W:** **Shell[SCALES]**
	RVCamp	**E:** **American Heritage Campground (.5 Miles)**, **Olympia Campground (.25 Miles)**
	ATM	**W:** **Shell**
	Other	**E:** **Washington State Patrol**
95		WA 121, Littlerock Maytown
	Food	**W:** **Farm Boy Restaurant**
	RVCamp	**E:** **Deep Lake Resort**
	Parks	**E:** **Maytown State Park**
(93)		**Rest Area (RR, Phones, Picnic, Vending, P; Southbound)**

EXIT		WASHINGTON
(91)		**Rest Area (RR, Phones, Picnic, Vending, P; Northbound)**
88AB		Jct. U.S. 12, Aberdeen, Tenino
	FStop	**W:** **Pacific Pride Commercial Fueling**, **Shell[*, LP] (CFN Fueling)**, **Texaco[*]**
	Gas	**W:** Arco[*]
	Food	**W:** **Dairy Queen**, **Golden Chinese (Texaco)**, Grand Mound Pizza & Deli, Little Red Barn, Maharaja Indian Restaurant, **Texaco**
	AServ	**W:** **Shell (CFN Fueling)**
	RVCamp	**E:** **Frank's RV Repair** **W:** **American RV Sales**, **Outback RV Park (2 Miles)**
	ATM	**W:** Key Bank, **Shell (CFN Fueling)**, Texaco, **Texaco**
82		Harrison Ave.
	Gas	**E:** Arco[*], Shell[*, D, 24] **W:** BP[*], Chevron[*, 24], Texaco[*]
	Food	**E:** Burger King[PLAY], Burgerville USA[PLAY], Casa Ramos Mexican, China Dragon, Dairy Queen, Divine Juices, Godfather's Pizza, Pizza Hut, Sharis Restaurant, Shell, TCBY, Wendy's, Yum Yum Teryaki **W:** Andree's, Arby's, Bill & Bee's, Country Cousin Family Restaurant, Denny's, Hickory House BBQ, Jack-In-The-Box, McDonald's, PaPa Murphy's Pizza, Subway, Taco Bell
	Lodg	**E:** Days Inn, Ferryman's Inn, Riverside Motel, TraveLodge **W:** Motel 6, Park Motel
	AServ	**E:** Q Lube **W:** Al's Auto Supply, Les Schwab Tires
	RVCamp	**E:** **Rotary Riverside Park** **W:** **Mid-way RV Park (1 Mile)**
	ATM	**E:** Arco **W:** BP, Centennial Bank, **Safeway Grocery**
	Other	**E:** Rite Aid Pharmacy, VF Outlet Stores (see our ad this page) **W:** **Factory Outlet Center**, **Safeway Grocery**
81		WA 507 North, Mellen St , Bucoda
	Gas	**E:** Shell[*], Texaco[*, D] (Greyhound Bus Pick-Up)
	Food	**E:** Buchanan's, King Solomon Restaurant, Piccadilly Pizza & Subs, Texaco (Greyhound Bus Pick-Up), The Winter Kitchen Restaurant
	Lodg	**E:** **Peppertree West Motel**
	AServ	**E:** Shell, Shell
	RVCamp	**E:** **Peppertree West Motor Inn & RV Park**
	Med	**W:** ✚ **Hospital**
	ATM	**E:** Texaco (Greyhound Bus Pick-Up)
79		Chamber Way, City Center
	Gas	**E:** Texaco[*, D] **W:** BP[*, D, LP] (Burger King, Taco Bell)
	Food	**E:** Chehalis Way Espresso, Plaza Jalisco Mexican **W:** BP (Burger King, Taco Bell), Burger King (BP), Hogi Yogi (BP), **K-Mart**, Little Caesars Pizza (K-Mart), McDonald's (Wal-Mart), Taco Bell (BP), **Wal-Mart[RX] (McDonald's, Tire & Lube)**
	AServ	**E:** **Goodyear Tire & Auto**, Mike's Auto Repair, Novus Auto Glass Repair, State Ave Auto & Muffler, Uhlmann's Toyota, Ford, Lincoln, & Mercury **W:** Wal-Mart, **Wal-Mart (McDonald's, Tire & Lube)**
	TServ	**E:** **Uhlmann Motors**
	RVCamp	**E:** **Uhlman's RV Center[LP]**
	ATM	**E:** Texaco
	Other	**E:** Chehalis Veterinary Hospital, **Visitor Information** **W:** **K-Mart**, **Wal-Mart[RX] (McDonald's, Tire & Lube)**
77		WA 6 West, Pe Ell, Raymond
	FStop	**E:** **Cemex Fueling[LP]**
	Gas	**E:** Arco[*]
	Food	**E:** Ice Cream & Espresso, The Dairy Bar, The

EXIT WASHINGTON

Picnic Patio
AServ E: Chehalis Muffler
ATM E: Arco
Parks W: **State Park (15 Miles)**
Other W: **State Police**

76 13th St
Gas E: Arco(*, 24), Chevron(*, 24)
Food E: **Denny's**, Jack-In-The-Box, Jade Garden Restaurant, **Kit Carson Restaurant**
Lodg E: Howard Johnson, **Relax Inn**
ATM E: Arco
Parks E: **Chehalis Recreation Park**
W: **Stan Hedwall Park (.25 Miles)**

72 Rush Road
FStop E: **Shell(*) (Taco Bell)**
W: **Pacific Pride Commercial Fueling**, **Texaco(*)**
Gas W: Chevron(*, D) (Hot Stuff Pizza, Cinnamon Street, Smash Hit Subs)
Food E: **McDonald's(PLAY)**, **Rib Eye Restaurant(24)**, **Shell (Taco Bell)**, Subway, **Taco Bell (Shell)**
W: Chevron (Hot Stuff Pizza, Cinnamon Street, Smash Hit Subs), Cinnamon Street (Chevron), Hot Stuff Pizza (Chevron), Smash Hit Subs (Chevron)
RVCamp E: **Dave's Country Canopy & RV Sales**
ATM E: **Shell (Taco Bell)**
W: **Texaco**

71 WA 508 East, Napavine, Onalaska
TStop E: **76(*, SCALES)**
FStop E: **CFN Card Lock**
Food E: **76**, One Eyed Jacks(24) (76)
TServ E: **76(SCALES)**, **76 Auto/Truck Plaza**, **KC Truck Parts**

68 U.S. 12 East, Morton, Yakima
FStop W: **Texaco(*, LP)**
Gas E: Arco(*), BP(*, D) (Visitors Information)
Food E: BP (Visitors Information), Spiffy's
W: **Mustard Seed Restaurant**
RVCamp E: **Chehalis KOA RV Park(LP) (.25 Miles)**, **KOA Kampground(LP)**
ATM E: Arco, BP (Visitors Information)
Parks E: **Louis & Clark State Park**, **Mount Ranier National Park**
Other E: **Visitor Information**

63 WA 505, Winlock, Toledo
Gas W: Shell(*, D, LP)
Lodg W: Sunrise Motel
ATM W: Shell, Shell
Other W: Visitor Information

60 Toledo

59 WA 506 West, Vader, Ryderwood
FStop E: **BP(*, D)**
W: **Texaco(*, LP)**
Food E: **BP**, Mrs. Beesley's
W: Country Cafe, Grandma's In'n'Out
Lodg E: Cowlitz Motel
RVCamp E: **Cowlitz RV Park**
W: **River Oaks RV Park (.5 Miles)**
ATM W: **Texaco**

57 Jackson Highway
TStop W: **Texaco(*, LP, SCALES, 24)**
Food W: **Gee Gee's Restaurant (Texaco TStop)**, **Texaco**
AServ W: **Texaco(24)**
TServ W: **Mack Truck & Trailer Parts**, **Texaco(SCALES, 24)**, **Texaco Truck Stop**
RVCamp W: **Camping**, **RV Park & Storage**
Other W: Freightliner Parts & Service

(55) **Rest Area (RR, Phones, Picnic, P; Northbound)**

(55) **Rest Area (RR, Phones, Picnic, P; Southbound)**

EXIT WASHINGTON

52 Barnes Dr, Toutle Park Road
RVCamp E: **Fox Park RV Park**

49 WA 411S to WA 504E, Toutle, Castle Rock
FStop E: **Texaco(*, LP)**
Gas E: Arco(*)
Food E: 49er Restaurant, Boyd's Coffee (Texaco), Burger King, El Compadre, Mount St Helens Motel, Papa Pete's, Rose Tree Restaurant, **Texaco**
Lodg E: **Motel 7 West**, Mount St Helens Motel, Timberland Inn and Suites
RVCamp E: **Mount St Helens RV Park (2 Miles)**, **Silver Lake Camping Area (6 Miles)**
ATM E: **Texaco**
Parks E: **Sea Quest State Park (5 Miles)**
Other E: **Mount St Helens Visitor Info Ctr**, Mount St. Helens Cinedome Theater

48 Bus Loop 5, Castle Rock

46 Headquarters Road
RVCamp E: **Cedars RV Park**

(44) **Weigh Station (Southbound)**

42 Ostrander Road, Pleasant Hill Road

40 North Kelso Ave

39 WA 4W, Kelso, Longview
Gas E: Arco(*), Shell(*)
Food E: Denny's, Double Tree Hotel, Hilander Restaurant (Bowling & Family Games), Jitters, Little Caesars Pizza, McDonald's(PLAY), Sharis Restaurant
W: Azteca, Burger King, Dairy Queen, Izzy's Pizza, Kesler's Restaurant, Red Lobster, Taco Bell
Lodg E: Double Tree Hotel, Motel 6, Super 8
W: Comfort Inn
AServ W: Q Lube, Sears
RVCamp E: **Brookhollow RV Park (1 Mile)**
ATM E: Arco, **Safeway Grocery**, Shell
W: Cowlitz Bank, Sea First Bank (Top Foods), **Top Foods Supermarket(24)**
Parks E: **Tam-O-Shanter Park**
Other E: Postal Emporium, Rite Aid Pharmacy, **Safeway Grocery**, **Tourist Info.**
W: **Target**, Three Rivers Cinemas, Three Rivers Eye Care, **Three Rivers Mall**, **Top Foods Supermarket**

36 WA 432W to WA 4, Longview, Long Beach Peninsula (Difficult Reaccess)
RVCamp E: **U-Neek RV Center**
Med E: **+ Hospital**
Other E: **State Police**

32 Kalama River Road
RVCamp E: **Camp Kalama RV Park**

30 Kalama (Difficult Reaccess)
Gas E: BP(*)
Food E: Bob Paul's Cafe, Burger Bar, Columbia Inn, Columbia Inn Restaurant, Kalama Cafe, Poker Pete's Pizza Parlor, The Key Bar & Grill
Lodg E: Columbia Inn
AServ E: Big A Auto Repair, Phil Poage's Transmission
RVCamp E: **Kalama RV & Marine**
W: **RV Park (More than .25 Miles)**
ATM E: Towlitz Bank
Parks E: **Peter D. Toteff Memorial Park**
Other E: City Police, Godfrey's Pharmacy, Hendrickson's Antiques & Deli, **Post Office**, The Kalama Market, The Little Bookstore

27 Todd Road, Port of Kalama
FStop E: **Texaco(*, LP)**
Food E: **Texaco**
RVCamp W: **Campground**

22 Dike Access Road

EXIT WASHINGTON

RVCamp W: **Columbia River Front RV Park (2 Miles)**

21 WA 503 East, Woodland, Cougar
Gas E: Arco(*), Chevron(*, 24), Shell(*, D, LP, 24), Texaco(*, D, LP)
Food E: **Brock's Oak Tree Restaurant**, Burgerville USA(PLAY), Casa Maria Mexican, Dairy Queen(PLAY), Figaro's Italian Kitchen, Rosie's Restaurant, South China Restaurant, Subway
Lodg E: Lewis River Inn Motel, **Woodlander Inn**
AServ W: Napa Auto
RVCamp E: **Woodland Shores RV Park**
ATM E: Shell
W: Columbia Bank, Sea First Bank
Other E: **Clean Wash Coin Laundry**, Coin Car Wash, **Hi-School Pharmacy**, Save On Foods
W: Tourist Info.

16 N.W. 319th St, La Center
FStop E: **Texaco(*, LP)**
ATM E: **Texaco**, **Texaco Fuel Stop**
Parks E: **Paradise Point State Park**

(16) **Weigh Station (Northbound)**

14 WA 501 West, NW 269th St, Ridgefield
FStop W: **Chevron(*)**
Gas E: Arco(*), BP(*)
Food E: **Country Junction Restaurant**
RVCamp E: **Big Fir RV Camp (4 Miles)**
ATM E: BP
W: **Chevron**

(13) **Rest Area (RR, Phones, Picnic, Vending, RV Dump, P; Southbound)**

(11) **Rest Area (RR, Phones, Picnic, Vending, RV Dump, P; Northbound)**

9 WA 502E, Northeast 179th St, Battle Ground
FStop W: **Chevron(*, LP)**
Food E: **Jollie's Restaurant(24)**
RVCamp E: **U-Neek RV Sales & Service(LP)**
W: **RV Park**
ATM W: 1st Independent Bank, **Chevron**

7 Northeast 134th St
FStop W: **Texaco Commercial Fueling(LP)**
Gas E: Astro(*, D), BP(*), Citgo(*)
W: Salmon Creek Wayside Market(*, D)
Food E: BP, Burger King(PLAY), Burgerville USA(PLAY), Grayhawk Espresso Bar (BP), JB's Roadhouse, McDonald's(PLAY), Round Table Pizza, Taco Bell
W: Salmon Creek Wayside Market
Lodg E: Comfort Inn, Shilo Motel
RVCamp E: **99 RV Park**, **Spring's RV Parts, Sales, & Service**
ATM E: Astro, BP, Citgo, Columbia Credit Union, Northwest National Bank, Washington Mutual
W: Salmon Creek Wayside Market, School Employees' Credit Union
Other E: 7-11 Convenience Store (Citgo), **Hi-School Pharmacy**, The Book Worm, The Letter Box, Zupan's Market
W: Mountain View Veterinary Hospital

5 Northeast 99th Street
Gas E: Arco(*), Citgo(*) (7-11 Convenience Store), Texaco(*, D)
W: Arco(*), Chevron(*, 24)
Food E: Burgerville USA, Domino's Pizza, Fat Dave's Restaurant
W: Bortolami's Pizzaeria, Clancy's Seafood Mexican, Pogy's Restaurant
AServ E: Gaynor's Automotives, Nissan/Kia Dealer, Protech Collision Repair
RVCamp E: **Custom RV Interiors & Sales, Tom**

Bold red print shows RV & Bus parking available or nearby

EXIT WASHINGTON

Corporation/ RV Service Center

ATM E: Arco, Citgo (7-11 Convenience Store)
W: Chevron, Northwest National Bank

Other E: 7-11 Convenience Store (Citgo), Cub Foods[24]
W: Albertson's Grocery[RX], Hi-School Pharmacy, Mail Biz, Mimi's Laundry, Premier Laundry

4 N.E. 78th St

Gas E: 76[*], Chevron[*, 24], Exxon[*, CW]
W: Shell[D, LP], Texaco[*, D]

Food E: Baskin Robbins, Bob's Supper Club, Burger King, Buster's Texas Style BBQ, Choi's Dynasty, KFC, McCully's Sports Pub & Grill, McDonald's[PLAY], Sakura Japanese Restaurant, Smokey's Pizza, Steak Burger[PLAY], The New Hong Kong Lounge, Totem Pole
W: Denny's, Figaro's Italian Kitchen, Kenny Roger's Roasters, Round Table Pizza, Sunrise Bagels, The City Grill, Wendy's, Yansing Chinese

Lodg E: Quality Inn, Value Motel
W: Best Western

AServ E: America's Tire Company, Car Mart, Chevron[24], Dusty's Auto Parts, Firestone Tire & Auto, Hazel Dell Muffler, Schuck's Auto Supply, Vancouver Dodge & Mazda
W: Shell

RVCamp E: Vancouver RV Park (.25 Miles)

ATM E: 1st Independent Bank, Riverview Savings Bank, Seafirst Bank
W: Safeway Grocery[RX], Washington Mutual

Other E: Fred Meyer Grocery, Hazel Dell Cinemas, Jiffy Mart, Locksmith, The Letter Box
W: Hall's Drugs, Laundry, Rite Aid Pharmacy, Safeway Grocery[RX], The Sea Store, Village Optical

3 Hazel Dell, Northeast Hwy 99, Main Street

Gas E: Chevron[*], Citgo[*], Texaco[D, CW]

Food E: A & W Drive-In, Baskin Robbins, Bob's Supper Club, McDonald's, Peachtree Restaurant & Pie House, Pizza Hut, Ragmuffin's Deli, Skipper's Seafood, Smokey's Hot Oven Pizza, Steakburger, Subway, Taco Bell, Taco Time
W: Hideaway Tavern

Lodg E: Kay's Motel, Quality Inn

AServ E: Chevron, Goodyear Tire & Auto, Les Schwab Tires, Midas Muffler & Brake, My Daddy's Muffler, Oil Can Henry's, Precision Tune & Lube, Schuck's Auto Parts, Tire Factory
W: Delco-Tech Service Center (Randy's Transmissions), Tech-tune Transmission

ATM E: U.S. Bank

2 WA 500E, 39th St, Orchards

1D WA 505, East - 4th Plain Blvd, Port of Vancouver

Food W: Dairy Queen, Hi-School Pharmacy, Main St. Diner (Hi-School Pharmacy)

AServ W: Clarke's European Car Service, Larson Tire Co

Other W: Hi-School Pharmacy

1C Mill Plain Blvd, City Center (Watch For One Ways)

Gas W: Chevron[*, 24]

Food W: Burgerville USA, Denny's

AServ W: Midas Auto Systems Experts

Parks E: Vancouver Central Park

Other E: State Police
W: Kinko's[24]

(0) Rest Area (RR, HF, Phones, P)

1AB WA 14 East, Camas, 1B- City Center, 6th Street

↑WASHINGTON

EXIT OREGON

↓OREGON

308 Jantzen Beach Center

Gas E: Chevron[*]
W: 76[*, D, 24]

Food E: Bayou Side Coffee Shop, Burger King, Eat Now, Safeway Grocery, Taco Bell
W: BJ's Pizza, Grill & Brewery, Barnes & Noble, Bradley's Bar & Grill, Chang's Mongolian Grill, Damon's, Denny's, McDonald's[PLAY], Newport Bay Restaurant, Plaid Pantry, Stanford's Restaurant & Bar, Starbucks Coffee, Subway (Plaid Pantry)

Lodg E: Double Tree Hotel, Oxford Suites
W: Double Tree

AServ E: Chevron, Chevron
W: 76, 76[24], Car Toys, Montgomery Ward

ATM E: Safeway Grocery, Wells Fargo
W: US Bank

Other E: Hayden Island Laundromat, Jantzen Automatic Car Wash, Rite Aid Pharmacy, Safeway Grocery
W: Barnes & Noble, Home Depot, Jantzen Beach Shopping Center, K-Mart, Plaid Pantry, Wunderland Games & Play Area

307 OR 99E, Martin Luther King Jr Blvd, Marine Drive

306B Interstate Ave, Delta Park , Expo Center

Gas E: 76[*, LP]

Food E: Burger King, Burrito House, Elmer's, Mar's Meadows, Shari's[24]

Lodg E: Best Western, Delta Inn[*]

AServ E: Baxter Auto Parts, Eric's Oilery

ATM E: 76, Builder's Square

Other E: Builder's Square

306A Columbia Blvd (Northbound, Difficult Reaccess)

RVCamp E: Portland Meadows RV Park (.75 Miles)

305AB U.S. 30, Lombard St (Northbound, Reaccess Southbound Only)

Gas W: Astro[D, LP, 24], Texaco[*, D]

Food W: Cam Ranh Bay Restaurant, Fred Meyer Grocery, KFC, McDonald's (Fred Meyer), Wendy's, Winchells Donuts

AServ E: Kelly Tires, Portland Tire Factory

ATM W: 7-11 Convenience Store[*], 7-11 Convenience Store, Texaco

Other W: 7-11 Convenience Store, Fred Meyer Grocery, Rite Aid Pharmacy

304 Portland Blvd

Gas W: Arco[*]

Food W: Nite Hawk Restaurant, Swan Garden

Lodg W: Viking Motel

Other W: Interstate Lanes

303 Killingsworth St, Swan Island

Food W: Aliby's Restaurant, Shamrock Restaurant[24], Subway, The Sub Shop

Lodg W: Knickerbocker Motel, Monticello Motel, Westerner Motel

AServ W: Mufflers Custom Exhaust

ATM W: U.S. Bank

Other W: Plaid Pantery

302C Greeley Ave, Swan Island (Difficult Reaccess)

302B I-405, U.S. 30, Beaverton, St Helens

302A Coliseum, Broadway - Weidler Street , Rose Quarter (Watch For One Ways)

Gas E: BP[*, CW], Texaco[*, D], Texaco[*, D]

Food E: Burger King[PLAY], Golden Palace Restaurant, KFC, McDonald's, Motor Moka Cafe, Ramada Plaza Hotel, Skipper's Seafood, Taco Bell, The Sandwich Experience, Traders Restaurant & Lounge (Ramada)

Lodg E: Ramada Plaza Hotel, TraveLodge

AServ E: Broadway Toyota, Coliseum Ford, Les Schwab Tires, Oil Can Henry's, Texaco

ATM E: 7-11 Convenience Store, 7-11 Convenience Store, Wells Fargo

Other E: 7-11 Convenience Store, Bee Rent-a-Car, Car Washman, Kinko's[24]

300 Jct I-84, U.S. 30E, Portland Airport, The Dalles

299B I-405, U.S. 26, City Center, Beaverton

299A U.S. 26 East, OR 43, Ross Island Bridge, Macadam Ave

298 Corbett Ave (Northbound, No Reaccess)

297 Terwilliger Blvd

Food W: Burger King[PLAY], Cafe Du Paris, KFC, La Costa Mexican, Norm's Garden Chinese

AServ W: Richardson Car Co

Med W: + VA Hospital

ATM W: Bank of America, U.S. Bank, Wells Fargo

Other E: Tryon Creek State Park (2.5 Miles)
W: Fred Meyer Grocery, Kaady Car Wash

296B Multnomah Blvd (Southbound, Reaccess Northbound Only)

296A Barbur Blvd (Southbound, Reaccess Northbound Only)

Gas W: Chevron[*, 24], Texaco

Food W: Golden Touch Family Restaurant, Humdinger Delicious Hamburgers, Manana Mexican Restaurant, Original Pancake House, Pizza Hut, Subway, Szechuan Restaurant

Lodg W: King's Row Motel, Portland Rose Motel

AServ W: Chevron, Chevron[24], Complete Automotive Repair, Jiffy Lube, Q-Lube, Texaco

ATM W: 7-11 Convenience Store[*], 7-11 Convenience Store, Key Bank

Other W: 7-11 Convenience Store, Capitol Hill Veterinary Hospital, Safeway Grocery[RX]

295 Capitol highway, Taylors Ferry Road (Northbound side no services within .25 mile)

FStop E: Pacific Pride Commercial Fueling

Gas E: Texaco[D, LP]

Food E: Boston Market Restaurant[PLAY], Dunkin Donuts, IHOP, Round Table Pizza, The Bagel Basket, The Sub Spot, The Thai Orchid
W: McDonald's, Taco Time, The Old Barn Restaurant, Wendy's

Lodg E: Hospitality Inn, The Ranch Inn Motel

AServ E: Metro Tire and Auto Repair, Oil Can Henry's, Texaco, Texaco
W: The Master Wrench

Other E: Kaady's Automatic Car Wash

294 Barbur Blvd

Gas W: BP, Texaco[*, LP, CW]

Food E: Angelo & Rose's
W: Arby's, Banning's Restaurant[24], Burger King, Buster's Texas BBQ, Carrows Restaurant, Dimsum, Hi Hat Northern Cantonese & American, KFC, Mazatland Mexican, New Port Bay Restaurant, Pizza Caboose, Sante Fe Burrito, Skipper's Seafood, Subway, Taco Bell, Tarra Thai II, Tong's Garden Restaurant

Lodg W: DAYS INN Days Inn, Howard Johnson's, Wayside Motor Inn

AServ W: BP, BP, Baxter Auto Parts, Les Schwab Tires, Poehler Automotives, Tigard Transmission

EXIT	OREGON
	Center
ATM	**W:** U.S. Bank
Other	**E:** **Barbur Blvd. Vet. Hospital**
	W: **Fred Meyer**
293	Haines St
292	OR 217, Tigard, Beaverton
Gas	**E:** Texaco(*, D)
Food	**E:** Applebee's, Best Teriyaki, Chevy's Mexican, Chili's, Hiro Sushi, Hunan Pearl, Max Market & Deli, Olive Garden, Stanford's Restaurant, Taco Bell
Lodg	**E:** Crown Plaza Hotel, Phoenix Inn, Residence Inn
ATM	**E:** Liberty Mutual, Portland Teachers' Credit Union, US Bank
Other	**E:** **Deseret Book**, Great Clips
291	Carman Drive, King City
Gas	**W:** Chevron(*), Shell(*, D, LP)
Food	**W:** A Place To Eat, Burgerville USA(PLAY), Domino's Pizza, Houlihan's, Muffin Break, Subway, Teriyaki Express
Lodg	**W:** Best Western, Courtyard Marriott
AServ	**W:** Chevron, Chevron, Peter's Auto Work
ATM	**W:** Centennial Bank
Other	**W:** Home Depot
290	Durham, Lake Oswego
Gas	**E:** 76(*), BP(D, LP), Chevron(*)
	W: Arco(*), Texaco(*, D, LP)
Food	**E:** Arby's, Baskin Robbins, Beaverton Bakery, Burger King, China Cafe, Dalton's Steakhouse, Denny's, Dotty's Deli, Fuddruckers, Lake Oswego Sub Stop, Miller's Homestead Restaurant, Skippers Seafood, Taco Bell, Winchells Donuts, Woo's Open Kitchen
	W: Koon Lok Chinese Restaurant, Pig N Pancake, Sneaker's Pub and Grill, Village Inn
Lodg	**E:** Motel 6, Motel 6
	W: Best Western, Quality Inn
AServ	**E:** Lake Oswego Transmission
	W: Car Quest Auto Parts, Texaco, Texaco
RVCamp	**E:** **Superior Inboard Repair**
ATM	**E:** Chevron, **Safeway Grocery(RX)**
Other	**E:** Borders Books & Music, Cascadia Eye Care, **Cat Care Veterinary Clinic**, Mail Boxes Etc, **Safeway Grocery(RX)**
289	Tualatin, Sherwood
Gas	**E:** Arco(*), Shell(*, LP, K), Texaco(*, CW)
Food	**E:** El Sol De Mexico, McDonald's, Mocha Madness, Sweetbriar Restaurant & Lounge
	W: Pizza Rush, Pogys Subs, Taco Bell, Wendy's
Lodg	**E:** Sweetbriar Restaurant & Lounge, The Sweetbrier Inn
AServ	**E:** Instant Oil Change, Shell
	W: **K-Mart**, K-Mart
RVCamp	**E:** **Trailer Park of Portland (.25 Miles)**
Med	**E:** **+ Legacy Meridian Hospital**
ATM	**E:** 7-11 Convenience Store(*)
	W: Bank Of America, Pacific One Bank, US Bank, Wells Fargo
Other	**E:** 7-11 Convenience Store, Kaady Car Wash, Meridian Park Veterinary Hospital
	W: Barber Shop, **Fred Meyer Grocery**, **K-Mart**, Postal Annex, **Safeway Grocery**, Super Cuts
288	to I-84, Jct I-205, Dalles, Seattle
286	Stafford, North Wilsonville
TStop	**E:** **Burns Brothers Travel Stop(*, SCALES) (Chevron)**
Gas	**E:** BP(*)
Food	**E:** **Burns Brothers Travel Stop (Chevron)**, Mrs. B's Homestyle (Burns Bros)
Lodg	**E:** **Burns Brothers Travel Stop (Chevron)**, **Burns West Motel**, Motel Orleans, Super 8
	W: Holiday Inn
AServ	**E:** **Burns Brothers Travel Stop (Chevron)**
TServ	**E:** **Burns Bros**
RVCamp	**E:** **Pheasant Ridge RV Park (.25 Miles)**

Most exits in California are not numbered. Boxes indicate mileage to Mexico border.

EXIT	OREGON
283	Wilsonville
FStop	**E:** **Pacific Pride Commercial Fueling**
Gas	**E:** 76(*)
	W: Shell(*, D)
Food	**E:** Anne's Bento Cafe, Arby's, Bagel Basket, Boston's Pub & Grill, Brew Ha Ha Coffee, Club House Deli, Coffee Break, Coffee's Gourmet Candy, Country Grains Bread Co., Denny's, Dotty's Bakery & Deli, La Isla Bonita, McDonald's(PLAY), Papa Murphy's Pizza, Paradise Grill, Portlandia Pizza, Royal Panda Restaurant, Shari's Restaurant, Subway, TCBY, Taco Bell, Wanker's Corner Cafe, Wendy's, Wok Inn, Zuka Juice
	W: Baskin Robbins, Burger King(24), Chili's, Fowler's Bakery & Deli, Kathy's Expresso, New Century Chinese
Lodg	**E:** Best Western, Comfort Inn, **Snooz Inn**
	W: Phoenix Inn
AServ	**W:** Shell
RVCamp	**W:** **Camping World (1.6 Miles)**
ATM	**E:** Bank of America, Commercial Bank, **Lamb's Thriftway Supermarket**, Washington Mutual
	W: **7-11 Convenience Store**, US Bank, Wells Fargo
Other	**E:** 20/20 Eye Care Center, Caldwell Banker, Eye Clinic, **Lamb's Thriftway Supermarket**, Plaid Pantry, Rite Aid Pharmacy, The Copy Center, The Letter Box, Town Center Car Wash, **Town Center Veterinary Clinic**, Village Main Veterinary Hospital
	W: **7-11 Convenience Store**, Book Rack, Car Wash(24), **Lowries I.G.A.**
282BA	Charbonneau District, Canby , 282A Canby, Hubbard
(282)	**Rest Area (RR, Phones, Picnic, RV Dump, P; Southbound)**
(282)	**Rest Area (RR, Phones, Picnic, RV Dump, P; Northbound)**
278	Donald, Aurora
TStop	**W:** **TA TravelCenters of America(*, CW, SCALES) (Shell)**
FStop	**E:** **Tesoro Alaska(*, LP, RV DUMP)**
	W: **Texaco(*, LP)**
Food	**W:** **TA TravelCenters of America (Shell)**
AServ	**W:** Bird Brains
TServ	**W:** **TA TravelCenters of America(SCALES) (Shell)**
RVCamp	**E:** **Isberg RV Park**
ATM	**E:** **Tesoro Alaska**
	W: **TA TravelCenters of America (Shell)**, **Texaco**
(274)	**Weigh Station (Southbound)**
(274)	**Weigh Station (Northbound)**
271	OR 214, Woodburn, Silverton
Gas	**E:** 76(*, 24), Arco(*), Chevron(*), Exxon(*, D, CW), Shell(*, D,

1290

CROWNE PLAZA
HOTELS RESORTS
Oregon • Exit 292 • 503-624-8400

CAMPING WORLD
Exit 283
26875 S.W. Boones Ferry Rd. • Wilsonville, OR
1-800-446-9039
1440

Bold red print shows RV & Bus parking available or nearby

EXIT OREGON

[LP] (Espresso Bar)

W: Texaco[*, D, LP]

Food E: **Burger King**[PLAY], Dairy Queen, Denny's, Formaggi Pizza, KFC, **McDonald's**[PLAY], Oregon Berry Restaurant, Patterson's, Taco Bell, Wendy's, Yun Wah Chinese Restaurant & Lounge

W: Texaco

Lodg E: Fairway Inn Motel, Holiday Inn Express, **Super 8**

W: Comfort Inn

AServ E: 76[24], Shell (Espresso Bar)

W: Chevrolet Dealer, Hershberger Chrsyler, Plymouth, Dodge & Jeep, Hillyer's Ford Dealership

RVCamp W: **Woodburn I-5 RV Park**

ATM E: First Security Bank, US Bank, **Wal-Mart (Vision Center)**

Other E: **Fairway Drugs**, Lynn's Market, **Wal-Mart (Vision Center)**

263 Brooks, Gervais

TStop W: **Pilot**[*, LP, SCALES] **(Taco Bell, Subway)**

Food W: **Subway (Pilot)**, **Taco Bell (Pilot)**

TServ W: **Pilot**[SCALES] **(Taco Bell, Subway)**

Parks W: **Williamette Mission State Park (4 Miles)**

260B Keizer

260A North Chemawa Road, Salem Parkway, OR 99E

258 OR 99E, Pacific Highway East

Gas E: BP[*, D]

W: Pacific Pride Commercial Fueling[*]

Food E: Figaro's, McDonald's, The Original Pancake House

Lodg E: Best Western, Sleep Inn

AServ E: Cottnan Transmissions, Mike's Auto Service

W: Stewart's Auto Supply

RVCamp E: **Highway Trailer Sales & Service**, **Trailer Park Village (.5 Miles)**

Med W: **✚ Hospital**

ATM E: BP

W: **Circle K Food Store**

Other E: Plaid Pantry

W: **Circle K Food Store**, **State Police**

256 Market St, Lancaster Mall (Continuous commerce on the east & west side)

Gas W: Arco[*], Pacific Pride Commercial Fueling, Texaco[*]

Food E: Best Teriyaki, Carl Jr's Hamburgers[PLAY], Chalet Restaurant, **Denny's**, Don Pedro, Dunkin Donuts, Elmer's Pancake & Steakhouse, Nacho's Mexican Restaurante, Santa Fe Burrito Company, Skipper's Seafood

W: Baskin Robbins, Canton Garden Chinese, McDonald's, Newport Bay Restaurant, O'Callahan's Restaurant (Quality Inn), Pietro's Engine House Pizza, Quality Inn, **Richard's Restaurant**, Rock-N- Rogers, Village Inn

Lodg E: Best Western

W: **Holiday Lodge**, Motel 6, **Phoenix Inn**, Quality Inn, Salem Inn, Shilo Inn, Super 8

AServ E: Les Schwab Tires, Midas Muffler & Brake

W: Auto Glass Express, Market Street Mazda & Isuzu, Salem Nissan, Texaco

RVCamp E: **Oak Park RV Village (1.5 Miles)**

ATM E: First Security Bank, **Fred Meyer Grocery**[RX] **(Mail Boxes Etc, Barber Shop)**

W: Arco, Wells Fargo

Other E: Car Wash, **Fred Meyer Grocery**[RX] **(Mail Boxes Etc, Barber Shop)**, Lancaster Mall, Suds City Depot

W: Coin Laundromat, **Jack's Grocery Store**, Wunderland Fun & Games

253 OR 22 North, Santiam Hwy, Stayton, Detroit Lake

Food W: Denny's

Lodg W: Best Western

AServ W: Roberson Chrysler/Plymouth

RVCamp E: **Salem Campground & RV's (.25 Miles)**

W: **Roberson RV Center**

Med W: **✚ Hospital**

Other E: Home Depot

W: Airport, Budget Car & Truck Rental, **Costco**, **Visitor Information**

252 Kuebler Blvd

Med W: **✚ Hospital**

249 Commercial Street (Northbound, Reaccess Southbound Only)

Med W: **✚ Hospital**

Other W: **Salem Historic Museum**

248 Sunnyside, Turner

FStop W: **Pacific Pride Commercial Fueling**

RVCamp W: **Forest Glen**

Other W: **Sunnyside Food Mart**

244 Jefferson

243 Ankeny Hill

242 Talbot Road

(241) **Rest Area (RR, Phones, Picnic, Vending, RV Dump, P; Southbound)**

(241) **Rest Area (RR, Phones, Picnic, Vending, RV Dump, P; Northbound)**

240 Hoefer Road

239 Dever - Conner

238 Jefferson, Scio

237 Viewcrest (Southbound, Reaccess Southbound Only)

235 Viewcrest

234AB OR 99E, Albany, Knox, Butte

Gas W: Arco[*], Chevron[*] (Tom Tom Deli)

Food W: Burger King[PLAY], Chevron (Tom Tom Deli), McDonald's[PLAY], Taco Bell (TCBY), **Tom Tom Restaurant**, Yaquina Bay Restaurant

Lodg W: Best Western, Comfort Inn

RVCamp E: **Knox Butte RV Park (.25 Miles)**

W: **Kamper Shoppe RV Center**[LP], **Parkview Estates RV Park**

Med W: **✚ Hospital**

ATM W: Arco

Other W: **K-Mart**

233 U.S. 20, Lebanon, Santiam Hwy, Sweet Home

TStop E: **BP**[*, SCALES]

FStop E: **Chevron**[*, LP, 24]

Gas W: Leathers Fuels[*, D], Plaza Gas, Texaco[LP]

Food E: **BP**, Lum Yuem Chinese, Snarky's

W: Abby's Legendary Pizza, **Appletree Family Restaurant (Valu-Inn)**, Baskin Robbins, Cameron's Restaurant, Carl Jr's Hamburgers, Chan Kam Kee Chinese, Elmer's Pancake & Steakhouse, Novak's Hungarian Restaurant, Skipper's Seafood, Smokehouse Cafe, Taco Time, **Valu-Inn**

Lodg E: Holiday Inn Express, Motel Orleans

W: **Valu-Inn**

AServ E: Lassen Toyota, Chevrolet & Geo Dealer, Mazda & Honda Dealership, Steve's Muffler Center

W: Albany Car Lab, Leathers Fuels, Les Schwab Tires, Texaco

TServ E: **Battam International**

RVCamp E: **B & L RV Center**, **Blue Ox RV Park**

ATM E: **Chevron**, Snarky's

W: Albany Quick Stop Market

Parks E: **Timber Lynn Park**

Other E: State Police

W: Albany Quick Stop Market, **Albertson's Grocery**, Rite Aid Pharmacy

228 OR 34, Lebanon, Corvallis

TStop E: **Texaco**[*, LP] **(Commercial Fueling Pacific Pride)**

FStop W: **Chevron**[*] **(CFN Commercial Fueling)**

Gas E: Leathers Fuels[*, D]

W: 76[*, LP, 24], **All Star**[LP], Arco[*], **Auto & Truck Service**[D, LP] **(24 hour towing)**, Shell[*, D, 24]

Food E: **Texaco (Commercial Fueling Pacific Pride)**

AServ E: Leathers Fuels

W: **Auto & Truck Service (24 hour towing)**

TServ W: **Auto & Truck Service (24 hour towing)**

ATM E: **Texaco (Commercial Fueling Pacific Pride)**

W: 76, Arco, **Chevron (CFN Commercial Fueling)**, Shell

216 OR 228, Brownsville, Halsey

TStop E: **BP**[*] **(Pioneer Villa, ATM)**

FStop W: **Texaco**[*] **(Subway & Taco Bell)**

Food E: **BP (Pioneer Villa, ATM)**, **Blimpie's Subs (Pioneer Villa)**, **Restaurant**[*] **(Pioneer Villa)**

W: Subway (Texaco), **Taco Bell (Texaco)**

Lodg E: **BP (Pioneer Villa, ATM)**, **Pioneer Villa**

AServ W: Larry's Auto Parts and Repair

TServ E: **BP (Pioneer Villa, ATM)**

ATM E: **Pioneer Villa**, **Pioneer Villa**

W: **Texaco (Subway & Taco Bell)**

209 Harrisburg, Junction City

Food W: **The Hungry Farmer**

TServ W: **Diamond Hill Truck & RV Repair**

RVCamp W: **Diamond Hill**

(206) **Rest Area (RR, Phones, Picnic, P; Southbound)**

(206) **Rest Area (RR, Phones, Picnic, P; Northbound)**

199 Coburg

TStop W: **T/A TravelCenters of America**[*, LP, RV DUMP, SCALES] **(Motel)**

Gas W: Shell[*, LP], Texaco[*, LP]

Food E: **LB (Country Squire Inn)**

W: **Country Pride**[LP] **(Travel America TStop)**, Shell, **The Hillside Grill**

Lodg E: **Country Squire Inn**

W: **T/A TravelCenters of America (Motel)**

AServ W: Texaco

TServ W: **Basin Tire**, **Cummins Diesel**, **Freight Liner**, **Lucas Truck Sales & Service**, **Marathon Coach Inc**

RVCamp E: **Coburg Hills RV Resort**, **RV Park**

W: **Destinations RV (.5 Miles)**, **Eugene Kamping World**, **Monaco Coach Corporation**

ATM W: Shell

Other E: **Road Runner Electronics**

195AB Junction City, Florence

Gas E: Arco[*], BP[*, D, LP], Chevron[*]

Food E: Denny's, Far Man Chinese & American Food, Fast Track Pizza, Gateway Chinese Buffet, Hodge Podge (Shilo Inn), IHOP, KFC, McDonald's[PLAY], Sharis Restaurant, Shilo Inn, Sizzler, Spencer's Restaurant & Brew House, Taco Bell, Taco Time

Lodg E: Best Western, Courtyard by Marriott, Double Tree Hotel, Gateway Inn, Motel 6, Motel Orleans, Pacific 9, Rodeway Inn, Shilo Inn

TServ E: **Stalick International Trucks**

ATM E: Arco, Dairy Mart, Western Bank

Other E: Dairy Mart, Kinko's

194AB OR 126, I-105, Springfield, Eugene

Bold red print shows RV & Bus parking available or nearby

EXIT		OREGON
192		OR 99, Eugene, Univ of Oregon (Northbound, Reaccess Southbound Only, Continuous commerce)
	Gas	W: BP(*, LP)
	Food	W: Black Angus Steakhouse (Quality Inn), Kim's Restaurant, Lyon's Restaurant, Quality Inn
	Lodg	W: Quality Inn
	AServ	W: Euro Asian Automotive, German Auto Service, Joe Romana Chevrolet
	Med	W: **+ Hospital**
	Other	W: **Hirons Pharmacy**, Mike's Farm Fresh
191		Glenwood, Springfield
	Gas	W: BP(*, D, LP), Texaco(*, D, LP)
	Food	W: Denny's
	Lodg	W: Motel 6
	TServ	E: **Pape Caterpillar Dealership**
189		30th Ave, South Eugene (Difficult Reaccess, Difficult access to the east side services)
	Gas	E: Texaco(*, D)
		W: Exxon(*, LP)
	Food	E: Subway (Texaco), Taco Bell (Texaco), Texaco
		W: Exxon, On the Go Espresso, The Old Smokehouse (Exxon)
	RVCamp	E: **Eugene Mobile Home Park (1.75 Miles)**, **Interstate 5 RV Service**
		W: **Shamrock Mobile Home Village (.5 Miles)**
	ATM	E: Texaco
188AB		OR 58, Willamette Hwy, Oakridge ,Klamath Falls
	TStop	W: **Goshen Truck Stop Tire Service(*)**
	Food	W: **Goshen Truck Stop Tire Service**, **Summers Cafe (Goshen TS)**
	AServ	W: The Auto Doctor
	TServ	W: **Roadrunner Tire Co**
	Other	W: Kumho Tires, R & D Propane
186		Goshen (Northbound, Reaccess Southbound Only)
182		Creswell
	Gas	W: Arco(*), BP(*, D, LP), Chevron, Texaco(*, D)
	Food	W: Apple Annie's, B & B Family Dining, Creswell Cafe and Deli, Dairy Queen, Donut Shop, Los Cabos, Mr. Macho's Pizza, Ray's U-Bake Pizza, Rita's Snack Shack, **TJ's Family Restaurant**, The Pizza Station
	Lodg	W: **Motel Orleans**
	AServ	W: Careco Automotive, Chevron, NAPA, The Tire Factory
	RVCamp	W: **KOA Campgrounds**, **Ruiz Repairs Auto Trucks & RVs**
	ATM	W: **Century Grocery Store**, Dari Mart, Dari Mart, Siuslaw Bank
	Other	W: **Century Grocery Store**, Coin Car Wash, **Creswell Vet. Clinic**, Dari Mart, Dari Mart, Visitor Information
(178)		**Rest Area (RR, Phones, Picnic, P; Southbound)**
(178)		**Rest Area (RR, Phones, Picnic, P; Northbound)**
176		Saginaw
174		Cottage Grove, Dorena Lake
	FStop	E: **Pacific Pride Commercial Fueling**
		W: **Chevron(*)**
	Gas	E: Chevron(*, D, LP)
	Food	E: Best Western, China Gardens Restaurant, Copper Rooster (Best Western), Cottage Restaurant, Subway, Taco Bell
		W: **Burger King**, Carl Jr's Hamburgers, KFC, McDonald's(PLAY), **Vintage Inn Restaurant**
	Lodg	E: Best Western
		W: Comfort Inn, Holiday Inn Express
	AServ	E: Chevron, Cottage Grove Chev, Pont, Olds, Lowther Chrysler Plymouth Dodge Jeep Eagle, South Valley Ford, **Wal-Mart(RX)**
	RVCamp	E: **RV Sales & Service**, **Village Green RV Park (.5 Miles)**
	Med	W: **+ Hospital**
	ATM	W: **Chevron**
	Other	E: The Bowling Green, **Wal-Mart(RX)**
172		6th Street, Cottage Grove Lk.
170		Bus OR 99, Cottage Grove (Northbound, Difficult Reaccess)
	Med	W: **+ Hospital**
163		Curtin , Lorane
	FStop	E: **Shell(*)**
	Gas	W: 76(*)
	Food	E: **Curtin Kitchen(24)**, **Shell**
		W: **The Coach House**
	Lodg	E: **Stardust Motel**
	TServ	W: **24 Hour Truck Repair**
	Parks	W: **Pass Creek Park**
	Other	E: **US Post Office**
162		Drain, Elkton, OR 38, OR 99
161		Anlauf, Lorane (Northbound, No Reaccess)
160		Salt Springs Road
159		Elk Creek, Cox Road
154		Elkhead, Yoncalla
150		Yoncalla, Red Hill
	RVCamp	W: **Trees of Oregon RV Park**
148		Rice Hill
	TStop	E: **Pilot(*, SCALES) (CFN Commercial Fueling)**
	FStop	E: **Pacific Pride Commercial Fueling**
	Gas	E: Chevron(*, LP, 24)
	Food	E: Homestead (Pilot), **Meggy's Restaurant**, **Pilot (CFN Commercial Fueling)**, Quickies Drive In, **Ranch Motel**, Subway (Pilot)
		W: K & R Drive-in
	Lodg	E: **Ranch Motel**
	AServ	E: Carl's Towing(24), **Economy Service Center (24 hour towing)**, Jim's Towing & Garage(24)
	TServ	E: **Economy Service Center (24 hour towing)**, **Northwest Diesel Service**
	ATM	E: Chevron, **Pilot (CFN Commercial Fueling)**
	Other	E: Laundromat
146		Rice Valley
(143)		**Rest Area (RR, Phones, Picnic, P; Southbound)**
(143)		**Rest Area (RR, Phones, Picnic, P; Northbound)**
142		Metz Hill
138		Oakland , OR 99 (Southbound, Reaccess Northbound Only)
136		OR 138 W, Sutherlin, Elkton
	Gas	E: BP(*, 24), Chevron(*), Texaco(*, D) (Subway)
		W: Astro(*, LP)
	Food	E: Burger King, McDonald's(PLAY), Subway (Texaco)
		W: Dairy Queen(PLAY), Taco Bell, West Winds(24)
	Lodg	E: Microtel Inn, Penny Wise Motel, Town & Country Motel
		W: **Best Budget Inn**
	AServ	E: BP(24), Chevron
		W: Astro, Blakely's Towing & Repair
	TServ	W: **Smalley Trucking & Diesel Center**
	RVCamp	E: **RV Sales & Service Center**
		W: **Hi-Way Haven RV Park (2 Miles)**
	ATM	W: West Winds
	Other	E: Mini Mart & Deli, Westwood Lanes Family Fun Center
		W: Visitor Information
135		Wilbur
	AServ	E: Mr.E Auto Sales, Mufflers, & Service
(130)		**Weigh Station (Southbound)**
129		Winchester,OR 99, North Roseburg
	TServ	E: **Southern Oregon Diesel**
	RVCamp	E: **Amacher Park**, **Kamper Korner(LP) (.3 Miles)**
127		Stewart Pkwy
	Med	W: **+ Hospital**
125		Roseburg, Garden Valley Blvd
	Gas	E: BP(*), Texaco(*, D, LP, 24)
		W: Chevron(*, 24), Gas(*), Shell(*, LP)
	Food	E: Brutke's Wagon Wheel Restaurant, Casey's Restaurant, KFC, Mi Familia Restaurant, Papa Murphy's Pizza, Purple Parrot Deli, Sandpiper (Windmill Inn), Schu-Mart Pizza and Subs(24), Taco Bell, Windmill Inn
		W: Arby's, Burger King, Fox Den, La Hacienda Mexican Restaurant, The Cellar 100 Deli, **Tom Tom Restaurant**, Wendy's, Yogurt Country
	Lodg	E: Comfort Inn, Motel Orleans, Windmill Inn
		W: Best Western
	AServ	E: BP, Mr. King's Auto Shop, Pennzoil Oil Change, Texaco(24), Van's Select Auto Service & Sales
		W: Schuck's Auto Supply, Shell, The Auto Tech
	RVCamp	E: **Jim,s Trailer Supply (.8 Miles)**
	Med	W: **+ Hospital**, **+ Roseburg VA Hospital**
	ATM	E: Schu-Mart Pizza and Subs, Texaco, Western Bank
		W: Bank of America, South Umpqua Bank
	Other	E: Bailey Veterinary Clinic, Bible Book Center, Champion Car Wash, **Coin Op Laundry**
		W: **Fred Meyer Grocery**, Garden Valley Cinema, Roseburg Valley Mall, Valley Opticians
124		OR 138, City Center, Diamond Lake
	Gas	E: BP(*, D, LP), Shell(*)
		W: Chevron(*)
	Food	E: Denny's
		W: Gay 90's Ice Cream, Subway, Taco Time(PLAY)
	Lodg	E: Dunes Motel, Holiday Inn Express, TraveLodge
	AServ	E: Shell
		W: Speedy Lube
	Med	W: **+ Douglas Community Hospital**
	ATM	W: **Anderson Place Market (US post office)**
	Other	E: **Visitor Information**
		W: 3d Coin Op Laundry, **Anderson Place Market (US post office)**, **Grocery Outlet**, While Away Books
123		Fairgrounds, Umpqua Park
	RVCamp	E: **Fairgrounds RV Park**
121		McLain Ave
120		Green District, Roseburg (Difficult Reaccess)
	Lodg	E: Shady Oaks Motel
	AServ	W: Chuck Swarm Auto Repair, Dunlop Tires
	TServ	W: **Transit Support Services**
	RVCamp	W: **Discount Auto & RV Repair**
119		OR 99, OR 42W, Winston Coos Bay
	FStop	W: **Texaco(*, D, CW, 24)**
	TWash	W: **Texaco(CW)**
	RVCamp	W: **Rising River RV Park (2 Miles)**, **Sheraton RV Park**, **Western Star**
113		Round Prairie, Clarks Branch Road
	Lodg	W: Quick Stop Motel & Market(*)
	TServ	W: **Doug's Diesel Inc**
	RVCamp	W: **On the River RV Park (2 Miles)**
112		**Dillard, Winston, Rest Area (RR, Phones, Picnic, P)**
	Food	E: **Rivers West South Umpqua Campground And RV Park (South Fork Lodge, Restaurant)**

Bold red print shows RV & Bus parking available or nearby

EXIT	OREGON
RVCamp	**E:** Rivers West South Umpqua Campground And RV Park (South Fork Lodge, Restaurant)
(112)	**Rest Area (RR, Phones, Picnic, P; Southbound)**
(111)	**Weigh Station (Northbound)**
110	Boomer Hill Road
108	Myrtle Creek
Food	**E:** Cross Creek Restaurant, Dairy Queen, Fat Elk Deli Cafe
Lodg	**E:** Rose Motel, South Umpqua Inn
AServ	**E:** Car Quest Auto Center, Chevron
RVCamp	**E:** Myrtle Creek RV Park
ATM	**E:** U.S Bank
Other	**E:** Mike's Books and Expresso
106	Weaver Road
103	Tri - City, Myrtle Creek
FStop	**W:** Chevron[*] (Pacific Pride Commercial Fueling)
Food	**W:** Chevron (Pacific Pride Commercial Fueling), McDonald's[PLAY]
Other	**E:** Nickel Bowl
102	Gazley Road
101	Riddle, Stanton Park
99	Canyonville, Crater Lake
TStop	**W:** Fat Harvey's Travel Center[*, LP, RV DUMP, SCALES]
Food	**E:** Burger King[PLAY]
Lodg	**E:** Riverside Lodge Motel, Seven Feathers Hotel & Gaming Resort, Valley View Motel
TServ	**W:** Fat Harvey's Travel Center[SCALES]
ATM	**W:** Fat Harvey's Travel Center
Parks	**E:** Stanton Park
Other	**E:** Cow Creek Indian Gaming Center
98	Canyonville, Days Creek
Gas	**E:** BP[*, D, LP], Texaco[*, D]
Food	**E:** Bella Donna, Bob's Country Junction
Lodg	**E:** The Inn
AServ	**E:** Dick's Pacific Hwy Garage & Towing[24] (24 hour towing), Napa Auto
	W: Bill's Tire Towing & Automotive[LP]
Med	**E:** ✚ Falk Family Urgent Care Medical Center
Other	**E:** Fast Stop Market, Gordon's Drugs[RX], Pioneer Indian Museum
95	Canyon Creek
88	Azalea, Galesville Reservoir
86	Quines Creek Road, Barton Road
Gas	**E:** Texaco[*, D, LP]
Food	**E:** Galesville Old Town Coffee, Heaven On Earth Restaurant, Oregon Apple Butter Farms
83	Barton Road (Northbound, Reaccess Southbound Only)
RVCamp	**E:** Meadow Wood RV Park (1.25 Miles)
(82)	**Rest Area (RR, Phones, Picnic, P; Southbound)**
(82)	**Rest Area (RR, Phones, Picnic, P; Northbound)**
80	Glendale
Gas	**W:** T & T[*]
Food	**W:** Lynn's Drive Inn
78	Speaker Road (Southbound, Reaccess Northbound Only)
RVCamp	**W:** Creekside[*, LP]
76	Wolf Creek (Southbound, Reaccess Northbound Only, Difficult Reaccess)
Gas	**W:** Texaco[*]
Food	**W:** Hungry Wolf Deli, Wolf Creek Tavern
RVCamp	**W:** Creekside RV Resort

EXIT	OREGON
Other	**W:** U.S. Post Office, Wolf Creek General Store
71	Sunny Valley
Gas	**E:** BP[*, LP]
Food	**W:** Aunt Mary's Cavern & Kitchen, Covered Bridge Cafe
Lodg	**E:** Sunny Valley Motel
RVCamp	**W:** KOA Camp
Other	**E:** Covered Bridge Country Store
66	Hugo
RVCamp	**E:** Joe Creek Waterfalls RV Park[LP]
(63)	**Rest Area (RR, Phones, Picnic, RV Dump, P; Southbound)**
(63)	**Rest Area (RR, Phones, Picnic, RV Dump, P; Northbound)**
61	Merlin
Gas	**W:** Texaco[*, D]
TServ	**W:** Pacific Truck & Trailer Service
Parks	**W:** Indian Mary County Park
Other	**W:** Colonial Building Supply, North Valley Animal Clinic
58	OR 99, I-199, Grant Pass , Crescent City
Gas	**W:** 76[*], Arco[*, 24], BP[D], Chevron[*], Gas 4 Less[LP] (U-Haul Rental), Shell[*], Texaco[*, D, LP], Towne Pump[CW]
Food	**W:** Angela's, Bee Gee's Restaurant, Burger King[PLAY], Carl Jr's Hamburgers, Della's Restaurant, Denny's, Lantern Grill, Maggie's Pizza, McDonald's[PLAY], Royal Vue, Senor Sam's Mexican Grill, Sizzler, Skipper's Seafood, Stanbrook's, Stars Restaurant (Royal Vue), Subway, Taco Bell, The Jelly Doughnut, Wendy's
Lodg	**W:** Golden Inn, Motel 6, Motel Orleans, Royal Vue, Shilo Inn Motel, Super 8
AServ	**W:** 76, Caveman Towing, Cray's Towing, Gas 4 Less (U-Haul Rental), Les Schwab Tires, Pennzoil Oil Change, Shell
RVCamp	**E:** Rogue Valley Overnighters (.25 Miles), The Tool Box (.25 Miles)
	W: Rogue Valley Overniters
ATM	**W:** Wells Fargo
Other	**W:** 4 Seasons Auto Wash, Coin Laundry, Grant's Pass Visitors Center, Hand Car Wash, Showtime Family Lanes, Solar Man Car Wash
55	East Grants Pass, Redwood Hwy
Gas	**W:** Arco[*]
Food	**W:** Elmer's Pancake & Steakhouse, Hamilton House Restaurant, Sharis, Taco Bell
Lodg	**W:** Best Western, Holiday Inn Express
AServ	**W:** Complete Auto & Truck Parts, United Auto Body
RVCamp	**W:** Daryl's RV Village (1.75 Miles), Siskiyou RV World (.25 Miles)
Other	**W:** Grocery Outlet, Wal-Mart
48	City of Rogue River
Gas	**E:** Arco[*], Exxon[*], Texaco[*, D, LP]
Food	**E:** Abby's Legendary Pizza, Cattleman's Saloon & Rib House, China House, Mr. Will's Place, Suzu-Ya Japanese, The Rogue Cafe
	W: Arnie's Fine Dining, Karen's Kitchen
Lodg	**W:** Best Western
AServ	**E:** Auto Works, Exxon, Texaco
RVCamp	**W:** Circle W RV Park (1 Mile), RV Park, River Park RV Resort (6.25 Miles), Whispering Pines RV Park
ATM	**E:** Evergreen Federal Bank, Valley of the Rogue Bank
Other	**E:** Dove Book Center
	W: Market Basket
45B	**Valley of the Rogue Park & Rest Area (RR, HF, Picnic, P)**

EXIT	OREGON
45A	OR 99, Savage Rapids Dam and Rogue River Route
Food	**E:** Rogue Riviera Supper Club
Lodg	**E:** Homestead on the Rogue
AServ	**E:** Tocher's Rods & Service
RVCamp	**E:** Cypress Grove RV Park[LP]
	W: Drifters Mobile Home Park
43	OR 99, OR 234, Gold Hill, Crater Lake
Food	**E:** Rock Point Bistro
Lodg	**E:** Rockpoint Motel & RV Park, Rogue River Guest House
40	Jacksonville, Gold Hill
Gas	**W:** BP[*]
Food	**W:** Gato Gordo Mexican, Sammy's Restaurant
RVCamp	**E:** KOA Campgrounds (.5 Miles), RV Park
	W: Dardanelle's RV Park, Lazy Acres Motel & RV Park (1.75 Miles)
35	OR 99, Central Pt., N. Medfore
33	Central Point
TStop	**E:** Pilot[SCALES, 24] (Taco Bell, Subway)
FStop	**W:** BP[*] (CFN Fueling)
Gas	**E:** Chevron[*, LP]
	W: Texaco[*, D, LP]
Food	**E:** Burger King[PLAY], Subway (Pilot), Taco Bell (Pilot)
	W: Abby's Legendary Pizza, Bee Gee's Restaurant, Central Express Sandwiches, McDonald's
RVCamp	**E:** Motor Home Rentals, Triple A RV Center (2 Miles)
	W: Central Point RV Service Center (1.5 Miles)
Other	**E:** The Rogue Valley Family Fun Center
30	OR 62, Medford, Crater Lake
TStop	**W:** Witham[*, SCALES] (Restaurant, Chevron)
Gas	**E:** Chevron[*, CW], Gas 4 Less[D, LP]
	W: Chevron[*, D], Exxon[*], Texaco[*, D, CW]
Food	**E:** Arby's, Carl Jr's Hamburgers[PLAY], Coyote Grill (Reston Hotel), Denny's, Elmer's Pancake & Steakhouse, IHOP, Pizza Hut, Reston Hotel, Stuft Pizza, Taco Bell, Taco Delite
	W: Burger King[PLAY], R & B Sandwich Factory, Red Lobster, Restaurant (Witham TStop), Skipper's
Lodg	**E:** Best Western, Comfort Inn, Reston Hotel, Rogue Regency Inn, Shilo Inn, Windmill Inn
	W: Motel 6, Rogue Regency Inn
AServ	**E:** Mastercraft Tires, Wholesale Auto Parts
	W: Exxon, Q Lube, Riverside Tire Center
TServ	**W:** Freightliner Dealer[SCALES], Witham[SCALES] (Restaurant, Chevron), Witham TStop
RVCamp	**E:** Lakewood Vista RV Resort
	W: Triple A RV Center (.5 Miles)
ATM	**E:** Washington Mutual
	W: US Bank
Other	**E:** Food 4 Less Supermarket[D, LP, 24] (Gas), Fred Meyer Grocery
	W: Rogue Valley Mall, Target
27	Medford, Barnett Road
Gas	**E:** Exxon[*, D], Shell[*, 24]
	W: Chevron[*], Texaco[*, D]
Food	**E:** Apple Annie's Family Restaurant, Krystal, Rock & Rod Diner
	W: Abby's Pizza, Burger King, Home Town Buffet, Jack-In-The-Box, KFC, Kim's, McDonald's, McGrath's Fish House, Roosters Homestyle Cooking, Sharis Restaurant, Starbucks Coffee, Stuft Pizza, Subway, Taco Bell, The Donut Factory, Zach's Deli
Lodg	**E:** DAYS INN Days Inn, Economy Inn, Horizon Motor Inn, Motel 6
	W: Capri Motel, Comfort Inn, Royal Crest Motel
AServ	**W:** Big O Tires, Chevron
Med	**E:** ✚ Rogue Valley Medical Hospital
ATM	**E:** Shell
	W: Fred Meyer (Washington Mutual), Liberty

Bold red print shows RV & Bus parking available or nearby

EXIT OREGON/CALIFORNIA

Federal Bank, Texaco, Western Bank
Other W: Fred Meyer (Washington Mutual), **Harry & David Grocery Store**, Mail Boxes Etc, Village Books

24 Phoenix
TStop E: **Petro**(LP, SCALES)
Gas E: Texaco(*, LP)
W: Exxon(*)
Food W: **McDonald's**
Lodg E: **Pear Tree Motel**
TServ E: **DSU Peterbilt**, **Petro**(SCALES)
RVCamp E: **DSU Peterbilt**, **Pear Tree Motel And RV Park**
W: **Holiday RV Park**
ATM W: **Ray's Food Place Grocery**
Other W: **Pear Three Factory Outlet Center**, **Ray's Food Place Grocery**

(22) **Rest Area (RR, Phones, Picnic, P; Southbound)**

21 Talent
TStop W: **Talent Truck Stop (Arco gas)**
Gas W: Arco(*)
Food W: **Talent Truck Stop (Arco gas)**, Talent Truck Stop Restaurant
AServ W: **Wal-Mart**
TServ W: **Talent Truck Stop (Arco gas)**
TWash W: **Talent Truck Stop (Arco gas)**
RVCamp W: **Oregon RV Roundup**
Parks W: **Lynn Newbrey Park**
Other W: **Wal-Mart**

19 Valley View Road, Ashland
FStop W: **Pacific Pride Commercial Fueling**
Gas W: Exxon(*, D, LP), Texaco(*, D)
Food W: Burger King(PLAY), Regency Inn, **Regency Inn**, Texaco
Lodg W: Best Western, **Regency Inn**
AServ W: Exxon
RVCamp W: **Ashland Regency Inn**, **Destinations RV (.5 Miles)**, **Eugene Kamping World RV Park (.25 Miles)**, **Regency Inn**
Med W: ✚ **Hospital**
Other W: Visitor Information

(18) **Weigh Station (Southbound)**

(18) **Weigh Station (Northbound)**

14 **OR 66, Ashland, Klamath Falls, Oregon Welcome Center**
Gas E: BP(*, LP), Chevron(*, D), Texaco(*, LP)
W: 76(*, 24), Arco(*), Exxon(*) (U-Haul Rental)
Food E: Copper Skillet
W: All American Ice Cream and Yogurt, Apple Cellar, Azteca, Chubby's, Jade Dragon, McDonald's, Oak Tree Restaurant, **Pizza Hut**, Taco Bell
Lodg E: Quality Inn, Vista Motel, Windmill Inn
W: Knight's Inn, Super 8
AServ E: BP
W: 76(24), Exxon (U-Haul Rental), Les Schwab Tires
ATM E: Texaco
W: Bank Of America
Other W: **Albertson's Grocery**, Bi-Mart, Mail Boxes Etc, Rite Aid Pharmacy(RX), Shop N Kart

11 OR 99, Siskiyou Blvd, Ashland (Northbound, Reaccess Southbound Only)

(9) Runaway Truck Ramp (Northbound)

(7) Runaway Truck Ramp (Northbound)

6 Mt Ashland
Food E: **Callahan's Dinner House & Country Store**
RVCamp E: **Siskiyou Lodge**

1 Siskiyou Summit (Northbound, Reaccess Southbound Only)

EXIT CALIFORNIA

↑OREGON

↓CALIFORNIA

Exit **(795)** Hilt
Gas W: Texaco(*)
Food W: Texaco

Exit **(792)** Bailey Hill Road

(791) Agricultural Inspection station (Southbound)

Exit **(790)** Hornbrook Hwy, Ditch Creek Road

Exit **(788)** Henley, Hornbrook
FStop E: **Chevron**(*, LP)

(786) **CA 96 ,Klamath River Hwy, Rest Area**

Exit **(782)** Vista Point (Southbound)

Exit **(777)** Yreka, Montague
FStop W: **USA Gasoline**(*, LP)
Food W: Casa Ramos Mexican, Claim Jumper's Family Restaurant, Ma & Pa's Restaurant
Lodg W: Gold Pan Motel, Super 8
RVCamp W: **Tandy's RV and Auto Service**
ATM W: **Ray's Food Place Grocery**, **USA Gasoline**
Other E: **Airport**
W: **Amerigas Propane**(LP), **Ray's Food Place Grocery**, **The Laundry Chute**, Visitor Information

Exit **(776)** Central Yreka (Watch for one-ways)
FStop E: **Pacific Pride Commercial Fueling**
Gas W: BP(*, LP), Chevron(*), Texaco(*)
Food W: A & W Drive-In (Texaco), Denny's, Grandma's House, Lavo's Mexican Restaurant, Ming's, Taco Time (Texaco), Texaco, The Daily Grind Coffee
Lodg W: Best Western
AServ W: All Pro Auto Parts, BP, Clayton Tire Center, Gary's Starter & Alternator Repair(24)
ATM W: Bank Of America, Scott Valley Bank, Texaco, Tri Counties Bank, US Bank
Other W: Visitor Information

Exit **(775)** CA 3, Fort Jones, Yreka
FStop E: **CFN Commercial Fueling**(24)
Gas W: Shell(*, D)
Food W: Burger King(PLAY), Carl Jr's Hamburgers(PLAY), Jerry's Restaurant, McDonald's(PLAY), Papa Murphy's Pizza, Subway, Taco Bell, The Old Boston Shaft Restaurant, Yogurt Etc.
Lodg W: **Amerihost Inn**, Motel 6, Motel Orleans
AServ E: Les Schwab Tires (Access from West frontage road)
W: Jim Wilson Ford Mercury & Lincoln, NAPA Auto Parts, Schuck's Auto Supply
RVCamp E: **Waiiaka Trailer Haven & RV Park (Access from West frontage road)**
Med W: ✚ **Hospital**
ATM W: **Raley's Supermarket**, Shell
Other W: Highway Patrol, **Raley's Supermarket**, **Wal-Mart**(RX)

Exit **(769)** Easy St., Shamrock Rd.
Gas W: Beacon(*, LP)
RVCamp W: **Campground**
ATM W: Beacon

Exit **(764)** Gazelle, Grenada
FStop E: **Shell**(*)
Lodg E: **Grenada Inn**
AServ E: Billy Tanner's Repair & Towing

Exit **(758)** Louie Road

(752) **Weed Airport Road, Rest Area**

EXIT CALIFORNIA

Inside Exit
Food W: **Porky Bob's BBQ**

(752) **Rest Area (Located within mile marker exit 752)**

Exit **(750)** Stewart Springs Road, Edgewood
RVCamp E: **Campground**
Other E: **Lake Shastina Recreation Area**

Exit **(746)** US 97, Klamath Falls, Central Weed
Lodg E: Motel 6
AServ E: Napa Auto
RVCamp E: **RV Park (Hi-Lo Motel)**
W: **Trailer Lane RV Park (1.25 Miles)**
Other E: **Ray's Food Place Grocery**

Exit **(746)** Central Weed Blvd, College Siskiyou
Gas E: BP(*), Chevron(*), Shell(*, D), Texaco(*)
Food E: Ellie's Espresso & Cafe, Hi-Lo Motel, The Y Restaurant
Lodg E: Hi-Lo Motel, The Townhouse Motel
AServ E: Bill's Garage & Towing, Chevron
RVCamp E: **RV Park (Hi-Lo Motel)**
ATM W: Scott Valley Bank
Other E: EZ Wash Laundry

Exit **(745)** South Weed Blvd
Gas E: Chevron(*, D, CW, 24)
Food E: Burger King, **McDonald's**, Taco Bell
Lodg E: **Comfort Inn**(LP), Holiday Inn Express, **Sis-Q Inn Motel**
RVCamp E: **Kellogg Ranch & RV Park**
ATM E: Chevron

Exit **(743)** Summit Drive, Truck Village Drive
FStop E: **Commercial Fueling Network**
Other W: **Grand Rental Station**(LP)

Exit **(741)** Abrams Lake Road
RVCamp W: **Camping**

Exit **(740)** Mount Shasta City (Southbound, Reaccess Northbound Only)

Exit **(739)** Central Mount Shasta
Gas E: Chevron(*), Texaco(*, D, CW)
Food E: Best Western, Black Bear Diner (Best Western), Burger King, Little Caesar's Pizza (Texaco), Round Table Pizza, Shasta's Family Restaurant, Subway, Suspender's BBQ, Texaco
Lodg E: Best Western
AServ E: Schuck's Auto Supply
RVCamp W: **Lake Siskiyou Campground**, **Mount Shasta RV Resort**
Med E: ✚ **Hospital**
ATM E: Scott Valley Bank, Texaco, Washington Mutual
Parks W: **Lake Siskiyou**
Other E: **Launderland Coin Laundry**, **Ray's Food Place Grocery**(RX), Rite Aid Pharmacy(RX), Suburban Propane

Exit **(737)** Mount Shasta City (Northbound, Difficult Reaccess)

Exit **(736)** CA 89, McCloud, Lawson Park
Lodg E: Swiss Holiday Lodge
RVCamp E: **McCloud Dance Country RV Park (10 Miles)**

(734) **Weigh Station, Inspection Center (Southbound)**

Exit **(733)** Mott Road, Dunsmuir Ave

Exit **(731)** Dunsmuir Ave, Siskiyou Ave
Food E: Best Choice Inn, Nicole's (Best Choice Inn)
Lodg E: Best Choice Inn
W: Cedar Lodge, Garden Motel

Bold red print shows RV & Bus parking available or nearby

EXIT — CALIFORNIA

Exit **(730)** Central, Dunsmuir
- **Gas** E: Shell[*]
  W: Texaco[*, D]
- **Food** W: Micki's Frostie, Shelby's Cafe
- **Lodg** E: Dunsmuir Inn, TraveLodge
  W: Cave Springs Motel
- **AServ** E: Napa Auto, Shasta Ford & Mercury Dealer, Shell
- **ATM** W: Texaco
- **Other** W: **Dunsmuir City Park**

Exit **(728)** Dunsmuir
- **Gas** E: 76[*, D]
- **AServ** E: Jim Kirby's Repair & Towing
- **ATM** E: 76

Exit **(727)** Crag View Drive, Railroad Park Road
- **Lodg** W: **Caboose Motel**
- **AServ** E: Dwight's Repair & 24 Hour Towing
- **RVCamp** E: **Rustic Park**[*, LP]
  W: **Railroad Park Resort (.5 Miles)**
- **Parks** W: **Railroad Park**

726 Soda Creek Road

Exit **(724)** Castella
- **Gas** W: Chevron[*, D]
- **Food** W: Chevron
- **RVCamp** E: **Cragview Valley Camp RV Park**
- **Parks** W: **Castle Crags State Park**
- **Other** W: **U.S. Post Office**

Exit **(723)** Vista Point (Northbound, Observation Area)

Exit **(722)** Sweetbrier Ave

Exit **(721)** Conant Road

Exit **(720)** Flume Creek Road

Exit **(718)** Sims Road
- **RVCamp** W: **Best In The West Resort**

Exit **(713)** Gibson Road

Exit **(711)** Pollard Flat
- **FStop** E: **Exxon**[*]
- **Food** E: **Exxon**
- **ATM** E: **Exxon**

Exit **(710)** La Moine

Exit **(706)** Vollmers

(704) **Rest Area (RR, Phones, Picnic; Southbound)**

Exit **(703)** Lakehead, Riverview Drive
- **Food** E: Klub Klondike
- **Lodg** E: Yukon Motel
- **AServ** E: C & J Automotive

Exit **(702)** Lakeshore Drive, Antlers Road
- **Gas** E: Shell[*, D, 24]
  W: 76[*, LP]
- **Food** E: Top Hat Cafe
  W: Pizza Station, The Wicker Chair Coffee Shop & Thrift Store
- **Lodg** E: Neu Lodge Motel
- **AServ** E: Shasta Lake Auto Repair[24], The Leftover Store
- **RVCamp** E: **Antler's RV Park & Campground (1.5 Miles), Lakehead Campground & RV Park, Lakeshore Villa RV Park (.5 Miles), Shasta Lake RV Resort & Campground (1.5 Miles)**
- **ATM** W: 76
- **Other** E: **U.S. Post Office**
  W: Jack's Market (76), Shasta County Sheriff

Exit **(698)** Salt Creek Road, Gilman Road
- **RVCamp** W: **Cascade Cove Resort RV Park (2 Miles), Salt Creek RV Park & Campground (1Miles), Trail In RVPark (.5 Miles)**

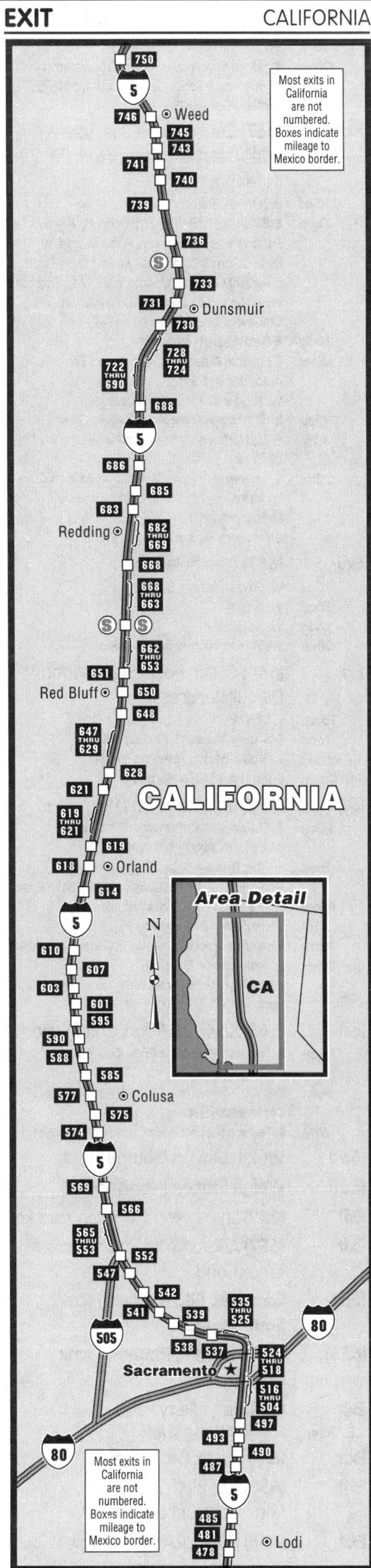

Exit **(694)** O'Brien, Shasta Caverns Road (Trucks not advised to go here)
- **RVCamp** W: **Campground**

Exit **(693)** Packers Bay Road

(693) **Rest Area (RR, Phones, Picnic; Northbound)**

692 Turntable Bay Road

Exit **(690)** Bridge Bay Road (No Trucks)
- **Food** W: Bridge Bay Restaurant, Tale of the Whale Restaurant
- **Lodg** W: Bridge Bay Motel
- **Other** W: **Bridge Bay Resort & Stores**

Exit **(688)** Fawndale Road, Wonderland Blvd
- **Lodg** E: Fawndale Lodge[LP]
- **RVCamp** E: **Fawndale Oaks RV Park**
  W: **Wonderland RV Park**[LP]

Exit **(686)** Mountain Gate, Wonderland Blvd
- **Gas** E: No Name[*] (You Save Market)
- **Food** E: Betty's Cafe
- **RVCamp** E: **Lake Shasta's Bear Mtn RV Resort, Mountain Gate RV Park (More than .25 Miles)**
  W: **Campground**
- **Other** E: **Visitor Information**

Exit **(685)** Shasta Dam Blvd, Shasta Dam
- **Gas** W: Chevron[*, D, LP], Texaco[*, D, LP]
- **Food** W: McDonald's, Taco Den, The Stage Stop Cafe
- **Lodg** W: Shasta Dam Motel
- **AServ** W: Chevron, Hob's Auto Body, Texaco

Exit **(683)** Pine Grove Ave
- **Gas** W: Exxon[*, D, LP]

Exit **(682)** Oasis Road
- **Gas** W: Arco[*]
- **AServ** W: All Wheel Alignment, Dick's Auto Repair, Twin View Service & Towing
- **RVCamp** E: **California RV Supply & Repair**
  W: **American Roads RVs**
- **ATM** W: Arco
- **Other** E: California Highway Patrol Post
  W: Harrison's Marine Center, Meyer's Marine Service Center, Reddy Performance Marine, Suburban Propane, Yamaha & Seadoo Dealer[LP]

Exit **(681)** Market St, Redding (Southbound, Reaccess Northbound Only)
- **FStop** W: **Exxon**[*, RV DUMP, 24]
- **Food** W: **Exxon**
- **AServ** W: Tire Cobbler
- **TServ** W: **CAT, Peterson's, Redding Freightliner**
- **ATM** W: **Exxon**

Exit **(680)** Twin View Blvd
- **FStop** W: **Pacific Pride Commercial Fueling, Redding Oil Co, Fischer Oil Co.**
- **Gas** E: 76[*, D, LP, 24]
- **Food** W: Michael's Sandwiches
- **Lodg** E: Motel 6
  W: Holiday Inn Select
- **AServ** W: California Auto Repair & Smog, State Tire Sales
- **RVCamp** W: **Northgate Mobile Park**
- **Other** E: Harley Davidson
  W: Meeks Building Center, Outboard Center, Shasta In Boards

680A CA 299 East, Burney, Alturas, Lake Blvd.
- **Gas** W: Texaco[*]
- **AServ** W: Gearen's Automotives, J&K Muffler
- **RVCamp** W: **KOA Campgrounds (.25 Miles), Redding RV Park (.5 Miles)**
- **ATM** W: Texaco

Bold red print shows RV & Bus parking available or nearby

EXIT	CALIFORNIA
Other	W: Shasta Lanes Bowling, Water Works Park
Exit	**(678)** CA 299 West, , Central Redding, Eureka-678 C
RVCamp	W: **Marina RV Park (2 Miles)**, **Sacramento River RV Park (2 Miles)**
Exit	**(678)** 678B CA 44, Hilltop Drive, Lassen Clarke
Exit	**(678)** Hilltop Drive, Lassen Clarke, Weaverville - 678A (Northbound, Difficult Reaccess)
Gas	E: Chevron(*)
Food	E: Applebee's, Chevy's Mexican, Double Tree Hotel, Express China, Holiday Inn, Italian Cottage Restaurant, Marie Callender's Restaurant, Misty's Restaurant & Lounge (Double Tree Hotel), Tokyo Garden, Winchells Donuts
Lodg	E: Double Tree Hotel, Holiday Inn, Motel 6, Oxford Suites, The Grand Manor Inn
AServ	E: Chevron
ATM	W: Bank Of America, Tri Counties Bank
Other	E: Tay-Van Car Wash(D)
	W: The Redding Mall
Exit	**(677)** Redding, Cypress Ave
FStop	W: **USA Gasoline(D, 24)**
Gas	E: 76(*), Chevron(*, 24), Exxon(*)
	W: 76(*), Beacon(*, LP), Shell(*)
Food	E: Black Bear Restaurant, **Burger King(PLAY)**, CR Gibbs (Best Western), Carl Jr's Hamburgers, Denny's, IHOP, KFC, McDonald's, Subarama, Szechuan, Taco Bell, Taco Shop, Wendy's
	W: Big Red's BBQ, California Cattle Company Steaks, Casa Lupe, Denny's, Lyon's Restaurant
Lodg	E: Best Western
	W: Motel 6, Vagabond Inn
AServ	E: 76, Chevron(24), Grand Auto Supply
	W: Big O Tires, Boyland Toyota, Lithia Chevrolet, Midas Muffler & Brake, Shasta Nissan, Shell
RVCamp	W: **Marina RV Park (2 Miles)**
ATM	E: 76, North Valley Bank, Wells Fargo Bank
Other	E: **Asher Animal Hospital**, **K-Mart**, **Longs Drugs**, Meeks Building Supply, WalGreens Pharmacy(24, RX)
	W: Country Bowl, Enterprise Rent-a-Car, U-Haul Center
Exit	**(675)** Bechelli Lane, Churn Creek Road
Gas	E: Arco(*), BP(*), Chevron(*, D, LP)
	W: Texaco(*, D)
Food	E: Cedar Tree Cafe, Cricket's Dinner House
	W: Texaco
Lodg	E: **Super 8**
AServ	E: BP
RVCamp	E: **Sacramento River RV Park**
ATM	E: Arco
Other	W: **Amerigas(LP)**
Exit	**(672)** Knighton Road, Redding Airport
TStop	W: **TA TravelCenters of America(*, LP, SCALES) (76 gas)**
Food	W: **TA TravelCenters of America (76 gas)**
TServ	W: **TA TravelCenters of America(SCALES) (76 gas)**
RVCamp	W: **Sacramento River RV Park (2 Miles)**
ATM	W: **TA TravelCenters of America (76 gas)**
Exit	**(669)** Riverside Ave
Exit	**(668)** Anderson (Southbound, Difficult Reaccess)
Gas	W: Chevron(*), Exxon(*, D), Texaco(LP)
Food	E: Burger King(PLAY), McDonald's, **The Big Taco**
	W: Bartell's Giant Burger, Golden Room Steakhouse, Koffee Korner Family Restaurant
AServ	W: Texaco
RVCamp	W: **RVs Unlimited**
ATM	W: Bank of America, Exxon
Other	E: Handy Spot Market(D) (Gas), Laundromat(24)
	W: Anderson Police, Shasta County Sheriff, Spotless Car Wash
Exit	**(667)** Central Anderson, Lassen Park, Bells Ferry Road, North St (Northbound)
Gas	E: 76(*, D, LP), Beacon(*)
Food	E: Bill's Take 'N Bake Pizza, Denny's, Jiffy 50's Deli Sandwiches & Ice Cream, Papa Murphy's, Perko's Family Restaurant, Round Table Pizza, Silver Star Chinese American, Subway, Taco Bell
	W: El Mariachi's, Frank's Old Fashoned Creamery, Good Times Pizza, KFC
Lodg	E: Best Western, **Valley Inn**
AServ	E: Franklin Auto Parts, Les Schwab Tires, Napa Auto, Quality Lube & Oil(CW)
	W: Kragen Auto Parts, Rick's Place
Med	E: ✚ **Anderson Medical Walk-In Clinic**
ATM	E: 76, North Valley Bank, **Safeway Grocery(RX)**, US Bank
Other	E: **Gateway Animal Clinic**, **Launderland Coin Laundry**, Rite Aid Pharmacy(RX), **Safeway Grocery(RX)**
	W: **Holiday Supermarket**
Exit	**(667)** Deschutes Road
Gas	W: Power Mart(*, D), Shell(*, D, CW)
Food	W: Arby's
Lodg	W: AmeriHost
Other	W: **Shasta Factory Stores Outlet**
Exit	**(664)** Cottonwood (Southbound, Difficult Reaccess)
FStop	E: **CFN(SCALES)**
Food	E: **Shasta Livestock Restaurant**
Lodg	E: **Alamo Motel**, **Travelers Motel**
RVCamp	E: **Frontier Mobile Home Park**
Exit	**(663)** Balls Ferry, Gas Point Road
Gas	E: Chevron(*, D), **Cottonwood Grocery(D)**
	W: 76(*, D, LP), **Arco(*, LP, RV DUMP)**
Food	E: Lilly's Donuts
	W: Eagles Nest Pizza, Jake's Cake & Bake Pizza
AServ	E: HHH Auto Parts, Jim's Auto Repair
ATM	W: **Holiday Grocery Store(RX)**
Parks	W: **Cottonwood Community Center and Park**
Other	E: **Cottonwood Grocery**
	W: **Holiday Grocery Store(RX)**, **Wash & Dry Coin Laundry**
Exit	**(662)** Bowman Road, Cottonwood
FStop	E: **Texaco(*, 24) (Pacific Pride Commercial Fueling)**
Food	E: A & W Restaurant, **Texaco (Pacific Pride Commercial Fueling)**
ATM	E: **Texaco (Pacific Pride Commercial Fueling)**
(661)	**Weigh Station (Southbound)**
(661)	**Weigh Station (Northbound)**
Exit	**(659)** Snively Road, Auction Yard Rd
Exit	**(657)** Auction Yard Road, Hooker Creek Road
(654)	**Rest Area (RR, Phones, Picnic; Southbound)**
(654)	**Rest Area (RR, Phones, Picnic; Northbound)**
Exit	**(653)** Jellys Ferry Road
RVCamp	E: **Bend RV Park(*) (2 Miles)**
Exit	**(651)** Wilcox Golf Road
Exit	**(650)** Red Bluff (Southbound, Reaccess Northbound Only)
Exit	**(648)** CA 36, CA 99S, Red Bluff, Chico
Gas	E: 76(*)
	W: 76(*, D, LP), No Name(*), USA(*, D, 24)
Food	E: Black Bear Diner, Burger King, KFC, **McDonald's(PLAY)**, Perko's
	W: Carl Jr's Hamburgers, Denny's, Egg Roll King, El Mariachi Mexican, Round Table Pizza, Shari's Restaurant, Subway, Wild Bill's Texas BBQ
Lodg	E: **Best Western**, Motel 6, **Super 8**
	W: Cinderalla Hotel, Goodnite Inn, Kings Lodge, **Red Bluff Inn**
AServ	W: Chief Auto Parts, Downtown Auto Repair
RVCamp	E: **Mendocino National Forest (.5 Miles)**, **Red Bluff RV Park (1 Mile)**
	W: **Idlewheels RV Park (GoodSam Park)**, **O' Nite Park (.5 Miles)**
ATM	E: 76
	W: USA
Other	W: **Antelope Veterinary Hospital**, **Coin Laundry**, **Food 4 Less(24)**
Exit	**(647)** Diamond Ave.- 647B (Southbound, Reaccess Northbound Only)
Exit	**(647)** Red Bluff - 647A (Difficult Reaccess)
Gas	E: Exxon(*)
	W: Arco(*, 24), Chevron(*, CW)
Food	E: **La Corona**
	W: Arby's, Italian Cottage, Jack-In-The-Box, Papa Murphy's, Pizza Hut, Yogurt Alley
Lodg	E: **Motel Orleans**
	W: Triangle Motel
AServ	E: **Yak- Yak Shack**
TServ	E: **Yak- Yak Shack**
Med	E: ✚ **Hospital**
ATM	E: Exxon
	W: **Raley's Supermarket(RX)**
Parks	E: **Ide Adobe Historical Park**
Other	W: **Raley's Supermarket(RX)**, **Wal-Mart (Tire & Lube Express)**
Exit	**(642)** Flores Ave, Proberta, Gerber (No Trucks Over 25 Tons)
Exit	**(636)** Tehama, Los Molinos, Gyle Road
Exit	**(633)** Richfield, Finnel Road
(632)	**Rest Area (RR, Phones, Picnic; Southbound)**
(632)	**Rest Area (RR, Phones, Picnic; Northbound)**
Exit	**(631)** Corning, Corning Rd.
Gas	E: 76(*), Chevron(*, 24), Jiffy(*)
Food	E: Burger King, Corning Restaurant, Francisco's Fine Mexican, Leslie's Deli, Marco's Pizza, **Olive Pit**, Papa Murphy's Pizza, Rancho Grande Mexican American, Round Table Pizza, Taco Bell
	W: **Bartell's Giant Burger**
Lodg	E: **7 Inn**, AmeriHost Inn, Corning Olive Inn Motel, Economy Inn, Olive City Inn
AServ	E: Corning Ford Dealership, Lyndon Johnson Dealership, Napa Auto, Reilly's Mufflers, Tires Plus
RVCamp	E: **Heritage RV Park(*, LP)**
	W: **Corning RV Park (.5 Miles)**
ATM	E: Chevron, **Safeway Grocery**
Other	E: **Clark's Drugstore(RX)**, Coin Car Wash, **Holiday Supermarket**, Java Lanes, **Launderland Coin Laundry**, Pay Less Drugs(RX), **Safeway Grocery**
Exit	**(629)** South Ave
TStop	E: **Burns Brothers Travel Stop(*, LP, SCALES)**, **Petro(*, SCALES)**
Food	E: **Burns Brothers Travel Stop**, **Iron Skillet(*) (Petro TStop)**, **McDonald's(PLAY)**, **Ms. B's**

Bold red print shows RV & Bus parking available or nearby

EXIT CALIFORNIA

Homestyle(*, LP, SCALES) (Burns Bros. TStop), Petro, Subway (Burns Bros), TCBY (Burns Bros)
Lodg E: Days Inn, Olive Tree Motel, Shilo Inn
AServ E: Linnet's Tire Shop
TServ E: Burns Bros TStop, Burns Brothers Travel Stop(SCALES), Corning Truck and Radiator Service, Petro(SCALES)
TWash E: Blue Beacon Truck Wash, Corning Truck Wash
RVCamp E: Heritage
ATM E: Burns Brothers Travel Stop
Other E: Ace Hardware
Exit **(628)** Liberal Ave
TServ W: I-5 Truck & Equipment
Exit **(621)** Road 7
Exit **(619)** CA 32, Chico, Orland
Gas E: Exxon(*), Shell(*)
W: 76(*, D), Sportsman's GasMart(*, LP)
Food E: Berry Patch Restaurant, Burger King
Lodg E: AmberLight Inn Motel, Orlanda Inn Motel
AServ E: Mike's Mufflers, Shell
RVCamp W: Black Butte RV Park, Green Acres (.5 Miles), Old Orchard RV Park
ATM E: Exxon
Exit **(618)** South St., Road 16
FStop E: Beacon(*) (CFN)
Food E: Pizza Factory
Lodg E: Orland Inn
Other E: Coin Laundry, Long's Drugs(RX)
Exit **(614)** Road 27
TServ E: William Erwin Trucking Sales & Service
Exit **(610)** Artois
(608) Rest Area (RR, Phones, Picnic, RV Dump, RV Water; Southbound)
(608) Rest Area (RR, Phones, Picnic, RV Dump, RV Water; Northbound)
Exit **(607)** Bayliss, Road 39
Exit **(603)** CA 162, Willows, Oroville
Gas E: Arco(*, 24), Chevron(*, 24), Shell(*, LP)
Food E: Burger King, Denny's(24), Eagle's Garden Chinese, Java Jim's Ice Cream, Jerry's Restaurant, KFC, McDonald's, Round Table Pizza, Santa Fe Grill, Subway, Taco Bell
W: Nancy's 24 Hour Cafe(24)
Lodg E: Best Western, Crossroads West Inn, Days Inn, Super 8
AServ E: Express Lube, Shell
Med E: + Glenn Medical Center
Other E: Hand Coin Car Wash, Highway Patrol
W: Wal-Mart(RX), Willows Airport(RX)
Exit **(601)** Road 57
Exit **(595)** Norman Road, Princeton
Parks E: Sacramento National Wildlife Refuge
Exit **(590)** Delevan Road
Exit **(588)** Maxwell (Southbound, Difficult Reaccess)
Exit **(585)** Stonyford, Maxwell
Food W: Chateau Basque Restaurant
RVCamp W: RV Park
Parks E: Delevan National Wildlife Refuge
Other W: Maxwell Country Market
(583) Rest Area (RR, Phones, Picnic; Southbound)
(583) Rest Area (RR, Phones, Picnic; Northbound)
Exit **(577)** CA 20, Colusa, Clear Lake
Med E: + Hospital

EXIT CALIFORNIA

Exit **(575)** Williams
FStop W: Shell (Pacific Pride Commercial Fueling)
Gas W: Arco(*), BP(*), Chevron(*, D, 24)
Food E: Carl Jr's Hamburgers(PLAY), Taco Bell
W: A & W Drive-In, Caliente Mexican Drive-in, Dairy Queen, Denny's, Granzella's Deli (Granzella's Inn), McDonald's, Piccadilli Pizza (Shell), Shari & Claire's Farmer Cafe, Shell (Pacific Pride Commercial Fueling), Wendy's
Lodg E: Holiday Inn Express
W: Granzella's Inn, Motel 6, Woodcrest Inn
AServ W: BP, Dave's Tire Service, Harper's Auto Repair (24 hour towing)
TServ W: Tanco (CAT)
RVCamp W: Almond Grove Mobile Home Park (.75 Miles)
ATM W: Shell (Pacific Pride Commercial Fueling)
Exit **(574)** Husted Road
FStop E: BC Petroleum (Automated Fueling)
Exit **(569)** Hahn Road
Exit **(566)** Arbuckle
Gas E: Shell(*, D)
Exit **(565)** College City (Difficult Reaccess)
FStop E: Pacific Pride
Gas E: 76(*, D), Chevron(*, D)
W: Beacon(*)
Food W: Beacon
AServ E: DeMarchi's
ATM W: Beacon
Other E: U.S. Post Office
Exit **(559)** County Line Road
(557) Rest Area (RR, Phones, Picnic; Southbound)
(557) Rest Area (RR, Phones, Picnic; Northbound)
Exit **(556)** Dunnigan
FStop E: Shell(*, LP)
Gas E: Chevron(*, 24), No Name(*)
W: 76(*)
Food E: Bill & Kathy's, Jack in the Box, No Name
Lodg E: Best Western, Value Lodge
Other E: Dunnigan General Store, U.S. Post Office
Exit **(553)** Road 8
TStop E: 76(*, LP, SCALES) (CFN Commercial Fueling)
FStop W: Beacon(*, LP, SCALES)
Food E: 76 (CFN Commercial Fueling), Aladero Coffee Shop (76 Truck Stop), Judy's Country Cafe
W: Beacon
Lodg E: Budget 8 Motel
TServ E: 76(SCALES) (CFN Commercial Fueling)
TWash E: 76 (CFN Commercial Fueling)
RVCamp E: Happy Time RV Park
Exit **(552)** Jct I-505, Winters, San Francisco (Southbound)
Exit **(547)** Zamora
FStop E: Texaco(*) (Pacific Pride Commercial Fueling)
Exit **(542)** Yolo
Exit **(541)** CA 16 West, Woodland
Exit **(539)** West St
Food W: Denny's
Exit **(538)** CA 113 North, Yuba City
FStop W: CFN
Gas W: Shell(*)
Food W: Denny's
Lodg E: Valley Oaks Inn
W: Best Western
Exit **(537)** CA 113 South, Davis

EXIT CALIFORNIA

Gas W: Exxon(*), Union 76(*)
Food W: Burger King, Denny's, McDonald's, Primo's Restaurant, Taco Bell
Lodg W: Comfort Inn, Motel 6, Phoenix Inn
AServ E: Lasher Auto Center
W: Art's Automotive, Bee Line Service
TServ W: J & J Trucker Repair
Other W: Canned Foods Grocery Outlet, K-Mart
Exit **(535)** Road 102
Gas E: Arco(*), Shell(*, D, CW)
W: Chevron(*)
Food E: Blimpie Subs & Salads (Shell), Jack in the Box, Shell, TCBY (Shell)
AServ E: Blakely Auto Repair, Rohwer Bros. Repair
TServ E: Cal West, Wesco Truck & Trailer Sales
TWash E: Truck Wash
Other E: Suburban Propane
Exit **(531)** Road 22, West Sacramento
(530) Rest Area (RR, Phones, Picnic; Southbound)
Exit **(528)** Airport
Exit **(525)** CA 99 to CA 70, Yuba City, Marysville (Difficult Reaccess)
Exit **(524)** Del Paso Road
Exit **(522)** Jct I-80, San Fransico, Reno
Exit **(521)** West El Camino Ave (Northbound, Reaccess Southbound Only)
Gas W: Exxon(*)
Food W: A-Mart Deli, Gourmet Wok, Jack-In-The-Box
Lodg W: Residence Inn
Exit **(520)** Garden Hwy -520B
Lodg W: Courtyard by Marriott
Parks W: Natomas Oaks Park
Exit **(520)** Richards Blvd -520A
Gas E: Chevron(*, 24)
W: Arco(*), Shell(*, CW, 24)
Food E: Buttercup Pantry, Hungry Hunter, Lyon's Restaurant(24), McDonald's, Monterey Seafood, The Rusty Duck
W: Perko's Cafe
Lodg E: Days Inn, Fountain Suites, Governor's Inn, Hawthorne Suites Hotel, Super 8
W: Best Western, Capital Inn, Crossroads Inn, La Quinta Inn, Motel 6
AServ E: Safelite Auto Glass
ATM E: Chevron
W: Arco, Motel 6
Parks W: Discovery Park
Exit **(519)** J St, Downtown Sacramento (Difficult Reaccess, Watch one-ways in the downtown area)
Food E: Denny's (Vagabond Inn), Hong King Lurn Restaurant, Lu Shan Chinese Buffet, Lucy's Place, Tokyo Restaurant, Vagabond Inn
Lodg E: Holiday Inn, Vagabond Inn
Other E: Downtown Plaza, United Artist Theaters
W: Old Sacramento South Historic Park
Exit **(518)** Q St - 518B
518A U.S. 50, Business I-80, San Francisco, CA 99 Jct., Fresno - 518A
Exit **(516)** Sutterville Rd
Exit **(514)** Fruitridge Rd, Seamas Ave - 514B
Exit **(514)** 43rd Ave - 514A (Southbound, Reaccess Northbound Only)
Other W: Green Haven Veterinary Hospital
Exit **(512)** Florin Rd

Bold red print shows RV & Bus parking available or nearby

EXIT CALIFORNIA

Gas E: Chevron[*], Shell[*, CW, 24]
Food E: ABC Bakery, Alicia's Mexican, Bill's Classic Yogurt, Land Park Bakery, Round Table Pizza
W: Burger King, Round Table Pizza, Sheri's Restaurant, Sonoma Valley Bagel, Subway
AServ E: Kragen Auto Parts, Shell[24]
ATM E: **Bel Air Grocery**, Sumitomo Bank, Washington Mutual
W: Bank of America, Cal Fed
Other E: **Bel Air Grocery**, **Long's Drugs**[RX]
W: Rite Aid Pharmacy[24, RX], **Super Saver Food**

Exit **(511)** Pocket Rd, Freeport, Meadowview Rd
Gas E: Shell[*, LP, CW, RV DUMP, 24]
Food E: **McDonald's**

Exit **(507)** Laguna Blvd
Gas E: 76[*, D, LP, CW], Chevron[*, LP], Shell[*, CW, 24]
Food E: Chevron, McDonald's (Chevron)
AServ E: Laguna Creek Auto Center
ATM E: 76, Chevron

Exit **(506)** Elk Grove Blvd

Exit **(504)** Hood Franklin Road

Exit **(497)** Twin Cities Road

Exit **(493)** Thornton, Walnut Grove
FStop E: **76**[*, LP]
AServ E: **76**
TServ E: **76**

Exit **(490)** Peltier Road

Exit **(487)** Turner Road

Exit **(485)** CA 12, Lodi , Rio Vista
TStop E: **Texaco Truck & Auto Plaza**[*, LP, SCALES, 24]
FStop E: **Arco**[*, LP]
Gas E: Chevron[*, D, LP], Exxon[*, D, LP]
Food E: Baskin Robbins (Exxon), Chevron, Exxon, **McDonald's**, Subway (Chevron), Taco Bell, **Texaco Truck & Auto Plaza**, Wendy's (Exxon)
RVCamp W: **Tower Park Marina Camping (5 Miles)**
ATM E: Chevron, Exxon, **Texaco Truck & Auto Plaza**

Exit **(481)** Eight Mile Road
RVCamp E: **KOA Campgrounds (5 Miles)**
Parks E: **Oak Grove Regional Park (Admission payment required)**

Exit **(478)** Hammer Lane
Gas E: 76[*], Arco[*, 24]
W: Exxon[*, 24]
Food E: Adalberto's Mexican, Bangkok, KFC, Little Caesars Pizza, Tandoori Nite's Fine Dining
W: Burger King, Chava's Taco House, Jack-In-The-Box, More Than Yogurt, Round Table Pizza, Subway, Taco Bell
Lodg W: Inn Cal
AServ E: Auto Parts Express
ATM E: 76, Arco
W: Subway
Other E: Car Wash, Colonial Plaza Vet Clinic, Roller Skating Rink, **S-Mart Foods**[RX], Suds City Laundromat, Wash Tub Laundry
W: Mail Boxes Etc

Exit **(477)** Benjamin Holt Drive
Gas E: Arco[*], Chevron[*, D, CW, 24]
W: Shell[*, D, 24]
Food E: Pizza & Deli (Quick Stop), Quick Stop
W: Lyon's, McDonald's, Round Table Pizza, Subway, Wong's Deli
Lodg E: Motel 6
AServ W: Shell[24]
ATM W: **7-11 Convenience Store**, Bank Of America, **Marina Grocery Store**
Other E: Quick Stop
W: **7-11 Convenience Store**, Le Bistro, **Marina Grocery Store**, **Village Veternarian Hospital**

EXIT CALIFORNIA

Exit **(475)** March Lane
Gas E: Citgo[*]
W: 76[*, D, 24]
Food E: Applebee's, Black Angus Steakhouse, Boston Market Restaurant, Carl Jr's Hamburgers, Denny's, El Torito Mexican, Jack-In-The-Box, Marie Callender's Restaurant, Straw Hat Pizza, Taco Bell, Testerosa Bar & Grill, Tony Roma's, Toot Sweets Bakery Cafe, Wendy's
W: Carrows Restaurant, **In-N-Out Hamburgers**
Lodg E: Radisson Inn, Traveler's Inn
W: La Quinta Inn, **Super 8**
ATM E: Citgo
W: 76
Other E: 7-11 Convenience Store (Citgo), **Longs Drugs**, Pack & Mail, Quick Stop Market, S-Mart Foods

Exit **(474)** Alpine Ave, Country Club Blvd (Services not accessible going southbound)
Gas E: Shell[*, LP]
W: Citgo[*], USA Gasoline[*, D, LP]
Food W: Baskin Robbins (USA Gasoline), Java Jim's (USA Gasoline), Subway (USA Gasoline), USA Gasoline
AServ E: Shell
ATM W: Citgo, **Safeway Grocery**[RX], USA Gasoline
Other W: 7-11 Convenience Store (Citgo), **Safeway Grocery**[RX]

Exit **(473)** Monte Diablo Ave
AServ W: AAMCO Transmission

Exit **(472)** Oak St, Fremont St (Southbound)
Gas W: Arco[*, 24]
Lodg W: Fremont River Inn
TServ W: **Cummins**
Med W: ✚ **Hospital**
ATM W: Arco

Exit **(471)** Pershing Ave. - 471C (Northbound)

471B Downtown Stockton, Fresno Ave, CA 4 East to CA 99 - 471B

Exit **(471)** CA 4, Charter Way - 471A
TStop W: **Vanco Truck/Auto Stop**[*, LP, SCALES] **(76/ Pacific Pride Commercial Fueling)**
Gas E: Chevron[*, 24], Shell[*, CW], Texaco[*, D, LP, CW, 24]
Food E: Burger King, Denny's, McDonald's
W: **Carrows Restaurant**, Taco Bell[24], **Vanco Truck/Auto Stop (76/ Pacific Pride Commercial Fueling)**
Lodg E: Best Western
W: **Motel 6**
AServ E: Pit Stop Tube & Lube, Transmission Service Center
W: Muffler Master
TServ W: **International Trucks**, **Peterbilt Dealer**, **Vanco Truck/Auto Stop**[SCALES] **(76/ Pacific Pride Commercial Fueling)**
ATM E: Chevron
Other E: Centromart, Delta Food Mart

Exit **(470)** Eighth St
Gas W: California Stop[*, D]
Lodg W: Econolodge
ATM W: California Stop
Parks E: **Harrell Park**

Exit **(469)** Downing Ave

Exit **(468)** French Camp
FStop E: **Exxon**[*] **(Pacific Pride Commercial Fueling)**
Food E: **Exxon (Pacific Pride Commercial Fueling)**, **Togo's (Exxon)**
Med E: ✚ **Hospital**
ATM E: **Exxon (Pacific Pride Commercial Fueling)**

EXIT CALIFORNIA

Exit **(467)** Mathews Road
FStop E: **Exxon**[*] **(CFN, J & L Auto Service)**
Food E: **Exxon (CFN, J & L Auto Service)**
AServ E: **American Tires & Co**, **Exxon (CFN, J & L Auto Service)**
TServ E: **American Tires & Co**
Med W: ✚ **Hospital**
Other E: **Peter's Market**

Exit **(466)** El Dorado St. (Northbound)
FStop E: **Exxon**[*] **(CFN, J & L Auto Service)**
Food E: **Exxon (CFN, J & L Auto Service)**
AServ E: American Tires & Co, **Exxon (CFN, J & L Auto Service)**
Other E: **Peter's Market**

Exit **(465)** Sharpe Depot, Roth Road
TServ E: **Kenworth Trucks**

Exit **(463)** Lathrop Road
Gas E: Chevron[*, LP, 24], Exxon[*]
Food E: Bella's Bakery, Papa's Pizza, Yan Yan Deli
Lodg E: DAYS INN **Days Inn (see our ad this page)**
RVCamp W: **Dos Reis (.5 Miles)**

Exit **(462)** Louise Ave
Gas E: Arco[*]
W: 76[*]
Food E: Carl Jr's Hamburgers, **Denny's**, Green Burrito, Jack-in-the-Box, McDonald's[PLAY], Taco Bell
Lodg E: Holiday Inn Express
ATM E: Arco, Bank of America
Parks W: **Mossdale Crossing County Park**

Exit **(460)** CA 120E, Monteca, Senora

Exit **(459)** Manthey Road (Southbound)

Exit **(458)** Jct I-580, Jct I-205, San Francisco (Southbound)

Exit **(457)** Defense Depot, Tracy

TRUCK OR LARGE VEHICLE PARKING
1214
DAYS INN®
14750 S. Harlan Rd
Lathrop, CA
Free Continental Breakfast
Outdoor Pool
Meeting/Banquet Facilities
Handicap Accessible
Coin Laundry
Pet Allowed
Interior Corridors
Steam & Sauna Room
25" Color TV with Video, Satellite Movies
Security Patrol Service
209-982-1959
FAX 209-982-4978
Lathrop Road Exit
California ¥ I-5 ¥ Exit 463

Bold red print shows RV & Bus parking available or nearby

EXIT CALIFORNIA

(Southbound, Reaccess Northbound Only)

Exit **(456)** Kasson Road
- FStop W: Commercial Fueling Network(24)

455B Mossdale Rd. (Northbound)
- Gas E: Texaco(*)

Exit **(452)** CA 33, Vernalis

Exit **(449)** CA132, San Francisco (West), Modesto (East)

Exit **(448)** Jct I-580 Northbound to Tracy & San Fransico

(447) **Rest Area (RR, Picnic, RV Dump, RV Water; Southbound)**

(447) **Rest Area (RR, Picnic, RV Dump, RV Water; Northbound)**

Exit **(437)** Westley
- TStop E: Westley Truck Stop(*, LP, SCALES) (CFN)
- Gas E: 76(*), 76(*, 24), Chevron(*, 24)
  W: Shell(*, D)
- Food E: Bobby Ray's Restaurant (Westley TS), McDonald's, Pepper Tree Restaurant, Westley Truck Stop (CFN)
  W: Ingram Creek Coffee Shop
- Lodg E: Budget Inn, Days Inn
- TServ E: Westley Truck Stop(SCALES) (CFN)
- TWash E: Westley Truck Stop (CFN)
- ATM W: Shell

Exit **(433)** Patterson
- Gas E: Arco(*, 24)
- Food E: Jack in the Box
- Med E: + Hospital
- ATM E: Arco

430 Vista Point (Northbound)

Exit **(427)** Crows Landing

Exit **(422)** Newman

Exit **(419)** Vista Point (Southbound)

Exit **(417)** CA140, Gustine, Merced
- Gas E: Shell(*, D, 24), Texaco(*, D)
- AServ E: Auto & Tire Service Center
- ATM E: Shell

(409) **Weigh Station (Southbound)**

(409) **Weigh Station (Northbound)**

Exit **(407)** CA 33, Santa Nella Blvd , Gilroy
- TStop E: Mid Cal 76 Auto/Truck Stop(*, LP, SCALES) (ATM)
- FStop W: Rotten Robby's Auto TruckPlaza(*, LP, SCALES) (Pacific Pride Commercial Fueling)
- Gas E: Texaco(*, D)
  W: Beacon(*, 24), Shell(*, 24)
- Food E: Burger King(PLAY), Carl Jr's Hamburgers, Del Taco(24), Mid Cal 76 Auto/Truck Stop (ATM), Pea Soup Andersen 's
  W: Denny's, McDonald's(PLAY), Taco Bell
- Lodg E: Best Western, Holiday Inn Express
  W: Motel 6, Ramada Inn
- TServ E: Mid Cal 76 Auto/Truck Stop(SCALES) (ATM)
- TWash E: Mid Cal 76 Auto/Truck Stop (ATM)
- RVCamp W: Santa Nella RV Park(LP)
- ATM E: Texaco
  W: Rotten Robby's Auto TruckPlaza (Pacific Pride Commercial Fueling), Shell
- Other W: Four Bay Golf Course & Restaurant

CAMPING WORLD®
San Martin Exit
13575 Sycamore Ave. • San Martin, CA
1-800-782-0061
1436

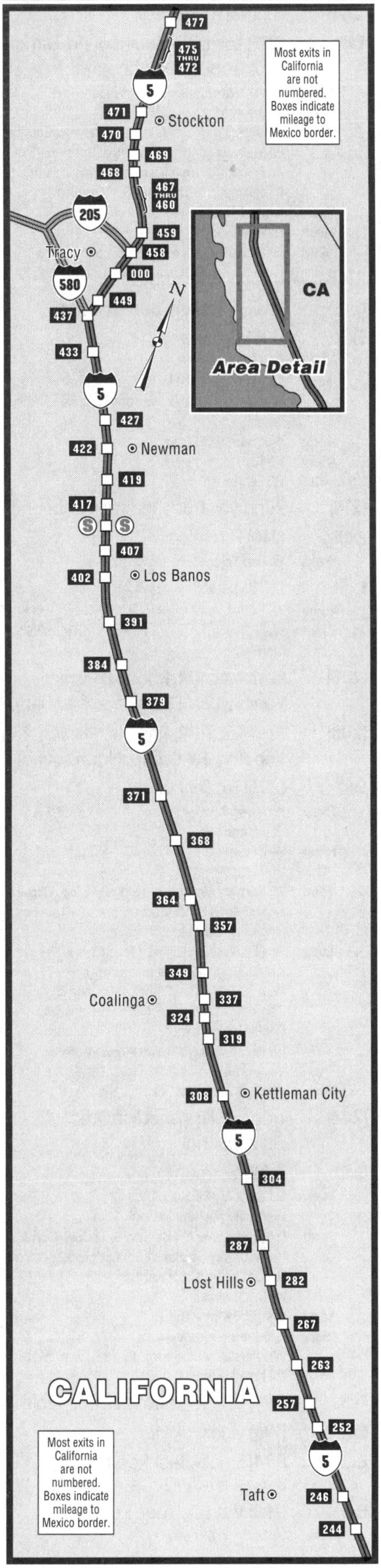

Most exits in California are not numbered. Boxes indicate mileage to Mexico border.

EXIT CALIFORNIA

Exit **(402)** Jct. CA 152, Monterey (West), Los Banos (East)
- RVCamp W: Camping World (see our ad this page)

Exit **(391)** CA165, Mercy Springs Rd
- Gas W: Shell(*)
- Med E: + Hospital

Exit **(390)** Dos Amigos Vista Pointe, (Northbound)

(387) **Rest Area (RR, Phones, Picnic, RV Water; Southbound)**

(387) **Rest Area (RR, Phones, Picnic, RV Water; Northbound)**

Exit **(384)** Nees Ave, Firebaugh
- FStop W: Texaco (CFN, 24hr Towing & Road Service)
- TServ W: Texaco (CFN, 24hr Towing & Road Service)

Exit **(379)** Shields Ave, Mendota

Exit **(371)** Russell Ave

Exit **(368)** Panoche Rd
- Gas W: Chevron(*, 24), Shell(*), Texaco(*, D)
- Food W: Apricot Tree Motel, Apricot Tree Restaurant, Foster's Freeze Hamburgers
- Lodg W: Apricot Tree Motel, Shilo Inn
- AServ W: Chevron(24), Texaco
- Other W: Shop Stop

Exit **(364)** Manning Ave, San Joaquin

Exit **(357)** Kamm Ave

Exit **(349)** CA 33N, Derrick Ave

337 CA 33 S, Coalinga,
- Med W: + Hospital

Exit **(333)** CA198, Lemoore, Hanford
- FStop E: CFN Fueling
- Gas E: Shell(*), Texaco(*, D, LP)
  W: 76(*, 24), Chevron(*), Mobil(*, D, LP)
- Food E: Harris Ranch Inn, Harris Ranch Restaurant (Harris Ranch Inn)
  W: Burger King, Carl Jr's Hamburgers(PLAY), Denny's(24), McDonald's, Oriental Express, Red Robin Restaurant, Taco Bell, Windmill
- Lodg E: Harris Ranch Inn
  W: Big Country Inn, Motel 6, Motel 6
- Med W: + Hospital
- ATM E: Shell, Texaco
  W: 76, Cal West Bank, Chevron, Mobil

Exit **(324)** Jayne Ave
- Gas W: Arco(*)
- RVCamp W: Sommerville's Almond Tree RV Park(LP)
- Med W: + Hospital
- ATM W: Arco
- Other W: Highway Patrol

(322) **Rest Area (RR, Phones, Picnic; Southbound)**

(322) **Rest Area (RR, Phones, Picnic; Northbound)**

Exit **(319)** CA.269, Lassen Ave, Avenal

Exit **(308)** Kettleman City, Paso Robles, Jct. Ca. 41
- FStop E: Beacon(*, D, SCALES)
- Gas E: 76(*, 24) (J & D Towing Service), Arco(*), Chevron(*, D, 24), Exxon(*, D), Shell(*, 24), Texaco(*, D)
- Food E: Burger King, Carl Jr's Hamburgers(PLAY), Exxon, In-N-Out Hamburgers, Jack-In-The-Box, Major's Bros. Farms Restaurant(24), McDonald's(PLAY), Subway (Exxon), TCBY (Exxon), Taco Bell

Bold red print shows RV & Bus parking available or nearby

EXIT CALIFORNIA

Lodg E: Best Western, Super 8
AServ E: Chevron[24], Kettleman City Tire & Repair Service[24]
RVCamp E: Kettleman RV Park[LP]
ATM E: Exxon

Exit **(304)** Utica Ave (Airport)

Exit **(287)** Twisselman Rd

Exit **(282)** CA 46, Lost Hills, Wasco
TStop W: Burns Brothers Travel Stop[*, LP] (24 hour road service)
Gas E: Texaco[*, D, LP]
W: 76[*], BP[*, 24], Beacon[*, D, 24], Chevron[*]
Food W: Burns Brothers Travel Stop (24 hour road service), Carl Jr's Hamburgers[PLAY], Denny's, Jack-In-The-Box
Lodg W: DAYS INN Days Inn, Motel 6
AServ W: 76
TServ W: Burns Brothers Travel Stop (24 hour road service)
RVCamp W: Koa RV Camp[LP]
ATM W: Beacon, Burns Brothers Travel Stop (24 hour road service)

Exit **(267)** Lerdo Hwy, Shafter

Exit **(265)** Buttonwillow, McKittrick (Southbound)

Exit **(265)** 7th Rd. (Northbound, Difficult Reaccess)
RVCamp W: Camping World (see our ad this page)

(264) **Rest Area (RR, Phones, Picnic, Vending; Southbound)**

(264) **Rest Area (RR, Phones, Picnic, Vending; Northbound)**

263 Jct. Ca. 58, Bakersfield
TStop E: Bruce's[*, SCALES], TA TravelCenters of America[*, SCALES] (76 gas)
FStop W: Exxon[*]
Gas E: Arco[*, 24], Chevron[*, 24], Mobil[*, D], Shell[*], Texaco[*]
Food E: A & W Restaurant (Bruce's), Bruce's, Burger King, Carl Jr's Hamburgers[PLAY], Country Pride Restaurant (TA TS), Denny's, McDonald's[PLAY], TA TravelCenters of America (76 gas), Taco Bell (TA TS), Willow Ranch Restaurant (Bruce's)
Lodg E: 1st Value Inn, Good Nite Inn, Motel 6, Super 8
AServ E: Chevron[24]
W: Exxon, Jeffrey Brothers (Exxon FS)
TServ E: TA TravelCenters of America[SCALES] (76 gas)
TWash E: Bruce's
ATM E: Bruce's, Mobil, TA TravelCenters of America (76 gas)

Exit **(252)** Stockdale Hwy
FStop E: Exxon[*, LP] (Restaurant)
Gas E: BP[*, 24], Shell[24]
Food E: Exxon (Restaurant), Jack-In-The-Box, Palm Tree Restaurant, Perko's Family Dining (Exxon FS)
Lodg E: Best Western, Econolodge
ATM E: Exxon (Restaurant)
Parks W: Tule Elk State Reserve
Other E: Highway Patrol

Exit **(246)** CA 43, Cast, Maricopa

Exit **(244)** CA 119, Pumpkin Center, Lamont

Exit **(238)** CA 223, Bear Mountain Blvd, Arvin

Exit **(234)** Old River Rd

Exit **(228)** Copus Rd

Exit **(225)** CA166, Maricopa, Mettler

EXIT CALIFORNIA

217B Junction CA.99 Bakersfield

Exit **(217)** Laval Rd - Southbound, Lamont Lake Isabella -Northbound
TStop E: T/A TravelCenters of America[*, SCALES]
Gas E: Chevron[*]
Food E: Burger King (TS of America), Chevron, Country Pride Restaurant (TS of America), Subway (TS of America), T/A TravelCenters of America, TCBY (TS of America), Taco Bell (TS of America)
TServ E: T/A TravelCenters of America[SCALES]
TWash E: Blue Beacon Truck Wash[24]
ATM E: Chevron, T/A TravelCenters of America

216B Lamont Lake Isabella

(216) **Weigh Station (Southbound)**

Exit **(215)** Grapevine
Gas W: 76[*], Texaco[*, D]
Food E: Denny's, Ranch House Coffee Shop
W: Farmers Table Restaurant, Taco Bell (Texaco), Texaco
Lodg W: Country Side Inn
AServ W: Texaco
ATM W: 76, Texaco

(214) Runaway Truck Ramp (Northbound)

Exit **(210)** Fort Tejon
Parks W: Fort Tejon State Historical Park

Exit **(209)** Lebec
AServ W: B & J Automotive Repair & Towing
Other W: Highway Patrol Office, Maybelline's Mini Mart

(208) **Rest Area (RR, Phones, Picnic, Vending, RV Dump; Southbound)**

(208) **Rest Area (RR, Phones, Picnic, Vending, RV Dump; Northbound)**

Exit **(205)** Frazier Park
TStop W: Flying J Travel Plaza[*, LP, SCALES] (Motel & Restaurant)
FStop W: Exxon[*]
Gas W: Texaco[D]
Food W: Cookery Restaurant (Flying J), Flying J Travel Plaza (Motel & Restaurant), Jack-In-The-Box, Smoke 'N Taco Latin Barbecue
Lodg W: Best Rest Inn (Flying J Truck Stop), Flying J Travel Plaza (Motel & Restaurant)
AServ W: Auto Parts Plus, Complete Foriegn & Domestic Auto Service, Neil's Radiator & Air Conditioning, Texaco, Tony's Auto Repair
ATM W: Exxon, Flying J Travel Plaza (Motel & Restaurant)
Other W: Highway Patrol Office

(204) Truck Brake Inspection Area (Southbound)

Exit **(202)** Gorman
Gas E: Chevron[*, D], Texaco[*, D]
W: Mobil[*] (24 hour towing)
Food E: Brian's Diner (Sizzler Motor Lodge), Carl Jr's Hamburgers, Sizzler Motor Lodge, Sizzler Steak House (Sizzler Motor Lodge)
W: McDonald's
Lodg E: Sizzler Motor Lodge
AServ E: Gorman Garage, Texaco
W: Interstate Auto Repair (Road Service), Mobil (24 hour towing)

Exit **(199)** CA 138, Lancaster, Palmdale

Exit **(198)** Quail Lake Rd

Exit **(194)** Smoky Bear Road
RVCamp W: Pyramid Lake RV Campground

Exit **(190)** Vista Del Lago Road
Other W: Visitor Information

EXIT CALIFORNIA

(184) Truck Brake Inspection Area (Southbound)

Exit **(182)** Templin Hwy (Steep Climb)

Exit **(177)** Lake Hughes Rd., Castaic (Steep Climb)
TStop E: Giant Truckstop[*, SCALES]
FStop E: Village Fuel Stop
Gas E: Citgo[*] (7-11 Convenience Store)
W: 76[*, 24], Mobil[*, D]
Food E: Burger King, Casa Lupe Plaza (Laundry), Foster Freeze, McDonald's[PLAY, 24], Zorbas
W: 76, Jack-In-The-Box[24], Taco Bell
AServ W: 5 Star Auto Clinic, 76[24]
ATM E: Citgo (7-11 Convenience Store), McDonald's, Ralph's Grocery, Village Fuel Stop
W: 76, Mobil
Other E: Casa Lupe Plaza (Laundry), Ralph's Grocery, Rite Aid Pharmacy[RX]

Exit **(176)** Parker Rd, Castaic (Northbound, Reaccess Southbound Only)
Gas E: Arco[*], Shell[*, CW, 24]
Food E: Cafe Mike Mexican American[24], Carl Jr's Hamburgers[PLAY], Tommie's Hamburgers, Vincenzo's Pizza, Wok's Cookin'
Lodg E: Castaic Inn, Comfort Inn, DAYS INN Days Inn
AServ E: Castaic Tire & Alignment, Street & Dirt Motorcycle Parts & Service
RVCamp E: Castaic Lake RV Park
ATM E: Arco, Shell
Other E: Dutch's Boat Service, U.S. Post Office, Veterinarian

Exit **(173)** Hasley Canyon Rd
Parks W: Wayside Honor Rancho Valverde Park

Exit **(172)** CA 126 West, Ventura

Exit **(171)** Rye Canyon Rd (Southbound)
Gas W: Shell[*, D, CW], Texaco[*, D] (CFN)
Food W: Baskin Robbins (Shell), Carving Cart Sandwich Shop (Shell), Jalapeno's Mexican (Shell), Rock Gourmet Pizza (Shell), Shell
ATM W: Shell

(170) **Weigh Station (Northbound)**

Exit **(170)** Magic Mtn Pkwy
Gas W: Chevron[*, 24]
Food W: El Torito Mexican, Hamburger Hamlet, Marie Callender's Restaurant, Red Lobster, Wendy's
Lodg W: Hilton/Garden Inn
ATM W: Chevron
Other W: Six Flags California

Exit **(169)** Valencia Blvd

Exit **(168)** McBean Pkwy
Food W: Baskin Robbins, Chili's, Chuck E Cheese's Pizza, Jamba Juice, Noah's New York Bagels, Starbucks Coffee, Subway, Wild Thyme Cafe & Bakery
Med E: ✚ Hospital
Other W: Mail Boxes Etc., Vons Food & Drug[RX]

Exit **(167)** Lyons Ave, Pico Canyon Rd
Gas E: 76[*], Chevron[*], Chevron[*], Texaco[*, D, LP, CW]
W: Arco[*], Mobil[*, D], Shell[*, D, 24]
Food E: Amaci Pizza & Pasta, Burger King[PLAY], Genghis Khan Mongolian BBQ, Pizza Esperienza, S & S Donuts, Tiny Naylors Restaurant[24], Vincendo's

3830 Saco Rd. • Bakersfield, CA
1-800-532-0897
1414

Bold red print shows RV & Bus parking available or nearby

EXIT	CALIFORNIA
	Pizza
	W: Blimpie's Subs (Mobil), Carl Jr's Hamburgers, Choy's Mesquite Broiler, Del Taco, Denny's, El Pollo Loco Mexican, Fortune Express, IHOP, In-N-Out Hamburgers, Jack-In-The-Box, Juice It Up, McDonald's(PLAY) (Wal-Mart), **McDonald's**(PLAY), Mobil, Outback Steakhouse, Subway, Taco Bell(PLAY, 24), **Wal-Mart (Vision Center)**
Lodg	W: Comfort Suites Hotel, Fairfield Inn, Hampton Inn, Residence Inn
AServ	E: 76, Chevron, Quality Motorcycle Accessories
	W: Jiffy Lube, Shell(24), **Wal-Mart (Vision Center)**
RVCamp	W: **Camping World (see our ad this page)**
ATM	W: Arco, Downy's Savings Bank (Hughes), **Hughes Family Market**(24, RX), **McDonald's**, Mobil
Parks	E: **William S. Hart Park**
Other	E: Kinko's(24)
	W: **Hughes Family Market**(RX), **Petsmart (Vet Smart)**, Stevenson Ranch Car Wash, **Wal-Mart (Vision Center)**
Exit	**(165)** Calgrove Blvd
Food	E: Carrows Restaurant
Parks	W: **Ed Davis Park**, **Towsley Canyon Park**
Other	W: Calgrove Kennel
162	CA14N, Palmdale, Lancaster
Exit	**(161)** Balboa Blvd, San Fernando Rd (Southbound, Difficult Reaccess)
160B	I-5 Truck Route North, CA 14
Exit	**(160)** Jct I-210, Pasadena
Exit	**(159)** Roxford St, Sylmar
Gas	E: Chevron(*), Mobil(*, D)
Food	E: Denny's(24), McDonald's
Lodg	E: Good Nite Inn, Motel 6
AServ	E: Chevron

RAMADA INN®
Burbank, CA
1733
818-843-5955
Restaurant/Lounge on Premises
Outdoor Pool
Meeting/Banquet Facilities
Handicap Accessible
Airport Shuttle
Free Parking
Free Cable TV/HBO/CNN/ESPN
In Room Movies & Nintendo Games
Jacuzzi Suites available
NBC • Universal Studios •
Walt Disney • Magic Mountain •
Rose Bowl • Dodgers Stadium
within minutes
2900 N. San Fernando Blvd
Burbank, CA 91504
I-5S Exit Buena Vista
I-5N Exit Buena Vista, Make 3 immediate R turns
CALIFORNIA • I-15 • EXIT Buena Vista

EXIT	CALIFORNIA
ATM	E: McDonald's
158B	Truck Bypass
Exit	**(158)** Junction I-405 S., San Diego Frwy, Santa Monica (Southbound)
Exit	**(157)** San Fernado, Mission Blvd
Gas	E: Mobil(*)
Food	E: Carl Jr's Hamburgers (Green Burrito), Christy's Donuts & Ice Cream, In-N-Out Hamburgers, Pollo Gordo
AServ	E: Chief Auto Parts, Earthbound Tire, Jiffy Lube, Tune-Up While You Wait
Med	E: ✚ **Hospital**
ATM	E: **AM & PM Market**, Mobil
	W: Purrfect Auto Service
Other	E: **AM & PM Market**
156C	Brand Blvd. San Fernando (Northbound)
Gas	E: Arco(24), Chevron(*), Shell
Food	E: Carnitas Michoacan, Taco Bell
AServ	E: Arco, Mission Hills Ford Truck
Other	E: **Coin Laundry**
Exit	**(156)** Junction CA118 E
Exit	**(156)** Paxton St
Gas	E: Shell(*, 24)
Food	E: Royal Donuts
Exit	**(154)** Van Nuys, Pacoima (Northbound)
Gas	E: 76(*)
Food	E: Cupido's, KFC, McDonald's(PLAY), Pizza Hut, Popeye's Chicken
	W: Domino's Pizza
AServ	E: 76, C & N Auto Repair, Chief Auto Parts, Discount Auto Parts
	W: Tune Up Masters
Other	E: Fiesta Car Wash, **Payless Foods**
Exit	**(154)** Terra Bella St. (Northbound, No Reaccess)
Exit	**(154)** Osborne St
Gas	E: Arco(*), Shell(*, 24)
	W: 76(*, 24)
Food	E: Daily Fresh Donuts, Papas & Tacos, Peter Piper Pizza, Wong's Kitchen
	W: Mi Taco, **Yummy Donuts**(24)
AServ	E: 76(*, 24), A&J Tires, Joe's Auto Repair
	W: 76(24)
ATM	W: 7-11 Convenience Store
Other	E: Coin Laundry, **Food 4 Less**, Pic'n Save, **Target**
	W: 7-11 Convenience Store, Auto Spa Car Wash, **Coin Laundry**, **United States Post Office**
Exit	**(153)** Branford St. (Northbound)
Exit	**(153)** CA170 S, Hollywood Frwy (Southbound)
Exit	**(153)** Sheldon St., Hospital
Food	E: Big Jim's Restaurant(24), Tacos & Burritos
	W: Karla's Restaurant
AServ	E: Art's Tires, Big O Auto Parts, Victor's Auto Service
Exit	**(152)** Lankershim Blvd., North Hollywood
FStop	E: **Texaco**(LP, SCALES, 24)
Food	E: The Donut Baker & Deli

CAMPING WORLD®
Lyons Ave. Exit
24901 W. Pico Canyon Rd. • Newhall, CA
1-800-235-3337
1439

EXIT	CALIFORNIA
AServ	E: Alfaro's Auto Service, Tune-Up While You Wait, Zap Auto Electric Zap
	W: Noki's Car Repair, Sunvalley, Trust Auto Repair
RVCamp	E: **Benchmark RV Center (.25 Miles)**
Exit	**(151)** Penrose St
FStop	W: **Timm Fuel & Tires**
AServ	W: Manning Fuel Gas & Diesel, Manning Tire
TServ	W: **Timm Fuel & Tires**
Exit	**(150)** Sunland Blvd., Sunvalley
Gas	E: 76(*), Mobil(*, 24)
	W: Exxon(*), Shell(*, 24)
Food	E: Acapulco Mexican, China King, Donut Star, El Pollo Loco, Georgio's Pizza, Royal Orchid Thai-Chinese
	W: Dimions, McDonald's(PLAY), Mi Taco, Sunland Donuts & Ice Cream
Lodg	E: Scottish Inn
AServ	E: 76, Mobil(24)
	W: Round's Auto Parts, Valley Auto Parts
ATM	E: 7-11 Convenience Store(*)
	W: McDonald's
Other	E: 7-11 Convenience Store, Maytag Laundry
	W: Maytag Coin Laundry
Exit	**(149)** Glenoaks Blvd. (Northbound)
Gas	E: Arco(*, LP)
Food	E: Cheo's Taco (Arco)
Lodg	E: Willow's Motel
AServ	E: R & S Auto Repair
Exit	**(149)** Hollywood Way, Burbank Airport
Gas	W: Texaco(*, D)
AServ	W: J & A Auto Center
Other	W: Uhaul(LP)
Exit	**(148)** Buena Vista St
Gas	W: Exxon(*)
Food	W: Jack in the Box, Whispers
Lodg	W: Ramada (see our ad this page), The Quality Inn, Whispers
Exit	**(147)** Scott Rd., Burbank (Reaccess Northbound Only)
Gas	E: Sevan(*)
Food	E: 1 Plus 1 Pizza, Eiffel Bakery, Mr Big Burger
Lodg	E: Bell Vista Motel, Scott Motel
AServ	E: Alpha Italia Service Center, In-Out Service Center(CW), Sevan
Other	E: **U.S. Post Office**
Exit	**(146)** Burbank Blvd.
Gas	W: Chevron(*, 24)
Food	E: Barragan's Mexican Restaurant, Baskin Robbins, El Mexicano, Harry's Family Restaurant(24), IHOP, In N Out Burger, Kenny Roger's Roasters, The Mipiace Italian Kitchen &Bakery
	W: **El Burrito**, Subway, The Place For Steaks
AServ	W: Discount Tire Center
RVCamp	W: **Fitzpatrick Trailer Service**
ATM	E: Home Savings Of America
Other	E: Discovery Zone, Save on Drugs
Exit	Verdugo Ave.
Food	E: Bobby McGee's, Bombay Bicycle Club, The Black Angus, The Wild Thyme Cafe
AServ	E: Acme Autoworks, Brake Masters
ATM	E: **Bank of America**, Washington Mutual Bank, Wells Fargo Bank
Other	E: **Bank of America**, Washington Mutual Bank, Wells Fargo Bank
146A	Olive Ave, Burbank Ave.
RVCamp	W: **Metro RV Inc.**
Exit	**(145)** Alameda Ave
Gas	W: Arco(*), Shell(*, CW, 24), United Gas(*)
Lodg	W: **Burbank Inn & Suites**
AServ	E: The Rackside Auto Center

Bold red print shows RV & Bus parking available or nearby

EXIT CALIFORNIA

W: Arco, United Gas
ATM W: Arco
Exit **(144)** Western Ave
FStop W: Mambo's Cafe
Gas W: Chevron[*, 24]
AServ W: Auto Repair, Bill Briggs Automotives
Other W: Western Drugs
Exit **(144)** Junction CA134, Glendate, Pasadeena
Exit **(142)** Colorado St
141B Griffith Park Dr (Southbound)
Exit **(141)** Los Feliz Blvd
Gas E: Arco[*]
Food E: Family Buffet Restaurant, Sun Hai Chinese
Lodg E: Los Feliz Motel
W: Travelodge (see our ad this page)
Other E: Darla's Vaccination Clinic for Animals, Los Feliz Animal Hospital, Los Feliz Drugs[RX]
Exit **(140)** Glendale Blvd
Gas E: 76[*, LP, 24], Shell[*]
W: Beacon[*, D], Riverside Service Station[*, LP, 24]
AServ E: 76[24]
W: Beacon, Classic Collision Center, Riverside Service Station[24]
Exit **(140)** Fletcher Dr (Southbound, Reaccess Northbound Only)
FStop W: Astro Family Restaurant, El Chico
Gas W: 76[*, 24], Arco[*], Chevron[*]
Food W: Rick's Drive In & Out, Rudolpho's Restaurant
AServ E: Saenz Auto Service
W: 76[24], Chevron, Distaso Automotive
ATM W: Arco
Other W: Animal Hospital
139 Junction CA2North, Glendale Freeway & Echo Park
Exit **(138)** Stadium Way
137 Junction CA110 North to Pasadena Frwy, South to Los Angeles
Exit **(136)** North Broadway, Pasadeena Ave
Exit **(135)** Main St. (Northbound)
Gas E: C & J Automotive
Food E: Blanca's Mexican, Burger Plus, Chinatown Express, Dino's Burgers, Honey Donuts, La Pizza Loca
AServ E: C & J Automotive, Daly Auto Parts, Tune Up Masters
Exit **(135)** Mission Rd. (Southbound)
Gas E: Chevron[*]
Food E: Jack in the Box

HOLLYWOOD TRAVELODGE
1257

1401 N. VERMONT
Cable TV with Free HBO
Pool • Guest Laundry
Restaurants within Walking Distance
Closest Travelodge to Dodgers Stadium
Universal Studios • Greek Theaters
HWY. 101, EXIT ON VERMONT
213-665-5735 • 800-578-7878
CALIFORNIA ▪ I-5 ▪ LOS FELIZ

EXIT CALIFORNIA

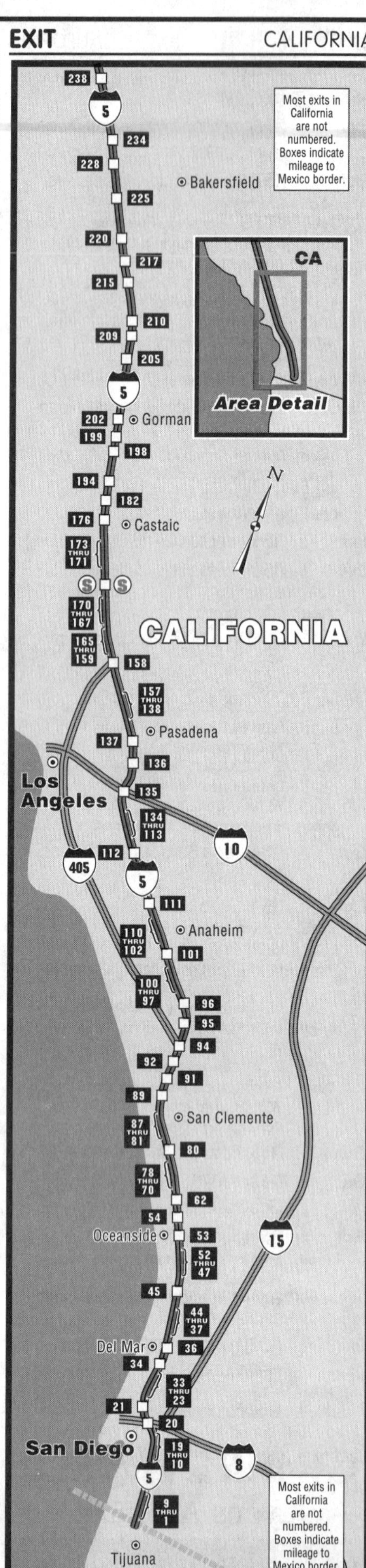

EXIT CALIFORNIA

AServ E: Auto Care Medic (Hospital), Stephen's Auto Service Center
Exit **(135)** Junction I-10, San Bernardino Freeway
Exit **(135)** Cesar Chavez Ave. (Northbound)
Gas W: Shell[*, 24] (Hospital)
Food E: El Pollo Loco, Shakeys Pizza
AServ E: Chief Auto Parts, PEP Boys Express
W: G & G Auto Repair, Hernandez Muffler, Shell[24] (Hospital)
Med W: + White Memorial Hospital
Exit **(134)** 4th St
Gas W: 76, Shell[24]
AServ W: L.A. Auto Service, Shell[24]
Parks W: Hollenbeck Park
133A Jct I-10E, CA 60, Santa Monica Frwy
Exit **(133)** Junction CA 60E Pamona
133B Soto St (Difficult Reaccess)
Gas E: Mobil
W: 76[24], Mobil[*, LP, CW]
Food E: Jim's Burgers, La Fortuna Bakery, Pioneer Chicken
W: El Pollo Loco, Jack-In-The-Box, McDonald's, Pepe Jones, Seafood Bay, Serena Bakery, Subway, The Orient Express, Winchells Donuts
AServ E: Mobil
W: 76[24]
ATM W: Bank Of America, Home Savings Of America
Other E: Coin Car Wash
W: Home Savings Of America
Exit **(132)** Grande Vista Ave (Northbound)
131B Calzona
Exit **(131)** Indiana St.
Exit Ditman (Southbound)
Gas W: Mobil[D, CW], Shell[*, CW]
Food W: Tacos & Burritos (Hospital)
AServ W: Auto Electric, Marco's Auto Parts, Mobil
130B Eastern Ave. (Northbound)
130 Jct I-710, South To Long Beach (Left Exit Northbound)
129B Triggs St
Food W: Denny's Restaurant
Lodg W: True-Value Inn
129A Atlantic Blvd
FStop W: Arco[24]
Food W: Steven's Steakhouse
Lodg E: Wyndham Garden Hotel
W: Bamby's Motel, Bob's Motel, Hines Motel, Rodeo Motel
AServ W: Paul's Automatic Transmission
Other E: Citadel Outlet Mall
Exit **(128)** Washington Blvd
Gas E: Chevron[*, D, LP]
Food E: JC's Bar & Grill (Commerce Hotel), McDonald's[PLAY]
Lodg E: Commerce Hotel
AServ E: Chevron, Firestone Tire & Auto
ATM W: Banco Popular
Other W: Banco Popular
127 Garfield Ave, Bandini Blvd
TServ W: Franklin Truck Parts
Other E: Home Depot
126B Slauson Ave to Montebello
FStop E: Shell[D]
Gas E: Shell[D]

Bold red print shows RV & Bus parking available or nearby

EXIT CALIFORNIA

W: Arco(*)
Food E: Burger King, Ozzie's Diner, Sandwich Plus
W: Denny's Restaurant, Jack in the Box
Lodg E: Four Corners Motel, Howard Johnson Hotel, Super 8
W: Ramada Inn, TraveLodge
AServ E: Shell
TServ E: ADC Truck Wash(D)
ATM W: Arco
Parks W: Veteran Memorial Park

126A Paramount Blvd, Downey
Food E: Florence Pizza, Granny's Donuts, Teriyaki Inn No. 8
ATM E: Circle K
Other E: Circle K

Exit **(125)** CA 19, Lakewood Blvd, Rosemead Blvd
Gas E: Arco(*), Mobil(*), Shell(*, 24)
Food E: Arthur's, Chateau Briand Restaurant, El Pedregal, Jose's Taco Delight, Olympic Donuts, Pepe's, Sam's Burgers
W: Chris & Pitt's BBQ, Drinx, Little Caesars Pizza, McDonald's, Penguin's Place, The Golden Wok Express
Lodg E: Econolodge
AServ E: Best Car Wash, Downey's Transmission, Mobil, R & A Auto Service(CW)
W: Downey Ford
Med E: ✚ Hospital
Other E: Northgate Supermarkets
W: Community Pharmacy(RX), Mailboxes Etc., Ralph's Food Market(24), Rider Truck Rental

123 Jct I-605

Buena Park, CA
DAYS INN
$34.99 +tax & up
Winter Rate
714-522-8461
800-374-4551
Bus and RV Parking
Outdoor Pool
Complimentary Disneyland Shuttle Service
Free Continental Breakfast
Many Newly Remodeled Rooms
Kids 12 & Under Stay & Eat Free
Free HBO, CNN, & ESPN
Extra Services Available
Discounts Available at Nearby Restaurants
Tickets Available for: Disneyland, Knott's Berry Farm, Magic Mountain, Raging Waters & Universal Studios (minimal service charge)
Discount reservations available for: Wild Bills, Medieval Times, Movieland Wax Museum, & Ripley's Believe-It-or-Not
7640 Beach Blvd • Buena Park, CA
Accessible from Freeway 91, Exit CA39/Beach Blvd South
California • I-5 • Exit Beach Blvd South

EXIT CALIFORNIA

Exit **(122)** Imperial Hwy, Pioneer Blvd
Gas E: Circle K(*)
W: 76(*, CW), Shell(*, CW)
Food W: Denny's Restaurant, Panda King Chinese Restaurant, Pizza Hut, Rally's Hamburgers, Sizzler Steak House, Southland Donuts, Taco Bell(24), Wienerschnitzel
Lodg W: Anchor Inn Motel, Comfort Inn, Keystone Motel, Towne House Motel, Westland Motel

122B Florence Ave, Downey (Difficult Reaccess)
Gas E: Mobil
Food E: Billie's, Birds Nest Chinese, Cherri's Donuts, Dragon Express, Express Pizza
AServ E: Chief Auto Parts, Mobil
W: Discount Auto Service, Massey Geo-Chevrolet-Cadillac
Other W: Sams Club

Exit **(121)** Norwalk Blvd, San Antonio Drive
Gas E: Shell(*)
Food W: Norwalk Grill
Lodg E: Marriott
AServ E: Shell
W: AC-DC Auto Electric
Other E: AMC Theaters

Exit **(120)** Rosecrans Ave, La Mirada
Gas E: Mobil(*, D), Shell(*, 24)
W: Arco(*)
Food E: Bakery, Big Saver Foods, Jim's Burgers, Mexican Restaurant
W: El Pollo Loco, Salt & Pepper Family Restaurant
AServ E: Best Best Tires, Car Wash(CW), Mobil
W: Budget Car & Truck Rental, Norwalk Lube, Sante Fe Nissan, Tune Up Masters
RVCamp W: Santa Fe Springs Motor Center

Exit **(119)** Carmenita Rd
Gas E: 76(*, D)
W: Arco(*), Mobil(*)
Food E: Bud's Submarine, Dippity Donuts, Jack-In-The-Box
W: Carl Jr's Hamburgers
Lodg E: Motel 6
W: Dynasty Suites, Super 8
AServ E: 76, Dean's Auto & Tire Center(D)
W: Mobil
TServ E: Carmenita Truck Center, Ford Trucks
RVCamp E: Cal-Western RV Supplies & Service(LP)
ATM W: Arco

118 Valley View Ave.
FStop W: Texaco(*, D, 24)
Gas E: Arco(*)
W: Chevron(*)
Food E: Carl Jr's Hamburgers, Holiday Inn, North Woods Inn Sandwiches
W: Blimpie Subs & Salads, El Pollo Loco, Fast Food China, Taco Tio, The Elephant Bar Restaurant, Winchell's-N-More
Lodg E: Holiday Inn
RVCamp W: Camping World (see our ad this page)

CAMPING WORLD®
Exit Valley View or Artesia
14900 S. Firestone Blvd. • La Mirada, CA
1-800-854-8422
1427

EXIT CALIFORNIA

AServ W: Texaco(24)
ATM W: Texaco, Well Fargo Bank
Other E: Gateway Five Theaters
W: Well Fargo Bank

Exit **(116)** Artesia Blvd
FStop E: 76(*, LP), Texaco(*, D)
W: Cardlock Fuels
Food E: Jerry's BBQ, Subway
Lodg E: Extended Stay America
AServ W: Gateway Chevrolet, La Mirada Auto Center
RVCamp W: Camping World
ATM E: Texaco

115 CA 39, Beach Blvd
Gas E: Arco(*), Chevron(*, 24)
Food E: China Gardens Restaurant, Copper Barrel Motel
W: Arby's, KFC, Korean BBQ, Pizza Hut
Lodg E: Copper Barrel Motel, Coral Motel
AServ E: Johnny's Auto Parts, Ken Grody Ford, Lew Webb's Toyota of Buena Park, Tire Pros
ATM E: Arco, Bank of America
Other E: Bank of America
W: Buena Animal Clinic, Coin Laundry, Enterprise Rent-a-Car, Food King Grocery Mart, Police Station

114C Manchester Ave. (Northbound)
114B Jct CA 91E, Riverside
RVCamp E: Lincoln RV Park (2 Miles)

113 Brookhurst St, La Palma Ave
Gas E: Chevron(*, 24)
W: Arco(*)
Food E: Dawn Donuts, Four Seasons Burger, Hatam Restaurant
AServ E: Guerrero Auto Repair
ATM W: Arco
Other W: Home Depot

112A Euclid St (Southbound)
Gas W: 76(*, 24), Arco(*), Mobil(*)
Food E: Baskin Robbins, Chris & Pitt's BBQ, Chubby's, Marie Callenders, Rubio's Baja Grill, Shangai Restaurant, Subway, Ten Ten Seafood Restaurant, The Fast Wok, Wendy's
W: Arby's, Big Dan's Donuts, Denny's, El Conejo Feliz Family Restaurant, Sav-On Drugs
Lodg W: Kettle Motor Hotel
AServ W: 76(24), Action Mufflers, Anaheim Chevrolet, Arco, Auto Trend Car Care Center, Bangla Motors, Car Wash, Discount Tires & Auto Repair, Harrington's -The Auto Care Professionals, Mills Ford, Mobil
Med E: ✚ Gateway Medical Center
ATM E: Calfed Bank, Home Savings Of America
W: Arco
Other E: Anaheim Plaza, Calfed Bank, Coin Laundry, King's Pharmacy, The Ranch Market, Wal-Mart
W: Laundry Stop, Sav-On Drugs

111B Loara St (Northbound, Same services as Euclid St)
AServ E: Wal-Mart
Other E: Anaheim Plaza, Petco, Wal-Mart

111A Lincoln Ave (Same services as Euclid and Loara Streets)
RVCamp E: Lincoln RV Park (2 Miles)

110C Ball Rd. (Southbound, Access to Disney Land)
Gas E: Chevron(*), Shell(*)
W: Arco(*)
Food E: Carrow's Restaurant, Poppy Cafe, Shakeys

EXIT CALIFORNIA

Pizza
W: Cuban Pete's Inn, The Spaghetti Station
Lodg **E:** Holiday Inn, The Anaheim Traffic Motel, The Courtesy Lodge, The Frontier Motel, The Ramada Limited
W: Best Western, Best Western, Budget Inn Motel, Days Inn, Sheraton Anaheim Hotel, Super 8, The Station Inn
AServ **E:** Harbor Auto Care
RVCamp **E:** **The Anaheim Harbor RV Park, Traveler's World RV Park**
ATM **W:** Arco
Other **E:** Corner Market

110B Freedman Way, Disney Land
Lodg **W:** Hawthorn Suites Ltd., Peacock Suites, Residence Inn
ATM **W:** 7-11 Convenience Store
Other **W:** 7-11 Convenience Store, Disney Land

110A State College Blvd., The City Drive
Food **E:** Del Taco, Hop City Steakhouse, The Catch
Lodg **E:** The Hilton Suites
W: The Country Side Inn, The Doubletree Hotel
Med **W:** ✚ **UCI Medical Center**
ATM **E:** The California State Bank
Other **E:** The California State Bank

109 Katella Ave, Anaheim Blvd.
Gas **E:** 76
W: Exxon
Food **E:** Courtyard Cafe, Fritz, Mr. Stox Fine Dining, Tweed's
W: Chinese Food, Cowboy Boogie, Del Taco, Donuts, Flaky Jake's Burgers, Ming Delight Restaurant, Persepolis, Thai Thai Restaurant
Lodg **E:** Comfort Inn, Ramada Inn
W: Alender Motel, Arenan, Crystal Suites, Little Boy Blue Motel, Peacock Suites, Rip Van Winkle Motel, Riviera Motel, Samoa Motel, Super 8 Motel (see our ad this page)
AServ **E:** 76
W: Cowboy Automotive, Exxon

107 CA 57N. to Pamona

106B Chapman Ave (Difficult Reaccess)
Food **E:** Burger King, Denny's
Lodg **E:** **Motel 6**
RVCamp **W:** **Ponderosa RV Park (.5 Miles)**

106A CA 22 East, Orange

105B Broadway, Main St
Food **E:** Polly's Pies
Lodg **E:** Red Roof Inn
Other **E:** **Main Place Santa Anna (Mall)**

105A 17th St., Penn Way
FStop **W:** **CFN**(LP)
Gas **E:** Shell(*, D, CW)
W: Chevron(*)
Food **E:** Country Harvest Buffet, IHOP, McDonald's(PLAY), Polloreno Pizza
W: Norm's Restaurant(24), Ruby Tuesdays, Yum Yum Coffee & Donuts
Lodg **E:** Howard Johnson
W: Aqua Motel
AServ **E:** Guaranty Chevrolet
W: Chevron
ATM **E:** McDonald's, Shell
W: 7-11 Convenience Store, Washington Mutual Bank
Other **E:** Coin Wash & Dry
W: 7-11 Convenience Store, San Wa Bank, Washington Mutual Bank

104 Santa Ana Blvd, Grand Ave

EXIT CALIFORNIA

Food **E:** Denny's
AServ **E:** Creagan Auto Parts, Parnelli Auto & Tire Service, United Engine
TServ **W:** **Tom's Truck Center**
Other **E:** Animal Hospital, **Target**
W: Car Wash(CW)

103 4th St , 1st St. (Access to Santa Ana Zoo)
Med **E:** ✚ **Kaiser Permanente**

102B CA55 South, Newport Beach

102A Newport Ave (Southbound, Difficult Reaccess)
FStop **E:** **Cardlock Fuels**
Gas **E:** Ultramar(*)
W: Thrifty(*)
Food **E:** Double Time Co., Jack in the Box, Rallys, Round Table Pizza, Sizzler
W: Arco(*, 24), Carl Jr's Hamburgers(PLAY), Donut King & Bakery, Taco Bell, The Green Burrito
AServ **E:** Car Wash, Tustin Transmission, Ultramar
W: Arco(24)
ATM **W:** Arco
Other **W:** Quinto's

Exit **(101)** Red Hill Ave
Gas **E:** Arco(*, CW), Arco(*), Mobil(*, D), Shell(*)
W: 76(*), Chevron(*, D, 24), Circle K(*)
Food **E:** D&N Donuts & Burgers, Del Taco, Denny's, Mario's Pizza, Seoul Garden BBQ
W: Minami Japanese Restaurant, R & R's Pizza, Taco Bell
Lodg **E:** Key Inn
AServ **E:** Arco, Mobil, Shell
W: 76, Arco(*), Car Wash
ATM **E:** Arco
W: Arco, Circle K

Anaheim/Disney

415 W. Katella Ave
Anaheim, CA 92802

1717

6 Restaurants in Walking Distance
Continental Breakfast
Kids Under 12 Stay & Eat Free
Heated Outdoor Pool • Jacuzzi
Free Local Calls
Coin Laundry
Disney Courtesy Shuttle
1 1/2 Blocks from Disneyland
Tours Available to all Major Sites

800-777-1123
714-778-6900

I-5 Exit Katella Ave. 2 Blocks West
CALIFORNIA • I-5 • EXIT 109

EXIT CALIFORNIA

Other **E:** **Coin Laundry, Drug Emporium**(24)
W: **Stater Bros. Grocery**

100B Tustin Ranch Road
Food **E:** McDonald's(PLAY)
AServ **E:** Goodyear Auto Center, Joe Macpherson Ford, Joe Macpherson Infinity, Joe Macpherson Mazda, Joe Macpherson Toyota, Lincoln Mercury, McLean Auto Dealer, Tustin Acura, Tustin Buick & Pontiac, Tustin Chevrolet, Tustin Dodge, Tustin Nissan
Other **E:** Costco, **K-Mart**

100A Jamboree Road
Gas **E:** 76(*, CW)
Food **E:** Black Angus Steakhouse, Busy Bee Oriental Food, Carl Jr's Hamburgers(PLAY), Dairy Queen, El Pollo Loco, In-N-Out Hamburgers, Jamba Juice, Koo-Koo-Roo, Macaroni Grill, Northwood Pizza, Red Robin, Rubio's Baja Grill, Sub Station II, Taco Bell, The Renaissance Coffee
AServ **E:** 76
Other **E:** Barnes & Noble, Bookstar, Home Depot, Starbucks Coffee, **Tustin Market Place**

Exit **(99)** Culver Drive
Gas **E:** Shell(*, 24)
W: Chevron(*)
Food **W:** Breadsmith, Carrows Restaurant, Caspian Restaurant, China Oasis, Denny's, Diho Bakery, Domino's Pizza, East Coast Bagel, India Cook House, Japanese Restaurant, Korean Restaurant, Milano's Italian Kitchen, Quan Thana Restaurant, Simply Pasta, Sumo Japanese Restaurant, ToGo's, Wendy's
AServ **E:** Shell(24)
W: Martin Bros. Auto Parts
ATM **W:** First Bank & Trust Co.
Other **E:** Police Station
W: Culver Pet Center, First Bank & Trust Co., First

128 Clean Comfortable Rooms

1266 23150 LAKE CENTER DRIVE
Lake Forest, CA

Renovated Rooms
Free Continental Breakfast
Outdoor Pool
Close to Beach
Tennis & Golf Close By
Corporate or Military Rates
Non-Smoking Rooms
Extended Stay Rates
Coin Laundry
Ample Free Parking
Microwave/Refrigerator Room Available
5 minutes to Irvine Spectrum
In-Room Coffee/Iron/Ironing Board
Satellite TV, HBO/CNN/ESPN
Walking Distance to Restaurant/Bar

I-5 exit on Lake Forest and turn left. Take a right on Rockfield and right on Boeing.

949-855-1000 • 800-591-9200
CALIFORNIA • I-5 • LAKE FOREST

Bold red print shows RV & Bus parking available or nearby

EXIT CALIFORNIA

Plus Bank, Mailboxes Etc., Pharmacy, Ralph's Food Center, **Sav-On Drugs**

Exit (97) Jeffrey Road
- **Food** W: A&J Restaurant, China Express, China Garden, El Conejo Mexican Food, Irvine Pizza, Japanese Restaurant, Jenny's Donuts & Croissants, O'Shine Cafe, S.W. Seafood & BBQ, The GoGo Cafe, The Nice Time Deli, The Pizza Exchange, Valley Cafe Coffee, Wienerschnitzel
- **AServ** W: 76(*, D)
- **ATM** W: Washing Mutual Bank
- **Other** W: **Arbor Animal Hospital**, Bank of America, **Camino Pet Hospital**, **Coin Laundry**, **Lucky Food Center**, **Thifty Drug & Discount**, Washing Mutual Bank

Exit (96) Sand Canyon Ave
- **Gas** W: 76(*, CW)
- **Food** W: Knowlwood, Season Ticket Sports Grill, Tia Juana's
- **Lodg** W: La Quinta Inn
- **AServ** W: 76
- **RVCamp** W: **El Toro RV Service Center(LP)**, **Traveland USA**
- **ATM** W: 76

95 Jct 133S, Laguna Beach (Southbound)

Exit (94) Alton Pkwy
- **Gas** E: Texaco(*, D)
- **Food** E: Arribal Cobo Grill, Bruegger's Bagel & Bakery, Carl Jr's Hamburgers, Quizno's Classic Subs, Starbucks Coffee, Subway (Texaco), TCBY (Texaco), Taco Bell (Texaco)
  W: Dave & Buster's, P.S. Chang's China Bistro
- **Lodg** E: Homestead Village
- **AServ** E: Costco
- **Med** W: **✚ Hospital**
- **ATM** E: Texaco
- **Other** E: Costco
  W: Barnes & Noble, Edward's 21 Cinemas, **Irvine Spectrum Center (Shopping Mall)**, Starbucks Coffee

93 Jct. I-405 Long Beach

92B Bake Pkwy., Lake Forest Dr.-Truck by-pass

Exit (92) Lake Forest Drive (To exit need to be in truck by-pass lane)
- **Gas** E: Texaco(*, D, LP), Texaco
  W: Chevron(*), Circle K(*), Shell(*, CW)
- **Food** E: Bodeckers Sandwiches, Burger King, California Wine Merchant Deli, Captain Creme (Adult Entertainment-must be at least 21yrs. old), Del Taco, Diho Chinese-Thai Restaurant, Donuts, Hungry Hunter, IHOP, Inka Grill Peruvian Cuisine, Mandarin Place, Mandarin Taste Restaurant & Lounge, McDonald's(PLAY), Subway, Taco Bell, Teriyaki House, The Original Peppino's Italian Family Restaurant, Uoko Japanese Cuisine, Vie a Paris French Bakery & Sandwiches
  W: Boomi's Teriyaki, Coco's Restaurant, Deli Bakery & Coffee House, McDonald's, Snooty Fox Cafe, Subway
- **Lodg** E: Best Western (Formosa Chinese Restaurant), El Toro Travelodge (see our ad opposite page)
  W: Comfort Inn
- **AServ** E: America's Tire Company, Beacon Bay Auto Wash, Econo Lube & Tire, Lake Forest Auto Service, Subaru Parts & Service, Texaco
  W: Hand Car Wash
- **ATM** E: Farmers Merchant Bank, Southern California Bank
  W: Circle K
- **Other** E: Enterprise Rent-a-Car, Farmers Merchant Bank, Federal Express, Hertz Car Rental, Southern California Bank
  W: Book's etc., Budget Rent-A-Car, Mail Biz Plus, Saddleback Suzuki Sea-doo

91 El Toro Rd.
- **Gas** E: Arco(*), Chevron(*), Mobile(*), Shell(*), Texaco(*, D, LP), USA Gasoline(*, D, LP, 24)
  W: 76(*), Chevron(*, D, 24), Shell(*)
- **Food** E: Arby's, Carmel's Restaurant, China Palms, Donut Shop, El Toro Ranch, Jack-In-The-Box, McDonald's, Mega Burgers, Numero Uno Pizzaria, Omar's Bakery Market, Red Lobster, Royal Donuts
  W: Carrows Restaurant, Don Jose's Mexican Restaurant, King's Fish House, Koo-Koo-Roo, Split Rock Tavern
- **Lodg** W: Laguna Hills Lodge
- **AServ** E: Master Care Auto Service, Shell, Texaco
  W: 76, Just Tires, Shell
- **ATM** E: Arco, Bank of America, Home Savings Of America, Texaco, USA Gasoline, Wells Fargo
  W: Home Savings Of America, Washing Mutual Bank
- **Other** E: **Sav-On Drugs(24)**, **Thrifty Drug**, Toro Laundromat
  W: Mall, Wallgreen's Pharmacy, Washing Mutual Bank

90 Alicia Pkwy
- **Gas** E: 76(D)
  W: 76(*, D, LP), Chevron(*, CW)
- **Food** E: Bakery Outlet, Casa Franco Mexican Food, Del Taco(24), Denny's, Mission Donuts, Piccadilly Pizza, Subway
  W: 20/20 Italian Cafe, Carl Jr's Hamburgers, Golden Baked Hams, Natraj Cuisine of India, P.J. Bernstein's New York Deli, Pancho Villas, Pasta Palace, Royal Donuts, Salsa Xpress Mexican Grill, Times Square Pizza, Togo's Eatery, Wendy's
- **AServ** E: America's Tire Company (Kragen's Auto Parts)
  W: 76, Buick Pontiac Mazda
- **ATM** E: La Jolla Bank, Wells Fargo
  W: Quick Stop Market
- **Other** E: **Target**
  W: Alicia's Pet Clinic, Mailboxes Etc., Mr. Good Books, Pic N' Save, Quick Stop Market, Thrifty Car Rental

Exit (89) La Paz Road
- **Gas** E: Arco(*), Mobil(*, LP)
  W: 76, Chevron(*), Ultramar(*)
- **Food** E: Diedrich's Coffee, KFC, Taco Bell
  W: Claim Jumper, D'Angelo's Trattoria Italian Restaurant, Elephant Bar Restaurant, Flamingo's Mexican Grill & Bar, McDonald's(PLAY), Outback Steakhouse, Spassos Family Italian Restaurant, Wienerschnitzel
- **Lodg** W: Holiday Inn
- **AServ** E: Mobil
  W: 76, Chevron, Ultramar, Winston Tire Co.
- **ATM** E: Arco, Bank of America, Downey Savings Bank, Wells Fargo
- **Other** E: **Animal & Bird Clinic**, **Lucky Food Center(24)** **(Sav-On Drugs & Bank of America)**
  W: Animal Hospital, Orange National Bank

Exit (87) Oso Pkwy.
- **Gas** E: 76(*, D, LP, 24)
- **Food** E: Carl Jr's Hamburgers
- **Lodg** E: Fairfield Inn
- **AServ** E: 76(24)

Exit (86) Crown Valley Pkwy
- **Gas** W: Chevron(*, D, CW)
- **Food** E: Coco's Restaurant, Jerry's Deli, King's Donut, Lucky 7 Oriental Food, TJ's Mexican Food & Cantina
- **AServ** E: 76(*), Arco(*), Chevron(*)
  W: AAMCO Transmission, Cape Auto Repair, **Carmer Collision & RV (see our ad this page)**, Econo Lube & Tune Mufflers & Brakes, Laguna Niguel Service Center, Suspension Plus, Tucker Tire Co. (Marvin's Automotive Service)
- **ATM** E: Arco, Bank of America, Home Savings Of America
- **Other** E: Downey Savings Bank, Mailboxes Etc., Mission Park Pet Hospital, Mission Viejo Mall
  W: Costco Wholesale Warehouse

Exit (85) Avery Pkwy
- **Gas** E: Texaco(*, D, CW) (Subway)
  W: Shell(*, D)
- **Food** E: Albertaco's Mexican(24), Carrows Restaurant, Del Taco, Gecko's, Jack-In-The-Box, La Ferme French Cuisine, Mandarin Dynasty, McDonald's, Tony Roma's
  W: A's Burgers, Buffy's Family Restaurant, In N Out Burger
- **Lodg** W: Laguna Inn & Suites
- **AServ** E: America's Tire Company, Freeway Auto Supply, Land Rover, Lexus, Mercedes Benz, Mission Tire Center, Mission Viejo Imports, Pro Auto Care
  W: Allen Oldsmobile-Cadillac-GMC Trucks
- **ATM** E: Fast Check Market & Deli, Texaco (Subway), Wells Fargo
- **Other** E: Acura, Enterprise Rent-a-Car, Fast Check Market & Deli, **Kinko's**

Exit (84) CA 72N to Long Beach (Northbound, Toll)

Exit (83) Junipero Serra Road
- **Gas** W: Shell(*, 24)
- **AServ** W: Shell(24), Ultramar(*, D)

Exit (82) CA 74, Ortega Hwy, to San Juan Capistrano
- **Gas** E: Shell(*, 24)
  W: 76(*)
- **Food** E: Ball Park Pizza, Denny's, O'Boy Burgers
  W: Boston Market Restaurant, Burger King, Carl Jr's Hamburgers, Carlo's Mexican Food, Del Taco(24), Diedrich's Coffee, Jack-In-The-Box, Marie Callender's Restaurant, McDonald's(24), Sizzler Steak House, Subway, Taco Bell, Upper Crust Pizza, Walnut Grove Restaurant
- **Lodg** E: Best Western
  W: Mission Inn
- **AServ** E: 76(*), Chevron(*, D), Ortega Hand Wash Car Wash, Shell(24), Texaco Express Lube
  W: 76, Chevron(*, 24)
- **ATM** W: 76, California Federal Bank, F&M Bank
- **Other** W: **Capistrano Historic Mission**, Mailboxes Etc., Mission Promenade, **Ralph's Food Center (Grocery Store)**

Exit (81) Camino Capistrano
- **Food** E: Carlton's Colorado Kitchen
  W: Baskin Robbins, Pranzare Italian Grill
- **ATM** W: Eldorado Bank, Glendale Federal, Wells Fargo

EXIT	CALIFORNIA
	Bank, Wells Fargo Bank
Other	**W:** Capistrano Pharmacy(RX), Mail Center, **Vons Grocery**
Exit	**(80)** CA 1, Pacific Coast Hwy., Camino Los Ramblas
Exit	**(78)** Camino de Estrella
Gas	**E:** 76(*, D, 24)
	W: Arco(*, D)
Food	**E:** Bakers Square Restaurant, Boston Market Restaurant, Carl Jr's Hamburgers, Golden Chicken, Juice Time, Ralph's Grocery (Union Bank of California), Rose Donuts & Sandwiches, Round Table Pizza, Rubio's Baja Grill, Starbucks Coffee, Subway, The Gourmet Bagel
AServ	**E:** 76(24)
	W: Arco
ATM	**E:** Home Savings Of America, Ralph's Grocery (Union Bank of California)
	W: Arco, Bank of America, Cal Fed Bank, Washington Mutual Bank
Other	**E:** Camino Veterinary Clinic, **Lucky Food Center**, Mailboxes Etc., **Sav-On Drugs**, Theater
	W: **K-Mart (Little Caesar's Pizza)**, Maytag Laundry
Exit	**(77)** Ave Pico
Gas	**E:** Mobil(*, CW)
	W: Chevron(*), Texaco(*, D, LP)
Food	**E:** Carrows Restaurant, McDonald's(PLAY)
	W: Burger Stop, Caterina's Yogurt, Coffee & Donuts, Denny's(24), Pick Up Stix, Pizza Hut, Stuft Pizza, Subway, Surfin' Chicken
AServ	**W:** Midas (San Clemente Auto & Tire Center), San Clemente Auto Collision, Stanley's Auto Repair
ATM	**W:** Del Taco, Eldorado Bank, First Plus Bank, Texaco
Other	**W:** Mailboxes Etc., **Sav-On Drugs**, The Pico Veterinarian Clinic
Exit	**(76)** Ave Palizada, San Clemente (Southbound, Difficult Reaccess)
Gas	**W:** Ultramar(*)
Food	**W:** Sonny's Pizza & Pasta
Lodg	**W:** Holiday Inn
AServ	**W:** Ultramar
ATM	**W:** 7-11 Convenience Store, Bank of America, Wells Fargo
Other	**W:** 7-11 Convenience Store, **Albertson's Grocery**
75	Ave Prasedio, San Clemente
Exit	**(74)** El Camino Real
Gas	**E:** Chevron(*, 24)
	W: 76(D), Mobil(*)
Food	**E:** Burrito Basket, El Mariachi, Surfin' Donuts Coffee House
	W: FatBurger, Hot Dog Heaven, Love Burger, Surfin' Donuts, Taco Bell, Tommy's Coffee Shop
Lodg	**E:** Budget Lodge, San Clemente Motel
AServ	**E:** 4 In Service Auto Repair, Chevron(24), Winston Tire Co.
	W: Kragen Auto Parts, Mobil, Top Tune
ATM	**E:** 7-11 Convenience Store
	W: 7-11 Convenience Store
Other	**E:** 7-11 Convenience Store, Buggy Bath Car Wash, **San Clemente Veterinary Clinic**, The Laundry Basket
	W: 7-11 Convenience Store, **Ralph's Grocery**
Exit	**(73)** Ave Calafia (San Clemente State Park)
Gas	**E:** 76(*, D), Shell(*, 24)
Food	**E:** China Beach Canteen, Coco's Restaurant, Jack-In-The-Box, Pedro's Tacos, Sugar Shack Cafe, The Beefcutter Restaurant
Lodg	**E:** C-Vu Motel, El Rancho Motel, La Vista Inn, Quality Inn, TraveLodge
	W: San Clemente Inn

EXIT	CALIFORNIA
AServ	**E:** 76, Dick Watson Auto Center, Shell(24), Winston Tire Co.
ATM	**E:** Shell
Exit	**(72)** Cristianitos Rd. (San Mateo Campground)
Food	**E:** **Carl Jr's Hamburgers**
Lodg	**E:** Carmela Motel, Comfort Suites Hotel
Parks	**W:** **San Clemente State Park**
Exit	**(71)** Basilone Rd, San Onofre
(67)	**Weigh Station**
Exit	**(63)** Vista Point (Southbound, Ocean Lookout)
Exit	**(62)** Las Pulgas Road
(57)	**Rest Area (RR, Phones, Picnic, Vending)**
Exit	**(54)** Oceanside Harbor Drive, Camp Pendleton
Gas	**W:** Chevron(*), Mobil(*, D, LP)
Food	**W:** Del Taco, Denny's, Jolly Roger, Monterey Bay Canners Fresh Seafood
Lodg	**W:** Days Inn, TraveLodge
AServ	**W:** Mobil
RVCamp	**W:** **Sandy Shores**
Other	**W:** Avis Rent-a-car, Carpenters Garage & Towing Service, Oceanside Harbor, Pend Market
53B	Coast Hwy., Oceanside
Gas	**W:** Arco(*), Shell(*, D, 24)
Food	**W:** Angelo's Burgers, Carrows Restaurant, Hamburger Heaven Cafe, Wienerschnitzel
Lodg	**W:** **Coast Inn**, Mira Mar Motel, Motel 9, **The Bridge Motel (Restaurant)**
AServ	**W:** Shell(24)
53A	Mission Ave, Downtown
Gas	**E:** Arco(*), Mobil(*, D)
Food	**E:** Burger King(PLAY), Jack-in-the-Box, Mission Donut House, Rally's Hamburgers, Taco Shop(24)
	W: Burger Joint, El Pollo Loco, Hemet Savings & Loan, Long John Silver, Mandarin Chinese, Manhattan's Giant Pizza
Lodg	**E:** Grandee Inn (Family Restaurant), Welton Inn
AServ	**E:** Bussey's Auto Service, Econo Lube & Tune
	W: Chief Auto Parts
ATM	**E:** Arco
	W: Bank of America, Home Savings Of America
Other	**E:** Police Station
	W: Rite Aid(RX)
Exit	**(52)** Oceanside Blvd (Highway Patrol Office)
Food	**E:** IHOP, Marsha's Deli, McDonald's, New Hong Kong, Pizza Hut
Lodg	**W:** Best Western
AServ	**W:** Texaco(*, D, LP, 24)
RVCamp	**W:** **Casitas Poquitos (.75 Miles)**, **Paradise By The Sea RV Park (.5 Miles)**
ATM	**E:** McDonald's, **Ralph's Grocery**
Other	**E:** Avis Rent-a-car, **Coin Laundry**, **Longs Drugs**, **Ralph's Grocery**, **Sav-on-Drugs**, **Vons Food Market**
Exit	**(51)** Cassidy St. (Southbound)
51C	Vista, San Marcos, CA 78 Escondido, Oceanside, Vista Way
Food	**W:** Hunter Steakhouse
51B	Jct CA 78, to Escondido
RVCamp	**E:** **Camping World (see our ad this page)**
	W: **Foretravel, Inc. (see our ad this page)**
51A	Las Flores Drive
Exit	**(50)** Carlsbad Village Drive, Elm Ave., Downtown

EXIT	CALIFORNIA
Gas	**E:** Shell(*, CW)
	W: 76(*, CW), Arco(*), Chevron(*, D), Texaco(*, D, LP, 24)
Food	**E:** Lotus Thai Bistro
	W: Al's n-the-Village Cafe, Alberto's Mexican(24), Carl Jr's Hamburgers, Carlsbad Country Bakery, Denny's, French Pastry Cafe, Giant New York Pizza & Pasta, Green Burrito, Jack-in-the-Box, KFC, Mikko Japanese Cuisine, Taco Bell
Lodg	**W:** Motel 6
AServ	**E:** Shell
	W: Chevron, Texaco(24)
ATM	**W:** Arco, Bank of Commerce, Eldorado Bank, Home Savings Of America, Union Bank of California
Parks	**E:** **Holiday Park**
Other	**W:** **Albertson's Grocery**(LP), Coin Laundry, El Camino Pharmacy(RX)
Exit	**(49)** Tamarack Ave
Gas	**E:** Chevron(*, 24), Texaco(*, D, 24)
	W: 76(*)
Food	**E:** Pizza Shuttle & Subs, Village Kitchen & Pie Shop
	W: Gerico's Family Restaurant
Lodg	**E:** Super 8, **Travel Inn**
AServ	**E:** Chevron(24), Texaco(24)
	W: 76
ATM	**E:** **Vons Grocery**
Other	**E:** **Coin Laundry**, Rite Aid(RX), **Vons Grocery**
	W: Dolphin Beach
Exit	**(48)** Cannon Road
AServ	**E:** Chrysler Auto Dealer, Ford Dealership, Hoehn Oldsmobile, Hoehn Porche-Audi-Acura, Jeep Eagle Dealer, Lexus Dealer, Lincoln Mercury, Mercedes Benz, Pontiac-GMC Trucks-Mazda, Rorick Buick, Toyota Dealer, Weseloh Chevrolet, Worthington Dodge
Exit	**(47)** Palomar Airport Rd.
FStop	**W:** **Texaco**(*, D, LP, 24)
Gas	**E:** Chevron(*, D, 24), Citgo(*) (7-11 Convienence Store), Mobil(*, CW)
Food	**E:** Carl Jr's Hamburgers, Denny's, Garden State Bagels, Greek Village Restaurant & Tavern, Orchard Cafe, Pea Soup Andersen's Restaurant (Gift Shop), Ruby's Diner, Starbucks Coffee, Subway, Taco Bell
	W: Claim Jumper, In-N-Out Hamburgers, Marie Callender's Restaurant, McDonald's, Sammy's

CAMPING WORLD®
Exit San Marcos Blvd.
off 78 Freeway
200 Travelers Way • San Marcos, CA
1-800-874-4346
1435

1055
Foretravel of California, Inc.
MOTORHOME
SALES • SERVICE • PARTS
Directions: From I-5 exit (Hwy 78 West). Go 2 miles West to Nordahl. South on Nordahl to West Mission Road. ½ mile East on West Mission Road.
1700 West Mission Road • Escondido, CA 92029
800.477.1310

Bold red print shows RV & Bus parking available or nearby

EXIT CALIFORNIA

California Woodfired Pizza
Lodg E: Holiday Inn, Motel 6
AServ E: Jiffy Lube(CW)
W: **Texaco**(24)
ATM E: Citgo (7-11 Convienence Store)
Other E: Carlsbad Company Stores, **Costco**, Hadley's Market, Postal Annex, Tip Top Meats

Exit (45) Poinsettia Ln., Aviara Pkwy.
Food W: El Pollo Loco, It's Coffee Time, Jack-In-The-Box, Panda Buffet, Raintree Restaurant (Inns of America), Subway
Lodg W: Carlsbad La Costa Lodge, Inns Of America, Motel 6, Ramada Suites
Med W: ✚ **Kaiser Permanente**
ATM W: Bank One, **Ralph's Grocery**(24), Union Bank of California
Other W: **All Cats Hospital**, Calvary Chapel Books, Mailboxes Etc., **Ralph's Grocery**, Rite Aid(RX), **Vision Center**

Exit (44) La Costa Ave
Gas W: Chevron(*, 24)
AServ W: Chevron(24)

Exit (43) Leucadia Blvd
Gas W: Shell(*, 24), Texaco(D, LP), Texaco(*, D, LP)
Lodg E: Holiday Inn Express
AServ W: Shell(24), Texaco
RVCamp W: **Trailer Rancho (1 Mile)**

Exit (41) Encinitas Blvd (Hospital)
Gas E: Arco(*), Chevron(*, CW, 24), Texaco(*, D, LP)
W: Shell(*, LP, CW)
Food E: Baskin Robbins, Coco's Restaurant, Del Taco, Gusto Trattoria, Honey Baked Ham, Stuft Pizza & Brewing Co., Super Donut no.1
W: Denny's (see our ad this page), Wendy's
Lodg W: DAYS INN Days Inn
AServ E: Arco, Mossy Nissan, Texaco
ATM E: Arco, Eldorado Bank
Other E: **Kinko's**, Lucky Food Center, **Sav-On Drugs**
W: Launderland Coin Laundry

40B Santa Fe Drive (Hospital)
Gas E: Shell(24)
W: 76(*, D, LP)
Food E: Carl Jr's Hamburgers, Green Burrito, Hide Away Cafe
W: Bagels by the Sea, Burger King (76), California Yogurt Company, NY Pizza House, The Great Wall Restaurant
AServ E: Shell(24)
Med W: ✚ **Scripps Memorial Hospital**
ATM E: 7-11 Convenience Store
W: Downey Savings Bank, **Vons Grocery**
Other E: 7-11 Convenience Store
W: **Lauderland Coin Laundry**, Postal Annex, Rite Aid(RX), **Santa Fe Animal Clinic**, **Vons Grocery**

40A Birmingham Drive

1064
Denny's
Open 24 Hours
760-942-0656
Where Value Hits a Grand Slam Everyday!
Denny s... good food and friendly service is just down the road!
Look for us in Encinitas, California
CALIFORNIA ▪ I-5 ▪ Encinitas Blvd. Exit

EXIT CALIFORNIA

Gas E: Chevron(*, 24), Texaco(*, LP, CW)
W: Arco(*)
Food E: Taco Bell(24)
Lodg E: Country Side Inn
AServ E: Texaco
ATM W: Arco

Exit (38) Manchester Ave
Gas E: 76(*)
AServ W: Budget Car & Truck Rental

Exit (37) Lomas Santa Fe Drive, Solano Beach
Gas W: Mobil(*), Texaco(*, D, CW)
Food E: Baskin Robbins, Einstein Bros Bagels, Foglanders Yogurt & Ice Cream, Pizza Nova, Roadhouse Grill, Samurai Restaurant
W: Cafe Europa Deli, Carl Jr's Hamburgers, Golden Bowl Chinese, Round Table Pizza, Sante Fe Co. Yogurt, Top of the Bagel
AServ W: Discount Tire Company, Texaco
ATM E: Mission Federal Credit Union, Wells Fargo, Wells Fargo Bank
W: Glendale Federal Bank, Mobil, Washington Mutual Bank
Other E: Postal Annex, **Vons Grocery**
W: ABC Veternary Hospital, Chronicles Christian Marketplace Bookstore, Nail Mania, **SAV On Drugs**, San Dieguito Pharmacy

36 Via De La Valle, Del Mar
Gas E: Chevron(*, CW), Mobil(*, D)
W: Arco(*)
Food E: Chevy's Mexican, Koo-Koo-Roo California Kitchen, McDonald's(PLAY), Milton's Deli, Papa Chino's Restaurante, Pick-Up-Stix, Taste of Thai, Tony Roma's
W: Denny's, Pampoe Mousse Grill, Red Tracton's Restaurant, The Fish Market
Lodg W: Hilton, Winner's Circle Resort
AServ W: Texaco(*, D)
ATM E: Bank of Commerce, Chevron, Grossmont Bank, Home Savings Of America
W: Arco
Other E: **Alberson's Grocery**(RX), Bookworks, Edward's Cinemas, Flower Hill Mall
W: **Del Mar Fairgrounds & Racetrack**

Exit (34) Del Mar Heights Road
Gas E: Texaco(*, D)
W: Citgo(D)
Food W: Golden Bagel Cafe, Greek Cuisine Cafe, Jack-In-The-Box, Jam's Yogurt, Le Bambou, Mexican Grill, O'Brien's Boulangerie, Rotisserie Chicken, The Juice Event
AServ E: Texaco
W: Citgo
ATM E: Wells Fargo
W: Bank of America
Other W: 7-11 Convenience Store, **Coin Laundry**, **Longs Drugs**, Postal Annex, **Vons Grocery**

33 Sorrento Valley Road (Northbound)

Exit (32) Carmel Valley Rd., Jct. CA 56E
Gas E: Arco(*, 24), Shell(*)
Food E: Taco Bell, Tio Leo's Mexican Restaurant
Lodg E: Doubletree Hotel
AServ E: Shell
ATM E: Arco

30 Jct I-805 S

29 Genesee Ave
Med E: ✚ **Scripps Memorial Hospital**

Exit (28) La Jolla Village Drive (Medical Center on west side)
Gas W: Mobil(*, D, CW)
Food E: Kiva Grill
W: Domino's Pizza, El Torito Mexican, Germain's

EXIT CALIFORNIA

Country Deli, Humphreys La Jolla Grill, International Market & Grill, Rock Bottom Restaurant & Brewery
Lodg E: Hyatt
W: Radisson
ATM W: City National Bank
Other W: Locksmith

27B Noble Dr. (Northbound, Reaccess Southbound Only)
Food W: BJ's, Cafe Cybernet, California Pizza Kitchen, Fin's Mexican Eatery, Garden State Bagels, Islands Burgers & Drinks, Jamba Juice, Mrs. Gooch's Cafe, Pasta Bravo, Peet's Coffee & Tea, Pick-Up Stix, Rubio's Baja Grill, Samson's Restaurant, Schlotzsky's Deli, Starbucks Coffee, T.G.I. Friday's, Whole Foods Market
ATM W: Bank Of America, Glendale Federal Bank, Wells Fargo, Wells Fargo
Other W: AMC 12 Theaters, **Kinko's**(24), **Ralph's Grocery**, **Sav-On Drugs**(24), Super Crown Bookstore, **Vision Center**

27 Gilman Drive, La Jolla Colony Drive
RVCamp W: **Trail RV Campground (1 Mile)**

26 CA 52E, San Clemente Canyon

25 Ardath Rd.

Exit (24) Balboa Ave., Garnet Ave. (Difficult Reaccess)
Gas W: 76(*), Citgo(*), Mobil(*)
Food W: In-N-Out Hamburgers, Manwai's Dragon House, Pizza & Deli, Sheldon's Cafe(24), Wienerschnitzel, Yum-Yum Donuts(24)
Lodg W: Comfort Inn
AServ W: 76, BMW & Mercedes Service, Bee Line Alignment & Brakes, Cal's Radiator & Tire Express, Discount Tire Company, Dualtone, Econo Lube & Tune, Jiffy Lube, Mission Bay Hand Car Wash, New Way Auto Service, Quiki Oil Change, Trans Masters & Auto Max, Winston Tire Company
RVCamp W: **Campland On The Bay (1.75 Miles)**
Med W: ✚ **Hospital**
ATM W: Citgo, Home Savings Of America
Other W: Camp Diego Canine Day Care

23 CA 274, Garnet Ave, Beaches, Grand Ave. (Reaccess Southbound Only)
Gas W: Shell
Food W: Kolbeh Restaurant
Lodg W: Sleepy Time Motel, Super 8, Trade Winds Motel, Western Shores Motel
AServ W: Guy Hill Cadillac, Massy Ford, Mossy Ford, Pacific Nissan, Shell
Med W: ✚ **Mission Bay Hospital**

Exit (21) Clairemont Drive, East Mission Bay Drive
Gas E: 76(*), Shell(*, CW)
Food E: J.R.'s Cafe California, Jack-In-The-Box, Petricca's Pizza
Lodg E: DAYS INN Days Inn
AServ E: 76, EZ Lube, Shell
RVCamp W: **De Anza Harbor Resort (1 Mile)**
ATM E: Wells Fargo
Other E: **Mission Bell Pharmacy**

20B Sea World Drive, Tecolote Road
Gas E: Shell(*, 24)
Food E: Andre's Patio Restaurant, Sardina's Italian Restaurant, Subway
Lodg E: Motel
AServ E: AAMCO Transmission, Joe Jr. Auto Repair, Pro Align Service, Shell(24), WPD Auto Parts, Worldwide Auto Parts
RVCamp E: **Morena Mobile Village**

EXIT CALIFORNIA

Other **W:** **Highway Patrol**, Mission Bay Park, **Sea World**

20A Jct I-8, CA 209, El Centro, Rosecrans St

19 Old Town Ave. (Marine Base)
Gas **E:** Arco(*), Shell
Food **E:** El Agave, Old Town Pizza
Lodg **E:** Ramada, TraveLodge, Vacation Inn, Western Inn
Other **E:** **Old Town Ave. State Park**
W: **Marine Base**

17 Washington St (Northbound)
Gas **E:** Chevron(*)
Med **E:** ✚ **Hospital**

16B Front St, to downtown San Diego, Civic Center (Southbound)
Gas **W:** Shell(*)
Lodg **W:** Holiday Inn, Radisson, Super 8
AServ **W:** Shell, Speedo Lube
Med **W:** ✚ **Hospital**

16A CA163N, Escondido

16 Pacific Hwy. (Northbound)

15C Sassafras St., Indian Street (Northbound)

15B Hawthorne St, San Diego Airport (Difficult Reaccess)

15 Sixth Avenue Downtown (Northbound)

14D CA 94E, Pershing Dr, B St

14C Imperial Ave (Northbound)

14 Jay Street (Northbound)

14B Crosby St
Food **W:** El Sarape, Imperial Express, Panchita's, Taco Shop
Lodg **W:** Econolodge
AServ **W:** Ace Radiator
Other **W:** **Coin Laundry**

14A Jct CA 75, Cornado (Toll)

13 National Ave, 28th St
Gas **W:** Texaco(*)
Food **W:** Burger King, El Pollo Loco, Long John Silver, McDonald's, Roberto's
AServ **E:** Chief Auto Parts
W: Texaco

12 Jct CA15, Riverside

11B Main St, National City Blvd (Difficult Reaccess)
Gas **E:** Mobil(LP), Shell
W: Chevron(*, D)
Food **E:** Keith's
Lodg **E:** Budget Inn, Ramada Limited
AServ **E:** Hopsing, Mobil, Shell
W: Sergio's Auto Electric, Welch Tire

11A 8th St, National City
Gas **E:** Thrifty(D)
Lodg **E:** Holiday Inn, Radisson
ATM **E:** Union Bank

10C Plaza Blvd., Downtown (No Reaccess)

10B Civic Center Drive (Reaccess Southbound Only)

10A 24th St
Food **E:** Denny's, In-N-Out Hamburgers

9 Jct CA 54E

EXIT CALIFORNIA

8 E St
Gas **E:** 76(*), Arco(*), Mobil
Food **E:** Aunt Emma's, Black Angus Steakhouse, Denny's, Little China Club, McDonald's, New Day (Royal Vista Inn), Pizza Junction, Royal China Palace, Taco Bell, Wendy's, Yum Yum Donuts
W: Anthony's Fish Grotto
Lodg **E:** **Best Western**, DAYS INN Days Inn, Motel 6, Royal Vista Inn, Traveler Motel Suites
W: Good Nite Inn
AServ **E:** Chief Auto Service, Hydro Spray Car Wash, Mobil
Other **E:** **IGA Grocery**

7 H St
Gas **E:** Arco(*), Chevron(CW), World(*)
Food **E:** BaJa Lobster, Casa Salsa, El Pollo Loco, Jack-In-The-Box, La Tostada
Lodg **E:** Early California Motel
AServ **E:** Chevron

6C J St, to Chula Vista Harbor
RVCamp **W:** **Chula Vista RV Resort & Marina (.25 Miles)**

6B L St

6A Palomar St
Gas **E:** Arco(*)
Lodg **E:** Palomar Inn

5 Main St

4B CA 75, Imperial Beach, Palm Ave
RVCamp **W:** **Bernardo Shores RV Park (2 Miles)**

4A Coronado Ave
Gas **E:** Chevron, Shell(LP)
W: Arco(*), Texaco(*, D)
Food **E:** Denny's, Dos Panchos
W: Mike's Giant New York Pizza
Lodg **E:** E-Z 8 Motel, San Diego Inn Motel, Travlers Motel
W: South Bay Lodge
AServ **E:** Chevron, Leo's Garage, Shell
W: Texaco, Texaco
Other **W:** **Nestor Pharmacy**

2B Jct CA 905, Tocayo Ave

2A Dairy Mart Road
Gas **E:** Arco(*)
Food **E:** Burger King, Carl Jr's Hamburgers, Coco's, McDonald's
Lodg **E:** Americana Inn & Suites, Motel 66, Valli-Hi Motor Hotel
RVCamp **E:** **LA Pacific**

1C Via de San Ysidro (Difficult Reaccess)
Gas **E:** 76, Chevron(*), Mobil(*), Shell(*)
W: Mini Mart Gas(*)
Food **E:** Amigos Tacos
W: KFC
Lodg **W:** Economy Motels of America, Motel 6
AServ **E:** 76
W: Chevron(*)
ATM **E:** Bank of America, Shell, Shell

1B Jct I-805

1A Camino de la Plaza
Food **E:** Burger King, El Pollo Authentic Mexican Chicken, Jack-In-The-Box, McDonald's, Mercado Sonora, Subway
W: Taco Bell
Lodg **E:** Gateway Inn, Holiday Lodge Motel, TraveLodge
AServ **W:** Border Tire
ATM **E:** Wells Fargo Bank
Other **W:** **Five Star Border Parking, San Diego Factory Outlet Center**

↑CALIFORNIA

Begin I-5

EXIT CALIFORNIA

Begin I-8

↓CALIFORNIA

0 Junction I-5 South

3 West Mission Bay Drive Sports Arena Blvd.

2 Junction I-5

4B Morena Blvd
Food **S:** Casa Guadalajara, Eric's Ribs & Steaks, Padre Trail Inn
Lodg **S:** Padre Trail Inn
AServ **S:** Stanco Automotive

Exit **(4)** Taylor St, Hotel Circle
Food **N:** D.W. Ranch, Hunter Steakhouse
Lodg **N:** **Comfort Inn**, **Hanalei Hotel**, **Motel 6**, Premier Inns

5A Hotel Circle
Gas **S:** Chevron(*, 24)
Food **N:** **Kelly's Steak House (Town & Country Hotel)**, Postcards American Bistro
S: Adam's Steak & Eggs, **Albi's Beef Inn (Travelodge)**, Amigo Spot Family Mexican Restaurant, Pam Pam Cafe & Grill (Days Inn), Ricky's (Hotel Circle Inn), Seven Seas Cafe (Best Western), Tickled Trout (Ramada Plaza), Valley Kitchen(*, 24)
Lodg **N:** **Handlery Hotel**, **Town & Country Hotel**
S: **Best Western**, DAYS INN **Days Inn**, **Econo Lodge**, **Holiday Inn Select**, Hotel Circle Inn & Suites (Ricky's), Howard Johnson, **Kings Inn (Amigo Spot Family Mexican Restaurant)**, **Quality Resort**, Ramada Plaza Hotel (Tickled Trout), Regency Plaza Hotel, **TraveLodge**, Vagabond Inn
Other **N:** Riverwalk Golf Club, Ryder Truck Rental, Thrifty Car Rental

5B Junction 163, Escondido, Downtown

5C Mission Center Road
Gas **S:** Arco(*)
Food **N:** Gourmet Bagger Sandwich Shop, Hooters, Koo-Koo-Roo California Kitchen, Mandarin Cuisine, McDonald's, Mini's Cafe
S: Benihana, Denny's, Hayama Restaurant, Love's (The Great Rib Restaurant), **Padre's Pub (Hilton)**, Wendy's
Lodg **S:** **Comfort Suites Hotel**, **Hilton**, **Radisson**, Ramada Limited
AServ **N:** Bob Baker Ford, Courtesy Chevrolet, Enterprise Rent-a-Car (Mission Valley Lincoln Mercury), Mission Valley Lincoln Mercury, Montgomery Ward
S: Arco, M2 Collision Center, Marvin Brown Cadillac, Buick, GMC Truck, & Hummer
Med **S:** ✚ **Urgent Care Clinic (Mission Valley Medical Center)**
ATM **N:** Home Savings Of America, Washington Mutual Bank
Other **N:** **Mission Valley Center Mall**, Park Valley Center (Mall), Valley Circle Theater

6A Texas St, Qualcomm Way
Gas **N:** Chevron(*, LP)
Food **N:** Bennigan's, Hogi Yogi Sandwiches & Frozen Yogurt, In-N-Out Burger, Pasta Bravo, Pick Up Stix, Rubio's Baja Grill, Taco Bell
S: Bully's East
AServ **N:** Chevron
ATM **N:** Bank of America

6B Junction I-805 N to Los Angeles, S to National City Tulla Vista

8A CA 15, 40th St Junction

8B Mission Gorge Road, Fairmount Ave

Bold red print shows RV & Bus parking available or nearby

EXIT	CALIFORNIA
Gas	N: Mobile(*, D, CW), Shell(*), Ultramar(*)
Food	N: Bagel King, Blarney Stone Pub Bar & Grill, Boll Weevil, Chili's, Hot Java, Osaka Japanese, Rally's Hamburgers, Szechuan Mandarin, Taco Bell
Lodg	N: Super 8
AServ	N: Mission Village Auto Care, Mobile, Quiki Oil Change, Rose Toyota, Shell, Ultramar
Med	N: Hospital
ATM	N: Mobile
Other	N: Adventure Outdoor & Travel Outfitters, Cush Honda, Hertz Car Rental, Home Depot
Exit	**(9)** Waring Road
Food	N: Nicolosi's Italian Restaurant, Patches Sports Bar & Grill (Good Nite Inn)
Lodg	N: Good Nite Inn, Motel 7, Villager Lodge S: Ramada Inn (see our ad this page)
Exit	**(10)** College Ave (San Diego State University)
Exit	**(11)** 70th St, Lake Murray Blvd
Gas	N: Shell(*, CW, 24) S: Texaco(*, D, LP, 24)
Food	N: Peppers Mexican, Subway S: D.Z. Akin's Bakery & Fountain, Denny's, Marie Callender's Restaurant
AServ	N: Prestigious Automotive S: Texaco(24)
Med	N: Hospital
13A	Fletcher Parkway
Gas	N: Texaco(*, D, CW)
Food	N: Baker's Square, Boston Market Restaurant, Broadway Pizza & Pasta, Chili's, De Nopoli's Mediterranean, McDonald's(24), Pick Up Stix S: Hungry Hunter
Lodg	N: **Comfort Inn, E-Z 8 Motel** S: **Motel 6**
AServ	N: Agua Clean Hand Car Wash, Costco

RAMADA INN®
1758 Chilton Conference Center
300 East 32nd Street • Yuma, AZ
520-344-1050
Special Tour Group Rate
Restaurant/Lounge on Premises
Full Breakfast Buffet
Kids Under 12 Stay Free
Meeting/Banquet Facilities
Cable TV w/HBO
Outdoor Pool
Coin Laundry
Refrigerators in Room
Pets Allowed • Airport Shuttle
Large Vehicle Parking
Exterior Corridors
Directions:
Traveling west from Tucson or Phoenix on I-8, Exit 32nd Street and our Inn is on right Traveling east from California on I-8, Exit 4th Ave to 32nd Street and our Inn is on the left.
ARIZONA • I-8 • EXIT 9

EXIT	CALIFORNIA
	Wholesale Warehouse, Express Oil Change S: Bob Shall Chevrolet Dealer
RVCamp	S: **Camperland, RV Peddler**
Med	N: **Kaiser Permanente**
ATM	N: 7-11 Convenience Store, Texaco, Wells Fargo, Western Financial California Bank
Other	N: 7-11 Convenience Store, **Coin Laundry**, Costco Wholesale Warehouse, Sports Nutrition(RX) S: Lucky Food Center
13B	Spring St., Downtown
Gas	S: Chevron(*, 24), Texaco(*, D, CW)
AServ	N: Auto Repair Specialists, Power Connection S: Tire Auto Center
ATM	S: Home Savings Of America, Texaco
Other	S: Police Station, **United States Post Office**
14A	Jackson Drive, Grossmont Blvd. (Difficult Reaccess)
Gas	N: Chevron(*, CW), Shell(*, 24)
Food	N: Beverages & More, Burger King, Carlos Murphy's, Chuck E Cheese's Pizza, Claim Jumper, Fuddruckers, Olive Garden, Pizza Nova, Red Lobster S: Chile Bandido, Honey Baked Ham, Jack-In-The-Box
AServ	N: Kragen Auto Parts, Shell(24), **Ward's Auto Express** S: Firestone Tire & Auto, Tune Craft
ATM	N: Bank of America, Glendale Federal Bank, Grossmont Bank, Home Savings Of America, Wells Fargo S: **Ralph's Grocery**
Other	N: **Grossmont Center Mall**, Kinko's(24), **Longs Drugstore, Target**, United States Post Office S: **Coin Laundry, Ralph's Grocery**
14B	La Mesa Blvd., Grossmont Center Dr. (No Reaccess)
Gas	S: 76(*)
Food	N: Claim Jumper, Pizza Nova, Submarina S: Marieta's Mexican
AServ	S: Discount Tire Company, Drew Ford, Drew Volkswagon, Hyundai
Med	N: **Grossmont Hospital**
ATM	N: Bank of America, Grossmont Bank, Washington Mutual Bank S: 76
15B	Junction CA125 S & CA125 N.
15A	Severin Dr., Fuerte Dr.
Food	S: Briganfine Seafood
Exit	**(16)** El Cajon Blvd (Eastbound, Reaccess Westbound Only)
Food	S: Wrangler BBQ Pit
Lodg	N: Days Inn
AServ	S: Auto Tech Automotive Repair, Cunningham BMW
Other	S: Enterprise Rent-a-Car

1065
Denny's
Open 24 Hours
619-447-2838
Where Value Hits a Grand Slam Everyday!
Denny s... good food and friendly service is just down the road!
Look for us in El Cajon, California
CALIFORNIA • I-8 • Mollison Ave. Exit

EXIT	CALIFORNIA
Exit	**(17)** Main St
Gas	N: Arco(*) S: 76, Chevron(*)
Food	N: Denny's(24), Javier's Sombrero Mexican(24)
Lodg	N: **Thriftlodge**
AServ	N: Banny Hom Automotive S: 76, Chevron, Earl Scheib Paint & Body, Mercedes BMW, Moffy Nissan, Village Auto Repair
ATM	N: 7-11 Convenience Store(24), Arco
Other	N: 7-11 Convenience Store
18A	Johnson Ave (Eastbound, Reaccess Westbound Only)
Food	N: Antonio's Hacienda, Burger King(PLAY), El Cotixan Mexican, Subway, Super Salsa, Tokyo Japanese Food & Sushi
AServ	N: Big O Tires, Bob Baker Chevrolet, Dorman's, Lexxus, Sear's Auto Center, Tipton Honda S: 4 Wheel Parts, AAMCO Transmission, Green's Brake and Alignment, Greg's Automotive, Saturn of El Cajon, Summit Transmissions
TServ	S: **Cummins Diesel**
ATM	N: Home Savings Of America, Navy Federal, World Savings Bank
Other	N: **Home Depot**, Mall, Petsmart (Vetsmart) S: Budget Rent A Car & Car Sales, **El Cajon Valley Animal Hospital**
18C	CA 67, Magnolia Ave, Civic Center
Gas	S: Texaco(*)
Food	S: Krispy's Donuts, Perry's Cafe, Rubio's Baja Grill, The Best Chinese Restaurant, Ultimate Pizzaria, Wienerschnitzel
Lodg	S: **Motel 6, TraveLodge**
AServ	S: T.L.C. Tire Stop, Texaco
Other	S: Discovery Zone, Enterprise Rent-a-Car, **Nudo's Pharmacy**, Regal Cinemas, Wells Quick Mart
Exit	**(19)** Mollison Ave
Gas	N: Chevron(*), Citgo(*) S: Arco(*)
Food	N: Denny's (see our ad this page), Winchells Donuts S: Taco Bell(24)
Lodg	N: **Best Western, Plaza International Inn** S: Super 8, Valley Motel
AServ	N: Chevron
ATM	N: Citgo S: Arco
Other	N: **Valley Coin Laundry**
Exit	**(20)** 2nd St, CA 54
FStop	S: **Pacific Pride Commercial Fueling**
Gas	N: Arco(*), Mobil(*) S: 76(*), Shell, Texaco(*, D)
Food	N: Julian's BBQ, Marechiaro's Italian Restaurant, Tijuana Taco Shop S: Arby's, Baskin Robbins, Boll Weevil, Carl Jr's Hamburgers, Chinese Cuisine, Cotixan Taco Shop, El Compadre(24), Finest Donuts, IHOP, Jack-In-The-Box, KFC, Subway, Taco Bell, Tyler's The Great Taste of Texas(24), Wings-N-Things
Lodg	S: Parkside Inn & Suites
AServ	N: Auto Doctor, Geni Car Wash, Midas Muffler & Brake, Mobil, Parts Plus, Run Rite Auto Service, Valley Automotive, Winston Tire Co S: 76, Car Wash, Firestone Tire & Auto, Instant Oil Change, Jiffy Lube, Worldwide Auto Parts
ATM	N: Bank Of America S: Texaco, Union Bank of California
Other	N: Mail Store S: Rite Aid(RX)
20B	East Main St. (Westbound, Reaccess Eastbound Only)
Gas	S: Arco(*)
Food	N: Pernicano's, R-U Hungry Pancake House
Lodg	N: **Budget Inn, Embasadora Motel, Fabulous 7 Motel, Ha'Penny Inns**

Bold red print shows RV & Bus parking available or nearby

EXIT CALIFORNIA

ASErv **N:** Decker's Auto Service, Ford Dealership
S: Arco, De La Fuente (Cadillac, Pontiac Dealership), **Touchless Car Wash**(CW)
RVCamp **N: Rick's RV Center, Vacationer's Travel**
S: El Capitan
Med **N: + Kaiser Permanente**
ATM **S:** Arco
Other **S: Kaelins Grocery**

Exit **(21)** Greenfield Drive, Crest
Gas **N:** Shell(*, LP, 24)
S: Mobil(*, D, LP), Texaco(*)
Food **N:** Jack's Deli, Janet's Cafe, Los Panchos Taco Shop, Marieta's Mexican, McDonald's(PLAY), Yum Yum Donuts
ASErv **N:** Chief Auto Parts, E & M Auto & Truck Service Inc., Riley's Auto Parts, Shell(24)
S: Mobil, Texaco
RVCamp **N: Circle RV Ranch (.25 Miles), The Vacationer Travel Trailer Park (.5 Miles)**
Med **N: + Hospital**
ATM **N:** 7-11 Convenience Store, Home Savings Of America, McDonald's
Other **N:** 7-11 Convenience Store, Abbey Clinic for Pets, Cajon Rancho Veternary Hospital, **State Police**

24A Los Coches Road, Lakeside
Gas **N:** Mobil(*, LP)
S: Shell(*, D, LP, CW) (Blimpie)
Food **S:** Blimpie's Subs (Shell), Giant New York Pizza & Pasta, McDonald's (Wal-Mart), McDonald's(PLAY), Panda Express, Subway, Taco Bell
ASErv **N:** Mobil
S: Tire & Lube Express (Wal-Mart), **Wal-Mart (Tire & Lube Express)**
RVCamp **N: Rancho Los Coches RV Park (.75 Miles)**
ATM **S:** Shell (Blimpie), **Vons Grocery**
Other **S:** Mailboxes Etc., **Vons Grocery, Wal-Mart (Tire & Lube Express)**

24B Lake Jennings Park Road
Gas **S:** Citgo(*)
Food **S:** Jilberto's Taco Shop, Marechiaro's (Italian)
RVCamp **N: Lake Jennings County Park (1 Mile)**
ATM **S:** Citgo
Parks **S: Flimm Springs State Park**

26 Map Stop (Phones; Westbound)

28 Harbison Canyon, Dunbar Lane

31 Alpine, Tavern Road
FStop **N: Alpine Express**(*, D)
Gas **N: Texaco**(*, D, LP, K, CW)
S: Citgo(*), Shell(*, LP, 24)
Food **S:** Alpine Frontier Deli, Alpine Mountain Yogurt & Ice Cream, **Carl Jr's Hamburgers**, Little Caesars Pizza, Long John Silver, Mananas Mexican, Ming's Dynasty, Ramone's Smoked BBQ, Steph's Donut Hole
Lodg **S: Country Side Inn**
ASErv **N: Texaco**
S: Shell(24)
ATM **S:** Washington Mutual Bank

Exit **(34)** Alpine Blvd, Willows Road (Ranger Station & Camping)

Exit **(37)** East Willows Road

Exit **(38)** Vista Point (Eastbound)

Exit **(40)** CA 79, Julian, Japatul Road

Exit **(46)** Pine Valley

Exit **(47)** Sunrise Highway

(51) **Rest Area (RR, Phones, Picnic)**

(51) **Buckman Springs Road, Rest Area & Camping (RV Dump)**

Exit **(53)** Cameron Station, Kitchen Creek Road

Exit **(61)** Crestwood Road, Live Oak Springs

Exit **(66)** CA 94, Campo (Camping)
Lodg **S:** Buena Vista Motel
Other **S:** Border Patrol Post

Exit **(70)** Jacumba
FStop **S: Texaco**(*, D, LP)
Gas **S:** Shell(*, LP, 24), **Texaco**(*, D)
ATM **S: Texaco**

Exit **(77)** Truck Brake Inspection Area (Eastbound)

Exit **(78)** In - Ko - Pah Park Road

Exit **(81)** Mountain Springs Road

Exit **(85)** Runaway Truck Ramp (Eastbound)

Exit **(88)** CA 98, Calexico (Difficult Reaccess)

Exit **(90)** Ocotillo Imperial Highway
FStop **N: OTU Fuel Mart**(*)
S: Desert FStop(*)
Gas **N: OTU Fuel Mart**(*)
Food **S: Desert Kitchen**
Lodg **N: Ocotillo Motel**(LP)
TServ **S: Desert FStop**
RVCamp **N: Ocotillo RV Park (Laundry Facility)**
ATM **S: Desert FStop**
Other **N:** Lazy Lizard Saloon (Bar only)

Exit **(101)** Dunaway Road

Exit **(108)** Drew Road, Seeley
RVCamp **N: Sunbeam Lake (Coffee shop)**
S: Country Mobile & RV Sales, Rio Bend

(109) **Rest Area (RR, Phones, Picnic, RV Dump)**

Exit **(112)** Forrester Road

Exit **(115)** Imperial Ave, El Centro
Gas **N:** Chevron(*, CW), Citgo(*, D, 24)
Food **N:** Del Taco, Denny's (Ramada Inn), KFC, Scribbles (Vacation Inn)
Lodg **N:** Ramada Inn
ASErv **N:** Chevron
RVCamp **N: Vacation Inn & RV Park (Restaurant, 1 Mile)**
ATM **N:** Citgo

Exit **(116)** CA 86, 4th St, El Centro
TStop **S: Mobil**(*, LP, SCALES) **(Millie's Kitchen)**
Gas **N:** Arco(*), Chevron(*), Citgo(*, D, 24), Texaco(*, D)
S: Mobil(*)
Food **N:** Carl Jr's Hamburgers, Jack-In-The-Box, La Fonda Mexican, McDonald's, Rally's Hamburgers
S: Happy Pizza Restaurant, **Millie's Kitchen (Mobil)**, Taco Bell
Lodg **N: Motel 6**
S: Best Western, E-Z 8 Motel
ASErv **N:** Chevron, Chief Auto Parts, Guerrero's Shop
S: Gene's Auto Service, Thomas Motor Company (Plymouth Dodge Jeep Eagle Honda Dealer)
RVCamp **S: Desert Trails RV Park & Country Club**
ATM **N:** Arco, Chevron, Citgo
S: Mobil (Millie's Kitchen)
Other **N:** El Sol Market, Uhaul(LP)
S: Max Food

Exit **(117)** Dogwood Road

Exit **(119)** CA 111S, Calexico, N to Brawley
RVCamp **N: Country Boys, Country Life RV Park (.25 Miles)**

Exit **(120)** Bowker Road

Exit **(126)** Orchard Road

Exit **(128)** Bonds Corner Road

Exit **(131)** CA 115
Gas **S: Mini Mart RV Park**(LP) **(Laundry Service)**
ASErv **S: Mini Mart RV Park (Laundry Service)**
RVCamp **S: Mini Mart RV Park (Laundry Service)**

Exit **(144)** CA 98

Exit **(147)** Brock Research Center Road

Exit **(151)** Gordons Well

(152) **Rest Area**

Exit **(153)** Grays Well Road

Exit **(160)** Ogilby Road

Exit **(164)** Sidewinder Road
Gas **S:** Shell(*, LP, RV DUMP)
RVCamp **S: Pilot Knob RV Park**(LP) **(.5 Miles)**

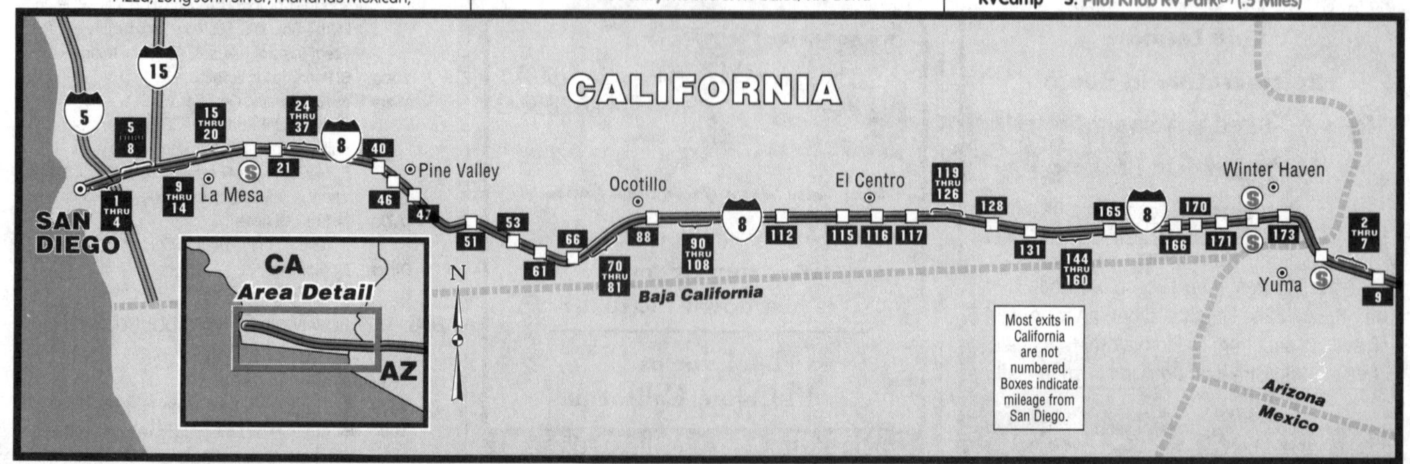

Bold red print shows RV & Bus parking available or nearby

EXIT CALIFORNIA

Other N: California Highway Patrol Post

(165) **California Agriculture Inspection & Weigh Station (Weigh Station Westbound Only)**

Exit **(166)** Algodones Road, Andrade

Exit **(170)** Winterhaven

RVCamp N: Sans End RV Park (1.25 Miles)
S: Rivers Edge RV Resort (.25 Miles)

Exit **(171)** Winterhaven 4th Ave.

Gas S: Circle K(*)

Food S: Jack-In-The-Box, Taco Mi Rancho, Yuma Landing

Lodg S: Best Western, Regal Lodge, Yuma Inn Motel

↑CALIFORNIA

↓ARIZONA

1 Giss Pkwy., Yuma (No commercial vehicles over 13,000 pounds)

Food S: California Bakery

Lodg S: Lee Hotel

RVCamp N: M & M RV Village (1.5 Miles)

Parks S: Uma Territorial Prison State Park (Historic Park)

Other S: Bandanna Books, First Capital Bank, US Post Office

(1) **Weigh Station**

2 US 95, 16th St

Gas N: 76(*)
S: Texaco(*, D)

Food N: Cracker Barrel, Denny's
S: Burger King(PLAY), McDonald's, SHONEY'S Shoney's

Lodg N: Best Western, DAYS INN Days Inn, La Fuente Inn & Suites, Motel 6, Shilo Inn Hotel (Restaurant & Lounge)
S: Comfort Inn, Motel 6, Super 8

AServ S: Apple's Garage

ATM N: 76
S: Burger King

Other S: Gila Veterinarian Clinic

3 AZ 280, Ave 3E, Yuma International Airport

FStop N: Texaco(*, SCALES, 24)

Food N: Dairy Queen (Texaco)

AServ S: Bingham Auto & Truck Park

TServ N: Texaco(SCALES, 24)
S: Bingham Auto & Truck Park, Diesel Components & Fuel Inspection

7 Araby Road

TServ S: Yuma Diesel Service

RVCamp S: Araby Acres (.75 Miles), Azure Sky RV Park (1.5 Miles), La Mesa RV, RV World & Truck Sales

Other S: Ryder (Laundry Center)

EXIT ARIZONA

9 Business Loop 8, 32nd St.

AServ S: Arizona Unlimited(LP), Richard's Foothills Auto Repair

RVCamp S: Arizona Unlimited, Sun Vista RV Resort (1 Mile)

Other S: Arizona West Veterinary Clinic

12 Fortuna Road

TStop N: Barney's Truck Stop(*, SCALES, 24) (Copper Miner's Restaurant)

FStop S: Texaco(*, LP)

Gas N: Chevron(*, 24)
S: 76(*, D)

Food N: Copper Miner's Restaurant (Barney's TStop), Jack-in-the-Box, Pizza Hut
S: Dairy Queen, Don Quijote, Subway

Lodg N: Courtesy Inn & Suites(LP)

AServ S: Big O Tires, Foothills Auto Parts

TServ N: Barney's Truck Stop(SCALES, 24) (Copper Miner's Restaurant)

RVCamp N: Caravan Oasis RV Park (.25 Miles), Las Quintas Oasis Senior Trailer Park (.5 Miles), Shangri-La RV Resort (.5 Miles)
S: Al's RV Service & Supplies, Blue Sky RV Park (.5 Miles, Laundry), Gila Mountain RV Park (1.5 Miles), Western Sands RV Park(LP), Westwind RV & Golf Resort (1 Mile)

ATM N: Barney's Truck Stop (Copper Miner's Restaurant), Chevron
S: Pioneer Supermarket

Parks S: Bonita Mesa RV Park, Southwest RV Sales

Other S: Coin Laundry, Desert Optical, Eckerd Drugs, Foothills Animal Hospital, Pioneer Supermarket

14 Foothills Blvd

Food S: Domino's Pizza, Mr. Fish & Chips, The Ice Cream Shoppe

RVCamp N: Foothill Village RV Park(LP), Fortuna De Oro RV Resort (.75 Miles), Sundance RV Park(LP) (.25 Miles)
S: S & H RV Parts and Service

ATM S: National Bank Of Arizona

Other S: Postal Mail Stop

17 Inspection Station (Eastbound)

21 Dome Valley

22 **Parking Area**

30 Ave 29 East, Wellton

RVCamp N: M & M RV Village (1.5 Miles), Tier Drop RV Park (.25 Miles)

37 Ave 36 East, Roll

42 Ave 40E, Tacna

Gas N: Chevron(*)

Food N: Basque Etchea Restaurant, Lu's Patio Cafe

Lodg N: Chaparral Motel(PLAY)

AServ N: Tipton Auto Supply

Other N: Tru Value Hardware(LP), U.S. Post Office

54 Ave. 52 E, Mohawk Valley

56 **Rest Area (RR, HF, Phones, Picnic, Vending, P)**

EXIT ARIZONA

67 Dateland

Gas S: Exxon(*, D, LP) (Vern's Tire Service)

Food S: Dateland Cafe(*, RV DUMP)

AServ S: Exxon (Vern's Tire Service), Vern's Tire Service

RVCamp S: Dateland Palms RV Village

ATM S: Dateland Cafe

73 Aztec

78 Spot Road

84 **Rest Area (RR, Picnic, Vending, P; Eastbound)**

85 **Rest Area (RR, Picnic, Vending, P; Westbound)**

87 Sentinel, Hyder

Gas N: No Name(*)

AServ N: No Name

102 Painted Rock Road

106 Paloma Road

111 Citrus Valley Road

115 AZ 85, Phoenix, Ajo (Difficult Reaccess)

RVCamp N: Wheel Inn, Wheel Inn (.25 Miles)

Med N: ✚ Gila Bend Primary Care

119 Business 8 West, Gila Bend

TStop N: Texaco(*, LP, RV DUMP, SCALES, 24) (Showers)

Food N: Exit West Cafe (Texaco)

Lodg N: Super 8

ATM N: Texaco (Showers)

123 **Rest Area (Picnic, P; Under construction)**

140 Freeman Road

144 Vekol Road

148 **Rest Area (Picnic, P)**

151 AZ 84 East, Maricopa Road, Stanfield

TStop S: Truck 19 Stop(LP) (Showers & mart)

Food S: Pullman Restaurant (TStop 19)

Lodg S: Pullman Motel (TStop 19)

RVCamp S: Saguaro RV Park

161 Stanfield Road

167 Montgomery Road

169 Bianco Road

172 Thornton Road, Casa Grande

Gas S: Blue Flame Corp.(LP)

Other S: Blue Flame Corp.

174 Trekell Road, Casa Grande

AServ S: Art's Radiator

Med N: ✚ Hospital (5 Miles)

178AB Jct I-10, Phoenix, Tucson

↑ARIZONA

Begin I-8

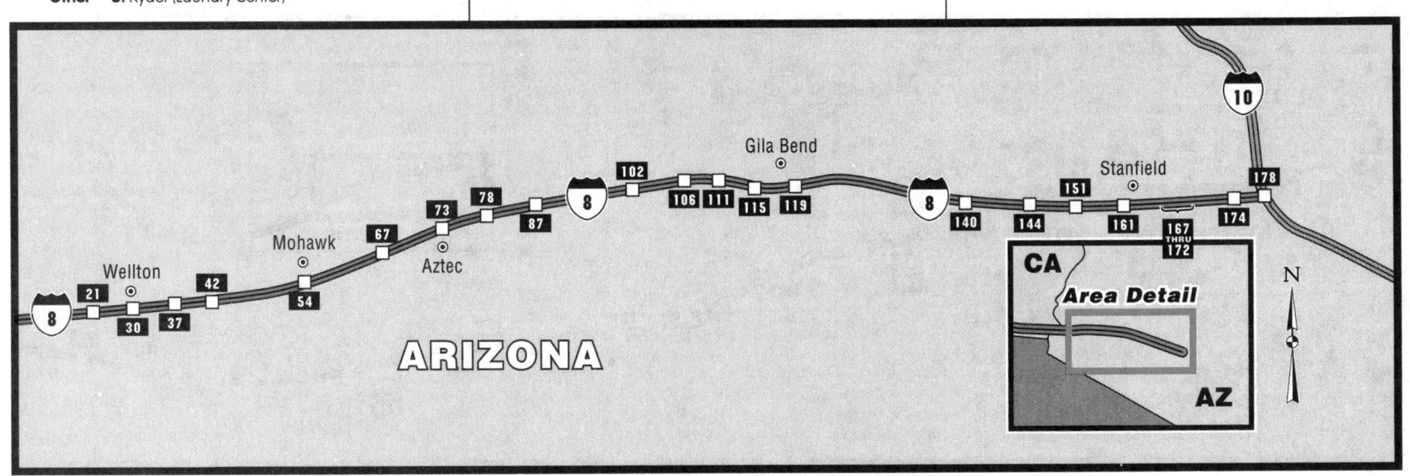

EXIT	CALIFORNIA
	Begin I-10
	↓CALIFORNIA
1A	4th St, 5th St
Gas	**S:** Arco[*]
Lodg	**S:** Double Tree Hotel, Police Station
AServ	**N:** Al's Tire Supply, Grigsby Automotive Service, Midas Muffler Shops, Sears Auto Center
ATM	**N:** San Wa Bank
Other	**N:** **Santa Monica Place (Mall)** **S:** Civic Center
1	Lincoln Blvd, S. CA 1
Gas	**N:** 76 **S:** Chevron[*, 24], Exxon[*], Shell[CW]
Food	**N:** Bay City Italian Deli & Bakery, Denny's, Norm's, Zipangu (Japanese) **S:** Domino's Pizza, Subway, Tommy's Hamburger's
AServ	**N:** Bay City's Auto Supply (AC Delco), Lincoln Auto Center, Paul's Transmission Service, Santa Monica Radiator, Tune Up Masters **S:** ABS Brake Supply, ACE Auto Pros, Firestone Tire & Auto, Lincoln Auto Repair, Shell
Other	**N:** Lincoln Blvd. Car Wash[CW] (76), **Vons Grocery**[RX] **S:** Kitty & Doggie Dunk, **V-Food Grocery**
1B	20th ST. (Eastbound, Reaccess Westbound Only)
Exit	**(3)** Cloverfield Blvd., 26th St. (Westbound, Reaccess Eastbound Only)
Gas	**N:** Arco, Shell
AServ	**N:** Arco, Bon Voyage Auto Body, German Car Service (VW, BMW, Porsche, Audi), Shell
Med	**N:** **+ Hospital**
2	Centinela Ave
Food	**S:** Wienerschnitzel
Lodg	**S:** TraveLodge
AServ	**N:** Golden Auto Body & Paint **S:** Morgan's Automotive Service, Peter's Foreign Auto Service
Other	**S:** Airport Pharmacy, California Map Center, V&S Market
Exit	**(4)** Bundy Dr. (Westbound, Reaccess Eastbound Only)
Food	**N:** Bo-Jay's Pizzeria, Chan Dare, Habayit Restaurant, Los Hermanos Lopez, Taco Bell, Teddy's Cafe, The Arsenal Fine Food, The Sushi House (Japanese)
AServ	**N:** Exclusive Jaguar Parts & Service, Pico Frame & Wheel Alignment, Westside Performance
Other	**N:** **9-1-1 Food Mart**, **Coin Op Laundry**, Cycle Products West

EXIT	CALIFORNIA
Exit	**(5)** Junction I-405 N. Sacramento, I-405 S. Santa Monica Airport
4	Overland Ave.
Gas	**S:** Arco[*], Mobil[*]
AServ	**S:** Jiffy Lube
Other	**N:** L.A. Public Library
Exit	**(7)** National Blvd. (Westbound, Reaccess Eastbound Only)
Gas	**N:** 76, Chevron[*]
Food	**N:** Emerald Cho's Chinese Restaurant, Subway, Thai Cheviot
AServ	**N:** 76, Chevron
Other	**N:** Coin Op Laundry, Rite Aid Pharmacy, **Vons Grocery**
Exit	**(7)** Robertson Blvd.
Gas	**N:** Chevron[*, 24], Mobil[CW]
Food	**N:** Domino's Pizza **S:** Adam's Deli, Del Taco, El Pollo Express, Golden China Restaurant, Grandma Lucia's Pizza, Hello Donuts & Ice Cream, Noah's Bagels, Tom's #5 Chili Burgers
Lodg	**S:** Metro Motel
AServ	**N:** Complete Auto Repair, EZ Lube, Midas Auto Systems Experts, RPM Auto Repair **S:** Butch's Truck & Auto Repair, Collision Expert, Fox Hills Buick Dealership, Hirji, Jack's Auto Service Center, Schrader Auto Parts (AC Delco)
Med	**S:** **+ Hospital**
Other	**N:** Pro Pet **S:** Office Max, **Save-On Drugs**
Exit	**(8)** La Cienega
Gas	**N:** Chevron[*, 24], Mobil[*]
Food	**N:** Pantry's Pizza, Yum Yum Donuts **S:** Subway
Lodg	**N:** Motel Sea Way **S:** King's Motel
AServ	**N:** 2001 Auto Body Group, Firestone Tire & Auto, Quality #1 Auto Repair **S:** AAA Muffler Shop, All West Auto Body, Delta Battery, L/M Motors Inc., La Cienaga Auto Center, Super Buy Tires
Med	**N:** **+ Hospital**
Other	**S:** Bob's Pharmacy[RX], Culver Auto Detail[CW], Giant Laundry Center
Exit	**(9)** Fairfax Ave, Washington Blvd.
Gas	**S:** Arco[*]
Food	**S:** McDonald's
AServ	**S:** Jiffy Lube
Exit	**(10)** La Brea Ave.
Gas	**N:** Shell[D] **S:** Chevron[*, 24]
Food	**S:** Laura's Mexican Deli
Lodg	**S:** Adams Motel
AServ	**N:** G&M Transmission, M.A.C. Auto Specialists, Pete's Golden Hands Auto Body, Shell **S:** Auto Parts Exchange, Chief Auto Parts, Mexico Auto Parts Foreign & Domestic, Three Amigos Auto Repair, West Adams Radiator

EXIT	CALIFORNIA
Exit	**(11)** Crenshaw Blvd.
Gas	**S:** Chevron[*, 24], Mobil, Thrifty[*]
Food	**S:** El Pollo Loco, Leo's Barbeque, McDonald's[PLAY], Taco Bell[24]
AServ	**S:** Mobil
Other	**S:** **Ace Hardware**
Exit	**(12)** Arlington Ave
Gas	**N:** Chevron, Mobil[*]
Food	**N:** Restaurant Yucatan
AServ	**N:** Bob's Tire Town, Jeff's Auto Repair, Chevron
Exit	**(13)** Western Ave
Gas	**S:** Chevron[24]
Food	**N:** 2 For 1 Pizza Co., Chabelita Ice Cream, Seafood, & Tacos, Daily Donut House, Hong Kong Express, McDonald's[PLAY], Panda Ski Fast Food
AServ	**N:** California Automotive & Transmission, Chief Auto Parts, Modern Auto Center **S:** Chevron[24], King's Transmission
Med	**S:** **+ Hospital**
Other	**N:** **Coin Laundry**, Fire Station, Star's Food Service
Exit	**(13)** Normandie Ave
Gas	**N:** Mobil **S:** Chevron, Shell[*], Texaco[*]
AServ	**N:** Mobil **S:** Chevron, Texaco
Exit	**(13)** Vermont Ave
Gas	**S:** Shell[*, 24]
Food	**N:** Burger King, Mandigo Restaurant, Super Donuts **S:** Jack-In-The-Box, La Barca Restaurant, Selaya Bakery, Tacos El Unico
AServ	**N:** Auto Electric Shop, Universal Auto Center **S:** Vermont Auto Plaza & Body Shop
Other	**N:** **Rite Aid Pharmacy**[RX] **S:** El Ranchito Market
Exit	**(14)** Hoover St
Gas	**N:** Mobil, Unified Gasoline **S:** Arco[*]
Food	**N:** King Donuts, Lucy's[24] (Mexican), Lucy's #1 (Mexican/American) **S:** La Fresa Bakery, Pete's Burgers, Rigo's Taco #5, Vera Cruz Mexican
AServ	**N:** John's Auto Body Repair, Mobil, Pep Boys Auto Center, Roble's Carboretor, Venegas Coffee Shop **S:** Arco
Other	**N:** Car Wash **S:** **Jerry's Market**, Lavanderia Coin Laundry, Market
Exit	**(15)** I-110 Harbor Fwy, CA 110, San Pedro, Downtown

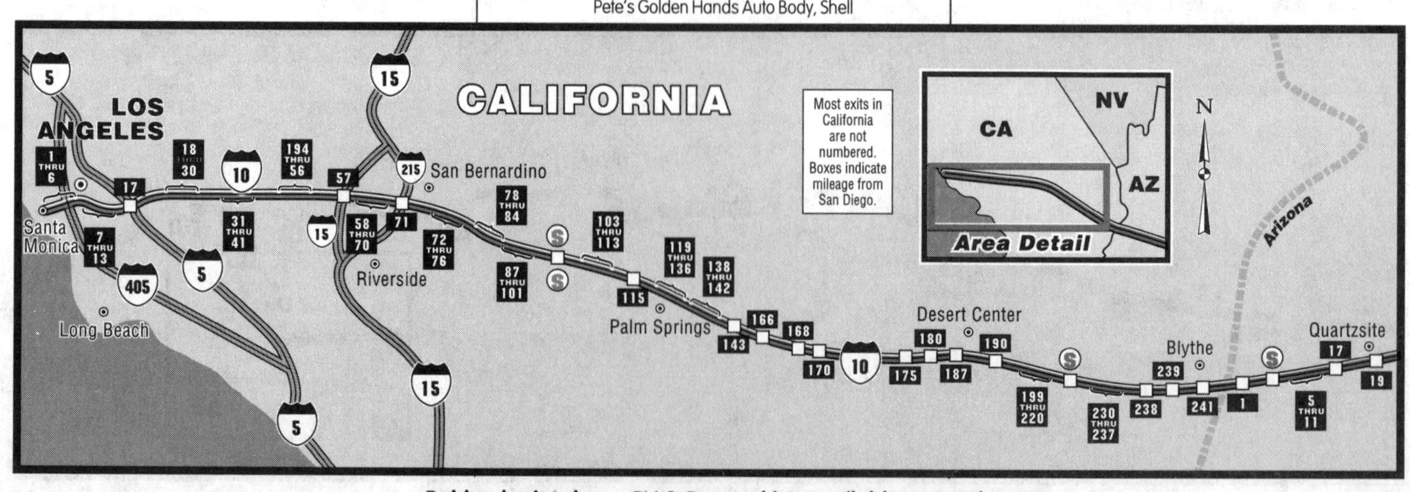

Bold red print shows RV & Bus parking available or nearby

EXIT CALIFORNIA

Exit **(15)** Grand Ave. (Eastbound, No Reaccess)
- Food **S:** Burger King, McDonald's(PLAY)

Exit **(15)** Los Angeles St. (Westbound)
- AServ **N:** Mufflers, Tires, & Alignment

Exit **(15)** Maple Ave. (Eastbound, No Reaccess)
- Food **S:** Chinese Food Bowl, El Pollo Loco, Greenwich Village Pizza
- AServ **S:** Kragen Auto Parts, Maple Auto Center
- Other **S:** **Launderland Coin Laundry**, Rite Aid Pharmacy

Exit **(15)** San Pedro St.
- Food **S:** China Town Fast Food, Gayle's Famous Burgers, Glady Goods Donuts & Ice Cream, Marisco's Seafood, Panaderia, Tortilleria Masa
- AServ **S:** Chief Auto Parts, NAPA Auto Parts
- Other **S:** Launderland Coin Laundry

Exit **(15)** Central Ave.
- Gas **N:** Shell
  S: Shell(CW)
- Food **S:** Ricas Tacos
- AServ **N:** Shell, Tune Up Masters
  S: Central Tire
- Other **N:** Fire Department

Exit **(15)** Alameda St.
- FStop **S:** **Alameda Petroleum Truck Stop(*, LP, SCALES)**, **Mobil(*, CW)**
- Gas **N:** 76(D)
- Food **N:** Green Taco, TV Cafe
  S: George's Charburgers, Jingle Donuts
- AServ **N:** 76
  S: Berlin Tire Center
- TServ **S:** **Alameda Petroleum Truck Stop(SCALES)**
- Med **S:** ✚ **Alameda Medical Group**

Exit **(17)** Santa Fe Ave, Mateo St.
- Gas **S:** Shell
- AServ **S:** Shell, Sunland Tire
- Other **S:** Fire Station, Mini Market(*, LP)

Exit **(18)** E CA 60, Pomona, I-5 S, Soto St, Santa Ana

Exit **(18)** 4th St.
- Gas **N:** 76
  S: Shell
- AServ **N:** Boyle Auto Repair, L.A. Auto Center, Memo's Auto Repair, Trejo's Radiator
  S: Shell

Exit **(19)** U.S. 101, Los Angeles

Exit **(19)** State St. (Difficult Reaccess)
- Gas **N:** 76(24)
- Food **N:** Fried Rice Express, Lupe's Deli (Mexican), Maria's Bakery, McDonald's, Panda Station, Yum Yum Donuts
- Med **N:** ✚ **Los Angeles County Univ. of S. Cal. Medical Center**

Exit **(19)** I-5 N. Golden State Fwy, Sacramento, U.S. 101 Los Angeles (Left Exit Westbound)

Exit **(19)** Soto St.
- Gas **N:** Shell
  S: Mobil(*), Shell
- Food **S:** Burger King, Orozcos Tacos, Taqueria La Guadalupana
- AServ **N:** Mercedes Body Shop
  S: Shell
- Med **N:** ✚ **LACUSC Medical Center**
- ATM **S:** Mobil, Shell
- Parks **N:** **Hazard Park**
- Other **S:** **Clean King Laundry**, Soto St. Market

EXIT CALIFORNIA

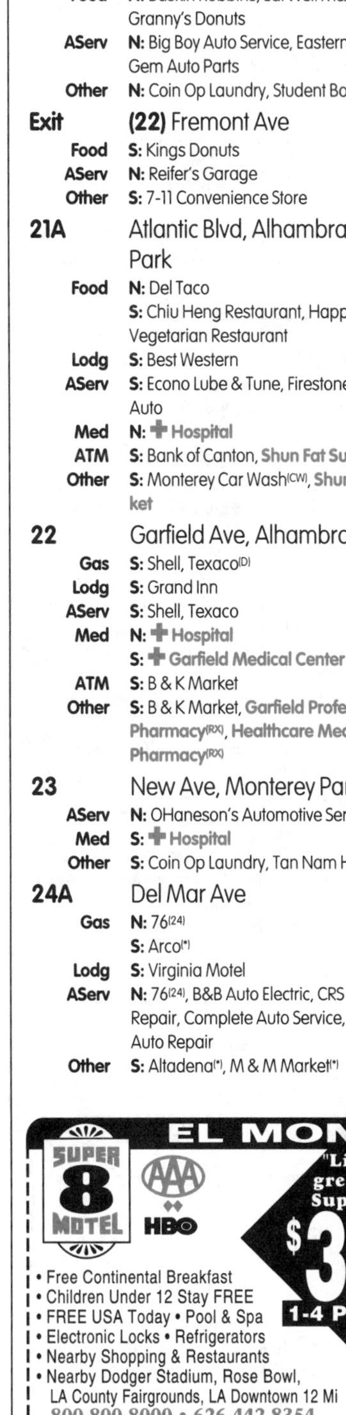

Exit **(20)** City Terrace Dr (Eastbound, Reaccess Westbound Only)
- AServ **S:** Vermont Auto Repair
- Other **S:** Coin Laundry

Exit **(21)** Eastern Ave.
- Gas **S:** Chevron, Mobil(*)
- Food **S:** McDonald's
- AServ **S:** Chevron

Exit **(21)** Jct I-710, Long Beach, Valley Blvd, Eastern Ave, Campus Rd.
- Food **N:** Baskin Robbins, Eat Well Mexican Food, Granny's Donuts
- AServ **N:** Big Boy Auto Service, Eastern Auto Service, Gem Auto Parts
- Other **N:** Coin Op Laundry, Student Bookmark

Exit **(22)** Fremont Ave
- Food **S:** Kings Donuts
- AServ **N:** Reifer's Garage
- Other **S:** 7-11 Convenience Store

21A Atlantic Blvd, Alhambra, Monterey Park
- Food **N:** Del Taco
  S: Chiu Heng Restaurant, Happy Family Vegetarian Restaurant
- Lodg **S:** Best Western
- AServ **S:** Econo Lube & Tune, Firestone All-American Auto
- Med **N:** ✚ **Hospital**
- ATM **S:** Bank of Canton, **Shun Fat Supermarket**
- Other **S:** Monterey Car Wash(CW), **Shun Fat Supermarket**

22 Garfield Ave, Alhambra
- Gas **S:** Shell, Texaco(D)
- Lodg **S:** Grand Inn
- AServ **S:** Shell, Texaco
- Med **N:** ✚ **Hospital**
  S: ✚ **Garfield Medical Center**
- ATM **S:** B & K Market
- Other **S:** B & K Market, **Garfield Professional Building Pharmacy(RX)**, **Healthcare Medical Pharmacy(RX)**

23 New Ave, Monterey Park
- AServ **N:** OHaneson's Automotive Service
- Med **S:** ✚ **Hospital**
- Other **S:** Coin Op Laundry, Tan Nam Hoa Supermarket

24A Del Mar Ave
- Gas **N:** 76(24)
  S: Arco(*)
- Lodg **S:** Virginia Motel
- AServ **N:** 76(24), B&B Auto Electric, CRS Complete Auto Repair, Complete Auto Service, D&H Complete Auto Repair
- Other **S:** Altadena(*), M & M Market(*)

EL MONTE
SUPER 8 MOTEL
AAA
HBO
"Life's great at Super 8"
$39.95* +tax
1-4 Persons
• Free Continental Breakfast
• Children Under 12 Stay FREE
• FREE USA Today • Pool & Spa
• Electronic Locks • Refrigerators
• Nearby Shopping & Restaurants
• Nearby Dodger Stadium, Rose Bowl, LA County Fairgrounds, LA Downtown 12 Mi
800-800-8000 • 626-442-8354
12047 Valley Blvd & 12040 Garvey Ave.
El Monte, CA 91732
*Must show ad at check-in. Based on availability. Not valid with other offer or during special events.
Directions: From I-10 W, Exit Garvey/Durfee Go Straight, motel on L. From I-10 E, Exit Valley/Peck Rd., N, Rt off Exit, R on Valley Blvd., Go Straight Motel on L.
1405 California • I-10 • Exit 28A

EXIT CALIFORNIA

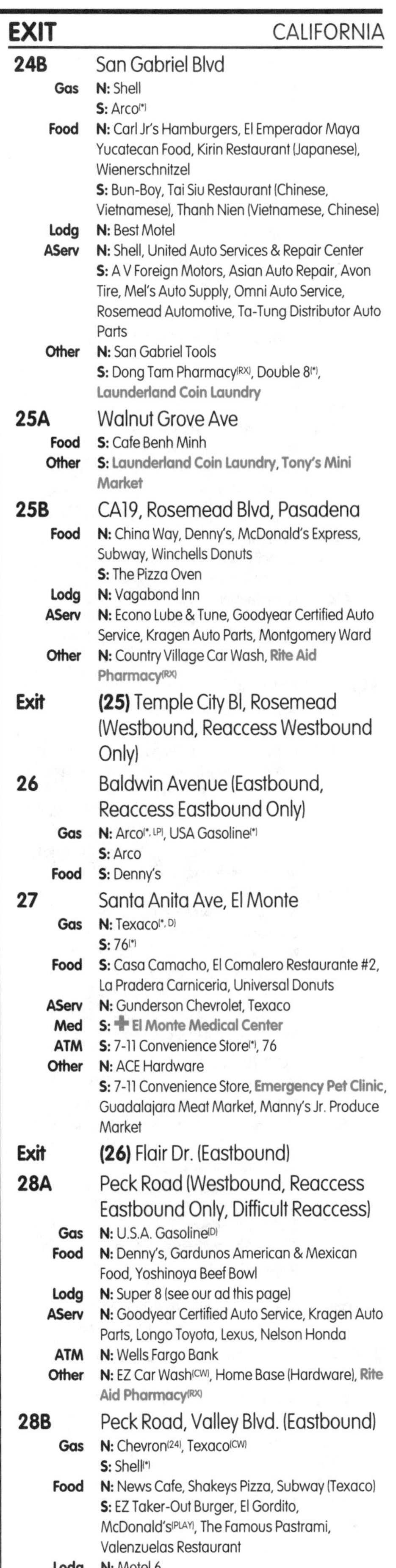

24B San Gabriel Blvd
- Gas **N:** Shell
  S: Arco(*)
- Food **N:** Carl Jr's Hamburgers, El Emperador Maya Yucatecan Food, Kirin Restaurant (Japanese), Wienerschnitzel
  S: Bun-Boy, Tai Siu Restaurant (Chinese, Vietnamese), Thanh Nien (Vietnamese, Chinese)
- Lodg **N:** Best Motel
- AServ **N:** Shell, United Auto Services & Repair Center
  S: A V Foreign Motors, Asian Auto Repair, Avon Tire, Mel's Auto Supply, Omni Auto Service, Rosemead Automotive, Ta-Tung Distributor Auto Parts
- Other **N:** San Gabriel Tools
  S: Dong Tam Pharmacy(RX), Double 8(*), **Launderland Coin Laundry**

25A Walnut Grove Ave
- Food **S:** Cafe Benh Minh
- Other **S:** **Launderland Coin Laundry**, **Tony's Mini Market**

25B CA19, Rosemead Blvd, Pasadena
- Food **N:** China Way, Denny's, McDonald's Express, Subway, Winchells Donuts
  S: The Pizza Oven
- Lodg **N:** Vagabond Inn
- AServ **N:** Econo Lube & Tune, Goodyear Certified Auto Service, Kragen Auto Parts, Montgomery Ward
- Other **N:** Country Village Car Wash, **Rite Aid Pharmacy(RX)**

Exit **(25)** Temple City Bl, Rosemead (Westbound, Reaccess Westbound Only)

26 Baldwin Avenue (Eastbound, Reaccess Eastbound Only)
- Gas **N:** Arco(*, LP), USA Gasoline(*)
  S: Arco
- Food **S:** Denny's

27 Santa Anita Ave, El Monte
- Gas **N:** Texaco(*, D)
  S: 76(*)
- Food **S:** Casa Camacho, El Comalero Restaurante #2, La Pradera Carniceria, Universal Donuts
- AServ **N:** Gunderson Chevrolet, Texaco
- Med **S:** ✚ **El Monte Medical Center**
- ATM **S:** 7-11 Convenience Store(*), 76
- Other **N:** ACE Hardware
  S: 7-11 Convenience Store, **Emergency Pet Clinic**, Guadalajara Meat Market, Manny's Jr. Produce Market

Exit **(26)** Flair Dr. (Eastbound)

28A Peck Road (Westbound, Reaccess Eastbound Only, Difficult Reaccess)
- Gas **N:** U.S.A. Gasoline(D)
- Food **N:** Denny's, Gardunos American & Mexican Food, Yoshinoya Beef Bowl
- Lodg **N:** Super 8 (see our ad this page)
- AServ **N:** Goodyear Certified Auto Service, Kragen Auto Parts, Longo Toyota, Lexus, Nelson Honda
- ATM **N:** Wells Fargo Bank
- Other **N:** EZ Car Wash(CW), Home Base (Hardware), **Rite Aid Pharmacy(RX)**

28B Peck Road, Valley Blvd. (Eastbound)
- Gas **N:** Chevron(24), Texaco(CW)
  S: Shell(*)
- Food **N:** News Cafe, Shakeys Pizza, Subway (Texaco)
  S: EZ Taker-Out Burger, El Gordito, McDonald's(PLAY), The Famous Pastrami, Valenzuelas Restaurant
- Lodg **N:** Motel 6
- AServ **N:** Auto Zone, Chevron(24), El Monte Auto Square (Honda, GMC Truck, Ford, Pont, Dodge), El Monte

EXIT		CALIFORNIA
		Nissan Service, Gunderson Nissan, Nelson Dodge, Star Tire (Texaco), Texaco
		S: All-Techs, El Monte Pontiac, GMC, El Monte Trailer Center, Lee Tires, Leeco Transmission, Park Auto Bake, Winston Tire
	Other	**N:** Ana Pharmacy(RX), El Monte Civic Center, Police
		S: Laundraland
29		Garvey, Durfee (Westbound, Difficult Reaccess)
	ASserv	**S:** J.I. Body Shop, Service Center Custom Auto Parts, Shellhappy
30		Jct I-605
32A		Frazier St. (Reaccess Westbound Only)
	Gas	**N:** Shell(24)
	Food	**N:** Taxcos Restaurant
	Lodg	**N:** Angel Motel, Aristocrat Motel
	AServ	**N:** Engine Depot, Independent Auto Repair
	Other	**N:** **7-11 Convenience Store**, Stop & Save Discount Store(*)
31A		Baldwin Park Blvd, Baldwin Park
	Gas	**N:** Chevron(*)
	Food	**N:** McDonald's (Chevron), Rosa Ristorante Italiano, Taco Bell
	AServ	**N:** "A" Mufflers, Brakes, & Transmissions
	RVCamp	**S:** **Altmans Winnebago**
	Other	**N:** **Food 4 Less**(24)
		S: Nichol's Lumber & Hardware (ACE Hardware)
31B		Francisquito Ave, La Puente
	Gas	**N:** Mobil, U.S.A. Gasoline(*)
		S: Chevron(*), Mobil
	Food	**N:** Baskin Robbins, Chano's Mexican, In-N-Out Burger, Jack-In-The-Box, Papa John's Pizza, Taco Ready, Yum Yum Donuts
		S: Carl Jr's Hamburgers, El Charro Meat Market, Hong Kong Fast Food, In-N-Out Burger, La Fogata Mexican, Los Tres Potrillos, Taqueria Las Amigos, Wienerschnitzel
	Lodg	**S:** TraveLodge
	AServ	**N:** Mobil, V&G Auto Service Center
		S: Chief Auto Parts, Mobil
	Other	**N:** Car Wash(CW), Jr. Market Place, Office Max, **Target**, Zacatecas Meats
		S: California Highway Patrol, **Franciscquito Laundry Mat**, Launderland Coin Laundry, Plaza Market, SCP The Propane People(LP)
32		Puente Ave
	Gas	**N:** Chevron(*, 24)
		S: Arco(*), Texaco
	Food	**N:** China Palace, Denny's, Guadalajara Grill, Happy Wok, McDonald's(PLAY), Milano Pizza, Tacos Las Palmas
		S: Chef's (Howard Johnson), Pepe's Restaurant
	Lodg	**N:** Motel 6, **Queens Lodge Motel**, Radisson
		S: Howard Johnson
	AServ	**S:** Dave Fallucca's Foreign & Domestic, Prestige Mercedes Benz Service, Texaco
	Med	**S:** ✚ **Hospital**
	Other	**N:** **Staples**, Visions Max Optometry
		S: Amber Animal Clinic, **U-Haul Center**(LP)
33A		W. Covina Pkwy, Pacific Ave
	Gas	**N:** 76(D, 24)
	Lodg	**N:** Covina Motel, Walnut Inn
	AServ	**N:** Carquest Auto Parts, Wesco Auto Service
		S: **Big K-Mart**
	Med	**S:** ✚ **Hospital**
	ATM	**S:** First Financial Federal Credit Union
	Other	**S:** **Big K-Mart**, **W. Covina Library**
33B		Sunset Ave, W.Covina (Westbound, No Reaccess)
	Med	**N:** ✚ **Hospital**
	Other	**S:** Police Station

EXIT		CALIFORNIA
33C		Vincent Ave, Glendora Ave.
	Gas	**N:** Chevron(*, LP, 24)
		S: 76(*, LP, CW), Exxon(CW), Mobil
	Food	**N:** Hungry Al's BBQ
		S: Applebee's, Chevy's Fresh Mex
	AServ	**N:** Chevron(24)
		S: Exxon, Jimmy's Muffler Service, Mobil, Plaza Radiator & Air Conditioner Repair, Tire Station
	ATM	**S:** Bank of America, Home Savings Of America, Pacific Western National Bank
	Other	**S:** Altadena(*), **Barnes & Noble Booksellers**, Discovery Zone(PLAY), Edward's 18 Cinema, Lens Crafters, Nevada Bob's Golf, **The Plaza (Mall)**, **U.S. Post Office**
34		CA 39, Azusa Ave
	Gas	**N:** 76(D), Arco(*)
		S: Mobil, Shell(*)
	Food	**N:** McDonald's, Taqueria La Fogata
		S: Carrows Restaurant(24)
	Lodg	**N:** El Dorado Motel, Super 8 (see our ad this page)
	AServ	**N:** Arco, Azusa Auto Parts, Econo Lube & Tune, Midas Muffler & Brake, West Covina Chrys, Plym, Jeep, Eagle
		S: Mobil, Shell, West Covina Auto Plaza (Saturn, Penske, Dodge), West Covina Nissan, West Covina Toyota
36		Citrus St, Covena
	Gas	**N:** Chevron(*, 24), Shell(24)
		S: 76(24)
	Food	**N:** Burger King(PLAY), IHOP, Old World Delicatessen, Seafood Bay, Subway
		S: Casa Jimenez (Mexican), Classic Hamburgers, Jackie's Cafe, The Pizza Den
	AServ	**N:** Chevron(24), Citrus Brake & Automotive, Eastland Transmission Service, Reynolds Buick, GMC Trucks, Seidner's Collision Center, Shell(24), Trojan Tire, West Covina Linoln Mercury
		S: 76(24), Crestview Cadillac
	Med	**N:** ✚ **Hospital**
	ATM	**N:** Foothill Independent Bank, San Wa Bank
	Other	**N:** Eastland Theater, **Longs Drugs**(RX), **Lucky Grocery Store**, Mail Boxes Etc., Optometry
		S: Tom's Pharmacy(RX)
36A		Barranca St.
	Food	**N:** Carl Jr's Hamburgers, Charlie Brown's Steak & Lobster, Chili's, MJ Ranch Dining House, Marie Callender's, Mariposa Restaurant, Monterey Bay Canners Fresh Seafood
		S: In-N-Out Burger, McDonald's(PLAY)
	Lodg	**S:** Comfort Inn
	AServ	**N:** Montgomery Ward's Automotive Center
	ATM	**N:** Bank of America, California State Bank, First Federal Savings, S.B.A. Loan System
	Other	**N:** Club Disney, **Target**
36B		Grand Ave.

Newly Renovated

SUPER 8 MOTEL

"In the heart of San Gabriel Valley"

626-969-8871

$39.99 And Up

- Free Continental Breakfast
- Kids 12 and under Stay Free
- Outdoor Jacuzzi • Exterior Corridors
- 25" Remote TV w/Free HBO
- Handicap Accessible
- Truck or Large Vehicle Parking
- Walking Distance to Restaurants

Special Rates for Tour Groups

I-10 Exit Azuza north 2.5 miles on left or I-210 Exit Azuza left, on left side 1449

California • I-10 • Exit 34 (Azuza Ave.)

EXIT		CALIFORNIA
	Gas	**N:** Chevron, Shell
	Food	**N:** Coco's, El Torito Mexican, Emperor Mongolian B-B-Q, House of Louie Chinese Restaurant, Magic Recipe
	Lodg	**N:** Best Western, Hampton Inn, Holiday Inn
	AServ	**N:** Chevron, Shell
37		Holt Ave, Barracan St
	Food	**N:** Blakes (Embassy Suites), Sizzling Kabob
	Lodg	**N:** Embassy Suites
	Parks	**N:** **Parque Xalapa**(PLAY)
40		Via Verde
	Other	**N:** Raging Waters (1 Mile)
39A		JCT I-210, Santa Anna, San Dinas, CA 71
42		Kellogg Dr
Exit		**(42)** South CA 57, West I-210 Pasadena, Orange Freeway Santa Anna; CA 71 South Corona
44AB		Dudley St, Fairplex Dr.
	Gas	**N:** 76(*, LP), Arco(LP)
		S: Mobil(*, D)
	Food	**N:** Denny's, Pamona Valley Mining Co.
	Lodg	**N:** Lemon Tree Motel
	AServ	**N:** 76
		S: Mobil
	RVCamp	**N:** **East Shore RV Park (1.75 Miles)**
	ATM	**N:** Arco
		S: **7-11 Convenience Store**
	Other	**N:** Mount Meadows Golf Course
		S: **7-11 Convenience Store**
Exit		**(45)** White Ave. (Eastbound, Reaccess Westbound Only)
	Gas	**S:** 76, Texaco
	Food	**S:** Bravo Burgers
	AServ	**S:** 76, Texaco
	Other	**S:** Carniceria(*), Coin Wash(CW), Fire Department
45		Garey Ave, Pamona, Orange Grove Ave.
	Gas	**S:** Arco(24), Chevron(*), Exxon(D), Shell(CW, 24)
	AServ	**S:** Arco(24), Exxon
	Med	**N:** ✚ **Pamona Valley Hospital Medical Center**
	ATM	**S:** Chevron
	Other	**S:** Garey Vision Center
46		Towne Ave.
	Food	**N:** Jack-In-The-Box, The Jelly Donut
	Other	**N:** Coin Car Wash(CW), Sunshine Coin-Op Laundry
47		Indian Hill Blvd, Claremont
	Gas	**N:** Mobil(*)
		S: Chevron(*), Shell(*)
	Food	**N:** B.C. Cafe (Howard Johnson), Baker's Square
		S: Burger King(PLAY), Chili's, In-N-Out Burger, McDonald's (Chevron), Round Table Pizza
	Lodg	**N:** Howard Johnson, TraveLodge
		S: Ramada Inn
	AServ	**S:** America's Tire Company
	ATM	**S:** **Lucky**(RX)
	Other	**N:** **Greyhound Bus Terminal**
		S: Claremont Car Wash(CW), **Lucky**(RX), Pic 'N' Save
48A		Monte Vista Ave.
	Gas	**N:** Texaco
	Food	**N:** Acapulco Mexican, Applebee's, Laissez Faire Espresso Tea Juice Bar, Olive Garden, Red Lobster, The Crescent City Creole Restaurant, Tony Roma's
	AServ	**N:** Texaco
	Med	**S:** ✚ **Hospital**, ✚ **U.S. Family Care Medical Center**(24)
	Other	**N:** **General Cinemas**, Lens Crafters
		S: Monte Vista Pharmacy(RX)
48B		Central Ave, Montclair

Bold red print shows RV & Bus parking available or nearby

EXIT — CALIFORNIA

Gas N: Texaco[24]
S: 76[*]
Food N: El Pollo Loco, McDonald's[PLAY], Starbucks Coffee, Subway, Theo's Cafe Greek & American
S: Johnny's Donuts, Long John Silver, S.C. Donuts, Wienerschnitzel
AServ N: Firestone Tire & Auto, Goodyear Certified Auto Service, Hi-Lo Auto Supply, Hi-Lo Auto Supply, Montgomery Ward, Texaco[24]
S: 76
Med S: ✚ **Hospital**
ATM N: PFF Bank & Trust, Washington Mutual
S: Paragon Gifts
Other N: Barnes & Noble Booksellers, **Montclair Plaza (Mall)**, **Office Depot**, Office Max, Petco
S: **K-Mart**, Paragon Gifts, The Wash Works Coin Laundry

49 Mountain Ave, Mount Baldy
Gas N: Mobil[*, LP], Texaco[*]
Food N: A & W Hot Dogs & More (Texaco), China Gate Restaurant, Denny's, El Torito, Honey Baked Ham, Mi Taco & Burgers, Picasso, San Biagio Pizza, Starbucks Coffee, Subway
S: Carl Jr's Hamburgers, San Remo Ristorante Italiano, Tacos Mexico[24]
Lodg N: Super 8
ATM N: **Pavilions Grocery**[RX]
Other N: Edward's Cinemas, Harbor Freight Tools, **Long's Drugstore**[RX], **Pavilions Grocery**[RX], Police Station, **Staples Office Superstore**, **The Home Depot**
S: **Food 4 Less**, **Target**, Toys R Us

50 CA 83, Euclid Ave, Upland, Ontario
Med S: ✚ **Hospital**

52 4th St
Gas N: Arco[*], Chevron[24], Shell[CW]
S: 76[*, LP], Gas, Texaco[*, D]
Food N: Burger King[PLAY], Carl Jr's Hamburgers, Domino's Pizza, Donut Star, Godinez Tacos, Jack-In-The-Box[24], Little Caesars Pizza (Big K-Mart)
S: China Express, Denny's, **KFC**, Taqueria El Portal, Yum Yum Donuts
Lodg N: Motel 6, Quality Inn, Red Carpet Motel
S: DAYS INN Days Inn
AServ N: Chevron[24]
ATM N: Arco
Other N: **Big K-Mart**[RX], Ontario Fire Dept.
S: Coin Op Laundry, **Jax Market**

53 Vineyard Ave, Airport
Gas S: Mobil, Texaco[*, D, 24]
Food S: Bombay Restaurant, **Cafe California (Good Nite Inn)**, Denny's, In-N-Out Burger, Rosa's Fine Italian Restaurant, Yoshinoya Beef Bowl
Lodg S: Best Western, Country Suites, Countryside Suites, Double Tree Hotel, DoubleTree Club Hotel, Express Inn, **Good Nite Inn**, Residence Inn, Super 8
AServ S: Mobil
Other S: Circle K Food Store[*]

54A Holt Blvd. (Westbound)
Food S: Marie Callender's Restaurant
Lodg S: Marriott, Residence Inn
TServ S: **Commercial Truck Center**
Other S: Ontario Convention Center

54 Archibald Ave
Gas N: Mobil[*, D, CW]
Food N: Burger Town USA, Joey's Pizza, Subway, Teriyaki Champ
Lodg N: Motel 6
ATM N: Mobil, Wescom Credit Union
Parks N: **Cucamonga Guasti Regional Park**[PLAY]
Other N: Circle K Food Store[*]

55 Haven Ave, Rancho Cucamonga
Gas N: Mobil[*, CW]
Food N: Holiday Inn
Lodg N: Hilton, Holiday Inn, La Quinta Inn
Other N: **Ontario Mills Mall**
S: Ontario International Airport

56 Milliken Ave
TStop S: **76 Auto/Truck Plaza**[*, LP, SCALES], **T/A TravelCenters of America**[*, SCALES]
Food N: Coco's
S: **Burger King (TA Truckstops)**, Buster's (76 Auto/Truck Plaza), **Country Pride Restaurant (TA Truckstops)**, Farmer's Boy Hamburgers, **Taco Bell (TA Truckstop)**
Lodg N: Country Suites, Amerisuites (see our ad this page)
AServ S: Chrome Shop
TServ S: **76 Auto/Truck Plaza**[SCALES], **T/A TravelCenters of America**[SCALES]
TWash S: **76 Auto/Truck Plaza**
Other N: **Ontario Mills Mall**

57 Jct I-15 , Barstow, San Diego

58 Etiwanda Ave, Valley Blvd.

60 Cherry Ave
TStop N: **Truck Town Truckstop**[*, SCALES, 24]
S: **Three Sisters Truck Stop**[*, SCALES]
Gas N: Arco[*], Mobil[*]
S: Circle K[*]
Food N: **Jack-In-The-Box**
S: Farmer Boy's Hamburgers
Lodg N: **Circle Inn Motel**
TServ N: **Big Rig Truck Repair**, **Diversified Truck Center**, **Trans-West Ford**, **Truck Town Truckstop**[SCALES, 24]
S: **Fontana Truck Auto Electric**, **Rush Truck Center (South Coast Peterbilt)**, **TIP Trailer**, **Western States Truck Repair**
TWash S: **Three Sisters Truck Stop**
ATM N: **Truck Town Truckstop**

62 Citrus Ave
Gas N: Ultramar
S: Arco[*]
Food N: Baker's[24], Superstar Donuts
AServ N: B & W Wheel Co., **Goodyear Commercial Tire Center**, Starpro Alternator, Starter
TServ N: **California Tool & Welding Supply**[LP], **Goodyear Commercial Tire Center**
ATM S: Arco
Other N: Citrus Market, Fontana Animal Supplies

63A Sierra Ave
Gas N: Arco[*, 24], Mobil[*, CW], Texaco[D, 24]
S: Circle K[*]
Food N: Arby's, Baker's, Billy T's Family Restaurant, Burger King, China Cook Chinese Restaurant, China Panda, Coco's, Denny's, Hacienda Mexican, Jack-In-The-Box, Little Caesars Pizza, McDonald's, Millie's, Sub Stop, Subway, Sun Fu Wah Chinese Kitchen, Taco Bell, Wienerschnitzel, Yoshinoya Beef Bowl
Lodg N: **Comfort Inn**, Motel 6, Valley Motel
AServ N: A-Boss, Chief Auto Parts, International Radiators, Pep Boys Auto Center, Texaco[24]
Med N: ✚ **Kaiser Permanente**
ATM N: Bank of America, **Vons Grocery**[RX]
S: Circle K
Other N: **Big K-Mart**, **Food 4 Less**, Mail' Etc., Ponderosa Car Wash, **Stater Bros. Grocery**, **Toys R Us**, Tru Value Hardware, **Vons Grocery**[RX]
S: **Target**

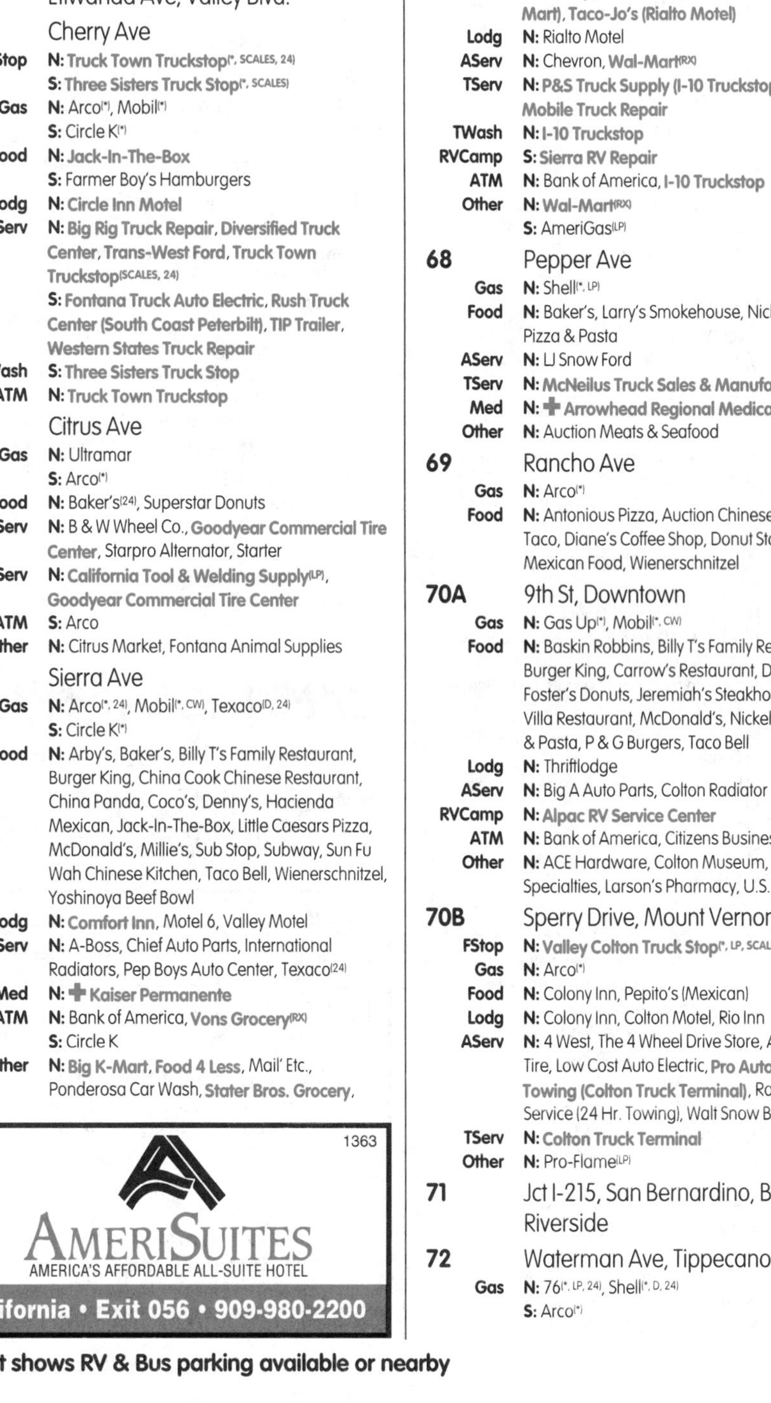

65 Cedar Ave, Bloomington
Gas N: Arco[*], Chevron[24], Mobil[*]
Food N: Baker's, Burger King[PLAY], Donut Star, El Mezquite Mariscos, El Rancho Grande Restaurant, Porky's Pizza, Taqueria La Mexicana
AServ N: 4 Wheel Drive Center, Advanced Auto Body & Paint, Alvidrez Tire Repair, Chevron[24], Classic Connection, Mobil, Precision Turbo Charger Co., R C Auto Repair, Young's Auto Service
RVCamp N: **Bloomington Mobile Home & RV Park (.25 Miles)**
Other N: Carter's Jr. Market, Public Library, Top Care Pharmacy[RX]

67 Riverside Ave, Rialto
TStop N: **I-10 Truckstop**[*, SCALES]
Gas N: Arco[*], Chevron
Food N: Burger King[PLAY], China Palace, Giovanni's Pizza, Hometown Buffet, **I-10 Cafe (I-10 Truckstop)**, Jack-In-The-Box, **McDonald's (Wal-Mart)**, **Taco-Jo's (Rialto Motel)**
Lodg N: Rialto Motel
AServ N: Chevron, **Wal-Mart**[RX]
TServ N: **P&S Truck Supply (I-10 Truckstop)**, **Tim's Mobile Truck Repair**
TWash N: **I-10 Truckstop**
RVCamp S: **Sierra RV Repair**
ATM N: Bank of America, **I-10 Truckstop**
Other N: **Wal-Mart**[RX]
S: AmeriGas[LP]

68 Pepper Ave
Gas N: Shell[*, LP]
Food N: Baker's, Larry's Smokehouse, Nickelodeon Pizza & Pasta
AServ N: LJ Snow Ford
TServ N: **McNeilus Truck Sales & Manufacturing**
Med N: ✚ **Arrowhead Regional Medical Center**
Other N: Auction Meats & Seafood

69 Rancho Ave
Gas N: Arco[*]
Food N: Antonious Pizza, Auction Chinese Food, Del Taco, Diane's Coffee Shop, Donut Star, El Rancho Mexican Food, Wienerschnitzel

70A 9th St, Downtown
Gas N: Gas Up[*], Mobil[*, CW]
Food N: Baskin Robbins, Billy T's Family Restaurant, Burger King, Carrow's Restaurant, Denny's, Foster's Donuts, Jeremiah's Steakhouse, KFC, La Villa Restaurant, McDonald's, Nickelodeon Pizza & Pasta, P & G Burgers, Taco Bell
Lodg N: Thriftlodge
AServ N: Big A Auto Parts, Colton Radiator
RVCamp N: **Alpac RV Service Center**
ATM N: Bank of America, Citizens Business Bank
Other N: ACE Hardware, Colton Museum, Dog Show Specialties, Larson's Pharmacy, U.S. Post Office

70B Sperry Drive, Mount Vernon Ave.
FStop N: **Valley Colton Truck Stop**[*, LP, SCALES]
Gas N: Arco[*]
Food N: Colony Inn, Pepito's (Mexican)
Lodg N: Colony Inn, Colton Motel, Rio Inn
AServ N: 4 West, The 4 Wheel Drive Store, A-1 Glass & Tire, Low Cost Auto Electric, **Pro Auto Service & Towing (Colton Truck Terminal)**, Ray's Auto Service (24 Hr. Towing), Walt Snow BF Goodrich
TServ N: **Colton Truck Terminal**
Other N: Pro-Flame[LP]

71 Jct I-215, San Bernardino, Barstow; Riverside

72 Waterman Ave, Tippecanoe
Gas N: 76[*, LP, 24], Shell[*, D, 24]
S: Arco[*]

EXIT CALIFORNIA

Food N: Black Angus Steakhouse, Bobby McGee's, Coco's, Guadalarharry's (Mexican), IHOP, La Potiniere (Hilton), Sizzler, Spoon's California Grill, T.G.I. Friday's, Yamazato of Japan
S: Burger King, Carl Jr's Hamburgers, Donut Factory[24], Gus Jr. Burgers, Popeye's Chicken, Surfer Joe's Pizza, Taco Bell
Lodg N: Comfort Inn, E-Z-8 Motel, Hilton, La Quinta Inn, Super 8, TraveLodge
AServ S: Island Auto Parts (AC Delco)
RVCamp S: **Camping World (see our ad this page)**
Other N: **Park Center Mall**
S: Marine Center Inc., Nevada Bob's Golf

73 Tippecanoe Ave, Anderson St.
Gas N: Arco[*, D], Shell[24]
S: 76
Food N: In-N-Out Burger[CW]
S: A & A Donut, BK Subs and Sandwiches, Baker's, Del Taco, HomeTown Buffet, KFC, Kool Kactus Cafe, Manileno Rice & Noodles, Napoli Italian
Lodg N: **Lomalinda Lodge**, University Inn Motel
AServ S: 76, Bob & Mike Lomalinda Automotive, On Target, Spreen Honda
ATM N: Shell
Other N: **Sam's Club**

74 Mtn. View Ave, Bryn Mawr
Gas N: Mobil[*, D, LP]
S: Arco[*]
Food S: Amie's Donuts, Farmer Boy's, Katie McGuire's Pie & Bake Shop, Subway
AServ S: Dee & Walt's Auto
RVCamp S: **Camping**
ATM S: Arco

75 California St
Gas S: Arco[*], Shell[*, 24]
Food S: Coffee, Coffee, Jack-In-The-Box, Jose's Mexican Food, Mr. You Chinese Food
RVCamp S: **Mission RV Park**
Other N: **Pharaoh's Lost Kingdom**, **San Bernardino County Museum**
S: **Food 4 Less**, KB Toy Works, Mail Boxes Etc., **Wal-Mart**[24, RX]

76 Alabama St. (Westbound)
Gas S: Flagg[*, 24], Texaco[*, D]
Food N: Denny's, Tom's #1 Chiliburgers
S: A & W Hot Dogs & More (Texaco), Del Taco, IHOP, Marie Callender's Restaurant, McDonald's[PLAY], Mr. J's Donuts, Nick's Burgers, Zabella's Mexican
Lodg N: 7 West Motel, Redlands Motor Inn, Super 8
S: Goodnite Inn
AServ S: Chief Auto Parts, Metro Nissan, Tom Bell Chevrolet
ATM S: Texaco
Other N: U-Haul[LP]
S: **Big K-Mart**

76A Tennesse St
Food S: Arby's, Baker's, Burger King[PLAY], **Carl Jr's Hamburgers**, Coco's Bakery & Restaurant, El Pollo Loco, Foster's Donuts[24], Long John Silver, Subway, Taco Bell
Lodg N: **Super 8 (see our ad this page)**
S: Best Western, Redlands Inn
AServ S: Redlands Ford
Med S: **✚ Hospital**

76B Jct. CA 30, Highland, To CA 330, Running Springs

78 CA 38, 6th St, Downtown
Gas N: Arco[*], Chevron[24]
Food N: Antonious Pizza, Donut n Burger
S: Boston Market Restaurant, Orange Garden Restaurant (Chinese), Pizza Stop, Subway
Lodg N: Budget Inn Motel, Stardust Motel

EXIT CALIFORNIA

AServ N: Chevron[24]
S: Kragen Auto Parts
Other N: Econowash Coin Laundry, **Stater Bros. Grocery**
S: **Albertson's Grocery**, Carlson Hardware, Orange Plaza Optometry, **Postal Annex +**, Redlands Chamber of Commerce

79 Cypress St (Difficult Reaccess)
Med S: **✚ Redlands Community Hospital**

80 Redlands Blvd, Ford Street
Gas S: Arco[*]
Food S: Gillen's Steak & Seafood, Griswold's Seafood

Exit **(81)** Wabash Ave. (Westbound, Reaccess Westbound Only)

82 Yucaipa Blvd, Oak Glen
Gas N: Arco[*], Chevron[24]
Food N: Antiques & Goumet Coffee, Baker's
AServ N: Chevron[24], Deshler's Specialties, European Automotive, Gateway Tires and Service
ATM N: Arco
Parks N: **Yucaipa Regional Park**
Other N: Antiques & Goumet Coffee

84A Live Oak Rd, Canyon Road
Food N: Cedar Mills Steaks, Seafood & Italian

(85) **Wildwood Safety Rest Area (RR, Phones, Picnic, Pet Walk)**

84B Yucaipa, County Line Rd.
Gas N: Fastrip[*, D], Texaco[LP]
Food N: CNI Coffee, Del Taco, Plaza Cafe (American, Mexican)
AServ N: Calimesa Tire Center, **Dinosaur Tire**, Golden's Auto Works & Upholstery, Morales Tire Auto Truck Repair, Parts Plus Auto Store, Texaco, Troyce's Automotive Shop
TServ N: **Dinosaur Tire**
Other N: Calimesa Pharmacy, **Coast to Coast Hardware**, **Laundromat**, Marv's Pet Grooming

87 Calimesa Blvd
Gas N: Arco[*], Shell[*, LP, CW, 24]
Food N: Burger King, Donut Hut, McDonald's, Taco Bell
Lodg N: Calimesa Inn Motel
ATM N: Redlands Federal Bank
Other N: Star Drug, **Stater Brothers Grocery**

CAMPING WORLD
Waterman S. or Waterman Exit
151 Redlands Blvd. • San Bernardino, CA
1-800-423-7569
1434

1501
SUPER 8 MOTEL
1160 Arizona Street
Redlands, CA
909-335-1612
Continental Breakfast
Denny's Restaurant on Premises
Heated Outdoor Pool
Cable TV/HBO/ESPN
Large Vehicle Parking
Laundry Services
Minutes to Pharaohs Lost Kingdom,
San Bernadino Museum, and
the San Manuel Indian Casino
CALIFORNIA • I-10 • EXIT 76A (ALABAMA)

EXIT CALIFORNIA

88 Singleton Road (Westbound)

89 Cherry Valley Blvd, Desert Lawn Dr.
RVCamp S: **El Rancho Brookside (1.75 Miles)**

(91) **Rest Area (RR, Picnic; Westbound)**

92 San Timoteo Canyon Road

93 CA 60, Riverside (Left Exit Westbound, Limited Access Highway)

94A CA 79, Beaumont Ave, Hamet, San Jacinto, Oak Glen, CA 60
Gas N: 76[*, LP], Arco[*]
Food N: Baker's, Donald's Burgers, Tacos, El Rancho, McDonald's[PLAY], Taco Shop, The Sandwich Shop, Yum Yum Donuts[24]
S: **Denny's**
Lodg N: Best Western, Budget Host Inn
AServ N: B & B Auto & Tire Service, Cash Boy Towing, Cherry Valley Automotive, D&S Auto Repair & Towing, Dick's VW, Foreign, & Domestic Repair, Lee's Auto Body & Auto Glass, Monte's Automotive, NAPA Auto Parts
RVCamp S: **Camping**
ATM N: 76, California State Bank, North County Bank
Other N: **Beaumont Antique Mall**, Beaumont Civic Center, Bible Bookstore, Save More Markets[*], Yamaha, Kawasaki (Motorcycles)

94B Pennsylvania Ave (Reaccess Eastbound Only)
Food N: Jimmy's (Mexican, American), Rusty Lantern Restaurant
Lodg N: Windsor Motel
AServ N: Bud's Automotive Center, Castillo's Auto Body, Transmission Repair, Tune & Lube Factory
RVCamp N: **Tom's RV Buy, Sale, Trade**
Other N: All Purpose Rentals[LP], Beaumont Auto Spa[CW], The Club House

95 Highland Springs Ave, Banning
Gas N: Arco[*, 24], Chevron[*], Ultramar[*, D, LP, 24]
S: Mobil[*, CW]
Food N: Burger King[PLAY], Denny's, Donut De-lite, Farmhouse Restaurant, Jack-In-The-Box, Little Caesars Pizza, Pizza "n" Pasta Lovers, Ramsey Burger #2, Subway
S: Baskin Robbins, Carl Jr's Hamburgers
AServ N: Highland Springs Car Wash & Express Lube[CW], Kragen Auto Parts
ATM N: **Stater Bros Grocery**
S: **Albertson's Grocery**, Downey Savings
Other N: Family Vision Care, Fire Department, **Food 4 Less**, Highland Springs Car Wash & Express Lube, Pet Depot, **Stater Bros Grocery**
S: **Albertson's Grocery**, **Big K-Mart**, California Highway Patrol

97 Sunset Ave
Gas N: Ultra Mar[*, D, 24]
Food N: Billy T's Family Restaurant, Chinese Table Restaurant, Domino's Pizza, Donut Factory, **Gramma's Kitchen**, Gus Jr's Famous Burgers, Maria's Market
AServ N: Auto Zone Auto Parts, Chief Auto Parts, Espinoza's Tire & Upholstery, Mountain Air Auto Care, Walter's VW Parts
RVCamp N: **Ray's RV Sales & Repairs**
ATM N: Redlands Federal Bank
Other N: ACE Hardware, **Banning Veterinary Hospital**, Coin-Op Launderland, K-9 Creations, **Rite Aid Pharmacy**[RX], **Sav-U-Foods**

98 22nd St, Banning
Gas N: Arco[*], Mobil[*]
Food N: Carl Jr's Hamburgers, Carrow's Restaurant, Del Taco, Grandpa's Corner Cafe, KFC, McDonald's, Pizza Hut, Ralibertos Mexican, Ramsey Burger, Sizzler Steak House, Taco Bell[24],

Bold red print shows RV & Bus parking available or nearby

EXIT CALIFORNIA

Wendy's
Lodg **N:** Days Inn, Days Inn, Sunset Motel, Super 8
AServ **N:** All Star Dodge, Chrysler, Eagle, Banning Muffler & Radiator, Carrera's Tire Shop, Winston Tire
ATM **N:** McDonald's
Other **N:** Shopping Basket(*)

99 CA 243, 8th St, Idlewild
Gas **N:** Ultra Mar(*, D, 24)
Food **N:** Ahloo Chinese Cafe, Banning Burgers Drive Thru, Banning Donut, Los Gallos Mexican, Paradise Pizza
Lodg **N:** Hacienda Inn, Peach Tree Motel
RVCamp **S:** Mobility Product & Design RV Repair, RV Repair
Med **N:** + Urgent Care Clinic
Other **N:** Banning Coin-Op Laundromat

100 Hargrave St, Idyllwild
FStop **N:** Texaco(*, LP)
Gas **N:** A Z Mini Mart & Gas(*), Shell(*, LP, CW, 24)
Food **N:** Consuelo's Mexican
Lodg **N:** Desert Star Motel, Monte Vista Motel
AServ **N:** Carlos Auto Repair, Parts Plus Auto Store, Stagecoach Wrecking Co.

(15) Weigh Station

101 Ramsey St. (Reaccess Eastbound Only)

(102) Weigh Station (Eastbound)

(102) Weigh Station, Inspection Station (Westbound)

103 Sports Road

104 Apache Trail

106 Fields Rd, Morongo Indian Reservation
Gas **N:** Chevron
Food **N:** McDonald's
Parks **N:** Morongo Indian Reservation & Casino
Other **N:** Desert Hill Premium Outlets

105 Apache Trail
FStop **N:** Shell(*, LP, CW, 24)
Food **N:** Hadley's Kitchen
ATM **N:** Hadley's Kitchen

111 Verbenia Ave
FStop **N:** Texaco(*), Texaco(*)
Food **N:** Burger King, Denny's, Wheel Inn(*)
AServ **N:** Drive Train LTD Tires, Drive Trains Limited Truck & Auto Repair
ATM **N:** Texaco, Wheel Inn
Parks **S:** Cabazon Park and Communtiy Center

112 Palm Springs, Hwy 111 (Eastbound)

(112) Rest Area (RR, Picnic; Eastbound)

(112) Rest Area (RR, HF, Picnic; Westbound)

113 White Water

115 CA 62, 29 Palms, Yucca Valley, Joshua Tree National Park (Difficult Reaccess)
Parks **N:** Joshua Tree National Park

119 Indian Ave, N Palm Springs
TStop **S:** Pilot(*, SCALES)
Gas **N:** 76(*), Arco(*, 24), Shell(*, LP)
Food **N:** Breakfast Sandwich Shop & Chinese Food, Denny's, Johnson's Donuts, Pub N Sub
S: Dairy Queen (Pilot), Wendy's (Pilot TS)
Lodg **N:** Motel 6
AServ **N:** NAPA Auto Parts, Shell
TServ **S:** Pilot(SCALES)
RVCamp **N:** Camping

EXIT CALIFORNIA

Med **S:** + Hospital
Other **N:** Buell American Motorcycles, Oroweat Bakery Thrift Store
S: Welding Shop (Pilot TS)

122 Palm Dr, Desert Hot Springs, Gene Autry Trail

125 Date Palm Dr
Gas **S:** Arco(*), Mobil(*, CW)
ATM **S:** Arco

129 Rancho Mirage, Cathedral City, Ramon Rd, Bob Hope Dr.
TStop **N:** Flying J Travel Plaza(*, LP, SCALES) (Conoco)
Gas **N:** Chevron(*, 24), Mobil(*, D, 24), Ultramar(*)
Food **N:** Burger King(PLAY), Carl Jr's Hamburgers, Del Taco, Denny's, In-N-Out Hamburgers, McDonald's(PLAY) (Flying J TS)
Lodg **N:** Travelers Inn(LP) (Flying J TS)
AServ **N:** Parkhouse Tire
TServ **N:** CB/Shine Shop
TWash **N:** Little Sister's Truck Wash (Flying J TS)
Med **S:** + Hospital
ATM **N:** Chevron
Other **N:** Animal Emergency Clinic, Animal Samaritans

130 Thousand Palms, Monterey Ave
Gas **N:** Arco(*)
S: Costco
AServ **S:** Costco

131 Cook St
RVCamp **S:** Emerald Desert Golf & RV Resort

136 Washington St, Country Club Dr
Gas **N:** Arco(*)
S: 76, Mobil(*)
Food **N:** Burger King(PLAY), Del Taco
S: Angelino's, Carl Jr's Hamburgers, Carmen's Mexican, Goody's Cafe, Lilli's Cuisine (Chinese), Pizza & Pasta (Angelino's), Pizza Hut, Subway, Swiss Donut (Angelino's), Teddy's Donuts, The Pantry Restaurant Home Cookin', Tutti Pasta
Lodg **N:** Motel 6
AServ **S:** 76, Tire Factory
RVCamp **N:** Camping (1 Mile)
ATM **S:** Circle K(*, LP)
Other **S:** Circle K, Pet Luv

138 Jefferson St
Other **S:** Highway Patrol Post

140 Monroe St, Central Indo
Gas **S:** 76(*), Shell(D, LP, CW)
AServ **S:** 76, Anaya's Transmission and Auto Repair
RVCamp **N:** Bob's RV Park (1 Mile)
Med **S:** + Hospital
ATM **S:** 76, Shell

141 Central Indio, Jackson St

1174

Special Rates for Tour Groups
Free Deluxe Breakfast
Free Cable TV with HBO/ESPN/CNN
Indoor Heated Pool & Spa
Bus & RV Parking • Guest Laundry
Free Local Calls
760-921-2300 • 800-HOLIDAY
CALIFORNIA • I-10 • EXIT 237

EXIT CALIFORNIA

RVCamp **N:** Camping

142 Auto Center Dr, Van Buren St, CA 111, Cabazon Indian Reservation
Lodg **N:** Holiday Inn Express

143 To CA86, To CA111 South, Brawley, Bus. 10, Dillon Road, Coachella, Indio
TStop **S:** Arco(*, SCALES)
Gas **N:** Chevron(*, LP), Shell(*, 24)
Food **S:** Mrs. B's (Arco TS), Taco Bell (Arco TS)
TServ **S:** Arco(SCALES)
TWash **S:** Arco
RVCamp **N:** Camping

(143) Rest Area (RR, HF, Phones, Picnic, RV Dump; Eastbound)

(144) Rest Area (RR, HF, Phones, Picnic, RV Dump; Westbound)

166 Frontage Road

168 Mecca, Twentynine Palms
Parks **N:** Joshua Tree National Park

170 Chiriaco, Summit
Gas **N:** Chevron(D, LP)
Food **N:** Chiriaco Summit Coffee Shop(*, 24)
Lodg **N:** Chiriaco Motel
AServ **N:** Chevron
RVCamp **N:** Dry Camping
Other **N:** General Patton Memorial Museum

175 Hayfield Road

180 Red Cloud Road

187 Eagle Mountain Road

190 CA177, Rice Rd., Desert Center , Parker, Needles
Gas **N:** Stanco(*)
Food **N:** Desert Center Cafe, Oasis
AServ **N:** Stanco
Parks **N:** Lake Tamarisk
Other **N:** Desert Center Market, U.S. Post Office(SCALES)

199 Corn Springs Road

215 Ford Dry Lake Road

(216) Rest Area (RR, HF, Phones, RV Dump)

220 Wileys Well Road

(224) Weigh Station (Westbound)

230 Airport, Mesa Dr
TStop **N:** 76 Auto/Truck Stop(*, SCALES)
S: Mesa Verde Truck Stop(*, 24)
Gas **N:** Chevron(*, D)
TServ **N:** 76 Auto/Truck Stop(SCALES)
RVCamp **N:** 76 Auto/Truck Stop
ATM **N:** Chevron
S: Mesa Verde Truck Stop

234 CA 78, Brawley, Neighbors Blvd, Ripley, Palo Verde
Gas **N:** Texaco(*)

237 Lovekin Blvd
Gas **N:** Mobil(*, D), Mobil, Shell(*)
S: 76(D), Arco, Chevron(*, D, 24), Texaco(*), Ultramar(*)
Food **N:** Carl Jr's Hamburgers(PLAY), Coffee Shop, Del Taco, Jack-In-The-Box, Java This Bakery & Gourmet Coffee, La Casita Dos Mexican Food, McDonald's(PLAY), Pizza Hut, Popeye's Chicken, Subway (Mobil)
S: Blythe Pizza, Burger King, Dairy Queen (Texaco), Denny's, KFC, Taco Bell, Town Square Cafe
Lodg **N:** Best Western, Comfort Inn, E-Z 8 Motel, EconoLodge, Hampton Inn, TraveLodge
S: Holiday Inn Express (see our ad this page).

EXIT CALIFORNIA/ARIZONA

Motel 6, Super 8
AServ N: Mobil, Shell
S: 76
Med S: ✚ Hospital
ATM N: Mobil
S: Chevron, Texaco
Parks S: Miller Park(PLAY)
Other N: Bandy's Pharmacy & Medical Supplies(RX), Blythe Cinema, Madd Jax Coin Laundry
S: Oscars Stop' Shop

238 Bus10, Blythe, 7th Street
Gas N: Chevron(*), Gas(*)
Food N: Blimpie Subs & Salads, Foster's Freeze Hamburgers, Pizza Place
Lodg N: Astro Motel, **Blue Line Motel and Trailer Park**, Budget Inn, Comfort Suites Hotel, Sea Shell Motel
AServ N: Chief Auto Parts, Larry Green Chrys, Plym, Dodge, Jeep, Eagle
Med N: ✚ **Blythe Ambulence Service**
ATM N: Gas
Other N: Albertson's Food Market, Cuzzies Car Wash, **Rite Aid Pharmacy(RX)**, Vision Care

239 U.S. 95, Intake Blvd, Needles
Gas N: Shell(*), Texaco(*), Ultramar, Value Gas(D, LP)
Food N: Ruperto's (Mexican), **Steaks 'N Cakes**
Lodg N: Desert Winds Motel, El Rancho Verde Motel
AServ N: Ultramar, Value Gas
TServ N: **Ramsey International (CAT, Cummins, Detroit Diesel)**
RVCamp N: **Burton's Mobil Home & RV Park (.5 Miles)**
Parks N: **Mayflower Park**
S: **MacIntire Park**

241 Inspection Station (Westbound, All Vehicles Stop)
RVCamp S: **Riviera Camping**

243 Riviera Dr.
RVCamp S: **Riveria RV Resort and Marina**

↑CALIFORNIA

↓ARIZONA

1 Ehrenberg, Parker
TStop S: **Flying J Travel Plaza(*, SCALES) (CB Shop)**
Food S: **Wendy's (Flying J TS)**
Lodg S: **Best Western (Flying J)**
TServ S: **Flying J Travel Plaza(SCALES) (CB Shop)**
TWash S: **Flying J Travel Plaza (CB Shop)**
RVCamp N: **River Lagoon Resort**, **Villa Verde RV Park**

(3) **Inspection & Weigh Station (Eastbound)**

(3) **Weigh Station (Westbound)**

(4) **Rest Area (RR, HF, Phones, Picnic, P; Eastbound)**

EXIT ARIZONA

(4) **Rest Area (RR, HF, Phones, Picnic, P; Westbound)**

5 Tom Wells Road
FStop N: **Beacon(*, SCALES)**
ATM N: **Beacon**

11 Dome Rock Road

17 U.S. 95, AZ95, Bus10, Quartzsite
TStop N: **Pilot Travel Center(*, SCALES)**
S: **Love's(*, D)**
Gas N: Mobil(*, LP, 24)
Food N: Burger King (Mobil), **Dairy Queen (Pilot TS)**, **McDonald's**, **Subway (Pilot TS)**, The Main Event
S: **A & W Hot Dogs & More (Love's TS)**, **Baskin Robbins (Love's TS)**, **Taco Bell (Love's TS)**
AServ N: **American Custom Tire**, Steve's Auto
TServ N: **American Custom Tire**
RVCamp N: **B-10 Campground (.75 Miles)**, **Camping**, **Desert Trails**, **RV Dump(LP)**
S: **Buzzard Gardens RV Park(LP)**, **Desert Gardens RV Park (.5 Miles)**, **RV Lifestyles Sales and Service**

19 U.S. 95, AZ 95, Yuma, Parker, Quartzsite
RVCamp N: **Quartzsite RV Park**
S: **Clouds Trailer Park(LP)**, **Desert Edge RV Park**

26 Gold Nugget Road

31 U.S. 60E, Wickenburg, Prescott (Difficult Reaccess)

45 Vicksburg Road, To AZ 72W, Vicksburg, Parker
TStop S: **Tomahawk Auto Truck Stop(*, LP, SCALES)**
Food S: **Cactus Grill (Tomahawk Truck Stop)**
TServ S: **Jobski's Diesel Repair & Towing**

(52) **Rest Area (RR, Picnic, Vending, P; Westbound)**

(52) **Rest Area (RR, Picnic, Vending, P; Eastbound)**

53 Hovatter Road

69 Ave 75E

81 Salome Road, Harquahala Valley Rd.

(86) **Rest Area (RR, Picnic, P; Westbound, Closed, Under Renovation)**

(86) **Rest Area (RR, Picnic, P; Eastbound, Closed, Under Renovation)**

94 411th Ave, Tonopah
FStop S: **Chevron(*)**, **Texaco(*, LP)**

EXIT ARIZONA

Food S: **Joe & Alice's Restaurant(24)**, **Subway (Texaco)**
AServ S: Ed's Tire & Towing
TServ S: **Tonopah Joe's & Alice'sTruck Service**
RVCamp S: **Saddle Mountain RV Park (.5 Miles)**
ATM S: **Chevron, Joe & Alice's Restaurant**
Other S: **U.S. Post Office**

98 Wintersburg Road
TStop S: **AmBest Truck Stop(*)**
TServ S: **Rip Griffin Travel Center**

103 339th Ave
TStop S: **Rip Griffin Travel Center(*, LP, RV DUMP, SCALES) (Texaco)**
Food S: **Pizza Hut (Rip Griffin TS)**, **Subway (Rip Griffin TS)**
TServ S: **Rip Griffin Travel Center(SCALES) (Texaco)**
TWash S: **Rip Griffin Travel Center (Texaco)**

109 Sun Valley Parkway, Palo Verde Road

112 AZ 85, To I-8, Yuma, San Diego

114 Miller Road, Buckeye
TStop S: **Love's Truck Stop(*, SCALES)**
Food S: **A & W Hot Dogs & More (Love's)**, **Baskin Robbins (Love's)**, Burger King(PLAY) (Love's), **Taco Bell (Love's)**

121 Jackrabbit Trail
Gas S: 76(*)

124 Cotton Lane, To AZ Loop 303
RVCamp S: **Cotton Lane RV & Golf Resort (.25 Miles)**, **KOA Campgrounds**

126 Pebble Creek Pkwy, Estrella Pkwy
Parks S: **Estrella Park (7 Miles)**

128 Litchfield Road, Luke Air Force Base
Gas N: Mobil(*, D)
S: Mobil(*)
Food N: Blimpie Subs & Salads (Mobil), **Cracker Barrel**, Denny's, Wendy's
S: Arby's, Schlotzsky's Deli
Lodg N: Holiday Inn Express
AServ S: Yates Pontiac, GMC Trucks
Med S: ✚ **Hospital**
ATM S: **Albertson's Grocery**
Parks N: **Litchfield Parks**
Other N: **Wig Wam Outlet Store**
S: **Albertson's Grocery**

129 Dysart Road, Avondale
Gas N: Chevron(*)
Food S: Jerry's Restaurant, Mazzone's Restaurant & Lounge, **McDonald's(PLAY)**, Waffle House
Lodg S: Comfort Inn, **Super 8**
AServ N: **Wal-Mart(RX)**
S: S&S Tire
Other N: **Wal-Mart(RX)**

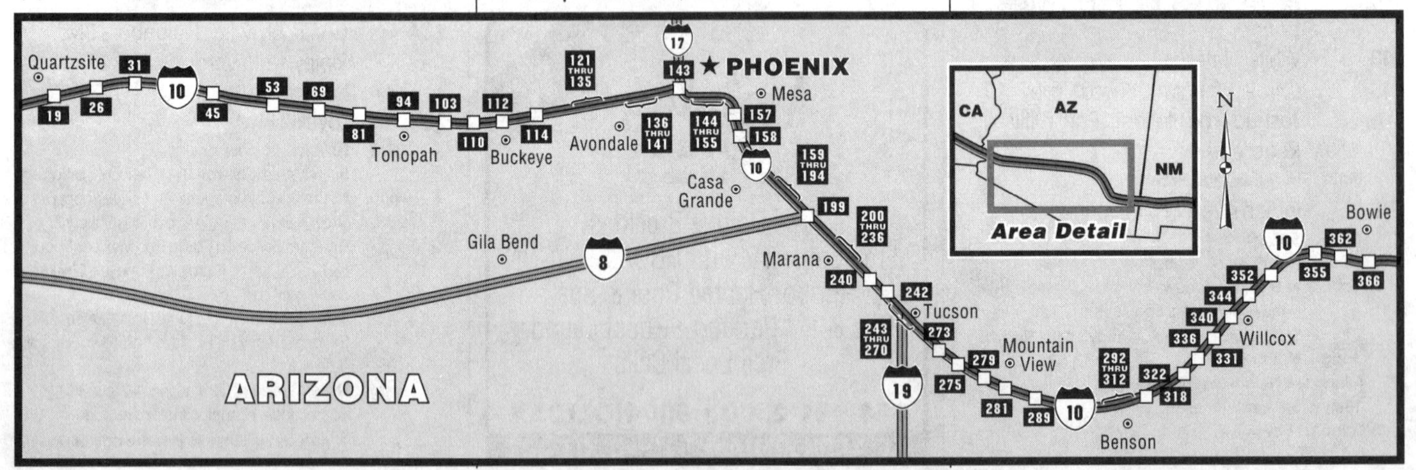

Bold red print shows RV & Bus parking available or nearby

EXIT ARIZONA

131 115th Ave, Cashion

132 107th Ave (Eastbound)

133A 99th Ave , 107th Ave., to AZ 101 Loop (Westbound)

134 91st Ave, Tolleson

135 83rd Ave
- Gas **N:** 76[*]
- Food **N:** Arby's, Burger King[PLAY], Jack-In-The-Box, Waffle House
- Lodg **N:** **EconoLodge**
- ATM **N:** 76
- Other **N:** Crystal Clean Car Wash[CW], **Sam's Club**

136 75th Ave
- Gas **N:** 76[*], Chevron[*, D, CW]
  S: Arco[*]
- Food **N:** Denny's
- AServ **N:** Pioneer Ford
- ATM **N:** 76
  S: Arco
- Other **N:** **Home Depot**, PetsMart, **Wal-Mart**[RX]

137 67th Ave
- Gas **N:** 76[*], Texaco[*, CW]
- ATM **N:** Texaco

138 59th Ave
- Gas **N:** 76[*, LP], Diamond Shamrock[*]
- Food **N:** Armandos Mexican[24]
  S: Waffle House, Whataburger[24]
- AServ **N:** Auto Zone Auto Parts
- TServ **S:** **Inland Kenworth**
- Other **N:** 7-11 Convenience Store, Weiss Guys Car Wash[CW]

139 51st Ave
- Gas **N:** Chevron[*, D, CW, 24], Citgo[*]
- Food **N:** Burger King, Domino's Pizza, Ed's Fish & Chips, La Fuente (Mexican), Las Cazuelas, Little China Restaurant, McDonald's[PLAY], Rice To You (Chinese), Sonic, Waffle House
  S: Carl Jr's Hamburgers, IHOP, Taco Bell
- Lodg **N:** Days Inn, Holiday Inn, Motel 6, Red Roof Inn
  S: Fairfield Inn, Hampton Inn, **Travelers Inn**
- AServ **N:** Discount Tire Company, Q-Lube, Tire Outlet (Bridgestone, Firestone)
- ATM **N:** Chevron
- Other **N:** Laundry, **Southwest Supermarkets**

140 43rd Ave
- Gas **N:** Citgo[*], Exxon[*, D, CW], Mobil[CW]
- Food **N:** Dunkin Donuts, KFC, Little Caesars Pizza, Mixteca (Mexican), Subway, Wendy's
- AServ **N:** AZ Accurate Transmission Specialist, Big O Tires, Midas Muffler & Brake, Mobil Lube Express
- ATM **N:** Citgo, Mobil
- Other **N:** **Food City**, Self Service Laundry, **Smitty's Supermarket**, **WalGreens Pharmacy**[RX]

142 27th Street (Eastbound)
- FStop **S:** **Pacific Pride (Credit)**
- Lodg **S:** Comfort Inn
- TServ **S:** **Arizona Great Basin Trucks Inc. (Detroit Diesel, Cummins, Volvo)**

141 35th Ave
- Gas **S:** 76[*], Texaco[*]
- Food **N:** Jack-In-The-Box, La Reyna Bakery, Rita's Mexican Food
- AServ **N:** R & Sons Auto Repair & Diesel
  S: S&G Auto Repair
- ATM **S:** Texaco
- Other **N:** ACE Hardware, **Southwest Supermarkets**

EXIT ARIZONA

143C U.S. 60, 19th St. (Westbound, Reaccess Eastbound Only)
- AServ **N:** AAPAK Automotive Air Parts & Kits, **Cryer King**
- TServ **N:** **Cryer King, Engine Warehouse (CAT, Cummins, Detroit)**
- Other **N:** Colliseum, Fairgrounds, Six Points Hardware & Electric (True Value)
  S: State Capitol

143AB I-17 North Flagstaff, I-17 South

144 7th Ave
- Gas **N:** 76[*]
  S: 76[*]
- Food **N:** Buffalo Brown's Wings and Things
  S: El Norteno (Mexican)

1829

RODEWAY INN

RODEWAY INN AIRPORT

124 S. 24TH ST. • PHOENIX, AZ

Restaurant/Lounge on Premises
Outdoor Pool • Exercise Room
Meeting/Banquet Facilities
Handicap Accessible
Truck/large Vehicle Parking
Airport Shuttle • Exterior Corridors

602-220-0044 • 800-228-2000

I-10E Exit 148 L on Jefferson
I-10E Exit 202 E to 24th St.

ARIZONA • I-10W • EXIT 150B

1667

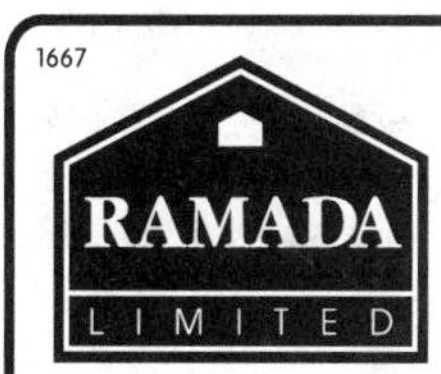

RAMADA LIMITED

RAMADA LIMITED
4120 E. Van Buren
Phoenix, AZ 85008

602-275-5746 • 800-272-6232

Minutes from Airport
Complimentary Shuttle Service to and from Airport & Nearby Restaurants
Free Deluxe Continental Breakfast
Outdoor Pool • Cable TV 67 Channels
Meeting/Banquet Facilities
Handicap Accessible
Truck/Large Vehicle Parking
Near Botanical Gardens
Visit Phoenix Zoo • Tempe Phoenix
See the Diamond Backs & Phoenix Suns at American West
See the Oakland A's @ the Municple Arena for Winter Camp
Free Tickets Available to the Nearby Dog Tracks
Papado Golf 2 mi
The Pueblo Grande Museum: Culture Park
Sun Devil's Stadium
Voice Mail & Data Port in Room

TOUR BUSES WELCOME

I-40 Exit 152S to E. Van Buren, Turn L Hotel 2 blocks on L

ARIZONA • I-10 • EXIT 152

EXIT ARIZONA

- Other **S:** Car Wash

145 Seventh St.
- Gas **N:** 76[*]
  S: 76[*], Texaco[*]
- Food **N:** Chico's Tacos, Einstein Bros Bagels, McDonald's, Starbucks Coffee, Subway, Whataburger[24]
  S: Taco de Juarez Mexican
- Med **N:** **Cigna Healthcare**
- ATM **N:** **ARCO Foods**[RX]
  S: Texaco
- Other **N:** **ARCO Foods**[RX]

146 16th St (Eastbound, Reaccess Westbound Only)
- Gas **S:** 76[*]
- Food **S:** Church's Chicken, Ramiro's Mexican Food[24], Taqueria 3 Amigos Restaurant
- AServ **S:** **Big K-Mart**
- Other **S:** **Big K-Mart**, The Wash & Dry Coin Laundry

147AB AZ 51N, Loop 202, Squaw Peak Pkwy (Limited Access Highway)

148 Jefferson St North, Washington St. South
- Food **N:** Carl Jr's Hamburgers
  S: Copper State Buffet, El Taurino Mexican & Spanish Food
- AServ **N:** Consolidated Tire Co.
  S: 20th St. Auto Parts
- Med **S:** **Hospital**
- Other **N:** Kachina Boats

149 Buckeye Road, Sky Harbor Center
- Food **N:** Roadhouse Restaurant (Rodeway Inn)
- Lodg **N:** Rodeway Inn
- AServ **N:** Charlie Case's American Car Care Center

150A Jct I-17N, Flagstaff

150B 24th St (Westbound, Reaccess Eastbound Only)
- Food **S:** Durado's (Best Western)
- Lodg **N:** Rodeway Inn Airport (see our ad this page)
  S: Best Western

151 University Dr.
- Lodg **N:** Extended Stay America, Holiday Inn Express, Radisson Hotel

152 40th St
- Gas **N:** Fina[D], Texaco[*]
  S: 76[*]
- Food **N:** The Sub Machine
  S: Burger King
- Lodg **S:** Ramada Limited Airport (see our ad this page)
- ATM **N:** Texaco
  S: Bank of America

153A AZ143N, Sky Harbor Airport
- Gas **S:** Texaco[*]
- Food **S:** A & W Hot Dogs & More (Texaco), Pine Cone Restaurant (Hampton Inn), Taco Bell Express (Texaco)
- Lodg **S:** Hampton Inn

153B Broadway Road, 52nd St (Difficult Reaccess)
- Lodg **N:** Comfort Suites Hotel, Ramada Plaza Hotel, Rodeway Inn

154 U.S. 60E, Scottsdale, Mesa-Globe (Limited Access Hwy)

EXIT ARIZONA

Lodg N: Days Inn (see our ad this page)
RVCamp N: Camping World (see our ad this page)

155 Baseline Road
Gas N: 76[*], Mobil, Texaco[*, D, LP]
Food N: Carl Jr's Hamburgers, Jack-In-The-Box (76), Rusty Pelican, SHONEY'S, Shoney's, Waffle House
S: Denny's, Enchilada's
Lodg N: AmeriSuites (see our ad this page), Fairfield Inn, Holiday Inn Express, Inn Suites Hotel, Residence Inn, Traveler's Inn
S: Hilton, Homestead Village
AServ N: Pro Auto Parts, Texaco
ATM N: 76
Other N: Arizona Mills Outlet Center

157 Elliot Road, Guadalupe
Gas S: Mobil[*]
Food N: Applebee's, Wendy's
S: Baskin Robbins, Caffe Boa, China Star Restaurant, KFC, Mathew's (Best Western), McDonald's[PLAY], Sarana Teppan Sushi Bar, Sub Factory, The Burrito Co.
Lodg N: Country Suites
S: Best Western, Quality Inn
AServ N: Autoplex
S: Checker Auto Parts
ATM S: Bank of America, Wells Fargo

158 Warner Road
Gas S: 76[*, D]
Other S: Fire Station

159 Ray Road
Gas S: Exxon[*, CW]
Food S: Cucina! Cucina!, El Paso BBQ, IHOP, Jack-In-The-Box, Jake's Pizza, Mimis Cafe, On The Border, Oscar's, Peter Piper Pizza, Romano's Macaroni Grill, Rubio's Baja Grill, Ruby Tuesday, TCBY, Valley Luna (Mexican), Wendy's
Lodg S: Extended Stay America
AServ S: Brake Masters, Sun Devil Auto Service
ATM S: Desert Schools Federal Credit Union
Other S: AMC 24 Theaters, Barnes & Noble Booksellers, Big K-Mart[RX], EyeMasters, Foothills Car Wash[CW], Hobby Town U.S.A., Kinko's Copies[24], Peppermint Bag, Petco

160 Chandler Blvd, Chandler
Gas N: Mobil[*, CW]
S: Chevron[*, CW]
Food N: Damon's, Denny's, Marie Callender's, Perkin's Family Restaurant, Pizza Hut (Mobil), Whataburger
S: Cousins' Sub's (Chevron), Cracker Barrel
Lodg N: Fairfield Inn, Hampton Inn, Homewood Suites Hotel, Red Roof Inn, Southgate Motel, Super 8, Wyndham Garden Hotel
S: Holiday Inn Express, HomeGate Studios & Suites, La Quinta
Med N: Hospital

162 Maricopa Road

164 Queen Creek Road, AZ 347S

167 Riggs Road, Sun Lakes

175 AZ587N, Chandler, Gilbert, Casa Blanca Road, Sacaton
RVCamp S: Camping

EXIT ARIZONA

(182) Rest Area (RR, Phones, Picnic, P; Eastbound)

(183) Rest Area (RR, Phones, Picnic, P; Westbound)

185 AZ187, AZ387, Sacaton, Florence
RVCamp S: Leisure Valley RV Park (2 Miles)

190 McCartney Road

194 AZ287, Bus. Loop 10, Casa Grande, Coolidge
Gas S: Arco[*], Chevron[*]
Food S: Burger King, Cracker Barrel, Dairy Queen (Chevron)
RVCamp S: Fiesta Grande an RV Resort (1.8 Miles)
ATM S: Arco
Other S: Factory Stores of America

198 AZ 84, Casa Grande
Food S: Wendy's
RVCamp S: Campground Buena Tierra
Other S: Tanger Outlet Center

199 Jct I-8W, San Diego

200 Sunland Gin Road, Arizona City
TStop N: Petro[*, SCALES] (ATM), Pilot Travel Center[*, SCALES] (Subway)
Gas N: Petro[*] (ATM)
S: Shell[*], Texaco[*, D]
Food N: Burger King, Eva's Mexican, Iron Skillet (Petro), Subway[SCALES] (Pilot)
S: Golden Restaurant (Motel 6)
Lodg N: Days Inn, Ramada Inn, Sunland Inn
S: Motel 6
AServ S: Shell, Texaco
TServ N: Petro[SCALES] (ATM), Rocha's Truck Tire & Diesel[24]
TWash N: Petro (ATM), Pilot Travel Center (Subway)
RVCamp N: Las Colinas MH-RV Resort (.25 Miles, Senior resort)
ATM N: Pilot Travel Center (Subway)

203 Toltec Road, Eloy
TStop S: T/A TravelCenters of America[SCALES]
FStop N: Circle K[*]
S: Pizza Hut
Gas N: Chevron[*]
S: Exxon[*]

333 W. JUANITA AVE.
MESA, ARIZONA
TRUCK/ LARGE VEHICLE PARKING
NEWLY RENOVATED
DAYS INN
1400
Restaurant on Premises
Free Deluxe Contential Breakfast, Local Calls & The Movie Channel
Kids Stay and Eat Free
Outdoor Pool • Spa & Sauna • Exercise Room
Meeting Facilities • Pets Welcome • Coin Laundry
Refrigerators in All Rooms • Interior Corridors
602-844-8900 • 800-674-8429
ARIZONA • I-10 • EXIT 154

EXIT ARIZONA

Food N: Carl Jr's Hamburgers, McDonald's[24], Mexican Food Restaurant, Waffle House
S: A & W Restaurant (TA Travel Center), Country Pride (TA Travel Center), Taco Bell (TA Travel Center)
Lodg N: Super 8, Tol Tec Inn (Mexican Restaurant)
AServ N: Service & Tire[24]
TServ N: Service & Tire[24], Truck Service[D]
S: T/A TravelCenters of America[SCALES]
TWash N: Circle K
S: T/A TravelCenters of America
ATM N: Chevron, Circle K
S: T/A TravelCenters of America
Other N: CB Radio Store

208 Eloy, St John Blvd, Sunshine Blvd.
TStop S: Flying J Travel Plaza[*, D, LP, RV DUMP, SCALES]
Gas S: Flying J Travel Plaza[*, D, RV DUMP]
Food S: Cookery (Flying J TStop)
TServ N: Regan's Diesel Service[24]
ATM S: Flying J Travel Plaza

211A AZ 84E; AZ 87S
RVCamp S: KOA Campgrounds (1 Mile)

211B AZ84W, AZ87N, Coolidge, Florence
Parks N: Casa Grande Ruins National Monument

212 Picacho (Westbound, Difficult Reaccess)
Gas N: Exxon[*, LP]
Lodg N: Motel 9, Picacho Motel
AServ N: Exxon
RVCamp S: KOA Campgrounds[*, LP]
Other N: U.S. Post Office

(217) Rest Area (RR, Picnic, P; Eastbound)

219 Picacho Peak Road
Gas N: Citgo[*]
Food N: Dairy Queen (Citgo)
S: Arizona Nut House, Picacho Peak Grill & Cantina
AServ S: No Name
RVCamp S: Picacho Peak RV Resort
Parks S: Picacho Peak State Park
Other S: Peak Convenience Mart

226 Red Rock

232 Pinal Air Park Road

236 Marana Road
Gas S: 76[*, LP], Chevron[*, D, LP] (Restaurant)
Food S: Don's Eats, Georgia's Family Restaurant, Pizza R & R Express
AServ S: NAPA Auto Parts, Pierce Auto Service
RVCamp S: Valley Of the Sun
ATM S: 76, Stockmen's Bank
Other S: Marana Grocery

240 Tangerine Road
RVCamp N: A Bar A Campgrounds (.25 Miles)

243 Cortaro, Avra Valley Road, Rillito

246 Cortaro Road
Gas S: Shell[*, D]
Food S: Burger King[PLAY], Cracker Barrel, McDonald's

248 Ina Road
Gas N: Chevron[*, 24], Citgo[*]
S: Exxon[*, LP], Texaco[*, D, LP]
Food N: Donut Wheel, Long John Silver, Perkins Family Restaurant[24], Waffle House
S: Denny's (Holiday Inn Express)
Lodg N: Motel 6
S: Comfort Inn, Holiday Inn Express, Red Roof Inn
AServ N: Car Quest Ina Auto Parts, Fletcher's Auto Service, Jiffy Lube, Spectrum Collision Center &

Bold red print shows RV & Bus parking available or nearby

EXIT ARIZONA

Car Wash
ATM S: Exxon, Texaco

250 Orange Grove
RVCamp N: The South Forty RV Ranch (.5 Miles)

Exit **(251)** Sunset Road (Eastbound, Difficult Reaccess)

252 El Camino Del Cerro, Ruth Rauss (Westbound)
TStop S: National(*, LP, 24)
Food S: Jenks Cafe(24), Mr. Catfish Restaurant, National
AServ S: Car Wash, Gonzo Auto Service, Star Automotive
TServ S: Industrial Radiator Service, National(24), Tire Industries, Truck & RV Wash
ATM S: Quick Mart
Other S: Quick Mart

254 Prince Road
Gas N: Citgo(*), Diamond Shamrock(*, D)
TServ N: Cummins Diesel
RVCamp N: Silent Wheels, Whispering Palms RV Trailer Park (.5 Miles)
ATM N: Citgo, Diamond Shamrock

255 AZ77N, Bus10, Miracle Mile
Gas N: Citgo(*)
Food N: Overpass Cafe
Lodg N: Dream House Motel, El Molino, Vista del Sol
AServ N: S&J Garage
TServ N: International Dealer, Tucson Truck Parts
RVCamp N: Romero RV Park, Sandy's RV Center(LP)
ATM N: Citgo

256 Grant Road
Gas S: 76(*)
Food N: Sonic Drive In
S: IHOP, Kenny Roger's Roasters, Waffle House
Lodg S: Budgetel Inn, Hampton Inn, Rodeway Inn (see our ad this page), Shoney's Inn
AServ S: Exxon(*)
RVCamp N: All RV Service Center Inc.(LP) (.8 Miles), Desert Diesel (.3 Miles)
ATM S: 76
Other N: Century Park Cinemas

257 Speedway Blvd.
Gas S: Arco(*)
AServ N: Gin's Oil Express, Lebo's Radiator, Rain Drop Alternator & Starter
ATM N: 7-11 Convenience Store
S: Arco
Parks S: Santa Cruz River Park
Other N: 7-11 Convenience Store

257A St. Mary's Rd.
Gas N: 76(*, D, LP)
S: Texaco(*, D, LP)
Food S: Burger King(PLAY), Denny's, Furr's Family Dining
Lodg S: La Quinta Inn
AServ N: 76
S: Texaco
ATM N: 76

258 Convention Center, Congress Street, Broadway
Gas N: 76(*)
Food N: Carlos Murphy's Mexican, Holiday Inn
S: Carl Jr's Hamburgers
Lodg N: Holiday Inn
S: Days Inn
ATM N: 76

259 22nd St, Starr Pass Blvd.
Food S: Kettle(24) (Holiday Inn Express), Waffle House
Lodg S: Comfort Inn, Holiday Inn Express, Howard Johnson (Restaurant), Motel 6, Super 8, Travel Inn
AServ S: El Campo

EXIT ARIZONA

260 I-19S, Nogales

261 4th Ave, 6th Ave, Bus 19
Gas N: Chevron(*)
Food N: Carrows Restaurant
S: Arby's, Bagels and Donuts, Burger King(PLAY), El Indio, Jack-In-The-Box, Maria's Fine Mexican Cuisine, McDonald's(PLAY)
Lodg N: Budget Inn, Econolodge, Star Motel
AServ N: Discount Tire Company
S: Midas, Pete's Auto Repair
Med S: VA Medical Center
Other S: McLellan's Drugs, Southwest Supermarkets

262 Park Ave, Benson Hwy.
Gas S: Arco(*), Chevron(*), Texaco(*, D)
Food S: JB's Restaurant (Howard Johnson), Navarone Restaurant, Philly's Finest, Waffle House
Lodg S: Howard Johnson(*), Motel 6, Motel 6, Rodeway Inn
AServ S: Chevron, Texaco
Med S: 7-11 Convenience Store
ATM S: Arco

263 Kino Pkwy. (Difficult Reaccess)
Med N: Hospital

264 Palo Verde Road
Food N: Carl Jr's Hamburgers, Denny's (Red Roof Inn)
S: All Star (Ramada Inn), Arby's, McDonald's
Lodg N: Crossland Economy Studios, Days Inn, Fairfield Inn, Holiday Inn, Red Roof Inn
S: Ramada Inn
RVCamp N: Camping World (see our ad this page)
S: Beaudry RV Center(LP), La Mesa
Med N: Hospital

265 Alvernon Way

267 Bus Loop10, Tucson Int Airport, Valencia Road

268 Craycroft Road
TStop N: Triple T Truck Stop(*, LP, CW, RV DUMP, SCALES)
Gas N: 76(*)
Food N: Triple T Truck Stop
TServ N: Triple T Truck Stop(SCALES)
S: Tucson Diesel Truck Repair
RVCamp N: Crazy Horse Campground (.25 Miles)

CAMPING WORLD®
Exit 264
3220 Irvington Rd • Tucson, AZ
1-800-298-1029
1838

EXIT ARIZONA

ATM N: 76, Triple T Truck Stop

269 Wilmot Road
AServ S: Wilmot Auto World
RVCamp N: Camping

270 Kolb Road
RVCamp S: Voyager

273 Rita Road
Parks S: Pima County Fair Grounds

275 Houghton Road
RVCamp N: Cactus Country RV Resort (.75 Miles)
Parks N: Saguaro National Monument

279 Vail Road, Wentworth Road
Parks N: Colossal Cave

281 AZ83S, Sonoita, Patagonia

289 Marsh Station Road

292 Empirita Road

297 J - Six, Ranch Road, Mescal Road
FStop N: Bell Gas(*, LP, 24)
AServ N: Big Sky Auto Repair, Hagen Auto & Tire Center

299 Skyline Road

302 AZ90, Fort Huachuca, Sierra Vista
Gas S: Shell(*, D)
Food S: McDonald's, Subway
Lodg S: Holiday Inn Express
ATM S: Shell
Parks S: Fort Huachuca National Historic Sight

303 Business Loop 10, AZ80, Benson Rd., Douglas (Eastbound)
Food S: Red's Cafe
AServ S: B & P Auto Repair, Super Suds Car Wash, Xpress Lube
RVCamp S: Pardner's RV Park
Other S: Benson Bowl

304 Ocotillo St.
Gas S: Chevron(*), Exxon(*)
Food N: Denny's
S: Burger King(PLAY), Plaza Restaurant (Exxon)
Lodg N: Days Inn, Super 8
S: Best Western
TServ S: Dutchman Diesel Service
RVCamp N: Benson I-10, KOA Campgrounds (.85 Miles)
S: A thru Z RV & Trailer Park, Butterfield RV Resort, Dillon's Corral & Sales, KOA Campgrounds (1 Mile), Quarter Horse RV Park (.75 Miles)
Med S: Hospital
Parks N: Red Barn RV Park(LP)
Other S: Louie's Groceries

306 AZ80, Bus10, Pomerene Road, Benson Road
Parks S: Douglas National Monument, Pato Blanco Lakes (1 Mile)

312 Sibyl Road
Gas S: Stuckey's(*, LP)

318 Dragoon Road

320 Rest Area (RR, Picnic, Vending, P; Eastbound)

(321) Rest Area (RR, Phones, Picnic, P; Westbound)

322 Johnson Road
Gas S: Citgo(*) (Dairy Queen)
Food S: Dairy Queen (Citgo)
Other S: The Thing? Museum (Citgo)

331 U.S. 191S, Douglas, Sunsites
Parks S: Cochise Strong Hold

336 Bus10, Willcox

Bold red print shows RV & Bus parking available or nearby

EXIT — ARIZONA

FStop	S: Exxon(*, LP)
AServ	S: Exxon
RVCamp	S: Fort Willcox Leisure Park (1.25 Miles)

340 AZ186, Rex Allen Dr, Fort Grant

TStop	N: Rip Griffin Travel Center(*, LP, RV DUMP, SCALES)
	S: Chevron(*)
FStop	S: Mobil(*)
Gas	S: 76(*)
Food	N: Subway (Rip Griffen's), Taco Bell (Rip Griffin's TStop)
	S: Burger King, KFC, McDonald's(PLAY), Pizza Hut, Plaza Restaurant (Chevron), R & R Pizza Express
Lodg	N: Super 8
	S: Best Western (Solarium), Days Inn, Motel 6
AServ	S: Big O Tires, Dick's Tire and Auto(LP)
TServ	S: Big O Tires, Chevron
TWash	N: 340 Truck Wash
RVCamp	N: Magic Circle
	S: Grande Vista RV Park (.5 Miles), Lifestyle RV Park (1 Mile)
Med	S: + Northern Cochise Hospital
ATM	N: Rip Griffin Travel Center
	S: 76, Chevron, Mobil
Parks	N: Chiri Cahua National Monument
Other	S: Bob's Grocery, Safeway Grocery(RX)

344 Bus10 loop, Willcox (Difficult Reaccess)

TServ	S: Ed's Truck Services, Willcox Diesel Service

352 U.S. 191N, Safford

355 U.S. 191N, Safford

362 Bus10, Bowie

RVCamp	N: Mt. View RV Park(D, LP) (.5 Miles)

366 Bus10 Loop, Bowie

Gas	N: Texaco(*)
Food	N: Baskin Robbins (Texaco), Subway (Texaco)
RVCamp	S: Alaskan RV Park
Parks	N: Fort Bowie Historic Sight

378 Bus Loop 10, San Simon

TStop	N: 4-K(*, RV DUMP, SCALES)
Gas	N: 4-K(*, RV DUMP), Texaco(*, LP)
Food	N: Kactus Cafe (4 Km)
AServ	N: Texaco
TServ	N: 4-K(SCALES)

382 Bus10, Portal Road, San Simon

(383) **Weigh Station (Eastbound)**

(384) **Weigh Station (Westbound)**

(388) **Rest Area (RR, Picnic, Grills, P; Eastbound, Under Construction)**

(389) **Rest Area (RR, Picnic, Grills, Vending, P; Westbound)**

EXIT — ARIZONA/NEW MEXICO

390 Cavot Road

↑ARIZONA

↓NEW MEXICO

3 Steins

5 NM80S, Road Forks

TStop	S: Desert West Travel Center, U.S.A. Truck Stop(*, SCALES)
Gas	S: Desert West Travel Center
Food	S: Shady Grove Restaurant & Mall (USA Truck Stop)
Lodg	S: Desert West (Restaurant)
AServ	S: Desert West Travel Center
TServ	S: U.S.A. Truck Stop(SCALES)
RVCamp	S: RV Park

11 NM338S, Animas

15 Gary

20B West Motel Dr

TStop	N: Love's Truck Stop(*, SCALES)
Food	N: A & W Hot Dogs & More (Love's Truck Stop), Denny's (Days Inn), Taco Bell (Love's Truck Stop)
Lodg	N: Days Inn & Suites
ATM	N: Love's Truck Stop
Other	N: Goldharl Outpost

20A **New Mexico Info. Center & Rest Area (RR, Phones, RV Dump, P; Eastbound)**

22 NM494, Main St.

Gas	N: Shell(CW)
	S: Chevron, Diamond Shamrock(*), Exxon(*, LP), Snappy Mart(*, 24), Texaco(*, D)
Food	N: Dairy Queen, McDonald's, Subway
	S: KFC, Kranberry's (Best Western), Motel 10, Pizza King
Lodg	S: Best Western, Holiday Inn Express, Motel 10, Super 8
AServ	S: Exxon
TServ	N: Ray's Tires
RVCamp	S: KOA Campgrounds
Parks	N: Gilla Cliff Dwellings
Other	N: Greyhound Bus Station, Saucedo's Supermarket

(24) **Weigh Station**

24 Bus Loop 10, E Motel Dr

Gas	N: Texaco(*)
AServ	N: DC Auto Repair, Turner Tire
RVCamp	N: Bill's Freeway RV Park (.25 Miles), New Freeway RV Park
	S: Chaparral Trailer Park (1 Mile)

EXIT — NEW MEXICO

29 Unnamed

34 NM113, Playas

42 Separ

FStop	S: Separ Gas
Gas	S: Chevron(*)
Food	S: Windmeal Diner
TServ	S: Separ Gas

49 NM146, Hachita, Antelope Wells

51 Continental Divide

(53) **Rest Area (RR, Picnic, RV Dump, P; Eastbound)**

55 Quincy

(61) **Rest Area (RR, Picnic, RV Dump, P; Westbound)**

62 Gage

FStop	S: Citgo(*)
Food	S: Dairy Queen (Citgo)
RVCamp	S: Butterfield Station

68 NM418

TStop	S: Savoy Truck Stop(*)
Gas	S: Stuckey's(*)
Food	S: Savoy Cafe (Savoy TStop)

81 BL10, West Motel Dr.

TStop	S: Deming Truck Terminal(*) (Restaurant), Truck Stop
Gas	S: Chevron(*, CW), Conoco(*), Diamond Shamrock(*, D), Texaco(*)
Food	S: Arby's, Burger Time, El Camino Real, Hong Kong Restaurant, Sonic
Lodg	S: Best Western, Budget Motel, Super 8, Wagon Wheel Motel, Western Motel (Restaurant)
AServ	S: Chevron, Texaco
TServ	S: Deming Truck Terminal (Restaurant)
RVCamp	S: 81 Palms (1 Mile), Jackson Ford-Lincoln Mercury, Inc. (1.1 Miles), Windy West RV Parts & Service
ATM	S: Conoco, Deming Truck Terminal (Restaurant)
Other	S: Fireworks

82A U.S. 180, Silver City

Gas	N: Fina(*, D)
	S: Exxon(*), Phillips 66(*)
Food	N: Blake's Lotaburger
	S: Burger King(PLAY), Cactus Cafe, China Restaurant, Coffee Pot Mexican Restaurant, Denny's, K-Bob's Steakhouse, Pizza Hut, Si Senor
AServ	S: Budget Tire Store(LP), Dunne's Automotive, Exxon, Harry's Auto Electric, PBQ Lube & Oil, Reyies Lube, Oil, & Tire Service, Tire Repair & Ten Minute Car Wash
RVCamp	S: Hitchin' Post RV Park
Other	N: Servi Gas(LP)

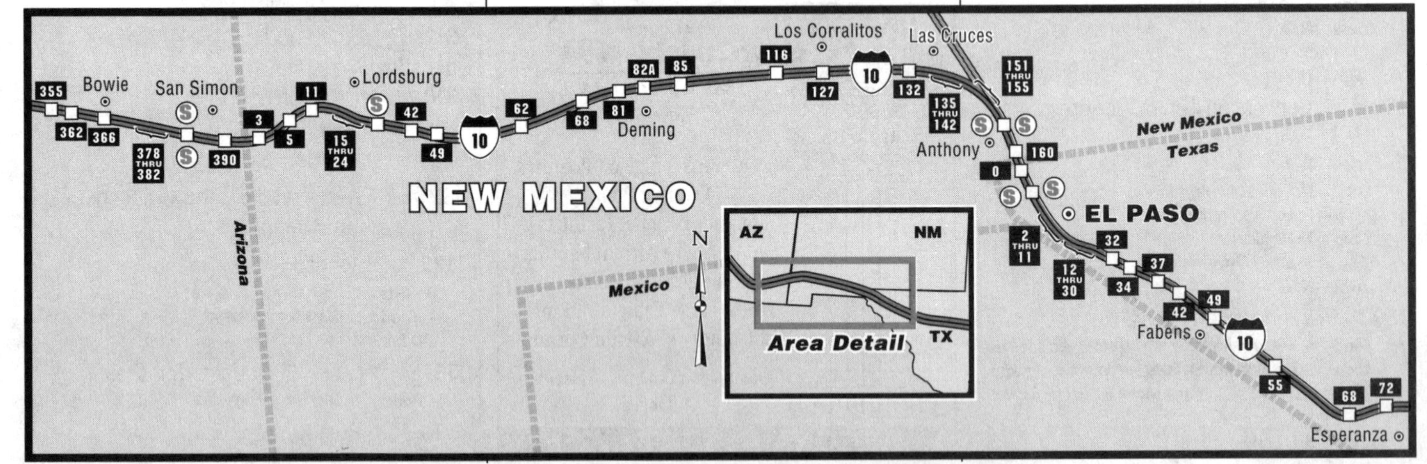

Bold red print shows RV & Bus parking available or nearby

EXIT NEW MEXICO

82B Cedar St
- Gas: N: Texaco(*, D, LP); S: Fina
- Food: S: KFC, La Fonda, Subway
- Lodg: S: Mirador Motel (Restaurant)
- AServ: S: C & C Auto Service, Checker Auto Parts, Fina, Fred's Radiator Service, NAPA Auto Parts
- ATM: S: **Furr's Grocery Store**
- Other: S: Deming Police Department, **Furr's Grocery Store**, Wash Land

85 Bus Loop 10, East Motel Dr.
- Gas: S: Chevron(*, D), Texaco(*, D, 24)
- Lodg: S: **Holiday Inn (Restaurant)**, Motel 6
- AServ: S: Chevron, Dodge Chrysler Plymouth
- RVCamp: S: **A Deming Roadrunner RV Park (1 Mile)**, **A Little Vineyard RV Park (1 Mile)**, **Dream Catcher**, **Sunrise RV Park (1 Mile)**, **Wagon Wheel RV Park (1 Mile)**

102 Akela
- Parks: S: **Rock Hound State Park**

116 NM549
- Gas: S: Gas Station(*)
- Food: S: **Old Fashioned Hamburgers**

Exit (121) Inspection Point (Westbound)

127 Corralitos Road
- Gas: N: **Chevron(*)**

132 Las Cruces International Airport
- TStop: S: **Loves Truck Stop(SCALES)**
- Food: S: Taco Bell Express (Love's TStop), Winchells Donuts (Love's TStop)
- ATM: S: **Loves Truck Stop**

135 U.S. 70E, West Picacho Ave.
- RVCamp: S: **Best View RV Park (1.5 Miles)**

139 NM292, Motel Blvd
- TStop: N: **Pilot Travel Center(*, SCALES)**, **T/A TravelCenters of America(*, SCALES, 24)**
- FStop: S: **Porter's**
- Gas: N: Shell(*); S: Chevron
- Food: N: **Subway (Pilot Travel Center)**

EXIT NEW MEXICO

- S: **Dick's Restaurant (Coachlight Motel)**
- Lodg: S: **Coachlight Motel**
- AServ: N: **T/A TravelCenters of America(24)**; S: Aguirre Auto Center, Chevron
- TServ: N: **T/A TravelCenters of America(SCALES, 24)**
- TWash: N: **Pilot Travel Center**, **T/A TravelCenters of America**
- RVCamp: S: **Coachlight RV Park**
- ATM: N: **Pilot Travel Center**

140 NM28, Mesilla, Historic Mesilla Plaza
- Gas: N: Chevron(*, 24); S: Conoco(*)
- Food: N: Blake's Lotaburger, Burger Time, **Cracker Barrel**, Dairy Queen, Domino's Pizza, Eddie's Bar & Grill (Best Western), **McDonald's(PLAY)**; S: Gadsden Purchase, Lantern Restaurant (Conoco), Truck Farm
- Lodg: N: **Best Western**, Budgetel Inn, **Hampton Inn**, **La Quinta Inn**, Vancouver Suites
- AServ: N: Chevron(24), On Sale Tire Stores Inc.
- RVCamp: N: **Camping World (see our ad this page)**; S: **Holiday RV Superstore(LP) (.2 Miles)**, **RV Doc's(LP)**, **S & H RV Home Center**, **Siesta (.5 Miles)**
- ATM: N: 1st National Bank

142 Main St , New Mexico State University
- Gas: N: Chevron, Chevron(*), Chevron(*), Diamond Shamrock(*, D, LP)
- Food: N: Blimpie's Subs (Chevron), Chilitos, **Dick's Restaurant**, Sunset Bar & Grill (Days Inn), Whataburger; S: Bravos Cafe, Karol's Candy Ranch, Sky's the Limit Coffee & Bakery
- Lodg: N: **Comfort Inn**, **Days Inn (see our ad this page)**, **Holiday Inn**, Holiday Inn Express, **Motel 6**, **Super 8**
- AServ: N: Adam's Turbo Lube, B & G Automotive, Chevron, Chevron, Saunder's Garage
- RVCamp: N: **Bogarts RV Service(LP)**, **Dalmont's RV & Trailer Corral**, **Trailor Corral**
- Med: N: **Hospital**
- ATM: N: Chevron
- Other: N: Motor Sports Dealer, Sheriff Dept.

Exit (145) Jct I-25 North, Albuquerque

151 Mesquite

155 NM227, Vado, Berino
- TStop: S: **Fina(*, LP, 24)**, **Golden West(*) (Restaurant)**, **Travel City(*, 24)**
- Food: S: **Hot Stuff Pizza (Fina TS)**, **Sally's Cafe (Fina TS)**, **Smash Hit Sub and Hot Stuff Pizza (Fina TStop)**, **Smash Hit Subs (Fina TS)**, **Travel City**
- TServ: S: **Fina(24)**, **Golden West (Restaurant)**, **Shop Truck & Tire Repair**, **Travel City(24)**
- RVCamp: N: **Vado RV Part**
- ATM: S: **Fina**

(159) **Weigh Station (Eastbound)**

(160) **Weigh Station (Westbound)**

162 NM 404, Anthony, Chaparral
- RVCamp: N: **El Paso- West RV Park (.5 Miles)**

(164) **New Mexico Welcome Center (RR, HF, Phones, Picnic, RV Dump, P; Westbound)**

EXIT NEW MEXICO/TEXAS

↑NEW MEXICO

↓TEXAS

0 Fm1905, Anthony
- TStop: N: **Flying J Travel Plaza(*, LP, SCALES)**
- Gas: N: **Flying J Travel Plaza(*)**; S: Chevron(*, D), **Exxon(*, D)**
- Food: N: **The Cookery (Flying J Travel Plaza)**; S: **Burger King (Exxon)**, Sundance Deli (Chevron)
- Lodg: N: **Super 8**; S: **Holiday Inn Express**
- AServ: N: **S & W Refrigeration**
- TServ: N: **S & W Refrigeration**
- TWash: S: **Truck Wash**
- ATM: N: **Flying J Travel Plaza**; S: Chevron, **Exxon**
- Other: S: **Big 8 Foods**, Synergy Gas(LP), **Wet N' Wild Water Park**

(0) **Texas Welcome Center, Rest Area (RR, Phones, P; Eastbound)**

Exit (1) Truck Check Station (Westbound)

2 Westway, Vinton
- FStop: N: **Petro: 2(*, RV DUMP, SCALES)**
- Gas: S: Circle N(*, 24)
- Food: N: **Blimpie Subs & Salads (Petro 2)**, La Parrilla Mexican, Rinconcito(24) (Mexicano), Tortilleria y Bakery, Westway Lounge & Bakery, Yvette's Bakery
- AServ: S: Vinton Auto Repair
- TServ: N: **Petrolube (Petro: 2)**
- Other: N: Westway Food Store

6 Loop 375, Trans Mountain Road, Canutillo Road
- FStop: N: **Texaco(*, 24)**
- Food: N: **TCBY (Texaco)**, **Taco Bell (Texaco)**
- Parks: N: **Franklin Mountain State Park**

8 Artcraft Rd.

9 Redd Road

11 TX 20, Mesa St
- Gas: N: Chevron(LP), Diamond Shamrock(*)
- Food: N: Carrows(24) (La Quinta Inn), Chili's, Ci Ci's Pizza, **Cracker Barrel**, Denny's, K-Bob's Steakhouse, Long John Silver, Mei Li's Chinese Food, Renelli's; S: **Burger King**, Luby's Cafeteria, McDonald's(PLAY), Peter Piper Pizza, Taco Cabana, Village Inn
- Lodg: N: **Best Value Inn**, Budgetel Inn, Comfort Inn, La Quinta Inn, Red Roof Inn; S: **Days Inn**, **Travelers Inn**
- AServ: N: Chevron, Pep Boys Auto Center; S: Complete Auto Repair, ProntoLube
- ATM: N: Chase Bank; S: El Paso Area Teachers Federal Credit Union, NationsBank
- Other: N: Bookmark Used Books, Nationwide Vision Center, **The Home Depot**, **Wal-Mart(24, RX) (Vision Center)**; S: 4 Seasons Coin Car Wash(CW), **Big 8 Foods**, El Paso Police Dept., **Sam's Club**

12 Resler Dr (Westbound, Reaccess Eastbound Only)

13 Sunland Park Dr, U.S. 85, Paisano Dr.
- Gas: S: Exxon
- Food: N: Carino's, HomeTown Buffet, Olive Garden, Red Lobster, T.G.I. Friday's; S: Carrera's (Holiday Inn)

EXIT TEXAS

Lodg S: Best Western, Comfort Suites Hotel, Holiday Inn (see our ad this page), Sleep Inn, Studio PLUS
AServ S: Exxon
ATM N: NationsBank
Other N: **Barnes & Noble**, **Office Depot**, **Sunland Park Mall**, **Target**

16 Executive Center Blvd
Food N: Ramada Inn, The Cafe (Ramada Inn)
Lodg N: Ramada Inn

18A Schuster Ave, UT El Paso
Med N: **Hospital**
Other N: University of Texas El Paso

18B Porfirio Diaz St, Franklin Ave.
Gas N: Circle K(*)
ATM N: Circle K

19A TX 20, Downtown Convention Center (Westbound, Difficult Reaccess)
Gas S: TraveLodge
Food S: China Pearl Express
Lodg S: International Hotel
AServ N: Dalton Brake & Alignment
S: AAMCO Transmission
ATM S: Bank CNB, NationsBank

19B Dowtown, Convention Center, Juarez Mexico International Port of Entry (Difficult Reaccess)
Lodg S: Hotel Gardner, TraveLodge Hotel
Med N: **Hospital**

19 Downtown, TX 20, Convention Center (Eastbound)
Food S: Jack-In-The-Box
Lodg S: International Hotel
ATM S: Sunwest Bank
Other S: **City Hall**, Old San Francisco Historic District

20 Dallas St (Westbound, Difficult Reaccess)
Gas N: Diamond Shamrock(*, D), Diamond Shamrock(*, D)
Food N: Amigos (Mexican), Church's Chicken, La Cuesta, Subway
AServ N: Sun City Tire & Wheel
ATM N: Diamond Shamrock, Diamond Shamrock

21 Piedras St
Gas N: Chevron(*)
Food N: Adriana's Restaurant, Anita's Restaurant, Baskin Robbins, Burger King, McDonald's(PLAY)
AServ N: Brantley Auto Center, Grand Prix Auto Service, Hi Tech Auto Center, Midway Body Shop
ATM N: Chevron
Other N: El Paso Police Headquarters, Q Food Mart, U.S. Post Office

EXIT TEXAS

22A Loop 478, Copla St
Gas N: Diamond Shamrock(*), Fina(*)
Food N: Church's Chicken, KFC, Tony's Place
S: La Colonial Tortilleria
AServ N: Copia Auto Service, One Stop Auto Service, Pilo's Automotive, Willie's Body Shop
S: Carberator Equipment of El Paso(LP), Frank Auto, Johnnie's Complete Collision Repair, R.E. Tires
ATM N: Diamond Shamrock, Fina
Other N: **Furr's Grocery Store**
S: Copia Fruit Stand, Economy Hardware & Plumbing

22B U.S. 54, Patriot Freeway, Alamogordo, Juarez, Fort Bliss (Limited Access Highway)

23A Raynolds St.

Kids Under 12 Eat Free!
1136
Holiday Inn®
Sunland Park & I-10 West
• Only Full Service Hotel with Restaurant and Two Bars on Westside • Across from Shopping Mall & Casino • Outdoor Pool with Heated Whirlpool • Luxury Accommodations with in Room Coffee, Iron and Ironing Board, Hairdryer, 25" Color Remote TV's HBO and Pay Per View Movies
915-833-2900 For Reservations: 800-HOLIDAY
EL PASO ,TEXAS • I-10 • EXIT 13

Knights Inn®
6308 Montana Ave.
El Paso, TX 79925
915-778-6661
Airway Blvd (north), go 1/4 mile turn left on Montana, go 1/4 mile and hotel is on the left.
¥ 5 Miles from Downtown & Mexico
¥ Non-Smoking Roooms
¥ Outdoor Pool
¥ Free Continental Breakfast
¥ Tours to Mexico
¥ 1/2 Mile from the Airport
¥ Free Laundry Service for Extended Stays
KN7992
TEXAS • I-10 • EXIT 23B

EXIT TEXAS

Food S: Arby's, Carmen's Restaurant
Lodg S: **Motel 6**
AServ S: Central Auto Supply
Med S: **Hospital**

23B Carlsbad, U.S. 62, U.S. 180 , Paisano Dr
Food N: Alexandro's Fine Mexican Food
Lodg N: Budget Inn, Knights Inn (see our ad this page)
AServ N: Casa Trowbridge Collision Center, El Paseo Auto Parts, V C Body Shop
S: Aldi Auto Transmissions, Chespy's, Day Transmission, Diesel Auto Electric Service, Plaza Transmission, Puasis Body Shop, Tech Auto Honda, Acura Service, Tune Automotive Center
Other N: U-Haul Center(LP)
S: **Animal Clinic**, **El Paso Zoo**

24A Trowbridge Dr. (Eastbound)
Gas S: Fina(*, D), Phillip 66(*, CW)
Food S: Bombay Bicycle Club, Denny's, El Mido Mexican Restaurant, Seafood Gallery, Yellow Rose Cafe (Quality Inn)
Lodg S: Embassy Suites, La Quinta Inn, Quality Inn, Sumner Suites
AServ S: Al's Muffler, Art's Muffler and Brake Shop, Bassett Tire & Service
ATM S: Fina, Montwood National Bank, Norwest Bank
Other S: Bassett Center Shopping Mall, Furr's Food Market

24B Geronimo Dr. (Eastbound)
Gas S: Fina(*, D), Phillips 66(*)
Food S: Bombay Bicycle Club, Denny's(24), El Nido
Lodg S: Embassy Suites, La Quinta Inn, Sumner Suites
AServ S: Art's Muffler and Brake Shop
ATM S: Fina

24 Geronimo Dr, Trowbridge Dr
Gas N: Chevron(24)
Food N: Furr's Cafeteria, Idle Spur Dining Room (Quality Inn), Seafood Galley, Yellow Rose Cafe (Quality Inn)
Lodg N: Quality Inn
AServ N: Bassett Tire and Service Store, Chevron(24)
ATM N: Norwest Bank
Other N: Amigo Laundry & Cleaners, **Bassett Center Shopping Mall**, Family Christian Stores, **Office Depot**, Springers Teaching Tools

25 Airway Blvd, El Paso Airport
TStop S: **El Paso Truck Terminal(*, 24) (Chevron)**
FStop S: **C R Auto Fuel(D) (Credit Card Only)**
Gas N: Shell(*, D, 24)
Food N: Holiday Inn, Jaxon's
Lodg N: Hampton Inn and Suites, Holiday Inn
AServ N: Hoi-Fox Infiniti, Acura, Hoi-Fox Mercedes Benz, Hoi-Fox Volkswagon
S: **El Paso Tire Center**
TServ N: **Great Basin GMC Truck Dealership**

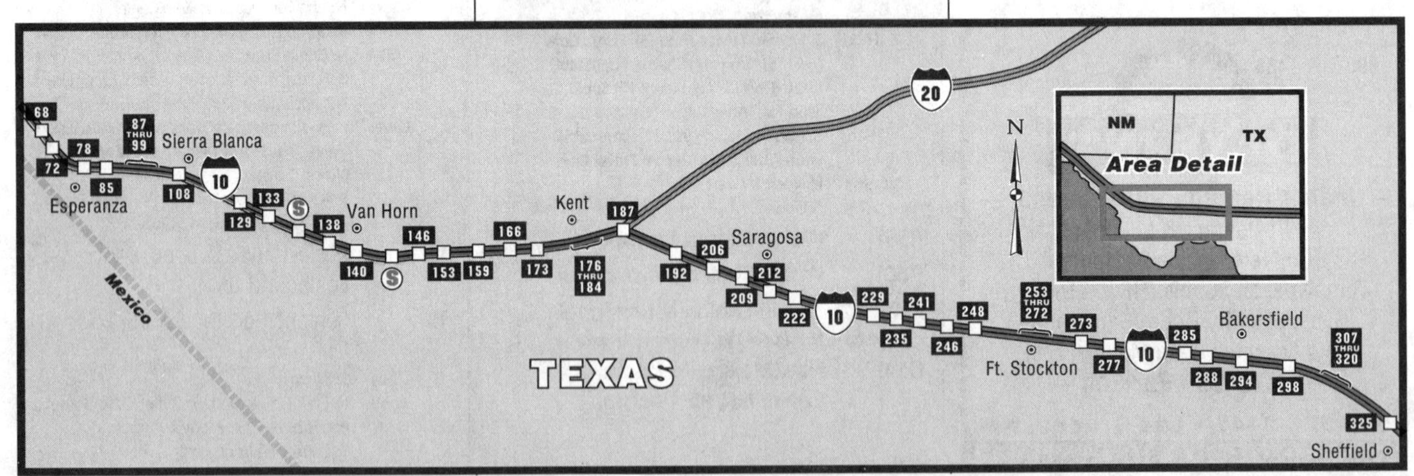

Bold red print shows RV & Bus parking available or nearby

EXIT TEXAS

(Peterbilt)
S: El Paso Tire Center, El Paso Truck Terminal(24) (Chevron)

ATM **N:** Government Employees Credit Union, Shell
S: El Paso Truck Terminal (Chevron)

Other **N:** Howdy's Food Mart

26 Hawkins Blvd.

Gas **N:** Chevron(*, D, CW), Diamond Shamrock(*, D)
S: Diamond Shamrock(*, D)

Food **N:** Arby's, Burger King, IHOP(24) (Howar Johnson), Luby's Cafeteria, Olive Garden, Red Lobster
S: China King's, McDonald's(PLAY), Terry's Pit BBQ, Village Inn Restaurant

Lodg **N:** Howard Johnson
S: Best Western

AServ **N:** Chevron, Montgomery Ward, Vintage Car & Lube(CW)
S: Spitzer Heavy Duty Parts

TServ **S:** Spitzer Heavy Duty Parts, United Trailer Repair

ATM **N:** Chevron, Diamond Shamrock
S: Diamond Shamrock

Other **N:** Cielo Bista Mall

27 Hunter Drive, Viscount Blvd (Eastbound, Reaccess Westbound Only)

Gas **N:** Diamond Shamrock(*, D, CW), Fina(*, 24)
S: Chevron(*), Exxon(*, D)

Food **N:** Asia Palace, Carrows, Doc's B-B-Que, Garden Buffet Restaurant, K-Bob's Steakhouse, Senor Fish, Taco Bell
S: Subway (Exxon), Whataburger(24)

Lodg **N:** DAYS INN Days Inn

AServ **S:** Hunter Automotive Service(LP, K), Las Americas Auto & Truck Supply

ATM **N:** Diamond Shamrock, Fina
S: Chevron, Exxon

Other **N:** Barnes & Noble, Dr. Nevins Eye World, Kwik Copy
S: El Paso Textbook Outlet, Food City, Freeway Pharmacy, Ranchland Laundry, U.S. Post Office, Uhaul(LP)

28A McRae Blvd

Gas **N:** Chevron(*, D, 24)
S: Chevron(*, CW), Fina(*, CW), Phillips 66(*)

Food **N:** Chico's Tacos, Five Star Mexican Bakery, Jack-In-The-Box, KFC, Pizza Hut
S: Gabriel's Cafe (Mexican)

AServ **N:** K-Mart(RX), Tune Up Masters
S: A-n-R Auto Repair, Gateway Performance Center, Saturn Dealership

ATM **S:** Fina

Other **N:** Discovery Zone(PLAY), K-Mart(RX), Office Max, Potter's Paperback Exchange, Toys R Us, WalGreens Pharmacy(24, RX)
S: Freeway Car Wash(CW), McRae Animal Hospital

28B Yarbrough Dr, Sumac Dr

Gas **N:** Chevron(24)
S: Diamond Shamrock(*, LP)

Food **N:** Beijing Lili (Chinese), Burger King, Dunkin Donuts(24), Long John Silver, McDonald's(PLAY), Peter Piper Pizza, Pistol Pete's Pizza (Wal-Mart), Subway, Wendy's, Whataburger(24)
S: Applebee's, La Malinche Cafe (Mexican), Pizza Hut, Quizno's Classic Subs

Lodg **N:** Travelers Inn
S: Budgetel Inn, Comfort Inn, Suburban Lodge

AServ **N:** Chevron(24), Midas Brake and Muffler

RVCamp **S:** Roadrunner RV Park, Parts, Sales, Service (.4 Miles)

Med **N:** + Columbia Medical Center East

ATM **N:** Wal-Mart(24, RX)
S: Diamond Shamrock

Other **N:** PetsMart, Wal-Mart(RX), Yarborough Plaza

EXIT TEXAS

29 Lomaland Dr. (Eastbound)

Gas **S:** Fina(*, CW)

Food **S:** Bakery, Hiney's Sports Restaurant

Lodg **S:** HomeGate Studios & Suites

ATM **S:** Fina

Other **S:** Barnett Harley-Davidson, Major Optical Vision Center

30 Lee Trevino Dr, Lomaland Dr

Gas **S:** Diamond Shamrock(*)

Food **N:** East Side Cafe, Mi Pueblito (Mexican), Oriental Hut

AServ **N:** Discount Tire Company, Firestone Tire & Auto, Hoi-Fox Toyota Service, Hoi-Fox Toyota, Lexus, Martin Tire Co., National Tire and Battery, R & S Paint & Auto Body, Shamaley Ford, Shamaley Isuzu, Super Center Muffler Shop, Trevino Transmissions
S: Story Nissan, Vista Chevrolet

TServ **N:** Wofford Truck Parts

ATM **N:** Sunwest Bank
S: Bank Of The West, Diamond Shamrock

Other **N:** The Home Depot(LP)
S: Eraser Dust, Movie One Cinema 12

32 FM 659, Zaragosa Road, George Dieter Road

FStop **S:** Diamond Shamrock(*)

Gas **N:** Chevron(*, D)
S: Chevron(*), Conoco

Food **N:** Whataburger(24)

TServ **S:** Border International Service (CAT, Cummins, International)

ATM **N:** Chevron
S: Chevron

Other **S:** Supro Energy(LP), Ysleta Vet. Clinic

34 Loop 375, Americas Ave

FStop **N:** Texaco(*)

Gas **N:** Chevron(*, 24), Diamond Shamrock(*, 24)

Food **N:** A & W Restaurant (Diamond Shamrock), Taco Bell Express (Texaco)

RVCamp **N:** Mission RV Park(LP), Mission RV Sales

ATM **N:** Chevron

Other **N:** El Paso Museum of History

37 FM 1281, Horizon Blvd

TStop **N:** Exxon(*, SCALES), Love's(*, D, SCALES, 24)
S: Petro(*, SCALES)

Food **N:** Bonita's (Exxon), Pizza Hut (Love's TStop), Subway (Love's TStop), Taco Bell (Love's TStop)
S: Blimpie Subs & Salads (Petro TS), Iron Skillet (Petro TS), McDonald's(PLAY)

TServ **N:** Cummins Diesel, El Paso Thermo King(24) (Freightliner), Exxon(SCALES)
S: Channel 17 CB Repair Shop, Expert Trailor Repair, P & I Fleet Service Truck Repair, Petro(SCALES), Sonny's Tires, Utility Trailer Southeast Sales, West Texas Great Dane Trailers

TWash **S:** Blue Beacon Truck Wash, Horizon

RVCamp **N:** Cummins Southwest Inc. (.25 Miles)
S: Sampson's RV Park (.5 Miles)

ATM **N:** Exxon
S: Petro

42 FM 1110, Clint, San Elizario

Gas **S:** Exxon(*, D)

Food **S:** Boll Weevil Restaurant (Cotton Valley Motel)

Lodg **S:** Cotton Valley Motel

RVCamp **S:** Cotton Valley RV Park (Cotton Valley Motel)

49 FM 793, Fabens

TStop **S:** Texas Red's Truck Stop(*)

Gas **S:** Texaco(*, D)

Food **S:** Lower Valley Cafe (Fabens Inn), Texas Restaurant(24) (Texas Red's Truck Stop)

Lodg **S:** Fabens Inn & RV Park

RVCamp **S:** Fabens Inn & RV Park

EXIT TEXAS

(50) Rest Area (RR, Picnic, P; Eastbound)

(51) Rest Area (RR, Picnic, P; Westbound)

55 Tornillo

68 Acala Road

72 Spur 148, Ft. Hancock

FStop **S:** Shell(*)

Gas **S:** Texaco(*)

Food **S:** Angie's Restaurant (Texaco)

Lodg **S:** Motel (Shell)

AServ **S:** McNary Garage

TServ **S:** McNary Garage

RVCamp **S:** RV Park

Other **S:** Fort Hancock Merchandise Co.

78 TX 20 West, McNary

81 FM 2217

85 Esperanza Road

87 FM 34

TStop **S:** Desert Outpost Truck Stop(*) (CB Shop)

TServ **S:** Desert Outpost Truck Stop (CB Shop)

RVCamp **S:** The Tiger RV (Desert Outpost TS)

ATM **S:** Desert Outpost Truck Stop (CB Shop)

95 Frontage Road (Eastbound, Reaccess Eastbound Only, Difficult Reaccess)

(98) Rest Area (Picnic, P; Eastbound)

(99) Picnic Area (Picnic, P; Westbound, Located at Exit 99, North Side)

99 Alsca Road

Exit **(102)** Inspection Station (Eastbound)

105 Bus. Loop 10 (Eastbound)

106 Bus. Loop 10 (Westbound)

107 FM 1111, Sierra Blanca Ave

FStop **N:** Exxon(*)

Gas **N:** Texaco(D)
S: Chevron(*)

Food **N:** Best Cafe, Chester Fried Chicken (Exxon), Chonas Ice Cream Parlor, Michael's Restaurant, The Sideline

Lodg **N:** El Camino Motel, Sierra Motel

AServ **N:** Texaco, Tony's Auto Parts, Wayne's Truck Shop(24), West's Value Auto Parts

TServ **N:** Texaco, Wayne's Truck Shop(24)

RVCamp **N:** High Country RV Park, Sierra Blanca RV & TR-PK

ATM **N:** Exxon

Parks **N:** Hueco Tanks State Park

Other **N:** Blanca Oasis Drugs & Fountain(RX), Guerra & Co. General Mercandise, Grocery, Hardware, R & G Grocery, RR Depot- Hudspeth County Museum, U.S. Post Office

108 Bus. Loop 10, Sierra Blanca (Caution Low Clearance 13'6")

129 Allamore, Hot Wells

133 Frontage Road (Westbound)

(136) Scenic Overlook (Picnic; Westbound)

(136) Weigh Station (Eastbound)

138 Golf Course Dr.

TStop **S:** Chevron(*)

Gas **S:** Exxon(*, LP)

Food **N:** Dairy Queen, Pizza Hut, Subway

Bold red print shows RV & Bus parking available or nearby

EXIT		TEXAS
		S: McDonald's(PLAY)
	Lodg	N: Best Western, Motel 6, Plaza Inn, Comfort Inn (see our ad this page)
		S: Holiday Inn Express, Super 8
	AServ	S: Chevron
	TServ	S: Chevron
	RVCamp	S: Eagle's Nest RV Park (.5 Miles)
	ATM	S: Chevron
	Other	N: Chamber of Commerce, Welsh's IGA Supermarket
140A		U.S. 90, TX 54, Van Horn Drive, Marfa
	TStop	S: Pilot Travel Center(*, SCALES)
	FStop	S: HH Gas(*)
	Gas	N: Texaco(*), Texaco(*, D)
		S: Conoco(*, D)
	Food	N: Burger King (Texaco), Leslie's BBQ
		S: Conoco, Papa's Pantry Cafe, Wendy's (Pilot Travel Center)
	AServ	N: Car Quest Auto Parts, N V Farm & Auto Parts, NAPA Auto Parts, Ramirez RV and Auto Shop, Texaco
	RVCamp	N: N V Farm & Auto Parts, Ramirez RV and Auto Shop
		S: KOA Kampground (.25 Miles)
	Med	N: ✚ Hospital
	ATM	N: Van Horn State Bank
	Parks	N: Carlsbad Caverns, Guadelupe Mountains
	Other	N: Culberson County Historical Museum, Frank's Supermarket, Hernandez Fruit Stand, Tru Value Hardware
140B		Bus. Loop 10, Ross Drive, Van Horn
	TStop	N: Love's(*, 24)
		S: Mountain View Truck & Travel Stop(*, LP) (RV Park)
	Gas	N: Chevron(*)
	Food	N: Sands Motel, Taco Bell (Love's)
	Lodg	N: Days Inn, Sands Motel, Comfort Inn (see our ad this page)
	AServ	N: A & A Repair(24), Whatley Tire Truck & Passenger Tire
	TServ	N: A & A Repair(24)
		S: Mountain View Truck & Travel Stop (RV Park)
	RVCamp	N: Eagles Nest RV Park (2 Miles), El Campo, El Campo RV Park
		S: Mountain View Truck & Travel Stop (RV Park)
	ATM	N: Love's
		S: Mountain View Truck & Travel Stop (RV Park)
(145)		Rest Area (RR, Picnic, P; Eastbound)
(145)		Rest Area (RR, Picnic, P; Westbound)
(145)		Weigh Station (Westbound)
146		Wild Horse Road
153		Michigan Flat
159		Plateau
	TStop	N: Citgo(*)
166		Boracho Station
173		Hurds Draw Road
176		TX 118, FM 2424, Kent, Fort Davis
	Gas	N: Chevron(*)
	AServ	N: Chevron
	Parks	S: Davis Mountains State Park (47 Miles)
	Other	N: Post Office
		S: McDonald Observatory (39 Miles)
181		Cherry Creek Road
	FStop	S: Chevron(*, 24)
184		Springhills
(185)		Rest Area (Picnic, Grills, P; Eastbound)
(185)		Picnic Area (Picnic, Grills, P; Westbound)
Exit		**(186)** I-10 East, San Antonio (Westbound)
Exit		**(187)** Junction I-20 East, Pecos
188		Griffin Road
192		FM 3078 East
206		FM 2903, Toyah, Balmorhea
	Parks	S: Balmorhea State Park
	Other	S: Lake Balmorhea
209		Bus. I-10, TX 17, Balmorhea, Fort Davis
	Parks	S: Balmorhea State Park, Davis Mountains State Park
212		TX 17, Pecos
	FStop	S: Fina(*)
	Food	S: Fina
	Parks	N: Picnic Area
(212)		Picnic Area (Picnic; Located at Exit 212, North Side)
214		FM 2448 (Westbound, Reaccess Eastbound Only, Difficult Reaccess)
222		Hoefs Road
229		Hovey Road
(233)		Rest Area (RR, Phones, Picnic, Grills, P; Eastbound)
(233)		Rest Area (RR, Phones, Picnic, Grills, P; Westbound)
235		Mendel Road
241		Kennedy Road
246		Firestone Road
248		U.S. 67, Alpine, FM 1776, Big Bend National Park
253		FM 2037, Belding
256		Bus. I-10 East, Fort Stockton
	FStop	S: Shell(*), Texaco(*)
	Food	S: Alpine Lodge Restaurant, Brazen Bean
	Lodg	S: Alpine Lodge, Best Western, Comfort Inn, Motel 6
	AServ	S: Fred's Auto & RV Repair
	TServ	S: H & H Truck Service
	RVCamp	S: RV Park (Texaco)
	Med	S: ✚ Hospital
257		U.S. 285, Pecos, Sanderson
	TStop	S: Exxon(*)
	FStop	S: Chevron(*)
	Food	S: McDonald's(PLAY)
	Lodg	S: Atrium West Inn Hotel & Suites, Days Inn, Holiday Inn Express, La Quinta Inn
	TServ	S: Exxon
	TWash	S: Exxon
	RVCamp	N: Comanche Land RV Park (.5 Miles)
	Other	N: Fort Stockton Golf Course
		S: Tourist Info. (McDonald's)
259B		TX 18, Monahan's
	FStop	N: Citgo(*), Shell(*)
	Gas	N: Texaco(*)
	Food	N: Burger King (Shell)
	RVCamp	N: I-10 RV Park
	Other	S: Annie Riggs Museum

1714

- Continental Breakfast
- Kids Under 12 Stay & Eat Free
- Outdoor Pool
- Pets Allowed
- Handicap Accessible
- Remote Control TV w/Free HBO
- Truck/Large VehicleParking
- Exterior Corridors

TEXAS ▪ I-10 (Bus.) ▪ Exit 138/140B

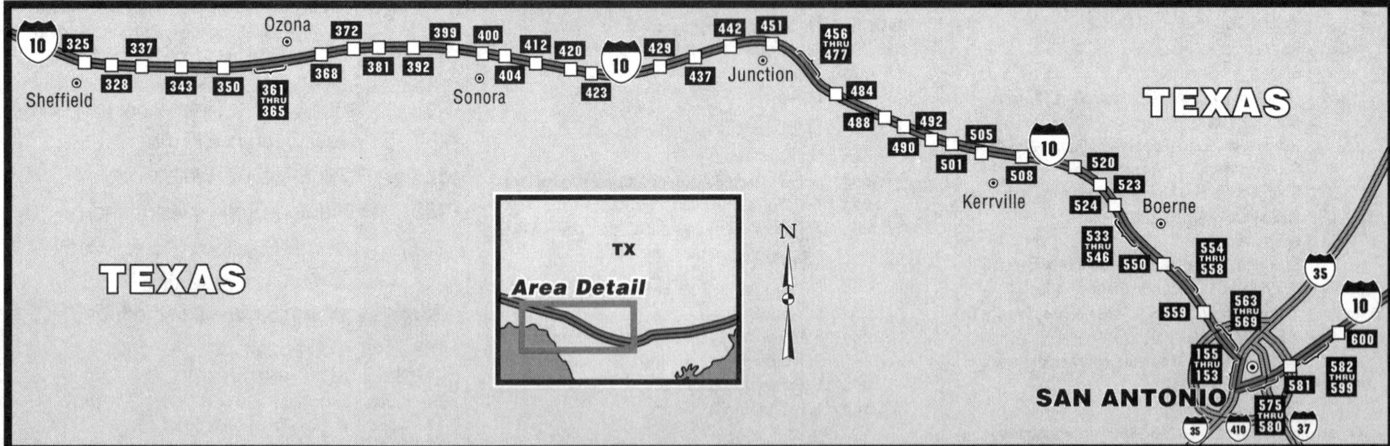

Bold red print shows RV & Bus parking available or nearby

EXIT TEXAS

259A FM 1053
AServ N: Garage & Wrecker Repair, Klassy Chassis Auto Body & Paint Repair
RVCamp N: I-10 RV Park (.25 Miles)

261 Bus. I-10, U.S. 385, Marathon, Fort Stockton
FStop N: Exxon(*)
Food N: TCBY (Exxon)
RVCamp N: A & M Camper Park (1 Mile)
S: Big Ben Park (139 Miles)
Med S: ✚ Hospital

264 Warnock Road
RVCamp N: KOA Kampground
S: Parkview RV Park (1.5 Miles)

272 University Road

273 U.S. 67, U.S. 385, San Angelo, McCamey

(273) Picnic Area (Picnic, P; Westbound, Located at Exit 273, North Side)

277 FM 2023

(279) Picnic Area (Picnic, P; Eastbound)

285 McKenzie Road

288 Ligon Road

294 FM 11, Bakersfield
Gas N: Exxon(*)
S: Chevron(*, D)

298 RM 2886

307 U.S. 190, FM305, McCamey, Iraan

(309) Rest Area (RR, HF, Phones, Picnic, Grills, P; Eastbound)

(309) Rest Area (RR, HF, Phones, Picnic, Grills, P; Westbound)

314 Frontage Road

320 Frontage Road

325 TX 290, TX 349, Iraan, Sheffield
Med N: ✚ Hospital
Parks S: Wild Life Viewing Area

328 River Road
FStop S: Phillips 66(*, D)
Lodg S: Peco's River Parking RV Park (Phillips 66)
RVCamp S: Peco's River Parking RV Park (Phillips 66)

337 Live Oak Road

343 TX 290 West, Sheffield

(346) Parking Area (Eastbound)

(349) Parking Area (Westbound)

350 RM 2398, Howard Draw Rd.

361 RM 2083, Pandale Road

363 RM 2398, Loop 466 Business, Ozona

365 TX 163, Sterling City, Comstock
Gas N: Chevron(*, D, CW), Texaco(*, D, 24), Town & Country(*, D)
S: Chevron(*), Phillips 66(*)
Food N: Burger King(PLAY), Country Kitchen (Town & Country), Dairy Queen(PLAY), Taco Bell, The Cafe Next Door
S: Poncho's Cafe (Mexican/American), The Burger Shoppe
Lodg N: Comfort Inn, Economy Inn
AServ N: NAPA Auto Parts
S: Joe's Tire Shop

EXIT TEXAS

RVCamp N: Economy Inn RV Park
ATM N: NB Motor Bank, Ozona National Bank, Town & Country
Other N: David Crockett Monument, Laundromat, Putt Putt, Tru Value Hardware

368 Loop 466 Business, Ozona

372 Taylor Box Road
TStop N: Circle Bar Auto/Truck Plaza(*, SCALES) (Chevron)
Food N: Circle Bar Steakhouse (Circle Bar TS)
Lodg N: Circle Bar Auto/Truck Plaza (Chevron)
TServ N: Circle Bar Auto/Truck Plaza(SCALES) (Chevron)
RVCamp N: Circle Bar RV Park (.25 Miles)

381 RM 1312 (Eastbound, Reaccess Westbound Only)

388 RM 1312 (Westbound, Reaccess Eastbound Only)

392 RM 1312, RM 1989, Caverns of Sonora Road

(394) Rest Area (RR, RV Dump, P; Eastbound)

(394) Rest Area (RR, RV Dump, P; Westbound)

399 Loop 467 Business, Sonora (Eastbound)

400 U.S. 277, San Angelo, Del Rio
FStop S: Circle K(*)
Gas N: Texaco(*, D)
S: Exxon(*, D), Shell(*, D)
Food N: Sutton County Steakhouse (Days Inn)
S: Dairy Queen, La Mexicana, Pizza Hut, Sonic Drive In
Lodg N: DAYS INN Days Inn
AServ N: I-10 Auto Ranch GM
S: Victor's Auto & Truck Parts
RVCamp S: Buster's RV Park
ATM S: Shell, Sutton County National Bank
Other N: Sonora Golf Club
S: Alco

404 Bus. Loop 467, Sonora
Med S: ✚ Hospital

412 RM 3130, Allison Road

420 Baker Road, RM 3130

(423) Parking Area (Eastbound)

(423) Parking Area (Westbound)

429 Harrell Road , RM 3130

437 Loop 291, Roosevelt (Eastbound)

438 Loop 291, Roosevelt (Westbound, Difficult Reaccess)

442 RM 1674, Loop 291, Fort McKavett (Difficult Reaccess)
Parks S: Fort McKavatt State Historic Park
Other N: Fort McKavett State Historic Site

445 FM 1674 (Eastbound)

451 RM 2291, Cleo Road

456 U.S. 83 North, Menard, U.S. 377, Mason, Junction, Rocksprings
FStop N: Chevron(*, 24)
Gas S: Exxon(*, D), Texaco(*)
Food N: Junction Restaurant, Tastee Freez
S: Come 'N' Git It(*), Dairy Queen
Lodg N: Comfort Inn
S: Slumber Inn
RVCamp S: KOA Kampground(LP) (.5 Miles)
Med S: ✚ Hospital

EXIT TEXAS

ATM N: Chevron
Parks S: Llano River State Park

457 FM 2169, Junction, Martinez Street
FStop N: Texaco(*)
Food N: Grandad's Corner Store BBQ (Texaco)
Lodg S: DAYS INN Days Inn
AServ N: Gonzalo's Auto Repair
RVCamp S: Lakeview Lazy Daze RV Park (2 Miles)
ATM N: Texaco

460 Bus Loop (Westbound, Reaccess Eastbound Only)

(461) Picnic Area (Picnic; Eastbound)

462 U.S. 83 South, Uvalde

465 RM 2169, Segovia
Gas S: Shell(*)
Food S: Best Western, Phillips 66(*)
Lodg S: Best Western, Cedar Hills Motel
TServ S: Phillips 66
RVCamp S: RV Park (Shell)
Other S: Laundromat (Shell)

472 Old Segovia Road, RM 479, RM 2169

477 East U.S. 290, Fredericksburg

484 Midway Road

488 TX 27, Mountain Home, Ingram

490 TX 41, Mountain Home, Rocksprings

492 RM 479
FStop S: Loan Oak Store(*)
RVCamp N: Camping
S: RV Campground

(497) Picnic Area (Picnic, Grills, P; Eastbound)

(497) Picnic Area (Picnic, Grills, P; Westbound)

501 RM 1338
RVCamp S: KOA Kampground (2 Miles)

505 RM 783, Harper, Ingram
Gas S: Exxon(*, D)
RVCamp S: Kerr Villa RV Park
ATM S: Exxon

508 TX 16, Kerrville
Gas N: Exxon(*, D)
S: Chevron(*), Phillips 66(*, D), Texaco(*, D), Town & Country(*, D)
Food S: Choo-Choo's BBQ, Dairy Queen(PLAY), Homestyle Restaurant (Executive Inn), McDonald's (Texaco), Subway (Chevron), Sunday House Restaurant (Best Western)
Lodg S: Best Western, Executive Inn, Quality Inn
AServ N: Cecil Atkission Chev, Pont, Olds, Buick, Cad, & Chev. Trucks, Exxon
RVCamp N: Hills of Kerrville RV Resort (1 Mile)
Med S: ✚ Hospital
ATM S: Chevron, Town & Country
Parks S: Kerrville Shreiner State Park (4 Miles)
Other N: Kerrville Camera Safari (Drive-Thru Wildlife Ranch)
S: Cowboy Artist Museum (4 Miles)

(514) Rest Area (RR, Picnic, Grills, Vending, RV Dump, P; Eastbound)

(514) Rest Area (RR, Picnic, Grills, Vending, RV Dump, P; Westbound)

520 RM 1341, Cypress Creek Road

523 North U.S. 87, San Angelo,

EXIT TEXAS

Fredericksburg
- **FStop** **S:** Texaco[*]
- **Gas** **S:** Exxon[*, D]
- **Food** **S:** Dairy Queen[PLAY]
- **Lodg** **S:** Motel
- **RVCamp** **S:** RV Park USA[LP]

524 Bus U.S. 87, Comfort

527 RM 1621, Waring

(529) Rest Area (Picnic, Grills, P; Eastbound)

(531) Picnic Area (Picnic, Grills, P; Westbound)

533 RM 289, Welfare

537 Bus. U.S. 87
- **RVCamp** **N:** American RV Storage, Sales, Service

538 Ranger Creek Road

539 Johns Road
- **Gas** **S:** Diamond Shamrock[*, D, 24]
- **RVCamp** **S:** Bell Hydro Gas[LP] (Butane)

540 TX 46, New Braunfels, Bandera
- **Gas** **N:** Exxon[*, D], H-E-B Grocery Store[RX], Texaco[*, CW]
- **Food** **N:** Church's Chicken, Dairy Queen, I Can't Believe It's Yogurt (Exxon), Little Caesars Pizza, Pizza Hut, Shang Hai Chinese Restaurant, Sunset Grill, Taco Bell (Exxon), Taco Cabana (H-E-B Grocery)
- **Lodg** **N:** Best Western
- **Other** **N:** H-E-B Grocery Store[RX], Parcel Express

542 Bus U.S. 87, Boerne (Westbound, Reaccess Eastbound Only)
- **RVCamp** **N:** Alamo Fiesta RV Resort[LP]

543 Boerne Stage Road, Cascade Caverns Road, Scenic Loop Road
- **FStop** **N:** Citgo[*]
- **Food** **N:** Cinnamon Street Bakery (Citgo), Hot Stuff Pizza (Citgo), Motel[24], Smash Hit Subs (Citgo)
- **Lodg** **N:** Motel
- **AServ** **N:** Jennings Anderson Ford
- **RVCamp** **N:** Alamo Fiesta RV Park (1 Mile)
- **Other** **N:** Cascade Caverns

546 Fair Oaks Pkwy, Tarpon Drive, Fair Oaks Ranch
- **Gas** **S:** Chevron[*], Exxon[*, LP]
- **Food** **S:** Flagstop Cafe (Exxon), Olde Tymer Jct. Cafe (Chevron)
- **RVCamp** **S:** Price Properties RV Park
- **ATM** **N:** Frost Bank
  S: Exxon
- **Other** **N:** County Line Country Store, Ellendale's Pet Grooming, Vet Clinic
  S: Fair Oaks Postal Exchange

550 Camp Stanley, RM 3351, Ralph Fair Road, Boerne Stage Rd.
- **FStop** **N:** Diamond Shamrock[*]
- **Food** **N:** Jalapenos Mexican (Diamond Shamrock)
- **ATM** **N:** Diamond Shamrock

551 Boerne Stage Road, Leon Springs
- **Gas** **N:** Diamond Shamrock[*]
- **Food** **N:** Romano's Macaroni Grill, Rudy's Country Store & BBQ
  S: Angelo Italian Restaurant, Las Palapas, Ping's Chinese Hunan
- **AServ** **S:** Leon Spring Automotive
- **ATM** **N:** Compass Bank
- **Other** **S:** Leon Springs Car Wash[CW], Mims Animal Hospital, Pet Hospital

554 Camp Bullis Road
- **FStop** **N:** Citgo[*]
- **Gas** **N:** Mobil City Auto Parts

EXIT TEXAS

- **Food** **N:** Casa-lux Restaurant
  S: Suzy's Home Cookin' (Rodeway Inn)
- **Lodg** **S:** Rodeway Inn
- **AServ** **N:** Mobil City Auto Parts
- **Parks** **N:** Raymond Russell Park
  S: Friedrich Wilderness Park

555 La Cantera Pkwy, Fiesta Texas
- **Gas** **S:** Shell[*, CW]
- **Food** **N:** Paleo's Mex-Cafe
- **ATM** **S:** Shell
- **Other** **N:** McCoy's
  S: Six Flags Fiesta Texas

556A Loop 1604, Anderson Loop (Divided Hwy)

556B Frontage Road

557 Spur 53, Univ. of Texas at San Antonio
- **Lodg** **N:** Best Western, EconoLodge, Howard Johnson Express, Super 8
- **AServ** **N:** Brake Check, Red McCombs, Smith Chevrolet
  S: AutoNation USA
- **ATM** **N:** Frost Bank

558 De Zavala
- **Gas** **N:** Mobil[*], Texaco[*]
- **Food** **N:** Barnacle Bill's (Seafood), Baskin Robbins, Bill

1291
AmeriSuites
AMERICA'S AFFORDABLE ALL-SUITE HOTEL
Texas • Exit 562 • 210-561-0099

Sleep Inn
8318 IH 10 West
San Antonio, TX
210-344-5400
800-893-9912
Special Tour Groups Rates
Bus & RV Parking
Deluxe Continental Breakfast
Expanded Satellite TV
Outdoor Pool
Coin Laundry
Iron/Full Size Iron Board/Hair Dryers/
Coffee Makers In Select Rooms
Interior Corridors
Kids Under 17 Stay Free w/Parent
Minutes away from Six Flags, Alamo, Sea World, Riverwalk, Shopping, Restaurants, Medical Center
Between Callaghan and Wurzbach Rd.
Aug 16-May 21 $35.95* 1-2 Persons/Single
May 22-Aug 15 $49.95* 1-2 Persons/Single
$20 Sire Charge Fri-Sat-from 5/22-8/15
1761 * Rooms based on availability.
TEXAS • IH-10 • EXIT 561

EXIT TEXAS

Miller BBQ, Blimpie Subs & Salads, Burger King[PLAY], Carrabba's Italian Grill, Chili's, E-Z's Brick Oven Grill, Joe's Crab Shack, McDonald's[PLAY], Outback Steakhouse, Sonic, Souper Salad, Starbucks Coffee, Subway (Texaco), Taco Bell, Taco Cabana
- **Lodg** **N:** Amerisuites (see our ad this page)
- **AServ** **S:** Wal-Mart[24] (Vision Center)
- **ATM** **N:** Allwas Bank, Compass Bank, Mobil, Security Service Federal Credit Union, Texaco
- **Other** **N:** 10 West Veterinary Hospital, Barnes & Noble Booksellers, H-E-B Grocery Store[RX], OfficeMax, Target, The Home Depot[LP], Total Vision Center
  S: Wal-Mart (Vision Center)

559 Woodstone Dr., South Loop 345, Fredericksburg Rd.
- **Food** **N:** La Madeleine French Bakery and Cafe, Marble Slab Creamery Ice Cream, Max's Restaurant, Deli, Bakery, On The Border (Mexican), Pearl Inn Chinese, Saltgrass Steakhouse
- **Lodg** **S:** Days Inn, HomeGate Studios & Suites, HomeStead Village Efficiencies
- **AServ** **N:** Cavender Buick, Gunn Collision Centers, Ken Batchelor Cadillac
  S: Alamo Cycle Complex (Honda, Kawasaki, Suzuki, Yamaha), Gunn Acura
- **Other** **N:** AMC 24 Theaters, Borders Books & Music, Kinko's[24], Pearl Vision Center
  S: Crystal Ice Palace, Travis Boating Center

560A Huebner Rd. (Eastbound)
- **Gas** **S:** Chevron[*, CW], Exxon[*, CW, 24]
- **Food** **S:** Bill Miller BBQ, Burger King[PLAY], Cracker Barrel, Jim's[24] (Hampton Inn)
- **Lodg** **S:** Hampton Inn
- **AServ** **S:** Midas Muffler & Brake
- **ATM** **S:** Chevron

560B Frontage Rd. (Eastbound)
- **ATM** **S:** USAA Bank

560C Medical Drive, Callaghan Rd. (Eastbound)
- **Food** **S:** Veladi Ranch Steakhouse
- **Lodg** **S:** Sleep Inn

561 Huebner Road
- **Gas** **N:** Fina[*]
- **Food** **N:** Pappasito's Cantina, Sea Island Shrimp House, The Honey Baked Ham Co.
- **Lodg** **N:** AmeriSuites, Homewood Suites Hotel, Omni Hotel, San Antonio Studio PLUS, Sleep Inn (see our ad this page)
- **AServ** **N:** Ancira Chrys, Plym, Jeep, Eagle, Nissan
- **ATM** **N:** Pentagon Federal Credit Union

Exit **(562)** Wurzbach Road
- **Gas** **N:** Exxon[D], Phillips 66[*]
- **Food** **N:** Bennigan's, China Palace, Fuddruckers, Golden Corral Family Steakhouse, Haagen Dazs Ice Cream, Hickory Hut BBQ, Jason's Deli, Mamma Ilardo's (Italian), Manhatten Bagel, Mercedes Hamburgers & Grill, Popeye's Chicken, Quizno's Subs, Schlotzsky's Deli, Starbucks Coffee, Taste of China, Texas Land & Cattle Steakhouse, Thai Orchid Cuisine
- **Lodg** **N:** Omni Hotel, Ramada Limited
- **AServ** **N:** Exxon, Xpress Lube
- **RVCamp** **N:** Xpress Lube
- **Med** **N:** Texas MedClinic
- **ATM** **N:** Albertson's Food Market, Bank of America, Bank of America, Froth Bank, NationsBank, Security Service Federal Credit Union
- **Other** **N:** Albertson's Food Market, Car Wash, Christ the King Bookstore, Colonies North Animal Hospital, Colonnade Vision Center, Eckerd Drugs[RX] (H-E-B), H-E-B Grocery Store[24, RX], Ironside Antiques Market, Office Depot, Package Express, Petco, The Ultimate

EXIT TEXAS

Cheesecake

Exit (563) Callaghan Road
- **Gas** N: Diamond Shamrock(*, CW), Mobil
- **Food** N: Fratelli's Caffe Italiano, Hui's Chinese, Las Palapas, Subway, Sun Harvest Market
- **AServ** N: Mobil, Red McCombs Ford, Red McCombs Mazda, Toyota Dealer
- **Other** N: Advanced Eye Care, Home Court America (Gym), Postal Web, Sun Harvest Market

564AB Junction I-410, Connally Loop

565A Crossroads Blvd., Balcones Heights Blvd.
- **Gas** N: Texaco(*)
- **Food** S: Church's Chicken, Main Street Pizza, Pasta, Ports O' Call (Seafood), SHONEY'S, Shoney's, Whataburger
- **Lodg** N: Comfort Suites Hotel; S: Rodeway Inn
- **AServ** S: Brake Check, Firestone, Montgomery Ward, Nogalitos Gear Transmission Service
- **RVCamp** S: **Morgan Building & Spas, Morgan RV's**
- **Other** S: **Builder's Square 2, Crossroads of San Antonio (Mall)**, The Sale & Ski Center

565B Westbound - First Park Ten Blvd.; Eastbound - Vance Jackson Rd., West Ave.
- **Gas** S: Exxon(*, CW), Texaco(*, D, CW)
- **Food** S: Kettle Restaurant (La Quinta Inn)
- **Lodg** S: La Quinta Inn
- **AServ** S: Texaco
- **ATM** N: NationsBank, San Antonio Credit Union
- **Other** S: **U.S. Post Office**

565C Vance Jackson Rd. (Westbound)
- **Gas** N: Datafleet Coastal(D) (Credit Only)
- **Food** N: Bill Miller BBQ
- **Lodg** N: Quality Inn
- **AServ** N: Kayser's Automotive Services (Datafleet)
- **Other** N: Fire Station, Westfall Branch Library

566A Westbound - West Ave.; Eastbound - Fresno Dr.
- **Gas** N: Diamond Shamrock(*), Exxon(*, D), Fina(*)
- **Food** N: Casa Del Carmen (Mexican), La Popular Bakery & Cake Shop, Whataburger(24)
- **AServ** N: All Tune & Lube, Econo Lube & Tune, Exxon, Full-Line Systems, Xpress Lube
- **ATM** N: Fina
- **Other** N: Laundry Kwik Wash

566B Fresno Dr., Hildebrand Ave, Fulton Ave
- **Gas** N: Diamond Shamrock(*); S: Conoco(*), Exxon(*, D, CW)
- **Food** N: Adelita Mexican Food; S: Dolce Bakery
- **Lodg** S: Galaxy Inn Motel
- **AServ** S: B.C. Garage, Hildebrand Auto Center, Turn Key Inc. Alternators, Starters
- **ATM** N: Diamond Shamrock; S: Citizen's State Bank
- **Other** S: Ben's Pharmacy(RX), Northside Opticians

567 Loop 345, Fredericksburg Road, Woodlawn Ave (Eastbound, Upper Level)
- **AServ** S: Northwest Paint & Body
- **Other** S: **Fredericksburg Rd. Animal Hospital**

567A Fulton Ave, Hildebrand Ave (Westbound, Upper Level)
- **Food** N: Kim Wah (Chinese/Mexican)
- **AServ** N: Don's Garage, Joe Nigro Garage & Towing
- **Other** N: Colborn Marines, Pronto Food Mart

567B Loop 345, Woodlawn Ave., Fredericksburg Rd., Fulton Ave., Hildebrand Ave. (Westbound, Lower Level)
- **Gas** N: Conoco(*)
- **Food** N: Garcia's Mexican Food
- **AServ** N: San Antonio Radiator & Paint Co.
- **Other** N: Keys & Locks Locksmith

568 Spur 421, Culebra, Bandera (Eastbound, Upper Level)
- **AServ** S: Alamo Radiator

568A Cincinnati Ave. (Westbound, Reaccess Eastbound Only, Lower Level)

568B Spur 421, Culebra Ave, Bandera (Westbound, Upper Level)
- **FStop** N: **Datafleet Coastal (Credit Only)**
- **AServ** N: Bexar Body Works

569 Colorado St. (Westbound, Lower Level)
- **AServ** N: Bear Wheel Aligning Company

569C Santa Rosa St., Downtown (Eastbound, Upper Level)
- **Med** S: **+ University Health Center Downtown**

570 North I-35 Austin (Eastbound, Upper Level)

Note: I-10 runs concurrent below with I-35. Numbering follows I-35.

156 West I-10, McDermott Freeway, North US 87 El Paso (Westbound, Upper Level)

155C West Houston St, Commerce St, Market Square (Southbound, Upper Level)
- **Gas** W: Pik Nik(*)
- **Food** W: Golden Star Cafe, Jailhouse Cafe, McDonald's
- **Lodg** W: Motel 6
- **Med** W: **+ University Health Center Downtown**
- **ATM** W: San Antonio City Employees Federal Credit Union

155B Westbound - Durango Blvd., Downtown; Eastbound - Frio St., Durango Blvd. (Difficult Reaccess, Access To Services Is Limited To The Direction Traveled)
- **Food** E: Bill Miller BBQ, Holiday Inn
- **Lodg** E: Courtyard by Marriott, Fairfield Inn, Holiday Inn, Residence Inn; W: Radisson Hotel
- **Med** E: **+ Santa Rosa Health Care**
- **ATM** E: **Stop N Go**, Wells Fargo
- **Parks** E: **San Antonio Missions National Historical Park (2.8 Miles)**
- **Other** E: **K-Mart(RX), San Antonio Police HQ, Stop N Go, The Market Square**; W: **Fire Station**

155A Spur 536, South Alamo St. (Southbound)
- **FStop** E: **Datafleet Coastal(D) (Datafleet Credit Card Only, No Attendant)**
- **Food** E: Church's Chicken, Wen Wah's Chinese
- **Lodg** E: Comfort Inn, Ramada Limited; W: Microtel Inn, River Inn Motel
- **AServ** E: Speed & Sport
- **Other** E: **US Post Office**

154B South Laredo St, Cevallos St
- **Gas** E: Exxon(*), Texaco(*)
- **Food** E: Eddie's Taco House, McDonald's(PLAY), Pizza Hut, Wendy's; W: Piedras Negras
- **Lodg** E: DAYS INN Days Inn
- **Other** W: **Gleason Veterinary Hospital**

154A Westbound-San Marcos St, Nogalitos St, Eastbound-Nogalitos St., Loop 353 (Difficult Reaccess)
- **Gas** E: J & L Food & Gas(*)
- **Food** E: Maria's Cafe, Tommy's Old San Antonio Cafe; W: Henry's Tacos To Go, Sunny's Ristorante Italiano
- **AServ** E: General Brake & Alignment, Hernandez Tire & Muffler
- **Other** W: **Collins Branch Garden Library, Fire Station, H-E-B Grocery Store**

153 West U.S. 90, Del Rio, East & West I-10, North & South U.S. 87 (Eastbound, Same as exit 572 Westbound)

Note: I-10 runs concurrent above with I-35. Numbering follows I-35.

572 South I-35 Laredo; West I-10 El Paso; North I-35, U.S. 87 Austin

573 Probandt St
- **Gas** S: Conoco(*), Diamond Shamrock(*)
- **Food** N: Bill Miller BBQ; S: El Ranchito Tortilleria, Eva's Cafe, Fiesta Bakery, Gyro's (Seafood, Burgers)
- **AServ** S: Atlas Auto Repair & Transmission, MWS Manufacturers
- **TServ** N: **Service Parts & Machine Co.**
- **ATM** S: Diamond Shamrock
- **Other** S: **Hernandez Grocery, San Antonio Missions National Historical Park**

574 Jct. I-37, U.S. 281, Corpus Christi, Johnson City

575 Pine St, Hackberry St.

576 New Brownfels Road, Gevers St
- **Gas** S: Diamond Shamrock(*, CW)
- **Food** S: McDonald's(PLAY)
- **ATM** S: Diamond Shamrock

577 U.S. 87 South, Roland Ave, Victoria
- **Food** S: Whataburger(24)

578 Pecan Valley Drive, MLK Drive
- **Gas** N: Phillips 66(*); S: Shell(*)
- **Other** N: Homestake Food Center, Little D's Washateria

579 Houston St, Commerce St.
- **Gas** N: Diamond Shamrock; S: Chevron
- **Lodg** N: Holiday Inn Express; S: DAYS INN **Days Inn**
- **ATM** N: Diamond Shamrock
- **Other** N: Police Station

580 W.W. White Road, Loop 13
- **Gas** N: Chevron(*, CW, 24), Fina(*); S: Texaco(*)
- **Food** N: Blue Bonnet Grill, El Jacalito Mexican, Hiley's Restaurant(24), Wendy's; S: Baysea's Fish Market III & Seafood Restaurant, McDonald's(PLAY), Phil Miller BBQ, Pizza Hut, **Super 8**
- **Lodg** N: Comfort Inn, Motel 6, **Scottsman Inn**; S: EconoLodge, Quality Inn, **Super 8**
- **AServ** N: Omalley's Tire Service; S: C & D Tire Shop, Drive Shaft Unlimited, Tieken Auto Service

Bold red print shows RV & Bus parking available or nearby

EXIT	TEXAS
TServ	**S:** Grande Ford Truck, Volvo Freightliner
RVCamp	**N:** San Antonio RV & MH Parts & Service (1.1 Miles)
Other	**N:** Brunswick Food Mart, Skyline Laundry
581	Jct. I-410, Connally Loop
582	Ackerman Road, Kirby
TStop	**N:** Pilot Travel Center(*, SCALES, 24) **S:** Petro(*, SCALES, 24) (Mobil)
Food	**N:** Arby's(24) (Pilot Travel Center TStop), Miss B's Cafe, T.J. Cinnamon's (Pilot) **S:** KFC, Petro (Mobil)
Lodg	**S:** Relay Station Motel
TServ	**N:** Buddy Storbeck's Diesel Service, Fruehouf, Santex International Trucks, Stewart & Stevenson San Antonio Branch, Toyo Tires, W W Tank & Trailor Parts, Western Star Trucks **S:** Petro(SCALES, 24) (Mobil)
TWash	**S:** Petro (Mobil)
583	Foster Road
TStop	**N:** Flying J Travel Plaza(*, LP, RV DUMP, SCALES)
Gas	**N:** Diamond Shamrock(*, CW, 24)
Food	**N:** Flying J Travel Plaza, Jack-In-The-Box(24)
TServ	**N:** Tire Distribution
RVCamp	**N:** Camping
ATM	**N:** Diamond Shamrock, Flying J Travel Plaza
585	FM 1516, Converse
TStop	**N:** Mobil Travel Center(*, LP, SCALES) (Laundromat, CB Shop)
Food	**N:** Winfield's
Lodg	**N:** Winfield's
TServ	**N:** Mobil Travel Center(SCALES) (Laundromat, CB Shop), Performance Trailor, Utility Trailor Sales **S:** Peterbilt Rush Truck Service(24), Rush Truck Center, Select Trucks Freight Liner
587	Loop 1604, Anderson Loop, Randolph AFB, Universal City
589	Graytown Road, Pfeil Road
TServ	**S:** Riske Fleet Service & Collision Repair
(590)	Rest Area (RR, Phones, Picnic, Grills, RV Dump, P; Eastbound)
(590)	Rest Area (RR, Phones, Picnic, Grills, RV Dump, P; Westbound)
591	Schertz, Fm1518
TStop	**N:** Exxon Travel Center(*, LP, SCALES, 24) (Truck Service)
Food	**N:** Farmers Restaurant (Exxon TStop)
Lodg	**N:** Exxon Travel Center (Truck Service)
TWash	**N:** Exxon Travel Center (Truck Service)
ATM	**N:** Exxon Travel Center (Truck Service)
593	FM 2538, Trainer Hale Road
TStop	**N:** Citgo Truck & Auto Plaza(*) **S:** Fina Truck Stop(*)

EXIT	TEXAS
Food	**N:** Dairy Queen(PLAY) (Citgo TStop) **S:** Fina Truck Stop
AServ	**N:** Citgo Truck & Auto Plaza
TServ	**N:** Citgo Truck & Auto Plaza **S:** Fina Truck Stop
ATM	**N:** Citgo Truck & Auto Plaza **S:** Fina Truck Stop
Other	**S:** 4 Watt CB Shop
595	Zuehl Road
597	Santa Clara Road
TServ	**N:** Brown Truck & Equip. Sales
599	FM 465, Marion
600	Schwab Road
601	FM 775, New Berlin, La Vernia
FStop	**N:** Mobil(*, 24)
Food	**N:** Arby's(24) (Mobil)
603	East U.S. 90, Alt. U.S. 90, Seguin (Eastbound)
RVCamp	**S:** RV Park (1.5 Miles), Russel RV Discount Parts & Service
604	FM 725
AServ	**N:** Quality Service Automotive
RVCamp	**S:** Bryan's Country RV Park (2 Miles)
Other	**N:** Allens Boats & Motors
605	FM 464
RVCamp	**N:** Camping
Other	**S:** Public Boat Ramp
607	TX 46, FM 78, New Braunfels, Lake McQueeney
Gas	**S:** Exxon(*)
Food	**S:** Bart's Old Town BBQ, Kettle, McDonald's
Lodg	**S:** Best Western, Super 8
609	Bus. TX 123, Austin St
FStop	**S:** Mobil(*)
RVCamp	**S:** Interstate RV Superstore, Shady Lane Mobil Home & RV Park
ATM	**S:** Mobil
Other	**S:** Sharp Propane Inc.(LP)
610	TX 123, San Marcos, Stockdale
TStop	**N:** Chevron Travel Center(*, 24)
Gas	**N:** Exxon(*, D)
Food	**N:** Adobe Cafe Mexican, Chester Fried Chicken (Chevron TS), Hot Stuff Pizza (Chevron TS), K&G Steakhouse, Madison's Restaurant (Holiday Inn), Subway (Chevron TS)
Lodg	**N:** Holiday Inn
TServ	**N:** Carter's Tire Center
ATM	**N:** Chevron Travel Center, Exxon
612	U.S. 90, Seguin
RVCamp	**N:** Dusty Oaks RV Park (3 Miles, Complete Facility)

EXIT	TEXAS
(615)	Weigh Station (Westbound)
(616)	Weigh Station (Eastbound)
617	FM 2438
620	FM 1104, Kingsbury
(621)	Rest Area (RR, Phones, Picnic, Grills, Vending, RV Dump, P; Eastbound)
(621)	Rest Area (RR, Phones, Picnic, Grills, Vending, RV Dump, P; Westbound)
625	Darst Field Road
TServ	**S:** Trucks of Texas
628	TX 80, Nixon, San Marcos
FStop	**N:** Diamond Shamrock(*, D)
Gas	**S:** Exxon
RVCamp	**N:** Riverbend RV Park (.25 Miles)
Med	**N:** + Hospital
632	U.S. 90, U.S. 183, Gonzales, Cuero, Luling, Lockhart
TStop	**N:** Love's(*, 24)
Food	**N:** Subway (Love's)
ATM	**N:** Love's
Parks	**S:** Palmetto State Park (5 Miles)
637	FM 794, Harwood
642	TX 304, Bastrop, Gonzales
RVCamp	**N:** Noah's Land RV Park (5.5 Miles)
Parks	**N:** Noah's Land Wild Life Park
649	TX 97, Waelder, Gonzales
653	U.S. 90, Waelder
Gas	**N:** Texaco(*, D)
ATM	**N:** Texaco
(657)	Picnic Area (Picnic; Eastbound)
(657)	Picnic Area (Picnic, P; Westbound)
661	TX 95, FM 609, Flatonia, Smithville, Moulton, Shiner
TStop	**N:** Mobil(*, 24) (Roadside)
Gas	**N:** Conoco **S:** Exxon(*), Shell(*, 24)
Food	**N:** Joel's BBQ (Conoco), Mi Ranchito, Stockman's Restaurant (Mobil TS) **S:** Dairy Queen(PLAY), Dan's BBQ (Exxon), Grumpy's Restaurant (Grumpy's Motor Inn), Homestyle Fried Chicken (Exxon)
Lodg	**S:** Grumpy's Motor Inn, Sav-Inn Antlers Inn
AServ	**N:** Flatonia Auto & Truck Repair
TServ	**N:** Flatonia Auto & Truck Repair, Mobil(24) (Roadside)
ATM	**N:** Conoco **S:** Dairy Queen

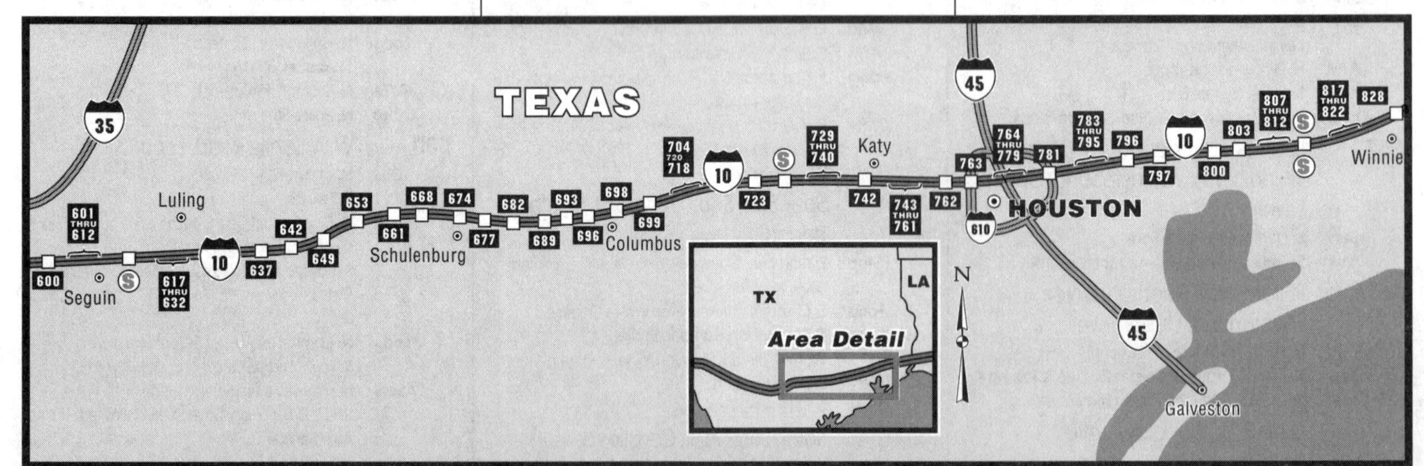

Bold red print shows RV & Bus parking available or nearby

EXIT		TEXAS
	Other	S: Maytag Washateria (Coin Laundry)
668		FM 2238, Engle
674		U.S. 77, Schulenburg, La Grange, Hallettsville
	FStop	S: Phillips 66(*)
	Gas	N: Chevron(*, D, CW, 24), Exxon(*, D)
		S: Diamond Shamrock(*), Exxon(*), Texaco(D)
	Food	N: Bar-B Q Smoke House, Chester Fried Chicken (Exxon), McDonald's(PLAY), Oakridge Restaurant
		S: Burger King, Dairy Queen, Diamond S Family Dining, Frank's Restaurant, Subway (Diamond Shamrock)
	Lodg	N: Oakridge Motor Inn
	AServ	S: Texaco
	RVCamp	S: Schulenberg RV Park (.25 Miles)(see our ad this page)
	ATM	N: Chevron
		S: Instant Cash
677		U.S. 90
	Food	N: Nannie's Biscuit and Bakery
	Other	N: Fostoria Glass Outlet
682		FM 155, Weimar
	Gas	N: Exxon(*, D), Texaco(*, D)
	Food	N: Dairy Queen, Texaco
	AServ	N: Exxon, Weimar Ford
	Med	N: ✚ Hospital
	ATM	N: Exxon
689		U.S. 90, Hattermann Lane
	RVCamp	N: Motorcoach RV Park
(692)		Rest Area (RR, Phones, Picnic, Grills, Vending, P; Eastbound)
(692)		Rest Area (RR, Phones, Picnic, Grills, Vending, P; Westbound)
693		FM 2434, Glidden
695		West TX 71, La Grange, Austin (Limited Access Hwy)
696		S. TX 71, Bus. TX 71, Columbus, EL Campo
	FStop	S: Diamond Shamrock(*)
	Gas	N: Chevron(*, D, CW, 24), Texaco(*)
		S: Exxon(*, D), Mobil(*, D)
	Food	N: Burger King, Denny's, Guadalajara Restaurant, Pizza Hut, Schobels' Restaurant, Whataburger(24)
		S: Church's Chicken (Mobil), McDonald's(PLAY), Sonic Drive In, Subway (Mobil)
	Lodg	N: Columbus Inn Motel
		S: Country Hearth Inn
	AServ	N: Columbus Ford Mercury
		S: Exxon
	RVCamp	S: Columbus RV Park & Campground
	Med	N: ✚ Hospital
	ATM	N: Texaco
		S: Exxon
	Other	N: H-E-B Pantry Foods, Wal-Mart(RX)
		S: Columbus Mini Golf
698		Alleyton Road, US 90, Columbus
	Gas	S: Shell(*, D) (see our ad this page)
	Food	N: Jerry Mikeska's BBQ
		S: Baskin Robbins (Shell), Grandy's (Shell), Taco Bell (Shell)
	AServ	S: Bob's Tire & Truck Service
	TServ	S: Bob's Tire & Truck Service
	ATM	S: Shell
699		(29) FM 102 Eagle Lake
	RVCamp	N: Happy Oaks RV Park (1 Mile)
	Parks	S: Wild Life Viewing Area
704		FM 949
709		FM 2761, Bernardo Road

EXIT		TEXAS
	Food	N: Texas Travel Stop and Grill
713		Beckendorff Road
	Other	S: Lonestar Raceway
716		Pyka Road
	TStop	N: Sealy(*)
	Food	N: Sealy
	TServ	N: Sealy
718		U.S. 90 (Eastbound, Reaccess Westbound Only)
720		TX 36, Sealy, Rosenberg, Bellville, Eagle Lake
	FStop	S: Mobil(*)
	Gas	N: Exxon, Texaco(*, D)
		S: Chevron(*, D, CW, 24), Shell(*, D, CW) (see our ad this page)
	Food	N: Dairy Queen, Hartz Chicken, McDonald's(PLAY), Sonic Drive In, Tony's Restaurant
		S: Buffet House (Chinese), Hinze's BBQ, KFC, Omar's, Pizza Hut, Subway, Taco Bell, Whataburger(24)
	Lodg	S: Best Western, Holiday Inn Express, Rodeway Inn
	AServ	N: Cliff Jones GM(LP), Hi/Lo Auto Supply
		S: Dowell Plymouth, Dodge, Eagle
	RVCamp	N: Airstream RV Sales & Service(LP)
	ATM	N: Tony's Restaurant
		S: Shell
	Other	N: U.S. Post Office
		S: Bill's Supermarket, Wal-Mart(RX)
721		U.S. 90
	AServ	N: West 10 Ford Mercury
	ATM	S: Outlet Center
	Other	S: Outlet Center
723		FM1458, San Felipe, Frydek
	TStop	N: Knox(*, SCALES, 24) (Coastal)
	Food	N: Subway (Knox TS)
	AServ	S: Riverside Tire Center
	TServ	N: Brown Truck Tire Center
		S: Riverside Tire Center
	ATM	N: Knox (Coastal)
	Parks	N: Stephen F. Austin State Park (3 Miles)
(726)		Weigh Station (Westbound)
725		Mlcak Rd. (Westbound)
730		Peach Ridge Road
(731)		Parking Area (Picnic, P; Left Exit)
731		FM 1489, Koomey Road, Simonton
	FStop	N: Exxon(*)
	Gas	N: Shell(*, CW, 24)
	Food	N: Texas Rose Family Restaurant (Travelers Inn), Villa Fuentes Mexican Restaurant
	Lodg	N: Brookshire Hotel, Travelers Inn
	AServ	S: Ford Truck Sales
	RVCamp	N: KOA Kampground(RV DUMP)
	Other	S: Brookshire Animal Clinic, Propane Co.(LP)
732		FM 359, Brookshire
	TStop	N: Ambest Houston West Travel Center(*, SCALES)
	FStop	N: Citgo
		S: Conoco(*, SCALES)
	Gas	N: Texaco(*)
		S: Chevron(*, CW), Coastal(*)
	Food	N: Ambest Houston West Travel Center, Charlie's Hamburgers, Joel's BBQ
		S: Burger King (Coastal), Jack-In-The-Box(24)
	Lodg	N: Brazos Valley Inn
	TServ	N: Ambest Houston West Travel Center(SCALES)
		S: Brookshire Truck and Trailor Parts
	TWash	S: Conoco
	ATM	N: Ambest Houston West Travel Center, Citgo
		S: Chevron
737		Pederson Road
740		FM 1463, Pin Oak Road
	Gas	S: Chevron(*)
	Food	S: Calli Chocolates & Coffee House, Chevron, Fruit Cup & More, Truffle Hound Gourmet
	Med	S: ✚ Columbia Katy Medical Center
	ATM	S: Chevron
742		West US 90, Katy; Katy - Fort Bend County Road, Rhodes Stadium
	FStop	S: Mobil(*)
	Gas	N: Citgo(*)
	ATM	N: Citgo
	Other	N: Police Station
743		Grand Pkwy, TX 99
	Food	S: Kettle
	Lodg	S: Best Western
	AServ	S: Atlas Auto Repair & Transmission, Professional Tire & Auto, Westside Chevrolet

1171
Schulenburg RV Park
Visit: Self-Guided Historic Painted Churches Tour
Walk To: • German/Czech Bakery • 7 Restaurants • Groceries
• 20/30/50 amps • Modern Jack
Good Sampark
(409) 743-4388
1-800-771-9955
65 NORTH KESSLER
Schulenburg, Tx 78956
E-mail: schurvpk@fais.net
http://schurvpk.fais.net
TEXAS ▪ I-10 ▪ EXIT 674

Show This Ad For A Free Cinnamon Roll
1507
Open 24 Hours
Easy Access
Shell
Taco Bell
Baskin Robbins
Clean Restrooms
Auto Diesel
Fast, Courteous Service
Plenty of Parking For RV's
Convenience Store • ATM
All Major Credit Cards
Checks Accepted
409-733-0000
TEXAS ▪ I-10 ▪ EXIT 698

1508
Open 24 Hours
Easy Access
Shell
Checks Accepted
ATM
Lottery
Clean Restrooms
Auto Diesel • Car Wash
Fast, Courteous Service
Convenience Store
All Major Credit Cards
409-885-2321
TEXAS ▪ I-10 ▪ EXIT 720

EXIT TEXAS

Other **S:** Houston Animal Clinic

745 Mason Road

Gas **S:** Diamond Shamrock(*, CW), Shell(*, CW, 24)
Food **S:** Black-Eyed Pea, Cancun Chef, Chick-Fil-A(PLAY), Chili's, China Inn Cafe, Hartz Chicken, Johnny Carino's Italian Kitchen, Landry's Seafood, Luby's Cafeteria, Marble Slab Creamery Ice Cream, Marco's, McDonald's(PLAY), Papa John's Pizza, Pizza Hut, Southern Maid Donuts, Taco Cabana
Lodg **S:** Holiday Inn Express, Ramada Limited, Super 8
AServ **S:** Discount Tire Company, Mike's Mufflers, Texan Ford
ATM **S:** Chase Bank
Other **S:** **Clubhouse Books, Eckerd Drugs(RX), Fed Ex Drop Box, Gerland's Food Store(24), Petco, Rejoice Christian Bookstore**, Stop-N-Fast Food Store

747 Fry Road

Gas **N:** Phillips 66(*), Shell(*, CW)
S: Chevron(*, CW), Diamond Shamrock(*, D), Shell(*, CW, 24)
Food **N:** Blimpie Subs & Salads, Burger King(PLAY), Dairy Queen, Daylight Donuts, Denny's, Hartz Chicken Buffet, McDonald's(PLAY), Pizza Hut, Sonic Drive In, Taco Bell, Texas Borders, Victor's Casa Garcia
S: Bo's Best BBQ (Shell), Boston Market Restaurant, El Chico, Fazoli's Italian Food, IHOP, Jack-In-The-Box(24), Omar's, Orient Express, Outback Steakhouse, Shipley Do-nuts, The Original Pasta Company, Wendy's
AServ **N:** Econo Lube & Tune, **Wal-Mart(RX) (Vision Center, 1-Hr Photo)**
ATM **N: Kroger Supermarket(24, RX)**, Phillips 66
S: Albertson's Grocery(24, RX), Community Bank, Diamond Shamrock, NationsBank, Shell
Other **N: Garden Ridge, Home Depot, Kroger Supermarket(RX)**, Kwik Kar Wash, Mail Boxes Etc, **Wal-Mart(RX) (Vision Center, 1-Hr Photo), WalGreens Pharmacy(24, RX) (1-Hr Photo)**
S: Albertson's Grocery(RX), Fox Photo 1-Hr Lab, Lowe's, PetsMart, Postmark Mail & Copies, Target

748 Barker - Cypress Road

Gas **N:** Mobil(*)
Food **S:** **Cracker Barrel**, Larry's BBQ
ATM **N:** Mobil
Other **N:** Airport

750 Park Ten Blvd. (Westbound)

Food **N:** Freddy's Breakfast & Lunch
Other **N: US Post Office**

751 TX 6, Addicks

Gas **N:** Texaco(*)
S: Chevron(*, 24), Texaco(*, D)
Food **N:** Cattleguard Restaurant, Holiday Inn Select, **Waffle House**
S: Burger Tex Burgers & Steaks, Charlie's Hamburger Joint, Denny's, Durango's, El Yucatan, Grisby Grill, Jack-In-The-Box(24), Kim House Hunan Cuisine, Lupe Tortilla(PLAY), Pasta Lo Monte's, Red Barn Creamery
Lodg **N:** Drury Inn, Holiday Inn Select, Homestead Village, Red Roof Inn
S: Fairfield Inn by Marriott, La Quinta Inn & Suites, Motel 6, Towne Place Suites
AServ **N:** Auto Check, **Sam's Club**
S: Texaco
RVCamp **S: Amerigas/John Varcados Exxon (2 Miles)**
ATM **S:** Wells Fargo
Other **N: Sam's Club**
S: U.S. Post Office

753A Eldridge Parkway, Addicks - Fairbanks Rd.

Gas **N:** Conoco(*, D, CW)
S: Diamond Shamrock(*, CW)

EXIT TEXAS

Food **N:** Shipley Do-nuts (Conoco)
Lodg **N:** Marriott
AServ **N:** Conoco
S: Kwik Kar Lube & Tune

753B Dairy - Ashford Road

Gas **S:** Exxon(*, D, CW)
Food **S:** Becks Prime, Cliff's & Otto's Burgers & BBQ, Palm Beach Club Restaurant (Hilton), Ryan's Steakhouse, SHONEY'S Shoney's (Shoney's Inn), Subway, Whataburger(24)
Lodg **S:** Hilton Inn, Shoney's Inn & Suites
AServ **S:** Don McGill Porsche, Audi, Ernie Guzman Pontiac GMC Trucks, McGinnis Cadillac, McGinnis Mitsubishi
ATM **S:** Bank United, CSB Community Bank, Exxon, Prime Bank
Other **S: Golf Warehouse, Produce Market & Vitamins**

754 Kirkwood

Gas **S:** Chevron(*, D), Shell(*, CW, 24)
Food **S:** Carrabba's Italian Grill, Dirty's Restaurant Bar, IHOP, Taco Cabana, The Original Pasta Co.
Lodg **S:** Hampton Inn
AServ **N:** Crown Dodge, Discount Tire Company, Don McGill Toyota, Honda, Acura Auto Repair, Infiniti Dealer, Mossy Nissan, Nils Sefeldt Volvo, Professional Car Care, Saturn of Houston, West Point Buick, West Point KIA, West Point Lincoln Mercury, West Side Lexus
S: Chevron, Mac Haik GMC Dealer
Other **S: Kirkwood Pharmacy(RX), Mountasia Fantasy Golf**

755 Wilcrest Dr., E. & W. Beltway 8, Frontage Rd

Gas **N:** Gas(*)
S: Exxon(*, 24), Sunny's(*), Texaco(*)
Food **N:** Sam's Deli Diner
S: China Plaza (La Quinta Inn), Jo Jos(24), McDonald's(PLAY, 24) (Exxon), Shipley Do-nuts (Exxon), Steak & Ale
Lodg **S:** La Quinta Inn
AServ **N:** Discount Collision, Jeff Haas Mazda, NTB
S: Texaco
ATM **S:** Exxon, Sunny's
Other **N: Washateria**
S: Joe's Golf House, Town & Country Mall

756A Beltway 8, N. & S. Frontage Roads (Westbound)

756B N. & S. Sam Houston Toll Way (Toll)

757 Gessner Road

Gas **N:** Chevron(CW) (Mr. Car Wash), Exxon(*)
S: Shell(*), Texaco(D, CW)
Food **N:** Asiana Garden, Ci Ci's Pizza, Golden King Chinese Buffet, Goodson's Cafe, Luther's BBQ, Schlotzsky's Deli, ThunderCloud Subs, Whataburger(24)
S: Champs Country Breakfast, Fuddruckers, Jason's Deli, Pappadeaux, Pappasitos Cantina, Romano's Macaroni Grill, Taste of Texas Restaurant
Lodg **S:** Candlewood Studio Hotel
AServ **N:** Brake Check, CSI Collision, Detail Lube Center, Exxon, Pep Boys Auto Center
S: Mac Haik Auto Service, Montgomery Ward, Sears
TServ **S: Mac Haik Auto Service**
Med **S: + Memorial Hospital Memorial City**
ATM **N:** Chase Bank
S: Sterling Bank, Wells Fargo
Other **N: Boater's World Discount Marine, Memorial Market**
S: Discovery Zone, Memorial City Shopping Mall, Office Depot, Petco Supplies, **Sony Theatres, WalGreens Pharmacy(RX)**

EXIT TEXAS

758A Bunker Hill Road, Memorial City Way

Gas **S:** Diamond Shamrock(*, D), Texaco(D)
Food **S:** Charlie's Hamburger Joint, Hunan Inn, Kobe Japanese Restaurant, La Fiesta, **Luby's Cafeteria**, Prince's Hamburgers (Days Inn), Quizno's Classic Sub, Shipley Do-nuts, Subway
Lodg **S:** Days Inn, Quality Inn
AServ **N:** Spring Branch Honda
S: Fixacar, Goodyear Tire & Auto, Texaco
ATM **S:** Compass Bank, Diamond Shamrock, Frost Bank
Other **S: American Pro-Line Golf, Bunker Hill Bowl, Eyemasters, Target, Toys R Us**

758B Blalock Road, Campbell Road, Echo Lane

Gas **S:** Chevron(*, CW)
Food **N:** Sonic Drive In
S: Baskin Robbins, McDonald's(PLAY, 24) (Chevron), Moveable Feast Natural Cafe, **Ninfas**, Three E's, **Villages Cafe (Kroger)**
AServ **N:** Adams Automotive, Lube Stop
S: Robert's Auto Works
Med **S: + Columbia West Houston Medical Center**
ATM **N: Fiesta Supermarket**
S: Chevron, **Stop N Go(*)**
Other **N: Fiesta Supermarket, Key Rexall Drugs(RX), The Photo Lab**
S: AAA Auto Club, Echo Lane Animal Clinic, Factory Eyeglass Outlet, Kroger Supermarket(24, RX), Postmark Mail, Stop N Go, United Optical, WalGreens Pharmacy(RX)

759 Campbell Rd. (Westbound)

Gas **N:** Phillips 66(*)
Food **N:** Bel Ami Croissant, Ciro's Cibi Italiani, General Joe's Chopstix, The Great Charcoal Chicken
Med **N: + Hospital**
Parks **N: City Hall(PLAY)**
Other **N:** Mail It!

760 Bingle Road, Voss Road

Gas **S:** Exxon(*, D), Texaco(D)
Food **S:** Good Co. Texas Bar-B-Q, Las Alamedas, Marie Callender's Restaurant, Pappy's, Saltgrass Steak House, Southwell's Hamburger Grill, Sweet Tomatoes, The Mason Jar, Ugo's Italian Grill
AServ **S:** Texaco
Med **N: + Hospital**
ATM **S:** NationsBank, Prime Bank
Other **S: Academy, Animal Emergency Clinic, Scuba, United Pharmacy(RX)**

761A Chimney Rock Road, Wirt Road

Gas **S:** Chevron(*, D, CW), Exxon(*, CW), Shell(*, CW)
Food **S:** 59 Diner, Dixie's Red Hot Roadhouse, McDonald's(PLAY), TCBY (Exxon)
Lodg **S:** La Quinta Inn
RVCamp **N: ABA Travel Park (1.5 Miles)**
ATM **S:** Chevron, Exxon, Prime Bank, Stopn Go
Other **S:** Stopn Go

761B Antoine Drive (Eastbound)

Food **S:** Denny's, Fuzzy's Pizza & Cafe, Mandola's Italian Restaurant, Papa John's Pizza, Whataburger(24)
Lodg **S:** HomeGate Studios & Suites
AServ **S:** NTB
ATM **S: Memorial Market**
Other **S: Hospital for Animals**, Mail Boxes Etc., **Memorial Market, Rei Sports Supplies, West Marine**

762 Silber Road, Post Oak Road, Antoine Dr.

Gas **N:** Chevron, Diamond Shamrock(*)
S: Shell(*, CW, 24)
Food **N:** Hunan Chef All Day Buffet, Steak Kountry Buffet, Wheel Burger
S: Aubrey's Ribs (Holiday Inn), Jack-In-The-Box,

Bold red print shows RV & Bus parking available or nearby

EXIT TEXAS

Shipley Do-nuts
Lodg **S:** Holiday Inn, Ramada Plaza Hotel
AServ **N:** Chevron, Courtesy Geo Chevrolet, Katy Freeway Tire (Firestone)
S: Courtesy Chevrolet
Med **N:** ✚ **Family Practice & Walk-In Clinic**
ATM **N:** Diamond Shamrock
S: Shell

763 I-610 North & South

764 Westcott St, Washington Ave, Katy Road
Gas **S:** Chevron[*, 24]
Food **N:** Denny's
S: IHOP, McDonald's
Lodg **N:** **Roadway Inn**
S: Scottish Inn
AServ **S:** Cooksey's West End Radiator
Parks **S:** **Memorial Park**

765A TC Jester Blvd
Gas **S:** Exxon[*], Texaco[*, D]
Food **N:** Perfecto Espresso & Tea
AServ **N:** Comet Tire, Discount Auto Parts Exchange
S: Engine Depot, Texaco
Other **N:** **City of Houston Fire Station**

765B N. Shepherd Dr., Patterson St., N. Durham Dr.
Gas **N:** Stewart's Walco Service[*]
S: Diamond Shamrock[*, D]
Food **N:** Wendy's
S: Hofbrau Steaks, Jax Grill, Pizzitola's BBQ
Lodg **N:** Howard Johnson
AServ **N:** ABC Auto Parts, Castl Transmissions, Midas Muffler & Brake, Stewart's Walco Service
ATM **N:** NationsBank
S: Diamond Shamrock
Other **N:** **Pet Vet Animal Hospital**

766 Studemont St., Heights Blvd. , Yale St. (Westbound)
Gas **N:** Chevron[*, 24]
S: Exxon[*, D]
AServ **N:** Kelley's Complete Car Care
S: Exxon

767A Yale St, Height Blvd, Studemont St. (Eastbound, Same Services As 766)

767B Taylor St

768AB 768A - I-45 N. Dallas, 768B - I-45 S. Galveston (Westbound, Left Exit Eastbound)

769A Downtown, Smith St (Eastbound)
Food **S:** All Street Deli, Longhorn Cafe, Palace Cafe
ATM **S:** Bank One, Chase Bank
Other **S:** **Alley Theater, The Jesse Jones Hall for the Performing Arts, The Theater District**, U.S. Post Office

769C McKee St, Hardy St, Nance St (Difficult Reaccess)
Parks **S:** **James Bute Park**

769B San Jacinto St., Main St.

770A US 59S Victoria, Dowtown (Left Exit Eastbound)

770C US 59 N Cleavand

770B Jensen Dr, Gregg St, Meadow St. (Difficult Reaccess)
TServ **N:** **Daniel Radiator**

771A Waco St
Food **N:** Chirps Chicken, Frenchy's Chicken
Lodg **N:** Sunrise Motel, Waco Motel
Other **N:** **Washateria**

EXIT TEXAS

S: **American Food Store & Washateria**

771B Lockwood Drive
FStop **S:** **Texaco[*]**
Gas **N:** Chevron[*, D, CW, 24], Mobil[*]
S: King Truck Stop[*, D]
Food **N:** McDonald's[PLAY]
S: Kozy Kitchen BBQ, Salotso's Pizza, Timmy Dang's Chicken
Lodg **S:** Palace Inn
AServ **N:** Auto Zone Auto Parts
S: **Texaco**
ATM **N:** Chase Bank, Chevron, **Fiesta Grocery**
Other **N:** **Eckerd Drugs[RX]**, **Fiesta Grocery**, Lyon's Pharmacy[RX], Texas State Optical, **WalGreens Pharmacy[RX] (1-Hr Photo)**

772 Kress St, Lathrop St
Gas **N:** Citgo[*], Conoco, Gas
S: Best Buy Food Mart[*]
Food **N:** Antonio's, Dixie Maid Hamburger, Domino's Pizza, Popeye's Chicken, Restaurant El Pariente, Samburger
S: Burger King[PLAY], Ostioneria 7 Mares #5, Porras Prontito
AServ **N:** Conoco, D & H Tire, Denver Harbor Auto Clinic, PEP Boys Express
ATM **N:** Citgo
Other **N:** Car Wash, **Matamoros Meat Market**, **Public Library**, **U Do Washeria (Coin Op Laundry)**, Wash & Vac Truck & Car Wash (Light Trucks)
S: **Kress Food Store**, **Lathrop Washateria**, **Russo's Food Market**

773A U.S. 90 Alt, N Wayside Drive (Reaccess Eastbound Only)
FStop **S:** **Coastal[*]**, **Mobil[*]**
Gas **S:** Shell[*, CW, 24]
Food **N:** Jack-In-The-Box, Whataburger[24]
S: Church's Chicken, Cozumel Taqueria
AServ **N:** **Wayside Auto & Truck Parts**
S: **Buddy Doyle's Diagnostic Car Clinic**, G & G Body Shop, J & T Parts & Repair, Quality Tire Service
TServ **N:** **Houston Truck Parts**, **Wayside Auto & Truck Parts**
S: **Buddy Doyle's Diagnostic Car Clinic**, **Mobil**
ATM **S:** **Mobil**, Mucho Mexico
Other **N:** Speedy Mart[*]

773B McCarty Drive
Gas **N:** Exxon[*, D], Shell[*, CW, 24]
Food **S:** Don Chile Mexican, Subway
AServ **N:** McCarty Auto Parts
TServ **N:** **Amigo Truck Parts[SCALES]**, **Depco Diesel Engine**, **Houston Freightliner**
S: **A-1 Public Scales[SCALES, 24]**, **A-1 Truck Parts & Equip.**, **Chalks Truck Parts Inc.**, **Mustang Truck Sales[SCALES]**, **Nick's Diesel Service**, **Randy's**, **Truck Wash 24 Hr (Oil Changes, etc)**
TWash **S:** **Truck Wash 24 Hr[24]**
Other **N:** **East Freeway Animal Clinic**

774 Gellhorn Drive (Eastbound)

775AB Junction I-610

776A Mercury Drive, Jacinto City, Galena Park
Gas **N:** Citgo[*], Mobil[*]
S: Diamond Shamrock[*, D, LP, 24], Mr. Mercury[*], Texaco[*, D, CW]
Food **N:** Burger King, East China Restaurant, McDonald's[PLAY], Pizza Inn, Taqueria Arandas
S: Dairy Queen, Donald Donuts, Luby's Cafeteria, Pizzini's, Steak & Ale, Taqueria Mi Jalisco
Lodg **N:** Best Western, Fairfield Inn, Hampton Inn, Premier Inn
AServ **N:** Citgo
TServ **N:** **Lakeview Volvo**

EXIT TEXAS

ATM **S:** Capital Bank, Diamond Shamrock, Prime Bank
Other **N:** Army Surplus
S: **Mercury Dr. Pharmacy[RX]**

776B John Ralston Road, Holland Ave, Jacinto City, Galena Park
Gas **N:** Chevron[*, D, 24], Mobil[*, D]
S: Eddie's Food Store[*]
Food **N:** Denny's, Golden River Chinese Buffet, Pappasitos, **The Raintree**
Lodg **N:** DAYS INN **Days Inn**, **La Quinta Inn**
AServ **N:** Chevron[24], Discount Tire Company, NTB
S: Discount Auto Service Center Inc., Murry's Auto Center, Parker Automotive Inc.
ATM **N:** **Fiesta Grocery**
Other **N:** **Fiesta Grocery**, **Kroger Supermarket[24]**, **Sunny's Food Store**, **Target**
S: **Jacinto City Animal Hospital**

778A FM 526, Pasadena, Federal Road (Westbound Says Normandy Street)
FStop **N:** **Conoco[*]**
Gas **N:** Diamond Shamrock[*, D, LP], Shell[*, CW, 24]
S: Diamond Shamrock[*, 24], Exxon, Shell[*, 24]
Food **N:** Casa Ole, El Imperial, Express Subs, **Golden Corral Family Steakhouse**, Jack-In-The-Box (Shell), KFC, Little Caesars Pizza, Long John Silver, Luby's Cafeteria, Pizza Hut, Popeye's Chicken, Subway, Taco Bell
S: Catfish Kitchen, Chili's, Church's Chicken, **James Coney Island**, Jo's Crab Shack, **McDonald's[PLAY]**, Ninfa's, Pappas Seafood House, Peking Bo, Taqueria Los Reyes
AServ **N:** Andrell Automotive
S: Exxon, Hi/Lo Auto Supply, Midas Muffler Shops
TWash **S:** **Truck Wash**
ATM **N:** Lone Star Bank, NationsBank
Parks **S:** **J.P. White Park[PLAY]**
Other **N:** **Eckerd Drugs[RX]**, **H-E-B Pantry Foods**, **Office Depot**, Sam Car Wash
S: **Auto Wash at the Truck Wash**, **Eastway Cinema 4**, Tinsel Town Theaters

778B Normandy St. (Eastbound)
FStop **S:** **Eastop[*]**
Food **S:** Taqueria Guanajuato
Lodg **S:** Bayou Motel, Normandy Inn
AServ **S:** Carquest Auto Parts, Ernesto Radiator, Fain's Auto Service & Parts, Market St. Used Auto Parts, Mauricio's, **Spurlock's Garage**
TServ **S:** **Spurlock's Garage**
Other **S:** **Animana Veterinary Center**, **Garcia & Associates Eye Clinic**

779A Westmont St. (Difficult Reaccess)
Gas **N:** Chevron[*]
Lodg **N:** **Interstate Motor Lodge**
Med **N:** ✚ **Columbia East Houston Medical Center**

779B Uvalde Road, Freeport St, Market St. (Westbound)
Gas **N:** Exxon[D], Mobil[*]
Food **N:** HoBo's, IHOP, Jack-In-The-Box, KFC, Poncho's Mexican Buffet, Shipley Do-nuts[24], Subway, Szechuan Wok
AServ **N:** Exxon, Meineke Discount Mufflers, Uvalde Mufflers
ATM **N:** Wood Forest National Bank
Other **N:** **ACE Hardware**, **Fire Department**, **Sellers Bros.**, **Texas State Optical**, **WalGreens Pharmacy[RX]**

780 Market St Road, Uvalde Rd, Freeport St
Gas **N:** Mobil[*], Texaco[*]
Food **N:** Nuevo Leon Meat Market
S: Black-Eyed Pea, Joe King Steakhouse, Marco's Mexican, **McDonald's (Wal-Mart)**, Whataburger[24]

EXIT TEXAS

Lodg N: Beaumont Hilton (see our ad this page)
AServ N: Crazy Don's Used Tires[24], Freeport Tire Service
S: Sam's Club, Wal-Mart[24, RX] (Optical, 1-Hr Photo)
ATM N: Texaco
S: Bank of America, Wal-Mart (Optical, 1-Hr Photo)
Other N: Bi-Rite Supermarket
S: Sam's Club, The Home Depot[LP], U-Haul Center[LP], Wal-Mart[RX] (Optical, 1-Hr Photo)

781A Beltway 8, Frontage Rd (Limited Access Hwy)
FStop S: Mobil[*]
AServ S: Baker Tire Co., Hanvy Auto Electric
TServ S: Baker Tire Co.
ATM S: Mobil

781B Beltway 8, Sam Houston Pkwy
Food N: Brewsky's (Holiday Inn)
Lodg N: Holiday Inn
Med N: + Columbia East Houston Medical Center

782 Dell Dale Ave. (Eastbound)
Gas N: Harper's[*]
Food N: Helen's Malts "N" Hamburgers, Mom's Kountry Cafe
Lodg N: Days Inn, Dell Dale Motel, I-10 Motel
S: Shady Glen Motel
AServ N: Dr. Rick's Auto Clinic
RVCamp N: Bob's LP Gas[LP], Channelview Supply Company
S: Channelview Supply Company[LP]
ATM N: The Pink Store Supermarket[24]
Other N: Bob's LP Gas[LP], Bud's LP Gas[LP], Let Carter's Cleaners (Laundry), The Pink Store Supermarket

783 Sheldon Road, Channelview
FStop N: Coastal[*, D]
Gas N: Diamond Shamrock[*], Shell[*, CW, 24]
S: Chevron[*, 24], Shell[*, 24]
Food N: Best Western, Burger King, Jack-In-The-Box[24], KFC, Pizza Hut, Pizza Inn, Popeye's Chicken, Subway, Taco Bell, Whataburger[24]
S: Captain D's Seafood, El Tejano, McDonald's[PLAY], Wendy's
Lodg N: Best Western, Leisure Inn, Super 8, TraveLodge Suites
AServ N: Auto Zone Auto Parts, Channelview Auto Supply, Discount Tire Company
S: Lyall Bros. Collision, Shell[24], Spiller's Automotive
TServ N: K-Rohn
ATM N: Coastal, Diamond Shamrock, Highlands State Bank, Shell
Other N: Eckerd Drugs[RX], Family Christian Stores, Gerland's Food Fair[24], US Post Office

784 Cedar Lane, Bayou Drive
Gas N: Citgo[*]
Food N: EconoLodge
S: I-10 Mexican Restaurant
Lodg N: EconoLodge, Magnolia Motel, Ramada Limited
TServ S: Channelview, Griffith Truck & Equip, Tommy's Truck Sales & Equip
RVCamp S: RV Outlet Mall
Other S: Land's Cycles

785 Magnolia Ave, Channelview
TStop N: Shell[*, SCALES]
S: Key Truck Stop[*, SCALES, 24] (Showers, Laundry)
FStop S: Kings[*]
Food N: Jack-In-The-Box, Shell
S: Key Truck Stop (Showers, Laundry)
TServ S: Guidry Equipment & Service, Highlands Diesel, Kings, Trak-ta-lube
TWash S: Kings
RVCamp S: Adventure RV

EXIT TEXAS

ATM N: Shell
S: Key Truck Stop (Showers, Laundry)
Other S: 4 G's Electronics

786 Monmouth Drive

787 Crosby - Lynchburg Rd, Spur 330
FStop N: Mobil[*]
Gas S: Phillips 66
Food S: Lynchburg Grill[24]
AServ S: Benders Radiator Shop
RVCamp N: Camping, Houston Leisure RV Park[LP] (.5 Miles)
S: Camping, San Jacinto State Park
ATM N: Mobil
S: Phillips 66
Parks S: San Jacinto State Park
Other N: Pet World, Stingray Marine

788 Spur 330, Baytown (Eastbound, Limited Access Hwy)

(788) Rest Area (RR, Phones, Picnic, Grills, Pet Walk, P; Eastbound)

(788) Rest Area (RR, Phones, Picnic, Grills, Pet Walk, P; Westbound)

789 Thompson Road, McNair
TStop S: T/A TravelCenters of America[*, 24]
FStop N: Delta Express[*, SCALES]
Food S: Country Pride (T of A)
AServ N: Reading Buick, Pontiac, GMC
TServ S: T/A TravelCenters of America[24]
ATM S: T/A TravelCenters of America

790 Ellis School Rd (Westbound)

791 John Martin Road, Wade Rd.

792 Garth Road
Gas N: Chevron[*, CW]
S: Racetrac[*], Shell[*, CW]
Food N: Burger King[PLAY], Cracker Barrel, Denny's, Jack-In-The-Box, Kettle, Red Lobster, Shoney's, Waffle House, Whataburger[24]
S: Lee Palace, McDonald's[PLAY], Pancho's, Piccadilly Cafeteria, Popeye's Chicken, Taco Bell, Tortuga, Wendy's
Lodg N: Best Western, Budgetel Inn, Hampton Inn, La Quinta Inn
S: Holiday Inn Express
AServ N: Casa Ford
S: Sears
RVCamp S: Terry Vaughn RVs
ATM N: Chevron
S: Bayshore National Bank
Other S: Cinema 6, San Jacinto Mall, Texas State Optical

793 North Main St
TStop S: Pilot Travel Center[*, SCALES] (Showers)
Food S: KFC Express (Pilot TS), Subway (Pilot TS)
AServ N: Baytown Nissan, Ron Craft Chrysler
Other S: Airport

795 Sjolander Road
TStop N: Pappa Truck Stop[*] (Showers)
Food N: Pappa Truck Stop (Showers)
AServ N: Pappa Truck Stop (Showers)

796A Frontage Rd. (Westbound)

796B Frontage Rd (Westbound)

797 TX 146, Mont Belvieu, Dayton, Baytown
TStop S: Mobil[*]
FStop N: Conoco[*], Texaco[*, CW]
Gas N: Chevron[*]
S: Exxon
Food N: Dairy Queen, Iguana Joe's, Pizza Inn, Subway, Waffle House
S: Jack-In-The-Box, Popeye's Chicken (Mobil TS)
Lodg N: Motel 6, Scanadian Inn
AServ S: Exxon
RVCamp S: KOA Kampground
Med S: + Hospital
ATM N: Conoco, Texaco
S: Mobil
Other N: Stop-N-Good Food Market
S: Able LP Gas Inc.[LP], Abshier-Meuth Animal Hospital

EXIT TEXAS

800 FM 3180

803 FM 565, Cove, Old River - Winfree

806 Frontage Rd (Eastbound)
Parks S: Wallisville Heritage Park
Other S: US Post Office, Wallisville Lake Project Ranger Station

807 Wallisville
Parks S: Wallisville Heritage Park
Other S: Wallisville Ranger Station

810 FM 563, Anahuac, Liberty
FStop S: Chevron[*, 24]
Food S: Blimpie's Subs (Chevron)
AServ S: Anahuac Auto
RVCamp N: Mobile Home Parking RV (8 Miles)
Other S: Stephenson Animal Clinic

811 Turtle Bayou Turnaround (Eastbound)
Food S: Grandma's Diner
RVCamp S: Turtle Bayou RV Park

812A Frontage Rd. (Westbound)
Gas S: Shell[*]
Food S: Shell
AServ S: Santos Ford
RVCamp N: RV Park

812 TX 61, Hankamer, Anahuac (Eastbound, Same Service As Exit 813)

813 TX 61, Hankamer
Gas S: Exxon[*, D]
ATM S: Exxon

(815) Weigh Station (Eastbound)

(815) Weigh Station (Westbound)

817 FM 1724

819 Jenkins Road
Gas S: Texaco[*]
Food S: Stuckey's (Texaco)

822 FM 1410

827 FM 1406

828 TX 73, 124, Winnie, Port Arthur (Eastbound)
Med S: + Hospital

829 FM 1663, Galvaston, Port Blvd., TX 73, TX 124, Winnie
FStop N: Exxon[*]
S: Phillips 66[*]
Gas N: Mobil[*, D], Texaco[*, D]
Food N: Blimpie Subs & Salads (Texaco), Burger King (Mobil), McDonald's, Taco Bell
S: AL T's Cajun, Hunan Chinese, Pizza Inn, Subway (Phillips 66), Waffle House
Lodg N: Holiday Inn Express
S: Best Western, Winnie Inn
AServ S: Vick's Road Service[24]
RVCamp N: RV Park
S: AL T's RV Park
ATM N: Texaco
S: Phillips 66, Winnie Banking Center

EXIT TEXAS

833 Hamshire Road
- FStop — N: **Chevron**(*)
- Food — N: **Bergeron's (Chevron)**

(837) **Parking Area (Picnic, Grills; Eastbound)**

(837) **Parking Area (Picnic, Grills, P; Westbound)**

838 FM 365
- Gas — N: Shell(*)
- RVCamp — N: **Lazy L Campground**

843 Smith Road

845 FM 364, Major Dr

846 Brooks Road (Eastbound, Reaccess Eastbound Only)

848 Walden Road
- TStop — S: **Petro**(*, SCALES) **(Mobil)**
- Gas — N: Texaco(*, D); S: Chevron(*, D, 24)
- Food — N: Pappadeaux Seafood Kitchen; S: Cheddar's, **Iron Skillet (Petro TS)**, Jack-In-The-Box, Jo's Crab Shack, Subway (Chevron), Waffle House
- Lodg — N: Holiday Inn; S: **Ramada Limited**
- TServ — N: **Performance Truck**
- TWash — S: **Petro (Mobil)**
- Parks — S: **Tyrrell Park**
- Other — N: **US Post Office**; S: **Tinsel Town USA Cinema**

849 U.S. 69 South, Washington Blvd, Port Arthur (Limited Access Hwy)

850 Washington Blvd.
- Gas — N: Exxon(*, D), Mobil(*, D); S: Chevron(*, CW)
- Food — N: Don's Seafood & Steakhouse, Miami Subs (Exxon), Outback Steakhouse, Post Oak Grill; S: Burger King (Chevron), Hilton
- Lodg — S: Courtyard by Marriott, Fairfield Inn, Hilton
- AServ — S: Auto Plex 2000, First Choice Auto Service, Kinsel Auto Ford, Mike Smith GMC, NTB, **Sam's Club**
- TServ — N: **Smart's Truck & Trailor Equip**
- RVCamp — S: **ABC Mobile Homes Supply**
- Other — S: **Animal Hospital, Sam's Club**

851 U.S. 90, College St
- Gas — N: Birdsongs(D, LP), Racetrac(*); S: Exxon(*, CW), Mobil(*), Shell(*, D)
- Food — N: Carrabba's Italian Grill, Fujiyama, Golden Corral Family Steakhouse, Waffle House; S: Burger King, Catfish Kitchen, China Hut, Dairy Queen(PLAY), Happy Buddha, Pig Stands Restaurant(24), Pizza Hut, SHONEY'S, Shoney's, Taste of China
- Lodg — N: Best Western, Comfort Inn, Roadrunner Motor Inn; S: Motel 6
- AServ — N: Binswanger Glass, Birdsongs, Hi/Lo Auto Parts, Magic Car & Lube Service; S: Firestone Tire & Auto, McDonald's Tire Center, Mobil, RX Seven Auto Repair, Super Shops
- RVCamp — N: **New World RV Sales & Service**
- Med — S: **+ Baptist Hospital**
- ATM — S: Chase Bank
- Other — N: **Dawson Marine, M & D Supply (Hardware), Sutherlands Building Supply**; S: **Cinema I & II, Office Depot, U-Haul Center**(LP), **WalGreens Pharmacy**(RX)

852A Laurel Ave (Westbound, Difficult Reaccess)
- Gas — N: Chevron(*, CW, 24), Texaco(*, D, CW)
- Food — N: Chili's, Willy Ray's BBQ
- ATM — N: Chevron, Texaco

852B Calder Ave, Harrison Ave, Gladys Ave
- Gas — N: Conoco(*); S: Chevron(*), E-Z Mart(*)
- Food — N: Bennigan's, Casa Ole, La Suprema, Olive Garden, Steak & Ale; S: Church's Chicken, Great China Restaurant, McDonald's, The Sports Page
- Lodg — S: DAYS INN Days Inn, La Quinta Inn
- AServ — S: Chevron
- Med — S: **+ St. Elizabeth Hospital**
- ATM — N: Chase Bank, Community Bank, PrimeBank
- Other — S: **Art Museum of S.E. Texas, StatCare Pharmacy**(RX), **Texas Marine**

853A U.S. 69 North, Lufkin (Limited Access Hwy)

853B 11th St (Difficult Reaccess)
- Gas — N: Fina(*); S: Conoco(*), E-Z Mart(*)
- Food — N: Denny's, Hoffbrau Steaks, Holiday Inn, Ninfa's, Red Lobster, The Ridgewood, Waffle House; S: Chula Vista, Luby's Cafeteria, Ramada Inn
- Lodg — N: Best Western, Holiday Inn (see our ad this page), Scottish Inns, Super 8, The Ridgewood, Travel Inn; S: Castle Motel (Laundromat), Ramada Inn
- ATM — S: E-Z Mart, Guaranty Federal Bank
- Other — N: **Market Basket**

853C 7th St (Eastbound)
- Gas — S: Shop N Go(*)

854 Spur 380, Babe Zaharias Museum, Fairgrounds
- Gas — N: Chevron(*); S: Exxon(D), Texaco(D)
- Food — N: Burger King(PLAY); S: McDonald's(PLAY)
- AServ — S: Exide Battery, Exxon, Fasulo Collision Repair, Neal Jacobs Automotive, Texaco
- RVCamp — S: **Morgan RVs Service & Sales**(D)
- Other — N: **Babe Didrikson Zaharias Museum**(PLAY)

1133

Beaumont Hilton

2355 I-10 South • Beaumont, TX 77705

Great Weekend Rates
Extended Cable
Fitness Center & Outdoor Pool
Restaurant & Lounge
Close to Shopping & Restaurants

Take Washington Blvd. Exit

409-842-3600 • Toll Free Reservations: 1-800-HILTONS

TEXAS ▪ I-10 ▪ EXIT 850

BEAUMONT MIDTOWN I-10

2095 N. 11th Street
Beaumont, TX 77703
409-892-2222 • 800-HOLIDAY

• Discount rates for tour groups • Coffee makers, irons & boards in some rooms
• In-room cable TV with pay-per-view movies
• Hollywood Dave's Lounge with nightly entertainment and dancing • 11th Street Grill
• Outdoor pool • Close to health club, jogging trail, tennis and golf

1465

855B Pine St., Magnolia Ave. (Difficult Reaccess)
- AServ — N: Automatic Transmission Service

855A US 90, Dowtown, Civic Center, Port of Beaumont

856 Old Highway (Eastbound)

857A Rose City West

857B The Workman Turnaround (Westbound)
- AServ — N: Moore's Auto Care

858A Rose City East (Eastbound)
- FStop — S: **E-Z Mart**(*)
- AServ — S: Freeway Auto Parts
- Other — S: **Progas**(LP)

858B The Asher Turnaround
- Food — N: Boomtown Restaurant
- RVCamp — N: **Boomtown USA RV & Fishing Park**

859 Bonner Turnaround (Eastbound)
- TServ — S: **Matthews Trucks & Equipment**

860A Dewitt Rd. (Westbound)
- AServ — N: ACE Auto Repair

860B West Vidor (Westbound, Reaccess Eastbound Only)
- Lodg — N: Greenway Motel
- AServ — N: Morris Moore

861A FM 105, Vidor
- Gas — N: Diamond Shamrock(*, D, 24), Fina(*, D), Shell(*, D); S: Conoco(*), Exxon(*, D)
- Food — N: Casa Ole, Dairy Queen(PLAY), Domino's Pizza, Donut Place, Dunkin Donuts (Shell), **Gary's Coffee Shop**, Jody Leigh's Restaurant & Ice Cream, **Little Caesars Pizza**, Mazzio's Pizza, McDonald's(PLAY), Steve's Country Kitchen, Waffle House; S: Burger King(PLAY), KFC, Pizza Hut, Sonic Drive In, Taco Bell, Whataburger(24)
- AServ — N: Ray's 24-Hr Towing; S: Gunstream's Tire & Alignment, Herrera's Collision & Towing, King's Transmission
- ATM — N: Community Bank, Diamond Shamrock, Orange Savings Bank; S: Exxon, Vidor State Bank
- Other — N: **Eckerd Drugs**(RX), **Price-Lo Grocery**; S: **Maytag Laundry, T and T Pharmacy**(RX)

861B Lamar St. (Westbound)
- FStop — N: **Conoco**(*)
- ATM — N: **Conoco**

861C Denver St. (Eastbound)

861D TX 12, Deweyville (Westbound)

862A Railroad Ave (Eastbound)

862B Old Hwy (Westbound)
- RVCamp — N: **Hodge RV Parts, Sales, & Service**

862C Timberlane Dr. (Eastbound)

864 FM 1132, 1135
- Food — N: Burrs Country Store & BBQ
- Lodg — N: Cacey Motel

865 Doty Rd. (Westbound)
- RVCamp — N: **Claiborne West Park**

867 Frontage Road (Eastbound)

EXIT — TEXAS

(867) Rest Area (RR, Phones, Picnic, Vending, P; Eastbound)

(867) Rest Area (RR, Picnic, Vending, P; Westbound)

869 FM 1442, Bridge City
- **RVCamp** **S:** Bridge City RV, Inc.(LP), Lloyd's I-10 RV Center

870 FM 1136
- **Gas** **N:** Stuckey's(*)
- **Food** **N:** Stuckey's

873 TX 62, TX 73, Bridge City, Port Arthur
- **TStop** **N:** Flying J Travel Plaza(*, LP, RV DUMP, SCALES)
- **FStop** **S:** Delta Express(*, SCALES)
- **Gas** **N:** Chevron(*, D)
  S: Diamond Shamrock(*, D), Texaco(*, D)
- **Food** **N:** Abba Mexican Restaurant, Flying J Travel Plaza, Hot Stuff Pizza (Chevron), Subway (Chevron), The Cookery (Flying J)
  S: Jack-In-The-Box, McDonald's, Waffle House
- **TServ** **N:** M & M Tire(24), Vic's Road Service(24)
- **TWash** **N:** M & M Tire
- **RVCamp** **N:** Oak Leaf RV Park Campground
- **ATM** **S:** Delta Express, Texaco

874A U.S. 90 Bus., Orange (Eastbound)
- **Food** **S:** JB's BBQ
- **RVCamp** **N:** Oak Leaf RV Park
- **Med** **S:** ✚ Hospital

874B Womack Rd. (Westbound)
- **AServ** **S:** Orange Chrysler, Dodge, Jeep
- **Other** **N:** McCoy's Building Supply Center

875 FM 3247, M. L. King Jr Drive
- **Food** **N:** Luby's Cafeteria
- **Med** **S:** ✚ Hospital

876 Adams Bayou, Frontage Rd
- **Gas** **N:** Mobil(*)
  S: Chevron(*)
- **Food** **N:** Cajun Cookery, Gary's Coffee Shop, Polo's (Ramada Inn), Waffle House
- **Lodg** **N:** Best Western, DAYS INN Days Inn, Holiday Inn Express, Kings Inn, Motel 6, Ramada Inn
- **AServ** **N:** Austin Lee GM
- **TServ** **N:** Bennett's Authorized Diesel Pump

877 TX 87, 16th St, Port Arthur
- **Gas** **N:** Chevron(*, CW), Diamond Shamrock(*)
  S: Shell(*)
- **Food** **N:** Little Caesars Pizza, Pizza Hut, Subway, Wyatt's Cafeteria
  S: Cody's, Dairy Queen(PLAY), Taco Bell
- **AServ** **N:** Chevron, Jerry's Specialty
  S: Hi-Lo Auto Supply (Parts), Modica Brothers Tire & Wheels
- **RVCamp** **S:** Costello RV Sales
- **ATM** **N:** First Bank & Trust Co., Hibernia, Market Basket Grocery

EXIT — TEXAS/LOUISIANA

  S: Shell
- **Other** **N:** Car Wash, Childs Building Supply, Eckerd Drugs(RX), Market Basket Grocery, North Orange Veterinary Clinic, Texas State Optical
  S: H-E-B Pantry Foods

878 U.S. 90 Bus, Orange (Livestock Inspection Station)
- **FStop** **N:** Mobil(*)
- **AServ** **S:** Rapid Road Service(24)
- **RVCamp** **N:** Cypress Lake RV Resort
- **Other** **N:** Air Boat Rides
  S: Pottery World

Exit **(879)** TX Travel Info Center (RR, Phones, Pet Walk, P; Westbound)

880 Sabine River Turnaround (Eastbound)
- **Other** **N:** Public Boat Ramp

↑TEXAS

↓LOUISIANA

1 Sabine River Turnaround (Westbound, Reaccess Eastbound Only)

(1) LA Tourist Info Center, Rest Area (RR, Phones, Picnic, RV Dump; Eastbound)

(2) Weigh Station (Westbound)

(2) Weigh Station (Eastbound)

4 U.S. 90, LA 109, Toomey, Starks
- **TStop** **N:** Cajun Auto/Truck Plaza(*) (Fuel-Shell), The Lucky Longhorn(*, RV DUMP, SCALES, 24) (Fuel-Diamond Shamrock, Truck Service)

1685

Holiday Inn®

LAKE CHARLES AREA

• Bus & RV Parking • Cable TV with HBO
• Outdoor Pool • Exercise Room
• Lobby Bar with Video Poker Machine
• Riverboat Casinos with Complimentary Shuttle Provided
• Coffeemakers in Rooms

318-528-2061 • 800-645-2425

LOUISIANA ▪ I-10 ▪ EXIT 20

EXIT — LOUISIANA

  S: Delta Truck Plaza(*) (Showers)
- **FStop** **N:** Exxon(*)
  S: Exxon(*)
- **Food** **N:** Bayou Gold, Cajun Auto/Truck Plaza (Fuel-Shell), Nevada Magic (No Minors, Cajun Auto TS), The Lucky Longhorn (Fuel-Diamond Shamrock, Truck Service)
  S: Best Western (Delta Truck Plaza), Delta Truck Plaza (Showers), Texas Pelican
- **Lodg** **N:** The Lucky Longhorn (Fuel-Diamond Shamrock, Truck Service)
  S: Best Western (Delta Truck Plaza)
- **TWash** **N:** The Lucky Longhorn (Fuel-Diamond Shamrock, Truck Service)
- **RVCamp** **S:** Texas Pelican RV Park (Washateria, Bath)
- **ATM** **S:** Exxon
- **Parks** **N:** Niblett Bluff Park

7 LA 3063, Vinton
- **FStop** **N:** Exxon(*, CW)
- **Food** **N:** Champ's Fried Chicken, Dairy Queen, The Lucky Delta
- **AServ** **N:** BJ's Auto Supply, Delta Tire & Lube, Exxon
- **RVCamp** **N:** KOA Kampground

8 LA 108, Vinton
- **FStop** **N:** E-Z Mart(*)
- **Gas** **N:** Chevron(*, D)
- **Food** **N:** Glenn's Mart Restaurant (Chevron)
- **RVCamp** **N:** KOA Kampground (.2 Miles)

(15) Rest Area (RR, Phones, Picnic, RV Dump; Westbound)

20 LA 27, Sulphur, Cameron
- **FStop** **S:** Speedway(*)
- **Gas** **N:** Canal(*), Circle K(*, 24), Exxon(*, D, CW), Shell(*, 24)
  S: Texaco(*, D, CW)
- **Food** **N:** Bonanza Steakhouse, Burger King(PLAY), Cajun Charlie's Seafood, Checkers Burgers, Hong Kong Chinese, Mr. Gatti's, Schillileagh's, SHONEY'S Shoney's, Subway, Taco Bell, Wendy's
  S: Pitt Grill, Pizza Hut, Seafood Caboose(24), Winkydoos
- **Lodg** **N:** Chateau Motor Inn, Hampton Inn, Holiday Inn (see our ad this page)
  S: Fairfield Inn, La Quinta Inn, Microtel Inn, Wingate Hotel
- **AServ** **N:** Insta Lube
  S: Kim's Radiator Service
- **RVCamp** **N:** Southern Mobile Home & RV Supply
- **ATM** **N:** First National Bank, Holiday Inn, Shell
- **Other** **N:** Stine Ace Hardware
  S: AmeriGas(LP)

21 LA 3077, DeQuincy
- **FStop** **S:** USA Super Stop(*)
- **Gas** **S:** Chevron(*)
- **Food** **N:** The Boiling Point
  S: Cajun Deli USA (USA Super Stop), Krispy

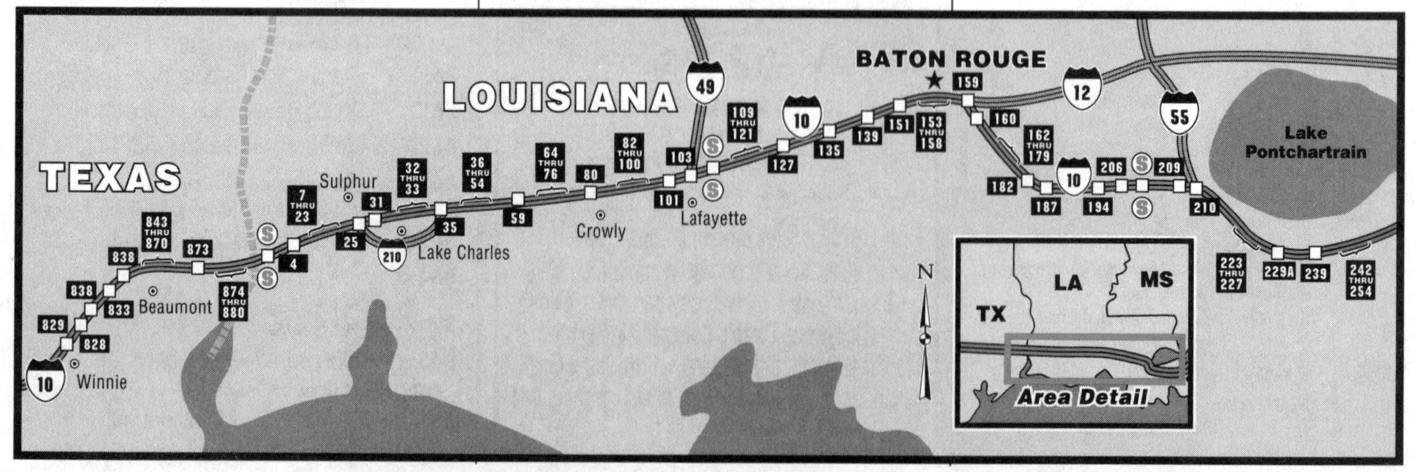

Bold red print shows RV & Bus parking available or nearby

EXIT LOUISIANA

Krunchy Chicken (USA FS), USA Super Stop
RVCamp **S: Hidden Ponds RV (1.65 Miles)**
Med **N: ✚ Hospital**
ATM **S: USA Super Stop**

23 LA 108, Industries, Sulfur
TStop **S: Texaco[*, 24]**
Gas N: Exxon[*, CW]
Food **N: Little Caesars Pizza (K-Mart), McDonald's[PLAY]**, Subway (Exxon)
S: **Cracker Barrel**, Waffle House, **Winners Choice[24] (Texaco TS)**
Lodg N: Comfort Suites Hotel
S: Super 8
TServ **S: Texaco[24]**
ATM N: Exxon, Hibernia
S: Texaco
Other **N: K-Mart[RX]**

25 I-210 East, Lake Charles Loop

26 Southern Road, Columbia, US 90W
Gas N: Circle K[*, 24]
Food **N: Chateau Charles Hotel & Suites**
Lodg **N: Chateau Charles Hotel & Suites**

27 LA 378, Westlake (Difficult Reaccess)
FStop **S: Conoco[*]**
Gas N: Circle K[*, 24], Fina[*, D], Shell[*, CW]
Food N: Burger King[PLAY], Dairy Queen
Lodg **S: The Inn At The Isle**
RVCamp **N: RV,s Plus, Inc. (2.3 Miles), Sam Houston Jones State Park (6 Miles)**
Parks **N: Sam Houston Jones State Park (6 Miles)**

29 LA 385, Business District, Tourist Bureau (Eastbound)
Other **S: Tourist Info.**

30A LA 385, N. Lakeshore Dr.
Gas N: Chevron[*]
Food N: Steamboat Bill's, Waffle House
Lodg N: Friendship Inn, Lakeview Motel, Travel Inn
S: Players Island Hotel
ATM N: Hibernia

30B Ryan St., Business District, Lake Charles Civic Center

31A US 90 Bus, Enterprise Blvd
Gas S: Texaco[*, CW]
Food S: Popeye's Chicken
Other **S: Pryce's Pharmacy[RX]**

31B U.S. 90 East To LA 14, Shattuck St. (Reaccess Eastbound Only)
TStop **N: Kings Ransom[*, SCALES] (Fuel-Texaco)**
Food **N: Kings Ransom (Fuel-Texaco)**
AServ S: Shattuck Street Garage
TServ **N: Kings Ransom[SCALES] (Fuel-Texaco)**

32 Opelousas St
Gas N: Conoco[*], Exxon[*]
Food **N: Nash's Superette**
Lodg S: Motel 6
Other **N: Nash's Superette, Willis Laundry Center**

33 U.S. 171 North, DeRidder To LA 14
Gas N: Chevron[*, CW], Racetrac[*, 24], Texaco[*, D, CW]
Food N: Burger King[PLAY], Church's Chicken, Taco Bell
Lodg N: Best Western, Comfort Inn, **Days Inn**
S: Motel 6
AServ N: Hi Lo Auto Parts
S: EJ's Automotive
ATM N: First National Bank, **Market Basket Grocery**
Parks **N: Sam Houston Jones State Park**
Other **N: Eckerd Drugs[RX], Market Basket Grocery, WalGreens Pharmacy[RX]**

34 I-210 West, Lake Charles Loop

35 **(34)** Junction I-210, Lake Charles Loop

36 LA 397, Creole, Cameron
TStop **S: Conoco Travel Plaza[*, SCALES] (FedEx Drop)**
Food **S: Conoco Travel Plaza (FedEx Drop)**
TServ **S: Conoco Travel Plaza[SCALES] (FedEx Drop)**
RVCamp **N: Jean Lafitte RV Park (1.5 Miles)**
S: James Mobile Campground (1 Mile)
Other **S: Double Diamond Casino (Conoco TStop)**

43 LA 383, Iowa
Gas S: Citgo[*], Shell[*, LP], Texaco[*, D, CW]
Food S: E T Express, Emery's Family Restaurant, Fausto's Fried Chicken, Gulf Fresh Seafood
ATM S: Citgo, **Factory Outlet Center**
Other **S: Factory Outlet Center**

44 U.S. 165, Alexandria
RVCamp **N: Mobile City Campground & RV Park**
S: AOK Campground (1.25 Miles)

48 LA 101, Lacassine
FStop **S: Exxon[*]**
Gas S: Citgo[*]
TServ **S: Exxon**

54 LA 99, Welsh
Gas S: Chevron[*], Citgo[*], Conoco[*], Exxon[*]
Food S: Cajun Tales, Citgo, Conoco, Dairy Queen, Perky's Pizza (Citgo), Sally's Subs (Citgo)
Med **S: ✚ Hospital**
ATM S: Conoco
Other **S: Welsh Municipal Airport**

59 LA 395, Roanoke

64 LA 26, Elton, Jennings, Lake Arthur
FStop **S: Shell[*, 24]**
Gas S: Fina[*], Texaco[*, D, LP, CW]
Food N: Donnie's Cooking (Sundown Inn), Golden Dragon
S: Blimpie Subs & Salads (Fina), Burger King[PLAY], Dairy Queen, McDonald's[PLAY] (Wal-Mart), Pizza Hut, SHONEY'S, Shoney's, **Sugar Mill (Holiday Inn)**, Taco Bell, Waffle House
Lodg N: Boudreaux Inn, Sundown Inn
S: **Holiday Inn**, Thrifty Inn
AServ S: Texaco, **Wal-Mart Supercenter[RX] (1-Hr Photo, Vision Center)**
RVCamp **N: Campground**
Med **S: ✚ Jennings Hospital**
ATM S: Fina, **Wal-Mart Supercenter (1-Hr Photo, Vision Center)**
Parks **N: Louisiana Oil & Gas Park**
Other **N: Visitor Information**
S: Airport, **Strand Theatre, Tupper Museum, Wal-Mart Supercenter[RX] (1-Hr Photo, Vision Center)**

65 LA 97, Evangeline, Jennings
TStop **S: Reed's I-10 Auto/Truck Plaza[*] (Fuel-Shell)**
Food **S: Reed's I-10 Auto/Truck Plaza (Fuel-Shell)**
Lodg S: Days Inn
TServ **S: Reed's I-10 Auto/Truck Plaza (Fuel-Shell)**

(67) **Rest Area (RR, Phones, Picnic, RV Dump, Pet Walk; Eastbound)**

(67) **Rest Area (RR, Phones, Picnic, RV Dump, Pet Walk; Westbound)**

72 Egan
Gas N: Cajun Cafe[D]
Food N: Cajun Cafe
S: Cajun Connection Restaurant
RVCamp **N: Cajun Heaven RV Park[LP] (.25 Miles)**
S: Trail's End Campground (1.5 Miles)

76 LA 91, Iota, Estherwood
TStop **S: Manuel's[*, 24] (Fuel-Conoco)**
TServ **S: Manuel's[24] (Fuel-Conoco)**
ATM **S: Manuel's (Fuel-Conoco)**

80 LA 13, Eunice, Crowley
TStop **N: Citgo Truck & Auto Plaza[*, SCALES]**
Gas N: Texaco[*, D, CW]
S: Chevron[*, D], Circle K Express[*, 24], Exxon[*, CW, 24]
Food N: Brodie's Place (Crowley Inn), **Rice Palace (Citgo TS)**, Waffle House
S: Burger King[PLAY], Exxon, KFC, McDonald's, Mr. Gatti's, P.J.'s Grill, Ponte Vecchio Italian, Sonic Drive In, Taco Bell
Lodg N: Best Western, Crowley Inn
AServ N: Thibodeaux Auto Repair
S: Auto Zone Auto Parts
TServ **N: Dubus Engine Co. Inc.**
ATM **N: Citgo Truck & Auto Plaza**
S: Chevron, First Bank & Trust Co.
Other **N: Crowley Veterinary Hospital**
S: Cinema IV, Rite Aid Pharmacy[RX]

82 LA 1111, East Crowley
Gas S: Murphey USA
Food **S: McDonald's (Wal-Mart)**, Wendy's
AServ **S: Wal-Mart Supercenter[24, RX] (Optical)**
Med **S: ✚ Hospital**
ATM **S: Wal-Mart Supercenter (Optical)**
Other **S: Wal-Mart Supercenter[RX] (Optical)**

87 LA 35, Church Point, Rayne
FStop **S: Mobil[*, 24]**
Gas N: Chevron[*, 24], Exxon[LP, 24]
S: Cypress[*, CW], Diamond Shamrock[*, CW], RK's[*], Shell[*]
Food N: McDonald's
S: Dairy Queen, Gabe's Cajun Food, Oasis, Popeye's Chicken, **Roland's Cajun Grill[24] (Mobil)**, Shannon's, Subway (Shell)
AServ N: Exxon[24]
S: Auto Tech & Fast Lube
ATM S: Shell
Other **S: City Police Dept., Eckerd Drugs[RX], The Rayne Chamber of Commerce & Agriculture, Winn Dixie Supermarket**

92 LA 95, Mire, Duson

97 LA 93, Cankton, Scott
Gas S: Texaco[*, D]
Food S: Church's Chicken (Texaco), Miss Helen's 100% Cajun
AServ **S: Gerald's Towing & Recovery**
TServ **S: Gerald's Towing & Recovery**
RVCamp **S: KOA Kampground[*, LP, PLAY] (Showers, Laundry)**
Other **S: Cajun Propane[LP]**

100 Ambassador Caffery Pkwy
Gas N: Exxon[*, D]
S: Chevron[*, CW, 24], Racetrac[*, 24], Texaco[*, D, CW]
Food S: Burger King[PLAY], Taco Bell, Waffle House, Wendy's
Lodg S: Hampton Inn, Microtel Inn
AServ **N: Sam's Club**
S: Daniell Battery, Robert's Auto Service
TServ **S: LaFayette Tire & Service, Tire Distribution, Treadco, Inc.**
Med **S: ✚ Hospital**
ATM S: Racetrac
Other **N: Sam's Club**

101 LA 182, Carencro, Lafayette
TStop **N: Lafayette Truck Stop[*, SCALES]**
FStop **N: Speedway[*]**
Gas N: Chevron[*], Texaco[*, D, CW]
S: Diamond Shamrock[*, CW], Shell[*, CW, 24], Texaco[*, D, CW]
Food **N: Lafayette Truck Stop**, McDonald's (Chevron), Waffle House
S: Cracker Barrel
Lodg N: Red Roof Inn
S: **Days Inn**, Quality Inn, St. Francis Motel
TServ **N: Lafayette Truck Stop[SCALES]**
ATM **N: Speedway**
Other S: New Spot Free Car Wash

EXIT LOUISIANA

103AB Junction I-49, U.S. 167, Opelousas, LaFayette
- **Gas** S: Shell(*), Texaco(*, D)
- **Food** S: Chopsticks Chinese, Kajun Restaurant (Lighthouse Inn), Kettle, La Fitte's (Rodeway Inn), **Waffle House**
- **Lodg** S: Fairfield Inn, Holiday Inn, La Quinta Inn, **Lighthouse Inn**, Rodeway Inn, Shoney's Inn, **Super 8 (see our ad this page)**
- **AServ** S: A-Abal Auto Service, Firestone Tire & Auto, **Montgomery Ward**
- **RVCamp** S: **Campground**
- **ATM** S: **Albertson's Food Market(RX)**, Texaco
- **Other** S: **Albertson's Food Market(RX)**, **Northgate Mall**, Rite Aid Pharmacy(RX)

(104) **Rest Area (RR, Phones, Picnic, RV Dump; Eastbound)**

(106) **Rest Area (RR, Phones, Picnic, RV Dump; Westbound)**

(108) **Weigh Station (Eastbound)**

(108) **Weigh Station (Westbound)**

109 LA. 328, Breaux Bridge
- **FStop** S: **Texaco(*, LP)**
- **Gas** N: Shell(*, D, 24)
  S: Chevron(*, CW), Delta Express(*), Mobil(*, D)
- **Food** N: Blimpie's Subs (Shell), Crawfish Kitchen Restaurant
  S: Baskin Robbins (Mobil), Burger King(PLAY), Burger Tyme, Popeye's Chicken (Chevron)
- **Lodg** S: Best Western
- **AServ** S: **Texaco**
- **RVCamp** N: **Campers Unlimited, Inc. (.1 Miles)**
  S: **Pioneer Campground**
- **ATM** N: Shell
  S: Delta Express, Mobil

115 LA 347, Cecilia, Henderson
- **TStop** S: **USA Truck Stop Chevron**
- **FStop** N: **Exxon(*) (Coin Laundry)**
  S: **Mapco Express(*)**
- **Gas** S: **Exxon(*, D, LP)**, Texaco(*)
- **Food** N: **Exxon (Coin Laundry)**, Landry's Seafood
  S: Dairy Queen (Texaco), Subway (Exxon), Texaco, Waffle House
- **AServ** S: **Exxon**
- **TServ** S: **Exxon**
- **ATM** S: **Mapco Express**
- **Other** N: Coin Laundromat (Exxon), **Exxon (Coin Laundry)**, Tourist Info.

(121) **Rest Area (RR, HF, Phones, Picnic, RV Dump; Eastbound)**

(121) **Rest Area, Welcome Center (RR, HF, Phones, Picnic, RV Dump; Westbound)**

121 Butte, La Rose
- **Gas** S: Summers C-Store
- **RVCamp** S: **Frenchman's Wilderness (.75 Miles)**

127 LA 975, Whiskey Bay

135 LA 3000, Ramah, Maringouin
- **Gas** N: P.J's Bait Shop(*), Texaco(*)
- **RVCamp** N: **False River RV Park**

(137) **Rest Area (RR, HF, Phones, Picnic, RV Dump; Eastbound)**

(137) **Rest Area (RR, HF, Phones, Picnic, RV Dump; Westbound)**

139 LA 77, Rosedale, Grosse Tete, Maringuin
- **TStop** N: **Texaco(*)**
  S: **Tiger Truckstop(*, D)**
- **Food** N: **Restaurant (Texaco)**, **Texaco**
  S: **Tiger Cafe (Tiger TS)**, **Tiger Truckstop**
- **AServ** N: Brock Hoeft Chevrolet GEO
- **TServ** S: **Tiger Truckstop**

151 LA. 415, to U.S. 90, Lobdell, Alexandria
- **TStop** N: **Fort Allen T/S(*)**
- **FStop** N: **Delta Express(*, SCALES)**
  S: **Shell(*, 24)**
- **Gas** N: Chevron(*), Exxon(*, D), Racetrac(*), Texaco(*)
- **Food** N: Burger King(PLAY), **Fort Allen T/S**, KFC, McDonald's, Popeye's Chicken, SHONEY'S Shoney's, Taco Bell, Waffle House
- **Lodg** N: DAYS INN Days Inn, Holiday Inn Express, Shoney's Inn
  S: Motel 6, **Ramada**, Super 8
- **AServ** N: **Wal-Mart(RX)**
- **RVCamp** N: **Cajun Country Campground (1.75 Miles)**

SUPER 8 MOTEL ®
1828

I-10 & I-49 Exit 103A

Lafayette

2224 NE Evangeline Thwy.
(318) 232-8826
1-800-800-8000

71 Unit Motel • Swimming Pool
24 Hour Front Desk • Cable w/Showtime
Free Local Calls • Free Coffee

Trucker, AAA & Senior Discounts

(151, continued)
- **ATM** N: **Delta Express**, Racetrac, Texaco
- **Other** N: **Wal-Mart(RX)**
  S: **LA. Tourist Information**

153 LA 1, Port Allen, Plaquemine
- **Gas** N: Chevron(*), Texaco(*, D, CW)
- **AServ** N: Russo's Auto Parts

155A LA 30, Nicholson Dr., Highland Dr. (Eastbound, Reaccess Westbound Only)
- **Gas** S: Mobil(*)
- **AServ** S: Mobil

155B I-110N, Business Dist., Metro Airport

155C Louise St.

156A Washington St. (Eastbound, Reaccess Westbound Only)

156B Dairymple Drive, LSU
- **Parks** S: **City Park Lake**

157A Perkins Road (Eastbound, Reaccess Westbound Only)
- **Gas** S: Phillips 66(*), Texaco(*, CW)
- **Food** S: O' Brian Crab House
- **AServ** S: Phillips 66
- **ATM** S: Texaco

157B Acadian Thruway
- **Gas** N: Citgo(*), Shell(*, CW)
  S: Mobil(*), Texaco(*, CW)
- **Food** N: Denny's, Perkee's Pizza (Shell), Ribs, Shell, Sully's Subs (Shell)
  S: Joe Muggs Coffee Shop, **Jubans Restaurant (Creo Cuisine)**, Lone Star Steakhouse, Outback Steakhouse
- **Lodg** N: Comfort Inn, La Quinta Inn
  S: **Courtyard by Marriott**
- **AServ** S: Mobil, Uniroyal, **Wal-Mart**
- **ATM** S: Bank One, Hancock Bank, Texaco
- **Other** S: **Books-A-Million**, **Eckerd Drugs**, **Wal-Mart**

158 College Drive
- **Gas** N: Speedway(*)
  S: Chevron(*, CW, 24), Texaco(*, CW)
- **Food** N: Hooters, Ruby Tuesday, Steam Room Grill, Sullivan's Steakhouse, Waffle House, Wendy's
  S: Applebee's, Burger King(PLAY), Chili's, Coffee Call, Gino's, Golden Gate Chinese, Great Wall Restaurant (Chinese), Koto Oriental, Picante Mexican Restaurant, Ruth's Chris Steakhouse, Simolina, The Factory Restaurant, The Station
- **Lodg** N: Corporate Inn, Hilton, Residence Inn
  S: Embassy Suites, Hampton Inn, Holiday Inn Express, Raddison Hotel, The Wilson Inn
- **AServ** N: Midas Muffler & Brake, Mineke Mufflers & Brakes
- **Med** S: + **Concord Hospital**

Bold red print shows RV & Bus parking available or nearby

EXIT LOUISIANA

ATM N: Bank One, Speedway, Union Planter's Bank
S: Albertson's Grocery(RX), Chevron, City National Bank, Hibernia, Regions Bank
Other S: Albertson's Grocery(RX), Office Depot, Rite Aid Pharmacy(RX), U.S. Post Office

159 Junction I-12, Hammond

160 LA 3064, Essen Lane
Gas S: Chevron(*), Exxon(*, CW), Racetrac(*)
Food S: Louisiana Pizza Kitchen
AServ S: NTB
Med S: + Our Lady of the Lake Regional Medical Center
ATM S: Racetrac
Other S: Rural Life Museum

162 Blue Bonnet Road
Gas S: Exxon(*), Racetrac(*, 24)
Food N: Albasha Greek, Cadillac Cafe, Trinity's Restaurant
S: Burger King(PLAY), Glynnwood, Ralph & Kacoos Seafood, Stray's Cheesecake Bakery
Lodg N: Quality Suites
S: AmeriSuites (see our ad this page)
AServ S: Sears Auto Center
Other N: Bluebonnet Veterinary Hospital
S: Mall of Lousianna

163 Siegen Lane
Gas N: Chevron(*, CW, 24), Racetrac(*, 24), Shell(*, CW)
Food N: Burger King, Holiday Inn, Kabob's Greek, Marble Slab Creamery Ice Cream, McDonald's, SHONEY'S Shoney's, Subway, Taco Bell, Waffle House
S: Chili's, Joe's Crab Shack(PLAY), Lowe's, McDonald's (Wal-Mart), Subway (Lowe's), Wal-Mart(RX) (Vision Center, One hour photo), Wendy's
Lodg N: Budgetel Inn, Holiday Inn, Motel 6
S: Courtyard by Marriott, Microtel Lodging and Suites
AServ S: Wal-Mart (Vision Center, One hour photo)
ATM N: Chevron
Other N: America's Best Contacts & Eyeglasses, K-Mart(RX), Office Depot, United Artist Theaters
S: Lowe's, Tinsel Town Cinemas, Wal-Mart(RX) (Vision Center, One hour photo)

166 LA 42, 427, Highland Road, Perkins Road
Gas S: Texaco(*, D, CW)
ATM S: Hancock Bank, Texaco
Other N: Water Amusement Park
S: Beth Claybourne Interiors and Antiques, LSU, Louisiana State Police Troop A

173 LA 73, Geismar, Prairieville
FStop N: Super Stop(*)
Gas S: Exxon(*, D, CW), Mobil(*)
Food S: Burger King(PLAY), Exxon, Krispy Kreme Doughnuts (Exxon), Mobil, Subway (In Mobil), TCBY (Exxon)
RVCamp S: Twin Lakes RV Park (1.6 Miles)

177 (178) LA 30, Gonzales, St. Gabriel
TStop N: USA Auto Truck Plaza(*, RV DUMP, SCALES)
Gas N: Shell(*, CW), Texaco(*)
S: Jet 24(*), Texaco(*, CW)
Food N: Burger King, Cajun Inn, Church's Chicken, McDonald's(PLAY), SHONEY'S Shoney's, Taco Bell, USA Auto Truck Plaza, USA Auto Truck Plaza, Waffle House
S: Cracker Barrel, Popeye's Chicken, Wendy's
Lodg N: Best Western, Budget Inn, Cajun Inn, DAYS INN Days Inn, USA Auto Truck Plaza
S: Comfort Inn
TServ N: USA Auto Truck Plaza, USA Auto Truck Plaza(SCALES)
RVCamp N: Vesta RV Park (1.9 Miles)

EXIT LOUISIANA

Med N: + Hospital
ATM N: Shell
Other N: Tourist Info.
S: Tanger Factory Outlet

179 LA 44, Gonzales, Burnside
TStop N: Red Man of Louisiana(*)
FStop N: Mobil(*)
Food N: Red Man of Louisiana
TServ N: Red Man of Louisiana
Med N: + Hospital
Other N: River Road Africa American Museum and Gallery

(180) Rest Area (RR, HF, Phones, Picnic, RV Dump; Northbound)

(180) Rest Area (RR, HF, Phones, Picnic, RV Dump; Southbound)

182 LA 22, Sorrento, Donaldsonville
TStop S: Square Deal(*, SCALES)
FStop S: PS Save(*, 24)
Food S: McDonald's
Other S: Tourist Info.

187 U.S. 61, Gramercy, Sorrento (Difficult Reaccess)

194 LA 641 South, Gramercy, Lutcher (Oak Valley and San Diego Plantations)

206 LA 3188, La Place
Med S: + Hospital

(207) Weigh Station (Eastbound)

(207) Weigh Station (Westbound)

209 U.S. 51, LaPlace, Hammond
FStop S: Speedway(*)
Gas S: Chevron(*, 24), Citgo(*), Shell(*, D, CW, 24)
Food S: McDonald's(PLAY), SHONEY'S Shoney's, Waffle House, Wendy's
Lodg S: Best Western
ATM S: Hibernia, Shell

210 Junction I-55 North, Hammond (Westbound)

220 Jct. 310S Boutte, Houma

EXIT LOUISIANA

221 Loyola Dr
Gas N: Circle K(*), Citgo(*), Exxon(*, D), Shell(*, CW), Texaco(*, CW), Timesaver(*)
S: Amoco(*), Chevron(*), Speedway(*)
Food N: Church's Chicken, Kenner's Seafood, McDonald's(PLAY), Popeye's Chicken, Rally's Hamburgers, Subway, Taco Bell, Tastee Donuts
S: Amoco, Wendy's
Lodg S: Sleep Inn
Med N: + Hospital
ATM N: Circle K, Shell, Timesaver
Other N: Economical Pharmacy, Get-N-Go, Sam's Club
S: Tourist Info.

223AB LA 49, Williams Blvd, New Orleans International Airport
Gas N: Texaco(*, D, CW)
S: Citgo(*), Exxon(*, CW), Shell(*, CW)
Food N: Jade Palace
S: A Bella's, Chez Pierre French Bakery, Daquiri, DAYS INN Days Inn, Denny's, Domino's Pizza, Franny's, Jazz Seafood and Steakhouse, McDonald's, Messina's Restaurant, Pizza Hut, Subway, Tasty Doughnuts
Lodg S: Contempra Inn, DAYS INN Days Inn, Holiday Inn Select, La Quinta, Park Plaza Inn, Radisson, TraveLodge
AServ N: La Marquis Ford, Speedee Oil Change
S: Goodyear, REM Tire and Car Care
ATM N: First American Bank
S: Citgo, Deposit Guaranty National Bank
Other S: U-Haul Center

224 Power Blvd. (Westbound, Reaccess Eastbound Only, Cannot go to the south side)
Lodg S: Days Inn (see our ad this page)
Other N: Schwegmann(24) (Texaco gas pumps)

225 Veteran's Blvd
Gas N: Chevron(*, CW)
S: EZ Serve(*), Shell(*, CW), Speedway(*)
Food N: Denny's
S: Bayou Cafe (Holiday Inn), Holiday Inn, Homeplate Cafe, Tiffin Inn Pancake House
Lodg N: La Quinta Inn
S: Evergreen Plaza Inn, Holiday Inn
AServ N: Courtesy Honda
S: Crescent City Nissan
ATM N: Chevron
Parks N: Lafreniere Park
Other N: Celebration Station

226 Clearview Pkwy, Huey Long Bridge
Gas N: Chevron(*, D, CW), Exxon
S: Chevron(*, CW), Circle K(*), Danny and Clyde's(*)
Food N: A&G Cafeteria, Campton Chinese Restaurant, Popeye's Chicken, Webster's
S: Burger King, C & W, Danny and Clyde's, Piccadilly Cafeteria, SHONEY'S Shoney's, Subway, TCBY
Lodg S: Shoney's Inn
AServ N: Exxon, Lucas Tires, Murphy-Grounds Cadillac
S: 5-Minute Oil Change, Crown Buick GMC Trucks, Firestone, Samco Auto Repairs
Med S: + Lakeside Hospital
ATM N: Bank One, First NBC Financial Center, Hibernia
S: Danny and Clyde's, Whitney Bank
Other N: K&B Drugs
S: Clearview Self-Serve Car Wash, Super Vision

228 Causeway Blvd, Mandeville
Gas N: Exxon(*, CW), Shell(*)
S: Exxon(*, CW), Phillips 66(D) (U-Haul Rental), Texaco(*), Timesaver(*)
Food N: Bennigan's, Burger King, Causeway Grill, Cucos Border Cafe, Doug's Place, Egg Roll House Chinese, Luther's Bar-B-Q, Outback Steak House,

EXIT	LOUISIANA
	Saia's Beef Room
	S: Bronx City Diner, Denny's, Holiday Inn, Manuel's, Pasta Kitchen (Holiday Inn)
Lodg	N: Best Western, Ramada Limited
	S: Extended Stay America, Holiday Inn, La Quinta, Quality Hotel, Residence Inn by Marriot
AServ	N: Meineke Discount Mufflers, Royal Oldsmobile,Mazda, GM
	S: Lakeside Collision Center, Rapid Oil Change
ATM	N: Shell
	S: Hibernia National Bank, Texaco, Timesaver
Other	N: Animal Hospital, **K-Mart(RX)**, **Lakeside Mall**, TF Chang's
	S: Best of America Car Wash
229	Bonnabel Blvd
230	Junction I-610,
231B	Florida Blvd, West End Blvd (Westbound, Difficult Reaccess)
231A	Metairie Road, City Park Ave
Other	S: New Orleans Museum of Art
232	U.S. 61, Airline Highway, Tulane Ave, Carrollton Ave (Difficult Reaccess)
Lodg	N: Budget Inn
234A	US Hwy 90, Super Dome Claybourne Ave, Westbank
Gas	S: Citgo(*), Gasco(*, D), Shell, Spur(*)
Food	S: Church's Chicken, Joe's PoBoys, Ms Hyster's Barbecue
Med	N: **+ VA Medical Center**
ATM	S: Spur
Other	S: Loyola University Tulane Ave, Speed Queen Coin Laundry
235C	U.S. 90 West, Claiborne Ave, Earhart Blvd (Westbound)
235B	U.S. 90 Business West, Canal St, Superdome (Westbound)
Gas	N: Econo Gas
Food	S: Pinky's Bar & Restaurant
Lodg	N: Pallas Wuite Hotel, Ramada, Roadway Inn
	S: Days Inn, Marriot Hotel, Radison Hotel, Sheraton Inn
Other	N: Discount Optical
	S: WalGreens Pharmacy
235A	Orleans Ave, Vieux Carre
Gas	S: Chevron(*)
Food	S: Peck's Steakhouse
Lodg	S: Clarion Carriage House Inn (see our ad this page)
Other	S: **Police Station**
236A	Esplanade Ave (Eastbound, Difficult Reaccess)
236B	LA39, North Claiborne Ave (Eastbound)
236C	Saint Bernard Ave, Downtown New Orleans (No Reaccess, Difficult Reaccess)
237	Elysian Fields Ave (Difficult Reaccess)
TStop	N: **Texaco(*) (Gallager)**
Other	N: Crescent Animal Clinic
238B	Junction I-610 West, Baton Rouge, New Orleans Int'l Airport (Westbound)
238A	Franklin Ave (Westbound, No Reaccess)
239AB	Louisa St S, Almonaster Blvd. E(239A) Louisa St N, Almonaster Blvd. W (239B) (Difficult Reaccess)
FStop	S: **Fuel Man**
Gas	N: Exxon(*, CW)
	S: Fina(*, D)
Food	N: Burger King, Daiquire's, Edward's, Gentilly Woods Restaurant (Knight's Inn), Knight's Inn, McDonald's, Pizza Hut, Popeye's Chicken, Rallys Hamburgers
	S: Fina
Lodg	N: Friendly Inn, Knight's Inn
AServ	N: Goodyear Tire & Auto, Maurice's Auto Repair, Precision Tune & Lube, Spee-Dee Oil Change, Toyota Service of New Orleans
ATM	N: Exxon, First NBC
Other	N: Coin Car Wash, **K-Mart**
240A	Downman Rd
RVCamp	S: **New Orleans Mardi Gras Campground**
240B	U.S. 90, Chef Highway
Gas	N: Amoco(*)
	S: Chevron(24), Citgo(*), Discount Zone, Shell
Lodg	N: Family Inns of America, Monte Carlo, Ramada Inn, Rest Inn, Super 8
AServ	S: Masters Auto and Transmission Repair, Meineke Discount Mufflers
RVCamp	N: **New Orleans Riverboat Travel Park**
	S: **Jude Travel Park & Guest House (8 blocks)**
Other	N: Riverboat Travel Park, U-Haul Center
241	Morrison Road
Gas	N: Exxon(*), Shell(*)
Food	N: Burger King
AServ	N: Pennzoil Oil Change, Shell
ATM	N: Exxon
Other	N: **Kenilworth Mall**, Rite Aid Pharmacy
242	Crowder Blvd
Gas	N: Chevron(*, CW)
	S: BP(*), Exxon(*)
Food	S: Bronx City Diner, Daquiri's, Four Seasons Cuisine, Lamar's, Mai Tai Restaurant, Rally's Hamburgers, Retails Seafood City Restaurant, SHONEY'S, Shoney's, Wendy's
Lodg	S: La Quinta Inn
ATM	S: Hibernia Bank
Other	S: **The Real Superstore**, WalGreens Pharmacy
244	Read Blvd
Gas	S: Exxon(D)
Food	N: Brown's Doughnut Shop, Jade East Chinese, Lama's, McDonald's(PLAY), Reid's Discount Market, Subway, Texas Barbecue Co, **Wal-Mart(RX) (One hour photo, optical center)**
	S: Days Inn, Dragon Palace, Popeye's Chicken, Wendy's
Lodg	S: Days Inn, Holiday Inn Express
AServ	N: Pennzoil Oil Change
	S: Crescent City Mazda Chrysler Plymouth Jeep Eagle, Exxon, Goodyear, Jazz City Lincoln Mercury, Midas Muffler
Med	S: **+ Hospital**, **+ Med First Medical Center**
ATM	N: Rite Aid Pharmacy
	S: Bank One, First NBC, WalGreens Pharmacy, Whitney
Other	N: Cinema 8, Delchamp's Supermarket, Gentilly Vet Hospital, Office Depot, Rite Aid Pharmacy, **Sam's Club**, **Wal-Mart(RX) (One hour photo, optical center)**
	S: Clear Vision Center, Eye Works, Fun Arcade, WalGreens Pharmacy
245	Bullard Ave
Gas	N: Chevron(*, CW)
	S: Exxon(*, CW), Shell(*, CW)
Food	N: Jamie's Seafood Restaurant, Kettle Inn, La Quinta Inn, Pizza Hut
	S: Burger King, KFC, Little Caesars Pizza, McDonald's, Schwegmann, SHONEY'S, Shoney's, Subway, Taco Bell
Lodg	N: La Quinta Inn
	S: Best Western
AServ	N: Honda Town, Metro Mitsubishi
	S: Bill Watson Ford, PEP Boys, Regency Buick GMC, The Nissan Way
RVCamp	S: **Sycamore Tree Travel Park (2 Miles)**
Med	S: **+ Lakeland Medical Center**
ATM	N: Chevron
	S: Schwegmann
Other	N: NAPA
	S: Home Depot, Starz Car Wash, Toys R Us
246A	Junction I-510 South
246AB	LA 47, Chalmette ,Mishoud, Nasa (No Reaccess)
248	Michoud Blvd (No Reaccess, Difficult Reaccess)
254	U.S. 11, Irish Bayou, North Shore Dr.
261	Oak Harbor Blvd, Eden Isles
263	**(264)** LA 433, Slidell
FStop	S: **Speedway(*, SCALES)**, **Texaco(*)**
Gas	N: Citgo(*), Exxon(*, LP, CW), Shell(*, CW)
Food	N: Check In-Check Out Deli, Pitt Grill(24), Ray's Bullpin Restaurant, Waffle House
	S: **Blimpie's Subs (Texaco FS)**, McDonald's(PLAY), **Speedway**, **Texaco**, The Brass Kettle, Wendy's
Lodg	N: Comfort Inn, Hampton Inn
AServ	N: A's Auto Repair, Exxon, Levi's Chevrolet, Taylor's Automotive Service Center
	S: Adrienne Vega's Ford Lincoln Mercury, Brian Harris Pontiac Buick GMC Truck, Brown's Mazda, Lakeshore Jeep Eagle, Chrysler Dodge, Slidell Toyota Isuzu
RVCamp	S: **KOA Campgrounds (.75 Miles)**, **Pine Crest RV Park (.2 Miles)**

The Historic French Market Inn

18th Century Charm in the heart of the French Quarter

$79.00 +tax
15% off Rack Rate if not available
Based on availability. Not valid with other discounts, holidays, or special events.

Free Continental Breakfast & Evening Cocktails
In Room Movies
Walking Tour of the French Quarter
Patio w/Pool, Hot Tub, Fountains
Free Movie & Sports Channels
Restaurant Nearby

888-211-3447 • 504-561-5621
501 Decatur St. • New Orleans, LA
I-10 Exit 235A (Orleans/Vieux Carre), Lt to French Quarter/Toulouse St. Rt on Decatur St. Hotel 1 block

Clarion Inn

LOUISIANA • I-10 • EXIT 235A

Bold red print shows RV & Bus parking available or nearby

EXIT LOUISIANA/MISSISSIPPI

Other N: Car Wash, Fort Pike State Comm Area (7 Miles)
S: **Slidell Factory Outlets**, Wild Bill's Fireworks

(265) **Weigh Station (Eastbound)**

(265) **Weigh Station (Westbound)**

266 U.S. 190, Slidel

TStop N: **76 Auto/Truck Plaza**(*, RV DUMP, SCALES), **Travel America Travel Center**(*, SCALES)
S: **T/A TravelCenters of America**(*, SCALES)

Gas N: Exxon(*, D), Shell(*, CW), Texaco(*, CW), USA(*)
S: Chevron(*, D, 24), Racetrac(*)

Food N: **76 Auto/Truck Plaza**, Arby's, Baskin Robbins, Burger King(PLAY), Carmelo's, China Wok, Denny's (Days Inn), Happy Dragon Chinese, KFC, Lone Star Steakhouse, McDonald's(PLAY), McDonald's, **Pete's Family Restaurant (76 Auto / Truck Stop)**, Pizza Hut, Rally's Hamburgers, SHONEY'S, Shoney's, Taco Bell, **Travel America Travel Center**, Wendy's
S: Applebee's, Big Easy Diner, **Cracker Barrel**, Daquiris and Creams, Outback Steakhouse, Ramada(D), Two Sister's Billiards and Cafe, Waffle House

Lodg N: Budget Host, DAYS INN Days Inn, Motel 6, SHONEY'S Shoney's
S: Econolodge, Interstate Plaza, King's Guest Lodge, La Quinta Inn, Oasis Budget Host, Ramada, **T/A TravelCenters of America**, Value Travel Inn

AServ S: Auto Triola's, Ernie's, Meineke Discount Mufflers, **Wal-Mart**(RX)

TServ N: **76 Auto/Truck Plaza**(SCALES), **Travel America Travel Center**(SCALES)
S: **T/A TravelCenters of America**(SCALES)

ATM N: **76 Auto/Truck Plaza**, USA
S: Racetrac

Other N: Coin Car Wash, **Office Depot**, **Schwegmann**(RX), U-Haul Center
S: **Wal-Mart**(RX)

267AB Junction I-59 North, Hattiesburg, Jct I-12W, Baton Rouge, Hammond

(269) **LA Tourist Info Center, Rest Area (RR, Phones, Picnic, RV Dump; Westbound)**

↑LOUISIANA

↓MISSISSIPPI

(1) **Weigh Station (Southbound)**

(1) **Weigh Station (Northbound)**

(2) **MS Welcome Center (RR, HF, Phones, Picnic, RV Dump, P; Westbound)**

2 MS. 607, NASA John C. Stennis Space Center

Other N: **Naval Oceanographic Center**, **Stennis Space Center**

(10) **Parking Area (Eastbound)**

13 MS 43, MS 603, Bay Saint Louis, Picayune

Gas S: Chevron(*, D), Conoco(*, LP), Exxon(*, D)

Food S: Conoco, Exxon, Subway (Exxon), Waffles (Conoco)

Lodg S: Motel (Conoco)

RVCamp S: **Bay Marina RV Park**, **Casino Magic RV Park**, **KOA Campgrounds**

Med S: **+ Hospital**

ATM S: Chevron, Conoco, Exxon

Parks N: **McLeod State Park**
S: **Buccaneer State Park**

EXIT MISSISSIPPI

16 Diamondhead

Gas N: BP(*), Chevron(*, CW)
S: Texaco(*)

Food N: BP, Blimpie's Subs (Chevron), Burger King(PLAY), Chevron, Dairy Queen, Domino's Pizza (BP), Dragon House of Hunan, Jackie O's Cafe, Robert's, Waffle House
S: O'Neal's Home of the Best Seafood, Pawpaw's (Texaco)

Lodg N: Diamond Head Resort (Ramada Inn)
S: Diamond Head Resort Community

ATM N: Caldwell Banker, Chevron, Hancock Bank, The People's Bank, Whitney

Other N: Diamond Head Animal Hospital, Diamondhead Supermarket, Pharmacy Discount Drugs
S: ACE Hardware, Super One Stop

20 DeLisle

Gas N: **Shell**(*), Spur(*)

Food N: **GiGi's (Shell)**, **Shell**

24 **(25)** Menge Ave

TStop N: **Amoco**(*, SCALES)

Gas S: Texaco(*)

Food S: Stuckey's (Texaco)

TServ N: **Amoco**(SCALES)

TWash N: **Amoco**

RVCamp S: **Campground**

28 Long Beach, Pass Christian

Gas S: Chevron(*), Citgo(*)

AServ S: Coastal Energy Tires

RVCamp S: **Magic River Camping**

ATM S: Citgo

31 Canal Road, Gulfport

TStop S: **Flying J Travel Plaza**(*, D, LP, RV DUMP, SCALES) **(Travel Store)**

FStop S: **BP**(*)

Food S: The Cookery Restaurant and Cafe (Flying J)

Lodg S: Crystal Inn

TServ N: **61 Tire Service (24 hour road sevice)**, **Dee's Tire Co Bridgestone Truck/Tire Service**, **I-10 Service and Parts**
S: **Flying J Travel Plaza**(SCALES) **(Travel Store)**

TWash N: **61 Tire Service (24 hour road sevice)**, **Russel's Truck Wash**

ATM S: **Flying J Travel Plaza (Travel Store)**

Other N: Go Cart Track

34AB U.S. 49, Gulfport, Hattiesburg, B-North, A-South

FStop N: **Speedway**(*, D)
S: **Fastlane**(*), **Shell**(*)

Gas N: Amoco(*, CW), Texaco(*, D)
S: Fast Lane(*), Murray USA, Texaco(*, D, CW)

Food N: **Hardee's**, Homestead, Waffle House
S: Applebee's, Arby's(24), Burger King, Holiday Inn, KFC, Krispy Kreme Doughnuts,

1783

1712 Beach Blvd.
Biloxi, MS
228-432-2000
800-446-4656

Continental Breakfast
Kids Under 17 Stay Free
Outdoor Pool • Exercise Room
Pets Allowed • Handicap Accessible
Interior Corridors
Across From the Beach
Microfrige Some Rooms
Casino Package/Casino Shuttle
Optional Jacuzzi Room (Higher Rate)
MISSISSIPPI • I-10 EXIT 46A

EXIT MISSISSIPPI

McDonald's(PLAY) (Walmart), Michael's Restaurant (Best Western), Morrison's Cafeteria, Rowdy's Roast Beef & Burgers, Schlotzsky's Deli, **Seaway Inn Best Western**, SHONEY'S, Shoney's, Subway, **Waffle House**, Wendy's

Lodg S: Best Western, Comfort Inn, Fairfield Inn, Hampton Inn, Holiday Inn, Holiday Inn Express, Motel 6, **Seaway Inn Best Western**, SHONEY'S Shoney's

AServ S: 10 Min. Oil Change, Pat Peck Nisson

Med S: **+ Hospital**

ATM N: Texaco
S: Deposit Guaranty National Bank, Fast Lane, **Fastlane**

Other N: Old Things Antiques
S: **Gus Port Factory Shops**, Home Depot, Kern Optical Lab, **Sam's Club**, **Wal-Mart Supercenter**(RX) **(Vision Center, One Hour Photo)**

38 Lorraine - Cowan Road, Barnard Bayou Industrial District

Gas N: Exxon(*), Speedway(*, LP), Texaco(*, D)

Food N: Captain Al's Restaurant, Domino's Pizza, Exxon, Subway (Exxon)

RVCamp S: **Gaywood RV Camp**

Med S: **+ Hospital**

ATM N: Exxon, Texaco

41 MS. 67, Woolmarket

Gas N: BP(*, LP)

TServ N: **Johnson Diesel Inc**

RVCamp S: **Mazalea Travel Park**(LP), **Parker's Landing RV Park (.25 Miles)**

44 Cedar Lake Road, Coast Coliseum

FStop S: **Shell**(*, RV DUMP)

Gas S: Citgo, Exxon(*, D)

AServ S: Cedar Lake Auto Parts, Worrell Auto Service

RVCamp S: **Kennedy Engine Co., Inc. (1.1 Miles)**

Med S: **+ Hospital**

ATM S: Exxon, Hancock Bank, **Shell**

Other N: Cedar Lake Hardware and Supply(LP, K) (U-Haul Available)
S: **Cedar Lake Animal Hospital**, Laser Knight

46AB I-110, MS 15, Biloxi, Keesler Air Force Base (Difficult Reaccess, B-North, A-South)

Gas N: Texaco(*, D)

Lodg S: Howard Johnson Express Inn (see our ad this page)

ATM N: Texaco

50 MS. 609S, Ocean Springs, St. Martin, Latimer

FStop S: **Speedway**(*, D, 24)

Gas N: Chevron(*), Texaco(*, CW)
S: Amoco(*, 24)

Food N: Pizza Inn (Texaco), Taco Bell (Texaco), Texaco
S: Amoco, **Blimpie's Subs (Speedway FS)**, Denny's, McDonald's (Amoco), **Waffle House**

Lodg N: Best Western, Super 8
S: DAYS INN Days Inn, Hampton Inn, Holiday Inn Express, Sleep Inn

ATM N: Chevron, Super 8, Texaco
S: Amoco, **Speedway**

Other S: **Blue Ridge Veterinary Clinic**

57 MS. 57, Fontainbleau, Vancleave

FStop S: **Texaco**(*, D)

Gas S: BP(*)

TServ S: **Texaco**

RVCamp N: **KOA Campgrounds**(LP, PLAY)

Other S: **Gulf Island National Seashore**

61 Gautier, Vancleave

RVCamp N: **Wonderland Park**
S: **Bluff Creek Camping**

Parks S: **Shepard State Park (1.5 Miles)**

Bold red print shows RV & Bus parking available or nearby

EXIT		MISSISSIPPI
	Other	N: Sand Hill Crane Wildlife Refuge Area
(64)		**Rest Area (RR, HF, Phones, Picnic, RV Dump, P; Northbound)**
(64)		**Rest Area (RR, HF, Phones, Picnic, RV Dump, P; Southbound)**
68		MS 613, Moss Point, Pascagoula
	FStop	N: **Citgo(*, D)**, **Conoco(*)**
	Gas	N: Texaco(*, D)
		S: Chevron(*)
	Food	N: KFC (Texaco), Texaco
	Lodg	N: Super 8 (see our ad this page)
	ATM	N: Texaco
	Other	N: Max Fishing Camp, Riverbend Camping

1273

SUPER 8 MOTEL

800-800-8000
228-474-1855

6824 Hwy 613
MOSS POINT, MS 39563

Continental Breakfast Included

Kids 12 and Under Stay & Eat Free
Outdoor Pool • Whirlpool
Remote TV, ESPN, HBO
24 Hour Front Desk
Free Local Calls
Pets Allowed
Handicap Accessible
Truck or Large Vehicle Parking
Interior Corridors

Tour Buses Welcome

Only 20 Minutes to Casino

MISSISSIPPI • I-10 • EXIT 68

NEW 103 ROOM FACILITY

4800 AMOCO DRIVE
Moss Point, MS
228-474-2100
800-962-1840

• Free Breakfast Bar • Free HBO
• Heated Whirlpool & Swimming Pool
• King with Jacuzzi • Double Queen Rooms
• Free Local Calls with Voice Mail Message System
• Within Walking Distance of Restaurants
• Interior Corridors

1229

MISSISSIPPI • I-10 • EXIT 69

Flagship Inn

4800 AMOCO DRIVE
Moss Point, MS
228-475-5000
800-522-5082

Michael's Lounge on Premises
Pool • Free Local Calls
Free HBO & ESPN
Free Coffee & Pastries In Our Lobby

1230

MISSISSIPPI • I-10 • EXIT 69

1231

SHULAR INN

6623 Highway 63 @ I-10
Moss Point, MS
228-475-8444
800-962-1820

Free Breakfast Bar In the Lobby
Large Screen TV's
Microwave, & Refrigerators
Easy Access to Restaurant & Fast Food Chains
On Premise Guest Laundry

MISSISSIPPI • I-10 • EXIT 69

EXIT		MISSISSIPPI/ALABAMA
69		MS. 63, East Moss Point, East Pacagoula (Hospital)
	FStop	S: **Amoco(*)**, **Cone Auto/Truck Plaza(D, SCALES)**
	Gas	N: Texaco(*, CW)
		S: Exxon(*)
	Food	N: Domino's Pizza (Texaco), Texaco
		S: Best Western, Burger King(PLAY), **Cone Auto/Truck Plaza**, **Cracker Barrel**, Exxon, Hardee's, **McDonald's(PLAY)**, Michael's Restaurant (Best Western), Pizza Hut, Quincy's Family Steakhouse, Subway (Exxon), Waffle House
	Lodg	N: Ashbury Suites
		S: Best Western (see oura d this page), Comfort Inn, Days Inn, **Hampton Inn**, Holiday Inn (see our ad this page), Shular Inn (see our ad this page)
	ATM	N: Texaco
		S: **Amoco**, **Cone Auto/Truck Plaza**
	Other	N: Airport
		S: Trucker and Traveler Center
(75)		**Weigh Station (Eastbound)**
(75)		**Welcome Center , Rest Area (RR, Phones, Picnic, RV Dump, P; Westbound)**
75		Franklin Creek Road
(77)		**Weigh Station (Westbound)**

↑MISSISSIPPI

↓ALABAMA

EXIT		ALABAMA
(1)		**Welcome Center, Rest Area (RR, HF, Phones, Picnic, RV Dump; Eastbound)**
4		AL. 188, Grand Bay
	TStop	N: **T/A TravelCenters of America(*, SCALES)**
	Gas	N: Citgo(*), Shell(*)
		S: Chevron(*, CW, 24)
	Food	N: Dairy Queen (Shell), Stuckey's (Shell), Waffle House
		S: Hardee's, Krispy Kreme Doughnuts (Chevron)
	TServ	N: **T/A TravelCenters of America**, **T/A TravelCenters of America(SCALES)**
	ATM	N: **T/A TravelCenters of America**
13		**(14)** Theodore, Dawes
	TStop	N: **Pilot Travel Center(*, D, SCALES)**
	Gas	N: Amoco(*, 24), Conoco(*), Shell(*, CW)
		S: Chevron(*)
	Food	N: **Krispy Kreme Doughnuts (Pilot TS)**, McDonald's (Amoco), Subway (Shell), Waffle House, **Wendy's (Pilot TS)**
	AServ	N: Economy Auto Center Inc
	RVCamp	S: **I-10 Kampground (.5 Miles)**

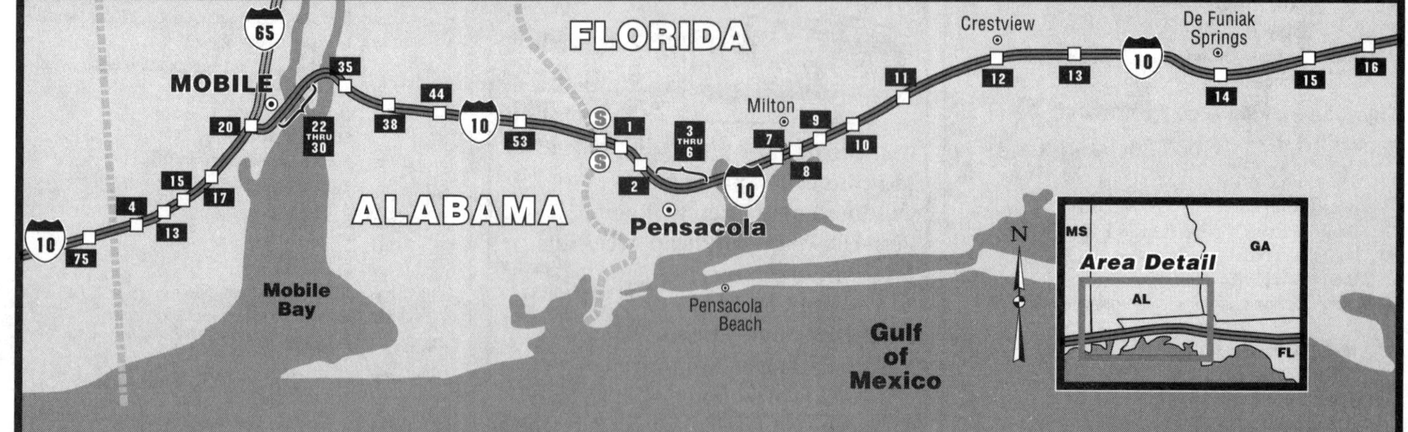

Bold red print shows RV & Bus parking available or nearby

EXIT	ALABAMA
ATM	N: Amoco
Other	N: **Mobile Greyhound Park**
15AB	U.S. 90, Theodore, Historic Mobile Pkwy., Tillman's Corner (15 B North, 15 A South)
FStop	S: **Texaco**(*, D)
Gas	N: Chevron(*, 24), Freeway(*), Racetrac(*, 24), Shell(*, CW)
	S: Chevron(*, CW, 24)
Food	N: Arby's, Checkers Burgers, China Town Restaurant, EL Toro, El Patio, Godfather's Pizza, KFC, McDonald's(PLAY), Neighbor's Seafood, Chicken and Vegetables, Orleans PoBoys, Papa John's Pizza, Popeye's Chicken, **Quincy's Family Steakhouse**, SHONEY'S Shoney's, Subway, Taco Bell, Waffle House
	S: Waffle House
Lodg	N: Best Western, Comfort Inn, DAYS INN Days Inn, Hampton Inn, Holiday Inn (see our ad this page), Motel 6, Red Roof Inn, Shoney's Inn, Super 8 (see our ad this page), TraveLodge
AServ	N: Goodyear, Mastercare by Firestone, Super Lube
	S: Bishop Automotives, PoBoy Tires and Towing, Ronnie's Mufflers and Brakes
RVCamp	N: **Bunkley RV Superstore (1 Mile), Pala Verde Mobile Home & RV Park**
ATM	N: Compass Bank, Regions Bank, SouthTrust Bank, Union Planter's Bank
	S: **Texaco**
Other	N: Auto Zone, **Delchamp's Supermarket**, Eye Glass Express, **Foodworld Grocery Store, K-Mart**(RX), Laundromat, Revco, Rite Aid Pharmacy, **Winn Dixie Supermarket**(RX)
	S: **B & R Camper Sales**, Don's Marine Service
17AB	AL 193, Dauphin Island, Tillman's Corner (Difficult Reaccess)
Gas	N: Citgo(*, CW)
Food	N: Blimpie's Subs (Citgo), Golden Corral Family Steakhouse
RVCamp	N: **PawPaw's**
Med	S: ✚ **Hospital**
Other	N: **Wal-Mart SuperCenter**(24, RX)
20	Junction I-65 N, Montgomery
22AB	Alabama 163, Dauphin Island Pkwy
Gas	S: Citgo(*), Exxon(*)
Food	N: Big Save Seafood
	S: Exxon, Subway (Exxon), Waffle House
Lodg	N: Motel 6
	S: Gone With The Wind Hotel
AServ	N: I-10 Auto Parts
TServ	S: **Truck Center**
23	Michigan Ave.
Gas	N: Exxon(*)
Lodg	N: Rodeway Inn
24	Broad St., Duval St. (Go under interstate to the south side and take the first left and another left to the north side services)
Gas	N: Chevron(*, CW, 24), Citgo(*, D)
Food	N: Citgo
AServ	N: Horace Auto Service, Sexton Garage
25	Virginia Street (Eastbound, Westbound it is 25B)
Gas	N: Texaco(*, D)
AServ	S: Ten-Tom Tires
25B	Virginia St
25A	Texas St. (Westbound, Difficult Reaccess)
26A	Canal St

EXIT	ALABAMA
Other	N: Civic Service
26B	Water St, Downtown Mobile
27	U.S. 90, U.S. 98, Government St., Battleship Pkwy
Food	S: Battleship Inn Best Western, Captain's Table
Lodg	S: Battleship Inn Best Western
Other	S: Battleship Memorial Park
30	U.S. 31, U.S. 90, U.S. 98, Battleship Pkwy, Spanish Fort
FStop	S: **Citgo**(*), **Texaco**(*, D)
Gas	S: Amoco(*), Hudson(*)
Food	S: Cock of the Walk Restaurant, Kimberly's (Ramada), Original Oyster House, Pier 4 Restaurant, Poor Man's, Ramada
Lodg	S: Ramada
Parks	S: **Battleship USS Alabama Park**

1582

Mobile, AL Bellingrath Gardens

- Free Breakfast Buffet Available
- Outdoor Pool with Spa
- Guest Laundry Facilities
- Executive Level
- Closest Full Service Hotel to Bellingrath Gardens

334-666-5600 • 800-465-4329

ALABAMA • I-10 • EXIT 15-B

5676 Tillmans Corner Pkwy
Mobile, AL 36619
334-666-0003

Sunday - Thursday Rates

** Special rates not valid during Holidays & Special Events.*

- Free Continental Breakfast
- Micro-Freeze in all Rooms
- Outdoor Pool • Coin Laundry
- Handicap Accessible
- Many Restaurants Nearby
- Free Local Calls
- Bus/Truck Parking Nearby
- Cable TV w/ Free HBO & 35 Channels
- Nearby Attractions: Bellingrath Gardens & USS Battleship Alabama

1559

ALABAMA • I-10 • EXIT 15B

EXIT	ALABAMA/FLORIDA
35AB	U.S. 98, U.S. 90, Daphne - Fairhope Spanish Fort
Gas	N: BP(*, LP)
	S: Citgo(*), Exxon(*, D), Shell(*)
Food	S: Arby's, Burger King(PLAY), Checkers Burgers, Domino's Pizza, McDonald's(PLAY), Nautilus, South China, Waffle House, Wendy's
Lodg	S: Eastern Shore Motel, Hampton Inn, Legacy Motel
Med	S: ✚ **Hospital**
ATM	N: BP
Parks	N: **Historic Blakeley State Park**
Other	S: Gayfers, Lakeforest Animal Clinic, Office Depot
38	**(39)** Alabama 181, Malbis
Gas	N: Amoco(*)
	S: Chevron(*)
44	Alabama 59, Loxley, Bay Minette
FStop	N: **Texaco**(*, SCALES)
	S: **Exxon**(*)
Gas	S: Chevron(*, D, CW)
Food	N: **Texaco**
	S: **Hardee's**, McDonald's(PLAY), **Waffle House**
Lodg	S: **Wind Chase Inn**
TServ	S: **Exxon, Truck Service (Exxon)**
TWash	S: **Truck Wash (Exxon)**
RVCamp	S: **Parkway RV Camp**
ATM	N: **Texaco**
Other	S: Gulf Shores Beaches and State Park
53	CR.64, Wilcox Road
TStop	N: **Oasis**(*, D, SCALES) **(BP)**
Gas	S: Chevron(*, 24), Outpost(*, D)
Food	N: **Mirage Restaurant (Oasis Travel Center), Oasis (BP)**
AServ	S: Chevron, Chevron(24)
TServ	N: **Oasis**(SCALES) **(BP), Oasis TS**(24) **(Wrecker Service), Truck Repair**(24)
RVCamp	N: **RV Repair**
	S: **Hilltop RV Park (.5 Miles)**
ATM	N: **ATM (Oasis Travel Center), Oasis (BP)**
	S: Chevron
Other	N: **Discount Fireworks, Styx River Water World**
(66)	**Welcome Center (RR, HF, Phones, Picnic, RV Dump; Westbound)**

↑ALABAMA

↓FLORIDA

(3)	**Weigh Station (Eastbound)**
(3)	**Weigh Station (Westbound)**
(2)	**Welcome Center (Eastbound)**
1	**(6)** U.S. 90 Alternate
FStop	N: **Speedway**(*, SCALES)
Food	N: **Speedway, Subway (Speedway)**
RVCamp	N: **Tall Oaks Campground**
ATM	N: **Speedway, Speedway**
2AB	**(7)** FL 297, Pine Forest Road, Pensacola Naval Air Station
Gas	N: Exxon(*)
	S: BP(*), Citgo(*, LP, 24), Texaco(*, D)
Food	N: Exxon
	S: Burger King, **Cracker Barrel**, Hardee's, McDonald's(PLAY), Waffle House
Lodg	N: Rodeway Inn
	S: Microtel, Ramada Limited, Sleep Inn
AServ	S: Interstate Air
RVCamp	N: **Tall Oaks Campground**
ATM	N: Exxon
	S: BP
3AB	**(10)** U.S. 29, Pensacola, Cantonment
FStop	N: **Mapco Express**(*, SCALES)

Bold red print shows RV & Bus parking available or nearby

EXIT FLORIDA

Gas **N:** Exxon(*), Parade(*, D)
S: Racetrac(*, 24), Shell(*)
Food **N:** Hardee's, Waffle House
S: Denny's, McDonald's(PLAY)
Lodg **S:** Days Inn, Econolodge
AServ **S:** Bob Tyler Toyota, Don Dawson Jeep Eagle
TServ **N:** Ryder Transportation Services
RVCamp **N:** Carpenter's Campers Inc.(LP) (1 Mile)
ATM **N:** Exxon, Mapco Express
S: Racetrac, Shell
Other **N:** Ryder Transportation Services
S: Greyhound Bus Station

4 **(12)** Junction I-110, Pensacola

5 **(13)** FL 291, Pensacola, University of West Florida

Gas **N:** Amoco(*, LP, 24), Chevron(*, CW), Texaco(*, D)
Food **N:** Arby's, Burger King, Captain D's Seafood, Denny's, McDonald's(PLAY), Peking Garden Chinese, Riccio's Pizza and Subs, SHONEY'S, Shoney's, TCBY, Taco Bell, Waffle House
S: Bennigan's, Chuck E Cheese's Pizza, Coconut Bay Restaurant, Cuco's Restaurant, Darryl's, First City Cafe (Holiday Inn), Holiday Inn, Los Rancheros, Pizza Hut, Steak & Ale, Tudo's Restaurant, Waffle House, Wendy's
Lodg **N:** La Quinta Inn, Motel 6, Shoney's Inn, Villager Lodge
S: Fairfield Inn, Hampton Inn, Holiday Inn, Marriot Residence Inn, Motel 6, Red Roof Inn, Super 8
AServ **S:** Master Care Auto Service, Tires Inc.
Med **N:** + Hospital
ATM **N:** AM South Bank
Other **N:** Big B Drugs, Food World Supermarket, Post Office, Storage Center (U-Haul)
S: Service Merchandise, U-Haul Center, United Artist Theaters, University Mall

6 **(16)** U.S. 90

Gas **N:** BP(*)
S: Exxon(*)
Food **S:** Dairy Queen (Exxon), Exxon, Ramada, Ramada
Lodg **S:** Ramada
ATM **N:** BP
S: Exxon

(20) **Parking Area**

7 **(22)** Avalon Blvd

Gas **N:** Shell(*)
Food **N:** McDonald's
AServ **N:** Michael Bratton Automotive
RVCamp **S:** By The Bay RV Park
Med **N:** + Hospital

8 **(26)** CR.191, Milton, Whiting Field, Bagdad

FStop **S:** T&B Food Store(*, 24)

EXIT FLORIDA

Gas **S:** Citgo(*)
Food **S:** Citgo, Dairy Queen (Citgo)
RVCamp **S:** Pelican Palms RV Park, Sunny Acres RV Resort
ATM **S:** Citgo, Citgo

9 **(28)** CR. 89, Milton

RVCamp **S:** Evans Cedar Lake RV Campground
Med **N:** + Hospital

(30) **Rest Area (RR, HF, Phones, Picnic; Westbound)**

(30) **Rest Area (RR, HF, Phones, Picnic; Eastbound)**

10 **(31)** CR87, Milton, Navarre, Fort Walton Beach

1 Minute to Beautiful Navarre Beach
Comfort Inn
8700 Navarre Pkwy
$69.00* May - August
$49.00* Sept. - April
*Rates with this Ad. Not Valid Holidays.
1209
Outdoor Pool
Free Continental Breakfast
Discount for Walk Ins Only
Pets Allowed, $5.00 per day
Handicapped Accessible
Great Restaurants Nearby
850-939-1761 • Reservations 800-868-1761
FLORIDA • I-10 • EXIT 10 South

HOLIDAY INN - NAVARRE BEACH
1575
Holiday Inn
I-10 • Exit 10
Navarre Beach, FL
Exit 10, Take Hwy. 87 South, Left on Hwy 98 to Navarre Beach Brdg.
850-939-2321
888-277-8667
$15 Off Sun - Thur May - Sept
7 Days Oct - Apr
On The Gulf
Indoor Heated Pool
Exercise Room
FLORIDA • I-10 • EXIT 10

EXIT FLORIDA

TStop **N:** Rolling Thunder Truck Stop(*)
Gas **S:** Amoco(*, LP), Chevron(*), RH Express(*, K)
Food **N:** Restaurant (Rolling Thunder TS)
Lodg **S:** Comrots Inn (see our ad this page), Holiday Inn (see our ad this page)
TServ **N:** Rolling Thunder Truck Stop, Wooten's Road Service
RVCamp **N:** Gulf Pines Resort
ATM **S:** RH Express
Parks **S:** Blackwater State Park
Other **N:** Ray Rich CB Shop

11 **(45)** CR189, Holt

FStop **S:** Shell(*, LP)
RVCamp **N:** Log Lake Road RV Park
S: Rivers Edge RV Campground (1.75 Miles)
Parks **N:** BlackWater River State Park

12 **(56)** FL 85, Crestview , Eglin AFB, Niceville, Ft. Walton Beaches

Gas **N:** Racetrac(*), Shell(*, D, LP)
S: Amoco(*, LP, 24), Citgo(*, LP, 24), Exxon(*)
Food **N:** Great China, McDonald's
S: Arby's, Cracker Barrel, Dairy Queen, Exxon, Hardee's, La Bamba Mexican, Nim's Garden Chinese, SHONEY'S, Shoney's, Subway (Exxon), Waffle House, Wendy's
Lodg **N:** Econolodge
S: Days Inn, Hampton Inn, Holiday Inn, Super 8
AServ **S:** Hub City Ford Mercury
RVCamp **S:** Holiday Lake Travel Park
Med **N:** + Hospital
ATM **N:** Racetrac
S: Exxon
Other **N:** Super Flea Open Air Mall, Wal-Mart(24, RX)

(58) **Rest Area (RR, HF, Phones, Picnic; Eastbound)**

(60) **Rest Area (RR, HF, Phones, Picnic; Westbound)**

13 **(70)** FL 285, Niceville, Eglin Air Force Base , Ft Walton Bches

TStop **S:** Lucky 13 Truck/Auto Plaza(*, SCALES)
FStop **N:** The Cola Cafe
Gas **N:** RaceWay(*)
Food **N:** The Cola Cafe
S: Lucky 13 Truck/Auto Plaza, Restaurant (Lucky 13), Subway (Lucky 13)
TServ **S:** Lucky 13 TS, Lucky 13 Truck/Auto Plaza(SCALES)
Med **N:** + Hospital
ATM **N:** RaceWay
S: Lucky 13 Truck/Auto Plaza, National Bank and Trust (Lucky 13)

14 **(85)** U.S. 331, De Funiak Springs, Freeport

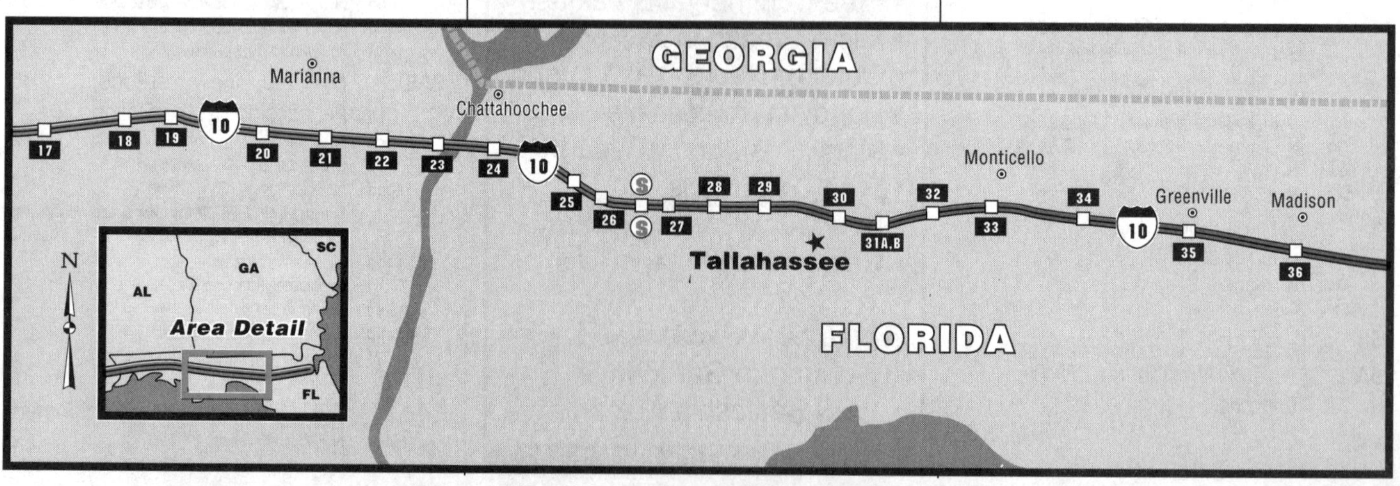

Bold red print shows RV & Bus parking available or nearby

EXIT FLORIDA

FStop S: **Exxon**[*]
Gas N: Amoco[*, LP], Chevron[*, 24]
S: Shell[*], Texaco[*]
Food N: Burger King[PLAY], McLain's Family Steakhouse, Waffle House
S: Best Western, **Exxon**, Hardee's, McDonald's[PLAY], **Taco Bell (Exxon FS)**
Lodg N: Budget Motel, DAYS INN Days Inn, Ramada Limited
S: Best Western
Med N: **+ Hospital**
S: **+ Health Facility**
ATM S: **Exxon**, Texaco
Other N: Chautauqua Winery

15 **(96) FL 81, Ponce De Leon, Rest Area**
FStop S: **Exxon**[*], **Texaco**[*]
Gas S: Amoco[*]
Food S: **Subway (Texaco)**, **Texaco**
Lodg S: Ponce de Leon Motor Lodge
RVCamp N: **Ponce de Leon Campground**, **Vortex Springs Resort**
ATM S: **Exxon**, **Texaco**
Parks N: **Ponce de Leon Springs State Recreation Area (No Camping)**

(96) **Rest Area (RR, HF, Phones, Picnic; Southside Of Exit 15)**

16 **(104)** CR. 279, Caryville

17 **(111)** FL 79, Bonifay, Panama City Beach
TStop N: **Simbo's Auto Truck Stop**[*]
FStop N: **Exxon**[*]
Gas N: Chevron[*]
Food N: **Hardee's**, McDonald's[PLAY], Pizza Hut, **Simbo's Steaks & Seafood (Citgo TS)**, Subway, Waffle House
Lodg N: **Econolodge**, Tivoli Inn Best Western
AServ N: Hightower Auto Parts
TServ N: **Simbo's Auto Truck Stop**
TWash N: **Simbo's Auto Truck Stop**
RVCamp N: **Hidden Lake Campground**
S: **Cypress Springs Campground**
Med N: **+ Hospital**
Other N: Kokopelli South Campground and RV Park

18 **(119)** FL 77, Chipley, Panama City
Gas N: Exxon[*, D, PLAY], Texaco[*]
S: Shell[*]
Food N: B&B Coffee House Wrecker, Burger King (Exxon), Exxon[PLAY], KFC, TCBY (Exxon), Taco Bell (Texaco), Texaco, Wendy's
S: Icecream Churn (Shell)
Lodg N: DAYS INN **Days Inn**, Holiday Inn Express, **Super 8**
Med N: **+ Hospital**
ATM N: Exxon, Texaco
Other N: Historic Chipley Antique Mall, **Wal-Mart**[RX]
S: **Falling Water State Recreation Area**

19 **(130)** U.S. 231, Panama City, Cottondale
FStop N: **Amoco**[*]
Gas N: BP, Chevron[*]
Food N: BP, **Hardee's**, Subway (BP)

(133) **Rest Area (RR, HF, Phones, Picnic; Westbound)**

(133) **Rest Area (RR, HF, Phones, Picnic; Eastbound)**

20 **(136)** FL 276, Marianna
FStop N: **Chevron**[*]
Med N: **+ Hospital**
Parks N: **Florida Caverns State Park**

21 **(142)** FL 71, Marianna, Blountstown
TStop S: **76 Auto/Truck Plaza**[*, SCALES] **(BP)**
FStop N: **Amoco**[*, 24]
S: **Speedway**[*]
Gas N: Shell[*, LP], Texaco[*, D]
Food N: Baskin Robbins, SHONEY'S Shoney's, Sonny's Barbecue, **Waffle House**
S: **76 Auto/Truck Plaza (BP)**, **McDonald's**
Lodg N: Comfort Inn, Hampton Inn, Holiday Inn
S: **Best Western**
TServ N: **Pilot**[SCALES]
S: **76 Auto/Truck Plaza**, **76 Auto/Truck Plaza**[SCALES] **(BP)**
RVCamp N: **Arrowhead Campsites (1.25 Miles)**
S: **Dove Rest RV Park & Campground**
Med N: **+ Hospital**
Parks N: **Florida Caverns State Park**

22 **(152)** FL 69, Grand Ridge, Blountstown

1553
$36 1-4 person with this Ad
DAYS INN
Within Minutes to Capitol Building, Florida State, A&M University, Civic Centre, Wakulla Springs, Greyhound & City Bus Terminal, Amtrack & Airport
Free Cable & HBO, Pool • Free Local Calls
Walking Distance to Restaurants • Outdoor Pool
Non-Smoking Rooms • Military & Corporate Discounts
Children Under 16 Stay Free with Parents
Complimentary Coffee/Donuts From 7-10am
— Mention Ad for Special Rate —
850-222-3219 • Tallahassee, FL
FLORIDA ▪ I-10 ▪ EXIT 28

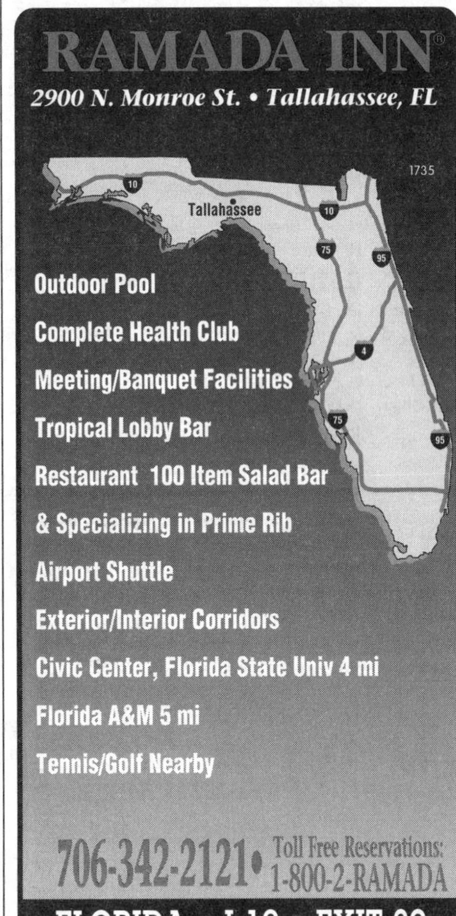

FStop N: **Chevron**[*]
Gas N: Exxon[*], Texaco[*]
Food N: **Chevron**, Icecream Churn (Texaco), Texaco, The Golden Skillet (Chevron)
Lodg N: Durden's Family Inn
Other N: **The Golden Lariat Western Store and Museum**

(155) **Rest Area (Westbound)**

(155) **Rest Area (Eastbound)**

23 **(158)** CR. 286, Sneads
Other N: Lake Seminole, **Three Rivers State Recreation Area**

(161) **Rest Area (RR, HF, Phones, Picnic; Westbound)**

(161) **Rest Area (RR, HF, Phones, Picnic; Eastbound)**

24 **(165)** CR.270 - A, Chattahoochee
Gas S: Texaco[*, D]
RVCamp S: **KOA-Chattahoochee**

25 **(174)** FL.12, Quincy, Greensboro
FStop N: **Amoco**[*], **Texaco**[*]
Food N: **Amoco**, **Burger King (Amoco)**
RVCamp N: **Beaver Lake Campground**

26 **(181)** FL 267, Quincy
Gas N: Texaco[*] (Ice Cream Churn)
S: BP[*, D], Shell[*, LP]
Food N: Icecream Churn (Texaco)
Lodg S: Holiday Inn Express
Med N: **+ Hospital**
Other S: **Lake Talquin Recreation Area**

27 **(192)** U.S. 90, Quincy, Midway, FSU, Florida A&M
TStop N: **Flying J Travel Plaza**[*, LP, RV DUMP, SCALES] **(Travel Store)**
Gas N: BP[*, LP]
Food N: BP, **Country Market (Flying J TS)**, **Flying J Travel Plaza (Travel Store)**, **Magic Dragon (Flying J TS)**, **Pepperoni Super Slice (Flying J TS)**
RVCamp N: **Tallahassee RV Service & Campground (5 Miles)**
Other S: Lakeside Travel Park (3.9 Miles)

(194) **Rest Area (RR, HF, Phones, Picnic; Westbound)**

(194) **Rest Area (RR, HF, Phones, Picnic; Eastbound)**

28 **(195)** FL 263, Capitol Circle, Regional Airport
Gas S: Chevron[*, CW], Shell[*, D]
Food S: Ice Cream Churn (Shell), Shell, Waffle House
Lodg S: Sleep Inn
Parks S: **Florida State Parks (.5 Miles)**
Other S: **Tallahassee Museum of History & Natural Science**

29 **(199)** U.S. 27, Havana, Tallahassee
Gas S: Amoco[*], Chevron[*], Texaco[*]
Food N: Burger King, Holiday Inn, Waffle House
S: Billy Jean Pancake House, China Super Buffet, Cracker Barrel, Crystal River Seafood Restaurant, Julie's Place, La Quinta Inn, SHONEY'S Shoney's, Sonny's BBQ, The Melting Pot
Lodg N: Best Inns, Comfort Inn, Hampton Inn, Holiday Inn, Microtel, Villager Lodge
S: Cabot Lodge, DAYS INN Days Inn, Econolodge, Howard Johnson, La Quinta Inn, Motel 6, Ramada(see our ad this page), Red Roof Inn, Shoney's Inn, Super 8
AServ S: Sun Tire
RVCamp N: **Big Oak RV Park**

Bold red print shows RV & Bus parking available or nearby

EXIT		FLORIDA
	Other	S: North Florida Animal Hospital, Visitor Information, Tallahassee Convention Visitor's Bureau (see our ad this page)
30		(202) U.S. 319, FL. 61, Thomasville, Tallahassee
	FStop	N: Dixie(*, 24)
	Gas	N: BP(*, D), Shell(*, D), Texaco(*, CW)
	Food	N: Baskin Robbins, Burgers N Bagels, Georgio's Restaurant, Hilton Inn, Hungry Howie's, King House Buffet Chinese, Manhattan Bagel, Philly Connection, Sonny's Barbecue, TCBY, Taco Bell, Wendy's
		S: Boston Market Restaurant, Miami Subs Grills, Outback Steakhouse, Steak & Shake, T.G.I. Friday's
	Lodg	N: Hilton Inn, Motel 6
		S: Cabot Lodge, Residence Inn
	AServ	N: Super Lube

Make Your Next Florida Trip an Eventful One in
TALLAHASSEE

Springtime Tallahassee
April 1999

Southern Shakespeare Festival
May 1999

Florida Folk Festival
May 1999

Caribbean Carnival
August 1999

Winter Festival
December 1999

Discover the natural, cultural and historical treasures of Tallahassee--Florida's Southern-Side Up.

Call our Sales Manager today for your FREE custom Group Tour Packet.
1-800-628-2866 ext. 49

Tallahassee Area
Convention and Visitors Bureau
200 West College Avenue
I-10 at Exit 29 • Tallahassee, FL 32302
www.co.leon.fl.us/visitors/index.htm

1775

EXIT		FLORIDA
	Med	S: Hospital, Seniors Health Care Tallahassee Community Hospital
	ATM	N: AM South Bank, FMB Bank, First Bank & Trust Co., NationsBank, Tallahassee State Bank
		S: Capital City Bank
	Parks	N: Alfred B. Maclay State Gardens
	Other	N: Discovery Zone, Eckerd Drugs, Publix Supermarket, Super Suds Car Wash
31AB		(208) U.S. 90, Tallahassee, Monticello
	FStop	S: Citgo(*, LP)
	Food	S: Cross Creek Restaurant
	Lodg	S: Seminole Inn Best Western
	RVCamp	S: Tallahassee RV Park
	ATM	S: Citgo, Citgo FS
32		(216) FL. 59
	TStop	S: BP(*, LP, SCALES, 24)
	FStop	S: Citgo(*)
	Gas	S: Amoco(*)
	Food	S: Amoco, BP, Joyner's (Amoco), Subway (Amoco FS)
	Lodg	S: BP
	TServ	S: BP(SCALES, 24), Big Bend Auto/Truck Plaza
33		(225) Monticello, Thomasville , US 19, Florida Georgia Pkwy
	FStop	S: Texaco(*)
	Gas	S: Chevron(*), Exxon(*), Shell(*, LP)
	Food	S: Arby's (Texaco Fs), Huddle House, Texaco, Wendy's (Exxon)
	Lodg	S: Days Inn, Super 8
	RVCamp	N: A Camper's World (.25 Miles)
		S: KOA Campgrounds
	ATM	S: Exxon, Texaco
	Other	S: Southern Trends and Antiques
34		(233) CR. 257
	Gas	N: Chevron(*), Fina(*) (U-Haul Rental)
(235)		Rest Area (RR, HF, Phones, Picnic; Westbound)
(235)		Rest Area (RR, HF, Phones, Picnic; Eastbound)
35		(242) U.S. 221, Greenville, Perry
	Gas	N: Texaco(*)
		S: BP(*)
	Food	N: Dairy Queen (Texaco), Texaco
	ATM	N: Texaco
36		(252) FL. 14, Madison, Perry
	Gas	N: Texaco(*)
	Food	N: Arby's (Texaco), Icecream Churn (Texaco), Texaco
	Med	N: Hospital
	Other	N: North Community College
37		(258) FL 53, Madison

EXIT		FLORIDA
	TStop	N: Texaco(*, SCALES)
	FStop	N: Amoco(*), Citgo(*, D), Citgo(*, D)
	Food	N: Amoco, Burger King (Amoco FS), Citgo, Dairy Queen (Texaco TS), Jimmy's Restaurant, Latrelle's Family Restaurant, Subway (Texaco), Taco Bell (Texaco TS), Texaco
	Lodg	N: Days Inn (see our ad this page), Holiday Inn Express, Super 8
		S: Deerwood Inn
	TServ	N: Citgo
	RVCamp	S: Frontier Territory RV Park (.75 Miles), Madison Campground (.25 Miles)
	Med	N: Hospital
	ATM	N: Amoco, Citgo, Texaco
	Parks	S: Dowling Park
	Other	S: Frontier Opry Hall
38		(262) CR. 255, Lee
	FStop	N: Exxon(*)

Family owned Restaurants and Motels

Frontier Territory is conveniently located within 5 minutes of our family-owned restaurants and motels. Enjoy a clean, comfortable room at the Days Inn or Super 8 Motels. And when you get hungry, feast on some delicious fare at Latrelle's Restaurant or Jimmie's Truck Stop and Restaurant. In the event your vehicle needs repair or servicing, we'll take good care of you at Jimmie's Firestone & Service Center.

Madison
I-10 • EXIT 37
904-973-3330

904-973-3115

Madison, FL
904-973-6267
I-10 Exit 37W

Monticello, FL
904-997-8888
I-10 Exit 33W

RV Camping
Full Hook-Ups, Dump Station
Picnic Tables • 60 ft. Waterslide
Private Showers & Restrooms
Fishing in Freshwater Lake

FLORIDA • I-10

Bold red print shows RV & Bus parking available or nearby

EXIT	FLORIDA
	S: Citgo[*]
Gas	**S:** Texaco[*]
Food	**S:** Citgo, Red Onion Grill (Citgo)
ATM	**S:** Citgo
Parks	**N:** Suwannee River State Park (12 Miles)
(265)	Rest Area (RR, HF, Phones, Picnic; Westbound)
(265)	Rest Area (RR, HF, Phones, Picnic; Eastbound)
(271)	Weigh Station, Agricultural Inspection (Westbound)
(271)	Weigh Station, Agricultural Inspection (Eastbound)
39	**(275)** U.S. 90, Live Oak, Lee
Gas	**S:** United 500[*, D]
AServ	**S:** United 500
Med	**S:** + Hospital
Parks	**N:** Suwannee River State Park
40	(384) U.S. 129, Live Oak, Jasper, Welcome Center
FStop	**N:** Spur[*]
Gas	**S:** BP[*] (U-Haul Rental), Chevron[*], Shell[*], Texaco[*]
Food	**S:** Huddle House, McDonald's[PLAY], TCBY (Taco Bell), Taco Bell, Waffle House, Wendy's
Lodg	**S:** Econolodge, Suwannee River Inn
AServ	**S:** Chevron, Chevron
RVCamp	**S:** Spirit of the Suwanne Campground
Med	**S:** + Hospital
ATM	**S:** Shell, Shell
Other	**N:** Spirit of the Suwannee Music Park & Campground **S:** Museum
(284)	Parking Area (Westbound)
41	**(293)** CR.137, Wellborn
(294)	Rest Area (RR, HF, Phones, Picnic; Eastbound)
(295)	Rest Area (RR, HF, Phones, Picnic; Westbound)
42A	**(297)** Junction I-75, Tampa
42B	Junction I-75 N, Valdosta
43	**(302)** U.S. 41, Lake City, White Springs
Gas	**N:** Amoco[*] **S:** Texaco[*]
Food	**S:** Ice Cream Churn (Texaco), Texaco
RVCamp	**N:** Kelly's RV Park
Med	**N:** + Hospital
ATM	**N:** Amoco
Parks	**N:** Stephen Foster Folk Center
44	**(304)** U.S. 441, Lake City, Fargo
FStop	**S:** Joy[*], Texaco[*]
Gas	**N:** BP[*], Chevron[*, D]
Lodg	**S:** Days Inn Days Inn
AServ	**N:** BP, BP
RVCamp	**N:** KOA-Lake City North (1 Mile)
Med	**S:** + Hospital
(318)	Rest Area (RR, HF, Phones, Picnic; Eastbound)
(318)	Rest Area (RR, HF, Phones, Picnic; Westbound)
45	**(324)** U.S. 90, Sanderson, Olustee
Gas	**S:** Exxon[*]
Other	**S:** Olustee Battlefield, Osceola National Forest
46	**(327)** CR. 229, Sanderson, Raiford
47	**(333)** FL.125, Glen, St. Mary

EXIT	FLORIDA
FStop	**N:** Exxon[*, 24]
ATM	**N:** Exxon, Exxon
48	**(336)** FL 121, Macclenny, Lake Butler
FStop	**N:** BP[*, D] **S:** Exxon[*, 24]
Gas	**N:** Exxon[*] **S:** Racetrac[*]
Food	**N:** Connie's Kitchen, Days Pizza, Hardee's, KFC, Larry's Giant Subs, McDonald's[PLAY], Pizza Hut, Subway, Taco Bell, Waffle House, Woody's Barbecue **S:** Burger King[PLAY], China Gardens Restaurant, Derek's Barbecue, Exxon
Lodg	**N:** Days Inn Days Inn **S:** Econolodge, Expressway Motel
AServ	**N:** Jiffy Lube
Med	**N:** + Hospital **S:** + Northeast Florida Hospital
ATM	**N:** BP, SouthTrust
Other	**N:** Baker Laundromat, Food Lion Supermarket, Okefenokee National Wildlife Refuge, Wal-Mart[RX], Winn Dixie Supermarket[24, RX]
49	**(337)** FL 228, Macclenny, Maxville
Med	**N:** + Hospital
Other	**N:** Phantom Fireworks
50	**(344)** U.S. 301, Baldwin, Starke
TStop	**S:** Jacksonville Unocal 76[*, SCALES] (Amoco)
FStop	**S:** Speedway[*, SCALES]
Gas	**S:** Exxon[*], Shell[*], Texaco[*]
Food	**S:** Burger King[PLAY], Jacksonville Unocal 76 (Amoco), McDonald's, Town & Country (Unocal 76 TS), Waffle House
Lodg	**S:** Best Western
TServ	**S:** Jacksonville Unocal 76[SCALES] (Amoco)
(351)	Rest Area (RR, HF, Phones, Picnic; Westbound)
(352)	Rest Area (RR, HF, Phones, Picnic; Eastbound)
51	**(352)** Whitehouse, Cecil Field
Gas	**N:** Chevron[*], Lil' Champ[*] **S:** Shell[*, D], Texaco[*]
Food	**N:** Chevron
RVCamp	**N:** Rivers RV Camp
ATM	**N:** Chevron
52	**(357)** Marietta
Gas	**N:** Gate[*], Texaco[*] **S:** Amoco[*, D]
Food	**S:** Bill's Diner, Domino's Pizza
TServ	**N:** Auto Masters
Other	**S:** Coin Car Wash, Lil'Champ Foodstore, Marietta Animal Hospital, Maytag Laundry
53	**(357)** Junction I-295, Savannah, St Augustine, Orange Park, International Airport
54	**(358)** FL 103, Lane Ave
FStop	**N:** Fleet Card
Gas	**S:** Chevron[*, CW, 24], Shell[*], Texaco[*, D, CW]
Food	**N:** Andy's Sandwich Shop, Ramada Inn, Tad's Restaurant (Ramada Inn) **S:** Cross Creek BBQ, Denny's, Hardee's, Lee's Dragon Chinese, Linda's Seafood, Piccadilly Cafeteria, Shoney's Shoney's
Lodg	**N:** Days Inn Days Inn, Ramada Inn (see our ad this page) **S:** Executive Inn, Paradise Inn, Super 8
ATM	**S:** Nation's Bank (Texaco), SunTrust Bank, Texaco
Other	**S:** Home Depot, Jax Lane's West Bowling Alley, Office Depot
55	**(359)** FL 111, Cassat Ave, Edgewood Ave
FStop	**N:** Amoco[*, D]
Gas	**N:** Hess[D] **S:** Racetrac[*]
Food	**N:** Amoco, Firehouse Subs (Amoco), Pat and Mike Restaurant **S:** Dunkin Donuts, Jason's Sandwich Shop, Krispy Kreme Doughnuts
AServ	**N:** HPD, Mr. Transmission **S:** Xpress Lube
ATM	**N:** Amoco
56	**(360)** Lenox Ave, Edgewood Ave (Westbound, Difficult Reaccess)
57	**(361)** FL129, McDuff Ave.
Gas	**S:** Amoco[*, D], Chevron[*]
Food	**S:** Chevron, Popeye's Chicken
AServ	**S:** Amoco, Amoco, McDuff Auto Center
ATM	**S:** Amoco
Other	**N:** Trinity Baptist College
58	**(362)** U.S. 17, Roosevelt Blvd (Westbound)
59	**(363)** Stockton St. , Riverside
Gas	**S:** Amoco[*, K], Gate[*, D]
Food	**N:** Mary Anne's Golden Fried Chicken
AServ	**N:** No Name
Med	**S:** + Hospital
ATM	**S:** Amoco
Other	**S:** Short Stop
60	**(363)** Junction I-95 S Jacksonville Beaches, Daytona Beach, I-95 N International Airport, Savannah, St Augustine

↑FLORIDA

Begin I-10

RAMADA® INN & SUITES

Redefining Hospitality

510 S. Lane Ave • Jacksonville, FL

1773

Free American Breakfast
Outdoor Pool
Live Entertainment
Restaurant/Lounge on Premises
Meeting/Banquet Facilities
Handicap Accessible
Exercise Room (Off Property)
Truck/Large Vehicle Parking
Coin Laundry
Exterior/Interior Corridors
Suites Include Microwaves
& Refrigerators

904-786-0500
800-272-6232
800-2RAMADA

FLORIDA ▪ I-10 ▪ EXIT 54

EXIT LOUISIANA

Begin I-12

↓LOUISIANA

1A Junction I-10 E

1B LA 1068 to LA 73, Jefferson Hwy, Drusilla Lane (Difficult Reaccess)
- **Gas** N: Texaco(*, D, CW)
- **Food** N: Drusilla Seafood, Fast Trac, Fresina, KarFra Bakery and Cafe, Mary Lee Donuts
- **AServ** N: Jiffy Lube, Tune Up Inc
- **Med** S: + Hospital
- **ATM** N: Bank One; S: Union Planters Bank
- **Other** N: Animal Ark, Auto Express Car Wash, Eckerd Drugs(RX), Hi Nabor, Jefferson Animal Hospital, Monkey Bizz

2A US 61 S, Airline Hwy
- **Lodg** N: Days Inn (see our ad this page)

2B Us 61 N, Airline Hwy, US 61 S
- **Gas** N: Exxon(*, D, CW), Shell(*); S: Circle K, Speedway(*), Texaco(D, CW)
- **Food** N: Applebee's, Cracker Barrel, Holiday Inn, McDonald's, New York Deli, Rafferty's (Holiday Inn), SHONEY'S Shoney's, Taste of China; S: Bonanno's Seafood, McDonald's, Waffle House
- **Lodg** N: Hampton Inn, Holiday Inn, Motel 6, Shoney's Inn, Sleep Inn; S: DAYS INN Days Inn, Plantation Inn
- **AServ** N: Exxon, Import One, PEP Boys, Robinson Bros Mercury/Lincoln/Ford; S: Duplessis Cadillac/GM, Volvo Specialist and Service
- **RVCamp** S: Morgan RV's
- **ATM** N: Whitney Bank; S: Circle K
- **Other** N: Celebration Station; S: Home Depot

4 Sherwood Forest Blvd
- **Gas** N: Exxon(*, CW), Jet 24(*), Texaco(*, D, CW); S: Chevron(*, CW, 24), Shell(*, CW, 24)
- **Food** N: Bamboo House, Burger King(PLAY), Chuck E Cheese's Pizza, Corfu Greek, Lebanese, Italian, Denny's, Egg Roll King, KFC, McDonald's(PLAY), Popeye's Chicken, Subway, Waffle House; S: Baskin Robbins, Daquiri Cafe, PIzza Hut, Taco Bell, The Daily Grind Coffee, The Ground Pati, The Pasta Garden, Todnuh's Barbecue
- **Lodg** N: Crossland Economy Studios, Red Roof Inn, Super 8; S: Quality Inn
- **AServ** N: Car Quest Auto Center, Firestone, Goodyear; S: Precision Tune
- **ATM** N: City National Bank; S: Citizen's Bank, Hancock Bank
- **Other** N: Eckerd Drugs(RX), Rite Aid(RX); S: East Gate Car Wash

6 Millerville Rd
- **Gas** N: Citgo(*)
- **Food** N: K-Mart(24, RX); S: Chris' Specialty Meats
- **AServ** N: K-Mart(24)
- **ATM** N: K-Mart, Whitney Bank (K-Mart)
- **Other** N: K-Mart(RX); S: ACE Hardware(LP)

7 O'Neal Ln.
- **Gas** N: Mobil(*, CW), Shell(*, CW, 24); S: Chevron(*, CW, 24), Exxon(*, D), Texaco(*, D, CW)
- **Food** S: Berthelot's O'Neal, Blimpie Subs & Salads, Burger King(PLAY), Little Caesars Pizza (Wal-Mart), Lonestar Steakhouse, McDonald's, Popeye's Chicken, Sonic, Subway, Taco Bell, Waffle House, Wendy's
- **AServ** S: Exxon, Wal-Mart Supercenter(24, RX) (One Hour Photo, Vision center, Tire Lube Express)
- **RVCamp** N: American RV's, Inc. (1.9 Miles), Knight's RV Park
- **Med** S: + Hospital
- **ATM** N: Union Planter's Bank; S: Bama 1 Bank (Wal-Mart), Hybernia, Regions Bank, Wal-Mart Supercenter (One Hour Photo, Vision center, Tire Lube Express)
- **Other** N: Hobby Lobby, Office Depot; S: Superfresh Grocery Store, Wal-Mart Supercenter(RX) (One Hour Photo, Vision center, Tire Lube Express)

1481
DAYS INN
$39*
10245 Airline Hwy • Baton Rouge, LA
Continental Breakfast Included
Outdoor Pool • Handicap Accessible
Meeting/Banquet Facilities
Truck/Large Vehicle Parking
Coin Laundry • Exterior Corridors
In Room Coffee • FREE Local Calls
Expanded Cable Station, HBO
Airline Hwy S 1/2 Mi S of I-12
504-291-8152
*Based on Availability.
Louisiana • I-12 • Exit 2A

10 LA 3002, Denham Springs
- **FStop** S: Speedway(*, SCALES)
- **Gas** N: Chevron(*), Circle K(*), Exxon(*), Racetrac(*, 24), Texaco(*, D, CW); S: Texaco(*)
- **Food** N: Burger King(PLAY), Cactus Cafe, Chinese Inn, Crawford's Family Restaurant (Catfish), Golden Corral Family Steakhouse, Jackpot Barbecue Southern Smokehouse, Mary Lee Donuts, McDonald's(PLAY), Popeye's Chicken, Subway, Waffle House, Wendy's; S: Church's Chicken (Speedway FS), Las Vegas Deli, Piccadilly Cafeteria, SHONEY'S Shoney's, Speedway
- **Lodg** N: Denham Springs Best Western; S: DAYS INN Days Inn
- **AServ** N: Firestone Tire & Auto, Michelin, Western Auto Parts America; S: All Star Dodge and Isuzu
- **TServ** S: Sam's Diesel
- **RVCamp** S: KOA Campgrounds (1 Mile)
- **Med** N: + Urgent Care Clinic
- **ATM** N: Chevron, Circle K, Exxon, Hancock Bank, Racetrac; S: Speedway
- **Other** N: Delchamp's Supermarket, Historic District and Antique Village (2 Miles), JJ Lee Optical, Louisiana Fireworks, Rite Aid(RX); S: Skate Haven

15 LA 447, Walker, Port Vincent
- **FStop** S: Chevron(*), Fina(*)
- **Gas** N: Shell(*, CW)
- **Food** N: Burger King(PLAY), McDonald's(PLAY), Waffle House
- **ATM** S: Chevron, Chevron, Fina
- **Other** N: Our House Antiques and Souveniers

19 Satsuma

22 LA. 63, Livingston, Frost
- **Gas** N: Conoco(*), Texaco(*, D)
- **AServ** N: Texaco, Texaco
- **RVCamp** S: RV Park

(28) Rest Area (RR, Phones, Picnic, RV Dump; Eastbound)

(27) Rest Area (RR, Phones, Picnic, RV Dump; Westbound)

29 LA 441, Holden
- **Gas** N: Coastal(*, D)
- **AServ** N: Bob's Auto and Truck Service

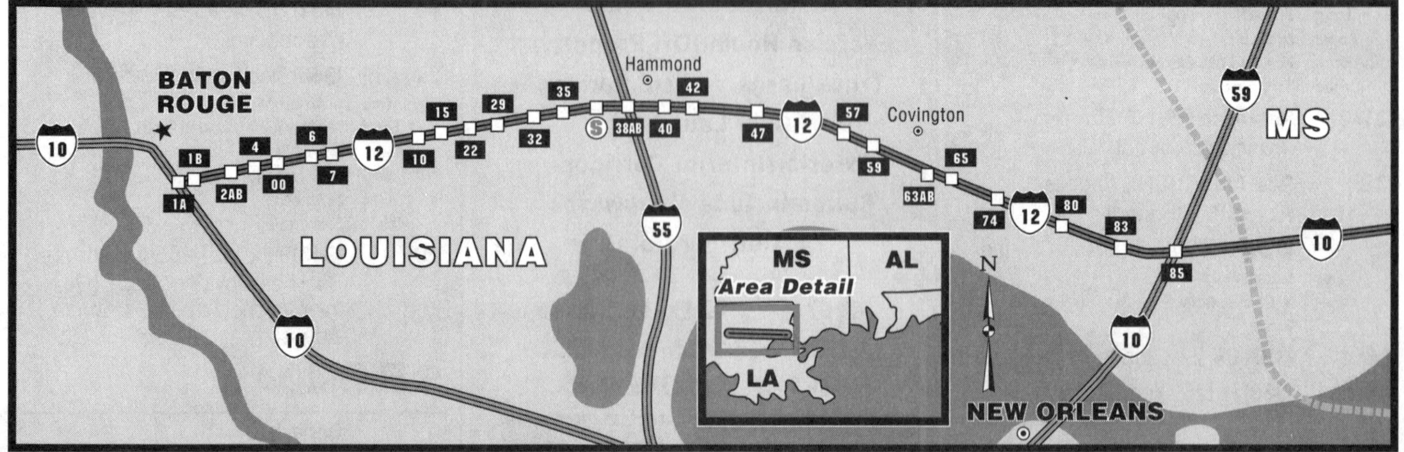

Bold red print shows RV & Bus parking available or nearby

EXIT LOUISIANA

32 LA 43, Albany, Springfield
- **Gas** N: Chevron(*)
  S: Citgo(*)
- **Food** N: Chevron
  S: Levi's Cafeteria

35 Baptist, Pumpkin Center
- **Gas** N: Exxon(*)
  S: Chevron(*)
- **AServ** S: C&S Automotive & Transmission Repair
- **RVCamp** N: **Punkin Park Campground (1.5 Miles)**
- **ATM** N: Exxon

(36) **Weigh Station (Eastbound)**

(36) **Weigh Station (Westbound)**

38AB Junction I-55, New Orleans, Jackson

40 U.S. Hwy 51 Bus., Hammond, Ponchatoula
- **TStop** S: **Petro**(*, SCALES), **Pilot Travel Center**(*, SCALES, 24)
- **Gas** N: Chevron(*, CW), Racetrac(*, 24), Shell(*), Texaco(*, D, CW)
  S: Shell(*, CW)
- **Food** N: Burger King(PLAY), China Garden, Cuscos Border Cafe, Denny's, McDonald's(PLAY), Morrisons Cafeteria, Pizza Hut, **Ryan's Steakhouse**, Taco Bell, Wendy's
  S: **Arby's (Pilot)**, **Iron Skillet (Petro)**, Krispy Kreme Doughnuts (Pilot), **Petro**, **Pilot Travel Center**, TJ Cinnamon's (Pilot), **Waffle House**
- **Lodg** N: Comfort Inn
  S: **Colonial Inn**
- **AServ** N: Hammond Tire and Rim, **Sears**, Sears
- **TServ** S: **Petro**, **Petro**(SCALES), **Speedco**(24), **Stewart Stevenson (Detroit Diesel, Allison Transmission, Thermo King)**
- **TWash** S: **Blue Beacon Truck Wash (Petro)**, **Petro**
- **RVCamp** S: **KOA Campgrounds**
- **Med** S: **✚ Hospital**
- **ATM** N: First Guarantee Bank, Racetrac, Racetrac
  S: **Pilot Travel Center**
- **Other** N: Cinema 2, Grand Prix Car Wash, **Hammond Square Mall**, Rite Aid(RX), **Sears**, U-Haul Center

42 LA. 3158, Airport
- **FStop** N: **Chevron**(*)
- **Food** N: **Chevron**, **The Lucky Dollar (Chevron)**
- **Lodg** N: **Friendly Inn**
- **TServ** N: **Chevron**
- **TWash** N: **Chevron**, **Hammond Truck Wash**
- **Other** N: Airport

47 LA. 445, Robert
- **RVCamp** N: **Hidden Oaks Campground**, **Jellystone Park Campground**, **Sunset Campground**
- **Parks** N: **Zemmurray Gardens**
- **Other** N: Global Wildlife Center

57 Goodbee, Madisonville, LA1077
- **Parks** S: **Fairview Riverside State Park**

59 LA21, Covington, Madisonville
- **Gas** N: Shell(*, CW)(see our ad this page), Spur(*)
- **Food** N: Burger King (Spur), McDonald's, Spur
- **Med** N: **✚ Hospital**
- **ATM** N: Shell, Spur
- **Parks** S: **Fairview Riverside State Park**

INTERSTATE EXIT AUTHORITY

The universal sign for the world's best-selling gasoline.

1548

Open 24 Hours | ATM | Shell | Touchless Car Wash | Pay at Pumps

Clean Restrooms
Fast, Courteous Service
Free Air & Water
$2 Off Carwash w/8 gal Purchase
Fully Stocked
Convenience Store
Fresh Hot Coffee
504-898-2674

LOUISIANA ▪ I-12 ▪ EXIT 59

Covington, Louisiana

1770

504-893-3580
I-12 • Exit 63B
Toll Free Reservations:
800-355-2000

- Well Lighted Parking For Buses
- 2 Restaurants
- Coffee & Liqueur Bar
- Indoor & Outdoor Pool
- Sports Bar
- In Room Movies • Electronic Keys
- Computer Data Ports in Each Room

LOUISIANA ▪ I-12 ▪ EXIT 63B

The universal sign for the world's best-selling gasoline.

1550

Open 24 Hours | Easy Access

Touch Less Car Wash | Pay at Pumps

Clean Restrooms
Fast, Courteous Service
Free Air, Water & Carwash
with 8 gal Purchase
Deli - Breakfast & Lunch
All Major Credit Cards & ATM
504-892-9112

LOUISIANA ▪ I-12 ▪ EXIT 65

(60) **Rest Area (RR, Phones, Picnic, RV Dump; Eastbound)**

(60) **Rest Area (RR, Phones, Picnic, RV Dump; Westbound)**

63A New Orleans via Causeway Toll Bridge (Toll)

63B U.S. 190, Covington, Mandeville, Bogalusa
- **Gas** N: Exxon(*, CW), Racetrac(*, 24), Shell(*, CW), Texaco(*, D, CW)
- **Food** N: Applebee's, Burger King(PLAY), Celebration (Holiday Inn), DaKota Restaurant (Best Western), Daiquiris and Creams, Denny's, Holiday Inn, Jo Mugg's (Books-A-Million), KFC, **McDonald's (Wal-Mart)**, Outback Steak House, Pasta Kitchen, SHONEY'S **Shoney's**, **Sicily's Pizza**, Subway, The Ground Pati, Waffle House, Wendy's
- **Lodg** N: Best Western, Courtyard by Marriott, Holiday Inn (see our ad this page)
- **AServ** N: **Wal-Mart SuperCenter**(RX)
- **RVCamp** N: **Calvin Klein Mobile Home and RV Center**
- **Med** S: **✚ Hospital**
- **ATM** N: **Albertson's Grocery**(RX), Deposit Guaranty National Bank, Hibernia Bank, Shell, **Wal-Mart SuperCenter**
- **Other** N: **Albertson's Grocery**(RX), **Books-A-Million**, Cinema 10, **Home Depot**, Northpark Car Wash, Office Depot, **Wal-Mart SuperCenter**(RX), Wild Cargo Pets

65 LA59, Abita Springs, Mandeville
- **Gas** N: Chevron(*, D, CW), Shell(*, CW)(see our ad this page)
  S: Spur(*, CW)
- **Food** N: Chevron, Subway (Chevron)
  S: Burger King(PLAY), **Winn-Dixie Marketplace**(24, RX)
- **ATM** N: Chevron, Shell
  S: **Winn-Dixie Marketplace**
- **Parks** S: **Fountain Bleau State Park**
- **Other** N: **Tourist Info.**
  S: **Winn-Dixie Marketplace**(RX)

74 LA. 434, St. Tammany, Lacombe

80 Airport Drive, North Shore Blvd
- **Gas** S: Chevron(*, CW, 24), Exxon(*, D)
- **Food** S: Burger King(PLAY), McDonald's(PLAY), Subway, TCBY, Taco Bell
- **AServ** S: Sears
- **RVCamp** N: **Camp Villere**
- **ATM** S: Chevron
- **Other** N: Airport
  S: Carmike Cinemas, **Delchamp's Supermarket**, **Northshore Square Mall**, Service Merchandise, Toys R Us

83 U.S. 11, Pearl River, Slidell
- **FStop** S: **Speedway**(*)
- **Gas** N: Chevron(*, CW, 24), Citgo, Exxon(*, D), Texaco(*)
  S: Shell(*, CW)
- **Food** N: McDonald's(PLAY), Waffle House
- **TServ** S: **Big T Tire Repair**
- **ATM** N: Texaco
  S: **Speedway**
- **Other** N: BrownSwitch Pet Hospital, **County Market Supermarket**, Live Oak Driving Range, McCoy's Building Supply Center

85ABC I-10 W. to New Orleans, I-59 N. to Hattysburg

↑LOUISIANA

Begin I-12

EXIT MONTANA

Begin I-15

↓MONTANA

(398) Canadian Border

397 Sweetgrass
- **Gas** W: Mars(LP), Sinclair(*)
- **Food** W: Glocca Morra Motel, Mars
- **Lodg** W: Glocca Morra Motel
- **Other** W: Duty Free Shop Ammex, US Post Office

(397) **Rest Area (RR, Phones, Picnic, P; West Side of Exit 397)**

394 Ranch Access

389 CR 552, Sunburst
- **Gas** W: Suta's Supply(D)
- **AServ** W: Suta's
- **Other** W: **Coin Laundry**, **Martin's Food Market**, **US Post Office**

385 Swayze Road

379 CR 215, CR 343, Kevin, Oilmont
- **Food** W: 4 Corners Bar & Cafe

373 Potter Road

369 Bronken Road

(367) **Weigh Station (RV Dump; Southbound)**

364 Bus Loop 15, Shelby
- **RVCamp** E: **Lake Sheloole Park (.5 Miles)**, **Lewis & Clark RV Park (1 Mile)**

363 U.S. 2, Shelby, Cut Bank, Port Of Shelby
- **TStop** E: **Exxon(*, 24) (Casino)**
- **Food** E: **Exxon (Casino)**, **Papa's Taco Fine Mexican Food**, **Pizza Hut**, **Subway (Exxon)**, **The Dixie Inn Casino Steakhouse**
  W: McDonald's
- **Lodg** E: **Comfort Inn**, **Crossroads Inn**
- **TServ** E: **Ed's Diesel Pump and Electric Service**
- **RVCamp** E: **Glacier Park**, **Horizon Park (1.5 Miles)**, **Lake Shel-oole**
  W: **Glacier RV Park**
- **Med** E: **+ Hospital**
  W: **+ Hospital**
- **ATM** E: **Exxon (Casino)**
- **Parks** W: **Glacier National Park**
- **Other** W: **Pamida Discount Center(RX)**

358 Marias Valley Road, Golf Course Road
- **RVCamp** E: **Camping**

352 Bullhead Road

348 MT 44, Valier Road
- **Parks** W: **Lake Francis Recreation Area (15 Miles)**

345 CR 366, Ledger Road, Tiber Dam

339 Bus Loop I-15, Conrad
- **FStop** W: **Exxon(*, D)**
- **Food** W: The Main Drive-In
- **Lodg** W: Motel, **Super 8 (Exxon)**
- **AServ** W: Conrad Auto and Tire, Van Motors Inc
- **TWash** W: **Robo Car and Truck Wash**
- **RVCamp** W: **Pondera RV Park (1 Mile)**, **Sunset RV Park**, **Westco Trailer Sales and Service(LP)**
- **Med** W: **+ Hospital**
- **Other** W: **Econo-Wash Coin Laundry**, **Lucky Lil's Casino (Exxon)**, **Robo Car and Truck Wash**

335 Midway Road, Conrad

328 CR 365, Brady
- **Food** W: The Red Onion Restaurant

321 Collins Road

EXIT MONTANA

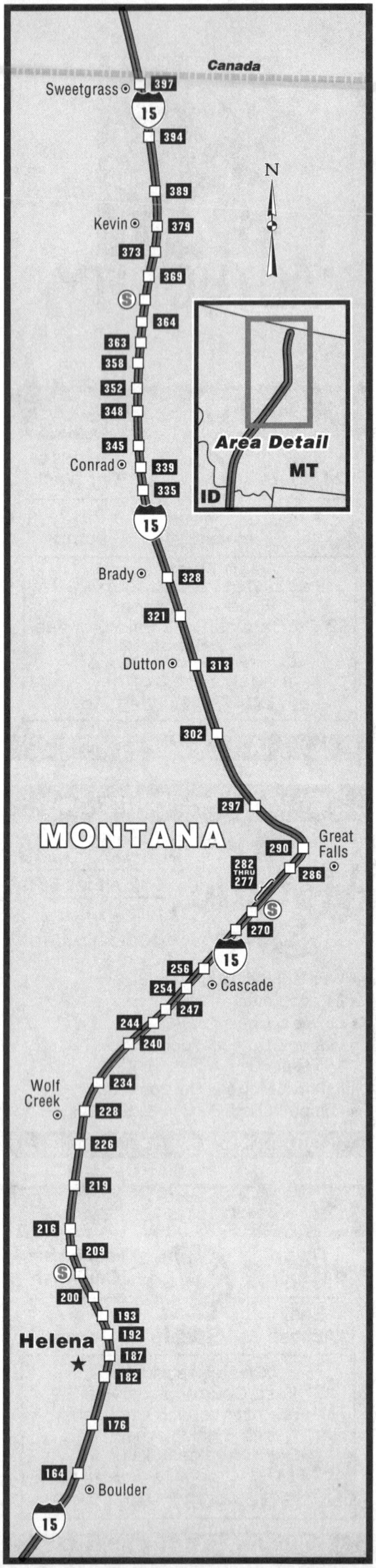

Canada
Sweetgrass 397 15 394 389 Kevin 379 373 369 364 363 358 352 348 345 Conrad 339 335 15 Brady 328 321 Dutton 313 302 297
N
Area Detail MT ID
MONTANA
290 Great Falls 282 THRU 277 286 270 15 256 Cascade 254 247 244 240 Wolf Creek 234 228 226 219 216 209 200 193 192 Helena 187 182 176 164 Boulder 15

EXIT MONTANA

(319) **Rest Area (RR, Phones, Picnic, P; Southbound)**

(319) **Rest Area (RR, Phones, Picnic, P; Northbound)**

313 CR 221, CR 379, Dutton, Choteau
- **FStop** W: **Conoco(*)**
- **Food** W: **Cafe Dutton**

305 Bozeman

302 CR 431, Power

297 Gordon

290 U.S. 89N, MT 200W, Missoula, Choteau
- **RVCamp** W: **Camping**

(286) **Parking Area (Southbound)**

286 Manchester

282 To U.S. 87N, N.W. Bypass (Southbound, Reaccess Northbound Only)
- **TStop** E: **Teton Truckstop(SCALES)**
- **Lodg** E: **Evergreen Motel**
- **TServ** E: **Metco Kenworth**

280 U.S. 87 N, Bus Loop 15, Central Ave West
- **TStop** E: **Flying J Travel Plaza(*, LP)**
- **Gas** E: **Sinclair(*)**, **Sinclair(*)**
- **Food** E: **Crossroads Cafe (Flying J)**, Double Barrell Family Dining, Ford's Drive-in, The Jack's Club Restaurant
- **Lodg** E: **Starlit Motel**
- **AServ** E: Car Quest Auto Center, **Wayland Tires**, Zenon's Autogon
- **TServ** E: **Cummins Diesel**, **Pronto Auto Parts**, **Wayland Tires**
- **TWash** E: **Big Sky Truck Wash**
- **RVCamp** E: **L'Neve Travel Trailer Park**

278 U.S. 89S, MT 200E, 10th Ave South (Loads Over 12' Wide Not Permitted)
- **Food** E: Quizno's Classic Subs
- **Lodg** E: Airway Motel
- **RVCamp** E: **Dick's RV Park (1 Mile)**, **KOA Campgrounds**
- **Med** E: **+ Hospital**
- **ATM** E: **Buttrey Big and Fresh(RX)**
- **Other** E: Barnes & Noble, **Buttrey Big and Fresh(RX)**, **Visitor Information**

277 International Airport
- **TStop** E: **Conoco(*, 24)**
- **Food** E: **Conoco**

(275) **Weigh Station (Northbound)**

270 CR 330, Ulm
- **Gas** E: Exxon(*, LP)
- **Food** E: Tinn Man Pizza Co.
  W: Griffin's Restaurant
- **ATM** E: Exxon
- **Parks** E: **Ulm Pishklin State Park**
- **Other** E: US Post Office

256 MT 68, Cascade

254 MT 68, Cascade

250 Local Access

247 Hardy Creek
- **RVCamp** W: **Camping**

(246) **Scenic View (Southbound)**

244 Canyon Access
- **RVCamp** W: **Camping (2 Miles)**
- **Other** W: **Boating (2 Miles)**

240 Dearborn
- **Food** W: Dearborn Inn

Bold red print shows RV & Bus parking available or nearby

EXIT MONTANA

RVCamp E: **Camping**

(240) Rest Area (RR, Phones, Picnic, P; Southbound)

(240) Rest Area (RR, Phones, Picnic, P; Northbound)

234 Craig
- **Gas** E: Gas[*]
- **Food** E: Hamm's Cafe
- **Lodg** E: Missouri River Trout Shop & Lodge
- **AServ** E: Rod's Motor Service
- **RVCamp** E: **Camping, Craig RV Camp & Recreation Area**

228 U.S. 287N, Augusta, Choteau

226 CR 434, Wolf Creek
- **Gas** E: Exxon[*, LP]
- **Food** E: Oasis Bar & Cafe; W: The Frenchman (and me) Cafe
- **Lodg** E: **Frenchy's Motel & Trailer Court**
- **AServ** E: J & R Auto Service
- **RVCamp** E: **Camping, Frenchy's Motel & Trailer Court**
- **Other** E: The Laundry Depot Coin Laundry; W: **US Post Office**

(222) Parking Area (RR, Phones, Picnic; Southbound)

(222) Parking Area (RR, Phones, Picnic; Northbound)

219 Spring Creek (Northbound, Reaccess Southbound Only)
- **RVCamp** E: **Camping**

216 Sieben

209 Gates Of The Mountains
- **Other** E: **Recreation Area**

(202) Weigh Station (Southbound)

200 CR 279, CR 453, Lincoln Road
- **Gas** W: Sinclair[*]
- **Food** W: Grub Stake Restaurant
- **RVCamp** W: **Lincoln Park Campground (.5 Miles)**
- **Parks** E: **Holter Lake, Houser Lake**

193 Bus Loop I-15, Cedar Street
- **Gas** W: Conoco[*], Exxon[*], Sinclair[*]
- **Food** W: Mother Lode Restaurant & Casino
- **AServ** E: Whalen Tire; W: Exxon, Pinnacle Auto Glass, Power Chevrolet
- **RVCamp** E: **Northern Energy Propane Sales[LP]**; W: **Branding Iron, Camping**
- **ATM** W: Mother Lode Restaurant & Casino
- **Other** E: **National Forest Ranger Station**, Veteran's Center, **Visitor Information**; W: **K-Mart[RX], US Post Office**

192 US 12E, US 287S, Townsend, East Helena; US 12W, Capitol Area (Southbound, Shares the same services as Exit 192A & 192B Northbound)
- **FStop** E: **Conoco[*, LP]**
- **Gas** E: Conoco[*, D]; W: Exxon[D], Mini Mart[*], Sinclair[*]
- **Food** W: Bullseye Casino & Restaurant, Burger King, Country Kitchen, Dairy Queen, JB's Restaurant, Jimmy B's Casino & Restaurant, KFC, Little Caesars Pizza, McDonald's, Pasta Pantry, Rack's, TCBY, Taco Bell, Taco Treat Mexican, Village Inn Pizza, Wendy's
- **Lodg** W: Jorgenson's Holiday Motel, Motel 6
- **AServ** W: Goodyear Tire & Auto, Muffler Shop, Toyota Dealer
- **RVCamp** E: **RV Center**
- **ATM** W: First Security Bank
- **Other** E: Car & Truck Wash, **Truck Permits**; W: **Bergum Drug's, Capital City Mall, Coin Laundry, Pet Supply Store, Safeway Grocery, State Museum, Terry's Food Store**

192B I-15 Business Loop, US 12 West, Capitol Area (Northbound)
- **Food** W: Country Harvest Restaurant, Overland Express
- **Lodg** W: Aladdin Motor Inn, Best Western, Comfort Inn, Days Inn, Fairfield Inn, Holiday Inn Express, Shilo Inn Motel, Super 8
- **Med** W: **+ Helena Medical Plaza, + Hospital**
- **ATM** W: **Albertson's Supermarket[RX]**, Helena Community Federal Credit Union
- **Other** W: AAA of Montana, **Albertson's Supermarket[RX]**

192A US 12 East, US 287 South, Townsend (Northbound)
- **Gas** E: BP[*]
- **Food** E: Burger King[PLAY]
- **RVCamp** E: **D & D RV Park Sales & Service**
- **ATM** E: BP, **Wal-Mart[RX]**
- **Other** E: **State Police, Tourist Info., Wal-Mart[RX]**

187 CR 518, Montana City, Frontage Road
- **Gas** W: Conoco[*]
- **Food** E: Papa Ray's Casino & Hugo Pizza; W: Big Sky Java Coffee, Exchange Restaurant, Jackson Creek Saloon
- **Lodg** W: Elkhorn Mountain Inn
- **AServ** W: Car Quest Auto Center
- **ATM** W: First Boulder Valley Bank
- **Parks** E: **Strawberry Mountain Recreation Area**
- **Other** W: Montana City Car Wash, US Post Office (Conoco)

182 Clancy
- **Food** W: Legal Tender Restaurant
- **RVCamp** E: **Alhambra RV Park[LP] (1 Mile)**
- **Parks** W: **National Forest Access, Park Lake (14 Miles)**
- **Other** W: **Clancy Creek**

(178) Rest Area (RR, Phones, Picnic, P; Southbound)

(177) Rest Area (P; Northbound)

176 Jefferson City
- **Other** W: **US Post Office**

164 MT 69, Boulder
- **FStop** E: **Exxon[*]**
- **TServ** E: **B L Cooper Inc**
- **RVCamp** E: **RC RV Park**
- **ATM** E: **Exxon**
- **Other** E: Car Wash[CW]

160 High Ore Road

156 Basin
- **RVCamp** E: **Camping**

151 Bernice, Bear Gulch Access, Boulder River Road
- **Other** W: **Camping**

138 Elk Park

134 Woodville

(131) Scenic Overlook (Southbound)

129 Jct East I-90, Billings; Jct. South I-15, West I-90, Butte (I-15 & I-90 run concurrent from exit 129 to exit 121. Numbering follows I-15)

127AB Harrison Ave
- **Gas** E: Conoco[*], Conoco[*], Exxon[*, D, CW]; W: Cenex[*, D, CW], Conoco[*], **Sinclair[*, RV DUMP]**
- **Food** E: 4 B's Restaurant[24], Arby's, Burger King, Godfather's Pizza, Joey's Seafood, KFC, McDonald's, Perkins Family Restaurant, Pizza Hut, Plaza Royale Restaurant, Ray's Place, Red Rooster Supper Club, Restaurant (Motel), Silver Bow Pizza, Subway, TCBY, Taco Bell, The Ponderosa Cafe, Uno's, Wendy's; W: Arctic Circle Hamburgers, Dairy Queen, Denny's, Derby Steakhouse, Domino's Pizza, El Taco Mexican Food, Hardee's, Hot Stuff Pizza (Cenex), John's, Little Caesars Pizza, Restaurant (War Bonnet Inn), Smash Hit Subs (Cenex), Taco John's, Top Deck
- **Lodg** E: Best Western, Comfort Inn, Days Inn, Mile High, Motel, Super 8; W: Holiday Inn Express, War Bonnet Inn
- **AServ** E: American Car Care Centers, Checker Auto Parts, Ford Dealership, GM Auto Dealership, Glenn's, Honda Dealer, Pennzoil Oil Change, **Wal-Mart**; W: Bob's Fast Lube, Champion Auto Parts Store, Nissan Dealer, Uniroyal Tire & Auto
- **ATM** E: American Federal Savings Bank, Conoco, Conoco, Exxon, First Citizens Bank, First National Bank, Norwest Bank; W: Cenex, Conoco
- **Other** E: **Butte Plaza Mall, Buttrey Food Grocery[RX], K-Mart, Optical, Wal-Mart[RX]**; W: **Downey Drug, Natural Healing, Safeway Grocery[24, RX]**

126 Montana Street
- **Gas** E: Conoco[*], Exxon[*, D]; W: Cenex[*], Sinclair
- **Food** E: Muzz & Stan's Food; W: Jokers Wild Casino & Restaurant (Chicken/BBQ Ribs), Winter Garden Lanes
- **Lodg** W: Eddy's Motel
- **AServ** W: Sinclair
- **RVCamp** W: **KOA Campgrounds**
- **Med** W: **+ Hospital**
- **ATM** E: Conoco
- **Other** W: **Dental Clinic, Safeway Grocery, Tourist Info.**

124 Jct I-115, Butte City Center

122 Rocker, Weigh Station
- **TStop** E: **Conoco[*, LP]**; W: **Flying J Travel Plaza[LP]**
- **Food** E: **4 B's Restaurant (Conoco), Arby's (Conoco TS)**; W: **Flying J Travel Plaza**
- **Lodg** W: **Rocker Inn**
- **AServ** E: **Rocker Repair[24]**
- **TServ** E: **Rocker Repair[24]**
- **ATM** E: **Conoco**; W: **Cash Machine (Flying J TS)**

121 I-15 South Idaho Falls, Jct. I-90 West Missoula (I-15 & I-90 End concurrency)

119 Hub Access, Silver Bow

116 Buxton

111 Feely

(109) Rest Area (RR, Phones, Picnic, P; Southbound)

(109) Rest Area (RR, Phones, Picnic, P; Northbound)

102 MT 43, Divide, Wisdom
- **Other** W: **Big Hole Battlefield Monument**

99 Moose Creek Road

93 Melrose
- **RVCamp** W: **Sportsman Motel RV Park (1 Mile)**

85 Glen

EXIT MONTANA/IDAHO

74 Apex, Birch Creek

63 Bus. Loop 15, MT 41, Dillon, Twin Bridges
- Lodg E: **Comfort Inn**
- RVCamp E: **Dillon KOA (1.5 Miles)**
- Med E: **+ Hospital**

62 Bus Loop 15, Dillon
- RVCamp E: **Southside RV Park**
  W: **Dillon KOA (1 Mile)**
- Med E: **+ Hospital, + Southwestern Montana Clinic**

59 MT 278, Jackson, Wisdom
- Parks W: **Bannack Ghost Town State Park**

56 Barrets
- TStop W: **Big Sky Truck Stop**[*, LP]
- RVCamp E: **Camping**
- Other W: **Laundry (Big Sky Truck Stop)**

(55) **Rest Area (RR, Picnic, P; Southbound)**

52 Grasshopper Creek (Reaccess Northbound Only)

51 Dalys (Southbound, Reaccess Northbound Only)

44 MTD 324, Clark Canyon Reservoir
- RVCamp E: **Arnstead Campground, Camping**
  W: **Camping**
- Parks W: **Recreation Area**

37 Red Rock

(34) **Rest Area (RR, Picnic, P; Northbound)**

(34) **Rest Area (RR, Picnic, P; Southbound)**

29 Kidd

23 Dell
- Gas E: Dell Mercantile[*]
- Food E: Yesterday's Cafe
- Lodg E: Red Rock Inn
- AServ E: Dell Garage

(16) **Weigh Station (Northbound)**

(16) **Weigh Station (Southbound)**

15 Lima
- Gas E: Exxon[*]
- Food E: Home Cooked Grub
- Lodg E: The Cafe Cabin, The Club Bar & Motel
- AServ E: Big Sky Tire, Sales, & Repair, Exxon
- RVCamp E: **Camping**
- Med E: **+ Ambulance Service**
- Other E: **I & J Market, US Post Office**

9 Snowline

0 Monida

↑MONTANA

↓IDAHO

190 Humphrey

184 Stoddard Creek Area
- RVCamp W: **Stoddard Creek Camp (1 Mile)**
- Other E: **Nez Perce Trail Historical Site**

180 Spencer
- Gas E: Opal
  W: Opal Mtn Showroom, **Spencer Bar & Grill**
- Food W: **Spencer Bar & Grill**
- Lodg E: Spencer Bed & Breakfast
  W: **Spencer Camping Cabins**

EXIT IDAHO

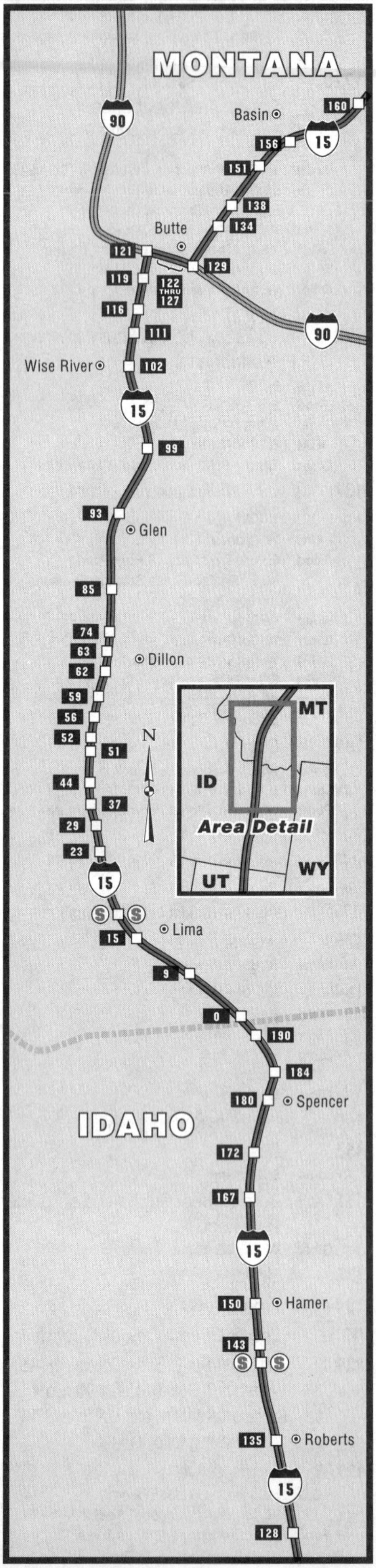

EXIT IDAHO

- RVCamp W: **Camping, Spencer RV Park**
- Other E: **Opal Mining Store**

172 US Sheep Experiment Station

167 I-22, CR A2, Dubois, Arco
- FStop E: **Exxon**[*] **(Showers), Phillips 66**[*, LP]
- Food E: Cow Country Kitchen, **Hot Stuffed Pizza (Phillips 66), Smash Hit Subs (Phillips 66)**
- AServ E: **Exxon (Showers)**
- RVCamp E: **Scoggins RV Camp**
- ATM E: **Exxon (Showers)**
- Other W: **Craters of the Moon National Monument, Nez Perce Trail**

(167) **Rest Area (RR, Picnic, P; Located at Exit 167)**

150 Hamer

143 ID 28, ID 33, Mud Lake, Rexburg

(143) **Weigh Station (Located at Exit 143, All Trucks Must Exit)**

135 ID 48, Roberts, Rigby
- TStop E: **Amoco**[*]
- AServ E: Mike's Tire Shop
- Other E: **Thriftway Food Stores, Tru Value Hardware**[LP]

128 Osgood Area, County Road
- FStop E: **Sinclair**[*, LP]

119 U.S. 20 East, Idaho Falls Air Terminal, City Center, West Yellowstone
- FStop E: **Texaco**[*, LP]
- Gas W: **Texaco**[*, LP, RV DUMP]
- Food E: Denny's, **Jaker's Steak, Ribs, & Fish House**, Outback Steakhouse, Quality Inn, Shilo Inn Hotel, **Snake River Smokehouse (Best Western)**, The Sandpiper Restaurant
- Lodg E: AmeriTel Inn, **Best Western**, Best Western CottonTree Inn, Quality Inn, Shilo Inn Hotel, **Super 8**
- AServ E: Aesco Automotive Electric & Supply Co
  W: **Texaco**
- TServ E: **Rumble's Diesel**
- RVCamp E: **KOA Campgrounds (.75 Miles)**
- ATM E: **Texaco**
  W: Westmark
- Other E: **Vietnam Memorial Monument**
  W: **Idaho State Police**

118 Bus. Loop 15, U.S. 20, Idaho Falls, Arco
- FStop E: **Kicks 66**[*], **Phillips 66**[*] **(C F N Commercial Fueling Network)**
- Gas E: Chevron
  W: **Amoco**[*], Flying J Travel Plaza[*], Phillips 66[*], Sinclair[*, CW]
- Food E: Applebee's, Arctic Circle Hamburgers, **Cedric's Restaurant**, Cinnamon Street Bakery (Kicks 66), **Hot Stuffed Pizza (Kicks 66)**, JB's Restaurant
  W: Arby's, Brady's Family Restaurant, Burger King, Dairy Queen, Fiesta Ole', Hong Kong Restaurant (Chinese & American), Leo's Place Pizza, Burgers, & Subs, Motel West, O'Ryan's Pizza, Subway, The Press Box Sports Bar & Restaurant
- Lodg W: Comfort Inn, Motel 6, Motel West
- AServ E: A-1 Automatic Transmission Co, Broadway Ford, Chevron, **Milfen Truck & Auto, Phillips 66 (C F N Commercial Fueling Network)**, The Parts Place
  W: **Amoco**, Pennzoil Oil Change
- TServ E: **Broadway Ford, Diesel Powered Truck Sales & Service, Milfen Truck & Auto**
  W: **Amoco**
- RVCamp W: **Amoco, Amoco**

Bold red print shows RV & Bus parking available or nearby

EXIT — IDAHO

Med	W: Family Emergency Center West
ATM	E: Kicks 66
	W: US Bank
Other	W: Skyline Car Wash(CW), Skyline Laundry Room, Western Union (Motel West)
113	New Sweden Road, Shelley
TStop	E: Exxon(*)
Food	E: Exxon
Lodg	E: Yellowstone Motel
TServ	E: Lake City International Cat, Detroit Diesel, Cummins, Lindsay Truck & Towing, Peterbilt Dealer
TWash	E: The Truck Wash(SCALES)
RVCamp	E: Sunnyside RV Camping (4.5 Miles)
Med	E: Hospital
Parks	E: Grand Teton National Park
108	Shelley-Firth, Area
(101)	Rest Area (RR, Phones, Picnic, Vending, P; Northbound)
(101)	Rest Area (RR, Phones, Picnic, Vending, P; Southbound)
98	Rose Area
93	Bus. Loop 15, U.S. 26, ID 39, Blackfoot, Aberdeen, Arco
FStop	E: Flying J Travel Plaza(*, LP)
Gas	E: Chevron(*, CW)
Food	E: Arctic Circle Hamburgers, Hogi Yogi Sandwiches & Frozen Yogurt, Homestead Family Restaurant, Little Caesars Pizza, McDonald's(PLAY), Mexican Bakery, Papa Murphy's Pizza, Pizza Hut, Rest for Less, Subway, Taco Bell, Wendy's
Lodg	E: Best Western, Rest for Less
AServ	E: 20th Century Ford Dodge & Mercury, Les Schwab Tires, Pro Lube
Med	E: Hospital
ATM	E: Albertson's Supermarket(RX), Flying J Travel Plaza, Zion's Bank
Other	E: Albertson's Supermarket(RX), Beehive Bookstore, Blackfoot Visitor's Center, Kesler's Supermarket, Rite Aid Pharmacy(RX), The Tub Coin Laundry, Wal-Mart(RX)
89	U.S. 91, Blackfoot
80	Fort Hall, Simplot Road
TStop	W: Sinclair(*)
Food	W: Melina's Oregon Trail (Sinclair)
Other	W: Shoshone-Bannock Tribal Museum, Trading Post Grocery, US Post Office
72	Jct I-86 West, Twin Falls
71	Pocatella Creek Road
FStop	W: Papa Kelsey's Food and Sub
Gas	E: Chevron(*, LP), Circle K(*), Phillips 66(*, CW)
	W: Exxon(*), Sinclair(*)
Food	E: Applebee's, Frontier Pies (Best Western), Jack-in-the-Box, Perkins, Subway, The Sandpiper
	W: Dairy Queen, Sizzler Steakhouse
Lodg	E: AmeriTel Inn (Sandpiper Restaurant), Best Western, Comfort Inn, Holiday Inn, Quality Inn (Restaurant), Super 8
AServ	W: Sinclair
RVCamp	E: KOA-Pocatello (1 Mile)
Other	W: Caldwell Banker, Fire Station, Norge Dry Cleaners, Rite Aid Pharmacy(RX), Wear Mart Food Centers
69	Clark St (No Trucks)
Med	E: Pocatello Regional Medical Center
	W: Bannock Regional Medical Center
67	Bus Loop 15, U.S. 30, U.S. 91, Pocatello (One Way Streets)
Gas	E: Exxon(*)
RVCamp	W: Cowboy RV Park (1 Mile)

EXIT — IDAHO/UTAH

Parks	E: Constitution Park
Other	E: Bo Works
63	Portneuf Area, Mink Creek Recreation Area
RVCamp	E: Mink Creek Recreation area
(59)	Weigh Station, Rest Area
58	Inkom, Pebble Creek Ski Area, Bus I-15 (Southbound, Difficult Reaccess)
Gas	W: Saloman's(D, LP)
57	Bus Loop I-15, Inkom (Northbound, Difficult Reaccess)
Gas	W: Sinclair(*)
Food	W: El Rancho
ATM	W: Sinclair
Other	W: Post Office
47	U.S. 30, Lava Hot Springs, Soda Springs, to Jackson, WY
TStop	E: Flying J Travel Plaza(*, LP, SCALES) (Conoco, Thad's REstaurant)
Gas	E: Conoco (Flying J)
44	Bus Loop I-15, McCammon. Jensen Rd.
40	Arimo
Other	E: United States Post Office Arimo, Idaho
36	Virginia
31	Downey, Preston
TStop	E: Flags West(*, LP, RV DUMP)
RVCamp	E: Flags West(LP)
(25)	Rest Area (RR, Phones, Picnic, Vending, P; Southbound)
22	Devil Creek Reservoir
RVCamp	E: Mountain Highland Park (Devil Creek Summit)
17	ID 36, Weston, Preston
Food	W: Gary's Deep Creek Inn
Lodg	W: Deep Creek Inn
13	ID 38, Malad
Gas	W: Phillips 66(*, D) (Cafe)
Lodg	W: Village Inn Motel
AServ	W: E-Z Coin & Automatic Car Wash
Med	W: Hospital
ATM	W: Phillips 66 (Cafe)
(7)	Rest Area (RR, Phones, Picnic, P; Northbound)
3	Woodruff, Samaria

↑IDAHO

↓UTAH

402	Portage
394	UT 13 South, Plymouth
TStop	E: Tri Valley Truck Stop(*)
Food	E: Subway (Tri Valley TStop)
392	I-84 West, Tremonton, Boise (Northbound)
387	UT 30 East, Riverside, Logan, Fielding
RVCamp	E: Camping
383	I-15 Loop, Tremonton, Garland
Med	E: Hospital
382	Jct I-84W, Boise (Southbound)
379	UT 13, I-15 Loop, Bus I-84, Tremonton, Garland

EXIT — UTAH

375	UT 240, to UT 13, Honeyville, Bear River
RVCamp	E: Crystal Hot Springs Camping
(370)	Rest Area (RR, Phones, Picnic, Vending, P; Southbound)
368	UT 13, 900 North St.
Parks	W: Bear River Bird Refuge
366	Forest St.
Parks	W: Bear River Bird Refuge
364	I-15 Loop, U.S. 89, 1100 South St.
RVCamp	E: Golden Spike RV Park (1 Mile)
Med	E: Hospital
(363)	Rest Area (RR, Phones, Picnic, Vending, P; Northbound)
361	Port of Entry & Weigh Station
360	UT 315, Willard, Perry
FStop	E: Flying J Travel Plaza(*, D, LP) (Country Market)
Food	E: Country Market (Flying J)
RVCamp	W: Camping
354	UT 126, U.S. 89, Willard
352	UT 134, Farr West, Plain City, North Ogden, Pleasant View
Gas	E: Maverick(*, PLAY)
Food	E: McDonald's, Subway
ATM	E: Maverick
349	Defense Depot, Harrisville
Gas	W: Texaco(*)
TServ	W: JM Bodily & Sons TService
347	UT 39, 12th Street
TStop	W: Pilot Travel Center(*, SCALES)
FStop	E: Flying J Travel Plaza(*)
Gas	E: Phillips 66(*, CW)
Food	E: Jeremiah's Restaurant
	W: Country Kitchen (Pilot), Dairy Queen (Pilot), Subway (Pilot), Taco Bell (Pilot)
Lodg	E: Best Western
	W: Sleep Inn
AServ	E: Steve's Car Care
TServ	W: General Diesel
Parks	E: Ogden Canyon Recreation Area
346	UT 104, 21st Street, Wilson Lane
TStop	E: Flying J Travel Plaza(RV DUMP, SCALES)
FStop	E: Chevron(*, CW)
	W: Texaco(*, D, RV DUMP)
Food	E: Arby's (Chevron), Big Z Restaurant, Cactus Reds (Comfort Suites), The Cookery Buffet
	W: Freeway Cafe
Lodg	E: Best Rest Inn, Big Z Motel, Comfort Suites Hotel
	W: Super 8
TServ	E: Flying J Travel Plaza, Lake City International, Ogden Diesel
RVCamp	W: Century RV Park & Campground
ATM	E: Flying J Travel Plaza
Other	E: Flying J Coin Laundry
345	UT 53, 24th Street, City Center, Fort Buena Ventura (Northbound, No Reaccess)
FStop	E: Sinclair(*)
Gas	E: Texaco(*)
344B	UT. 79 West
344	UT 79 East
343	I-84 East, Cheyenne (Southbound)
342	UT 26, I-84 East, Riverdale (Northbound, Reaccess Southbound Only)
Gas	E: Conoco(D)
	W: Phillips 66(*, D, LP, CW)

Bold red print shows RV & Bus parking available or nearby

EXIT UTAH

Food **E:** Applebee's, Boston Market Restaurant, Chili's, McDonald's (Wal-Mart)
W: ABC Chinese Cuisine, Arby's Roast Town, Burger Bar, Chinese Gourmet, Dairy Queen, Gade Terrace, JB's Restaurant, KFC, Lee's Fish & Rice, Lucky China, Star Burger, Subway, Taco Time, Tafoya Brother's Pizza, Warrens

Lodg **E:** Motel 6
W: Circle R Motel

AServ **W:** Big O Tires, Buffalo Bros Tire Outfitters, Discount Tire Company, Midas Muffler & Brake, Q-Lube

ATM **W:** Key Bank, Phillips 66

Other **E:** **Target**, **Wal-Mart**
W: **Animal Care Vet**, **Standard Optical**, Super Serve Coin Car Wash

341 UT 97, Roy, Sunset, Hill Air Force Base (Difficult Reaccess)

Gas **W:** Citgo[*], Roy's 66, Sinclair[*, CW]

Food **W:** Arby's, B.C. Chicken, Blimpie's Subs, Burger King[PLAY], Denny's, Domino's Pizza, J B's Restaurant, KFC, Los Petates Mexican Tacos, Lucky China, McDonald's[PLAY], PaPa Murphy's Pizza, Pizza Hut, Taco Bell, Taco Time, Wendy's

AServ **W:** David Early Tires, Brakes, Lube, Q Lube, Roy's 66

ATM **W:** Citgo, First Security Bank, Golden West, Washington Mutual

Other **E:** Air Force Museum
W: **Albertson's Food Market**[24, RX], Rite Aid Pharmacy, Standard Optical

338 UT 103, Clearfield, West Point

Gas **W:** Chevron[*, CW], Conoco[*, CW]

Food **W:** Arby's, Carl Jr's Hamburgers, KFC, **McDonald's**, Subway, Taco Bell

Lodg **W:** Crystal Cottage Inn, Super 8

AServ **W:** Big O Tires

ATM **W:** Chevron, Conoco

Other **E:** Hill AFB Entrance

336 Freeport Center, Clearfield

Gas **E:** Circle K[*], Texaco[D, LP, CW]

AServ **E:** Texaco

RVCamp **E:** **JP's Texaco**

335 UT 108, Freeport Center, Syracuse

FStop **E:** **Phillips 66**[*, LP, CW]

Gas **E:** No Name[*, CW, 24]

Food **E:** Carl Jr's Hamburgers, Chili's, **Cracker Barrel**, Golden Corral Family Steakhouse, Holiday Inn Express, JB's Restaurant, Quizno's, San Francisco Sourdough Pizza, Schlotzsky's Deli, **Super Target**[RX]

Lodg **E:** Fairfield Inn, Hampton Inn & Suites, Holiday Inn Express, La Quinta Inn

AServ **E:** Grandma's Tires, Tunex
W: Ford Dealership

Med **E:** ✚ **IHC Healthcenter**
W: ✚ **Davis Hospital & Medical Center**

ATM **E:** No Name, **Phillips 66**
W: Zion's Bank

Other **E:** Barnes & Noble, **Super Target**[RX]

334 UT 232 to UT 126, Layton

Gas **W:** Flying J Travel Plaza[*, D, CW]

Food **E:** Denny's, Garcia's Mexican Food, McDonald's[PLAY], Olive Garden, Red Lobster, Sizzler Steak House, Training Table Gourmet Burgers, Wendy's
W: Blimpie's Subs, Burger King, Einstein Bros Bagels, Empire Chinese Buffet, Famous Chicken, Fuddruckers, Godfather's Pizza, Home Town Buffet, KFC, Kenny Roger's Roasters, Lone Star Steakhouse, Sconecutter Scones, Sandwiches, & Fries, SHONEY'S Shoney's, Taco Bell

Lodg **E:** Travelers Inn

AServ **W:** **Cutrubus**, Layton Lube Too[CW] (Pennzoil), Merrill's Auto, Home, & Business Glass, National Tire and Battery, Safelite Auto Glass, Simmons Auto Repair

RVCamp **W:** **Cutrubus**

Med **W:** ✚ **Health & Wellness Clinic**

ATM **E:** First Community Bank, Key Bank, Washington Mutual
W: Barnes Banking Company

Other **E:** **Layton Hills Shopping Mall**
W: Eye Clinic for Animals, Magic Touch Car Wash[CW] (Layton Lube Too), **Optical (ShopKo)**, **Petsmart**, **Reams Grocery**, **Sam's Club**, **ShopKo Grocery**[RX], **Wal-Mart**[RX]

332 North Business Loop I-15 to UT 126, Layton, Kaysville (Northbound)

Food **W:** Little Orient Restaurant

AServ **W:** Performance Truck Accessories

331 UT 273, Kaysville

Gas **E:** Chevron[*, D, CW], Kick's 66[*, CW], Phillips 66[*]

Food **E:** Joanie's, McDonald's (Chevron)

AServ **E:** Xpress Automotive, Xpress Lube
W: First Choice Cars

RVCamp **W:** **Blaine RV Sales & Service (.75 Miles)**

Med **E:** ✚ **Tanner Clinic**

Other **E:** **Albertson's Food Market**[RX]

(329) Parking Area (Northbound)

(329) Parking Area (Southbound)

327 UT 225, Lagoon Dr., Farmington

326 U.S. 89 North to East I-84, South Ogdon, to UT 225, Lagoon Dr., Farmington (Northbound, Difficult Reaccess)

RVCamp **E:** **Lagoon's Pioneer Village Campground**

325 UT 227, Lagoon Drive, Farmington (Northbound)

RVCamp **E:** **Lagoon's Pioneer Village Campground**, **Lagoon's RV Park & Campground (1 Mile)**

322 Centerville

FStop **E:** **Phillips 66**[*, D, CW]

Gas **E:** Chevron[*, D, CW], Phillips 66[*, D, CW]

Food **E:** Arby's, Burger King, Dairy Queen, Del Taco, Lone Star Steakhouse, Longhorn Cafe (Chevron), McDonald's[PLAY], Subway, **Super Target**[RX], Taco Bell

AServ **E:** Big O Tires, Ray's Muffler Service

ATM **E:** **Phillips 66**

Other **E:** Super Car Wash[CW], **Super Target**[RX]

321 U.S. 89 South, 500 West (Left Exit Northbound)

Gas **E:** Chevron[*, CW, 24], Conoco, Phillips 66[CW], Texaco[*]

Food **E:** Alicia's Cafe

AServ **E:** Action Alternator and Starters, Conoco, Phillips 66, Walton's Brake & Tire Co.

RVCamp **E:** **Bontivilla Trailer Park**

320AB UT 68, 500 South, Bountiful

FStop **W:** **Phillips 66**[*]

Gas **E:** Amoco[*, LP, CW], Texaco[*, D]

Food **E:** Blimpie's Subs, Christopher's Seafood & Steak, Chuck-A-Rama Buffet, Galaxy Diner, KFC, McDonald's[PLAY], PaPa Murphy's Pizza, Renny's Charbroiled Drive-Thru, San Francisco Sourdough Pizza, Sizzler Steak House, Su Casa Mexican, Subway, Taco Bell, The Deli at 5th, Winger's American Diner, Zbees Juice

AServ **E:** AA Auto Glass, Auto Zone Auto Parts, Big O Tires, C J Auto Works, CGC Central Glass Company, Carl's European Car Service, Checker Auto Parts, David Early Tires, Diamond Glass, Firestone Tire & Auto, Grandma's Tires, Lodder's Auto Repair, Marque Body & Paint, Meineke Discount Mufflers, Midas Muffler & Brake, Parts

Bold red print shows RV & Bus parking available or nearby

EXIT UTAH

Plus Auto Service, Q Lube, Ray's Muffler Service, Safelite Auto Glass
W: Dave Roberts Auto Service

RVCamp **E:** **Smitty's RV**

Med **E:** **Benchmark Regional Hospital**, **Bountiful Family Wellness Center**

ATM **E:** Barnes Banking Company, US Bank

Other **E:** Animal Clinic at Fifth South, Animal Medical Clinic, **Barnes & Noble**, Bountiful Small Animal Hospital, Car Wash, Deseret Bookstore, East Bay Car Wash & Detail(CW), **Optical (Shopko)**, **Shopko Grocery**(RX), Super Wash Car Wash(CW)

318 UT 93, North Salt Lake, Woods Cross

FStop **E:** **Chevron**(*, D, LP, CW)

Gas **E:** Sinclair(*), Texaco(*)

Food **E:** Arby's, Atlantis Burgers, Cutler's Grill, Hostess Bakery Outlet, McDonald's(PLAY), Pizza Hut, Subway, Village Inn, Wendy's, Wok & Roll (Chinese, American, Philipino)
W: Denny's, Larena's Restaurant (Mexican)

Lodg **E:** Best Western
W: Hampton Inn, Motel 6

AServ **E:** Jerry Seiner Buick, GMC Trucks, Ken Garff Bountiful Motors, Nation Wide Auto Glass, Tunex

RVCamp **E:** **Barber RV Sales & Service (.7 Miles)**

ATM **E:** Key Bank, **Smith's Food & Drug**(24, RX), US Bank, Wells Fargo

Other **E:** **K-Mart**(RX), **Smith's Food & Drug**(RX), Wilson Veterinarian Hospital

317 Center St. (Southbound, Reaccess Northbound Only)

316 I-215, Belt Route, Salt Lake International Airport (Southbound)

315 U.S. 89 South, Beck

314 2300 North, Warm Springs Road

313 900 West (Southbound, Reaccess Northbound Only)

312AB 600 North, 6th North

Gas **E:** Conoco(*)

Lodg **E:** Gateway Motel

RVCamp **W:** **Camping**

Med **W:** **Hospital**

311 Junction I-80W, Salt Lake International Airport, Reno

310 6th So. St, City Center (Difficult Reaccess)

Gas **E:** Chevron(*, CW), Circle K(*), Phillips 66(*), Sinclair(*)

Food **E:** "J" Burger, Albertos Mexican, Best Western, Denny's, Hilton, Iggy's Sports Grill, McDonald's, Quality Inn, Quality Inn

Lodg **E:** Best Western, Cavanaugh's Hotel, Crystal Inn, Hampton Inn, Hilton, Motel 6, Quality Inn, Quality Inn, Quality Inn, Super 8, TraveLodge

AServ **E:** Brigham Street Service, Mark Miller Toyota

ATM **E:** Sinclair

Other **E:** Brewvies Cinema & Pub

309 13th So. St, 21st So. St. (Difficult Reaccess)

Gas **E:** Citgo(*)

Food **E:** Cafe Trang (Vietnamese, Chinese), China Pearl, Main Street Cafe (Holiday Inn), Miquelita's Mexican

Lodg **E:** Diamond Inn, Holiday Inn

AServ **E:** Atex Automatic Transmission, Classics & More Sales & Service, Ford Superstore, Ken Garff Honda, Lelis Automatic Transmission Service Inc., Meineke Discount Mufflers, Midas, Rick Warner Mazda, Nissan, Saturn of Salt Lake, Steve Harris Motors, Utah Auto Parts
W: Japanese Auto Repair

EXIT UTAH

308 21st So. St. (Difficult Reaccess, Limited Access Hwy)

Food **E:** McDonald's

Other **E:** **Home Depot**, U-Haul(LP)

307 Junction I-80E, to U.S. 40, Denver, Cheyenne (Exit under construction)

306 UT171, 33rd S St, South Salt Lake

Gas **E:** Citgo(*)

Food **E:** Goldbar Saloon

Lodg **E:** Days Inn

AServ **E:** AAMCO Transmission, Automotive Utilities, Berlin Tire Services, Best Rate Mufflers, Tires, & Exhaust

RVCamp **E:** **Keith's Trailer Park**

ATM **E:** Citgo

304 UT 266, 45th S St, Murray, Kearns (Exit under construction)

Gas **E:** Chevron, Phillips 66(*, CW)
W: Shell, Texaco(*)

Food **E:** Imperial Garden, McDonald's, Super Grinders Sandwiches
W: Denny's, Rocky's Deli

Lodg **W:** Hampton Inn, Quality Inn

AServ **E:** Checker's Auto Parts, Midas Muffler

Other **E:** **Zim's Craft Supply**
W: **Eagle Hardware & Garden**

303 UT173, 53rd S St, Murray, Kearns

Gas **W:** Chevron(*, LP, CW), Conoco(*, LP, CW)

Food **W:** Golden Isle Chinese, Hogi Yogi (Chevron), PaPa Murphy's Pizza, Schlotzsky's Deli, Tio's Fine Mexican

Lodg **W:** Reston Inn

Med **E:** **Hospital**

ATM **W:** **Smith's Food & Drug**(RX), Utah Central Credit Union

Other **W:** **Smith's Food & Drug**(RX), The Eye Doctor

302 Junction I-215

301 UT48, Midvale, 72nd S St (Exit under condtruction)

Gas **E:** Hart's, Phillips 66(*), Standard(CW), Texaco(*, LP)

Food **E:** Cafe Silvestre Mexican, Denny's, KFC, McDonald's, Midvale Mining Company

Lodg **E:** Best Western, Days Inn, Discovery Inn, La Quinta Inn, Motel 6

298 UT209, 90th S St, Sandy, West Jordan

Gas **E:** Sinclair(*)
W: Maverick(*, LP), Texaco(*, LP)

Food **E:** Arby's, The SconeCutters Sandwiches, Scones, & Fries

Lodg **E:** Comfort Inn

AServ **E:** Butterfield Ford Dealership, David Early Tires
W: Advantage Auto Service, K & K Custom Auto Body (Texaco), NTB National Tire & Battery, Techna-Glass

RVCamp **E:** **Ardell Brown's Quail Run RV Park (.5 Miles)**

Med **E:** **Hospital**

ATM **E:** Guardian State Bank
W: Maverick

297 106th St, Sandy, South Jordan (Exit under construction)

Gas **E:** Conoco(*), Phillips 66(*, CW)

CAMPING WORLD®
Exit 294
13111 S. Minuteman Dr. • Draper, UT
1-800-294-1240
1422

EXIT UTAH

Food **E:** Carver's Prime Rib, Jade Garden Chinese, SHONEY'S, Shoney's, T.G.I. Friday's, **Village Inn**
W: Denny's

Lodg **E:** Best Western, Courtyard by Marriott, Hampton Inn
W: Sleep Inn, Super 8

AServ **E:** Conoco, Utah Auto Mall Chevrolet Olds

ATM **E:** Bank One, Zion's First National Bank

Other **E:** **Locksmith**, **Shopping Mall**

295 U.S. 89N, Sandy

Lodg **E:** Holiday Inn Express

Other **E:** **Factory Stores of America**

294 UT 71, Draper, Riverton

Gas **E:** Flying J(*, D, CW), Texaco(*, CW)

Food **E:** Arctic Circle Hamburgers(PLAY), Guadalahonky's Mexican, Neal's Charcole Broiler, Zuka Juice

Lodg **E:** TraveLodge

RVCamp **E:** **Camping**, **Camping World (1 Mile) (see our ad this page)**, **Holiday Camping**, **Mountain Shadows RV Park (2 Miles)**, **Quality RV Service**

ATM **E:** Smith's Food & Drug(RX), Texaco

Other **E:** **Factory Stores of America**, Smith's Food & Drug(RX)

291 UT 140, Bluffdale, Draper

287 UT 92, Highland, Alpine

Gas **W:** Amoco(*, D, CW, 24)

Food **W:** **Burger King (Amoco)**

Parks **E:** **Timpanogos Cave**

285 South US 89, Lehi

AServ **E:** Gears Tramission Repair

RVCamp **W:** **Yates Travel Trailers Sales & Service**

282 UT73 West, Lehi

Gas **W:** Chevron(*, D, LP, CW), Phillips 66(*)

Food **E:** Carnivores Sandwiches, One Man Band Diner
W: All American Deli, Arctic Circle (Hamburgers), Dreyers Ice Cream (Phillips 66), KFC Express (Chevron), McDonald's(PLAY), New York Burrito, Pizza Hut (Chevron), Subway, Wendy's (Phillips 66)

Lodg **E:** Motel 6
W: Best Western, Super 8

AServ **E:** Mountain Valley Automotive Specialties, The Auto Works
W: Big O Tires, Chevron

TServ **E:** **Rex's Diesel**

RVCamp **E:** **A-1 Travel Trailer & Vehicle Sales**

ATM **W:** **Albertson's Food Market**(24, RX), Bank Of American Fork, Phillips 66, Zion Bank

Other **E:** Curt's Propane(LP)
W: **Albertson's Food Market**(RX)

281 Main St

FStop **E:** **Hart's**(*)

Med **E:** **Hospital**

279 Pleasant Grove, 5th East, American Fork (Service More Then 1 Mile Away)

Food **E:** **McDonald's (Wal-Mart)**, Taco Bell

Lodg **E:** Quality Inn

AServ **W:** Utah Valley Auto Mall

RVCamp **E:** **American Campgrounds (.25 Miles)**, **RV Park**, **Stuarts RV Sales & Service**

Med **E:** **Hospital**

Other **E:** **Vision Center (Wal-Mart)**, **Wal-Mart**(RX)

(278) **Rest Area (P; Northbound)**

(278) **Rest Area (P; Southbound)**

276 Lindon

TStop **W:** **Conoco**(*, SCALES)

FStop **W:** **Texaco**(*)

AServ **W:** Certified Transmission & Drive Trained Clinic, RJ's Tire, Towing, & Auto

275 UT 52, to U.S. 189, 8th St. North

FStop **E:** **C F N Commercial Fueling Network**(*)

EXIT UTAH

Gas E: Phillips 66[*, D, CW] (Natural Gas for Autos)
AServ W: Dave Adam's Auto Body Collision & Painting
TServ W: **Six States Distributors Inc**
Med E: ✚ **Hospital**
Parks E: **Provo Canyon, Sundance Recreation Park**
Other E: **Highway Patrol Post**

274 Center St
Gas E: Citgo[*], Conoco[*, CW]
Food E: The Pizza Pipeline (Water Sports)
AServ W: Alpine Auto Air & Accessories
Med E: ✚ **Hospital**
ATM E: Citgo, Conoco
Other E: FedEx Center, The Cookie Factory Convenience Store, The Pizza Pipeline (Water Sports)
W: Security First Car Wash[CW]

272 University Parkway
Gas E: Amoco[*, CW], Shell[*, 24], Sinclair[*]
Food E: McDonald's, **McDonald's (Wal-Mart)**, Subway
Lodg E: Hampton Inn
AServ E: Saturn Of Orem
ATM E: Shell, **Wal-Mart**[RX]
Other E: **Wal-Mart**[RX]

268 UT114, Center St.
Gas W: Amoco[*], Conoco[*]
Food W: Hot Stuffed Pizza (Amoco), The Great Steak Sandwich Co
Lodg W: Econolodge
AServ W: Conoco
RVCamp W: **KOA Campgrounds (.75 Miles), Lakeside RV Campground (2 Miles)**
Med E: ✚ **Hospital**
W: ✚ **Hospital**
Parks W: **Utah Lake**
Other W: **The Park Pharmacy**[RX]

266 U.S. 189N, University Ave. (Difficult Reaccess)
Gas E: Chevron[*, CW, 24], Circle K[*], Texaco[*, D, LP, CW]
Food E: Arby's, Bayside Bagel, Hogi Yogi, Joe Vera's Mexican, McDonald's[PLAY], Ruby River Steak House (Holiday Inn), Sizzler Steak House
Lodg E: Colony Inn Suites, Fairfield Inn, Hampton Inn, Holiday Inn, Howard Johnson, **Motel 6**, National 9 Inn, Sleep Inn, Super 8
AServ E: **Sam's Club**[RX]
ATM E: Bank One, Texaco
Parks E: **Seven Peaks Recreation Area**
Other E: **K-Mart**[RX], **Optical (Sam's Club), Sam's Club**[RX]

265 UT75, Springville
TStop E: **Flying J**[*, LP, SCALES]
Food E: **Flying J**
Lodg E: Best Western
TServ E: **Flying J**[SCALES]
TWash E: **Flying J**

263 UT77, Springville, Mapleton
Gas W: Chevron[*, D, LP, CW, 24]
Food W: Arby's (Chevron), **Cracker Barrel**, Juice World (Chevron)
RVCamp W: **Quality RV Center, RV Service & Repair**

261 U.S. 89 East, U.S. 6, Price, Manti
Gas E: Chevron[*, D, LP]
Food E: Arby's, Burger King, Cinnamon Street Bakery (Chevron), Hot Stuffed Pizza (Chevron), McDonald's[PLAY], Scoops Ice Cream, Smash Hit Subs (Chevron), Subway, Taco Time
Lodg E: **Holiday Inn Express**
AServ E: Expressway Lube
RVCamp E: **Miller's Trailer Sales**
ATM E: Chevron
Other E: **K-Mart**[RX], **Storehouse Market**

260 UT 156, Price, Spanish Fork
Gas E: Amoco[*, D, CW], Chevron[*]
W: Conoco[*, D]
Food E: Arctic Circle, KFC, Little Caesars Pizza, North's Star Buffet, Taco Bell
W: Hickory Kist
AServ W: Barber Bros Chevrolet
RVCamp W: **Barber Bros RV Center**
Other E: **Maceys Food & Pharmacy**[RX], **Optical (ShopKo), Seagull Books & Tapes, ShopKo Grocery**[RX]

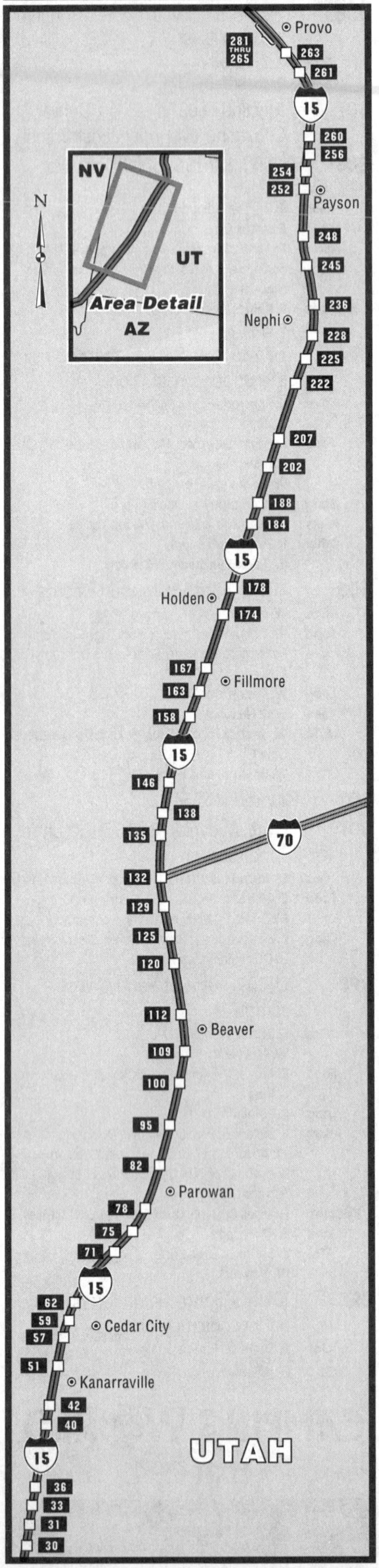

256 UT164, Benjamin

254 UT115, Payson
TStop E: **Flying J Travel Plaza**[*, LP, CW, SCALES]
Gas E: Texaco[*, D]
Food E: **McDonald's**[PLAY], Subway
Lodg E: Comfort Inn
Med E: ✚ **Hospital**
ATM E: **Payson Market**[RX], Texaco
Other E: **Payson Market**[RX], **Travel Agency (Payson Market)**

252 Payson
FStop E: **Chevron**[*, D, LP]

248 U.S. 6W, Santaquin
Gas W: Amoco[*, LP], Conoco[*], Texaco[*, D, CW]
AServ W: Rocky Mountain Tire
ATM W: Amoco, Texaco

245 So. Santaquin

236 UT 54, Mona

228 Bus. Loop I-15, Nephi. Delta
Med W: ✚ **Hospital**

225 UT131, Nephi, Manti, Moroni, Ephriam
Gas E: Amoco[*, LP]
W: **Phillips 66**[*]
Food E: Taco Time
W: **Wendy's (Phillips 66)**
AServ E: Amoco
RVCamp E: **KOA Campgrounds**
Med E: ✚ **Hospital**
W: ✚ **Hospital**
ATM W: **Phillips 66**

222 To I-70, Salina, Richfield, UT 28, Levan, Gunnison, Mt. Nebo Scenic Loop
TStop E: **Sinclair**[*, LP, SCALES]
W: **Flying J Travel Plaza**[*, LP, RV DUMP, SCALES]
FStop E: **Texaco**[*]
Gas E: Chevron[*]
Food E: **Burger King, Denny's, Hogi Yogi (Sinclair)**, JC Mickelson's Restaurant, **Subway**
W: **Pepperoni's (Flying J), The Cookery (Flying J)**
Lodg E: Motel 6, **Roberta's Cove Motor Inn, Super 8**
TServ E: **Doyle's Diesel Cummins, Sinclair**[SCALES]
RVCamp W: **High Country RV Camp (.5 Miles)**
Med W: ✚ **Hospital**
ATM E: **Sinclair**
W: **Flying J Travel Plaza**

207 UT 78E, Mills, Lavan

202 Yuba Lake
RVCamp E: **Camping**

188 U.S. 50E, Scipio, to I-70, Salina, Richfield
FStop E: **Amoco**[*], **Chevron**[*]
Food E: **Hillside Farms Restaurant (Amoco)**
Lodg E: **Amoco**
AServ E: Sam's Diesel & Auto

184 Ranch Exit

178 U.S. 50 to Delta, Holden
Parks W: **Great Basin National Park**

174 U.S. 50, Delta, Holden

Parks W: The Great Basin National Park

167 Bus. Loop I-15, Fillmore, Rest Area (P)
- FStop W: Texaco(*)
- Gas E: Chevron(*)
- Food E: Best Western
  - W: Subway (Texaco)
- Lodg E: Best Western
- RVCamp E: Wagon West Campground (1 Mile)

163 I-15 Loop, UT 100, Fillmore (More Services 2-4 Miles)
- FStop E: Chevron(*) (CFN Commercial Fueling Network, Natural Auto Gas)
  - W: Phillips 66(*)
- Food E: Hogi Yogi Sandwiches & Yogurt, The Taco Maker
  - W: Burger King (Phillips 66)
- AServ E: Chevron (CFN Commercial Fueling Network, Natural Auto Gas)
- RVCamp E: KOA Campgrounds (.5 Miles)
- Med E: ✚ Hospital
- Other E: Superwash Car Wash

158 UT133, Meadow, Kanosh
- FStop E: Texaco(*)
- Gas E: Chevron
- Food E: Chester Fried Chicken (Texaco)
- AServ E: Chevron
- Parks E: Meadow Creek Canyon

(151) Parking Area (Northbound)

(151) Parking Area, View Area (Southbound)

146 Kanosh

138 Ranch Exit

(137) Rest Area (RR, (P); Southbound)

135 Historic Cove Fort

132 Jct I-70E, Richfield, Denver

129 Sulphurdale

(126) Rest Area (RR, Phones, (P); Northbound)

125 Ranch Exit

120 Manderfield

112 To UT21, Bus. Loop 15, Beaver, Milford
- FStop E: Chevron(*)
- Gas E: Arco(*, 24), Conoco(*), Sinclair (Country Inn Motel)
  - W: Amoco(*, D) (Towing)
- Food E: Arby's, Garden of Eat 'N (Best Western), McDonald's(PLAY), Subway
  - W: Wendy's
- Lodg E: Best Western, Country Inn Motel
  - W: Super 8
- AServ E: Arco(24), Conoco, RV, Auto, & Diesel Repair
  - W: Amoco (Towing)
- TServ E: Diesel RV Repair, RV, Auto, & Diesel Repair
- RVCamp E: Diesel RV Repair, KOA Kampground (1 Mile), RV, Auto, & Diesel Repair
- ATM E: Arco, Chevron, McDonald's
  - W: Amoco (Towing)
- Other E: Great Basin National Park

109 I-15 Loop, UT 21, Beaver, Milford
- Gas E: 76(*, LP, RV DUMP), Texaco(*, D)
  - W: Chevron(*, 24)
- Food E: Burger King (Texaco), Taco Time
  - W: Chevron, Kan Kun Restaurant (Mexican), Timberline Inn (Quality Inn)
- Lodg W: Quality Inn
- AServ E: 76, Texaco
  - W: Chevron(24)

EXIT UTAH

- RVCamp E: 76, Delano Motel & RV Camp (2 Miles), United Beaver Camperland
  - W: RV, and Auto and Diesel Repair & Towing
- Med E: ✚ Hospital
- ATM W: Chevron
- Parks E: Great Basin National Park, Minersville State Park

100 Ranch Exit

95 UT20, U.S. 89, Panguitch, Kanab, Circleville

(87) Rest Area (RR, Phones, Picnic, (P); Southbound)

(87) Rest Area (RR, Phones, Picnic, (P); Northbound)

82 UT 271, Paragonah

78 Business Loop 15, UT143, Parowan, Paragonah
- TStop W: Burns Brothers Travel Stop(*, LP)
- Food E: Swiss Village Restaurant (Best Western)
  - W: Subway (Burns Bros. TS), Taco Bell (Burns Bros. TS)
- Lodg E: Best Western

75 Bus. Loop 15, UT 143, Parowan, Paragonah
- Other E: Bryan Head Ski Resort, Cedar Brakes, Fairgrounds, Petroglyths

71 Summit, Enoch
- TStop W: Sunshine(*, LP)
- Food W: Sunshine
- TServ W: Sunshine

62 Bus. Loop 15 To UT 14, Cedar City, UT 130, Minersville, Milford
- TStop W: JR's Truck Stop(*, SCALES) (Texaco)
- FStop W: Sinclair(*, D)
- Gas W: Texaco(*)
- Food W: La Villa #1 Authentic Mexican Food, Steaks 'n' Stuff
- Lodg W: TraveLodge
- AServ W: Texaco
- TServ W: Color Country Diesel Inc.
- RVCamp E: Country Aire RV Park (.75 Miles)
- Med E: ✚ Hospital
- ATM W: JR's Truck Stop (Texaco)
- Parks E: Iron Mission State Park (2 Miles)

59 UT56, Cedar City
- Gas E: Amoco(*), Chevron(*), Conoco(*, D), Maverik Country Store(*), Phillips 66(*, D, LP, CW), Sinclair(*), Texaco(D)
  - W: Texaco(*, D, LP)
- Food E: Arby's, Burger King, Denny's, KFC, McDonald's(PLAY), SHONEY'S, Shoney's, Taco Bell, Wendy's
  - W: Bristlecone Restaurant (Holiday Inn), Subway
- Lodg E: Abbey Inn, Comfort Inn, EconoLodge
  - W: Holiday Inn, Motel 6, Super 8
- AServ E: Texaco
  - W: Texaco
- RVCamp E: KOA-Cedar-City (2 Miles), Sizzler (1 Mile)
- ATM E: Conoco, Maverik Country Store
- Parks E: Iron Mission State Park (2 Miles)
- Other E: Spot Free Car Wash(CW)

57 I-15 Loop, to UT 14, Cedar City
- Gas E: Texaco(*)
  - W: Chevron(*, D)
- Food W: A & W Restaurant (Chevron)
- Lodg E: DAYS INN Days Inn
- AServ E: Condie's Auto Wrecking & Repair, Superior Service Center
- RVCamp E: KOA Campgrounds
- Med E: ✚ Hospital

EXIT UTAH

- Parks E: Bryce Canyon, Cedar Brakes, Navajo Lakes, Ducks Creek

51 Kanarraville, Hamilton Fort

(44) Rest Area (RR, HF, Phones, Picnic, (P); Northbound)

(44) Rest Area (RR, HF, Phones, Picnic, (P); Southbound)

42 New Harmony, Kanarraville

40 Kolob Canyons
- Parks E: Zion National Park Kolob Canyons

36 Ranch Exit

33 Ranch Exit

31 Pintura

30 Browse

27 UT17, Toquerville, Hurricane

23 Leeds, Silver Reef (Difficult Reaccess)
- Food E: Catfish Charlie's
- RVCamp E: Harrisburg Lakeside Resort (2 Miles), Leeds RV Park (.8 Miles), Zion West RV Park
- Other E: La Bodega Market, Laundromat, Leeds Post Office

16 UT 9, Hurricane, Grand Canyon, Lake Powell
- RVCamp E: Harrisburg RV Park
- Parks E: Grand Canyon, Lake Powell

10 Washington City, Middleton Dr
- FStop W: Texaco(*, LP) (RV Tires)
- Gas E: Amoco(*, D), Phillips 66(*, D)
  - W: Arco(*, 24)
- Food E: Bishop's (Red Cliff Inn), Botness Eatery & More, Burger King, Little Caesars Pizza, Red Cliffs Inn
- AServ E: Quick Lube & Wash(CW)
  - W: Texaco (RV Tires)
- TServ W: Texaco (RV Tires)
- RVCamp E: Redlands RV Park(CW)
  - W: St. George Campground (.5 Miles)
- ATM E: Albertson's Grocery(RX), Zion's First National Bank
  - W: Texaco (RV Tires)
- Other E: Albertson's Grocery(RX), PostNet

8 Business Loop 15 To UT18, St George Blvd, Santa Clara
- Gas E: Shell(*), Texaco(*)
  - W: Chevron(*, CW, 24), Sinclair(*, LP) (Fleet Fueling), Texaco
- Food E: Carl Jr's Hamburgers, Chili's, Chuck-A-Rama Buffet, Cold Stone Ice Cream, Red Lobster, Red Rock Bagels, SHONEY'S, Shoney's, Village Inn
  - W: Burger King, Denny's(24), Frontier Pies Restaurant, Wendy's
- Lodg E: Hampton Inn, Ramada, Shoney's Inn
  - W: Comfort Inn, DAYS INN Days Inn, Motel 6, TraveLodge
- AServ W: Bracken's Auto Tech, Bradshaw/Weeks Auto Mart, Econo Lube & Tune, Sinclair (Fleet Fueling), Texaco
- TServ W: Dixie Diesel Service & Towing (Cummins)
- TWash W: Dixie Diesel Service & Towing (Cummins)
- RVCamp E: Settler's RV Park (.5 Miles)
  - W: St George RV Service, St. George RV Park
- ATM E: Texaco
- Other E: Little Professor's Book Center, Staple's, Zion Factory Stores
  - W: The Movie

6 Jct I-15, Bus., UT18, Bluff St
- Gas E: Arco(*, 24), Chevron(*, D, LP), Texaco(*, LP)
  - W: Hii Ton Inn, Texaco(*)
- Food E: A & W Restaurant (Texaco)
  - W: Burger King, Claimjumper Steakhouse, Dairy

EXIT UTAH/ARIZONA/NEVADA

Queen, Denny's[24], JB's Restaurant, McDonald's, Tony Roma's (Hii Ton Inn)

Lodg **E:** Fairfield Inn, Sleep Inn
W: Best Western, Budget 8 Motel, Budget Inn, Claridge Inn, Comfort Suites Hotel, Hii Ton Inn, Quality Inn, The Bluffs

AServ **E:** Chevron, Newby Buick, Pont, Olds, GMC Trucks, Transport Tire Service, Willies Auto Parts
W: Painter's Sun Country Chrys, Plym, Eagle, Dodge, St. George Car Wash, Stanger Toyota, Stephen Wade Chev, Cad, Nissan, Stephen Wade Honda, Mazda

RVCamp **E:** McArthur's Temple View RV Resort (.25 Miles)
W: Temple View RV Park, Vacation World RV Center

ATM **W:** Texaco

Other **W:** Dixie Eye Center, Fiesta Fun Family Fun Center, Painter's RV & Boat, St. George Car Wash

4 Bloomington

FStop **E:** Shell[*, CW, 24]
Gas **W:** Chevron[*]
Food **E:** Burger King (Shell)
W: Big Apple Bagels, Stewmans Steakhouse, Taco Bell (Chevron)
ATM **E:** Shell
W: Chevron
Other **W:** Purple Crown Bookstore

(2) Welcome Center, Rest Area (RR, Picnic, P; Northbound)

1 Utah Port of Entry & Weigh Station

↑UTAH

↓ARIZONA

(28) Parking Area (Southbound)

27 Black Rock Road

(24) Check Station for Buses & Trucks

18 Cedar Pocket, Virgin River Canyon Recreation Area

9 Farm Road

8 Littlefield, Beaver Dam

↑ARIZONA

↓NEVADA

(123) Rest Area (RR, HF, Phones, Picnic, P)

122 Mesquite, Bunkerville

FStop **W:** 76[*, D]
Gas **E:** Chevron[*, 24], Texaco[*]
Food **E:** Arby's (Texaco), Blimpie Subs & Salads, Burger King[PLAY], Denny's, Jack in the Box, Pizza Hut, Subway (Chevron)
Lodg **E:** Budget Inn, Mesquite Star Hotel & Casino
W: Holiday Inn, Rancho Mesquite, Virgin River Casino & RV Park
RVCamp **E:** Desert Skies RV Resort (1.5 Miles)
W: Virgin River Casino & RV Park
ATM **E:** Chevron
Other **E:** Smith's Food & Drug[24, RX]
W: Cinema & Bowling Alley (Virgin River Casino & RV)

(122) Nevada Welcome Center (Located At Exit 122, East Side)

120 Mesquite, Bunkerville

Food **E:** Casablanca Resort & Casino, Oasis Resort Hotel & Casino

Most exits in California are not numbered. Boxes indicate mileage from San Diego.

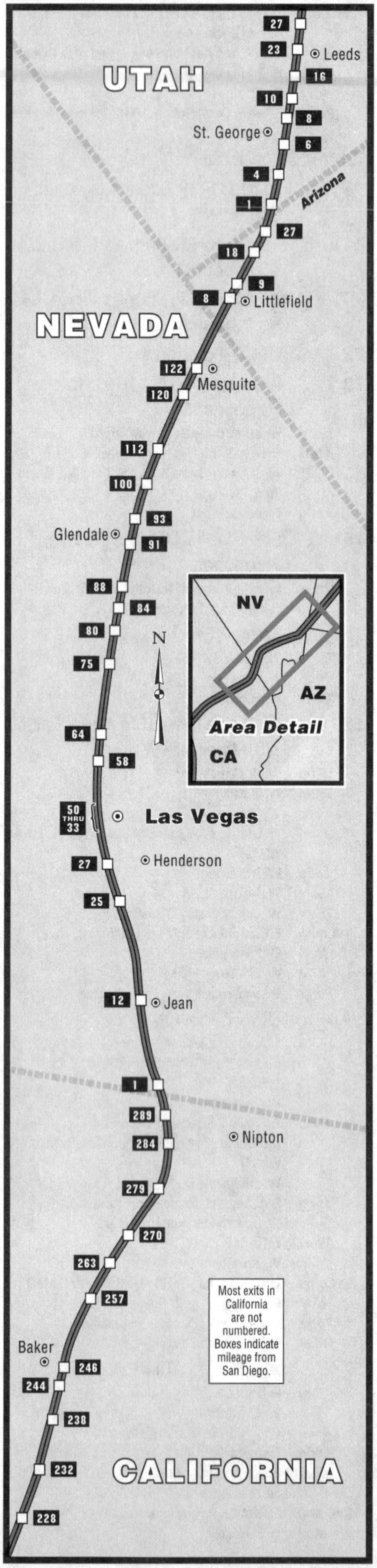

EXIT NEVADA

Lodg **E:** Casablanca Resort & Casino, Oasis Resort Hotel & Casino
RVCamp **E:** Casablanca Resort RV Park, Oasis RV Park (.5 Miles)

112 NV 170, Riverside, Bunkerville

(110) Truck Parking (Northbound)

(110) Truck Parking (Southbound)

100 Carp, Elgin

(96) Truck Parking (Northbound)

(96) Truck Parking (Southbound)

93 NV169, Overton, Logandale

Parks **E:** Lake Mead National Recreation Area
Other **E:** Lost City Museum

91 NV168, Glendale, Moapa (Southbound)

Gas **W:** Arrowhead Food Mart[*], Chevron
Food **W:** Chevron
Lodg **W:** Glendale Motel[24]
AServ **W:** Arrow Car & Truck Tire
TServ **W:** Arrow Car & Truck Tire

90 NV 161, Glendale, Moapa (Northbound, Same Exit as Exit 91)

88 Hidden Valley

(87) Truck Parking (Southbound)

(87) Truck Parking (Northbound)

84 Byron

80 Ute

75 NV 169E, Valley of Fire, Lake Mead

Other **E:** Lake Mead National Recreation Area (23 Miles), Moapa Tribal Enterprises, Valley of Fire State Park (18 Miles)

64 U.S. 93N, Pioche, Ely, Great Basin Hwy, Apex, Caliente, Alamo

Exit **(61)** Check Station (Southbound)

58 NV 604, Apex, Nellis AFB

54 Speedway Blvd, Hollywood Blvd

Other **E:** Las Vegas Motor Speedway

50 Lamb Blvd

RVCamp **W:** Hitchin' Post RV Park (2 Miles)

48 Craig Road

TStop **E:** Pilot Travel Center[*, SCALES]
Gas **E:** Chevron[*, CW, 24], Mobil[*]
Food **E:** Dairy Queen (Pilot TS), Interstate Grill & Bar[24], Jack in the Box, KFC Express (Pilot TS), Pizza Hut (Pilot TS), Speedway Bar & Grill, Subway (Mobil), Subway (Chevron), Winchells Donuts (Mobil)
AServ **E:** A & F Auto Shop, Dat's The Brakes, First Gear Transmission Service Inc., Grubs Tire Service, Wolf Audi & VW Auto Repair
RVCamp **E:** Hitchin' Post RV Park (2 Miles)
ATM **E:** Interstate Grill & Bar, Pilot Travel Center

46 Cheyenne Ave

TStop **W:** ADC Truck Stop[*] (Natural Gas), Flying J Travel Plaza[*, LP, RV DUMP]
Gas **W:** Citgo[*, D]
Food **W:** McDonald's, The Cookery (Flying J Travel Plaza)
Lodg **W:** Comfort Inn
AServ **W:** Interwest Rebuilders
TServ **W:** Flying J Travel Plaza, Las Vegas Kenworth, CAT, Cummins, Detroit Diesel, Las Vegas Truck Center (Freightliner, Cummins, Detroit Diesel), Purcell Tire Co.
TWash **W:** ADC Truck Stop (Natural Gas), Las Vegas Kenworth, CAT, Cummins, Detroit Diesel
RVCamp **W:** Big Tex Nevada Inc.

Bold red print shows RV & Bus parking available or nearby

EXIT NEVADA

ATM W: Citgo

45 Lake Mead Blvd
- **AServ** W: Amigo's Auto Repair, Drive Train Services Shop, Las Vegas Auto & Truck Salvage
- **RVCamp** W: Camping World (see our ad this page)
- **Med** E: Hospital

44 Washington Ave (Southbound)

43 D Street (Northbound)
- **Food** E: Daniel's Short Stop (Best Western)
- **Lodg** E: Best Western
- **AServ** E: A-1 Radiator & Auto Service, AC Delco

42AB U.S. 95 North Reno; I-515, U.S. 93, U.S. 95 South, Phoenix, Dowtown Las Vegas (Limited Access Hwy)

41 Charleston Blvd.
- **Gas** W: 76(*), Texaco(*, D), Texaco(*, LP)
- **Food** W: Carl Jr's Hamburgers, McDonald's(PLAY), Wendy's
- **AServ** W: Texaco
- **Med** W: University Medical Center
- **ATM** W: 76

40 Sahara Ave, Convention Center
- **Gas** E: 76(CW, 24)
  W: Texaco(*, D, LP, 24), Texaco(*, D, LP)
- **Food** E: Bixby's Cafe (TraveLodge), Red Hot City
  W: Blimpie Subs & Salads, Burger King (Palace Station), Carrows Restaurant(24), Denny's, Fresh Blend Smoothy Juice Bar, Landry's Seafood, Palace Station Hotel & Casino, Romano's Macaroni Grill, The Old Coffee Mill
- **Lodg** E: TraveLodge
  W: Palace Station Hotel & Casino
- **AServ** E: 76(24), Desert Transmission, Las Vegas Auto Parts (Delco), Purcell Tire Co., Superior Tire Inc.
  W: Texaco
- **TServ** E: Presidio Truck & Brake, Purcell Tire Co.
- **RVCamp** E: Purcell Tire Co., Sahara RV Center
- **ATM** W: Nevada Financial Center

39 Spring Mtn. Road

38AB Flamingo Road
- **Food** W: Rio Hotel & Casino
- **Lodg** E: Bally's Hotel & Casino, Barbary Coast Hotel & Casino, Crowne Plaza Hotel Resorts (see our ad this page), Bellagio, Caesars Palace Hotel & Casino, Chanel, Flamingo Hilton Hotel & Casino
  W: Rio Hotel & Casino

37 Tropicana Ave.
- **FStop** W: King 8 Truck Plaza(LP, SCALES)
- **Gas** W: Arco(*, 24), Standard(*, D, 24)
- **Food** E: Excalibur Hotel & Casino, Tropicana Hotel & Casino
  W: Howard Johnson, IHOP, In-N-Out Hamburgers, Jack-In-The-Box, McDonald's, Wendy's
- **Lodg** E: Excalibur Hotel & Casino, MGM Grand Hotel & Casino, Monte Carlo, New York New York
  W: Budget Suites,AmeriSuites (see our ad this page), Howard Johnson, King 8 Hotel & Casino, Motel 6
- **TServ** W: J & S Diesel Service
- **ATM** W: Arco, McDonald's

36 Russell Road
- **Gas** W: Chevron(*, D, 24)
- **ATM** W: Chevron

34 Jct I-215E, McCarran Airport, Las Vegas Blvd. (Limited Access Hwy)

33 NV160, Blue Diamond, Pahrump, Red Rock, Death Valley
- **TStop** W: T/A TravelCenters of America(*, LP, SCALES)

EXIT NEVADA

- **Gas** W: Chevron(*, D, 24)
- **Food** W: Jack in the Box, Silverton Hotel/Casino RV Park (.25 Miles), T/A TravelCenters of America
- **Lodg** W: Firebird Motel, Silverton Hotel/Casino RV Park (.25 Miles)
- **AServ** W: T/A TravelCenters of America
- **TServ** W: T/A TravelCenters of America(SCALES)
- **RVCamp** E: Destiny's Oasis Las Vegas (.5 Miles), Oasis RV Resort
  W: Silverton Hotel/Casino RV Park (.25 Miles)
- **ATM** W: Chevron
- **Other** E: Belz Factory Outlet World

27 NV146, Henderson, Lake Mead

25 Sloan

(13) Truck Inspection Station (Northbound)

12 NV161, Jean, Goodsprings, Nevada Welcome Center (RR, Phones)
- **FStop** E: Mobil(*)
- **Gas** W: Shell(*, 24)
- **Food** E: Burger King (Gold Strike Hotel), Gold Strike Hotel & Casino, Miss Olga's Ice Cream Parlor (Gold Strike Hotel)
  W: Nevada Landings Hotel & Casino

CAMPING WORLD
Exit 45 Lake Mead Blvd
1600 S. Boulder Hwy. • Henderson, NV
1-800-646-4093
1425

1293
CROWNE PLAZA
HOTELS RESORTS
Nevada • Exit 38AB • 702-369-4400

1366
AMERISUITES
AMERICA'S AFFORDABLE ALL-SUITE HOTEL
Nevada • Exit 37 • 702-369-3366

FASHION OUTLET
LAS VEGAS
100 WORLD CLASS DESIGNERS.
OUTLET PRICES.
1254
I-15 AT STATELINE, PRIMM
888-424-6898

EXIT NEVADA/CALIFORNIA

- **Lodg** E: Gold Strike Hotel & Casino
  W: Nevada Landings Hotel & Casino
- **ATM** W: Shell

(12) Nevada Welcome Center (RR, Phones; Located At Exit 12, East Side)

(1) Rest Area (RR, HF, Phones, P)

1 State Line, Primm
- **TStop** W: Whiskey Pete's Truck Stop(SCALES)
- **Gas** E: 76
- **Food** E: McDonald's, Primm Valley Resort & Casino
  W: Whiskey Pete's Casino
- **Lodg** E: Buffalo Bill's Resort & Casino, Primm Valley Resort & Casino
  W: Whiskey Pete's Casino
- **RVCamp** E: Primadonna RV Village, Primm Valley Resort & Casino
- **Other** E: Amusement Park (Buffalo Bill's Resort & Casino),
  W:Fashion Outlet of Las Vegas (see our ad on this page)

↑NEVADA

↓CALIFORNIA

289 Yates Well Road

284 Nipton Road

279 Bailey Road

(278) Truck Brake Inspection Area (Northbound)

270 Cima Road
- **Gas** E: Gas(*, D)

(269) Rest Area (RR, Picnic; Northbound)

(269) Rest Area (RR, Picnic; Southbound)

263 Halloran Summit Road
- **FStop** E: Hilltop Mart(*)
- **AServ** E: Mr. D's Tire Service

257 Halloran Springs Road
- **FStop** E: Lo-Gas(*)
- **Food** E: Lo-Gas

246 Baker (Reaccess Northbound Only)
- **AServ** W: Arnold's Market & Garage

244 CA 127, Death Valley, Kelbaker Road
- **Gas** W: 76(*), Arco(*), Chevron(*), Mobil(*)
- **Food** W: Bun Boy Restaurant, Del Taco, Denny's (Mobil), Los Dos Torito's (Mexican), The Mad Greek
- **Lodg** W: Arnie's Royal Hawaiian Hotel, Bun Boy Motel, Motel
- **RVCamp** W: Baker Hardware Complex & RV Center, Clark's Mobile Home Park
- **ATM** W: 76, Chevron, Will's Country Store(*)
- **Other** W: Mojave Desert Information Center, Will's Country Store

238 Zzyzx Road

232 Rasor Road
- **FStop** E: Goodspeed & Sons(*, 24)
- **AServ** E: Goodspeed & Sons(24)

228 Basin Road

219 Afton Rd, Dunn

(218) Rest Area (RR; Northbound)

(218) Rest Area (RR; Southbound)

211 Field Road

204 Harvard Road
- **Gas** W: Jeremy's(*, 24)

EXIT — CALIFORNIA

ASERV W: Jeremy's[24]
RVCamp E: Twin Lakes RV Park (5 Miles)

196 Minneola Rd
FStop W: Rustlers[*]
Gas W: Mobil[D]
Food W: Minneola Travel Store (Rustlers)
AServ W: Mobil
Other W: Calico Early Man Archeological Site

Exit (195) Agricultural Inspection Station (Southbound)

194 Yermo Road (Reaccess Northbound Only)

192 Calico Road, Yermo Road
Food E: International American & Chinese Food

189 Ghost Town Road
FStop E: Vegas Truck Stop[*]
W: Shell[*]
Gas E: AMPM
W: Texaco[*]
Food E: Peggy Sue's Diner
W: Jenny Rose Restaurant
Lodg E: Calico Motel
RVCamp W: KOA Kampground (.5 Miles)
ATM E: Vegas Truck Stop
Other W: Calico Ghost Town (3 Miles)

187 Ft. Irwin Road
Gas W: 76[*, D]
RVCamp W: Camping

184 Old CA 58 West, Bakersfield

182 East Main St, Needles, I-40, Route 15 Bus.
Gas E: Chevron[*], Mobil[*, D], Shell
W: Arco[*], Chevron[*], Shell[*, 24]
Food E: Donut Star[24], Hollywood Cafe, McDonald's, StarWok Express[24], Tom's Burgers
W: Burger King[PLAY], Cactus Kitchen (Holiday Inn), Carl Jr's Hamburgers[PLAY], Coco's Bakery & Restaurant, Del Taco, Di Napoli's Firehouse Italian Eatery, IHOP, Jack-In-The-Box, Long John Silver, Sizzler Buffet, Court, & Grill, Taco Bell, The Green Burrito[PLAY]
Lodg E: Best Western, Gateway Motel
W: Comfort Inn, Holiday Inn, Motel, Quality Inn, Super 8
AServ E: Shell
TServ W: Public Scales
ATM E: Mobil
W: Arco, Shell, Taco Bell
Other W: Wallace Theatres

181B Jct I-40, Needles

181 CA 247, Barstow Road
Gas E: Ultramar[*]
Food E: Pizza Hut
W: Little Caesars Pizza (Big K-Mart)
AServ W: Chief Auto Parts
Parks W: Centennial Park
Other W: Big K-Mart, Fire Station, Food 4 Less

Exit L Street

179 W. Main St, Lenwood, CA 58, Bakersfield (Limited Access Hwy)
RVCamp W: Desert Moon RV Camp

176 Lenwood Road
TStop W: Rip Griffin Travel Center[*, SCALES] (Texaco)
FStop W: Arco[*, RV DUMP], Pilot[*]
Gas E: 76[*], Chevron[*], Exxon[*], Mobil[*]
Food E: Arby's, Baskin Robbins, Carl Jr's Hamburgers[PLAY], Del Taco, Denny's, El Pollo Loco, Hana Grill (Japanese), Harvey House, In-N-Out Hamburgers, KFC, Panda Express, Quigley's Restaurant, Starbucks Coffee, Subway, Wendy's (Exxon)
W: Dairy Queen[24] (Pilot), McDonald's, Subway (Rip Griffin TS)
Lodg W: Good Nite Inn
TServ W: Rip Griffin Travel Center[SCALES] (Texaco)
TWash W: Little Sisters Truck Wash
ATM E: Wendy's (Exxon)
Other E: Factory Merchant Outlets, Tanger Outlet Center

173 Outlet Center Dr.

168 Hodge Rd

163 Wild Wash Road

159 Boulder Road

152 Bell Mountain, Stoddard Wells Road

151C Stoddard Wells Road
Gas W: 76[*, D], Mobil[*], U.S. Gas[*, D, LP] (Towing)
Food E: Peggy Sue's Restaurant
W: Denny's
Lodg W: Motel 6, Queens Motel, TraveLodge
AServ E: J & J Auto Repair & Towing
W: Mobil, U.S. Gas (Towing)
RVCamp E: KOA Kampground (.25 Miles)
Parks W: Grady Trammel Park

151B E Street

151A CA 18, D Street, Apple Valley

150 Mojave Drive
Gas E: 76[*, D]
W: Chevron[24], Kwik-Stop[*]
Food W: Mojave One Stop Donuts Plus Sandwich, Mollie's Country Cafe
Lodg E: Budget Inn
W: Economy Inn, Mojave Village Motel, Sunset Inns
AServ E: 76
W: A-Quality Automotive Repair, Central Transmissions, Chevron[24]
ATM W: John's Market
Other E: Fairgrounds
W: John's Market

149 Roy Rogers Drive
Gas E: Texaco[*, D]
W: Arco[*]
Food E: A & W Hot Dogs & More (Texaco), Chinese Food, Hometown Buffet, IHOP, Jack-In-The-Box, Pic 'N' Save, TCBY (Texaco)
ATM E: Desert Community Bank
Other E: Asian Market, Coin Op Laundry, Costco Wholesale Warehouse, Fairgrounds, Food 4 Less[24], Harley Davidson Motorcycles, Skate-N-Sport

148 Palmdale Rd, CA 18 West
Gas E: Texaco[*, D]
W: Mobil[*], Shell[*, CW], Thrifty[*, 24]
Food E: Anton's Cafe, Baker's, Best Western, Casa Delicias Mexican, Denny's, H & C BBQ, KFC, Richie's Real American Diner, Rocks Club
W: Buzze's Pizza Circus, Chateau Chang Seafood & Steaks, China Food Express, Coco's, Del Taco, Hole in One Donuts, Little Caesars Pizza, Long John Silver, Oriental Gardens Chinese, Sanara Japanese Restaurant, Subway, Taco Bell, The Brass Pickle, The Grumpy Englishman, The Oak Room (Holiday Inn)
Lodg W: Budget Inn, E-Z 8 Motel, Holiday Inn
AServ E: Rancho Motor Co. (Nissan, Olds, Cad, GMC Trucks), Victorville Motors (Chrys, Plym, Dodge, Dodge Trucks)
W: Sunland Ford
RVCamp W: Kamper's Korner (1.25 Miles)
ATM E: Texaco
W: Mobil
Other E: Chamber of Commerce
W: Civic Center Hand Wash[CW], Frame-N-Lens, Movies 7, Target

146 Lucerne Valley, Bear Valley Rd, Apple Valley
Gas E: Arco[*], Citgo[*], Mobil[*, CW], Shell[*, CW, 24]
Food E: Bagels R Bagels, Burger King[PLAY], Carl Jr's Hamburgers[PLAY], Carpino's Pizza Palace, Del Taco, Donuts "N" Deli, John's Incredible Pizza Co., KFC, Long John Silver, Marie Callender's, McDonald's, Panda Express, Steer 'N Stein Restaurant, TNT's Cafe, The Green Burrito
W: El Tio Pepe Mexican, Greenhouse Cafe, Red Lobster, Tony Roma's
Lodg E: Days Inn, EconoLodge, Super 8, Thrifty Z Inn
AServ E: America's Tire Company, American TransWorld & Auto Care, Bear Valley Firestone
RVCamp E: American TransWorld & Auto Care, Range RV Sales & Service
ATM E: Citgo
Parks E: Mojave Narrows Regional Park (7 Miles)
Other E: Golden Companion Animal Hospital, Victor Bowl
W: The Mall of Victor Valley

145 Hesperia, Main St
Gas E: Shell[*], Texaco[*, D], Ultramar[*]
W: Arco[*, 24]
Food E: A & W Hot Dogs & More (Texaco), Burger King, Dairy Queen (Ultramar), E-Z Burger (Ultramar), In-N-Out Burger, Jack-In-The-Box, Popeye's Chicken (Texaco)
W: Bob's Big Boy
RVCamp W: Camping[*], Desert Willow RV Park
ATM E: Texaco
W: Arco
Other E: Pizza Factory Express (Ultramar)

139 Jct U.S. 395, Bishop, Adelanto
TStop W: Newton's Outpost[*, LP, SCALES]
Food W: Old Outpost Cafe (Newton's Outpost TS)
TWash W: Action Truck Wash (Newton's Outpost)

136 Oak Hill Road
Gas E: Arco[*], Texaco[*, 24]
Food E: Summit Inn Cafe
AServ E: Texaco[24]
RVCamp W: Oak Hill RV Village

131 CA 138, Palmdale, Silverwood Lake
Gas W: 76[*], Texaco[*, D]
Food E: McDonald's, Tiffiny's C.S.
W: Del Taco (76)
AServ E: Northern Sun Automotive
W: Texaco
TServ E: Northern Sun Automotive
ATM E: McDonald's
Parks E: Silverwood Lake State Recreational Area (10 Miles)

(129) Weigh Station (Southbound)

(129) Weigh Station (Northbound)

127 Cleghorn Rd.

Exit Kenwood Ave.

123 Jct I-215S, San Bernardino (Limited Access Hwy)

Exit Glen Helen Pkwy.

119 Sierra Ave
Gas W: Arco[*, 24], Shell[*]
Other W: Litle Creek Recreation Area

115 Lake Arrowhead, CA 30, Big Bear, Highland Ave

113 Baseline

112 CA 66, Foothill Blvd.

Bold red print shows RV & Bus parking available or nearby

EXIT CALIFORNIA

Food **E:** Claimjumper Restaurant, Golden Spoon, In-N-Out Hamburgers, Stuffed Bagel, Subway, Taco Bell, Wienerschnitzel
AServ **E:** Costco Wholesale Warehouse, Oil Max, **Wal-Mart**[24]
Other **E:** **Food 4 Less**, Mail Boxes Etc, Office Depot, Optometry, PetsMart, **Wal-Mart**

110 4th St
Gas **W:** Mobil[*, D, CW], Texaco[*, D, CW]
Food **W:** Cucina Cucina Italian Cafe, Rubio's Baja Grill, Starbucks Coffee, Subway (Mobil), Tokyo Tokyo (Japanese)
Lodg **W:** AmeriSuites
AServ **W:** Mobil
ATM **W:** Mobil, Texaco
Other **W:** Edwards 22 Cinemas, Juice Stop, **Ontario Mills Mall**, Ultra Screen Theater

109 Jct I-10 Los Angeles, San Bernardino

108 Jurupa Ave
Gas **W:** Arco[*]
Food **W:** Carl Jr's Hamburgers
AServ **E:** The Ontario Auto Center (Penske, Honda), The Ontario Auto Center (GMC Trucks, Pont, BMW, Volvo, Sub, VW, Dodge, Isuzu, Jeep, Daewoo)
W: Citrus Ford Motors
ATM **W:** Arco
Other **E:** Sun Country Marine
W: Scandia Amusement Park

106 CA 60, Riverside, Los Angeles (Limited Access Hwy)

103 Limonite Ave

100 Sixth St, Norco Dr.
Gas **E:** Arco[*], Chevron[*, CW, 24]
W: Arco[*], Ultramar[D]
Food **E:** Jack-In-The-Box, McDonald's[PLAY]
W: **Country Junction**
Lodg **E:** Ramada Limited (see our ad this page)
ATM **E:** Chevron
W: Arco
Other **W:** Community Center

98 Second St, Norco
Gas **W:** Shell[*, 24]
Food **W:** Burger King, Cougar Den Pizzeria, Donut, In-N-Out Burger, Norco Subs, Sizzler Steakhouse, Texas Loosey's (Steaks, Ribs), Wienerschnitzel
Lodg **W:** Howard Johnson
AServ **W:** Frahm Dodge, Hemborg Ford, Norco Center Car Wash[CW], Norco Chrys, Plym, Jeep, Eagle, Norco Mitsubishi, Phillips Pontiac, Mazda
TServ **W:** **Fernandes Truck & Auto Center**
TWash **W:** **Car Wash & Truck Wash**[CW]
RVCamp **W:** **RV Parts & Supplies**
Med **W:** **✚ Hospital**
Other **W:** 7-11 Convenience Store, Brunswick Classic Lanes, **Car Wash & Truck Wash**, Norco Center Car Wash

Exit Yuma Dr.
Gas **W:** Texaco[*, D]
Food **W:** A & W Hot Dogs & More (Texaco), Dairy Queen, Gus Jr's Famous Burgers, Mangia Italian Fruit Ice, McDonald's[PLAY], TCBY (Texaco), Wendy's
ATM **W:** **Lucky, Save-On Drugs**[RX]
Other **W:** **Lucky, Save-On Drugs**[RX], **Staple's, Target**

96 Jct CA 91, Riverside, Beach Cities (Limited Access Highway)

95 Magnolia Ave
FStop **E:** **Down's Commercial Fueling (Credit Only)**
Gas **W:** Mobil[*], Shell[*, CW]
Food **W:** Baskin Robbins, Burger King[PLAY], Carl Jr's Hamburgers[PLAY], Coffee Town, Dalia's Pizza, Fifth Ave. Bagel, Little Caesars Pizza, Lotus Garden Chinese, McDonald's, Pizza Palace, Sizzler Steak House, Subway, The Sub Pub, Zendejas Mexican
AServ **W:** Kragen Auto Parts
ATM **W:** McDonald's, **Ralph's Grocery**, Redlands Federal Bank
Other **W:** Mail Boxes Etc., Post Box Plus, **Ralph's Grocery, Rite Aid Pharmacy**[RX], **Save-On Drugs**[RX], **Stater Bros. Grocery Store**

93 Ontario Ave
Gas **W:** Arco[*]
AServ **W:** Pete's Tire

92 El Cerrito Road

91 Cajalco Road

90 Weirick Road

86 Temescal Canyon Road, Glen Ivy
Gas **W:** Arco[*, D, 24]
Food **W:** Carl Jr's Hamburgers[PLAY], **The Original Tom's Farmer's Market**[*]
Other **W:** **The Original Tom's Farmer's Market**

85 Indian Truck Tr.
Other **E:** Lake Corona

81 Lake St, Alberhill

78 Nichols Road
Gas **W:** Arco[*]
Other **W:** **Outlet Stores**

77 CA 74, Central Ave, Perris, San Juan Capistrano
Gas **E:** Arco[*], Chevron[*], Mobil[*, CW]
Food **E:** Douglas #23 Burgers, Off Ramp Cafe
ATM **E:** Chevron

75 Rt. 15 Bus, Main St.
Gas **W:** 76[*], Circle K[*], Lake Gas[*]
Lodg **W:** Elsinore Hot Springs Hotel

1725

RAMADA
LIMITED

1248 W. Sixth Street
Corona, CA 91720

Continental Breakfast
Outdoor Pool/Heated Jacuzzi
Kitchen Units Available
Golf Nearby
MeetingRooms
Guest Laundry
In Room Coffee, Hair dryer, Iron, Microwave
Nearby Fine Dining/
Shopping/Fast Food

909-272-4900

CALIFORNIA • I-15 • EXIT 100

EXIT CALIFORNIA

AServ **W:** 76, Lake Elsinore Tire & Auto Center, Lear Auto Body & Towing, Superior Muffler
Other **W:** **Van's Coin Laundry**

73 Railroad Canyon Road, Diamond Drive
Gas **E:** 76[*]
W: Arco[*], Chevron[24], Mobil[*, D]
Food **E:** Denny's, Donut Depot, El Pollo Loco, In-N-Out Hamburgers, KFC, Latte Express Coffee, **McDonald's (Wal-Mart)**, Peony Chinese
W: Burger King[PLAY], Carl Jr's Hamburgers, Chinese Food, Don Jose's Mexican Restaurant (Mexican), Ice Cream, Mammy's Grill, McDonald's[PLAY], Pizza Hut, Sizzler Steak House, Subway, Taco Bell, The Green Burrito, Vincenco's Olive, Vista Donuts, Wild Weenies
AServ **E:** **Wal-Mart**[RX] **(Vision Center)**
W: Express Tire, Firestone Tire & Auto
Med **W:** **✚ Urgent Care Family Practice**
ATM **E:** 76, World Savings
W: Bank of America
Other **E:** Mail Boxes Etc., **Vons Grocery**[RX], **Wal-Mart**[RX] **(Vision Center)**
W: 7-11 Convenience Store, Frame N Lens, Hostess Bakery Outlet, Post & Parcel, **Save-On Drugs**[RX]

71 Bundy Canyon Road, Sedco Hills
Gas **W:** Arco[*]
ATM **W:** Arco
Other **E:** Torres Car Wash & Detail[CW]

69 Baxter Road, Wildomar

68 Clinton Keith Road
Med **E:** **✚ Inland Valley Regional Medical Center (.75 Miles)**

65 California Oaks Rd., Kalmia St
Gas **E:** Shell[CW, 24]
W: Arco[*]
Food **E:** Bearly Sweets, Burger King[PLAY], Carl Jr's Hamburgers[PLAY], Dairy Queen, KFC, Molcasalsa (Shell), Numero Uno Pizza (Shell)
W: Jack-In-The-Box
AServ **E:** Chief Auto Parts
ATM **E:** **Albertson's Grocery**[RX]
W: Arco
Other **E:** **Albertson's Grocery**[RX], Postal Connections

64 Murrieta Hot Springs Road
Gas **W:** Texaco[*]
Food **W:** IHOP, McDonald's[PLAY], Popeye's Chicken (Texaco), Subway (Texaco)
Med **E:** **✚ Hospital**
ATM **W:** Texaco
Other **W:** PetsMart, Pic 'N' Save, Staple's, **The Home Depot**

62 Jct. to I-215, Riverside, San Bernardino (Northbound)

61 CA 79 N, Winchester Rd.
Gas **W:** Arco[*], Chevron[D], Mobil[*]
Food **E:** Baskin Robbins, Carl Jr's Hamburgers, Coco's, Little Caesars Pizza (Big K-Mart), Mandarin Express (Chinese), Mexicana, Pam's Donuts, Sub-marina, Taco Bell, The Green Burrito
W: Bangkok Chef, Burger King, Chico's Tecate Grill, Dairy Queen, Del Taco[PLAY], El Pollo Loco, El Rancho Nuevo, Ernie B's Hoagie's, Graziano's Italian, Jack-In-The-Box, Little Chung King, Margarita Grill, New York Pizzeria, Pasquale's Italian, Rocky Cola Cafe, Stadium Pizza, Tony Roma's, Vera's Italian
Lodg **W:** **Comfort Inn**
AServ **E:** America's Tire Company, Express Tire, Kragen Auto Works, Xpress Lube
W: M & M Tire, Mobil, Winston Tire
RVCamp **W:** **Richardson's RV Center**

EXIT		CALIFORNIA
	Med	**E:** ✚ **Walk In Clinic**
	ATM	**E:** Home Savings Of America, Quick Stop Food Stores, Union Bank of CA **W:** Fast Freddy's(*)
	Other	**E:** AAA Auto Club, **Big K-Mart**, **Food 4 Less**(24), Optometry, Pack 'n' Mail, Quick Stop Food Stores, See's Candy **W:** Candy Stop, **El Rancho Animal Hospital**, Emergency Pet Clinic, Fast Freddy's, Kinko's Copies, Lady of the Lake Books, Mail Mart, Nevada Bob's Golf, Rancho Car Wash(CW) (Mobil), **Stater Bros. Grocery**, Surf N Sport, Temecula Eye Center
59		Rancho California Road, Temecula
	Gas	**E:** Arco(*) **W:** 76(*, D), Chevron, Mapco(D)
	Food	**E:** Black Angus Steakhouse, Chesapeake Bagel, Chili's, Claimjumper Restaurant, Del Taco, Katie McGuire's Pie & Bake Shop, Oscar's, Rockin' Baja Lobster, Round Table Pizza, Starbucks Coffee, Subway, The Harvest Cafe (Embassy Suites) **W:** Denny's, Domino's Pizza, KFC, McDonald's(PLAY), Mexico Chiquito, Nick's Super Burgers, Olde Town Donuts & Pastry, Penfold's Cafe & Bakery, Steak Ranch Restaurant, Taco Bell, Togo's Eatery
	Lodg	**E:** Embassy Suites **W:** Best Western, Motel 6
	AServ	**W:** Automotive Electrical Electronic, Chevron
	ATM	**E:** Bank of America, Fallbrook National Bank, **Vons Grocery**, Wells Fargo Bank **W:** 76
	Parks	**E:** **Temecula Duck Pond**
	Other	**E:** **Albertson's Grocery**, Postal Place, The Movie Experience, **Vons Grocery** **W:** Coin Op Laundry & Car Wash, Fortner Hardware Co., Visitor Information
58		CA 79 S, Temecula, Indio, Warner Springs
	Gas	**E:** Mobil(*) **W:** Texaco(*, D)
	Food	**E:** Carl Jr's Hamburgers, Donut Depot, Pizza Company, Sophie's Ice Cream **W:** Alberto's Mexican(24), Baskin Robbins (Texaco), Colombo's, Hungry Howie's (Texaco), Wienerschnitzel (Texaco)
	Lodg	**W:** **Ramada Inn**
	AServ	**W:** Xpress Tire
	RVCamp	**W:** **Temecula Valley RV Sales**
(53)		**Inspection & Weigh Station (Northbound, All Vehicles Stop)**
Exit		**(52)** Rainbow Valley Blvd
(52)		**Weigh Station (Southbound, Located At Rainbow Valley Blvd. Exit On West Side)**
51		Mission Road, Fallbrook
	Med	**W:** ✚ **Hospital**
46		CA 76, Pala, Oceanside
	Gas	**W:** Mobil(*), **Pala Mesa Market**(LP)
	Food	**W:** **Nessy Burgers**
	Lodg	**W:** La Estancia Inn
	Other	**E:** Bonsall Palomar Mountain **W:** **Pala Mesa Market**

CAMPING WORLD
Exit San Marcos Blvd.
off 78 Freeway
200 Travelers Way • San Marcos, CA
1-800-874-4346
1441

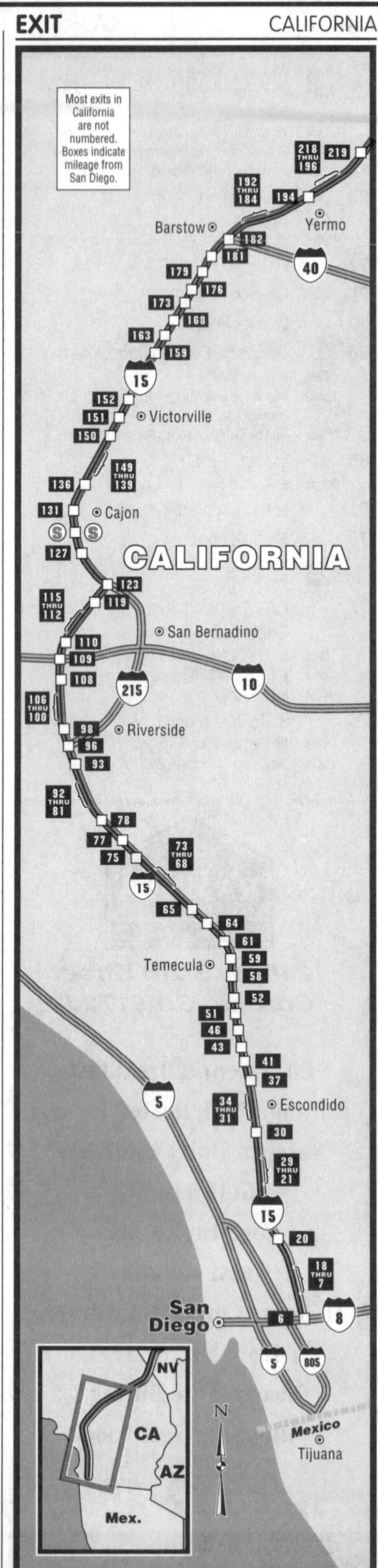

EXIT		CALIFORNIA
43		Old Hwy 395, West Lilac Road
41		Gopher Canyon Road, Old Castle Road
	Food	**E:** Castle Creek Country Club (Public)
	RVCamp	**E:** **All Seasons Campground**
	Other	**E:** Castle Creek Country Club (Public)
37		Deer Springs Road, Mountain Meadow Road
	Gas	**W:** Arco(*)
	ATM	**W:** Arco
	Other	**E:** Welk Resort Center **W:** Fire Station
34		Centre City Pkwy, Escondido (Southbound)
33		El Norte Pkwy, Escondido
	Gas	**E:** Mobil(*, CW), Shell(*, CW, 24) **W:** 76(LP), Circle K(*)
	Food	**W:** Big Apple Bagels, Donut Star, Graciano's Pizza Restaurant, Rosa #1 Pizza, Royal Dragon Chinese, Wendy's
	Lodg	**E:** Best Western
	AServ	**E:** Express Tire Goodyear, Precision Tune & Lube **W:** 76
	RVCamp	**E:** **Escondido RV Resort**(LP)
	ATM	**E:** Mobil **W:** **Vons Grocery**(RX)
	Other	**W:** Cal Postal, El Norte Veterinary Clinic, Lens 4 Less, **Vons Grocery**(RX)
32		CA 78, Oceanside, Ramona (Limited Access Highway)
	RVCamp	**E:** Camping World (see our ad this page)
31		Valley Pkwy, Downtown, Escondido
	Gas	**E:** Arco(*) **W:** Parkway Express(*, D), Shell(CW)
	Food	**E:** Chili's, Gilbey's, McDonald's(24), Rock N' Jenny's Italian Subs, The Olive Garden, Yogurt & Ice Cream Garden, Yoshinoya Beef Bowl **W:** Barbecues Galore, Burger King(PLAY), Carl Jr's Hamburgers, Coco's Bakery & Restaurant, Del Taco, Fogerty's, Joey's Only Seafood, La Falsa, Starbucks Coffee, TGI Steaks, Ribs, Seafood, Taco Bell, Taco Jr.
	Lodg	**W:** Comfort Inn, Holiday Inn Express
	AServ	**E:** Econo Lube & Tune
	Med	**E:** ✚ **Hospital** **W:** ✚ **Immediate Family Medical Care**
	ATM	**E:** Arco **W:** 7-11 Convenience Store
	Other	**E:** **Barnes & Noble Booksellers**, Joshua's Book Store, Petco, West Coast Eye Care **W:** 7-11 Convenience Store, Lens Crafters, Pearl Vision Center, Postal Annex, Staple's, **Target**
30		9th Ave, Auto Park Way, Escondido
	Food	**W:** Applebee's, **Hestons**, Joey's Only Seafood, Peking Panda Chinese
	AServ	**E:** Escondido Motors (Mercedes Benz)
	Other	**W:** Frame-N-Lens, **Target**, Toys R Us
Exit		Felicita Rd.
29		Bus. Route 15, City Centre Pkwy, Escondido (Northbound, Reaccess Southbound Only)
27		Via Rancho Pkwy
	Gas	**E:** Chevron(*), Shell(*, CW, 24) **W:** Texaco(*, D)
	Food	**W:** Bagel's & Spuds (Greek), Bobaluchi's, McDonald's(PLAY), Panda King (Chinese), Smoothie King, Subway (Taco Bell), T.C. Santa Fe, Taco Bell (Subway), Tony's Spunky Steer
	ATM	**E:** Chevron
	Parks	**W:** **Felicita Park (1 Mile)**

EXIT	CALIFORNIA
Other	**E:** Farmer's Market, **North County Fair Shopping Mall**
	W: Lake Hodges, Mail Box Annex
25	W. Bernardo Drive, Pomerado Road
Other	**W:** Lake Hodges
24	Rancho Bernardo Road, Lake Poway
FStop	**W: Texaco**[*]
Gas	**E:** Arco[*, 24]
	W: 76[*], Shell[CW]
Food	**E:** Bakery LaFayette, Baskin Robbins, Heidi's Frogen Yozurt, Juice Connection, Starbucks Coffee, Sub-marina, Taco Shop, The Coffee Merchant, The Incredible Egg, Valentino's Pizzeria
	W: The Elephant Bar
Lodg	**W:** Holiday Inn
AServ	**W:** Shell, **Texaco**
ATM	**E:** Bank of America, Home Savings Of America, Wells Fargo Copy & Postal Center
Other	**E:** Dr. Lee & Lee Optometry, Fire Station, **Mail Boxes Etc**, Postal Annex, **Rite Aid Pharmacy**[RX], **U.S. Post Office**, **Vons Grocery**
23	Bernardo Center Drive
Food	**E:** Burger King[PLAY], Denny's, El Torito, Fortune Cookie Restaurant, Passage To India, Quizno's Classic Sub, Rubio's Baja Grill, Sesame Donuts, Spices Thai Cafe, Taco Bell
AServ	**E:** Firestone Tire & Auto, Future Automotive Volvo, Toyota, Mazda, Goodyear Tire & Auto, Instant Oil Change, Pettey's Auto Service Ford, Lincoln, Mercury, R.B. German Automotive (Merc, Porsche, Audi, BMW, Volvo, VW), R.B. Tire & Brake, Secor's GM Service & Import, Transmasters
ATM	**E:** Companion Care Veterinarian, Point Loma Federal Credit Union
Other	**E:** Companion Care Veterinarian
22	Camino del Norte
Med	**E:** ✚ **Hospital**
21	Carmel Mountain Road
Gas	**E:** Chevron[*, CW]
	W: Chevron[*, 24]
Food	**E:** Athens Market Cafe, Baskin Robbins, Bruegger's Bagel & Bakery, Cafe 66, Cafe Luna, California Pizza Kitchen, Carl Jr's Hamburgers[PLAY], Chevy's Mexican, Ching Fun, Heidi's Frozen Yogurt, Marie Callender's, Olive Garden, Schlotzsky's Deli, Sesame Donuts, Sombrero Mexican, Subway, Swensen's Ice Cream, T.G.I. Friday's, Wendy's
	W: Dragon Wok
Lodg	**E:** Residence Inn
	W: Carmel Highland Doubletree Resort
AServ	**W:** Chevron[24]
ATM	**E:** USA Federal Credit Union
Other	**E: Borders Books & Music**, Pacific Theaters, Pearl Vision Center, Petco, Staple's, **U.S. Post Office**
	W: 7-11 Convenience Store
20	CA 56W, Ted Williams Pkwy (Limited Access Hwy)
18	Poway Rd, Rancho Penasquitos Blvd.
Gas	**W:** 76[LP], Mobil[*, LP], Shell[*, CW, 24]
Food	**W:** Burger King[PLAY], IHOP, Little Caesars Pizza, McDonald's[PLAY], New Manila Bakery & Market, Subway, Taco Bell
Lodg	**W:** La Quinta Inn, Ramada Limited
AServ	**W:** 76
ATM	**W: 7-11 Convenience Store**[24]
Other	**W: 7-11 Convenience Store**
17	Mercy Road, Scripps Poway Pkwy
16	Mira Mesa Blvd.
Gas	**W:** Shell[CW]
Food	**E:** C's Ice Cream & Deli, Chuck E Cheese's Pizza, Crane's Restaurant, D'Valerio Family Bakery, Denny's, Don Lucio's Taco Shop, Filippi's Restaurant, Golden Crown (Chinese), Panda Fuji Restaurant, Pizza Hut, Sesame Donuts, Taco Bell, The Deli Express, Yummy Yogurt
	W: Applebee's, Dairy Queen, Fins A Mexican Eatery, Golden State Seafood, Hungry Howie's Pizza, In-N-Out Burger, Starbucks Coffee, Subway
Lodg	**E:** Quality Suites
AServ	**W:** Instant Oil Change
Med	**E:** ✚ **Family Physicians Urgent Care**
ATM	**E:** Navy Federal Credit Union
	W: Ralph's Grocery, Shell
Other	**E: Medco Drugs**[RX], Scripps Ranch Optometric Center, Sieu Thai 79 Supermarket
	W: Mail Boxes Etc., Petco, **Ralph's Grocery**
15	Caroll Canyon Road
Food	**E:** Canyon Grill, Mieki Sushi
Other	**E:** Optometry
14	Palmerado Road, Miramar Road
Gas	**W:** Arco[D], Chevron[*, CW], Mobil[*, CW], Shell[*, CW, 24], Texaco[*, D, 24]
Food	**W:** Keith's Restaurant[24], Maxwell's (Days Inn), The Bread Basket (Holiday Inn)
Lodg	**W:** Best Western, Days Inn, Holiday Inn Select
AServ	**W:** Texaco[24]
ATM	**W:** Bank of America
13	Miramar Way
Exit	South CA 163 (Southbound, Limited Access Hwy)
12	CA 52 (Limited Access Hwy)
10	Clairemont Mesa Blvd
Food	**W:** El Roberto's Taco Shop
ATM	**W:** Navy Federal Credit Union
9	Balboa Ave, CA 274, Tierrasanta Blvd
Gas	**E:** Chevron
Food	**E:** Ambio Italian, Boston Market Restaurant, Coffee Bean, Round Table Pizza, Subway
ATM	**E:** Home Savings Of America
8	Aero Drive
Gas	**W:** Arco[*, 24], Shell[*, CW]
Food	**E:** Popeye's Chicken
	W: Del Monto Italian, Del Taco, Einstein Bros Bagels, El Berto's, Fong Fong, Holiday Inn, Jack-In-The-Box, **McDonald's (Wal-Mart)**, McDonald's[PLAY], Sizzler Steak House, Star Bucks Coffee, Submarina, TCBY, Taco Bell[24]
Lodg	**W:** Holiday Inn
AServ	**W:** Shell, **Wal-Mart**
ATM	**W:** McDonald's
Other	**W:** PetsMart, **Vons Food & Drug**, **Wal-Mart**
7	Friars Rd.
Med	**E:** ✚ **Hospital**
Other	**W: Jack Murphy Stadium**
6	Jct. I-8; East I-8 El Centro; West I-8 Beaches, Camino del Rio South

↑CALIFORNIA

Begin I-15

Notes:

EXIT	GEORGIA

Begin I-16

↓GEORGIA

1 (0) To I-75 S., Valdosta (Westbound)

2 (1) U.S. 23, U.S. 129, GA 49, Spring St., Milledgeville
- Gas N: Fina[*] (Ryder Truck Rental)
  S: Amoco[*], Conoco[*, D, LP], Exxon[*]
- Food N: El Sombrero, Hong Kong Express, Krispy Kreme Doughnuts, **Kroger Supermarket**[RX], McDonald's, Nu-Way Hamburgers, Papa John's Pizza, Subway
  S: Burger King, Checkers Burgers, Pizza Hut, Wendy's
- AServ N: Attaway Tire, Fina (Ryder Truck Rental)
- Med S: ✚ **Georgia Medical Center**
- ATM N: **Kroger Supermarket**
- Other N: **Baconfield Pharmacy**, CVS[RX], **Kroger Supermarket**[RX], U-Haul Center
  S: **Greyhound Bus Station**

3 (1) GA 22, to U.S. 129, to GA 49, 2nd Street, Macon (Westbound, Difficult Reaccess, Easiest reaccess is to go to exit 4)
- Lodg S: Crowne Plaza Hotel
- Med N: ✚ **Coliseum Hospital**
  S: ✚ **Georgia Medical Center**, ✚ **Middle Georgia Hospital**
- ATM S: First Liberty Bank, Security National Bank
- Other N: Macon Coliseum

4 (2) U.S. 80, GA 87, Martin Luther King Blvd., Coliseum Drive
- Gas S: Fina[*, D, LP, K], Safety-Oil[D]
- Med N: ✚ **Coliseum Hospital**
- Parks S: **Central City Park**
- Other N: **Ocmulgee National Monument**, Old Mill Antiques
  S: **African American Museum**, Central City Park Antiques, **Georgia Music Hall of Fame**, **Tourist Info.**

5 U.S. 23, U.S. 129, Golden Isles Highway, Ocmulgee East Blvd
- FStop S: **Exxon**[*, LP]
- Gas S: Texaco[*, CW]
- Food S: **Exxon**, **Sam's Country Kitchen (Exxon)**, Subway (Texaco), Texaco, Waffle King
- Other N: Airport, **Georgia Forestry Center**

6 (11) Sgoda Road, Huber
- FStop N: **Fina**[*]

7 (18) Bullard Road, Jeffersonville

8 (24) GA 96, Jeffersonville, Tarversville
- FStop N: **Citgo**[*, LP]
  S: **BP**[*, LP]
- Food N: **Chester Fried Chicken (Citgo)**, **Citgo**
  S: **BP**, Huddle House (BP)
- Lodg S: Days Inn logo **Days Inn (see our ad this page)**
- AServ N: **Citgo**, Crossroads Auto Service (Citgo)
- Other S: **Museum of Aviation**

9 (27) GA 358, Danville

10 (32) GA 112, Montrose, Allentown
- FStop S: **Chevron**[*]
- Food S: **Me-Ma's**
- TServ S: **Tread Stop**

11 (39) GA 26, Cochran

12 (42) GA 338, Dudley, Dexter

(44) **Rest Area (RR, Phones, Picnic, Vending, RV Dump; Eastbound)**

(46) **Rest Area (RR, Phones, Picnic, Vending, RV Dump; Westbound)**

13 (49) GA 257, Dublin
- TStop S: **Fina**[*]
- Gas N: Chevron[*]
- Food S: **Fina**
- TServ S: **Fina**, **LJL Truck Center**
- Med N: ✚ **Hospital**
- ATM N: Chevron
  S: **Fina**

14 (51) U.S. 319, U.S. 441, McRae, Dublin
- FStop N: **Amoco**[*, 24], **Exxon**[*], **Speedway**[*, LP, K]
- Gas N: BP[*], Texaco[*, CW]
- Food N: **Amoco**, Arby's, BP, Buffalo's Cafe, Burger King[PLAY], **Holiday Inn**, KFC[24] (Amoco), Krispy Kreme Doughnuts (BP), McDonald's[PLAY], **Pizza Hut (Holiday Inn)**, SHONEY'S **Shoney's**, Subway (BP), TCBY, Taco Bell, **Waffle House**, Wendy's

912-945-3785
Jeffersonville, GA
DAYS INN
• Contential Breakfast
• Kids Under 18 Stay Free
• Outdoor Pool
• Pets Allowed
• Handicap Accessible
• Truck/Large Vehicle Parking
• Exterior Corridors
• Iron & Ironing Board
1724
GEORGIA ▪ I-16 EXIT 8

- Lodg N: Comfort Inn, Days Inn logo Days Inn, **Holiday Inn**, **Shoney's Shamrock Inn Dublin**, Super 8
- Med N: ✚ **Hospital**
- ATM N: **Exxon**
- Parks S: **Little Ocmulgee State Park**
- Other N: **Georgia State Patrol Post**
  S: Dublin Antique Mall

15 (54) GA 19, Dublin, Glenwood, East Dublin
- Med N: ✚ **Hospital**

16 (59) GA 199, East Dublin, Lothair

17 (67) GA 29, Soperton, Vidalia
- FStop S: **Texaco**[*]
- Gas S: Chevron[*]
- Food S: **Huddle House**, **Texaco**
- AServ N: MS Garage
- Other S: **Tourist Info.**

18 (71) GA 15, GA 78, Soperton, Adrian
- Gas N: Chevron[*, LP]
- Food N: Chevron, **Front Porch BBQ (Chevron)**
- ATM N: Chevron

19 (78) U.S. 221, GA 56, Swainsboro

20 (84) GA 297, Vidalia
- TServ N: **I-16 Truck Sales & Equipment**

21 (89) U.S. 1, Swainsboro, Lyons
- FStop N: **Phillips 66**[*]
- Gas N: BP[*]
- Food N: Barbecue Bill's, **Phillips 66**, Seafood Sally's
- TServ N: **I-16 Service**, **Phillips 66**

22 (98) GA 57, Stillmore, Reidsville, Cobbtown
- FStop S: **Amoco**[*]
- Gas S: Chevron[*, D]
- Food S: **Amoco**
- ATM S: Chevron
- Parks S: **Gordonia Altamaha State Park**
- Other S: Wiregrass Trail

23 **(104) GA 23, GA 121, Metter, Reidsville, Welcome Center**
- FStop N: **BP**[*, LP, 24], **Phillips 66**[CW]
  S: **Texaco**[*]
- Gas N: Exxon[*], Shell[*, LP]
- Food N: Burger King, Dairy Queen, Hardee's[PLAY], Huddle House, **Joe Mac's BBQ**, KFC, **McDonald's**[PLAY], Subway, Taco Bell, Village Pizza, Waffle House, **Western Steer Family Steakhouse**
- Lodg N: **Comfort Inn**, Days Inn logo Days Inn, **Holiday Inn**, Metter Inn
- AServ N: **BP**[24], Discount Tires & Auto Parts, Jimmy Franklin Chevrolet, Oldsmobile, **Phillips 66**, Williams Tire Center
- TServ N: **Phillips 66**

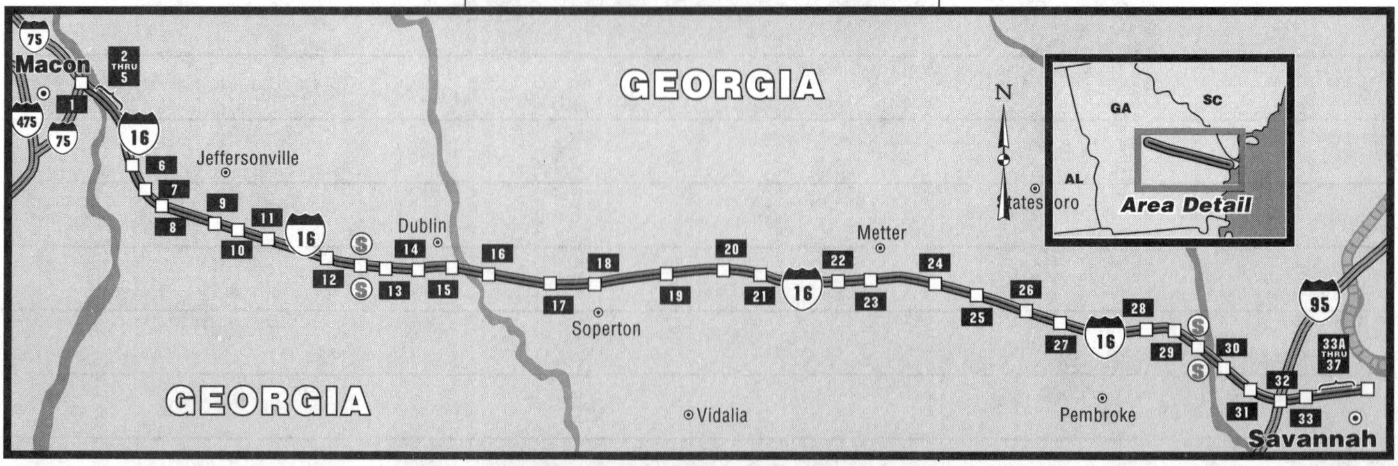

Bold red print shows RV & Bus parking available or nearby

EXIT	GEORGIA
Med	N: ✚ Hospital
ATM	N: Metter Banking Co., Pineland State Bank
Parks	N: **George L. Smith State Park**
Other	N: Guido Gardens, **Rite Aide Pharmacy**[RX] **(One-Hour Photo)**
24	**(111)** Pulaski - Excelsior Road
TStop	S: **Citgo**[*]
Food	S: **Citgo**
TServ	S: **Citgo**
RVCamp	S: **Beaver Run (.3 Miles)**
25	**(117)** U.S. 25, U.S. 301, Statesboro, Claxton, Jones Lane Hwy.
FStop	N: **Chevron**[*, LP, SCALES, 24]
	S: **El Cheapo**[*] **(Shell)**
Food	S: **El Cheapo (Shell)**
Lodg	S: **Red Carpet Inn**
ATM	S: **El Cheapo (Shell)**
26	**(126)** GA 67, Pembroke, Fort Stewart
FStop	S: **Chevron**[*, D]
Food	S: **Huddle House**
RVCamp	S: **Oasis Campground**
Other	S: **Fort Stewart Museum**
27	**(132)** Ash Branch Church Road
28	**(137)** GA 119, Springfield,

Howard Johnson Lodge

Howard Johnson Lodge 912-232-4371

Restaurant/Lounge on Premises
Newly Appointed Guest Rooms
Outdoor Pool • Cable TV
Poolside Rooms w/Private Balcony
Daily Historic District Tours
In Room Movies
Near Savannah Historic District,
River Street and Beaches

224 W. Boundary St. • Savannah, GA 1823

GEORGIA ▪ I-16 ▪ EXIT 36

EXIT	GEORGIA
29	**(143)** U.S. 280, to U.S. 80
FStop	S: **BP**[*], **Chevron**[*, D]
Food	S: **Chevron**, Country Cafe (Chevron)
ATM	S: **BP**
(144)	**Weigh Station (Eastbound)**
(144)	**Weigh Station (Westbound)**
30	**(148)** Old River Road, to U.S. 80
31	**(152)** GA 17, Bloomingdale Rd.
32AB	**(157)** I-95 South to Jacksonville, Brunswick, I-95 North to Florence
33	**(160)** GA 307, Dean Forest Rd
33A	**(162)** Chatham Parkway
34AB	**(164)** Jct.I-516, Lynes Pkwy, U.S. 80, U.S. 17, GA 21 (To Limited Access)
35	**(165)** GA 204, 37th Street (Eastbound)
36	**(166)** U.S. 17, GA 25, Gwinnett Street, Louisville Rd (Eastbound)
Lodg	N: Howard Johnson (see our ad this page)
37AB	**(166)** Martin Luther King Blvd, Montgomery St (Eastbound)
Gas	N: Enmark, Speedway[*]
Food	S: Burger King, Popeye's Chicken, Wendy's

↑GEORGIA

Begin I-16

I-17 S →

EXIT	ARIZONA
	Begin I-17

↓ARIZONA

EXIT	ARIZONA
341	McConnell Drive, Flagstaff (Northbound)
Gas	W: Chevron[*], Circle K[*], Mobil, Texaco[*]
Food	W: Coco's, Del Taco, Denny's, Fazoli's Italian Food, Olive Garden, Perkins Family Restaurant[24], Pizza Hut, Red Lobster, Ruby Lew's Home Cooking, Sizzler
Lodg	W: AmeriSuites (see our ad this page), EconoLodge, Fairfield Inn, Hampton Inn, Hilton, La Quinta Inn, Quality Inn
AServ	W: Mobil
ATM	W: Texaco
Other	E: **Northern Arizona University**
	W: **Big K-Mart**, Mountain Sports, **Wal-Mart**
340AB	East I-40 Winslow, Albuquerque, West I-40 Williams, Los Angeles
339	Lake Mary Rd, Mormon Lake (Northbound, Reaccess Northbound Only)
Gas	E: Texaco[*, LP]
Food	E: Texaco
337A	AZ 89A South, Old Creek Canyon, Pulliam Airport, Sedona
Parks	W: **Fort Tuthill Park**
Other	E: Pulliam Airport
333	Kachina Blvd, Mountainaire Rd
Gas	W: 76[*]
Food	W: Subway (76)
Parks	W: **Dr. R.O. Raymond County Park**[PLAY]
331	Kelly Canyon Rd
328	Newman Park Rd
326	Willard Springs Rd
(324)	**Rest Area (RR, Picnic, Ⓟ; Southbound)**
(324)	**Rest Area (RR, Picnic, Ⓟ; Northbound)**
322	Pinewood Blvd, Munds Park
Gas	E: Chevron[*, D, LP], Shell[*, D]
	W: Exxon[*, LP]
Food	E: Lone Pine Restaurant
Lodg	E: Motel In The Pines
AServ	E: Chevron
	W: Ye Old Town Garage
RVCamp	W: **Munds Park RV Campground (.1 Miles)**
ATM	E: Chevron, Shell
Other	E: **U.S. Post Office**
320	Schnebly Hill Rd
317	Fox Ranch Rd
315	Rocky Park Rd
(312)	**Scenic View (Southbound)**
306	Stoneman Lake Rd
Exit	**(300)** Runaway Truck Ramp (Southbound)
298	AZ 179 North, Sedona, Oak Creek Canyon
(296)	**Rest Area (Ⓟ; Southbound)**
(296)	**Rest Area (RR, HF, Picnic, Ⓟ; Northbound)**
293	Cornville, McGuireville, Montezuma Well, Lake Montezuma, Rimrock
Gas	E: Bever Creek
	W: 76[*, D]
Food	E: **Inge's McGuireville Cafe**
	W: **Beaver Hollow Cafe**
AServ	E: American Automotive, Bever Creek

EXIT	ARIZONA
289	Camp Verde, Middle Verde Rd, Camp Rd
RVCamp	E: **Krazy K RV Park (2 Miles)**
287	AZ 260, To AZ 89A, Cottonwood, Payson, Jerome-Clarkdale
Gas	E: Mobil[*, D], Texaco[*, D]
	W: Chevron[*, D]
Food	E: Baskin Robbins (Texaco), Blimpie Subs & Salads (Mobil), **Burger King**[PLAY], Dairy Queen, Denny's, **McDonald's**, Pizza Hut, Subway (Texaco), Taco Bell
Lodg	E: Comfort Inn, **Microtel Inn**, **Super 8**
RVCamp	E: **Crazy K RV Park**
Parks	E: **Fort Verde State Park (2 Miles)**
	W: **Dead Horse State Park (15 Miles)**, **Jerome State Park (22 Miles)**
Other	E: Montezuma's Castle (7 Miles), **Montezuma's Castle (Tourist Info)**
	W: Tuzigoot National Monument (16 Miles)
285	Gen. Crook Tr, Camp Verde
278	AZ 169, Cherry Rd, Prescott
268	Dugas Rd, Orme Rd
262AB	AZ 69 North, Cordes Junction Rd, Prescott, Acrosanti
FStop	E: **Texaco**[*, LP]
Gas	E: Chevron[*]
Food	E: **McDonald's**, **Subway (Texaco)**
	W: Papa's Place Steakhouse
Lodg	E: **Motel & RV Park**
AServ	E: **Texaco**
RVCamp	E: **Motel & RV Park**
ATM	E: **Texaco**
259	Bloody Basin Rd, Crown King
256	Badger Springs Rd
(252)	**Sunset Point Rest Area (RR, HF, Phones, Picnic, RV Dump, Ⓟ; Northbound)**
(252)	**Sunset Point Rest Area, Brake**

EXIT		ARIZONA
		Check Area (RR, HF, Phones, Picnic, Vending, RV Dump, Ⓟ; Southbound)
248		Bumble Bee
244		Bus Loop 17, Black Canyon City, Squaw Valley Rd, Dog Track Rd.
	Food	E: Squaw Peak Steakhouse
	ATM	E: Squaw Peak Steakhouse
242		Bus Loop 17, Rock Springs, Black Canyon City
	Gas	W: Chevron(*) (Towing)
	Food	W: Rock Springs Cafe
	RVCamp	E: KOA Campgrounds (.5 Miles)
	ATM	W: Rock Springs Cafe
236		Table Mesa Rd
232		New River
	Gas	E: Jack Ass Acres
	Other	W: Lake Pleasant
229		Desert Hills Rd
	Food	W: Arizona Factory Shops
	Other	W: Arizona Factory Shops
225		Pioneer Rd
	Food	W: Pioneer Cafe
	RVCamp	W: Pioneer RV Park
223		AZ 74, Carefree Hwy, Wickenburg
218		Happy Valley Rd
217		Pinnacle Peak Rd
	RVCamp	E: Phoenix Metro RV Park
217B		Deer Valley Rd., Rose Garden Lane
	FStop	W: Texaco(*, D, LP)
	Gas	E: Exxon(*, LP), Texaco(*, D) W: 76(*)
	Food	E: Burger King, McDonald's(PLAY), Wendy's W: Cracker Barrel, Denny's, Mia's Homestyle Restaurant & Lounge
	Lodg	W: Days Inn
	AServ	E: Anderson's Auto Service, Deer Valley Transmissions, Exxon, Firebird Tire Service, Gardener Foreign Car Repair, Lyons Auto Center, Sheps Automotive W: Foreign & Domestic Auto Repair, NAPA Auto Parts, Texaco
	RVCamp	E: Exxon, Leisure Time Services RV Rental

RAMADA PLAZA HOTEL

METROCENTER

12027 N. 28th Drive
Phoenix, AZ

602-866-7000 • 800-566-8535

- Restaurant/Lounge on Premises
- Outdoor Heated Pool • Exercise Room
- Convenient to Metrocenter, Golf, Tennis, Amusement Park, & Factory Outlet
- Pets Allowed • Interior Corridors
- Handicap Accessible
- Truck/Large Vehicle Parking
- Meeting/Banquet Facilities

1672

ARIZONIA • I-17 • Exit 209 (Catcus Rd.)

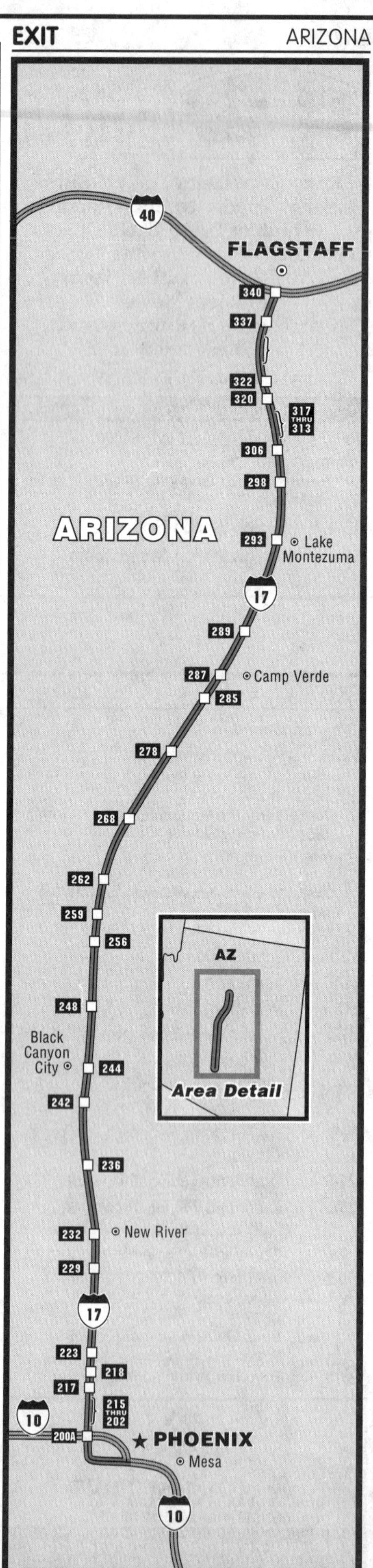

EXIT		ARIZONA
	Other	W: Grime Stop(CW)
217A		Rose Garden Lane (Northbound)
215		AZ Loop 101 (Limited Access Highway)
	RVCamp	E: AmeriGas/Deer Valley Exxon(LP) (.3 Miles)
214AB		Yorkshire Dr, Union Hills Dr
	Gas	E: 76(*), Diamond Shamrock(*) W: Arco(*, 24)
	Lodg	W: Homestead Village, Sleep Inn, Wyndham Garden Hotel
	RVCamp	E: Desert Shadows Travel Trailer Resort (.5 Miles)
	Med	W: ✚ John C. Lincoln Hospital (.5 Miles)
	ATM	E: Diamond Shamrock
212AB		Bell Rd, Racetrack, Sun City
	Gas	E: Exxon(LP) W: 76 (Danny's Family Car Wash), Mobil(*, CW)
	Food	E: Coco's Bakery & Restaurant, Waffle House W: Applebee's, Chill Out Yogurt, Denny's, Fran's Deli & Coffee, Hometown Buffet, Hooter's, Kyoto Bowl (Japanese), Native New Yorker, Que Pasa (Mexican), Santisi Bros. Pizzeria, Sizzler Steak House, Sub Factory & Pizza
	Lodg	E: Best Western, Fairfield Inn, Motel 6 W: Red Roof Inn
	AServ	E: Bell Lexus, Ford, Big O Tires, Exxon, Midway Chev, Isuzu, Geo W: Danny's Family Car Wash(CW) (76)
	ATM	W: Hooter's, M & I Thunderbird Bank, Smitty's One Stop Shop
	Other	W: Albertson's Grocery(RX), Danny's Family Car Wash (76), Mr. Books, Pak Mail, Popular Outdoor Outfitters, Sam's Club, Smitty's One Stop Shop, Super Saver Cinema 8
211		Greenway Rd
	Lodg	E: Embassey Suites, La Quinta Inn
	Med	E: ✚ Deer Valley Medical Center
	ATM	E: 7-11 Convenience Store
	Other	E: 7-11 Convenience Store
210AB		Thunderbird Rd
	Gas	E: 76(*) W: Exxon
	Food	E: Barro's Pizza, Magic Bowl Chinese, Wendy's
	AServ	E: Jiffy Lube W: Exxon
	ATM	E: 76
	Other	E: Home Depot, WalGreens Pharmacy(RX) W: Deer Valley Lanes
209		Cactus Rd
	Gas	W: Chevron, Citgo(*)
	Food	W: Anzio's Italian Restaurant, Blimpie Subs & Salads (The Brass Armadillo), Cousins' Sub's, Denny's, Oliva's Mexican, Shangri-La
	Lodg	W: Ramada Plaza (see our ad this page)
	AServ	W: Chevron, Tire Outlet
	ATM	W: Bashas' Grocery
	Other	W: Bashas' Grocery, Royal Pet Boutique, Supermat Laundromat, The Bent Cover Bookstore, The Brass Armadillo Antique Mall
208		Peoria Ave
	Gas	W: Mobil(LP)
	Food	W: Bennigan's, Black Angus Steakhouse, Burger King, China Inn, Coco's Bakery & Restaurant, El Torito (Mexican), Islands Hamburgers, Kiawe Grill, Mamma Mia Ristorante (Italian), Peter Piper Pizza, The Olive Garden, Whataburger, Wyndham Metrocenter Hotel
	Lodg	E: Amerisuites (see our ad this page), Comfort Suites Hotel, Crowne Plaza Hotel, Homewood Suites Hotel W: Premier Inns, Wyndham Metrocenter Hotel
	AServ	W: Fletcher's Auto Service, Master Care Auto Service, Mobil, Q-Lube
	ATM	W: Bank of America

Bold red print shows RV & Bus parking available or nearby

EXIT ARIZONA

Other **E:** Rose Moffard Sports Complex
W: **Barnes & Noble Booksellers**, Petco, Staple's Office Superstore

207 Dunlap Ave
Gas **E:** 76(*, D)
W: Exxon(*, CW)
Food **E:** Blimpie Subs & Salads, Fuddruckers
W: Denny's, Schlotzsky's Deli, Subway
Lodg **E:** Sheraton, TraveLodge
AServ **E:** AAMCO Transmission
W: Midas Muffler, Mr. Clutch
Med **E:** **+ Dunlap Medical**
ATM **W:** Exxon
Other **W:** America's Best Contacts & Eyeglasses, Castle's Coasters Golf & Arcade, International Golf Discount, Metro Center Shopping Mall, Office Max, **Toys R Us**

206 Northern Ave
Gas **E:** Exxon
Food **E:** Burger King, Denny's, Los Compadres (Mexican), Marie Callender's (Buffet)
W: Dairy Queen, Furrs Cafeteria, New Yorker Family Restaurant, Village Inn Restaurant, Winchells Donuts
Lodg **E:** Hampton Inn
W: Motel 6, Travelers Inn
AServ **E:** Exxon
W: **Big K-Mart(RX)**
ATM **E:** Wells Fargo Bank
Other **E:** **Desert Dave Books**, Eye Clinic for Animals
W: **Big K-Mart(RX)**, Car Wash, **Northern Animal Hospital**

205 Glendale Ave
Gas **E:** Gas(*)
W: 76(*), **Exxon(*, D, LP)**
Food **E:** Q's BBQ & Pit Stop, The Question Soul Food
W: Abalberto's (Mexican), Jack-In-The-Box, Mexico Lindo
AServ **E:** Auto Electric of Arizona, Sun Transmission
W: Checkers Auto Parts, Dynamite Tire Co., Herb's Garage, I-17 Body Shop Collision
RVCamp **W:** **Covered Wagon RV Park (.5 Miles)**
ATM **W:** 7-11 Convenience Store(24), 76
Other **E:** Car Wash, Circle K(*, LP), **Emergency Animal Clinic**
W: 7-11 Convenience Store, Acme Cycle, B & D Motorcycle Service, Pueblo Coin-Op Laundry(24)

204 Bethany Home Rd.
Gas **E:** 76(*, LP), Arco(*)
W: Exxon
Food **E:** Brad's Fish & Chips, Isberto's Mexican Food, McDonald's(PLAY)
W: Burger King, Chu's Cathay (Chinese), Joe's Coffee Shop, Pier De'Orleans Steaks, Pizza Wings & Things, The Bagel Hut
AServ **W:** Jake's Auto Service, Japanese Engines, Lee Myles Transmissions, Q-Lube, Southwest Emission Repairs, Tune Up While You Wait
RVCamp **W:** **RV Park (.5 Miles)**
Med **E:** **+ Pheonix Baptist Hospital**
ATM **E:** Arco
Other **E:** Bethany West Laundromat
W: Bethany West Kennels, Car Wash Company(CW), Savers The Thrift Dept. Store, **Southwest Supermarkets**, Super Kleen Laundry, The Laundry Basket

203 Camelback Rd.
Gas **W:** Mobil, **Texaco(*)**
Food **E:** Burger King, Country Boys Restaurant(24), Denny's
W: European Bistro Restaurant, Jack in the Box, McDonald's Express, Taco Bell, Treulich's
Lodg **W:** **Comfort Inn**
AServ **E:** Bill Luke Chrys, Plym, Jeep, Eagle, Dodge, Childress Buick, KIA, Discount Tire Company, NAPA Auto Parts
W: Lou Grubb Chevrolet, Mobil, **Texaco**, Town & Country Detail Center
RVCamp **W:** **Amerigas/Stahl's Camelback & Fwy Texaco(LP)**, **Texaco**, **Welcome Home RV Park**
Med **E:** **+ Phoenix Baptist Hospital**

202 Indian School Rd
Gas **E:** Arco(*)
W: Texaco(*)
Food **E:** Filiberto's Mexican
W: Burger Town, Hunter Steakhouse, J.B.'s Restaurant, Marisco's Ensenada, Wendy's
Lodg **W:** Motel 6, Super 8
AServ **E:** Arizona & Collision, Engine House
W: Texaco
RVCamp **E:** **Arizona Trailer Sales**, **Little Dealers World Of Shells & Campers**
ATM **E:** Arco
W: 7-11 Convenience Store
Other **E:** AMF Thunderbird Lanes
W: 7-11 Convenience Store

201 To U.S. 60 West, Thomas Rd
Gas **E:** Chevron(*)
Food **E:** Arby's, Denny's, Jack-In-The-Box(24), McDonald's (Chevron), Roman's Pizza, Taco Bell
W: Burger King
Lodg **E:** Days Inn, E-Z In Motel, **La Quinta Inn**
AServ **E:** Just Brakes
W: Phoenix International Body & Paint
RVCamp **W:** **Pecan Grove (.75 Miles)**
Other **E:** Circle K(*), Petco, Phoenix Fire Station

200A Jct. I-10 Tucson, Los Angeles
200B McDowell Rd, VanBuren St.
Food **W:** Whatasub
AServ **E:** **Asco Parts, Truck & Trailer Service(24)**, Purcell's Western States Tires
TServ **E:** **Asco Parts, Truck & Trailer Service(24)**
W: **Southwest Peterbilt, GMC Trucks**
Other **W:** Chip's Machine Shop Service

199B State Capitol, Jefferson St., Adams St, Van Buren St.
Gas **E:** Circle K(*)
W: Circle K(*)
Food **E:** Jack-In-The-Box
W: Asia Express, Burger Shop, Pete's Fish & Chips
Lodg **E:** Coconut Grove Motel, K Motel
AServ **W:** Bill's Radiator, Penny Pincher Auto Parts, Pep Boys Auto Center
TServ **W:** **Truck Stuff**
ATM **E:** Bank One
Other **W:** **Southwest Grocery Store**

199A Grant, Buckeye Rd.
AServ **E:** Victor's Auto Service
W: Ron's Used Pick Up Parts
RVCamp **W:** **Joplin RV Sales**

198 Buckeye Rd
Food **E:** Horseshoe Restaurant
AServ **E:** **Arizona Auto & Truck**, Arizona Auto Parts, Rogelio's Auto Repair (American/Japanese)
TServ **E:** **Arrow Truck Sales**, **Carrillo's Truck Parts**, **Donaldson Equipment Sales & Salvage**, **United Truck & Equipment Water Trucks**

197 19th Ave, Durango St, State Capitol, U.S. 60
FStop **E:** **FoodFuel(*)**
Food **E:** Whataburger(24)
AServ **E:** AAA Recon Transmissions Etc.
TServ **E:** **Intech Equipment & Supply(LP)**
W: **Arizona Truck & Trailer**, **Arizona Truck Center**, **Williams Detroit Diesel**
ATM **E:** **FoodFuel**
Other **E:** State Capitol

196 7th Ave, Central Ave
Food **E:** Burger King

195B 7th St, Central Ave.
FStop **E:** **Pacific Pride Commercial Fueling (Credit)**
Gas **E:** Exxon(*, LP, 24)
Food **E:** Diamond Plate Restaurant (E-Z 8 Motel), McDonald's(PLAY), Samyra's Restaurant, Taco Bell(24)
Lodg **E:** **E-Z 8 Motel**
AServ **E:** Burley's Service, P & M Tire Service, Ramon's Auto Repair
TServ **E:** **Arizona Truck & Equipment Repair**
RVCamp **E:** **Desert West Coach**
ATM **E:** Exxon

195A 16th St.
Other **W:** State of Arizona Dept. of Public Safety

194 I-10 West Sky Harbor International Airport, To AZ 51, Squaw Peak Pkwy (Southbound)

↑ARIZONA

Begin I-17

Bold red print shows RV & Bus parking available or nearby

EXIT ARIZONA

Begin I-19

↓ARIZONA

99 AZ 86, Ajo Way
- **Gas** E: Shell[*]
  W: Chevron
- **Food** E: Eegee's, La Bella China Restaurant, Original Hamburger Stand, Subway, Taco Bell
- **AServ** E: El Campo Tire Center
- **RVCamp** W: **Rincon Country West (1 Mile)**
- **ATM** E: Bank 1, Norwest Bank, Wells Fargo
- **Other** E: Fry's Food & Drug, Nationwide Vision Center, Ocso Drug, Santa Cruz Lanes, U.S. Post Office
  W: **Desert Museum Old Tucson**, **Santa Cruz River Park**

98 Irvington Rd.
- **Gas** E: Arco[*]
- **Food** E: Little Mexico
  W: McDonald's[PLAY]
- **AServ** E: Sonora Motors Inc., Super Wash
- **ATM** E: Arco, **Smith's Food & Drug[RX]**
- **Parks** W: **Santa Cruz River Park**
- **Other** E: **Smith's Food & Drug[RX]**
  W: Home Depot

95A Valencia Rd. East, Tucson Int. Airport

95B Valencia Rd. West

92 San Xavier Rd.

87 Papago Rd.

80 Pima Mine Rd.

75 Helmet Peak Rd.

69 Bus 19 N. Duval Mine Rd., Sahuarita
- **Gas** W: 76[*, D, CW]
- **Food** E: Denny's, Pizza Hut, Subway
  W: Arby's, Burger King, Dairy Queen (76), Green Valley Lanes
- **Lodg** W: Holiday Inn Express
- **AServ** W: 76, Big O Tires, Jim Click Ford Mercury Lincoln, Super Wash
- **RVCamp** W: **Greenvalley RV Resort**
- **ATM** E: World Savings
  W: 76, Green Valley Lanes
- **Other** E: **Basha's Grocery**, Multiplex Theater, **Wal-Mart**
  W: Green Valley Lanes

65 Esperanza Blvd., Green Valley
- **Gas** E: Texaco[*]
  W: Exxon[*, LP]
- **Food** W: Arizona Family Restaurant, Armando's Italian, China View, Kelly's Ice Cream & Yogurt, Old Chicago Deli
- **Lodg** W: Best Western
- **AServ** E: Texaco
  W: Exxon
- **ATM** W: Arizona Bank, Bank Of America, Bank One, **WalGreens Pharmacy**
- **Other** W: ABCO Foods[CW], Budget Rent-A-Car, Green Valley Mall, Green Valley Vision, **WalGreens Pharmacy**

63 Continental Rd.
- **Gas** W: Exxon[*] (Hot Stuff Pizza)
- **Food** E: **Madera Canyon**
  W: China Vic, Exxon (Hot Stuff Pizza), **Java-Lena Coffee & Expresso**, KFC, Kelly's Ice Cream, Mama's Kitchen, McDonald's, Mesquite Willy's, Safeway Grocery, Taco Bell
- **Lodg** E: **Madera Canyon**
- **AServ** W: Exxon (Hot Stuff Pizza), Fletcher's Auto Service
- **ATM** W: Arizona Bank, Bank One, Bank of America, Commercial Federal Bank, Norwest Bank, Safeway Grocery, State Savings Bank, Wells Fargo Bank
- **Other** E: **Madera Canyon, US Post Office**
  W: Book Store, Mailboxes Etc., Pacific Century Savings Bank, Your Cleaners

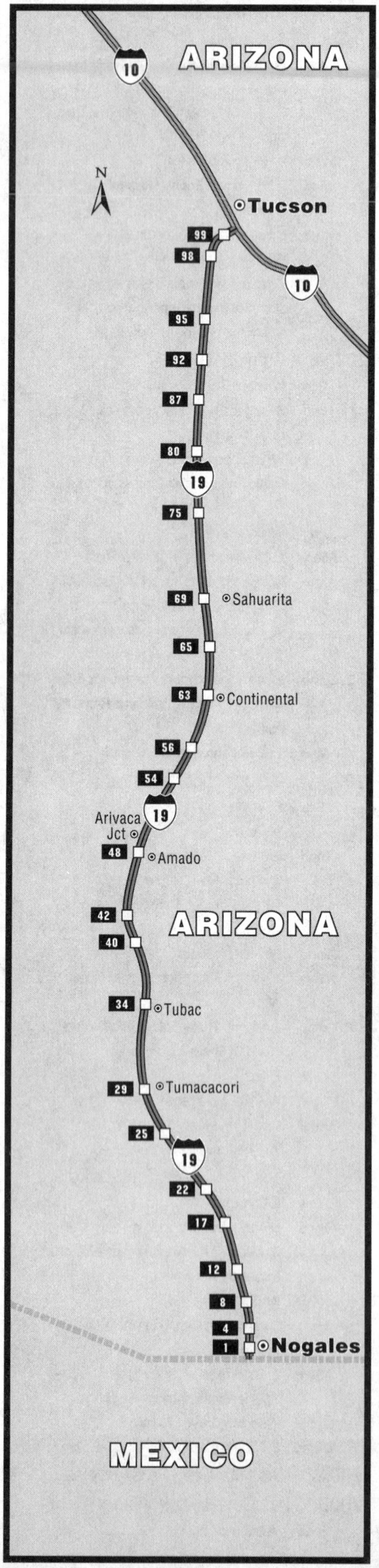

EXIT ARIZONA

EXIT ARIZONA

56 Canoa Rd.

(54) **Rest Area (RR, Phones, Picnic, P)**

48 Arivaca Rd., Amado
- **Gas** W: Amado Market
- **Food** W: Amado's Pizza, Cow Palace, Longhorn Grill
- **Lodg** E: Amado Inn (Cafe)
- **RVCamp** E: **Mountain View RV Park (1.75 Miles)**
- **Other** W: Amado Market, Laundry Mat, U.S. Post Office

42 Agua Linda Rd., Amado

40 Chavez Siding., Tubac

34 Tubac
- **Other** E: **Tubac Presidio State Park**

29 Tumacacori Carmen
- **Other** E: **Tumacacori National Historical Park**

25 Palo Parado Rd.

22 Peck Canyon Rd.

17 Rio Rico Dr., Yavapai Dr.
- **Gas** W: Chevron[*]
- **Food** W: The Bandits Rendezvous
- **Lodg** W: Rio Rico Resort
- **AServ** W: Chevron
- **ATM** W: Bank Of America, Garrett's Supermarket
- **Other** W: Garrett's Supermarket, **Rio Rico Laundry Mat**

12 AR. 289, Ruby Rd

8 NM82 Bus. Loop 19, Nogales (Left Exit Westbound, Reaccess Northbound Only, Difficult Reaccess)
- **RVCamp** E: **Mi Casa**

4 AZ189, Mariposa Rd., Mexico Truck Route
- **Gas** E: 76[*, D], Chevron[*, D]
  W: **Shell[*]**
- **Food** E: Arby's, **Barrow's (Super 8)**, China Star, Dairy Queen (Chevron), Formosa, KFC, **McDonald's[PLAY]**, Yokohama Rice Bowl
  W: **Carl Jr's Hamburgers**, Famous Fan's Fun Food & Spirits
- **Lodg** E: **Super 8**
- **AServ** W: Ed Moses Chrysler Dealer
- **ATM** E: Bank 1, Bank of America, Norwest Bank, **Safeway Grocery**
  W: **Shell**
- **Other** E: **K-Mart**, Mariposa Mall, **Safeway Grocery**, **Veterans Market Grocery**, **Wal-Mart**, **WalGreens Pharmacy**

1 Western Ave., Nogales
- **Med** W: **+ Carondelet Holy Cross Hospital**
- **Other** E: **Coin Laundry**

↑ARIZONA

Begin I-19

Bold red print shows RV & Bus parking available or nearby

EXIT TEXAS

Begin I-20

↓TEXAS

3 Stocks Road

7 Johnson Road

13 McAlpine Road

22 Fm2903, Toyah
- TStop N: Toyah Auto/Truck Stop[*, 24]
- Gas S: Texaco[*, D]
- Food N: Roses, Toyah Auto/Truck Stop
- TServ N: Toyah Auto/Truck Stop[24]
  S: Pete's Garage and Tire Service
- Other N: U.S. Post Office

(25) Picnic Area (Picnic, P; Eastbound)

(25) Parking Area (Picnic, P; Westbound)

29 Shaw Road

33 Fm869

37 Bus20E, Pecos

39 TX17, Fort Davis, Balmorhea
- AServ N: Eagle Tire Service
- TServ S: C&L Deisel, Truck Repair and Engine Service
- Med N: ✚ Hospital
- Other N: Depot 2 Grocery & Deli

40 Country Club Dr, Pecos (Difficult Reaccess)
- Gas S: Chevron[*]
- Food S: Alpine Lodge (Best Western), Subway (Chevron)
- Lodg S: Best Western
- AServ S: GM, Chevrolet, Buick
- RVCamp S: Trapark RV Park (1.5 Miles)
- Parks S: Maxey Park
- Other N: Dept. Of Public Safety

42 U.S. 285, Carlsbad, Fort Stockton
- TStop N: Flying J Travel Plaza[*, RV DUMP, SCALES]
- Gas N: Exxon[D], Texaco[*, D]
- Food N: McDonald's, Purple Sage Restaurant (Quality Inn), The Cookery (Flying J)
- Lodg N: Motel 6, Quality Inn
- AServ N: Custom Muffler & Lube[LP], Exxon
  S: Hecktor's Tire & Wrecker Service[24]
- TServ N: Flying J Travel Plaza[SCALES]
- ATM N: Flying J Travel Plaza
- Other N: Wal-Mart

44 Pecos, Collie Rd

49 Fm516, Barstow

52 Barstow, Bus20W

58 Frontage Road

66 Fm1927, TX115, Pyote, Kermit
- Gas N: Pyote Grocery & Gas[*]
- Other N: U.S. Post Office

(69) Rest Area (RR, Picnic, P; Eastbound)

(69) Rest Area (RR, Picnic, P; Westbound)

70 Spur65

73 Fm1219, Wickett
- TStop S: National Truck Stop[*, D]
- FStop N: Fina[*]
- Food S: National Truck Stop
- AServ S: Jim's Auto & Truck Repair
- TServ N: Tire Shop
  S: Jim's Auto & Truck Repair
- ATM N: Fina

EXIT TEXAS

- S: National Truck Stop

76 Bus20E, Monahans

79 Loop464

80 TX18, Kermit, Fort Stockton
- FStop N: Exxon[*]
  S: Fina[*], Phillips 66[*, LP]
- Gas N: Chevron[*, D, 24]
  S: Diamond Shamrock[*], Texaco
- Food N: Dairy Queen[PLAY], McDonald's[PLAY]
  S: Country Kitchen (Fina), Taco Bell (Fina)
- Lodg S: Best Western, Texan Inn
- AServ N: Exxon
  S: Dempseys Auto Repair, Southwest Transmission, Texaco
- ATM S: Diamond Shamrock, Fina
- Other N: Alco, Lowe's Foods[RX], Ted's Car Wash
  S: U Haul Rental

83 Bus20 W, Monahans

86 TX41, Monahans Sandhill State Park

93 Fm1053, Ft. Stockton

101 Fm1601, Penwell
- TStop S: Texas Interstate Truck Stop[*]
- Food S: Country Kitchen Cafe (TStop)
- TServ S: Penwell Enterprises, Texas Interstate Truck Stop

(103) Parking Area (Eastbound)

(103) Parking Area (Westbound)

(104) Weigh Station (Available Both Directions)

104 Fm866, FM 1936, Goldsmith, Meteor Crater Road

112 Fm1936, Odessa, Bus. Loop 20 (Difficult Reaccess)
- FStop N: Citgo[*]

113 TX302, Loop338, Kermit, Meteor Crater Road

115 Fm1882, County Road W
- Gas N: Fina[*]
- Food N: Country Kitchen (Fina)
- TServ N: Five Star Diesel Repair
- Other N: Texas Department Of Public Safety

116 U.S. 385, Andrews, Crane
- FStop S: Phillips 66[*]
- Gas N: Chevron[*, D, 24], Town & Country[*]
  S: Texaco[*]
- Food N: Country Kitchen (Town & Country), Dairy Queen, La Margarita, La Union Tortilla
- Lodg N: Best Western, EconoLodge, Villa West Inn
  S: Motel 6
- AServ N: Superior Auto & Truck Repair
- TServ N: Superior Auto & Truck Repair
- RVCamp S: Billy Sims Trailer Town
- Med N: ✚ Hospital
- ATM N: Chevron, Town & Country
  S: Phillips 66
- Parks N: Comanche Trail Park

118 Fm 3503, Grandview Ave
- Gas N: Shell[*]
- TServ N: Cummins Diesel (.2 Miles), Freightliner of Odessa, Harbison-Fisher, Kirkland Bros., West Texas Peterbilt-Odessa
- RVCamp N: Cummins Diesel (.2 Miles), I-20 Sales & Service, Miller's RV Specialists
- ATM N: Shell

121 Loop 338, Odessa

126 Fm1788, Midland Int Airport
- TStop N: Warfield Truck Terminal[*, CW, SCALES, 24]

EXIT TEXAS

- Gas N: Chevron[*, 24], Fina[*, D]
- Food N: Warfield Truck Terminal
- TServ N: Warfield Truck Terminal[SCALES, 24]
- TWash N: Warfield Truck Terminal[CW]
- RVCamp N: KOA-Midessa (1.5 Miles)
- ATM N: Fina
- Other N: Confederate Air Force Museum

131 Loop 250, TX158
- Lodg N: TraveLodge
- RVCamp N: Midland RV Campground (1.5 Miles)

134 Midkiff Road
- FStop N: Chevron[*, D, 24] (Gas Card Fueling), Texaco[*]
  S: Patriot Oil[*, D, 24]
- Food N: Subway (Chevron)
- RVCamp N: Bo's RV Center
- ATM N: Chevron (Gas Card Fueling)

136 TX349, Rankin, Lamesa
- FStop N: Phillips 66[*] (Pacific Pride Commericial Fueling)
  S: Eddins-Walcher[D, LP], Exxon[*]
- Gas N: Shell[*]
  S: Chevron[*, D], Fina[*]
- Food N: McDonald's[PLAY], Sonic Drive In
  S: Burger King (Exxon), Country Kitchen (Fina)
- Lodg N: Comfort Inn, Super 8
- AServ S: Chevron
- ATM N: Fiesta Foods[RX], Shell
  S: Exxon, Fina
- Other N: Fiesta Foods[RX]

137 Old Lamesa Rd.

138 TX158, Greenwood, Garden City, Fm715
- FStop N: Eddins-Walcher[LP], Frank's Fuel, Texaco[*]
  S: Fina[*]
- Gas N: Phillips 66[*]
- Food N: KD's BBQ, Phillips 66, Whataburger
  S: Country Kitchen (Fina), Taco Bell (Fina)
- AServ N: Big 3 Tire And Automotive Center
- ATM S: Fina

(141) Rest Area (RV Dump, P; Eastbound)

(142) Rest Area (RV Dump, P; Westbound)

143 Frontage Road (Eastbound)

144 Bus20, Midland, TX 250 Loop

151 Fm829

154 Bus. 20, Stanton

156 TX137, Stanton, Lamesa
- TStop S: Diamond Shamrock[*, D]
- FStop S: Fina[*, LP]
- Gas N: Chevron[*]
  S: Exxon[*, D, LP]
- Food N: Guys (Chevron)
  S: Country Kitchen (Diamond Shamrock), Dairy Queen, Subway (Diamond Shamrock)
- AServ S: Exxon
- Med S: ✚ Hospital
- ATM S: Diamond Shamrock, Exxon, Midland American Bank

158 Loop154, Stanton, BUS20W

165 Fm 818

(167) Picnic Area (Picnic; Eastbound)

(168) Picnic Area (Picnic; Westbound)

169 Fm 2599

171 Moore Field Road

172 Cauble Road

174 Bus 20E, Big Spring

EXIT	TEXAS
Gas	S: Exxon(*)
Med	S: Hospital
Parks	S: Big Spring McMahon Wrinkle Air Park
Other	S: Airport
176	Andrews, Link TX 176
177	U.S. 87, San Angelo, Lamesa
TStop	N: Rip Griffin Travel Center(*, SCALES)
FStop	S: Chevron(*)
Gas	N: Exxon(*, D)
	S: Fina(*, CW)
Food	N: Burger King (Exxon), Country Fare (Rip Griffen), Subway (Rip Griffen), Sunrise Grill (EconoLodge)
	S: Casa Blanca, Country Kitchen (Chevron), Dairy Queen, McDonald's(PLAY), Sub City (Chevron)
Lodg	N: Best Western, EconoLodge, Motel 6
TServ	N: Rip Griffin Travel Center(SCALES)
	S: Don's Tire & Truck Repair, Quality Truck Tires
Med	N: Hospital
ATM	N: Exxon, Rip Griffin Travel Center
	S: Chevron
178	TX350, Snyder
Gas	N: Texaco(*, D)
179	Bus. 20 W., Big Spring (Watch for One Way Streets)
Gas	S: Fina(*), T&T Hickory House BBQ, Texaco(*)
Food	S: College Park Cafe, Dairy Queen, Dell's Cafe, Denny's(24)
Lodg	S: Comfort Inn, Days Inn, Super 7 Motel
ATM	S: Fina
Other	S: College Automatic Laundry, Price Fyghter
181A	FM 700, Airport
AServ	N: Big Springs Auto Electric
RVCamp	N: Hillside RV Park
Med	S: Hospital
Other	S: Big Spring Airport
181B	Refinery Road
Parks	N: Big Springs State Park
182	Midway Road
RVCamp	S: Suburban East RV & Mobile Park (.5 Miles)
184	Moss Lake Road, Sand Springs
Gas	N: Phillips 66(*, D, LP), Texaco(*, D)
	S: Lakeway Grocery(*)
Food	S: Lakeway Grocery
RVCamp	S: Suburban East RV & Mobile Park (1.25 Miles), Whip-In Campground
186	Salem Road, Sand Spring
188	FM 820, Coahoma Road
Gas	N: Chevron(*), Fina(D, CW), Fowler's
Food	N: Dairy Queen
Lodg	N: Motel
AServ	N: Fowler's, Multi-Mile Tires, Robert's Auto Service
TServ	N: Clausen Truck Service
ATM	N: Chevron, First Bank of West Texas
Other	N: Car Wash, Little Sooper Market, U.S. Post Office
189	McGregor Road
190	Snyder Field Road
191	Rest Area (RR, Phones, Picnic, P; Eastbound)
192	FM 821
194A	East Howard Field Road
194B	Frontage Rd
195	Frontage Road
199	Latan Rd.
200	Conaway Road
(204)	Rest Area (RR, Phones, Picnic, P; Westbound)
206	FM 670, Westbrook, Bus. Loop 20
FStop	N: Citgo(*)
207	Bus. 20
Gas	S: Conoco(*, D)
209	Born Road
210	FM 2836
Gas	S: Fina(*, D)
Parks	S: Lake Colorado City State Park (6 Miles)
212	FM 1229
213	Bus20E, Colorodo City
215	FM 3525, 80 John Wallace Unit, Dick Ware Unit
216	TX 208 N, Snyder, Colorado City
FStop	N: Chevron(*)
Gas	N: Exxon(*, D), Texaco(*), Texaco(*)
	S: Henderson's(*), Phillips 66(*, D)
Food	N: Dairy Queen(PLAY), McDonald's (Exxon), Subway (Chevron), Texaco
	S: Burger King(PLAY) (Phillips 66), Henderson's, Pizza Hut, Sonic Drive In, USA Burritos, Villa Inn Motel, Villa Restaurant (Villa Inn)
Lodg	N: Days Inn
	S: Villa Inn Motel
AServ	N: Cooper Tires
Med	S: Hospital
ATM	N: Exxon
	S: First Bank of West Texas, First National Bank, Phillips 66
Other	S: Alco, Big A Auto Parts, Coin Car Wash, Sheets Eye Clinic, The Medicine Place(RX)
217	TX 208 S, San Angelo
TStop	S: Homeward Bound(*)
Food	N: Platter Restaurant
	S: Collum's Restaurant, Feed Store BBQ, Ft. Wood Cafe, Homeward Bound
AServ	S: Homeward Bound
TServ	S: Homeward Bound
RVCamp	S: Camping
Other	S: Matlock Farm Supply and Butane Services(LP)
219A	Country Club Rd
219B	Bus. 20 W., Colorado City (Southbound)
220	FM1899
221	Lasky Road
223	Lucas Road
224	Bus. 20, Lorraine
225	FM 644
226A	Fm644N
226B	Bus Loop 20, Loraine
227	Narrell Road
(228)	Picnic Area (Picnic, P; Eastbound)
(229)	Picnic Area (Picnic, P; Westbound)
230	FM 1230
235	Bus. 20, Roscoe
TStop	S: Truck & Travel Stop(*, SCALES) (ATM)
Food	S: Truck & Travel Stop (ATM)
AServ	S: Truck & Travel Stop (ATM)
TServ	S: Truck & Travel Stop(SCALES) (ATM)
236	FM 608, Roscoe
Gas	N: Conoco(*), Texaco(*, D, LP), Town & Country(*, D)
Food	N: Country Kitchen (Town & Country)
	S: Dairy Queen
AServ	N: Langston Automotive
ATM	N: Conoco, Town & Country
Other	S: Audio Plus CB Radio Repairs and Sales
237	Cemetery Road
238A	U.S. 84W, Roscoe, Lubbock, Snyders
238B	Blackland Road
238C	Frontage Rd.
239	May Road
Other	S: A-1 Auto Parts
240	TX170, City Airport, 170 loop
241	Bus. 20, Sweetwater
242	Hopkins Road
TStop	S: T/A TravelCenters of America(*, SCALES)
Food	S: Chester Fried Chicken (TA), Country Pride

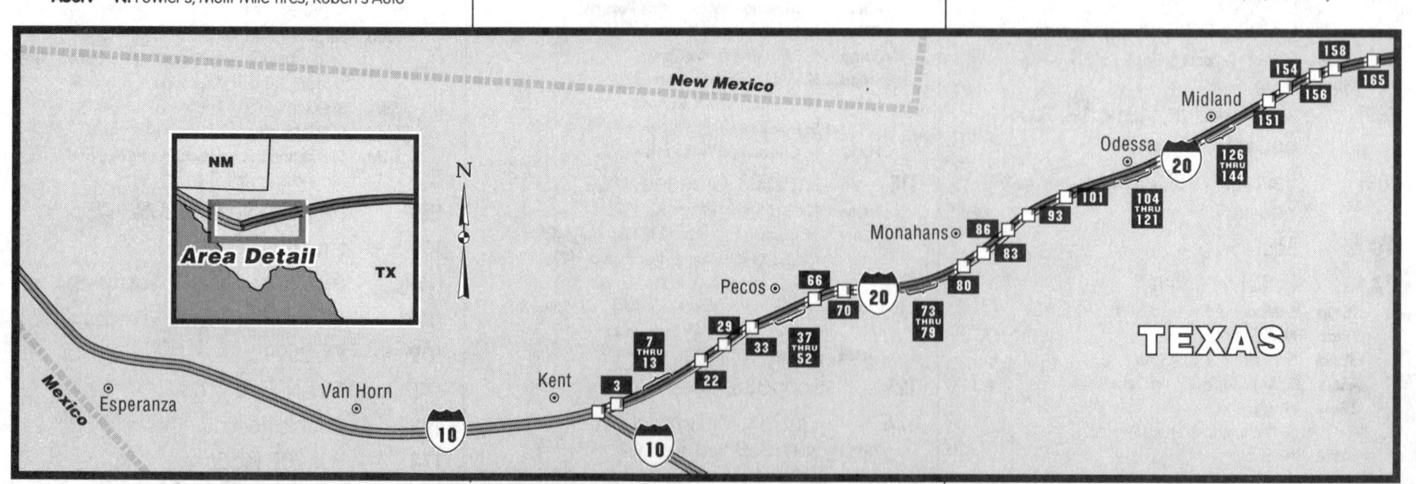

Bold red print shows RV & Bus parking available or nearby

EXIT — TEXAS

(TA), Pizza Hut (TA)
TServ **S:** Cummins Diesel, Jim's Truck and Alignment Service, T/A TravelCenters of America(SCALES)
TWash **S:** I-20 Truck Wash
ATM **S:** T/A TravelCenters of America

243 Robert Lee St., Hillsdale Road
RVCamp **N:** Bewley's RV Service
Other **N:** Bentley RV Service

244 TX 70 S., TX 70 Bus., Sweetwater, San Angelo
FStop **N:** Fina(*)
Gas **N:** Diamond Shamrock(*, D), Fina(*, D, 24), Texaco(*, D)
S: Chevron(*), Fina(*), Texaco(*, D)
Food **N:** Buck's Steaks and BBQ, Buck's Steaks and BBQ, Dairy Queen, Kettle, McDonald's(PLAY)
S: Buck's Steaks and BBQ, Golden Fried Chicken, Jack's Family Steak House, Ranch House Motel, Roadhouse Cafe (Best Western), Schlotzsky's Deli, TCBY, Taco Bell
Lodg **N:** Holiday Inn (see our ad this page), Motel 6, Sweetwater Inn
S: Best Western, Comfort Inn, Ranch House Motel
AServ **N:** Bledsoe Ford, Diamond Shamrock
S: Toliver Auto Plaza Chevrolet, Pontiac, Oldsmobile, Buick
RVCamp **N:** Mobile Park, Sweetwater RV Park
S: Chabarral, Sweetwater RV Park
Med **N:** ✚ Rolling Plains Memorial Hospital
ATM **S:** Fina, First National Bank, Texaco
Other **S:** Holiday Bowl, IGA Store, K-Mart, Laser Wash, Lawrence Supermarket

245 Arizona Ave.

246 Alabama Ave

247 Bus. 20, TX 70 N., Sweetwater, Roby

249 FM1856

251 Eskota Road

255 Adrian Road

256 Stink Creek Road

(257) Rest Area (RR, Phones, P; Westbound)

(257) Rest Area (RR, Phones, P; Eastbound)

258 White Flat Road

259 Sylvester Road

261 Bus.20, Trent
FStop **N:** Texaco(*)
AServ **N:** Texaco

262 FM 1085
FStop **S:** Fina(*, D)
AServ **N:** Lindsey Garage(24)

263 Bus.20

264 Noodle Dome Road

266 Derstine Road

267 Bus. 20, Merkel

269 FM 126
FStop **S:** Fina(*, 24)
Gas **S:** Lawrence Brothers(*), Texaco(*, D)
Food **N:** Bizkits Grill, Subway
S: Dairy Queen, Merkle Motel, Mesquite Bean Barbeque, Mr. G's Pizza
Lodg **N:** Save Inn
S: Merkle Motel
AServ **S:** Badger Lube(CW), Merkle Auto Service, Texaco, Tra-Tech Auto Center
Other **S:** Coin Operated Car Wash, Coin Operated Laundry, Lemens LP Gas(LP)

270 Bus. 20, FM 1235, Merkel
TStop **N:** Wiley's Texaco(*)
FStop **N:** Texaco(*)
Gas **N:** Diamond Shamrock(*)
Food **N:** Texaco, Wiley's Texaco
TServ **N:** I-20 Tire Service for Trucks and Cars
TWash **S:** Truck & Car Wash(CW)
ATM **N:** Diamond Shamrock, Texaco

272 Wimberly Road

274 Wells Lane

277 FM 707, Bus. 20, Tye
TStop **N:** Flying J Travel Plaza(*, LP, SCALES)
Gas **S:** Fina(*), Texaco(*, D)
Food **N:** Country Market & Cafe (Flying J), Magic Dragon (Flying J), Pepperoni's the Superslice (Flying J)
AServ **S:** Texaco

Newly Renovated

I-20 • Exit 244
500 Georgia Street
Sweetwater, TX
915-236-6887
24 Hour Restaurant & Lounge
25" Color TV w/Free HBO
Outdoor Pool • Coin Laundry
AAA, AARP, Special Tour Group Rates
Large Area for Truck/RV Parking
Easy Access to I-20
1142
TEXAS ▪ I-20 ▪ Exit 244

1139
RAMADA INN®
3450 South Clack • Abilene, Texas
147 Beautifully Decorated Rooms
2000 sq ft. of Banquet/Meeting Space
Outdoor Pool • Enclosed Jacuzzi
Serving Full Cook-to-Order Breakfast
Bar (Serving Dinner from 5pm-10pm)
Room Service (5pm-10pm)
Group & Corporate Rates Available
915-695-7700 • 800-676-7262
TEXAS ▪ I-20 ▪ Hwy 83/84 ▪ EXIT SW Dr.

HOTEL SHUTTLE
1132

• Free Cable TV with HBO
• Free Deluxe Continental Breakfast
• Guest Laundry • Hotel Shuttle
• Non-Smoking Rooms Available
• Bus, RV, and Truck Parking
• In Room Coffee Makers
915-673-5271 For Reservations: 800-588-0072
TEXAS ▪ I-20 ▪ EXIT 288

RVCamp **N:** Tye RV Park (.25 Miles)
ATM **N:** Flying J Travel Plaza
Other **S:** Poppy's Antique Mall and Museum

278 Bus. 20, Tye
TStop **S:** Wes-T-Go(*, SCALES, 24) (Truck Service)
FStop **N:** Conoco(*)
Food **S:** Wes-T-Go (Truck Service), Wes-T-Go Restaurant
TServ **N:** 278 Alternators-Starter, Griffin's Refrigeration Truck and Trailer Repair(24), Shuman Equipment Company
S: Hughes GMC & Volvo Trucks
TWash **S:** 278 Truck Wash, Wes-T-Go (Truck Service)
RVCamp **N:** Tye RV Park (.5 Miles)
ATM **N:** Conoco
S: Wes-T-Go (Truck Service)

279 Bus. 20, U.S. 84, Abilene

280 Fulwiler Road

282 FM 3438, Shirley Road, Dyess AFB
Lodg **S:** Motel 6
RVCamp **S:** Camping, KOA Kampground

283AB US 83, US 277N, Anson (Difficult Reaccess)
Lodg **S:** Ramada Inn-Abilene (see our ad this page)

285 Old Anson Road, Impact
Gas **N:** Texaco(*)
S: Texaco(*, D)
Food **N:** Charolette Belle (Travel Inn)
Lodg **N:** Travel Inn
ATM **N:** Texaco
S: Texaco
Other **N:** Coin Car Wash

286AB U.S. 83 N & S, Bus. Rt., Abilene
Gas **S:** Fina(*), Fisca(*)
Food **S:** Budget Host
Lodg **S:** Budget Host, Econolodge
AServ **S:** Auto Brokers Sales and Service, Fina, Fina
TServ **N:** Firestone GCR Tire and Truck Service

286C FM 600
FStop **N:** Diamond Shamrock(*), Fina(*)
Gas **S:** Chevron(*, D)
Food **N:** Denny's
S: Bobbie's Home Cooking
Lodg **N:** La Quinta Inn
ATM **N:** Diamond Shamrock, Fina

288 TX 351, Albany
FStop **N:** Diamond Shamrock(*), Fina(*)
Gas **N:** Chevron(*)
Food **N:** Dairy Queen(PLAY), Kettle(24) (Days Inn), Skillet's Restaurant, Subway (Fina)
Lodg **N:** Comfort Inn, DAYS INN Days Inn, Holiday Inn Express, Roadway Inn, Rodeway Inn
S: Holiday Inn (see our ad this page), Super 8
Med **S:** ✚ Hospital
ATM **N:** Diamond Shamrock, Fina

290 TX36, Loop322, Cross Plains
Other **S:** Abilene Zoo, Airport

292A Bus. 20, Abilene

292B Elmdale Road
Food **S:** The Gym Diner
TServ **N:** Guerrero's Truck Repairs and Body Work, Herb's Truck Service and Repairs
RVCamp **S:** Abeline Campground
Other **S:** Abilene East Drive Range, Duke's RV

294 Buck Creek Road
RVCamp **S:** Abilene RV Park (1 Mile)

(296) Rest Area (Phones, P; Eastbound)

(297) Rest Area (RR, Phones, Picnic, P; Westbound)

EXIT — TEXAS

297 FM 603

299 FM 1707, Hays Rd.

300 FM 604 N, Spur 189, Cryde
- **Food** S: Red's BBQ, The Smoking Pit
- **AServ** N: Jander's Auto Repair
  S: Rose & Sons Automotive and Used Cars
- **RVCamp** S: **White's Shady Oak**
- **ATM** S: People's State Bank
- **Other** S: Coin Operated Laundromat, HW Lemen's LPG[LP]

301 FM604, Spur 189S, Cherry Lane, Clyde
- **FStop** S: **Texaco[*, D, 24] (Allsups Doughnuts and BBQ)**
- **Gas** N: Chevron[*, 24]
  S: Fina[*]
- **Food** N: Whataburger[24]
  S: Allsups Doughnuts and BBQ (Texaco), **Dairy Queen[PLAY]**, Pizza House, **Texaco (Allsups Doughnuts and BBQ)**
- **Lodg** N: Derrick Motel
- **TWash** S: **301 Truck Wash**
- **ATM** N: Chevron
  S: Fina, First National Bank
- **Other** N: Callahan County Veterinary Clinic, Hawk Top Campers, Rattlesnake Exhibit
  S: **Falk Pharmacy[RX]**, **Lawrence Bros. Supermarket**

303 Union Hill Road
- **Food** S: **Ann's Country Kitchen**

306 Bus. 20, FM 2047, Baird (Difficult Reaccess)
- **AServ** N: Hanner Chevrolet, Pontiac, GMC, Geo, Hanner Jeep and Eagle

307 U.S. 283, Albany, Coleman
- **FStop** S: **Conoco[*] (Pizza Pro)**
- **Gas** S: Fina[*, D] (Allsups Doughnuts and BBQ)
- **Food** N: **Dairy Queen**
  S: Allsups Doughnuts and BBQ, **Conoco (Pizza Pro)**, Fina (Allsups Doughnuts and BBQ), Pizza Pro (Conoco), Robertson's, Union Pacific BBQ
- **Lodg** N: **Baird Motor Inn & Campground**
- **RVCamp** N: **Baird Motor Inn & Campground**
- **ATM** S: **Conoco (Pizza Pro)**, Fina (Allsups Doughnuts and BBQ)

308 Bus.20 West

310 Finley Road

313 FM 2228

316 Brushy Creek Road

319 FM 880 S
- **Gas** N: Conoco[*, D]
- **Food** N: Spur and Sportsman
- **Other** N: Hitch-N-Post Convenient Store, **U.S. Post Office**

320 FM 880 N, FM 2945, Moran

322 Cooper Creek Road

324 Scranton Road

(327) **Picnic Area (P; Eastbound)**

(329) **Picnic Area (Picnic; Westbound)**

330 TX 206, Cisco, Cross Plains
- **FStop** N: **Chevron[*]**
- **Food** N: **White Elephant (Chevron)**
- **Lodg** N: **Best Western**
- **RVCamp** N: **Everett's RV Park (1.5 Miles)**
- **ATM** N: **Chevron**

332 U.S. 183, Cisco, Brownwood, Breckenridge
- **FStop** N: **Citgo[*, D]**
  S: **Fina[*, D]**
- **Food** N: **Binger's Ranch House Restaurant**, Dairy Queen, **Sisco Steak House**, Sonic Drive In
- **Lodg** N: **Oak Motel**
- **AServ** N: T&G's Auto Repair
  S: Hanner Dealership
- **RVCamp** N: **Everett RV Park (.5 Miles)**
- **ATM** N: **Citgo**
  S: **Fina**
- **Other** N: Sisco Car Wash

337 Spur 490

340 TX 6, Gorman, Breckenridge
- **FStop** N: **Texaco[*]**
  S: **Texaco[*, 24] (Red Star Cafe)**
- **Gas** N: Chevron[24]
- **Food** N: Ramona's Mexican
  S: Red Star Cafe (Texaco)[24], **Texaco (Red Star Cafe)**
- **AServ** N: Chevron[24], Mangum Automotive and Electric, Triple A Transmission Service
  S: **Texaco[24] (Red Star Cafe)**
- **Med** N: **+ Hospital**
- **ATM** S: **Texaco (Red Star Cafe)**

343 FM 570, TX 112, Lake Leon
- **Gas** N: Fina[*] (Subway), Texaco[*, D]
  S: Exxon[*, D, CW]
- **Food** N: **Dairy Queen[PLAY]**, Fina (Subway), **Harry Jordan Steak House**, Home Cooked BBQ, Ken's Chicken-N-Fish, **McDonald's[PLAY]**, Sonic Drive In, Subway (Fina), TCBY, Taco Bell, The Asia Restaurant
  S: Burger King (Exxon), Kettle (Ramada), Pulido's Mexican
- **Lodg** N: **Super 8**
  S: **EconoLodge**, Ramada
- **AServ** N: **Mangum Service Center[24]**
  S: Davis Chrysler Plymouth Jeep Eagle Dodge
- **TServ** N: **Mangum Service Center[24]**
- **RVCamp** N: **Super 8**
- **Med** N: **+ Hospital**
- **ATM** N: Fina (Subway)
  S: Exxon
- **Other** N: **David's Supermarket, Wal-Mart**

347 FM 3363, Olden

349 FM 2461, Loop 254, Lake Leon, Ranger College
- **FStop** N: **Love's Country Store[*] (Pizza Hut and Subway)**
- **Gas** S: Fina[*]
- **Food** N: **Dairy Queen, Love's Country Store (Pizza Hut and Subway), Pizza Hut (Love's FS), Subway (Love's FS), Winchells Donuts (Love's FS)**
  S: Fina, Last Chance BBQ
- **Lodg** N: Days Inn
- **ATM** N: **Love's Country Store (Pizza Hut and Subway)**

351 Desdemona Blvd. (Eastbound)

352 Blundell Street (Westbound)

354 Loop 254 W
- **AServ** N: Freddy's Garage and Wrecker Service

358 No Name (Westbound, Reaccess Westbound Only, Difficult Reaccess)

361 TX 16, Strawn, De Leon

(362) **Rest Area (Picnic, P; Westbound, Reaccess Westbound Only)**

(363) **Rest Area (Picnic, P; Eastbound)**

363 Tudor Road (Reaccess Eastbound Only)

367 TX 108, Thurber, Mingus
- **Food** N: Smokestack Restaurant
  S: **New York Hill**

370 TX 108, Gordon, Stephenville, FM 919
- **TStop** N: **Conoco[*, SCALES] (ATM)**
- **FStop** N: **Texaco[*]**
  S: **Citgo[*] (Long Horn Inn Motel and Restaurant)**
- **Food** N: **Conoco (ATM)**
  S: **Longhorn Inn**
- **Lodg** S: **Citgo (Long Horn Inn Motel and Restaurant), Longhorn Inn**
- **TServ** N: **Clay's Little Radio Shack, Conoco[SCALES] (ATM), I-20 Diesel Service Truck Repair**
- **RVCamp** S: **Longhorn Inn**
- **ATM** N: **Conoco (ATM)**

373 TX 193
- **FStop** N: **Chevron[*]**
- **Food** N: **Chevron**, Trolly 373 Restaurant (Chevron)
- **AServ** S: Dave's Garage

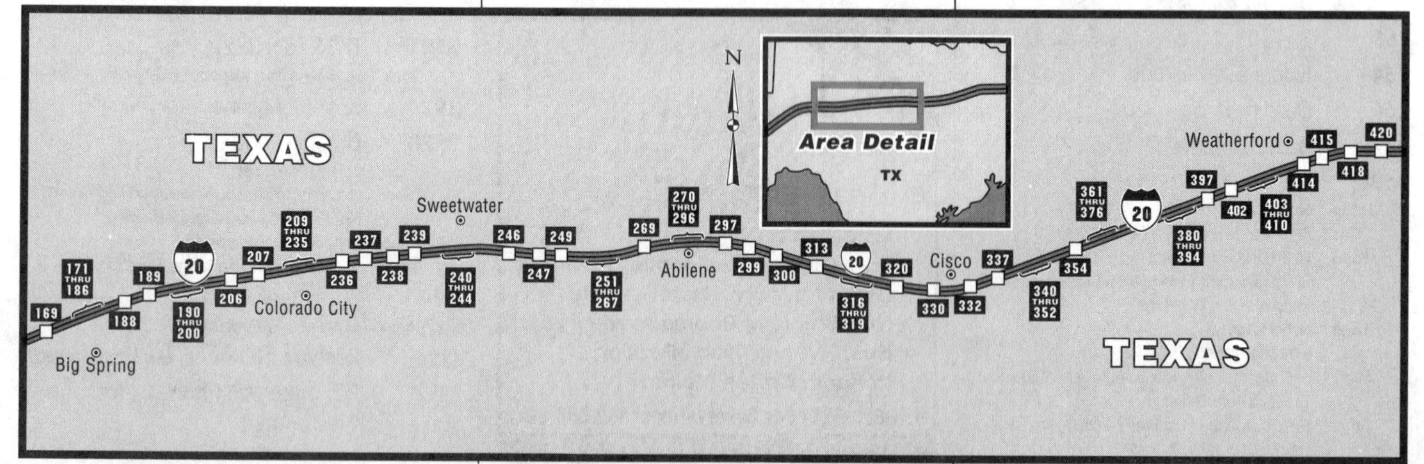

Bold red print shows RV & Bus parking available or nearby

EXIT TEXAS

376 Panama Road, Blue Flat Road

380 FM 4, Palo Pinto, Lipan-Santo
- **FStop** S: Roadrunner
- **Gas** S: Roadrunner Cafe
- **Food** S: Roadrunner Cafe
- **RVCamp** S: Windmill Acres RV Park

386 U.S. 281, Stephenville, Mineral Wells
- **FStop** N: Chevron(*) (Billy Jean's Restaurant)
- **Gas** N: Fina(*)
- **Food** N: Billie Jane's Restaurant (Chevron), Chevron (Billy Jean's Restaurant), Fina
- **Other** N: Brazos Rattlesnake Ranch and Petting Zoo, Camping

389 Rest Area (P; Eastbound)

390 Rest Area (RR, Phones, P; Westbound)

391 Gilbert Pit Road

394 FM 113, Millsap (Difficult Reaccess)
- **FStop** N: Fina(*)
- **RVCamp** N: Joe's RV Park(*)

397 FM 1189, Brock
- **Gas** N: Diamond Shamrock(*, D, 24)
- **Food** N: Diamond Shamrock
- **AServ** N: Rick's Tire Service

402 Weatherford, Spur 312 E (Eastbound)
- **RVCamp** N: Buxton's Diamond B RV Park (.5 Miles)

403 Dennis Road (Westbound, Reaccess Eastbound Only)

406 Old Dennis Road, S. Bowie Dr.
- **TStop** N: Conoco(*, RV DUMP)
- **Food** N: Wayside (Conoco)
- **Lodg** N: Wayside Motel (Conoco)
- **TServ** N: Conoco
- **TWash** N: Conoco
- **RVCamp** S: Safari Camping
- **ATM** N: Conoco

407 FM 1884, Tin Top Road
- **RVCamp** S: Weatherford Kampground(LP) (1 Mile)

408 TX 171, FM 51, Granbury, Cleburne
- **Gas** N: Exxon(*, CW), Mobil(*, LP)
  S: Exxon(*, D), Texaco(*, D)
- **Food** N: Golden Corral Family Steakhouse, Grandy's, McDonald's(PLAY), McDonald's (Wal-Mart), Schlotzsky's Deli, Taco Bell
  S: Burger King(PLAY) (With Texaco), Waffle House
- **Lodg** S: Hampton Inn, Holiday Inn Express, Super 8
- **AServ** N: Wal-Mart SuperCenter(RX) (Vision Center)
- **ATM** N: Mobil, Wal-Mart SuperCenter (Vision Center)
  S: Texaco
- **Other** N: Sand's Propane Inc.(LP), Wal-Mart SuperCenter(RX) (Vision Center)

409 Clear Lake Road, FM 2552 N., Sante Fe Rd.
- **TStop** N: Petro(*, SCALES)
- **Gas** S: Chevron(*)
- **Food** N: Armondos Mexican Food, Domino's Pizza, Iron Skillet (Petro), Jimmy's Catfish Seafood Restaurant (Best Western), Jimmy's Pancake-N-Waffle House (Best Western), La Fiesta
- **Lodg** N: Bed and Bath (Petro), Best Western
- **TServ** N: Petro(SCALES), Weatherford
- **TWash** N: Blue Beacon Truck Wash, Reata Car & Truck Wash
- **Med** N: + Hospital
- **ATM** N: Petro
- **Other** N: Reata Car & Truck Wash

410 Bankhead Hwy
- **TStop** S: Love's Truck Stop(*, SCALES)
- **Food** S: Baskin Robbins (Love's), Subway (Love's), Winchells Donuts (Love's TS)
- **ATM** S: Love's Truck Stop

413 Lake Shore Dr. (Eastbound)
- **Gas** S: Chevron(D)
- **AServ** S: Chevron

414 U.S. 180, Weatherford, Mineral Wells, Hudson Oaks
- **Gas** N: Phillips 66(*), Racetrac(*, 24), Texaco(*, D)
- **Food** N: Cowboy's BBQue and Rib Co., Dairy Queen, Jack's Restaurant, Sonic
- **AServ** N: Hook's Lincoln Mercury, Jerry's Chevrolet, Jerry's Nissan, Jerry's Oldsmobile, Pontiac, GMC, Southwest Toyota, Texaco
- **ATM** N: Phillips 66, Racetrac, Texaco

415 Mikus Road, Annetta Road
- **FStop** S: Citgo(*)
- **Gas** S: Texaco(*, LP)
- **Food** N: Mr. Jim's Pizza
  S: Drivers Diner (Citgo)
- **RVCamp** S: RV 's(LP)
- **ATM** S: Caldwell Banker, Citgo, Texaco
- **Other** N: Discount Fireworks

(417) Weigh Station (Westbound)

418 Willow Park, Ranch House Road
- **FStop** N: Fina(*)
- **Gas** S: Texaco(*, D)
- **Food** N: Fina, Piccadilly Pizza (Fina), Pizza Hut, Subway
  S: Chicken Express Restaurant, McDonald's(PLAY), Texaco
- **Lodg** S: Ramada Limited
- **AServ** S: Red River
- **RVCamp** S: Cowtown RV Park (1 Mile)
- **ATM** N: Fina, Texas Bank
  S: Texaco, Winn Dixie Supermarket(24, RX)
- **Other** N: Brookshire's, Tackett Pharmacy(RX)
  S: Aledo Veterinarian Clinic, Winn Dixie Supermarket(RX)

(419) Weigh Station (Eastbound)

420 FM 1187, Aledo, Farmer Road
- **RVCamp** N: Camping

421 Jct I-30, Downtown, Ft. Worth (Eastbound)

425 Markum Ranch Road

426 FM 2871, Chapin School Road

428 Jct. I-820 N.

429A U.S. 377, Granbury
- **Gas** S: Chevron(*, CW, 24), Exxon(*, CW), Racetrac(*, 24)
- **Food** S: Dairy Queen, Domino's Pizza, McDonald's(PLAY), Pappa Johns Pizza, Racetrac, Waffle House, What A Burger(24)
- **ATM** S: Albertson's Grocery (Nationsbank ATM)(LP, RX), Chevron
- **Other** S: Albertson's Grocery (Nationsbank ATM)(RX), Animal Hospital, Eckerd Drugs(*)

429B Winscott Road
- **FStop** N: Overland Express(*, D)
- **Gas** S: Diamond Shamrock(*), Texaco(*)
- **Food** N: Chester Fried Chicken, Cracker Barrel, Overland Express
  S: Eagle's Doughnuts, Texaco
- **ATM** S: First National Bank of Texas, Texaco

431 Bryant Irving Rd.
- **Gas** N: Mobil(*, CW)
  S: Exxon(*, CW)
- **Food** N: Perrotti's Pizza, Pizzahut
  S: Black Eyed Pea, Blue Moon Creamery Ice Cream and Candy, Colonial Cafe, Cypress Hamburger Grill, Exxon, International House of Pancakes, Lone Star Oyster Bar, Outback Steakhouse, Piccadilly Pizza (Exxon), Razzoo's Cajun Cafe, Sharky's Texas Sports Bar, Subway, Szechuan, Texas To The Bone, The Noble Bean, Wingstop
- **Lodg** S: Amerisuites (see our ad this page), La Quinta Inn, Studio Plus
- **ATM** N: Citizens National Bank, Mobil
  S: Bank One, Wells Fargo
- **Other** N: Country Day Pharmacy(RX), Loews Theaters
  S: Tom Thumb Grocery Store(24, RX)

432 TX 183, Southwest Blvd.
- **Gas** N: Exxon(*)
- **Food** N: Black Eyed Pea, Chicken Express Restaurant, Piccadilly Pizza (Exxon), Tony Lama
  S: International House of Pancakes, Saltgrass Steakhouse
- **Lodg** N: Hampton Inn
- **ATM** N: Chicken Express Restaurant
- **Other** N: Discovery Zone, Home Depot
  S: Lowes

433 Hulen St
- **Gas** N: Texaco(*, D)
- **Food** N: Bagel Chain, Grady's, Honey Baked Ham, Olive Garden, Russell Stover's Candies, Souper Salad, Starbucks Coffee, Subway, TCBY, Tia's Texan Mexican Food
  S: Bennigan's, Colter's Barbecue, JO JO's, Jack-In-The-Box, McDonald's(PLAY), Red Lobster
- **AServ** S: Montgomery Ward
- **ATM** N: Frost Bank
  S: Bank One, Bank of America
- **Other** N: Albertson's Grocery(LP, RX), Office Depot, Petsmart
  S: Bookstop, Borders Books & Music, Hullen Mall, Pearl Vision Center, United Artist Cinema 10

434A Granbury Drive, South Drive
- **Gas** S: Citgo(*)
- **Food** S: Charbroiler Steakhouse, Doughnuts, Hunan Chinese Restaurant, Ming Wok, Poncho's Mexican Buffet
- **AServ** S: Wedgewood Tire Auto Repair
- **ATM** S: Citgo
- **Other** S: Eckerd Drugs(*, RX), Fort Worth Police Department, US Post Office, Wedgewood Animal Hospital, Wedgewood Bowl Bowling Alley, Wedgewood Theater

434B Trail Lake Drive
- **Gas** S: Citgo(*, 24), Exxon(*)
- **AServ** S: Citgo(24), Don Perry's Garage
- **ATM** S: Exxon, Southwest Bank
- **Other** S: Antique Mall of Wedgewood

435 McCart Ave, West Creek Dr
- **Gas** N: Fina(*, D, LP)
  S: Fina(*, CW), Mobil
- **Food** S: Busy B's Bakery, Hoy Pan, Mexico Real
- **AServ** N: Bolen's Automotive
  S: Discount Tire Company, Mobil
- **ATM** N: Fina
  S: Fina
- **Other** N: Quick Wash, South Hills Animal Hospital, Speedway Coin Car Wash

436A Fm731, Crowley Road, James Ave

EXIT TEXAS

Gas **N:** Conoco(*, D)
S: Chevron(*, CW, 24)
Food **S:** Crowley Doughnuts, Ralph's Breakfast and Barbecue, Taco Bell, Vegas Grill, What a Burger
AServ **N:** Gibco Auto Sales and Service
S: Southwest Auto Repair, Transmission Masters
ATM **S:** Chevron
Other **S:** Coin Laundry

436B Hemphill St
Gas **N:** Texaco(*, D, CW)
AServ **S:** Bruce Lowrie Chevrolet
ATM **N:** Terry's Foodmart, Texaco
Other **N:** Terry's Foodmart

437 Jct. I-35W, Fort Worth, Waco

438 Oak Grove Road
Gas **S:** Conoco(*, 24), Texaco(*)
Other **S:** Car Wash, Lucy's Minimart

439 Campus Dr
AServ **N:** Meador Chrysler Plymoth, Meador Oldsmobile, Nichol's Ford
Other **S:** **Sam's Club**

440A Wichita St
Gas **N:** Chevron(*, 24)
S: Fina(*), Total(*)
Food **N:** McDonald's, Taco Bell, Wendy's
S: Chicken Express Restaurant, What A Burger
ATM **N:** Chase Bank, Chevron
Other **N:** Student Bookstore

440B Forest Hill Dr
Gas **S:** Citgo(*), Texaco(*, D)
Food **S:** Braum's Ice Cream, Captain D's Seafood, Ci Ci's Pizza, Jack In The Box, Luby's Cafeteria, Schlotzsky's Deli, Subway
Lodg **S:** Comfort Inn
Other **S:** Animal Clinic of Forest Hill, Chief Auto Parts, **Eckerd Drugs**(*), Eckerd Pharmacy(RX), **Kroger Supermarket**(RX), U. S. Pharmacy(RX), WalGreens Pharmacy(RX), Winn Dixie Supermarket(24, RX)

441 Anglin Drive Hartman Lane
Gas **N:** Texaco(*, D, CW)
S: Conoco(*, LP)
AServ **S:** CHB Auto Repair
ATM **S:** Conoco
Other **S:** C-Doo Watercrafts

442A 287Bus, Mansfield Hwy, Kennedale

442B Jct. I-820, 287N, Downtown Fort Worth

443 Bowman Springs Road (Westbound)

444 U.S. 287, Waxahachie

445 Green Oaks Blvd, Little Road , Kennedale
Gas **N:** Chevron(*, CW, 24), Conoco(*, LP), Mobile(*),

EXIT TEXAS

Texaco(*, CW)
S: Chevron, Citgo(*)
Food **N:** Arby's, Boston Market Restaurant, Braum's, Bubba's Bagel Nosh, KFC, Ole Spanish Mexican Grill and bar, Papa John's Pizza, Sacred Grounds Coffee House, Sweet Success Bakery, Taco Bell, Tai-pan Chinese Buffet, What a Burger
S: Cheddar's Casual Cafe, Harrigans Grill and Bar, Hibachi 93 Japanese Steakhouse, International House of Pancakes, Kracker Seafood, Mandarin Garden Chinese Restaurant, McDonald's(PLAY), Mulligan's 19th Hole, Natural Foods Market and Deli, No Frills Grill, Pancho's Mexican Food, Pasta Oggi & Pizza, Sno-Hut Snowcones, Sonic, Southern Maid Donuts, Steak and Ale, Subway, Taco Bueno, Waffle House
AServ **N:** Mastercare by Firestone
S: Jiffylube
ATM **N:** Bank 1, Bank United, Bank of America, Conoco, **Minyard Supermarket**(RX), NationsBank, NationsBank, Norwest Banks, Well's Fargo
S: Citgo, Security Bank Of Arlington
Other **N:** AMC 8 Theaters, **Albertson's Grocery Store**(RX), **Eckerd Drugs**(24, RX), I-20 Animal Medical Center, **Minyard Supermarket**(RX), Washmaster (hand and automated carwash)
S: Animal Doctor, Brightwash Laundry, Chief Auto Parts, Coin Operated Carwash, Doctor Right (pharmacy)(RX), Loews Theaters, Shirley's Pets 'n Xtras, **Winn Dixie Supermarket**

447 Park Springs Road, Kelly - Elliott Road
Gas **S:** Exxon(*, CW), Fina(*, CW)
Food **S:** Pizzahut Express

448 Bowen Road
Gas **N:** Conoco(*, LP), Shell(*, CW)
S: Texaco(*, D, CW)
Food **N:** Bobby Valentine Sports Gallery, **Cracker Barrel**
ATM **N:** Conoco
Other **N:** United Artist Theaters

449 Fm157, Cooper St, Arlington
Gas **S:** Conoco(*, D), Fina(*, D, CW)
Food **N:** Bennigan's, Black Eyed Pea, Chili's, Chuys Tex Mex Restaurant, Grandy's, Jason's Deli, La Madeleine French Bakery and Cafe, McDonald's(PLAY), Red Lobster, Schlotzsky's Deli
S: Applebee's, Arby's, Burger Street, Chick-Fil-A, El Phoenix, Hometown Buffet, Macaroni Grill, Olive Garden, T G I Friday's
Lodg **N:** Best Western, Holiday Inn Express
S: Homestead Village, Suburban Lodge
AServ **S:** Buz Post Pontiac Issuzu Gmc, Hilcher Ford, National Tire and Battery, Vandergriff Chevrolet
RVCamp **N:** **Treetops RV Village (.75 Miles)**
ATM **N:** Cirrus 24 Hour Bank, Comerica Bank

EXIT TEXAS

S: Chase Bank, Fina
Other **N:** Baptist Bookstore, Barnes & Noble Bookstore, Pearl Vision 1 Hour Service, Toys R Us, **US Post Office**
S: Boating World and Supreme Golf, **Home Depot**, **K-Mart**(RX), Putt Putt Golf and Games and Batting Cages, **Wal-Mart**(RX)

450 Matlock Road
FStop **N:** **Fina**(*, D)
Gas **S:** Citgo(*), Diamond Shamrock(*, LP, CW), Texaco(*, CW)
Food **N:** International House of Pancakes, Iron Skillet, Mercado Juarez Cafe, On The Border Cafe, Outback Steakhouse, Spaghetti Warehouse Italian Grill, Tony Roman
S: Joe's Pizza & Pasta, Saltgrass Steakhouse
Lodg **N:** Hampton Inn
Med **N:** **+ Hospital**
ATM **N:** Compass Bank, Frost Bank
S: Citgo, Diamond Shamrock
Other **N:** Kinko's Copies, **The Parks Mall**

451 Collins St New York Ave.
Gas **N:** Exxon(*, CW), Mobil(*, D, CW), Racetrac(*)
S: Diamond Shamrock(*, CW), Texaco(*)
Food **N:** Jack In The Box, Pizzahut Express
S: McDonald's(PLAY)
AServ **N:** Hiley Mazda, Saturn Dealership, Vandergriff Acura
ATM **N:** Exxon, Racetrac
S: Diamond Shamrock
Other **N:** Cimmaron Pottery
S: **Davis Nissan**, U. S. Post Office

453A TX 360, Dallas, Fort Worth, Airport

453B S H 360S Watson Road

454 Great Southwest Pkwy
FStop **N:** **Conoco**(*)
Gas **N:** Chevron(*, CW, 24)
S: Diamond Shamrock(*, D, LP), Exxon(*), Texaco(*, D, CW)
Food **N:** Kentucky Fried Chicken, McDonald's(PLAY), Taco Bell, Tex's Roadhouse, Wendy's
S: Arby's (Stop & Go), Burger King(PLAY), Doughnuts, Sal's Pizza and Subs, Subway
Lodg **N:** DAYS INN Days Inn
S: Comfort Inn
AServ **S:** AutoNation USA, Discount Tire Company
ATM **S:** Diamond Shamrock, Exxon, Independent National Bank
Other **S:** **Winn Dixie Supermarket**(24, RX)

456 Carrier Pkwy
Gas **S:** Mobil(*, CW)
Food **N:** Benny's Bagels, Chick-Fil-A(PLAY), Don Pablo's Mexican Kitchen, The Original Taco Cabana
S: Boston Market Restaurant, Brass Bean Coffee Shop, Chili's, Denny's, Little Caesars Pizza, McDonald's(PLAY), Subway, Ton's Mongolian Grill

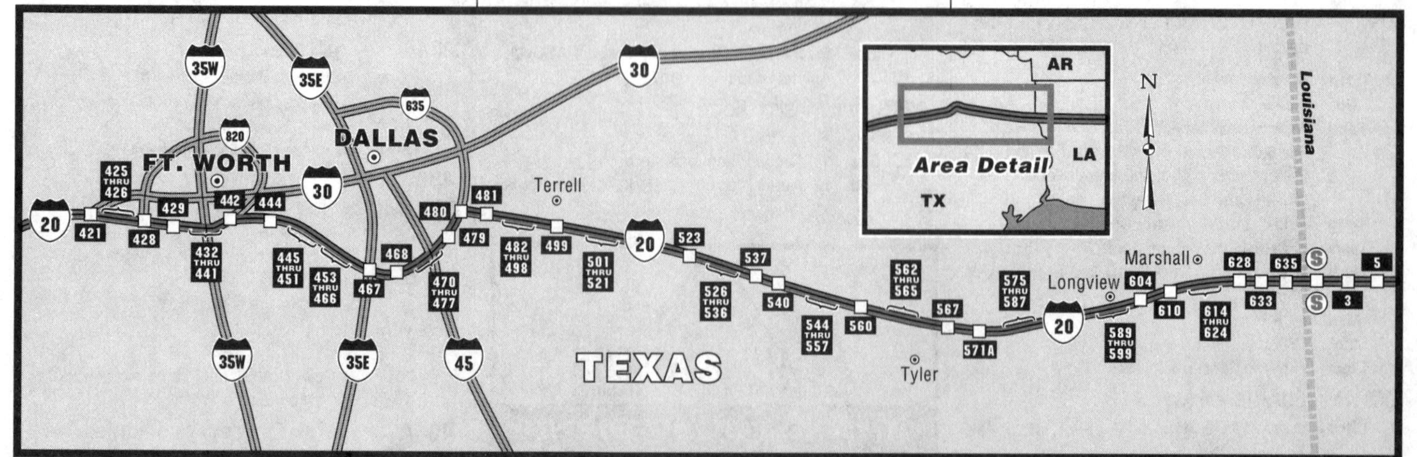

Bold red print shows RV & Bus parking available or nearby

EXIT TEXAS

AServ S: City Garage
ATM S: Mobil, Nationsbank
Other N: **Home Depot**, **Target**
S: **Albertson's Grocery**(LP, 24, RX), Alex's Car Wash, **Movies 16 Theater**, **United Artist Theaters**, **WalGreens Pharmacy**

457 FM 1382, Grand Prairie, Cedar Hill
Gas N: Diamond Shamrock(*), Texaco(*, CW)
S: Racetrac(*, 24)
Food N: TCBY (Diamond Shamrock), Taco Bell (Diamond Shamrock), Waffle House
S: Jack-In-The-Box
ATM N: Diamond Shamrock
S: Racetrac
Parks N: **Cedar Hill State Park & Joe Pool Lake**

458 Mt. Creek Parkway

460 Spur 408 (Difficult Reaccess)

461 Cedar Ridge Drive
Gas S: Diamond Shamrock(*, LP, CW), Racetrac(*)
ATM S: Diamond Shamrock, Racetrac

462B North Main St
Gas S: Citgo, Exxon, Shell, Texaco(*, D), Total(*)
Food S: Arby's, Captain D's Seafood, Chow-Line Buffet, Church's Chicken, Jack-In-The-Box, K.C. Doughnuts (Texaco), Long John Silver, Los Lupes, O Doughnuts, Popeye's Chicken, Taco Bell, Webb's BBQ, Whataburger(24), Williams Chicken
Lodg S: Motel 6
AServ S: Car Quest Auto Center, Citgo, Exxon, Firestone Tire & Auto, Goodyear, Shell
ATM S: **Kroger Supermarket**(24, RX), Western Bank & Trust
Other S: Discount Bakery, Fox Photo 1-Hr Lab, **Jiffy Wash Coin Laundry**, **Knick Knacks**, **Kroger Supermarket**(RX), Kwik Kar Wash

463 Cockrell Hill Road, Camp Wisdom Road
FStop N: **Chevron**(*, CW, 24)
Gas N: **Chevron**(*, CW, 24), Exxon(*, CW)
S: Diamond Shamrock(*)
Food N: Bennigan's, Catfish King, Denny's, Halls Chicken, Papa John's Pizza, Rice Garden Chinese, Steak & Ale, Taco Bueno, Taco Cabana Mexican Patio Cafe(24), Texas Tux (Holiday Inn)
S: Burger King(PLAY), Donut Palace, Olive Garden, Owen's Restaurant, Red Lobster
Lodg N: Hampton Inn, Holiday Inn, Lexington Hotel Suites, Motel 6, Royal Inn
AServ N: Allen Samuel's Ford, Midas Muffler & Brake, Red Bird Jeep and Eagle, Red Bird Nissan
S: Red Bird Pontiac, Red Bird Toyota
Other N: Joshua's Christian Bookstore, Speed's, **Texas Drug Warehouse Pharmacy**(RX)
S: **K-Mart**(RX), **Medifirst Walk-in Clinic**, **Target**

464A U.S. 67 N., Dallas

464B U.S. 67 S., Cleburne

465 Hampton Road, Wheatland Road
Gas N: Texaco(*, D)
S: Chevron(*), Racetrac(*, 24)
Food S: Arby's, Cheddar's Casual Cafe, Jack-In-The-Box, McDonald's(PLAY) (Chevron), Sonic Drive In, Spring Creek BBQ, Taco Bell, Wendy's
Lodg S: Comfort Inn
AServ S: Davis Dealership, GMC Trucks, & Buick, Hyundai Davis Dealership, Lincoln Mercury Dealer, **Sam's Club**, Saturn of Duncanville Dealership
Med S: ✚ **Hospital**
ATM S: Racetrac
Other S: **Home Depot**, Lowe's, **Sam's Club**

466 South Polk St
Gas N: Citgo(*), Texaco(*, D)

EXIT TEXAS

Food N: Citgo, Dairy Queen, W.B.S.Catfish and Hamburgers, Western Barbeque
Other N: Coin Car Wash, **Sun Brite Coin Laundry**

467A Jct. I-35 East, North Dallas

467B I-35 East, South Waco

468 Houston School Road

470 TX 342, Lancaster Road
TStop N: **Pilot Travel Center**(*, RV DUMP, SCALES)
Gas N: Chevron(*, CW, 24)
S: Racetrac(*, 24), Texaco(*)
Food N: **Wendy's (Pilot)**
S: **McDonald's**(PLAY), Williams Chicken
Lodg S: DAYS INN Days Inn
TServ S: **Dallas Truck Wash**, **Goodyear Tire & Auto**
TWash S: **Dallas Truck Wash**
Med N: ✚ **Veterans Affairs Hospital**
ATM N: Chevron, **Pilot Travel Center**
S: Racetrac

472 Bonnie View Road
TStop N: **Flying J Travel Plaza**(*, 24)
Food N: **Layover Restaurant**, **The Cookery (Flying J)**
Lodg N: Ramada Limited
TServ N: **Flying J Travel Plaza**(24)
TWash N: **Flying J Travel Plaza**, **United Truck Wash**(24)

473AB 473A - N I-45 Dallas, 473B - S I-45 Houston

474 TX 310 N

476 Dowdy Ferry Road (Reaccess Eastbound Only)

477 St. Augustine Road

479B U.S. 175 E., Kaufman

479A U.S. 175 W., Dallas

480 I-635 North

481 Seagoville Road
Gas N: Beasley's Grocery(*, RX), Total(*)
Food N: Smith Donuts (Beasley's), Taco Bell (Total)
S: **Lindy's Family Restaurant**
ATM N: Total

482 Belt Line Road
RVCamp S: **Countryside RV & Mobile Home Park**(RV DUMP)

483 Lawson Road., Lasater Road

487 FM 740, Forney

490 FM 741

491 FM 2932, Helms Tr. Road

493 FM 1641

498 FM 148

499A To US 80W Dallas, Forney, Mesquite (Westbound, Reaccess Eastbound Only)

499B Rose Hill Road

501 TX 34, Terrell, Kaufman
FStop S: **Total**(*)
Gas N: Chevron(*, 24), Exxon(*)
S: Citgo(*), **Overland Express**(*)
Food N: **America's Kitchen**, **Best Western**, **Big E. Checkered Flag Cafe**, Burger King, Jr.'s Hamburgers, Hot Dogs, & BBQ, Puerto Escondido, Schlotzsky's Deli, Waffle House
S: Citgo, **McDonald's**(PLAY), Wendy's
Lodg N: **Best Western**, **Classic Inn**, DAYS INN Days Inn, Holiday Inn Express, **Motel 6**
S: Super 8
Med N: ✚ **Hospital**
ATM N: Exxon
S: **Overland Express**, **Total**

EXIT TEXAS

Other N: Airport
S: **Tanger Factory Outlet**

503 Wilson Road
TStop S: **Rip Griffin Travel Center**(*, RV DUMP, SCALES) **(Fuel-Texaco, Barber, Showers, Laundry)**
Food S: **Pizza Hut (Rip Griffin TS)**, **Rip Griffin Travel Center (Fuel-Texaco, Barber, Showers, Laundry)**, **Subway (Rip Griffin TS)**
TServ S: **Rip Griffin Travel Center**(SCALES) **(Fuel-Texaco, Barber, Showers, Laundry)**
RVCamp S: **Rip Griffin Travel Center**

506 FM 429, FM 2728, College Mound Road

509 Hiram Road
FStop S: **Phillips 66**(*, D)
Food S: **McDonald's Bar-B-Q (Phillips 66)**

(510) **Rest Area (RR, Picnic, Grills, Vending, P; Eastbound)**

(511) **Rest Area (RR, Picnic, Grills, Vending, P; Westbound)**

(511) **Weigh Station (Eastbound)**

(511) **Weigh Station (Westbound)**

512 FM 2965, Hiram - Wills Point Road
RVCamp S: **Dallas Hi Ho Campground**

516 FM 47, Lake Tawakoni
Gas S: Diamond Shamrock(*, D), Robertson's(*, D)
Food S: Diamond Shamrock, **Interstate Motel**(24), Robertson's
Lodg S: **Interstate Motel**
AServ S: Bass Auto Clinic

519 Turner - Hayden Road
AServ N: J & P Auto Service

521 Myrtle Cemetery Road., Myrtle Springs Road
Food S: **Canton Jubilee Superb Buffet**
AServ S: Tommy's Garage and Wrecker Service
RVCamp S: **Marshall's RV Centers Inc.**(LP)

523 TX 64, Wills Point
RVCamp N: **Action RV Park (1 Mile)**, **Camping**, **Canton Campground & RV Park**(LP) **(1 Mile)**

526 FM 859, Edgewood
Food S: Crazy Cow BBQ & Steakhouse
RVCamp S: **First Monday Trade Days Campground (1 Mile)**
Parks N: **Edgewood Heritage Park**

527 TX 19, Emory, Canton
FStop S: **Fina**(*), **Overland Express**(*)
Gas N: Citgo(*, 24), Texaco(*, 24)
S: Chevron(*, D, CW, 24), Shell(*, CW)
Food N: Burger King(PLAY), Jewel's Restaurant & Steakhouse, Ranchero Restaurant, **Whataburger**
S: Crazy Cow BBQ & Steakhouse, Dairy Queen, Genya's Kitchen, **Jerry's Pizza**, Juanita's Family Mexican, **McDonald's**(PLAY), Taco Bell, Two Senorita's Mexican, World Famous Hamburgers(24)
Lodg N: Holiday Inn Express, Ramada Limited, **Super 8**
S: **Best Western**, DAYS INN Days Inn
AServ S: Canton Motors Ford Mercury, Chevron(24)
TServ S: **Western Star Trucks**
RVCamp S: **Armstrong's Outback RV Park (.25 Miles)**, **Canton Inn & RV Park**, **Jerry's RV Parts & Service**, **RV Service**
ATM N: Citgo
S: **Overland Express**, Shell
Other S: Automatic Gas Co. Inc.(LP), **Farmers LP Gas Co.**(LP), Jerry's Car Wash, Texas Freshwater

EXIT TEXAS

Fishery (33 Miles)

528 FM 17
Other S: Old Mill Marketplace (see our ad this page)

530 FM 1255
Parks N: First Monday Park

533 Colfax Oakland Road
TStop N: Citgo(*, 24)
Food N: Blimpie Subs & Salads (Citgo), Citgo, Pizza for Less (Citgo), TCBY (Citgo)
S: RV Park
TServ N: Citgo(24)
RVCamp S: RV Park
ATM N: Citgo

536 Tank Farm Road

537 FM 773, FM 16

(537) Rest Area (RR, Phones, Picnic, Grills, Vending, RV Dump, P; Eastbound)

(537) Rest Area (RR, Phones, Picnic, Grills, Vending, RV Dump, P; Westbound)

540 FM 314, Van
Gas N: Exxon(*, D)
Food N: Dairy Queen
Lodg N: Van Inn
AServ N: Exxon

544 Willow Branch Road
FStop N: Conoco(*, 24) (CB Shop, Road Service)
AServ N: Conoco(24) (CB Shop, Road Service)
TServ N: Conoco(24) (CB Shop, Road Service)
RVCamp N: Willow Branch RV Park(RV DUMP) (1 Mile)

(546) Weigh Station (Eastbound)

(546) Weigh Station (Westbound)

548 TX 110, Grand Saline
FStop S: Chevron(*)
Gas N: Exxon(*)
ATM S: Chevron
Other N: YWAM Go Center

552 FM 849
Gas N: Chevron(*, 24)
RVCamp S: Camping
ATM N: First Service Bank, Lindale State Bank
Other N: Elliott's Pharmacy(RX), Hide-A-Way Small Animal Clinic

554 Harvey Road
RVCamp S: Tyler 554 Campground on I-20 (1 Mile)

556 U.S. 69, Lindale, Mineola, Tyler
FStop N: Total(*)
Gas N: Racetrac(*)
S: Chevron(*), Texaco(*, 24)
Food N: Burger King, Juanita's Family Mexican, McDonald's(PLAY), Paco's Mexican, Subway, Taco Bell
S: Dairy Queen (Texaco), Econo Inn Express
Lodg N: Comfort Inn, Executive Inn
S: Econo Inn Express
ATM N: Racetrac, Total
S: Texaco
Other N: Tourist Info.
S: Latif's Antique, Reliable Propane(LP)

557 Jim Hogg Road
FStop N: Texaco(*)
Food N: Tio's Restaurant

560 Lavender Road

562 TX 14, Tyler State Park, Hawkins
Food N: Bodacious Bar-B-Q
RVCamp S: Blue Jay Camp (4 Miles)

EXIT TEXAS

Parks N: Tyler State Park (2 Miles)

565 FM 2015, Driskill, Lake Road

567 TX 155, East Texas Center, Gilmer, Winona, Big Sandy
Lodg S: DAYS INN Days Inn
Med S: + Univ. Texas Health Center

571A U.S. 271, Glan Border
Gas S: Chevron(*)

571B FM 757, Starrville, Omen Road

(573) Parking Area (Picnic; Eastbound)

(573) Parking Area (Picnic; Westbound)

575 Barber Road

579 Joy - Wright Mountain Road

1054

Foretravel of Texas, Inc.

MOTORHOME
SALES • SERVICE • PARTS

Directions: I-20, exit #589, (Hwy 259) go 65 miles South to Nacogdoches, Texas

811 NW Stallings Drive • Nacogdoches, TX 75964
800.955.6226

EXIT TEXAS

TStop N: Diamond Shamrock(*)
Gas S: Fina(*)
Food N: Diamond Shamrock, Hickory Ridge Cafe
AServ N: Tire Place
TWash N: Red Devil Truck Wash

582 FM 3053, Liberty City, Overton
Gas N: Exxon(*, D), Fastrac(*, D), Texaco(*)
Food N: Crazy Bob's BBQ, Dairy Queen, Daylight Donuts, Pizza Boy, Subway (Exxon)
Lodg S: Thrifty Inn
AServ N: Hog-Eye Auto Parts
ATM N: Fastrac
Other N: Aquajet Car Wash, Security Mail Service, Soapbox Laundry, Spot Free Rinse Car Wash

583 TX 135, Kilgore, Overton
Gas N: E-Z Mart(*)
Food N: Liberty City Cafe

587 TX 42, Kilgore, White Oak
FStop S: Chevron(*)
Gas N: Diamond Shamrock(*)
Food N: Bodacious Bar-B-Q, Maxey Brothers Grill
S: Ragen Cajun

589AB U.S. 259, TX 31, Kilgore, Henderson, Longview (Left Exit Westbound, Limited Access Hwy)
RVCamp S: Foretravel of Texas (see our ad this page)

591 FM 2087, FM 2011
TServ S: Master Aligners of 18 Wheelers
RVCamp S: Pine Meadows Campground(RV DUMP)

595AB TX 322, FM 1845, Loop 281, Estes Parkway, Longview
Gas N: Chevron(*, D), Diamond Shamrock, Exxon(LP), Texaco(*, D)

The Village Shops • The Mountain Shops • The Pavilions

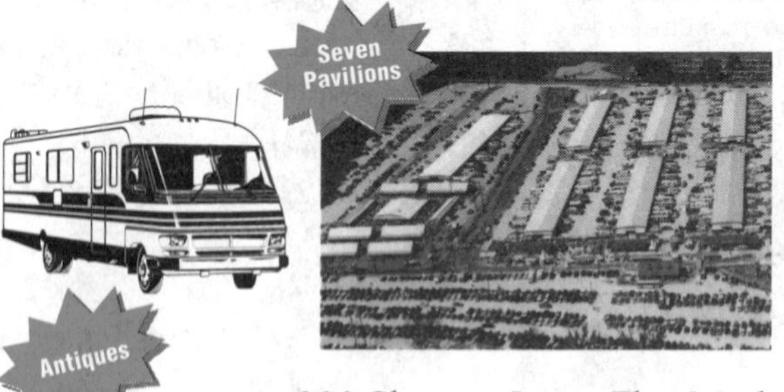

800 Shops • Large Flea Market
RV Rallies & Tour Buses Welcome - Easy Access
Vendor Spaces Available • 50 Acres of Convenient Parking
Bed and Rest Overnight Accommodations
RV Rental Spaces Available all Month

Music

Open the 1st Fri, Sat, & Sun. preceding the 1st Monday of the month

HWY 64 East Canton, TX
www.oldmillmarketplace.com
903-567-5445

1843

TEXAS ▪ I-20 ▪ EXIT 528

EXIT — TEXAS

S: Chevron[*, D], Fina[*, D]
Food N: Applewood's (Holiday Inn), Dairy Queen, Denny's, KFC, Lupe's Mexican, McDonald's[PLAY], Pizza Hut, Subway (Chevron), Waffle House
S: Kettle
Lodg N: Days Inn, EconoLodge, Holiday Inn, Longview Inn, Stratford House Inns
S: Hampton Inn, La Quinta Inn, Motel 6
AServ N: Exxon

596 U.S. 259 North, TX 149, Eastman Road, Carthidge
FStop N: **Texaco**[*, D]
Gas N: Exxon[*, D]
S: Total[*]
Food N: Burger King, Exxon, Grandy's[*] (Exxon), **Taco Bell (Texaco)**, Whataburger[24]
S: Arby's (Total)
Lodg N: TraveLodge
TServ N: **Twin States Truck Inc.**
Med N: **Hospital**
ATM N: Exxon, **Texaco**
Parks S: **Martin Lake State Park**
Other N: Car Wash

599 Loop 281, FM 968
TStop S: **National Truck Stop**[*] **(Fina Fuel)**
FStop S: **Pennzoil Oil Change**[*], **Phillip 66**[*]
Gas S: Exxon[*]
Food S: **National Truck Stop (Fina Fuel)**
TServ N: **East Texas Truck Equipment, Fluid Power Service, Michelin Dealer, Texas Kenworth Co., Truck Parts World**
TWash S: **Truck Wash**
RVCamp N: **Gum Springs RV Travel Trailor Park, Texas Quick RV Park & Campground**
S: **Phillip 66, RV Park, Wanda's Kountry Korner RV Park**

604 FM 450, Hallsville
Gas N: Chevron[*, D]
RVCamp N: **450 RV Park Hitchin' Post (Laundry), Lake O the Pines**
ATM N: Chevron

(608) **Rest Area (RR, Phones, Picnic, Grills, Vending, P; Eastbound)**

(608) **Rest Area (RR, Phones, Picnic, Grills, Vending, P; Northbound)**

610 FM 3251

614 TX 43, Marshall, Kado Lake
Parks S: **Martin Creek Lake State Park (18 Miles)**

617 U.S. 59, Marshall, Carthage
TStop S: **Texaco**[*, SCALES]
FStop S: **Diamond Shamrock**[*]
Gas N: Exxon[*, 24], Texaco[*]
S: Chevron[*, D, 24], Total[*]
Food N: Catfish Express, Domino's Pizza, Elmwood

RAMADA INN®
1745
903-938-9261
Restaurant/Lounge on Premises
Continental Breakfast
Kids Under 12 Eat & Stay Free
Outdoor Pool • Exercise Room
Handicap Accessible
Golf (within 2 mi)
Truck/Large Vehicle Parking
Coin Laundry • Interior Corridors
35 mi to Shreveport
5301 E. End Blvd. S. • Marshal, TX 75672
TEXAS ■ I-20 EXIT 617

EXIT — TEXAS/LOUISIANA

Cafeteria (Ramada Inn), Golden Corral Family Steakhouse, McDonald's[PLAY], Schlotzsky's Deli, The Hot Biscuit (Best Western), Waffle House
S: Days Inn, **Maverick Inn, Texaco**
Lodg N: Best Western, Economy Inn Express, Holiday Inn Express, **Ramada Inn (see our ad this page)**
S: **Comfort Inn**, Days Inn, Motel 6, Super 8
AServ N: Chevrolet, Oldsmobile Dealership
TWash S: **Texaco**
RVCamp N: **Camping, Hilltop RVPark**

620 FM 31, Elysian Fields

624 FM 2199, Scottsville

628 Frontage Rd.

633 FM 134, FM 9
Gas N: Texaco[*, 24]
Food N: Robertson's Hams
RVCamp S: **Camping (.7 Miles)**

635 Spur 156, Waskom
Gas N: Chevron[*, D], Texaco[*]
Food N: Dairy Queen, Jim's Bar-B-Q & Catfish
AServ N: Buddy's Auto Service
ATM N: Chevron, First State Bank
Other N: **Tiller Veterinary Clinic**

(636) **TX Welcome Center (RR, Phones, RV Dump, P; Westbound)**

(636) **Truck Parking Area (Eastbound)**

↑TEXAS

↓LOUISIANA

(1) **Weigh Station (Eastbound)**

(1) **Weigh Station (Westbound)**

(2) **LA Welcome Center (RR, Phones, Picnic, RV Dump; Eastbound)**

3 South U.S. 79, LA 169, Mooringsport, Carthage Texas
TStop S: **Flying J Travel Plaza**[*, RV DUMP, SCALES]
Food S: The Cookery (Flying J)
Other N: **Boothill Speedway**

5 North U.S. 79, U.S. 80, Greenwood
TStop N: **Kelly's Truck Terminal**[LP, SCALES]
FStop N: **Texaco**[*]
Food N: **Kelly's Truck Terminal, The Derrick Restaurant (Country Inn)**
Lodg N: **Country Inn, Kelly's Truck Terminal**
RVCamp N: **Kelly's RV Park, Kelly's Truck Terminal**
ATM N: **Texaco**

8 U.S. 80, LA 526 East, Industrial Loop
TStop S: **Petro**[*]
FStop S: **Speedway**[*]
Gas S: Chevron[*, D]
Food S: **Iron Skillet Restaurant (Petro TS)**
Lodg N: **Red Roof Inn**
TServ N: **Shreveport Truck Center**[24], **United Engine**
RVCamp N: **Randy's Travel Town**
S: **Campers RV Center**[LP] **(1.9 Miles), KOA Kampground**

10 Pines Road
Gas N: Fina[*, 24]
S: Exxon[*], Shell[*, D, CW]
Food N: Dairy Queen, Pizza Hut, Subway, Western Sizzlin'
S: Blimpie Subs & Salads (Exxon), Burger King[PLAY], **Cracker Barrel**, Grandy's, KFC, McDonald's[PLAY], Nicky's Mexican Restaurant, TCBY (Exxon), Taco Bell, Wendy's
Lodg S: Fairfield Inn by Marriott, La Quinta Inn & Suites
AServ S: Exxon, Minit Oil Change, Xpress Lube
RVCamp S: **KOA Kampground (1.75 Miles)**

EXIT — LOUISIANA

ATM N: Hibernia National Bank
S: Deposit Guaranty National Bank
Other N: **Brookshire's Grocery Store**
S: **Eckerd Drugs**[RX], **Kroger Supermarket, U.S. Post Office, Wal-Mart SuperCenter**[24, RX]

11 I-220 East, LA 3132 East, Alexandria

13 Monkhouse Dr., Airport
Gas S: Chevron[*, CW, 24], Exxon[*, D], Texaco
Food N: Denny's, Kettle Restaurant, Leon 's Bar-B-Que
S: Ramada Inn, Subway (Exxon), Waffle House
Lodg N: Best Value Inn & Suites, **Days Inn (see our ad opposite page)**, EconoLodge, Holiday Inn Express, Plantation Inn
S: Best Western, Pelican Inn Airport Station, Ramada Inn, Super 8
AServ S: Texaco
ATM N: Regions Bank
Other S: **Shreveport Airport**

14 Jewella Ave
Gas N: Mobil[*], Pennzoil Oil Change[*, 24], Texaco[*, CW]
Food N: Burger King[PLAY], Church's Chicken, John's Seafood, McDonald's, Popeye's Chicken, Subway, Taco Bell, Whataburger
Lodg N: **Jo-dan Motel**
AServ N: Auto Zone Auto Parts, Brake-O Brake Shop, John's Repair[CW], Pennzoil Oil Change
ATM N: Hibernia, Pennzoil Oil Change
Other N: **County Market Total Discount Foods, Eckerd Drugs**[RX], **Medic Pharmacy, Rite Aid Pharmacy**[24, RX], **Super 1 Foods**

16A U.S. 171, Hearne Ave.
Gas N: Texaco[*, CW]
S: Exxon[*], Fina[*], Texaco[*, D, LP]
Food N: South Made Donuts
S: KFC
AServ N: Computer Tune-A-Car, Service Tire Inc.
S: Exxon
Med N: **LSU Medical Center, WK Medical Center**
Other N: **Caddo Animal Clinic, Medic Pharmacy**[RX]
S: Superior Hand Wash & Detail

16B U.S. 79, U.S. 80, Greenwood Road
Gas S: Mobil[*]
Food S: El Chico's Mexican, Rusty's Family Restaurant
Lodg S: Sundowner West
AServ S: Ed's Muffler Shop
Med N: **WK Medical Center**
ATM N: Hibernia Bank
Other S: **U.S. Post Office**

17A Linwood Ave, Lakeshore Dr.
Gas S: Mobil[*]
AServ N: Jordan Auto Parts
S: Dixie Imported Auto Parts, Used Tires, Windshields Of America (Mobil)
Other S: **Arkla Natural Gas Vehicle Refueling Station (.46 Miles), Davis Tool & Tarp, Scuba Training School**

17B I-49 South, Alexandria

18A Common St., Line Ave. (Eastbound, Reaccess Westbound Only, Difficult Reaccess)
Gas S: Texaco
AServ S: Joe Rachal Transmissions, Texaco
Med S: **Dr.'s Hospital, Schumpert Medical Center**
ATM S: Hibernia

18C Fairfield Ave (Difficult Reaccess)
Gas S: Circle K[*, LP]
Food N: Fertitta's Deli
AServ S: Under Car Service Specialists, Uniroyal Tire & Auto, Walker's Auto Spring
Med N: **Schumpert Medical Center**

EXIT LOUISIANA

ATM S: Circle K

18D Common St, Louisiana Ave (Westbound)

19A North U.S. 71, Spring St, South LA 1, Market St. (Westbound)

Lodg N: Best Western, Holiday Inn

19B Traffic St (Eastbound)

Food N: Jacob's Well Coffee House

AServ N: A & R Automotive Service, Chevrolet Dealer

Other N: Casino Pride Arcade

20C US 71 South, Barksdale Blvd (Eastbound)

Gas S: Mobil[*]

Food S: Southern Maid Donuts Cafe

AServ S: Martin's Auto Electric

20B LA 3, Benton Rd (Eastbound, Reaccess Eastbound Via Old Minden)

Gas S: Exxon[*, CW]

Food S: Blimpie's Subs, Burger King, Johnny's Pizza House, McDonald's, Podnuh's Bar-B-Q, Poncho's Mexican Buffet, Posados Cafe, Ralph & Kacoo's Seafood, SHONEY'S Shoney's (Shoney's Inn), Subway, TCBY, What A Burger[24]

Lodg S: Shoney's Inn

AServ S: Doug's Pit Stop Import Service, Mazda, Volks, Audi, Porsche, Western Auto

ATM S: Bank One, Exxon, Hibernia

Other S: **Book Rack**, **Inspiration Christian Bookstore**, **US Post Office**

20A Isle of Capri Blvd, Hamilton Rd

Gas N: Circle K[*], Speedway[*], Texaco[*]
S: Chevron

Food S: Lucky Garden (Ramada Inn)

Lodg S: Ramada Inn

AServ N: Regency Tire
S: Chevron

ATM N: Circle K

21 LA 72, To U.S. 71South, Old Minden Rd

Gas N: Circle K Express[*, 24], Exxon[*, CW]
S: Racetrac[*]

Food N: Adam's Restaurant (Holiday Inn), Blimpie Subs & Salads, Burger King[PLAY], El Chico Mexican Restaurant, Kettle Restaurant[24], Ralph & Kacoo's Restaurant, Shoney's Inn, TCBY
S: Dragon House (Chinese)

Lodg N: Holiday Inn, La Quinta Inn, Shoney's Inn
S: DAYS INN **Days Inn (see our ad this page)**, Motel 6

AServ N: Volkswagen Dealer

22 Airline Dr., Barksdale AFB

Gas N: Chevron[*], Circle K[*], Citgo[*, CW]
S: Circle K[*], Exxon[*, D, CW], Texaco[*, D, LP, CW]

Food N: Arby's, Backyard Burgers, Bagel Shop, Burger King, Captain D's, Chili's, China Inn, Chuck E Cheese's Pizza, Freeda's Full House Saloon, Grandy's, Little Caesars Pizza, Luby's Cafeteria, McDonald's (Chevron), Notini's Italian, Pizza Hut, Popeye's Chicken, Red Lobster, Sonic Drive in, Taco Bell, **Waffle House**
S: Darrell's Grill & Restaurant, David Beard's Catfish & Seafood, Outback Steakhouse

Lodg N: Best Western, Crossland, Isle Of Capri Hotel, Rodeway Inn
S: Red Carpet Inn

AServ N: Firestone, **K-Mart**[RX], Midas Muffler & Brake, Minute Oil Change, Pep Boys Auto Center
S: Time-It-Lube, Tune-A-Car

Med N: **+ Hospital**

ATM N: **Albertson's Food Market**[RX], Bank One, Circle K, Citgo, Deposit Guaranty National Bank, Regions Bank
S: Bank One

Parks N: **Cyprus Black Bayou Recreation Area**

Other N: **Albertson's Food Market**[RX], Books-A-Million, **Eckerd Drugs**[RX], **K-Mart**[RX], **Office Depot**, **Pierre Bossier Mall**, Regal Cinema's, **Rite Aid Pharmacy**[RX], USA Drugs[RX], Vision 4 Less

Toll Free Reservations:
800-329-7466

DAYS INN 1152

Bossier City, LA
200 John Wesley Blvd.
I-20 • Exit 21 • 318-742-9200
Free Continental Breakfast
Bus Parking • Tour Pkgs
Outdoor Pool
Near Casinos
Free HBO/ESPN/CNN

Newly Renovated

Shreveport, LA
4935 W. Monkhouse Dr.
I-20 • Exit 13 • 318-636-0080
Free Continental Breakfast
Bus Parking • Tour Pkgs
Free HBO/ESPN/CNN
Near Riverboat Casinos
Near Airport

nta ABA AMERICAN BUS ASSOCIATION

LOUISIANA • 2 LOCATIONS

23 Industrial Dr

FStop S: **Chevron**[*, D]

Gas N: Circle K[*], Phillips 66[D], Texaco[*, D]
S: Road Mart[*]

Food N: Burger King[PLAY], Country Kitchen, Greenway's Harvest Buffet, McDonald's[PLAY], Popeye's Chicken (Texaco), Taco Bell

Lodg N: Horseshoe Le Boss'ier Hotel
S: Quality Inn

ATM N: Circle K

Other S: **State Police**

26 I-220 West Bypass, Louisiana Downs Racetrack

33 LA 157, Haughton, Fillmore

Gas N: Phillips 66[*]

AServ S: Haughton Auto Repair

RVCamp N: **Hilltop Campground (1.9 Miles)**
S: **Lake Bistineau State Park**

Parks N: **Bodcau Recreational Area (1.75 Miles)**
S: **Lake Bistineau State Park**

(36) **Rest Area (RR, Phones, Picnic, Grills, RV Dump, Pet Walk; Eastbound)**

(36) **Rest Area (RR, Phones, Picnic, Grills, Vending, RV Dump, Pet Walk; Westbound)**

38 Goodwill Road, Ammunition Plant

TStop S: **Fina**[*]

Food S: **Rainbow Diner (Fina Truck Stop)**

44 LA 7, Cotton Valley, Springhill

Gas N: Bud's

Food N: **Bayou Inn Catfish & Steak**, **Hamburger Happiness**, **Southern Maid Donuts**

47 LA 7, S U.S. 371, Minden, Sibley

Gas N: Chevron[*, D], Mobil[*, D], Texaco[*]

Food N: Exacta Inn

Lodg N: Best Western, Exacta Inn

AServ N: Clark's Pro Detailing, Eli's Tire

Parks S: **Lake Bistineau State Park (17 Miles)**

49 LA 531, Dubberly, Minden

TStop N: **Truckers Paradise**[*, 24]

Food N: **Truckers Paradise**

TServ N: **Petchak's Truck & Tire Repair**

ATM N: **Truckers Paradise**

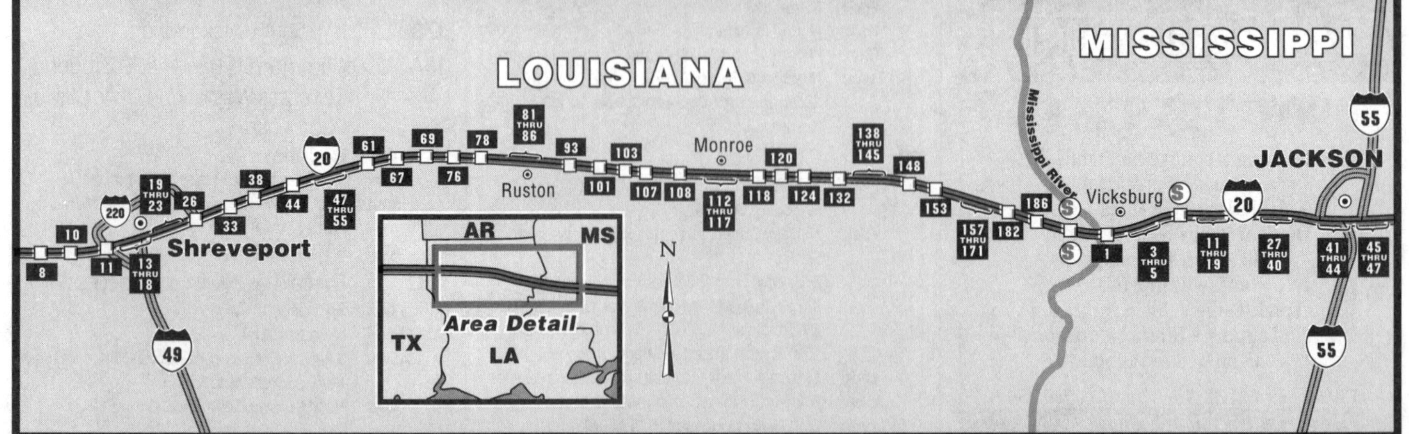

Bold red print shows RV & Bus parking available or nearby

EXIT		LOUISIANA
52		LA 532, Dubberly, To U.S. 80
	FStop	S: Chevron(*)
	Gas	S: Texaco(*)
55		U.S. 80, Ada, Taylor
(58)		Rest Area (RR, Phones, Picnic, RV Dump, Pet Walk; Eastbound)
(58)		Rest Area (RR, Phones, Picnic, Vending, RV Dump; Westbound)
61		LA 154, Gillsland, Athens
	Parks	N: Lake Claiborne State Park (17 Miles)
67		LA 9, Arcadia, Homer
	Gas	S: Texaco(LP)
	Food	S: J&J Express
	AServ	S: Texaco
	Parks	N: Lake Claiborne State Park (16 Miles)
69		LA 151, Arcadia, Dubach
	FStop	S: Fina(*)
	Gas	S: Exxon(*), Texaco(*)
	Food	S: Country Folks Kitchen, Nob Hill Inn, Pronto Pizza, Snuffy's Pizza, Sonic Drive In, Subway
	Lodg	S: Days Inn, Nob Hill Inn
	AServ	S: Arcadia Tire & Service, NAPA Auto Parts
	ATM	S: Texaco
	Other	S: Brookshire's Grocery Store, Car Wash, Factory Outlet Center, Freds Drug Store(RX)
76		LA 507, Simsboro
78		LA 563, Industry
81		Grambling, LA 149, Grambling State University
	Gas	S: Clark(*, D), Exxon(*), Texaco(*)
	Food	S: Church's Chicken (Clark)
84		LA 544, Ruston
	Gas	N: Mobil(*, D)
		S: Chevron(24), Citgo(*, CW, 24), Exxon(*), Texaco(*, D)
	Food	S: Domino's Pizza, Johnny's Pizza, Pizza Inn, Subway, TCBY
	Lodg	S: Super 8 (see our ad this page)
	AServ	S: Chevron(24)
85		U.S. 167, Ruston, Dubach (One Way Street)
	Gas	N: Chevron(*, CW, 24), Citgo(*), Shell(*, CW)
		S: Texaco(*)
	Food	N: Baskin Robbins, Burger King(PLAY), Captain D's Seafood, I Can't Believe It's Yogurt (Citgo), Maxwell's (Holiday Inn), McDonald's(PLAY), Peking, Pizza Inn, SHONEY'S, Shoney's, Subway (Citgo), Wendy's
		S: Pizza Hut
	Lodg	N: Days Inn, Hampton Inn, Holiday Inn
		S: Best Western

SUPER 8 MOTEL
318-255-0588
800-800-8000
1101 Cooktown Rd.
Ruston, LA
Continental Breakfast
Kids Under 12 Stay Free
Outdoor Pool • Jacuzzi Rooms Avail
Handicap Accessible • Coin Laundry
Bus/Sm Truck Parking
Cable TV w/HBO
Restaurants Nearby • Exterior Corridors
Micro-Fridge in All Rooms 1814
LOUISIANA • I-20 • Exit 84

EXIT		LOUISIANA
	AServ	S: Snappy Lube, Taylor's Tire
	Med	S: Hospital
	ATM	N: Bank One, CentralBank, Citgo, Community Trust Bank
	Other	N: Super 1 Foods
86		LA 33, Ruston, Farmerville
	Gas	N: Hwy. 33(*), Shell(*, CW)
		S: Texaco(*)
	Food	N: Cowboy's BAR-B-Q, Log Cabin Smokehouse
	Lodg	N: Comfort Inn, Ramada Limited
	AServ	N: Ruston Chrysler Plymouth Dodge Jeep Eagle, Xpress Lube
	RVCamp	N: Tri-Lake Marine & RV
	ATM	N: Community Trust Bank, Shell
	Other	N: Pack & Mail
		S: The Soap Opera Coin Laundry
93		LA 145, Choudrant, Sibley
	FStop	N: Texaco(*)
	Gas	S: Chevron(*, CW)
	Food	S: Down Home Cafe
	TServ	N: Texaco
(95)		Rest Area (RR, Phones, Picnic, RV Dump, Pet Walk; Eastbound)
(97)		Rest Area (RR, Phones, Picnic, RV Dump, Pet Walk; Westbound)
101		Calhoun, Downsville, LA 151
	TStop	S: Shell(*, D, 24)
	Food	S: Shell
	TServ	S: Shell(24)
103		U.S. 80, Calhoun
	TStop	N: USA Truck Stop Chevron(*)
	Gas	N: Stop N Shop(*)
	Lodg	N: Avant West Motel
	AServ	N: Bridgestone Tire & Auto
	TServ	N: Collman's Truck City
	TWash	N: Calhoun Super Truck Wash
107		Camp Road, Ouachita Parish 25
108		LA 546, Cheniere, To U.S. 80
	Gas	N: Texaco(*)
	RVCamp	N: Carters Camping Center Sales & Service
112		Well Road
	Gas	N: Shell(*, CW), Texaco(*)
	Food	N: McDonald's, Sonny
	AServ	N: Big A Auto Parts Claiborne, Ray's Garage & Tire Service, Xpress Lube
	RVCamp	S: I-20 Trailor Camp
	ATM	N: CentralBank
	Other	N: Claiborne IGA, Cooper Veterinary Hospital
114		LA 617, Thomas Road
	FStop	S: Exxon(*), Texaco(*)
	Gas	N: Racetrac(*), Texaco(*)
		S: Citgo(*, CW)
	Food	N: Chick-Fil-A, Chile Verde Mexican Bar & Grill, KFC, McDonald's(PLAY), Pizza Q, Popeye's Chicken, River West Seafood, SHONEY'S, Shoney's, Subway, TCBY, Taco Bell, Waffle House
		S: Baskin Robbins (Citgo), Chili's, Cracker Barrel, Donut Shop, K-Mart Supercenter(24, RX) (Grocery Store), Kettle, Logan's Roadhouse Steaks & Ribs, Lone Star Steakhouse, Outback Steakhouse, Peking Chinese, Sonic Drive In, Waffle House, Western Sizzlin'
	Lodg	N: Shoney's Inn, Super 8 (see our ad this page)
		S: Best Western, Holiday Inn Express, Red Roof Inn
	AServ	N: Wal-Mart Supercenter(24, RX), Xpress Lube
		S: Firestone, K-Mart Supercenter(24) (Grocery Store), Sears
	Med	N: Glenwood Regional Medical Center
	ATM	N: Hibernia Bank, Wal-Mart Supercenter
		S: Citgo, Exxon

EXIT		LOUISIANA
	Other	N: Tinsel Town Theaters, Wal-Mart Supercenter(RX)
		S: K-Mart Supercenter(RX) (Grocery Store)
115		LA 34, Stella St, Mill St
	Gas	N: Citgo(*)
	AServ	N: Muffler Shop, Westside Imports
116B		Bus. US 165, LA 15, to Civic Center, Jackson Street (Eastbound)
	Gas	S: Citgo(CW)
	Food	S: Popeye's Chicken
	AServ	S: Citgo, Muffler Center
	Med	N: St. Francis Medical Center
116A		Fifth St
	Gas	N: Circle K(*)
	AServ	N: Tire Town, Welker Auto Inc. Diagnostics
117A		Hall St (Eastbound)
	Food	S: Guest House Inn
	Lodg	S: Guest House Inn
	Med	S: St. Francis Medical Center
117B		LA 594, Texas Ave
117C		Bus. US 165, LA 15, Civic Center (Westbound)
	Med	N: St. Francis Medical Center
	Other	N: Monroe Civic Center, Police Dept
117D		South 2nd St, Layton Ave (Westbound)
118AB		U.S. 165, Bastrop, Columbia
	Gas	S: Chevron(*, 24), Citgo(*), Exxon(*), Shell(*, CW), Texaco(*)
	Food	N: Bobbisox (Holiday Inn), Kettle(24) (La Quinta)
		S: Captain D's, Haskell's Donuts, KFC, McDonald's, Podnuh's BBQ, Popeye's Chicken, Wendy's, Western Sizzlin
	Lodg	N: Holiday Inn, La Quinta Inn, Stratford House Inns
		S: Hampton Inn, Motel 6, Ramada Limited
	AServ	N: Cooper Jeep Eagle Buick GMC, Interstate Dodge Dodge Trucks
	TServ	N: Monroe Mack Sales Louisiana Kenworth, Scott Truck & Tractor
		S: Harrison Truck Repair
	ATM	S: Central Bank
	Other	S: Car Wash
120		Garrett Rd, Monroe Airport
	FStop	N: Citgo Travel Plaza(*)
	Gas	N: Shell(*)
		S: Exxon(*, D)
	Food	N: Olive Garden, Pizza Hut
	Lodg	S: Best Western, Days Inn
	AServ	N: Firestone, Sears Auto Center
	RVCamp	S: Monroe's Shiloh Camp Resort (1.5 Miles), Pecanland RV Park
	ATM	N: Citgo Travel Plaza

The Pride of Super 8 1791

SUPER 8 MOTEL
318-325-6361
1101 Glenwood Drive
West Monroe, LA
Group Rates Available
• Kids Under 12 Stay Free
• Outdoor Pool
• Handicap Accessible
• Truck/Large Vehicle Parking
• Exterior Corridors
• Free Local Calls
• Many Restaurants Nearby
• Cable TV w/HBO/ESPN
I-20, Exit14, Thomas Rd., Rt at 2nd light on Glenwood Dr.
LOUISIANA • I-20 • EXIT 114

Bold red print shows RV & Bus parking available or nearby

EXIT LOUISIANA

S: Exxon
Other N: Pecanland Mall
S: Sam's Club

124 LA 594, R Sage Wildlife Area, Millhaven
FStop N: E-Z Mart(*)
RVCamp N: RV Park
Other N: LA State Police

132 LA 133, Columbia, Start
Gas N: Exxon(*)

138 LA 137, Archibald, Rayville
TStop N: Pilot Travel Center(*)
FStop N: Cannon's Handee Korner(*, LP)
S: Citgo(*)
Gas S: Exxon(*)
Food N: Burger King(PLAY), Dairy Queen (Pilot TS), Johnny's Pizza, McDonald's(PLAY), Sports Grill, Wendy's (Pilot TS)
S: Cottonland Inn, Popeye's Chicken, Subway (Citgo), TCBY (Citgo), Waffle House
Lodg N: Days Inn
S: Cottonland Inn
AServ S: Goodyear
TServ N: Lee's Truck Service(24)
RVCamp S: Cottonland Inn, Cottonland RV Park
Med N: Richardson Medical Center
ATM N: Richland State Bank
Other N: Car Wash, Kaye's Food Market, Wal-Mart(RX)
S: Dupeire Animal Clinic

141 LA 583, Bee Bayou Road
FStop N: Texaco(*)
TServ N: Atkins Tire Repair, Bee Bayou Truck Service(24) (Texaco)
ATM N: Texaco

145 LA 183, Richland Parish 202, Holly Ridge

148 LA 609, Dunn

(150) Rest Area (RR, Phones, Picnic, RV Dump, Pet Walk; Eastbound)

(150) Rest Area (RR, Phones, Picnic, RV Dump, Pet Walk; Westbound)

153 LA 17, Winnsboro, Delhi
TStop N: Jubilee Truck Stop(*, 24)
Gas N: Exxon(*), Texaco
S: Texaco(*)
Food N: Big Sid's, Dairy Queen, Pizza Hut, Subway, Taco Bell (Jubilee Truck Stop)
S: Best Western
Lodg S: Best Western, Hotel
AServ N: Exxon, Texaco
TServ N: Interstate Engine(24)
TWash N: Jubilee Truck Stop
Other N: Brookshire's Grocery, Freds Drug Store(RX)

157 LA 577, Waverly
FStop N: Tiger Truck Stop(*, 24)
Food N: Tiger Truck Stop

171 U.S. 65, Vidalia, Tallulah, Newellton
TStop S: T/A TravelCenters of America(*, SCALES), Tallula Truck Stop(*)
FStop N: Shell(*)
Gas N: Citgo(*)
S: Texaco(*)
Food N: McDonald's(PLAY), Wendy's
S: Country Pride (TA), T/A TravelCenters of America, Tallula Truck Stop
Lodg N: Days Inn, Super 8
TWash S: Tallula Truck Stop
ATM N: Shell

173 LA 602, Richmond
RVCamp S: Roundaway RV Park

EXIT LOUISIANA/MISSISSIPPI

182 Mound, LA 602

(184) Rest Area (RR, Phones, Picnic, Grills, RV Dump; Eastbound)

(184) Rest Area (RR, Phones, Picnic, Grills, RV Dump; Westbound)

186 U.S. 80 West, Delta
FStop N: Texaco(*)
S: Chevron(*, 24)
Food S: Blimpie Subs & Salads (Chevron)
ATM S: Chevron

(187) Weigh Station (Westbound)

(187) Weigh Station (Eastbound)

↑LOUISIANA

↓MISSISSIPPI

1A Washington St, Warrenton Rd, MS Welcome Center (P)
Gas N: Exxon(*, D), Shell(*, D, LP)
Food N: Delta Point River Restaurant, Goldie's Trail BAR-B-QUE
S: Waffle House
Lodg N: Delta Point Inn
S: Ramada Limited, Ridgeland Inn
AServ N: Automatic Transmission Service
RVCamp N: Isle of Capri RV Park (.5 Miles)
ATM N: Exxon, Shell
Parks N: Navy Circle & Grant's Canal (2 Miles)
Other N: Kar Kleen Car Wash(CW)

1B U.S. 61 South, Natchez (Left Exit Westbound)
RVCamp S: River City RV Park (1.25 Miles)

1C Halls Ferry Rd.
Gas N: Chevron(*, 24), Exxon(*)
S: Fast Lane(*), Shell(*, CW)
Food N: Burger King
S: Baskin Robbins(PLAY), Captain D's Seafood, Goldies Express BAR-B-QUE, Hardee's, Little Caesars Pizza, Popeye's Chicken, Shipley's Do-Nuts, SHONEY'S, Shoney's, Subway, Taco Casa, Wendy's
Lodg N: Guesthouse Inn
S: Days Inn, EconoLodge, Fairfield Inn by Marriott
AServ S: Discount Auto Parts, Xpress Lube
Med N: Columbia Vicksburg Medical Center, Hospital
ATM S: Deposit Guaranty National Bank, Fast Lane, Miss Money, Trustmark National Bank
Other N: Durst Discount Drugs(RX)
S: K-Mart(RX), Kar-Kleen Car Wash, Kroger Supermarket(24, RX)

1116
VICKSBURG FACTORY OUTLETS
VICKSBURG, MISSISSIPPI
4000 South Frontage Road • 601-636-7434
Across I-20 From The National Park
Monday-Saturday 9am-9pm
Sunday Noon-6pm
Bass Company Store • Boot Country • Bon Worth
Bugle Boy • Casual Corner • Claire's Boutique
Corning Revere • Duck Head • J. Richard's Deli
Dress Barn • Factory Brand Shoes
Famous Brands Housewares • Florsheim Shoes
Full Size Fashions • L'eggs Hanes Bali Playtex
Capacity • The Collage • Paper Factory • Publisher's Outlet
Rue 21 • Sunglass Hut • Tools & More
Tots-to-Teens • Van Heusen Direct • Welcome Home
MISSISSIPPI • I-20 • EXIT 5B

EXIT MISSISSIPPI

3 Indiana Ave
Gas N: Texaco(*, D, CW)
S: Chevron(*, CW), Shell(*, CW)
Food N: Blimpie Subs & Salads (Texaco), McDonald's(PLAY), Pizza Hut, Sun Garden Restaurant, Taco Casa, Waffle House
S: Heavenly Ham, KFC, Ponderosa Steakhouse
Lodg N: Best Western, Delux Inn
S: Quality Inn
AServ N: Atwood Chevrolet, Olds, Geo, Delta Ford
S: Buick, Pontiac, Cadillac, GMC Truck Dealer
ATM S: Shell
Other N: Battlefield Discount Drugs(RX), Rite Aid Pharmacy(RX), Super Value Foods

4AB West Clay Street, Downtown Vicksburg
Gas N: Chevron(*)
S: Texaco(*)
Food N: Gernetts Restaurant (Holiday Inn), Levi's Cafe, Waffle House
S: Battlefield Inn, Cracker Barrel, Maxwell's Restaurant, McAlister's Gourmet Deli, Oasis(24) (Scottish Inns), Pizza Inn, The Dock Seafood
Lodg N: Hampton Inn, Holiday Inn, Super 8
S: Battlefield Inn, Comfort Inn, Scottish Inns
AServ S: Rivertown Toyota Jeep Eagle Lincoln Mercury
RVCamp N: Vicksburg Battlefield Kampground (Laundry, Store, Pool, Hookups; .5 Miles)
S: Battlefield Inn
Med S: Hospital
Parks N: Vicksburg National Military Park
Other S: Sun-Up Laundry, Vicksburg Factory Outlets

5AB U.S. 61 North, MS 27 South, Rolling Fork, Utica, Yazoo City (Left Exit Eastbound)
FStop N: Shell(*)
Gas N: Conoco(*, D, LP)
S: Texaco(*, D, CW)
Food S: Beechwood Inn, Blimpie Subs & Salads(D) (Texaco), Rowdy's Restaurant, Taco Bell (Texaco)
Lodg S: Beechwood Inn, Hillcrest Inn
AServ N: Conoco
ATM N: Shell, Trustmark National Bank
S: Texaco
Other S: Vicksburg Factory Outlets (see our ad this page)

(6) Parking Area (Eastbound)

(7) Weigh Station (Eastbound)

11 Bovina
FStop N: Texaco(*, D, LP, RV DUMP)
Food S: Restaurant
AServ S: Import Automotive Specialist
RVCamp N: Clear Creek Campground and RV Park (Laundromat)
ATM N: Texaco

15 Flowers

19 MS 22, Flora, Edwards
FStop S: Conoco(*, D)
Gas S: Texaco(*)
Food S: Dairy Queen (Texaco)
Lodg S: Relax Inn
RVCamp N: Askew's Landing Campground (2.5 Miles)

27 Bolton
Gas N: Chevron(*)

34 Natchez Trace Parkway

35 Clinton - Raymond Road
TStop S: Conoco
Gas N: Chevron(*, LP), Phillips 66(*, CW), Texaco(*, CW)
Food N: Pizza Inn (Texaco)
S: Conoco

Bold red print shows RV & Bus parking available or nearby

EXIT MISSISSIPPI

AServ N: Chevron, Texaco
TServ S: Conoco
ATM N: Phillips 66

36 Springridge Road
Gas N: BP[*], Shell[*, LP]
S: Exxon[*, D, LP], Texaco[*, D, CW]
Food N: McDonald's[PLAY], Taco Bell, Waffle House
S: Baskin Robbins (Exxon), Popeye's Chicken, Shoney's, Xan's Diner
Lodg N: Days Inn
S: Hampton Inn, Holiday Inn Express
RVCamp S: Springridge RV Park
ATM N: BP, Kroger Supermarket[RX], Shell
S: Exxon, Texaco
Other N: Kroger Supermarket[RX], Quality Car Wash
S: Animal Hospital of Clinton, United Artist Theaters

40AB MS 18 West, Raymond, Robinson Road
Gas N: Phillips 66, Shell[*, D], Spur[*, D, 24]
S: Max Gas[*]
Food N: Mazzio's Pizza, Pizza Hut, Popeye's Chicken, Wendy's
S: Waffle House
Lodg S: Comfort Inn
AServ N: Car Care Clinic
S: Wal-Mart SuperCenter[24, RX]
Med S: Hospital
ATM N: Spur
S: Max Gas, Trustmark Bank
Other N: Car Wash, Office Depot
S: Wal-Mart SuperCenter[RX]

41 I-220, U.S. 49, N. Jackson, Yazoo City (Left Exit , Limited Access Hwy)

42AB Ellis Ave
Gas N: BP[*, CW], Shell[*, CW]
S: Conoco[*, D], Exxon[*], Pump & Save Gas
Food N: Burger King, Denny's, Hunan Garden, McDonald's[PLAY], Ponderosa Steakhouse, Popeye's Chicken, Wendy's
S: Dairy Queen, Pizza Hut
Lodg N: Barren's (Ramada Inn), Best Western, Camelot Inn, Days Inn, EconoLodge, Holiday Inn (see our ad this page), Ramada Inn, Scottish Inns, Sleep Inn, Stonewall Jackson Motor Lodge
AServ N: Auto Zone Auto Parts, Firestone, Midas Muffler & Brake, Mr. Transmission, Wilson Dodge
Med S: Hospital
ATM N: Deposit Guaranty National Bank
Other S: Sac & Save Food & Drug[RX]

43AB Terry Road
Gas N: A & M Food Mart[*], Shell[*, 24]
Food N: Kim's Seafood Restaurant, Krystal
Lodg N: Tarrymore Motel
S: La Quinta Inn
AServ N: Delta Muffler & Exhaust, Randy's Auto, Southern Auto Supply
RVCamp N: S & S Apache Camping Center Sales & Service
ATM N: Deposit Guaranty National Bank
Other N: Rexal Drugs[RX]

44 Junction I-55 South, New Orleans (Left Exit Westbound)

45A Gallatin St.
Gas N: Chevron[*], Dixie Gas[*], S & S Mini Service, Texaco[*]
Lodg N: Crossroads Inn
AServ N: Anglin Tire Co, Cowboys Used Tires, Gentry's Body Shop, Smith Automatic Transmission, Xpress Lube
S: Regency Toyota, Nissan, Mitsubishi
Other N: Camping, Duncan's Discount Marine, Jackson Animal Clinic
S: Animal Health Products, Magnolia Animal Hospital

EXIT MISSISSIPPI

45B US 51N, State St
AServ N: AAMCO Transmission, Fowler Buick, Fowler GMC Truck, Freeman Auto Service, Paul Moak Pontiac, Volvo, Honda

46 Junction I-55 & I-20
TServ S: Cummins Mid South, Inc. (1 Mile)
RVCamp S: Cummins Mid South, Inc. (1 Mile)

47 U.S. 49 South, Hattiesburg, U.S. 80 Flowood
TStop N: Flying J Travel Plaza[*, LP, RV DUMP, SCALES]
Food N: Country Market (Flying J TS), Flying J Travel Plaza, Western Sizzlin'
Lodg N: Days Inn, TraveLodge
AServ N: Graves & Stoddard's Toyota, Nissan, Honda & Mazda

48 MS 468, Pearl
FStop N: Speedway[*, LP]
S: Chevron[*, 24]
Gas N: BP[*, K, CW], Conoco[*, LP], Shell[*, CW]
S: Texaco[*, D]
Food N: Arby's, Burger King, Cracker Barrel, Deli (Speedway), El Charro Mexican, Frisco Deli, McDonald's[PLAY], Popeye's Chicken, Schlotzsky's Deli, Shoney's, Sonic Drive in, Speedway, USA Bumpers Drive-In, Waffle House
Lodg N: Best Western, Budgatel Inn, Comfort Inn, Econolodge, Fairfield Inn, Holiday Inn Express
S: Days Inn
AServ N: E-Z Lube[CW], High Tech Transmissions
ATM N: Conoco, Deposit Guaranty National Bank, Shell
Other N: Car Wash, Delton Moore Drugs

52 MS 475, Jackson Int'l Airport
Gas N: Chevron, Exxon[*, D, LP]
Food N: Waffle House
S: Taylor's Fish House
Lodg N: Howard Johnson, Ramada Limited
TServ N: Peterbilt Dealer
ATM N: Exxon

54 Crossgates Blvd, Greenfield Road
Gas N: Amoco[*, LP, CW], BP[*, CW], Exxon[*, CW]
Food N: Domino's Pizza, Dunkin Donuts (BP), KFC, Kismet's (Greek), Papa John's Pizza, Pizza Hut, Waffle House, Wendy's
Lodg N: Ridgeland Inn
AServ N: Brandon Discount Glass, Crossgates Tire & Auto, Fowler Buick & GMC Truck, Goerlich Mufflers, Goodyear Tire & Auto, Gray-Daniels Ford, Jet-Lube
Med N: Rankin Medical Center
ATM N: Kroger Supermarket[RX]
Other N: Carwash, Kroger Supermarket[RX], Polks Discount Drugs

56 U.S. 80, Downtown Brandon
Gas S: BP[*, D, CW], Exxon[*], Texaco[*, D, CW]
Food N: Annie B's Family Grill, McDonald's[PLAY], Sonny's

Holiday Inn

JACKSON SOUTHWEST

2649 Highway 80 West
Jackson, Mississippi 39204

601-355-3472
800-HOLIDAY

• Close to downtown's cultural, arts and historic districts • Excellent shopping a short drive away • Remington's full-service restaurant • In-room cable TV with premium news, sports and movie channels • Outdoor pool • 18-acre grounds with recreation/sports areas

1466

EXIT MISSISSIPPI

Real Pit Bar-B-Q, Taco Bell
S: Blimpie's Subs (Texaco), Dairy Queen[PLAY], Orie's Kuntry Kitchen, Sonic Drive In, Texaco
Lodg S: Days Inn
AServ N: Auto Zone Auto Parts, Brandon Radiator Supply, Ozene Cumberland Body Shop
S: Brandon Discount Tire, Delta Muffler & Brake, Havoline Express Lube, Pete's Tire Service & Brakes
ATM N: Community Bank
S: Exxon, Texaco
Parks S: Ross Barnett Park
Other N: Brandon Police Dept

59 U.S. 80, East Brandon

68 MS 43, Pelahatchie, Puckett
FStop N: Chevron[*, 24], Conoco[*, LP, CW, RV DUMP, 24]
S: MGM Fuel Center BP[*, LP]
Gas S: Ol' Yeller[*]
Food N: Chevron, Stuckey's Express (Chevron), Subway (Chevron)
TWash N: Conoco[CW]
RVCamp N: Camping
ATM N: Chevron, Conoco

(75) Rest Area (RR, Phones, Picnic, Grills, Vending, RV Dump, RV Water, Pet Walk, P; Westbound)

77 13, Morton, Puckett
TStop N: Phillips 66[24] (CB Shop)
Gas N: Phillips Farm & Garden[*, D]
Food N: Phillips Farm & Garden, Southern BBQ & Stuff (Phillips Farm & Garden)
TServ N: 77 Truck Repair Garage[24] (Towing)
Med N: Hospital
Parks N: Roosevelt State Park (.5 Miles, Camping)
Other N: National Forest Trail

80 481, Morton, Raleigh

88 35, Forest, Raleigh
TStop S: Chevron[*, 24]
FStop N: Amoco[*, D, LP], Shell[*, D]
Gas N: BP[*, D], Quik Stop[*, D], Shell[D]
Food N: Bar-B-Q Ribs (Quik Stop), Best Western, Quik Stop, Wendy's
S: Chevron, Santa Fe Steak House, Stuckey's Express (Chevron)
Lodg N: Best Western, Comfort Inn, Days Inn
AServ N: Auto Lube & Tune-Ups
Med N: Hospital
ATM N: Amoco, Shell, Shell
Other N: Car Wash
S: Bienville National Forest Info Center

(91) Rest Area (RR, Phones, Picnic, Grills, Vending, RV Dump, Pet Walk, P; Southbound)

96 Lake

100 U.S. 80, Lake, Lawrence
TStop N: BP[*, 24]
Food N: BP
ATM N: BP

109 MS 15, Newton, Philadelphia, Decatur, Union
FStop N: Texaco[*]
S: Citgo[*]
Gas S: Chevron[*, D, 24], Conoco[*, D, LP, CW]
Food N: BoRo Family Restaurant, Spanky's (Texaco), Texaco, Wendy's (Texaco)
S: Hardee's, McDonald's[PLAY]
Lodg N: Thrifty Inn
S: Days Inn
Med S: Hospital
ATM N: Texaco
S: Citgo, Conoco
Parks N: Turkey Creek Water Park

115 MS 503, Hickory, Decatur

EXIT MISSISSIPPI

121 Chunky
- **Food** N: Chunky Junction Seafood (Thurs-Sun)

129 U.S. 80 West, Lost Gap, Meehan Junction
- **Gas** S: Spaceway(*, CW)
- **Food** S: Grill King (Spaceway), Spaceway

Exit (130) I-59 South, Laurel

Note: I-20 runs concurrent below with I-59. Numbering follows I-59.

150 U.S 11, N19, Philadelphia, Meridian Airport
- **TStop** E: **Stuckey's Express**(*, D)
  W: **Phillips 66**, **Twin Cities Truck Stop**
- **FStop** E: **Amoco**(*, LP)
- **Gas** W: No Name(*)
- **Food** E: **Stuckey's Express**, **Subway (Stuckey's Express)**
  W: **Phillips 66**
- **TServ** W: **International**, **Phillips 66**, **Tire Centers Inc.**, **Waters Int. Truck**
- **ATM** E: **Amoco**
- **Parks** W: **Lake Okatibee Park**

151 49th Avenue, Valley Rd, Meridian

152 29th Avenue (Difficult Reaccess)
- **FStop** W: **Amoco**(*), **Chevron**(*, D, 24)
- **Food** E: Royal Inn Motel
- **Lodg** E: Royal Inn Motel
  W: Ramada Limited
- **ATM** W: **Chevron**

153 U.S 145S, 22nd Avenue, Quitman, Downtown Meridian
- **TStop** E: **Red Hot Truck Stop**
- **Gas** E: Chevron(*, D, 24), Conoco(*, D, LP, CW, RV DUMP), Exxon(*, D, LP), Shell
  W: Amoco(*, 24), BP(*)
- **Food** E: Best Western, Depot (Best Western), Morrison's Cafeteria, **Red Hot Truck Stop**, Waffle House
  W: Barnhill's, Burger King, Captain D's Seafood, El Chico Mexican Restaurant, Hardee's, KFC, McDonald's(PLAY), SHONEY'S, Shoney's, Wendy's
- **Lodg** E: Astro Motel, Best Western, Budget 8 Motel, Budgetel Inn, Econolodge, **Holiday Inn Express**, **Motel 6**, **Sleep Inn**
- **AServ** E: Coin Car Wash, Nelson Hall Hyundai Chevrolet, **Patco Inc.**, Shell
  W: Firestone Tire & Auto, Goodyear Tire & Auto, Tire Center
- **TServ** E: **Patco Inc.**
- **Med** E: ✚ **Hospital**
- **ATM** E: Conoco, Exxon
  W: Citizens National Bank, Union Planters Bank
- **Other** W: **Foodmax Grocery**, K&B Drugs, **Medi Save Pharmacy**, **Optical**

154AB Hwy 19 S, Hwy 39 North, Naval Air Station, De Kalb, Butler AL
- **Gas** E: Chevron(*, D, CW), Conoco(*, D, LP, CW)
  W: Amoco(*, D), BP(*, D, CW), Shell(*, CW) (see our ad this page)
- **Food** E: Chesterfield's, China King, Luby's Cafeteria, Mazingo's, McDonald's, O'Charley's Restaurant, Popeye's Chicken, Red Lobster, Ryan's Steakhouse, Taco Bell
  W: Applebee's, Backyard Burgers, **Cracker Barrel**, Denny's(24) (Holiday Inn), Greenbriar (Howard Johnson), Holiday Inn, Mr C's Rancho, Waffle House
- **Lodg** E: Comfort Inn
  W: DAYS INN Days Inn, Hampton Inn, Holiday Inn, Howard Johnson, Relax Inn, Rodeway Inn, **Super 8**, Western Motel
- **AServ** E: Express Lube, Sears
  W: Bill Ethridge Lincoln Mercury Isuzu, Johnson Dodge, Meridian Honda, Premier Paint & Body, Sellers Olds Cadillac
- **TServ** E: **Truckers Supply Co. (Parts)**
  W: **Stribling Equipment Empire Truck**
- **RVCamp** W: **Campground RV And Trailer Park (2 Miles)**, **Ethridge RV Center**(LP) **(.4 Miles)**, **Jen's Discount Furniture Mobil Home Parts**
- **ATM** E: Chevron, Citizen National Bank, Conoco
  W: Howard Johnson, Shell(*, CW), Shell
- **Other** E: **Bonita Lake Mall**, **K-Mart**(RX), Meridian Shop Plaza, **Wal-Mart**(RX)
  W: **Old South Antique Mall**

157A US 45S, Quitman

157B US 45N, Macon, Quitman (Difficult Reaccess)

160 Russell
- **TStop** E: **T/A TravelCenters of America**, **Travel Center**(*, SCALES) **(BP)**
  W: **Amoco**(*, LP, SCALES)
- **Food** E: **T/A TravelCenters of America**, Travel Center, **Travel Center (BP)**
- **TServ** E: **Travel Center**(SCALES) **(BP)**
- **RVCamp** W: **Nanabe Creek Campground (1 Mile)**
- **ATM** E: **Travel Center (BP)**
  W: **Amoco**

(164) **Rest Area, Welcome Center (RR, Phones, RV Dump, P; Westbound)**

165 Toomsuba
- **TStop** E: **Fuel Mart**(*, SCALES)
- **FStop** W: **Travla Texaco**(*, D, 24)
- **Gas** W: Shell(*) (see our ad this page)
- **Food** E: Arby's (Fuel Mart), **Fuel Mart**
  W: **Travla Restaurant (Texaco)**, **Travla Texaco**
- **RVCamp** E: **KOA Campgrounds (1.75 Miles)**
- **ATM** W: **Travla Texaco**
- **Other** W: Coin Car Wash

169 Kewanee
- **TStop** E: **Kewanee One Stop**(*)
- **FStop** E: **Red Apple**(*)
  W: **Dixie**
- **Food** E: **Kewanee One Stop**, **Restaurant (Kewanee One Stop)**

(170) **Weigh Station (Eastbound)**

(170) **Weigh Station (Westbound)**

↑ MISSISSIPPI

↓ ALABAMA

(1) **Rest Area (RR, Phones, RV Dump; Eastbound)**

1 U.S 80 East, Cuba, Demopolis
- **TStop** W: **Phillips 66**
- **Gas** E: Chevron(*), Dixie(*)
- **Food** W: **Phillips 66**

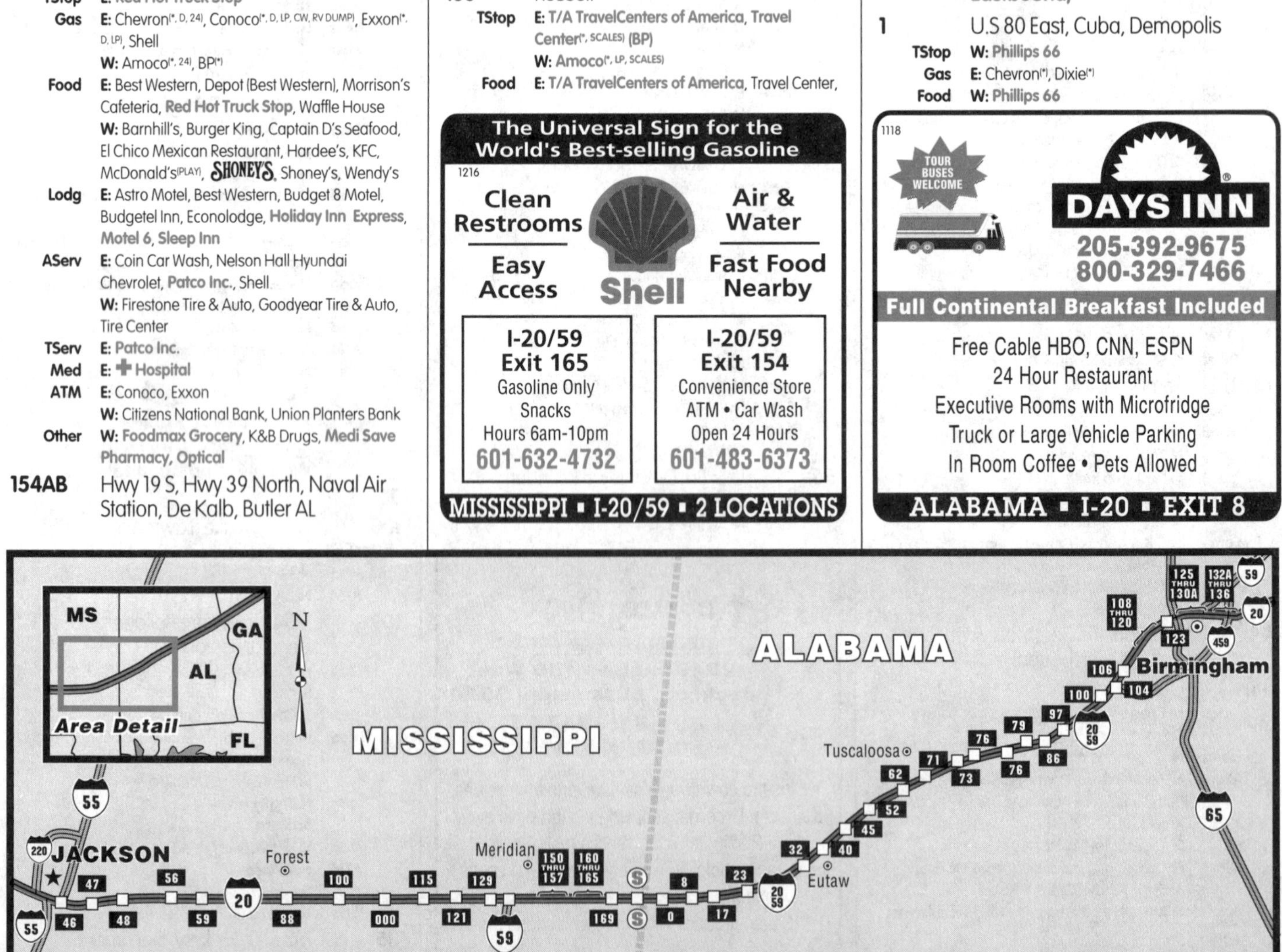

1216
The Universal Sign for the World's Best-selling Gasoline
Clean Restrooms
Easy Access
Shell
Air & Water
Fast Food Nearby
I-20/59 Exit 165
Gasoline Only
Snacks
Hours 6am-10pm
601-632-4732
I-20/59 Exit 154
Convenience Store
ATM • Car Wash
Open 24 Hours
601-483-6373
MISSISSIPPI • I-20/59 • 2 LOCATIONS

1118
TOUR BUSES WELCOME
DAYS INN
205-392-9675
800-329-7466
Full Continental Breakfast Included
Free Cable HBO, CNN, ESPN
24 Hour Restaurant
Executive Rooms with Microfridge
Truck or Large Vehicle Parking
In Room Coffee • Pets Allowed
ALABAMA • I-20 • EXIT 8

Bold red print shows RV & Bus parking available or nearby

EXIT	ALABAMA
8	AL 17, York
TStop	**E:** BP(*, SCALES)
Food	**E:** BP
Lodg	**E:** Days Inn (see our ad this page)
TServ	**E:** Dun-Rite Truck Wash (BP)
TWash	**E:** BP
Med	**E:** Hospital
17	AL 28, Livingston, Boyd
TStop	**E:** Noble Truck Stop(*, SCALES)
FStop	**E:** Exxon(*, D), Texaco(*)
Gas	**E:** BP(*, 24), Chevron(*, 24)
Food	**E:** Burger King, Chevron, Exxon, Noble Truck Stop, Pizza Hut, Royal Waffle King (Noble TS), Subway (Chevron)
Lodg	**E:** Comfort Inn, Western Inn
TServ	**E:** Dickey's 24hr Shop Lube & Repair (Noble)
ATM	**E:** Chevron
23	Gainesville, Epes
32	Boligee
FStop	**W:** BP(*)
Gas	**E:** Chevron(*, 24)
Food	**E:** Chevron, Subway (Chevron) **W:** BP
Parks	**W:** Boligee Park
(38)	Rest Area (RR, Phones, RV Dump; Eastbound)
(39)	Rest Area (RR, Phones; Westbound)
40	AL 14, Eutaw, Aliceville
Med	**E:** Hospital (2 Miles)
Other	**W:** Visitor Information
45	Union
FStop	**E:** Amoco(*)
Food	**E:** Hardee's, Southfork Restaurant(24) **W:** Cotton Patch Restaurant
Lodg	**E:** Western Inn
AServ	**E:** Auto Value (Parts)
52	U.S 11, U.S 43, Knoxville
FStop	**W:** SpeedStop(*)
62	Fosters
71A	AL 69S, Moundville (Difficult Reaccess)
Gas	**E:** Exxon(*, D)
Food	**E:** Arby's, IHOP, Lone Star Steakhouse, Outback Steakhouse, Pizza Hut, Waffle House, Wendy's
Lodg	**E:** Courtyard by Marriott, Fairfield Inn, Jameson Inn
AServ	**E:** Quality Jeep Eagle
Other	**E:** K-Mart, Lowe's (Hardware)
71B	Junction I-369, AL 69 North, Tuscaloosa
Other	**W:** Tuscaloosa Convention and Visitor's Bureau (see our ad this page)
73	U.S 82, McFarland Blvd
FStop	**W:** BP(*)
Gas	**E:** Amoco, Exxon(*, LP), Texaco(*, D, CW) **W:** BP(*, D), Chevron(*), Parade(*, CW), Phillips 66(*), Racetrac(*), Shell(*, CW)
Food	**E:** Chili's, Guthrie's Chicken, Hardee's, Huddle House, Joe Mugs (Books-A-Million), Jordan Homestyle Restaurant, KFC, Logan's Roadhouse Steaks & Ribs, McDonald's(PLAY), Piccadilly Cafeteria, Pizza Hut, Quincy's Family Steakhouse, Sonic Drive In, Subway, Taco Bell, Taco Casa, Trey Yuen, Wendy's **W:** Burger King, Captain D's Seafood, Denny's, Ezell's Catfish Cabin, Fortune Garden, Krystal, Long John Silver, O'Charley's, Shoney's, Shoney's, Sneaky Peeks (Chevron), Waffle House
Lodg	**E:** Comfort Inn, Country Inn & Suites, Days Inn, La Quinta Inn, LaQuinta Inn, Motel 6, Ramada Inn, Super 8 **W:** Best Western, Holiday Inn, Master's Inn, Shoney's Inn, TraveLodge
AServ	**E:** Amoco, Carport Auto Service, SouthTrust Bank, Townsend Ford, Townsend Glass, Tuscaloosa Isuzu **W:** Barkley's Pontiac, GMC, O.K. Tire Service, Postle's Auto Service, Tuscaloosa Motor Parts
Med	**E:** Family Care Medical Center & Cancel **W:** Hospital
ATM	**E:** AM South, Amoco, Exxon, Region Bank **W:** Racetrac
Parks	**E:** Lake Lurene State Park **W:** Bowers Park
Other	**E:** Books-A-Million (Coffee Shop), Delchamp's Supermarket, Food World, Harkco Super Drug, McFarland Mall, Rite Aid Pharmacy, Sam's Club, Spiffy's Car Wash(CW), Walmart Super Center(24, RX) (Vision Center), Winn Dixie Supermarket(RX) **W:** Christian Book & Gift Store, Ramey Animal Hospital
76	U.S 11, East Tuscaloosa, Cottondale
TStop	**E:** 76 Auto/Truck Plaza(SCALES), Baggett's
Gas	**E:** Texaco(*, D, LP) (Wrecker Service) **W:** Citgo(*), Shell(*, D)
Food	**E:** Baggett's **W:** Burger King, Cracker Barrel, Knight's Inn
Lodg	**E:** Sleep Inn **W:** Key West Inn, Knight's Inn
AServ	**E:** Baggett's, Texaco (Wrecker Service) **W:** Donnie Bryant Transmission
TServ	**E:** 76 Auto/Truck Plaza(SCALES), Baggett's
TWash	**E:** 76 Auto/Truck Plaza
RVCamp	**E:** Country Roads RV Sales & Service(LP) (1 Mile) **W:** Sunset II Travel Park
ATM	**E:** 76 Auto/Truck Plaza **W:** Shell
Other	**W:** Geer Bros. Camper Sales and Service
77	Cottondale
TStop	**W:** T/A TravelCenters of America(*, RV DUMP, SCALES)
Gas	**W:** Amoco(*)
Food	**W:** Country Pride (Truck Stops Of America), McDonald's(PLAY) (Amoco), Subway (Truck Stops Of America), T/A TravelCenters of America, Taco Bell (Truck Stop)
Lodg	**W:** Hampton Inn, Microtel Inn
AServ	**E:** Troy's Honda Parts
TServ	**W:** T/A TravelCenters of America(SCALES)
TWash	**W:** T/A TravelCenters of America
79	U.S 11, University Blvd, Coaling
RVCamp	**N:** Candy Mountain RV Park (4.5 Miles)
(85)	Rest Area (Eastbound)
(85)	Rest Area (RR, HF, Phones, Picnic, Vending, RV Dump, Pet Walk)
86	Brookwood, Vance
TStop	**W:** Shell(*) (Restaurant)
Food	**W:** Shell (Restaurant)
TServ	**W:** Shell, Shell (Restaurant)
RVCamp	**E:** Candy Mountain RV Park (4.5 Miles), Lakeside RV Park
89	Mercedes Dr
97	U.S 11 South, AL 5 South, West Blocton, Centerville
FStop	**E:** Amoco(*), Texaco(*, LP)
Gas	**E:** Shell(*, LP)
Food	**E:** Dot's Farmhouse, KFC
ATM	**E:** Amoco
100	Abernant, Bucksville
TStop	**E:** Petro(*, D)
Gas	**E:** Exxon(*, LP), Phillips 66(*, D), Texaco(*, LP)

Tuscaloosa!

The Perfect Off-Road Experience.

Not only is Tuscaloosa home of the new Mercedes off–road vehicle but also home of the perfect off–road experience for your group.

You can tour the Mercedes-Benz Visitors Center and Factory. Enjoy an historic tour of the University of Alabama campus, or tour the Alabama Museum of Natural History, and the Paul W. "Bear" Bryant Museum. You can also view the world renowned Warner Art Collection that includes precious works ranging from primitive, to classical, to modern. Or visit Moundville Archaeological Park and experience the life of Native Americans who lived here during prehistoric times.

Tuscaloosa's cultural and relaxing environment also provides 27 hotels and countless fine restaurants. So call today and let us help you put together the perfect off–road experience.

P.O. Box 3167 • Tuscaloosa, AL 35403
(205) 391-9200 • 1-800-538-8696
FAX (205) 391-2125 or
visit our web site at http://www.tcvb.org

1668

Travelodge

QUALITY ACCOMMODATIONS AT BEARABLE RATES

- 165 Guest Rooms with Coffee Makers/Hair Dryers
- Complimentary Continental Breakfast
- 4 Spacious Meeting/Banquet Rooms
- Full Food and Beverage Catering
- Expanded Cable TV Featuring Showtime, ESPN and CNN

3920 E. McFarland Blvd. (Exit 73 I-20/59)
Tuscaloosa, AL 35405
205-553-1550

EXIT ALABAMA

W: Citgo[*, LP]
Food E: Iron Skillet (Petro), Petro
W: Family Deli & Grill
AServ E: McKinney Wrecker 24 Hr.
TServ E: Petro
RVCamp W: KOA-Mccalla/Tannehill (6 Miles)
Med E: ✚ Tannehill Valley Medical Center
ATM E: Phillips 66
Parks E: Tannehill Ironworks Historical State Park

104 Rock Mountain Lakes
TStop E: Flying J Travel Plaza[*, RV DUMP]
Food E: Flying J Travel Plaza
ATM E: Flying J Travel Plaza

106 Junction I-459 North, Gadsden, Atlanta

108 U.S 11, AL 5, Academy Drive
Gas E: BP[*, LP, CW], Shell[*]
Food E: Burger King[PLAY], Little Caesars Pizza, McDonald's (Wal-Mart), Omelet Shop, Wal-Mart SuperCenter[RX]
W: McKluskies, Quincy's
Lodg E: Days Inn (see our ad this page), Masters Inn, Ramada Inn (see our ad this page)
W: Best Western
AServ E: Shell, Tire & Lube Express (Wal-Mart), Wal-Mart SuperCenter
Med E: ✚ Hospital
ATM E: BP
W: South Trust Bank
Other E: Baskin Robbins (Wal-Mart), Drugs for Less, Wal-Mart SuperCenter[RX], Winn Dixie Supermarket

112 18th St, 19th St, Bessemer
Gas N: Amoco
S: Amoco[*], Chevron[*, CW]
Food N: Jack's Hamburgers, Roller Coaster
S: Bob Sykes BBQ, Captain's Place Seafood, KFC, Muffalettas Italian Foods
AServ N: O.K. Tire & Battery Co.
S: Big A Auto Parts, City Auto Parts
ATM S: Chevron
Other N: Mick's True Value Hardware[LP]
S: Bessemer National Park, Bessemer Pet Clinic

113 18th Avenue, Brighton, Lipscomb
TStop E: Speedway[*]
Food E: McDonald's, Speedway
AServ W: Alabama Alignment & Spring Peterbilt of Birmingham Inc.
ATM E: Speedway

115 Jaybird Rd, Midfield, Pleasant Rd

118 Valley Rd, Fairfield
Lodg E: Fairfield Inn, Villager Lodge
AServ E: Alton Jones Auto Service, Fairfield Transmission, National Tire & Battery Warehouse, Penske Auto Service, Scogin Bros Auto Repair, Valley Road Auto Parts
TServ E: Truck & Diesel Repair
ATM E: AmSouth Bank
Other E: Home Depot[LP]

119A Lloyd Nolan Pkwy
Gas E: Exxon, Texaco[*]
W: Amoco[*, D], Chevron[*], Chevron[*, 24]
Food E: Omelet Shoppe
W: Burger King, McDonald's[PLAY], Mrs Winner's Chicken, Subway, Taco Bell, Wingo's Buffalo Wings, Wingo's Buffalo Wings
AServ E: Exxon, Sharp Auto Supply
W: CloverLeaf Auto Center
TServ E: B&W Wrecker, Big Mo Alignment Center
Med E: ✚ Hospital
Other E: Carwash

RAMADA INN®
205-424-9780

Hot Breakfast
Outdoor Pool
Restaurant/Lounge on Premises
Meeting Facilities
Golf Nearby
Pets Allowed

1720

Bessemer, AL

205-424-6078

Continental Breakfast
Outdoor Pool/Jacuzzi/Exercise Room
Restaurant/Lounge on Premises
Truck Parking
Meeting/Banquet Facilities

ALABAMA • I-20/59 • Exit 108

EXIT ALABAMA

119B Avenue 1 (Westbound, Difficult Reaccess)

120 20th St, Ensley Avenue, Alabama State Fair Complex (Difficult Reaccess)
Gas E: BP[*, 24], Jiffy Mart #4[*]
W: Crown[*, D, CW, 24]
Food W: KFC
AServ E: Jim Burke Chevrolet, Limbaugh Toyota
ATM W: Crown
Other E: Washing Well Coin Laundry

121 Bush Blvd, Ensley
Gas W: Citgo[*], Exxon[*, LP]
Food W: Fat Burger
ATM W: Exxon

123 U.S 78, Jasper, Arkadelphia Rd (Difficult Reaccess)
Gas W: Amoco[*], Chevron[*], Shell[*, CW, 24]
Food W: Denny's (La Quinta Inn), Popeye's Chicken
Lodg W: La Quinta Inn
AServ W: AAMCO Transmission
Med E: ✚ Hospital
ATM W: Amoco, Chevron

124A Junction I-65 South, Montgomery (Left Exit Southbound)

124B Junction I-65 North, Nashville, Huntsville

125 22nd Street, Downtown (Left Exit)
Food W: Sophia's Deli
Lodg W: Best Western, Sheraton
Other W: AL Sports Hall of Fame, Birmingham Jefferson Civic Center, Boutwell Auditorium, Tourist Info.

125A 17th St, Downtown Birmingham (Northbound, Reaccess Southbound Only, Difficult Reaccess)
Gas E: Gem[*]
Food E: Burger King
Other E: AL School of Fine Arts, Fire Department

125B 22nd St, Downtown Birmingham, Art Museum, Civic Center (Northbound, No Reaccess, Difficult Reaccess, Same Services As Exit 125)
Food E: Burger King

126A U.S. 31, U.S 280, Carraway Blvd
Gas W: Citgo[D]
Food E: KFC
W: Church's Chicken, Ed's Diner, Rally's Hamburgers
AServ W: Citgo

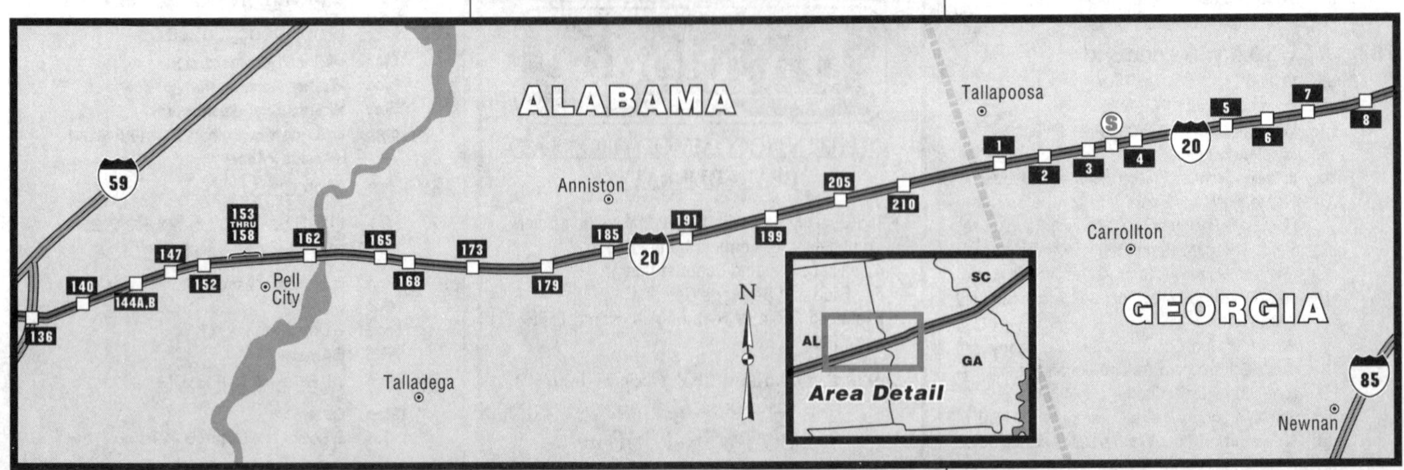

Bold red print shows RV & Bus parking available or nearby

EXIT — ALABAMA

Med E: Hospital

126B 31st St, Sloss Furnaces, Civic Ctr

Gas W: Circle K[*], Texaco[*]
Food W: McDonald's, Sol's Hotdogs
TServ E: Alabama Trailer Co., Commercial Truck Sales, Freightliner[SCALES], Kurt's Truck Parts, Liberty Truck Sales & Service
Other E: Used Vehicle Sales
W: Sani-Clean Laundromat

128 AL 79, Tallapoosa St, Tarrant

Gas W: Shell[*, CW]

129 Airport Blvd

Gas E: Exxon[*], Shell[*, CW, 24], Texaco[*]
Food E: Blimpie's Subs (Texaco), Hardee's, Holiday Inn, Huddle House, Sammy's Sandwich Shop
W: Clairon
Lodg E: Days Inn, Holiday Inn
W: Clairon
ATM E: Shell
Other E: Coin Operated Car Wash, Woodlawn Mart
W: Airport

Note: I-20 runs concurrent above with I-59. Numbering follows I-59.

130 Junction I-59 North, Gadsden

130B U.S. 11 South, 1st Ave (Reaccess Eastbound Only)

RVCamp N: Colonial Center

130A U.S. 11 North, 1st Ave (Difficult Reaccess)

132A to U.S. 78, Oporto Road

132B to U.S. 78, Montevallo Road

133 to U.S. 78, Kilgore, Memorial Dr

135 to U.S. 78, Old Leeds Road

136 Junction I-459, Montgomery, Tuscaloosa, Gadsden

140 U.S. 78, Leeds

Gas S: Chevron[*, CW, 24]

144AB U.S. 411, Leeds, Moody, Odenville

FStop S: Speedway[*, LP, K]
Gas N: BP[*, CW], Racetrac[*, 24], Shell[*] (Subway)
S: Exxon[*, LP, CW], RaceWay[*]
Food N: Arby's, Bamboo House Chinese, Cracker Barrel, Milo's, Pizza Hut, Subway (Shell), Waffle House, Wendy's
S: Burger King, Captain D's Seafood, Guadalajara Jalisco Mexican, Hardee's, KFC, McDonald's[PLAY], Taco Bell, Waffle House
Lodg N: Comfort Inn, Super 8 Motel (see our ad this page)
S: Days Inn
AServ N: Xpress Lube
S: Advance Auto Parts, Auto Clean Car Wash[CW], Auto Zone Auto Parts
RVCamp N: Holiday Travel
ATM N: Regions Bank, Winn Dixie Supermarket[RX] (Region's Bank)
Other N: Open Book Bookstore, Winn Dixie Supermarket[RX] (Region's Bank)

147 Brompton

TServ S: Alabama Outdoors[LP]
RVCamp S: Alabama Outdoors
Other S: Alabama Outdoors, Camp Winnataska

152 Cook Springs

Other N: Worldsong Camp

153 U.S. 78 West, Chula Vista

156 Eden, US 78 E, Pell City

FStop S: Exxon[*, CW]
Gas S: Amoco[*, CW, 24], Chevron[*, LP, 24]

158 U.S. 231, Ashville, Pell City (Logan Martin Lake available)

Gas S: BP[*, CW]
Food S: Burger King, Waffle House
Lodg S: Ramada Limited
AServ S: Pell City Ford Lincoln Mercury
RVCamp N: Lakeside Landing RV Park & Campground
Med S: Hospital
Other N: Feline Campers
S: Antique Mall

162 U.S. 78, Riverside, Pell City (Logan Martin Lake available)

Gas S: BP[*], Phillips 66[*]
Food S: Pancake House
Lodg S: Best Western (Hungry Bear Restaurant)

1808

1/2 Mi N of I-20 on US 411
Exit 144B going E, Exit 144A going W
205-640-7091
800-800-8000
$42.64 +tax Ask for Exit Authority Rate
• Continental Breakfast
• Kids Under 12 Stay Free
• King Beds in Single
• Handicap Accessible
• Cable TV/Showtime, ESPN, CNN
• Whirlpool Bathtubs Available
Fully Remodeled
2451 Moody Parkway • Moody, AL
Not valid on special events & holidays.
ALABAMA • I-20 • EXIT 144B

1539

SEE HISTORY ON WHEELS
Trace NASCAR's first 50 years through dozens of vehicles, exhibits, and displays of memorabilia from NASCAR.

UNOCAL 76 OFFICIAL SPONSOR
Open Daily 8 am - 5 pm
Speedway Boulevard • Talladega, Alabama
For a Free Brochure call (205) 362-5002
www.MotorsportsHallofFame.com
ALABAMA • I-20 • EXIT 168 & 173

RVCamp N: Safe Harbor RV Park
Other N: Riverside Cleaners and Laundry
S: Alan Battle's Riverside Marina (Stern Drive and Inboards)

165 Embry, Cross Roads

TStop S: I-20 Texaco Truckstop[*, SCALES] (Restaurant, McCane's Motel)
FStop S: Speedmart[*]
Food S: Broiler Room (I-20 TS), Huddle House
Lodg S: McCaig's Motel
TServ S: Bobby Orr Tire Shop & Garage
Other N: Palm Harbor Homes[LP]

168 AL. 77, Talladega, Lincoln

FStop N: Conoco[*, LP]
S: Pace Car[*, D]
Gas S: Bill's Gas[LP], Chevron[*, D], Texaco[*] (Burger King, Baskin Robbins)
Food N: Jack's[PLAY]
S: Baskin Robbins, Burger King[PLAY] (Texaco), Gateway Restaurant[24], McDonald's[PLAY], Rippin Ribs (Chevron)
Lodg S: McCaig Motel
RVCamp N: Dogwood Campground
Other S: International Motor Sports Hall of Fame (see our ad this page)

173 Eastaboga

Gas S: Shell[*], Texaco[*]
Food S: Dairy Queen[*] (Texaco), Stuckey's (Texaco)
ATM S: Shell
Other N: Nascar Collegiate Outlet
S: International Motor Sports Hall of Fame (see our ad this page)

179 Munford, Coldwater

Other N: Anniston Army Depot

185 AL 21, Oxford, Anniston

FStop S: Mapco Express[*, SCALES], Texaco[*] (Subway, Baskin Robins, Food Mart)
Gas N: Amoco (Auto Service), BP[*, D, CW], Chevron[*, D, CW, 24], Exxon[D], Texaco[*, D] (Quick Oil and Lube)
S: Exxon[*, LP], Racetrac[*, 24], Shell[*]
Food N: Applebee's, Arby's, Burger King[PLAY], Captain D's Seafood, Domino's Pizza, Los Mexicanos, McDonald's[PLAY], O'Charley's, Pizza Hut, Quincy's Family Steakhouse, Shoney's, Taco Bell, Western Sizzlin'
S: Chick-Fil-A[PLAY], Huddle House, Waffle House
Lodg N: Days Inn, Holiday Inn, Howard Johnson, Red Carpet Inn
S: Comfort Inn, Econolodge, Hampton Inn, Motel 6, TraveLodge
AServ N: Exxon, Firestone Tire & Auto
TServ S: Cobb Automotive Truck Center
Med N: Hospital
ATM N: AmSouth, BP, Colonial Bank, Regions Bank
S: Exxon, Mapco Express, Shell
Other N: Anniston Museum of Natural History, Books-A-Million, Car Wash, Gregerson's Supermarket[RX] (WEstern Union), Kid's Depot, Martin's Family Clothing Store, Quintard Mall
S: Food Outlet of Oxford, Mulberry Corner Antiques, U.S. Post Office, Wal-Mart Supercenter[24, RX] (Vision Center)

188 (189) to U.S. 78, Oxford, Anniston

FStop N: Skinner's Super Stop[*, LP]
Gas N: Supermart[*, CW] (KFC), Texaco[*] (Subway)
Food N: Cracker Barrel, Lone Star Steakhouse, Wendy's
Lodg N: Jameson Inn, Sleep Inn, Wingate Inn
AServ N: Golden Springs Tire & Service Center
ATM N: Colonial Bank, Texaco (Subway)

191 to U.S. 78, U.S. 431, Talladaga Scenic Hwy, Chehaw State Park

Parks S: Cheaha State Park

Bold red print shows RV & Bus parking available or nearby

EXIT ALABAMA/GEORGIA

199 AL 9, Heflin, Hollis,Talladaga National Forest ,Talladaga Scenic Biway
- FStop N: **Texaco[*, D, LP, K] (Taco Bell, Subway, Food Mart)**
  S: **Citgo[*]**
- Gas S: Chevron[*, CW, 24]
- Food N: **Hardee's, Pop's Char Burgers, Subway[*] (Texaco), Taco Bell (Texaco FS)**
  S: **Huddle House**
- Lodg N: **Howard Johnson**

205 AL 46, Ranburne
- FStop N: **BP[*, 24] (Tires Only), Texaco[*]**
- TServ N: **BP[24] (Tires Only)**
- ATM N: **BP (Tires Only)**

(209) **Weigh Station (Westbound)**

210 **(211)** Abernathy
- Other N: Fireworks Direct Factory Outlet
  S: **Stateline Fireworks**

(214) **AL Welcome Center, Rest Area (RR, HF, Phones, Picnic, RV Dump; Westbound)**

↑ALABAMA

↓GEORGIA

(1) **GA Welcome Center , Rest Area (RR, HF, Phones, Picnic, RV Dump; Eastbound)**

1 **(5)** GA 100, Tallapoosa, Bowdon
- TStop S: **Noble Truck Plaza[*, SCALES] (Citgo Gas, Janet's Restaurant)**
- FStop N: **Shell[*, 24]**
  S: **Owen's (Big O's Restaurant), Pilot[24] (KFC, Taco Bell, Travel Center)**
- Gas N: Exxon[*]
  S: BP[*] (Huddle House)
- Food N: Waffle House
  S: Dairy Queen, Huddle House, **Janet's Country Restaurant (Noble)**
- Lodg S: Comfort Inn
- TServ S: **Noble Truck Plaza[SCALES] (Citgo Gas, Janet's Restaurant)**
- TWash S: **Big O FS**
- ATM N: Exxon, **Shell**

2 **(9)** Waco Rd

3 **(12)** U.S. 27, Bremen, Carrollton
- FStop N: **Texaco[*, LP]**
  S: **BP[*, LP]**
- Gas S: Amoco[*, D]
- Food N: Arby's, **McDonald's[PLAY]**, Wendy's
  S: Waffle House
- Lodg N: **Days Inn**, Hampton Inn
- TServ S: **I-20 Truck Stop**
- Med N: **✚ Hospital**
- ATM N: **Texaco**, Texaco FS
  S: Amoco, **BP**
- Parks S: **John Tanner State Park**

(15) **Weigh Station (Westbound)**

4 **(19)** GA 113, Temple, Carrollton
- Food N: **Hardee's**

5 **(24)** GA.61, GA. 101, Villa Rica, Carrollton (State Patrol Office)
- FStop N: **Shell[*] (NationsBank)**
- Gas N: Racetrac[*, 24]
- Food N: Arby's, Domino's Pizza, El Torito, **Hardee's**, KFC, Krystal, McDonald's[PLAY], Pizza Hut, Subway, Taco Bell, Waffle House, Wendy's
- Lodg N: Comfort Inn, **Super 8 (see our ad this page)**

EXIT GEORGIA

- Med N: **✚ Hospital**
- ATM N: Nation's Bank (Shell), Racetrac, **Shell (NationsBank)**
- Other N: CVS Pharmacy[RX], **Ingles Supermarket**

6 **(26)** Liberty Rd, Villa Rica
- TStop S: **Leathers Truck Stop[*, SCALES]**
- Food S: **Restaurant (Leathers Truck Stop)**
- Lodg S: Night's Inn
- TServ S: **Leaters TS**
- TWash S: **Leathers TS**
- ATM S: **Leathers Truck Stop**

7 **(31)** Post Rd
- FStop S: **Texaco[*]**
- ATM S: **Texaco, Texaco FS**

8 **(34)** GA 5, Douglasville
- Gas N: Fina[*, LP]
  S: Chevron[*, D, CW, 24]
- Food N: Hooters, Huddle House, Uncle Bud's River Cafe
  S: Baskin Robbins, Chili's, Chinese Pagoda, Dunkin Donuts, El Rodeo Mexican, Folks, IHOP, KFC, Long John Silver, McDonald's[PLAY], Monterrey Restaurant, Philly Connection, Ruby Tuesday, SHONEY'S, Shoney's, Szchuan Village restaurant, Waffle House, Wendy's
- Lodg N: Quality Inn, Sleep Inn
- AServ N: Southerlin Honda
- Med N: **✚ Parkway Immediate Care**
- ATM S: Chevron, First Union, NationsBank, SunTrust, Wachovia Bank
- Other S: CVS[RX], **Eckerd Drugs**, Goody's, Home Depot, **K-Mart, Pearl Vision Center (Optometry)**, Quality's Food Depot, **Wolf Camera**

9 **(36)** Chapel Hill Rd. (Hospital)
- Gas S: Amoco[*, CW, 24] (McDonald's Express), QuikTrip[*]
- Food S: McDonald's (Amoco), Outback Steakhouse,

Truck/Large Vehicle Parking

Super 8 Motel
Villa Rica, GA
770-459-8888

• Continental Breakfast Included
• Outdoor Pool • Golf Nearby
• Meeting/Banquet Facilities
• Pets Allowed • Interior Corridors
• Restaurants Nearby

1536

GEORGIA • I-20 • EXIT 5

RAMADA LIMITED
770-949-3090

Truck/ Large Vehicle Parking

Free Continental Breakfast
Restaurant & Golf Nearby
Kids Under 12 Stay Free
Meeting/Banquet Facilities
Indoor Pool & Spa • Suites Available
Pets Allowed ($15 Charge)
Handicap Accessible
Coin Laundry • Interior Corridors
8315 Cherokee Blvd • Douglasville, GA

1601

GEORGIA • I-20 • EXIT 10

EXIT GEORGIA

  Waffle House
- Lodg S: Hampton Inn
- Med N: **✚ Douglas Hospital**

10 **(38)** GA 92, Fairburn Rd, Douglasville (Hospital)
- Gas N: BP[*, CW], Chevron[*, 24], Texaco[*, D, CW]
  S: Amoco[*], Shell[*, D]
- Food N: Burger King[PLAY], Captain D's Seafood, Cracker Barrel, House Of Ming, KFC, Krystal[24], Pagoda Express, Pizza Hut, SHONEY'S, Shoney's, Taco Bell, Waffle House
- Lodg N: **Best Western**, Days Inn, Holiday Inn Express, **Ramada Limited (see our ad this page)**
- AServ S: ABS Automotive, Amoco
- Med N: **✚ Hospital**
- ATM N: Suntrust, Texaco
  S: Shell
- Other N: Storage Trust (Uhaul rental)

11 **(42)** Lee Rd., Lithia Springs
- FStop N: **Citgo[*, LP]**
  S: **Speedway[*, LP]**
- Food N: **Hardee's, Icecream Churn (Citgo FS)**
  S: Waffle House
- AServ N: Lee Road Transmission
- ATM N: **Citgo**
  S: **Speedway, Speedway**

(42) **Weigh Station (Eastbound)**

12 **(43)** GA 6, Thorton Rd, Austell, Powder Springs (Sweetwater Creek State Park, Atlanta Airport, Camp Creek Pkwy, Columbia parkway Medical Center)
- Gas N: Amoco[*, CW, 24], Exxon[*, CW], Phillips 66[*, CW], Racetrac[*]
- Food N: Blimpie's Subs, Burger King[PLAY], Chick-Fil-A, Dunkin Donuts, **Hardee's**, International House of Pancakes, McDonald's[PLAY], SHONEY'S, Shoney's (Shoney's Inn), Subway, Taco Bell, The Olive Tree, Waffle House
- Lodg N: Budget Inn, **Hampton Inn**, Knight's Inn
  S: Fairfield Inn
- AServ N: John Blakely
  S: AutoNation, Douglas County dodge, The Champions, Westside Mitsubishi, Toyota
- RVCamp N: **Atlanta Camp RV Park**
- Med N: **✚ Parkway Medical Center**
- ATM N: Racetrac, Suntrust
- Parks S: **Sweetwater Creek State Park**
- Other N: CVS[RX], Royal Laundry
  S: AutoNation

(43) **Weigh Station**

13BA Six Flags Dr., Riverside Pkwy.
- Gas N: Amoco[*, LP] (Church's Chicken), Conoco[*] (Quik-Pick), QT[*, 24] (First Union)
  S: Coastal[*, LP]
- Food N: Big Mac's Phily Cheesesteaks, Church's Chicken (Amoco), Denny's, Hot Wings, Lester's Cafe, Seven Flags Chinese Restaurant, Waffle House
- Lodg N: La Quinta Inn
  S: Days Inn, Sleep Inn
- RVCamp N: **Arrowhead RV Park**
- ATM N: Amoco, First Union, QT (First Union)
- Other N: A-1 Mini Storage (U-Haul), E-Z CarWash, Parkview Coin Laundry, Quik-Pick Convenient Store
  S: **Sam's Club, Six Flags Over Georgia**

13C **(47)** Riverside Pkwy, Six Flags Pkwy (Westbound, West Access By Access Rd)
- FStop N: **Amoco[*, D]**
- Gas N: Mark Inn

Bold red print shows RV & Bus parking available or nearby

EXIT GEORGIA

Lodg **N:** Mark Inn
TServ **N:** **Sunbelt Power Cat. Truck Engine Parts & Service**
RVCamp **N:** **Arrowhead Campground**
Other **S:** **Six Flags Over Georgia**

14 **(49)** GA 70, Fulton Industrial Blvd, Fulton County Airport
FStop **N:** **Happy Stores**(*)
S: **Mapco Express**(*)
Gas **N:** Racetrac(*) (NationsBank)
S: Amoco(*), Chevron(CW, 24), Racetrac(*), Texaco(*), UFO(D)
Food **N:** Baskin Robbins, Captain D's Seafood, Checkers Burgers, Dairy Queen, Dunkin Donuts, EJ's, Hardee's, Krystal, Mrs. Winner's, Subway (Ramada), Waffle House, Wendy's
S: Arby's, Blimpie's Subs, Burger King(PLAY), McDonald's, Roma Sub Express, Waffle House, Wency's Cafe
Lodg **N:** Fulton Inn, Masters Inn, Ramada Inn (see our ad this page), Suburban Lodge
S: Comfort Inn, Executive Inn, Mark's Inn, Red Roof Inn, Super 8
AServ **S:** Quality Automotive Service
ATM **N:** NationsBank (RaceTrac), Racetrac (NationsBank)
S: Mapco Express, Racetrac
Other **N:** **Fulton County Airport**
S: Office Depot, **U-Haul Center**(LP)

15A **(49)** Junction I-285 South, Macon, Montgomery

15B **(49)** Junction I-285 North, Chattanooga, Greenville

16 **(50)** GA 280, Hightower Rd
Gas **S:** Exxon(*, D)

17 **(51)** GA 139, Martin Luther King Jr. Dr
Gas **N:** Citgo(*), Texaco(D)
S: The Right Stuff(*)
Food **S:** Unity Restaurant
AServ **N:** Citgo, Texaco
S: Holt Auto Parts
Other **N:** **Coin Laundry**

18 **(52)** Langhorn Street, Cascade Road (Westbound, Reaccess Eastbound Only)

19 **(52)** Ashby St., West End (Difficult Reaccess)
Gas **S:** BP(*, CW), Exxon(*)
Food **S:** Chinese Kitchen, Church's Chicken, Dipper Dan Ice Cream, Italian Sub & Salad, Krispy Kreme Doughnuts, Momo's Pizza & Pasta, New York Subs, Pizza Hut, Popeye's Chicken, Taco Bell, West Inn Cafeteria
ATM **S:** Capitol City Bank, First Union, NationsBank, SouthTrust, Wachovia Bank
Other **S:** **A & P Supermarket**, **Hardy's Market**, **West End Mall**, **Western Union**

20 **(53)** Lee St., Ft. McPherson, Atlanta University Center (Westbound)
Other **S:** **Fed Ex Drop Box**

21 **(54)** U.S. 19, U.S. 29, McDaniel St., Whitehall St. (Eastbound, Reaccess Westbound Only)

22 **(55)** Windsor St., Spring St., Stadium, Georgia World Congress Center

23 **(56)** Junction I-75, I-85, Macon, Montgomery, Chattanooga, Greenville

EXIT GEORGIA

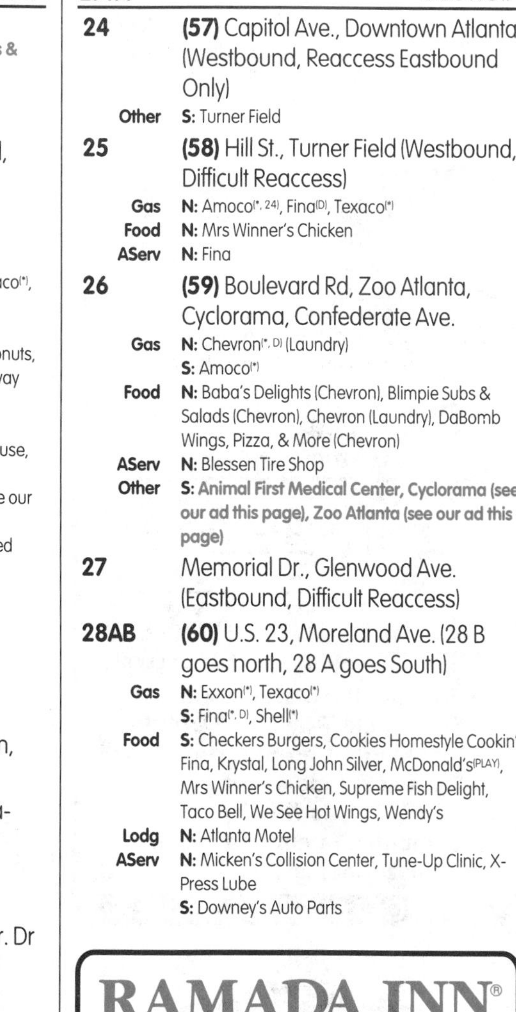

24 **(57)** Capitol Ave., Downtown Atlanta (Westbound, Reaccess Eastbound Only)
Other **S:** Turner Field

25 **(58)** Hill St., Turner Field (Westbound, Difficult Reaccess)
Gas **N:** Amoco(*, 24), Fina(D), Texaco(*)
Food **N:** Mrs Winner's Chicken
AServ **N:** Fina

26 **(59)** Boulevard Rd, Zoo Atlanta, Cyclorama, Confederate Ave.
Gas **N:** Chevron(*, D) (Laundry)
S: Amoco(*)
Food **N:** Baba's Delights (Chevron), Blimpie Subs & Salads (Chevron), Chevron (Laundry), DaBomb Wings, Pizza, & More (Chevron)
AServ **N:** Blessen Tire Shop
Other **S:** **Animal First Medical Center**, **Cyclorama (see our ad this page)**, **Zoo Atlanta (see our ad this page)**

27 Memorial Dr., Glenwood Ave. (Eastbound, Difficult Reaccess)

28AB **(60)** U.S. 23, Moreland Ave. (28 B goes north, 28 A goes South)
Gas **N:** Exxon(*), Texaco(*)
S: Fina(*, D), Shell(*)
Food **S:** Checkers Burgers, Cookies Homestyle Cookin', Fina, Krystal, Long John Silver, McDonald's(PLAY), Mrs Winner's Chicken, Supreme Fish Delight, Taco Bell, We See Hot Wings, Wendy's
Lodg **N:** Atlanta Motel
AServ **N:** Micken's Collision Center, Tune-Up Clinic, X-Press Lube
S: Downey's Auto Parts

RAMADA INN®

Six Flags
4225 Fulton Industrial Blvd.
Cable TV
Outdoor Swimming Pool
Restaurant & Lounge with Entertainment
Room Service
In-Room Movies
Gift Shop
Free Parking on Premises
404-691-4100
Toll Free: 1-800-645-5723
1614
GEORGIA ▪ I-20 ▪ EXIT 14

CYCLORAMA 1728
Civil War Museum
The Atlanta Cyclorama is an historical landmark in The South. Come experience The Battle of Atlanta.
Located next to Zoo Atlanta off I-20 at Exit 26
GRANT PARK • 800 Cherokee Ave., SE, Atlanta • 404-624-1071
GEORGIA ▪ I-20 ▪ EXIT 26

Experience a beautiful wildlife park less than a mile from downtown.
SEE OUR AD ON I-75
1236.2
GEORGIA ▪ I-20 ▪ EXIT 26

EXIT GEORGIA

ATM **N:** Exxon
S: NationsBank
Other **N:** Discount Auto Parts

29 **(61)** Maynard Terrace, Memorial Dr (Eastbound, No Reaccess)

30 **(62)** Glenwood Ave., GA 260
Gas **N:** Texaco(*)

31 **(63)** Flat Shoals Rd (Eastbound, Reaccess Westbound Only)
Gas **N:** Amoco(*), Citgo(*), Texaco(*, LP, CW)

32 **(64)** Gresham Rd, Flat Shoals Road (Difficult Reaccess)
Gas **N:** Phillips 66(*)
S: Amoco(*, 24), Citgo(*), Shell(*)
Food **S:** Bigelow's Bar & Grill, Church's Chicken, G&G BBQ, Mamie's Soul Food
AServ **S:** Brakes & Wheels, Road King Tire Service, Smith's Auto Repair
Med **S:** ✚ **Southside Health Care Inc.**
ATM **N:** Phillips 66
S: Amoco
Other **N:** Mayuri Food Mart
S: **Buy Rite Pharmacy**(RX), **Coin Laundry**, Super Soaper Coin Car Wash

33 **(65)** GA 155, Candler Rd, Decatur
Gas **N:** BP(*, LP), Hess(*)
S: Amoco(*, CW), Chevron(*, 24)
Food **N:** Dundee's Cafe, Dynasty Chinese, Long John Silver, Pizza Hut, Red Lobster, Supreme Fish Delight, Wendy's
S: Arby's, Burger King(PLAY), Chester Fried Chicken (Chevron), Chevron, China Cafeteria, Chit-Chat Sports Bar & Grill, Church's Chicken, Dunkin Donuts
Lodg **N:** EconoLodge
S: Candler Inn, Villager Lodge
AServ **N:** Tune-Up Clinic
S: Advance Auto Parts, Firestone Tire & Auto, Mitchell Tire Company, Pep Boys Auto Center, Rich's Auto Center
Med **S:** ✚ **Emory Clinic**, ✚ **Grady Medical Center**
ATM **S:** Citizen's Trust Bank, First Union Bank, SunTrust Bank, Wachovia Bank
Other **N:** A-1 Food Store, **CVS Pharmacy**(RX), Twiner Car Wash, **U-Haul Center**
S: **Coin Laundry**, **Kroger Supermarket**(RX), **South Dekalb Mall**, Super Soaker Car Wash, **Toys R Us**, **Winn Dixie Supermarket**

34 **(66)** Columbia Drive (Eastbound, Reaccess Westbound Only)
Gas **N:** Phillip 66(*), Texaco(*)
S: Fina(*)
Food **S:** Fina, Subway (Fina)
AServ **N:** Columbia Emissions Inspection(CW)
Other **N:** **New Deal Convenient Store**

35AB **(67)** Junction I-285, Macon, Greenville

36 **(68)** Wesley Chapel Rd, Snapfinger Rd
Gas **N:** Exxon(*, D), Texaco(*, D, CW)
S: Amoco(*, CW, 24), Chevron(*, 24), Crown(*, CW), Speedway(*, D, LP, K)
Food **N:** Chick-Fil-A(PLAY), China Cafeteria, Church's Chicken, Dudley's Food & Spirit (Motel 6), KFC, Motel 6, Waffle House, Wendy's
S: Burger King, Dairy Queen, Dragon Chinese Restaurant, McDonald's, Supreme Fish Delight
Lodg **N:** Motel 6
S: DAYS INN Days Inn
AServ **N:** Goodyear Certified Auto Service, NTB, Q Lube
S: Car Wash & Detailing, Friendly Auto Finance, Jiffy Lube, Precision Tune

Bold red print shows RV & Bus parking available or nearby

EXIT GEORGIA

ATM **N:** SouthTrust Bank, Wachovia Bank
S: Chevron, Tucker Federal Bank

Other **N:** **CVS Pharmacy(RX)**, **Coral Sands Animal Hospital**, **Home Depot**, **Ingles Supermarket**, **Wal-Mart(RX)**
S: Car Wash & Detailing

37 Panola Rd

Gas **N:** Exxon(*, D), QuikTrip(*, D, 24)
S: Amoco(*, 24), Exxon, Stop N Shop(*)

Food **N:** Brandon's Restaurant, Burger King(PLAY), Checkers Burgers, McDonald's(PLAY), **Waffle House**
S: Amoco, Domino's Pizza

Lodg **N:** La Quinta Inn, Super 8 (see our ad this page)
S: Sleep Inn

AServ **S:** Exxon

ATM **N:** Citizen's Trust Bank, QuikTrip, Suntrust
S: Stop N Shop

38 Evans Mill Rd, Lithonia

FStop **S:** **Speedway(*, D)**

Gas **N:** Amoco(*, CW), Chevron(*, CW, 24), Texaco(*)

Food **N:** Captain D's Seafood, KFC, Mamie's Kitchen, McDonald's, Pizza Hut, Simply Tasteful, Taco Bell, Waffle House, Wendy's
S: Dairy Queen, Golden Palace 2, Krystal, Snuffy's, Waffle House

Lodg **S:** Howard Johnson

ATM **N:** Chevron, Convenient Store(LP) (U-Haul Distributor)
S: **Speedway**

Other **N:** Convenient Store (U-Haul Distributor), Eastgate Car Wash
S: **Ace Hardware (U-Haul Distributor)**, **CVS Pharmacy(RX)**

39 **(73)** GA 124 West, U.S. 278, Turner Hill Rd

FStop **N:** **US Discount(*)**

Gas **N:** Amoco(*)

AServ **N:** Cars R Us

ATM **N:** **US Discount**

40 **(76)** Sigman Rd

FStop **N:** **Circle K(*, LP)**

Food **N:** **Waffle House**

AServ **N:** J.R.'s Auto & Tire, Power Motors

Med **N:** ✚ **Hospital**

ATM **N:** **Circle K**

Other **N:** Rondell Rental Center(LP)
S: Georgia State Patrol Post

(76) **Weigh Station, Rest Area (Eastbound)**

41 **(78)** West Ave., Conyers

Gas **N:** Speedway(*, LP, K), Texaco(*, D, LP)
S: Exxon(*)

Food **N:** American Deli, Dairy Queen, Domino's Pizza, Donna Marie's Pizza, Golden Palace Chinese, Holiday Inn, Mrs Winner's Chicken, Subway
S: Longhorn Steakhouse, McDonald's(PLAY), Quik-Chick, Waffle House

Lodg **N:** Holiday Inn, Rich Field
S: Comfort Inn

AServ **N:** Car Country, Midas Muffler, Western Auto
S: Buick Pontiac Lou Sobh, Conyers Auto Finance, Conyers Mazda, Conyers Nissan, John Miles Chrysler Plymouth Jeep, Town & Country Mitsubishi, Wheels Inc.

TServ **N:** **Tough Truck**
S: **Ryder Transportation Services**

RVCamp **S:** **Coach & Camper of 20East**, **Crown RV Center**, **Super 1 RV Center**, **Trailer Sales & Service**

ATM **N:** FNB Bank, Sun Trust Bank

Other **N:** **Coin Laundry**, Conyers Historic District, **Conyers Pharmacy(RX)**, **Piggly Wiggly**

SUPER 8 MOTEL
Super 8 Motel
5354 Snapfinger Park Dr.
770-987-5128
Located Behind Burger King
- Free Continental Breakfast
- Free Cable TV with HBO/ESPN
- Smoking & Non-Smoking Rooms
- Rollaway Beds & Cribs
- Golf & Tennis Nearby
- Computer/Telephone Jacks
- Jacuzzi Rooms

1237
GEORGIA ▪ I-20 ▪ EXIT 37

1113

I-20 Exit 42, Conyers • 770-483-8838
- Free Continental Breakfast
- Free Local Calls
- 25'' Cable TV • HBO
- Outdoor Pool
- In Room Coffee Maker & Iron

GEORGIA ▪ I-20 ▪ EXIT 42

S: **Conyers Animal Hospital**, L & H Personal Storage, **Reagan Home Care Pharmacy(RX)**

42 **(82) GA 138, Conyers, Monroe, Welcome Center**

FStop **N:** **Speedway(*)**

Gas **N:** Amoco(*, 24), BP(*, D, CW, 24), QuikTrip(*, 24)
S: Racetrac(*, 24), Texaco(*, D)

Food **N:** Amoco, Baby Cakes Bakery, Bruster's Old Fashion Ice Cream, Crabby Bill's, **Cracker Barrel**, Golden Corral Family Steakhouse, Hard Luck Cafe, IHOP, McDonald's (Wal Mart), O'Charley's, Outback Steakhouse, Papa's Country Cafe, **Wal-Mart Supercenter(RX)**
S: Applebee's, BJ's Country Kitchen, Boston Market Restaurant, Burger King, Checkers Burgers, Chili's, City Slickers, El Charro's Mexican, Folks, Hardees, Hooters, JR Cricket's Bar & Grill, Krystal, Long John Silver, Morrison's, Nagaya Japanese Sushi Bar, Pizza Hut, Shades, Taco Bell, Waffle House, Yenshing Garden Chinese

Lodg **N:** Conyers Motor Inn, Days Inn, Hampton Inn (see our ad this page), La Quinta Inn, Ramada, The Jameson Inn
S: Intown Suites, Suburban Lodge

AServ **N:** BP(24), John Miles Chevrolet, **Wal-Mart Supercenter**
S: Bickerson Automotive, Conyers Tire Service, Conyers Toyota, Hinton's, Mighty Muffler, NTB, Sim's Radiator Service, Town & Country Dodge

TServ **N:** **Trammel Truck Sales**

Med **N:** ✚ **Hospital**

ATM **N:** Amoco, Wachovia Bank, **Wal-Mart Supercenter**
S: First Union Bank, NationsBank, Racetrac, Regions Bank, Suntrust Bank, Texaco

Other **N:** **Home Depot**, NAPA Auto Parts, **Pearl Vision Center**, **PetsMart**, Smith O'Kelley Auto Parts, **Wal-Mart Supercenter(RX)**
S: **Animal Hospital**, **Billy Bob's Skating**, Buddy's Bubble Car Wash, **CVS Pharmacy(RX)**, **Coin Laundry**, **Drug Emporium(RX)**, **Eckerd Drugs(RX)**, **K-Mart(RX)**, **Quality Food Depot(SCALES)**, Regal Wash & Valvoline Lube

(82) **Weigh Station (Westbound)**

43 **(84)** GA 162, Salem Rd

Gas **S:** Amoco(*, CW), BP(*), Chevron(*, 24), Citgo(*, LP), Racetrac(*)

Food **S:** Burger King(PLAY), Hardee's, Waffle House

AServ **N:** Atlanta Tire Specialist, Courtesy Ford
S: BJ McDaniel Auto Service

TServ **N:** **Leer Truck Service**

ATM **S:** BP, Racetrac

Other **S:** **Eckerd Drugs(RX)**

44 **(88)** Almon Rd, Porterdale

Gas **N:** Chevron(*, LP)

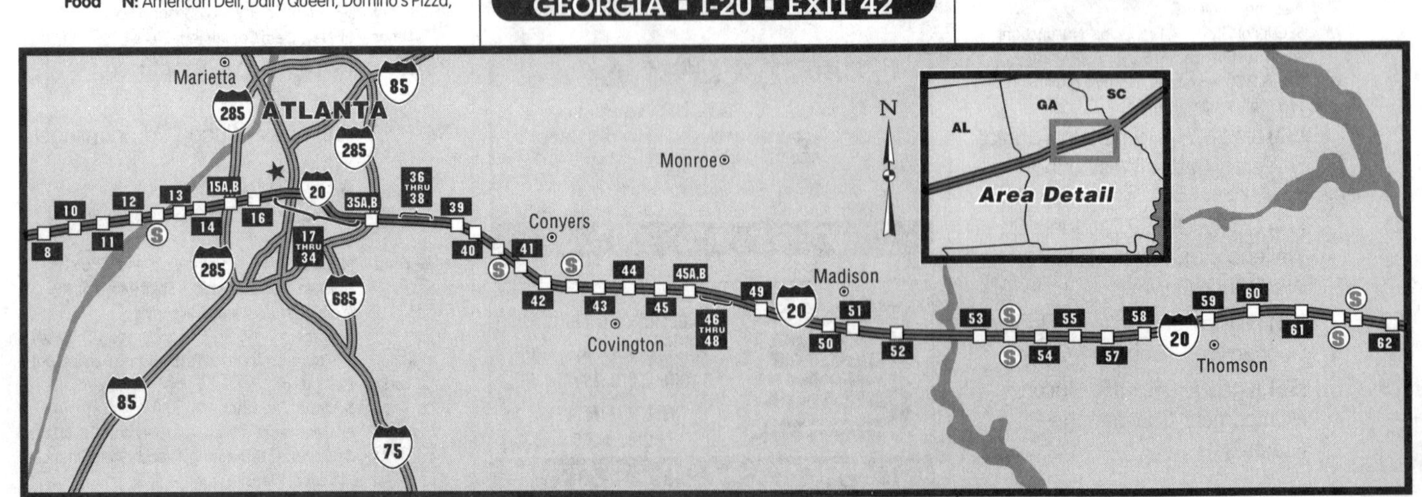

Bold red print shows RV & Bus parking available or nearby

EXIT	GEORGIA
RVCamp	S: Riverside Estates RV Park (.5 Miles)
45	**(90)** U.S. 278 East, Covington, Oxford
Gas	S: Exxon(*, D), Racetrac(*)
Food	S: Arby's, Captain D's Seafood, Chen's Chinese, Domino's Pizza, El Arrollo Mexican, KFC, SHONEY'S, Shoney's, South Star Family Restaurant, Sports Bar & Grill, Taco Bell, Waffle House
Lodg	S: The Crest
AServ	S: Advance Auto Parts, Ginn Chevrolet Oldsmobile, Henry's Fast Lube, Statham Tire Co.
ATM	S: Racetrac, Winn Dixie Supermarket
Other	S: Ingles Supermarket, K-Mart(RX), Winn Dixie Supermarket
45A	**(92)** Alcovy Rd
FStop	N: Circle K(*)
Gas	N: Chevron(*, LP)
Food	N: Alcovy Station Restaurant, Chevron, Pippin's BBQ, Waffle House
Lodg	N: Best Western, DAYS INN Days Inn (see our ad this page), EconoLodge, Holiday Inn Express
Med	S: + Hospital
Other	N: Rollin Hills Skating Arena S: Tourist Info.
46	**(93)** GA 142, Hazelbrand
FStop	S: Exxon(*)
Gas	S: Texaco(*, LP)
Lodg	S: The Jameson Inn
TServ	S: Bridgestone
Med	S: + Hospital
ATM	S: Exxon
Other	S: Sigman Veterinary Clinic
47	**(98)** GA 11, Monroe, Monticello, Social Circle, Mansfield
48	**(101)** U.S. 278
Other	N: State Headquarters Wildlife Resources Division
(103)	Rest Area (RR, HF, Phones, Picnic, RV Dump; Eastbound)
49	**(106)** Rutledge, Newborn
Gas	N: Chevron(*, D)
Parks	N: Hard Labor Creek State Park
(108)	Rest Area (RR, Phones, RV Dump; Westbound)
50	**(113)** GA 83, Madison, Monticello
Gas	N: BP(*, LP)
Med	N: + Hospital
ATM	N: BP
Other	N: Georgia State Patrol Post, Historic Madison
51	**(115)** U.S. 441, GA 129, Rock Eagle, Madison, Eatonton
TStop	S: TA TravelCenters of America(*, SCALES) (BP gas)
FStop	N: Exxon(*, CW, 24) S: Fuel Mart(*)
Gas	N: Amoco(*, 24), Chevron(*, LP), Racetrac(*) S: Texaco(*, LP)
Food	N: Arby's, Burger King(PLAY), Chevron, Davis Brothers Southern Cookin', Hardee's, KFC, McDonald's(PLAY), Pizza Hut, Subway (Chevron), Waffle House, Wendy's S: China Way (Ramada Inn), Country Pride Restaurant (TA TS), Popeye's, Chicken (TA TS), Ramada Inn, TA TravelCenters of America (BP gas), Taco Bell (TA TS), Waffle House
Lodg	N: Comfort Inn, DAYS INN Days Inn, Hampton Inn S: Holiday Inn Express (see our ad this page), Ramada Inn, Super 8
AServ	N: Phil Cook Chevrolet, Pontiac, Oldsmobile, GMC Truck
TServ	S: Southern Road Service, TA TravelCenters of America(SCALES) (BP gas)
RVCamp	S: Talisman RV Resort (1.5 Miles)
Med	N: + Hospital
ATM	N: Chevron S: Texaco
Other	N: African American Museum, Cultural Center, Heritage Hall, Tourist Info. S: Rock Eagle
52	**(121)** Buckhead
Gas	S: Phillip 66(*, D, LP)
53	(130) Greensboro, Eatonton, Lake Oconee Pkwy., GA 44, Weigh Station
FStop	S: Chevron(*, LP, 24)
Gas	N: Amoco(*, LP, 24), BP(*)
Food	N: BP, McDonald's(PLAY), Pizza Hut, Subway (BP), Waffle House, Zaxby's
Lodg	N: Jameson Inn, Microtel Inn
Med	N: + Hospital
ATM	N: Amoco S: Chevron
(130)	Weigh Station (Eastbound)
(130)	Weigh Station (Westbound)
54	**(137)** GA 77, GA 15, Siloam, Union Point, Sparta
FStop	S: Amoco(*, D, LP)
Gas	S: Exxon(*)
Med	S: + Hospital
ATM	S: Amoco
55	**(148)** GA 22, Crawfordville, Sparta
FStop	N: Amoco(*) S: Chevron(*, LP) (Laundromat)
Food	S: Chevron (Laundromat)
Lodg	S: Chevron (Laundromat)
TServ	S: Chevron (Laundromat)
Parks	N: A.H. Stevens State Park (2 Miles)
56	**(154)** U.S. 278, Warrenton, Washington
57	**(159)** Norwood
58	**(165)** GA 80, Camak
59	**(172)** U.S. 78, GA 17, Thomson, Washington, Lincolnton
FStop	N: Chevron(*) S: Amoco(*, CW), Citgo(*, D), Fuel City(*, LP, SCALES, 24)
Gas	N: BP(*) S: Racetrac(*, 24), Texaco(*)
Food	N: BP, Krispy Kreme Doughnuts (BP) S: Amoco, Arby's, Blimpie Subs & Salads (Fuel City), Burger King(PLAY), Dairy Queen (Amoco), Fuel City, Long John Silver, McDonald's(PLAY), Pizza Hut, Plantation House (Best Western), SHONEY'S, Shoney's, Taco Bell, Waffle House, Wendy's, Western Sizzlin', White Columns Inn (Best Western)
Lodg	S: EconoLodge, Holiday Inn Express, Ramada Limited, White Columns Inn (Best Western)
AServ	N: Classic South Pontiac, Oldsmobile, GMC Trucks, Ford, Mercury, Thomson Chrysler Plymouth, Dodge, Jeep Eagle
Med	S: + Hospital
ATM	N: Chevron S: Amoco, Citgo, Fuel City, Racetrac
Other	N: Georgia State Patrol Post, Historic Washington Wilkes
60	**(175)** GA 150
TStop	N: Samuels Truck Stop(*, SCALES) (Amoco gas)
Food	N: Samuels Truck Stop (Amoco gas)
Lodg	N: DAYS INN Days Inn
TServ	N: Samuels Truck Stop(SCALES) (Amoco gas)
ATM	N: Samuels Truck Stop (Amoco gas)
Parks	N: Mistletoe State Park
(182)	Rest Area (RR, Phones, RV Dump; Eastbound)
(182)	Rest Area (RR, Phones, RV Dump; Westbound)
61	**(183)** U.S. 221, Appling, Harlem
AServ	N: Colpepper Ford
Other	N: Clarks Carroll Lake
(187)	Weigh Station (Eastbound)
(187)	Weigh Station (Westbound)
62	**(190)** GA 388, Grovetown
FStop	S: Amoco(*, 24)
Gas	S: BP(*)
ATM	S: Amoco
Parks	N: Patriot Park
Other	N: Fairgrounds S: Fort Gordon
63	**(194)** GA 383, Belair Rd, Dyess

1610
DAYS INN
Continental Breakfast
Outdoor Pool
Restaurants Nearby
Handicap Accessible
Exterior Corridors
Jacuzzi Suites Available
Free Cable TV w/HBO
Close to Stone Mountain, Atlanta Int'l Raceway & Int'l Horse Park
770-788-8919
Covington, GA
GEORGIA • I-20 • EXIT 45A

1235
Holiday Inn EXPRESS
$40 Single
• Free Breakfast Bar
• Free Newspaper
• Free Local Calls • Free HBO/ESPN
• Non-Smoking Rooms Available
• Pool • Meeting Room
706-342-3433 • Madison, GA
GEORGIA • I-20 • EXIT 51

EXIT GEORGIA

Parkway

FStop **N:** Smile Gas[*, CW]
S: Speedway[*, LP]

Gas **N:** Circle K[*, LP], Exxon[*, LP]
S: Amoco[*, D, 24]

Food **N:** Burger King, Exxon, Popeye's Chicken, Smile Gas, TCBY (SMilesGas), Taco Bell (Exxon), Waffle House
S: Amoco, Cracker Barrel, Dairy Queen (Amoco), Huddle House, Stuckey's (Amoco), Waffle House

Lodg **N:** Villager Lodge
S: Best Western, EconoLodge, Ramada Limited, Wingate Inn

TServ **S:** Carroll Tire Inc.

ATM **N:** Smile Gas, Southtrust
S: Amoco, Speedway

Other **N:** Coin Car Wash, Funsville

63A **(195)** Wheeler Road

FStop **S:** Smile Gas[*, LP]

Food **S:** Blimpie Subs & Salads (SMilesGas), Smile Gas

ATM **S:** CSRA Federal Credit Union, Smile Gas

64AB **(197)** Junction I-520 South,Bobby Jones Expressway- 64A GA 232 West, Bobby Jones Expwy- 64B (64A-South services)

Gas **N:** Racetrac[*]

Food **N:** Applebee's, Checkers Burgers, China Pearl, Heavenly Ham, McDonald's (Wal-Mart), Ruby Tuesday, Waffle House, Wal-Mart[RX]
S: Chili's

Lodg **N:** Comfort Inn, Howard Johnson, Suburban Lodge
S: Sheraton Inn

AServ **N:** Wal-Mart

Med **N:** ✚ Martinez Urgent Care
S: ✚ Hospital

Other **N:** Bi-Lo Grocery[24], Eye Glass World Express, Home Depot, Home Quarters Warehouse, Joshua Christian Bookstore, Roller Skating Rink, Sams Club Warehouse, Wal-Mart[RX]
S: Fort Gordon

65 **(200)** GA 28, Washington Rd, Augusta

Gas **N:** BP[*, CW], Racetrac[*]
S: Circle K[*, CW], Crown[*, LP], Shell[*, LP], Smile Gas[*, D], Smile Gas[*]

Food **N:** Burger King, Captain D's Seafood, Damon's Ribs, Days Inn, Empress Chinese Supper Buffet (Days Inn), McDonald's[PLAY], Pizza Hut, Rhinehart's Oysters & Seafood, Sho Gun Japanese Steakhouse, SHONEY'S, Shoney's, Veracruz Mexican Restaurant, Waffle House
S: Bojangles, Fazoli's Italian Food, Hooter's, Joe Muggs Coffee, Krispy Kreme Doughnuts, Michael's Fine Food, Outback Steakhouse, Red Lobster, Shangri-La Chinese, TBONZ Steakhouse, Taco Bell, Teresa's Mexican Restaurant, Waffle House

Lodg **N:** Courtyard by Marriott, Days Inn, Hampton Inn, Holiday Inn, Homewood Suites Hotel, La Quinta, Master's Inn, Radisson Suites, Scottish Inns, Shoney's Inn, Sunset Inn, TraveLodge
S: EconoLodge, Fairfield Inn, Knight's Inn, Motel 6, West Bank Inn

AServ **S:** Amoco Touchless Car Wash (Quaker State Fast Lube), Firestone Tire & Auto

ATM **S:** Circle K, Crown, First Union Bank, NationsBank, Shell, Smile Gas, Smile Gas, Suntrust Bank

Other **S:** Amoco Touchless Car Wash (Quaker State Fast Lube), Books-A-Million, CVS Pharmacy[RX], Drug Emporium[RX], Master's Cleaners, Westside Animal Hospital

66 **(200)** GA 104, River Watch Pkwy, Augusta

Lodg **N:** Ameri Suites
S: Amerisuites (see our ad this page), Comfort Inn (see our ad this page)

AServ **S:** Steve's Auto Service

Other **S:** Augusta Richmond County Civic Center, National Science Center for Discovery, Tourist Info.

(201) **GA Welcome Center (RR, Phones, RV Dump; Westbound)**

↑GEORGIA

EXIT SOUTH CAROLINA

↓SOUTH CAROLINA

(1) **SC Welcome Center (RR, Phones; Eastbound)**

1 SC 230, N. Augusta

FStop **S:** Smile Gas[*, K]

Food **N:** Fox Creek Junction[24]
S: Blimpie's Subs (SMilesGas), Smile Gas, Tastee Freez (SMilesGas), Waffle House

AServ **S:** Kinsey's Auto

ATM **N:** Fox Creek Crossing
S: Smile Gas

Other **N:** Fox Creek Crossing, Legends of South Carolina
S: Holton's I-20 Marine, Wacky Wayne's Fireworks, Wildlife Viewing Area

5 U.S. 25, SC 121, Edgefield, Johnston

FStop **N:** Fuel City[*, LP, SCALES] (SMilesGas)
S: Speedway[*, LP]

Gas **N:** BP[*, LP], Shell[*]
S: Exxon[*, LP]

Food **N:** Blimpie Subs & Salads (Fuel City), Burger King[PLAY], Fuel City (SMilesGas), Hardee's, Hot Stuff Pizza (Fuel City), Huddle House, Number 1 Chinese Buffet, Shell, Sonic American
S: Waffle House

AServ **N:** BP

RVCamp **N:** Mobile Home Estates (.13 Miles)

Other **N:** Coin Laundry, Winn Dixie Supermarket[24, RX]
S: Town & Country Party Shop

11 Road 144, Graniteville

Other **N:** Sage Mill Industrial Park

18 SC 19, Aiken, Johnston

FStop **S:** Exxon[*], Shell[*]

Food **S:** Blimpie Subs & Salads (Shell), Exxon, Ramada Inn, Shell, Subway (Exxon), Waffle House

Lodg **S:** Deluxe Inn, Ramada Inn

Med **S:** ✚ Hospital

Other **S:** Hopeland Gardens

(20) **Parking Area (Eastbound)**

(20) **Parking Area (Westbound)**

22 U.S. 1, Aiken, Ridge Spring

FStop **S:** Smile Gas[*, D, K]

Gas **S:** BP[*, LP], Racetrac[*], Shell[*, LP, K]

Food **S:** Blimpie Subs & Salads (Shell), Eddie Pepper's Great Mexican Food (SMilesGas), Hardee's, Hot Stuff Pizza (SMilesGas), McDonald's[PLAY], Pizza King, Shell, Smile Gas, Waffle House

Lodg **S:** Days Inn, Holiday Inn Express

ATM **S:** Racetrac, Smile Gas

Other **S:** Airport

29 Road 49

33 SC 39, Wagener, Monetta

FStop **N:** Shell[*, K]
S: BP[*]

Food **S:** BP, Huddle House (BP)

(35) **Weigh Station (Eastbound)**

39 U.S. 178, Batesburg, Pelion, Leesville

FStop **N:** Exxon[*, K]

1295

Georgia • Exit 66 • 706-733-4656

Medical Center
1455 Walton Way
Augusta, GA 30901
706-722-2224 • 800-228-5150
Deluxe Continental Breakfast
Outdoor Pool
Meeting/Banquet Facilities
Handicap Accessible
Bus and RV Parking
Coin Laundry
Exterior Corridors
In Room Micro-Fridge & Coffee
25" TV Cable/HBO
Exit Riverwatch Pkwy East,
Right on 15th St. Left on Walton Way
1547
GEORGIA ▪ I-20 ▪ EXIT 66

EXIT SOUTH CAROLINA

S: Citgo Hill View Truck Stop(*)
Food S: Citgo Hill View Truck Stop
RVCamp S: Cedar Ponds Campground (1.5 Miles)
ATM N: Exxon
S: Citgo Hill View Truck Stop

44 Road 34, Gilbert
TStop N: 44 Truck Stop(*) (Citgo gas, restaurant)
Food N: 44 Restaurant (44 TS)
TServ N: 44 Truck Stop (Citgo gas, restaurant)
TWash N: 44 Truck Stop (Citgo gas, restaurant)
ATM N: 44 Truck Stop (Citgo gas, restaurant)

(48) Parking Area (Eastbound)

(48) Parking Area (Westbound)

51 Road 204
FStop N: Texaco(*, 24)
S: Amoco International Auto Truck Plaza(*, 24) (CB Repair)
Food N: Subway (Texaco), Texaco
AServ S: Amoco International Auto Truck Plaza(24) (CB Repair)
TServ S: Amoco International Auto Truck Plaza(24) (CB Repair)
ATM N: Texaco
S: Amoco International Auto Truck Plaza (CB Repair)

(53) Weigh Station (Westbound)

55 SC 6, Lexington, Swansea
FStop S: Exxon(*, LP)
Gas N: Texaco(*)
S: Citgo(*)
Food N: Hardee's, Planet Venus Bar & Grill
S: Bojangles, Golden Town Chinese, McDonald's(PLAY), Subway, Waffle House
Lodg S: Ramada Limited (see our ad this page)
RVCamp N: John's RV Sales & Service(LP)
ATM N: BB&T Bank, Texaco
S: Exxon, Wachovia Bank
Other N: Antique Shop, Car Quest Auto Center, Lake Murray Dam
S: CVS Pharmacy(RX), Piggly Wiggly, Winn Dixie Supermarket(24, RX)

58 U.S. 1, Columbia Airport, West Columbia, Univ of South Carolina
FStop N: Texaco(*, K, 24)
Gas N: Citgo(*, CW)
Food N: Citgo, Columbo Frozen Yogurt (Citgo), Krispy Kreme Doughnuts (Citgo), Subway (Texaco), Texaco, Waffle House
S: Meat'n Place Ribs & BBQ
ATM N: Citgo, Texaco
Other S: Four Oaks Farm, West Columbia Airport

61 U.S. 378, West Columbia
FStop S: Amoco(*, K)
Gas S: Phillips 66(*, LP)
Food S: Golden Nugget Restaurant(24), Waffle House
Med S: Hospital
ATM S: Amoco

63 Bush River Road
Gas N: BP(*, LP, CW)
S: Exxon(*, CW)
Food N: Burger King(PLAY), Cracker Barrel, Market Point Mall, Steak-Out, Subway, Wings & Ale
S: El Chico Mexican Restaurant, Fuddruckers, Key West Grill, The Villa (Italian), Waffle House
Lodg N: TraveLodge
S: Best Western, Knight's Inn, Sheraton, Sleep Inn
ATM N: BP
S: Exxon, Palmetto Trust Federal Credit Union
Other N: CVS Pharmacy(RX), Hemrick's, Market Point Mall, Waccamaw
S: Kinko's Copies(24), Major League Lanes (Bowling)

64AB Junction I-26 East, Columbia,

64B- Junction I-26, U.S. 76 West, Spartanburg

65 U.S. 176, Broad River Road
Gas N: BP(*, CW)
S: Racetrac(*)
Food N: Applebee's, Bojangles, Monterrey Mexican, Treasures(24), Waffle House
S: Arby's, Burger King, Captain Tom's Seafood, Church's Chicken, Cracker Jack's Food & Drink, Hooter's, KFC, Lizard's Thicket Country Cookin, McDonald's, Pizza Hut, Sandy's famous Hotdogs, Taco Bell, Taco Cid
Lodg N: Quality Inn
S: American Inn, La Quinta Inn, Royal Inn
AServ N: AAMCO Transmission, All Tune & Lube, Guardian Tire & Service Center
S: Pep Boys Auto Center, Precision Tune & Lube, Q Lube
ATM N: First Citizens Trust
Other N: National Pride Car Wash, Snappy Carwash
S: Service Merchandise

68 SC 215, Monticello Road, Jenkinsville
FStop N: Exxon(*, LP)
Gas N: Amoco(*), Texaco(*, D, LP)
S: Shell(*, 24)
Food N: Culler's Restaurant, Virginia's Grill
S: Shell, Subway (Shell), Sunrise
AServ N: P & C Enterprises Tire Service
ATM N: Exxon, Texaco

70 U.S. 321, Fairfield Road, Winnsboro
TStop S: Flying J Travel Plaza(*, LP, RV DUMP, SCALES) (Conoco Gas)
Gas S: Exxon(*)
Food S: Flying J Travel Plaza (Conoco Gas), Hardee's, The Cookery Restaurant & Buffett (Flying J)
Lodg S: Super 8
ATM S: Exxon, Flying J Travel Plaza (Conoco Gas)
Other S: B & B Treasures

71 U.S. 21, North Main St
TStop N: Carolina Travel Center(*, SCALES)
FStop N: United(*, 24) (Truckers Chapel)
Gas N: BP(*, K, CW)
S: Shell(*)
Food N: Carolina Country Cafe (Carolina TS), Carolina Travel Center, McDonald's(PLAY), Pizza Hut (Carolina TS), Subway (Carolina TS), United (Truckers Chapel)

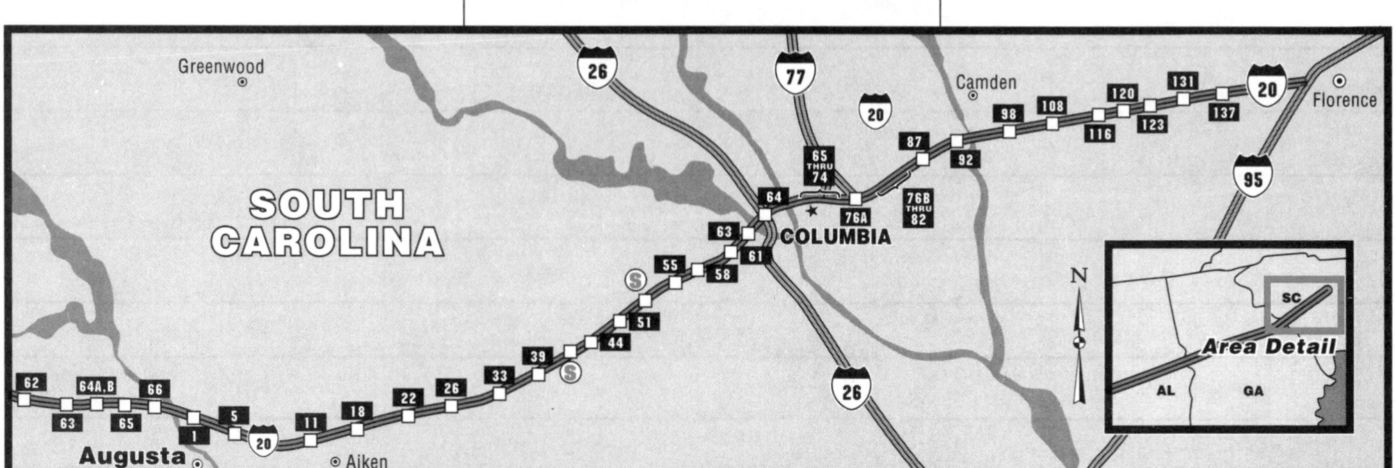

EXIT	SOUTH CAROLINA
	S: Bert's Grill and Diner
Lodg	**N:** Days Inn
TServ	**N:** **Carolina Travel Center**(SCALES), **Columbia Commercial Tire Center, Gerald Freight & Tires Inc.**
ATM	**N:** **United (Truckers Chapel)**
	S: First Citizens Bank
72	SC 555, Farrow Road
73AB	SC 277, Junction I-77, Charlotte, Columbia (Eastbound)
74	U.S. 1, Two Notch Road, Fort Jackson
Gas	**N:** BP(*, CW)
	S: Citgo(*, LP, CW, 24)
Food	**N:** Chili's, Fazoli's Italian Food, Holiday Inn, Hops Restaurant & Bar, International House of Pancakes, Lizard's Thicket Country Cookin, Mc Kenna's (Holiday Inn), Outback Steakhouse, Quality Inn, Tara's Restaurant (Quality Inn), Waffle House
	S: Applebee's, Baskin Robbins, Bojangles, Captain D's Seafood, Honey Baked Ham, Maurice's BBQ, Miami Subs & Grill, Quincy's Family Steakhouse, Roadhouse Grill, SHONEY'S Shoney's
Lodg	**N:** AmeriSuites (see our ad this page), Comfort Inn, Hampton Inn, Holiday Inn, Microtel Inn, Motel 6, Quality Inn, Red Roof Inn
AServ	**S:** NAPA Auto Parts, Precision Tune, Q Lube
ATM	**S:** Citgo, NationsBank, NationsBank
Other	**N:** Home Depot, **Sesqui Centennial State Park**
	S: Fireworks, Joshua's Christian Books, **Lowe's**, Sansberry Eye Center, Shops of O'Neil Court, The Book Dispensery
76AB	Alpine Rd., Fort Jackson, Junction I-77, Charlotte, Charleston

EXIT	SOUTH CAROLINA
80	Clemson Road
Gas	**N:** BP(*, CW), Exxon(*, K, CW), Shell(*, LP)
Food	**N:** Bojangles (Shell), **McDonald's**, Shell, **Waffle House**
ATM	**N:** Exxon
Other	**N:** **CVS Pharmacy**(RX)
82	Road 53, Pontiac, Pierce Road
87	Elgin, White Pond Road
FStop	**N:** **BP**(*), **Texaco**(*, K)
AServ	**N:** Regal Auto Care
92	U.S. 601, Lugoff, Camden
TStop	**N:** **Pilot Travel Center**(*, SCALES, 24)
Gas	**N:** Shell(*, LP)
Food	**N:** Dairy Queen (Pilot), Hardee's, **Pilot Travel Center**, Subway (Pilot), Waffle House
Lodg	**N:** **Days Inn**
RVCamp	**S:** **Columbia/Camden RV Park (.7 Miles)**
ATM	**N:** **Pilot Travel Center**
(93)	**Rest Area (RR, Phones, Picnic, Vending; Eastbound)**
(93)	**Rest Area (RR, Phones, Picnic, Vending; Westbound)**
98	U.S. 521, Camden, Sumpter
Gas	**N:** Exxon(*, D)
Med	**N:** **Hospital**
ATM	**N:** Exxon
Parks	**N:** **Revolutionary War Park**
101	Road 329
108	Manville , Jamestown

1296
AMERISUITES
AMERICA'S AFFORDABLE ALL-SUITE HOTEL
South Carolina • Exit 74 • 803-736-6666

EXIT	SOUTH CAROLINA
Gas	**N:** Shell(*)
	S: Citgo(*, CW)
AServ	**N:** Frankie's Garage & Wrecker Service
ATM	**S:** Citgo
116	U.S. 15, Bishopville, Hartsville, Sumter
FStop	**N:** **Shell**(*, 24)
Food	**N:** KFC (Shell), **McDonald's**(PLAY), **Shell**, Waffle House
Lodg	**N:** **Econolodge**
AServ	**S:** **Slater's (S. 1 Mile, tires, service, towing)**
TServ	**S:** **Slater's (S. 1 Mile, tires, service, towing)**
RVCamp	**S:** **Slater's (S. 1 Mile, tires, service, towing)**
ATM	**N:** **Shell**
120	SC 341, Lynchburg, Bishopville, Lake City
FStop	**S:** **Citgo**(*, LP)
Food	**S:** **A Taste of Country (Citgo)**, **Citgo**
Lodg	**S:** **Bishopville Motel**(24)
123	Road 22, Lamar, Lee State Park
FStop	**N:** **Amoco**(*)
Parks	**N:** **Lee State Park (1 Mile)**
(129)	**Parking Area (Eastbound)**
(129)	**Parking Area (Westbound)**
131	U.S. 401, SC 403, Timmonsville, Darlington, Lamar
FStop	**N:** **Phillips 66**(*, 24)
Gas	**N:** Exxon(*)
Food	**N:** **Phillips 66**
TServ	**N:** **Handee's Truck Shop (Phillips 66)**, **Phillips 66**(24)
137	SC 340, Darlington
Gas	**S:** BP(*)
AServ	**N:** B&B Auto Shop
141AB	Junction I-95 N, SC 327 Myrtle Beach, Fayetteville, I-95S , Savannah

↑SOUTH CAROLINA

Begin I-20

Notes:

EXIT		ILLINOIS/KENTUCKY
		Begin I-24

↓ILLINOIS

7 Goreville, Tunnel Hill
- FStop N: **Citgo**(*, D)
- RVCamp S: **Camping**

14 U.S. 45, Vienna, Harrisburg

16 IL 146, Vienna, Golconda
- Gas S: Amoco(*, 24), Citgo(*), Shell(*, 24)
- Food N: **Budget Inn (Restaurant)**
  S: Dairy Queen
- Lodg N: **Budget Inn (Restaurant)**
  S: Ramada
- AServ S: Amoco, Cagle's Tire and Wheel
- ATM S: Shell
- Other S: Collins Car Wash, **South Illinois Propane Gas**(LP)

27 New Columbia, Big Bay

37 U.S. 45, Metropolis, Brookport, Rest Area
- TStop N: **Veach's Service**(*, D)
  S: **BP**(*, D, SCALES, 24)
- Food S: Pizza Hut, **Ponderosa Steakhouse**
- Lodg S: Best Inns of America, Comfort Inn, **Metropolis Inn**
- TServ S: **BP**
- ATM S: BP

(37) IL Welcome Center (RR, Phones, Vending, P)

↑ILLINOIS

↓KENTUCKY

3 Kentucky 305, Paducah
- TStop N: **Citgo**(D) **(Truck Fuel Only)**
  S: **Pilot Travel Center**(*, CW, SCALES)
- FStop S: **Pilot Travel Center**(*, CW, SCALES)
- Gas N: Ashland(*)
  S: BP(*, D)
- Food N: El Maguey Mexican, Huddle House, Leroy & Lita's Restaurant, Slim's BBQ
  S: Mia Via Pizza (Pilot Tstop), **Subway (Pilot FS)**, Waffle Hut(24)
- Lodg N: **Comfort Inn**, Ramada Limited, Super 8
  S: Budgetel Inn
- TServ N: **Citgo**
- RVCamp S: **Fern Lake Campground (.25 Miles)**
- ATM N: Citgo

4 U.S. 60, Bus. Loop 24, Wickliffe, Paducah
- Gas N: Shell(*)
  S: Ashland(*), BP(*)

EXIT		KENTUCKY

- Food N: Applebee's, Burger King, Double Happiness Chinese, McDonald's, O'Charley's, Outback Steakhouse
  S: Atlanta Bread Company, Captain D's, Chong's Chinese, Chuck E Cheese's Pizza, Cracker Barrel, Denny's, Domino's Pizza (Ashland), El Chico Mexican Restaurant, Fazoli's Italian Food, Godfather's Pizza, Hardee's, Logan's Roadhouse Steaks & Ribs, Olive Garden, Pizza Hut, Red Lobster, Ryan's Steakhouse, Steak N' Shake, Subway, Taco Bell(PLAY), The Pasta House Company, Wendy's
- Lodg N: Courtyard Inn, **Days Inn**, Drury Inn, **Holiday Inn Express**, Motel 6, **Westowne Inn**
  S: Best Inns of America, Comfort Suites Hotel, Drury Suites, **Hampton Inn**, Peartree Inn
- AServ S: Goodyear Tire & Auto, **Sam's Club**, **Wal-Mart Supercenter**(RX)
- ATM S: Citizens Bank and Trust
- Other N: Doctors Valu Vision
  S: **Kentucky Oaks Mall**, **Sam's Club**, **Wal-Mart Supercenter**(RX)

7 U.S. 62, U.S. 45, Mayfield, Bardwell, Welcome Center
- FStop N: **Shell**(*, D, 24)
  S: **BP**(*, K) **(US 62)**
- Gas N: Pet-tro(*)
  S: Shell(*, CW) (US 62)
- Food N: Baskin Robbins (Pet-tro), **Burger King**(PLAY), Subway (Pet-tro), Taco Bell
  S: Arby's, **BP (US 62)**, KFC, McDonald's(PLAY), Sonic, Taco John's
- Lodg S: Denton Motel, Sunset Inn
- AServ S: Express Lube, **Kmart**(RX)
- Med N: **+ Lordes Hospital**
- ATM N: Pet-tro
  S: BP, Citizens Bank and Trust
- Other S: All Seasons Car Wash(24), **Kmart**(RX), Payless Drugs, Petzone

(7) KY Welcome Center (RR, Phones, Vending)
- Gas N: **Ashland**(*, D), Shell(*, D)
- Food N: Burger King (Ashland), Subway (Ashland), Taco Bell (Ashland)
  S: Arby's, McDonald's, Sonic
- Lodg S: Sunset Inn
- AServ S: K-Mart

Sponsored by Interatate America and Ramada Inn, Limited and Plaza Hotels of Kentucky

RAMADA

For information on how you can sponsor a child call 800-556-7918

KENTUCKY ■ I-24

EXIT		KENTUCKY

- Med N: **+ Hospital**
- Other S: Coin Car Wash, **K-Mart**

11 KY 1954, Husband Road, Paducah
- Lodg N: **Paducah Inn (Best Western)**
- TServ N: **Hartman's Truck & Equip. Service**

16 U.S. 68, Business 24, Paducah
- TStop S: **BP/AmBest**(*, D, SCALES)
- Gas S: Citgo(*)
- Food S: **Southern Pride (BP/AmBest)**
- AServ S: Citgo, Citgo
- TServ S: **Bridgestone Truck Service (BP/AmBest)**
- ATM S: **BP/AmBest**

25AB Purchase Pkwy, Fulton, Calvert City (Toll)

27 U.S. 62, Calvert City, KY Dam
- TStop S: **Coastal Travel Plaza**(*, SCALES)
- Gas N: Ashland(*, D), **BP**(*)
- Food N: KFC, **McDonald's**(PLAY), Willow Pond Restaurant
  S: **Coastal Travel Plaza**, Doug's Country Cafe (Coastal Travel Plaza)
- Lodg N: **Foxfire Motor Inn**
- TServ N: **Freightliner Dealer**
  S: **Bridgestone Tire & Auto**, **Coastal Travel Plaza**(SCALES)
- RVCamp N: **Cypress Lakes RV Park (.5 Miles)**, **KOA Campgrounds (1.25 Miles)**

31 KY 453, Grand Rivers, Smithland
- Gas N: Amoco(*, D)
  S: BP(*, D)
- Food N: Blimpies (Amoco)
  S: BP, **Mrs. Scarletts Restaurant**
- Lodg S: Best Western
- ATM S: BP
- Other S: Lakes Area Tourist Information

(34) Rest Area (Westbound)

(36) Weigh Station

40 U.S. 62, U.S. 641 Kuttawa, Eddyville
- FStop S: **Sunshine Travel Center**(*, D) **(Sunshine Restaurant)**
- Gas S: **BP**(*), Shell(*)
- Food N: Mary Major's Homestyle with Seafood Buffet
  S: Burger King (Shell), Sunshine Restaurant, **Sunshine Travel Center (Sunshine Restaurant)**, Taco Bell (Shell), Wendy's (BP)
- Lodg N: Relax Inn
  S: **Days Inn**, **Hampton Inn**
- ATM S: BP, Shell, Sunshine Travel Center

42 West KY Pkwy. East, Princeton, Elizabethtown

45 KY 293, Princeton
- FStop S: **Chevron**(*, D)
- Food S: Hot Stuff Pizza (Chevron), Smash Hit Subs

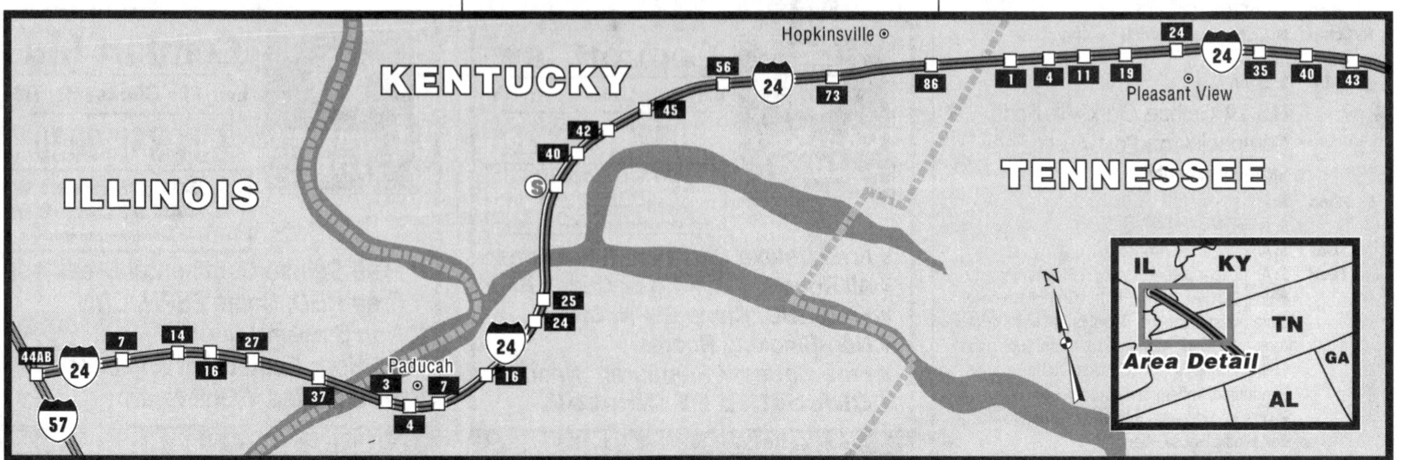

EXIT	KENTUCKY/TENNESSEE
	(Chevron)
RVCamp	N: R.V. Park
	S: Holiday Hills Resort (2 Miles), Indian Point RV Park (1.3 Miles), Lake Barkley RV Resort (1 Mile)
56	KY 139, Cadiz, Princeton
FStop	S: Chevron[*, 24]
RVCamp	S: Rock Castle RV Resort and Campground
65	U.S. 68, KY 80, Cadiz, Hopkinsville (Kentucky State Park Resort And Recreational Area)
FStop	S: Coastal[*, D] (Souvenir)
Gas	S: BP[*], Phillips 66[*, D], Shell[*, 24]
Food	S: Broad Bent Cafe (Coastal), Hardees, Sherlocke's Buffet and Grill Restaurant
Lodg	S: Country Inn, Holiday Inn Express, Knight's Inn, Lakeway Motel
AServ	S: Lakeland Chevrolet, Taber's Towing and Recovery Service
Med	S: ✚ Hospital
ATM	S: Phillips 66
Other	S: Tourist Info.
73	KY 117, Newstead, Gracey
86	U.S. Alt. 41, Hopkinsville, Ft. Campbell, Pennyrile Pky., Oak Grove
TStop	S: Flying J Travel Center[*, LP] (Conoco Fv), Pilot Travel Center[*, LP, SCALES]
FStop	N: Chevron[*, SCALES]
Gas	S: Amoco[*, 24]
Food	N: Taco Bell (Chevron)
	S: Burger King (Amoco), Country Market Restaurant (Flying J), Magic Dragon Chinese Eatery (Flying J), Pepperoni's Super Slice (Flying J), Pilot Travel Center, Subway (Pilot), The Great American Food (Pilot), Waffle House
Lodg	S: Budgetel Inn, Comfort Inn (see our ad this page), DAYS INN Days Inn (see our ad this page)
TServ	S: Pilot Travel Center
ATM	N: Chevron
	S: Amoco
89	KY 115, Oak Grove, Pembroke (Jefferson Davis Monument)
(93)	KY Welcome Center (RR, HF, Phones, Vending; Westbound)

↑KENTUCKY

↓TENNESSEE

EXIT	TENNESSEE
(1)	TN Welcome Center (RR, Phones; Eastbound)
1	TN 48, Clarksville, Trenton
FStop	N: Shell[*, D, K]
Gas	S: Exxon[*, LP, K]
Food	S: Ice Cream Corner (Exxon)
RVCamp	N: Clarksville RV Park & Campground[LP] (.25 Miles)
ATM	S: Exxon[*]
4	U.S. 79, Guthrie, Clarksville (Fort Campbell Army Post, Austin Peay State University)
FStop	N: BP[*, K]
	S: Speedway[*, LP]
Gas	S: Amoco[*, LP, CW], Amoco[LP]
Food	S: Amoco, Applebee's, Arby's, Burger King, Cracker Barrel, Hunan Garden Chinese Buffet, Krystal, Logan's Roadhouse Steaks & Ribs, Long John Silver, McDonald's, Miami Subs and Grill, O'Charley's, Olive Garden, Outback, Ponderosa, Rafferty's, Red Lobster, Rio Bravo, Ryan's Steak House, SHONEY'S Shoney's, Taco Bell, Waffle House, Wendy's
Lodg	S: Best Western, Comfort Inn, DAYS INN Days Inn (see our ad this page), Econolodge, Fairfield Inn, Hampton Inn, Holiday Inn, Microtel Inn and Suites, Motel 6, Ramada Limited, Royal Inn, Shoney's Inn, Super 8 (see our ad this page), TraveLodge, Wingate Inn
AServ	S: Q-Lube
TServ	S: Goodyear Tire & Auto
RVCamp	N Clarksville RV Sales and Service Center
ATM	S: Amoco, Amoco, BP, Heritage Bank, Speedway
Other	S: Governor's Square Mall, K-Mart[RX], Sam's Club, Value Vision, Wal-Mart[24, RX] (Food Court)
8	TN 237, Rossview Rd.
11	TN 76, Adams, Clarksville
FStop	N: Texaco[*, LP]
	S: Amoco[*, D, LP, 24]
Gas	S: Citgo[*], Phillips 66[*, D] (Days Inn)
Food	S: Homeplace Restaurant (Days Inn), Subway (Citgo), Waffle House
Lodg	S: Comfort Inn (see our ad this page), DAYS INN Days Inn, Holiday Inn Express
ATM	S: Amoco, Citgo
19	TN 256, Maxey Road, Adams
TStop	N: Phillips 66
FStop	S: Shell[*, LP]
Gas	N: BP[*]
Food	N: Phillips 66, Phillips 66
TServ	N: Phillips 66, Phillips 66
TWash	N: Phillips 66
24	TN 49, Springfield, Ashland City
FStop	N: Delta Express[*, LP, K]
Gas	N: Amoco[*], Texaco[*]
	S: Shell[*, LP]
Food	N: Buffet Pizza (Amoco)
ATM	N: Delta Express
	S: Piggly Wiggly
Other	S: Piggly Wiggly
31	TN 249, New Hope Road (Nashville Zoo)
TStop	S: BP[*, LP]
Gas	N: Shell[*, LP]
Food	S: Buddy's Chop House Steak, Chicken and Fish
TServ	S: BP
ATM	S: BP Tstop
Other	S: Self Service Car Wash
35	U.S. 431, Joelton, Springfield
Gas	S: Amoco[*, K], BP[*, LP, CW]
Food	S: Country Junction, McDonald's[PLAY], Subway (BP)
Lodg	S: DAYS INN Days Inn
RVCamp	S: OK Campground
Med	N: ✚ Hospital
ATM	S: Amoco

Closest Hotel to Ft. Campbell

1071

212 Auburn Hills
Oakgrove, KY
502-640-3888

- Continental Breakfast Included
- Kids 12 and under Stay & Eat Free
- Outdoor Pool • Handicap Accessible
- Tour Buses Welcome • Local Calls Free
- Remote TV with HBO/ESPN
- Corporate/Military Rates
- Kitchenettes Rooms Available
- Non-Smoking Rooms • Exterior Corridors
- Special Group/Extended Stays Rates

NEW

KENTUCKY • I-24 • EXIT 86

NEW HOTEL

Comfort Inn
Exit 86 • Oak Grove, KY
502-439-3311

20% Discount With Ad at Check In
Not valid with any other discount

¥ Free Deluxe Continental Breakfast
¥ All Rooms with King or Queen Beds
¥ Free HBO, Cable ESPN, CNN
¥ Non-Smoking Rooms
¥ Free Coffee ¥ Restaurant Nearby
¥ Closest to FT Cambell

1072

KENTUCKY • I-24 • EXIT 86

1124

130 WESTFIELD COURT

SWIMMING POOL
CABLE TV-HBO/ESPN
FREE CONTINENTAL BREAKFAST
RESTAURANTS NEARBY

931-552-1155 • Clarksville, TN

TENNESSEE • I-24 • EXIT 4

Super 8 Motel
3065 Wilma Rudolph Blvd.
615-647-2002

- Indoor Heated Pool
- Cable TV with HBO
- Deluxe Continental Breakfast
- Restaurants Nearby

1123

TENNESSEE • I-24 • EXIT 4

Comfort Inn
Exit 11 • Clarksville, TN
931-358-2020

20% Discount With Ad at Check In
Not valid with any other discount

¥ Free Deluxe Continental Breakfast
¥ Free HBO, Cable ESPN, CNN
¥ Non Smoking Rooms
¥ 24 Hour Restaurant Adjacent
¥ Free Coffee ¥ Golf Nearby

AAA

1073

TENNESSEE • I-24 • EXIT 11

EXIT TENNESSEE

Other S: Coin Operated Laundromat

40 TN 45, Old Hickory Blvd

Gas N: Citgo Quick Mart(*, D), Phillips 66(*)

Food N: Family Restaurant (Super 8 Motel), Subway (Citgo)

Lodg N: Super 8

ATM N: Citgo

43 TN 155, Briley Pky., to Opryland

44AB Junction I-65, Nashville

Note: I-24 runs concurrent below with I-65. Numbering follows I-65.

83A I-24 East, I-40 East, Knoxville, Chattanooga

83B I-40 West, South I-65, Memphis, Birmingham

84 Arena, Shelby Ave

Gas W: Exxon(*)

Food W: Gersthaus

Lodg W: Econolodge, Ramada Limited

AServ W: Napa Auto, Standard Motor Parts

Other E: **Lynn Drugs, Martin's Grocery**

W: **Prop Shop & More**

85 James Robertson Parkway, State Capitol (Difficult Reaccess)

TStop W: **TravelCenters of America**(RV DUMP, SCALES)

Gas E: Mapco Express, Shell(*, CW)

W: Cone(*)

Food W: **Country Pride (TravelCenters)**, Gersthaus Restaurant, Mrs. C's, SHONEY'S, Shoney's, **Subway (TravelCenters)**

Lodg W: Best Host Motel, Econolodge, Ramada Limited

AServ E: Amoco, Coin Car Wash

Nashville, TN

1126

615-833-6860
800-55-ECONO

Full Continental Breakfast • Lounge on Premises
Kids Under 12 Stay & Eat Free
Outdoor Pool • Exterior Corridors
Meeting/Banquet Facilities
Pets Allowed (Extra $) • Handicap Accessible
Truck/Large Vehicle Parking
Close to Nashville's Major Attractions
Grand Ole Opry Packages Available

Ask About Daily Tours

I-24, Exit Harding Place W, L between Gameland & Shell Station

NORTH CAROLINA • I-77 • EXIT 6A

1125

Quality Inn
Exit 59 • Antioch
615-731-8441
800-228-5151

Full Continental Breakfast
Kids Under 12 Eat & Stay Free
Lounge on Premises
Outdoor Pool • Golf Range Nearby
Handicap Accessible • Exterior Corridors
Truck/Large Vehicle Parking
Starwood Amphiltheatre, Hickory Mall & Other Points of Interest Close By

Sight Seeing Tours

TENNESSEE • I-24 • EXIT 59

EXIT TENNESSEE

W: Vogely & Todd Collision Repair Experts

TServ W: **TravelCenters of America**

ATM E: Mapco Express

Other E: Main Street Auto Wash

W: **Country Hearth Bread, Bakery Thrift Store, Performing Arts Center, State Capitol, Tourist Info.**

85A U.S. 31 E., N. Ellington Pkwy, Spring St.

FStop E: **Cone**(*), **Pacific Pride**

Gas E: Spur(*, D)

Lodg E: Best Western (Metro Inn), DAYS INN Days Inn

AServ E: Jefferson Street Car Care

W: NAPA Auto Parts, Nashville Tansmission Parts, Todd's Auto Parts

TServ E: **Pacific Pride**

Other W: Burnette's Truck Wash, **U-Haul Center**(LP)

85B Jefferson St. (East Side Services Are The Same As In Exit 85A)

Gas W: Spur

Lodg W: Best Western, DAYS INN Days Inn

86 Junction I-265 Memphis

87AB U.S. 431, Trinity Lane

TStop E: **Pilot Travel Center**(SCALES)

Gas E: Circle K(*, LP)

W: Amoco(*, D, K, CW), BP(*, D, CW), Exxon(*, D), Texaco(*, D)

Food E: **Arby's (Pilot)**, Candle Light Restaurant, Chuch's Chicken, Krystal(24), Sonic, TJ Restaurant, White Castle Restaurant

W: Burger King, Captain D's Seafood, Chugers Restaurant, Club Paradise, Denny's(24), Gabe's Lounge, Jack's BAR-B-QUE, Lockers Sports Grill, McDonald's, Ponderosa, SHONEY'S, Shoney's, Taco Bell, The Broken Spoke Cafe (Ramada Inn), Track 1 Cafe (Rain Tree Inn), Waffle House

Lodg E: **Cumberland Inn (Pilot TS)**, Key Motel, Red Carpet Inn, Savoy Motel, Scottish Inns, Trinity Inn

W: Comfort Inn, DAYS INN Days Inn, Econolodge, Hallmark Inn, Hampton Inn, **Holiday Inn Express**, Knight's Inn, Liberty Inn, Motel 6, Oxford Inn, Rain Tree Inn, Ramada

AServ E: Bobby's Tire Service, Gary's, The Tire Store

W: Exxon

RVCamp E: **Holiday Mobile Village (.5 Miles), RV and Camper Corral Truck Accessories**

ATM W: BP

Parks E: **Trinity Park (Mobil Home Park)**

Other E: Coin Car Wash, National Car Wash, **Sweeney's Food Town Gocery Store, Trinity Gas Co. Inc**(LP), **US Post Office**

Note: I-24 runs concurrent above with I-65. Numbering follows I-65.

Note: I-24 runs concurrent below with I-40. Numbering follows I-40.

211AB Jct. I-65, I-24, I-40, Louisville, Huntsville

212 Fesslers Lane (Difficult Reaccess)

FStop S: **Citgo**(*, LP), **Mapco Express**(*, LP), **Texaco**(*, CW)

Food S: Burger King, Krystal (Citgo), La Fiesta, Lee's Famous Recipe Chicken, McDonald's, Mrs. Winner's, Sonic Drive in, Southern Way Cafe, Wendy's

Lodg S: Drake Motel, Lee Motel, Music City Motor Inn

AServ N: Bridgestone, Southeastern Brake

S: Chevrolet Dealer, Mercedes Dealership

TServ N: **Goodyear Tire & Auto, Neely Coble Sunbelt Truck Center**

S: **Tredaco Truck Service**

Med N: **+ Hospital**

S: **+ Hospital**

ATM S: **Citgo, Mapco Express, Texaco**

EXIT TENNESSEE

213A Junction I-24 East, West I-40, Knoxville, Chattanooga

213B Junction I-24 West, Junction I-40 West, Nashville

Note: I-24 runs concurrent above with I-40. Numbering follows I-40.

52AB 52A - I-24W, I-40W, Nashville 52B - I-40E, Knoxville

52 U.S. 41 South, Murfreesboro Road

Gas N: BP(*, CW), Texaco(*)

Food N: Dad's Place (Ramada Inn), Denny's, Lin's Garden Chinese Restaurant (Quality Inn), Ramada Inn, Waffle House

S: Teasers

Lodg N: DAYS INN Days Inn, Quality Inn, Ramada Inn

S: Midway Motel

AServ S: Dixie Motor, Master Muffler, Music City Dodge Inc.

TServ N: **Cummins Diesel**

S: **Fruehauf, Kile International Trucks**

ATM N: First American Bank, Texaco

53 Junction I- 440 West & I-24

54AB TN 155, Briley Parkway (Difficult Reaccess, Limited Access)

Gas S: Shell(*)

AServ S: Shell

Parks S: **Grassmere Wildlife Park**

56 Route 255, Harding Place

Gas N: Amoco(*, D, CW, 24), Exxon(*, CW), Mapco Express(*, D, LP), Texaco(*, D)

S: Mapco Express(*), Shell

Food N: Applebee's, Church's Chicken, City Cafe, Denny's(24) (Pear Tree Inn), Drury Inn, Golden House Chinese, KFC, Long John Silver, McDonald's, Mikado Japanese Steakhouse, Schlotzsky's Deli (Drury Inn), Subway, Taco Bell, Teasers Sport Grill, Waffle House, Wendy's, White Castle Restaurant

S: Burger King, **Hooters**, Spiffy's Restaurant Lounge, **Uncle Bud's Catfish, Chicken And Such**, Waffle House

Lodg N: Drury Inn, HoJo Inn, Motel 6, Pear Tree Inn, Suburban Lodge, Super 8

S: Econolodge (see our ad this page), Motel 6

AServ S: Shell

Med S: **+ Hospital**

ATM N: Amoco, Mapco Express

Other N: **Safeway Grocery, Sam's Club**

S: **Supermarket**

57AB Antioch, Haywood Lane

Gas N: Amoco(D, K), Kwik Sak(*, LP, K)

S: Exxon(*, LP), Phillips 66(*, CW)

Food N: Blimpie Sub & Salads, Fat Mo's, Georgia's Coast Pizza, Steak, & Burgers, Golden Donuts, Hardee's, Mama Taori's Pizza, Pizza Hut, Rio Grande Mexican & Salvadorian Restaurant, Waffle House, Whitt's BBQ

S: Chanello's Pizza, Exxon, Pocono's Grill Cafe & Deli, TCBY (Exxon), Taco Bell (Exxon)

AServ N: Amoco, Car Quest Auto Center

TServ N: **Peterbilt Dealer**

Med N: **+ Antioch Medical Center (Walk-Ins Welcome)**

ATM N: Kwik Sak

S: Exxon

Other N: **Food Lion, JML Market**(*), **Jumbo Washette Coin Laundry**, Pop's Antioch Car Wash, **The Book Trader**, U-Wash Car Wash, **WalGreens Pharmacy**(RX)

S: **Apache Trail Animal Hospital, Quick Stop Food Mart**(*, LP)

EXIT — TENNESSEE

59 TN 254, Bell Road
- **Gas** N: BP(*), Shell(*)
  S: Amoco(*, LP, K), BP(*, D, CW), Texaco(*, D, LP, CW)
- **Food** N: Applebee's, Arby's, Burger King, Chuck E Cheese's Pizza, Courtyard Cafe, Cracker Barrel, KFC, Logan's Roadhouse Steaks & Ribs, McDonald's(PLAY), Nathan's Italian Restaurant (Ramada Inn), O'Charley's, Panda Garden, Pizza Hut, Red Lobster, TGI Friday
  S: Casa Fiesta Mexican Restaurant (Quality Inn), Evergreen Chinese, Olive Garden, SHONEY'S Shoney's, Waffle House
- **Lodg** N: DAYS INN Days Inn, Ramada Inn
  S: Knight's Inn, Quality Inn (see our ad this page), The Quarters Motor Inn
- **AServ** N: Firestone Tire & Auto
  S: Gary Force Acura, Texaco, Valvoline Oil Change
- **TServ** N: **Bill Heard**
- **ATM** N: First American, First Union, Union Planter's National Bank
  S: Texaco
- **Other** N: Hickory Hollow Cinemas, **Hickory Hollow Shopping Mall**, **Horner-Rauch Optical Superstore**, Kinko's Copies, Pier 1 Imports
  S: **Pet Med**, **Target**

60 Hickory Hollow Parkway (Difficult Reaccess)
- **Food** N: El Toreo, Wendy's
- **Lodg** N: Hampton Inn, Holiday Inn
- **AServ** N: Bill Heard Chevrolet

62 TN 171, Old Hickory Boulevard
- **FStop** N: **Speedway**(*, D, LP), **T/A TravelCenters of America**
- **Gas** N: Amoco(*, D, CW), Texaco(*, D)
- **Food** N: Amoco, Blimpie's Subs(*) (Amoco), Waffle House
- **Lodg** N: Best Western (Music City Inn)
- **TServ** N: **76**(SCALES) **(Music City TS)**
- **ATM** N: **Speedway**, Texaco

64 Waldron Road, La Vergne
- **TStop** N: **417 Travel Center**(*, SCALES, 24)
- **FStop** N: **Speedway**(*, RV DUMP, SCALES)
- **Gas** N: Exxon(*), Marathon(*, K), Speedway(*)
  S: Mapco Express(*, LP)
- **Food** N: **417 Travel Center**, Anna Lee's, Arby's, **Hardee's**, **Krystal**, **McDonald's**(PLAY), Perkin's Family Restaurant, **Subway (Speedway)**, Subway (417 Travel Center), Taco Bell (417 Travel Center), **Waffle House**, Waffle House, Zoomerz Broasted Chicken Deli
  S: **Daisy's Kitchen (Driftwood Inn)**, Pizza Neatza, Rice Bowl II
- **Lodg** N: Comfort Inn (see our ad this page), Holiday Inn, Tennesee Mountain Inn
  S: **Driftwood Inn**
- **TServ** N: **417 Travel Center**(SCALES, 24), **International**
- **RVCamp** N: **Music City Campground (1.9 Miles)**, **RV Service (1 Mile, 7 days)**
- **ATM** N: **417 Travel Center**, Exxon
- **Other** S: Car Wash

66AB TN 266, Sam Ridley Pkwy, Smyrna
- **Gas** N: Texaco(*, D, LP, K)
  S: Amoco(*, D, K)
- **Food** N: Baskin Robbins (Texaco), Texaco, The Catfish House Seafood, Chicken, Steaks
- **Lodg** S: Comfort Inn
- **RVCamp** N: **R.V. Service (1.25 Miles)**
- **ATM** N: Texaco
  S: Bank

70 TN 102, Lee Victory Pky, Almaville Rd, Smyrna
- **Gas** S: Amoco(*, D, LP, K), Citgo(*, LP, CW), Exxon(*, D, K), Mapco Express(*, D, LP, K)
- **Food** S: McDonald's
- **RVCamp** N: **Nashville I-24 Campground**, **New Smyrna Campground**
- **ATM** S: Amoco

74 TN 840 East, Knoxville (Reaccess Westbound Only, Difficult Reaccess)

78AB TN 96, Franklin, Murfreesboro
- **Gas** N: Phillips 66(*, D, LP), Shell(*, LP), Texaco(*), USA
  S: Amoco(*, LP, K, CW), BP(*, K, CW), Chevron(*, D, 24), Exxon(*, D, LP)
- **Food** N: Backyard Burgers, Baskin Robbins, Burger King (Texaco), **Cracker Barrel**, Don Pablo's Mexican, El Chico, IHOP, KFC, McDonald's, Murfree's Restaurant (Holiday Inn), O'Charley's (Steak & Ribs), Outback Steakhouse, Red Lobster, Ryan's Steakhouse, Subway, Texaco, Waffle House, **Wal-Mart Supercenter**(24, RX), Wendy's
  S: Corky's Ribs & BBQ, Hardee's, Waffle House
- **Lodg** N: Best Western, Comfort Inn, Country Inn & Suites, Garden Plaza Hotel, Hampton Inn, Holiday Inn, Microtel Inn, Motel 6, Super 8, Wyngate Inn
- **AServ** N: Parkway Auto & Tire Service, Shell
  S: Auto Glass Service, **Sam's Club**
- **Med** N: **+ Hospital**
- **ATM** N: First American Bank, SunTrust Bank, Texaco
  S: Amoco, Cavalry Bank, Exxon
- **Other** N: **Golf USA Fun Park**, **Stones River Mall**, **Wal-Mart Supercenter**(RX), **William's Animal Hospital**
  S: Auto Pride Car Wash, **Sam's Club**

81AB U.S. 231, Murfreesboro, Shelbyville
- **FStop** N: **Uncle Sandy's BP**(*)
  S: **Pacific Pride**, **Phillips 66**(*, LP, CW)
- **Gas** N: Amoco(D), Racetrac(*)
  S: Citgo(*, LP, K), Mapco Express(*, D, LP, K), Texaco(*, D, LP)
- **Food** N: Arby's, Burger King(PLAY), Cracker Barrel, King's Table Restaurant, Krystal, Ponderosa, Shang Hai Chinese Restaurant, SHONEY'S Shoney's, The Parthenon Steakhouse, Waffle House, Wendy's
  S: McDonald's(PLAY), **Pacific Pride**, Q's Country Cookin' (Howard Johnson), Subway, Waffle House, Whitt's BBQ
- **Lodg** N: DAYS INN **Days Inn (see our ad this page)**, Ramada Inn, **Scottish Inns**, Shoney's Inn, TraveLodge
  S: Howard Johnson, Quality Inn, Safari Inn
- **AServ** N: Car Wash Auto Pride, Dodge Dealer
  S: Neill Sandler Toyota
- **Med** N: **+ Hospital**
- **ATM** S: Citgo, **Phillips 66**, Texaco
- **Other** N: Car Wash, **Direct Factory Outlet Fireworks Supermarket**, **Keepsake Antique Mall Center**
  S: Car Wash, **Laundry (Coin Laundry)**

86 Buchanan Road

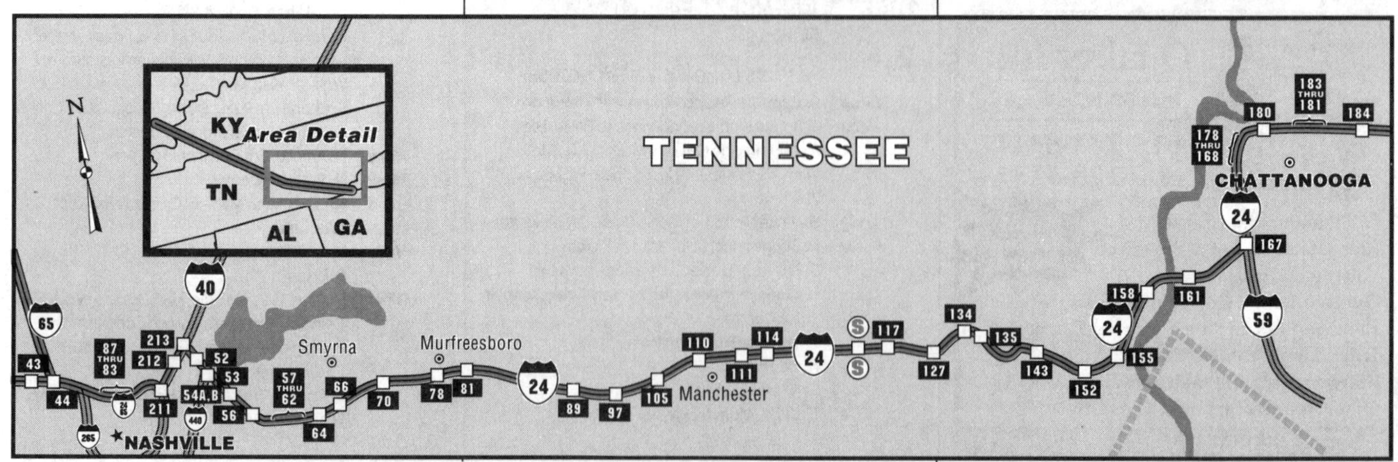

Bold red print shows RV & Bus parking available or nearby

EXIT TENNESSEE

- FStop — S: Citgo Danny's Food & Fuel Plaza(*, K)
- Gas — N: Texaco(*)
- Food — N: Restaurant (Texaco), Texaco; S: Citgo Danny's Food & Fuel Plaza, Huddle House (Citgo)
- TServ — N: Truck Tire & Service(24) (Wrecker Service)
- Other — N: Crazy J's Fireworks & Hot Grill

97 TN 64, Beechgrove Road, Shelbyville
- Gas — N: Beech Grove General Store(*, LP, K); S: Phillips 66(*)
- AServ — N: The Import Clinic
- Other — N: Parker's Quick Mart(*), US Post Office

105 U.S. 41, Manchester
- FStop — N: BP(*)
- Gas — N: Texaco(*, D); S: Amoco(LP, K)
- Food — N: Ranch House Restaurant
- AServ — N: Best Tire Co.
- RVCamp — S: KOA Campgrounds (8 Miles), Whispering Oaks Campground (1 Mile)
- ATM — N: BP

110 TN 53, Manchester, Woodbury
- FStop — S: Texaco(*, D, K)
- Gas — N: BP(*, K), Exxon(*, LP), Phillips 66(*)
- Food — N: Cracker Barrel, Davy Crockett's Roadhouse, Exxon, Floyd's Family Restaurant, TCBY (Exxon), The Oak Family Restaurant; S: Los 3 Amigos, Waffle House
- Lodg — N: Ambassador Inn & Luxury Suites, Days Inn, Hampton Inn
- AServ — S: Hulletts Service Center(24) (Towing), Hulletts Service Center
- TServ — S: Hulletts Service Center(24) (Towing)
- Med — N: Hospital
- ATM — N: BP, Exxon, Phillips 66; S: Texaco
- Parks — S: Old Stone Fort State Park

111 TN 55, Manchester, McMinnville
- Gas — N: Amoco(*, D, LP, K, 24), Chevron(*, D, K), Citgo(*, LP); S: BP(*, D, K)
- Food — N: Citgo, TCBY (Citgo); S: J & G Pizza & Steakhouse, Porky's Pit BBQ
- AServ — S: Bunch Tire Co.
- Med — N: Hospital; S: Hospital
- ATM — N: Amoco, Citgo
- Parks — N: Rock Island State Park (37 Miles); S: Old Stone Fort State Park (3 Miles), Tim's Ford State Park (23 Miles)

114 U.S. 41, Manchester
- TStop — N: Jiffy Truck/Auto Plaza(*, K, SCALES) (Showers)
- Gas — N: Phillips 66(*, D), Texaco(*, D, LP); S: BP(*), Exxon(*, LP), RaceWay(*, 24)
- Food — N: Jiffy Truck/Auto Plaza (Showers), Longfellow's Family Restaurant (Ramada Inn), Trucker's Inn Cafe (Jiffy T/A Plaza); S: Arby's, Burger King(PLAY), Captain D's Seafood, Exxon, KFC, McDonald's(PLAY), SHONEY'S, Shoney's, TCBY (Exxon), Taco Bell, Waffle House, Wendy's
- Lodg — N: Ramada Inn, Scottish Inns, Super 8, Trucker's Inn (Jiffy T/A Plaza); S: Budget Motel, Holiday Inn, Red Carpet Inn
- AServ — N: Roberts Nissan/Toyota; S: Auto Zone Auto Parts, Bobby Vann Chevrolet/Geo
- RVCamp — N: KOA Kampground(LP) (.5 Miles)
- ATM — N: Jiffy Truck/Auto Plaza (Showers); S: Bi-Lo Grocery, Exxon
- Other — N: Arrowhead Aerospace Museum, Train Toy WWII Museum; S: Bi-Lo Grocery, Wal-Mart(LP, RX)

(116) Weigh Station (Eastbound)

(116) Weigh Station (Westbound)

117 U.S. Air Force, Arnold Center, Tullahoma, UT Space Institute

EXIT TENNESSEE

(120) Parking Area (Eastbound, Trucks Only)

(120) Parking Area (Westbound, Trucks Only)

127 US 64, TN 50, Pelham, Winchester
- Gas — N: Amoco(*, D, LP), Phillips 66(*, D, LP), Texaco(*); S: Exxon(*, D, LP)
- Food — N: Stuckey's (Texaco), Texaco
- Parks — S: Tim's Ford State Park

(134) Rest Area (Eastbound)

(134) Rest Area (RR, Phones, Picnic, Vending, Pet Walk; Westbound)

134 U.S. 41A, Monteagle, Sewanee
- Gas — N: Exxon, The Depot(*, LP); S: Chevron(*, D, LP), Citgo(*, LP), Texaco(*, D, PLAY)
- Food — N: Papa Ron's Pizza; S: Hardee's(PLAY), Jim Oliver's Smokehouse Restaurant & Trading Post, Waffle House
- Lodg — S: Budget Host Inn, Jim Oliver's Smokehouse Lodge
- AServ — N: Exxon; S: Denton's Wrecker Service, Monteagle Firestone
- ATM — S: Citgo
- Parks — N: South Cumberland State Park
- Other — N: Flea Market & Antique Mall; S: Piggly Wiggly Grocery

135 U.S. 41 North, Monteagle, Tracy City
- TStop — N: 76 Monteagle Truck Plaza(SCALES)
- FStop — N: Citgo(*, D, K), Phillips 66(*, LP, K)
- Food — N: 76 Monteagle Truck Plaza, Citgo, Pop's Happyland Restaurant & Truck Stop
- Lodg — S: Days Inn
- AServ — N: 76 Monteagle Truck Plaza, Auto Sure
- TServ — N: 76 Monteagle Truck Plaza(SCALES)
- TWash — S: I-24 Truck Wash

(136) Truck Inspection Station

Exit (137) Runaway Truck Ramp

(139) Runaway Truck Ramp

143 Martin Springs Road
- FStop — N: Chevron(*)

152 U.S. 41, U.S. 64, U.S. 72, Kimball, S. Pittsburg
- Gas — N: Amoco(*), Phillips 66(*) (TN/AL Fireworks), Racetrac(*)
- Food — N: Arby's, China Inn, Domino's Pizza, KFC, Krystal, Long John Silver, McDonald's(PLAY), Pizza Hut, SHONEY'S, Shoney's, Subway, Taco Bell, Waffle House, Wendy's; S: Bubba's Down Home Pizza, Oscar's BBQ
- Lodg — N: Budget Host Inn Kimball Motor Lodge, Days Inn, Holiday Inn Express
- AServ — N: Jentry Geo/GM/Chevrolet, Wal-Mart(RX)
- Med — S: Hospital
- ATM — N: Citizen's State Bank, Pioneer Bank
- Other — N: Bi-Lo Grocery(RX), Eye Ear Optical,

1478

Comfort Inn

Exit 175 • Chattanooga, TN

423-821-1499

800-228-5150

Comfort Inn

- Continental Breakfast Included
- Kids 12 and under Stay & Eat Free
- Outdoor Pool • Indoor Heated Pool
- Handicap Accessible • Free HBO
- Jacuzzi Room Extra • Pets Allowed
- Ruby Falls & Warehouse Row Outlet 2 miles
- Tennessee Aquarium & Lookout Mountain 3 miles
- Many exciting attractions and restaurants close by

Truck/Large Vehicle Parking

I-24 Exit 175 Hotel located behind Hardees Restaurant

Tennessee ¥ I-24 ¥ Exit 175

EXIT TENNESSEE/GEORGIA

Laundromat, New Tennessee Alabama Fireworks(*), Tennessee Fireworks Factory (Amoco), Wal-Mart(RX)

155 TN 28, Jasper, Dunlap, Whitwell
- Gas — N: Amoco(*, D)
- Food — N: Hardee's, Western Sizzlin'
- Lodg — N: Acuff Country Inn
- Med — S: Columbia Grandview Medical Center
- ATM — N: Amoco
- Other — N: Fireworks Supermarket(24)

158 TN 27, Nickajack Dam, Powells Crossroads
- FStop — N: Phillips 66(*) (Accessible Via Both Sides); S: Phillips 66(*, D) (Accessible Via Both Sides)
- Gas — N: Texaco(*, K)
- RVCamp — S: Camping (3 Miles)
- Other — N: Tennessee/Alabama Fireworks (Accessible Via Both Sides); S: Tennessee/Alabama Fireworks (Accessible Via Both Sides)

(160) Rest Area (Eastbound)

(160) Rest Area (RR, HF, Phones, Picnic, Vending, Pet Walk; Westbound)

161 TN156, Haletown, New Hope
- Gas — S: Chevron(*) (Big Daddy's Fireworks)
- AServ — S: Glenn's Wrecker Service(24)
- RVCamp — S: Smith's Camp on the Lake Campground
- Other — S: Big Daddy's Fireworks(*)

167 Junction I-59 South, Birmingham

↑TENNESSEE

↓GEORGIA

169 Georgia 299 to U.S. 11, Wildwood
- FStop — N: $av-A-Ton(*, LP); S: Amoco(*, SCALES, 24), Cone Auto/Truck Plaza(*)
- Gas — S: Racetrac(*)
- Food — S: Amoco, Subway(24) (Amoco), TCBY(24) (Amoco)
- ATM — S: Amoco, Cone Auto/Truck Plaza, Racetrac

↑GEORGIA

↓TENNESSEE

(172) Rest Area (RR, Phones, Vending, Pet Walk)

174 Junction U.S. 11, U.S. 41, U.S. 64, Lookout Valley & Mtn.
- FStop — S: Amoco(*, LP)
- Gas — S: BP(*), Exxon(*, 24)
- Food — N: Waffle House; S: BP, Circle C Breakfast & Vegtables, Cracker Barrel, Taco Bell, Waffle House
- Lodg — N: Days Inn, Holiday Inn; S: Best Western, Bugetel Inn, Comfort Inn & Suites, Econolodge, Fricks Motel, Hampton Inn, Ramada Limited, Royal Inn, Super 8
- RVCamp — N: Barren Mountain (1.9 Miles), Raccoon Mtn, Crystal Caverns, Campground (1.3 Miles); S: Lookout Valley RV Park (.5 Miles)
- ATM — S: Exxon
- Other — N: State Highway Patrol

175 Browns Ferry Road, Lookout Mtn, US 11, US 64 (Eastbound, Difficult Reaccess)
- FStop — S: Conoco(*, LP, K)
- Gas — N: Citgo(*, LP), Exxon(*); S: Texaco(*, LP)
- Food — N: Knight's Inn, Restaurant (Knights Inn); S: Hardee's(PLAY)
- Lodg — N: Knight's Inn; S: Comfort Inn (see our ad this page)

EXIT TENNESSEE

- **ATM** N: Citgo
- **Other** N: CVS Pharmacy[RX], Food Lion Supermarket, Lookout Valley Post Office, Revco Drugs

178 U.S. 27 N, Lookout Mtn, Downtown Chattanooga, Market Street (Reaccess Westbound Only, Difficult Reaccess)
- **FStop** N: Amoco[*, K]
- **Gas** N: Amoco, BP[*]
- **Food** N: Chatt's Restaurant (Stadium Inn), Dino's Restaurant (Knights Inn), Knight's Inn, Malone's, Stadium Inn
- **Lodg** N: Days Inn, Knight's Inn (see our ad this page), Stadium Inn
- **AServ** N: Amoco, Ford, Nisson Dealership, Grant Auto Glass Co., Midas Muffler & Brake, Mountain View Ford, Nissan
- **TServ** N: Ford Truck Dealer
- **Other** N: Mr. C's Meats & Things, Tennessee Aquarium; S: Fabric Care Center Coin Operated Laundry, Historical Chattanooga Choo-Choo

180A TN 8 North, Rossville Blvd, Central Ave (Difficult Reaccess)
- **FStop** S: Speedway[*]
- **Gas** S: Racetrac[*]
- **Food** N: Hot'Lanta
- **AServ** N: Universal Tire; S: Baker's Transmission & Muffler
- **Other** N: Car Wash, Hy's Car Wash, Hy's Car Wash

180B U.S. 27 South, Rossville Blvd (Difficult Reaccess)
- **FStop** S: Speedway[*]
- **Gas** S: Phillips 66[*, LP], Racetrac[*]
- **Food** S: Juke Box Players Cafe, Long John Silver, Speedway
- **AServ** S: Baker's Transmission & Muffler, Roy's Tire Service, Scenic City Auto Repair (NAPA)
- **Med** S: Medical Care Center (Walk-Ins Welcome)
- **Other** S: Eyear One Hour Optical

181 Fourth Ave
- **Gas** N: Amoco[*, K], Citgo[*, K], Exxon[D], Pure[*]; S: Citgo[*]
- **Food** N: Burger King[PLAY], Central Park Burgers, Hardee's, Krystal, Mick's 24 Hour Diner, Quality Inn, Waffle House
- **Lodg** N: Quality Inn
- **AServ** N: Lancaster Auto Parts, Mr. Transmission, One Stop Auto Parts, Yates Wrecker Service[24]
- **TServ** N: Mack Trucks Cummins, Cat, & Mercedes; S: City Truck & Trailer Parts
- **Med** N: Hospital
- **ATM** N: First Tennessee Bank
- **Other** N: Animal World Boarding & Supplies; S: Stewart's Coin Laundry

181A U.S. 41 South, East Ridge (Eastbound, Reaccess Westbound Only, Difficult Reaccess)
- **Gas** N: Amoco[*]
- **Food** N: Central Park, Hardee's, Krystal; S: Ridge Cut Cafe (King's Lodge), Westside Grille & Bar
- **Lodg** S: Gateway Motel, King's Lodge
- **TServ** N: Doug Yate's Wrecker Service, Thermo-King
- **Med** N: Hospital

183A (184) Belvoir Ave, Germantown Road (Westbound)

184 Moore Road, Chattanooga (Difficult Reaccess)
- **AServ** S: K-Mart
- **Med** S: Hospital
- **Other** S: K-Mart[RX], Winn Dixie Supermarket[RX]

185AB Junction I-75

↑TENNESSEE

Begin I-24

EXIT WYOMING

Begin I-25

↓WYOMING

(300) Jct I-90, Gillette

299 U.S. 16, Buffalo
- **FStop** W: Big Horn Travel Plaza[*], Cenex[*]
- **Gas** E: Cenex, Conoco, Texaco[*]
- **Food** W: Bozeman Restaurant, Crossroads Inn, Dash Inn Restaurant, Econolodge, Hardee's, McDonald's, Pizza Hut, Real Hickory B-B-Q, Subway, Taco John's, The Breadboard Sub Shop
- **Lodg** E: Comfort Inn; W: Crossroads Inn, Econolodge, Motel Wyoming, Super 8
- **RVCamp** E: KOA Campgrounds (.25 Miles); W: Indian Campground (1 Mile)
- **Med** W: Hospital
- **ATM** W: Big Horn Travel Plaza, Cenex
- **Other** E: Buffalo Veterinarian Clinic; W: Squeeky Kleen Car Wash

298 Business I-25, Business U.S. 87, Buffalo
- **Gas** W: Sinclair
- **Other** W: Visitor Information

291 Trabing Road

280 Middlefork Road, Crazy Woman

(274) Parking Area

265 Reno Road

254 Kaycee, Mayoworth, Barnum, Sussex, Rest Area (RR, Phones, Picnic, RV Dump, RV Water)
- **FStop** W: Sinclair[*, LP]
- **Gas** E: Texaco[*, D, CW]
- **Food** E: Country Inn Dining, Hole in the Wall Restaurant, The Feed Rack Cafe; W: Subs on the Run (Sinclair)
- **AServ** E: Tom's Tire Service & Repair Towing & Car Wash
- **RVCamp** E: Kaycee RV Park
- **ATM** E: Texaco
- **Other** E: Kaycee Grocery Market, US Post Office

(254) Rest Area (RR, Phones, Picnic, RV Dump)

249 TTT Road

246 Powder River Rd.

235 Tisdale, Mountain Rd.

227 WY387N, Midwest, Edgerton

223 Kaycee

(219) Parking Area

Knights Inn

2100 South Market Street

Cable TV
Outdoor Swimming Pool
Dino's Restaurant Hideaway
Lounge with Live Music
Room Service
In-Room Movies
Chattanooga Aquarium Nearby
Golf Nearby

423-265-0551

1616

TENNESSEE • I-24 • EXIT 178

EXIT WYOMING

216 Ranch Road

210 Horse Ranch Creek Road

197 Ormsby Road

191 Wardwell Road, Bar Nunn
- **Gas** W: Texaco[*]
- **RVCamp** W: Antelope Campground, KOA Campgrounds (2 Miles)

189 U.S. 20, U.S. 26, Shoshoni, Port of Entry, Teton Yellowstone National Parks

188B WY220W, Poplar Street
- **Gas** W: Exxon[*]
- **Food** E: El Jarro (Mexican), JB's Restaurant; W: Casper's Restaurant[24], Dairy Queen
- **Lodg** E: Hilton Inn, Kelly Inn, Motel 6
- **RVCamp** W: Camping, Stalkup's RV Superstore (1.2 Miles)
- **Other** W: Car Wash, Truck & Car[24], Casper Planetarium, Nicolaysen Art Museum

188A Center Street
- **FStop** E: Texaco[CW]
- **Gas** E: Conoco[*, D], Mini Mart[*]; W: Cenex[*]
- **Food** E: Benham's Restaurant, Chef's Coop, Taco John's; W: Denny's, Parkway Plaza Hotel & Convention Center, Subway
- **Lodg** E: Hampton Inn, Holiday Inn, National 9 Inn Showboat Motel; W: Days Inn, Parkway Plaza Hotel & Convention Center
- **AServ** E: Dave's Auto Service Center, Texaco, Wyoming Glass; W: Service Center Car Wash
- **Other** W: Casper Chamber of Commerce Tourist Info.

187 McKinley Street
- **Gas** E: Mini Mart[*]
- **Lodg** E: Ranch House Motel
- **AServ** E: DCB Auto Repair, Pride Auto Repair; W: Auto Dynamics Engine Rebuilders, Auto Electric Equipment Co.
- **RVCamp** W: Maxes RV Service
- **Med** W: Hospital
- **Other** E: Aamco Transmissions, Jerry's Detail & Car Wash

186 Bus. Loop I-25, U.S. 20, U.S. 26, U.S. 87, North Beverly St., Bryan Stock Trail
- **Gas** W: Texaco[D]
- **Food** W: Plow's Diner, Western Grill
- **Lodg** W: Best Western, Colonial House Motel
- **AServ** E: ABC Towing, Bert's Auto & Truck Repair; W: Checker Auto Parts, Chevrolet White's Mountain, Pat's Body Shop, White's Mountain GEO
- **TServ** E: ABC Towing, Stewart & Stevenson Detroit Diesel
- **RVCamp** W: Rec-Vee RV Service
- **Med** W: Hospital
- **Other** E: Wyoming Highway Patrol; W: Sweetheart Bread Bakery Outlet

185 WY 258, East Casper, Evansville
- **TStop** W: Flying J Travel Plaza[*, LP, SCALES]
- **FStop** E: Texaco[*]
- **Gas** E: Citgo[*], Phillips 66[CW]; W: Exxon[*], Mini Mart[*]
- **Food** W: Arby's, Burger King, Hardee's, KFC, McDonald's[PLAY], Original Hamburger Stand, Perkins Family Restaurant, Pizza Hut, Taco Bell, Taco John's, The Cookery (Flying J), Wendy's
- **Lodg** E: Shiloh Inn Motel; W: 1st Interstate Inn

Bold red print shows RV & Bus parking available or nearby

EXIT WYOMING

AServ E: Phillips 66
W: Decker Auto Glass, Eastridge Autoplex Mercury/Lincoln, Lube Express, Uniroyal Tire & Auto
RVCamp E: **KOA Campgrounds**
W: **Casper KOA (1 Mile)**
Med W: **+ Hospital**
ATM W: Norwest Banks
Other E: Car Wash
W: Eastridge Car Wash, **Eastridge Mall**, **K-Mart(RX)**, **Sam's Club**, **Wal-Mart(RX)**

182 WY 253, Broox, Hat Six Road
FStop E: **Exxon(*, 24)**,
Food E: **Exxon**
TStop E: **Hat Six Travel Plaza (see our ad this page)**,
Parks E: **Edness K. Wilkins State Park**

(171) **Parking Area**

165 Glenrock
RVCamp E: **Deer Creek Village Campground**

160 Bus Loop I-25, U.S. 87, U.S. 20, U.S. 26, East Glenrock
Other E: **Camping**

156 Bixby Rd.

154 Barber Rd.

(153) **Parking Area (Southbound)**

151 Natural Bridge

150 Inez Road

146 La Prele Road
RVCamp W: **Camping**

140 To WY 59, Douglas, Gillette
Gas E: Conoco(*, 24), Gas for Less(*, LP)
Food E: Arby's, Best Western, La Costa (Mexican), McDonald's(PLAY), Subway (Conoco)
Lodg E: Best Western, **Super 8**
RVCamp E: **KOA Campgrounds (.5 Miles)**, **Lonetree Village RV Park**
Med E: **+ Hospital**
ATM E: Conoco
Other E: Car Wash

135 Bus I-25, Douglas
TStop E: **Sinclair(*, 24)**
Food E: Country Inn Restaurant
Lodg E: 1st Interstate Inn, Alpine Inn
TServ E: **Bud's Field Service & Truck Repair**, **Sinclair**

(129) **Parking Area**

126 **U.S. 18, U.S. 20E, Lusk, Rest Area (RV Dump)**

(126) **Rest Area (RR, HF, Phones, Picnic, RV Dump)**

111 Glendo

Open 24 hrs, 7 Days a Week
1533
Hat Six Travel Plaza
307-234-0504
24 Hr Convenience Store
and Restaurant
RV Dump & Water
Gas, Diesel, Propane
Showers, Coin Laundry, ATM
Truck Wash, CB Repair
Casper, Wyoming
WYOMING ▪ I-25 ▪ EXIT 182

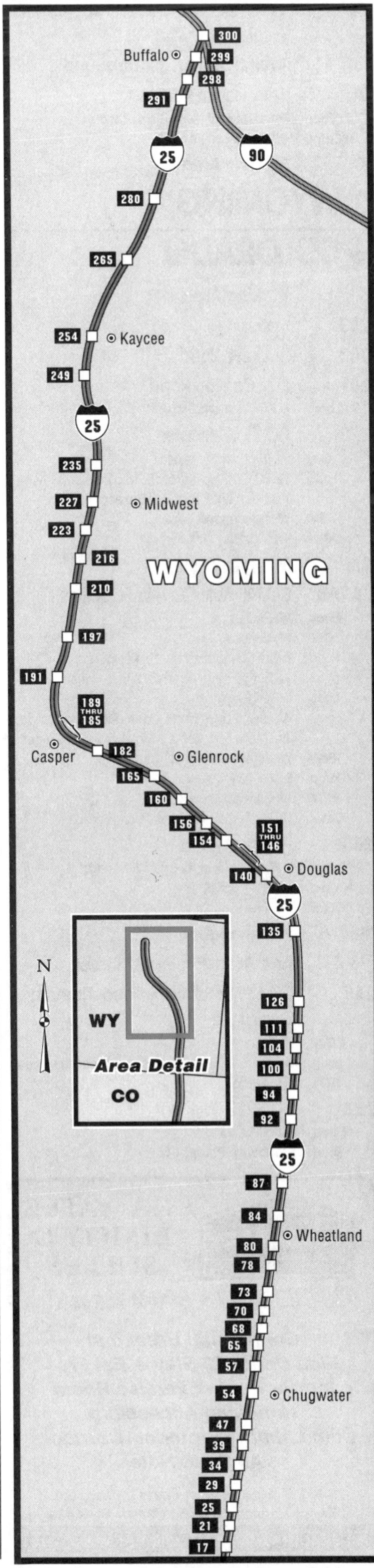

EXIT WYOMING

FStop E: **Sinclair(*)**
Food E: Corner Cafe, Rooster's Steakhouse
Lodg E: **Howard's Motel (Sinclair)**
RVCamp E: **Lakeview Motel & Campgrounds (.5 Miles)**
Parks E: **Glendo State Park (4 Miles)**
Other E: Fireworks, **Howard's General Store**, U.S. Post Office

104 Ranch Road, Little Bear

100 Cassa Rd.

94 El Rancho Road
RVCamp W: **4 W Ranch Campground**

92 U.S. 26, Guernsey, Torrington (Left Exit Southbound)
RVCamp E: **RV Camping**
Parks E: **Fort Laramie National Historic Site**, **Guernsey State Park**

(91) **Rest Area (RR, HF, Picnic, RV Dump)**

87 Johnson Road

84 Laramie, River Rd.

80 Wheatland
Food E: Pizza Hut, Timberhaus
Lodg E: **Best Western**
AServ E: Bob Ruwart GMC, Wheatland Jeep
RVCamp E: **Arrowhead RV Park**
Med E: **+ Hospital**
Other E: North Sixteenth Coin Laundry

78 Bus Loop I-25, U.S. 87, Wheatland
FStop E: **Co-Op(*)**
W: **Conoco(*)**, **Exxon(*)**
Gas E: Texaco(*, D)
Food E: Arby's, Bl Restaurant, Burger King, Terra Grano Pizza, Vimbo's Motel
Lodg E: Motel 6, Plains Motel, Vimbo's Motel
AServ E: **Co-Op**
TServ E: **Co-Op**
RVCamp W: **Mountain View Park**
Med E: **+ Hospital**
ATM E: **Co-Op**
W: **Conoco**
Other E: Look Dad Fireworks, **Platte County Visitor's Center**, WY Hwy. Patrol

73 WY 34W, Laramie

70 Bordeaux Road

68 Antelope Road

66 Hunton Rd.

(65) **Parking Area**

65 Slater Road

57 Chugwater, TY Basin Road

54 I-25 Business, Chugwater
FStop E: **Sinclair(*, D)**
Food E: **Buffalo Grill (Buffalo Lodge)**
Lodg E: **Buffalo Lodge**
RVCamp W: **Camping (12.5 Miles May-Oct)**
ATM E: **Sinclair**
Other E: Fireworks

47 Bear Creek Road

39 Little Bear Community

34 Nimmo Road

29 Whitaker Road

25 No Access

21 Ridley Road, Little Bear Road

17 U.S. 85N, Torrington (Left Exit Southbound)

16 WY 211, Horse Creek Road

Bold red print shows RV & Bus parking available or nearby

EXIT WYOMING/COLORADO

13 Vandehei Ave
- **Gas** E: Mini Mart(*, 24)
  - W: Total(*, D, 24)
- **ATM** E: Mini Mart
  - W: Total

12 Central Avenue
- **Gas** E: Conoco(*)
- **Food** E: Central Cafe
- **Lodg** E: Quality Inn
- **Med** E: ✚ Hospital
- **Other** E: Airport
  - W: Cheyenne Visitor's Center

11 Randall Ave, Warren AFB - Gate 1
- **Other** W: Warren AFB

10B Happy Jack Road, Warren AFB - Gate 2

10D Missile Drive
- **Lodg** E: Luxury Inn, Motel 6
- **AServ** E: Fassett-Nickel Toyota, Ford Fassett-Nickel, Halladay Motors Olds, Cad, GMC, Suz, Tyrrell-Doyle Honda, Windshields America
- **RVCamp** E: Hy Land Park

9 U.S. 30, West Lincolnway
- **TStop** E: Conoco(*, LP, SCALES)
  - W: Little America(*, LP)
- **Food** E: Denny's(24)
  - W: Little America Hotel (Golf Course)
- **Lodg** E: Days Inn (see our ad this page), Econo Lodge, La Quinta Inn
  - W: Little America Hotel (Golf Course)
- **AServ** E: Tyrrell-Doyle Chevrolet
  - W: Little America
- **TServ** E: Conoco(SCALES), Wyoming CAT
  - W: Little America
- **Med** E: ✚ Hospital
- **ATM** E: Conoco

8B Jct I-80W, Laramie

8D Jct. I-80E to U.S. 85 Omaha

7 I-25 Business, College Drive, Wyoming Welcome Center (RR, Phones, Picnic, RV Dump, RV Water)
- **TStop** W: Flying J Travel Plaza(*, LP, SCALES)
- **FStop** E: Total(*, LP)
- **Food** E: Subway (Total)
  - W: McDonald's, The Cookery (Flying J)
- **Lodg** W: Comfort Inn
- **TServ** E: Art's Truck Repair (Total)
- **ATM** E: Total
  - W: Flying J Travel Plaza
- **Other** E: Fire King Fireworks, Fireworks
  - W: Frank Norris Jr. Travel Center

Cheyenne's Best Rates/Location

Cheyenne, Wy
307-778-8877
800-DaysInn

1397

Free Deluxe Continental Breakfast,
HBO & Local Calls
Restaurant Nearby
Kids Stay & Eat Free
Pets Welcome • Interior Corridors
Exercise Equipment • Hot Tub & Sauna
Truck or Large Vehicle Parking

WYOMING ¥ I-25 Exit 9

EXIT COLORADO

(7) WY Welcome Center (RR, Phones, Picnic, RV Dump)

(6) Weigh Station (Northbound)

2 Terry Ranch Rd.
- **Food** E: Restaurant (Terry Bison Ranch)
- **RVCamp** E: Terry Bison Ranch(*)

(0) Parking Area

↑WYOMING

↓COLORADO

(296) Parking Area

293 Carr

288 Buckeye Road

281 Owl Canyon Road
- **RVCamp** E: KOA Campgrounds(LP)

278 CO 1S, Wellington
- **Gas** W: Mini Mart(*), Texaco(*, CW)
- **Food** W: Burger King (Texaco), Pizza Palace, Subway, T-Bar-Inn Cafe, Taco Bell (Texaco)
- **ATM** W: Independent Bank
- **Other** W: U.S. Post Office

271 Mountain Vista Dr.

269AB CO 14E Ault, CO 14W Ft. Collins
- **FStop** W: Phillips 66(*)
- **Gas** W: Conoco(*)
- **Food** E: The Chenz and Mrs. C's Restaurant
  - W: Burger King, Denny's, Waffle House
- **Lodg** E: Mulberry Inn
  - W: Days Inn, Ft. Collins Plaza Inn, Holiday Inn, Motel 6, National 9 Motel, Sleep Inn, Super 8
- **TServ** W: Schwinzell's Truck Repair
- **RVCamp** E: Lee's RV Center & Service(LP)
- **ATM** W: Conoco
- **Other** W: FedEx Center, United Parcel Service

268 Prospect Road
- **RVCamp** E: Powder River RV Sales & Service
- **Med** W: ✚ Hospital
- **Other** W: AmeriGas Co.(LP)

(267) Weigh Station

(266) Rest Area (RR, Picnic, Grills)

265 CO 68W, Harmony Road, Timnath, Severance
- **Gas** W: Texaco(*)
- **Lodg** W: Ramada Limited Suites (see our ad this page)
- **ATM** W: Texaco

262 CO 392E, Windsor
- **FStop** E: Phillips 66(*, CW)
- **Food** E: Subway (Phillips 66)

1663

RAMADA LIMITED SUITES

970-282-9047 • 800-2 RAMADA

Continental Breakfast
Kids Under 12 Stay & Eat Free
Indoor Pool • Exercise Room
Handicap Accessible
Coin Laundry • Interior Corridors
All Suite Hotel

4001 S. Mason St. • Fort Collins, CA
Exit on Harmony W 4 mi to Mason St. N 1 mi

COLORADO • I-25 • EXIT 265(HARMONY WEST)

EXIT COLORADO

- **TServ** W: GMC Trucks
- **ATM** E: Phillips 66

259 Airport Road
- **Other** W: Airport

257AB U.S. 34E Greeley, U.S. 34W Loveland, Welcome Center (Difficult Reaccess)
- **Gas** E: Total(*, D)
  - W: Sinclair(*)
- **Food** E: Taco Bell (Total)
  - W: Cracker Barrel, IHOP, Lone Star Steakhouse
- **Lodg** W: Best Western Coach House Resort, Hampton Inn
- **RVCamp** E: Alpine Valley Motor RV Sales
  - W: Big Red RV (3 Miles), Loveland RV Village (1 Mile)
- **Med** W: ✚ Hospital
- **ATM** E: Total
- **Parks** W: Boyd Lake State Park, Estes Park, Rocky Mountain National Park
- **Other** W: Rocky Mountain Outlet Stores

255 CO 402W, Loveland (Difficult Reaccess)

254 CO 60W, Campion (Difficult Reaccess)
- **TStop** E: Johnson's Corner
- **Lodg** E: Budget Host Inn
- **TServ** E: Johnson's Corner
- **RVCamp** E: Johnson's Corner Camp(*, LP)
  - W: Murdock Trailer Sales

252 CO 60E, Johnstown, Milliken

250 CO 56W, Berthoud

245 Mead

243 CO 66, Lyons, Longmont, Platteville
- **Gas** E: Texaco(*, D)
- **Food** E: Blimpie's Subs (Phillips 66), Pizza Restaurant Scotts 66
- **AServ** E: J.W. Brewer Tire Co.
- **RVCamp** E: K & C RV Inc.(LP) (Frontage road)
- **Parks** W: Rocky Mountain National Park

240 CO 119W, Longmont
- **FStop** W: Conoco(*, SCALES), Texaco(*, LP, SCALES)
- **Gas** W: Total(*, D, LP)
- **Food** W: Arby's, Burger King, McDonald's, Pizza Hut (Texaco), Restaurant (Travelodge), Subway (Conoco), Taco Bell, The Little Oasis Restaurant, Waffle House
- **Lodg** W: Comfort Inn, Days Inn, First Interstate Inn, Super 8, TraveLodge
- **AServ** W: M 'N' S Garage
- **TServ** W: Freightliner
- **TWash** W: Truck Wash
- **RVCamp** E: Stevinson RV Center
  - W: Del Camino RV Sales & Service
- **Med** W: ✚ Hospital
- **ATM** W: Conoco, Texaco
- **Parks** W: Barbour Ponds State Park

235 CO 52, Frederick, Firestone, Eldora, Dacono, Ft. Lupton, Niwot
- **TStop** W: Phillips 66

232 Erie
- **RVCamp** E: Trailers USA (Frontage Rd)

229 CO 7, Lafayette, Brighton
- **RVCamp** E: Denver North Campground Good Sam Park

223 CO 128W, 120th Ave
- **Gas** E: Diamond Shamrock(*, CW), Sinclair, Texaco(LP, CW)
  - W: Conoco(*, LP, CW), Total(*, LP, CW)
- **Food** E: Applebee's, Damon's (Holiday Inn), Lone Star Steakhouse

Bold red print shows RV & Bus parking available or nearby

EXIT COLORADO

	W: Cracker Barrel, Jade City Chinese Cafe, Subway, Village Inn Restaurant, Wendy's
Lodg	E: Days Inn, Hampton Inn, Holiday Inn, Radisson, Sleep Inn
	W: Comfort Suites Hotel, La Quinta Inn, Super 8
AServ	E: Sinclair, Texaco
ATM	E: Diamond Shamrock
	W: Conoco, Total
Other	W: Op Urgent Care, Optical
221	104th Ave, Northglenn
Gas	E: Conoco(*, LP, CW), Total(*, D, LP)
	W: Citgo(*), Conoco(*, LP, CW), Texaco(*, D)
Food	E: Burger King, Denny's, IHOP, Subway, Texas Roadhouse, Winchells Donuts
	W: Applebee's, Black-Eyed Pea, Coco's, Oil Can Harry's, Taco Bell
Lodg	W: Ramada Limited
AServ	W: Firestone, Goodyear, O'meara Ford
ATM	E: Total, World Savings
	W: Citgo, US Bank
Other	E: Tejal International Foods
	W: **Northglenn Mall**
220	Thornton Pkwy
Med	E: ✚ **Columbia North Medical Center**
219	84th Ave, Federal Heights
Gas	E: Conoco(*, LP, CW)
	W: Coastal(*)
Food	E: Arby's, Bonanza Steakhouse, Goodtime's, Waffle House
	W: Burger King, Donut's Plus, New Skillets, Tokyo Bowl (Japanese), Village Inn
AServ	E: A-1 Independent Service & Repair, Auto Trim Design, Karas Auto Body, North Valley Firestone
	W: Econo Lube & Tune, Mobile Air, Power Brake of Metro Denver
Med	E: ✚ **Hospital (1.2 Miles)**
	W: ✚ **Hospital (1.7 Miles)**
Other	E: Radio Shack Outlet Store, **WalGreens Pharmacy**
	W: Hmong Mini Store (Oriental Grocery), **The Vet's Animal Hospital**
217	U.S. 36W, Boulder (Difficult Reaccess)
Gas	W: Fairway Oil
Food	W: Subway
AServ	W: Chesrown Chevrolet, Denver Toyota
Other	W: 711
216AB	Jct I-76E Fort Morgan; I-76W Grand Jct.
215	58th Ave
FStop	W: **Total(*)**
Gas	E: Amoco(*, LP, CW)
Food	E: Continental Cafe (Kabobs, Steaks, Gyros, Hamburgers), Los Dos Pepe's (Mexican), Wendy's
	W: Colorado Cafe, **Taco Bell (Total)**
Lodg	E: Quality Inn
	W: Super 8
AServ	E: Amoco, Luxer Mazda New & Used Parts & Service
	W: Checker Auto Parts Warehouse
RVCamp	E: **Lite-Craft Campers**
Other	E: **Mapleton Grocery & Deli Inc.**
	W: World of Sleep Outlet Store
214AB	Jct I-70, Limon, Grand Junction (Difficult Reaccess)
Food	W: Holiday Inn, TraveLodge, Village Inn
Lodg	W: Holiday Inn, TraveLodge, Village Inn
213	Park Ave, W 38th St, Coors Field
Gas	E: Amoco(*)
	W: Texaco(D)
Food	E: Denny's, McDonald's (Amoco)
	W: Jake's Restaurant (Regency Hotel)
Lodg	E: La Quinta Inn

EXIT COLORADO

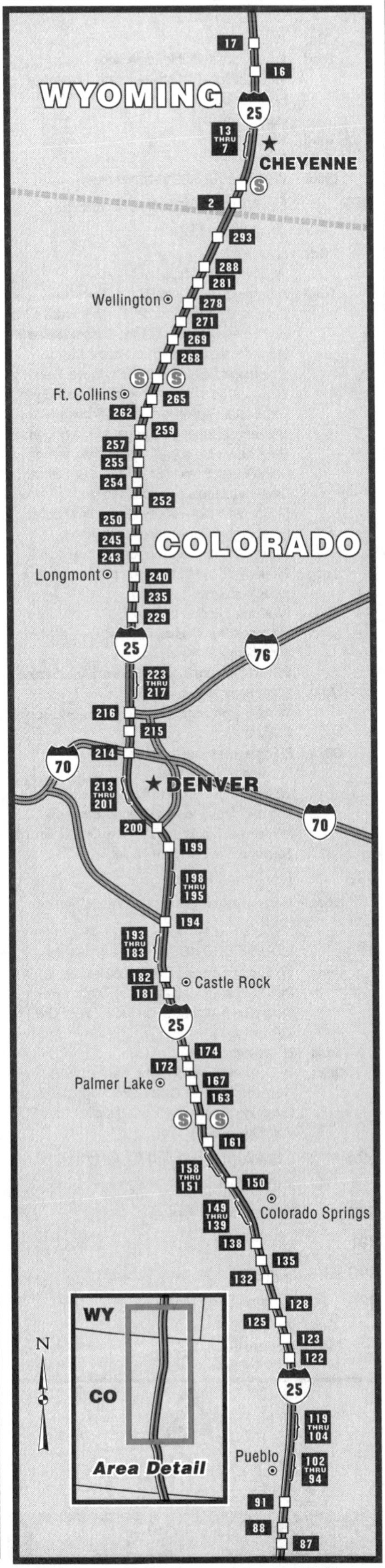

EXIT COLORADO

	W: Regency Hotel, Rosedale Motel, Town & Country Motel
AServ	W: Texaco
Other	E: Coors Field
212C	20th St
Other	E: Coors Field
212A	Speer Blvd.
Gas	W: Conoco(*, D), Texaco(D)
Food	W: La Loma (Mexican)
Lodg	W: Budget Host Inn, Residence Inn, Super 8
AServ	W: Alignment Brake Service, Conoco, Texaco
Other	E: Elitch Gardens Amusement Park, Forney Historic Transportation Museum
211	23rd Ave
Other	E: **The Children's Museum**
210C	Auraria Pkwy (Difficult Reaccess)
210B	17th Ave
Lodg	W: Ramada
Other	W: **Denver Sports Complex**
210A	U.S. 40, Colfax Ave (Reaccess Northbound Only, Difficult Reaccess)
209C	8th Ave, Zuni Street
Lodg	E: Motel 7
AServ	E: Ledezma Tire & Wheel, Stadium Auto Parts
209AB	U.S. 6, 6th Ave (Limited Access Hwy)
208	CO 26, Alameda Ave. (Southbound)
FStop	W: **Conoco(*, CW)**
Lodg	W: Motel 5
AServ	W: High Country Transmissions, J.D. Byrider, Mobil Auto Glass
Parks	W: **Valverde Park**
207B	U.S. 85 S, Santa Fe Drive, To CO 26, Alameda Ave.
Gas	E: Amoco(*, LP), Total(*, D)
Food	E: Burger King, Denny's
AServ	E: Amoco
	W: Swiss Tire & Automotive Service
Other	E: **Home Depot**
207A	Lincoln St, Broadway
Gas	W: Texaco(*)
Food	E: Friends Cafe, Griff's Hamburgers
	W: Sunny Chine Cafe
AServ	E: Econo Lube & Tune, Performance Radiator, Zimmer Auto Parts
	W: Denver Discount Tire Service, General Tires, Jim Paris Tire City
ATM	W: Colorado National Bank
Other	E: **Tru Value Hardware**
206B	Emerson St, Washington St
Food	E: **Wild Oats Market & Cafe**
	W: Pearl Street Ice Cream & Deli
Med	E: ✚ **Hospital**
ATM	W: 7-11 Convenience Store
Other	E: **Wild Oats Market & Cafe**
	W: 7-11 Convenience Store, Premier Pet Grooming
206A	Downing St (Northbound, Reaccess Southbound Only, Difficult Reaccess)
205AB	University Blvd
Gas	W: Conoco(*, LP)
Food	W: Bruegger's Bagel & Bakery, Donuts Plus, Isle Of Singapore, Juice Stop, Keefan MidEast Restaurant, Red Dragon Chinese, Starbucks Coffee, Subway, The Border Mexican Restaurant
Med	W: ✚ **University Park Medical Center**
Other	E: Denver Police
	W: **University Park Medical Center(RX)**, **WalGreens Pharmacy(RX)**
204	CO 2, Colorado Blvd

Bold red print shows RV & Bus parking available or nearby

EXIT COLORADO

Gas **E:** Conoco[*, CW], Texaco[*, CW]
Food **E:** Bennigan's, Bruegger's Bagel & Bakery, Grisanti's Italian, Jamba Juice, Le Peep Restaurant, Little Caesars Pizza, Logan Farms Honey Hams, Red Coral Chinese, Saigon Terrace (Vietnamese), Subway, Village Inn, Village Inn
W: Denny's, KFC, Perkins Family Restaurant, Taco Shop, Wang's Chinese Cuisine
Lodg **E:** Fairfield Inn
W: La Quinta Inn
AServ **W:** Windshields America
ATM **E:** **Safeway Grocery**[24, RX], VectraBank
W: Norwest Banks
Other **E:** FedEx, Mail Boxes Etc, One Hour Optical, Rei Sports Supplies, **Safeway Grocery**[RX], Toys R Us, Vista Optical
W: **Albertson's Grocery**[LP, RX], **Colorado Center (Theaters), U.S. Post Office**

203 Evans Ave
Food **E:** Entenmann's Bakery Outlet
W: Wok USA (Chinese)
Lodg **E:** **Rockies Inn**
W: Cameron Motel
AServ **E:** Al's Autohaus Mercedes Benz, Big O Tires, House of Mufflers & Brakes, Pro Star Mercedes Service
W: Car Quest Auto Parts, Discount Muffler & Brake, Freeway Ford, Xpress Lube
Other **W:** **Jerusalem Market**

202 Yale Ave
Gas **E:** Diamond Shamrock[*], Sinclair
W: Total[*, D]
Food **E:** Bagel Stop, Fazoli's Italian Food, Pizza Hut, Taco Bell
W: Sam Wilsons Restaurant
Other **E:** **Safeway Grocery**
W: **King Soopers Grocery**

201 U.S. 285, CO 30, Hampden Ave
Gas **E:** Amoco[CW], Amoco[*], Conoco[*, LP, CW], Texaco[*, CW]
W: Conoco[*], Texaco
Food **E:** Expresso Drive-Thru Cafe, Jackson's All American Sports Grill, New York Bagel Boys Inc., Piccolo's (Italian/Mexican), Quality Inn, Skillets (Quality Inn), Sushi Boat Restaurant
W: Burger King, Starbucks Coffee
Lodg **E:** Marriott, Quality Inn
AServ **E:** Amoco, Just Brakes, Texaco
ATM **E:** Community Bank, **King Soopers Grocery**[24]
Other **E:** Animal Hospital, Fire Station, **King Soopers Grocery**, United Artist Theaters
W: **Safeway Grocery**

200 Jct North I-225 to I-70, Limon (Left Exit Southbound)
Lodg **W:** AmeriSuites (see our ad this page)

199 CO 88 West, Belleview Ave, Littleton
Gas **E:** Amoco, Phillips 66[LP]
W: Conoco[*, CW], Total[*, D, LP]
Food **E:** DTC Broker, Gandhi (Indian), Garcia's Mexican Food, Gasho Japanese Steakhouse, La Chine L'Oriental Gourmet Szechuan, Tosh's Hacienda Restaurant, Wendy's
W: European Cafe Al Fresco, McDonald's, Mountain View Restaurant, Taco Bell
Lodg **E:** Marriott
W: DAYS INN Days Inn, Holiday Inn Express, HomeGate Studios & Suites, Homestead Village, Super 8
AServ **E:** Amoco, Phillips 66
W: Grease Monkey, Midas Muffler & Brake
ATM **E:** Norwest Banks, Smith Barney
W: Total
Other **E:** Kinko's[24]
W: **Mountain View Miniature Golf**

EXIT COLORADO

198 Orchard Road
Gas **W:** Texaco[*, D]
Food **E:** Del Frisco's Double Eagle Steakhouse
W: Great Bagel & Coffee Express (Texaco), Le Peep Restaurant, Quizno's Subs, Taco Bell Express (Texaco)
Lodg **W:** Hilton
ATM **E:** Key Bank
Other **W:** Orchard Road Christian Center

197 Centennial Airport, CO 88 East, Arapahoe Road
Gas **E:** Amoco[LP]
W: Barn Store[*], Phillips 66[*, D, CW]
Food **E:** Bennigan's, Country Dinner Playhouse, Denny's, El Parral Mexican, Gunther Toody's, Ho Ho (Chinese), Las Brisas, **Little Caesars Pizza (K-Mart)**, Mama Louise Italian Pizza & Pasta, Schlotzsky's Deli, Subway, Sushi Wave, Wendy's
W: Arby's, Baja Fresh Mexican Grill, Black Eyed Pea, Boston Market Restaurant, Brook's Steakhouse, Bruegger's Bagel & Bakery, Carl's FF Deli, Chevy's Mexican, Chipotle Mexican Grill, Dairy Queen, Einstein Bros Bagels, Goodtimes Drive-Thru Burgers, Grisanti's Italian, McDonald's, Nick-N-Willy's Pizza, Red Robin Hamburgers, Ruby Tuesday, Stanford's Restaurant, Subway, Taco Bell[24], The Egg & I
Lodg **E:** Courtyard by Marriott, Hampton Inn, Motel 6, Woodfield Suites
W: Marriott Residence Inn
AServ **E:** Amoco, Don Massey Cadillac, Olds, **K-Mart Supercenter**[24, RX]
W: Firestone Tire & Auto, Raceway Auto Service
ATM **E:** Key Bank, Norwest Banks
W: **Albertson's Grocery**[LP] **(C-Store)**, First Bank & Trust Co.
Other **E:** Eagle Hardware & Garden, **K-Mart Supercenter**[RX], **Target**
W: **Albertson's Grocery (C-Store)**, All Season's Rental[LP], Arapaho Golf & Tennis, **Barnes & Noble**, Mail Boxes Etc, One Hour Optical, Optical Boutique, The Complete Angler

196 Dry Creek Road
Lodg **E:** Best Western, Homestead Village, Ramada Limited

195 County Line Road
Food **W:** Champs Americana, Crocodile Cafe, Jason's Deli, PF Chang's Chinese Bistro, Tommy Wok (Asian Food), Wahoo's Fish Taco, Z Tejas Grill, Zuka Juice
Lodg **E:** Inverness Hotel & Golf Club
Other **W:** **Borders Books & Music, Centennial Promenade (Mall), Office Max, Park Meadows Shopping Center**, Rei Sports Supplies, **Toys R Us**, Vista Optical

194 CO 470, Tollway E470, Grand Junction

193 Lincoln Ave, Parker

191 Unnamed

190 Surrey Ridge

188 Castle Pines Pkwy
Gas **W:** Total[*]
Food **W:** Pizza (Total)

1297
AMERISUITES
AMERICA'S AFFORDABLE ALL-SUITE HOTEL
Colorado • Exit 194 • 303-804-0700

EXIT COLORADO

ATM **W:** Bank West, Total
Other **W:** Fire Station

187 Happy Canyon Road

184 Founders Pkwy, Meadows Pkwy
Gas **E:** Texaco[*, D, CW]
Food **E:** Carl Jr's Hamburgers (Texaco), Cozzoli's Pizza Pasta, Juice Stop
W: McDonald's
ATM **E:** First Bank & Trust Co., **King Soopers Grocery**[LP, 24], Texaco
W: Norwest Banks
Other **E:** **King Soopers Grocery**, Pearl Vision Center
W: **Castle Rock Factory Shops**

183 U.S. 85 North, Sedalia, Littleton

182 Wilcox St., Wolfensberger Rd
Gas **E:** Amoco, Phillips 66[D], Western[*]
W: Diamond Shamrock[*], Texaco[*, LP, CW]
Food **E:** Bagel Stop, China Dragon, Little Caesars Pizza
W: Burger King, KFC, McDonald's[PLAY], Mr. Manners Country Restaurant, Sharis Restaurant, Taco Bell, Village Inn, **Wendy's**
Lodg **E:** Castle Pines Motel
W: Comfort Inn, Holiday Inn Express, Super 8 (see our ad this page)
AServ **E:** Amoco
W: Boyer Tire & Service, Castle Chrys, Plym, Jeep, Dodge, Eagle, Castle Rock Motors, Double B Auto Repair, Goerlich Mufflers, NAPA Auto Parts
TServ **W:** **Trailers USA**
ATM **W:** Diamond Shamrock
Other **E:** Aquarius Dive & Travel, Car Wash[CW], Colorado State Patrol, **Veterinary Hospital**
W: Barnyard Pet Shop, Castle Rock Veterinary Clinic, Malibu Car Wash[CW], Rent-X[LP], Xtreme Polaris

181 Wilcox St, Plum Creek Pkwy, To CO 86, Franktown
FStop **E:** **Western**[*, LP]
Gas **E:** Citgo[*], Sav-o-mat
Food **E:** Pizza Hut
AServ **E:** Big A Auto Parts, Big O Tires, Medved Brutyn Ford, Linc, Mercury, Midas Brakes, Mufflers, Alignment
ATM **E:** Citgo, First Bank & Trust Co.
Other **E:** **Wal-Mart**[RX]

174 Tomah Road
RVCamp **W:** **KOA Kampground**[LP]
Other **E:** Iron Horse Stables

173 Larkspur (Southbound)

172 Larkspur, Southlake Gulch Rd.

(170) **Rest Area (RR, Phones, Picnic, Vending; Southbound)**

(170) **Rest Area (RR, Phones, Picnic,**

1020 Park St.
Castle Rock, CO
303-688-0880
SUPER 8 MOTEL
1518
• Continental Breakfast
• Walk to Restaurants
• Nearby Shopping
• 24 hr Front Desk Service
• Pets Allowed (with permission)
• Cable TV w/HBO
• Free local Calls
• Bus/Truck Parking
Trucker's Discount
COLORADO ▪ I-25 ▪ EXIT 182

EXIT COLORADO

Vending; Northbound)

167 Greenland Road

163 County Line Road

(161) Weigh Station (Southbound)

(161) Weigh Station (Northbound)

161 CO 105, Woodmoor Dr., Monument, Palmer Lake

FStop W: Conoco(*, LP, CW)

Gas E: Amoco(LP)
W: Citgo(*), Texaco(D, LP)

Food W: Boston Market Restaurant, Burger King(PLAY), Columbine Gardens Chinese, Daylight Donuts, Josh & John's Ice Cream, Lots A' Bagels, Mandarin House Chinese, McDonald's(PLAY), Monument Pizza, Pizza Hut, Subway, Taco Bell, The Mug (Mexican), Village Inn

Lodg E: Falcon Inn

AServ E: Amoco
W: Rampart Car Care, Rocky Mountain Oil Change Center, Texaco

RVCamp W: Lake Of The Rockies Retreat & Camping Resort (.75 Miles), Ray Diggins (1 Mile)

ATM E: People's National Bank
W: Citgo, Norwest Bank, Safeway Grocery(LP, 24, RX)

Other W: Laundromat, Safeway Grocery(RX)

158 Baptist Road

FStop W: Total(*, SCALES)

Food W: Total

ATM W: Total

Other E: Brookhart's Building Centers

156AB Gleneagle Drive, North Entrance U.S. Air Force Academy

Other E: Western Museum of Mining & Industry
W: U.S. Air Force Academy North Entrance

(152) Parking Area, Scenic Area (Southbound)

151 Briargate Pkwy, Black Forest

Other E: Focus on the Family Visitor Center

150B South Entrance to Air Force Academy

150A CO 83, Academy Blvd

Gas E: Farmcrest Milk Store, Total(*, D, CW)

Food E: Captain D's Seafood, Chevy's Mexican, Cracker Barrel, Denny's, IHOP, KFC, McDonald's(PLAY), Quizno's Subs (Total), Schlotzsky's Deli, Village Inn, Wendy's

Lodg E: Comfort Suites Hotel, Days Inn, Drury Inn, Radisson, Red Roof Inn, Sleep Inn, Super 8

AServ E: Econo Lube & Tune, Midas Muffler & Brake

ATM E: Farmcrest Milk Store

Other E: Colorado Springs Police Dept., Wal-Mart(RX) (Vision Center)
W: U.S. Air Force Academy

149 Woodmen Road

Food E: Carrabba's Italian Grill, Hardee's
W: Old Chicago Pasta & Pizza, Outback Steakhouse, T.G.I. Friday's, Tao Tao Restaurant

Lodg W: Embassy Suites, Fairfield Inn, Hampton Inn, Holiday Inn Express, Microtel Inn

ATM E: ENT Federal Credit Union

Other W: AMC 6 Theaters

148A Business Loop 25 South, Nevada Ave (Left Exit Southbound)

AServ E: Front Range Radiator

TServ E: Mountain View Motors

RVCamp E: Morris RV Sales & Service, Peak View Camp (.75 Miles)

148B Corporate Centre Drive (Southbound, Reaccess Southbound Only)

EXIT COLORADO

Food W: New South Wales Restaurant

Lodg W: Comfort Inn, Extended Stay America

147 Rockrimmon Blvd

Gas W: Texaco(*, LP, CW)

Food W: Marriott

Lodg W: Marriott

AServ W: Texaco

ATM W: Air Academy Federal Credit Union, UMB Bank

Other W: Pro Rodeo Hall of Fame

146 Garden of the Gods Road

Gas E: Amoco(*), Texaco(*, D, CW)
W: Conoco(*, CW)

Food E: Antonio's Pasta & Seafood, Denny's, Hardee's, McDonald's(PLAY)
W: Alpine Chalet (Days Inn), Applebee's, Black Eyed Pea, Dunkin Donuts, Holiday Inn, Subway, Taco Bell, The Hungry Farmer, Village Inn Restaurant

Lodg E: La Quinta Inn
W: Days Inn, Holiday Inn, Quality Inn, Sumner Suites, Super 8

AServ E: Amoco
W: Action Auto Repair

TServ E: High Country Truck Specialists (Volvo)

RVCamp E: K & C RV Inc.

Med E: EmergiCare Family Medical Center

ATM W: Conoco

Other E: Diver's Reef Scuba Shop, Kaylor Marine

145 CO 38 East, Fillmore St

Gas E: Total(*)
W: Conoco(*), Texaco(*, D)

Food E: Lucky Dragon Chinese
W: A & W Restaurant (Texaco), Waffle House

Lodg E: Motel 7, Ramada Inn
W: Best Western, Motel 6, Super 8

AServ E: Auto Tech Plaza(LP), Express Auto Glass
W: Super Lube

RVCamp E: Adventures In RV's (1 Mile, Sales & Rental), Auto Tech Plaza

Med E: Hospital

Other E: Sterling Harbor Marina, Tackle Shop
W: Car Wash(CW)

144 Fontanero St (Reaccess Northbound Only)

143 Uintah St

Gas E: 7-11 Convenience Store(*)

Med E: Hospital

142 Bijou St, Central Business District

Gas W: Total(*)

Food W: Best Western, Denny's

Lodg W: Best Western

AServ E: Firestone Tire & Auto

ATM W: 711

Other E: Public Library
W: 711

141 U.S. 24 West, Cimarron St, Manitou Springs, Pikes Peak

Lodg W: Holiday Inn Express

RVCamp W: Dee's RV (1.75 Miles), Godfield Campground (2 Miles)

Other W: Wal-Mart(RX)

140B U.S. 85 South, Tejon St, Nevada Ave, To CO 115, 122, Broadmor, Canon City

Gas W: Circle K(*), Conoco(*)

Food E: Grindelwald German Deli, Old Heidelberg Cafe
W: Jamie's English Connection

AServ E: Black & White Auto, Colorado Springs Jeep, Eagle, Chrys, Peerless Tyre
W: Colorado Springs Jeep, Eagle, Infiniti, Saab, Scania Dealership, Liberty Toyota, NAPA Auto Parts, Phil Long Mitsubishi, Reilly Buick GMC Trucks, Sports Car City 2

Other W: The Ski Shop

EXIT COLORADO

140A Business Loop 25 North, Nevada Ave (Northbound)

Food W: Conway's Red Top Hamburgers, Go Yang Geep Korean (Sun Springs Motel), KFC, La Casita (Mexican), Shogun Express, Subway, Taco Bell, Wendy's, Yakitori's Japanese

Lodg E: 4 U Motel, Big Horn Lodge, Chateau Motel, Colorado Springs Motel, Howard Johnson Express, Nevada Motel
W: EconoLodge, Sun Springs Motel

AServ E: Axle Xpert, Colorado Springs Jeep, Chrys, Plym, Tire King
W: Colorado Auto Repair, D & J Auto Tech, Gray's Tire & Auto, Meineke Discount Mufflers, Midas Muffler & Brake

Parks E: Dorchester Park(PLAY)

Other E: Power Wash(CW)
W: Coin Laundry, High Country Custom Cycles, King's One Hour (Laundromat), The Rocky Mountain Motorcycle Museum

139 Peterson AFB, Airport, U.S. 24 East, Limon (Limited Access Hwy)

138 CO 29, Circle Drive, Colorado Springs World Arena

Gas E: Conoco(*, LP, CW), Texaco(*, D)
W: Citgo(*)

Food E: Las Palmeras III (Days Inn), Sheraton
W: Arby's, Baskin Robbins, Burger King, Carrabba's Italian Grill, Chili's, Denny's, Hardee's, Outback Steakhouse, Village Inn Restaurant

Lodg E: Days Inn, Sheraton
W: Budget Inn, Double Tree Hotel, Fairfield Inn by Marriott, Hampton Inn, La Quinta Inn, Residence Inn

AServ W: Pott's Radiator Service

ATM W: Cheyenne Mountain Bank, Citgo

Other W: OfficeMax, Target, Total Vision Eye Care

135 CO 83, Academy Blvd, Fort Carson

132 CO 16, Widefield, Security

RVCamp E: Colorado RV Services, KOA Columbine Campground (1 Mile), KOA Kampground (.75 Miles)

128 Fountain Security

TStop W: Texaco(*, SCALES)

Gas E: Citgo(*)

Lodg E: Ute Motel
W: Interstate Inn

AServ E: One Stop Auto Repair

TServ W: Texaco(SCALES)

TWash W: Texaco

ATM E: Citgo

Other E: Jesse's Seven Day Flea Market

125 Ray Nixon Road

123 Unnamed

122 Pikes Peak International Roadway

Other W: Pikes Peak International Roadway

119 Midway

116 County Line Road

(115) Rest Area (RR, Phones, Picnic, Vending, RV Dump; Northbound)

114 Young Hollow

(112) Rest Area (RR, Phones, Picnic, Vending, RV Dump; Southbound)

110 Pinon

TStop W: Pinon Truck Stop(*)

EXIT COLORADO

Lodg W: Pinon Truck Stop
TServ W: Chiarito's (Pinon Truck Stop)

108 Bragdon

106 Porter Draw

104 Eden
TServ W: Wagner Caterpillar
RVCamp E: Empiregas[LP]
Other E: All Star Gas[LP]

102 Eagleridge Blvd
Gas E: Total[*, D, CW]
Food W: Cracker Barrel, IHOP
Lodg W: Comfort Inn, EconoLodge, Hampton Inn, La Quinta, National 9 Motel, Wingate
TServ W: Kenworth Dealer
Med W: ✚ Emergicare
ATM E: Total
Other E: Home Depot, Sam's Club
W: Federal Express

101 U.S. 50 West, Canon City, Royal Gorge
FStop W: Total[*]
Gas W: Conoco[*, CW]
Food E: Captain D's Seafood, Denny's
W: Applebee's, Arby's, Black Eyed Pea, Boston Market Restaurant, Burger King, Country Kitchen, Golden Corral Family Steakhouse, Little Caesars Pizza (K-Mart), McDonald's[PLAY], Red Lobster, Santa Fe Cafe (Holiday Inn), Taco Bell, Wendy's, Willy Bob's Restaurant (Pueblo Motor Inn)
Lodg E: Sleep Inn
W: DAYS INN Days Inn, Holiday Inn Express (see our ad this page), Motel 6, Pueblo Motor Inn
AServ W: K-Mart[RX], Western Auto Parts America
Med W: ✚ EmergiCare Medical Clinic
ATM W: Conoco, Total, U.S. Bank
Other W: K-Mart[RX], Outpost Harley Davidson Inc., Visitor Information

100B 29th St
Gas E: Peerless Tyre
W: Amoco[LP], Diamond Shamrock[*, D], Sinclair[*, LP]
Food E: Country Buffet, KFC, Mandarin, Panda Buffet, Peter Piper Pizza
W: 29th Street Submarine Sandwiches, Don's Cafe, Rosario's Italian, Sinclair
Lodg W: Bel Mar Motel
AServ E: Montgomery Ward Auto Center, Peerless Tyre
W: Amoco, Five Star Muffler & Brakes, Grease Monkey, Hamid's Complete Auto Service
ATM E: C U Service Centers, King Soopers Grocery[24], Norwest Banks
W: Safeway Grocery
Other E: Blue Flame Gas Inc.[LP], King Soopers Grocery, Mail Boxes Etc., Pueblo Mall, Pueblo Mall Cinemas
W: Auto Glow Car Wash[CW], Safeway Grocery

Special Tour Group Rates

1190

Holiday Inn EXPRESS

Complimentary Breafast Bar
Complimentary Welcome Reception
Indoor Pool • Spa • Exercise Room
Free Local Phone Calls
Handicap Accessible

Located on Historic Santa Fe Trail

719-384-2900 • La Junta, CO

Colorado • I-25 • Exit 101

EXIT COLORADO

100A U.S. 50 East, La Junta
AServ E: Belmont Tire

99B 13th St, Santa Fe Ave
Food W: City Diner, Siagon Garden (Chinese, Seafood)
Lodg W: Travelers Motel
AServ W: Diodosio Pontiac, Isuzu, Hedrick-Landrum Nissan, Pueblo Motive Services Pronto Auto Parts, Spradley Chevrolet, Wil Coxson Buick, Cad, GMC Trucks
Med W: ✚ Hospital
Parks W: Mineral Place Park

99A TO CO 96, 6th St (Southbound)
Food W: Best Western, Cornell's Cafe, Taco Bell, Wendy's
Lodg W: Best Western, Brambletree Inn
AServ W: Vidmar Mazda, Olds, Chrys, Plym, Jeep, Eagle
Other W: YMCA

98B TO CO 96, 1st St
Gas W: Total[*]
Food W: Cafe Bimba, Carl Jr's Hamburgers, Jubilee Inn, Martinez Mexican Foods, Nacho's, Patty's Restaurant, Quizno's Subs, Rendezvous Restaurant & Lounge, Smitty's Green Light Grand Cafe
AServ W: Pueblo Auto Parts
ATM W: Minnequa Bank, U.S. Bank
Other E: Rainbo Bakery Store
W: El Pueblo Museum, Ice Arena, Pueblo Chamber of Commerce, Pueblo Convention Center, Sangre Dedcristo Conference Center & Children's Museum, Stein's Fine Food, The Drug Store & Soda Fountain

98A Bus. U.S. 50 East, La Junta
FStop E: Cliff Brice Commercial Fueling[24]
W: Texaco[*, D]
Food W: Sonic Drive In
AServ W: Discount Batteries & Tire, Gem Star Auto Electric Service, Lassiter Automotive Engineering, Moore Automotive
Other W: Pet Paradise

97B Abriendo Ave
Gas W: Texaco[*]
Food W: Pizza King & Subs
Other W: Bargain Books

97A Central Ave, Northern Ave, Minnequa Bus. District
Gas W: Total[*]
Food W: Cuca's Authentic Mexican, El Nopal, Jorge's Sombrero, Liz's Cafe (Mexican), Mi Pueblito (Mexican), Pasta Cottage (Italian Carry Out), Taco Bell Express (Total)
AServ W: All Pro Auto Parts, B & F One Stop Auto Repair, Jim's Automotive & Light Diesel Repair, Larry's Transmission, Motor Service & Parts, Routt Auto Service, Southwest Auto Service
ATM W: Minnequa Bank, Total
Other W: Fire Station, Minnequa Car Wash[CW], Tool City

96 Indiana Ave, Minnequa Ave. (Difficult Reaccess)
Gas W: Fuzzy's Gas & Goodies, Texaco[*]
Med W: ✚ Hospital

95 Illinois Ave (Southbound, No Reaccess)

94 CO 45 North, Pueblo Blvd.
Gas W: Total[*, D]
Food W: El Corral Cafe, Taco Bell Express (Total)
AServ E: 5 J's Auto Parts
RVCamp W: Forts Mobile Home & RV Park
ATM W: Total
Parks W: Lake Pueblo State Park

EXIT COLORADO

91 Stem Beach
Lodg W: Motel

88 Burnt Mill Road

87 Verde Road

83 Unnamed

(82) Parking Area (Southbound)

(82) Parking Area (Picnic; Northbound)

77 Cedarwood

(74) Rest Area (Located At Exit 74, On West Side)

74 CO 165W, Colorado City, Rye, San Isabel
FStop E: Total[*]
Food E: Taco Bell Express (Total)
W: Greenhorn Mountain Resort
Lodg W: Greenhorn Mountain Resort
AServ E: Total
RVCamp E: KOA Kampground (.25 Miles)
Other W: Rocking R Country Store

71 Graneros Road

67 Apache

64 Lascar Road

60 Huerfano

Exit **(59)** Point of Interest

59 Butte Road

56 Redrock Road

55 Airport Road

52 CO 69 W, Gardner, Westcliffe
FStop W: Phillips 66[*]
Gas W: Diamond Shamrock[*]
Food W: Best Western
Lodg W: Best Western, Budget Host Inn
AServ W: Phillips 66
RVCamp W: Birco RV Service (.75 Miles), Country Host RV Park (.25 Miles), Dakota Campground (.75 Miles)
Parks W: Lathrup State Park

50 CO 10, El Junta
Food E: Chef Liu's Chinese Food
Med W: ✚ Hospital
Other W: Lathrop State Recreation Area (4 Miles)

49 North Bus Loop 25, To West U.S. 160, Walsenburg, Alamosa
Parks W: Lathrop State Park

42 Rouse Road, Pryor

41 Rugby Road

(37) Rest Area (RR, Picnic, Grills, Vending, RV Dump; Southbound)

(37) Rest Area (RR, Picnic, Grills, Vending, RV Dump; Northbound)

34 Aguilar
TStop E: AMNTO Food Fuel[*] (Amoco)
ATM E: AMNTO Food Fuel (Amoco)

30 Aguilar Road

27 Ludlow
Other W: Ludlow Massacre Memorial

23 Hoehne Road

18 El Moro Road

15 U.S. 160 East, Kit Carson Trail, To U.S. 350 East, La Junta
Gas W: Texaco[*, D]

Bold red print shows RV & Bus parking available or nearby

EXIT	COLORADO/NEW MEXICO
Food	E: Burger King W: Frontier Motel
Lodg	E: Super 8 W: Frontier Motel
Other	E: Eye Care, Super Save Discount Foods, Wal-Mart(RX)
14B	Bus Loop 25, Trinidad Bus. Loop (Southbound)
Gas	W: Amoco, Phillips 66(D), Texaco
AServ	W: Amoco, Armstrong Big A Auto Parts, J M Tire Inc. Car Care Center, Phillips 66, Texaco
Other	W: J.R.'s Country Store, Spot Free Car Wash(CW), Trinidad True Value Hardware
14A	CO 12 West, Cuchara, La Veta, Colorado Welcome Center
Gas	E: Texaco(*) W: Conoco(LP), Diamond Shamrock(*, D, CW)
Food	E: McDonald's(PLAY), Pizza Hut, Taco Bell W: Dairy Queen, Domino's Pizza, El Capitan Italian & Mexican, Monte Leone's Deli, Nana & Nano's Past House, Piccadilly Pizza & Subs (Diamond Shamrock)
Lodg	W: Prospect Plaza Motel
AServ	W: Conoco
Med	E: + Hospital
ATM	W: First National Bank
13B	U.S. 160, U.S. 350, Main St
Gas	E: Conoco(*, LP, CW)
Food	E: Days Inn Days Inn
Lodg	E: Days Inn Days Inn, Inn on the Sante Fe Trail Bed & Breakfast
AServ	E: Car Quest, Trinidad Tire
Med	E: + Hospital
ATM	E: Conoco
Other	E: Carnegie Public Library, Police Station, Safeway Grocery, The Ultimate Car Wash(CW)
13A	Trinidad
Food	E: Best Western, Chef Liu's Chinese Food
Lodg	E: Best Western
RVCamp	E: Cawthon Campground & Motel (.75 Miles)
Other	E: Trinidad Lanes Bowling Alley
(11)	Weigh Station (Located At Exit 11, East Side)
11	Weigh & Check Station, Bus. Loop 25, Trinidad Bus. Loop, Starkville, Santa Fe Trail
FStop	E: Texaco(*, LP)
Food	E: Bob & Earl's Family Restaurant W: Country Kitchen (Holiday Inn)
Lodg	E: Budget Host Inn, Budget Inn W: Holiday Inn
AServ	W: Circle Chevrolet Buick
RVCamp	E: Biggs RV Park (Budget Host Inn), Budget Inn, Exit 11 RV Park (.25 Miles), Summit RV Park (Budget Inn)
8	Spring Creek
6	Gallinas
2	Wootton
(1)	Scenic Overlook (Northbound)

↑COLORADO

↓NEW MEXICO

EXIT	NEW MEXICO
(460)	Weigh Station (Southbound, Located At Exit 460)
(460)	Rest Area (RR, Picnic, P; Northbound, Located At Exit 460)
460	Unnamed
RVCamp	E: Cedar Rail Campground & RV Park (.5 Miles)
454	Bus Loop 25, Raton
452	NM 72 East, Raton
Gas	W: Conoco(*)
Lodg	W: Mesa Vista Motel
Med	W: + Hospital
ATM	W: Conoco
Parks	E: Sugarite State Park (5 Miles)
Other	W: Everything From A to Z
451	U.S. 64, U.S. 87 East, Raton, Clayton
TStop	E: Total(*)
FStop	E: Texaco(*)
Gas	E: Chevron, Diamond Shamrock(*) W: Conoco(*), Phillips 66, Texaco(*)
Food	E: Domingo's (Summerland RV Park), Hooter Brown's Restaurant (Total), Subway (Diamond Shamrock) W: All Seasons Family Restaurant, Arby's, Dairy Queen, Holiday Classic Motel, McDonald's(PLAY), Sands Restaurant (Best Western)
Lodg	W: Best Western, Comfort Inn, Harmony Manor Motel, Holiday Classic Motel, Motel 6, Super 8, Travel Motel
AServ	E: Chevron, Raton Auto Truck Service W: Phillips 66, Texaco
TServ	E: Raton Auto Truck Service, Total
RVCamp	E: Summerland RV Park(LP) W: KOA-Raton (1 Mile)
ATM	E: Texaco, Total
Parks	W: Capulin Volcano
Other	E: Capulin Volcano National Monument
450	I-25, Raton
FStop	W: Diamond Shamrock(*, K)
Food	W: Sonic Drive In
Lodg	W: Holiday Inn Express
RVCamp	W: KOA-Raton (1.5 Miles)
Med	W: + Hospital
Other	W: Mesa Vista Veterinary Hospital
446	U.S. 64 West, Taos, Cimarron, Eagle Nest, Angel Fire
435	Tinaja
(434)	Rest Area (RR, HF, Picnic, RV Dump, P; Southbound)
(434)	Rest Area (RR, HF, Picnic, RV Dump, P; Northbound)
426	NM 505, Maxwell, Maxwell Lakes
419	NM 58, Cimarron, Eagle Nest, Red River, Angel Fire
TStop	E: Texaco Truck/Auto Stop(*, D, SCALES)
Food	E: Russell's (Texaco TS)
TServ	E: Oliver's Tire Co. (Texaco TS)
414	Springer
Gas	E: Conoco(*), Diamond Shamrock, Phillips 66(D), Texaco(*)
Food	E: El Taco Mexican, Minnie's Dairy Delite, Smokeys Cafe, Stockman's Cafe
Lodg	E: Cozy Motel, Oasis Motel, The Brown Hotel
AServ	E: Road King Tires
Other	E: Tourist Info.
412	I-25 Springer, U.S. 56, 412 East, Clayton, NM 21, NM 468
404	NM 569, Colmor, Charette Lakes
393	Levy
387	NM120, Wagon Mound, Roy, Ocate
Gas	E: Chevron(*), Phillips 66(*, D)
Food	E: Levi's Cafe
AServ	E: Phillips 66
(375)	Rest Area (RR, HF, Picnic, RV

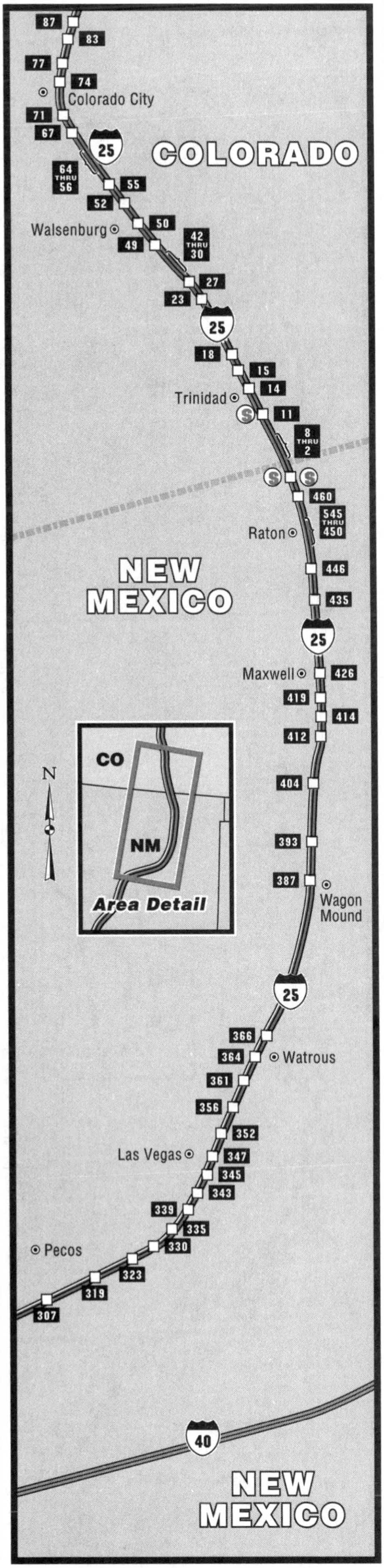

Bold red print shows RV & Bus parking available or nearby

EXIT	NEW MEXICO
	Dump, P; Southbound)
(374)	**Rest Area (RR, HF, Picnic, RV Dump, P; Northbound)**
366	NM 161, NM97, Watrous, Valmora
Other	W: **Fort Union National Monument**
364	NM 97, NM 161, Watrous, Valmora
361	Unnamed
(360)	**Rest Area (P; Southbound)**
(360)	**Rest Area (P; Northbound)**
356	Onava
352	Airport
347	Las Vegas
Gas	W: **Texaco[*, LP] (Inn of Las Vegas)**
Food	W: **Inn of Las Vegas**
Lodg	W: **Comfort Inn, Inn of Las Vegas**
AServ	W: **Texaco (Inn of Las Vegas)**
Parks	W: **Storrie Lake State Park**
345	NM 65, NM 104, University Ave, Bus. Loop 25
Gas	W: Fina[*], Texaco[*, 24]
Food	W: Fina, Mexican Kitchen
AServ	W: NAPA Auto Parts, Quality Chevrolet
Med	W: **+ Hospital**
ATM	W: Fina
Other	W: Rough Riders Museum
343	Business Loop 25, Las Vegas, To NM518, Storrie Lake Mora
AServ	E: BF Goodrich
339	U.S. 84 South, Romeroville, Santa Rosa
Gas	W: Texaco[*, D]
RVCamp	E: **KOA Kampground (.5 Miles)**
335	Tecolote
330	Bernal
(325)	**Rest Area (P; Southbound)**
(325)	**Rest Area (P; Northbound)**
323	NM 3 South, Villanueva
Gas	E: Shell[*]
Parks	E: **Villanueva State Park**
319	San Juan, San Jose
RVCamp	W: **Pecos River Campground**
307	NM 63, Rowe, Pecos
Parks	W: **Pecos National Historic Park**
Other	W: **Pecos National Monument**
299	NM 50, Glorieta, Pecos
297	Valencia
294	Canoncito at Apache Canon
RVCamp	W: **KOA Kampground (.5 Miles)**
290	U.S. 285 South, Clines Corners,Eldorado, Lamy
Gas	W: Fina
RVCamp	W: **Rancheros RV Park (1 Mile)**
284	Old Pecos Trail, NM 466
Med	W: **+ Hospital**
282	U.S. 84, U.S. 285, St. Francis Dr, Sante-Fe Plaza, Espanola, Los Alamos, Taos (Eastbound-Limited Access Hwy)
Gas	W: Giant Food Store[*, D, LP]
278	NM14, Cerrillos Road, Madrid
Lodg	W: Ramada Inn (see our ad this page)
RVCamp	W: **Al's RV Center (.5 Miles)**

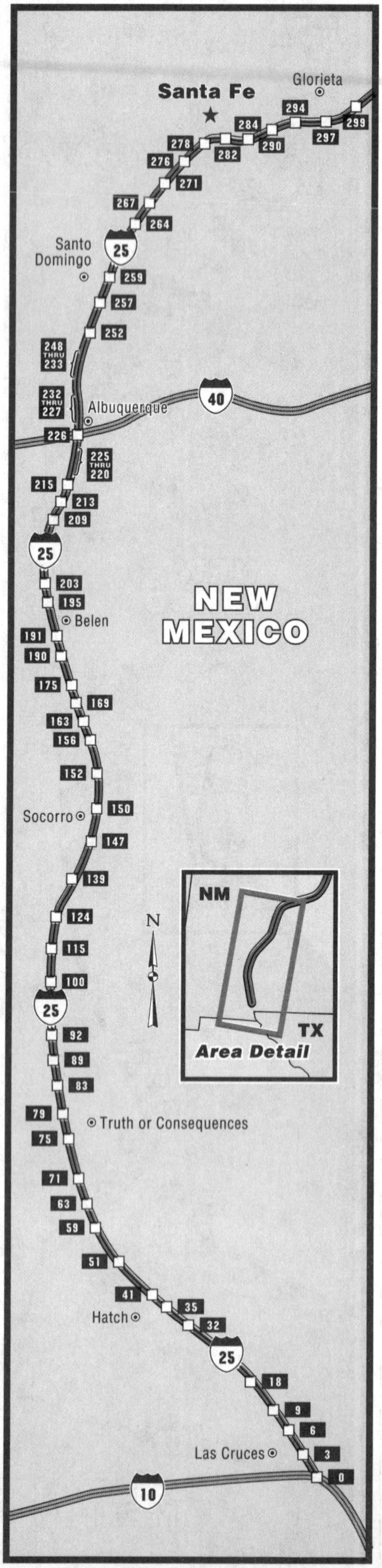

EXIT	NEW MEXICO
Other	W: **Sante Fe Premium Outlets**
276AB	NM 599, NM 14, Madrid
271	CR 50F, La Cienega
(268)	**Rest Area (RR, HF, Phones, Picnic, RV Dump, P; Northbound)**
267	No Name (Northbound)
264	NM 16, Cochiti Pueblo
259	NM 22, Santo Domingo Pueblo, Pena Blanca
Gas	W: Phillips 66[*, D]
Other	W: **Cochiti Lake Recreation Area (11 Miles)**
257	Budaghers
252	San Felipe Pueblo
248	Algodones
242	NM 44 West, NM 165 East, Rio Rancho, Bernalillo, Farmington, Placitas, Cuba
Gas	W: Conoco[*, D]
Food	W: **Donut Hole**, McDonald's[PLAY], Taco Bell
Lodg	W: **Super 8**
RVCamp	W: **KOA Kampground**
Parks	W: **Coronado State Park**
240	NM 473, Bernalillo
RVCamp	W: **Albuquerque KOA Campground (1 Mile)**
234	NM 556, Tramway Road, 2nd - 4th Street
Gas	W: Phillips 66[*, D]
ATM	W: Phillips 66
Other	E: Bien Mur Indian Market Center
233	Alameda Blvd
Gas	E: Chevron[*, LP, CW, 24]

Sante Fe, NM
1653
Ramada Inn
505-471-3000
Restaurant/Lounge on Premises
Room Service
Kids Under 12 Stay Free
Outdoor Pool • Golf Nearby
Meeting/Banquet Facilities
Pets Allowed • Exterior Corridors
Handicap Accessible
Truck/Large Vehicle Parking
Alpine & Nordic Skiing
Sports Bar/Comedy Club/ /Near Casino
2907 Cerrillos Rd. • Sante Fe, NM 87505
NEW MEXICO • I-25 • EXIT 278

ALBUQUERQUE
1679
AMBERLEY SUITE
HOTEL
• 2-3 Room Suites• Meeting Facilities
• FREE Buffet Breakfast
• Fully Equiped Kitchens
• Microwave Ovens • Refrigerators
• Wet Bars • Built-in Coffee Makers
• Cozy Living & Dining Areas
• Gift Shop • Restaurant • Lounge
• Heated Pool • Whirlpool • Exercise Room
505-823-1300
7620 Pan American Frwy N.E.
NEW MEXICO • I-25 • EXIT 231

Bold red print shows RV & Bus parking available or nearby

EXIT	NEW MEXICO
Food	E: Burger King(PLAY)
Lodg	E: Comfort Inn & Suites
	W: Ramada Limited
AServ	E: American Toyota
232	NM 423, Paseo del Norte
RVCamp	E: Osburn's RV Service & Storage
231	San Antonio Ave, Ellison Rd.
Food	E: Cracker Barrel, The Kettle (La Quinta Inn)
Lodg	E: La Quinta Inn, Quality Suites, Amberly Suite Hotel (see our ad this page), Howard Johnson Express Inn (see our ad this page)
	W: Budgetel, Crossland Economy Studios, Hampton Inn
AServ	W: University Mazda, Volkswagon, SAAB
230	San Mateo Blvd, Osuna Rd.
Gas	E: Chevron, Texaco(*, D)
	W: Diamond Shamrock(*, D)
Food	E: McDonald's(PLAY), Taco Cabana, Village Inn Pancake House, Winchells Donuts
Lodg	E: Wyndham Garden Hotel
AServ	E: Chevron, Firestone, Lee Galles Cadillac, Olds, Lexus, Premier Motor Cars Porsche, Mercedes, Audi
Med	E: Presbyterian Northside
ATM	W: Diamond Shamrock
Other	E: Bound To BE Read
229	Jefferson St
Food	E: Carrabba's Italian Grill, Landry's Seafood, Outback Steakhouse
228	Montgomery Blvd, Montano
Gas	E: Diamond Shamrock(*), Texaco(*, CW)
Food	E: Taco Bell Express (Texaco)
	W: Wendy's
AServ	E: Discount Tire
Med	E: Hospital
ATM	E: Norwest Bank
Other	W: Water Theme Park
227B	Comanche Blvd, Griegos
Gas	W: Phillips 66(*)
Food	W: Chester Fried Chicken (Phillips 66)
Other	E: U.P.S.
	W: Comanche Car Wash(CW)
227A	Candelaria Road, Menaul Blvd
TStop	E: Fina(*) (CB Repair), T/A TravelCenters of America(*, SCALES)
Food	E: Duke City (Fina), Liberty Cafe (Motel 76), Milly's Restaurant
	W: Waffle House
Lodg	E: Comfort Inn, Motel 1, Motel 76, Super 8 (see our ad on I-40 at Exit 166, NM)
	W: A-1 Motel, Red Roof Inn
AServ	E: Southwest Automotive Paints & Supplies
TServ	E: Albuquerque Truck Center (Ford, Kenworth, Cummins, CAT), Fina (CB Repair), T/A TravelCenters of America(SCALES)
TWash	E: Fina (CB Repair)
	W: Express Truck Wash(CW)
226	Junction I-40, Santa Rosa, Grants
225	Lomas Blvd
Food	E: JB's Restaurant (Plazá Inn)
Lodg	E: Plaza Inn
AServ	E: Ford Supercenter, Melloy Dodge
Med	E: Hospital
224B	Dr. Martin Luther King Jr. Ave., Central Ave.
Food	W: Milton's Restaurant (Mexican)
Lodg	E: Crossroads Motel
	W: Downtown Travel Inn, Imperial Motel, Lorlodge, Stardust Inn
Med	W: St. Joseph's Medical Center
224A	Lead Ave, Coal Ave, Central Ave. (One Way Streets)
Gas	E: Texaco(*)
	W: Diamond Shamrock(*)

EXIT	NEW MEXICO
Med	E: Presbyterian Hospital
ATM	E: Texaco
Parks	E: Roosevelt Park
223	Avenida, Cesar Chavez
Lodg	E: Motel 6
222B	Gibson Blvd
222A	Gibson Blvd, Kirtland AFB, Airport
Gas	E: Phillips 66(*, CW), Pump-N-Save(*)
Food	E: Burger King(PLAY)
Lodg	E: Budgetel Inn, Radisson Inn
Med	E: Hospital
221	Sunport Blvd, Airport
Lodg	E: AmeriSuites (see our ad this page)
Other	E: Historic Former Terminal Building, U.S. Post Office
220	Rio Bravo Blvd
215	NM 47, Broadway
Gas	E: Conoco(*, D)
RVCamp	W: Isleta Lakes & Recreation Area (1.25 Miles)
Other	E: Isleta Lakes & Recreation Area (1 Mile), Police Station (Conoco)
213	NM 314, Isleta Blvd.
Gas	W: Chevron(*, D, CW)
Food	W: Subway (Chevron)
ATM	W: Chevron
209	NM 45, Isleta, Pueblo, NM 314, NM 317
203	NM 6, Los Lunas
Gas	E: Chevron(*, D), Diamond Shamrock(*)
Food	E: Hot Stuff Pizza (Chevron)
Lodg	E: Comfort Inn, Days Inn
191	NM 548, Sosimo, Padilla Blvd
Food	W: La Mirada Inn & RV Park (.75 Miles), Rio Grande Diner
Lodg	W: Best Western, La Mirada Inn & RV Park (.75 Miles), Oak Tree Inn
RVCamp	W: La Mirada Inn & RV Park (.75 Miles)
190	Bus. Loop 25, Belen
Gas	E: AKIN(D, LP)
AServ	E: AKIN
RVCamp	E: KOA Campgrounds, La Marada
175	U.S. 60 East, Bernardo, Mountainaire
Gas	E: Didio's Mini Mart(*)
RVCamp	W: Kiva RV Park
169	La Joya State Game Refuge

1367

AMERISUITES
AMERICA'S AFFORDABLE ALL-SUITE HOTEL
New Mexico • Exit 221 • 505-242-9300

ALBUQUERQUE
1678
Howard Johnson
EXPRESS INN
- Brand New in 1996
- Free Continental Breakfast
- Fax & Copy Services
- Free Cable with HBO
- Kids Stay Free
- Heated Outdoor Pool
- Exercise Room

505-828-1600
7630 Pan American Frwy N.E.
NEW MEXICO • I-25 • EXIT 231

EXIT	NEW MEXICO
RVCamp	W: Kiva RV Park (1 Mile)
(166)	Rest Area (RR, Picnic, P; Southbound)
(166)	Rest Area (RR, Picnic, Vending, P; Northbound)
163	San Acacia
156	Lemitar
Food	W: Coyote Moon Cafe
152	Escondida
150	U.S. 60W, Bus. Loop 25, Socorro, Magdelena
Gas	W: Chevron(*, CW), Exxon(*, D)
Food	W: Burger King, K-Bob's Steakhouse (Super 8 Motel), McDonald's(PLAY), Sonic Drive In
Lodg	W: Holiday Inn Express, Super 8
AServ	W: Exxon, Viva Motors Chev, Pont, Olds, Buick, Chrys, Dodge
147	U.S. 60 West, Bus. Loop 25, Socorro, Magdalena
Gas	W: Exxon(*)
Food	W: Arby's
Lodg	W: Motel 6
AServ	W: Dean Tires
RVCamp	W: Casey's RV Park(LP), KOA Campgrounds(LP)
ATM	W: Exxon
Other	W: Car Wash
139	U.S. 380 East, San Antonio, Carrizozo
RVCamp	E: Night Owl RV Park
124	San Marcial
Other	E: Bosque Del Apache Refuge
115	NM107
TStop	E: Santa Fe Diner & Truck Stop & RV Park(*, RV DUMP)
AServ	E: Santa Fe Diner & Truck Stop & RV Park
RVCamp	E: Santa Fe Diner & Truck Stop & RV Park(RV DUMP), Sante Fe RV Park
(113)	Rest Area (RR, HF, Phones, Picnic, P; Southbound)
(113)	Rest Area (RR, HF, Phones, Picnic, P; Northbound)
100	Red Rock
92	Mitchell Point
89	NM 181, NM 52, Cuchillo, Monticello
83	NM 181 NM, 52 Cuchillo, Monticello
Exit	(82) Border Patrol Inspection Station (All Vehicles Exit)
79	Bus. Loop 25, Truth or Consequences
Gas	E: Chevron(D)
Food	E: K-Bob's Steakhouse, McDonald's(PLAY)
Lodg	E: Best Western, Super 8
AServ	E: Chevron
RVCamp	E: Lakeside RV Park (2 Miles)
Parks	E: Elephant Butte Lake State Park
(75)	Picnic Area (Picnic; Located at Exit 75, East Side)
75	Bus. Loop 25, Truth or Consequences (Difficult Reaccess)
Gas	E: Chevron(*), Diamond Shamrock(*)
Food	E: Cafe Rio
Lodg	E: Rio Grande Motel
AServ	E: Auto Doctor Body Shop, Mechanic Shop, Dayton Tires
TServ	E: Truck Tires
RVCamp	E: Broadway RV Park (1.6 Miles), R.J. RV Park (1.25 Miles), Shady Corner RV Park (.5 Miles)
Med	E: Hospital
ATM	E: Chevron, Diamond Shamrock
Other	E: U.S. Post Office
71	Las Palomas
(67)	Rest Area (Picnic; Southbound)
(67)	Rest Area (Picnic, P; Northbound)

EXIT NEW MEXICO

- **63** NM 152, Hillsboro
  - **Gas** E: Texaco(*, LP)
  - **RVCamp** E: **KOA Kampground**
  - **Parks** E: **Caballo Lake State Park**
- **59** Caballo-Percha State Parks
- **51** Garfield
- **41** NM 26 West, Hatch
  - **RVCamp** W: **Happy Trails RV Park (1 Mile)**
- **35** NM 140 West, Rincon
- **32** Upham
- (27) **Scenic Overlook (Picnic; Northbound)**
- **Exit** **(26)** Inspection Station (Northbound, All Vehicles Stop)
- (23) **Rest Area (RR, HF, Picnic, Vending, P; Southbound)**
- (23) **Rest Area (RR, HF, Picnic, Vending, P; Northbound)**
- **19** Radium Springs
  - **RVCamp** W: **HOA RV Park**
  - **Parks** W: **Leasburg State Park (1 Mile)**
  - **Other** W: **Fort Selden State Monument (1 Mile)**
- **9** Dona Ana
  - **Gas** W: Chevron(*), Citgo(*), **Diamond Shamrock**(*)
  - **RVCamp** W: **ValVerde Mobil Park**
  - **ATM** W: Chevron, **Diamond Shamrock**
  - **Other** E: **Ben Archer Health Center**
- **6AB** U.S. 70, U.S. 82, Alamogordo, Las Cruces
  - **Gas** E: Texaco(*, CW)
    W: Diamond Shamrock(*, D, LP)
  - **Food** E: IHOP
    W: Burger Time
  - **RVCamp** W: **S & H RV Center (.2 Miles)**
  - **Med** E: **+ Mesilla Valley Hospital**
  - **Parks** W: **Leasburg State Park (14 Miles)**
  - **Other** E: **K-Mart**, Lucky Sav-On, Mail Boxes Etc., Yamaha ATVs, Motorcycles, Watercraft
    W: **Fort Selden State Monument Historic Ruins (14 Miles)**, Haydens True Value Hardware, Las Cruces Border Patrol Station, **WalGreens Pharmacy**(RX)
- **3** Lohman Ave
  - **Food** E: Applebee's, Burger King(PLAY), Chili's, Golden Corral Family Steakhouse, Jack-In-The-Box, KFC, **Luby's Cafeteria (Mall)**, Red Lobster, Village Inn Restaurant
    W: Arby's, McDonald's(PLAY)
  - **Lodg** E: Hilton
  - **AServ** E: Discount Tire Company, Sears Auto Center
    W: **Montgomery Ward**, **Wal-Mart**(RX) **(Vision Center)**
  - **RVCamp** E: **American RV & Marine (.35 Miles)**
  - **ATM** E: **Albertson's Food Market**(RX), Bank of America, **Citizens Bank of Las Cruces (Mall)**, Norwest Bank, Sierra Bank
    W: **Wal-Mart (Vision Center)**
  - **Other** E: **Albertson's Food Market**(RX), Cinema 8, **Mesilla Valley Mall**, **Office Max**, **Target**
    W: Golf USA, Hasting's Books, Music, Video, **Montgomery Ward**, **Toys R Us**, **Wal-Mart**(RX) **(Vision Center)**
- **1** University Ave
  - **Food** W: **Dairy Queen**, Lorenzo's Italian, McDonald's
  - **Lodg** W: Comfort Suites Hotel, Sleep Inn
  - **Med** E: **+ Memorial Medical Hospital**
  - **ATM** E: Bank of Rio Grande
  - **Other** E: New Mexico State Univ. Golf Course, State Police
    W: New Mexico State University
- **0** Jct. I-10, El Paso, Tucson

↑NEW MEXICO

Begin I-25

EXIT NORTH CAROLINA

Begin I-26

↓NORTH CAROLINA

- **1** Junction I-40, Canton, Knoxville, NC 191 to Blue Ridge Pwky.
- **2** NC 191, to Blue Ridge Parkway
  - **Food** S: Cookies N Creme, Harbor Inn, Little Caesars Pizza, Long John Silver, Ryan's Steakhouse, Subway, Taco Bell, Waffle House
  - **Lodg** N: Hampton Inn, Wingate Inn
    S: Comfort Suites Hotel (see our ad this page)
  - **AServ** N: Jim Barkley Toyota, Saturn of Ashville
  - **RVCamp** N: **Bear Creek Campground**
    S: **North Mills Recreation Area, Powhaton Camping**
  - **Other** N: **Biltmore Estates, Super Petz (Pet owners warehouse)**
    S: **Biltmore Square Mall, Ingles Supermarket, K-Mart, Ridgefield Mall, U.S. Post Office**
- **6** NC 280, Skyland
  - **Gas** N: Amoco(*, D, LP)
  - **Food** N: Eat Rite Cafe, Hardee's, SHONEY'S Shoney's, Shoney's Inn, Waffle House
    S: Cider Mill Restaurant & Pub
  - **AServ** N: Airport Connection Auto Service
  - **Other** N: **W.N.C. Vetninarian Hospital**
- **9** NC 280, Brevard, Arden, Asheville Regional Airport
  - **Gas** N: BP(*, D, CW), Texaco(*)
    S: Amoco(*, D, CW)
  - **Food** N: Arby's, McDonald's, Waffle House
  - **Lodg** N: Budget Motel, DAYS INN Days Inn, **Econolodge**, Holiday Inn
    S: Fairfield Inn
  - **AServ** N: Appletree Honda, L.B. Smith Volvo

TRUCK/LARGE VEHICLE PARKING
Comfort Suites
828-665-4000
800-622-4005
FREE CONTINENTAL BREAKFAST
1408
Restaurant on Premises
Kids 12 and under Stay & Eat Free
Outdoor Pool • Exercise Room
Meeting/Banquet Facilities
Pets Allowed • Coin Laundry
Handicap Accessible
Airport Shuttle • Interior Corridors
In Room Coffee/Refridg/
Iron & Ironing Board/Hairdryer
North Carolina • I-26 • Exit 2

Free Continental Breakfast
Quality Inn & Suites
GOLD AWARD WINNER
Quality Inn
Inn & Suites
201 Sugarload Road
Hendersonville, NC 28792
828-692-7231 • 800-228-5151
Restaurant/Lounge on Premises
Jacuzzi, 2 Room, & Business Suites
Indoor Heated Pool • Fitness Room
Sauna/Whirlpool/Jacuzzi
FREE Local Calls • Modem Hook-up
Handicap & Non-smoking Rooms
Pets Allowed Some Rooms
Indoor Mini Putt-Putt • Game Room
Truck or Large Vehicle Parking
AAA
1287
North Carolina • I-26 • Exit 18A

EXIT NORTH CAROLINA

  - **ATM** N: Texaco
  - **Other** S: **Ashville Regional Airport**
- (10) **Rest Area (RR, Phones, Picnic, Vending)**
- **13** U.S. 25, Fletcher, Mountain Home
  - **TStop** S: **Skyway**(*, SCALES)
  - **Gas** S: Exxon(*), Phillips 66
  - **Food** N: Hardee's
    S: Burger King, **Huddle House, Skyway Restaurant**
  - **AServ** S: Phillips 66
  - **TServ** S: **Skyway TStop, Will's CD Shop**
  - **Med** S: **+ Park Ridge Hospital**
  - **ATM** S: Skyway
- (15) **Weigh Station**
- **18AB** U.S. 64, Hendersonville, Bat Cave
  - **FStop** N: **Shell**(*, D)
  - **Gas** N: Chevron(*), Texaco(*, D, LP)
    S: Exxon(*, D)
  - **Food** N: A Day in the Country (Bakery & Coffee shop), Fireside Restaurant, Waffle House
    S: Applebee's, Arby's, Baskin Robbins, Bojangles, Bunyan's Road House, Burger King, Checkers Burgers, Denny's, Hardee's, KFC, Lon Sen Chinese, Long John Silver, McDonald's, Savannah Beach Grill, Schlotzsky's Deli, Subway, Taco Bell
  - **Lodg** N: **Best Western**, Hampton Inn, Quality Inn (see our ad this page), Ramada Limited
    S: Comfort Inn, DAYS INN Days Inn
  - **AServ** N: Chevron, Hendersonville Tire & Oil, I-26 Auto Supply
    S: Carolina Tire Co., Penske Auto Service, Qlube
  - **RVCamp** N: **Apple Valley Travel Park (1.5 Miles), Mountain Camper Sales & Servoce**
    S: **Lazy Boy Travel Park (1.25 Miles)**
  - **ATM** S: First Citizen's Bank
  - **Other** S: **Allan's Pharmacy, Blue Ridge Mall, Eckerd Drugs, Ingles Supermarket, K-Mart, Mail Boxes Etc, Wal-Mart, Winn Dixie Supermarket**
- **22** Upward Road, Hendersonville
  - **RVCamp** N: **Lakewood RV Resort (.5 Miles), Rite-Way Services, Twin Ponds (Open year round)**
    S: **Park Place RV Park (.5 Miles), Town Mountain Travel Park (1 Mile)**
- **23** U.S. 25, to U.S. 176 (Closed)
- **28** Saluda
  - **FStop** S: **Amoco**(*)
  - **Gas** S: Texaco(*, LP)
  - **Lodg** N: Heaven's View Motel
  - **AServ** S: **Hipps Garage**
  - **TServ** S: **Hipps Garage**
  - **Other** S: **The Apple Mill (Cidar Mill Museam)**
- **36** NC 108, U.S.74, Columbia, Tryon, Lake Lour, Chimney Rock
  - **Gas** N: BP(*), Texaco(*)
    S: Amoco(*, LP)
  - **Food** N: BP, Blimpie Subs & Salads (Texaco), Burger King (BP), Chester Fried Chicken (Texaco), Hardee's, McDonald's(PLAY), Subway, Texaco
    S: KFC, Sow Sun Chinese
  - **Lodg** S: DAYS INN Days Inn
  - **Med** S: **+ Hospital**
  - **ATM** N: Texaco
    S: **Bi-Lo Grocery**
  - **Other** N: **CVS Pharmacy**(RX), **Food Lion Supermarket**
    S: **Bi-Lo Grocery**
- (36) **NC Welcome Center (RR, Phones, Picnic, Vending; Westbound)**

↑NORTH CAROLINA

Bold red print shows RV & Bus parking available or nearby

EXIT SOUTH CAROLINA

↓SOUTH CAROLINA

1 SC 14, Landrum
- **FStop** S: BP(*)
- **Food** S: Denny's
- **AServ** S: BP
- **Other** S: Ingles Supermarket

(3) **SC Welcome Center (RR, Phones, Vending; Eastbound)**

5 SC 11, Campobello, Chesnee
- **FStop** N: Citgo(*)
- **Gas** N: Lil' Cricket(*)
  S: Spur(*) (Fireworks Superstore)
- **Food** N: Aunt M's (Citgo FStop), Citgo
- **ATM** N: Citgo, Lil' Cricket

(9) **Parking Area (Eastbound)**

(9) **Parking Area (Westbound)**

10 SC 292, Inman
- **FStop** N: Conoco(*, SCALES)
- **Food** N: Conoco, Krispy Kreme Doughnuts (Conoco), Subway (Conoco FStop)
- **ATM** N: Conoco

15 U.S. 176, Inman
- **FStop** N: Fuel City(*, SCALES) (SMilesGas)
  S: Exxon(*)
- **Gas** N: Fast Stop(*)
- **Food** N: Waffle House
  S: Blimpie Subs & Salads (Exxon FStop), Exxon
- **AServ** N: NIX Tires, Alignment, & Brakes
- **ATM** N: Fast Stop, Fuel City (SMilesGas)
- **Other** N: Hickory Hill Antiques

16 John Dodd Road, Wellford
- **FStop** N: Citgo(*)
- **Food** N: Aunt M's (Citgo FStop), Citgo
- **Other** N: Red Star Fireworks

17 New Cut Road
- **Gas** S: Citgo(*), Speedway(*, LP)
- **Food** S: Burger King, Fatz Cafe, Hardee's, McDonald's(PLAY), Waffle House
- **Lodg** S: Comfort Inn, Days Inn, EconoLodge, Howard Johnson Express Inn
- **RVCamp** S: Spartanburg Cunninghan RV Park (1 Mile)
- **Other** S: Foothills Factory Stores

18AB Jct. I-85 South to Greenville - 18A, Jct. I-85 North to Charlotte - 18B

19AB Junction I-85 Business Loop North, Spartanburg Jct. I-85 Bus. Loop South

21BA U.S. 29 North, Spartanburg, U.S. 29 South, Greer (21A to Greer, 21B to Spartanburg)
- **Gas** N: Crown(*, LP), Exxon(*)
  S: Citgo(*, D, K), Texaco(D)
- **Food** N: Aloha Oriental Dining, Chick-Fil-A, Exxon, Hardee's, Long John Silver, O'Charley's, Pizza Hut, Quincy's Family Steakhouse, Sub Station II, Subway (Exxon), Wendy's
  S: Applebee's, Aunt M's (Citgo), China Buffett, Citgo, McDonald's(PLAY), Piccadilly, Prime Buffett Bakery Steaks, Steakout, Taco Bell
- **AServ** N: Firestone Tire & Auto, Goodyear Tire & Auto, Jiffy Lube, K-Mart(24, RX), Sears
  S: Spartan Automotive, Western Auto
- **ATM** N: BB&T Bank, NationsBank, Wachovia Bank
  S: American Federal
- **Other** N: Eckerd Drugs(RX), K-Mart(RX), West Gate Mall
  S: Books n Stuff, Ingles Supermarket, Lowe's, Sam's Club, Wal-Mart(RX) (Vision center, one hour photo), West Wash

22 SC 296, Reidville Road, Spartanburg
- **Gas** N: Exxon(*, LP)
  S: BP(*, CW), Hess(*, D)
- **Food** N: Arby's, Hong Kong Express, Ice Cream & Coffee Beans, Little Caesars Pizza, Outback Steakhouse, Waffle House
  S: A Latte Coffee, Burger King(PLAY), Denny's(24), Domino's Pizza, Hardee's(PLAY), TCBY, Waffle House
- **Lodg** S: Sleep Inn, Super 8
- **AServ** N: B.F. Goodrich, Exxon
  S: Century BMW, Dave Edward's Toyota, Reidville Road Auto Service, Rick's Auto Service(CW), Xpress Lube
- **ATM** N: American Federal Bank, CPM Federal Credit Union, Palmetto Bank
  S: First Union Bank
- **Other** N: Mail Boxes Etc, Putt-Putt & other games, Wynnsong Cinema's

1660

Comfort Inn
Exit 52 • Clinton, SC
864-833-5558

- Restaurant Adjoining Building
- Deluxe Continental Breakfast
- Kids Under 18 Eat & Stay Free
- Meeting Facilities
- Coin Laundry
- Truck/Large Vehicle Parking
- Outdoor Pool • Handicap Accessible

SOUTH CAROLINA ▪ I-26/I-385 ▪ EXIT 52

- S: Bi-Lo Grocery(RX), CVS Pharmacy(RX), Red Star Fireworks

28 U.S. 221, Spartanburg, Moore
- **Gas** N: Shell(*, LP)
- **Food** N: Krispy Kreme Doughnuts (Shell), Shell, Subway (Shell), Walnut Grove Seafood (Open evening hrs. Thurs - Sun)
- **RVCamp** N: Pine Ridge Campground
- **Med** N: ✚ Hospital
- **Other** N: Walnut Grove Plantation

35 Road 50, Woodruff
- **FStop** S: Citgo(*, 24)
- **Food** S: Citgo, Family Restaurant(24) (Citgo)
- **Med** S: ✚ Hospital
- **ATM** S: Citgo

38 SC 146, Woodruff
- **Food** N: Big Country Restaurant

41 SC 92, Enoree
- **Gas** S: Phillips 66(*, LP)

(43) **Parking Area (Picnic; Eastbound)**

(43) **Parking Area (Picnic; Westbound)**

44 SC 49, Cross Anchor, Union

51 Junction I-385, Laurens, Greenville (Westbound, Left Exit Westbound)

52 SC 56, Cross Anchor, Clinton
- **FStop** N: Speedway(*, K, SCALES)
  S: Phillips 66(*, D)
- **Gas** S: Texaco(*)
- **Food** N: Blue Ocean Seafood Restaurant, McDonald's, Waffle House
  S: Hardee's, Waffle House, Wendy's
- **Lodg** N: Comfort Inn (see our ad this page)
  S: Days Inn, Holiday Inn, Traveler's Inn
- **TServ** N: Carolina Transportation Inc.(24) (Truck Wrecker & Truck Trailor Service)
- **TWash** N: Carolina Transportation Inc. (Truck Wrecker & Truck Trailor Service)
- **ATM** N: Speedway

54 SC 72, Clinton
- **FStop** S: Texaco(*, LP, K)
- **Med** S: ✚ Hospital

60 SC 66, Whitmire, Joanna
- **FStop** S: BP(*)
- **Gas** S: Chevron(*)
- **Food** S: 60 Truck Stop Restaurant
- **AServ** S: BP
- **RVCamp** S: KOA Kampground(LP) (.6 Miles)

(63) **Rest Area (RR, Phones, Picnic, Vending; Westbound)**

(63) **Rest Area (RR, Phones, Picnic, Vending; Eastbound)**

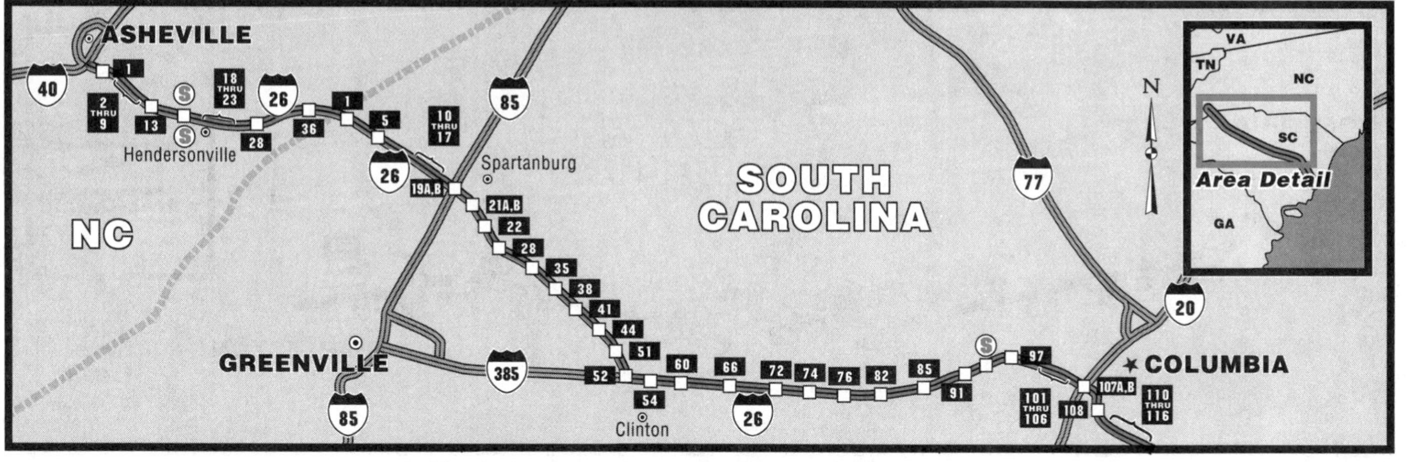

EXIT — SOUTH CAROLINA

66 Road 32, Jalapa

72 SC 121, Whitmire, Union
- **Gas** N: Shell(*) (see our ad this page)
- **Med** S: Hospital

74 SC 34, Newberry, Winnsboro
- **FStop** N: **Shell**(*, 24)
  S: **Texaco**(*)
- **Gas** N: BP(*, K)
- **Food** N: Bill & Fran's, Mickey's (Shell), **Shell**
  S: **Waffle House**
- **Lodg** N: Best Western
  S: Days Inn (see our ad this page)
- **Med** S: **Hospital**
- **ATM** N: Fun Time Video, **Shell**
  S: **Texaco**
- **Other** N: Fun Time Video

76 SC 219, Newberry
- **Other** S: Newberry Opera House

(81) **Weigh Station (Eastbound)**

82 SC 773, Pomaria, Prosperity
- **FStop** N: **Amoco Travel Plaza**(*, SCALES)
- **Food** N: **Amoco Travel Plaza**, **BJ's Diner**, Subway (Amoco)
- **AServ** N: **Craig Hipps Truck Service**
- **TServ** N: **Craig Hipps Truck Service**
- **RVCamp** N: **Flea Market Campground**
- **Other** N: **Jockey Lot Flea & Farmers Market**

(84) **Parking Area (Eastbound)**

85 SC 202, Pomaria, Little Mountain

(88) **Parking Area (Westbound)**

91 Road 48, Chapin
- **FStop** S: **Texaco**(*, LP, K)
- **Gas** S: Amoco(*, K)
- **Food** S: **Capital City Subs & Salad (Texaco)**, McDonald's(PLAY), **Texaco**
- **ATM** S: Texaco, **Texaco**

(94) **Weigh Station (Westbound)**

97 U.S. 176, Peak
- **FStop** S: **Amoco**(*, K, 24)
- **RVCamp** S: **Smokewood Campground, Wood Smoke Campground (.9 Miles)**

101 U.S. 76, U.S. 176, Ballentine, White Rock
- **Gas** S: Amoco(*, LP), BP(*, CW)
- **Food** S: Baskin Robbins, Burger King, Waffle House
- **AServ** S: BP
- **ATM** S: BB&T Bank(24)

102 SC 60, Irmo (Westbound, Reaccess Eastbound Only)
- **Food** S: Cookies by Design, Papa John's Pizza, TCBY
- **Other** S: **Piggly Wiggly Supermarket**

EXIT — SOUTH CAROLINA

103 Harbison Blvd
- **Gas** S: Amoco(*)
- **Food** N: Applebee's, Hop's Restaurant & Bar
  S: **Bagle Works**, **Baker's Row Cafe**, Blimpie Subs & Salads, Chick-Fil-A, Chili's, Joe Mug Coffee, McDonald's(PLAY), Olive Garden, Outback Steakhouse, Ruby Tuesday, Rush's Hamburgers, Sonic Drive In, Subway, **Wal-Mart Supercenter**(24, RX) **(Vision center, one hour photo)**
- **Lodg** N: Hampton Inn
- **AServ** S: **Wal-Mart Supercenter**(24) **(Vision center, one hour photo)**
- **Med** S: **Baptist Medical Center**
- **ATM** S: BB&T Bank, First Union Bank, NationsBank
- **Other** N: **Home Depot**, **Lowe's**
  S: Barnes & Noble, **Best Buy**, **Bi-Lo Grocery**, **Books-A-Million**, Bookstore, **Columbiana Centre Mall**, **Phar Mor Drugs**(RX), Sansbury Eye Center, Toys R Us, **Wal-Mart Supercenter**(RX) **(Vision center, one hour photo)**

104 Piney Grove Road
- **FStop** N: **Speedway**(*, LP)
- **Gas** N: Shell(*) (see our ad this page)
  S: Exxon(*, CW)
- **Food** N: **Hardee's**, Waffle House
- **Lodg** N: Comfort Inn, **EconoLodge**
- **AServ** N: Dick Smith Infiniti, Dick Smith Nissan, Hampton Pontiac Buick, Jiles Auto Repair, Saturn of Columbia
- **RVCamp** N: **Holiday Camper**
- **ATM** N: Shell, **Speedway**
  S: Exxon
- **Other** N: Coin Laundromat, **Sam's Club**

106AB St Andrews Rd. (106B goes North, 106A goes South)
- **Gas** N: Exxon(*)

50 Thomas Griffin Rd
Newberry, SC 29108

DAYS INN

Truck/ Large Vehicle Parking

1587

Restaurants Nearby
Continental Breakfast
Kids Under 12 Stay Free
Meeting/Banquet Facilities
Pet Allowed ($5 charge)
Handicap Accessible
Exterior Corridors
Golf/Tennis Nearby

803-276-2294 • Newberry, SC

South Carolina • I-26 • Exit 74

EXIT — SOUTH CAROLINA

- S: BP(*, D, CW), Circle K(*), Hess(*, D)
- **Food** N: BB's Steak & Ribs, Chick-Fil-A (Kroger), Chuck E Cheese's Pizza, IHOP, **Kroger Supermarket**(RX), Papa John's Pizza
  S: Burger King, Domino's Pizza, Garrett's Grill, Lowcountry Cafe, Mauric's BBQ, McDonald's, Pizza Hut, Pizza Hut, Sandy's Hot Dogs & Icecream, Steak & Ale, Sub Station II, Taste of China Hut, WG's Chicken Wings, Waffle House, Wendy's, Western Steer Family Steakhouse
- **Lodg** N: Motel 6
  S: Holiday Inn Express, Red Roof Inn
- **AServ** S: NTB
- **ATM** S: NationsBank, Wachovia Bank
- **Other** N: **Kroger Supermarket**(RX)
  S: **Eckerd Drugs**(RX), **Piggly Wiggly Supermarket**

107AB Junction I-20, Florence, Augusta

108 Junction I-126, Bush River Road, Columbia
- **Gas** N: Texaco(*, K, CW)
  S: RaceWay(*), Speedway(*, LP)
- **Food** N: Blimpie Subs & Salads, Captain D's Seafood, China Town, Hardee's, McCarey's Bar & Grill, Schlotzsky's Deli, SHONEY'S, Shoney's
  S: Catman & Lulu's (HOJO), Howard Johnson
- **Lodg** N: Budgetel Inn, Villager Lodge
  S: Howard Johnson, Junction Inn
- **AServ** N: **K-Mart**(RX), Master Care Auto Service, Midas Muffler & Brake
- **ATM** N: First Union Bank, Texaco, Wachovia Bank
- **Other** N: **Dutch Square Mall**, Dutch Square Theaters, Franks Car Wash, H Ruben Vision Center, **K-Mart**(RX), Vision Works
  S: **Corley Lock & Key**, M&M Car Wash, **Target**

110 U.S. 376, Lexington, West Columbia
- **Gas** N: Texaco(*, D)
  S: BP(*, CW)

The universal sign for the world's best-selling gasoline.

Open 24 Hours | Shell | ATM & Pay at Pump
Easy Access | | Restaurant Adjacent

Clean Restrooms
Fast, Courteous Service
Air & Water
Convenience Store with Fresh Hot Coffee & Fountain Drinks
All Major Credit Cards

803-276-6662

1495

SOUTH CAROLINA • I-26 • EXIT 104/74

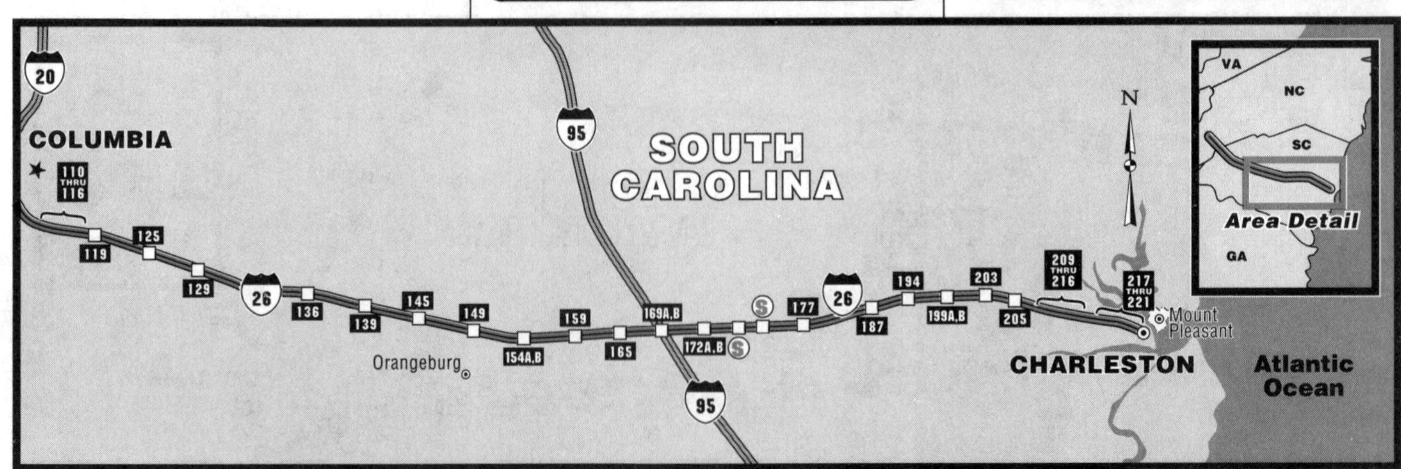

EXIT — SOUTH CAROLINA

Food N: Burger King(PLAY), Grecian Garden Restaurant, McDonald's(PLAY), Millinder's BBQ, Pizza House, Pizza Hut, Quincy's Family Steakhouse, **Ramada**, Rush's Hamburgers, Waffle House
S: Bojangles, Hardee's, Pizza Hut
Lodg N: Hampton Inn, **Ramada**
S: Executive Motel
Med S: ✚ **Lexington Medical Center**
ATM N: BB&T, Texaco
S: Wachovia Bank
Other N: **Sunset Drugs**(RX), **U.S. Post Office**, West Columbia Animal Clinic

111AB U.S. 1, Lexington, West Columbia
Gas N: Racetrac(*)
Food N: Domino's Pizza, Dragon City Chinese, **Hardee's**, Holiday Inn, Magnolia's (Holiday Inn), Sonic Drive In, Terry's Diner
Lodg N: Delta Motel, Holiday Inn, Super 8 (see our ad this page)
TServ N: **Williams Detroit Diesel**
Other S: Lowe's, U-Haul Center

113 SC 302, Columbia Airport, Cayce
Gas N: Amoco(*)
S: Racetrac(*, 24), Smile Gas(*, D, K, 24)
Food N: Cherry's Bar & Grill
S: Burger King, Denny's, SHONEY'S Shoney's, Waffle House
Lodg N: Best Western, Knight's Inn, **Masters Inn**
S: Comfort Inn, DAYS INN **Days Inn**
AServ N: Peake's Auto & Tire
S: NAPA Auto Parts
TServ N: **Kenworth/Cherokee**
ATM S: Racetrac, Smile Gas

115 U.S. 321, U.S. 21, U.S. 176, Cayce, Columbia
TStop S: **Pilot Travel Center**(*, SCALES)
FStop S: **United**(*)

1110

I-26 • Exit 145A
Orangeburg • 803-531-6400
• Free Deluxe Continential Breakfast
• Free Local Calls
• 25" Cable TV's with HBO
• Outdoor Pool • Fitness Center
• In Room Iron & Coffee Makers
• Whirlpool Rooms Available
SOUTH CAROLINA • I-26 • EXIT 145A

Gas N: Racetrac(*, 24)
Food N: **Waffle House**
S: **Dairy Queen (TS)**, Great China Restaurant, Hardee's, **McDonald's**(PLAY), **Pilot Travel Center**, Shooters Grill & Pub, Steak & Eggs House, Subway, **United**, **Wendy's (TS)**
Lodg S: Ramada Limited
AServ N: Scott's Automotive
S: Firestone Tire & Auto
ATM N: Racetrac
S: **United**
Other S: **Piggly Wiggly Supermarket**

116 I-77 to Charlotte, Fort Jackson

119 U.S. 21, U.S. 176, Dixiana
FStop N: **BP**(*, D)
S: **Citgo**(*), **The Depot**(*) **(Shell Gas)**
Food S: **Maggie Mae's Cafe**(24), Subway (The Depot), TCBY (The Depot), **The Depot (Shell Gas)**
TServ S: **South Carolina Transport**
ATM S: **Citgo**

(122) **Rest Area (RR, Phones, Picnic, Vending; Eastbound)**

(122) **Rest Area (RR, Phones, Picnic, Vending; Westbound)**

125 **Road 31, Gaston, Rest Area**
TServ N: **Trailer Services**, **Wolfe's Truck & Trailer Repair**

129 U.S. 21
Gas N: Shell(*)

136 SC 6, North Swansea St.
FStop N: **Exxon**(*) **(Fireworks, Briar Patch Restaurant)**
Food N: **Briar Batch (Exxon)**
AServ N: **Exxon (Fireworks, Briar Patch Restaurant)**
TServ N: **Exxon (Fireworks, Briar Patch Restaurant)**
ATM N: **Exxon (Fireworks, Briar Patch Restaurant)**

139 Road 22, St Matthews
FStop S: **Citgo**(*)
Food S: Stuckey's (Citgo)
TServ N: **Truck Tire & Service**
RVCamp S: **Campground**

145AB U.S. 601, St Matthews, Orangeburg
FStop S: **Speedway**(*, LP)
Gas S: Amoco(*), Exxon(*), Texaco(*)
Food S: **Hardee's**, KFC, **McDonald's**(PLAY), Rita's Food & Spirits, Waffle House
Lodg S: Carolina Lodge, Comfort Inn, DAYS INN Days Inn, Hampton Inn (see our d this page), Howard Johnson, **Southern Lodge**
ATM S: Exxon

149 SC 33, Orangeburg, Cameron

(150) **Rest Area (RR, Phones, Picnic, Vending; Eastbound)**

CHARLESTON, S.C.
1516
DAYS INN
$39.95 Sun-Thur 1-2 Person
$43.95 Fri-Sat 1-2 Person
Based on Availability
I-26 • Exit 203

(152) **Rest Area (RR, Phones, Picnic, Vending; Westbound)**

154AB U.S. 301, Orangeburg, Santee
FStop S: **BP**(*), **Texaco**(*, K)
Food N: DAYS INN **Days Inn**
Lodg N: DAYS INN **Days Inn**
AServ S: S&R Garage

159 Road 36, Bowman
TStop N: **Speedway**(*, SCALES) **(Laundromat, CB Doctor)**
AServ N: **Speedway (Laundromat, CB Doctor)**
TServ N: **Bowman Truck Service**, **Speedway**(SCALES) **(Laundromat, CB Doctor)**
ATM N: **Speedway (Laundromat, CB Doctor)**

165 SC 210, Bowman
TStop S: **Texaco**(*, SCALES) **(ATM)**
FStop N: **Exxon**(*)
S: **BP**(*)
Food S: **BP**, Blimpie Subs & Salads (Texaco), Carolina Cafe (BP), **Texaco (ATM)**
AServ S: **Texaco (ATM)**
TServ S: **Texaco**(SCALES) **(ATM)**

169AB Junction I-95, Savannah, Florence

172AB U.S. 15, Santee, St George
TStop S: **Dixie Boy**(*, LP, K, SCALES, 24) **(Amoco gas)**
FStop N: **I-26 Coffee Shop**
Food S: **Dixie Boy (Amoco gas)**
AServ S: **Dixie Boy**(24) **(Amoco gas)**
ATM S: **Dixie Boy (Amoco gas)**

(173) **Weigh Station (Eastbound)**

(174) **Weigh Station (Westbound)**

177 SC 453, Holly Hill, Harleyville
FStop S: **BP**(*, LP)
Food S: **BP**, The Finishing Mill (BP)
ATM S: **BP**

187 SC 27, Ridgeville, St. George

194 Road 16, Jedburg

199AB Alternate U.S. 17 , Mocks Corner, Summerville - 199B North, Lincolnville- 199A South
TStop N: **Citgo**(*, CW)
FStop N: **Speedway**(*, LP, K)
S: **Pacific Pride**(*, LP, K) **(Amoco)**
Gas N: Hess(*, D)
S: BP(*)
Food N: **Citgo**, **Ruthy's Diner (Citgo)**
S: Bojangles, Burger King(PLAY), Fazoli's Italian Food, Hardee's(PLAY), Huddle House, **Pacific Pride (Amoco)**, Perkins Family Restaurant, Ryan's Steakhouse, SHONEY'S Shoney's, TCBY (Pacific Pride), Waffle House
Lodg S: **Comfort Inn**, EconoLodge, **Economy Inn**, Hampton Inn, Holiday Inn Express
AServ N: McElveen Pontiac, Buick, GMC Trucks
TServ N: **Blanchard**, **Carolina Truck & Equipment**
TWash N: **Citgo**(CW)
ATM N: **Citgo**
S: First Citizens Bank, First Federal of Charleston, **Pacific Pride (Amoco)**
Other S: **Wal-Mart**(RX)

(202) **Rest Area (RR, Phones, Picnic, Vending; Westbound)**

203 College Park Road, Ladson, Exchange Park
FStop N: **Speedway**(*, LP)
Gas N: **BP**(*, CW)
Food N: **McDonald's**, Waffle House
Lodg N: DAYS INN **Days Inn (see our ad this page)**
RVCamp S: **KOA Campgrounds (1.8 Miles)**
Parks S: **Exchange Park**

EXIT	SOUTH CAROLINA
Other	S: College Park Veterinarian
(204)	Rest Area (RR, Phones, Picnic, Vending; Eastbound)
205BA	U.S. 78 W, Summerville- 205A, 205 B U.S. 78 E
Gas	N: Shell(*, LP)
RVCamp	S: KOA Campgrounds (1 Mile)
Med	N: Columbia Trident Med Center
ATM	N: First Citizens Bank, NationsBank
208	U.S. 52, Goose Creek, Moncks Corner (Difficult Reaccess)
209	Ashley Phosphate Road
Gas	N: Exxon(*, CW), Shell(*) S: Citgo(*, LP), Hess(*), Racetrac(*)
Food	N: Blimpie Subs & Salads (Exxon), Exxon, Hardee's, Krispy Kreme Doughnuts, Taco Bell, Waffle House, Wendy's S: Bojangles, Cracker Barrel, Domino's Pizza, IHOP, Kobe Japanese Restaurant, McDonald's(PLAY), SHONEY'S Shoney's, Waffle House
Lodg	N: Best Western, Red Roof Inn, Residence Inn, Studio PLUS, Super 8 S: Fairfield Inn, Howard Johnson, La Quinta Inn, Motel 6, Suburban Lodge
AServ	N: Gene Reed Toyota, Master Care Auto Service, Monroe Muffler & Brakes
ATM	N: First Citizen's Bank, Shell, South Trust Bank
Other	N: Carolina Ice Palace, Home Depot, Lowe's S: Animal Hospital
211AB	Aviation Ave, Air Force Base, Redmount Rd.
FStop	S: Speedway(*, D)
Gas	N: Amoco(*), Exxon(*, CW), Shell(*)
Food	N: Arby's, Burger King, China Garden, China Town, Church's Chicken, Grandy's, Huddle House, KFC, Mongolian BBQ, Old Country Buffet, Papa John's Pizza, Pizza Inn, Schlotzsky's Deli, Sea Fare, Subway, Wendy's S: Waffle House
Lodg	N: Masters Inn, Radisson S: Budget Inn, Holiday Inn, Knight's Inn, TraveLodge
AServ	N: Amoco, Pep Boys Auto Center
RVCamp	N: Fain's RV Park (.4 Miles) S: Campground
ATM	N: SC Federal Credit Union, Wachovia Bank
Other	N: Sam's Club S: Airport, United Artist Theaters
212A	Hanahan, Redmont Rd. (Westbound, Reaccess Eastbound Only)
Gas	N: Hess(D)
Food	N: Captain Tang's, KFC, Mongolian BBQ, Papa John's Pizza, Taco Bell, Tom Portaro's Italian
AServ	N: Advance Auto Parts, Albritton's Coastal Transmission Service, Altman Dodge, Auto Zone Auto Parts, Engine Exchange, Grease Monkey, J & R Automotive Service, Jell's Tires, Jones Ford, Muffler Shop
ATM	N: Wachovia Bank S: NationsBank
Other	N: Coin Laundry, Fox Theater, Vet Center
212BC	Junction I-526W, Savannah, Mt. Pleasant
213	Montague Ave, Mall Drive
Gas	S: Ashley's(*, D), Citgo(*)
Food	N: Piccadilly Cafeteria, Red Lobster S: Bojangles, Day Break Restaurant (Days Inn), Days Inn, Hess (Bojangles), Waffle House
Lodg	N: Hilton S: Comfort Inn, Days Inn, Extended Stay America, Orchard Inn, Quality Suites, Ramada
AServ	N: Montgomery Ward S: Ashley's
TServ	S: Cummins Onan
ATM	N: First Federal of Charleston, NBSC
Other	S: Visitor Information
215	SC 642, Dorchester Road
Gas	N: Hess(D) S: Amoco(*, LP, K)
Food	N: Hardee's, Harold's Lunch Time, Howard Johnson S: Alex's Restaurant(24), EconoLodge, Quarter House Restaurant (EconoLodge)
Lodg	N: Howard Johnson S: EconoLodge, Villager Lodge
Other	N: Coin Laundry, Greyhound Bus Station
216AB	SC 7, Cosgrove Ave (216A goes South, 216B goes North)
Food	N: Oriental Food and Gift Shop
Med	N: Roper Medical Center
217	North Meeting St (Eastbound)
218	Spruill Ave, Naval Base (Westbound, Reaccess Eastbound Only)
219B	Morrison Dr., East Base Street (Eastbound, Reaccess Westbound Only)
Gas	N: Shell(*, D)
Food	N: Huddle House
AServ	N: Sam's Star Service, Shell
ATM	N: Sam's Star Service
219A	Rutledge Ave , The Citadel (Eastbound, Reaccess Westbound Only)
220	Port Terminal, Columbus Street, Union Pier (Westbound, No Reaccess)
221AB	U.S. 17S, King St, Savannah - 221A, U.S. 17 North , Mt. Pleasant- 221B
Med	S: Hospital

↑SOUTH CAROLINA

Begin I-26

I-27 S →

EXIT	TEXAS
	Begin I-27

↓TEXAS

EXIT	TEXAS
124	Junction I-40 , Amarillo
123B	Jct. I-40W Tucumcari; I-40E South U.S. 287 Oklahoma City, Ft. Worth (Northbound)
123A	26th Ave. (Northbound)
Gas	E: Citgo(*), Conoco(*)
AServ	E: J & R Transmissions
123	26th Ave.
Food	W: Burritos Gordo
122B	34th Ave, Tyler St.
Gas	E: Texaco(*)
Food	E: Sonic Drive-In
ATM	E: NationsBank
122A	FM 1541, Washington St, Parker St, Moss Lane
Gas	W: Texaco
Food	W: Taco Bell
Lodg	E: Amarillo Motel
AServ	E: Elite Wheel, Tire & Trailers W: Texaco
Other	W: Maxor Pharmacies(RX)
121B	Hawthorne Dr, Austin St. (Southbound)
FStop	W: Texaco(*, D, CW)
AServ	W: Scottie's Transmission
121A	Georgia St
Gas	E: Phillips 66(*, CW)
Food	E: Jeff's Grand Burger
AServ	E: Brown Pontiac, GMC Trucks, Circle 4 Transmissions, Dwayne's Quick Auto Service, Mastercraft Automotive Services, Quality Nissan Dealership, Southwest Honda Dealership, Street Mazda, Toyota
Other	W: Texas Department Of Public Safety
120B	45th Ave
Gas	E: Fina(*, D, K) W: Diamond Shamrock(*)
Food	W: Abuelo's Mexican, Burger House, Hardee's, Luby's Cafeteria, The Doughnut Stop
Lodg	E: American Motel
AServ	E: Beauchamp Motors, Carr Automotive W: Caprock, High Plains Transmission, Quality Tire & Service
TServ	W: Roberts Truck Center (Kenworth)
RVCamp	E: Jack Sisemore Travelland
Other	W: Colonial Veterinary Clinic, Panhandle Car Wash(CW)
120A	Republic Ave. (Southbound)
119B	Western St, 58th Ave (Southbound)
Gas	W: Gasman(*), Texaco(*, D)
Food	W: Pizza Hut
RVCamp	W: RV Sales & Service
ATM	W: Texaco, Western Bowl
Other	W: Payless Cashway Hardware, U.S. Post Office, Western Bowl
119A	Hillside Rd West (Southbound)
119	Hillside Rd, Western St.
Gas	E: Phillip 66(*, 24)
AServ	E: Aardvark Automotive, Five Star Transmission
ATM	E: Phillip 66
Other	E: Centergas(LP), Homeland Grocery Store, Jack's Marine Service, Parker Boats
117	Bell St.
Gas	W: Texaco(*, LP)
Food	W: Long John Silver
Other	E: Spot Free Rinse Car Wash(CW) W: Veterinarian
116	Loop 335, Hollywood Rd
FStop	E: Love's(*, 24)
Food	E: McDonald's, Waffle House
Lodg	E: Days Inn
115	Sundown Lane
113	McCormick Rd
Gas	W: Texaco(*)
AServ	E: Ron Clark Ford
RVCamp	W: Family Camping Service Center(LP)
112	FM2219
FStop	W: Citgo(D)
111	Rockwell Rd

Bold red print shows RV & Bus parking available or nearby

EXIT TEXAS

Gas E: Fina
ASErv E: Midway Chevorlet
110 West Texas A & M University, U.S. 87S, U.S. 60W, Canyon, Hereford (Southbound)
109 Buffalo Stadium Rd.
108 West U.S. 60, Hereford, FM 3331, Hunsley Rd.
106 TX 217, Canyon
RVCamp E: **Palo Duro RV Park**
Parks E: **Palo Duro Canyon State Park (10 Miles)**
103 FM1541, Cemetery Rd. To TX217 East
99 Hungate Rd
(97) **Parking Area (P; Southbound)**
(97) **Parking Area (P; Northbound)**
96 Dowlen Rd.
94 FM285, Wayside
92 Haley Rd
90 FM1075
88 U.S. 87, FM1881, Happy
83 FM2698
82 FM214
77 U.S. 87, Tulia
75 NW 6th St
74 TX86, Tulia
TStop W: **Rip Griffin's Faststop[*] (Texaco)**
Food W: **Grandy's (Rip Griffin's TS), Subway (Rip Griffin TS)**
Lodg W: **Best Western**
ATM W: **Rip Griffin's Faststop (Texaco)**
(79) **Parking Area (Southbound)**
(69) **Parking Area (Northbound)**
68 FM928
63 FM145
61 U.S. 87, Kress
56 FM788
54 FM3183
53 Bus. Loop 27
51 Quincy St
50 TX194
Med E: **+ Hospital**
49 U.S. 70
FStop E: **Diamond Shamrock[*]**
Gas E: Texaco[*, D]
W: Chevron[*, CW], Conoco[CW], Shell[*, D]
Food E: China Dragon, Far East Restaurant, Field House Sandwich Shop, Furr's Family Dining, Kettle[24], Subway (Texaco)
W: Burger King, Casa Ole, Chicken Express Restaurant, McDonald's[PLAY], Mr Gatti's Pizza, Sabrie's Seafood, Subway, Taco Villa, The Donut Shop

Antique Capital of the Southwest
1148

I-27 • Exit 49
Plainview, TX
806-293-9454

Executive King Suites
Outdoor Pool
Continental Breakfast
Kettle Restaurant on Property
Lounge on Premises
AAA, AARP, Special Tour Group Rates
45 min. to Canyon outdoor theatre
TEXAS ▪ I-27 ▪ EXIT 49

EXIT TEXAS

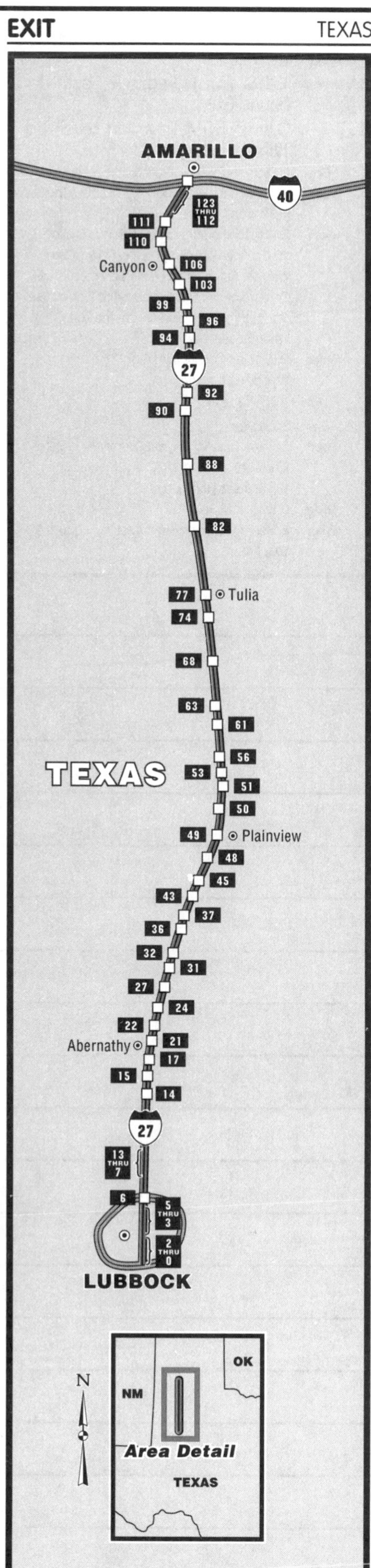

EXIT TEXAS

Lodg E: **Best Western (see our ad this page)**, Days Inn
W: **Holiday Inn Express**
AServ E: Jack Morris Ford, Lincoln, Mercury, Toyota Dealer
W: Conoco
ATM E: **Diamond Shamrock**, Texaco, **United Supermarket**
Other E: **Llano Estacado Museum, Revco[RX], United Supermarket**
W: **Eye Wear Outlet**, JC Penney Outlet Store, **K-Mart[RX], Wal-Mart[RX]**
48 FM3466
45 Bus. Loop 27, Plainview
43 FM2337
41 County Rd
38 Main St, Hale (Southbound)
37 FM1914, Cleveland St
Gas W: Fina[*, 24], Phillips 66[*]
Food E: Dairy Queen
W: Tom's Restaurant
AServ W: Roy's Automotive, Waller's Garage
Med W: **+ Hospital**
Parks W: **Park**
Other W: Century Hardware, Fire Station, Hale Center Public Library, **Pay-N-Save Grocery**
36 FM1424, Main Streete
Med W: **+ Hospital**
32 West FM37
31 East FM37
(28) **Rest Area (RR, Phones, Picnic, Grills, P; Southbound)**
(28) **Rest Area (RR, Phones, Picnic, Grills, P; Northbound)**
27 County Rd
24 FM54
RVCamp W: **RV Park**
22 Loop369, Abernathy (Southbound)
21 FM2060, Main Street, FM 597
Gas W: Co-Op[LP], Conoco[*], Fina[*, 24]
Food W: Dairy Queen, Poppy's Pizza, Rocking R Steakhouse
AServ W: Patton's Parts Place
ATM W: Fina, First State Bank
Other W: Fire Department, Library, **Pinson Pharmacy**, Struv's True Value Hardware, **U.S. Post Office**
20 FM597, Abernathy (Northbound)
17 CR 53
15 Loop461, New Deal (Southbound)
14 FM1729
13 Loop461, New Deal
12 CR 58 (Northbound)
11 FM1294, Shallowater
10 Keuka St
9 Lubbock International Airport
Other E: Lubbock International Airport
8 FM2641, Regis St, Airport Passenger Terminal
Other E: Lubbock International Airport
7 Yucca Lane
6B Loop 289 (Southbound, Limited Access Hwy)
Lodg W: Texas Motor Inn
RVCamp E: **Pharr Rv**
6A Spur 326, Ave Q (Southbound)
Lodg W: El Tejas Motel
6 Loop 289 (Northbound, Limited Access Hwy)
RVCamp E: **Pharr's RV Camp**
5 Ave H, Municipal Dr (Southbound)

EXIT TEXAS

1146

Best Western

Present this ad at check in & Receive 20% Off the Regular Rate

Best Western Lubbock Regency

Free Deluxe Continental Breakfast

Coffee Makers in All Rooms

Lubbock's Largest Indoor Pool with Whirlpool,

Sauna & Complete Recreation Area

806-745-2208 • Reservations 1-800-588-5677

TEXAS ▪ I-27 ▪ EXIT 1B

AServ **W:** Owen's Auto & Electric

Parks **W:** Aztlan Park

4 U.S. 82, 4th St, Crosbyton, Bus. U.S. 87, Brownfield

Gas **W:** Gas(*)

Food **W:** Rhodes Cafe

EXIT TEXAS

AServ **W:** Service Auto

3A 13th St, Ave. H (Reaccess Southbound Only)

3 U.S. 62, TX114, Floydada, Levelland, 19th St, Depot District

Gas **E:** Diamond Shamrock, Town & Country(*)

Food **W:** Bleachers, Legendary Stubb's BBQ, The Depot Restaurant

AServ **E:** Wilkison Radiator Shop, William's Brake & Tune **W:** Continental Battery Factory Outlet, Great Western Automotive Sales & Service, Lubbock Carburetor and Electric, Rick's Tire Warehouse, Star Automotive Wharehouse, The Parts Wharehouse

Other **E:** Winnie's Car Sparkle Wash(CW) **W:** Cactus Theater

2 34th St, Ave H

Gas **E:** Chevron(*, 24)

Food **E:** Pete's Drive In, Town & Country Food Stores (Chevron) **W:** Mr. Lee's Hamburgers

Lodg **E:** Budget Motel

AServ **E:** Henry's Radiator & Automotive, Lubbock Axle, York Tire

EXIT TEXAS

Other **W:** Imperial Coin Laundry, Raff & Hall Drug

1C 50th St (Southbound)

Food **W:** Bryan'Steaks, Country Plate Diner, Dairy Queen(PLAY), Josie's Restaurant, KFC, Long John Silver, Subway, Wienerschnitzel

AServ **W:** Stone's Tire & Auto Center

Other **W:** **U.S. Post Office**

1B East U.S. 84, Slaton, Post, South U.S. 87, Tahoka, Loop 289 (Southbound)

Lodg **W:** Super 8, Best Western (see our ad this page)

1A 50th St, Loop289W

Gas **E:** Buddy's

Food **E:** El Jalapeno, Jo Jo's Jumbo Burger

AServ **E:** B & R Muffler & Brake, Beevers Radiator Shop

Other **E:** Pronto Mart(*)

1 Bus. U.S. 87, 82nd St, U.S. 84, Loop 289, Littlefield

Gas **W:** Chevron(*), Conoco(*, D)

0 98th St

↑TEXAS

Begin I-27

Notes:

Bold red print shows RV & Bus parking available or nearby

EXIT — NORTH DAKOTA

Begin I-29

↓NORTH DAKOTA

(215) U.S./Canadian Border

215 ND 59, County 55, Neche, Pembina
TStop E: Gastrak(*, LP, RV DUMP, SCALES)
FStop E: The Trad 'N' Post(*)
Food E: The Depot Cafe
ATM E: Gastrak, The Trad 'N' Post
Other E: Ammex Duty Free Shop, Dumoulin Church Historic Site, The Pembina Museum

212 Unnamed

208 CR1, Bathgate

203 U.S. 81, ND 5, Hamilton, Cavalier, Hallock, Weigh Station
TStop W: Joliette Express Truck Stop(*, 24)
Food W: Restaurant(*) (Joliette)
Parks W: Icelandic State Park (25 Miles)

(203) Weigh Station (Located at Exit 203)
TStop W: Joliette Express(*, LP)
Parks W: Icelandic State Park (25 Miles)

200 Unnamed

196 CR 3

193 Unnamed

191 CR 11, St. Thomas

187 ND 66, Drayton, Donaldson
FStop E: Cenex(*), Northdale Oil Amoco(*)
Gas E: Spur(*)
Food E: Cinnamon Street Bakery (Cenex), Dairy Queen, Dakota Junction Diner, Hot Stuff Pizza (Cenex), Smash Hit Subs (Cenex)
Lodg E: Motel 66, Red River Motel
AServ E: Car Quest
TServ E: Helm International
TWash E: Drayton
RVCamp E: Catfish Haven Campground, Red River Camping

184 Drayton
RVCamp E: Camping

180 Unnamed

(179) Rest Area (RR, HF, Phones, Picnic, RV Dump; Left Exit Both Directions)

176 ND 17, Grafton
RVCamp W: Campground
Med W: ✚ Unity Medical Center

172 Unnamed

168 Warsaw, Minto

164 Unnamed

161 ND 54, CR 19, Oslo, Ardoch

157 Unnamed

152 U.S. 81, Manvel, Gilby
FStop W: Town Mart(*, D, LP)

145 N. Washington St

141 U.S. 2, Gateway Drive
TStop W: Long Haul Truck Stop(*, SCALES), StaMart(*, LP, RV DUMP, SCALES) (Pacific Pride Commercial Fueling)
FStop E: Sinclair(*)
Gas E: Amoco(*, CW, 24)
Food E: Burger King(PLAY), G.F. Goodribs Steakhouse, Highway Host American Family Restaurant, Holiday Inn, McDonald's, Ramada Inn
W: Perkins Family Restaurant
Lodg E: Econolodge, Holiday Inn, Ramada Inn, Roadking Inn, Rodeway Inn, Select Inn
W: Prairie Inn

EXIT — NORTH DAKOTA

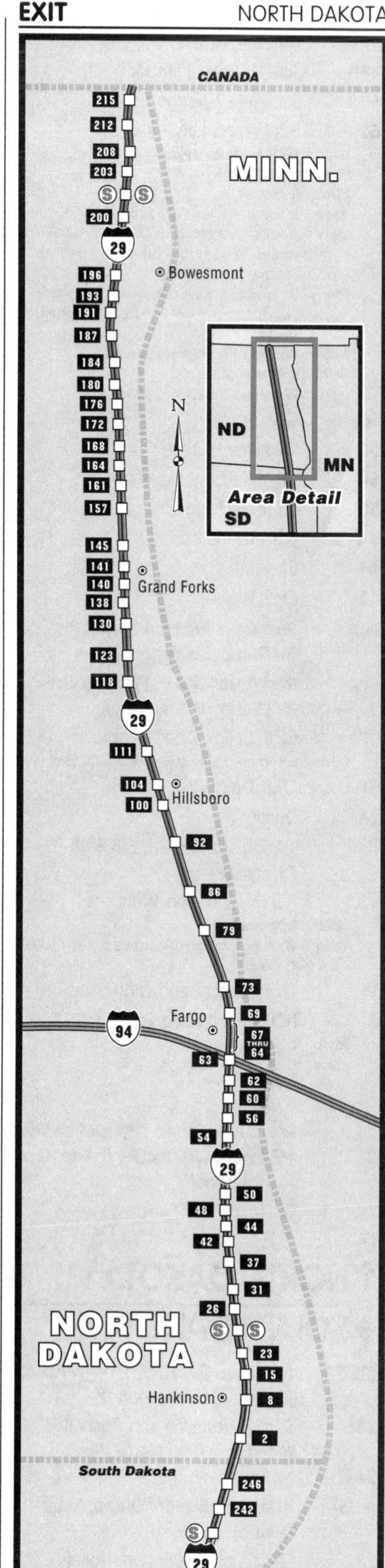

EXIT — NORTH DAKOTA

AServ E: Amoco(24), Big A Auto Parts, Big Wheel Auto Stores, Hansen Ford, Smitty's Transmission
W: Advance Body Works
TServ E: Forks Freightliner
W: Cummins, Thermo King, Long Haul Truck Stop(SCALES)
RVCamp W: Budget RV Service, Key RV
Med E: ✚ Hospital
ATM E: Amoco, First National Bank, Sinclair
W: Long Haul Truck Stop, StaMart (Pacific Pride Commercial Fueling)
Parks W: Turtle River State Park (19 Miles)
Other E: Cleanerama Car Wash, Cleanerama Coin Laundry, Suburban Propane(LP), Tourist Info.

140 DeMers Ave, City Center, Grand Forks
Gas E: Amoco(*)
AServ E: NAPA (Amoco)
Med E: ✚ Hospital

138 Bus. U.S. 81, 32nd Ave South
TStop W: Conoco(*, LP, RV DUMP)
Gas E: Holiday(*, LP, CW), Super Pumper(*, CW)
Food E: Subway (Holiday)
W: I-29 Cafe (Conoco), Subway (Conoco)
Lodg E: Country Inn Suites, Days Inn, Fairfield Inn by Marriott, Roadking Inn
AServ E: National Muffler
RVCamp W: Campground
ATM E: Holiday
W: Conoco
Other W: Kindness Animal Hospital

130 CR 81, ND 15, Thompson

123 Reynolds

(120) Weigh Station (Southbound)

(120) Weigh Station (Northbound)

118 Buxton

111 ND 200 West, Mayville, Cummings

104 Hillsboro
FStop E: Cenex(*, LP)
Gas E: Amoco(*)
Food E: Burger King (Cenex), Cinnamon Street Bakery, Country Hearth Family Restaurant, Eddie Pepper's Mexican Restaurant (Amoco), Hot Stuff Pizza (Amoco), Smash Hit Subs
Lodg E: Hillsboro Inn
RVCamp E: Hillsboro Campground, No Name RV Camp(LP, PLAY)
Med E: ✚ Hospital
ATM E: Amoco, The Goose River Bank
Other E: Speed Queen Coin Laundry

100 ND East 200, Alternate West 200, Blanchard, Halstead

(99) Rest Area (RR, HF, Phones, Picnic, RV Dump; Southbound)

(99) Rest Area (RR, HF, Phones, Picnic, RV Dump; Northbound)

92 Grandin
FStop E: Co-Op Farmland(*)
W: Stop & Shop(*)
Food E: Rendezvous Bar & Grill
AServ E: Co-Op Farmland

86 Gardner
FStop W: Sinclair(*)

79 Argusville

(74) Rest Area (RR, HF, Phones, Picnic, RV Dump, Pet Walk; Southbound)

(74) Rest Area (RR, HF, Phones, Picnic,

Bold red print shows RV & Bus parking available or nearby

EXIT NORTH DAKOTA

RV Dump, Pet Walk; Northbound)

73 Harwood
- FStop E: Cenex[*, LP]
- Food E: Cenex

69 County Route 20

67 Bus U.S. 81, 19th Ave North
- Med W: ✚ VA Hospital

66 12th Ave North
- Gas E: Stop 'N Go[*]
- AServ W: OK Tire Store
- TServ W: Interstate Detroit Diesel, Northwest Truck & Trailer, OK Tire Store, Power Brake Midwest Inc.
- ATM E: Stop 'N Go
- Other E: Whale Of A Wash[CW] (Car Wash)
  W: UPS

65 U.S. 10, Downtown Fargo, West Fargo
- FStop W: Cenex[*]
- Gas E: Amoco[*, CW]
  W: Mobil[*, D]
- Food E: Valley Kitchen
  W: Best Western, Embers, Hardee's, Subway (Cenex)
- Lodg W: Best Western
- AServ E: Dave's I-29 Service Ctr, Doctor Motor Worx, NAPA Auto Parts, Transmission City
  W: AAMCO Transmission, Car Quest Auto Center, Clint's Car Care Center, Corwin Chrys, Plym, Dodge, Lunde Linc, Merc, Jeep, Eagle, Mobil, Tim Corwin GM, Buick, Toyota, Valley Ford, Volvo
- TServ W: Ardo Mack, Ford Wallwork Truck Center, Detroit, Cummins, Cat, Hall Truck Service, Nelson International, W.W. Wallwork Truck Center, Kenworth
- RVCamp E: Bernie's Camper Corral, McLaughlin's RV (1 Mile)
- ATM E: Amoco
  W: Cenex
- Other E: Surplus Tractor Parts, Valley Veterinarian Hospital

64 13th Ave South, East 13th Ave Downtown, West 13th Ave, 38th St. Southwest Shopping Center
- FStop E: Sinclair[*, LP], Sta-Mart[*]
- Gas E: Amoco[CW, 24]
- Food E: Best Western, Borna's Bagel Bakery, Burger King, Cactus Jack's Saloon, Chuck E Cheese's Pizza, Giovanni's Pizza, Green Mill, Mr. Steak, Nine Dragons (Chinese), Perkins Family Restaurant, Ponderosa Steakhouse
  W: Arby's, Chi-Chi's Mexican Restaurant, Chili's, Fuddruckers (Hamburgers), Grandma's Saloon & Deli, Holiday Inn, Mandarin Chinese, McDonald's[PLAY], Paradiso Mexican, Pizza Hut, Randy's Restaurant, T.G.I. Friday's, Taco Bell, The Rock (Pizza & Mexican), Valentino's Ristorante
- Lodg E: Americinn Motel, Best Western, Comfort Inn, Comfort Suites Hotel, Country Suites, Econolodge, Hampton Inn, Motel 6, Motel 75, Super 8
  W: Comfort Inn, DAYS INN Days Inn, Fairfield Inn by Marriott, Holiday Inn, Holiday Inn Express, Red Roof Inn, Select Inn
- AServ E: Amoco[24], Schumacher Goodyear
  W: Midas
- ATM E: Cash Wise Foods Grocery[RX], Sinclair, Sta-Mart
  W: Community First, Gate City Federal Savings Bank, US Bank
- Other E: Cash Wise Foods Grocery[RX], Pearl Vision Center
  W: Barnes & Noble, Hornbacher's Groceries,

EXIT NORTH/SOUTH DAKOTA

West Acres Mall

63B Jct. I-94 West Bismark

63A Jct. East I-94 Fargo

62 32nd Ave South
- TStop W: Flying J Travel Plaza[*, LP, SCALES] (Lodging)
- FStop E: GasMart[*, K, CW]
- Gas E: Amoco[*, CW]
- Food E: Country Kitchen, PaPa John's Pizza
- AServ E: ABRA, Certicare Repair Center, Jiffy Lube
  W: Brad Ragan Inc, Goodyear, Thermo King Radiator Isuzu, Diesel
- TServ W: Brad Ragan Inc, Goodyear, Cummins, Flying J Travel Plaza[SCALES] (Lodging), Peterbilt Dealer
- TWash W: Flying J Travel Plaza (Lodging)
- ATM E: Amoco, GasMart
  W: Flying J Travel Plaza (Lodging)

60 CR 6, Frontier

56 Wild Rice, Horace

54 CR 16, Oxbow, Davenport

50 CR 18, Hickson

48 ND 46, Kindred

44 Christine

42 CR 2, Walcott

(40) Rest Area (RR, HF, Phones, Picnic, RV Dump; Southbound)

(40) Rest Area (RR, HF, Phones, Picnic, RV Dump; Northbound)

37 CR 4, Colfax, Abercrombie
- Other E: Fort Abercrombie Historic Site (7 Miles)

31 CR 8, Galchutt

26 Dwight

(24) Weigh Station (Left Exit Both Directions)

23 ND 13, Mooreton, Wahpeton
- Med E: ✚ Hospital
- Other W: Bagg's Bonanza Farm Interpretive Center (2 Miles)

15 CR 16, Great Bend, Mantador

8 ND 11, Hankinson, Fairmount
- FStop E: Moblie[*]
- AServ E: Moblie
- TServ E: Moblie
- ATM E: Moblie

(3) Rest Area, Tourist Information (RR, HF, Phones, Picnic, RV Dump; Northbound)

2 CR 22

1 Ct 1E

↑NORTH DAKOTA

↓SOUTH DAKOTA

(251) Rest Area (RR, HF, Phones, Picnic, RV Dump; Southbound)

246 SD 127, New Effington, Rosholt
- Parks W: Sica Hollow State Park (24 Miles)

242 No Name

(235) Weigh Station (RV Dump; Southbound)

232 SD 10, Sisseton, Browns Valley

EXIT SOUTH DAKOTA

- FStop E: Phillips 66[*]
- RVCamp W: Camp Dakota (.5 Miles)
- Med W: ✚ Hospital
- Parks W: Fort Sisseton (25 Miles), Roy Lake State Park (25 Miles)

224 Peever
- Gas E: No Name[*, D]
- Parks W: Pickerel Lake (16 Miles)
- Other W: Sioux Tribal Headquarters

(213) Rest Area (RR, HF, Phones, Picnic, RV Dump)
- Parks E: Hartford Beach State Park (17 Miles)

213 SD 15, Wilmot (RR, Phones, Picnic)
- Parks E: Hartford Beach State Park (17 Miles)
- Other E: Highway Patrol

207 U.S. 12, Summit, Aberdeen
- FStop E: Conoco[*]
- Food E: Hot Stuff Pizza (Conoco)
- Other W: Blue Dog State Fish Hatchery, Waubay National Wildlife (19 Miles)

201 Twin Brooks

193 SD 20, South Shore, Stockholm
- RVCamp E: Camping (6 Miles)

185 Waverly

180 Bramble Park Zoo, Municipal Airport

177 U.S. 212, Watertown, Kranzburg
- TStop E: Sinclair[*, SCALES]
- FStop W: Conoco[*]
- Food W: Country Kitchen (Country Inn & Suites), Hot Stuffed Pizza (Conoco), McDonald's
- Lodg E: Stone's Inn
  W: Comfort Inn, Country Inn & Suites
- TServ E: Sinclair[SCALES]
- TWash E: Sinclair
- Med W: ✚ Hospital
- ATM E: Sinclair
  W: Conoco
- Other W: Redlin Arts Center, Sandy Shore Recreation Area (10 Miles)

164 SD 22, Castlewood, Clear Lake
- Med E: ✚ Hospital (10 Miles)

(160) Rest Area (RR, HF, Phones, Picnic, RV Dump; Southbound)

(160) Rest Area (RR, HF, Phones, Picnic, RV Dump; Northbound)

157 Brandt

150 SD 15, SD 28, Toronto, Estelline
- Parks W: Lake Poinsett Rec Area (24 Miles)

140 SD 30, White, Bruce
- Parks W: Oakwood Lakes State Park (12 Miles)

133 US 14 Bypass, Volga, Arlington, De Smet
- Other W: Laura Ingles Wilder Homestead (43 Miles)

132 Bus. I-29, U.S. 14, Brookings, Huron, Lake Benton
- FStop E: Cenex[*]
  W: Amoco[*, CW, 24]
- Gas W: Citgo[*, CW]
- Food E: Burger King (Cenex)
  W: Country Kitchen, Dairy Queen, Hardee's, Holiday Inn, KFC, Little Caesars Pizza (K-Mart), Perkins Family Restaurant
- Lodg E: Super 8
  W: Best Western, Comfort Inn, Holiday Inn
- AServ W: Amoco[24], Big O Tires, Car Quest Auto Center, Nagel's Body Shop, Paula Motors Chev, Pont, Olds, Buick, Cad, GMC Trucks
- RVCamp E: A & D Campers

EXIT SOUTH DAKOTA

Med W: ✚ Hospital
ATM W: First National Bank
Other W: K-Mart(RX), Visitor Information, Wal-Mart(RX)

127 SD 324, Elkton, Sinai

(121) Rest Area (RR, Phones, Picnic, Vending, RV Dump; Southbound, Located at Exit 121)

(121) Rest Area (RR, Phones, Picnic, Vending, RV Dump; Northbound, Located at Exit 121)

121 Nunda, Ward (RR, Phones, Picnic, RV Dump, Pet Walk)

114 SD 32, Flandreau

109 SD 34, Madison, Colman, Egan
TStop W: Texaco(*)
FStop W: Sinclair(*, LP)
Food W: Sinclair
TServ W: Eich's Truck Repair & Service
ATM W: Texaco
Parks W: Lake Herman State Park (24 Miles)
Other W: South Dakota State Museum

104 Trent

(103) Parking Area (Southbound)

(102) Parking Area (Northbound)

98 Dell Rapids, Chester

94 Lyons, Baltic, Colton

86 Renner, Crooks

84B Jct. I-90 West

84A Jct. I-90 East

83 SD West Airport, 60th St. North
TServ E: Holcomb Freightliner Inc.

81 Arena & Convention Center, Russell St. (Low Clearance-15ft 4in)
Gas E: Amoco(*, CW)
Food E: Best Western, Brimark Inn, Rollin' Pin Family Dining
Lodg E: Best Western, Brimark Inn, Kelly Inn, Motel 6, Northwestern Ramkota Inn
AServ E: Sioux Brake & Equipment
RVCamp E: Schaap's Traveland
Other E: Highway Patrol

79 SD 42, 12th St, Fairgrounds
FStop W: Cenex(*, LP, SCALES)
Gas E: Amoco(*) (Casino)
W: Citgo(*)
Food E: Chris' Grill & Restaurant, Wendy's
W: Hardee's, Victory Lane Homecooked Meal
Lodg E: Ramada Limited
W: Sunset Motel
AServ E: Automated Systems, K-Mart, Kent's, Saturn of Sioux Falls, Terry Schulte NAPA, Chev, Subaru, Mitsubishi
W: City Glass, Select Motors, Sioux Falls Tire
TServ W: Wheelco Brake & Fruehaus
RVCamp W: Tower Campground, Weeg RV & Mobile Park
Med E: ✚ Hospital
ATM E: Amoco (Casino)
Parks E: Sioux River Waterslide Park
Other E: K-Mart, Sioux River Amusement Park
W: Great Plains Zoo & Museum (1 Mile), USS South Dakota Battleship Memorial (1 Mile)

78 26th St
Lodg E: Hampton Inn
W: MainStay Suites

77 41st St

EXIT SOUTH DAKOTA

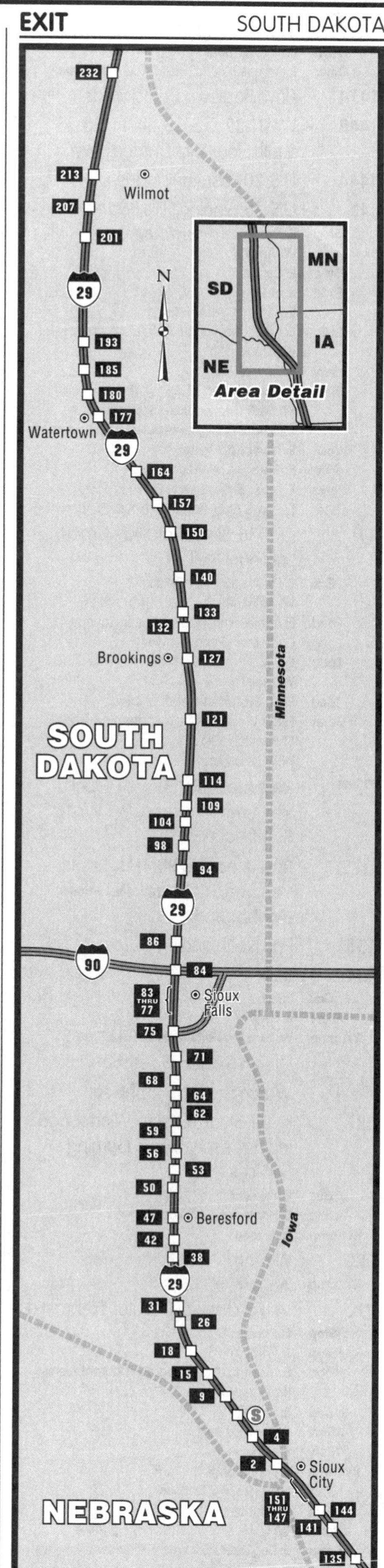

EXIT SOUTH DAKOTA

Gas E: Amoco(*, CW)
W: Texaco(*, D, LP)
Food E: Arby's, Carlos O'Kelly's Mexican Cafe, Chi Chi's Mexican Restaurant, Embers, Fryn' Pan, KFC, McDonald's, Pizza Hut, Red Lobster, T.G.I. Friday's, Taco Bell, Wendy's
W: Burger King, Denny's, Denucci's Pizza, Godfather's Pizza, Perkins Family Restaurant
Lodg E: Best Western, Comfort Suites Hotel, Empire Inn, Fairfield Inn by Marriott, Microtel Inn & Suites, Radisson Inn, Residence Inn, Super 8
W: AmericInn, Budgetel Inn, Days Inn, Select Inn
AServ E: Abra Auto Body & Glass, Batteries Plus, Kennedy Transmission, Mazda BMW, Sam's Club, Sioux Falls Ford
ATM E: BankFirst, Valley Bank
Parks E: Falls Park
Other E: Barnes & Noble Booksellers, Econo Foods, Fast Car Wash(CW), Petco Supplies & Fish, Sam's Club, Sunshine Supermarket, The Empire Mall, Wal-Mart(RX)

75 Jct. I-229

73 Tea
TStop E: Texaco(*)
Food E: Pat's Steakhouse
AServ E: Kohler Bros Auto, Midwest Tire & Muffler, Inc.
W: Auto Check
RVCamp W: Red Barn Campground (1 Mile)
Other W: Antique Mall

71 Tea, Harrisburg
AServ E: Lund
TServ E: Lund
RVCamp W: Red Barn RV Park (1.5 Miles)

68 Parker

64 SD 44, Worthing, Lennox
AServ W: Southtown Chev, Pont, Buick

62 U.S. 18 East, Canton (Low Clearance Under Bride 14ft.7in)
FStop E: Phillips 66(*)
Lodg E: Charlie's Motel
ATM E: Phillips 66

59 U.S. 18 West, Davis, Hurley

56 Fairview
Parks E: Newton Hills State Park (12 Miles)

53 Viborg

50 Centerville, Hudson

47 SD 46, Irene, Beresford; Hawarden, IA; Ft. Randall Dam
TStop W: Cenex(*, LP)
FStop E: Sinclair(*) (Casino)
Gas E: Ampride(*), Cenex(*)
Food E: Bert's Lounge, Emily's Family Restaurant, Hot Stuffed Pizza (Cenex), The Good Times Pizza & Pub
W: Truck Town Cafe (Cenex)
Lodg E: Crossroad's Motel, Starlite Motel
AServ E: Ampride, Dan Cotton Chevrolet, Jet Service Center
TServ W: Cenex
TWash W: Cenex
RVCamp E: Windmill RV Campground (Laundry Facilities, .5 Miles)
ATM E: Cenex, Jubilee Foods Supermarket, Sinclair (Casino)
Other E: Great American Car Wash(CW), Jubilee Foods Supermarket

42 Alcester, Wakonda

(41) Parking Area (Southbound)

38 Volin

Bold red print shows RV & Bus parking available or nearby

EXIT SOUTH DAKOTA/IOWA

Parks E: Union County State Park (1.5 Miles)

31 SD 48, Spink, Akron

26 SD 50, Vermillion, Yankton (RR, Phones, Picnic)
FStop W: Conoco(*)
Other E: State Police
W: Shrine Music Museum (7 Miles)

18 Elk Point, Burbank
Gas E: Amoco(*, LP, CW), Phillips 66(*)
Food E: Cody's Homestead Steakhouse Lounge & Cafe, Dairy Queen
Lodg E: HomeTown Inn
ATM E: Amoco

15 Bus. Loop I-29, Elk Point

9 SD105, Jefferson
FStop E: Amoco(*)
ATM E: Amoco

4 McCook
RVCamp W: Sioux City North KOA Campground (.75 Miles)

(3) Weigh Station (Northbound)

2 SD 105N, North Sioux City
FStop E: Ampride(*)
Gas E: Amoco(*)
W: Casey's General Store(*), Citgo(*, CW)
Food E: Ampride, Bakery Outlet, McDonald's, Pronto Hot Fresh Pizza (Amoco), Taco John's
W: Homemade Pizza To Go (Casey's General Store), Taco Bell (Citgo), Tacos To Go (Casey's General Store)
Lodg W: Apple Inn, Comfort Inn, Hampton Inn, Super 8
RVCamp W: Cott's Campground
ATM E: Amoco
Other E: Outpost Optical, US Post Office

1 Dakota Dunes
Gas W: Citgo(*, D, LP, CW)
Food W: Chix Chicken Station (Citgo), Hot Stuffed Pizza (Citgo), The First Edition II (Beef & Seafood)
Lodg W: Country Inn & Suites
ATM W: First Financial Bank

↑SOUTH DAKOTA

↓IOWA

151 IA 12 North, Riverside Boulevard

(149) Rest Area (RR, Phones, Picnic, Vending)

149 Hamilton Boulevard, Welcome Center
Gas E: Conoco(*, CW, 24)
Food E: Horizon Restaurant
W: Johnny's On the River
Lodg E: Holiday Inn
AServ E: Jiffy Lube
Parks W: Chris Larsen Jr Park

148 South Sioux City, NE; South U.S. 77, Bus. U.S. 20

147B Bus. U.S. 20, South IA 12, Bus. District (Reaccess Southbound Only, Difficult Reaccess)
Gas E: Amoco(*, CW), Holiday(*, LP)
Food E: Arby's, Hardee's, Perkins Family Restaurant, Riverboat Inn, Stage Coach Mexican, The Little Chicago Deli
Lodg E: Best Western, Hilton Inn, Riverboat Inn
AServ E: Chevrolet, Firestone, Midas Muffler, Speedy Lube
Med E: ✚ Central Medical Building

EXIT IOWA

ATM E: Norwest Bank
Other E: Antique Mall, US Post Office, WalGreen's

147A Floyd Boulevard, Stockyards

144B West I-29, U.S. 20, South U.S. 75, South Sioux City (Divided Hwy)

144A U.S. 20 East, Fort Dodge

143 U.S. 75, Singing Hills Blvd
TStop E: Texaco(*, SCALES) (Lodging)
W: Amoco(*, SCALES)
FStop E: Cennex(*)
Food E: McDonald's
W: Amoco, Wendy's
Lodg E: AmericInn, Budgetel Motel, Days Inn
W: Amoco
AServ E: Sam's Club
TServ E: Texaco(SCALES) (Lodging), Thermo-King
W: Bridgestone, Diesel Specialties, International, Kenworth, Peterbilt Dealer, Volvo
TWash E: Texaco (Lodging)
ATM E: Texaco (Lodging)
Parks E: Lewis & Clark State Park
Other E: Sam's Club, Sargeant Floyd Monument

141 CR D38, Sioux Gateway Airport, Sargeant Bluff
Gas E: Phillips 66(*, D, CW), Texaco(*, D, LP)
W: Amoco(*, D, LP)
Food E: Aggies Smoked BBQ, Cheers Lounge, Godfather's Pizza, Subway
Lodg E: Rath Inn
W: Motel 6
Med E: ✚ Grandview Medical Clinic
Other E: Car Wash, Mrs C's Laundromat, Nissen Chiropractic Clinic
W: Air Museum

(139) Rest Area (RR, Phones, Picnic, Vending, RV Dump, Pet Walk; Southbound)

(139) Rest Area (RR, Phones, Picnic, Vending, RV Dump, Pet Walk; Northbound)

135 Port Neal Landing

134 Salix
Gas E: Citgo(*)
AServ E: Citgo
RVCamp W: Bigelow Park-Brown's Lake (2 Miles)

(132) Weigh Station (Southbound)

(132) Weigh Station (Northbound)

127 IA 141, Sloan, Casino, Winnebago Indian Reservation & Gaming Services
Gas E: Texaco(*, D)
Lodg E: Homestead Inn, Rodeway Inn
RVCamp E: Texaco

120 Whiting
RVCamp W: Camping

112 IA 175, Oanwa; Decatur, Nebraska
TStop E: Conoco(*)
FStop E: Phillips 66(*)
Food E: McDonald's, Michael's Restaurant, Oehler Brothers, Subway (Phillips 66)
Lodg E: Super 8
AServ E: Don's Exhaust
TServ E: Conoco
RVCamp E: Interchange RV Park
Med E: ✚ Hospital (2 Miles)
ATM E: Conoco
Parks W: Lewis & Clark State Park (2 Miles)
Other E: Dug Dale's Car Wash(CW), Onawa Antiques, Pamida Grocery
W: Indian Reservation, Keel Boat Exhibit

EXIT IOWA

(109) Rest Area (RR, Phones, Picnic, RV Dump; Southbound)

(109) Rest Area (RR, Phones, Picnic, RV Dump; Northbound)

105 CR E 60, Blenco

95 IA 301, Little Sioux
RVCamp W: Woodland Campground

(92) Rest Area-Parking Only (Southbound)

(92) Rest Area-Parking Area (Northbound)

89 IA 127, Mondamin

82 IA 300, CR F50, Modale

(80) Rest Area (RR, Phones, Picnic, Grills, RV Dump; Southbound)

(79) Rest Area (RR, Phones, Picnic, Grills, RV Dump; Northbound)

75 U.S. 30, Missouri Valley, Blair NE
FStop E: Texaco(*)
Gas E: Phillips 66(*, CW)
W: Amoco(*, D), Conoco(*)
Food E: McDonald's, Subway, Tailor Made Pizza & Subs (Texaco)
W: Burger King(PLAY), Copper Kettle (Conoco), Oehler Bros
Lodg W: Days Inn, Rath Inn, Super 8
AServ E: Bob Anderson Ford Mercury
W: A & G Auto And Truck Repair, Ratigan Chev, Pont, Olds, Buick, Dodge, Jeep, Geo
TServ W: A & G Auto And Truck Repair
Med E: ✚ Hospital (2 Miles)
ATM E: Texaco
Other W: De Soto Refuge, May West Antiques Crafts & Gifts, Steamboat Exhibit

(74) Weigh Station (Southbound)

(73) Weigh Station (Northbound)

72 IA 362, Loveland, State Park, Weigh Station
FStop E: Conoco(*)

71 Jct. I-680 East, Des Moines

66 Honey Creek
FStop W: Phillips 66(*, LP)
Food W: Iowa Feed & Grain Company (Phillips 66)
RVCamp W: Honey Creek Campground (.5 Miles)

61B Jct. I-680 West, North Omaha

61A IA 988 East, Crescent

56 IA 192 South, Bus. District, Council Bluffs (Southbound, Left Exit)

55 North 25th St.
Gas E: No Name(*), Pump-N-Munch Too(*), Sinclair(*, 24)
Food E: The Dairy Fair
Lodg E: Garden Inn
AServ E: Steffes Motor Sales & Service
Other E: Car Wash(CW)

54B North 35th St.

54A G. Ave. (Southbound)

53B Jct. I-480 West, US 6, Omaha (Left Exit Westbound)

53A Riverboat Casino, 9th Ave, Harvey's Blvd.
Gas E: Phillips 66(*), Texaco(*, CW), Total(*)

Bold red print shows RV & Bus parking available or nearby

EXIT	IOWA
Food	E: Mighty Mo Subs (Total)
	W: Harvey's Casino Hotel
Lodg	E: Days Inn
	W: Harvey's Casino Hotel
RVCamp	W: **Friendship Park (.5 Miles)**
52	Riverboat Casino, Nebraska Ave., Dog Track Casino
Gas	E: Conoco[*, D, LP, CW]
Food	E: Conoco
	W: Holiday Inn
Lodg	E: Comfort Suites Hotel
	W: Ameristar Casino & Lodging, Holiday Inn
51	Jct. I-80W. Omaha

Note: I-29 runs concurrent below with I-80. Numbering follows I-80.

EXIT	IOWA
1B	**South 24th St, Council Bluffs, Welcome Center**
TStop	E: **Pilot**[*, SCALES], **Texaco**[*]
Gas	E: Amoco[CW], Sinclair[*]
Food	E: **Arby's (Pilot TS)**, **Burger King (Texaco TS)**, Happy Chef, Happy Chef Restaurant, Leisure Lounge, **TJ Cinnamon's (Pilot TS)**
Lodg	E: **Best Western**, **Interstate Inn**, **Super 8**
AServ	E: Amoco, **Goodyear**
TServ	E: **Boyer's Diesel**, **Goodyear**, **Peterbilt**, **Stoughton Trailers**
TWash	E: **Texaco**
ATM	E: **Pilot**, **Texaco**
Other	E: **Bluff Run Casino**, Hops CB & Stereo
	S: Western Historic Trail Ctr & Welcome Ctr
3	IA 192, Council Bluffs, Lake Manawa
TStop	S: **Travel Centers of America**[*, D, LP, K, SCALES, 24] **(Country Pride Restaurant)**
Gas	S: Total[*]
Food	S: Burger King, Cracker Barrel - Settle Inn, Dairy Queen, Golden Corral Family Steakhouse, Hardee's, Long John Silver, McDonald's[PLAY], Perkin's Family Restaurant, Red Lobster, Sam's Club[*], Subway, Taco Bell, **Travel Centers of America (Country Pride Restaurant)**
Lodg	S: Cracker Barrel - Settle Inn, Econo Lodge, Fairfield Inn, Motel 6
AServ	S: Dodge Bluff Dodge, Edwards-O'Neill Hyundai, Edwards-O'Neill Old Cadillac and Subaru, Lake Manawa Nissan, McMullen Ford, Rhoden Pontiac Buick GMC Trucks Suzuki, Sam's Club, Toyota Bluff Lincoln-Mercury, **Wal-Mart**[24, RX]
TServ	S: **Great Dane Trailers/Jim Hawk Truck Trailers**, **Larry's Diesel Truck and CB Radio**[D], **Travel Centers of America**[SCALES, 24] **(Country Pride Restaurant)**, **V&Y Truck and Trailer Service**[24]
TWash	S: **Larry's Diesel Truck and CB Radio**
ATM	S: Total, **Travel Centers of America (Country Pride Restaurant)**, US Bank
Other	S: Sam's Club, **Wal-Mart**[RX]
4	Jct I-80 East, Des Moines, I-29 South Kansas City

Note: I-29 runs concurrent above with I-80. Numbering follows I-80.

EXIT	IOWA
48	Jct. I-80 East, Des Moines; I-29, I-80 West, Council Bluffs, Omaha
47	U.S. 275, IA 92, Lake Manawa
42	IA 370, Bellevue
TServ	W: **Vander Haag's**
(37)	**Rest Area (RR, Phones, Picnic, RV Dump; Northbound)**
(37)	**Rest Area (RR, Phones, Picnic, RV Dump; Southbound)**

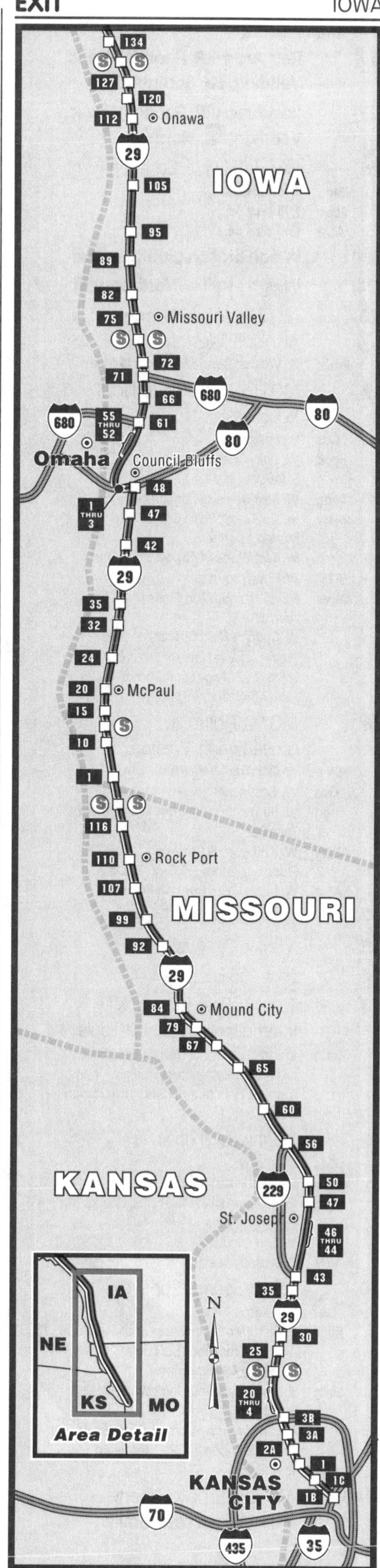

EXIT	IOWA/MISSOURI
35	U.S. 34 East, Glenwood, Red Oak
FStop	W: **Amoco**[*]
Food	W: **Bluff View Cafe (Amoco)**
Lodg	W: Bluff View Motel
AServ	W: **Napa Auto (Amoco)**
Other	W: Antiques
32	U.S. 34 West, Plattsmouth, Pacific Jct
24	CR L31, Bartlett, Tabor
20	IA 145, McPaul, Thurman, Forney Lake
15	CR J26, Percival
(11)	**Weigh Station (Northbound)**
10	IA 2, Sidney, Nebr City
Parks	E: **Waubonsie State Park (5 Miles)**
3	IA192, Lake Manawa
RVCamp	S: **Tomes Country Club Acres (1.5 Miles)**
1	IA 333, Hamburg
Gas	W: Citgo[*, D]
Med	E: **+ Hospital**

↑IOWA

↓MISSOURI

EXIT	IOWA/MISSOURI
(121)	**Weigh Station (Southbound)**
(121)	**Weigh Station (Northbound)**
116	CR A & B, Watson
AServ	E: **Don's Auto & Truck Salvage**
TServ	E: **Don's Auto & Truck Salvage**
110	U.S. 136, Rock Port, Phelps City
TStop	W: **Amoco**[*, CW, SCALES], **Phillips 66**[*, SCALES]
FStop	E: **Conoco**[*]
Gas	E: Texaco[*, D, LP]
Food	E: **Hardee's (Conoco)**
	W: **Cinnamon Street Bakery (Amoco TS)**, **Hot Stuffed Pizza (Amoco TS)**, **McDonald's**, **Smash Hit Subs (Amoco TS)**, **Trails End Restaurant (Phillips 66)**
Lodg	E: Rockport Inn
	W: Oak Grove Inn
AServ	W: **Amoco**
TServ	W: **Amoco**[SCALES]
TWash	W: **Amoco**[CW]
RVCamp	W: **KOA Campgrounds (.5 Miles)**
ATM	W: **Amoco TS**, **Phillips 66**
(110)	**Rest Area (RR, Phones, Picnic, Vending, P; Southbound)**
107	MO 111, Langdon, Rock Port
Lodg	W: Elk Motel
AServ	W: Auto Image
99	CR W, Corning
FStop	E: **Citgo**[*]
AServ	E: **Citgo**
92	U.S. 59, Craig, Fairfax
84	MO 118, Mound City, Bigelow
Gas	E: Conoco[*], Phillips 66[*, D, LP, K], Total[*, D]
Food	E: Breadeaux Pisa, **Hardee's**, Phillips 66, Quacker's
AServ	E: Laucamper Motors, Phillips 66
ATM	E: Cameron Savings & Loan
Other	E: Dancing Horse Antiques, Roger's Pharmacy[RX], Thomas Market, Wash-N-Dry Laundromat
(81)	**Rest Area (RR, Phones, Picnic, Vending, P; Northbound)**
(81)	**Rest Area (RR, Phones, Picnic,**

Bold red print shows RV & Bus parking available or nearby

EXIT		MISSOURI
		Vending, P; Southbound)
79		U.S. 159, Rulo
	TStop	E: Phillips 66(*, RV DUMP, SCALES)
	Lodg	E: Phillips 66
	AServ	E: Squaw Creek Plaza
	TServ	E: Phillips 66(SCALES), Squaw Creek Plaza
	TWash	E: Phillips 66
	ATM	E: Phillips 66
	Other	W: Squaw Creek National Wildlife Refuge
75		U.S. 59, Oregon
67		U.S. 59 North, Oregon
65		U.S. 59, Fillmore, CR RA
60		CR CC, Hwy K, Amazonia
56B		Jct. I-229 South, St. Joseph
56A		U.S. 71, U.S. 59 North, Maryville
53		U.S. 59, Bus. U.S. 71, Savannah, St. Joseph
	TServ	E: St Joseph Diesel, Inc
	RVCamp	E: AOK Campground (.75 Miles), M & L Lucky See Lake, Walnut Grove Camping
	Other	W: Jesse James Antique Mall
50		U.S. 169, St. Joseph, King City
47		MO 6, Frederick Blvd., Clarksdale
	Gas	E: Conoco(*, LP) W: Amoco(*, CW), Texaco(*, D), Total(*, D)
	Food	E: Country Kitchen, Stan's Golden Grill W: Applebee's, Burger King, Carlos O'Kelly's Mexican, Denny's, Perkins, Red Lobster, Sizzler Steak House, The Ground Round, Wyatt's Cafeteria
	Lodg	E: Days Inn, Drury Inn W: Budget Inn, Hampton Inn, Pony Express Motel, Ramada Inn, Super 8
	AServ	W: Anderson Ford, Firestone Tire & Auto, Freeway Chevrolet, Midas, Parts America, Texaco
	ATM	E: Provident Bank W: First Bank CBC, North American Savings Bank, Texaco, Total
	Other	W: Osco Drugs, Tourist Info.
46AB		U.S. 36, St. Joseph, Cameron (Difficult Reaccess)
	RVCamp	W: Beacon RV Park (.9 Miles)
44		Bus. Loop I-29, U.S. 169, St. Joseph, Gower
	TStop	W: Texaco(*, SCALES)
	Gas	E: King(*, LP)
	Food	E: Kathy's Kafe, St. Joe Prime Meat Co., Subway W: McDonald's(PLAY)
	Lodg	E: Best Western
	TServ	E: Dave's Diesel Service W: Texaco(SCALES)
	Other	E: Simply Clean Car & Truck Wash, Suburban Propane(LP)
43		Jct. I-229, Downtown St. Joseph
35		CR DD, Faucett
	TStop	W: Farris Truckstop(*, LP, K, SCALES)
	Food	W: Subway (Farris TStop)
	Lodg	W: Farris Truckstop
	TServ	W: Farris Truckstop(SCALES)
	TWash	W: Farris Truckstop
	ATM	W: UMB Bank
30		Hwy. Z, Hwy. H, Dearborn, New Market
	FStop	E: Conoco(*)

EXIT		MISSOURI
	ATM	E: Conoco
(27)		**Rest Area (RR, Phones, Picnic, Vending, P; Southbound)**
(27)		**Rest Area (RR, Phones, Picnic, Vending, P; Northbound)**
25		Hwy. U, Hwy. E, Camden Point
	FStop	E: Phillips 66(*)
	Food	E: Phillips 66
	ATM	E: Phillips 66
(24)		**Weigh Station (Southbound)**
(24)		**Weigh Station (Northbound)**
20		MO 273, MO 371 North, Atchison, Weston
	Parks	W: Weston Bend State Park (5 Miles)
19		MO HH, Platte City (Difficult Reaccess)
	Gas	W: Phillips 66
	Food	W: Dairy Queen, Red Dragon 2 Chinese, Sidekick's
	Lodg	W: Best Western, Comfort Inn
	AServ	W: Car Quest, Platte City Ford, Tony Marten's Dodge
	RVCamp	W: Best Western Airport Inn RV Park
	ATM	W: Liberty Savings
	Other	E: I-29 Antique Mall, Platte Falls Wildlife Area W: Country Mart Grocery, Eckerd Pharmacy, Eye Care Midwest, IGA Food Store, The Village Laundromat, Tru Value Hardware(LP), US Post Office
18		MO 92, Platte City, Leavenworth, Weston
	FStop	W: QuikTrip(*, SCALES, 24)
	Gas	W: Gas Mart(*)
	Food	W: Burger King, McDonald's, Subway, Taco Bell
	AServ	W: Kwik Lube & Car Wash, Saturn Of Platte City, Sonny Hill GMC Trucks
	ATM	W: Platte Valley Bank, QuikTrip
17		Jct. I-435 South , Topeka
15		Mexico City Ave.
14		Jct. I-435 East
13		To I-435 East, Kansas City International Airport St. Louis
	Lodg	E: Best Western, Comfort Suites Hotel, Extended Stay America, Fairfield Inn by Marriott, Holiday Inn, Wyndham Garden Hotel
12		Northwest 112th St
	Gas	E: Amoco(*)
	Food	E: Hilton Hotel
	Lodg	E: Hampton Inn, Hilton Hotel, Holiday Inn Express W: Econolodge
	ATM	E: Bank Of Weston
10		Tiffany Springs Parkway
	Gas	E: Texaco(*, D, CW)
	Food	E: Deli & More, Final Approach Pub, Jade Garden, Smokebox BBQ Cafe W: Cracker Barrel
	Lodg	E: Embassy Suites, Homewood Suites Hotel W: Courtyard by Marriott, Drury Inn & Suites, Ramada Inn, Residence Inn
	ATM	E: Texaco
9AB		MO 152, Topeka, Liberty (Difficult Reaccess, Limited Access Hwy)

EXIT		MISSOURI
8		Northwest Barry Road
	Gas	E: Total(*, D, LP, CW) W: Phillips 66(*, CW), QuikTrip(*, CW)
	Food	E: 54th Street Grill, Applebee's, Bagel & Bagel, Boston Market Restaurant, Carlito's Mexican, Chili's, China Wok, Lamar's Donuts, Lone Star Steakhouse, On The Border Mexican, Subway, Tres Hombres Mexican, Wendy's, Winstead's, Woids W: Barry's BBQ, Daylight Donuts, Long John Silver, McDonald's, Minsky's Pizza, Outback Steakhouse, Rainbow Restaurant
	Lodg	W: Motel 6, Super 8
	Med	E: ✚ St. Luke's Northland Hospital
	ATM	E: Food 4 Less, Mercantile Bank W: UMB Bank
	Other	E: Animal Clinic, Barry Woods Crossing, Eckerd Drugs(24), Food 4 Less, Russell Stover Candy, The Boardwalk Square
6		Northwest 72nd St, Platte Woods
	Gas	E: Sinclair(D) W: Quik Trip(*)
	Food	W: KFC, PaPa John's Pizza, Pizza Hut
	AServ	E: Sinclair
	Other	E: Animal Hospital W: K-Mart
5		MO 45 North, Northwest 64th St.
	Gas	W: Texaco(*, CW)
	Food	W: Hen House Grocery Store(RX), IHOP, Johnny O'Quigley's, Little Caesars Pizza, McDonald's, Paradise Grill, Pete's Inn, Pizza Hut
	Med	W: ✚ Parkville Primary Care
	ATM	W: Hen House Grocery Store, Midland Bank
	Other	W: By The Book Book Store, Cat Clinic, Colonial Bakery Store, Eckerd Pharmacy, Eye Care, Hen House Grocery Store(RX), Lasus, Osco Drugs(RX)
4		Northwest 56th Street
3C		CR.A, Riverside (Southbound, Difficult Reaccess)
3B		Jct. I-635 South, Kansas, North I-29, U.S. 71, St. Joseph (Left Exit)
3A		County Road AA, Waukomis Drive (Northbound)
2A		U.S. 169 North, Smithville (Difficult Reaccess, Limited Access Hwy)
1		U.S. 69, Vivion Road (Southbound)
	Food	E: Lamar's Donuts
	AServ	E: Courtsey Chevrolet, Cadillac, Jack Miller Chrysler Plymouth, Northtown Mercury Lincoln, Northtown Mitibushi
	Other	E: Price Chopper Supermarket, Venture Discount Store
1D		MO 283S, Oak Trfwy, Vivion St.
	AServ	E: Courtesy Chevrolet, Jack Miller Chrysler Plymouth
1C		Gladston, North Oak Trfwy (Reaccess Southbound Only, Difficult Reaccess)
	Food	E: Deli Depot, Lemar's Donuts
	AServ	E: Northtown Lincoln, Mercury, Volkswagon
	ATM	E: Mercantile Bank
	Other	E: Price Chopper Supermarket
1B		Jct. I-35 North, Des Moines (Southbound)
1A		Davidson Road

↑MISSOURI

Begin I-29

Bold red print shows RV & Bus parking available or nearby

EXIT	TEXAS

Begin I-30

↓TEXAS

Exit **(1)** Jct. I-20 West, Weatherford, Abilene (Westbound)

1B Linkcrest Dr.
- **FStop** **S:** **Mobil(*)**
- **Gas** **S:** Chevron(*, D), Fina(*, D), Phillips 66(*), Wheel in West(*)
- **Food** **S:** Joseifina's Mex Cafe
- **ATM** **S:** Fina

2 East Spur 580

3 RM2871, Chapel Creek Blvd.
- **Other** **S:** Eagle Quest Golf Center

5A Alemeda St. (Eastbound)

5BC Junction I-820

6 Las Vegas Trail
- **Gas** **N:** Chevron(*, CW), Highway Oil
  S: Citgo(*), Diamond Shamrock(*), Exxon(*, CW), Texaco(*, D, CW)
- **Food** **N:** Amigos Tex-Mex, McDonald's (Chevron), Waffle House
  S: Denny's, Donut Deli, Vegas Grill
- **Lodg** **N:** DAYS INN Days Inn
  S: Comfort Inn, Motel 6, TraveLodge Suites
- **AServ** **S:** Chief Auto Parts, Garry McKinney KIA, Subaru
- **ATM** **S:** Exxon, Vegas Food Store
- **Other** **N:** **Ridgmar Animal Hospital**
  S: **E-Z Wash Laundry**, Vegas Food Store

7A Cherry Lane
- **Gas** **N:** Conoco(*, D), Texaco(*)
- **Food** **N:** Chuck E Cheese's Pizza, Ci Ci's Pizza, IHOP(24) (La Quinta Inn), Luby's Cafeteria, Papa John's Pizza, Ryan's Steakhouse, Subway, Wendy's
- **Lodg** **N:** La Quinta Inn, Super 8
  S: Hampton Inn
- **AServ** **N:** **Big K-Mart(RX)**, Hi/Lo Auto Supply, Texas Motors Ford Dealership
- **Other** **N:** **Big K-Mart(RX)**, **Home Depot**, Louis DelHomme Marine, **Toys R Us**
  S: Pak 'N' Mail, **Target**

7B TX183, Spur 341, NAS Ft. Worth, JRB, Green Oaks Rd. (Difficult Reaccess)
- **Food** **N:** Applebee's, Blimpie Subs & Salads, TGI Fridays
- **Lodg** **S:** Best Western
- **AServ** **N:** National Tire and Battery, Sam's Club (with Michelin Tire and Battery)
  S: Grubbs Infinity, Nissan, Oldsmobile, and GM, West Loop Mitsubishi
- **ATM** **N:** **Albertson's Grocery Store(LP, 24, RX) (NationsBank ATM)**
- **Other** **N:** **Albertson's Grocery Store(RX) (NationsBank ATM)**, **Ridgmar Mall**, Sam's Club (with Michelin Tire and Battery), U-Haul
  S: Rollerland Skate

8A Green Oaks Rd. (Westbound, If you are traveling west on I-30 you will see this exit, but if you are going east you have to use exit 7B to get to Green Oaks Rd)
- **Food** **N:** Applebee's, Blimpie Subs & Salads, TGI Friday's
- **AServ** **N:** NTB
- **ATM** **N:** **Albertson's G(RX)**
- **Other** **N:** **Albertson's G(RX)**, Joshua's Christian Bookstore, Office Depot, Parcel Plus

8B Ridgmar Blvd, Ridglea Ave.
- **Gas** **N:** Texaco(*)
- **ATM** **N:** Texas Bank

8C Green Oaks Rd
- **Food** **N:** Applebee's, T.G.I. Friday's
  S: Chinese Cuisine Buffet, Tommy's Hamburgers
- **AServ** **N:** National Tire and Battery, Sear's Auto Care
- **Other** **N:** **Albertson's Grocery**, **Joshua's Book Store**, **Nieman Marcus**, **Ridgmar Mall**

8D TX183S (Westbound, This exit is westbound only, but if you are eastbound you get to TX183 by taking 7B)
- **Lodg** **S:** Best Western

9A Bryant-Irvin Rd.
- **Gas** **S:** Texaco(*, LP)

9B U.S. 377S, Camp Bowie Blvd, Horne St
- **Gas** **S:** Citgo(*), Fina(*, D)
- **Food** **N:** Uncle Julio's
  S: Dunkin Donuts, Edmondson's Fried Chicken, Scoops N Cakes, Subway, Szechuan Restaurant (Chinese), Taco Bueno, Tejano Cafe
- **AServ** **S:** Just Brakes
- **Med** **S:** **+ Camp Bowie Medical Center**
- **ATM** **S:** Citgo, Comerica Bank
- **Other** **S:** **Camp Bowie Animal Clinic**

10 Hulen St.

11B Montgomery St.
- **Gas** **N:** Citgo(*)
  S: Texaco(*, D, CW)
- **Food** **N:** Cafe Jazz, The Market On Montgomery St.
  S: Railhead Smokehouse, Whataburger
- **AServ** **N:** Eastman Automotive Service Garage
  S: Bob's Auto Supply
- **Other** **N:** **Kwik Wash Coin Laundry**

12A University Dr, City Parks
- **Gas** **S:** Conoco(*, D)
- **Food** **S:** Ol' South Pancake House, Romano's Macaroni Grill
- **Lodg** **S:** Fairfield Inn, Ramada Inn
- **RVCamp** **N:** **Fort Worth Midtown RV Park (1.25 Miles)**
- **Parks** **N:** **Ft. Worth Botanic Park**, **Trinity Park**

12B Rosedale St. (Eastbound, Reaccess Westbound Only)
- **Gas** **S:** Fina(*)
- **Med** **S:** **+ Hospital**
- **ATM** **S:** Fina

12C Forest Park Blvd
- **Food** **N:** Pappadeaux Seafood Kitchen, Pappasitos Cafe
- **ATM** **N:** Colonial Savings Bank

Exit **(13)** 15th Ave. (Difficult Reaccess)

13 Ballinger St, Summit Ave. (Difficult Reaccess)
- **Other** **N:** **Kay Pharmacy(RX)**

14 TX199, Henderson St. (Difficult Reaccess)
- **Gas** **N:** Chevron(*)
- **Food** **N:** Ambrosia Restaurant (Care-A-Lot-Inn), Domino's Pizza
- **Lodg** **N:** The Care-A-Lot-Inn
- **Med** **S:** **+ Hospital**
- **ATM** **N:** Bank of Commerce

Exit **(14)** Cherry St, Downtown (Eastbound, Left Exit Eastbound, Difficult Reaccess)
- **ATM** **N:** Bank One
- **Other** **N:** Fire Department

Exit **(14)** Commerce St.
- **Food** **N:** Bali Grill & Seafood Restaurant (Ramada Plaza Hotel), Rodeo's Steakhouse
- **Lodg** **N:** Park Central Hotel, Ramada Plaza Hotel
- **Other** **N:** Fort Worth Tarrant County Conv. Center

Exit **(14)** Commerce St, Downtown, Jones St.

14A Westbound: Junction I-35W, Denton, Waco Eastbound: I-35W, U.S. 377N, U.S. 287 N, I-35W South Waco

15AB Eastbound: U.S. 287, Loop TX 180, Lancaster Ave. Westbound: North I-35W, U.S. 287 Denton

16AB Riverside Dr. (Westbound)
- **Gas** **S:** Food Mart(*, D)
- **Food** **S:** Glady's Soul Food

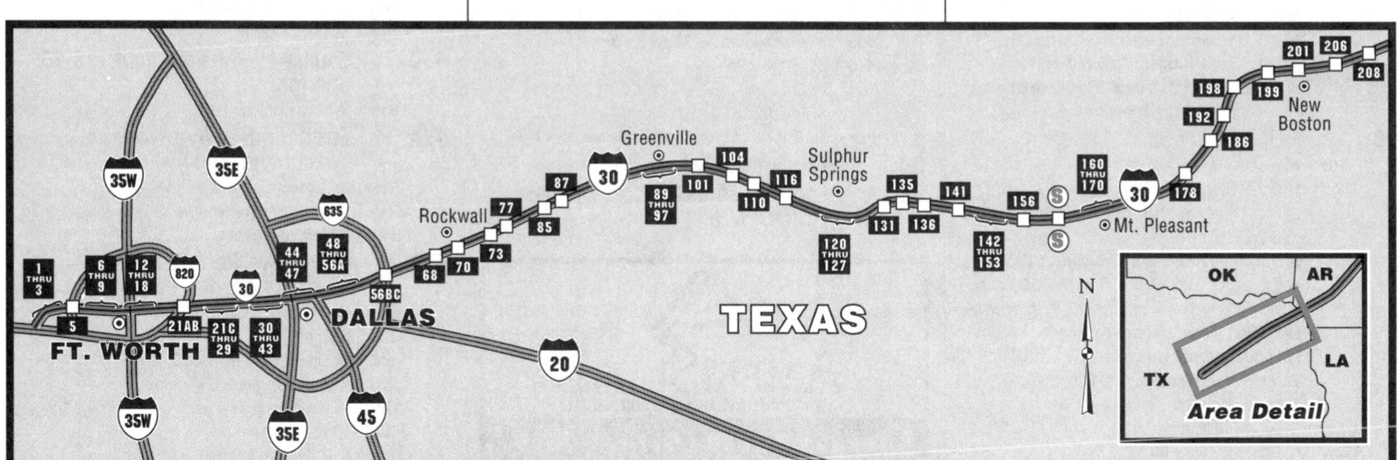

Bold red print shows RV & Bus parking available or nearby

EXIT TEXAS

Lodg **S:** Great Western Inn
AServ **N:** AB's Like New Used Parts, Continental Auto Salvage
ATM **S:** Food Mart
Other **S:** East Lancaster Animal Hospital, Heavenly Kleen Detail Shop

16C Beach St.
Lodg **S:** Comfort Inn, Holiday Inn
ATM **S:** Bank One

18 Oakland Blvd.
Gas **N:** Phillips 66(*, CW), Texaco(*, D, CW)
Food **N:** Alcatraz Cafe, Burger King, Taco Bell, Waffle House
Lodg **N:** Motel 6
AServ **N:** Texaco
ATM **N:** Taco Bell

19 Brentwood Stair Rd (Eastbound)
Gas **N:** Texaco(*)
S: Citgo(*), Texaco
Food **N:** Chuy's, Doughnuts, Italy Pasta and Pizza, Memphis Sizzin Wings, Rickshaw
S: A Taste of Europe, Lino's Mexican, Lombada Foodstore and Deli
AServ **S:** Texaco, Transmission Depot
ATM **N:** Woodhaven National Bank
Other **S:** Coin Car Wash, Fort Worth Municipal Golf Course

21AB Junction I-820

21C Bridgewood Dr.
Gas **N:** Mobil(*, CW)
S: Conoco(*)
Food **N:** Luby's Cafeteria, Subway
S: Catfish Cove, Whataburger(24)
AServ **N:** Mastercare Car Service (Firestone)
ATM **N:** **Kroger Supermarket**(RX)
S: Bank of America
Other **N:** **Kroger Supermarket**(RX), Pack Optical, **Woodhaven Pet Clinic**
S: Mrs. Baird's Bread Store, Optometrist

23 Cooks Lane

24 Eastchase Pkwy.
Gas **S:** Chevron(*, CW, 24), Texaco(*, CW)
Food **S:** IHOP, McDonald's(PLAY), Schlotzsky's Deli, Subway, Taco Bell, Wendy's, Whataburger
AServ **N:** Eastchase Village Carmax
ATM **S:** Texaco
Other **S:** **Crown Books**, **PetsMart**, **Target**, Toys R Us, United Artist Theater

26 Fielder Rd

27 Lamar Blvd, Cooper St
Gas **N:** Mobil(*, CW)
S: Citgo(*), Texaco(*, CW, 24)
Food **N:** Hong Kongo, Jack-in-the-Box, Subway
S: Burger King(PLAY)
AServ **N:** Kwik Kar Lube & Tune
ATM **N:** Bank One, Mobil
S: Citgo, Security Bank, Texaco
Other **N:** ACE Hardware, Crossroad's Animal Clinics, **Eckerd Drugs**, **Kroger Supermarket**(24)
S: **Arlington North Animal Clinic**, **Coin Laundry (Cooper Minimart)**, Cooper Minimart

28 TX157, Collins St.
Gas **N:** Mobil(*, LP, CW), Shell(*, CW)
Food **N:** Bagel Company, Boston Market Restaurant, La Madeleine French Bakery and Cafe, Piccolo Mondo, Waffle House
S: Black Eyed Pea, Chili's, Coffee Haus, Colter's Barbecue, Country Kitchen, Cozy Mel's, El Chico, French Bakery, Gas Pipe Restaurant, Harrigan's Grill & Bar, Hooter's, Joe's Crab Shack, Pappadeaux Seafood Kitchen, Portofino Restaurant, TGI Friday's, Taco Buenos, Taco Cabana, Tony Roma's, Wendy's
Lodg **S:** Courtyard by Marriott
AServ **N:** Don Davis Ford, Mercury, Lincoln, Don Davis Mitsubishi, Ford, Merc., Moritz Cadillac, BMW, Pennzoil Oil Change, Shell
Other **N:** Kodak Photo 1, **Six Flags Over Texas**, **Wet N' Wild Water Park**
S: Barnes & Noble Booksellers, **Drug Emporium**(RX), Joshua's Christian Bookstore, Loew's Theaters

28B Nolan Ryan Expressway, The Ballpark In Arlington (Eastbound)
Food **S:** Cozumels, Joe's Crab Shack
Lodg **S:** Courtyard by Marriott, Marriot Hotel

29 Ballpark Way
Gas **S:** Fina(*, CW)
Food **N:** Romano's Macaroni Grill
S: On the Border Mexican Cafe, Texas Land & Cattle Steakhouse
Lodg **S:** Marriott, Rodeway Inn
ATM **N:** Bank Of America
Other **N:** Hurrican Harbor (Water Park)
S: Six Flags Over Texas, **The Ballpark at Arlington (Texas Rangers)**

30 TX360, Six Flags Dr, D/FW Airport
Gas **N:** Exxon(*, D)
S: Exxon(*, D), Texaco(*, CW), Texaco(*, D, CW), Total(*)
Food **N:** McDonald's
S: Bennigan's, Cheddar's, China City, Garden Palace Fresh Seafood and Lounge, Humperdinks, Luby's, Mariano's Mexican, McDonald's, Ninfa's, Owens Restaurant, Poncho's Mexican Buffet, Slamer's Neighbor-hood Sports Grill, Smoothie King, Steak & Ale, Subway
Lodg **N:** Radisson Suite Hotel
S: Amerisuites (see our ad this page), Budgetel Inn, La Quinta Inn, Ranger Inn Suites, Sleep Inn, Value Inn Motel
ATM **S:** Nationsbank, Total
Other **S:** Kwik Copy, **Six Flags Mall**, **Six Flags Over Texas**, **US Post Office**

32 NW19th St
Gas **N:** Diamond Shamrock(*, LP), Exxon
S: Fina(*, D), Mobil(*, CW)
Food **N:** Donuts, Mr. Jim's Pizza
S: Denny's (La Quinta Inn), Donut Palace, Long John Silver, McDonald's(PLAY), Pearl Chinese, Pizza Hut, Subway, Taco Bell, The Earl of Sandwich, Whataburger(24)
Lodg **S:** La Quinta Inn
ATM **N:** Diamond Shamrock
S: Fina, Norwest Bank
Other **S:** Car Wash(CW), L & K Carwash, North Grand Prarie Animal Clinic

34 Belt Line Rd
Gas **N:** Chevron(*, CW)
S: Diamond Shamrock(*, CW), Fina(*, D, CW), RaceTrac(*)
Food **N:** Chevron, Days Inn, Ramada Inn
S: Blimpie Subs & Salads (Fina), TCBY (Fina)
Lodg **N:** Days Inn, Motel 6, Ramada Inn
Med **S:** **+ Hospital**
ATM **N:** Chevron
S: RaceTrac
Other **N:** **Palace Of Wax**, **Ripley's Believe It or Not**

36 MacArthur Blvd.

38 Loop12 (Difficult Reaccess, Limited Access Hwy)

41 Hampton Rd South (Reaccess Westbound Only, Same Services as Exit 42)
Gas **S:** Exxon(*), Texaco(*, CW)
Food **S:** Dairy Queen, Jack In The Box, Luby's Cafeteria, Wendy's
Lodg **S:** Miramar Hotel
AServ **S:** Al's Auto Service (Goodyear)
ATM **S:** **Mineyard's Grocery Store**, Nationsbank
Other **S:** AutoZone, Charlies Laundry, Elrod's Cost-Plus Foods, **Mineyard's Grocery Store**

42 Hampton Rd, Westmoreland Rd. (Reaccess Westbound Only, Same services as exit 41)
Gas **S:** Exxon(*), Texaco(*, CW)
Food **S:** Dairy Queen, Jack-In-The-Box, Luby's Cafeteria, Pastry, Subway (Exxon), Wendy's
Lodg **S:** Miramar Hotel
AServ **S:** Al's Auto Service (Goodyear), Auto Zone, Santos Radiator Service
ATM **S:** **Minyard Supermarket**
Other **S:** Charlie's Laundry, Elrod's Cost-Plus Foods, **Minyard Supermarket**

43AB Sylvan Ave. (Westbound)
Gas **N:** Dairy Mart(*, D)
Food **N:** Pitt Grill, The Golf Club Bar and Grill
Lodg **N:** Alamo Plaza Hotel Courts, Budget Travel Inn Motel
AServ **N:** C & W Automatic Transmission Shop, Dallas County Auto Service, O.K. Auto Center, The Little Garage
Med **S:** **+ Hospital**
ATM **N:** Bank One
Other **N:** **U.S. Post Office**(24)

44A Westbound: I-35E North Denton, Ft. Worth; Eastbound: Beckley Ave (Reaccess Westbound Only)
Food **S:** Lone Star Donuts
AServ **N:** JR Turbyfill Inc., Oxendine Transmission, Reem Auto Garage
S: Drive Shaft King
TServ **N:** **Performance Truck Tires**
Med **S:** **+ Hospital**

44B I-35E South Waco, Industrial Blvd.

45 Junction I-35E North Denton, Commerce Street, Downtown (Eastbound)

45A Lamar St, Griffin St. (Eastbound, Difficult Reaccess)
Lodg **S:** Ramada Plaza Hotel

Exit **(45)** Ervay St. (Westbound, Difficult Reaccess)
Lodg **S:** Ambassador Hotel

46A Downtown Central Expressway (Left Exit Westbound)
Food **S:** McDonald's
Lodg **S:** Ambassador Hotel
Parks **S:** **Old City Park**

46B South I-45 Houston; North U.S. 75 Sherman
Food **S:** Macdonalds

47A Eastbound: 1st Ave, Fair Park Westbound: 2nd Ave.
Gas **S:** Texaco(*)
AServ **N:** McGregor Automotive
Parks **S:** **Fair Park (State Fair)**

47B Carroll Ave, Peak St, Haskell Ave. (Eastbound)
Gas **N:** Diamond Shamrock(*)
S: Fina(*)
Food **N:** Only The Name Fried Chicken
S: Joe's Burgers, Joe's Seafood
AServ **N:** Hercules Muffler and Radio Service, J & J Lantas
Other **S:** Rutherford Animal Clinic

Bold red print shows RV & Bus parking available or nearby

EXIT TEXAS

48C Peak St, Haskell Ave, Carroll Ave. (Westbound)
- **Gas** N: Diamond Shamrock(*)
- **Food** N: Eggroll Hut, Gracielas Bakery, Jilberto's Mexican, Taqueria Pinocho, The Only Name Fried Chicken Has Changed
- **AServ** N: Branch's Discount Auto Parts, Hamm's Discount Tire, Hercules Muffler & Radiator, J & J Llantas, Lonestar Auto Service

48A Eastbound: TX78, E. Grand Ave, Barry Ave, Munger Blvd. Westbound: Munger Blvd. (Reaccess Eastbound Only)
- **Food** S: Azteca Restaurant
- **AServ** S: Primos Garage
- **Other** S: F & D Auto Parts, Gator Wash(CW)

48B Eastbound: TX78, Winslow St, East Grand Ave. Westbound: Winslow St.
- **Gas** N: Citgo(*) (Super Seven Big Subs), Fina(*), Mobil(*), Texaco(*, D)
  S: Phillips 66(*), Shell(*)
- **Food** N: 3-Guys Chinese Food and Hamburgers, Brownie's Restaurant, Chucho's Mexican, Church's Chicken, Citgo (Super Seven Big Subs), El Taquito Cafe, La Acapulquena
- **AServ** N: Chief Auto Parts, Mobil, Pennzoil Oil Change
  S: Napa Auto
- **ATM** N: Comerica Bank
  S: Stop n Go (NationsBank)
- **Other** N: Chief Auto Parts, **Eckerd Pharmacy(RX)**, Fire Station, **Foodland Grocery(*)**, Swif Wash Coin Laundry, **Texas Foodland Grocery Store**
  S: Stop n Go (NationsBank)

49A Dolphin Rd.
- **Gas** N: Texaco(*)
- **Food** N: Hickory Roasted Chicken, Polo Bueno Hickory Roasted Chicken
- **Lodg** N: Eastern Hills Motel, Regency Motel, Welcome Inn
- **AServ** N: Freddie's Transmission Service, Ken's Muffler's and Shocks
- **ATM** N: Texaco
- **Other** N: Super Discount Food Mart(*)

49B Lawnview Ave, Samuell Blvd (Eastbound)
- **Lodg** S: Lawnview Motel
- **AServ** S: Al's Automotive, Bill King's Brake-O
- **Other** S: U-Haul Custome Hitches

50 Furguson Rd, Samuell Blvd. (Same services as exit 49B)
- **Gas** N: Diamond Shamrock(*), Texaco(*)
- **Lodg** N: Fair Park Inn
  S: Lawnview Motel
- **AServ** S: Brake-O
- **Other** S: U-Haul(LP)

51 Highland Rd, Jim Miller Rd.
- **Gas** N: Exxon(*, D)
  S: RaceTrac(*), Texaco(*, CW)
- **Food** N: America's Kitchen Kettle, Denny's, Kettle, McDonald's(PLAY)
  S: Burger King, Captain D's, Captain D's Seafood, Casa Cavazos, Ci Ci's Pizza, Donuts, East Ocean Chinese, Formosa Express (Chinese), Furr's, Gentile's Casa D'Italia, Grandy's, KFC, Pizza Hut, Pizza Inn, Sonny #2 BBQ, Subway, Taco Bell, Wendy's
- **Lodg** N: La Quinta Inn
  S: Holiday Inn Express, Red Roof Inn
- **AServ** N: Exxon, Exxon
  S: Chief Auto Parts, First Automotive Services, Goodyear Certified Auto Service, Jim Miller Stop
- **ATM** N: Exxon, First Citizens Bank
  S: Compass Bank, Guaranteed Federal Bank, Versateller
- **Other** S: B-Z Mart, **Eckerd Drugs**, Laundry Kwik Wash, Optical Clinic, Pet Purr-Fection, The Mail Centre, Village Hardware

52A Saint Francis Ave.
- **Gas** N: Citgo(*)
- **Food** N: Denny's (La Quinta Inn), Luby's Cafeteria
- **Lodg** N: Comfort Inn, Motel
- **AServ** N: Big Toe Towing(24)
  S: Skyline Ford
- **ATM** S: Compass Bank
- **Other** S: **Buckner Terrace Animal Clinic**

52B Loop 12 (Eastbound)
- **Gas** N: Racetrac(*)
- **Food** N: Pizzagetti, Subway, Wok Delite
  S: **Big K-Mart(RX) (Little Ceaser's Pizza)**, Whataburger(24)
- **AServ** N: Fowler Toyota
  S: **Big K-Mart (Little Ceaser's Pizza)**, Pemske Auto Center, **Sam's Club (with tire service)**
- **Other** N: Aladin Carwash, **Tom Thumb Grocery Store(RX)**
  S: **Big K-Mart(RX) (Little Ceaser's Pizza), Sam's Club (with tire service)**

52C East U.S. 80, Terrell (Eastbound, Limited Access Hwy)

53 Loop 12, Buckner Blvd. (Westbound)

54 Big Town Blvd.
- **TStop** S: **TA TravelCenters of America(*, SCALES) (Dunkin Doughnuts)**
- **Gas** N: Citgo(*), Shell(*, CW), Texaco(*)
- **Food** N: Her Donut and Bakery Shop, Lillis Cafe Mexicano
  S: **Country Pride (TA Travel Centers of America), TA TravelCenters of America (Dunkin Doughnuts), Villa Inn(24)**
- **Lodg** N: Best Western
  S: Tia's Motel, **Villa Inn**
- **AServ** N: Fowler Toyota
- **TServ** S: **Cummins Southern Plains, Inc. (.25 Miles), TA TravelCenters of America(SCALES) (Dunkin Doughnuts)**
- **TWash** S: **Big Town Truck Wash**
- **RVCamp** S: **Cummins Southern Plains, Inc. (.25 Miles), Holiday World RV Center**
- **ATM** N: Citgo
- **Other** N: Coin Laundry (Texaco), Consumer's Speedy Laundry, Eastfield Bookstore
  S: Farmers Market

55 Motley Dr.
- **Gas** N: Texaco(*, D)
  S: Chevron(*)
- **Food** N: Golden Ox Cafe
- **Lodg** N: Astro Inn, Ramada Limited
- **AServ** N: Stewart's Automotive
- **Med** S: ✚ **Mesquite Community Hospital**
- **ATM** S: Chevron

56A Gus Thomasson Rd, Galloway Ave (Eastbound)
- **Gas** N: Diamond Shamrock(*), Fina(*)
  S: Citgo(*)
- **Food** N: Fina, KFC
  S: Baskin Robbins, China 1st, Dickey's BBQ Pit, Jumbo China, Luby's Cafeteria, Southern Maid Donuts, Subs Miami Grill, Subway, The Feedbag, Wendy's
- **Lodg** S: Delux Inn
- **AServ** S: Firestone Tire & Auto, Midas Muffler & Brake, Rodeo Dodge, Tune-Up Masters
- **RVCamp** S: **Mesquite Camper Sales & Service**
- **ATM** S: Citgo, **Kroger Supermarket(RX) (Bank of America ATM)**
- **Other** S: **Kroger Supermarket(RX) (Bank of America ATM)**, United Artists Town East 6

56CB Junction I-635

57 Northwest Dr. (Construction)
- **Gas** N: Total(*, D)
  S: Fina(*, LP)
- **Food** S: Jack-In-The-Box
- **ATM** N: Total

58 Rosehill, Garland, Beltline Rd (Difficult Reaccess, Exit under constructon)
- **Gas** N: Conoco(*), Mobil(*, D, CW), Total(*, LP)
  S: Exxon(*, D), Shell(*, CW)
- **Food** N: China City, Denny's, Donut Palace, KFC, Little Caesars Pizza, Long John Silver, McDonald's, Spaghetti Warehouse, Subway, Taco Bell, Taco Bueno, Whataburger
  S: Baker's Ribs, Buck's Pizza, Burger King, Dairy Queen, Grandy's, Waffle House, Wok One
- **Lodg** S: DAYS INN Days Inn, Motel 6
- **AServ** N: Chief Auto Parts
  S: Exxon, Exxon
- **ATM** N: **Albertson's Grocery Store (NationsBank)**, Mobil, Mobil
  S: Bank Of America, Bank of Texas, MPACT, Shell
- **Other** N: **Albertson's Grocery Store (NationsBank)**, Chief Auto Parts, Interstate 30 Animal Hospital
  S: Coin Operated Carwash, **Kroger Supermarket(24, RX), Petmobile Pet Hospital**

59 Rose Hill Rd (Exit under construction)

60 Bobtown Rd (Exit Under construction)
- **Gas** N: Mobile(*, CW) (Picadilly Pizza), Texaco(*)
- **Food** N: Catfish King, Jack In The Box, Mobile (Picadilly Pizza)
- **ATM** N: Texaco
- **Other** N: Fin and Feather (boat service)

61 Zion Rd.
- **FStop** N: **Conoco(*)**
- **Food** S: Cafe Filipinas, Dice's pizza and Subs Express Delivery, Lakepoint China Restaurant

62 Chaha Rd.
- **Gas** S: Diamond Shamrock(*, LP) (Taco Bell), Texaco(*)
- **Food** N: Martinez Mexican Foods, Sunrise Square Restaurant
  S: Diamond Shamrock (Taco Bell), Texaco
- **Lodg** N: Best Western
- **ATM** S: Texaco

64 Dalrock Rd, Rowlett
- **Gas** N: Diamond Shamrock(*, CW)
- **ATM** N: Diamond Shamrock
- **Other** S: Bayview Marina, Dalrock Fishing Pier Marina

67C Frontage Rd. (Eastbound)
- **Other** S: **Lakeside Veterinary Clinic, The Home Depot**

67AB FM 740, Ridge Rd, Village Dr, Horizon Blvd.
- **Gas** N: Chevron(*, CW, 24), E-Z Mart(*, CW), Mobil(*, CW)
  S: Texaco(*), Total(*)
- **Food** N: Arby's, Burger King(PLAY), **Cajun Catfish**, Grandy's, L Trevino's Mexican, McDonald's, Schlotzsky's Deli, Waffle House, Wendy's
  S: Applebee's, Boston Market Restaurant, Chili's, Culpeppers, Donut Palace, El Chico Mexican Restaurant, Jack-In-The-Box, Papa John's Pizza, Pizza Getti, Quizno's Classic Sub (Total), Rockwall Country Cafe, Starbucks Coffee, Subway, TCBY, Taco Bell
- **AServ** N: Goodyear Tire & Auto, Kwik Kar Lube & Tune, **Wal-Mart(24, RX) (Vision Center)**
  S: Discount Tire Company
- **ATM** N: Bank of America, Chevron, Mobil, Schlotzsky's Deli
  S: **Albertson's Grocery(24, RX) (NationsBank)**, American National Bank, **Kroger Supermarket(RX) (Bank Of America)**, Lakeside National Bank
- **Other** N: Home Depot, **Wal-Mart(RX) (Vision Center)**
  S: **Albertson's Grocery(RX) (NationsBank), Eckerd Drugs(RX), Kroger Supermarket(RX) (Bank Of America)**, Lakeside Veterinary Clinic, Movies 8, **Ridge Road Animal Hospital, Roma's Pre-read Books, Target**, The Vision Gallery, Wolf Camera

EXIT TEXAS

68 TX205, Rockwall, Terrell
- TStop — **S:** 76 Auto/Truck Plaza[*, LP, SCALES]
- Gas — **N:** RaceTrac[*], Shell[*, CW], Texaco[*], Texaco
  S: Total[*]
- Food — **N:** Braum's, Dairy Queen, Donna's Kitchen, Granma's Fried Chicken, KFC, Luigi's Italian, Mr. Jim's Pizza, Pizza Hut, Wan Fu, Whataburger[24]
  S: Taco Bell (Total)
- Lodg — **N:** Super 8
- AServ — **N:** Carquest Auto Parts, Carquest Auto Parts and Service, Lakeside Chevrolet, Pro Lube, Rockwall Ford, Mercury, Texaco[D], Texaco
- TServ — **S:** 76 Auto/Truck Plaza[SCALES]
- ATM — **N:** RaceTrac
  S: 76 Auto/Truck Plaza
- Other — **N:** Coin Operated Carwash, Mrs. Baird's Bread Store, Rockwall Veterinary Hospital

69 Frontage Rd.

70 FM549
- AServ — **N:** Special D Automotive
- TServ — **N:** Jerry's Diesel Service
- Other — **N:** Mother-H and RVs, Rockwell Marine and Fiberglass Repair
  S: Four Seasons RV Sales and Service

73 FM551, Fate

77A FM548, Royse City
- Gas — **N:** Mobil[*, K], Texaco[*, D, CW]
  S: Conoco[*]
- Food — **N:** Boothill Grill
- Lodg — **N:** Sun Royse Inn
- AServ — **N:** Royse Center Tire Co.

77B FM35
- FStop — **N:** Exxon[*], Knox[*, SCALES, 24]
- Gas — **N:** Diamond Shamrock[*]
- Food — **N:** Big Bad John's BBQ & Soul Food, Sexton's Old Fashioned Burgers, Soulman's BBQ, Subway (Knox)
- AServ — **N:** Crumpton Auto Repair, Johnson's Auto & Wrecker Repair
- ATM — **N:** Exxon
- Other — **N:** Coin Operated Car Wash

79 FM2642

83 FM1565

85 FM36, Caddo Mills
- AServ — **S:** C.A.M.S. Auto Service
- RVCamp — **N:** Dallas Northeast Campground

88 FM1903, Caddo Mills
- FStop — **S:** Fina[*]
- Food — **S:** The Caddo Pancake House (Fina)
- TServ — **S:** R & K 24-Hr. Truck Repair

89 FM1570
- Lodg — **S:** Meadowview Motel, Motel

93AB TX34 North, Bus. U.S. 67, Greenville
- Gas — **N:** Jim Dandy[*]
  S: Chevron[*, D, CW]
- Food — **N:** Applebee's, Ci Ci's Pizza, IHOP, Ryan's Steak House, Schlotzsky's Deli, Subway, TCBY, Taco Bell, Taco Bueno, Wendy's
  S: Cracker Barrel, Denny's, Luby's, Red Lobster, The Spare Rib
- AServ — **N:** Joe Gibson Olds, Cadillac, Steve Gerard Pont, Buick, GMC Trucks
  S: Greenville Ford, Merc, Lincoln
- Med — **N:** Hospital 3 miles
- ATM — **N:** Alliance Bank
  S: Chevron, Wal-Mart[24, RX] (Vision Center)
- Other — **N:** Crossroad's Mall
  S: Honda & Yamaha Motorcycles, Wal-Mart[RX] (Vision Center), Greenville Convention and Visitor's Center (see our ad this page)

94A U.S. 69, U.S. 380, Denison, McKinney
- FStop — **S:** Fina[*]
- Food — **N:** Country Kitchen

EXIT TEXAS

- Lodg — **N:** Days Inn, Royal Inn
- AServ — **N:** Petty's Auto Service Center
  S: Jackson Mazda, Jackson Plym, Jeep, Dodge, Dodge Trucks
- ATM — **N:** Lone Oak State Bank
  S: Benchmark Bank, Fina
- Other — **N:** Library, Super 1 Foods, Western Auto Parts America
  S: Majestic 8 Theaters

94B Bus. U.S. 69, Emory
- FStop — **N:** Total[*]
- Gas — **N:** Citgo[*], Fisca
  S: Chevron[*, CW], Exxon[*]
- Food — **N:** Kettle[24] (Best Western), Taco Bell (Total)
  S: Arby's, Catfish King, McDonald's[PLAY], Tiffany's Restaurant (Holiday Inn)
- Lodg — **N:** Best Western, Days Inn, Royal Inn
  S: Comfort Inn, Economy Inn, Holiday Inn, Motel 6, Super 8
- AServ — **N:** D & L Tire Service
  S: Exxon
- ATM — **N:** Total
  S: Chevron
- Other — **N:** Animal Medical Center, Putters Paradise
  S: Bob's Car Wash

95 Division Street
- Med — **S:** Glenn Oaks Hospital

96 Bus. U.S. 67, Loop 302

95A Frontage Rd (Westbound, Reaccess Westbound Only)
- Lodg — **N:** Budget Inn, Dream Lodge Motel

97 Lamar St.
- Gas — **N:** Exxon[D]
  S: Fina[*]
- Lodg — **S:** Sunrise Motel & RV Park
- AServ — **N:** Exxon, Wall's Auto Service
- RVCamp — **S:** Sunrise, Sunrise Motel & RV Park
- ATM — **N:** Exxon
- Other — **S:** Greenville Animal Hospital, Hilltop Bowl

101 TX24, TX50, FM1737, Commerce, Paris
- FStop — **N:** Phillips 66[*]
- Lodg — **N:** Country Inn Motel
- Other — **N:** Cooper Lake (25 Miles), Pippin's Propane Gas[LP]

104 FM513, Campbell, Lone Oak

110 FM275, FM2649, Cumby
- Gas — **N:** Phillips 66[*]
  S: Texaco[*]
- Food — **S:** Duvall Motel
- Lodg — **S:** Duvall Motel
- AServ — **N:** Interstate Battery
- Other — **N:** Cumby Car Wash[CW]

112 FM499 (Westbound)

116 U.S. 67, FM2653, Brashear Rd

120 Bus. U.S. 67

- Puddin Hill Store
- American Cotton Museum
- 500 + motel rooms, B&B
- restaurants, shopping & fun!

Greenville Chamber of Commerce
P.O. Box 1055 • Greenville, TX 75403-1055
903/455-1510 • tourism@greenville-chamber.org

EXIT TEXAS

122 TX19, Emory
- TStop — **S:** Phillips 66[*]
- FStop — **S:** Phillips 66[*]
- Gas — **N:** Chevron[*]
- Food — **S:** Phillips 66
- TServ — **S:** Larry Vititow's, Phillips 66
- RVCamp — **N:** Hillcrest Village Mobile Home & RV Park
  S: I-30 RV Sales and Service (1 Mile), Shady Lake RV Park (2 Miles)
- Med — **N:** Hospital (4 Miles)
- ATM — **S:** Phillips 66, Phillips 66
- Other — **N:** Cooper Lake State Park
  S: Sulphur Springs Veterinary Clinic

123 FM2297, League St.
- Gas — **N:** Chevron[*], Phillips 66[CW], Texaco[*]
- TServ — **N:** G & L Truck Service, Service Trucking Inc

124 TX11, TX154, Sulphur Springs, Quitman
- Gas — **N:** Diamond Shamrock, Exxon[*], Phillips 66[*, 24], Total[*]
  S: Shell[*, D, LP], Texaco[*]
- Food — **N:** Catfish King, KFC, Northcutt's Donuts, Peddler's Pizza, Pitt Grill[24], Sonic Drive-In, Subway, Ta Molly's Mexican, Western Sizzlin'
  S: Baskin Robbins (Grandy's), Bodacious BBQ, Braum's, Burger King[PLAY], China House, Furr's Cafeteria, Grandy's, Jack-In-The-Box, K-Bobs Steakhouse, McDonald's[PLAY], Pizza Inn, Shell, Taco Bell
- Lodg — **N:** Royal Inn
  S: Holiday King Motel
- AServ — **N:** Chief Auto Parts, Chrysler, Plymouth, Dodge Dealer, Dealer's Choice Automotive, Diamond Shamrock, Gober & Merrell Chev, Buick, GMC Trucks, I-30 Radiator Shop, Jack's Tire Service, Phillips 66[24]
  S: Discount Wheel and Tire Co., Pennzoil Oil Change, Tire Town
- ATM — **N:** Alliance Bank, City National Bank, First National Bank
  S: Shell
- Other — **N:** Car Wash[CW], Classic Lanes, Shelton's Propane[LP], Spring Village Laundromat, Suburban Propane[LP], U.S. Post Office
  S: Eckerd Drugs[RX], Lum's Car Wash, Tire Town

125 Frontage Rd (Westbound, Reaccess Westbound Only)

126 FM1870, College St.
- Gas — **S:** Exxon[*]
- Lodg — **S:** Country Folks Inn
- AServ — **S:** Firestone Tire & Auto[24]

127 Bus. U.S. 67, Loop 301
- FStop — **S:** Chevron[*, CW]
- Gas — **S:** Texaco[*]
- Food — **N:** Monroe's (Holiday Inn)
  S: Burton's Family Restaurant (Best Western)
- Lodg — **N:** Budget Inn, Holiday Inn
  S: Best Western
- AServ — **S:** Chevron
- Med — **N:** Hospital
- Other — **S:** Car Wash

131 FM69

135 U.S. 67 North

136 FM269, Weaver Rd
- Gas — **N:** Phillip 66[*]
- AServ — **N:** Weaver Automotive

141 FM900, Saltillo Rd
- FStop — **N:** Exxon[*]

142 County Line Rd (Eastbound)

(143) Rest Area (RR, Phones, Picnic, Grills, Vending, P; Eastbound)

(143) Rest Area (RR, Phones, Picnic, Grills, Vending, P; Westbound)

146 TX37, Clarksville, Winnsboro

Bold red print shows RV & Bus parking available or nearby

EXIT	TEXAS
FStop	S: Texaco[*]
Gas	N: Exxon[*]
	S: Chevron[*, LP]
Food	S: Barn Stormer's Restaurant, Burger King[PLAY], Cypress Glen, Dairy Queen
Lodg	S: Cypress Glen, Super 8
AServ	N: Crowston's Auto Service
	S: Mt. Vernon Tire, Pennzoil Oil Change[CW], Perry's Tires
Med	N: Hospital
ATM	S: Chevron, Franklin National Bank
Other	S: Kwik Kleen Car Wash[CW], Tom Scott Lumberyard, Ace Hardware
147	Spur 423
FStop	N: Love's[*]
Food	N: Subway (Love's), Taco Bell (Love's)
Lodg	N: Mount Vernon Motel
AServ	N: Big A Auto Parts, Turner Auto Repair
	S: Lone Star Tire
Other	S: Shelton's Propane[LP]
150	Ripley Rd
153	Spur 185, Winfield, Millers Cove
TStop	N: Citgo Truck Stop[*] (CB Shop)
Gas	N: Chevron[*]
	S: Citgo[*, D]
TServ	N: C Truck Repair, Citgo Truck Stop (CB Shop), Cummins Diesel
TWash	N: Citgo Truck Stop (CB Shop)
RVCamp	N: RV Park
Other	N: Coin Laundry (Citgo TS)
156	Frontage Rd
(157)	Weigh Station (Eastbound)
(157)	Weigh Station (Westbound)
160	FM1734, U.S. 271, Paris, Pittsburg
FStop	S: Texaco[*, 24]
Gas	S: Exxon[*, D]
Food	N: Two Senoritas
	S: El Chico Mexican Restaurant, Elmwood Cafeteria (Holiday Inn), Gameday Sports Grill (Holiday Inn), Western Sizzlin'
Lodg	S: Comfort Inn, Days Inn, Holiday Inn
AServ	S: AC Automotive & Transmission
ATM	S: Texaco
162A	U.S. 271, FM1402, FM2152, Mt. Pleasant
FStop	S: Total[*, D] (Subway)
Gas	N: Chevron[*, D, CW]
	S: Shell[*], Texaco[*]
Food	N: Blaylock BBQ, Lakewood Motel, Pitt Grill[24] (Lakewood Motel)
	S: Alps Restaurant (Best Western), Burger King[PLAY], McDonald's[PLAY], Subway (Total)
Lodg	N: Lakewood Motel
	S: Best Western
RVCamp	N: KOA Kampground
Med	S: Titus Regional Medical Center
ATM	S: Shell
Other	S: TX Department of Public Safety
162B	Bus. U.S. 271, FM 1402, FM 2152, Mt. Pleasant
165	FM1001
FStop	S: Chevron[*]
170	FM1993
Gas	N: Mobil[*, D]
178	U.S. 259, De Kalb, Daingerfield, Omaha
186	FM561
(190)	Rest Area (P; Eastbound)
(190)	Rest Area (P; Westbound)
192	FM990
FStop	N: Fina[*]
Food	N: Pitt Grill (Fina)
TServ	N: Burkett Tire[24]
198	TX98

EXIT	TEXAS
199	U.S. 82, Dekalb, Clarksville
Gas	N: Phillips 66[*]
201	TX8, New Boston
FStop	N: Texaco[*], Total[*, D]
	S: Overland Express[*, D]
Gas	S: E-Z Mart[*], Exxon[*]
Food	N: Pitt Grill (Tex Inn)
	S: Arby's (Overland Express), Burger King (Exxon), McDonald's[PLAY], Pizza Hut, Taco Delite
Lodg	N: Tex Inn
	S: Best Western, Bostonian Motor Inn
AServ	N: Coleman Chevrolet, Chrysler, Plym, Dodge
RVCamp	N: Eaves MH & RV Park (.25 Miles)
	S: RV Park (.5 Miles)
Med	S: Hospital
ATM	S: Overland Express
206	Spur 86, Red River Army Depot
208	FM560, Hooks
TStop	N: Hooks Truckstop[*, SCALES], Love's[*, SCALES, 24]
FStop	S: Total[*]
Gas	S: Gas[*], Quality Fuel[*, CW]
Food	N: Browning's Main Street Cafe, Love's
	S: Dairy Queen[PLAY], Quality Fuel, Taco Bell (Total)
Lodg	N: Hooks Truckstop
AServ	S: HTS Automotive, Hook's Tire Service, KRP Tire Repair[24]
TServ	N: Hooks Truckstop[SCALES]
RVCamp	N: Hook's Camper Center (1 Mile)
ATM	S: Gas, Quality Fuel, Total
Other	S: Coin Car Wash, Coin Laundry[24], Rehkopf's Food Store
212	Spur74, Lonestar Army Ammunition Plant
Gas	S: Texaco[*]
213	FM2253, Leary
218	FM989, Nash
Gas	S: Exxon[*]
Food	S: Burger King[PLAY] (Exxon), TCBY (Exxon)
TServ	S: Volvo Dealer (CAT, Cummins, Detroit Diesel)
Other	S: U.S. Post Office
220A	U.S. 59 South, Houston, Wright Patman Lake (Limited Access Hwy)
220B	FM559, Richmond Rd
Gas	N: Exxon[*, CW], Texaco[*]
	S: Chevron, Total[*]
Food	N: Bob's Smokehouse BBQ, Burger King, Cracker Barrel, Dairy Queen, Domino's Pizza, Pancho's Mexican, Pizza Hut, Popeye's Chicken (Texaco), Quizno's Classic Sub, Ta Molly's, Taco Bell, Texas Roadhouse
	S: Arby's, Baskin Robbins, Chili's, Chocolitiera, Grandy's, Lee's China, McDonald's[PLAY], Subway
AServ	S: Chevron, Jiffy Lube, Sears
Med	N: Hospital
ATM	N: Hibernia
	S: Albertson's Grocery[RX], Hibernia, State First

INDOOR POOL & RECREATION CENTER

• 210 guest rooms including three suites • In-room cable TV, free HBO, Pay-per view movies, hair dryer and coffee maker • Full service Red Lobster® restaurant • Texas A&M - Texarkana • Perot Theatre, Ace of Club House and Four States Fairgrounds all within five miles

Holiday Inn
TEXARKANA I-30

5100 N. Stateline Road
Texarkana, Arkansas 71854
870-774-3521 • 800-HOLIDAY

1464

EXIT	TEXAS/ARKANSAS
	National Bank, Teacher's Credit Union
Other	N: Movies 12, Sam's Club, Super 1 Foods[RX], Vision 4 Less
	S: Albertson's Grocery[RX], Animal Clinic, Books-A-Million, Books-A-Million, Central Mall, Fant Optical, Office Depot, Pier 1 Imports, Target, Texarkana Eye Associates
222	TX93, FM1397, Summerhill Rd
Gas	N: Shell[*, CW], Total[*]
	S: Texaco[*]
Food	N: Applebee's[*], Burger Tyme (Shell), CJ's, Kona Ranch Steaks & Seafood, McDonald's, Subway (Total), Waffle House
	S: Bryce's Cafeteria, Martha's (Ramada Inn), Ramada Inn, Southern Grill (Ramada)
Lodg	N: Motel 6
	S: Ramada Inn
AServ	N: Orr Honda Dealer
TServ	N: Heintschel Truck Tire Center, Texarkana Truck Center (CAT, Cummins, Detroit Diesel)
RVCamp	N: Andrews Recreation Center
Med	N: Hospital (.5 Miles)
ATM	N: Shell, State First National Bank
Other	S: 24 Hr. Advanced Car Wash Systems, Inc.
(223)	Texas Welcome Center, Rest Area (RR, Picnic, P; Westbound)
223AB	U.S. 71, State Line Ave, Ashdown
TStop	S: Texarkana Auto/Truck Stop[*, 24] (CB Shop)
Gas	N: E-Z Mart[*, LP], Shell[*], Texaco
	S: E-Z Mart[*, LP], Exxon[*, CW], Mobil, Racetrac[*], Texaco[*], Total[*, D]
Food	N: Best Western, Denny's, IHOP, Red Lobster (Holiday Inn), SHONEY'S, Shoney's (Shoney's Inn), Waffle House
	S: Backyard Burgers, Baskin Robbins, Bennigan's, Best Western, Burger King, Cattleman's Steakhouse, Ci Ci's Pizza, Doc Alexander's, El Chico Mexican Restaurant, Harriett's Restaurant (Knights Inn), KFC, La Carreta, Little Caesars Pizza, Long John Silver, McDonald's[PLAY], Mi Pueblo, Pizza Inn, Schlotzsky's Deli, Subway, TCBY, Taco Bell, Taco Tico, Texarkana Auto/Truck Stop (CB Shop), The Kettle (La Quinta), The King's Row Restaurant (Best Western), Tombo's BBQ, Western Sizzlin', Whataburger
Lodg	N: Best Western, Budgetel Inn, Four Points Hotel Sheraton, Hampton Inn, Holiday Inn (see our ad this page), Holiday Inn Express, Shoney's Inn, Super 8
	S: Best Western, Comfort Inn, Days Inn, EconoLodge, Howard Johnson Express (Texarkana Auto/Truck Stop), Knight's Inn, La Quinta Inn, Villager Lodge
AServ	N: Cooper Tires, Jo Esco Tire Co., Texaco
	S: Chevrolet Dealer, Mobil
TServ	N: Dayton Tires[24], State Line Tire
	S: Texarkana Auto/Truck Stop[24] (CB Shop), Texas Kenworth Co.
TWash	S: Texarkana Auto/Truck Stop (CB Shop)
RVCamp	N: Northgate RV Park
Med	N: Hospital (3 Miles)
	S: Hospital (3 Miles)
ATM	N: Shell
	S: Long John Silver, Total
Other	S: Baptist Bookstore, Mail Boxes Etc., Wal-Mart[RX]

↑TEXAS

↓ARKANSAS

EXIT	
1	Jefferson Ave
Lodg	S: Motel 6
AServ	S: Auto Glass Pro
(1)	Welcome Center (RR, Phones,

EXIT ARKANSAS

Picnic, Vending, P; Eastbound)
RVCamp N: Fred & Jack Trailer Sales Inc. (2 Miles)
2 AR245, Airport
FStop N: Overland Express(*), Total(*)
S: BP(*)
Food N: A & W Hot Dogs & More (Overland Express), Chester Fried Chicken (Total), Taco Bell (Total)
S: Peggy Sue's Cafe
RVCamp N: Overland Express
ATM N: Overland Express
7 AR108, Mandeville
TStop N: Flying J Travel Plaza(*, LP, RV DUMP, SCALES)
Food N: Mi Mi & Papa's Burgers, Red Barn BBQ, The Cookery (Flying J TS)
TServ N: Exit 7 Tire (CB Shop), TWA Truck Wash
TWash N: TWA Truck Wash
RVCamp N: KOA Kampground (.5 Miles)
12 U.S. 67, Fulton (Eastbound, Reaccess Westbound Only)
18 Fulton
FStop N: BP(*)
Food N: BP
TServ N: BP
(25) Weigh Station (Eastbound)
(25) Weigh Station (Westbound)
30 U.S. 278, Hope, Nashville
Gas N: Phillips 66
S: Texaco(*, D)
Food N: Little B's Mexican & Steakhouse, Western Sizzlin' (Best Western)
S: Burger King(PLAY), Catfish King, Days Inn(24), McDonald's(PLAY), Taco Bell, Texaco
Lodg N: Best Western, Holiday Inn Express, Super 8
S: Days Inn (see our ad this page)
AServ S: John Hays Chevrolet, Pope Ford, Mercury, Lincoln, Wal-Mart(RX)
RVCamp S: Fair Park RV Park (2 Miles)
Med S: ✚ Hospital
ATM S: Texaco
Parks N: Old Washington Historic State Park (8 Miles)
Other N: Airport
S: Wal-Mart(RX)
31 AR29, Hope
FStop N: Shell(*), Texaco(*)
Gas S: Exxon(*), Texaco(*), Total(*)
Food N: Pit Grill (Friendly Inn), Quality Inn, Russell's Smokehouse, The Spinning Wheel (Quality Inn)
S: KFC, Smokhouse BBQ, Total
Lodg N: Friendly Inn, Hope Village Inn & RV Park, Quality Inn
S: Economy Inn
AServ S: Exxon
TServ N: Texaco
RVCamp N: Hope Village Inn & RV Park
ATM N: Shell, Texaco
Other N: AR State Police, Kwik Klean Car Wash(CW)
36 AR299, Emmet
44 U.S. 371, AR24, Prescott
TStop S: Exit 44 Truck Stop(*, SCALES)
Food S: Norman's 44 (Exit 55 Truck Stop)
Lodg S: EconoLodge, Split Rail Inn
TServ S: Exit 44 Truck Stop(SCALES)
TWash S: Exit 44 Truck Stop
ATM S: Exit 44 Truck Stop
46 AR19, Prescott, Magnolia
FStop N: Citgo(*, 24), Phillips 66(*, D)
Gas S: Texaco(*, D)
AServ S: Texaco
TServ N: Citgo(24), U.S. Express
ATM N: Citgo
Parks N: Crater of Diamonds State Park (31 Miles)
54 AR51, Okolona, Gurdon
(56) Rest Area (RR, Picnic, Vending, P; Eastbound)

EXIT ARKANSAS

(57) Rest Area (RR, Picnic, Vending, P; Westbound)
63 AR53, Gurdon
TStop N: Citgo(*, 24), Southfork Truck Stop(*, D)
Gas S: Shell(*, D)
Food N: Southfork Restaurant(24) (Citgo)
S: Shell
AServ S: I-30 Automotive
TServ N: Citgo(24), Southfork Truck Stop
ATM N: Citgo, Southfork Truck Stop
69 AR26E, Gum Springs
73 AR8, AR26, AR51, Arkadelphia
Gas N: Citgo(*, D), Shell(*, CW)
S: Exxon(*, D, LP), Texaco(*), Total(*)
Food N: Stuckey's (Shell), Western Sizzlin'
S: Andy's Restaurant, Burger King, Mazzio's Pizza, TCBY, Taco Tico
AServ N: Automo "Bill's"
S: Auto Zone Auto Parts
Med S: ✚ Baptist Medical Center
Parks N: Crater of Diamonds State Park
Other N: Coin Car Wash
S: All Care Family Discount Pharmacy(RX), Hardman Ace Hardware
78 AR7, Caddo Valley, Arkadelphia, Hot Springs
FStop N: Fina(*, LP, SCALES, 24) (Mid Arkansas Truck Plaza (truck service)), Shell(*, LP), Total(*)
Gas S: Exxon(*, D, CW), Texaco(*)
Food N: A & W Hot Dogs & More (Total), Total
S: Bowen's (Best Western), Exxon, McDonald's, Pig Pit BBQ, SHONEY'S, Shoney's, Subway (Exxon), Taco Bell, Waffle House, Wendy's
Lodg S: Best Western, Days Inn, EconoLodge, Holiday Inn Express, Quality Inn, Super 8
TServ N: Fina(SCALES, 24) (Mid Arkansas Truck Plaza (truck service)), Mid-Ark Truck Plaza
RVCamp N: KOA Kampground(LP) (1.2 Miles)
ATM S: Citizen's First Bank (Exxon), Elk Horn Bank
Parks N: Grey Lake Resort State Park (6 Miles), Hot Springs National Park (29 Miles)
Other S: Skateland
83 AR283, Friendship
FStop S: Shell(*)
AServ S: Shell
91 AR84, Social Hill
Gas S: Social Hill Country Store(*)
RVCamp S: Social Hill RV Park
(93) Rest Area (RR, Phones, Picnic, Grills, Vending, P; Left Exit Both Directions)
97 AR84, AR171
98AB U.S. 270, Malvern, Hot Springs
FStop S: Fina(*), Shell(*)
Gas S: Phillips 66(*)
Food N: Fishnest

1101

1500 N. Hervey
25" Cable TV with HBO
Outdoor Swimming Pool
Continental Breakfast
24 Hr Coffee in Lobby
"Watermelon Capital of the World"
Golf & Tennis Nearby
Birth Place of President Clinton
870-722-1904
ARKANSAS • I-30 • Exit 30

EXIT ARKANSAS

S: Mazzio's Pizza, Phillips 66, Shell, Waffle House
Lodg N: Super 8
S: Economy Inn
Med S: ✚ Hospital
ATM S: Fina
Other S: Rockport Muffler and Auto Sales, RV Sales and Service
106 Old Military Rd
TStop S: JJ's Truck Stop(SCALES, 24) (Fina)
Food S: JJ's Truck Stop (Fina)
Lodg N: JJ's Motel
S: JJ's Truck Stop (Fina)
TServ S: JJ's Truck Stop(SCALES, 24) (Fina)
RVCamp N: JB's RV Park & Campground (.36 Miles)
111 U.S. 70 West, Hot Springs
Parks N: Hot Springs National Park
Exit (112) AR Police Hwy. Inspection Station (Westbound)
114 U.S. 67 South, Benton Services Center
TServ N: Rentch Equipment Co.
116 Benton, Sevier St.
Gas N: Shell(*, D, LP), Sinclair(*), Texaco(*, D)
S: BP(*), Texaco(*, LP)
Food N: Ed and Kay's Family Restaurant, Hunan Place (Chinese), Pines Drive-In
S: Daylight Donuts, El Cena Casa, No Name Original BBQ, Texas Style Chili Co.
Lodg N: Troutt Motel
S: Capri Motel
AServ N: Benton Brake and Front End
S: Benton Auto Electric, Benton Transmissions, Britt's Tire Repair, Brown's Small Engine Parts and Service, Texaco
Other N: Jerry's CB Radio, Outdoors Inc.
S: Breitweiser's Meat Market, Bud's Roller Rink, Fun Wash Express Coin Laundry, Saline County Airport
117 AR5, AR35
Gas N: Conoco(*, D, LP), Shell(*, D, LP, 24)
Food N: Denny's (Ramada Inn), Pinky's Family Restaurant, Pizza Hut, Waffle House
S: Arby's, KFC, Tasty Freeze
Lodg N: Best Western, EconoLodge, Ramada Inn, The Cedarwood Inn
Med S: ✚ Hospital
ATM S: Superior Federal Bank
Other N: Club Pet, Floods of Suds 2(CW), Kids Sports Fun & Fitness Club, Thunder Road Grand Prix
118 Congo Rd
FStop N: Phillips 66(*, CW)
Gas N: Citgo(*, D), Texaco(*, D)
S: Citgo(*, CW), Exxon(LP), Shell(*, D, LP, CW), Shell(*, D)
Food N: Brown's Country Store
S: Dairy Queen, Denton's Trotline Buffet, Dizzy's Grill, Doug's Donuts, Olive Zoe's Bakery, Sergio's Pizza, SHONEY'S, Shoney's, Sonic, TCBY, Taco Bell, Tia Wanda Mexican, Western Sizzlin'
Lodg N: Scottish Inns
S: Days Inn
AServ N: Donnie's Foreign Car Service, Precision Brake, Williams Tire Service
S: AR Auto Repair, Carter Tire, Exxon, Greased Lightening, Quaker State Oil & Lube, Razorback Quick Lube, Tire Town, Whitfield Tire
TWash N: Phillips 66(CW)
RVCamp N: I-30 Travel Park (Service Road; 1.9 Miles)
Other S: Congo Road Animal Clinic, Fun Wash Coin Laundry (Shell), Saugey's Antique Mall, Wal-Mart(24, RX)
121 Alcoa Rd
Gas N: Texaco(*, D, CW)
AServ N: Brazil's Auto Repair, J & S Auto Repair, Lander's United Auto Mart, Landers Chrys, Plym, Dodge, & Truck Center, NAPA Auto Parts
S: Brett Morgan Chev, Oldsmobile, Freeway Ford,

EXIT	ARKANSAS
	Mercury, Lincoln
TServ	N: Ramsey Truck & Equipment Sales
RVCamp	S: I-30 Travel Park(LP) (Service Road; .8 Miles)
ATM	N: Texaco
123	AR183, Bryant, Bauxite, Reynolds Rd.
FStop	S: Total(*, LP)
Gas	N: Phillips 66(CW)
	S: Exxon(*, D, LP), Phillips 66(*, D, CW)
Food	N: Cinnamon Street Bakery (Phillips 66), Cracker Barrel, Domino's Pizza, Eddie Pepper's Mexican Restaurant (Phillips 66), Hot Stuff Pizza (Phillips 66), Pasta Plus, Smash Hit Subs (Phillips 66), Taste of D-Light (Oriental)
	S: Chinese On the Go, Little Caesars Pizza, McDonald's(PLAY), Ole South Pancake House, Sergio's Pizza, Sonic, Subway, Taco Bell, Wendy's
Lodg	N: Holiday Inn Express
	S: Super 8
AServ	S: Bryant Brake & Tire, Exxon
ATM	N: Mercantile Bank, Phillips 66
	S: Union Bank of Benton, Union Bank of Bryant
Other	N: Bryant Veterinary Clinic
	S: Bryant Laundromat, Coin Car Wash, Foster's(RX), Reynolds Road Animal Clinic, U.S. Post Office
126	AR111, County Line Rd, Alexander
FStop	N: Shell(*, CW)
Gas	N: Citgo(*, LP)
	S: Mapco Express(*, LP)
Food	N: KFC, Taco Bell, Wagon Wheel
	S: Pit Stop BBQ
AServ	N: Car Quest Auto Parts, Eddie's Auto Parts
	S: Hyundai Southland, Universal Mechanical Services
Other	N: Car Wash(CW), Expo Center
	S: I-30 Speedway, Moix RV
128	Mabelvale West, Otter Creek Rd.
Gas	S: Phillips 66(*)
Food	S: Michael's (La Quinta Inn)
Lodg	S: La Quinta Inn
AServ	S: Purcell Tire Co.
Med	N: Hospital
	S: Southwest Hospital
Other	S: Fire Station
129	Junction I-430N
Lodg	N: AmeriSuites (see our ad this page)
130	AR338, Baseline Rd, Mabelvale
Gas	N: Mapco Express(*)
	S: Phillips 66(*)
Food	N: Frontier Diner (King Motel), The Hawg Diner (Jones Harley Davidson)
Lodg	N: Cimarron Inn, King Motel
AServ	S: BF Goodrich, Hamm Diesel Electric
TServ	S: Hamm Diesel Electric
ATM	S: Phillips 66
Other	N: Jones Harley Davidson Motorcycles

EXIT	ARKANSAS
131	South Chicot Road (Eastbound, Reaccess Eastbound Only, Only services the east side of the interstate along the frontage rd)
Food	S: Luby's Cafeteria, McDonald's, Plantation Inn, Ryan's Steakhouse, Waffle House
Lodg	S: Knight's Inn, Plantation Inn, Regal Inn, Super 7 Inn
AServ	S: Terry Auto Care
TServ	S: United Engines Inc. (Detroit Diesel, Allison Transmission)
RVCamp	S: Camper Caps
Other	S: Camper Capps RV Center, Walmart(24, RX)
132	U.S. 70B, University Ave. McDaniel Dr. (Limited Access Hwy)
Lodg	S: Plantation Inn
133	Geyer Springs Rd.
Gas	N: Exxon(*, LP, 24), Fuel Mart(*)
	S: Phillips 66(*), Total(*, D)
Food	N: Church's Chicken, Cuisine Of China, Sim's BBQ, Sonic, Subway, Tony's Chinese Restaurant
	S: Arby's, Burger King, El Chico Mexican Restaurant, KFC, Pizza Inn, Taco Bell, Waffle House, Western Sizzlin'
Lodg	S: Comfort Inn, Hampton Inn, Super 8
AServ	N: Razorback Transmission, Roy Rogers Foreign Car Parts, Steve's Speed & Truck Outlet
	S: Goodyear Certified Auto Service, Toxic Performance & Off-Road
ATM	N: Exxon
	S: First Commercial Bank, NationsBank
Other	N: Coin Operated Car Wash, Grooming Table, U.S. Post Office
	S: AR State Police
134	Scott Hamilton Dr., Stanton Rd.
Gas	S: Exxon(*, D)
Food	S: Waffle House
Lodg	S: Motel 6, Red Roof Inn
ATM	S: Exxon
135	65th St
FStop	N: Exxon(*, D, 24)
Gas	N: Mapco Express(*), Texaco(*, D, CW)
Food	N: Days Inn
	S: Denny's (La Quinta Inn)
Lodg	N: Days Inn
	S: La Quinta Inn
AServ	S: Transmission Express

EXIT	ARKANSAS
TServ	N: Cummins Diesel
138AB	Junction I-440E, Little Rock National Airport, U.S. 65S, U.S. 167S, Pine Bluff, El Dorado
139A	AR365, Roosevelt Rd
Gas	N: Exxon
	S: Texaco(*)
AServ	N: Autocare, Exxon
	S: NAPA Auto Parts
ATM	N: Exxon
	S: Nationsbank
Other	N: Coin Car Wash, State Fair Grounds
	S: Kroger Supermarket(RX)
139B	Junction I-630
140A	9th Street
Gas	N: Exxon(*, D), Shell(*, CW), Texaco(*, D)
	S: Fuelman(*), Phillips 66(*)
Food	N: Pizza Hut, Waffle House
Lodg	N: Best Western
	S: Masters Inn Economy
AServ	N: Exxon
TServ	S: International From Navastar
ATM	N: Exxon
	S: First Commercial Bank
Parks	N: McArthur Park(PLAY)
Other	N: Fire Department
	S: Rexall Drugs(RX), Skyline Detail(CW)
140B	6th St
Gas	N: Exxon(*, D)
	S: Phillips 66(*)
Lodg	N: Best Western
AServ	N: Exxon
TServ	S: Diamond International Trucks
TWash	S: I-30 Tank Wash & Public Scales(SCALES)
Other	N: U.S. Post Office
141A	AR10, Cantrell Rd, Markham St
141B	U.S. 70E, Broadway
Gas	N: Exxon(*, CW), Shell(*), U.S. Fuel(LP)
	S: Total(*, D)
Food	N: Burger King
	S: Arby's, KFC, McDonald's, Popeye's Chicken, Wendy's
AServ	N: Three Star Muffler Shop
	S: Fleet Tire Service, The Maintenance Center
ATM	N: NationsBank
Other	N: U-Haul(LP)
142	15th St
Gas	S: Phillips 66(*)
Other	N: Ideal Coin Laundry
143AB	I-40W, U.S. 65N, AR 107, Ft. Smith; U.S. 67N, U.S. 167N, I-40E, Memphis

↑ARKANSAS

Begin I-30

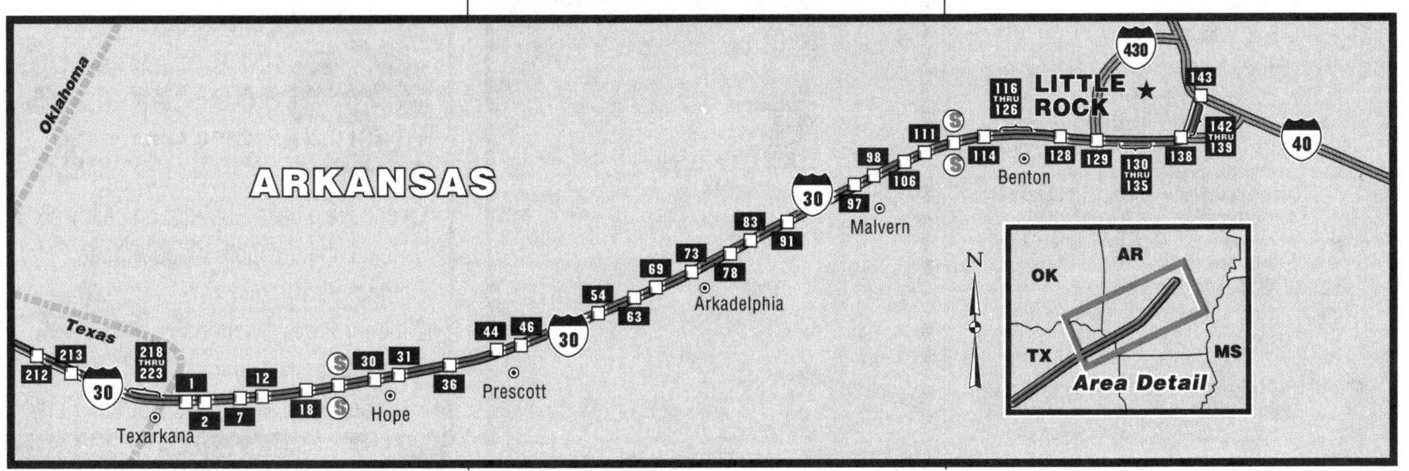

EXIT | MINNESOTA

Begin I-35

↓ MINNESOTA

258 21st Ave E
- **Gas** E: Amoco(CW), ICO(*, D), Spur(*, D), Spur(*, LP), SuperAmerica(*, D)
- **Food** E: Big Apple Bagels (Spur), Blackwoods Grill, Burger King, KFC, McDonald's, Perkin's Family Restaurant, Pizza Hut, Spur, Subway, Taco John's, Wendy's
- **Lodg** E: **Best Western (see our ad this page)**, Chalet Motel, Viking Motel
- **AServ** E: Amoco
- **ATM** E: SuperAmerica
- **Other** E: **Duluth Veterinary Hospital**

256B Lake Ave, 5th Ave. West
- **Gas** E: ICO(*)
- **Food** E: Belasarro's Italian, Burger King, Canal Park Inn, Dairy Queen (ICO), Grandma's Garden Bar & Grill, ICO, Little Angie's Cantina, Old Chicago Pizza, Red Lobster, Subway, Taste of Saigon, The Blue Note Cafe, The Green Mill, Timber Lodge Steakhouse
- **Lodg** E: Canal Park Inn, Comfort Suites Hotel, Hampton Inn, Hawthorne Suites, The Inn on Lake Superior
  W: Holiday Inn, The Radisson
- **ATM** E: **Dewitt Point Seitz Marketplace**
- **Other** E: **Dewitt Point Seitz Marketplace**, Lake Superior Maritime Visitors Center
  W: **Hospital**

256A Mesaba St., Superior St.
- **Food** E: Holiday Inn, The Greenery (Holiday Inn), The Porter's (Holiday Inn)
- **Lodg** E: Holiday Inn, Radisson Inn
- **Med** E: ✚ **Hospital**

255B I-535, U.S. 53S to Wisconsin

255A U.S. 53, 21st Ave West

254 27th Ave West
- **Gas** W: Amoco(*, CW), Phillips 66(LP), Spur(*, D)
- **Food** W: Amoco, Burger King (Amoco), Duluth Grill, Subway
- **Lodg** W: Motel 6
- **AServ** W: Amoco, Amoco, Dave's Automatic Transmission, Duluth Tire, Ford Dealership, Phillips 66
- **TServ** W: **Cummins North Central, Inc. (1.25 Miles)**
- **RVCamp** W: **Cummins North Central, Inc. (1.25 Miles)**
- **ATM** W: Duluth Grill

253B 40th Ave
- **FStop** W: **Amoco**(*, LP)
- **Food** W: **Amoco**, Hot Stuff Pizza (Amoco), Mean Gene's Burgers (Amoco), Perkin's Family Restaurant
- **Lodg** W: Comfort Inn, Super 8
- **ATM** W: Norwest Bank

253A U.S. 2, Wisconsin

252 Central Ave
- **Gas** W: Conoco(*, D), Holiday(*, LP, CW)
- **Food** W: Conoco, Domino's Pizza, Jade Fountain Restaurant (Chinese & American), KFC, Little Caesars Pizza, McDonald's, Pizza Hut, Sammy's Pizza & Restaurant, Subway, Taco Bell (Conoco), The Gopher Restaurant, The Italian Village
- **AServ** W: Bumper to Bumper Auto Parts, Leland Spirit Valley Auto Body
- **Med** W: ✚ **West Duluth Med-Dental**
- **ATM** W: Conoco, First Bank & Trust Co., Holiday, Pioneer National Bank, **Super 1 Foods Grocery**, Western National Bank, Western National Bank
- **Other** W: **Gentle Dentist**, **Grand Avenue Veterinary Clinic**, **K-Mart**(RX), **Spirit Valley Laundromat**, Spirit Valley Optical, **Super 1 Foods Grocery**, U.S.

EXIT | MINNESOTA

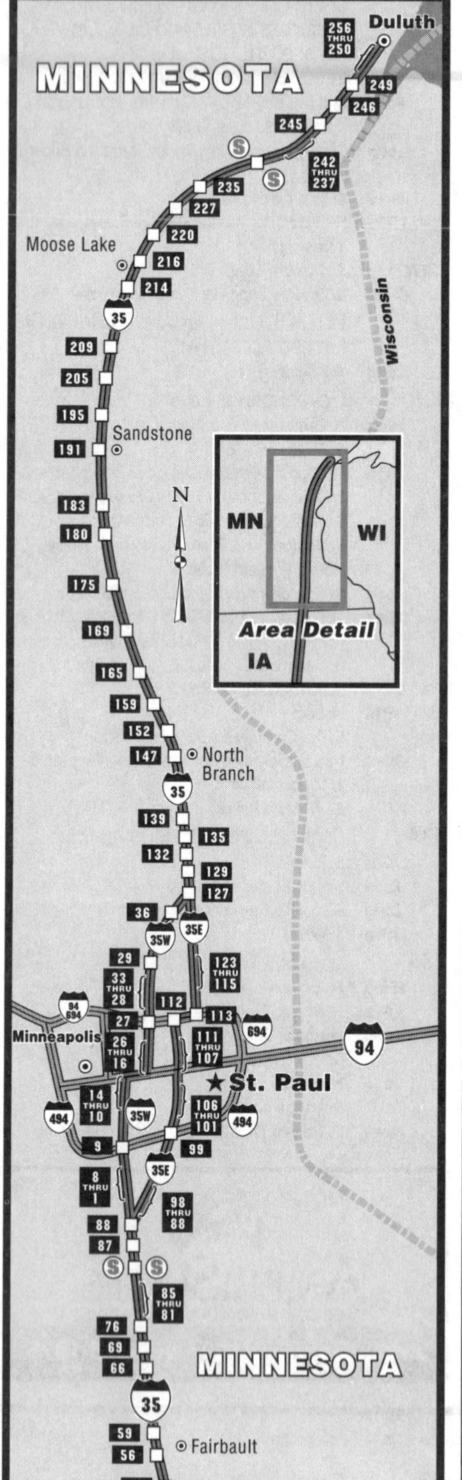

EXIT | MINNESOTA

- Post Office, **WalGreens Pharmacy**(RX)

251B MN 23 South, Grand Ave (Left Exit)
- **Food** W: Danish Bakery & Deli, The Sunshine Cafe
- **AServ** E: Auto Glass Specialist
- **TServ** E: **Freightliner Trucks**
- **RVCamp** W: **Indian Point Campground (1.5 Miles)**

251A Cody St (Northbound, Reaccess Southbound Only)
- **Lodg** E: Allendale Motel, Motel
- **RVCamp** E: **Indian Point Campground**
- **Other** E: **Lake Superior Zoo**

250 U.S. 2W, Proctor, Grand Rapids

249 Boundary Ave
- **FStop** E: **Holiday**(*, D, LP)
- **Gas** W: Phillips 66(*, LP)
- **Food** E: McDonald's
  W: Country Kitchen
- **Lodg** E: Country Inn & Suites, Sundown Motel (Access Road)
  W: Spirit Mountain Lodge
- **RVCamp** E: **Campground**
  W: **Spirit Mountain Campground (1 Mile)**
- **ATM** E: Holiday
  W: Phillips 66, Phillips 66
- **Other** E: **Spirit Mountain Recreation Area**
  W: **Rest Area, Full Facilities**

246 CR13, Midway Road, Nopeming
- **Food** W: Dry Dock Restaurant

245 CR61
- **Food** E: Buffalo House Restaurant
- **RVCamp** E: **Campground**

242 CR1, Esko, Thomson
- **Gas** E: Amoco(*)
- **ATM** E: Amoco

239 MN 45, Scanlon, Cloquet
- **Gas** W: Conoco(*, LP)
- **Food** W: Blimpie Subs & Salads (Conoco), Conoco, **Golden Gate Motel**, River Inn, The Pantry Restaurant
- **Lodg** W: **Golden Gate Motel**
- **AServ** W: Kolar Chevrolet Pontiac Olds Buick GM
- **RVCamp** E: **KOA Kampground**
- **ATM** W: Conoco, Conoco
- **Parks** E: **J Cooke State Park**

237 MN 33, Cloquet
- **Med** W: ✚ **Hospital**

235 MN 210, Cromwell, Carlton
- **TStop** E: **76**(*, K), **Stage Stop Truck Stop**(*, LP) **(Amoco gas, 24 hour road service)**
- **FStop** E: **Amoco**(*)
- **Food** E: **76**, **Junction Oasis (76)**, Stage Stop Restaurant
  W: Black Bear Casino

1189

Edgewater

Best Western

218-728-3601
800-777-7925

**2400 London Rd.
Duluth, Minnesota**

- Overlooking Lake Superior on Lakewalk
- 9 Hole Minature Golf, Video Arcade, Outdoor Playground
- 2 Indoor Pools, Whirlpool, Sauna, Exercise Room
- Free Breakfast/Manager's Cocktail Party

Minnesota ▪ I-35 ▪ Exit 258

EXIT MINNESOTA

Lodg — E: AmericInn, Royal Pines Motel
W: Black Bear Hotel (Casino)
TServ — E: Stage Stop Truck Stop (Amoco gas, 24 hour road service), Truck Center
TWash — E: Stage Stop Truck Stop (Amoco gas, 24 hour road service)
Parks — E: Jay Cooke State Park (5 Miles)

227 CR4, Mahtowa
RVCamp — E: Campground

(225) Rest Area (RR, HF, Phones, Picnic; Northbound)

220 CR6, Barnum
Gas — W: Amoco(*, LP)
Food — W: Restaurant (Amoco), Wind Tree North Restaurant
Lodg — W: North Woods Motel
RVCamp — E: Bear Lake County Campground
ATM — W: Amoco
Other — W: Munger Trail

216 MN 27, Moose Lake (Southbound, Reaccess Northbound Only)
RVCamp — W: Moose Lake City Park (1.25 Miles)
Med — W: ✚ Hospital

214 MN 73, Moose Lake
FStop — W: Conoco(*, D, LP)
Food — W: Conoco, Subway (Conoco)
RVCamp — E: Camping
W: Moose Lake City Park (1.25 Miles), Red Fox Campground (.25 Miles)
Med — W: ✚ Hospital (2 Miles)
ATM — W: Conoco, Conoco
Parks — E: Moose Lake State Park (.25 Miles)
Other — W: Sioux, Moose Munger Trails

209 CR46, Sturgeon Lake
Gas — E: Phillips 66(*, LP)
Food — E: Cafe (Phillips 66), Red Oak Inn
Lodg — W: Sturgeon Lake Motel
RVCamp — E: Campground
W: Campground
ATM — E: Phillips 66

(208) Rest Area (RR, HF, Phones, Picnic; Southbound)

205 CR43, Willow River, Bruno
FStop — W: Citgo(*)
Food — W: Cafe (Citgo), Citgo
AServ — W: Citgo
RVCamp — W: Campground
ATM — W: Citgo

(198) Rest Area (RR, HF, Phones, Picnic; Northbound)

195 MN 18, MN 23E, Finlayson, Askov, Sandstone
Gas — E: 76(*), Amoco(*)
Food — E: Amoco, Banning Junction Cafe (Amoco), Cafe (76)
Lodg — E: Super 8
RVCamp — E: Banning State Park (.5 Miles), Camping
W: Camping
ATM — E: Amoco
Parks — E: Banning State Park (.5 Miles)
Other — E: Tourist Info.

191 MN 23E, Sandstone
FStop — E: Conoco(*, CW, 24)
Gas — E: Amoco(LP, CW)
Food — E: Amoco, Conoco, Hot Stuff Pizza (Amoco)
Lodg — E: Sandstone 61 Motel
Med — E: ✚ Hospital
ATM — E: Amoco, Conoco
Other — E: Gate Family Health Clinic(RX)

183 MN 48, Hinckley

EXIT MINNESOTA

Gas — E: Conoco(*), Holiday(*, D, LP, 24)
W: Amoco(*, CW), Little Store(*), Mobil(*, CW), Phillips 66(*)
Food — E: Baskin Robbins, Burger King, Dairy Queen, Grand Hinckley Inn, Hardee's, Subway, Taco Bell, Tobies Bakery, Tobies Restaurant
W: Cassidy's Restaurant, Firehouse Bar & Lounge, Jeffrey's Bakery, Phillips 66, White Castle Restaurant (Phillips 66)
Lodg — E: DAYS INN Days Inn, EconoLodge, Grand Hinckley Inn, Holiday Inn Express
W: Best Western
AServ — W: Hinckley Automotive
RVCamp — E: Grand Casino Hinckley RV Resort (1 Mile)
Med — E: ✚ Pine Medical Center & Hinkley Walk-In Clinic
ATM — E: Conoco, Conoco, Holiday, Holiday
W: Little Store, Phillips 66
Parks — E: St. Croix State Park
Other — E: Casino (Grand Hinckley Inn), Coin Laundry
W: Hinckley Fire Museum, Tourist Info.

180 MN 23W, CR61, Mora

175 CR 14, Beroun
FStop — E: Total(*, D, LP)

171 (172) CR 11
FStop — E: Super America(*, LP)
Food — E: McDonald's
RVCamp — W: Camping
ATM — E: Super America, Super America

169 MN 324, CR 7, Pine City
FStop — E: Amoco(*, LP)
Gas — E: Holiday(*, D, LP)
Food — E: Hardee's, KFC, Pizza Hut, Pizza Pub, Red Shed Restaurant, Subway
AServ — E: Mercury Ford Dealership
ATM — E: Amoco, Holiday, Holiday
Other — E: Jubilee Grocery, Pamida Grocery(RX), Public Beach, Tourist Info., Wal-Mart(RX)

165 MN 70, Rock Creek, Grantsburg
FStop — W: Total(*)
Food — E: Chalet Motel, Tim's Crossroads
W: Rock Creek Cafe (Total), Total
Lodg — E: Chalet Motel
TServ — E: Tim's Crossroads
RVCamp — E: Campground
ATM — W: Total
Other — W: Federated Propane(LP)

159 MN 361, County 1, Rush City
FStop — E: Conoco(*, LP) (Greyhound Bus Station), Tank & Tackle(*)
Gas — E: 76(*)
Food — E: Baskin Robbins (Conoco), Burger King (Conoco), Conoco (Greyhound Bus Station)
RVCamp — W: Campground (2 Miles)
Med — E: ✚ Hospital
ATM — E: Tank & Tackle
Other — E: Coin Laundry, Super Fair Foods

(154) Rest Area (RR, HF, Phones, Picnic, Pet Walk; Northbound)

152 CR10, Harris

147 MN 95, Cambridge, North Branch
FStop — E: Conoco(*, LP, K, CW)
Gas — E: Amoco(K), Casey's General Store(*), Holiday(*, D, LP), Phillips 66(*, LP), Total(*, D, LP)
Food — E: Amoco, Holiday, Homemade Pizza To Go (Casey's), Hot Stuff Pizza (Holiday), McDonald's(PLAY), Subway, The Oak Inn Restaurant
W: Burger King(PLAY)
Lodg — E: Crossroads Motel
AServ — E: Auto Care, Auto-Tech, Car Quest Radiator Repair, GM Auto Dealership (Frontage Rd), NAPA Auto Parts

EXIT MINNESOTA

W: Anderson & Kroch Ford Dealership, Central Chev Chrysler Dealer
TServ — E: Freightliner Dealer (Frontage Rd)
RVCamp — W: Campground (6 Miles)
Med — E: ✚ Wild River Med Clinic
ATM — E: Conoco, Holiday, Holiday, Merchant State Bank
W: Community National Bank, Tanger Factory Outlet
Parks — E: Wild River Park (14 Miles)
Other — E: Happy Wheels Car Wash, Super Value Grocery Store
W: North Branch Cinemas, Tanger Factory Outlet

139 County 19, Stacy
Gas — W: Conoco(*)
Food — W: Hot Stuff Pizza (Conoco)
Other — W: Sunrise Grocery Store

135 U.S. 61, CR22, Wyoming
FStop — E: 76(*, LP), Amoco(*, LP)
W: Fina(*, LP, CW)
Food — E: Dairy Queen, Subway
W: Village Inn Restaurant
AServ — E: Auto Glass Plus, Car Quest Auto Center
RVCamp — E: Campground (2 Miles)
W: Campground (10 Miles)
Med — E: ✚ Hospital
ATM — E: Subway
W: Fina, Fina
Other — E: Alumacraft Boat Service
W: Animal Hospital

132 U.S. 8, Taylors Falls, Difficult Reaccess (Northbound, Reaccess Southbound Only, Divided Hwy)

131 CR2, Forest Lake
Gas — E: Amoco(*), Holiday(*, D, LP), Super America(*, D, LP, CW)
W: Holiday(*, D, LP)
Food — E: Arby's, Burger King, Cheung Sing Chinese, Hardee's, Hot Stuff Pizza (Holiday), KFC, McDonald's, McDonald's (Wal-Mart), Perkins Family Restaurant, Sparro's Pizza & Subs, Subway, Taco Bell
W: Famous Dave's BBQ, Little Caesars Pizza (K-Mart), Taco Bell
Lodg — E: Americinn Hotel
W: Country Inn 7 Suites
AServ — E: Amoco, Big Wheel Auto Parts, Car X, Champion Auto Stores, Crown Auto, Jems Service Center, Metcalf Service Auto, RV, Truck, Northern Auto Service, Tire Plus, Wal-Mart
W: Abra Auto Body & Glass, Chrysler Auto Dealer, Dave's Car & Truck Repair, Ford Dealership, GM Auto Dealership, Koppy Motors, Northlake Used Motors, Novack GM Dealer, Quaker State Oil & Lube, Valvoline Oil Change
Med — E: ✚ Hospital
ATM — E: Amoco, Amoco, Holiday, Holiday, Super America, Super America, TCF Bank Of Minnesota
W: Holiday
Other — E: 12st Corner Car Wash, Broadway Car Wash, New Wave Laundry Mat & Tanning Salon, Rainbow Foods Grocery, Wal-Mart(RX) (Optical)
W: K-Mart(RX)

(131) Rest Area (Southbound)

129 MN 97, County 23
FStop — W: Conoco(*)
Food — W: Hot Stuff Pizza (Conoco), Smash Hit Subs, Trout Air Restaurant
TServ — E: A+ Radiator Service, Columbus Truck Service
RVCamp — E: Campground
W: Campground 1 mile
ATM — W: Conoco

128 Weigh Station

EXIT MINNESOTA

127 I-35E Merges With I-35W, East St Paul, West Minneapolis (Southbound)

Note: I-35 runs concurrent below with I-35E. Numbering follows I-35E.

123 CR14
- **FStop** W: Amoco(*, CW)
- **Gas** W: Texaco(*, LP)
- **Food** W: Amoco, Azzini's Italian (Amoco), Pizza & Subs
- **AServ** W: ADL Inc. Muffler Brakes Tires
- **TServ** W: ADL Inc. Muffler Brakes Tires
- **RVCamp** E: Otter Lake RV Center
- **ATM** W: Texaco, Texaco
- **Other** E: Otter Lake Animal Care Center
  W: Star Express Car Wash, Super Car Wash

120 CRJ (Reaccess Southbound Only)
- **Gas** W: Mobil(CW)
- **Food** W: Circus Foods (Mobil), Cousins' Sub's (Mobil), Mobil, Picadilly Pizza (Mobil), TCBY (Mobil)
- **Other** W: The White Bear Township Theater

117 CR 96
- **Gas** E: SuperAmerica(*, D, LP), Total(*, LP)
  W: Amoco(*, CW), PDQ(*)
- **Food** E: Burger King, Fioni Italian Cafe (Total), Georgie V's, Total
  W: Applebee's, Arby's, Boston Market Restaurant, Hardee's, Little Caesars Pizza, McDonald's(PLAY), Sbarro's Pizza, Subway, Tia Pan
- **Lodg** E: AmericInn
- **AServ** E: Goodyear Tire & Auto
  W: Amoco, Tires Plus, Valvoline Oil Change
- **Med** W: ✚ Northeast Medical
- **ATM** W: Cub Foods(24, RX), Cub Foods, PDQ, PDQ
- **Other** W: Cub Foods(RX), Northeast Dental, U.S. Post Office, WalGreens Pharmacy(RX)

115 CRE
- **Gas** E: Amoco(*), Citgo(*), SuperAmerica(*, D, LP), Total(*)
- **Food** E: Citgo, Perkin's Family Restaurant, Ruberto's Italian Restaurant
  W: McDonald's (Wal-Mart), Wal-Mart(RX) (Vision Center)
- **AServ** E: Amoco
  W: Wal-Mart, Wal-Mart (Vision Center)
- **ATM** E: Amoco, Amoco, Super America, SuperAmerica
- **Other** W: Optical (Wal-Mart), Target(RX), Wal-Mart(RX) (Vision Center)

113 I-694W, U.S. 10 (Left Exit)

112 Little Canada Road
- **Gas** E: 76(*, LP), Citgo
  W: Sinclair(*)
- **Food** W: Rocco's Pizza, Sinclair
- **AServ** E: 76, Citgo
- **ATM** W: Sinclair
- **Other** W: Dental Clinic, Tom Thumb C-Store

111AB MN 36E, Stillwater 111A, 111B MN 36W

110B Roselawn Ave

110A Wheelock Parkway, Larpenteur Ave
- **Gas** E: Amoco(*, LP), Total(*, LP)
  W: Sinclair(*)
- **Food** E: Roadside Pizza, Subway
  W: Champp's
- **AServ** E: Amoco, Amoco
  W: Sinclair, Sinclair
- **ATM** E: Amoco, Total, Total

109 Maryland Ave
- **Gas** E: 76(*), Citgo, SuperAmerica(*)

EXIT MINNESOTA

- **Food** E: Phou Dia Oriental Market
  W: Wendy's
- **AServ** E: 76, Citgo, Pete's Auto Repair, Tires Plus Performance Center
  W: K-Mart, K-Mart, Maryland Ave. Auto Sales & Repair
- **ATM** E: Super America, SuperAmerica
- **Other** E: NHIA Grocery Store (Asian & Mexican Foods)
  W: Capital City Animal Hospital, K-Mart

108 Pennsylvania Ave
- **AServ** W: Apex Auto Salvage New & Used Parts

107A I-94E Junction

106C 11th St, State Capitol (Northbound, Reaccess Southbound Only)
- **Med** E: ✚ St. Joseph's Hospital
- **Other** E: The Science Museum of Minnesota

106B Kellogg Blvd (Reaccess Southbound Only)
- **Lodg** E: Days Inn
- **Other** E: Civic Center

106A Grand Ave (Reaccess Southbound Only)
- **Gas** E: Mobil(*)
- **Food** E: Burger King
- **AServ** E: Mobil, Mobil
- **Med** E: ✚ Richie Medical Plaza

105 St. Clair Ave (Southbound, Reaccess Northbound Only)

104C Victoria St, Jefferson Ave (Southbound, Reaccess Northbound Only)

104A Randolph Ave
- **Gas** W: Total(*)
- **Food** E: Rooster's Deli

103B MN 5, West 7th St
- **Gas** E: Holiday(*, D, LP)
  W: SuperAmerica(*, D)
- **Food** E: Burger King, J.R. Mac's Grill
- **AServ** E: Champion Crown Auto Service, Crown Auto, Highland General Training Auto Parts with Car Quest, Len's Automotive Service
  W: Midas
- **ATM** E: Holiday
  W: Super America
- **Other** W: U.S. Post Office

103A Shepard Road (Northbound, Reaccess Southbound Only)

102 MN 13, Sibley Highway
- **Gas** W: Amoco(*, CW), Holiday(*, LP)
- **Food** E: China Delight, Moose Country Restaurant
  W: Amoco
- **ATM** W: Holiday, Holiday
- **Parks** E: City Park
- **Other** E: Just Paws Pet Store, The Parkview Cat Clinic

101AB MN 110
- **Gas** W: General Tire Company, SuperAmerica(*)
- **AServ** W: General Tire Company
- **ATM** W: Dakota Bank, SuperAmerica

99AB I-494

98 CR26, Lone Oak Road
- **Gas** W: Amoco(*), Fina(*, LP, CW)
- **Food** W: American Hero's Sandwiches, Costello Coffee, Cracker Barrel, Joe Censor's Bar & Grill
- **Lodg** E: Homestead Village
  W: Hampton Inn, Residence Inn
- **ATM** W: Fina
- **Other** W: Dental Clinic

EXIT MINNESOTA

97AB CR 31, CR 28, Pilot Knob Road, Yankee Doodle Road
- **Gas** E: Citgo(CW), Holiday(*), Phillips 66(*, CW), Super America(*, D)
  W: Amoco(*, LP, CW), Conoco(*), Super America(*, LP), SuperAmerica
- **Food** E: Applebee's, Arby's, Big Apple Bagels, Burger King, Chili's, Hardee's, He He Chinese Food, Hun Nan's Chinese Garden, KFC, McDonald's, Ole Chicago, Perkins Family Restaurant, Pizza Hut, Schlotzsky's Deli, Taco Bell, Wendy's
  W: Al Baker's, Arby's, Best Steak House, Blimpie Subs & Salads, Burger King, D'Amico & Sons, Dairy Queen, Domino's Pizza, Double T Deli, Dragon Palace Chinese Food, Hobie's, Houlahans, Italian Pie Shoppe, John Hardy BBQ, Maggie's Cafe, New China Buffet, Pablo's, Papa John's, Que Viet, Quizno's Subs, Sidney's, Stuart Anderson Cattle Co., The Best Steakhouse
- **Lodg** E: Fairfield Inn
  W: Best Western, Extended Stay America
- **AServ** E: Abra, All Imports & Domestic Auto Service, Auto Maul, Car X Mufflers & Brakes, Firestone Tire & Auto, Goodyear Tire & Auto, Jiffy Lube(CW), Kennedy Transmission, Phillips 66, Precision Tune, Tires Plus
  W: Amoco, Amoco, NAPA Auto Parts, NAPA Auto Parts
- **TServ** E: Tires Plus
- **Med** E: ✚ Eagan Medical Center
- **ATM** E: First Bank & Trust Co., Holiday, Holiday, Super America, US Bank
  W: Amoco, Byerly's Grocery, Firststar Bank, Norwest Bank, Signal Bank, Super America, Super America, SuperAmerica, TCs Bank
- **Other** E: Companion Animal Hospital, Kinko's Copies, Kohl's Department Store, Mermaid's Car Wash, Petco, Rainbow Foods Grocery, Wal-Mart(RX), WalGreens Pharmacy(RX), Yankee Eye Clinic
  W: AAA Office, Byerly's Grocery, Carribou, Eagan's Cinema's, Pet's Food Outlet, Sterling Optical

94 CR30, Diffley Road
- **Gas** W: Conoco(*, LP, CW)
- **Other** W: Groom Dale Pets Salon

93 CR32, Cliff Road
- **Gas** W: Total(*, LP, CW)
- **Food** W: Anna Chung (Chinese), Baker's Square, Baskin Robbins, Boston Market Restaurant, Broadway Pizza, Burger King, Dairy Queen, Davanni's Pizza & Hoagie's, Green Mill, KFC, McDonald's, Pizza Hut, Taco Bell
- **Lodg** W: Hilton, Holiday Inn Express
- **AServ** W: Big Wheel Auto Store, Meineke Discount Mufflers, Tires Plus, Valvoline Oil Change
- **RVCamp** E: Lebanon Hills Campground (2 Miles)
- **Med** E: ✚ Park Nicollett Medical Clinic
- **ATM** W: Bremer ATM, Cub Foods(24), Dakota Bank, First American Bank, Firstar Bank
- **Other** W: Car Wash, Cub Foods, Dental Clinic, Dental Clinic, GNC, Heartland Pets, Now Med Ctr, Pak Mail, Pet Clinic, Post Office, TLC Pet Grooming, Target(RX), WalGreens Pharmacy(RX)

92 MN 77, Cedar Ave (Divided Hwy)
- **Gas** W: Amoco(*, LP, CW), Holiday(*, LP), Super America(*, D, CW)
- **Food** W: Broadway, Caribou Coffee, Cherokee Sirlion Room Sports Bar, Hardee's, Hung Wong Chinese, J Doodlittle Air Cafe, KFC, McDonald's(PLAY)
- **Lodg** W: Sleep Inn
- **AServ** W: Amoco, Precision Tune
- **ATM** W: Amoco, Dakota Bank, Super America
- **Other** E: Zoo

90 CR11

Bold red print shows RV & Bus parking available or nearby

EXIT MINNESOTA

Gas **E:** PDQ(*), QuikTrip(*, D, LP, CW)
ATM **E:** PDQ, PDQ
Other **E:** **Valley View Pet Hospital**

88B CR42
Gas **W:** Amoco(*, CW), PDQ(*)
Food **E:** Sioddie's Italian
W: Arby's, Burger King, China Seas, Fuddruckers, Marie Callender's Restaurant, McDonald's, Old Country Buffet, Sbarro Pizza, The Ground Round
Lodg **W:** Country Inn, Fairfield Inn, Holiday Inn
AServ **W:** Midas Muffler & Brake
Med **W:** ✚ **Ridge Point Medical**
ATM **W:** PDQ, The Richfield Bank
Other **E:** **Brylie's Grocery & Restaurant**, Pets Mart
W: **Animal Hospital**

Note: I-35 runs concurrent above with I-35E. Numbering follows I-35E.

Note: I-35 runs concurrent below with I-35W. Numbering follows I-35W.

36 CR23
FStop **E:** **Amoco**(*, LP)
ATM **E:** **Amoco**, Fina

33 CR17, Lexington Ave
Gas **E:** Amoco(*, LP)
ATM **E:** Amoco
Other **E:** Pets Supply Warehouse

32 CR52, 95th Ave NE
Other **W:** **National Sports Center**

31B Lake Drive, CRI, 85th Ave (Northbound)

31A CR J, MN118 (Northbound, Divided Hwy)

30 MN 118 (Reaccess Northbound Only, Difficult Reaccess)

29 CR I

28C U.S. 10, CR H (Southbound, Reaccess Southbound Only)
Gas **W:** Amoco(*, CW)
Food **W:** KFC, McDonald's, Perkins Family Restaurant, R. J. Riches Family Restaurant, Taco Bell
Lodg **W:** Mounds View Inn
AServ **W:** Saturn
ATM **W:** Amoco
Other **W:** Car Wash, Car Wash

28B U.S. 10, St. Paul (Southbound, Reaccess Northbound Only)

28A MN 96
Parks **W:** **Long Lake Regional Park**

27AB Junction I-694

26 CRE2
Gas **W:** Tank-n-Tummy(*)

25B CR 88 (Southbound, Reaccess Northbound Only)
Food **W:** Picadilly Pizza (Total)
ATM **W:** Total
Other **E:** **Ken's Market**

25A CR D
Gas **E:** Spur(*)
W: PDQ Food Store(*), SuperAmerica(D, CW), Total(*, D)
Food **E:** Higher Ground Gristles Coffee Shop
W: Kien Giang Chinese/Vietnamese Restaurant, Main Event Restaurant, McDonald's(PLAY), Perkin's Family Restaurant, Subway
Lodg **E:** Fairfield Inn, Residence Inn

EXIT MINNESOTA

TServ **E:** **American Semi Parts & Services**
ATM **W:** PDQ Food Store, SuperAmerica, Total
Other **E:** Ken's Market

24 CRC
Food **E:** Burger King, DAYS INN Days Inn, Grove's (Ramada Inn), India Palace (Days Inn), Ramada
Lodg **E:** DAYS INN Days Inn, Ramada
W: Comfort Inn
AServ **E:** Harmon Auto Glass
W: Danny Hacker's Rosedale Dodge Trucks, GM Auto Dealership, McCarthy's Oldsmobile GM, Rosedale Chevrolet Geo, Rosedale Chrysler Plymouth, Rosedale Hyundai
TServ **E:** **Cummins Diesel**
W: **Casco**, **Chesley Freightliner**, **Mack Truck Dealer**, **Ryder Transportation Service**
Other **E:** **Suburban Animal Hospital**

23A MN 280

23B MN 36, Cleveland Ave (Left Exit)

22 Industrial Blvd, St. Anthony Blvd
Food **E:** Sheraton, The Anchorage (Sheraton), The Nectary
Lodg **E:** Sheraton
Other **E:** **U.S. Post Office**

21A County 88, Stinson Blvd
Gas **E:** Easy Stop(D, CW)
Food **E:** Blimpie Subs & Salads (Easy Stop), Easy Stop, Taco John's (Easy Stop)
W: Burger King(PLAY), Country Kitchen, Donut Connection, Leeann Chin Chinese, McDonald's, Taco Bell
AServ **E:** Mettler Auto Parts
TServ **E:** **Boyer Ford Trucks**, **Boyer Truck Parts**, **MidWest Great Dane**, **Northstar International**
ATM **E:** Easy Stop
W: **Rainbow Foods Grocery**, TCS Bank
Other **W:** Mail Boxes Etc., PetsMart, **Rainbow Foods Grocery**, **Target**(RX)

21B Johnson St (Northbound, Reaccess Southbound Only, Same west services as 21A)

19 E. Hennepin Ave (Northbound)

18 4th St SE, University Ave
Gas **E:** Amoco
Food **E:** Hardee's
Lodg **E:** Gopher Campus Motor Lodge
AServ **E:** Amoco
ATM **W:** Ralph & Jerry's
Other **W:** Gopher Cleaners, Ralph & Jerry's

17CB Washington Ave - 17C, 17B I-94W, 11th Ave.
Gas **W:** Mobil(CW)
Lodg **E:** Holiday Inn
AServ **W:** Mobil
ATM **W:** Mobil

17A MN 55, Hiawatha Ave. (Southbound, Reaccess Northbound Only)
Lodg **E:** Holiday Inn

16A Junction with I-94 (Northbound)

14 35th St, 36th St
Gas **W:** SuperAmerica(*, D)
AServ **W:** Wrongo's Auto Repair
ATM **W:** SuperAmerica

13 46th St
Gas **E:** Mobil
W: 76(*), Amoco(*, CW), Mobil
Food **E:** Mobil
W: Bruegger's Bagel & Bakery, Fresh Wok Chinese, KFC, Mobil, Papa John's Pizza, Pepito's, Subway

EXIT MINNESOTA

AServ **E:** Mobil(*), Mobil
W: 76, Hawkins Service Inc, Mobil
Other **W:** Packaging Store, **Snyder's Drugs**(RX)

12B Diamond Lake Road
Gas **W:** Holiday(*, D, LP)
Food **W:** Cathay's Chow Mein, Chinese Restaurant, Steep & Brew, The Best Steakhouse
AServ **W:** ATS Auto Repair, Big Wheel Auto, Diamond Lake Auto
ATM **W:** Holiday
Other **W:** **ACE Hardware**(LP), **Towns Edge Cleaners/ Coin Laundry**, **U.S. Post Office**

12A 60th St (Reaccess Northbound Only)
Food **W:** CinTia of Mexico, Hong Kong Restaurant (Chinese), Perkin's Family Restaurant
AServ **W:** Meineke Discount Mufflers, World Wide Auto Body & Martin Motors
ATM **W:** **Cub Foods**(RX), Cub Foods
Other **W:** **Cub Foods**(RX), Nicollet Car Wash

11B MN 62E, Airport (Left Exit)

11A Lyndale Ave (Reaccess Northbound Only)
Gas **E:** Food-N-Fuel(*), Texaco(*, LP)
Food **E:** Mister Donut, Pizza Hut
AServ **E:** Champion, Nelvin's Auto Body
ATM **E:** Food-N-Fuel
Other **E:** **Dental Clinic**, **Northstar Paint & Body Supply**, **Wood Ave Veterinary**

10B MN 62W, I-35W, Albert Lea (Difficult Reaccess)

10A CR53, 66th St

9C 76th St (Southbound, Reaccess Northbound Only)
ATM **W:** Tom Thumb
Other **W:** Tom Thumb

9AB Jct I-494

8 82nd St
AServ **W:** GM Auto Dealership (Frontage Rd), Harold's Chevrolet, Infiniti, Saturn

7B 90th St

7A 94th St
Gas **E:** Amoco(*, CW)
Lodg **W:** Holiday Inn
AServ **E:** Amoco, Bloomington Auto & Tire
ATM **E:** Amoco, Amoco
Other **E:** **Bloomington Rental Ctr**(LP)

6 98th St, CR 1
FStop **W:** **Super America**(*, D)
Gas **E:** Indian Joe's(*), Sinclair, Total(*)
Food **E:** Applebee's, Baker's Square, **Byerly's Grocery**, Chinese Restaurant, Deli Supreme, Godfather's Pizza, Lee Ann Chin, McDonald's, New China Buffet, Subway, Wendy's, White Castle Restaurant
W: Denny's
AServ **E:** Champion Auto, Ford Dealership
W: A-1 Body
Med **E:** ✚ **Fairview Oxboro Clinic**
ATM **E:** **Byerly's Grocery**, Firstar Bank, Norwest Bank, Total, US Bank
Other **E:** **Bloomington Drugs**, **Byerly's Grocery**, Kinko's, Mail Boxes Etc., Post Office, WalGreens Pharmacy

5 106th St

4B Black Dog Rd
AServ **W:** Burnsville Volkswagon
Parks **E:** **National Wildlife Refuge**

4A Cliff Road
AServ **E:** Dodge of Burnsville

EXIT MINNESOTA

W: Volkswagen Dealer
Other E: **Mystic Lake Casino, Zoo**

3AB MN 13, Shakopee
Gas E: Phillips 66[*, CW]
W: Sinclair
Food W: Burger King, House of Wu
Lodg E: Quality Inn
AServ W: AAMCO Transmission, Champion, Jeep Eagle Dealer, Sinclair
ATM E: Phillips 66
Other E: AAA Office, River Ridge Pet Clinic
W: **Best Buy**, Mr. Sparkle Truck & Car Wash

2 Burnsville Parkway
Gas E: 76[*, LP], Citgo[*, LP], Fina[*, D], Oasis Market & Convenience Store[LP]
W: Amoco, Standard[*, D]
Food E: Benchwarmer Bob's, Denny's, Hardee's, Little Caesars Pizza
W: Chinese Gourmet, Embers, Timberlodge Steakhouse
Lodg W: Days Inn, Prime Rate Motel, Red Roof Inn, Super 8
AServ E: 76, Citgo
W: Standard
ATM E: Fina, Firstar Bank, Oasis Market & Convenience Store
Other W: **Quik Mart**

1 County 42, Crystal Lake Road (Southbound, Reaccess Northbound Only)
Gas E: Amoco[*, CW], PDQ[*]
W: Sinclair[*, D]
Food E: Arby's, Burger King[PLAY], China Seas, Ciatti's Italian, Dakota County (Holiday Inn), Fuddruckers, Ground Round Restaurant, Marie Callender's Restaurant, McDonald's[PLAY], Old Country Buffet, Sparro Pizza, Taco Bell, The Ground Round
W: Applebee's, Asia Grille, Baker's Square, Bescio's Italian, Champp's, Chi Chi's Mexican Restaurant, Chili's, Chung King Garden, Godfather's Pizza, Macaroni Grill, Mandarian Garden, Olive Garden, Red Lobster, TGI Friday's
Lodg E: Country Inn, Fairfield Inn, Hampton Inn, Holiday Inn
AServ W: Car X Mufflers & Brakes, Ford Dealership, Goodyear Tire & Auto, Grossman Chevrolet, Jiffy Lube, Sears, Sinclair, Valvoline Oil Change
Med E: **Hospital**
ATM E: PDQ, PDQ, Richfield Bank & Trust
W: Norwest Bank, U Bank
Other E: **Benson Optical**, Cross Roads Animal Clinic, **Dental Clinic, Petsmart**
W: America's Best Contacts & Eyeglasses, Burnsville Center, **Kinko's Copies, Kohl's Department Store, Office Max**, Professional Vet Clinic of MN, **Target**[RX], **Toys R Us**, UA Movies

Note: I-35 runs concurrent above with I-35W. Numbering follows I-35W.

88A Junction I-35EW (Northbound)

87 Crystal Lake Road (Southbound, Reaccess Southbound Only)
Gas W: QuikTrip[*, D, LP]
AServ W: Burnsville Lincoln Mercury, Nissan, Buick, Toyota of Burnsville
Other W: Mini Golf

86 CR 46 (Southbound)
Gas E: Quik Trip[*, D, CW], Super America[D, LP, CW]
ATM E: Quik Trip, Super America

85 MN50, CR 5 (Southbound)
Gas E: Amoco[*, LP, CW], Sinclair[*, LP], Super America[*, D, CW], Tom Thumb[*, D]
W: Holiday[*, D, LP, CW]
Food E: Burger King[PLAY], Dairy Queen, Domino's Pizza, Fudge Shoppe, Lakeview Chinese, One Mean Bean Coffee Shop, Pizza Hut, Subway, TAK Shing Chinese, Taco Bell
W: **Cracker Barrel**
Lodg E: Comfort Inn, Finely Host Inn
W: Americinn
AServ E: Big Wheel, Goodyear Tire & Auto, Meals Farm Fleet[D, K], Rapid Oil Change, Valvoline Oil Change
Med E: **Urgent Care Clinic**
ATM E: First National Bank, Marquette Lakeville, Olive Family Foods, Super America, Tom Thumb
W: Holiday
Other E: Mail Boxes Etc., Mr. Sparkle Truck & Car Wash, Olive Family Foods, Snider Family Pharmacy, Southfork Animal Clinic, Touchless Car Wash

84 185th St W (Southbound, Reaccess Northbound Only)

81 CR70, Lakeville, Farmington
FStop E: **MegaStop**[*, CW]
Food E: Grimes Stone Family Restaurant, **JL Pizza, McDonald's**[PLAY], **Subway**, Tacoville, Winslow Steak & Pasta
Lodg E: **Motel 6**, Super 8
TWash E: **Mega Stop**
ATM E: MegaStop, **MegaStop**
Other E: Canine Grooming

76 CR2, Elko, New Market
FStop E: **Phillips 66**[*, LP]
TServ E: **Phillips 66**

(76) **Rest Area (RR, Phones, Picnic, Vending; Southbound)**

69 MN19, Northfield, New Prague
FStop W: **Conoco**[LP, CW, SCALES]
Gas E: Phillips 66[*, LP]
Food E: Bridgeman's Soda Fountion
W: **Big Steer/Conoco**
Med E: **Hospital (7 Miles)**

66 CR1, Dundas, Montgomery

59 MN21, Fairbault, Le Center
FStop E: **Texaco**[*]
Food E: Country Kitchen, Lavender Inn, Restaurant (Lavender Inn), Restaurant/Texaco, Truckers Inn Restaurant (Lavender Inn)
Lodg E: Americinn Motel, Best Western, Super 8 Motel Trucker's Complex
RVCamp W: **Camping**

56 MN60, Fairbault, Waterville
FStop W: **Conoco**[*]
Gas E: Amoco[*]
Food E: Amoco, Bernie's Grill (Amoco), China Cafe, Perkin's Family Restaurant
W: Dairy Queen, **Happy Chef**
Lodg W: Select Inn
AServ E: Chevrolet & Buick, Goodyear, Harry's Brown Dodge Oldsmobile, Steffenes Chrysler, Jeep
W: Car Quest Auto Center
TServ E: **Tires Plus**
W: **Cumming Truck Service**
RVCamp E: **Camping Fairbault (2 Miles Good Sams Camp), Robert Lake Campground & Resort**
W: **Camp Faribo (1.5 Miles)**
Med E: **Hospital**
ATM E: State Bank of Fairbault
W: **Conoco**
Other E: **4 More Grocery Store**, Cinema 6, **Fairbault West Mall, Hi-Vee Grocery Store (24 hours), Wal-Mart**[RX]

55 Fairbaut (Eastbound, Reaccess Southbound Only)
Food E: Altequilia Mexican Food, Broaster Restaurant
Lodg E: Knight's Inn

48 CR12, CR23, Medford
Food W: **McDonald's**[PLAY]
Other W: **Outlet Center**

45 CR9, Clinton Falls
Lodg W: Comfort Inn
Other W: **Cabella's, Heritage Hall Museum**

43 26th St, Airport Road

42B U.S. 14 CR 45, Waseca
FStop W: **Amoco**[*, LP, K, CW, SCALES]
Gas E: Sinclair[*, D, LP, 24]
Food E: Graces Mexican American, Kernel Restaurant, **McDonald's**[PLAY], Sinclair
W: **Amoco, Happy Chef, Perkins Family Restaurant, Restaurant (Ramada Inn)**
Lodg E: Budget Host Inn
W: Best Budget Inn, Best Western, **Ramada Inn, Super 8**
AServ E: Auto Glass Specialist, Champion Auto Stores, Ford, Lincoln, Mercury Dealer, Gleason's Auto Service
TServ E: **NAPA**
ATM E: **Cash Wise Foods Grocery**[LP, RX] **(24 hours)**, Wells Federal Bank
Parks E: **Rice Lake State Park**
Other E: **Cash Wise Foods Grocery**[RX] **(24 hours), Wal-Mart**[RX]

41 Bridge St
FStop W: **Budget Oil Company Commerical Fueling**[*]
Gas E: Citgo[*, D, LP, CW]
Food E: Applebee's, **Arby's**, Burger King, Dairy Queen, KFC, Subway, Subway, Taco Bell
Lodg E: Americinn, Country Inn & Suites
AServ E: Pit's Stop Quick Lube
Med E: **Hospital**
ATM E: Citgo, Citgo
Other W: **Target**[RX]

40 U.S. 218, U.S. 14, Owatonna Rochester
RVCamp E: **Camping**
Med E: **Hospital**

(35) **Rest Area (RR, Phones, Picnic, Vending)**

32 CR 4, Hope
RVCamp E: **Hope Oak Knoll Campground (.75 Miles)**
Other E: **Camping**

26 MN30, Blooming Prairie, New Richland
FStop W: **Texaco**
Gas E: Cinnex[*]
Food E: Cinnex, **Restaurant/Amoco**
W: **Restaurant/Texaco**
TWash W: **Texaco**

22 CR35, Geneva, Hartland
RVCamp W: **Lowry Grove (1.25 Miles)**

18 MN251, Hollandale, Clarks Grove
FStop W: **Gas**[*, LP], **Phillips 66**[*, LP]

14 35th St, 36th St
Gas W: Super America[*]

13AB Junction I-90, Sioux Falls, La Crosse
Gas E: Mobil[*]
W: 76[*], Amoco[*, CW]
Food W: Bruegger's Bagel & Bakery, KFC, Papa John's, Subway
AServ E: Mobil
W: 76, Hawkins Serv Inc

12 U.S. 65, I-35 Business, Albert Lea
AServ W: CrossRoad Chevrolet Trucks, Motor Supply Co. Auto Parts
TServ W: **Interstate Motor Trucks Cummins**

EXIT	**MINNESOTA/IOWA**
11A	International Airport
11	CR46
TStop	**E:** T/A TravelCenters of America(*, LP, SCALES)
Food	**E:** McDonald's, Trails Restaurant
RVCamp	**W:** KOA Campgrounds
Med	**W:** + Hospital
Parks	**E:** Myre-Big Island State Park (.5 Miles)
8	U.S. 65, Albert Lea, Glenville
TServ	**W:** Cross Road's, Diesel Specialist of Albertlee, R&R Truck Repairs
TWash	**W:** Tim's Spotting Service
RVCamp	**W:** Albert Lee RV & Marine(LP)
5	CR13, Twin Lakes Glenville
RVCamp	**W:** Camping
2	CR5
(1)	**Welcome Center, Rest Area (RR, Phones, Picnic, Vending, RV Dump)**

↑MINNESOTA

↓IOWA

214	CR105, Lake Mills, Northwood
(213)	**IA Welcome Center, Rest Area (RR, Phones, Picnic; Southbound)**
(212)	**Weigh Station**
208	CR A38, Joice, Kensett
203	IA9, Manly, Forest City
FStop	**W:** Amoco(*, D)
RVCamp	**W:** RV Mobility Sales & Service, Winnebago Industries (see our ad this page)
197	CR B20
Parks	**E:** Lime Creek Nature Center (8 Miles)
(196)	**Rest Area (RR, Phones, Picnic, Vending, RV Dump)**
194	U.S. 18, Clear Lake, Mason City
FStop	**E:** Coastal(*, D, RV DUMP) **W:** Conoco(*, D, SCALES)
Gas	**W:** Casey General Store(*), Kum & Go(*, LP)
Food	**E:** Coastal **W:** Bennigan's (Best Western), Blimpie Subs & Salads, Burger King, Casey General Store, Conoco, Dairy Queen, Denny's, KFC, McDonald's, Perkins Family Restaurant, Pizza Hut
Lodg	**W:** AmericInn, Best Western, Budget Inn Motel
Med	**E:** + Hospital
193	CR B35, Clear Lake, Mason City
FStop	**E:** Amoco(*, D, LP)
Gas	**W:** Phillips 66(*)
Food	**E:** Happy Chef
Lodg	**E:** Super 8
AServ	**E:** Amoco **W:** Jim Hanson Ford, Lake Chevrolet
188	CR B43, Burchinal
182	CR B60, Swalendale, Rockwell
180	CR B65, Thornton
RVCamp	**W:** Campground
176	CR C13, Sheffield, Belmond
170	CR C25, Alexander
165	IA3, Hampton, Clarion
FStop	**E:** Texaco(*, D)
Food	**E:** Dudley's
TServ	**E:** Texaco
ATM	**E:** Texaco

EXIT	**IOWA**
159	CR C47, Dows
151	CR R75, Woolstock
147	CR D20
144	Blairsburg
TStop	**E:** Phillips 66(RV DUMP) **W:** AmBest(*, SCALES) (Amoco)
FStop	**E:** Phillips 66(*)
Food	**E:** Boondocks Motel(*), Phillips 66 **W:** AmBest (Amoco), Trump Restaurant (Amoco)
Lodg	**E:** Best Western
TServ	**E:** Phillips 66
ATM	**E:** Phillips 66
142AB	U.S. 20E, Waterloo
139	CR D41, Kamrar
133	IA175, Jewell, Eldora
FStop	**W:** Cinnex
Gas	**W:** Phillip 66(*)
Other	**W:** Car Wash, US Post Office
128	CR D65, Randall, Stanhope
Parks	**W:** Little Wall State Park (5 Miles)
124	Story City
FStop	**W:** Phillips 66(*, D), Texaco(*, LP)
Food	**W:** Dairy Queen, Godfather's Pizza, Happy Chef, McDonald's, Pizza Hut, Subway, Valhalla Restaurant
Lodg	**W:** Super 8, Viking Motor Inn
AServ	**W:** Gookin Ford
RVCamp	**W:** Gookin RV Center, Whispering Oaks Campground (.5 Miles)
ATM	**W:** Story County Bank & Trust
Other	**W:** Factory Stores of America
123	IA221, CR E18, Roland, McCallsburg

EXIT	**IOWA**
(120)	**Rest Area (RR, Phones, Picnic, Vending, RV Dump; Northbound)**
(119)	**Rest Area Southbound (RR, Phones, RV Dump; Southbound)**
116	CR E29
113	13th St, USDA Veterinary Lab, Ames
Gas	**W:** Amoco(*), Kum and Go(*, D)
Food	**W:** Best Western, Burger King
Lodg	**W:** Best Western
Med	**W:** + Hospital
Other	**W:** Vet Lab
111AB	U.S. 30, Ames, Nevada
TStop	**W:** Texaco(*)
Food	**W:** Happy Chef, Texaco
Lodg	**W:** AmericInn, Comfort Inn, Hampton Inn, Heartland Inn, Super 8
TServ	**W:** Texaco
RVCamp	**E:** Campground
ATM	**W:** Texaco
(106)	**Weigh Station**
102	IA210, Slater, Maxwell
96	Elkhart
(94)	**Rest Area (RR, Phones, Picnic, Vending)**
92	1st St
Gas	**W:** Amoco(*, D, CW), Kum and Go(*), QuikTrip(*, 24)
Food	**W:** Applebee's, Arby's, Burger King, Casey's Tacos, Duffey's Bar & Grill (Best Western), Fazoli's Italian Food, Happy Chef, KFC
Lodg	**W:** Best Western, DAYS INN Days Inn, Heartland Inn, Super 8
AServ	**W:** Amoco, Amoco, Goodyear, O'Riley's Auto Parts

Tour 60 of the most productive acres in Iowa.

See how Winnebago Industries builds motor homes. Witness production of the entire line of Winnebago, Itasca, Rialta, Vectra and Luxor motor homes. You'll see how Winnebago Industries took the determination that made Iowa's agricultural acreage great and created a plant that makes excellent motor homes. From April through October you can tour the 60-acre plant Monday through Friday at 9 a.m. and 1 p.m. All ages are welcome on the free tour. If your group is larger than six, please make reservations by calling us at 1-800-643-4892, ext. 1.

To reach Winnebago Industries, take 1-35 to exit 203 (15 miles south of the Minnesota border). Go west on Iowa Highway 9 for 15 miles and you'll reach Forest City, Iowa the home of Winnebago Industries.

Be well informed when you visit your local dealer. Tour the Winnebago Industries motor home manufacturing facilities!

WINNEBAGO INDUSTRIES

1396

IOWA ▪ I-35 ▪ EXIT 203

EXIT IOWA

ATM W: Brenton Bank
Other W: Classic Car Wash, Super Wash, **Wal-Mart**[24, RX]

90 IA 160, Bondurant, Ankeny Industrial Area
FStop W: **Casey's**[*]
Food E: Chips Chicken
W: **Burger King**[PLAY], **Casey's**, **McDonald's**[PLAY]
Lodg E: Country Inn, Holiday Inn Express
AServ W: Karl's Chevrolet
TServ W: **Snyder Truck Service**

87B Junction I-80W

Note: I-35 runs concurrent below with I-80. Numbering follows I-80.

136 U.S. 69, East 14th St, Ankeny
FStop S: **Casey's General Store**[*, D], **QuikTrip**[*, SCALES]
Gas N: Amoco[*, D, CW], Phillips 66[*, CW], Sinclair[*, D]
Food N: Bonanza Steakhouse, Bontels Restaurant, Country Kitchen, Okoboji, Red Baron (Best Western)
S: Broadway Diner, **Casey's General Store**, **Magic Food Restaurant**, **QuikTrip**
Lodg N: Best Western, Motel 6
S: 14th Street Inn
AServ N: Sinclair
S: Farm & Country Tires and More[LP], Ford Truck
TServ N: **McKenna Truck Center**
S: **Housvay Mack Trucks**, **James W. Bell Cummins**, **Ruan Truck Sales**
RVCamp N: **Cummins Great Plains (.4 Miles)**
ATM S: **Casey's General Store**
Other N: **K-Mart**[RX]

135 IA 415, 2nd Ave, Polk City
Gas S: Coastal[*], QuikTrip[*, K]
TServ N: **Interstate Detroit Diesel**
S: **Freightliner Dealer**
Other N: Iowa State Patrol

131 IA 28, Merle Hay Road, Urbandale
Gas N: Coastal[*, D], QuikTrip[*]
S: Amoco[*, D, LP, CW, 24], QuikTrip[*], Sinclair[*, LP]
Food N: North Inn Diner (The Inn), Pagiai's Pizza, The Inn
S: Arby's, Bennigan's, Burger King, Denny's, Embers[24], Famous Dave's BBQ, Hostetler's BBQ, McDonald's, Perkins Family Restaurant, The Ground Round, Wendy's
Lodg N: Best Inns of America, The Inn
S: Comfort Inn, DAYS INN Days Inn, Four Points Hotel Sheraton, Holiday Inn, Roadway Inn, Super 8
AServ N: Jordan Motors, Super Lube[CW]
S: All Pro Auto Center, Car Star Collision Repair, Ford, Hummelis Nissan, Lincoln, Mercury, Sinclair, Stevens Foreign & Domestic, Toyota
Med S: + **VA Hospital**
ATM S: US Bank
Other N: Animal House, Village Animal Hospital
S: Animal Medical Clinic, Carmike Cinemas, Discovery Zone, **Touchless of Merle Hay**[CW]

129 NW 86th St., Camp Dodge
Gas N: Heartland Pantry[*] (Phillips 66)
Other N: Wynnsong Cinema's

127 IA 141, Grimes, Perry
FStop N: **Phillips 66**[*, D, LP]
Food N: Subway
RVCamp N: **Cutty's RV Park**

126 Douglas Ave, Urbandale
TStop N: **Pilot Travel Center**[SCALES, 24]
Gas S: Phillips 66[*, CW]
Food N: **Pilot Travel Center**
S: Dragon House
Lodg S: DAYS INN **Days Inn**, **Econolodge**
TServ N: **Pilot Travel Center**[D, SCALES]

EXIT IOWA

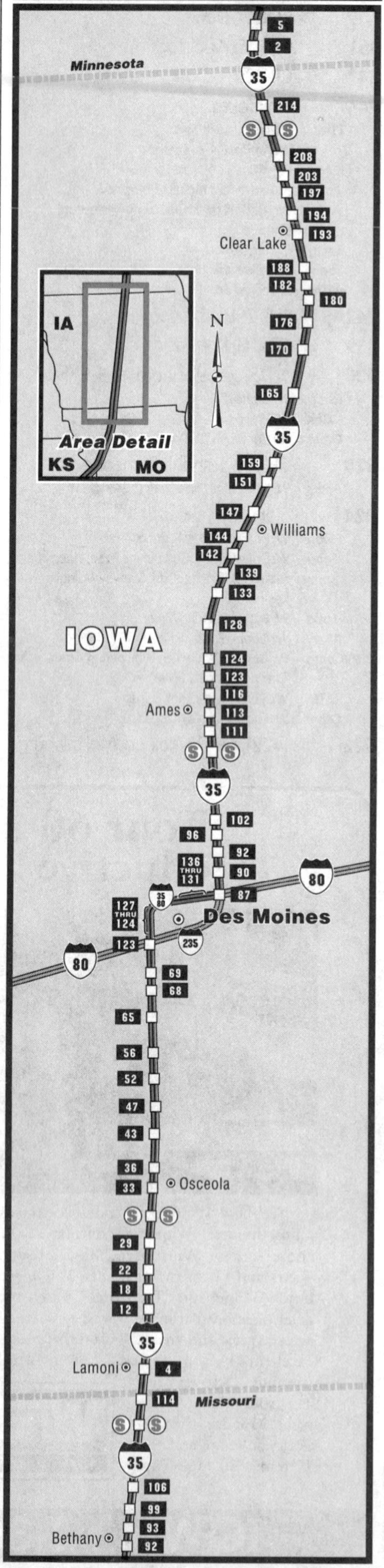

Minnesota
Clear Lake
Williams
IOWA
Ames
Des Moines
Osceola
Lamoni
Missouri
Bethany
IA
KS
MO
Area Detail
N

EXIT IOWA

TWash N: **Pilot Travel Center**
ATM N: **Pilot Travel Center**, **Pilot Travel Center**

125 **U.S. 6, Hickman Road, Adel, Welcome Center**
TStop N: **Flying J**[*, LP]
Food N: **Flying J**
S: Iowa Machine Shed (Comfort Suites)
Lodg S: Comfort Suites Hotel, Four Points Hotel Sheraton, Sleep Inn
AServ S: GMC Trucks, Goodyear Tire & Auto, Oldsmobile, Honda Dealer
TServ S: **Goodyear**

124 University Ave, Clive
Gas N: Amoco[*, CW], Kum & Go[*, CW], Quik Trip[*]
S: Phillips 66[*, CW, 24]
Food N: Cracker Barrel, Mustard's Rib Restaurant
S: Applebee's, Baker's Square, Big Apple Bagels, Chatter's Casual Cafe, Chili's, Cucos Mexican Cafe, Damon's (Holiday Inn), McDonald's, Outback Steakhouse, Palmer's Deli, The Tavern
Lodg N: Budgetal Inn, Country Inn Suites
S: Courtyard by Marriott, Fairfield Inn, Heartland Inn, Holiday Inn, Residence Inn, The Inn, Wildwood Lodge
Med S: + **Urgent Care Clinic**
ATM S: Banker's Trust, State Employees Credit Union

123B I-35 & I-80 split

Note: I-35 runs concurrent above with I-80. Numbering follows I-80.

69AB West Des Moines, Grand Ave

68 IA 5, Des Moines Airport
Parks E: **Blank Park Zoo (2 Miles)**

65 CR G14, Cumming, Norwalk

56 IA 92, Indianola, Winterset
FStop W: **Kum & Go**[*, D] **(Texaco)**
Gas W: Total[*, D]
Food W: Piccadilli Pizza (Texaco), SF Tapp's Hitchin Post Grill
AServ W: Anderson's Auto Service & Sales, Total
ATM W: **Kum & Go (Texaco)**
Other W: US Post Office

52 CR G50, St. Charles, St. Marys
Other W: Covered Bridge 2 miles

(51) **Rest Area (Southbound)**

47 CR G64, Truro

43 IA 207, New Virginia
Gas E: Conoco[*, D, LP]
W: Total

36 IA 152

33 U.S. 34, Osceola, Creston
TStop E: **AM Pride**[*, D, SCALES]
FStop E: **AM Pride**[*, D, SCALES, 24]
Gas E: Texaco[*]
Food E: AM Pride, Byers Restaurant (Texaco), Hardee's, McDonald's, Pizza Hut, Subway
Lodg E: Best Western, Holiday Inn Express, Super 8
AServ E: Chrysler Auto Dealer, Craig's Car Wash, Goodyear Tire & Auto, O'Reilly Auto Parts, T&H Tire Cooper Tires
TServ E: **AM Pride**, **Cooper's Tire Service**, **Pallaton Truck Service**
TWash E: **AM Pride**
ATM E: **AM Pride**, American State Bank, Clark County State Bank
Other E: Iowa State Patrol

(33) **Rest Area (RR, Phones, Picnic, Vending, RV Dump)**

(31) **Weigh Station**

Bold red print shows RV & Bus parking available or nearby

EXIT — IOWA/MISSOURI

29 CR H45

22 IA 258, Van Wert

18 CR J20, Grand River, Garden Grove

12 IA 2, Leon, Mount Ayr
- **FStop** **E:** Texaco[*, LP]
- **Food** **E:** Country Corner Restaurant (Texaco)

(7) **Rest Area (RR, HF, Phones, Picnic, Vending, RV Dump)**

4 **U.S. 69, Lamoni, Davis City, Iowa Welcome Center**
- **Gas** **W:** Amoco[*, D, LP]
- **Food** **W:** Quilt Country Restaurant
- **Lodg** **W:** Chief Lamoni Motel, Super 8
- **AServ** **W:** Gary's One Stop
- **TServ** **W:** Gary's One Stop
- **ATM** **W:** Amoco
- **Parks** **E:** Nine Eagle's Park (9 Miles)

↑IOWA

↓MISSOURI

114 U.S. 69 Lamoni
- **FStop** **W:** Conoco[*, D, RV DUMP]
- **TServ** **W:** Conoco
- **RVCamp** **W:** Camping

(110) **Weigh Station**

106 CR N, Blythedale, Eagleville
- **TStop** **E:** Eagleville Truckstop[*, D, SCALES]
- **FStop** **W:** Texaco[*, D]
- **Gas** **E:** Conoco[*]
- **Lodg** **E:** Eagles Landing Motel
- **TServ** **E:** Eagleville Truckstop
- **RVCamp** **W:** Eagle Ridge RV Park (1.25 Miles), I-35 RV Park & Campground (.2 Miles)

99 CR A, Ridgeway
- **RVCamp** **W:** Eagle Ridge

93 U.S. 69, Spur, Bethany
- **RVCamp** **W:** Hadden Camping[RV DUMP]

92 U.S. 136, Bethany, Princeton
- **FStop** **E:** Conoco[*, D], Phillips 66[*]
- **Gas** **W:** Amoco[*, D], QuikTrip[*, D]
- **Food** **W:** Country Kitchen, Dairy Queen, Hardee's, Russel Stover Candy, Subway, Toot Toot Restaurant, Wendy's
- **Lodg** **E:** Best Western
  W: Super 8
- **AServ** **W:** Bethany All Pro Auto Parts, Hensley Chevrolet, Oldsmobile, Buick Dealer
- **RVCamp** **E:** Chick's RV Camping
- **Med** **W:** ✚ Hospital
- **ATM** **E:** Phillips 66

210 Platte Clay Way
Kearney, MO 64060

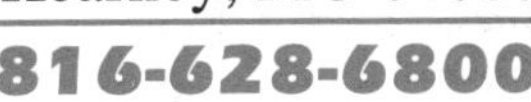

SUPER 8 MOTEL

- Continental Breakfast Included
- Kids Under 12 Stay & Eat Free
- Truck/Large Vehicle Parking
- Handicap Accessible • Interior Corridors
- Gourmet Coffee 24 Hours • Pets Allowed
- Cable TV, 32 Channel & HBO
- King & Queen Beds • Jacuzzi Suites
- Kansas City Events 20 minutes

1543

MISSOURI • I-35 • EXIT 26

EXIT — MISSOURI

MISSOURI

KANSAS

EXIT — MISSOURI

- **W:** QuikTrip
- **Other** **E:** 24 Hour Laundromat (Chick's Mini Mart)
  W: Laundry, Tourist Info., Wal-Mart Supercenter[RX]

88 MO 13, Bethany, Gallatin

84 CR H, CR AA, Gilman City

(81) **Rest Area (RR, Phones, Picnic, P)**

80 CR B, CR N, Coffey

78 CR C, Pattonsburg

72 CR DD

68 U.S. 69, Pattonsburg

64 MO 6, Gallatin, Maysville

61 U.S. 69, Winston, Jamesport
- **FStop** **E:** Texaco[*, LP]
- **Food** **E:** Restaurant (Texaco)

54 U.S. 36, Busi Loop 35, Hamilton, Cameron
- **FStop** **E:** AM Pride[*], Amoco[*]
- **Gas** **W:** Total[*]
- **Food** **E:** AM Pride, McDonald's, Subway (Amoco)
  W: Bread Dougl Pizza, Burger King[PLAY], Dairy Queen, KFC, Ma & Pa's Kettle
- **Lodg** **E:** Best Western, Comfort Inn, Crossroads Inn[SCALES]
  W: DAYS INN Days Inn, EconoLodge, Holiday Inn Express, Super 8
- **AServ** **E:** Knowell Goodyear
  W: Ford, Mercury Dealership, Quick Lube & Car Wash, Red X Motors (Oldsmobile, Chevrolet, Buick, GM)
- **ATM** **W:** Farmer State Bank, Missouri Federal Savings Bank, The Cameron Savings & Loan
- **Other** **E:** Pony Express Regional Tourist Information Center
  W: Country Mart Food Store, Wal-Mart Supercenter

52 Bus Loop 35, CR BB, Cameron (Northbound, Reaccess Southbound Only)

48 U.S. 69, Cameron, Wallace State Park
- **Gas** **W:** Total[*, D]
- **Parks** **E:** State Park (2 Miles)

40 MO 116, Polo, Lathrop
- **FStop** **E:** Phillips 66[*, D]
- **Gas** **E:** Total[*]
- **Food** **E:** Country Cafe (Phillips 66)
- **ATM** **E:** Phillips 66

(35) **Rest Area (RR, Phones, Picnic, P; Southbound)**

(34) **Rest Area (RR, Phones, Picnic, P; Northbound)**

33 CR PP, Lawson, Holt
- **FStop** **W:** Conoco[*, D], Phillips 66[*, D]
- **Lodg** **W:** Holt Steel Inn
- **AServ** **E:** Anderson's Garage
- **RVCamp** **E:** J J Campground (1.35 Miles)

26 MO 92, Kearney, Excelsior Springs
- **TStop** **W:** Kearney Truck Plaza[*, D, SCALES, 24]
- **Gas** **E:** Phillips 66[*], Texaco Star Mart[*, D]
- **Food** **E:** McDonald's, Sonic Drive In, Taco Bell (Texaco Star Mart)
  W: Donuts Plus, Hardee's, Hunan Garden Chinese, Kearney Truck Plaza, Legends Sports Grill, Pizza'N More, Subway
- **Lodg** **E:** Super 8 (see our ad this page)
- **AServ** **E:** Quaker State Oil & Lube
  W: Chevrolet, Geo Dealership
- **TServ** **W:** Kearney Truck Plaza

Bold red print shows RV & Bus parking available or nearby

EXIT MISSOURI

ATM E: Carnie Trust Co., Texaco Star Mart
W: Pony Express Bank
Other E: Kearney Vision Center
W: **John's Super Grocery Store**

(23) **Weigh Station**

20 U.S. 69, MO 33, Excelsior Springs
Gas E: Blue Light(*)
Med E: ✚ **Liberty Hospital**

17 MO 291, CR A, Liberty, KCI Airport
Gas W: Phillips 66(*, LP, CW)
AServ E: Motorcad Repair
ATM W: Phillips 66

16 MO 152, Liberty
Gas E: Texaco(*, LP)
W: Phillips 66(*, CW)
Food E: Boston Market Restaurant, Carlitos Mexican Restaurant, El Cerro Grande Mexican Restaurant, Greaser's Burgers, Hunan Garden Chinese, KFC, Perkins Family Restaurant, Pizza Hut, Ponderosa Steak House, Wendy's
W: Applebee's, Burger King, Country Kitchen, **Cracker Barrel**, Golden Corral Family Steakhouse, McDonald's, Waffle House, **Wal-Mart**(RX)
Lodg E: Best Western, Super 8
W: Fairfield Inn
AServ E: Adam's Muffler & Brake, Firestone Tire & Auto, Gary Crossley's ford, Heartland Geo, Chevrolet, Parts America Auto Parts
W: Hart's Auto Repair, Wal-Mart Tire & Lube
RVCamp E: **AAA RV Sales, Miller's Kampark**
ATM E: Commerce Bank, **Hy Vee Grocery and Pharmacy**(RX), NationsBank, Platte Valley Bank, UMB Bank
Other E: Eckerd Drugs, **Hy Vee Grocery and Pharmacy**(RX), **K-Mart**(RX), Liberty 8 Theatre, Spotless Car Wash
W: **Wal-Mart**(RX)

13 U.S. 69, Pleasant Valley (Northbound)
Gas E: Sinclair(*, LP, CW) (Food: Hot Stuff Pizza), Texaco(*, LP, CW), Total(*, D)
W: Conoco(*)
Food E: Hot Stuff Pizza (Sinclair), Sinclair (Food: Hot Stuff Pizza), Texaco
AServ E: Budget Auto Repair, Frank's Tow & Service, Outback Body Shop
RVCamp E: **I-35 Parts & Accessories**
ATM W: Conoco

12B I435 to North to St. Josephs

12A Jct. I-435S, St. Louis

11 U.S. 69, Vivion Road
Gas W: QuikTrip(*), Total(*)
Food W: Alfredo's Place Mexican Restaurant, Big Burger, Church's Chicken, R B BBQ, Sonic Drive In, Subway
AServ W: Riley's Auto Parts
ATM W: Mercantile Bank
Other W: Animal Hospital, Bob's Automatic Car Wash, Doggie Den, **Foxwood Drugs Pharmacy**, **Timber Ridge Park**, US Post Office

10 North Brighton Ave (Northbound, Reaccess Southbound Only, Difficult Reaccess)
Gas W: QuikTrip(*), Total(*)
Food W: Big Burger, Church's Chicken, Sonic Drive-In, Subway
AServ W: O' Reilly Auto Parts
Other W: **Foxwood Drugs**

9 MO 269, Chouteau Trafficway
Gas E: Phillips 66(*, CW), Sinclair(*)
AServ E: Sinclair

EXIT MISSOURI/KANSAS

ATM E: Phillips 66

8C MO 1, Antioch Road
Gas E: Citgo(*), Sinclare(*, LP)
W: Phillips 66(*, CW)
Food E: Country Girl, Domino's Pizza
W: Waffle House
Lodg E: Best Western, Inn Towne
AServ E: Acton Auto Service
W: Antioch Car Wash(CW)
ATM E: Citgo

8B Jct. I-29 North U.S. 71 North, Kansas City International Airport, St. Joseph, I-35 North Des Moines

8A Parvin Road
Gas E: Texaco(*, LP, CW), Total(*, D)
Food W: TraveLodge, Trevaly's Family Restaurant, Vito's On the Hill
Lodg W: TraveLodge
AServ E: O' Reilly Auto Parts
Other E: Thrifty Coin Laundry

6AB Armour Rd. MO 210 East, North Kansas City
FStop E: **Total**(*, K)
Gas W: Phillips 66(*, CW), Texaco(*, LP, CW)
Food E: Arby's, Captain D's Seafood, McDonald's, SHONEY'S Shoney's, TJ Cinnamon's
W: American Inn, Krispy Kreme Doughnuts (Texaco), Pizza Hut, Taco Bell, Wendy's
Lodg E: DAYS INN Days Inn
W: American Inn, Country Hearth Inn & Suites
AServ E: Northtown Auto Clinic
Med W: ✚ **Omni Family Medicine Health South**
ATM E: NationsBank
W: First Federal Bank
Other E: **Soap & Suds Deli & Grocery**

5B 16th Ave. (Northbound)

5A Levee Rd., Bedford St. (Difficult Reaccess)

4B Front St

4A U.S. 24, The Paseo (Southbound)
Gas E: Citgo(*), Phillips 66
W: Phillips 66(*)
Food E: Chubbies
W: McDonald's
Lodg E: Capri Motel
W: Admiral Motel, Royale Inn
AServ E: Phillips 66, Thoroughbred Ford

3 Junction I-70

2F Oak St, Grand - Walnut

2D Maine - Delaware, Wyandotte St

2C Broadway, US 169N

2W 12th St

2G JCT 29

2H US 24, MO 9

2U Junction I-70E, I-670, St.Louis

1D 20th St

1C Pennway (Northbound, Difficult Reaccess)

1B 27th St, Broadway (Left Exit)

1A Southwest Trafficway

↑MISSOURI

↓KANSAS

235 Cambridge Circle

EXIT STKANSASATE

234 U.S. 169, 7th St. Trafficway, Rainbow Blvd.
RVCamp E: **Central States Special Products (1.7 Miles)**

233A SW Blvd, Mission Road

233B 37th Ave

232B Rowland Park, 18th St Expressway, Roe Ave, US69N

232A Lamar Ave
Gas E: QuikTrip(*), Total(*, LP)

231A Junction I-635, South U.S. 69, Metcalf Ave

231B South U.S. 69, Metcalf Ave.

230 Antioch Road (Northbound, Reaccess Northbound Only)

229 Johnson Dr
Gas W: Conoco(*, D)
Food E: Chile's, PaPa John's Pizza
AServ E: Country Hill Auto Sales, Johnson County Automotive (NAPA), Weaver's Auto Body
RVCamp W: **Walnut Grove RV Park (.5 Miles)**
ATM W: Conoco
Other W: Old Shawnee Town

228B East U.S. 56, North U.S. 69, Shawnee, Mission Pkwy.
Gas E: Texaco(*, LP, CW)
Food E: Checkers Burgers, IHOP, Krispy Kreme Doughnuts (Texaco), Rio Bravo (Mexican), SHONEY'S Shoney's, Taco Bell, Winstead's
Lodg E: Comfort Inn, Drury Inn, Homestead Village
AServ E: Texaco
ATM E: Mercantile Bank, Texaco
Other E: **Big K-Mart**(RX), Shawnee Mission Animal Hospital

228A 67th St
Food E: Burger King(PLAY)
Lodg E: Fairfield Inn by Marriott

227 75th St
Gas E: Circle K(*, LP)
W: Citgo(*), Total(*, D)
Food E: McDonald's, Perkins Family Restaurant
W: Sonic Drive In, Wendy's
AServ E: Ziebart
W: Quaker State Oil & Lube
Med E: ✚ **Shawnee Mission Medical Center**
ATM W: Citgo
Parks W: **Streamway Park**
Other E: **Georgetown Pharmacy**, **Gerry Optical**, Johnson County Animal Clinic

225B U.S. 69 South, Overland Pkwy

225A 87th St Pkwy, Overland Park
Gas W: New Wave(D, LP), Phillips 66(*, CW)
Food W: KFC, Longbranch Steakhouse
AServ E: Maaco, Santa Fe Body Shop
W: Econo Lube & Tune, NTB National Tire & Battery
ATM E: UMB Bank
W: New Wave

224 95th St
Gas E: Phillips 66(*, CW)
W: Conoco(*), Total(*, D, LP)
Food E: Applebee's, Bagel and Bagel, Denny's, Holiday Inn, McDonald's, Steak & Ale
Lodg E: DAYS INN Days Inn, Holiday Inn, **Howard Johnson**, La Quinta Inn, Motel 6, Super 8
AServ E: Parts America
W: Auto Zone, Professional Auto Care
ATM W: Total
Other E: Dept. Of Wildlife & Parks, Oasis Convenient Store, **Sam's Club**

EXIT KANSAS

222AB Junction I-435

220 119th St

- **Gas** E: Texaco[*, CW]
- **Food** E: Baskin Robbins, Burger King[PLAY], China Cafe, Eat At Joe's, Honey Baked Ham, Krispy Kreme Doughnuts (Texaco), Long John Silver, Machine Shed Restaurant, McDonald's[PLAY], Pickerings Restaurant, Rio Bravo (Mexican), Roadhouse Ruby's, Subway, Wendy's
- **Lodg** E: Hampton Inn
- **ATM** E: Commerce Bank, Mercantile Bank, Texaco
- **Other** E: PetsMart, **Super Target**[RX], Tourist Info.

218 Sante Fed

- **Gas** E: Amoco[*, CW, 24]
  W: Amoco[*, CW], Phillips 66[*, CW], QuikTrip[*, 24]
- **Food** E: Back Yard Burgers, Baskin Robbins, Golden Bowl Chinese, Mexican, Perkins Family Restaurant, Winstead's
  W: Denny's
- **Lodg** W: **Best Western**
- **AServ** E: Instant Oil Change Valvoline, McCarthy Auto Group, Olathe Ford
  W: Parts America, **Ridgeview Auto Plaza**, Robert Brogden Pontiac, Buick, GMC Trucks, Team Auto Repair Center
- **TServ** W: **Ridgeview Auto Plaza**
- **ATM** E: Amoco, First National Bank, NationsBank
  W: Amoco, Bank of Blue Valley, Capital Federal Savings, Phillips 66, QuikTrip
- **Other** E: Valu Foods
  W: Car Wash[CW], Olympic Car Wash[CW]

217 Old Hwy 56 (Reaccess Northbound Only)

- **Food** W: Looney's Grill & Bar

215 U.S. 169 South, KS7, Paola

- **TStop** W: **Texaco**[*, LP, SCALES]
- **Gas** E: Phillips 66[*, CW, 24]
- **Food** W: Applebee's, **Blimpie's Subs (Texaco)**, Burger King[PLAY], Country Kitchen, **Krispy Kreme Doughnuts (Texaco)**, **McDonald's**[PLAY], Red Lobster, **Wendy's**
- **Lodg** W: Holiday Inn, Microtel Inn
- **Med** W: ✚ **Olathe Medical Center**
- **ATM** E: Phillips 66
  W: **Texaco**
- **Other** W: **Great Plains Great Mall**

(213) Motor Vehicle Inspection Station

210 U.S. 56, Gardner

- **Gas** W: Phillips 66[*, CW]
- **Food** W: McDonald's[PLAY], Waffle House
- **Lodg** W: Super 8
- **ATM** W: Phillips 66

207 Gardner Road

- **Gas** W: Conoco[*, D]
- **RVCamp** W: **Olathe RV Center**

202 Edgerton

198 KS 33, Wellsville

- **Gas** W: Total[*]

193 Le Loup Road, Baldwin

- **Food** W: McKenzie's Country Cafe

187 Bus. U.S. 50, KS 68, Ottowa, Paola

- **FStop** W: **Phillips 66**[*]
- **Gas** W: Fill R Up[*, D]
- **ATM** W: **Phillips 66**

185 15th St, Ottowa

- **Lodg** W: DAYS INN Days Inn
- **Med** W: ✚ **Hospital**

183B U.S. 59 North, Ottawa, Lawrence

- **FStop** W: **Phillips 66**[*]
- **Gas** W: Amoco[*, CW], Citgo[*], Conoco[*, LP, CW, 24]

EXIT KANSAS

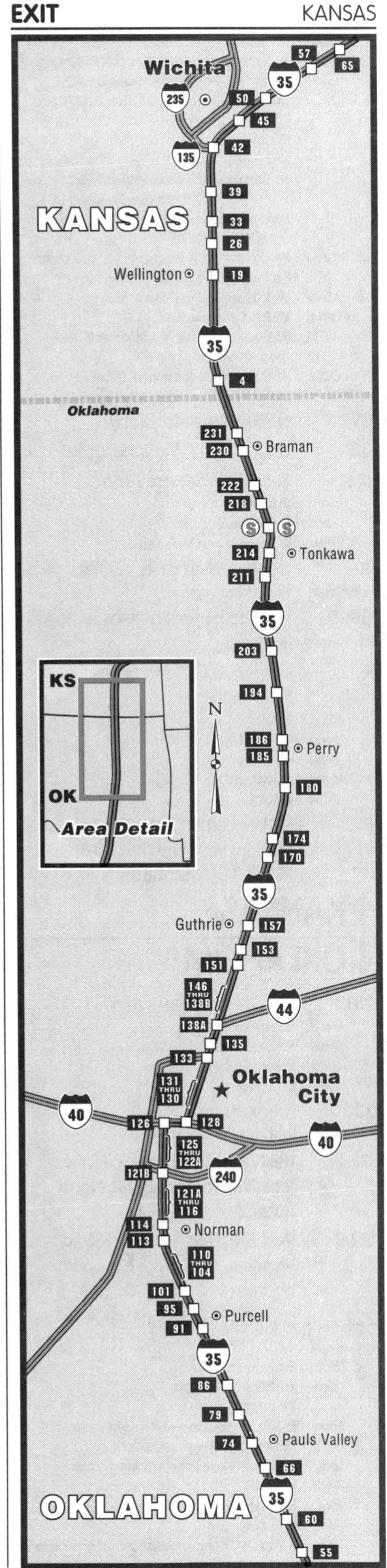

EXIT KANSAS

- **Food** W: Burger King, Country Kitchen, Long John Silver, McDonald's[PLAY], Sirloin Stockade, Taco Bell, **Wal-Mart**[24, RX], Wendy's
- **Lodg** W: **Best Western**, **EconoLodge**, Holiday Inn Express
- **AServ** W: Big A Auto Parts, **Wal-Mart**[24]
- **TWash** W: **Car Wash & Truck Wash**[CW]
- **ATM** W: Amoco, **Country Mart Food Store**, Kansas State Bank
- **Other** W: **Car Wash & Truck Wash**, **Country Mart Food Store**, On Cue Music, Books, Movies, **Wal-Mart**[RX]

182B Ottawa, (Difficult Reaccess)

182A County Road

176 Homewood

- **RVCamp** W: **Homewood RV Park & Campground**

(175) **Rest Area (RR, Phones, Picnic, Vending, RV Dump, P; Northbound)**

(175) **Rest Area (RR, Phones, Picnic, Vending, RV Dump, P; Southbound)**

170 KS 273, Williamsburg, Pamona

- **Gas** W: Davey and Gails Convenience Store

162 KS 31South, Waverly

160 KS 31North, Melvern

155 U.S. 75, Burlington, Lyndon

- **TStop** E: **T/A TravelCenters of America**[*, LP, SCALES], **Total**[*]
- **Lodg** E: Beto Inn
- **TServ** E: **Lebos Garage (TA TS)**
- **Other** E: **John Redman Reservoir**
  W: **Melvern Lake**

148 KS 131, Lebo

- **FStop** E: **Coastal**[*]
- **Food** E: Cafe
- **Lodg** E: Universal Inn

141 KS 130, Neosho Rapids, Hartford

138 County Road

135 Thorndale

- **RVCamp** W: **Camping**

133 U.S. 50, 6th Ave

- **Food** E: McDonald's, Pizza Hut
- **Lodg** E: Budget Host Inn (.75 Miles)

131 Burlingame Road, 12th Ave

- **Gas** E: Amoco[*], Coastal[*]
- **Food** E: Burger King[PLAY], Hardee's[PLAY], Mr. Goodcents Subs
- **AServ** E: American Car Care Centers, Amoco
- **ATM** E: Admire Bank, Coastal, NationsBank
- **Other** E: Dillon's Groceries

130 KS 99, Merchant St

- **Gas** E: Phillips 66[D]
- **Lodg** E: University Inn
- **AServ** E: Phillips 66
- **Med** E: ✚ **University Medical Center**

128 Industrial Road

- **FStop** W: **Phillips 66**[*, CW, SCALES]
- **Gas** E: Conoco[*, D], Total[*]
  W: Texaco[*]
- **Food** E: Arizona Vic's, Burger King, Coburn's Family Restaurant, Noah's Food & Spirits
  W: **Cracker Barrel**, Golden Corral Family Steakhouse, McDonald's, Taco Bell, **Wendy's (Phillips 66)**
- **Lodg** E: Comfort Inn, Motel 6, Ramada Inn
  W: Fairfield Inn by Marriott
- **AServ** E: Goodyear Kansasland Tire, Western Auto

Bold red print shows RV & Bus parking available or nearby

EXIT KANSAS

W: Wal-Mart(RX) (Vision Center)
TWash W: Hydra King(CW)
ATM E: Commerce Bank & Trust, NationsBank
W: Texaco
Other E: Carroll's Entertainment Superstore, Food 4 Less Grocery(24), Otto Car Wash
W: Hydra King, Wal-Mart(RX) (Vision Center)

127 Jct I-335, U.S. 50 West, North KS 57, Ottawa, Kansas Turnpike, Topeka, Wichita
TStop W: Martin's Truck Service(SCALES)
FStop E: Phillips 66(*, D, LP)
Gas E: Amoco, Conoco(*, D)
Food E: Arby's, Hardee's(PLAY), Mazzio's Pizza, Western Sizzlin'
W: Ranch House Cafe
Lodg E: Best Western, DAYS INN Days Inn, Super 8
W: Ranch House
AServ E: Amoco, Napa Auto
TServ W: Martin Truck Service, CAT
RVCamp W: Emporia RV Park (.75 Miles), KOA Campgrounds
ATM E: First National Bank, Phillips 66
Other E: Car Wash, Laundromat (Phillips 66)

127B To U.S. 50, KS 57, Emporia (Northbound)

(97) Mattifield Green Service Area (Left Exit)
FStop B: Coastal(*, D)
Food B: Hardee's
ATM B: Coastal

92 KS 177, Cassoday

76 U.S. 77, El Dorado North, Nick Badwey Plaza
Parks E: El Dorado State Park

71 KS 254, KS 196, El Dorado, Augusta
Gas E: Phillips 66
Food E: Burger King, Chin's Chinese Restaurant, Golden Corral Family Steakhouse, KFC, McDonald's, Moe's BBQ, Pizza Hut, Sub & Stuff Sandwich Shop
Lodg E: Best Western, Heritage Inn, Super 8
AServ E: All Pro Auto Parts, Jarvis Auto Supply, Wal-Mart(RX)
ATM E: Commerce Bank, NationsBank
Other E: Coin Laundry, Wal-Mart(RX)

(65) Towanda Service Area
FStop B: Coastal(*)
Food B: Hardee's
ATM B: Coastal
Other B: Tourist Info.

57 Andover, 21st Street

53 KS 96, Wichita (Difficult Reaccess, Limited Access Hwy)

50 U.S. 54, U.S. 400, Kellogg Ave
Gas W: Coastal(*)
Food W: Grandy's, Marriott, SHONEY'S Shoney's, Steak & Ale
Lodg W: Comfort Inn, DAYS INN Days Inn, Fairfield Inn, Hampton Inn, Marriott, Residence Inn by Marriot, Rodeway Inn, Scotsman Inn, StudioPlus, Super 8, Wyndham Garden Hotel
AServ W: Discount Auto Glass, Joe Self Chev, BMW, Geo, NTB National Tire & Battery, Pep Boys Auto Center
ATM W: Coastal
Other W: K-Mart(RX), U.S. Post Office

45 KS 15, Wichita K-15

42 Jct I-135, I-235, U.S. 81, 47th Street (Toll)

EXIT KANSAS/OKLAHOMA

Gas W: Coastal(*, CW), Phillips 66(*, CW)
Food W: Applebee's, Azteca Mexican, Braum's Ice Cream(PLAY), Dairy Queen, Dillon's Food Market(RX) (Chinese Food), Domino's Pizza, Erby's Pizza, Evergreen Chinese American Cuisine, Godfather's Pizza, Heritage Restaurant, KFC, Little Caesars Pizza, Long John Silver, McDonald's, Mr. Goodcents Subs, Pizza Hut, Potbelly's Family Restaurant, Spaghetti Jack's, Spanglers, Sub & Stuff Sandwich Shop, Subway, Super Wok, Taco Bell, Taco-Tico
Lodg W: Comfort Inn, El Rancho Motel, Holiday Inn Express, Red Carpet Inn, The Heritage Inn
AServ W: K-Mart(RX), O'Reilly Auto Parts
RVCamp W: R & D Camperland
ATM W: Coastal, Dillon's Food Market (Chinese Food), Phillips 66
Other W: Checkers Supermarket, Dillon's Food Market(RX) (Chinese Food), K-Mart(RX)

39 U.S. 81, Haysville, Derby

33 U.S. 81, KS 53, Mulvane, Belle Plaine

(26) Belle Plain Service Area
FStop B: Coastal(*)
Food B: Hardee's
Other B: Travel Information Center

19 U.S. 160, Wellington, Winfield
RVCamp W: KOA Campgrounds

(19) Toll Plaza, End of Kansas Turnpike (Toll)

4 U.S. 166, U.S. 81, Arkansas City, South Haven
FStop E: Total(*)
Food E: Piccadilly Pizza (Total)
Lodg E: Economy Inn
AServ E: Strickland Road Service
ATM E: Total

(1) KS Welcome Center, Weigh Station, Rest Area (RR, Phones, Picnic, P; Northbound)

↑KANSAS

↓OKLAHOMA

231 U.S. 177, Braman
FStop E: Conoco(*, SCALES)
Food E: Kanza Cafe
Lodg E: Kanza Motel
ATM E: Conoco

230 Braman Road
FStop W: Texaco(*)

(226) Rest Area (RR, Phones, Picnic, Vending, RV Dump, P; Northbound)

(226) Rest Area (RR, Phones, Picnic, Vending, RV Dump, P; Southbound)

222 (219) OK 11, Blackwell, Medford, Alva, Newkirk
FStop E: Conoco(*)
Gas E: Phillips 66(*), Texaco(*, D)
W: Texaco(*)
Food E: Braum's Ice Cream(PLAY), Kettle Restaurant, McDonald's, Plainsman Restaurant, Subway
Lodg E: Comfort Inn, DAYS INN Days Inn
AServ E: Texaco
Med E: + Hospital
ATM E: Conoco
Other E: Top Of Oklahoma Museum, Whites Factory

EXIT OKLAHOMA

Outlet Center

218 Hubbard Road

(217) Weigh Station (Northbound)

(217) Weigh Station (Southbound)

214 (212) U.S. 60, Lamont, Ponca City.
FStop W: Phillips 66(*)
Food W: Conestoga Restaurant
Lodg W: New Western Inn Motel
AServ W: Steve's Auto Service
RVCamp W: Woodland RV Park

211 Fountain Road
TStop E: Love's(*)
Food E: Pizza Hut (Love's)
TServ E: Wilkins Okla Truck Supply
ATM E: Love's

(210) Parking Area (Northbound)

(210) Parking Area (Southbound)

203 OK 15, Billings, Marland
TStop E: Conoco(*)
Food E: Dairy Queen (Conoco)
Other E: Coin Operated Laundry(D) (Conoco)

(196) Parking Area (Northbound)

(195) Parking Area (Southbound)

194AB U.S. 64, U.S. 412, Stillwater, Tulsa, Enid, Cimmarron Turnpike (Difficult Reaccess)

186 U.S. 64 East, Perry, Fir St
FStop E: Diamond Shamrock(*)
W: Conoco(*, SCALES)
Food E: Braum's Ice Cream, McDonald's(PLAY), Subway (Diamond Shamrock), Taco Mayo (Mexican)
Lodg W: DAYS INN Days Inn
Med E: + Hospital
Other E: Cherokee Strip Museum

185 U.S. 77, Perry, Covington
TStop W: Texaco(*)
Gas E: Phillips 66(*)
Food E: Best Western
Lodg E: Best Western
W: Texaco
TServ W: Texaco
RVCamp W: Sooner's Corner RV Park & Motel, Texaco
ATM W: Texaco

180 Orlando Road

174 OK 51, Stillwater, Hennessey
FStop E: Phillips 66, Texaco(*)
AServ E: Texaco

(173) Parking Area (Southbound)

(171) Parking Area (Northbound)

170 Mulhall Road
FStop E: Sinclair(*)
AServ E: Sinclair

157 OK 33, Guthrie, Cushing
FStop W: Texaco(*)
Gas E: Sinclair(D, LP)
W: Phillip 66(*)
Food W: Best Western (RV Hookups), Burger King(PLAY), Chester Fried Chicken To Go (Phillips 66), Dairy Queen, El Rodeo Mexican (Texaco), Texaco
Lodg W: Best Western (RV Hookups), Interstate Motel
AServ E: Sinclair
W: Phillip 66
RVCamp W: Best Western (RV Hookups), Best Western Territorial Inn & RV Park, Cedar Valley Golf and Recreation Area (4 Miles)
Med W: + Hospital (4 Miles)

EXIT	OKLAHOMA
ATM	W: Texaco
Other	W: Oklahoma Territorial Museum (2 Miles)
153	U.S. 77, Guthrie (Northbound, Reaccess Southbound Only)
151	Seward Road
FStop	E: Conoco
Food	E: Lazy E. Arena Cafe (Conoco), Stuckey's (Conoco)
RVCamp	E: K @ J RV Park (.5 Miles)
ATM	E: Conoco
(149)	Rest Area (RR, Phones, Picnic, P)
(149)	Weigh Station (Northbound)
(149)	Weigh Station (Southbound)
146	Waterloo Road
FStop	E: Conoco(*, LP)
Food	E: County Line Cafe
ATM	E: Conoco
143	Covell Road
142	Danforth Rd (Northbound, No Reaccess)
141	US 77 South, Second St, OK 66, Edmond, Tulsa
Parks	E: Central State Park, Edmond Park
Other	E: Arcadia Lake
140	SE 15th St
Parks	E: Arcadia Spring Creek Park
139	SE 33rd St
138D	Memorial Road
138C	Sooner Road
138B	Kilpatrick Turnpike
138A	Jct I-44 E, Tulsa
137	NE 122nd St
TStop	W: Flying J Travel Center(*, LP, SCALES)
FStop	E: Texaco(*) (CB Repair), Total(*)
	W: Love's Country Store(*, SCALES), Texaco(*)
Food	E: Kettle (Texaco FS)
	W: Carl Jr's Charbroiled Hamburgers (Texaco), Cracker Barrel, Magic Dragon Chinese (Flying J Travel Center), McDonald's, Oklahoma Trading Post, Pepperoni's Pizza (Flying J Travel Center), Subway (Love's), Taco Bell (Love's), Waffle House
Lodg	E: Motel 6
	W: Comfort Inn, Days Inn (see our ad this page), Motel 6, Quality Inn, Red Carpet Inn
AServ	W: Interstate Auto Repair, Interstate Battery (RV Campground Good Sam Park)
TWash	W: Oasis Truck Wash
RVCamp	W: RV Campground Good Sam Park(LP)
ATM	W: Love's Country Store, Texaco
Other	W: Tourist Info.
136	Hefner Road
Gas	W: Conoco(*)
Food	W: Homemade Italian Specialties
Other	W: Frontier City (Amusement Park)
135	Britton Road, NE 93rd St
134	Wilshire Blvd, NE 78th St
TStop	W: Texaco(*, SCALES)
Lodg	W: EconoLodge
TWash	W: Texaco
ATM	W: Texaco
133	State Capitol, Jct. I-44 W, Lawton, Amarillo
132B	NE63rd St.
Gas	E: Conoco(*, D)
Food	E: Braum's, Derby's

EXIT	OKLAHOMA
Lodg	E: Super 8
RVCamp	W: ACME RV Service
Other	E: Animal Clinic
132A	NE 50th St
Parks	W: Remington Park
Other	W: Museum, Zoo
131A	NE 36th St, Forest Park
Other	W: 45th Infantry Division Museum
130	U.S. 62E, NE 23rd St
Gas	E: Conoco(*, D), Total(*, D)
Food	E: Country Club BBQ
129	NE 10th St
128	Jct I-40 E, Fort Smith (Left Exit Southbound)
127	Eastern Ave
TStop	N: Petro Travel Plaza(*, SCALES), Pilot(*, SCALES, 24)
Gas	N: Texaco(*)
Food	N: Gary Dale's BBQ, Iron Skillet Restaurant (Petro Travel Plaza), Waffle House, Wendy's (Pilot)
Lodg	N: Best Western, Central Plaza Hotel & Convention Center
TWash	N: Blue Beacon (Petro Travel Plaza)
RVCamp	N: Lewis RV Center Sales & Service
126	Jct I-40, Jct I-235N, Edmond, Amarillo, Wichita, Fort Smith
125B	SE 15th St
Gas	E: Conoco(*, D), Total(*, D)
Food	E: Choice Restaurant(24) (Howard Johnson Express), El Sombrero, Skyliner Restaurant(24), Subway (Conoco)
Lodg	E: Howard Johnson Express
TServ	W: Oklahoma Truck Supply
ATM	E: Conoco

Oklahoma City
1611
DAYS INN
— Children Under 12 Stay Free —
— Full Service Restaurant on Premises —
— Free Local Calls —
— Free HBO —
— Banquet for 345 —
— Free Continental Breakfast —
— Outdoor Swimming Pool —
— Coffee Makers in Hotel Rooms —
— 152 Remodeled Rooms —
405-677-0521 • Oklahoma City
OKLAHOMA ▪ I-35 ▪ EXIT 124B

Oklahoma City
DAYS INN
405-478-2554
Toll Free Reservations:
800-329-7466
• 47 Large Spacious Deluxe Suite Rooms with Refrigerators & Microwaves
• Jacuzzi Suites Available
• Heated Indoor Swimming Pool
NEW
• Free Continental Breakfast
• Will Rogers World Airport - 22 Miles
• Oklahoma University - 5 Miles
• In Room Movies Block Buster
• Pennington Park & OK Zoo - 5 Miles
• Frontier City - 2 Blocks
1188
OKLAHOMA ▪ I-35 ▪ EXIT 137

EXIT	OKLAHOMA
125A	SE 25th St., SE 29th St. (Southbound)
Gas	W: Phillips 66(*, CW)
Food	W: Mama Lou's Restaurant(24)
RVCamp	W: McClain's RV
ATM	W: Phillips 66
124B	SE 29th St, SE 25th St. (Northbound)
Food	E: Days Inn, Denny's, McDonald's, Taco Bell, Waffle House
Lodg	E: Days Inn (see our ad this page), Plaza Inn, Royal Inn, Super 8
124A	Grand Blvd
Food	W: Drover's Inn
Lodg	W: Drover's Inn, Executive Inn
AServ	W: Gary's Auto Center
RVCamp	W: McClain's RV Superstore(LP)
123B	SE 44th St
Gas	E: Conoco(*), Stax Gas(*)
Food	E: Domino's Pizza, Lucy's Restaurant(24), Sonic Drive In
	W: Pizza 44, Sunset Grill, Taco Mayo
Lodg	E: Courtesy Inn & Suites
AServ	W: Auto Pro, Rod's Car Shop
Med	W: Hospital, PM Clinic Minor Medical Emergency Plus
ATM	E: Stax Gas
Other	W: Sav-A-Lot Grocery
123A	SE 51st St
Gas	E: Conoco
Food	W: Southgate Inn
Lodg	E: Best Value Inn
	W: Southgate Inn
AServ	W: Cherokee Tire
TServ	W: Cherokee Tire
RVCamp	E: Roadrunner RV Park
122B	SE 59th St, Hillcrest St
FStop	W: Stax Gas(*), Total(*, RV DUMP)
Gas	E: Texaco(*, D)
	W: Stax Gas(*)
AServ	E: Championship Transmission Auto Repair
	W: ITG Automotive
RVCamp	E: Briscoes RV Park(*, LP, K)
ATM	W: Total
122A	SE 66th St
Gas	W: 7-11 Convenience Store(*)
Food	E: Burger King, Charles' Place (Ramada Inn), Luby's Cafeteria, McDonald's(24), Ramada Inn, Taco Bell
	W: Arby's
AServ	E: Cooper Tires
ATM	W: 7-11 Convenience Store
Other	E: Crossroads Mall, Discovery Zone, Eyemart Express
121B	Jct I-240, OK 3, U.S. 62W, Lawton
121A	SE 82nd St
Food	W: Denny's
Lodg	W: La Quinta Inn, Red Carpet Inn
AServ	W: Classic Auto Parts
120	SE 89th St
FStop	E: Total(*, SCALES)
	W: Love's Country Store(*, 24)
Food	E: Hot Stuff Pizza (Total FS), Smash Hit Subs (Total FS)
	W: Carl Jr's Hamburgers, Mom's Bar-B-Que, Subway (Love's Country Store)
ATM	E: Total
Other	W: Superior Coin Car Wash
119B	N 27th St
Gas	E: Texaco(*)
	W: Phillips 66(*)
Food	E: Best Western
	W: Pickle's Restaurant
Lodg	E: Best Western

Bold red print shows RV & Bus parking available or nearby

EXIT OKLAHOMA

RVCamp **W:** Wholesale RV's
119A Shields Blvd (Northbound, Left Exit)
118 N12th St, Main St, N 5th St
Gas **E:** Stax Gas[*, CW], Texaco, Total[*, D]
W: Texaco[*, CW]
Food **E:** Harry Bear's Restaurant, Hong Kong Wok, Mazzio's Pizza, Sonic Drive In
W: Arby's, Braum's, Grandy's, KFC, Las Fajitas, Long John Silver, Mama Lou's[24], McDonald's[PLAY], Papa John's Pizza, Pizza Hut, Taco Bell, Wendy's, Western Sizzlin'
Lodg **E:** Super 8
W: Comfort Inn, Days Inn, Motel 6
AServ **E:** Texaco, Total
W: Auto Zone Discount Auto Parts
ATM **E:** Stax Gas
Other **E:** Dolly Madison Bakery, Maytag Coin Laundry
117 OK37, S 4th St, Main St., N 5th St.
Gas **E:** Texaco[D]
W: Jerry's Foods[*], Total[*, D, CW]
Food **E:** China Doll Chinese
W: Mr Burger, The Donut Delight
AServ **E:** Moore Kar Kare, Texaco
W: Total
Med **W:** + Moore Medical Center
Other **W:** Moore Veterinary Hospital, Southgate Drug[RX], U.S. Post Office
116 S 19th St
FStop **E:** Conoco[*, D]
Gas **E:** Conoco[*, D]
W: Wal-Mart Supercenter[24, RX] (1 Hr Photo)
Food **E:** Braum's Hamburgers, Carl Jr's Hamburgers, Country Vittles Buffet, Dairy Queen, HB Burgermaker, McDonald's[PLAY], Taco Bell
W: Burger King[PLAY]
Lodg **E:** Microtel Inn & Suites
AServ **E:** Firestone, Moore Auto
W: Wal-Mart Supercenter[24] (1 Hr Photo)
ATM **W:** Wal-Mart Supercenter (1 Hr Photo)
Other **W:** Wal-Mart Supercenter[RX] (1 Hr Photo)
114 Indian Hill Road, 179th St
RVCamp **E:** Kerr Country
113 U.S. 77 S, Franklin Road (Southbound, Left Exit Southbound)
112 Tacumsa Rd.
110 Robinson St
Gas **E:** Albertson's Grocery[24, RX], Petro - Self-Service
W: Conoco[*]
Food **E:** Carl Jr's Hamburgers[PLAY], Sonic Drive In, Taco Bell
W: Arby's, Braums[PLAY], Cracker Barrel, Domino's Pizza, Gabriel's, Hunan Chinese, Jama's Italian, Outback Steakhouse, Pizza Hut, Pizza Shuttle (Conoco), Ryan's Steakhouse, Subway, Waffle House
Lodg **W:** Holiday Inn
AServ **E:** Ferguson Pontiac, Buick, GMC Trucks, Fowler Toyota, Dodge, Jeep Eagle, Lincoln Mercury Dealer, Q Lube, Riddles Ford
W: Auto Valet
ATM **E:** Albertson's Grocery
Other **E:** Albertson's Grocery[RX]
W: AMC Theaters, Hollywood's Theaters
109 Main St
Gas **E:** Phillips 66[*, CW], Texaco[*, D, CW]
W: Conoco[*, D, CW]
Food **E:** Denny's (Guest Inn), Golden Corral Family Steakhouse, Praire Kitchen, Waffle House
W: Applebee's, Baskin Robbins, Bellini's Italian Grill, Burger King[PLAY], Charleston's, Chili's, Don Pablo's Mexican, El Chico, McDonald's[PLAY], Olive Garden, On The Border, Red Lobster
Lodg **E:** Days Inn, EconoLodge, Guest Inn, Super 8 (see our ad this page), TraveLodge
W: Fairfield, Hampton Inn
AServ **E:** Ferguson Dodge, Hibdon Tire, Marc Heitz Oldsmobile, Cadillac, Spencer Chevrolet, Texaco, Travis Chrysler Plymouth
W: Pig Red Kia & Isuzu, Sears, Wal-Mart[RX]

EXIT OKLAHOMA

ATM **E:** Citizens Bank, Phillips 66
W: Bank of Oklahoma
Other **E:** Target
W: Barnes & Noble, Borders Books & Music, Eyemart Express, Home Depot, Mail Boxes Etc., Office Max, PetsMart, Posh Wash, Shopping Mall, Wal-Mart[RX]
108B OK 9E, OK 74A, Lindsey St, Tecumseh, Univ of Oklahoma
Gas **E:** Conoco[*, LP, CW], Phillips 66[*], Sinclair
Food **E:** Arby's, Arthur's (Ramada), Bo Bo's Chinese, Braum's, China Star, Del Rancho's Hamburger, Goldie's Grill, KFC, Schlotzsky's Deli, Subway, Taco Bell[24], Taco Bueno
W: Village Inn
Lodg **E:** Ramada Inn (see our ad this page)
W: La Quinta
AServ **E:** Fast Lube, Midas Muffler Shop, O'Rilley Auto

1873

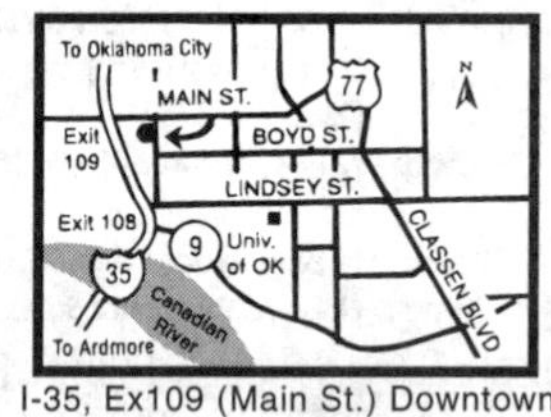

I-35, Ex109 (Main St.) Downtown
2600 W. Main St
Norman, OK
$45.00* +tax
1-4 Persons
Continental Breakfast
Kids Under 12 Stay Free
Indoor Pool/Hot Tub
Exercise Room/Sauna
Meeting/Banquet Facilities
Pets Allowed • Coin Laundry
Truck/Large Vehicle Parking
Exterior/Interior Corridors
Satellite TV w/HBO
Game Room
405-329-1624
Pricing not valid for special events, holidays & weekends. No other discounts can be combined with the above special.
OKLAHOMA • I-35 • EXIT109

1260
RAMADA INN®
1200 24th Ave. SW • Norman, OK 73072
• Restaurant & Lounge On-Site
• In-Room Coffeemakers
• Fitness Room
• Coin Laundry
• Free Local Calls
• Free Cable TV & HBO
• Outdoor Pool & Sundeck
• Easy Access off I-35(108B Exit)
Newly Renovated
$38.00
Valid with coupon at check-in. Based on availability. Not valid with other discounts or during holidays or special events.
405-321-0110 • Toll Free Reservations: 1-800-500-9869
OKLAHOMA • I-35 • EXIT 108B

EXIT OKLAHOMA

Parts, Ron's Automotive, Sinclair
ATM **E:** Phillips 66
Other **E:** Coin Car Wash, Luxury Wash Laundry, Skateland
108A OK 9 E, Tucumseh
Gas **E:** Phillips 66[*, D]
Lodg **E:** Residence Inn, ThunderBird Lodge
TServ **E:** B & H Machine Co.
Other **E:** Parkside Animal Hospital
106 OK 9W, Chickasha, New Castle, Blanchard
FStop **W:** Conoco[*, 24], Love's Country Store[*, 24]
Food **W:** Burger King (Conoco), Taco Bell (Love's Country Stores)
TServ **E:** Mid-Continent Truck Sales
ATM **W:** First American Bank & Trust Co.
104 OK 74S, Goldsby, Washington
FStop **W:** Total[*]
Gas **W:** Texaco[*, D]
Food **W:** Hydes Smokehouse BBQ, Libby's Kitchen
AServ **W:** Andrew's Service Center, Texaco
TServ **W:** Andrew's Service Center
RVCamp **E:** Floyd's RV Center
101 Ladd Road
98 Johnson Road
FStop **E:** Texaco[*]
RVCamp **E:** Alamo RV Park
95 U.S. Hwy 77, Purcell, Lexington (Left Exit Southbound)
Med **E:** + Hospital
91 OK 74, to OK 39, Purcell, Lexington, Maysville
FStop **W:** Texaco[*]
Gas **E:** Phillips 66[*, D], Total[*, D]
Food **E:** Beaver's Restaurant (EconoLodge), McDonald's[PLAY]
W: Blimpie Subs & Salads (Texaco)
Lodg **E:** EconoLodge
AServ **E:** Elliott's Automotive
ATM **W:** Texaco
86 OK 59, Wayne, Payne
79 OK145E, Paoli
74 Kimberlin Road
72 OK 19, Pauls Valley, Maysville, Lindsey, Ada
TStop **E:** Total[*, SCALES, 24] (Road Service)
FStop **W:** Love's Country Store[*, 24] (CB Shop), Phillips 66[*]
Food **E:** Ballard's Drive In, Braum's, Carl Jr's Hamburgers, Denny's, KFC, McDonald's, Punkin's BBQ, Subway, Taco Mayo, Total (Road Service), Valley Cafe (Total)
W: A & W Hot Dogs & More (Love's FS), Mr. P's BBQ, Steaks, & Fish
Lodg **E:** Amish Inn Motel, Days Inn, Garden Inn Motel, Sands Inn
AServ **E:** John Winkler Buick, Pontiac, Cadillac, Chrysler, Plymouth
TServ **E:** Total[SCALES, 24] (Road Service)
TWash **W:** Rusty's Truck Wash
RVCamp **E:** Pecan RV Park
ATM **E:** Total (Road Service)
W: Phillips 66
Other **E:** Super H Foods
70 Airport Road
Med **E:** + Hospital
Other **E:** Airport
66 OK 29, Wynnewood, Elmore City
TStop **E:** Kent's Truck Stop - Citgo[*, D]
Gas **W:** Texaco[*]
Food **E:** Kent's Truck Stop - Citgo
W: Texaco
Lodg **E:** Kent's Truck Stop - Citgo
TServ **E:** Kent's Truck Stop - Citgo
64 OK 17A East, Wynnewood
FStop **W:** Fina[*]
RVCamp **W:** Royal Coach RV Service[LP]
60 Ruppe Road
(57) **Rest Area (RR, HF, Phones, Picnic, RV Dump, P; Southbound)**
(58) **Rest Area (RR, Phones, Picnic, RV**

Bold red print shows RV & Bus parking available or nearby

EXIT		OKLAHOMA
		Dump, (P); Northbound)
55		OK 7, Davis, Duncan, Sulphur, Ada
	FStop	E: Phillips 66(*, D), Total(*)
	Food	E: A & W Hot Dogs & More (Phillips 66)
	RVCamp	W: Oak Hill RV Park
	ATM	E: Phillips 66
	Parks	E: Chickasaw National Recreation Area
	Other	E: Arbuckle Lake
(53)		Weigh Station (Both Directions)
51		U.S. 77, Turner Falls Area
	Gas	W: Sinclair
	Food	W: The Trout Place
	Lodg	E: Arbuckle Motel
		W: Canyon Breeze Motel (RV Hookups)
	RVCamp	E: Martins Rv Park
	Parks	E: Turner Falls Park (1 Mile)
	Other	E: Arbuckle Wilderness (1 Mile)
		W: Cedarville Botanical Gardens (1 Mile)
(49)		Scenic View (Southbound)
47		U.S. 77, Turner Falls Area
43		Dougherty, Springer
(46)		Scenic View (Northbound)
42		OK53W, Comanche
	FStop	W: Diamond Shamrock(*)
40		U.S. 77, OK 53, Autrey, Ardmore Airpark
	FStop	E: Total(*, LP, RV DUMP)
33		OK 142, Ardmore
	FStop	E: Fuel Man(*)
	Gas	E: Phillips 66(*, 24)
	Food	E: Ponders (Guest Inn)
	Lodg	E: Days Inn, Guest Inn, Super 8
	ATM	E: Phillips 66
32		12th St
	FStop	W: Love's Country Store(*, D, LP, SCALES)
	Food	W: Baskin Robbins (Love)
	Med	E: ✚ Memorial Hospital (1 Mile)
31B		U.S. 70W, OK 199, Waurika, Lane Grove, Ardmore
	Gas	W: Conoco(*, D), Total(*, D)
	Food	W: Calvin's Cove
	AServ	W: Billingsly Ford Mercury Nissan, McCulloh Olds Cadillac
	Other	W: Westwood Animal Hospital
31A		OK199 E, Ardmore
	Gas	E: Conoco(*), Sinclair(*, D), Texaco(*, D), Total(*)
	Food	E: Burger King(PLAY), Cattle Rustler's, Classic Interurban Grill, Denny's (Holiday Inn), El Chico Mexican Restaurant, KFC, Pecos Red's Roadhouse, Pizza Hut, Praire Kitchen, SHONEY'S, Shoney's
	Lodg	E: Best Western, Comfort Inn, Dorchester Inn, Hampton, Holiday Inn, Motel 6
	Other	E: Carmike Cinemas, Owner's Coin Car Wash
29		U.S. 70E, Madill, Ardmore
	Other	E: Hardy Murphey Colliseum
24		OK 77 S
	FStop	E: Total(*)
	Gas	E: Wilderness Way
	Food	E: Two Sister's Kountry Cafe (Red River Livestock Market), Wilderness Way
	RVCamp	E: KOA Kampground
	Parks	E: Lake Murray State Park (3 Miles)
21		Oswalt Road
	RVCamp	W: KOA Kampground(LP)
15		OK 32, Marietta, Ryan
	TStop	E: Total(*)
	Gas	E: Sinclair
		W: Phillips 66(*), Texaco(*)
	Food	E: Carl Jr's Hamburgers, Denim's Restaurant, Pizza Hut, Robertson's Bisquits & Sandwiches, Sonic Drive In, Total
		W: Hickory House BBQ, Subway (Phillips 66)
	AServ	E: Anderson Ford, Jones Auto Repair, Sinclair
	TServ	E: Total
	RVCamp	W: Grey Rock
	ATM	E: Bank of Love Co., Total, Winn Dixie Supermarket
		W: Phillips 66
	Parks	E: Lake Texoma State Park

EXIT		OKLAHOMA/TEXAS
	Other	E: Winn Dixie Supermarket
5		OK153, Thackerville
	RVCamp	W: Indian Nation RV Park
(4)		Rest Area (RR, Phones, Picnic, (P); Southbound)
(3)		OK Info Center, Rest Area (RR, Phones, RV Dump, (P); Northbound)
1		U.S. 77N

↑OKLAHOMA

↓TEXAS

EXIT		TEXAS
504		Frontage Road (Northbound)
(503)		Parking Area ((P); Northbound)
(502)		TX Info Center, Rest Area (RR, Phones, (P); Southbound)
501		TX 1202
	Gas	W: Conoco(*)
	Food	W: Hilltop Cafe, Wayne Harper's Steaks, Seafood, & BBQ
	AServ	E: Glenn Polk Ford
	RVCamp	W: Gainesville Factory Shop
	ATM	W: Conoco
	Other	W: Gainesville Factory Shop
500		Fm 372, Gainesville
	TStop	E: Gainesville Truck Stop(*)
		W: Texaco(*, SCALES, 24)
	Food	E: Gainesville Truck Stop
		W: Texaco
	TServ	E: Gainesville Truck Stop
		W: Texaco(SCALES, 24)
	TWash	E: Gainesville Truck Stop
	ATM	W: Texaco
499		Frontage Road (Northbound)
	FStop	E: Little Red's(*)
	Food	E: Denny's
	Lodg	E: Bed & Bath Inn, Budget Host Inn, Comfort Inn
	ATM	E: Little Red's
498B		U.S. 82W, Wichita Fallls
	Gas	E: Conoco, Diamond Shamrock(*, D, 24), Exxon(*, D), Texaco(*)
		W: Exxon(*, D)
	Food	E: Waffle Inn
		W: Bamboo Garden
	Lodg	E: 12 Oaks Inn
		W: Best Western, Days Inn (see our ad this page), Texas Motel
	AServ	E: CBJ Tire & Alignment Firestone, Conoco, Exxon, King's Garage
		W: Brown Chevrolet, Pontiac, Buick
	Med	E: ✚ Hospital
	ATM	E: Diamond Shamrock, Texaco
	Other	E: Car Wash, Coin Laundry, Gainesville Optical
		W: Animal Clinic, Enderby(LP)
498A		U.S. 82E, Sherman (See Services On

1102

KIDS EAT FREE

Cable TV With HBO

Restaurant on Premises

Swimming Pool

Golf & Tennis Nearby

940-665-5555

TEXAS ▪ I-35 ▪ Exit 498B

Bold red print shows RV & Bus parking available or nearby

EXIT		TEXAS

498B)

497 Frontage Road
Gas E: Conoco(*)

496B TX 51, California St, Decatur
Gas E: Conoco(*, D), Diamond Shamrock(*, 24), Mobil(*)
W: Texaco
Food E: Braum's, Burger King(PLAY), Grandy's, Holiday Inn, McDonald's, Taco Bell, Taco Mayo, Wendy's
Lodg E: Holiday Inn
AServ E: Glenn Polk Chrysler, Plymouth, Dodge, Oldsmobile, Cadillac, Osbornes Hardware
W: Texaco
Other E: Osbornes Hardware, **Scivally's Grocery**(RX)
W: **Frank Buck Zoo**

496A Weaver St. (Northbound, Trucks Prohibited)

495 Frontage Road (Southbound)

494 TX1306

(492) **Rest Area (RR, Phones, Picnic, Grills, Vending, RV Dump, P; Southbound)**

491 Spring Creek Road

(490) **Rest Area (RR, Phones, Picnic, Grills, Vending, P; Northbound)**

488 Hockley Creek Road

487 FM 922, Valley View (Difficult Reaccess)
FStop W: **Chevron**(*)
Food W: Dairy Queen
ATM W: **Chevron**
Other W: **U.S. Post Office**

486 Frontage Road, FM 1307

485 Frontage Road (Southbound, Reaccess Southbound Only)

483 TX 3002, Lone Oak Road
RVCamp E: **RV Ranch Sales & Service**(LP)

482 Chisam Road

481 View Road

480 Lois Road

479 Belz Road
Lodg E: **Sanger Inn**
AServ E: Beard's Motors(24)
RVCamp E: **North Village Campground**

478 Fm 455, Pilot Point, Bolivar
Gas E: Phillips 66(*), Texaco(*, CW)
W: Chevron(*)
Food E: Dairy Queen, Dos Amigo's, Kirby's BBQ
W: Subway (Chevron), Wimpy's Burgers & Salads
AServ W: Jim McNatt Chevrolet
TServ W: **Cowboy Truck Repair**
ATM E: Texaco
W: Chevron, GNB Bank, Sanger Bank
Parks E: **Ray Roberts State Park**
Other E: Cleaners Laundromat
W: **Bruss IGA Grocery Store**

477 Bus 35, Keeton Road
Gas E: Phillips 66(*)
W: Diamond Shamrock(*, D)
Food E: Cattle Rustler's, Mr. Gatti's
AServ E: Parts Plus, Sanger Radiator & Welding

475B Rector Road

475A TX 156, Krum (Southbound, Reaccess Southbound Only)

474 Cowling Turnaround (Northbound)

EXIT		TEXAS

473 TX 3163, Milam Road
FStop E: **Love's Country Store**(*)
ATM E: **Love's Country Store**

472 Ganzer Road

471 U.S. 77, Fm1173, Loop 288, Denton, Krum
TStop E: **T/A TravelCenters of America**(*, SCALES)
W: **Citgo Truckstop**(*, CW, SCALES)
FStop W: **Fina**(*)
Food E: **T/A TravelCenters of America**
W: **Citgo Truckstop**
TServ E: **T/A TravelCenters of America**(SCALES)
W: **Citgo Truckstop**(SCALES), **Denton Drive Train**
TWash W: **Citgo Truckstop**(CW)
RVCamp W: **Camping World Inc. (1 Mile)**
Med W: **+ Hospital**

470 Loop 288 (Northbound)
Food E: Good Eats
Lodg W: **Excel Inn**, Motel 6
RVCamp W: **Camping World (see our ad this page)**
Med W: **+ Denton Regional Medical Center**
ATM E: **Denton Factory Stores**
Other E: **Denton Factory Stores**, **Denton Visitor Center**

469 U.S. 380, Decatur, McKinney
FStop W: **Conoco**(*)
Gas E: Chevron(*)
W: Diamond Shamrock(*), Shell(*, CW), Texaco(*, D)
Food E: **Cracker Barrel**, McDonald's
W: Dairy Queen, **Denny's**, Waffle House
Lodg W: **EconoLodge**
AServ W: Shell
Med W: **+ Hospital**
ATM E: Chevron
W: Texaco

468 Fm 1515, Airport Road, West Oak St (Southbound)
Med E: **+ Denton Community Hospital**

Note: I-35 runs concurrent below with I-35E. Numbering follows I-35E.

467 Jct I-35W South, Fort Worth

466B Ave D
Gas E: Exxon(*)

Group Rates Available
1200
RAMADA
FANTASY/SUITES
820 SOUTH I-35E • DENTON, TEXAS
Located Close to Texas Motor Speedway
University of North Texas &
Texas Women's University
TOUR BUSES WELCOME
60 Channel Cable TV • Truck Parking • Pool
Restaurant & Bar on Site • Mirowave & Refrigerator
In Room Coffee, Iron & Hair Dryer's
Close to Shopping & Many Restaurants
E-Z on & off Access to Interstate
940-387-0591 • Toll Free Reservations: 1-800-2-RAMADA
TEXAS • I-35E • EXIT 465A

CAMPING WORLD
Exit 470
5209 I-35 North • Denton, TX
1-800-527-4812
1420

EXIT		TEXAS

Food E: IHOP(24), McDonald's
Lodg W: Radisson Hotel
ATM E: Exxon, **Sack & Save**(RX)
Other E: **Sack & Save**(RX)

466A McCormick St
FStop E: **Phillips 66**(*)
Gas E: Citgo(*), **Phillips 66**(*), Texaco(*, D, CW)
W: Fina(*)
Food E: 2.99 Oriental Express, Bread of Heaven, Burger King, Milano's Italian, NY Subway, Pancho's Mexican Buffet, Siam House, Swenson's Ice Cream, The Cup
Lodg E: Royal Inn & Suites
AServ W: A-1 Auto Body & Repair
ATM E: Bank One, Quick Stop, Texaco
Other E: Coin Laundromat, Quick Stop

465B U.S. 377, Fort Worth Drive
FStop W: **Piggly Wiggly**
Gas E: Citgo(*, D), Diamond Shamrock(*)
W: Citgo(*), Conoco(*, D), Phillips 66, Total(*, D)
Food E: Kettle Restaurant(24), Taco Bueno, Whataburger(24)
W: Frosty, JR Pockets, Mi Ranchito, Outback Steakhouse, Smoke House BBQ, Sonic Drive In, Taco Bell (Total)
Lodg E: La Quinta Inn
W: Days Inn, Desert Sands Motor Inn
AServ E: Tommy's Hi Tech Auto
W: **A & T Truck & Trailer Repair**(D), All Tune & Lube, American Trim & Glass, Lee's Transmission, Phillips 66, Ray's E-Z Lube
ATM E: Citgo, Texas Bank
W: Conoco, Total
Other W: **Piggly Wiggly**

465A Fm 2181, Teasley Lane
Gas E: Citgo(*)
W: Fina(*, D), Shell(*), Texaco(*)
Food E: Applebee's, Braum's Restaurant(PLAY), Golden China, KFC, Little Caesars Pizza, Pizza Hut
W: Olive 'O Branch Pizza, Ramada Inn
Lodg W: **Ramada Inn (see our ad this page)**, Super 8
AServ E: Chief Auto Parts
W: Shell
ATM E: Citgo
Other E: **Winn Dixie Supermarket**(24, RX)
W: Car Wash

464 Pennsylvania Drive
Food E: JJ Pizza
Lodg E: Holiday Inn
AServ E: Carquest Parts Center, Denton Chrysler Plymouth, Pep Boys Auto Center
ATM E: First State Bank

463 Loop 288
Gas W: Mobil(*, D, CW)
Food E: Arby's, Burger King, Cafe China, Ci Ci's Pizza, Colters BBQ, Grandy's, Jason's Deli, Long John Silver, Smoothie King, TCBY, Taco Bell, Wendy's
W: Black Eyed Pea, Chili's, Donut Palace, Jack-In-The-Box, Luby's Cafeteria, Pizza, Red Lobster, Red Pepper, Schlotzsky's Deli, Tia's Texmex, Uncommon Ground Coffee
AServ E: Discount Tire, Goodyear Tire & Auto, Midas Muffler & Brake, Montgomery Ward, Sears, USA Lube & Tune
ATM E: Bank One, **Kroger Supermarket**(24, RX)
W: **Albertson's Supermarket**, Red Lobster
Other E: EyeMasters, **Golden Triangle Mall**, Heritage Car Wash, **Kroger Supermarket**(RX), Petco, **Target**
W: **Albertson's Supermarket**, **Southridge Pet Hospital**

462 State School Road, Mayhill Road
Gas E: Fina(*)
W: Exxon(*, 24)

EXIT TEXAS

Food **W:** Brier Inn
ASserv **E:** Eckert Hyundai
W: Jane's Wood Auto Park

461 Shady Shores Road, Post Oak Dr.
ASserv **W:** Huffines Mazda, Kia, Lence Nissan
RVCamp **E:** **McClain's RV Superstore**
ATM **W:** Lake Cities Bank

460 Corinth
Gas **E:** Chevron[*]
ASserv **E:** Chevron
RVCamp **E:** **McLain's RV**[LP]
W: **KOA Kampground**

459 Frontage Road
RVCamp **W:** **KOA Campgrounds**[LP, CW]

458 Fm 2181, Swisher Road, Lake Dallas, Hickory Creek
Gas **E:** Phillips 66[*]
W: Chevron[*], Exxon[*, CW]
Food **W:** Exxon, Genti's Pizza & Pasta, Jack-In-The-Box, McDonald's (Chevron), Mr. Gatti's, Wendy's (Exxon)
ASserv **W:** Kwik Kar Lube & Tune
ATM **E:** Phillips 66
W: **Albertson's Supermarket**[24, RX], Chevron
Other **W:** **Albertson's Supermarket**[RX], National Nail Center, Vet Clinic

457AB Lake Dallas (Northbound)
Gas **E:** Chevron[*], Citgo[*], Phillips 66[*, 24], Texaco
Food **E:** Chubby Burger's & More, Enrique's Place Mexican, Godfather's Pizza (Citgo), Ozzie's Donuts, Sonic Drive in, Subway
ATM **E:** Chevron, Citgo, Texaco

455 McGee Lane
Gas **W:** Snap-E-Sack
RVCamp **E:** **Tower Bay RV Park**

454B Highland Village, Rest Area (P; Southbound)
Parks **W:** **Copparas Branch Park**

454A Road 407, Justin
Gas **E:** Citgo[*], Diamond Shamrock[*], Phillips 66
W: Fina[*, D, CW], Texaco[*]
Food **E:** Al's Chuck Wagon BBQ
W: Blum's Donuts, Domino's Pizza, Fina, McDonald's[PLAY]
ASserv **E:** Phillips 66, Royal Tire
W: Kwik Kar Oil & Lube[CW]
ATM **W:** Fina, Texaco
Other **W:** Spot Free Car Wash

453 Valley Ridge Blvd
ASserv **E:** **Village Ford**
RVCamp **E:** **Buddy Gregg Motor Homes, Inc., May's RV's (.25 Miles)**
Other **W:** **Home Depot, Lowe's**

452 Fm 1171, Flower Mound
Gas **E:** Lewisville Quick Stop, Mobil[*, CW]
W: Exxon[*, D], Shell[*, 24]
Food **E:** Taco Bueno
W: Blimpie Subs & Salads, Chick-Fil-A[PLAY], Ci Ci's Pizza, Denny's[24], Golden Corral Family Steakhouse, Grandy's, McDonald's[PLAY], Smoothie Factory, Taco Bell, Taco Cabana, Wendy's, Whataburger[24]
Lodg **E:** Holiday Inn Express
ASserv **E:** Lewisville Quick Stop
W: All Tune & Lube, Atlas Transmission, Chief Auto Parts, KClinic, Midas Muffler & Brake, **Sam's Club, Wal-Mart**[RX] **(Vision Center, 1 Hr. Photo)**
Med **E:** **+ Hospital**
W: **+ Prime Care Medical Clinic**
ATM **E:** Bank One, First Federal Bank
W: NationsBank, Omni American Federal Credit Union

EXIT TEXAS

Other **W:** Petco, **Sam's Club, Wal-Mart**[RX] **(Vision Center, 1 Hr. Photo)**

451 Fox Ave
Gas **E:** Texaco[*, D, CW]
W: Chevron[*, CW, 24], Diamond Shamrock[*]
Food **E:** Braum's Ice Cream
W: Black Eyed Pea, **Cracker Barrel**, El Chico Mexican Restaurant, Southern Maid Donuts, Taqueria Guadalhara
Lodg **W:** Hampton Inn, Microtel
ASserv **E:** Just Brake's
RVCamp **E:** **Avion Sales & Service**

450 TX 121, Grapevine, McKinney
Gas **E:** Citgo[*], Racetrac[*]
W: Chevron[*, CW], Conoco[*], Fina[*], Texaco[*, D, CW]
Food **E:** Marshalls BBQ, Owen's Restaurant, Pancho's
W: Burger King[PLAY, 24], Chili's, Church's Chicken, Furr's Family Dining, Long John Silver, Ming Garden Chinese, **Ninfa's**, Roma Pasta House, Subway, Taco Bell, Tia's Tex-Mex, Waffle House
Lodg **E:** Pines Motel, Ramada Inn
W: DAYS INN Days Inn, Spanish Trails Inn, Super 8
ASserv **E:** Bob's Tire & Auto Center, Huffines Dodge, Oliver's
W: All State Transmission, Firestone Tire & Auto, Kwik Kar Lube & Tune, Saturn Dealer
ATM **W:** Chevron, Fina, **Kroger Supermarket**[24, RX]
Other **E:** **Lewisville Animal Hospital**
W: **Eckerd Drugs**[RX], Eye Glass Repair, Jet Spray Car Wash, **Kroger Supermarket**[RX]

449 Corporate Drive
Gas **W:** Exxon[*, CW], Fina[*]
Food **E:** On the Border Cafe, Water Street Seafood Co.
W: Fresco Pasta, Seafood, Good Eats Grill, Jack-In-The-Box, Kettle, Outback Steakhouse, Pizza Inn (Exxon), Quizno's Classic Sub (Exxon), TCBY (Exxon)
Lodg **E:** Motel 6
W: La Quinta Inn
ASserv **E:** Huffines Chevrolet, GM
W: Jim McNatt Honda, Service King
RVCamp **W:** **Treetops RV Village (.75 Miles)**
Other **E:** **United Artist Theaters**
W: BBQ Galore[LP]

448A Fm 3040, Round Grove Road, Hebron Pkwy
Gas **W:** Exxon[*, CW]
Food **E:** Chuck E Cheese's Pizza, Olive Garden, Razzoo's Cajun Cafe, Saltgrass Steakhouse, Souper Salad
W: Applebee's, Barnes & Noble, Carino's, Chick-Fil-A[PLAY], Cotton Patch Cafe, Einstein Bros Bagels, IHOP, Jason's Deli, Lover's Eggroll, McDonald's[PLAY], Omaha Steaks, Pizza Hut (Exxon), Schlotzsky's Deli, Spring Creek BBQ, TCBY (Exxon), Taco Cabana, Wendy's
Lodg **E:** Homewood Suites Hotel
ASserv **E:** Auto Nation USA, **Montgomery Ward**
W: Discount Tire Company
Med **E:** **+ Metro Medical Associates, + Trinity West Medical Plaza**
ATM **W:** Compass Bank, Texas Commerce Bank
Other **E:** Book Stop, **Garden Ridge Home Decorations & Crafts, PetsMart**
W: Baptist Bookstore, Barnes & Noble, Borders Books & Music, Office Depot, **Office Max**, Pack N Mail, Pearl Vision Center, **Target**

448B Spur 553 (Southbound)
Food **W:** Don Pablo's Mexican, Red Lobster, Romano's Macaroni Grill, T.G.I. Friday's, Tony Roma's
Lodg **W:** Comfort Inn, Country Inn Suites, Residence Inn
ASserv **W:** Sears
Other **W:** **Vista Ridge Mall**

446 Frankford Rd., Trinity Mills Rd.

EXIT TEXAS

Gas E: Racetrac[*]
RVCamp E: **North Dallas RV Sales & Service**

445 Trinity Mills Road (Northbound)
AServ W: Vista Ridge Pontiac, GMC
RVCamp W: **North Dallas RV Sales & Service**

444 Whitlock Lane, Sandy Lake Road
Gas E: Texaco[*, CW]
W: Chevron[*, CW]
Food E: Taco Bell, Tommy's BBQ
W: Lite Bites Deli, McDonald's
Lodg W: Deluxe Inn
AServ E: Stanley's Garage
RVCamp W: **Sandy Lake RV Park (.5 Miles)**
Other W: Sandy Lake Amusement Park

443C Frontage Rd. (Northbound)
AServ W: American Collision Center

443B Belt Line Road, Crosby Road
Gas E: Conoco[*, D], Racetrac[*]
W: Texaco[D]
Food E: Blimpie Subs & Salads (Conoco), La Pasadita, Praire House Restaurant, The Bakery Sandwich Shop
W: The Pocket Place Sandwich Shop
AServ E: NTB, Town Auto Service, Valley View Foreign Car Service, Van's Chevrolet
W: B&B Radiator & Muffler, Big A Auto Parts, Texaco
ATM E: Conoco
W: Texaco

443A Crosby Road
Gas E: Shell[*, CW]
AServ E: Lee Jarmon Ford

442 Valwood Parkway
Gas E: Highway Oil[*], Superfuels, Texaco[*, D]
W: Fina[*, D]
Food E: Dairy Queen, Denny's, El Chico Mexican Restaurant, Elena's Tortillas, Grandy's, Jack-In-The-Box, Red Line Burgers, Taco Bueno, Waffle House
Lodg E: Comfort Inn, Guest Inn, Howard Johnson, Red Roof Inn
AServ E: Alan Express Oil & Lube, Hill Tire Co. (Firestone), Metro Plex, Payless Auto Service, Texaco
W: A-1 Transmission, American Transmission, Pennzoil Oil Change

441 Valley View Lane
Gas W: Exxon[*], Mobil[*, CW]
Food E: Angel's Family Restaurant, The China Restaurant
W: JoJo's Bakery and Restaurant
Lodg W: Best Western, DAYS INN Days Inn, **EconoLodge**, La Quinta Inn
AServ E: Bob Hackler Transmission, JT Xpress, Pruitt's Automotive
W: Exxon
ATM W: Bank One, Exxon, Mobil

440BC Junction I-635 East & West
Lodg E: AmeriSuites (see our ad this page)

439 Royal Lane
Gas E: Fina[*], Texaco[*]
W: Chevron[*, CW]
Food E: McDonald's, Royal Wok Chinese (At Fina), Seoul Garden Restaurant (Fina), Wendy's, Whataburger
W: Donut, Jack-In-The-Box, Momy Kinchi Restaurant, Nam-Gang Japanese Korean Restaurant, Royal BBQ
AServ E: Ken's Muffler Shop, Royal Lane Service Center, Tune Up Masters
ATM E: Fina, Texaco
Other E: **Pharmacare Drugs[RX]**
W: Animal Clinic

438 Walnut Hill Lane
Gas E: Mobil[*, CW], Shell[*, CW, 24]
W: Citgo[*], Texaco[*, D]
Food E: Bennigan's, Burger King[24], Denny's, Hunan Cafe, Monterrey Jack, Old San Francisco Steak House, Paul's Porterhouse Steaks and Seafood, TGI Friday, Trail Dust Steak House, Wild Turkey
Lodg E: Drury Inn, Hampton Inn
RVCamp W: **Morgan RVs**
ATM E: Mobil
W: Texaco
Other E: Don Carter's All Star Lanes West Bowling Alley
W: Malibu

437 Manana (Northbound, Reaccess Southbound Only)

436 Loop 12, Spur 348

434B Regal Row
Gas E: Chevron[*, CW, 24]
Food E: Denny's, Whataburger[24]
W: Regal Plaza Cafe, Regal Sandwich
Lodg E: La Quinta Inn
W: Fairfield Inn by Marriott
ATM E: Chevron

434A Empire Central
Gas E: Shell[*, CW, 24]
W: Exxon[*, CW]
Food E: McDonald's, Wendy's
W: Exxon, Hot Stuff Pizza (Exxon), Schlotzsky's Deli, Taco Bell
ATM W: Exxon

433B Mocking Bird Lane, Dallas, Love Field Airport
Gas E: Mobil[*], Texaco[*, CW]
W: Chevron[*], Exxon[*, CW]
Food E: Jack-In-The-Box
W: Chevron, Church's Chicken, Exxon, McDonald's (Chevron), Wendy's (Exxon)
Lodg E: Candlewood Suites, Crowne Plaza, **Holiday Inn**, Residence Inn, Sheraton Suites (see our ad this page)
TServ W: **Cummins Southern Plains, Inc. (1.1 Miles)**
RVCamp W: **Cummins Southern Plains, Inc. (1.1 Miles)**
ATM E: Mobil
Other W: Fox Photo 1-Hr Lab

432B Road 356, Commonwealth Dr.
Lodg W: Delux Inn, Studio PLUS

AServ E: Bill King's Brake-O
Other E: Optical Mart

432A Inwod Road
Gas E: Exxon[*, D, CW]
W: Fina[*, D], Texaco[*]
Food W: Ninfa's Mexican, Whataburger[24]
Lodg W: Embassy Suites
AServ E: Friendly Chevrolet
W: Texaco
Med E: ✚ **South Western Medical Center**, ✚ **St. Paul's Medical Center**
ATM W: Fina
Other W: Alladin Car Wash

431 Motor St
Gas E: Mobil[*, CW]
W: Shell[*, CW]
Food E: JoJo's
W: Stemons Wok, Zuma
Med E: ✚ **Hospital**
ATM E: Mobil

430C Wycliff Ave.
Lodg E: Renaissance Hotel
W: Wilson World Hotel & Suites

430B Market Center Blvd
Food W: Denny's, Georgio's (Best Western), Holiday Inn, Las Brisas
Lodg W: Best Western, Courtyard by Marriott, Fairfield Inn, Holiday Inn, Ramada, Sheraton Suites, Wyndham Garden Hotel
Other E: **World Trade Center**

430A Oak Lawn Ave
Gas W: Texaco[*, D]
Food W: Medieval Times (Food & Entertainment)
ATM W: Texaco

429A To I-45, US 75 Sherman
Lodg E: AmeriSuites (see our ad this page)

429B Continental Ave, Commerce St
Gas W: Exxon[*, D], Shell[*, CW, 24]
Food E: Planet Hollywood, Spaghetti Warehouse, TGI Friday
W: Burger King, McDonald's, Popeye's Chicken, US Subs
Lodg E: AmeriSuites
Other E: West End Market Place

429C Hi Line Drive (Northbound, Reaccess Southbound Only, Difficult Reaccess)

429D Tollway North (Northbound, No Reaccess)

428A Jct. I-30 E., Texarkana

428B Commerence Street, Reunion

428D Jct. I-30W

427A Colorado Blvd

427B Industrial Blvd
Food E: Mr. Hamburger

427C Junction I-30, Cadiz St.

426C Jefferson Ave

426B East 8th St, TX 180W
Gas E: Texaco[*, D]
W: Shell

1840
Dallas Texas
Sheraton Dallas Brookhollow HOTEL
• Free HBO, CNN, ESPN
• Complimentary Parking
• Restaurant & Sports Bar
• Outdoor Pool
• Free Local Calls
• Minutes From Westend Market Place • Shopping
• Downtown • the Arts District
214-630-7000 • 800-442-7547
TEXAS ▪ I-35 ▪ EXIT 433B

Bold red print shows RV & Bus parking available or nearby

EXIT TEXAS

Food W: James Grill
Lodg E: Classic Motor Lodge
W: La Santa, Sunvalley Hotel
AServ E: Gerard Motors(24) (Towing)
W: USA Tire & Incorp.

426A Ewing Ave
Food E: Roy's Place
Lodg E: Courtsey Inn
W: Circle Inn
AServ E: State Radiator & Air Conditioning Service
W: Good Taylor Honda, Pontiac, Trucks
Parks E: Dallas Zoo

425C Marsalis Ave, Ewing Ave
Gas E: Chevron(*, 24)
W: Diamond Shamrock(*), Mobil(*)
Lodg E: Dallas Inn Motel
ATM W: Diamond Shamrock
Parks E: Dallas Zoo
Other W: Wash N Dry Laundry

425B Beckley Ave, 12th St (Difficult Reaccess)
Gas W: Chevron, Exxon(*)
ATM W: Bank of America, NationsBank, Swiss Avenue Bank

425A Zang Blvd., Beckley Ave (North-bound, Same Services As 425 B)

424 Illinois Ave
Gas E: Chevron(24), Citgo(*)
W: Exxon(*)
Food E: Down Beat Seafood, Hercules Hamburgers, KFC, Williams Fried Chicken
W: Church's Chicken, IHOP, Jack-In-The-Box, Little Caesars Pizza, Sonic Drive in, Subway, Taco Bell
Lodg W: Oak Tree Inn
AServ E: Bud and Ben Mufflers
W: Exxon, Factory Brake Centers, Midas Muffler & Brake
ATM E: Chevron, Citgo
Other E: Coin Car Wash
W: Eckerd Drugs(RX)

423B Saner Ave
Food W: Ben's Family Restaurant
Lodg W: Westiner Motel
AServ W: Express Tire
Other W: Optical Clinic

423 U.S. 67, Cleburne

422BA Beckley Ave, Overton Rd., Kiest
Gas W: Shell(*)
Food W: McDonald's(PLAY)
Lodg E: Interstate Motel
W: Dallas Inn
AServ W: Shell
ATM W: Main Bank

421AB Junction Loop 12, Ann Arbor Ave.
Gas E: Racetrac(*, 24), Texaco(*, D)
Food W: Luby's Cafeteria
Lodg E: Howard Johnson's Express Inn
W: Sunbelt Motel
AServ W: Jess Auto Body
ATM E: Racetrac

421A Ann Arbor Ave, RD 12 Loop

420 Laureland Road
Gas W: Fina(*), Mobil(*, CW)
Food W: Blimpie Subs & Salads (Mobil), Perky's Pizza (Mobil), Smokey BBQ
Lodg E: Master's Suite Motel, Southern Comfort
W: Embassy Motel, Holiday Motel
AServ W: Discount Auto, Wins Auto
ATM W: Fina

419 Camp Wisdom Road
Gas E: Exxon(*, CW)
W: Chevron(*, 24), Shell(*, CW, 24)
Food W: McDonald's(PLAY)
Lodg E: Oak Cliff Inn
W: Sun Crest Inn
AServ E: L & M Muffler, Ronnie's Auto Care
RVCamp E: Good Luck RV Camp
ATM W: Chevron, Shell
Other E: Coin Car Wash
W: Kwik Kar Wash

418AB 418A - 20 W To Fort Worth 418B- 20 E To Schieveport

417 Wheatland Road, Danieldale Road

416 Wintergreen Road
Gas W: Citgo(*)
Food W: Cracker Barrel, El Chico, Waffle House
Lodg W: Best Western, Holiday Inn, Red Roof Inn
AServ E: Southwest Auto Service
TServ E: Wreck Truck Repair
ATM W: Citgo

415 Pleasant Run Road
Gas E: Chevron(*, CW), Racetrac(*, D), Texaco(*, D)
W: Exxon(*, D), Mobil(*, CW)
Food E: Benavides Restaurant, Chow Line, Chubby's, Grandy's, Subway, Waffle House
W: Antojitos Mexican, Burger King(PLAY), China Dynasty, KFC, Long John Silver, Luby's Cafeteria, McDonald's(PLAY), On The Border, Taco Bueno, Wendy's
Lodg E: Great Western Inn, Royal Inn, Spanish Trails Motel
AServ E: All Pro Transmission, Hilltop Chrysler, Plymouth, Napa Auto, Pep Boys Auto Center
W: Chuck Fairbank Chevrolet, Doug Stanley Ford, Firestone Tire & Auto
Other E: Movies 14
W: K-Mart(RX), Kroger Supermarket(24)

414 Road 1382, De Soto, Belt Line Road
Gas W: Conoco(*, D), Texaco(*, D, 24)
Food E: Whataburger(24)
W: Joe's Pizza
Lodg E: Comfort Inn
AServ E: Wal-Mart(RX) (Vision Center, 1 Hr. Photo)
W: Conoco
Other E: Wal-Mart(RX) (Vision Center, 1 Hr. Photo)

413 Parkerville Road
Gas W: Total(*)
Food W: Taco Bell (With Total), Total
AServ W: All Star Transmission, Jim McNatt Honda, SWS Trucks & Sales Service, Tires & Wheels
ATM W: Total

412 Bear Creek Road , Glen Heights
Gas W: Texaco(*, D, CW)
Food W: Dairy Queen (Texaco), Jack-In-The-Box, Texaco
RVCamp W: Dallas Hi Ho Campground (2 Miles)
ATM W: Texaco
Other W: Countryside Animal Clinic

411 FM 664, Ovilla Road
Gas E: Exxon(*, D, CW), Racetrac(*)
W: Exxon(*), Phillips 66(*), Texaco(*, D)
Food E: Church's Chicken (Exxon), Exxon, McDonald's(PLAY), TCBY (Exxon), Taco Bell (Exxon)
W: Hot Stuff Pizza (Exxon), Smash Hit Subs (Exxon)
AServ E: Flores Repair
W: Perry's Tires, Tom's Auto Repair
ATM E: Exxon, Main Bank
W: Exxon
Other E: Eckerd Drugs(RX)
W: Adkins Animal Service, Steve's Optical

410 Red Oak Road
FStop E: Coastal(*)
Food E: Baskin Robbins (Coastal), Denny's, Subway (Coastal)
Lodg E: Days Inn
RVCamp W: Hilltop Travel Trailors

408 U.S. 77

406 Sterrett Road
TServ E: Frontera Truck Parts

405 Road 387
Gas E: Chevron(*)
ATM E: Chevron

404 Lofland Road

403 U.S. 287, Corsicana, Fort Worth
AServ E: Carlisle Chevrolet, Oldsmobile, Cadillac
W: Buick Pontiac GMC Trucks, Thornbill Ford, Mercury

401B U.S. 287 Business, Road 664, Waxahachie
Food E: Comfort Inn
Lodg E: Comfort Inn
AServ W: Heartland of Waxahachie
Med E: Hospital

401A Brookside Road
Food E: TraveLodge
Lodg E: Ramada Limited, TraveLodge
Med E: Hospital
Other W: Brookside Animal Hospital

399B Road 1446

399A Road 66, 876, CR 1446
Gas E: Diamond Shamrock(*)
W: Chevron(*), Texaco(*, D)
Lodg E: Texas Inn Motel
AServ E: Diamond Shamrock, Total Automotive

397 U.S. 77, Waxahachie

(393) Rest Area (RR, Phones, Picnic, Grills, Vending, P; Southbound)

(393) Rest Area (RR, Phones, Picnic, Grills, Vending, P; Northbound)

391 Road 329, Forreston Road

386 TX 34, Italy, Ennis
FStop E: Texaco(*)
Food E: Blimpie Subs & Salads (With Texaco), Dairy Queen
AServ E: Chris'v&v Auto Service

384 County Road

381 Road 566, Milford Road

377 Road 934

374 Road 2959, Carl's Corner
FStop W: Carl's FS(*) (Fina)

Note: I-35 runs concurrent above with I-35E. Numbering follows I-35E.

Note: I-35 runs concurrent below with I-35W. Numbering follows I-35W.

85A Jct I-35, Dallas/Ft. Worth

84 TX 1515, Bonnie Brae St

82 TX 2449, Ponder

79 Crawford Road

76 TX 407, Argyle, Justin
Gas W: Citgo(*, D)
RVCamp W: Corral City Campground

(75) Picnic Area (Picnic; Southbound)

(75) Picnic Area (Picnic; Northbound)

EXIT		TEXAS
74	Fm1171, Lewisville, Flower Mound	
70	TX114, Dallas, Bridgeport	
	Other	W: **Texas Motor Speedway**
68	Eagle Pkwy	
67	Alliance Blvd	
66	Haslet, Westport Pkwy	
	Gas	W: Mobil(*, D, CW)
	Food	W: Cactus Flower Cafe, Joe's Pizza (Mobil), Mobil, Sonny Bryan's Smokehouse, Subway, TCBY (Mobil), Wendy's (Mobil)
	ATM	W: Mobil
	Other	W: Fort Worth Alliance Airport
65	TX170E	
64	Golden Triangle Blvd, Keller Hicks Road	
63	Park Glen Blvd.	
60	Jct U.S. 287N, U.S. 80N, Decatur	
59	Jct I-35W North, Denton, US 287	
58	Western Center Blvd	
	Gas	E: Citgo(*)
	Food	E: Braum's, Chili's, Christen's Grill & Bar, Domino's Pizza, Donut Palace, Wendy's
57A	Jct I-820E	
56B	Jct I-820W, Melody Hills Dr (Left Exit)	
56A	Meacham Blvd	
	Gas	W: Mobil(*, CW)
	Food	W: **Cracker Barrel**, Holiday Inn, J & J Donuts, McDonald's, Roma Deli Pizza
	Lodg	E: Comfort Inn, La Quinta Inn W: Hampton Inn, Holiday Inn
	ATM	E: Mercantile Bank of Ft. Worth
54C	33rd St, Long Ave	
	Lodg	W: Motel 6
	AServ	E: **Discount Auto Parts Exchange**, Goodyear Tire & Auto W: **Dick Smith Auto Parts**
	TServ	E: **Cummins Onan**, **Kenworth Dealer**, **Robertson Fleet Service**, **Tarrant Truck Center** W: **Dick Smith Auto Parts**
	Med	E: **Puelma Medical Clinic**
54B	TX183W, Papurt St	
	TStop	W: **Circle K Truck Stop**(*, D)
	TServ	E: **Bridgestone Tire & Auto** W: **Truck Center of Fort Worth**
54A	TX183E, NE 28th St, Papurt St.	
	Gas	W: Quik Stop(*)
	Food	W: Big Boss's
	Lodg	W: **Motel Classic Inn**
	TServ	E: **Bridgestone Tire & Auto** W: **Mid Continent Truck & Auto**
	TWash	W: **Mid Continent Truck & Auto**
	ATM	W: Quik Stop, The National Bank of Texas
53	Northside Dr, Yucca Ave	
	Gas	E: Texaco(*, D)
	Food	W: Mercado Juarez Cafe
	Lodg	W: Country Inn & Suites
	Other	W: **Camping**
52D	Carver St (Northbound, Reaccess Southbound Only)	
52C	Pharr St	
	TServ	W: **Freightliner Dealer**(24), **Southwest International**, **CAT,Cummings**
52B	Spur347W, Belknap St	
52A	Belknap St, TX 121 North, Fort Worth Airport	

EXIT		TEXAS
50	Jct I-30, U.S. 287S, U.S. 377S	
49B	Rosedale St	
	Food	E: Frank's BBQ, Little John's BBQ W: Edmondson's Fried Chicken
	AServ	E: Low Cost Auto Tire Center
	Med	W: **VA Hospital**
49A	Allen St., Rosedale St (Northbound, Difficult Reaccess)	
	Gas	W: Chevron, Shell(*, 24)
	AServ	W: Chevron
	Med	W: **Hospital**
48B	Morning Side Dr (Southbound)	
48A	Berry St	
	Gas	E: Chevron(*), Citgo(*) W: Racetrac(*)
	Food	E: McDonald's (Chevron)
	AServ	E: Economy Tires
	Other	E: **Sack & Save Warehouse Food Store**
47	Ripy St	
	Lodg	W: Astro Inn
	AServ	W: A-1 Automotive
46B	Seminary Drive	
	Gas	E: Racetrac(*) W: Diamond Shamrock(*), Texaco(*, D, CW)
	Food	E: Grandy's, Jack-In-The-Box(24), Long John Silver, Sonic Drive In, Taco Bell, Whataburger(24), William's Chicken W: Denny's, IHOP, Peony Chinese Restaurant, Wendy's
	Lodg	E: Days Inn, Delux Inn, Motel 6, TraveLodge
	AServ	E: NAPA Auto Parts W: Firestone Tire & Auto, **Longhorn Dodge Truck Stop Truck Accessories**, M & J Radiator, Pep Boys Auto Center, Sears Auto Center
	TServ	W: **Longhorn Dodge Truck Stop Truck Accessories**
	ATM	W: Diamond Shamrock, NationsBank
	Other	E: Pearl Vision Center, Texas State Optical W: **Animal Clinic**, Dollar Cinema, **Eckerd Drugs**(RX) **(Mall)**, **Fiesta Supermarket**, **Optical Clinic**, **Town Center Mall**, VisionMart
46A	Felix St	
	Gas	E: Mobil(*)
	Food	E: Pulido's Mexican, **Southoaks Motel** W: Burger King(PLAY), McDonald's(PLAY)
	Lodg	E: **Southoaks Motel**
	AServ	W: Longhorn Dodge
	Other	W: **U.S. Post Office**
45B	Junction I-20 East, Abilene, Dallas	
45A	Junction I-20 West	
44	Altamesa Blvd	
	Gas	W: Citgo(*), Texaco
	Food	W: Cha Cha's, **The Rig Steak House**, **Waffle House**
	Lodg	E: Holiday Inn W: Best Western, Comfort Suites Hotel, Motel 6, Ramada Limited
	AServ	W: Texaco
	RVCamp	W: **Happy Camper RV Sales**
	ATM	E: Norwest Bank
43	Sycamore School Rd (Southbound)	
	Gas	W: Exxon(*, CW)
	Food	W: Beefer's Breakfast & Burgers(24), Joe's Pizza, Subway, Taco Bell, Whataburger(24)
	Other	W: **Hallmark Pharmacy**(RX)
42	Everman Parkway, Sycamore School Rd.	
	Gas	E: Exxon(*, CW, 24)
	ATM	E: Bank One, Exxon

EXIT		TEXAS
41	Risinger Road	
	AServ	W: Terrell Automotive
	RVCamp	W: **Boats & Motors**, **Morgan's RV**
40	Garden Acres Drive	
	FStop	E: **Love's Country Store**(*)
	Food	E: **A & W Hot Dogs & More (Love's FS)**, **Subway (Love's FS)**
	Lodg	E: Budget Motel
	RVCamp	W: **C&S RV World**
39	TX 1187, McAllister Road, Rendon - Crowley Road	
	Gas	W: Citgo(*, D, CW, 24), Diamond Shamrock(*, D, LP)
	Food	W: Taco Bell (Citgo)
	Med	E: **Huguley Hospital**
	Other	W: **Hollywood's Theaters**
38	Alsbury Blvd	
	Gas	E: Chevron(*, D, CW, 24) W: Citgo(*), Texaco(*), Texaco(*, LP, CW, 24)
	Food	E: **Cracker Barrel**, JB's BBQ, McDonald's(PLAY), Old Country Steak House W: Arby's, Burger King, Denny's, Grandy's, Pancho's
	Lodg	E: Super 8
	AServ	E: Southtown Ford W: Kwik Kar Lube and Tune, Lynn Smith Chevrolet
	ATM	E: Chevron W: Citgo, Educational Employee Credit Union, First National Bank
	Other	E: **Gene Harris Petroleum Inc.**(LP), **Lowe's** W: **Albertson's Supermarket**(LP, 24, RX), **Animal Hospital**, **K-Mart**(RX), **Vision Mart**
37	TX 174, Cleburne, Wilshire Blvd (Southbound)	
36	Spur 50, Renfroe St, FM 3391, TX 174, Burleson St.	
	FStop	E: **Citgo**(*)
	Gas	E: Mobil(*, CW) W: Chevron(*, LP), Diamond Shamrock(*, D), Fina(*, D)
	Food	E: Brangus, Waffle House
	Lodg	E: Comfort Suites Hotel, Days Inn
	AServ	E: **Citgo**, Paul's Auto & Noah's Parts W: Diamond Shamrock, Shelby's Automotive
	ATM	E: **Citgo**, First State Bank of Texas
	Other	W: **Bransom Grocery**, West Pharmacy(RX)
34	Briaroaks Rd (Southbound)	
	RVCamp	W: **Camping**
(34)	**Rest Area (RR, Phones, Picnic, Grills, P; Southbound)**	
32	Bethesda Road, Briar Oaks Rd.	
	Gas	E: Citgo(*)
	Food	E: **Five Star Inn**
	Lodg	E: **Five Star Inn**
	RVCamp	W: **Country Junction RV Park**
(31)	**Rest Area (RR, Phones, Picnic, Grills, P; Northbound)**	
30	TX 917, Joshua, Mansfield	
	Gas	W: Citgo(*, D), Texaco(*, K)
	Food	W: Snappy Jack's (Texaco)
	AServ	W: **Discount Auto Salvage Exchange**
	RVCamp	E: **Capri Campers & RV**
27	CR707/604	
	RVCamp	E: **All Star RV Park**, **Anacira Pace**, **Arrow**, **Ancira Travel Villa**, **Motor Homes**, **Travel Trailer**
26A	U.S. 67, Cleburne, Dallas	
	FStop	E: **Citgo**(*)
	Food	E: Pop's Honey Fried Chicken (Citgo), Pop's Honey Fried Chicken (Citgo)
	RVCamp	W: **Campground**
26B	Bus 35 W, Alvarado (Southbound,	

Bold red print shows RV & Bus parking available or nearby

EXIT TEXAS

Left Exit)

24 U.S. 35 West, TX 1706, 3136, Alvarado, Maple Ave
- **Gas** E: Chevron(*)
- **Food** E: Alvarado House
- **AServ** E: Bill Lowrey's Motors, Turner's Automotive
- **RVCamp** W: McLain's RV

21 Greensfield, Barnesville Road

17 TX 2258
- **RVCamp** E: Dotsco Parts & Service

16 CR 201
- **RVCamp** E: Camping
  W: Camping (2 Miles)

15 TX 916, Grandview, Maypearl
- **Gas** W: Diamond Shamrock(*, D, LP, CW)
- **Food** W: Rick's Texas BBQ
- **ATM** W: Diamond Shamrock

12 TX 67

8 TX 66, Itasca
- **FStop** E: Chevron(*)
  W: Citgo(*, D)
- **Food** E: Brianna's Pizza Cafe (Chevron)
  W: Dairy Queen
- **AServ** W: Lloyd Ford
- **ATM** E: Chevron
  W: Citgo
- **Other** W: Picnic Area (Phone)

7 TX 934
- **Other** E: Picnic Area (Northbound)

3 TX 2959, Hillsboro Airport

Note: I-35 runs concurrent above with I-35W. Numbering follows I-35W.

371 Junction I-35E Dallas, I-35W Ft. Worth (Left Exit Northbound)

370 North U.S. 77 , Spur 579

368B FM 286 (Southbound)
- **Gas** W: Chevron(*), Diamond Shamrock(*, D, CW)
- **Food** W: Braum's, Dairy Queen(PLAY), El Conquistador, Pizza Hut
- **Lodg** W: Best Western, Comfort Inn
- **ATM** W: Chevron, Diamond Shamrock

368A TX 22, TX 171, FM 286, Whitney, Corsicana
- **FStop** E: Love's(*, SCALES, 24) (Citgo)
  W: Shell(*)
- **Gas** E: Citgo(*)
  W: Citgo(*), Exxon(*), Mobil(*, CW)
- **Food** E: American Restaurant (Hillsboro Outlet Center), Arby's, Black-Eyed Pea, Burger King, Golden Corral Family Steakhouse, Grandy's, Lonestar Cafe, McDonald's(PLAY), Roze's Cafe (Ramada Inn), Subway (Love's FS), Taco Bell
  W: KFC, Schlotzsky's Deli, Thunderbird Motel, Whataburger(24)
- **Lodg** E: Holiday Inn Express, Ramada Inn
  W: Thunderbird Motel
- **AServ** W: Dobbs & Co. Pontiac, Buick, & GMC Trucks, Wal-Mart SuperCenter(24, RX) (Vision Center, 1 Hr. Photo), Westside Motors Chevrolet
- **Med** W: ✚ Hospital
- **ATM** E: Citgo
  W: Norwest Bank, Shell, Wal-Mart SuperCenter (Vision Center, 1 Hr. Photo)
- **Other** E: Hillsboro Outlet Center, Super Skate
  W: Super Clean Car Wash & Laundry, Wal-Mart SuperCenter(RX) (Vision Center, 1 Hr. Photo)

367 FM 3267, Old Bynum Rd

EXIT TEXAS

364B TX 81, Hillsboro (Left Exit Northbound)

364A FM 310
- **FStop** E: Chevron(*)
  W: Knox Coastal(*, LP, SCALES)
- **Gas** E: Texaco(*)
- **Food** W: Up In Smoke BBQ
- **ATM** E: Chevron
  W: Knox Coastal

362 Chatt Road

359 FM 1304
- **FStop** W: Mobil(*, 24)
- **Food** W: Arby's(24) (Mobil)
- **TServ** W: Mobil(24)
- **ATM** W: Mobil

358 FM 1242 East, Abbott
- **Gas** E: Exxon(*)
- **Food** E: Turkey Shop Cafeteria
- **TWash** W: Abbott Truck Wash

356 Abest Road

355 County Line Road
- **RVCamp** E: KOA Kampground

354 Marable St
- **RVCamp** E: Waco North-KOA
- **Med** E: ✚ Hospital
- **Other** E: West Gas Service(LP)

353 FM 2114, West
- **Gas** E: Circle K(*), Citgo(*, D), Fina(*), Shell(*)
  W: Citgo(*), Exxon(D)
- **Food** E: Dairy Queen, Jaime's Restaurant, Little Czech Bakery, Old Czech Smoke House, Pizza House
- **AServ** E: Sykora Ford Dealership
  W: Alvin's Body Shop & Supply, Damron City Service Goodyear, Exxon, Gerrel Bolton Geo Chevrolet
- **Med** E: ✚ Hospital
- **ATM** E: Citgo, Shell

351 FM 1858
- **Food** W: West Auction Check America Restaurant

349 Wiggins Road

347 FM 3149, Tours Road

346 Ross Road
- **TStop** E: Shell(*, 24)
  W: Fina(*) (Showers, Truck Wash)
- **Food** E: BLT's Restaurant (Shell TS), Chicken Express Restaurant (Shell TS), Dogs N Suds Express (Shell TS)
- **Lodg** W: Fina (Showers, Truck Wash)
- **AServ** W: EZ Pickens Auto Ranch Inc.
- **TServ** W: Fina (Showers, Truck Wash), M and M Tire Sales, Pickens Truck Sales & Parts
- **ATM** E: Shell
  W: Fina (Showers, Truck Wash)

DAYS INN®
Special Rates for Tour Groups
- Continental Breakfast
- Outdoor Pool
- Pets Allowed (charge per pet)
- Handicap Accessible
- 60 Channels & 2 HBO Channels
- Truck/Large Vehicle Parking
- Exterior Corridors

1744

254-799-8885 • 800-329-7466

TEXAS • I-35 • EXIT 338B

EXIT TEXAS

(345) Parking Area (Picnic, P; Northbound)

345 Old Dallas Road
- **TServ** E: Texas Truck
- **Other** E: Heart of Texas Speedway

343 FM 308, Elm Mott
- **TStop** E: Texaco(*, SCALES)
- **Gas** E: Fina(*, D)
  W: Chevron(*, D, 24)
- **Food** E: Country Cafe (Texaco TS), Dairy Queen(PLAY), Dee's Deelicious Donuts, Eddie Ray's Smokehouse
  W: Heitmiller Family Steakhouse
- **AServ** E: A & D Tires
- **TServ** E: Texaco(SCALES)
- **TWash** E: Texaco
- **ATM** E: Texaco
- **Other** W: Coin Laundromat, Elm Mott Grocery, U.S. Post Office

342B Bus. South U.S. 77
- **RVCamp** W: Northcrest Manor Travel Trailer Park(LP)

342A FM 2417, Northcrest
- **FStop** W: Diamond Shamrock(*) (Laundry)
- **Gas** E: Citgo(*)
- **Food** W: Dairy Queen
- **Lodg** W: Every Day Inn
- **AServ** W: Chuck's Automotive Repair
- **Other** E: TX State Technical College - Waco, Texas Department Of Public Safety

341 Craven Ave, Lacy, Lakeview
- **Gas** E: Chevron(*)
  W: Mobil(*)
- **AServ** W: Chief Auto Parts
- **ATM** W: Mobil

340 Meyers Lane (Northbound)

339 FM 3051 To S. TX 6, Loop 340, Lake Waco, Lakeshore Dr
- **FStop** E: Texaco(*)
- **Gas** E: Diamond Shamrock(*, D)
- **Food** E: Casa Ole, El Conquistador, Luby's Cafeteria, McDonald's (Wal-Mart), Pizza Hut, Popeye's Chicken, Shipley Do-nuts, Sonic, Wendy's, Whataburger(24)
  W: Burger King, Cracker Barrel, KFC, McDonald's(PLAY)
- **Lodg** W: Hampton Inn
- **AServ** E: Kwik Kar Oil & Lube, Wal-Mart Supercenter(24, RX) (Vision Center, 1-Hr Photo)
  W: Carquest Auto Parts
- **ATM** E: American Bank, Texaco
  W: Winn Dixie Supermarket(RX)
- **Other** E: Genie Car Wash, Pharmacy Plus(RX), U.S. Post Office, Wal-Mart Supercenter(RX) (Vision Center, 1-Hr Photo)
  W: Brown's Hardware, Hollywood's Theaters, Winn Dixie Supermarket(RX)

338B Behrens Circle, Bell Mead
- **FStop** W: Texaco(*, LP)
- **Gas** E: Gas Station(*)
- **Food** W: Blue Bonnet Cafe(24), Neighbor's Restaurant
- **Lodg** W: Days Inn (see our ad this page), Delta Inns, Knight's Inn, Motel 6, Royal Inn
- **AServ** E: Superior Car Care
- **Other** E: Mrs. Baird's Thrift Store
  W: Eckerd Drugs(RX), Food Basket IGA

338A U.S. 84, To TX 31, Waco Drive, Bellmead
- **Gas** E: Fina(*), H-E-B
  W: Ace(*), Texaco(*)
- **AServ** E: Auto Zone Auto Parts, Pickens Auto Parts, Sam's Club
- **ATM** E: Fina

EXIT		TEXAS
	Other	E: **H-E-B Grocery Store**[RX] **(1-Hr Photo), Lynn's La Vega Pharmacy, Sam's Club**
337B		Business North U.S. 77, Elm Ave
	AServ	W: Bill's Discount Tire Service, Busy Bees Auto Care Center
337A		Business South U.S. 77
336		**Forrest St**
	Gas	W: Chevron[*]
	Food	W: Chevron
335C		MLK Jr. Blvd,Lake Brazos Pkwy
	Gas	E: Texaco[*, D, LP]
	Food	E: **Holiday Inn**, Paquito's Cantina & Grill
		W: Damon's (Hilton), Dock's River Front
	Lodg	E: **Holiday Inn**, Howard Johnson
		W: EconoLodge, Hilton, Victorian Inns
	Med	W: **✚ Hospital**
	Other	E: **Brazos Golf Range**
		W: **Cameron Park Zoo, The Waco Suspension Bridge**
335B		FM 434, Fort Fischer, University Parks Drive
	Food	E: Baskin Robbins, Eggroll House, SHONEY'S, Shoney's, Thai Orchid
		W: Arby's, Jack-In-The-Box, Playhouse Cafe
	Lodg	W: Lexington Inn, Residence Inn
	RVCamp	E: **Fort Fischer Park**
	ATM	W: Bank of America
	Parks	E: **Fort Fischer Park**
	Other	E: **Convenient Food Mart, Gov. Bill & Vera Daniels Village, The Ferrell Center (Sports Arena for U. of Baylor), The Texas Sports Hall of Fame, The University of Baylor Info Center**
		W: **Fire Department, Waco Convention & Visitors Bureau (see our ad this page)**
335A		4th - 5th Sts.
	Gas	E: Exxon[*, D], Texaco[*, D]
		W: Diamond Shamrock[*, D], Mobil[*, CW]
	Food	E: Cafe China Super Buffet, Exxon, IHOP, Subway (Exxon), TCBY (Exxon), Taco Bueno
		W: Long John Silver, McDonald's[PLAY], Sonic, Taco Bell, Taco Cabana[24], The Pineapple Grill (Clarion), Wendy's, Whataburger[24], Wrap & Roll Cafe
	Lodg	E: Best Western
		W: Clarion
	AServ	E: Exxon
	ATM	E: Exxon, Texaco
	Other	W: **The Dr. Pepper Museum**
334B		8th St (Northbound)
	Food	E: Denny's (La Quinta Inn), Lee's Vietnamese, Pizza Hut
	Lodg	E: La Quinta Inn[24]
	ATM	E: Bank of America
	Other	E: **Rother's Bookstore, The University of Baylor**
334A		18th - 19th Streets (Under Construction)
	Gas	E: Chevron[*], Shell[*], Texaco[*, D]
	Food	E: Burger King[PLAY], La Jaivita, Schlotzsky's Deli
	Lodg	E: Budget Inn, Comfort Inn, Super 8
	Other	E: **Harley Davidson Motorcycles**
334		US 77 South, 17th - 18th Sts.
	Gas	E: Chevron[*], Mobil[*], Texaco[*]
		W: Chevron[*], Phillips 66[*, D], Texaco
	Food	E: Burger King[PLAY], La Jaivita, Schlotzsky's Deli, Vitek's BBQ
		W: Alvin Sandwich Shop, Dairy Queen, George's Steaks, Seafood, BBQ, Mexico Lindo
	Lodg	E: Budget Inn, Comfort Inn, Super 8
	AServ	W: Makowski Automotive, Texaco
	Med	W: **✚ Hillcrest Baptist Medical Center**
	Other	E: Genie Car Wash
		W: **Startex Propane**[LP]

EXIT		TEXAS
333A		Loop 396, La Salle Ave, Valley Mills Dr
	Gas	W: Racetrac[*, 24]
	Food	E: El Chico, Elite Cafe, Trajillo's Mexican
		W: Gold-N-Crisp Chicken, Papa John's Pizza
	Lodg	E: Economy Hotel, Motel 6
		W: Mardi Gras Motel
	AServ	E: Waco Isuzu, Kia, Subaru
		W: **Cen-Tex Brake & Spring**, Jenkins Radiator Shop, Marsteller Mercury, Lincoln, Ford, Dodge, Jeep Eagle, Precision Tune, Tracy's Auto Sales
	TServ	E: **Allen-Jenson Inc.**
		W: **Cen-Tex Brake & Spring, Driveline Shop, Duncan Truck Sales**[24] **(Freightliner)**
331		New Road
	Gas	E: Citgo[*, D]
	Lodg	E: Astro Motel, **Best 4 Less Motel, New Road Inn**, Relax Inn
	TServ	E: **Central Texas International Inc.**
	Med	W: **✚ VA Hospital**
	Other	W: **Cottonwood Country Club Golf Course, Heart O' Texas Fair Complex**
330		TX 6, Loop 340, Meridian, Robinson (Limited Access Hwy)
328		FM 2063, FM 2113, Hewitt
	Gas	W: Diamond Shamrock[*, D], Texaco[*, CW]
	ATM	W: Diamond Shamrock
325		FM 3148, Robinson Road
	TStop	W: **Shell**[*, 24] **(Showers)**
	Food	W: **Pizza Inn (Shell TS), Shell (Showers), Subway (ShellTS), TCBY (Shell TS)**
	TServ	E: **Mid-Tex Truck Repair**
		W: **US Tire Co.**[24] **(Road Service)**
	ATM	W: **Shell (Showers)**
323		FM 2837 (Southbound)
	Food	W: Chicken Express Restaurant, Coyote Ranch Cafe, D's Speedy Pizza
	Other	W: **U.S. Post Office**
322		FM 2837, Lorena
	FStop	E: **Diamond Shamrock**[*]
	Gas	W: Chevron[*, D]
	Food	E: Dakota Steakhouse
	AServ	E: Cook's Automotive
	ATM	W: Chevron
319		Woodlawn Road
(318)		**Parking Area (Picnic, Grills; Southbound)**
(318)		**Rest Area (RR, Phones, Picnic, Grills, P; Northbound, Located At Exit 318B)**
318B		Bruceville (Southbound)
	Gas	W: Fina[*, D] (Laundry)
	RVCamp	E: **Trail's End (1 Mile)**
		W: **KOA Kampground (27 Miles)**
318A		Bruceville, Frontage Rd. (Reaccess Southbound Only)
	Gas	E: Chevron
	TServ	W: **Joe KinCannon Truck Tire Retreading**
	RVCamp	E: **Bruceville RV Park**
	Other	W: **U.S. Post Office**
315		TX 7, FM 107, Moody Marlin
	FStop	W: **Texaco**[*]
	Gas	W: Fina, Mobil[*]
	Food	W: **I Can't Believe It's Yogurt (Texaco)**, Lil' Orky's Cafe, **Pizza Hut (Texaco), Red Line Burgers (Texaco), Texaco**
	AServ	W: Fina
	ATM	W: Mobil, **Texaco**
	Parks	W: **Mother Neff State Park**
	Other	W: **Pelzel Foods**

Bold red print shows RV & Bus parking available or nearby

EXIT		TEXAS
314		Old Blevins Road
311		Big Elm Road
308		FM 935, Troy
	Gas	E: Texaco(*)
		W: Diamond Shamrock(*), Exxon(*)
	Food	E: Phelan's Restaurant
		W: Hot Stuff Pizzeria (Exxon)
	AServ	E: Texaco
	ATM	W: Exxon
	Other	E: Coin Operated Laundry, U.S. Post Office
306		FM 1237, Pendleton
	FStop	E: Love's(*, RV DUMP) (Citgo Fuel)
	Food	E: A & W Hot Dogs & More (Love's TS), Subway (Love's TS)
	RVCamp	E: Campground
	ATM	E: Love's (Citgo Fuel)
305		Berger Road
	TStop	W: Willie's 305 Truck Stop(*, SCALES) (Fina)
	FStop	E: Phillips 66(*)
	TServ	E: Gray International
		W: Goodyear Tire & Auto, Temple Diesel Service(24)
	TWash	W: Willie's 305 Truck Stop (Fina)
	RVCamp	W: Camping
304		Loop 363
	Gas	W: Diamond Shamrock(*, D)
	TServ	W: Temple Freightliner
	ATM	W: Diamond Shamrock
303B		Mayborn Civic & Convention Center (Northbound)
	Other	E: Cultural Activities Center, Frank W. Mayborn Civic & Convention Center
303A		Spur 290, FM 1143, Industrial Blvd, North 3rd St
	Gas	E: Citgo(*), Diamond Shamrock(*)
	Food	E: Why Poncho's?
		W: Continental Motel
	Lodg	E: Texas Sands Motel
		W: Continental Motel
	ATM	E: Cash Card, Citgo, Diamond Shamrock
302		Nugent Ave
	Gas	E: Exxon(*, D), Texaco(*, D)
		W: Chevron(*)
	Food	W: Denny's, Drake's (Ramada Inn), Ramada Inn
	Lodg	E: Comfort Suites Hotel, EconoLodge, Holiday Inn Express
		W: Days Inn, Motel 6, Ramada Inn, Stratford House Inns
	AServ	E: Green's Garage
	TServ	E: Green's Garage
	RVCamp	W: Bird Creek Mobile Home Parking (Overnight)
	ATM	E: Exxon, Texaco
		W: Chevron
301		TX 53, FM 2305, Central Ave, Adams Ave
	Gas	E: Diamond Shamrock(*, D), Texaco
	Food	E: Arby's, Grandy's, KFC, Long John Silver, McDonald's(PLAY), Mr. Gatti's Pizza, Pizza Hut, Schlotzsky's Deli, SHONEY'S Shoney's, Subway, Taco Bell, Wendy's, Whataburger(24)
		W: Czech Heritage Bakery
	Lodg	E: La Quinta Inn
	AServ	E: Becker's Radiator Service, Griffin Body Shop, Johnson Bros. Ford, Texaco
		W: Olson Auto Clinic, Temple Alternator & Starter Service, Temple Mercury Jeep Lincoln Dealer
	Med	E: + Hospital
	ATM	E: Temple Santa Fe Credit Union
		W: Albertson's Grocery(24, RX), Cash Card(24)
	Parks	W: Sammon's Park & Golf Course
	Other	E: Eckerd Drugs(RX), Gils Auto Shine(CW), H-E-B(RX) (1-Hr Photo), Robertson's Laundry
		W: Albertson's Grocery(RX), Temple Veterinary Hospital of Western Hills
300		Ave H, 49th - 57th Streets
	Gas	E: Shell(*), Texaco, Texaco(*)
		W: Texaco(*)
	Food	E: Clem Mikeska's BBQ, Clem Mikeska's Soup & Salad, DeVinchi's Steak & Hoagie, Gina's Pizza, Jack 'N' Jill Donuts, Las Casas, RDJ's Burger In A Flash, Rylander's Hamburgers, Sorge's Italian
	Lodg	E: Oasis Motel
		W: Temple Inn
	AServ	E: Action Auto Glass, Big 3 Auto Supply, Bostick Tire & Auto Repair, Harmon Glass, Slim Kotrla, Temple Collision Center, Texaco, Young Dodge Dealer
		W: Carquest Auto Parts, Temple Auto Glass, Temple Grinding Co. Auto Parts
	ATM	E: Texaco
	Parks	W: Sammons Park & Golf Course
	Other	E: Railroad Pioneer Museum, Temple Wonder Wash, Triple Clean Car Wash(CW)
299		East U.S. 190, Loop 363, TX 36, Gatesville, Cameron
	Gas	E: Diamond Shamrock(*), Phillips 66(*), Shell(*), Texaco(*, D, CW)
		W: Exxon(*, D), Texaco(*)
	Food	E: Doyle Phillips Steak House, El Conquistador, Jack-In-The-Box, Luby's Cafeteria, NY Bagel Cafe
	Lodg	E: Budget Inn, Regency Inn
		W: A Rebel Inn
	AServ	E: Ringler Chevrolet Toyota Geo
		W: Exxon, Friend Tire, J & S Custom Paint & Body
	ATM	E: Bank One, Bank of America, Phillips 66
		W: Texaco
	Other	E: K-Mart(RX), Putter Golf (Mini-Golf)
		W: Marine Outlet
298		Frontage Road (Northbound)
	RVCamp	E: Ancira Motor Homes
	Other	E: Scuba Plus
297		FM 817, Midway Drive
	Gas	E: Citgo(*, D)
		W: Diamond Shamrock(*, D)
	Food	E: Lil-Tex Family Restaurant(24)
	Lodg	E: Super 8
	AServ	E: Shelton Volvo, Nissan Dealership
		W: Tranum Buick, Pontiac, GMC, Tranum VW GMC Truck Dealer
	Other	E: Snippers Pet Grooming
		W: Fed Ex Drop Box, Laser Wash(CW, 24)
294B		FM 93, 6th Ave, University of Mary Hardin Baylor
	Gas	E: Texaco(*, D, CW)
		W: Shell(*, D, CW)
	Food	E: McDonald's(PLAY), Perky's Pizza (Texaco)
		W: Best Western, Subway
	Lodg	W: Best Western
	AServ	E: Belton Auto Repair
		W: Jerry's Radiator Shop, M & B Auto Repair
	ATM	E: Texaco
	Parks	W: Heritage Park
	Other	E: Mike's Complete Auto Detail(D), Totally Scuba Training Center
		W: Bell County Veterinary Hospital, University of Mary Hardin Baylor
294A		Spur 253, Central Ave, Downtown
	Gas	W: Diamond Shamrock(*), Shell(*), Texaco(*, D)
	Food	W: Bobby's Burgers, J. Pleasant's Eatery, Pizza Hut, Pizza Plus, Sam's Great Southwest Restaurant, Schoepf's Old Time BBQ, Sonic Drive In, TCBY (Shell), Taco Bell (Shell), Whataburger(24)
	Lodg	W: Ramada Limited
	AServ	W: Auto Zone Auto Parts, Big 3 Auto Supply, Rick's Tire Service, Shine Bros. & Associate

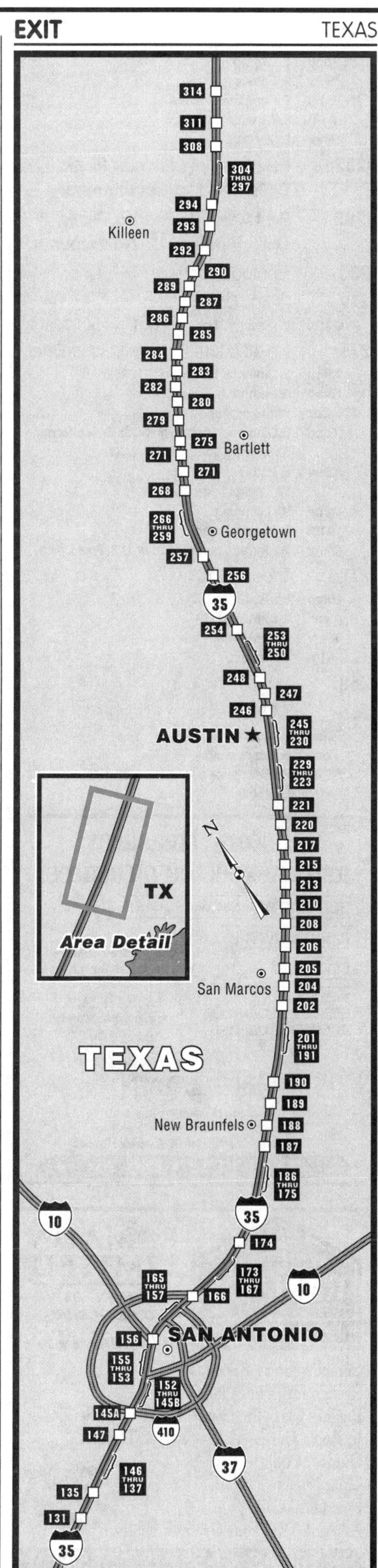

Bold red print shows RV & Bus parking available or nearby

EXIT		TEXAS
	Goodyear, Western Auto	
ATM	W: Compass Bank, Shell, Texaco	
Other	W: Bell County Museum, The Medicine Shoppe(RX)	
293B	TX 317, FM 436, Main St (Southbound)	
Gas	W: Citgo(*)	
Food	W: Ernie's Fried Chicken	
Other	W: Sea Horse Car Wash, South Main Washateria	
293A	West U.S. 190, TX 317, FM 436, Killeen, Fort Hood	
TStop	E: Diamond Shamrock(*, 24)	
Gas	E: Exxon(*, D), Fina(*, D), Smith Bros. Miller Hts. Grocery(*)	
Food	E: Diamond Shamrock, Pat's Cafe	
Lodg	E: Budget Host Belton Inn	
TServ	E: Diamond Shamrock(24)	
TWash	E: Diamond Shamrock	
292	Loop 121	
Gas	W: Mobil(*, D)	
Food	W: Bakery Street (Mobil), Blimpie's Subs (Mobil), I Can't Believe It's Yogurt (Mobil), Oxbow Steakhouse & BBQ, Tia Rita's Tacos (Mobil)	
Lodg	E: Bloom's Motel	
AServ	W: Fisher-Vincent Ford	
RVCamp	W: KOA Kampground (1.5 Miles), Sunbelt RV Center Service & Sales (1.5 Miles)	
ATM	W: Mobil	
Other	E: Brown Boat & Motor Repair W: Expo Center	
290	Shanklin Road	
TServ	W: Capital Truck & Equipment Co.	
RVCamp	W: KOA Kampground (1 Mile), Sunbelt RV Center (1 Mile)	
Other	E: Mr. Marine Boat Sales	
289B	Frontage Road (Northbound)	
289A	Tahuaya Road	
AServ	E: Hi-Way Auto Parts	
287	Amity Road	
286	FM 1670, Stillhouse Hollow Lake	
Other	W: Salado Veterinary Hospital	
285	FM 2268, Salado	
Gas	W: Chevron(*)	
Food	E: Samm's Family Restaurant W: Cowboy's BBQ, Robertson's Choppin Block	
AServ	E: Pronto Auto Service	
ATM	E: Brookshire Bros. Grocery, Compass Bank W: Chevron	
Other	E: Brookshire Bros. Grocery, Fletcher's Books & Antiques, Village Pharmacy(RX)	
284	Stagecoach Road	
Gas	E: Exxon(*) W: Mobil(*, D)	
Food	E: Burger King (Exxon), Cathy's Boardwalk Cafe, Old Town Salado & Patio Cafe, Pietro's Italian, Pink Rose Tea Room, Salado Square Cafe, Strawberry Patch, The Gathering Place, The Range Restaurant, The Salado Mansion W: Dairy Queen, Lucey's Place	
Lodg	E: Halley House Bed & Breakfast, Stage Coach Inn, The Inn at Salado, The Old Granary W: Super 8	
ATM	E: Exxon, First State Bank W: Mobil	
Other	E: Central Texas Area Museum, U.S. Post Office	
283	FM 2268, Salado, Holland, Stagecoach Rd.	
282	FM 2115, FM 2843	
TStop	E: Texaco(*, LP)	

EXIT		TEXAS
Food	E: Texaco	
TServ	E: Texaco	
RVCamp	E: Camping (2 Miles)	
ATM	E: Texaco	
Other	E: Sky Dive	
(282)	Rest Area (RR, Phones, Picnic, Grills, Vending; Southbound)	
(281)	Rest Area (RR, Phones, Picnic, Grills, Vending, P; Northbound)	
280	Frontage Road	
279	Prairie Dell	
RVCamp	W: Emerald Lake RV Park (Approx. 1 Mile)	
275	FM 487, Jarrell, Bartlett, Schwertner	
TStop	E: Diamond Shamrock(*, LP, SCALES)	
FStop	E: Exxon(*)	
Gas	W: Texaco(*)	
Food	E: Diamond Shamrock, Doc's Cafe (Diamond Shamrock), Joe's Country BBQ	
AServ	E: Exxon W: Central Texas Chevy Parts	
RVCamp	W: Camping	
ATM	E: Diamond Shamrock	
Other	W: Jarrell Country Market, U.S. Post Office	
271	Theon Road	
FStop	W: Texaco(*)	
AServ	E: RPM Tires	
TServ	E: RPM Tires	
ATM	W: Texaco	
268	FM 972, Walburg	
266	TX 195, Florence, Killeen	
FStop	E: Mobil(*)	
Food	E: Arby's (Mobil)	
AServ	W: Georgetown Interstate Transmission	
ATM	E: Mobil	

1479
Historic treasures and unexpected pleasures!
HISTORIC DOWNTOWN SQUARE
CANDLE FACTORY
CAVE
FAMILY FUN
ACCOMMODATIONS
Call for free Visitors Fun Pack, ask for a coupon book!
1.800.436.8696
www.georgetown.org
GEORGETOWN
TEXAS
ESTABLISHED 1848
Georgetown Convention & Visitors Bureau
TEXAS • I-35 • EXIT 261

1160
RAMADA LIMITED
RAMADA
LIMITED
1400 N. I-35
ROUND ROCK, TX
512-255-4437
Complimentary Breakfast
Restaurant/Lounge Next Door
Busines Class Program • Fax & Copy Service
In Room Coffee-Makers & Hair Dryers
Outdoor Pool
Cable, HBO
Free Local Calls
AAA, AARP Tour Group Friendly
Special Tour Group Rates
TEXAS • I-35 • EXIT 254

EXIT		TEXAS
264	Bus Loop I-35, Lakeway Drive, Austin Ave	
AServ	E: Stone's Quality Automotive	
RVCamp	E: The Live Oaks at Berry Creek (1 Mile)	
Other	W: Georgetown Airport	
262	Road 2338, Lake Georgetown, Andice, FM 971, Granger (Northbound Exit Number Is 261A)	
Gas	E: Diamond Shamrock(*), Gas Station(*, D) W: Phillips 66, Texaco(*)	
Food	E: Burger King(PLAY), McDonald's(PLAY), Pizza Hut, Quizno's Classic Sub, Schlotzsky's Deli, Short Stop, Sonic, Subway W: Chuck Wagon, Dairy Queen, La Quinta Inn, Little Caesars Pizza, Little River Cafe (La Quinta Inn), Popeye's Chicken, Taco Bueno, Whataburger(24)	
Lodg	W: DAYS INN Days Inn, La Quinta Inn	
AServ	E: Fox Auto Parts, The Georgetown Tire Center W: Phillips 66	
ATM	E: Albertson's Grocery(RX), Austin Area Teachers Federal Credit Union, Diamond Shamrock W: Texaco, Union State Bank	
Other	E: Albertson's Grocery(RX), Budget Opticals, Eckerd Drugs(RX), Fast Forward Mail, Tim's Book Shop	
261	TX 29, Taylor, Burnet	
FStop	W: Chevron(*, D)	
Gas	E: Texaco(*, D, CW)	
Food	E: Taco Bell(PLAY)	
AServ	E: Wal-Mart(RX) W: Chevron	
ATM	E: Texaco	
Other	E: Georgetown Convention & Visitors Bureau (see our ad this page), H-E-B Grocery Store(RX), Wal-Mart(RX)	
260	RM 2243, Leander	
Gas	W: Chevron(*), Circle K(*), Diamond Shamrock(*)	
Food	W: Lupita's Mexican, Marvin's Countertop Cafe, Page House Bed & Breakfast, Sverre's Donuts	
Lodg	W: Comfort Inn, Page House Bed & Breakfast	
AServ	E: A-1 Automotive	
Med	E: + Georgetown Medical Center	
ATM	W: Chevron, Circle K	
Other	E: Gus's Drugs(RX), U.S. Post Office W: Animal Hospital	
259	I-35 Bus Loop, Georgetown (Difficult Reaccess)	
RVCamp	W: RV Outlet Mall	
Other	E: Candle Factory W: Inner Space Cavern	
257	Westinghouse Road	
(256)	Rest Area (RR, Phones, Picnic, Grills, Vending, P; Southbound)	
256	RM 1431, Chandler Road	
(255)	Rest Area (RR, Phones, Picnic, Grills, Vending, Pet Walk, P; Northbound)	
254	I-35 Bus Loop, FM 3406	
Gas	E: Chevron W: Phillips 66(*, D)	
Food	E: Giovanni's Italian Restaurant, Hayloft Steakhouse, Lone Star Cafe, McDonald's(PLAY) W: Bennigan's, Cracker Barrel, Denny's, Golden Corral Family Steakhouse, Johnny Carino's Italian Kitchen, Kona Ranch Steaks & Seafood	

Bold red print shows RV & Bus parking available or nearby

EXIT TEXAS

Lodg **W:** Ramada Limited (see our ad this page)
AServ **E:** Chevron, Classic Pontiac, Honda
ATM **E:** Bank of America
W: Texas Heritage Bank
Other **E:** Interstate Bowl, Movies 8, Skate Center

253A Frontage Rd (Southbound)

Gas **W:** Exxon[*, D], Shell[*, CW, 24]
Food **W:** Hunan Lion, Poke Jo's BBQ, Popeye's Chicken, Taco Bell, Thundercloud Subs
Lodg **W:** The Inn at Brushy Creek
ATM **W:** Chase Bank, Shell
Other **W:** Eckerd Drugs[RX], TX State Optical, U.S. Post Office

253 US 79, Taylor

FStop **E:** Shell[*, D]
Gas **E:** Diamond Shamrock[*, D, CW]
W: Texaco[*, D, CW]
Food **E:** Arby's, Baskin Robbins, Castaways Steakhouse, Dairy Queen, Damon's, KFC, Long John Silver, Short Stop, Sirloin Stockade
W: IHOP, K-Bob's Steakhouse, La Margarita
Lodg **E:** Best Western
W: La Quinta Inn, Ramada Limited, Sleep Inn
AServ **E:** Austin Datsun Repair, Auto Zone Auto Parts, Hester Auto Radiator, Rick's Auto Parts
W: Bishop Automotive Machine, Longhorn Foreign & Domestic
ATM **E:** Bank One, Compass Bank, Heartland Bank, Shell
Other **E:** H-E-B[RX], Mail Boxes Etc.

252B RM 620

Gas **E:** Texaco[*, D, CW]
W: New York Deli[*, D]
Food **E:** Golden Fried Chicken, Ole Taco
W: Frank's Fish Grill, Grandy's, Great American Frozen Custard, Little Caesars Pizza, McDonald's[PLAY], New York Deli, Peking Palace, Wendy's
AServ **E:** Kwik Kar Oil & Lube
W: K&S Automotive
Med **W:** ✚ Hospital
ATM **E:** First Texas Bank, Norwest Bank
W: Alberson's Grocery[24, RX]
Other **E:** Round Rock Travel & Tours
W: Alberson's Grocery[RX], Putt-Putt Golf & Games

252A McNeil Road

Gas **W:** Phillips 66[*, CW]
Food **E:** Bob's BBQ etc., Brewmoon Cafe & Pub, Ci Ci's Pizza, Delaware Sub Shop, Golden Palace, Whataburger[24]
ATM **E:** Austin Area Teachers Federal Credit Union
Other **E:** Antique Mall of Texas, Pet Hospital
W: Animal Hospital

251 Bus Loop I-35, Round Rock

Gas **E:** Citgo[*], Diamond Shamrock[*, CW]
W: Exxon[*], Texaco
Food **E:** Jo's Crab Shack
W: Bagel Tree, Burger King[PLAY], China Wall Restaurant, Jack-In-The-Box, Jambalaya, Luby's Cafeteria, TCBY, Taco Cabana[24]
Lodg **W:** Rodeway Inn & Suites
AServ **E:** AAMCO Transmission, Auto Tech, Brake Check, Genie Lube Express, Meineke Discount Mufflers
W: E & T Automotive, NTB, Precision Tune, Texaco
ATM **W:** First State Bank, Texaco
Other **E:** Car Wash
W: Fed Ex Drop Box, Hasting's Books, Music, Video, Optical Outlets, Tomlinson's Pet Food & More, WalGreens Pharmacy[RX] (1 Hr Photo)

EXIT TEXAS

250 FM 1325

Gas **E:** Mobil[*, D]
W: Texaco (Xpress Lube), Xpress Lube
Food **E:** Alcapone's Italian, Applebee's, Boston Market Restaurant, Buffet Palace, Chick-Fil-A[PLAY], Chili's, Dickey's BBQ Pit, El Chico, Jason's Deli, Jo's Crab Shack, Lamp Post Pizza, McDonald's[PLAY], McDonald's (Wal-Mart), Short Stop, Souper Salad, Star of India, Subway, Taco Bell
Lodg **W:** Baymont Inn
AServ **E:** Lamb's Tire & Auto, Pro Auto Body (Towing), Wal-Mart Supercenter[24, RX] (Vision Center, 1 Hr. Photo)
W: Xpress Lube
RVCamp **E:** Texas Camper Corral, Travel Town Texas
ATM **E:** NationsBank
Other **E:** Emeral Green's Golf Complex, EyeMasters, Mail Boxes Etc., Office Max, PetsMart, Target, The Home Depot[LP], Wal-Mart Supercenter[RX] (Vision Center, 1 Hr. Photo)
W: Doc Holiday's Car Wash, Garden Ridge Shopping Mall

248 Grand Ave Parkway

FStop **E:** Circle K[*]
ATM **E:** Circle K
Other **E:** Certified Propane Inc. & Truck Wash[LP], Tinsel Town USA Cinema

247 FM 1825, Pflugerville

Gas **E:** H-E-B (H-E-B Grocery), Racetrac[*]
W: Exxon[*, CW]
Food **E:** Jack-In-The-Box, Taco Cabana
AServ **W:** Purcell Auto/Truck Service Center
TServ **W:** Diesel Tech Parts & Service, Purcell Auto/Truck Service Center
ATM **W:** Exxon, Texas Heritage Bank
Other **E:** H-E-B Grocery Store[24, RX] (1-Hr Photo)

246 Dessau Road, Howard Lane

Gas **E:** Shell[*, D], Texaco[*]
W: Diamond Shamrock[*, D, CW, 24]
Food **E:** Dunkin Donuts (Shell)
ATM **E:** Texaco

245 FM 734, Parmer Lane, Yager Lane

Gas **W:** Citgo[*]
AServ **W:** Van's Auto Parts
Med **W:** ✚ Hospital
ATM **W:** Citgo

244 Yager Lane (Northbound)

243 Braker Lane

Gas **E:** Diamond Shamrock[*, 24]

1819
FAIRFIELD INN
Marriott
63 Bright, Attractive Guest Rooms
Free Continental Breakfast
Heated Indoor Pool & Exercise Room
Hot Coffee & Tea, Free 24 Hours
Ample Free Parking • Guest Laundry
Two Convenient Locations on I-35!
Austin North — I-35 • Exit 238B — 512-302-5550
Austin South — I-35 • Exit 230 — 512-707-8899
TEXAS ▪ I-35 ▪ EXIT 238B & 230

EXIT TEXAS

W: Citgo[*], Texaco[*]
Food **E:** C & B BBQ, Jack-In-The-Box, Subway, Tropical Heat Cafe & Bar, Whataburger[24], Zazquez Taco
W: Gunther's
Lodg **W:** Austin Motor Inn, Walnut Forest Motel
AServ **E:** Austin Braker Automotive
W: AusTex, Tire Mart
ATM **W:** Citgo, Norwest Bank
Other **E:** Animal Clinic

241 Rutherford Lane, Rundberg Lane

Gas **E:** Diamond Shamrock[*], Exxon[*, CW], Phillips 66[*]
W: Chevron[*, 24], Conoco[*], Texaco[*, CW]
Food **E:** Dairy Queen, Golden China Restaurant, Jack-In-The-Box, Mr. Gatti's Pizza, Old San Francisco Steakhouse, Taquerias Arandas
W: Mr. India Palace
Lodg **E:** HomeGate Studios & Suites, Ramada Inn
W: Austin Village Motor Inn, Budget Inn, Howard Johnson, Motel 6
AServ **E:** Exxon, Henna Chevrolet, Texas Alternator Service
W: A-One Discount Tire, J.C. 's Motor World, Nortek Auto Repair, Xpress Lube[CW]
ATM **E:** Diamond Shamrock, Exxon
W: Chevron, Conoco
Other **E:** Koin Wash
W: Affordable Car Wash, Golf

240B N. U.S. 183, Research Blvd. (Limited Access Hwy)

240A S. U.S. 183, Anderson Ln., Lampasas, Lockhart (Southbound)

Gas **W:** Conoco[*, D], Diamond Shamrock[*], Exxon[*, CW]
Food **W:** American Grill Bandstand, Bennigan's, Burger Tex, Denny's, Koffee 'N Ice Kream, Mason Jar, Ninfa's, Outback Steakhouse, Rocky's Grill (Red Roof Inn), Souper Salads, Stringfield's (Four Points Hotel), Taj Palace
Lodg **W:** Best Western, Chariot Inn, Comfort Inn, Four Points Hotel Sheraton, Holiday Inn Express, La Quinta Inn, Motel 6, Red Roof Inn, Sumner Suites, Super 8, TraveLodge
AServ **W:** Henna Motor Co., Longhorn Glass
TServ **W:** Austin Drive Train
ATM **W:** Conoco, Diamond Shamrock, Frost Bank
Other **W:** General Cinemas, Lucky 7 Food Mart

240 US 183 (Northbound)

Gas **E:** Fisco[*]
Food **E:** Chili's
Lodg **E:** DAYS INN Days Inn, Hampton Inn
RVCamp **W:** McClain's RV Superstore[LP]

239 St. Johns Ave (Northbound)

Food **E:** Fuddruckers, Owens Restaurant, Pappadeaux, Pappasito's, Savannah's (Holiday Inn), SHONEY'S Shoney's
Lodg **E:** Doubletree Hotel, Drury Inn, Holiday Inn, Homestead Village
AServ **E:** Heart of Texas Dodge
Other **E:** Malibu Grand Prix, The Home Depot[LP], U.S. Post Office

238B East U.S. 290, West FM 2222, Houston

Food **E:** China Star, El Racho Grande (EconoLodge), Palmeras, Texas Land & Cattle Steakhouse
W: Bombay Bicycle Club, Cafe Serranos, Carrabba's Italian Grill, Carrows Restaurant, China Cafe, IHOP, Lonestar Cafe, Ma Ferguson's (Hilton), Smoothie King, TJ Cinnamons Bakery, Thai Village
Lodg **E:** Austin Studio Plus, Fairfield Inn (see our ad this page), EconoLodge, Embassy Suites, Red Lion Hotel
W: Drury Inn, Fairfield Inn, Hilton, La Quinta Inn,

Quality Inn, Super 8 (see our ad this page)
AServ **E:** American Collision Center, Roger Beasley Volvo
Other **W:** Highland Mall, Lincoln Theatre, Office Depot

238A Reinli St, Clayton Ln (Southbound Reads 51st St)
Gas **E:** Chevron[*, 24]
W: Texaco[*]
Food **E:** Amaya's Taco Village, Ci Ci's Pizza, Grandy's, India Cuisine, McDonald's[PLAY]
W: Baby Acapulco, El Paraiso (Rodeway Inn), The Captain's
Lodg **W:** Austin Rio Motel, Bad Griesbach, Courtyard by Marriott, Fairfield Inn by Marriott, Motel 6, Ramada Limited, Rodeway Inn
AServ **E:** Brake Check, Firestone Tire & Auto, Montgomery Ward, Western Auto
W: AC Auto Electric, Interstate Automotive, Trans-Care Transmission Parts
ATM **E:** Bank One
W: Bank One
Other **E:** OfficeMax, Texas State Optical, Toys R Us, WalGreens Pharmacy[RX] (1-Hr Photo)

237B 51st St, Cameron Road (Upper Level)
Gas **E:** Shell[*], Yemco Petroleum[*, LP]
ATM **E:** Shell

237A Airport Blvd, 51st St, Cameron Rd, 38 1/2 St (Upper Level - No Services)
Gas **W:** 1st Evening[*], Diamond Shamrock[*, D], Texaco
AServ **W:** Airport Auto Supply, Goodyear, Sears Auto, Texaco, The Oil Works
ATM **W:** 1st Evening, Diamond Shamrock, H-E-B[RX]
Other **E:** Academy, U-Haul Center[LP]
W: H-E-B[RX]

236B 38 1/2 St
Gas **E:** Chevron[*], Gas[*]
W: Texaco[*, D, CW]
Food **E:** Little Caesars Pizza, Pato's, Short Stop Hamburger
W: Jades Chinese
AServ **E:** Hi/Lo Auto Supply, Van's Auto Parts
W: Dura-Tune
Med **W:** ✚ Hospital
ATM **E:** Chevron, Fiesta Grocery[24]
W: NationsBank
Other **E:** Austin Outdoor Gear & Guidance, Fiesta Grocery, Monarch Food Mart
W: Hancock Golf Course

236A 26th - 32nd Streets
Food **E:** Stars Cafe[24]
W: Enchiladas Y Mas
Lodg **E:** Days Inn
W: Rodeway Inn (see our ad this page)
Med **W:** ✚ St. David's Medical Center
Other **W:** Austin Veterinary Hospital

235C University of Texas, 15th & MLK Blvd, State Capitol

235B Manor Road, 26th St

235A 15th Street - Martin Luther King Blvd, State Capital (Southbound)
Med **W:** ✚ Brackenridge Hospital, ✚ Children's Hospital of Austin (Upper Level Access)
Other **W:** Lyndon Baines Johnson Library & Museum, The University of Texas

234C 6th - 12th Streets, State Capitol
Gas **E:** Chevron, Exxon[*], Texaco[*]
W: Texaco[*, D]
Food **E:** Angie's, Ben's Long Branch BBQ, Milagro
W: Capitol Cafe (La Quinta Inn), Serranos
Lodg **E:** Super 8
W: La Quinta Inn, Marriott
AServ **E:** Armadillo Auto Repair, Chevron
Med **W:** ✚ Hospital
ATM **E:** Chevron, Exxon, Texaco
W: Austin Municipal Federal Credit Union, Texaco
Other **E:** Eckerd Drugs
W: Historic Sites and Museums

234B Cesar Chavez St, 2nd - 4th Sts., 8th - 3rd Sts. (8th-3rd Streets Are Southbound Only)
Gas **W:** Mobil[*]
Food **W:** High Lite Cafe, O'Shucks Tomales, The Boiling-Pot Restaurant
Lodg **W:** Omni Hotel, Sheriton Suites
AServ **E:** East First Auto Supplies
W: Bethke, Empire Automotive
ATM **W:** Mobil

2900 IH-35N
Austin, TX
512-477-6395
AT UNIVERSITY
AAA
Sun thru Thur Only
$49.00*
1-2 Persons
*Must show ad at check-in. Not Valid with other offers & on special events.
FREE Continental Breakfast
Remote Cable TV w/HBO, CNN, ESPN & TBS
Free Local Calls & Parking
Non-Smoking Rooms Avail.
Outdoor Pool
LBJ Library & Univ of Texas 2 blocks
1762
I-35 (lower level) at intersection of 26th St., Exit #236A.
TEXAS ▪ I-35 ▪ EXIT 236A Lower Level

1659

SUPER 8
Highland Mall
IH-35 • Austin, TX
512-467-8163

Deluxe Continental Breakfast
Outoor Pool
Meeting/Banquet Facilities
Handicap Accessible
Exercise Room
Truck/Large Vehicle Parking
Coin Laundry
Interior Corridors
Restaurants & Mall Nearby
Free Local Calls
6000 Middle Fiskville Road
TEXAS ▪ I-35 ▪ EXIT 238B

Other **E:** Public Library
W: Fire Department, O. Henry House & Museum, Police HQ

234A Cesar Chavez St, Holly St (Southbound)
Food **W:** IHOP, Iron Works
AServ **W:** Austin Foreign Car Center
Other **W:** Austin Convention Center, Visitor Information

233A 1st - 4th Streets

233BC Unnamed (Northbound)
Gas **E:** Shell[*]
ATM **E:** Shell

233 Town Lake, Riverside Drive
Gas **E:** Diamond Shamrock[*]
W: Chevron[*, CW, 24]
Food **E:** Wok 'N Gold
W: The Pecan Tree (Holiday Inn)
Lodg **E:** HomeGate Studios & Suites
W: Holiday Inn
RVCamp **W:** Pecan Grove RV Park (Approx. 2 Miles)
Other **W:** Public Boat Ramp

232B Woodland Ave (Northbound)

232A Oltorf St., Live Oak
Gas **E:** Citgo[*], Fisco[*], Texaco[*, CW]
W: Chevron[*, CW], Texaco
Food **E:** Carrows Restaurant, Kettle, Luby's Cafeteria, Mr. Gatti's Pizza, Sonic
W: Denny's, Marco Polo Restaurant
Lodg **E:** Austin Motel, Exel Inn, La Quinta Inn, Motel 6, Ramada Limited, Super 8
W: Clarion Inn
AServ **E:** Tuneup Masters
W: Chevron, Texaco
Other **W:** Dallas Cowboy's Training Camp, Quality Vision Eyeware, Whip In[*]

231 Woodward St., St. Edwards Univ. (Southbound)
Food **E:** Country Kitchen (Holiday Inn)
Lodg **E:** Holiday Inn

230A St. Elmo Rd (Southbound)
AServ **W:** Beasley Mazda Kia, Cen-Tex Nissan, Hendrix GMC Trucks, McMorris Ford, NTB, Red McCombs Toyota, Roger Beasley South Kia, South Point Jeep, Eagle, Lincoln, Mercury, South Point Pontiac, Cadillac, Southstar Dodge

230B US 290 West, TX 71, Ben White Blvd. (Southbound)
Food **W:** Bill Miller BBQ, Burger King, IHOP, Pizza Hut, Taco Cabana
Lodg **W:** Days Inn, Hawthorn Suites, La Quinta Inn
AServ **W:** Howdy Honda
Med **W:** ✚ Hospital

230 U.S. 290 West, TX 71, Ben White Blvd, St Elmo Rd (Northbound)
Gas **E:** Texaco[*, D, CW]
Food **E:** Saigon Kitchen (Best Western), Subway (Best Western)
Lodg **E:** Best Western, Fairfield Inn (see our ad on previous page), Hampton Inn, Homewood Hotel, The Omni Hotel
ATM **E:** NationsBank
Other **E:** Celebration Station

229 Stassney Lane (Must Be Exited At 228 Services Are the Same)
Lodg **E:** Courtyard by Marriott, Fairfield Inn, Red Roof Inn, Residence Inn
AServ **E:** Sam's Club, Wal-Mart[24, RX] (Optical, Photo)
RVCamp **E:** KOA Campgrounds
Other **E:** Celebration Station, Sam's Club, Wal-Mart[RX]

EXIT TEXAS

(Optical, Photo)

228 William Cannon Drive
- **Gas** E: Citgo(*), Diamond Shamrock(*), Exxon(*, CW), Shell(*, D)
  W: Texaco(*, D)
- **Food** E: Applebee's, I Can't Believe It's Yogurt (Shell), McDonald's(PLAY), Sonic Drive in, Subway, Taco Bell, TiaRita's Tacos (Shell)
  W: Burger King(PLAY), Delaware Sub Shop, KFC, Long John Silver, Mr. Gatti's Pizza, Peter Piper Pizza, Taco Cabana, Thai Kitchen, Wendy's, Whataburger(24)
- **AServ** E: Chief Auto Parts, Discount Tire Company, Gillman Hyundai, Gillman Mitsubishi, Prestige Chrysler
  W: Capitol Chevrolet Geo, Firestone, **Hackney Automotive & Truck Service**, Western Auto
- **TServ** W: **Hackney Automotive & Truck Service**
- **RVCamp** E: **Austin Capitol-KOA Kampground(LP)**
  W: **South Austin**
- **ATM** E: Citgo, Diamond Shamrock, Exxon, Shell
  W: Texaco
- **Other** E: **H-E-B(24, RX) (1-Hr Photo)**, **K-Mart(RX)**, **Target**, **Texas State Optical**
  W: **Academy Sports & Outdoors**, **Century Veterinary Hospital**, **Eckerd Drugs(RX)**, NOW Optical Outlet

227 Slaughter Lane, TX Loop 275, South Congress Ave.
- **Gas** W: Diamond Shamrock(*, D)
- **RVCamp** E: **Austin Capitol-KOA**
- **ATM** W: Diamond Shamrock

226 FM 1626, Slaughter Creek Overpass
- **Gas** E: Texaco(*, D, CW)
- **RVCamp** W: **Marshall's Traveland Sales**

225 Onion Creek Parkway
- **Gas** E: Diamond Shamrock(*)
- **RVCamp** W: **Marshall's Traveland**
- **ATM** E: First American Bank

223 FM 1327

221 Loop 4, Buda
- **TStop** E: **Dorsett 221(SCALES) (Phillips 66)**
- **Gas** W: Chevron(*, 24), Texaco(*, D, CW)
- **Food** E: **Dorsett 221 (Phillips 66)**
  W: Taco El Paso
- **Lodg** E: **Interstate Inn (Phillips 66 TS)**
- **AServ** E: **Dorsett 221 (Phillips 66)**, **Ford Truck City**
  W: A-Line Auto Parts
- **TServ** E: **Carlstead Truck & Bus**, **Dorsett 221(SCALES) (Phillips 66)**, **Ford Truck City**
- **ATM** W: First American Bank

220 FM 2001, Niederwald
- **Food** E: Hinojosa Express
- **RVCamp** E: **First RV Service**
  W: **Crestview RV Park & Center(LP)**

217 Loop 4, Buda
- **FStop** E: **Conoco(*)**
- **Gas** W: Diamond Shamrock(*, D), Exxon(D)
- **Food** E: **Burger King (Conoco)**
  W: Pizza Hut (Diamond Shamrock)
- **AServ** W: Exxon
- **TServ** E: **K D Truck Parts**
- **RVCamp** W: **Interstate RV**
- **ATM** E: **Conoco**

215 Bunton Overpass

213 FM 150, Kyle
- **Gas** E: Diamond Shamrock(*, D)
  W: Conoco(*), Texaco(*)
- **Food** E: Dairy Queen
  W: Blanco River Pizza Co., Chicken Willies, Panaderia Mexicana Kyle Bakery, Paradise Restaurant, Railroad BBQ, Taqueira Loredo
- **AServ** W: 4 Way Auto Repair Shop(24), J & R Tire Service(24)
- **ATM** E: Diamond Shamrock, Instant Cash
  W: Balcones Bank, Conoco, Wells Fargo
- **Other** E: **Mr. T Washateria (Diamond Shamrock)**
  W: **Bon-Ton Grocery**, **Center Grocery**, **Kyle Drug Store(RX)**, **U.S. Post Office**

(212) **Rest Area (RR, Phones, Picnic, Grills, Vending, P; Northbound)**

(211) **Weigh Station (Northbound)**

(211) **Rest Area (RR, Phones, Picnic, Grills, Vending, P; Southbound)**

(211) **Rest Area (RR, HF, Picnic, Grills, Vending, P; Northbound)**

210 Yarrington Road
- **RVCamp** W: **Plum Creek RV Resort(LP)**

208 Blanco River

206 Loop 82, Aquarena Springs Dr
- **Gas** E: Conoco(*), Diamond Shamrock(*, D)
  W: Exxon(*, D), Mobil(*, D), Shell(*, CW), Texaco(*)
- **Food** W: Casa Ole, Kettle Restaurant, Popeye's Chicken, SHONEY'S, Shoney's, Sonic
- **Lodg** W: Comfort Inn, Executive House Inn, Howard Johnson, La Quinta Inn, Motel 6, Ramada Limited, Stratford House, Super 8, University Inn
- **RVCamp** E: **United RV Park(LP) (.5 Miles)**
- **ATM** E: Diamond Shamrock
- **Other** E: **Texas Natural Aquarium Aquarena Springs (.5 Miles)**
  W: **Super Klean Laundromat**, **Tourist Info.**

205 TX 80 To TX 21 Luling, TX 12 To TX 142 Wimberley, Lockhart.
- **Gas** E: Diamond Shamrock(*, D), Exxon(*), Mobil(*, D), Racetrac(*, 24), Shell(*, D)
  W: Diamond Shamrock(*), H-E-B
- **Food** E: Arby's, Baysea's Fish Market III & Seafood Restaurant, Casa Pico, **Dairy Queen(PLAY)**, Fushak's BBQ, J J's Flame-Broiled Hamburgers, **McDonald's (Wal-Mart)**, Schlotzsky's Deli, Subway
  W: August Moon, Burger King(PLAY), Church's Chicken, Donut Palace, Firs Family Dining, Gill's Fried Chicken, Imperial Garden, KFC, Long John Silver, **McDonald's(PLAY)**, Pizza Hut, Sirloin Stockade, Taco Cabana, Wendy's
- **Lodg** W: Best Western, DAYS INN Days Inn, Microtel Inn, Rodeway Inn, Shoney's Inn, Southwest Motor Lodg
- **AServ** E: Grease Monkey, **Wal-Mart SuperCenter(RX) (Vision Center, 1 Hr. Photo)**
  W: Starr Lube, The Brake Shop
- **ATM** E: Diamond Shamrock, Frost Bank, Racetrac, **Wal-Mart SuperCenter (Vision Center, 1 Hr. Photo)**
- **Other** E: Bright Wash Car Wash, **Cinema 5**, Coin Laundromat, **Eckerd Drugs(RX)**, **Hastings Bookstore**, Mail & More, **S.W. Vision Optical**, **Tickle Blagg Animal Hospital**, **Wal-Mart SuperCenter(RX) (Vision Center, 1 Hr. Photo)**
  W: **H-E-B Grocery Store(RX)**, Laser Wash, **Springtown Animal Hospital**

204 West Loop 82, East TX 123, San Marcos, Seguin (Texas State University)
- **FStop** E: **Texaco(*)**
  W: **Texaco(*, LP)**
- **Gas** E: Conoco(*), Diamond Shamrock(*), Phillips 66(*, D, CW)
  W: Conoco(*, D, K), Diamond Shamrock(*)
- **Food** E: Burger King, Chili's, Golden Corral Family Steakhouse, Luby's Cafeteria, McDonald's(PLAY), Red Lobster, Whataburger(24)
  W: Dairy Queen, Guadalupe Street Smokehouse, Hacienda Gonzalez, Hong Kong Restaurant, Panda King, Taqueria La Fonda
- **Lodg** E: Holiday Inn Express
  W: EconoLodge
- **AServ** E: Chuck Nash Jeep Eagle Dodge, Pennzoil Oil Change, Red Simon Ford Mercury, Rudy's Automotive
  W: Auto Zone Auto Parts, Carquest Auto Parts, Ellison's Auto Repair & Windshield, Fritz's Muffler Shop, NAPA Auto Parts, Quik Align, Saucedo's Wrecker Service(24)
- **TServ** W: **Texaco(CW)**
- **Med** E: **+ Hospital**
- **ATM** W: Diamond Shamrock
- **Other** E: **La Palma Grocery**, **San Marcos Skate Center**
  W: Budget Opticals

202 FM 3407, Wonder World Dr
- **Gas** W: Diamond Shamrock(*, D)
- **Food** W: Pizza Hut (Diamond Shamrock)
- **Med** E: **+ Central TX Medical Center**
- **ATM** E: NBC Bank of Texas
- **Other** E: **Lowe's Home Improvement Warehouse(LP)**
  W: **Wonder World**

201 McCarty Lane

200 Center Point Road
- **Gas** W: Diamond Shamrock(*, D)
- **Food** E: Food Court (San Marcos Factory Shops), Lone Star Cafe, Outback Steakhouse, **Subway (Tanger Outlet)**, Taco Bell, Wendy's
  W: **Antique Outlet Center**, Centerpoint Station, Whataburger
- **Lodg** W: AmeriHost Inn
- **ATM** E: Food Court (San Marcos Factory Shops), **Tanger Factory Outlet**
  W: Diamond Shamrock
- **Other** E: **San Marcos Factory Shops**, **Tanger Factory Outlet**
  W: **Antique Outlet Center**

199A Posey Road

196 FM 1102, York Creek Rd.

195 Watson Lane, Old Bastrop Rd.

193 Kohlenberg Rd., Conrads Rd.
- **TStop** W: **Rip Griffin Travel Center(*, LP, PLAY, SCALES) (Shell)**
- **Food** W: **A & W Drive-In (Rip Griffin TS)**, **Rip Griffin Travel Center(PLAY) (Shell)**, **Subway (Rip Griffin TS)**
- **TServ** W: **Rip Griffin Travel Center(SCALES) (Shell)**

191 TX 306, TX 483, Canyon Lake
- **FStop** W: **Exxon(*)**
- **Gas** E: Fina(*, D)
  W: Mobil(*, CW)
- **Food** W: Burger King(PLAY), I Can't Believe It's Yogurt (Mobil), Mesquite Smoked BBQ (Mobil), Mobil, Pizza Hut (Mobil)
- **AServ** W: Garland Automatic Transmission
- **RVCamp** W: **Maricopa Ranch Resort**
- **ATM** W: Mobil

190C Post Rd (Southbound)
- **Other** W: **Tourist Info.**

190B S. Bus. Loop I-35, New Braunfels (Southbound)
- **Gas** W: Conoco(*, D)
- **AServ** W: Conoco
- **RVCamp** W: **Wayside RV Park**

190A Frontage Rd (Southbound)
- **Lodg** W: Best Western, Comfort Suites Hotel

190 North U.S. 35, South Bus Loop (Northbound)
- **RVCamp** E: **Evergreen RV Sales & Services**, **I-35 RV Park**

EXIT	TEXAS
	& Campground
189	**TX 46, Loop 337, Seguin, Boerne**
Gas	E: Shell[*, D], Texaco[*, D, CW, 24]
	W: Chevron[*, D, 24], Diamond Shamrock[*]
Food	E: Luby's Cafeteria, Oma's Haus
	W: Applebee's, Breustedt Haus, IHOP, Longhorn Grill, McDonald's[PLAY], Molly Joe's, New Braunfels Smokehouse, Shipley Do-Nuts, Skillet's Restaurant, TCBY, Taco Bell, Taco Cabana[24], Wendy's
Lodg	E: Oak Wood Inn, Super 8
	W: Days Inn, Dwight's Motel, Edelweiss Inn, Fountain Motel, Hampton Inn, Holiday Inn, Old Town Inn, Rodeway Inn
ATM	E: Shell, Texaco
	W: Chevron
Other	E: Comal Animal Clinic, Home Depot, K-Mart[RX]
188	**Frontage Road**
Food	W: DC's Restaurant, Ryan's Steakhouse
Lodg	W: Lucky Star Motel
AServ	W: Best Deal Tires 24-Hr Road Service
RVCamp	W: New Braunfel's RV Park
ATM	W: New Braunfel Factory Stores
Other	W: Hasting's Books, Music, Video, New Braunfel's Factory Stores, O'Neal's Cinemas
187	**FM 725, Seguin Ave, Lake McQueeny**
Gas	E: Chevron[*, 24], Diamond Shamrock[*]
	W: Conoco[*, K], Exxon
Food	E: Arby's, Burger King[PLAY], Cancun Cafe, China Kitchen Restaurant & Bar, Ci Ci's Pizza, Donut Palace, Long John Silver, Whataburger[24]
	W: AJ's Fast Food, Adobe Cafe, Dairy Queen, Hill Country Inn, Jack-In-The-Box, Keno's BBQ & Smokehouse, Peking Restaurant
Lodg	W: Budget Host Inn, Hill Country Inn
AServ	E: AAMCO Transmission, Precision Tune & Lube, Q Lube
	W: B & C Service Center (NAPA), Delux Glass & Mirror, Exxon
RVCamp	W: Mobile Home & RV Parts
Med	W: + Hospital (2 Miles)
Other	E: E-Z Wash #2, Handy Andy Supermarket, Polly's Pet Shop, Texas State Optical
186	**Walnut Ave**
Gas	E: Diamond Shamrock[*, D, CW], Exxon[*]
	W: Conoco[*], H-E-B, Texaco[*, D, CW]
Food	E: Don Juan's, McDonald's (Wal-Mart), McDonald's[PLAY], Popeye's Chicken, Subway (Exxon)
	W: KFC, Mr. Gatti's, Papa John's Pizza, Schlotzsky's Deli, Shanghai Inn, Shipley Do-nuts
Lodg	E: Ramada Limited
AServ	E: Maxwell Chevrolet, Wal-Mart Supercenter[24, RX] (1-Hr Photo, Vision Center)
	W: Auto Zone Auto Parts, Brinkkoeter's, Complete Automotive, Morris Glass Co., Rick's Muffler & Hitch Center, Xpress Lube
RVCamp	E: RV Service (Wal-Mart)
ATM	E: Diamond Shamrock, Exxon, Randolph-Brooks Federal Credit Union, Wal-Mart Supercenter (1-Hr Photo, Vision Center)
	W: H-E-B Grocery Store[RX], Texaco, Texstar Bank
Other	E: Wal-Mart Supercenter[RX] (1-Hr Photo, Vision Center)
	W: Country Clean Coin-Op Laundry, H-E-B Grocery Store[RX], Mail It Plus, Target, Tru Value Hardware, Vivroux Toy & Sporting Goods, Walnut 6 Cinema
185	**S Bus. Loop 35, FM 1044, New Braunfels**
Food	W: Butcher Boy Meat Market
AServ	W: RN Tire Service, Z's 24-Hr Tow Service
Other	W: Car Wash, Coin Laundry

EXIT	TEXAS
184	**Loop 337, FM 482, Ruekle Road**
Gas	E: Texaco[*, D, 24]
Food	E: Blimpie Subs & Salads (Texaco), Texaco
RVCamp	E: Hill Country RV Resort
ATM	E: Texaco
Other	W: Fire Department
183	**Solms Road**
Gas	W: Exxon[*]
182	**Engel Road (Northbound Closed Due to Construction)**
Food	W: Mesquite Pit Junction
AServ	W: World Car Mazda
RVCamp	E: Stahmann RV Sales
	W: Appleman RV Outlet, W W RV Service Center
Other	W: Bird Park, Snake Farm
180	**Schwab Road (Closed Due to Construction)**
(179)	**Rest Area (RR, Phones, Picnic, Grills, Vending, RV Dump, Pet Walk, P; Southbound)**
(179)	**Rest Area (RR, Phones, Picnic, Grills, Vending, RV Dump, Pet Walk, P; Northbound, Closed For Construction)**
178	**FM 1103, Cibolo, Hubertus Road**
Gas	E: Shell[*]
RVCamp	E: Happy Camper RV Sales, Rancho Vista Park
177	**FM 482, FM 2252**
Food	E: Mario's Cafe
RVCamp	W: Stone Creek RV Park, Stone Creek RV Park[LP]
175	**FM 3009, Natural Bridge Caverns Road, Roy Richard Dr.**
FStop	W: Diamond Shamrock[*]
Gas	E: Diamond Shamrock[*, D, CW], H-E-B
	W: Texaco[*, D, CW]
Food	E: Bill Miller BBQ, La Pasadita, McDonald's[PLAY], Taco Cabana
	W: Abel's Diner, Arby's, Denny's, Diamond Shamrock, Jack-In-The-Box, Subway (Diamond Shamrock), Wendy's
Lodg	W: Atrium Inn
ATM	E: Diamond Shamrock, State Bank & Trust
	W: Diamond Shamrock, Texaco
Other	E: Garden Ridge Animal Hospital, H-E-B Grocery Store[RX], Mail Boxes Etc
	W: Natural Bridge Caverns (8 Miles), Natural Bridge Wildlife Ranch (8 Miles), Texas Pecan Candy
174B	**Schertz Parkway**
RVCamp	E: Oak View Mobile Home Park
	W: Beryl's RV Sales Center, Crestview RV Sale
ATM	E: Schertz Trust Bank
174A	**FM 1518, Selma, Schertz**
AServ	E: Gillman Honda, Saturn of San Antonio N.E.
Other	W: Ronnie's Marine, Tex-All Boat Co.
173	**Olympia Parkway, Old Austin Road**
172	**Loop 1604, Anderson Loop**
171	**TX 218, Pat Booker Road, Universal City, Randolph AFB (Northbound)**
AServ	E: Jordan Ford, Red McCombs Nissan
RVCamp	E: ABC RV & Mobile Home Park (2 Miles)
170B	**Toepperwein Road**
Food	E: Kettle Restaurant, Subway, Whataburger[24]
Lodg	E: La Quinta Inn
AServ	E: Gunn Chevrolet
Med	E: + Northeast Methodist Hospital

EXIT	TEXAS
Other	E: Live Oak Pharmacy[RX], My Buddy, Village Oaks Pharmacy[RX]
170A	**Judson Road**
Gas	E: Texaco[*, D, CW]
	W: Exxon[*, CW]
Lodg	W: Holiday Inn Express
AServ	E: Gunn Auto Park, Universal Toyota
	W: Sam's Club, Universal Mazda Subaru
ATM	E: Texaco
Other	W: Sam's Club
169	**O'Connor Road**
FStop	E: Conoco[*, 24]
	W: Texaco[*, SCALES]
Gas	E: Gas[*]
	W: Diamond Shamrock[*, CW, 24], Racetrac[*, 24]
Food	W: Chester Fried Chicken (Texaco), Hong Won Chinese Buffet, Jack-In-The-Box, Jim's Restaurant, K-Mart[24, RX], Little Caesars Pizza (K-Mart)
Lodg	W: EconoLodge
AServ	W: K-Mart[24], Kwik Kar Lube & Tune, Martinez Tire & Muffler Shop
RVCamp	W: Camping
ATM	E: Conoco
	W: Diamond Shamrock
Other	W: K-Mart[RX]
168	**Weidner Road**
Gas	E: Bank Card Self Service, Diamond Shamrock[*, D], Exxon[*, 24]
	W: Chevron[*, 24]
Lodg	E: Days Inn
	W: Ramada Inn, Super 8
AServ	E: Gunn Dodge
	W: Carburetor Shop
TServ	W: Grande Trucks
RVCamp	W: Interstate RV
ATM	E: Diamond Shamrock
	W: Chevron
Other	W: Harley Davidson
167A	**Randolph Blvd (Southbound)**
Food	W: Best Western
Lodg	W: Best Western, Classic Inn & Suites, Days Inn, Motel 6, Ruby Inn
AServ	W: Yang's Auto Repair
167B	**Starlight Terrace (Southbound)**
167	**Starlight Terrace (Northbound)**
Gas	E: Diamond Shamrock[*]
AServ	E: Ford Automotive & Performance, Performance Automotive & Transmission, Uncle Sam's Auto Repair
ATM	E: Diamond Shamrock
166B	**Randolph Blvd, Windcrest (Northbound)**
Gas	E: Diamond Shamrock[*, D, CW], Stop N Go[*]
Food	E: Healthy Habits Cafe, Mongolia Restaurant, Saigon Gardens
RVCamp	E: Traveltown Texas
ATM	E: Diamond Shamrock, Stop N Go
Other	E: Christ the King Bookstore, Joe Harrison Motor Sports, Skateland
166	**I-410 West, South Loop 368**
165	**FM 1976, Walzem Road, Windcrest**
Gas	E: Texaco[*, D, CW]
	W: Mobil
Food	E: Applebee's, Burger King, China Cafe, Chuck E Cheese's Pizza, Church's Chicken, Jim's, Marie Callender's Restaurant, McDonald's (Wal-Mart), Mr. Goodcents Subs & Pastas, Olive Garden, Red Line Hamburgers, Red Lobster, Shoney's, Shoney's, Taco Cabana[24], Wendy's
	W: Sonic
Lodg	E: Drury Inn, Hampton Inn
AServ	E: AutoExpress (Montgomery Ward), Discount

Bold red print shows RV & Bus parking available or nearby

Tire Center, Firestone Tire & Auto, **Wal-Mart(RX) (1 Hr Photo , Vision Center)**
W: Mobil, NTB
ATM E: Frost Bank, Security Service Federal Credit Union
W: Randolph-Brooks Federal Credit Union
Other E: **Builder Square, OfficeMax, Pearl Vision Center, PetsMart, Sports Authority, The Home Depot(LP), Toys R Us, Wal-Mart(RX) (1 Hr Photo , Vision Center), Windsor Optical, Windsor Park Mall**
W: **Baseball City**, La Placida Food Mart

164 Eisenhower Road
Gas E: Exxon(*, D, CW)

164B **(163)** Rittiman Road
Gas E: Exxon(*, CW), Mobil(*), Racetrac(*), Texaco(*, D, CW)
W: Chevron(*, D), Diamond Shamrock(*, D), Otto Food Mart(*)
Food E: Burger King, Church's Chicken, **Cracker Barrel**, Denny's, Kettle Restaurant(24), McDonald's(PLAY), Red Line Burgers, Sam Won Garden, Taco Cabana(24), Whataburger(24)
W: Bill Miller BBQ, Cristan's Tacos #5, Simply The Best Cafe, Wendy's
Lodg E: Comfort Suites Hotel, Knight's Inn, La Quinta Inn, Motel 6, Motel 6, Scotsman Inn, Super 8
AServ E: C & J Automotive, Goll Auto Service, MAACO Auto Body, Tire Shop
TServ E: **Onan Cummins**
ATM E: Exxon
W: Chevron, Diamond Shamrock, Otto Food Mart
Other E: **Rittiman Animal Hospital**

163C Holbrook Rd, Binz - Englemann Rd (Southbound)
Med W: ✚ **Brook Army Medical Center (Ft. Sam Houston)**

163AA South I-410 (Southbound, Left Exit Southbound)

163B Petroleum Drive

162 I-410 South, Loop 13, W.W. White, FM 78, Kirby (Northbound)
Lodg W: Comfort Inn

161 Binz - Englemann Road (Northbound)
Food W: Holiday Inn
Lodg W: Holiday Inn, Quality Inn & Suites
AServ E: Jim Buffaloe Automotive
TServ E: **Southwest Brake & Alignment**
Med W: ✚ **Brook Army Medical Center**

160 Splash Town Drive, Coliseum Rd (Access To Services Varies On Direction Traveled)
Food W: Casey's BBQ, Los Pinos
Lodg E: Delux Inn
W: Days Inn, Super 8, TraveLodge
Other E: **Splash Town Water Park**

159B Walter St., Fort Sam Houston, Colliseum Rd. (Difficult Reaccess)
FStop E: **Diamond Shamrock(24)**
Food E: C & C Tacos, J & E Drive-Inn, McDonald's(PLAY)
W: Drop Zone Cafe, Flores Drive-In
Lodg W: Howard Johnson
AServ E: Aarco Transmission
RVCamp E: **KOA Kampground**
ATM E: **Diamond Shamrock**
Other W: **Fort Sam Houston**

159A New Braunfels Ave
Gas E: Exxon(*, D), Texaco(*, D, CW)
W: Chevron(*), Diamond Shamrock(*)
Food W: Bill Miller BBQ, Johnny's Mexican Restaurant, Johnny's Seafood, TNK Oriental Restaurant
Lodg W: Park Inn Suites
AServ W: Atlas Body Shop
ATM W: Diamond Shamrock
Other W: **Historical Fort Sam Houston, San Antonio Botanical Center (1 Mile)**

158C Loop 368, North Alamo St, Broadway (Southbound)
AServ E: Bowers Brake & Alignment

158B South I-37, South US 281, Corpus Christi (Southbound)

158 I-37, U.S. 281 S, U.S. 281 N, Corpus Christi, Johnson City (Northbound)

157C St. Mary's St, Loop 368, Broadway (Northbound)
Food E: El Nogal
Lodg E: Super 8
AServ E: Gene's Brake & Alignment, Malin's Auto Repair
Other E: **Fire Station, Hickey Animal Clinic Emergency Hospital, San Antonio Museum of Art**

157B McCullough Ave, Brooklyn Ave (Upper Level)
Gas E: Diamond Shamrock(*)
Food E: Audry's Mexican
Med E: ✚ **Baptist Medical Center**
W: ✚ **Metropolitan Methodist Hospital**
ATM E: Diamond Shamrock
W: NationsBank
Other E: **San Antonio Museum of Art**
W: **Your Eyes Optical**

157A San Pedro Ave., Main Ave., Lexington Ave.
Gas W: Diamond Shamrock(*, CW)
Food W: Cristan's Tacos, Jack-In-The-Box, Luby's Cafeteria, McDonald's(PLAY), Pizza Hut, Rodeway Inn, Taco Bell, Wendy's
Lodg W: Rodeway Inn
AServ W: Fred Luderus Tire Service, Quality Paint & Body, Tuneup Masters
Med E: ✚ **Baptist Medical Center**
ATM E: Compass Bank
W: Diamond Shamrock
Other E: **Madison Square Medical Building Pharmacy(RX)**
W: **Polo's Photo 1-Hr Photo, WalGreens Pharmacy(RX)**

156 West I-10, McDermott Freeway, North US 87 El Paso (Westbound, Upper Level)

155C West Houston St, Commerce St, Market Square (Southbound, Upper Level)
Gas W: Pik Nik(*)
Food W: Golden Star Cafe, Jailhouse Cafe, McDonald's
Lodg W: Motel 6
Med W: ✚ **University Health Center Downtown**
ATM W: San Antonio City Employees Federal Credit Union

155B Westbound - Durango Blvd., Downtown; Eastbound - Frio St., Durango Blvd. (Difficult Reaccess, Access To Services Is Limited To The Direction Traveled)
Food E: Bill Miller BBQ, Holiday Inn
Lodg E: Courtyard by Marriott, Fairfield Inn (see our ad this page), Holiday Inn, Residence Inn
W: Radisson Hotel
Med E: ✚ **Santa Rosa Health Care**
ATM E: **Stop N Go**, Wells Fargo
Parks E: **San Antonio Missions National Historical Park (2.8 Miles)**
Other E: **K-Mart(RX), San Antonio Police HQ, Stop N Go, The Market Square**
W: **Fire Station**

155A Spur 536, South Alamo St. (Southbound)
FStop E: **Datafleet Coastal(D) (Datafleet Credit Card Only, No Attendant)**
Food E: Church's Chicken, Wen Wah's Chinese
Lodg E: Comfort Inn, Ramada Limited
W: Microtel Inn, River Inn Motel
AServ E: Speed & Sport
Other E: **US Post Office**

154B South Laredo St, Cevallos St
Gas E: Exxon(*), Texaco(*)
Food E: Eddie's Taco House, McDonald's(PLAY), Pizza Hut, Wendy's
W: Piedras Negras
Lodg E: Days Inn
Other W: **Gleason Veterinary Hospital**

154A Westbound-San Marcos St, Nogalitos St, Eastbound-Nogalitos St., Loop 353 (Difficult Reaccess)
Gas E: J & L Food & Gas(*)
Food E: Maria's Cafe, Tommy's Old San Antonio Cafe
W: Henry's Tacos To Go, Sunny's Ristorante Italiano
AServ E: General Brake & Alignment, Hernandez Tire & Muffler
Other W: **Collins Branch Garden Library, Fire Station, H-E-B Grocery Store**

153 West U.S. 90, Del Rio, East & West I-10, North & South U.S. 87 (Upper Level Southbound)

152B Malone Ave, Theo Ave
Gas W: Diamond Shamrock(*), Texaco(*, D)
Food E: Taco Cabana(24)
AServ E: Liberty Transmission & Gear Co.
W: Mack's Transmission Service
ATM W: Diamond Shamrock, Texaco

152A Division Ave
Gas E: Chevron(*, CW)
W: Exxon(*, CW), Phillips 66(*)
Food E: Bill Miller BBQ, Whataburger(24)
W: Victoria Tortilla & Tamale Factory
Lodg E: Holiday Inn Express
AServ W: Backus Radiator Works, Coxco Transmission, Guerrero's Tire Shop
ATM E: Chevron
Other E: Car Wash, **Pan Am Pharmacy**
W: **Pablo's Grocery**

EXIT		TEXAS
151		Southcross Blvd
	Gas	E: Citgo(*), Shop "N" Save(*)
		W: Texaco(*, D, CW)
	Food	E: Centeno Market (Flea Market)
		W: Taco Jalisco
	RVCamp	E: Camping
	ATM	E: Citgo
	Other	E: Centeno Market (Flea Market)
150B		Loop 13, Military Dr, Kelly AFB, Lackland AFB
	Gas	E: Chevron(*, D, CW, 24), Texaco(*)
		W: Exxon(*, CW), Mobil(*)
	Food	E: Casa Dos Pedros, Denny's(24), Jang's Chinese, Pizza Hut, Pizza Rio Buffet, Sonic, Subway, Taco Cabana(24)
		W: Hungry Farmer Steakhouse, Hungry Italian Steakhouse, Jack-In-The-Box, Long John Silver, McDonald's(PLAY), Popeye's Chicken, Red Line Hamburgers, SHONEY'S, Shoney's, Southfork Restaurant, Uncle Barney's Old Fashioned Hamburgers, Wendy's
	Lodg	E: La Quinta Inn
	AServ	E: Auto Zone Auto Parts, Brake Check, Discount Tire, Eagle Auto Glass, Macias Tire Shop, Thad Ziegler
	Med	E: + Family Pracice Minor Emergency
	ATM	E: Chevron
		W: Bank One, Mobil, San Antonio Teacher's Credit Union
	Other	E: Alamo City Optical, Century Plaza Theatres, EyeMasters, Ram's Texas Car Wash, U-Haul Center(LP)
		W: Eckerd Drugs(RX), H-E-B(RX) (1 Hr Photo), Office Depot, Toys R Us
150A		Zarzamora St
	FStop	W: Coastal Datafleet (Credit Card Only)
	Gas	E: Diamond Shamrock(*)
	Food	E: Berta's Mexican Cafe
		W: Chelsea Street Grill (Mall), Food Court (Mall), KFC, Luby's Cafeteria (Mall)
	AServ	W: Firestone Tire & Auto, Sears Auto Center
	ATM	E: Diamond Shamrock
		W: Albertson's Food Market(RX)
	Other	E: Rios Meat Market #4
		W: Albertson's Food Market(RX), Skate Time, South Park Mall
149		Hutchins Blvd. (Southbound)
	Med	W: + Hospital
148B		Palo Alto Road (Left Exit Northbound)
	FStop	W: Phillips 66(*)
	Gas	W: Save N Go(*)
	Other	W: Kwik Wash Laundry
148A		Spur 422, TX 16 South, Poteet (Northbound)
147		Somerset Road
146		Cassin road
145B		North Loop 353 (Left Exit Northbound, Difficult Reaccess)
	AServ	W: A-1 Auto Parts, A-1 Imports, A-Alpha Import Co., ABA Parts, Alamo City Imports, Alamo Imports, All Foreign Auto Parts, Apache Auto Parts, Auto World, Benzes & BMW Recyclers, Cristobal Auto Parts, E & D Complete Auto Parts, Laredo Auto & Truck Parts, Million Auto Parts, NICA Motors & Parts, Ozone Air
	TServ	W: A-1 Auto Parts, A-Alpha Import Co., ABA Parts, International Truck Parts, Inc., Interstate Truck Sales, Laredo Auto & Truck Parts
145A		I-410, TX 16
144		Fischer Road
	TStop	E: Diamond Shamrock(*, SCALES) (Fax Machine)

EXIT		TEXAS
	Food	E: Subway (Diamond Shamrock TS)
	Lodg	E: D&D Motel
	RVCamp	E: Hidden Valley RV Park & Camp (Store, Laundry, Full Hookups, .5 Miles)
142		Medina River Turnaround (Northbound)
	TServ	E: Gene's Truck Parts
	RVCamp	E: Uresti's Camper Sales & Truck Accessories
141		Benton City Road, Von Ormy
	TStop	W: Texaco(*, 24)
	Food	W: Mario's Cafe (Texaco TS), Texaco, Von Ormi Ice House(*)
	ATM	W: Texaco
	Other	E: AJM Food Store, US Post Office
140		Loop 1604, Anderson Loop, Somerset, Sea World, Fiesta
	FStop	E: Exxon(*, 24)
	Food	E: Burger King(PLAY)
	ATM	E: Exxon
139		Kinney Road
	AServ	E: A & J's Auto Parts
	RVCamp	E: Camping
137		Shepherd Road
	Gas	W: JC's Food Mart(*, D)
135		Luckey Road
131		FM 3175, FM 2790, Benton City Rd, Lytle
	Gas	W: Conoco(*, D), H-E-B, H-E-B Supermarket(RX)
	Food	W: Dairy Queen, La Villa Restaurant (Best Western), Lytle Taco House, Mr. Pizza
	Lodg	W: Best Western
	AServ	E: Heritage Tires(LP), Lytle Auto Parts
	ATM	E: Lytle State Bank
		W: Conoco
	Other	W: H-E-B Supermarket(RX)
(129)		Rest Area (RR, Phones, Picnic, Grills, Vending, RV Dump, P; Southbound)
(129)		Rest Area (RR, Phones, Picnic, Grills, Vending, RV Dump, P; Northbound)
127		FM 471, Natalia
124		FM 463, Bigfoot Road
	AServ	E: Chaparral Ford
122		TX 173, Hondo, Jourdanton
	FStop	E: Calame Store(*, D, K), Exxon(*)
	Gas	W: Chevron(*, D)
	Food	E: Bob's BBQ
		W: Subway (Chevron), Triple-C Steak House
	Lodg	W: Country Corner Motel
	AServ	E: Brown Chevrolet Geo
	RVCamp	E: Nine Oaks Camper Park
	ATM	E: Calame Store, Exxon
		W: Triple-C Steak House
121		North TX 132, Devine (Northbound)
	RVCamp	E: Campground
(118)		Weigh Station (Southbound)
(118)		Weigh Station (Northbound)
114		FM 462, BigFoot, Yancey, Moore
	Gas	E: Diamond Shamrock(*, D)
		W: The Moore Store(*, D)
	Food	E: Roitas Taco
		W: The Moore Store
	AServ	E: Auto Service
		W: The Pit
	TServ	W: The Pit
	Other	W: Frio County Sheriff, US Post Office

EXIT		TEXAS
111		U.S. 57, Eagle Pass
104		South Bus Loop I-35
101		FM 140, Charlotte, Uvalde
	FStop	W: Conoco(*, 24)
	Gas	E: Chevron(*)
	Food	E: Cowpokes BBQ
		W: Blimpie Subs & Salads (Conoco), Chester Fried Chicken (Conoco), Porterhouse Restaurant (Budget Inn)
	Lodg	E: Rio Frio Motel, Royal Inn
		W: Budget Inn
	AServ	E: Brooks GMC Trucks
		W: Vega Tire & Road Service(24)
	TServ	W: Vega Tire & Road Service
	ATM	W: Conoco
	Other	E: Animal Clinic
99		Bus Loop I-35, FM 1581, Pearsall, Divot
	Other	W: Ferrell Gas(LP)
(93)		Picnic Area (Picnic, Grills; Southbound)
(93)		Picnic Area (Picnic, Grills, P; Northbound)
91		North Spur 581, FM 1583, Derby
86		South I-35 Bus. Loop
85		FM 117, Batesville
	FStop	W: Exxon(*, 24)
	Food	W: Dairy Queen, La Pasadita (Safari Motel)
	Lodg	E: Pacho Garcia Motel
		W: Safari Motel
84		TX 85, Charlotte, Carrizo Springs
	FStop	W: Diamond Shamrock(*), Texaco(*, 24) (Cleo's Travel Center)
	Food	W: Campbell House Restaurant (Executive Inn), Chester Fried Chicken (Diamond Shamrock), Church's Chicken (Texaco)
	Lodg	W: Executive Inn
	AServ	E: NAPA Auto Parts, Tindall Chevrolet Pontiac Geo
	Med	E: + Hospital
	ATM	E: Dilley State Bank
		W: Diamond Shamrock, Texaco (Cleo's Travel Center)
	Other	E: Super S Foods
82		I-35N Bus Loop, County Line Road, Dilley
77		FM 469, Millett
74		Gardendale
67		FM 468, Big Wells
	FStop	E: Diamond Shamrock(*, 24) (Cleo's Travel Center)
	Gas	E: Country Store, Exxon(*, D)
	Food	E: Church's Chicken (Diamond Shamrock), Country Store, Dairy Queen, Hot Stuff Pizza (Exxon), Log Cabin Restaurant, Wendy's (Exxon)
	Lodg	E: Cotulla Executive Inn, Rodeway Inn
	TServ	E: Valentine's(24)
	TWash	E: Catulla Truckwash
	RVCamp	W: RV Park
	ATM	E: Diamond Shamrock (Cleo's Travel Center), Exxon
65		North Bus. Loop I-35, Cotulla
63		Elm Creek Interchange
(59)		Parking Area (Picnic; South-

Bold red print shows RV & Bus parking available or nearby

EXIT TEXAS

bound)

(59) **Parking Area (Picnic, P; Northbound)**

56 FM 133, Artesia Wells, Catarina
- **Gas** E: Adam's Grocery(*)
- **Other** E: U.S. Post Office

48 Caiman Creek Interchange

39 Bus. 35, TX 34, Encinal

38 TX 44, Bus Loop I-35, Encinal (Reaccess Southbound Only)

32 San Roman Interchange

27 Callaghan Interchange
- **RVCamp** W: **Ancira Travel Villa**

22 Webb Interchange

18 U.S. 83N, Carrizo Springs, Uvalde, Eagle Path, Del Rio
- **RVCamp** W: **Camping (2 Miles)**

Exit **(14)** Inspection Station - US Border Patrol Station, All Traffic (Northbound, Southbound Is Parking Area)

13 Uniroyal Interchange
- **TStop** E: **Pilot**(*, SCALES)
- **Food** E: **Country Cooker (Pilot TS), Subway (Pilot)**
- **TWash** E: **Pilot**
- **ATM** E: **Pilot**

10 Port Laredo (Northbound)

8 FM 3464; Bob Bullock Loop, Loop 20

7 Shiloh Dr., La Cruces Dr. (Southbound)
- **Other** E: Texas Travel Information

4 FM 1472, Del Mar Blvd, Santa Maria Ave.
- **FStop** W: **Fina**
- **Gas** E: Chevron, Coastal(*, 24), Exxon(D)
  W: Carlos Puente Food Store(*), Texaco(*, D, 24)
- **Food** E: Applebee's, Ci Ci's Pizza, El Metate, La Cucina Galante Ristorante, Las Asadas(24), McDonald's(PLAY), Tokyo Garden, Whataburger(PLAY)
  W: Danny's Restaurant, Ernie's Smokehouse
- **Lodg** E: Hampton Inn
  W: Executive House Hotel, Motel 6
- **AServ** E: Chevron, Exxon
- **RVCamp** E: **Casa Norte Trailer Park, RV Camp, Town North RV Park (1 Mile)**
- **ATM** E: **Albertson's Grocery**(RX)
  W: International Bank of Commerce
- **Other** E: **Albertson's Grocery**(RX), **Book Mark Books, Border Patrol Sector HQ, J & A Pharmacy**(RX), **Mail Boxes Etc, North Creek United Artists Theatres,** Oliveira's Pharmacy(RX), **Target Greatland**
  W: **AAA Auto Club**

3B Mann Road

CAMPING WORLD®
Bryan Road Exit
1325 E. Expressway 83 • Mission, TX
1-800-628-6753
1429

EXIT TEXAS

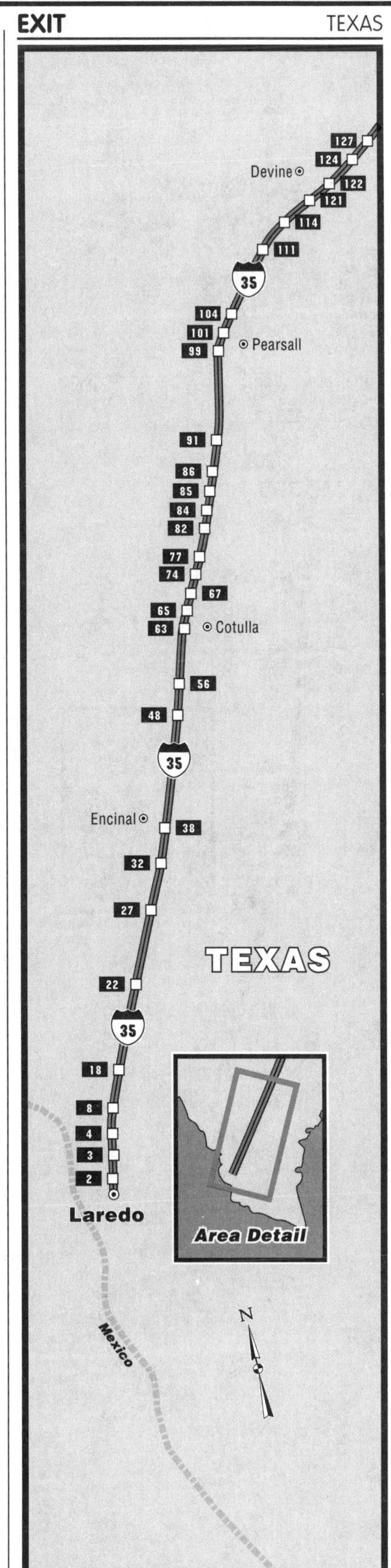

EXIT TEXAS

- **Gas** E: Exxon(CW)
- **Food** E: El Taco Tote, La Palapa Mexican, Luby's Cafeteria (Mall), Tony Romas Ribs (Mall)
  W: Chili's, Golden Corral Family Steakhouse, Kettle, Subway, Taco Palenque Jr.(PLAY)
- **Lodg** W: Family Gardens Inn, Motel 6
- **AServ** E: **Montgomery Ward**, Powell-Watson, Sames Honda Subaru
  W: **Wal-Mart**(24, RX) **(1-Hr Photo)**
- **Med** E: **Columbia Doctor's Hospital**
- **ATM** E: IBC, NBC Bank of Laredo
  W: Loredo National Bank, South Texas National Bank
- **Other** E: Mail Boxes Int., **Mall Del Norte, Maverick Market**
  W: **Builder Square, Movies 12, OfficeMax, Toys R Us, Wal-Mart**(RX) **(1-Hr Photo)**

3A San Bernardo Ave, Calton Road
- **Gas** E: Texaco(*, D)
  W: Phillips 66(D)
- **Food** E: **Chinese Kitchen (H-E-B)**, Emperor Garden, Fuddruckers, Long John Silver, Luby's Cafeteria, Peter Piper Pizza, Sirloin Stockade
  W: Acapulco Steak & Shrimp(PLAY), Baskin Robbins, Burger King(PLAY), Dunkin Donuts, El Pollo Loco(PLAY), McDonald's(PLAY), Ming Dynasty, Pizza Hut, Popeye's Chicken, Taco Palenque(PLAY, 24), Wendy's, **Whataburger**(PLAY)
- **Lodg** W: Best Western, Gateway Inn, La Hacienda Motor Hotel, Monterey Inn, Red Roof Inn
- **AServ** E: NAPA Auto Parts, Pep Boys Auto Center
  W: Goodyear Tire & Auto, **Sam's Club**
- **ATM** E: Norwest Banks
  W: International Bank of Commerce
- **Other** E: **H.E.B. Mercado Grande**(RX), **K-Mart**(RX) **(1-Hr Photo), Mail Boxes Etc,** Religious Good Center, **TX State Optical, Yo Books & Games**
  W: **Sam's Club**

2 U.S. 59, Freer, Corpus Christi, Houston, Laredo Intnl. Airpt
- **Gas** E: Conoco(*), Diamond Shamrock(*), Texaco(*)
  W: Coastal(*), Exxon(*, D), Phillips 66(*, D)
- **Food** E: Gallegos, Jack-In-The-Box(24), Mariscos El Pescador
  W: Burger King (Exxon), Church's Chicken, Denny's, Pan American Courts Cafe, Quick Bite, The Holiday Bakery, The Shrimp Royal
- **Lodg** W: El Courtez Motel, Haynes Motel, La Fonda Motel, La Quinta Inn, Mayan Inn
- **AServ** E: Frontera Auto Parts, Laredo Auto Air & Radiator Shop, Lopez Transmission
  W: Auto Zone Auto Parts, Phillips 66, Rodriguez Tire Shop
- **TServ** E: **Murillo Truck & Trailer**
- **ATM** E: Conoco, Texaco
  W: Exxon
- **Parks** E: **Lake Casa Blanca State Park**
- **Other** E: **Chito's**
  W: **Coin Laundry**

1AB Park St., Sanchez St., Scott St., Washington St. (Southbound)
- **Gas** W: Conoco(*, D)
- **Food** E: La Saberia
  W: Favarato's, La Casita(24), La Paisana II, Pizza Hut, Poncheria La Mexicana, Popeye's Chicken
- **Lodg** W: Courtyard by Marriott, Holiday Inn
- **AServ** W: City Radiator, Guzman Auto Parts, Roy's Auto Center, Rubio Auto Electric Shop, Tire Center of Laredo, Villa Auto Service II
- **RVCamp** E: **Camping World (see our ad this page)**
- **Med** E: **Hospital**
- **ATM** W: Conoco

↑TEXAS

Begin I-35

EXIT	TEXAS

Begin I-37

↓TEXAS

142AB 142A - N. I-35, Austin, 142B - S. I-35, Laredo (Northbound)

141C McCullough Ave, Nolan Street (Southbound)
- **Gas** **W:** Chevron[*, CW]
- **Food** **W:** Oasis Cafe, TraveLodge
- **Lodg** **W:** TraveLodge
- **AServ** **W:** ACE Break Service, Auto Air & Axle, Auto Value Parts Store, Automotive Accidents, Cavender Cadillac, Downtown Auto Parts, Downtown Auto Repair, Grayson St. Garage, Nix Alignment

141B Houston Street, The Alamo (Southbound)
- **Gas** **W:** Coastal[*]
- **Food** **W:** Burger King, Fuddruckers, GM Steakhouse, Haagen Dazs Ice Cream, Morton's, Pizza Hut, Taco Bell
- **Lodg** **W:** Crockett Hotels, DAYS INN Days Inn, Hampton Inn, Holiday Inn, Homewood Hotel, Hyatt, Ramada Inn, Residence Inn by Marriott, The Hilton, The Menger Hotel
- **AServ** **W:** Bob's Auto Service
- **Other** **W:** **Alamo Visitor Center, Fire Station, IMAX Theater, King's X Toy Soldiers, Antiques, Ripley's Believe It or Not, Rivercenter**

141A Commerce Street, Downtown (Southbound)
- **Food** **W:** Denny's, Landry's Seafood House, Marriott, **The Tower of the Americas**
- **Lodg** **W:** La Quinta Inn, Marriott
- **Other** **W:** **AMC Rivercenter Theaters, Rivercenter Drugstore**[RX], **The Hemisfair Plaza, The Tower of the Americas**

141 Commerce St, Downtown, The Alamo, St. Paul's Square, Amtrac Rail Station (Northbound)
- **Food** **E:** Aldaco's
- **Lodg** **E:** Red Roof Inn
- **AServ** **E:** Theo's Brake & Tire
- **Other** **E:** Amtrac Rail Station, **The Alamodome**

140B Durango Blvd, Alamodome, La Vallita
- **Food** **E:** Bill Miller BBQ, Ray's Mexican
- **Other** **E:** **Alamodome, Piknik Foods**

140A Florida Street, Carolina Street
- **FStop** **W:** **Datafleet Coastal (Datafleet Credit Cards Only)**
- **Gas** **E:** Fina[*, D]
  W: Coastal[*, D]
- **Food** **W:** Eagle's Nest Cafe
- **Other** **W:** **Pick-N-Pay Grocery Store**

139A I-10, US 90, US 87, El Paso, Houston, Victoria del Rio

139 Fair Ave., Hackberry St.
- **Gas** **E:** Chevron
  W: Exxon[*], Texaco[*, 24]
- **Food** **E:** Dairy Queen, KFC, Peter Piper Pizza, Red Line Burgers, Taco Bell
  W: Texaco
- **AServ** **E:** Brake Check, Chevron
- **ATM** **W:** Texaco
- **Other** **E:** **The Home Depot**[LP]

138A New Braunfels Ave, Southcross Blvd
- **Gas** **W:** Exxon[*, CW]
- **Food** **E:** Hong Kong Buffet Restaurant, Luby's Cafeteria, McDonald's[PLAY], Pizza Hut, SHONEY'S Shoney's, Taco Cabana[24], Wendy's
  W: Burger King[PLAY], Sonic

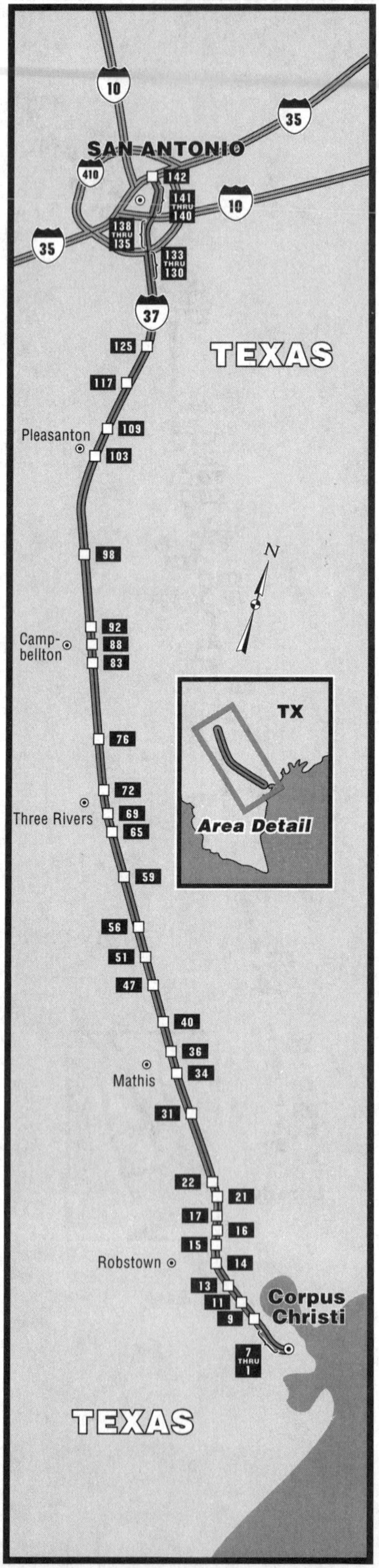

EXIT	TEXAS

- **AServ** **E:** Auto Express (Montgomery Ward), Full Service Auto Parts Warehouse, Terry's Auto Repair
- **ATM** **E:** Bank of America, Frost Bank
- **Other** **E:** **McCreless Mall**, Movies 9

137 Hot Wells Blvd
- **Gas** **E:** Exxon
- **Food** **E:** Taco Hut
  W: IHOP
- **AServ** **E:** Exxon
  W: Hot Wheels Automotive Repair & Sales
- **ATM** **E:** NationsBank
- **Other** **E:** **Fire Station**

136 **(135)** Pecan Valley Drive
- **Gas** **E:** Coastal[*, D]
- **Food** **E:** Beijing Express, Church's Chicken, KFC, La Popular Bakery & Cake Shop, Neptunes Seafood House, Pizza Hut
- **AServ** **E:** Joe's Tires & Wheels, One Stop Car Care
- **ATM** **E:** **Handy Andy Grocery**
- **Other** **E:** Delco Coin Vehicle Wash, **Eckerd Drugs**[RX], **For Your Convenience Store, Handy Andy Grocery, Mail Pack, Mission Cleaning Center (Laundromat), Ponderosa Bowl**

135 Loop 13, Military Dr, Brooks AFB
- **Gas** **E:** Diamond Shamrock[*]
  W: Diamond Shamrock[*, 24], H-E-B
- **Food** **E:** New China Restaurant
  W: Burger King[PLAY]
- **AServ** **E:** Goodspeed's Collision, Stanley's Radiator Shop[CW]
- **ATM** **E:** Diamond Shamrock
  W: Diamond Shamrock
- **Other** **W:** **H-E-B Grocery Store**[24, RX] **(1-Hr Photo), K-Mart**[RX]

133 Jct. I-410, South & North U.S. 281, Connally Loop, San Antonio, Johnson City

132 South US 181, Floresville (Southbound, Reaccess Northbound Only)
- **Gas** **E:** Fina[*, D], Stop N Go[*], Texaco[*]
- **ATM** **E:** Fina

132A Spur 122 (Northbound, Reaccess Southbound Only)
- **Gas** **E:** Diamond Shamrock[*, D]
- **ATM** **E:** Diamond Shamrock

130 Southton Road, Donop Road, Braunig Lake
- **TStop** **E:** **Diamond Shamrock Travel Center**[*, RV DUMP, SCALES]
- **Gas** **W:** Texaco[*]
- **Food** **E:** **Braunig Lake Cafe (Diamond Shamrock TS), Diamond Shamrock Travel Center**
- **ATM** **E:** **Diamond Shamrock Travel Center**
- **Other** **E:** **Braunig Lake (2 Miles), I-37 Flea Market**

127 San Antonio River Turnaround, Lake Braunig

125 Loop1604, Anderson Loop, Elmendorf
- **FStop** **E:** **Conoco**[*]
  W: **Fina**[*]
- **Gas** **W:** Exxon[*, D]
- **Food** **E:** **Burger King (Conoco)**, Mi Reina
  W: Hot Stuff Pizza (Exxon), Smash Hit Subs (Exxon)
- **ATM** **E:** **Conoco**
  W: **Fina**

122 Priest Road, Mathis Road
- **Other** **E:** Jack's Corner Store

120 Hardy Road

117 FM 536

113 FM 3006, Pleasanton

(112) **Rest Area (Picnic, Grills, P; Southbound)**

Bold red print shows RV & Bus parking available or nearby

EXIT	TEXAS
(112)	**Rest Area (Picnic, Grills, P; Northbound)**
109	TX 97, Pleasanton, Floresville
FStop	**E:** JP's Superstop[*] (Chevron)
Food	**E:** Shorty's Place #3
AServ	**E:** Atascosa Auto Dealer
RVCamp	**E:** Camping
ATM	**E:** JP's Superstop (Chevron)
Other	**W:** Tourist Info.
106	Coughran Road
104	Spur 199, Leal Road (Northbound, Difficult Reaccess)
TStop	**E:** Kuntry Korner[24] (Diamond Shamrock)
FStop	**E:** Bubba's Fuel Stop[*, 24] (Citgo)
Food	**E:** Dairy Queen, Kuntry Korner (Diamond Shamrock)
Lodg	**E:** Kuntry Korner (Diamond Shamrock)
AServ	**E:** Bubba's Fuel Stop[24] (Citgo)
TServ	**E:** Bubba's Fuel Stop[24] (Citgo)
ATM	**E:** Kuntry Korner (Diamond Shamrock)
103	North US 281, Pleasanton (Southbound)
98	FM 541, McCoy, Poth
92	Alt. U.S. 281, Campbellton, Whitsett (Southbound)
88	FM 1099 To FM 791
83	FM 99, Whittsett, Karnes City, Peggy
FStop	**E:** Texaco[*]
	W: Exxon[*] (Deli)
Gas	**W:** Chevron[*, D]
Food	**E:** The Sandwich Shop (Texaco)
	W: Chevron, Exxon (Deli)
AServ	**E:** Cypret's Garage
ATM	**W:** Exxon (Deli)
(82)	**Rest Area (RR, Phones, Picnic, Grills, P; Southbound)**
(78)	**Rest Area (RR, Phones, Picnic, Grills, P; Northbound)**
76	FM 2049, Whitsett
(75)	**Weigh Station (Southbound)**
(74)	**Weigh Station (Northbound)**
72	U.S. 281 South, Three Rivers, Alice
69	TX 72, Three Rivers, Kenedy
TStop	**W:** Wolffs Travel Stop[*, 24] (Diamond Shamrock)
Food	**W:** Wolffs Travel Stop (Diamond Shamrock)
TServ	**W:** Wolffs Travel Stop[24] (Diamond Shamrock)
ATM	**W:** Wolffs Travel Stop (Diamond Shamrock)
Parks	**W:** Choke Canyon State Park
65	FM 1358, Oakville
Gas	**E:** Texaco[*]
	W: Chevron[*]
Food	**E:** Van's BBQ (Texaco)
	W: Chevron
Other	**W:** US Post Office (Chevron)
59	FM 799
56	U.S. 59, George West, Beeville
FStop	**W:** Chevron[*], Exxon[*]
Food	**W:** Best Tech's BBQ & Catering, Burger King (Exxon), TCBY (Chevron)
ATM	**W:** Chevron, Exxon
Other	**W:** Junction Convenient Store
51	Hailey Ranch Road
47	FM 3024, FM 534, Swinney
Gas	**W:** Brown's Country Store[*]
RVCamp	**W:** KOA Kampground (4 Miles)
(43)	**Parking Area (Southbound)**
(41)	**Parking Area (Northbound)**
40	FM 888
RVCamp	**W:** KOA Kampground

EXIT	TEXAS
36	TX 359, Skidmore
Gas	**W:** Exxon[*, D], Exxon[D]
Food	**W:** El Taco Loco, Pizza Hut, Ranch Motel
Lodg	**W:** Mathis Motor Inn, Ranch Motel
AServ	**W:** Compos New & Used Tires, Exxon
RVCamp	**W:** Camping, Hill-Tech Marine, KOA Kampground (9 Miles), Mathis Motor Inn, Mathis Motor Inn & RV Park
Parks	**W:** Lake Corpus Christi State Recreational Area
34	TX 359 West
Food	**W:** CW Cafe
AServ	**E:** C&C Auto Service
RVCamp	**W:** Sunrise Beach RV Park (see our ad this page)
Parks	**W:** Lake Corpus Christi State Recreational Area
Other	**W:** Wash & Vac (Car Wash)
31	TX 188, Sinton, Rockport
22	FM 796, Edroy, Odem
Other	**W:** U.S. Post Office
20B	Cooper Road
Gas	**E:** I-H 37 Shortstop[*]
(19)	**Rest Area (RR, Phones, Picnic, Grills, Vending, P; Southbound)**
(19)	**Rest Area (RR, Phones, Picnic, Grills, Vending, P; Northbound)**
17	U.S. 77 North, Victoria, Sinton, Odem (Difficult Reaccess)
16	Nueces River Park
Parks	**W:** Nueces River Park
Other	**E:** Public Boat Ramp
	W: City of Corpus Christi Tourist Info Center
15	Sharpsburg Road, Red Bird Lane
14	U.S. 77, Kingsville, Red Bird Ln., Robstown
TStop	**W:** Sun Mart #114[*, SCALES] (In Robstown on U.S.77)
13B	Sharpsburg Rd. (Northbound)
13A	Callicoatte Rd
Food	**W:** Mother's Pizza
AServ	**W:** Don's Automotive Service
Other	**E:** Hilltop Bowl
11B	FM 24, Violet Rd., Hart Rd.
Gas	**E:** Conoco[*]
	W: H-E-B
Food	**E:** Chinese Kitchen (H-E-B), Roadhouse Restaurant
	W: McDonald's[PLAY], Whataburger[24]
Lodg	**W:** Best Western
ATM	**E:** Conoco
Other	**W:** H-E-B Grocery Store[RX] (1-Hr Photo)
11A	FM 3386, McKinsey Road

SUNRISE BEACH RV PARK
1406
Longest Freshwater Pier in Texas
• Shaded Full Hookups
• Grassy Tent Area
• Launching Ramps
• Groceries • Ice
• Bait • Laundry
512-547-3004
Fax 512-547-7722
1 Mile of Shoreline on Lake Corpus Christi
34 Mi NW of Corpus Christi
359 To Corpus Christi 37 Mathis Park Road 25 359 N
TEXAS ▪ I-37 ▪ EXIT 34

EXIT	TEXAS
RVCamp	**W:** RV Sales & Service (1 Mile)
10	Carbon Plant Rd
9	FM 2292, Up River Rd, Rand Morgan Rd
Gas	**W:** Texaco[*, D]
7	Tuloso Road, Suntide Road, Clarkwood Rd.
RVCamp	**W:** Camping
6	Southern Minerals Road
5	Corn Products Road
FStop	**W:** Petro Fleet (Pay w/credit card only)
Food	**W:** Kettle Restaurant, Racetrack Hotel & Suites, TraveLodge
Lodg	**W:** Racetrack Hotel & Suites, Red Roof Inn, Super 8, TraveLodge
TServ	**E:** French-Ellison Truck Center[*, D]
ATM	**W:** TraveLodge
4B	Lantana Street, McBride Lane (Southbound)
Lodg	**W:** Motel 6
4A	TX 358, NAS - CCAD Padre Island, CC Airport (Northbound)
4	TX 44, C.C. International Airport, TX 358, Padre Island (Northbound)
3B	McBride Lane, Lantana Street (Northbound)
Food	**E:** Marco's (Hampton Inn)
Lodg	**E:** Hampton Inn
3A	Navigation Blvd
FStop	**E:** Texaco[*]
	W: Coastal Datafleet[24] (Credit Card Only, No Attendant), Petro Fleet[24] (Automated Fueling, Credit Cards Only)
Gas	**W:** Exxon[*, D, CW]
Food	**W:** Bill Miller BBQ, DAYS INN Days Inn, Denny's
Lodg	**E:** Val-U Inn Motel
	W: Comfort Inn, DAYS INN Days Inn, La Quinta Inn
AServ	**W:** Creager Tire, Richard's Auto, Winston Warehouse Auto & Truck Parts
TServ	**W:** Creager Tire, Winston Warehouse Auto & Truck Parts
ATM	**W:** Exxon
2	Up River Road
RVCamp	**E:** Hatch RV Park (1.25 Miles)
	W: Camping
1E	Lawrence Drive, Neuces Bay Blvd
Gas	**W:** Citgo[*]
1D	Port Ave , Brown Lee Blvd, Port of Corpus Christi (Southbound)
Gas	**W:** Coastal[*, D, K]
Food	**W:** El Regio Mexican Restaurant, Vick's Hamburgers
AServ	**W:** Carl Kuehn's Central Auto Body, General Tire Service, Gulf Radiator
ATM	**W:** Frost Bank
1C	TX 286, Crosstown Expressway
1B	Brownlee Blvd, Port Ave (Northbound)
Gas	**W:** Chevron[*]
Food	**W:** Taqueria Banda's
AServ	**W:** Eddie Villarreal & Son, Shaffer's Muffler
1A	Buffalo Street, City Hall (Southbound)
ATM	**W:** American Bank, Mercantile Bank
Other	**W:** Public Library, US Post Office
1	(0) U.S. 181, TX 35, Portland
Other	**W:** CC Beach, Texas State Aquarium, USS Lexington

↑TEXAS

Begin I-37

EXIT WISCONSIN

Begin I-39

↓WISCONSIN

208 WI 64, WI 17, Merrill, Antigo (Low Bridges)
- **Gas** W: Mobil[*, D]
- **Food** W: 3's Company, **Burger King**, Diamond Dave's Taco, McDonald's, Pine Ridge Restaurant
- **Lodg** W: Best Western, Super 8
- **AServ** W: Pine Ridge Quick Lube
- **RVCamp** W: **Camping**
- **Med** W: ✚ **Hospital**
- **ATM** W: River Valley State Bank
- **Other** W: BP Car Wash, **Wal-Mart**

205 Bus 51, Merrill
- **TStop** E: **Union 76 Truck Stop**[*, D]

197 CR WW, Brokaw (Low Bridge)
- **Gas** W: Citgo[*]

194 CR U, US51, CR K, Wassau (Low Bridges)
- **Gas** E: Kwik Trip[*]
- **Food** E: **McDonald's**, Philly's Subs, Taco Bell
- **ATM** E: Kwik Trip
- **Other** E: Car Wash

193 Bridge Street (Low Bridge)

192 WI59, WI 52, Wassau, Abbotsford (Difficult Reaccess)
- **Gas** E: 29 Super, Mobil[*, D]
- **Food** E: American Country Cafe, Applebee's, Big Apple Bagels, Captain's Steak, Counsin's Subs, George's Restaurant, Little Caesars Pizza, McDonald's, Pizza Chef, Subway
  W: Burger King, Fender's Frozen Custard, Hardees, Schlotzsky's Deli, The 25 10 Family Restaurant
- **Lodg** E: Budgetel Inn, Exel Inn, Hampton Inn, Marlene Motel, Ramada Inn, Super 8
- **AServ** E: Horak's
  W: Pennzoil Oil Change
- **ATM** E: Security Bank
- **Other** E: **Midwest Dental**
  W: White Water Car Wash

191 Sherman Street (Difficult Reaccess)
- **TServ** W: **Mike's Trucks Accessories, Northwest Trucks International Dealer**

190 CR NN
- **Gas** W: Citgo[*, D, CW], Mobil[*]
- **Food** E: Emma Krumbees
  W: Shakeys Pizza, Subway
- **Lodg** E: Wausau Inn
  W: Best Western, Hoffman's House
- **ATM** E: First Star Bank
  W: Citgo
- **Other** E: **Dental Clinic**
  W: **Wisconsin Station Patrol**

188 CR N
- **TStop** E: **Amoco**[*, SCALES]
- **Gas** E: Spur[*]
- **Food** E: Java City Bagels, McDonald's, Rosati's Pizza, Wendy's
- **Lodg** E: DAYS INN Days Inn
- **AServ** E: Exhaust Pros
- **TServ** E: **Cummins Diesel, Ryder Truck Rental**

EXIT WISCONSIN

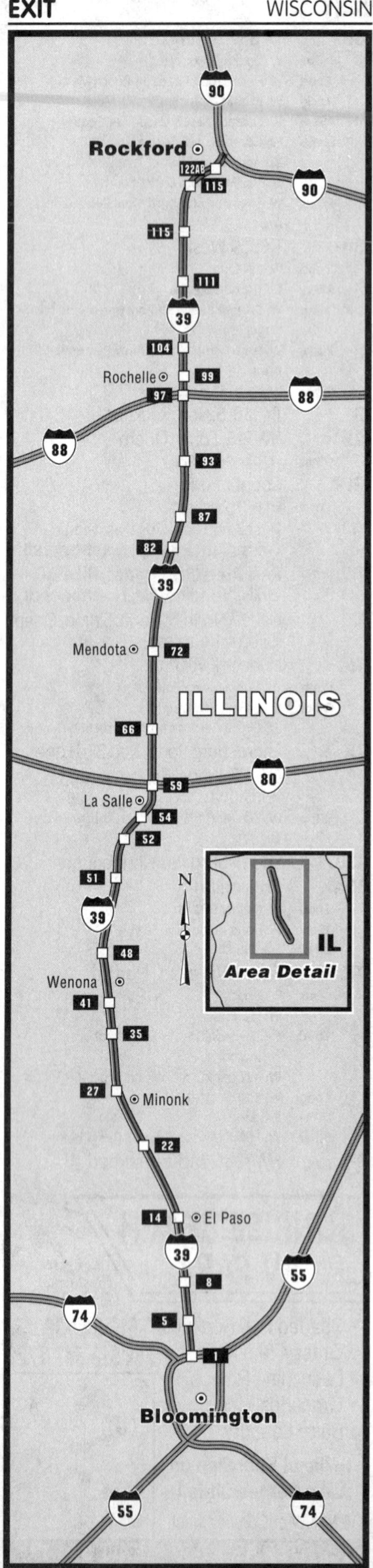

EXIT WISCONSIN

- **RVCamp** E: **Kings Campers & Service**
- **ATM** E: Marathon Savings Bank
  W: M&I State Bank
- **Parks** W: **Rib Mountain State Park**

187 WI 29, GreenBay, US51

185 Bus 151, Rothschild Wausau

(183) **Parking Area (Southbound)**

181 Maple Ridge Road

179 WI 53, Mosinee, Elderon
- **Gas** W: Amoco[*], Shell[*, D, CW]
- **Food** W: Hardees, McDonald's, The Stage's
- **Lodg** W: Amerihost Inn
- **ATM** E: River Valley State Bank
  W: Amoco
- **Other** E: **Middle Wisconsin Airport**

(178) **Parking Area (Northbound)**

175 WI 34, Knowlton, Wisconsin Rapids

171 CR DB Knowlpon DuBay

165 CR X

164 **Weigh Station**

161 Bus 51, Stevens Point
- **Gas** W: Amoco[*], Kwik Trip[*], Super America[*, D]
- **Food** W: Burger King, China Garden, Country Kitchen, Domino's Pizza, Fender's, Hardees, Hunan Chinese, KFC, McDonald's, Michelle Restaurant, Olympic Family Restaurant, Perkin's Family Restaurant, Pizza Hut, Pointer's Family Restaurant, Ponderosa Steakhouse, Rocky Rococo Italian, Subway, Taco Bell, Topper's Pizza
- **Lodg** W: Comfort Suites Hotel, Holiday Inn, Point Motel, Super 8, The Road Star Inn
- **ATM** W: Kwik Trip, Super America
- **Other** W: **Coin Laundry, K-Mart**[RX]

159 WI 66 Stevens Point, Rosholt
- **Gas** W: Kwik Trip[*]
- **TServ** W: **Mock Truck Repair Service**
- **ATM** W: Kwik Trip

158 US 20 Stevens Point, Waupaca
- **Gas** E: Mills Fleet Farms[CW], Mobil[*, D, CW]
  W: Amoco[*, CW]
- **Food** E: Applebee's, Colver's Frozen Dessert, McDonald's, SHONEY'S Shoney's, Taco Bell, Wendy's
  W: Cafe Royal, Hilltop Grill
- **Lodg** E: Fairfield Inn
  W: Best Western, Budgetel Inn
- **AServ** E: Mills Fleet Farms
- **ATM** E: Mobil
- **Other** E: **Target, Wal-Mart**

156 CR HH Whiting

153 CR B Clover Amherst
- **Gas** W: Amoco[*], Mobil[*, D, CW]
- **Food** W: Blake's Family Restaurant, Burger King (Amoco)
- **Lodg** W: Americinn

EXIT WISCONSIN/ILLINOIS

ATM W: Wood County National Bank

151 WI 54, Wisconsin Rapids, Waupaca
- **Gas** E: Phillips 66(*, D)
- **Food** E: Four Star Family Restaurant, Shooters
- **Lodg** E: Days Inn, Elizabeth Inn

143 CR W Bancroft, Wisconsin Rapids
- **Gas** E: Citgo(*, D)

138 CR D, Almond

136 WI 73, Plainfield, WI Rapids
- **TStop** E: **Plainfield Truck Stop**(*)
- **FStop** E: **Amoco**(*, D)
- **Lodg** E: R&R Motel
- **AServ** E: BF Goodrich
- **TServ** E: **Amoco**

131 CR V, Hancock
- **Gas** E: Phillips 66(*)

(126) **Weigh Station (Left Exit)**

124 WI 21, Coloma, Necedah
- **Gas** E: Mobil(*, D)

(117) **Rest Area (RR, Picnic, Vending, RV Dump)**

113 CR E, CR J, Westfield
- **FStop** W: **Mobil**(*)
- **Gas** W: Amoco(*), Union 76(*, CW)
- **Food** W: Bob's & Kay Family Inn, Brakebush Chicken, **Hardees**, **McDonald's**, Pioneer Restaurant, Subway
- **Lodg** E: Sandman Motel
  W: Pioneer Motor Inn
- **ATM** W: Amoco, Montello State Bank

106 WI82, WI 23 Oxford, Montello
- **Food** E: Rissen's Family Restaurant
- **Lodg** E: Crossroads Motel

104 CR D, Packwauklee

100 WI23, CR P, Endeavor
- **Gas** E: US

92 US51, Portage
- **Gas** E: Kwik Trip(*)
- **Food** E: Culver's Frozen Custard, Hardees, KFC, McDonald's, Taco Bell
- **Lodg** E: Best Western, Ridge Motor Inn, Super 8
- **ATM** E: First Star, Kwik Trip
- **Other** E: **K-Mart**, **Wal-Mart**

89AB WI16, WI127, Portage, WI Dells
- **FStop** N: **76**(*, D)

87 WI 33, Portage

85 Cascade Mt. Rd.

↑WISCONSIN

↓ILLINOIS

122B U.S. 20, Belvidere

122A Harrison Ave
- **FStop** W: **Marathon Gas**(*, D)
- **Gas** W: Citgo(*), Mobil(*)
- **Food** W: Baker's Square, Cherryville Mall, Kegel's Diner, **Marathon Gas**, TGI Friday
- **AServ** W: Batteries Plus, Cherryville Tire & Auto (Goodyear), F&F Tire World, Lub Bachrodt Jeep/Eagle, Chevrolet, Isuzu, NTB, Sear's (Jiffy Lube), Team Tire Plus
- **ATM** W: Alpine Bank(24), Cherryville Mall, **Marathon Gas**, Mobil
- **Other** W: Cherryville Mall, Cherryville Theatre, Competition Grand Prix (Go Kart Track), Golf & Games, Magic Waters Amusement Park, Perryville Pet Hospital, Petland (Animal Clinic), Sear's (Jiffy Lube), Super Wash, The Cherry Bowl (Bowling)

EXIT ILLINOIS

121 U.S. 20, Rockford, Shreveport, Belvidere (Left Exit Northbound)

115 **(121)** Baxter Rd
- **TStop** E: **Maggio's Truck Center**(*, D, SCALES)
- **TServ** E: **Maggio's Truck Center**(SCALES)
- **TWash** E: **Maggio's Truck Center**
- **ATM** E: **Maggio's Truck Center**

111 IL 72, Byron, Genoa

(108) **Tollaway Oasis (Toll)**
- **Gas** B: **Mobil**
- **Food** B: McDonald's

107 IL38, IL23, Annie Gidden Rd., Dekalb
- **Lodg** N: Super 8

104 IL 64, Oregon Sycamore

99 IL 38, Rochelle, DeKalb
- **TStop** W: **Petro**(*, CW, SCALES)
- **Gas** W: Amoco(*, LP)
- **Food** W: **Petro**, **The Iron Skillet (Petro)**, **Wendy's**
- **Lodg** W: Amerihost Inn, **Super 8**
- **TServ** W: **Petro**(SCALES)
- **TWash** W: **Petro**(CW)
- **Med** W: **+ Hospital**

97AB East I-88 Tollway, West Moline, Rock Island

93 Steward

87 U.S. 30, Sterling, Rock Falls, Aurora
- **RVCamp** W: **Jellystone Park Campground (16 Miles)**
- **Parks** E: **Shabbona Lake State Park**

(86) **Rest Area (RR, HF, Phones, Picnic, RV Dump; Westbound)**

(86) **Rest Area (RR, HF, Phones, Picnic, RV Dump, P; Eastbound)**

82 Paw Paw
- **RVCamp** E: **Smith's Stonehouse Park (10 Miles)**

EXIT ILLINOIS

72 U.S. 34, Mendota, Earlville
- **FStop** W: **Amoco**(*, SCALES), **Shell**(*, D)
- **Food** W: **Amoco**, **Buster's Family Restaurant (Amoco)**, McDonald's
- **Lodg** W: Comfort Inn, **Super 8**
- **Med** W: **+ Hospital**
- **ATM** W: **Shell**

66 U.S. 52, Troy Grove
- **RVCamp** E: **KOA Campgrounds**

59AB I-80 Junction to Chicago & Des Moines

57 U.S. 6, Ottawa, La Salle - Peru
- **Gas** W: Casey's General Store(*)
- **RVCamp** W: **Camping**

54 Oglesby
- **Gas** E: **Amoco**(*), Shell(*)
- **Food** E: Baskin Robbins, Delaney's Family Restaurant, Dunkin Donuts, **Hardee's**(PLAY), McDonald's, Subway
- **Lodg** E: **Days Inn**, Holiday Inn Express
- **AServ** E: J. Dorni K. Auto Body
- **RVCamp** E: **Starved Rock Lake State Park**
- **ATM** E: **Amoco**, Illinois State Bank, Shell
- **Parks** E: **Starved Rock Lake State Park**

52 IL 251, La Salle - Peru

51 IL 71, Oglesby, Hennepin

48 Tonica
- **Gas** E: Amoco(*, D, LP)
- **Food** E: **J & J Truck Repair**(*)
- **AServ** E: Amoco
- **TServ** E: **J & J Truck Repair**

41 IL 18, Henry, Streador

35 IL 17, Lacon, Wenona
- **FStop** E: **Amoco**(*, D)
- **Food** E: **Amoco**, Burger King (Amoco), **Buster's Family Restaurant**
- **Lodg** E: **Super 8**
- **ATM** E: **Amoco**

27 Minonk

22 IL 116, Peoria, Pontiac

14 U.S. 24, Peoria, El Paso
- **Gas** E: Freedom(*, D, LP), Shell(*, CW)
- **Food** E: **Carl Jr's Hamburgers**(PLAY), **Dairy Queen**(PLAY), **McDonald's**(PLAY), Monical's Pizza, Shell, Subway (Shell), **Woody's Family Restaurant**
- **Lodg** E: **Days Inn**
  W: **Super 8**
- **AServ** E: Feeney Oil With Goodyear, Heller Lincoln, Mercury, Dodge, NAPA Auto Parts
- **RVCamp** E: **Hickory Hill Camping (4 Miles)**
- **ATM** E: Flanagan's State Bank, Freedom, **IGA Grocery**(LP)
- **Other** E: Doc's Drugs, **IGA Grocery**, Vision Doctor Healthcare

8 IL 251, Kappa, Lake Bloomington Rd
- **RVCamp** W: **Camping**
- **Parks** W: **Comlara Park Evergreen Lake**
- **Other** E: Lake Bloomington

5 **(7)** Hudson
- **Other** E: Casey's General Store

2 **(4)** Business U.S. 51, Bloomington Normal

1 Jct. I-55, I-39

↑ILLINOIS

Begin I-39

EXIT	CALIFORNIA
	Begin I-40

↓CALIFORNIA

EXIT	
1	I-15 San Bernandino, Las Vegas; E. Main St., Montaro Road
Gas	**S:** Arco(*), Texaco(*, D, LP)
Food	**N:** Frosty's Donuts, Straw Hat Pizza
Lodg	**N:** Best Western
AServ	**S:** Texaco, **Wal-Mart**(RX)
ATM	**S:** Jack's Market(*)
Other	**N: Barstow Mall**
	S: Jack's Market, **Wal-Mart**(RX)
3	Marine Corps Logistics Base
Lodg	**N:** Rodeway Inn
TServ	**S: Woodard Diesel Service**
Other	**N:** Marine Corps Base
4	Nebo St (Eastbound, Reaccess Westbound Only)
7	Daggett
AServ	**N:** Interstate Fleet Service(LP)
RVCamp	**N: Desert Springs RV Park**(*, LP) **(2 Miles)**
12	Barstow-Daggett Airport
19	Newberry Springs
FStop	**N: Ultramar**(*)
Gas	**S:** Kelly's Market(*)
RVCamp	**S: Twin Lake RV Park**
23	Fort Cady Road
FStop	**N: Wesco**(*, 24)
RVCamp	**S: Twin Lakes RV Park (3 Miles)**
(28)	**Rest Area (RR, HF, Phones; Eastbound)**
(28)	**Rest Area (RR, HF, Phones, Picnic; Westbound)**
32	Hector Road
50	Ludlow, Amboy, 29 Palms
FStop	**S: Ludlow Truck Stop**(*)
Gas	**N:** 76(*)
	S: Chevron(*, 24)
Food	**S: Ludlow Coffee Shop**
Lodg	**S: Ludlow Motel**
AServ	**S: Ludlow Truck Stop**
78	Amboy, Kelso, Kelbaker Road
RVCamp	**N: Camping**
100	Essex, Essex Road
Parks	**N: Providence Mtn. State Rec. Area**
(105)	**Rest Area (RR, HF, Phones, Picnic; Eastbound)**
(105)	**Rest Area (RR, HF, Phones, Picnic; Westbound)**
107	Goffs Road, Essex
FStop	**N: Hi Sahara Oasis**(*, 24)
115	Mountain Springs Road, Amboy, 29 Palms
120	Water Road
133	U.S. 95, Searchlight, Las Vegas
139	Lake Havasu City, London Bridge, River Road Cutoff (Reaccess Westbound Only)
RVCamp	**N: KOA Kampground**
141	Bus 40, West Broadway, River Road (Reaccess Westbound Only)
FStop	**S: Arco**(*, 24), **Chevron**(*), **Texaco**(*, LP)
Gas	**S: Mobil**(*)
Food	**S:** California Pantry(24) (Best Western), Carl Jr's Hamburgers, **Dairy Queen (Texaco)**, **Taco Bell**, The Green Burrito, **Wagon Wheel Restaurant (Arco)**
Lodg	**S:** Best Chalet Inn, Best Western, Best Western Colorado River Inn
AServ	**N:** Southwestern Tire(24)
	S: Broadway Tire, **Mobil**, **Texaco**
TServ	**N: Goodyear Diesel Repair & Towing**
RVCamp	**N: KOA Campgrounds (1.5 Miles)**
	S: Mobil
ATM	**S: Arco**
142	Needles, J Street, Downtown, Bullhead City
Gas	**N:** 76(*, 24)
Food	**N:** Jack-In-The-Box, **McDonald's**
	S: Denny's
Lodg	**N: Travelers Inn**
	S: DAYS INN Days Inn & Suites, **Motel 6**
AServ	**N:** 76(24), Big Foot Country Big A Auto Parts
RVCamp	**N: Needles Marina RV Park (1.5 Miles)**
Med	**N: Hospital**
ATM	**N:** Bank of America
Other	**N:** Mini Mart(*), Needles Point Pharmacy(RX)
143	South U.S. 95, East Broadway, Blythe
FStop	**N: Chevron**(*, D), **Texaco**(*, D, LP)
Gas	**N:** Arco(*, 24), Shell(*)
Food	**N:** Burger King, Vito's Pizza
Lodg	**S: Super 8**
AServ	**N:** Harah's Auto Repair (Towing), Needles Radiator, Muffler, Welding, Shell, **Texaco**
	S: TransTec Transmission
ATM	**N:** Arco
Other	**N: Basha's Supermarket**, Maytag Laundry, **Thrifty Food Store**
	S: Riverview Airport
147	Five Mile Road

EXIT	CALIFORNIA/ARIZONA
Exit	**(149)** Inspection Station (Eastbound, All Vehicles Stop)
Exit	**(149)** Inspection Station (Westbound, All Vehicles Stop)
153	Park Moabi Road
155	Topock, Oatman

↑CALIFORNIA

↓ARIZONA

EXIT	
1	Topock, Lochlin , Bull Head City, Golden Shores, Oatman
2	Needle Mountain Road
(3)	**Weigh Station (Westbound)**
(3)	**Weigh Station (Eastbound)**
9	AZ 95S, Lake Havasu City, Parker
Lodg	**N:** Holiday Inn (see our ad this page)
Parks	**S: Lake Havasu State Park**
13	Franconia Road
20	Gem Acres Road
(23)	**Rest Area (RR, HF, Phones, Picnic, Vending, P; Eastbound)**
(23)	**Rest Area (RR, HF, Phones, Picnic, Vending, P; Westbound)**
25	Alamo Road
FStop	**N: Micro-Mart**(*)
Food	**N: Micro-Mart**
26	Proving Ground Road
Lodg	**S:** Whiteng Brothers Motel

1193

520-855-4071

Holiday Inn®

245 London Bridge Rd.
Lake Havasu City, AZ

Special Tour Group Rates

Full Service Restaurant & Lounge
Outdoor Pool & Spa • Lakefront
Meeting/Banquet Facilities
Within Walking Distance of London Bridge
Quaint English Village Shopping Nearby
Airpot Shuttle
Beauty Shop & Valet Service

ARIZONIA • I-40 • Exit 9

Bold red print shows RV & Bus parking available or nearby

EXIT	ARIZONA
Other	S: Ford Proving Grounds
28	Old Trails Road
37	Griffith Road
44	AZ 66E, Oatman Road, McConnico Rd.
TStop	S: Crazy Fred's[*]
TServ	S: Crazy Fred's
48	U.S. 93 to AZ 68, Beale St, Las Vegas, To U.S. 66, Kingman
TStop	N: T/A TravelCenters of America[*, SCALES]
FStop	N: Pilot Travel Center[*, 24], Shell[*]
Gas	N: Exxon[*, LP, RV DUMP], Woody's[*]
	S: Chevron[*, D, CW, 24]
Food	N: Country Pride Restaurant (TA Travel Centers of America), House of Chan (Chinese/ American), Subway (Pilot)
	S: Calico's Restaurant, Carl Jr's Hamburgers
Lodg	S: Arizona Inn, Motel 6
AServ	S: Chevron[24]
TServ	N: T/A TravelCenters of America[SCALES]
RVCamp	S: Chevron, Fort Beale RV Park[LP], One Stop RV Service (.2 Miles)
ATM	N: Shell
Other	S: Chamber of Commerce, Mohave Museum of Art and History
51	Stockton Hill Road
Gas	N: Arco[*], Chevron[*]
	S: 76[*, LP], Texaco[*, D]
Food	N: KFC, Subway, Taco Bell, Uncle Kings Chinese Mandarin
	S: Baskin Robbins, Dairy Queen, Golden Corral Family Steakhouse, Little Caesars Pizza, Pizza Hut, The Bread Basket
AServ	N: Checker Auto Parts, Wal-Mart[24], Winston Tire
	S: Q-Lube
Med	N: + Kingman Regional Medical Center
ATM	N: Albertson's Grocery[RX]
Other	N: Albertson's Grocery[RX], Wal-Mart
	S: Cleaners Laundromat, Hastings Bookstore, Safeway Grocery, Sav-On Drugs[RX]
53	AZ 66, Bus Loop 40, Andy Devine Ave, Kingman
TStop	N: Flying J Travel Plaza[*, LP, RV DUMP, SCALES]
Gas	N: Shell[*, D] (see our ad this page), Terrible Herbst[*, 24]
	S: Exxon, Sinclair[*, D]
Food	N: Arby's, Burger King[PLAY], Denny's, Jack-In-The-Box, McDonald's, Pizza Hut, The Cookery (Flying J)
	S: JB's Restaurant
Lodg	N: 1st Value Inn, Motel 6, Silver Queen Motel, TraveLodge (see our ad this page)
	S: Best Western, Best Western King's Inn, Comfort Inn, Days Inn, Holiday Inn, Lido Motel, Mohave Inn
AServ	S: D & J Holiday Service Center, Dunlop Tires, Exxon, Sinclair
RVCamp	N: Circle "S" Campground & RV Park (see our ad this page)
	S: Exxon, Good Sam's RV Park, Quality Stars
Other	N: Big K-Mart[RX]
59	D W Ranch Road
66	Blake Ranch Road
TStop	N: Petro[*, LP, SCALES, 24], Texaco[*, CW] (CB Shop)
	S: Beacon[*, 24]
Food	N: Iron Skillet (Petro TS), Stage Stop (Texaco TS)
	S: Beacon
TServ	N: Bob's Refrigeration (Carrier, Thermoking), Capital Diesel Repair (CAT, Cummins, Detroit), Petro[SCALES, 24], Speedo[24]
TWash	N: Blue Beacon (Petro TS), Texaco[CW] (CB Shop)
RVCamp	N: Blake Ranch RV Park[LP]
ATM	N: Texaco (CB Shop)

EXIT	ARIZONA
71	Jct. U.S. 93S, Wickenburg, Phoenix
79	Silver Springs Road
87	Willows Ranch Road
91	Fort Rock Road
96	Cross Mountain Road
103	Jolly Road
109	Anvil Rock Road
121	AZ 66, Bus Loop 40, Seligman
123	AZ 66, Bus Loop 40, Seligman, Peach Springs
FStop	N: Shell[*]
Gas	S: Chevron[*, D, LP, 24]
Food	S: Chevron, Subway (Chevron)
RVCamp	N: KOA Campgrounds (1 Mile)

NEWLY REMODELED!
1076
Travelodge
3275 E. ANDY DEVINE AVE.
Free In Room Coffee
Remote TV HBO/ESPN/CNN
Free Local Calls
Heated Pool & Spa
Coin Operated Laundry
RV/Bus/Truck Parking
85% Non Smoking Rooms
Exit 53, Andy Devine Ave., Then East 1 Block, Motel is on your Left
AAA
520-757-1188 • 800-578-7878
ARIZONA • I-40 • EXIT 53

CIRCLE S Campground & RV Park
1091
2360 Airway Ave. • Kingman, AZ

• Pull-Thru Sites
• Large "Cool" Pool
• Clean, Modern Restrooms w/ Showers
• Modern Laundry Facilities
• Close to Golf, Tennis & Fitness Center
• Good Sam, KOA, AAA, AARP Discounts Honored
$11.99 + tax
520-757-3235
Directions: I-40 (exit 51) 1/4 Mile N on Stockton Hill Rd. then 3/4 mile on Airway Ave. From I-40 (Exit 53) 1/4 N on Andy Devine then left on Airway Ave. 1 1/2 mile entrance on left.
ARIZONA • I-40 • EXIT 53

The Universal Sign for the World's Best-selling Gasoline
1258
Open 24 Hours

"TCBY." Treats
Diesel
Pay at the Pump
Convenience Store
All Major Credit Cards
ATM
Tour Buses Welcome
"Route 66" Souvenirs
520-757-5676
ARIZONA • I-40 • EXIT 53

EXIT	ARIZONA
ATM	S: Chevron
Parks	N: Grand Canyon Caverns Supai
139	Crookton Road, AZ 66
144	Bus Loop 40, Ash Fork, AZ 66
FStop	S: Chevron[*, LP], Exxon[*]
Food	S: Piccadilli Pizza & Subs (Chevron)
Lodg	N: Ash Fork Inn
AServ	S: Chevron
TServ	N: Diesel Repair
RVCamp	N: KOA Campgrounds (Behind Ashfork Inn)
	S: Hillside RV Park[RV DUMP]
ATM	S: Chevron
146	AZ 89 South, Bus Loop 40, Ash Fork, Prescott
TStop	N: Ted's Bull Pen[*, SCALES]
Gas	N: Bell[*], Mobil
Food	N: Fernows Ranchouse Cafe (Ted's Bull Pen)
AServ	N: Mobil
TServ	N: Ted's Bull Pen[SCALES]
148	County Line Road
149	Monte Carlo Road
FStop	N: Monte Carlo Truck Stop
TServ	N: Monte Carlo Truck Stop
151	Welch Road
Exit	**(156)** Safety Pull-Out (Westbound)
157	Devil Dog Road
161	Bus Loop 40, Williams, Grand Canyon, Country Club Road
Gas	S: Shell[*]
Food	S: Denny's
Lodg	S: Best Western, Days Inn
RVCamp	N: Camping
ATM	S: Shell
Parks	N: Cateract Lake
163	Williams, Grand Canyon
Gas	N: Chevron[*, D]
	S: Mobil[*, D], Texaco[*, D]
Food	N: Subway (Chevron)
	S: Buckles Family Restaurant (Texaco), Doc Holiday Steakhouse (Holiday Inn), Jack in the Box, McDonald's
Lodg	N: Fairfield Inn
	S: Arizona Welcome Inn & Suites, Holiday Inn, Howard Johnson Express
AServ	S: Mobil
ATM	N: Chevron
	S: Mobil, Texaco
Parks	S: Grand Canyon Railway Depot
165	AZ 64, Bus Loop 40, Red Lake, Williams, Grand Canyon
RVCamp	S: Railside RV Ranch (1.5 Miles)
167	Garland Prairie Road, Circle Pines Road
RVCamp	N: KOA Campgrounds (.5 Miles)
171	Pittman Valley Road, Deer Farm Road
Food	S: Quality Inn
Lodg	S: Quality Inn
178	Parks Road
RVCamp	N: Ponderosa Forest RV Park
(181)	Rest Area (RR, HF, Phones, Picnic, P; Eastbound)
(182)	Rest Area (RR, HF, Phones, Picnic, P; Westbound)
185	Bellemont, Transwestern Road, Camp Navajo
TStop	N: Texaco[*]

Food N: Pizza Hut (Texaco TS), Subway (Texaco TS)
TServ N: Wertz Tire Center (Texaco TS)

190 A-1 Mountain Road

191 U.S. 89N, Bus Loop 40, Flagstaff, Grand Canyon
RVCamp N: Woody's Camp (2 Miles)

192 Flagstaff Ranch Road

195A Jct. I-17S, U.S. 89A, Sedona, Phoenix

195B AZ 89N, Flagstaff, Grand Canyon
Lodg N: AmeriSuites (see our ad this page)

198 Butler Ave, Flagstaff
TStop S: Little America[*, RV DUMP] (Sinclair)
FStop N: Pacific Pride
Gas N: Exxon[*], Giant[*, D, 24], Shell
S: Mobil[*]
Food N: Country Host Restaurant (Super 8 Motel), Denny's, McDonald's, The Kettle (Howard Johnson)
Lodg N: EconoLodge, Holiday Inn, Howard Johnson, Motel 6, Motel 6, Ramada Limited, Super 8, TraveLodge
S: Little America (Sinclair)
AServ N: NAPA Auto Parts, Shell
TServ S: Little America (Sinclair)
RVCamp S: Black Bart's RV Park
ATM N: Exxon
S: Mobil
Other N: Sam's Club

201 U.S. 89, Bus. Loop 40, Page, Grand Canyon, Country Club Dr.
Gas S: Mobil[*]
Lodg S: Residence Inn
RVCamp N: Flagstaff Service Center[LP]
Med N: Hospital, Walk In Clinic
ATM S: Mobil
Other N: Flagstaff Mall, Wupatki Sunset Crater National Monument
S: Continental Laundry

204 Walnut Canyon National Momument
Other S: Walnut Canyon National Monument

207 Cosnino Road (No Trucks Over 13 Tons)

211 Winona
FStop N: Texaco[*, LP]
AServ N: Texaco
ATM N: Texaco

219 Twin Arrows
TStop S: Twin Arrows Trading Post[*]
Food S: Twin Arrows Trading Post

225 Buffalo Range Road

230 Two Guns
RVCamp S: Two Guns RV Camp

233 Meteor Crater Road
FStop S: Mobil[*, D]
RVCamp S: Meteor Crater RV Park
Other S: Meteor Crater Natural Landmark (6 Miles)

(235) Rest Area (RR, HF, Phones, Picnic, P; Eastbound)

(236) Rest Area (RR, HF, Phones, Picnic, P; Westbound)

239 Meteor City Road, Red Gap Ranch Road

245 AZ 99, Leupp

252 AZ 87 South, Bus. Loop 40, Winslow, Payson
Gas S: Mobil, Shell[*, D], Texaco[*, D]
Food S: Burger King, Hot Stuff Pizza (Texaco), Smash Hit Sub (Texaco)
Lodg S: Days Inn, Delta Motel
AServ S: Mobil, R & M Auto Repair, Randy's Garage
RVCamp S: Glen's RV Shop, Sonoma Trailer Park
Other S: Old Trails Museum

253 North Park Dr, Winslow
TStop N: Pilot Travel Center[*, RV DUMP, SCALES]
FStop N: Chevron[*, CW]
Gas S: 76[*]
Food N: Arby's (Pilot TS), Captain Toni's Pizza (Pilot TS), Denny's[24], Pizza Hut, Senor D's Mexican (Pilot TS)
S: KFC, McDonald's[PLAY], Subway, Taco Bell
Lodg S: Best Western, Comfort Inn, EconoLodge
AServ N: O'Haco's Big O Tire
S: NAPA Auto Parts
TWash N: Pilot Travel Center
Med N: Hospital
S: Hospital
ATM S: 76, Basha's Grocery
Other N: Laundromat, Visitor Information, Wal-Mart
S: Basha's Grocery, Handee Laundromat & Car Wash[CW], Safeway Grocery[RX]

255 Bus. Loop 40, Winslow
TStop S: Flying J Travel Plaza[*, LP, RV DUMP, SCALES]
Gas N: Shell[*]
Food N: Freddie's Burger Shack (Shell)
S: The Country Market (Flying J TS)
AServ S: Cake Chev, Chrys, Plym, Dodge, Jeep, Eagle
RVCamp N: Freddie's RV Park (Shell)

257 AZ 87 N, Second Mesa
Parks N: Homolovi Ruins State Park

264 Hibbard Road

269 Jackrabbit Road
Gas S: Stop n Go[*]

274 Bus. Loop 40, Joseph City

277 Bus. Loop 40, Joseph City
FStop N: Love's[*]
Food N: A & W Hot Dogs & More (Love's FS), Subway (Love's FS)
Parks S: Cholla Lake County Park

280 Hunt Road, Geronimo Road

1302
AMERISUITES
AMERICA'S AFFORDABLE ALL-SUITE HOTEL
Arizona • Exit 195B • 520-774-8042

Holiday Inn EXPRESS
I-40 • Exit 286
Holbrook, AZ
520-524-1466
• Complimentary Breakfast Bar
• Indoor Pool & Jacuzzi
• Guest Laundry
• Free Parking • Gift Shop
• Meeting Facilities
• Free Cable TV
1179
ARIZONA ▪ I-40 ▪ EXIT 286

283 Perkins Valley Road, Golf Course Road
TStop S: Texaco[*, LP]
Food S: Country Host (Texaco)
AServ S: Texaco
ATM S: Texaco

285 South AZ 77, East U.S. 180, Show Low, Holbrook, Rest Area (Picnic, P)
Lodg S: Best Western

286 Holbrook, Bus. Loop 40
Gas N: Diamond Shamrock[*, D]
S: Chevron[D], Exxon[*, D, 24]
Food N: Burger King, Road Runner Cafe
S: Dairy Queen
Lodg N: Holiday Inn Express (see our ad this page)
S: El Rancho
AServ S: Chevron, Tate's Auto Center Chrys, Eagle, Dodge, Ford, Lincoln, Merc
RVCamp N: OK RV Park

289 Bus. Loop 40, Holbrook
Gas N: Chevron[*, 24]
Food N: Denny's, Jerry's Restaurant (Comfort Inn)
Lodg N: Best Western, Comfort Inn, Days Inn, EconoLodge, Motel 6, Ramada Limited, TraveLodge
RVCamp N: KOA Campgrounds
S: KOA Campgrounds (1.25 Miles)

292 AZ 77 N, Keams Canyon
TStop N: Holbrook Truck Plaza[*, RV DUMP, SCALES] (Shell)
Food N: Arizona Country Cafe[24] (Holbrook Truck Plaza), Burger King (Holbrook Truck Plaza), Pizza Express (Holbrook Truck Plaza)
AServ N: Holbrook Truck Plaza (Shell)
TServ N: Holbrook Truck Plaza[SCALES] (Shell)
TWash N: Red Baron Truck Wash[SCALES] (Holbrook Truck Plaza)
RVCamp N: Holbrook Truck Plaza[RV DUMP] (Shell)
Other N: Coin Laundry (Holbrook Truck Plaza)

294 Sun Valley Road
Gas S: Trading Post[*]
Food S: Restaurant
Lodg S: Desert Garden Motel
AServ S: Trading Post
RVCamp N: Root 66 RV Park & Campground

300 Goodwater

303 Adamana Road

311 Petrified Forest National Park, Painted Desert
Parks N: Petrified Forest National Park

320 Pinta Road

325 Navajo
Gas S: Texaco[*, D]
Food S: Subway (Texaco)

330 McCarrell Road

333 U.S. 191 N, Chambers, Ganado
FStop S: Exxon[*]
Food S: Best Western
Lodg S: Best Western

339 U.S. 191S, Sanders, St. Johns
Other N: U.S. Post Office

(340) Weigh Station (Eastbound)

(340) AZ Inspection Station, Weigh Station (Westbound)

341 Ortega Rd.
Gas N: Shell[*]
ATM N: Shell
Other N: Ortega Indian Center

Bold red print shows RV & Bus parking available or nearby

EXIT	ARIZONA/NEW MEXICO
343	Querino Road
346	Pine Springs Rd.
348	St. Anselm Rd, Houck
Gas	N: Chevron
Food	N: Pancake House Restaurant, Taco Bell Express (Pancake House Restaurant)
AServ	N: Chevron
Other	N: Fort Courage Trading Post
351	Allentown Road
Food	N: Taco Bell Express (Indian City)
Other	N: Chee's Indian Store, Indian City
354	Hawthorne Road
357	Indian Hwy 12N, Lupton, Window Rock
AServ	S: Scotty's Auto, RV, & Truck Service
TServ	S: Scotty's Auto, RV, & Truck Service
RVCamp	S: Scotty's Auto, RV, & Truck Service
Other	N: Shirley's Trading Post[LP], U.S. Post Office
359	Grants Road, Lupton, Welcome Center
TStop	N: Speedy's[*]
Gas	S: Texaco[*]
Food	N: Tee Pee Trading Post Restaurant
TServ	N: Speedy's
ATM	N: Speedy's
Other	N: Chaparral Trading Post, State Line General Store, Yellow Horse Trading Post S: Ortega's Indian Market (Texaco)

↑ARIZONA

↓NEW MEXICO

EXIT	NEW MEXICO
(3)	Rest Area (RR, Phones, Picnic, P; Eastbound)
(3)	Rest Area (RV Dump, P; Westbound)
8	Defiance, Manuelito
(9)	Weigh Station (Westbound)
(11)	Weigh Station (Eastbound)
16	Bus. Loop 40, NM 118, W. Gallup
TStop	N: TA TravelCenters of America[*, SCALES] (Shell), Texaco[*, SCALES]
FStop	N: Love's[*]
Gas	S: Chevron[*], Gas Man[*], Phillips 66[*], Texaco[*]
Food	N: A & W Hot Dogs & More (Love's FS), Baskin Robbins (Love's FS), Blimpie Subs & Salads (TA Travel Centers of America), Country Pride Restaurant (TA Travel Centers of America), Subway (Love's FS) S: Carriage Inn (Comfort Inn)
Lodg	N: Howard Johnson (TA Travel Centers of America) S: Comfort Inn, Days Inn, Microtel Inn, Motel 6, TraveLodge, Travellers Inn
AServ	S: Phillips 66
TServ	N: Augie's Truck Service (Detroit, CAT, Cummins), TA TravelCenters of America[SCALES] (Shell), Texaco[SCALES]
TWash	N: Blue Beacon (TA Travel Centers of America), Blue Beacon Truck Wash (TA Travel Centers of America)
RVCamp	S: KOA Kampground (1 Mile)
Other	N: West 66 Laundromat
20	Munoz Blvd, U.S. 666 N, NM602 S, Shiprock, Zuni
Gas	N: Giant[*, D, 24], Malco[*, CW], Shell[*]
Food	N: Blake's Lotaburger, Cracker Barrel, Furr's Family Dining, Hong Kong Restaurant, McDonald's[PLAY]
Lodg	N: Holiday Inn Express
AServ	N: American Car Care Centers, Car Quest Auto Parts, Midas Muffler & Brake
RVCamp	S: Chapperal Mobile Inn
Med	S: ✚ Hospital
ATM	N: Norwest Banks, Safeway Grocery
Other	N: Big K-Mart, Laundromat, Mail Boxes Etc., Rio West Mall, Safeway Grocery, Troy's Laundromat, Wal-Mart S: Airport
22	Miyamura Dr, Montoya Blvd
Gas	S: Armco[*], Shell[*], Texaco
Food	S: Avalon Restaurant (Chinese/American), Baskin Robbins, Church's Chicken, Creamland, El Rancho Hotel, Panz Alegra Restaurant, Taco Bell
Lodg	S: Arrowhead Lodge, Blue Spruce Lodge, El Rancho Hotel, Lariat Lodge, Redwood Lodge, Zia Motel
AServ	S: Big O Tires, Texaco
Parks	N: Miyamura State Park
Other	N: Harold Runnels Swimming Complex S: Cal-Mar The Market Scene
(22)	New Mexico Welcome Center (RR, Picnic, RV Dump; Located at Exit 22 On the North Side)
26	Bus. Loop 40, E. 66 Ave.
FStop	N: Chevron[*, D]
Gas	S: Gas Man[*]
Food	N: Denny's
Lodg	N: Sleep Inn
Med	S: ✚ Gallup Hospital
Parks	N: Red Rock State Park
Other	N: Gallup Indian Plaza
31	Fort Wingate Army Depot, Church Rock
33	NM 400, McGaffey, Fort Wingate
36	Iyanbito
39	Refinery
TStop	N: Giant[*, LP, RV DUMP, SCALES] (Conoco)
Food	N: A & W Hot Dogs & More (Giant TS), Pizza Hut (Giant TS), Taco Bell (Giant TS)
TServ	N: Giant[SCALES] (Conoco)
TWash	N: Giant (Conoco)
(39)	Rest Area (RV Dump, P)
44	Coolidge
47	Continental Divide
Gas	N: Chevron[*]
Other	N: Continental Divide Gift Shop, Indians Market S: U.S. Post Office
53	NM 371, NM 612, Crownpoint, Chaco Canyon Farmington, Thoreau
AServ	N: Herman's Garage
RVCamp	N: St. Bonaventure Mission RV Park (.5 Miles)
Other	N: Red Mountain Market & Deli
63	NM412, Prewitt, Bluewater State Park
Gas	N: Conoco
RVCamp	N: Grants West Campground (.5 Miles)
Parks	S: Bluewater State Park
72	Bluewater Village
Gas	N: Citgo[*]
Food	N: Dairy Queen (Citgo)
79	NM122, NM605, Milan, San Mateo, U.S. 509
TStop	S: Petro[*, SCALES]
FStop	N: Love's[*] S: Pacific Pride Commercial Fueling (Credit Only)
Food	N: Taco Bell (Love's FS) S: Iron Skillet Restaurant (Petro TS)
Lodg	N: Crossroads Motel
AServ	N: Truck Auto Repair
TServ	N: Truck Auto Repair S: Baker Diesel Repair (Cummins, Thermoking), Petro[SCALES]
RVCamp	N: Bar-S RV Park (.25 Miles) S: Baker Diesel Repair (Cummins, Thermoking)
Parks	S: Chaco Culture State Park
Other	N: Milan Super Market S: CB Shop, Zuni Mountain Golf Course
81AB	NM53S, Grants, San Rafael
Food	N: KFC, McDonald's[PLAY]
RVCamp	S: Blue Spruce RV Park, Cibola Sands RV Park (.25 Miles)
Med	N: ✚ Hospital
Parks	S: Zuni Sands Canyon
85	NM122, NM547, Bus. Loop 40, Grants, Mt. Taylor
Gas	N: Chevron[*, 24], Pump n Save, Shell, Texaco[*, D]
Food	N: 4 B's Restaurant, EconoLodge, House of Pancakes, New Mexico Steakhouse (Best Western)
Lodg	N: Best Western, Days Inn, EconoLodge, Holiday Inn Express, Motel 6, Super 8, TraveLodge
AServ	N: Shell
RVCamp	S: Lavaland RV Park
ATM	N: Texaco
89	NM 117, Quemado
Gas	N: Citgo[*]
Food	N: Stuckey's (Citgo)
Other	S: El Malpais National Conservation Area (10 Miles)
(93)	Rest Area (RV Dump, P; Eastbound)
96	McCartys
100	San Fidel
102	Acomita, Acoma, Sky City, Rest Area (RR, Phones, Picnic, P)
Gas	N: Acoma Gas[*, 24]
Med	S: ✚ Hospital
Other	N: Laundromat (Acoma Gas)
(102)	Rest Area (RR, Phones, Picnic; Located At Exit 102 on the South Side)
(103)	Rest Area (P; Westbound)
104	Cubero, Budville
108	Casa Blanca, Paraje
Gas	S: Conoco[*, D]
Other	S: Casa Blanca Laguna Pueblo Commercial Center
(113)	Scenic View (P; Eastbound)
(113)	Scenic View (Westbound)
114	NM124, Laguna
117	Mesita
126	NM6, Los Lunas
131	Canoncito

EXIT	NEW MEXICO
140	Rio Puerco
FStop	**N:** **Chevron**[D]
Gas	**S:** Citgo[*]
Food	**S:** **Dairy Queen, Stuckey's**
AServ	**N:** **Chevron**
149	Paseo, Del Volcan, Central Ave, Albuquerque
FStop	**S:** **Chevron**[*], **Diamond Shamrock**[*]
TServ	**N:** **Freightliner Dealer (Cummins, Detroit Diesel)**
	S: **Chevron**
TWash	**S:** **Truck & Trailer Wash**
RVCamp	**N:** **Enchanted Trails Camping Resort**[LP] **(1.25 Miles)**
	S: **American RV Park (.5 Miles)**
Other	**N:** **Double Eagle Airport**
153	98th St
TStop	**S:** **Flying J Travel Plaza**[*, LP, RV DUMP, SCALES]
Food	**S:** **Magic Dragon Chinese (Flying J TS), Pepperoni's (Flying J TS), The Country Market (Flying J TS)**
154	Unser Blvd.
155	Rio Rancho, Coors Road
Gas	**S:** Chevron[*, CW, 24], Texaco[*, LP, CW]
Food	**N:** Cuco's Mexican Kitchen
	S: Denny's, Furr's Family Dining, McDonald's[PLAY], Taco Bell
Lodg	**S:** Comfort Inn, DAYS INN Days Inn, Holiday Inn Express, La Quinta, Motel 6, Motel 6, **Motel 76, Super 8 (see our ad next page)**, Village Inn
RVCamp	**N:** **Albuquerque West Campground**
Other	**S:** U-Haul[LP]
157A	NM194, Rio Grande Blvd.
Gas	**N:** Diamond Shamrock[*], Texaco[*]
	S: Standard Chevron[*, 24], Texaco[*, CW]
Food	**N:** Burger King[PLAY] (Texaco), Jr.'s BBQ, Seafood House & Pub
	S: Albuquerque Grill (Best Western), Gold Coast Coffee House, Manhattan on the Rio Grande Deli, Rio Grande Cantina
Lodg	**S:** Best Western, Sheraton Inn
AServ	**N:** Martin's Tire Shop
	S: Rio Grande Automotive
ATM	**S:** Standard Chevron
Other	**S:** Mail Boxes Etc.
157B	12th St
Other	**S:** Indian Pueblo Cultural Center
158	8th St, 6th St
FStop	**N:** **Love's**[*, 24]
Gas	**S:** Diamond Shamrock[*]
Food	**N:** **Subway (Love's)**
AServ	**S:** Five Foreign Auto Parts, National Auto Body Parts
TServ	**N:** **Big West Truck Sales & Service (UD, Iveco)**

EXIT	NEW MEXICO
Other	**N:** U-Haul[LP], **WalGreens Pharmacy**[RX]
159A	2nd St, 4th St
Gas	**N:** Conoco[*]
	S: Brewer Oil Co. (Automated Fueling)
Food	**N:** Furr's Family Dining
	S: Tony's Pizza & Restaurant, Village Inn
Lodg	**S:** Interstate Inn, Traveler's Inn
AServ	**N:** Perfection Plus
	S: Ray's Automotive & Truck Service
TServ	**S:** **Great Basin Volvo (MAC, Cummins, CAT, Detroit Diesel)**
Parks	**S:** **Corondo Park**
159B	Jct. I-25S, Belen (Left Exit Westbound)
159C	I-25N, Santa Fe (Left Exit Eastbound)
160	Carlisle Blvd.
Gas	**N:** Texaco[*]
	S: Circle K[*], Speedy's, Texaco[*, D, LP]
Food	**N:** Blake's Lotaburger, Rudy's Country Store & BBQ
	S: **Burger King**[PLAY], Subway (Texaco), Winchells Donuts
Lodg	**N:** EconoLodge, Homestead Village, Motel 6, Radisson Hotel, Residence Inn
AServ	**N:** Goodyear Certified Auto Service
	S: **K-Mart**, Speedy's, Texaco
ATM	**N:** Texaco

1138

RAMADA INN®

25 Hotel Circle N.E. • Albuquerque, NM

Centrally Located for Easy Access
to All Points of Interest!
Restaurant & Lounge on Premises
Remote Cable TV/HBO Pay Per View & Nintendo
Coffeemakers In-Room/Guest Laundry
Outdoor Pool & Jacuzzi
Children Under 18 Stay Free with Parents
Bus, RV & Truck Parking Free!

505-271-1000 • Toll Free Reservations: 1-800-435-9843

NEW MEXICO • I-40 • EXIT 165

EXIT	NEW MEXICO
Other	**N:** Police Department, **Wal-Mart**[RX]
	S: Blue Cross Animal Clinic, **K-Mart, Spin Cycle Coin Laundry, WalGreens Pharmacy**[RX]
161AB	San Mateo Blvd.
Gas	**N:** Phillips 66[LP], Texaco[*]
	S: Plateau[*]
Food	**N:** Boston Market Restaurant, Denny's, Einstein Bros Bagels, K-Bob's Seafood and Steaks, Keva Juice, Starbucks Coffee
Lodg	**N:** La Quinta Inn
AServ	**N:** Bob Raught's Auto Repair, Phillips 66
Other	**N:** Popular Outdoor Outfitters, The Pavilions at San Mateo, Vista Optical
162AB	Louisiana Blvd
Food	**N:** American Grille & Bar (Marriott), Bennigan's, Garduno's, Japanese Kitchen, Le Peep Restaurant, Romano's Macaroni Grill, Shoney's, Steak & Ale, T.G.I. Friday's
Lodg	**N:** AmeriSuites (see our ad this page), Marriott, Winrock Inn
ATM	**N:** Norwest Banks
Other	**N:** **Borders Books & Music**, General Cinema Park Square, **Toys R Us, Winrock Shopping Mall**
	S: **National Atomic Museum**
164AB	Wyoming Blvd. (Westbound Access Ramp Is Under Construction)
Gas	**N:** Circle K[*], Phillips 66[*, CW]
AServ	**N:** NAPA Auto Parts, Plains Auto Refrigeration & Repair
	S: Carl Malone Toyota, Garcia Honda, Garcia Infiniti, Rich Subaru, KIA, Mazda, Ford, Isuzu, Zangara Dodge
RVCamp	**N:** **Travelland RV Center**
Med	**N:** ✚ **Presbyterian Caseman Hospital**
ATM	**N:** Phillips 66
Other	**N:** **Wyoming Animal Hospital**
164C	Lomas Blvd, Wyoming Blvd. (Westbound, Services At Exit 164AB Are Accessed By This Exit)
165	Eubank Blvd.
Gas	**N:** Chevron[*, 24], Diamond Shamrock[*, D], Phillips 66[*], Texaco[*]
Food	**N:** Applebee's, JB's Restaurant (Howard Johnson), Jose Olson's (Ramada Inn), Owl Cafe, Sonic Drive In
	S: Boston Market Restaurant, Burger King, Taco Bell, Wendy's
Lodg	**N:** EconoLodge, Holiday Inn Express, Howard Johnson, **Ramada Inn (see our ad this page)**
RVCamp	**S:** **American Holiday RV (1 Mile)**
ATM	**N:** Phillips 66
Other	**N:** Builder's Square Hardware, **Office Max, Target**
	S: Albuquerque Eye Care, Home Base Hardware[LP], Mr. Ship N' Chek, **Office Depot**,

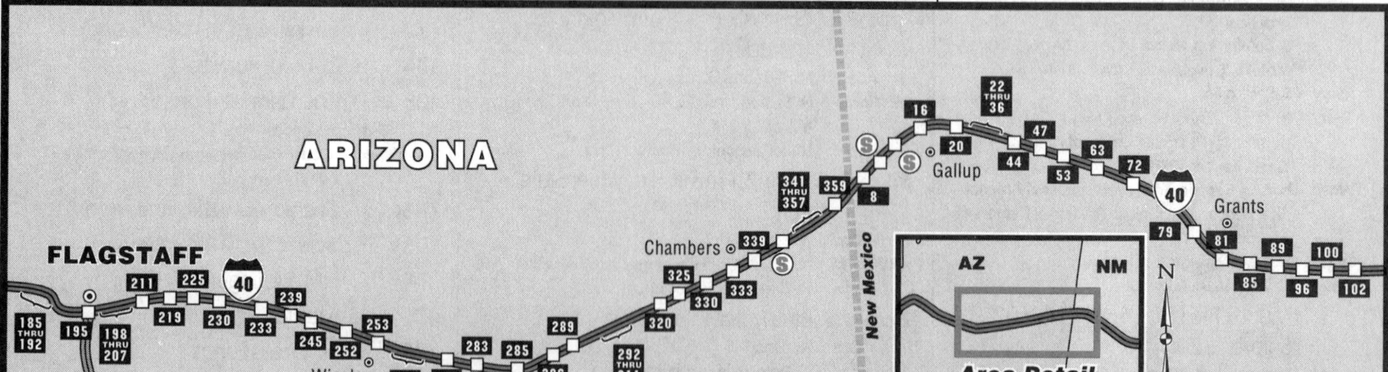

Bold red print shows RV & Bus parking available or nearby

EXIT	NEW MEXICO
	PetsMart, Sam's Club, Wal-Mart(24) (Vision Center)
166	**Juan Tabo Blvd**
Food	N: Black Eyed Pea, Burger King, Carrows, Imperial Lion, Olive Garden
	S: Chen's (Chinese), Dragon City Chinese, Wienerschnitzel
Lodg	N: Park Inn, Super 8 (see our ad this page)
RVCamp	S: Action RV Specialists(LP), All Systems RV Repair, American RV & Marine (.5 Miles), KOA Campgrounds, Myers RV Center
ATM	N: NationsBank
	S: Furr's Grocery Store, Norwest Bank
Other	N: Hobby Lobby, Roller King
	S: Citation Car Wash(CW), Furr's Grocery Store
167	**NM 556, Tramway Blvd**
Gas	S: Chevron(*, 24), Fina(*, 24), Texaco(*, CW)
Food	S: Albuquerque Grill (Best Western), Burger King(PLAY) (Texaco), Casa de Pancakes, Einstein Bros Bagels, McDonald's, Starbucks Coffee, Subway, TCBY (Texaco), The Four Hills Cafe (Comfort Inn), Waffle House
Lodg	S: Best Western, Canyon Motel, Comfort Inn, Days Inn, Deluxe Inn & Suites, EconoLodge, Motel 6
RVCamp	N: Best Western Motor Inn & RV Park (.25 Miles)
ATM	S: Money, Smith's(RX)
Other	S: Albertson's Grocery(RX), Duds 'N Suds Coin Laundry, Mail Boxes Etc., Smith's(RX), United Artists
170	**Carnuel**
175	**NM337, NM14, Cedar Crest, Tijeras**
RVCamp	N: Camping
ATM	S: Norwest Bank
Parks	N: Sandia Crest Recreation Area
	S: Cibola National Forest
Other	S: Canyon Crossroads Animal Hospital, Public Library, Sandia Ranger Station, U.S. Post Office
176	**NM14, San Antonio, Tijeras**
178	**Zuzax**
Gas	S: Chevron(K)
AServ	S: Chevron
RVCamp	S: Hidden Valley Resort
181	**NM217, Sedillo**
187	**NM344, Edgewood**
FStop	S: Phillips 66(*, D, LP)
Gas	N: Citgo(*), Conoco
	S: Diamond Shamrock(*), Fina(*)
Food	N: Dairy Queen (Citgo)
	S: Chester Fried Chicken (Fina), Homerun Pizza, Homestead Restaurant, Pizza Barn, Stuckey's (Diamond Shamrock)
AServ	N: Conoco
	S: Under Car Express Lube
RVCamp	S: Red Arrow
ATM	N: Citgo
	S: Diamond Shamrock
Other	N: Edgewood Volunteer Fire Dept. & Ambulance Service
	S: Edgewood Grocery, The Book Source, U.S. Post Office
194	**Bus. Loop 40, Moriarty West, Rt 66**
TStop	S: Rip Griffin Travel Center(*, SCALES)
Gas	S: Chevron(*, 24)
Food	S: Arby's, McDonald's(PLAY), Pizza Hut (Rif Griffin TS), Subway, Taco Bell, Touch Down Pizza
Lodg	S: Days Inn, Howard Johnson, Super 8
TServ	S: Rip Griffin Travel Center(SCALES)
RVCamp	S: Happy Trails Campground (.25 Miles), Ralph's Repair, Texaco Gas
ATM	S: Moriarty IGA Foods
Other	S: Moriarty IGA Foods

EXIT	NEW MEXICO
196	**NM41, Howard Cavasos Blvd, Estancia, Santa Fe**
Gas	S: Circle K(*, D), Phillips 66
Food	S: Blake's Lotaburger, Chubby's Restaurant
Lodg	S: Sands Motel, Siesta Motel
AServ	S: A & V Tire Sales & Auto Service, Phillips 66
ATM	S: Circle K
Parks	S: Moriarty Neighborhood Park
Other	S: Moriarty Historical Museum
197	**Bus. Loop 40, Moriarty East, Rt. 66 (Reaccess Eastbound Only)**
TStop	S: Ted's Truck Center(*, LP)
Food	S: Bull Pen Restaurant (Ted's Truck Center)
TServ	S: Continental Express Inc., Ted's Truck Center, West Truck Service
RVCamp	S: Camping
203	**Unnamed Exit**
Food	S: El Vaquero(24)
Lodg	S: Long Horn Ranch Motel
RVCamp	N: Zia RV Park
Other	S: Exit 203 CB Shop
(207)	**Rest Area (RR, Picnic, P; Eastbound)**
(207)	**Rest Area (RR, HF, Picnic, RV Dump, P; Westbound)**
208	**Wagon Wheel**
Gas	N: Texaco
Lodg	N: Wagon Wheel Motel
AServ	N: Texaco
218	**U.S. 285, Vaughn, Santa Fe, Clines Corners, Encino**
FStop	N: Chevron(*, 24)
Gas	N: Clines Corners Travel Center(*) (Shell)

1786

SUPER 8 MOTEL

Three Great Locations

Albuquerque East

- Pets Allowed (w/permission)
- Handicap Accessible
- Coin Laundry
- Interior Corridors

450 Paisano, NE
505-271-4807 800-800-8000
I-40, Exit 166 North

Albuquerque West

- Truck Parking
- Handicap Accessible
- Interior Corridors

6030 Iliff Rd., NW
505-836-5560 • 800-800-8000
I-40, Exit 155 South

Albuquerque

- Truck Parking
- Handicap Accessible
- Interior Corridors

2500 University Blvd, NE
505-888-4884 • 800-800-8000
I-25, Exit 227A East

New Mexico

EXIT	NEW MEXICO
Food	N: Clines Corners Travel Center (Shell)
226	**Unnamed Exit**
230	**NM 3, Encino, Villanueva**
234	**Unnamed Exit**
Gas	N: Citgo(*)
Food	N: Dairy Queen (Citgo)
239	**Unnamed**
243	**Milagro**
FStop	N: Chevron(*)
(251)	**Rest Area (RR, Picnic, RV Dump, P; Eastbound)**
(251)	**Rest Area (RR, Picnic, RV Dump, P; Westbound)**
252	**Unnamed Exit**
256	**U.S. 84N, Las Vegas, NM219, Pastura**
263	**San Ignacio**
267	**Colonias**
Gas	N: Texaco
Food	N: Tex-Mex Cafe (Texaco)
273	**U.S. 54, Bus. Loop 40, NM U.S. 66, Santa Rosa, Vaughn**
AServ	S: Ortega's RV & Auto Repair
RVCamp	S: Ortega's RV & Auto Repair, Ramblin' Rose RV Park (1 Mile), Sundown RV Paark
275	**Santa Rosa**
Gas	N: Phillips 66(*, 24), Texaco(*)
	S: Diamond Shamrock, Exxon(*)
Food	N: Burger King (Texaco), McDonald's, Santa Fe Grille
	S: Sun N Sand Motel
Lodg	N: Best Western, Days Inn, Ramada Limited, TraveLodge
	S: Sun N Sand Motel, Super 8
RVCamp	N: Donnie's RV Park
	S: KOA-Santa Rosa (.25 Miles), Ramblin' Rose RV Park (1 Mile)
Med	S: + Hospital
Parks	S: Park Lake(PLAY)
Other	N: NM State Police, Route 66 Restaurant (Steaks/ Mexican)
277	**U.S. 84S, Ft. Sumner**
TStop	S: TA TravelCenters of America(*, SCALES) (CB Shop)
FStop	N: Texaco(*)
Gas	N: Chevron(*, D)
Food	N: Chix Chicken Station (Chevron), Cinnamon Street Bakery (Chevron), Dairy Queen, Golden Dragon Chinese, Hot Stuff Pizza (Chevron), Silver Moon
	S: Country Pride (TA Travel Centers of America), Subway (TA Travel Centers of America)
Lodg	N: Budget Inn, Comfort Inn, Holiday Inn Express, Motel 6
AServ	N: Texaco
TServ	S: Big Rig Truck Service(24), TA TravelCenters of America(SCALES) (CB Shop)
TWash	S: Joe's (TA Travel Centers of America)
RVCamp	N: KOA Campgrounds (1 Mile), Texaco
284	**Unnamed Exit**
291	**Cuervo**
Gas	S: Cuervo Gas
AServ	S: Cuervo Gas
300	**NM129, Newkirk**
FStop	N: Phillips 66(*)
Gas	S: Vista Mini Mart(*, D)
Parks	N: Conchas Lake State Park
Other	N: U.S. Post Office
(301)	**Rest Area (RR, Picnic, RV Dump, P;**

EXIT	NEW MEXICO
	Eastbound)
(301)	**Rest Area (RR, Picnic, P; Westbound)**
311	Montoya
321	Palomas
Gas	S: Texaco(*)
Food	S: **Dairy Queen (Texaco), Stuckey's (Texaco)**
ATM	S: Texaco
329	U.S. 54, NM U.S. 66, Bus. Loop 40, Tucumcari Blvd.
TStop	N: **Shell**(*)
Food	N: **Shell Cafe (Shell TS)**
TServ	N: **Shell**
331	Camino del Coronado
332	NM209, NM104, 1st Street
FStop	N: **Exxon**(*)
Gas	S: Texaco
Food	N: Blake's Lotaburger, K-Bobs (Best Western), KFC, **McDonald's, Subway (Exxon)**
Lodg	N: Best Western, Days Inn, Microtel Inn
AServ	S: Texaco
Med	N: **Dan C. Trigg Memorial Hospital, Hospital**
ATM	N: **Exxon**
Other	S: **NM State Police**
333	U.S. 54E, Ute Lake State Park, Dalhart, Mountain Road
FStop	N: **Love's**(*, 24)
Food	N: **Taco Bell Express (Love's)**
AServ	N: Bill's Auto Service
RVCamp	N: **KIVA Park (1.25 Miles), Mountain Road RV Park (.5 Miles)**
335	Bus. Loop 40, Tucumcari Blvd.
Gas	N: Chevron(*), Conoco(*, D, LP, 24), Shell, Texaco(*)
Lodg	N: Comfort Inn, **EconoLodge**, Holiday Inn, Howard Johnson, Motel 6, Super 8
AServ	N: Shell
RVCamp	S: **KOA Campgrounds (.5 Miles)**
339	NM278
343	Unnamed Exit
356	NM469, San Jon
FStop	N: **Citgo**(*, LP)
Gas	S: Texaco(*, D)
Food	N: **KFC (Citgo), Taco Bell Express (Citgo)** S: Burger King (Texaco)
TServ	N: **Citgo**
(357)	**Weigh Station (Eastbound)**
(357)	**Weigh Station (Westbound)**
361	Bard
369	NM93S, NM392N, Endee
(373)	**NM Welcome Center (RR, HF,**

EXIT	NEW MEXICO/TEXAS
	Phones, Picnic, RV Dump, P; Westbound)

↑NEW MEXICO

↓TEXAS

0	Bus. Loop 40, Glenrio
(12)	**Picnic Area (Picnic, P; Eastbound)**
18	Gruhlkey Road, FM2858
Gas	S: Texaco(*)
Food	S: **Stuckey's (Texaco)**
22	TX214, Bus. Loop 40, Adrian (Difficult Reaccess)
Gas	S: Phillips 66(*)
28	Landergin
(31)	**Picnic Area (Picnic, P; Eastbound)**
35	East Bus. Loop 40, Vega
Lodg	S: Best Western
36	U.S. 385
FStop	N: **Conoco**(*) S: **Texaco**(*)
Gas	N: Phillips 66(*)
Food	N: **Dairy Queen**
Lodg	N: Comfort Inn
RVCamp	S: **Texas Quick Stop & Campgrounds**
ATM	S: **Texaco**
37	West Bus. Loop 40, Vega
42	Everett Road
49	Fm809, Wildorado
Gas	S: **Diamond Shamrock**(*, LP), Phillips 66(LP)
Food	S: Jesse's Cafe
Lodg	S: Texan Motel
(53)	**Parking Area (P; Eastbound)**
54	Adkisson Road
RVCamp	S: **Adkisson**
57	Fm2381, Bushland
RVCamp	S: **Camping**
Other	S: U.S. Post Office
60	Arnot Road
FStop	S: **Love's**(*)
Food	S: **A & W Hot Dogs & More (Love's), Subway (Love's)**
Other	S: Texas Trading Company
62A	Hope Road, Helium Rd.
RVCamp	S: **Amarillo West View RV Park, Sun-Down Campground (1 Mile)**
62B	Bus. Loop 40E, Amarillo Blvd.

EXIT	TEXAS
	(Reaccess Westbound Only)
64	Loop 335, Soncy Rd.
Food	N: Joe's Crab Shack S: Applebee's, Legends Steakhouse, On The Border Mexican Cafe, Ruby Tuesday
AServ	N: Mr. Automotive
Parks	S: **Palo Duro Canyon State Park (25 Miles)**
Other	S: **Barnes & Noble Booksellers**, Builder's Square, High Plains Christian Bookstore, **PetsMart, Target**, Toys R Us, **U.S. Post Office**
65	Coulter Dr
Gas	N: Phillips 66(*)
Food	N: Arby's, Golden Corral Family Steakhouse, Hud's, Luby's Cafeteria, My Thai Chinese, Taco Bell, The Donut Stop, Waffle House S: Chuck E Cheese's Pizza, Fortune Cookie (Chinese), Hoffbrau Steaks, Outback Steakhouse
Lodg	N: Comfort Inn, Days Inn, La Quinta Inn, **Motel** S: Ramada Inn
AServ	N: Firestone Tire & Auto, Westgate Chevrolet
RVCamp	N: **Motel** S: **Interstate Motel**
Med	N: **Midstate Medical**
ATM	N: Amarillo National Bank S: Amarillo National Bank, Herring National Bank
Other	S: Landstuhl Christian Book & Gift, U.A. Cinema Six, **Westgate Mall**
66	Bell St, Wolflin Ave, Avondale St.
Gas	N: Citgo(*, D), Diamond Shamrock(*) S: Chevron, Texaco(*, CW)
Food	N: Subway, Toucan Sportz Club & Grill S: King and I Thai Food
Lodg	N: Fairfield Inn, HomeGate Studios & Suites, Motel 6, Residence Inn
AServ	N: Big A Auto Parts S: Chevron
Med	S: **Family Medical Clinic**
ATM	N: Amarillo Federal Credit Union S: Bank One, NationsBank, Texaco
Other	N: Bakery Thrift Shop, Dale's Grand Burger, Tripp's Harley Davidson Motorcycles S: **Albertson's Grocery**
67	Western St, Avondale
Gas	N: Citgo, Phillips 66(*, CW), Texaco(*)
Food	N: Black Eyed Pea, Burger King, Chowders Seafood Grill, McDonald's(PLAY), Sonic, Taco Bell, Time Out BBQ S: Catfish Shack, Furr's, IHOP, Olive Garden, Taco Cabana, Waffle House
AServ	S: Firestone Tire & Auto, Montgomery Ward
ATM	N: Texaco S: Amarillo National Bank
Other	N: **Amarillo Bowl** S: Texas State Optical
68A	Julian Blvd, Paramount Blvd (Exit is

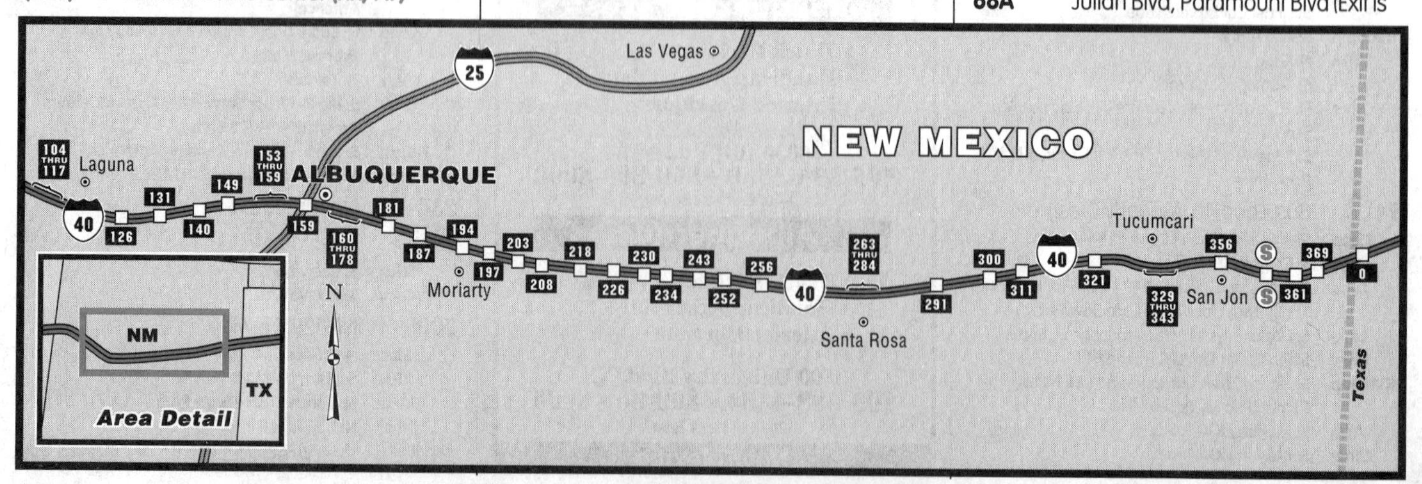

Bold red print shows RV & Bus parking available or nearby

EXIT	TEXAS
	closed Westbound due to Construction)
Food	**S:** Bennigan's, Bless Your Heart, Buns Over Texas, Calico County, Denny's[24], El Chico, Hattie's Cafe, Kabuki Japanese Steakhouse, Kettle, Lettuce Works, Long John Silver, Occasions Elegant Dining, Orient Express, Peking Restaurant (Chinese), Pizza Planet, Red Lobster, Ruby Tequila's, Steak & Ale, Western Sizzlin'
Lodg	**S:** Comfort Suites Hotel, Holiday Inn Express, Motel 6, TraveLodge
AServ	**S:** Mr. Muffler, Pit Stop
68B	Georgia St (Exit is closed Eastbound due to Construction)
Gas	**N:** Shell[*], Texaco[*]
Food	**N:** Dyer's BBQ, Gardski's, Macaroni Joe's Pasta House, Schlotzsky's Deli, Subway (Shell)
Lodg	**N:** Ambassador Hotel
ATM	**N:** Amerillo National Bank
69A	Crockett St (Westbound)
69B	Washington St, Amarillo College
Gas	**S:** Phillips 66[*, CW], Texaco[*]
Food	**N:** Arnold Burger
	S: Donuts
AServ	**N:** Tony's Service
	S: Jesse's Discount Auto Parts (CarQuest)
ATM	**S:** First National Bank
Other	**N:** **Albertson's Grocery**[RX]
	S: **Eckerd Drugs**[RX]
70	Jct I-27S, U.S. 60, Pampa, Downtown, U.S. 87, U.S. 287, Dumas, Canyon, Lubbock
71	Ross-Osage St, Arthur St.
Gas	**N:** Diamond Shamrock[*, CW], Diamond Shamrock[*], Shell[*], Texaco[*]
	S: Texaco[*]
Food	**N:** Burger King, Grandy's, Long John Silver, McDonald's[PLAY], Popeye's Chicken, Schlotzsky's Deli, SHONEY'S Shoney's, Tacos Garcia, The Brass Lantern (Holiday Inn), Wienerschnitzel
	S: Arby's, Denny's, La Fiesta (Mexican), Taco Bell, Wendy's
Lodg	**N:** **Coach Light Inn**, Comfort Inn, DAYS INN Days Inn, Holiday Inn (see our ad this page)
	S: Hampton Inn, La Quinta Inn, **Traveler's Inn**
AServ	**N:** Texaco
	S: John Chandler Ford, Hyundai, Plains Chevrolet, Geo
ATM	**S:** Amarillo National Bank
Other	**S:** **Sam's Club, U.S. Post Office**
72A	Loop 395, Nelson St, Quarter Horse Dr, Tee Anchor Blvd.
Gas	**S:** Chevron, Diamond Shamrock[*], Shell[*, D]
Food	**N:** Carolyn's Place (TraveLodge), **Cracker Barrel**, KFC, Pizza Hut (Ramada Inn)
Lodg	**N:** Budget Host, Ramada Inn, Sleep Inn, Super 8, TraveLodge
	S: **Camelot Inn**
AServ	**S:** Chevron, Pro 1 Automotive
Other	**N:** **American Quarter Horse Museum**
72B	Grand St, Bolton St.
Gas	**N:** Lonestar, Texaco[*]
	S: Phillips 66[*, CW], Yukon[*, D]
Food	**N:** Chicho's Cafe, Henk's BBQ, The Donut Stop
	S: Braum's Ice Cream, McDonald's, Pizza Hut, Sonic, Subway, Taco Cabana, Taco Villa
Lodg	**S:** Motel 6
AServ	**N:** Grand Battery & Electric, Lonestar, Payless Autoplex
	S: Parts America, **Wal-Mart**[24, RX] **(Vision Center)**
ATM	**N:** NationsBank
	S: Phillips 66
Other	**N:** H & L Foods, Harold's Farmers Market
	S: **United Supermarket**[RX], **Wal-Mart**[RX] **(Vision Center)**
73	Eastern St, Bolton St.
FStop	**S:** **Pacific Pride Commercial Fueling**[D]
Gas	**N:** Diamond Shamrock[*, D, LP]
	S: Chevron[*, D, LP], Citgo[*]
Lodg	**S:** Best Western
AServ	**N:** Ray Stoors Automotive
	S: Repair
TServ	**S:** **Amarillo Thermoking, Cummins, Onan Dealership, Treadco, Inc.**
RVCamp	**N:** **Village East**
	S: **Cummins Southern Plains, Inc. (.2 Miles)**
ATM	**N:** Diamond Shamrock
Other	**N:** CB Shop, Sharp's Honda, Suzuki, Yamaha, **Trucker's Store**
74	Whitaker Road
FStop	**S:** **Love's**[*, 24]
Food	**N:** **Big Texan Steak Ranch Motel**
Lodg	**N:** **Big Texan Steak Ranch Motel**
	S: **Coachlight Inn**
TServ	**S:** **Amarillo Truck Center, West Texas Peterbilt**
TWash	**S:** **Blue Beacon, West Texas Peterbilt**
RVCamp	**N:** **The Village East RV Park (1 Mile)**
75	Loop 335, Lakeside Dr.
TStop	**S:** **Petro**[*, SCALES]
Gas	**N:** Phillips 66[*], Shell[*]
Food	**N:** Country Barn (BBQ, Steak), Waffle House
	S: **Iron Skillet Restaurant (Petro TS)**
Lodg	**N:** Quality Inn & Suites, **Radisson Inn, Super 8**
TServ	**N:** **Bypass Service, Diesel Mechanics, Lakeside Trailer Repair, Trinity Trailer Sales Inc.**
	S: **Petro**[SCALES]
TWash	**S:** **Blue Beacon (Petro TS)**
RVCamp	**N:** **Overnite Trailer Inn**[LP]
Other	**S:** Billy's Boat-Ramp
76	Spur 467, International Airport
TStop	**N:** **Flying J Travel Plaza**[*, RV DUMP, SCALES]
Food	**N:** **The Cookery (Flying J TS)**
TServ	**N:** **Planet Truck Wash**[24]
TWash	**N:** **Planet Truck Wash**
Other	**N:** CB Shop
Exit	**(76)** Texas Travel Information Center
77	FM1258, Pullman Rd.
TStop	**N:** **Pilot Travel Center**[*, SCALES]
	S: **Texaco**[*, SCALES]
Food	**N:** **Arby's (Pilot TS)**
	S: **Pepper Mill Restaurant (Texaco)**
TServ	**S:** **Amarillo Branch Stewart & Stevenson (Detroit Diesel, Allison, Heister), Peek Industrial Tractor Parts Co., Texaco**[SCALES]
TWash	**S:** **Texaco**
78	U.S. 287S, Fort Worth (Eastbound)
80	Spur 228
RVCamp	**N:** **AOK RV Camp**
81	FM1912
TStop	**S:** **T/A TravelCenters of America**[*, SCALES, 24]
FStop	**N:** **Texaco**[*]
Food	**S:** **Country Fresh Restaurant (TA Travel Centers of America), Subway (TA Travel Centers of America)**
TServ	**S:** **T/A TravelCenters of America**[SCALES, 24], **West Texas CAT**
85	Durrett Rd, Old U.S. 66, West Bus. Loop 40, Amarillo Blvd.
(87)	**Rest Area (RR, Picnic, P; Eastbound)**
(87)	**Rest Area (RR, Picnic, Grills, P; Westbound)**
87	FM2373
89	FM2161, Old U.S. 66

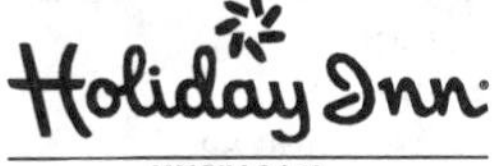

AMARILLO I-40

1911 I-40 East
Amarillo, Texas 79102
806-372-8741 ¥ 800-HOLID

• Holidome family recreation center with heated indoor pool, sauna, whirlpool, fitness room, putting green, foose-ball, ping-pong, video games and sundeck • Full-service restaurant • Brass Rail Lounge • Room service • Close to the Civic Center and downtown Amarillo • Minutes from the city golf course, shopping, the fairgrounds and the American Quarter Horse Heritage Museum

1463

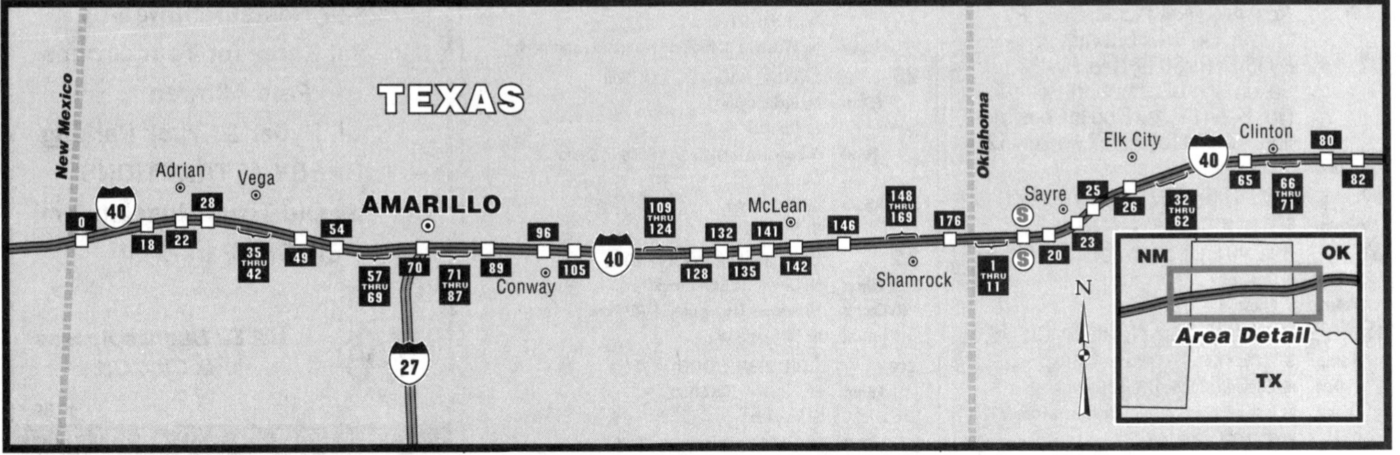

Bold red print shows RV & Bus parking available or nearby

EXIT TEXAS

96 TX207, Conway, Panhandle
- **FStop** **N:** Love's(*)
- **Gas** **S:** Shell(*)
- **Food** **N:** A & W Hot Dogs & More (Love's FS), Taco Bell (Love's FS)
  - **S:** L.A. Motel, The Conway Restaurant (S & S Motor Inn)
- **Lodg** **S:** L.A. Motel, S&S Motor Inn
- **AServ** **S:** Shell
- **ATM** **N:** Love's

98 South TX 207, Claude

105 FM2880

(107) Parking Area (P; Westbound)

109 FM294

110 East Bus. Loop 40, Groom, Old U.S. 66

112 FM295, Groom

113 FM2300, Groom
- **Gas** **S:** Texaco(*, D)
- **Food** **S:** Dairy Queen
- **Lodg** **S:** Chalet Inn

114 West Bus. Loop 40
- **AServ** **N:** Tower Garage(D)
- **TServ** **N:** Tower Garage

121 North TX 70, Pampa

124 South TX 70, Clarendon
- **Gas** **N:** Conoco(D)
- **RVCamp** **N:** Groom McLean Campground (Conoco)

128 FM2477, Lake McClellan Rd.
- **Parks** **N:** Wild Life Viewing Area

(129) Picnic Area (Picnic, P; Eastbound)

(131) Picnic Area (Phones, Picnic, P; Westbound)

132 Johnson Ranch Road

135 FM291, Alanreed , Old U.S. 66
- **Gas** **S:** Conoco(*, D)
- **Lodg** **S:** Conoco
- **AServ** **S:** Bill's Auto & RV Repair
- **RVCamp** **S:** Bill's Auto & RV Repair
- **Other** **S:** U.S. Post Office

141 Bus. Loop 40, McLean

142 TX273, FM3143, McLean
- **FStop** **N:** Texaco(*)
- **AServ** **N:** Kirk's Auto Service and Supply (CarQuest)
- **RVCamp** **N:** Country Corner RV Park (Texaco), Windmill RV Park (.25 Miles)

143 Bus. Loop 40, McLean (Westbound)
- **Other** **N:** Veterinary Clinic

146 County Line Road
- **RVCamp** **S:** Camping

148 FM1443, Kellerville
- **RVCamp** **S:** Camping

(149) Rest Area (RR, Picnic, P; Eastbound)

(149) Rest Area (RR, Picnic, Grills, RV Dump, P; Westbound)

152 FM1547, FM3075, Lela, FM453, Pakan Road (Eastbound: Exit 157 Has Been Closed Due to Construction. Access To Exit 157 via Exit 152)
- **Gas** **S:** Gas Station(*)

157 Fm1547, Fm3075, Lela (Westbound)
- **RVCamp** **S:** West 40 Camp Area (2 Miles)

161 Bus. 40 East, Shamrock, Old Rte 66
- **Gas** **S:** Chevron(D)
- **AServ** **S:** Chevron

163 U.S. 83, Wheeler, Wellington, Old U.S. 66
- **FStop** **S:** Phillips 66(*, CW), Texaco(*, D, LP)
- **Gas** **N:** Chevron, Conoco, Texaco(*, D)
- **Food** **N:** Irish Inn (Best Western), Mitchell's Family Restaurant, Pizza Hut

EXIT TEXAS/OKLAHOMA

- **S:** Dairy Queen, McDonald's, Subway (Phillips 66), Western Motel
- **Lodg** **N:** Best Western
  - **S:** Western Motel
- **AServ** **N:** Chevron, Conoco, Texaco
  - **S:** C & H Supply
- **Med** **S:** + Hospital
- **ATM** **S:** Phillips 66
- **Other** **N:** Neigbors Ace Hardware

164 Bus. Loop 40 West, Shamrock (Westbound)

167 FM2168, Daberry Road
- **TStop** **N:** Texaco(*)
- **Food** **N:** Butch's Restaurant (Texaco TS)
- **AServ** **N:** Texaco
- **TServ** **N:** Texaco
- **RVCamp** **N:** Texaco

169 FM1802

(173) Picnic Area (Picnic, P; Eastbound)

Exit **(176)** Livestock Inspection Area (Westbound)

176 Spur 30E, Texola

↑TEXAS

↓OKLAHOMA

1 Texola
- **TStop** **S:** Diamond Shamrock(*)
- **Food** **S:** The Windmill Restaurant (Diamond Shamrock)
- **RVCamp** **S:** Double D Campground
- **Other** **S:** U.S. Post Office

5 Bus. Loop 40E, Honeyfarm Road, Hollis

7 OK30, Erick, Sweetwater
- **FStop** **N:** Texaco(*, D)
  - **S:** Love's(*, 24)
- **Food** **N:** Cal's Country Cooking
  - **S:** A & W Hot Dogs & More (Love's), Cowboys, Taco Bell (Love's)
- **Lodg** **N:** Comfort Inn
  - **S:** DAYS INN Days Inn (see our ad this page)
- **TServ** **S:** CB Shop Tires

(9) OK Welcome Center (RR, Phones, Picnic, RV Dump, P; Eastbound)

(9) Rest Area (RR, Phones, Picnic, RV Dump, P; Westbound)

11 Bus. Loop 40W, Erick

Exit **(13)** Check Station (All Trucks Exit)

Exit **(13)** Check Station (All Trucks Exits)

14 Hext Road

20 U.S. 283, Bus. Loop 40E, S 4th St, Mangum
- **Parks** **N:** Washita Battlefield National Landmark

23 OK152, Main St, Cordell
- **FStop** **N:** Phillips 66(*)
  - **S:** Texaco(*, D)
- **Food** **S:** Junction Restaurant(24) (Steak, Seafood, Mexican)
- **AServ** **N:** Phillips 66
  - **S:** Texaco

25 Bus. Loop 40W, N 4th St.
- **FStop** **N:** Diamond Shamrock(*)
- **RVCamp** **N:** Recess Travel Stop & RV Park
- **Med** **N:** + Hospital

26 Cemetery Road
- **FStop** **N:** Citgo(*, D) (CB Shop)
  - **S:** Texaco(*, 24)
- **Food** **N:** Bud's American Cafe(24) (Citgo)

EXIT OKLAHOMA

- **S:** Carl Jr's Hamburgers (Texaco)
- **AServ** **N:** Tire Repair
- **TServ** **S:** Texaco(24)

32 OK 34S, East Bus. Loop 40, Elk City, Mangum, Carter (Left Exit Eastbound)

34 Merritt Road
- **TServ** **N:** DARR Equipment Co. (CAT)

38 OK6, S Main St, Altus, Elk City
- **FStop** **N:** Conoco(*, D)
  - **S:** Phillips 66(*, D)
- **Gas** **S:** Gill's Catfish & Steaks
- **Food** **N:** Arby's, Denny's (Ramada), Long John Silver, McDonald's, Taco Mayo, Western Sizzlin'
  - **S:** Holiday Inn
- **Lodg** **N:** Ramada Inn
  - **S:** EconoLodge, Holiday Inn, Quality Inn (see our ad this page)

580-526-3315
ERICK, OK
DAYS INN
I-40 and Hwy. 30
AAA Member
• Truck Parking
• Free Continental Breakfast
• 36 Channel Remote TV w/Showtime
• Senior Citizen & AARP Rates
• Taco Bell & A&W Across the Street
• Group Rates • 10% off Rack Rates
• Restaurant across the Street
• 24 hr Gas Station/Truck Stop
1782
OKLAHOMA ▪ I-40 ▪ EXIT 7

Quality Inn
30% AARP Discount
405-225-8140
800-228-5151
Indoor Heated Pool & Hot Tub
In Room Coffee
Free Local Calls
Free 9 Item Continental Breakfast
24 hr Restaurant Nearby
Special Rates for Tour Groups
Pets Allowed
U-Haul, Ryder & Truck Parking
NEARBY ATTRACTIONS
Elk City Old Town Museum-2 mi
Elk City Park-5 mi
AAA
102 BJ Hughes Access
Elk City, OK
1789
OKLAHOMA ▪ I-40 ▪ EXIT 38

Bold red print shows RV & Bus parking available or nearby

EXIT OKLAHOMA

- **AServ** S: Phillips 66
- **RVCamp** N: Elk Creek RV Park
- **ATM** N: Conoco
- **Parks** S: Quartz Mountain State Park
- **Other** N: Gene's Fin & Feather Marine, Puckett's Grocery

40 E. 7th St

41 OK34N, Woodward (Left Exit Eastbound)
- **FStop** N: Love's(*, 24)
- **Gas** N: Conoco(*, D)
- **Food** N: Home Cooking Cafe (Budget Host), Kettle, Super 8 (see our ad this page)
- **Lodg** N: Budget Host Inn, DAYS INN Days Inn, Knight's Inn, Motel 6, Super 8 (see our ad this page), TraveLodge
- **RVCamp** N: Elk Run RV Park (.25 Miles), Fun Junction RV Park
- **Med** N: Hospital
- **Other** N: Skate Place

47 Canute
- **Gas** S: Texaco(*)
- **Food** S: Ann's Route U.S. 66 Pizza & Subs, Domino Express
- **Lodg** S: Sunset Inn
- **AServ** S: Gordon's Oil & Lube
- **Other** S: U.S. Post Office

50 Clinton Lake Road
- **Gas** N: KOA Kampground(LP)
- **RVCamp** N: KOA Campgrounds

53 OK 44, Foss, Altus
- **FStop** S: Texaco(*)
- **AServ** S: Texaco
- **TServ** S: Texaco
- **Parks** N: Foss Resevoire

57 Stafford Road

61 Haggard Road

62 Parkersburg Road
- **Gas** N: Conoco(*, D, LP)

65 Bus. Loop 40 East, Gary Blvd, Clinton (Reaccess Westbound Only)
- **Food** N: Long John Silver, McDonald's, Pancake Inn (TraveLodge), Taco Mayo
- **Lodg** N: Best Western, TraveLodge, Treasure Inn
- **AServ** N: Atwoods, Jay's Tires
- **Other** N: Atwoods, K-Mart(RX)

65A 10th St, Neptune Dr
- **FStop** S: Phillips 66(*)
- **Food** N: Braum's Ice Cream & Dairy Store, KFC, Lupita's Mexican, Oakwood (Holiday Inn), Pizza Hut, Subway
- **Lodg** N: Holiday Inn, Relax Inn, Super 8; S: Budget Inn
- **AServ** N: Ed DeLong Pontiac, Buick, GMC Trucks; S: L M Garage(24), Phillips 66
- **RVCamp** S: Wink's RV Park

66 U.S. 183, S. 4th St, Cordell
- **AServ** S: McKinsey Ballard Ford, Merc, Chrys, Dodge

69 Bus. Loop 40W, Clinton

71 Custer City Road
- **FStop** N: Love's(*, 24)
- **Food** N: A & W Hot Dogs & More (Love's), Cherokee Trading Post Restaurant, Taco Bell (Love's)

80 OK54, Weatherford, Thomas, Colony/Corn (Eastbound, Reaccess Westbound Only)
- **Gas** N: Conoco(*, D), Texaco(LP)
- **Food** N: Little Mexico
- **Lodg** N: EconoLodge

EXIT OKLAHOMA

- **AServ** N: Texaco

80A Bus. Loop 40 East, E. Main St. (Eastbound, Reaccess Westbound Only)

82 Bus. Loop 40W, E Main Street (Difficult Reaccess)
- **Gas** N: Citgo(*, CW), Conoco(*, D, 24), Phillips 66(D), Texaco
- **Food** N: Baskin Robbins (Citgo), Carl Jr's Hamburgers, Cinnamon Street Bakery (Citgo), City Diner, Eddie Pepper's Mexican Restaurant (Citgo), Hot Stuff Pizza (Citgo), Jerry's Restaurant, K-Bob's Steakhouse, KFC, Mazzio's Pizza, McDonald's, Pizza Hut, Smash Hit Subs (Citgo), Starvin' Marvin Pizza, Subway, The Dutchman
- **Lodg** N: DAYS INN Days Inn
- **AServ** N: Auto Zone Auto Parts, Conoco(24), O' Reilly

Large Vehicle Parking

1781

SUPER 8 MOTEL

2820 S. Hwy 81
El Reno, OK

405-262-8240
800-262-8240

Continental Breakfast
Restaurant Next Door
Kids Under 12 Stay Free
Outdoor Pool • Free Local Calls
Pets Allowed • Handicap Accessible
Coin Laundry • Exterior Corridors
Remote Control Cable TV w/HBO

OKLAHOMA ▪ I-40 ▪ EXIT 125

Truck/Bus Parking

1759

SUPER 8 MOTEL

2801 E. Hwy 66
Elk City, OK 73644

580-225-9430
800-800-8000

Restaurant on Premises
Lounge Nearby
Donut & Coffee
Free Local Calls
Cable TV w/HBO/ESPN/CNN
Kids Under 12 Stay Free
Outdoor Pool
Tennis/Golf Nearby
Pets Allowed
(with permission only)
Coin Laundry
Interior Corridors
Near Old Town Museum

I-40 Exit 41 to Traffic Light, N on 34 to Access Rd, Turn R to Motel

OKLAHOMA ▪ I-40 ▪ EXIT 41

EXIT OKLAHOMA

Auto Parts, Phillips 66, Texaco, Western Wheel & Tire
- **Med** N: Hospital
- **ATM** N: Bank First, Southwest National Bank, Wal-Mart(RX)
- **Other** N: Imperial Coin Car Wash(CW), United Supermarket, Wal-Mart(RX)

84 Airport Road
- **Gas** N: Total(*)
- **AServ** N: Cummins Buick, Pont, GMC, Chrys, Plym, Dodge, Jeep, Total
- **Other** N: General Tom Stafford Space Museum (2 Miles)

88 OK58, Hydro, Carnegie
- **Gas** N: Texaco
- **AServ** N: Texaco

(94) Picnic Area (Picnic; Westbound)

95 Bethel Road

101 U.S. 281, OK 8, Anadarko, Watonga, Hinton, Roman Nose, Geary
- **TStop** S: Biscuit Hill Truck Stop(*) (Texaco)
- **FStop** S: Phillips 66(*)
- **Lodg** S: Phillips 66
- **TServ** S: Big Foot CB & Tire Shop
- **Parks** N: Roman Nose State Park; S: Red Rock Canyon State Park (5 Miles)
- **Other** N: Public Picnic Area

104 Methodist Road

108 Spur U.S. 281N, Geary, Watonga
- **TStop** N: Cherokee Texaco(*, CW, RV DUMP)
- **FStop** S: Love's(*, 24)
- **Food** N: Cherokee Texaco
- **Lodg** N: Cherokee Texaco
- **TServ** S: Tire Shop (CB Shop)
- **RVCamp** N: KOA Kampground; S: Good Life RV Resort
- **ATM** N: Cherokee Texaco
- **Other** N: I-40 Lighthouse Christian Book Shoppe; S: Indian Trading Post

(111) Picnic Area (Picnic, P; Eastbound)

115 U.S. 270W, Calumet

119 Bus. Loop 40E, El Reno

123 Country Club Road, El Reno
- **FStop** S: Phillips 66(*, D)
- **Gas** N: Conoco(*), Texaco(*, CW)
- **Food** N: Baskin Robbins (Texaco), Braum's Ice Cream, Carl Jr's Hamburgers, Donuts, KFC, Little Caesars Pizza, Long John Silver, McDonald's(PLAY), Pizza Hut, Red Sun Chinese, Taco Bell; S: Denny's, Sirloin Stockade
- **Lodg** S: Best Western, DAYS INN Days Inn, Red Carpet Inn
- **AServ** N: Wal-Mart(24, RX)
- **RVCamp** S: Best Western, Hensley's Best Western RV Park
- **Med** N: Hospital
- **ATM** N: American Heritage Bank, Texaco
- **Other** N: TSC Tractor Supply Co. (Hardware), Wal-Mart(RX)

125 U.S. 81, Chickasha, El Reno
- **Food** N: Brass Apple, Hwy BBQ Grill
- **Lodg** N: Ramada Limited, Super 8 (see our ad this page), Western Sands Motel
- **AServ** N: Diffee Ford, Lincoln, Mercury

(129) Weigh Station (Westbound)

(129) Weigh Station (Eastbound)

130 Banner Road
- **Gas** N: Texaco(*, D)

132 Cimarron Road

EXIT OKLAHOMA

136 OK92, Yukon, Mustang
Gas N: Conoco[*, D], Texaco[*, D, CW]
Food N: Braum's Ice Cream[PLAY], Carl Jr's Hamburgers[PLAY], Harry's American Grill and Bar, KFC, Long John Silver, McDonald's
RVCamp N: **Boyd Chevrolet of Yukon (.2 Miles)**
Other N: Hasting's Bookstore, Movies 5, **Wal-Mart[24, RX]**

138 OK4, Yukon, Mustang
Gas S: Conoco[*], Stax[*]
Food N: Denny's, Miller's Crossing
S: Blimpie Subs & Salads (Conoco), Sonic Drive-In
Lodg N: Comfort Inn
ATM S: Conoco, **Homeland Grocery Store**
Other S: **Homeland Grocery Store**

140 Morgan Road (Eastbound)
TStop N: **T/A TravelCenters of America[*, SCALES]**
S: **Flying J Travel Plaza[*, LP, RV DUMP, SCALES]**
FStop S: **Love's[*, 24]**
Food N: **T/A TravelCenters of America**
S: Grandy's, Sonic, **Subway (Love's)**
TServ N: **Double L Car and Truck Tires[24]**, **T/A TravelCenters of America[SCALES]**
TWash N: **Double L Car and Truck Tires**
ATM S: **Love's**

142 Council Road
TStop S: **T/A TravelCenters of America[*, RV DUMP, SCALES]**
Gas N: Sinclair[*, 24], Texaco[*]
Food N: Braum's Ice Cream, McDonald's, Stan's BBQ, Taco Bell, Waffle House, Wendy's
S: **Burger King (TA Travel Centers of America)**, **Country Pride (TA Travel Centers of America)**, **T/A TravelCenters of America**
Lodg N: Best Budget Inn
S: **EconoLodge**
AServ S: Superior Chassis Auto Repair
TServ S: **J & J Fleet Service**, **Oklahoma Transport Refridgeration**, **T/A TravelCenters of America[SCALES]**
TWash S: **TruckoMat Truck Wash (TA Travel Centers of America)**
RVCamp N: **Motley RV Repair (.5 Miles)**
S: **Council Road RV Park**
Med N: **+ Hospital**
ATM N: Texaco

143 Rockwell Ave
Gas S: Interstate Gas & Grocery[*, D, LP]
Lodg N: Rockwell Inn
S: **Sands Motel & A-OK RV Park**
TServ N: **Truck Pro**
RVCamp N: **McClain's RV Superstore[LP]**
S: **Rockwell RV Park**, **Sands RV Park**
ATM N: All America Bank
Other N: TF Enterprises (CB Shop)

144 MacArthur Blvd.
FStop S: **Sinclair[*]**
Gas N: Texaco[*]
S: Texaco[*]
Food S: Ruby's Restaurant Country Grill (Quality Inn), Signature Cuisine (Italian/American)
Lodg S: Quality Inn, Super 10 Motel, TraveLodge
TServ N: **Cummins Onan Diesel[D]**, **Southwest Trailers & Equipment**
S: **Oklahoma Kenworth Dealership[24]**, **Rush Truck Center (Peterbilt & Volvo)**, **Thompson Diesel Specialists**
ATM S: Texaco
Other S: **Garden Ridge**, Sam's Club

145 Meridian Ave.
TStop N: **Freightliner**
Gas N: Conoco[*, CW], Texaco[*, D, CW]
S: Phillips 66[*], Total[*, D]
Food N: Applewood's, Boomerang Grille, Denny's, Junie's Sports Bar & Grill (American), McDonald's[PLAY], Outback Steakhouse, Radisson Inn, Shorty Small's Ribs, Steak & Ale
S: Bennigan's, Burger King[PLAY], Calhoun's Bar and Grill (La Quinta), **Cracker Barrel**, Kettle, Shoney's, Shoney's
Lodg N: Best Western, Budget Host Inn, Extended Stay America, **Howard Johnson Express Inn (see our ad this page)**, AmeriSuites (see our ad this page)

1304

Oklahoma • Exit 145

RECENTLY RENOVATED
1810

400 S. Meridian Ave • Oaklahoma City, OK
Outdoor Pool • Kids Under 12 Stay Free
Free Continental Breakfast
Truck/Large Vehicle Parking
Airport Shuttle • Interior Corridors
Many Restaurants in Walking Distance
In Room Coffee, Refrigerator • Coin Laundry
Free HBO/Cable/Local Calls • Pets Allowed
Microwave Available (No charge)
405-943-9841 • 800-458-8186
I-40, Exit 145N 1/2 Block. Hotel on Right
OKLAHOMA ▪ I-40 ▪ EXIT 145

Oklahoma City
1635

Special Tour Packages & Rates
Continental Breakfast
Outdoor Pool
Meeting/Banquet Facilities
Pets Allowed
Free Local Calls
Satellite TV
Handicap Accessible
Tennis/Golf Nearby
Bus Parking
Airport Shuttle
Coin Laundry

405-947-8721
OKLAHOMA ▪ I-40 ▪ EXIT 145

Radisson Inn, Red Roof Inn, Super 8, Traveler's Inn
S: Clarion Hotel, Comfort Inn & Suites, Courtyard by Marriott, **Days Inn (see our ad this page)**, Executive Inn, La Quinta Inn, Motel 6, Motel 6, Sleep Inn
ATM N: Texaco
S: First Oklahoma Bank
Other S: Celebration Station

146 Portland Ave. (Eastbound, Reaccess Westbound Only)
Other N: Whitewater Bay (Water Park)

147A Jct I-44W, South Bypass, Lawton, Dallas (Left Exit)

147B Jct I-44E, OK3W, Tulsa, Wichita (Left Exit Eastbound)

147C May Ave, Fair Park (Westbound, Reaccess Eastbound Only)
Gas N: Total[*]
Food N: Chubby's Old Time Diner
AServ N: Southwest Pickup Salvage, Willard's Batteries
TServ N: **Truck Repair**

148A Agnew Ave, Villa Ave
FStop N: **Fuelman (Automated Fuel)**
Gas S: Total[*, CW]
Food S: **Braum's Ice Cream**, Taco Bell (Total), The Rib Stand
AServ N: Aging & Older Imports (Parts), Delta Transmissions
S: Freddie's Discount Tires, Mobile Auto Repair, Mr. Pickup
TServ N: **HD Copeland International**, **Lub-A-Truck**, **Sooner State Used Trucks**
Other S: Thompson Inland Marine

148B Pennsylvania Ave (Eastbound)
TServ S: **HD Copeland International**

148C Virginia Ave. (Westbound, Reaccess Eastbound Only)

149A Western Ave, Reno Ave. (Difficult Reaccess)
Gas S: Gas[*, D], Phillips 66[*, D]
Food S: Burger King
AServ S: Lumas Batteries
TServ S: **Commercial Trailer & Parts**

149B Classen Blvd. (Westbound, Difficult Reaccess)
Gas N: Total[*, D, CW]
Food N: McDonald's, Subway (Total), Taco Bell

150A Walker Ave. (Eastbound, Difficult Reaccess)
Gas S: Phillips 66[*]

150B Harvey Ave (Eastbound, Difficult Reaccess)
Other S: **U.S. Post Office**

150C Downtown, Robinson Ave (Westbound, Difficult Reaccess)
AServ N: **Fred Jones Ford Truck**
TServ N: **Fred Jones Ford Truck**

151A Lincoln Blvd (Eastbound)

151B Jct I-35S, Dallas

151C I-35N, OK Health Center, State Capital, Edmond

Note: I-40 runs concurrent below with I-35. Numbering follows I-35.

127 Eastern Ave
TStop N: **Petro Travel Plaza[*, SCALES]**, **Pilot[*, SCALES, 24]**

Bold red print shows RV & Bus parking available or nearby

EXIT OKLAHOMA

Gas N: Texaco[*]
Food N: Gary Dale's BBQ, Iron Skillet Restaurant (Petro Travel Plaza), Waffle House, Wendy's (Pilot)
Lodg N: Best Western, Central Plaza Hotel & Convention Center
TWash N: Blue Beacon (Petro Travel Plaza)
RVCamp N: Lewis RV Center Sales & Service

128 Jct I-40 E, Fort Smith (Left Exit Southbound)

Note: I-40 runs concurrent above with I-35. Numbering follows I-35.

154 Scott St, Reno Ave.
Gas N: Conoco[*], Sinclair
S: 7-11 Convenience Store[*], Phillips 66[*, CW]
AServ N: Sinclair
RVCamp S: G & G RV Parts & Service
Other N: Comet Go-Cart Rides

155A Sunny Lane Road, Del City
FStop N: Total[*]
Gas S: Stovall's
Food S: Braum's, Pizza Hut
AServ N: Jim's Auto Center
S: Stovall's
Med S: ✚ Lassater Clinic
Parks N: Ray Trent Park[PLAY]
Other N: Murphy's Car Wash[CW], U-Haul[LP]

155B SE15th St, Del City, Midwest City
Gas N: Texaco[*, D, CW]
Food S: Ashley's Country-Style Cookin'
AServ S: Instant Radiator Exchange
ATM N: Baker's Supermarket[RX], Texaco
Other N: Baker's Supermarket[RX]
S: Fire Station

156A Sooner Road
Gas N: Conoco[*, CW], Texaco[*]
Food N: Bristol Station, Cracker Barrel, TD Rays
Lodg N: Clarion Inn, Comfort Inn, Hampton Inn, La Quinta Inn, Sixpence Inn

156B Hudiburg Rd.
Lodg S: Motel 6
AServ S: Hudiburg Chev, Pont, GMC
ATM N: Tinker Credit Union
Other N: Planet Bowl

157A SE 29th St, Mid-West City (Eastbound, Reaccess Westbound Only)
AServ S: Joe Cooper Truck Center (Ford)
Other S: Sam's Club

157B Air Depot Blvd.
FStop N: Texaco[*, CW]
Gas N: Conoco[*, D]
Food N: Al's Diner (Super 8 Motel), Asian Cuisine, Mr. Spriggs BBQ & Burgers, Pizza Inn
Lodg N: Super 8
AServ N: NAPA Auto Parts, O'Reilly Auto Parts, S & S Muffler Center
Med N: ✚ Hospital, ✚ Hospital
ATM N: FNB Bank, Texaco
Other N: Midwest Farm & Home Pet Vet Supply
S: Tinker Air Force Base

157C Eaker Gate - Tinker Air Force Base, Welcome Center
Gas N: Diamond Shamrock[*]
Food N: Eggroll Express Chinese, Jim's BBQ, Sub Stop
Lodg N: Sheffield Inn
AServ N: Firestone Tire & Auto

159A Hruskocy Gate - Tinker Air Force Base

159B Lancer Gate, Liberator Gate, Marauder Gate - Tinker Air Force Base, Douglas Blvd
Gas N: Conoco[*, D], Phillips 66[*, CW]
S: Conoco[*]
Food N: Acropolis Greek Restaurant, Denny's, McDonald's[PLAY], Sonic, Subway, Taco Bell
RVCamp N: Eastland Hills Campground, Lee's RV Service, Universal RV
ATM N: Phillips 66
Other N: Highlander Center Coin Laundry

162 Anderson Road
Other N: Lundy's[LP]

165 Jct I-240 West, Lawton, Dallas, Amarillo (Westbound)

166 Choctaw Road
TStop S: Bruce's AM Best Travel Plaza[SCALES] (Texaco)
FStop N: Love's[*]
Food N: Taco Bell Express (Love's)
RVCamp N: KOA Kampground (.75 Miles)
ATM N: Love's
S: Bruce's AM Best Travel Plaza (Texaco)

169 Peebly Rd.

172 Harrah, Newalla Road

176 OK102N, McLoud Road
FStop S: Carl and Velma's General Store[*, D]
Gas S: Love's[*, 24]
Food S: Curtis Watson's Restaurant

178 OK102S, Bethel Acres, Dale
FStop S: Kerr McGee[*]

181 U.S. 177, U.S. 270, OK3W, Stillwater, Tecumseh, Shawnee (Limited Access Hwy)
Gas S: Conoco[*, D]
Food S: Mia Casa Mexican

185 OK3E, Shawnee, Kickapoo St.
Gas S: Phillips 66[*, CW]
Food N: Luby's Cafeteria, Red Lobster, Taco Bueno
S: Charlie's Chicken, McDonald's, SHONEY'S Shoney's
Lodg S: Hampton Inn
AServ N: Wal-Mart (Shawnee Mall)
Med N: ✚ Hospital
ATM S: Phillips 66
Other N: Shawnee Mall, Wal-Mart (Shawnee Mall)
S: Lowe's Hardware

186 OK18, Shawnee, Meeker
Gas N: Citgo[*, D], Texaco[*]
Food N: City Lights (Ramada Inn), Denny's
Lodg N: American Inn, Days Inn, Motel 6, Ramada Inn
S: TraveLodge

192 OK9A, Earlsboro
FStop S: Texaco[*, LP]
Food S: Biscuit Hill Restaurant
Lodg S: Rodeway Inn

(197) Rest Area (RR, Phones, Picnic, RV Dump, P; Eastbound)

(197) Rest Area (RR, HF, Phones, Picnic, RV Dump, P; Westbound)

200 U.S. 377, OK99, Prague, Seminole
TStop N: Phillips 66[*, RV DUMP, SCALES, 24]
FStop S: Citgo[*], Conoco[*, D], Love's[*, 24]
Food S: Robertson's Hams, Round-Up RV Park, Subway (Love's)
TServ N: Phillips 66[SCALES, 24]
RVCamp S: Round-Up RV Park
ATM N: Phillips 66

212 OK56, Wewoka, Cromwell
FStop N: Conoco[*]
Gas S: Texaco[*, D]
Food S: Texaco
AServ N: Danny's Auto Center
RVCamp S: Camping

217 OK48, Bristow, Holdenville
FStop S: Total[D]
Gas N: Total[*]
Food S: Derrick Cafe
AServ S: Total
RVCamp N: Camping
Other N: Historical Museum (Total)

221 OK27, Okemah, Wetumka
TStop S: K-Bar[*, 24]
FStop N: Conoco[*], Total[*]
S: Love's[*]
Gas S: Texaco[*]
Food N: Aspen Restaurant, Mazzio's Pizza, Sonic, Subway (Total)
S: A & W Hot Dogs & More (Love's), K-Bar, Taco Bell (Love's)
Lodg N: OK Motor Lodge
AServ N: Big A Auto Parts
TServ S: K-Bar[24], Truck Shop
RVCamp S: Bleeker's RV Park
Med S: ✚ Hospital
ATM N: Conoco
Other N: Car Wash[CW]

227 Clearview Road

231 U.S. 75S, Weleetka
FStop N: Phillips 66[*]
Food N: Cowpoke's Cafe[24]

237 U.S. 62, U.S. 75, Henryetta, Bus. Loop 40
FStop N: Kelloggs Handy Mart[*], Texaco[*]
Food N: Cal Creek Ranch House Restaurant[24]
S: Hungry Traveler
Lodg N: Sleepy Traveler Motel, Trail Motel
S: Super 8
AServ N: Texaco
TServ N: Sanford's Truck Wash
Med N: ✚ Hospital
ATM N: Texaco

240AB Indian Nation Turnpike, Dallas, U.S. 62E, U.S. 75N, Henryetta, McAlester, Okmulgee, Tulsa
Gas N: Citgo
Lodg N: Gateway Inn, Le Baron Motel
AServ N: Citgo
Med N: ✚ Hospital

247 Tiger Mt. Road

(251) Rest Area (P; Eastbound)

(251) Rest Area (P; Westbound)

255 Pierce Road
RVCamp N: KOA Kampground (.5 Miles)

259 OK150, Fountainhead Road
Gas S: Citgo[LP], Lakeway Station & Store[*], Texaco[*]
Lodg S: Best Western
AServ S: Citgo, Lakeway Station & Store
Parks S: Fountain Head State Park

262 To U.S. 266, Lotawatah Road
FStop N: Conoco[*]
Gas N: Phillips 66[*]
ATM N: Conoco

264AB U.S. 69, Eufaula, Muskogee (Limited Access Hwy)

265 Bus. U.S. 69, Checotah
FStop N: Texaco[*]
S: Citgo[*], Phillips 66[*, D, LP]
Food S: Sub San Express (Citgo), Taco Shack (Citgo)

Bold red print shows RV & Bus parking available or nearby

EXIT	OKLAHOMA
Lodg	**S:** Budget Host Inn
AServ	**N:** Texaco
RVCamp	**N:** Checotah Holiday Park
Other	**S:** Thomas Marine
270	Texanna Road, Porum Landing
FStop	**S:** 10(*)
278	U.S. 266, OK2, Warner, Muskogee
FStop	**N:** Texaco(*, LP)
Food	**N:** Big Country Restaurant (Western Sands Motel)
Lodg	**N:** Western Sands Motel
(283)	Parking Area (Eastbound)
284	Ross Road
286	Muskogee Turnpike, Muskogee, Tulsa
287	OK100N, Webbers Falls, Gore
FStop	**N:** Love's(*, 24)
Food	**N:** Charlie's Chicken, Subway (Love's), Taco Bell Express (Love's)
Lodg	**N:** Super 8
AServ	**N:** Firestone Service & Tire (CB Shop)
TServ	**N:** Firestone Service & Tire (CB Shop)
ATM	**N:** Love's
Other	**N:** Brewers Bend Lock & Dam (8 Miles), OK Trading Post, Webber Falls Lake (8 Miles)
291	OK10N, Gore, Carlile Road
Parks	**N:** Green Leaf State Park (13 Miles), Ten Killer Reacreation Area (14 Miles)
Other	**N:** Cherokee Nation Information Center (2 Miles)
297	OK82N, Vian, Tahlequah
Gas	**N:** Phillips 66(*, CW)
Parks	**S:** Sequoia Wild Life Area
303	Dwight Mission Road, Blue Ribbon Downs
308	U.S. 59, Bus. Loop 40, Sallisaw, Poteau, Blue Ribbon Downs
FStop	**N:** Phillips 66(*)
	S: Texaco(*, SCALES)
Gas	**N:** Total(*)
Food	**N:** Braum's, Dana's Restaurant, Jr's Dinner Bell (Best Western), McDonald's, Phillips 66, Western Sizzlin'
Lodg	**N:** Best Western, McKnight Motel, Super 8
RVCamp	**S:** KOA Kampground (.5 Miles)
ATM	**S:** Texaco
Parks	**N:** Brushy Lake State Park (8 Miles)
311	U.S. 64, Sallisaw, Stilwell
TStop	**N:** Fina(*)
Gas	**N:** Phillips 66(*), Texaco(*)
Food	**N:** Pizza Hut, Simple Simon's Pizza, Taco Mayo, The Fig Tree Restaurant (Fina)

EXIT	OKLAHOMA/ARKANSAS
Lodg	**N:** EconoLodge
Parks	**N:** Brushy Lake State Park (10 Miles), Sequoyah's Cabin
(313)	OK Welcome Center (RR, HF, Phones, Picnic, RV Dump, P; Westbound)
(316)	Rest Area (RR, HF, Phones, Picnic, RV Dump, P; Eastbound)
321	OK64B North, Muldrow
TStop	**N:** Texaco(*, 24)
	S: Curt's Oil Co.(*)
Food	**N:** Texaco
	S: Carolyn's Restaurant
Lodg	**S:** Gold Crown Motel (Curt's Oil Co.)
TServ	**S:** Kerr's Truck Wash
TWash	**S:** Kerr's Truck Wash
325	U.S. 64, Roland, Ft. Smith
TStop	**N:** Total(*, SCALES)
FStop	**S:** Conoco(*, CW)
Gas	**S:** Fina(*)
Food	**N:** Best Western, Total
	S: McDonald's (Conoco)
Lodg	**N:** Best Western, DAYS INN Days Inn
	S: Interstate Inn
AServ	**S:** Fina
ATM	**N:** Total
Other	**S:** Fort Smith National Historic Site (6 Miles)
330	OK64D South, Dora, Ft. Smith (Eastbound, Reaccess Eastbound Only)

↑OKLAHOMA

↓ARKANSAS

1	Dora, Ft. Smith (Westbound, Difficult Reaccess)
(2)	AR Welcome Center (RR, Phones, Picnic, P; Eastbound)
3	Lee Creek Road
5	AR59, Van Buren, Siloam Springs (AR59 Closed To Trucks)
TStop	**S:** AmBest Texco(*, SCALES)
FStop	**S:** Texaco(*)
Gas	**N:** Exxon(*), Total(*, D)
	S: Citgo(*)
Food	**S:** Big Jake's Cattle Co. Steakhouse, Braum's Ice Cream(PLAY), Hardee's(PLAY), Little Caesars Pizza, Mazzio's Pizza, Subway, Taco Bell, Waffle House, Wendy's
Lodg	**N:** Holiday Inn Express

EXIT	ARKANSAS
	S: Motel 6, Super 8
AServ	**S:** Crawford County Ford Dealership, Texaco
TServ	**N:** Arkansas Kenworth, Peterbilt of Van Buren
TWash	**S:** AmBest Texco
RVCamp	**S:** Outdoor Living Center(LP), Overland RV Park
ATM	**S:** Citizen's Bank
Parks	**N:** Lee Creek Dam Tailwater Recreation Area
7	I-540S, U.S. 71S, Van Buren, Fort Smith (Limited Access Hwy)
(9)	Weigh Station (Westbound)
(9)	Weigh Station (Eastbound)
12	AR540N, Fayetteville, Lake Ft. Smith State Park (Limited Access Hwy)
Parks	**N:** Lake Ft. Smith State Park
13	U.S. 71, Alma
TStop	**S:** Gold Truck Stop(*, SCALES)
FStop	**S:** Citgo(*)
Gas	**N:** BP(*), Exxon(*), Phillips 66(*, D), Shell(*)
	S: Total(*)
Food	**N:** Burger King, KFC, Mazzio's Pizza, Meadors Motor Inn, Taco Bell
	S: Braum's, McDonald's, Ozark Restaurant (Gold Truck Stop), Piccadilly Circus Pizza & Subs (Citgo), Sonic, Subway
Lodg	**N:** Alma Inn, Meadors Motor Inn
	S: DAYS INN Days Inn
AServ	**N:** Exxon
	S: O'Reilly Auto Parts
TServ	**S:** Gold Truck Stop(SCALES), Ideal Motor Co.
TWash	**S:** Gold Truck Stop
RVCamp	**N:** Alma RV Park, KOA-Fort Smith/Alma (2.5 Miles)
Med	**S:** ✚ Quick Care Immediate Medical Care
ATM	**N:** Bank of the Ozarks
	S: Citgo, Citizen's Bank
Parks	**N:** Lake Ft. Smith State Park
	S: Clear Creek Park
Other	**S:** Alma Pharmacy(RX), CV's Family Foods
20	Dyer, Mulberry
FStop	**N:** Conoco(*, D)
	S: Citgo(*)
Gas	**S:** Texaco
TServ	**S:** Semi Trailer Repair
24	AR215, Mulberry
Parks	**S:** Vine Prairie Park (4 Miles)
35	AR23, Ozark, Huntsville
Med	**S:** ✚ Hospital
Parks	**S:** Aux Arc Park (5 Miles)
(35)	Rest Area (RR, HF, Phones, Grills, P; Eastbound)
(36)	Rest Area (RR, Phones, Picnic, P; Westbound)

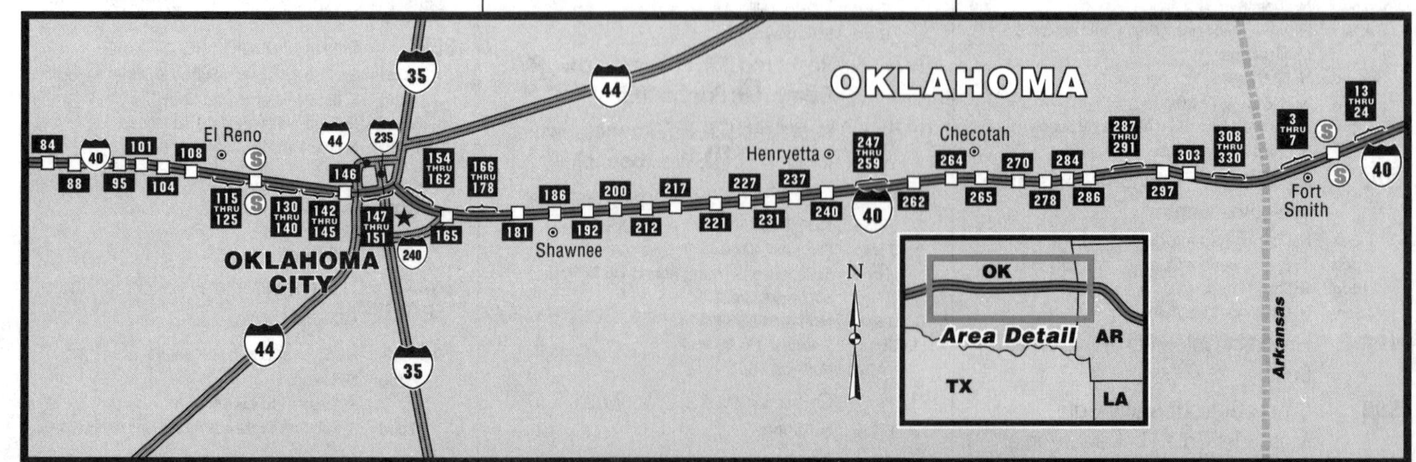

Bold red print shows RV & Bus parking available or nearby

EXIT ARKANSAS

37 AR219, Ozark
- **FStop** S: Love's(*)
- **Food** S: A & W Hot Dogs & More (Love's), Subway (Love's)
- **RVCamp** S: McNutt RV Park (.5 Miles), Ozark Crafts & Marketplace & RV Park (.75 Miles)
- **Med** S: Hospital
- **ATM** S: Love's

41 AR186, Altus
- **RVCamp** S: Camping

47 AR164, Coal Hill, Hartman

55 U.S. 64, Clarksville, AR109, Scranton
- **FStop** S: Exxon(*)
- **Gas** N: Citgo(*, D), Exit 55 Grill, Phillips 66(*, D)
- **Food** N: BBQ Steak & Carrot Cake, Hardee's(PLAY), Lotus Chinese
  S: Hot Stuff Pizza (Exxon), Smash Hit Subs (Exxon), Western Sizzlin'
- **Lodg** N: Days Inn, Hampton Inn
- **AServ** N: U-Haul
- **Other** N: Clarksville Cinema
  S: AR State Police

57 Clarksville

58 AR103, AK21, Clarksville
- **TStop** S: Texaco(*)
- **Gas** N: Phillips 66(*), Texaco(*)
- **Food** N: KFC, Mazzio's Pizza, McDonald's(PLAY), Ole South Pancake House, Wendy's, Woodard's Family Restaurant
  S: South Park Restaurant (Texaco TS)
- **Lodg** N: Best Western, Comfort Inn, Economy Inn, Super 8
- **AServ** N: J & S Tire Center, Johnson Chev, Olds, Buick, Pontiac, Tailer Road Oil X-Change
  S: Whitson-Morgan Ford, Merc, Chrys, Plym, Dodge, Jeep
- **TServ** S: Texaco
- **Med** N: Hospital
- **Parks** S: Spadra Park & Marina (2.5 Miles)
- **Other** N: The Gazebo Mall (Antiques)
  S: Yarbrough Orchards (Farmer's Market)

64 U.S. 64, Lamar
- **Gas** S: Texaco(*, D, LP)
- **RVCamp** S: Dad's Dream RV Park (Texaco)

67 AR315, Knoxville

(68) Rest Area (RR, Phones, Picnic, Grills, Vending, P; Eastbound)

(70) Parking Area (Picnic, P; Westbound)

74 AR333, London

78 U.S. 64, Russellville, Lake Dardanelle State Park (Eastbound, Reaccess Westbound Only)
- **Med** S: Hospital
- **Parks** S: Lake Dardanelle State Park (2 Miles)

81 AR7, Russellville
- **Gas** N: Conoco(*, D, LP)
  S: Exxon(*, D), Texaco(*, D, CW), Texaco(*, CW)
- **Food** N: Coffee Mill Cafe, The Supper Club, Waffle House
  S: Burger King, Cracker Barrel, New China, Ole South Pancake House, Pizza Inn, SHONEY'S Shoney's (Best Western), Subway, The Dixie Cafe, Waffle House(24)
- **Lodg** N: Motel 6, Ramada Limited, Sunrise Inn
  S: Best Western, Budget Inn, Hampton Inn, Holiday Inn, Southern Inn, Super 8
- **AServ** N: Conoco
- **RVCamp** N: Outdoor Living Center RV Park, Outdoor Living Center(LP)

EXIT ARKANSAS

- **Med** N: Hospital
- **ATM** S: Texaco
- **Other** N: Bower Marine
  S: Antique Mall, Arkansas Tech University, Lake Dardanell State Park, Russellville Christian Center

84 U.S. 64, AR331, Russellville
- **TStop** N: Flying J Travel Plaza(*, LP, RV DUMP, SCALES)
- **FStop** N: Texaco(*)
  S: Mapco Express(*) (see our ad this page)
- **Gas** S: Texaco(*, CW)
- **Food** N: The Cookery (Flying J TS)
  S: Baskin Robbins (Mapco Express), Hardee's, McDonald's, Perkin's Family Restaurant (Mapco Express)
- **Lodg** S: Comfort Inn
- **AServ** N: Texaco
  S: Wal-Mart
- **TServ** N: Barton's Freightliner Sales & Parts
  S: Diamond International Trucks (Detroit Diesel, Cummins, CAT)
- **TWash** N: Flying J Travel Plaza
- **ATM** N: Texaco
  S: Mapco Express, Texaco
- **Other** S: Lowe's Hardware, U.P.S., Wal-Mart

88 Pottsville
- **TServ** S: Gala Creek Truck Center
- **Other** S: Gala Creek Wildlife Management (5 Miles)

94 AR105, Atkins
- **FStop** S: Phillips 66(*, D)
- **Gas** N: BP(*, D), Citgo(*, D)
- **Food** N: Chicken & More, Hardee's (BP), Sonic Drive-In, Subway (Citgo), Tastee Burger, The Pizza Meister
  S: Loner Drive-In
- **AServ** S: Ron's Auto Repair
- **TServ** N: J & I Truck Accessories
- **TWash** S: General Jack's Water Works
- **ATM** N: BP
  S: First Arkansas Valley Bank
- **Other** S: Medicine Shoppe, Sav-On-Foods, U.S. Post Office

101 Blackwell

107 AR95, Morrilton
- **FStop** N: Citgo(*, LP, CW)
  S: Love's(*)
- **Gas** S: Phillips 66(*), Shell(*)
- **Food** N: Chester Fried Chicken (Citgo), Scottish Inns
  S: A & W Hot Dogs & More (Love's), Baskin Robbins (Love's), Mom and Pop's Waffles (Shell), Morrilton Drive-In, Yesterday's Restaurant & Bar
- **Lodg** N: Scottish Inns
  S: Days Inn
- **RVCamp** N: KOA Kampground (.5 Miles)

108 AR9, Morrilton

EXIT ARKANSAS

- **Gas** S: Phillips 66(*), Shell(*)
- **Food** S: KFC, McDonald's, Pizza Hut, Pizza Pro, Subway, Sweeden's Betterburger, Waffle House (Super 8 Motel)
- **Lodg** S: Super 8
- **AServ** S: Lentz Truck Shop & Car Care Parts, McConnell-Dew Chev, Pont, Olds, Buick, GMC Trucks
- **TServ** S: Lentz Truck Shop & Car Care Parts
- **Med** S: Conway Co. Hospital
- **ATM** S: Morrilton Security Bank
- **Parks** S: Petit Jean State Park (21 Miles)
- **Other** S: Brown Animal Hospital, Fire Station, Splash Car Wash(CW)

(109) Rest Area (RR, HF, Phones, Picnic, P; Eastbound)

(109) Rest Area (RR, HF, Phones, Picnic, P; Westbound)

112 AR92N, Plumerville
- **Gas** N: Total(*, LP)
- **Food** N: Payton Creek Catfish House Too

117 Menifee

124 AR25N, Conway (Reaccess Westbound Only)
- **Gas** S: Mocking Bird(*, LP), Texaco(*, D)
- **Food** S: Mr. Goodcents Subs and Pasta
- **Med** S: Hospital
- **Other** S: Animal Care Veterinary Center, Christian Book Outlet, Fire Station, PK's Bait Shop(LP), Pet Country

125 U.S. 65N, U.S. 65B S, Conway, Greenbrier, Harrison
- **Gas** N: Conoco(*, D), Shell(*, D), Texaco(*, CW)
  S: Citgo(*, CW), Exxon(*)
- **Food** N: China Town, Cracker Barrel, El Acapulco, El Chico Mexican Restaurant, Hardee's, McDonald's, Ole South Family Restaurant(24), Subway (Texaco)
  S: Backyard Burgers, Baskin Robbins(PLAY), Burger King(PLAY), Fazoli's Italian Food, Hart's Seafood, Holiday Inn, McAlister's Gourmet Deli, McDonald's (Wal-Mart), Ryan's Steakhouse, Waffle House, Wendy's
- **Lodg** N: Comfort Inn
  S: Holiday Inn, Motel 6, Super 8
- **AServ** S: Conway Tire & Battery, McKaskle Tire Service
- **ATM** N: First National Bank, First National Bank, Superior Federal Bank
  S: First Community Bank, NationsBank
- **Other** N: Cinema 6, Hastings, The Wildside Pet Store, Visioncare Arkansas
  S: Lowe's Hardware, Wal-Mart(24, RX)

127 U.S. 64, Conway, Vilonia, Beebe
- **Gas** N: Citgo(*, CW)
  S: RaceTrac(24), Texaco(*, D, CW), Total(*, LP)
- **Food** N: Frontier Diner (Best Western), Waffle House
  S: Burger King, Dillon's Steakhouse & Grill, Happy Inn Chinese, Hardee's, KFC, McDonald's, Shipley Donuts, Subway (Texaco), Taco Bell, Western Sizzlin'
- **Lodg** N: Best Western, Days Inn, Economy Inn, Hampton Inn, Ramada Inn
  S: Knight's Inn
- **AServ** N: Honda World, Jodi Brown Pont, Olds, GMC Trucks, Buick, John Walters Chevrolet, Karpro Auto Parts, Smith Ford, Linc, Mercury, Tires For Less
  S: Auto Zone Auto Parts, Country Cousins Muffler Shop
- **RVCamp** N: Moix RV
- **ATM** S: Kroger Supermarket(RX)
- **Other** S: Alco Discount Store, Faulkner 6 Cinema, Hobby Lobby, Kroger Supermarket(RX)

EXIT ARKANSAS

129 U.S. 65B, AR286, Conway
- **FStop** S: **Mapco Express**(*, LP)
- **Gas** S: Exxon(*)
- **AServ** S: Midas Muffler & Brake
- **Parks** S: **Toad Suck Park**
- **Other** S: Duncan Outdoors Inc.

Exit **(133)** AR Hwy. Police Inspection Station (Westbound, All Trucks Must Exit)

Exit **(133)** AR Hwy. Police Inspection Station (Eastbound, All Trucks Must Exit)

135 AR89, AR365, Mayflower
- **Gas** N: Phillip 66 - Bates Field & Stream Inc.(*)
  S: Fina(*), Sinclair(*)
- **Food** S: Glory B's Catfish, Mayflower Diner
- **AServ** S: R's Tires
- **RVCamp** N: **Mayflower RV (2 Miles)**

142 AR365, Morgan, Maumelle
- **FStop** N: **Shell**(*, LP), **Total**(*)
  S: **Texaco**(*, SCALES)
- **Food** N: **Taco Bell (Total)**
  S: **A & W Hot Dogs & More (Texaco)**, BJ'S Family Buffet, **I-40 Restaurant**, KFC, McDonald's, Subway, Waffle House
- **Lodg** N: DAYS INN Days Inn
  S: Comfort Suites Hotel
- **TWash** S: **Texaco**
- **RVCamp** N: **Lazy S RV Park**
- **Other** N: Kodiac CB Shop, Worldwide Optical

147 Jct I-430S, Texarkana

148 AR 100, Crystal Hill Road
- **FStop** S: **Citgo**(*)
- **Gas** N: Texaco(*)
  S: Total(*, LP)
- **RVCamp** S: **KOA-Little Rock North (1 Mile)**
- **Other** N: Hatchet Jack's Bait & Tackle(LP)

150 AR176, Burns Park, Camp Robinson, Camp Pike
- **RVCamp** N: **Campground**
  S: **Burns Park (.25 Miles)**
- **Parks** N: **Burns Park**
  S: **Burns Park**
- **Other** S: NLR Animal Shelter

152 AR365, Levy, AR 176 East (Reaccess Westbound Only)
- **Gas** N: Conoco(*)
- **Food** N: Dixie Pig, Eggroll Express Chinese, Jo-Jo's BBQ, Sonic Drive-In, U.S. Pizza Co.
- **AServ** N: Bryant Bro's Service Center, CB Auto Parts
- **Med** S: ✚ **Baptist Memorial Medical Center**, ✚ **VA Medical Center**

EXIT ARKANSAS

- **ATM** N: Mercantile Bank
- **Other** N: Art's Marine, Eye Clinic, Fire Station, Mainline Cycle Parts & Accessories, My Pet Shop, Stanley Hardware

153A AR107N, JFK Blvd, Main St
- **Gas** N: Shell(*, CW)
  S: Exxon(*, CW)
- **Food** S: Bonanza Steakhouse, Country Kitchen (Ramada Inn), Hardee's, Shipley Do-Nuts, Waffle House
- **Lodg** N: Masters Inn
  S: Country Inn & Suites, Hampton Inn, Holiday Inn, Motel 6, Ramada Inn
- **ATM** N: NationsBank, Shell
- **Other** N: Park Hill Pet Clinic
  S: Dolly Madison Bakery, North Little Rock Police Dept., **Robertson's Pharmacy**(RX), **U.S. Post Office**, Wash-Away(CW)

153B West I-30, U.S. 65S, Little Rock

154 Lakewood (Eastbound, Reaccess Westbound Only)

155 U.S. 67, U.S. 167N, Jacksonville
- **Food** N: SHONEY'S Shoney's

157 AR161, Prothro Road
- **TStop** N: **Mid-State Truck Plaza**(SCALES)
- **FStop** S: **Citgo**(*)
- **Gas** N: Conoco(*), Exxon
  S: Texaco(*, D), Total(*, D)
- **Food** S: Burger King, Fred's Place, **McDonald's**, Taco Bell, Waffle House
- **Lodg** S: **Masters Inn**, **Super 8**
- **AServ** N: Exxon
- **TWash** N: **Mid-State**

159 Jct I-440W, LR River Port, Texakana

161 AR391, Galloway
- **TStop** S: **76 Auto/Truck Plaza**(*, D, LP, SCALES) **(Showers)**, **Pilot Travel Center**(SCALES) **(Cars Only)**, **TruckoMat**(D, SCALES)
- **FStop** N: **Love's Country Store**(*, D)
- **Gas** S: Shell
- **Food** N: **A & W Drive-In (Love's)**, **Taco Bell (Love's)**
  S: **Dairy Queen (Pilot)**, **Subway (Pilot)**
- **TServ** S: **76**
- **TWash** S: **76**, **Blue Beacon Truck Wash**

165 Kerr Road

169 AR15, Remington Road, Cabot

(170) Truck Inspection Station

175 AR31, Lonoke
- **FStop** N: **Citgo**(*, D)
  S: **Total**(*, D)
- **Gas** S: Shell(*, D)
- **Food** N: **McDonald's**(PLAY)

EXIT ARKANSAS

  S: KFC, Taco Bell
- **Lodg** N: DAYS INN Days Inn
  S: **Economy Inn**
- **ATM** N: Citgo

183 AR13, Carlisle
- **FStop** S: **Conoco**(*, D), **Phillips 66**(*, D)
- **Gas** S: Exxon, Texaco(*)
- **Food** S: **KFC (Phillips 66)**, Nick's BBQ & Catfish, Pizza & More, **Pizza Masters Express (Conoco)**
- **Lodg** S: **Best Western**
- **ATM** S: Conoco

193 AR11, Hazen, Des Arc, Stuttgart, De Vaees, Clarendon
- **TStop** S: **Shell**(*, D) **(Showers, Overnight Parking)**
- **Gas** N: Exxon(*)
- **Food** N: Exxon Restaurant
- **Lodg** S: Super 8

(198) **Rest Area (RR, Phones, P)**

(199) **Rest Area (RR, Vending, P; Westbound)**

202 AK33, Biscoe

216 U.S. 49, AR17, Brinkley, Cotton Point, Helena, Jonesboro
- **RVCamp** N: **Super 8 Motel and RV Park**
  S: **Good Sam's RV Park**, **Heritage Inn Camper Park**

221 AR78, Wheatley, Marianna
- **TStop** N: **Holmes Truckstop**(*, D), **Phillips 66**(*, D)
- **FStop** S: **Delta Express**(*, D), **Shell Super Stop**(*, D)
- **Gas** N: Exxon(*)
- **Food** S: **KFC (Shell)**, **Subway (Delta Express)**
- **TServ** N: **Holmes Auto Service and Truck Service**, **I-40 Truck and Tire Repair Shop**, **Tire Center (Phillips 66)**
- **TWash** N: **Holmes**

233 AR261, Palestine
- **FStop** S: **Citgo**(*, D), **Fina**(*)
- **Gas** N: Loves(*)
- **Food** N: Subway
  S: **Citgo Restaurant**
- **AServ** S: 24 Hour Tire Shop
- **RVCamp** S: **Camping**

(235) **Rest Area (RR, Phones, P; Eastbound)**

(236) **Rest Area (RR, Phones, P; Westbound)**

241A AR1S, Forrest City, Wynne
- **Gas** S: Citgo(*, CW), Exxon(*), Phillips 66(*), Texaco(*)
- **Food** S: Bonanza Steakhouse, Hardees, **McDonald's**, **McDonald's (Wal-Mart)**, Pizza Hut, Simons Old South Pancake House, Subway, Taco Bell, Waffle

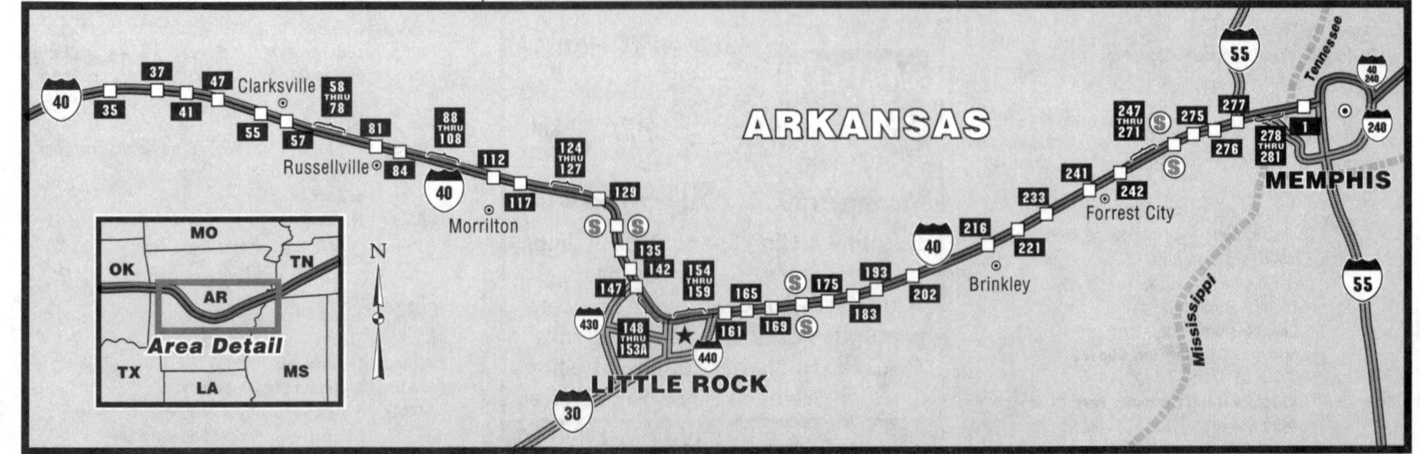

Bold red print shows RV & Bus parking available or nearby

EXIT ARKANSAS

House
Lodg S: Best Western, Colony Inn
ATM S: First National Bank
Other S: Edward's Food Giant, Fred's Discount Pharmacy, Kroger Supermarket, Pay Less Shoe Store, Wal-Mart Supercenter

241B AR1N, Wynne
RVCamp N: Days Inn RV Park (1 Mile)

242 AR284, Crowley's Ridge Road
Med N: ✚ Hospital
Parks N: Village Creek State Park

(243) Rest Area (RR, HF, Phones, Picnic, Vending, P)

247 AR38E, Widener, Hughes
TServ N: Truck Outlet Goodrich Tires

256 AR75, Parkin
FStop N: Delta Express(*, D)
Parks N: Parkin Archeological State Park

260 AR149, Earle
TStop N: T/A TravelCenters of America(SCALES)
FStop N: BP, Phillips 66(*)
Gas S: Texaco(*, CW)
Food N: Country Pride, Subway
Lodg N: Best Western
TServ N: T/A TravelCenters of America(SCALES)
TWash N: BP
RVCamp N: KOA-Memphis West/Shell Lake(*, SCALES)
Other S: Coin Car Wash

265 Marianna Elaina Rd.

271 AR147
FStop S: P J's(*)
Gas S: Exxon(*, D), Texaco(*, D)
Food S: PJ's

(273) Weigh Station

(274) Rest Area (RR, HF, Phones, Picnic, P; Westbound)

275 AR118, Airport Road, West Memphis Airport

276 AR76, Rich Road, Missouri Street (Difficult Reaccess)
Food S: McDonald's (In Walmart)
AServ S: Wal-Mart
Other S: Wal-Mart

277 Junction I-55, N. Blytheville, St Louis (Difficult Reaccess)

278 7th St, West Memphis, AR191
TStop S: Memphis Gateway Auto/Truck Plaza(*, SCALES)
FStop S: Love's(*, 24)
Gas S: Citgo(*)
Food N: Blimpie's Subs (Citgo)

1286

Open 24 Hours

870-732-1340

Gasoline & High Speed Diesel Pumps
Full Service Restaurant
Truck Accessories • Private Showers
Laundry Facilities • ATM Machines
D.A.T. Load Boards • Sandwich Shop
Certified Scales • Copy & Fax Services
ARKANSAS • I-40 • EXIT 280

EXIT ARKANSAS/TENNESSEE

S: Catfish Island, I Can't Believe It's Yogurt (Memphis Gateway TS), McDonald's (Wal-Mart)
Lodg S: Ramada Inn
TServ S: Memphis Gateway Auto/Truck Plaza
RVCamp S: Tom Sawyer's RV Park
ATM S: Love's
Other S: Wal-Mart(24)

279A Ingram Blvd (Difficult Reaccess)
Gas N: BP(*)
S: BP, Citgo(*, CW), Shell(*)
Food N: Delta Point (Days Inn), Grandy's (Days Inn), Little Italy Pizza (Days Inn)
S: Cinnamon Street Bakery (Citgo), Earl's Restaurant, Eddi Pepper's Mexican (Citgo), Holiday Inn Restaurant (Holiday Inn), Hot Stuff Pizza (Citgo), Smash Hit Subs (Citgo), Waffle House, Waffle House
Lodg N: Classic Inn, Comfort Inn, DAYS INN Days Inn
S: Classic Inn, DAYS INN Days Inn, Econolodge, Hampton Inn, Holiday Inn, Holiday Inn, Howard Johnson, Motel 6, Motel 6, Relax Inn, Relax Inn
AServ N: BP
RVCamp S: Rikard & Sons, Inc. (.7 Miles)
Other N: Southwind Greyhound Park
S: Coin Laundry

279B Junction I-55, South Memphis, Jackson, MS

280 Dr Martin Luther King Jr Dr (S. Side Services Are Same As Those On I-55, Ex. 4 East Side)
TStop S: Flying J Travel Plaza(*, LP, RV DUMP, SCALES), Petro(*, SCALES) (Showers, CB Shop, MS Carriers Recruiting Office)
FStop N: Fina(*) (Showers), Mapco(*, LP) (see our ad this page)
S: Pilot Travel Center(*, D, SCALES)
Food S: Dairy Queen (Pilot TS), Iron Skillet Restaurant (Petro TS), KFC, McDonald's, Subway (Pilot TS), Taco Bell
Lodg S: Best Western, Deluxe Inn, Express Inn, Super 8
AServ N: Goodyear Tire & Auto
TServ N: Goodyear Tire & Auto, Riggs Cat Truck Engine Service
S: Bridgestone Tire & Auto (Petro TS), Jim's & Son Truck Service & Parts, Landstar Service Center
TWash S: Blue Beacon Truck Wash (Petro TS), Mr. Clean Truck Wash, XVIII Wheeler's Truck Wash(24)
Other N: Best Tarps
S: CB Shop

281 AR 131, Mound City Road (Westbound)

↑ARKANSAS

↓TENNESSEE

(1) Riverside Dr, Front St, Welcome Center
Food N: TJ Mulligan's
S: Gridiron Restaurant (Comfort Inn)
Lodg S: Comfort Inn, DAYS INN Days Inn (see our ad this page)
Med S: ✚ Hospital
Parks S: Confederate Park, Jefferson Davis Park
Other N: The Pyramid

1A 2nd Street, 3rd Street
Food S: Highpoint Grill
Lodg S: Comfort Inn
Med S: ✚ St Joseph's Hospital

EXIT TENNESSEE

Other S: Memphis Convention Center Complex

1B US 51, Danny Thomas Blvd
Med N: ✚ St. Joseph Hospital, ✚ St. Jude Children's Research Hospital

1C US 51 South, Danny Thomas Blvd (Westbound, Services Same As Previous Exit B)

1D US 51 N, Danny Thomas Blvd (Services Same As Previous Exit B)
Lodg S: Ronald McDonald House

1E I-240 S, Jackson MS, Madison Ave

1FG TN 14, Jackson Ave
Gas S: Exxon(*), Mapco Express(*)
Lodg N: Rainbow Inn
AServ S: Donn's Transmission
ATM S: Mapco Express
Other N: Super Value Foods(RX)
S: Car Wash

2 Chelsea Ave, Smith Ave (Difficult Reaccess)
Gas N: K Corner Grocery
AServ S: Used & Recycled Auto Parts
TServ N: Memphis Trucks Parts and Equipment Inc

2A U.S. 51, Millington (Left Exit Northbound)

3 Watkins St
Gas N: Amoco(*, 24), Citgo(*), Coastal, Gas Express(*, D), Oil City USA(*), Total(*)
S: Gas Express(*)
Food N: Oriental Market Restaurant
Other N: Coin Op Laundry
S: Southern Style Fish Market

5 Hollywood St
Gas N: Mapco Express(*)
Food N: Moma's Bar-B-Q
ATM N: First Bank Tennessee, Mapco Express
Other N: WalGreens Pharmacy

6 Warford St, New Allen Road

8 Raleigh, TN 14
Gas S: Texaco(*, CW)
Food S: Central Park, Taqueria La Fogata
Lodg N: Comfort Inn
AServ S: Auto Zone, Transmission Service, Uneeda Auto Glass
Med N: ✚ Raleigh Methodist Hospital
ATM S: Texaco
Other S: Jackson Grocery & Deli, Peoples' Pharmacy, Rub A Duds Laundromat

10 TN 204, Covington Pike
Gas N: Pump & Save
Food N: McDonald's(PLAY), Wendy's

Bold red print shows RV & Bus parking available or nearby

EXIT TENNESSEE

AServ N: Cadillac Dealer, Covington Pike Dodge, Covington Pike Honda, Covington Pike Tire & Auto Service, Covington Pike Toyota, Gossett Jeep/Eagle, Gossett Mitsubishi, Gossett VW, Gwatney Olds Chev, Homer Skelton Mazda, Kia, Jim Keras Buick & Nissan, Pat Patterson Volvo, Sunrise Pontiac/GMC

Other N: **Mega Market Supermarket**, **Sam's Club**

12C Jct I-240E, East I-40, Nashville

Lodg N: Elvis Presley's Heartbreak Hotel (see our ad this page)
S: **Comfort Inn (see our ad this page)**

12B Sam Cooper Blvd (Difficult Reaccess)

12A Summer Ave, U.S. 64, 70, 79

FStop N: **Mapco Express**(*, D, LP)

Gas N: Texaco(*, D, CW)
S: Amoco, Exxon(*), Texaco

Food N: Luby's Cafeteria, Pappy & Jimmy's Restaurant, Waffle House
S: Arby's, Great China Restaurant, McDonald's, Nam King, Pizza Hut, Poncho's (Mexican), Wendy's, Western Sizzlin'

Lodg N: Holiday Inn Express

AServ N: Lewis Ford, Mr. D's Service
S: Amoco, Bill King's Brake-O, Dayton Tires, Firestone Tire & Auto, Goodyear Tire & Auto (Penske), **K-Mart**, Texaco, Zellner Alignment

ATM N: **Mapco Express**, Texaco, Union Planters Bank
S: National Bank of Commerce

Other N: Permiter Center
S: **Bookcase Paper Back Books**, Car Wash, **Cloverleaf Animal Clinic**(RX), **Cloverleaf Pharmacy**, Great China Food Market, **K-Mart**, **Piggly Wiggly**

12 Sycamore View Road, Bartlett

Gas N: Texaco(*, D, LP, CW), Total(*, D)
S: Amoco(*, LP), BP(*, CW), Exxon(*), Mapco Express(*)

Food N: Captain D's, **Cracker Barrel**, Holiday Inn, KFC, McDonald's, Mrs Winner's Chicken, Perkins Family Restaurant, Shoney's, Sonic Drive in, Taco Bell, Waffle House, Willie Moffatt's
S: Blimpie's Subs (Mapco), Burger King, Celebration Station Food & Fun, Celebration Station, Cuisine Of India, Denny's, Eagle's Nest Sports Grill, Fortune Inn Chinese, Great World, Gridley's BBQ, Subway, Tops Bar-B-Q, Wendy's

Lodg N: Budgetel Inn, Drury Inn, Hampton Inn, Holiday Inn, Howard Johnson Express Inn, Red Roof Inn
S: Best Western, Comfort Inn, Days Inn, Fairfield Inn, La Quinta Inn, Memphis Inn, Motel 6, Super 8

AServ N: Cardova Tire & Automotive, Jiffy Lube, Midas Muffler & Brake
S: Express Lube

ATM N: First Tennessee Bank, Texaco, Union Planter's Bank
S: BP, Mapco Express

RVCamp N: **Camping World (see our ad this page)**

Other N: Animal Clinic, **Fred's Grocery Store**, **Piggly Wiggly**, Sicamore View Car Wash
S: Celebration Station

13 Walnut Grove Rd

Lodg N: Holiday Inn Express (see our a d this page)

14 Whitten Road

Gas N: BP(*, CW), Mapco Express(*)
S: Citgo(*, D, 24), Stuckey's(*)

Lodg S: Stuckey's, Villager Lodge

ATM N: Mapco Express

15AB Appling Rd.

16 TN 177, Germantown

Gas N: BP(*, CW)

Food N: Alexander's Restaurant, Bahama Breeze, Blimpie Subs & Salads, Chick-Fil-A(PLAY), Chili's, Danver's Restaurant, Find Grind, IHOP, Logan's Roadhouse Steaks & Ribs, McDonald's(PLAY), On the Border Cafe, Red Lobster, Taco Bell, Tellini Italian, The Melting Pot, Wendy's

Lodg N: Hampton Inn
S: Best Suites, AmeriSuites (see our ad this page)

AServ N: Chevrolet Dealer, Ford Dealer

ATM N: First Tennessee Bank, **Seessel's Grocery**, Southern Security

Other N: **Baptist Bookstore**, **Barnes & Noble**, Bommons Shopping Center, Malco, **Office Max**, Pier 1 Imports, **Seessel's Grocery**, **Target**, WalGreen's, **Wolfchase Galleria Shopping Mall**

18 U.S. 64, Somerville, Bolivar (Difficult Reaccess)

Gas N: Exxon(*, LP, CW)
S: Amoco(*, LP, 24), Circle K(*, LP), Citgo(CW), STP

Food N: Bresler's Ice Cream (Exxon), Burger King (Exxon), Don Pablo's Mexican, Exxon, **McDonald's (Wal-Mart)**, Schlotzsky's Deli
S: Backyard Burgers, Pizza Hut, Wang Garden

Lodg N: **Holiday Inn Express (see our ad this page)**

AServ N: Sears, **Wal-Mart**

Med S: **Hospital**

ATM N: Exxon
S: Amoco, Circle K, SouthTrust Bank

Other N: **Wal-Mart**
S: **Kroger Supermarket**(RX), **Pet Health Center (Veterinary Clinic)**

20 Canada Road, Lakeland

FStop N: BP(*, D)

Gas N: Amoco, Discount Gas(*, D, LP)
S: Exxon(*, D, LP)

Food N: Waffle House
S: Exxon, Subway (Exxon), TCBY (Exxon), The Cotton Cabin

CAMPING WORLD
Exit 12 off Briley Pkwy
2622 Music Valley Dr. • Nashville, TN
1-800-831-0111
1431

Comfort Inn
Exit 12C • Collierville, TN
901-853-1235
• Free Deluxe Continental Breakfast
• Cable TV with Free HBO/CNN/ESPN
• Restaurant within Walking Distance
• Outdoor Pool
• Bus & Truck Parking
• Free Local Phone Calls
1182
TENNESSEE • I-40 • EXIT 12C

GRACELAND
ELVIS PRESLEY'S
Heartbreak HOTEL™
3677 Elvis Presley Boulevard
Memphis, TN 38116
901-332-1000
Graceland tour/hotel packages available
1750
Memphis I-40 to 240 south to I-55 south exit 5B

Memphis, Tennessee
1561

• 108 Spacious Rooms & Suites
• Free Self Service Breakfast Bar
• Free Local Phone Calls/Fax
• Free Premium Channel
• Refrigerators & Work Desks in Each Room, Microwaves Available
901-372-0000 For Reservations: 800-HOLIDAY
TENNESSEE • I-40 • EXIT 18

1305

Tennessee • Exit 16 • 901-680-9700

Fayetteville, Arkansas
1562

• Free Cable with HBO & Showtime
• Free Continental Breakfast
• Business & Game Room
• Free Entree on Mon, Wed, Thurs, Sat.
• Free Local Calls & Faxes
• Special Rates for Tour Groups
501-444-6006 For Reservations: 800-465-4329
ARKANSAS • I-40 • EXIT 13

FREE CONTINENTAL BREAKFAST

Super 8
Lakeland, Memphis, TN
800-800-8000
901-372-4575
1211
• Kids Under 12 Stay Free
• Free HBO Remote Color TV
• Laundry Room
• Fax and Copy Service Available
• Refrigerator/Microwave Available
• Near: Belz Factory Outlet Mall, Wolfchase Galleria, Restaurants & Cinema
TENNESSEE • I-40 • Exit 20

Bold red print shows RV & Bus parking available or nearby

EXIT TENNESSEE

Lodg N: Days Inn, Relax Inn, Super 8 (see our ad this page)
RVCamp S: KOA Campgrounds (1 Mile)
Other S: Belz Factory Outlet

25 TN 205, Airline Road, Arlington, Collierville
Gas N: Exxon[*, D]
Food N: Subway (Exxon)

35 TN 59, Covington, Somerville
FStop S: BP[*]
Food S: BP, Longtown Cafe (BP)
Other S: The CB Shop

42 TN 222, Stanton, Somerville
Gas S: Exxon[*, D], Phillips 66[LP]
Food S: Exxon
Lodg N: Countryside Inn
AServ N: Carl's Garage & Wrecker
S: Phillips 66

47 TN 179, Stanton - Dancyville Road
TStop S: PTP Stop[*]
TServ S: PTP Stop

(49) Weigh Station (Eastbound)

(50) Weigh Station (Westbound)

52 TN 76, TN 179, Koko Road, Whiteville
Gas S: KoKo Community Market[*], Phillip's Quick Stop[*]

56 TN 76, Brownsville, Somerville
FStop S: Exxon[*, D]
Gas N: Amoco[*], Citgo[*, D, 24]
S: BP[*, 24]
Food N: Baskin Robbins, Dairy Queen, Fiesta Garden, KFC, McDonald's[PLAY], Taco Bell
S: Huddle House (Exxon)
Lodg N: Best Western, Comfort Inn, Days Inn, Holiday Inn Express
ATM N: Citgo
S: Exxon
Other S: Headquarters for the Hatchie National Wildlife Refuge

60 TN 19, Mercer Road
AServ N: Auto Service
TServ S: Simmons Truck Tire Service[24]

66 U.S. 70
FStop S: Fuel Mart[*, SCALES]
Gas S: Citgo[*, D, K]
Food S: Blimpie's Subs (Fuel Mart)
Lodg S: Motel 6

68 TN 138, Providence Road
TStop S: 76 Auto/Truck Plaza[SCALES] (BP Fuel)
Gas N: Amoco[*, D]
S: Citgo[*]
Food S: 76 Auto/Truck Plaza (BP Fuel), Union Restaurant (76 TS)
Lodg N: Econolodge
TWash S: Al's Truck Wash
RVCamp S: Joy-O RV Park[D]
ATM N: Amoco
S: 76 Auto/Truck Plaza (BP Fuel)

(73) Rest Area (RR, Phones, Picnic, Vending, Pet Walk; Eastbound)

(74) Rest Area (RR, Phones, Picnic, Pet Walk; Westbound)

74 Lower Brownsville Road (RR, HF, Picnic, Pet Walk)

76 TN 223 South, McKellar - Sipes Regional Airport

79 U.S. 412, Jackson (Difficult Reaccess)

1767
Discount Home Decorating Center
Areas Largest Selection of In-stock Merchandise
• Bedspreads • Wallpaper
• Window Blinds • Lamps
• Rugs • Comforters
• Wicker • Fabric
Plus much, much, more...
Stop by and visit us.
HUMBOLDT
OUTLET STORES
N. 14th Ave., Humboldt, TN 800-714-3881
Hours: Mon-Sat, 9am-5:30pm or 800-658-1160
TENNESSEE • I-40 • EXIT 80AB

SUPER 8 MOTEL
Super 8 Motel
2295 N. Highland
Jackson, TN 38305
901-668-1145
• Remote Control Cable TV-HBO-ESPN-CNN
• Continental Breakfast
• Exercise Room • Meeting Room
• Free Local Calls • Bus Parking
• Shoney's & Po Folks within Walking Distance
1085
TENNESSEE • I-40 • EXIT 82A

FStop S: Citgo[*, CW]
Gas S: BP, Citgo[*, D, CW], Exxon[*], Tanana, Volunteer Oil Co.[D]
Food S: GG's Restaurant
Lodg S: Days Inn
AServ S: Auto Glass & Door, BP, Citgo
RVCamp S: Jackson Mobile Village & RV Park (.25 Miles)
ATM S: Exxon
Parks S: Penson Mounds State Park
Other S: Madison Wholesale Co.

80AB US 45 Bypass, Milan, Jackson
Gas S: Amoco[*, CW], BP[*, LP, CW], Citgo[*, D, LP, CW], Citgo[*], Phillips 66[*, D, LP]
Food N: Chick-Fil-A[PLAY], Chili's, Five & Diner, IHOP, KFC, Lone Star Steakhouse, Peking, Schlotzsky's Deli
S: Applebee's, Arby's, Barn Hill's Country Cafe, Baudo's Italian American, Best Western, Burger King, Cheese Factory, Comfort Inn, Dunkin Donuts, El Chico Mexican Restaurant, Holiday Inn, Hugh's Pit Bar-B-Q, Logan's Roadhouse Steaks & Ribs, McDonald's, Mrs Winner's Chicken, O'Charley's, Old Town Spaghetti Store, Pizza Hut, Sonic Drive-In, Subway, Taco Bell, Village Inn Pizza, Waffle House
Lodg S: Best Western, Budget Inn, Casey Jones Station Inn, Comfort Inn, Days Inn, Econolodge, Fairfield Inn, Garden Plaza Hotel, Hampton Inn, Holiday Inn
AServ N: Quaker State Oil & Lube
S: K-Mart, King Tire Co, Midas Muffler & Brake
Med N: Hospital
ATM S: First American, First South Bank, First Tennessee Bank, The Bank of Jackson, Union Planters Bank, Volunteer Bank
Other N: Dan's Factory Outlet (see our ad this page), Kinko's[24], Sam's Club, Wal-Mart[RX] (Vision Center)
S: Casey Jones Village & Railroad Museum, K-Mart

82AB U.S. 45, Jackson
Gas S: Citgo[*, D, LP], Exxon[*], Racetrac[*]
Food N: Cracker Barrel
S: Barley's Brew House & Eatery, China Palace, Dairy Queen, Pizza Hut, Po Folks, SHONEY'S Shoney's, Suede's Restaurant (Sheraton Inn), Taco Bell, Village Inn Pizzeria & Grill, Waffle House
Lodg N: Microtel
S: Budgetel Inn, Quality Inn, Ramada Limited, Sheraton Inn, Super 8 (see our ad this page), Traveller's Motel
Med N: Hospital
ATM S: Union Planters Bank
Other N: Tennessee Highway Patrol
S: Animal Clinic, IGA Food Store, The Clean Machine Coin-Op Laundry

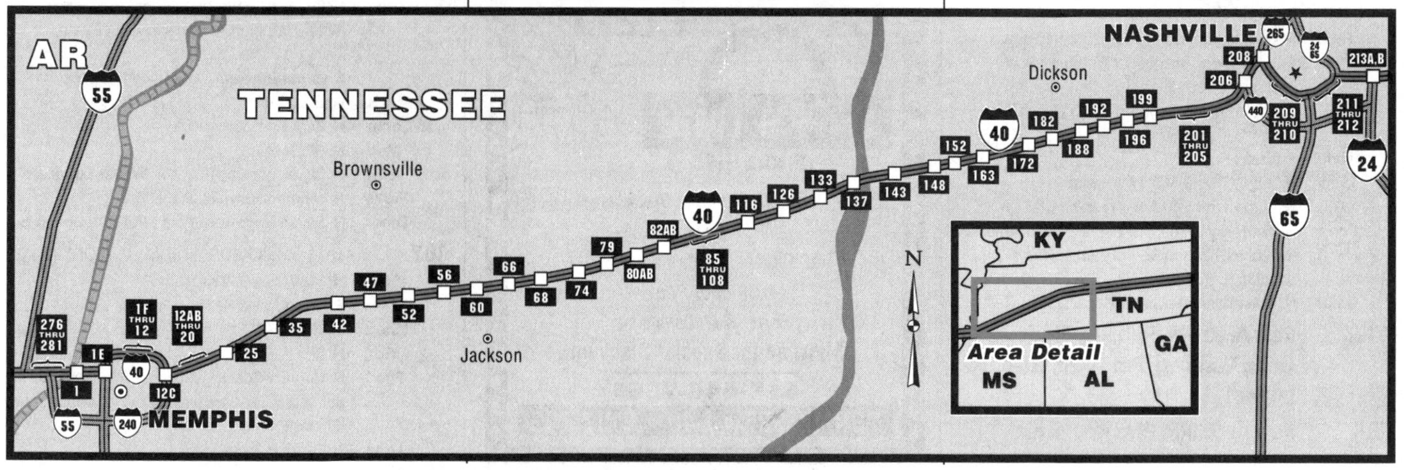

EXIT	TENNESSEE
85	Christmasville Road, Dr. F. E. Wright Drive, Jackson
FStop	N: **Amoco**[*], **Exxon**[*, LP]
Gas	N: **Amoco**[*, D, K]
Food	N: **Amoco, Subway (Amoco)**
Lodg	N: Howard Johnson Express Inn
TServ	N: **Kenworth of Tennessee**
Parks	S: **Pringles Park**
87	U.S. 70, U.S. 412, Huntingdon, McKenzie
FStop	S: **Texaco**[*, D, K]
Gas	N: Citgo[*, D, LP]
	S: Exxon[*, D]
Food	N: Ben's & Hammond's Pit Bar-B-Q
ATM	N: Citgo
Other	N: **Antique Mall**, Catherine's Collectibles
93	TN 152, Law Road, Lexington
FStop	S: **Texaco**[*, K]
Gas	N: Phillips 66[*, K]
101	TN 104
Gas	N: Exxon[*] (Wrecker Service)
ATM	N: Exxon (Wrecker Service)
(102)	**Parking Area (Westbound)**
(103)	**Parking Area, Weigh Station (Phones; Eastbound)**
108	TN 22, Huntington, Lexington, Parkers Crossroads
FStop	N: **Citgo**[*, LP, K], **Phillips 66**[*]
Gas	N: Amoco[*], BP[*, K]
	S: Duckies[*] (Fireworks), Exxon[*], **Texaco**[*]
Food	N: **Bailey's Restaurant**[24], Little Denice Pizza
	S: **Cotton Patch Restaurant (Tourist Info)**, Subway (Duckies)
Lodg	N: **Knight's Inn**
	S: **Best Western**
AServ	N: Tire Shop[K]
RVCamp	N: **Beach Lake Campground, Parker's Crossroads Campground (1.25 Miles)**
Med	S: **+ Hospital**
ATM	N: BP, **Citgo**, First Bank & Trust Co., **Phillips 66**
Parks	S: **Natchez Trace State Park (2 Miles), Pickwick Landing (65 Miles), Shiloh Park (51 Miles)**
Other	N: **Civil War Tour**
116	TN 114
RVCamp	S: **Bucksnort Campground**
Parks	S: **Natchez Trace State Park**
Other	N: **Maple Lake (3.5 Miles), Spring Valley Golf (7 Miles)**
126	TN 69, U.S. 641, Camden, Paris, Parsons
TStop	N: **North 40 Auto/Truckstop**[*, SCALES], **Sugar Tree**
FStop	S: **BP**[*, LP, K], **Shell**[*]
Gas	N: Amoco[*, LP], Exxon[*, D, LP], Texaco[*, D]
	S: Citgo[*]
Food	N: Burger Barn, North 40 Restaurant, Subway (Exxon), **Sugar Tree**, Sugar Tree Truck Stop Restaurant, TCBY (Exxon)
	S: Apple Annie's (Days Inn), Dairy Queen (Citgo), Stuckey's (Citgo)
Lodg	S: Days Inn
TServ	N: **B & W Diesel, Wilson's Repair**
ATM	N: Exxon, **North 40 Auto/Truckstop**
Parks	N: **Kentucky Lake, Lake Barkley, Land Between the Lakes, Nathan Bedford Forest, Paris Landing State Parks**
Other	N: **Patsy Cline Memorial Plane Crash**
(130)	**Rest Area (RR, Phones, Picnic, Grills, Vending, Pet Walk; Eastbound)**
(131)	**Rest Area (RR, Phones, Picnic, Grills, Vending, Pet Walk; Westbound)**
133	TN 191, Birdsong Road
RVCamp	N: **Birdsong Resort & Marina**
Other	S: Tennessee Wildlife Refuge
137	Cuba Landing
FStop	S: **Citgo**[*]
Food	S: **Carfish Restaurant**
RVCamp	N: **Camping**
Other	N: **Cuba Landing Marina (Full Service Marina Store & Deli)**
143	TN 13, Linden, Waverly, Lobelville, Buffalo
TStop	N: **Tyland**
FStop	N: **Phillips 66**[*, D], **Pilot Travel Center**[*, SCALES]
Gas	N: BP[D], Phillips 66, Shell[*, D]
	S: Exxon[*], Texaco[*]
Food	N: **Buffalo River Grill**, Country Kitchen, **Log Cabin Restaurant (Best Western), Loretta Lynn's Kitchen, McDonald's**, Phillips 66, **Subway (Tyland)**, TNT BBQ
	S: Annabelle's Place, South Side Restaurant
Lodg	N: **Best Western**, Buffalo Inn, **Days Inn (see our ad this page), Holiday Inn Express, Super 8**
	S: **Best Budget Motel**
AServ	N: BP
	S: **Barnett's Towing**[24]
TServ	S: **Barnett's Towing**[24]
RVCamp	N: **KOA Kampground**[LP] **(.25 Miles)**
ATM	N: **Phillips 66**
Other	N: Loretta Lynn Dude Ranch
148	TN50, Centerville, Barren Hollow Road, Turney Center
Gas	S: Texaco[*]
152	TN 230, Bucksnort
Gas	N: BP[*, D]
Food	N: **Rudy's Resturaunt**
Lodg	N: **TraveLodge**
RVCamp	S: **Camping Guide Service**
163	TN 48, Centerville, Dickson
Gas	N: Citgo[*, K], Phillips 66[*, D, LP, K]
	S: Shell[*, LP]
AServ	N: Citgo, Phillips 66
RVCamp	S: **Tanbark Campground (.5 Miles)**
Other	S: **CB Shop**
(170)	**Rest Area (RR, Phones, Picnic, Vending, Pet Walk; Eastbound)**
(170)	**Rest Area (Westbound)**
172	TN 46, Centerville, Dickson
TStop	N: **Mapco Express**[*, LP, SCALES] **(see our ad this page)**
Gas	N: Amoco[*, D, LP, 24], BP[*, LP], Shell[*], Texaco[*, PLAY] (Burger King, Baskin Robbins)
	S: Chevron[*, 24], Exxon[*, D, LP, K]
Food	N: Arby's, BP, Baskin Robbins[PLAY] (Burger King), Burger King[PLAY] (Texaco), **Cracker Barrel**, Key West Cafe, McDonald's[PLAY], **Steak 'N Shake (Mapco Express TS)**, Subway (BP), Texaco[PLAY] (Burger King, Baskin Robbins), Waffle House, Wang's China
Lodg	N: Bugetel, Comfort Inn, **Econolodge**, Eye 40 Motel, Hampton, **Knight's Inn**, Quality Inn, Ramada Limited, Super 8
	S: **Days Inn (see our ad this page), Holiday Inn**
RVCamp	N: **KOA Kampground**
Med	N: **+ Hospital**
ATM	N: BP, Burger King (Texaco), **Mapco Express**
Parks	N: **Montgomery Bell State Park**
Other	N: **Seven Flags Race Park - Put-Put, Go-Karts**
182	TN 96, Dickson, Fairview, Franklin
TStop	N: **New Hwy 96 Truck Stop**[*, LP]
	S: **Flying J's**[*, LP, SCALES]
FStop	S: **BP**[*, D, 24]
Gas	N: BP[*, 24], Citgo
Food	N: **Country Cooking (Citgo TS)**, Phantom 309
	S: Country Cookin (Flying J's), Flying Dragon Eatery (Chinese), **Flying J's**, Pepperoni's Super Slice
Lodg	N: **Dickson Motel**

1846
childreach
U.S. MEMBER OF PLAN INTERNATIONAL
Sponsored by Interatate America and Ramada Inn, Limited and Plaza Hotels of Tennessee
RAMADA
For information on how you can sponsor a child call 800-556-7918
TENNESSEE ▪ I-40

1199
DAYS INN
15415 Hwy. 13 South
Hurricane Mills, TN
AAA
24 Hour Deluxe Continential Breakfast
Direct TV - 8 Channels
Free Local Calls • Call Attendant
In Room Coffee • Tours-On Site
In House Laundry
Electronic Locks • Double Queen Rooms
800-841-5813
I-40, Exit 143 on Rte 1 Hwy 13
TENNESSEE ▪ I-40 ▪ EXIT 143

1285
MAPCO Express
Open 24 Hours
Famous for Steak n Shake Steakburgers
615-446-4600
Gasoline & High Speed Diesel Pumps
Full Service Restaurant
Truck Accessories • Private Showers
Laundry Facilities • ATM Machines
D.A.T. Load Boards • Sandwich Shop
Certified Scales • Copy & Fax Services
TENNESSEE ▪ I-40 ▪ EXIT 172

1070
DAYS INN
Dickson
Show This Ad for 30% Discount
— FREE Continental Breakfast —
— FREE Local Calls —
— 42 Channel Cable TV w/HBO —
— Outdoor Pool —
— Cracker Barrel & McDonald's adjacent —
— Show ad for Special Discount —
615-446-7561
TENNESSEE ▪ I-40 ▪ EXIT 172

Bold red print shows RV & Bus parking available or nearby

EXIT TENNESSEE

TServ N: GTF Tire & Maintenance Service, New Hwy 96 Truck Stop, Two Feathers Truck Center
ATM N: BP, New Hwy 96 Truck Stop
S: BP
Parks N: Montgomery Bell State Park (16 Miles)

188 TN 249, Kingston Springs Road, Ashland City
TStop S: Petro-2[*, LP, SCALES]
Gas N: BP[*, D, K], Mapco Express[*, LP, K], Shell[*, D, K]
Food N: Arby's (Shell), Blimpie Subs & Salads (Mapco Express), Miss Sadie's Diner, Pizzeria (EconoLodge), Restaurant, Shell
S: Pizza Hut (Petro), Quick! Skillet (Petro-2)
Lodg N: Best Western, Econolodge, Scottish Inns
TServ S: Petro-2[SCALES]
ATM N: Cheatham State Bank, Mapco Express, Shell
S: Petro-2
Other N: US Post Office, Vegas Coin Laundry
S: Kingston Springs Animal Hospital

192 Natchez Trace Parkway
Parks N: Newsoms Mill State Park (2 Miles)

196 U.S. 70 South, Bellevue, Newsom Station
Gas N: Mapco Express[*, LP]
S: BP[*, LP, CW], Mapco Express[*, D, LP], Shell[*, 24], Texaco[*, D, CW]
Food N: SHONEY'S, Shoney's
S: Applebee's, Baskin Robbins, McGillicudy's Restaurant, PIzza Hut, Pasgetti's, Sir Pizza, Subway, Taco Bell, Waffle House, Wendy's
Lodg S: Hampton Inn
AServ S: Firestone Tire & Auto, Shell[24]
Med S: + Baptist Bellevue Medical Center
ATM S: BP, First America, First Union, Texaco
Other N: Regal Cinemas
S: Bellevue Center Mall, Bruno's Grocery & Pharmacy[RX], Piggly Wiggly Supermarket, The Galleria Shopping Center, U.S. Post Office, WalGreens Pharmacy[24, RX]

199 TN 251, Old Hickory Blvd
Gas N: Texaco[*, D, LP, CW]
S: Mapco Express[*, LP]
Food S: Mapco Express, Subway (Mapco Express), Waffle House
ATM N: Texaco
S: Mapco Express
Other S: Putt-Putt Golf & Games, Rojo Red's Car Wash, Sam's Club, Touchless Automatic Car Wash

201AB U.S. 70E, Charlotte Pike
Gas N: Exxon[*, D, LP, CW], Phillips 66[*, D, CW], Texaco[*, D]
Food N: Cracker Barrel, Star Bagel Company, Waffle House
Lodg N: Hallmark Inn
S: Howard Johnson
AServ S: Ron Haul Auto & Truck Repair
TServ S: Ron Haul Auto & Truck Repair
ATM N: Exxon, Texaco
Other N: Drew's Market, West Meade Veterinary Clinic

204 TN 155, Briley Pkwy, Robertson Ave, White Bridge Road
Gas N: Exxon[*], Texaco[*, D, K]
S: Citgo[*, D, LP], Phillips 66[*, D, LP], Texaco
Food S: Burger King, Church's Chicken, Domino's Pizza, KFC, Las Palmas Mexican, New China Buffet, SHONEY'S, Shoney's, Sir Pizza, Uncle Bud's Catfish, Chicken, & Such, Waffle House, White Castle Restaurant[24]
Lodg S: Budgetel Inn, Daystop Inn, Super 8
AServ N: Texaco
S: Auto Value Parts Store, Carquest Auto Parts, NTB, NTB National Tire & Battery, Pep Boys Auto Center, Performance Ford, Phillips 66, Precision Tune & Lube, Q Lube, Texaco
ATM N: Exxon
S: First Union, WalGreens Pharmacy[RX]
Other S: Kroger Supermarket[24, RX], Save-A-Lot Food Stores, WalGreens Pharmacy[RX]

205 46th Ave, West Nashville
Gas S: Amoco[*, D, K, CW], Mapco Express[*, LP]
Food N: Harley Davidson
S: McDonald's
Other S: US Post Office

206 Junction I-440 East, Knoxville (Difficult Reaccess)

207 Jefferson St. (Reaccess Westbound Only)
Gas N: Circle K[*]
Food N: Lee's Famous Recipe Chicken, Mrs Winner's, Marie's Country Kitchen, Mrs Winner's Chicken, Sir Pizza, Subway, Wendy's
Med N: + Hospital
Other N: Rapid Mart

208 Junction I-265, Louisville

209 Charlotte Ave, Church St
Gas S: Amoco[*, D, K], Exxon[*, CW]
Food N: Shoney's
S: Farooge Chicken, Subway
AServ N: Chrysler, Plymouth
S: Car Plus
Med S: + Hospital
Other N: Tenn Oriental Market
S: Haddox Pharmacy

209A US 70S, US 431 Broadway (Westbound)
Gas S: Amoco

209B U.S. 70 South, U.S. 431, Demonbreun St
Gas N: Exxon[*, D, CW]
S: Texaco[*, D, CW]
Food N: McDonald's
S: Church's Chicken
Lodg N: Union Station Hotel
AServ N: Firestone, Hippodrome Oldsmobile Nissan, Master Care Auto Service, Truck Tire Service
S: Chevrolet, Mitsubishi Dealer, Pontiac, GMC, Subaru, Suzuki, Toyota, White Tire Sales & Service
ATM S: Texaco

210A Junction I-65 South, I-40 West, Louisville, Knoxville (Eastbound)

210B Junction I-65 North (Eastbound)

210C U.S. 31 A South, U.S. 41 A, 4th Ave, 2nd Ave (Difficult Reaccess)
Med N: + Hospital

25% off Rack Rate
Briley Parkway/
1 mile s. of I-40
1098
DAYS INN
— Closest Days Inn To Opryland —
— Full Service —
— Restaurant & Lounge —
— Beautiful Outdoor Pool —
— Pay Per View Movies & Nintendo —
— Free Parking —
— AAA & AARP Rates —
— Gift Shop & Tour Desk —
615-361-7666 • Nashville, TN
TENNESSEE • I-40 • EXIT 215

Other S: Cumberland Science Museum

211AB Jct. I-65, I-24, I-40, Louisville, Huntsville

212 Fesslers Lane (Difficult Reaccess)
FStop S: Citgo[*, LP], Mapco Express[*, LP], Texaco[*, CW]
Food S: Burger King, Krystal (Citgo), La Fiesta, Lee's Famous Recipe Chicken, McDonald's, Mrs. Winner's, Sonic Drive in, Southern Way Cafe, Wendy's
Lodg S: Drake Motel, Lee Motel, Music City Motor Inn
AServ N: Bridgestone, Southeastern Brake
S: Chevrolet Dealer, Mercedes Dealership
TServ N: Goodyear Tire & Auto, Neely Coble Sunbelt Truck Center
S: Tredaco Truck Service
Med N: + Hospital
S: + Hospital
ATM S: Citgo, Mapco Express, Texaco

213A Junction I-24 East, West I-40, Knoxville, Chattanooga

213B Junction I-24 West, Junction I-40 West, Nashville

213 U.S. 41, Spence Lane, Murfreesboro Rd (Difficult Reaccess)
Gas N: Texaco[*, D, K, CW]
Food S: Dad's Place (Ramada Inn), The Down Under Bar & Grill (Days Inn), Waffle House
Lodg S: DAYS INN Days Inn, Ramada Inn
TServ N: Kenworth of Tennessee
S: Cummins Diesel

215AB TN 155, Briley Pkwy
Gas S: Phillips 66[*], Shell[*, CW]
Food S: Daisy Cafe (Howard Johnson), Denny's[24], Howard Johnson, Shell, Steak-Out
Lodg N: Holiday Inn Select, La Quinta, Marriott
S: DAYS INN Days Inn (see our ad this page), Howard Johnson, Ramada Inn, Villager Lodge
Other S: Opryland

216A TN 255, Donelson Pike, International Airport
Gas N: Amoco[*, D, CW], BP[*, CW], Racetrac[*], Texaco[*]
Food N: KFC, McDonald's, SHONEY'S, Shoney's, Subway (Texaco), Waffle House, Wendy's
Lodg N: Budgetel Inn, Hampton Inn & Suites, Holiday Inn Express, Red Roof Inn, Super 8, Wyndham Garden Hotel
AServ N: Amoco, K-Mart
ATM N: Racetrac
Other N: K-Mart, Piggly Wiggly Supermarket
S: Airport

216B TN255, S Cargo, Donelson Pike, International Airport (Southbound)
Food S: Waffle House

216C TN255, Airport (Northbound)
Gas N: Amoco[*, D, CW], BP[*, LP, CW], Parmart Texaco[*, D], Racetrac[*]
Food N: Arby's, Backyard Burgers, Blimpie Subs & Salads, Burger King[PLAY], Darfons, KFC, Los Padres, McDonald's, Parmart Texaco, Ruby Tuesday, SHONEY'S, Shoney's, Subway (Texaco), Taco Bell, Wendy's
Lodg N: Budgetel Inn, Hampton Inn Suites, Holiday Inn Express, Red Roof Inn, Super 8, Windham Garden Hotel
AServ N: Advanced Auto Parts, Amoco, K-Mart[RX]
ATM N: BP, WalGreen's[24, RX]
Other N: Coin Car Wash, K-Mart[RX], Kinko's Copies[24], Piggly Wiggly, WalGreen's[RX]

219 Stewart's Ferry Pike, J. Percy Priest Dam
Gas N: Mapco Express[*, LP, K]

EXIT TENNESSEE

S: Mapco Express[*, D, LP, K], Texaco[*, D, CW]
Food S: Cracker Barrel, Dragon Palace, Mapco Express, New York Experience, Subway (Mapco Express), Uncle Bud's Catfish, Chicken, & Such, Waffle House
Lodg S: Best Western, Days Inn, Family Inns of America, Howard Johnson, **Sleep Inn**
ATM N: Mapco Express
S: Texaco
Other S: B & E Laundry, Touchless Automatics Car Wash

221A TN 45, Old Hickory Blvd, The Hermitage, Central Pike (Eastbound)
Gas N: **Mapco Express**[*, LP, K], Racetrac[*], Shell[*]
S: **Mapco Express**[*, LP], Speedway[*, LP], Texaco[*, D, LP]
Food N: Dairy Queen[PLAY], Hardee's, K.O.'s Pizza & Sandwiches, Waffle House
S: Dairy Queen[PLAY], Express Pizza
Lodg N: Comfort Inn, Holiday Inn Express, Ramada Limited
S: Comfort Inn, Ramada Inn
Med N: + **Summit Hospital**
ATM N: **Mapco Express**
S: **Mapco Express**, Speedway
Other N: Car Wash
S: Car Wash

226 TN 171, Mount Juliet Road
Gas N: BP[*, LP], Citgo[*, LP], Mapco Express[*, D, LP, K], Texaco[*, D, LP]
S: Mapco Express[*, D, LP, K]
Food N: Arby's, BP, Captain D's Seafood, McDonald's (BP)
S: **Cracker Barrel**, Waffle House
ATM N: BP, Mapco Express
S: Mapco Express
Other N: Car Wash, **Squeeky Clean Coin Laundry**

232 TN 109, Gallatin
TStop N: **Mapco Express**
Gas N: Amoco[*, K]
Food N: Baskin Robbins (Mapco Express), Granny's (Amoco), **Mapco Express**
TServ N: **Utility Of Tennessee**
RVCamp S: **Countryside RV Park**

235 TN 840 West, Chattanooga, Murfreesboro (Difficult Reaccess, Limited Access Highway)

238 U.S. 231, Lebanon, Murfreesboro
TStop S: **Mapco Express**[*, D, LP, K] **(see our ad this page)**
FStop S: **Cone**[*, LP, K]
Gas N: Amoco[*, 24], BP[*], Exxon[*], Pilot Travel Center[*, D, LP, K], Shell[*, CW] (see our ad this page)
Food N: Amoco, Arby's (Amoco), Chum's (Shell), **Cracker Barrel**, Don Dola Restaurant, **Hardee's**, **McDonald's**[PLAY], **McDonald's (Wal-Mart)**, Mrs Winner's Chicken, Pizza Hut, Ponderosa, SHONEYS, Shoney's, Subway, Sunset Family Restaurant (Scottish Inns), Taco Bell, Uncle Bud's Catfish, Chicken, & Such, Waffle House, Wendy's
S: Baskin Robbins (Mapco Express), **Mapco Express**, O'Charley's Restaurant, **Outlet Village of Lebanon**
Lodg N: Best Western, Comfort Inn, Hampton Inn, Holiday Inn Express, Scottish Inns, Shoney's Inn
S: **Days Inn**, Knight's Inn, **Super 8**
AServ N: **Wal-Mart Supercenter**[24]
RVCamp S: **Shady Acres (2 Miles)**, **Timberline Campground (.7 Miles)**
ATM N: BP, Pilot Travel Center
S: **Mapco Express**
Parks S: **Cedars of Lebanon State Park (6 Miles)**
Other N: **Wal-Mart Supercenter**
S: **Outlet Village of Lebanon**

239AB U.S. 70, Lebanon, Watertown
TStop S: **Uncle Pete's Super Truck Stop**[*, D, SCALES, 24]
Gas N: Amoco[*, K], Racetrac[*]

The universal sign for the world's best-selling gasoline.

Chum's Convenience Stores

1247

210 Knoxville Ave.
Lebanon, TN 37087

Shell

615-444-1114

Fresh Hot Coffee!

Open 24 Hours • Car Wash
ATM • Deli
Walmart Supercenter(200Yards)
Card Readers
Hotels & Fast Food Nearby

TENNESSEE • I-40 • EXIT 238

1283

Open 24 Hours

31 Baskin Robbins. Where Wonders Never Cease.

615-453-8866

Gasoline & High Speed Diesel Pumps
Full Service Restaurant
Truck Accessories • Private Showers
Laundry Facilities • ATM Machines
D.A.T. Load Boards • Sandwich Shop
Certified Scales • Copy & Fax Services

TENNESSEE • I-40 • EXIT 238

The universal sign for the world's best-selling gasoline.

1250

Shell

T-N-T Market
Hwy 53 North
Gordonsville, TN 38563

615-638-8600

Fresh Hot Coffee!

ATM • Diesel
Full Line Deli
Card Reader
Hotel & Fast Food Nearby

TENNESSEE • I-40 • EXIT 258

1248

Comfort Inn
of Gordonsville
479 Gordonsville Hwy

615-683-1300

- *Cable TV with HBO*
- *Restaurant Nearby*
- *Outdoor Pool • Jacuzzi*
- *Truck Parking*
- *Efficiencies Available*
- *Free Continental Breakfast*
- *Handicapped Facilities*

TENNESSEE ¥ I-40 ¥ EXIT 258

Food S: **Four Winds Truckstop**, **Uncle Pete's Super Truck Stop**
AServ S: **I-40 BP**[24] **(Towing)**
TServ S: **I-40 BP**[24] **(Towing)**
TWash S: **Emoglo Truck Wash**
Med N: + **Hospital**
ATM N: Racetrac
S: **Uncle Pete's Super Truck Stop**

245 Linwood Road
FStop N: **BP**[*, LP]
ATM N: **BP**

(252) **Parking Area, Weigh Station (Eastbound)**

(252) **Rest Area, Weigh Station (Westbound)**

254 TN 141, Alexandria

258 TN 53, Carthage, Gordonsville, Hartsville
Gas N: Amoco[*, D, K], Shell (see our ad this page)
S: BP[D, K], Citgo[*, D, K], Keystop[*, D]
Food N: McDonald's[PLAY], Timberloft (Family Dining)
Lodg N: **Comfort Inn (see our ad this page)**
AServ S: BP
Med N: + **Hospital**
ATM S: Keystop

(267) **Rest Area (RR, HF, Phones, Picnic, Vending, RV Dump, Pet Walk; Eastbound)**

(267) **Weigh Station (Westbound)**

268 TN 96, Buffalo Valley Road, Center Hill Dam
Lodg N: Buffalo Bill's Motel, Market & General Store
Parks S: **Edgar Evins State Park (4 Miles)**
Other N: **Buffalo Bill's Market & General Store**
S: **US Post Office**

273 TN 56, Smithville, McMinnville
Gas S: BP[D, K], Phillips 66[*]
Food S: **Rose Garden Restaurant**
AServ S: BP
Parks S: **Edgar Evins State Park**
Other S: Antique Center, **Appalachian Center for Crafts (6 Miles)**, **Center Hill Dam (8 Miles)**, Joe L Evans Craft Center, **US Post Office**

276 Old Baxter Road
Gas N: T-Tommy's[*, D, 24]
S: Texaco[*]
AServ N: T Tommy's I-40 Auto & 24-Hour Wrecker Service, T-Tommy's[24]
Other S: The Old Home Place (Antique Center)

280 TN 56 North, Baxter, Gainesboro
RVCamp N: **Camp Discovery (24 Miles)**
Parks N: **Burgess Falls State Park**
Other N: Dale Hollow Dam

286 TN 135, South Willow Ave., Cookville
TStop N: **Cumberland Truck Center**
FStop N: **Exxon**[*, CW], **Racetrac**[*, D, 24], **Shell**[*, CW]
S: **Pacific Pride**, **Texaco**[*, D, LP]
Gas N: BP[*]
S: Amoco[*, LP, K]
Food N: China One Express & Gifts, Hardee's, Waffle House
S: **Rice's Restaurant (Star Motor Inn)**
Lodg S: **Star Motor Inn**
AServ N: Auto Glass Service, Cookeville Nissan, Cumberland Chrysler Center, Cumberland Toyota, KIV, Mike Williams Goodyear
TServ N: **Walker Diesel**
Med N: + **Hospital**
ATM N: First American
Parks S: **Burgess Falls State Park**
Other N: **Family World Bookstore**, **U.S. Post Office**
S: **Touchless Automatic Car & RV Wash**

287 TN 136, Cookeville, Sparta
TStop S: **Exxon**[*, K, 24] **(Showers)**
FStop S: **Exxon**, **Pilot Travel Center**[*, LP, K]
Gas N: Amoco[*, CW], Chevron[*, D], Excalibur Car Wash,

EXIT	TENNESSEE
	Shell(*, CW), Texaco(*, D, LP)
Food	**N:** Baskin Robbins, Burger King, Captain D's Seafood, China Star Chinese Restaurant, Cracker Barrel, Dairy Queen, Dairy Queen, El Sombrero, El Tapatio (Best Western), Finish Line Subs & Such (Amoco), Long John Silver, McDonald's, Nick's (Executive Inn), Pizza Hut, Ponderosa, Ryan's Steakhouse, Sade & Dora's (Holiday Inn), Schlotzsky's Deli, SHONEY'S, Shoney's, Subway, TCBY (Amoco), Tumbleweed, Uncle Bud's Catfish Chicken & Such, Waffle House, Wendy's
	S: Blimpie Subs & Salads (Pilot), Gondola Pizza, KFC, Pilot Travel Center, Waffle House
Lodg	**N:** Best Western, Comfort Suites Hotel, DAYS INN Days Inn, Executive Inn, Hampton, Holiday Inn, Key West, Ramada Limited, Super 8
	S: Econolodge
AServ	**N:** Class A, Cookeville Transmission, Ron's Auto Repair
ATM	**S:** Exxon (Showers), Exxon, Pilot Travel Center
Parks	**S:** Fall Creek Falls (43 Miles), Rock Island State Park (29 Miles)
Other	**N:** Cokeville Mall, Excalibur Car Wash, Horner-Rausch Optical Co. Superstore, Optical Superstore, TN Highway Patrol
288	**TN 111, Livingston, Sparta**
TStop	**S:** Mid Tenn. Auto/Truck Plaza(*, RV DUMP, SCALES, 24)
Gas	**S:** Shell(*, D, K)
Food	**S:** Huddle House(24), Mid Tenn. Auto/Truck Plaza, Subway (Mid Tenn. TS)
Lodg	**S:** Knight's Inn
TServ	**S:** Mid Tenn. Auto/Truck Plaza(SCALES, 24)
Parks	**N:** Standing Stone State Park (31 Miles)
	S: Fall Creek Falls, Rock Island
290	**U.S. 70 North, Cookeville**
Gas	**S:** Amoco(*, D, LP, K)
Food	**S:** Grady's Resturaunt (Alpine)
Lodg	**S:** Alpine Lodge & Suites
300	**U.S. 70 North, TN 84, Monterey, Livingston**
Gas	**N:** Citgo(*, D, K), Phillips 66(D, K)
Food	**N:** Hardee's, The Coffee House Emporium
Lodg	**S:** The Garden Inn At Bee Rock
AServ	**N:** Phillips 66
Parks	**S:** Pickett Park & Big South Fork
301	**U.S. 70 North, TN 84, Monterey, Jamestown**
Gas	**N:** Amoco(*, D, K)
Food	**N:** Mountain Top Grill (Amoco), Subway
AServ	**N:** LTL Discount Tire Auto & Truck Service(24) (Emergency Road Service)
TServ	**N:** LTL Discount Tire Auto & Truck Service(24) (Emergency Road Service)
Other	**N:** Monterey Food Center(*)
(307)	**Parking Area, Weigh Station**
311	**Plateau Road**
Gas	**N:** Chevron(*, D)
	S: BP(*, D), Exxon(*, K)
Food	**N:** Chevron
RVCamp	**S:** Plateau Recreation Vehicle Service
317	**U.S. 127, Crossville, Jamestown, Pikeville**
Gas	**N:** BP(D, K), Citgo(*, D), Exxon(*, D, K, CW), Shell(*, D, CW)
	S: Amoco(*, D, K), Phillips 66(*, D, K) (CB Shop), Texaco(*)
Food	**N:** Blimpie's Subs (Shell), Exxon, Huddle House(24), Shell, Subway (Exxon)
	S: Cracker Barrel, Ryan's Steakhouse, SHONEY'S, Shoney's, Waffle House
Lodg	**N:** Best Western, Hampton Inn, Ramada Inn
	S: DAYS INN Days Inn, Heritage Inn, Scottish Inns
AServ	**N:** BP
	S: Chevrolet, Oldsmobile Dealership
ATM	**N:** Exxon
	S: Amoco
Parks	**N:** Pickett State Park (46 Miles)
	S: Cumberland Mountain State Park (7 Miles)
320	**TN 298, Genesis Road, Crossville**
TStop	**S:** BP(*)
Gas	**S:** Shell(*, LP, 24)
Food	**N:** Halcyon Days, Stone Haus Winery (Restaurant)
	S: BP, Catfish Cove, Dairy Queen (BP TS), Pizza Hut (BP TS)
AServ	**N:** Lacks Auto Repair
TServ	**S:** Universal Tire
Other	**N:** Antique Village Mall & Shops
	S: Factory Outlet Center
322	**TN 101, Peavine Road, Crossville**
Gas	**N:** BP(*, LP, K), Exxon(*, D, K), Phillips 66(*)
Food	**N:** Bean Pot (BP), Exxon, Hardee's, McDonald's(PLAY), TCBY (Exxon)
RVCamp	**N:** Beanpot Holiday Trav-L-Park (1.5 Miles), Roam & Roost RV Campground (see our ad this page) (4.5 Miles)
	S: KOA Kampground (7.1 Miles)
ATM	**N:** BP, Exxon
Parks	**S:** Cumberland Mtn State Park
(324)	**Rest Area (RR, Picnic, Vending, Pet Walk; Eastbound)**
(327)	**Rest Area (RR, HF, Phones, Picnic, RV Dump; Westbound)**
329	**U.S. 70, Crab Orchard**
FStop	**N:** BP(*, D)
Gas	**N:** Exxon(*)
Food	**N:** S&H General Store Home Cooking
AServ	**N:** Exxon
Other	**N:** US Post Office
(336)	**Parking Area, Weigh Station (Eastbound)**
338	**TN 299 South, Westel Road, Rockwood**
TStop	**S:** East-West Truckstop(*, LP, K, 24)
Gas	**N:** BP(D, K)
	S: Texaco(*, K)
AServ	**N:** BP
TServ	**S:** East-West Truckstop(24)
TWash	**S:** East-West Truckstop
RVCamp	**S:** Campground
340	**TN 299 North, Airport Road**
347	**U.S. 27, Harriman, Rockwood**
Gas	**N:** Phillips 66(*, D, 24)
	S: BP(*), Exxon(*, D), Shell(*, LP)
Food	**N:** Cancun Mexican Restaurant, Cracker Barrel, Hardee's, KFC, Long John Silver, McDonald's(PLAY), Pizza Hut, Taco Bell, Wendy's
	S: Dairy Queen(24) (Shell), Exxon, Shell, SHONEY'S, Shoney's, TCBY (Exxon)
Lodg	**N:** Best Western
	S: Holiday Inn Express, Scottish Inns
AServ	**N:** Hensley Tire
Med	**N:** + Harriman City Hospital, + Roane Medical Center(24) (2 Miles)
ATM	**S:** Shell
Parks	**N:** Big South Fork National Recreation Area, Frozen Head State Park
Other	**N:** Rugby
350	**TN 29, Midtown**
Lodg	**S:** Mid-town Motel
AServ	**S:** C & S Tune-Up, Midtown Tire
RVCamp	**S:** Peterson's
Other	**S:** United Cities Propane Gas
352	**TN 58 South, Kingston**
Gas	**S:** Exxon(*, D, K, 24), RaceWay(*), Shell(*, LP, K, CW)
Food	**N:** Knight's Inn
	S: Dairy Queen, Handee Burger, Hardee's, McDonald's(PLAY), Petro's Hot Dogs (Raceway), RaceWay, Subway, Taco Bell
Lodg	**N:** Knight's Inn
	S: Comfort Inn
AServ	**N:** The Auto Place (NAPA Auto Parts)
	S: Dayton Tires (Wrecker Service), Terry's Service Center
ATM	**S:** NationsBank, Shell
Other	**S:** Car Wash, Coin Operated Laundry, Harrell's Foodliner Grocery, US Post Office
355	**Lawnville Road**
FStop	**N:** Aztec(*, D, LP, K), Texaco(*, LP, K)
ATM	**N:** Aztec
356AB	**TN 58N, Oak Ridge, Gallaher Road**
FStop	**N:** Penny's Restaurant Fine Food (Family Inns of America)
Gas	**N:** BP(*, D)
Food	**N:** BP, Family Inns of America, Huddle House (Days Inn)
Lodg	**N:** DAYS INN Days Inn, Family Inns of America
RVCamp	**N:** 4 Seasons Campground(LP)
ATM	**N:** BP
Other	**N:** Huling's Market & Deli (BP)
360	**Buttermilk Road**
RVCamp	**N:** Soaring Eagle Campground(LP)
(363)	**Parking Area (Phones; Eastbound)**
(363)	**Parking Area (Westbound)**
364	**U.S. 321, TN 95, Lenoir City, Oak Ridge**
Gas	**N:** Shell(*)
Food	**N:** Shell
RVCamp	**N:** Cross-Eyed Crickett Campground (2 Miles), Melton Hill Dam (.5 Miles)
368	**Junction I-75 South & I-40, Knoxville, Chattanooga**
369	**Watt Road**
TStop	**N:** Flying J Travel Plaza(*, LP, SCALES)
	S: Petro Travel Plaza(*, SCALES), T/A TravelCenters of America(*)
Gas	**S:** BP(*)
Food	**N:** Flying J Travel Plaza, The Cookery (Flying J Travel Plaza)
	S: Burger King (Truckstop of America), Iron Skillet Restaurant(24) (Petro TS), Perkins (TA), Petro Travel Plaza, Pizza Hut (TA)
TServ	**S:** Petro Travel Plaza(SCALES)
TWash	**S:** Petro Travel Plaza
Other	**S:** Knoxville Travel Center, 76
(372)	**Weigh Station (Eastbound)**
(372)	**Weigh Station (Westbound)**
373	**Campbell Station Road, Farragut**
FStop	**N:** Texaco(*, D, K, CW)
Gas	**N:** Amoco(*)
	S: BP(*, LP, CW), Pilot Travel Center(*, D, LP, K), Speedway(*, K)
Food	**S:** Applecake Tearoom, Applewood, Cracker Barrel, Hardee's
Lodg	**N:** Comfort Suites Hotel, Super 8
	S: Budgetel Inn, Holiday Inn Express
RVCamp	**N:** Buddy Gregg Motor Homes, Inc.
ATM	**N:** Texaco
	S: Pilot Travel Center

Roam & Roost RV Campground

Very Clean, Quiet Country Setting
25 Sites Full Hook-ups
30-50 AMPS • Pull Thru's
Parking Pads & Patios
Slide-Outs, Awnings Welcome
Easy In . . . Easy Out
Coaches to 40'
Fishing • Lake

931-707-1414

I-40 Exit 322 N 3.6 mi Right 1/4 mi
255 Fairview Dr • Crossville, TN 1877

Tennessee • I-40 • Exit 322

Bold red print shows RV & Bus parking available or nearby

EXIT		TENNESSEE
	Other	S: Appalachian Antiques, Campbell Station Antiques, Station West
374		TN 131, Lovell Rd
	TStop	N: TravelCenters of America(*, SCALES)
		S: Pilot Travel Center(*, K, SCALES)
	Gas	N: Amoco(*, D, 24), BP(*, CW), Marathon(*, D), Texaco(*, CW)
		S: Citgo (Wrecker Service), Speedway(*)
	Food	N: Country Pride (TravelCenters of America), McDonald's(PLAY), Prince Deli, Taco Bell (TravelCenters of America), TravelCenters of America, Waffle House
		S: Arby's, Krystal(24), Pilot Travel Center, SHONEY'S, Shoney's, Wendy's (Pilot Travel Center)
	Lodg	N: Best Western, Knight's Inn, Travelodge (TravelCenters of America)
		S: DAYS INN Days Inn, Motel 6
	AServ	S: Citgo (Wrecker Service)
	TServ	N: TravelCenters of America(SCALES)
	ATM	N: BP
		S: Pilot Travel Center
376B		Jct. I-40 & I-140
376A		TN 162 North, Oak Ridge
	Med	N: + Hospital
378AB		Cedar Bluff Road
	Gas	N: Amoco(*), Pilot(*, LP, K), Texaco(*), Weigel's Farm Store(*, K) (Amoco)
		S: Exxon(*, CW)
	Food	N: Arby's, BelAir Grill, Burger King(PLAY), Cedar Grill, Cracker Barrel, Dunkin Donuts, El Mercado (Mexican Market), Holiday Inn Select, Jigger's Restaurant (Ramada Inn), KFC, Long John Silver, McDonald's, Papa John's, Pilot, Pizza Hut, Prince Deli & Sports Bar, Quizno's Subs, Ramada Inn, Stefano's Chicago Style Pizza, Taco Bell (Pilot), The Soup Kitchen, Waffle House, Wendy's
		S: Applebee's, Bob Evan's Restaurant, Corky's Ribs & BBQ, Denny's, Grady's, Hops Restaurant, Outback Steakhouse, Pizza Hut
	Lodg	N: Hampton Inn, Holiday Inn Select, Ramada Inn, Scottish Inns
		S: Best Western, Courtyard by Marriott, Extended Stay America, La Quinta Inn, Microtel Inn, Red Roof Inn, Residence Inn, Signature Inn, Wyndham Garden Hotel
	AServ	N: Texaco
		S: Harry Lane KIA Chrysler Plymouth
	Med	N: + Hospital
		S: + Metro Medical (Primary Care)
	ATM	N: Amoco, BankFirst, First American, First Tennessee Bank, Food City Grocery(LP), Pilot, SunTrust Bank, Weigel's Farm Store (Amoco)
		S: Tenn. Credit Union, Union Planter's National Bank
	Other	N: Coin Laundry, El Mercado, Food City Grocery
		S: CVS Pharmacy(24), Celebration Station, The Marketplace (Mall)
379		Gallaher View Rd, Walker Springs Road, Bridgewater Road
	Gas	N: Aztex(*, D, LP) (Texaco), Exxon(*, LP)
		S: BP(*, D, LP, CW)
	Food	N: Subway (Exxon)
		S: Can Ton Restaurant (Chinese), Joe Muggs Coffee Shop, Mrs Winner's Chicken, Old Country Buffet, SHONEY'S, Shoney's
	AServ	N: Sam's Club, Wal-Mart(24, RX)
		S: Firestone Tire & Auto, Goodyear Tire & Auto, Jim Codgdil Dodge, Ted Russell Ford, Ted Russell Nissan
	Med	S: + Park Med Ambulatory Care Walk-In Medical Center
	ATM	N: Exxon
		S: Union Planters Bank
	Other	N: Sam's Club, Wal-Mart(RX)
		S: Books-A-Million, CVS Pharmacy(RX), Pet Supply, Walker Springs Plaza Shopping Center, Winn Dixie Supermarket(24, RX)
380		U.S. 11, U.S. 70, West Hills
	Gas	S: BP(*, CW), Conoco(*, LP), Texaco(*, D)
	Food	S: Backyard Burgers (Conoco), Borders Books, Music & Cafe, Conoco, Cozumels (Mexican Grill), Dunkin Donuts (Conoco), KFC, Kaya Korean Restaurant, Romano's Macaroni Grill, Steak & Shake, Steak-Out Char-Broiled Delivery, Subway, Taco Bell
	Lodg	S: Comfort Hotel, Howard Johnson
	AServ	S: BP, Capettas Auto Trim, NTB, Penske
	ATM	S: Conoco, First American Bank, First Tennessee Bank, First Vantage Bank Of Tennessee, Food Lion, SunTrust, Texaco
	Other	S: Bi-Lo Grocery, Borders Books, Music & Cafe, Food Lion, K-Mart, Kingston Pike Pet Hospital, Kohl's, PetsMart, State Hwy Patrol, West Town Mall
383		Papermill Dr
	FStop	S: Pilot(*, LP, K)
	Gas	S: BP(*, LP, CW), Citgo(*), Spur(*)
	Food	N: Holiday Inn
		S: Smokey Market Deli, Spur, Waffle House
	Lodg	N: Holiday Inn
		S: Super 8
385		North Junction I-75, I-40, East Junction I-640, Lexington, Knoxville
386A		University Ave, Middlebrook Pike (Eastbound, Services Same As 386B)
	AServ	N: Gene's Alignment Service
	TServ	S: Post & Co. The Truck Body People
	Other	N: Pharmacy
386B		U.S. 129, Alcoa Hwy, Airport, Smoky Mountains
	Lodg	N: Expo Inn
	TServ	S: Post & Co. The Truck Body People
387		TN 62, 17th St - 21st St, Western Ave
	Gas	N: Western Ave Tire & Service Center
	Lodg	N: Expo Inn
	AServ	N: Gene's Alignment Service, Western Ave Tire & Service Center
	TServ	N: Gene's Alignment Service
	Med	N: + Medical Center
		S: + Fort Sanders Regional Medical Center
	Parks	N: World's Fair Park
	Other	S: Coin Laundry(24)
387A		Junction I-275 North, Lexington
388A		to US 441 South, James White Pkwy, Downtown (Limited Access Hwy)
389A		U.S. 441 North, Broadway (Limited Access Hwy)
	Gas	S: BP(*, LP, CW), Spur(K)
	Food	S: Oriental Garden Chinese Restaurant, Taco Bell
	AServ	S: Transmissions
	ATM	S: SunTrust
	Other	S: Belew Rx Drugs, Kroger(RX)
389B		Fifth Avenue (Westbound)
390		Cherry St
	FStop	N: Texaco(*, CW)
	Gas	N: Citgo(*), Pilot(*, K), Weigel's Farm Store(*)
		S: Buy Quick Market(*), Exxon(*, CW)
	Food	N: Citgo, Country Table Restaurant, Hardee's, Krispy Kreme Doughnuts, Red Carpet Inn
	Lodg	N: Red Carpet Inn
	AServ	N: Ford Parts Unlimited, Goodyear Tire & Auto
		S: Advance Auto Parts, AllRight Service Center, Cherry Street Automotive, Ron's Import Auto Parts
	ATM	N: Citgo, Pilot
392AB		U.S. 11 W, Rutledge Pike
	Gas	S: BP(*, LP, CW)
	Food	N: Ron's Tavern, The Cookhouse
		S: Hardee's, SHONEY'S, Shoney's, The Lunch House Restaurant
	Lodg	S: Family Inns of America
	AServ	S: Atkins & Son Transmission, Quicko Mufflers, Shocks
	TServ	N: Cummins Diesel, Disney Tire Company, East Tennessee Tire, Freightliner Dealer, International Dealer, Kenworth, Quick Serve, Suspentions Unlimited, TK's Truck Service, Wheels & Brakes Inc.
	Parks	S: Chilhowee Park, Knoxville Zoo
	Other	S: TVA and I Fairgrounds
393		West I-640 to North I-75, Lexington
394		U.S. 11 East, U.S. 25 West, U.S. 70, Asheville Highway
	Gas	N: BP(*, CW)
		S: Phillips 66(*), Texaco(*, D)
	Food	S: Waffle House
	Lodg	S: DAYS INN Days Inn (see our ad this page)
	AServ	N: K-Mart
	ATM	S: Texaco
	Other	N: Food Lion Supermarket, K-Mart
398		Strawberry Plains Pike
	FStop	N: Amoco(*, D, K, CW, 24), Phillips 66(*, K)
		S: Pilot(*, K, SCALES) (Showers), Speedway(*, SCALES)
	Gas	N: BP(*, D, LP, K, CW), Shell(*)
		S: Citgo(*), Geigel
	Food	N: Amoco, Baskin Robbins (Amoco), McDonald's(PLAY), Phillips 66, Pizza Hut (Phillips 66), TCBY (BP), Waffle House, Wendy's
		S: Arby's, Burger King (Pilot), Citgo, Cracker Barrel, Dairy Queen (Pilot), KFC, Krispy Kreme Doughnuts, Krystal(24), Perkins Family Restaurant, Pilot (Showers), Speedway, Starlite Diner, Subway (Pilot)
	Lodg	N: Comfort Inn, Country Inn & Suites, Hampton Inn (see our ad this page), Holiday Inn Express, Ramada Limited, Super 8
		S: Fairfield Inn

1639
$57.60 2-4 Persons
Hampton Inn
EAST KNOXVILLE
• Free multi-choice continental breakfast
• Some rooms with jacuzzi & whirlpool
• Indoor & outdoor pool • Exercise room
• Free HBO • 25" TV
Strawberry Plains Pike at I-40
423-525-3511 • 800-HAMPTON
Add $10 Fri-Sat from June-Oct & Special Events.
TENNESSEE • I-40 • EXIT 398

Bold red print shows RV & Bus parking available or nearby

Located at the intersection
of fun and excitement.

You could wear yourself out just thinking about everything that awaits in action-packed Pigeon Forge, in the Smoky Mountains of Tennessee. Live shows, outlet stores, fun dining, family activities. We're also home to Dollywood, the theme park that's perfect for folks of all ages. For a free travel planner, call 1-800-365-6993 or visit us online at www.pigeon-forge.tn.us.

1637

EXIT		TENNESSEE
	ATM	N: Amoco, First American Bank, McDonald's S: Citgo, Speedway
402		Midway Road
407		TN 66, Pigeon Forge, Gatlinburg, Sevierville (Dollywood)
	Gas	N: Texaco(*) S: Amoco(*) (Fireworks Supercenter), BP(*), Texaco(*, CW)
	Food	S: BP, Dairy Queen (BP), Ole Southern Pancakes, Pizza Inn Express (BP), Subway, Wendy's
	Lodg	N: Econolodge, Super 8 (see our ad this page), S: Best Western, Comfort Inn, Days Inn (see our ad this page), Super 8 (see our ad this page),, Quality Inn
	RVCamp	N: KOA Kampground (.5 Miles) S: Foretravel Sales (see our ad this page), Services, Parts, Smoky Mountain Campground (.25 Miles)
	ATM	S: Texaco
	Parks	S: Great Smoky Mountain National Park
412		Deep Springs Road, Douglas Dam
	TStop	N: Sunshine Travel Center(*, LP, K, SCALES) S: TR Auto/Truck Plaza(*, SCALES) (CB Shop)
	Food	N: Apple Valley Cafe (Sunshine Travel Center), Sunshine Travel Center S: TR Auto/Truck Plaza (CB Shop)
	TServ	S: TR Auto/Truck Plaza(SCALES) (CB Shop)
	ATM	N: Sunshine Travel Center
	Other	S: Mt View CB Sales
415		U.S. 25 West, U.S. 70, Dandridge
	FStop	S: Texaco(*, D, K)
	Food	S: Wild Bill's Texas BBQ (Thurs thru Sun)
	ATM	S: Texaco
417		TN 92, Dandridge, Jefferson City (Cherokee Dam)
	TStop	N: 417 Travel Center(LP, SCALES, 24) (Exxon)
	Gas	N: Marathon(*) S: Amoco(*, D, LP, K), Shell(*, D, 24)
	Food	N: Anna Lee's Restaurant, Baskin Robbins (417 Travel Center TS), Hardee's, McDonald's(PLAY), Perkins(24), Subway (417 Travel Center), Taco Bell (417 Travel Center TS) S: Shell, SHONEY'S Shoney's, Wendy's (Shell)
	Lodg	N: Tennessee Mountain Inn S: Best Western, Comfort Inn (see our ad this page), Super 8
	TServ	N: 417 Travel Center(SCALES, 24) (Exxon)
	ATM	S: Shell
(419)		Rest Area (RR, HF, Phones, Picnic, Vending, RV Dump; Eastbound)
421		I-81 North & I-40, Bristol
424		TN 113, Dandridge, White Pine
	FStop	N: Marathon(*, K)
	Gas	N: Amoco(*, K)
	RVCamp	S: Douglas Lake Campground (1 Mile), Fancher's Campground
	ATM	N: Marathon
	Other	N: L & N Produce
(425)		Rest Area (RR, HF, Phones, Picnic, Vending, Pet Walk; Westbound)
432AB		432A - US 411 S, Sevierville 432B - US 25 W, US 70 E, Newport
	FStop	N: Exxon(*, D) S: Texaco(*, D, CW)
	Gas	S: Amoco(*), Citgo(*, K), Shell(*, K, CW)
	Food	N: Kathy's Family Restaurant, Lois's Country Kitchen Restaurant S: Family Farm Restaurant (Family Inn), Family Inns of America
	Lodg	N: Comfort Inn, Relax Inn S: Family Inns of America

Super 8 Motel
523 E. Parkway Hwy. 321
423-436-9750
To Gatlinburg- Go to traffic light #3 Go left (East Parkway) Go 1/2 mile and Super 8 on left at traffic light.
- Free Continental Breakfast
- Outdoor Jacuzzi/New Outdoor Pool
- Fireplace In Room
- Scenic Smoky Mountain View
- Dollywood Nearby
- Convention Center & Ski Resort 1 mile
- Tour Buses Welcome

1504
TENNESSEE • I-40 • EXIT 407

1056

MOTORHOME
SALES • SERVICE • PARTS

Directions: I-40 exit 407 (Hwy 66) Go 200 yards South on Hwy 66, turn Left on Foretravel Drive ¼ mile.

195 Foretravel Drive • Kodak, TN 37764
800.678.2233

Super 8 Motel
Exit 407 • Sevierville, TN
423-429-0887
- Cable TV with HBO & ESPN
- Heated Pool • Free Local Calls
- Exercise Room with Whirlpool Bath
- Most Units have 2 Bedrooms/ All King & Queen
- Nearest Super 8 to I-40
- Near Dollywood, Music Road, Smoky Mtns. National Park
- Bus Parking-Dump Station

1185
TENNESSEE • I-40 • EXIT 407

1590

423-397-2090
800-228-5150
- Continental Breakfast
- Kids Under 12 Stay & Eat Free
- Outdoor Pool
- Handicap Accessible
- Exterior Corridors

620 Green Valley Drive • Dandridge, TN 37725
Tennessee • I-40 • Exit 417

1594

GREAT LOCATIONS TO CHOOSE FROM!

PIGEON FORGE
(423) 453-4707
Toll Free Reservations:
1-800-645-3079

INTERSTATE
(423)933-7378
Toll Free Reservations:
1-800-348-4652

SEVIERVILLE
(423) 428-3353
Toll Free Reservations:
1-800-590-4861

INTERSTATE
(423) 933-4500
Toll Free Reservations:
1-800-304-3915

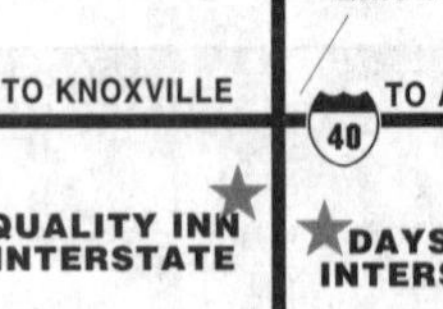

$5 OFF regular room rates per night
AAA & Seniors An Extra 10% Discount

TENNESSEE • I-40 • EXIT 407

Bold red print shows RV & Bus parking available or nearby

EXIT		TENNESSEE
	ASErv	N: Liberty Ford Mercury, Newport Tire Center
	TServ	N: Newport Truck & Trailer Repair
	RVCamp	N: TMC Campground
		S: KOA Campgrounds (2 Miles)
	ATM	N: Exxon
		S: Amoco, Texaco
	Other	S: Newport Animal Clinic
435		U.S. 321, TN 32, Newport, Gatlinburg
	Gas	N: Dixie Pawn Shop, Exxon(*, D, LP), Marathon(*, K), Texaco(*, CW)
		S: Amoco(*), BP(*, K), Bi-Lo Grocery(*, CW)
	Food	N: Arby's, Baskin Robbins (Exxon), Burger King(PLAY), Exxon, Hardee's, KFC, La Carreta, McDonald's(PLAY), Pizza Hut, Pizza Plus, Pride Of The Mountain Pancake & Waffle House, Sagebrush Steakhouse, SHONEY'S, Shoney's, Taco Bell
		S: BP, Cracker Barrel, Cracker Barrel, Ryan's Steakhouse, Shiners Bar-B-Q (Best Western), TCBY (BP), Waffle House, Wendy's
	Lodg	N: Bryant Town Motel, Motel 6
		S: Best Western, Family Inns of America, Holiday Inn
	ASErv	N: Cosby Highway Service Center
		S: Calibur Express Lube, Pennzoil Oil Change, Wal-Mart Supercenter(RX)
	Med	N: + Hospital
	ATM	N: Exxon, First Union Bank, National Bank of Newport
	Other	N: Cinema 4, Town & Country Drugs(RX)
		S: CVS Drugstore(RX), Save-A-Lot Food Stores, Wal-Mart Supercenter(RX)
440		U.S. 321 South, TN 73, Wilton Springs Road, Gatlinburg
	FStop	N: Coastal(*, 24)
	Food	N: Coastal
	TServ	N: Frank's Truck Repair
(441)		Weigh Station
443		Foothills Pkwy, Great Smoky Mtns National Park, Gatlinburg
(446)		TN Welcome Center (RR, HF, Phones, Picnic, RV Dump; Westbound, No Trucks)
447		Hartford Road
	Gas	S: Exxon(*, K)
	ASErv	S: Exxon
	RVCamp	N: Tripple Creek Campground
	Other	S: Pigeon River Outdoors, Smoky Mtn River Company (White Water Rafting), The Hartford Outpost(*), U.S. Post Office, USA Raft, Wild Water Rafting, Pigeon River Rafting Center
451		Waterville Road

EXIT		TENNESSEE/NORTH CAROLINA
		↑TENNESSEE
		↓NORTH CAROLINA
7		Harmon Den
(11)		NC Welcome Center (RR, Phones; Eastbound)
15		Fines Creek
20		U.S. 276, Maggie Valley
	FStop	S: Exxon(*, D, K)
	Gas	S: Amoco(*, D, LP, K)
	Food	S: Shoney's
	ASErv	S: T&T Enterprises
	RVCamp	S: Creekwood Farm RV Park (1 Mile)
	ATM	S: Amoco

1628

COME PLAY IN THE MOUNTAINS.

The Great Smoky Mountains are smokin' with non-stop excitement. That's because Harrahs Cherokee Casino is here with thrilling, heart-racing action 24 hours a day. We've got all your favorite games in video format like Double Diamonds, Red, White & Blue and Sizzling Sevens, all with the added skill feature of a second spin to win. Plus, Video Blackjack, Video Poker and Video Craps. Bring your appetite to any one of three first-class restaurants. And be sure to catch world-class entertainment appearing throughout the year in the comfort of our spacious Cherokee Pavilion theater. For general tourist information or accommodations in Cherokee, call 1-800-438-1601. Just take Route 441 to Cherokee, in North Carolina's Great Smoky Mountains. For our entertainment schedule or for more information, call 1-800-HARRAHS®.

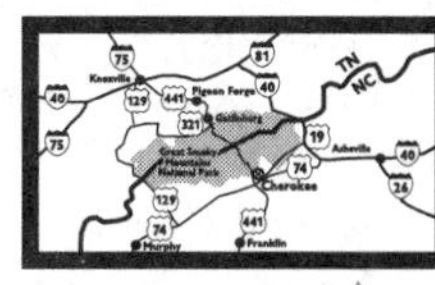

Your biggest nights happen here.℠

Must be 18 or older. Know When to Stop Before You Start® Gambling Problem? Call 1-800-522-4700. ©1998, Harrah's Entertainment, Inc. An Enterprise of the Eastern Band of Cherokee Indians.

EXIT		NORTH CAROLINA
	Parks	S: Great Smoky Mountain National Park (.5 Miles)
24		NC 209, Lake Junaluska, Hot Springs
	TStop	N: Pilot Travel Center(*, SCALES)
		S: 76 Auto/Truck Plaza(*, SCALES), Citgo
	Food	N: Country Cooker (Pilot TS), Pilot Travel Center
		S: 76 Auto/Truck Plaza, Citgo
	Lodg	N: Pilot Travel Center
	ASErv	S: 76 Auto/Truck Plaza
	TServ	N: Pilot Travel Center(SCALES)
		S: 76 Auto/Truck Plaza(SCALES)
	Med	S: + Hospital
27		U.S. 19, U.S. 23, West U.S. 74, Clyde, Waynesville (Difficult Reaccess)
	Med	S: + Hospital
	Parks	S: Great Smoky Mountain National Park
	Other	S: Ghost Town, Maggie Valley, Cherokee, Harrah's Casino (see our as this page)
31		NC 215, Canton
	FStop	S: Amoco(*, K, CW)
	Gas	S: BP(D), Exxon(*, 24), Texaco(*, D)
	Food	N: Western Steer Family Steakhouse
		S: Arby's (Texaco), Burger King, Exxon, McDonald's (Exxon), Taco Bell, Texaco
	Lodg	N: EconoLodge
		S: Comfort Inn
	ASErv	S: An-ton Chevrolet Pontiac Oldsmobile Buick, BP, Ken Wilson Ford
	ATM	S: Amoco, Texaco
	Other	S: Auto Pride Car Wash, Ingles
33		Newfound Rd., Leicester
37		Candler
	TStop	N: Travelport(*, SCALES)
	Gas	N: Amoco(*, K)
		S: Exxon(*, D, LP, K)
	Food	N: Buck Horn Restaurant (Travelport TS), Travelport
		S: DAYS INN Days Inn, Restaurant (Days Inn)
	Lodg	S: DAYS INN Days Inn
	ASErv	N: Brad Ragan Inc. Truck Tire Center
	TServ	N: Brad Ragan Inc. Truck Tire Center
	RVCamp	S: Big Cove Campground (2.7 Miles), KOA Kampground (.7 Miles)
(41)		Weigh Station (Westbound)
(41)		Weigh Station (Eastbound)
44		U.S. 19, U.S. 23, US 74, West Asheville, Enka - Candler
	Gas	N: Amoco(*, CW), Exxon(*, LP, K), Shell(*, D, LP)
	Food	N: Best Western, Burger King(PLAY), Cracker Barrel, Cracker Barrel, El Chapala, Popeye's Chicken, Shell, Sub Station II (Shell), Waffle House, Wendy's
		S: McDonald's(PLAY), Ramada Plaza Hotel, Ramada Plaza Hotel, SHONEY'S, Shoney's

EXIT NORTH CAROLINA

Lodg **N:** Best Western, Comfort Inn, Red Roof Inn, Sleep Inn, Super 8
S: Budget Motel, Ramada Plaza Hotel
AServ **N:** Auto Repair, Chevrolet Dealer, Mercedes, Chrysler, Oldsmobile Dealer, Smokey Mountain Auto Service
ATM **N:** Amoco, Shell

46A Junction I-26 East, East US 74, Hendersonville, Spartanburg, Hickory

46B Junction I-240, Asheville (Eastbound)

47 NC 191, West Asheville, Farmer's Market
Gas **S:** Phillips 66(*, D, K)
Food **S:** Moose Cafe
AServ **S:** The Tire Station
TServ **S:** Carolina Tractor (CAT)
RVCamp **N:** Asheville-Bear Creek RV Park (.5 Miles)
Other **S:** US Post Office, WNC Farmer's Market

50 U.S. 25, Asheville, Biltmore Estate
Gas **N:** Texaco(*, D)
Food **N:** Arby's, Biltmore Dairy Bar & Grill, Bruegger's Bagel & Bakery, Chatt's Restaurant (Howard Johnson), Howard Johnson, The Criterion Grill
S: Apollo Flame Pizza & Subs, Golden Cricket, Huddle House(24)
Lodg **N:** Holiday Inn Express, Howard Johnson, Plaza Motel, Quality Inn, Sleep Inn
AServ **S:** Sony Auto Sound
Med **N:** + Hospital (Trama Center)
ATM **N:** NationsBank
Other **S:** Office of the Sheriff Buncombe County, The Book Rack

53AB 53A - US 74A E, Blue Ridge Pky; 53B - I-240, US 74AW, Asheville
Other **N:** NC Nature Center

55 to U.S. 70, East Asheville
Gas **N:** Amoco(*), Citgo(*, D, K, CW)
Food **N:** Arby's, Citgo, Country Kitchen, Dragons' (Days Inn), Poseidon Steak & Seafood, Subway (Citgo), Waffle House
Lodg **N:** Best Inns of America, Days Inn (see our ad this page), EconoLodge, Holiday Inn, Motel 6, Super 8
RVCamp **N:** Azalea Country Campground (Full Hookups), RC RV Propane Filling Station, Taps RV Park (.2 Miles)
Med **N:** + VA Hospital
ATM **N:** Citgo
Other **N:** GO Grocery Outlet
S: Billy Graham Training Center, The Cove, Folk Art Center

59 Swannanoa
FStop **N:** Exxon(*, D, LP, K) (Coin Operated Laundry)
Gas **N:** Amoco(LP), Citgo(*), Texaco(*)
Food **N:** Admiral's Pizza Restaurant, Athen's Pizza, Breakfast Shop (Exxon FS), Burger King(PLAY), Citgo, Perry's Famous Southwestern BBQ, Subway (Citgo), Swannanoa Restaurant, TCBY (Citgo), Wannanoa
AServ **N:** Carolina Tire Co., Chandler's Auto Service, Goodyear, Phillips Automotive (Foreign & Domestic), Texaco
RVCamp **N:** KOA Campgrounds (1.5 Miles), Miles RV Center & Campground(LP)
S: Mama Gertie's Hideaway Campground (.5 Miles)
Med **N:** + St Joseph's Urgent Care (7 Days a Week)
ATM **N:** NationsBank, NationsBank
Other **N:** Classic Auto Museum, Coin Laundry, Ingles Supermarket, Kerr Drugs, US Post Office

64 NC 9, Black Mountain, Montreat
Gas **N:** Texaco(*, LP)
S: Phillips 66(*)
Food **N:** Pizza Hut, Subway (Texaco), Texaco
S: Campfire Steaks Buffet, Denny's, Huddle House, KFC, McDonald's(PLAY), Mountain BBQ, Taco Bell, Wendy's
Lodg **S:** Comfort Inn
AServ **N:** Black Mountain Chevrolet Geo
ATM **N:** First Union Bank, Texaco
Other **N:** Black Mountain Antique Mall, Visitor Information
S: Chimney Rock (20 Miles), Eckerd Drugs(RX), Ingles Supermarket

65 U.S. 70, Black Mountain (Westbound, Reaccess Eastbound Only)
FStop **N:** Chevron(*)
Gas **N:** Citgo(*)
Food **N:** Franks Roman Pizza, No. 1 China, Olympic Flame Restaurant, Pizza Express, Tong Sing
Lodg **N:** Super 8
Other **N:** Coin Laundry, Food Lion

66 **Ridgecrest**

Exit **(69)** Information Station (Eastbound, Trucks Going Eastbound Must Exit)

72 U.S. 70, Old Fort (Southbound)

73 Old Fort
Gas **N:** BP(*, LP, K)
S: Exxon, K-Max(*), SuperTest(*, D)
Food **N:** Hardee's
S: McDonald's
AServ **N:** Big Rig Tire & Brake, Old Fort Auto Parts (NAPA)
S: Ellis Auto Service, Exxon, Parts Plus
RVCamp **S:** Camping

75 Parker Padgett Road
FStop **S:** Citgo(*)
Food **S:** Citgo, Dairy Queen (Citgo)

81 Marion, Sugar Hill Road
FStop **N:** Chevron(*, LP, 24)
Gas **N:** Amoco(*, K, 24)
AServ **N:** Dixie Auto & Truck Repair
TServ **N:** Dixie Auto & Truck Repair, H & A Truck Repair Inc
Med **N:** + McDowell Hospital

(82) **Rest Area (RR, HF, Phones, Picnic, Grills, Vending, RV Dump; Westbound)**

(82) **Rest Area (RR, HF, Phones, Picnic, Vending; Eastbound)**

83 Ashworth Road

85 U.S. 221, Marion, Rutherfordton
FStop **S:** Shell(*, D, K)
Gas **S:** BP(*, D)
Food **S:** Carolina Chocolatiers Ice Cream, Park Inn, Western Steer Family Steakhouse
Lodg **S:** Park Inn, Scenic Inn, Super 8
Parks **N:** Mt. Mitchell State Park (Approx 20 Miles)

1068
DAYS INN
1500 Tunnel Road
Ashville, North Carolina
Full Continental Breakfast Included
Restaurant on Premises
Outdoor Pool
Kids Stay & Eat Free
Pets Allowed
Handicap Accessible
704-298-5140 • 800-329-7466
North Carolina • I-40 • Exit 55

86 NC 226, Marion, Shelby
RVCamp **N:** Hidden Valley Campground & Recreation Park (2 Miles)

90 Nebo - Lake James
FStop **N:** Exxon(*)
S: Amoco(*, LP, K)
Food **N:** Exxon
TServ **N:** Davis Wrecker Of Marion NC
Parks **N:** Lake James State Park
Other **N:** National Forest Ranger Station

94 Dysartsville Road, Lake James

96 Kathy Road

98 Causby Road, Glen Alpine

100 Glen Alpine, Jamestown Road
Gas **N:** Amoco(*, LP, K, 24)
Food **N:** Asian & American
AServ **N:** BG Diversified Glass, Martin Family Ford Lincoln Mercury
ATM **N:** Amoco

103 U.S. 64, Morganton, Rutherfordton
Gas **N:** Exxon(*, LP, CW, 24), Texaco(*, D, LP, K)
S: BP(*), Conoco(*), Racetrac(*), SuperTest(*, D)
Food **N:** Max' Mexican Eatery, Tastee Freez
S: Captain D's Seafood, Checkers Burgers, Denny's, Dragon Garden Chinese, Hardee's, KFC, Subway, Taco Bell
AServ **S:** Carolina Tire Co., Goodyear, Xpress Lube
ATM **N:** Exxon
S: First Citizens Bank
Other **N:** Sen. Sam J. Ervin Jr. Library & Museum, Western Piedmont Community College
S: Food Lion Supermarket, Ingles Supermarket, Wal-Mart(RX)

104 Enola Road
Gas **S:** BP(*, LP, K)
ATM **N:** State Employees Credit Union
S: BP
Other **N:** Burke County Sheriff's Office, Highway Patrol

105 NC 18, Morganton, Downtown
Gas **N:** Amoco(*), Exxon(D)
S: QM(*), Texaco(*, LP)
Food **N:** Arby's, Hardee's, Mr. Omelet, Peking Express Chinese, Pizza Inn, Quincy's Family Steakhouse, SHONEY'S, Shoney's, Wendy's
S: Harbor Inn Seafood Restaurant, Sagebrush Steakhouse
Lodg **N:** Hampton Inn, Red Carpet Inn
S: DAYS INN Days Inn, Holiday Inn, Sleep Inn
AServ **N:** Exxon, Rooster Bush Pontiac, Cadillac, GMC Trucks
Med **N:** + Broughton Hospital, + Grace Hospital
ATM **S:** Texaco
Parks **S:** South Mountain State Park
Other **N:** Vitamin's & Such

106 Bethel Road
FStop **S:** Exxon(*, LP, 24)
Food **S:** Timberwood (Rainbow Motel)
Lodg **S:** Rainbow Motel
AServ **N:** I-40 Auto Parts

107 NC 114, Drexel

111 Valdese

112 Mineral Springs Mtn Road, Valdese

113 Rutherford College, Connelly Springs
FStop **N:** Phillips 66(*, D, K)

EXIT NORTH CAROLINA

AServ **N:** Paramount Ford, Paramount Pontiac
Med **N:** Hospital
Other **N:** Speedway

116 Icard
FStop **S:** Conoco[*, LP, K]
Food **S:** Burger King[PLAY], Granny's Kitchen[24] (Icard Inn)
Lodg **S:** Icard Inn[24]
ATM **S:** Conoco
Other **S:** Icarda Wash, US Post Office

118 Old NC 10
Gas **N:** Exxon[*, LP, K], Texaco[*, D, LP]
ATM **N:** Texaco

119AB Hildebran, Henry River
Gas **N:** Texaco[*, LP]
Food **N:** Hardee's, Subway (Texaco), Texaco

123 U.S. 70, U.S. 321, NC 127, Hickory, Lenoir (Limited Access Hwy)

125 Hickory
Gas **N:** Exxon[*, D, LP], Racetrac[*]
S: Shell[*]
Food **N:** Bojangles, Dragon Inn (Chinese), Exxon, Golden Corral Family Steakhouse, Monterey Cafe, Rock-ola Cafe, Subway (Exxon), The Peddler Steakhouse and Lounge, Tripps, Western Steer Family Steakhouse
S: Cracker Barrel, Fuddruckers, Hardee's, J & S Cafeteria, Kobe Japanese Restaurant, Krispy Kreme Doughnuts, Outback Steakhouse, Ragazzi's, Red Lobster, Sagebrush Steakhouse, Schlotzsky's Deli, Steak & Ale, The Stockyard & Co. Grille, Waffle House
Lodg **N:** Red Roof Inn
S: Comfort Suites Hotel, Fairfield Inn, Hampton Inn, Holiday Inn Select, Sleep Inn
AServ **N:** Lube Works, Mercedes, Safelite Auto Glass, Saturn of Hickory
S: Armstrong Ford, Midas Muffler & Brake, Servco[*, D, LP, CW]
ATM **N:** Racetrac
S: Shell
Other **N:** Waterworks Car Wash
S: Aldi, Celebration Bookstore, Food Lion Supermarket, Hickory Metro Trade Center, Office Max, Piedmont Center (Holiday Inn Select), Valley Hills Regional Mall

126 To 70 US Newton, Hickory

128 Fairgrove Church Road
FStop **S:** Citgo[*, D, LP, K]
Gas **N:** Amoco[*, LP, K], Texaco[*, LP]
S: Exxon (Credit Card Only), Phillips 66[*, D]
Food **N:** McDonald's, Waffle House
S: Arby's[PLAY], Bennett's Smokehouse & Saloon, Burger King[PLAY], Harbor Inn Seafood, Mr. Omelet, SHONEY'S, Shoney's, Thai Orchid, Wendy's
Lodg **S:** Best Western, DAYS INN Days Inn
TServ **S:** Volvo, GM Dealer
Med **N:** Hospital
Other **S:** Highway Patrol

130 Old U.S. 70
Food **N:** Domino's Pizza, No.1 Kitchen, Subway
Other **N:** City of Conover Fire Dept, Countryside Pet Hospital, Firefighters Museum, K-Mart[RX], Lowe's Foods[LP, 24], US Post Office

131 NC 16, Conover, Taylorsville
Gas **N:** Amoco[*, LP, CW], Texaco[*, D, LP]
Lodg **N:** Holiday Inn
RVCamp **N:** Lake Hickory RV Resort (9.6 Miles)
Other **N:** Jet-Kleen Car Wash

133 To U.S. 70 To U.S. 321, Rock Barn Road, Newton
TStop **S:** Wilco Travel Plaza[*, LP, SCALES] (Showers)
Gas **N:** Exxon[*, D, LP, K, CW]
Food **S:** D J's Diner, Stuckey's Express (Wilco TS), Subway (Wilco TS), Taco Bell (Wilco TS), Wilco Travel Plaza (Showers)

135 Claremont
Gas **S:** Texaco[*, LP, 24]
Food **S:** Buffet Pizza (Texaco), Flapjacks Country Cookin, Texaco
Lodg **S:** Super 8
Other **S:** Lowe's Foods

(136) Rest Area (RR, HF, Phones, Picnic, RV Dump; Eastbound)

(136) Rest Area (RR, HF, Phones, Picnic, RV Dump; Westbound)

138 Oxford School Road, Catawba, West NC 10
FStop **N:** Exxon[*, LP]
S: Texaco[*, D, K]
ATM **S:** Texaco
Other **S:** Murray's Mill State Historic Site

141 Sharon School Road
Other **S:** Buffalo Shoals Golf

(143) Weigh Station (Eastbound)

(143) Weigh Station (Westbound)

144 Old Mountain Road
FStop **N:** Chevron[*, LP, K]
S: Texaco[*]
Gas **N:** BP[D]
S: B&B Quick Stop[*, D, K]
Food **N:** Troy's 50's
AServ **N:** BP

146 Stamey Farm Road
TStop **S:** Homer's Truck Stop[*, SCALES] (CB Shop)
Food **S:** Homer's Truck Stop (CB Shop)
TServ **S:** Homer's Truck Stop[SCALES] (CB Shop)
ATM **S:** Homer's Truck Stop (CB Shop)
Other **S:** Airport

148 US 64, NC 90, West Statesville, Taylorsville
Gas **N:** Citgo[*, D], Exxon[*, K]
S: Traveller's
Food **N:** Arby's, Burger King[PLAY], Country Cafe, McDonald's, Prime Sirloin, Subway, Village Inn Pizza
Lodg **N:** Economy Inn
AServ **S:** CG Towing, Dowell's Auto Parts, Traveller's
ATM **N:** Citgo
Other **N:** CVS[RX], Car Wash, Ingles Supermarket

150 NC 115, Statesville Downtown, Wilkesboro
FStop **N:** BP[*, K]
Gas **N:** Citgo[*, D], Shell[*]
S: Amoco[*]
Food **N:** Little Caesars Pizza
AServ **S:** Amoco
RVCamp **N:** Jerry Lathan's RV World[LP]
Other **N:** Animal Hospital of Statesville Northside, Riverfront Antique Mall

151 U.S. 21 East, Statesville, Harmony
Gas **N:** Citgo[*, D, CW]
S: BP[*, D, CW], Exxon[*, LP]
Food **N:** Applebee's, Bojangles, Burger King[PLAY], Cracker Barrel, Golden Corral Family Steakhouse, Italian Oven, KFC, Long John Silver, McDonald's[PLAY], Pizza Inn, Quincy's Family Steakhouse, Red Lobster, Sagebrush Steakhouse, Schlotzsky's Deli, Taco Bell, The Italian Oven, Wendy's
S: Carolina Cafe & Donut, Hardee's[PLAY], Huddle House, Lotus Pier Restaurant & Lounge, Szechuan Chinese, Waffle House
Lodg **N:** Sleep Inn
S: EconoLodge, Hampton Inn, Holiday Inn Express, Masters Inn Economy
AServ **N:** The Lube Doctor
S: Cannon Motors Inc. Volkswagon
Med **S:** Iredell Memorial Hospital, Urgent Care Family Practice (7 days a week)
ATM **N:** Bi-Lo Grocery, First Union Bank
S: BB&T Bank
Other **N:** Arts & Science Museum, Bi-Lo Grocery, CVS, Wal-Mart[24, RX] (One Hr Photo)
S: Statesville Coin Laundry

152AB Junction I-77, Elkin, Charlotte

153 U.S. 64 (Eastbound)
Gas **S:** Rickie's[*, LP, K]
Food **S:** Ice Cream Churn

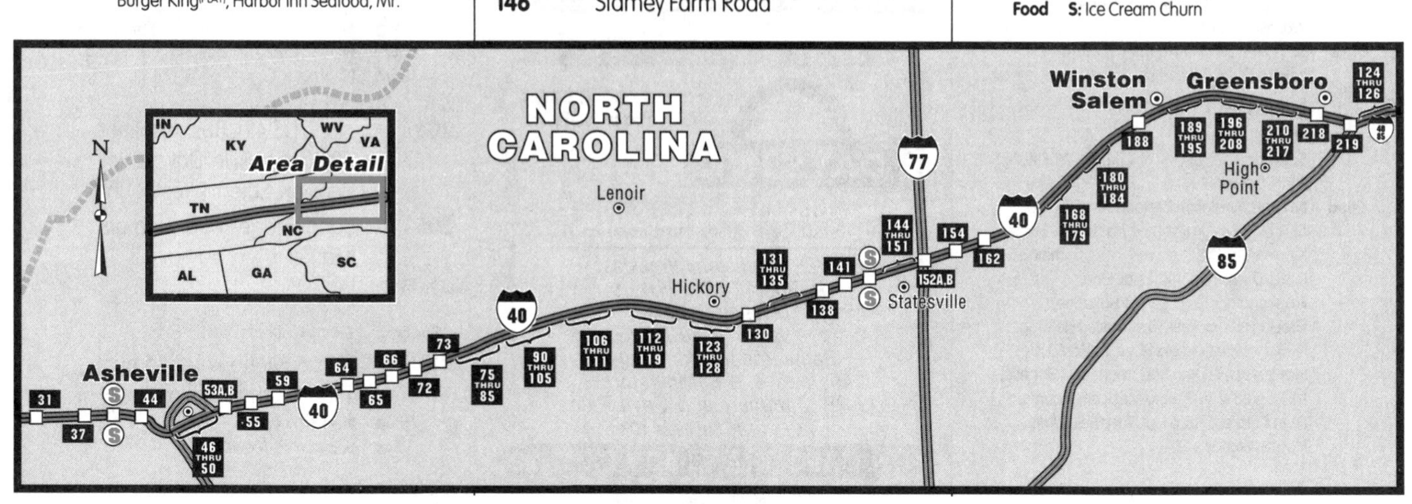

EXIT NORTH CAROLINA

Lodg **S:** Hallmark Inn
TServ **S:** Carolina Truck & Tractor
Other **S:** Animal Hospital of Statesville

154 Old Mocksville Rd
Gas **S:** Citgo(*, D, LP, K)
Food **S:** Jay Bee's
AServ **S:** Bill Martin Tire
Med **N:** Columbia Davis Medical Center

162 U.S. 64
Gas **S:** Texaco(*)
RVCamp **S:** Midway Campground Resort (.5 Miles)

168 U.S. 64, Mocksville
FStop **S:** Amoco(*, D, LP, K)
Gas **N:** Mobil(*, LP, K)
RVCamp **N:** Lake Myers RV Resort
ATM **S:** Amoco

170 U.S. 601, Mocksville, Yadkinville
TStop **N:** 76 Auto/Truck Plaza(*, SCALES), Horn's Auto Truck Plaza(SCALES)
FStop **S:** BP(*, D, LP, K)
Gas **N:** Citgo(D, LP)
S: Amoco(*), Texaco(*, LP)
Food **N:** 76 Auto/Truck Plaza, Good Kitchen Rest. (76 Auto TS), Horn's Auto Truck Plaza
S: Burger King(PLAY), Highway Inn, Pizza Hut, Wendy's, Western Steer Family Steakhouse
Lodg **S:** Comfort Inn (see our ad this page), Highway Inn
AServ **N:** Citgo
S: BP
TServ **N:** 76 Auto/Truck Plaza(SCALES), Horn's Auto Truck Plaza(SCALES)
TWash **N:** 76 Auto/Truck Plaza, Horn's Auto Truck Plaza
Med **S:** Hospital
ATM **S:** Cashpoint, Texaco

174 Farmington Road
Gas **N:** Exxon(*, D)
AServ **N:** Exxon
Other **N:** Davie County Large Animal Hosp.

(177) Rest Area (RR, Phones, Picnic, Grills, Vending; Eastbound)

(177) Rest Area (RR, Phones, Picnic, Grills, Vending; Westbound)

180 NC 801, Bermuda Run, Tanglewood
Gas **S:** Chevron(*, D, LP, K), Citgo(*, K), Shell(*, K)
Food **S:** Subway (Citgo), Venezia Pizzeria & Italian
AServ **S:** Chevron, Quick Lube Service Station (Chevron), Shell
RVCamp **S:** Tanglewood Park (1 Mile)
ATM **S:** First Union, Mocksville Savings Bank, Wachovia Bank
Other **S:** CVS(RX), Food Lion Grocery Store(RX), Village Way Veterinary

184 Lewisville, Clemmons
Gas **N:** Shell(*, K), Texaco(*)
S: Amoco(*, CW), BP(*, LP, CW), Citgo(D, LP, 24), Etna(*, D, LP, K), Exxon(*, D)
Food **N:** I Bambini Italian Restaurant, KFC
S: Arby's, Baskin Robbins, Biscuitville, Burger King(PLAY), Cracker Barrel, Domino's Pizza, Dunkin Donuts (Etna), Etna, Frauenhofer's Ice Cream & Bake Shop, Grecian House Rest, JB's Toasted Hot Dogs, K-Mart, Little Caesars Pizza (K-Mart), Little Richard's Lexington BBQ, Mandarin Chinese, McDonald's, Mi Pueblo Mexican, Mountain Fried Chicken, Pizza Hut, Taco Bell, Waffle House, Wendy's

EXIT NORTH CAROLINA

Lodg **N:** Holiday Inn Hotel & Suites
S: Ramada, Super 8
AServ **N:** Shell
S: Citgo(24)
ATM **N:** NationsBank
S: Amoco, Central Carolina Bank, First Citizens Bank
Other **N:** Animal Hosp of Clemmons, Car Wash
S: Clemmons Coin Laundromat, Food Lion Grocery Store(24), K-Mart, Solid Rock Christian Bookstore, Streetcar's Full Service Car Wash (Etna)

188 Junction I-420 & I-40 East Business, U.S. 421, Winston - Salem (Difficult Reaccess)
Lodg **S:** Days Inn (see our ad this page)

189 U.S. 158, Stratford Road to Hanes Mall Blvd
Gas **S:** BP(*), Shell(*)
Food **N:** Bojangles, Chili's, Olive Garden, Red Lobster, Taco Bell, The Honey Baked Ham Co., Western Steer Family Steakhouse
S: Applebee's, Burger King, Macaroni Grill, Romanos Macaroni Grill, Subway, Village Tavern
Lodg **N:** Best Western
S: Extended Stay America, Hampton Inn, La Quinta, Sleep Inn
AServ **N:** NTB
Med **S:** Forsyth Memorial Hospital
ATM **S:** NationsBank, Shell
Other **N:** Family Bookstores, Hanes Mall, Office Max
S: Barnes & Noble, PetsMart, Sam's Club

190 Hanes Mall Blvd (Westbound, Difficult Reaccess)
Food **N:** Don Pablo's Mexican (Mexican), O'Charley's
S: Burger King(PLAY), Cookies By Design, Corbins, Lone Star Steakhouse, NY Bagel & Deli, Outback Steakhouse, Oyster Bay Seafood Restaurant
Lodg **S:** Comfort Suites Hotel, Microtel Inn
AServ **N:** Firestone
S: America's Home for Car Service (Firestone)
Med **S:** Northside Hospital, Prime Care Medical Clinic
Other **N:** Hanes Mall
S: CVS Drugstore, Food Lion

Mention this ad for 10% Discount*
Comfort Inn
Exit 170 • Mocksville, NC
336-751-7310
800-852-0035
• Free Deluxe Continental Breakfast
• Cable TV with Free HBO/CNN/ESPN
• Free Local Calls • Data Port Phones
• Outdoor Pool • Truck/Bus Parking
• Non-Smoking Rooms
• Restaurants within Walking Distance
• Evening Cappuccino 6-8pm
*Some Restrictions Apply
1459
NORTH CAROLINA ▪ I-40 ▪ EXIT 170

1219
336-760-4770
Winston-Salem
DAYS INN
— Adjacent to Hanes Mall —
Largest Indoor Shopping Mall in NC
— FREE Continental Breakfast —
— In-Room Coffee Makers —
— Meeting Rooms —
— Cable TV w/HBO —
— Some Rooms With King Bed, Microwave, & Refrigerator —
— AARP, Commercial & Gov't Rates —
I-40, Exit 188 Business 40
N. CAROLINA ¥ I-40 ¥ EXIT 188

EXIT NORTH CAROLINA

192 Peters Creek Pkwy, Downtown, NC 150
Gas **N:** Wilco(*, D, K)
S: Texaco
Food **N:** Bojangles, Boston Market Restaurant, Burger King(PLAY), Char's, Checkers Burgers, Country Roadhouse, Dragon Inn, IHOP, Little Caesars Pizza, Monderry, Monterrey, SHONEY'S, Shoney's, Subway, TJ's Deli, Taco Bell
S: Libbey Hill Seafood, McDonald's(PLAY)
Lodg **N:** Innkeeper
AServ **N:** Baity's Discount Tire Sales, Dunrite, Liberty Lincoln Mercury, Parkway Ford, Precision Tune
S: Advance Auto Parts, Flow Buick BMW, Forsyth Honda, Saturn of Winston-Salem, Texaco
ATM **N:** BB&T Bank, NationsBank
Other **N:** Cinema 6, Eckerd Drugs(RX), Lowes Foods(24), Magnum Auto Wash, Office Depot, Phar Mor Drugs(RX)
S: Harris Teeter Supermarket, K-Mart

193C Silas Creek Pkwy, S. Main St (Westbound)

193AB U.S. 52, NC 8, Mount Airy, Lexington

195 U.S. 331 NC 109, Thomasville, Clemonsville Road
Gas **N:** Easton Grocery(*)

196 U.S. 311 South, Highpoint (Limited Access Rd)

201 Union Cross Road
Food **N:** Burger King(PLAY), China Cafe, Jerry's Pizza
Other **N:** CVS Drugstore(RX), Food Lion Supermarket

203 NC 66, Kernersville, Highpoint
Gas **N:** Amoco(*, D, CW), Citgo(*, D)
S: Shell(*, LP, K)
Food **N:** Citgo, McDonald's(PLAY) (Citgo)
S: Krispy Kreme Doughnuts, Shell
Lodg **N:** Sleep Inn
AServ **N:** Auto Choice, Merchant's Tire & Auto
ATM **N:** Amoco, Citgo
S: Shell

206 North US 421, Business Loop 40, Kernersville, Downtown Winston, Salem (Westbound)

208 Sandy Ridge Road, Farmers Market
FStop **N:** Exxon(*)
S: Citgo(*, D, K)
RVCamp **S:** Out-of-Doors Mart

210 NC 68, Highpoint, Piedmont, Triad International Airport
FStop **N:** Phillips 66(*, D)
Gas **S:** Exxon(*, D), Mobil(*)

EXIT NORTH CAROLINA

Food N: Arby's, Hardee's, Mr. Omelet(24), Wendy's (Days Inn)
S: Bojangles, McDonald's, Pollo Pizza & Pasta, SHONEY'S Shoney's, Subway
Lodg N: Best Inns of America, DAYS INN Days Inn
S: Candlewood Suites, Comfort Suites Hotel, Hampton Inn, Motel 6, Ramada, Red Roof Inn
TServ N: Ford Truck, Kenworth, Piedmont Automotive Center
S: Piedmont Peterbuilt Inc
ATM N: Phillips 66
S: BB&T, Central Carolina Bank, Mobil

212 Chimney Rock Road
TServ S: Carolina Tractor, Covington Diesel

213 Jamestown
Gas N: BP(*, D, CW)
S: Pace Olive Mtn Halal Market(*)
Food N: Damon's (Radisson)
Lodg N: Radisson Inn
ATM N: BP
Other S: Guilford Jamestown Animal Hospital

214AB Wendover Avenue
Gas N: Exxon(*, D), Texaco(*, D)
Food N: Blimpie's Subs, Burger King, Country's BBQ, Herbie's Breakfast, K & W Cafeteria, Queen's Gardens Chinese, Ruby Tuesday, TCBY, Waffle House
S: Applebee's, Bojangles, Chick-Fil-A(PLAY), Cracker Barrel, Fuddruckers, Golden Corral Family Steakhouse, IHOP, Kabuto Japanese Steak House and Sushi Bar, McDonald's(PLAY), Red Lobster, SHONEY'S Shoney's, Steak 'N Shake, Subway, T.G.I. Friday's, Tripps, Wendy's
Lodg N: Extended Stay America, Innkeeper, Microtel
S: AmeriSuites (see our ad this page, Courtyard by Marriott, Lodge America, Shoney's Inn
AServ N: Bob Dunn Isuzu, Volvo Dealer
S: Econo Lube & Tune, Foreign Cars Italia, Sam's Club, Wal-Mart(RX)
ATM N: Wachovia Bank
Other N: Celebration Station, Staple's
S: Sam's Club, Wal-Mart(RX)

216 Greensboro, Colliseum Area, NC 6. (Eastbound, Left Exit, Reaccess Westbound Only)

217 Coliseum Area, High Point Road
Gas N: Exxon(*)
S: Crown(*, LP, CW)
Food N: Bennigan's, Biscuitville, Blue Marlin Seafood, Burger King(PLAY), Chili's, Grady's American Grill, Hooter's (Howard Johnson), India Mahal Restaurant, Jack Astor's Grill, Lone Star Steakhouse, Olive Garden, Po Folks, Shoney's
S: Darryl's, Don Pablo's Mexican, Houlihan's, McDonald's(PLAY), Waffle House(24), Wendys
Lodg N: Howard Johnson, Park Lane Hotel, Red Roof Inn, Super 8, TraveLodge(SCALES)
S: Best Western, Comfort Inn, DAYS INN Days Inn, Drury Inn, EconoLodge, Fairfield Inn, Hampton Inn, Holiday Inn, Residence Inn
AServ S: C & C Auto, NTB, Southern Airbrake & Equipment Co
ATM N: First Citizen's Bank
Other N: Office Depot
S: Borders Books & Music, Car Wash, Joseph S. Koury Convention Center

218AB 218A - US 220 to I-85 Asheboro

EXIT NORTH CAROLINA

218B

219 Junction I-85 South, US 29 South, US 70 West, Charlotte

Note: I-40 runs concurrent below with I-85. Numbering follows I-85.

124 Randleman Road
Gas E: BP(*, CW), Exxon, Texaco(*, K, 24)
W: Amoco(*, 24), Shell(*, K)
Food E: BP, Blimpie Subs & Salads (BP), Cafe 212, Cookout, Mayflower's Seafood Restaurant, Quincy's Family Steakhouse, Waffle House, Wendy's
W: Arby's, Ben's Diner, Burger King(PLAY), Captain D's Seafood, China Town Express, Dairy Queen, Jed's BBQ, KFC, McDonald's(PLAY), Pizza Hut, Sub Station II, Taco Bell, The Spring Valley Restaurant
Lodg E: Cavalier Inn
W: Budget Motel, Southgate Motor Inn
AServ E: Exxon, Korman Auto Works BMW, Porsche, Mercedes
W: Grease Monkey, Meineke Discount Mufflers, Precision Tune, Reed Tires Inc.
TServ E: Cummins Diesel
ATM E: Machine (Texaco)
W: Amoco, Wachovia Bank
Other E: The Optical Place
W: Dry Clean America, Eckerd Drugs(RX), Food Mart, New Globe Car Wash

125 South Elm - Eugene Street, Downtown Greensboro
FStop E: Amoco(*, K, CW, 24)
Gas E: Amoco(*, D, CW), Texaco(*, D)
W: Citgo(*, LP), Crown(*)
Food E: Big City Pizza, Howard Johnson, Torero's Mexican Restaurant (Howard Johnson)
W: BT's Sandwich Cafe Express, Sonic Drive in, VIP Express Chinese
Lodg E: Cricket Inn, DAYS INN Days Inn, Howard Johnson, Howard Johnson, Super 8
W: Homestead Lodge, Ramada Inn
AServ E: Shep's Towing & Recovery
W: Auto Zone Auto Parts, Superior Auto Parts Store
TServ E: Alice - Chalmers Lift Trucks
ATM E: Amoco
W: Cashpoint, Citgo
Other W: Auto Zone Discount Auto Parts, Coin Op Laundromat, Coint Laundry, Food Lion Grocery Store, Kerr Drugs(RX), Visitor Information

126 U.S. 421 South, Sanford, MLK Jr. Drive, Siler City
Gas E: Exxon(*)
Food E: Biscuitville, Burger King, Domino's Pizza, Golden Pizza, McDonald's(PLAY), Old Hickory's Barbecue, Pizza Pronto, Subway, Szechuan Chinese Restaurant, Wendy's
AServ E: Advantage Auto Stores, Exxon,

1306
AMERISUITES
AMERICA'S AFFORDABLE ALL-SUITE HOTEL
North Carolina • Exit 214A • 910-852-1443

EXIT NORTH CAROLINA

Goodyear Tire & Auto, Hall Tire Company, Tom's Tire & Auto
ATM E: BB&T Bank, Cashpoint
Other E: A-1 Convenience Store, Advance Auto Parts, Bi-Lo Grocery, Buchannan's Discount Drugs(RX), CVS Pharmacy(RX), Carolina Pride Car Wash, Food Lion Grocery Store, Post Office, Revco Drugs

127 U.S. 29 North, U.S. 70 East, U.S. 220, U.S. 421, Reidsville, Danville (Northbound, No Reaccess)

128AB NC 6 to North US 29 to US 222 North, East Lee St.
Gas W: BP(*), Phillips 66
Food W: BP, Blimpie Subs & Salads (BP), Krispy Kreme Doughnuts (Phillips 66), Phillips 66
Lodg W: Holiday Inn Express
TServ W: Hertz Penske
RVCamp E: Greensboro Campground (1.5 Miles)
ATM W: BP, Phillips 66

130 McConnell Road
Gas E: Texaco(*)
AServ E: Harrison's, Texaco
Other W: Replacements Unlimited Fine China Retail Store

132 McLeansville, Mtn Hope Church Road
Gas W: Handi Pik(*), Shell(*, CW), Texaco(*, D)
AServ W: Shell, Texaco
ATM W: Shell

135 Rock Creek Dairy Road, Sedalia
Gas W: Citgo(*)
Food W: McDonald's(PLAY)
Other W: Charlotte Hawkin's Brown Memorial, Food Lion

138 NC 61, Gibsonville, Whitsett
TStop W: TA TravelCenters of America(*, SCALES) (ATM, Lodging)
Gas W: BP (TravelCenters of America)
Food W: Burger King (TA), Country Pride Restaurant (TravelCenters of America), Popeye's Chicken (TA), TA TravelCenters of America (ATM, Lodging)
Lodg W: Adesta Lodging (TA), Day Stop (TravelCenters of America)
TServ W: TA TravelCenters of America(SCALES) (ATM, Lodging), Truck Service (TravelCenters of America)
TWash W: Piedmont Truck Wash, TA TravelCenters of America (ATM, Lodging)
ATM W: Machine (TravelCenters of America)

(140) Rest Area (RR, HF, Phones, Picnic; Northbound)

(140) Rest Area (RR, HF, Phones, Picnic; Southbound)

141 Elon College
Gas E: Amoco(*), BP(*), Shell(*, LP)
W: Phillips 66(D)
Food E: Bogey's Sports Bar & Grill, IHOP, International House of Pancakes, Mayflower's Seafood Restaurant, Outback Steakhouse, Shea Restaurant
W: Applebee's, Arby's, Bedrock Cafe, Best Western of Burlington, Bojangles, Burger King, Chick-Fil-A, Cookout, Cracker Barrel, Errichiello's Pizza, Golden Corral Family Steakhouse, K-

EXIT	NORTH CAROLINA
	Mart Supercenter(24, RX), Little Caesars Pizza (K-Mart), O'Charley's, **Rockola Restaurant (Best Western)**, Sal's Italian, Subway, The Summit Restaurant, The Village Grill
Lodg	E: Hampton Inn
	W: **Best Western, Best Western of Burlington**, Country Suites by Carlson, Courtyard by Marriott, Super 8
AServ	W: Burlington Motors Ford, Mercury, Lincoln, Jiffy Lube, Phillips 66, Phillips 66
Med	E: **+ Alamance Regional Medical Center, + Hospital**
ATM	W: First State Bank, Wachovia Bank
Other	E: Lake Mackintosh Marina
	W: **Burlington Animal Hospital**, Elon Home for Children, **K-Mart, K-Mart Supercenter(RX), Wal-Mart(24, RX) (One hour photo, vision center)**
143	NC 62, Alamance
Gas	W: Circle K(*), Exxon(*, CW)
Food	E: **Hardee's**, Waffle House
	W: Cutting Board Steakhouse, Libby Hill Seafood, Nick's Cuisine, Ramada Inn, The Cutting Board
Lodg	W: Ramada Inn (O'Hara's Restaurant), Ramada Inn
AServ	W: Big Shirley Mitsubishi, Big Shirley Oldsmobile, Cadillac, GM, Dick Shirley Chevrolet, Stearn's Ford
ATM	W: CCB Bank, Cashpoint, Central Carolina Bank, Circle K, Exxon
Other	E: **Alamance Historical Museum, Burlington Outlet Mall**, JR's Cigars Superstore
	W: Alamance State Historic Site, **Eckerd Drugs(RX), Food Lion Grocery Store, Plaza Veterinary Hospital**
145	NC 49, Liberty, Burlington, Downtown
FStop	E: **Texaco**(*, LP, CW)
Gas	E: Speedway(*, LP), Starvin Marvin
	W: BP(*, CW)
Food	E: Captain D's Seafood, SHONEY'S Shoney's
	W: Bojangles, Burger King, China Inn Buffett, Hardee's, Hot Shots Grill & Bar, KFC, Quincy's Family Steakhouse, Ship Ahoy Restaurant, Subway, Waffle House
Lodg	E: DAYS INN Days Inn, Motel 6
	W: **Comfort Inn**, Holiday Inn, Scottish Inn
AServ	E: **Texaco**
	W: Nichole's Dodge
ATM	E: **Texaco**
	W: CCB Bank
Other	E: NC Highway Patrol
	W: **Antique Mall, Burlington Outlet Center, Eckerd Drugs(RX), Food Lion Grocery Store**, Nicholas Dodge, Tanger Outlets
147	NC 87, Graham, Pittsboro
FStop	W: **Citgo**(*)
Gas	E: Servco(*, D) (Coin Laundry)
	W: Citgo, Exxon(*, D, CW), Texaco(*)
Food	E: Arby's, Bojangles, Burger King, Domino's Pizza, Las Brisas Mexican Restaurant, Pizza Hut, **Sagebrush Steakhouse**, Subway, TCBY, Wendy's
	W: Biscuitville, Golden China, **Hardee's**, McDonald's(PLAY), Taco Bell
AServ	E: County Ford, Edwards Tire, Stearns Chevrolet
ATM	E: Centura Bank, Mid Carolina Bank
	W: BB&T Bank, Central Carolina Bank, Community Saving Bank, NationsBank,

EXIT	NORTH CAROLINA
	Wachovia Bank
Other	E: CVS Pharmacy(RX), **Cobert Vision Center**, Coin Laundry, Highway Patrol Post, Snow Camp, **Winn Dixie Supermarket**
	W: **Flowers Foods**, Lowe's Foods, South Court Pharmacy, **Tarheel Drugs(RX)**, Vintage Advantage Antiques
148	NC 54, Chapel Hill, Carrboro, Graham
FStop	E: **BP**(*)
Gas	E: Amoco(*, 24), Country Store Gas(*), Quality(LP)
Food	E: Waffle House
	W: Doug's Cafe (EconoLodge), EconoLodge
Lodg	W: EconoLodge, Embers Motor Lodge
ATM	E: Amoco, **BP**
Other	W: The Challenge Golf Course
150	Haw River , Green Level
TStop	W: **Flying J Travel Center**(*, SCALES), **Wilco(SCALES) (Travel Plaza)**
FStop	W: **Flying J, Wilco (Citgo)**
Food	W: **Dairy Queen (Wilco), Flying J Travel Center, Krispy Kreme Doughnuts (Wilco), Stuckey's (Wilco), The Cookery (Flying J), Wendy's (Wilco)**
TServ	W: **Flying J Travel Center(SCALES)**
TWash	W: **Flying J Travel Center**
Other	W: Alamance Community College
152	Trollingwood Road
TStop	E: **Speedway**(*, LP, SCALES)
FStop	W: **Amoco(*), Fuel City(*)**
Gas	W: **Amoco**(*)
Food	E: **Country Kitchen Restaurant (Speedway), Speedway**
	W: **Golden Nugget Restaurant**
ATM	E: **Speedway**
	W: **Fuel City**
153	NC 119, Mebane
FStop	E: **BP, Citgo**
	W: **Exxon**
Gas	E: **BP**(*)
	W: **Exxon**(*)
Food	E: **BP, KFC (BP), Pizza Hut (BP), Taco Bell (BP)**
	W: Baldwin's Best Too Restaurant, **Burger King (Exxon)**, Domino's Pizza, **Exxon**, Oyster Bar, Subway, Yum Yum's Chinese Food
Lodg	E: Hampton Inn
ATM	E: **BP**
	W: Cashpoint, **Exxon**
Other	W: **CVS Pharmacy(RX), Food Lion Grocery Store, Piedmont Veterinary Clinic**, The Laundry Basket
154	Mebane
FStop	E: **Pacific Pride Commercial Fueling(*, LP) (Shell gas)**
	W: **Texaco**(*)
Gas	W: Amoco
Food	E: Blimpie Subs & Salads (Pacific Pride), **Pacific Pride Commercial Fueling (Shell gas)**
	W: **McDonald's(PLAY)**
Lodg	W: Budget Inn
AServ	W: Amoco
Other	W: Mebane-Oaks Car Wash, **Peaches & Cream Children's Outlet, Winn Dixie Supermarket**
157	Buckhorn Road
FStop	E: **Amoco**(*)
(159)	**Weigh Station (Southbound)**

EXIT	NORTH CAROLINA
(159)	**Weigh Station (Northbound)**
160	Efland
FStop	W: **Texaco**(*)
Gas	W: **BP**(*, D)
Food	W: Missy's Grill
AServ	W: BP
ATM	W: **Texaco**
161	To U.S. 70, NC 86
	Note: I-40 runs concurrent above with I-85. Numbering follows I-85.
259	Junction I-85 ,Durham
261	Hillsborough
263	New Hope Church Road
266	NC 86
270	U.S. 15, U.S. 501, Chapel Hill, Durham
Food	N: Bob Evan's Restaurant, Outback Steakhouse, Philly Steak
Lodg	N: Comfort Inn
	S: Red Roof Inn
AServ	N: Swedish Imports
Med	N: **+ Hospital**
	S: **+ Hospital**
Other	N: Barnes & Noble Booksellers, **Duke University, Home Depot, New Hope Cummins Mall**, UNC
273AB	NC 54, Durham, Chapel Hill
Gas	S: BP(*, LP), Texaco(*, D)
Food	S: Hardee's, New China, Pizza A Mante
ATM	S: BP, NationsBank
Other	S: Animal Hospital, Mardi Gras Bowling
274	NC 751, Jordan Lake Road
276	Fayetteville Road
Gas	N: Exxon(*), Kick's 66(*)
Food	N: A & W Restaurant (Kicks 66), China Cafe, Kick's 66, Little Caesars Pizza, Subs Etc., TCBY, Waffle House, Wendy's
ATM	N: Exxon
Other	N: **Eye Care Center, Harris Teeter Supermarket**, Rose's Discount Department Store
278	NC 55 to NC 54, Apex, World Trade Center
Gas	S: Crown(*, LP), Exxon(*, CW)
Food	N: **Waffle House**
	S: Arby's, Bojangles, Briggs, Burger King, Chinese, Country Junction, El Dorado Mexican, Ginger Inn Chinese, Jamacian Restaurant, Jersey Mike's Subs, KFC, McDonald's(PLAY), Miami Subs Grills, Oh Brian's, Papa John's Pizza, Parkside Bagel, Philly Steak Factory, Philly Subs, Pizza Hut, Schlotzsky's Deli, Shor Sezchuan, Subway, Taco Bell, U.S. Market Rotisserie, Wendy's
Lodg	N: Doubletree Guests Suites, Fairfield Inn, Innkeeper Motel, La Quinta Inn, Red Roof Inn
	S: Courtyard by Marriott, Homestead Village, Residence Inn
AServ	S: A & A Tire & Automotive, Best Transmission, Econo Lube & King, Ingold Tire, Precision Tune & Lube, Quick 10 Oil Change Center
ATM	S: CCB Bank, South Bank, Triangle Bank
Other	N: World Trade Center
	S: **CVS(RX), Coin Laundry, Eckerd Drugs, Food Lion Supermarket, Parkwood Animal Hospital, Winn Dixie Supermar-**

EXIT	NORTH CAROLINA
	ket
279AB	North Carolina 147, Durham, Alexander Drive (279B goes to the north, 279A goes to the south)
Med	**N:** ✚ Hospital
280	Davis Dr
Lodg	**S:** Radisson
ATM	**S:** Cintura Bank, First Citizen's Bank, First Union, NationsBank, Wachovia Bank
281	Miami Blvd
Gas	**S:** BP(*), Shell(*, 24)
Food	**S:** Krispy Kreme Doughnuts (Shell), Shell
Lodg	**N:** Marriot, Wyndham Garden Hotel **S:** HomeGate Studios & Suites, Homewood Suites
Med	**S:** ✚ Park Medical Center
282	Page Road
Food	**S:** Holiday Inn
Lodg	**S:** Comfort Suites Hotel, Holiday Inn, Sheraton, Wingate Inn
283B	Jct I-540, to U.S. 70
284	Airport Blvd
Gas	**S:** Amoco(*, D), Shell(*)
Food	**S:** Amoco, Hot Stuff Pizza (Amoco), Indian Palace Restaurant, Munchies Grill (Amoco), Smash Hit Subs (Amoco), Waffle House, Wendy's
Lodg	**S:** Budgetel Inn, Courtyard by Marriott, DAYS INN Days Inn, Extended Stay America, Fairfield Inn, Hampton Inn, La Quinta Inn, Microtel
Other	**S:** Triangle Factory Shops
285	Morrisville, Aviation Pkwy
RVCamp	**S:** Lake Crabtree Country Park
287	Cary, Harrison Avenue
Gas	**S:** Shell
Food	**S:** Burger King, Chick-Fil-A, Manhattan Gourmet Deli, McDonald's, NY Pizza, Newton's West, Shanghai Garden Chinese (Shell), Shell, Wendy's
Med	**S:** ✚ Med Stop Walk-In (Harrison Square)
ATM	**S:** First Union, Shell, Wachovia Bank
Parks	**N:** William B Umstead State Park
Other	**S:** Sam's Club
289	to U.S. 1 North, Raleigh Downtown, Wade Avenue (Difficult Reaccess)
Med	**N:** ✚ Hospital
Other	**N:** NC Highway Patrol
290	NC 54, Cary
Gas	**E:** Circle K(*), Circle K(*, LP), Crown(*), Servco(*, CW)
Food	**E:** Anedeo Italian, BoJangles, Dairy Queen, McDonald's, Mike's Subs, Pizza Hut, Subway, Taco Bell, Ten Ten Chinese, Village Inn Pizza Parlor, Wendy's
Lodg	**E:** Hampton Inn
AServ	**E:** Clark West Auto Parts, Jiffy Lube, Meineke Discount Mufflers **W:** Peniske Oil
ATM	**E:** First Union **W:** Wachovia Bank
Other	**E:** Coin Laundry, Econo Food Mart **W:** K-Mart
291	Cary, Cary Town Blvd.
293BA	U.S. 1, U.S. 64, Raleigh, Wake Forest, Sanford, Asheboro,

EXIT	NORTH CAROLINA
	Jordan Lake, Junction I-440 (293B goes north, 293A goes south)
Other	**S:** Crossroads Plaza, South Hills Mall
295	Gorman St
Gas	**N:** Exxon(*, CW)
ATM	**N:** Exxon
297	Lake Wheeler Road
Gas	**N:** Exxon(*) **S:** Citgo(*, D, CW)
Food	**N:** Burger King (Exxon), Exxon, Farmers Market Restaurant
Med	**N:** ✚ Hospital
ATM	**N:** Farmers Market Restaurant
298BA	U.S. 401, U.S. 70, NC 50, Fayetteville, Raleigh, Downtown, South Saunders Street
Gas	**N:** Shell(*) **S:** Crown(*), Servco(*, CW)
Food	**S:** Home Chinese Restaurant, KFC, SHONEY'S Shoney's
Lodg	**N:** Red Roof Inn **S:** Claremont Inn, Inn Keeper
ATM	**S:** Crown
Other	**S:** Car Quest Auto Center, Sam's Club
299	Person St, Hammond Road
300AB	Rock Quarry Road, Martin Luther King Memorial Garden
Gas	**S:** Texaco(*, LP)
Food	**S:** Burger King(PLAY), Hardee's, PTA Pizza, Subway
ATM	**S:** M&F Bank, Texaco
Other	**N:** MLK Gardens **S:** Coin Laundry, Eckerd Drugs(RX)
301	East U.S. 64, Jct I-440N (Left Exit Eastbound)
303	Jones Sausage Road
FStop	**S:** Texaco(*)
ATM	**S:** Texaco
306AB	U.S. 70, Smithfield, Garner
Gas	**S:** Fina(*) (Bait Shop)
312	NC 42, Clayton, Fuquay-Varina, Wilson
FStop	**N:** Exxon(*, LP) **S:** Texaco(*, LP)
Gas	**S:** Amoco(*, LP, CW, 24), BP(*), Citgo(*, D, LP)
Food	**N:** Cracker Barrel, Exxon, Krispy Kreme Doughnuts (Texaco), Smithfield's BBQ & Chicken, Wendy's (Exxon) **S:** Amoco, BP, Bojangles, Burger King (BP), Citgo, Huddle House (BP), Jimmy's Pizza Time, KFC, Lil' Dino's Subs,

INTERSTATE EXIT AUTHORITY

EXIT	NORTH CAROLINA
	McDonald's(PLAY), Ribs-R-Us, Shane's Pizza (BP), Subway (Amoco), Taco Bell, Waffle House
Lodg	**N:** Jameson Inn
Med	**S:** ✚ Quick Med
ATM	**S:** Amoco, Citgo, First Citizens Bank, Four Oaks Bank & Trust, Texaco, Wachovia Bank
Other	**S:** Animal Hospital, CVS Pharmacy(RX), Coin Laundry, Eye Deals, Food Lion Grocery Store
319	NC 210, Smithfield, Angier, McGee's Crossroad
FStop	**N:** Texaco(*, 24)
Food	**N:** Blimpie Subs & Salads (Texaco), Texaco
ATM	**N:** Texaco
(324)	**Rest Area (Eastbound)**
(324)	**Rest Area (RR, Phones, Picnic; Westbound)**
325	NC 242, to U.S. 301, Benson
FStop	**S:** BP(*)
328AB	Junction I-95, Benson, Smithfield
334	NC 96, Meadow
341	NC 50, NC 55, to U.S. 13, Newton Grove
Gas	**S:** BP(*, CW)
Food	**S:** McDonald's (BP)
ATM	**S:** BP
343	U.S. 701, Clinton
Other	**N:** Bentonville Civil War Battleground
348	Suttontown Road
355	NC 403, Faison, Goldsboro, Clinton
364	NC 24 to NC 50, Warsaw, Clinton, Turkey
FStop	**S:** Amoco(*), BP(*), Texaco(*, LP)
Gas	**S:** Citgo(*, CW), Phillips 66(*)
Food	**S:** Bojangles, McDonald's, Smithville Chicken & B-Que, Subway, Waffle House, Wendy's
(364)	**Rest Area (RR, Phones, Picnic, Vending)**
369	U.S. 117, Warsaw, Magnolia
373	NC 903, Magnolia, Kenansville
Med	**N:** ✚ Hospital
Other	**N:** Liberty Hall/Cowan Museum
380	Rose Hill, Greenevers
Gas	**S:** Citgo(*, CW)
384	NC 11, Wallace, Teachey, Kenansville
385	NC 41, Wallace, Beulaville, Chinquapin
RVCamp	**N:** Campground
390	U.S. 117, Wallace, Burgaw
398	NC 53, Burgaw, Jacksonville
Med	**S:** ✚ Hospital
408	NC 210, Hampstead, Rocky Point, Topsail Island Beaches
FStop	**S:** Exxon(*)
Food	**S:** Paul's Place Restaurant(*)
RVCamp	**S:** Campground
Med	**S:** ✚ Medical Care Center
Other	**S:** Farmer's Market
414	Castle Hayne, Brunswick County Beaches.
420	NC 132 North, Gordon Road
RVCamp	**S:** Camelot Campground

↑ NORTH CAROLINA

Begin I-40

EXIT WISCONSIN

Begin I-43

↓WISCONSIN

192AB Jct 41, U.S. 141, Marinet, Appleton
Lodg E: Days Inn (see our ad this page)

189 Atkinson Dr.
Other W: Jubilee Foods Grocery

187 Webster Ave, East Shore Dr
FStop W: Shell(*, D, CW)
Food W: McDonald's, Wendy's
AServ W: Berna's Auto Sales & Service
ATM W: Shell
Other E: Amusement Park, Wildlife Sanctuary
W: Car Wash

185 U.S. 54, 57, Sturgeon Bay, Algoma (Difficult Reaccess)

183 WI V, Mason St
Lodg E: AmeriHost
Med W: ✚ Hospital

181 WI JJ, Eaton Road, Manitowoc Rd
FStop E: Citgo(*, D, LP)
Food E: Blimpie's Subs, Gallagher's Pizza, GiGi's, Hardee's
AServ E: Dorsch Ford, Red Engine & Service
ATM E: Citgo, First National Bank
W: Food Festival(24)
Other E: Town & Country Pet Grooming
W: Food Festival

180 WI 172, To WI 32, A. Straubel Ave., Arena Stadium (Difficult Reaccess)

178 U.S. 141, WI 29, Cnty Road MM, Bellevue, Kewaunee
TStop W: Amoco(LP, SCALES)
Food E: Redwood Inn Food & Cocktails
W: Amoco, Restaurant (Amoco)
TServ W: Amoco(SCALES)
RVCamp E: Shady Acres Campsites (1.75 Miles)

171 WI 96, Cnty Rd. KB, Greenleaf, Denmark
FStop E: Citgo(*)
Food E: McDonald's, Uncle Subs With Pizza
TServ E: Citgo
Other E: Steve's Cheese

(168) Rest Area (RR, Phones, Picnic, Vending, RV Dump; Southbound)

(168) Rest Area (RR, Phones, Picnic, Vending, RV Dump; Northbound)

164 WI 147, CR Z, Maribel, Two Rivers
TStop W: Citgo(*)
Food W: Cedar Ridge Restaurant (see our ad this page)
TServ W: Citgo
RVCamp E: Devils River Campers Park (1.8 Miles)
Parks E: County Park
Other E: Hidden Valley Ski

160 CR K, Kellnersville

157 CR V, Mishicot, Francis Creek, Hillcrest Road
FStop E: BP(*)
Food E: BP, Lyla's Deli (BP), Rolo's Diner (BP)
TServ E: All American Transport

154 WI 310, U.S. 10, Two Rivers, Appleton

152 WI 42, U.S. 10, CR JJ Manitowoc, Sturgeon Bay
Other W: Pine Crest Historical Village (3 Miles)

149 U.S. 51, WI 42, Manitowoc, Fond du Lac
FStop E: Shell(*, D)
Food E: Applebee's, Country Kitchen, Fazoli's, Perkins Family Restaurant, Wendy's
Lodg E: Comfort Inn, Holiday Inn, Super 8, Westmoor Motel
AServ E: AllCar Automotive Center, First Chrysler, Dodge, Jeep, Tietroske Buick, Pontiac
Med E: ✚ Hospital
ATM E: Shell
Other E: Auto Car Museum, Wal-Mart(LP, RX), Wisconsin Maritime Museum

144 CR C, St Nazianz, Newton
FStop E: Mobil(*, D)

(142) Weigh Station (Southbound)

137 Cnty Road XX, Kiel, Cleveland
FStop E: Citgo(*, D)
Food E: Cleveland Family Restaurant
ATM E: Citgo

128 WI 42, Sheboygan, Howards Grove
FStop E: Interstate Inn(*)
W: Citgo(*, D)
Food E: Hardee's, Highway Bakery & Coffee Shop
W: Citgo, Cousins' Sub's (Citgo)
Lodg E: Comfort Inn
TServ E: Pumps Tire
ATM W: Citgo
Other E: Big Wheel Skate Center, Super Wash

126 WI 23, Sheboygan, Kohler
Food E: Applebee's, Big Apple Bagels, Cousins' Sub's, Culver's Ice Cream, Hardees, McDonald's, New China 8 Restaurant, Ponderosa Steak House, Rococo Pizza, Taco Bell
Lodg E: Super 8
AServ E: All Car Automotive, Batteries Plus, Dick Brantmier Ford, Mercury, Lincoln, Firestone Tire &

920-498-8088
Green Bay, WI
DAYS INN
Lambeau Field
1978 Holmgren Way
Green Bay, WI
• Restaurants Adjacent
• Kids Under 18 Stay Free
• Indoor Pool & Jacuzzi
• In Room Coffee Makers
• Bus Parking • AAA & AARP Rates
• Lambeau Field, Packer's Hall of Fame, Brett Faure's Steakhouse - 1 Block
Special Tour Group Rate
1195
I-43 • Exit 180 • Follow Arena/Stadium signs. Right Packer Dr. • 8 miles from Exit 180
Wisconsin • I-43 • Exit 192AB

Visit Our Mini Farm Pond and Trail

1475
6 AM - 10 PM Daily
920-863-8691
800-881-8691
Call for Trout Boil Dates April thru Oct
Located halfway between Green Bay and Manitowoc on I-43, Exit 164
Maribel, WI 54227

Wisconsin • I-43 • Exit 164

Bold red print shows RV & Bus parking available or nearby

EXIT	WISCONSIN
	Auto, Goodyear, Sear's, Van Horn-Wieland Oldsmobile Hunda
Med	**E:** St. Nicholas Hospital
ATM	**E:** Associated Bank, Community Bank
Other	**E:** Cinema, Coin Operated Laundry, Memorial Mall, Piggly Wiggly, Putt Putt, Go Kart, Shopko Grocery(RX) (Optical), Wal-Mart, WalGreens Pharmacy(RX)
123	WI 28, Sheboygan, Sheboygan Falls
FStop	**E:** Citgo
Gas	**E:** Mobil(*)
Food	**E:** Cruisers Frozen Custard & Jumbo Burgers, McDonald's (Mobil), Mobil, SHONEY'S, Shoney's, Wendy's
Lodg	**E:** Americinn, Holiday Inn Express
TServ	**E:** Mark Wardt Sales & Service
ATM	**E:** Mobil
Other	**E:** Harley Davidson Sales & Service
120	Cnty Rd. V, Cnty Rd. OK, Waldo Sheboygan
FStop	**E:** Phillips 66(*)
Food	**E:** Hill Farm Restaurant
Lodg	**E:** The Parkway Motel
TWash	**E:** Hydro Truck Wash
RVCamp	**W:** Horn's Sales & Service(LP) (1.1 Miles)
Parks	**E:** Kohler-Andrae State Park
116	Cnty Road AA, Foster Road, Oostburg
113	WI 32, Cnty Rd. LL, Cedar Grove
TStop	**W:** Hy-Way (Citgo)
TServ	**W:** Hy-Way (Citgo)
107	Cnty Road D, Belgium, Lake Church
TStop	**W:** How Deda Truck Stop(*, SCALES) (Showers)
Gas	**W:** Amoco(*, CW), Mobil(*, LP)
Food	**W:** Amoco, Bic's Place, Dairy Queen (Amoco), Hobos Korner Kitchen (How Deda Truck Stop), How Deda Truck Stop (Showers), Mobil, Piccadilli Pizza
Lodg	**W:** Americinn Motel
AServ	**W:** Belgium Service Center (NAPA)
TServ	**W:** How Deda Truck Stop(SCALES) (Showers)
ATM	**W:** Amoco
Parks	**E:** Herrington Beach State Park
100	WI 32, West Cnty Rd. 8, Fredonia, Port Washington
Gas	**E:** Citgo(*, D)
Food	**E:** Arby's, Burger King, McDonald's, Subway **W:** Niesletts Country Inn
AServ	**E:** Goodyear Tire & Auto, Quicky Lube
Other	**E:** Eye Center, Pet Supply, Sentry Foods Grocery Store
97	Jct WI-57N, to Plymouth (Left Exit Northbound)
96	WI 33, Saukvill, Port Washington
Gas	**E:** Mobil(*) **W:** Amoco(*)
Food	**W:** Bublitz's Family Restaurant, Hardee's, Subway
Lodg	**W:** Super 8
AServ	**E:** Erniezon Schledorn Buick, Chrysler, Plymouth, Pontiac, GM, Schmit Brothers Ford, Mercury, Lincoln **W:** Albinger
ATM	**E:** Piggly Wiggly **W:** Port Washington State Bank
Other	**E:** Piggly Wiggly, Squeaky Clean Car Wash, Wal-Mart(LP, RX) **W:** Coin Laundry
93	Cnty. Rd. B, North WI 32, Port Washington, Grafton
92	Cnty Rd. Q, WI 60, Grafton
FStop	**W:** Citgo(*)
Food	**E:** Ghostown Tavern & Restaurant **W:** Citgo, Dairy Queen (Citgo)
89	Cnty Road C, Cedarburg
Gas	**W:** Mobil(*)
Med	**W:** Hospital

EXIT	WISCONSIN
ATM	**W:** Mobil
85	West WI 167, South WI 157, Mequon Road, Thiensville
Gas	**W:** Amoco(*), Citgo(*, D), Mobil(*, CW)
Food	**W:** Boulangerie Cafe & Bakery, Bread Smith, Chancery, Dairy Queen, Damon's, Einstein Bros Bagels, Freddy's Frozen Custard & Jumbo Hamburgers, La Anh Palace (Chinese), McDonald's(PLAY), Subway, Wendy's, Wooden Goose Cafe
Med	**E:** Hospital
ATM	**W:** Amoco, First Star, Kohl's Food Emporium, M&L Bank, Norwest Bank, Ozaukee Bank
Other	**W:** Kohl's Food Emporium, Lake Shore Eye Care, Mail Boxes Ect., Mequon Pharmacy(RX), Pick & Save, Stein Optical Express, Vision Care Center, WalGreen's
83	Port Washington Rd (Reaccess Southbound Only, Difficult Reaccess)
Parks	**E:** High & Richard Smith JCC Family Park(PLAY)
82B	Brown Deer Rd.
82A	WI 32 East Brown Deer Rd., WI 100
Gas	**E:** Amoco(*, LP), PDQ(*)
Food	**E:** Bonnie Ellen's Nuts & Candy House, Cousins' Sub's, Daily's Cafe & Expresso, Hanna Sushi Bar, Heinemann's Restaurant, James Take Away Food, Jonathan's Bagels, McDonald's, PDQ, Pizza Hut, The Speakeasy & Judy's Kitchen, Victor's Coffee & Tea
ATM	**E:** Amoco, Bank One, First Star, Great Midwest Bank, M&I Bank, TCF Bank
Other	**E:** Kohl's Food Emporium, Osco Drugs, U.S. Post Office, Vision Care Center
80	Good Hope Road
Lodg	**E:** Residence Inn
Med	**E:** Hospital
78	Silver Spring Dr
Gas	**E:** Amoco(*), Mobil(*) **W:** Amoco(*, LP), Mobil
Food	**E:** Annie's American Cafe, Boston Market Restaurant, Brubaker's, Burger King, Cousins' Sub's, Denny's, Hardee's, Kopps Frozen Custard, Little Caesars Pizza, McDonald's(PLAY), Pappa John's Pizza, Schlotzsky's Deli, Subway, Taco Bell, The Ground Round, Wong's Wok **W:** Applebee's, The Ground Round, Tumbleweed Southwest Grill
Lodg	**E:** Budgetel Inn, Exel Inn, Woodfield Suites
AServ	**E:** Car X Mufflers & Brakes, Mobil, Nodell, Quaker State Oil & Lube **W:** Firestone, Goodyear, Mobil, Sear's
Med	**E:** Hospital
ATM	**E:** Security Bank **W:** First Star Bank, Mutual Savings Bank
Other	**E:** Echo Bowl, Pet Supplies, Stein Optical Express, Ye Old RX(RX) **W:** Bayshore Mall, City Animal Hospital, Kohl's Food Emporium, WalGreen's(RX)
77AB	Hampton Ave.
Food	**E:** Sally's Coffee Shop
Lodg	**E:** Hilton Inn, North Shore Inn
76AB	WI 57, 190, Green Bay Ave, Capitol Dr
75	Atkinson Ave, Keef Ave
Gas	**E:** Mobil(*) **W:** Amoco
AServ	**E:** Pennzoil Oil Change
74	Locust St
Gas	**E:** Amoco
Food	**E:** Burger King
AServ	**E:** Uniroyal Tire
Other	**E:** Milwaukee Police Station
73C	North Ave
Food	**W:** Wendy's
73A	WI 145, 4th St, Broadway (Reaccess Southbound Only)
72C	Civic Center, Wells St, Kilbourn Ave

EXIT	WISCONSIN
Med	**W:** Hospital
72B	Jct I-94 West Madison
72A	Jct I-94 East
	Note: I-43 runs concurrent below with I-94. Numbering follows I-94.
311	WI 59, National Ave., 6th St. (Southbound, Reaccess Westbound Only)
312A	Lapham Blvd., Mitchell, Beecham
Gas	**S:** Amoco(*), Citgo(*)
AServ	**S:** Amoco
ATM	**S:** Citgo
312B	Beecher St., Lincoln Ave.
Gas	**S:** BP(*, D), Citgo(*, D)
ATM	**S:** Citgo
314A	Holt Ave.
Gas	**N:** Citgo(*, D)
Food	**N:** Dairy Queen (Pik & Save), Pik & Save(RX) (Vision Mart), Subway (Pik & Save), Taco Loco (Pik & Save)
Med	**S:** Hospital
ATM	**N:** Pik & Save (Vision Mart)
Other	**N:** Builder Square(LP), Pik & Save(RX) (Vision Mart)
314B	Howard Ave.
Gas	**N:** Clark(*), Mobil(*), Shell(*, CW)
Food	**N:** Copper Kitchen, George Webb Restaurant, Ho Ho Chinese Food, Peppe's Pizza
AServ	**N:** Mobil
ATM	**N:** Clark, First Star, Mutual Savings Bank
Other	**N:** Tru Value Hardware(LP), WalGreens Pharmacy(24)
316	Jct I-43, I-894W, Beloit
	Note: I-43 runs concurrent above with I-94. Numbering follows I-94.
	Note: I-43 runs concurrent below with I-894. Numbering follows I-894.
10AB	I-94 Chicago, I-43/94 Dowtown Milwaukee
9AB	U.S. 41, 27th St
Gas	**E:** Amoco, Citgo(*, LP), Mobil(*, LP)
Food	**E:** Arby's, Burger King, Chancery (Suburban), Cousins Submarines, Mandarin Garden Chinese, Pizza Hut, Spring Garden Restaurant, Super Saver **W:** Hardee's(PLAY), McDonald's(PLAY), Taco Amego Mexican Restaurant
Lodg	**E:** Suburban Motel **W:** Hospitality Inn
AServ	**E:** Amoco, Car Star, Citgo, Dodge City Auto, Valvoline Oil Change, Wisconsin Auto Parts **W:** Arrow Oldsmobile, GMC, Braeger Chevrolet Parts & Service, Midas Muffler & Brake, Parts America, Quaker State Oil & Lube, Scrub & Dub Auto Wash (Penske Oil Change)
Med	**W:** Hospital
ATM	**E:** Great Midwest Bank, Guaranty Bank, Super Saver **W:** First Star
Other	**E:** K-Mart, Puppy World, Target **W:** Olympic Lanes (Bowling), Scrub & Dub Auto Wash (Penske Oil Change), Triple A Offices
8A	WI 36, Loomis Road
Gas	**E:** Amoco(*, CW), Citgo(*, D, LP, CW)
Food	**E:** Los Mariachoi's (Mexican) **W:** George Webb Restaurant
AServ	**W:** Bill Maynard's Auto Service, Pennzoil Oil Change
Other	**E:** WalGreens Pharmacy(*)
7	60th St
Gas	**E:** Super America(*, LP) **W:** Speedway(*, LP)
Food	**E:** Mineo's Italian
AServ	**W:** North Star Automotive Sales & Service
Med	**W:** Urgent Care Clinic

← N I-43

EXIT	WISCONSIN
ATM	**E:** Credit Union, Super America
Other	**E:** WalGreens Pharmacy(RX)
	W: Coin Operated Laundry
5B	76th St.- 84th St.
5A	WI 24, Forest Home Ave. (Reaccess Southbound Only, Difficult Reaccess)
Gas	**E:** Citgo(*, D)
Food	**E:** Lychee Garden Chinese & American, Wendy's
AServ	**E:** Citgo, Jason's Auto Repair, QLube Quaker State
ATM	**E:** Jewel Grocery
Other	**E:** Jewel Grocery
4	Junction I-43 & I-894
2	National Avenue
1	WI59
Gas	**W:** SuperAmerica(*, D)
Food	**E:** Dicken's Grille
	W: Burger King, McDonald's, Steakhouse 100, Yick-Sing
AServ	**E:** Wisconsin Auto Parts
	W: Meineke Discount Mufflers
ATM	**W:** SuperAmerica
Other	**W:** WalGreens Pharmacy

Note: I-43 runs concurrent above with I-894. Numbering follows I-894.

EXIT	WISCONSIN
61	894N, U.S. 45 (Left Exit Northbound)
60	U.S. 45, WI 100, 108th St
59	Laton Ave. WI-100 (Left Exit Northbound)
AServ	**E:** D&A Car Care
57	Moorland Road
Gas	**E:** Super America(*, LP)
Other	**E:** Ridge Cinemas
54	Cty. Road Y, Racine Ave.
FStop	**E:** Citgo(*, LP)
Food	**E:** Citgo, Subway (Citgo)
ATM	**E:** Citgo
50	WI 164, Waukesha, Big Bend
Gas	**W:** Arms Express(*, D)
Food	**W:** Antonio's Deli, Arms Express, McDonald's
ATM	**W:** Arms Express, Citizen's Bank
43	WI 83, Waterford, Mukwonago
FStop	**E:** Mobil(*)
Gas	**W:** Citgo(*)
Food	**W:** Dairy Queen, Imperial House Chinese, Shannahans Sandwiches/Coffee Shop, Taco Bell
Lodg	**W:** Sleep Inn
RVCamp	**E:** Countryview Campground
Med	**W:** + Childcare Clinic
ATM	**E:** Mobil
Other	**W:** Wal-Mart(RX)
38	WI 20, East Troy Waterford
TStop	**W:** Citgo(*, LP)
Gas	**W:** Amoco(*, LP, CW), J&L Oil(*)
Food	**W:** Burger King, Citgo, Family Kitchen Restaurant, Rona Pizza, Subway (Citgo)
AServ	**W:** Bumper to Bumper, Frasona Plymouth, Dodge, Truck
TServ	**W:** Citgo
ATM	**W:** Citgo
Other	**W:** Drive-N-Shine (Car Wash)
36	WI 120, East Troy
Gas	**W:** Side View Plaza(D)
33	Bowers Road
(33)	**Rest Area (RR, Phones, Picnic, RV Dump; Southbound)**
(33)	**Rest Area (RR, Phones, Picnic, RV Dump; Northbound)**
29	WI 11, Elkhorn, Burlington
27AB	U.S. 12, Lake Geneva, Madison
TServ	**E:** Stuard Truck Service
Med	**E:** + Hospital
25	WI 67, Elkhorn, Williams Bay
FStop	**E:** Mobil(*, CW)
Lodg	**E:** AmericInn
AServ	**E:** Tasch Chevrolet, Buick, GMC, Tasch Chrysler, Plymouth, Dodge, Jeep
	W: Crosby Automotive Repair (AAA)
TServ	**W:** ECO Complete Transportation
RVCamp	**E:** Dehann RV Sales & Service(LP) (.25 Miles)
Other	**E:** Elkhorn Animal Clinic
21	WI 50, Delavan, Lake Geneva
Gas	**W:** Mobil(*, LP)
Food	**W:** Burger King, Cousins' Sub's, KFC, McDonald's(PLAY), Pizza Hut, SHONEY'S, Shoney's, Subway, Taco Bell, Wendy's
Lodg	**W:** Super 8
AServ	**W:** Country Ford, Crest Cadillac
ATM	**W:** First Star, Pick & Save, Piggly Wiggly
Other	**E:** Geneva Lakes Kennel Club
	W: K-Mart(RX), Pick & Save, Piggly Wiggly, ShopKo(RX) (Optical), WalGreens Pharmacy
17	Highway X, Delavan
Gas	**W:** Gas(*, D, LP)
Food	**W:** A & W (Gas), Bresler's Ice Cream (Gas), Gas, Little Caesars Pizza (Gas)
ATM	**W:** Gas
15	U.S. 14, Darien Whitewater, Janesville
Gas	**E:** Citgo(*)
Food	**E:** West Wind Diner
TServ	**E:** Robert Henson Trucking
Med	**E:** + The Darian Medical Ctr.
ATM	**E:** Amcore Bank
6	WI 140, Clinton, Avalon
Gas	**E:** Citgo
Food	**E:** Citgo, Subway (Citgo)
AServ	**E:** Tom Beck Ford
ATM	**E:** AM Core Bank, Citgo
2	Highway X, Hart Road
1AB	Jct I-90, Madison, Chicago

↑ WISCONSIN

Begin I-43

I-44 E →

EXIT	TEXAS
	Begin I-44

↓ TEXAS

EXIT	TEXAS
1A	U.S. 277 S, Abeline (Westbound)
Food	**N:** Arby's
Lodg	**N:** EconoLodge, Four Points Hotel Sheraton
	S: Holiday Inn
AServ	**S:** Action Battery Center
Med	**N:** + Hospital
Other	**N:** City Police
1B	Scottland (Eastbound)
Gas	**S:** Citgo(*)
Lodg	**N:** Four Points Motel by Sheraton
	S: Scottland Park Motel
1C	Texas Travel Info. Center
Gas	**S:** Citgo(*)
Other	**N:** Travel Info.
	S: J.S. Bridwell Agricultural Center
1D	Bus. 287
Gas	**N:** Conoco(*), Texaco
Food	**S:** Pioneer
Lodg	**N:** River Oaks Inn
TServ	**S:** International Harvester
2	Maurine St
Gas	**N:** Fina(*)
	S: Fina(*, D), Texaco(D)
Food	**N:** China Star, Dairy Queen, Denny's, El Chico Mexican Restaurant, Long John Silver, Whataburger
Lodg	**N:** Hampton Inn, La Quinta Inn, Super 8, Travelers Inn
	S: Comfort Inn, DAYS INN Days Inn, Motel 6
AServ	**S:** Herb Easley Nissan, Volvo, Volkswagon, GM, Chev, Texaco
3B	Spur 325, Sheppard
3A	US 287, Vernon, Amarillo (Left Exit)
3C	Hwy. FM 890, Municipal Airport
Gas	**N:** Diamond Shamrock(*, D)
ATM	**N:** Diamond Shamrock
	S: Food Lion(24, RX)
Other	**S:** Food Lion(RX)
4	City Loop
5	Access Rd. (Eastbound)
5A	Hwy FM 3492, Shepperd AFB, Missile Rd, Dept. of Safety
Food	**S:** TePee Restaurant
6	Bacon Switch Rd
7	East Rd
(10)	**Rest Area (RR, Phones, P; Westbound)**
(10)	**Rest Area (RR, Phones, P; Eastbound)**

EXIT	TEXAS/OKLAHOMA
11	Hwy FM 3429, Daniels Rd
12	TX 240, Burk Burnett
Gas	**N:** Diamond Shamrock(*), Fina(*, D, CW)
	S: Conoco(*), Phillips 66(*)
Food	**N:** Braum's Ice Cream, Carl Jr's Hamburgers, Golden Fried Chicken, Mazzio's Pizza, McDonald's(PLAY), Whataburger
Lodg	**N:** Ranch House Motel
	S: Twilight Motel
AServ	**N:** Car Quest, Larry Landrum Chev, Pont, Olds, Pruitt Ford
	S: Ed's Tire Mart, Phillips 66
ATM	**N:** Fina
13	TX Spur 383, Glendale St.
Food	**N:** Circle BBQ
Other	**N:** Sav A Lot Food Stores, Wal-Mart(RX)
14	Loop 267, East Third St.
Other	**N:** KOA Campgrounds

↑ TEXAS

↓ OKLAHOMA

EXIT	OKLAHOMA
1	OK 36, Grandfield
5	North U.S. 277, U.S. 281, Jct. US.70, Waurika, Randlett, County Road
20	OK 5, Walters

EXIT	OKLAHOMA
(20)	**Elmer Graham Plaza, Welcome Center (RR, HF, Phones, Picnic)**
FStop	B: **Texaco**(*)
Food	B: **McDonald's**(PLAY)
30	OK 36, Geronimo, Faxon, Frederick
33	US Bus. 281, 11th St
Other	N: **Hospital**
36A	OK 7, Lee Blvd, Duncan
FStop	N: **Fina**(*), **Sun Country**(*)
Food	N: Big Chef Coffee Shop, KFC, **Truck Stop Restaurant**
Lodg	N: Motel 6
AServ	N: Exhaust Shop, **Fina**
TServ	N: **Alford's Truck Service**
37	Gore Blvd
Food	N: **Cracker Barrel**, Mike's Sports Grill S: Howard Johnson
Lodg	S: Howard Johnson
Med	N: **+ USPHS Indian Hospital**
Other	N: Dept. Of Public Safety S: Native Sun Waterpark
39A	Cache Road (Difficult Reaccess, Limited Access Hwy)
Gas	N: Conoco(*), Phillips 66
Lodg	N: Ecomony Inn, Super 9 Motel, Travel Inn
AServ	N: Midas Muffler
39B	Bus281, Lawton
40A	U.S. 62 West, Cache, Altus, Rogers Lane
Lodg	N: **Super 8 (see our ad this page)**
40B	U.S. 62 W, Cache, Altus
40C	Gate Two
41	Ft. Sill Key Gate
Other	N: **Ft. Sill Museum**
45	OK 49, Medicine Park, Carnegie
FStop	N: **Love's**(*)
Food	N: **A & W Drive-In (Love's)**, Burger King(PLAY), **Subway (Love's)**
ATM	N: **Love's**
Other	N: Comanche Tribal Complex
46	East US 62, North US 277, US 281, Elgin, Apachee, Anadarko (Eastbound, Difficult Reaccess)
53	U.S. 277, Elgin, Fletcher, Sterling, Lake Ellsworth
FStop	N: **Phillips 66**(*)
Gas	S: Fina(*) (Vehicle Inspection Center), Total(*)
AServ	S: Fina (Vehicle Inspection Center)
Other	S: Car Wash(CW)

EXIT	OKLAHOMA
(60)	**Parking Area (Picnic, P; Eastbound)**
62	Fletcher, Elgin, Sterling
(63)	**Parking Area (Picnic, P; Westbound)**
79	Toll Booth (Toll)
80	U.S. 81, Chickasha, Duncan
Food	N: Arby's, Braum's Ice Cream, McDonald's(PLAY), Peking Dragon, Pizza Hut, Taco Mayo S: Burger King, Jake's Ribs, Western Sizzlin
Lodg	N: **Best Western**, Ranch House Motel S: Days Inn, Delux Inn, Royal American Inn
AServ	S: Ralph & Sons Olds, GMC Trucks, Steve Lacefield Chev, Pont, Buick, **Wal-Mart**(RX)
ATM	S: **Wal-Mart**

EXIT	OKLAHOMA
Other	N: **Eckerd Drugs**, Sundance Car Wash(CW), Vision Center S: Bonanza Car Wash(CW), **Wal-Mart**(RX)
83	U.S. 62, Chickasha (Toll)
Med	N: **+ Hospital**
(85)	**Service Area**
FStop	B: **Texaco**(*)
Food	B: **McDonald's**(PLAY)
(97)	**Parking Area (Picnic, P; Westbound)**
98	Toll Plaza (Toll)
(99)	**Parking Area (Picnic, P; Eastbound)**
107	U.S. 62 S, Newcastle
FStop	S: **Conoco**(*)
Food	S: **Burger King (Conoco)**
ATM	S: **Conoco**
107A	Indian Hills Rd (Westbound)
108	OK 37, Tuttle, Minco
Gas	N: Phillips 66(*, CW)
Food	N: Braum's Ice Cream, Hardee's, Mazzio's Pizza, Subway
AServ	N: Tri-City Quick Lube
ATM	N: Phillips 66, Sooner State Bank
Other	N: **Wal-Mart**(RX)
108A	Frontage Rd (Westbound, No Reaccess)
109	SW 149th St
Food	S: JR's Pub and Grill
110	OK 37 East, Moore
Gas	S: Diamond Shamrock(*)
111	SW 119th St
AServ	N: Lindsay's Auto Services
112	SW 104th St
FStop	N: **Texaco**(*)
Food	N: **Hi-Way Grill (Texaco)**
ATM	N: **Texaco**
113	SW 89th St
FStop	S: **Love's Country Store**(*, D, CW, 24)
Gas	S: Total(*, D)
ATM	S: **Love's Country Store**, Total
114	SW 74th St
Gas	S: 7-11 Convenience Store(*), Sinclair, Stax(*), Texaco(*), Total(*, D, CW)
Food	S: Braum's, Burger King, Captain D's Seafood, Crocketts Smokehouse, Perry's Restaurant, Taco Bell
Lodg	S: Cambridge Inn
AServ	S: Sinclair
ATM	S: Sinclair, Stax, Total

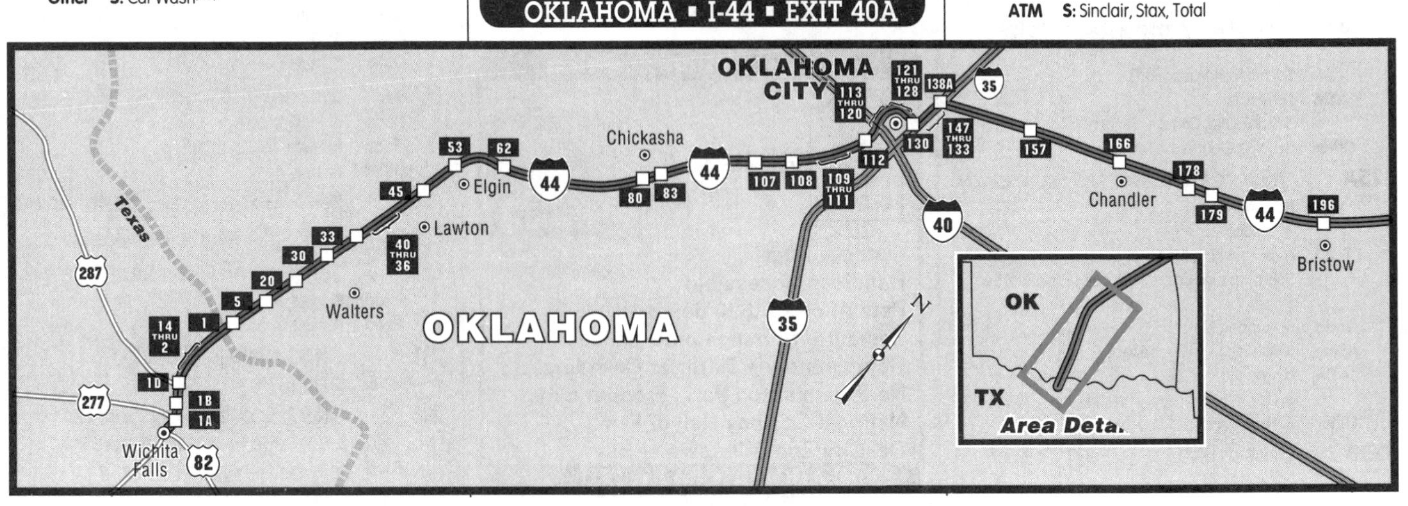

EXIT OKLAHOMA

115 Jct I-240 E, US 62 E, OK 3 E, Fort Smith

116A SW 59th St
- **Gas** **S:** Conoco[*], Stax's[*]
- **Food** **S:** Pizza Inn, Pizza King, Sonic Drive in, Taco Mayo, Winchells Donuts
- **ATM** **S:** Bank One, Stax's

116B Airport Rd (Left Exit , Difficult Reaccess)

117A SW 44th Street

117B SW44th St

118 OK 152 W, SW 29th St
- **Gas** **N:** Texaco[*]
- **Food** **S:** Burger King[PLAY], KFC, McDonald's[PLAY], Taco Bueno
- **AServ** **S:** Long's Paint & Body Shop
- **Other** **S:** Sooner Food Market, WalGreen's[RX]

119 SW 15th St

120B Jct. I-40E, Fort Smith

120A Jct. I-40 W, Amarillo (Left Exit)

121A NW 10th St, Fair Park (Eastbound, Difficult Reaccess)

121B NW 10th Street (Westbound, Difficult Reaccess)
- **Gas** **N:** Stax[*]
- **AServ** **N:** Crackmasters Windshield Cracks Repaired
- **ATM** **N:** Stax

122 NW 23rd St
- **Gas** **N:** 7-11 Convenience Store[*], Conoco[*, CW]
  S: Conoco[*, CW]
- **Food** **N:** Church's Chicken, Egg Roll King, Long John Silver, Taco Mayo
  S: Arby's, Sonic
- **AServ** **N:** Hibdon Tire Center, Lee Auto Service, Roadpro Auto Parts
  S: Big O Tires
- **ATM** **N:** 7-11 Convenience Store, Conoco
  S: Conoco
- **Other** **S:** Metro Car Wash Depot[CW], Super Coin Laundry

123A NW 36th St
- **Gas** **N:** Stax[*, D], Total[*]
- **ATM** **N:** Stax, Total

123B OK 66 W, Warr Acres Bethany

124 North May Ave
- **Gas** **N:** Texaco[*]
  S: Conoco[*], Texaco[*]
- **Food** **N:** Dairy Queen, Deckers Restaurant, Subway (Texaco)
  S: Milini's Pizza, Wendy's
- **Lodg** **N:** Days Inn, Super 8 (see our ad this page)
- **AServ** **N:** City Glass, Lynn Hickey Dodge, O'Reilly Auto Parts
  S: Dub Richardson Ford
- **ATM** **N:** Texaco
  S: Bank One, Conoco, Texaco
- **Other** **S:** Swiss Cleaners & Laundry

125A OK 3A to Penn Ave., NW Expressway
- **Gas** **N:** Conoco[*]
  S: Texaco[*]
- **Food** **N:** Burger King (Conoco)
  S: Braum's Ice Cream[PLAY], Coit's Cafe Root Beer Stand
- **Lodg** **S:** Habana Inn
- **AServ** **S:** Joe Esco Tire Co., Texaco
- **ATM** **N:** Conoco
  S: Homeland Grocery Store[RX]
- **Other** **S:** Homeland Grocery Store[RX]

125B Classen Blvd.

EXIT OKLAHOMA

- **Food** **S:** Courtyard by Marriott, McDonald's, Richmond Hotel
- **Lodg** **S:** Courtyard by Marriott, Richmond Hotel
- **AServ** **N:** Auto Express
- **Other** **N:** Car Wash[CW], Penn Square Mall

126 Western Ave
- **Gas** **S:** Conoco[*]
- **Food** **N:** Deep Fork Grill
- **ATM** **S:** Conoco
- **Other** **S:** An-Son Car Wash

127 Junction S. I-235, Oklahoma City Downtown, Jct. U.S. 77, Edmond

128A Lincoln Blvd, State Capitol (Difficult Reaccess)
- **Gas** **S:** Total[*]
- **Food** **S:** Holiday Inn Express
- **Lodg** **S:** Holiday Inn Express, Oxford Inn
- **ATM** **S:** Total

128B Kelley Ave.
- **Gas** **N:** Conoco[*], Total[*, D, CW]
- **Food** **N:** Sonic Drive In, Subway (Total)
- **ATM** **N:** Total
- **Other** **N:** Cowboy Hall of Fame

129 Martin Luther King Ave.
- **Food** **S:** McDonald's
- **Lodg** **S:** Ramada Inn

130 Junction I-35 S to I-40 Dallas

Note: I-44 runs concurrent below with I-35. Numbering follows I-35.

133 State Capitol, Jct. I-44 W, Lawton, Amarillo

134 Wilshire Blvd, NE 78th St
- **TStop** **W:** Texaco[*, SCALES]
- **Lodg** **W:** EconoLodge
- **TWash** **W:** Texaco
- **ATM** **W:** Texaco

135 Britton Road, NE 93rd St

136 Hefner Road
- **Gas** **W:** Conoco[*]
- **Food** **W:** Homemade Italian Specialties
- **Other** **W:** Frontier City (Amusement Park)

137 NE 122nd St
- **TStop** **W:** Flying J Travel Center[*, LP, SCALES]
- **FStop** **E:** Texaco[*] (CB Repair), Total[*]
  W: Love's Country Store[*, SCALES], Texaco[*]
- **Food** **E:** Kettle (Texaco FS)
  W: Carl Jr's Charbroiled Hamburgers (Texaco), Cracker Barrel, Magic Dragon Chinese (Flying J Travel Center), McDonald's, Oklahoma Trading Post, Pepperoni's Pizza (Flying J Travel Center), Subway (Love's), Taco Bell (Love's),

Large Vehicle Parking

SUPER 8 MOTEL

405-946-9170

$32.88* 1-2 Persons

*Not valid with anyother offer.

Outdoor Pool
Handicap Accessible
Pets Allowed ($20 deposit)
Restaurant/Lounge on Premises
Coin Laundry • Exterior Corridors
Near Remington Park, Frontier City, National Cowboy Hall of Fame, OK City Zoo, Whitewater Bay

OKLAHOMA • I-44 • EXIT 124

EXIT OKLAHOMA

Waffle House
- **Lodg** **E:** Motel 6
  W: Comfort Inn, Days Inn, Motel 6, Quality Inn, Red Carpet Inn
- **AServ** **W:** Interstate Auto Repair, Interstate Battery (RV Campground Good Sam Park)
- **TWash** **W:** Oasis Truck Wash
- **RVCamp** **W:** RV Campground Good Sam Park[LP]
- **ATM** **W:** Love's Country Store, Texaco
- **Other** **W:** Tourist Info.

138A Jct I-44 E, Tulsa

Note: I-44 runs concurrent above with I-35. Numbering follows I-35.

(153) Parking Area (Phones, Picnic, P; Westbound)

(153) Parking Area (Phones, Picnic, P; Eastbound)

(156) Service Area (Southbound)

(157) Service Area (Westbound)

158 **(157)** OK 66, Wellston (Eastbound, Reaccess Westbound Only)

166 OK 18, Chandler, Cushing
- **Gas** **S:** Phillips 66[*]
- **Food** **S:** Tastee Freeze
- **Lodg** **S:** EconoLodge
- **AServ** **S:** Phillips 66

(167) Service Area (Eastbound)

171 Rest Area (Phones, Picnic, P; Eastbound)

(178) Service Area

179 OK 99, Stroud, Drumright
- **FStop** **S:** Conoco[*]
- **Gas** **N:** Citgo[*]
  S: Stax[*]
- **Food** **N:** Best Western
  S: El Nino Mexican, Mazzio's Pizza, McDonald's, Sonic Drive In, Specialty House Family Restaurant, Taco Mayo
- **Lodg** **N:** Best Western
- **ATM** **N:** Citgo
  S: Stax
- **Other** **N:** Book Warehouse, Tanger Outlet Center

(183) Toll Plaza (Toll)

(189) Parking Area (Picnic; Eastbound)

(192) Parking Area (Picnic; Westbound)

196 OK 48, Bristow, Lake Keystone
- **Gas** **S:** 7-11 Convenience Store[*], Phillips 66[*, D]
- **Food** **S:** Pizza Hut, Steer Inn, Taco Mayo
- **Lodg** **S:** Carolyn Inn
- **AServ** **S:** Wal-Mart[RX]
- **Other** **S:** Wal-Mart[RX]

(196) Service Area (Eastbound)
- **FStop** **B:** Phillips 66[*]
- **Food** **B:** McDonald's
- **Other** **B:** Tourist Info.

(204) Parking Area (Picnic; Eastbound)

(205) Parking Area (Picnic; Westbound)

(207) Service Area (Westbound)
- **FStop** **B:** Phillips 66[*]
- **Food** **B:** McDonald's

211 OK 33, Kellyville, Sapulpa
- **Gas** **S:** Phillips 66[*, D]

215 OK 97, Sapulpa, Sand Springs
- **Gas** **S:** 7-11 Convenience Store[*], Phillips 66[*, D]
- **Food** **S:** Margie's Restaurant

EXIT OKLAHOMA

Med **S:** Hospital

222A 49th W Ave
- **FStop** **S:** QuikTrip(*, SCALES), Texaco(*, SCALES)
- **Food** **N:** Carl Jr's Hamburgers(PLAY), Mama Lou's Restaurant(24), Marvin's Food Warehouse, Monterey's Mexican
  S: Arby's, McDonald's(PLAY), SHONEY'S, Shoney's, Subway (Texaco), Waffle House, Wendy's (Quick Trip)
- **Lodg** **N:** Gateway Motor Hotel, Motel 6, Super 9 Inn, Tulsa Inn
  S: Traveler's Inn
- **AServ** **S:** Service Tire & Battery
- **TServ** **N:** Mack Truck Sales
  S: Cummins, Cat, Detroit Diesel, Freightliner Dealer(24), Kenworth(24), Peterbilt
- **ATM** **S:** QuikTrip, Texaco
- **Other** **N:** May's Drugs(RX)

222B 55th Place (Eastbound, Difficult Reaccess)
- **Food** **S:** DAYS INN Days Inn
- **Lodg** **S:** DAYS INN Days Inn

222C 56th Street (Westbound, Same Services as Exit 222A)
- **Food** **N:** Mama Lou's, Montery's
- **Lodg** **N:** Crystal Motel, Gateway Motor Inn, Super 9 Motel, Tulsa Inn, Western Capri Motel
- **TServ** **N:** Oklahoma Truck Supply

223A Junction I-244 E, Downtown Tulsa

223B 51st Street

223C 33rd W Ave
- **Gas** **S:** Phillips 66(*)
- **Food** **N:** Braum's Ice Cream, Little Caesars Pizza
- **ATM** **S:** Phillips 66

224 Union Ave., Elwood Ave., U.S. 75, G Okmulgee, Bartlesville
- **Gas** **N:** Citgo(*), QuikTrip(*), Total(*, CW)
- **Food** **N:** Arnold's, KFC, Linda-Mar Drive-In, Mazzio's Pizza, Pizza Hut, Subway
  S: The Last Great American Diner(24)
- **Lodg** **S:** Rio Motel, Roadside Inn
- **TServ** **S:** Thermo King
- **RVCamp** **S:** Warrior Campground
- **ATM** **N:** QuikTrip, Warehouse Market Discount Foods(RX)
- **Other** **N:** Coin Laundry, Warehouse Market Discount Foods(RX)

225 Elwood Ave (Westbound)
- **Lodg** **S:** Old Capitol Motel
- **AServ** **N:** GM Auto Dealership

226A Riverside Dr
- **Lodg** **S:** Country Garden Inn
- **AServ** **N:** GM Auto

81 Newly Renovated Guest Rooms & Suites 1812

Howard Johnson

4724 South Yale Tulsa, OK

918-496-9300 • 800-I GO HOJO

Free Continental Breakfast
Denny's on Property (24 hrs)
Outdoor Pool (Seasonal)
Cable TV w/HBO/ESPN/CN
In Room Coffee
Guest Laundry

GOLD MEDAL PROPERTY

AAA Approved

OKLAHOMA • I-44 • EXIT 229

EXIT OKLAHOMA

226B Peoria Ave
- **Gas** **N:** Conoco(*, D, CW)
  S: Gas Stop, Texaco(*, CW)
- **Food** **N:** Burger Street, Church's Chicken, Ci Ci's Pizza, Panda Super Buffet, Philly's Steaks & Burgers, Pizza Hut, The Shez Palace Club (Super 8 Motel), Waffle House
  S: Braum's Ice Cream, Burger King, Golden Palace (Chinese), Kelly's Restaurant, Ron's Hamburgers
- **Lodg** **N:** Super 8 (see our ad this page)
- **AServ** **N:** Conoco
  S: Auto Zone Auto Parts, Gary's Automotive Service, Gas Stop, Meineke Discount Mufflers
- **ATM** **N:** NationsBank
  S: Texaco
- **Other** **S:** Antique Mall, Buy for Less Grocery(RX), Couch Pharmacy(RX), May's Drug Store

227 Lewis Ave
- **Gas** **S:** Conoco, Stax(*)
- **Food** **S:** Stuffers U.S.A. (Steaks, Sandwiches), Turnpike Lounge
- **AServ** **S:** Conoco, Hibdon Tire Centers, Victory Auto Care
- **RVCamp** **S:** Interstate RV Park(LP)
- **ATM** **S:** Stax
- **Other** **S:** Blue Monday Laundry

228 Harvard Ave
- **Gas** **N:** Texaco(*, D, CW)
  S: 51st Street Auto Clinic, Phillips 66(*) (Credit Card Only)
- **Food** **N:** Best Western Trade Winds East, Best Western Trade Winds Central, Black Jack's, SHONEY'S, Shoney's, Subway
  S: Baskin Robbins, Blimpie's Subs, Chili's, Grille

SUPER 8 MOTEL

Super 8 Motel

1347 E. Skelly Drive
Tulsa, OK 74105

918-743-4431

Outdoor Pool
Lounge on Premises
Restaurant Nearby
Free Local Calls
25" Remote Control Cable TV w/HBO/ESPN/CNN
Queen & King Size Beds
Exterior Corridors
Near Gilcrease Museum & Tulsa Fairgrounds
Military, Senior, Truckers Discount
Group Rates offered
Downtown Convention Center 3 mi

1755

OKLAHOMA • I-44 • EXIT 226B

EXIT OKLAHOMA

Fifty-one, Happy Cricket Bodean Seafood, Jamil's Family Dining, Lanna Thai Restaurant, Little Caesars Pizza (Big K-Mart), Long John Silver, Mario's Pizzeria, McDonald's, Osaka Steakhouse of Japan, Papa John's Pizza, Pickle's Pubs, Rick's Cafe Americain, Viet-Huong Vietnamese Cuisine
- **Lodg** **N:** Best Western Trade Winds East, Best Western Trade Winds Central, Towers Hotel & Suites
  S: Holiday Inn Express
- **AServ** **N:** Jiffy Lube
  S: 51st Street Auto Clinic, Big K-Mart(RX), Tulsa Automotive Repair
- **Med** **N:** S. Harvard Medical Clinic
- **ATM** **N:** Spirit Bank, Texaco
  S: Albertson's Grocery(RX), Bank of Oklahoma Transfund
- **Other** **S:** Albertson's Grocery(RX), Big K-Mart(RX), Edgewood Veterinarian Hospital, Novel Idea Discount Books, U.S. Post Office

229 Yale Ave.
- **Gas** **N:** Texaco
  S: Phillips 66(*), QuikTrip(*)
- **Food** **S:** Applebee's, Arby's, Burger King, Denny's, Don Pablo's Mexican, Joseph's Steak House & Seafood, Outback Steakhouse, Subway
- **Lodg** **S:** Budgetel Inn, Comfort Inn, Howard Johnson (see our ad this page), Holiday Inn Select Hotel (see our ad this page)
- **AServ** **N:** Texaco
  S: Dean Bailey Oldsmobile, Phillips 66
- **Med** **S:** Hospital, St. Francis Hospital
- **ATM** **N:** Texaco
  S: QuikTrip
- **Other** **S:** Celebration Station Food & Fun, Spot-Not Car Wash

230 41st St., Sheraton Rd.
- **Gas** **N:** Texaco(*, LP, CW)
- **Food** **N:** All American Cafe, Whataburger
- **Lodg** **S:** Quality Inn
- **AServ** **N:** Goodyear Tire & Auto
  S: APS
- **Med** **S:** Children's Medical Center
- **ATM** **N:** Texaco
- **Other** **N:** Harmon Science Center, PetsMart

231 Jct. U.S. 64, OK 51, Muskogee, Broken Arrow, 31st St. Memorial Dr.

232 Memorial Drive, E31 St. (Services are shared with Exit 231)
- **Gas** **N:** Phillips 66(LP)
  S: Texaco(*, CW)
- **Food** **N:** Country Inn, Whataburger
  S: A & W Drive-In (Texaco), Cracker Barrel, McDonald's
- **Lodg** **N:** Ramada Inn
  S: Courtyard by Marriott, Embassy Suites,

I-44, Yale Exit

5000 E. Skelly Dr. • Tulsa, OK

Restaurant/Lounge on Premises
Outdoor Pool • Exercise Room
Meeting/Banquet Facilities
Pets Allowed (Fee Assessed)
Handicap Accessible
Truck/Large Vehicle Parking
Airport Shuttle • Coin Laundry
Exterior/Interior Corridors

918-622-7000 • 800-836-9635 1830

OKLAHOMA • I-44 • EXIT 229

EXIT		OKLAHOMA
		Extended Stay America, Super 8
	ASery	N: Phillips 66
		S: Reliable Chevrolet
	ATM	S: Texaco
	Other	S: Oklahoma Eye Center
233		East 21 Street (Westbound, No Reaccess)
	Food	S: El Chico
	RVCamp	N: **Estes Park (1 Mile)**
		S: **Dean's RV Super Store**
	Other	S: **K-Mart**
234		U.S. 169, Broken Arrow, Owasso
234B		Garnett Rd.
	Gas	S: QuikTrip(*)
	Food	N: Hardee's, Mazzio's Pizza
		S: Braum's Ice Cream
	Lodg	N: Garnett Inn, Motel 6, Statford House Inn
	AServ	N: Jiffy Lube
	Other	N: **May's Drugstore(RX), Red Bud Supermarket**
234A		U.S. 169, Broken Arrow, Owasso (Westbound)
235		East 11th Street
	Food	N: Carl Jr's Hamburgers, Fajita Rita's, Mazzio's Pizza, Sonic Drive In
		S: Denny's, EconoLodge, Taco Bueno
	Lodg	N: Executive Inn, Garnett Inn, Motel 6, Super 8
		S: EconoLodge, National Inn
	AServ	S: Freedom Oil Change
236A		129th Ave. East, Admiral Place (Westbound)
236B		West Jct. I-244, Downtown Tulsa (Westbound)
238		161st East Ave
	TStop	N: **Bruce's Tulsa Truck Plaza(*, SCALES) (CB Shop)**
	FStop	S: **QuikTrip(*)**
	Food	S: Arby's, Burger King
	Lodg	S: Microtel
	AServ	S: Brad's Auto Parts Center
	TServ	N: **Bruce's Tulsa Truck Plaza(SCALES) (CB Shop), Cummins(D)**
	RVCamp	N: **Cummins**
	ATM	S: **QuikTrip**
240A		OK 167 North, 193rd East Ave
	TStop	N: **Diamond Shamrock(*, SCALES)**
	FStop	N: **Git 'N Go(*)**
	Gas	S: Citgo(*), Texaco(*)
	Food	N: **Git 'N Go, McDonald's(PLAY)**, Pauline's Buffet, Pizza Hut, Taco Mayo, **Waffle House**, Wendy's
		S: A & W Drive-In (Texaco), Lot-A-Burger, Mazzio's Pizza, Mike's Coney Island Hot Dogs, Rex Chicken Express (Texaco), Sonic Drive In, Subway, Sunrise Donut
	Lodg	N: **Traveler's Inn**
	AServ	S: NAPA Auto Parts
	TServ	N: **Diamond Shamrock(SCALES)**
		S: **Cooper Tires Auto Repair**
	RVCamp	N: **KOA Campgrounds (.5 Miles)**
		S: **Complete RV & Truck Repair, Thurman Traveland**
	ATM	N: **Git 'N Go**
		S: Citgo, Texaco
	Other	S: Car Wash(CW), **Homeland Grocery Store(RX)**
240B		U.S. 412 East, Choteau, Siloam Springs
241		I-44 E Turnpike to Joplin, OK 66 East, Catoosa, Claremore
255		OK 20, Claremore, Pryor
	Gas	N: Phillips 66(*, D), Texaco
	Food	N: Hugo's Family
	Lodg	N: Motel Claremore, Walker Motel
	AServ	N: Texaco
	Med	N: **+ Hospital**
	Other	N: J.W. Davis Gun Museum, Will Roger's Memorial
(256)		**Parking Area (Picnic; Westbound)**
(269)		**Parking Area (Picnic; Eastbound)**
269		OK 28, Adair, Chelsea
(271)		**Parking Area (Picnic; Westbound)**
283		U.S. 69, Big Cabin, Adair, Vinita

EXIT		OKLAHOMA/MISSOURI
	TStop	N: **Big Cabin Truck Plaza(*, SCALES)**
	Lodg	N: Super 8
	TServ	N: **Big Cabin Truck Plaza(SCALES), Franks & Son Inc.**
	TWash	N: **Truck Wash**
(286)		Toll Plaza (Toll)
(288)		**Service Area (Westbound)**
	FStop	N: **Phillips 66(*)**
	Food	N: **McDonald's**
(288)		**Service Area (Eastbound)**
	FStop	S: **Phillips 66(*)**
	Food	S: **McDonald's**
289		U.S. 66, U.S. 69, Vinita
	Gas	N: Total(*, D)
		S: Sinclair(D)
	Food	N: Braum's, McDonald's, Pizza Hut, Subway
	Lodg	N: Lewis Motel, Vinita Inn
	Other	N: **Wal-Mart**
(299)		**Parking Area (Picnic; Eastbound)**
302		U.S. 59, U.S. 69, Afton, Fairland, Grove
(310)		**Parking Area (Picnic; Westbound)**
(312)		**Parking Area (Picnic; Eastbound)**
313		OK 10, Miami
	FStop	N: **Citgo(*, D)**
	Food	N: Best Western
	Lodg	N: Best Western, Super 8
	AServ	N: Wrecker & Garage 24 Hrs.
		S: Key Chrys, Plym, Dodge
	RVCamp	N: **Miami RV & Mobile Home Community**
	Other	N: The Miami Tribe of Oklahoma Info. Center
(314)		**Service Area, Welcome Center (Westbound)**
	FStop	N: **Phillips 66(*)**
(315)		**OK Information Center, Rest Area (RR, P; Westbound)**

↑OKLAHOMA

↓MISSOURI

EXIT		MISSOURI
1		U.S. Hwy. 400, U.S. 166, Baxter Springs, Kansas
(1)		**Rest Area, Mississippi Info. Center (RR, Phones, Picnic, Vending, P; Westbound)**
(1)		**Rest Area, Mississippi Info. Center (RR, Phones, Picnic, Vending, P; Eastbound)**
(3)		**Weigh Station (Westbound)**
(3)		**Weigh Station (Eastbound)**
4		MO 43 South, Seneca, Joplin
	TStop	S: **Petro(*, LP, SCALES), Pilot Travel Center(*, SCALES)**
	Food	S: **Blimpie's Subs (Petro), Dairy Queen (Pilot)**, McDonald's, **Wendy's (Pilot)**
	Lodg	S: Sleep Inn
	TServ	N: **Peterbilt of Joplin**
		S: **4 State Trucks, Petro(SCALES), Pilot Travel Center(SCALES)**
	TWash	S: **Petro**
	RVCamp	S: **KOA Campgrounds(*, LP) (.13 Miles)**
6		North MO 43, MO 86, Business Loop I-44, Joplin, Racine
	Gas	N: Citgo(*)
		S: Texaco(*)
	Food	N: Eagle Drive-In
	AServ	N: The Muffler Shop
		S: Texaco
	RVCamp	S: **Ozark Sunrise Expeditions (2 Miles)**
	Med	N: **+ Hospital**
	ATM	N: Citgo
8A		Bus. U.S. 71 South, Range Line Road, Joplin Airport
	FStop	S: **Citgo(*, LP)**
	Gas	N: Amoco(*, CW), Conoco(*), Phillips 66(*), Texaco(*)
	Food	N: Beefmaster's, Bob Evan's Restaurant, Country Kitchen, Denny's, Gringos Mexican, Holiday Inn, McDonald's, Olive Garden, Roadhouse Ruby's,
		Ruby Tuesday's, Steak 'N Shake, Waffle House
		S: **Cracker Barrel**
	Lodg	N: Best Inns of America, Best Western (see our ad this page), Comfort Inn, Days Inn, Drury Inn, Fairfield Inn by Marriott, Hampton Inn, Holiday Inn, Howard Johnson, Ramada Inn, Riviera Roadside Motel, Super 8
		S: Microtel Inn & Suites
	AServ	N: Amoco, NAPA Auto Parts, Phillips 66, **Sam's Club**
		S: **Citgo**
	TServ	S: **Trucks R Us(24)**
	RVCamp	S: **Wheelen RV Center**
	ATM	N: Conoco, Texaco
	Other	N: **Food 4 Less(24), Sam's Club**
11AB		U.S. 71 S, Fayetteville, U.S. 71 North
	TStop	N: **Flying J Travel Plaza(*, RV DUMP, SCALES)**
15		MO 66, West I-44 Bus. Loop, 7th Street (Westbound, Reaccess Eastbound Only)
	RVCamp	N: **RV Park**
18A		Alt. U.S. 71, Diamond
	Gas	S: **Citgo(*, D, LP) (Ballard's Campground)**
	RVCamp	N: **4 State RV Sales, Coachlight**
		S: **Ballard's Campground (.5 Miles)**
18B		U.S. 71 North, Kansas City
	RVCamp	N: **Coachlight Campground (.75 Miles)**
22		County Rd 10
	FStop	S: **Xpress(*)**
	TServ	S: **Bill's Truck & Tire Service**
	ATM	S: **Xpress**
26		MO 37, Bus. 44, Sarcoxie, Reeds
	Gas	S: Amoco(*)
29		MO U, Sarcoxie, La Russell
	Gas	S: Citgo(*)
	Food	S: Citgo
	Lodg	S: Rebel's Inn, Sarcoxie Motel
	AServ	S: Jim's Garage, Mitch's Garage
	RVCamp	N: **B & E Trailer Sales, WAC RV Park Good Sam Park (.5 Miles)**
	Other	N: **Ozark Village**
		S: Nickorbobs Crafts Mall
33		MO 97 South, Pierce City
	FStop	S: **Sinclair(*)**
	Food	S: **Sinclair**
38		MO 97, Stotts City
	Gas	N: Massie's Superstop(*, D)
	AServ	N: Massie's Superstop
44		MO H, Bus Loop 44, Mt. Vernon, Monett
	RVCamp	N: **Mid America RV Park (.5 Miles)**
46		MO 39, MO 265, Mount Vernon, Aurora
	TStop	N: **Sinclair(*, CW, SCALES), TA TravelCenters of America(*, SCALES) (Auto Service)**
	Gas	N: Phillips 66(*)
		S: Total(*)
	Food	N: Dalmas Family Restaurant, Hardee's, KFC,

1144

Best Western

Best Western - Hallmark Inn

— Deluxe Continental Breakfast —

— Free HBO & Free Local Calls—

— Exercise Facility • Guest Laundry —

— Swimming Pool —

— Denny's Restaurant Adjacent —

417-624-8400 • Reservations 1-800-825-2378

MISSOURI • I-44 • EXIT 8B

Bold red print shows RV & Bus parking available or nearby

EXIT — MISSOURI

Mazzio's Pizza, **McDonald's**, Simple Simons Pizza, Sonic Drive-In, Taco Bell, Tin Lizzie Restaurant
Lodg N: Best Western, Budget Host, Mid-West Motel
S: Comfort Inn
AServ N: Auto Parts, Bill Dowdy Motors, L & N Tire Center & Wheel Alignment
TServ N: **TA TravelCenters of America[SCALES] (Auto Service)**
TWash N: **Sinclair[CW]**, **TA TravelCenters of America (Auto Service)**
Med N: **✚ Mount Vernon Family Medical Center**
ATM N: **Food Fair Grocery Store**, **TA TravelCenters of America (Auto Service)**
S: Total
Other N: **Food Fair Grocery Store**
S: **Nana's Antique Mall**

49 MO 174, Chesapeake
(52) **Rest Area (RR, HF, Phones, Picnic, P; Westbound)**
(52) **Rest Area (RR, HF, Phones, Picnic, P; Eastbound)**
57 CR O, MO 96, Halltown (Westbound, Reaccess Eastbound Only)
58 CR Z, CR 0, Halltown (Difficult Reaccess)
FStop S: **Conoco[*]**
Lodg S: Scandinavian Motel
AServ N: Owen's Auto Service
S: Joe's Junction Auto Repair
61 CR K, CR PP
TStop N: **Total[*, SCALES]**
Lodg N: **Total**
AServ N: **Total**
ATM N: **Total**
Other N: **Nifty 50's Antique Mall**
67 CR T, CR N, Bois D'Arc, Republic
FStop S: **Citgo[*]**
Gas S: Conoco[*]
Food S: Ozark Travel Restaurant
ATM S: Conoco
70 CR B, CR MM
RVCamp S: **KOA Campgrounds (1 Mile)**
Other S: Wilson's Creek National Battlefield
72 MO 266, Bus Loop 44, Chestnut Expressway
FStop S: **Seven Gables[*]**
Food S: Seven Gables
Lodg S: Best Budget Inn
AServ N: Bridgestone Tire & Auto
S: Lacey's Dent Clinic
TServ S: **Wilson Truck Repair**
RVCamp N: **Travellers RV Park**
S: **KOA Campgrounds (1.5 Miles)**, **Traveler's Park Campground (.2 Miles)**
75 U.S. 160, West Bypass, Willard
77 MO 13, Kansas Expressway, Bolivar (Difficult Reaccess)

EXIT — MISSOURI

Gas S: Citgo[*], Hocker Oil Company, Phillips 66[*, D], QuikTrip[*]
Food S: **McDonald's[PLAY]**, Rally's Hamburgers, Subway, Uncle Boo's Bar & Grill, Waffle House
Lodg S: EconoLodge
AServ S: **Wal-Mart[24, RX]**
RVCamp S: **Thomas & Sons Camper Sales (1.2 Miles)**
ATM S: Citgo, Phillips 66, QuikTrip, **Wal-Mart**
Other N: Fantastic Caverns, Ozark Empire Fairgrounds, Zoo
S: **Wal-Mart[RX]**
80A Bus Loop 44, Glenstone Ave
Gas S: Amoco[*], Conoco[*], Phillips 66[*, D], Texaco[*], Total[*, D]
Food N: Waffle House
S: A & W Restaurant (Total), Bob Evan's Restaurant, Breakaway (Total), Country Kitchen, Denny's, SHONEY'S Shoney's
Lodg N: Microtel Inn, Quality Inn, Super 8

1141
RAMADA LIMITED
417-337-5207
Continental Breakfast
Outdoor Pool
King Size 2 Person Jacuzzi
Kids Under 12 Stay Free
Restaurant Next Door
AAA, AARP, Tour Group Rates
Free Local Calls
Tennis/Golf Nearby
2316 Shepard of the Hills Expressway
BRANSON, MO
MISSOURI • I-44 • EXIT 82AB

EXIT — MISSOURI

S: Bass Country Inn, Best Western, Best Western, Best Western Coach House Inn, Comfort Inn, Days Inn, Drury Inn & Suites, Economy Inn, Executive Inn, Fairfield Inn by Marriott, Holiday Inn, Holiday Inn, Knight's Inn, Red Roof Inn, Scottish Inns, Sheraton Motel, Village Inn
AServ N: Interstate Auto Service
S: Amoco, Conoco, Texaco
Med N: **✚ Doctor's Hospital**
S: **✚ Doctors Hospital**
ATM S: Total
Other S: **North Town Mall**
80B CR H, Pleasant Hope (Same Services As Exit 80A, North Services)
82AB U.S. 65, Branson, Sedelia (Difficult Reaccess, Divided Hwy)
Gas S: Amoco[*, D], Conoco[*, D]
Food S: **Waffle House**
Lodg S: American In, **Ramada Grand (see our ad this page)**, **Ramada Limited (see our ad this page)**
TServ S: **Kenworth, Peterbilt Dealer, Southwest Missouri Truck Center**
ATM S: Amoco
Other S: **Highway Patrol Headquarters**
84 MO 744
88 MO 125, Fair Grove, Strafford
TStop N: **TravelCenter of America[*, SCALES]**
FStop N: **Phillips 66[*, LP, SCALES]**
Gas S: Citgo[*, LP]
Food N: Country Pride Restaurant (TravelCenter of America), **McDonald's[PLAY]**, **Phillips 66, Subway (TravelCenter of America)**
S: Mekong Inn (Chinese)
Lodg S: Super 8
TServ N: **Phillips 66[SCALES]**, **TravelCenter of America[SCALES]**
TWash N: **18 Wheeler Truck Wash**
RVCamp S: **AmeriGas/Greene County[LP] (1 Mile)**, **Strafford RV Park[LP] (.25 Miles)**
ATM N: **Phillips 66**
S: Citgo, Empire Bank
Other S: **Exotic Animal Paradise (3 Miles)**
(89) **Weigh Station (Both Directions)**
96 CR B, Northview
RVCamp N: **Oak Rest RV Campground**
100 CR W, MO 38, Marshfield
Gas N: Amoco[*]
S: Conoco[*], Phillips 66[*, D], Texaco[*, D, LP]
Food N: Tiny's Smokehouse
S: Beijing Cafe, Country Kitchen, Dairy Queen, KFC, McDonald's[PLAY], Pizza Inn, Subway, Taco Bell
Lodg N: Fair Oaks Motel, Plaza Motel
S: Holiday Inn Express
AServ N: Marshfield Motor Co. GM, Ford
S: Goodyear Tire & Auto, **Wal-Mart[RX]**
RVCamp N: **Fountain Plaza Mobile Home and RV Park (3.5 blocks)**

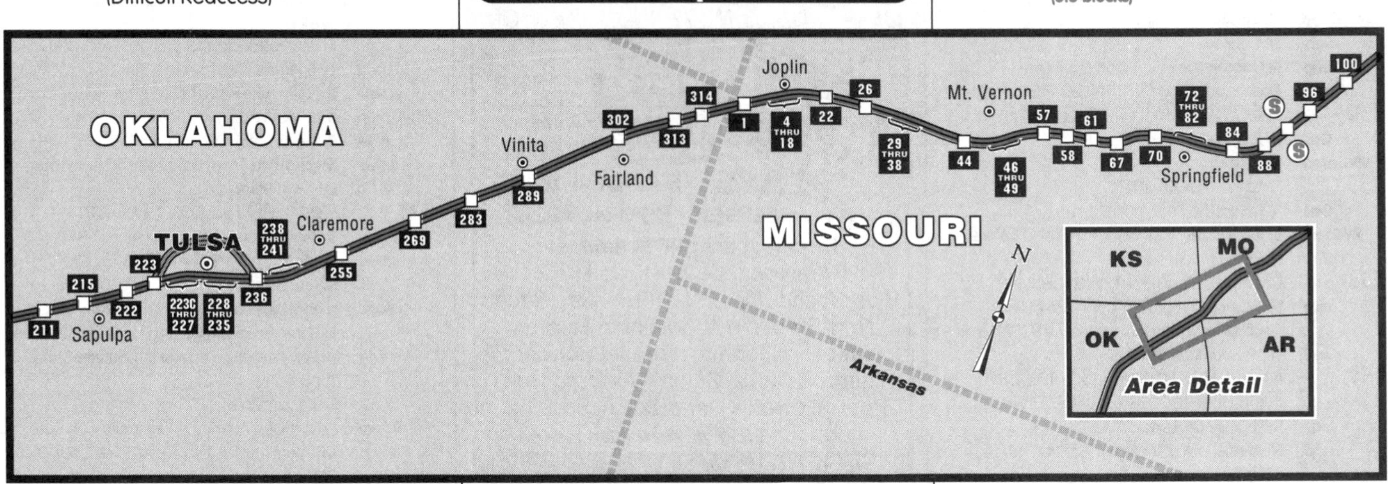

EXIT MISSOURI

ATM N: Amoco
S: Conoco, Phillips 66, Texaco
Other N: Antique Mall, Empire Gas(LP)
S: Bible Bookstore, Eye Clinic, Hurricane Bay Car Wash, Stanley's Rx Express(RX), Wal-Mart(RX)

107 County Rd

(110) Rest Area (RR, Phones, Picnic, P; Westbound)

(110) Rest Area (RR, Phones, Picnic, P; Eastbound)

113 CR Y, CR J, Conway
FStop N: Shell(*)
Gas N: Phillips 66(*)
Food N: McShanes Restaurant

118 CR A, CR C, Phillipsburg
Gas N: Conoco(*, D, LP)
S: Phillips 66(*), Texaco(*)
ATM S: Texaco

123 County Rd
RVCamp S: KOA Campgrounds (.5 Miles)

127 Bus Loop 44, Lebanon
TStop N: Texaco(*, LP, SCALES)
Gas N: MFA Oil, Phillips 66(*)
Food N: Quality Inn, Waffle House
Lodg N: EconoLodge, Hampton Inn, Quality Inn, Scottish Inns, Super 8
AServ N: Kelly Tires, MFA Oil
TServ N: Texaco(SCALES)
TWash N: Texaco
ATM N: Texaco

129 MO 5, MO 32, MO 64, Lebanon, Hartville
Gas S: Amoco(*), Conoco(*, D)
Food N: Burger King(PLAY), Long John Silver, SHONEY'S, Shoney's, Western Sizzlin'
S: Captain D's Seafood, Hardee's, La Mexican Kitchen, Pizza Hut, Stonegate Station, Wal-Mart(24, RX) (Optical)
Lodg S: Brentwood Motel
AServ S: Goodyear, JSC Super Center (NAPA)
Med N: + Hospital
ATM S: Amoco, Central Bank South, Commerce Bank, Conoco, Mercantile Bank
Other N: Factory Stores Walnut Bowls, Lake of the Ozarks
S: Lebanon Books, Wal-Mart(RX) (Optical)

130 Bus. Loop 44, CR MM
Gas N: Phillips 66(*), Total(*)
Food N: Bell Restaurant, What's Cookin
Lodg N: Best Western, Forest Manor Motel, Holiday Motel, Munger Moss Motel
RVCamp N: Forest Manor Motel & Campground (.25 Miles)
ATM N: Phillips 66, Total
Other N: Wrink's Market Grocery Store

135 CR F, Sleeper

140 CR T, CR N, Stoutland
FStop S: Phillips 66(*)
Food S: Midway Restaurant

145 MO 133, CR A & B, Richland
TStop N: Conoco(*)
TServ N: Conoco
RVCamp S: Gasconade Hills Resort (1.5 Miles), Gasconade RV Park (1.5 Miles), RV Parking

150 MO 7, CR P, Richland , Laquey
Gas N: Amoco(*)
RVCamp N: Amoco

153 MO 17, Buckhorn
Gas S: Texaco(*)
RVCamp S: Glen Oaks RV Park Good Sam Park (.25 Miles)
Other N: Gypsy Trail Antiques

156 CR H, Bus Loop 44, Waynesville
RVCamp N: Covered Wagon RV Park (1.75 Miles), Roubidoux Springs Campground (1.75 Miles)
Med N: + Roubidox Clinic

159 MO 17, Bus Loop 44, Saint Robert (Difficult Reaccess, Divided Hwy)
Gas S: Phillips 66(*), Texaco(*)
Food N: Aussie Jack's Steaks and Seafood
S: Alpine Haus

EXIT MISSOURI

Lodg S: Alpine Haus, Motel Ozark
AServ N: Skyline Welding Auto Service
S: Mid Missouri Motors Pont, Olds, Jeep, Eagle, Texaco
Med S: + Mercy Medical Group

161 CR Y, Bus Loop 44, Ft. Leonard Wood
FStop S: Total(*)
Gas N: Conoco(*)
S: MFA Oil
Food S: Captain D's Seafood, KFC, Lily's, McDonald's(PLAY), Taco Bell, Waffle House, Wendy's
Lodg S: Budget Inn, EconoLodge, Motel DeVille, Ramada Inn, Ranch Motel
Med S: + Mercy Medical Group
ATM S: Total

163 MO 28, Dixon
TStop N: 28 Truck Port(*) (Phillips 66)
Gas S: Amoco, Conoco(*, D)
Food S: Country Cafe
Lodg S: Best Western, DAYS INN Days Inn, Super 8
AServ S: Amoco
TServ N: 28 Truck Port (Phillips 66)
RVCamp S: Covered Wagon RV Park, Good Sam Park (Super 8 Motel), Super 8

169 CR J

172 CR D, Jerome
Other N: Camping

176 Sugar Tree Rd
Lodg N: Vernelle's Motel
RVCamp S: Camping

(178) Rest Area (RR, Phones, P; Westbound)

(178) Rest Area (RR, Phones, P; Eastbound)

179 CR C & T, Doolittle, Newburg
FStop S: Citgo(*)
Food S: Cookin' From Scratch (Citgo)
ATM S: Citizen's Bank

184 U.S. 63 South, Bus Loop 44 East, Rolla
Gas S: Conoco(D, CW), Moto Mart(*), Phillips 66(*), Shell(*, D), Texaco (Truck & Auto Towing)
Food S: Hero's Pizza & Subs (Moto Mart), Howard Johnson, Lucky House Chinese, Papa Meaux's (Cajun), SHONEY'S, Shoney's, Sirloin Stockade
Lodg S: Best Western, DAYS INN Days Inn, EconoLodge, Holiday Inn Express (see our ad this page), Howard Johnson, Ramada Inn, Super 8, Wayfarer Inn, Western Inn, Zeno's Steakhouse & Motel
AServ S: Conoco, Texaco (Truck & Auto Towing)
Med S: + Hospital
ATM S: Citizen's Bank of Newburg, Moto Mart
Other S: Tourist Info.

185 CR E, Rolla
Food S: Dairy Queen, Hardee's, Subway, Taco Bell
Med S: + Hospital
Other N: Highway Patrol Post

186 U.S. 63, MO 72, Rolla, Jefferson City

1166
Holiday Inn EXPRESS
I-44 • Exit 184
1507 Martin Springs Dr.
Rolla, Missouri
573-364-8200
800-HOLIDAY
Free Continental Breakfast
Free Local Calls • Free HBO
Kids 18 and Under Stay Free with Parent
Non-Smoking & Adjoining Rooms
Meeting Rooms • Guest Laundry
Remote Cable Color TV • Data Port
Pets Allowed • Handicap Accessible
I-44 - Exit 184, S.W. on Martin Springs Drive
MISSOURI • I-44 • EXIT 184

EXIT MISSOURI

Gas N: Sinclair(*, LP)
S: Amoco(*, D), Christopher Automotive, Conoco(*), Shell(*)
Food N: Steak 'N Shake
S: Denny's, Dunkin Donuts, Fortune Inn Chinese, Lee's Famous Recipe Chicken, Waffle House
Lodg N: Drury Inn, Sooter Inn
S: American Motor Inn, Budget Motel
AServ N: Dayton Tires
S: Christopher Automotive, Ozark
TServ N: Dayton Tires
ATM S: Amoco, Shell
Other N: Memoryville U.S.A. (Gifts)

189 CR V
FStop S: Conoco(*) (CB Shop)
Food S: Conoco (CB Shop)
TServ S: Conoco (CB Shop)
RVCamp N: RV Park
ATM S: Conoco (CB Shop)

195 MO 68, MO 8, Saint James, Salem
FStop S: Delano(*, K)
Gas N: Conoco(*, D), Mobil(*, CW)
S: Food Mart(*), Phillips 66(*)
Food N: McDonald's, Pizza Hut, Ruby's Ice Cream, Subway, Taco Bell (Mobil)
Lodg N: Comfort Inn, Economy Inn
S: Finn's Motel
AServ N: Bumper to Bumper, Conoco
S: Phillips 66
ATM S: Town & Country Bank
Other N: Maytag Coin Laundry, St. James Eye Care, Tourist Info.
S: Country Mart Grocery, Crystal Clean Car Wash(CW)

203 CR F, CR ZZ
RVCamp N: Eaglewood RV Park (.25 Miles)

208 (6) MO 19, Cuba, Owensville, Steeleville
TStop N: Texaco(*, SCALES) (Auto Service)
Gas N: Citgo(*)
S: Casey's General Store, Mobil(*, LP, CW)
Food S: Chester Fried Chicken, Hardee's(PLAY), Homemade Donuts To Go (Casey's General Store), Homemade Pizza To Go (Casey's General Store), McDonald's(PLAY), Ozark Ice Cream, Subway
Lodg N: Best Western, Super 8
AServ S: Chevrolet Dealer, Jim's Motors, NAPA Auto Parts, Road Pro American Auto Supply
TServ N: Texaco(SCALES) (Auto Service)
TWash N: Texaco (Auto Service)
ATM N: Texaco (Auto Service)
S: Casey's General Store, People's Bank of Cuba
Other S: Maytag Coin Laundry

210 CR UU

214 CR H, Leasburg
Gas N: Mobil(*, D, K)
Parks S: Onondaga Cave State Park (7 Miles)

218 CR C, CR J, CR N, Bourbon
Gas N: Citgo(*, D, K)
S: Mobil(*, LP, K)
Food S: Henhouse Restaurant, Scoop 'N' Snacks Ice Cream
Lodg N: Budget Inn
AServ S: NAPA Auto Parts, Triple J's Auto Glass
RVCamp S: Boubon RV Center Sales & Service
ATM S: Mobil, Town & Country Bank
Other S: Car Wash, Town & Country Supermarket, U.S. Post Office

225 North MO 185, CR D, Sullivan
TStop S: Bobber Texaco Travel Center(*, SCALES)
Gas N: Mobil(*, CW), Shell(*)
S: Arro Gasoline(*)
Food N: Best Western, Jack in the Box, Ramada Inn
S: Homer's Deli BBQ, Lucky House Chinese, Sonic
Lodg N: Best Western, Ramada Inn, Sunrise Motel, Super 8
S: Sullivan Motel
AServ S: Car Quest Auto Parts, Federated Auto Parts, J & K Custom Muffler, Jerry Meier Buick, Chev, Olds, GMC

Bold red print shows RV & Bus parking available or nearby

EXIT	MISSOURI
TServ	S: Bobber Texaco Travel Center[SCALES]
ATM	N: Mobil
Other	S: Sudsy Coin Laundry, V W CB Sales
226	MO 185 South, Oak Grove, Sullivan
TStop	N: Flying J[*, LP, SCALES]
Gas	S: Phillips 66[*]
Food	N: Magic Dragon Chinese (Flying J), Pepperoni's Pizza (Flying J)
	S: Burger King[PLAY] (Phillips 66), Golden Corral Family Steakhouse, Hardees[PLAY], KFC, McDonald's, SHONEY'S, Shoney's, Steak 'N Shake, Taco Bell, Wal-Mart SuperCenter[24, RX]
AServ	S: Goodyear, Wal-Mart SuperCenter[24]
RVCamp	S: KOA Campgrounds (1.5 Miles)
ATM	N: Flying J
	S: Bank of Sullivan
Parks	S: Meramec State Park
Other	S: Wal-Mart SuperCenter[RX]
230	CR JJ, CR W, Stanton
Gas	N: No Name[D, LP]
	S: Phillips 66[*, D]
Food	N: Rooo'sters Bar & Grill
	S: The Cavern City Hideout Restaurant & Motel
Lodg	N: Stanton Motel
	S: Delta Motel, The Cavern City HideoutMotel
RVCamp	S: KOA Campgrounds
Other	S: Antique Toy & Truck Museum, Jesse James Museum, U.S. Post Office
(235)	Rest Area (RR, Phones, P; Left Exit Both Directions)
(238)	Weigh Station (Westbound)
(238)	Weigh Station (Eastbound)
239	MO 30, CR AB, CR WW, St. Clair
Gas	S: Shell[*]
Food	S: Jim's Country Diner
AServ	S: AFI Muffler Auto & Electric, American Auto Supply
TServ	N: Robbins Truck Repair
240	MO 47, St. Clair, Union
Gas	N: Phillips 66[*, D], Sinclair[*]
	S: Mobil[*, D, K, 24]
Food	N: Burger King
	S: Hardee's, McDonald's, Subway
Lodg	S: Budget Lodging, Super 8
AServ	S: Mobil[24]
ATM	S: Mobil
Other	N: Daniel Boone's Home (17 Miles)
242	CR AH
247	U.S. 50 West, CR AT, CR O, Union (Difficult Reaccess)
RVCamp	N: Bourbeuse Mobil Park & Camp, Pine Oak Creek RV Park & Campground (1 Mile)
	S: Shady Jack's Camp
Parks	N: Camping
	S: Robertsville State Park (5 Miles)
Other	N: Flea Market
251	MO 100, Washington
TStop	N: Fuel Mart[*, SCALES]

EXIT	MISSOURI
FStop	N: Mr. Fuel[*, K, SCALES]
Gas	N: Citgo[*], Conoco[*, LP], No Name[*]
Food	N: Blimpie's Subs (Fuel Mart), Burger King (Citgo), Ike's, The Pizza Maker
TServ	N: I-44 Service Center (Towing)
TWash	N: McCoy's Truck Wash
ATM	N: Citgo, Fuel Mart, Mr. Fuel
253	MO 100 East, Gray Summit
Gas	S: Phillips 66[*, LP]
Lodg	S: Best Western, Gardenway Motel
257	Bus Loop I-44, Pacific
Gas	S: Citgo[*], Conoco[*], Mobil[*, D, CW], Motomart[*, CW]
Food	S: Hardee's[PLAY], McDonald's, Taco Bell
Lodg	S: Holiday Inn Express
AServ	N: Presley's Glass Auto, Commercial, Residential
	S: B J's Automotive Service, Bessinger's Automotive, NAPA Auto Parts
Med	S: ✚ Pacific Health Center
ATM	S: Motomart, Security Pacific Bank
261	Allenton
FStop	S: Phillips 66[*, LP]
Gas	S: Shell[*, CW]
Food	N: Denny's, Lion's Choice Roast Beef
Lodg	N: Oak Grove Inn, Ramada Inn, Red Carpet Inn
AServ	S: Long Ford
RVCamp	N: KOA Campgrounds (.5 Miles), Yogi Bear Camp Resort (.5 Miles)
ATM	S: Phillips 66
Other	N: Six Flags Over Mid America
264	MO 109, CR W, Eureka
Parks	N: Babler Memorial State Park
265	Williams Rd
266	Lewiss Rd
269	Antire Rd, Beaumont
272	MO 141, Fenton, Valley Park
FStop	S: Citgo[*]
Gas	N: Motomart[D]
	S: Shell[*, CW]
Food	N: Hero's Pizza & Subs (Motomart)
	S: Burger King, McDonald's[PLAY], Steak 'N Shake, Taco Bell
AServ	S: Pennzoil Oil Change
ATM	N: Motomart
	S: Citgo
Other	S: Wet Willy's Waterslide
274	Bowles Ave
Gas	S: Citgo[*, D], QuikTrip[*]
Food	S: Cracker Barrel, SHONEY'S, Shoney's, Tubby's Grilled Subs (Citgo), White Castle
Lodg	S: Drury Inn, Holiday Inn Express, Motel 6, Pear Tree Inn
ATM	S: Commerce Bank, QuikTrip
Other	S: Police Substation (Quick Trip), Sears Parts & Service
275	Yarnell Rd (Westbound)
276AB	Junction I-270, Memphis, Chicago
277A	MO 366 East, Watson Rd
277B	U.S. 61, U.S. 67, U.S. 50, Lindbergh Blvd.

EXIT	MISSOURI
Gas	N: Shell[*]
	S: Shell[*, CW], Vickers Gas & Food Market[*]
Food	N: Richard's Ribs, The China Buffet
	S: Bob Evan's Restaurant, Burger King[PLAY], Denny's, Helen Fitzgerald's, Holiday Inn, House of Hunan (Chinese), Steak 'N Shake, Viking Restaurant
Lodg	N: Best Western, Howard Johnson
	S: Comfort Inn, DAYS INN Days Inn, Holiday Inn, Ramada Inn
AServ	N: Jiffy Lube
	S: Kelly's Tires & Auto Center, Midas Muffler
Med	N: ✚ Hospital
ATM	N: Shell
	S: Shell
Other	S: Nature Center, The Plaza at Sunset Hills Mall
278	Big Bend Rd
Gas	S: Conoco[*, D], QuikTrip[*], Sinclair[*]
AServ	S: Conoco
Other	S: Animal Hospital, Hydrojet Coin Car Wash
280	Elm Ave
Gas	N: Amoco[*]
AServ	N: Amoco
282	Murdoch Ave, Laclade Station Rd (Difficult Reaccess)
Gas	N: Amoco, Clark's[*], Mobil[*]
Food	N: Dairy Queen, Hunan Wu's (Chinese)
AServ	N: Amoco, Jiffy Lube, Mobil
283	Shrewsberry Ave. (Westbound)
284A	Jamieson Ave
284B	Arsenal Rd. (Westbound)
286	Hampton Ave
Gas	N: Amoco[*], Clark's[*]
	S: Shell[*, CW], Sinclair[*]
Food	N: Chinese Express, Denny's, Hardee's, Imo's Pizza, Jack in the Box, McDonald's[PLAY], Steak 'N Shake, Subway, Taco Bell
	S: Hardee's, Hunan Cafe, Sing Lee Wok Chinese (Chinese)
Lodg	S: Holiday Inn, Red Roof Inn
AServ	N: Amoco
Other	N: St. Louis Zoo
287	Kings Highway
Gas	N: Amoco[*, CW]
AServ	N: Amoco
288	Grand Blvd., Downtown St. Louis
Med	N: ✚ Incarnate Word Hospital
289	Jefferson Ave
Gas	N: Citgo[*]
Food	N: Subway
	S: McDonald's, Taco Bell
290A	Junction I-55 South, Memphis
290B	Junction I-55, I-70 West, I-64 East, U.S. 40, 18th Street

↑MISSOURI

Begin I-44

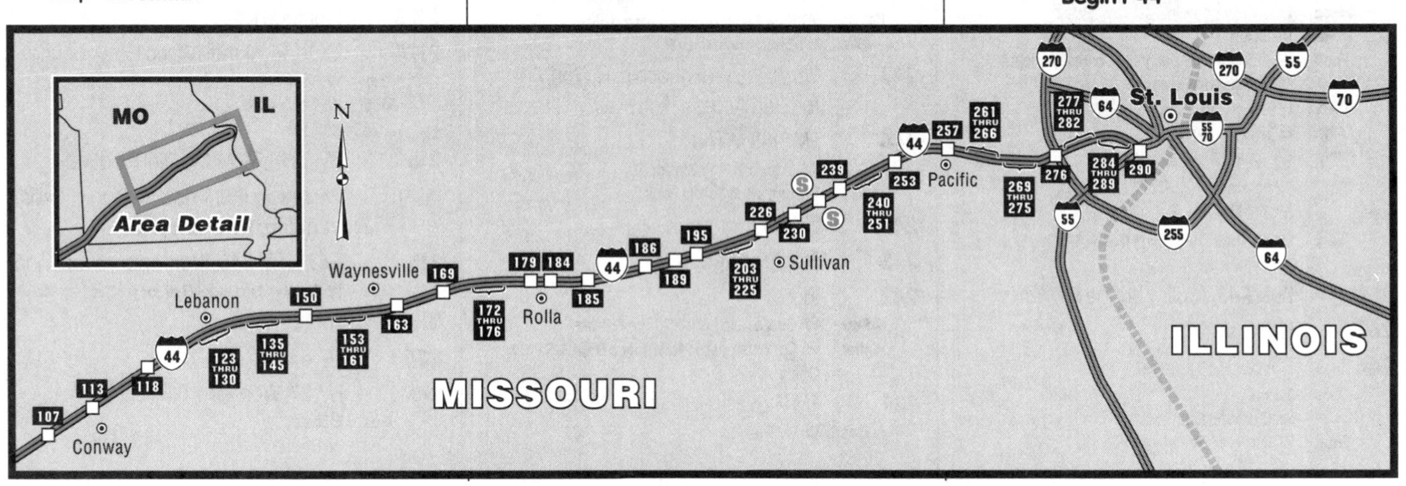

I-45 S →

EXIT TEXAS

Begin I-45

↓TEXAS

284A I-30

283 US 175 East, Kaufman, MLK Jr. Blvd, Fair Park (Southbound)
- **Gas** W: Diamond Shamrock(*), Shell
- **Food** W: Hardeman's Bar-B-Q, KFC, Taco Bell
- **Lodg** W: Motel Winnway
- **AServ** W: Chief Auto Parts, House of Parts, P D's Tire Service, Shell
- **ATM** W: Diamond Shamrock
- **Other** W: **Friedman's Pharmacy**

283A Lamar Street
- **Gas** W: Gas(*, D)
- **Food** W: Gilbert's Fast Food & Grocery
- **Other** E: **Hasty Grocery**

283B Fair Park, Pennsylvania Ave, MLK Jr Blvd (Northbound)

281 Overton Road (Southbound)
- **AServ** E: Taylor Auto Supply (IAPA)

280 Linfield Street, Illinois Avenue
- **Gas** W: Texaco(*, D)
- **Lodg** E: Linfield Motel, Star Motel
- **AServ** E: International Paint & Body
- **TServ** E: **Body Shop, DIS 24 Hr Tire & Break Service**
- **ATM** W: Texaco

279 Loop 12 (Limited Access Highway, Northbound Is 279AB)

277 Simpson Stuart Road
- **Gas** W: Chevron

276AB 276A - I-20 West Fort Worth 276B - I-20 East Shreveport

274 Dowdy Ferry Road, Hutchins
- **FStop** W: **Afco (Automated Fueling)**
- **Gas** E: Exxon, Texaco(*, D, LP)
- **Food** E: **Tooters Diner (Gold Inn)**
  W: Dairy Queen, **The Smith's Restaurant**
- **Lodg** E: **Gold Inn**
- **AServ** E: Exxon
- **ATM** W: NationsBank
- **Other** W: **Eagle Bus Parts**

273 Wintergreen Road
- **TServ** W: **Frank Prasifka & Sons Tire Service**

272 **Fulgham Road Truck Check Station, Weigh Station**
- **Food** E: Texas Rose Restaurant & Club

271 Pleasant Run Road

270 Belt Line Road, Wilmer
- **FStop** E: **Texaco(*), Total(*)**
- **Gas** W: Exxon(*, CW)
- **Food** W: Dairy Queen, Delightful Donuts, Monopoly Pizza, Subway (Exxon)
- **AServ** E: **Texaco**
- **ATM** E: **Total**
- **Other** W: Car Wash, **Laundromat, Mac's Supermarket, Police Station, US Post Office**

269 Mars Road
- **TServ** E: **Industrial Truck Parts (Texas Star Truck Sales), Texas Star Truck Sales**

268 Bus. I-45, Malloy Bridge Rd, Ferris

267 Frontage Road

266 FM 660, 5th Street
- **Gas** E: Fina(*, D)
  W: Diamond Shamrock(*)
- **Food** W: Dairy Queen
- **ATM** E: Commercial State Bank, Fina
  W: Diamond Shamrock
- **Other** E: **Get 'N Go Food Store**

264 Wester Road
- **TServ** E: **T & H Bus Repair**
  W: **G & S Truck & Equipment**

263A Loop 561, Trumbull

262 Risinger Rd.

260 Bus. I-45, Palmer (Northbound Is Called Hampel Rd)
- **Other** E: **Tri-State Semi-Tractor Driving School**

259 FM 813 to FM 878
- **TServ** W: **I-45 Truck & Trailer Repair Inc. (Goodyear)**
- **Other** W: **US Post Office**

258 Parker Hill Road
- **TStop** W: **Knox(*, SCALES) (Fuel-Coastal, FedEx Drop), Mobil(*) (FedEx Drop)**
- **Food** W: **BLT's Breakfast, Lunch & Treats (Mobil TS), Chicken Express Restaurant (Mobil TS), Dogs 'N Suds Express (Mobil TS), Subway (Knox TS)**
- **Lodg** W: **Palmer House Motel**
- **ATM** W: **Knox TS, Mobil TS**

255 FM 879, Garrett
- **FStop** W: **Chevron(*)**
- **Gas** E: Diamond Shamrock (Northbound Access Only)
- **ATM** W: **Chevron**

253 Bus. Loop I-45, Ennis
- **Gas** W: Texaco(*, D)
- **AServ** W: JR Auto Ranch
- **Med** W: **✚ Hospital**
- **Other** W: **Veterinary Clinic**

251 TX 34, Kaufman Italy
- **Gas** E: Fina(*), Texaco(*, D)
  W: Chevron(*, D), Exxon(*, CW)
- **Food** E: Donuts, McDonald's(PLAY)
  W: Arby's, Braum's Hamburgers & Ice Cream, Dairy Queen, Golden Corral Family Steakhouse, Jack-in-the-Box, KFC, Mr. Gatti's Pizza (Chevron), Taco Bell, Waffle House, What A Burger
- **Lodg** E: Holiday Inn Express
  W: **Ennis Inn**, Quality Inn
- **AServ** W: Allen Samuel's Autoplex, Terry Gregory Ford, Mercury, **Wal-Mart**
- **RVCamp** W: **Jeff's RV Campground (Showers)**
- **ATM** W: Chevron, Exxon
- **Other** E: **Golf Store**
  W: **Chamber of Commerce, Wal-Mart(RX)**

249 Unnamed
- **TStop** W: **Ennis Truck Stop(*) (CB Shop)**
- **FStop** W: **Total(*)**
- **Food** W: **Ennis Truck Stop Restaurant (Ennis Truck Stop)**
- **TServ** W: **Doherty's Bros. Truck(24) (Wrecker Service & Truck Repair)**
- **TWash** W: **Blue Beacon Truck Wash (Total)**
- **ATM** W: **Ennis Truck Stop, Total**

247 US 287N, Waxahachie, Ft Worth (Limited Access Highway)

246 FM 1183, Alma
- **Gas** W: Chevron(*, D), Phillips 66(*)
- **AServ** W: Tom's Bait & Auto Parts

244 FM 1182

243 Frontage Road

242 Rice
- **AServ** W: Gary's Auto Parts, OLJ Tire & Brake
- **Other** W: Car Wash, **Mini Mart, Police Dept, US Post Office**

239 FM 1126
- **Gas** W: Phillips 66(*)

238 FM 1603
- **TStop** E: **Fina(*, 24)**
- **Food** E: **Blimpie's Subs (Fina TS)**
- **AServ** E: H & H Auto Parts
- **TServ** E: **C&E Truck Tire & Road Service(24)**
- **RVCamp** E: **RV Park (Fina TS)**
- **ATM** E: Fina Truck Stop

237 Frontage Road

235B Bus. I-45, Corsicana (Southbound, No Exit 235 B Northbound, Only Exit 235)

235A Frontage Road (Southbound, Known As Only Exit 235 Northbound)

232 Roane Road

231 TX 31, Waco, Athens (Navarro College)
- **Gas** E: Mobil, Texaco(*)
  W: Chevron(*), Exxon(*, D)
- **Food** E: **Sandy's Restaurant (Colonial Inn)**
  W: **Bill's Fried Chicken**, Charlie's Bar-B-Q, **Cisco's Mexican Grill**, Dairy Queen, McDonald's(PLAY)
- **Lodg** E: **Colonial Inn**
- **AServ** E: Carl White Chevrolet, Mobil
  W: Berry Chrys, Plym, Dodge, Jeep, Eagle, Brinson Ford
- **Med** W: **✚ Hospital**
- **Other** E: **Navarro Pecan Company with Factory Outlet Store**

229 US 287 South, Palestine (Richland Chambers Reservoir)
- **Gas** E: Shell(*, D)
- **Food** W: **El Patio (Ramada Inn)**, Fish Camp Catfish & Seafood Dinners, **Hallmark Restaurant (Days Inn)**, Waffle House
- **Lodg** W: DAYS INN **Days Inn, Ramada Inn, Royal Inn, Travelers Inn**
- **Other** E: **Factory Outlet Center, Texas Department Of Public Safety**

228B Frontage Road (Northbound Reads North Bus. I-45, Corsicana)
- **FStop** E: **Phillips 66(*)**

228A 15th Street (Northbound)
- **FStop** E: **Phillips 66(*)**

225 FM 739, Angus, Mustang
- **FStop** W: **Citgo(*, D)**
- **Gas** E: Bennies, Chevron(*), Exxon(*, D)
  W: Shell(*)
- **Food** E: Bennies Old Fashioned Hamburgers (Bennies Gas Station)
- **RVCamp** W: **Camper Depot (1 Mile), Richland Chambers Reservoir**

221 Unnamed

220 Frontage Road

219B Frontage Rd

219A TX 14, Richland, Mexia (Southbound)
- **Gas** W: Shell(*)
- **Food** W: B & J's Cafe
- **ATM** W: Shell

218 FM 1394, Richland (Northbound)

(217) **Rest Area (RR, Phones, Picnic, Grills, Vending, RV Dump, P)**

213 TX 75, FM 246, Worthman, Streetman
- **Gas** W: **Exxon(*) (No Diesel Fuel for Trucks)**, Texaco(*, D)

211 FM 80, Kirvin

206 FM 833

198 FM 27, Wortham, Fairfield
- **Gas** E: Shell(*)
  W: Exxon(*)

Bold red print shows RV & Bus parking available or nearby

EXIT TEXAS

Food E: Real Pit Bar-B-Q (Shell)
W: First Stop Food & Grill (Exxon)
Lodg W: **Budget Inn**
RVCamp W: **Budget Inn RV Park**
Med E: **✚ Hospital**

197 US 84, Fairfield, Teague
FStop W: **Shell**[*], **Texaco**[*, D]
Gas E: Exxon[*], Fina[*], Texaco[*, D]
Food E: Dairy Queen, Jack-in-the-Box, **McDonald's**[PLAY], Ponte's Diner, Sam's Chicken & Bar-B-Q, **Sam's Restaurant**, Something Different Restaurant, Subway, Texas Burger
W: **I-45 Coffee Shop**, **Pizza Hut**, **Sammy's Restaurant**
Lodg W: Regency Inn, **Sam's Motel**
AServ E: Bossier Chev, Chev. Trucks, Chrys, Plym, Dodge, NAPA Auto Parts (Bossier), Rutherford 24 Hr. Mechanic, Tire, Service, Towing
W: Fairfield Ford, Mercury
TServ W: **Sandra's Tire Service (Shell)**
Other E: Roadster Car Wash

189 TX 179
TStop E: **Conoco**[*] **(Showers)**, **Fina**[*, 24]
Gas E: Chevron[*]
Food E: **Dew Cafe**[24] **(Fina TS)**, **Restaurant (Conoco)**
W: **Tatum's Bar-B-Q**
TServ E: **Conoco**
ATM E: **Conoco**

(187) **Parking Area (Picnic, P)**

180 TX 164, Groesbeck

178 US 79, Buffalo
FStop W: **Diamond Shamrock**[*] **(FedEx Drop)**, **Mobil**[*, 24]
Gas E: Conoco, Texaco[*]
W: Chevron[*]
Food E: Pizza Inn, **Weathervane Restaurant**
W: **Arby's (Mobil)**, Dairy Queen, Pitt Grill, Pop's BBQ, Rainbow Restaurant, **Texas Burger**
Lodg W: Best Western, **Economy Inn**
AServ E: Buffalo Body Shop & Car Wash
W: Triangle Tire
ATM W: **Diamond Shamrock**
Other E: **Brookshire Bros. Grocery**

(166) **Weigh Station (Southbound, Under Construction)**

164 TX 7, Centerville
FStop W: **Woody's Diesel Express (Showers, No Auto Fuel)**
Gas E: Diamond Shamrock[*], Texaco[D]
W: Exxon[*], Shell[*]
Food E: Country Cousin's Barbecue, Texas Burger, Woody's Smoke House (Diamond Shamrock)
W: Dairy Queen, Jack-in-the-Box, Mama Mike's, Piccadilly Circus Pizza (Shell), Woody's Smoke House & Bakery (Shell)
Lodg E: **Days Inn**
AServ E: Texaco
ATM W: Exxon

(159) **Parking Area (Picnic, P)**

156 FM 977, Leona
FStop W: **Diamond Shamrock**[*]
Gas W: Exxon[*, D]
Food E: **Crystal's Skillet**
W: D-K Diner

(155) **Parking Area (Picnic, P; Northbound)**

152 TX OSR, Normangee
FStop W: **Chevron**[*, D]
Food W: Chuckwagon, **Yellow Rose Cattle Co.**
Other W: **Old West Town (Yellow Rose Cattle Co)**, **Yellow Rose Arena**

146 TX 75, Madisonville

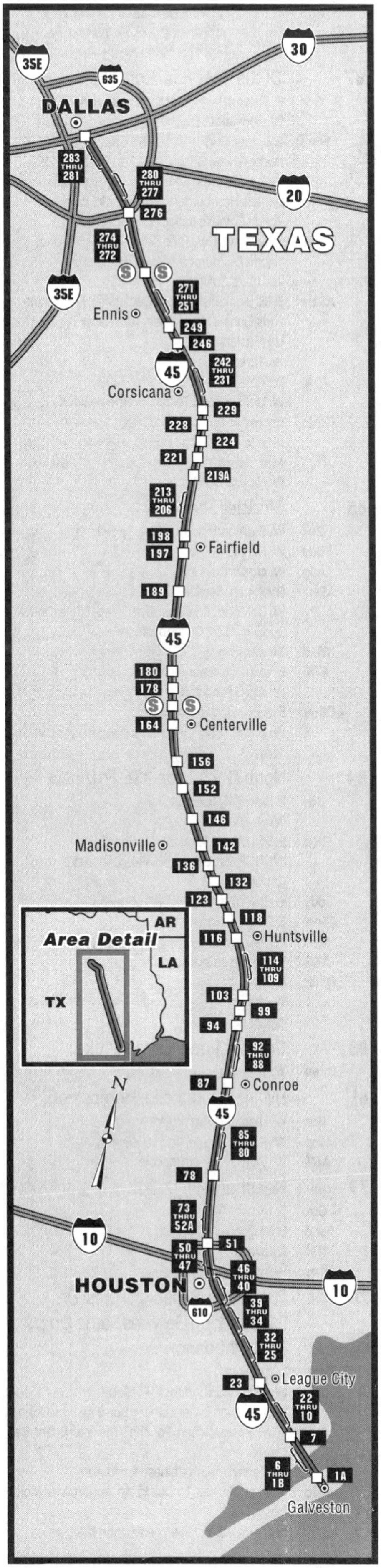

EXIT TEXAS

142 US 190, TX 21, Bryan, Crockett, Madisonville
FStop E: **Chevron**[*, D], **Exxon**[*]
W: **Diamond Shamrock**[*, D, 24]
Gas E: Texaco[*, D, CW]
W: Shell[*]
Food E: Church's Chicken, **Corral Cafe**, **Eddie Pepper's Great Mexican Food (Exxon)**, **Hot Stuff Pizza (Exxon)**
W: J W **Cattleman's**, McDonald's, **Pizza Hut**, Sonic, Subway (Shell), Texas Burger
Lodg E: **Best Western**
W: **Budget Motel**
AServ E: **Chevron**
W: Carquest, Drake's Service Center, Madisonville Ford, Mercury, & Ford Trucks
TServ E: **Chevron**
Med W: **✚ Hospital**
ATM E: **Chevron**, **Exxon**, Texaco

136 Spur 67

132 FM 2989

(126) **Rest Area (RR, Picnic, Grills, Vending, RV Dump, Pet Walk, P; Southbound)**

(124) **Rest Area (P; Northbound)**

123 FM 1696

(121) **Weigh Station (Phones; Northbound)**

118 TX 75, Huntsville (Sam Houston State Univ. & Museum)
TStop W: **Citgo Truck & Auto Plaza**[*, SCALES] **(FedEx Drop)**
Food E: **Hitchin' Post Restaurant (Texaco TS)**
W: **Blimpie's Subs (Citgo Truck/Auto Plaza)**, **Burger King (Citgo T/A Plaza)**, **Country Kitchen (Citgo T/A Plaza)**
AServ E: **Texaco TS**[24]
TServ E: **Texaco TS**[24]
W: **Citgo Truck & Auto Plaza**
TWash E: **Truck Wash (Texaco TS)**
Other E: **Huntsville Municipal Airport**

116 TX 30, East US 190, Huntsville (Lake Livingston)
Gas E: Diamond Shamrock[*, D]
W: Chevron[*, CW], Exxon[*, D], Shell[*], Texaco[*, CW], Texaco[*, D]
Food E: Church's Chicken, El Chico Mexican Restaurant, Golden Corral Family Steakhouse, Imperial Garden, Kettle, McDonald's[PLAY], Mr. Gatti's Pizza, Popeye's Chicken, TCBY, Tejas Cafe & Bar, Texas Burger, The Junction Steaks & Seafood, What A Burger[24]
W: Bullwinkle's Restaurant, Burger King, Chili's, Denny's, Jose's Restaurant, KFC, Shipley Do-nuts, Subway
Lodg E: Comfort Inn, Econolodge, La Quinta Inn, Motel 6
AServ E: Huntsville Chrysler, Dodge, Jeep, & Dodge Trucks
Med W: **✚ Hospital**
ATM E: Citizen's Bank
W: Exxon, First National Bank West, Guaranty Federal Bank, NationsBank, Texaco
Other W: **Hastings Books, Music, Video**, **Kroger Supermarket**[24, RX], **Mail Boxes Etc**, Maurel Car Wash, **Sam Houston Optical**, **Today's Vision**, **WalGreens Pharmacy**, **West Hill Mall**

114 FM 1374, Huntsville
Gas E: Corner Pantry[*, D], Fina[*, D]
W: Chevron, Diamond Shamrock[*]
Food E: Dairy Queen[PLAY]
W: Casa Tomas Mexican Restaurant, **Country Inn III Steakhouse**
Lodg E: Rodeway Inn
W: Sam Houston Inn
AServ E: Hillcrest Ford, Lincoln, Mercury Dealership

EXIT TEXAS

	W: Chevron
Med	**W:** Huntsville Memorial Hospital
ATM	**E:** Corner Pantry, Fina
Other	**W:** Slaughter Drugs
112	TX 75
Gas	**E:** Citgo[*]
Other	**E:** Sam Houston Statue Visitor Center
113	TX 19, Huntsville, Crockett (Northbound)
109	Park 40, Huntsville State Park
RVCamp	**W:** Huntsville State Park[RV DUMP]
Parks	**W:** Huntsville State Park (.25 Miles)
Other	**E:** Sam Houston Statue with Visitor Center
(105)	Rest Area (Phones, Picnic, Grills, P)
103	TX 150, FM 1374, FM 1375, New Waverly (Southbound)
FStop	**W:** Citgo[*]
Gas	**W:** Texaco[*]
AServ	**W:** Texaco
Other	**W:** Sam Houston National Forest District Office
102	TX 150, FM 1374, FM 1375, New Waverly (Northbound)
98	**(99)** Danville Rd., Shepard Hill Rd.
Food	**W:** Squeeky's Place BBQ
RVCamp	**E:** The Fish Pond RV Park[RV DUMP]
94	FM 1097, Willis
Gas	**W:** Chevron[*], Texaco[*, D]
Food	**E:** Jack-in-the-Box, Sonic
	W: McDonald's
AServ	**E:** Isaacks Auto Diagnostics & Car Exhaust
92	FM 830, Seven Coves Rd, Panorama Village
RVCamp	**W:** Camping[RV DUMP]
91	League Line Road
Gas	**W:** Citgo[*]
Food	**E:** Wendy's
	W: Cracker Barrel
Other	**E:** Conroe Texas Outlet Center
90	FM 3083, Teas Nursery Road
Parks	**E:** Montgomery County Park (3 Miles)
88	Wilson Road, Loop 336 To Navasota, Cleveland
Gas	**E:** Diamond Shamrock[*, D], Exxon[*, CW, 24], Shell[*, CW]
	W: Chevron[*, CW, 24]
Food	**E:** Arby's, Burger King[PLAY], China Delight, Domino's Pizza, Donut Shoppe, Grandy's, Hofbrau Steaks, Hooks Casual Seafood Restaurant, Little Caesars Pizza, Margarita's Mexican Restaurant, McDonald's[PLAY], Papa John's Pizza, Rainbow Cafe, Shipley Do-nuts, Sonic, Subway, What A Burger[24]
	W: Casa Ole Mexican, Honey-B-Ham, Hunan Village Restaurant, I Can't Believe It's Yogurt, KFC, Leaf N' Ladle Garden Cafe, McDonald's (Wal-Mart Supercenter), Ryan's Steakhouse, The Black-Eyed Pea
AServ	**E:** Discount Brake & Muffler, Discount Tire Company, Goodyear Tire & Auto, Pennzoil Oil Change, Professional Car Care Express Tire Service
	W: Sam's Club, Wal-Mart
ATM	**E:** Bank of America, Diamon Shamrock, Guaranty Federal Bank, Klein Bank
	W: First Bank of Conroe, Klein Bank, Randall's Food & Drugs, Wal-Mart Supercenter
Other	**E:** Animal Hospital Of Conroe Inc., Cinema 6, Hastings Books, Music, & Video, Kroger Supermarket[24, RX], Montgomery College, Timber Lane Washateria, WalGreens Pharmacy (1-Hr Photo)
	W: Academy Sports & Outdoor Supplies Store, Eye Land, For Heaven's Sake Christian Bookstore, Pet's Paw Animal Hospital, Randall's Food & Drugs[RX] (1 Hr Photo), Sam's Club, Wal-Mart Supercenter[RX] (Vision Center, 1-Hr Photo)
87	TX 105, FM 2854, Conroe
Gas	**E:** Chevron[*, D, 24], Diamond Shamrock[*], Exxon[*]
	W: Coastal[*, D], Exxon[*, CW], Texaco
Food	**E:** Burger King[PLAY], Church's Chicken, Ci Ci's Pizza, Donut Wheel, ElT'son's Chicken Tender & Tasty, Jack-in-the-Box[24], Kettle, La Carreta Taqueria, Luther's Hamburgers Bar-B-Q, McDonald's[PLAY], Panda Chinese Buffet, Popeye's Chicken, Schlotzsky's Deli, Taco Bell, Taqueria Vallarta, Village Restaurant[24], Wyatt's Cafeteria
	W: Luby's Cafeteria
AServ	**E:** Bill Blankenship, Ford Dealership, Fred's Auto Parts, Sunset Auto Repair, Tom Kelley Tire Co., Tune Up Masters
	W: Xpress Lube
ATM	**E:** Bank One
	W: NationsBank, Texas Commerce Bank
Other	**E:** Car Service Center, Eckerd Drugs[24] (1-Hr Photo), Kroger Supermarket[RX], Lifechek Drug, Mail Depot, Texas State Optical, US Post Office
	W: Maurel Car Wash
85	Gladstell Street
Gas	**W:** Diamond Shamrock[*, D], Texaco[*, D]
Food	**W:** Malt-N-Burger
Lodg	**W:** Days Inn, Motel 6
AServ	**E:** AAA Tire Service[24]
	W: DeMontrond Chrys, Plym, Jeep, Eagle, Dodge, Cadillac, Olds, Gullo Toyota
Med	**W:** Hospital
ATM	**E:** Texas Commerce Bank
	W: A & H Foodstore
Other	**E:** Barnacle Bill's Marine
	W: A & H Foodstore, Texas Department Of Public Safety
84	North TX 75, Loop 336, Frazier St.
Gas	**E:** Exxon[*, D], Texaco[D]
	W: Shell[*, CW]
Food	**E:** San Miguel Taqueria Mexican
	W: IHOP, Pizza Hut, Shoney's, Taco Cabana[24]
Lodg	**E:** Holiday Inn, Ramada Limited
AServ	**E:** Exxon, Texaco
Med	**W:** Columbia Conroe Regional Medical Center
ATM	**W:** Albertson's Grocery
Other	**E:** U-Haul Center[LP]
	W: Albertson's Grocery[24, RX], K-Mart[RX], Mail Boxes Etc
83	Crighton Road, Camp Strake
Other	**W:** Animal Emergency Clinic
81	FM 1488, Magnolia, Hempstead
Gas	**W:** Diamond Shamrock[*, D]
RVCamp	**W:** Camper Land Sales & Service
ATM	**W:** Diamond Shamrock
79	Needham Rd, TX 242
Gas	**E:** Texaco[*, D]
Food	**E:** McDonald's (Texaco)
ATM	**E:** Texaco
Other	**W:** Montgomery College
78	Tamina Rd, Research Forest Dr, Shenandoah (Services Same On Exit 77 Northbound)
FStop	**E:** Conoco[*]
Gas	**W:** Diamond Shamrock[*, D], Mobil[*]
Food	**E:** Cafe China Buffet, Luther's Bar-B-Q, Papa John's Pizza, Pasta Kitchen, Poncho's Mexican Buffet, Red Lobster
	W: Denny's, Win's Chinese Restaurant
Lodg	**W:** Hampton Inn, La Quinta Inn, Roadrunner Motor Inn
AServ	**E:** Knee's Automotive Volkswagon & American
Med	**W:** Hospital
ATM	**E:** Compass Bank
	W: Diamond Shamrock
Other	**E:** A-Med Medical Supply, Cinema 4, Office Depot, Woodland's Bowl
	W: Mail Boxes Etc, Shenandoah Animal Clinic
76	Woodlands Pkwy, Robinson Rd., Oak Ridge North, Chateau Woods
Gas	**W:** Texaco[*, D, CW]
Food	**E:** Long John Silver
	W: Chili's, Guadalajara Mexican Grill & Bar, Jack-in-the-Box, Luby's Cafeteria, The Black-Eyed Pea
Lodg	**W:** Courtyard by Marriott, Drury Inn
AServ	**E:** Bill Blankenship (Firestone)
ATM	**W:** Compass Bank, NationsBank
Other	**E:** Drive Pro Golf Shop
	W: Barnes & Noble, Target, The Woodlands Mall, Toys R Us, US Post Office
73	Rayford Road, Sawdust Road
Gas	**E:** Conoco[*], Shell[*]
	W: Shell[*, CW, 24], Texaco[*, D, CW]
Food	**E:** Baskin Robbins, Hartz Chicken Buffet, Hydens Restaurant & Oyster Bar, Jack-in-the-Box, Manuel's Mexican, McDonald's[PLAY], Popeye's Chicken, Sonic, Tam's Restuarant, Thomas Bar-B-Q
	W: 19th Hole Grill & Bar, Bagel Express, Bei Jing Chinese Restaurant, Ci Ci's Pizza, Giuseppe's Restaurant, Grandy's, Greek Tony's, Ninfa's, Oscar's Creamery, Papa's Icehouse, Fishfry, Rookies Sports Bar & Grill, Sam's Cafe & Restaurant, Shipley's Do-Nuts, Smoothie King, Subway, Sundale Donuts, Supreme Soup & Salad, What A Burger, Woodlands House Chinese, Z K's Cafe
Lodg	**W:** Red Roof Inns
AServ	**E:** AAMCO Transmission, Auto Zone Auto Parts, Hi-Lo Auto Supply, Kelly Tire, Meineke Discount Mufflers, Quick Lube & Sticker
	W: Discount Tire Company, Express Lube, Fast Lube
RVCamp	**W:** Great Parks (.25 Miles)
Med	**E:** Primary Medical Clinic (Minor Emergency/7 Days A Week)
ATM	**E:** Conoco, Woodforrest National Bank
	W: Bank of America, Kroger Supermarket, Texas Commerce Bank
Other	**E:** Academy (Outdoor Store), Boats Unlimited, Golf Balls Unlimited, News/Craft Books, Photo Hut, Quick Clean Car Wash, Swing Masters Golf Shop
	W: Golf USA, H-E-B Pantry Foods, Just Cats Veterinary Hospital, Kroger Supermarket[24, RX], Nesbit's Cleaners & Laundry, Rainbow Car Wash, Today's Vision, WalGreens Pharmacy, Woodlands Pet Clinic
73A	**(72)** Frontage Road, Hardy Toll Rd South (Southbound)
TStop	**W:** Mobil[*] (1-Hr Photo)
Food	**W:** Restaurant (Mobil TS)
TServ	**W:** King of the Road Heavy Repair & Tires
ATM	**W:** Mobil TS
72	Unnamed (Southbound)
AServ	**W:** Bruce Automotive
70B	Spring - Stuebner Road
Other	**E:** Island Mist Spas[LP]
70A	Spring - Cypress Road, FM 2920, Tomball
Gas	**E:** Exxon[*, CW]
	W: Chevron[*, D], Racetrac[*], Shell[*, CW, 24], Texaco[*, D]
Food	**E:** Charlie's Neighborhood Grill, El Palenque Mexican, Hartz Chicken Buffet, McDonald's[PLAY], Pizza Hut, Subway, Sun Li Chinese Restaurant, Wendy's
	W: Burger King, Chinese Wok, Taco Bell, What A Burger[24]
AServ	**E:** C & L Tire Co. Inc., Hi-Lo Auto Supply

Bold red print shows RV & Bus parking available or nearby

EXIT	TEXAS
	W: Spring Body Shop
RVCamp	E: **Campground(RV DUMP)**
ATM	E: Wells Fargo
	W: Compass Bank
Other	E: **Birds of Paradise Pet Store, Kroger Supermarket(24, RX), Northland Optical, Splash Town USA (Water Theme Park), Spring Center Animal Clinic, US Post Office, WalGreens Pharmacy (1-Hr Photo)**
	W: **Spring Animal Hospital, U-Haul Center(LP)**
69	Louetta Rd., Holzwarth Rd
Gas	W: Chevron(*)
Lodg	W: Motel 6, TraveLodge
AServ	W: Planet Ford
Other	W: **The Home Depot(LP)**
66	FM 1960, Addicks, Humble
Gas	E: Chevron(*), Racetrac(*), Texaco(*, CW)
	W: Exxon(*, CW)
Food	E: Chinese Restaurant East Bow, Pour House Restaurant
	W: Bennigan's, Champs(24), Grandy's, Hooters, James Coney Island, Lasagna House III, Marco's Mexican, McDonald's(PLAY), Ninfa's Mexican, Outback Steakhouse, Pizza Hut, Red Lobster, Steak & Ale, Subway, The Original Pasta Co.
Lodg	W: HomeStead Village Efficiencies, La Quinta Inn
AServ	E: AutoNation USA, Detail Lube Center
	W: All Tune & Lube, NTB
ATM	E: First Educator's Credit Union, Texaco
	W: **Kroger Supermarket**, Wells Fargo
Other	E: **Golf World Driving Range**, Mr. Car Wash (Chevron)
	W: **Book Nook, Golfsmith Golf Center, Kroger Supermarket(24, RX), Mail Boxes Etc, OfficeMax, Pet City Discount Center, Venture, WalGreens Pharmacy(24)**
64	Richey Road
TStop	W: **45 Travel Center(*) (Citgo, Truckers Lounge)**
Food	W: **Restaurant(24) (45 Travel Center)**
Lodg	E: Holiday Inn, Lexington Hotel Suites
	W: **Bunkhouse (45 Travel Center)**
AServ	E: Carmax, Discount Tire Co. of Texas, **Sam's Club**
	W: Gunther's Auto Repair
TWash	W: **45 Travel Center**
ATM	W: **45 Travel Center**
Other	E: **Sam's Club**
63	Airtex Drive, Rankin Rd
RVCamp	E: **Demontrond Motorhomes**
62	Kuykendahl, Rankin Road (Closed Due To Construction)
61	Greens Road
Gas	E: Mobil(*)
Food	E: Blimpie's Subs, Brown Sugar Bar-B-Q, Chef Lin's Hunan, Fajitas A Sizzlin' Celebration, Fuddruckers, IHOP, Imperial Dragon Chinese Restaurant, Jack-in-the-Box, McDonald's, Monterey's Tex Mex Cafe, Pizza Inn, Souper Salad, Wendy's, Zero's Sandwich Shop
	W: Burger King(PLAY), Chinese Palace Restaurant, Ginger Chinese Cafe, Kiraku Sushi Bar, Luby's Cafeteria, Marco's Mexican, Rocky's Subs, Subway, Supreme Soup & Salad, TCBY, The Black-Eyed Pea
Lodg	E: (DAYS INN) Days Inn, Wyndham Garden Hotel
	W: Budgetel Inn
AServ	E: **Auto Express Montgomery Ward**
RVCamp	E: **Morgan RV's (1 Mile), Royal Coach Village (.25 Miles)**
ATM	E: NationsBank, NationsBank
	W: Bank United
Other	E: **Greenspoint Mall, Today's Vision Optometrist**
	W: **Kroger Supermarket(24), Office Depot, Petco Supplies & Fish, Target**
60B	Beltway 8, West Sam Houston Tollway
60A	Beltway 8, Frtg Rd, Intercontinental Airport
60D	Beltway 8, FM 525, Airport
Food	W: Marco's Mexican Restaurant, Supreme Soup & Salad, TCBY
Other	E: **Greenspoint Mall**
	W: **Office Depot, Petco Supplies & Fish**
59	West Road
Gas	E: E-Z Serve(*), Shell(CW)
	W: Exxon(*, CW), Shell(*, CW)
Food	E: McDonald's(PLAY)
	W: Blimpie's Subs (Exxon), **Little Caesars Pizza (K-Mart), McDonald's (Wal-Mart)**, TCBY (Exxon), Taco Bell, What A Burger(24)
AServ	E: Bob Lunsford's Honda, Carquest Auto Parts, Midas, Shell
	W: **K-Mart**, Pep Boys Auto Center, **Wal-Mart**
Other	E: **Pier 45 Marine**
	W: **Academy Outdoors (Outdoor Store), K-Mart(RX), Wal-Mart(24)**
57B	TX 249, West Mount Houston Rd
Gas	E: Exxon(*, D), Mobil(*)
	W: Shell(*, CW)
Food	E: Church's Chicken (Mobil), Taquito Joe
	W: Pizza Inn, Sonic
Lodg	W: **Green Chase Inn**
AServ	E: Discount Tire Company
	W: Landmark Chevy Trucks, Northwood Lincoln Mercury Dealer
Other	E: **Kroger Supermarket**
	W: **Eckerd Drugs(24), Stop n Get(*), Washateria**
57A	Gulf Bank Road
FStop	E: **Mobil(*)**
Gas	E: Conoco(*)
	W: Diamond Shamrock(*)
Food	E: Ricardo's Mexican
Lodg	W: (DAYS INN) **Days Inn**
AServ	E: Hidden Valley Wrecker, In & Out Auto & Marine Repair, Joey Co Engines, New & Used Reproduction Parts
	W: Archer Chrysler Plymouth Dealer, Archer Jeep Eagle, Landmark Geo Chevrolet
RVCamp	E: **Smith RV Rentals**
ATM	E: Conoco, Texas Commerce Bank
	W: Diamond Shamrock
Other	E: **Cahill Veterinary Clinic, In & Out Auto & Marine Repair**
	W: **Barber Boats**
56B	Spur 261, Shepherd Dr, Little York Rd (Southbound)
Gas	W: Mobil(*), Shell(*, CW)
Food	W: Arby's (Mobil), Denny's, Luby's Cafeteria
Lodg	W: Gulf Wind Motel, Houston Motor Inn
AServ	W: All Tune & Lube, Archer Mazda, Brandt Auto Truck & Equipment Sales, Duron Tires, Fred Haas Toyota, Lifetime Warranty Transmission, Lone Star Ford, Q-Lube, Saturn of Houston North Frwy, Western Auto
Other	W: **WalGreens Pharmacy**
56A	Canino Rd (Northbound)
RVCamp	E: **Best Buy RV Sales & Service, Holiday World RV Center**
55B	Little York Rd (Northbound)
FStop	E: **Coastal(*, CW)**
Gas	E: Chevron(*), Exxon, Fina(*)
Food	E: Church's Chicken, Ocean Fish Market & Restaurant, Sam's Country Bar-B-Q, What A Burger(24)
AServ	E: Exxon, Rick's Auto, Wholesale Wheel & Tire
TWash	E: **Coastal**
ATM	E: Chevron, **Coastal**
Other	E: **Price Buster Foods, Travis Boats**
55A	Parker Rd., Yale St.
Gas	E: Mobil(*), Northtown Service(D, LP), Shell(*)
	W: Shell
Food	E: Schlotzsky's Deli
	W: Hartz Chicken, Long John Silver
Lodg	E: Olympic Motel
AServ	E: Bap Geon Imported Car & Truck Parts, Northtown Service
	W: Dave Cory Trucks, Fact-O-Bake Body & Paint Shop, Shell
RVCamp	E: **Atlas Supply of Texas (.75 Miles), Atlas Supply of Texas (.8 Miles)**
Med	E: **+ Columbia North Houston Medical Center**
ATM	W: Merchant's Bank
Other	E: **ACE Pharmacy, Army Surplus, Parkway Optical, Parkway Pharmacy**
	W: **Parker Food Mart**
54	Tidwell Road
Gas	E: Best Food Market(*), Exxon(*, CW)
	W: Chevron(*, 24), Circle A(*), Shell(*, CW)
Food	E: Aunt Bea's Restaurant(24), China Border (Chinese Buffet), Connie's Seafood, Lee's Inn Chinese & Vietnamese, Pancho's Mexican Buffet, Pizza Inn, Subway, Taco Cabana, Thomas Bar-B-Q
Lodg	W: **Guest Motel**, Scottish Inns, **South Wind Motel**
AServ	E: Tex-Star Motors
	W: AAMCO Transmission, North Freeway Body Shop
TServ	W: **Rush Truck Center**
RVCamp	W: **Ron Hoover Co.'s RV Center**
ATM	E: J.M. Grocery Store & Deli, Municipal Employees Credit Union
	W: Chevron
Other	E: **Bakery Outlet, Eckerd Drugs, J. M. Grocery Store & Deli, Washaway Laundry (Coin Laundry)**
	W: **Red Stone Food Mart, U-Haul Center(LP)**
53	Airline Drive
Gas	E: Chevron(*, D), Conoco
	W: Citgo(*)
Food	W: What A Burger(24)
Lodg	W: Villa Provencial Motor Inn
AServ	E: Conoco, Discount Tire Center, **Montgomery Ward**, Stop n Go, Tuneup Masters
ATM	E: Chevron
Other	E: **Fiesta Grocery(RX), Northline Mall**
	W: Car Care Car Wash (Hand Wash), **First Stop Store, Glen Burnie Washateria**
52B	Crosstimbers Road
Gas	E: Shell(*, CW), Texaco(*, D)
	W: Chevron(*), Exxon(*), Mobil(*), N.N. Food Store(*)
Food	E: Baskin Robbins, China Inn Restaurant, Ci Ci's Pizza, Denny's, Hungry Farmer Bar-B-Q, Jack-in-the-Box, James Coney Island, KFC, Long John's Donuts, McDonald's(PLAY), Piccadilly Cafeteria, Pizza Hut, Sonic, Taco Bell, Texas Seafood Chinese Restaurant
	W: Monterey's, Restaurant (Howard Johnson), Wendy's
Lodg	W: Economy Lodge, Howard Johnson, Luxury Inn, The Silver Glo Motel
AServ	E: 3-A Auto Service, AJ's Grease Rack, **Montgomery Ward**, Tire Station, Western Auto
	W: Crosstimbers Muffler & Brake Service, Llantas Tires, M & G Used Auto Sales, Meineke Discount Mufflers, National Engine & Supply, Nick's International Auto Care
RVCamp	W: **Felton's RV Service (.5 Miles)**
ATM	E: Navigation Bank Northline Branch, Shell, Texas Commerce Bank
Other	E: **Cinema I-IV, Foot Locker Outlet, Northline Mall, Price Buster Foods (Grocery), Texas State Optical**
52A	Frontage Road (Southbound)
Lodg	W: Guest Inn, Super 8
51	Junction I-610
50	Cavalcade Street, Patton Street

EXIT TEXAS

(Northbound Is Exit 50AB)

TStop E: **Pilot[*, SCALES]**

Gas E: Chevron[*, 24], Diamond Shamrock[*], Exxon, Texaco[*, CW]

Food E: Casa Garay Carnes Asadas, Dairy Queen, Laredo Taqueria, Sol Y Mar Restaurant, **Wendy's (Pilot TS)**

Lodg W: DAYS INN Days Inn

AServ E: Reparacion de Radiadores
W: National Auto Parts, Unidos Auto Service

TServ E: **Embry Isuzu Truck Center, Pilot Travel Center**

TWash E: **Pilot Travel Center**

ATM E: **Pilot Travel Center**

Other E: **39 Cent Bakery Outlet Store, Grocery World[RX]**, O'Banions Car Wash, **Quick Food Store**
W: Car Wash, **Snap Groceries, Texas Groceries, Washateria (Coin-Op Laundry)**

49B North Main Street, Houston Avenue

Gas W: Exxon[*, D, CW], Texaco[*]

Food E: Casa Grande Mexican Restaurant & Club
W: Domino's Pizza, Food Court Express (Exxon), Hunan Bo Restaurant, KFC, McDonald's[PLAY], Shipley Do-Nuts, Subway, What A Burger[24]

AServ W: Hi/Lo Auto Supply

Other W: **La Fiestita II Food Market, Simon's United Drugs**

49A Quitman Street (Southbound, Reaccess Northbound Only)

Gas W: Stop N Go[*]

AServ W: Illusion Mechanic Shop

48AB 48A - I-10 East, Beaumont, 48B - I-10 West, San Antonio (Left Exit Both Directions)

47D Dallas Ave, Pierce Ave (Southbound)

47C McKinney Street (Left Exit Southbound, Difficult Reaccess)

Food W: Downtown Soup & Salad, Foley's Deli Express, James Coney Island, Luther's Bar-B-Q, Mandarin Hunan Cuisine Restaurant, Massa's Restaurant, McDonald's, Souper Sandwich, Zero's Sandwich Shop

Lodg W: Doubletree Hotel, Hyatt Regency

Other W: **Fox Photo 1-Hr Lab, Houston Public Library, Music Hall, Prescription House, The Heritage Society, The Jesse Jones Hall for the Performing Arts, Theatre District, United Parcel Service**

47B Houston Ave, Memorial Dr, Theatre District (Northbound)

AServ E: Firestone Tire & Auto, Knapp Chevrolet

47A Allen Parkway (Left Exit Both Directions, Difficult Reaccess)

46AB US 59, TX 288, Lake Jackson, Freeport, Cleveland (Left Exit Both Directions)

45A Scott Street (Northbound Is Exit 45)

Food E: Blimpie's Subs (Texaco), Creole Fried Chicken

AServ E: University Firestone

ATM E: Texaco

Other E: **Joe's Washateria, Lavenderia**

44C Cullen Blvd (Southbound)

Food W: Burger King, McDonald's[24], Wendy's

Other W: **University of Houston**

44B Calhoun Street (Southbound)

Other W: **University of Houston**

44A Elgin - Lockwood Cullen Blvd. (Northbound)

Gas E: Diamond Shamrock[*, D]

ATM E: Diamond Shamrock

43B Tellepsen St, Schlumberger St (Northbound)

43A s Road (Phones)

Gas W: 6-Eleven[*]

Food E: Fiesta The Original Loma Linda, Luby's Cafeteria, Tel-45 Kitchen
W: Panaderia Taqueria

EXIT TEXAS

AServ W: Auto-Air Wholesale Parts, Sales, Service, Galvan's Tire Service, Hernan's Transmissions, Juan Tire Service, Lidstone Garage, M & N Mechanic Shop

42 US 90 Alt., S. Wayside Drive (Southbound)

Gas W: Exxon[*]

Food W: Jack-in-the-Box, **Little Caesars Pizza (K-Mart)**, McDonald's[PLAY], **Monterey's Tex-Mex Cafe**

Lodg W: Josephine Motel, Sunset Inn

AServ W: Galvan's Tire Service, Juarez Tire Service

Other W: **K-Mart[RX]**

41B Broad Street, Griggs Road, Alt US 90, S. Wayside Dr (Southbound)

Gas E: Diamond Shamrock[*], Shell[*, CW]
W: Conoco[*], Jack's Mini Mart[*, 24], Mobil[*]

Food E: **Swifty's Bar-B-Que (Red Carpet Inn)**, Taqueria Arandas
W: **Little Caesars Pizza (K-Mart)**, Mary Lee Donuts[24], Morelia Taqueria y Refresqueria

Lodg E: Gulf Freeway Inn, Houtex Inn, Red Carpet Inn

AServ E: Fiesta Paint, Body, & Auto Glass
W: Casey's Paint & Body Shop, Don Rucker Tire Co.

Med E: **✚ Clinical Santa Ana (Minor Emergencies Clinic)**

Other W: **K-Mart[RX], Sellers Bros. Grocery Store**

41A Woodridge Dr (Southbound)

Gas W: Shell[*, CW]

Food W: Church's Chicken, Dot Coffee Shop[24], Grandy's, King Hoagie N' Rice, McDonald's[PLAY], Pappas Bar-B-Q, Pizza Hut, Schlotzsky's Deli, Taqueria Mexico, Wendy's

AServ W: Bayway Lincoln, Mercury, Subaru, Body Shop, Cabell Chevrolet, Mazda, Geo

ATM W: Savings of America, Shell, Texas Commerce Bank

Other W: **4 Less Food Store, Gulfgate Animal Hospital, Gulfgate Mall, Snow White Laundromat, Stop N Go**

40 Jct.I-610

40A Frontage Rd (Northbound)

40B E.I-610 To TX 225, Pasad., S. TX 35, W.I-610 Pearland, Alvin (San Jacinto Battleground State Park, Battleship Texas)

40C I-610 West (Left Exit Northbound)

39 Park Place Blvd, Broadway Blvd

Gas E: Gas Station[*], Texaco[*]
W: Phillips 66[*], Shell[*], Texaco[*]

Food E: Dante Italian Cuisine, Del Sol Bakery, Ice Cream, Deli, & Gifts, Kim Long Restaurant, La Ojarasca Bakery, Nuevo Mexico, Taquerias Del Sol, Tony Mandola's Blue Oyster Bar
W: Blimpie's Subs (Texaco), Kelley's Country Cookin', Mac's Chicken & Rice, May Moon Cafe, Noemi's Tacos, Sun Sai Gai Restaurant

AServ E: Crafts Car Center Auto Parts, Gulf Gate Auto Sales, Jimenez Auto Repair, Texaco, Trans Auto Body Complete Auto Repair, Tygco Cars N' Vettes
W: Earl Scheib Paint & Body, Kelly's Auto Repair & Tire, Texaco

Other E: **Food Valley Grocery, P & P Washateria, Public Library**
W: **Food Picante, Park Place Pharmacy, US Post Office, Washateria**

38B Bellfort Avenue, Howard Dr. (Southbound, East Services Are At Exit 38)

Gas W: Citgo[*, D, 24]

Food W: Don Tako, Luby's Cafeteria, Taj Mahal Restaurant

AServ W: Pep Boys Auto Center

Other W: **A&M Grocery**, Car Wash, **Food Spot, Hobby Airport, St. Mary's Washateria**

38 TX 3, Monroe Road, Howard Dr.

Gas E: Chevron[*, D, CW], Diamond Shamrock[*], Exxon[*, D], Shell[*], Stopn Go[*]
W: Chevron[*], Get nGo[*], Texaco[*, D]

EXIT TEXAS

Food E: Dairy Queen, Halbrook's Bar & Grill, Jack-in-the-Box, Keiko Seafood, Lam's Chinese Restaurant, Ninfa's Mexican, Old Galveston Seafood Restaurant, Snowflake Donuts, The Captain's Half Shell Oyster Bar, Tijuana's Tex-Mex Grill, Wendy's
W: Luby's Cafeteria, Luther's Bar-B-Q, Omega Restaurant[24], Oriental Gourmet, Subway

Lodg W: Quality Inn & Suites, Smile Inn

AServ E: Carquest Parts Center, Chevron
W: Firestone Tire & Auto

RVCamp E: **Best Buy RV**

ATM E: Bank One, Diamond Shamrock
W: Chevron

Other E: **Glenbrook Animal Clinic, Hobby Skate, Wikler Food Market, Winkler Food Mart & Deli**
W: **Best Marine, Hobby Airport**

36 College Avenue, Airport Blvd

Gas E: Shell[*, CW, 24]
W: Exxon[*, CW], Texaco[*, D, CW]

Food E: Aranda's Panaderia Bakery, Dairy Queen, Shipley Do-nuts, Taqueria Arandas, Thirst Parlor, Waffle House, Yummy Chow
W: Damon's (Holiday Inn), Denny's, Kettle, Lucky Dragon Restaurant, McGrath's, Taco Cabana

Lodg E: Airport Inn, DAYS INN Days Inn
W: Comfort Inn, Courtyard by Marriott, Drury Inn, Holiday Inn, La Quinta Inn, Red Roof Inn, Sumner Suites, Super 8, Travel Inn

AServ E: Castl Transmission & Auto Care, Kari's Garage, Trans City Transmission
W: Fleet Transmission Exchange & Repair, Gulf Freeway Auto Service, Lone Star Automotive, Millennium Autohouse

RVCamp E: **Eastex Camper Sales**

ATM W: Comerica Bank

Other E: **Boots Follmar Marine, Davis Food City, Union Drive-In Grocery**
W: **Boat Stuff, Hobby Airport, R & M The Car Specialist (Car Detail), Stopn Go[*], Supertrac Games**

35 Edgebrook Dr, Clearwood Dr

Gas E: Chevron[*, 24], Exxon, Racetrac[*]
W: Shell[*]

Food E: Burger King, Burger Mart, Chine One Restuarant, Grandy's, Jack-in-the-Box[24], Popeye's Chicken, Subway, Taco Bell
W: James Coney Island, Mary Lee Donuts, McDonald's[PLAY], Pizza Hut, What A Burger[24]

AServ E: David McDavid KIA, Exxon, Gulf Freeway Pontiac GMC Trucks, Master Care Auto Service

RVCamp E: **Terry Vaughn RV's, Thompson RV**
W: **Lone Star RV[LP]**

ATM E: Bank One, Bank of America
W: Shell

Other E: **Animal Emergency Clinic S.E., Eckerd Drugs, Fiesta, Office Depot, See-N-Focus, WalGreens Pharmacy**

34 South Shaver Rd, Almeda - Genoa Rd

Gas E: Conoco
W: Chevron[*, CW, 24], Exxon[*], Mobil[*]

Food W: Burger King[PLAY], General Joe's Chopstix, Pancho's Mexican Buffet, Sciortino's Deli, Wendy's

AServ E: Carlie Thomas Chrys, Plymouth, Jeep, Eagle, Charlie Thomas Acura, Charlie Thomas Hyundai, Isuzu, Conoco, Houston-Pasadena Foreign Car Service, Jay Marks Toyota, McDavid Honda, Saturn of Houston
W: David McDavid Olds, Nissan, Discount Tire Company, NTB, Western Auto

RVCamp W: **Holiday World**

ATM W: Wells Fargo

Other E: **Almeda Super Rink, Roy's Gas Grills[LP]**
W: **Almeda Mall, Baptist Bookstore**, Coin Car Wash, **OfficeMax, R H Tropical Fish & Pets, Toys R Us, Venture**

Bold red print shows RV & Bus parking available or nearby

EXIT TEXAS

33 Fuqua Street, Beltway 8 Frtg Rd.
- **Gas** **E:** Stopn Go[*]
  W: Texaco[*, D, CW]
- **Food** **E:** Blimpie's Subs (Diamond Shamrock), Chili's, Fuddruckers, King Bo, Luby's Cafeteria, Mexico Lindo, Olive Garden, Schlotzsky's Deli, T.G.I. Friday's
  W: Black-Eyed Pea, Boston Market Restaurant, Brown Sugar Bar-B-Q, Casa Ole, Ci Ci's Pizza, Golden Corral Family Steakhouse, Joe's Crab Shack[PLAY], Lillie's Cantina, Little Caesars Pizza, Long Horn Cafe, Loong Wah, Seafood Plus, Sing Lee Restaurant, Steak & Ale, Subway, TCBY, Taco Bell, Tejas Cafe, What A Burger
- **AServ** **E:** Bayway Lincoln Mercury
  W: AutoNation USA, **Sam's Club**, The Tire Station
- **ATM** **E:** Diamond Shamrock, Stopn Go, Texas Commerce Bank
  W: Bank of America
- **Other** **E: Medicine Man Pharmacy, Sony Theaters, United Optical**
  W: Almeda Mall, Eckerd Drugs, Golf Superstore, Longhorn Golf, Randalls Food & Drugs[24], Sam's Club, Sears Hardware[LP], Texas State Optical, The Home Depot[LP]

32 Sam Houston Tollway

31 FM 2553, Scarsdale Blvd, Beltway 8 Frontage Rd.
- **Gas** **W:** Exxon[*], Shell[*, CW, 24] (CNG Natural Gas)
- **Food** **W:** Dairy Queen[PLAY], Danny's Donuts and Kolaches, McDonald's[PLAY], Perry's Grill & Steakhouse, Pho Cong Ly
- **ATM** **W:** Exxon, My Quang Market
- **Other** **E: Stop & Sock Driving Range**
  W: My Quang Market, Scarsdale Pharmacy, Stop & Gone Groceries

30 FM 1959, Ellington Field, Dixie Farm Road
- **Gas** **E:** Conoco[*]
- **AServ** **E:** Clear Lake Dodge, Dodge Trucks
- **RVCamp** **W: Morgan Building & Spas**
- **Med** **W: Hospital**
- **ATM** **W:** First Community Bank
- **Other** **E: Laundromat**

29 FM 2351, Friendswood, Clear Lake City Blvd (Space Center Houston)
- **Parks** **E: Clear Lake Recreational Center**
- **Other** **E: Space Center Houston**

27 El Dorado Blvd
- **Gas** **E:** Texaco[*, CW]
- **Food** **E:** Dairy Queen[PLAY]
- **ATM** **E:** Texaco
- **Other** **E:** Car Wash, **Fire Station, Space Center Houston**
  W: Texas Ice Stadium (Public Ice Skating)

26 Bay Area Blvd
- **Gas** **W:** Shell[*]
- **Food** **E:** Kettle, Pappas Seafood House, Red Lobster, The Original Taco Cabana
  W: Bennigan's, Burger King, Chuck E Cheese's Pizza, Denny's, Marie Callender's Restaurant, McDonald's, Steak & Ale
- **Lodg** **E:** Best Western
- **AServ** **E:** Discount Tire Company, Pro Tech Collision Repair Ctr
  W: Sears
- **Med** **E: Columbia Clear Lake Regional Medical Center**
- **ATM** **W:** NationsBank, Savings of America
- **Other** **E: Barnes & Noble, Boaters World, Discovery Zone, Sony Theatres, Space Center Houston, Venture**
  W: Baybrook Mall, Bookstop, Eyemasters, OfficeMax, Pet Vet Animal Hosp., PetsMart, Target, Toys R Us

EXIT TEXAS

25 NASA Rd. 1, FM 528, NASA, Alvin
- **Gas** **E:** Conoco[*, CW], Stopn Go[*]
- **Food** **E:** Cesar's Cantina, Chili's, Ci Ci's Pizza, Crazy Cajun Bayou Steakhouse, Enzo's, King Food, Logan Farms Honey-Glazed Hams, Marco's Mexican Restaurant, Mason Jar, Saltgrass Steakhouse, Simply Yogurt, Waffle House
  W: Dairy Queen, Hans Mongolian BBQ, Hooters, Luther's Bar-B-Q, Subway, The Boat
- **Lodg** **E:** Comfort Inn (see our ad this page), **Motel 6**
- **AServ** **E:** Western Auto
  W: Stickerstop, **Wal-Mart**
- **ATM** **E:** Bank of America, Stopn Go
  W: Wal-Mart
- **Parks** **W: Challenger 7 Memorial Park**
- **Other** **E: Dollar Cinema, General Cinemas, Joshua's Christian Bookstore, Office Depot, Scuba, Space Center Houston, Space Center Souvenirs, The Home Depot**
  W: Wal-Mart[24, RX]

23 FM 518, Kemah, League City
- **Gas** **E:** Racetrac[*], Texaco[D, 24]
  W: Exxon[*], Mobil[*]
- **Food** **E:** Ashley's Donuts, Burger King, Jack-in-the-Box[24], KFC, Little Caesars Pizza, New Hunan Buffet, Pancho's Mexican, Subway, Taqueria Arandas, The Pardise Restaurant
  W: Bonny's Donuts, **Cracker Barrel**, Hartz Chicken, McDonald's[PLAY], Taco Bell, Waffle House, Wendy's
- **Lodg** **W:** Super 8
- **AServ** **E:** Auto Air, Q-Lube, Texaco
  W: Auto Chek
- **RVCamp** **W: All Star RV Park (.5 Miles)**
- **ATM** **W:** Merchant's Bank
- **Other** **E: Academy (Outdoor Store), Box Get, Eckerd Drugs, Kroger Supermarket[24, RX], M & H One-Hr Photo, Mass Mailing Systems, Pets To Luv, WalGreens Pharmacy**
  W: Discount Mini Mart, New Concept Veterinary Clinic

22 Calder Drive, Brittany Bay Blvd
- **RVCamp** **W: Safari Mobile Home Community (1.5 Miles)**
- **Other** **W: Lazer Marine Inc.**

20 FM 646, Santa Fe
- **Other** **W: Public Golf Course**

19 FM 517, Dickinson, San Leon Hughes Rd
- **Gas** **E:** Diamond Shamrock[*], Shell[24]
  W: Exxon[*, CW], Texaco[*, D, CW]
- **Food** **E:** Jack-in-the-Box, Monterey's Tex-Mex Cafe, Pizza Inn, Szechuan Garden Chinese
  W: KFC, Kettle[24], McDonald's[PLAY], Pizza Hut, Subway, Taco Bell, Wendy's, What A Burger[24]
- **Lodg** **W:** El Rancho Motel
- **AServ** **E:** Gay Pontiac, GMC Trucks, Shell
- **ATM** **E:** Guaranty Federal Bank
  W: Exxon
- **Other** **E: Eckerd Drugs, Food King Grocery Store, Speed Queen Laundry (Coin-Op)**
  W: Animal Care Clinic of Dickinson, Kroger Supermarket[24], Mail Boxes Etc, Oasis Pets, WalGreens Pharmacy (1-Hr Photo)

17 Holland Road

16 FM 1764 East, Texas City, College of the Mainland (Southbound)
- **Med** **W: Hospital**

1712
281-332-1001 • 800-228-5150
Comfort Inn
Deluxe Continental Breakfast • Indoor Pool
In Room Coffee Maker • Restaurant/Lounge
Cable TV w/ HBO, Cinemax, Showtime, CNN
Microfriuge • Many Nearby Attractions
750 W. NASA Rd #1
Webster, TX
I-45S Exit 25E on NASA 2nd light turn L
TEXAS • I-45 • EXIT 25

EXIT TEXAS

15 FM 1764 West, FM 2004, Hitchcock Mall of the Mainland Pkwy
- **Gas** **E:** Shell[*]
  W: Mobil[*], Texaco[*, D]
- **Food** **E:** Jack-in-the-Box
  W: Waffle House, What A Burger[24]
- **Lodg** **E:** Fairfield Inn, Hampton Inn
- **RVCamp** **W: Camping**
- **Med** **E: Hospital**
- **ATM** **W:** Mobil, Texaco, Texas First Bank
- **Other** **E: Mall of the Mainland**

13 Johnny Palmer Rd, Delany Rd
- **Lodg** **W:** Holiday Inn, Pelican Inn
- **RVCamp** **E: Lazy Days RV Campground (2 Miles)**
- **ATM** **W:** Factory Outlet Center
- **Other** **W: Factory Outlet Center**

12 FM 1765, LaMarque
- **Gas** **W:** Chevron[*, CW, 24], Texas Discount Gasoline[*]
- **Food** **W:** Jack-in-the-Box, Kelley's Country Cookin', Sonic
- **AServ** **W:** All Pro Automotive, Bunch's Engine Machine Service, Robby's Full Service Auto Repair
- **RVCamp** **W: Li'L Thicket Travel Park (.25 Miles), Mainland Camper Sales**
- **Other** **W: LaMarque Police Dept.**

11 Vauthier Road

10 FM 519, Main Street
- **FStop** **W: Texaco[*]**
- **Gas** **E:** Stopn Go[*]
- **Food** **E: McDonald's[PLAY]**
- **AServ** **E:** MCH Truck & Auto Repair
- **ATM** **E:** Stopn Go
- **Parks** **W: Highland Bayou Park, Mahan Park**
- **Other** **E: LaMarque Police Dept.**

9 Frontage Rd (Southbound)

8 Frontage Rd (Northbound)

7 TX3, TX 146, TX 6, Texas City, Bayou Vista, Hitchcock (Left Exit)
- **Gas** **W:** Diamond Shamrock[*], Texaco[*]

7C Frontage Rd (Northbound)

6 Frontage Road (Southbound)

5 Frontage Road

4 Village of Tiki Island
- **Gas** **W:** Conoco[*, D, 24]
- **Food** **W:** The Grill (Teakwood Marina)
- **ATM** **W:** Conoco
- **Other** **E: Salty's Bait, Tackle**
  W: Public Boat Ramp, Teakwood Marina

1C FM 188, TX 275, Harborside Drive, Teichman Rd. (Port Of Gavelston)
- **FStop** **E: Chevron[*, D], Texaco[*]**
- **Gas** **E:** Conoco[*, D]
- **AServ** **E:** Bob Pagan Toyota, Ford, Rick Perry's Nissan, Plym, Dodge Trucks
- **TServ** **E: NCI Diesel Service**
- **ATM** **E: Texaco**
- **Other** **W: Payco Marina**

1B 71st Street
- **Lodg** **E:** Motel 6
- **AServ** **E:** Galveston Auto Center
- **Other** **W: Galveston Marine Center**

1A Spur 342, 61st Street, West Beach
- **Gas** **W:** Exxon[*, D]
- **Food** **W:** The Diner On 61st Street
- **Lodg** **W:** Days Inn
- **AServ** **W:** Hicks Automotive
- **RVCamp** **W: Camping**
- **ATM** **W:** Exxon
- **Parks** **W: Washington Park Recreation Area**
- **Other** **W: Galveston County 61st Street Public Boat Ramp**

↑TEXAS

Begin I-45

EXIT LOUISIANA

Begin I-49

↓LOUISIANA

206 I-20 & I-49 Junction, Dallas, Monroe
205 Kings Hwy
Gas W: Diamond Shamrock(*, CW)
Food E: Mall St. Vincent
W: Long John Silver, McDonald's(PLAY), Smokey Joe's Rib Shack, Subway, Taco Bell
AServ E: Sears
Med W: ✚ Louisiana State University Medical Center, ✚ Shriners Hospital for Children
ATM E: Bank One
Other E: Mall St. Vincent, Tourist Info.
W: Biomedical Research Institute
203 Hollywood Ave, Pierremont Rd.
Gas W: Fina(*)
Food W: Lee's Country Kitchen
Other E: Boyce's Pet Land, Fairfield Grocery & Market
202 LA 511E, 70th Street
Gas W: Chevron(*), Circle K(*)
Food W: John's Seafood, Sonic
AServ E: Grant's Automotive
W: 70th Street Radiator Shop, J & J Auto Repairs, Kaddo Alternator & Starter Shop
ATM E: Bank One
W: Circle K
Other E: Medic Pharmacy(RX)
201 LA 3132 To Dallas To Texarkana (Limited Access Hwy)
199 LA 526, Bert Kouns - Industrial Loop, LSU Shreveport
FStop E: Chevron(*)
Gas E: Citgo(*)
Food E: Arby's (Chevron), Burger King(PLAY), KFC, Taco Bell, Wendy's
ATM E: Community Bank
Other E: The Home Depot(LP)
191 DeSoto Parish16, Stonewall
186 LA 175, Kingston, Fierson
177 LA 509, Carmel
TStop E: Country Auto Truck Stop(*)
Food E: Country Auto Truck Stop
172 U.S. 84, Mansfield, Grand Bayou
169 Asseff Road
162 US 371, LA 177, Pleasant Hill, Coushatta
155 LA 174, Ajax, Lake End
FStop W: Spauldings(*)
RVCamp W: Country Livin RV Camp(LP)
148 LA 485, Allen, Powhatan
142 Parish 547, Posey Road
138 LA 6, Many, Natchitoches
TStop W: Lott's O' Luck Truck Stop(*, 24)
Gas E: Exxon(*, 24), Shell(*, 24)
W: Jet 24(*), Texaco(*, D)
Food E: SHONEY'S, Shoney's
W: Burger King(PLAY), Jet 24, Lott's O' Luck Truck Stop, McDonald's
Lodg E: Best Western
W: Comfort Inn
RVCamp W: Nakatosh Campground (.2 Miles)
Med E: ✚ Hospital
ATM W: Jet 24
Other W: Kisatchie National Forest District Office
132 LA 478
127 LA 120, Flora, Cypress
119 LA 119, Derry, Gorum, Cloutierville
Other E: Cane River Plantation
113 LA 490, Chopin
107 Lena
103 LA 8 West, Flatwoods
FStop E: Texaco(*)

EXIT LOUISIANA

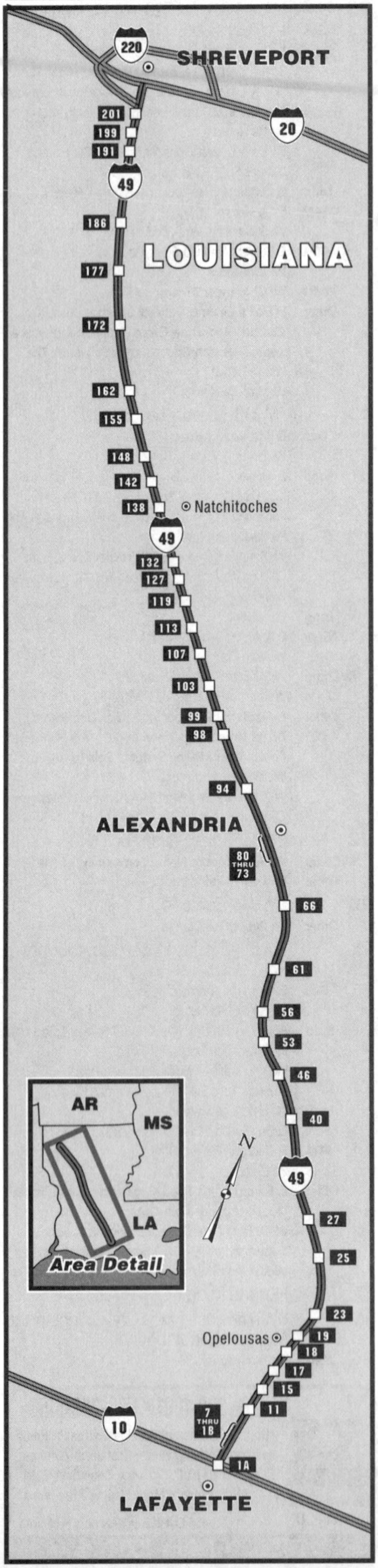

EXIT LOUISIANA

Other E: Cotile Lake (8.6 Miles)
W: Youth Rodeo
99 LA 8 East, LA 1200, Boyce
Gas E: Best Source(*)
Food E: Best Source
Other E: Police Station
98 LA 1, Boyce (Reaccess Southbound Only)
94 Rapides Parish 23, Rapides Station Rd
Gas E: Shari Sue's(*)
Other E: Louisiana Boating Center
90 LA 498, Air Base Road, Alexandria International Airport
FStop W: Chevron(*, 24)
Gas W: Mobil(*, D), Texaco(*)
Food W: Burger King(PLAY), Krystal (Mobil), McDonald's(PLAY)
Lodg W: Guesthouse Inn, Howard Johnson Express, La Quinta Inn
RVCamp W: Cabana Mobile Estates & RV Park (.25 Miles)
Parks E: England Air Park
Other W: Airport
86 US 71, US 165, MacArthur Dr
Gas E: Chevron(*, D), Fina(*, D)
AServ E: Goodyear
85B Monoe St., Medical Center Drive
Med E: ✚ Rapides Regional Medical Center
85A 10th St., Downtown, Alexandria, To LA 1, Elliot St
AServ E: M & T Automotive
Other E: Alexandria Fire Dept., Alexandria Library, Alexandria Police Dept.
84 North US 161, LA 28, LA 1, Pineville Expwy, Casson St.
83 Broadway Avenue
Gas E: Fina(*, D), Lesser(*)
80 U.S. 71, U.S. 167, MacArthur Drive, Alexandria
73 LA 3265, Woodworth
FStop W: Exxon(*, 24)
Food W: Blimpie's Subs (Exxon)
ATM W: Exxon
Other W: Indian Creek Recreation Area
66 LA 112, Forest Hill, Lecompte
Food W: Nell's Cajun Kitchen (Thurs-Sun)
61 U.S. 167, Turkey Creek, Meeker
Other E: Lloyd Hall Plantation
56 LA 181, Cheneyville
53 LA 115, Bunkie
Med E: ✚ Hospital (6 Miles)
46 LA 106, St. Landry
Parks E: Chicot State Park
40 LA 29, Ville Platte
Gas E: Texaco
(34) Rest Area (RR, Picnic, Grills, Pet Walk; Southbound)
(34) Rest Area (RR, Picnic, Grills, RV Dump, Pet Walk; Northbound)
27 LA 10, Lebeau
25 LA 103, Washington, Port Barre
23 U.S. 167, LA 744, Ville Platte
TStop E: Gold Rush Truck Stop(*) (Fuel-Texaco)
Food E: Gold Rush Truck Stop (Fuel-Texaco)
Med W: ✚ Hospital
19AB U.S. 190, Baton Rouge, Opelousas
Gas W: Mobil(*)
AServ W: Automotive Masters
Med W: ✚ Opelousas General Hospital
ATM W: Mobil
Other W: Jim Bowie Museum, Ray's Grocery
18 LA 31, Cresswell Lane
Gas W: Chevron(*)
Food E: The Back Porch Cafe
W: Burger King(PLAY), Cresswell Lane Restaurant,

EXIT		LOUISIANA
		Domino's Pizza, McDonald's[PLAY], Mr. Gatti's Pizza, Ryan's Steakhouse, Subway, Wendy's
	Lodg	W: Best Western
	AServ	E: Sterling Plymouth
		W: Danny's Tire World, Diesi Pontiac, Greased Lightening[CW] (Oil Change), Wal-Mart[RX]
	ATM	W: American Bank, Chevron
	Other	W: Cinema-IV, Delchamp's Supermarket, Eckerd Drugs[RX], Rite Aid Pharmacy[RX], Wal-Mart[RX], Whipps Family Pharmacy[RX]
17		Judson Walsh Drive
	Gas	E: Texaco[*, D, LP]
	Food	E: Texaco
	Lodg	E: Bed & Breakfast
	ATM	E: Texaco
15		LA 3233, Harry Guilbeau Road
	Lodg	W: Quality Inn
	Med	W: + Columbia Doctors Hospital of Opelousas
11		LA 93, Sunset, Grand Coteau
	TStop	E: Citgo Truck & Auto Plaza[*, 24]
	Gas	E: Chevron[*], Exxon[*]
	Food	E: Beau Chene[24] (Citgo TS), Popeye's Chicken (Exxon)
	RVCamp	W: Courvelle RV
	ATM	E: Bank of Sunset
	Other	E: Baronne Veterinary Clinic, St. Cyr Clinic & Pharmacy[RX]
7		LA 182
	Food	E: Prudhomme's Cajun Cafe
	Lodg	W: Acadian Village Inn
	AServ	W: Victory
4		LA 726, Carencro
	Gas	W: Chevron[*, D]
	Food	W: Burger King[PLAY], Popeye's Chicken (Chicken)
	AServ	W: PPG Collision Repair Center
	TServ	W: Acadiana Mack & LA Kenworth
	ATM	W: First National Bank
	Other	W: Carencro Eye Clinic, US Post Office
2		LA 98, Gloria Switch Road
	Gas	E: Chevron[*], Citgo[*], Shell[*]
		W: Texaco[*]
	Food	E: Blimpie's Subs (Citgo)
		W: Church's Chicken (Texaco), Picante
	AServ	E: All American & Foreign Used Parts & Cars, Ben's Auto Repair
	RVCamp	E: Floyd's RV Park, Jackie Edgar RV Center Inc., Trade Winds Camping Center
	ATM	W: Texaco
	Other	E: LA Museum of Military History, The Book Rack
1B		Point Des, Mouton RD
	TStop	W: Golden Palace Truck Stop[*, 24]
	Gas	E: Exxon[*], Texaco[*, D]
	Food	E: Fish & Game Grille (Plantation Inn), Subway (Texaco)
		W: Golden Palace Truck Stop
	Lodg	E: Plantation Motor Inn
	AServ	W: M & J Services, Ronnie's Car Care
	TServ	W: International Trucks
	RVCamp	E: Gauthier Homes & RV Center, Gauthier Mobile Homes
	ATM	E: Exxon, Texaco
	Other	E: Louisiana State Police Region II HQ
1A		I-10 West, Lake Charles
	Food	E: The Tropics (Plantation Motor Inn)
		W: Golden Palace (Golden Palace TS)
	AServ	W: Stelly's Auto Repair
	TServ	W: Stelly's Auto & Truck Repair
	ATM	W: Golden Palace TS
(0)		I-10 East, Baton Rouge

↑LOUISIANA

Begin I-49

I-55 S →

EXIT		ILLINOIS
		Begin I-55

↓ILLINOIS

EXIT		ILLINOIS
293D		Martin Luther King Dr
	Gas	E: Amoco
	Med	E: + Hospital
293C		N255, U.S. 41 Lakeshore Dr. (Reaccess Northbound Only)
293B		Junction I-90/94 East, Indiana (Southbound)
	Gas	E: Amoco
	Food	E: McDonald's
	Lodg	W: Hyatt
	Med	E: + Mercy Hospital, + Michael Reese Hospital
293A		Cermak Road, Chinatown
292		Junction I-90/94 West To Wisconsin, I-90/94 East To Indiana (Westbound)
290		Damen Ave, Ashland Ave. (Reaccess Southbound Only, Difficult Reaccess)
289		California Ave (Northbound)
	FStop	E: Speedway[*, RV DUMP]
	Gas	E: Clark
	Food	E: Red Top Grill, Speedway, Subway (Speedway)
	TWash	E: Trucker's Oil Pros
	ATM	E: Clark, Speedway
288		Kedzie Ave (Southbound, Reaccess Northbound Only)
	Food	E: Best Kosher Restaurant For Truckers
	Other	E: Car Wash
287		Pulaski Road
	Food	E: Burger King
	AServ	E: A&B Automotive (Towing)
286		Cicero Ave., IL 50
	Gas	E: Amoco[*]
	TServ	E: Great Dane Trailer Service, Mr. N. Truck Repair, Team Semi-Trailer Repair
285		Central Ave
	Gas	E: Amoco[*], Citgo[*]
	Food	E: Donald's Hot Dogs, Steak & Egger[24]
	TServ	E: International Truck
	ATM	E: Amoco, Citgo
283		IL 43, Harlem Ave
	Gas	E: Shell[*]
	Food	E: Arby's, Burger King, Dunkin Donuts, Subway, Tam's Mandarin
	ATM	E: Shell
	Other	E: Joe & Frank's Grocery, Met Radiator, Minuteman Press, WalGreens Pharmacy[RX]
282AB		IL 171, 1st Ave. (Difficult Reaccess)
279AB		U.S 12, U.S 20, U.S 45, LaGrange Road (Difficult Reaccess)
277AB		Junction 294, Wisconsin, Indiana (Toll)
276C		Joliet Road
276AB		County Line Road
	Food	E: China King Restaurant, Gia Italian Bisto, Kirsten's Danish, Mack's & Erma's Restaurant
	Lodg	E: Best Western, Extended Stay America
	TServ	E: Roadworthy Truck
	ATM	E: Harris Bank
		W: First National Bank
	Other	E: Post Met
274		IL 83, Kingery Rd
	Gas	E: Shell[*, LP, 24]
		W: Amoco[CW], Marathon[*] (Wrecker), Mobil[*, CW], Shell
	Food	E: Dunkin Donuts, Joel Falco's Pizza
		W: Baker's Square, Blueberry Hill Pancakes, Bono's Lunch Buffet, Delrh Chicken Basket, Denny's, Dunkin Donuts, Holiday Inn, Kerry Piper Irish Pub, Patio (Ribs, Beef, Burgers), Pazzo Pizzeria, Pina's Italian Deli, Salvador's Mexican, Tassio's Porterhouse Restaurant, Triple Play Pizza, Willby's Restaurant (Holiday Inn)
	Lodg	W: Budgetel Inn (Tractors Only/No Trailers), Fairfield, Holiday Inn, Red Roof Inn
	AServ	E: Buridge Car Care
		W: Amoco, Marathon (Wrecker), Shell, Total Tire, West Town Auto Supply, Willowbrook Ford
	TServ	W: The House of Trucks
	ATM	W: American National Bank, Heritage Bank
	Other	E: Buridge Animal Clinic
		W: Kinko's, Minuteman Press, Pak Mail
273AB		Cass Ave
	Gas	W: Shell[*, CW]
	Food	W: Ripples Dining
	ATM	W: NAB Bank, Shell, West Suburban Bank
271AB		Lemont Road
	Gas	W: Shell[*, LP, CW]
	ATM	W: Shell
269		Junction I-355 North, S Joliet Road (Toll)
	TServ	E: Kenworth
267		IL 53, Bolingbrook
	TStop	E: 76 Auto/Truck Plaza[*, SCALES]
	Gas	E: Amoco[*, 24]
		W: Shell[*], Speedway[*, LP]
	Food	E: 76 Auto/Truck Plaza, Bob Evan's Restaurant, Buno's Great Food Fun Place, McDonald's[PLAY], Restaurant (76)
		W: Arby's, Baskin Robbins, Bert's Soul Food & BBQ, Brooster's Chicken, Cheddar's Casual Cafe, Denny's, Family Square Restaurant, Golden Chopsticks, Harold's Rib & Chicken, IHOP, KFC, LaLo's Mexican Food, Little Caesars Pizza, Maurie's Table (Pizza), McDonald's, Mom's Italian Beef & Ribs, Subway, White Castle Restaurant
	Lodg	E: Comfort Inn, Ramada Limited, Super 8
		W: Holiday Inn
	AServ	E: Ed James Chevrolet, GM, Village Ford
		W: Goodyear, Merlin Muffler & Brake, Trak Auto
	TServ	E: 76 Auto/Truck Plaza[SCALES], Arrow Truck

EXIT ILLINOIS

Sales, Northwest Trucks
RVCamp W: **Camping World (1.2 Miles)(see our ad this page)**
Med W: **+ Ogdon Medical Clinic**
ATM E: Midwest Savings
W: Shell, Speedway
Other W: Aldi, Coin Operated Laundry, **Dominic's Grocery**[RX], Eye Ful Tower Optical, Home Town Pantry, Mailboxes Etc., **Wal-Mart**[RX] **(Vision Center)**, **WalGreens Pharmacy**

(265) **Weigh Station (Southbound)**

(265) **Weigh Station (Northbound)**

263 Weber Road
Gas E: Citgo[*]
W: Shell[*, CW]
Food W: Cracker Barrel, Wendy's
Lodg W: Country Inn & Suites, Howard Johnson
ATM E: Citgo
W: Shell

261 IL 126 West, Plainfield (Reaccess Southbound Only)

257 U.S 30, Aurora, Joliet
TStop W: **Clark's**[*, LP, SCALES]
Gas E: Shell[*]
W: Amoco[*]
Food E: Applebee's, Burger King, Diamans Family Restaurant, Lone Star Steakhouse, McDonald's[PLAY], Old Country Buffet, Pizza Hut, Red Lobster, Steak & Shake, Subway, TGI Friday, Taco Bell, Wendy's
W: **Clark's**, Restaurant (Clark's), Subway (Clark's)
Lodg E: **Comfort Inn**, Fairfield Inn, Hampton Inn, Motel 6, **Ramada**, Super 8
AServ E: Discount Tire Company, NTB, Sears (Jiffy Lube), Volvo
ATM E: Cash Station, First America
W: **Clark's**
Other E: Home Depot[LP], **Joliet Mall**, **K-Mart**[RX], Pets Mart, Phar Mor Drugs, **Target**

253 U.S 52, Joliet, Shorewood
Gas E: Amoco[*, LP], Shell[*]
W: Amoco[*, D, LP]
Food E: **Days Inn**, Jimmy's (Days Inn), **McDonald's**, Wendy's
W: Burrito King
Lodg E: **Days Inn**, **Elks Motel**, Fireside Resort, Wingate Inn
AServ E: Amoco, Ron Tirapelli Suzki, Ford
RVCamp E: **Rick's RV**
Med E: **+ Hospital**
ATM W: Amoco
Other E: Landmark Full Service Car Wash

251 IL 59, Shorewood, Plainfield (Northbound, Reaccess Southbound Only)
Food W: Maryland Fried Chicken, Pizza
AServ W: Absolute Truck Repair, Northwest Muffler & Brake, Smothers Auto, Electric, Alternators & Starters, Surwood Lube & Service Goodyear
Other W: Car Wash, K's C-Store

250AB Junction I-80, Des Moines, Toledo (Difficult Reaccess)

248 U.S 6, Moriss, Joliet
Gas E: Speedway[*, LP]
W: Amoco[*, LP]
Food E: Country Manor Inn Restaurant, Ivo Express Grill (Italian)
W: Amoco, McDonald's (Amoco)
Lodg E: **Manor Motel**
AServ E: BMS Auto Tech
TServ E: **Juliet Mac Sales & Service**
ATM E: Speedway, Tri-County Bank

EXIT ILLINOIS

CAMPING WORLD
Exit 267
620 S. Woodcreek Dr. • Bolingbrook, IL
1-800-621-1038
1416

W: Amoco

247 Bluff Road, Channahon
TServ E: **Fruehauf**

245 Arsenal Road

241 Wilmington
RVCamp W: **Des Plaines State Conservation Area (1 Mile)**
Other E: Milliken Lake

240 Lorenzo Road
TStop W: **Citgo**[*]
FStop E: **Phillips 66**[*]
Food W: **Citgo, River Restaurant (Citgo)**
Lodg W: Motel 55
ATM W: **Citgo**
Parks E: **Lorenzo State Park**

238 IL 129 South, Braidwood (Reaccess Northbound Only)
RVCamp E: **Fossil Rock Recreation Area (1.5 Miles)**

236 IL 113, Coal City, Kankakee
Gas W: Clark[*, LP, K]
Food E: The Good Table
AServ E: Chucks Bzaka Motors, Plymouth, Eagle, Dodge
RVCamp E: **Fossil Rock Recreation Area**
W: **Coal Valley RV Park**, **EZ Living RV Sales & Service**[LP]
ATM W: Clark

233 Reed Road
Gas E: Marathon[*]
Lodg E: **Sands Motel**
AServ E: Marathon

227 IL 53, Gardner
Gas W: Amoco[*]
TServ E: **Cooper Truck/Auto (Diesel)**
Parks W: **State Park (Wildlife, Fishing)**

220 IL 47, Morris, Dwight
FStop E: **Amoco**[*], **Clark**[*], **Fuel 24**[*, D]
Food E: **Amoco, Burger King (Amoco)**, Dwight's Restaurant (Chinese), **McDonald's**[PLAY], Pete's Pancake House, Subway
Lodg E: **Super 8, Traffic Inn**
ATM E: **Amoco, Clark**

217 IL 17, Streator, Kankakee, Dwight
TStop E: **Shell**[*]
Gas E: Marathon
Food E: Dairy Queen, Harvest Table Restaurant (Shell TS), **Shell**, Stark Family Restaurant
AServ E: Dempsey, Chyrsler, Plymouth, Dodge, Jeep, Eagle, Marathon, NAPA Auto Parts
TServ E: **Rt 66 Truck/Automotive Center, Shell**
ATM E: **Shell**
Other E: Doc's Discount Drug, Tru Value Hardware[LP]

209 Odell
Gas E: Amoco
AServ E: Amoco

201 IL 23, Pontiac, Streator
TServ W: **International, Gray's Garage (Wrecker)**
RVCamp E: **4H Camping (April - November)**

197 IL 116, Pontiac, Flanagan
FStop E: **Amoco**[*, D]
Gas W: Citgo[*]
Food E: Aldi Grocery Store, **Arby's**, **Burger King**[PLAY],

EXIT ILLINOIS

Busters Family Restaurant, Taco Bell, Wendy's
Lodg E: **Comfort Inn**, Holiday Inn Express, Super 8
AServ E: Auto Zone Auto Parts, Heller Lincoln, Mercury, Dodge, Lynn Chevrolet, Buick, Geo, **Wal-Mart**[RX]
Med E: **+ Hospital**
ATM E: Bank of Pontiac
W: Citgo
Other E: Police Department, Super Wash, **Wal-Mart**[RX]

(194) **Rest Area (RR, Phones, P; Southbound)**

(193) **Rest Area (RR, HF, Phones, Picnic, P; Northbound)**

187 U.S 24, Chenoa, El Paso
Gas E: Amoco[*, D], Casey's General Store, Citgo[*, CW], **Shell**[*]
Food E: **Chenoa Family Restaurant**, **McDonald's**[PLAY] **(Citgo)**
Lodg E: Super 8
AServ E: Shelby Chevrolet
ATM E: **Shell**
Other E: **Coin Car Wash**

178 Lexington
Gas E: Amoco
Food E: Amoco, PIzza Hut
ATM E: Amoco

171 Towanda

167 I-55 S Bus Veteran's Pkwy, Airport
Med E: **+ Hospital**

165 Bus U.S 51, Bloomington, Normal
Gas E: Amoco[*, CW], Shell[*]
Food E: Denny's
Lodg E: Best Western, **Holiday Inn**, Motel 6, Super 8
AServ E: Amoco
TServ W: **Central Illinois Truck Kenworth**, **Cummins Mid-States Power, Inc. (.6 Miles)**, **International Truck**, **Volvo**
RVCamp E: **Sales**
W: **Cummins Mid-States Power, Inc. (.6 Miles)**
Other E: Illinois Basketball Hall of Fame, Soooo C-Store

164 I-39, U.S 51, Rockford

163 Junction I-74 West, Champaign, Peoria

160AB U.S 150, Il 9, Pekin, Market St
TStop E: **76 Auto/Truck Plaza**[*, SCALES], **Pilot Travel Center**[SCALES, 24]
FStop E: **Speedway**[*, LP, K]
Gas E: Amoco[*], Freedom[*, D, LP], Phillips 66[*], Shell[*]
Food E: **76 Auto/Truck Plaza**, Arby's, Burger King, Carl Jr's Hamburgers[PLAY], **Cracker Barrel**, India Garden Cuisine of India, KFC, **McDonald's**[PLAY], **Pilot Travel Center**, Subway, Taco Bell, Yen Ching (Chinese)
W: Country Inn & Suites by Carlson, Country Kitchen (Country Inn & Suites), Steak 'N Shake
Lodg E: **Best Inns of America**, Comfort Inn, Days Inn, EconoLodge, Quality Inn & Suites
W: Country Inn & Suites by Carlson
AServ E: NAPA, Shell
W: Blain's Farm & Fleet With Auto Service
TWash E: **Blue Beacon**, **Touchless Auto Car Wash**[CW]
ATM E: **76 Auto/Truck Plaza**, Bank One, First America, Phillips 66, Shell, **Speedway**
W: First of America
Other E: Aldi Supermarket
W: Bloomington/Normal Factory Outlet Stores

157B Bus I-55, U.S 51, Veteran's Pkwy, Airport
Gas E: Shell[*, LP]
Food E: Knight's Inn
Lodg E: Knight's Inn, Parkway Inn
Med E: **+ Hospital**

Bold red print shows RV & Bus parking available or nearby

EXIT	ILLINOIS
Other	**E:** Miller Park Zoo/Golf Course
157A	Jct I-74 E, U.S 51, Indianapolis, Decatur, West- Chicago, Peoria
154	Shirley
(149)	**Rest Area (RR, Phones, Picnic, Vending, P)**
145	US 36 McLean, Heyworth
TStop	**W: AmBest[*, SCALES] (Phillips 66, Mobil)**
Gas	**W:** Citgo[*, LP]
Food	**W: AmBest (Phillips 66, Mobil)**, Citgo, McDonald's (Citgo)
Lodg	**W:** Super 8
TServ	**W: AmBest[SCALES] (Phillips 66, Mobil)**
RVCamp	**E: Quality RV Supercenter**
ATM	**W:** Citgo
140	Atlanta, Lawndale
FStop	**W: Phillips 66[D]**
Food	**W: Country Aire Restaurant**
Lodg	**W: I-55 Motel**
AServ	**W:** NAPA Auto Parts
RVCamp	**E: Campground (May-October)**
133	Lincoln, I-55 Bus, Landale
RVCamp	**E: Camping**
Med	**E: + Hospital**
127	Junction I-155 , Peoria, Hartsburg
126	IL 10, IL 121, Lincoln, Mason City
FStop	**E: Phillips 66[*, SCALES]**
Food	**E:** A & W Drive-In, Bonanza Steakhouse, Burger King, Long John Silver, Maverick Steakhouse, **McDonald's[PLAY]**, **Phillips 66**, Steak & Shake, Taco Bell, The Tropics, Wendy's
Lodg	**E:** Comfort Inn, Crossroads Motel, Holiday Inn Express, Red Wood Motel, Super 8, The Lincoln Country Inn
AServ	**E:** Auto Zone Auto Parts, Pennzoil Oil Change, **Wal-Mart Supercenter[RX]**
Med	**E: + Hospital**
ATM	**E:** Illini Bank
Other	**E:** Aldi, Animal Nutrition Warehouse, Camping, **Eagle Country Supermarket**, Logan Cty Fairground, Postville Courthouse (State Historic Site), **Wal-Mart Supercenter[RX]**
123	Lincoln, Bus I-55, Logan Cty Fairground
Med	**E: + Hospital**
119	Broadwell
RVCamp	**E: Camping**
115	Elkhart
Gas	**W:** Shell[*]
AServ	**W:** Shell
109	Williamsville, New Salem St
Gas	**E:** Shell[*]
AServ	**E:** Shell
Other	**E:** IGA
(107)	**Weigh Station (Southbound)**
105	I-55 Bus., Sherman (Reaccess Southbound Only)
Gas	**W:** Amoco, Shell[*]
Food	**W:** Antonio's Pizza, Cancun Mexican, Sam's Too Italian, Subway
AServ	**W:** Amoco
RVCamp	**W: Camping (3 Miles)**
ATM	**W:** Williamsville State Bank
Other	**W:** Car Wash
(104)	**Rest Area (RR, HF, Phones, Picnic, P; Southbound)**
(102)	**Rest Area (RR, HF, Phones, Picnic, P; Northbound)**

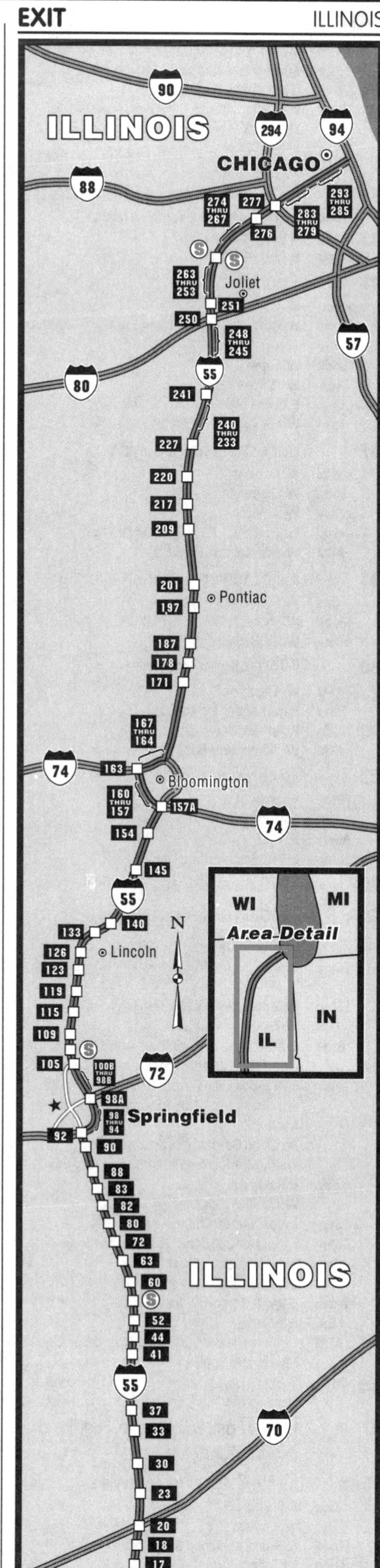

EXIT	ILLINOIS
100B	Sangamon Ave., Clinton, Capitol Airport, Springfield
Gas	**W:** Shell[*, D, LP, CW], Speedway[*, D, LP]
Food	**E:** Citgo
	W: Arby's, Burger King, Hardee's, Parkway Cafe
Lodg	**W:** Ramada Limited
TServ	**E: Kenworth[SCALES]**
Other	**W: Ferrellgas Liquid Propane**
100A	IL 54, Clinton, Junction Sangamon Avenue
TStop	**E: Citgo[*, D]**
Gas	**W:** Amoco[*, CW], Shell[*, D, CW, 24], Speedway[*, D]
Food	**E: Citgo**
	W: Arby's, Burger King, **Coffee Cup Cafe**, Juke Box Junction, Parkway Cafe
Lodg	**W:** Northfield Inn & Suites, Ramada
AServ	**W: Collision Craft**, Jim's Auto Service
TServ	**E: American Truck Lube, Citgo, RTR (Ryder Truck), Volvo, Kenworth**
	W: Collision Craft, Mid-Illinois, OTR Truck Collision Center
TWash	**W: OTR Truck Collision Center**
RVCamp	**W: Camping (2 Miles)**
ATM	**E: Citgo**
	W: Speedway
Other	**E:** Camp Butler National Cemetery
	W: Fun Park With Golf (Putt-Putt), King Pen Lane
98B	IL 97 West, Clear Lake Avenue
98A	Junction I-72 East, U.S 36 East, Decatur, Champaign, Urbana
96A	IL 29 South, Taylorville
Gas	**W:** 76[D], Citgo
Food	**W:** Burger King, Godfather's Pizza, Jolly Tamale, Nichole's Restaurant
Lodg	**W:** Red Roof Inn, Super 8
AServ	**W:** Auto Zone, Giuffre (Buick, Volvo, Isuzu), Green on Dirsken (Hunda, Audi), HP Mazda, Nissan (With Trucks), Rich Wagoner Dodge, S & K Pontiac, Springfield Mitsubishi
ATM	**W:** BankOne, Citgo, Cub Food, Shop "N" Save
Other	**W:** Capital Complex, Cub Food, Korean War Memorial, Landmark Ford, Lincoln Sites, Quality Car Wash, Shop "N" Save, Vietnam Veterans Memorial
96B	IL 29 North, S Grand Avenue, Springfield
94	Stevenson Road, Eastlake Dr, Springfield
Gas	**W:** Amoco[*, CW], Shell[*, LP, CW]
Food	**W:** Arby's, Bob Evan's Restaurant, Bombay Club, California Bar & Deli, DAYS INN Days Inn, Denny's, Gallina Pizzeria, Hide Out Steak & Bar, Long John Silver, Maverick's Family Steakhouse, McDonald's, Mountain Jack's Steakhouse, Red Lobster, Steak & Shake, Taco Bell, Taste of Thai (Chinese), Wendy's
Lodg	**W:** Comfort Suites Hotel, Crown Plaza, DAYS INN Days Inn, Drury Inn & Suites, Hampton Inn, Holiday Inn, Peartree Inn (Drury), Signature Inn, Stevenson Inn
AServ	**W:** Amoco, Friendly's Chevrolet
RVCamp	**W: Mr Lincoln's RV Parts & Accessories, Mr. Lincoln's Campground (1 Mile)**
ATM	**W:** Amoco, First National Bank, Shell
Other	**W:** CVS Drugstore, Capital City Shopping Ctr, Center City Theaters
92AB	U.S 36 West, I-55 Business, 6th St., Jacksonville, Junction (Left Exit Northbound, Reaccess Northbound Only, Difficult Reaccess)
Food	**W:** Heritage House Smorgasbord, Illini Inn,

EXIT ILLINOIS

Legends (Ramada), McDonald's, Ramada, Reflections (Illini Inn), **Southern View Motel**
Lodg **W:** Illini Inn, Ramada, **Southern View Motel**, Super 8
AServ **W:** 66 Fast Lube, Auto Glass
RVCamp **W: Mr. Lincoln's Campground**
Med **W: ✚ Hospital**
Other **W:** Car Wash

90 Toronto Road, Springfield
Gas **E:** Amoco(*), Shell(*, LP)
Food **E:** Antonio's Pizza, Burger King, **Cracker Barrel**, **Hardee's**, Hen House Restaurant (Motel 6), McDonald's, Muchachos Mexican, Subway
Lodg **E:** Budgetel Inn, **Motel 6**, Ramada
AServ **E:** Amoco
Med **E: ✚ Doctor's Hospital**
ATM **E:** First Bank of America, Prairie State Bank, Shell
Other **E:** Car Wash

88 Eastlake Dr., Chatham
RVCamp **E: KOA Campgrounds**
W: Holiday Trav-L-Park(LP) (2 Miles)
Other **E: Lincoln Memorial Garden & Nature Center**, **State Police**, **State Police Training Academy**

83 Glenarm

82 IL 104, Pawnee, Auburn
FStop **W: Mobil(*, D)**
Food **W:** Barb's Deli, **Mobil**
Lodg **W:** Punkins Mansion
TServ **W: Mobil**
ATM **W: Mobil**
Parks **E: Csangchris State Park**

80 Divernon
Gas **W:** Citgo(*, LP), Phillips 66(*, D, LP)
Food **W:** Phillips 66
TWash **W: Truck Wash**
ATM **W:** Citgo
Other **W:** Car Wash

72 Farmersville, Girard
FStop **W: Mobil(*, D, CW)**
Gas **W:** Shell(*)
Food **W: Mobil**, Shell, **Subway (Mobil)**, TCBY
Lodg **W: Art's Motel**
TServ **E: Trucking Tarps**, **Trucks Auto & Repair**
ATM **W: Mobil**
Other **W:** Truck & Car Wash (Mobil)

(65) **Rest Area (RR, Phones, Picnic, Vending, Pet Walk, P)**

63 IL 48, IL 127, Raymond, Waggoner, Morrisonville, Taylorville

60 IL 108, Carlinville
FStop **W: Shell(*)**
Food **W:** Captain's Table (Holiday Inn), **Holiday Inn**, **Moonlight Cafe (Moonlight Motel)**, **Shell**
Lodg **W: Holiday Inn**, **Moonlight Motel (Moonlight Cafe)**
RVCamp **E: Kamper Kompanion Campground (.5 Miles)**
Other **W:** Moonlight Antiques

(56) **Weigh Station (Northbound)**

52 IL 16, Gillespie, Litchfield, Hillsboro, Mattoon
Gas **E:** Amoco(*, CW), Casey's General Store, Coastal(*)
Food **E:** Amoco, Ariston, Hardee's, Jubelt's Bakery, **Long John Silver (Bus Parking Available)**, Maverick Steakhouse, McDonald's(PLAY), Pizza Hut, **Ponderosa**, Taco Bell, Wendy's
Lodg **E: Best Western**, **Super 8**
AServ **E:** McKay Auto Parts, Neal Tire & Battery, Snappy Lube
TServ **E: Goodyear Tire & Auto**
RVCamp **E: Rain Maker Campground (8.5 Miles)**
Med **E: ✚ Hospital**

EXIT ILLINOIS

ATM **E:** Bank & Trust Company, First National Bank, **Kroger Supermarket(LP)**, McDonald's, NationsBank
Other **E:** Cinema, **Kroger Supermarket**, Medicine Shoppe, Skyview Drive In, Sportsman's Park, **Wal-Mart(RX)**
W: State Police

44 IL 138, Benld, Mount Olive, White City
Food **E: CrossRoads Restaurant**, Scheepps
Lodg **E: Budget 10 Motel**
RVCamp **E: Camping**

41 Staunton
FStop **W: Phillips 66(*, D, PLAY)**
Food **W: Dairy Queen(PLAY)**, **Diamond's Cafe (Phillips 66)**, **Phillips 66(PLAY)**
Lodg **W:** Super 8
TServ **W: Phillips 66**
RVCamp **E: Camping**
ATM **W: Phillips 66**

37 Livingston, New Douglas
Gas **W:** Amoco(*, D)
Lodg **W:** Country Inn
AServ **W:** Amoco
RVCamp **E: Shady Oak Campground (4 Miles)**
ATM **W:** First National Bank

33 IL 4, Staunton, Lebanon, Worden
Gas **W:** Schlechte's
Food **W:** Shooter's Grill
AServ **W:** Schlechte's

30 IL 140, Alton, Greenville
Gas **W:** Citgo, Shell(*)
Food **E:** Inn Keeper, Inn Keeper
Lodg **E:** Inn Keeper
ATM **W:** Hamel State Bank, Shell

23 IL 143, Edwardsville, Marine
FStop **E: Citgo(*, D)**
Gas **E:** Mobil(*)
AServ **E:** Mobil
RVCamp **E: Red Barn Rendezvous**

20B I-270 West, Kansas City

20A Junction I-70, Indianapolis

18 IL 162, Troy
TStop **E: Amoco Auto/Truck Stop(*, SCALES, 24)**, **Pilot/Shell(SCALES)**
FStop **W: Andrea's Cafe (Scottish Inn)**
Gas **W:** Mobil(*, D)
Food **E: Amoco Auto/Truck Stop**, Arby's (Pilot), Burger King, Dairy Queen, Hardee's, Imo's Pizza, Jack-In-The-Box, Little Caesars Pizza, **McDonald's**, **Pilot/Shell**, Pizza Hut, Subway, TJ Cinnamon's (Pilot)
W: China Garden, **Cracker Barrel**, Randy's Restaurant, **Scottish Inns**, Taco Bell
Lodg **E: Relax Inn**
W: Scottish Inns, **Super 8**
AServ **E:** Valvoline Oil Change
TServ **E: Arrow Truck Sales**, **Speedco Truck Lube(24)**, **XV111 Wheeler's Truck Wash**
W: Freightliner Dealer
TWash **E: XV111 Wheeler's Truck Wash**
Med **E: ✚ Hospital**
ATM **E: Amoco Auto/Truck Stop**, Magna Bank, Merchantile Bank
Other **E:** Car Wash, **Super Valu Grocery(LP)**, Tru Value Hardware(LP)

17 U.S 40 East, Saint Jacob, Highland (Northbound)

15AB IL 159, Collinsville, Maryville
Gas **E:** Phillips 66(*, D)
W: Conoco(*)
Food **E:** Sharky's Seafood & Crabhouse
Lodg **W:** EconoLodge

EXIT ILLINOIS/MISSOURI

AServ **W:** Capital X 2 Collision, Conoco
Other **E:** AmeriGas(LP)

(14) **Weigh Station (Southbound)**

11 IL 157, Collinsville, Edwardsville
Gas **E:** Amoco(*) (Wrecker Service), Shell(*, CW)
W: Moto Mart(*, D)
Food **E:** China Palace, Denny's (Pear Tree Inn), Hardee's(PLAY), Long John Silver, McDonald's(PLAY), Pizza Hut, The Pub Lounge & Grill, TraveLodge, Waffle House, Wendy's
W: Applebee's, Arby's, Bob Evan's Restaurant, Boston Market Restaurant, Burger King, Cancun Mexican, Dairy Queen(PLAY), **Holiday Inn**, Pete's Ice Cream & Fudge Factory, Ponderosa, Porter's (Holiday Inn), SHONEY'S, Shoney's, Steak & Shake, White Castle Restaurant
Lodg **E: Best Western**, DAYS INN Days Inn, Howard Johnson, Motel 6, Pear Tree Inn, TraveLodge
W: Comfort Inn, Drury Inn, Fairfield Inn, Hampton Inn, **Holiday Inn**, Ramada Limited, Super 8
AServ **E:** Amoco (Wrecker Service), Midas Muffler & Brake
W: Dave Kroft Chrysler, Dodge, Jeep Eagle, GMC, Pontiac
TServ **E: Gateway Industrial**
ATM **W:** Magna Bank
Other **E:** Animal Emergency Care, Asiana Cafe (TraveLodge), Car Wash, Carri-lite Sales & Service, Cinema
W: 4 Seasons Auto Wash, **Convention Center**, Fun Factory Putt Putt, **State Police**

10 Junction I-255, I-270, Memphis

9 Black Lane (Northbound)

6 IL 111, Great River Road, Wood River, Washington, Park
Gas **E:** Clark(*, D)
Food **E:** Gateway Pit Stop & Motel
Lodg **E:** Gateway Pit Stop & Motel, Rainbo Court Motel
RVCamp **E: Safari RV Park**
Other **E: Cahokia Mounds Historic Sight**, **Foodland Supermarket(RX)**
W: Horseshoe Lake State Park

4B IL 203, Fairmont City

4A IL 203, Granite City
TStop **W: America's Best Truck Stop(*, SCALES) (Texaco)**
Food **W: America's Best Truck Stop (Texaco)**, Big Duga's Restaurant(SCALES) (America's Best Truck Stop), Burger King, Pizza Hut (America's Best Truck Stop), Taco Bell (America's Best Truck Stop)
AServ **W: America's Best Truck Stop (Texaco)**
TServ **W: America's Best Truck Stop(SCALES) (Texaco)**
Other **W: Gateway International Raceway**, **Volvo Dealer**

3 Exchange Ave (Southbound, Reaccess Northbound Only)

2 Junction I-64, IL 3, St Clair Avenue, Louisville

2A ML King Bridge, Downtown St Louis (Southbound, Reaccess Northbound Only)

2B 3rd Street (Southbound, Reaccess Northbound Only)

1 IL 3, Sauget (Southbound, Reaccess Northbound Only)

↑ILLINOIS

↓MISSOURI

EXIT MISSOURI

209B Jct I-70 West

209A North/East I-64, I-55, I-70, U.S. 40 to Illinois

208 7th St (Reaccess Westbound Only, Difficult Reaccess)
- **Food** E: Burger King, Dairy Queen, McDonald's Express, St Louis Bread
- **TServ** E: **Broadway Ford**[SCALES]
- **Other** E: **Farmer's Market**

207B West I-44, Lafayette St (Reaccess Southbound Only, Difficult Reaccess, Reaccess Tucker St)

207A Gravois Ave, 12th St (Reaccess Southbound Only, Difficult Reaccess, 207A Is The Same As 290C On I-44)
- **Gas** E: Citgo[*, D]
- **Food** E: A-1 Wok Restaurant, Jack-In-The-Box

290C 12th St, Gravois Ave
- **Gas** E: Citgo[*, D]
- **Food** E: A-1 Wok Restaurant, Jack-In-The-Box[24]

206C Arsenal St
- **Gas** W: Shell[*]
- **Food** W: Gus' Pretzel Shop
- **Other** W: **Metro. Police Station (Shell)**

206B Broadway 3200 So. (Northbound)
- **Gas** E: Citgo[*, LP, K]
- **AServ** E: Broadway Auto Radiator, Broner Generator Service

206A Potomac St (Northbound, Reaccess Southbound Only, Difficult Reaccess)

205 Gasconade St (Southbound, Reaccess Northbound Only)
- **Med** W: **✚ Alexian Bros. Hospital**

204 Broadway S
- **Gas** E: Mobil[*]
  W: Clark[*, LP], Sinclair[*]
- **Food** W: Hardee's, McDonald's
- **AServ** E: Mobil
- **Other** W: WalGreens Pharmacy[RX]

203 N-Virginia St, S-Bates St (Difficult Reaccess)
- **Gas** W: Standard Amoco
- **ATM** W: 7-11 Convenience Store
- **Other** W: 7-11 Convenience Store

202C Loughborough Avenue (Reaccess Southbound Only, Difficult Reaccess)
- **Other** W: **Schnucks 24 hr Supercenter**

202B Germania Avenue (Reaccess Northbound Only)

202A Carondelet Blvd (Northbound, Reaccess Southbound Only)

201B Weber Road (Southbound, Reaccess Northbound Only)

201A Bayless Avenue
- **Gas** E: Amoco[*, 24], Crystal Clean Car Wash & Auto Care[CW]
  W: Amoco[24] (Wrecker), Citgo[*] (7-11 Convenience Store), Shell[24]
- **Food** E: McDonald's, St Andrew's Restaurant
  W: China Wok, Jack-In-The-Box, Subway, Taco Bell
- **AServ** E: Crystal Clean Car Wash & Auto Care
  W: A to Z Auto Parts, Amoco[24] (Wrecker), BF Goodrich
- **ATM** W: Citgo (7-11 Convenience Store), NationsBank
- **Other** E: **Bayless Hardware**[LP]

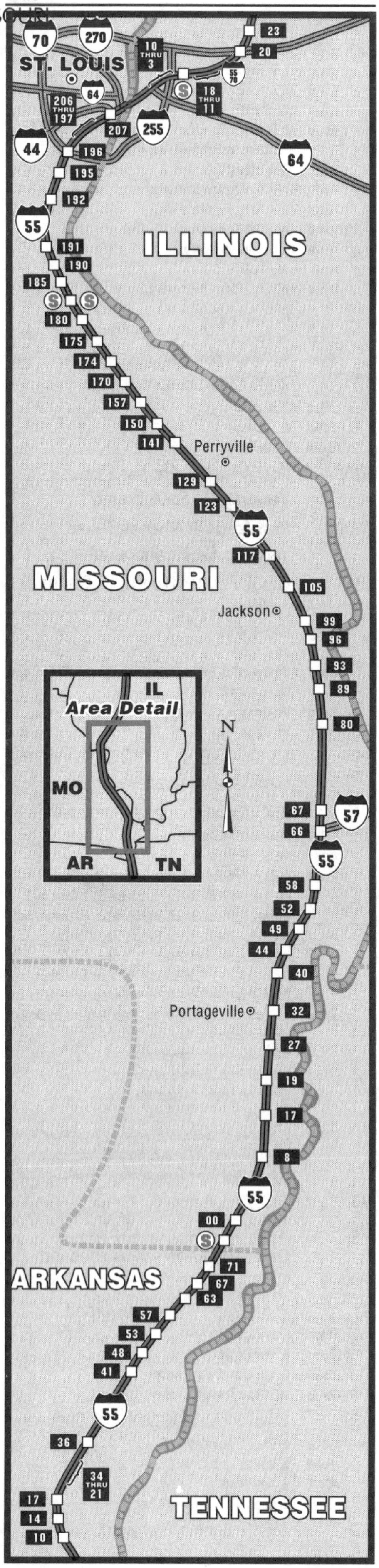

EXIT MISSOURI

W: **Eberhart Pharmacy, Maytag Laundry (Coin Laundry), Sav-A-Lot Grocery**

200 Union Road (Southbound, Reaccess Northbound Only)

199 Reavis, Barracks Road
- **Gas** E: Shell[*]
- **Food** E: Papa's Steakhouse
- **AServ** E: Reavis Auto Repair, Shell
- **ATM** E: Mercantile Bank
- **Other** E: **V & E Pet Grooming & Supplies**

197 U.S 61, U.S 50, U.S 67, Lindbergh Blvd
- **Gas** E: Amoco[*], Phillips 66[*, CW]
- **Food** E: Holiday Inn, Hot Shots Sports Bar & Grill, KFC, Shoney's, Tucker's Place
- **Lodg** E: Holiday Inn

196AB 196A - I-255E, Chicago, US 61, 67, 190B - I-270W, Kansas

195 Butler Hill Road
- **Gas** E: Citgo[*]
  W: Sinclair[*, LP]
- **Food** W: Burger King, Frailey's Southtown Grill, Hardee's, Taco Bell, Waffle House
- **Lodg** E: Holiday Inn
- **AServ** W: 55 Tires & Service
- **ATM** E: Citgo
  W: Magna Bank, **Schnucks Grocery Store**
- **Other** W: **Schnucks Grocery Store**

193 Meramec Bottom Road
- **Gas** E: QuikTrip[*]
- **Food** E: **Cracker Barrel**
- **Lodg** E: Best Western
- **AServ** E: Extra Mile Service
- **ATM** E: Southern Commercial Bank

191 MO 141, Arnold Fenton
- **Gas** E: Citgo[*], QuikTrip[*], Shell[*, 24]
  W: Phillips 66[*, D]
- **Food** E: Applebee's, Cecil Whittaker's Pizzeria, Denny's (Drury Inn), Hardee's, McDonald's[PLAY], SHONEY'S, Shoney's, Steak 'N Shake
  W: Pasta House
- **Lodg** E: Drury Inn
- **AServ** W: Best Auto
- **ATM** E: Mercantile Bank
- **Other** E: **K-Mart, National Grocery**[24, RX], **Schnucks Supercenter**[24, RX]

190 Richardson Road
- **Gas** E: Citgo[*, D, CW]
  W: Shell[*, D, K, CW]
- **Food** E: Domino's Pizza, Ponderosa, Sonic, White Castle Restaurant
  W: Blimpie Subs & Salads (Shell), McDonald's[PLAY], Pizza Plus
- **AServ** E: Reuther Ford & Mazda
- **ATM** E: Heartland Bank, Lemay Bank
  W: Shell
- **Other** E: Car Wash, **Sav-A-Lot Grocery**

186 Imperial, Kimmswick
- **Gas** E: Shell[*, CW]
- **AServ** E: Lambert's Custom Muffler
- **ATM** E: Southern Commercial Bank
- **Other** W: **Mastadon Historic Site**

185 Barnhart, Antonia, RT. M
- **Gas** W: Citgo[*, LP]
- **Food** E: Tressel Cafe
- **RVCamp** W: **KOA Kampground (2.5 Miles)**
- **ATM** W: Citgo
- **Other** W: **U.S. Post Office**

(184) **Weigh Station (Southbound)**

(184) **Weigh Station (Northbound)**

Bold red print shows RV & Bus parking available or nearby

EXIT — MISSOURI

180 Rt Z, Hillsboro, Pevely
- TStop W: **McStop[*, SCALES] (Phillips 66)**
- FStop W: **Mr Fuel[*]**
- Gas E: Coastal[*, 24], Sinclair[*, D]
- Food E: Bobby Tom's BBQ, **Burger King**, Domino's Pizza, Subway, The Kitchen[24]
  W: **McDonald's (McStop)**
- Lodg W: Gateway Inn
- AServ E: Pevely Plaza Auto Parts
- RVCamp W: **KOA Campgrounds (2.5 Miles)**
- ATM E: Coastal
- Other E: Maytag Coin Laundry, **Sav A Lot Food Stores**

178 Business Loop I-55, Herculaneum
- TStop E: **QT[*, SCALES]**
- Food E: **Wendy's (Truck Stop)**
- AServ W: Sapaugh Chev, Olds, Cad, Buick, Pont, GMC Trucks
- Other W: **Animal Clinic**

175 Festus, Crystal City, Route A
- FStop E: **Phillips 66[*]**
  W: **Coastal[*]**
- Gas W: Citgo[*, D] (7-11 Convenience Store)
- Food E: Bob Evan's Restaurant, Captain D's Seafood, Dohack's Family Restaurant, Fazoli's Italian Food, Imo's Pizza, McDonald's[PLAY], **Steak 'N Shake**, Taco Bell, White Castle Restaurant
  W: **Hardee's, Hot Stuff Pizza (Coastal)**, Waffle House
- Lodg E: **Drury Inn**, Holiday Inn
  W: **Budgetel Inn**
- AServ E: Parts America
- ATM E: Commerce Bank
- Other E: **Schnucks Grocery Store[LP]**

174B US 67 South, Park Hills
- AServ W: Pippin Towing, Auto & Truck Repair[24]
- Med E: **+ Hospital**

174A U.S 67 North, U.S 61 Crystal City, Festus
- Med E: **+ Hospital**

170 U.S 61
- FStop W: **Citgo[*, K]**
- Food W: Laddie Boys Restaurant

162 Rt DD, Rt 00
- Food W: The Corner Grill

(160) **Rest Area (RR, Phones, Picnic, P; Southbound)**

(160) **Rest Area (RR, Phones, Picnic, P; Northbound)**

157 Rt Y, Bloomsdale
- FStop W: **Texaco[*]**
- Gas W: Phillip 66[*]
- AServ E: Bloomsdale Tire

154 Rt 0, St Genevieve, Rocky Ridge

150 MO 32, Rt B, Rt A, Ste. Genevieve, Farmington
- Gas E: Amoco[*, 24]
- Food E: **Dairy Queen[PLAY]**
- Med E: **+ Hospital**
- ATM E: Amoco
- Parks W: **Hawn State Park (11 Miles)**

143 Rt M, Rt N, Ozora
- FStop W: **J & N Truck Stop[*]**
- Gas W: Citgo[*]
- Food W: Subway (Citgo)
- Lodg W: **Family Budget Inn (J & N Truck Stop), J & N Truck Stop**
- TServ W: **J & N Truck Stop**
- Other W: Coin Laundromat

141 Rt Z, St Mary

135 Rt M, Brewer

EXIT — MISSOURI

- Other E: Empire Gas[LP]

129 MO 51, Perryville
- FStop E: **Phillip 66[*]**
- Gas E: Amoco[*]
  W: Shell[*, D]
- Food E: Burger King, KFC, **McDonald's[PLAY]**, Taco Bell
  W: **Colonial Inn Best Western**, Dairy Queen[PLAY], Kelly's (Best Western)
- Lodg W: **Colonial Inn Best Western**, Comfort Inn
- AServ E: Amoco, Ford Dealer
- RVCamp W: **KOA Kampground (1 Mile)**
- ATM E: Union Planters Bank
  W: Shell
- Other W: **Wal-Mart[24] (Grocery Store)**

123 Rt B, Biehle
- FStop W: **Phillips 66[*]**
- Food W: **Country Kettle (Phillips 66), Phillips 66**

117 Rt KK, Old Appleton
- Gas E: Sewing's
- Food E: Sewing's
- AServ E: Sewing's

(110) **Rest Area (RR, Phones, Picnic, Vending, P; Southbound)**

(110) **Rest Area (RR, Phones, Picnic, Vending, P; Northbound)**

105 U.S 61, Business Loop I-55, Fruitland, Jackson
- FStop E: **Phillips 66[*]**
  W: **Citgo[*]**
- Food W: **Bavarian Halle (Drury Inn), Bert's B-B-Q, Dairy Queen**, Pizza Haus
- Lodg W: **Drury Inn & Suites**
- ATM W: **Citgo**

99 US 61, I-55 Bus. 55, MO 34, Cape Girardeau, Jackson

96 Rt K, Cape Girardeau, Gordonville
- Gas E: Amoco[*], Citgo[*, D]
  W: Shell[*, 24]
- Food E: Blimpie Subs & Salads, Burger King, Cedar Street Restaurant & Bar (Drury Lodge), **Cracker Barrel**, El Chico, Great Wall Chinese, Pizza Inn, Red Lobster, Ruby Tuesday, Ryan's Steakhouse, Shoney's, Steak 'N Shake, Taco Bell
  W: Hardee's[PLAY], Heavenly Ham, **McDonald's (Wal-Mart)**, McDonald's[PLAY], Outback Steakhouse
- Lodg E: Drury Lodge, Holiday Inn, Pear Tree Inn by Drury, Victorian Inn
  W: Drury Suites, Hampton Inn
- Med E: **+ St Francis Medical Center**
- ATM E: Capaha Bank, Mercantile Bank
  W: Shell
- Other E: **Barnes & Noble**, Pier 1 Imports, **West Park Mall**
  W: Cape West 14 Cinema, **Sam's Club**, Staple's, **Target, Wal-Mart Supercenter[24, RX] (McDonald's)**

95 MO. 74 E., IL Rt. 146

93 MO74, Dutchtown, U.S 61, Cape Girardeau (Reaccess Southbound Only)

91 Rt AB, Cape Girardeau, Airport
- TStop E: **Phillips 66[*, SCALES]**
- Food E: **Phillips 66**
- TServ E: **Midwest Diesel, Raben**
- RVCamp W: **Cape Town RV Sales**

89 US 61, Rt. M, Rt. K, Scott City, Chaffee
- Gas E: Citgo[*], Texaco[*]
- Food E: Burger King, Dairy Queen
- AServ E: Auto Parts
- ATM E: Citgo, Union Planter's Bank

80 MO 77, Benton, Diehlstadt

EXIT — MISSOURI

67 U.S 62, Sikeston, Bertrand
- FStop E: **Citgo[*], Phillips 66[*]**
- Gas W: Amoco, Citgo[*]
- Food E: JD's Steakhouse & Saloon
  W: **Hardee's, Lambert's**, Queen House Chinese, Ramada, SHONEY'S, Shoney's
- Lodg E: Best Western, Red Carpet Inn
  W: Country Hearth Inn, Drury Inn, Holiday Inn Express, Ramada, **Super 8**
- AServ W: Amoco
- TServ E: **Volvo Dealer**
  W: **Chevrolet Dealer**
- RVCamp E: **Hinton Park Camping (2 blocks), Town & Country RV Park (1.5 Miles)**
- ATM E: **Phillips 66**
  W: **Piggly Wiggly Supermarket**
- Other W: **Miner Fire Station, Piggly Wiggly Supermarket**, S & S Propane[LP], **Sikeston Factory Outlet Stores**

66B I-57S, U.S 60W, Poplar Bluff
- TServ W: **Duckett Truck Center (Freightliner Services)**

66A Junction I-57 North, East U.S 60, Chicago

58 MO 80, Matthews, East Prairie, Toll Ferry to Kentucky
- TStop E: **T/A TravelCenters of America[SCALES]**
  W: **Flying J Travel Plaza[*, LP, RV DUMP, SCALES]**
- Food E: **Country Pride (TA TS), Taco Bell (TA TS)**
  W: **Flying J Travel Plaza**

52 Rt P, Kewanee
- FStop E: **Amoco[*]**
  W: **Citgo[*]**

49 U.S 61, U.S 62, Business Loop I-55, New Madrid
- FStop E: **BP[*]**
- Food E: **BP**

44 U.S 61, U.S 62, New Madrid, Howardville

(42) **Rest Area (RR, Phones, Picnic, Vending, P; Southbound)**

(42) **Rest Area (RR, Phones, Picnic, Vending, P; Northbound)**

40 Rt EE, Marston, St Jude Road
- TStop E: **Pilot Travel Center[*, SCALES]**
- FStop W: **Amoco[*], Phillips 66[*]**
- Food E: **Arby's (Pilot TS)**
  W: Cottonboll Inn, Granny's Kitchen, **Jerry's Cafe (Amoco)**, Smash Hit Subs (Phillips 66)
- Lodg E: **Super 8**
  W: Budget Inn
- AServ W: Jerry's Diesel & Auto Repair

32 MO 162, Portageville
- FStop W: **Amoco[*, 24], McDonald's**
- Gas W: Kaycee's[*]
- Food W: Gary's Bar-B-Q

27 Rt K, Rt. A, Rt BB, Wardell
- RVCamp E: **KOA Kampground (3 Miles)**

19 U.S 412, MO 84, Hayti, Caruthersville
- FStop E: **Conoco[*], Phillips 66[*]**
  W: **Total[*, SCALES]**
- Gas E: Exxon[*]
  W: Amoco[*, 24], Conoco[*], Gas[*]
- Food E: **Blimpie Subs & Salads (Conoco), Hardee's, McDonald's**, Pizza Hut
  W: Apple Barrel Restaurant[24] (Pear Tree Inn), Dairy Queen, **Pear Tree Inn by Drury**, Subway (Amoco)
- Lodg E: **Comfort Inn**, Holiday Inn Express
  W: **Pear Tree Inn by Drury**
- RVCamp W: **KOA Kampground (6 Miles)**
- Med W: **+ Hospital**

Bold red print shows RV & Bus parking available or nearby

EXIT	MISSOURI/ARKANSAS
ATM	E: Conoco, Exxon, Phillips 66
17A	Junction I-155, U.S 412, Dyersburg, TN
14	Rt J, Rt H, Rt U, Caruthersville, Braggadocio
(10)	Weigh Station
8	MO 164, U.S 61, Steele
Gas	E: Duckie's Phillips 66(*)
ATM	E: Duckie's Phillips 66
4	Rt E, Cooter, Holland
(3)	Rest Area (RR, Phones, Picnic, Vending, P)
1	U.S 61, Rt O, Holland
FStop	E: Raceway(*, D, LP)
Gas	W: Coastal(*)

↑MISSOURI

↓ARKANSAS

EXIT	ARKANSAS
(71)	Weigh Station (Southbound)
71	AR 150
Gas	W: Citgo(*)
(68)	Welcome Center, Rest Area (RR, Phones, Picnic, Vending, P; Southbound)
67	AR 18, Armorel/Hickman Rd., Blytheville
FStop	E: Mapco Express(*) W: Pacific Pride with Exxon Gas(*, D)
Gas	W: Amoco(*), Texaco(*)
Food	E: Ginny's Kitchen (Mapco Express), Harry's Steaks, Seafoods, Ruben's Delli (Mapco Express) W: Big Daddy's Bar and Grill (Holiday Inn), Blimpie's (Amoco), Bonanza, El Alcapulco (Comfort Inn), Great Wall Chinese Restaurant (Hampton Inn), Grecian Steak House, Hardee's, KFC, Mazzio's Pizza, McDonald's(PLAY), Olympia, Perkin's Family Restaurant, Piccadilly Circus Pizza (Pacific Pride), Pizza Inn, SHONEY'S Shoney's, Sonic Drive In, Subway, TCBY, Taco Bell, Wendy's
Lodg	E: DAYS INN Days Inn W: Comfort Inn, Drury Inn, Hampton Inn, Holiday Inn
TServ	E: Mid-America International Trucks
Med	W: + Hospital
ATM	E: Mapco Express W: Amoco, Farmer's Bank & Trust, First National Bank, Pacific Pride with Exxon Gas
Other	W: Malco Cinema, Penny Pincher Coin Operated Car Wash, Wal-Mart(RX)
63	U.S 61, Blytheville
TStop	W: Citgo Travel Center(*, RV DUMP, SCALES) (CB Repair)
FStop	E: Total(*)
Gas	W: Dodge's Store(*, K), Shell(*, CW), Texaco(*, D, LP, K)
Food	W: Baskin Robbins (Citgo Tstop), Dodge's Store, Knights of the Road (Citgo Tstop), Krystal's (Shell), Popeye's Chicken, Tasty Freeze (Shell)
Lodg	W: Best Western, Delta K Motel
AServ	W: Texaco
TServ	W: Citgo Travel Center(SCALES) (CB Repair)
RVCamp	W: Knights of the Road RV Park (Service Road)
Med	W: + Hospital
ATM	W: Shell
57	AR 148, Burdette
53	AR 158, Luxora, Victoria
48	AR 140, Osceola
FStop	E: Texaco(*)
Gas	E: Amoco(*)
Lodg	E: Best Western, Holiday Inn Express
AServ	E: Amoco
Med	E: + Hospital
(45)	Rest Area (RR, Picnic, P; Northbound)
44	AR 181, Wilson, Keiser
41	AR 14, Marie, Lepanto
36	AR 181, Bassett, Evadale
(35)	Rest Area (RR, Phones, Picnic, P; Southbound)
34	AR 118, Joiner, Tyronza
23AB	23A - AR 77 S, Turrell; 23B - US 63 N, Marked Tree, Jonesboro
Gas	W: Citgo(*)
Food	W: Baskin Robbins (Citgo), Hot Stuff Pizza (Citgo)
ATM	W: Citgo
21	AR 42
FStop	W: Fuelmart(*, LP, SCALES)
17	AR 50, Jericho
14	Crittendon Co. AR 4
FStop	E: Citgo(*, SCALES)
Gas	W: Citgo(*)
Food	E: Eddie Pepper's Great Mexican Food (Citgo), Hot Stuff Pizza (Citgo), Smashit Subs (Citgo)
RVCamp	W: Best Holiday Trav-L Park-Memphis(LP) (Service Road)
10	US 64W, Marion, Sunset, Wynne
FStop	E: Mapco Express(*) W: Total(*, D)
Gas	E: Avery's(*), BP(D), Citgo(*, LP, CW), Exxon(*, D) W: Odie's(*, LP), Shell(*, CW)
Food	E: Avery's, Baskin Robbins (Citgo), Big John's Restaurant, Exxon, Ford's Family Restaurant, Hardee's, Smash Subs (Citgo), Sonic Drive In
Lodg	E: Hallmarc Inn W: Best Western, Journey Inn
AServ	E: BP W: Allensworth Transmission Service, Keith's Auto Service
ATM	E: Citizen's Bank, Exxon, Fidelity National Bank, Union Planter's Bank
Parks	W: Parkin Archaeological State Park (23 Miles)
Other	E: Big A Auto Parts, Big Star, Marion Discount Pharmacy
(9)	Weigh Station
8	West I-40, Little Rock
7	AR 77, Missouri St.
Gas	W: Exxon(*, CW), Mapco(*, LP), Texaco, Total(*, LP)
Food	W: Baskin Robbins, Bonanza, Burger King, Domino's Pizza, Howard's Donuts, Krystal, McDonald's, Mrs Winner's Chicken, Pizza Inn, SHONEY'S Shoney's, Subway
Lodg	W: Ramada Inn
AServ	W: Don Gage's Auto, Goodyear Tire & Auto, Mr. Fast Lube, Texaco
ATM	W: Fidelity National Bank, Union Planter's Bank
Other	W: Holiday Plaza Lanes Bowling, Kroger Supermarket, WalGreens Pharmacy, Wonder Hostess Bakery Thrift Shop

Note: I-55 runs concurrent below with I-40. Numbering follows I-40.

EXIT	ARKANSAS/TENNESSEE
278	AR 191, 7th St
TStop	N: AmBest
FStop	N: Love's
Gas	S: Flashmart(*)
Food	N: Catfish Island, Cracker Barrel S: Blimpie Subs & Salads (Flashmart)
TWash	N: Blue Beacon
279A	Ingram Blvd
Gas	N: Citgo(*, CW), Shell(*)
Food	N: Earl's Hot Biscuits, Waffle House S: Grandy's
Lodg	N: Econolodge, Hampton Inn, Holiday Inn, Howard Johnson, Motel 6, Relax Inn S: Classic Inn, Comfort Inn, DAYS INN Days Inn
Other	S: Southland Greyhound Park
279B	I-40E, Memphis, Nashville, I-55S, Memphis, Jackson Miss
FStop	E: Citgo(*)
Gas	E: BP, Citgo(LP, CW), Shell(*)
Food	E: Delta Point, Earl's Restaurant, Eddie's Peppers Mexican Great Restaurant, Grendy's Restuarant, Smash Hit Subs (Citgo), Waffle House(LP, CW) I: Bakery (Citgo), Hot Stuff Pizza (Citgo)
Lodg	E: Classic Inn, Comfort Inn, DAYS INN Days Inn, Hampton Inn, Holiday Inn, Howard Johnson, Motel 6, Relax Inn

Note: I-55 runs concurrent above with I-40. Numbering follows I-40.

EXIT	ARKANSAS/TENNESSEE
4	Dr Martin Luther King Jr Drive, Southland Drive
TStop	E: Flying J Travel Plaza(*, LP, RV DUMP, SCALES), Mapco Express, Petro(*, SCALES) (Showers, Truck Security)
FStop	E: Fina(*), Pilot Travel Center(*, SCALES)
Gas	W: Citgo(*)
Food	E: Cookery (Flying J), Dairy Queen (Pilot), KFC, McDonald's(PLAY), Perkin's Family Restaurant (Mapco Express), Restaurant (Pilot), Subway (Pilot), Taco Bell W: Pancho's Mexican
Lodg	E: Best Western, Deluxe Inn, Express Inn, Super 8
AServ	W: Bridgestone Tire & Auto, Howard Ford Truck & Car Center
TServ	E: Goodyear, Petro(SCALES) (Showers, Truck Security), Speedco(LP, SCALES)
TWash	E: Petro (Showers, Truck Security), XVIII Wheeler's Truck Wash(24)
ATM	E: Flying J Travel Plaza
3B	US 70, Broadway Blvd (Northbound)
Lodg	E: Budget Inn
3A	AR 131, Mound City Rd (Northbound)
TServ	E: Prostop Truck & Trailer Repair
1	Bridgeport Road (Northbound)

↑ARKANSAS

↓TENNESSEE

EXIT	TENNESSEE
12C	Metal Museum Dr.
Food	W: River Bluff Inn
Lodg	W: DAYS INN Days Inn (see our ad this page), River Bluff Inn
RVCamp	W: Mississippi River RV Park(*)

1627
DAYS INN
$39.95
1-2 Persons
Restaurant on Premises • Continental Breakfast
Outdoor Pool • Exercise Room
Meeting/Banquet Facilities
Pets Allowed • Airport Shuttle
Handicap Accessible
Truck/Large Vehicle Parking
Coin Laundry • Exterior Corridors
Downtown Memphis 1 mile
TOUR BUSES WELCOME
901-948-9005 • 800-325-2525
TENNESSEE • I-55 • EXIT 12C

EXIT TENNESSEE

12B Riverside Drive
- **Gas** E: Texaco[*]
- **Food** W: Elvis Presley's Memphis Restaurant (see our ad this page)
- **AServ** E: Texaco
- **Other** E: National Civil Rights Museum

12A US 61, 64, 70, 79 E Crump Blvd
- **TServ** E: G & W Diesel Services Inc.
- **Other** E: Fast Check Food Store & Deli

11 McLemore Ave, Presidents Island

10 South Parkway, Memphis
- **Food** E: Morrison's Restaurant
- **TServ** W: Haygood Truck & Trailer Parts
- **Parks** W: Dr Martin Luther King Jr Riverside Park

9 Mallory Ave., Memphis
- **TServ** E: Fruehauf, Great Dane Trailors Sales & Service, Scully Parts & Service

8 Horn Lake Rd (Reaccess Southbound Only, Difficult Reaccess)

7 US 61S, Vicksburg
- **Gas** E: Amoco, Exxon[*]
- **Food** E: Family Dining, Interstate Bar-B-Q, Lot-A-Burger
- **AServ** E: Amoco, Anderson[CW], Art's Master Muffler

6AB Interchange between I-240 E. & I-55 N
- **Parks** W: Fuller St Park
- **Other** W: Indian Museum

5AB U.S 51, Elvis Presley Blvd. South, Brooks Road, Graceland
- **Gas** E: Mapco Express[*, LP]
- **Food** E: Brooks' Court Fine Dining (Howard Johnson), Dad's Place (Ramada Inn), Grid Iron Restaurant[24] (Days Inn), Shoney's
  W: "Q" Inn, Kettle Restaurant[24], Peking Inn, Tastee Bar-B-Q, Tony's Restaurant (Graceland)
- **Lodg** E: Comfort Inn, Days Inn, Days Inn, Howard Johnson, Ramada Inn, TraveLodge
  W: "Q" Inn, Graceland Inn, Motel 6, Elvis Presley's Heartbreak Hotel (see our ad this page)

EXIT TENNESSEE/MISSISSIPPI

- **AServ** W: Advance Muffler, Bob's Honda Dealership, Coleman Taylor Transmissions, Graceland Dodge, NAPA Auto Parts
- **TServ** E: Barton Parts & Service (Freightliner)
- **RVCamp** E: Cummins Mid-South (.7 Miles)
  W: D&N Camper Sales, Davis Motor Home Mart, KOA Campgrounds (.5 Miles)
- **Med** W: ✚ Hospital
- **ATM** E: Mapco Express
  W: National Bank of Commerce
- **Other** W: U.S. Post Office

(3) TN Welcome Center (RR, Phones, Vending, Pet Walk; Northbound)

2AB U.S. 5, TN 175E, Shelby Dr, White Haven, Capleville
- **Gas** E: Amoco[*, 24], Circle K[*], Texaco[*, D, CW], Total[*]
  W: BP[*, CW], Circle K[*], The Working Man's Friend
- **Food** W: Adams Family Restaurant (Mexican), Burger King[PLAY], CK's Coffee Shop[24], Central Park, Mrs Winner's Chicken, Pizza Inn, Ruby's Family Restaurant, Soul Food Express (Homestyle Cooking), Wing King- Hamburgers
- **Lodg** E: Knight's Inn, Super 8
- **AServ** W: Goodyear Tire & Auto, Shaw's Auto Glass Co., Xpert Tune
- **ATM** E: Circle K, Texaco
  W: Circle K, First American
- **Other** E: Coin Car Wash, Dean's Coin-Op Laundry
  W: Car Wash, Car Wash, Leith's Coin Laundry, Piggly Wiggly Supermarket (Western Union), Super D Drugs, Super Value Foods

↑TENNESSEE

↓MISSISSIPPI

291 Southaven, State Line Rd
- **Gas** E: BP[*, LP, CW], Pump 'n Save
  W: Amoco[*], Exxon[*, D], Texaco[D]
- **Food** E: Baskin Robbins, Burger King[PLAY], CK's Coffee Shop, Chinese Chef, Exlines' Pizza, Harlow's Donuts, K-Mart[24, RX] (One Hr Photo), Little Caesars Pizza, McDonald's[PLAY], Pizza Hut, Poncho's Mexican, SHONEY'S, Shoney's, Subway, Tops Bar-B-Q, Waffle House, Yesterday Cafe
  W: Captain D's, Dale's, El Porton Mexican, KFC, Mrs Winner's Chicken, Rally's Hamburgers, Sonic, Taco Bell, Wendy's
- **Lodg** E: Best Western, Comfort Inn, Holiday Inn Express, Shoney's Inn
- **AServ** E: Firestone Tire & Auto, Goodyear, K-Mart[24] (One Hr Photo)
  W: Amoco, Speedy Auto Glass, Texaco, Valvoline Oil Change, Xpert tune
- **ATM** E: BP, K-Mart (One Hr Photo), Trustmark National Bank
  W: Bank of Mississippi, Deposit Guaranty National Bank, The People's Bank, Union Planter's Bank
- **Other** E: Bookstore (Christian), Jitney Premier Grocery[24, RX], K-Mart[RX] (One Hr Photo), Kroger Supermarket[24, RX], Wal-Mart[24, RX], WalGreens Pharmacy[RX]
  W: Freds Drug Store, Oliver Drug[RX], Rite Aid Pharmacy, Seessel's Grocery, Southaven Police Dept

289 MS 302, Horn Lake, Olive Branch, S. Southaven, Goodman Rd
- **FStop** W: Phillips 66[*, LP, K, CW]
- **Gas** E: BP[*, CW], Shell[*, D, CW]
  W: Shell[*, D]
- **Food** E: Burger King[PLAY], IHOP, Krystal[24], O'Charley's, Steak & Shake
  W: Applebee's, Arby's, Cracker Barrel, Great Wall, Hardee's, KFC, Papa John's, Popeye's Chicken, Ryan's Steakhouse, Taco Bell, Waffle House, Wendy's
- **Lodg** E: Hampton Inn

EXIT MISSISSIPPI

  W: Days Inn, Days Inn, Ramada Limited, Sleep Inn
- **AServ** E: Country Ford, E & M Auto & Truck Service Inc., Ferguson's Auto Service Inc. (NAPA Auto Care Service Center), Instant Oil Change, Pontiac, GMC Dealership
  W: Abra Auto Body, Dale's Auto
- **TServ** E: E & W Auto & Truck Service
- **Med** E: ✚ Baptist Memorial Hospital De Soto
- **ATM** E: BP, Deposit Guaranty National Bank, Shell, Trustmark National Bank
  W: Kroger Supermarket[RX], Shell
- **Other** E: Antique Mall
  W: Kroger Supermarket[RX]

287 Church Rd
- **Gas** W: Shell[*, D]
- **ATM** W: Shell

(285) Weigh Station

(285) Weigh Station

284 Nesbit Road
- **Gas** W: BP[*], Citgo[*]
- **Food** W: Happy Daze Dairy Bar
- **AServ** E: Jimmy Gray Oldsmobile/Chevrolet/Geo
- **Other** W: Car Wash, US Post Office

280 Hernando, Arkabutla Lake, MS 304
- **Gas** E: BP
  W: Chevron[*, D, LP, CW], Shell[*, D, CW], Total[*, LP, 24]
- **Food** E: The Lowe Sports Cafe
  W: Church's Chicken, Colemans Bar-B-Q, McDonald's, Pizza Hut, Pizza Inn, Subway (Chevron), Taco Bell (Total), Total
- **Lodg** E: Days Inn, Days Inn (see our ad this page), Hernando Inn, Super 8
- **AServ** E: BP
  W: Bryant Tire & Service Center, Delta Muffler, NAPA Auto Parts
- **RVCamp** W: Memphis South Campground & RV Park (1.5 Miles)
- **ATM** W: Deposit Guaranty National Bank, Shell, Trustmark National Bank
- **Other** W: Piggly Wiggly Supermarket

(279) MS Welcome Center (RR, Phones, Picnic, RV Dump, Pet Walk, Ⓟ; Westbound)

(276) Rest Area (RR, Phones, Picnic, RV Dump, Pet Walk, Ⓟ; Eastbound)

271 MS 306, Coldwater, Independence
- **Gas** W: Amoco[*]
- **RVCamp** W: Arkabutla Lake (14 Miles, Camping)

265 MS 4, Senatobia, Holly Springs
- **TStop** W: Rascal's Travel Plaza[SCALES] (BP)
- **FStop** W: Fuel Mart[*]
- **Gas** W: Comet[CW, 24], Exxon[*], Texaco[*, LP, CW]
- **Food** W: Colemans Bar-B-Q, Domino's Pizza, KFC, McDonald's, New China Buffet, Pizza Hut, Rascal's Travel Plaza (BP), Senatobia Inn, Subway, Taco Bell, Wendy's, Western Sizzlin'
- **Lodg** W: Comfort Inn, Senatobia Inn
- **AServ** W: Clear Vision Auto Glass, Texaco, Tommy

DAYS INN
1272
• Outdoor Pool
• Coffee Available 24 Hours
• Free Continental Breakfast
• 20 Miles to Casinos
601-429-0000 • Hernando, MS
MISSISSIPPI • I-55 • EXIT 280

Bold red print shows RV & Bus parking available or nearby

EXIT MISSISSIPPI

Heafner Pontiac Buick GMC Trucks
TServ W: Rascal's Travel Plaza(SCALES) (BP)
TWash W: Comet(CW)
Med W: Senatobia Community Hospital
ATM W: Exxon
Other W: City Drugs(RX), Coin Operated Laundry, Community Discount Pharmacy, Freds Drug Store(RX), Porters Grocery

257 MS 310, Como
Gas W: Bob Payne's Como Marine(*)
Other E: North Sardis Lake

252 MS 315, Sardis
FStop E: Chevron(*, CW)
Gas E: Amoco(*, D), Texaco(*, D, LP)
W: BP(D) (Towing), Phillips 66(*, LP)
Food E: Lake Inn, Pop's Piggy Place Bar-B-Q, Restaurant (Lake Inn), Scooters
W: Happy Days (Best Western)
Lodg E: Gulf Travel Lodge, Lake Inn, Super 8
W: Best Western
AServ E: NAPA Auto Parts, Sardis Glass Co, Simmerman Auto Service
W: BP (Towing)
RVCamp E: Sardis Lake (1 Mile)
Med W: Hospital
ATM E: Amoco, Texaco
Parks E: John W Kyle Park

246 MS 35, N Batesville
FStop W: Texaco(*)
Food W: Maggie T's (Texaco), Texaco
Other E: Sardis Dam (8 Miles)

243B MS 6, Batesville (Westbound)
FStop W: Phillips 66(*)
Gas W: Exxon(*, D)
Food W: Burger King, Cracker Barrel, Dairy Queen, Food Court (Factory Outlet)
Lodg W: AmeriHost Inn, Comfort Inn, Days Inn, Hampton Inn
ATM W: First Security Bank
Other W: Bookstore, Factory Stores of Mississippi, Promises & Praises Christian Bookstore

243A MS 6, Oxford, Batesville (Eastbound)
FStop E: Texaco(*, D, LP)
Gas W: Exxon(*, D), Fast Lane(*, D), Phillips 66(*, D)
Food W: Burger King(PLAY), Cracker Barrel, Dairy Queen, Hardee's, KFC, Sonic Drive In, Taco Bell
Lodg W: AmeriHost Inn, Comfort Inn, Days Inn, Hampton Inn, Ramada Limited
Med W: Hospital
ATM E: Texaco
W: Fast Lane, First Security Bank
Other W: Factory Outlet Center, Food World(24), U.S. Post Office, Wal-Mart(RX)

(239) Rest Area (RR, Picnic, RV Dump, Pet Walk, P)

237 Pope, Courtland
FStop E: Amoco(*, LP)
Food E: Amoco

233 Enid
Gas W: Benson's Grocery Store(*)
RVCamp E: Enid Lake (1 Mile)

227 MS 32, Oakland, Water Valley
FStop W: Chevron(*, LP)
Food W: Country Catfish
AServ W: 32/55 Service, Ashmore's Wrecker Service
TServ W: 32/55 Service, Ashmore's Wrecker Service
RVCamp E: George Payne Cossar State Park
Parks E: George Payne Cossar State Park

220 MS 330, Coffeeville, Tillatoba Rd
TStop E: Conoco(*, LP)
Food E: All American Restaurant (Conoco TS)
TServ E: Conoco
ATM E: Conoco

211 North MS 7, Scenic Route 333, Coffeeville
FStop W: Texaco(*, LP)
Food W: Chester Fried Chicken (Texaco), Texaco

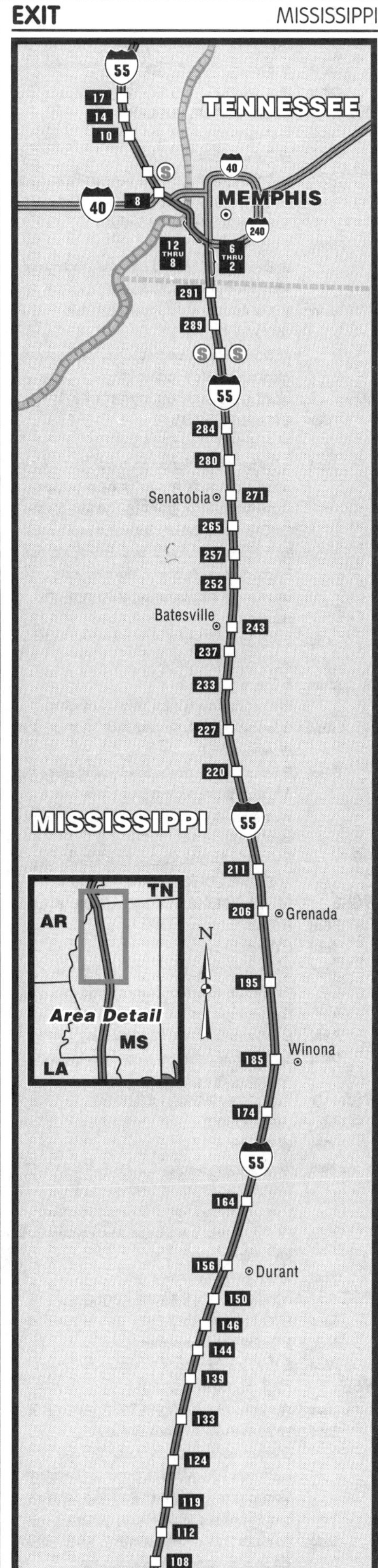

EXIT MISSISSIPPI

RVCamp E: Oxbow RV Park

208 N. Grenada - Papermill Rd.

206 South MS 7, MS 8, Grenada, Greenwood
FStop E: Shell(*, D)
Gas E: Exxon(*), Racetrac(*), Texaco(*)
W: Texaco(24) (Hilltop Inns)
Food E: Beef House, Best Western, Burger King, Domino's Pizza, Fiori's Italian, French Quarter (Holiday Inn), Grand Palace Chinese, Holiday Inn, Hot Stuff Pizza (Shell), Jake & Rip's Bar-B-Q, Steaks, & Catfish, McAlister's Gourmet Deli, McDonald's (Wal-Mart Supercenter), Pizza Hut, Pizza Inn, Ragtime Bar & Grill, Shell, Shoney's, Shoney's, Subway, TCBY, Taco Bell, Wal-Mart Supercenter(24, RX), Wendy's, Western Sizzlin'
Lodg E: Best Western, Comfort Inn, Days Inn, Hampton Inn, Holiday Inn, Ramada Limited
W: Hilltop Inns
AServ E: Kirk Auto Co. Merc/Lincoln/Ford/Toyota, Wal-Mart Supercenter(24)
W: B & L Service Center, Marter Brothers
RVCamp E: Lake Grenada
Med E: Hospital
ATM E: Exxon, Shell, Wal-Mart Supercenter
Parks E: Grenada Lake's Hugh White State Park
Other E: U.S. Post Office, Wal-Mart Supercenter(RX)

(202) Parking Area (RV Dump; Northbound)

199 New

195 MS 404, Duck Hill
Other W: Camp McCain Army Training

185 US 82, Winona, Greenwood
Gas E: Exxon(*), Pat's Kwik Stop(*) (Shell), Shell(*), Simply Irresistable(*), Texaco(*, LP)
Food E: Baskin Robbins (Texaco), McDonald's, Sharon's Family Restaurant (Relax Inn), TCBY (Exxon)
Lodg E: Days Inn, Magnolia Inn, Relax Inn
Med E: Hospital
ATM E: Exxon

174 MS 430, MS 35, Vaiden, Carrollton
TStop E: AmBest 35-55 Truck Plaza(SCALES) (Chevron)
Gas E: BP(*, CW), Comet, Shell(*, D)
W: Texaco(*) (Stuckey's)
Food E: Pizzazz Pizza
W: Chester Fried Express (Texaco), Texaco (Stuckey's)
Lodg E: 35-55 Motel
AServ E: NAPA Auto Parts
TWash E: AmBest 35-55 Truck Plaza (Chevron)
RVCamp E: Vaiden Campground
ATM E: 35-55 Motel, AmBest 35-55 Truck Plaza (Chevron)
Other E: T & H Laundromat

(173) Rest Area (RR, Phones, Picnic, Grills, RV Dump, Pet Walk, P; Westbound)

164 West
FStop W: West Truck Stop(*)
TServ W: West Truck Stop

(163) Rest Area (RR, HF, Phones, Picnic, Grills, RV Dump, Pet Walk, P; Eastbound)

156 MS 12, Durant, Lexington, Kosciusko
FStop E: Texaco(*, LP)
Lodg E: Super 8
Med E: Hospital

150 Holmes County State Park
Parks E: Holmes County State Park (1.5 Miles)
Other E: Camping

146 MS 14, Goodman, Ebenezer

144 MS17, Pickens, Lexington
TStop E: Texaco(LP, SCALES, 24)
FStop W: BP Fuel Center(*, LP)
Food W: Lakeside Restaurant, MGM Restaurant, North Fork Restaurant
Lodg W: Motel

EXIT MISSISSIPPI

ATM E: Texaco
W: BP Fuel Center
Other W: Little Red School House
139 MS 432, Pickens, Yazoo City, Benton
133 Vaughan
Other E: Casey Jones Museum
124 16, North Canton, Yazoo City
(120) Parking Area (Phones, Picnic; Southbound)
119 MS 22, Canton, Flora
TStop E: Chevron(*, RV DUMP, 24)
Gas E: Amoco(*, D), BP(*), Exxon(*, D), Shell(*), Texaco(*, D)
Food E: Amoco, Chevron, McDonald's(PLAY), Pizza Hut, Popeye's Chicken, Subway (Amoco), Two Rivers Restaurant (Steak & Seafood), Wendy's
Lodg E: Days Inn, Econolodge, Holiday Inn Express
AServ E: Briggs Ford
Med E: Hospital
ATM E: Chevron, Texaco
(117) Rest Area (Phones, Picnic, P; Eastbound)
112 Gluckstadt
FStop E: Amoco(*, LP), Mac's Gas(*, D)
Lodg E: Howard Johnson
RVCamp W: Camper Corral(LP) (Sales & Service)
ATM E: Amoco
108 MS 463, Madison
Gas E: Shell(*), Texaco(*, D, LP, CW)
Food E: Blimpie's Subs (Texaco), Burger King, Texaco
ATM E: Shell, Texaco
105B Ridgeland, Old Agency Road
Gas E: Chevron(*, D)
105A Natchez Trace Pkwy
104 Junction I-220, West Jackson
103 County Line Road, Ridgeland
Gas E: BP(*, CW), Chevron, Exxon(*, D, CW)
Food E: Applebee's, Chick-Fil-A(PLAY), Copeland's, Furr Transmission, Grady's, Hardee's, Huntingtons Grille, Ice Cream Shoppe, On The Border (Mexican), Pickles & Ice Cream, Ralph & Kacoo's Restaurant, Ramano's Macaroni Grille, Roadhouse Grille, SHONEY'S, Shoney's, The Honey Baked Ham Co., Wok On The Run
W: Kim Long Chinese Cuisine, Olive Garden, Red Lobster, Smoothie Q (Ice Cream & Sandwich Shop), Subway
Lodg E: Cabot Lodge Bed & Breakfast, Hilton, Plaza Hotel, Red Roof Inn, Shoney's Inn, Studio PLUS
W: Comfort Suites Hotel, Motel 6
AServ E: Fur Transmission, Hallmark Toyota, Midas Muffler & Brake, North Park Acura Mazda, The Pit Stop Auto Service & Repair, Watson Quality Ford
W: Capitol Sports Center
Parks E: Ross Barnett Reservoir
Other E: Baptist Bookstore, Barnes & Noble, Books, Bibles & Shirt Supplies, Mail Boxes Etc, Office Max, Pier 1 Imports, Sam's Club
W: Eyemart Express (1 Hr Service), Office Depot, Optometrist, PetsMart, Super Dollar X Stores(RX), Target
102B Beasley Road, Adkins Blvd.
Gas E: Chevron(*, D), Chevron(*)
Food E: Cracker Barrel, Kenny Roger's Roasters, Lone Star Restaurant, Outback Steakhouse, Subway, The Wok Shoppe
W: K-Mart(RX), McDonald's(PLAY)
AServ E: Chevron, Discount Auto Parts
W: K-Mart, Penske
Med E: Methodist Medical Center (No Emergency Room)
ATM E: Chevron
Other W: K-Mart(RX)
102A Briarwood Dr., Jackson
Gas E: Amoco(*)
W: Pump & Save
Food W: Chili's Grill & Bar, Chuck E Cheese's Pizza, Perkins Family Restaurant, Steak & Ale, Steam Room Grill (Lobster Steak & Seafood)
Lodg E: La Quinta Inn
W: Best Suites of America, Extended Stay America, Hampton Inn, Holiday Inn Select
AServ E: Dixie Auto Glass, Van-Trow Oldsmobile Volkswagon
W: Big Ten Tires 10, Blackwell Chevrolet, Blackwell Import Motors Merc Porsche
100 Northside Dr, Meadowbrook Rd
Gas E: Chevron(*), Sprint Mart(*)
W: Amoco(*, LP), Exxon(*, D, CW), Shell(*)
Food E: Golden Dragon Restaurant, Logan Farms Honey Hams, McDonald's(PLAY), Old Tyme Deli & Bakery, Pizza Hut, Pizza Inn, SHONEY'S, Shoney's, Steak-Out Charbroiled Delivery, Subway, We Love Yogurt
W: Bennigan's, Domino's Pizza, IHOP(24), Marcel's Steak & Seafood, Pizza Hut, Sam's Westside Restaurant & Bar, Stamps Super Burger, Waffle House
Lodg E: Highland Village
W: Knight's Inn, Super 8
AServ E: Chevron
W: Car Quest Auto Center, Safelite Auto Glass
ATM E: Deposit Guaranty National Bank, Trustmark Bank
W: Amoco, Shell
Other E: Beemon Drugs, McDade's Seafood & Deli, Red Arrow Car Wash, Super D Drug Store
W: Eyecare Plus, Highlander Coin-Op Laundry, Minit Mart Groceries
99 Meadowbrook Road, Northside Dr East, Old Cantan Rd (Northbound)
98BC MS 25 North, Carthage, Lakeland Dr
Gas E: Shell(*)
Food E: Crawfish Hut
Med W: St Dominic-Jackson Health Services (Hospital, Med Offices, Mental Health, MS Heart Center)
Parks E: LeFleur's Bluff State Park (Camping, 1 Mile)
Other E: Agriculture & Forestry Museum, Mississippi Sports Hall Of Fame
98A Woodrow Wilson Dr (Left Exit Westbound)
Gas W: Conoco(*, LP)
Med W: Arthritis, Surgery & Outpatient Rehab, Blair E. Batson Hospital for Children, Columbia Surgicare Of Jackson, Lakeland Medical Center, Univ of Mississippi Medical Center, VA Medical Center
Other W: Miss. Highway Patrol
96C Fortification St (Difficult Reaccess)
Food E: The Bel-Haven Bar & Grill
Lodg E: Residence Inn by Marriott
Med E: Mississippi Sports & Orthopedic Center
96B High St., State Capitol
Gas W: Homer's Bar-B-Q Store(*), Shell(*), Texaco(*, D, CW)
Food W: Blimpie's Subs (Texaco), Burger King, Chimneyville Station, Dairy Queen, Dennery's Restaurant, Dunkin Donuts, Emporium Restaurant (Ramada Inn), Ramada Inn, SHONEY'S, Shoney's, Taco Bell, Texaco, Waffle House, Wendy's
Lodg W: Days Inn, Hampton Inn & Suites, Holiday Inn Express, Ramada Inn, Red Roof Inn
AServ E: Herrin-Gear Autoplex Saturn, Chev, Infin, Lexus, Infiniti of Jackson
ATM W: Shell, Texaco
Other W: Antique Mall & Flea Market, Miss. State Fairgrounds
96A Pearl St., Downtown (Difficult Reaccess)
Other W: Miss. Museum of Art, Natural Science Museum, Old Capitol Museum
94 Jct I-20E, US49S, Meridian, Hattiesburg

Note: I-55 runs concurrent below with I-20. Numbering follows I-20.

45A Gallatin St.
Gas N: Chevron(*), Dixie Gas(*), S & S Mini Service, Texaco(*)
Lodg N: Crossroads Inn
AServ N: Anglin Tire Co, Cowboys Used Tires, Gentry's Body Shop, Smith Automatic Transmission, Xpress Lube
S: Regency Toyota, Nissan, Mitsubishi
Other N: Camping, Duncan's Discount Marine, Jackson Animal Clinic
S: Animal Health Products, Magnolia Animal Hospital
45B US 51N, State St
AServ N: AAMCO Transmission, Fowler Buick, Fowler GMC Truck, Freeman Auto Service, Paul Moak Pontiac, Volvo, Honda

Note: I-55 runs concurrent above with I-20. Numbering follows I-20.

92C West I-20, U.S 49, Vicksburg, Yazoo City (Left Exit)
92B U.S 51 North, State St, Gallatin St
92A McDowell Road
Gas W: Dixie(*), Hwy Oil(*), Shell(*, CW, 24), Texaco(*, D)
Food W: China Wok, Golden Glazed Donuts, Thai House Restaurant (Super 8 Motel), Waffle House
Lodg W: Super 8
TServ E: Jackson's Truck & Trailor Repair
90B Daniel Lake Blvd.
Gas W: Shell(*, LP)
ATM W: Shell
90A Savanna St
Gas W: Spur(*)
Food E: Charlie's Restaurant (Save Inn)
W: Bo Don's Seafood Restaurant
Lodg E: Rodeway Inn, Save Inn
AServ E: Rick's Pro Truck & Auto
RVCamp W: Camping
88 Elton Road
Gas E: Chevron(*, LP, CW), Exxon(*, D)
Food E: Chester Fried Chicken (Exxon), Subway (Exxon)
ATM E: Chevron, Exxon
Other E: Car Wash
85 Byram
Gas E: Chevron(*, 24)
W: Bill's(D), Pump & Save, Texaco(*, D, LP, CW)
Food E: Krystal (Chevron)
W: Blimpie Subs & Salads (Texaco), Golden Glazed Donuts, Hong Kong Restaurant, Pizza Hut, Popeye's Chicken, Subway, Taco Bell, Wendy's
Lodg W: Days Inn
AServ W: Davis Tire & Auto
ATM W: Bank of Mississippi, Texaco, Union Planter's Bank
Other W: Jitney Jungle, Super D Drug Store(RX)
81 Wynndale Road
TServ E: Fulgham's Auto & Truck Repair
78 Terry

Bold red print shows RV & Bus parking available or nearby

EXIT	MISSISSIPPI
FStop	E: Texaco(*)
Gas	E: Conoco(*)
	W: Mac's(*)
Food	E: Church's Chicken (Texaco), Conoco
Other	E: Car Wash
72	US 51, MS 27, North Crystal Springs, Vicksburg
FStop	E: Phillips 66(*)
Food	E: Louise's Pit BBQ, McDonald's(PLAY)
AServ	E: Ford, Lincoln, Mercury Dealer, Lewis Tire & Auto Service
Other	E: Blossman Inc. Propane(LP)
68	South Crystal Springs
Gas	E: Gas
Other	E: Copiah Animal Hospital
65	Gallman
Gas	E: Citgo(*)
Food	E: Dairy Queen (Citgo), Stuckey's (Citgo)
61	MS 28, Hazlehurst, Fayette
Gas	E: Exxon(*, CW), Phillips 66(*, CW), Pump 'n Save
Food	E: Burger King, J & B BBQ, KFC, McDonald's(PLAY), Pizza Hut, Stark's Restaurant, Subway (Exxon), Wendy's, Western Sizzlin
Lodg	E: Ramada Inn, Western Inn Express
AServ	E: Discount Auto Parts
Med	E: ✚ Hospital
Other	E: Jitney Jungle, Wal-Mart(RX)
59	South Hazlehurst
56	Martinsville
(54)	Rest Area (RR, Phones, Picnic, Grills, RV Dump, P; Southbound)
(54)	Rest Area (RR, Phones, Picnic, Grills, RV Dump, P; Northbound)
51	Wesson
TStop	W: Country Junction Truckstop(*)
TServ	W: Country Junction Truckstop
RVCamp	W: Country Junction Truckstop (Full Hookups), Country Junction Truckstop
Parks	E: Lake Lincoln State Park
48	Mt. Zion Road
42	North Brookhaven
TStop	E: Phillips 66(*)
FStop	E: Shell(LP)
Food	E: Ernie's Diner (Phillips 66 TS), Phillips 66
AServ	E: Shell
RVCamp	E: Circle N Campground (Hookups)
40	To MS 550, Downtown Brookhaven
Gas	E: BP(*, D), Chevron(*, CW, 24), Exxon(*), Texaco(*, D)
Food	E: Bowie BBQ, Cracker Barrel, Dairy Queen, Little Caesars Pizza, McDonald's (Wal-Mart), McDonald's, Pizza Hut, SHONEY'S, Shoney's, Subway (Exxon)

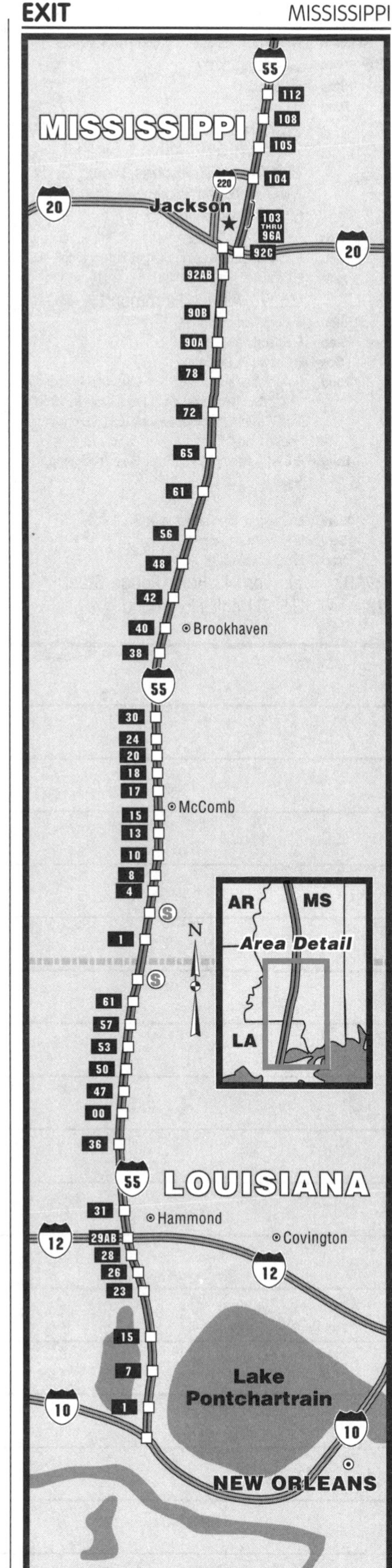

EXIT	MISSISSIPPI/LOUISIANA
Lodg	E: Best Western, Comfort Inn, Days Inn, Hampton Inn, Howard Johnson
AServ	E: Allbritton Sullivan Ford
Other	E: Wal-Mart Supercenter(24, RX) (Vision Center)
	W: Animal Medical Center
38	U.S 84, South Brookhaven, Natchez, Monticello, Meadville
FStop	W: Chevron(*, 24), Hickory Hill Grocery
Food	W: Busy B's
AServ	W: Chevron(24)
30	Bogue Chitto, Norfield
FStop	E: Shell(*)
Med	W: ✚ Southwest Mississippi Regional Medical Center
24	Lake Dixie Springs, Johnstons Station
(23)	Parking Area (Southbound)
20AB	U.S 98 West, Summit, Natchez
FStop	E: BP(*)
	W: Phillips 66(*)
Gas	E: Texaco(*, D)
	W: Exxon(*)
Food	E: BP
	W: A & W Hot Dogs & More (Exxon), Summit Smokehouse & Casey's Kitchen
18	MS 570, Smithdale Road, North McComb
FStop	W: Chevron(*, CW)
Food	E: McDonald's, Piccadilly Cafeteria
AServ	E: Wal-Mart SuperCenter(24, RX)
	W: Ford, Lincoln, Mercury Dealer
Med	E: ✚ Hospital
ATM	W: Chevron
Other	E: Edgewood Mall, Wal-Mart SuperCenter(RX)
17	Delaware Ave, Downtown McComb
Gas	E: BP(*, D), Citgo(*)
	W: Exxon(*)
Food	E: Dairy Queen, Wendy's
	W: Krystal (Exxon)
Lodg	E: Comfort Inn, Holiday Inn
	W: Best Western
AServ	E: Quality Oil & Lube
	W: Delaware Motors Chrysler Plymouth Toyota
ATM	E: Deposit Guaranty National Bank
15AB	U.S 98 East, MS 24 West, Tylertown, Liberty
FStop	W: BP(*, 24)
13	Fernwood Road
TStop	W: Fernwood Truckstop(*, SCALES) (Conoco)
Food	W: Fernwood Truckstop (Conoco)
Lodg	W: Rodeway Inn
TServ	E: Interstate Supply
Parks	W: Percy Quin State Park (1 Mile)
10	MS 48, Magnolia
RVCamp	E: Camping
8	MS 568, Gillsburg, Magnolia
4	Chatawa
(3)	MS Welcome Center (Northbound)
(2)	Weigh Station (Southbound)
(2)	Weigh Station (Northbound)
1	MS 584, Osyka, Gillsburg
RVCamp	W: Camping

↑MISSISSIPPI

↓LOUISIANA

(65)	LA Tourist Info, Rest Area (RR, Phones, Picnic, RV Dump; Southbound)
(64)	Weigh Station (Northbound)

Bold red print shows RV & Bus parking available or nearby

EXIT		LOUISIANA
61		LA 38, Kentwood, Liverpool
	FStop	**E:** Chevron(*)
		W: Texaco(*)
	Gas	**E:** Texaco(D)
	Food	**E:** Chicken Little, Sonic Drive In
	AServ	**E:** Kentwood Ford Mercury Dealership, Texaco
	RVCamp	**W:** Great Discovery Camp (2.7 Miles)
	ATM	**W:** Texaco
	Other	**E:** Brown Morris Pharmacy(RX), Kentwood Plaza, Sunflower Grocery
(59)		Weigh Station (Southbound)
57		LA 440, Tangipahoa
	RVCamp	**E:** Camp Moore
	Other	**E:** Camp Moore Museum
53		LA 10, Fluker, Greensburg
50		LA 1048, Arcola
	FStop	**E:** Texaco(*)
47		LA 16, Amite, Montpelier
	TStop	**W:** Citgo Auto/Truck Plaza(*, SCALES)
	Gas	**W:** Shell(*), Texaco(*)
	Food	**E:** Burger King, KFC, McDonald's(PLAY), Mike's Catfish Inn
	Lodg	**W:** Colonial Inn Motel
	RVCamp	**E:** Camping
	Med	**E:** + Hospital
41		LA 40, Independence
	Gas	**E:** Conoco(*)
	Food	**E:** The Kingfish

EXIT		LOUISIANA
	RVCamp	**W:** Indian Creek Campground (1.75 Miles)
36		LA 442, Tickfaw
	FStop	**E:** Chevron(*)
	Food	**E:** Chevron
(33)		Rest Area (RR, Phones, Picnic, Grills, Pet Walk; Southbound, Closed)
(33)		Rest Area (RR, Phones, Picnic, Grills, RV Dump, Pet Walk; Northbound)
32		LA 3234, Wardline Rd.
	Gas	**E:** Citgo(*, LP, 24), Texaco(*)
	Food	**E:** Blimpie Subs & Salads (Citgo), Burger King(PLAY)
	ATM	**E:** Citgo
31		U.S 190, Albany, Hammond
	TStop	**E:** Fleet Truck Stop(*, 24)
	FStop	**E:** Speedway(*)
	Gas	**E:** Chevron(*), Exxon(*, D)
	Food	**E:** Applebee's, Blimpie Subs & Salads (Speedway), Cracker Barrel, Fleet Truck Stop, Red Room (Best Western), Subway (Exxon), TCBY (Exxon), Waffle House
	Lodg	**E:** Best Western, Econo Motel, Fleet Truck Stop, Super 8
		W: Motel
	AServ	**E:** Chevron, Tire Centers Inc.
	TServ	**E:** Fleet Truck Stop(24)
	Med	**E:** + Hospital
29AB		Junction I-12, Baton Rouge, Slidell
28		U.S. 51 North, Hammond

EXIT		LOUISIANA
	Food	**E:** Cajun Connection Restaurant (Ramada Inn)
	Lodg	**E:** Ramada Inn
	TServ	**E:** Big Wheel Diesel Repair
	RVCamp	**E:** KOA Campgrounds (1.25 Miles)
	Med	**E:** + Hospital
	Other	**E:** Tourist Info.
26		LA 22, Ponchatoula, Springfield
	Gas	**E:** Chevron(*, D), Conoco(*, D), Shell(*)
	Food	**E:** Burger King, China King, KFC, McDonald's(PLAY), Popeye's Chicken, Sonic Drive In, Wendy's
	AServ	**E:** Gateway Ford
	Med	**E:** + Hospital
	ATM	**E:** First Guarantee Bank, Hancock Bank, Shell
	Other	**E:** Tony Turbo Car Wash, Winn Dixie Supermarket, Wolfe Lumber & Supply(LP)
23		U.S 51 Bus, Ponchatoula
22		Frontage Road (Difficult Reaccess)
15		Manchac
7		Ruddock
1		U.S. 51, Junction I-10, La Place, Baton Rouge, New Orleans
	FStop	**E:** Speedway(*)
	Gas	**E:** Chevron(*), Citgo(*), Shell(*, CW)
	Food	**E:** SHONEY'S, Shoney's, Waffle House, Wendy's
	ATM	**E:** Hibernia Bank, Speedway

↑ LOUISIANA

Begin I-55

Notes:

Bold red print shows RV & Bus parking available or nearby

EXIT | ILLINOIS

Begin I-57

↓ILLINOIS

359 Junction I-94, Chicago, Indiana

357 IL 1, Halsted St
- **Gas** E: Amoco[*, CW], Mobil[*]
  W: Shell[*]
- **Food** W: McDonald's

355 111th St
- **Gas** W: Amoco[*, 24]

354 119th St

353 127th St, Burr Oak Ave
- **Gas** E: Amoco[*], Mobil[*], Shell[*, LP]
  W: Amoco[*, 24], Gas City[*, D]
- **Food** E: Burger King[PLAY], Dillinger's Gyros Etc., McDonald's[24], Subway
- **Lodg** E: **Super 8 (See our ad this page)**
- **AServ** E: Amoco, Firestone Tire & Auto, Goodyear Tire & Auto, Mobil, Mobil
  W: Meineke Discount Mufflers
- **ATM** E: Shell
- **Other** E: **Auto Parts Inc.**

350 IL 83, Sibley Blvd, 147th St
- **Gas** E: Citgo[*], Marathon[*], Mobil
  W: BP[*, K]
- **Food** E: Alfa Gyros, BBQ and Tacos
- **AServ** E: Murray's Discount Auto Stores
  W: Fair Muffler
- **ATM** W: BP
- **Other** E: **Key Market Grocery Store**, New Laundry Coin Operated Laundry

348 U.S. 6, 159th St
- **Gas** E: King[*, D], Marathon[*, D, 24]
  W: Citgo[*, D, LP, CW]
- **Food** E: Anthony Michael's Burritos, Baskin Robbins, Burger King, Hung's Garden, McDonald's, New Wok, Subway, Taco Bell, USA #1 Family Restaurant[24], White Castle Restaurant
- **Lodg** E: Highway Motel, Holiday Inn Express
- **AServ** E: Bajan Auto Repair, Firestone Tire & Auto, Rowe's Auto Repair, Value Plus Mufflers
  W: Quik Lube (Citgo)
- **ATM** E: Suburban Bank
  W: Citgo
- **Other** E: **Markham Animal Clinic, Post Office, WalGreens Pharmacy**

346 167th St
- **FStop** E: **Minuteman**[*, D, LP, K]
- **Gas** E: Amoco[*, CW]
  W: Shell[*]

345AB Junction I-80, Indiana, Iowa (Difficult Reaccess)

342AB Vollmer Road
- **Gas** E: Shell[*, 24]

EXIT | ILLINOIS

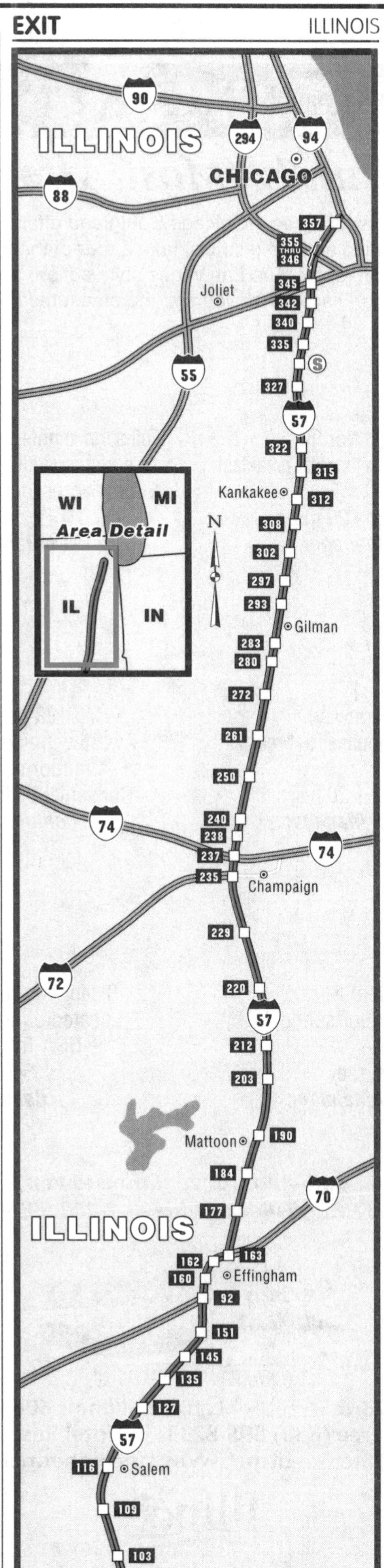

EXIT | ILLINOIS

- **ATM** E: Shell
- **Other** W: White Hen Pantry

340AB U.S. 30, Lincoln Highway
- **Gas** E: Mobil[*]
- **Food** E: Alcove Fine Dining (Holiday Inn), Applebee's, Baker's Square, Cafe De Plaza (Holiday Inn), Chi Chi's Mexican Restaurant, Chuck E Cheese's Pizza, **Cracker Barrel**, Fuddruckers, J.N. Michael's, Liang's Buffet, Old Country Buffet, Olive Garden, Pizza Hut, Subway, The Great American Bagel, Wendy's
- **Lodg** E: Budgetel Inn, Hampton Inn, Holiday Inn
- **AServ** E: Firestone, Goodyear Tire & Auto, Pep Boys
- **ATM** E: Harris Bank, La Salle Bank
- **Other** E: **Lincoln Shopping Mall, Sam's Club, Target**[RX], **Wal-Mart**[RX]

339 Sauk Trail
- **Gas** E: Amoco[*, CW], Shell[*]
- **Food** E: Bozo's Hot Dogs, McDonald's[PLAY]
- **ATM** E: White Hen Pantry
- **Other** E: **White Hen Pantry**[24]

335 Monee, Manhattan
- **TStop** E: **Petro Truck Plaza**[*, SCALES]
- **FStop** E: **Amoco**[*, D], **Speedway**[*, SCALES]
- **Food** E: **Burger King**[PLAY], Hardees (Speedway), **Leo's Gyros & Ribs**, Max's Red Hots, Pizza Hut (Petro Travel Plaza), Subway (Amoco), Windy City (Petro Travel Plaza)
- **Lodg** E: Country Host Inn, Super 8
- **AServ** E: Amoco
- **TServ** E: **Petro Truck Plaza**
- **TWash** E: **Blue Beacon Truck Wash**
- **ATM** E: Petro Travel Plaza, Speedway, **Speedway**

(332) **Rest Area (RR, Phones, Picnic, RV Dump, P)**

(330) **Weigh Station**

327 Peotone, Wilmington
- **Gas** E: Shell[*]
- **Food** E: Dairy Queen (Shell), **McDonald's**, Taco Bell (Shell)

322 Manteno
- **Gas** E: Amoco[*], Phillips 66[*]
- **Food** E: Hardee's, McDonald's (Amoco), Subway (Phillips)
- **Lodg** E: Comfort Inn
- **ATM** E: Amoco, Phillips 66

315 IL 50, Bradley, Kankakee, Bourbonnais
- **Gas** E: Shell[*]
  W: Amoco[*, D, LP]
- **Food** E: Burger King (Shell), **Cracker Barrel**, Lone Star, Old Country Buffet, Pizza Hut, Red Lobster, White Castle Restaurant
  W: Applebee's, Bakers Square Restaurant, Boston Market Restaurant, Bradley Inn (Restaurant), Denny's, Hardee's, Mancino's Pizza, **McDonald's**, Mongolian Buffet, Sirloin Stockade, Steak & Shake, Subway, Taco Bell
- **Lodg** E: Fairfield Inn, Hampton Inn, Holiday Inn Express, Lees Inn
  W: Bradley Inn (Restaurant), Motel 6, Super 8
- **AServ** E: Blain's Farm and Fleet, Midas Muffler & Brake, Sears Auto Service
  W: Hove Nissan, Buick, K-Mart
- **RVCamp** E: **Mirrielees RV Center (.5 Miles)**
- **ATM** E: Shell
  W: Amoco
- **Other** E: Hidden Cove Family Fun Park, **Northfield Square Mall, Target**[RX]
  W: **K-Mart**[24, RX], Petco, Supertrak Warehouse Auto Parts, **Wal-Mart**[LP, 24, RX]

312 IL 17, Kankakee, Momence
- **Gas** W: Clark[*, D], Shell[*]
- **Food** W: McDonald's, Poor Boy Restaurant, Subway, Uncle Johnnis
- **Lodg** W: Days Inn
- **AServ** E: Taylor Chrysler, Plymouth, Dodge
  W: Best Muffler and Brake, Dubois Auto Electrical,

NEXT EXIT: CHICAGO SOUTHLAND

Chicagoland's "Most Affordable" Region!

Located just minutes away from downtown Chicago, Chicago Southland offers easy accessibility, affordable rates and entertainment galore! Visit our charming antique districts, take a tour of the Frank Lloyd Wright Home and Studio, tee off in the Midwest's largest golf region, or for pure Las Vegas style action, take a cruise aboard one of our Riverboat Gaming Casinos. Discover for yourself the pleasures of the Southland.

SOUTH HOLLAND
From I-80/I-294 exit Halsted Street North
Free in-room coffee maker & room delivered Continental breakfast
Free local calls
McCormick Place - downtown Chicago - 20 miles
Contact: Mary Macht, General Manager
(708) 596-8700

MATTESON
Exit I-57 at U.S.30 East (Lincoln Highway)
Free in room coffee maker & room delivered Continental breakfast
Free local calls
McCormick Place - downtown Chicago - 20 miles
Contact: Marie Robinson, General Manager
(708) 503-0999

TINLEY PARK
From I-80 Take exit #148B to Harlem North
Indoor greenhouse pool/spa with outdoor sundeck
Complimentary breakfast
Near World Music Theatre, Odyssey
Contact: David Thometz, General Manager
(708) 633-1200

HOMEWOOD HOTEL
Full service hotel, indoor/outdoor pool, whirlpool, health room
Banquets/weddings/meetings/seminar facilities for up to 550
Easy access for Chicago highways, public transportation
Restaurant/lounge, free full breakfast
Contact: Charlene Simpson, Manager
(708) 957-1600

ALSIP
193 beautifully renovated guest rooms
Award winning Allgauer's Grill and Stone's Throw Bar
Indoor pool, game room and exercise room
Conveniently located at I-294 and Cicero Avenue exit
Contact: Jacqui Parzy, Director of Sales
(708) 371-7300, ext. 621

LANSING
Clean, comfortable recently '98 remodeled rooms
Located on I-80 & exit 161 North Torrence Avenue
Free USA Today paper & local & 800 phone service
Bob Evans Restaurant adjacent
Contact: Gene, General Manager
(708) 895-9570

Call the Chicago Southland Convention and Visitors Bureau today for a FREE Visitors Guide at 1-888-895-8233.

CONVENTION & VISITORS BUREAU

2304 173rd Street ❖ Lansing, Illinois 60438-6006
(708) 895-8200 ❖ Toll Free (888) 895-8233 ❖ Hotel Reservations (800) 920-2266
E-mail: lrcscvb@lincolnnet.net ❖ http://www.Lincolnnet.net/Chicago-Southland-CVB

1776

EXIT ILLINOIS

Just Lube, Route 17 Complete Auto Service
TServ E: Mobile Powerwash Service
W: International Truck
ATM W: Clark, Shell
Other W: Coin Operated Car Wash and Laundromat, WalGreens Pharmacy

308 U.S. 45, U.S. 52, Kankakee
FStop W: Fleet Fuel
Gas W: Phillips 66(*, D)
Food E: Redwood Inn
Lodg W: Fairview Motel
AServ E: Kankakee Springs Service Auto and Truck
TServ E: Raymond's Truck, Trailer and Tire Repair Service, Ted's Truck Sales

302 Chebanse
Gas W: BP(*, D)
Food W: Hot Stuff Pizza (BP)
AServ W: Mike's Service
TServ W: Ken's Truck Repair
ATM W: BP
Other W: United States Post Office

297 Clifton
Gas W: Phillips 66(*, D)
Food W: Dairy Queen (Phillips 66), Taco John's Express (Phillips 66)
ATM W: Phillips 66, Phillips 66

293 IL 116, Pontiac, Ashkum
Food W: The Loft
AServ E: Meier Brothers Tire, Yokohama Tires
ATM E: Central Bank

283 U.S. 24, Gilman, Chatsworth
TStop E: Apollo Travel Center Citgo(*, D), K & H Truck Plaza(*, D, SCALES)
FStop W: Phillips 66(*, LP)
Gas E: Shell(*, D)
Food E: Baby Bulls Family Restaurant (Apollo Travel Center), Dairy Queen, Gillman Restaurant, K & H Truck Plaza Restaurant, McDonald's
W: Subway (Phillips 66)
Lodg E: Budget Host Inn, Days Inn, Super 8
AServ E: Alignment Unlimited, Brown's Hardware and Auto Parts
TServ E: Apollo Travel Center, K & H Truck Plaza
ATM E: Apollo Travel Center, K & H Truck Plaza
W: Phillips 66
Other E: Coin Car Wash, Docs Drugs and Grocery Mart

280 Onarga, Roberts, IL 54
Gas E: Phillips 66(*, D, CW) (Coin Laundry)
RVCamp W: Lake Arrowhead Campground

272 Buckley , Roberts

(269) Rest Area (RR, Phones, Vending, RV Dump, P; Southbound)

(268) Rest Area (RR, Phones, Vending, RV Dump, P; Northbound)

261 IL 9, Paxton, Gibson City
FStop W: Amoco(*)
Gas W: Amoco(*)
Food E: Hardees, Monical's Pizza, Pizza Hut, Subway
W: Country Garden Restaurant
Lodg W: Paxton Inn
AServ E: Auto Laundry Car Wash, Shields Geo, Chevrolet, Pontiac, Buick. Cadillac, GMC, Oldsm, Specchio Motors, Ford
ATM E: Farmer's & Merchant Bank
W: Amoco
Other E: Auto Laundry Car Wash

250 U.S. 136, Rantoul, Fisher
Gas E: Amoco(*), Shell(*, 24)
Food E: Days Inn, Long John Silver, McDonald's(PLAY), Red Wheel Pancake & Steak House, Taco Bell
Lodg E: Best Western, Days Inn, Super 8
AServ E: Tatman's Auto Body
TServ E: Grand Tool Equipment

EXIT ILLINOIS

ATM E: Amoco, Bank of Rantoul, Shell

240 Market St
TStop E: Amoco(*) (CB Shop)
TWash E: Amoco (CB Shop)
RVCamp W: D & W Camping and Fishing Lake (.75 Miles)

238 Olympian Dr., Champaign
FStop W: Mobil(*, D, LP)
Food W: Dairy Queen (Mobil)
ATM W: Mobil

237AB Junction I-74 Peoria, Indianapolis (Difficult Reaccess)

235AB Junction I-72 (Difficult Reaccess)

229 Savoy, Monticello
FStop E: Speedway(*)

(222) Rest Area (RR, Phones, P; Southbound)

(221) Rest Area (RR, Phones, Picnic, Vending, P; Northbound)

220 U.S. 45, Pesotum, Tolono
Gas W: Citgo(*)
Food W: Lakeside Resturaunt
Other E: State Police

212 U.S. 36, Tuscola, Newman
TStop W: Dixie Trucker's Home(*, D, SCALES), Pilot Travel Center(*, D, SCALES)
FStop E: Fuel Mart(*)
Food W: Burger King, Dixie Restaurant (Dixie Truckers Home), Hardee's, Manchu Wok (Factroy Outlet), McDonald's(PLAY), Rocky Mountain Chocolate, Sabarros Pizza (Factory Outlet), Sara Lee (Factory Outlet), Subway (Pizza), TCBY (Factory Outlet), Taco Bell Express (Factroy Outlet)
Lodg W: Ameri Host Inn, Cooper Motel, Holiday Inn Express, Super 8
AServ W: Dixie Trucker's Home, IGA Grocery(CW), Tuscola Auto Parts
TServ W: Dixie Trucker's Home(SCALES)
RVCamp E: Campground (East)
ATM W: Dixie Trucker's Home, Tuscola National Bank
Other W: Factory Outlet Center, IGA Grocery, The Car Wash

203 IL 133, Arcola, Paris
FStop E: Citgo(*)
Gas W: Marathon(*, LP), Phillips 66(*, LP), Shell(*)
Food W: Dairy Queen, Hardee's(PLAY), Hen House, Subway
Lodg W: Amish Country Inn, Arcola Inn, Comfort Inn
AServ E: Jerry's Radiator Shop, Key Auto & Diesel Repair(CW)
W: Hal's Wrecker and Service
TServ E: I-57 Truck and Trailer Repair
RVCamp W: Arcola Camper Stop (.25 Miles)
Other W: Acola Car Wash

190AB IL 16, Mattoon, Charleston
Food W: Alamo Steak House, Cody's, Country Kitchen, Little Caesars Pizza (Big K-Mart), McDonald's(PLAY), Osco Pharmacy(RX), Pondorosa, Steak & Shake, Taco Bell (Cross County Mall), Wendy's
Lodg W: Fairfield Inn, Hampton Inn, Ramada Inn, Super 8
AServ W: Big K-Mart(RX), Sear's
Med E: + Hospital
ATM W: Central National Bank
Parks E: State Park
Other W: Big K-Mart(RX), Clyde Animal Clinic, Cross Country Mall, Illinois Express Eyecare, Osco Pharmacy(RX), Wal-Mart Supercenter(RX) (Wal-Mart Optical, Tire Center, Express Lube), WalGreens Pharmacy(RX)

184 U.S. 45, IL 121, Toledo, Mattoon
Gas W: Marathon(*, D)
Food W: McDonald's(PLAY)
Lodg W: Budget Inn(PLAY), Motel 57
AServ W: Marathon

EXIT ILLINOIS

177 U.S. 45, Neoga
FStop E: Shell(*)
Gas E: Citgo(*), Shell(*)
RVCamp W: Howard Mobile Home Park and Overnight Camping (.25 Miles), Over Night Campground

(167) Rest Area (RR, Phones, Picnic, RV Dump, P; Southbound)

(166) Rest Area (RR, Phones, Picnic, RV Dump, P; Northbound)

163 Junction I-70 East, Indianapolis

162 U.S. 45, Sigel, Effingham
Gas E: Moto Mart(*)
W: Citgo(*), Shell(D)
Food W: Trailways Restaurant
Lodg W: Budget Host Inn
AServ W: Shell
RVCamp W: Camp Lakewood (2 Miles)
ATM W: Citgo

160 IL 32, IL 33
TStop W: Bobbers Truck Plaza(*, RV DUMP, SCALES), Trucks America Truck Plaza(*, SCALES)
Gas E: Amoco(*), Shell
W: Phillips 66, Shell(*, D)
Food E: Dixie Cream Donut Shop, Little Caesars Pizza, Papa John's Pizza, Pizza Hut
W: Arby's, Blimpie's Subs, Bobber Restaurant, Bonanza Steakhouse, Burger King(PLAY), Cracker Barrel, Denny's, El Rancherito, K Square Food Court, KFC, Long John Silver, McDonald's (Inside Wal-Mart), McDonald's, Ramada Inn, Ryan's Steakhouse, Steak & Shake, Stix B B Q, Subway (Shell), T.G.I. Friday's, Taco Bell, Trucks America, Wendy's
Lodg E: Amerihost Inn, Hampton Inn
W: Best Inns of America, Budgetel Inn, Econolodge, Ramada
AServ E: Auto Zone Auto Parts, Shell
W: Ken Diepholz Ford, Mercury, Lincoln, Phillips 66
TServ W: Bobbers Truck Plaza, Speedco Truck Service, Trucks America
TWash W: Trucks America
RVCamp W: Camp Lakewood (West 1 Miles)
Med E: + Hospital
ATM E: Amoco, Crossroads Bank, First Mid- Illinois
W: Bobbers Truck Plaza, Illinois Community Bank
Other E: Aldi Grocery Store, Effingham Veterinary Clinic, Ever Clean Car Wash, K-Mart, Kroger Supermarket(24), Rollin Hill Laundromat, Super X Pharmacy
W: Factory Outlet Center

159 Effingham
TStop E: 76 Auto/Truck Plaza(LP, SCALES)
W: Petro(SCALES, 24), Truck-O-Mat(SCALES)
FStop E: Speedway(*, RV DUMP, SCALES)
Gas E: Amoco(*, CW), Clark, Phillips 66(*, D, CW), Shell(*, 24), Speedway(*, D, SCALES)
Food E: Domino's Pizza, G Wilkes Bar and Grill, Golden China Restaurant, Hardee's, Little Caesars Pizza, Niemerg's Family Dining, Spaghetti Shop, Subway, The China Buffet
W: Petro
Lodg E: Abe Lincoln Hotel, Comfort Suites Hotel, Days Inn, Holiday Inn, Howard Johnson, Paradise Inn, Quality Inn
W: Best Western
AServ E: Amoco, Effingham Tire Center, Firestone Tire & Auto, Pennzoil Oil Change, Shell
TServ E: 76 Auto/Truck Plaza, Effingham/International Truck Sales, Firestone Tire & Auto
W: Petro
TWash E: 76 Auto/Truck Plaza
W: Truck-O-Mat
Other E: Car Wash, Sav-A-Lot Grocery

157 I-70 West, St. Louis, Indianapolis (Left

EXIT		ILLINOIS
		Exit Northbound)
151		Watson, Mason
145		Edgewood
	Gas	**E:** Citgo(*)
	ATM	**E:** Citgo
135		IL 185, Farina, Vandalia
	FStop	**E:** Shell(*, LP)
	AServ	**E:** Engel Bros. Ford
	RVCamp	**W:** S & S RV Sales & Service
	ATM	**E:** Shell
127		Patoka, Kinmundy
	TStop	**E:** Marathon(*)
	Food	**E:** Granny's (Marathon), Pizza (Marathon)
	TServ	**E:** Kinmundy Diesel & Auto Repair (Marathon)
116		U.S. 50, Salem, Sandoval
	FStop	**W:** Phillips 66(*)
	Gas	**E:** Amoco(*, 24), Clark(*, K, 24), Shell(*)
	Food	**E:** Austin's Fried Chicken, Burger King(PLAY), Golden Corral Family Steakhouse, Hunan's Garden Chinese Restaurant, KFC, Kim's Chinese Restaurant, Long John Silver, McDonald's, Pizza Hut, Pizza Man, Subway, Taco Bell, Wendy's
		W: Denny's (Holiday Inn)(see our ad this page)
	Lodg	**E:** Budget Inn
		W: Comfort Inn, Holiday Inn, Super 8
	AServ	**E:** Auto Zone Auto Parts, Lander's Tire & Automotive Center, Max Dye Chrys, Plym, Dodge, Jeep, Olds, Pont, GMC, Pennzoil Oil Change, Salem Auto Supply, Shell
		W: Chris Chev, Buick, Joe Hotze Ford, Mercury, Salem Tire Center
	TServ	**W:** Joe Hotze Ford, Mercury, Salem Tire Center
	Med	**E:** ✚ Hospital
	ATM	**E:** NationsBank
	Parks	**E:** Steven Forbes State Park (17 Miles)
	Other	**E:** Brandy's(RX), Mad Pricer Grocery Store, Rapid Roy's Car Wash, Wal-Mart(RX), Westgate Car Wash
		W: AmeriGas(LP)
(114)		**Rest Area (RR, Phones, Picnic, Vending, P; Northbound)**
109		IL 161, Centralia
	Gas	**W:** Phillips 66(*, D)
	Food	**W:** Biggie's (Phillips 66)
	ATM	**W:** Phillips 66
103		Dix
	FStop	**E:** Marathon(*, D)
	Food	**E:** Austin's Restaurant, Piccadilly Pizza (Marathon)
	Lodg	**E:** Scottish Inns
	TServ	**E:** AC Delco
96		Jct. I-64
95		IL 15, Mt. Vernon, Ashley
	TStop	**W:** 76 Auto/Truck Plaza(*, SCALES, 24)
	FStop	**W:** Huck's(*, SCALES)
	Gas	**E:** Amoco(*, 24), Hucks Food Store(*), Phillips 66(*, CW), Shell, Speedway(*)

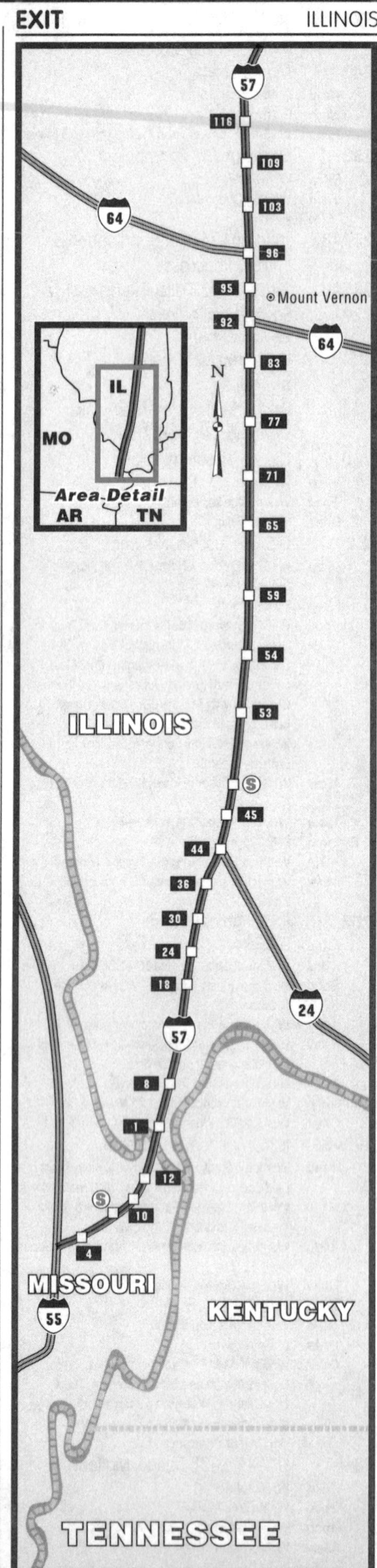

EXIT		ILLINOIS
		W: Shell(*), Shell(*)
	Food	**E:** Big-O's BBQ, Bonanza Steakhouse, Burger King, China Buffet, Cobbler's Restaurant (Ramada Inn), Denny's, El Rancherito, Fazoli's Italian Food, Hardees(PLAY), KFC, Little Caesars Pizza, Long John Silver, Pizza Hut, Pizza Pro (Kroger), Steak & Shake, Subway, Taco Bell, Triple E BBQ, Waffle's and More, Wendy's
		W: Applebee's, Arby's, Burger King, Caroline's (Holiday Inn), Cracker Barrel, McDonald's(PLAY), Shell
	Lodg	**E:** Best Inns of America, Best Western, Drury Inn, Motel 6, Ramada Inn, Super 8, Thrifty Inn
		W: Comfort Inn, Hampton Inn, Holiday Inn
	AServ	**E:** Midas Muffler & Brake, Phillips 66, Shell
		W: Tyler Pontiac, Buick, Cadillac, and GMC Trucks, Tyler Toyota
	TServ	**W:** 76 Auto/Truck Plaza, Truck Centers Inc, with Freightliner(24), XVIII Wheelers(24)
	RVCamp	**W:** Quality Times (.75 Miles)
	Med	**E:** ✚ Care First, ✚ Hospital
	ATM	**E:** Amoco, Bank of Illinois, Citizen's Bank, First National, Huck Food Store, Kroger, Merchantile Bank, NationsBank, Phillips 66
		W: Citizens Bank (Hampton Inn), Huck's, Shell, Shell, Truckstop
	Other	**E:** Country Fair Grocery(RX), K-Mart(RX), Kroger Supermarket(24, RX)
		W: Wal-Mart Supercenter(24, RX) (Tire Center)
92		I-64 East, Louisville (Difficult Reaccess)
83		Ina
	FStop	**E:** BP(*, LP)
	RVCamp	**E:** Sherwood Camping Resort (1.75 Miles)
(79)		**Rest Area (RR, Phones, P; Southbound)**
77		IL 154, Sesser
	RVCamp	**E:** Benton Best Holiday Trav-L-Park (.75 Miles)
		W: Gun Creek Recreation Area (.75 Miles)
(73)		**Rest Area (RR, Phones, Picnic, Pet Walk, P; Northbound)**
71		IL 14, Benton, Christopher
	Gas	**E:** 500 Platolene(D), Citgo(*), Coastal(*), Han-dee Mart(*, LP)
		W: Shell(*, D)
	Food	**E:** Gray Plaza Family Restaurant(24), Hardee's, Pizza Hut, Wendy's
		W: Bonanza Steakhouse, Full Moon House Chinese Restaurant, McDonald's(PLAY), Subway, Taco John's
	Lodg	**E:** Days Inn, Gray Plaza Motel, Super 8
	AServ	**E:** Pennzoil Oil Change, Southern Illinois Auto Repair
	RVCamp	**E:** Benton-KOA (1.13 Miles)
	Med	**E:** ✚ Hospital
	ATM	**E:** Southpointe Bank
		W: Combank, Shell
	Other	**E:** America's Best Car Wash, Super Wash Automatic Car Wash
		W: Big John's Grocery Store, Revco, Wal-Mart(24, RX)
65		IL 149, West Frankfort, Zeigler
	Gas	**E:** Amoco(*, 24), Citgo(*, D), Clark On The Go(*, LP, K), Shell(*, LP, 24) (Ice Cream Churn)
	Food	**E:** Dixie Creme Doughnuts, Hardee's, Hungry's Pancake House, KFC, Long John Silver, Mike's Drive-In, Pizza Inn, Shell (Ice Cream Churn)
		W: McDonald's(PLAY), Triple E Plus Steakhouse
	Lodg	**E:** Gray Plaza
		W: HoJo Inn
	AServ	**E:** Big A Auto Parts, Carquest, Speed Lube
		W: Weeks Chevrolet, Pontiac
	ATM	**E:** Amoco, Banterra Bank
	Other	**E:** Car Wash, Franklin County Animal Hospital
		W: K-Mart, Kroger Supermarket, Revco Drugs
59		Johnston City, Herrin
	Gas	**E:** Shell(*, 24) (No Trucks)
	Food	**E:** Hardee's

Bold red print shows RV & Bus parking available or nearby

EXIT — ILLINOIS

AServ E: KIP's Tires
RVCamp E: Campground
Med W: ✚ Hospital

54AB IL 13, Carbondale, Murphysboro, Marion
TStop W: Marion Truck Plaza[*, D, SCALES] (BP)
Gas E: Citgo[*, D, CW], Pet-tro, Phillips 66[*, CW]
W: Amoco[*]
Food E: Arby's, Fazoli's, Hardee's, KFC, La Fiesta Mexican Restaurant, Long John Silver, Nong Chen Chinese, Papa John's Pizza, Pizza Hut, Subway, Tequilas Mexican Restaurant, Wendy's, Western Sizzlin
W: Applebee's, Bob Evan's Restaurant, Burger King, Embers (Marion Hotel), McDonald's[PLAY], Ryan's Steakhouse, Sonic Drive In, Steak 'N Shake, Taco Bell, Waffle House
Lodg E: Days Inn, Gray Plaza Motel, Ramada Limited
W: Best Inns of America, Drury Inn, Hampton Inn, Marion Hotel and Conference Center, Motel 6, Super 8
AServ E: Instant Oil Change, Marion Ford Collision Center and Dealership
W: Foley-Sweitzer Pontiac, Oldsmobile, Buick, GMC Trucks
ATM E: Bank of Marion, Bantera Bank, Central Bank, Charter Bank, Citizens Bank, Kroger, NationsBank, Phillips 66
W: Amoco, Bank of Marion, Banterra
Other E: Kroger Supermarket[24, RX]
W: Sam's Club, Target, Wal-Mart[LP, RX]

53 Main St, Marion
Gas E: 76[*, D], Coastal[*], Shell[*]
W: Motomart[*, 24]
Food E: Dairy Queen
W: 20's Hideout Steakhouse, Cracker Barrel, Trudie's Mug Root Beer
Lodg E: Motel Marion
W: Budgetel, Comfort Inn, Comfort Suites Hotel
AServ E: 76, Marion Toyota, Mitsubishi Body Shop
RVCamp E: Motel Marion Campground (.25 Miles)
Med E: ✚ Hospital, ✚ VA Hospital
ATM E: Shell
W: Motomart
Other W: Laundromat (Motomart)

47 Wiegh Station (Southbound)

(46) Weigh Station (Northbound)

45 IL 148, Herrin
TServ W: Doc's Diesel Repair
RVCamp E: Camping

44AB Junction I-24 East, Nashville

40 Goreville Road, Scenic Overlook
FStop W: Scenic Ridge Plaza[*, D, LP, 24] (Citgo)
RVCamp E: Camping, Hilltop Campgrounds
Parks E: Fern Clyffe State Park

36 Lick Creek Road
AServ E: Carter's Garage

(32) Rest Area (RR, Phones, P; Southbound)

(31) Rest Area with Tourist Information (RR, Phones, Vending, P; Northbound)

30 IL 146, Anna, Vienna
FStop W: Shell[*, LP]
Food W: The Omelet Hut (Shell)
AServ W: Martin's Auto Service

24 Dongola Road
Gas W: Shell[*, LP]
ATM W: Shell
Other W: Coin Op Laundry (Shell)

18 Ullin Road
Gas W: BP[*]
Food W: Cheeko's[24]
Lodg W: Cheekwood Inn (Best Western)
AServ W: BP
Other E: Olmsted Locks & Dam
W: State Police

8 Mounds Road
FStop E: K & K Auto & Truck Stop[*]
AServ E: K&K
TServ E: K&K

1 IL 3 to U.S. 51, Cairo
TStop E: Cairo Truck Stop (BP)
Gas E: Amoco[*, D, 24]
Lodg E: Days Inn
TServ E: Cairo Truck Stop (BP)
RVCamp E: Camping
W: Camping

EXIT — ILLINOIS/MISSOURI

Med E: ✚ Medical Care Center

↑ILLINOIS

↓MISSOURI

(18) Weigh Station

12 U.S. 62, US 60, MO 77, Charleston, Wyatt
TStop E: Sunshine Travel Center[*, SCALES]
FStop E: Phillips 66[*]
W: The Flag Stop
Food E: Apple Valley Cafe (Sunshines Travel Center)
W: Charleston Restaurant (Charleston Inn Motel), KFC
Lodg E: Economy Motel
W: Charleston Inn Motel (The Flagstop TS)
ATM E: Sunshine Travel Center

10 MO 105, Business Loop I-57, Charleston, East Prairie
TStop E: Pilot[*, SCALES, 24]
FStop E: MFA Oil[LP]
Gas E: Boom-land[*] (Fireworks)
W: Casey's General Store[*] (Doughnuts)
Food E: Subway (Pilot), Wally's Chew-Chew (Boomland)
W: Casey's General Store (Doughnuts), China Buffet, Dairy Queen, McDonald's, Pizza Hut
Lodg W: Comfort Inn
TServ E: M & M Truck Repair[24], Pilot
W: Truck Parts
TWash E: Pilot
RVCamp E: Camping, Sam's Camping
ATM E: Pilot
W: First Securities State Bank, Union Planter's Bank
Other W: Town & Country Supermarket[LP], Wal-Mart[RX]

4 Route B, Bertrand
FStop E: BP[*]
Food E: BP

1AB 1A - I-55 South, Memphis, 1B - I-55 North, St Louis

0 Junction I-55, I-57

↑MISSOURI

Begin I-57

I-59 S →

EXIT — GEORGIA

Begin I-59

↓GEORGIA

4 **(19)** West I-24 Nashville

3 **(18)** Slygo Rd, New England
Gas W: Citgo[*, LP, CW]
AServ W: Avalanche Auto
RVCamp W: KOA Kampground (1.7 Miles)
ATM W: Citgo

2 **(12)** GA 136, Trenton
Gas E: Chevron[*, CW], Citgo[*, LP], Exxon[*, D]
W: Amoco[*], Citgo[*, D]
Food E: Burger King, Deli Dipper (Sandwich & Ice Cream), Hardee's, McDonald's[PLAY], Pizza Hut, Subway
W: Huddle House, Little Caesars Pizza, TCBY (Amoco), Taco Bell
Lodg E: Days Inn
AServ E: Chevron, NAPA Auto Parts, Smith's Auto Parts
RVCamp E: Lookout Lake Camping (7 Miles)
ATM E: Citgo, Citizens Bank & Trust Inc., Exxon
W: Amoco, Citgo
Parks E: Cloudland Canyon State Park
Other E: Bi-Lo Grocery[RX], CVS Pharmacy[RX], Chamber of Commerce, Family Dollar Store, Ingles Supermarket, Ponder Valu-Rite Pharmacy, Revco
W: Food Lion

1282

Open 24 Hours

706-462-2455

Gasoline & High Speed Diesel Pumps
Full Service Restaurant
Truck Accessories • Private Showers
Laundry Facilities • ATM Machines
D.A.T. Load Boards • Sandwich Shop
Certified Scales • Copy & Fax Services
GEORGIA ▪ I-59 ▪ EXIT 1

EXIT — GEORGIA/ALABAMA

(11) Parking Area, Scenic View (Westbound)

(11) Weigh Station (Eastbound)

1 **(4)** Rising Fawn
TStop W: Mapco Express[*, SCALES] (see our ad this page)
FStop E: Citgo[*]
Gas W: Amoco[*]
Food W: Blimpie Subs & Salads (Amoco), Cafe[SCALES], Mapco Express, Perkins Family Restaurant (Mapco), TCBY (Amoco)
ATM E: Citgo
W: Amoco, Mapco Express
Other W: Fox Mountain Trout Farm (1.5 Miles)

↑GEORGIA

↓ALABAMA

(241) AL Welcome Center (RR, HF, Phones, Picnic, RV Dump, RV Water, Pet Walk; Westbound)

EXIT ALABAMA

239 To U.S 11, Sulphur Springs Rd
Lodg E: Freeway Motel
RVCamp E: **Sequoyah Caverns & Campground (3.5 Miles)**

231 AL 40, AL 117, Hammondville, Valley Head, Stevenson, Bridgeport
Gas W: Texaco(D, LP)
AServ W: Texaco
RVCamp E: **Sequoyah Caverns Campground (5.3 Miles)**
Other E: Antique

222 U.S 11, Fort Payne
Gas E: Shell(*)
W: Citgo(*, LP), Exxon(*), Texaco(*, LP)
Food W: **Waffle King**(24)
AServ W: Airport Tire & Auto Service, Exxon, Williams Garage & Wrecker Service
ATM W: Texaco
Other W: Gary's TV & Appliance Outlet

218 AL 35, Fort Payne, Rainsville, Scottsboro
TStop W: **Pure, Pure Truck Plaza**
Gas E: Conoco(*, LP)
W: Exxon(*, CW), Shell(*)
Food E: Captain D's Seafood, Central Park, Pizza Hut, SHONEY'S, Shoney's, Taco Bell
W: Burger King(PLAY), Hardee's, **Huddle House**, **Pure**, Quincy's Family Steakhouse, Waffle House (Quality Inn), **Wal-Mart Supercenter**(24, RX) **(One Hr Photo)**
Lodg W: DAYS INN Days Inn, Holiday Inn Express, Quality Inn
AServ W: Ford Dealership, **Wal-Mart Supercenter**(24) **(One Hr Photo)**
TServ W: **Pure, Pure Truck Plaza**
Med W: ✚ **Dekalb Baptist Medical Center**
ATM E: Conoco
W: Carwash, Exxon
Parks E: **De Soto State Park**
Other W: Carwash, **Food World**, **K-Mart**(RX), **Wal-Mart Supercenter**(RX) **(One Hr Photo)**

205 AL 68, Collinsville, Crossville
FStop W: **Texaco**(*, LP)
Gas E: Chevron(*), Pure(D)
W: Shell(*), Texaco(*, D, LP)
Food E: **Big Valley Restaurant**, **Howard Johnson Inn**, Jack's(PLAY)
Lodg E: **Howard Johnson Inn**
AServ E: Pure
ATM W: Shell

188 AL 211, To U.S 11, Noccalula Falls, Gadsden
FStop W: **Amoco**(*)
Gas E: Chevron(*)
W: I-59 Echo(*, K)
Food E: Noccalula Station Restaurant
RVCamp E: **Noccalula Campgrounds**

183 **(184)** U.S 278, U.S 431, Gadsden, Attalla
FStop E: **Amoco**(*)
Gas E: Shell(*), Texaco(*, LP)
W: Amoco(*), Chevron(*, LP, 24), Exxon(*, CW), Texaco(*)
Food E: **Hardee's**, Magic Burger, Waffle House, Wendy's
W: Itallia Food Market (Fresh Fruits & Vegetables Homestyle Cooking), **KFC**, McDonald's(PLAY), Pizza Hut, Quincy's Family Steakhouse, SHONEY'S, Shoney's, Subway, Taco Bell
Lodg E: Columbia Inn, **Holiday Inn Express**, **Rodeway Inn**
W: Econolodge
AServ E: Attalla Auto Parts
W: Cook's Auto Body Shop, Exxon, Texaco, Truck & Trailer
ATM E: The Exchange Bank of AL
W: Texaco
Other E: **AL State Troopers Gadsden Post**, Catfish Bill's

EXIT ALABAMA

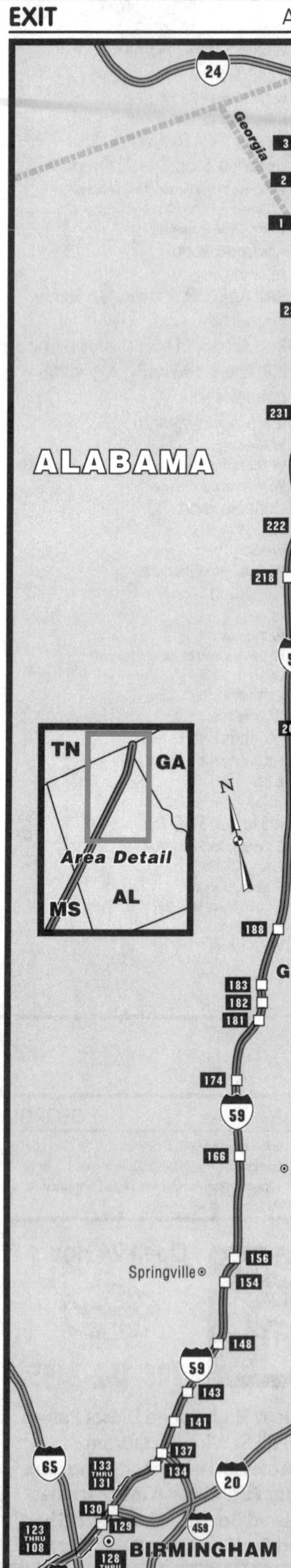

EXIT ALABAMA

Fish & Seafood Market
W: Coin Operated Car Wash, **Sunbeam Bakery Thrift Store**

182 Junction I-759, Gadsden

181 AL 77, Attalla, Rainbow City
FStop W: **BP**(*)
Food W: Dairy Queen, Hardee's, Subway
Lodg E: DAYS INN **Days Inn**
ATM W: **BP**
Other E: Federal Express, **Flowers Bakery Thrift Store**

174 Steele
FStop W: **Chevron**(*, D), **Spur**(*, SCALES)
Food W: **Spur**
TServ E: **Steele City Truck Stop (Truck & Tire Service)**
W: **J-K Truck Service, Spur**(SCALES)

(167) **Rest Area (RR, Phones, Picnic, Vending, RV Dump, Pet Walk; Westbound)**

166 U.S. 231, Oneonta, Ashville
FStop E: **Exxon**(*)
W: **Texaco**(*)
Gas E: Chevron(*, LP, 24)
Food W: **Taco Bell (Texaco)**, **Texaco**
Other W: **Horse Pins Forty**

(165) **Rest Area (RR, HF, Phones, Picnic, RV Dump; Eastbound)**

156 AL 23, Saint Clair Springs, Springville

154 AL 174, Springville, Odenville
Gas W: Chevron(*, LP, CW, 24), Texaco(*, CW)
Food W: Jack's Hamburgers(PLAY), McDonald's, Sneeky Peeks (Texaco), Texaco
ATM W: Texaco

148 To U.S. 11, Argo
Gas E: Amoco(*, D), BP(*, LP, K), Citgo(*, D)
Food E: Argo Cafe
AServ E: Code 3 Automotive, Dunaway, Rapid Auto and Quick Lube
Other E: **Argo Animal Clinic**, **Argo Optical**, **Argo True Value Hardware**, **Buckeye Grocery**(K)

143 Deerfoot Pkwy, Mt Olive Church Rd (Reaccess Southbound Only, Difficult Reaccess)

141 Trussville, Pinson, Grayson Valley
FStop E: **Amoco**(D, CW)
Gas E: BP(*, D, CW), Exxon(*), Shell(*)
W: Chevron(*, CW, 24), Shell(*)
Food E: Big Dragon Chinese Restaurant, **Cracker Barrel**, Lone Star Steakhouse, McDonald's(PLAY), Papa John's Pizza, Pizza Hut, Shell, Subway (Shell), Taco Bell, **Waffle House**, Wendy's
W: Burger King(PLAY), Dairy Queen, **Little Caesars Pizza (K-Mart)**, Paul's Hot Dogs, Ruby Tuesday, Wall Street Deli & TCBY
AServ W: Express Lube
ATM E: Exxon
W: Chevron, Compass Bank, SouthTrust Bank, **Western Supermarket**
Other E: Chiropractic, Orthodontic
W: CVS Pharmacy(RX), **K-Mart**(RX), **Western Supermarket**

137 Junction I-459 South, Tuscaloosa, Montgomery (Left Exit Westbound, Trucks with more than six wheels must use I-459 through Birmington)

134 To AL 75, Roebuck Pkwy
Gas W: Amoco(*), BP(*, D), Chevron(*, CW, 24), Citgo(*), Shell(*, 24)
Food W: Baskin Robbins, Chick-Fil-A, Chuck E Cheese's Pizza, Denny's, Guadalajara Mexican Restaurant, Johnny's Ray's, Krystal(24), McDonald's(PLAY), Milo's Hamburgers, Mrs Winner's Chicken, O' Charley's, Pioneer Cafeteria, Steak & Ale, Waffle House
Lodg W: Parkway Inn

Bold red print shows RV & Bus parking available or nearby

EXIT ALABAMA

ASERV W: Amoco, Citgo, K-Mart[RX], Marty's Transmission, NTB National Tire & Battery, Penske, Roebuck Honda, Roebuck Parts & Auto Service
Med W: Hospital
ATM W: Amoco, Citgo, Colonial Bank, Compass Bank, SouthTrust Bank
Other W: CVS Pharmacy[24], K-Mart[RX], Pearl Vision

133 4th Ave S (Northbound, Reaccess Southbound Only)
Gas E: Citgo
Food E: Arby's, Catfish Cabin Seafood Family Restaurant, El Ringos Restaurant, Johnny Ray's, Joy's Fish & BBQ, Papa John's Pizza, Pasquale's Pizza, Sneeky Pete's Hot Dog, Wok Cuisine
AServ E: Citgo, Goodyear, Roebuck Chrysler Plymouth Jeep Eagle
ATM E: Compass Bank, SouthBank, Winn Dixie Supermarket[RX]
Parks E: Don A. Hawkins Park
Other E: Bruno's Bakery, Car Wash, Chiropractic, Dental Center, Drugs for Less, Kmart[RX], Pearl Vision, Rite Aid Pharmacy, Roebuck's Shopping City Mall, Total Eye Care, U.S. Post Office, Winn Dixie Supermarket[RX]

132 U.S 11, 1st Ave N
Gas E: Amoco, Chevron[D, LP, CW], Exxon[*, CW], Racetrac
W: Exxon
Food E: Jo & Deb's, Rally's Hamburgers, Subway
W: Double Dog Dare, El Placio, Krispy Kreme Doughnuts
Lodg W: Anchor Motel, El Rancho Motel
AServ E: East Lake Auto Parts
W: Exxon
RVCamp E: Dandy RV Parts & Sales (1/3 Mile)
ATM E: Amoco, Chevron, Exxon, Racetrac
Other E: Dog & Cat Hospital
W: Ethridge Car Wash, Hardware Store[LP, RX], Hudds Assoc Foods, Meat Locker, Pet Food IAMS

131 Oporto - Madrid (Northbound, Difficult Reaccess)
Gas E: Exxon[*, CW]
Food E: Andrew's Bar-B-Q, Burger King, Church's Chicken, Rally's Hamburgers, Taco Bell
AServ E: East Lake Tire Center, NAPA Auto Parts
RVCamp E: Dandy RV Parts & Service
ATM E: Exxon
Other E: Convenience Store, Wood's V & S Drugs

130A US 11 South, 1st Ave N (Northbound)
Food E: Captain D's Seafood, McDonald's, Mrs Winner's Chicken
Lodg E: Motel American, Relax Inn, Sky Inn
AServ E: Auto Painting Body & Repair
Other E: Merita Bakery Thrift Store

130B US 11 North, 1st Ave N (Northbound)
Gas E: Amoco, Chevron[*]
Lodg E: Bama Motel
AServ E: Auto Zone Auto Parts, Eastern Alternator & Starter Service, SouthTrust, Westwood Auto Parts
RVCamp E: Colonial RV
Other E: Fire Station, Food Fair, Western Union

130 Junction I-20 East, Atlanta
Gas S: Exxon[*], Shell[CW], Texaco[*]
Food N: Restaurant (Ramada Inn)
S: Blimpie's Subs, Huddle House
Lodg N: Ramada Inn (Restaurant)
S: DAYS INN Days Inn, Holiday Inn
AServ S: Airport Car Wash (Self Wash)

129 Airport Blvd
Gas E: Exxon[*], Shell[*, CW, 24], Texaco[*]
Food E: Blimpie's Subs (Texaco), Hardee's, Holiday Inn, Huddle House, Sammy's Sandwich Shop
W: Clairon
Lodg E: DAYS INN Days Inn, Holiday Inn
W: Clairon
ATM E: Shell

EXIT ALABAMA

Other E: Coin Operated Car Wash, Woodlawn Mart
W: Airport

128 AL 79, Tallapoosa St, Tarrant
Gas W: Shell[*, CW]

126B 31st St, Sloss Furnaces, Civic Ctr
Gas W: Circle K[*], Texaco[*]
Food W: McDonald's, Sol's Hotdogs
TServ E: Alabama Trailer Co., Commercial Truck Sales, Freightliner[SCALES], Kurt's Truck Parts, Liberty Truck Sales & Service
Other E: Used Vehicle Sales
W: Sani-Clean Laundromat

126A U.S. 31, U.S 280, Carraway Blvd
Gas W: Citgo[D]
Food E: KFC
W: Church's Chicken, Ed's Diner, Rally's Hamburgers
AServ W: Citgo
Med E: Hospital

125 22nd Street, Downtown (Left Exit)
Food W: Sophia's Deli
Lodg W: Best Western, Sheraton
Other W: AL Sports Hall of Fame, Birmingham Jefferson Civic Center, Boutwell Auditorium, Tourist Info.

125B 22nd St, Downtown Birmingham, Art Museum, Civic Center (Northbound, No Reaccess, Difficult Reaccess, Same Services As Exit 125)
Food E: Burger King

125A 17th St, Downtown Birmingham (Northbound, Reaccess Southbound Only, Difficult Reaccess)
Gas E: Gem[*]
Food E: Burger King
Other E: AL School of Fine Arts, Fire Department

124B Junction I-65 North, Nashville, Huntsville

124A Junction I-65 South, Montgomery (Left Exit Southbound)

123 U.S 78, Jasper, Arkadelphia Rd (Difficult Reaccess)
Gas W: Amoco[*], Chevron[*], Shell[*, CW, 24]
Food W: Denny's (La Quinta Inn), Popeye's Chicken
Lodg W: La Quinta Inn
AServ W: AAMCO Transmission
Med E: Hospital
ATM W: Amoco, Chevron

121 Bush Blvd, Ensley
Gas W: Citgo[*], Exxon[*, LP]
Food W: Fat Burger
ATM W: Exxon

120 20th St, Ensley Avenue, Alabama State Fair Complex (Difficult Reaccess)
Gas E: BP[*, 24], Jiffy Mart #4[*]
W: Crown[*, D, CW, 24]
Food W: KFC
AServ E: Jim Burke Chevrolet, Limbaugh Toyota
ATM W: Crown
Other E: Washing Well Coin Laundry

119B Avenue I (Westbound, Difficult Reaccess)

119A Lloyd Nolan Pkwy
Gas E: Exxon, Texaco[*]
W: Amoco[*, D], Chevron[*], Chevron[*, 24]
Food E: Omelet Shoppe
W: Burger King, McDonald's[PLAY], Mrs Winner's Chicken, Subway, Taco Bell, Wingo's Buffalo Wings, Wingo's Buffalo Wings
AServ E: Exxon, Sharp Auto Supply
W: CloverLeaf Auto Center
TServ E: B&W Wrecker, Big Mo Alignment Center

EXIT ALABAMA

Med E: Hospital
Other E: Carwash

118 Valley Rd, Fairfield
Lodg E: Fairfield Inn, Villager Lodge
AServ E: Alton Jones Auto Service, Fairfield Transmission, National Tire & Battery Warehouse, Penske Auto Service, Scogin Bros Auto Repair, Valley Road Auto Parts
TServ E: Truck & Diesel Repair
ATM E: AmSouth Bank
Other E: Home Depot[LP]

115 Jaybird Rd, Midfield, Pleasant Rd

113 18th Avenue, Brighton, Lipscomb
TStop E: Speedway[*]
Food E: McDonald's, Speedway
AServ W: Alabama Alignment & Spring Peterbilt of Birmingham Inc.
ATM E: Speedway

112 18th St, 19th St, Bessemer
Gas N: Amoco
S: Amoco[*], Chevron[*, CW]
Food N: Jack's Hamburgers, Roller Coaster
S: Bob Sykes BBQ, Captain's Place Seafood, KFC, Muffalettas Italian Foods
AServ N: O.K. Tire & Battery Co.
S: Big A Auto Parts, City Auto Parts
ATM S: Chevron
Other N: Mick's True Value Hardware[LP]
S: Bessemer National Park, Bessemer Pet Clinic

108 U.S 11, AL 5, Academy Drive
Gas E: BP[*, LP, CW], Shell[*]
Food E: Burger King[PLAY], Little Caesars Pizza, McDonald's (Wal-Mart), Omelet Shop, Wal-Mart SuperCenter[RX]
W: McKluskies, Quincy's
Lodg E: DAYS INN Days Inn, Masters Inn, Ramada Inn
W: Best Western
AServ E: Shell, Tire & Lube Express (Wal-Mart), Wal-Mart SuperCenter
Med E: Hospital
ATM E: BP
W: South Trust Bank
Other E: Baskin Robbins (Wal-Mart), Drugs for Less, Wal-Mart SuperCenter[RX], Winn Dixie Supermarket

106 Junction I-459 North, Gadsden, Atlanta

104 Rock Mountain Lakes
TStop E: Flying J Travel Plaza[*, RV DUMP]
Food E: Flying J Travel Plaza
ATM E: Flying J Travel Plaza

100 Abernant, Bucksville
TStop E: Petro[*, D]
Gas E: Exxon[*, LP], Phillips 66[*, D], Texaco[*, LP]
W: Citgo[*, LP]
Food E: Iron Skillet (Petro), Petro
W: Family Deli & Grill
AServ E: McKinney Wrecker 24 Hr.
TServ E: Petro
RVCamp W: KOA-Mccalla/Tannehill (6 Miles)
Med E: Tannehill Valley Medical Center
ATM E: Phillips 66
Parks E: Tannehill Ironworks Historical State Park

97 U.S 11 South, AL 5 South, West Blocton, Centerville
FStop E: Amoco[*], Texaco[*, LP]
Gas E: Shell[*, LP]
Food E: Dot's Farmhouse, KFC
ATM E: Amoco

89 Mercedes Dr

86 Brookwood, Vance
TStop W: Shell[*] (Restaurant)
Food W: Shell (Restaurant)
TServ W: Shell, Shell (Restaurant)

Bold red print shows RV & Bus parking available or nearby

EXIT ALABAMA

RVCamp E: Candy Mountain RV Park (4.5 Miles), Lakeside RV Park

(85) Rest Area (RR, HF, Phones, Picnic, Vending, RV Dump, Pet Walk)

(85) Rest Area (Eastbound)

79 U.S 11, University Blvd, Coaling

RVCamp N: Candy Mountain RV Park (4.5 Miles)

77 Cottondale

TStop W: T/A TravelCenters of America[*, RV DUMP, SCALES]

Gas W: Amoco[*]

Food W: Country Pride (Truck Stops Of America), McDonald's[PLAY] (Amoco), Subway (Truck Stops Of America), T/A TravelCenters of America, Taco Bell (Truck Stop)

Lodg W: Hampton Inn, Microtel Inn

AServ E: Troy's Honda Parts

TServ W: T/A TravelCenters of America[SCALES]

TWash W: T/A TravelCenters of America

76 U.S 11, East Tuscaloosa, Cottondale

TStop E: 76 Auto/Truck Plaza[SCALES], Baggett's

Gas E: Texaco[*, D, LP] (Wrecker Service)
W: Citgo[*], Shell[*, D]

Food E: Baggett's
W: Burger King, Cracker Barrel, Knight's Inn

Lodg E: Sleep Inn
W: Key West Inn, Knight's Inn

AServ E: Baggett's, Texaco (Wrecker Service)
W: Donnie Bryant Transmission

TServ E: 76 Auto/Truck Plaza[SCALES], Baggett's

TWash E: 76 Auto/Truck Plaza

RVCamp E: Country Roads RV Sales & Service[LP] (1 Mile)
W: Sunset II Travel Park

ATM E: 76 Auto/Truck Plaza
W: Shell

Other W: Geer Bros. Camper Sales and Service

73 U.S 82, McFarland Blvd

FStop W: BP[*]

Gas E: Amoco, Exxon[*, LP], Texaco[*, D, CW]
W: BP[*, D], Chevron[*], Parade[*, CW], Phillips 66[*], Racetrac[*], Shell[*, CW]

Food E: Chili's, Guthrie's Chicken, Hardee's, Huddle House, Joe Mugs (Books-A-Million), Jordan Homestyle Restaurant, KFC, Logan's Roadhouse Steaks & Ribs, McDonald's[PLAY], Piccadilly Cafeteria, Pizza Hut, Quincy's Family Steakhouse, Sonic Drive In, Subway, Taco Bell, Taco Casa, Trey Yuen, Wendy's
W: Burger King, Captain D's Seafood, Denny's, Ezell's Catfish Cabin, Fortune Garden, Krystal, Long John Silver, O'Charley's, SHONEY'S, Shoney's, Sneaky Peeks (Chevron), Waffle House

Lodg E: Comfort Inn, Country Inn & Suites, DAYS INN Days Inn, La Quinta Inn, LaQuinta Inn, Motel 6, Ramada Inn, Super 8
W: Best Western, Holiday Inn, Master's Inn, Shoney's Inn, TraveLodge

AServ E: Amoco, Carport Auto Service, SouthTrust Bank, Townsend Ford, Townsend Glass, Tuscaloosa Isuzu
W: Barkley's Pontiac, GMC, O.K. Tire Service, Postle's Auto Service, Tuscaloosa Motor Parts

Med E: ✚ Family Care Medical Center & Cancel
W: ✚ Hospital

ATM E: AM South, Amoco, Exxon, Region Bank
W: Racetrac

Parks E: Lake Lurene State Park
W: Bowers Park

Other E: Books-A-Million (Coffee Shop), Delchamp's Supermarket, Food World, Harkco Super Drug, McFarland Mall, Rite Aid Pharmacy, Sam's Club, Spiffy's Car Wash[CW], Walmart Super Center[24, RX] (Vision Center), Winn Dixie Supermarket[RX]
W: Christian Book & Gift Store, Ramey Animal Hospital

71B Junction I-369, AL 69 North, Tuscaloosa (Difficult Reaccess)

EXIT ALABAMA

Tuscaloosa!

The Perfect Off-Road Experience.

Not only is Tuscaloosa home of the new Mercedes off–road vehicle but also home of the perfect off–road experience for your group.

You can tour the Mercedes-Benz Visitors Center and Factory. Enjoy an historic tour of the University of Alabama campus, or tour the Alabama Museum of Natural History, and the Paul W. "Bear" Bryant Museum. You can also view the world renowned Warner Art Collection that includes precious works ranging from primitive, to classical, to modern. Or visit Moundville Archaeological Park and experience the life of Native Americans who lived here during prehistoric times.

Tuscaloosa's cultural and relaxing environment also provides 27 hotels and countless fine restaurants. So call today and let us help you put together the perfect off–road experience.

P.O. Box 3167 • Tuscaloosa, AL 35403
(205) 391-9200 • 1-800-538-8696
FAX (205) 391-2125 or
visit our web site at http://www.tcvb.org

1668

QUALITY ACCOMMODATIONS AT BEARABLE RATES

- 165 Guest Rooms with Coffee Makers/Hair Dryers
- Complimentary Continental Breakfast
- 4 Spacious Meeting/Banquet Rooms
- Full Food and Beverage Catering
- Expanded Cable TV Featuring Showtime, ESPN and CNN

3920 E. McFarland Blvd. (Exit 73 I-20/59)
Tuscaloosa, AL 35405
205-553-1550

EXIT ALABAMA/MISSISSIPPI

71A AL 69S, Moundville (Difficult Reaccess)

Gas E: Exxon[*, D]

Food E: Arby's, IHOP, Lone Star Steakhouse, Outback Steakhouse, Pizza Hut, Waffle House, Wendy's

Lodg E: Courtyard by Marriott, Fairfield Inn, Jameson Inn

AServ E: Quality Jeep Eagle

Other E: K-Mart, Lowe's (Hardware)

62 Fosters

52 U.S 11, U.S 43, Knoxville

FStop W: SpeedStop[*]

45 Union

FStop E: Amoco[*]

Food E: Hardee's, Southfork Restaurant[24]
W: Cotton Patch Restaurant

Lodg E: Western Inn

AServ E: Auto Value (Parts)

40 AL 14, Eutaw, Aliceville (Tombevillock & Dam, Visitor)

Med E: ✚ Hospital (2 Miles)

Other W: Visitor Information

(39) Rest Area (RR, HF, Phones, Picnic, Vending, RV Dump, RV Water, Pet Walk; Westbound)

(38) Rest Area (RR, HF, Phones, Picnic, Vending, RV Dump, RV Water, Pet Walk; Eastbound)

32 Boligee

FStop W: BP[*]

Gas E: Chevron[*, 24]

Food E: Chevron, Subway (Chevron)
W: BP

Parks W: Boligee Park

23 Gainesville, Epes

17 AL 28, Livingston, Boyd

TStop E: Noble Truck Stop[*, SCALES]

FStop E: Exxon[*, D], Texaco[*]

Gas E: BP[*, 24], Chevron[*, 24]

Food E: Burger King, Chevron, Exxon, Noble Truck Stop, Pizza Hut, Royal Waffle King (Noble TS), Subway (Chevron)

Lodg E: Comfort Inn, Western Inn

TServ E: Dickey's 24hr Shop Lube & Repair (Noble)

ATM E: Chevron

8 AL 17, York

TStop E: BP[*, SCALES]

Food E: BP

Lodg E: DAYS INN Days Inn

TServ E: Dun-Rite Truck Wash (BP)

TWash E: BP

Med E: ✚ Hospital

1 U.S 80 East, Cuba, Demopolis

TStop W: Phillips 66

Gas E: Chevron[*], Dixie[*]

Food W: Phillips 66

(1) Rest Area (RR, HF, Phones, Picnic, RV Dump; Eastbound)

↑ALABAMA

↓MISSISSIPPI

(170) Weigh Station (Westbound)

(170) Weigh Station (Eastbound)

169 Kewanee

TStop E: Kewanee One Stop[*]

FStop E: Red Apple[*]
W: Dixie

Food E: Kewanee One Stop, Restaurant (Kewanee One Stop)

165 Toomsuba

TStop E: Fuel Mart[*, SCALES]

EXIT MISSISSIPPI

FStop	**W:** Travla Texaco(*, D, 24)
Gas	**W:** Shell(*)
Food	**E:** Arby's (Fuel Mart), Fuel Mart
	W: Travla Restaurant (Texaco), Travla Texaco
RVCamp	**E:** KOA Campgrounds (1.75 Miles)
ATM	**W:** Travla Texaco
Other	**W:** Coin Car Wash

(164) Rest Area, Welcome Center (RR, Phones, Picnic, RV Dump, RV Water, Pet Walk, P; Westbound)

160 Russell

TStop	**E:** T/A TravelCenters of America, Travel Center(*, SCALES) (BP)
	W: Amoco(*, LP, SCALES)
Food	**E:** T/A TravelCenters of America, Travel Center, Travel Center (BP)
TServ	**E:** Travel Center(SCALES) (BP)
RVCamp	**W:** Nanabe Creek Campground (1 Mile)
ATM	**E:** Travel Center (BP)
	W: Amoco

157B US 45N, Macon, Quitman (Difficult Reaccess)

157A US 45S, Quitman

154AB Hwy 19 S, Hwy 39 North, Naval Air Station, De Kalb, Butler AL

Gas	**E:** Chevron(*, D, CW), Conoco(*, D, LP, CW)
	W: Amoco(*, D), BP(*, D, CW), Shell(*, CW)(see our ad this page)
Food	**E:** Chesterfield's, China King, Luby's Cafeteria, Mazingo's, McDonald's, O'Charley's Restaurant, Popeye's Chicken, Red Lobster, Ryan's Steakhouse, Taco Bell
	W: Applebee's, Backyard Burgers, Cracker Barrel, Denny's(24) (Holiday Inn), Greenbriar (Howard Johnson), Holiday Inn, Mr C's Rancho, Waffle House
Lodg	**E:** Comfort Inn
	W: Days Inn, Hampton Inn, Holiday Inn, Howard Johnson, Relax Inn, Rodeway Inn, Super 8, Western Motel
AServ	**E:** Express Lube, Sears
	W: Bill Ethridge Lincoln Mercury Isuzu, Johnson Dodge, Meridian Honda, Premier Paint & Body, Sellers Olds Cadillac
TServ	**E:** Truckers Supply Co. (Parts)
	W: Stribling Equipment Empire Truck
RVCamp	**W:** Campground RV And Trailer Park (2 Miles), Ethridge RV Center(LP) (.4 Miles), Jen's Discount Furniture Mobil Home Parts
ATM	**E:** Chevron, Citizen National Bank, Conoco
	W: Howard Johnson, Shell(*, CW), Shell
Other	**E:** Bonita Lake Mall, K-Mart(RX), Meridian Shop Plaza, Wal-Mart(RX)
	W: Old South Antique Mall

153 U.S 145S, 22nd Avenue, Quitman,

The Universal Sign for the World's Best-selling Gasoline

1215

Clean Restrooms | Air & Water | Easy Access | Fast Food Nearby

Shell

I-20/59 Exit 165
Gasoline Only
Snacks
Hours 6am-10pm
601-632-4732

I-20/59 Exit 154
Convenience Store
ATM • Car Wash
Open 24 Hours
601-483-6373

MISSISSIPPI • I-20/59 • 2 LOCATIONS

EXIT MISSISSIPPI

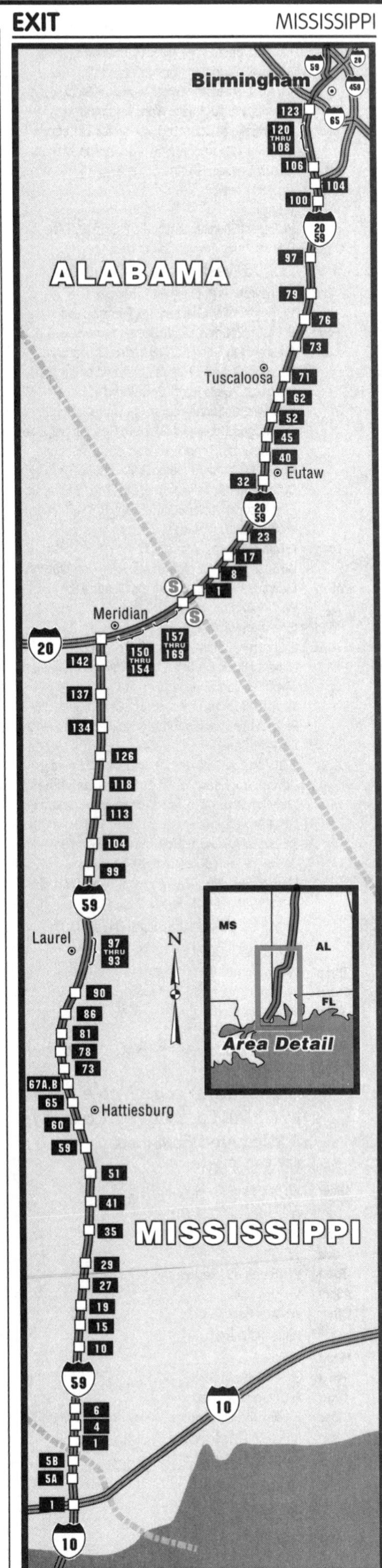

EXIT MISSISSIPPI

Downtown Meridian

TStop	**E:** Red Hot Truck Stop
Gas	**E:** Chevron(*, D, 24), Conoco(*, D, LP, CW, RV DUMP), Exxon(*, D, LP), Shell
	W: Amoco(*, 24), BP(*)
Food	**E:** Best Western, Depot (Best Western), Morrison's Cafeteria, Red Hot Truck Stop, Waffle House
	W: Barnhill's, Burger King, Captain D's Seafood, El Chico Mexican Restaurant, Hardee's, KFC, McDonald's(PLAY), SHONEY'S, Shoney's, Wendy's
Lodg	**E:** Astro Motel, Best Western, Budget 8 Motel, Budgetel Inn, Econolodge, Holiday Inn Express, Motel 6, Sleep Inn
AServ	**E:** Coin Car Wash, Nelson Hall Hyundai Chevrolet, Patco Inc., Shell
	W: Firestone Tire & Auto, Goodyear Tire & Auto, Tire Center
TServ	**E:** Patco Inc.
Med	**E:** Hospital
ATM	**E:** Conoco, Exxon
	W: Citizens National Bank, Union Planters Bank
Other	**W:** Foodmax Grocery, K&B Drugs, Medi Save Pharmacy, Optical

152 29th Avenue (Difficult Reaccess)

FStop	**W:** Amoco(*), Chevron(*, D, 24)
Food	**E:** Royal Inn Motel
Lodg	**E:** Royal Inn Motel
	W: Ramada Limited
ATM	**W:** Chevron

151 49th Avenue, Valley Rd, Meridian

150 U.S 11, N19, Philadelphia, Meridian Airport

TStop	**E:** Stuckey's Express(*, D)
	W: Phillips 66, Twin Cities Truck Stop
FStop	**E:** Amoco(*, LP)
Gas	**W:** No Name(*)
Food	**E:** Stuckey's Express, Subway (Stuckey's Express)
	W: Phillips 66
TServ	**W:** International, Phillips 66, Tire Centers Inc., Waters Int. Truck
ATM	**E:** Amoco
Parks	**W:** Lake Okatibee Park

148 **(130)** I-20 West, New Orleans, Laurel (Left Exit Northbound)

142 Savoy, Dunn's Falls

137 North Enterprise, Stonewall

134 MS 513, South Enterprise, Rose Hill

FStop	**E:** BP(*)

126 MS 18, Pachuta, Rose Hill, Quitman

FStop	**E:** Amoco(*), BP(*)

118 Vossburg, Paulding, Stafford Springs, Waukaway Springs

113 MS 528, Heidelberg, Bay Springs

TStop	**E:** J.R.'s Truckstop(*, CW, RV DUMP)
FStop	**E:** Stuckey's Express(*)
Gas	**E:** Exxon(*, D), Shell(*)
	W: Texaco(D, LP)
Food	**E:** Flyin Pig BBQ, Hot Stuff Pizza (Stuckey's Express), J.R.'s Truckstop, Pizza Inn (Exxon), Subway (Exxon)
AServ	**W:** Texaco
ATM	**E:** Stuckey's Express

(109) Parking Area (Southbound)

(106) Parking Area (Northbound)

104 Sandersville, Sharon

99 U.S. 11, Laurel

FStop	**E:** T & B Curb(*)
Food	**E:** Days Inn
Lodg	**E:** Days Inn, Magnolia Motel
TServ	**E:** T & B Curb
RVCamp	**E:** KOA Campgrounds (1.25 Miles)

97 U.S. 84 East, Waynesboro, Chantilly St.

EXIT MISSISSIPPI

FStop E: Chevron(*), Doc's Food 'N Fuel Center(*)
Gas W: BP(*, D), Texaco(*)
Food E: Hardee's, Subway (Chevron)
W: KFC, Out Back BBQ & Grill, Vic's Biscuits & Burgers
Lodg E: Doc's Food 'N Fuel Center

96B MS 15 South, Cook Ave

96A 4th Ave, Masonite Rd
Gas E: Blues(*)

95C Beacon St
Gas E: BP(*, D, K), Chevron(*, D), Texaco(*, CW)
W: Pump & Save
Food W: Burger King, Chuck's Wagon Buffet, Church's Chicken, McDonald's(PLAY), Old Mexico Restaurant, Popeye's Chicken
Lodg W: Town House Motel
ATM W: Central Sunbelt Federal Credit Union
Other W: Cinema 5 (Mall), Lauren Rogers Museum of Art, Sawmill Square Mall, Synergy Gas(LP)

95AB U.S 84 West, MS 15 North, 16th Ave
Gas W: Amoco(*), Exxon(*, D, CW), Shell(*, D)
Food W: SHONEY'S, Shoney's, Taco Bell, Waffle House, Wendy's
Lodg W: Econolodge, Holiday Inn Express, Quality Inn
AServ W: Discount Auto Parts, KIA of Laurel, Shell
Med W: + South Central Regional Medical Center
ATM W: Bank of Mississippi, Central Sunbelt Federal Credit Union, Trustmark National Bank
Other E: Blossman Inc. Propane(LP)
W: Dicket's Drugs(RX)

93 South Laurel, Fairgrounds, Industrial Park
TStop W: American Food Truck Stop(*) (Fuel-Citgo)
FStop W: Shell(*, CW)
Gas W: Exxon(*, D)
Food W: American Food Truck Stop (Fuel-Citgo), Chix Food Station (Shell), Hardee's, Hot Stuff Pizza (Shell), Subway (Exxon)
AServ E: Paul's Discount Glass, Tires, Muffler, Rebel Alternator Service
ATM W: Trustmark National Bank
Other E: Mississippi National Guard
W: Smith's Sunbeam Bread Store

90 U.S 11, Ellisville Blvd
FStop W: Dixie Gas(*, 24)
Food E: Charlie's Catfish House
AServ E: Joe's Service Center(*, D, LP), Poole Wheel Service, Roger's Auto Parts
W: White's Auto Electric
TServ W: Industrial Services Diesel Repair
Other E: Shaffer's Optical Express

88 MS 29, MS 588, Ellisville
FStop E: Chevron(*)
Gas W: Shell, Woody's Total Discount Fuel & Tires(*, D)
Food E: Country Girl Kitchen, KFC, McDonald's(PLAY), Subway
W: Po' Boy!
AServ E: Cooksey's Used Tire, Ellisville Auto Parts (NAPA)
W: Hanna's Auto Repair, Shell, Woody's Total Discount Fuel & Tires
ATM E: Chevron
Other E: Alexander's Hardware, Food Tiger

85 MS 590, Ellisville, State School
FStop W: Triple T Junction(*) (Spur)
AServ W: Triple T Automotive
Other E: Jones County Jr. College

80 Moselle

78 Sanford Rd

76 Hattiesburg - Laurel Regional Airport
Other W: Hattisburg-Laurel Airport

73 Monroe Rd

69 Eatonville Rd, Glendale

67AB U.S. 49, Hattiesburg, Collins, to MS Gulf Coast
FStop W: Amoco(*), Smith Quick Shop(*), Speedway(*)
Gas E: Exxon(*), Shell(*)
W: Chevron(*), RaceWay(*), Shell(*), Stuckey's Express(*)
Food E: Arby's, Burger King(PLAY), Cracker Barrel, Farmer's Market Buffet, KFC, Krystal, Louie's (Holiday Inn), McDonald's(PLAY), Pizza Hut, Subway (Shell), Summit Restaurant (Comfort Inn), Waffle House
W: Northgate Diner (Best Western), Stuckey's Express, Waffle House, Ward's Hamburgers
Lodg E: Budget Inn, Cabot Lodge, Comfort Inn, DAYS INN Days Inn, Holiday Inn, Howard Johnson, Motel 6, Quality Inn, Scottish Inns, Super 8
W: Best Western
ATM E: Shell
W: Deposit Guaranty National Bank, Stuckey's Express
Other E: Hattisburg Convention Center

65AB U.S. 98 West, Hardy St, Columbia
Gas E: Chevron(*, D, 24), Shell(*, D, CW), Texaco(*)
W: Amoco(*, CW), Chevron(*, CW), Pump & Save
Food E: Baskin Robbins, Ci Ci's Pizza, Creative Cuisine, Crescent City Grill, Hub City Coffee Co., Janaly's Pizza, Mr Gatti's, Mr. Jim's Pizza, Panino's Italian, Pizza Hut, Purple Parrot Cafe, Ward's
W: Chili's, Columbo Yogurt (Chevron), It's Yogurt, Jo's Muggs (Books-A-Million), La Fiesta Brava, Little Caesars Pizza, Lone Star Steakhouse, Mandarin House, O'Charley's, Outback Steakhouse, Peking Garden, Red Lobster, Rocket City Diner, Shipley Donuts, Smokehouse BBQ (Chevron), TCBY (Amoco), Waffle House, Wendy's
Lodg E: Fairfield Inn by Marriott
W: Budget Inn, Comfort Suites Hotel, Hampton Inn
AServ E: Carquest Auto Parts, Goodyear, University Quick Lube
W: K-Mart Supercenter(24, RX)
Med E: + Immediate Care
ATM E: Chevron, Community Bank, Deposit Guaranty National Bank, Great Southern National Bank, Union Planters Bank
W: Amoco, Bank of Mississippi, Central Sunbelt Federal Credit Union, Citizens National Bank, Union Planter's Bank
Other E: 20/20 Eye Care Center, Angie's Pet Palace, Davis Animal Hospital, Eckerd Drugs, Lighthouse Christian Bookstore, Roses, Stewart's Camera & 1-Hr Photo, Sunflower Food Store, U.S. Post Office
W: Books-A-Million, Hattisburg Convention Center, K-Mart Supercenter(RX), Rite Aid Pharmacy(RX), Sac & Save Foods, Super D Drug Store(RX), Super Valu Foods

60 U.S. 11, South Hattiesburg (William Carey College)
TStop W: Chevron(*, 24)
FStop W: Amoco(*)
Food W: Chevron
AServ W: B & B Road Service
TServ W: B & B Road Service(24), Chevron(24), K & K Truck Trailor Parts, Inc.(24)

59 U.S. 98 East, Lucedale, Mobile, to U.S. 49 MS Gulf Coast (Limited Access Hwy)

(56) Parking Area (Southbound)

51 MS 589, Purvis
Other W: Little Black Creek Water Park

41 MS 13, Lumberton
FStop W: Conoco(*)
Gas W: BP(LP)
Food W: Alma's I-59 Restaurant
AServ W: BP
Other W: Bass Pecan Co.

35 Hillsdale Rd
FStop E: Pure(*)
Food E: Deli Express (Pure)
Lodg E: Georgetowne Inn
Other E: Hillsdale Golf Course (Georgetowne Inn)

29 MS 26, Poplarville, Wiggins

27 MS 53, Poplarville, Necaise

19 Millard

15 McNeill
TStop W: McNeill Truck Stop(*, 24)
Food W: McNeill Truck Stop

EXIT MISSISSIPPI/LOUISIANA

Lodg W: McNeill Truck Stop

(13) Parking Area (P; Southbound)

10 Carriere
TStop E: Hilda's I-59 Truckstop(*) (Fuel-Phillips 66)
Food E: Hilda's I-59 Truckstop (Fuel-Phillips 66)
TServ W: McNeill Service Center
ATM E: Hilda's I-59 Truckstop (Fuel-Phillips 66)

(8) Parking Area (P; Northbound)

6 MS 43 North, North Picayune
Gas W: Chevron(*)
Lodg W: Budget Host, Majestic Inn
Med W: + Hospital
ATM W: Chevron, First National Bank
Other W: Berry Veterinary Clinic, Cinema IV, Eckerd Drugs(RX), Winn Dixie Supermarket(RX)

4 MS 43 South, Picayune, Kiln
Gas E: Murphey USA
W: Exxon(*, D, CW), Shell(*, D), Spur(*), Texaco(*, D)
Food E: Baskin Robbins (Wal-Mart), McDonald's (Wal-Mart)
W: Backyard Burgers (Exxon), Burger King(PLAY), Domino's Pizza, Fruizil Smoothie's & Yogurt (Texaco), Hardee's, Piccadilly Circus Pizza (Exxon), SHONEY'S, Shoney's, Subway (Texaco), Waffle House
Lodg W: Comfort Inn, DAYS INN Days Inn, Heritage Inn
AServ E: Bill Garrett Chev Dealer, Greg's Tire & Service Center, Wal-Mart Supercenter(24, RX) (Optical)
W: Auto Zone Auto Parts, Dub Herring Chrysler
RVCamp E: Campground
W: Paw-Paw's Camper City
ATM E: Wal-Mart Supercenter (Optical)
W: Bank Plus, First National Bank of Picayune
Parks W: Crosby Aboretum Industrial Park
Other E: The Crosby Arboretum, Wal-Mart Supercenter(RX) (Optical)
W: Eye Center, Pet Depot

(2) MS Welcome Center, Rest Area (RR, Phones, Picnic, Grills, RV Dump, P; Northbound)

(1) Weigh Station (Northbound)

(1) Weigh Station (Southbound)

1 U.S. 11, MS, 607, Nicholson, NASA John C. Stennis Space Ctr.
FStop W: Chevron(*, D)
AServ W: Croney's Auto Repair
Other E: John C. Stennis Space Ctr. (6 Miles), Naval Oceanographic Center

↑ MISSISSIPPI

↓ LOUISIANA

11 Pearl River Turnaround

5B Honey Island Swamp (No Access to East Side of Interstate)

5A LA 41 Spur, Pearl River (No Access to East Side of Interstate)
Food W: Corner Cafe
TServ W: Kabco Parts & Service
Other W: Wally's Gators

3 U.S. 11 South, Pearl River Town, S. LA 1090

(1) LA Tourist Info, Rest Area (RR, Phones, Picnic, RV Dump; Southbound)

1BC I-10, New Orleans, Bay, St. Louis (Southbound)

1A I-12 West, Hammond (Southbound)

↑ LOUISIANA

Begin I-59

Bold red print shows RV & Bus parking available or nearby

EXIT		MISSOURI/ILLINOIS

Begin I-64

↓MISSOURI

40C West I-44, South I-55

↑MISSOURI

↓ILLINOIS

1 IL 3 South, Sauget, West I-70, Great River Rd IL, Cahokia

2A Downtown St. Louis via MLK Bridge

2B 3rd Street
- **Med** S: ✚ Hospital

3 North I-55, East I-70, Chicago, Indianapolis (Difficult Reaccess)

4 Baugh Avenue, 15th Street (Difficult Reaccess)

5 25th Street

6 Kingshighway, IL 111
- **Gas** N: Amoco(*, 24), Shell(*) (Towing)
- **Food** N: Munchie's (Soul Food), Popeye's Chicken
  S: Stoplight Restaurant (Ethnic)
- **Lodg** N: Econo Inn Motel
- **AServ** N: Shell (Towing)
  S: Norton's Automotive
- **Parks** S: Frank Holten State Park

7 I-255, U.S. 50, Chicago, Memphis

9 IL 157, Caseyville, Centreville
- **FStop** S: Shell(*, LP)
- **Gas** N: Phillips 66(*, D)
  S: Amoco(*, 24)
- **Food** N: Hardee's(PLAY)
  S: Cracker Barrel, Domino's Pizza, McDonald's(PLAY), Taco Bell
- **Lodg** S: Best Inns of America, Days Inn(see our ad this page), Motel 6, Quality Inn & Suites
- **AServ** N: Vehicle Doctor (Towing)
- **ATM** S: Amoco
- **Other** S: Our Lady of the Snows Shrine 6

12 IL 159, Belleville, Collinsville
- **Gas** N: CFN(*, D, CW)
  S: Amoco(*, CW), Mobil(*)
- **Food** N: Applebee's, Blimpie Subs & Salads, Carlos O'Kelly's Mexican Cafe, Damon's, Houlihan's Restaurant & Bar, Joe's Crab Shack, Lotawata Creek Southern Grill, Olive Garden, Red Lobster, SHONEY'S Shoney's, T.G.I. Friday's (Ramada Inn)
  S: Arby's, Boston Market Restaurant, Burger King, Casa Gallardo, Chili's, China Buffet, Chuck E Cheese's Pizza, Denny's, IHOP, Little Caesars Pizza (K-Mart), Long John Silver, McDonald's(PLAY), Old Country Buffet, Pasta House, Ponderosa, Quizno's

EXIT		ILLINOIS

Classic Subs, Ruby Tuesday's, Show-Me's Seafood, Steak 'N Shake, Taco Bell, The Honey Baked Ham Co., The Square Meal (Mall Food Court), White Castle Restaurant
- **Lodg** N: Best Western, Drury Inn, Fairfield Inn, Hampton Inn, Ramada Inn, Super 8
- **AServ** N: Saturn of Metro East
  S: Auto Tire, Dobb Tire & Auto, Firestone Tire & Auto, In & Out Auto Center, Jiffy Lube, K-Mart(RX), National Tire & Battery, Parts America, Sears
- **ATM** S: Central Bank, First Financial Bank, Magna Bank
- **Other** N: St. Clair's Cinema
  S: American Vision Center, K-Mart(RX), Lens Crafters, National Market(RX), Petco, St. Clair Square Mall, Target, U.S. Post Office, WalGreens Pharmacy(24, RX)

14 O'Fallon
- **Gas** N: Shell(*, 24)
- **Food** N: Japanese Garden Steakhouse, Steak 'N Shake
  S: Dairy Queen, Hardee's, Jack-In-The-Box, KFC, Lion's Choice Roast Beef, Lone Star Steakhouse, McDonald's(PLAY), Mr. Goodcents Subs and Pasta, Super Smokers BBQ, Taco Bell, Western Sizzlin'
- **Lodg** N: Extended Stay America, Holiday Inn Express, Sleep Inn
  S: EconoLodge, Ramada Limited
- **AServ** N: Jack Schmitt Nissan, Olds, Cad, Volks, Schantz Ford
  S: Auffenberg Chrys, Plym, Jeep, Eagle, Auffenberg Hyundai, Auffenberg Mazda, Auffenberg Mitsubishi, Auffenberg Suzuki, Subaru, Full Circle Automotive, Sam's Club, Wal-Mart(24, RX)
- **ATM** N: Shell, Union Bank of IL
  S: MidAmerica Bank
- **Other** S: Home Depot(LP), O'Fallon 15 Cine, PetsMart, Sam's Club, Wal-Mart(RX)

(17) Weigh Station (Eastbound)

1817
DAYS INN
8950 Trucker Drive
— 55 CLEAN, COMFORTABLE ROOMS —
FREE CONTINENTAL BREAKFAST
JACUZZI ROOMS AVAILABLE
OUTDOOR POOL • GOLF NEARBY
ACROSS FROM
CRACKER BARREL & TACO BELL
618-397-4200 • Caseyville, IL
ILLINOIS ▪ I-64 ▪ EXIT 9

EXIT		ILLINOIS

19AB U.S. 50, IL 158, West O'Fallon, Scott AFB
- **FStop** N: Motomart(*, D)
- **Food** N: Hero's Pizza & Subs (Motomart), Schiappa's Italian
  S: Ivory Chopsticks
- **Lodg** N: Comfort Inn
- **Med** S: ✚ Hospital
- **ATM** N: Motomart

23 IL 4, Mascoutah, Lebanon

(24) Rest Area (RR, Phones, Picnic, Vending, Pet Walk, P; Eastbound)

(25) Rest Area (RR, Phones, Picnic, Vending, Pet Walk, P; Westbound)

27 IL 161, New Baden
- **FStop** N: Shell(*, D, 24)
- **AServ** N: Hemann Chevrolet
- **ATM** N: Shell

34 Albers, Damiansville

41 IL 177, Okawville
- **FStop** S: Amoco(*)
- **Food** S: Burger King (Amoco TS), Dairy Queen(PLAY), Hen House
- **Lodg** S: Super 8
- **AServ** S: Gary's Tire Service Center
- **TServ** S: Gary's Tire Service Center
- **Other** S: Heritage House Museum

50 IL 127, Carlyle, Nashville
- **TStop** S: Conoco(*, SCALES, 24)
- **FStop** S: Shell(*, 24)
- **Food** S: Little Nashville (Conoco TS), McDonald's
- **Lodg** S: Best Western
- **TServ** N: Norrenbern Truck Service
  S: Gary's Tire (Conoco TS)
- **ATM** S: Conoco

61 US 51, Centralia, Ashley

69 Woodlawn

73 I-57 North, Chicago (Left Exit Eastbound)

Note: I-64 runs concurrent below with I-57. Numbering follows I-57.

95 IL 15, Mt Vernon, Ashley
- **TStop** W: 76 Auto/Truck Plaza(*, SCALES, 24)
- **FStop** W: Huck's(*, SCALES)
- **Gas** E: Amoco(*, 24), Hucks Food Store(*), Phillips 66(*, CW), Shell, Speedway(*)
  W: Shell(*), Shell(*)
- **Food** E: Big-O's BBQ, Bonanza Steakhouse, Burger King, China Buffet, Cobbler's Restaurant (Ramada Inn), Denny's, El Rancherito, Fazoli's Italian Food, Hardees(PLAY), KFC, Little Caesars Pizza, Long John Silver, Pizza Hut, Pizza Pro (Kroger), Steak & Shake, Subway, Taco Bell, Triple E BBQ, Waffle's and More, Wendy's

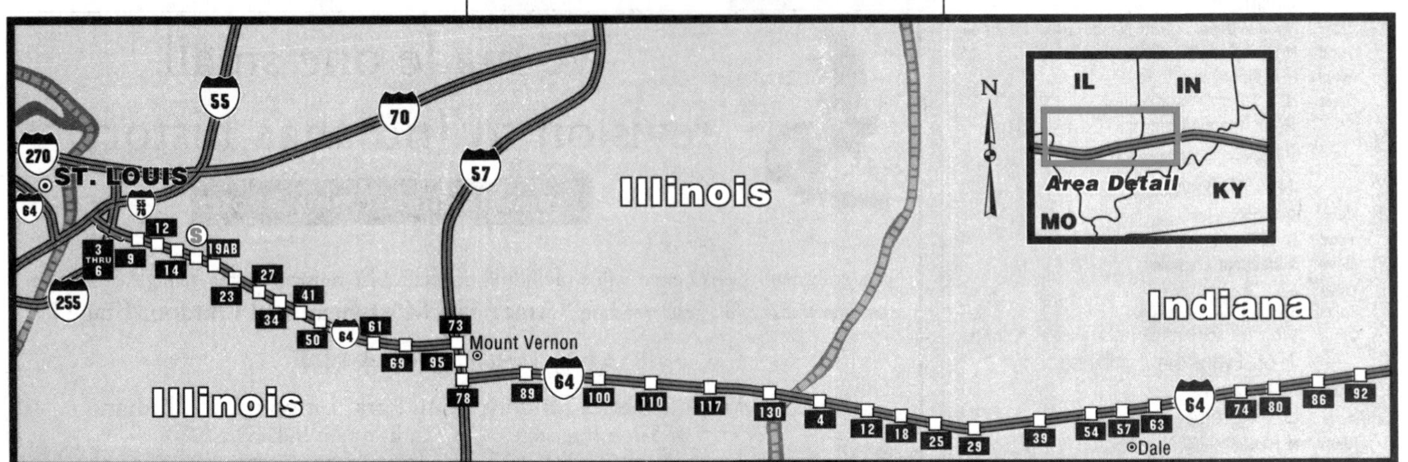

Bold red print shows RV & Bus parking available or nearby

EXIT ILLINOIS/INDIANA

W: Applebee's, Arby's, Burger King, Caroline's (Holiday Inn), Cracker Barrel, McDonald's[PLAY], Shell
Lodg E: Best Inns of America, Best Western, Drury Inn, Motel 6, Ramada Inn, Super 8, Thrifty Inn
W: Comfort Inn, Hampton Inn, Holiday Inn
AServ E: Midas Muffler & Brake, Phillips 66, Shell
W: Tyler Pontiac, Buick, Cadillac, and GMC Trucks, Tyler Toyota
TServ W: 76 Auto/Truck Plaza, Truck Centers Inc, with Freightliner[24], XVIII Wheelers[24]
RVCamp W: Quality Times (.75 Miles)
Med E: ✚ Care First, ✚ Hospital
ATM E: Amoco, Bank of Illinois, Citizen's Bank, First National, Huck Food Store, Kroger, Merchantile Bank, NationsBank, Phillips 66
W: Citizens Bank (Hampton Inn), Huck's, Shell, Shell, Truckstop
Other E: Country Fair Grocery[RX], K-Mart[RX], Kroger Supermarket[24, RX]
W: Wal-Mart Supercenter[24, RX] (Tire Center)

Note: I-64 runs concurrent above with I-57. Numbering follows I-57.

78 I-57 South, Memphis (Westbound)
80 IL 37, Mt. Vernon
RVCamp S: Sherwood Camping
(82) Rest Area (P; Eastbound)
(86) Rest Area (RR, Phones, Picnic, Vending, P; Westbound)
89 Belle Rive, Bluford
100 IL 242, Wayne City, Mc Leansboro
FStop N: Marathon[*]
AServ N: Marathon
110 U.S. 45, Norris City, Fairfield
RVCamp S: Barnhill Campground
117 Burnt Prairie
FStop S: BP[*]
Food S: Chuckwagon Charlie's (BP)
AServ S: Whetstone Marina & Auto Service
130 IL 1, Grayville, Carmi
FStop N: Shell[*, 24]
S: Phillips 66[*]
Food N: Best Western
Lodg N: Best Western
RVCamp N: Beall Woods State Park (10 Miles)
ATM N: Best Western
Parks N: Bobeall Woods State Park (10 Miles)
(131) Rest Area (RR, Phones, Picnic, P; Westbound)

↑ILLINOIS

↓INDIANA

4 Griffin
Gas N: Griffin Depot[*, D] (Farm Bureau Co-Op), Phillips 66
Food N: Griffin Depot (Farm Bureau Co-Op)
AServ N: Phillips 66
Other N: U.S. Post Office
(7) Rest Area, Welcome Center (RR, Phones; Eastbound)
12 IN 165, Poseyville
FStop S: Citgo[*]
Food S: T's Restaurant
AServ S: Broerman Chevrolet
TWash S: Car & Truck Wash[24]
Parks S: Harmonie State Park
Other S: Car & Truck Wash, New Harmony Historic Area
18 IN 65, Evansville, Cynthiana
FStop S: Moto Mart[*]
25AB U.S. 41, Terre Haute, Evansville
TStop N: Pilot[*, SCALES, 24]

EXIT INDIANA

S: Busler's Pennzoil[*, SCALES, 24]
Gas S: Amoco[*]
Food N: Wendy's (Pilot TS)
S: Arby's, Burger King, McDonald's
Lodg S: Amoco Motel, Comfort Inn, Days Inn (see our ad this page), Holiday Inn Express, Super 8
TServ S: Busler's Pennzoil[SCALES, 24]
TWash N: Pilot
S: Busler's Pennzoil
RVCamp N: Weather Rock Campground (1.5 Miles)
ATM N: Pilot
S: Amoco
Other S: Indiana State Police
29A I-164, IN 57 South, Evansville, Henderson KY
29B IN 57 North, Petersburg
FStop N: Sunoco[*]
Food N: Subway (Sunoco), TCBY (Sunoco)
ATM N: Sunoco
39 IN 61, Boonville, Lynnville
Gas N: Shell[*]
Food N: BBQ Cafe, East L.A. Restaurant
RVCamp N: Camping
ATM N: Lynnville National Bank
Other N: Barnie's Market, Main Street Video & Pizza, U.S. Post Office
S: Warrick County Museum (10 Miles)
54 IN 161, Tennyson, Holland
RVCamp S: Camping
57 U.S. 231, Dale, Jasper, Huntingburg
TStop N: AmBest[*, SCALES, 24]
Gas S: Shell[*, 24]
Food S: Denny's
Lodg N: Scottish Inns (Am Best TS)
S: Baymont Inn
TServ N: AmBest[SCALES, 24]

1217
812-473-7
Evansville
DAYS INN®
AAA Approved
• Cleanest Hotel off the Exit
• Outdoor Pool • Free Parking
• Jacuzzi Rooms Available
• All Interior Corridors
• Cable TV with Free HBO
5 Sunburst Quality Award Winner
South on U.S. 41. Go East on Loyd Expressway 1/4 mile Green River Rd. exit and Days Inn on left
INDIANA ¥ I-64 ¥ EXIT 25

EXIT INDIANA

RVCamp N: G & S Mobile Home & RV Service & Supply (1 Mile)
ATM N: AmBest
Parks S: Lincoln State Park
Other S: Lincoln Amphitheater (June-August)(see our ad this page), Lincoln Boyhood National Memorial, Mega Maze Water Wars, Mini Golf
(59) Rest Area (RR, Phones; Westbound)
(58) Rest Area (RR, Phones; Eastbound)
63 IN 162, Santa Claus, Ferdinand
RVCamp S: Camping
Parks N: Ferdinand State Forest
72 IN 145, Bristow, Birdseye
Gas S: Possum Junction General Store[24]
AServ S: Rightway Diesel Service (Possum Junction General Store)
79 IN 37 South, Tell City
RVCamp S: Camping
Parks S: Hoosier National Forest Recreational Facilities
(80) Parking Area (Eastbound)
(81) Parking Area (Westbound)
86 IN 37N, Sulphur, English
Parks N: Patoka Lake
S: Hoosier National Forest (2 Miles)
92 IN 66, Leavenworth, Marengo
TStop S: Amy's Place Citgo[*], BP[*, SCALES], Shell[*, SCALES]
Gas S: Carefree Indiana Restaurant[24] (Days Inn)
Food S: Carefree Indiana Restaurant (Days Inn), Country Style Restaurant[*, 24] (Shell TS), Kathy's Kitchen (BP TS), Krispy Kreme Doughnuts (Shell TS), Taco Bell Express (BP TS)
Lodg S: Cavern Inn (BP TS), Days Inn
TServ S: BP[SCALES]
ATM S: BP
Other N: Marengo Cave
S: Wyandotte Cave
105 IN 135, Palmyra, Corydon
Gas N: Citgo[*, D], Shell[*]
S: Amoco[*, D, 24], Five Star[*], Swifty[*, D]
Food N: Broaster's Chicken (Citgo), Frisch's Big Boy
S: Arby's, Burger King, Country Folk's Buffet, Dairy Queen, Lee's Famous Recipe Chicken, Long John Silver, McDonald's (Wal-Mart), McDonald's, Papa John's Pizza, Ponderosa, Sassy's Subs & Such (Amoco), Subway, Taco Bell, Waffle & Steak, Wendy's
Lodg N: Best Western
S: Budgetel Inn, Holiday Inn Express
AServ S: Heritage Ford, Mercury, Wal-Mart Supercenter[RX] (Vision Center)
Med S: ✚ Hospital
ATM S: First Federal Financial Center, Wal-Mart Supercenter (Vision Center)
Other S: Corydon Cinemas, Shireman Farm Market, Wal-Mart Supercenter[RX] (Vision Center)

1277

We made one small revision to Indiana's history.
Lincoln couldn't sing a note.
For a complete theatre experience including tickets to the musical drama *Young Abe Lincoln* or *The Music Man* performed on **"America's Most Beautiful Outdoor Stage"**
CALL 1-800-264-4ABE
Lincoln Amphitheatre, Lincoln State Park, Lincoln City, Indiana
Exit 57 on Interstate 64 in Southwestern Indiana.

Bold red print shows RV & Bus parking available or nearby

EXIT INDIANA/KENTUCKY

113 Lanesville
(115) **IN Welcome Center, Rest Area (RR, Phones, Picnic; Westbound)**
118 IN 62, IN 64W, Georgetown
- **FStop** N: **Marathon**[*, LP, K, 24]
- **Gas** N: Shell[*, K]
  S: Marathon[*]
- **Food** N: Korner Kitchen, McDonald's, Pizza King
- **AServ** S: Marathon
- **ATM** N: Harrison County Bank, Shell
- **Other** N: The Drug Store, **Thriftway Supermarket**

119 U.S. 150 West, Greenville
- **FStop** N: **Citgo**[*, D]
- **Gas** N: Amoco[*], Ashland[*]
- **Food** N: **Broaster's Chicken (Citgo FS)**, China King, Dairy Queen, Domino's Pizza, Papa John's Pizza, Pizza City, Subway, Tumbleweed Mexican Food
- **AServ** N: Quick Stop Oil Change
- **Med** N: ✚ **Floyd Memorial Hospital**
- **ATM** N: Ashland, NBD Bank, National City Bank, **Rite Aid Pharmacy**[RX]
- **Other** N: Automatic Car Wash[CW], Jay C's Food Store, **Rite Aid Pharmacy**[RX]

121 Junction I-265 East, To I-65 (Left Exit Eastbound)
123 IN 62 East, New Albany
- **Gas** N: Amoco[*, 24]
  S: BP[*, LP]
- **Food** S: Waffle & Steak
- **Lodg** S: **Holiday Inn Express**
- **AServ** N: Guaranteed Auto Parts, Mike Smith's Firestone
- **Med** N: ✚ **Hospital**
- **ATM** N: Bank One, PNC Bank, Regional Bank
  S: BP

↑ INDIANA

↓ KENTUCKY

1 Junction East I-264, Shively
3 U.S. 150 East, 22nd St.
- **Gas** S: Chevron[*], Dairy Mart[*], Shell[*, 24]
- **Food** S: Dairy Queen, McDonald's
- **AServ** S: Shell[24]
- **ATM** S: Chevron

4 9th Street, Roy Wilkins Avenue
5A Junction I-65, Nashville, Indianapolis
5B 3rd Street, Downtown Louisville (Westbound, Difficult Reaccess)
- **Food** S: City Wok, Marketplace Bar & Grill, Subway
- **Other** S: **Louisville Science Center**, **Louisville Slugger Museum & Visitor Center**

6 Junction I-71, Cincinnati
7 U.S. 42, U.S. 60, Mellwood Ave

EXIT KENTUCKY

- **Gas** N: Speedway[*, D, LP, K]
- **Food** N: J.K.'s Corner Grill, Picasso, Sugardoe Cafe
  S: Hall's Cafeteria
- **AServ** N: Bob Collett Auto Wreckers, Collett Bros. Auto Parts
- **Other** N: **Thomas Edison Museum**

8 Grinstead Drive
- **Gas** S: $ave, BP[*], Chevron
- **Food** S: August Moon, K.T.'s Restaurant & Bar
- **AServ** S: BP, Chevron
- **Other** S: **Pets Galore**

10 Cannons Ln. Bowman Field Airport
12 Junction I-264, Watterson Expwy
15 KY 1747, Jeffersontown, Middletown, Hurstbourne Lane
- **Gas** N: Amoco[*, CW], BP[*, CW], Shell[*, LP, CW]
  S: BP[*, D, CW], Thornton's Food Mart[*, D]
- **Food** N: Arby's, Benihana, Bob Evan's Restaurant, Burger King, Joe's O.K. Bayou, McDonald's, Olive Garden, Sichuan Gardens Chinese, Skyline Chili, Steak-out, Subway, T.G.I. Friday's, Tumbleweed Mexican Food
  S: Applebee's, **Au Bon Pain (DoubleTree Club Hotel)**, Balihai Chinese Restaurant, Blimpie's Subs, Dairy Queen, Damon's, Hardee's, O'Charley's, Shalimar Indian Restuarant, SHONEY'S, Shoney's, Wendy's, Yen Ching Chinese
- **Lodg** N: Blair Wood, Courtyard by Marriott, Fairfield Inn, Holiday Inn, Red Roof Inn, AmeriSuites (see our ad this page)
  S: DAYS INN Days Inn, DoubleTree Club Hotel, Hampton Inn, Marriott, Red Carpet Inn, StudioPLUS, Wilson Inn & Suites
- **AServ** N: BP, Chevron
  S: Swobe Auto Center
- **ATM** N: Bank One, National City Bank, PNC Bank
- **Other** N: **60 Min. Photo**, **AAA Auto Club - Kentucky**, **Fragile Pack (Shipping)**, **Kroger Supermarket**, **Revco Drugs**
  S: **EYE Mart**, **Wal-Mart**

17 Blankenbaker Road, Industrial Park
- **Gas** S: BP[*], Chevron[*, CW, 24], Thornton's Food Mart[*, D]
- **Food** S: Arby's, Burger King, **Cracker Barrel**, HomeTown Buffet, McDonald's, Subway (Thornton's), Waffle House
- **Lodg** S: Candlewood, Comfort Suites Hotel, Microtel Inn, Regency (Best Western), Sleep Inn

EXIT KENTUCKY

- **ATM** S: BP, Bank of Louisville
- **Other** S: **Sam's Club**

19AB 19A - S.I-265, KY 841, G.Snyder Fwy 19B - N.I-265, KY 841, G.Snyder e
(24) **Rest Area (RR, Phones, Vending; Eastbound)**
28 Veechdale Road, Simpsonville
- **TStop** N: **Pilot Travel Center**[*, SCALES]
- **Gas** S: BP[*]
- **Food** N: **Subway**[24] **(Pilot)**

(29) **Rest Area (RR, Phones, Vending; Westbound)**
32AB KY 55, Taylorsville, Shelbyville
- **Gas** N: Shell[*]
- **Food** N: Arby's, Parkside Deli & Grocery (Shell)
- **Lodg** N: Best Western, DAYS INN **Days Inn**
- **AServ** N: Brinkhaus Buick, Pontiac, GMC Trucks (light)
- **Med** N: ✚ **Hospital**
- **Parks** S: **Taylorsville Lake State Park**
- **Other** N: **Shelby Lanes**

35 KY 53, Shelbyville
- **Gas** N: BP[*, D, LP], Chevron[D]
- **AServ** N: Chevron

(38) **Weigh Station**
43 KY 395, Waddy, Peytonia
- **TStop** S: **76 Auto/Truck Plaza**[*, LP, SCALES]
- **Food** S: **Hot Stuff Pizza (76)**, **Restaurant (76 Auto/TruckStop)**
- **TServ** S: **76**
- **TWash** S: **76**
- **Other** S: **Laundromat (76)**

48 KY 151, US 127 S, Lawrenceburg, Grafenburg
- **Gas** S: Chevron[*, K], Shell[*]
- **Food** S: Subway (Shell)
- **ATM** S: Chevron

53AB U.S. 127, Frankfort, Lawrenceburg
- **Gas** N: Chevron[*], Shell[*]
- **Food** N: Applebee's, Chili's, Fazoli's, Frisch's Big Boy, O'Charley's, Sassy's Subs & Stuff (Chevron), Steak 'N Shake
- **Lodg** N: Hampton Inn
- **AServ** N: **Wal-Mart Supercenter**[RX]
- **Med** N: ✚ **Hospital**
- **Other** N: Cinema 6, **Kroger Supermarket**, Pet Store, **Wal-Mart Supercenter**[RX], **Winn Dixie Supermarket**

58 U.S. 60, Frankfort, Versailles
- **Gas** N: Citgo[*, D], Shell[*]
- **Food** N: DaVinci's (Best Western)
- **Lodg** N: Best Western
- **AServ** N: Justice Auto Glass Co.
- **ATM** N: Shell

(61) **Rest Area (Eastbound)**

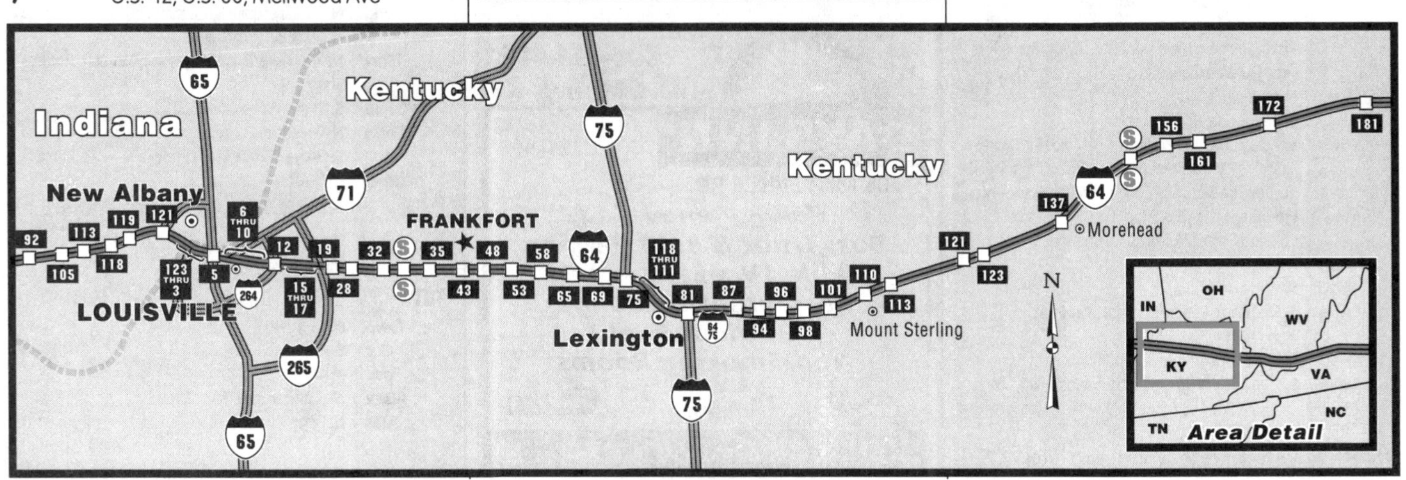

EXIT KENTUCKY

(61) **Rest Area (RR, Phones, Picnic, Vending, Pet Walk; Westbound)**

65 To KY 341, U.S. 62, Midway, Versailles
- ASErv S: Midway Auto Service

69 U.S. 62E, Georgetown

75 Junction I-75, Cincinnati

Note: I-64 runs concurrent below with I-75. Numbering follows I-75.

115 KY 922, Bluegrass Pkwy, Lexington
- FStop E: Exxon(*, CW)
  W: Chevron(*)
- Gas E: Shell(*, LP, CW)
- Food E: Cracker Barrel, McDonald's, Subway (Shell), Waffle House
  W: Denny's, The Mansion Restaurant (Marriot), The Post Restaurant (Holiday Inn)
- Lodg E: Knight's Inn, La Quinta Inn, Wyndham Garden Hotel
  W: Holiday Inn, Marriott
- AServ W: Chevron
- ATM W: Chevron
- Other E: Kentucky Horse Park
  W: Griffin Gate Golf Club (Marriot)

113 U.S. 27, U.S. 68, Paris, Lexington
- FStop E: Chevron(*), Shell(*)
  W: BP(*), SuperAmerica(*, K)
- Gas W: Marathon(*, LP)
- Food E: Days Inn, Fazoli's Italian Food, Shoney's, Subway (Chevron)
  W: Sigee's Restaurant (Harley Hotel), Waffle House
- Lodg E: Days Inn, Red Roof Inn
  W: Harley Hotel
- AServ W: BP
- Med W: + Hospital
- ATM W: SuperAmerica, Whitaker Bank
- Other E: Tourist Info.
  W: Joyland Bowl

Note: I-64 runs concurrent above with I-75. Numbering follows I-75.

81 Junction I-75 South, Richmond, Knoxville

87 KY 859, Lexington Army Depot, Blue Grass Station

94 KY 1958, Van Meter Rd, Winchester
- TStop N: Shell(*, D, SCALES, 24) (Showers, Fax Machine)
- FStop S: Speedway(*, D, LP, K, 24)
- Gas N: Chevron(24)
  S: BP(*, D), Somerset(D, K)
- Food N: Shell (Showers, Fax Machine)
  S: Applebee's, Arby's, Cantuckee Diner Inc., Domino's Pizza, El Rio Grande Mexican, Fazoli's Italian Food, Gators, Hardee's(PLAY), KFC, Lee's Famous Recipe Chicken, Long John Silver, Magarita's Traditional Mexican, McDonald's, Pizza Hut, Rally's Hamburgers, SHONEY'S Shoney's, Sir Pizza, Southern Maid Donuts, Subway, Tacos Too, Time Out Steakhouse, Waffle House, Wendy's
- Lodg N: Days Inn
  S: Budget Inn, Red Carpet Inn
- AServ S: Auto Zone Auto Parts, Bypass Auto Hardware, Hatfields Plymouth Jeep Dodge Trucks (Light Trucks), Paynter Tire & Service Center, Pitt-Stop Auto Service, Pro Lube Plus(CW), S & S Tire, T & D Auto, Ted's Collision Center, Valvoline Oil Change
- TWash N: Truck Wash
- Med S: + Hospital
- ATM S: PNC Bank, People's Commercial Bank, Speedway
- Parks S: Fort Boonesbough State Park
- Other S: Blue Line Car Wash, Coin Car Wash, Maytag Laundry, Prescott Books, Rite Aid Pharmacy(RX), Sav-A-Lot Grocery

96AB 96A - KY 627S, Winchester, 96B - KY 627N, Paris, North
- TStop N: 96 Truck Stop(*)
- FStop N: Sunoco(*)
- Gas S: Ashland(*)
- Lodg S: Hampton Inn, Holiday Inn
- AServ S: Ashland, Casey Geo Chevrolet Olds
- TServ N: 96 Truck Stop, Sunoco
- Other N: Fire Station

98 Campton, Mountain Pkwy, Prestonsburg, Junction (Eastbound, Reaccess Westbound Only, Difficult Reaccess)
- Parks N: Natural Bridge State Park

(98) **Rest Area (RR, Phones, Picnic, Vending, Pet Walk; Eastbound)**

101 U.S. 60

(108) **Rest Area (RR, Phones, Picnic, Vending, Pet Walk; Westbound)**

110 U.S. 460, KY 11, Mt. Sterling, Paris
- Gas N: Chevron(24)
  S: BP(*, D), Exxon(*), Shell(*, CW)
- Food N: Cracker Barrel
  S: Arby's, Burger King, Exxon, Golden Corral Family Steakhouse, Hardee's(PLAY), Jerry's Restaurant, KFC, Lee's Famous Recipe Chicken, Long John Silver, McDonald's(PLAY), Peking Chinese, Pizza Hut, Rio's Steakhouse & Lounge (Days Inn), SHONEY'S Shoney's, Subway (Exxon), Taco Bell, Wendy's
- Lodg N: Fairfield Inn
  S: Budget Inn, Days Inn(see our ad this page)
- AServ N: Chevron(24)
  S: Advance Auto Parts
- Med S: + Hospital
- ATM S: Shell, Traditional Bank
- Other S: Crystal Clean Car Wash, Food Lion

113 U.S. 60, Mt. Sterling
- FStop N: Citgo Truck & Auto Plaza(*, LP, K)
- Food N: Super Express Stop(K) (Citgo)
- ATM N: Citgo Truck & Auto Plaza, Super Express Stop (Citgo)

121 KY 36, Frenchburg, Owingsville
- FStop N: Citgo(*, K), Sunoco(*)
- Gas N: BP(*, D, K), Shell
- Food N: Citgo, Dairy Queen, Kountry Kettle, McDonald's, Shell, Subway (Shell), Toms' Pizza Shop
- ATM N: Owingsville Banking Co., Sunoco
- Other N: No Touch Automatic Car Wash, Owingsville Drug(RX), Town & Country Car Wash

123 U.S. 60, Owingsville, Salt Lick
- Gas N: 76(D, K)
- AServ N: 76
- RVCamp S: Cave Run Lake (12 Miles)
- ATM N: 76

606-498-4680
Mt. Sterling, KY
DAYS INN
Toll Free Reservations:
800-329-7466
705 MAYSVILLE RD.
Newly Renovated
Bus, Truck & Boat Parking
Cable TV • Easy Access
Restaurant & Lounge
Outdoor Pool
Non-Smoking Rooms
ABA American Bus Association
1154
KENTUCKY • I-64 • EXIT 110

133 KY 801, Farmers, Sharkey
- FStop S: BP(*, LP)
- Parks S: Cave Run Park, National Forest Recreation Area

137 KY 32, Morehead, Flemingsburg
- FStop S: Exxon(*)
- Gas N: Shell(D)
  S: Chevron(*, D, 24), Citgo(*, LP)
- Food N: Boomerang's Bar & Grill, China Garden, Cutter's Roadhouse, Tacos Too!
  S: Baskin Robbins (Exxon), Hardee's, Holiday Inn, KFC, Lee's Famous Recipe Chicken, Ponderosa, SHONEY'S Shoney's, Subway
- Lodg S: Best Western, Days Inn, Holiday Inn, Mountain Lodge, Shoney's Inn & Suites, Super 8
- AServ N: Trademore Tire Service
  S: Major Brands Tire & Auto Service, Michelin Tire
- Med S: + Hospital
- ATM N: Citizen's Bank
  S: Citgo, Trans Financial Bank
- Other N: Kroger Supermarket, On Cue Music, Books & Movies, Tuttle's Coin Laundry
  S: All American Car Wash, Food Lion, KY State Police, Pine Crest Plaza, Wal-Mart

(141) **Rest Area (RR, Phones, Picnic, Grills, Vending, Pet Walk)**

(141) **Rest Area (RR, Phones, Picnic, Grills, Vending; Westbound)**

(148) **Weigh Station (Eastbound)**

(148) **Weigh Station (Westbound)**

156 KY 2 To KY 59, Olive Hill, Vanceburg
- FStop S: Sunoco(*) (CB Repair)
- Gas S: Citgo
- Food S: Deli (Sunoco)
- AServ S: Citgo, Sunoco (CB Repair)

161 U.S. 60, Olive Hill
- FStop S: Exxon(*, K, SCALES)
- Gas N: Citgo(*)
- Food S: Exxon
- TWash S: Truck Wash
- Parks N: Carter Caves State Resort Park(*) (5 Miles)
- Other N: U.S. Post Office
  S: Car Wash

172 KY 1, KY 7, Grayson, Maysville
- TStop N: Super Quick(*, LP, CW, 24), Truck Stop(*, LP)
- FStop N: Pondarosa
  S: Pilot Travel Center(*, SCALES)
- Gas S: Ashland(*), Chevron(*, D, LP), SuperAmerica(*, LP, K)
- Food N: Eagle's Nest Restaurant, KFC, Long John Silver, Loredo's, Pondarosa, SHONEY'S Shoney's, Truck Stop, Western Steer Family Steakhouse
  S: A & W Drive-In (SuperAmerica), Arby's, Baskin Robbins (SuperAmerica), Burger King, Dairy Queen, McDonald's(PLAY), Pizza Hut, Subway, SuperAmerica, Taco Bell, Wendy's (Pilot)
- Lodg N: Country Squire Inn, Days Inn, Econolodge, Holiday Inn Express
- TServ N: Interstate Truck Supply Inc, Marcum Radio/CB Shop
- RVCamp S: Camp Webb (10 Miles)
- Parks N: Greenbow Lake State Resort Park
  S: Grayson Lake State Park
- Other N: K-Mart(RX)

(173) **KY Welcome Center (RR, Phones, Picnic, Grills, Vending, Pet Walk; Westbound)**

181 U.S. 60
- FStop N: Citgo(*, LP)
- Gas S: Rich(*)
- Food N: Citgo
- AServ N: Sixty four sixty, Tires "R" Us
- ATM N: Citgo

Bold red print shows RV & Bus parking available or nearby

EXIT KENTUCKY/WEST VIRGINIA

7216 US 60 • Ashland, KY
606-928-9501
800-843-5644
Local Resv.# 800-497-7560
1839
• Free Continental Breakfast • Outdoor Pool
• In-Room Safes • Refrigerators in All Rooms
• Fax & Copier Service • Free Cable TV with HBO/SVI Entertainment (Pay Per View)
• Free Access to Physical Fitness Center
• Truck Parking on Lot • Restaurants Close By
• Free Coffee in Rooms • All Rooms On Ground Floor
• Local Calls Free • AT&T Phone Service
4-7/10 Miles from I-64 on Right
KENTUCKY ▪ I-64 ▪ EXIT 185

185 KY 180, Cannonsburg, Ashland
- Gas N: Chevron(*)
- Lodg N: Knights Inn (see our ad this page)
- RVCamp S: Hidden Valley Campground (1.75 Miles)
- Other N: KY State Patrol Post

191 U.S. 23, Ashland, Louisa, Catlettsburg
- Lodg N: Ramada Limited
- Med N: Hospital

↑KENTUCKY

↓WEST VIRGINIA

1 U.S. 52 South, Kenova, Ceredo
- Gas N: Exxon(*), Sunoco(*, D)
- Other S: Glass Factory Tours, Tri State Airport

6 U.S. 52 North, West Huntington, Chesapeake (OH)
- Gas N: Marathon(*), SuperAmerica(*, D, CW)
- Food N: Blimpie Subs & Salads (SA), Pizza Hut, SuperAmerica
- Med N: Madison Ave VA Medical Center

8 WV 152 South, WV 527 North, 5th St East
- Food S: Dairy Queen, Laredo Texas Steakhouse
- Other N: Animal Hospital, Huntington Museum of Art
  S: Hills Plaza West

(10) WV Welcome Center (RR, Phones, Vending; Eastbound)

11 WV 10, Hal Greer Blvd, Downtown
- RVCamp S: Beach Fork State Camp (8.5 Miles south)
- Med N: Hospital

15 U.S. 60, 29th St East
- FStop N: Go Mart(*)
- Gas N: Chevron
  S: Exxon(*)

RAMADA LIMITED
304-562-3346
800-726-7016
Continental Breakfast
Restaurant on Premises
Kids Under 12 Stay Free
Outdoor Pool
Meeting/Banquet Facilities
Pets Allowed
Handicap Accessible
Truck/large Vehicle Parking
Exterior Corridors
Special Rates for Tour Groups!
1671
419 Hurricane Creek Rd. • Hurricane, WV
Centrally located between Charleston & Huntington
WEST VIRGINIA ▪ I-64 ▪ EXIT 34

EXIT WEST VIRGINIA

- Food N: Arby's, Jolly Pirate Donuts(24), Nanna's Country Restaurant, Omelette Shoppe, Wendy's
  S: Fazoli's Italian Food, Golden Corral Family Steakhouse, McDonald's(PLAY), Orient Express Chinese, SHONEY'S, Shoney's, Taco Bell
- Lodg N: Colonial Inn Motel, Traveler's Motel
  S: DAYS INN Days Inn, Red Roof Inn
- Med N: Hospital
- ATM N: Go Mart
  S: Bank One
- Other S: CVS(RX), Office Depot, Wal-Mart(RX)

20 U.S. 60, Barboursville, Mall Road
- Gas N: Exxon(*, D)
  S: BP(*), Exxon(*)
- Food N: Applebee's, Bob Evan's Restaurant, Fiesta Bravo (Mexican), Logan's Roadhouse Steaks & Ribs, McDonald's, Olive Garden, Wendy's
  S: Billy Bob's Pizza Wonderland, Cracker Barrel, Fiesta Bravo, Gino's Pizza & Spaghetti, Lone Star Steakhouse, Outback Steakhouse, Sonic Drive In, Subway, TCBY
- Lodg N: Comfort Inn
  S: Hampton Inn, Ramada Limited
- RVCamp S: Foxfire Resort Camping (5.6 Miles)
- ATM S: BP
- Other N: Drug Emporium, Huntington Mall, Office Max
  S: Maytag Coin Laundry, Moore's Car Wash(24)

28 U.S. 60, Milton
- Gas S: Ashland(*, LP, K), Exxon(*), Go Mart(*), Rich(*)
- Food S: Bubba's Deli & Roadkill, Dairy Queen, Gino's Pizza & Spaghetti House, Go Mart, Krispy Kreme Doughnuts (Go Mart), McDonald's, Pizza Hut, Tudor's Biscuit World, WV Fried Chicken (Go Mart)
- RVCamp S: Foxfire Resort (3.4 Miles)
- ATM S: Bank One, Huntington Banks of WV
- Other S: Milton Animal Hospital, Milton Car Wash, Nicholas Cleaners & Coin Laundry, Save-A-Lot Food Stores

34 Hurricane, WV 19
- Gas S: Chevron(D), Go Mart(*), Sunoco(D, K, CW)
- Food S: China Town, Gino's Pizza & Spaghetti, McDonald's, Nancy's, Pizza Hut, Subway, Tudor's Biscuit World
- Lodg S: Ramada Limited (see our ad this page)
  S: Chevron, Hurricane Motors(CW), Sunoco

(35) Rest Area (Eastbound)

(35) Rest Area (RR, Phones, Picnic, Vending; Westbound)

(38) Weigh Station (Eastbound)

(38) Weigh Station (Westbound)

39 WV 34, Teays Valley, Winfield
- TStop S: 76 Auto/Truck Plaza(*) (Showers)
- FStop N: Go Mart(*)
- Gas N: BP(*)
  S: Chevron(*, D), Go Mart(*)
- Food N: Applebee's, Arby's (BP), BP, Baskin Robbins (BP),

1275
Comfort Inn
Exit 47 • Charleston, WV
304-776-8070
800-798-7886
• Free Deluxe Continental Breakfast
• Kids 12 and Under Stay & Eat Free
• Outdoor Pool
• Lounge on Premises
• Meeting/Banquet Facilities
• Handicap Acessible
• Airport Shuttle • Interior Corridors
• Restaurant Next Door
Truck or Large Vehicle Parking
West Virginia ▪ I-64 ▪ Exit 47

EXIT WEST VIRGINIA

Bob Evan's Restaurant, Go Mart, Half Time Cafe, Hardee's, Jade House of Chinese, Krispy Kreme Doughnuts (Go Mart)
  S: 76 Auto/Truck Plaza (Showers), Blimpie's Subs (Go Mart), Burger King(PLAY), Captain D's Seafood, China Chef, Fazoli's Italian Food, Gino's Pizza & Spaghetti, Go Mart, KFC, McDonald's(PLAY), Paul Bunyan Restaurant(SCALES) (76 Auto/Truck Stop), Schlotzsky's Deli, SHONEY'S, Shoney's, Subway, TCBY, Taco Bell, Tudor's Biscuit World, Wendy's
- Lodg N: DAYS INN Days Inn, Red Roof Inn
- Med S: Health Plus, Hospital
- ATM N: BP, Go Mart
  S: Kroger Supermarket(24, RX), OneValley Bank, United National Bank
- Other N: Big Bear Food & Grocery(RX), Hills Foodstore, Teays Valley Laundry Center (Coin Laundry)
  S: K-Mart(RX), Kroger Supermarket(RX), Rite Aid Pharmacy

44 U.S. 35, St Albans

45 WV 25, Nitro
- TStop N: Pilot(*, SCALES)
- Gas S: BP(*, D, K), Pennzoil Oil Change(*)
- Food N: Arby's (Pilot), Pilot
  S: Checkers Burgers, Deihl's Deli & Grill, Gino's Pizza, McDonald's, Subway, Tudor's Biscuit World
- Lodg S: Best Western
- ATM S: BP

47 WV 622, Cross Lanes, Goff Mtn Road
- Gas N: Chevron(*, CW, 24), Exxon(*), Go Mart(*), SuperAmerica(*)
- Food N: Bob Evan's Restaurant, Captain D's Seafood, Gino's Pizza & Spaghetti House, Pizza Hut, Rice Bowl Chinese, Taco Bell, Tudor's Biscuit World, Wendy's
  S: Arby's, Char House, Cracker Barrel, KFC, SHONEY'S, Shoney's
- Lodg N: Motel 6
  S: Comfort Inn (see our ad this page)
- Other N: Rite Aid Pharmacy(24, RX)
  S: Wal-Mart(RX)

50 WV 25, Institute (Difficult Reaccess)
- Gas S: Go Mart(*)
- Food S: Andy's Grill, Go Mart, Krispy Kreme Doughnuts
- Parks S: Shawnee Regional Park
- Other S: US Post Office

53 WV 25/25, Roxalana Rd, Dunbar
- Gas S: Go Mart(*)
- Food S: Captain D's Seafood, Fiesta, Go Mart, Graziano's Pizza, Krispy Kreme Doughnuts (Go Mart), McDonald's(PLAY), SHONEY'S, Shoney's, Subway, Wendy's
- Lodg S: Super 8, TraveLodge
- Other S: Aldi Food Store, CVS Drugstore, Dunbar Animal Hospital, Kroger Supermarket, Rite Aid Pharmacy(RX), Wanda's Car Wash

54 U.S. 60, MacCorkle Ave, South Charleston
- Gas S: Ashland(*)
- Food N: TCBY
  S: Bob Evan's Restaurant, Husson's Pizza, KFC, McDonald's, Taco Bell, Wendy's
- Lodg S: Red Roof Inn
- RVCamp N: Cummins Cumberland, Inc. (.6 Miles)
- Med S: Thomas Memorial Hosp
- Other S: Sav-A-Lot Grocery, West Va State Police HQ

55 Kanawha Turnpike (Westbound, Difficult Reaccess)

56 Montrose Dr, South Charleston
- Gas N: Chevron(*, D, CW), Citgo(*), Exxon(*, D), SuperAmerica(*, 24)
- Food N: Baskin Robbins, Blimpie Subs & Salads, Chevron, Hardee's(24), Krispy Kreme Doughnuts, Ramada, Restaurant (Ramada); SHONEY'S, Shoney's
- Lodg N: Microtel Inn, Ramada, Wingate Inn

Bold red print shows RV & Bus parking available or nearby

EXIT WEST VIRGINIA

ATM N: Chevron, Citgo, Exxon
Other N: Avalon Dog & Cat Hospital, Car Wash

58A U.S. 119 South, Oakwood Road (Difficult Reaccess)

58B U.S. 119 North, Virginia Street Civic Center (Eastbound)

Gas N: BP
Food N: Arby's
S: Captain D's Seafood, Elk River Town Center Inn, Fifth Quarter Steak & Seafood, Joey's BBQ, Long John Silver, Mack's Restaurant & Lounge (Elk River Town Center Inn), SHONEY'S, Shoney's, Wendy's
Lodg S: Elk River Town Center Inn, Hampton Inn, Holiday Inn, Town Center Inn
AServ N: BP, Jiffy Lube, Sportcar Clinic, Turner Transmissions
S: Sear's Auto Care
ATM N: Huntington Banks of WV
Other N: Car Wash, Mountaineer Pride Car Wash, US Post Office, Valley West Veterinary Hosp
S: Center Of Town Car Wash, Charleston Civic Center, Phillip's Animal Center

58C U.S. 60, Washington Street, Civic Center

Gas N: Chevron[CW], Exxon, Go Mart[*], Rich
Food N: Country Junction Restaurant, Dutchess Bakeries, Go Mart, Husson's Pizza, Tudor's Biscuit World
S: Allie's American Grill
Lodg S: Embassy Suites, Marriott
AServ N: Exxon, Garrett Tire Center
Med S: ✚ Columbia St Francis Hospital
ATM N: Go Mart, OneValley
Other N: Car Wash, FasChek Food Market, Kroger[RX], Pharmacy Express, Rite Aid Pharmacy
S: Charleston Civic Center

59 Junction I-77, Junction I-79, Huntington, Parkersburg

Note: I-64 runs concurrent below with I-77. Numbering follows I-77.

101 Junction I-64 & I-72, Huntington

100 Broad St, Capitol St (Difficult Reaccess)

Gas W: Chevron
Food W: Cagney's, Embassy Suites, Heart O' Town, Outback Steak House, Pavilion Cafe (Heart O' Town), Quarrier Diner, Young's Food House
Lodg W: Cagney's, Embassy Suites, Heart O' Town
AServ W: Chevron, Firestone Tire & Auto, Ziebart TidyCar
Med W: ✚ Charleston Area Medical Center, ✚ Columbia St Francis Hospital
ATM W: Huntington Banks
Other W: Capitol Market

99 WV 114, Greenbrier St, State Capitol

Gas W: Chevron[*], Exxon[*, D]
Food W: Domino's Pizza, Fire House No 4, New China Restaurant, Rally's Hamburgers, Subway, Wendy's
ATM W: Bank One, Chevron
Other W: Airport, West Virginia State Capitol Building

98 WV 61, 35th Street Bridge (Southbound, Toll)

Food W: Shoney's

97 WV 60, Kanawha Blvd, Midland Trail

96 U.S. 60 East, Belle (Difficult Reaccess)

Food E: Gino's Italian, Tudor's Biscuit House
W: Dano's
Lodg W: Budget Host Inn

95 WV 61, MacCorkle Ave

FStop E: Go Mart[*]
Gas W: Exxon[*, D]
Food E: Applebee's, Bob Evan's Restaurant, Go Mart, Graziano's Italian, Krispy Kreme Doughnuts, Lone Star Steakhouse, McDonald's, Taco Bell, Wendy's
W: Burger King, Cancun Mexican Restaurant, Captain D's Seafood, Chi Chi's Mexican Restaurant, Hooters, Ponderosa Steak House, Taco Bell
Lodg E: Days Inn, Knight's Inn, Motel 6, Red Roof Inn
AServ E: Advance Auto Parts, K-Mart[RX], W H Service Center
W: Brake Shop, Danny's Service Center, Subaru Dealer
ATM E: Bank One, Go Mart
W: Bank One, Kroger Supermarket[24, RX], One Valley Bank
Other E: K-Mart[RX]
W: Hills Grocery Store, Kanawha Mall, Kroger Supermarket[RX]

89 WV 61, WV 94, Marmet, Chesapeake

FStop E: Exxon[*, D, K]
Gas E: Go Mart[*], Sunoco[*, K]
Food E: Craddocks 60's Cafe, Gino's Pizza, Hardees[24], Subway (Exxon), Tudor's Biscuit World
AServ E: Hudson's Auto Repair, NAPA Auto Parts
ATM E: Exxon, Go Mart, Kroger Supermarket[24, RX]
Other E: Kroger Supermarket[RX], Rite Aid Pharmacy[RX]

85 US 60, Hwy 61, Chelyan, Cedar Grove (Toll)

Gas E: No Name[*, D]
AServ E: No Name, Paul White Chevrolet Geo

(83) Toll Plaza C (Toll)

79 Sharon, Cabin Creek Rd

74 WV 83, Paint Creek Rd

(72) Travel Plaza (RV Dump; Northbound)

FStop N: Exxon[D, RV DUMP]
Food N: Hot Dog City, Roy Rogers (Travel Plaza), TCBY (Travel Plaza)
ATM N: Exxon

(69) Rest Area (RR, Phones)

66 WV 15, Mahan

FStop W: Sunoco[*]

60 WV 612, Mossy, Oak Hill

Gas E: Exxon[*, D]
Food E: Miss Ann's Fancy Food
AServ E: Exxon
RVCamp E: Camping (Full Hookup)
ATM E: Exxon
Parks E: Plum Orchard Lake Park

(56) Toll Plaza (Toll)

54 WV 23, WV 2, Plum Orchard Lake, Pax

Gas E: BP[*]
W: Exxon[*, D, K]
Food W: Long Branch[K]
Parks E: Plum Orchard Lake Park (Public Fishing Area)

48 U.S. 19, Summersville, North Beckley (Toll)

(45) Travel Plaza (Southbound)

FStop W: Exxon[RV DUMP] (Tamarack TP)
Food W: Mrs Fields Cookies (Tamarack TP), Sbarro Italian (Tamarack TP), TCBY (Tamarack TP), Taco Bell (Tamarack TP)
Other W: Tamarack Huge Craft Center (Tamarack TP)

44 WV 3, Harper Rd, Beckley

FStop W: Go Mart[*]
Gas E: Chevron[*, D, LP, K, CW], Exxon[*, D], Shell[*]
W: BP[*, CW]
Food E: Applebee's, Beckley Pancake House, Bennett's Smokehouse & Saloon, Bojangles (Shell), Dairy Queen, Morgan's, Omelet Shoppe, Outback Steak House, Pizza Hut, Pizza Inn (Shell), Shell, TCBY (Shell)
W: BP, Baskin Robbins (BP), Bob Evan's Restaurant, Cracker Barrel, Fox's Pizza, Pasquale Mira (Days Inn), Subway (BP), Texas Steakhouse, Wendy's
Lodg E: Comfort Inn, Courtyard by Marriott, Fairfield Inn, Holiday Inn, Howard Johnson, Motor Lodge, Super 8, The Courtyard By Marriott
W: Country Inn and Suites, Days Inn, Hampton Inn, Shoney's Inn
RVCamp W: Lake Stephens
Med E: ✚ Doctors Immedia Care (7 Days/Week, No Appt), ✚ Hospital
ATM E: Chevron, Exxon, Shell
W: Go Mart
Other E: CVS Drugstore[RX]

42 WV 16, WV 97, Mabscott, Robert C Byrd Dr (Difficult Reaccess)

Parks E: Twin Falls Resort Park

40 Junction I-64 East, Lewisburg

Note: I-64 runs concurrent above with I-77. Numbering follows I-77.

121 Junction I-77 South, Bluefield

124 U.S. 19, East Beckley, Eisenhower Dr. (Limited Access)

125 WV 307, WV 9/9, Beaver, Airport Road

FStop N: Shell[*]
Food N: Bojangles (Shell), TCBY (Shell)
Lodg N: Sleep Inn
ATM N: Shell

129 WV 9, Shady Spring, Grandview Road

Gas S: Exxon[*, D]
Parks N: New River Gorge National River Grandview
S: Little Beaver State Park

133 WV 27, Bragg, Pluto Road

Exit (136) Runaway Truck Ramp (Eastbound)

Exit (137) Runaway Truck Ramp (Westbound)

139 WV 20, Sandstone, Hinton

Gas S: Ashland[*]
Parks S: Bluestone Pipestem Resort Park

143 WV 20, Green Sulphur Springs, Meadow Bridge

Gas N: Boyd's Store[*]

Exit (147) Runaway Truck Ramp (Westbound)

150 WV 29/4, Dawson

156 U.S. 60, Midland Trail, Sam Black Church

Gas N: Exxon[D], Shell[*, D, K]
AServ N: Exxon

161 WV 12, Alta, Alderson

FStop S: Exxon[*]
Food S: Grandpaw's Rest (Exxon)
RVCamp S: Campground (14.5 Miles)

169 U.S. 219, Lewisburg, Ronceverte

Gas S: Exxon[*], Shell[*]
Food S: Arby's, Hardee's, McDonald's (Wal-Mart), SHONEY'S, Shoney's, Subway, TCBY (Shell), Western Sizzlin'
Lodg N: Days Inn
S: Brier Inn Motel & Convention Center, Super 8
Med S: ✚ Hospital
ATM S: Exxon, Greenbriar Valley National Bank
Other S: Wal-Mart[RX]

175 U.S. 60, Caldwell, White Sulphur Springs, WV 92

FStop N: Shell[*, 24]
Gas N: Chevron[*, LP, 24], Exxon
Food N: Granny's House Restaurant (Sleeper Motel), McDonald's, Subway (Shell), Wendy's
Lodg N: The Sleeper Motel
AServ N: Exxon, Shell[24]
TServ N: Mountain International, Shell[24]
RVCamp S: Greenbriar Mountainaire Campground (1 Mile), Greenbriar State Forest (2 Miles), Shaw Mi-Del-Eca Village (2 Miles)

EXIT WEST VIRGINIA/VIRGINIA

Parks **N:** Greenbriar State Forest Cavern Tours

(179) **WV Welcome Center (RR, Phones, RV Dump; Westbound)**

181 U.S. 60, WV 92, White Sulphur Springs

Gas **N:** Pennzoil Oil Change

Food **N:** April's Pizzeria Restaurant, Blake's Rest & Lounge (Old White Motel), Hardee's[PLAY]

Lodg **N:** Budget Inn, The Old White Motel

S: All State Motel (Coin Laundry)

AServ **N:** NAPA Auto Parts, Pennzoil Oil Change

RVCamp **S:** All State Motel (Coin Laundry), Twilight Overnight Camping (.5 Miles)

Other **N:** Food Lion Supermarket

183 VA 311, Crows (Eastbound, Reaccess Westbound Only)

↑WEST VIRGINIA

↓VIRGINIA

1 Jerry's Run Trail

Other **N:** Allegheny Trail

(2) **VA Welcome Center (RR, Phones, Pet Walk; Eastbound)**

7 CR 661 (Difficult Reaccess)

10 U.S. 60 East, VA 159 to South VA 311, Callahan

Gas **S:** Marathon[D]

14 VA 154, Covington, Hot Springs

Gas **N:** Coastal[*], Exxon[*]

Food **N:** Arbys (Exxon), Baskin Robbins (Exxon), Wendy's

Lodg **N:** Town House Motel

16 U.S. 60 West, U.S. 220 North, Covington, Hot Springs

Gas **N:** Exxon, Texaco[*, 24]

Food **N:** Best Western, Burger King, Dugout Bar & Grill, Marion's Cafe, Western Sizzlin

S: Comfort Center, Long John Silver, McDonald's[PLAY]

Lodg **N:** Best Western, Knights Court, Pinehurst Motel

S: Comfort Inn

AServ **N:** Exxon

S: K-Mart

Other **S:** K-Mart

21 VA 696 , Low Moor

Med **S:** ✚ Allegheny Regional Hospital

24 U.S. 60 East, U.S. 220 South, Clifton Forge

Other **S:** Allegheny Highlands Arts & Crafts Center

27 U.S. 60 West Bus., U.S. 220 South,

EXIT VIRGINIA

CR 629, Clifton Forge

Gas **S:** Citgo[*, D, LP, K], Texaco[*]

TServ **N:** Forrest Park Truck & Equip Inc

Parks **N:** Douthat State Park

29 VA 269 East, VA 42 North

Gas **S:** Exxon[*, D]

Food **S:** Triangle Restaurant (Exxon)

AServ **S:** Triangle Auto Tires

35 VA 269, CR 850, Longdale Furnace

Food **S:** Old Stacks

43 CR 780, Goshen

Other **S:** National Forest Scenic Byway

50 U.S. 60, CR 623, Kerrs Creek, Lexington

55 U.S. 11 to VA 39, Lexington, Goshen

Gas **N:** Exxon[D, K]

S: Texaco[*, D]

Food **N:** Burger King, Crystal Chinese Food, Naples Pizza, Pasta, & Subs

S: Golden Corral Family Steakhouse, Redwood Family Restaurant, SHONEY'S, Shoney's, Texaco

Lodg **N:** Best Western, Colony House Motel, Super 8

S: Comfort Inn, EconoLodge, Holiday Inn

RVCamp **N:** Long's Campground

Med **S:** ✚ Hospital (2.5 Miles)

ATM **S:** Crestar Bank

Other **N:** Wal-Mart[RX]

S: Kroger Supermarket[LP, RX]

56 Junction I-81 South, Roanoke (Eastbound)

75 7th St to Norfolk

Note: I-64 runs concurrent below with I-81. Numbering follows I-81.

191 Junction I-64 West, Lexington, Charleston

Food **W:** Shoney's

195 U.S. 11, Lee Hwy

TStop **W:** Shell[*, D]

Gas **W:** Citgo

Food **E:** Maple Hall

W: Aunt Sara's Pancake House

Lodg **E:** Maple Hall

W: Howard Johnson, Ramada, Red Oaks Inn

(199) **Rest Area (RR, Phones; Southbound)**

200 VA 710, Fairfield

205 VA 606, Raphines, Steeles Tavern

213 U.S. 11, Greenville

217 VA 654, Mint Spring, Stuarts Draft

220 VA 262, U.S. 11, Staunton (Exit To Ltd Access)

221 Junction I-64 East (Southbound)

Note: I-64 runs concurrent above with I-81. Numbering follows I-81.

EXIT VIRGINIA

87 Junction I-81 North, Staunton, Lexington (North To Winchester, South Roanoke, Harrisonburg)

Other **N:** Museum Of American Frontier Culture, Robert E. Lee Burial Grounds, Staunton Historic Dist, Stonewall Jackson Burial Grounds, Woodrow Wilson Birthplace

91 VA 608, Fisherville, Stuarts Draft

Gas **S:** Exxon[*, 24]

Food **S:** McDonald's

AServ **N:** Eddie's Tire

S: Eddie's Tire

Med **N:** ✚ Augusta Medical Center

Other **N:** Woodrow Wilson Rehab Ctr

94 U.S. 340, Waynesboro, Stuarts Draft

Gas **N:** Citgo[*], Exxon[D]

S: Pennzoil Oil Change[*]

Food **N:** KFC, SHONEY'S, Shoney's, Wendy's, Western Sizzlin'

Lodg **N:** Best Western, DAYS INN Days Inn, Holiday Inn Express, Super 8

AServ **N:** Exxon

S: Ladd Auto Repair

Other **S:** Moss Museum, Waynesboro Outlet Village

96 VA 624, Waynesboro, Lyndhurst (Trucks Use Lower Gear)

TServ **S:** Overnight Truck Facility

RVCamp **N:** The North Forty RV Campground

Other **N:** Sherando Lake, George Washington Nat'l Forrest

99 U.S. 250, Afton, Waynesboro

Gas **S:** Chevron[*]

Food **S:** Howard Johnson

Lodg **N:** Colony House Motel, Redwood Lodge

S: Howard Johnson, The Inn at Afton

Other **N:** Appalachian Trail Crossing

S: Blue Ridge Parkway, Shenandoah National Park, Tourist Info., Wintergreen Ski

(105) **Rest Area (RR, Phones, Picnic, Vending; Eastbound)**

107 U.S. 350, Crozet

RVCamp **S:** Misty Mountain Camp Resort (1 Mile)

(113) **Rest Area (RR, Phones, Picnic, Vending; Westbound)**

114 VA 637, Ivy

118AB U.S. 29, Charlottesville, Lynchburg (Culpepper)

Other **N:** University Info Ctr

120 VA 631, 5th St, Charlottesville

Gas **N:** Exxon[*], Texaco[*, LP]

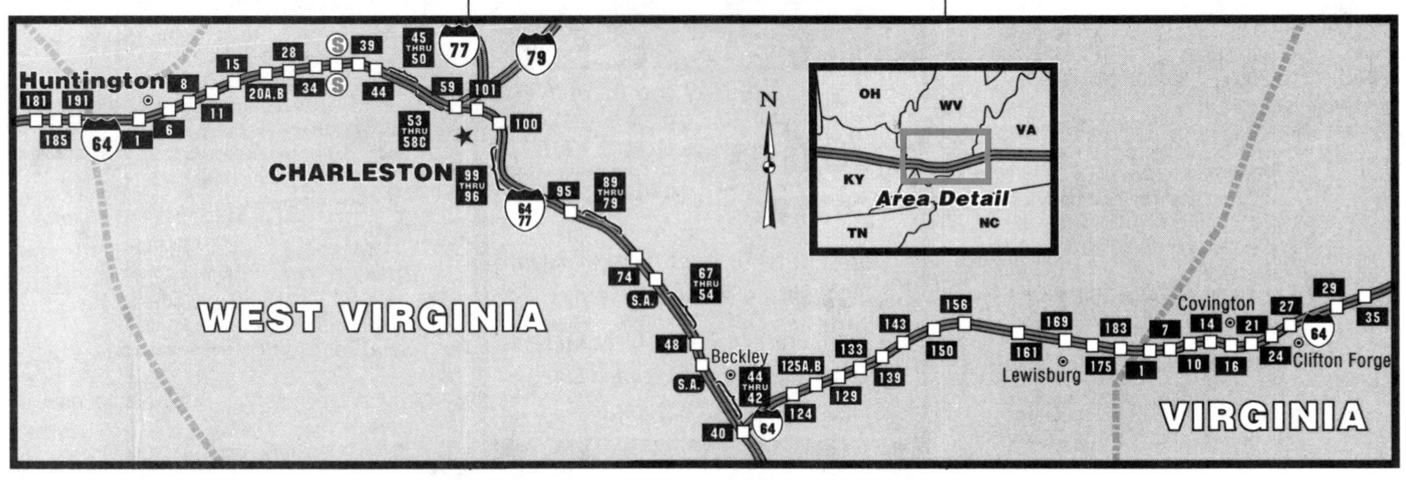

EXIT VIRGINIA

Food N: Domino's Pizza, Hardee's, Henry's Restaurant, Jade Garden (Chinese)
Lodg N: **Holiday Inn(see our ad this page)**
AServ N: Texaco
ATM N: F&M Bank, Nationsbank (Texaco)
Other N: Coin Car Wash, **Pet Motel & Salon**

121 VA 20, Charlottesville, Scottsville
Gas N: Amoco(*), **Chevron(*)**
Food N: Blimpie's Subs (Amoco), **Holiday Food & Deli**, Moore's Creek Restaurant
AServ N: Chevron, Shull's Wrecker Service
RVCamp S: **KOA Campgrounds (9.6 Miles)**
Med S: **+ Hospital**
Other S: **Ashlawn (James Monroe's Home)**, **Jefferson Vinyard Tour**, **Monticello (Thomas Jefferson's Home)**, **Monticello Visitor Center**

124 U.S. 250, Charlottesville, Shadwell, Jefferson Hwy
Food S: Ramada Inn
Lodg S: Ramada Inn
Med N: **+ Hospital**

129 VA 616, Keswick, Boyd Tavern

136 U.S. 15, Gordonsville, Palmyra (Zions Cross Roads & Fork Union)
FStop S: **Amoco(*)**, **Citgo**
Gas S: Exxon(*, D), RaceWay(*, LP), Texaco(*)
Food S: Burger King (Exxon), **Crescent Inn Restaurant**, McDonald's (Amoco), Zion Cross Roads Market & Deli
Lodg S: Zion Cross Roads Motel
Other S: **Crossroads Market**

143 VA 208, Louisa, Ferncliff
Gas S: Citgo(*, D), Exxon(D, LP)
RVCamp N: **Small Country Camping (7 Miles)**
ATM S: Citgo
Other N: **Ferncliff Market**
S: **Ferncliff Market (Citgo)**

149 VA 605, Shannon Hill

152 VA 629, Hadensville

159 U.S. 522, Gum Spring, Mineral
FStop N: **Exxon(*, D, CW) (Picnic Area)**
Gas S: Citgo(*)
Food N: **Emhardt Hot Dogs (Exxon)**
S: Junction Restaurant
AServ N: Gum Springs Auto Service
S: Excel
TServ N: **Gum Springs Truck Service**
ATM S: Citgo
Other S: **Perish Grocery**

167 VA 617, Oilville, Goochland
FStop S: **Amoco(*, LP) (Picnic)**
Food S: **Bullet's (Amoco)**
ATM S: Amoco

(168) **Rest Area (RR, Phones, Picnic, Vending; Westbound)**

(169) **Rest Area (RR, Phones, Picnic, Vending; Eastbound)**

173 VA 623, Rockville, Manakin
FStop S: **Texaco(*)**

177 Junction I-295, Washington, Norfolk, Williamsburg

178AB US 250, Richmond, Short Pump
FStop N: **Texaco(K, CW)**
Gas S: Amoco(*)
Food N: Boychick's Deli, Chesapeake Bagel, Crab House, Dairy Queen, DeFazio Of Innsbrook (Steaks, Pasta), Hickory Ham, Hunan Express, Leonardo's Pizza, Manhattan Bagel, Mulligan's, Parkside Cafe, Sharkie's, Starbucks Coffee, Thai Garden, Zack's Frozen Yogurt
S: Casa Grande, Grill & Cafe, Hot Stuff Pizza (Amoco), **McDonald's (Wal-Mart)**, Taco Bell, Wendy's
Lodg N: AmeriSuites (see our ad this page), Hampton Inn, Homestead Villas
AServ N: Auto Import Serv All In One Detail, Carmax, Firestone Tire & Auto (Master Care), Import Auto House, Jiffy Lube, Universal Ford
S: Car Quest Auto Center, Richard's Auto Repair, Short Pump Tire & Exhaust
Med S: **+ Patient Walk In Clinic**
ATM N: Fidelty Federal, First Union Bank, Jefferson National Bank, Signet Bank
S: Commerce Bank, Crestar Bank
Other N: **Auto Port Shopping Center**, **Dog's & Cat's World**, **Fed Ex Drop Box**, **Great Land Hess Pharmacy**, **Innsbrook Pavalion**, **Innsbrook Shopping Ctr**, **Mail Room**
S: **Target**, **Wal-Mart**

180AB Gaskins Road
FStop N: **East Coast(*, D, LP, K)**
Gas N: Amoco(*), Exxon(*), Texaco(*)
S: Citgo(D, LP), Texaco(*)
Food N: Applebee's, Bistro's Pantry, **Blimpie's Subs (East Coast)**, China Express, Golden Corral Family Steakhouse, Jimmy's American Deli, McDonald's, Ruby Tuesday
AServ N: **Costco**, Goodyear Tire & Auto, Haynes Jeep & Eagle
S: Citgo
ATM N: Central Fidelity Bank. First Virginia Bank, Nationsbank
Other N: **Circuit City Corral Plaza**, **Commonwealth Eyeglasses**, **Deep Run Animal Clinic**, **LeGourmet Bakery**, **Lexington Commons Shopping Ctr**, **Pet Center**, **Phar Mor Drugs**, **UKrops(RX) (Supermarket)**
S: **7-11 Convenience Store**, **Breeze Convience Store**, **Coin Operated Laundry**

181AB Parham Road
Food N: Shoney's
Med N: **+ Hospital**
S: **+ Patient First Walk-In**
ATM N: First Virginia Bank, Jefferson Nat'l Bank

183 U.S. 250, Broad St, Glenside Dr
Gas N: Amoco, Citgo(*, CW), Crown(*, LP, CW), Exxon(*, D), Merritt, Shell(CW)
S: Amoco(*), Chevron(*), Shell, Texaco(*, D, CW)
Food N: Aunt Sara's Pancake House, Awful Arthur's Seafood, Bennigan's, Blue Marlin Seafood, Bob Evan's Restaurant, Bojangles, Brothers Italian Restaurant & Pizza, Bullets' Burgers & More, Burger King, Casa Grande Mexican Restaurant, China Buffet, China Inn, Friendly's, Fuddruckers, Hooters, Indian Foods & Flavor, Italian Kitchen West, Kabuto Japanese Steak House and Sushi Bar, Little Caesars Pizza, Lone Star Steakhouse, McDonald's, Morrisons Cafeteria, Mozzarella's Cafe, Old Country Buffett, Olive Garden, Outback Steakhouse, Peking Garden, Piccadilly Cafeteria, Pizza Hut, Red Lobster, SHONEY'S Shoney's, Steak & Ale, Subway, T.G.I. Friday's, Taco Bell, Thai Dynasty (Thai/American), The Wood Grill (Steaks & Seafood), Vietnam Harbor Restaurant, Waffle House, Wendy's
S: Arby's, Bill's BBQ, Chinese Restaurant, **Denny's**, Dunkin Donuts (Chevron), El Maddador Restaurant, Full Kee Restaurant, Holiday Inn, House of Hunan, McDonald's, Me-Kong Restaurant, Mexico Restaurant, Taco Bell, Toppings Pizza & Subs
Lodg N: Comfort Inn, Embassy Suites, Fairfield Inn, Quality Inn, SHONEY'S Shoney's, Super 8
S: Courtyard by Marriott, DAYS INN Days Inn, Holiday Inn, Hyatt
AServ N: Amoco, Capitol Ford Lincoln, Mercury, Exxon, George Toyoto, Haywood Clark Pontaic Buick, Hutch's Body Shop, Jiffy Lube, K-Mart, Lawrence Dodge, Merchant's Tire & Auto, Midas, Mitsubishi/Honda Dealer, Royal Oldsmobile, Saturn, Trak Auto, Volvo Dealer
S: Advance Auto Parts, Alan Tire Goodyear, All Tune & Lube, Amoco, Baugh Auto Body, Dominion Chevrolet, Import Auto House, Muffler Shop, Shell
ATM N: Central Fidelity Bank, First Union Bank, First Virginia Bank, Hanover Bank, Jefferson Nat'l Bank, Nationsbank, Signet Bank
S: Crestar Bank, First Virginia Bank
Other N: **7-11 Convenience Store**, **A&A Convenience**, **Allied Animal Hospital**, **CVS Pharmacy**, **Coin Operated Laundry**, **Fountain Square Shopping**, **K-Mart**, **Krops Pharmacy**, **Merchant's Walk Shopping Ctr**, **Old Town Shopping Ctr**, **Petsmart**, **Richmond Lock & Safe**, Western Wash Car Wash, **Winn Dixie Supermarket**
S: **7-11 Convenience Store**, **Ambassador Dog & Cat Hospital**, **Coin Laundry (Horsepin Convience)**, **Crestview Food Store**, **Horsepin Convience**, **Rolling Hills Super Center**, **UniMart Convience Store**, **WalGreens Pharmacy**, **Westwood Shopping Ctr**

185 U.S. 33, Staples Mill Road, Dickens Road (Difficult Reaccess)
Gas S: Shell
Food N: Shoney's
AServ S: Shell
Med S: **+ Hospital**
ATM S: Central Fidelity Bank
Other S: **7-11 Convenience Store**

186 Junction I-195 South

187 Junction I-95 North, Washington (Left Exit Eastbound)

Note: I-64 runs concurrent below with I-95. Numbering follows I-95.

79 Junction I-64, I-195 South, Charlottesville

78 Boulevard
Gas E: Citgo
W: Amoco(*, D), Lucky(*, LP)
Food E: Holiday Inn, Zippy's BBQ
W: Bill's Virginia BBQ, Taylor's Family Restaurant (Days Inn)
Lodg E: Diamond Lodge and Suites, Gadnes Restaurant, Holiday Inn
W: DAYS INN Days Inn
TServ W: **Dolan International**
ATM W: Jefferson National Bank (Lucky)
Other W: **Tourist Info.**, **US Marine Museum**

76B U.S. 1, U.S. 301, Belvidere
Med W: **+ Belvidere Medical Center**
Other W: **Maggie Walker Historical Site**, **VA War Memorial**

76A Chamberlayne Ave (Northbound)
Gas E: Citgo
Food E: Burger King, Captain D's Seafood, Dunkin

1308
AMERISUITES
AMERICA'S AFFORDABLE ALL-SUITE HOTEL
Virginia • Exit 178B • 804-747-9644

1407

Closest Hotel To Monticello, Ashlawn Highland & Michie Tavern
• We Feature In Room Coffee Makers
• Free HBO, ESPN & Extended Cable
• Outdoor Pool • Restaurant
VIRGINIA • I-64 • EXIT 120

Bold red print shows RV & Bus parking available or nearby

3 Star Rated

- Full Service Colonial Style Hotel
- Hotel 1/4 Mile from Colonial Williamsburg
- Surrounded By 42 Acres of Beautiful Landscaped Grounds
- Tennis Courts, Pools, Outdoor Pavilion featuring Special Events
- All Guest Rooms Feature Colonial Decor
- Lombardis Pizzeria & Game Room
- 1776 Tavern Featuring Crableg & Shrimp Buffet

757-220-1776 • 800-446-2848

Special Rates $99

Holiday Inn 1776

1149

WILLIAMSBURG, VIRGINIA ▪ I-64 ▪ EXIT 238

EXIT VIRGINIA

	Donuts, Hawks Bar-B-Que And Seafood, McDonald's
Lodg	E: Belmont Motel
AServ	E: Emrick Chevrolet, Napa Auto, Texaco[*, D, K]
Other	E: **7-11 Convenience Store, Easters Convenience Store**

Note: I-64 runs concurrent above with I-95. Numbering follows I-95.

190	Junction I-95 South
192	U.S. 360, Mechanicsville
Gas	N: Amoco[CW, 24], Lucky Convience, Texaco[D] (Wrecker Service)
	S: Chevron[D, CW]
Food	N: Church's Chicken, KFC, McDonald's, Murrey's Steak & Seafood, Ocean Seafood Market
	S: Stuarts Seafood Take-Out

EXIT VIRGINIA

AServ	N: Texaco
	S: Tuffy, Weaver Transmission
Other	N: **Community Pride Food Store, Lucky Coin Operated Laundry, Lucky Convience Store, Mathematics and Science Center, Repair and Towing, Strawberry Hill, Western Union**
	S: **Cheek & Shockley RV, Coin Operated Laundry (Chevron)**
193AB	VA 33, Nine Mile Road
Gas	N: Amoco[*, D], Exxon[*]
Food	N: Shoney's
AServ	N: Amoco
TServ	N: **Capitol Freightliner Sales and Services**
Med	S: **Hospital**
195	Laburnum Ave, VA 33, US60, VA5
Gas	N: Mobil, Shell
Food	S: Applebee's, China King, Subway, Taco Bell
AServ	N: Mobil, Shell

1394

In Historic Williamsburg
Toll Free Reservations:
800-446-9228

Busch Gardens Williamsburg & Water Country
We offer over 600 rooms in the heart of Williamsburg!
Patrick Henry Inn is a full service hotel with conference facilities.
Just 1/2 Block from Colonial Williamsburg Historic Area & 5 min. to Busch Gardens Williamsburg. All rooms feature 2 extra long double beds, climate control, AM/FM clock radio, remote control cable TV and more!

Visit us at any of our 3 Locations on I-64

Best Western Patrick Henry Inn • 757-229-9540
Best Western Williamsburg (Exit 242A) • 757-229-3003
Best Western Colonial Capitol Inn • 757-253-1222

VIRGINIA • I-64 • EXIT 238

EXIT VIRGINIA

ATM	S: Central Fidelity Bank, Jefferson National Bank
Other	N: **James River Plantation**
	S: **Eye Care Center, Fish Tail Pet Store, Puppy Love Pet Care Center, Rite Aide Pharmacy**
197AB	VA 156, Airport Dr, Highland Springs, Sandston
FStop	S: **East Coast[*, LP]**
Gas	S: BP[*]
Food	S: Best Western, Bullet's, Burger King, Ma & Pa's Country Diner, Mexico Restaurant, Pizza Hut, Waffle House
Lodg	S: Best Western, Days Inn, Econolodge, Hampton Inn, Holiday Inn, Legacy Inn, Motel 6, Super 8
AServ	S: **Central Virginia Auto Sales**, Town & Country Auto Sales and Truck Center
TServ	N: **Penske Truck Center**
ATM	S: Central Fidelity
Other	S: **7-11 Convenience Store[*, 24], VA Aviation Museum**
200	Junction I-295, U.S. 60, Washington D.C., Rocky Mount NC
FStop	N: **Exxon[*, 24]**
Gas	N: Amoco[*, LP]
	S: Texaco[*, LP]
Food	N: Fast Mart Cafe, Nava's Pizza
	S: McDonald's (Texaco)
AServ	N: Amoco
ATM	N: Citizens and Farmers Bank
Other	N: **Food Lion Grocery Store, New Kent Crossing Supermarket, Post Office (Amoco), Revco Drugs**
	S: **Lipscomes Hardware, Winn Dixie Supermarket[RX]**
(203)	**Weigh Station**
205	VA 33E, VA 249W, to U.S. 60, Bottoms Bridge, Quinton
FStop	N: **Exxon[*, D, 24]**
Gas	N: Amoco[*, D, LP] (Wrecker Service)
	S: Texaco[*, LP]
Food	N: Nava's Pizza
	S: McDonald's (Texaco)
AServ	S: Texaco[LP]
ATM	N: Citizens & Farmers Bank
Other	N: **Food Lion Grocery Store, New Kent Crossing Supermarket, Revco Drugs**
	S: **Lipscones Hardware Store, U.S. Post Office, Winn Dixie Supermarket[RX] (Deli)**
211	VA 106, Talleysville, Prince George
(213)	**Rest Area (RR, Phones, Picnic, Vending)**
214	VA 155, New Kent, Providence Forge
RVCamp	S: **Ed Allen's Campground (9.9 Miles)**
220	VA 33 East, West Point
Gas	N: Exxon[*, D, K]
227	VA 30, to VA 60, Toano, Williamsburg
FStop	S: **Texaco[*]**
Gas	S: Shell[LP]
Food	S: **McDonald's (Texaco FS), Stuckey's[LP] (Shell)**
RVCamp	S: **Williamsburg Campsites (6.5 Miles)**
231AB	VA 607, Croaker, Norge
Gas	N: Citgo[*]
Parks	N: **York River State Park**
234AB	199 &VA 646, Lightfoot
RVCamp	N: **Camp Skimono, KOA Campgrounds (1 Mile), KOA Campgrounds (1.5 Miles)**
	S: **Fair Oaks Campground (.75 Miles), Kin-Kaid Kampground (1 Mile)**
Other	N: **Old Dominion Oprey**
238	VA 143, Camp Peary, Colonial Williamsburg, to U.S. 60
Lodg	N: **Best Western (see our ad this page)**
	S: **Holiday Inn (see our ad this page)**
RVCamp	S: **Anvil Campground**
Med	N: **Hospital**
Parks	S: **Water Mill Park**
Other	N: **Cheatham Annex**
242AB	VA 199, Colonial Pkwy , Williamsburg
Food	N: Days Inn
Lodg	N: **Days Inn**
Other	N: **Water Country USA Water Park, Yorktown**
	S: **Busch Gardens**
243	VA 143 West, Williamsburg (Left Exit

EXIT	VIRGINIA
	Westbound, Difficult Reaccess)
247AB	VA 238, Yorktown, Lee Hall (Westbound)
Gas	N: BP[*, D], Citgo[*]
AServ	N: BP
ATM	N: BP
250AB	VA 105, Fort Eustis Blvd , Ft Eustis, Yorktown
RVCamp	N: **Campground**
Parks	N: **Newport News Park**
Other	N: **US Army & Transportation Museum**
255AB	VA 143, Jefferson Ave, Newport News, Williamsburg
FStop	N: **Mobil**[*, D]
Gas	S: Citgo[*, D], Exxon[*, D]
Food	N: Shoney's
	S: Applebee's, Burger King, Cheddar's Casual Cafe, Chick-Fil-A, **Cracker Barrel**, Don Pablo's Mexican Kitchen, KFC, Krispy Kreme Doughnuts, McDonald's, Nappo Suschi Bar Restaurant (Japanese), Outback Steakhouse, Samuri Steaks & Seafood, Subway, Waffle House, Wendy's
Lodg	S: Comfort Inn, Hampton Inn
AServ	N: AAMCO Transmission, Hall Acura, Suttle Cadillac, Oldsmobile, GMC Trucks
	S: Exxon, Tires of America
RVCamp	N: **Newport News Park Campsites (1 Mile)**
ATM	S: Crestar Bank, NationsBank (FedEx/UPS)
Other	N: **Newport New Int'l Airport**, **Sam's Club**, **Wal-Mart Supercenter**
	S: **7-11 Convenience Store**[*], **Dr. Roy Martin Optical**, **Home Quarters**, **Jefferson Green Shopping Ctr**, **N H Northern Hardware Store**, **Patrick Henry Mall**
256AB	Oyster Point Road, Poquoson Rd, Victory Blvd
Gas	N: Citgo[*, CW]
Food	N: Burger King, Chesapeake Bagel Bakery, Empress Chinese, Fuddruckers, Hardees, Kenny Roger's Roasters, Pizzaria Uno, Spaghetti Warehouse, Subway
AServ	N: **K-Mart**, Kramer Tire
ATM	N: Cenit Bank, First VA Bank, Old Point Nat'l Bank
Other	N: **Farm Fresh Grocery**, **K-Mart**[24, RX], **Mail Boxes Etc**, **Village Square Shopping Center**
258AB	U.S. 17, J Clyde Morris Blvd, Yorktown
FStop	S: **East Coast**[*, LP, K]
Gas	N: Amoco[*, D, K], Exxon[*], Shell[*, D, K, CW]
	S: Citgo[*, D], Exxon[*, D, CW], Texaco[*, LP]
Food	N: Chanello's Pizza, Domino's Pizza, Glass Pheasant Tea Room, Grandstand Grill, Hauss' Deli, New China Express, Spring Garden (Chinese), Waffle House
	S: Belgin Waffle And Family Steakhouse, Bo Dines Hickory Hut Bar-B-Que, Captain's Rail, Don's Bar-B-Que, Egg Roll King (Chinese), El Mariachi Mexican, Hong Kong Restaurant, Joe & Mimma's Pizza, Philly's Sub, Pizza Hut, Rally's Hamburgers, Sammy and Angelo's Steak and Pancake House, Subway, Taco Bell, Wendy's
Lodg	N: Budget Lodge, Host Inn, Ramada, Super 8
	S: **Motel 6**, Omni Hotel
AServ	N: Advance Auto Parts, Casey's All State Car Sales, Import Car Service, Shell
	S: Car Matic, Casey Chevrolet, Casey Honda, Charlie Faulk Auto Dealer, David's Towing, Dent Doctor, Dunlop Tires, Jiffy Lube, Mike's Q-Lube, Mizer Muffler and Brakes
Med	S: ✚ **Hospital**, ✚ **Sentara Urgent Care**
ATM	N: Central Fidelity Bank, Credit Union
	S: First Federal Savings Bank, First Union Bank, Nationsbank (7-11 Convenience Store), Peninsula Trust Bank
Other	N: **7-11 Convenience Store**, **Animal Hospital**, **Bay Berry Village Shopping Center**, **Coin Laundry**, **Food Lion Grocery Store**, **Kiln Creek Shopping Ctr (UPS Drop Box)**, **Mag's Deli and Ice Cream**, **Mariners Fine Art Center**, **Pac-N-Mail**, **Rips Convience Store**
	S: **7-11 Convenience Store**[24], Charlie's Car Wash, **Coin Op Laundry**, **Newport Square Shoppng Center**, **Pet Supply Store**, **Revco Drugs**, **Rite Aide Pharmacy**, **Super Fresh Grocery**, **Tourist Info.**, **Virginia Living Museum**
261A	Hampton Roads Center Pkwy
Gas	N: Citgo[*], Exxon[*, D, CW], Shell[*]
	S: Amoco[*], Exxon, Texaco[*, CW]
Food	N: Andrea's Pizza, Applebee's, Blimpie's Subs (Shell), Boston Market Restaurant, Burger King, Carmela's Pasta Cafe, Chi Chi's Restaurant, Chili's, China Garden, Darryl's Restaurant And Tavern, Daswiener Works, Daybreak Restaurant (Days Inn), Denny's, Dunkin Donuts, East Japanese Restaurant, Fay's Chinese, Golden Corral Family Steakhouse, Golden Palace Chinese, Holiday Inn, Hooters, IHOP, KFC, Larry's Oyster Bar, McDonald's, Mongolian BBQ, Olive Garden, Olive Garden, Picadilly, Pizza Hut, Rally's Hamburgers, Red Lobster, Schlotzsky's Deli, Steak & Ale, Subway, Szechuan Chinese Food, TCBY, Taco Bell, The Grate Steakhouse, Waffle House, Wendy's
	S: Arby's, Burger King, Captain George's Seafood, Domino's Pizza, Great Family Restaurant (BBQ, Subs, Pasta), High's Ice Cream, Krispy Kreme Doughnuts, MiPiseo Mexican Food, Old Country Buffett, Papa John's Pizza, Pizza Hut, Sammy and Nicks Family Steakhouse, Szechuan Pan Mongolian BBQ Beef, The Kettle Restaurant[24], Tommy's Restaurant, Waffle House
Lodg	N: Comfort Inn, Days Inn, Fairfield Inn, Hampton Inn, Holiday Inn, Red Roof Inn
	S: Econolodge, La Quinta Inn
AServ	N: Advance Auto Parts, Firestone Tire & Auto, Freedom Ford, Hamptons Chevrolet, Joseph Automotive, Napa Auto, Pomoco
	S: AAMCO Transmission (Wrecker Service), Amoco, Auto Repair Fast Stop, Big Al's Mufflers & Brakes, Birds Auto Repair, Brakes Parts Auto Speciality, Car Quest Auto Center, Christian Auto Repair, Copeland Auto Plaza, Dr Motor Works Engine Repair, Eurato European Repair (Diesel Service), Jiffy Lube, Midas Muffler & Brake, Montgomery Ward, Paul Tysinger Nissan, Pep Boys Auto Center, R & D Carburator, Tread Quarters Tires, **Western Auto**, Williams Honda Used Cars, Windshields Of America
TServ	S: **Watsons Petroleum and Repair**
Med	N: ✚ **Hospital**
	S: ✚ **Mercury West**[RX], ✚ **Riverside Medical Care Ctr**
ATM	N: BB&T Banking, Crestar, First Union Bank, First Virginia Bank, First Virginia Bank (Wal-Mart), Langley Credit Union, Nationsbank, Old Point Nat'l Bank, Super Fresh Supermarket
	S: Crestar Bank
Other	N: **Almost A Bank (Check Cashing Services)**, Car Wash, **Casey's Marine Boat Repair**, **Coliseum Mall (UPS Drop Box)**, **Eye to Eye Optical**, **Food Lion Supermarket**, **Langley Air Force Base**, **Lenscrafters Eyeglasses**, **National Optical**, **Pearl Express**, **Pet World**, **Phar Mor Drugs**, **Super Fresh Supermarket**, **Target**, **Wal-Mart Supercenter**[RX] **(Vision Ctr)**
	S: **7-11 Convenience Store**[24], **Better Vision Ctr**, **Coliseum Business Center**, **Farm Fresh Supermarket**, **Goodman Hardware**, **Greenwood Shopping Ctr**, **Mercury Animal Hospital**, **Sandy Bottom Nature Park**, Scrub A Dub Car Wash, **Todds Center**

WILLIAMSBURG • VIRGINIA

SURROUNDING WILLIAMSBURG WITH A HOST OF FINE HOTELS

We offer you more choices than anyone in Williamsburg...all within minutes of every major attraction, outlet shopping and championship golf. Accommodations from well appointed, newly renovated rooms to comfortable two-room suites with amenities like indoor and outdoor pools, fitness centers and jacuzzis, all at very affordable rates! Let Newport Hospitality Group be your host for your Williamsburg vacation adventure.

Starting at $49^{00}

- Ramada Inn & Conference Center
- Quality Suites Williamsburg
- Quality Inn Historic
- Hampton Inn Williamsburg
- Hampton Inn Historic Area
- Quality Inn Lord Paget
- Comfort Inn & Suites

1-800-444-4678

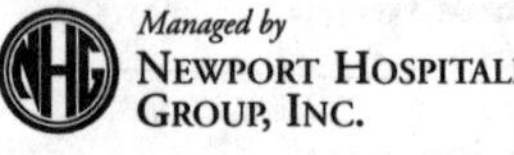

Managed by NEWPORT HOSPITALITY GROUP, INC.

Web Site: www.wmbg.com/nhg • E-mail: nhg@wmbg.com

1212

EXIT VIRGINIA

262B Hampton Roads Center Pkwy (Westbound)

263AB U.S. 258, VA 134, Mercury Blvd, James River Bridge

- **Gas** **N:** Exxon(*, CW), Shell(*, CW)
  S: Amoco(*)
- **Food** **N:** Blimpie's Subs, Boston Market Restaurant, Chi Chi's Mexican Restaurant, Chili's, China Garden, Darryl's, Days Inn, Denny's, Dunkin Donuts, Golden Corral Family Steakhouse, Holiday Inn, KFC, McDonald's, Olive Garden, Pizza Hut, Rally's Hamburgers, Red Lobster, Steak & Ale, Taco Bell, The Grate Steak, Waffle House, Wendy's
  S: La Quinta Inn, Old Country Buffet, Waffle House
- **Lodg** **N:** Comfort Inn, Courtyard by Marriott, Days Inn, Fairfield Inn, Hampton Inn(see our ad this page), Holiday Inn(see our ad this page), Quality Inn, Red Roof Inn
  S: Econolodge, La Quinta Inn, Travelodge (see our ad this page)
- **AServ** **N:** Coliseum Mercury, GM Auto Dealership, Thompson Ford
  S: All Tune & Lube, Big Al's Mufflers & Brakes, Copland Toyota, Volvo, Nissan, Montgomery Ward, Pep Boys Auto Center, Western Auto
- **Med** **S:** ✚ Riverside Medical Care Walk-In/ Pharmacy (Open 7 Days a Week)
- **ATM** **N:** First VA Bank, Langley Federal Credit Union
  S: Crestar Bank
- **Other** **N:** Coliseum Mall, Riverdale Shopping Center, Super Fresh Grocery, Wal-Mart
  S: Farm Fresh Grocery

264 Junction I-664 South, Downtown Newport News, Pembrook Pkwy

- **Gas** **S:** Citgo(*)
- **AServ** **S:** Rod's Transmission

320 ROOMS
800-842-9370

1565
• Tivoli Gardens Full Service Restaurant
• Garden Court Lounge
• 16,000 sq.ft. Meeting Space
• Indoor Pool/Exercise Room
• 1 Block from Mall & Restaurants
• Shuttle Service
Hampton Newport News Area
VIRGINIA • I-64 • EXIT 263B

132 Rooms
1567

757-838-8484
• Free Deluxe Continental Breakfast
• All Rooms Coffee Maker, Ironing Board and Iron
• Free Local Calls
• Mall and Restaurants, 1 Block
Hampton Newport News Area
VIRGINIA • I-64 • EXIT 263B

- **ATM** **S:** Citgo

265C Armistead Ave, Langely AFB (Eastbound, Reaccess At 265A)

265AB VA 134, VA 167, La Salle Ave

- **Gas** **N:** Citgo
- **Lodg** **N:** Super 8
- **AServ** **N:** Citgo
- **Med** **S:** ✚ Hospital

267 U.S. 60, VA 143, Settlers Lodge Rd

- **Gas** **N:** Citgo(*, D)
- **Food** **N:** Grill (Citgo), Krispy Kreme Doughnuts (Citgo)
  S: Burger King, Subway Station
- **Med** **S:** ✚ Hospital
- **ATM** **S:** NationsBank (Collegiate Bookstore)
- **Other** **S:** Coin Laundry, Tourist Info., VA Air & Space Museum

268 VA 169, Ft Monroe, Mallory St

- **FStop** **N:** Exxon(*), Onmark(*)
- **Gas** **N:** Texaco(*)
- **Food** **N:** Hardee's, Little Chicago Pizza, McDonald's
  S: Strawberry Banks
- **Lodg** **S:** Strawberry Banks
- **AServ** **N:** Texaco
- **Med** **S:** ✚ Hospital
- **ATM** **N:** First Union Bank, Old Point Nat'l Bank, Onmark
- **Other** **N:** Ft Monroe

(271) Vehicle Inspection - All Vehicles Over 10'6" Wide

272 West Ocean View Ave, Willoughby Spit (No Thru Trucks)

- **Food** **S:** Fisherman's Warf
- **Lodg** **S:** Days Inn(see our ad this page)

273 4th View St, Ocean View

- **Gas** **O:** Exxon(*, D, LP)
- **Lodg** **O:** Chesa-Bay Motel, Econolodge
- **Other** **I:** Norfolk Visitor Info Center

Marina Beach
FISHING PIERS ▪ PRIVATE BEACHES
Restaurant on Premises
Continental Breakfast Included
Kids 12 and Under Stay Free
Outdoor Pool • Beachfront
Meeting/Banquet Facilities
Pets Allowed • Coin Laundry
Truck or Large Vehicle Parking
Exterior Corridors
1084
757-583-4521 • Norfolk, VA
VIRGINIA • I-64 • EXIT 272

Newport News, Virginia
1564
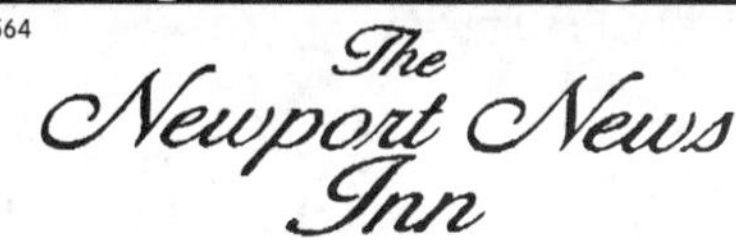

6128 Jefferson Ave.
Newport News, VA 23605
162 Rooms
In Room Coffee • Outdoor Pool
Non-Smoking Rooms Available
Inside Access
Free Local Calls • Guest Laundry
757-826-4500
VIRGINIA • I-64 • EXIT 263A

- **O:** Sarah Constant Beach

274 Bay Ave, Naval Air Station (Westbound)

276A Jct I-564, U.S. 460, Granby St, Naval Base (To VA165 Little Creek Rd, To 406 Terminal Blvd)

- **Gas** **O:** Amoco(D), Exxon(*, D, CW)
- **Food** **O:** Kin's Wok II, McDonald's, Mister Jim's Submarines, Oh! Brian's Restaurant, Old Virginia Hams, Papa John's Pizza, Reaino's Restaurant, Saigai Restaurant, Subway, TJ Super Subs, Taco Bell, Taste-N-See (Donuts, Pizza, Subs), The Pancake House, Wendy's, Zero's Mister Submarine
- **AServ** **O:** Auto Zone Auto Parts, Firestone Tire & Auto, Import Car Wash, Nationwide Safety Brake Service
- **Med** **O:** ✚ Hospital
- **ATM** **O:** BT&T Bank, Central Fidelity (Farm Fresh Supermarket), Centura Bank (Haniford Drugs), Crestar Bank, First Union Bank, Life Savings Bank, Nationsbank
- **Parks** **I:** Virginia Zoological Park
- **Other** **O:** 7-11 Convenience Store, Almost A Bank (Check Cashing), Coin Operated Laundry, Eckerd Drugs, Farm Fresh Supermarket, Haniford Drugs, Locksmith, Optical, Parrott Island (Pets), Pearl Vision Center, Revco Drugs, Super Fresh Food Store, Wards Corner Mall

276B Junction I-564, to VA 406

276C VA 165, U.S. 460 West, Little Creek Road

277AB VA 168, Tidewater Drive

- **Gas** **I:** Amoco, Citgo(*, LP)
  O: Citgo(*), Crown(CW), Exxon(*), Shell(CW)
- **Food** **I:** Carolino Seafood, Hunan Express
  O: Arby's, Bamboo Hut, Captain D's Seafood, Fortune Dragon (Chinese Dragon), Hardee's, Kings Seafood, Little Caesars Pizza (K-Mart), No Frill Grill, Open House Diner, Philly Cheesesteak House, Rotisserie Lite, TCBY
- **AServ** **I:** Amoco, Hy-Tech Auto Service, Re-King Tires
  O: Advantage Auto Store, All Tune & Lube, Carburator Clinic, Cinder Tire, Exxon, Maaco, Napa Auto, Penske (K-Mart), Tune-Up Plus
- **Med** **I:** ✚ Tidewater Walk-In Medical Center
- **ATM** **O:** Central Fidelity Bank (Rack-N-Sack Supermarket), NationsBank
- **Other** **O:** Coin Op Laundry, Eckerd Drugs, K-Mart(RX), Rack-N-Sack Supermarket, SSS Car Wash, Veterinary Clinic

278 VA 194 South, Chesapeake Blvd

279AB Norview Ave, Norfolk Int'l Airport

- **Gas** **O:** Shell(*, LP) (Wrecker Service)
- **Food** **O:** Franco's Italian Restaurant & Pizza, New China Restaurant, Pizza Hut
- **AServ** **O:** J&M Tire Mart
- **Other** **O:** Bromlee Shopping Center, Eckerd Drugs, Food Lion Supermarket, K-Mart(24), Norfolk Botanical Gardens

281 VA 165, Military Highway (Difficult Reaccess)

- **Gas** **I:** Exxon(D, CW)
  O: Amoco
- **Food** **I:** Hilton, Yings Chinese & American
  O: Andy's Pizza House, House of Eggs, Pappy's Hacienda, Stone Horse Restaurant, Tidewater Seafood, Wendy's
- **Lodg** **I:** Hampton Inn, Hilton
  O: Econolodge
- **AServ** **I:** Calvary Repair, Firestone Tire & Auto
  O: AAMCO Transmission, Atlantic Auto Repair & Service, Cider Tire, ED's Auto Repair, Green Grifford Nissan/ Chrysler/ Plymouth/ Saab, Inco Transmission, Ingrams Used Auto Parts, Planet Cars, Tidewater Transmission, Windshields Of America

EXIT		VIRGINIA
	Other	**O:** Airport, Coin Operated Laundry, Robo Car Wash
282		U.S. 13N, N Hampton Blvd, Chesapeake Bridge Tunnel
	TStop	**O:** Big Charlie's Truck Plaza(*, SCALES)
	Food	**O:** Quality Inn
	Lodg	**O:** Quality Inn
284AB		Junction I-264, VA 44, Virginia Beach, Newtown Rd
	Food	**O:** Quality Inn
	Lodg	**O:** Clarion Hotel, Comfort Inn, Days Inn, Holiday Inn, LaQuinta Inn, Quality Inn, Ramada Limited (see our ad this page), Ramada Plaza Resort (see our ad this page), Murphy's Emerald isle Motel (see our ad this page)
286AB		Indian River Road
	Gas	**I:** Amoco(*, CW), Citgo(*, D), Exxon(*, LP), Shell(*, CW), Shell(*, LP, CW), Texaco(*, D, CW, 24) **O:** Citgo, Exxon(*, D), Texaco(*, LP)
	Food	**I:** Catherine's Restaurant, Egg Roll King, Hardee's **O:** Arby's, Captain D's Seafood, China Garden, El Cantine Mexican Restaurant, Famous Uncle Al's Hotdogs & Fries, Fiesta Han Oriental (Philippina Fast Food), Golden Corral Family Steakhouse, IHOP, KFC, Lagoona Bakery, Leone's Seafood, McDonald's, Outback Steakhouse, Pizza Hut, Rally's Hamburgers, Riverpoint Deli and Pizzeria, SHONEY'S Shoney's, Subway, TCBY, Taco Bell, Thomasinna Pizzeria, Waffle House
	Med	**O:** Patient First Walk-In
	ATM	**I:** Central Fidelity Bank, Life Savings Bank **O:** Bank of Hampton Rd
	Other	**I:** 7-11 Convenience Store, Family Vision Ctr, Indian River Pet Grooming **O:** 7-11 Convenience Store, Animal Hospital, Farm Fresh Supermarket, K-Mart(RX), Optical Ctr, Pac-N-Mail Postal Service, Pet Land, Revco, University Shops
289AB		Greenbrier Pkwy (Difficult Reaccess)
	Gas	**I:** Amoco(*, D, CW), Citgo(*, D, CW), Exxon(CW) **O:** Amoco, Citgo(*), Mobil(*, D)
	Food	**I:** Bancho Grande Mexican, Beijing Restaurant, Burger King, Chevy's, Cugini's Pizza, Deli, Denny's, Hot Dog Deli, Johnson's BBQ, McDonald's, Oriental Cuisine (Thailand, Philippine, Chinese), Pizza Hut, Subway, Village Grill, Wendy's **O:** Anna's Bar & Grill, KFC, S&D Seafood, Taco Bell
	Lodg	**I:** Hampton Inn, Suburban Lodge, Wellsley (see our ad this page) **O:** Econolodge
	Med	**O:** Hospital
	Other	**I:** 7-11 Convenience Store, All Pets Pleasures (Pet Supplies), Food Lion Grocery Store(24), K-Mart, National Optical, Parkview Shopping Center, Phar Mor Drugs, VA State Police **O:** Eckerd Drugs, Food Lion Supermarket (Deli, Bakery), Midway Shopping Ctr, Midway Vetenarian Hospital, Rainbow Coin Operated Laundry
290AB		VA 168, Battlefield Blvd, Great Bridge
	FStop	**O:** Amoco(*, D, CW)
	Gas	**O:** Texaco(*, LP, CW)
	Food	**N:** Shoney's **O:** 2 Mom's Cafe, Anthony's Deli & Grill, Applebee's, Bagel Works, Blimpie's Subs (Texaco), Chanello's Pizza, Chick-Fil-A, Chuck E Cheese's Pizza, Dunkin Donuts (Days Inn), Golden Corral Family Steakhouse, Hardee's, Honey Glazed Ham & Bread Shop, Joey's Pizza, Maxwell's, Ryan's Steakhouse, Taco Bell, Waffle House, Wendy's
	Lodg	**O:** Days Inn, Super 8
	AServ	**O:** Sam's Club
	TServ	**I:** Mack's Truck
	Other	**O:** 7-11 Convenience Store, Animal Clinic, Battlefield Market Place, Dept of Motor Vehicles, Eastern Lock & Key, H-Q Center, Lowe's Super Center, Sam's Club (Optical), U.S. Post Office, Volvo Parkway Shopping Ctr, Wal-Mart
291		Junction I-464, VA 104, to U.S. 17, Norfolk, Elizabeth City
292		VA 190, Dominion Blvd, to VA 104 (Westbound)
	Gas	**I:** Texaco(*) **O:** Mobil(*)
	Food	**I:** Hardee's, No. One Chinese Food
	Other	**I:** Food Lion Supermarket (Deli, Bakery), Food Mister Jim's Subs, Pizza & Wings
296		U.S. 17, Portsmouth, Elizabeth City
	RVCamp	**O:** Campground
	Other	**I:** Deep Creek Veterinary Hospital
297		U.S. 13, U.S. 460, Military Hwy
	Gas	**I:** Exxon(*)
299A		Junction I-264E, Portsmouth, Norfolk
299B		Jct I-664, U.S. 13, U.S.58, U.S. 460, Bowershill, Suffolk

↑VIRGINIA

Begin I-64

Murphy's Emerald Isle Motel

Virginia Beach, VA

All 2 Room Suites
Outdoor Pool
Meeting/Banquet Facilities
Handicap Accessible
Exterior Corridors
Beachfront (1Block)
RODEWAY INN coming soon

757-428-3462 • 1005 Pacific Ave.

VIRGINIA • I-64 • EXIT 284AB

1309

Value Never Looked This Good!

Virginia • Exit 289A • 757-366-0100

Virginia Beach, VA

1281

RAMADA LIMITED

3108 Atlantic Ave
Virginia Beach, VA
757-425-7730
800-677-4500

Free Continental Breakfast
Kids Under 12 Stay & Eat Free
Outdoor Pool & Kiddie Pool
Meeting Facilities • Handicap Accessible
Internet Access Site • Seasonal Sundeck
Special Rates for Groups • Bus Parking
Walk to Restaurants & Attractions
Across Street From Boardwalk & Beach

I-64 to SR 44E to end, L on Atlantic Ave & 10 Blocks on L

VIRGINIA • I-64 • EXIT 284

RAMADA PLAZA RESORT OCEANFRONT

Oceanfront at 57th St.
Virginia Beach, VA
757-428-7025

Restaurant & Lounge on Premises
Outdoor & Indoor Pool • Exercise Room
Meeting/Banquet Facilities • Airport Shuttle
Handicap Accessible • Interior Corridors
Truck/Large Vehicle/Bus Parking
Beachfront

1279

I-64 to RT44E, Ends at 21St., L on Pacific Ave go to 57th St.

VIRGINIA • I-64 • EXIT 284

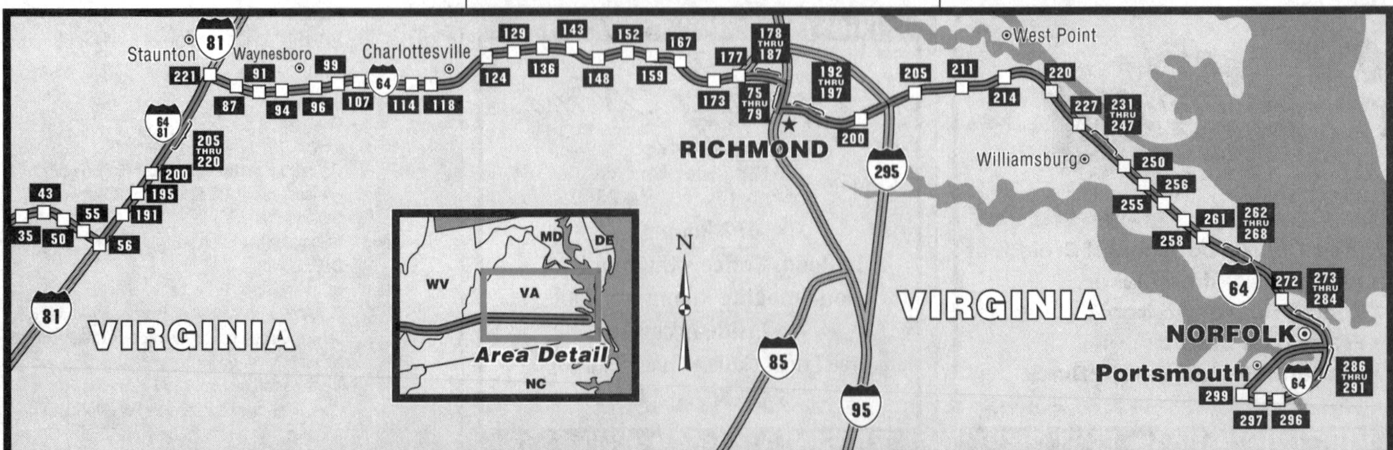

Bold red print shows RV & Bus parking available or nearby

EXIT INDIANA

Begin I-65

↓INDIANA

262 Junction I-90, Chicago, Ohio (Toll)
261 U.S. 6, 15th Ave, Gary
Gas W: 76 Station(*)
259AB Junction I-80, Junction I-94, Chicago, Ohio
258 U.S. 6 Bus., Ridge Rd.
Gas E: Mobil(*), Speedway(*, D, LP)
W: K & G(*, 24), Shell(*)
Food E: Diner's Choice Family Restaurant
AServ E: Widco Transmission
W: Jerry's Towing Service, Quality Brake & Muffler, USA Muffler Shop
ATM W: Shell
255 61st Ave, Merrillville, Hobart
FStop E: Speedway(*, LP)
Gas E: Amoco(*, LP, CW, 24), Mobil(*, CW), Phillips 66(*)
W: Coastal(*), Shell(*, CW, 24)
Food E: Blimpie's Subs (Mobil), Cracker Barrel, McDonald's
W: Burger King
Lodg E: Comfort Inn, Dollar Inn, Lee's Inn
AServ E: Shaver Chevrolet
W: Auto Zone Auto Parts
Med E: ✚ Hospital
ATM E: Amoco, Mobil
W: Wise Way Supermarket(RX)
Other W: Osco Drugs(*, RX), Wise Way Supermarket(RX)
253AB U.S. 30, Merrillville, Valparaiso
FStop W: Amoco(*, 24)
Gas E: Amoco(*, 24)
W: Gas City(*, LP), Shell(*, CW), Speedway(*, LP)
Food E: Angelo's Italian American Restaurant, Bakers Square Restaurant, Bob Evan's Restaurant, Boston Market Restaurant, Casa Gallardo Mexican, Dairy Queen, McDonald's(PLAY), Old Country Buffet, Olive Garden, Popeye's Chicken, Red Lobster
W: Arby's, Checkers Burgers, Colorado Steakhouse, Denny's, Hooters, New Moon Chinese, Rio Bravo, White Castle Restaurant
Lodg E: DAYS INN Days Inn, Economy Inns of America, Extended Stay America, Knight's Inn, La Quinta Inn, Motel 6, Super 8
W: Dollar Inn, Fairfield Inn, Hampton Inn, Holiday Inn Express, Radisson, Red Roof Inn, Residence Inn
AServ E: Amoco(24)
W: Amoco, Big K-Mart(RX)
Med W: ✚ Hospital, ✚ Prompt Medical Care
ATM W: Gas City, Gas City, Speedway
Other E: Southlake Mall
W: Big K-Mart(RX), Century Consumer Mall
247 U.S. 231, Crown Point, Hebron
Gas W: Mobil(*)
Med W: ✚ Hospital
Other E: Vietnam Veterans Memorial
(241) Weigh Station
240 IN 2, Lowell, Hebron
TStop E: Mobil(*, D, LP, SCALES)
FStop E: Shell(*)
W: Marathon(*)
Gas E: Citgo(*)
Food E: Blimpie's Subs (Mobil), Burger King (Shell)
W: USA Interstate Restaurant (Marathon)
Lodg E: Super 8
TServ E: Mobil(SCALES)
ATM E: Mobil, Shell
Other W: Indiana State Police Post
(231) Rest Area (RR, Phones)
230 IN 10, Roselawn, Demotte
Gas W: Amoco(*), Shell(*)
Food W: Renfrow's Hamburgers, Subway (Shell)
AServ W: Car Quest Auto Center
RVCamp W: Oak Lake Campground (1 Mile), Rose RV Sales & Service, Yogi Bear Camp Resort
ATM W: Amoco
Other W: Fagen Pharmacy(RX), Roselawn Star

EXIT INDIANA

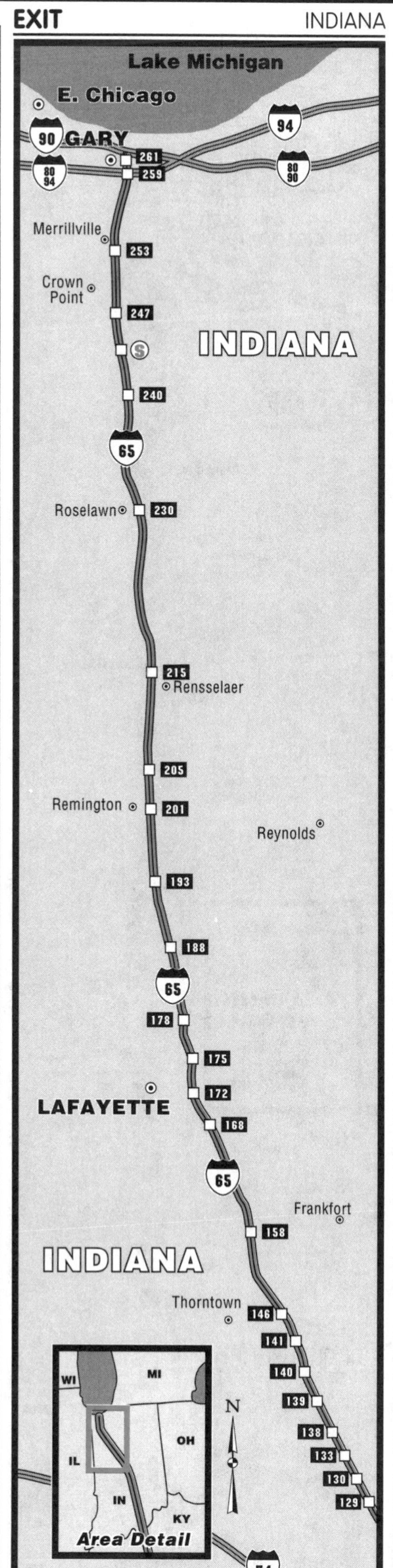

EXIT INDIANA

Supermarket
215 IN 114, Morocco, Rensselaer
TStop W: Tree Trail Truck Stop(*, SCALES, 24)
FStop E: Amoco(*, 24)
Food E: Dairy Queen, KFC, McDonald's, Scotty's Family Restaurant
W: Burger King, Tree Trail Restaurant
Lodg E: Holiday Inn Express, Interstate Motel
W: Mid-Continent Inn
TServ W: Cooper's Tire Service, Tree Trail Truck Stop(SCALES, 24)
ATM E: Amoco
W: Tree Trail Truck Stop
205 U.S. 231, Remington, Rensselaer
TStop E: Travellers Plaza(*)
Gas E: Marathon(*)
Food E: Traveller's Plaza
Lodg E: Knight's Inn
AServ E: Marathon
Med E: ✚ Hospital
ATM E: Travellers Plaza TS
201 U.S. 24, U.S. 231, Remington, Wolcott
TStop W: 76 Auto/Truck Plaza(*, D, SCALES, 24)
FStop W: Citgo(*), Speedway(*, D, SCALES, 24)
Food W: McDonald's, Subway (Speedway)
Lodg W: Holiday Inn
TServ W: 76 Auto/Truck Plaza(SCALES, 24)
ATM W: Citgo, Speedway
(195) Rest Area (RR, Phones, Picnic)
193 U.S. 231, Chalmers, Wolcott (Exit under construction)
Gas E: Shell(*)
Food E: Dairy Queen, Wayfara Restaurant (Shell)
188 IN. 18, Fowler, Brookston
178 IN 43, West Lafayette, Brookston
Gas E: Gas of America(*, LP), Phillips 66(*, D, LP), Shell(*)
Food E: Burger King (Shell), McDonald's(PLAY), Subway (Phillips 66), Taco Bell (Gas of America)
Lodg E: Holiday Inn, Super 8
ATM E: Gas of America, Phillips 66, Shell
Other E: Indiana State Police Post
175 IN 25, Lafayette, Delphi
Gas E: Citgo(*, LP)
RVCamp E: Camping
Other W: Creekside Animal Hospital
172 IN 26, Lafayette, Rossville
FStop W: Speedway(*, D, LP)
Gas E: Meijer
W: Amoco(*, CW, 24), Shell(*, 24)
Food E: Cracker Barrel, Steak 'n Shake, White Castle & Church's Chicken
W: Arby's, Bob Evan's Restaurant, Burger King, Chili's, Damon's Place for Ribs (Ramada), Denny's, Hour Time Great Food (Radisson), McDonald's(PLAY), Mountain Jack's, Olive Garden, SHONEY'S, Shoney's, Spageddie's Italian Kitchen
Lodg E: Budget Inns of America (see our ad this page), Comfort Suites Hotel, Holiday Inn Express, Lee's

Budget Inn Of America
139 Frontage Rd • Lafayette, IN
Complimentary Coffee & Pastry Daily
Fax & Copier Services • Direct Billing
Beverage & Ice Machines • Great Room Rates
Guest Laundry Facilities
Non-Smoking Rooms
Game & Video Room
Cable T.V. with ESPN & HBO
Pay Per View Movies
765-447-7566
1675
INDIANA ▪ I-65 ▪ EXIT 172

Bold red print shows RV & Bus parking available or nearby

EXIT INDIANA

Inn
W: Dollar Inn, Fairfield Inn, Homewood Suites, Knight's Inn, Radisson Inn, Ramada, Red Roof Inn, Signature Inn
Med W: Hospital
ATM E: Meijer
W: Lafayette Bank nad Trust
Other E: Meijer Food Court[*, D, LP, K, 24], Visitor Information
168 IN 38, Lafayette, Dayton
FStop E: Mobil[*, LP]
158 IN 28, Attica, Frankfort
FStop E: Amoco[*, 24]
Gas E: Marathon[*]
Food E: Amoco
TServ E: Amoco
RVCamp W: Camping
Med E: Hospital
ATM E: Amoco
(150) Rest Area (RR, Phones, Picnic; Southbound)
(148) Rest Area (RR, Phones, Picnic; Northbound)
146 IN 47, Thorntown, Sheridan
141 U.S. 52, Lafayette Ave. (Left Exit)
140 IN 32, Lebanon, Crawfordsville
FStop W: McClure[*]
Gas E: Amoco[*, CW]
W: Shell[*, CW]
Food E: Ice Cream Paradise, White Castle Restaurant
W: Arby's, Burger King, KFC, McDonald's, Ponderosa, Steak 'n Shake, Subway, Taco Bell
Lodg E: Comfort Inn
W: Dollar Inn, Lee's Inn, Super 8
AServ E: Amoco, Beason's Mufflers, Goodyear Tire & Auto, Hoffman's Auto Service, Mike's Body Shop and Garage, Petro's Tires
TServ W: Bob's Towing Recovery
TWash W: Interstate Speed Truck Wash
Med E: Hospital
ATM E: Amoco
W: Shell
Other E: Auto Zone Auto Parts, Sparkle Kleen Coin Laundry
139 IN 39, Lizton, Lebanon
Gas E: Gas of America[*, D, LP, K, CW]
Food E: Wendy's
W: Old Chicago Family Restaurant, Venues (Holiday Inn)
Lodg W: Holiday Inn
ATM E: Gas of America
138 Lebanon (Difficult Reaccess)
Gas E: Citgo[*, LP], Shell[*]
AServ E: Gene Lewis Ford
ATM E: Citgo, State Bank
Other E: Lebanon Bowling Center
133 IN 267, Brownsburg, Whitestown
130 IN 334, Zionsville, Whitestown
TStop W: T/A TravelCenters of America[*, SCALES]
FStop E: Crystal Flash[*, LP]
Gas E: Phillips 66[*]
Food E: Stuckey's (Phillips 66), Subway (Crystal Flash)
W: Country Pride Restaurant (T A Travel Center), Shelley's Eatery
TServ W: T A Travel Plaza
ATM E: Crystal Flash
129 Junction I-465 East, U.S. 52 East
124 71st St
Parks W: Eagle Creek State Park
123 Junction I-465 South, To Indianapolis Inter. Airport
121 Lafayette Road
Gas W: Amoco[*, CW], Meijer Food[D, LP, K, 24], Shell[*, CW]
Food W: Applebee's, Chaz's Steakhouse, Claude and Annies, India Palace, Sizzling Wok, Subway, TCBY
Lodg E: Lee's Inn
W: Dollar Inn
AServ W: Collins Mercury, Lincoln, Collins Mitsubishi, Collins Nisson, Collins Oldsmobile, Isuzu, Discount Tire Company, Don Sisk Pontiac, Hubler Acura, Indy Lube, Kennedy Jeep, Eagle, Chrysler, McKinny

EXIT INDIANA

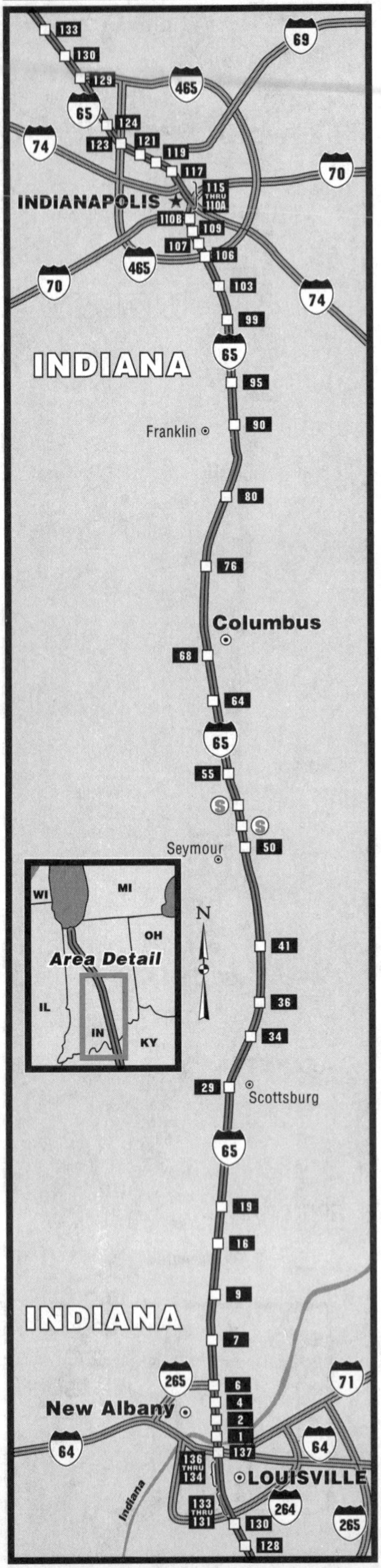

EXIT INDIANA

Transmission, PEP Boys, Saturn of Indianapolis, Speedway North Auto Parts & Pro. Auto Repair, Stitzer Buick, GMC Trucks, Tire Barn, Tom Wood Kia Center and Toyota
Med W: Hospital
ATM W: Amoco, Meijer Food
Other W: Eye World Optical Company, Georgetown Animal Hospital, Lenscrafters, Meijer Food, Mike's Express Coin Car Wash, NAPA Auto Parts
119 38th St. East, State Fairgrounds
117 Martin Luther King Jr. St. (Southbound)
ATM W: Bank One
116 29th St., 30th St. (Northbound)
115 21st St.
Gas E: Shell[*]
Med E: Hospital
114 Dr. Martin Luther King Jr. St., To West St.
Food W: Best Taste Chinese Buffet, Donato's Pizza, Hardee's, Papa John's Pizza, Subway, Taco Bell
Med W: Hospital
113 U.S. 31, IN 37, Meridian St.
Food E: Candlelight (Howard Johnson)
Lodg E: Howard Johnson
AServ E: Jiffy Lube (Midas), Midas, Payton Motors
Med E: Hospital
112A Junction I-70 East, Columbus, Ohio
111 Michigan St., Ohio St., Fletcher ave.
110A East St. (Difficult Reaccess)
Gas E: Citgo[*, D, K]
W: Speedway[*, K]
Food E: Burger King
110B Junction I-70 West, St. Louis
109 Raymond St
Gas W: Speedway[*, LP, K]
Food W: Griner's Sub Shop, His n Hers, Roselyn Drive-in Bakery
AServ W: Baggett Tire Service
Med E: Hospital
Other E: Tucker State Pharmacy[RX]
W: CVS Pharmacy[RX], Safeway Grocery
107 Keystone Ave.
Gas E: Speedway[*, K]
W: Amoco[*, CW, 24], Speedway[*, LP, K]
Food W: Burger King, McDonald's[PLAY], Subway, The Point After
Lodg E: Dollar Inn
W: Holiday Inn Express
AServ W: Amoco, Peters Auto Service, Q Lube
Med E: Hospital
ATM W: Amoco, Bank One, Cub Foods, NBD Bank, Speedway
Other W: Cub Foods[24, RX], South Keystone Animal Clinic
106 Junction I-465, Junction I-74
103 Southport Road
Gas E: Amoco[*, 24], Meijer[*, D, LP, K], Shell[*, CW, 24]
W: Big Foot[*, LP], Citgo[*], Speedway[*, D, LP]
Food E: Dog n Suds Drive-In, Krispy Kreme Doughnuts (Shell), McDonald's (Amoco), Noble Roman's, Schlotzsky's Deli
W: Bob Evan's Restaurant, Bobby Joe's Beef and Brew, Burger King, Cracker Barrel, KFC, McDonald's[PLAY], Steak 'n Shake, Taco Bell (Speedway), Waffle & Steak, Wendy's
Lodg W: Best Western, Comfort Inn and Suites, Courtyard, Dollar Inn, Fairfield Inn, Hampton Inn, Signature Inn, Super 8
AServ E: Q Lube
Med E: Hospital
ATM E: Amoco, First of America Bank (Meijer), NBD
W: Fifth Third Bank, Speedway
Other E: Meijer Grocery, Department Store[24], Mike's Car Wash
99 Greenwood
TStop E: Phillips 66[*, SCALES]
Gas W: Amoco[*, 24], Citgo[*], Shell[*, CW, 24], The Village Pantry[*, LP], Tobacco Road[*]
Food E: Chester Fried Chicken (Phillips 66)

Bold red print shows RV & Bus parking available or nearby

EXIT	INDIANA
	W: Arby's, Bob Evan's Restaurant, Hardee's(PLAY), Jonathan Byrd's Cafeteria, Mark Pai's China Gate, McDonald's(PLAY), SHONEY'S, Shoney's, Subway, TCBY, Taco Bell, Waffle & Steak, White Castle Restaurant
Lodg	**W:** Comfort Inn, Greenwood Inn, Lee's Inn
AServ	**E:** Searcy Body Shop
	W: Q Lube
TServ	**E:** Phillips 66
RVCamp	**W:** Stout's RV Sales & Service
Med	**W:** + Hospital
ATM	**E:** Phillips 66 Tstop
	W: Bank One, Citgo, Key Bank, Shell, The Village Pantry
Other	**W:** Low Cost Drug Store, Sam's Club, Vale Vista Animal Hospital
95	Whiteland
FStop	**E:** Marathon(*, LP, SCALES)
	W: Pilot(*, SCALES, 24), Speedway(*, LP)
Food	**E:** Kathy's Kitchen (Marathon)
	W: Arby's (Pilot), Country Kitchen (Speedway Tstop)
AServ	**E:** Bleake's Auto
TServ	**W:** Scott Truck Systems Inc.(24) (Trailer Repair, Wrecker Service)
ATM	**W:** Speedway Tstop
90	IN 44, Shelbyville, Franklin
Gas	**W:** Amoco(*), Shell(*)
Food	**W:** Burger King, Library Steakhouse (Days Inn), McDonald's(PLAY), Subway, Waffle & Steak
Lodg	**W:** Carlton Lodge, Days Inn, Howard Johnson, Quality Inn, Super 8
ATM	**W:** Amoco
80	IN 252, Flat Rock, Edinburgh
Gas	**W:** Shell(*)
76AB	U.S. 31, Taylorsville, Columbus
FStop	**E:** Shell(*)
Gas	**W:** Citgo(*, D), Thorntons(*, D)
Food	**E:** KFC, Waffle & Steak
	W: Arby's, Cracker Barrel, Hardee's(PLAY), McDonald's(PLAY), Snappy Tomato Pizza (Citgo), Subway (Citgo)
Lodg	**E:** Comfort Inn
	W: Best Western Horizon Inn, Hampton Inn, Holiday Inn Express
TServ	**W:** Kenworth of Columbus, Suburban Tire, White River Truck Repair
RVCamp	**W:** Driftwood RV Park
ATM	**E:** Irwin Union Bank
	W: Centra
Other	**W:** Prime Outlets at Edinburgh
(74)	Rest Area (RR, Phones, Picnic; Southbound)
(72)	Rest Area (RR, Phones, Picnic; Northbound)
68	IN 46, Columbus, Bloomington, Nashville
Gas	**E:** Amoco(*, D, 24), Big Foot(*), Shell(*), Speedway(*, LP)
	W: Marathon, Swifty(*)
Food	**E:** American Cafe (Ramada), Burger King, McDonald's
	W: Arby's, Bob Evan's Restaurant, Bobby G's (Days Inn), SHONEY'S, Shoney's, Taco Bell, Wendy's
Lodg	**E:** Holiday Inn, Ramada, Super 8
	W: Courtyard, Days Inn (see our ad this page), Dollar Inn, Knight's Inn
ATM	**W:** Centra
64	IN 58, Walesboro, Ogilville
Gas	**W:** Marathon(*, D, LP)
TServ	**E:** Cummins
RVCamp	**W:** Columbus Woods N Waters Campground (1.5 Miles)
55	IN 11, Jonesville, Seymour
Gas	**E:** Marathon(LP)
AServ	**E:** Marathon
(51)	Weigh Station
50AB	U.S. 50, Seymour, North Vernon, Brownstown

EXIT	INDIANA
Gas	**W:** Amoco(*, 24), Shell(*), Sunoco(*, LP)
Food	**W:** Arby's, Burger King(PLAY), Cracker Barrel, Long John Silver, Ponderosa, Ryan's Steakhouse, SHONEY'S, Shoney's
Lodg	**E:** Days Inn, Econolodge
	W: Holiday Inn, Knight's Inn, Lee's Inn
AServ	**W:** Wal-Mart(24, RX)
Med	**W:** + Hospital
ATM	**W:** Wal-Mart
Other	**W:** Wal-Mart(RX)
41	IN 250, Uniontown, Crothersville
FStop	**W:** Marathon(*, LP)
36	U.S. 31, Crothersville, Austin
Gas	**E:** Shell(*, LP, K)
	W: BP(*, LP, CW)
Food	**W:** Beef Boys
34AB	IN 256, Austin
FStop	**W:** Fuel Mart(*, D)
Gas	**E:** Big Foot(*, K)
Food	**E:** Dairy Bar
	W: A & W Drive-In, The Home Oven
ATM	**E:** Big Foot
Parks	**E:** Clifty Falls State Park
29	IN 56, Scottsburg, Salem
Gas	**E:** Amoco(*, D, CW, 24), Moto Mart(*, K, 24), Speedway(*, D, LP, K)
	W: Shell(*)
Food	**E:** Burger King(PLAY), Mariann Restaurant, Ponderosa, Taco Bell
	W: Arby's, Long John Silver, McDonald's(PLAY), Sweet Tooth, Waffle & Steak, Wendy's
Lodg	**E:** Mariann Motel
	W: Dollar Inn, Scottsburg Best Western
AServ	**E:** Grease Pit Oil Change & Lube
	W: Wal-Mart(24, RX) (Vision Center)
RVCamp	**E:** Ashmoor RV Campground (1.25 Miles)
ATM	**E:** Bank One
Other	**E:** Touchless Auto Car Wash

1468

Over 300 Units In Stock!
Award Winning Service
The Nation's Largest Indoor RV Showroom
520 Marriot Drive
Clarksville, IN
1-800-583-5685
1-812-282-7718
Exit 1 (Stansifer Ave.) 1 Mile North of Louisville
Indiana • I-65 • Exit 1

812-376-9951
Columbus, IN
DAYS INN
Toll Free Reservations:
800-329-7466
1270

• Free Continental Breakfast
• Newly Renovated Rooms
• Executive King Size Beds
• Cocktail Lounge
• Free HBO/ESPN/CNN • Game Room
• Located Near Little Nashville Opry
INDIANA • I-65 • EXIT 68

EXIT	INDIANA
	W: Wal-Mart(RX) (Vision Center)
(22)	Rest Area (RR, Phones)
19	IN 160, Henryville, Charlestown
Gas	**E:** Big Foot(*), Citgo(*), Shell(*)
Food	**E:** Dairy Queen, Schuler's, Stuckey's (Citgo)
16	Memphis Rd
TStop	**W:** Davis Brothers Travel Plaza(*, D, SCALES)
Food	**W:** Cleo's Buffet (Davis Bro. TS)
TWash	**W:** Bay Truck Wash
RVCamp	**E:** Customers First RV Inc.
	W: Customers First Inc.
9	IN 311, Sellersburg, New Albany
Gas	**E:** Five Star(*), Swifty(*)
	W: Dairy Mart(*, LP)
Food	**E:** Arby's, Dairy Queen
	W: Burger King(PLAY), McDonald's, Taco Bell
AServ	**E:** Car America
ATM	**E:** Bank One
	W: Dairy Mart
Other	**E:** Classic Car Wash, Coin Laundry(24), Disbro's Drugs
	W: State Police
7	IN 60, Salem, Cementville, Hamburg
TStop	**E:** Davis Brothers Travel Plaza(*, D, SCALES) (Ashland Gas)
FStop	**W:** BP(*, LP, CW, 24)
Food	**E:** Cleo's Country Kitchen (Davis Bro. TS)
	W: KFC
Lodg	**W:** Days Inn
ATM	**E:** Davis Bro. TS
Other	**W:** Care-Pets Animal Hospital
6B	I-265 West, to I-64, New Albany
6A	IN 265 East, Clark Maritime Ctr.
4	U.S. 31 North, IN 131 S, Clarksville, Cementville
TStop	**E:** Big Foot Auto/Truck(*, D, LP, K, SCALES) (Shell)
Gas	**E:** Thornton's(*, D, LP)
Food	**E:** Big Foot Auto/Truck (Shell), Subway (Thornton's)
	W: Applebee's, Arby's, Blimpie Subs & Salads, Bob Evan's Restaurant, Burger King, Captain D's Seafood, Damon's, Denny's, Don Pablo's Mexican, Fazoli's Italian Food, Hooters, Jerry's Restaurant, O'Charley's, Outback Steakhouse, Red Lobster, SHONEY'S, Shoney's, Steak 'n Shake, Texas Roadhouse, Wendy's
Lodg	**E:** Crest Motel
	W: Best Western, Colonial Inn, Dollar Inn, Hampton Inn
AServ	**W:** Carriage Ford, NTB, Sears Auto Center
TServ	**W:** Goodyear Tire & Auto, Mac
RVCamp	**W:** Premier Sales & Service
ATM	**E:** Big Foot Auto/Truck (Shell), Thornton's
	W: Bigg's Foods(24, RX)
Other	**W:** Bigg's Foods(RX), Greentree Mall, River Falls Car Wash, River Falls Mall, Target, Wal-Mart(LP, 24)
2	Eastern Blvd, Clarksville
Gas	**W:** Amoco(*, CW), Chevron(D), Dairy Mart(*, LP), Sav-A-Step(*), Shell(*)
Food	**W:** Restaurant Omelet Shop(24), Ryan's Steakhouse, The Hungry Pelican
Lodg	**E:** Days Inn, Motel 6, Super 8
	W: Econolodge, Knight's Inn, Rivers Edge Hotel, Star Motel
AServ	**W:** AAMCO Transmission, Chevron
TWash	**E:** McDuffy's
Med	**W:** + Immediate Care Center (7 Days/Wk, 9am to 9 pm)
ATM	**W:** NBD, PNC Bank
Other	**E:** U-Haul Center(LP)
	W: Drug Emporium, McClures Drugs, SVS Vision
1A	West New Albany (Northbound)
1	IN 62 E., Stansifer Ave., Clarksville, New Albany, U.S. 31 S (Stansifer Ave)
Gas	**E:** Thornton's(*)
Lodg	**W:** Holiday Inn
RVCamp	**W:** KOA Kampground(LP) (.25 Miles), Tom Stinnett RV (see our ad this page)

EXIT INDIANA/KENTUCKY

Med E: ✚ Clark Memorial Hospital
Other E: All American Car Wash, Daily's 24-Hr Foodmart[24], Farm Bureau Co-op[LP, K], WalGreens Pharmacy[RX] (1-Hr Photo)
0 IN 62 E, Jeffersonville (Difficult Reaccess)
Gas E: Chevron[CW], Thornton's[*, LP]
Food E: China Palace, Hardee's, McDonald's, Thornton's, Waffle Steak
Lodg W: Ramada Inn
AServ E: Bales Jeep Eagle Chrysler Plymouth Nissan Hyundai, Chevron, NAPA Auto Parts, Ross Bros. Automatic Transmission Service, Uniroyal Tire & Auto
Med E: ✚ Hospital
ATM E: NBD
Other W: Falls of the Ohio

↑INDIANA

↓KENTUCKY

137 Jct. I-71, I-64, Cincinnati, Lexington, St. Louis
136C Muhammed Ali Blvd.
Gas W: Chevron[*, D], Shell[*]
Food E: Long John Silver
Lodg W: Club Hotel by Doubletree, The Hyatt, The Inn at Jewish Hospital, TraveLodge
AServ E: Firestone
W: Midas
Med E: ✚ Jewish Hospital
W: ✚ Norton Hospital Emergency
Other E: Napa Auto
W: Visitor Information
136B Brook St. (Northbound)
Gas E: Chevron[*, D, 24], Shell[*]
Food E: Chung King Chinese American Restaurant
Lodg E: Days Inn, The Inn at Jewish Hospital by Marriot
Med E: ✚ Jewish Hospital
ATM E: Shell
136A Broadway, Chestnut St. (Northbound)
Gas E: Chevron[*, 24]
W: Thornton's[*, D]
Food E: Chopsticks, KFC, Pacific Rim Cafe, Subway, Taco Bell
W: McDonald's, Pesto's
Lodg W: Holiday Inn
AServ E: Broadway Chevrolet, Brown Brothers Cadillac, Classic Wash and Lube, Louisville Frame and Fender Auto Service, Monarch Lincoln Mercury
Med E: ✚ Kosair Children's Hospital, ✚ Louisville Medical Center, ✚ University Children's Health Center
ATM E: P & C Bank
Other E: Delight Car Wash Center
W: WalGreens Pharmacy[RX]
135 St. Catherine, Old Louisville (Spalding University)
Gas E: Amoco[*, CW], Shell[*, 24]
Food W: Dizzy Whiz Hamburgers, Ermin's French Bakery & Cafe
ATM E: Shell
Other W: Coin Operated Laundry, Quick Stop Market & Deli
134 KY 61 S, Arthur St (Southbound, Difficult Reaccess)
Gas W: Amoco[*, D]
Lodg W: Days Inn
Other W: Charles Heitzman Bakery
134AB 134A - KY 61N, Jackson St, 134B - Woodbine St (Northbound, Difficult Reaccess)
Other E: Fire Station, Jerry's Grocery
133AB Alt. US - 60, Eastern Parkway, Univ of Louisville
Gas W: BP[*, D, LP, CW]
Food E: Denny's, Papa John's Pizza, Subway
W: McDonald's
AServ E: Huber Tire
Other E: Sav-A-Step Food Mart
132 Crittenden Dr., Fair/Expo Ctr. Gates 2, 3, 4 (Southbound)
FStop W: BP[*, D, LP]
Food W: Burger King
TServ W: Hubbard Tire Service, Trail Mobile
ATM W: BP
Other W: Kentucky Kingdom Fair/Expo Ctr.
131AB 131A - I-264E, W Watterson Expwy Airpt; 131B - Fair Expo Ctr
130 KY 61, Preston Highway, Grade Lane
Gas E: BP[*, LP]
Food E: Bob Evan's Restaurant, Domino's Pizza, Pepper Shaker Chilli, Waffle House
Lodg E: Red Roof Inn, Super 8
AServ E: Big-O Tires, Instant Oil Change, Louisville Brake & Mufflers, Preston Auto Supply
Other E: U-Haul Center[LP]
128 KY 1631, Fern Valley Road
Gas E: BP[D, LP], Big Foot[*], Chevron[*, 24], Thornton's Food Mart[*, D, LP, K]
Food E: Arby's, Bojangles, Frisch's Big Boy, Hardee's, McDonald's, Outback Steakhouse, SHONEY'S, Shoney's, Substation II, Subway (Thornton's), Waffle House
Lodg E: Holiday Inn, Signature Inn, Thrifty Dutchman
AServ E: BP
ATM E: Thornton's Food Mart
127 KY 1065, Okolona, Fairdale
Food E: Texas Roadhouse
W: McDonald's[PLAY]
125AB Junction I-265, KY 841 - Gene Snyder Freeway
121 KY 1526, Brooks Road
TStop W: Pilot Travel Center[*, SCALES, 24]
Gas E: Chevron[*, K]
W: Amoco[*, 24], BP[*, D], Shell[*]
Food E: Arby's, Burger King, Cracker Barrel, Sassy's Subs & Such (Chevron)
W: Waffle House
Lodg E: Budgetel Inn, Fairfield Inn by Marriott
W: Comfort Inn, Hampton Inn, Holiday Inn Express
ATM E: Chevron
W: Pilot Travel Center, Shell
117 KY 44, Shepherdsville, Mount Washington
FStop W: Amoco[*, D, LP, 24], Chevron[*, 24]
Gas E: BP[*, LP], Shell[*]
W: Super America[*, D, LP]
Food E: Hardee's[PLAY], Pizza Hut (BP), The Kitchen Family Rest. (Days Inn)
W: Arby's, Bearno's Little Sicily Pizza, Burger King, Dairy Queen, Doughnut Express, Fazoli's Italian Food, Great Wall Chinese Restaurant, KFC, Little Szechuan Chinese Restaurant, Long John Silver, McDonald's[PLAY], Mr. Gatti's Pizza, Papa John's Pizza, Rio's Steakhouse, SHONEY'S, Shoney's, Subway, Taco Bell, Waffle House, Wendy's, White Castle Restaurant
Lodg E: Best Western, Days Inn
W: Motel 6, Super 8
AServ W: Hardy & Mooney Auto & Tractor Supplies, Price's Auto Parts & Machine Shop
RVCamp E: KOA Campgrounds (1.5 Miles)
ATM E: BP
W: Super America, Winn Dixie Supermarket
Parks E: Taylorsville Lake State Park
Other W: Kart Kountry (Go Karts, Mini Golf), Louisville Optical, Rite Aide Pharmacy (1 Hr Photo), Speed Queen Laundry (Coin Operated), Winn Dixie Supermarket
116 KY 480 to KY 61
FStop E: Shell[*, D, K]
Gas W: Barnyard[*, D, K], Citgo[*, K]
Other W: Leisure Life RV Sales and Service
(113) Rest Area (RR, HF, Phones, Picnic; Southbound)
112 KY 245, Clermont, Bardstown
Gas E: Shell[*]
ATM E: Shell
105 KY 61, Lebanon Junction, Boston
TStop W: Davis Brothers Travel Plaza[*, SCALES] (Shell Fuel, Travel Store)
Gas W: 105 Plaza[*]
ATM W: Davis Brothers Travel Plaza (Shell Fuel, Travel Store)
102 KY 313 to KY 434, Radcliff, Vine Grove
94 U.S. 62, KY 61, Elizabethtown
Gas E: Citgo[*, D, LP, K, CW], Shell[*, 24]
W: Chevron[*, D, 24], SuperAmerica[*, D, LP]
Food E: Denny's (Days Inn), KFC, Waffle House, White Castle Restaurant[24]
W: Atrium Gardens (Comfort Inn), Burger King[PLAY], Cracker Barrel, Ryan's Steakhouse, SHONEY'S, Shoney's, Texas Roadhouse, Uncle Bud's River Cafe, Wendy's
Lodg E: Days Inn[PLAY], Super 8
W: Comfort Inn, Hampton Inn, Holiday Inn, Motel 6, Ramada Limited
RVCamp E: KOA Campgrounds (1.25 Miles)
Med W: ✚ Hospital
ATM E: Citgo
W: SuperAmerica
93 Bardstown, Bluegrass Parkway, Lexington
RVCamp E: KOA Kampground
91 U.S. 31 West, KY 61, Western KY Pkwy, Elizabethtown, Paducah
TStop E: Big T Truck Stop[*, SCALES] (Citgo fuel)
Gas E: Chevron[*, 24], Shell[*, D]
W: Citgo[D]
Food E: High Tide Cafe (Commonwealth Lodge), Long John Silver, Omelet House
W: Jerry's Restaurant[24]
Lodg E: Bluegrass Inn, Budget Holiday Motel, Commonwealth Lodge, Heritage Inn
W: Best Western, Roadway Inn
AServ E: Big T Truck Stop (Citgo fuel), Chevron[24]
W: Citgo
ATM E: Shell
W: First Citizens Bank
Other E: Pittstop Car Wash[24]
(89) Weigh Station
86 KY 222, Glendale
TStop W: Country Style Plaza[*, SCALES, 24] (Texaco)
FStop E: Speedway[*, LP]
Lodg W: Glendale Economy Inn
AServ E: Glendale Automotive
RVCamp E: Glendale Campground (1 Mile)

Sponsored by Interstate America and Ramada Inn, Limited and Plaza Hotels of Kentucky
RAMADA
For information on how you can sponsor a child call 800-556-7918
KENTUCKY • I-65

EXIT	KENTUCKY
ATM	E: Speedway W: Country Style Plaza (Texaco)
(82)	Rest Area (RR, HF, Phones, Picnic; Southbound)
(81)	Rest Area (RR, HF, Phones, Picnic; Northbound)
81	KY 84, Sonora, Abe Lincoln Birthplace
TStop	E: Davis Brothers Travel Plaza(SCALES) (Ashland Gas)
FStop	E: Citgo(*, LP)
Gas	E: BP(*) W: Ashland(*, K), Shell(*, K)
AServ	W: Sonora Garage Inc.
RVCamp	E: Avery's Campground (4 Miles)
Other	W: US Post Office
76	KY 224, Upton
Gas	E: Chevron(*, D), Citgo(*), Sleepy Hollow Motel(*) (Ashland Gas)
Food	E: Citgo, Stuckey's (Citgo)
Lodg	E: Sleepy Hollow Motel (Ashland Gas)
71	KY 728, Bonnieville
65	U.S. 31 W, Munfordville
FStop	E: BP(*, D)
Gas	E: Citgo(D), Texaco(*) W: Chevron(*, D, 24), Shell(*)
Food	E: Dairy Queen, McDonald's(PLAY), Pizza Hut, Sheldon's Country Fixens (Texaco), Sonic, Subway (BP) W: Cave Country Restaurant
Lodg	E: Super 8
AServ	E: Citgo
ATM	E: BP
Other	E: Houchens Food Stores
58	KY 218 to KY 335, Horse Cave
FStop	W: Chevron Driver's Travel Mart(*)
Gas	W: BP(*), Marathon(*, D), Shell(*)
Food	W: Chevron Driver's Travel Mart, Pizza Hut (Chevron)
Lodg	W: Budget Host Inn, Hampton Inn
AServ	W: Marathon
RVCamp	W: KOA Kampground
ATM	W: Chevron Driver's Travel Mart
(55)	Rest Area (RR, HF, Phones, Picnic; Southbound)
53	KY 70, KY 90, Cave City, Glasgow

CAMPING WORLD®
Exit 28
134 Beech Bend Rd. • Bowling Green, KY
1-800-635-3196
1417

RAMADA INN®
4767 Scottsville Rd. • Bowling Green, KY
Restaurant/Lounge on Premises
Continental Breakfast • 25" TV w/HBO
Kids Under 12 Stay & Eat Free
Outdoor Pool • Exercise Room
Coffee Makers in Rooms • Coin Laundry
Pets Allowed • Handicap Accessible
Meeting/Banquet Facilities
Truck/Large Vehicle Parking
Interior Corridors
Special Tour Group Rates
Welcome Reception For All Tours
502-781-3000
1774
KENTUCKY • I-65 • EXIT 22

EXIT KENTUCKY

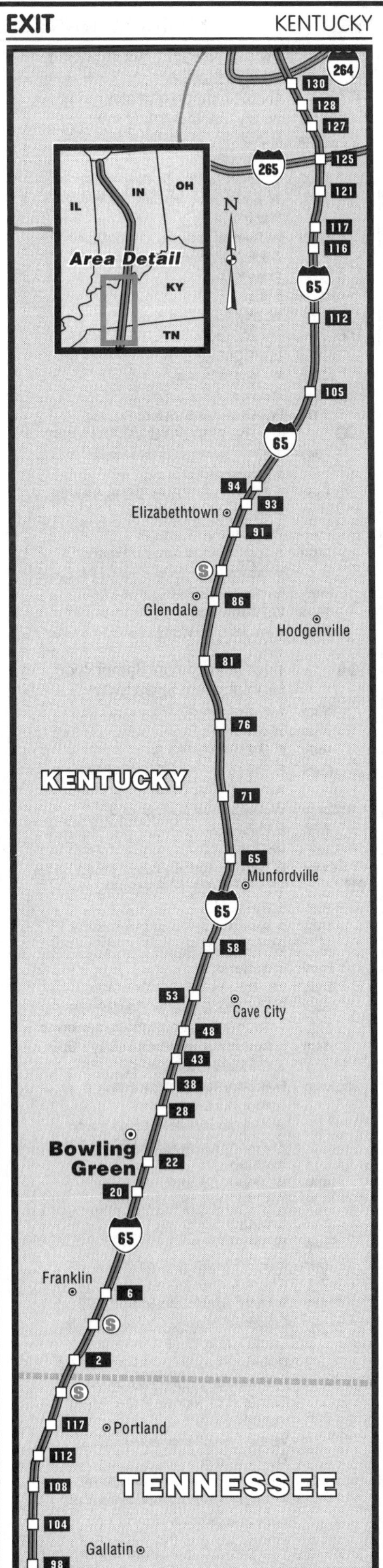

EXIT	KENTUCKY
Gas	E: Amoco(*, D), BP(*, CW), Chevron(*, D, 24), Jr. Food Stores(*), Shell(*, D), Super America(*) W: Shell(*, D, LP, K)
Food	E: Amoco, Baskin Robbins (BP), Burger King(PLAY) (BP), Caveman Pizza and Subs, Country Kitchen (Quality Inn), Hickory Villa Family Restaurant, Hillside Family Restaurant, Jerry's Restaurant, KFC, Long John Silver, McDonald's(PLAY), Pizza Hut, Rio's Roadhouse, Sassy's Subs (Amoco), Subway (Jr. Food Stores), Taco Bell, Wendy's W: Puerto Vallarta Mexican, Watermill Restaurant
Lodg	E: Comfort Inn, Days Inn, Executive Inn, Holiday Inn Express, Kentucky Inn (Best Western), Quality Inn, Super 8
AServ	E: Chevron(24) W: Shell
RVCamp	W: Mammoth Cave Jellystone Park(LP) (.75 Miles), Mammoth Cave National Park (10 Miles), Primitive Camping, Singing Hills Camping
Med	E: Hospital
Parks	E: Barren River Lake State Resort Park W: Mammoth Cave National Park
Other	W: Guntown Mountain Visitor Attraction, Mammoth Cave Wax Museum, Onyx Cave, Smith's Country Store, Ye Olde Fudge Shop
48	KY 255, Park City, Brownsville
FStop	E: Shell(*)
Gas	E: Citgo
Lodg	E: Parkland Motel
AServ	E: Citgo
TServ	E: Park City Service Center
RVCamp	W: Diamond Caverns Camping
Parks	W: Mammoth Cave National Park
43	Cumberland Parkway Toll Road, Glasgow, Somerset
Parks	W: Barren River Lake State Resort Park
(40)	Rest Area (RR, Phones, Picnic, Vending, Pet Walk)
38	KY 101, US 68, Scottsville, Smith Grove (Historic Victorian Site On West Side)
TStop	W: BP(SCALES)
Gas	W: Chevron(*, D, K, 24), Kentucky Souvenirs(*, D), Shell(*)
Food	W: Donita's Country Diner, McDonald's
Lodg	W: Bryce Motel
TServ	W: BP(SCALES)
Other	W: Cee Bee Food Store
36	U.S. 68, KY 80, Oakland (Northbound, Difficult Reaccess)
(30)	Rest Area (RR, Phones, Picnic; Southbound)
28	To U.S. 31 West, Bowling Green
Gas	W: BP(*), Shell(*, CW, 24)
Food	W: Blimpie's Subs (Shell), Hardee's(PLAY), Jerry's Restaurant, Shell, Wendy's
Lodg	W: Continental Inn (Best Western), Country Hearst Inn, Value Lodge
RVCamp	W: Camping World (see our ad this page)
ATM	W: Shell
Other	W: National Corvette Museum
22	U.S. 231, Scottsville, Bowling Green
Gas	E: Chevron(*, D), Citgo(*, LP), Shell(*, CW) W: BP(*, CW), Chevron(*, D, 24), Exxon(*), Racetrac(*), Texaco(*)
Food	E: Cracker Barrel, Cross Roads Grill (Ramada Inn), Denny's (Best Western), Domino's Pizza, Hardee's, Old Kentucky Home Country Hams, Ryan's Steakhouse, Tabatha's Country Inn, Waffle House W: Applebee's, Arby's, Bob Evan's Restaurant, Burger King(PLAY), China Buffet, Ci Ci's Pizza, Fazoli's Italian Food, G. D. Ritzy's, Garfield's, Hometown Buffet, Hops, Kroger(LP) (Deli), Krystal, Little Caesars Pizza, McDonald's(PLAY), Outback Steakhouse, Pizza Hut, Ponderosa, Puerta Vallarta, Red Lobster, Shoney's, Subway, The

EXIT KENTUCKY

1289

MAPCO Express

Open 24 Hours

31 Baskin Robbins Ice Cream & Yogurt

502-586-9544

Gasoline & High Speed Diesel Pumps
Full Service Restaurant
Truck Accessories • Private Showers
Laundry Facilities • ATM Machines
D.A.T. Load Boards • Sandwich Shop
Certified Scales • Copy & Fax Services

KENTUCKY ▪ I-65 ▪ EXIT 6

Blue Moose (Holiday Inn), Waffle House, Wendy's, White Castle Restaurant(24)

Lodg E: Best Western, Comfort Inn, DAYS INN Days Inn, Econolodge, Fairfield Inn, Microtel Inn, Quality Inn, **Ramada Inn (see our ad this page), Super 8**
W: Budgetel Inn, Drury Inn, **Greenwood Executive Inn**, Hampton Inn, **Holiday Inn**, Motel 6, **News Inn**, Scottish Inns

AServ E: Chevron
W: Chevron(24), Greenwood BMW, Ford, Lincoln, Mercury

RVCamp W: **KOA Kampground (1.5 Miles)**

ATM W: Exxon, First American Bank, **Kroger (Deli)**, National City Bank, Transfinancial Bank

Other W: CVS Drugstore(RX), Greenwood Car Wash, **Greenwood Mall, Houchens Food Store, K-Mart(RX), Kroger (Deli)**, Pets & More, **Tourist Info., Walmart Supercenter(LP, RX)**

20 William H. Natcher Toll Road, Bowling Green, Owensboro

6 KY 100, Scottsville, Franklin

TStop W: **)Mapco Express(SCALES)(see our ad this page)**

FStop E: **Bluegrass Auto/Truck Stop(*, SCALES) (Citgo fuel)**
W: **Speedway(*, LP, K, SCALES, 24)**

Gas E: BP(*, D)

Food E: **Original Ole South Diner (BP TS)**
W: **Baskin Robbins (Mapco), Loretta Lynn's Kitchen, Subway (Speedway), Wendy's (Mapco)**

Lodg W: DAYS INN **Days Inn**, Super 8

TServ W: **Bluegrass Tire & Truck Repair(24), Petro Lube**

RVCamp W: **KOA Kampground(LP)**

Med W: **+ Hospital**

ATM E: **Bluegrass Auto/Truck Stop (Citgo fuel)**

(4) **Weigh Station (Northbound)**

2 U.S. 31 West, Franklin

TStop E: **Flying J Travel Plaza(*, LP, SCALES) (CB Shop)**

FStop E: **Keystop(*) (Texaco)**
W: **BP(*, D)**

Gas E: **Conoco(*) (Flying J Travel Plaza)**

Food E: **Burger King (Keystop), Country Market (Flying J TS), Magic Dragon Chinese Eatery (Flying J TS), Pepperoni's the Superslice (Flying J TS)**
W: **Cracker Barrel, Huddle House**, Lotto Land Market & Grill, McDonald's, SHONEY'S, Shoney's, Waffle House

Lodg E: Hampton Inn
W: **Comfort Inn**, Franklin Executive Inn, Holiday Inn Express, **Ramada Limited**

ATM W: Lotto Land Market & Grill

(1) **KY Welcome Center (RR, Phones, Picnic, Vending, Pet Walk; Northbound)**

↑KENTUCKY

↓TENNESSEE

(121) **TN Welcome Center (RR, Phones,**

EXIT KENTUCKY/TENNESSEE

Picnic, Vending; Southbound)

(119) **Weigh Station**

117 TN 52, Orlinda, Portland

TStop W: **Jiffy Truck-Auto Plaza(*, SCALES)**

Gas E: Shell(*, D, K)
W: Amoco(*, D, K)

Food W: **Red River (Jiffy Truck-Auto Plaza)**

Lodg W: **Budget Host Inn (Jiffy Truck-Auto Plaza)**

TServ W: **Bumper to Bumper Truck Repair (Jiffy Truck-Auto Plaza), Jiffy Truck-Auto Plaza(SCALES)**

ATM E: Shell
W: **Jiffy Truck-Auto Plaza**

112 TN 25, Gallatin, Cross Plains, Springfield

FStop W: **Mapco Express(*, LP, K)**

Gas W: Exxon(*, K)

ATM W: Delta Express, **Mapco Express**

108 TN 76, Springfield, White House

Gas E: BP(*, LP), Nervous Charlies Market(*, D)
W: Amoco(*, D, K)

Food E: **Dairy Queen, Dinner Bell Restaurant, Hardee's**, McDonald's(PLAY)
W: Red Lantern (Days Inn)

Lodg E: Comfort Inn, Holiday Inn Express
W: DAYS INN **Days Inn (see our ad this page)**

AServ E: Baskin Body Shop, Xpress Lube

Med W: **+ Hospital**

Other E: Precision Car Wash, **United States Post Office**

104 TN 257, Ridgetop, Bethel Road, Highland Rim Speedway

TStop E: **Phillips 66(LP, SCALES)**

Gas W: Shell(*, D, 24)

Lodg E: **Motel (Phillips 66 TS)**

TServ E: **Phillips 66(SCALES), Ridgetop 24-Hr Service (Phillips 66 TS)**

RVCamp W: **Owl's Roost Campground(LP)**

ATM E: **Phillips 66**
W: Shell

Other E: **Ridgetop Laundry (Motel, Phillips 66 TS)**

98 U.S. 31 West, Millersville, Springfield

Gas E: Amoco(*, D), Raceway(*), Shell(*, D, LP, 24)
W: Amoco(*, D, K, 24)

Food E: Waffle House

Lodg W: **Economy Inn**, Graystone Motel

AServ E: 31W Truck Tire Center, Goodlettsville Collision & Car Care, Ken's Wrecker Service

TServ E: **David's Garage (Shell), Fatboy's Truck & Tire Repair Service(24)**

RVCamp E: **Holiday Rest Nashville Family Campground (2 Miles)**
W: **Greystone Motel & Campground, KOA Campgrounds, Nashville I-65 North (.5 Miles)**

ATM W: Amoco, Amoco

97 TN 174, Long Hollow Pike, Goodlettsville

FStop W: **Citgo(*, D, LP, K)**

Gas E: BP(*, CW), Exxon(*, D, CW), Mapco Express(*, D, LP, K)

Food E: Arby's, Blimpie Subs & Salads (BP), Captain D's Seafood, Chef Market Cafe, China Express, **Cracker Barrel**, Domino's Pizza, KFC, Little Caesars Pizza, McDonald's(PLAY), SHONEY'S, Shoney's (Shoney's Inn), Subway, Waffle House, Wendy's
W: Bob Evan's Restaurant, Hardee's, Krystal(24), Sonic

Lodg E: Comfort Inn(see our ad this page), Econolodge, Hampton Inn, Holiday Inn Express, Red Roof Inn, Shoney's Inn

EXIT TENNESSEE

W: Budgetel Inn, Motel 6

AServ W: Xpress Lube(CW)

Med E: **+ Goodlettsville Family Care Center (No Appt. Necessary), + St. Thomas' Health Services**

ATM E: Annie from Union Planters Bank, BP, **Kroger Supermarket(24, RX)**, Mapco Express
W: **Citgo**, Union Planters Bank

Other E: **K-Mart(LP, RX), Kroger Supermarket(RX), US Post Office**
W: Eckerd Drugs(*, RX), Sunshine Car Wash

96 Two Mile Parkway, Goodlettsville

Gas E: BP(*, D, CW), Shell(*, LP, CW), Texaco(*, D)
W: Amoco(*, 24), Phillips 66

Food E: Bailey's Sports Grille, Checkers Burgers, Chili's, Chuck E Cheese's Pizza, Cooker, El Chico Mexican Restaurant, Hooter's, Krystal(24), Las Palmas Mexican, Lee's Famous Recipe Chicken, Mrs. Winner's, McDonald's, Mr. Gatti's Pizza, O'Charley's, Pargo's, Pizza Hut, Ruby Tuesday, SHONEY'S, Shoney's, Subway, Uncle Bud's Catfish, Chicken, & Such, Waffle House, Wendy's

Lodg E: DAYS INN Days Inn, Rodeway Inn, Super 8

AServ E: Bob Williams Llincoln-Mercury, Crest Cadillac, Firestone Tire & Auto, Goodyear Tire & Auto, NTB, Trickett Honda, Trickett Oldsmobile, Universal Tire
W: Don Harris Auto Service Center (Phillips 66), Phillips 66

ATM E: First American, NationsBank, Old Hickory Credit Union, Tennessee Teachers Credit Union, Union Planters

Comfort Inn
925 Conference Drive
615-859-5400

AAA ◆◆

• Cable TV/Show Time
• Heated Indoor Pool
• Free Deluxe Continental Breakfast
• In-Room Whirlpool Suites with Refrigerator & Microwave
• Near All Major Attractions
• 10 minutes from Airport & Opreyland

Goodlettsville, TN 1122

TENNESSEE ▪ I-65 ▪ EXIT 97

1204

$32

DAYS INN

Free Deluxe Breakfast
Truck Parking
Cable TV with Remote Control
Free Local Calls
Outdoor Pool • Free Ice
Near Restaurant
615-672-3746 • White House, TN

TENNESSEE ▪ I-65 ▪ EXIT 108

Bold red print shows RV & Bus parking available or nearby

EXIT TENNESSEE

Bank, WalGreens Pharmacy(RX)

Other E: **Pearl Vision Center, Rivergate Mall, Target**, WalGreens Pharmacy(RX)

95 TN 386, Vietnam Veteran's Blvd., Hendersonville, Gallatin (Limited Access Hwy)

92 TN 45, Madison, Old Hickory Blvd, Old Hickory Dam

Med E: **✚ Hospital**

90A TN 155W, Briley Pky (Difficult Reaccess)

90B **(89)** U.S. 31 West, U.S. 41, TN 155, Dickerson Pike, Briley Pky, Opryland

Gas E: Citgo(*, LP)

Food E: Arby's, Burger King, Lee's Famous Recipe Chicken (Mrs. Winner's Chicken and Biscuits),

2306 Brick Church Pike
Nashville, TN
615-226-9560
Quality Inn
Newly Remodeled Rooms
Inn & Suites
Deluxe Continental Breakfast
Denny's on Premises
Kids Under 12 Stay Free
Truck/Large Vehicle Parking
Outdoor Pool • 25" TV w/FREE HBO
In Room Coffee • Small Pets Allowed
Handicap Accessible • Exterior Corridors
Sun-Thur $42
Fri-Sat $48
Expiration Date 11-99
1715
TENNESSEE • I-65 • EXIT 87B

Opryland

Super 8 North
3320 Dickerson Rd
Nashville, TN
615-226-1897
800-800-8000
Continental Breakfast
Outdoor Pool
Handicap Accessible
Truck/Large Vehicle Parking
Interior Corridors
1511
TENNESSEE • I-65 • EXIT 90

Senior Citizen Disc.
615-226-4600

1198
• Swimming Pool & Exercise Room
• Secured Indoor Corridors
• Special Rates for Tour Groups
• Guest Laundry • Free Parking
• Nintendo in Each Room
• Complimentary Breakfast Each Morning
TENNESSEE • I-65 • EXIT 87

EXIT TENNESSEE

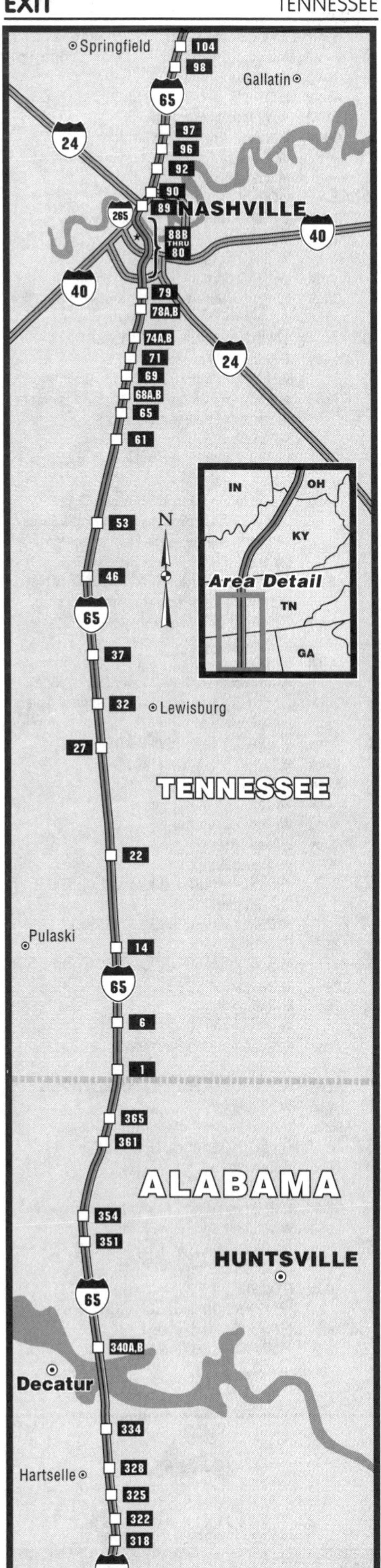

EXIT TENNESSEE

McDonald's(PLAY), Pizza Hut, Taco Bell, Waffle House, Wendy's

Lodg E: Days Inn, Econolodge, Super 8(see our ad this page)

AServ E: Advance Auto Parts

ATM E: Citgo

Other E: **H.G. Hill Foodstores, Speed Queen Laundry (Coin Laundry)**

88AB Junction I-24 West, Clarksville, Fort Campbell Army Post

87AB U.S. 431, Trinity Lane

TStop E: **Pilot Travel Center**(SCALES)

Gas E: Circle K(*, LP)

W: Amoco(*, D, K, CW), BP(*, D, CW), Exxon(*, D), Texaco(*, D)

Food E: **Arby's (Pilot)**, Candle Light Restaurant, Chuch's Chicken, Krystal(24), Sonic, TJ Restaurant, White Castle Restaurant

W: Burger King, Captain D's Seafood, Chugers Restaurant, Club Paradise, Denny's(24), Gabe's Lounge, Jack's BAR-B-QUE, Lockers Sports Grill, McDonald's, Ponderosa, SHONEY'S, Shoney's, Taco Bell, The Broken Spoke Cafe (Ramada Inn), Track 1 Cafe (Rain Tree Inn), Waffle House

Lodg E: **Cumberland Inn (Pilot TS)**, Key Motel, Red Carpet Inn, Savoy Motel, Scottish Inns, Trinity Inn

W: Comfort Inn, Days Inn, Econolodge, Hallmark Inn, Hampton Inn, **Holiday Inn(see our ad this page) Express**, Knight's Inn, Liberty Inn, Motel 6, Oxford Inn, Rain Tree Inn, Ramada see our ad this page), **Quality Inn & Suites (see our ad this page)**

AServ E: Bobby's Tire Service, Gary's, The Tire Store

W: Exxon

RVCamp E: **Holiday Mobile Village (.5 Miles), RV and Camper Corral Truck Accessories**

ATM W: BP

Parks E: **Trinity Park (Mobil Home Park)**

Other E: Coin Car Wash, National Car Wash, **Sweeney's Food Town Gocery Store, Trinity Gas Co. Inc**(LP), **US Post Office**

86 Junction I-265 Memphis

85B Jefferson St. (East Side Services Are The Same As In Exit 85A)

Gas W: Spur

Lodg W: Best Western, Days Inn

85A U.S. 31 E., N. Ellington Pkwy, Spring St.

FStop E: **Cone**(*), **Pacific Pride**

Gas E: Spur(*, D)

Lodg E: Best Western (Metro Inn), Days Inn

AServ E: Jefferson Street Car Care

W: NAPA Auto Parts, Nashville Tansmission Parts, Todd's Auto Parts

TServ E: **Pacific Pride**

Other W: Burnette's Truck Wash, **U-Haul Center**(LP)

85 James Robertson Parkway, State Capitol (Difficult Reaccess)

TStop W: **TravelCenters of America**(RV DUMP, SCALES)

Gas E: Mapco Express, Shell(*, CW)

1412 Brick Church Pike
Cable TV
Restaurant & Lounge with
Live Country Music
Room Service
Fitness Center
4 Meeting Rooms
Grand Ole Opry & Opyland Nearby
Golf Nearby
Free Parking on Premises
800-544-6385
Toll Free Reservations: 1-800-2-Ramada
1615
TENNESSEE • I-65 • EXIT 87B

Bold red print shows RV & Bus parking available or nearby

EXIT TENNESSEE

- W: Cone[*]
- **Food** W: Country Pride (TravelCenters), Gersthaus Restaurant, Mrs. C's, SHONEY'S Shoney's, Subway (TravelCenters)
- **Lodg** W: Best Host Motel, Econolodge, Ramada Limited
- **AServ** E: Amoco, Coin Car Wash
- W: Vogely & Todd Collision Repair Experts
- **TServ** W: TravelCenters of America
- **ATM** E: Mapco Express
- **Other** E: Main Street Auto Wash
- W: Country Hearth Bread, Bakery Thrift Store, Performing Arts Center, State Capitol, Tourist Info.

84 Arena, Shelby Ave
- **Gas** W: Exxon[*]
- **Food** W: Gersthaus
- **Lodg** W: Econolodge, Ramada Limited
- **AServ** W: Napa Auto, Standard Motor Parts
- **Other** E: Lynn Drugs, Martin's Grocery
- W: Prop Shop & More

83B I-40 West, South I-65, Memphis, Birmingham

83A I-24 East, I-40 East, Knoxville, Chattanooga

82B I-40 West, Memphis (Left Exit Northbound)

82A North I-65, East 1-40, Louisville, Knoxville

81 Wedgewood Ave
- **Gas** W: BP[*, CW], Citgo[*], Exxon[*]
- **Food** W: Burger King[PLAY], Mrs Winner's Chicken
- **AServ** E: Village Tire & Auto Service
- W: Hubcap Aanie
- **ATM** W: Citgo, Exxon
- **Parks** W: Reservoir Park

80 Junction I-440, Memphis, Knoxville

79 Armory Drive (Nashville School Of Law)
- **Other** E: 100 Oaks Mall, The Home Depot[LP]

78AB TN 255, Harding Place
- **Gas** E: Amoco[D], Mapco Express[*, LP], Texaco[*, LP], Texaco
- **Food** E: Bei Jing Chinese Restaurant, Cracker Barrel, Cuban Cuisine Restaurant, Darryl's, Mama Mia's Italian Restaurant, Santa Fe Cantina & Cattlemen's Club, Waffle House
- **Lodg** E: La Quinta Inn, Ramada Inn, Red Roof Inn
- **AServ** E: Amoco, Sidco Auto Parts, Texaco
- **Med** E: ✚ Hospital
- **ATM** E: Mapco Express
- **Parks** E: Grassmere Wildlife Park
- **Other** E: Brooks Pharmacy[RX]

74AB TN 254, Old Hickory Blvd, Brentwood
- **Gas** W: Shell[*, CW], Texaco[*, D]
- **Food** E: Captain D's Seafood, Holiday Inn, SHONEY'S Shoney's, Waffle House
- W: Corky's Ribs & BBQ, Mrs Winner's Chicken, O'Charley's, Pargo's Restaurant, Wendy's
- **Lodg** E: AmeriSuites(see our ad this page), Holiday Inn, Steeple Chase Inn, Wilson Inn & Suites
- W: Hampton Inn, Travelers Rest Inn
- **AServ** W: Valvoline Oil Change
- **Med** E: ✚ Hospital
- **ATM** W: Union Planters Bank

71 TN 253, Concord Road, Brentwood

69 TN 441, Moores Lane
- **Gas** E: Mapco Express[*, D, CW]
- W: Amoco[*, CW], Speedway[*, LP, CW]
- **Food** E: Baskin Robbins (Mapco Express), Blimpie Subs & Salads[*] (Mapco Express), Canyon Cafe, Copeland's of New Orleans, Cozumels, Joe's Crab Shack, Outback Steakhouse, Shogun, Sportsman Lodge, Tony Roma's Famous for Ribs
- W: Back Yard Burgers, Chili's, Honey Baked Ham, J. Alexander's Restaurant, Logan's Roadhouse Steaks & Ribs, McDonald's[PLAY],

EXIT TENNESSEE

- Peking Palace, Red Lobster, Rio Bravo, Romano's Macaroni Grill, Schlotzsky's Deli, TCBY, Taco Bell
- **Lodg** W: Sleep Inn
- **AServ** E: Lexus Dealer
- **ATM** W: Amoco, NationsBank
- **Other** E: Bruno's Grocery[RX], PetsMart
- W: Carmike Cinemas, Cool Springs Galleria Mall, Pier 1 Imports, Target

68AB Cool Springs Blvd
- **Food** W: Canton Buffet, Las Palmas Mexican
- **Lodg** W: Hampton Inn & Suites
- **AServ** W: Saturn of Cool Springs
- **ATM** W: AM South Bank, First Union Bank
- **Other** W: Kroger Supermarket[LP], Staple's The Office Superstore

65 TN 96, Franklin, Murfreesboro
- **Gas** E: Exxon[*, CW], Texaco[*, D, LP]
- W: BP[*, LP, CW], Mapco Express[*, LP], Shell[*, CW]
- **Food** E: Cracker Barrel, Log Cabin Restaurant (Texaco), Old New York Pizzeria, Sonic, Steak 'N Shake
- W: Hardee's, KFC, SHONEY'S Shoney's, Waffle House, Wendy's
- **Lodg** E: Bugetel Inn, Comfort Inn, Days Inn, Howard Johnson Express, Quality Inn & Suites
- W: Best Western (Franklin Inn), Holiday Inn Express
- **AServ** E: Cain Buick, Pontiac, GMC Trucks, Chevrolet, Oldsmobile Dealership, Reed's Auto Service
- **Med** E: ✚ Franklin Family Walk-In Clinic, ✚ Williamson Medical Center
- **ATM** E: Exxon
- W: AM South Bank, BP, Mapco Express, Shell
- **Other** E: Food Lion Supermarket, Pet Product Center, Pop's Car Wash

61 TN 248, Peytonsville Road
- **TStop** E: 76 Auto/Truck Plaza[*] (BP)
- **FStop** E: Speedway[*]
- **Gas** W: Cone[*, LP, K], Mapco Express[*, LP]
- **Lodg** W: Goose Creek Inn
- **AServ** E: Reed's Towing
- **ATM** W: Mapco Express

53 TN 396, Saturn Parkway, Columbia, Spring Hill

(49) Parking Area, Weigh Station (Northbound)

46 U.S. 412, TN 99, Columbia, Chapel Hill
- **TStop** W: Texaco
- **Gas** E: Chevron[*, LP]
- W: BP[*], Exxon[*]
- **Food** E: Bear Creek Family Restaurant
- W: Burger King (Exxon), Texaco
- **Lodg** W: EconoLodge, Holiday Inn Express, Relax Inn
- **Med** W: ✚ Hospital
- **Parks** E: Henry Horton State Park (12 Miles)

37 TN 50, Columbia, Lewisburg
- **Gas** W: Texaco[*, LP]
- **Med** E: ✚ Hospital
- **Other** E: TN Walking Horse Association Headquarters
- W: James K. Polk Home-Historic Site

32 TN 373, Columbia, Lewisburg, Mooresville Hwy
- **Gas** E: Exxon[*]

27 TN 129, Lynnville, Cornersville
- **RVCamp** E: Texas "T" Campground

(25) Parking Area (Southbound, Trucks Only)

EXIT TENNESSEE/ALABAMA

(24) Parking Area (Northbound, Trucks Only)

22 U.S. 31A, Lewisburg, Cornersville
- **TStop** E: The Tennessean[*]
- **FStop** W: BP[*], Mapco Express[*, LP, K]
- **Gas** W: Exxon[*]
- **Food** E: The Tennessean
- **Lodg** E: EconoLodge
- **AServ** W: BP
- **TServ** E: Truck Summit Tires
- **ATM** W: Mapco Express

14 U.S. 64, Pulaski, Fayetteville
- **FStop** E: BP[*], Texaco[*]
- **Food** E: Sarge's Shack, The Sands Restaurant (Super 8 Motel)
- **Lodg** E: Super 8
- **AServ** E: Texaco
- **RVCamp** E: KOA Kampground[LP] (.25 Miles, Mini Mart, Laundry)
- **Parks** W: David Crockett State Park (30 Miles)

6 TN 273, Elkton, Bryson Road
- **TStop** E: Shady Lawn Truck Stop[*, SCALES] (Phillips 66)
- **Food** E: Shady Lawn Truck Stop (Phillips 66)
- **Lodg** E: Economy Inn, AmeriSuites (see our ad this page)
- **TServ** E: Shady Lawn Truck Stop[SCALES] (Phillips 66)
- **ATM** E: Shady Lawn Truck Stop (Phillips 66)

(3) TN Welcome Center (RR, HF, Phones, Picnic, RV Dump; Northbound)

1 U.S. 31, TN 7, Pulaski, Lawrenceburg
- **Gas** E: Chevron[*], Exxon[*, D, LP]
- **ATM** E: Exxon

↑TENNESSEE

↓ALABAMA

365 AL 53, Ardmore
- **Gas** E: Texaco[*]
- **Lodg** E: Budget Inn

(364) Rest Area (RR, HF, Phones, Picnic, RV Dump; Southbound)

361 Elkmont
- **TStop** W: Charlie's TS[*] (Amoco)
- **FStop** W: Exxon[*, LP]
- **Food** W: Charlie's TS (Amoco)
- **AServ** W: Morris Garage[24]
- **TServ** W: Charlie's TS (Amoco), Morris Garage[24]

354 U.S. 31 South, Athens
- **Med** W: ✚ Hospital

351 U.S. 72, Athens, Huntsville
- **Gas** E: Exxon[*], Racetrac[*, 24], Shell[*]
- W: Chevron[*, CW, 24]
- **Food** E: Cracker Barrel, Heidelberg Cafe, McDonald's[PLAY], Subway (Shell), Waffle House, Wendy's
- W: Hardee's, Krystal, SHONEY'S Shoney's
- **Lodg** E: Best Western, Comfort Inn, Hampton Inn, Holiday

1579

DAYS INN

Free HBO • Free Coffee • Free Truck Parking
Pool • Ceiling Fans • Guest Laundry
Micro/Freeze • AARP, Corp.& Govt. Discounts

Athens I-65 Exit 351 205-233-7500	**Jasper** I-20/59 Exit 123 I-65 Exit 299 205-221-7800
Guntersville I-59 Exit 183 205-582-3200	**Tenton, GA** I-59 Exit 2 706-657-2550

Alabama/Georgia • 4 LOCATIONS

Bold red print shows RV & Bus parking available or nearby

EXIT ALABAMA

Special Rates for Tour Groups

Holiday Inn® HOTEL & SUITES

HOLIDOME INDOOR RECREATION CENTER

1186

Decatur, AL

Full Service Restaurant with Room Service
In Room Coffee Makers
Ample Free Parking • Guest Laundry
Indoor Outdoor Heated Pool
Holidome Game Room Area
Remote Control 25" Cable TV
Fitness Center in Hotel

256-355-3150 For Reservations: 800-553-3150

ALABAMA ▪ I-65 ▪ EXIT 340A

Comfort Inn

Huntsville, AL

256-533-3291
800-221-2222

- All Rooms Mini-Suites
- Free Continental Breakfast
- Outdoor Swimming Pool
- Meeting/Banquet Facilities
- Business Rate Program
- Truck Parking
- Cable TV with Free Showtime

AAA ◆◆◆

1524

ALABAMA ▪ I-65/I-565 ▪ EXIT 340AB

1535

70 Marco Drive
Priceville, AL 35603

256-355-2525
800-800-8000

- Free Deluxe Continental Breakfast
- Outdoor Pool
- Queen or Kings Beds Available
- Coin Laundry • Exterior Corridors
- In Room Refrigerator, Microwave & Dataport Phone • Handicap Accessible
- 25" Remote Color TV w/HBO

I-65 to HWY 67 East, Take First L Hotel on L

ALABAMA ▪ I-65 ▪ EXIT 334

1402

Open 24 Hours

Perkins Family Restaurant
We make it special for you

31 Baskin Robbins. Where Wonders Never Cease.

205-353-5252

Gasoline & High Speed Diesel Pumps
Full Service Restaurant
Truck Accessories • Private Showers
Laundry Facilities • ATM Machine
D.A.T. Load Boards • Sandwich Shop
Certified Scales • Copy & Fax Services

ALABAMA ▪ I-65 ▪ EXIT 334

EXIT ALABAMA

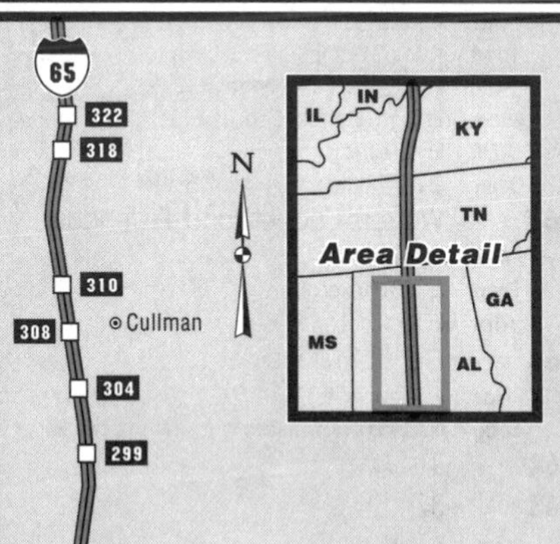

EXIT ALABAMA

	Inn Express
	W: Days Inn(see our ad this page), TraveLodge
ATM	E: Exxon
Other	E: Athens Limestone Veterinary Hospital
340AB	Junction I-565, AL 20, Decatur, Huntsville (Space & Rocket Center)
Gas	W: Racetrac[*, 24], Texaco[*, D, CW]
Lodg	E: Holiday Inn (see our ad this page),
	W: Comfort Inn (see our ad this page)
Other	W: Chip Shot Golf Range
334	AL 67, Priceville, Decatur, Somerville
TStop	W: Mapco Express[*](see our ad this page)
FStop	E: Racetrac[*]
Gas	E: Amoco[*, D]
	W: BP[*, D], Chevron[*, LP]
Food	W: Baskin Robbins (Mapco Express), Dairy Queen, Hardee's, Libby's Catfish & Diner Home Cooking, McDonald's[PLAY], Perkin's Family Restaurant (Mapco Express), Southern Bar-B-Q, Waffle House
Lodg	E: Days Inn, Super 8(see our ad this page)
RVCamp	W: Hood Tractor & RV Center
ATM	W: BP, Chevron
328	AL 36, Hartselle
Gas	W: Chevron[*, D], Shell[*]
Food	W: Homestyle Bar-B-Q, Huddle House
AServ	W: Chevron
Med	W: + Hospital
325	Thompson Road, Hartselle
322	Falkville, Eva
FStop	E: BP[*, LP]
ATM	E: BP
318	U.S. 31, Lacon, Vinemont
Gas	E: Texaco[*, D]
Food	E: Dairy Queen (Texaco), Stuckey's (Texaco)
Lodg	E: Lacon Motel

1655

Prattville, AL

334-365-6003
I-65 EXIT 310
Continental Breakfast
Outdoor Pool
Restaurant within 5 mi
Handicap Facilitieis
Cable TV

Cullman, AL

256-734-1240
800-228-5150
I-65 EXIT 179
Continental Breakfast
Outdoor Pool
Restaurant within 5 mi
Handicap Facilitieis
Cable TV

ALABAMA ▪ I-65

EXIT ALABAMA

310 AL 157, Cullman, Moulton
Gas E: Amoco[*, CW], Conoco[*, D], Shell[24]
W: BP[*, D], Exxon[*]
Food E: Burger King, Cracker Barrel, Denny's, McDonald's, Morrison's Cafeteria, Taco Bell, Waffle House
Lodg E: Best Western, Comfort Inn(see our ad this page), Hampton Inn
W: Super 8
AServ W: Exxon
RVCamp W: Cullman Campground (2.5 Miles)
Med E: Hospital
ATM W: BP

308 U.S. 278, Cullman, Double Springs, Ave Maria Grotto
Gas W: Chevron[*]
Food E: Omelet Shoppe (Days Inn)
W: Bryant's Seafood (Howard Johnson)
Lodg E: Days Inn
W: Howard Johnson

304 AL 69, Cullman, Good Hope
TStop E: Shell[*, SCALES]
Gas E: BP[*], Exxon[*, D], Texaco[*, D]
W: Citgo[*, D]
Food E: Hardee's, Jack's Restaurant (Shell), Maxine's (Ramada Inn), Miguel's Mexican, Waffle House
Lodg E: Holiday Inn Express, Ramada Inn
TServ E: Good Hope Truck & Wrecker Service, Truck Express Lube
RVCamp E: Good Hope Campground (.5 Miles)
Med E: Hospital

(302) Rest Area (RR, HF, Phones, Picnic, RV Dump; Southbound)

(302) Rest Area (RR, HF, Phones, Picnic, RV Dump; Northbound)

299 AL 69 South, Jasper, Dodge City
FStop W: Conoco[*]
Gas W: Amoco[*, D, K, 24], Pure[*, LP], Texaco[*, D]
Food W: Conoco, The Pizza Place
W: Days Inn(see our ad this page
TServ W: Conoco, Lee's Truck Service

292 AL 91, Hanceville, Arkadelphia
TStop W: Shell[*]
Food W: Shell
Lodg W: Shell
TWash W: Shell
RVCamp E: Country Park RV & Camping (1.4 Miles)

289 Empire, Blount Springs
Gas W: Texaco[*]
Food W: Dairy Queen (Texaco), Stuckey's (Texaco)
Parks W: Rickwood Caverns State Park (3 Miles)

287 U.S. 31 North, Garden City, Blount Springs
Gas E: Citgo[*]
Food E: Citgo

284 U.S. 31 South, AL 160 East, Hayden Corner, Rickwood Caverns State Park
Gas E: Conoco[*, LP], Phillips 66[D], Shell[*, CW]
ATM E: Community Bank, Shell

282 Warrior, Robbins
Gas E: BP[*], Chevron[*, LP]
W: Amoco[*, 24]
Food E: Hardee's, McDonald's[PLAY] (BP), Pizza Hut, Taco Bell
ATM E: BP, Chevron

281 Warrior

280 To U.S. 31, Warrior

275 To U.S. 31, Morris

272 Mount Olive Road
Gas W: Chevron[*, 24]
RVCamp E: Gardendale Kampground (.8 Miles)

271 Fieldstown Road

EXIT ALABAMA

Gas E: Racetrac[*]
Food E: Milo's Hamburgers, Subway
W: Cracker Barrel
AServ E: Serra Chevrolet Geo
ATM E: Racetrac
Other E: Delchamp's Supermarket, Wal-Mart[RX]

267 Walkers Chapel Road, Fultondale
Gas E: Texaco[*, CW]
Food E: TCBY (Texaco)
ATM E: Texaco

266 U.S. 31, Fultondale
Gas E: Chevron[*, 24]
Lodg E: Days Inn(see our ad this page), Super 8

264 41st Ave

263 32nd Ave
Gas E: Shell[*, CW]
W: Amoco[*, LP], Exxon[*, CW]

Quality Hotel
260 Goodwin Crest Dr.
Birmingham, AL
205-290-8000
800-841-7078
$39.95 +tax
1-4 People
Based on availability. Not valid with other discounts, holidays, or special events.
Restaurant/Lounge on Premises
Free American Breakfast
Free Parking • Cable TV
In Room Coffee Makers
Health Club/Swimming Pool
Laundry Facilities • Free Local Calls
Birmingham's New Choice
1772
I-65N Exit 254A turn L at Traffic Light on Osmoor Rd.
I-65S Exit 256A R on Osmoor Rd.After exiting onto Osmoor Rd., Next R onto Vulcan Rd. Go thru traffic light and continue on Bagby Drive. Turn R onto Goodwin Crest Dr. 1st driveway on L
ALABAMA • I-65 • EXIT 256A

1719
DAYS INN
Prattville, AL
(Exit 186)
334-365-3311
Continental Breakfast
Outdoor Pool
Restaurant/Lounge off Premises
Golf/Tennis Nearby
Truck Parking
Meeting Facilities
Fultondale, AL
(Exit 266)
205-849-0111
Restaurant/Lounge on Premises
Outdoor Pool/Jacuzzi
meeting/Banquet Facilities
Tennis/Golf nearby
Truck Parking
Cable TV w/HBO/ESPN
ALABAMA • I-65 • Exit 186/266

EXIT ALABAMA

Food E: Hardee's
Lodg E: Apex Motel
ATM W: Exxon

262B Finley Blvd
FStop E: Phillips 66[*], South Star Fuel Center[*, SCALES] (Texaco)
W: Mapco Express[*]
Gas E: Amoco[*, 24]
W: Chevron[*, 24]
Food W: Captain D's Seafood, McDonald's
ATM W: Chevron, Mapco Express

262A 16th Street
Other E: Hand Car Wash

261AB Junction I-20, Junction I-59, Tuscaloosa, Gadsden, Atlanta

260 U.S. 11, 3rd Ave. N.
Gas E: Amoco[*, CW], Shell[*], Texaco[*]
W: Chevron[*, CW]
Food E: Hardee's, Mrs. Winner's (Texaco), Sneaky Peeks (Texaco)
Lodg E: Villager Lodge
W: Adams Inn
AServ E: Alignment by Ingram, Nissan Dealership
W: Lou's Automotive Service, Possel Tire & Auto
ATM E: Shell, Texaco

259B 4th Ave South (Southbound, Difficult Reaccess)
Food W: Ted's Cafeteria

259A 6th Street South (Southbound)

259 University Blvd. (Northbound)
Gas W: Chevron[*, CW, 24]
Food E: Waffle House (Best Western)
Lodg E: Best Western
AServ W: Mazda Dealer

258 Green Springs Ave

256AB Oxmoor Road, Homewood
Gas E: Exxon[*, D], Shell[*, CW]
W: BP[*], Chevron[*, 24]
Food E: Blimpie Subs & Salads (Shell), Burger King, El Polecio, Los Compadres, Lovoy's Italian American, Paw Paw Patch
W: Bennigan's, Fifth Quarter Steak & Seafood, Hardee's, Jim 'N Mix, Jitterbugs (Holiday Inn), SHONEY'S, Shoney's (Shoney's Inn)
Lodg E: Howard Johnson
W: Comfort Inn, Fairfield Inn, Holiday Inn, Microtel, Red Roof Inn, Shoney's Inn, Super 8, Quality Inn (see our ad this page)
AServ E: Goodyear
TServ W: Southland International Truck
ATM E: Compass Bank, Shell
Other E: Food World, K-Mart[RX], Rentals Judge

255 Lakeshore Dr.
Gas E: BP[*, CW]
Food W: Boston Market Restaurant, Chick-Fil-A, Chili's, IHOP, Landry's Seafood, Lone Star Steakhouse, Mr. Wang's Restaurant, O'Charley's, Taco Bell, Tony Roma, Wendy's
Lodg W: Best Suites
Med E: Hospital
ATM E: BP
W: Compass Bank, Regions Bank
Other W: Bruno's Supermarket, Sam's, Wal-Mart SuperCenter

254 Alford Ave

252 U.S. 31 Montgomery Highway
Gas E: BP[*, CW], Chevron[*, CW, 24], Shell[*, CW]
W: Amoco[*, LP]
Food E: Arby's, Captain D's Seafood, Comfort Inn, Johnny Ray's Restaurant, Milo's Hamburgers, Pizza Hut, Ranch House BBQ, Solazteca Mexicna Restaurant (Vestavia Motor Lodge),

Bold red print shows RV & Bus parking available or nearby

EXIT	ALABAMA
	Waffle House
	W: Burger King, El Palacio Mexican, Kenny Roger's Roasters, Manderin Chinese, McDonald's(PLAY), Sarris Seafood & Steaks, Simmering Pot (Holiday Inn), Waffle House (Days Inn)
Lodg	**E:** Comfort Inn(see our ad this page), Hampton Inn, Vestavia Motor Lodge
	W: Days Inn, Holiday Inn
AServ	**E:** Express Lube, NAPA Auto Parts, Royal Saturn, Shell, Vulcan Ford/Lincoln/Mercury
	W: Express Lube, Mr. Transmission
Med	**E:** ✚ **Hospital**
ATM	**W:** Amoco, Compass Bank
Other	**E:** Circle K Food Store, **Vestavia Animal Clinic**
	W: Coin Car Wash
250	to U.S. 280, Junction I-459, Atlanta, Gadsden, Tuscaloosa
247	Valleydale Road , County Hwy17, Helena Hoover
Gas	**E:** BP(*, CW)
	W: Shell(*, LP)
Food	**E: Big Mo's Pizza, Granny's Country Kitchen,** Hardee's, Tin Roof BBQ
Lodg	**W:** La Quinta Inn
AServ	**E:** Goodyear Tire & Auto
	W: Shell
ATM	**E: Food World Supermarket (South Trust Bank), SouthTrust Bank (Food World)**
	W: First National Bank
Other	**E:** CVS(RX), **Emergency Pet Care, Food World Supermarket (South Trust Bank),** Lowe's
246	AL 119, Cahaba Valley Road (Oak Mountain State Park)
FStop	**W: Amoco**(*), **Speedway**(*, LP)
Gas	**W:** BP(*, LP, CW, 24), Shell(*, LP, CW)
Food	**W:** Applebee's, Arby's, Captain D's Seafood, Chick Fil A, Cock of the Walk Restaurant, **Cracker Barrel,** Dairy Queen, **McDonald's**(PLAY), O' Charley's, Peaches n Cream, Pizza Hut, SHONEY'S, Shoney's, Taco Bell, Waffle House, Wendy's
Lodg	**W:** Best Western, Comfort Inn, Holiday Inn Express, Ramada Limited, Sleep Inn, **TraveLodge**
AServ	**W:** Driver's Mart, Express Lube
ATM	**W: Speedway**
Parks	**W: Oak Mountain State Park**
242	Pelham, Helena (Hospital, Camp)
FStop	**E: Chevron**(*, D, 24), **Exxon**(*, LP)
AServ	**W:** Sunbelt Rental(LP)
TServ	**W: Diesel Tractor Trailer Sales Inc**
RVCamp	**W: Birmingham South KOA**
238	U.S. 31 Alabaster ,Saganoff (Hospital)
Gas	**E:** BP(*, D, LP)
	W: Chevron(*, D), Shell(*, LP), Texaco(*, CW)
Food	**E:** Chester Fried Chicken (BP), Icecream Churn (BP)
	W: Snow Hut, Waffle House
Med	**W:** ✚ **Hospital**
ATM	**W:** Texaco
234	Shelby County Airport (University of Montevallo)
Gas	**W:** Chevron(*, LP, 24)
Food	**W:** Blimpie Subs & Salads (Chevron)
ATM	**W:** Chevron, Chevron
231	U.S. 31, Calera, Montevallo
Food	**W:** Kathleen's Restaurant
RVCamp	**E: Burton Camper Sales, Parts & Service**
Other	**E:** Rolling Hills Conference Center
228	AL. 25, Calera (Briar Field State Park)
FStop	**E: Citgo**(*, D), **Texaco**(*, LP, CW)
Food	**E:** Hog Heaven BBQ
Lodg	**E: Best Western, Days Inn**
ATM	**E: Texaco**
219	Jemison, Thorsby (Peach Queen Campground, Park and Ride)
TStop	**E: Porter's Truckstop**(*)
FStop	**E: Headco Food Mart**(*) **(Ice cream and yogurt)**
Gas	**E:** Chevron(*, 24)
	W: Shell(*, LP) (Ice cream churn)
Food	**E:** Porter's Family Restaurant
	W: Icecream Churn (Shell), **Smokey Hollow Restaurant**
TServ	**E: Porter's Truck & Road Service**
RVCamp	**E: Peach Queen Campground (.5 Miles)**
ATM	**E:** Chevron, Chevron
(214)	**Rest Area (RR, Phones, Picnic, RV Dump; Southbound)**
(214)	**Rest Area (RR, Phones, Picnic, RV Dump; Northbound)**
212	AL. 145, Clanton, Lay Dam, Wilsonville, 4-H Center
FStop	**W: Headco Food Mart**(*)
Gas	**E:** Chevron(*)
	W: BP(*, 24)
Food	**W: Icecream & Yogurt Shop (Headco Food Mart),** Peach Tower Restaurant
TServ	**W: I-65 Tire and Sevice**
Med	**W:** ✚ **Hospital**
Other	**E:** Jean's Marina
	W: Headley's Fruits and Vegetables
208	Clanton, Lake Mitchell
FStop	**W: Exxon**(*)
Food	**W:** Heaton Pecan Farm, SHONEY'S, **Shoney's**
Lodg	**W:** SHONEY'S, **Shoney's**
ATM	**W:** Exxon
205	U.S. 31, AL 22, Clanton, Verbena

Comfort Inn

BIRMINGHAM

1485 Montgomery Hwy

FREE Deluxe Continental Breakfast

159 Spacious Interior Corridor Rooms

25" Remote Control TV's

Meeting/Banquet Facilities (up to 250)

Fax & Copy Service Available

Outdoor Pool/Wading Pool for Kids

FREE Local Calls & Newspaper

Convenient to: Galleria Mall, Golf Courses, Hoover Metropolitan Stadium, Jefferson Civic Center, Downtown and much more.

100% SATISFACTION GAURANTEE

205-823-4300

1157

ALABAMA • I-65 • EXIT 252

EXIT	ALABAMA
	(Confederate Memorial Park)
FStop	**E: Shell**(*, LP)
	W: BP(*, D)
Gas	**E:** Amoco(*)
	W: Chevron(*, 24)
Food	**E:** Ice Cream Churn, McDonald's(PLAY), Teach Park Gray and Sons Farm, Tink's Restaurant, Waffle House
	W: Burger King(PLAY), Captain D's Seafood, Durbin's Farm and Market, **Hardee's,** Heaton Pecan Farm, KFC, Subway, Taco Bell
Lodg	**E:** Best Western, **Holiday Inn,** Scottish Inns
	W: Key West Inn
AServ	**W:** Southside Auto Repair
ATM	**E:** Amoco
Other	**E:** Shadows Antiques
	W: Suburban Gas Inc(LP)
200	Verbena, Billingsley
FStop	**E: BP**(*, LP)
Gas	**W:** Texaco(*) (Stuckey's, Dairy Queen)
Food	**W:** Dairy Queen (Texaco), Stuckey's (Texaco)
RVCamp	**W: Holly Hill Plantation Travel Park**
186	U.S. 31, Pine Level, Prattville (Hospital)
Gas	**W:** BP(*, D, LP), Chevron(*), Conoco(*, D)
Food	**W: Days Inn,** Icecream Churn (BP)
Lodg	**W: Days Inn(see our ad opposite page)**
Parks	**E: Confederate Memorial Park**
Other	**W:** SHilton county Fruit Basket and Nursery
181	AL. 14, Prattville, Wetumpka
FStop	**E: Chevron**(*, D, 24)
Gas	**W:** Conoco(*, D, LP)
Food	**W: Cracker Barrel**
Lodg	**W:** Best Western, Comfort Inn
Med	**W:** ✚ **Hospital**
179	Millbrook, Prattville
FStop	**W: Amoco**(*, D)
Gas	**W:** BP(*, D, CW), Citgo(*), Exxon(*, LP), Shell(*, CW, 24)
Food	**E:** Fantail, Igor's
	W: Hardee's, McDonald's(PLAY), SHONEY'S, Shoney's, Waffle House
Lodg	**W:** Comfort Inn (see our ad on page 277), Econolodge, Hampton Inn, Holiday Inn
AServ	**E:** Buckey's Transmission and Performance
RVCamp	**E: K & K Park & Campground**(*, LP) **(W/RV Sales & Service), K & K RV Park**
Other	**E:** Bennet's Antiques, Ludder's Antiques, Sara's Antique Mall, Sister's Antique Emporium
176	AL. 143, Millbrook (Northbound, No Reaccess)
173	North Blvd., To U.S. 231 (Difficult Reaccess, Montgomery Zoo, only goes to the east side)
172	Downtown, Clay St.. (Maxwell Air Force Base)
Gas	**E:** Amoco(K), Petro Plus(*)
Other	**E:** Visitor Information
171	**(170)** Junction I-85 North, Atlanta
170A	Fairview Ave (Huntington College)
Gas	**E:** Spur(*)
	W: Exxon(*, CW)
Food	**E:** Joe's, McDonald's(PLAY)
	W: Ellis's Seafood, **Hardee's**
AServ	**E:** Auto Zone Auto Parts, B.F. Goodrich, Coleman's Auto Service
RVCamp	**W: Cummins Alabama Inc. (.8 Miles)**
Other	**E:** A & S Hand Car wash, Bargain Town, **CVS Drugstore,** EZ Dash Laundromat, The Wash House (Laundromat)
	W: Calhoun Foods Grocery
169	Edgemont Ave (Southbound, Reaccess Northbound Only)
Gas	**E:** Amoco(*, CW)
168	U.S. 80 E., U.S. 82, to U.S. 31, to U.S. 331, South Blvd (Hospital)
TStop	**E: 76 Auto/Truck Plaza**(*), **T/A TravelCenters of America**(*, LP)
FStop	**W: Speedway**(*, D)

Bold red print shows RV & Bus parking available or nearby

EXIT ALABAMA

Gas E: BP(*, CW), Entec(*, D)
W: Amoco(*, CW), Chevron(*, 24), Shell(*, D)
Food E: 76 Auto/Truck Plaza, Arby's, Burger King(PLAY), Captain D's Seafood, McDonald's(PLAY), Pizza Hut, SHONEY'S, Shoney's, Taco Bell, Waffle House, Willy's Dinnette (Knight's Inn)
W: Hardee's, Holiday Inn, Omellete House, Quincy's Family Steakhouse, Subway (Shell), Waffle House, Wendy's
Lodg E: Best Western, Knight's Inn, Travel Inn Motel, Diplomat Inn (see our ad this page)
W: Comfort Inn, DAYS INN Days Inn, Econotel, Holiday Inn, Inn South, Peddler's Inn (The Watering Trough)
Med E: ✚ Hospital
W: Amoco
Other E: Greyhound Trails

167 U.S. 80 West, Selma (Difficult Reaccess, Airport)

164 U.S. 31, Pintlala, Hope Hull (KOA Campground)
FStop E: **Safeway Truck Plaza**(*, SCALES)
Gas E: Amoco(*), Texaco(*)
W: BP(*), Chevron(*, 24)
Food E: Huddle House (Rodeway Inn)
W: Burger King (BP), Krispy Kreme Doughnuts (BP)
Lodg E: **Rodeway Inn**
RVCamp E: **KOA-Montgomery (.25 Miles)**
ATM E: Amoco
W: BP, REgion Bank (BP)

158 To U.S. 31, Pintlala, Tyson, Hayneville
Gas E: Texaco(*)
Food E: Dairy Queen (Texaco), Stuckey's (Texaco)

151 AL. 97, Davenport, Letohatchee, Lowndesboro, Hayneville
FStop W: **Amoco**(*, D)
Gas W: BP(*)
Other E: Country Squire Flea Market

142 AL.185, Fort Deposit, Logan
Gas E: BP(*, D, LP)
W: Chevron(*)
Food E: Fort Restaurant, **Priester's Pecans**

(134) **Rest Area (RR, HF, Phones, Picnic, RV Dump; Westbound)**

(134) **Rest Area (RR, HF, Phones, Picnic, RV Dump; Eastbound)**

130 AL. 10 Truck Route E., AL. 185, Greenville
Gas E: BP(*, LP), Chevron(*, CW), Phillips 66(*, D), Shell(*)
W: Exxon(*), Phillips 66(*)
Food E: Arby's, Captain D's Seafood, Golden Corral Family Steakhouse, Hardee's, KFC, McDonald's(PLAY), Pizza Hut, The Nineteenth Green Restaurant (Holiday Inn), Waffle House, Wendy's
W: Bates House of Turkey, Burger King, **Cracker Barrel**, Giuseppi's Restaurant & Lounge, SHONEY'S, Shoney's, Subway (Phillips 66), Taco Bell
Lodg E: **Econolodge**, Holiday Inn, **Thrifty Inn**
W: Best Western, Hampton Inn, Jameson Inn

EXIT ALABAMA

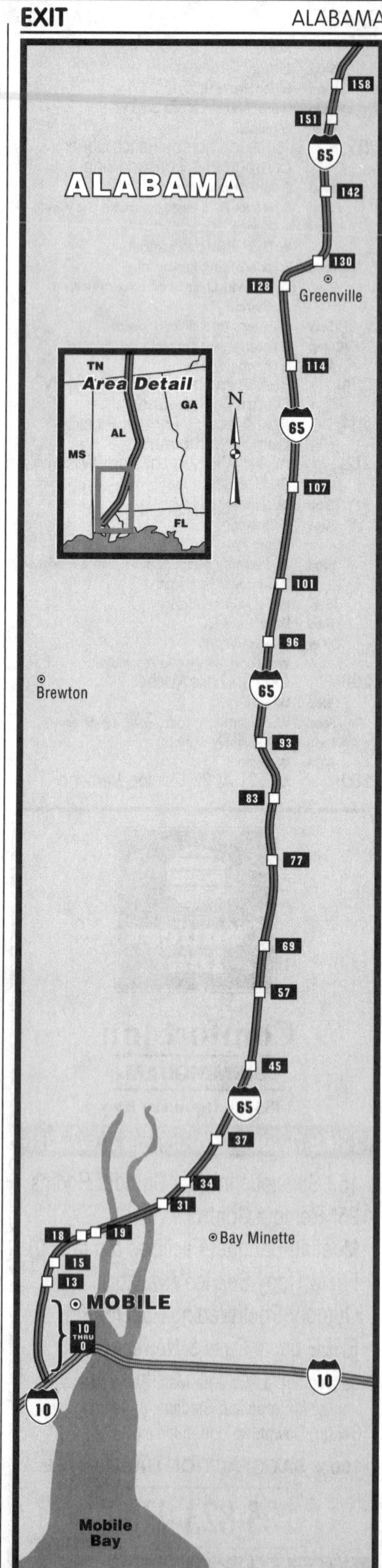

EXIT ALABAMA

ATM E: Colonial Bank, First National Bank of Greenville, The People's Bank and Trust Company
W: Camellia City Bank
Other E: Auto Pride Car Wash, CVS(RX), Fred's Dollar Store, Gladys Scay Gallery, High Cotton Antiques and Gifts, Rite Aid Pharmacy, Speed Queen Coin Laundry
W: **Wal-Mart**(RX) **(Tire and lube service)**, **Winn Dixie Supermarket**(24, RX)

128 AL. 10 Truck Route W, Greenville, Pine Apple (Hospital)
Gas E: Exxon(*), Shell(*)
W: Amoco(*)
Food E: Shell, **Smokehouse Country Kitchen (Shell)**
Med E: ✚ **Hospital**

114 AL.106, Georgiana, Starlington
Gas W: **Amoco**(*), Chevron(*)
Food W: **Amoco FS**
Med E: ✚ **Hospital**
Other E: **Hank Williams Museum**

107 Grace, Garland

101 Awassa
FStop E: **BP**(*, D)
W: **Exxon**(*, D)

96 AL 83, Evergreen, Midway (Reid State Technical College)
Gas E: Chevron(*, CW, 24), Shell(*)
W: BP(*, CW)
Food E: **Burger King**(PLAY), Hardee's, KFC, **McDonald's**, Taco Bell
W: Pizza Hut
Lodg W: DAYS INN **Days Inn**, **The Evergreen Inn**
ATM W: BP

93 U.S. 84, Evergreen, Monroeville, Brewton (Overnight Camping, Pine Crest Park (3/10 mi))
Gas E: Exxon(*)
W: BP(*, D) (Towing Service)
RVCamp E: **Pinecrest Park Camping (.2 Miles)**

(89) **Rest Area (RR, HF, Phones, Picnic, RV Dump; Southbound)**

(85) **Rest Area (RR, HF, Phones, Picnic, RV Dump; Northbound)**

83 Castleberry, Lenox
FStop E: **Texaco**(*) **(Louise's Family Restaurant)**
Gas E: Exxon(*, D, LP)
Food E: Louise's Restaurant
RVCamp E: **Country Sunshine RV Parking and Camping (3.6 Miles)**

77 AL 41, Brewton, Repton
FStop W: **Amoco**(*, D), **Shell**(*, 24) **(Stuckey's Express)**, **Texaco**(*, D)
Gas E: BP(*)
Food W: Ranch House Restaurant
ATM W: **Shell (Stuckey's Express)**
Other W: Stuckey's Express

69 AL 113, Flomaton, Wallace, Barnett Crossroads
FStop E: **Texaco**(*, D)
W: **Conoco**(*, D) **(Hot Stuff Pizza, AM South Bank)**
Gas E: Phillips 66(*)
Food W: **Hot Stuff Pizza (Conoco)**, **Huddle House**
ATM W: AM South, **Conoco (Hot Stuff Pizza, AM South Bank)**

57 AL. 21, Atmore, Uriah
FStop E: **Exxon**(*, D)
Gas W: BP(*)
Food E: Creek Family Restaurant (Best Western)
Lodg E: **Best Western**
ATM E: **Exxon**
W: BP

54 County Hwy 1 (Camping, Indian Reservation)

45 Rabun, Perdido
Gas W: Chevron(*), Harville's(*, D)
Food W: Harville's Cafe
AServ W: Rolins Tire Service

Bold red print shows RV & Bus parking available or nearby

EXIT ALABAMA

37 AL. 287, Gulf Shores Parkway, Bay Minette, Rabun (Faulkner State Community College)
TStop E: Jones Truck Stop[*, 24] (Spur)
Gas E: Chevron[*, 24] (Delissimo)
Food E: Delissimo Pizza, Subs, & Breakfast (Chevron), Jones Truck Stop
RVCamp E: R-V Parking
ATM E: Chevron (Delissimo)
Other E: R-V Parking
W: Camp Pine Treat

34 AL 59, Bay Minette, Stockton
Med E: Hospital

31 AL. 225, Stockton, Spanish Fort (Historic Blakely State Park, Confederate Memorial Battlefield)
FStop W: Conoco[*, D]
Food W: Conoco, Hot Stuff Pizza (Conoco)
ATM W: Conoco
Parks E: Historic Blakeley State Park

22 Creola
RVCamp W: Mobile North River Delta-KOA (12.5 Miles)

19 U.S. 43, Satsuma, Creola (I-65 RV camp grounds 1.6mi)
FStop E: Chevron[*, D, CW] (Krispy Kreme)
Food E: Chevron (Krispy Kreme), Krispy Kreme Doughnuts (Chevron)
Lodg E: Days Inn (see our ad this page)
RVCamp W: I-65 Campground (1 Mile)

15 Saraland, Citronelle
Gas W: Circle K[*, LP], Citgo[*, D]
Food W: Citgo, Hot Stuff Pizza (Citgo)
ATM W: AM South (Citgo), Citgo

13 AL. 158, AL. 213, Eight Mile, Saraland (Chickasabogue Park, University of Mobile)
FStop E: Texaco[*]
Gas E: BP[*, CW]
W: Exxon[*]
Food E: Krystal (Texaco), SHONEY'S Shoney's, Texaco, Waffle House
W: Blimpie Subs & Salads (Exxon), Exxon, Pizza Inn Express (Exxon)
Lodg E: Comfort Inn(see our ad this page), Days Inn, Holiday Inn Express (see our ad this page)
W: Best Western
RVCamp W: Chickasabogue Park
ATM E: BP, Bank One (BP), Texaco
Other E: Eye World, Wal-Mart Supercenter[RX]

10 West Lee St, Chickasaw
Gas E: Conoco[*], Shell[*], Spur[*]
Food E: Cajun Country Fried Chicken (Spur), Conoco, Hot Stuff Pizza (Conoco), Shell, Spur, Subway (Shell)
ATM E: AM South (Conoco), Conoco, Shell

9 Prichard, Downtown Mobile , Junction I-165 S

8AB U.S. 45 North, Citronelle (West), US 45 S, Pritchard (East) (Westbound)
FStop W: Ride With Pride[*, 24] (U-Haul Rental)
Gas E: Chevron[*, 24], Fred Eaton Service Station, Gas For Less[*], Texaco[*, CW]
W: Amoco[*], Exxon[*], Spur[*, D]
Food E: Church's Chicken
W: Burger King, Domino's Pizza, McDonald's[PLAY]
RVCamp E: Cummins Alabama Inc.
ATM W: Ride With Pride (U-Haul Rental)
Other E: American Supermarket, Food Tiger Supermarket, Port City Cleaners
W: American Coin Car Wash, Eight Mille Animal Clinic

5B U.S. 98, Moffett Road (Robert Trent Jones Golf Trail)
FStop W: Speedway[*, D, LP]
Food E: Burger King, Church's Chicken, Quincy's Family Steakhouse, Sub King
W: Dolly Madison, Hardee's
Lodg W: Super 8
AServ E: Brown and Keahey, Mr. T's
W: Brown and Duke Radiator Service, Richard's Garage[24], Southern Auto Repair & Transmission
RVCamp W: Seven Oaks RV Park (.5 Miles)
Other E: Advance Auto Parts, Wes Building Materials
W: Rough Wate Marine

5A Spring Hill Ave.
Gas E: Amoco[24], Shell
W: Chevron[*, D], Exxon[*], Petro[*], Texaco[*, D, CW]
Food E: Burger King, Church's Chicken, Dreamland BBQ, McDonald's[PLAY], Sub King
W: Hennessy's, Waffle House
Lodg W: Extended Stay America
AServ E: Big Ten Tires, Cockrell's Body Shop[24], Duitt's Battery, Hunt Automotive (BMW Service), L & M Tires, Professional Body and Paint, Southern Transmission, Super-Lube
W: Chevron, Chevron
ATM E: Shell

HUNTSVILLE
1525
DAYS INN
— Complimentary Continental Breakfast —
— Remote Control Cable TV —
— 2 Swimming Pools —
— In-Room Movies —
— Walk to 24 Hour Restaurant —
— Up to 120 person Meeting Room —
— 256-536-7441 —
ALABAMA ▪ I-565 ▪ EXIT 19A

1169
Comfort Inn
Comfort Inn
Exit 13 • Saraland, AL
334-675-0100
• Free Continental Breakfast
• Restaurant Nearby
• Outdoor Swimming Pool
• Business Rate Program
• Refrigerator / Microwaves
• Govt. Military Program
• Pets Prohibited
• Jacuzzi Rooms Available
• Cable TV • Golf Nearby

Holiday Inn EXPRESS
Holiday Inn Express
Exit 13 • Saraland, AL
334-679-8880
• Free Continental Breakfast
• Restaurant Nearby
• Outdoor Swimming Pool
• Business Rate Program
• Refrigerator / Microwaves
• Govt. Military Program
• Meeting Room
• Pets Prohibited
• Jacuzzi Rooms Available
• Cable TV • Golf Nearby
ALABAMA ▪ I-65 ▪ EXIT 13

W: Exxon
Other W: Eye Care Center

4 Dauphin St (Mobile Museum and Art, Springhill College)
Gas E: Amoco[*, D], BP[*, CW]
Food E: Baskin Robbins, Checkers Burgers, Cracker Barrel, Godfather's Pizza, Hong Kong Island Chinese, Krystal, McDonald's, Popeye's Chicken, Subway, Taco Bell, The New French Cafe, Waffle House, Wendy's
W: SHONEY'S Shoney's
Lodg E: Comfort Suites Hotel, Econolodge, Red Roof Inn
W: Best Inns of America, Best Suites of America
Med W: Spring Hill Medical Complex
ATM E: BP, Colonial Bank, South Alabama Bank of Mobile
W: Colonial Bank, Whitney Bank
Other E: Baptist Bookstore, Clardy Contact Lens Center, Dauphin St Veterinary Clinic, Dauphin Street Cinema, Delchamp's Supermarket, Downey's Book and Gift, Rite Aid Pharmacy, Van's One Hour Photo Center

3AB Airport Blvd
Gas E: Chevron[*, CW]
W: Econ[*, D], Phillips 66, Texaco[*, D, CW]
Food E: Hooter's, Morrison's, Piccadilly Cafeteria, Schlotzsky's Deli, Wendy's
W: All Seasons Restaurant (Best Western), Arby's, Billiard's, Caba Beach Club (Ramada), Chili's, Darryl's Restaurant, Delhi Palace, Denny's, El Chico Mexican Restaurant, Hickory Ham, House of Chin, Japanese Imperial Steakhouse, Joe's Crab Shack[PLAY], Little Saigon Food & Deli, Lone Star Steakhouse, Los Rancheros, Mozzarella's, Mulligan's Food Spirits (Holiday Inn), O' Charley's, Olive Garden, Outback Steak House, Paddy O'Toole's Grub and Grocery, Sonic Drive in, Sub Zone, Waffle House, Wan Fu
Lodg W: Best Western (Bradbury Suites), Courtyard by Marriott, Days Inn, Drury Inn, Fairfield Inn, Family Inns of America, Hampton Inn, Holiday Inn, La Quinta Inn, Motel 6, Ramada(see our ad this page), Residence Inn, Suburban Lodge
Med W: American Family Medical Care
ATM E: AM South, Mobile Educator's Credit Union, Union Planter's Bank
W: Texaco, Whitney
Other E: Barnes & Noble, Bel Aire Mall, Books-A-Million, Carmike Cinemas, Joe Bullard Mitsubishi, Lowe's, Springdale Mall
W: Animal Hospital, Babies R Us, Boat/United States Marine Center, Circuit City, Discovery Zone, Home Depot, Mobile Police Department, NAPA, Office Depot, Office Max, Phar Mor Drugs, Sam's Club, U-Haul Center[LP], Wal-Mart[24]

1AB U.S. 90, Government Blvd
Gas E: Chevron
W: Hudson
Food E: Royal Knight
W: Bama Bells Restaurant (Rest Inn), Waffle House
Lodg E: Howard Johnson
W: Rest Inn
AServ E: AAMCO Transmission, Bay Chevrolet/Geo, Chevron, Classic Dodge, Dean McCrary, Grady Buick, Mazda, BMW, Hyundai, Isuzu, Gulf Coast Chrysler, Plymouth, Jeep, Eagle, Lexus of Mobile, Robinson Bros Lincoln/Mercury, Saturn of Mobile, Springhill Toyota, Treadwell Ford, Treadwell Honda
W: Atrecx Transmission, Claxton Automotive Center, M & S Automotive, Michelin, Precision Tune, TNT Auto Parts
Other W: Putt Putt Golf Course

0 Junction I-10 West, Mississippi , I-10 East to Florida

↑ALABAMA

Begin I-65

EXIT	VIRGINIA

Begin I-66

↓VIRGINIA

1AB Jct I-81, Roanoke, Winchester (Westbound)
6 U.S.340, U.S. 522, Winchester, Front Royal
- **Food** S: McDonald's
- **RVCamp** N: Fishnet Campgrounds (2.1 Miles)
  S: Gooney Creek Campground (1.4 Miles), KOA Campgrounds, Poe's South Fork Campground (1.25 Miles)
- **Med** S: ✚ Hospital
- **Parks** S: Shenandoah Nat'l Park
- **Other** S: Skyline Caverns, Skyline Dr

13 VA79, to VA55, Linden, Skyline Dr, Front Royal
- **Gas** S: Chevron(*), Mobil(*, LP)
- **Food** S: The Apple House
- **RVCamp** S: Campground
- **Parks** S: Shenandoah Nat'l Park
- **Other** N: Apple Mountain Lake
  S: Skyline Caverns, Skyline Dr, Tourist Info.

18 VA688, Markham
23 VA73, to U.S.17N, to VA55W, Delaplane, Paris (Reaccess Westbound Only)
27 VA 55E, VA 647, Marshall
- **FStop** N: Chevron
- **Gas** N: Exxon(*, D, LP)
- **Food** N: Joe's Pizza & Subs, Main Street Deli
- **AServ** N: Chevron
- **ATM** N: Exxon

28 U.S.17, Marshal, Warrenton
- **Gas** N: Amoco(*, D)
- **Food** N: McDonald's (Amoco)
- **Med** S: ✚ Hospital
- **ATM** N: Amoco

31 **(245)** The Plains, Old Tavern
40 U.S.15, Haymarket, Leesburg
- **FStop** S: Citgo(*, LP), Sheetz(*, D, 24)
- **RVCamp** N: Yogi Bear Camp Resort
  S: Mountain View Campground
- **ATM** S: Citgo, Sheetz
- **Other** S: Nisson Pavilion

43AB U.S.29, Gainesville, Warrenton
- **Gas** S: Exxon(*, D), Mobil, Racetrac(*, 24), Texaco(*, D, LP)
- **Food** S: Joe's Pizza & Subs
- **RVCamp** S: Hillwood Camping Park (1 Mile), Wildwood Camping Park (1.1 Miles)
- **Other** S: 7-11 Convenience Store

44 VA 234, Manassas
47 VA234, Manassas
- **Gas** N: Texaco(*, LP)
  S: Amoco(24), Exxon(*, 24), Racetrac(*, 24), Shell(*, CW, 24), Sunoco(*, 24)
- **Food** N: Cracker Barrel
  S: Bob Evan's Restaurant, Burger King(PLAY), McDonald's(PLAY), Pargo's, Pizza Hut, SHONEY'S, Shoney's, Subway, TGI Friday, Zi Pani Breads Cafe
- **Lodg** N: Courtyard by Marriott, Holiday Inn
  S: Best Western, DAYS INN Days Inn, Hampton Inn, Red Roof Inn, Super 8
- **Med** S: ✚ Altmed Medical Center (3 Miles)
- **RVCamp** S: Camping World
- **ATM** S: Amoco, Exxon
- **Parks** N: Splash Down Water Park
- **Other** N: Manassas Nat'l Battlefield Park
  S: Bowl America, Discovery Zone, Manassas Museum, Petco, Visitor Information, Wal-Mart(RX)

(49) VA Welcome Center, Rest Area (RR, Phones, Picnic, Pet Walk; Westbound)
(49) VA Welcome Center (RR, Phones, Picnic, Pet Walk; Eastbound)
52 U.S.29, Centreville
- **Gas** S: Mobil(*)
- **Food** S: BBQ Country, Baskin Robbins, Hunan Dynasty, Long Star Steakhouse, McDonald's, Pizza Hut, Ruby Tuesday, The Shade Tree
- **RVCamp** N: Campground
- **Med** S: ✚ Urgent Care Clinic
- **ATM** S: Chevy Chase Bank, Mobil
- **Parks** N: Bullrun Park
- **Other** S: Centreville Square Animal Hospital, Centrewood Plaza, Giant Food & Pharmacy(RX), Mail Boxes Etc

53 VA28, Centreville
- **Parks** S: Ellanor C Lawrence

Econo Lodge®
Metro in Arlington
703-538-5300
800-785-6343
Minutes to DC
Minutes Walk to Metrorail
6800 Lee Highway
Arlington, VA
1129
Free Continential Breakfast
Ask For New Rooms
Kids 18 and Under Stay & Eat Free
Handicap Accesible
Coin Laundry • Data Ports
Interior Corridors • Hot Tub Rooms
HBO, ESPN, CNN • Tour Pick Up
VIRGINIA ▪ I-66 ▪ EXIT 69

CAMPING WORLD®
Exit 47
10850-B Baits Ford Rd • Manassas, VA
1-800-377-7664
1777

- **Other** S: Walney Visitor Ctr

55AB VA7100, Fairfax Cty Pkwy, Reston, Herndon, Springfield
- **Med** N: ✚ Hospital, ✚ Urgent Care Clinic (Fairlakes Ctr)

57AB U.S.50, Fairfax, Winchester
- **Lodg** N: Holiday Inn
- **Other** N: Fair Oaks Shopping Center
  S: National Firearms Museum

60 VA123, Fairfax, Vienna
- **Gas** S: Exxon(*), Shell(*, 24)
- **Food** N: Bob Evan's Restaurant
  S: Alexander's (Holiday Inn), Bonbay Bistro, Fuddruckers
- **Lodg** S: Holiday Inn
- **Med** S: ✚ Emergency Medical Care, ✚ Hospital
- **ATM** S: Exxon, NationsBank
- **Other** S: Rite Aid Pharmacy(RX)

62 VA 243, Nutley St, Vienna
- **Gas** S: Exxon
- **Food** S: Domino's Pizza, Hunan Szechuan, McDonald's
- **AServ** S: A.K. Auto, Exxon
- **ATM** S: Chevy Chase Bank, First Union Bank, Safeway Grocery
- **Other** S: CVS Pharmacy, Discovery Zone, Pan Am Shopping Ctr, Safeway Grocery

64AB Jct I-495, to Baltimore, Richmond
66 VA7, Leesburg Pike, Falls Church
- **Gas** N: Exxon(*), Mobil
  S: Xtra(*, D)
- **Food** N: Dunkin Donuts (Exxon), Leda Pizza
  S: Baskin Robbins, KFC, Long John Silver, New World Chinese Restaurant, Pizza Hut, Roy Rogers, Starbucks Coffee, Subway
- **AServ** N: Mobil
  S: Don Bayer Volvo, Precision Tune & Lube, Speedee Muffler King, Track Auto
- **ATM** N: Exxon
  S: Chevy Chase Bank
- **Other** N: Idylwood Shopping Plaza, US Post Office
  S: CVS Pharmacy, Falls Church Animal Hospital, Giant Food Store(RX)

68 West Moreland St
69 U.S.29, VA237, Washington Blvd, Lee Hwy
- **Food** S: La Cote D'or Cafe
- **Lodg** S: Econolodge(see our ad this page)
- **AServ** S: All Tune & Lube, Don Auto Service
- **ATM** S: First VA Bank
- **Other** S: Suburban Animal Hospital

71 VA120, Glebe Rd, VA237, Fairfax Dr
- **Lodg** S: Holiday Inn
- **Med** S: ✚ Hospital

72 U.S. 29, Lee Hwy, Spout Run Pkwy (Difficult Reaccess)
73 Rosslyn, Key Bridge (Difficult Reaccess)
75 to Jct I-395, to U.S.1, VA110S, Alexandria
76 E Street

↑VIRGINIA

Begin I-66

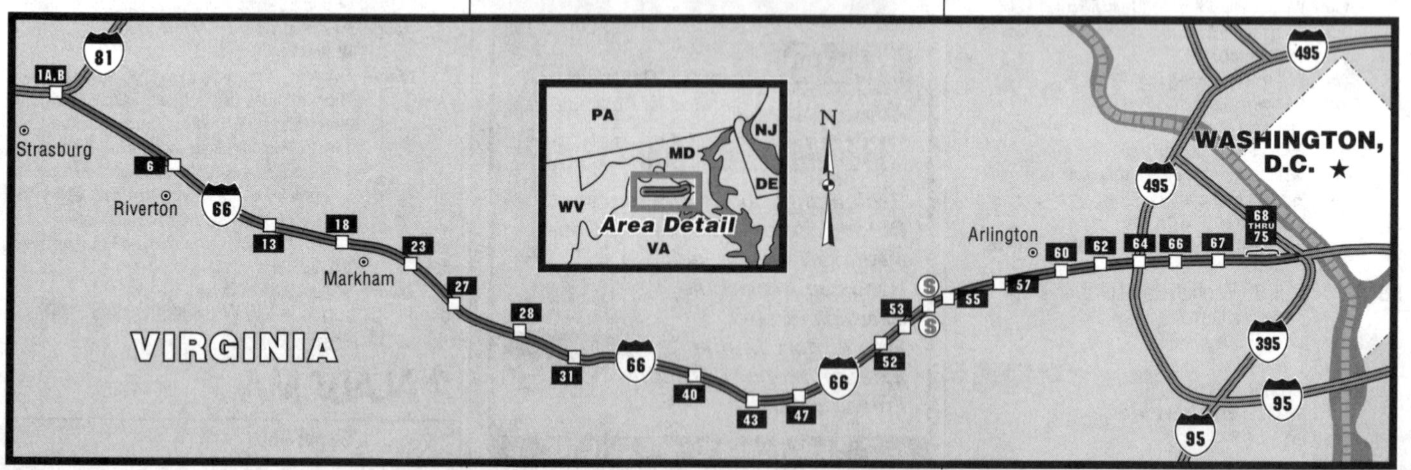

Bold red print shows RV & Bus parking available or nearby

EXIT WEST VIRGINIA

Begin I-68

↓WEST VIRGINIA

0 Jct I-79N, to Washington, South to Fairmont (Left Exit Southbound)

1 U.S. 119, University Ave, Downtown
- **Food** N: Neighbors Food and Spirit
- **Lodg** N: Comfort Inn(see our ad this page), Ramada
- **Parks** S: Tygart State Park

4 WV 7, Sabraton
- **Gas** N: Exxon(*)
- **Food** N: Blimpie's Subs (Exxon), McDonald's(PLAY), Pizza Hut, Ponderosa
- **AServ** N: NAPA Auto Parts, Parts America
- **ATM** N: One Valley Bank
- **Other** N: Kroger Supermarket(RX)

7 WV705, Airport, Pier Pont Rd
- **Gas** N: Exxon(*)
  S: 76(*, CW)
- **Food** S: Tiberio's Italian
- **Med** N: ✚ Hospital
  S: ✚ Cheat Lake Urgent Care
- **ATM** N: Huntington Bank

10 WV 857, Cheat Lake, Fairchance Road
- **FStop** N: BP(*, D)
- **Food** N: Ruby & Ketchys Restaurant
  S: AJ's On The Fairway
- **ATM** N: BP, Bruceton Bank
- **Other** S: Golf Course

15 WV 73/12, Coopers Rock
- **RVCamp** N: Chestnut Ridge Park, Sand Springs Camping Area
- **Parks** S: Coopers Rock State Forest (1.5 Miles)

23 WV 26, Bruceton Mills
- **TStop** N: Little Sandy's Truckstop(*)

1813

Comfort Inn

225 Comfort Inn Dr.
Morgantown, WV
304-296-9364
800-228-5150

Restaurant/Lounge on Premises
Outdoor Pool • Exercise Room w/Whirlpool
Meeting/Banquet Facilities
Handicap Accessible • Interior Corridors
In Room Movies
Coffee Available 24 hrs
White Water Rafting Nearby
Tour Bus Parking

West Virginia • I-68 • Exit 1

EXIT WEST VIRGINIA/MARYLAND

- **FStop** N: Ashland(*)
- **Gas** N: Country Store
- **Food** N: Country Fixins, Little Sandy's Truckstop, The Mill Place
- **Lodg** N: Mapleleaf Hotel
- **AServ** N: Murphy's Garage
- **RVCamp** N: Glade Farm Campground (6 Miles)
- **ATM** N: Ashland, Bruceton Bank, Little Sandy's Truckstop, West Banco
- **Other** N: US Post Office

29 WV 5, Hazelton Road
- **Gas** N: Mobil(*, D)
- **Food** S: Casteel's Dairy King
- **TServ** N: Mel's Truck Sales
- **RVCamp** S: Big Bear Lake Campgrounds (3 Miles), Pine Hill Campground

↑WEST VIRGINIA

↓MARYLAND

4 MD 42, Friendsville
- **FStop** N: Citgo(*)
- **Gas** N: Amoco(D)
- **Food** N: Citgo, Tabor's Restaurant
- **RVCamp** S: Campground
- **Other** S: Maryland History Heritage Museum and Library

(6) MD Welcome Center (RR, Phones, Picnic, Vending; Eastbound)

14 U.S. 219 South, U.S. 40 West, Oakland, Uniontown
- **TStop** N: Keyser Ridge TS
- **FStop** N: Citgo(*)
- **Food** N: Keyser Ridge TS, McDonald's
- **Lodg** N: Keyser Ridge TS
- **TServ** N: Menges Trucking and Repair
- **ATM** N: Keyser Ridge TS
- **Parks** S: Deep Creek Lake Recreational Area State Park
- **Other** N: Tourist Info.

19 MD495, Grantsville, Swanton
- **Gas** N: Exxon(*, D), Mobil(*)
- **Food** N: Casselman's Restaurant, Hey Pizza!
- **Lodg** N: Casselman's Restaurant
- **AServ** N: Billy Bender Chevrolet, Sumners Auto Parts Inc.
- **ATM** N: 1st United Nat'l Bank, American Trust Bank
- **Other** N: Beachy's Pharmacy, Buckel's Laundromat, U.S. Post Office

22 U.S. 219 North, Meyersdale (PA)
- **TStop** N: BP(*, SCALES)
- **FStop** N: Exxon
- **Gas** S: Amoco(*, LP, CW)
- **Food** N: BP, Burger King(PLAY), Chester Fried Chicken (BP TS), Hilltop Delight Restaurant, Subway
- **Lodg** N: Little Meadows Motel Lake and Campgrounds
  S: Holiday Inn

EXIT MARYLAND

- **AServ** N: Exxon, Napa Auto
- **Parks** S: New Germany State Park, Savage River State Forest
- **Other** N: Food Land Supermarket, Rite Aide Pharmacy

24 Lower New Germany Rd, US 40 Alternate
- **Parks** S: Big Run State Park, New Germany State Park/ Forest, Savage River State Forest

29 MD 546, Finzel
- **RVCamp** N: Mason Dixon Campground (4 Miles)

(31) Weight Station (Eastbound)

33 Midlothian Road, Frostburg
- **AServ** S: Knieriem Tires

34 MD 36, Westernport, Frostburg
- **Parks** S: Dans Mountain State Park

39 U.S. 40 Alt., La Vale Rd (Westbound)
- **Gas** N: Amoco(CW), Citgo(D), Exxon
- **Food** N: Best Western, Burger King, Denny's, KFC, Little Caesars Pizza, Long John Silver, McDonald's
- **Lodg** N: Best Western, Scottish Inns, Super 8
- **AServ** N: Advance Auto Parts, Amoco, Citgo, Exxon, Midas Muffler
- **ATM** N: First Peoples Credit Union, HNB National Bank
- **Other** N: La Vale Pharmacy(RX)

40 **(39)** Truck Rt 220 South, La Vale , Vocke Road (Difficult Reaccess)
- **Gas** N: BP(*, LP), Mobil
- **Food** N: Arby's, Bob Evan's Restaurant, D'Atri Restaurant, Dairy Queen, Kenny Roger's Roasters, Wendy's
  S: Chi- Chi's, Kenny's Diner, Ponderosa
- **Lodg** S: Oaktree Inn
- **AServ** N: Mobil
  S: Kelly's Tires
- **Med** N: ✚ Hospital, ✚ Sports Medicine Center
- **ATM** N: American Trust Bank
  S: American Trust Bank
- **Parks** N: First Toll Gate House
- **Other** N: Diamond Shine Automatic Car Wash, La Vale Pharmacy, Revco Drugs(RX), State Police
  S: Country Club Mall, Wal-Mart(24, RX) (Vision Center)

41 Seton Dr, to MD49 (Westbound, Reaccess Eastbound Only, Difficult Reaccess)
- **Med** N: ✚ Sacred Heart Hospital

42 U.S. 220 South, Greene St (Eastbound, No Trucks Or Buses)
- **Gas** N: Exxon
- **AServ** N: Exxon

43A Johnson St , to WV 28Alt
- **Gas** N: Citgo, Sheetz(*, LP, 24)
- **Food** N: Fox's Pizza, Oxford House Restaurant
- **AServ** N: Citgo
- **Med** N: ✚ Hospital

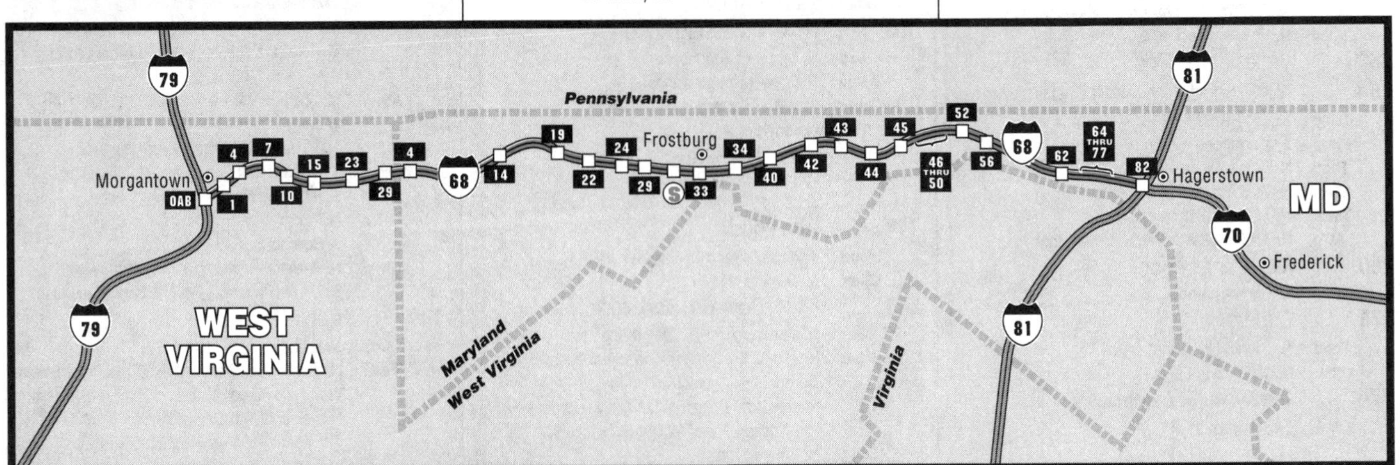

Bold red print shows RV & Bus parking available or nearby

← W I-68

EXIT — MARYLAND

Other N: Tourist Info.
43B MD 51, Industrial Blvd, Airport
Gas S: Amoco, Citgo(*, D, CW)
Food S: Dunkin Donuts, Roy Rogers, Taco Bell, Wendy's
Lodg N: Holiday Inn
AServ S: Amoco, Citgo
ATM N: First National Bank of Maryland
43C Downtown (Westbound)
43D Maryland Ave.
Gas S: Texaco(*, D)
Food S: Subway (Texaco)
Med S: + Hsopital
ATM S: Texaco
44 U.S. 40 Alt, Baltimore Ave, Willow Brook Rd
45 Hillcrest Dr
FStop S: BP(*, LP)
46 U.S. 220 North, Bedford
Food N: DaVinci's Pizzaria
S: J.B.'s Steak Cellar, Masons Barn, Uncle Tucker's
Lodg N: Cumberland Motel
TServ N: CHP Truck Parts
Other N: Crossroads Animal Hospital, Premier Car Wash
47 MD 144, Old National Pike (Westbound)

EXIT — MARYLAND

50 Pleasant Valley Road, Rocky Gap State Park
RVCamp N: Campground
Parks N: Rocky Gap State Park
Other N: Tourist Info.
52 MD 144 East, National Pike
56 MD 144, National Pike, Flintstone
Gas S: Citgo(*), VanMeters(*)
Food S: Dawn's Country Diner
AServ S: Citgo
ATM S: Citgo
Other S: U.S. Post Office
62 U.S. 40, Scenic Rt, Fifteen Mile Creek Road
64 **M. V. Smith Road, Scenic Overlook (Phones)**
Parks S: Green Ridge State Forest Hdqtrs
68 Orleans Road
FStop N: Citgo(*)
AServ N: Bellegrove Auto Service, Citgo
RVCamp S: Campground
Other S: CNO Canal
72 U.S. 40 Scenic, High Germany Road, Swain Road

EXIT — MARYLAND

FStop S: Amoco(*)
74 U.S. 40 East Scenic, Mtn Road (Eastbound Reaccess Via US 40)
(74) Sideling Hills Exhibit Center (RR, Phones, Picnic, Vending)
(75) Runaway Truck Ramp
77 U.S. 40 Scenic, MD 144, Woodmont Road
RVCamp S: Happy Hills Campground
82A I-70 West Exit 1B, US 522, Breezwood, Hancock Winchester (Left Exit Westbound)
Gas S: Gary's, Same Pipeline, Sheetz(*, 24)
Food S: Fox's Pizza, Pizza Hut
Lodg S: Econolodge
RVCamp S: Happy Hills Campground
82B US 40 E., Hagerstown
82C I-70 W, US 522 N, Breezwood
82ABC Jct I-70, U.S. 522, U.S. 40 East, Breezewood, Winchester (Eastbound)

↑MARYLAND

Begin I-68

I-69 S →

EXIT — MICHIGAN

Begin I-69

↓MICHIGAN

199 Business Loop 69, Port Huron
AServ S: Sam's Club
Other S: K-Mart(*, 24, RX), Sam's Club
198 Junction I-94W to Detroit, I-94 E to Canada (Left Exit Eastbound)
196 Wadhams Road
FStop N: By-Lo(D, LP, K)
Gas N: Marathon(*, D, K), Shell(*, D, K)
Food N: French's Bakery & Cafe, Hungry Howie's Pizza & Subs, McDonald's, Wadhams Country Kitchen, Wadhams House of Pizza
RVCamp N: KOA Campgrounds (.75 Miles), Pete's Camping Service(LP) (2 Miles)
Med N: + Mercy Family Care
ATM N: Old Kent, Speedy Q Market
Other N: Car Wash, Coin Laundry, Speedy Q Market, Wadhams Pharmacy
194 Barth Road
RVCamp N: Fort Trodd Campground (Good Sam Park)
Med N: + Humane Society Animal Clinic
189 Wales Center Road
184 MI 19, Sandusky, Richmond
TStop N: 76(*, D, LP, SCALES) (24hr Restaurant)
FStop S: Marathon(*, D, LP, K)
Food N: Bisco's, Diane's Kitchen
AServ N: 76 (24hr Restaurant)
TServ N: 76(SCALES) (24hr Restaurant)
ATM N: 76 (24hr Restaurant), Old Kent Bank
180 Riley Center Road
RVCamp N: Campground
176 Capac
Food N: Country Side Banquet Hall
Other N: Kapec Food Center
174 **Rest Area (RR, Phones, Picnic; Southbound)**

EXIT — MICHIGAN

168 MI 53, Imlay City, Almont
FStop N: Amoco(*, D, CW), Total(*, D, LP)
Food N: Big Boy, Dairy Queen, Little Caesars Pizza, Taco Bell (Total), Wah Wong Chinese, Wendy's
Lodg N: Super 8
AServ N: Chrysler Auto Dealer, Ford Dealership, GM Dealer, Pennzoil Oil Change, Quality Farm & Fleet, Total
Med N: + Mercy Family Center
ATM N: Amoco, Total
Other N: Coin Laundry, IGA Food Store, Lapeer Vision Center, Newark Car Wash, Pamida Grocery(RX)
163 Lake Pleasant Road, Atpica
161 **Rest Area (RR, Phones, Picnic; Northbound)**
159 Wilder Road
155 MI 24, Pontiac, Lapeer
Gas S: Mobil(*, D)
AServ S: Pontiac Buick GM Dealer
RVCamp N: Camping
Med N: + Hospital
Other S: Lapeer Eye Clinic
153 Lake Nepessing Road
Food N: Michael's Roadhouse
AServ N: Pioneer Transmissions
RVCamp S: Hilltop Campground (1.25 Miles)
ATM N: Farm Credit Services
Other N: Lake Nepessing Road Convenience Store, Propane Parker, Serrell Gas
S: Country Club & Golf Course, Golf Land
149 Elba Road
Food S: Woody's Pizza (Country Market)
Other S: Country Market
145 MI 15, Davison, Clarkston
Gas N: Marathon(*, LP, K), Shell(*, D, K), Speedway(*, LP)
Food N: Arby's, Big Boy, Big John's Steak & Onion, Burger King, Country Boy(24), Cruiser's Drive-Thru, Hungry Howie's Pizza & Subs, Italia Gardens, KFC, Little Caesars Pizza, McDonald's, Taco Bell
Lodg N: Comfort Inn

EXIT — MICHIGAN

AServ N: Davidson Automotive, Jim Waldron Pontiac Buick GMC Trucks, Q Lube, Robo Car and Truck Wash, Ross Automotive
RVCamp N: American Recreation Vehicles (1.3 Miles)
Med S: + Dunckel Veterinary Hospital, + Hospital, + McLaren Medical Center
ATM N: 7-11 Convenience Store, NBD Bank, Shell, Speedway
S: Dort Credit Union
Other N: 7-11 Convenience Store, Eye Care Associates, Rite Aide Pharmacy(24), Sparkle Buggy Car Wash
S: Davidson Athletic Club
143 Irish Road
Gas S: Marathon(*)
Food S: McDonald's (Marathon)
AServ N: Bubble's Galore Car Wash
ATM S: Marathon
Other S: 7-11 Convenience Store, Coin Laundry (Marathon)
141 Belsay Road
Gas N: Shell(*, D, K)
Food N: Little Caesars Pizza (K-Mart), McDonald's, McDonald's (Wal-Mart), Taco Bell
S: Bootlegger's Bar & Grill, Country Kitchen, Little Caesars Pizza, Packy's Pizza, Paliani's Italian, Scotti's Fish & Chips
AServ N: J & L Auto Cleaners, K-Mart(RX), Shell, Wal-Mart(RX)
S: Beaver Auto Parts & Service
RVCamp S: Bud's Trailer Center, Inc. (.8 Miles)
Med S: + Genesy's Medical Bldg
ATM N: Flint's Credit Union
S: National Bank of Detroit
Other N: K-Mart(RX), Kessel Grocery, Wal-Mart(RX)
S: Rite Aid Pharmacy, Sparkle Buggy Car Wash
139 Center Road, Flint
Gas N: Speedway(*, D), Total(*, D, LP)
Food N: Applebee's, Boston Market Restaurant, Empire Wok, Halo Burger, Mapleleaf Family Restaurant (Travelodge), Old Country Buffet, Olympic Grill, Ponderosa, Subway, Tubby's Grilled Subs,

Bold red print shows RV & Bus parking available or nearby

EXIT — MICHIGAN

Wendy's
S: Bob Evan's Restaurant, China 1, Walli's Restaurant
Lodg N: TraveLodge
S: Super 8, Walli's Motor Lodge
AServ N: Auto Works, Goodyear Tire & Auto
S: Pro Style Auto
Med S: ✚ McLaren Occupation & Urgent Care Center
ATM N: Speedway
S: Farmer Jack's Supermarket(RX)
Other N: Coin Laundry, Courtland Shopping Center, Home Depot, Sear's Optical, VG's Grocery(RX)
S: Farmer Jack's Supermarket(RX), SVS Vision Optical, Staples Office Superstore, Target

138 MI 54, Dort Highway
FStop N: Total(*, D, LP)
Gas N: Amoco, Sunoco(D, K)
S: Speedway(*), Sunoco (Express Lube)
Food N: Big John's Steak & Onion, Dunkin Donuts (Total), Grape Vine, Pumpernik's Bagel Factory, Rally's Hamburgers, Roaches Bar & Grill, Sizzler Grill & Bar, Ya Ya's Flame Broiled Chicken
S: Big Boy, Bill Knapp's Restaurant (see our ad this page), Hot 'N Now Hamburgers, KFC, McDonald's, Subway, Taco Bell
Lodg S: Travel Inn
AServ N: Amoco, Canrock Tire Co.
S: Design Auto Trim, Midas Muffler & Brake, Paul's Auto Service, Pontiac Buick GM Dealer, Ross Oil Change & Car Wash, Semmens Transmission, Sunoco (Express Lube), Tuffy Auto Center
Med N: ✚ Hospital
ATM N: Amoco, Citizens Bank, Michigan National Bank
Other N: AmTrack Train Station, Eascor Animal Hospital, Rite Aide Pharmacy, Southern Pride Car Wash
S: U-Haul Center(LP)

137 Junction I-475, Saginaw, Detroit

136 Saginaw Street, Downtown
Food N: Italia Gardens
AServ S: Michigan Glass Service
Med N: ✚ Hurley Trauma Center
S: ✚ American Red Cross

135 Hammerberg Road
Other N: Swartz Golf Course

133 Junction I-75, U.S. 23, Saginaw, Ann Arbor, Detroit

131 MI 121, Bristol Road
Food W: Burger King, Long John Silver, Mem's Oriental Food, Subway
AServ E: Goodyear Tire & Auto
W: Valley Tire & Service
ATM W: Chemical Bank, Michigan National Bank
Other E: Airport
W: Complete Eye Care

129 Miller Road
Gas E: Marathon(*)
Food E: Arby's, McDonald's
W: O'Tooles
AServ E: Marathon
Other W: Gander Mountain Outdoor Sportsmen Center

128 Morrish Road
Gas E: Amoco(*, CW, 24)
Med E: ✚ McLaren Family Care
Other E: Sport Creek Horse Racing

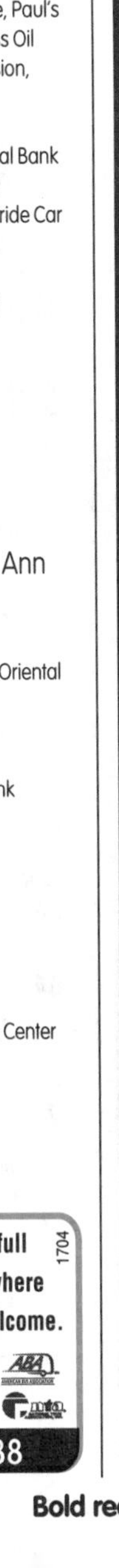

Bill Knapp's Restaurant
Bill Knapp's is a casual, full service family restaurant where Motorcoaches are always welcome.
Open daily at 11:00 am
Over 50 locations throughout: Michigan • Ohio • Indiana
810-234-8657 - Flint
MICHIGAN • I-69 • EXIT 138
1704

EXIT — MICHIGAN

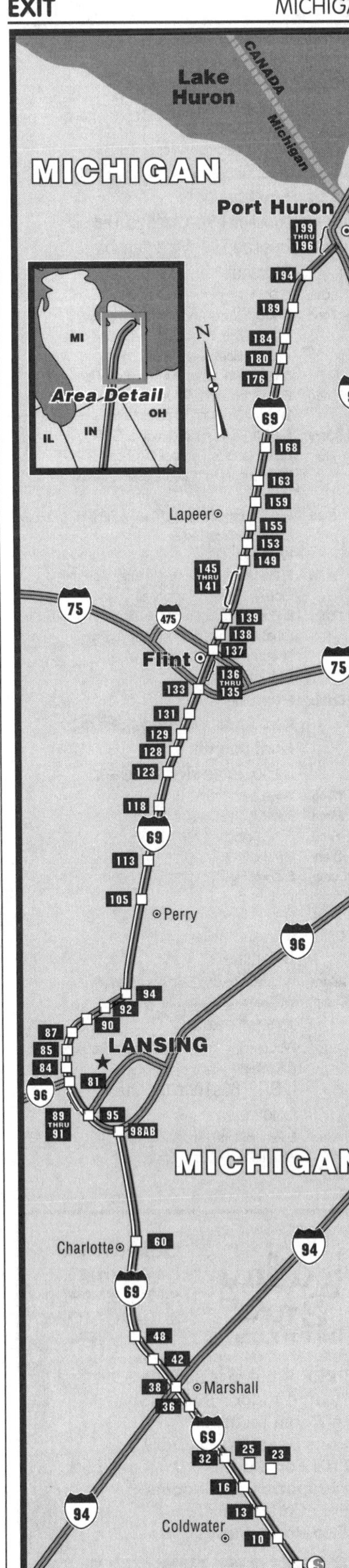

EXIT — MICHIGAN

(126) Rest Area (RR, Phones, Picnic, Vending; Northbound)

123 MI 13, Saginaw
RVCamp S: Holiday Shores (2 Miles)
Other N: Arnie's Convenient Store

117 Junction 75/69 , Flint, Port Huron

118 MI 71, Corunna, Durand
FStop E: Shell(*, D, LP)
Gas E: Total(*, LP)
W: Mobil(*)
Food E: Dutch Hollow Golf Club, Hardee's, McDonald's, Subway
W: London's Bakery Shoppe
AServ W: Durand Mobil Service
RVCamp E: Camping, Rainbow RV Sales Parts & Service
Other E: Carter's Food Center, Dutch Hollow Golf Club, Rite Aid Pharmacy(RX)

113 Bancroft
RVCamp S: Camping

105 MI 52, Perry, Owosso
TStop E: Joe's(*, D, LP, K)
Gas E: Citgo(*, CW), Shell(*, CW)
Food E: Burger King, Cafe Sports, Dunkin Donuts (Citgo), Joe's, McDonald's, Pizza (Citgo), Taco Bell (Shell), Tasty Twist, West Side Deli
Lodg E: Heb's Inn
AServ E: Galaxy Auto Center
RVCamp E: Camping
ATM E: Citgo, Joe's, Shell
Other E: Rite Aid Pharmacy(RX)
W: Perry Animal Clinic

(100) Rest Area (Eastbound)

98 Woodbury Road, Laingsburg, Shaftsburg
RVCamp E: Moon Lake Campground (1 Mile)
Other E: Sam's Snapper LP Service(LP)

94 East Lansing
Gas E: Admiral(*, D, K), Speedway(*, LP, K)
Food E: Your Family Restaurant
Lodg E: Willow Lakes Motel
AServ E: Davis Collision Center
RVCamp E: Gillette Trailer Center(LP) (.7 Miles)
Parks E: Lake Lansing Park
Other E: Brite Reflection Car Wash, Sav A Lot Food Stores, Thermo Gas(LP)

92 Webster Road, Bath

90 U.S. 127 South, East Lansing, Jackson (Westbound)

89 U.S. 127 South, East Lansing, Jackson

87 U.S. 27, Clare, Lansing
FStop W: Total(*, D, LP)
Gas E: Speedway(*, LP)
W: Marathon(*, CW), Standard(*, CW, 24)
Food W: Arby's, Bob Evan's Restaurant, Burger King, Dunkin Donuts (Standard Gas), Little Caesars Pizza, McDonald's, Subway
Lodg W: Sleep Inn
AServ E: Pennzoil Oil Change(CW)
W: Annie Raye Chevrolet, GM Auto Dealership
RVCamp W: RV Sales & Service
Med W: ✚ Delta Medical Center
ATM W: Community First Bank(24), Lansing Automakers Federal Credit Union, Michigan National Bank
Other E: Lansing Factory Outlet Stores, Outlet Mall
W: Animal Hospital, Car Wash, L & L Food Center(RX)

85 DeWitt

84 Airport Road

Exit (82) 69 North becomes 69 East

81 Junction I-96 West, Grand Rapids (Southbound)

Bold red print shows RV & Bus parking available or nearby

EXIT MICHIGAN

91 Junction North I-69, U.S. 27, Flint, Clare

93AB Junction I-69 Business Loop, MI 43, Saginaw Highway
- **Gas** **E:** Shell(*, CW), Total(*, D)
  W: Amoco(*, CW, 24)
- **Food** **E:** Burger King, Denny's, Frank's Press Box, Hoffman House (BestWestern), **McDonald's**, Roxy's (Best Western), T.G.I. Friday's (Holiday Inn)
  W: **Cracker Barrel**, Dunkin Donuts (Amoco)
- **Lodg** **E:** Best Western, Fairfield Inn, Hampton Inn, **Holiday Inn**, Motel 6, Quality Inn, Quality Suites, Red Roof Inn, Residence Inn
- **AServ** **W:** Crippen Oldsmobile, GMC Dealer, Regency Olds/ GMC Trucks/ Mazda
- **Med** **E:** **+ Westside Medical Center**
  W: **+ Hospital**
- **ATM** **E:** Michigan National Bank, Total
- **Other** **W:** **TFC-Farm, Home, Auto**

95 JCT I-496, Downtown Lansing

98AB Junction I-69 South

72 I-96 East, Detroit

70 Lansing Road
- **Food** **E:** **Mary's Truckstop**, Tom
- **Other** **E:** **State Police**

66 MI 100, Potterville, Grand Ledge
- **Gas** **W:** Amoco(*, CW, 24), BP(*)
- **Food** **W:** Charlie's Bar & Grill, McDonald's
- **AServ** **W:** Amoco(24), Auto Value Parts Store, **Potpouri Trailer & Leasing**
- **TServ** **W:** **Potpouri Trailer & Leasing**
- **ATM** **W:** BP, Independent Bank
- **Other** **W:** Mr. Clean Car Wash, **Wildern's Pharmacy(RX)**

61 Lansing Road
- **FStop** **E:** **Mobil(*, D, K) (Pacific Pride)**
  W: **Quality Dairy(*, CW, 24)**
- **Gas** **E:** Total(*, D, K)
  W: Speedway(*, D, LP, K)
- **Food** **E:** **Mobil (Pacific Pride)**
  W: **Arby's**, Arctic Creamery, **Big Boy**, Charlotte Country Club, Hot N' Now Hamburgers, KFC, Little Caesars Pizza, Mancino's Pizza, Pizza Hut, **Quality Dairy**, Taco Bell, Wendy's
- **Lodg** **E:** Goldie's Motel, Sundown Motel
- **AServ** **E:** Beacon Sales, Team One Chevrolet Olds, Tire City
  W: Candy Ford, Car Quest Auto Center, Davis Pontiac, Eaton's Auto Body, Martin Jeep Eagle, Master Muffler & Kelly Tires
- **TServ** **E:** **Gra-Bell Truck Line**
- **Med** **W:** **+ Hospital**
- **ATM** **E:** Lansing Automakers Federal Credit Union, **Mobil (Pacific Pride)**
  W: **Quality Dairy**
- **Other** **E:** **Carter's Grocery, K-Mart(RX)**, **Lowe Brother's & Dad Inc.(LP)**, **RX Optical, Wal-Mart(RX)**
  W: Charlotte Car Wash, **Pet Corner, Sav-A-Lot Grocery**

60 MI 50, Charlotte, Eaton Rapids
- **Lodg** **W:** **Super 8**
- **Med** **W:** **+ Hospital**

57 I-69 Business Loop, Cochran Road, Charlotte
- **RVCamp** **E:** **Campground**
- **Other** **W:** **Town & Country Animal Hospital**

51 Ainger Road
- **RVCamp** **E:** **Camping**

48 MI 78, Bellevue, Olivet
- **RVCamp** **E:** **Camping**

42 N Drive North
- **Gas** **W:** Citgo(*, D, LP, K)
- **AServ** **W:** J & S Automotive Repair

(41) **Rest Area (RR, Phones, Picnic; Southbound)**

38 Junction I-94, Chicago, Detroit

36 Bus Loop 94, Michigan Ave, Marshall
- **Gas** **E:** Shell(*, CW)
- **Food** **E:** **Arby's**, Bake Apple Bagels, **Big Boy**, **Burger King**, Cinnamon City (Shell), Coffee Beanery (Shell), **Little Caesars Pizza (K-Mart)**, **McDonald's**, Pizza Hut, Taco Bell, **Wendy's**
- **Lodg** **E:** AmeriHost Inn, Arbor Inn
  W: Bear Creek Inn, Imperial Motel
- **AServ** **E:** Brian Banfield's Automotive, Caron Chevrolet Olds, Pennzoil Oil Change
  W: Boshears Ford, Kool Classic Chrysler Plymouth
- **Med** **E:** **+ Marshall Medical Center, + Oak Lawn Medical Center**
  W: **+ Hospital**
- **ATM** **E:** **Carter's Food Center(24)**, Chemical Bank, Marshall Savings Bank, Shell
- **Other** **E:** **Carter's Food Center, K-Mart(RX)**, Marshall Lanes, Mission Car Wash, **Rite Aid Pharmacy(RX)**, Westside Car Wash

32 F Drive South
- **RVCamp** **E:** **Camping**

(28) **Rest Area (RR, Phones, Picnic; Northbound)**

25 MI 60, Three Rivers, Jackson
- **TStop** **E:** **Pekon(*, D, SCALES)**
- **FStop** **E:** **BP(*, D, K)**, **Sunoco(*, D, LP)**
- **Food** **E:** **BP**, Dairy King, **McDonald's**
- **TServ** **E:** **Pekon(SCALES)**
- **RVCamp** **E:** **Camping**
  W: **Camping**
- **ATM** **E:** **BP, Pekon, Sunoco**
- **Other** **E:** **Acme Propane(LP)**

23 Tekonsha
- **AServ** **W:** Ernie's Towing, Seltner's Auto Tech
- **RVCamp** **W:** **Camping**

16 Jonesville Road
- **RVCamp** **W:** **Camping, Ferris RV Sales and Service(LP) (1.5 Miles)**

13 U.S. 12, Bus Loop 69, Quincy, Coldwater
- **Gas** **E:** Pennington(LP), Speedway(*, D, K)
  W: Amoco(*, CW), Citgo, Speedway(*, D, K), Sunoco(*, CW)
- **Food** **E:** Bob Evan's Restaurant, Mancino's
  W: Arby's, Burger King, Charlie's, **Cold Water Garden Restaurant**, Elias Brothers Restaurant, Hot 'N Now Hamburgers, **KFC**, Little Caesars Pizza, McDonald's, Pizza Hut, Ponderosa Steakhouse, Subway, TCBY, Taco Bell, Wendy's
- **Lodg** **E:** Little King Motel
  W: Cadet Motor Inn, **Holiday Inn Express(see our ad this page)**, Quality Inn, Super 8
- **AServ** **E:** Discount Auto Parts, **Haylett Service Center**, One Stop Auto Finance, Quaker State Oil & Lube
  W: Max Larsen Ford Lincoln Mercury, Midas Muffler & Brake
- **RVCamp** **E:** **Haylett Service Center**
- **Med** **W:** **+ Hospital**
- **ATM** **E:** Branch County Federal, Century Bank
  W: Coldwater Banking Center, First of America, Southern Michigan
- **Other** **E:** Clean Vehicles Car Wash, **Farmer Jack Grocery(RX)**, Maytag Coin Laundry, RX Optical, **Sav-A-Lot Grocery, Wal-Mart(RX)**
  W: **Coldwater Recreation Bowling Lanes, K-Mart**

1061
Holiday Inn EXPRESS®
Coldwater
I-69 Exit 13
517-279-0900
800-HOLIDAY
- FREE Breakfast Bar
- Heated Indoor Pool & Spa
- In-Room Jacuzzis
- Coin Operated Laundry
- Free Local Calls
- Dataports in all Rooms
- Free Coffee and Tea
- Two Room Suites

SAVE 15%
MICHIGAN • I-69 • EXIT 13 West

EXIT MICHIGAN/INDIANA

10 Business Loop 69, Coldwater

(8) **Weigh Station (Northbound)**

(6) **Welcome Center (RR, Phones, Picnic, Vending; Northbound)**

3 Copeland Road, Kinderhook
- **Gas** **W:** BP(*, K)
- **AServ** **W:** **Advanced Auto & Truck (Wrecker)**
- **TServ** **W:** **Advanced Auto & Truck (Wrecker)**
- **RVCamp** **E:** **Camping**

↑MICHIGAN

↓INDIANA

157 Lake George Road, Jamestown, Orland
- **TStop** **E:** **Mobil(*, D, LP, SCALES, 24)**
  W: **Shell(*, D, K, SCALES, 24)**
- **FStop** **W:** **Speedway(*, LP, K, SCALES)**
- **Food** **E:** **Baker Street Family Restaurant (Mobil)**, JO JO's (Mobil), **Subway (Mobil)**
  W: Hardee's (Speedway), Red Arrow (Shell), **Shell**
- **Lodg** **E:** **Lake George Inn (Mobil), Mobil**
  W: **Redwood Lodge**
- **TServ** **E:** **Mobil(SCALES, 24)**
  W: **Damiros Truck Sales, Gulick Volvo Truck Dealership**
- **RVCamp** **W:** **Yogi Bear Camp Resort**

156 Junction I-80/90, Chicago, Toledo (Toll)

154 IN 127 to IN 727, Angola
- **Food** **E:** Holiday Inn
- **Lodg** **E:** Budgeteer Motor Inn, Holiday Inn
  W: Pokagon Motel
- **RVCamp** **E:** **Oak Hill Camping, Yogi Bear Camp Resort**
- **Parks** **W:** **Pokagon State Park**
- **Other** **E:** Pokagon Falls Miniature Golf Course

150 County Road. 200 West, Lake James, Crooked Lake
- **Gas** **W:** Pennzoil Oil Change(*), Shell(*, D, K)
- **Food** **W:** Ice Cream Cove
- **RVCamp** **W:** **Boyd's Fairground, Fawn Forest Campground, Stuben County**

Bold red print shows RV & Bus parking available or nearby

EXIT	INDIANA
	Campgrounds & Beach
Other	**W:** Crooked Creek, Dry Dock Marine Center
148	U.S. 20, Angola, Lagrange
FStop	**E:** Speedway[*, LP, K]
Gas	**E:** Amoco[*, LP], Marathon[*, D]
Food	**E:** Amoco, Subway (Amoco)
	W: Best Western, West Edge Bar & Grill (Best Western)
Lodg	**W:** Best Western
RVCamp	**E:** Cook's Happy Acres RV Park (1 Mile)
Med	**E:** ✚ Hospital
ATM	**E:** Amoco
(144)	Rest Area (RR, Phones, Picnic; Southbound)
140	IN 4, Hamilton, Ashley, Hudson (Exit under construction)
Gas	**W:** Marathon[*]
134	U.S. 6, Kendallville, Waterloo
FStop	**W:** Marathon[*, K, 24]
ATM	**W:** Marathon
129	IN 8, Auburn, Garrett
Gas	**E:** Amoco[*], Gas America[*, LP], Marathon[*]
Food	**E:** Ambrosia, Amoco, Arby's, Auburn Bed & Breakfast, Bob Evan's Restaurant, Burger King, Dairy Queen, Dunkin Donuts (Amoco), Fazoli's Italian Food, KFC, McDonald's[PLAY], Pizza Hut, Ponderosa Steakhouse, Taco Bell, Wal-Mart[RX] (Vision center, one hour photo), Wendy's
Lodg	**E:** Auburn Bed & Breakfast, Country Hearth Inn, Holiday Inn Express, Super 8
AServ	**E:** Auto Zone Auto Parts, Marathon, Wal-Mart (Vision center, one hour photo)
RVCamp	**E:** Ben Davis RV Sales
Med	**E:** ✚ Hospital
ATM	**E:** Gas America
Other	**E:** Auburn-Cord-Duesenburg Museum, Classic Car Wash, Wal-Mart[RX] (Vision center, one hour photo)
	W: Ryder Truck Rental
126	Garrett, Auburn
RVCamp	**W:** KOA Kampground
Other	**E:** Kruse Auction Park
(124)	Rest Area (RR, Phones, Picnic, Vending; Southbound)
(124)	Rest Area (RR, Phones, Picnic, Vending; Northbound)
116	IN 1 North, Dupont Road, Leo-Teeterville
Gas	**E:** Amoco[*, CW, 24]
	W: BP[*, D, CW], Speedway[*, LP, K]
Food	**E:** Amoco, Burger King (Amoco)
	W: Bob Evan's Restaurant
Med	**W:** ✚ Dupont Medical Center
ATM	**E:** Amoco
Other	**W:** Dupont Medical Park Pharmacy[RX]
115	Jct I-469, US 30 E
112AB	Coldwater Road (112A west, 112B east)
Gas	**E:** Amoco[*, D, CW]
Food	**E:** Arby's[24], Bill Knapp's Restaurant (see our ad this page), Chi-Chi's Mexican Restaurant,

EXIT	INDIANA
	Coldwater, Angola, Auburn, Fort Wayne, Huntington, Marion, Muncie, Anderson, Indianapolis
	MICHIGAN, INDIANA
	Area Detail: MI, OH, IL, IN

EXIT	INDIANA
	Cork 'N Cleaver Steak & Seafood, DeBrand Gourmet Chocolate Shop, Don Hall's Factory Steakhouse, House of Hunan Chinese, Krispy Kreme Doughnuts, Lone Star Steakhouse, Marriott, Old Country Buffet, Papa John's, Red River Steak & BBQ (Marriott), Taco Cabana, Wendy's, Zesto Ice Cream
Lodg	**E:** Marriott, Sumner Suites
Other	**E:** Coliseum, Discovery Zone, Longe Optical, Wal-Mart[LP, RX], WalGreens Pharmacy[RX]
111AB	U.S. 27 South,, Fort Wayne, 111A (East) IN 3 North, Kendallville 111B (West)
Gas	**E:** Shell[*, CW]
	W: Amoco[*], BP[*, D, LP]
Food	**E:** Days Inn, Denny's, Happy Days (Days Inn)
	W: Amoco, Cracker Barrel, Dog n Suds, Golden China (Signature Inn), KFC, McDonald's[PLAY], Richard's Restaurant, Signature Inn, Subway (Amoco)
Lodg	**E:** Days Inn, Residence Inn
	W: Budgetel Inn, Courtyard by Marriott, Dollar Inn, Don Hall's Guest House, Economy Inn, Fairfield Inn, Fort Wayne Studio PLUS, Hampton Inn & Suites, Lee's Inn, Signature Inn
AServ	**E:** Don Ayres Pontiac GM, Fort Wayne Nissan, Infiniti of Fort Wayne
Other	**E:** Lincoln Museum, Science Central
109AB	U.S. 30 West, U.S. 33 North, Fort Wayne (109B west, 109A east)
TStop	**E:** Fort Wayne Truck Center (Kenworth), Fort Wayne Truck Plaza[*, SCALES] (Citgo gas)
FStop	**E:** OTR Premium Fuel[SCALES] (Ray's TW)
Food	**E:** Azar's Big Boy, Fort Wayne Truck Plaza (Citgo gas), McDonald's, Subway (Fort Wayne Truck Plaza), The Point Restaurant (Fort Wayne TS), Value Lodge
Lodg	**E:** Best Inns of America, Comfort Inn, Dollar Inn, Holiday Inn, Knight's Inn, Motel 6, Red Roof Inn, Value Lodge
TServ	**E:** Cummins Diesel, Goodyear Tire & Auto, International Navistar, Thermo King of Indiana, Vermeer of Indiana, Western Star, Whiteford Truck Center
TWash	**E:** Fort Wayne Truck Plaza (Citgo gas), OTR Premium Fuel (Ray's TW), Ray's Truck Wash
Med	**E:** ✚ Hospital
ATM	**E:** Fort Wayne Truck Plaza (Citgo gas)
Other	**E:** Children's Zoo
105AB	IN 14 West, Fort Wayne, South Whitley (105B west, 105A, east)
Gas	**E:** Shell[*, CW], Speedway[*, LP]
Food	**E:** John Kolptenstein (Ramada Inn), Ramada, Speedway, Steak 'N Shake
Lodg	**E:** Ramada
AServ	**E:** Fort Wayne Toyota
ATM	**E:** Three Rivers Federal Credit Union
Other	**E:** Meijer Grocery[24]
102	U.S. 24 West, Huntington, Fort Wayne
Gas	**W:** Amoco[*, 24], Marathon[*]
Food	**W:** Applebee's, Arby's, Bob Evan's Restaurant, Captain D's Seafood, Carlos O'Kelly's Mexican, Don Hall's Tavern & Coventry, Expresso Bakery, McDonald's, Pizza Hut, Strazlo's, Wendy's, Zesto

Bold red print shows RV & Bus parking available or nearby

EXIT	INDIANA
Lodg	E: Extended Stay America, Hampton Inn
	W: Best Western, Comfort Suites Hotel
AServ	W: Southwest Automotive Service Center(CW)
Med	E: ✚ Hospital
ATM	W: Fort Wayne National Bank, NBD Bank, Norwest Banks
Other	W: Coventry 13 Cinemas, Indiana State Police Post, Longe Optical, Mail Boxes Etc., Perfection Auto Wash, Scott's Grocery, WalGreens Pharmacy(RX)
99	Lower Huntington Road
Other	W: Hoosier Propane(LP)
96A	IN 469, U.S. 24 East, U.S. 33 South 96A east, Lafayette Center Road 96B West
(93)	**Rest Area (RR, Phones, Picnic, Vending; Southbound)**
(89)	**Rest Area (RR, Phones, Picnic, Vending; Northbound)**
86	U.S. 224, Markle, Huntington, Decatur, Bluffton, Huntington Reservoir
Gas	E: Sunoco(*)
Med	W: ✚ Hospital
Other	W: Huntington Reservoir
(80)	**Weigh Station (Southbound)**
78	IN 5, Warren, Huntington, Salimoni Reservoir
TStop	W: Citgo Truck & Auto Plaza(*, SCALES) (Citgo gas)
Gas	E: Sunoco(*, D)
	W: Clark(*)
Food	E: Chester's Fried Chicken (Sunoco), Sunoco
	W: Citgo Truck & Auto Plaza (Citgo gas), Clark, Hoosier-land Restaurant, McDonald's, Subway (Clark)
Lodg	E: Huggy Bear Motel
TServ	W: Citgo Truck & Auto Plaza(SCALES) (Citgo gas)
Med	W: ✚ Hospital
ATM	W: Citgo Truck & Auto Plaza (Citgo gas), Clark
Other	W: Salimoni Reservoir
73	IN 218, Van Buren, Warren, Berne
64	IN 18, Marion, Montpelier
FStop	W: Marathon(*, LP)
RVCamp	E: Camping
Med	W: ✚ Hospital
59	U.S. 35, IN 22, Gas City, Upland
Food	E: Burger King
Lodg	E: Best Western
RVCamp	E: Mar-Brook Camping (2.25 Miles), Sports Lake Campground (1.75 Miles)
	W: Post 95 Lake Campground
55	IN 26, Hartford City, Fairmount
Gas	E: Marathon(*) (Boomers Fireworks)
Other	W: Home of James Dean
(50)	**Rest Area (RR, Phones, Picnic, Vending; Southbound, Motorist Info Center)**
(50)	**Rest Area (RR, Phones, Picnic, Vending; Northbound, Motorist Info Center)**
45	U.S. 35 South, IN 28, Alexandria, Muncie, Albany
TStop	E: Standard Auto Truck Plaza(*) (Hoosier Heartland Travel Center)

EXIT	INDIANA
Food	E: Standard Auto Truck Plaza (Hoosier Heartland Travel Center), Taco Bell (Standard Auto Truck Plaza)
TServ	E: Standard Auto Truck Plaza (Hoosier Heartland Travel Center)
ATM	E: Standard Auto Truck Plaza (Hoosier Heartland Travel Center)
41	IN 332, Muncie, Frankton
Gas	E: Amoco(*, D, K)
AServ	W: Jack Smith & Sons RV Service
Med	E: ✚ Hospital
Other	E: Airport
34	IN 32, Indiana 67 North, Muncie, Anderson
TStop	W: Travel Plaza Truck Stop(*, SCALES)
FStop	E: Speedway(*, SCALES)
	W: Gas America(*, LP, K)
Gas	E: Shell(*)
	W: Q Lube(K)
Food	E: Arby's, Burger King (Shell), Hardee's (Speedway), Indiana Factory Shops, Krispy Kreme Doughnuts (Shell), Noble Roman's Pizza Express (Shell), Shell, Speedway, Taco Bell
	W: Cleo's Restaurant (Truckstop), McDonald's, Subway, Third Generation Pizza, Travel Plaza Truck Stop, Wendy's
Lodg	E: Budget Inn
	W: Super 8
AServ	W: Q Lube
TServ	W: Travel Plaza Truck Stop(SCALES)
TWash	W: Travel Plaza Truck Stop
Med	W: ✚ Hospital
ATM	E: Shell, Speedway
Parks	W: Mound State Park
Other	E: Indiana Factory Shops
26	IN 9 North, Indiana 109 South, Anderson
Gas	E: Meijer(*, K, 24)
	W: Amoco(*), Marathon(*, D, CW)
Food	E: Ryan's Steakhouse
	W: Baskin Robbins, Bob Evan's Restaurant, Burger King, Chen's Buffet, Country Store Dinner & Gifts, Cracker Barrel, Grindstone Charley's Restaurant, Lone Star Steakhouse, Old Country Buffet, Red Lobster, Ruby Tuesday, Steak 'N Shake, Subway, Waffle & Steak, Wendy's
Lodg	E: Dollar Inn
	W: Best Inns of America, Holiday Inn, Lee's Inn, Motel 6, Sterling House Ramada Inn
TServ	W: Freightliner Trucks
Med	W: ✚ Hospital
ATM	E: Meijer
	W: Payless Supermarket(24, RX)
Parks	W: Hoosier Park
Other	E: Visitor Information
	W: Applewood Raceway, Applewood's 6 Cinemas, Payless Supermarket(RX), Putt Putt Golf & Games, Target
22	IN 67 South, Indiana 9 South, Anderson, Pendleton
Med	W: ✚ Hospital

EXIT	INDIANA
Other	E: State Police
19	IN 38, Pendleton, Noblesville
Gas	E: Marathon(*, D)
Food	E: Dairy Queen, Krispy Kreme Doughnuts (Marathon), Marathon, McDonald's(PLAY), Subway
RVCamp	W: Pine Lake Camping
ATM	E: Marathon
14	IN 13, Lapel, Fortville
TStop	W: Pilot Travel Center(*, SCALES, 24)
Food	W: Pilot Travel Center, Subway (Pilot)
RVCamp	W: Glowood Campground (5 Miles)
ATM	W: Pilot Travel Center
10	IN 238, Noblesville
5	116th St, Fishers, Conner Prairie Settlement
Gas	W: Shell(*, CW), Village Pantry(*, LP, K)
Food	W: McDonald's(PLAY), Pantry Chicken (Village Pantry), Pantry Pizza (Village Pantry), Village Pantry
ATM	W: Village Pantry
Other	W: Indianapolis Boat Company Inc.
3	96th Street
Gas	E: Amoco(*), Meijer Gas(*, LP), Shell(*, LP, CW)
	W: Village Pantry(*, D, LP, K, 24)
Food	E: Applebee's, Blimpie Subs & Salads, Cracker Barrel, Freshen's Yogurt, Ho Lee Chow Chinese, Italiana's Pasta, Pizza, & Vino, McDonald's(PLAY), Muldoon's Grill, Noble Romans Pizza, Ruby Tuesday, Steak 'N Shake, Wendy's
	W: Arby's, Burger King, Schlotzsky's Deli, Taco Bell
Lodg	E: Holiday Inn, Holiday Inn Express
	W: Residence Inn
AServ	E: Auto Nation USA
	W: Indy Lube, Monroe Muffler & Brakes, Q-Lube
ATM	E: Meijer Supermarket(24), National City Bank, Shell
	W: Village Pantry
Other	E: Cord Camera, Harold Christian Bookstore, Kinko's(24), Marsh Supermarket(RX), Meijer Supermarket, Sam's Club, United Artist Theaters, VCA Crosspointe Animal Hospital, Wal-Mart(RX)
	W: Mike's Car Wash
1	82nd Street, Castleton
Gas	W: Marathon(*), Shell(*)
Food	E: Pizza Hut
	W: Cancun Mexican, Charleston's, Fairfield Inn, Krispy Kreme Doughnuts, Le Peep Restaurant, Loon Lake Lodge Food (Fairfield Inn), Marathon, Skyline Chili
Lodg	E: American Inn Motel, Dollar Inn, Omni Hotel
	W: Days Inn, Fairfield Inn, Hampton Inn
AServ	W: Car X Mufflers & Brakes, Marathon, Shell, Wax Works Air Conditioning Systems
Med	E: ✚ Community North Hospital
ATM	W: Marathon, National Bank of Indianapolis
Other	E: Avalon Animal Clinic, Dr. Aziz Pharmacy(RX), Lowe's
	W: Castleton Antiques, Coin Car Wash, Sparkling Image Car Wash
0	Junction I-465

↑INDIANA

Begin I-69

Bold red print shows RV & Bus parking available or nearby

EXIT UTAH

Begin I-70

↓UTAH

Exit **(0)** I-15 North, Fillmore, Salt Lake; I-15 South, Beaver, Las Vegas

1 Historic Cove Fort
- Other N: Historic Cove Fort

8 Ranch Exit

Exit **(13)** Truck Brake Test Area (Eastbound)

17 Fremont Indian Museum
- RVCamp S: Castle Rock Campground
- Other N: Visitor Information

23 U.S. 89 South, Panguitch, Kanab
- Gas S: Shell

26 Joseph, Monroe, UT 118
- Gas S: Shell(*)
- RVCamp S: Flying U RV Campground

32 Elsinore, Monroe, Mt. Road
- Gas S: Chevron(*, CW)
- ATM S: Chevron
- Other S: Mystic Hot Springs (5.7 Miles)

37 Richfield, Bus Loop I-70, Sevier Valley
- RVCamp S: Jr. Munchie's, KOA Campgrounds (1.5 Miles)
- Med S: ✚ Hospital

40 Business Loop 70, Richfield
- TStop S: Flying J Travel Plaza(*, LP, RV DUMP)
- Gas S: Chevron(*) (Natural Gas for Vehicles)
- Food S: Arby's, Chuckwagons Steakhouse, Subway
- Lodg S: Super 8
- AServ S: Bob's Complete Auto Truck & RV Service, Chevron (Natural Gas for Vehicles), Pennzoil Oil Change
- TServ S: Bob's Complete Auto Truck & RV Service
- RVCamp S: Bob's Complete Auto Truck & RV Service
- Med S: ✚ Sevier Valley Hospital
- Parks S: Capital Reef, Fish Lake

48 UT24, Sigurd, Aurora, Capitol Reef
- Gas S: Cedar Ridge Station(*)
- Parks S: Capital Reef National Park, Fish Lake

54 North U.S. 89, Business Loop I-70 North, Salina, Salt Lake, U.S. 50 West. Delta, Reno
- TStop N: Amoco(*, 24) (Towing)
- FStop N: Chevron(*), Texaco(*) (Towing)
- Gas N: Shell(*)
- Food N: Best Western, Burger King (Chevron), Denny's (Amoco TS), Shell, Subway
- Lodg N: Best Western, Budget Host (Amoco TS), Safari Motel (Shell), Scenic Hills Motel
- AServ N: Amoco(24) (Towing), Texaco (Towing)
- TServ N: Amoco(24) (Towing), Wheeler CAT Service

EXIT UTAH

- Center
- RVCamp N: Butch Cassidy Campground (.5 Miles), Butch Cassidy RV Camp, Salina Creek RV Camp Good Sam Park, Texaco (Towing)
- ATM N: Amoco (Towing), Chevron

61 Gooseberry Road

72 Ranch Exit

(84) Rest Area (P; Eastbound)

(84) Rest Area (P; Westbound)

89 UT72, UT10, Price, Loa, Emery
- Parks S: Capital Reef National Park

97 Ranch Exit

Exit **(102)** View Area (RR, P; Westbound)

(102) View Area, Rest Stop (RR, P; Eastbound)

105 Ranch Exit

Exit **(113)** View Area (P; Westbound)

Exit **(113)** View Area (P; Eastbound)

114 Moore

Exit **(120)** View Area (P; Westbound)

Exit **(120)** View Area (P; Eastbound)

129 Ranch Exit

Exit **(136)** Brake Test Area (Eastbound)

Exit **(139)** Runaway Truck Ramp (Eastbound)

Exit **(141)** View Area (Westbound)

Exit **(141)** View Area (Eastbound)

Exit **(142)** Runaway Truck Ramp (Eastbound)

Exit **(144)** View Area (P; Westbound)

147 UT24 West, Hanksville, Capitol Reefs, Lake Powell Goblin Valley
- Parks N: Capital Reef National Park, Lake Powell

156 U.S, 6 West, U.S. 191 North, Price, Salt Lake

158 Business Loop 70, Green River, UT 19
- FStop N: Conoco(*)
- Gas N: Chevron(*, D, 24)
- Food N: Arby's (Conoco)
- RVCamp N: KOA Green River Campground

162 Bus. Loop 70, UT19, Green River

173 Ranch Exit

(180) Rest Area (P; Eastbound)

EXIT UTAH/COLORADO

180 U.S. 191, Moab, Crescent Junction
- FStop N: Amoco(*)
- Food N: Crescent Junction Cafe
- Parks S: Canyon Land Arches National Park

(183) Rest Area (P; Westbound)

(183) Rest Area (P; Eastbound)

185 Thompson
- FStop N: Texaco(*, D)

(187) Rest Area (RR, Picnic, P; Westbound)

190 Ranch Exit

202 UT128, Cisco, Moab

212 Cisco, Bookcliffs

220 Ranch Exit

225 Westwater

226 View Area (RR, Picnic; Westbound)

↑UTAH

↓COLORADO

2 Rabbit Valley
- Parks N: Dinosaur Quarry Trail

11 Mack

(14) Weigh & Check Station (Westbound)

(14) Weigh & Check Station (Eastbound)

15 CO139 North, Loma, Rangely
- Parks N: Highline Lake State Park

(19) Colorado Welcome Center, Rest Area (RR, Phones, Picnic, RV Dump; Located at Exit 19, South Side)

19 CO 340 East, U.S. 6, Fruita, Colorado Welcome Center (RR, Phones, Picnic)
- TStop S: Conoco(*, LP)
- Gas N: Conoco(*, D)
  S: Texaco(*, D)
- Food N: Burger King, Dinosaur Pizza, Java Junction, Marge's Frozen Custard, Munchies Pizza & Deli, Park Hotel, Pizza Pro, Poncho's Via 2 Mexican, The Health Basket
  S: McDonald's(PLAY), Starvin Arvin's (Conoco), Wendy's (Texaco)
- Lodg N: Balanced Rock Motel, Park Hotel
  S: Super 8
- AServ N: Car Quest, NAPA Auto Parts
- RVCamp S: Fruita Monument RV Park(LP) (.25 Miles)
- Med N: ✚ Family Healthwest Hospital
- ATM N: Community First National Bank, Conoco

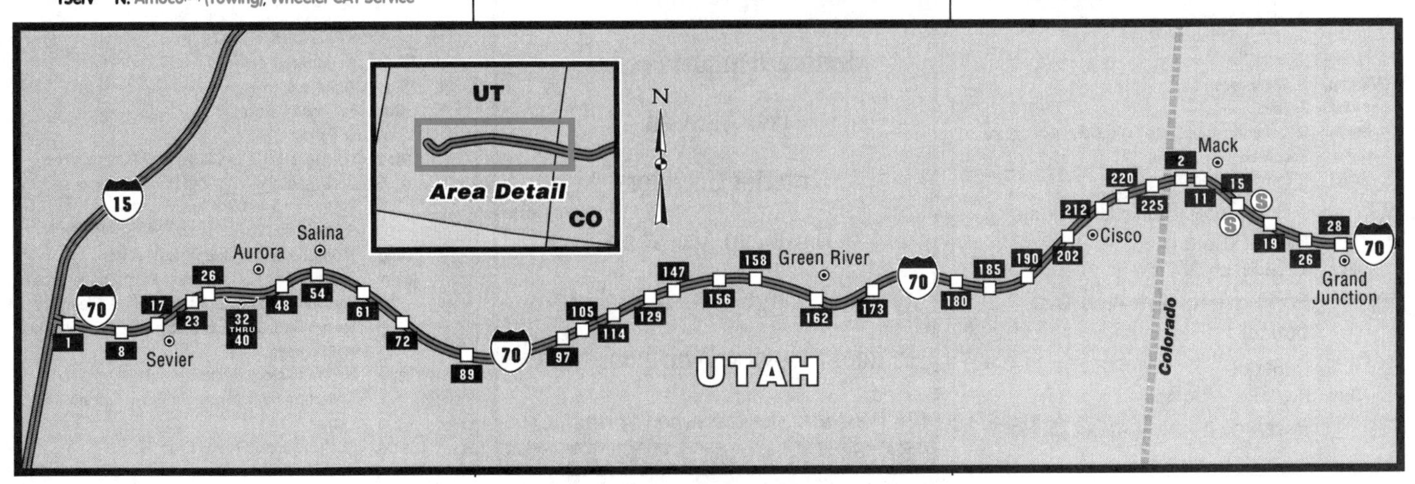

EXIT COLORADO

S: Conoco, Texaco
Parks N: Colorado National Monument, Triangle Park
Other N: Car Wash(CW), City Market Supermarket(24, RX), Go-fer Foods (Conoco), U.S. Post Office
S: CO Monument Trading Co, Colorado National Monument, Dinamation's Dinosaur Discovery Museum

26 Business Loop I-70, U.S. 6, U.S 50, Grand Junction, Delta, Montrose, 22 Road
FStop S: Conoco(*) (Pacific Pride Commercial Fueling)
Food S: Auto's (Westgate Inn)
Lodg S: Westgate Inn
TServ N: Dodd Diesel
S: Alcan Springs, Freightliner(24)
RVCamp N: Junction West RV Park (.5 Miles)
S: Mobile City RV Park (1.5 Miles)
ATM S: Conoco (Pacific Pride Commercial Fueling)
Other S: Walker State Wildlife Area

28 24 Road, Redlands Pkwy
TServ N: Kenworth(24)
RVCamp N: Camping
S: Camping

31 Horizon Dr, Grand Junction
Gas N: Amoco(*, CW), Texaco(*, D)
S: Conoco(*, D, CW), Phillips 66(*, CW)
Food N: Lenny's Grid-iron Family Restaurant, Oliver's (Grand Vista Hotel), Pantuso's Restaurant & Lounge, Starvin' Arvin's (Ramada Inn), WW Peppers, Wendy's
S: Applebee's, Burger King, Denny's, Good Pastures Restaurant (Days Inn), Shanghai Garden (Chinese), Taco Bell
Lodg N: Best Western, Comfort Inn, Grand Vista Hotel, Holiday Inn, La Quinta Inn, Ramada Inn
S: Best Western, Budget Host Inn, Country Inns of America, Days Inn (see our ad this page), Hilton, Super 8, Travelers Inn
AServ N: Amoco, Zarlingo's Automotive Service Center
Med N: ✚ Grand Junction Women's Clinic
S: ✚ Hospital
ATM S: Alpine Bank, Conoco, Phillips 66
Parks N: BLM National Forest Information
Other N: U.S. Post Office
S: Visitor Information

37 Business Loop I-70 West, To U.S. 6, Clifton, Grand Junction, Delta, To U.S. 50 South, Montrose
RVCamp S: KOA-Grand Junction (1 Mile)

42 To U.S. 6, Palisade (Eastbound)

44 I-70 Bus Loop, Palisades (Westbound, Reaccess Eastbound Only)

46 Cameo

47 Colorado River State Park, Island Acres
TStop S: Total(*, LP)
Food S: Rosie's Restaurant (Total)
Lodg S: Total
RVCamp N: Campground
ATM S: Total
Parks N: Colorado River State Park, Island Acres State Rec. Area
Other S: Fawn's Gift Shop

49 South CO65 to East CO330, Grand Mesa, Collbran
Other S: Powder Horn Ski Area

(50) Parking Area, View Area (Eastbound)

62 DeBeque
AServ N: Wild Horse Auto Repair(LP)

(75) Rest Area (Located At Exit 75, North Side)

75 Parachute, Battlement Mesa
Gas N: Sinclair(*, D, LP), Texaco(*, LP)
S: Total(*)
Food N: Hot Stuff Pizza (Texaco), Jim's & Bonnie's Outlaws, Outlaw's Restaurant(24), Sage Cafe, Smash Hit Subs (Texaco)
S: Taco Bell (Total)
Lodg N: Super 8
ATM N: Texaco
Other N: Rest Area, The Trading Post, The Valley Store(*), U.S. Post Office
S: Battlement Mesa, Parachute Fire Dept., Parachute Police Station, Valley Car Wash(CW)

81 Rulison

87 Meeker, West Rifle

(90) Rest Area (Located At Exit 90, North Side)

90 CO13 North, Rifle, Meeker, Rest Area (RR, Phones, Picnic, Vending, RV Dump)
Gas S: Conoco(*, 24), Phillips 66(*, D)
Food S: Burger King(PLAY), Hot Stuff Pizza (Conoco), McDonald's(PLAY), Phillips 66, Red River Inn(24), Shanghai Garden, Smash Hit Subs (Conoco)
Lodg S: Red River Inn, Rusty Cannon Motel
Med N: ✚ Hospital
ATM S: Conoco, Phillips 66
Other N: Visitor Information (Rest Area)

94 Garfield County Airport Road

97 Silt
Gas N: Conoco(*), Tim's Tools(D)
Food N: Gil-fer Deli (Conoco), Piccadilly Pizza, Pizza Pro, Silt Bar Cafe, Subs (Conoco), Trail Inn Pizza & Subs
Lodg N: Red River Motel
AServ N: Reed's Auto Service
RVCamp S: Viking RVPark & Camping (.75 Miles)
ATM N: Conoco
Parks N: Harvey Gap State Park
Other N: Fire Station, Tru Value Hardware (Tim's Tools)

105 New Castle, Apple Tree
FStop S: Phillips 66(*, LP) (C F N Commercial Fueling Network)
Gas N: Conoco(*, D)
Food N: Burning Mountain Grill, Subway
RVCamp S: Burning Mountain RV Park
ATM N: Alpine Bank, City Market(RX), Conoco
Other N: City Market(RX), Wash By-U Car Wash(CW)

107 River Bend Parking Area (Southbound)

109 Canyon Creek

111 South Canyon

114 West Glenwood
TStop N: Conoco(*, LP, 24)
FStop N: Amoco(*, LP, 24)
Gas N: Citgo(*), Texaco(*, D, 24)
S: Conoco(*, D, CW)
Food N: Burger King, Dairy Queen, I-70 Cafe (Conoco), Los Desperados, Marshall Dillons Steakhouse Restaurant (1st Choice Inns)
S: Hot Stuffed Pizza (Conoco), Smash Hit Subs
Lodg N: 1st Choice Inns, Budget Host Motel
AServ N: Big O Tires, Car Quest Auto Parts, Cooper Tires, Country General Tires, El Dorado Tires, Glenwood Springs Ford, Lincoln, Mercury, Henry Taylor's Auto & RV Center
RVCamp N: Ami's Acres Campground (1 Mile), Campground (1 Mile), Henry Taylor's Auto & RV Center
ATM N: Alpine Bank, Amoco, Citgo, Texaco

5 Sunburst Quality Award Winner
AAA Approved
1267
DAYS INN
1-800-790-2661 or 1-800-DAYS INN
970-245-7200
Standard, King Rooms, Suites
Non-Smoking/Special Needs Rooms
Wheelchair Accessible
Children Under 12 Free
AAA & CAA Discounts
Special Rates:
Seniors, Bus Tours, Business Travelers
Electronic Key System
Interior Corridors
Pool
Free Color TV: HBO, ESPN, CNN
Free Coffee/USA Today/Local Calls
Good Pastures Restaurant In Building
733 Horizon Dr., GRAND JUNCTION
COLORADO • I-70 • EXIT 31

1664
Glenwood Springs
Ramada Inn®
& Suites
970-945-2500 • 800-332-1472
Restaurant/Lounge on Premises
Indoor Pool/Hot Tub
Exercise Room
Meeting/Banquet Facilities
Pets Allowed
Interior Corridors
Handicap Accessible
Truck/Large Vehicle Parking
In Room Movies, Whirlpool, Suites
124 West 6th St. • Glenwood Springs, CO
COLORADO • I-70 • EXIT 116

EXIT COLORADO

S: Conoco
Parks N: **Sister Lucy Downey Park**
Other N: Glenwood Springs Emergency Services, **Glenwood Springs Mall, K-Mart (Mall)**, US Post Office

(114) **Rest Area (Eastbound)**

116 CO 82 East, Glenwood Springs, Aspen
Gas N: Amoco, Conoco(*), Texaco(*, D)
Food N: A & W Drive-Thru, Dairy Kreme, Daylight Donuts, Denny's, KFC, Mancinelli's Pizza & Subs, Rosi's Bavarian Restaurant (Glenwood Motor Inn), Smokin' Willies Mountain Smoked BBQ, Village Inn
Lodg N: Best Western, Glenwood Motor Inn, Hampton Inn, Holiday Inn Express, Hot Springs, Hotel Colorado, **Ramada Inn (see our ad opposite page)**, Silver Spruce Motel, Starlight Lodge
AServ N: Amoco, Audi, Big Horn Motors Toyota, Elk Mountain Motors Nissan, Volkswagon, The Pit Stop(CW), Toyota Big Horn Motors
Med N: **Hospital**
ATM N: Conoco
Other N: **Hot Springs Pool**, Snow Mass Ski Area, **Sunlight Mountain**

(119) **Rest Area (RR, Phones, Picnic; Located At Exit 119, South Side)**

119 **Rest Area (RR, Phones, Picnic)**
RVCamp S: **Rock Gardens Campground**

121 Grizzly Creek To Hanging Lake

(121) **Rest Area (RR, Phones, Picnic; Located At Exit 121, South Side)**

123 Shoshone (Reaccess Westbound Only)

125 Hanging Lake (Eastbound, Difficult Reaccess)

129 **Bair Ranch, Rest Area (RR, HF, Phones, Picnic)**

(129) **Rest Area (RR, Phones, Picnic; Located At Exit 129, South Side)**

133 Dotsero

140 Gypsum
Gas S: Texaco(*, D)
Food S: Arturo's Restaurant (Mexican, American), La Tienda Mexicana
AServ S: **SS Auto & Truck Repair**
TServ S: **SS Auto & Truck Repair**
Other S: Touch Free Car Wash(CW), WSC Supply(LP)

(147) **Rest Area (Located At Exit 147, South Side)**

147 Eagle
FStop S: **Amoco**(*, D, CW)

EXIT COLORADO

Gas N: Texaco(*, D, CW)
S: Conoco(*, LP)
Food N: Bagelopolis, Burger King, Taco Bell (Texaco), Tienda Arcoiris
S: Conoco, **Jackie's Olde West**, Sage Brush Cafe & Bar, Subway (Amoco)
Lodg N: AmericInn, Holiday Inn Express
S: Best Western, Suburban Lodge
AServ S: American Eagle Tire & Automotive Center
RVCamp S: **Eagle RV Park Upon Vail**
ATM N: **City Market**(RX)
S: Alpine Bank
Other N: **Carniceria Aquario Mercado Mexicano, City Market**(RX), **Information Center**
S: **Castle Peek Veterinary Service**, Eagle Laundry, Eagle River Anglers, **Historical Museum**, Summit Lumber Co., Tru Value Hardware, Truck Parking, **U.S. Post Office**

157 CO 131 North, Wolcott, Steamboat Springs

(160) **Scenic Overlook-Wilmore Lake (Westbound)**

(163) **Rest Area (Located At Exit 163, South Side)**

163 Edwards
FStop S: **Texaco**(*, CW)
Food S: **Jerry's Deli (Texaco)**, Sacred Grounds Coffee House
AServ S: **Texaco**
Other S: **North Star Center (Shopping)**, The Pet Spot Grooming & Supplies

167 Avon, Beaver Creek, Arrowhead (Many Services More Than Half A Mile From The Exit)
Gas N: Coastal(*, 24)
Food N: Pizza Hut
S: Andre's Bistro & Restaurant (Christie Lodge), Burger King, Chicago Pizza, CoHo Grill, Denny's, Jitters N' Shakes, Lodge at Avon Center(*), Masato's Japanese, Pazzo's Pizzeria, Seasons, Starbucks Coffee, Subway (Christie Lodge), Subway
Lodg S: Christie Lodge, Comfort Inn, Lodge at Avon Center, Seasons, The Stratford on Avon
AServ N: Goodyear Golden Eagle Service Center
Med S: **Colorado Mountain Medical**
ATM N: Coastal
S: 1st Bank, Alpine Bank, Norwest Bank, **Wal-Mart**(RX), WestStar Bank Center
Other S: **Annex Shopping Center, Beaver Creek Ski Area**, Green's Machines Coin-Op Laundry, **North Mall & South Mall**, Shopping Mall (The Lodge at Avon), **U.S. Post Office, Wal-Mart**(RX)

171 West U.S. 6, U.S. 24 East, Minturn,

EXIT COLORADO

Leadville
Parks N: **National Forest**
Other N: **Cooper Ski Area**

173 Vail, West Entrance
Gas N: Phillips 66(*, CW), Texaco(*, D)
S: Conoco(*, D, LP)
Food N: Dairy Queen, Jackalope Cafe & Cantina, McDonald's, Mickey's Mountain Pizza, Poppy Seeds Bakery, Subway, Taco Bell, The Dancing Bear (West Vail Lodge), Wendy's
Lodg N: West Vail Lodge
S: Marriot Streamside at Vail
AServ N: Texaco
S: Conoco
ATM N: Texaco
Other N: 7-11 Convenience Store, **Safeway Grocery**
S: Recreation Path

176 Vail, Lions Head
Gas S: Amoco(*)
Food S: Holiday Inn, Vail Gateway Plaza
Lodg S: Evergreen Lodge, Holiday Inn, Lodge at Vail, Sonnen Alp Resort, The Chateau at Vail, Vail Village Inn
AServ S: Amoco
Med S: **Hospital**
ATM S: 1st Bank, Amoco, Vail Gateway Plaza, WestStar Bank
Other S: **Colorado Ski Museum, Craig's Market**, Town of Vail Municipal Center, Vail Gateway Plaza

180 Vail, East Entrance

Exit **(183)** Runaway Truck Ramp (Westbound)

Exit **(186)** Runaway Truck Ramp (Westbound)

(189) **Truck Parking, Truck Check Station (Westbound)**

(190) **Rest Area (Westbound)**

(190) **Rest Area (Eastbound)**

195 CO 91 South, Copper Mountain, Leadville
Gas S: Conoco(*, D)
Lodg S: Copper Mountain Ski Resort
ATM S: Conoco

(197) **Scenic Area**

198 Officers Gulch

201 Frisco, Main Street, Breckenridge
Food S: Blue Spruce Inn, El Rio Cantina & Grill
Lodg S: Bighorn, Blue Spruce Inn, Cedar Lodge, Creekside Inn, Woodbridge Inn
Other S: Frisco Ski Area (1 Mile), **Tourist Info., US Post Office**, Vail Pass 10 Mile Canyon Natl. Rec. Trail

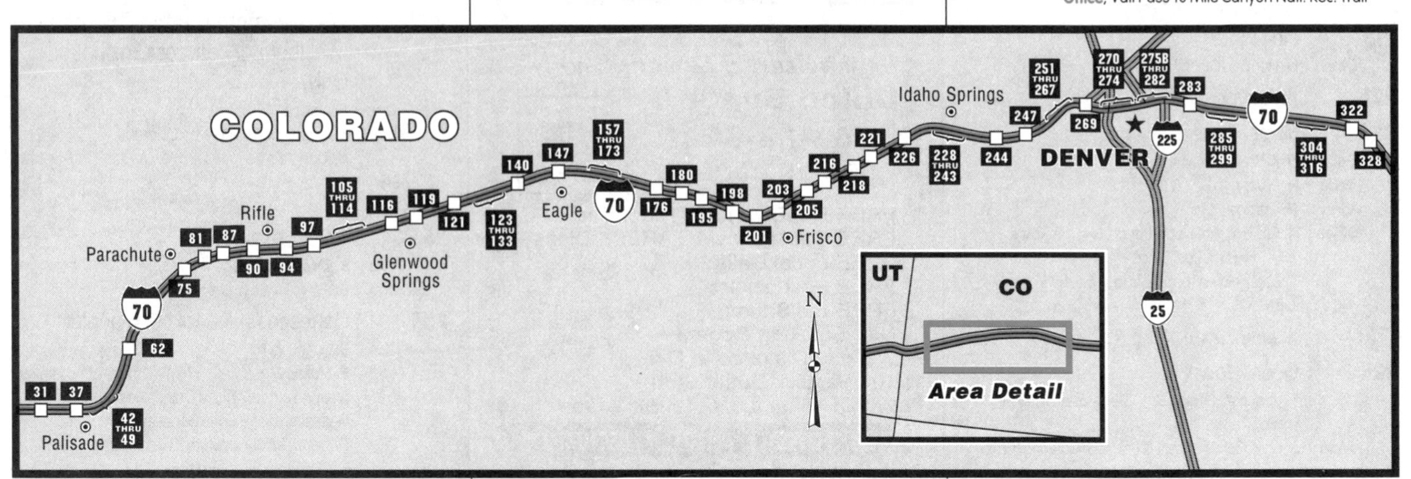

Bold red print shows RV & Bus parking available or nearby

EXIT COLORADO

Head

203 CO 9 South, Frisco, Breckenridge
- **Gas** **S:** Diamond Shamrock[*, D], Texaco[*]
- **Food** **S:** A & W Drive-In, China Szechuan, Claimjumper Restaurant, Country Kitchen, KFC, Pizza Hut, Subway
- **Lodg** **S:** Alpine Inn, Best Western, Holiday Inn, Microtel Inn, Summit Inn, Towers At Lakepoint
- **AServ** **S:** Big O Tires, NAPA Auto Parts, Texaco
- **TServ** **S:** Texaco
- **RVCamp** **S:** Tiger Run RV Resort
- **Med** **S:** + Emergency Medical Care
- **ATM** **S:** Community First National Bank, Diamond Shamrock, Norwest Banks, Safeway Grocery[RX], Wal-Mart[RX]
- **Other** **S:** Car Wash[CW], Custom Eyes, Dillon Dam & Recreation Center, Safeway Grocery[RX], Ski Shop, Tourist Info., Wal-Mart[RX]

(203) Scenic Overlook - Lake Dillon (Westbound)

205 U.S. 6 East, CO 9 North, Silverthorne, Dillon
- **Gas** **N:** Bradley[*, D], Citgo[*], Conoco[*], Food Mart[*, D], Texaco[*]
  S: Coastal[*], Total[*]
- **Food** **N:** Denny's, Domino's Pizza, Good Times Burgers (Texaco), Mint Steaks & Seafood, Old Chicago (Hampton Inn), Quizno's Subs, Village Inn, Wendy's
  S: Arby's, Blue Moon Baking Co, Burger King, Cactus Cantina, Dairy Queen, Dragon Chinese Restaurant, McDonald's, Nick-N-Willy's Pizza, Pizza Hut, Subway, Sunshine Cafe, Virgin Islands Lounge
- **Lodg** **N:** Days Inn (see our ad this page), First Interstate Inn, Hampton Inn, Luxury Inn & Suites
  S: Super 8 (see our ad this page)
- **AServ** **N:** Auto Body
  S: Golden Eagle Service Center
- **ATM** **N:** Citgo, Community First National Bank, Texaco
  S: 1st Bank, City Market Supermarket[RX], Total
- **Other** **N:** Blue Valley Ski Rentals, Car Wash[CW], Factory Outlets, Prime Outlets at Silverthorne
  S: Best-Wash Laundromat, City Market Supermarket[RX], Columbine Outfitters, Mail Boxes Etc, Mountain Sports Outlet, Silverthorne Factory Outlet, The Yankee Doodler Book Shop, Virgin Island Ski Rental, Wilderness Sports

Exit **(209)** Runaway Truck Ramp

Exit **(212)** Runaway Truck Ramp (Westbound)

(214) Rest Area (Westbound)

(214) Rest Area (Eastbound)

216 U.S. 6 West, Loveland Pass
- **Other** **S:** Loveland Valley Ski Area

218 No Name
- **Other** **N:** Herman Gulch Trail Head

221 Bakerville

226 Silver Plume
- **Food** **N:** KP Cafe
- **Lodg** **N:** Bruery Inn Bed & Breakfast
- **AServ** **N:** Garage
- **Other** **N:** City Hall, Fire Department, George Rowe Museum, U.S. Post Office
  S: Georgetown Loop Railroad, Silver Plume Historic Site

(226) Scenic Overlook (Eastbound)

228 Georgetown
- **Gas** **S:** Conoco[*], Phillips 66[*] (Gerogetown Market), Total[*]
- **Food** **S:** Chris Cakes Bakery & Pancake Catering, Crazy Horse Restaurant, Dairy King, Georgetown Station Cafe, Pizza Crossing, Swiss Inn, Taco Bell Express (Total)
- **Lodg** **S:** Super 8, Swiss Inn
- **AServ** **S:** Phillips 66 (Gerogetown Market)
- **Other** **S:** Fire Station, Georgetown Market, Historic Georgetown, Visitor Information

232 U.S. 40 West, Empire, Granby
- **Parks** **N:** Rocky Mountain National Park
- **Other** **N:** Berthoud Pass Ski Area, Silver Creek Ski Area, Winter Park Ski Area

233 Lawson (Eastbound)

(234) Weigh Station, Check Station (Located at Exit 234 On South Side)

234 Downieville, Dumont, Lawson
- **FStop** **N:** Conoco[*] (Restaurant)
- **Food** **N:** Burger King[PLAY], Subway (Conoco)
- **TServ** **N:** Allied West, Truck Repair & Towing[LP]
- **Other** **N:** Breeze Ski Rentals, Mad Adventures Rafting, Telemark Ski Rental

235 Dumont (Westbound)
- **Other** **N:** Dumont Fire Station, U.S. Post Office

238 Fall River Rd, St. Mary's Glacier
- **Parks** **N:** St. Mary's Glacier (12 Miles)

239 Business Loop 70 East, Idaho Springs, Stanley Rd. (Reaccess Westbound Only)
- **Food** **N:** The Sandwich Mine
- **Lodg** **N:** Blair Motel
- **AServ** **N:** Silver City Automotive & Towing[24]
- **RVCamp** **S:** Camping
- **Other** **N:** Circle of Animals Veterinary Hospital

240 CO 103, Mount Evans

DAYS INN Silverthorne, Colorado
Summit County's
Best Rates/Best Location
FREE...Continental Breakfast
Encore Movie Channel • Local Calls
Hot Tub & Sauna • Interior Corridors
Kitchenettes • Suites • Fireplaces
Wet Bars • Refrigerators
Pets Welcome • Large Vehicle Parking
970-468-8661 • 800-DAYS INN 1399
COLORADO • I-70 • EXIT 205

"In the Heart of Summit County"
Dillon Super 8
970-468-8888
800-800-8000
SUPER 8 MOTEL
FREE Hot Beverage/Toast Bar
FREE Cable TV w/STARZ! & Disney
FREE Local Calls
FREE Ski Lockers
FREE Ski Shuttle
Non-Smoking Rooms
Walking Distance to Over
100 Factory Outlet Stores
Within 15 minutes of 5 Ski Areas
10% Off with this ad.
1117
COLORADO • I-70 • EXIT 205

- **Gas** **N:** Phillips 66[D], Texaco[*, D]
- **Food** **N:** Donnelly's Bakery Shop, Espresso Bar, Gold Mine Restaurant (Steak), Java Mountain Roasters, Main Street Restaurant, Mountain Pies by Beau-Je's (Colorado Style Pizza), Picci's Bakery & Pizza, Pittsburgh Mine Company (Mexican/American), Skippers Ice Cream Parlor, The Bagelry, The Buffalo Restaurant & Bar (BBQ, Burgers, Pizza), The Lodge, WestWinds Lounge & Restaurant
- **Lodg** **N:** Miner's Pick Bed & Breakfast, The Lodge Bed & Breakfast
- **AServ** **N:** A & B Garage, A-OK Auto Clinic, Chuck's Auto Service, Jim Hudson Chevrolet, Olds, & Geo, Phillips 66
- **RVCamp** **N:** Indian Springs Resort (.5 Miles)
  S: Cottonwood RV Campground & Mobile Home Park
- **Med** **S:** + Chicago Creek Family Clinic Ugent Care
- **ATM** **N:** First State Bank
- **Parks** **S:** Arapaho National Forest
- **Other** **N:** Antiques, Clear Creek Veterinarian Clinic, Coin Laundromat, Espresso Bar, Gingerbread Bookstore, Idaho Springs City Hall, K & R Hardware, Outback Outfitters, U.S. Post Office
  S: Clear Creek Ranger Station, Fire Station, Mount Evans (28 Miles), Visitor Information

241A Bus. Loop 70 West, Idaho Springs
- **Gas** **N:** Conoco[*], Phillips 66[*], Texaco[*, D, LP, 24] (Towing)
- **Food** **N:** 6 & 40 Restaurant (6 & 40 Motel), A & W Drive-In, Flip Side Diner, King's Derby Restaurant (JC Suites), Marion's of the Rockies, Sunrise Donuts, Wildfire Restaurant (Italian, Mexican, American)
- **Lodg** **N:** 6 & 40 Motel, JC Suites, National 9 Inn, Peoriana Motel
- **AServ** **N:** Allied Towing[24], Phillips 66, Texaco[24] (Towing)
- **TServ** **N:** Allied Towing
- **Other** **N:** Arena Sports Inc., Car Wash[CW], Colorado State Patrol, Ferrell Gas[LP], Maison De Ski

241B Idaho Springs, CR 314 (Westbound)

243 Hidden Valley

244 U.S. 6, To CO119, Golden, Blackhawk, Central City (Left Exit Eastbound, Reaccess Westbound Only)
- **Food** **N:** Kermitts Food & Spirits

247 Beaver Brook, Floyd Hill (Eastbound, Reaccess Westbound Only)
- **Food** **S:** Floyd Hill Restaurant & Coffee Outlet Store

248 Beaver Brook, Floyd Hill (Westbound, Reaccess Eastbound Only)
- **Other** **S:** Animal Hospital

251 El Rancho, Evergreen (Reaccess Westbound Only, Same as Westbound Exit 252)

252 CO 74, Evergreen Pkwy, El Rancho (Westbound, Reaccess Eastbound Only)
- **Gas** **S:** Amoco[*]
- **Food** **S:** Burger King, El Rancho Colorado, McDonald's[PLAY]
- **AServ** **S:** Wal-Mart[RX]
- **Other** **S:** Alpine Rescue Team, Wal-Mart[RX]

253 Chief Hosa
- **Lodg** **S:** Chief Hosa Lodge[*]
- **RVCamp** **S:** Chief Hosa Campground

254 Genesee Park, Lookout Mountain
- **Gas** **S:** Conoco[*, LP]
- **Food** **S:** Buffalo Moon Coffee & Mercantile, Chart House Steaks, Seafood, Diced Onions Restaurant, Genesee Towne Cafe, Genesee Towne Cafe, Genesee's Country Store, Guido's Pizza

Bold red print shows RV & Bus parking available or nearby

EXIT COLORADO

Parks S: Genesee Park
Other N: Boettcher Mansion, Buffalo Bill's Grave
S: Genesee Veterinary Hospital, Genesee's Country Store, U.S. Post Office

256 Lookout Mtn, Mother Cabrini Shrine Rd

Exit **(256)** Runaway Truck Ramp (Eastbound)

259 Business Loop 70, U.S 40, Golden, Morrison, CO 26 East, Red Rock Parks
FStop N: Conoco(*)
Food N: Maggio's Italian Eatery
RVCamp N: Dakota Ridge RV Park (1 Mile)
Parks S: Matthew Winters Park, Red Rocks
Other S: Point of Geological Interest

260 CO 470, Colorado Springs (Limited Access Hwy)

261 U.S. 6 East, W 6th Ave (Eastbound, Difficult Reaccess, Limited Access Hwy)

262 Business Loop I-70, U.S. 40, To U.S. 6, W. Colfax Ave
Gas N: Sinclair(*, D, 24)
S: Conoco
Food N: Q Up BBQ
S: Daybreak Restaurant (Days Inn)
Lodg S: DAYS INN Days Inn, Holiday Inn, Mountain View Inn, Pleasant Valley Motel
AServ N: AC Transmission, Lawson's Paint Body Car Service, Lawson's Towing, Mobil Mechanic Subaru, Planet Honda
S: Conoco, Stevinson Chevrolet, Stevinson Toyota, Lexus
RVCamp N: Dakota Ridge RV Park (2 Miles)
S: Golden Terrace Villages & RV Resort (1.5 Miles), Stevinson RV Sales
Other N: Alpenglow Mountain Sport Inc., Fire Station, Golden Wings Hang Gliding, U-Haul(LP)

263 Denver West Blvd
Food N: American Grill (Marriott), Goldfields (Marriott), Pizza Hut (Marriott)
S: Alfalfa's Market, Einstein Bros Bagels, Healthy Habits, Macaroni Grill, On The Border Mexican, Outback Steakhouse, Tokyo Joe's Healthy Fast Japanese, Yanni's Sports Grill, Zuka Juice
Lodg N: Marriott
S: Denver West Marriott, Holiday Inn
ATM S: Key Bank
Other S: Barnes & Noble, Denver West Village (Mall), United Artist Theaters, Visto Optical

264 Youngfield St, W 32nd Ave
Gas S: Amoco(*, LP, CW), Conoco(*, CW), Diamond Shamrock(*)
Food N: Country Cafe (La Quinta Inn), La Quinta Inn
S: Chili's, Chipotle Mexican Grill, Dairy Queen, Juice Stop, Las Carretas Mexican Restaurant, McDonald's, Oriental Kitchen, Starbucks Coffee, Subway, Taco Bell, Taj Mahale Cuisine of India
Lodg N: La Quinta Inn
AServ S: Amoco, Applewood Auto Body Inc
RVCamp S: Camping World (see our ad this page)
ATM S: Norwest Banks
Other S: Belmont Animal Clinic, King Soopers Grocery(RX), Petsmart, Vision Center (Wal-Mart), Wal-Mart(RX), WalGreen's(RX), Wally's Quality Meats

265 CO 58 West, Golden, Central City (Limited Access Hwy)

266 CO 72, Ward Road, W 44th Ave
TStop S: T/A TravelCenters of America(*, LP, SCALES)
Gas N: Texaco(*, D, CW)
S: Total(*)
Food S: Palancar Reef, Quality Inn
Lodg S: Quality Inn
AServ N: Car Care Center
S: JW Brewer Tire, L & R Ford Specialists
TServ S: T/A TravelCenters of America(SCALES)
RVCamp S: Camping World, RV America Sales & Service, RV Repair Annex Prospect RV Park
ATM S: T/A TravelCenters of America, Total
Other S: Abner's Market, Heinies Market

267 CO 391, Kipling St
Gas N: Amoco(*, CW), Standard(*, CW), Texaco(*, D)
S: Conoco(*, LP, CW), Phillips 66(*, CW)
Food N: Burger King, Cactus Cafe, Carl Jr's Hamburgers (Texaco), Denny's, Furr's Family Dining, Lil' Nick's Mex-Italia, Luke's (Steak), Pigskins Sports Saloon, Subway
S: Holiday Inn Express, Taco Bell, Village Inn, Winchells Donuts
Lodg N: American Motel, Motel 6
S: 17 Inn, Holiday Inn Express, Motel 6, Super 8
AServ N: High Country Auto Body, M & M Glass, Walker Transmissions
RVCamp S: Ketelsen Campers RV Service, Morgan RV's
Med N: + Red Rocks Health Campus
S: + Hospital, + Primera Healthcare
ATM N: 7-11 Convenience Store, Amoco, Foothills Bank
S: Phillips 66
Other N: 7-11 Convenience Store, Kipling Car Wash, Lasting Impressions Book Store, Sierra Vista Lanes
S: Larson's Ski & Sport

269A CO 121, Wadsworth Blvd

CAMPING WORLD®
Exit 264
4100 Youngfield St. • Wheat Ridge, CO
1-800-222-6795
1421

Food N: Alamos Verdes Mexican, Applebee's, Bennett's BBQ & Steaks, Bennigan's, Burger King, Chinese Restaurant, Country Buffet, Fazoli's Italian Food, IHOP, Lone Star Steakhouse, McDonald's(PLAY), Namiko's Oriental, New York Burrito Gourmet Wrap, Red Robin Burger & Spirit Emporium, Schlotzsky's Deli, Subway, Taco Bell, Wok King Chinese
S: New Canton Chinese
AServ N: A & T Muffler, Auto FX, Econo Lube & Tune, Parts America & Brakes Plus
S: Discount Tire Company, Grease Monkey, Pep Boys Auto Center
Med N: + Hospital
ATM N: First National Bank, Norwest Banks
S: 1st Bank
Parks S: Johnson Park
Other N: Home Depot, Mail Boxes Etc., Office Depot, Sam's Club, Vista Optical, Walden Books

269B Junction I-76, I-70 East, Denver, Fort Morgan

270 CO 95, Harlan St, Sheridan Blvd.
Gas N: Texaco(*, D, CW)
Food S: El Paraiso Mexican
AServ N: Texaco
S: Montgomery Ward Auto Center, Seyfer Automotive
ATM S: Bank One, Union Bank & Trust Lakeside
Other S: Lakeside Center Mall

271A **(270)** CO 95, Sheridan Blvd (Westbound)

271B Lowell Blvd, Tennyson (Reaccess Eastbound Only, Difficult Reaccess)
Gas N: Phillips 66
AServ N: Phillips 66
Other N: Boater's Choice Marine Accessories, Busy B Coin Laundry

272 US 287, Federal Blvd
FStop N: Amoco(*, CW)
Gas N: Bradley(*), Sinclair(*)
S: Conoco(*, LP, CW)
Food N: 49 Cent Hamburger Stand, Burger King, Good Times Drive Thru Burgers, Luethy's Kitchen, McCoy's Family Restaurant(24), McDonald's(PLAY), Pizza Hut, Subway, Village Inn, Wendy's, Wienerschnitzel, Winchells Donuts
S: Los Palmeras II Mexican Restaurant
Lodg N: Motel 6
S: La Denver Inn
AServ N: Amoco, De Luna's Tire Service, Del Gado Automotive Service, Goodyear Tire & Auto, Penske Auto Center, The Tire Store
RVCamp N: Camping
ATM N: MegaBank
Other N: Hi-Performance Car Wash(CW), K-Mart(RX)

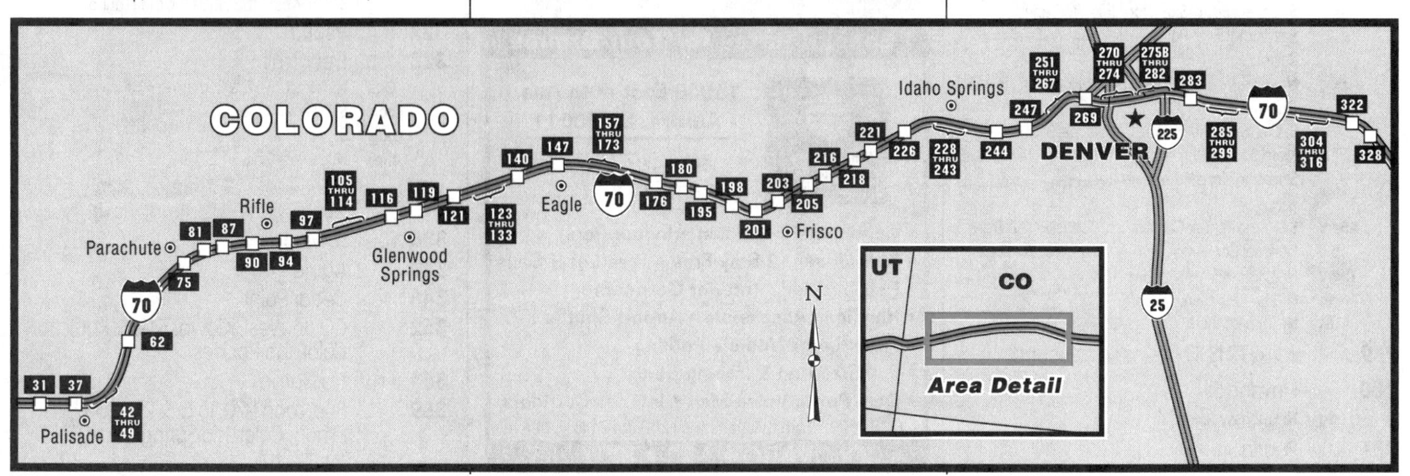

Bold red print shows RV & Bus parking available or nearby

EXIT	COLORADO
273	Pecos St
Gas	**S:** Circle K[*]
Food	**S:** Fat Boy's Sub & Pizza, Pompinio's Restaurant
AServ	**N:** Westside Auto Repair
	S: Denver Engine & Transmission Exchange, Pecos Auto Center
ATM	**N:** Safeway Grocery[RX]
	S: Circle K
Other	**N:** Butts Rental[LP], Family Dollar Store, Safeway Grocery[RX], Tru Value Hardware
	S: U.S. Post Office
274	Junction I-25, Fort Collins, Colorado Springs
275A	Washington St (Westbound)
275B	CO265, Brighton Blvd, Coliseum (Difficult Reaccess)
Gas	**N:** Citgo[*] (7-11 Convenience Store)
Food	**N:** Cindy Lynn Cafe
AServ	**N:** Auto & Truck Parts Warehouse
ATM	**N:** Citgo
Other	**N:** Public Library
	S: Corres Field
275C	York St, Josephine St
276A	Steele St., Vasquez Blvd
TStop	**N:** Pilot Travel Center[*, K, SCALES]
Gas	**S:** Citgo[*]
Food	**N:** Dairy Queen, Wendy's (Pilot)
	S: Burger King
Lodg	**N:** Western Motor Inn
AServ	**S:** NAPA Auto Parts
TServ	**N:** Colorado Mack, Ford Trucks, Fruehauf, Goodyear Tire & Auto, Peterbilt Dealer, Volvo Trucks of Colorado
TWash	**N:** Pilot Travel Center
ATM	**N:** Pilot Travel Center
	S: Citgo
Other	**N:** Vasquez Scale[SCALES]
276B	CO2, to US - 6E, US 85N Colorado Blvd
Gas	**S:** Diamond Shamrock[*], The Lowest
Food	**N:** El Toro Mexican, Silver Bullet Lounge & Restaurant
AServ	**N:** J.W. Brewer Tire Company
ATM	**N:** The Bank of Cherry Creek
	S: US Bank
277	Dahlia St., Holly St., Monaco St. (Reaccess Eastbound Only)
278	CO35, Quebec St
TStop	**N:** Sapp Brothers[*, CW, SCALES]
FStop	**N:** Goodyear Tire & Auto
Gas	**S:** Amoco
Food	**N:** Burger King (Sapp Brothers), Denny's, Great American Restaurant (Sapp Brothers), Red Apple Restaurant (Quality Inn)
	S: Capers Bistro (Stapleton Hotel), Morgan's Restaurant (Four Points Motel), Summerfield's Restaurant
Lodg	**N:** Economy Inn (Sapp Bros TS), Hampton Inn, Quality Inn
	S: Courtyard by Marriott, Doubletree, Four Points Motel, Holiday Inn, Metro Inn, Renaissance Hotel, Stapleton Plaza Hotel, Comfort Inn (see our ad this page)
AServ	**S:** Alamo Rent-A-Car, Amoco, Budget Rent A Truck, National Car Rental, Rent-A-Vette, Wyatt Towing
TServ	**N:** Goodyear Tire & Auto
TWash	**N:** Sapp Brothers
ATM	**N:** Sapp Brothers
279	Jct I-270 N, Ft Collins (Westbound)
280	Havana St
Lodg	**N:** Embassy Suites
281	Peoria St
Gas	**N:** Conoco[*, D, CW]
	S: Amoco[*, CW], Total[*, D]
Food	**N:** Best Western, Blimpie's Subs, McDonald's[PLAY]
	S: Bennett's Bar-B-Que Pit, Church's Chicken, Denny's, Ho Ho Chinese Food, IHOP, Old Santa Fe Mexican, Subway, Taco Bell, The Airport Broker Restaurant, Waffle House, Wendy's
Lodg	**N:** Best Western, Drury Inn, Village Inn
	S: La Quinta Inn, Motel 6, Rodeway Inn, Traveler's Inn
AServ	**S:** Goodyear Tire & Auto
ATM	**N:** Citywide Bank, US Bank
Other	**S:** North-East Animal Hospital
282	Junction I-225S, Colorado Springs, Aurora
283	Chambers Road
Gas	**S:** Phillips 66[D], Total[*]
Food	**N:** Budget Motel
	S: Burger King, Taco Bell (Total)
Lodg	**N:** Budget Motel, Holiday Inn, Sleep Inn (see our ad this page), Amerisuites (see our ad this page)
AServ	**S:** B A Baldwin Automotive, NAPA, Phillips 66
RVCamp	**S:** B A Baldwin Automotive, NAPA
285	Airport Blvd.
TStop	**S:** Flying J Travel Plaza[*, LP, SCALES]
Food	**S:** Country Market (Flying J), Magic Dragon

1312

AMERISUITES
AMERICA'S AFFORDABLE ALL-SUITE HOTEL
Colorado • Exit 284 • 303-371-0700

1081

Comfort Inn
I-70 Central
Exit 278 • Denver, CO
303-393-7666
- Free Continental Breakfast
- Free Local Calls, Airport Shuttle
- Free USA Today & Parking
- Guest Laundry
- Restaurant Adjacent
- Seasonal Heated Pool
- Special Rates for Tour Groups

1/2 mile south on Quebec turn right on 36th Ave.
COLORADO • I-70 • EXIT 278

Special Rates for Tour Groups
1784

Sleep Inn
15900 East 40th Ave.
Aurora, Co 80011
303-373-1616
800-753-3746
- Continental Breakfast • Indoor Pool
- Kids Under 12 Stay Free • Free Local Calls
- Pets allowed • Interior Corridors
- Handicap Accessible • Airport Shuttle
- Truck/Large Vehicle Parking
- Full Size Iron & Ironing Board
- Data Ports, Voice Mail • Interior Corridors

I-70, Exit 203 Turn Lt Chambers Rd, Turn Rt to 40th Ave.
COLORADO • I-70 • EXIT 283

EXIT	COLORADO
	Chinese (Flying J), Pepperoni's (Flying J's)
Lodg	**S:** Comfort Inn, Crystal Inn
286	CO 32, Tower Road
288	I-70 Bus. Loop, U.S. 40, U.S. 287, Colfax Ave (Left Exit Westbound)
289	Gun Club Rd
292	CO 36, Air Park Rd
FStop	**S:** Conoco[*]
Food	**S:** 99th Aero Squadron BBQ
295	Bus Loop I-70 North, Watkins
TStop	**N:** Tomahawk Auto/Truck Plaza[*, LP] (Chapel)
FStop	**N:** Sinclair[*]
Food	**N:** Interstate Truckstop Restaurant, Lu Lu's Restaurant (Tomahawk), Tomahawk Auto/Truck Plaza (Chapel)
Lodg	**N:** Country Manor Motel
TServ	**N:** Tomahawk Auto/Truck Plaza (Chapel)
TWash	**N:** Tomahawk Auto/Truck Plaza (Chapel)
Other	**N:** US Post Office (Tomahawk), US Post Office
299	Manila Rd
FStop	**S:** Total[*]
Food	**S:** Taco Bell (Total)
ATM	**S:** Total
304	CO 79 North, Bennett
TStop	**N:** Hank's Truck Stop[*]
TServ	**N:** Hank's Truck Stop
305	**Kiowa, Rest Area (RR, Phones, Picnic; Eastbound, Reaccess Eastbound Only)**
(306)	**Rest Area (Westbound, Reaccess Westbound Only)**
310	Strausburg
Gas	**N:** Amoco[*], No Name, Tri-Valley Gas[LP]
Food	**N:** Cafe, Hank's Lounge, Hometown Pizza, The Pizza Shop
Lodg	**N:** Strausburg Inn
AServ	**N:** Harv's Diesel & Auto Repair, John's Repair Oil & Lube, NAPA Auto Parts, Stanley Tradition Auto Service
TServ	**N:** Harv's Diesel & Auto Repair
RVCamp	**N:** KAO Campground[RV DUMP] (.25 Miles)
ATM	**N:** First National Bank
Other	**N:** Corner Market, Ferrell Gas[LP], Laundromat, US Post Office
316	U.S 36, Byers
Gas	**N:** Sinclair[*]
	S: Amoco[*, D, CW]
Food	**S:** Byer's Pizza Place, Country Burger, Golden Spike Inn
Lodg	**N:** Longhorn Motel
	S: Lazy 8 Motel
AServ	**S:** Amoco
TServ	**N:** Cummins Diesel
ATM	**N:** First National Bank
Other	**N:** Byers General Store[RX]
	S: Car Wash, The Wash Tub Coin Laundry
322	Peoria
328	Deer Trail
Gas	**N:** Texaco[*, D], The Corner[*, D]
Food	**S:** Deertrail Cafe
Lodg	**S:** Motel
Other	**N:** US Post Office
(332)	**Rest Area (RR, Phones, Picnic, Vending; Westbound)**
336	Lowland
340	Agate
348	Cedar Point
352	CO 86 West, Kiowa, Scenic Route to Colorado Rockies
354	No Name
359	Bus. Loop I-70, to U.S. 24, CO 71, Limon, Colorado Springs, East 40, South 287

Bold red print shows RV & Bus parking available or nearby

EXIT	COLORADO
TStop	S: Texaco(*, SCALES)
FStop	S: Total(*, D)
Gas	S: Texaco(*)
Food	S: Arby's, Fireside Restaurant, McDonald's, Subway (Texaco)
Lodg	S: Best Western, Comfort Inn, Econolodge, Holiday Inn Express, Super 8
TServ	S: Texaco(SCALES)
TWash	S: Texaco
ATM	S: Texaco
Other	S: State Police
(360)	Weigh Station (Westbound)
(360)	Weigh Station (Eastbound)
361	To CO 71, Limon
TStop	S: Flying J Travel Plaza(*)
FStop	S: Conoco(*, LP), Texaco(*)
Food	S: Dairy Queen, Pizza Hut, Wendy's (Texaco)
Lodg	S: Preferred Motor Inn, Travel Inn
AServ	S: NAPA Auto Service
RVCamp	S: KOA Campgrounds
ATM	S: Texaco
363	US40, US 287, Hugo, Kit Carson, Limon, Colorado Springs
Med	S: Hospital (13 Miles)
371	Genoa, Hugo
AServ	N: Dean's Garage
Med	S: Hospital (9 Miles)
376	Bovina
383	Arriba
FStop	N: Phillips 66(*, D)
Lodg	N: Motel
RVCamp	N: Old West Campground
Parks	N: Old West Campground
(383)	Rest Area, Tourist Information Center (RR, Phones, Picnic; Westbound, Located at Exit 383, South Side)
(383)	Rest Area, Tourist Information Center (RR, Phones, Picnic; Eastbound, Located at Exit 383, South Side)
395	Flagler
FStop	S: Country Store(*)
Gas	N: Total(*, D, LP), W N LP Gas Service(LP)
Food	S: Pat's Cafe (Home Style)
Lodg	N: Little England Motel
AServ	N: J & J Auto & Truck Service, NAPA Auto Parts S: Country Store
RVCamp	N: Little England Motel & RV Park, Little England Motel
ATM	S: Country Store
Other	N: W N LP Gas Service
405	CO 59, Seibert
FStop	S: Burian Fuel, Seibert Travel Plaza(*)
Food	S: A & W Restaurant (Seibert Travel Plaza)

EXIT	COLORADO/KANSAS
AServ	S: S & E
RVCamp	N: Gortons Campground
412	Vona
419	Stratton
FStop	N: Ampride(*), Conoco(*)
Food	N: Dairy Treat, Freshway Subs & Salads (Ampride)
Lodg	N: Best Western (Truck Parking Nearby), Claremont Inn (Truck Parking Nearby)
RVCamp	N: Good Sam Park (Conoco), Marshall Ash Village RV Park, Trail's End Campground
ATM	N: Ampride
Other	N: Classic on Wheels Museum
429	Bethune
437	Bus Loop I-70, U.S 385, Rays, Burlington Way
TStop	N: Conoco(*)
Gas	N: Total(*, D)
Food	N: Arby's, Burger King, Interstate House Restaurant (Conoco), McDonald's, Pizza Hut, Sonic Drive In, Taco Bell Express (Total), TraveLodge, Westen Motor Inn
Lodg	N: Chaparral Motor Inn (Budget Host), Comfort Inn, Super 8, TraveLodge, Westen Motor Inn
Med	N: Hospital
ATM	N: Total
(438)	Welcome Center, Rest Area, Tourist Information (RR, Phones, Picnic, Vending; Westbound)
438	U.S. 24, Rose Ave. (RV Dump)
FStop	N: Sinclair(*) S: Amoco(*, 24)
Gas	N: Red Front(*), Texaco(*)
Lodg	N: Hi-Lo Motel, Kit Carson Motel
TServ	S: The Truck Shop
RVCamp	N: Campland
Med	N: Hospital
Parks	N: Bonny State Recreation Area
Other	N: Otter Wash Car Wash(CW)

↑COLORADO

↓KANSAS

EXIT	KANSAS
(0)	Weigh Station (Eastbound)
1	KS 267, Kanorado
(7)	KS Welcome Center, Rest Area (RR, Phones, Picnic, Grills, RV Dump, RV Water, P; Eastbound)
9	Ruleton
12	Caruso
17	U.S 24 Bus., KS 27, St Francis, Sharon Springs
TStop	S: Texaco(*, SCALES)
FStop	N: Phillips 66(*, LP) S: Total(*, SCALES)
Gas	N: Amoco(*), Conoco(*)
Food	N: Best Western, Howard Johnson, KFC (Taco Bell), McDonald's, Pizza Hut (Phillips 66), Subway, Taco Bell (KFC), Wendy's S: A & W Drive-In (Total), Apple Trail (Texaco)
Lodg	N: Best Western, Comfort Inn, Howard Johnson, Motel 6, Super 8 S: New Trail Travel Center Motel
RVCamp	S: Mid-America Camp Inn (.25 Miles)
Med	N: Hospital
ATM	N: Phillips 66, Wal-Mart SuperCenter(24, RX)
Other	N: Gibson's Discount Center(RX), Wal-Mart SuperCenter(RX)
19	Goodland
FStop	N: Conoco(*, D) (Picnic Area)
RVCamp	N: KOA Campgrounds (.75 Miles)
Other	N: High Plains Museum
27	(36) KS 253, Edson
36	KS 184, Brewster
Gas	N: Citgo(*), Total
Food	N: Stuckey's (Citgo)
45	U.S. 24, Levant
(48)	Rest Area (RR, Phones, Picnic, Grills, RV Dump, P; Westbound)
(48)	Rest Area (RR, Phones, Picnic, Grills, RV Dump, P; Eastbound)
53	KS 25, Atwood, Leoti
TStop	N: Conoco(*)
FStop	N: Amoco(*) S: Total(*)
Gas	N: Phillips 66(*)
Food	N: Arby's(PLAY), Burger King(PLAY), Dairy Queen (Conoco), Long John Silver, McDonald's, Old Depot Restaurant, Ramada Inn, Sirloin Stockade, Subway, Taco Johns S: Village Inn
Lodg	N: Days Inn, Ramada Inn, Super 8, Welk Um Inn S: Best Western (Truck Parking Nearby), Comfort Inn
TServ	N: Central Detroit Diesel-Allison, Cummins Diesel, Diesel Equipment Specialists, Inc. (2.5 Miles)
RVCamp	N: Bourquin's RV Park & Farm Market, Diesel Equipment Specialists, Inc. (2.5 Miles), RV Park And Campground At Bourquins' (.5 Miles)
ATM	N: Phillips 66
Other	N: Wal-Mart(RX) S: Whites Factory Outlet Center
54	Country Club Dr
RVCamp	N: Camping
Med	N: Hospital
62	Mingo

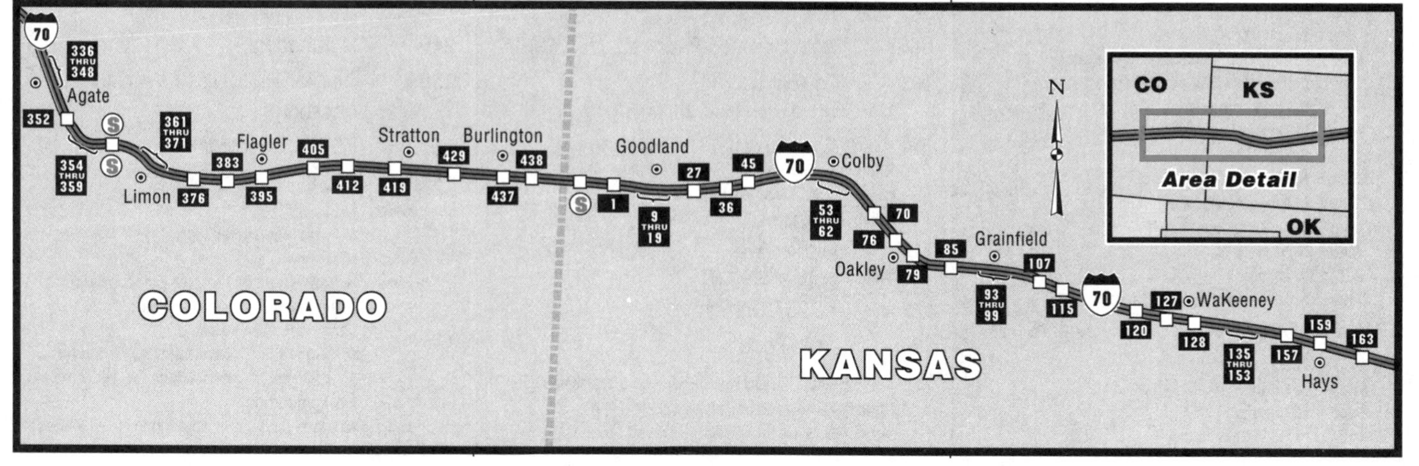

Bold red print shows RV & Bus parking available or nearby

EXIT		KANSAS
70		U.S. 83, Rexford
	FStop	S: Conoco[*], Phillips 66[*]
	Food	S: Colonial Steakhouse
	Lodg	N: Inn
	AServ	S: Dan's Service Center
	TServ	S: Phillips 66
	TWash	S: Phillips 66
	RVCamp	S: Camp Inn RV Park[LP]
	Med	N: Hospital
	Other	S: Antiques, Prairie Dog Town Museum
(72)		Rest Area (RR, Phones, Picnic, RV Dump, P)
76		U.S 40 West, Oakley, Sharon Springs
	TStop	S: Texaco[*, SCALES]
	Gas	S: Phillips 66 (Tourist Info)
	Lodg	S: 1st Interstate Inn
	TServ	S: Texaco[SCALES]
	Med	S: Hospital
79		Campus Road
85		KS 216, Grinnell
	Gas	S: Texaco[*]
	Food	S: Dairy Queen (Texaco), Stuckey's (Texaco)
93		KS 23, Grainfield, Gove
	FStop	N: Conoco[*]
	AServ	N: B's Ultimate Finish Car & Truck Service, Conoco, Shaw Motor Company Ford
	TServ	N: B's Ultimate Finish Car & Truck Service, Conoco
95		KS 23N, Hoxie, Grainfield
(97)		Rest Area (RR, Picnic, RV Dump, P; Westbound)
(97)		Rest Area (RR, Picnic, RV Dump, P; Eastbound)
99		KS 211, Park
107		KS 212, Castle Rock Road, Quinter
	FStop	N: Phillips 66[*]
		S: Conoco[*]
	Food	N: Budget Host Motel
		S: Dairy Queen, Pizza
	Lodg	N: Budget Host Motel
	AServ	N: Phillips 66
	RVCamp	N: Sunflower Camp RV Park[LP]
	Med	N: Hospital
	ATM	S: Conoco
115		KS 198 North, Banner Rd., Collyer
	FStop	N: Phillips 66[*]
	AServ	N: Phillips 66
120		Voda Rd
127		Bus. US 40, US 283, WaKeeney, Ness City
	TStop	S: Amoco[*, SCALES, 24]
	FStop	N: Phillips 66[*]
	Gas	S: Conoco[*, D]
	Food	N: Jade Garden Chinese, M-W Restaurant, McDonald's (Phillips 66), Pizza Hut
		S: Restaurant (Best Western), Subway (Conoco)
	Lodg	N: Kansas Country Inn
		S: Best Western
	AServ	N: Kent's Radiator
	TServ	S: Amoco[SCALES, 24]
	RVCamp	S: KOA Campgrounds[RV DUMP]
	Med	N: Hospital
	ATM	S: Amoco
	Other	S: Bove's Antiques
128		US 283 North, US 40, WaKeeney, Hill City
	FStop	N: Conoco[*, 24]
	Food	N: Conoco
	Lodg	N: Budget Host Motel
	Med	N: Hospital
(131)		Rest Area (RR, Picnic, Vending, RV Dump, P; Eastbound)
(133)		Rest Area (RR, Picnic, Vending, RV Dump, P; Westbound)
135		KS 147, Ogallah
	FStop	N: Schreiner
	Food	N: Restaurant (Schreiner)
	AServ	N: Schreiner
	TServ	N: Goodyear Tire & Auto (Schreiner)
	Parks	S: Cedar Bluff State Park
140		Riga Road
145		KS247, South Ellis
	Gas	S: Casey's General Store[*], Texaco[*]
	Food	S: Alloway's Restaurant (Tastee-Freez), Casey's General Store, Homemade Pizza To Go (Casey's General Store), The Depot Supper Club
	Lodg	S: Ellis House Inn
	AServ	S: D & B Body Shop, Texaco
	Other	S: Antiques, Ellis Railroad Museum, Town & Country Car Wash, Walter P. Chrysler Boyhood Home & Museum
153		Yocemento Ave
157		U.S 183, Bypass South, Hays, LaCrosse
	Lodg	S: General Hays Inn
	Other	S: Fort Hays Sternberg Museum, Frontier City Museum & Antiques, Old Fort Hays Museum, Tourist Info.
159		U.S 183, Hays, Plainville
	FStop	N: Total[*]
		S: Conoco[*], Phillips 66[*, D]
	Gas	S: Amoco[*], Texaco[*]
	Food	N: Applebee's, Carlos O'Kelly's Mexican
		S: Arby's, Conoco, Country Kitchen, Golden Corral Family Steakhouse, Hardee's (Texaco), Long John Silver, McDonald's, Papacito's Pizza & Subs, Pheasant Run Pancake Inn, Village Inn Pancake House
	Lodg	N: Comfort Inn
		S: Days Inn, Econolodge, Hampton Inn, Holiday Inn, Motel 6, Super 8
	AServ	N: Advantage Glass Plus, Hay's Ford, Lincoln, Mercury, Toyota, Lewis Paint & Collison, Wheels 'N Spokes
		S: Coker's Auto Body Repair, George's Car & Truck Service, MacDonald Chevrolet, Mazda, & GM Dealer, Wal-Mart[RX]
	TServ	S: George's Car & Truck Service
	TWash	S: Conoco
	Med	S: Hospital
	ATM	S: Amoco, NationsBank
	Other	S: Old Historic Ft. Hays (4 Miles), The Mall, Wal-Mart[RX]
161		Commerce Parkway
	Med	N: Hospital
(162)		Rest Area (RR, Phones, Picnic, P)
163		Toulon Ave
	TServ	N: Lang Diesel Truck & Tractor Repair
168		KS 255, Victoria
	FStop	S: Ampride[*]
	AServ	S: AAA Mobil Glass & Body
	Other	S: Antiques
172		Walker Ave
	Food	S: Walker Shed Cafe
175		KS 257, Gorham
180		Balta Road
184		US 281, Bus. US 40, Russell, Hoisington
	FStop	N: Amoco[*, 24], Phillips 66[*, D, RV DUMP]
	Food	N: Fossil Station Mesquite Grill (Phillips 66), McDonald's, Meridy's, Pizza Hut, Russell's Inn, Subway
	Lodg	N: Days Inn, Russell's Inn, Super 8
	AServ	N: Heartland Auto Body, Killian Auto Repair, Roger's Towing & Transport, Ten Minute Auto Lube
	RVCamp	N: Campground, Docks Boat & RV Service, Dumler Estates RV Park, Triple J RV Park
	Med	N: Hospital
	ATM	N: Amoco, Phillips 66
	Other	N: Oil Patch Museum, Russell Veterinarian Service
(187)		Rest Area (RR, Phones, Picnic, RV Dump, P; Westbound)
(187)		Rest Area (RR, Phones, Picnic, RV Dump, P; Eastbound)
189		Russell, Pioneer Rd, Bus US40
193		Bunker Hill Road
	TStop	N: Total[*]
	ATM	N: Total
	Other	N: Wilson Lake Wildlife Area
199		KS 231, Dorrance
	Gas	S: Kerr McGee[*]
	Parks	N: Wilson Lake (6 Miles)
206		KS 232, Wilson, Lucas
	FStop	S: Texaco[*, LP]
	Gas	N: Conoco[*]
	Food	N: Conoco
	ATM	S: Texaco
	Other	N: Garden of Eden (16 Miles), Kansas Originals Market Folk Art Crafts, Tourist Info.
		S: CB Shop
209		Sylvan Grove
216		Vesper
	Gas	S: Texaco[*]
	Food	S: Dairy Queen (Texaco), Stuckey's (Texaco)
219		KS 14S, Ellsworth
	FStop	S: Conoco[*]
	AServ	S: Conoco
	TServ	S: Conoco
221		KS 14 North, Lincoln
(223)		Rest Area (RR, RV Dump, Pet Walk, P; Westbound)
(224)		Rest Area (RR, RV Dump, Pet Walk, P; Eastbound)
225		KS 156, Ellsworth, Great Bend
	FStop	S: Texaco[*, LP]
	AServ	S: Texaco
233		Beverly, Carneiro
238		Brookville, Tescott
244		Hedville, Culver
	Food	S: Outpost Restaurant Family Dining
	RVCamp	N: Sundowner West Park (.5 Miles)
249		Halstead Rd
250A		Junction I-135, U.S 81, Wichita, Lindsborg
250B		US 81N, Concordia
252		KS 143, Nineth St, Salina
	TStop	N: Petro 2[*, SCALES]
		S: Bosselman Travel Center[*, SCALES]
	FStop	N: Amoco[*]
	Food	N: Baskin Robbins, Bayards Cafe Family Dining, Dairy Queen, Denny's, McDonald's, Pizza Hut (Petro), Wendy's (Petro)
		S: Blimpie's Subs (Bosselman TS), Grandma Max's Restaurant (Bosselman TS), Mid-America Inn, Ramada Inn
	Lodg	N: Days Inn, Holiday Inn Express, Motel 6,

Bold red print shows RV & Bus parking available or nearby

EXIT KANSAS

Salina Inn, Super 8
S: Best Western, Ramada Inn
AServ **N:** Amoco
TServ **N:** Inland Truck Parts, Kansas Truck Center, Freightliner
S: Stewart's International Truck, Detroit Diesel
TWash **N:** Petro 2
RVCamp **N:** Salina-KOA Kampground (.5 Miles)
ATM **N:** Amoco

253 Ohio St., Bicentennial Center
TStop **S:** Flying J Travel Plaza(*, LP, SCALES)
TServ **S:** Kenworth
TWash **S:** Flying J Travel Plaza
RVCamp **N:** Webster Conference Campground

260 Niles Road, New Cambria

(265) Rest Area (RR, Phones, Picnic, RV Dump, P; Westbound)

(265) Rest Area (RR, Phones, Picnic, RV Dump, P; Eastbound)

266 KS 221, Solomon
TServ **S:** Chuck Henry Sales
TWash **S:** Chuck Henry Sales

272 Fair Rd.
RVCamp **S:** Econo RV Park

275 KS 15, Abilene Clay Ctr
Gas **S:** Amoco(*), Phillips 66(*, CW)
Food **N:** Dairy Queen
S: Baskin Robbins (Amoco), Best Western Abilene's Pride, Blimpie's Subs (Amoco), Burger King, Evergreen Chinese, Green Acres Restaurant, McDonald's, Pizza Hut, Sirloin Stockade (Best Western), Subway
Lodg **S:** Best Western, Best Western Abilene's Pride, Super 8
AServ **S:** Auto Zone Auto Parts, Green Ford, Lincoln, Merc, Plym, Eagle, Dodge Trucks, Jeep, Holm Chev, Pont, Olds, Buick, Cad, GM
Med **S:** + Hospital
ATM **S:** UMB Bank
Other **S:** Ricco Pharmacy(RX), Trails End Car Wash(CW), West Plaza Country Mart

277 Jeep Rd.

281 KS 43, Enterprise
Gas **N:** Four Seasons RV Acres Campground RV Sales & Service(*, D, LP)
RVCamp **N:** Campground, Four Seasons RV Acres Campground RV Sales & Service

286 KS 206, Chapman
Gas **S:** Citgo(*, D)
Food **S:** Subway (Citgo)
ATM **S:** Citgo

290 Milford Lake Road

(294) Rest Area (RR, Picnic, RV Dump, P; Westbound)

(294) Rest Area (RR, Picnic, RV Dump, P; Eastbound)

295 US 77 West, KS 18, Marysville, Herrington
Med **N:** + Hospital
Other **N:** Milford Lake

296 US 40 Bus., Washington St
Gas **N:** Coastal(*), Texaco(*, D)
Food **N:** Country Kitchen, Dairy Queen, Denny's, McDonald's(PLAY), Sirloin Stockade, Subway, TCBY
Lodg **N:** Comfort Inn, DAYS INN Days Inn, Ramada Limited
RVCamp **N:** Junction City RV Park (.5 Miles)
Med **N:** + Hospital
ATM **N:** Central National Bank, Coastal, Texaco
Other **N:** Food 4 Less

298 East St, Chestnut St
FStop **N:** Texaco(*, LP)
Food **N:** Burger King (Texaco), Taco Bell
Lodg **N:** Holiday Inn Express
AServ **N:** Wal-Mart(RX)
ATM **N:** Falley's Food(24), Texaco, Wal-Mart
Other **N:** Falley's Food, Wal-Mart(RX)

299 J Hill Road, Flinthills Blvd
Gas **N:** Texaco, Total(*)
Food **N:** Stacy's, Tyme Out Lounge (Steaks, Great Western Inn)
Lodg **N:** Best Western, Econolodge, Great Western Inn
AServ **N:** Big A Flinthill's Auto Parts, Texaco
TServ **N:** Texaco

300 Bus US 40, KS 57, Council Grove
Lodg **N:** Dreamland Motel, Sunset Motel

301 Ft Riley, Marshallfield (Exit under construction)
Other **N:** Custer House, First Teritorial Capital, US Cavalry Museum

303 KS 18, Ogden, Manhatten

304 Humboldt Creek Road

307 McDowell Creek Road

(309) Rest Area (RR, Picnic, RV Dump, P; Westbound, Under construction)

(309) Rest Area (RR, P; Eastbound, Under construction)

311 Moritz Rd.

313 KS 177, Manhattan, Council Grove
FStop **N:** Phillips 66(*)

316 Deep Creek Rd

318 Frontage Road

323 Frontage Road

324 Wabaunsee Road

328 KS 99, Wamego, Alma, Skyline Millcreek Scenic Dr
FStop **N:** Gas-N-Go(*)
ATM **N:** Gas-N-Go

(329) Weigh Station & Motor Carrier Inspection (Westbound)

(329) Weigh Station & Motor Carrier Inspection (Eastbound)

330 KS 185, McFarland

332 Spring Creek Road

333 KS 138, Paxico
Gas **N:** Fields of Fair Winery
RVCamp **N:** Mill Creek RV Park Good Sam Park (1 Mile)

335 Snokomo Road

(336) Rest Area (RR, Phones, Picnic, RV Dump, P; Left Exit Both Directions)

338 Vera Road
Gas **S:** Texaco(*)
Food **S:** Dairy Queen (Texaco), Stuckey's (Texaco)

341 KS 30, Maple Hill, St Marys
FStop **S:** Amoco(*, LP)
TServ **S:** Amoco
ATM **S:** Amoco

342 Eskridge Road, Keene Road

343 Frontage Road

346 Willard, Rossville, Dover

347 West Union Road

350 Valencia Road

351 Frontage Road

353 KS 4, Eskridge

355 Junction I-470, US 75 South

356 Wanamaker Road
TStop **S:** Topeka Travel Plaza(*, LP, SCALES)
Gas **S:** Citgo(LP), Phillips 66(*, D)
Food **S:** Burger King, Quizno's Subs (Citgo), The Roost Family Restaurant (Topeka TS), Vista Hamburgers
Lodg **N:** Amerisuites (see our ad this page)
S: ClubHouse Inn, Econo Lodge, Motel 6, Super 8
AServ **S:** Autocare Ford, Linc, Merc, Phillips 66
TServ **S:** Topeka Travel Plaza(SCALES)
TWash **S:** Topeka Travel Plaza
ATM **S:** Mercantile Bank
Other **N:** Kansas History Center & Museum (1 Mile)
S: Food for Less, Western Hills Veterinarian Hospital

357A Fairlawn Road
Gas **S:** Miller Mart(*, D), Phillips 66(*, CW)
Food **S:** Michelle's (Holiday Inn)
Lodg **S:** Holiday Inn, Motel 6

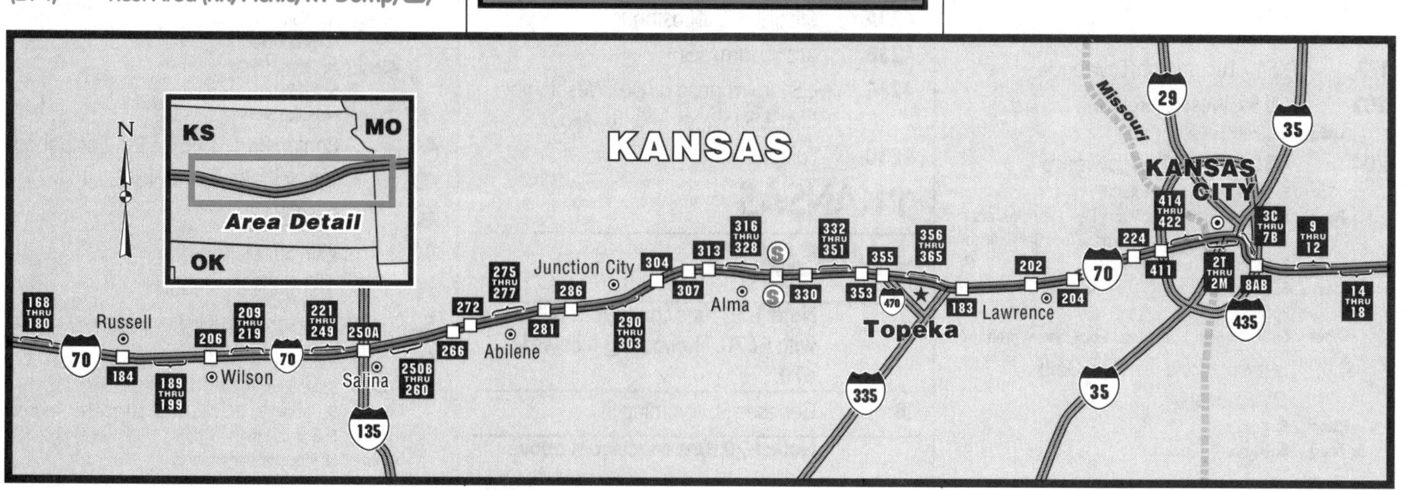

EXIT KANSAS

- AServ S: Interstate Batteries
- Other S: Zoo-Rainforest

357B Danbury Lane (No Reaccess)

358 US 75, KS 4, Gage

- Gas S: Conoco[D]
- Food S: Judy's Soft Serve & Snacks
- AServ S: Conoco
- Other S: Kansas Hwy Patrol

358A US 75 North (Westbound)

- Med S: + Hospital

358B Gage Blvd (Westbound)

- Gas S: Conoco[D]
- Food S: Judy's Soft Serve & Snacks
- AServ S: Conoco
- Other S: Kansas Hwy Patrol

359 MacVicar Ave

361A 1st Ave, Topeka Blvd (Eastbound, Reaccess Westbound Only)

361B 3rd St, Monroe St

362A 4th St. (Westbound)

- Gas S: Amoco[*, LP, CW]
- Food S: The Downtowner Restaurant
- Lodg N: Ramada Inn
- AServ N: Car Care of Topeka

362B 8th Ave, Downtown Topeka

362C 10th Ave, Madison St., State Capitol

- Lodg N: Days Inn
- TServ N: KCR International Trucks

363 Adams St, Branner Trfwy

364A California Ave

- Gas S: Conoco[*, D]
- Food S: Rosa's Mexican, Tacos El Sol
- AServ S: Heartland Automotive, Heartland Automotive #2
- RVCamp N: Jay Roberts RV Sales & Service
- Other S: Highland Park Animal Clinic

364B US 40, KS 4, Carnahan Ave, Deer Creek Trfwy

365 21st St, Rice Road

Note: I-70 runs concurrent below with KSTNPK. Numbering follows KSTNPK.

182 JCT East I-70, Kansas Turnpike, Laurens, Kansas City; I-470, I-335, Kansas Turnpike South, Emporia, Wichita

(183) Service Plaza (Left Exit Both Directions)

- FStop B: Conoco[*]
- Food B: Hardee's[PLAY]

197 KS 10, Lecompton, Lawrence

202 US 59, West Lawrence

- Lodg S: Ramada Inn

204 US 24, US 59, East Lawrence

- Gas S: Citgo[*, D], Texaco[*], Total[*, D]
- Food S: Burger King[PLAY], Fat Man's Restaurant, Juicers, Sonic Drive-In, Subway (Texaco), Taco Bell (Texaco)
- Lodg S: Bismarck Inn, J Hawk Motel
- AServ S: Lawrence Batter, Mike's Auto Sales, O' Reilly Auto Parts
- Other S: Downtown Outlet Mall, Publishers Warehouse

(209) Service Plaza (Left Exit Both Directions)

- FStop B: Conoco[*]
- Food B: Hardee's (Conoco)

EXIT KANSAS/MISSOURI

224 KS 7, to US 73, Bonner Springs, Leavenworth

- Other N: Historic Ft Leavenworth (.25 Miles)

Note: I-70 runs concurrent above with KSTNPK. Numbering follows KSTNPK.

410 110th St.

411AB Junction I-435

414 78th St

- Gas N: QuikTrip[*]
- S: Phillips 66[*, LP]
- Food N: Cracker Barrel
- Lodg S: American Motel
- Med N: + Hospital

(414) Parking Area (Westbound)

(414) Parking Area (Eastbound)

(415) Kansas State Motor Vehicle Inspection Station (All Trucks Required to Stop)

415A 65th St, Riverview St, US 40 East (Limited Access Hwy)

415B US 40 West, State Ave (Limited Access Hwy)

415 US Hwy 40, State Ave (Westbound, Limited Access Hwy)

417 57th St

418AB Junction I-635

419 Park Dr, 38th St

420A Junction US 69 South, 18th St Expwy

420B 18th St North

- TStop N: Phillips 66[*]
- Gas N: No Name
- Food N: Chicken To Go (Phillips 66)
- Lodg N: Eagle Inn
- AServ N: Larry's
- TServ N: Phillips 66
- TWash N: Phillips 66
- Med N: + Hospital

421A Railroad Yard (Westbound)

421B Jct I-670

422A North US 69, South US 169, 7th St Trfwy

- RVCamp S: Central States Special Products

422B US 169, 7th Street Trfwy (Westbound)

422C Service Rd.

422D Central Ave.

- Med N: + Hospital

423A 5th St (Left Exit Eastbound)

423B 3rd St, James St

423C US 24, Minnesota Ave., Washington Blvd, US 169, Jct. I-70, Topeka

423D Fairfax District

↑KANSAS

↓MISSOURI

Note: I-70 runs concurrent below with I-670. Numbering follows I-670.

1B Genesee St, Wyoming St

Note: I-70 runs concurrent above with I-670. Numbering follows I-670.

EXIT MISSOURI

2A I-35 South, Wichita

2B Beardsley Rd

2C US 169, Broadway

2D Main St, Delaware St, Wyendot St

2E Illinois North, Oak St.

2F Oak St, Grand Ave., Walnut St. (Westbound, Difficult Reaccess)

2G Jct I-29, I-35 Topeka, US 71; East I-70, Des Moines; St. Joseph, U.S. 40, U.S. 71 St. Louis, U.S. 24 (Left Exit)

2H East U.S. 24, North MO 9, Admireable Blvd (Difficult Reaccess)

2K Harrison St., Troost Ave. (Difficult Reaccess)

2L Alternate I-70, West I-670, South I-35, Topeka, Wichita (Left Exit)

Note: I-70 runs concurrent below with I-670. Numbering follows I-670.

2M I-70, U.S 40, U.S 71, end I-670

2N Junction I-29, I-35, U.S 71

Note: I-70 runs concurrent above with I-670. Numbering follows I-670.

2P 13th Street, Downtown

Note: I-70 runs concurrent below with I-670. Numbering follows I-670.

2R Central St, Convention Center

2T Junction I-35S Wichita

Note: I-70 runs concurrent above with I-670. Numbering follows I-670.

3A The Paseo

- Gas S: Amoco[*]
- AServ S: Car Wash[CW], Fulton's Body Shop & Tow Service, General Tires, Quaker State Oil & Lube, Tommie's Auto Care, Weld Wheels Tire & Wheel Center, Wheel Warehouse

3C U.S. 71 South, Prospect Ave

- Gas N: Service Oil Co.
- Food N: Church's Chicken
- S: McDonald's
- AServ N: Service Oil Co.
- S: A & Reds Transmission Parts
- Other N: Police Station

4A Benton Blvd., Truman Rd. (Eastbound)

4B 18th St (Difficult Reaccess)

4C 23rd St

5A 27th Street

5B 31st Street (Eastbound)

5C Jackson Ave. (No Reaccess)

6 Van Brunt Blvd

- Gas S: Amoco[*, CW], Total
- Food S: Checker's, KFC, McDonald's, Pizza Hut, Taco Bell
- Lodg S: Ball Park Inn
- AServ N: Precision Performance

Bold red print shows RV & Bus parking available or nearby

EXIT	MISSOURI
	S: Porters Auto Glass, Total
Med	S: ✚ VA Medical Center (.5 Miles)
Other	S: Osco Drug, Ross Miller Laundry
7A	31st St
AServ	N: Able Auto Salvage, Dependable Auto Salvage S: All Star Auto Parts
RVCamp	N: Heart Mobile Village(*, LP)
Other	N: Laundromat (Heart Mobile Village)
7B	Manchester Trafficway
TServ	N: Arrow Truck Sales S: U.S. Truck Source Inc.
8AB	Junction I-435, Des Moines, Wichita
9	Blue Ridge Cutoff, Sports Complex
Gas	S: Amoco(*, CW)
Food	N: Denny's S: Alison House Restaurant (American), Taco Bell
Lodg	N: Adam's Mark Hotel, Drury Inn S: Holiday Inn
Med	S: ✚ Humana Medical Health Care, ✚ Stadium Medical Center
ATM	S: Amoco, UMB Bank
Other	S: MO Tourist Info. Center, Royal Stadium (Kansas City Chiefs)
10	Sterling Ave. (Eastbound, Services are the same as the South Side Services of Exit 11)
11	U.S. 40, Blue Ridge Blvd, Raytown
Gas	N: Circle K(*, LP) S: Amoco, Sinclair(*, 24), Sinclair(*, LP)
Food	N: Burger King, Long John Silver, Subway S: Chi Chi's Mexican Restaurant, Ridgewood Doughnuts, Winchells Donuts
AServ	N: A-1 Hubcap & Wheel, Quaker State Oil & Lube S: Amoco, Broome Cadillac, Olds, Montgomery Ward Auto Center (Blue Ridge Mall)
RVCamp	N: Stadium RV Park (.75 Miles)
ATM	S: Blue Ridge Bank & Trust Co., First Federal Bank, Sinclair
Other	N: Speed Queen Coin Laundry S: Blue Ridge Shopping Mall, Cosentino's Apple Market
12	Noland Rd
Gas	N: Texaco(*, LP, CW), Total(*, D) S: Phillips 66(*, CW)
Food	N: A & W (Texaco), Chuck E Cheese's Pizza, Denny's, Gold China, Hardee's, SHONEY'S, Shoney's S: Arby's, Baskin Robbins, Burger King(PLAY), China Palace, Country Kitchen, Fuddruckers, KFC, Krispy Kreme Doughnuts, McDonald's(PLAY), Red Lobster, Taco Bell, Wendy's
Lodg	N: Super 8 S: American Inn, Howard Johnson, Red Roof Inn
AServ	N: Independent Alignment & Auto Service, Jack Schorr's Auto Service, Noland Rd. Transmission S: Harmon Auto Glass, Team Tires Plus
ATM	N: Bank of Jacomo, NationsBank S: Bannister Bank
Other	N: Car Wash(CW), Coin Laundry, Osco Drugs(24, RX) S: Price Chopper Grocery, Wild Bird Center Pet Store
14	Lee's Summit Road
Food	S: Cracker Barrel
15A	Jct. I-470, MO 291 South, Lee's Summit
15B	MO 291, North Liberty (Limited Access Hwy)
Med	N: ✚ Hospital
18	Blue Springs, Woods Chapel Rd., Lake Tapawingo, Fleming Park
Gas	N: Amoco(CW) S: Conoco(*, CW), Little General Convenience Store(*), Phillips 66(*, LP), QuikTrip(*)

EXIT	MISSOURI
Food	S: King Dragon Chinese, McDonald's(PLAY), Perkins Family Restaurant, Taco Bell, Waffle House
Lodg	N: American Inn, Interstate Inn
AServ	N: Amoco S: Blue Spring Ford Body Shop, Dave Arnold Nissan Trucks, Phillips 66, Pro Lube of America(CW)
ATM	S: IGA Supercenter, UMB Bank
Other	S: IGA Supercenter, Laundromat (IGA Supercenter), Rainbow Car Wash(CW)
20	MO 7, Lake Lotawana, Blue Springs
FStop	S: Conoco(*)
Gas	N: Phillips 66(*, D, CW), Sinclair S: Amoco(*, 24), Texaco(*)
Food	N: Bob Evan's Restaurant, Hardee's, Mr. Goodcents Subs & Pasta, New York Burrito, T. Rider's Bar & Grill S: Applebee's, Blimpie's Subs, China City, Denny's, Godfather's Pizza, Krispy Kreme Doughnuts (Texaco), Long John Silver, McDonald's, Russell Stover's Candies, Simply Sicilian, Subway, TCBY, Texas Tom's (Mexican), White Castle Restaurant, Winstead's
Lodg	N: Motel 6, Ramada Limited, Sleep Inn, Super 8 S: Hampton Inn, Holiday Inn Express
AServ	N: O'Reilly Auto Parts, Sinclair, Valvoline Oil Change S: Molle Chevrolet
ATM	N: Mercantile Bank, Phillips 66, Price Chopper Grocery(24), Sterling National Bank S: Amoco, Texaco
Other	N: ACE Hardware(LP), PETS Supply, Price Chopper Grocery S: Humana Pharmacy, Medicine Shoppe Pharmacy, O.H. Gerry Optical, Owner's Pride Car Wash
21	Adams Dairy Parkway
24	U.S. 40, Hwy AA, Hwy BB, Grain Valley, Buckner
TStop	N: Phillips 66(*, LP, RV DUMP, SCALES)
FStop	N: McShop(*, K) S: Pilot(*, LP, SCALES)
Food	N: Appletrail Restaurant (Phillips 66) S: Pic-N-Save, Subway (Pilot)
Lodg	N: TraveLodge S: Kozy Inn
RVCamp	N: RV Service S: Good Sam's RV Park(LP) (1.25 Miles), RV Service, Trailside Camper's Inn of K. C. (.25 Miles, Frontage road)
ATM	N: Phillips 66
28	Hwy F, Hwy H, Levasy, Oak Grove
TStop	N: T/A TravelCenters of America(*, SCALES) S: Oak Grove 70(*, SCALES)
FStop	S: QuikTrip(*, SCALES)
Food	N: Pizza Hut (TA TravelCenters of America), Popeye's Chicken (TA TravelCenters of America) S: Blimpie's Subs (Oak Grove 70), Country Kitchen (Oak Grove 70), Hardee's, McDonald's, PT's Family Restaurant, Subway, Wendy's (Oak Grove 70)
Lodg	N: DAYS INN Days Inn S: Econolodge
TServ	N: T/A TravelCenters of America(SCALES) S: Oak Grove 70(SCALES), Speedo Oil Change
TWash	N: T/A TravelCenters of America S: Oak Grove 70
RVCamp	N: KOA Kampground (.25 Miles)
ATM	N: T/A TravelCenters of America S: Oak Grove 70, QuikTrip
31	Hwy D, Hwy Z, Bates City, Napoleon
FStop	S: Citgo(*)
Gas	S: Amoco(*), Phillips 66 (Western Union), Total
Food	S: Taco Bell (Total), The Bates City BBQ
Lodg	N: I-70 Lodge & Motel
AServ	S: B & T Auto Service, Bob's Action Auto Service
TServ	S: B & T Auto Service, MidAm Truck Service, Transtar

EXIT	MISSOURI
RVCamp	N: I-70 RV Park
ATM	S: Phillips 66 (Western Union), Total
Other	S: Army/Navy Surplus Store (Amoco)
(36)	Weigh Station (Eastbound)
(36)	Weigh Station (Westbound)
37A	Outlet Mall, Action Road (Eastbound, Reaccess Westbound Only)
Food	S: Izzy's Pizza, Wendy's
AServ	S: Heritage Ford, Chrys, Plym, Dodge, Jeep
ATM	S: First State Bank
Other	S: Prime Outlets at Odessa
37	MO 131, Odessa, Wellington (Eastbound, Reaccess Westbound Only)
FStop	N: Phillips 66(*)
Gas	N: Amoco(D, CW), Total(*)
Food	N: Hardee's, McDonald's(PLAY), Morgan's Restaurant, Pizza Hut, Sonic, Subway, Taco Bell
AServ	N: Amoco, Hill's Rebuilding Alternators & Starters, O'Reilly Auto Parts
ATM	N: Total
Other	N: Odessa Motor Lodge, Thriftway Grocery
38	MO 131 South, Odessa (Reaccess Eastbound Only, Difficult Reaccess)
Gas	S: Amoco(D), Odessa One Stop, Phillips 66(*), Sinclair, Total(*)
Food	S: McDonald's, Morgan's Restaurant, Pizza Hut, Sonic Drive in, Subway, Taco John's, Wendy's
Lodg	S: Odessa Motorlodge
AServ	S: Amoco, Sinclair
ATM	S: Total
Other	S: Book Store Outlet, Keene's Super Store
41	Hwy M, Hwy O, Lexington
45	Hwy H, Mayview
49	MO 13, Higginsville, Warrensburg
Gas	N: Amoco (Towing)
Food	N: Best Western
Lodg	N: Best Western S: Odessa Motor Lodge, Super 8
AServ	N: Amoco (Towing)
TServ	N: Iron Horses of Higginsville
RVCamp	S: Interstate RV Park Good Sam Park (.25 Miles)
52	MO T, Aullville
(57)	Rest Area (RR, Phones, Picnic, P; Westbound)
(57)	Rest Area (RR, Phones, Picnic, P; Eastbound)
58	MO 23, Concordia, Waverly
TStop	N: T/A TravelCenters of America(*, CW, SCALES)
FStop	S: Break Time MFA Oil Co.(*), Conoco(*)
Gas	S: Texaco(*)
Food	N: KFC, McDonald's(PLAY), Pizza Hut (TA TravelCenters of America), Subway (TA TravelCenters of America), TCBY (TA TravelCenters of America) S: Biffle's Smokehouse BBQ, Cree Mee Freeze, Gambino's Pizza, Hardee's, On the Run Pizza, Subs, & Tacos (Conoco)
Lodg	S: Best Western, DAYS INN Days Inn, Golden Award Motel
AServ	S: Mike's Automotive & Muffler Shop, NAPA Auto Parts
TServ	N: T/A TravelCenters of America(SCALES)
ATM	S: Concordia Bank, Conoco, Texaco
Other	S: Car Wash, IGA Food Store, Insight Eye Care, The Central State Car Wash(CW)
62	CR Y & CR V V, Emma
FStop	N: Sinclair(*)
Food	N: Country Motel, Lazy J Arena Malfunction Junction Restaurant (Sinclair)
Lodg	N: Country Motel

Bold red print shows RV & Bus parking available or nearby

EXIT MISSOURI

RVCamp N: Malfunction RV Park
ATM N: Sinclair

66 MO 127, Sweet Springs, Mt. Leonard
Gas S: Break Time Phillips 66[*, D], Poor Boys[*, D]
Food S: Break Time Phillips 66, Brownsville Station Family Dining, People's Choice Restaurant (People's Choice Motel)
Lodg S: People's Choice Motel
AServ S: Advanced Transmission, NAPA Auto Parts, Wrench & Wrecker
ATM S: Break Time Phillips 66
Other S: Greyhound Bus Stop (Break Time, Phillips 66)

71 CR K, CR EE, Houstonia

74 CR YY
TStop N: Betty's Truck Stop Restaurant & Motel[*] (Towing)
S: Amoco, Standard[*] (Towing)
Lodg N: Betty's Truck Stop Motel
AServ N: Betty's Truck Stop Restaurant & Motel (Towing)
TServ S: Amoco, Standard (Towing)
ATM N: Betty's Truck Stop Restaurant & Motel (Towing)

78AB U.S. 65, Sedalia, Marshall (Difficult Reaccess, Divided Hwy)
FStop S: Break Time[*]
Food S: Cafe (Break Time), Countryside Palace
RVCamp N: Lazy Daze Campground (1 Mile)

84 CR J
Gas N: Citgo[*]
Food N: Dairy Queen (Citgo)

89 CR K North, Blackwater
Gas N: MFA Oil Co.
Lodg S: Rustic Acres Motel
AServ S: Bill's Garage, NAPA

98 MO 135, MO 41, Arrow Rock, Pilot Grove
FStop S: Conoco[*]
Gas S: Texaco[*, D]
Food S: The Dogwood Restaurant (Conoco)
TServ S: Thermo King
ATM S: Conoco
Other N: Arrow Rock Historic Site
S: Antique Mall (Conoco)

101 MO 5, Ashley Road, Boonville, Tipton
Gas S: Texaco[*]
Food N: Russell Stover Candy
Lodg N: Comfort Inn
AServ S: Frontier Motors
Other S: State Police

103 CR B, Boonville, Main St, Bunceton
TStop S: Shell[*, LP, RV DUMP]
FStop S: Amoco[*, LP]
Gas N: Phillips 66[*, D], Texaco[*]
Food N: Ice Cream Churn (Texaco), McDonald's[PLAY], Subway (Texaco), Taco Bell
S: Restaurant (Shell)
Lodg N: Days Inn, Super 8
S: Motel
AServ S: Central MO Tire & Towing Service
TServ S: Central MO Tire & Towing Service
RVCamp S: Bobber Lake Campground
ATM S: Shell

(104) Rest Area (RR, Phones, Picnic, Vending, P; Westbound)

106 Bus Loop 70, MO 87, Boonville, Bingham Rd, Prairie Home, New Franklin
Gas N: Conoco[*, D], Texaco[*, D]
Lodg N: Atlasta Motel

EXIT MISSOURI

111 MO 179, MO 98, Overton, Wooldridge
Gas S: Phillips 66[*, D, LP]
AServ S: The MO River Tire Co. (Phillips 66)

115 CR BB North, Rocheport
Gas S: No Name[*]
Food N: Lesbourgeois
Lodg N: Missouri River Inn
Other S: Antiques

117 CR J, CR O, Harrisburg, Huntsville

121 U.S. 40, MO 240, CR UU, Fayette
TStop N: Midway Travel Center[*, RV DUMP, SCALES]
Food N: Backdoor Lounge (Midway Travel Center)
Lodg N: Budget Inn
TServ N: Goodyear (Midway Travel Center)
ATM N: Budget Inn

124 MO 740, CR E Columbia, Stadium
Gas S: Shell[*]
Food S: Applebee's, Days Inn, G & D Family Steakhouse, Holiday Inn Select, Old Chicago (Pasta & Pizza), Red Lobster, Ruby Tuesday's, TCBY, Taco Bell, Wendy's
Lodg S: Budgetel Inn, Days Inn, Drury Inn, Holiday Inn Select (see our ad this page), Motel 6
AServ S: Joe Machens Toyota, BMW, Isuzu
ATM S: Commerce Bank, Shell, Union Planter's Bank
Other S: Columbia Mall, K-Mart[RX]

125 West Blvd
Gas S: Citgo, Conoco[*]
Food S: Fazoli's Italian Food, Hardee's, Olive Garden, Outback Steakhouse, Perkins Family Restaurant, Ryan's Steakhouse
Lodg S: EconoLodge
AServ S: AA Auto Repair, Citgo, Firestone Tire & Auto, University Chrysler Center (Chrys, Plym)
ATM S: Price Chopper Discount Food Center
Other S: Price Chopper Discount Food Center, West Blvd. Car Wash[CW]

126 Providence Rd. Downtown, MO 163, Broadway Blvd. Downtown
Gas N: Amoco[*, D, CW], Conoco[*], Texaco[*]
S: Amoco[CW], Break Time MFA Oil[*]
Food N: Country Kitchen, Denny's, Holiday Inn, SHONEY'S Shoney's
S: Burger King, George's Pizza & Steakhouse, McDonald's, Pizza Hut, Taco Bell, Town & Country Lanes Restaurant
Lodg N: Holiday Inn, Motel 6, Red Roof Inn
AServ N: Albert Buick, GMC Trucks, Conoco, McKnight Tire
S: AA Compact Auto Repair, Cornell Motors Inc. (Mercury, Lincoln), Perry/Legend Collision Repair Center
Med S: University of MO Ellis Fischel Cancer Center (.75 Miles)
ATM S: Break Time MFA Oil, First National Bank

1570
Holiday Inn SELECT Executive Center
I-70 • Exit 124
Columbia, MO
573-445-8531
800-HOLIDAY
• 24 Hour Restaurant & Room Service
• Indoor & Outdoor Pool
• Free Local Calls
• Coffeemaker in Rooms
• Iron/Ironing Board in Rooms
• Adjacent to Columbia Mall
• Special Rates for Tour Groups
MISSOURI • I-70 • EXIT 124

EXIT MISSOURI

Other S: Columbia Pet Center, Kilgore's Medical Pharmacy[RX]

127 MO 763, Range Line St
Gas N: Break Time MFA Oil[*]
S: Phillips 66[*, D]
Lodg N: Ramada Inn, TraveLodge
S: Super 7 Motel
AServ N: Dodge City Motors (Hyundai, Dodge Trucks), Legend GM, Olds, Pont, Cad, Mazda, Mercedes Benz, Ziebart TidyCar

128 Bus. Loop I-70 West, Columbia (Left Exit, No Reaccess)

128AB U.S. 63, Jefferson City, Moberly, Bus. Loop I-70, Columbia
Gas N: QuikTrip[*]
S: Break Time MFA Oil[*, D]
Food N: Bob Evan's Restaurant, Cracker Barrel, KFC, McDonald's[PLAY], McDonald's[PLAY], Steak 'N Shake, Taco Bell, Wendy's
S: Haymarket Restaurant & Lounge, Hong Kong Square
Lodg N: Fairfield Inn by Marriott, Hampton Inn, Super 8
S: Best Western, Comfort Inn, Howard Johnson Express
Med S: Columbia Regional Hospital, Keene Medical
ATM N: QuikTrip
S: Best Western, Break Time MFA Oil, Nowell's IGA Market
Other S: Nowell's IGA Market

131 Lake Of The Woods Road
FStop N: Shell[*]
Gas S: Shell[*, LP]
Food N: J J's Cafe (Shell)
ATM N: Shell

133 CR Z, Centralia
Other N: Loveall's RV's Center

137 CR J, CR DD, Millersburg
Gas S: Phillips 66[*]
Food S: Dairy Queen (Phillips 66)
TServ S: Columbia Freightliner Service
ATM S: Phillips 66
Other S: Little Dixie Wildlife Area (4 Miles), Walnut Bowl Factory Store

144 CR M, CR HH, Hatton
RVCamp S: Crooked Creek Campground (1.75 Miles)

148 U.S. 54, Mexico, Fulton
TStop S: Gasper's Truck Stop[*], Petro[*, RV DUMP, SCALES]
FStop N: Phillips 66[*]
S: Mack Stop of Mid Missouri[*], Shell[*]
Food N: Taco Bell
S: Iron Skillet Restaurant (Petro), McDonald's[PLAY], Subway (Shell)
Lodg S: Comfort Inn, Days Inn, Frontier Motel, Super 8
TServ S: Gasper's Truck Stop, Petro[SCALES]
TWash S: 18 Wheeler Truck Wash
ATM N: Phillips 66
S: Gasper's Truck Stop, Shell
Other N: Nostalgia-Ville, U.S.A., U.S. Post Office
S: Lake of the Ozarks, Ozarkland

155 CR A, CR Z, Calwood, Bachelor

161 CR YY, CR D, Williamsburg
TStop S: Shell[*]
Food S: Buffet Pizza (Shell)
TServ S: Ray's Tires & Truck Parts (Shell)

(167) Rest Area (RR, Phones, P; Eastbound)

(170) Rest Area (Westbound)

170 MO 161, CR J, Montgomery City,

EXIT MISSOURI

Danville, Mineola
- FStop **N:** Phillips 66 Fuel Stop(*, K)
- RVCamp **S:** Kan-Do Kampground & RV Park (1 Mile), Lazy Daze Campground (1 Mile)
- Other **N:** Grahan Cave State Park (2 Miles)

175 MO 19, Hermann, New Florence, Wellsville, Montgomery City
- FStop **N:** Amoco(*), Shell(*)
- Gas **N:** Phillips 66(*)
- Food **N:** Hardee's (Amoco), Maggie's Cafe, McDonald's, Royal Inn
- Lodg **N:** Royal Inn
- RVCamp **S:** The Crosroads RV Park
- ATM **N:** Phillips 66, Shell
- Other **N:** Clarence Cannon Dam, Mark Twain Lake

179 CR F North, High Hill
- FStop **N:** Breaktime MFA Oil(*)
- Lodg **S:** Budget Motel, Colonial Inn

183 CR Y, CR NN, CR E, Jonesburg
- FStop **S:** Texaco(*, D)
- Gas **S:** Amoco(*)
- Food **S:** The Dairy Barn
- Lodg **S:** Rose's Sleeping Rooms Weekly Rentals
- AServ **S:** Schwartz Automotive
- RVCamp **N:** KOA Campgrounds (1 Mile)
- ATM **S:** Amoco
- Other **S:** The Market Basket Supermarket

188 CR A, CR B, Truxton
- TStop **S:** Flying J Travel Plaza(*, LP, RV DUMP, SCALES)
- Food **S:** The Cookery (Flying J Travel Plaza)
- Lodg **S:** Collier Hospitality Inn
- TServ **S:** The 188 Pit Stop(24)

193 MO 47, Hawk Point, Warrenton
- Gas **N:** Citgo(*, K), Phillips 66(*, D), Sinclair(LP)
  S: Amoco(*, D), Conoco(*, K), Texaco(*, D)
- Food **N:** Burger King, Hunan Style, Jack-In-The-Box, McDonald's(PLAY), Pizza Hut, Ron's Family Restaurant, Waffle House
  S: Buck's Pizza, Hardee's, KFC, Taco Bell
- Lodg **S:** Motel 6
- AServ **N:** Fred Vollmer Ford Inc., Sinclair
  S: Auto Zone Auto Parts, Gastorf & Schrumpf GM, Chev, Pont, Olds
- Med **N:** ✚ Doctors Hospital Family Medicine
- ATM **N:** Phillips 66
  S: Amoco, Mercantile Bank, Texaco
- Other **N:** Moser's Food Market, Wal-Mart, Wonder Hostess Bakery & Thrift Shop
  S: Coin Laundry

(199) Rest Area (RR, Phones, Picnic, Vending, P; Eastbound)

(199) Rest Area (RR, Phones, Picnic, Vending, P; Westbound)

EXIT MISSOURI

199 CR H, Wright City (Difficult Reaccess)
- Food **S:** Fast & Company
- AServ **N:** NAPA, General Tires, Wright Car Care
- TServ **S:** Missouri Truck Centers (Volvo, Cummins)

200 CR F, CR H, CR J, Wright City (Westbound, No Reaccess)
- FStop **N:** Shell(*, LP, K)
- Gas **S:** Phillips 66(*)
- Food **S:** Big Boy's, Chester Fried Chicken To Go (Phillips 66), Hot Stuff Pizza (Phillips 66), Ice Cream Churn (Wright Stop), Wright Stop
- Lodg **S:** Super 7 Inn
- AServ **S:** Auto Body, Bob's Repair, B & T Auto Service
- ATM **S:** Farmers & Merchants Bank
- Other **S:** Economy Supermarket

203 CR T, CR W, Foristell
- TStop **N:** T/A TravelCenters of America(*, LP, SCALES)
- FStop **N:** Mr. Fuel(*, SCALES)
  S: Texaco(*)
- Food **N:** The Ice Cream Churn (TA TravelCenters of America)
  S: 50's East Cafe
- Lodg **N:** Best Western
- TServ **N:** T/A TravelCenters of America(SCALES)
- ATM **N:** T/A TravelCenters of America

(204) Weigh Station (Eastbound)

(204) Weigh Station (Westbound)

208 Pearce Blvd
- Gas **S:** Amoco(*, CW), Texaco(D, LP)
- Food **S:** Hardee's, Ruggeri's Ristorante'
- Lodg **S:** Super 8
- AServ **S:** Grease Monkey 10-Minute Lube, Swantner Motor Company, Texaco
- RVCamp **S:** Pinewoods Park (.5 Miles), Swantner Motor Company
- Med **N:** ✚ Doctor's Hospital
- ATM **S:** First Bank & Trust Co.
- Other **N:** WalGreen's(RX)
  S: Schnucks Grocery Store(RX), Wal-Mart(RX)

209 CR Z, Church St, New Melle (Difficult Reaccess)

210AB U.S. 40, U.S. 61, Wentzville, Hannibal (Difficult Reaccess, Divided Hwy)
- Food **N:** Southern-Air
- Lodg **N:** Collier Hospitality Inn, Howard Johnson, Ramada Limited

212 CR A
- Gas **S:** Citgo(*, D, LP) (Aviation Gasoline)
- Food **S:** Bommarito West Pizza & Pasta (Citgo)
- RVCamp **N:** Freedom RV

214 Lake Saint Louis
- Gas **S:** Phillips 66(*, D, LP), Shell(*, CW)

EXIT MISSOURI

- Food **S:** Cutter's at the Wharf, Denny's, Hardee's, Spillway Grill & Bar, Subway
- Med **S:** ✚ LakeSide Medical Center, ✚ St. Joseph's Hospital West
- ATM **S:** First Bank & Trust Co., Mercantile Bank, Shell
- Other **S:** IGA Food Store, Police Department, Wharf Pharmacy(RX)

216 Bryan Road, North Outer Road
- Gas **S:** QuikTrip(*)
- Lodg **N:** Super 8
- AServ **N:** Scheppe Auto Body
- TServ **N:** Mid America Peterbilt

217 CR K, CR M, O'Fallon
- Gas **N:** Clark's(K), Huck's(*, LP), Mobil, Vicker's(*, LP)
  S: Citgo(*, D, K), Phillips 66(*, D), Shell(*, CW)
- Food **N:** Baskin Robbins, Blimpie's Subs, Burger King(PLAY), Hardee's, Jack-In-The-Box, Ponderosa Steakhouse, Rally's Hamburgers, Sonic, Taco Bell, Waffle House
  S: Domino's Pizza, KFC, Lion's Choice Roast Beef, Little Caesars Pizza, McDonald's(PLAY), Pantera's Pizza, Pizza Hut, Roadhouse Express, SHONEY'S, Shoney's, Stefanina's Pizzeria, Subway
- AServ **N:** Firestone Tire & Auto, Jiffy Lube, Mobil, Valvoline Oil Change
  S: AutoTire Car Care Centers, Button Automotive Machine Shop & Parts, Meineke Discount Mufflers, Midas Muffler & Brake, The Body Shop
- ATM **N:** Huck's, Mercantile Bank, NationsBank
  S: Citgo, Commerce Bank, Mercantile Bank, Phillips 66, Shell
- Other **N:** Eye Care Center
  S: Aldi Grocery Store, K-Mart(RX), Schnucks Supersaver(RX), Shop 'n Save Grocery, WalGreens Pharmacy(24, RX)

220 MO 79, Elsberry, Louisiana, Clarksville
- Gas **S:** Amoco(*, CW)
- Food **S:** Hardee's
- RVCamp **N:** Cherokee Lake
- ATM **S:** Amoco

222 (223) MO C, Mid Rivers, Mall Drive
- FStop **N:** QuikTrip(*)
- Gas **S:** Mobil(*, CW)
- Food **N:** Burger King, Eat at Joe's Crab Shack
  S: Arby's, Bob Evan's Restaurant, Cecil Whittaker's Pizzeria, China Wok, Domino's Pizza, Jack-In-The-Box, McDonald's(PLAY), Olive Garden, Ruby Tuesday's, Steak 'N Shake, Subway, Wendy's
- Lodg **S:** Drury Inn
- AServ **N:** Lou Fusz Chevrolet
  S: Instant Oil Change, NTB
- ATM **S:** First Bank & Trust Co., Mercantile Bank, Mobil, NationsBank
- Other **S:** Dierbergs Food & Drugs(RX), Dierbergs Mid Rivers Center Mall, Mid River Mall, One Way Book Shop

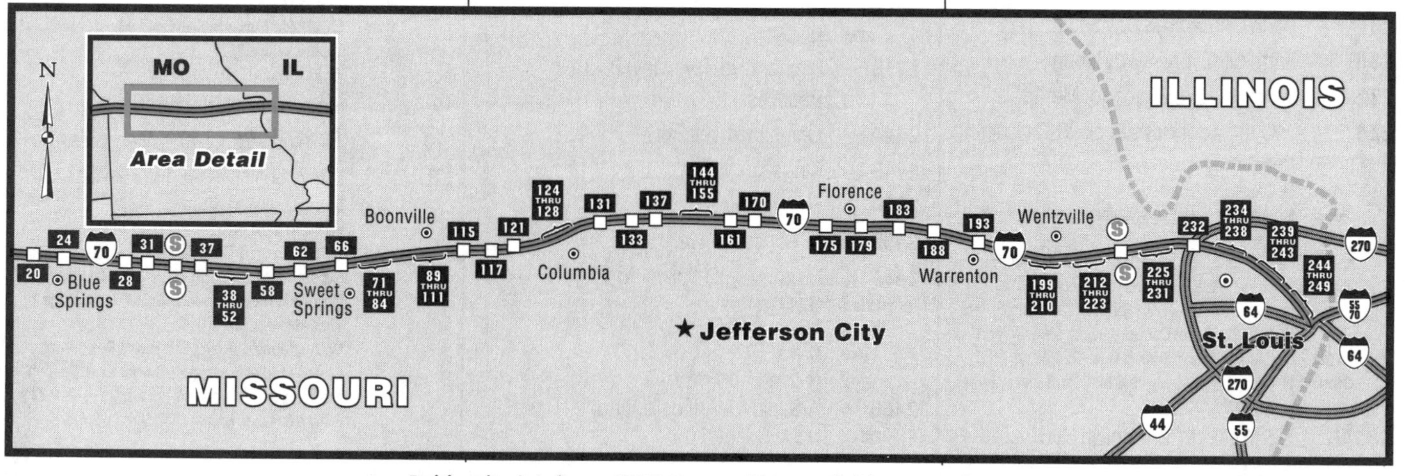

EXIT MISSOURI

224 MO 370 East (No Reaccess, Limited Access Hwy)

225 Cave Springs, Truman Rd.
- **Gas** **N:** Amoco(*, CW), Citgo(*, D)
  S: Conoco(LP), Mobil(*)
- **Food** **N:** Wendy's
  S: Denny's, Lion's Choice Roast Beef, McDonald's(PLAY), Steak 'N Shake
- **Lodg** **N:** Knight's Inn
- **AServ** **S:** Conoco
- **ATM** **N:** Amoco
  S: St. John's Bank & Trust Co.
- **Other** **S:** Cataract & Eye Disease Specialist

227 Zumbehl Road
- **Gas** **N:** Texaco(*)
  S: Huck's(*)
- **Food** **N:** Burger King, Rural Route Country Cookin', Sara's Donuts & Cafe
  S: Applebee's, Bob Evan's Restaurant, Captain D's Seafood, Fratelli's Ristorante, Hardee's, Jack-In-The-Box, Oriental Palace (Chinese), Popeye's Chicken, Quizno's Subs, Shogun (Japanese), St. Louis Bread Company, Taco Bell
- **Lodg** **N:** **EconoLodge**
  S: Red Roof Inn
- **AServ** **S:** Jiffy Lube
- **ATM** **N:** Texaco
  S: Huck's, UMB Bank
- **Other** **N:** Hucks Food Store, Save-A-Lot Food Stores, **Standard Drugs(RX)**
  S: **Dierbergs Bogey Hills Plaza (Mall), Regency Square Mall**

228 MO 94, First Capitol Dr, Weldon Springs
- **Gas** **N:** Clark
  S: Shell(*, CW)
- **Food** **N:** Arby's, Imo's Pizza, Lil' Bear Waffle Shop, Papa John's Pizza, Steak 'N Shake, The Arctic & Equator Ice Cream, Wendy's
  S: Gingham's Home Style, Time Out Pub
- **AServ** **N:** Parts America, Sunset Auto Parts
- **Other** **S:** **County Veterinary Hospital**

229AB Bus Loop I-70 North, 5th St
- **Gas** **N:** Amoco(*, CW)
  S: Phillips 66(*), QuikTrip(*)
- **Food** **N:** Blimpie Sub & Salads, Denny's, McDonald's(PLAY), Subway, Waffle House
  S: Chicago Style Pizza (Phillips 66), **Cracker Barrel**, Noah's Ark Motor Inn Crown Motel
- **Lodg** **N:** Budgetel Inn, Ramada Limited, The Charles Inn
  S: Fairfield Inn by Marriott, Noah's Ark Motor Inn Crown Motel
- **AServ** **N:** Meineke Discount Mufflers
- **ATM** **S:** QuikTrip
- **Other** **N:** First State Capitol, GrandPa's Food Store(RX), **WalGreen's(24, RX)**

231A Earth City Expressway South

231B Earth City Expressway North

232 Junction I-270, Chicago, Memphis

234 MO 180, St Charles Rock Rd (Difficult Reaccess)
- **Gas** **N:** Citgo(*)
- **Food** **N:** Hatfield's & McCoy's Southern Cooking, Imo's Pizza
- **AServ** **N:** Harman Glass, Hood's Towing & Auto Repair, Jiffy Lube, Mark Twain Transmission, Meineke Discount Mufflers, NTB, Niehaus Tire & Auto, Sparrs Hi-Tech Computer Car Care, Windshields & More
- **ATM** **N:** Citgo, St. John's Bank & Trust Co.
- **Other** **N:** **Grandpa's Grocery Store(RX), Northwest Animal Hospital**

235AB U.S. 67 North, Lindbergh Blvd

EXIT MISSOURI

- **Gas** **N:** Shell(*, CW, 24)
- **Food** **N:** CungKing Garden, Duffy's Irish Pub, Henry the 8th Inn & Lodge, Holiday Inn, Howard Johnson
  S: Massa's Italian, T.G.I. Friday's (Radisson)
- **Lodg** **N:** EconoLodge, Henry the 8th Inn & Lodge, Holiday Inn, Howard Johnson, Linair Motel, Scottish Inn, Stanley Cour-Tel Motel
  S: Embassy Suites, Home Stead Village, Radisson Hotel
- **AServ** **S:** K & B Express Lube

235C CR B, Cypress Road, Hunter Road

236 Lambert, St. Louis Airport
- **Gas** **S:** Amoco(*)
- **Food** **S:** Hampton Inn, Marriot
- **Lodg** **S:** Drury Inn, Hampton Inn, Hilton, Marriot
- **Med** **S:** **+ Daughters of Charity National Health System**

237 MO 115 East, Natural Bridge Road (Westbound)
- **Gas** **S:** Phillips 66(*, CW)
- **Food** **S:** Del Taco, Denny's, Jack in the Box, London & Sons Winghouse, Waffle House, Wendy's
- **Lodg** **S:** Renaissance Hotel
- **AServ** **S:** Car Repair Co.
- **Other** **S:** **Tienda Mexicana El Caporal Grocery**

238A Lambert-St Louis Airport

238C Junction I-170 North

238B Junction South I-170 (Left Exit)

239 N. Hanley Road
- **Gas** **S:** Amoco(*, CW)
- **Food** **N:** Jack-In-The-Box

240AB Hwy N, Florissant Rd (Short Access Ramp)
- **Gas** **N:** Amoco(*), Clark Mini Mart(*)
- **Food** **N:** Dairy Queen, Donuts & Coffee, McDonald's (Amoco)
- **AServ** **N:** Dwight's Muffler, Lesco, Maaco
- **Other** **N:** **Coin Laundry, WalGreen's(RX)**

241A Bermuda Rd.

241B CR U, Lucas & Hunt Road
- **Gas** **N:** Shell(*, CW)
- **ATM** **N:** Shell

242AB Jennings Station Road (Difficult Reaccess)
- **Gas** **N:** Texaco(*, D, K)
  S: Shell(*, 24)
- **Food** **N:** Roma Pizza
- **AServ** **S:** Auto Alarm & Car Stereo Protection 24

243 Goodfellow Blvd
- **FStop** **N:** **Phillips 66(*, K)**
- **Gas** **N:** Shell(*, CW)
- **Food** **N:** Chester Fried Chicken To Go (Shell)
- **AServ** **N:** Louis Auto Radiator Service, Northside Glass Co.
- **ATM** **N:** Shell

243B Bircher Blvd, Riverview Blvd (No Reaccess)

244A Union Blvd (Left Exit)

244B Kingshighway

245A Shreve Ave

245B W Florissant Ave

246A Broadway, O-Fallon Park
- **FStop** **N:** **Phillips 66(*)**
- **Gas** **N:** Amoco
- **AServ** **N:** **Phillips 66**
- **TServ** **N:** **Freightliner Dealer**

246B Adelaide Ave (Eastbound)
- **Other** **N:** **Saveway Food Co.**

EXIT MISSOURI/ILLINOIS

247 Grand Ave, Grand Blvd
- **Gas** **N:** Citgo(*, D, K)

248A Salisbury St, McKinley Bridge
- **Gas** **S:** Amoco, Mobil(*, D)
- **AServ** **S:** Amoco
- **TServ** **N:** **Tom's Truck Repair**
- **ATM** **S:** Amoco, Mobil

248B Branch St (No Reaccess)
- **FStop** **N:** **North Broadway Truck Stop**

248 Natural Bridge Rd., Broadway

249A Madison St.

249C Broadway

249D Broadway (Eastbound)

249 Junction I-55, I-70 West

↑MISSOURI

↓ILLINOIS

Note: I-70 runs concurrent below with I-55. Numbering follows I-55.

1 IL 3, Sauget (Southbound, Reaccess Northbound Only)

2B 3rd Street (Southbound, Reaccess Northbound Only)

2A ML King Bridge, Downtown St Louis (Southbound, Reaccess Northbound Only)

2 Junction I-64, IL 3, St Clair Avenue, Louisville

3 Exchange Ave (Southbound, Reaccess Northbound Only)

4A IL 203, Granite City
- **TStop** **W:** **America's Best Truck Stop(*, SCALES) (Texaco)**
- **Food** **W:** **America's Best Truck Stop (Texaco)**, Big Duga's Restaurant(SCALES) (America's Best Truck Stop), Burger King, Pizza Hut (America's Best Truck Stop), Taco Bell (America's Best Truck Stop)
- **AServ** **W:** **America's Best Truck Stop (Texaco)**
- **TServ** **W:** **America's Best Truck Stop(SCALES) (Texaco)**
- **Other** **W:** **Gateway International Raceway, Volvo Dealer**

4B IL 203, Fairmont City

6 IL 111, Great River Road, Wood River, Washington, Park
- **Gas** **E:** Clark(*, D)
- **Food** **E:** Gateway Pit Stop & Motel
- **Lodg** **E:** Gateway Pit Stop & Motel, Rainbo Court Motel
- **RVCamp** **E:** **Safari RV Park**
- **Other** **E:** **Cahokia Mounds Historic Sight, Foodland Supermarket(RX)**
  W: Horseshoe Lake State Park

9 Black Lane (Northbound)

10 Junction I-255, I-270, Memphis

11 IL 157, Collinsville, Edwardsville
- **Gas** **E:** Amoco(*) (Wrecker Service), Shell(*, CW)
  W: Moto Mart(*, D)
- **Food** **E:** China Palace, Denny's (Pear Tree Inn), Hardee's(PLAY), Long John Silver, McDonald's(PLAY), Pizza Hut, The Pub Lounge & Grill, TraveLodge, Waffle House, Wendy's
  W: Applebee's, Arby's, Bob Evan's Restaurant, Boston Market Restaurant, Burger King, Cancun Mexican, Dairy Queen(PLAY), **Holiday Inn**, Pete's Ice Cream & Fudge Factory, Ponderosa, Porter's

Bold red print shows RV & Bus parking available or nearby

EXIT		ILLINOIS
		(Holiday Inn), Shoney's, Shoney's, Steak & Shake, White Castle Restaurant
	Lodg	E: Best Western, Days Inn, Howard Johnson, Motel 6, Pear Tree Inn, TraveLodge W: Comfort Inn, Drury Inn, Fairfield Inn, Hampton Inn, Holiday Inn, Ramada Limited, Super 8
	AServ	E: Amoco (Wrecker Service), Midas Muffler & Brake W: Dave Kroft Chrysler, Dodge, Jeep Eagle, GMC, Pontiac
	TServ	E: Gateway Industrial
	ATM	W: Magna Bank
	Other	E: Animal Emergency Care, Asiana Cafe (TraveLodge), Car Wash, Carri-lite Sales & Service, Cinema W: 4 Seasons Auto Wash, Convention Center, Fun Factory Putt Putt, State Police
(14)		Weigh Station (Southbound)
15AB		IL 159, Collinsville, Maryville
	Gas	E: Phillips 66(*, D) W: Conoco(*)
	Food	E: Sharky's Seafood & Crabhouse
	Lodg	W: EconoLodge
	AServ	W: Capital X 2 Collision, Conoco
	Other	E: AmeriGas(LP)
17		U.S 40 East, Saint Jacob, Highland (Northbound)
18		IL 162, Troy
	TStop	E: Amoco Auto/Truck Stop(*, SCALES, 24), Pilot/Shell(SCALES)
	FStop	W: Andrea's Cafe (Scottish Inn)
	Gas	W: Mobil(*, D)
	Food	E: Amoco Auto/Truck Stop, Arby's (Pilot), Burger King, Dairy Queen, Hardee's, Imo's Pizza, Jack-In-The-Box, Little Caesars Pizza, McDonald's, Pilot/Shell, Pizza Hut, Subway, TJ Cinnamon's (Pilot) W: China Garden, Cracker Barrel, Randy's Restaurant, Scottish Inns, Taco Bell
	Lodg	E: Relax Inn W: Scottish Inns, Super 8
	AServ	E: Valvoline Oil Change
	TServ	E: Arrow Truck Sales, Speedco Truck Lube(24), XVIII Wheeler's Truck Wash W: Freightliner Dealer
	TWash	E: XVIII Wheeler's Truck Wash
	Med	E: Hospital
	ATM	E: Amoco Auto/Truck Stop, Magna Bank, Merchantile Bank
	Other	E: Car Wash, Super Valu Grocery(LP), Tru Value Hardware(LP)
20A		Junction I-70, Indianapolis
20B		I-270 West, Kansas City

Note: I-70 runs concurrent above with I-55. Numbering follows I-55.

EXIT		ILLINOIS
15		Junction I-55 North, I-270 West
21		IL 4, Lebanon, Staunton
	FStop	N: A.D.R Service(D, 24) (Towing)
	Gas	N: Mobil(*)
	TServ	S: Dorsey Trailor Service
24		IL 143, Marine, Highland
	Med	S: Hospital
(26)		Rest Area (RR, Phones, Picnic, P; Eastbound)
(27)		Rest Area (RR, Phones, Picnic, Vending, P; Westbound)
30		IL 143, U.S 40, Highland, Pierron
	Gas	S: Shell(*, 24)
	Food	S: Blue Springs Cafe
	TServ	S: Cheveron Truck Service (Towing)
	RVCamp	S: Tomahawk Campground (Jan-Dec., 7.5 Miles south)
	Med	S: Hospital
	ATM	S: Shell
	Other	S: Propane Plus(LP)
36		US 40 E, Pocahontas
	Gas	S: Amoco(*, D, 24)
	Food	S: Powhatan Hotel
	Lodg	S: Powhatan Hotel, Tahoe Motel, Wikiup Motel
	AServ	S: Phillips 66(LP)
	TServ	S: Shuster Repair Auto Truck & Tire(24)
41		Greenville, East U.S 40 (Eastbound)
45		IL 127, Greenville, Carlyle Lake, Carlyle
	FStop	N: Shell(*, D, 24)
	Gas	N: Amoco(*), Phillips 66(*, D)
	Food	N: Best Western, Chang's Chinese Restaurant, KFC, Lu-Bob's Restaurant, McDonald's(PLAY) S: Circle B Steak House
	Lodg	N: 2 Acres Motel, Best Western, Budget Host Inn, Super 8
	AServ	N: Amoco, Greenville Ford, Mercury, Wayne's Auto World
	RVCamp	N: Campground
	ATM	N: Phillips 66, Shell
52		Mulberry Grove, Keyesport
	FStop	N: Citgo(*, D, LP)
	TServ	N: Elliot Truck Service, Firestone
	RVCamp	N: Timber Trails Camping (1.75 Miles) S: Cedarbrook RV & Camper Park (1 Mile South, April-Nov. 1)
61		U.S 40, Vandalia
	Food	S: Pondorosa
	Lodg	S: Ramada Limited
	TServ	S: NAPA Auto Parts
	ATM	S: Pondorosa
	Other	S: Wal-Mart(RX)
63		U.S 51, Vandalia, Pana

EXIT		ILLINOIS
	Gas	S: Amoco(*, CW), Clark(*, D, LP), Marathon(*, LP)
	Food	N: Chuckwagon Restaurant, Long John Silver S: Dairy Queen, Hardee's(PLAY), Jay's Family Dining, KFC, McDonald's(PLAY), Pizza Hut, Subway, Wendy's
	Lodg	N: Days Inn S: Jay's Inn, TraveLodge
	Med	S: Hospital
	ATM	S: Citizen's Bank, FNB Bank, Marathon, National Bank
	Other	N: Vandalia Animal Clininc S: Aldi Supermarket, Star Car Wash, The Medicine Shoppe, Tourist Info.
68		U.S 40, Brownstown, Bluff City
	RVCamp	N: Mid-State Camper Sales (2.4 Miles), Okaw Valley Kampground (April - October)
(72)		Weigh Station
76		St Elmo
	Gas	N: Phillips 66(*)
	Food	S: Country Harvest Restaurant
	RVCamp	N: Bales Timber Line Lake, Vail's Timberline Lake Camping (2.5 Miles north, April-Nov.)
82		IL 128, Altamont
	FStop	S: Phillips 66(*, D, LP)
	Gas	N: Asgro Planter's Farm Center, Citgo(*, CW), Marathon(*), Speedway(*, D)
	Food	N: Best Western, Dairy Bar, McDonald's, Stuckey's (Citgo), Subway (Citgo)
	Lodg	N: Altamont Hotel, Best Western S: Super 8
	ATM	N: Citgo
(87)		Rest Area (RR, Phones, Picnic, Vending, RV Dump, P; Eastbound)
92		Junction I-57 Chicago, Memphis

Note: I-70 runs concurrent below with I-57. Numbering follows I-57.

EXIT		ILLINOIS
159		Effingham
	TStop	E: 76 Auto/Truck Plaza(LP, SCALES) W: Petro(SCALES, 24), Truck-O-Mat(SCALES)
	FStop	E: Speedway(*, RV DUMP, SCALES)
	Gas	E: Amoco(*, CW), Clark, Phillips 66(*, D, CW), Shell(*, 24), Speedway(*, D, SCALES)
	Food	E: Domino's Pizza, G Wilkes Bar and Grill, Golden China Restaurant, Hardee's, Little Caesars Pizza, Niemerg's Family Dining, Spaghetti Shop, Subway, The China Buffet W: Petro
	Lodg	E: Abe Lincoln Hotel, Comfort Suites Hotel, Days Inn, Holiday Inn, Howard Johnson, Paradise Inn, Quality Inn W: Best Western
	AServ	E: Amoco, Effingham Tire Center, Firestone Tire & Auto, Pennzoil Oil Change, Shell
	TServ	E: 76 Auto/Truck Plaza, Effingham/International

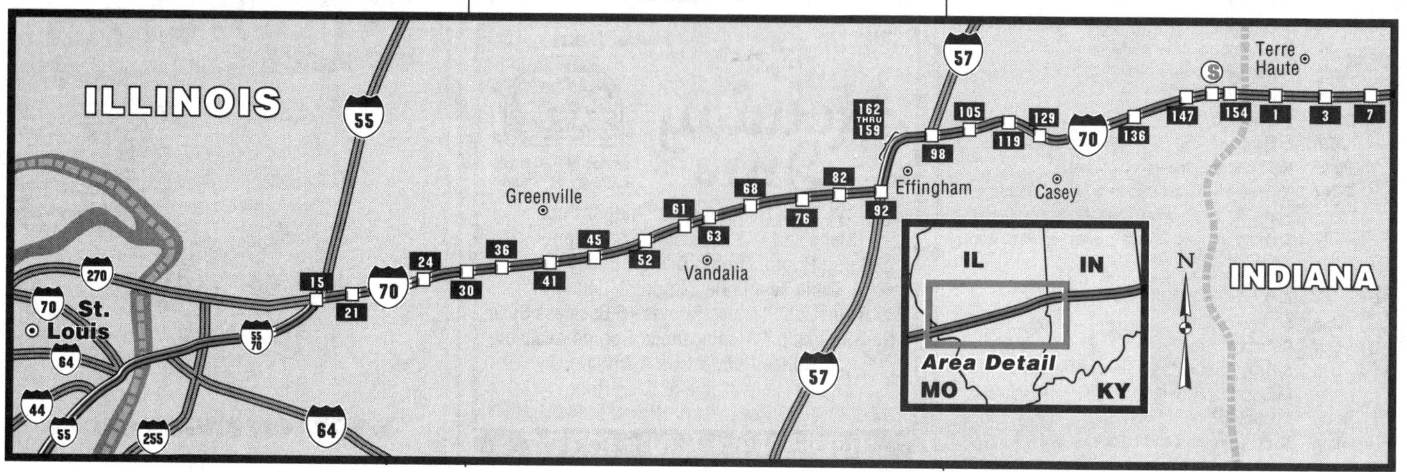

Bold red print shows RV & Bus parking available or nearby

EXIT		ILLINOIS
		Truck Sales, Firestone Tire & Auto
		W: Petro
	TWash	E: 76 Auto/Truck Plaza
		W: Truck-O-Mat
	Other	E: Car Wash, Sav-A-Lot Grocery
160		IL 32, IL 33
	TStop	W: Bobbers Truck Plaza(*, RV DUMP, SCALES), Trucks America Truck Plaza(*, SCALES)
	Gas	E: Amoco(*), Shell
		W: Phillips 66, Shell(*, D)
	Food	E: Dixie Cream Donut Shop, Little Caesars Pizza, Papa John's Pizza, Pizza Hut
		W: Arby's, Blimpie's Subs, Bobber Restaurant, Bonanza Steakhouse, Burger King(PLAY), Cracker Barrel, Denny's, El Rancherito, K Square Food Court, KFC, Long John Silver, McDonald's (Inside Wal-Mart), McDonald's, Ramada Inn, Ryan's Steakhouse, Steak & Shake, Stix B B Q, Subway (Shell), T.G.I. Friday's, Taco Bell, Trucks America, Wendy's
	Lodg	E: Amerihost Inn, Hampton Inn
		W: Best Inns of America, Budgetel Inn, Econolodge, Ramada, Days Inn (see our ad I-74 IL at exit 159)
	AServ	E: Auto Zone Auto Parts, Shell
		W: Ken Diepholz Ford, Mercury, Lincoln, Phillips 66
	TServ	W: Bobbers Truck Plaza, Speedco Truck Service, Trucks America
	TWash	W: Trucks America
	RVCamp	W: Camp Lakewood (West 1 Miles)
	Med	E: Hospital
	ATM	E: Amoco, Crossroads Bank, First Mid- Illinois
		W: Bobbers Truck Plaza, Illinois Community Bank
	Other	E: Aldi Grocery Store, Effingham Veterinary Clinic, Ever Clean Car Wash, K-Mart, Kroger Supermarket(24), Rollin Hill Laundromat, Super X Pharmacy
		W: Factory Outlet Center
162		U.S. 45, Sigel, Effingham
	Gas	E: Moto Mart(*)
		W: Citgo(*), Shell(D)
	Food	W: Trailways Restaurant
	Lodg	W: Budget Host Inn
	AServ	W: Shell
	RVCamp	W: Camp Lakewood (2 Miles)
	ATM	W: Citgo

Note: I-70 runs concurrent above with I-57. Numbering follows I-57.

EXIT		ILLINOIS
98		Junction I-57 North, Chicago
105		Montrose, Teutopolis
	Gas	S: Amoco(D), Shell(*, 24)
	Lodg	S: Motel Montarosa
	AServ	S: Amoco
119		IL 130, Greenup, Charleston
	FStop	S: BP(*)
	Gas	S: Amoco(*, LP, K), Phillips 66(*)
	Food	S: Dairy Queen, Dutch Pan Restaurant, Hot Stuff Pizza (Amoco), Subway (Phillips 66)
	Lodg	S: BudgetHost Inn
	AServ	S: Bud Mitchell's Chevrolet
	RVCamp	S: Camping
	ATM	S: Phillips 66
	Parks	N: Fox Ridge State Park (11 Miles)
	Other	N: Lincoln Log Cabin Home (17 Miles), Moore Home State Memorial (17 Miles)
		S: Hydro Spray Car Wash(CW), Sam Parr State Park (20 Miles)
129		IL 49, Casey, Kansas
	FStop	S: Citgo(*)
	Gas	S: Amoco(*, CW)
	Food	S: Dairy Queen (Citgo), Hardee's(PLAY), KFC, McDonald's, Pizza Hut, Richard Farm Restaurant
	Lodg	S: Comfort Inn
	RVCamp	N: KOA Kampground(LP) (.5 Miles, Sales & Service)

EXIT		ILLINOIS/INDIANA
136		Martinsville
	RVCamp	S: Camping
147		IL 1, Marshall, Paris
	FStop	S: Phillips 66(*)
	Gas	S: Jiffy(*, D, K, 24), Shell(*)
	Food	N: Ike's Great American Restaurant
		S: Burger King(PLAY), Hardee's, McDonald's(PLAY), Subway (Shell), Wendy's
	Lodg	S: Peak's Motor Inn, Super 8
	AServ	S: Phillips 66
	RVCamp	S: Camping
	ATM	S: Jiffy, Phillips 66, Shell
	Parks	S: Lincoln Trail State Park (5 Miles)
(149)		Rest Area (RR, Phones, Picnic, Vending, P; Westbound)
(151)		Weigh Station (Westbound)
154		U.S. 40 West
	Other	S: South Forks Convenience Plaza(*)

↑ILLINOIS

↓INDIANA

EXIT		INDIANA
1		U.S. 40 East, West Terre Haute, Terre Haute (Left Exit Eastbound, Reaccess Westbound Only)
(2)		Rest Area, Welcome Center (RR, Phones, Picnic, Vending, RV Dump; Eastbound)
3		Darwin Road, West Terre Haute
7		U.S. 41, U.S. 150, Terre Haute, Evansville
	Gas	N: Amoco(*, CW, 24), Big Foot(*), Marathon(*, CW), Thornton's(*)
		S: Jiffy(*, 24), Shell(*), Speedway(*, LP)
	Food	N: Applebee's, Bob Evan's Restaurant, Cracker Barrel, Dunkin Donuts, Fazoli's Italian Food, Little Caesars Pizza, Lone Star Steakhouse, Pizza City, Pizza Hut, SHONEY'S, Shoney's, Steak 'N Shake(24), Texas Road House, Tumbleweed Southwest Bar & Grill
		S: Apple Club (Holiday Inn), Arby's, Baskin Robbins, Buffalo Wild Wings Grill, Chi Chi's Mexican Restaurant, Dairy Queen, Denny's, Food Court (Mall), Garfield's, Great China Buffet, Hardee's, Jade Garden Chinese, Laughner's Cafeteria, Long John Silver, McDonald's, Olive Garden, Outback Steakhouse, Panda Garden, Papa John's Pizza, Pizza Inn, Ponderosa, Rally's Hamburgers, Red Lobster, Royal Fork Buffet, Subway, Sycamore Grove (Holiday Inn), Taco Bell, Wendy's
	Lodg	N: Comfort Suites Hotel, Dollar Inn, Drury Inn, Fairfield Inn, Knight's Inn, Pear Tree Inn, Signature Inn, Super 8
		S: Best Western, Holiday Inn (see our ad this page),

1255

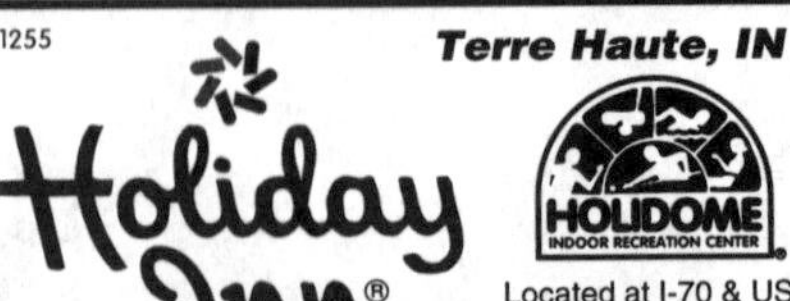

Terre Haute, IN

Holiday Inn®

HOLIDOME INDOOR RECREATION CENTER

Located at I-70 & US Highway 41 South

We are a Holidome with Indoor Pool, Mens and Womens Sauna, Whirlpool, Game Room, Fitness Center, Pool Tables, Table Tennis Restaurant & Lounge

230 Renovated Sleeping Rooms • 5 Business Suites

Non-Smoking & Handicapped Rooms Available

Coffee Pots & Iron & Ironing Boards Available In Each Room

812-232-6081 For Reservations: 800-HOLIDAY

INDIANA • I-70 • EXIT 7

You Should See Us Now

If you haven't been in Terre Haute for a while, you're in for some surprises. We have nearly 1700 hotel rooms to accommodate travelers of every budget. And there's a slew of exciting new restaurants to tempt you—from fast family fare to an evening-long dining experience. Besides all this, there's a buzz in the air. New stores are springing up on street corners where you probably remember vacant lots. Old stores are sprucing up, relocating, getting a new lease on life. And Indiana State University, St. Mary-of-the-Woods College and Rose-Hulman continually add to their facilities, making them even more beautiful campuses than before.

So come on back to Terre Haute, take a look around, and even plan to catch up with some old friends—because friendliness is something that hasn't changed around here. **For more information on things to do and see call us at:**

1740

www.terrehaute.com

Bold red print shows RV & Bus parking available or nearby

EXIT		INDIANA
		Motel 6
	ASserv	N: Auto Zone Auto Parts, Burger Plymouth, Jeep, Eagle, Marathon, Midas, Quaker State Oil & Lube, Southern Indiana Tire
		S: Bowen Olds, GMC Trucks, Mazda, McCord Goodyear Tire & Auto, Sears, Suson Pont, Buick, Cad, Toyota, Vigo Dodge
	Med	S: ✚ Ambucare Clinic, ✚ Hospital
	ATM	N: Amoco, Marathon, Thornton's
		S: 1st National Bank & Trust, Citizen's Bank, Jiffy, Kroger Supermarket(RX), Shell
	Other	N: Dr. Tavel 1 Hr. Optical, Mike's Market, U.S. Post Office
		S: Cinemas, EYE Mart, Great American Car Wash, Honey Creek Animal Hospital, Honey Creek Mall, Kroger Supermarket(RX), Pearl Vision, Pet Food Center, Pet Land, Pharmor(RX), Sam's Club, Sand & Paw Pet Shop
11		IN 46, Bloomington, Terre Haute
	TStop	N: Pilot Travel Center(*, LP, K, SCALES, 24)
	Gas	N: Thornton's Food Mart(*)
	Food	N: Arby's (Pilot), Burger King(PLAY), McDonald's, TJ Cinnamon's (Pilot)
	TServ	N: Russ Fisher Truck Parts
	RVCamp	S: KOA Kampground(LP) (.5 Miles)
	ATM	N: Pilot Travel Center, Thornton's Food Mart
	Parks	N: Hawthorne Park
23		IN 59, Brazil, Linton
	TStop	S: AmBest(*, SCALES, 24) (Shell)
	FStop	S: Speedway(*, LP, SCALES)
	Gas	S: Sunoco(*, D, LP)
	Food	S: Brazil 70 Restaurant (Am Best TS), Burger King, Ike's Great American Restaurant, Rally's Hamburgers (Sunoco), Subway (Speedway)
	Lodg	S: Howard Johnson Express (see our ad this page)
	AServ	N: Red Bird Garage
	TServ	N: Red Bird Garage
		S: AmBest(SCALES, 24) (Shell)
	Med	N: ✚ Hospital
	ATM	S: AmBest (Shell), Speedway, Sunoco
37		IN 243, Putnamville
	Parks	S: Lieber State Recreation Area
41		U.S. 231, Greencastle, Cloverdale
	TStop	S: Cloverdale Travel Plaza(*, SCALES, 24) (Citgo)
	Gas	S: Amoco(*, D, CW), Shell(*)
	Food	N: Long Branch Steakhouse Saloon
		S: Burger King, Chicago Pizza, Hardee's, KFC, McDonald's, Subway (Cloverdale TS), Taco Bell, The Touring Car Dining Room, Wendy's
	Lodg	N: Midway Motel
		S: Briana Inn, Days Inn, Dollar Inn, Holiday Inn Express, Quality Inn
	AServ	N: Darren's I-70 Service, Thompson's Collision Center
		S: Andy Mohr Chevrolet Trucks, Big A Clover Tire & Auto Repair, Shell
	TServ	S: Cloverdale Travel Plaza(SCALES, 24) (Citgo)
	TWash	S: Cloverdale Travel Plaza (Citgo)
	RVCamp	N: Cloverdale RV Park (1 Mile)
	Med	N: ✚ Hospital
	ATM	S: Amoco, Cloverdale Travel Plaza (Citgo), First National Bank, McDonald's
51		CR 1100 West
	TStop	S: Little Point Truckstop(*) (Phillips 66)
	Gas	S: Koger's Country Mart(*, 24)
	AServ	S: Curtis Garage & Wrecker Service(24)
	TServ	S: Curtis Garage & Wrecker Service(24), Koger's Garage & Wrecker Service
	RVCamp	S: Curtis Garage & Wrecker Service
59		IN 39, Belleville, Monrovia
	TStop	S: Blue & White(*, SCALES), TA TravelCenters of America(*, SCALES) (76)
	Gas	N: Marathon(*, D)

Budget Inn
Of America EAST SIDE
6850 East 21st St. • Indianapolis, IN
Complimentary Coffee & Pastry Daily
Fax & Copier Services • Direct Billing
Beverage & Ice Machines • Great Rooms Rates
Guest Laundry Service Facilities
Non-Smoking Rooms • King Leisure Rooms
Game & Video Room
Beverage & Ice Machines
FREE ESPN & HBO
317-353-9781 1677
INDIANA • I-70 • EXIT 89

I-70 • Exit 23
Brazil, IN
812-446-2345
• Free Continental Breakfast
• Newly Renovated
• Free Large Vehicle Parking
• Cable TV
• Non-Smoking Rooms
• Farm Setting
See deer from room! 1119
INDIANA • I-70 • EXIT 23

EXIT		INDIANA
	Food	S: Country Pride (TA Travel Centers of America), Happ's Place (Blue & White)
	Lodg	N: Canary Motel
	TServ	S: Blue & White(SCALES), TA TravelCenters of America(SCALES) (76)
	TWash	S: Indy Truck Wash, Cars, RV, Buses, etc.
	ATM	N: Marathon
		S: Blue & White, TA TravelCenters of America (76)
	Other	S: Indy Truck Wash, Cars, RV, Buses, etc.
(64)		Rest Area (RR, Phones, Picnic, Vending; Westbound)
(64)		Rest Area (RR, Phones, Picnic, Vending; Eastbound)
66		IN 267, Plainfield, Mooresville
	Gas	N: Amoco(*, 24), Shell(*, CW, 24), Speedway(*, D), Thornton's(*, LP, K)
	Food	N: Arby's, Bob Evan's Restaurant, Burger King(PLAY), Cracker Barrel, Dog n Subs Drive-In, Golden Corral Family Steakhouse, Koyo Japanese Steakhouse, McDonald's(PLAY), Perkins Family Restaurant, Ritter's Frozen Custard, Royal Line Pizza, Steak 'N Shake, Subway, The Coachman, Wendy's, White Castle Restaurant
	Lodg	N: AmeriHost Inn, Days Inn, Holiday Inn Express, Lee's Inn & Suites, Super 8
	ATM	N: Shell, Speedway
73A		Junction I-465 South, I-74 East
73B		Junction I-465 North, I-74 West
75		Airport Expwy to Raymond St
77		Holt Road
	TServ	S: Cummins Mid-State Power, Inc. (.1 Miles)
78		Harding St
79A		West St
79B		Illinois St, McCarty St
80		I-65 South, Louisville
83A		Michigan St, Indianapolis (Westbound)
83B		Junction I-65 North
85AB		Rural St, Keystone Ave
	Food	S: McDonald's
87		Emerson Ave
	Med	S: ✚ Hospital
89		Junction I-465 eastbound, Shadeland Ave.
	Lodg	S: Budget Inn of America (see our ad this page)
90		Jct I-465
91		Post Road, Fort Harrison
	Gas	N: Marathon(*)
		S: Amoco(*, CW, 24), Clark(*), Shell(*)

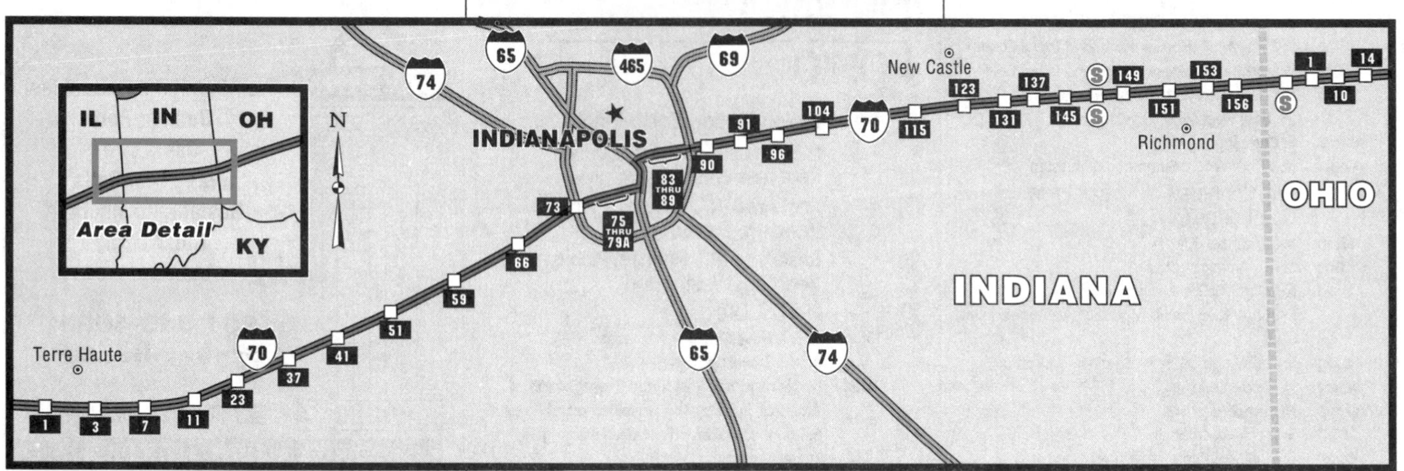

Bold red print shows RV & Bus parking available or nearby

EXIT INDIANA

Food — N: Cracker Barrel, Eat at Joe's Crab Shack, Marathon, Outback Steakhouse, Steak 'N Shake, Wendy's
S: Dollar House Chinese Restaurant, Hardee's, **La Tapatia (Quality Inn), Quality Inn**, Taco Bell, Waffle & Steak
Lodg — N: Budgetel Inn, Suburban Lodge
S: Dollar Inn, **Quality Inn**, Super 8
ATM — N: Marathon
S: Bank One
Other — N: **Lowe's**
S: Bubble Bright Car Wash, **CVS Pharmacy**[RX], **Indiana State Police Post, Marsh Grocery, State Police Museum, The Cave**

96 Mount Comfort Road
TStop — S: **Pilot Travel Center**[*, SCALES]
FStop — N: **Speedway**[*, SCALES]
Gas — S: Shell[*, 24]
Food — S: **Great American (Pilot), McDonald's, Pilot Travel Center**
RVCamp — S: **KOA Kampground (.25 Miles)**
ATM — S: **Pilot Travel Center**, Shell
Other — S: **Mount Comfort Airport**

104 IN 9, Maxwell, Greenfield
Gas — N: Gas America[*, LP]
S: Gas America[*, D, LP, K], Sunoco[*, LP, K]
Food — S: Bob Evan's Restaurant, SHONEY'S, Shoney's, White Castle Restaurant
Lodg — S: Comfort Inn, Dollar Inn, Holiday Inn Express, Lees Inn, **Super 8**
RVCamp — N: **Camping**
S: **Camping**
Med — S: ✚ **Hospital**
ATM — N: Gas America
S: Gas America

(107) **Rest Area (RR, Phones, Picnic, Vending; Eastbound)**

(114) **Rest Area (RR, Phones, Picnic, Vending; Westbound)**

115 IN 109, Wilkinson, Knightstown
FStop — N: **Gas America**[*]
Food — N: **Gas America, Gas Grill Family Restaurant (Gas America)**
RVCamp — N: **Gas America Services Campground, Yogi Bear Camp Resort (.5 Miles)**
ATM — N: **Gas America**

123 IN 3, New Castle, Spiceland
TStop — S: **BP**[*]
FStop — S: **Marathon**[*, D, K]
Gas — N: Shell[*, 24], Speedway[*]
Food — N: Denny's[24], Speedway
S: **BP**
Lodg — N: DAYS INN Days Inn
RVCamp — N: **Camping**
Med — N: ✚ **Hospital**
ATM — S: **Marathon**
Other — N: **Indiana Basketball Hall of Fame**

131 Wilbur Wright Road, New Lisbon
TStop — S: **Marathon**[*] **(Hoosier Heartland Travel Center)**
Gas — S: **Marathon**[*] **(Hoosier Heartland Travel Center)**
Food — S: **Country Harvest (Marathon), Marathon (Hoosier Heartland Travel Center)**
RVCamp — S: **Camping**
Other — N: **Wilber Wright Birthplace & Museum**

137 IN 1, Connersville, Hagerstown, Cambridge City
TStop — S: **Marathon**[*, K, SCALES]
Gas — S: Gas America[*], Shell[*, LP]
Food — N: Dutch Mill Cheese Shoppe (Amish)
S: **Burger King (Shell), Marathon, McDonald's**, Shell
Lodg — S: Cambridge City Inn[*] (Marathon), **Marathon**
AServ — N: Road One Towing
RVCamp — N: **Camping**
ATM — S: Gas America, Shell
Other — S: Martindale State Fishing Area

EXIT INDIANA/OHIO

(144) **Rest Area (RR, Phones, Picnic, Vending; Eastbound, Motorist Info Center)**

(144) **Rest Area (RR, Phones, Picnic, Vending; Westbound, Motorist Info Center)**

145 Centerville
Gas — N: Amoco[*]
Food — N: Amoco, **Dairy Queen (Amoco), Stuckey's (Amoco)**
Lodg — N: **Super 8**
AServ — N: Goodyear Truck Service
RVCamp — S: **Big Bear Campground**

149AB U.S 35 North, IN 38 West, Williamsburg Pike (149A south, 149B north)
AServ — N: **Pardo's Auto & Truck Service**
S: Westside Auto Service

151AB U.S 27, Chester Blvd (151A south, 151B north)
Gas — S: Shell[*], Sunoco[*, LP]
Food — N: Fricker's
S: Burger King, Carver's Family Dining Restaurant, Frisch's Big Boy, McDonald's (Shell), Pizza Hut, Richard's, Shell, Subway, Wendy's
Lodg — S: Super 8
RVCamp — N: **Best Buys Rv's, KOA Kampground**
Med — S: ✚ **Hospital**
ATM — S: Star Bank
Other — S: Avery's Express Wash, **Richmond Municipal Airport (8 Miles)**

153 IN 227, Union City
RVCamp — N: **Grandpa's Farm (2 Miles)**
S: **Deer Ridge Camping Resort**[LP] **(.5 Miles)**

156AB **U.S 40 West, National Road - 156A, 156B U.S. 40 East, Lewisburg Ohio, Welcome Center**
TStop — N: **Petro**[*, LP, CW, SCALES, 24] **(ATM)**
FStop — N: **Fuel Mart**[*, K]
Gas — N: Swifty[*]
S: Amoco[*, CW, 24], Shell[*, 24]
Food — N: **Baskin Robbins (Petro), Fuel Mart, Iron Skillet (Petro), Petro (ATM)**
S: Amoco, Bob Evan's Restaurant, **Cracker Barrel, McDonald's**, Red Lobster, Ryan's Steakhouse, Steak 'N Shake, White Castle Restaurant (Amoco)
Lodg — N: **Fairfield Inn**
S: DAYS INN Days Inn, Dollar Inn, Knight's Inn, Lee's Inn
AServ — S: Victory Cadillac, Chevrolet, Nissan
TServ — N: **Petro**[SCALES, 24] **(ATM)**
RVCamp — N: **Archway Campground (.75 Miles)**
Med — S: ✚ **Hospital**
ATM — S: Shell
Other — N: Shelton World's Largest Fireworks Store
S: Cinemas, **Lowe's**, Putt Putt & Batting Cages, **The Skate, U-Haul Center**

↑INDIANA

↓OHIO

(1) **Weigh Station (Eastbound)**

1 U.S 35 East, Eaton (Eastbound, Reaccess Westbound Only)

(3) **Rest Area (RR, Phones, Picnic, Vending; Eastbound)**

(3) **Rest Area (RR, Phones, Picnic, Vending; Westbound)**

10 U.S 127, Greenville
TStop — N: **T/A TravelCenters of America**[*, SCALES]
S: **Pilot Travel Center**[*, SCALES, 24]
Food — N: **Country Pride Restaurant (TravelCenters of America), Subway, T/A TravelCenters of America**
S: **Country Cooker, Dairy Queen (Pilot), Pilot Travel Center**

EXIT OHIO

Lodg — S: **EconoLodge**
Other — N: **Highway Patrol**

14 Ohio 503, Lewisburg, West Alexandria
Gas — N: Sunoco[*, K, CW]
S: Marathon[*, LP]
Food — N: Covered Bridge Restaurant (Super Inn), Dari-Twist, Subway (Sunoco), Sunoco, Super Inn
S: Marathon
Lodg — N: Super Inn
ATM — N: Lewisburg Bank, Sunoco
S: Marathon
Other — N: **Brennan's Grocery**

21 County Road 533, Brookville
FStop — S: **Speedway**[*]
Gas — S: BP[*]
Food — S: **Arby's**, KFC, **McDonald's**[PLAY], Rob's Family Dining, **Speedway, Subway (Speedway)**, Waffle House, **Wendy's**
Lodg — S: DAYS INN **Days Inn (see our ad this page)**
AServ — S: BP, Boose Chevrolet GM
ATM — S: Milton Federal Savings Bank

24 Ohio 49 North, Clayton, Phillipsburg
AServ — N: Tim Williams Auto Sales
RVCamp — S: **KOA Campgrounds (.5 Miles)**
Other — N: **Clayton Animal Hospital**

26 Ohio 49 South, Trotwood, Miami Valley CTC, Englewood (Reaccess Westbound Only)

29 Ohio 48, Englewood
FStop — N: **Cummins Diesel**
Gas — N: BP[*, LP], Sunoco[*, LP, K, CW]
S: Meijer[*, K]
Food — N: Bob Evan's Restaurant, Frisch's Big Boy, Perkin's Family Restaurant
S: McDonald's[PLAY], Steak 'N Shake, Waffle House
Lodg — N: Dollar Inn, Hampton Inn, Holiday Inn, Motel 6
S: Cross Country Inn
ATM — N: Sunoco
Parks — N: **Englewood Metro Park**
Other — S: **Meijer Grocery**[24]

32 Dayton International Airport, Vandalia
Other — N: Airport

33AB Junction I-75 South, Dayton 33A, Junction I-75 North, Toledo 33B

36 OH 202, Huber Heights, Old Troy Pike
FStop — N: **Speedway**[*, SCALES]
Gas — N: Speedway[*]
S: BP[*], Sunoco[*, K]
Food — N: Applebee's, Fazoli's Italian Food, Frisch's Big Boy, Kenny Roger's Roasters, Ruby Tuesday, Steak 'N Shake, Taco Bell, Uno Chicago Bar & Grill, **Waffle House**, Wendy's
S: Arby's, Bob Evan's Restaurant, Burger King, Cadillac Jack Sports Bar & Grill, Cold Beer & Cheeseburgers, Friendly's, Golden Nugget Chinese, Gourmet Sandwich Shop, Bagels, Long

1560
DAYS INN
Free Continental Breakfast
Outdoor Pool
Cable TVe
Free Local Calls
Restaurants nearby
Golf Nearby
AAA Approved
937-833-4003
Brookville, OH
Bus Parking Available
OHIO ▪ I-70 ▪ EXIT 21

Bold red print shows RV & Bus parking available or nearby

EXIT		OHIO
		John Silver, McDonald's, Old Country Buffet, Skyline Chili, Subby's Sandwich Shop, White Castle Restaurant
	Lodg	N: Super 8
		S: Days Inn
	AServ	N: Jiffy Lube, Wal-Mart(RX)
		S: BP
	ATM	N: Cub Foods(24, RX), Speedway
		S: Bank One, Citizens Federal, Citizens Federal, Huntington Bank, National City Bank, School Employees' Credit Union
	Other	N: Cub Foods(RX), Little Professor's Book Center, Mail Boxes Etc., PetsMart, Target(RX), Wal-Mart(RX)
		S: Carpenter Shop Christian Bookstore, K-Mart(RX) (Penske), Kroger Supermarket(RX), Revco Drugs(RX), Showcase Cinemas, Spot Free Car Wash
38		OH 201, Brandt Pike
	Gas	N: Amoco(*)
		S: Shell(*, CW)
	Food	S: Denny's, Waffle House
	Lodg	S: Comfort Inn, TraveLodge
	ATM	N: Amoco
	Other	N: Barney Rental(LP), Carriage Hill Reserve & Farm (1 Mile)
41AB		OH 4, OH 235, Fairborn, New Carlisle
	Gas	N: BP(*, D)
	Food	N: BP, Dunkin Donuts (BP), Wendy's
	TServ	N: Freightliner Trucks, Kenworth
	RVCamp	S: Camping
	ATM	N: BP
	Other	S: Wpafbusaf Museum
44AB		I-675 South, Fairborn, Cincinnati, Medway
47		OH 4, Springfield, Donnelsville, Enon (Eastbound, Reaccess Westbound Only)
	RVCamp	N: Enon Beach Campground
48		Enon, Donnelsville (Westbound, Reaccess Eastbound Only)
52AB		52A U.S 68 South, 52B U.S. 68 North Urbana, Xenia
	RVCamp	N: Bass Lake Family Recreation & Campground (2 Miles)
	Other	N: Springfield Municipal Airport
54		OH72, Cedarville
	Gas	N: BP(*, 24), Shell(*, CW, 24), Sunoco(*, D)
		S: Swifty(K)
	Food	N: Arby's, Bob Evan's Restaurant, Cassano's Pizza & Subs, Chen Dynasty Chinese Restaurant, Cracker Barrel, Denny's, Hardee's, KFC, Long John Silver, McDonald's, Panda Chinese, Perkin's Family Restaurant, Ponderosa, Rally's Hamburgers, Subway, Wendy's
	Lodg	N: Hampshire Motel, Holiday Inn, Imperial House Motel, Ramada Limited
	Med	N: Hospital

EXIT		OHIO
	ATM	N: Shell
	Other	N: Drug Castle(RX), Fulmer Grocery(24)
		S: Springield Airport
59		OH 41, South Charleston
	FStop	S: Prime Fuel(*) (Clark Gas)
	Gas	S: BP(*, LP)
	Food	S: BP
	Med	N: Hospital
	ATM	S: BP, Prime Fuel (Clark Gas)
	Other	S: Antique Mall, Clark County Fairgrounds, Zip In Drive Through Convenience Store(*) (BP)
62		U.S 40, Springfield
	Gas	N: Speedway(*, LP)
	Food	S: Pizza Pause
	Lodg	N: Harmony Motel
	AServ	N: Suburban Automotive
	RVCamp	S: Beaver Valley Resort (.2 Miles), Crawford's Campground (1.5 Miles)
	Parks	N: Buck Creek State Park
	Other	N: Heart Of Ohio Antique Center, Knight's Antiques, State Police
		S: Tomorrow's Stars Music Park
66		OH 54, Catawba, South Vienna
	FStop	N: Fuel Mart(*, K)
	Gas	S: Speedway(*, K)
	RVCamp	S: Crawfords Campground
(71)		Rest Area (RR, Phones, Picnic, Vending; Eastbound)
(71)		Rest Area (RR, Phones, Picnic, Vending; Westbound)
72		OH56, Mechanicburg, London, Summerford
	AServ	N: Summerford Truck Auto Repair
	Med	S: Hospital
	Other	S: Madison County Fairgrounds
79		U.S 42, Plain City, London
	TStop	S: TA TravelCenters of America(SCALES) (Shell gas,

1796

- Continental Breakfast
- Restaurant on Premises
- Meeting Facilities
- Free Cable/HBO
- Queen Beds
- Jacuzzi Rooms Available
- Truck Parking

1070 Dublin-Grandview Ave • Columbus, OH

OHIO ▪ I-70 ▪ EXIT 96

EXIT		OHIO
		truck wash)
	FStop	N: Circle-K(*)
		S: Speedway(*, SCALES)
	Gas	N: BP(*, LP)
		S: Sunoco(*, 24)
	Food	N: Olde Iron Kettle, Waffle House
		S: Blimpie Subs & Salads (Speedway), McDonald's, Pizza Hut (TA), Popeye's Chicken (TA TS), Speedway, TA TravelCenters of America (Shell gas, truck wash), Taco Bell, Wendy's
	Lodg	S: Holiday Inn Express, Trail's Inn
	RVCamp	N: RV Headquarters
	Med	S: Hospital
	ATM	S: Sunoco, TA TravelCenters of America (Shell gas, truck wash)
	Other	N: CB Shop
80		OH29, West Jefferson
	Other	S: OH State Patrol Post
85		OH 142,Plain City, Georgesville Road
91AB		Hilliard, New Rome
	Gas	N: Meijer(*, LP), Shell(*, LP), SuperAmerica(*, D)
		S: BP(*, CW), Marathon(*, D, LP, CW)
	Food	N: AA China, Applebee's, Arby's, Burger King, Coffee Cafe, Danoto's Pizza, Fazoli's Italian Food, McDonald's (Wal-Mart), McDonald's(PLAY), Outback Steakhouse, Perkin's Family Restaurant, Subway, Taco Bell, Wal-Mart(RX), Wendy's, White Castle Restaurant
		S: Bob Evan's Restaurant, Marathon, Minelli's Pizza, Steak 'N Shake, Subway (Marathon)
	Lodg	N: Cross Country Inn, Hampton Inn, Motel 6, Red Roof Inn
		S: Best Western
	AServ	N: Havaland Instant Oil Change, Monroe Muffler & Brakes, Wal-Mart
	TServ	N: CAT, Fyda Freightliner, GMC Trucks
	ATM	N: National City Bank
		S: BP, Marathon
	Other	N: Meijer Grocery(24), Movies 10, PetsMart, Sam's Club, Wal-Mart(RX)
		S: Ohio Expo Center, Ohio State Fair
93AB		93A Jct-270 South, Cincinnati, 93B Junction I-270 North, Cleveland
94		Wilson Road
	Gas	N: United Dairy Farmers(*, K)
		S: BP(*, CW), Shell(*, CW), Speedway(*, LP)
	Food	S: McDonald's, Waffle House
	Lodg	S: EconoLodge
	ATM	N: United Dairy Farmers
		S: BP, Speedway
	Other	S: Anchor Car Wash, Ziebart Car Wash
95		Hague Ave (Westbound, Reaccess Eastbound Only)
96		Grandview Ave (Eastbound, Left Exit Eastbound)
	Lodg	N: Howard Johnson Inn (see our ad this page)

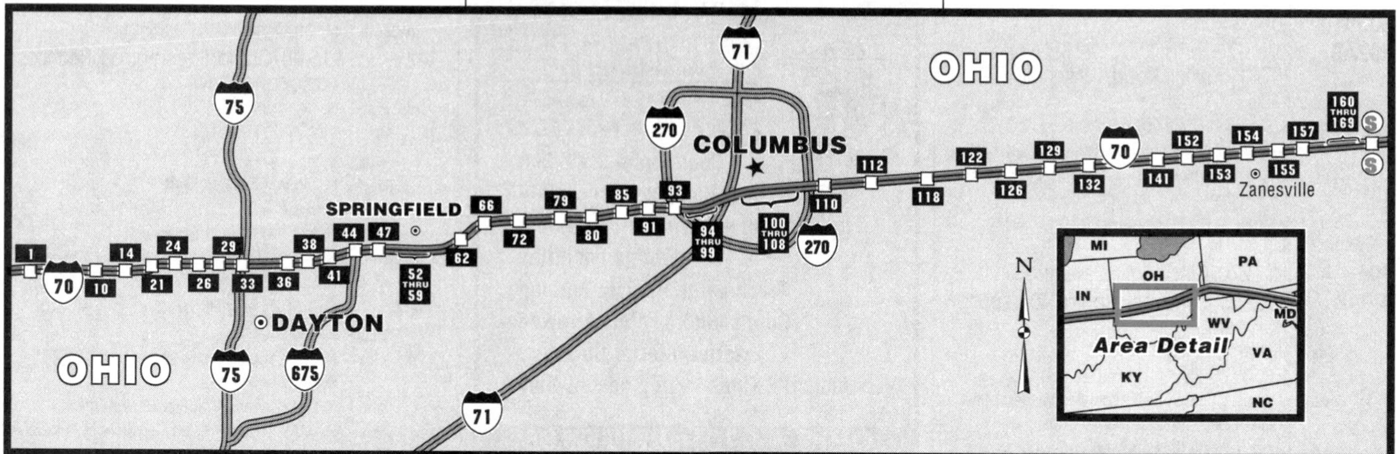

Bold red print shows RV & Bus parking available or nearby

EXIT		OHIO
97		U.S 40, West Broad St
	Gas	N: Amoco[*]
	Food	N: Burger King, Great China Express, KFC, McDonald's, Subway, Taco Bell, Tim Horton's, Wendy's, White Castle Restaurant
	Lodg	N: Days Inn
	ATM	N: National City Bank
	Other	N: CVS Pharmacy[RX], Cooper Stadium, U-Haul Center[LP], U.S. Post Office
98A		U.S 62, Ohio 3, Grove City, Central Ave., Sullivant Ave. (Westbound, Reaccess Eastbound Only)
98B		OH 315 North, Mounds St. (Westbound, Reaccess Eastbound Only)
99A		Jct I-71, Cincinnati
99B		OH 315 North, Dublin Rd., Rich St., Towne St.
99C		Rich St, Towne St (Eastbound)
100B		U.S 23 , 4th St, Livingston Ave
	ATM	N: Federal Credit Union
	Other	N: German Village, Greyhound Bus Station, Santa Maria Visitor's Center, Veteran's Memorial Auditorium & Exhibition Hall & Convention
100A		U.S 23 South, Front St , High St (Westbound)
101A		JctI-71N, to Cleveland (Left Exit Eastbound)
101B		18th St (Eastbound, Reaccess Westbound Only)
	Med	S: ✚ Children's Hospital
102		Miller Ave, Kelton Ave
	Other	S: Rite Aide Pharmacy
103A		Main St , Bexley (Services Same As Exit 103B)
	Gas	N: 76, BP[*, CW], Thornton's[*] S: Rich, Shell[CW]
	Food	N: Domino's Pizza, JC's Bakery, Long John Silver, Mr Hero, Peking Dynasty, Subway, Taco Bell S: McDonald's, Rally's Hamburgers, White Castle Restaurant
	AServ	N: Ernie's, Muffler King, Speedee Muffler
	ATM	N: National City Bank
	Other	N: Car Wash, Conison's Grocery, Deli Delicious C-Store
103B		Alum Creek Dr, Livingston Ave
	Gas	N: BP[*, LP, CW], Thornton's[*] S: Rich, Shell[*, CW]
	Food	N: Chinese Cuisine, Long John Silver, Mr Hero, Taco Bell, Wendy's S: McDonald's, Rally's Hamburgers, White Castle Restaurant
	AServ	N: Ernie's Brake & Automotive, Sports & Imports
	ATM	N: Thornton's
	Other	N: Bexley Spot Free Car Wash
105A		U.S 33 East, Lancaster (Reaccess Westbound Only)
105B		James Road
107AB		OH 317 South - 107A, OH 317 North - 107B Hamilton Road, Whitehall
	Gas	S: Citgo[*, D, LP], Shell[*, D, K]
	Food	S: Bennigan's (Four Points Hotel), Bob Evan's Restaurant, Four Points Hotel Sheraton, Red Lobster
	Lodg	S: Four Points Hotel Sheraton, Holiday Inn, Knight's Inn, Residence Inn, Suburban Lodge
	AServ	S: Citgo
	Other	S: Toys R Us
108		Jct I-270, Cincinnati, Cleveland
110AB		Brice Road, Reynoldsburg (110A south, 110B north)
	Gas	N: Shell[*] S: BP[*, LP], Meijer[*, D, K], United Dairy Farmers[*]
	Food	N: Abner's Country Restaurant (Best Western), Best Western, Bob Evan's Restaurant, Cantina Del Rio (Super 8 Motel), Chi Chi's Mexican Restaurant, Shoney's, Subway, Super 8, Tee Jaye's, Waffle House S: BP, Boston Market Restaurant, Burger King, China Paradise, Frisch's Big Boy, KFC, Mark Pi's Express, McDonald's, Perkin's Family Restaurant, Ponderosa, Subway, Taco Bell, Waffle House, White Castle Restaurant
	Lodg	N: Best Western, Cross Country Inn, La Quinta Inn, Red Roof Inn, Studio PLUS, Super 8 (see our ad this page) S: EconoLodge, Motel 6
	AServ	N: Shell S: All Tune & Lube, Firestone Tire & Auto, Germaine Toyota, Honda East, Key Oldsmobile, Lindsay Acura, Meineke Discount Mufflers, NTB, Precision Tune & Lube, Sprint Lube
	RVCamp	S: Farber Recreational Vehicles
	ATM	N: Bank One, Dairy Mart Convenience Store, Star Bank S: Kroger Supermarket[24, RX], United Dairy Farmers
	Other	N: Dairy Mart Convenience Store S: Anderson's General Store, Babies R Us, Bryce Outlet Store, Coin Car Wash, Drug Emporium[RX], Half Price Books Records Magazines, JC Penney Outlet Store, Kinko's[24], Kroger Supermarket[RX], Magic Mountain Golf & Games, Meijer Grocery[24], Publisher's Outlet, Sam's Club, Super Saver Cinema 8
112AB		OH 256, Pickerington, Reynoldsburg (112A south, 112B north)
	Gas	N: Shell[*, CW], Sunoco[*, D, LP] (Ryder Truck Rental) S: SuperAmerica[*, LP]
	Food	N: Lenox Inn, McDonald's (Shell), Shell S: Arby's, Blimpie Subs & Salads, Cracker Barrel, Damon's Ribs, Jinxing Chinese, Massey's Pizza, Montana Mining Co. Steakhouse & Saloon, Noelle's Chocolate, Schlotzsky's Deli, TCBY, Wendy's
	Lodg	N: Lenox Inn S: Hampton Inn
	AServ	N: Sunoco (Ryder Truck Rental) S: Faslube
	ATM	S: Bank One
	Other	S: CVS Pharmacy[RX], Marcus Cinema Pinkerington
118		OH 310, Pataskala
	Gas	N: Sunoco[*] (24 hour towing) S: Duke[*, D, K]
	AServ	N: Sunoco (24 hour towing)

1847
childreach
U.S. MEMBER OF PLAN INTERNATIONAL
Sponsored by Interatate America and Ramada Inn, Limited and Plaza Hotels of Ohio
RAMADA
For information on how you can sponsor a child call 800-556-7918
OHIO • I-70

1721
NEW PROPERTY
SUPER 8 MOTEL
6480 Birchview Dr.
Reynoldsburg, OH
614-866-8000
800-800-8000
Continental Breakfast
Handicap Accessible
Indoor Pool • Spa • Exercise Room
Meeting Facilities
Truck/Large Vehicle Parking
Coin Laundry • Pets Allowed
Exterior/Interior Corridors
Jacuzzi • Kings • Fireplace • Lobby
Exit 110B N to Eastgreen Blvd, follow signs to hotel
OHIO • I-70 • EXIT 110B

EXIT		OHIO
	TServ	S: International Truck Service
	ATM	N: Sunoco (24 hour towing)
	Other	S: Red Barn Flea Market, TC Antiques & Toys Mall
122		OH 158, Kirkersville, Baltimore
	TStop	S: Flying J Travel Plaza[*, SCALES]
	Food	S: Country Market Restaurant (Flying J), Flying J Travel Plaza, Magic Dragon Chinese (Flying J), Pepperoni's Pizza (Flying J)
	Other	S: Ohio Pyro Fireworks
126		OH 37, Granville, Lancaster
	TStop	N: Pilot Travel Center[*, SCALES] S: TA TravelCenters of America[*, SCALES] (Showers, Barber shop, cb shop)
	FStop	N: Certified[*, LP, K]
	Gas	N: Shell[*] S: Sunoco[*, LP, K]
	Food	N: Dairy Queen (Pilot), Pilot Travel Center, Shell, Sub Express (Shell) S: Country Pride (TA TS), TA TravelCenters of America (Showers, Barber shop, cb shop)
	Lodg	S: Buzz Inn Steakhouse, Motel 76
	TServ	S: TA TravelCenters of America[SCALES] (Showers, Barber shop, cb shop)
	TWash	S: TA TravelCenters of America (Showers, Barber shop, cb shop), Truck-O-Mat
	RVCamp	N: Airport RV Park-R/C Aviation Country Club (.5 Miles), Campground (1.7 Miles) S: KOA Campgrounds (3.6 Miles)
	ATM	N: Pilot Travel Center
	Other	N: National Trail Raceway (2 Miles)
129AB		OH 79, Buckeye Lake, Newark (129A south, 129B north)
	TStop	S: Duke's Travel Plaza[*] (Amoco gas)
	Gas	S: Amoco[*] (CB shop), BP[*, LP], Shell[*]
	Food	S: Burger King, Dairy Creem, Duke's Family Restaurant (Duke's TS), Duke's Travel Plaza (Amoco gas), McDonald's[PLAY], Shell, TCBY (Shell), Taco Bell, Wendy's
	Lodg	S: Duke Inn, Duke's Travel Plaza (Amoco gas)
	AServ	S: A-1 Auto Parts
	TServ	S: Duke's Travel Plaza (Amoco gas)
	TWash	S: Beechridge Truck Wash
	RVCamp	S: KOA Kampground (1.5 Miles)
	ATM	S: Cardinal Grocery[LP], Shell
	Other	S: Cardinal Grocery, Tourist Info.
(131)		Rest Area (RR, Phones, Picnic; Eastbound)
(131)		Rest Area (RR, Phones, Picnic; Westbound)
132		OH 13, Newark, Thornville, Somerset, New Lexington
	Gas	S: BP[*], Shell[*, K, 24]
	AServ	S: BP
	RVCamp	N: Camping
	ATM	S: BP
141		OH 668, Brownsville, Gratiot (Eastbound, Reaccess Westbound Only)
	RVCamp	N: Campground
142		U.S 40, Gratiot (Westbound, Reaccess Eastbound Only)
	RVCamp	N: Campground
152		U.S 40, Zanesville
	Gas	N: Shell[*, D, K]
	Food	N: Big Boy, McDonald's[PLAY]
	Lodg	N: Super 8
	TServ	N: Hartman's Truck Center
	RVCamp	N: National Trail Campground (10 Miles, U.S.40)
	ATM	N: Shell
153A		OH 60 N., Ohio 146 W, State St
	FStop	S: Pacific Pride
	Gas	N: BP[*, D], SuperAmerica[*, D, 24] S: BP[*, D]
	Food	N: Dairy Queen, Picnic Pizza Italian Eatery
	AServ	N: AAMCO Transmission, Ken Brown's Auto Service

Bold red print shows RV & Bus parking available or nearby

EXIT — OHIO

S: BP
Med N: Hospital
ATM N: SuperAmerica
Parks N: Dillon State Park

154 Fifth St
Other S: Tourist Info.

155 OH 60, OH 146 East, Seventh St.
Gas S: Exxon[*, LP]
Food N: Bob Evan's Restaurant, Olive Garden, Red Lobster, SHONEY'S, Shoney's, Tumbleweed Restaurant
S: Best Western, Cracker Barrel, Exxon, Maria Adornetto Italian, Subway, Wendy's (Exxon), William's Bakery
Lodg N: Comfort Inn, Fairfield Inn, Hampton Inn
S: Amerihost Inn, Best Western, Thrift Lodge
RVCamp N: Wolfie's Family Kamping (2 Miles)
Med N: Hospital
Other N: Pick 'N Save Supermarket

157 OH 93, Adamsville
Gas N: Duke[*, LP, 24]
S: BP, Marathon[*], Shell[*, D, LP, K]
Food S: East Pike Donut & Food, Marathon, Shell
AServ S: BP
RVCamp S: KOA Kampground (.9 Miles)
Other S: A & A Car Wash, Highway Patrol (2 Miles), Hittle Roofing[LP], Pottery

160 OH 797, Airport
Gas S: BP[*], Shell[*, LP]
Food S: Earl's Village Pizza, McDonald's[PLAY], Wendy's
Lodg S: Clara Belle Motel, DAYS INN Days Inn, Holiday Inn, Red Roof Inn
Other S: Clara Belle's Antiques, Highway Patrol

(163) Rest Area (RR, Phones, Picnic; Westbound)

164 U.S 22, U.S 40, Norwich
Gas N: Shell[*]
Lodg N: Baker's Motel
Other N: National Road & Zane Gray Museum, Ohio Pottery

169 OH 83, Cumberland, New Concord
Gas N: BP
AServ N: BP
RVCamp N: Camping

(173) Weigh Station (Eastbound)

(173) Weigh Station (Westbound)

176 U.S 22, U.S 40, Cambridge
Food N: Chal's Ribs & Steak
Lodg N: Cambridge Delux Inn, Fairdale Inn
AServ N: Berger's Garage
RVCamp N: Camping
Other N: Highway Patrol, Pritchard-Laughlin Civic Center

178 OH 209, Cambridge, Byesville
FStop S: Speedway[*, K]
Gas N: BP[*, D], Shell[*, D]
Food N: Best Western, Big Boy, Bob Evan's Restaurant, Bonanza Steakhouse, Cracker Barrel, Deer Creek Motel, Deer Creek Steak House (Deer Creek Motel), Holiday Inn, J & K On The Hill (Best Western), KFC, Rax, The Forum, The Parkway Restaurant (Holiday Inn)
S: Blimpie Subs & Salads (Speedway), Burger King, Speedway
Lodg N: Best Western, DAYS INN Days Inn, Deer Creek Motel, Holiday Inn, TraveLodge
S: AmeriHost Inn
AServ N: Shell
RVCamp S: Spring Valley Campground (1 Mile)
Med N: Hospital
ATM N: BP
S: Speedway
Other N: Kroger Supermarket[24], Rite Aid Pharmacy[RX], Tourist Info.
S: Cambridge Municipal Airport (2 Miles), K-Mart[RX]

EXIT — OHIO

180AB Jct I-77, Marietta, Cleveland
Parks N: Salt Fork State Park

186 U.S 40, OH 285, Senecaville, Old Washington
TStop S: Shenandoah Truckstop[D] (Citgo)
FStop S: Go-Mart[*, D]
Gas N: Shell[*, K]
Food S: Shenandoah Truckstop (Citgo)
Lodg S: Shenandoah Inn
TServ S: Shenandoah Truckstop (Citgo)
RVCamp N: Campground
ATM S: Go-Mart, Shenandoah Truckstop (Citgo)

(190) Rest Area (RR, Phones, Picnic; Eastbound)

193 OH 513, Quaker City
FStop N: Fuel Mart[*, D, K, SCALES]
Gas N: BP[*], Shell[*]
Food N: Delizio's (BP)
TServ N: R & R Truck Repair

198 CR 114, Fairview

202 OH 800, Dennison, Barnesville
Gas S: Citgo[*]
AServ N: Jade Inc.
S: Citgo
Med S: Hospital
Parks N: Egypt Valley Wildlife Area

204 U.S 40 East, National Road, CR 100 (Eastbound, Reaccess Westbound Only)

208 OH149, Morristown, Belmont
FStop N: BP[*, D]
Gas S: Marathon[*, D, K]
Food N: Schlepp's, Sub Express (BP)
S: Wees' Drive-In
AServ N: Ford Dealership, Paradox
RVCamp N: Jamboree Valley Campground
S: Barkcamp State Park, Camping, Valley View Campgrounds
Med N: Morristown Clinic
ATM N: BP
Parks S: Barkcamp State Park
Other N: Morristown Pharmacy[RX]
S: Crooked Creek Golf Course

(211) Rest Area (RR, Phones, Picnic; Eastbound)

(211) Rest Area (RR, Phones, Picnic; Westbound)

213 U.S 40, OH 331, Flushing (Difficult Reaccess)
Gas S: Citgo[*], Exxon[*, D, K], Marathon[*, LP]
Lodg S: Twin Pines Motel
AServ S: Marathon
TWash S: Valley One Auto Semi Wash[CW]
RVCamp N: Fine Day Campground, Starky's Camping (1 Mile)
S: Valley View Campgrounds
Other N: Sheriff Dept.
S: Airport, East Richland Automotive Supply, Hillendale Golf Course

215 U.S 40, National Rd.
Food N: Burger King, Domino's Pizza, Subway, Wen Wu Chinese
Med N: Za Primary Care Outpatient Clinic
ATM N: Belmont National Bank, Riesbeck's Supermarket
Other N: Riesbeck's Supermarket, Valley Skate Center

216 OH 9, St. Clairsville
Gas N: BP[*]
S: Ashland
AServ N: BP
S: Ashland
Other N: Car Wash

218 Mall Road, Banfield Road
Gas N: Exxon[*, D]

EXIT — OHIO/WEST VIRGINIA

S: U.S.A.[D]
Food N: Applebee's, Arby's, Boston Market Restaurant, Burger King, Chang Buffet, Denny's[24], Eat N Park, McDonald's (Wal-Mart), Outback Steakhouse, Pizza Hut, Red Lobster, Shoney's, TJ Cinnamon's, Taco Bell, Undo's (Hampton Inn), West Texas Roadhouse
S: Big Boy, Big K-Mart[RX], Bob Evan's Restaurant, Bonanza Steakhouse, Little Caesars Pizza (K-Mart), Long John Silver, McDonald's, Rax
Lodg N: Hampton Inn, Knight's Inn, Red Roof Inn, Super 8
AServ N: Auto Zone Auto Parts, Midas Muffler & Brake, Wal-Mart[24, RX] (Vision Center), White Side Chevrolet, Pontiac, Oldsmobile, Buick, White Side Service Center
S: Auto World, NTB, Sears, Sun Super Savigns Center
RVCamp N: Stewart's RV Center[LP]
ATM N: Kroger Supermarket[24, RX], Steel Valley Bank, WesBanko
S: Belmont National, Wheeling National Bank
Other N: Kroger Supermarket[RX], Pets Supply Plus, Sam's Club, Wal-Mart[RX] (Vision Center)
S: Big K-Mart[RX], Ohio Valley Mall, Revco Drugs[RX]

219 Jct I-470E, Bellaire, Washington, PA

220 U.S.40, National Rd, CR 214
Gas N: Citgo[*, K, CW, 24] (Towing), Exxon[*, D, K]
S: Marathon[*] (Econo Oil Change)
Food S: Habaneros Grill & Bar (Days Inn)
Lodg N: Plaza Motel
S: DAYS INN Days Inn
AServ N: Citgo[24] (Towing)
ATM N: Exxon

225 U.S.250 W. OH 7, Bridgeport
Gas N: Citgo[*, D, K], Star Fire Express[*, K], Sunoco[*, D, 24]
S: Exxon[*], Gulf, Marathon[*]
Food N: Papa John's Pizza, Pizza Hut
S: Domino's Pizza
AServ N: Citgo, Meineke Discount Mufflers
S: Exxon, Gulf
Med N: East Ohio Regional Hospital
ATM N: Belmont National Bank
S: Citizen's Bank
Other S: Car Wash[24]

Note: I-70 runs concurrent below with I-470. Numbering follows I-470.

1 Banfield Road, Maoo Road (Difficult Reaccess)

3 County Road 214

6 Ohio 7, Bridgeport, Bellaire (Difficult Reaccess)

↑OHIO

↓WEST VIRGINIA

1 U.S 250, WV, Wheeling, Moundsville2
Food S: Best Western
Lodg S: Best Western
Med S: Hospital

2A WV 88 N, Oglebay Park (Northbound)
Gas N: Exxon[*]
Food N: Big Boy, Bob Evan's Restaurant, Boots Texas Road House, Hardee's[24], Long John Silver, Tj's
Lodg N: Hampton Inn
AServ N: Marheska, WA Wilson Auto Glass
Med N: Hospital
ATM N: Exxon, Kroger Supermarket[LP, 24, RX], WesBanco
Parks N: Oglebay Park
Other N: Kroger Supermarket[RX], Minit Car Wash, Revco Drugs[*, RX]

EXIT WEST VIRGINIA

Note: I-70 runs concurrent above with I-470. Numbering follows I-470.

0 Zane Street, Wheeling Downs, Dog Track, Wheeling Island (Reaccess Eastbound Only)
- **Gas** **N:** Exxon[*, D, LP, K]
- **Food** **N:** Abbey's Restaurant, Dairy Queen, KFC
- **ATM** **N:** Convenient Food Mart, Exxon, Wheeling National Bank
- **Parks** **N:** Camp Carlisle
- **Other** **N:** Arcade, Convenient Food Mart

1A WV 2, Main St., Downtown
- **Food** **N:** O'Renegan's
  S: Bill's Hamburger, Koffee Shop, Riverside Restaurant (Best Western), Subway
- **Lodg** **S:** Best Western
- **ATM** **S:** Bank One
- **Other** **S:** Rite Aid Pharmacy[RX]

1B U.S.250S, WV 2, South Wheeling, Moundsville

2B Washington Ave
- **Food** **S:** Sigaretti's
- **Med** **S:** ✚ Hospital

(4) **Weigh Station (Eastbound)**

(4) **Weigh Station (Westbound)**

4 WV 88 S, Elm Grove (Eastbound, Reaccess Westbound Only)
- **Gas** **S:** Amoco[*, D], BP[*, D, LP, K], Exxon[*, D]
- **Food** **S:** Dairy Queen, Di Carlo's Pizza, Jaybo's
- **Lodg** **S:** Grove Terrace Motel
- **AServ** **S:** Amoco, Exxon
- **ATM** **S:** Belmont National Bank, WesBanco

5 U.S 40, Elm Grove, Triadelphia, WV 48
- **Gas** **N:** Citgo[*, D]
- **Food** **N:** Christopher's, Pizza Hut, Subway, Wendy's
  S: Amigo's Mexican, Domino's Pizza, McDonald's
- **AServ** **N:** America Auto Parts Pros, Quality Farm & Fleet[LP]
  S: Fed One Bank
- **ATM** **N:** Citgo, Wheeling National Bank
- **Other** **N:** Quality Farm & Fleet, Rite AidePharmacy[RX]
  S: Coin Laundromat, The Medicine Shoppe[RX]

5A Junction I-470, Columbus, Wheeling

11 WV41, Dallas Pike
- **TStop** **N:** TravelCenters of America[*, SCALES]
  S: Dallas Pike TS[*, D]
- **Gas** **S:** BP[*, LP, K, CW], Exxon[*]
- **Food** **N:** Country Pride (TravelCenters of America), Windmill Lounge (TravelCenters of America)
  S: A & W Hot Dogs & More (Dallas Pike),

1088

— 106 Newly Renovated Rooms —
Non-Smoking Rooms
Full Service Restaurant & Lounge
Outdoor Pool
Special Group Rates
Truck & Bus Parking
— Jacuzzi Rooms —
304-547-0610 • Triadelphia, WV
WEST VIRGINIA ▪ I-70 ▪ EXIT 11

EXIT WEST VIRGINIA/PENNSYLVANIA

Cherokee Trading Post, Dairy Queen (BP), Taco Bell Express (Dallas Pike)
- **Lodg** **N:** Days Inn (see our ad this page)
  S: Holiday Inn
- **TServ** **N:** Little Dragon CB Shop, Ohio Valley Scale & Equipment, TravelCenters of America[SCALES]
  S: Dallas Pike TS
- **TWash** **N:** Americas Truck Wash[SCALES]
- **RVCamp** **N:** Camping
  S: Dallas Pike Campground[LP] (.5 Miles)
- **ATM** **S:** Dallas Pike TS

(13) **WV Welcome Center (RR, Phones, Picnic, RV Dump; Westbound)**

↑WEST VIRGINIA

↓PENNSYLVANIA

1 West Alexander
- **Gas** **S:** Texaco[*]
- **Food** **N:** Watson's Pizza Ice Cream
- **AServ** **S:** Texaco

(5) **PA Welcome Center (RR, Phones, Picnic, Vending; Eastbound)**

2 **(6)** PA 231, Claysville
- **TStop** **S:** Petro[*, D, SCALES]
- **Gas** **N:** Exxon[*, LP]
- **Food** **S:** I Can't Believe It's Yogurt (Petro), Kings Family Restaurant (Petro), Sbarro Italian (Petro)
- **Lodg** **S:** Petro
- **AServ** **S:** Petro
- **ATM** **N:** Exxon
  S: Petro

3 **(11)** PA 221, Taylorstown
- **Gas** **N:** Amoco[*, D]
- **Food** **N:** Cc's Restaurant
- **AServ** **N:** Amoco

4 **(14)** U.S 40, Chestnut St
- **Gas** **S:** Amoco, BP[*], Exxon[*, 24]
- **Food** **N:** Bonanza Steakhouse, Hogie Haven, Stone Crab Inn
  S: Big Boy, Blimpie Subs & Salads (BP), Denny's, Donut Connection, Hardee's[24], Long John Silver, McDonald's[PLAY], Pizza Hut, Taco Bell, Wendy's
- **Lodg** **N:** Noce Motel, Pugh's Motel
  S: Days Inn, Interstate Motel, Ramada, Red Roof Inn, Washington Motor Inn
- **AServ** **N:** A & M Glass
  S: Amoco, Sears
- **TServ** **N:** Moving & Storage[SCALES]
- **ATM** **N:** Foodland Grocery
  S: BP, Exxon, PNC Bank, Washington Federal Savings
- **Other** **N:** BJ's Brushless Car Wash, Chestnut Laundry Depot, Foodland Grocery

5 **(16)** Jessop Place
- **Gas** **N:** Dean's Oil Co.[*, D, LP, K]
- **AServ** **N:** City Auto Reconditioning, Larry Cock's Auto Sales & Auto Repair[D, 24] (Towing)
  S: Beem's Collision Parts

6 **(17)** PA 18, Jefferson Ave
- **Gas** **N:** Gulf[*, D, CW], Texaco[*, D]
- **Food** **N:** Chinese Kitchen, Dairy Queen, Firinci's Pizza, McDonald's, Ten Different Hot Dogs
  S: 4-Star Pizza, Burger King, Krency's
- **AServ** **N:** All Pro Auto Parts, Pennzoil Oil Change
  S: Jefferson Auto
- **Med** **N:** ✚ Emergency Medical Center
  S: ✚ Hospital
- **ATM** **N:** Co Go's Convenience Store, Washington Federal Savings
  S: Foodland Grocery[RX]
- **Other** **N:** Co Go's Convenience Store, Coin Laundry, Rite

EXIT PENNSYLVANIA

Aid Pharmacy[RX]
  S: Distar Autograph, Foodland Grocery[RX], Viehmann Pharmacy[RX], Wonder Hostess Bakery & Thrift Shop

(18) Jct I-79 North - Pittsburgh

7AB **(19)** U.S 19, Murtland Ave
- **Gas** **S:** Amoco[*], BP[*, D, CW], Exxon, Sunoco[*], Texaco[*]
- **Food** **S:** Big Boy, Bob Evan's Restaurant, Burger King, China Feast, Donut Connection, Eat N Park, Jade Inn, KFC, Long John Silver, McDonald's, Papa John's Pizza, Pizza Hut, SHONEY'S, Shoney's, Taco Bell, The Italian Oven
- **Lodg** **S:** Hampton Inn, Motel 6
- **AServ** **S:** Amoco, Baer's Buick, Exxon, Firestone Tire & Auto, Midas Muffler, Monroe Muffler & Brakes, Tire America
- **Med** **S:** ✚ Hospital
- **ATM** **S:** Dollar Bank, Mellon Bank, National City Bank, PNC Bank
- **Other** **S:** K-Mart, State Police, Thrift Drug, Wal-Mart[RX] (Vision Center), Washington Mall

8 **(19)** PA 136, Beau St
- **RVCamp** **N:** KOA Campgrounds

Exit **(21)** Jct I-79 South, Waynesburg, Morgantown

9 **(25)** PA 519, Eighty Four, Glyde
- **TStop** **S:** Toot-N- Scoot[*, D, K, 24] (ATM)
- **Gas** **S:** Amoco[*, K]
- **Food** **S:** Toot-N- Scoot (ATM)
- **AServ** **S:** Eighty Four Auto Sales, Toot-N- Scoot[24] (ATM)
- **TServ** **S:** Toot-N- Scoot[24] (ATM)
- **RVCamp** **N:** Robert L. Jones RV Parts & Service
- **ATM** **S:** Amoco

10 **(28)** Dunningsville
- **Food** **S:** Avalon Motor Inn
- **Lodg** **S:** Avalon Motor Inn

11 **(30)** Kammerer
- **Food** **N:** Carlton Motel
- **Lodg** **N:** Carlton Motel
- **Parks** **N:** Mingo Creek County Park

12A **(33)** PA 917, Ginger Hill

12B **(33)** PA 917, Bentleyville, Ginger Hill
- **TStop** **S:** Pilot Travel Center[*, D, K, SCALES, 24]
- **Gas** **S:** Amoco[*]
- **Food** **N:** King of the Hill Restaurant
  S: Burger King, Dairy Queen (Pilot), Lounge & Grill, McDonald's, Subway (Pilot)
- **AServ** **S:** Advance Auto Parts, Tregembo Ford
- **TWash** **S:** Pilot Travel Center
- **RVCamp** **N:** Campground 70 (.75 Miles)
- **Med** **S:** ✚ Southwest Medical Center
- **ATM** **S:** Amoco, National City Bank, Pilot Travel Center
- **Other** **S:** Giant Eagle Food Store, Rite Aid Pharmacy[RX]

13 **(35)** PA 481, Monongahela, Centerville
- **Med** **N:** ✚ Hospital

14 **(36)** Lover (Westbound, Reaccess Eastbound Only)

15AB **(38)** PA 43, Toll Road South, CA (Toll)

16 **(40)** Speers
- **Gas** **S:** Exxon[*]
- **Food** **N:** Lorraine's Family
- **AServ** **S:** Exxon
- **RVCamp** **N:** Camping
  S: Bethany Christian Campground (1 Mile)

17 **(41)** PA 88, Charleroi, Allenport
- **Gas** **N:** Amoco[*], Texaco[*, D, K, 24]
- **Food** **N:** KFC, Pizza Hut (Texaco), Sub Express (Amoco), Taco Bell (Texaco)
  S: Campy's Pizza & BBQ, Snooters's
- **Med** **N:** ✚ Hospital

Bold red print shows RV & Bus parking available or nearby

EXIT PENNSYLVANIA

ATM N: National City Bank
Other N: Car Wash

18 **(41)** PA 906, Belle Vernon , Monessen
ASErv S: Wince Auto & Truck Repair
TServ S: Wince Auto & Truck Repair
Med N: + Monn Valley Hospital

19 **(42)** North Belle Vernon (Difficult Reaccess)
Gas S: BP(*), Sunoco(*, D, 24)
Food S: Dairy Queen, Hardees (BP)
AServ S: Roley Body Shop
ATM S: BP
Other S: Duritza's Grocery(LP)

19A Monessen (Difficult Reaccess)

20AB **(43)** PA 201, to PA 837, Denora, Fayette City
Gas N: Val's(*)
S: Exxon(*), Sunoco(*, 24)
Food S: Best Val-U Motel, Big K-Mart, Burger King, Denny's, Dunkin Donuts (Exxon), KFC, Little Bamboo Chinese, Little Caesars Pizza, Long John Silver, McDonald's (Wal-Mart), McDonald's, Peking Buffet (Best Val-U Motel), Redd Dawgs All Star Clubhouse, Subway, Wendy's
Lodg S: Best Val-U Motel
AServ S: Advance Auto Parts, Kelly Auto Parts and Service, Penske, Wal-Mart Supercenter(RX) (Supermarket, Vision Center)
Med N: + Hospital
ATM S: First Federal Savings, McDonald's, Naional City Bank, PNC Bank, Shop "N" Save, Wal-Mart Supercenter (Supermarket, Vision Center)
Other N: Coin Car Wash
S: Aqua Jet Car Wash, Big K-Mart, Eckerd Drugs(RX), Giant Eagle Supermarket, Shop "N" Save, Union Laundromat, Wal-Mart Supercenter(RX) (Supermarket, Vision Center)

21 **(44)** Arnold City

22AB **(46)** PA 51, Pittsburgh, Uniontown
FStop S: Texaco(*, D, 24) (Commercial Fueling)
Gas N: Exxon(*)
Food N: Howard Johnson
S: Cedar Brook Golf Course(*), Holiday Inn, The Main Course (Cedar Brook Golf Course)
Lodg N: Budget Host, Howard Johnson
S: 5 M's Hotel, Cedar Brook Golf Course, Holiday Inn, Knotty Pine Motel
AServ N: Exxon
ATM S: Texaco (Commercial Fueling)
Parks N: Cedar Creek Park
Other S: Cedar Brook Golf Course

23 **(49)** Smithton
TStop N: Shell(*, D, SCALES) (ATM), Smithton Truckstop(*, D, K, SCALES)

EXIT PENNSYLVANIA

Food N: Ethyl Creek (Shell TS), Old Farmhouse Pizza & Hoagies, Shell (ATM), Silly Corral Brass Saddle, Smithton Truckstop, Someone Donut (Smithton TS)
TServ N: Shell(SCALES) (ATM)
S: Truck of Western PA Sales, Parts & Service
TWash N: Shell (ATM), Smithton Truckstop
ATM N: Smithton Truckstop
Other N: Motor Dome Speedway

24AB **(51)** PA 31, West Newton, Mt Pleasant

25 **(53)** Yukon
RVCamp N: KOA Campgrounds (.75 Miles)

25A **(54)** Madison
FStop S: Atlantic(*, D), Citgo(D)
AServ S: Citgo
TServ S: Atlantic
RVCamp N: Camping (1 Mile)
Other S: Larry's CB Shop (Atlantic)

26 **(57)** New Stanton
Gas N: Exxon(*), Sheetz(*, LP, K, 24), Sunoco(*)
S: BP(*, D), Sunoco(*, D, 24)
Food N: Bob Evan's Restaurant, Donut Chef, Eat N Park, KFC, McDonald's, Pagano's Family Restaurant, Pepperidge Restaurant (Ramada), Pizza Hut, Subway, Szechuan Wok, Wendy's
S: Cracker Barrel, La Tavola Ristorante
Lodg N: Budget Inn, Comfort Inn, Days Inn (see our ad this page), Howard Johnson, Ramada Inn, Super 8
S: New Stanton Motel
AServ S: BP, New Stanton Auto Sales
RVCamp N: Campground
ATM N: Exxon, Mellon Bank, Sheetz, Southwest Bank
Other N: Coin Car Wash
S: New Stanton Pharmacy(RX)

DAYS INN 724-925-3591
New Stanton, Pennsylvania 1412
• Restaurant/Lounge on Premises
• Outdoor Pool • Exercise Room
• Meeting/Banquet Facilities
• Coin Laundry
Located at the Intersection of I-70 & PA. Turnpike, Exit #8 (I-76)
Pennsylvania ▪ I-70 ▪ Exit 26

EXIT PENNSYLVANIA

Note: I-70 runs concurrent below with I-76. Numbering follows I-76.

8 **(75)** Jct I-70W, U.S. 119, PA 66 N, New Stanton, Greensburg, Wheeling WV (Toll)
RVCamp S: Fox Den Acres Campground (2 Miles)

(78) New Stanton Service Plaza (Westbound)
FStop W: Sunoco(*)
Food W: King's Family, McDonald's
ATM W: Machine

9 **(91)** Donegal, PA 31, PA 711, Legonier, Uniontown (Toll)
FStop S: Citgo(*)
Gas S: Exxon(*, D), Sunoco, Texaco(*)
Food N: Laurel Highlands Lodge, Tall Cedars Inn
S: Candlelight Family, Dairy Queen
Lodg N: Laurel Highlands Lodge
S: Days Inn, Donegal Motel
AServ S: Sunoco
RVCamp S: Donegal Campground (.5 Miles), Laurel Highland Campgrounds (.75 Miles), Mountain Pines Campground (3 Miles), Pioneer Park Campground (11 Miles)
ATM S: PNC Bank
Parks S: Kooser State Park, Laurel Hills State Park, Laurel Ridge State Park, Ohiopyle State Park

(94) Parking Area (Picnic; Westbound)

10 **(110)** U.S. 219, Somerset, Johnstown (Toll)
TStop S: Jim's Auto/Truckstop(*)
Gas N: Quick Fill, Sheetz(*), Your Car Wash
S: Exxon(*)
Food N: Hoss's Steakhouse, Kings Family Restaurant, Pizza Hut, Taco Bell
S: Arby's, China Garden, Dairy Queen, Dunkin Donuts, Eat N Park, Holiday Inn, Jim's TS, KFC, Little Caesars Pizza, Long John Silver, Maggie Mae's Cafe, McDonald's, Myron's Restaurant, Pine Grill, Ramada Inn, Subway, Summit Diner, Wendy's, Yogurt Ice Cream Classics
Lodg N: Dollar Inn, Economy Inn
S: Best Western, Budget Host Inn, Budget Inn, Days Inn, Economy Inn, Hampton Inn, Holiday Inn, Knight's Inn, Ramada
AServ N: Dumbaulds Tire, Ford Dealership, Mardis Chrysler Plymouth, Midas Muffler & Brake, Speedy Lube
TServ N: Mulhollen
S: Jim's Auto/Truckstop
TWash N: Your Car Wash
Med S: + Hospital
ATM S: Jim's TS
Other N: Coin Car Wash, Horizon Outlet Center

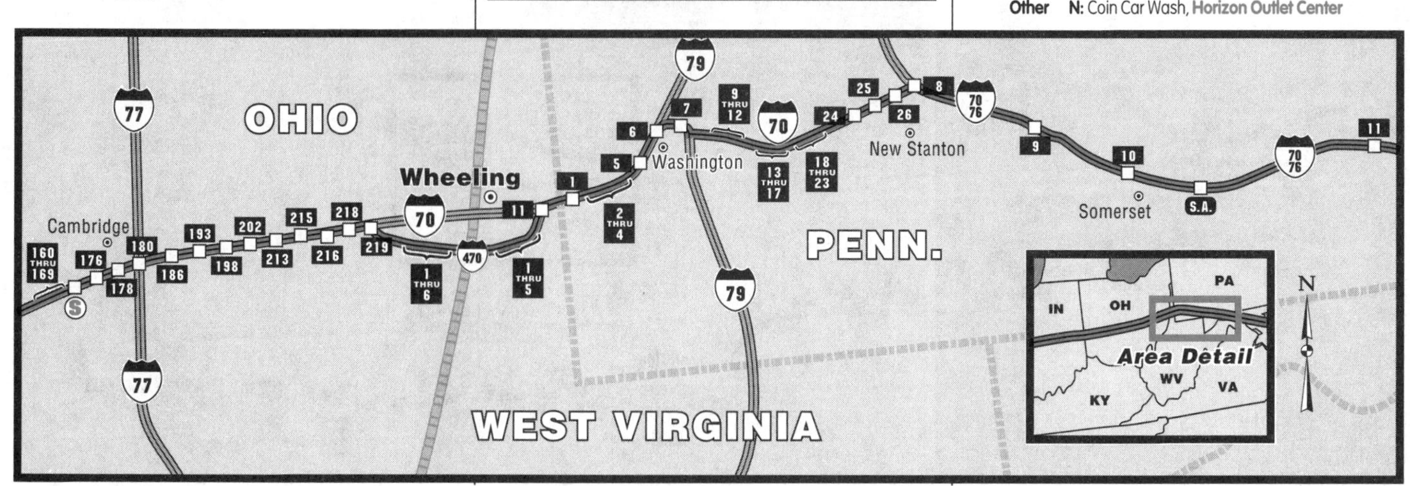

EXIT PENNSYLVANIA

S: Clean Water Car Wash, Coin Laundry, Visitor Information

(112) **Somerset Service Plaza**
FStop **B:** Sunoco(*)
Food **B:** Bob's Big Boy, Hershey's Ice Cream, Roy Rogers, TCBY
W: Burger King, Hershey's Ice Cream, TCBY
AServ **B:** Sunoco
ATM **B:** ATM

11 **(146)** U.S. 220, Bedford, Altoona, Johnstown (Toll)
FStop **N:** Amoco(*), BP(*)
Gas **N:** Sunoco(*, D), Texaco(*, D, LP)
Food **N:** Baskin Robbins, Budget Inn (Sunoco), Burger King, Chester Fried Chicken (BP), China Inn, Clara's Place (Best Western), Denny's, Dunkin Donuts, Ed's Steakhouse, Hardee's, Hoss's Steak & Sea House, Long John Silver, McDonald's (Amoco), Pizza Hut, Sub Express, The Arena (Quality Inn), The Country Apple Restaurant (EconoLodge)
Lodg **N:** Best Western, Budget Inn, Econolodge, Host Inn, Midway Motel, Quality Inn, Super 8
S: Motor Town House
TServ **N:** Mack Truck
RVCamp **S:** Friendship Village Campground
ATM **N:** BP
Other **S:** Visitor Information

(147) **North Midway Service Plaza**
FStop **B:** Sunoco(*)
Food **B:** Hershey's Ice Cream, KFC, Mrs Fields Cookies, Sbarro Italian, TCBY
AServ **B:** Sunoco
ATM **B:** PNC Bank

12 **(161)** U.S. 30, Everett, Breezewood, to I-70 East, Hagerstown (Toll)
TStop **S:** All American 76 Truck Plaza(*, SCALES), T/A TravelCenters of America(*, SCALES)
Gas **S:** Amoco (TA), BP(*), Citgo(*), Exxon(*, D), Sheetz(*), Sunoco(*), Texaco(*)
Food **N:** Breeze Manor Restaurant (Quality Inn), McDonald's, Prime Rib Restaurant (Ramada Inn)
S: Arby's, Arthur Treacher's Fish & Chips, Blimpie's Subs (Am Best), Bob Evan's Restaurant, Bonanza Steakhouse, Burger King, Dairy Queen(*, SCALES) (TA), Deli Cafe (Sunoco), Family House Restaurant (Bus Parking), Gateway Restaurant (TA), Hardee's, Hershey's Ice Cream (Am Best), KFC, Little Caesars Pizza (TA), McDonald's, Oven Fresh Bakery (TA), Perkins Family Restaurant (Am Best), Pizza Hut, Post House Cafeteria (Am Best), Stuckey's Express (Exxon), Subway, Taco Bell, Taco Maker (Am Best), Uncle Bud's Pizza (Am Best), Wendy's
Lodg **N:** Pan Am Motel, Quality Inn, Ramada Inn
S: Best Western, Breezewood Motel, Comfort Inn, Econolodge (TA), Penn Aire Motel, Wiltshire Motel
TServ **S:** AmBest, T/A TravelCenters of America
RVCamp **N:** Breezewood Campground (.25 Miles)
ATM **S:** Sunoco, T/A TravelCenters of America

(172) **Sideling Hill Service Area (RV Dump)**
FStop **B:** Sunoco(*)
Food **B:** Bob's Big Boy, Burger King, Pretzel Time, TCBY
AServ **B:** Sunoco
ATM **B:** PNC Bank
Other **B:** RV Dump Station, Tourist Info.

13 **(179)** U.S. 522, McConnelsburg, Mount Union (Toll)
Gas **N:** Amoco(*), Exxon(*)
Food **N:** Fort Family Restaurant
Lodg **N:** Downe's Motel #2
S: Downe's Motel
AServ **N:** Amoco
Med **N:** ✚ Hospital
Other **N:** State Police

14 **(189)** PA 75, Fort Loudon, Willow Hill (Toll)
Food **S:** TJ's Restaurant
Lodg **S:** Willow Hill Motel

15 **(201)** PA 997, Blue Mountain, Shippensburg, Chambersburg (Toll)
Gas **S:** Johnnies
Food **S:** Johnnies
Lodg **S:** Blue Mountain Brick Motel, Kenmar Motel

Note: I-70 runs concurrent above with I-76. Numbering follows I-76.

28 **(149)** U.S 30 to I-76, PA Turnpike

DAYS INN
Scenic Mountain View
Continental Breakfast 1794
Free HBO • Free Local Calls
Meeting/Banquet Facilities
Handicap Accessible • Interior Corridors
Truck/Large Vehicle Parking
Easy On-Off I-75
30 min. from White Tail Ski Resort
Tour Bus & Travel Packages
814-735-3836 • Warfordsburg, PA
Pennsylvania • I-70 • Exit 31

TStop **S:** AmBest Truck Stop(*), TravelCenters of America(*, SCALES)
FStop **S:** BP(*)
Gas **S:** Exxon(*), Sunoco(*, D), Texaco(*, LP)
Food **N:** Prime Rib (Ramada Inn)
S: 76 Auto/Truck Plaza, Arby's, Arthur Treacher's Fish & Chips, Bob Evan's Restaurant, Bonanza Steakhouse, Burger King, China Bamboo, Comfort Inn, Dairy Queen, Deli Cafe (Sunoco), Dunkin Donuts, Family House Restaurant, Gateway Restaurant (TS of America), Hardee's, KFC, Little Caesars Pizza, McDonald's, Pizza Hut, Post House Cafe, Taco Bell, Wendy's
Lodg **N:** Quality Inn, Ramada
S: Best Western, Breezewood Motel, Comfort Inn, Econolodge (TravelCenters Of America), Penn Aire Motel, Wiltshire Motel
AServ **N:** Sac Inc
S: BP
TServ **S:** 76 Auto/Truck Plaza(*), TravelCenters of America
RVCamp **S:** Breezewood Campground (4 Miles), Brush Creek Campground (4 Miles), Camping, Crestview Campground (4 Miles)
ATM **S:** TravelCenters of America

29 **(150)** U.S 30 West, Everett (Low Clearance-14'3")
Food **S:** The Wildwood Inn
Lodg **S:** Hi-Way Motel, Panorama Motel, Ritchey's Redwood Motel, Stonewall Jackson Motel, Wildwood Inn
RVCamp **S:** Hide Away Campground

30 **(154)** PA 915, Crystal Spring
Gas **S:** Atlantic
Food **N:** Dutch Hausn and Restaurant
Lodg **N:** Motel 70
TServ **N:** Fischer's Major Repairs
RVCamp **S:** Brush Creek Campground (.5 Miles)
Other **S:** Country C-Store, Post Office

(156) **Rest Area (RR, Phones, Picnic, Vending; Eastbound)**

31 **(158)** PA 643, Town Hill
TStop **N:** Town Hill Truckstop- Texaco(*, LP, RV DUMP, SCALES)
Food **N:** Days Inn
Lodg **N:** Days Inn (see our ad this page)

32 **(166)** PA 731, Amaranth

33 **(171)** U.S 522 North, Warfordsburg
Gas **N:** Exxon(*)
Food **N:** Nan's Kettle
AServ **N:** Beatty's

(172) **PA Welcome Center (RR, Phones,**

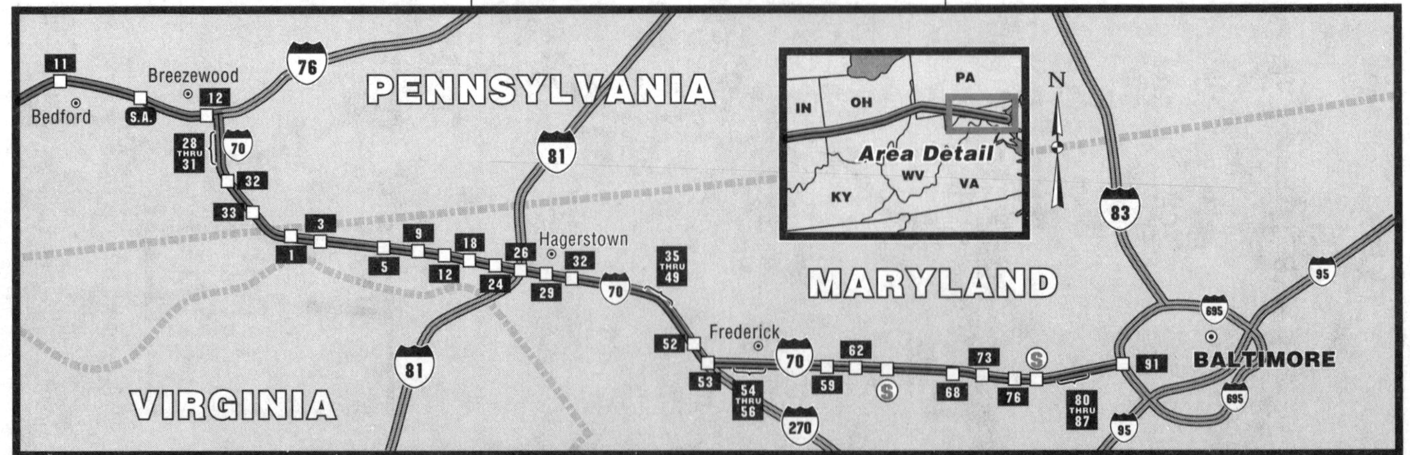

Bold red print shows RV & Bus parking available or nearby

EXIT	PENNSYLVANIA/MARYLAND
	Picnic, Vending)

↑PENNSYLVANIA

↓MARYLAND

1A Jct I-68, U.S 40 West, Cumberland (Left Exit Westbound)

1B U.S 522 South, Hancock, Winchester (Left Exit Westbound)
- Gas S: Gary's, Sheetz(*)
- Food S: Fox's Pizza, Pizza Hut
- Lodg S: Comfort Inn, Hancock Motel
- RVCamp S: Happy Hills Campground
- Other S: Sav-A-Lot Grocery

3 MD 144, Hancock (Left Exit Westbound)
- TStop S: Hancock Truckstop(*) (Amoco)
- Gas S: BP(*, D), Citgo(*, D, LP), Hancock Truckstop(*) (Amoco)
- Food S: Little Sandy's Restaurant (Hancock TS)
- TServ S: Hancock Truckstop (Amoco)
- ATM S: Home Federal Savings Bank
- Other S: Coin Car Wash

5 MD 615 (Left Exit)

9 U.S 40, Indian Springs (Left Exit, Difficult Reaccess)

12 MD 56, Big Pool, Indian Springs
- RVCamp N: Indian Springs Campground (1 Mile)
- Parks S: Fort Frederick State Park (1 Mile)

18 MD 68, Clear Spring
- Gas N: Amoco(*), BP(*)
  S: Exxon(*, D)
- Food N: Al's Pizza (BP), Chester Fried Chicken (BP), McDonald's
- AServ S: Exxon
- ATM N: American Trust Bank, BP

24 MD 63, Williamsport, Huyett
- AServ N: Keefer's Towing and Repair Service
- RVCamp S: KOA Campgrounds (2 Miles)
- Other S: CNO Canal

26 Jct I-81, Roanoke, Harrisburg

29 MD65, Sharpsburg, Hagerstown
- FStop S: Shell(*)
- Gas N: Mobil(*, CW, 24), Sunoco(*, D, CW)
- Food S: Blimpie's Subs (Shell), Burger King(PLAY), Hot Stuff Pizza (Shell), McDonald's(PLAY), Wendy's
- RVCamp S: Yogi Bear Camp Resort
- ATM S: Shell
- Other N: Prime Outlets at Hagerstown
  S: Antdem Battlefield, Sharpsburg Battlefield

32AB U.S 40, Hagerstown
- Lodg N: Comfort Suites Hotel, Days Inn (see our ad on I-81, Exit 6A, MD), Four Points Sheraton
- AServ N: Younger Mercedes Dealer
  S: Hagerstown Honda, Sharrett Volkswagon Oldsmobile, Mazda
- Med N: ✚ Hospital

35 MD 66, Boonsboro, Smithsburg
- RVCamp N: Camping
  S: Camping
- Parks S: George Washington State Park
- Other N: Albert Powell Fish Hatchery

(39) Welcome Center, Rest Area (RR, Phones, Picnic, Vending, RV Dump, Pet Walk)

42 Maryland 17, Myersville, Middletown Road
- FStop S: Amoco(*)
- Gas N: Exxon(*, LP), Sunoco(D, 24)
- Food N: McDonald's(PLAY)
- AServ N: Sunoco(24)
  S: Amoco
- ATM N: Exxon
- Parks N: Gambrill State Park (6 Miles), Greenbrier State Park (4 Miles)

48 US 40 E, Frederick (Difficult Reaccess)
- Gas N: Mobil(D)
- Food N: Barbara Fritchie Fine Dining, Bob Evan's Restaurant, Burger King, Dairy Delight (Ice Cream & Subs), House of Kobe Japanese, Masser's Motel, McDonald's(PLAY)
- Lodg N: Masser's Motel
- AServ N: Golden Mile, Mobil
- Med N: ✚ Hospital
- ATM N: 7-11 Convenience Store, Weis Grocery & Pharmacy(RX)
- Other N: 7-11 Convenience Store, Aurorua Car & Van Wash, Weis Grocery & Pharmacy(RX), West Fredrick Animal Hospital

49 U.S 40 Alternate, Braddock Heights, Middletown (Westbound, Difficult Reaccess)
- Parks S: Washington Monument State Park
- Other N: MD State Police

52 U.S 340 West, U.S 15, Charles Town, Gettysburg

53 Jct I-270 to Washington

54 MD 355 to MD 85, Market St, Frederick
- TStop N: Frederick I-70 Truck City(*, SCALES)
- FStop S: Mobil(*), Southern States(*)
- Gas S: Exxon(*, D)

- Food N: Frederick I-70 Truck City
  S: Burger King(PLAY), Checkers Burgers, Dunkin Donuts, El Paso Restaurant, Papa John's Pizza, Wendy's
- Lodg N: I-70 Motor Inn (Fredrick TS), Crown America (see our ad this page),
  S: Econolodge, Days Inn (see our ad this page)
- AServ S: AAMCO Transmission, Ideal Hyundai, Buick, GMC Trucks, Precision Tune & Lube, S&S Tires, SSK Lincoln, Mercury, Audi, Saturn Dealership, Wal-Mart(RX)
- TServ N: Frederick I-70 Truck City(SCALES)
  S: S&S Tires
- ATM N: Frederick I-70 Truck City
- Other S: Wal-Mart(RX)

55 South St, Frederick
- TServ S: Donald B Rice Tire Co

56 MD144, Patrick St
- Gas N: Citgo(*, LP), Sheetz(*, 24)
- Food N: Bejing Chinese, Belles' Pit Beef, Roy Rogers
- TServ N: Grimes Truck Center
- RVCamp S: Triangle Outdoor World Sales & Services
- ATM N: F&M Bank, SCN Bank

59 MD 144 (Westbound, Reaccess Eastbound Only)

62 MD 75, Libertytown, Hyattstown
- Gas N: Mobil(*, CW, 24)
- Food N: Domino's Pizza, Little George's Deli, McDonald's
- ATM N: F & M Bank, Mobil
- Other N: Food Lion Supermarket, Medicine Plus Pharmacy(RX)

(64) Weigh Station (Eastbound)

(67) Truck Parking Area (Eastbound, No Cars)

68 MD 27, Damascus, Mount Airy
- Gas N: Amoco(*, D)
  S: Exxon(*, D, 24)
- Food N: Chong Yet Yin Chinese, Roy Rogers, TCBY, Zeller's Buffet
- AServ S: Exxon(24)
- ATM N: First Bank of Frederick, Super Fresh Food Market(RX), Union Nat'l Bank, Westminister Bank
- Other N: Rite Aid Pharmacy, Safeway Grocery, Super Fresh Food Market(RX)

73 MD 94, Woodbine, Lisbon
- Food N: McDonald's, Mr Teddy's Restaurant & Deli, Pizza Hut
- RVCamp N: Ramblin' Pines (4 Miles)
- ATM N: Sandy Spring Nat'l Bank, Westminster Bank
- Other N: Harvest Fare Supermarket, Woodbine Animal Hospital

76 MD 97, Westminster, Olney, Cookesville
- Food S: Cooksville Cafe

(78) Weigh Station (Westbound)

80 MD 32, Sykesville, Clarksville

82 U.S 40, Ellicott City (Eastbound, Reaccess Westbound Only)

83 Marriottsville Road (Westbound, Reaccess Eastbound Only)

87AB U.S 29, to MD 99, Columbia, Washington

91AB Jct I-695, to I-95

94 Security Blvd N, Park & Ride

↑MARYLAND

Begin I-70

Bold red print shows RV & Bus parking available or nearby

EXIT OHIO

Begin I-71

↓OHIO

247B Junction I-90 West
247A West 14th St, Clark Ave (Northbound, Limited Access)
246 Dennison Ave (Southbound, Left Exit)
245 U.S. 42, Pearl Rd, West 25th St , Fulton Rd.
- Gas W: Clark Gas(*, K)
- Food E: China Town, Little Caesars Pizza, Phoenix Coffee House, Wendy's
  W: Marvin's Deli
- AServ W: Bargo's Service Center
- Med W: + Hospital
- ATM E: American Cash Express
- Other E: CVS Pharmacy(RX), Convenience Food Mart, Murray's Discount Auto Store, Spin Cycle Coin Laundry, Zoo

244 Denison Ave, West 65th St (Northbound, Left Exit Northbound)
242 West 130th St (Northbound sign reads 242AB)
- Gas W: BP(*), Sunoco(*)
- Food W: Dairy Mart, Little Caesars Pizza (Dairy Mart)
- AServ W: Sunoco
- ATM W: Sunoco
- Other W: City of Cleveland Police, Dairy Mart

240 West 150th St
- Gas E: Marathon(*), Shell(*, 24), Sunoco
  W: BP(*, CW)
- Food E: China Chef, Denny's, Jimmy C's, Marriot
  W: Country Kitchen, Holiday Inn, Oriental Palace, Winners (Holiday Inn)
- Lodg E: Marriot
  W: Budgetel Inn, Holiday Inn
- AServ E: Goodyear (Marathon), Lube Stop, Marathon, Shell(24), Sunoco
- ATM E: Charter 1 Bank, National City Bank, Star Bank
- Other E: Mark's Grocery Store
  W: Soft Cloth Car Wash

239 Ohio 237 South, Airport, Berea (Southbound, Left Exit)
238 Junction I-480, Airport, Toledo, Youngstown
237BA to Ohio 17, Brookpark Road, Engle Road, Snow Road (237B goes to the west, 237A goes to the east)
- Lodg E: Best Western, Fairfield Inn

235 Bagley Rd, Berea, Middleburg Heights
- Gas W: BP(*, D), Shell(*), Speedway(*)
- Food E: Bob Evan's Restaurant
  W: Burger King, Damon's, Denny's, Dunkin Donuts, Friendly's, Golden Corral Family Steakhouse, Hong Kong Palace, McDonald's, Olive Garden, Penn Station East Coast Subs, Perkins Family Restaurant, Pizza Hut, Taco Bell
- Lodg E: Harvey Hotel
  W: Comfort Inn, Cross Country Inn, Hampton Inn, Middleheights Studio Plus, Motel 6, Radisson, Red Roof Inn, Residence Inn
- AServ E: BP Pro Care
  W: Gene Norris Olds, K-Mart(RX), Lube Stop, Shell
- Med W: + Hospital
- ATM W: Speedway
- Other W: K-Mart(RX), Rapid Car Wash

234 U.S. 42, Parma Heights, Strongsville
- Gas E: Shell(CW), Sunoco(*)
- Food E: House of Hunan Chinese, Islander Grill, Mr Hero Cheese Steaks, Santo's Pizza
- Lodg W: La Siesta Motel

EXIT OHIO

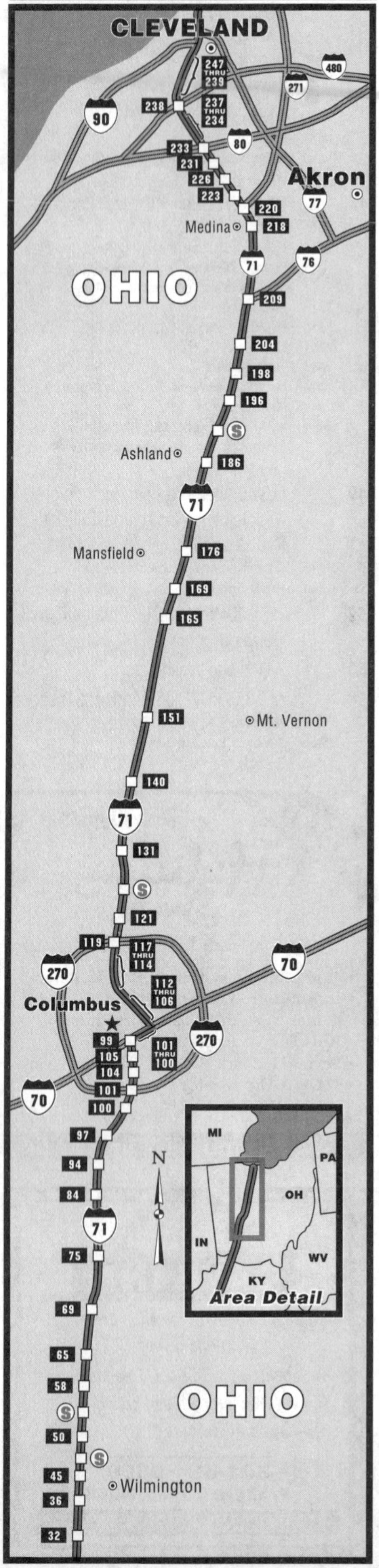

EXIT OHIO

- AServ E: Saturn Dealership, Shell, Sunnyside Audi, Porsche,Honda
- ATM E: Convenient Food Mart, Sunoco
- Other E: Briar Cliff Party Center Restaurant & Lounge, Convenient Food Mart
  W: Builders Square, Coin Car Wash, Wal-Mart(RX)

233 Jct I-80, OH Tnpk, Youngstown, Toledo (Toll)
231AB OH 82, Strongsville, Royalton
- Gas E: Shell(*, CW, 24)
  W: BP(*, LP, CW), Marathon(*, CW), Sunoco(*)
- Food E: Holiday Inn
  W: Country Kitchen, Longhorn Steakhouse, Mr Steak, Romano's Macaroni Grill
- Lodg E: Holiday Inn, Red Roof Inn
- AServ W: BP, Lube Stop, Marathon, Meuller Tire, Midas Muffler & Brake, Sunoco
- Med W: + Cleveland Clinic Hospital
- ATM W: Marathon
- Other E: River Run Raquet Club
  W: Medic Drugs(RX), South Park Center Mall

226 OH303, Brunswick
- FStop E: Pacific Pride(*, 24) (Amoco gas)
- Gas W: BP(*), Marathon(*, CW), Sunoco(*, D)
- Food E: Denny's, Pizza Hut
  W: Big Boy, Bob Evan's Restaurant, Burger King, Friendly's, McDonald's, Taco Bell, Wendy's
- Lodg W: Howard Johnson, Sleep Inn
- RVCamp E: Camping World (see our ad this page),
- AServ E: Brunswick Toyota/ Chrysler/ Plymouth
  W: K-Mart(RX), Marathon, Norris Ford
- TServ E: Goodyear Truck Tire Center, Williams Carrier Detroit Diesel Allison
- ATM E: Pacific Pride (Amoco gas)
  W: Bank One
- Other E: Countryside Animal Hospital
  W: Country Counter Food& Drug Store(RX), K-Mart(RX)

(225) Rest Area (RR, Phones, Picnic; Northbound)
(224) Rest Area (RR, Phones, Picnic; Southbound)
222 OH 3 , Medina
- Other W: Highway Patrol, Medina County Fairgrounds

220 Jct I-271 North, Erie, Pennsylvania (Northbound)
218 OH 18, Akron, Medina
- Gas E: BP(*, D), Citgo(*, D), Shell(*, CW, 24), Speedway(*), Sunoco(*, D, LP)
- Food E: Big Boy, Burger King, Cracker Barrel, Dairy Queen, Holiday Inn Express, McDonald's, Medina Best Western, Medina Family (Holiday Inn Express), On Tap Bar & Grill (Suburbanite Motel), Perkins Family Restaurant, Speedway, Suburbanite Motel, Sunoco
  W: Arby's, BW-3 Grill & Pub, Bob Evan's Restaurant, Pizza Hut
- Lodg E: Holiday Inn Express, Medina Best Western, Suburbanite Motel
  W: Cross Country Inn
- AServ E: Toth Olds/GMC Trucks
  W: Chesrown Medina Honda, Norris Pontiac/ Buick/Dodge
- Med W: + Hospital

CAMPING WORLD®
Exit 226
1244 Industrial Pkwy. N. • Brunswick, OH
1-800-528-4566
1419

Bold red print shows RV & Bus parking available or nearby

EXIT OHIO

209 Jct I-76, U.S. 224, Lodi, Akron (Services On U.S.224)
- **TStop** W: 76 Auto/Truck Plaza(*, SCALES), TA TravelCenters of America(*, SCALES) (Truck service)
- **FStop** W: Speedway(*, K)
- **Food** W: 76 Auto/Truck Plaza, Blimpie's Subs (Speedway), Country Kitchen (Speedway), Country Pride (TravelCenters of America), McDonald's, Speedway, TA TravelCenters of America (Truck service), Taco Bell (Speedway)
- **Lodg** W: HoJo Inn (TravelCenters of America), TA TravelCenters of America (Truck service)
- **TServ** W: 76 Auto/Truck Plaza(SCALES)
- **TWash** W: 76 Auto/Truck Plaza, Blue Beacon Truck Wash (TA TS), TA TravelCenters of America (Truck service)
- **RVCamp** W: Chippewa Valley Camping (.7 Miles)
- **ATM** W: Speedway
- **Other** W: Chippewa Lake, Seville

204 OH 83, Lodi, Wooster
- **FStop** E: BP(*, D), Khalsa's Gas/Diesel(*)
- **Gas** E: Duke(*), Shell(*, LP)
- **Food** E: Duke, Khalsa's Gas/Diesel, Taco Bell (Duke)
- **Lodg** E: The Plaza Motel
- **AServ** E: Bear's Towing
- **Med** W: ✚ Hospital
- **Other** W: Prime Outlets at Lodi

198 OH 539, West Salem, Congress
- **RVCamp** W: Town & Country Camp Resort (1.9 Miles)

(197) Rest Area (RR, Phones, Picnic, Vending; Southbound)

(197) Rest Area (RR, Phones, Picnic, Vending; Northbound)

196 OH301, West Salem (Northbound, Reaccess Southbound Only)

(190) Weigh Station (Southbound)

186 U.S. 250, Ashland, Wooster
- **TStop** W: TA TravelCenters of America(*, SCALES) (BP gas)
- **Gas** E: Citgo(*, D)
- **Food** E: Grandpa's Village Deli Sandwiches, H & B Coffee Gifts & Crafts, Perkins Family Restaurant
  W: Country Pride (TravelCenters of America), Denny's, McDonald's, TA TravelCenters of America (BP gas), Wendy's
- **Lodg** W: Amerihost Inn, Days Inn, TraveLodge
- **TServ** W: TA TravelCenters of America(SCALES) (BP gas)
- **RVCamp** E: Hickory Lake Campground (7.2 Miles)
- **Med** W: ✚ Hospital
- **Other** E: Sweeties Jumbo Chocolates
  W: Highway Patrol

(180) Rest Area (RR, Phones, Picnic; Northbound)

(180) Rest Area (RR, Phones, Picnic; Southbound)

176 U.S. 30, Mansfield, Wooster
- **Gas** E: Marathon(*)
- **Food** E: EconoLodge, Ike's Great American Restaurant (EconoLodge)
- **Lodg** E: EconoLodge
- **Other** E: Antique Mall

173 OH 39, Mansfield, Lucas

169 OH 13, Mansfield, Bellville
- **Gas** E: BP(*, D, K)
  W: Citgo(*)
- **Food** E: BP, Cracker Barrel, Daugherty's Family
  W: Arby's, Bob Evan's Restaurant, Burger King, Denny's, McDonald's, SHONEY'S, Shoney's, Taco Bell
- **Lodg** E: Budgetel Inn
  W: Super 8 (see our ad this page), TraveLodge
- **AServ** E: BP
- **Med** W: ✚ Hospital

EXIT OHIO

- **ATM** E: BP
- **Parks** E: Mohican State Park (19 Miles)
- **Other** E: Ski Area
  W: Clothing Outlet, OH State Patrol, Tourist Info.

165 OH 97, Lexington, Bellville
- **FStop** E: Speedway(*)
- **Gas** E: BP(*, CW), Shell(*, D, 24)
- **Food** E: Burger King, Der Dutchman, Doc's Family Restaurant, McDonald's, Speedway
  W: Dinner Bell Restaurant, Wendy's
- **Lodg** E: Comfort Inn, Motel, Ramada Limited (see our ad this page), Star Inn
  W: Mid-Ohio Motel
- **RVCamp** E: Blue Lagoon Campground (8 Miles), Honey Creek Campground (8 Miles), Yogi Bear Camp Resort (8 Miles)
- **ATM** E: BP
- **Parks** E: Mohican State Park (14 Miles)

151 OH 95, Mount Gilead, Fredericktown
- **TStop** E: Duke(*, SCALES) (24 hr. Laundromat)
- **FStop** W: BP(*, D)
- **Gas** E: Marathon(*, K)
  W: Sunoco(*, 24)
- **Food** E: Gathering Family Restaurant, McDonald's, Wendy's
  W: Leaf Family
- **Lodg** E: Best Western Executive Inn, Duke (24 hr. Laundromat)
- **TServ** E: Duke(SCALES) (24 hr. Laundromat)
- **RVCamp** W: KOA Campgrounds (.5 Miles)
- **Med** W: ✚ Hospital
- **Parks** W: Mt Gilead State Park
- **Other** E: Highway Patrol

140 OH 61, Mount Gilead, Sunbury
- **Gas** W: Amoco(*), Sunoco(*)
- **Food** E: Sam's Deli
  W: Amoco, Ole Farmstead Inn, Subway (Sunoco), Sunoco, TCBY (Sunoco), Taco Bell (Sunoco)

RAMADA LIMITED
1000 Comfort Plaza Dr.
Bellville, OH 44813
419-886-7000
Free Deluxe Breakfast Buffet
Kids Under 12 Stay & Eat Free
Indoor Pool • Exercise Room
Meeting/Banquet Facilities
Handicap Accessible • Coin Laundry
Truck/Large Vehicle Parking
Golf Nearby • Interior Corridors
Restaurant Nearby
1591
OHIO ▪ I-71 ▪ Exit 165

(419) 756-8875
1-800-800-8000
Continental Breakfast • HBO
Movies On Demand • Kids 12 & Under Free
Suites • Many Restaurants Nearby
Free Local Calls • Massage Showerheads

EXIT OHIO

- **AServ** E: Brown's (24 hour towing)
- **ATM** W: Amoco, Sunoco

131 U.S.36, OH 37, Sunbury, Delaware, Ohio Wesleyan University
- **TStop** E: Flying J Travel Plaza(*, RV DUMP, SCALES) (Conoco gas)
- **FStop** E: Speedway(*, LP)
- **Gas** W: BP(*, D, CW), Shell(*, 24), Sunoco(*, D)
- **Food** E: Blimpie Subs & Salads (Speedway), Burger King(PLAY), Flying J Travel Plaza (Conoco gas), Speedway, The Cookery (Flying J)
  W: Arby's, Bob Evan's Restaurant, Subway, Taco Bell, Waffle House, Wendy's
- **Lodg** W: Hampton Inn, Holiday Inn
- **AServ** W: Sunoco
- **RVCamp** E: Camping
- **Med** W: ✚ Hospital
- **ATM** E: Speedway
  W: McDonald's
- **Parks** W: The Alum Creek State Park (6 Miles)

(130) Weigh Station (Northbound)

(128) Rest Area (RR, Phones, Picnic, Vending; Southbound)

(128) Rest Area (RR, Phones, Picnic, Vending; Northbound)

121 Polaris Parkway
- **Gas** E: BP(*, CW), Shell(*, LP, CW)
- **Food** E: BP, Blimpie Subs & Salads (BP), McDonald's, Polaris Grill
  W: Max & Erma's Restaurant, Wendy's
- **Lodg** E: Wingate Inn
- **Other** E: Polaris Amphitheater

119AB Junction I-270, Indianappolis, Wheeling

117 OH 161, Worthington, New Albany
- **Gas** E: BP(*)
  W: Super America(*)
- **Food** E: Caddo's (Days Inn), Days Inn, Max & Erma's Restaurant, TeeJay's Country Place Restaurant
  W: Best Western Columbus North, Bob Evan's Restaurant, Casa Fiesta Authentic Mexican Cuisine, China Jade, Crazy Louie's, Damon's, Domino's Pizza, Elephant Bar Restaurant, Helmsley Hotel, Houlihan's, Jiro-Cho, Mark Pi's Express, McDonald's, New House of Mandarin, O Tani Japanese, Pasta Petite, Pizza Hut, Sigee's Restaurant (Helmsley Hotel), Sky Line Chili, Stains Seafood & Steaks (Best Western), Subway, Thai Palace, The French Market, Waffle House, Wendy's
- **Lodg** E: Comfort Inn, Days Inn, Holiday Inn Express, Knight's Inn, Motel 6
  W: Best Western Columbus North, Cross Country Inn, EconoLodge, Extended Stay America, Hampton Inn, Helmsley Hotel, Paramount Hotel, Ramada Limited, Residence Inn, Super 8, The Truman Club Hotel
- **AServ** E: Firestone L&M Car Care Center
  W: Best Way Auto Care
- **Med** E: ✚ Hospital
- **ATM** E: BP, Bank One
- **Other** E: Carfagna's Italian Grocery Store, Fantasy Golf
  W: Coin Laundry, Sony Theaters Cinema

116 Morse Rd, Sinclair Rd
- **Gas** E: BP(*, LP, CW), Super America(*, LP, K)
  W: BP(*)
- **Food** E: Cloak & Dagger Dinner Theater, Niki's Restaurant
  W: SHONEY'S, Shoney's
- **Lodg** E: Fairfield Inn
  W: Cross Country Inn, Radisson Hotel, Red Roof Inn
- **AServ** E: Bob Daniel's Buick
  W: National Tire & Battery
- **Med** E: ✚ Health South Medical Clinic
- **Other** E: Family Fun Center

EXIT OHIO

W: Car Wash Express
115 Cooke Rd
114 North Broadway
Gas W: BP[*], Sunoco[*, D]
Med W: Hospital
Parks W: Columbus Park of Roses
113 Weber Rd
Gas W: Speedway[*]
Food W: Speedway
Other E: Nickles Bakery Thrift Store
W: Car Quest Auto Parts
112 Hudson St
Gas E: BP[*, LP, CW], Payless Auto Service[*], Shell[*, CW]
Food E: Wendy's
AServ E: John's Used Tires, Payless Auto Service
Med W: Hospital
Other E: A & B Locksmith, Miracle Car Wash
111 17th Ave
Food W: McDonald's
Lodg W: Days Inn
Other W: Ohio Historical Society Library & Museum, Ohio Village
110B 11th Ave
110A 5th Ave (Southbound)
Gas E: Sunoco[*, D]
W: BP[*], Shell[*, CW, 24]
Food E: KFC, White Castle Restaurant
W: Church's Chicken, Mr. Big's Smokehouse BBQ, Rally's Hamburgers, Wendy's
AServ E: Keen's Body Shop
W: Romero's Brake Service
Med W: Dr.'s Hospital North
ATM W: BP
Other W: Auto Zone Auto Parts
109A Junction I-670 , Airport
109B Leonard Ave, OH 3, Cleveland Ave
109C Spring St (Southbound, Left Exit Southbound)
108B U.S. 40, Broad St
108A U.S. 33, Main St (Southbound)
107 Junction I-70 E, Wheeling (Southbound, Left Exit Southbound)
106B Duppitin Rd., Rich Street, Towne Street
106A Junction I-70 West (Northbound, Left Exit Northbound)
105 Greenlawn Ave
Gas W: Fast and Fair Mini Mart[*]
RVCamp W: Greenlawn RV Sales & Service
Med E: Hospital
Parks E: Columbus Recreation & Parks
Other W: Cooper Stadium
104 OH 104, Frank Rd
101 Jct I-270, Wheeling, Indianapolis, Scioto Downs, Urban Crest, Buela Park
100 Stringtown Rd, Grove City
FStop W: Certified[*, LP, K]
Gas E: BP[*]
W: Speedway[*, LP, CW], Sunoco[24]
Food E: Bob Evan's Restaurant, Church's Chicken, Hampton Inn, Peddler Lounge (Hampton Inn), Ramada, White Castle Restaurant
W: Burger King, Captain D's Seafood, China Bell (Value Inn), Cracker Barrel, Cricket's Pub & Grill (Heritage Inn), Fazoli's Italian Food, Heritage Inn, KFC, McDonald's, Perkins Family Restaurant, Rally's Hamburgers, SHONEY'S, Shoney's, Tee Jaye's, Waffle House, Wendy's
Lodg E: Best Western Executive Inn, Cross Country Inn, Hampton Inn, Microtel Inn, Ramada
W: Comfort Inn, Heritage Inn, Red Roof Inn, Saver Motel, Value Inn
ATM E: BP
Parks W: Garden Ganz Park
Other W: Aldi Grocery Store
97 OH 665, London - Groveport Rd
Gas E: Dairy Mart[*], Sunoco[*]
Food E: Dairy Mart, Taco Bell (Dairy Mart), Tim Horton's,

EXIT OHIO

Wendy's
TServ E: Peterbilt Parts & Service
W: RW Diesel Service &Repair
ATM E: Dairy Mart, Sunoco
Other W: Evans Market Convenience Store, Fore Star Golf Center
94 U.S. 62, OH 3, Orient, Harrisburg
Gas E: BP[*, LP]
W: Shell[*], Sunoco[*]
AServ W: Shell
ATM W: Sunoco
84 OH 56, London, Mount Sterling
Gas E: BP[*, LP], Sunoco[*, LP]
Food E: BP, Subway (BP), Sunoco
Lodg E: Royal Inn
Parks E: Deer Creek State Park
75 OH 38, Midway, Bloomingburg
Gas W: Sunoco[*, LP]
ATM W: Sunoco
69 OH 41, OH 734, Jeffersonville , Washington CH
Gas W: BP[*], Shell[*]
Food W: Arby's, BP, Shell, Subway (Shell), TCBY (Shell), Wendy's, White Castle Restaurant (BP)
Lodg W: Amerihost Inn
RVCamp E: Walnut Lake Campground
Med E: Hospital
ATM W: BP
Other W: Prime Outlets at Jeffersonville II
(68) Rest Area (RR, Phones, Picnic, Vending; Southbound)
65 U.S. 35, Washington Court House, Xenia, Jamestown
TStop E: TA TravelCenters of America[*, SCALES] (BP gas)
W: TA TravelCenters of America[*, SCALES] (Roadrunner CB Shop, BP gas)
FStop E: Amoco[*], Circle K[*]
Gas E: Shell[*, 24]
Food E: Bob Evan's Restaurant, Burger King, Circle K, Country Pride (TA TS), Dairy Queen (Circle K), KFC, McDonald's[PLAY], SHONEY'S, Shoney's, TA TravelCenters of America (BP gas), Taco Bell, Waffle House, Wendy's
W: Country Pride (TravelCenters of America), TA TravelCenters of America (Roadrunner CB Shop, BP gas)
Lodg E: AmeriHost Inn, Hampton Inn
W: Dollar Inn
TServ E: TA TravelCenters of America[SCALES] (BP gas)
W: TA TravelCenters of America[SCALES] (Roadrunner CB Shop, BP gas)
RVCamp W: Camping
Med E: Hospital
ATM E: Amoco
Other E: Prime Outlets at Jeffersonville I
58 OH72, Jamestown, Sabina
(54) Weigh Station (Southbound)
50 U.S. 68, Wilmington
FStop W: Shell[*, D], Speedway[*]
Gas W: BP[*, D]
Food W: BP, Dairy Queen (BP), L&K Motel, McDonald's[PLAY], Speedway, Subway (Speedway)
Lodg W: L&K Motel
AServ W: Sandy's Towing & Tire Service
TServ E: Roberts Truck Parts & Service (Only RL Carriers)
W: Goodyear, Sandy's Towing & Tire Service
Med E: Hospital

Bill Knapp's RESTAURANT
Open daily at 11:00 am
Bill Knapp's is a casual, full service family restaurant where Motorcoaches are always welcome.
1702
Over 50 locations throughout: Michigan • Ohio • Indiana
513-398-4444 - Cincinnati
OHIO • I-71 • EXIT 25NB/25ASB

EXIT OHIO

(49) Weigh Station (Northbound)
45 OH73, Waynesville
Gas E: BP[*], Marathon[*]
Food E: BP
RVCamp E: Thousand Trails Campground (2 Miles)
Med E: Hospital
ATM E: Marathon
Parks W: Caesar Creek State Park (5 Miles)
Other W: Caesar Creek Flea Market
36 Wilmington Rd
RVCamp E: Camp Swonkey, Olive Branch Campground (.25 Miles)
Parks E: Fort Ancient & Campground
Other E: Fort Ancient State Memorial
(34) Rest Area (RR, Phones, Picnic, Vending; Southbound)
(34) Rest Area (RR, Phones, Picnic, Vending; Northbound)
32 OH123, Morrow, Lebanon
Gas E: BP[*, LP], Marathon[*]
Food E: Country Kitchen
RVCamp W: Camping
Other E: Fort Ancient State Memorial, Little Miami Canooing, Morgan's Canoe & Outdoor Center (3 Miles)
W: Lebanon Raceway, Warren County Fairgrounds
28 OH48, South Lebanon
Other W: Highway Patrol Post
25AB OH 741 North, Kings Island, Mason (25B to the west, 25A to the east)
Gas E: Shell[*], Speedway[*, LP]
W: AmeriStop[*], BP[*]
Food E: Bill Knapp's Restaurant (see our ad this page), McDonald's[PLAY], Taco Bell
W: AmeriStop, Bob Evan's Restaurant, Burger King, Corky's Pizzeria & Deli (AmeriStop), Frisch's Big Boy, Perkins Family Restaurant, Skyline Chili, Subway (AmeriStop), Waffle House, Wendy's
Lodg E: Comfort Suites Hotel
W: Hampton Inn, Holiday Inn Express, Microtel Inn
AServ W: BP
RVCamp E: Kings Island Campground, Yogi Bear Camp Resort (1 Mile)
ATM E: Speedway
Other E: Kings Island Amusement Park, Showcase Cinemas
W: The Beach
24 Western Row Rd, King's Island Drive (Northbound, Reaccess Southbound Only)
Other E: Kings Island Amusement Park
19 Mason Montgomery Rd, Fields Ertel Rd
Gas E: Sunoco[*]
W: AmeriStop[*], BP[*, CW], Marathon[*, 24], Shell[*, CW]
Food E: Arby's, Bennigan's, Bob Evan's Restaurant, Cracker Barrel, Fazoli's Italian Food, Frisch's Big Boy, Grand Oriental, KFC, McDonald's, Pizza Tower, Ponderosa Steakhouse, Taco Bell, White Castle Restaurant
W: Applebee's, BP, Blimpie Subs & Salads (BP), Dragon Chinese Buffet (Quality Inn), Fire Glazed Ham & The Swiss Colony, Fuddruckers, Johnny Chan Chinese, Lone Star Steakhouse, Marriott, O' Charley's, Quality Inn, River City Grill (Marriott), Skyline Grill, Snappy Tomato Pizza, Steak 'N Shake, Subway, Tumble Weed, Waffle House, Wendy's
Lodg E: Comfort Inn, Signature Inn
W: Budgetel Inn, Country Hearth Inn, Days Inn, Marriott, Quality Inn, Red Roof Inn
AServ E: Firestone Tire & Auto, King's Auto Mall, Tire Discounters
W: BP Pro Care, Jack Sweeney Auto Center
Med W: Children's Hospital
ATM E: Fifth Third Bank, First National Bank, Sunoco, United Dairy Farmer C-Store
W: BP, Biggs Hyper Mart[RX] (Grocery), Fifth Third Bank, Shell

Bold red print shows RV & Bus parking available or nearby

EXIT — OHIO

Other E: **Kings Veterinary Hospital**, **Kroger Supermarket**(RX), **United Dairy Farmer C-Store**
W: **Biggs Hyper Mart**(RX) **(Grocery)**, **Cord Animal Hospital**, **Lowe's**, **Night Flight**

17AB Jct I-275, to I-75, OH 32 (17A Junction I-275 East to OH 32, 17B Junction I-275 West to I-75)

15 Pfeiffer Rd., Blue Ash, Montgomery
Gas W: BP(*, CW)
Food W: BP, Blue Ash Best Western, Bob Evan's Restaurant, Cafe 71 (Best Western), Subway
Lodg W: Blue Ash Best Western, Red Roof Inn
Med E: ✚ **Hospital**
Other W: Airport

14 Ronald Reagan Cross County Hwy., OH 126

12 U.S. 22, OH. 3, Montgomery Rd. , Madera, Silverton
Gas E: BP(*, D), Shell(CW)
Food E: Arby's, Bob Evan's Restaurant, China Island Restaurant, Lone Star Steakhouse, Rio Bravo Cantina, Subway, T.G.I. Friday's
W: Dick Clark's American Bandstand Grill, Johnny Rockets, Max & Erma's, McDonald's
Lodg E: Harley Hotel
AServ E: Shell
W: Firestone Tire & Auto
Med W: ✚ **Hospital**
ATM E: BP, Bank One, Fifth Third Bank, Provident Bank
W: Key Bank
Other E: Half Price Books
W: BP Soft Cloth Car Wash, **Discovery Scientific Amusement**, **Kenwood Towne Centre Mall**, Lens Crafters, Toys R Us

11 Kenwood Rd, Madeira (Northbound, Reaccess Southbound Only)
Gas W: Chevron(*)
Food W: Burger King, Graeter's Ice Cream, I Can't Believe It's Yogurt, KFC, Wendy's, Wok & Roll Chinese
AServ W: Firestone Tire & Auto
Med W: ✚ **Hospital**
ATM W: Bank One, PNC
Other W: Barnes & Noble

10 Stewart Rd. (Northbound, Reaccess Southbound Only)
Gas W: Marathon(*, D, LP)
ATM W: Marathon

9 Redbank, Fairfax (Reaccess Northbound Only, Goes to the east)

8 Ridge Ave., Kennedy Ave.
Gas W: Marathon(*), Speedway(*, D, LP, K)
Food W: Denny's, Gold Star Chili, Houligan's (Howard Johnson), Howard Johnson, **K-Mart**, Krispy Kreme Doughnuts, Little Caesars Pizza (K-Mart), Long John Silver, McDonald's(PLAY), Rally's Hamburgers, Subway, Taco Bell, Wendy's
Lodg E: Red Roof Inn
W: Howard Johnson
AServ W: John Nolan Sales & Service (Ford), **K-Mart**, Tire Discounters
ATM W: Marathon, PNC, Speedway
Other W: Builder's Square, **K-Mart**, **Sam's Club**, Value City, **Wal-Mart**(RX) **(Vision center, one hour photo)**

7 Ohio 562, Norwood (Difficult Reaccess)

6 OH 561, Smith Rd., Edwards Rd.
Gas E: SuperAmerica(*, D, LP)
W: Shell(*, CW, 24)
Food E: Gold Star Chili
AServ W: Car X Mufflers & Brakes, Midas Muffler
ATM E: Greater Cincinnati School Employees' Credit Union

5 Dana Ave. (Reaccess Northbound Only)
Other W: C & G Compressed & Natural Gas Fuel

3 Taft Rd (Southbound, Difficult Reaccess)
Food W: White Castle Restaurant

EXIT — OHIO

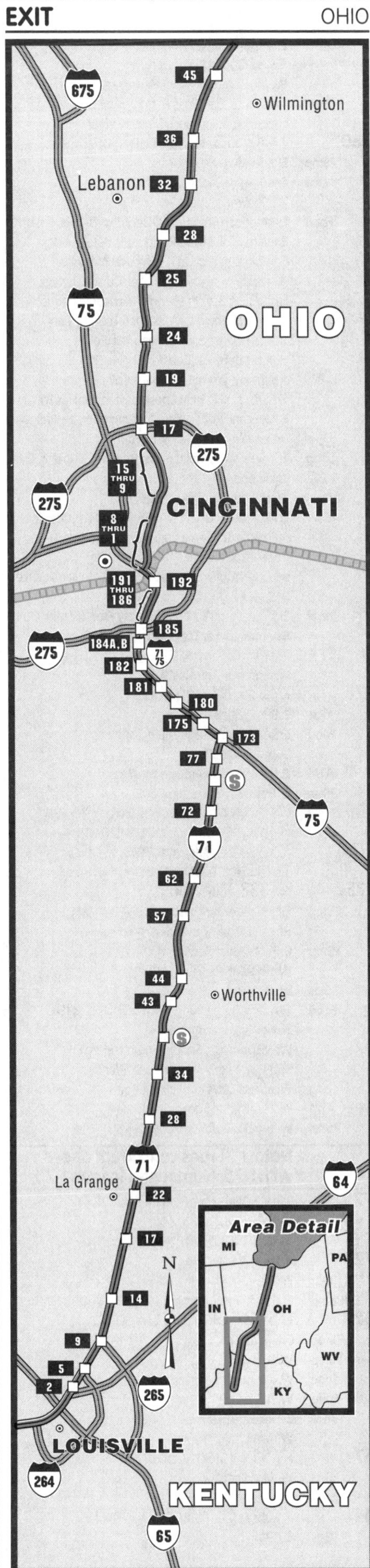

EXIT — OHIO/KENTUCKY

AServ W: Midas Muffler & Brake
Med W: ✚ **Hospital**
Other W: Cincinnati Zoo

2 U.S. 42 North, Reading Rd, Florence Ave (Difficult Reaccess)

1K Junction I-471 South, Newport KY, U.S. 50, U.S. 52 East, Columbia Parkway (Northbound)

1J Jct I-471 South, Newport, KY

Note: I-71 runs concurrent below with I-75. Numbering follows I-75.

1H Ezzard Charles Dr, Liberty Street (Northbound)

1G River Road, Linn Street, U.S. 50 West
Food W: Frisch's Big Boy, Taco Bell, Wendy's
Lodg W: Holiday Inn
ATM W: Fifth Third Bank, Star Bank

1F Seventh St
Gas W: Ashland(D), Sunoco(*)
Food W: Chili Company(24)
Lodg W: Holiday Inn
AServ W: Fuller Ford, Walt Sweenew GMC Trucks
ATM W: Ashland, Provident Bank, Three Star Bank

1E Fifth Street

Note: I-71 runs concurrent above with I-75. Numbering follows I-75.

1D Main St

1C Vine St, Covington Ky (Left Exit Southbound)

1B Elm Street, 3rd Street, Pete Rose Way

1A Jct I-75 N, Dayton (Must take southbound in order to get to 1G & 1H)

↑OHIO

↓KENTUCKY

Note: I-71 runs concurrent below with I-75. Numbering follows I-75.

192 Fifth St, Covington, Newport
Gas E: BP(D, CW), Shell(*, D, CW), SuperAmerica(*, D, LP)
W: Deli Direct
Food E: Burger King, Frisch's Big Boy, Gold Star Chili, McDonald's, Perkins Family Restaurant, River Front Pizza, Skyline Chili, Subway, Taco Bell, Waffle House, Waterfront South Beach Grill, White Castle Restaurant
W: **Willy's Sports Cafe**
Lodg E: **Holiday Inn**, **Quality Inn**
W: Hampton Inn
AServ E: Smith Muffler Shop, Smith Quick Lube
W: Ford Dealership Ridgeview
Other E: Dairy Mart, **Mainstrasse Village & N. KY Visitor Ctr.**, Tourist Info.

191 Twelfth St, Pike St, Covington
AServ E: Jeff & Sons 24-Hr Towing, Marshall Dodge Body Shop
Med E: ✚ **Hospital**
W: ✚ **Hospital**
Other E: AmeriStop Food Store, **Coin Laundry**, **Zimmer Hardware**

190 Jefferson Ave

189 KY 1072, Kyles Lane, Fort Wright, Park Hills
Gas W: BP(*, D), Marathon(*, D), Shell(*, CW), SuperAmerica(*, LP)
Food W: Fort Wright Restaurant, Frisch's Big Boy, Grandpa's Gourmet Ice Cream & Coffee House, Hardee's, Stefano's Pizza, Sub Station II
Lodg W: Lookout Motel
AServ W: Marathon, Roger Kuchle Garage & Body Shop

188AB 188A - Dixie Hwy South, Ft Mitchell; 188B - Dixie Hwy North, Ft Mitchell
Gas E: Sunoco(*, K, 24)
Food E: **Skyline Chili**
W: D'Andrea's (Ramada Inn), Indigo Bar & Grill,

EXIT		KENTUCKY
		Pizza Hut, Restaurant (Holiday Inn)
	Lodg	W: DAYS INN Days Inn, Holiday Inn, Ramada Inn
	ATM	E: PNC Bank
	Other	E: Kroger Supermarket
		W: Thriftway Food & Drug(24), WalGreens Pharmacy(RX)
186		KY 371, Buttermilk Pike
	Gas	E: Ashland(*), BP(*, K, CW), Citgo
		W: BP(*, CW), Shell(*), Sunoco(*, D, CW)
	Food	E: Burbank's Real BBQ & Ribs, Chaucers Coffee Shop (The Crossbow's Tavern), Dairy Queen (Citgo), Gatehouse Tavern (Gatehouse Inn), Graeter's Ice Cream, Jacqueline's Steak & Ribs, Montoyas Mexican, Oriental Wok (Chinese/American), The Crossbow's Tavern
		W: Arby's, Bob Evan's Restaurant, Boston Market Restaurant, Burger King, Cookies By Design, Domino's Pizza, Donato's Pizza, Dunkin Donuts, Fazoli's Italian Food, Goldstar Chili, Marx Hot Bagels, McDonald's, Outback Steakhouse, Papa John's Pizza, Papadino's Pizza, Penn Station, Sandwich Block Deli, Subway, The Canyon Grill
	Lodg	E: Cross Country Inn, Gatehouse Inn, The Drawbridge Inn
	AServ	E: Ashland
		W: Jiffy Lube, Menninger Auto Body
	ATM	E: Citgo, First National Bank, The Drawbridge Inn
		W: Fifth Third Bank, PNC Bank, Shell, Star Bank, Sunoco
	Other	E: Oldenberg Brewery Tours & Museum
		W: Animal Hospital, CVS Pharmacy, Drug Emporium, IGA Food Store, Royal Touch Car Wash, WalGreens Pharmacy
185		Junction I-275, Airport
184AB		KY 236, Erlanger
	Gas	E: BP(*), Citgo(*)
		W: Ashland(*, D), Marathon(*), Speedway(*)
	Food	E: BP, Double Dragon Oriental Cuisine, Rally's Hamburgers (BP)
		W: Carriage House Restaurant (Comfort Inn), Peels Palace (HoJo), Subway (Ashland), The Finish Line (Days Inn), Waffle House
	Lodg	W: Comfort Inn, DAYS INN Days Inn, EconoLodge, HoJo Express Inn
	Med	W: + Hospital
	Other	W: Eyeware Frame Repair
182		KY 1017, Turfway Road
	Gas	E: BP(*)
	Food	E: Frisch's Big Boy, Krispy Kreme Doughnuts, Lee's Famous Recipe Chicken, Penn Station, Ryan's Steakhouse
		W: Applebee's, Cracker Barrel, Fuddruckers, Grand Cafe (Commonwealth Hilton), Italianno's, Longhorn Steakhouse, Ming Garden (Chinese), O'Charley's, Rafferty's, Shells Seafood, Steak 'N Shake, Tumbleweed (Mexican), Wendy's
	Lodg	E: Courtyard by Marriott, Fairfield Inn, Signature Inn
		W: Commonwealth Hilton, Hampton Inn
	Med	W: + St. Luke's Hospital
	ATM	E: BP, Crawford Insurance
		W: Star Bank
	Other	E: Family Fun Center, Thriftway Marketplace(24, RX)
		W: Sam's Club, Turfway Park (Horse Races), Wal-Mart(24)
181		KY 18, Florence, Burlington
	TStop	E: T/A TravelCenters of America(*, LP, SCALES)
	Gas	E: Speedway(*, LP), Swifty(*, K)
		W: BP(*, LP, CW), Citgo(*)
	Food	E: Country Pride Restaurant (TA TravelCenters of America), Goodfellow's Distinctive Dining, Waffle House
		W: Goldstar Chili, Hardee's, La Rosa's (Italian), Lone Star Steakhouse, Taco Bell
	Lodg	E: Best Western, Cross Country Inn
	AServ	E: LTD Mobile Glass Auto Glass Specialist
		W: Airport Ford, Dodgeland Dodge, Jiffy Lube (Sear's), Pro Care (BP), Suber's Auto Repair, Toyota Towne

EXIT		KENTUCKY
	Other	E: Angel Animal Hospital, Fundome Skating Rink, Speed Queen Coin Laundry
		W: Big K-Mart(RX), CVS Pharmacy(RX), Drug Emporium, Eye Glass Factory, Mall, Suburban Lodge, World of Sports Fitness Center
180		KY 42, U.S. 127, Union, Florence
	FStop	E: Speedway(*, D, LP, K)
	Gas	E: BP(*, D, CW), Thornton's(*, LP)
		W: Chevron(*), Shell(*, CW)
	Food	E: American Prime (American), Bar-B-Q Pit, Baskin Robbins, Bob Evan's Restaurant, Burger King, Captain D's Seafood, Casino Real Mexican (Ramada Inn), Chinese Buffet, Dunkin Donuts, Frisch's Big Boy, Jalepeno's (Mexican), Long John Silver, McDonald's, Mess Bar & Lounge, Penn Station Cheese Steaks, Pizza Hut, Rally's Hamburgers, Red Lobster, Skyline Chili, Sub Station II, Subway, Warm Ups Sports Cafe, Wendy's
		W: Arby's, KFC, Little Caesars Pizza, Perkins Family Restaurant, Ponderosa, T.J. Cinnamon's, Waffle House, White Castle Restaurant
	Lodg	E: Knight's Inn, Motel 6, Ramada Inn, Super 8, The Wildwood Inn
		W: Holiday Inn, TraveLodge
	AServ	E: Mr. Transmission, Quaker State Oil & Lube, The Auto Bath Self Serve Car Wash, Value-rated Used Cars at Rock Castle
		W: Car X Mufflers & Brakes, Midas Muffler & Brake, NTB, Quick Stop Oil Change
	Other	E: Classic Car Wash(CW), Fantasy Frontier Mini Golf, Go Karts, Lazer Tag, Ultimate Detail Shop (Thornton's)
		W: Florence Animal Clinic
178		KY 536, Mt Zion Road
	Gas	E: BP(*, D), Shell(*, D)
	Food	E: Rally's Hamburgers (BP), Thriftway Supermarket(RX)
	ATM	E: Shell, Thriftway Supermarket
	Other	E: Thriftway Supermarket(RX)
(177)		KY Welcome Center (RR, Phones, Picnic, Vending; Southbound)
(176)		Rest Area (RR, Phones, Picnic, Vending; Northbound)
175		KY 338, Richwood
	TStop	E: TravelCenters of America(*, SCALES) (BP)
		W: Pilot Travel Center(*, SCALES)
	FStop	E: Pilot Travel Center(*, SCALES)
		W: Shell(*, LP, CW, 24)
	Gas	W: BP(*, 24)
	Food	E: Arby's, Burger King, Taco Bell Express (TA TravelCenters of America)
		W: McDonald's, Snappy Tomato Pizza (BP), Subway (Pilot), Waffle House, Wendy's
	Lodg	W: DAYS INN Days Inn, Econolodge
	ATM	W: Huntington Banks, Shell
	Parks	W: Big Bone Lick State Park

Note: I-71 runs concurrent above with I-75. Numbering follows I-75.

EXIT		KENTUCKY
77		Junction I-75 South, Lexington (Northbound)
(75)		Weigh Station (Southbound)
72		KY 14, Verona
	Gas	E: Chevron(*, D)
	RVCamp	E: Oak Creek Campground (5.3 Miles)
62		U.S. 127, Glencoe, Owenton
	TStop	E: Exit 62 Truck Plaza(*, LP)
	FStop	W: Ashland(*)
	Food	W: Ashland
	Lodg	W: Ashland
	ATM	E: Exit 62 Truck Plaza
		W: Ashland
57		KY 35, Warsaw, Sparta
	Gas	W: Marathon(*)
	RVCamp	E: Camping
44		KY 227, Carrollton, Worthville
	Gas	E: BP(*, LP)

EXIT		KENTUCKY
		W: Ashland(*), Chevron(*, D), Shell(*, 24)
	Food	W: Arby's, Burger King, KFC, McDonald's(PLAY), Shell, Taco Bell, Waffle House
	Lodg	W: DAYS INN Days Inn, Hampton, Holiday Inn Express, Super 8
	Med	W: + Hospital
	Parks	W: General Butler State Resort Park
43		KY 389 to KY 55, English, Prestonville
(35)		Weigh Station (Northbound)
34		U.S. 421, Bedford, Cambellsburg
	Gas	W: Ashland(*, D, K), Marathon(*)
	Food	W: Cody's Burgers & Shakes
	AServ	W: JR's Auto & Truck Repair
28		KY 153, KY 146, Sligo, New Castle, to U.S. 42, Bedford
	TStop	E: Davis Brothers Truck Stop(*, SCALES) (Citgo gas)
		W: Pilot Travel Center(*, SCALES, 24)
	FStop	E: Marathon(*, D)
	Gas	E: No Name(*) (Bait shop)
	Food	E: Cleo's (Davis Bro. TS), Davis Brothers Truck Stop (Citgo gas), No Name (Bait shop), Taylor's Dairy Bar
		W: Pendelton Food Mart Hickory Smoked BBQ, Pilot Travel Center, Subway (Pilot)
	ATM	E: Davis Brothers Truck Stop (Citgo gas), Marathon
22		KY 53, Ballardsville, La Grange
	Gas	E: Ashland(*, D, LP), BP(*, 24), Super America(*, D)
		W: Chevron(*), Swifty(*)
	Food	E: Burger King, Lucky Dragon Chinese, Ponderosa Steakhouse, Rally's Hamburgers (Super America), SHONEY'S Shoney's, Super America, Waffle House, Wendy's
		W: Arby's, Cracker Barrel, Dairy Queen, Domino's Pizza, KFC, Long John Silver, McDonald's(PLAY), Taco Bell
	Lodg	E: Best Western (Luxberry), DAYS INN Days Inn, Holiday Inn Express
		W: Super 8
	AServ	E: Big O Tires, Wal-Mart(24, RX)
		W: Barney's Auto, NAPA Auto Parts, Smiser-Carter Chevrolet, Olds, Buick, Geo
	Med	E: + Tri County Baptist Hospital
	Other	E: Wal-Mart(RX), Wash Master
		W: Kentucky State Police, La Grange Auto Bath, LaGrange Animal Hospital, Oldham 8 Theatres, Rite Aide Pharmacy(RX), U.S. Post Office
18		KY. 393, Buckner
17		KY 146, Buckner
	Gas	W: Shell(*), Thornton's Fuel Mart(*, LP)
	AServ	E: Tri County Ford Lincoln Mercury
	ATM	W: PNC Bank
	Other	W: Kentucky State Police, U.S. Post Office
14		KY 329, Crestwood, Pewee Valley, Brownsboro
	Gas	E: Chevron(*, 24), Shell(*)
(13)		Rest Area (RR, Phones, Picnic; Southbound)
(13)		Rest Area (RR, Phones, Picnic; Northbound)
9AB		Jct I-265, KY 841, Gene Snyder Freeway
5		Jct I-264, Watterson Exprwy.
2		Zorn Ave.
	Gas	W: BP(*, LP, CW), Chevron(*)
	Food	W: Chevron
	Lodg	W: Rivermont Hotel
	Med	E: + Hospital, + Veteran's Hospital
	Other	W: Marine Sales & Service, Riverfront Country Club, Water Tower Museum
1A		I-64 West, St Louis (Southbound)
1B		I-65 Indianapolis, Nashville (Southbound, Left Exit Southbound)

↑ KENTUCKY

Begin I-71

Bold red print shows RV & Bus parking available or nearby

EXIT ILLINOIS

Begin I-72

↓ILLINOIS

(4) JCT US 36, I-172 North to Quincy

10 IL 96, Hull, Payson

20 IL 106, Barry
- **FStop** S: **Phillips 66**[*, D]
- **Gas** S: Shell[*, D], Standard[D]
- **Food** S: **Wendy's**
- **ATM** S: Barry Community Bank, **Phillips 66**
- **Parks** S: **PASA Park**

31 New Salem, Pittsfield
- **RVCamp** S: **Camping (5 Miles)**

35 US 54, IL 107, Griggsville, Pittsfield
- **RVCamp** S: **Campground**, **Pine Lake Camping**
- **Med** S: **✚ Hospital**
- **Other** N: Tourist Info.

46 IL 100, Bluffs, Detroit

52 IL 106, Winchester

60 US 67, Jacksonville, Berardstown

64 US 67, Alton, Jacksonville (Hospital, North)
- **AServ** S: RV Sales & Service

68 to IL 104, Jacksonville (Hospital)

76 IL 123, Ashland, Alexander

82 New Berlin

91 Wabash Ave., Loami

93 IL 4, Springfield, Chatham (Northbound)
- **Gas** N: Huck's[*, LP]
- **Food** N: Applebee's, Bakers Square Restaurant and Pies, Best Buffet, Damon's Clubhouse, Den Chili, **Hardee's**, Jeffrey's Speciality Sandwiches, Kenny Roger's Roasters, McDonald's[PLAY], Ned Kelly's Steakhouse, Perkin's Family Restaurant, Subway, **Taco Bell**, The Gathering Place
- **Lodg** N: Comfort Inn, Courtyard Inn, Fairfield Inn, Sleep Inn
- **AServ** N: Carwash City (Auto, Self Service), **Wal-Mart**[RX]
- **ATM** N: Huck's, Magna Bank
- **Other** N: Batteries Plus, Carwash City (Auto, Self Service), Kinko's[24], Parkway 8 Cinemas, Sparkling Clean Car Wash, **Target**[RX], **Wal-Mart**[RX]

Note: I-72 runs concurrent below with I-55. Numbering follows I-55.

92AB U.S 36 West, I-55 Business, 6th St., Jacksonville, Junction (Left Exit Northbound, Reaccess Northbound Only, Difficult Reaccess)
- **Food** W: Heritage House Smorgasbord, Illini Inn, Legends (Ramada), McDonald's, Ramada, Reflections (Illini Inn), **Southern View Motel**
- **Lodg** W: Illini Inn, Ramada, **Southern View Motel**, Super 8
- **AServ** W: 66 Fast Lube, Auto Glass
- **RVCamp** W: **Mr. Lincoln's Campground**
- **Med** W: **✚ Hospital**
- **Other** W: Car Wash

94 Stevenson Road, Eastlake Dr, Springfield
- **Gas** W: Amoco[*, CW], Shell[*, LP, CW]
- **Food** W: Arby's, Bob Evan's Restaurant, Bombay Club, California Bar & Deli, Days Inn, Denny's, Gallina Pizzeria, Hide Out Steak & Bar, Long John Silver, Maverick's Family Steakhouse, McDonald's, Mountain Jack's Steakhouse, Red Lobster, Steak & Shake, Taco Bell, Taste of Thai (Chinese), Wendy's
- **Lodg** W: Comfort Suites Hotel, Crown Plaza, Days Inn, Drury Inn & Suites, Hampton Inn, Holiday Inn, Peartree Inn (Drury), Signature Inn, Stevenson Inn
- **AServ** W: Amoco, Friendly's Chevrolet
- **RVCamp** W: **Mr Lincoln's RV Parts & Accessories, Mr. Lincoln's Campground (1 Mile)**
- **ATM** W: Amoco, First National Bank, Shell
- **Other** W: CVS Drugstore, Capital City Shopping Ctr, Center City Theaters

96B IL 29 North, S Grand Avenue, Springfield

96A IL 29 South, Taylorville
- **Gas** W: 76[D], Citgo
- **Food** W: Burger King, Godfather's Pizza, Jolly Tamale, Nichole's Restaurant
- **Lodg** W: Red Roof Inn, Super 8
- **ATM** W: BankOne, Citgo, Cub Food, Shop "N" Save
- **Other** W: Capital Complex, Cub Food, Korean War Memorial, Landmark Ford, Lincoln Sites, Quality Car Wash, Shop "N" Save, Vietnam Veterans Memorial

98A Junction I-72 East, U.S 36 East, Decatur, Champaign, Urbana

Note: I-72 runs concurrent above with I-55. Numbering follows I-55.

103AB Junction I-55, North - Chicago, South - St. Louis, Jackson, I-72 West
- **FStop** N: **Baskin Robbins**
- **Gas** N: Amoco[*, 24], Shell[*, D, LP]
- **Food** N: **Hardee's**, Hunan Express, Little Caesars Pizza (K-Mart), Marrio's Pizza, Mc Donalds[PLAY], Shell, Subway, Taco Bell, WalGreens Pharmacy[RX], Wendy's
- **Lodg** N: Park View Motel
- **ATM** N: Amoco, Bank One, Shell
- **Other** N: Gas Town Carwash, **K-Mart**[RX], Super Shine Car Wash, WalGreens Pharmacy[RX]

104 Camp Butler
- **AServ** N: Dave's Auto Body

108 Riverton, Dawson

114 Buffalo, Mechanicsburg

122 Mt. Auburn, Illiopolis

128 Niantic

133AB US 36 E - Decatur, Harristown, US 51 S - Pana (Left Exit Both Directions)
- **Med** N: **✚ Hospital**

138 IL-121 Decatur, Lincoln, Warrensburg (Hospital, southbound)

141AB US 51 - Decatur, Bloomington (Hospital 141A)
- **Gas** N: Shell[*, D, LP, 24]
- **Food** N: Applebee's (Hickory Point Mall), Cheddar's, Country Kitchen Restaurant, **Cracker Barrel**, Hardee's, Home Town Buffet, McDonald's[PLAY], Steak N' Shake
  - S: Arby's, Burger King, China Buffet, El Rodeo, Subway
- **Lodg** N: Budgetel Inn, Comfort Inn, Country Inn & Suites, Fairfield Inn, Hampton Inn, Ramada Limited
  - S: **Sam's Club, Wal-Mart**[LP, RX] **(Tire Service, Lube, Vision Center)**
- **Med** N: **✚ Gailey Eye Clinic (Hickory Point Mall)**
- **ATM** N: Hickory Point Bank & Trust, Mutual Bank[24]
  - S: First National Bank
- **Other** N: GC Theaters 12, **Hickory Point Mall**, Super Wash[CW]
  - S: Petcare, **Sam's Club, US Post Office, Wal-Mart**[RX] **(Tire Service, Lube, Vision Center)**

144 IL 48 Dacatur, Oreana
- **FStop** N: **Oasis**
- **Food** N: **Restaurant (Oasis)**

150 Argenta

(156) **Rest Area (RR, Phones, Picnic, Vending, P)**

156 IL-48, Sisco, Weldon
- **RVCamp** S: **Campground**

164 Bridge Street (Camping 8 miles south from exit)
- **Parks** S: **Allenton Park, 4-H Memorial Park**

166 IL-105 W, Market Street
- **Gas** S: FT Fast Stop[*, D]
- **Food** S: Taco Bell
- **Lodg** S: Best Western, Montecello Gateway Inn
- **Med** S: **✚ Hospital**
- **ATM** S: FT Fast Stop

169 White Heath Road
- **Parks** N: **Lodge Park**

172 IL-10 Clinton

176 I-47 Mahomet

182AB Junction I-57, South - Memphis, North - Chicago

↑ILLINOIS

Begin I-72

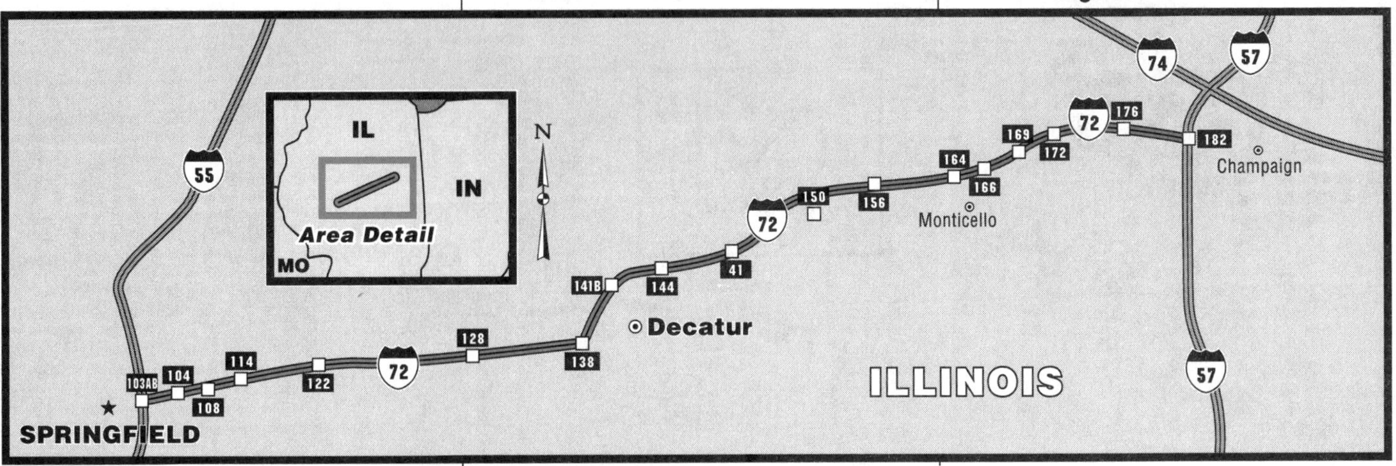

EXIT IOWA/ILLINOIS

Begin I-74

↓IOWA

1 53rd Street, Hamilton Tech College
- **Gas** N: Citgo(*, CW)
- **Food** S: Steak 'N Shake, **Target(RX) (Super Food Center)**
- **AServ** N: Citgo
- **ATM** N: Williams Tower
  S: **Target (Super Food Center)**
- **Other** S: Pets Mart, Staple's, **Target(RX) (Super Food Center)**

2 U.S. 6, Spruce Hill Drive, Kimberly Road
- **Gas** N: Phillips 66(*)
  S: Hy-Vee Food Store
- **Food** N: KFC, Old Chicago
  S: Applebee's, Bob Evan's Restaurant, Burger King, Country Kitchen, Godfather's Pizza, Red Lobster, St Louis Bread
- **Lodg** N: Courtyard By Marriott, Heartland, Jumers Castle Inn, Signature Inn, Super 8
  S: DAYS INN Days Inn, Hampton Inn
- **AServ** N: Phillips 66
  S: John Keady Pontiac, Buick, Cadillac, **Sam's Club**, The Grease Spot
- **ATM** S: Norwest Bank
- **Other** N: **U-Haul Center(LP)**
  S: Bowling Alley, E Suds Car Wash, Lowe's, Petco, **Sam's Club**, **Wal-Mart(RX)**

3 Middle Road, Locust Street
- **Gas** N: Phillips 66(*)
- **Food** N: Bishop's Cafeteria, Bruegger's Bagel & Bakery, Duck's Creek Family Restaurant, Fortune Garden (Chinese), Long John Silver, McDonald's(PLAY), Subway, Taco Bell
- **Lodg** N: EconLodge
- **AServ** N: Goodyear, Phillips 66
- **ATM** N: First Mid West Bank
- **Other** N: Ducks Creek Plaza, WalGreens Pharmacy(RX)

4 U.S. 67, Grant Street, State Street, Riverfront
- **Gas** N: Amoco(*), Clark, Conoco(*, CW), Phillips 66(*), Sinclair
  S: Coastal
- **Food** N: Conoco, Conoco Deli, Paddle Wheel Restaurant, Ross's 24 Hour Restaurant
  S: Dairy Queen, Village Inn Restaurant, Waterfront Deli
- **Lodg** N: Traveler Motel
  S: City Center Motel
- **AServ** N: Big A Auto Part Store, Phillips 66
- **ATM** N: Conoco

↑IOWA

↓ILLINOIS

EXIT ILLINOIS

1 (5) River Dr. (Eastbound, Difficult Reaccess)
- **Med** S: ✚ **Hospital**

2 7th Avenue, Civic Center, Riverfront
- **Other** S: Fire/Police Dept

3 23rd Avenue
- **Gas** S: Amoco
- **Food** N: Hardee's
  S: Hardee's, Hungry Hobo, Whitey's Ice Cream

4AB IL 5, John Deere Rd
- **Gas** N: Amoco(*)
- **Food** N: Applebee's, Blimpie's Subs, Burger King, Chi Chi's Mexican Restaurant, Old Country Buffet, Stashu Deli/Pizza, Steak & Shake, **Wal-Mart SuperCenter(RX) (Vision)**, Wendy's, Wok River Plaza
  S: Garfield Restaurant, Long John Silver, McDonald's, Miss Mammie's Catfish House, Pizza Hut, Subway, Super China Buffet, The Winner's Circle, Wendy's, Yen Ching
- **Lodg** N: Exel Inn
  S: Best Western, Comfort Inn, Fairfield
- **AServ** N: McLaughlin Cadillac, Isuzu, Oldsmobil, Montgomery Ward, Tires Plus
  S: Bud Mills, Geo, Goodyear, Key Pontiac, Buick, Truck, Master Care Auto Service, Sear's, Sexton Ford
- **Med** S: ✚ **Hospital**
- **ATM** N: Amoco, Black Hawk State Bank, Mississippi Valley Credit Union, Southeast National Bank
  S: BankOne, First Of America Bank
- **Other** N: Batteries Plus, Car Wash, Lowe's(LP), Mall With Foodcourt, Office Max, Office Max, **Wal-Mart SuperCenter(RX) (Vision)**
  S: America's Best Contacts & Eyeglasses, Black Hawk Historic Site, Mailboxes & Parcel Depot, Petco, WalGreens Pharmacy(RX), Water Works Car Wash

(5) **Weigh Station (Eastbound)**

5AB IL 6, US 6, Moline, Quad City Airport (Left Exit Northbound, Exits To Exit Four)
- **Gas** N: Citgo(*)
- **Food** N: Benders (LaQuinta Inn), La Quinta Inn, McDonald's, Skyline Inn Ribs and Catfish, The Omlet Shop
- **Lodg** N: Hampton Inn, Holiday Inn Express, La Quinta Inn, **Motel 6**

(8) **Weigh Station (Westbound)**

(8) Junction I-80, Chicago, Des Moines

(14) Jct I-80

24 IL 81, Kewannee, Cambridge

(28) **Rest Area (RR, Phones, Picnic, Vending, RV Dump, P; Eastbound)**

(30) **Rest Area (RR, Phones, Picnic, Vending, RV Dump, P; Westbound)**

EXIT ILLINOIS

32 IL 17, Woodhull, Alpha
- **TStop** S: **Woodhull Truck Plaza(*, D, SCALES)**
- **FStop** N: **Citgo(*, D, LP)**
- **Gas** N: Texaco
- **Food** N: **Homestead Restaurant (Texaco)**
- **TServ** S: **Woodhull Truck Plaza(SCALES)**
- **RVCamp** S: **Shady Lakes**
- **Med** N: ✚ **Woodhull Clinic**
- **ATM** S: **Woodhull Truck Plaza**

46AB US 34, Kewanee, Monmouth
- **TServ** N: **Nichols Diesel Service**
- **Med** S: ✚ **Hospital**

48AB East Galesburg, Galesburg
- **FStop** S: **Mobil(*, D, LP)**
- **Gas** S: Phillips 66(*)
- **Food** N: Tavern of the Severence (Jumer's Continental Inn)
  S: A & W Drive-In, Four Stars Family Restaurant, KFC, Pizza Hut
- **Lodg** N: Jumer' Continental Inn
  S: Holiday Inn Express
- **ATM** S: Harvey
- **Other** S: **Harvey Grocery Store(*, RX)**, Southward's Car Wash

51 Knoxville
- **FStop** S: **Amoco(*)**, **Citgo(*, LP)**
- **Food** S: **Hardee's**, **McDonald's**
- **Lodg** S: Super 8
- **ATM** S: Citgo

54 U.S. 150, IL97, Lewistown
- **RVCamp** N: **Galesburg East Best Holiday Trav-L-Park (.5 Miles)**

(62) **Rest Area (Phones, Picnic, Vending, P)**

71 IL 78, Canton, Kewannee

75 Brimfield, Oak Hill

82 Kickapoo, Edwards Road
- **FStop** N: **Shell(*, LP, K)**
- **Gas** N: Mobil(*)
- **Food** N: **Jubilee Cafe**
- **Parks** N: **Jubilee State College Park (North)**
  S: **Wildlife Prarie Park (South)**

87AB Jct I-474, IL 6, Indianapolis, Chillicote

89 U.S. 150, War Memorial Drive (Northbound)
- **Gas** N: Amoco(*, CW), Clark(*, D, 24)
- **Food** N: Arby's, Burger King, China Buffett, Dunkin Donuts, Kenny Roger's Roasters, Khoury's Cusine, McDonald's, Ming Shee Chinese Restaurant, Ned Kelly's Restaurant, Perkins Family Restaurant(24), Red Lobster, Schlotzsky's Deli, Steak & Shake, Subway, **WalGreens Pharmacy(24, RX)**
- **Lodg** N: Comfort Suites Hotel, Courtyard by Marriott, Fairfield Inn, Holiday Inn, Red Roof Inn, Residence Inn, Signature Inn, Super 8
- **AServ** N: Amoco, Jim McComb Chevrolet, Geo, Neil

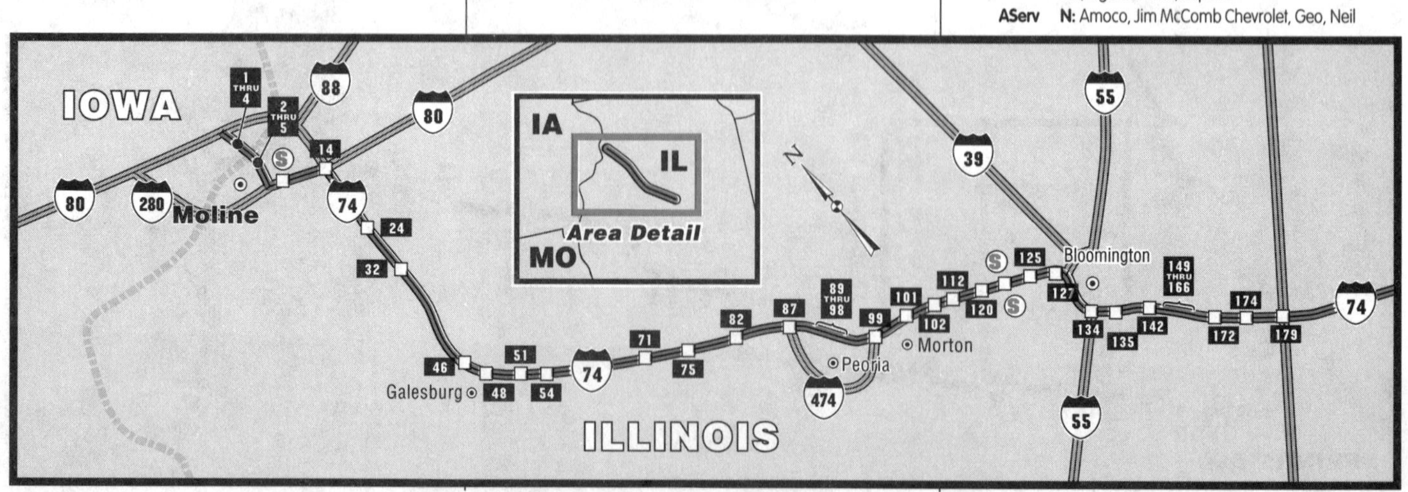

Bold red print shows RV & Bus parking available or nearby

EXIT ILLINOIS

Norton Pontiac, Cadillac, Northwoods Firestone, Parkway Chrysler, Plymouth, Subreau, Wal-Mart(RX)
ATM **N:** Amoco, CEFCU, Clark, Magna Bank
Other **N:** Eyeglasses World Express, Meadowbrook Veternary Clinic, Northwoods Mall, Pak N Mail, Thompons Food Basket(*, 24), Wal-Mart(RX), WalGreens Pharmacy(RX), Water Works Car Wash

90 Gale Ave

91 University Street
AServ **N:** Midas
Other **N:** Tri-County Animal Emergency Clinic

92A IL 88, Knoxville Ave. (Westbound, Left Exit)
Gas **S:** Amoco(*)
Food **S:** Arby's, Carl Jr's Hamburgers
Lodg **S:** Townehouse Motel
AServ **S:** Amoco, Firestone

92 Glendale Avenue (Difficult Reaccess)
AServ **S:** Harmon Auto Glass, Mytee Muffler
Med **N:** + Saint Frances Medical Center
S: + Methodist Medical Center
ATM **S:** Bank One
Other **S:** Tourist Info.

93A Jefferson Street

93B U.S. 24, IL 29, Washington Street, Adams Street (No Reaccess, Difficult Reaccess)
Lodg **S:** Budget Motel, Mark Twain Hotel
AServ **S:** Sears Automotive
ATM **S:** CEFCU

94 IL 40, Industrial Spur (Difficult Reaccess)

95A North Main Street
Gas **S:** Amoco(*, CW)
Food **S:** Applebee's, Blimpie's Subs, Bob Evan's Restaurant, Long John Silver, Youssef's Deli
Lodg **N:** Hampton Inn
S: Mark Twain House, Motel 6
AServ **N:** Firestone Tire & Auto
S: Goodyear Tire & Auto
Other **S:** Kroger Supermarket(RX), Wal-Mart Supercenter(RX)

95B IL 116, Metamora

95C U.S. 150 East Camp St.
Gas **N:** Site
Food **N:** Subway
Lodg **N:** Super 8

96 IL 8, East Washington Street

98 Pinecrest Drive

99 Jct I-474

101 Jct I-155 S, Lincoln

102 Morton
Gas **N:** Amoco(*, LP), Phillips 66(*, D)
S: Shell(*)
Food **N:** Blimpie's Subs (Phillips 66), Burger King, Cracker Barrel, Dunkin Donuts (Phillips 66), Phillips 66, Taco Bell
S: McDonald's(PLAY), Subway (Shell)
Lodg **N:** Comfort Inn, Days Inn, Holiday Inn Express, Knight's Inn
ATM **S:** Shell

112 IL 117, Goodfield
FStop **N:** Shell(*, D, LP, 24)
AServ **N:** Amoco
RVCamp **N:** Yogi Bear Camp Resort (1.75 Miles)
ATM **N:** Goodfield State Bank (Amoco)

(115) Rest Area (RR, Phones, Picnic, Vending, RV Dump, P)

120 Carlock
Gas **N:** Amoco(*, LP)
Food **N:** Country Side Family Restaurant
AServ **N:** Amoco

EXIT ILLINOIS

RVCamp **N:** KOA-Tall Corn (1.75 Miles)

(123) Weigh Station

125 U.S. 150, Mitsubishi Motor Way

127 Jct I-55

Note: I-74 runs concurrent below with I-55. Numbering follows I-55.

160AB U.S 150, Il 9, Pekin, Market St
TStop **E:** 76 Auto/Truck Plaza(*, SCALES), Pilot Travel Center(SCALES, 24)
FStop **E:** Speedway(*, LP, K)
Gas **E:** Amoco(*), Freedom(*, D, LP), Phillips 66(*), Shell(*)
Food **E:** 76 Auto/Truck Plaza, Arby's, Burger King, Carl Jr's Hamburgers(PLAY), Cracker Barrel, India Garden Cuisine of India, KFC, McDonald's(PLAY), Pilot Travel Center, Subway, Taco Bell, Yen Ching (Chinese)
W: Country Inn & Suites by Carlson, Country Kitchen (Country Inn & Suites), Steak 'N Shake
Lodg **E:** Best Inns of America, Comfort Inn, Days Inn, EconoLodge, Quality Inn & Suites
W: Country Inn & Suites by Carlson
AServ **E:** NAPA, Shell
W: Blain's Farm & Fleet With Auto Service
TWash **E:** Blue Beacon, Touchless Auto Car Wash(CW)
ATM **E:** 76 Auto/Truck Plaza, Bank One, First America, Phillips 66, Shell, Speedway
W: First of America
Other **E:** Aldi Supermarket
W: Bloomington/Normal Factory Outlet Stores

157B Bus I-55, U.S 51, Veteran's Pkwy, Airport
Gas **E:** Shell(*, LP)
Food **E:** Knight's Inn
Lodg **E:** Knight's Inn, Parkway Inn
Med **E:** + Hospital
Other **E:** Miller Park Zoo/Golf Course

Note: I-74 runs concurrent above with I-55. Numbering follows I-55.

157A I-74 and US 51 to Indianapolis, Decatur

134A Jct I-55, Chicago, Memphis

134B I-55 Business, Veterans Parkway

135 U.S. 51, U.S. 51 Bus, Decatur, Bloomington
Gas **N:** Phillips 66(*)

142 Downs

149 Le Roy
FStop **S:** Shell(*, D)
Gas **N:** Amoco(*)
Food **S:** Woody's Restaurant (Shell)
Lodg **S:** Super 8
ATM **S:** Shell

Toll Free Reservations: 800-329-7466 Days Inn
800-433-7966 Econo Lodge

DAYS INN

— Continental Breakfast —
— FREE HBO • ESPN • WGN • CNN —
— Sprinkler in Rooms —
— Spa • Sauna • Jacuzzi • King & Queen Beds —
— Guest Laundry Facilities —
— Conference Room • Direct Dial Phones —
— Handicap Room • Major Credit Cards —

Champaign
217-356-6873
I-74 • EXIT 181 South

Farmer City
309-328-9434
I-74 • EXIT 159

Econo Lodge
Effingham
217-347-7131
I-57&70 • EXIT 160

1080

ILLINOIS • I-57&70 • 1 LOCATION
ILLINOIS • I-74 • 2 LOCATIONS

EXIT ILLINOIS

152 U.S. 136, Rantoul, Heyworth

(156) Rest Area (RR, Phones, P)

159 IL 54, Farmer City, Gibson City
Lodg **S:** Budget Motel, Days Inn (see our ad on this page)

166 Mansfield
FStop **S:** Amoco(*, D)

172 IL 47, Gibson City, Mahomet
Gas **S:** Apollo(*), Clark(*, LP)
Food **S:** Bull Dog Pizza, Hardee's, Hen House, Monical's Pizza, Subway, The Treetop Family Dining
Lodg **S:** Heritage Inn
AServ **S:** NAPA Auto Parts
RVCamp **S:** R & S Sales & Service, Inc.(LP) (1.5 Miles)
ATM **S:** Busey Bank
Other **S:** Courtesy Coin Laundry, IGA Store(LP), JR's Car Wash

174 Prairie View Rd. Lake of the Woods Road
FStop **N:** Mobil(*, LP)
Gas **N:** Amoco(*, 24)
Food **N:** Subway (Mobil)
RVCamp **N:** Champaign Sportsmen's Club Campgrounds (.5 Miles), Tincup Campers' Park (1 Mile)

179AB Junction I-57 Chicago, Memphis, To I-72 Decatur (Difficult Reaccess)

181 Prospect Avenue
Gas **N:** Meijer(*, D, LP, K)
S: Amoco(*, CW), Clark(*, LP), Freedom, Mobil(*, CW)
Food **N:** Applebee's, Best Wok, Burger King(PLAY), Cheddar's, Chili's, Damon's, Fazoli's Italian Food, Hardee's, HomeTown Buffet, Lone Star Steakhouse, Meijer Grocery(24), Outback Steakhouse, Ryan's Steakhouse, Steak 'N Shake, Subway, Wendy's
S: Arby's, Dos Reales, Great Wall Buffet, Hong Kong, K-Mart Supercenter(24, RX), KFC, Long John Silver, Red Lobster
Lodg **N:** Drury Inn & Suites
S: Days Inn (see our ad this page), EconoLodge
AServ **N:** AAMCO Transmission, AOK Transmission, Parts America, Prospect Hyundai, Prospect Mitsubishi, Sam's Club, Sellers Collision Center, Wal-Mart(LP, RX) (Vision Center)
S: Car X & Jiffy Lube, K-Mart Supercenter(24), Midas Muffler & Brake, NAPA Auto Parts, Saturn of Champagne, Tire Barn Warehouse
TServ **S:** Prairie International
RVCamp **N:** Campground
ATM **N:** Busey Bank, Meijer Grocery
S: Amoco, Clark, First of America Bank, Mobil
Other **N:** GKC Beverly Theater, Lowe's(LP), Mail Boxes Etc., Meijer Grocery, PetsMart, Sam's Club, Target(RX), Wal-Mart(RX) (Vision Center)
S: K-Mart Supercenter(RX)

182 Neil Street
Gas **S:** Mobil(*)
Food **N:** Bob Evan's Restaurant, Chi Chi's Mexican Restaurant, Denny's, Fortune House Super Deluxe Chinese Buffet, Grandy's, McDonald's(PLAY), Olive Garden, Taco Bell
S: Perkins Family Restaurant
Lodg **N:** Budgetel Inn, Comfort Inn, Courtyard by Marriott, Extended Stay America, Fairfield Inn, La Quinta Inn, Red Roof Inn, Super 8
S: Howard Johnson
AServ **N:** Marketview Car Wash(CW), Marketview Lube (Pennzoil), Sear's, Shelby Dodge, Jeep, Eagle, Sullivan Park Hill Chev, Chrys, Cad, Volvo
S: Bickers Auto Repair, NTB
ATM **N:** Bank Champaign
Other **N:** Bard Optical, Lens Crafters, Market Place Mall, Osco Drugs(RX)

183 Lincoln Ave.

EXIT ILLINOIS

Gas S: Phillips 66(*, D, CW), Speedway(*, LP)

Food S: The Grand Ball Room (Holiday Inn), Urbana Garden Family Restaurant

Lodg S: Holiday Inn, Ramada Limited, Sleep Inn

TServ N: Firestone & Interstate Batteries, Grider Truck Repair, Interstate Trailor Inc. Service & Parts

Med S: ✚ Hospital

ATM S: Phillips 66

Other S: Franco's Restaurant

184AB U.S. 45, Rantoul, Cunningham Ave.

Gas S: Freedom(*, D, LP), Shell(*), Speedway(*)

Food S: Cracker Barrel, Ned Kelly's Steakhouse, Steak 'N Shake, Taco Bell Express (Speedway)

Lodg N: Park Inn International

S: Best Western, Motel 6

AServ N: Bernie's Tire, Blain's Farm & Fleet

S: Complete Automotive Repair & Quick Lube, Pro Tech Motors, Ron's Truck & Auto Repair, Shell, TK Service Center, Tatman's Auto Body

TServ N: Bernie's Tire

ATM S: Freedom

Other N: Amerigas(LP)

S: Beaumont Small Animal Clinic, Sav-A-Lot Food Store(RX), TJ's Coin Laundry, Urbana Tourist Info.

185 IL 130, University Avenue

192 St. Joseph

FStop N: Marathon

Food S: Dairy Queen

AServ N: Marathon

TServ N: Marathon

Other S: Ultimate Shine Car Wash

197 IL 49 South, Royal, Ogden

Gas S: Citgo(*, D, LP)

Food S: Godfather's Pizza (Citgo), Ogden Family Restaurant, Subrageous Subs (Citgo)

200 IL 49, Rankin, Fithian

206 Oakwood, Potomac

TStop N: Shell(*, SCALES, 24)

S: Knoll's Oakwood Truck Plaza(*, SCALES) (Marathon)

Gas S: Phillips 66(*, LP)

TServ N: Shell(SCALES, 24)

ATM N: Shell

S: Knoll's Oakwood Truck Plaza (Marathon)

(207) Rest Area (RR, Phones, Picnic, Vending, P; Westbound)

210 U.S. 150, ML King Dr.

Food N: The Little Nugget Trading Post & Restaurant

AServ S: Tommy House Tire

TServ S: Tommy House Tire

RVCamp N: Campground

Med N: ✚ Hospital

Other N: Kickapoo State Park, The Little Nugget Trading Post & Restaurant

214 G Street

Gas S: Shell(*)

215AB U.S. 150, Gilbert Street, IL 1, Georgetown Rd.

Gas N: Citgo(*, D), Speedway(*, LP)

S: Speedway(*)

EXIT ILLINOIS/INDIANA

Food N: Arby's, Central Park Hamburgers, Coach's All American Bar and Grill (Days Inn), Hardee's, Long John Silver, McDonald's(PLAY), Pizza Hut, Steak 'N Shake, Taco Bell

S: Burger King, Monical's Pizza, Subway

Lodg N: Best Western, Days Inn

AServ N: Bass Tire Co., Care Muffler Shop, Quicklube

S: Auto Zone, Royal Pontiac, Buick, GMC

RVCamp S: Travel Trailers Sales & Service Inc.(LP) (1 Mile)

Med N: ✚ Hospital

ATM S: Palmer Bank

Other S: Aldi Supermarket, Eagle's Country Market, Harley Davidson Dealership

216 Bowman Avenue, Perrysville Rd

FStop N: Mobil(*, LP)

Gas N: Citgo(*, LP)

Food N: Godfather's Pizza (Citgo), Subrageous Subs (Citgo)

RVCamp S: Danville Motor Homes Park & Campground

ATM N: Mobil

220 Lynch Road

FStop N: Amoco(*)

Food N: Big Boy, Stanley's (Budget Suites), The Rose (Budget Suites)

Lodg N: Best Western, Budget Suites & Inn, Comfort Inn, Fairfield Inn, Ramada Inn, Super 8

ATM N: Amoco

↑ILLINOIS

↓INDIANA

(1) Welcome Center (RR, Phones, Picnic, Vending; Eastbound)

4 IN 63, West Lebanon, Newport

TStop N: Pilot(*, SCALES)

Food N: Beef House, Dairy Queen (Pilot)

8 Covington

Gas N: Shell(*)

Food N: Overpass Pizza

AServ N: Warrick Motor Co. (Ford, Mercury)

Other N: Petro Lane(LP)

15 U.S. 41, Attica, Veedersburg

Parks S: Turkey Run State Park

(19) Weigh Station (Westbound)

(19) Weigh Station (Eastbound)

(23) Rest Area (RR, Phones, Picnic, Vending; Eastbound)

(23) Rest Area (RR, Phones, Picnic, Vending; Westbound)

25 IN 25, Wingate, Waynetown

RVCamp S: Camping

34 U.S. 231, Linden, Crawfordsville

Gas S: Amoco(*, 24), Gas America(*), Shell(*)

Food S: Burger King, Holiday Inn, McDonald's

Lodg S: Comfort Inn, Days Inn, Dollar Inn, Holiday Inn, Super 8

AServ S: Northridge Auto Service, Twin City Collision

TServ S: Citgo Auto/Truck Plaza(*, SCALES), Hoosier Truck Tech

RVCamp S: KOA Kampground (1 Mile)

EXIT INDIANA

Med S: ✚ Hospital

ATM S: Bank One, Citgo Auto/Truck Plaza, Gas America

39 IN 32, Crawfordsville

52 IN 75, Advance, Jamestown

RVCamp S: Campground

(57) Rest Area (RR, Phones, Picnic, Vending; Eastbound)

(57) Rest Area (RR, Phones, Picnic, Vending; Westbound)

58 IN 39, Lebanon, Lizton

Gas N: Phillips 66(*)

Food S: Drive-Through Restaurant

AServ N: Phillips 66

S: Scott's Auto Service

Med S: ✚ Hospital

ATM S: State Bank Of Lizton

61 Pittsboro

TStop S: Blue & White(*, SCALES)

Food S: Hap's Place (Blue & White TS)

TServ S: Blue & White(SCALES)

ATM S: Blue & White

66 IN 267, Brownsburg

FStop S: Speedway(*)

Gas N: Phillips 66(*), Shell(*, CW, 24)

S: Amoco(*, D)

Food N: Boulder Creek Dining Co., Hardee's, La Charreada Mexican Restaurant, Pizza King

S: Arby's, Blimpie Subs & Salads, Burger King, China's Best Buffet, Elegance Restaurant, Green Street Station, Little Caesars Pizza (Big K-Mart), McDonald's(PLAY), Noble Roman's Pizza, Papa John's Pizza, TCBY, Taco Bell, Wendy's

Lodg N: Holiday Inn Express

S: Dollar Inn

AServ N: Big O Tires, Q Lube

S: Mears Automotive Tire & Service

ATM N: State Bank, Union Federal

S: First Indiana Bank, Hendrick's County Bank, Kroger Supermarket(24, RX), National City Bank, Speedway

Other N: Car Wash(CW)

S: Big K-Mart(RX), CVS Pharmacy(RX), Kroger Supermarket(RX), Mail Boxes Etc.

Note: I-74 runs concurrent below with I-465. Numbering follows I-465.

16AB U.S. 136, Crawfordsville Road, I-74 West, Peoria

Gas I: Big Foot(*, LP), Shell(*, CW)

Food I: Arby's, BW3's Buffalo Wild Wings Grill & Bar, Buffalo Wild Wings Grill, Burger King, Denny's, Dip n Deli Ice Cream, El Rodeo Authentic Mexican Cuisine (HoJo Inn), Hardee's, Long John Silver, McDonald's, NCL Cafeteria, Taco Bell, Union Jack Family Dining & Pub, Wendy's

Lodg I: Dollar Inn, HoJo Inn, Motel 6, Red Roof Inn

AServ I: Goodyear Tire & Auto, Jiffy Lube

ATM I: Big Foot, NBD Bank

Other I: Family Vision Care, Mail Boxes Etc., Marsh Grocery Store(LP, 24, RX), Self Serve Laundry, Speed

EXIT INDIANA

Queen Laundry, **U.S. Post Office, Village Pantry Grocery**(LP)

14AB Tenth St.

Gas **O:** Gas America(*), Shell(*)

Food **I:** Pizza Hut, Wendy's

O: Gas America, Subway (Gas America)

Med **I:** **+ Hospital**

ATM **I:** **Cub Foods**(24, RX)

O: First Indiana Bank, Shell

Other **I:** **Cub Foods**(RX), **Lowe's**(LP)

13AB U.S. 36, Danville, Rockville Rd.

Gas **O:** Speedway(*)

Food **O:** Bob Evan's Restaurant

Lodg **I:** Comfort Inn, Sleep Inn

AServ **I:** **Sam's Club**

O: Indy Lube

Other **I:** Convenient Food Mart, **Sam's Club**

12AB U.S. 40 East, Washington St., Plainfield

Gas **I:** Amoco(*, 24)

O: Big Foot(*, LP), Phillips 66(*, D, CW, 24), Shell(*)

Food **I:** Checkered Flag Tavern & Cafeteria, Fazoli's Italian Food, Taco Bell, White Castle Restaurant

O: Airport Deli, Arby's, Burger King, Dunkin Donuts, Hardee's, KFC, **Little Caesars Pizza (K-Mart)**, Long John Silver, McDonald's, Noble Roman's Pizza, Noble Romans Pizza Express (Philiips 66), Omelet Shoppe, Phillips 66, Pizza Hut, SHONEY'S Shoney's, Smiley's Pancake & Steak, Steak 'N Shake, Subway, TCBY (Phillips 66), Wendy's

Lodg **O:** Dollar Inn

AServ **I:** ACE Auto Service, Speedway Auto Parts

O: Advance Automotive, Brandy's, Burt Nees Tire (Firestone), Car X Mufflers & Brakes, Goodyear Tire & Auto, Midas Muffler & Brake, Q-Lube, Tire Barn(24)

ATM **I:** Amoco

O: Big Foot, National City Bank

Other **I:** Airport Animal Emergency Center, **Central Ace Hardware**(LP), **Coin Laundry**(PLAY), **Osco Drugs**(RX), **U-Haul Center**(LP), **WalGreens Pharmacy**(24, RX)

O: **Big K-Mart**(RX), Classy Car Wash, Patriotic Fireworks, Smiley's Car Wash, **Target**, Western Bowl Bowling Alley

11AB Airport Expressway, International Airport

Gas **I:** Marathon(*, D), Speedway(*, LP)

Food **I:** Adam's Mark Hotel, DAYS INN Days Inn, Denny's(24), JoJo's Restaurant (La Quinta), La Quinta Inn, PK's (Days Inn), Quincy's (Adam's Mark Hotel), Schlotzsky's Deli, The Library Steakhouse & Pub, The Marker (Adam's Mark Hotel), Waffle & Steak

Lodg **I:** Adam's Mark Hotel, Budgetel Inn, Courtyard by Marriott, DAYS INN Days Inn, Extended Stay America, Fairfield Inn, Hampton Inn, La Quinta Inn, Motel 6, Residence Inn

O: Holiday Inn Select, Ramada Inn

AServ **I:** Marathon

TServ **I:** **Speedway International**

ATM **I:** NBD Bank, Speedway

Other **O:** Airport

9AB 9A - Junction I-70 East, Indianapolis, 9B - I-70 West, St. Louis,Terra Haute

8 IN 67 South, Kentucky Ave., Mooresville Rd.

Gas **O:** Speedway(*, LP, K), Swifty(K)

Food **O:** KFC

Med **I:** **+ Hospital**

7 Mann Rd. (Westbound, Reaccess Eastbound Only)

4 IN 37 South, Harding St., Martinsville, Bloomington

TStop **I:** **Pilot Travel Center**(*, SCALES, 24)

O: **Flying J Travel Plaza**(*, LP) **(Conoco gas)**

Gas **O:** Citgo(*, CW)

Food **I:** **Bender's Restaurant (EconoLodge)**, EconoLodge, **Krispy Kreme Doughnuts (Pilot)**, **Omelet Shoppe, Pilot Travel Center, Wendy's (Pilot)**

O: **Flying J Travel Plaza (Conoco gas), Hardee's, McDonald's**, Taco Bell, **Waffle & Steak**, White Castle Restaurant

Lodg **I:** **Dollar Inn**, EconoLodge, **Super 8**

O: **Knight's Inn**

TServ **I:** **Peterbilt Dealer**

O: **Flying J Travel Plaza (Conoco gas), Freightliner Dealer, Greent's Truck Service, International Navistar, J & E Tire, Paul's Trailer Service Inc., Speedco Thirty Minute Truck Lube**

TWash **O:** **Flying J Travel Plaza (Conoco gas)**

RVCamp **O:** **Kamper Korner (1.5 Miles)**

Med **I:** **+ Hospital**

Other **I:** Classy Chassy Go Go

2AB 2A - U.S. 31, IN 37 North, Indianapolis, (outside) 2B - U.S. 31 South East St. (Inside)

Gas **O:** Big Foot(*), Shell(*, CW)

Food **I:** Baskin Robbins, Old Country Buffet, Pizza Hut, Steak & Ale

O: Bob Evan's Restaurant, Denny's, Heritage Smorgasbord, Red Lobster, SHONEY'S Shoney's

Lodg **O:** Comfort Inn, Economy Inn, Holiday Inn Express, Quality Inn, Ramada Limited, Red Roof Inn

AServ **I:** Midas Muffler & Brake

ATM **I:** Bank One, First Indiana Bank, **Kroger Supermarket**(RX)

O: Shell

Other **I:** **CVS Pharmacy**(RX), **Kroger Supermarket**(RX)

53BA Junction I-65, Louisville, Indianapolis (53A goes north to Indianapolis, 53B goes south to Louisville)

52 Emerson Ave., Beech Grove

Gas **I:** Amoco(CW), Marathon(*), Shell(*)

O: Shell(*, CW, 24), Speedway(*, LP, K) (Fireworks Stand)

Food **I:** Expo Bowl, KFC

O: Egg Roll, Fazoli's Italian Food, Fuji Yama Japanese Steakhouse, McDonald's(PLAY), Pizza Hut, **Ramada (Conference Center)**, Steak 'N Shake, Sunshine Cafe(24), White Castle Restaurant

Lodg **I:** Motel 6

O: Holiday Inn, **Ramada (Conference Center)**, Red Roof Inn, Super 8

AServ **I:** Amoco, Grime Stopper Car Wash, Marathon

O: Emerson Grove Tire Service by Goodyear, Indy Lube (Ryder Truck Rental), Rama Car Wash & Lube

Med **I:** **+ Hospital**

ATM **O:** Speedway (Fireworks Stand), Teacher's Credit Union

Other **I:** Expo Bowl, GreatTimes Amusement, Grime Stopper Car Wash

49AB Junction I-74 East, U.S. 421 South

Note: I-74 runs concurrent above with I-465. Numbering follows I-465.

94AB Jct I-465, U.S.421 N, I-74 W

96 Post Rd

FStop **N:** **Pacific Pride**(*, LP) **(Marathon gas)**

Gas **S:** Amoco(24), Shell(*)

Food **N:** **McDonald's, Pacific Pride (Marathon gas), Subway (Pacific Pride)**

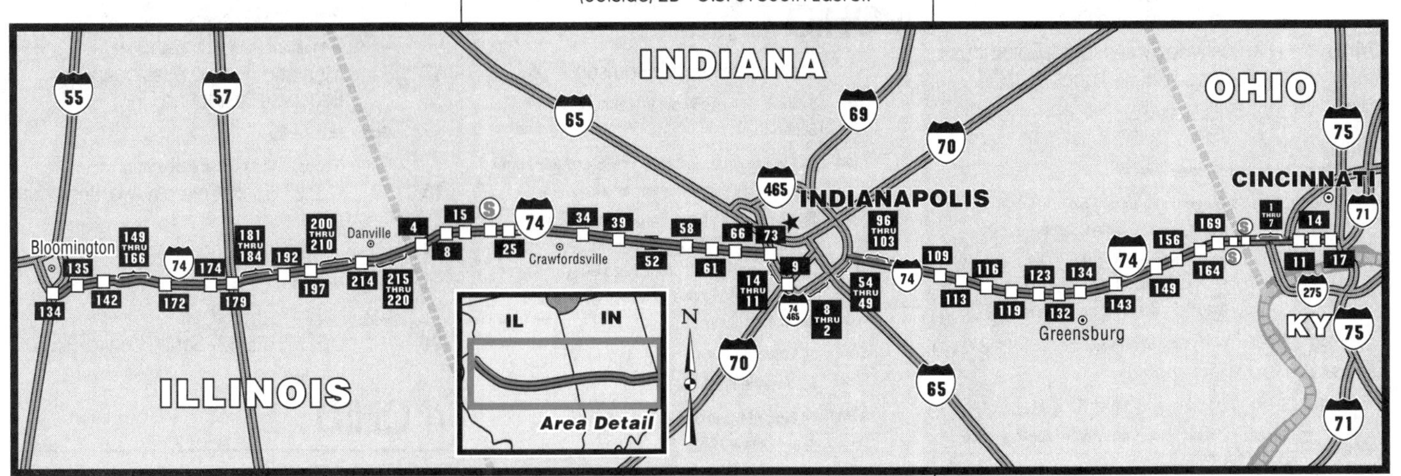

EXIT — INDIANA

S: Olisgo's Mexican Restaurant
Lodg N: Dollar Inn
AServ S: Amoco[24], Mahoney Chevrolet (Trans Drive Foriegn & Domestic Transmission Specialist)
ATM N: Pacific Pride (Marathon gas)
Other N: Wanamaker
S: Marion County Fairgrounds

99 Acton Road

101 Pleasant View Road
Gas N: Marathon[*]
AServ N: Marathon
ATM N: Key Bank
Other N: Don's Marine Service, Pleasant View One Stop

103 London Road, Boggstown

109 Fairland Road
RVCamp S: Fairland Recreation Park
Other N: Chevyville Municipal Airport, National Guard Armory
S: Brownie's Marine

113 IN 9, Shelbyville, Greenfield
Gas S: Mr T's[*, 24] (Coin laundry), Shell[*, CW]
Food S: McDonald's, Ramada, Vern Flemmings (Ramada Inn), Waffle House
Lodg S: Comfort Inn, Holiday Inn Express, Ramada, Super 8
Med S: Hospital
ATM S: Shelby County Savings, Shell

116 IN 44, Shelbyville, Rushville
FStop N: Big Foot[*, 24]
Food S: Arby's, Bavarian Haus, Bob Evan's Restaurant, China Inn, El Rodeo Authentic Mexican Cuisine, SHONEY'S, Shoney's
Lodg S: Lees Inn
AServ S: Hubler Ford/Lincoln/Mercury
Med S: Hospital
ATM N: Big Foot
S: Centra Credit Union
Other N: Shelbyville Animal Clinic
S: Aldi Food Store, CVS Pharmacy[RX], New Life Christian Resource Center

119 IN 244, Milroy, Andersonville
AServ N: I-74 Auto Center & Towing

123 Saint Paul, Middletown
RVCamp S: Camping

132 U.S. 421, Greensburg (Eastbound, Reaccess Westbound Only)

134AB IN 3, Rushville, Greensburg, Columbus (34A goes south, 34B goes north)
FStop S: Pacific Pride Commercial Fueling[*, CW] (Shell gas)
Gas S: Big Foot[*], Speedway[*, K]
Food S: Arby's, Burger King, Frisch's Big Boy, Great Wall Chinese, K-Mart[RX], KFC, Little Caesars Pizza (K-Mart), Mang's Family[24], McCamment's Steakhouse, McDonald's, Papa John's Pizza, Subway, Taco Bell, Waffle House, Wendy's
Lodg S: Belter Motel, Best Western (Pines Inn), Lees Inn
AServ S: Don Meyer Ford Mercury
ATM S: Fifth-Third Bank, Irwin Union Bank, Jay C Grocery, Pacific Pride Commercial Fueling (Shell gas), Speedway

EXIT — INDIANA/OHIO

Other S: Advance Auto Parts, Buggy Bath Car Wash, Jay C Grocery, K-Mart[RX], Wal-Mart[RX]

143 New Point, St Maurice
TStop N: Ross Point Hossier Heartland Travel Center[SCALES] (Marathon gas)
Food N: Hossier Pride Restaurant, Ross Point Hossier Heartland Travel Center (Marathon gas)
TServ N: Ross Point Hossier Heartland Travel Center[SCALES] (Marathon gas)
RVCamp N: Camping (7 Miles)

149 IN 229, Batesville, Oldenburg
Gas N: Shell[*]
S: Amoco[*, CW]
Food N: China Wok, McDonald's, Subway, Wendy's
S: Arby's, Dairy Queen, Hardee's, KFC, La Rosa's Italian
Lodg N: Hampton Inn
S: DAYS INN Days Inn
AServ N: Pennzoil Oil Change
Med S: Hospital
ATM N: FCN Bank, People's Trust Bank, Shell
S: Amoco
Other N: Kroger Supermarket[RX], Pimida Discount Center, The Strawberry Cottage
S: Revco Drugs[RX]

(152) Rest Area (RR, Phones, Picnic, Vending; Eastbound)

(152) Rest Area (RR, Phones, Picnic, Vending; Westbound)

156 IN 101, Sunman, Milan
AServ S: Todd Wrecker Service & Tire Repair[24] (24 hour road service)
RVCamp S: Thousand Trails (2 Miles)

164 IN 1, Lawrenceburg, St Leon
Gas N: Citgo[*], Shell[*, D, K]
S: BP[*, D]
Food N: Christina's Family, Citgo, Tiny Town Pizza (Citgo)
S: BP, Blimpie Subs & Salads (BP)
AServ N: Shell
ATM S: BP

169 U.S.52 West, Brookville

(171) Weigh Station (Westbound)

↑INDIANA

↓OHIO

1 New Haven Road, Harrison
Gas S: Shell[*, CW], Speedway[*, LP, K], Sunoco[*], SuperAmerica[*, D]
Food N: Bigg's Hypermarket[RX], Cracker Barrel, McDonald's (Bigg' Hypermarket)
S: Arby's, Back's Deli[*], Burger King, El Cayote Southwestern Grill (Quality Inn), Hardee's[PLAY], KFC, Perkin's Family Restaurant, Pizza Hut, Quality Inn, Sunoco, Waffle House, Wendy's, White Castle Restaurant (Sunoco)
AServ N: Kesserling Ford
S: Firestone Tire & Auto
ATM N: Bigg's Hypermarket
S: Back's Deli, Sunoco

EXIT — OHIO

Other N: Bigg's Hypermarket[RX]
S: Auto Parts Warehouse Outlet, Back's Deli, CVS Pharmacy[RX], Harrison Police Station

(2) Weigh Station (Eastbound)

3 Dry Fork Road
FStop S: Chevron[*, D], Shell[*, CW]
Gas N: Citgo[*]
S: BP[*, LP]
Food S: Burger King (Shell), Shell
Lodg S: Motel Deluxe
AServ S: Hirlinger Chevrolet Dealership
RVCamp N: Miami Whitewater Forest Campground (1 Mile)
ATM S: Shell
Other N: Miami Whitewater Forest (1 Mile)
S: Cincinnati S.W. Veterinary Clinic, Suburban Propane[LP]

5 Jct I-275 South , to KY

7 OH 128, Hamilton, Cleves
Gas N: BP[*, D], Shell[*, D, K]
Food N: Wendy's
S: Angelo's Pizza
AServ N: Don's Miami Town

9 Jct I-275 North , to I-75, Dayton

11 Rybolt Road, Harrison Pike
Gas S: Sunoco
Food S: Angilo's Pizza, Dante's Restaurant (Imperial)
Lodg S: Imperial House
AServ S: Sunoco
ATM S: Oak Hills Savings & Loan
Other S: Ameristop Convenience Store

14 North Bend Road, Cheviot
Gas N: Ameristop[*], Shell[CW], Speedway[*], SuperAmerica[*, D]
S: BP[*, LP]
Food N: Dairy Queen, Dunkin Donuts, McDonald's, Papa John's Pizza, Rally's Hamburgers, Skyline Chili, Subway, Wendy's
S: Bob Evan's Restaurant
Lodg S: Tri Star Motel
AServ N: Jim's Auto Clinic, Midas Muffler & Brake, Quaker State Oil & Lube, Shell, Tuffy Auto Center, Valvoline Oil Change
Med N: Hospital
ATM N: Fifth Third Bank, Key Bank, The Provident Bank (Thriftway Food & Drug)
Other N: Complete Pet Mart, Sam's Club, Thriftway Food & Drug, WalGreens Pharmacy
S: Monford Heights Animal Clinic

17 Montana Avenue (Westbound, Reaccess Eastbound Only)
Gas N: BP[*, CW]
Other N: Dairy Mart Convenience Store

18 U.S. 27 North, Colerain Ave, Beekman St

19 Elmore St, Spring Grove Ave
Gas N: Sunoco[*]
ATM N: Sunoco

20 U.S. 27, U.S. 127 South, Central Pkwy (No trucks)

↑OHIO

Begin I-74

Bold red print shows RV & Bus parking available or nearby

EXIT | MICHIGAN

Begin I-75

↓MICHIGAN

394 **Easterday Ave, Sault Locks, Rest Area, Welcome Center**
- Gas W: USA(*, D)
- Food E: **McDonald's**
- Lodg E: Holiday Inn Express
- Med W: **✚ Hospital**
- ATM W: USA
- Other E: Canada Toll Bridge, Lake Superior State University

392 Bus 75, Three Mile Road, Sault Ste. Marie
- FStop E: **76**(*, D, LP)
- Gas E: Amoco(*), **Mobil**(*, CW), Shell(*), USA Mini-Mart(*, D, K)
- Food E: Albie's, **Arby's**, **Burger King**, **La Senorita Mexican**, **Wendy's**
- Lodg E: Best Western, Comfort Inn, **Ramada Inn (see our ad this page)**
- AServ E: Reno's Car Care, Sadler GM Dealership
- RVCamp E: **Camping**, **Chippewa Campground (1 Mile)**
- Med E: **✚ Hospital**
- ATM E: North Country Bank & Trust, USA Mini-Mart
- Other E: Don D. Lanes Bowling, **Glen's County Market**, JC Penney, **Kewadin Casinos (see our ad this page)**, **MI State Police & Sheriff Dept**, **Sault Tribe Indian Reservation**, **Tourist Info.**, **Wal-Mart**(RX)
  W: Sears

(389) **Rest Area (RR, Phones, Picnic, Vending; Northbound)**

386 MI 28, Newberry, Munising
- Food E: Sharolyn Restaurant
- Lodg E: Sharolyn Motel, Sunset Motel
- RVCamp W: **KOA Campgrounds**
- Parks W: **Brimley State Park**

379 Gaines Hwy, Barbeau Area
- RVCamp W: **Clear Lake Campground (1.5 Miles)**

378 Kinross
- Gas E: **Amoco**(*)
- Food E: Frank & Jim's Italian/American, Kinross Cafe
- RVCamp E: **Kinross RV Park West (1 Mile)**
- Other E: **Airport**, Kinross 4H Center-Horseraces

373 MI 48, Rudyard, Pickford
- Food W: Clyde's Drive-In
- AServ W: Rudyard Collision Repair
- TServ W: **Gaylor Trucking**(CW)

359 MI 134, DeTour Village, Drummond Isand
- Lodg W: Christmas Motel

1688

RAMADA INN®

Convention Center

Restaurant/Lounge on Premises
Kids Under 18 Stay Free
Indoor Pool • Exercise Room
Meeting/Banquet Facilities
Handicap Accessible
Truck/Large Vehicle Parking
Interior Corridors • Pets Allowed
Casino Packages - Casino Shuttle

906-635-1523 • 800-432-5903

MICHIGAN • I-75 • EXIT 392

Kewadin Means North... And So Much More

KEWADIN CASINOS
SAULT STE. MARIE
300 ROOM HOTEL
INDOOR POOL
GAME ROOM
VEGAS STYLE GAMING
LIVE ENTERTAINMENT
SPECIALTY SHOPS
DREAM CATCHER'S RESTAURANT

KEWADIN CASINOS
ST. IGNACE
VEGAS STYLE GAMING
GIFT SHOPS
DELI

CALL:
1-800-KEWADIN
FOR INFORMATION ON ALL FIVE UPPER PENINSULA LOCATIONS!
SAULT STE. MARIE
MANISTIQUE
CHRISTMAS
ST. IGNACE
HESSEL

EXIT | MICHIGAN

352 MI 123, Newberry, Tahquamenon Falls

348 Mackinaw Trail, Hwy. 63, Salut Reservation (National Forest Campground)
- Gas E: Shell(*)
- Food E: Shores Pizzaria
- Lodg E: Birchwood Motel, Carey's Motel, Cedar's Motel, Great Lakes Motel, Northern Aire Budget Inn, Pines Motel, Rock View Motel, Sand's Motel
- RVCamp E: **Castle Rock Mackinac Trail Campark (.5 Miles)**, **KOA Campgrounds (6 Miles)**, **National Forest Campground (6 Miles)**
- Other W: **Castle Rock Tourist Attraction**(*)

344AB Bus I-75, St. Ignace
- TStop W: **St Ignace Truck Stop**(*, D, LP, 24)
- Gas W: Holiday(*), Shell(*, D)
- Food E: Northern Lights
  W: **Big Boy**, **Burger King**, Clyde's Drive-In, **McDonald's**, **St Ignace Truck Stop**, Subway (Shell), Up North Restaurant
- Lodg E: Aurora Borealis Motel, Normandy Motel, Quality Inn, Roadway Inn, St Ignace Inn
  W: **Howard Johnson**, **Super 8**
- RVCamp W: **KOA Campgrounds (2 Miles)**
- Med E: **✚ Hospital**
- ATM E: **Glen's Market**(24)
  W: First of America(24), Shell
- Parks E: **Straits State Park**
- Other E: Bowl Gateway Lanes, **Glen's Market**, **Mackinaw Island Ferry & Fish Market**
  W: Marquette Museum, St. Ignace Golf & Country Club

(346) **Rest Area, Scenic Turnout (Southbound)**

1268

Present this ad and Receive 15% Off

MACKINAW CITY'S BEST VALUE HOTELS

ABA & NTA MEMBERS

— Deluxe Jacuzzi Suites—
— Bridge View & Lake View Rooms —
— Special Facilities —
— Non-Smoking Rooms Available—
— Indoor Pool, Spa & Sauna —
616-436-5252 EXIT 339

RAMADA INN® CONVENTION CENTER
— Indoor Pool, Spa & Sauna —
— Special Facilities —
— Non-Smoking Rooms Available —
— Free HBO—
— Restaurant and Sportsbar On-site—
616-436-5535 EXIT 338

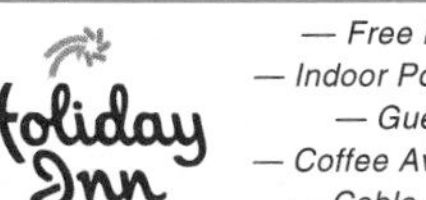

— Free Breakfast Bar —
— Indoor Pool, Spa & Sauna —
— Guest Laundry —
— Coffee Available 24 Hours —
— Cable • HBO • ESPN —
616-436-7100 EXIT 339

— Indoor Pool & Spa —
— Fresh AM Coffee —
— Family Units Available —
— Free HBO —
— Downtown Location —
616-436-8961 EXIT 339

Mackinaw City, MI • I-75

EXIT	MICHIGAN
344	**Rest Area**
343	Bridgeview (Southbound, Reaccess Westbound Only)
339	Jamet St (Note: Beware High Winds)
Gas	E: Amoco(*, D), Mobil, Total(*, D)
	W: **Shell(*)**, **Sunoco(CW)**
Food	E: Audie's Family Restaurant, Burger King, Chinese Restaurant, Cunningham's Family Restaurant, Dairy Queen, El Senor's Mexican, Joanne's Fudge, KFC, Mama Mia's Pizzeria, McDonald's, Pancake Chef, Parkside Bridgeview Room, Squealy Downing's Family Restaurant, Subway
	W: Darrow's Family Restaurant, The Fort Restaurant
Lodg	E: Budget Host, Downing's Downtown Motel, Econolodge, La Mirage Motel, Motel 6 (see our ad Pg. 325), Riviera Motel, Super 8 (see our ad Pg. 325)
	W: Bridgeview Motel, Chalet Motel, Fort Mackinaw Motel, Holiday Inn Express (see our Pg. 325), Trails End Inn, Vindel Motel
AServ	W: **Sunoco**
RVCamp	E: **Tee Pee Campground (1 Mile)**
	W: **Shell**, **Sunoco**, **Sunoco**
ATM	E: Federal Credit Union(24), First of America
Parks	W: **Wilderness State Park**
Other	E: **Colonial Michilimackinac**, **IGA Grocery**, Macinaw Crossing Shopping Center
	W: Wash & Dry Coin Laundry
(338)	**Welcome Center, Rest Area (RR, Phones, Picnic, Vending)**
337	MI 108, Nicolet St, Mackinaw City
FStop	E: **Citgo(*, D, LP)**
Food	E: Christopher's Home Cooking, Mario's Ristorante
	W: Neath The Birches
Lodg	E: Anchor Budget Inn, Beach Comber Motel, Best Western, Best Western, Best Western, Cherokee Shores Inn, Chippewa Motor Lodge, Comfort Inn, DAYS INN Days Inn (see our ad this page), Econo Lodge, **Hamilton Inn Select**, Howard Johnson, Huron Motel, Quality Inn, Ramada Limited, Starlite Budget Inn, Sundown Motel, Surf Motel, TraveLodge, Water Front Inn
	W: Americana Motel, Flamingo Hotel, Rambler's Motel, Valru, White Birches Motel
AServ	E: **Citgo**
RVCamp	E: **Camping**, **Macinaw City Camping**
	W: **KOA Campgrounds (1.5 Miles)**
Parks	W: **Wilderness State Park**
328	**Rest Area (RR, HF, Phones, Picnic; Southbound)**
326	CR 66, Cheboygan, Cross Village
FStop	E: **Hilltop Bar & Grill**
Gas	E: Marathon(*)
Med	E: ✚ **Hospital**
Other	E: **Seashell City Gift Shop**
	W: Wheelock's Boat & RV Storage
322	CR 64, Pellston, Cheboygan
AServ	E: Holton's LP Gas Co.
Med	E: ✚ **Hospital**
Other	E: **Blarney Castle Oil Company(LP)**
317	**Rest Area, Scenic View, Nature Trail (RR, Phones, Picnic, Vending; Northbound)**
313	MI 27 North, Topinabee, Cheboygan
AServ	E: Stoyka Service Center, Tri-Rivers Collision
RVCamp	E: **Indian River RV Resort & Campground (1.5 Miles)**, **KOA Campgrounds**
Med	E: ✚ **Judy's Dog Boarding & Grooming**
Other	E: RV Storage
310	MI 68, Rogers City, Indian River
Gas	W: Amoco(D), **Shell(*) (Restaurant)**
Food	W: BC Pizza, Breadeaux Pizza, **Burger King**, Christopher's Family Dining, Dairy Queen, Don's Country Chicken & Pizza, Flip & Slice Deli, Ice Cream & Fudge Carousel, Paula's Cafe, Wilson's River Edge Restaurant
Lodg	E: Holiday Inn Express (see our ad this page)
	W: Coach House Motel, Indian River Motel, Reid's Motor Court
AServ	W: Dan's Auto Repair, Inland Transmission, Jack's Auto Repair, Mobile Service(CW), Pollard's Quick Lube
RVCamp	E: **Camping**
	W: **Camping**
ATM	W: Citizen's National Bank, First of America
Parks	W: **Burt Lake State Park (.25 Miles)**
Other	W: Big Bear Adventure Golf, **Coin Laundry**, Conquest Auto Parts, **Ken's Village Market**, Optim Eyes, Pat & Gary's Convenient Store(LP), Tuscarora Township Police
301	CR 58, Wolverine
FStop	E: **Marathon(*, D, LP, K)**
Food	E: **County Line Restaurant**
RVCamp	E: **Camping**
	W: **Camping**
Med	E: ✚ **Wolverine Medical Center**
290	Vanderbilt
Gas	E: 76(*, D), Mobil(LP, K)
	W: Amoco(*)
Food	E: Darcy's Bar, Olde Town Pizza & Restaurant, Restaurant
AServ	E: 76
ATM	E: Gateway Restaurant
Other	E: **Grocery Store**

Save 10%
1060
I-75 • Exit 310
Indian River, MI
616-238-3000
800-HOLIDAY
Holiday Inn EXPRESS
• Free Breakfast Bar
• Heated Indoor Pool & Spa
• In-Room Jacuzzis
• Meeting Facilities
• Coin Laundry
• 27 Mi. to Mackinac Island
• Cross in the Woods (World's Largest Crucifix) 2 Miles
MICHIGAN • I-75 • EXIT 310

Bold red print shows RV & Bus parking available or nearby

EXIT MICHIGAN

(287) Rest Area (RR, Phones, Picnic, Vending; Southbound)

282 Gaylord, Alpena, MI 32
- FStop W: Citgo(*, D), Marathon(*, D)
- Gas E: Amoco(*, D, CW), Clark(*), Holiday(*, LP), Phillips 66(*), Total(*, D, LP)
  W: BP(*), Shell(*, D)
- Food E: Arby's, Baskin Robbins, Big Buck Brewery & Steakhouse, Breadeaux Pizza, Burger King, Dairy Queen (Glen's Market), Dan's Pizza Plus, Dunkin Donuts, KFC, La Senorita, McDonald's, Red Rose American-Chinese Cuisine, Subway, TCBY, Total(*, LP), Wendy's
  W: Big Boy, Bob Evan's Restaurant, Flap Jack Shack, Little Caesars Pizza, Mobil(D), Pastie's Subs & Salads, Pizza Hut, Ponderosa, Taco Bell, Willie's Ribs
- Lodg E: Comfort Inn, Holiday Inn, Microtel Inn & Suites, Super 8 (see our ad this page)
  W: DAYS INN Days Inn, Hampton Inn, Super 8
- AServ E: Bill's Auto Service
  W: Arthur's Auto Parts & Sales, Fred's Garage, Midas Muffler & Brake, Mobil, Monte's Auto Wash, Quaker State Oil & Lube
- TServ W: Gaylord Truck Wash, Northern Michigan Kenworth Dealer
- RVCamp W: Burnside RV(LP) (.4 Miles), Gaylord Alpine Campground (.5 Miles), Weller Truck Parks
- Med E: ✚ Hospital
  W: ✚ Medical Care Center
- ATM E: First National Bank of Gaylord, Glen's Market(24, RX), Northwestern Savings Bank & Trust, Old Kent Bank, Total
  W: Citgo
- Parks E: Bavarian Falls Park
  W: Valley Truck Parts
- Other E: Glen's Market(RX), Norman's Sports Goods, Rite Aid Pharmacy(*), Town Country Car Wash
  W: Buy-Low Foods, GFS Grocery, Wal-Mart(24, RX)

279 Bus Loop 75, Downtown Gaylord, Old 27
- FStop E: Marathon(*, D), Mobil(*, D, LP, K)
- Gas E: Shell(*)
- Food E: Burger King(PLAY), Busia's Polish Kitchen Home Cooking, Dowker's Deli, Mama Leone's Italian, Subway
  W: Schlang's Bulvarian Inn
- Lodg E: Brentwood Inn, Econolodge
- AServ E: Alpine Service Center, Jim Wernig & Express Oil Change, Nissan of Gaylord
  W: 76 Station, Rick's Auto
- RVCamp E: Gaylord RV Service(LP), Moore's RV Supply
  W: Camping
- ATM E: Marathon

277 Rest Area (RR, Phones, Picnic,

Tour Buses Welcome

SUPER 8 MOTEL

Super 8 Motel

1042 West Main St.
Gaylord, MI

517-732-5193

1269

- Free Continental Breakfast
- Indoor Pool
- Free HBO, ESPN
- Sauna/Spa/Excercise Room

AAA
ABA & NTA MEMBERS

"Super Rooms at Super Rates!"

Show this ad for 15% Off

MICHIGAN ▪ I-75 ▪ Exit 282

EXIT MICHIGAN

Vending; Northbound)

270 Waters, Otsego Lake State Park
- TStop E: Mobil(D) (Restaurant)
- Food W: Countryside Cafe, Keg Bar W/ Great Food, McDonald's, The Trading Post Deli & Pizza(*)
- Lodg W: Alan's Roost
- AServ W: Waters Garage
- TServ W: Northern Tank Truck Service
- RVCamp W: Camping
- Parks W: Otsego Lake State Park
- Other W: DJ's IGA Grocery, Waters RV Storage & Sales(LP)

264 Lewiston, Frederic
- RVCamp W: Camping
- Parks E: Hartwick Pine State Park
  W: National Propane Co.

262 Rest Area (RR, Phones, Picnic, Vending; Southbound)

259 Hartwick Pines Road, MI 93
- RVCamp E: Campground
  W: Campground
- Parks E: Hartwick Pines State Park (1 Mile)
- Other W: Department of Natural Resources(CW)

256 North Down River (Southbound, Reaccess Northbound Only)
- Med W: ✚ Hospital
- Other W: Animal Hospital

254 Business Loop 75, MI 72, Traverse City, Downtown Grayling (Left Exit Northbound)
- FStop W: Mobil(*, D)
- Gas W: Phillips 66(*), Total(*, D, LP)
- Food W: Big Boy, Burger King, China West, Dairy Queen, KFC, Little Caesars Pizza, McDonald's, Patti's Towne House, Subway, Taco Bell, Wendy's
- Lodg W: Aquarama Motor Lodge, Holiday Inn
- AServ W: Carquest Auto Center, Ford-Mercury Dealership (Auto Parts), Parts Plus, Upper Lakes Tire, Wagenwheel Cleaning Center(CW) (Laundry)
- TServ W: Wagenwheel Cleaning Center (Laundry)
- ATM W: 7-11 Convenience Store, Chemical Bank, Citizens Bank, Empire National Bank
- Other W: 7-11 Convenience Store, Ace Hardware, Country Club & Golf Course, Glen's Supermarket(RX), K-Mart, Mini Mall, NAPA Auto Parts, Rite Aid Pharmacy(*)

252 Rest Area (RR, Phones, Picnic, Vending; Northbound)

251 4 Mile Road
- FStop W: Total(*, D, LP, K) (Shower, laundry)
- Lodg W: Super 8
- TServ W: Red Eagle Community CB Shop
- RVCamp E: Camping
  W: Campground
- ATM W: Total (Shower, laundry)
- Other W: Fox Run Country Club

249 U.S. 27 South, Claire, Lansing (Southbound, Reaccess Northbound Only)

244 North Higgins Lake State Park
- Gas W: Sunoco(*, D, LP)
- RVCamp W: Higgins Hills RV Park (1.25 Miles)
- Other W: CCC Museum

239 Bus Loop 75, MI 18, South Higgins Lake, Roscommon
- RVCamp E: Camping
  W: Camping
- Parks W: State Park

EXIT MICHIGAN

235 Rest Area (RR, Phones, Picnic, Vending; Southbound)

227 MI 55 W, Houghton Lake, Cadillac, Prudenville
- Food E: Maple Valley Restaurant

222 Old 76, St Helen
- RVCamp E: Camping

215 Business Loop 75, MI 55 East, West Branch
- FStop E: Atherton's Soup & Chicken, Total(*, D, LP, K)
- Gas E: Welcome Motel
- AServ E: Gene's Garage, Pontiac Buick Dealer, Total
- Med E: ✚ Hospital, ✚ Ryder(LP), ✚ West Branch Veterinary Services

212 Bus Loop 75, Cook Road, West Branch
- TStop W: DeShano's(D, LP) (Showers)
- FStop E: Big Boy(D), Marathon(*, D) (Honker Travel Center)
- Gas E: Shell(*, 24)
  W: DeShano's(D) (Showers)
- Food E: Arby's, Big Boy, Burger King, McDonald's, Ponderosa Steakhouse, Taco Bell, Wendy's
  W: North Country Junction (BP Fuel Stop)
- Lodg E: Holiday Inn(*), Super 8
- RVCamp E: Camping
  W: Camping
- Med W: ✚ Hospital
- ATM E: Marathon (Honker Travel Center)
  W: DeShano's (Showers)
- Other E: Tanger Factory Outlet

210 Rest Area (RR, Phones, Picnic, Vending; Northbound)

202 MI 33, Alger, Rose City
- Gas E: Mobil(*, D, LP, K), Shell(*)
- Food E: Hot Stuff Pizza (Shell), Subway (Shell), Taco Bell (Shell)
- RVCamp E: Camping
- ATM E: Shell

201 Rest Area (RR, Phones, Picnic, Vending; Southbound)

195 Sterling Road
- RVCamp E: Camping

190 MI 61, Gladwin, Standish
- Gas E: Standard(*, LP)
  W: Mobil(*)
- AServ W: John's Auto Repair
- Med E: ✚ Hospital

188 U.S. 23, Standish, Alpena
- RVCamp E: Cedar Springs Campground

181 Pinconning Road, Pinconning
- FStop W: Sunoco(*, D, LP, K)
- Gas E: Mobil(*), Shell(*)
- Food E: McDonald's (Shell), Peppermill
- TServ W: T & T Repairs
- RVCamp E: Camping
- Med E: ✚ Peppermill Lanes
- ATM E: Shell
  W: Sunoco

175 Rest Area (RR, Phones, Picnic, Vending; Northbound)

173 Linwood Road, Linwood
- Gas E: Mobil(*)

168 Beaver Road
- Gas W: Mobil(*)
- ATM W: Mobil
- Parks E: Bay City State Park (5 Miles)

164 to MI 13, Wilder Road, Kawkawlin

EXIT		MICHIGAN
	Gas	E: Meijer Superstore(*, D, LP, K, 24)
	Food	E: Bill Knapp's Restaurant (see our ad this page), Spad's Pizza
	Lodg	W: Americann Motel & Suites
	Med	E: Hospital
		W: Powerhouse Gym
	Other	E: Coin Car Wash, Meijer Superstore
162AB		U.S.10 West, Midland, Bay City, MI 25
	Med	E: Hospital
160		MI 84, Saginaw Road
	Gas	E: Mobil(*), Shell(*)
		W: Amoco(*), Citgo(*), Marathon(*, D, CW)
	Food	E: Dunkin Donuts (Shell), Subway (Mobil)
		W: Bergers Fine Food, Burger King, Howard Johnson's Restaurant, McDonald's, Michigan Dhaus
	Lodg	W: Bay Valley Hotel & Resort, Best Western
	RVCamp	W: International RV World(LP)
	ATM	W: Citgo, Citizens Bank, Marathon
158		Rest Area (RR, Phones, Picnic, Vending; Southbound)
155		Junction I-675, Downtown Saginaw
154		MI 13, Zilwaukee (Difficult Reaccess)
	Gas	E: Total(*)
	AServ	E: Great Lakes Transmission & Auto Repair
		W: Pines Tree Service & Landscaping
	Other	E: Paddy's Car Wash
153		MI 13, East Bay City Rd
151		MI 81, Caro, Reese
	FStop	E: Sunoco(*, D, LP, K)
	AServ	W: Outer Drive, Robinson's Auto Clinic, Williamson Tire
	TServ	E: Tri-City Suspension & Brake, Upper Lakes Tire
		W: Coty's Truck Wash, Freightliner Equipment Corp.
	ATM	E: Sunoco
	Other	E: Express Stop (Sunoco)
		W: Express Mart, PNF Market
150		Junction I-675 North, Downtown Saginaw
149AB		MI 46, Holland Ave, Sandusky
	Gas	W: BP, Fisca, Sunoco(*), Total(*, D, K)
	Food	E: Back Street Saloon & Eatery, Tradition Restaurant
		W: Arby's, Big Boy, Big John's Steak & Onion, Burger King, Ern's Seafood, Little Caesars Pizza (K-Mart), McDonald's(PLAY), Porter's Restaurant (Holiday Inn), Speedway(*, D), Taco Bell, Texan T Restaurant, Wendy's
	Lodg	E: Roadway Inn, Holiday Inn (see our ad this page)
		W: Holiday Inn, Knight's Inn, Red Roof Inn
	AServ	W: Car Wash
	TServ	W: Detroit Diesel & Ellison Transmission, Ryder
	Med	E: Hospital
	ATM	W: First of America, Speedway
	Other	E: Browne Airport
		W: Auto Wash, K-Mart(RX), Kessel Grocery
144AB		Bridgeport, Frankenmuth
	TStop	W: 76 Auto/Truck Plaza(*, D, K, RV DUMP, SCALES)
	FStop	E: Speedway(*, D, LP, K, SCALES), Total(*, D)
		W: Mobil
	Gas	E: Shell(*)
	Food	E: A & W Drive-In (Total), Blimpie's Subs (Shell), Freeway Fritz (Shell), TCBY (Shell)
		W: Apple Creek Family Restaurant (76 TS), Arby's, Big Boy, Burger King, Cracker Barrel, Dunkin Donuts (Mobil), Little Caesars Pizza, McDonald's, Peking City Chinese & American, Render's, Sbarro, Subway, Taco Bell, Wendy's
	Lodg	W: Budgetel Inn, Days Inn, Motel 6
	TServ	W: 76 Auto/Truck Plaza(SCALES)
	TWash	W: 76 Auto/Truck Plaza

EXIT		MICHIGAN
	Med	W: Bridgeport Food Center
	ATM	E: Total
		W: 76 Auto/Truck Plaza, NBD Bank
	Other	E: Parker's Propane(LP)
(143)		Rest Area (RR, HF, Phones, Picnic; Northbound)
138		Weigh Station
136		MI 54, MI 83, Birch Run, Frankenmuth
	FStop	E: Mobil(*, D, K)
		W: Sunoco(*, D), Total(*, D)
	Gas	E: Citgo(*, D), Shell(*)
		W: Amoco(*, CW), Citgo(*), Sunoco(*, D)
	Food	E: Bar & Grill, Dally's Pizza, Dixie Dave's Old Dixie Inn, Dunkin Donuts (Shell), Exit Restaurant, Halo Burger, KFC, Subway
		W: A & W Drive-In, Applebee's, Arby's, Bob Evan's Restaurant, Burger King (Amoco), McDonald's, Schlotzsky's Deli, Shoney's, Shoney's, Tony's Restaurant (Truck parking nearby), Wendy's
	Lodg	E: Best Western, Comfort Inn, Hampton Inn, Holiday Inn Express, Super 8
		W: Country Inn & Suites
	AServ	E: Conquest Auto Parts, Cotten Tire Center, HS Gray Garage (24 Hr. Towing), J & B Quick Oil Change
		W: Suski Chevrolet & Buick
	RVCamp	W: Campground
	ATM	E: Mobil
		W: Amoco, Citgo
	Other	E: Fents Laundry
		W: Prime Outlets at Birch Run (see our ad this page), NHL Skate, Outlet Mall
131		MI 57, Clio, Montrose
	Gas	E: Sunoco(*)
		W: Amoco(*), Mobil(*, 24)
	Food	E: Arby's, Burger King, KFC, McDonald's, Oriental Express (Chinese), Subway, Taco Bell, Twins Pizza, Pasta, & More
		W: Big Boys, Dunkin Donuts (Amoco), McDonald's, Wendy's
	Lodg	E: Econolodge
	AServ	E: Chevrolet, Clio Chrysler Dealership, Expressway Ford Dealership
		W: Mike's Auto Service, Skip's Auto Service
	Med	E: McLaren Family Care (Urgent Care)
129		Rest Area (RR, Phones, Picnic, Vending)
126		Mount Morris
	TStop	E: BP(*, LP, K, SCALES)
	FStop	W: Amoco(*, D)
	Food	E: Burger King (BP)
		W: McDonald's (Amoco)
	AServ	W: NAPA Auto Parts, Tucker's Car Wash & Co.
	RVCamp	E: Timberwolf Campground (11 Miles), Wolverine Campground (14 Miles)

1192
Holiday Inn®
HOLIDOME INDOOR RECREATION CENTER
517-755-0461
Saginaw, MI
TOUR BUSES WELCOME
• Lounge with Entertainment
• Restaurant on Premises
• Kids 12 and Under Stay & Eat Free
• Banquet Rooms
• Holidome w/Indoor Pool
• Close to Frankenmuth
• 15 Mi from Birchrun Factory Outlet
Michigan • I-75 • Exit 149B

Bill Knapp's Restaurant
Open daily at 11:00 am
Bill Knapp's is a casual, full service family restaurant where Motorcoaches are always welcome.
Over 50 locations throughout: Michigan • Ohio • Indiana
1802
810-695-6722 Grand Blanc
MICHIGAN • I-475 • EXIT 2

EXIT		MICHIGAN
		W: Bell Fork Lift(LP) (LP Gas available)
	ATM	W: Amoco
125		Junction I-475, Downtown Flint
	Food	W: Bill Knapp's Restaurant (see our ad this page)
122		Pierson Road, Flushing
	Gas	E: Amoco(*, CW), Clark(*), Marathon(*, 24), Total(*, D, LP)
		W: Meijer Grocery(*, D, LP, 24)
	Food	E: China 1 Buffet, KFC, McDonald's, Moy Kong Express, Papa's Gyro's, Subway, Walli's Restaurant
		W: Arby's, Bill Knapp's Restaurant (see our ad this page), Bob Evan's Restaurant, Burger King, Cracker Barrel, Denny's, Halo Burger, Long John Silver, Pizza Hut, Ramada Inn, Red Lobster, Taco Bell, Wendy's, Ya Ya's Flame Broiled Chicken
	Lodg	E: Super 8, Walli's Motor Lodge
		W: Budgetel Inn, Knight's Inn
	AServ	E: Archie's Auto & Truck Service, Auto Brake Collision, Goodyear Tire & Auto, Marathon(24), Master's Automotive, Muffler Man, Murray's Discount Auto Store, Total, Tuffy Auto Center
		W: Discount Tire Company, Valvoline Oil Change
	RVCamp	E: Moore's Mobile Home & RV Supplies
	ATM	E: Amoco
		W: Meijer Grocery
	Other	E: Coin Laundry, Double D Super Market, K-Mart(RX)
		W: Meijer Grocery, Soccer Zone
118		MI 21, Corunna Road, Owosso
	FStop	E: Jolly Olive
	Gas	E: Sunoco(*, CW)
		W: MSI(*), Mobil(*)
	Food	E: Bada Lebanese West, Big John's Steak & Onion, Hardee's, King Chinese Buffet, The Whisper Restaurant
		W: David's Pizza, Domino's Pizza, Happy Valley Restaurant, Valley Pub (Economy Motel)
	Lodg	W: Economy Motel
	AServ	E: D & V Collision, Garrison's Hitch Center, Sunoco
		W: Car Quest Auto Center, Mobil, Muffler Man, Q Lube & Wash Center, Wal-Mart(RX)
	Med	E: Hospital
	ATM	E: Old Kent
	Other	E: Asian Supermarket, Kessel Grocery, Rite

PRIME OUTLETS
BIRCH RUN
Over 100 Designer Outlet Stores and Food Court
Jones New York • Liz Claiborne • Nike
Ask for your FREE COUPON BOOK
1854
414-857-2101
MICHIGAN • I-75 • EXIT 136

Bill Knapp's Restaurant
Open daily at 11:00 am
Bill Knapp's is a casual, full service family restaurant where Motorcoaches are always welcome.
Over 50 locations throughout: Michigan • Ohio • Indiana
1700
810-732-2240 - Flint
517-684-2913 - Bay City
MICHIGAN • I-75 • Exit 122/164

Bold red print shows RV & Bus parking available or nearby

EXIT — MICHIGAN

Aide Pharmacy
W: Sam's Club, Wal-Mart(RX), Whirly Ball Fun Center

117B Miller Road
- **Gas** E: Speedway(*, D, LP), Sunoco(*)
  W: Amoco(*), Marathon(*), Red Roof Inn
- **Food** E: Applebee's, Arby's, Bennigan's, Bill Knapp's Restaurant (see our ad this page), Chi Chi's Mexican Restaurant, Cottage Inn Pizza, Coty's Westside Diner, Don Pablo's Mexican, Fuddruckers, KFC, Laredo Texas Steakhouse, McDonald's, Subway
  W: Big Boy Restaurant, Bob Evan's Restaurant, Burger King(PLAY), Chuck E Cheese's Pizza, Dunkin Donuts (Marathon), Honey Baked Ham, Mancino's Pizza, McDonald's (Amoco), Olive Garden, Pizza Hut, Salvatore Scallopini, Wendy's
- **Lodg** E: Comfort Inn, Motel 6, Sleep Inn
  W: Howard Johnson (see our ad this page), Super 8
- **AServ** E: K-Mart(RX), Meineke Discount Mufflers, National Tire & Battery, Sunoco, Tuffy Auto Center, Valvoline Oil Change
  W: Fast Eddie's Oil Change & Car Wash, Midas Muffler & Brake, Pep Boys Auto Center
- **Med** E: ✚ Medical Care Center
- **ATM** E: Citizens Bank, Speedway
  W: Amoco, Federal Credit Union
- **Other** E: K-Mart(RX), New Vision, Pet Supplies Plus, Rite Aide Pharmacy, Sav-A-Lot Grocery
  W: Animal Hospital, Best Buy, Builder Square, Pet Care Superstore, Rack It Billiards & Games, Target (Mini mall), Town & Country Bowling

117A Junction I-69, Lansing, Port Huron

116AB Bishop International Airport, Bristol Road (Southbound)
- **Gas** E: Amoco, Total(*, D)
- **Food** E: Beechtree & American Grill, Capitol Coney Island Family Restaurant, Imperial Coney Island, McDonald's
- **Lodg** E: Days Inn Days Inn (Restaurant)
- **AServ** E: Amoco, Auto Zone Auto Parts
- **ATM** E: Amoco, Credit Union
- **Other** E: Super K Convenience Store & Deli
  W: Bishop International Airport

111 Junction I-475 (Northbound)
- **Food** E: Bill Knapp's (see our ad opposite page)

Bill Knapp's Restaurant
Bill Knapp's is a casual, full service family restaurant where Motorcoaches are always welcome.
Open daily at 11:00 am
Over 50 locations throughout: Michigan • Ohio • Indiana
810-239-4609 - Flint
1699
MICHIGAN ▪ I-75 ▪ EXIT 117/117B

Howard Johnson
G-3277 Miller Rd.
Flint, MI 48507
810-733-5910
800-446-4656
- Continental Breakfast
- Kids Under 12 Stay Free
- Outdoor Pool
- Meeting/Banquet Facilities
- Pets Allowed
- Handicap Accessible
- Truck/Large Vehicle Parking
- Coin Laundry
- Exterior Corridors

1766
Michigan ▪ I-75 ▪ Exit SB117/NB117B

EXIT — MICHIGAN

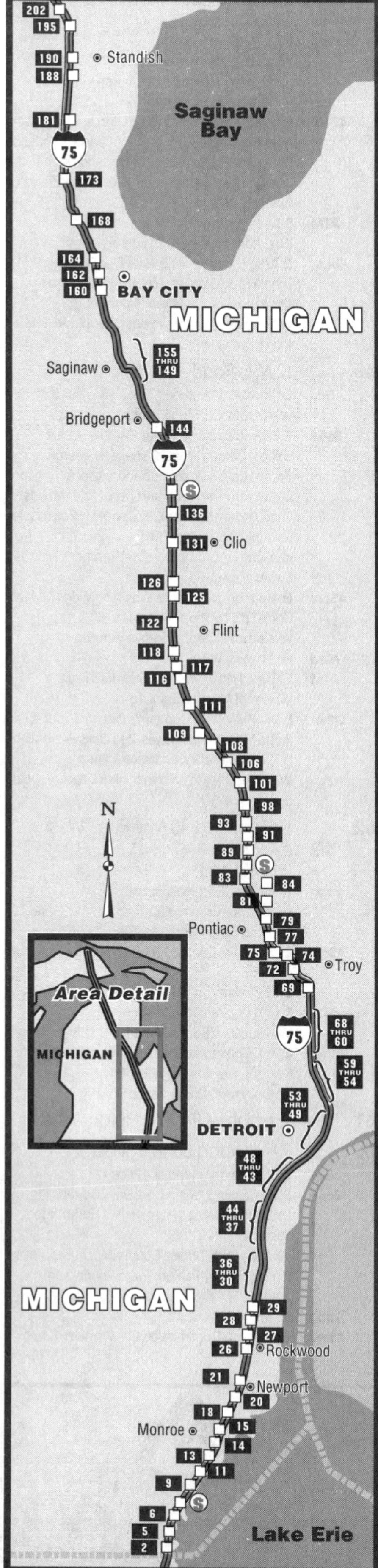

EXIT — MICHIGAN

Bill Knapp's Restaurant
Bill Knapp's is a casual, full service family restaurant where Motorcoaches are always welcome.
Open daily at 11:00 am
Over 50 locations throughout: Michigan • Ohio • Indiana
810-695-6722 Grand Blanc
1802
MICHIGAN ▪ I-475 ▪ EXIT 2

109 MI 54, Dort Hwy, Burton
- **FStop** E: Kid's Castle Pizza & Fun Center
- **Food** E: Mobil(*, D)
- **Other** E: Food Castle Grocery

108 Holly Road
- **Gas** E: Sunoco(*)
- **Lodg** E: Amerihost Inn
- **AServ** E: Sunoco, Toyota Dealer
- **Med** W: ✚ Genesys Health Park

106 Segena Rd., Grand Blanc (Southbound)
- **Gas** N: Clerk(*, LP)
- **Food** N: Fajitas Tex Mex Cafe, Warwick Inn
- **Lodg** E: Temp Home

101 Grange Hall Road, Fenton
- **AServ** E: Ackie's Auto Sales
- **RVCamp** E: Yogi Bear Camp Resort(LP)
- **Parks** E: Groveland Oaks County Park, Holly State Recreation Area (2 Miles)
  W: Seven Lakes State Park

98 East Holly Road
- **Gas** E: Mobil(*, D, LP)
- **RVCamp** E: Pifer

(97) Rest Area (RR, Phones, Picnic, Vending; Northbound)

(95) Rest Area (RR, Phones, Picnic, Vending; Southbound)

93 U.S. 24, Dixie Hwy, Waterford
- **Food** E: Clarkston Coney Cafe
- **AServ** E: Saturn Dealership, Town & Country Dodge
  W: Clarkston's Chrysler Plymouth Dealership
- **Parks** W: Indian Springs Metro Park, Pontiac Lake Recreation Area

91 MI 15, Clarkston, Davison
- **Gas** E: Citgo(*, D)
  W: Shell(*, D, 24)
- **Food** W: LB's Muffins & Yogurt, Mesquite Creek Restaurant
- **AServ** W: Clarkston Muffler & Brake
- **Med** W: ✚ St. Joseph's Mercy Hospital
- **ATM** W: Shell
- **Other** W: Clarkston Vision

89 Sashabaw Road
- **Gas** E: Shell(*, CW)
  W: Amoco(*) (Towing)
- **Food** W: Dunkin Donuts, Little Caesars Pizza, Little Dana's Deli & Pizza, Mike's Oasis Family Dining, Subway, Wai Hong Chinese
- **AServ** E: Shell
  W: Amoco (Towing), Clarkston Auto Body
- **ATM** W: The State Bank
- **Parks** E: County Park
- **Other** E: Pine Knob Golf Course Center
  W: Arbor Drugs(RX), Foodtown Grocery, Independence Animal Hospital

(86) Weigh Station (Southbound)

(86) Weigh Station (Northbound)

84AB Baldwin Ave
- **Gas** W: Mobil(*)
- **Food** E: Big Boy

83AB Joslyn Rd.
- **Food** W: Little Caesars Pizza
- **AServ** W: K-Mart(RX)
- **ATM** W: First of America

Bold red print shows RV & Bus parking available or nearby

EXIT MICHIGAN

Other **W:** Food Town Grocery, K-Mart[RX], Mulligan's Golf Center

81 MI 24, Lapeer (Difficult Reaccess)

Parks **E:** Bald Mt. Recreation Area

79 University Dr, Auburn Hills, Rochester

Gas **E:** Amoco[*, CW]
W: Speedway[*, D, LP, K]

Food **E:** Bristoni's Italian, Domino's Pizza, Dunkin Donuts, Hershel's Deli, Subway
W: Big Buck Brewery & Steakhouse, Bistro 75 (Holiday Inn Select), McDonald's, Mountain Jack's Steakhouse, Taco Bell

Lodg **W:** AmeriSuites (see our ad this page), Candlewood Suites, Courtyard by Marriott, Fairfield Inn by Marriott, Hampton Inn, Holiday Inn Select (see our ad this page), Motel 6

RVCamp **W:** A & S Sales Center[LP] (1.2 Miles)

Med **E:** ✚ Hospital, ✚ Urgent Care Clinic
W: ✚ Havenwood Hospital

ATM **E:** Motor Parts Special Credit Union
W: Speedway

Other **E:** Eye Care
W: Car Wash[CW]

78 Chrysler Drive (Reaccess Southbound Only)

Gas **W:** Mobil[*]

Food **W:** Arby's, Burger King, Relli's

Lodg **W:** Hilton Suites, Wyngate Inn

AServ **W:** Metro 25 Tire

Other **E:** Chrysler World Headquarters
W: Pontiac Silver Dome

77AB MI 59, Utica, Pontiac

75 Square Lake Road, Pontiac, 75 Bus. Loop (Left Exit)

Med **W:** ✚ Hospital

74 Adams Road

AServ **E:** Pontiac Silver Dome

72 Crooks Road

Food **E:** Charley's Crab, De Soto Diner (Hilton), Hilton
W: Cookers Foreign Grill

Lodg **W:** Doubletree Guest Suites

ATM **W:** National Bank of Detroit

69 **(4)** Big Beaver Road

Gas **W:** Amoco[*, CW], Shell[*]

Food **E:** Shula's Steakhouse (Marriot)
W: Denny's, Einstein Bros Bagels, O'Grady's (Drury Inn), Papa Romano's Pizza, Ruth's Chris Steakhouse, T.G.I. Friday's

Lodg **E:** Marriot
W: Drury Inn

ATM **E:** D & N Bank

Other **E:** Champ's Food

67 Rochester Road

Gas **E:** Mobil

Food **E:** Big Boy, Burger King, Leo's Coney Island, Mr. Pita's, Ram's Horn
W: Mountain Jack's Steakhouse, Wall Street Restaurant (Holiday Inn)

Lodg **W:** Holiday Inn, Red Roof Inn

AServ **E:** Cottman Transmissions, Mobil
W: Belle Tire, Michelin

ATM **E:** First Federal of Michigan, First of America, Michigan National Bank

Other **E:** Rite Aid Pharmacy

65AB 14 Mile Road, Clawson

Gas **E:** Mobil[*], Shell[*]

Food **E:** Astro Lanes Bowling Alley, Bob Evan's Restaurant, Chi Chi's Mexican Restaurant, Chili's, Denny's, McDonald's[PLAY], Sign of the Beef Carver, Steak & Ale, Taco Bell, Wendy's
W: Applebee's, Bennigan's, Big Fish Too, Grecian Place, McDonald's, New York Coney Island, Outback Steakhouse

Lodg **E:** Motel 6, Red Roof Inn
W: DAYS INN Days Inn, Extended Stay America, Fairfield Inn, Hampton Inn, Knight's Inn, Residence Inn by Marriot

AServ **E:** Firestone Mastercare Car Service, Foresters Auto Wash & Oil Change, Four Seasons Radiator, Goodyear Tire & Auto, NTB, Oakland Dodge Truck Service, Sears, Unique Auto Care, Ziebart's Tidy Car

ATM **E:** Michigan National Bank
W: Credit Union[24], First Federal

Other **E:** Astro Lanes Bowling Alley, Doc Eye World, Fannie Mae Candies, Madison Place Mall, Oakland Mall, Oakland Plaza, Sears
W: Eyeglass Factory, Oakland Foodland, Rite Aid Pharmacy[RX]

63 12 Mile Road

Gas **E:** Clark[*, D], Marathon[*], Total[*, CW]
W: Marathon[*], Mobil[*], Total[*]

Food **E:** Betty Ross 2 Finer Foods, Blimpie Subs & Salads, Golden Wheel Chinese Restaurant, Green Lantern Pizza, Hacienda Azteca Mexican Restaurant, Leo's Country Oven, Major Majic's Pizza, Marinelli's Pizza, McDonald's, Red Lobster, Sero's Family Dining, TCBY
W: Denny's, Dunkin Donuts (Marathon), Friends Family Dining

AServ **E:** Auto Lab, Master Car Wash[CW], Midas Muffler, Uncle Ed's Oil Shop
W: Chevrolet Dealer, Sparks Tune-up

Med **W:** ✚ Hospital

ATM **E:** Clark, First of America, Standard Federal
W: First of America Bank, Total

Other **E:** Big K-Mart[RX], Dunham's Discount Sports, Oak Ridge Market, Optim Eyes, Red Oaks Recreation, U.S. Post Office, Veterinarian Center
W: Arbor Drugs[RX], Farmer Jack Grocery, Gold's Gym

62 11 Mile Road, 10 Mile Road West

Gas **E:** Mobil[*, CW]
W: Citgo[*], Mobil[*]

Food **E:** Boodles, Domino's Pizza
W: Jim's Ice Cream, KFC, Taco Bell, Tim Horton's Coffee & Baked Goods[24], Tubby's Sub Shops

AServ **E:** Matt's Tire Center, S & J Auto Service, Tuffy Auto Center
W: Belle Tire

ATM **E:** 7-11 Convenience Store
W: Citgo, First Bank of America

Other **E:** 7-11 Convenience Store, Animal Health Services, Heights Car Wash[CW]
W: Dairy Mart Convenience Store

61 Junction I-696, Port Huron, Lansing

60 9 Mile Road, John R Street

Gas **W:** Marathon[*, D], Mobil[*], Price

Food **E:** Burger King, China One, Dairy Queen, McDonald's, Nick's Pizza, Rally's Hamburgers, Subway
W: Dairy Park, Dunkin Donuts (Mobil), Elias Bros Big Boy, End of the Park, Pizza Connection, Wendy's

Lodg **E:** Quality Inn

AServ **E:** Advance Transmission Co., Western Auto Service

1314
AMERISUITES
AMERICA'S AFFORDABLE ALL-SUITE HOTEL
Michigan • Exit 79 • 810-475-9393

EXIT MICHIGAN

W: Hazel Park Collision Center, Shorts Auto Parts

ATM **W:** First of America, Mobil

Other **E:** 19 Hole Miniature Golf, Farmer Jack Grocery[RX], Harmony House Grocery, Rite Aid Pharmacy[RX], U.S. Post Office

59 8 Mile Road, MI 102

Gas **E:** Oklahoma
W: Clark[D], Marathon

Food **E:** Coney Island Restaurant

AServ **E:** Good Wheels Auto Sales & Service, New Tires Auto Center, Oklahoma

RVCamp **E:** J Kelly Propane Filling Station
W: Campers Paradise

Med **W:** ✚ Bi-Country Walk-in Clinic

58 7 Mile Road

Gas **E:** Clark[*, D]
W: Amoco[*, D]

Food **E:** Wngyuen Chinese

Other **E:** Coin Laundry, Imperial Pharmacy[RX]

57 McNichols Road

Gas **E:** BP[*, D, K]
W: BP[*, D]

Food **E:** KFC, LA Koney Family Restaurant[24], Taco Bell
W: Motor City Coney Island[24]

AServ **E:** McCormick Auto & Truck Repair
W: Donia Auto Service (BP), Kelly Tires

56AB Oakland Park, Highland, Davison Frwy.

55 Holbrook Ave, Caniff Ave (Reaccess Southbound Only)

Food **W:** KFC, Taco Bell

Med **E:** ✚ Hospital

54 East Grand Blvd, Clay Ave

Gas **W:** Shell[*]

Food **W:** Super Coney Island Restaurant

AServ **W:** Shell

Other **W:** Market Street

53B Ford Frwy, I-94, Port Huron, Chicago

53A Warren Ave

Gas **E:** Mobil, Shell[*]
W: Amoco[*, 24]

Food **E:** Bianca's Coney Island Restaurant
W: Little Caesars Pizza

Med **W:** ✚ Detroit Medical Center, ✚ Hutzel Hospital Medical

ATM **W:** Farmer Jack's Grocery

Other **W:** Farmer Jack's Grocery

52 Mack Ave

Gas **E:** Shell[*]

Food **E:** McDonald's

Med **W:** ✚ Detroit Medical Center

ATM **E:** Shell

51C Junction I-375, Chrysler Frwy

Please Request Exit Authority Rate
Holiday Inn SELECT
Entertainment Hub
I-75, North Exit 79
Auburn Hills, MI
248-373-4550
800-HOLIDAY
• Free Parking
• Movies-On-Demand
• Free HBO/CNN/TNT/ESPN
• Bristo 75 Restaurant & Lounge/Pizza Hut
• Indoor Pool, Jacuzzi & Sauna
• Fitness Center
• Close to Silverdome, Palace and Pine Knob
• 3 Miles from Great Lakes Crossing Mall & Canterbury Village
1841
MICHIGAN • I-75 • EXIT 79

Bold red print shows RV & Bus parking available or nearby

EXIT | MICHIGAN

51B Gratiot Ave (Left Exit)

51A MI 11, Woodward Ave, John R. Brush Street (Reaccess Northbound Only)

50 Grand River Ave
Gas W: Amoco
Lodg W: Viking Motel

49B MI 10, Lodge Frwy. (Northbound)

49A MI 10, Lodge Freeway, Rosa Parks Blvd, Civic Center
Gas E: Shell[*, 24]
W: Mobil[*]
Food E: Home Free Restaurant, Maxies Deli, White Castle Restaurant
AServ E: Firestone Mastercare Car Service, Fort-Trumbuli Auto Care, Goodyear Tires, Shell[24]
Med W: ✚ **Hospital**

48 Junction I-96, Jeffries Frwy, Lansing

47B Bridge to Canada, Lafayette Blvd
FStop E: **Canadian Border**[*]
Other E: **Canadian Border**

47A MI 3, Clark Ave
Gas E: Mobil[*, CW, 24]
W: Marathon[*, D]
Other W: La Plaza Market

46 Livernois Ave, Downtown Detroit
FStop E: **Marathon**[*]
Food E: KFC, Oscar's Coney Island Restaurant[24], Taco Bell, Taco Mart
W: Lafayette Market

45 Fort St, Springwells Ave
Gas E: BP[*, D], Marathon[D]
W: Mobil[*]
Food W: Hungarian Village, McDonald's
AServ E: Marathon

44 Dearborn Ave (Reaccess Southbound Only)
Gas E: Citgo[*, D, K]
Food E: **All-American Market**
AServ E: Sam's Auto Craft
Other E: **All-American Market**, Aunt Ries Market

43AB Rouge, MI 85, Fort St, Schaefer Hwy
Gas E: Amoco[*], BP[*, K], Sunoco[*]
W: Marathon
ATM E: Amoco

42 Outer Dr, Melvindale, Ecorse
FStop W: **Quick Fuel**[*]
Gas E: Mobil[*]
W: Amoco[*, 24]
Food E: Mickey's 2 Coney Island Restaurant
Med E: ✚ **Oakwood Downriver Medical Center**
ATM E: Coamerica Bank
Other E: 99 Cent More or Less Food Mart

41 Lincoln Park, MI 39, Southfield Hwy
Gas W: Mobil[*, D]
Food E: A & W Drive-In, Bangkok Star (Authentic Thai), Bill's Place, Lincoln Coney Island Restaurant, Park Restaurant Family Dining
W: Dunkin Donuts, Long John Silver, McDonald's
AServ E: Murray's Auto Parts, Pep Boys Auto Center, Quality Car Wash[CW]

EXIT | MICHIGAN

W: Jiffy Lube, **Sears**
ATM W: **Kroger Supermarket**[RX], Michigan National Bank
Other E: Arbor Drugs[RX], Car Wash[CW], **Coin Laundry**, Lincoln Park Skating Center
W: Doc's Eye Exam, **Kroger Supermarket**[RX], Laundromat, **Rite Aid Pharmacy**[*, 24, RX], **Sears**

40 Dix Hwy
Gas E: Citgo[*, CW], Clark
W: Shell[*, CW], Total[*, LP]
Food E: Ponderosa Steakhouse, Toma's Coney Island Restaurant
W: Burger King, Dairy Queen, Dunkin Donuts, Long John Silver, McDonald's, Pizza Hut, Rally's Hamburgers, Spad's Pizza, Taco Bell
Lodg W: Holiday Motel
AServ E: Downriver Springs Service, Global Car Care Express Lube, **K-Mart**[24, RX], Lincoln Park Foreign Cars, Tuffy Auto Center
W: Auto Glass, Belle Tires, Downriver Alignment, Firestone Tire & Auto, Jiffy Lube, Midas Muffler & Brake, Top Value Muffler Shop
Med E: ✚ **Health One Medical Center**
ATM W: Shell
Other E: **Arbor Drugs**, Car Wash, **K-Mart**[RX]
W: **Foodland Grocery**, **Kroger Supermarket**[RX]

37 Metropolitan Airport, Allen Road, North Line Road
Gas E: Speedway[*], Total[*]
Food E: **Charlie's Chop House (Holiday Inn)**, Yum Yum Donuts
W: Arby's, **Bill Knapp's Restaurant (see our ad this page)**, **Burger King**, IM Thursties Tavern, Jonathan B, McDonald's, Nifty 50's
Lodg E: **Holiday Inn**
W: **Budgetel Inn**, Cross Country Inn
AServ E: Lube N More
W: K & N Engineering Clutches, Love Days Quality Quick Service, Ramchargers Automotive
Med E: ✚ **Hospital**, ✚ **Oakwood Health Care Center**
ATM E: Total
Other E: **Sam's Club**
W: **Andy's Farmer Market**, Car Wash, Fireside Shop[LP]

36 Eureka Road, Wyandotte
Gas E: Shell[*] (Towing), Total[*]
Food E: Bob Evan's Restaurant, Denny's, Dono's Prime Time, Ryan's Steakhouse, TJ's Sports Bar & Grill (Ramada Inn), Trovano's Pizzeria
W: Baker's Square Restaurant, Hooters, Little Daddy's Parthenon & Coney Island, Mountain Jack's Steakhouse, Schlotzsky's Deli, SHONEY'S **Shoney's**
Lodg E: **Ramada Inn**, Super 8
W: Red Roof Inn
AServ E: Pennzoil Oil Change, Quality Image Service Center, Shell (Towing)
W: Discount Tire Company
Med E: ✚ **Red Cross Center**
W: ✚ **Medical Care Center**, ✚ **Metro Rehab Physical Therapy**
ATM E: Old Kent Bank, Standard Federal, Total
Other E: Optim Eyes, **Southwest Animal Hospital**
W: **Cross Creek Mall**, **Home Depot**, **S & M Pharmacy**[RX], **Southland Mall**, Sports Authority

35 U.S. 24, Telegraph Road (Left Exit)

34AB Sibley Road, Dix Hwy
Gas E: Total[*, LP]
W: Shell[*]
Food E: **Main Street Country Bar & Grill**, Sibley & Allen Deli Sandwiches
W: Baskin Robbins (Shell), Dunkin Donuts (Shell), Subway (Shell)
Lodg E: Southland Motor Lodge

EXIT | MICHIGAN

RVCamp W: **General Trailer RV Center**[LP] **(1.1 Miles)**
ATM E: First America Bank
W: Shell
Other E: Par-Fection Profession Golf Center & Deli
W: Mitch's Market

32 West Road, Trenton, Woodhaven
TStop E: **Citgo**[*, D, SCALES]
Gas E: **Miejer**[*, D, LP], Mobil, Total[*, D, LP]
W: Amoco[*, CW], Shell[*, CW, 24]
Food E: **Birch Tree Cafe (Citgo)**, **Burger King**, Christoff's Family Restaurant, Church's Chicken, Dunkin Donuts, Good Fellas Pizza, **Pizza Hut**, Subway, Taco Bell, Uncle Harry's Family Dining, Wendy's, White Castle Restaurant
W: **Amigo's Mexican Restaurant**, Country Skillet, Domino's Pizza, **Dynasty Restaurant (Chinese, Best Western)**, Kwan's Chop Suey, **McDonald's**
Lodg W: **Best Western**, Knight's Inn
AServ E: All Pro Transmission, Belle Tire, Firestone Mastercare Car Service, Guardian Car Care, **K-Mart**[RX], Lube Max Two, Midas Muffler, Mobil, Precision Tune, Rodgers Chevrolet
TServ E: **Citgo**[SCALES]
TWash E: **Citgo**
RVCamp E: **Team 60 Lakes**
Med E: ✚ **Henry Ford Medical Center**
ATM E: Old Kent Bank
W: Old Kent Bank, Shell, Standard Federal
Other E: **Customs Info. Center**, **K-Mart**[RX], **Kroger Supermarket**, **Miejer**, Optim Eyes, Payless Shoe Source, **Pet Supplies Plus**, Rainbow Auto Wash[CW], **Sears Hardware**[LP], **Super Suds Coin Laundry**, **Target**, Westwood Auto Wash[CW]
W: West Market, Woodhaven Laundromat, **Woodhaven Pharmacy**[RX]

29AB Flat Rock, Gibraltar
Gas W: Marathon[*]
Lodg W: Sleep Inn
AServ E: Jimmy's Auto Body Repair
W: Superior Ford Dealership
Med E: ✚ **Hospital**
Parks E: **Lake Erie Metro Park**

28 MI 85, Front St.

27 North Huron River Dr, Rockwood
Gas E: Total[*, K]
W: Speedway[*, D]
Food E: Benito's Pizza, D & D, Diner & Pizza, Dominex Pizza & Subs, Huron River Inn, Marco's Pizza
W: Riverfront Family Restaurant
ATM E: Old Kent Bank, Total
Other E: **Food Town Grocery**, **Rite Aid Pharmacy**, Speed Wash Laurndomat, **U.S. Post Office**

26 South Huron River Dr, South Rockwood
Gas E: Sunoco[*, D]
Food E: Dixie Cafe, Drift In
ATM E: Monroe Bank & Trust
Other E: Stan's Car Wash[CW], **U.S. Post Office**

21 Newport Road, Newport
FStop W: **Total**[*, D]
AServ E: Cornett's Auto Service
ATM E: Monroe Bank & Trust

20 Junction I-275 North, Flint, Metro Airport

18 Nadeau Road
FStop W: **Pilot Travel Center**[*, D, K, SCALES]
Food W: **Arby's (Pilot)**

15 Dixie Hwy
TStop W: **BP**[*, D]
FStop W: **Speedway**[*, D, LP]
Gas E: Shell[*]
Food E: **Bob Evan's Restaurant**, Burger King, Dixie

Bill Knapp's Restaurant
Open daily at 11:00 am
Bill Knapp's is a casual, full service family restaurant where Motorcoaches are always welcome.
1698
Over 50 locations throughout: Michigan • Ohio • Indiana
734-281-9948 - Southgate
MICHIGAN • I-75 • EXIT 37

EXIT	MICHIGAN/OHIO
	Skillet (EconoLodge), **Red Lobster**
	W: **Big Boy**, **Cracker Barrel**, **Denny's**, **McDonald's**, Subway, Timco's (Holiday Inn), Wendy's
Lodg	**E:** Cross Country Inn, EconoLodge, Hometown Inn
	W: **Holiday Inn**, Knight's Inn
TServ	**W:** **Great Lakes Western Star Truck Service**
RVCamp	**E:** **Camping**
Med	**W:** **+ Hospital**
Parks	**E:** **State Park**
Other	**E:** Raisin River Golf Club
	W: Historic Monroe Vietnam Veterans Memorial
14	Elm Ave
Other	**W:** Riverfront Store, Sheriff Dept.
13	Front St , Monroe
11	La Plaisance Road, Downtown Monroe, Bolles Harbor
Gas	**W:** Amoco(*, CW), Speedway(*, LP, K)
Food	**W:** **Burger King**, **McDonald's**(PLAY)
Lodg	**W:** AmeriHost Inn, Comfort Inn
AServ	**W:** Auto Trim
Med	**W:** **+ Hospital**
ATM	**W:** Monroe Bank & Trust
Other	**E:** Bolles Harbor Marina, Yuri Party Shop & Docks
	W: **Horizon Outlet Center**, **State Police**, Time Out Go-Karts
(10)	**Rest Area, Welcome Center (RR, Phones, Picnic, Vending; Northbound)**
9	South Otter Creek Road, La Salle
Other	**E:** Right House Marina
	W: **American Heritage Antique Mall**
(8)	**Weigh Station (Southbound)**
(8)	**Weigh Station (Northbound)**
6	Luna Pier
FStop	**E:** **Sunoco**(*, D, LP, K, 24)
Gas	**W:** BP(*)
Food	**E:** Gander's, **Here's The Scoop Ice Cream (Sunoco)**, **McDonald's (Sunoco)**, Piasano's Pizza
ATM	**E:** Monroe Bank & Trust, **Sunoco**
Other	**E:** Luna Pier, Luna Pier Coin Car Wash(CW), **Luna Pier Market**
5	Erie Road
2	Erie, Temperance

↑MICHIGAN

↓OHIO

EXIT	OHIO
210	OH 184, Alexis Road
FStop	**W:** **BP**(*, LP), **Speedway**(*, D, LP, SCALES)
Gas	**W:** **Meijer**(*, D, LP, K, 24)
Food	**W:** **Blimpie Subs & Salads (Speedway)**, **Burger King**, **McDonald's (Meijer)**, **McDonald's**, **Taco Bell**, Wendy's
TServ	**W:** **TIP**
ATM	**W:** **BP**
Other	**W:** **All American Coach Co. (see our ad this page)**, **Meijer**
209	Ottawa River Road (Reaccess Southbound Only)
Gas	**E:** BP(*, LP, CW), Citgo(*, D, LP, 24), Sunoco(*, LP)
Food	**E:** Anchor Inn, Breakwater Cafe, Hinkles Donuts, Little Caesars Pizza, Marco's Pizza, New China Chinese
ATM	**E:** BP, Citgo, Key Bank, Sunoco
Other	**E:** **Food Town Supermarket**, **Food Town Supermarket**, **Rite Aid Pharmacy**(RX), **Shoreland Animal Hospital**, Speed Queen Coin Laundry,
	Suder Medical Center
208	Junction I-280 South, Cleveland
207	LaGrange St, Stickney Ave
206	Phillips Ave
205B	Berdan Ave
Food	**W:** Burger King, Mancy's Steakhouse, Pizza Hut, Rudy's Hot Dogs, Subway
Med	**E:** **+ Hospital**
ATM	**W:** Key Bank
Other	**W:** **Rite Aid Pharmacy**(24, RX)
205A	Willys Pkwy, Jeep Pkwy
204	Junction I-475 West to U.S. 23, Maumee, Ann Arbor (Left Exit)
203B	U.S. 24, Detroit Ave, Monroe Street
Gas	**E:** Gas(K)
	W: BP(*, CW), Citgo
Food	**W:** KFC, King's Garden Chinese, **McDonald's**, Rally's Hamburgers, **Wendy's**
AServ	**W:** Brad's Auto Parts, Howard's (Citgo)
ATM	**W:** Huntington Bank
Other	**W:** Cash Connection, **Rite Aid Pharmacy**(RX), **Save-A-Lot Food Stores**
203A	Bancroft St
Med	**E:** **+ Hospital**
202AB	South Washington Street, Downtown, Collingwood Blvd
Food	**W:** **McDonald's**
AServ	**W:** **Murray's Auto Parts**
Med	**E:** **+ Hospital**
Other	**W:** **CVS Pharmacy**(RX), **Prestige Car Wash**(CW) **(CVS Pharmacy)**
201AB	To OH 25, Collingwood Ave (Difficult Reaccess)
Food	**E:** Old Roadhouse Inn
RVCamp	**W:** **Creekside Mobile Village**
Other	**E:** Gary Street Supermarket
200	South Ave , Kuhlman Dr
199	OH 65, Rossford , Miami St
Food	**E:** **Palm's Cafe (EconoLodge)**
Lodg	**E:** **EconoLodge**
AServ	**E:** Miami Motors
198	Wales Road, Oregon Road, Northwood
FStop	**E:** **Shell**(*)
Gas	**E:** Speedway(*, LP)
Food	**E:** Comfort Inn & Suites, Coney Island, Kayvon's Grill, **Subway (Shell)**
Lodg	**E:** Comfort Inn & Suites
ATM	**E:** Key Bank
197	Buck Road
Gas	**W:** **BP**(*, D, LP), Sunoco(D, LP)
Food	**E:** Buck Road Plaza Deli, Tim Horton's Baked Goods(24), **Wendy's**
	W: **Denny's**, Ike's Great American Restaurant (Super 8 Motel), **McDonald's**
Lodg	**W:** **Knight's Inn**, **Super 8**
AServ	**W:** Sunoco
ATM	**W:** **BP**
Other	**W:** **Interstate Lanes**
Exit	**(195)** Jct. I-80/90
195	OH 795, Millbury
Gas	**E:** BP(*, D, LP, CW)
Lodg	**E:** **The Courtyard by Marriot**
ATM	**E:** BP
193	U.S. 20, U.S. 23, Perrysburg, Fremont
FStop	**E:** **BP**(*, D, CW)
	W: **Marathon**(*, CW)
Gas	**E:** **Sunoco**(*, D, LP)
Food	**E:** **Bob Evan's Restaurant**, **Burger King**, **Cracker Barrel**, **Croy's Supper Club**, Fricker's, Frisch's Big Boy, Jed's BBQ & Brew, Kao's Golden Gate Restaurant (Szechuan/Mandarin), **McDonald's**, **Ralphie's Burgers**, Ranch Bake & Seafood, St. Patrick's Restaurant (French Quarter Hotel), Stinger's Cafe, Subway, **Taco Bell**, Wendy's
Lodg	**E:** **Best Western**, **Days Inn (see our ad this page)**, **French Quarter Hotel**, **Holiday Inn Express**
	W: Budgetel Inn
AServ	**W:** Auto Zone Auto Parts, **Ray's Towing Service (Marathon)**
RVCamp	**E:** **KOA Campgrounds (7 Miles)**
Med	**W:** **+ Perrysburg Medical Center**
ATM	**E:** **BP**, **Kroger Supermarket**(RX), **Sunoco**
	W: Huntington Bank, Mid-America National Bank & Trust Co.
Other	**E:** **Big K-Mart**(RX), **Kroger Supermarket**(RX), The Fitness Club
192	Junction I-475, U.S. 23 North, Maume, Ann Arbor (Left Exit)
187	OH 582, Haskins, Luckey
Food	**E:** Central Inn
181	OH 64, OH 105, Bowling Green, Pemberville
FStop	**E:** **Citgo**(*)
	W: **Speedway**(*, D, K)
Gas	**W:** BP(*, LP, CW), Citgo(*, D, LP, K), Sunoco(*, LP), SuperAmerica(*, LP, 24)
Food	**W:** Big Boy, Blimpie Subs & Salads (SuperAmerica), **Bob Evan's Restaurant**, **Burger King**, Chi Chi's Mexican Restaurant, **Domino's Pizza**, **Fricker's**, **Hunan Palace Chinese**, Kaufman's Restaurant (Quality Inn & Suites), Little

ALL AMERICAN COACH CO.
1680
5080 Alexis Rd. • Sylvania, OH 43560
Sales ★ Service ★ Rentals
Coachmen • Allegro • Pace-Arrow
Tioga • Cherokee • Georgetown
419-885-4601
Directions:
I-75, Exit Alexis Rd. W 7 miles
I-475, Exit Hwy 23, Exit Monroe St. E 1 mi
ALL AMERICAN COACH
Alexis Rd.
Monroe St. Exit
Corey Rd
Monroe St.
OHIO • I-75 • EXIT 210

Perrysburg, Ohio
1107
DAYS INN
Award Winning Property
Days Inn of Toledo/Perrysburg
Outstanding Accommodations & Service
Walk to Over 18 Restaurants & Shopping
Extensive Complimentary Continental Breakfast
In-Room Coffeemakers, Free HBO/ESPN/CNN
Welcoming Over 200 Tour Groups Each Year
E-Z on-off at I-75 & U.S. 20, Exit 193
419-874-8771 • 800-329-7466
OHIO • I-75 • EXIT 193

Bold red print shows RV & Bus parking available or nearby

EXIT OHIO

Caesars Pizza, McDonald's, Pizza Hut, Ranch Steak & Seafood, Subway (Citgo), **Threacher's Fish & Chips**, **Wendy's**
Lodg W: Best Western, **Buckeye Budget Motor Inn**, Days Inn, **Quality Inn & Suites**
Med W: **Hospital**
ATM W: BP, Citgo, MidAm University Banking Center, Sunoco, SuperAmerica
Other W: **Bowling Green State University**, **Greenwood Coin Laundry**

179 U.S. 6, Napoleon, Fremont

(179) **Rest Area (RR, Phones, Picnic, Vending; Southbound)**

(179) **Rest Area (RR, Phones, Picnic, Vending; Northbound)**

(176) **Weigh Station (Northbound)**

171 OH 25, Cygnet
Gas E: Marathon
AServ E: Marathon

168 Eagleville , Quarry Road
FStop E: **Fuel Mart**(*, D, K)

167 OH 18, North Baltimore, Fostoria
TStop E: **Petro**(*, SCALES)
FStop W: **Citgo**(*, D)
Gas E: **Mobil (Petro Truckstop)**
Food E: **McDonald's**, **Pizza Hut (Petro Truckstop)**, Pizza Hut
W: **Denny's**(24)
Lodg W: **Crown Inn**
AServ W: Bernie's Auto Service (Towing)
TServ E: **Petro**(SCALES)
W: **Azor Truck Equipment**
TWash E: **Petro**
Other W: **Robert's IGA**

164 OH 613, Van Buren, Leipsic, Fosteria, McComb
FStop W: **Pilot Travel Center**(*, D, LP, K, SCALES)
Food E: The Fillin' Station, **Van Buren State Park**(*, LP) **(1 Mile)**
W: **Dairy Queen (Pilot)**, **Subway (Pilot)**, **Taco Bell (Pilot)-**
RVCamp E: **Pleasant View Recreation (Van Buren State Park)**

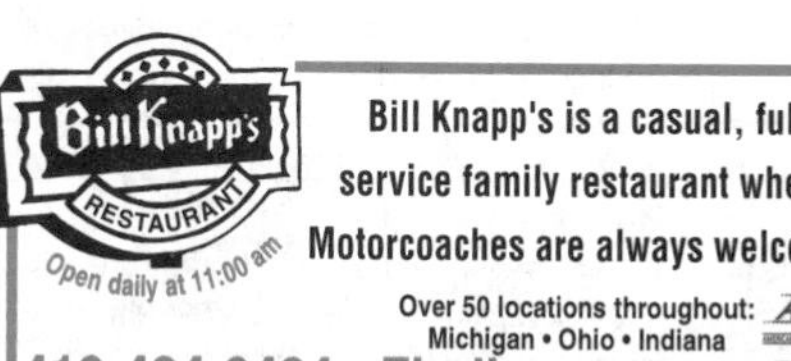
Bill Knapp's Restaurant
Open daily at 11:00 am
Bill Knapp's is a casual, full service family restaurant where Motorcoaches are always welcome. 1703
Over 50 locations throughout: Michigan • Ohio • Indiana
419-424-9434 - Findlay
OHIO • I-75 • EXIT 157

1143
DAYS INN
Restaurant & Lounge
Outdoor Pool
Bus Parking
Banquet & Meeting Facilities
Exercise Room
— Jacuzzi Suite —
419-423-7171 • Findlay, OH
OHIO • I-75 • EXIT 157

EXIT OHIO

Parks E: **Van Buren State Park (1 Mile)**

(162) **Weigh Station (Southbound)**

161 Township Road 99
AServ W: Dick's Automotive Service
RVCamp E: **Campground**
Med E: **Physician's Plus Urgent Care**
Other E: **Ohio State Patrol Post**
W: **Jeffrey's Antique Mall**

159 **(160)** U.S. 224, OH 15, Ottawa, Tiffin
Gas E: BP(*, D, LP, CW), Marathon(*, LP), Swifty(*, K)
W: **Shell**(*, D)
Food E: Archie's Too, Bob Evan's Restaurant, Burger King, Domino's Pizza, **McDonald's**, **Ming's Great Wall (Chinese)**, Pizza Hut, Ponderosa Steakhouse, **Rally's Hamburgers**, Ralphie's Burgers, SHONEY'S, **Shoney's**, **Subway**, Taco Bell, The Spaghetti Shop, The Yogurt Parlor, Wendy's
W: **Cracker Barrel**, Jac & Do's Pizza
Lodg E: **Cross Country Inn**, **Ramada Inn**, Rodeway Inn, **Super 8**
W: Country Hearth Inn, Hampton Inn, **Holiday Inn Express**
AServ E: Rainbow Muffler
W: Easter Tire, Kill Brake & Wheel Co., Lloyd Treadway Chrys, Plym, Dodge Dealer, Two to Four Auto
TServ W: **Hyway Trucking Co.**, **Peterbilt Dealer**
ATM E: Bank One
W: **Shell**
Other E: **AMF Sportsman Lanes**, Colonial Coin Laundry(24), Findlay Auto Wash, **Great Scott's Food Store**(24), **Rite Aid Pharmacy**
W: Putt-Putt Golf

157 OH 12, Columbus Grove, Findlay
TStop W: **Ohio West Truck Plaza**(*, SCALES)
FStop W: **Pacific Pride Commercial Fueling**
Gas E: Citgo(*, D, 24), Marathon(*, CW)
W: BP(*)
Food E: **Bill Knapp's Restaurant (see our ad this page)**, Blimpie Subs & Salads (Marathon), Imperial Dining Room (Days Inn), Nathan's (Citgo), Noble Roman's Pizza (Marathon), TCBY (Citgo)
W: **Fricker's**, **Ohio West Country Griddle (Ohio West Truckstop)**, Pilgrim Family Restaurant
Lodg E: **Days Inn (see our ad this page)**
W: **EconoLodge**
AServ W: BP
TServ W: **Exit 157 Garage**, **MAC Trucks**, **Miami Industrial Trucks**, **Rent O Wreck**
RVCamp W: **Rent O Wreck**
ATM E: Car Wash(CW), Marathon, **Wolfies Roasted Nuts, Deli**
Other E: Westside Car Wash, **Wolfies Roasted Nuts, Deli**
W: The Findley Animal Care Center

156 U.S. 68 South, OH 15 East, Carey
Food E: Rose Villa Supersteaks
W: BMK Drive-In, Dairy Queen
AServ E: Wrecker Bear Towing
Med E: **Hospital**
Other E: Hancock Air Terminals

(153) **Rest Area (RR, Phones, Picnic, Vending; Southbound)**

(153) **Rest Area (RR, Phones, Picnic, Vending; Northbound)**

145 OH 235, Mount Cory
RVCamp E: **Twin Lakes Park Campground**(LP) **(.6 Miles)**

142 **(143)** OH 103, Arlington, Bluffton
FStop W: **Shell**(*, LP)
Gas E: Citgo(*, D), **Sunoco**(*, LP)

EXIT OHIO

W: Marathon(*)
Food E: **Denny's**
W: **Arby's**, **KFC**, **McDonald's**, **Subway**, Taco Bell
Lodg E: Bluffton Inn
AServ W: Superb Wash Coin Operated Car Wash(CW)
Med W: **Hospital**
ATM W: Marathon, **Shell**
Other E: Bluffton Flying Service
W: Fireworks

140 Bentley Road, Bluffton, Bluffton College
Food W: Dari Freeze
Med W: **Blanchard Valley Regional Health Center (Blufton College)**, **Hospital**

135 **(136)** To U.S. 30, Upper Sandusky, Delphos
TStop E: **Citgo**(*, D, K, SCALES)
W: **Flying J Travel Plaza**(*, D, LP, RV DUMP, SCALES)
FStop E: **Speedway**(*, D, LP)
Food E: **Blimpie Subs & Salads (Speedway)**, **Grandma's Pantry Restaurant (Citgo)**, **Subway (Citgo)**
W: **The Cookery (Flying J Travel Plaza)**
TServ E: **Citgo**(SCALES)
W: **Northwest Ohio Towing & Recovery**
ATM E: **Citgo**, **Speedway**
W: **Flying J Travel Plaza**

134 OH 696, Napoleon Road, Beaverdam (Reaccess Southbound Only)

130 Blue Lick Road
Gas E: Citgo(*, K)
Food E: Subway (Citgo), Taco Maker (Citgo), The Rail Station Restaurant (Ramada Inn)
W: General T's Pizza & Ice Cream
Lodg E: **Ramada Inn**
Other E: Dream Marine Boat Repair
W: Blue Lick General Store

127AB **(128)** OH 81, Lima, Ada
Gas W: BP(*)
Food W: Choices Fine Food & Drink, **Darihutt**, **Waffle House**
Lodg W: Adkinson's Motel, Comfort Inn, **Days Inn**, **EconoLodge**
AServ W: A-1 Towing, Executive Motors of Lima, Five Acres Auto Recycling, Kenny's Wrecking, Livingston Tire & Service Center
TServ E: **Truck & E.R. Trailer**
W: **Lima Tank Wash**, **Tomlinson Truck Service**, **Western Ohio Truck & Equipment**
Other E: Hi Point Convenience Store, Hostess Thrift Store

125AB OH 309, OH 117, Kenton, Lima
TStop W: **Lima Truck Plaza**(*, D, K)
Gas E: BP(*, D, CW), Speedway(*, LP)
W: Shell
Food E: Arby's, Big Boy, Bob Evan's Restaurant, **Burger King**, Captain D's Seafood, **Cracker Barrel**, Hunan Garden, **Little Caesars Pizza (K-Mart)**, **McDonald's**, **Olive Garden**, Pat's Donuts & Kreme, Pizza Hut, **Ponderosa Steakhouse**, Rally's Hamburgers, **Red Lobster**, **Ryan's Steakhouse**, **Taco Bell**, W.S. Grinder's Sandwich Shop, **Wendy's**
W: Kewpee Hamburgers, SHONEY'S, **Shoney's**, The Spaghetti Shop
Lodg E: **Hampton Inn**, **Holiday Inn**, **Motel 6**
W: East Gate Motel, Economy Inn, Super 8
AServ E: Parts of America, **Sam's Club**
W: Quaker State Oil & Lube, Shell
TServ W: **Lima Truck Plaza**
Med W: **Hospital**
ATM E: AmeriCom, Bank One, Fifth Third Bank
W: Union Bank

Bold red print shows RV & Bus parking available or nearby

EXIT		OHIO
	Other	E: Coin Car Wash, K-Mart(RX), Pharm Pharmacy(RX), Ray's Marketplace(24), Sam's Club
		W: Eastside Coin Laundry, Econowash Coin Laundry, Sav-a-lot Food Store
124		4th St
122		**(123)** OH 65, Lima, Ottawa
	FStop	W: Shell(*, D, K, 24)
	AServ	W: Grismer's Firestone & Michelin Tire Co, S & S Volvo, GMC Trucks
	TServ	W: Buckeye Truck Center, Freightliner Dealer, S & S Volvo, GMC Trucks
	TWash	W: Steam's (Freightliner)
	Other	W: Airport (3 Miles), U.S. Post Office
120		**(121)** Breese Road, Fort Shawnee
	FStop	W: Citgo(*, LP, K)
	Gas	W: Speedway(*, LP)
	Food	W: Buckeye Broasted Foods, Dixie Dairy Stand, Old Barn Deli & Bakery
	Lodg	W: Tourest Motel
	AServ	W: Mike Muleski's Body Shop, Shawnee Motors Sales, South Dixie Car & Truck Wash
	TServ	W: South Dixie Car & Truck Wash
	Other	W: AmeriGas(LP), Golf Carts Video & Putt-Putt, Lima Bargain Center
118		**(119)** Cridersville, National Road
	FStop	W: Fuel Mart(*)
	Gas	W: Speedway(*, LP)
	Food	W: Endless Endeavors Restaurant, Padrone's Pizza & Subs, Pat's Donuts & Creme, Subway (Fuel Mart)
	ATM	W: Bank One
	Other	E: Fraco Service Center Honda, Suzuki
		W: Baker Animal Hospital, Cridersville Laundry, Dave's Market Grocery
114		Rest Area (RR, Phones, Picnic, Vending; Southbound)
(114)		Rest Area (RR, Phones, Picnic, Vending; Northbound)
113		OH 67, Wapakoneta, Uniopolis
	AServ	W: Miswoncer Chev, Olds, The Gate's Bros. County Glass Shop
111		**(112)** Bellefontaine St, Wapakoneta
	TStop	E: L & G Auto/Truck Stop(*, LP, SCALES)
	Gas	W: BP(*, LP, CW), Citgo(D), Shell(*, CW)
	Food	E: Dodge City Restaurant, Mickey's Restaurant (L & G Truck Stop)
		W: Arby's, Burger King, Captain D's Seafood, Dairy Queen, KFC, Lucky Steer Restaurant, McDonald's, Pizza Hut, Ponderosa, Taco Bell, The Chalet Restaurant (Holiday Inn), Waffle House, Wendy's
	Lodg	E: DAYS INN Days Inn
		W: Dollar Inn, Holiday Inn, Super 8
	AServ	E: Kinstle & Western Star Truck
		W: Advance Auto Parts, Pennzoil Oil Change
	TServ	E: Kinstle & Western Star Truck, L & G Auto/Truck Stop(SCALES)
	TWash	E: L & G Auto/Truck Stop
	RVCamp	E: Glacier Hill Lakes(LP) (3.2 Miles), KOA Campgrounds, Twin Lakes Resort
	ATM	W: Fifth Third Bank
	Other	W: Astro Bowling Lanes, Big Bear Plus Grocery, Family Dollar, Lunar Kitchen Putt, Neil Armstrong Air and Space Museum, The Clean Scene Coin Laundry & Car Wash
110		U.S. 33, St Marys, Bellefontaine
	AServ	E: Interstate Battery
	RVCamp	E: KOA Campgrounds (.9 Miles)
	Other	E: Ohio State Patrol Post
104		**(105)** OH 219, Botkins
	Gas	W: Marathon, Sunoco(*, D)

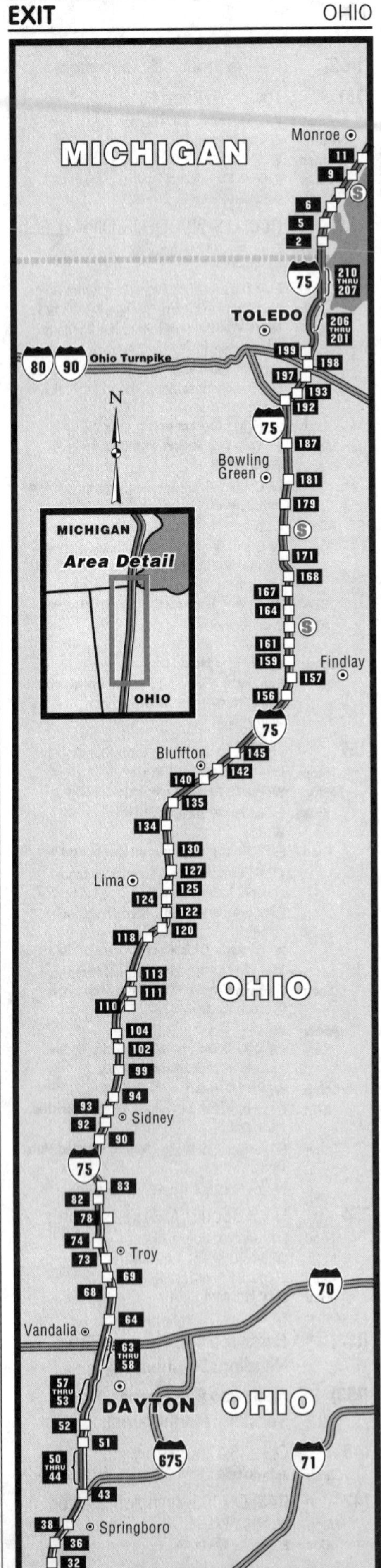

EXIT		OHIO
	Food	W: Kinningers Restaurant, Little John's Lounge & Restaurant (Budget Host Inn)
	Lodg	W: Budget Host Inn
	AServ	W: Firestone Tire & Auto, Kennedy's Garage, Marathon
	ATM	W: Sunoco
	Other	W: Coin Op Laundry & Car Wash(CW) (Kinningers)
102		**(103)** OH 274, New Bremen, Jackson Center
	AServ	E: Howell's Body Shop (24 Hr. Towing)
	Other	W: Inn Between Grocery
99		**(100)** OH 119, Anna, Minster
	TStop	E: 99 Truckstop(*, SCALES), Sav-a-Ton(*, K)
	Gas	W: Gas America(*, LP), Sunoco(*, K, 24)
	Food	E: Apple Valley Cafe (Sav-a-Ton), Cafe 99 (99 Truckstop)
		W: Subway, Wendy's
	AServ	W: Lee Tires
	TServ	E: L & O Inc. Truck Service (99 Truckstop)
		W: ARMS Inc., CB Shop
	TWash	W: 5 Star Truck Wash
	ATM	W: Gas America
94		CR 25A, Sidney East
	Lodg	E: Motel La Belle
93		OH 29, St Marys, Sidney
	RVCamp	W: Camp Qtokee, Campground
92		OH 47, Bus Loop 75, Versailles, Sidney
	Gas	E: Shell(*, CW), Speedway(*, LP)
		W: Amoco(*, D), BP(*), Sunoco(*, D, LP)
	Food	E: Arby's, Auto Millie's Bakery Outlet, China Garden, East of Chicago Pizza Co., Pub Lounge & Restaurant, Razzelbury's Ice Cream, Subway, Taco Bell, Wendy's, Winger's
		W: Big Bear Bakery & Deli, Bob Evan's Restaurant, Burger King, KFC, Marco's Pizza, McDonald's (Wal-Mart), McDonald's, Michael Anthony's Grill (Days Inn), Mom's Bakery, Pepito's Mexican (EconoLodge), Perkins Family Restaurant, Pizza Hut, Ponderosa, Rally's Hamburgers, The Country Squire Restaurant (Holiday Inn), Waffle House
	Lodg	W: Comfort Inn, DAYS INN Days Inn, EconoLodge, Holiday Inn
	AServ	E: Auto Zone, NAPA Auto Parts
		W: Amoco, Don's Knasel Collision, Pennzoil Oil Change, Sidney Ford
	Med	E: ✚ Wilson Memorial Hospital
	ATM	W: Bank One, Fifth Third Bank, Star Bank, The Provident Bank
	Other	E: Coin Laundry, Dairy Mart, Holiday Lanes, Sav-a-lot Food Store, Sidney Plaza, The Pharm Pharmacy, Wash U Up Coin Laundry
		W: Aldi Supermarket, CVS Pharmacy, Go For It Go-karts, Mini-golf, Batting Cage, Kroger Supermarket(RX), Super Wash Car Wash, Wal-Mart(RX) (Vision Center)
90		Fair Road, Sidney
	Gas	E: Sunoco(*, D, LP, K)
	Food	E: The Fairington Restaurant
	AServ	E: G & H Night & Day Towing
		W: Edco Automotive
	RVCamp	W: Campground
	Med	E: ✚ Fairington Medical Building
83		**(84)** CR 25A
	Food	W: J J's Restaurant (Knights Inn)
	Lodg	W: Knight's Inn, Piqua Motel
	AServ	W: Dan Hemm Olds, Cadillac, Dayton Tires, Paul Sherry Chrys, Jeep, Dodge, Paul Sherry Conversion Van & Truck Center-Chev, Piqua Quick Lube, Piqua Wheels Alignment & Body Shop
	RVCamp	W: Paul Sherry RV Center

Bold red print shows RV & Bus parking available or nearby

EXIT OHIO

Med W: Hospital
Other W: Brell Aire Bowling & Billiards

82 U.S. 36, Urbana, Piqua

Gas E: BP[*]
W: Speedway[*, LP, K]
Food E: Arby's, China East, Duff's Smorgasboard, KFC, Long John Silver, Ponderosa, Rax, Taco Bell, Wendy's
W: Bob Evan's Restaurant, Burger King (Hill's), El Sombrero Mexican Restaurant (HoJo Inn), Food Court (Mall), McDonald's[PLAY], Red Lobster
Lodg W: Comfort Inn, HoJo Inn
AServ E: BP, Complete Tire & Auto (Goodyear), Pennzoil Oil Change, Sears Auto Center
Med E: Kienle Medical Center, St. Joseph's Children's Treatment Center
W: Hospital
Other E: Piqua Mall
W: Aldi Supermarket, Eye Mart, Hill's[RX], Miami Valley Centre Mall

(81) Rest Area (RR, HF, Phones, Picnic, Vending, RV Dump; Southbound)

(81) Rest Area (RR, HF, Phones, Picnic, Vending, RV Dump; Northbound)

78 CR 25A

Med E: Upper Valley Medical Center

74AB OH 41, Covington, Troy, Hobart Arena

Gas E: BP[*, D, LP]
W: Meijer[*, D, LP, K], Shell[*, CW], Speedway[*, LP]
Food E: Bagel Boomers Deli, Bonato's Pizza, China Garden Buffet, Little Caesars Pizza, Long John Silver, McDonald's, Perkins Family Restaurant, Pizza Hut, Sally's Cafe, Subway
W: Applebee's, Bob Evan's Restaurant, Burger King, C J's High Marks (Hampton Inn), Dairy Queen, Fazoli's Italian Food, Friendly's, Frisch's Big Boy, KFC, McDonald's (Wal-Mart), Steak 'N Shake, Tokyo Peking Restaurant
Lodg W: Fairfield Inn by Marriott, Hampton Inn, Holiday Inn Express, Knight's Inn, Residence Inn by Marriot
AServ E: Trojan Tire
W: Auto Zone

1848
childreach
U.S. MEMBER OF PLAN INTERNATIONAL
Sponsored by Interatate America and Ramada Inn, Limited and Plaza Hotels of Ohio
RAMADA
For information on how you can sponsor a child call 800-556-7918
OHIO ▪ I-75

1754
SUPER 8 MOTEL
Super 8 Motel
1330 Archer Drive
Troy, OH 45373
937-339-6564
Continental Breakfast
Kids Under 12 Stay Free
Outdoor Pool
Restaurants Nearby
Handicap Accessible
Truck/Large Vehicle Parking
Pleasant Hill Civil War Hero Monument, Air Force Museum, Ludlow Fall Nearby
OHIO ▪ I-75 ▪ Exit 73

EXIT OHIO

Med E: Hospital, Upper Valley Family Care
W: Med First
ATM E: National City Bank, Star Bank
W: Fifth Third Bank
Other E: Pro Care Vision Center, Super Petz Food Store, The Pharm Deep Discount Drugs, Troy Animal Hospital & Bird Clinic
W: CVS Pharmacy, Gemini Eye Care, Meijer[24, RX], Sear's Hardware, Troy Towne Center Mall, Wal-Mart[RX] (Vision)

73 OH 55, Troy, Ludlow Falls

Gas E: Amoco[*], BP[*, LP]
Food E: Mel-O-Dee Restaurant, Papa John's Pizza, Waffle House
Lodg E: Motel 6, Quality Inn & Suites, Super 8 (see our ad this page)
Med E: Hospital
ATM E: Kroger Supermarket[RX]
Other E: Fantastic Sams Pet Store, Kroger Supermarket[RX]

69 CR 25A

Gas E: Dairy Mart[*, LP], Marathon[*, LP], Starfire Express[*, D]
Food E: Taco Bell Express (Dairy Mart)
AServ E: Dave's Arbogast Buick, Pont, GMC Truck, Troy Ford Dealership
ATM E: Marathon

68 OH 571, West Milton, Tipp City

Gas E: BP[*, D, LP, CW], Shell[*, CW, 24], Speedway[*]
W: Citgo[*, D], SuperAmerica[*, D, 24]
Food E: Burger King, Cassano's Pizza & Subs, Chin's Ginger Grill (Asian), Domino's Pizza, Hong Kong Kitchen, McDonald's[PLAY], Subway, Taco Bell
W: Arby's, Blimpie Subs & Salads (SuperAmerica), Frisch's Big Boy, Tipp O'the Town Family Restaurant, Wendy's
Lodg W: Heritage Motel, Holiday Inn Express
AServ E: Cars Plus Honda, Goodyear Tire & Auto, Honda Dealer
W: Citgo, Sears Parts & Service
Med E: Upper Valley Pediatric Care
ATM E: National City Bank, Star Bank
W: Bank One, Fifth Third Bank, SuperAmerica
Other E: ACE Hardware[LP], CVS Pharmacy[RX], Chmiel's Grocery
W: English Veterinary

64 Northwoods Blvd

63 U.S. 40, Vandalia, Donnelsville

Gas E: SuperAmerica[*, D, K]
W: BP[*, D, LP], Shell[*, CW], Speedway[*, D]
Food E: Bunkers Bar & Grill, Dragon China, Fricker's, Gliders Soup, Salad, & Sandwiches
W: Arby's, Jim's Donut Shop, KFC, McDonald's, Original Rib House, Pizza Hut, Subway, TW's Smokehouse, Taco Bell, Wendy's
Lodg E: Crossroads Motel
W: Cross Country Inn
AServ E: Beau Townsend Collision Center, Jon Rankin Auto Sales, Vandalia Auto Clinic
W: Muffler Brothers
ATM E: Kroger Supermarket[RX]
W: Key Bank, Monroe Federal Savings, Shell
Other E: Kroger Supermarket[RX], Royal Z Bowling Lanes
W: Ken's Pharmacy, Vandalia Animal Clininc

61AB Junction I-70, Indianapolis, Columbus, Dayton International Airport

60 Little York Road, Stop Eight Road

Gas W: Sunoco[*, K]
Food E: Subway
W: Arby's, Bennigan's, Bob Evan's Restaurant, Cooker's Bar & Grill, Cracker Barrel, Lone Star Steakhouse, Max & Erma's, Northern Palace Chinese, O'Charley's, Olive Garden, Red Lobster, Ryan's Steakhouse, Sante Fe Restaurant & Cantina (Ramada Inn), Wendy's
Lodg E: Residence Inn
W: Comfort Inn, Days Inn, Fairfield Inn by Marriott, Howard Johnson, Knight's Inn, Motel 6, Ramada Inn, Red Roof Inn
AServ E: Frank V. Imports Volvo, BMW, NTB, Stereo On Wheels
W: Ken's Auto Service
TServ W: International Trucks
Other W: Highway Patrol, Sam's Club

58 Needmore Road, Hara Arena, Hwy Patrol, Airforce Museum

FStop W: Speedway[*, LP, K], SuperAmerica[*, D, LP, K]
Gas E: BP[*, D, LP], Shell[*, CW]
W: Clark[LP], Sunoco[D], Swifty[K]
Food E: Airway Billiards Bar & Grill, Entemann's Thrift Cake Bakery, Fisch's Big Boy, Hardee's, McDonald's (Shell)
W: Arby's, Burger King, Captain D's, Cassano's Pizza & Subs, China Gate Restaurant, Church's Chicken, Domino's Pizza, Formosa Chinese, Friendly's, George's Family Restaurant, IZU Japanese Restaurant, Long John Silver, McDonald's, New Peking Restaurant (Mandarin/Szechwan), Rally's Hamburgers, Subway (Speedway), Taco Bell (SuperAmerica), Waffle House, Yogurts
Lodg E: Quality Inn
W: Ramada Inn (see our ad this page)
AServ E: Cooper Tires, Frank Weiss Auto Repair, Goodyear Tire & Auto, Past Forward Auto Restoration, Tires Unlimited
W: Auto Zone Auto Parts, Brownie's Auto Service, Coke's Auto Imports, Jiffy Lube, Midas Muffler & Brake, Needmore Service Center, Parts America, Pro Trim Auto & Truck Accessories, Safelite Auto Glass, Spot Free Rinse Car Wash[CW], Wagon Wheel Auto Sales
TServ W: Harris Travel Trailer Service
RVCamp W: Harris Travel Trailer Service
Med W: Needmore Medical Center, Northridge Health Center Child Health
ATM E: BP
W: Bank One, Kroger Supermarket[RX], National City Bank, Speedway, SuperAmerica
Other W: CVS Pharmacy, Ideal Coin Operated Laundry, Kroger Supermarket[RX], Northridge Animal Clinic, Payless Shoe Source

57B Wagner Ford Road, Siebenthaler Road

Gas E: Sunoco[*, LP, 24]
W: Speedway[*, D], United Dairy Farmers[*]
Food W: Denny's, Dixie Deli, Little Caesars Pizza, Marian's Piazza, On the Circle Restaurant, Subway
Lodg E: Holiday Inn
W: Best Western, EconoLodge
AServ W: Frank Johnson Carborator, Magnum Auto Sales & Auto Repair, Traffic Circle Tires
RVCamp W: Onan Power Systems
ATM W: Advance America Cash Advance Center
Other W: Odd Lots, Rite Aid Pharmacy

57A Neva Dr (Northbound, Reaccess Southbound Only)

Food W: Bakers A.K.A. Dave's World, Dixie Deluxe Donuts, Gabe's Sports Bar & Grill, Monte's Roast Beef
Lodg W: Traveler's Motel
AServ W: Craftmaster's Van & Truck
Other W: Bakers A.K.A. Dave's World

56AB Stanley Ave (Southbound)

FStop E: Amoco[*, D]

EXIT OHIO

Gas W: 76[*, D], BP[*]
Food E: Ohio Pizza Outlet
W: Gold Star Chili, Golden Nugget Pancake, McDonald's, Rally's Hamburgers, Taco Bell, Wendy's
Lodg W: Dayton Motor Hotel, Plaza Motel, Royal Motel
TServ E: **North Dayton Truck Service**
ATM W: 76, Bank One
Other W: Coin Car Wash

55B Keowee St North, Leo St (Northbound)
FStop W: **Clark**[*, D]
Gas E: Sunoco
W: BP[*]
Food W: Golden Nugget Pancake, Goldstar Chili, Great Steak & Potato Co., **Jack's Drive-In**, **McDonald's**, Rally's Hamburgers, Taco Bell, Wendy's
Lodg W: **Plaza Motel**, **Royal Motel**
AServ E: Champion Auto Service, R & Z Domestic & Foreign, Sunoco
W: Corner Mechanic
ATM W: Bank One, **Clark**
Other W: Self Service Car Wash[CW]

55A Keowee Street
Gas W: BP[*]
Food W: Rally's Hamburgers, Royal Z Bowling Lanes
AServ E: Big Muffler Shop #4
W: Corner Mechanic, L OK Body Shop
ATM W: Bank One
Other W: Family Dollar Store, Genuine Auto Parts, Parkside Food Mart, Royal Z Bowling Lanes, St. Francis Thrift Store

54C OH 4, Springfield

54B OH 48, Main St, Downtown Dayton
Gas W: BP[*]
Food E: Chili King Restaurant
W: Dayton Nut & Candy Company, Louie's Chicken
AServ E: Car Wise, **White Allen Chevrolet**, White Allen Honda
W: W.B. Walker Olds, Walker Bros. Jaguar
Med W: ✚ **Hospital**
Other E: **Russ's Market**[24]

54A Grand Ave

53AB OH 49, Salem Ave, First St, Third St

53A Sinclair College, Dayton Convention Center (Reaccess Northbound Only)
Gas W: Ashland[CW], BP[*, D], Speedway[*, LP], SuperAmerica[*, D, LP]
Food W: Bedrock Steakhouse, Cowloon Kitchen (Szechuan/Cantonese), KFC, McDonald's, Pizza Hut, Taco Bell, Wendy's
AServ E: Bill's Transmission
W: Bubble Brush Car Wash[CW]
ATM W: National City Bank, SuperAmerica
Other W: Duds & Suds Laundry (SuperAmerica), **U.S. Post Office**, Woody's Deli, Bakery, Seafood

52B U.S. 35, Eaton, Xenia

52A Albany St, Stewart St

51 Nicholas Road, Edwin C. Moses Blvd, Sun Watch Indian Village, Univ. of Dayton
Gas W: BP[*, D], **Shell Express**
Food W: **McDonald's**, Tropical Falls Restaurant
Lodg W: **EconoLodge**
Med E: ✚ **Hospital**
ATM W: BP
Other E: Univ. of Dayton Arena

50B OH 741, Springboro Road
Med E: ✚ **Hospital**

50A Dryden Road, U.S. Air Force Museum
Gas E: SuperAmerica[*]

EXIT OHIO

Food W: **Gus's Restaurant & Grocery**, In Between Carry-Out & Sandwich Shop, TJ's Restaurant (Super 8 Motel)
Lodg W: **Holiday Inn**, **Super 8**
AServ E: Broadway Car Care
W: Eric's Auto Sales
Other E: **Dayton Emergency Veterinary Clinic**, Moraine Civic Center

47 Moraine, Kettering, OH 741 (Reaccess Southbound Only)
Gas E: Clark[LP], Sunoco[*, K]
W: Citgo[*, D, K]
Food E: 4200 Place Cheese Steaks, Dixie Dairy Dreem, Domino's Pizza, **Fricker's World Famous Wings**, Frisch's Big Boy, Mandarin Garden Chinese, Penn Station, Treasure Island Supper Club, Waffle House
Lodg E: Parkview Inn, Parkview Inn, Villager Lodge
AServ E: Cottman Transmissions, Mr. Prescription (MAACO), Precision Tune Auto Care, **Slone's Automotive Car & RV Care**, Specialty Motorwerks
W: Brownie's Independent Transmission, Bruce Miller Auto & Towing, Daddy Myan Drive-Thru (Citgo), Honda of Troy Yamaha, Suzuki, Honda, LTD Mobile Glass Auto Glass Specialist, Meineke Discount Mufflers, Toy Store Ford & Dodge
RVCamp E: **Slone's Automotive Car & RV Care**
W: **Campground**
Med E: ✚ **Hospital**
Other E: **CF Holiday Park**, Quick and Clean Car Wash[CW]
W: Police Department

44 OH 725, Miamisburg, Centerville, West Carrollton
Gas E: BP[*, LP, CW], Shell[*], Speedway[*]
W: BP[*, LP], Marathon[*, D], Shell
Food E: Applebee's, **Bistro Restaurant (DoubleTree Guest Suites)**, Blimpie Subs & Salads, **Burger King**, Captain D's Seafood, **Chi Chi's Mexican Restaurant**, Chuck E Cheese's Pizza, **Delphine's Steak, Seafood, & Ribs (Holiday Inn)**, Denny's, Dunkin Donuts, Friendly's, Grindstone Charley's Restaurant, KFC, Lone Star Steakhouse, McDonald's, Olive Garden, Peking Express (Chinese), Pizza Hut, Ponderosa, Rally's Hamburgers, **Rocky's (Holiday Inn)**, Skyline Chili, Taco Bell, Wendy's
W: **Alex's Restaurant (Best Western)**, **Bob Evan's Restaurant**, China Hut, Long John Silver, Luciano's Pizza, Perkins Family Restaurant, Pizza Hut, **Samurai Sword Steakhouse (Japanese/American)**
Lodg E: **DoubleTree Guest Suites**, **Holiday Inn**, Motel 6, Residence Inn by Marriot, **The Courtyard by Marriot**
W: Best Western, Byers Inn, DAYS INN Days Inn (see our ad this page), **Knight's Inn (see our ad this page)**, Red Roof Inn, **Signature Inn**
AServ E: BP, Custom Lube and Oil, Firestone Tire & Auto, Jiffy Lube, Mazda Dealer, Nissan, Pro Care (BP), Speedy Muffler, Tire Discounters
W: Amoco Transmission, Interstate Drive-Thru (Marathon), Interstate Ford Dealer, Marathon, Q-Lube, Shell
Med E: ✚ **The Neighborhood Doctor (Urgent Care Facility)**
W: ✚ **Sycamore Hospital**
ATM E: Key Bank, National City
W: Fifth Third Bank, Star Bank
Other E: **Dayton Mall**, Fantastic Sams Pet Store & Reptile House, **Super Pets**, Super Pets
W: Miami Valley Indoor Golf, **Rite Aid Pharmacy**, **Twin Maples Veterinary Hospital**

EXIT OHIO

43 Junction I-675 North, Columbus

38 OH 73, Springboro, Franklin
Gas E: BP[*], Sunoco[D]
Food E: **Arby's**, China Garden Buffet, Goldstar Chili, I Can't Believe It's Yogurt, KFC, Long John Silver, Malachi Deli & Catering, **McDonald's**, **Perkin's Family Restaurant**, Subway, **T.J. Cinnamon's**, Taco Bell, Wendy's
W: Frisch's Big Boy, Village Station Steak & Seafood[24]
Lodg E: Holiday Inn Express
W: EconoLodge, Knight's Inn
AServ E: Restoration Station, Springboro Automotive, Sunoco
W: Interstate Auto Mart, Muffler Brothers, NAPA Auto Parts
RVCamp W: **4X4 Phonetics Jay Sales**
ATM E: First National Bank, National City Bank
W: Community National Bank
Other E: **Animal Medical Center**, **Coast to Coast Hardware**, **Kroger Supermarket**, Tota Vision Centers

36 OH 123, Franklin, Lebanon
TStop E: **Citgo**[*, LP, SCALES]
FStop E: **Speedway**[*, LP]
Gas W: BP[*, LP, CW]
Food E: **Brickhouse Lounge (Royal Inn)**, **Hardee's (Speedway)**, **McDonald's**, **Waffle House**
Lodg E: **Royal Inn**, **Super 8**
AServ E: **Adesa of Cincinatti & Dayton**
TServ E: **Adesa of Cincinatti & Dayton**, **Bridgestone**

Bill Knapp's RESTAURANT
1701
Bill Knapp's is a casual, full service family restaurant where Motorcoaches are always welcome.
Open daily at 11:00 am
Over 50 locations throughout: Michigan • Ohio • Indiana
513-424-2454 - Middletown
OHIO • I-75 • EXIT 32

Knights Inn South
Knights Inn
937-859-8797
800-843-5644
• Free Continental Breakfast
• Kids Under 12 Stay Free
• Meeting/Banquet Facilities
• Outdoor Pool • Exterior Corridors
• Pets Allowed • Handicap Accessible
• Exercise Facility Off Property
• Truck/Large Vehicle Parking
$34.50 1-3 Persons w/coupon at check in
1882 185 Byers Road • Miamisburg, OH
OHIO • I-75 • EXIT 44

Bold red print shows RV & Bus parking available or nearby

EXIT — OHIO

(Citgo), The Lube Zone
TWash — E: Truck Wash
ATM — W: BP
Other — W: The Practice Center Golf Range

32 — OH 122, Middletown
FStop — W: Meijer(*, LP, K, 24)
Gas — E: BP(*, LP), Duke(*, LP)
Food — E: BP, McDonald's, Waffle House
W: Applebee's, Bamboo Garden (Chinese Gourmet), Bill Knapp's Restaurant (see our ad opposite page), Bob Evan's Restaurant, Boston Market Restaurant, Cracker Barrel, Hardee's, KFC, Lone Star Steakhouse, Old Country Buffet, Olive Garden, Ponderosa Steakhouse, Shell's Seafood, Steak 'N Shake, Wendy's
Lodg — E: Best Western, Comfort Inn, Ramada Inn, Super 8
W: Fairfield Inn by Marriott, Garden Inn & Suites, Holiday Inn Express
AServ — E: Cronin Ford, Merc, Lincoln, MAACO Auto Body
W: Goodyear Tire & Auto, Jiffy Lube, Tire Discounters
Med — W: Doctor's Urgent Care Clinic
ATM — W: Boston Market Restaurant, Kroger Supermarket(LP, RX), Mid First Credit Union
Other — E: Honda, Kawasaki, Yamaha Motorcycles, Put Put Golf & Games, RV & Truck Parking Lot
W: Kroger Supermarket(RX), Meijer, Middletown Crossing, Pearl Vision Center, Super Pets, Towne Mall

29 — OH 63, Monroe, Lebanon
TStop — E: Stoney Ridge Truck Plaza(*, SCALES)
FStop — W: Sunoco(*, 24), SuperAmerica(*, LP)
Gas — E: Shell(*)
W: BP(*, D, LP)
Food — E: Tim Horton's Baked Goods, Waffle House, Wendy's
W: Gold Star Chili, McDonald's, Perkin's Family Restaurant, Sarah Jane's Country Cookin', Subway (SuperAmerica)
Lodg — E: Days Inn (see our ad this page), Stoney Ridge Truck Plaza
W: EconoLodge, Hampton Inn
AServ — W: Gregor's Auto Detailing, Monroe Car Care Center
TServ — E: Bishop's Truck Care(24)
TWash — E: Bishop's Truck Care
ATM — E: Stoney Ridge Truck Plaza
W: Sunoco, SuperAmerica
Other — E: Rob's Audio Concepts CB Service
W: Splash Auto Bath(CW)

(28) — Rest Area (RR, Phones, Picnic, Vending; Southbound)

(28) — Rest Area (RR, Phones, Picnic, Vending; Northbound)

22 — Tylersville Road, Hamilton, Mason
FStop — W: Speedway(*, LP, K)
Gas — E: Amoco(*, LP), BP(*), United Dairy Farmers
W: Meijer(*, D, LP, 24), Shell(*, CW)
Food — E: Arby's, Boston Market Restaurant, Fazoli's Italian Food, Gold Star Chili, KFC, Long John Silver, McDonald's, Pizza Hut, Taco Bell, Waffle House
W: Bruegger's Bagel & Bakery, O'Charley's, Steak 'N Shake
Lodg — E: Rodeway Inn
AServ — E: Goodyear & Dave Kutney Tire, Mastercare Car Service, Michel's Tire, Quaker State Oil & Lube
W: Car X Mufflers & Brakes, Oil Express, Tire Discounters, Wal-Mart(24, RX) (Pharmacy)
ATM — E: BP, Fifth Third Bank, United Dairy Farmers
W: Enterprise Federal, Shell, Star Bank (Meijer), Star Bank
Other — E: Thunderbird Exlress Auto Wash(CW)
W: Complete Pet Mart, Meijer, Sear's Hardware(LP), Wal-Mart(RX) (Pharmacy)

21 — Cin-Day Road
Gas — W: BP, Shell(24), United Dairy Farmers(*, D, K)
Food — E: Frisch's Big Boy
W: Amigo's Mexican, China Fun, La Rosa's, Papa John's Pizza
Lodg — E: Holiday Inn Express
W: Knight's Inn
AServ — W: BP, Shell(24)
ATM — W: United Dairy Farmers
Other — W: Pfister Animal Hospital

19 — Entre Center Blvd.

16 — Junction I-275, to I-74, I-71, Indianapolis, Columbus
Lodg — W: Argosy Casino & Hotel (see our ad this page)

15 — Sharon Road, Sharonville, Glendale
Gas — E: Ashland(*), BP(*, LP), Chevron(*, D), Marathon(*, D), Shell
W: Sunoco(*, 24)
Food — E: Bob Evan's Restaurant, Burbank's Real BBQ, Frisch's Big Boy, Pizza Hut, Skyline Chili, Spanky's (Holiday Inn), Waffle House
W: Arby's, Bombay Bicycle Club, Captain D's Seafood, Chuck E Cheese's Pizza, Long John Silver, Lotus Buffet Oriental Restaurant, McDonald's, Osaka Japanese, Penn Station Steak & Sub, Red Dog Saloon, Shogun, Subway, Taco Bell, Tahan Mongolian BBQ, Texas Roadhouse, Wendy's, Windjammer Restaurant
Lodg — E: Best Western, Fairfield Inn by Marriott, Hampton Inn, Holiday Inn, Red Roof Inn, Woodfield Suites
W: Comfort Inn, Econolodge, Extended Stay America, Marriott, Red Roof Inn, Residence Inn, Signature Inn, Super 8
AServ — E: Burnett Rent-A-Car, Firestone Tire & Auto, Marathon, Marathon, Shell, Shell
W: Instant Oil Change, Safelite Auto Glass, Top Value Muffler Shops
TServ — E: Dent Spring Truck Service & Co.
ATM — E: Ashland
W: Fifth Third Bank
Other — E: Burnett Rent-A-Car, Golden Tee Golf Center, Malibu Grand Prix
W: Maytag Laundry, Princeton Marine Sales & Service

14 — OH 126, Neumann Way, Woodlawn, Evendale
Gas — W: Swifty(K)
Food — W: Raffel's (Quality Inn)
Lodg — W: Quality Inn
TServ — W: Triton Transport Service
ATM — W: Fifth Third Bank

13 — Shepherd Lane, Lincoln Heights
Gas — W: Citgo
Food — W: Taco Bell, Wendy's
AServ — W: Cooke's Garage (Citgo)
Other — W: I-75 Check Cash

12 — Lockland, Reading (Difficult Reaccess)
Gas — W: Marathon(*, D)
Food — W: Hot Stuff Pizza (Marathon), Marathon
ATM — W: Marathon

10B — Arlington Heights, Galbraith Rd.
Gas — W: Sunoco(*, LP), SuperAmerica(*, D, LP)
Food — E: Howdi's Home Cooking
Lodg — E: Ramada Inn (see our ad this page)
AServ — E: First America Auto Center, McCluskey's, Tire Discounters
ATM — W: Sunoco, SuperAmerica
Other — E: Louis Animal Hospital

10A — OH 126, Ronald Reagan Hwy (No Reaccess)
Gas — E: BP(*, D, CW), Shell(*)
Food — E: Burger King
AServ — E: Midas Muffler & Brake
ATM — W: Huntington Bank (SuperAmerica), Sunoco

9 — OH 4, OH 561, Paddock Road, Seymour Ave.
Gas — W: Speedway(D, LP)
Food — W: White Castle Restaurant(24)
AServ — W: Conley Buick, McDonald's Frame & Axle Collision Repair, Rod's Auto Body
Other — W: Hamilton County Fair

8 — Elmwood Place, Towne St (Northbound, Reaccess Northbound Only)

7 — To Norwood, OH 562, I-71 (Exit To Limited Access Hwy)

$69 ROOMS AND UP
based on availability
Prices vary by season
RESTAURANTS • BUFFET • ENTERTAINMENT
Argosy Casino & Hotel
Call 1-888-ARGOSY-7
Must be 21. Photo I.D. required. Guaranteed admission with reservations only. ©1998 by Indiana Gaming Co. L.P. All rights reserved. www.argosycasino.com
I-275 West to Exit 16, Lawrenceburg, IN

1622

513-539-2660
Jacuzzi Rooms & Suites Available
Indoor Pool
Continental Breakfast
Restaurants Nearby
Meeting Facilities
Golf/Tennis Nearby

120 Senate Drive • Monroe, OH 45050
OHIO • I-75 • Exit 29

1596
RAMADA INN®
and Conference Center
Restaurant/Lounge on Premises
Kids Under 12 Stay Free
Outdoor/Indoor Pool • Exercise Room
Meeting/Banquet Facilities • Interior Corridors
Coin Laundry • Pet Allowed (charge)
Golf Nearby Truck/Large Vehicle Parking
Cincinnati Zoo, Kings Island, & Cinergy Stadium Nearby
Cable TV w/HBO, ESPN, CNN
513-821-5111 • 7965 READING ROAD CINCINNATI, OH 45237
OHIO • I-75 • EXIT 10B

Bold red print shows RV & Bus parking available or nearby

EXIT — OHIO

6 Mitchell Ave, St Bernard
- **Gas** E: Marathon[*], Shell, Speedway[*]
  W: BP[*, LP]
- **Food** E: KFC, Taco Bell
  W: McDonald's, Rally's Hamburgers
- **AServ** E: Jim's Auto Electric, Marathon, Shell
  W: Michel Tires, Sander Ford, Superior Honda Service
- **Med** E: ✚ **Hospital**
- **ATM** W: BP
- **Other** W: Don's Self Serve Car Wash

4 Junction I-74 W, U.S. 52 W, U.S. 27 N, Indianapolis

3 University of Cincinatti, Hopple Street
- **Gas** E: BP[*, D, LP], Shell[*, CW]
  W: Marathon
- **Food** E: Blimpie Subs & Salads (BP), **C.W. Donuts**, Camp Washington Chili, U.S. Chili's
  W: Frisch's Big Boy, Sunflower Coffee Shop, The Cave Lounge & Deli, White Castle Restaurant
- **Lodg** W: Budget Host, Interstate Motel, TravelLodge
  E: **Days Inn (see our ad this page)**
- **AServ** W: Jiffy Lube, Kristen Sunnley Service, Marathon
- **Med** E: ✚ **Good Samaritan Hospital**
- **ATM** E: Shell
  W: **Dairy Mart**
- **Other** W: **Dairy Mart**, Parkway Auto Wash[CW]

2B Harrison Ave (Left Exit Northbound)
- **Gas** W: BP[*]
- **Food** W: Blimpie Subs & Salads (BP), McDonald's
- **ATM** W: BP

2A Western Ave, Liberty St (Southbound)
- **Food** W: Gold Star Chili

1H Ezzard Charles Dr, Liberty Street (Northbound)

Cincinnati, OH

1532

513-559-0400

Continental Breakfast Included
Outdoor Pool
Meeting/Banquet Facilities
Handicap Accessible
Interior Corridors
Restaurant & Cincinnati Zoo Nearby

2880 Central Parkway • Cincinnati, OH 45225

OHIO • I-75 • EXIT 3

513-241-8660

• Free Parking
• Simmering Pot Restaurant
• Outdoor Pool &
• Whirlpool Suites
• Kids Stay & Eat Free
• AAA & AARP Discount
• Guest Laundry & Valet

1455

If Exit I-75N, Exit Linn St.
If Exit From I-75S, Exit Freeman Ave.

EXIT — OHIO/KENTUCKY

1G River Road, Linn Street, U.S. 50 West
- **Food** W: Frisch's Big Boy, Taco Bell, Wendy's
- **Lodg** W: Holiday Inn (see our ad this page)
- **ATM** W: Fifth Third Bank, Star Bank

1F Seventh St
- **Gas** W: Ashland[D], Sunoco[*]
- **Food** W: Chili Company[24]
- **Lodg** W: Holiday Inn
- **AServ** W: Fuller Ford, Walt Sweenew GMC Trucks
- **ATM** W: Ashland, Provident Bank, Three Star Bank

1E Fifth Street

1D Main Street

1C Covington, KY; Vine Street
- **Other** E: **Cinergy Stadium**

1B Pete Rose Way

1A I-71 North, I-471, U.S. 50 E, US 52 E; Columbus Parkway

↑OHIO

↓KENTUCKY

192 Fifth St, Covington, Newport
- **Gas** E: BP[D, CW], Shell[*, D, CW], SuperAmerica[*, D, LP]
  W: Deli Direct
- **Food** E: Burger King, Frisch's Big Boy, Gold Star Chili, McDonald's, Perkins Family Restaurant, River Front Pizza, Skyline Chili, Subway, Taco Bell, Waffle House, Waterfront South Beach Grill, White Castle Restaurant
  W: **Willy's Sports Cafe**
- **Lodg** E: **Holiday Inn**, **Quality Inn**
  W: Hampton Inn
- **AServ** E: Smith Muffler Shop, Smith Quick Lube
  W: Ford Dealership Ridgeview
- **ATM** E: BP, Preston Financial Group, Shell
  W: Deli Direct
- **Other** E: Dairy Mart, **Mainstrasse Village & N. KY Visitor Ctr.**, Tourist Info.

191 Twelfth St, Pike St, Covington
- **AServ** E: Jeff & Sons 24-Hr Towing, Marshall Dodge Body Shop
- **Med** E: ✚ **Hospital**
  W: ✚ **Hospital**
- **Other** E: AmeriStop Food Store, **Coin Laundry**, **Zimmer Hardware**

190 Jefferson Ave

189 KY 1072, Kyles Lane, Fort Wright, Park Hills
- **Gas** W: BP[*, D], Marathon[*, D], Shell[*, CW], SuperAmerica[*, LP]
- **Food** W: Fort Wright Restaurant, Frisch's Big Boy, Grandpa's Gourmet Ice Cream & Coffee House, Hardee's, Stefano's Pizza, Sub Station II
- **Lodg** W: Lookout Motel
- **AServ** W: Marathon, Roger Kuchle Garage & Body Shop
- **ATM** W: AmeriStop[*], Fifth Third Bank, Guardian Savings Bank, Huntington Banks, Shell
- **Other** W: AmeriStop

188AB 188A - Dixie Hwy South, Ft Mitchell; 188B - Dixie Hwy North, Ft Mitchell
- **Gas** E: Sunoco[*, K, 24]
- **Food** E: **Skyline Chili**
  W: D'Andrea's (Ramada Inn), Indigo Bar & Grill, Pizza Hut, Restaurant (Holiday Inn)
- **Lodg** W: Days Inn, Holiday Inn (see our ad this page), Ramada Inn
- **ATM** E: PNC Bank
- **Other** E: **Kroger Supermarket**
  W: **Thriftway Food & Drug**[24], **WalGreens Pharmacy**[RX]

EXIT — KENTUCKY

186 KY 371, Buttermilk Pike
- **Gas** E: Ashland[*], BP[*, K, CW], Citgo
  W: BP[*, CW], Shell[*], Sunoco[*, D, CW]
- **Food** E: Burbank's Real BBQ & Ribs, Chaucers Coffee Shop (The Crossbow's Tavern), Dairy Queen (Citgo), Gatehouse Tavern (Gatehouse Inn), Graeter's Ice Cream, Jacqueline's Steak & Ribs, Montoyas Mexican, **Oriental Wok (Chinese/American)**, The Crossbow's Tavern
  W: Arby's, Bob Evan's Restaurant, Boston Market Restaurant, Burger King, Cookies By Design, Domino's Pizza, Donato's Pizza, Dunkin Donuts, Fazoli's Italian Food, Goldstar Chili, Marx Hot Bagels, McDonald's, Outback Steakhouse, Papa John's Pizza, Papadino's Pizza, Penn Station, Sandwich Block Deli, Subway, The Canyon Grill
- **Lodg** E: Cross Country Inn, Gatehouse Inn, **The Drawbridge Inn**
- **AServ** E: Ashland
  W: Jiffy Lube, Menninger Auto Body
- **ATM** E: Citgo, First National Bank, **The Drawbridge Inn**
  W: Fifth Third Bank, PNC Bank, Shell, Star Bank, Sunoco
- **Other** E: **Oldenberg Brewery Tours & Museum**
  W: **Animal Hospital**, **CVS Pharmacy**, **Drug Emporium**, **IGA Food Store**, Royal Touch Car Wash, **WalGreens Pharmacy**

185 Junction I-275, Airport
- **Lodg** W: **Argosy Casino & Hotel (see our ad this page)**

184AB KY 236, Erlanger
- **Gas** E: BP[*], Citgo[*]
  W: Ashland[*, D], Marathon[*], Speedway[*]
- **Food** E: BP, Double Dragon Oriental Cuisine, Rally's Hamburgers (BP)

1411

NEWLY RENOVATED

2100 Dixie Hwy. • Ft. Mitchell, KY

• Holidome • Recreation Facility
• Guest Laundry & Valet
• Simmering Pot Restaurant
• Kids Stay & Eat Free

606-331-1500

KENTUCKY • I-75 • EXIT 188B

Bold red print shows RV & Bus parking available or nearby

EXIT | KENTUCKY

W: **Carriage House Restaurant (Comfort Inn)**, Peels Palace (HoJo), Subway (Ashland), **The Finish Line (Days Inn)**, Waffle House

Lodg W: **Comfort Inn**, Days Inn, **EconoLodge (see our ad this page)**, **HoJo Express Inn**

Med W: **Hospital**

ATM E: BP, Heritage Bank

Other W: Eyeware Frame Repair

182 KY 1017, Turfway Road

Gas E: BP(*)

Food E: Frisch's Big Boy, Krispy Kreme Doughnuts, Lee's Famous Recipe Chicken, Penn Station, Ryan's Steakhouse

W: Applebee's, **Cracker Barrel**, Fuddruckers, Grand Cafe (Commonwealth Hilton), Italianno's, Longhorn Steakhouse, Ming Garden (Chinese), O'Charley's, Rafferty's, Shells Seafood, Steak 'N Shake, Tumbleweed (Mexican), Wendy's

Lodg E: Courtyard by Marriott, Fairfield Inn by Marriott, Signature Inn

W: Commonwealth Hilton, Hampton Inn

Med W: **St. Luke's Hospital**

ATM E: BP, Crawford Insurance

W: Star Bank

Other E: **Family Fun Center**, **Thriftway Marketplace**(24, RX)

W: **Sam's Club**, **Turfway Park (Horse Races)**, **Wal-Mart**(24)

181 KY 18, Florence, Burlington

TStop E: **T/A TravelCenters of America**(*, LP, SCALES)

Gas E: Speedway(*, LP), Swifty(*, K)

W: BP(*, LP, CW), Citgo(*)

Food E: **Country Pride Restaurant (TA TravelCenters of America)**, Goodfellow's Distinctive Dining, Waffle House

W: Goldstar Chili, Hardee's, La Rosa's (Italian),

Florence, Kentucky

1458

Holiday Inn®

• Outdoor Pool
• Guest Laundry & Valet
• Simmering Pot Restaurant
• Kids Stay & Eat Free
• AAA & AARP Discounts
• Special Tour Rates Available

606-371-2700

KENTUCKY ▪ I-75 ▪ EXIT 180

1226

Econo Lodge®

Erlanger, KY

633 Donaldson Rd

• Free Coffee
• Free Local Calls
• 3 mi to Cincinnati Airport
• Jacuzzi Room Available
• Restaurant Close By
• Cable TV/HBO

606-342-5500

KENTUCKY ▪ I-75 ▪ EXIT 184B

EXIT | KENTUCKY

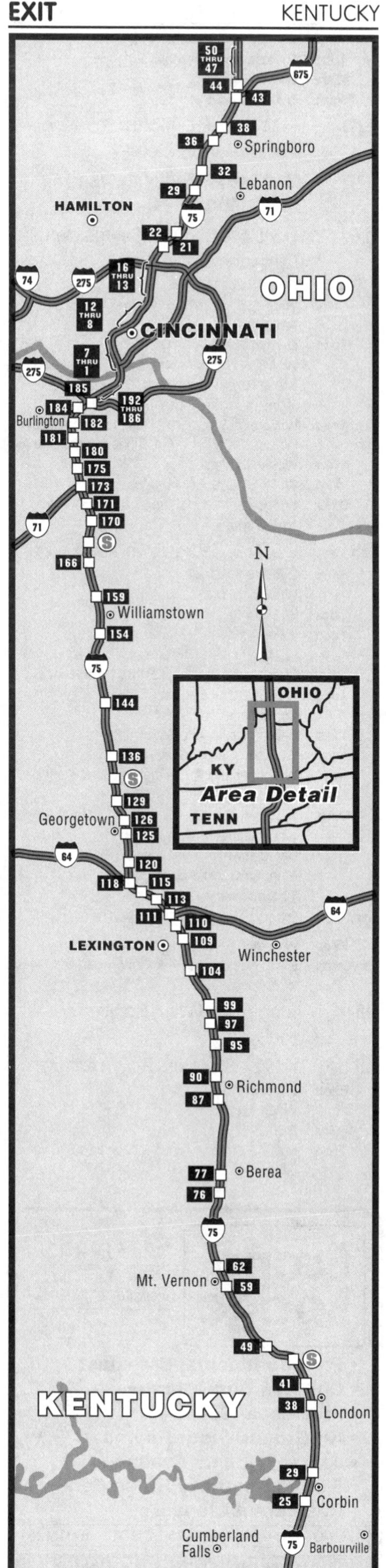

EXIT | KENTUCKY

Lone Star Steakhouse, Taco Bell

Lodg E: Best Western, Cross Country Inn

AServ E: LTD Mobile Glass Auto Glass Specialist

W: Airport Ford, Dodgeland Dodge, Jiffy Lube (Sear's), **Pro Care (BP)**, Suber's Auto Repair, Toyota Towne

TServ E: **T/A TravelCenters of America**(SCALES)

W: **Pro Care (BP)**

ATM W: Fifth Third Bank

Other E: **Angel Animal Hospital**, **Fundome Skating Rink**, **Speed Queen Coin Laundry**

W: **Big K-Mart**(RX), **CVS Pharmacy**(RX), Drug Emporium, Eye Glass Factory, **Mall**, Suburban Lodge, World of Sports Fitness Center

180 KY 42, U.S. 127, Union, Florence

FStop E: **Speedway**(*, D, LP, K)

Gas E: BP(*, D, CW), Thornton's(*, LP)

W: Chevron(*), Shell(*, CW)

Food E: American Prime (American), Bar-B-Q Pit, Baskin Robbins, Bob Evan's Restaurant, Burger King, Captain D's Seafood, **Casino Real Mexican (Ramada Inn)**, Chinese Buffet, Dunkin Donuts, Frisch's Big Boy, Jalepeno's (Mexican), Long John Silver, McDonald's, Mess Bar & Lounge, Penn Station Cheese Steaks, Pizza Hut, Rally's Hamburgers, Red Lobster, Skyline Chili, Sub Station II, Subway, Warm Ups Sports Cafe, Wendy's

W: Arby's, KFC, Little Caesars Pizza, Perkins Family Restaurant, **Ponderosa**, T.J. Cinnamon's, Waffle House, White Castle Restaurant

Lodg E: Knight's Inn, Motel 6, **Ramada Inn**, **Super 8**, The Wildwood Inn

W: Holiday Inn (see our ad this page), TraveLodge

AServ E: Mr. Transmission, Quaker State Oil & Lube, The Auto Bath Self Serve Car Wash, Value-rated Used Cars at Rock Castle

W: Car X Mufflers & Brakes, Midas Muffler & Brake, NTB, Quick Stop Oil Change

ATM E: Fifth Third Bank, **Speedway**

W: Shell

Other E: Classic Car Wash(CW), **Fantasy Frontier Mini Golf**, **Go Karts**, **Lazer Tag**, Ultimate Detail Shop (Thornton's)

W: **Florence Animal Clinic**

178 KY 536, Mt Zion Road

Gas E: BP(*, D), Shell(*, D)

Food E: Rally's Hamburgers (BP), **Thriftway Supermarket**(RX)

ATM E: Shell, **Thriftway Supermarket**

Other E: **Thriftway Supermarket**(RX)

(177) **KY Welcome Center (RR, Phones, Picnic, Vending; Southbound)**

(176) **Rest Area (RR, Phones, Picnic, Vending; Northbound)**

175 KY 338, Richwood

TStop E: **TravelCenters of America**(*, SCALES) **(BP)**

W: **Pilot Travel Center**(*, SCALES)

FStop E: **Pilot Travel Center**(*, SCALES)

W: **Shell**(*, LP, CW, 24)

Gas W: BP(*, 24)

Food E: Arby's, Burger King, **Taco Bell Express (TA TravelCenters of America)**

W: McDonald's, Snappy Tomato Pizza (BP), **Subway (Pilot)**, Waffle House, Wendy's

Lodg W: Days Inn, Econolodge

TServ E: **Bridgestone Tires**

ATM W: Huntington Banks, **Shell**

Parks W: **Big Bone Lick State Park**

173 Jct I-71 South, Louisville

171 KY 14, KY 16, Walton, Verona

TStop W: **Flying J Travel Plaza**(*, LP, RV DUMP, SCALES)

Bold red print shows RV & Bus parking available or nearby

(Conoco)
Gas E: BP(*), Citgo
Food W: The Cookery (Flying J TS)
AServ E: Citgo
TServ W: STI Towing and Truck Repair, TMI, Truck Lube Center(24)
TWash W: Blue Beacon Truck Wash, Truck Lube Center
RVCamp W: Delightful Days RV Center, Oak Creek Campground (1 Mile)
ATM W: The Bank of Kentucky
Parks W: Big Bone Lick State Park
Other W: Bullock Pen Lake (8 Miles), CB Shop

(168) **Weigh Station (Southbound)**

166 KY 491, Crittenden
FStop W: Chevron(*, 24)
Gas E: Ashland(*, K), BP(*), Citgo
W: Shell(*)
Food E: A & W Drive-In (Ashland), Taco Bell Express (Ashland)
W: B & E's Log Cabin Restaurant, Subway (Shell)
AServ E: Citgo, Crittenden Auto Sales, Grant County Auto & Truck Service
TServ E: Grant County Auto & Truck Service
RVCamp E: KOA Campgrounds(LP)
ATM E: Eagle Bank, Grant County Deposit Bank
Other E: Kentucky State Patrol Post

159 KY 22, Dry Ridge, Owenton
Gas E: Ashland(*), BP(*), Shell(*, CW)
W: I-75 Gas, Marathon(*)
Food E: Arby's, B-52 BBQ, Burger King (BP), Family Fare Home Cookin', KFC, McDonald's, Pizza Hut, Taco Bell, Waffle House, Wendy's
W: SHONEY'S, Shoney's, The Country Grill
Lodg E: Dry Ridge Motor Inn, Super 8
W: Big $avings Motel, Holiday Inn Express
AServ W: Dry Ridge Toyota, I-75 Gas
RVCamp W: Dry Ridge Camper Village (1 Mile)
ATM E: Eagle Bank, Shell
Other E: Kentucky State Patrol Post
W: Dry Ridge Outlet Center, Sav-A-Lot Grocery

154 KY 36, Owenton, Williamstown
Gas E: BP(*)
W: Ashland(*, D, K, CW), Citgo(D)
Food E: The Copper Kettle (HoJo Inn)
W: Ashland
Lodg E: DAYS INN Days Inn, HoJo Inn
AServ W: Citgo, Monarch Tires
Med W: ✚ Hospital
ATM W: Ashland
Parks E: Kincaid Lake State Park, Kincaid Lake State Park

144 KY 330, Corinth, Owenton
TStop E: Marathon(*)
Gas E: Ashland(*, K), Taylor's Grocery(*, LP)
W: BP(*)
Food E: Noble's (Marathon)
W: Free Way Restaurant
Lodg W: K-T Motel
AServ E: Sechrest Garage (Marathon)
TServ E: Sechrest Garage (Marathon)
ATM E: Ashland, Eagle Bank, Marathon
Other W: K-T Auto Parts

136 KY 32, Sadieville
Gas W: Chevron
AServ W: Chevron

(131) **Weigh Station (Northbound)**

129 KY 620
TStop E: Pilot Travel Center(*, SCALES, 24)
W: Speedway(*, LP, K, SCALES)
Gas W: Shell(*)
Food E: Great American Buffet (Pilot), Subway (Pilot TS)
W: Hardee's (Speedway TS)
Lodg E: DAYS INN Days Inn, Motel 6
TServ E: American Eagle
TWash E: American Eagle

(127) **Rest Area (RR, Phones, Vending, Pet Walk; Northbound)**

(127) **Rest Area (RR, Phones, Vending, Pet Walk; Southbound)**

126 U.S. 62, to U.S. 460, Georgetown, Cynthiana
FStop E: Standard(*, LP, 24)
W: BP(*, CW), Marathon(*, LP), Shell(*, CW), Super America(*)
Food E: Frisch's Big Boy, McDonald's
W: A & W (Super America), Cracker Barrel, Fazoli's Italian Food, KFC, SHONEY'S, Shoney's, Waffle House
Lodg W: Comfort Suites Hotel, Hampton Inn, Holiday Inn Express, Microtel Inn, Shoney's Inn, Super 8
AServ W: Ford Dealership
ATM W: BP, Shell, Super America
Other W: Factory Stores of America Outlet Center, Tourist Info.

125 U.S. 460, Georgetown, Paris
FStop E: BP(*, LP, CW), Shell(*, LP)
W: Dairy Mart(*)
Gas W: Swifty(*)
Food E: Flag Inn
W: Dairy Queen, Little Caesars Pizza, Long John Silver, Reno's Roadhouse, Taco Bell, Wendy's
Lodg E: Econolodge, Flag Inn
W: Winner's Circle Motel
AServ E: Georgetown Auto Repair
W: Exhaust Pro & Speedy Lube
ATM W: Farmer's Bank, Georgetown Bank, Kentucky Bank
Other E: Country World Flea Market
W: Dr. Clark Cleveland - Veterinarian, Georgetown Antique District, K-Mart(RX), Mancino's Pizza & Grinders, Winn Dixie Supermarket(RX)

120 KY 1973, Ironworks Pike
FStop W: Citgo(*, SCALES)
RVCamp E: Kentucky Horse Park Campground (.6 Miles)
Med W: ✚ Hospital

118 Junction I-64 West, Frankfort, Louisville

115 KY 922, Bluegrass Pkwy, Lexington
FStop E: Exxon(*, CW)
W: Chevron(*)
Gas E: Shell(*, LP, CW)
Food E: Cracker Barrel, McDonald's, Subway
(Shell), Waffle House
W: Denny's, The Mansion Restaurant (Marriot), The Post Restaurant (Holiday Inn)
Lodg E: Knight's Inn, La Quinta Inn, Wyndham Garden Hotel
W: Holiday Inn, Marriott
AServ W: Chevron
ATM W: Chevron
Other E: Kentucky Horse Park
W: Griffin Gate Golf Club (Marriot)

113 U.S. 27, U.S. 68, Paris, Lexington
FStop E: Chevron(*), Shell(*)
W: BP(*), SuperAmerica(*, K)
Gas W: Marathon(*, LP)
Food E: DAYS INN Days Inn, Fazoli's Italian Food, Shoney's, Subway (Chevron)
W: Sigee's Restaurant (Harley Hotel), Waffle House
Lodg E: DAYS INN Days Inn, Red Roof Inn
W: Harley Hotel
AServ W: BP
Med W: ✚ Hospital
ATM W: SuperAmerica, Whitaker Bank
Other E: Tourist Info.
W: Joyland Bowl

111 Junction I-64 East, Winchester, Ashland

110 U.S. 60, Lexington
FStop W: SuperAmerica(*, D), Thornton's(*, D, LP)
Gas W: Shell(*, CW)
Food W: Arby's, Bob Evan's Restaurant, Cracker Barrel, Krispy Kreme Doughnuts (Thornton's), McDonald's, SHONEY'S, Shoney's, Thornton's, Waffle House, Wendy's
Lodg W: Best Western, Bluegrass Suites, Comfort Inn, Country Inn & Suites, Hampton Inn, HoJo Inn, Holiday Inn, Holiday Inn Express, Microtel, Motel 6, Super 8
RVCamp W: Hall's Campers & Motorhomes(LP) (2.3 Miles)
Med W: ✚ Hospital
ATM W: SuperAmerica, Thornton's

108 Man O' War Blvd
Gas E: Shell
Food E: Applebee's, Burger King (Shell), Fazoli's Italian Food, Long John Silver (Shell), TGI Friday's
Lodg E: Courtyard by Marriott
Med W: ✚ Hospital
ATM E: Star Bank
Other E: Goody's, Hamburg Pavilion Shopping Ctr, Kids Zone (Shell), Meijer Superstore, Target

104 KY 418, Athens, Lexington
FStop E: Shell(*)
W: SuperAmerica(*, LP, K)
Gas E: Exxon(*)
W: BP(*, D, CW), Shell(*)
Food E: Baskin Robbins (Exxon), Dunkin Donuts (Exxon), Shell, Waffle House, Wendy's (Exxon)
W: Jerry's Restaurant, Subway (SuperAmerica), Taco Bell (SuperAmerica)
Lodg E: Comfort Suites Hotel, DAYS INN Days Inn, EconoLodge, Holiday Inn
Med W: ✚ Hospital
ATM W: Shell, SuperAmerica

99 N. U.S. 25, N. U.S. 421, Clays Ferry

97 South U.S. 25, South U.S. 421
TStop E: Clays Ferry Travel Plaza(*, SCALES) (Exxon, Showers, CB Repair)
Food E: Clays Ferry Travel Plaza (Exxon, Showers, CB Repair), Restaurant (Clays Ferry TS), Subway (Clays Ferry TS)
AServ E: Super Value Auto Mart
TServ E: Clays Ferry Travel Plaza(SCALES) (Exxon, Showers, CB Repair)

1227
Econo Lodge
I-75 • Exit 126
3075 Paris Pike
Georgetown, KY 40324
502-863-2240
• Free Continental Breakfast
• Children Under 18 Free
• Free Local Calls
• All Ground Floor Rooms
• Jacuzzi Rooms Available
• 5 mi to Kentucky Horse Park
• Restaurant Close By
New Senior Rooms Available
I-75 NORTH — EXIT125, I-75 SOUTH — EXIT 126
GEORGETOWN • I-75 • KENTUCKY

EXIT	KENTUCKY

RVCamp E: Clay's Ferry Campground (2 Miles)
W: Clays Ferry Landing Campground & RV Park (1.5 Miles)

95 KY 627, Winchester, Boonesborough
FStop W: Shell(*, LP, K)
Gas E: BP(*, D, K)
Food E: BP, Blimpie's Subs (BP), McDonald's(PLAY)
W: Burger King (Shell), Shell
ATM E: BP
W: Shell
Parks E: Boonesborough State Park (5 Miles)
Other W: Whitehall State Historic Site (2 Miles)

90BA U.S. 25, U.S. 421, Richmond
Gas E: Shell(*, 24)
W: BP(*, D, K), Citgo(*), Exxon(*, 24), Marathon(*, LP), Pennzoil Oil Change(*), Shell(*, D)
Food E: Cracker Barrel, Western Sizzlin'
W: Arby's (Exxon), Citgo, Dairy Queen, Dunkin Donuts (Citgo), Exxon, Frisch's Big Boy, Hardee's (Citgo), Pizza Hut, Waffle House
Lodg E: Best Western, HoJo Inn, Knight's Inn, Motel 6, Roadstar Inn, TraveLodge
W: Days Inn, Super 8
AServ W: NTB, Pennzoil Oil Change
RVCamp W: Interstate RV Outlet
ATM E: Shell
W: Bank One, Citgo, Exxon, People's Bank of Madison County
Other W: $uper-$ave Food Stores, Auto Wash, Keene Land Coin Laundry

87 KY 876, Lancaster, Richmond
Gas E: Amoco(*), Chevron(*, LP, CW, 24), Citgo(D, K, 24) (Wrecker Service Auto & Diesel), Dairy Mart(*), Exxon(*), Shell(*, D)
W: BP(*, D, LP, K), Dairy Mart
Food E: Denny's, Dunkin Donuts, Lydia's The Landing Rest., Pizza Hut, SHONEY'S Shoney's, Subway, Waffle House, Wok-N-Go Chinese
W: Reno's Roadhouse, Ryan's Steakhouse, Steak 'N Shake
Lodg E: EconoLodge, Holiday Inn, Quality Quarters Inn
W: Hampton Inn
AServ E: Citgo(24) (Wrecker Service Auto & Diesel), University Tire Center
W: BP
Med E: Hospital
ATM E: Bank One, Shell
Other E: All Creature's Small Animal Hospital, Kentucky State Patrol Post

(83) Rest Area (RR, Phones, Picnic, Grills, Vending, Pet Walk; Southbound)

(83) Rest Area (RR, HF, Phones, Picnic, Grills, Vending, Pet Walk)

77 KY 595, Berea
Gas W: BP(*, D, K, 24), Shell(*, D)
Food W: Columbia's Mountain Grill (Steaks, Chicken & Ribs), Denny's, Taco Bell(24) (BP)
Lodg W: Days Inn, Holiday Inn Express
Med E: Hospital
Other E: Tourist Info.

76 KY 21, Berea
FStop W: Spur(*)
Gas E: BP(CW), Citgo(*), Shell(*), Speedway(*)
W: BP(*), Chevron(*, LP, 24), Marathon(*, D)
Food E: Arby's, Burger King(PLAY) (Shell), Citgo, Dairy Queen(*) (Citgo), Dinner Bell Restaurant, Hometown Cafeteria, Long John Silver, McDonald's(PLAY), Papa John's Pizza, Pizza Hut, Shell, Stuckey's (Citgo), Sweet Betty's Restaurant, Wanpen Oriental Cuisine, Wendy's, Won Thai Restaurant
W: China Sea Restaurant, Lee's Famous Recipe Chicken, Pantry Family Restaurant
Lodg E: Holiday Motel, Howard Johnson, Super 8
W: EconoLodge, Mountain View Motel
AServ E: BP, Jenning's Auto Parts, NAPA Auto Parts, Wal-Mart(RX)
W: Madison County Dodge Chrysler Plymouth
TServ W: 76, Powell's Wrecker Service, Spur
RVCamp W: Covered Wagon RV Park-Full Hookups, Oh Kentucky Campground (.25 Miles), Walnut Meadow Campground (.5 Miles)
Med E: Hospital
ATM E: Berea National Bank, Shell
Other E: Wal-Mart(RX)
W: Maytag Coin Laundry

62 U.S. 25 to KY 461, Renfro Valley, Mt. Vernon
TStop E: Derby City Truck Stop(*, 24)
Gas E: Shell(*)
W: Ashland(*), BP(*), Shell(*, LP)
Food E: Derby City Truck Stop, Hardee's, Renfro Valley Motel, Restaurant (Derby City Truck Stop)
W: Ashland, BP, Blimpie's Subs (BP), Dairy Queen, Denny's, McDonald's, Rock Castle Steakhouse, Shell, Subway (Shell), Taco Bell (Ashland), Wendy's
Lodg E: Renfro Valley Motel
W: Days Inn, EconoLodge
TServ E: Derby City Truck Stop(24)
RVCamp E: KOA Kampground (1.5 Miles), Renfro Valley RV Park (.25 Miles)
Med W: Hospital
ATM E: Shell
W: BP, Shell
Other W: Big South Fork National River Rec. Area, Lake Cumberland

59 US 25, Livingston, Mt Vernon
TStop E: Spur
Gas E: BP(*), Burr Hill(*, D), Quality Gasoline(*, D, K) (Sunoco), Spur Hill(*, D, LP, K)
W: Peg's Food Mart(*, D, K)
Food E: Jean's Restaurant, Kastle Inn Motel, Pizza Hut, Restaurant (Kastle Inn Motel)
Lodg E: Kastle Inn Motel
W: Super 8
AServ W: Hwy 25 Cleanup Shop
TServ E: Spur Hill
RVCamp E: Nicel'y Campground (.5 Miles)
ATM W: Peg's Food Mart

49 KY 909 to US 25, Livingston
FStop W: 49er Fuel Center(*, D, 24), Shell(*)
Food W: Kentucky Grub Diner(24) (49er Fuel Center)

(41) Weigh Station

(41) Weigh Station

41 KY 80, Somerset, London, Daniel Boone Parkway (Toll Rd)
TStop W: London Auto/Truck(SCALES) (BP)
FStop W: Citgo(*)
Gas E: Chevron(*, K, 24), Marathon(*)
W: Chevron(*), Citgo(*, D, LP), Shell(*, CW)
Food E: Arby's, KFC, Rax Gold Star Chili, Zachary's Family Restaurant (Best Western)
W: Chevron, Homestyle Cookin (London TS), Jerry's Restaurant, Kontry Kookin, London Auto/Truck (BP), Long John Silver, McDonald's(D) (Chevron), Shell, Shiloh Roadhouse, Subway (Shell), Wendy's
Lodg E: Best Western, Economy Inn, Holiday Inn Express, Red Roof Inn, Sleep Inn, Super 8
W: Budget Host Inn
TServ W: Kron International
RVCamp W: Westgate RV Camping
Med E: Hospital
ATM W: Chevron, Dog Patch Trading Post(LP), Shell
Parks E: Levi Jackson State Park
Other E: Kentucky State Police
W: Dog Patch Trading Post, Tourist Info., Wilderness Rd Info Center

38 KY 192, London, to Daniel Boone Pkwy
FStop E: Shell(*, LP)
Gas E: BP(*, D), SuperAmerica(*)
W: Shell(*, LP, K), Texaco(*)
Food E: Arby's (Shell), Burger King(PLAY), Charcoal (Days Inn), Days Inn, Fazoli's Italian Food, Frisch's Big Boy, Hardee's, McDonald's (Wal-Mart), Rally's Hamburgers (SuperAmerica), Ruby Tuesday (Comfort Suites), Shell
Lodg E: Comfort Suites Hotel, Days Inn, Hampton Inn, Microtel
RVCamp E: Levi Jackson State Park Camping (4 Miles)
Med E: Hospital
ATM E: Shell
W: Shell
Parks E: Levi Jackson State Park
Other E: US Post Office, Wal-Mart Supercenter(24, RX)
W: Lake Cumberland London Dock (21 Miles), Laurel Lake Holly Bay (18 Miles), Laurel River Lake

29 U.S. 25, U.S. 25 East, Corbin, Barbourville
TStop E: 76 Auto/Truck Plaza(*, SCALES, 24), Citgo(*)
FStop E: Pilot Travel Center(*, D, K, SCALES), Speedway(*, LP, SCALES)
Gas E: BP, Exxon(*)
W: Amoco(*, D, 24), Chevron(*, D), Shell(*, LP, CW)
Food E: Burger King(PLAY), Pilot Travel Center, Quality Inn, Restaurant (Quality Inn), SHONEY'S Shoney's, Subway (Pilot), Western Sizzlin', Western Steer Family Steakhouse
W: Amoco, Cracker Barrel, Krystal (Amoco), Sonny's Real Pit Bar-B-Q
Lodg E: Baymont Inn & Suites (see our ad this page), Quality Inn, Super 8
W: Budgetel Inn, Fairfield Inn, Knight's Inn
AServ E: BP
TServ E: Lens Truck Garage (Pilot Truck Stop)
TWash E: 76 Auto/Truck Plaza, Jiffy Truck Wash
RVCamp W: KOA Campgrounds (.5 Miles)
ATM E: 76 Auto/Truck Plaza, Speedway
Other E: Antique Mall, Discount Christian Bookstore
W: Greyhound Bus Station

25 U.S. 25 West, Corbin
FStop W: BP(*, D)
Gas E: Shell(*, CW), Speedway(*, LP)
W: Exxon(*, D), Shell(*, CW)
Food E: Corbin Burger House, Jerry's Restaurant, McDonald's
W: Arby's, Baskin Robbins (Exxon), Buddy's Bar-B-Q (Exxon), Exxon, Rino's Roadhouse

BAYMONT
INN & SUITES
CORBIN
1558
FREE Continental Breakfast
In-Room Coffee
FREE Local Calls • FREE Showtime
25" Remote Control TV with Cable
Heated Indoor Pool & Spa
Interior Corridors with Electronic Card Locks
In Room Safe
Adjacent to Cracker Barrel Restaurant
Discounts for AAA • CAA • CSA • AARP
606-523-9040 • 800-428-3438
KENTUCKY • I-75 • EXIT 29

EXIT KENTUCKY/TENNESSEE

Lodg E: Country Inn & Suites by Carlson, Days Inn, Red Carpet Inn
W: Best Western, Holiday Inn, Levi Jackson State Park
AServ E: Complete Auto & Truck Repair(24)
TServ E: Complete Auto & Truck Repair(24)
Med W: + Hospital
ATM E: Shell, Speedway
W: Shell
Parks E: Levi Jackson State Park (15 Miles)
W: Cumberland Falls State Resort Park (15 Miles)
Other E: S & H Towing Service(24)

15 U.S. 25 West, Williamsburg
Gas W: Chevron(D), Shell(*)
AServ W: Chevron, Jayne's Tire Company
Other W: Grove Recreation Area & Marina (15 Miles)

11 KY 92, Williamsburg
FStop W: Mapco Express(*, LP, RV DUMP, SCALES) (see our ad this page)
Gas E: BP(*, D), Direct, Exxon(*, LP), Shell(*, LP)
W: Amoco(*), Shell(*, D, K)
Food E: Arby's, BP, Dairy Queen, Hardee's(PLAY), KFC, McDonald's(PLAY), Pizza Hut, Subway (BP)
W: B J's Restaurant(24), Baskin Robbins (Mapco Express), Buffet Pizza (Shell), Long John Silver, Mapco Express, Restaurant (Williamsburg Motel), Shell, Wendy's (Mapco)
Lodg E: Cumberland Inn (see our ad this page), Holiday Inn Express
W: Best Western, Williamsburg Motel
AServ E: 10 Lube, Paul Steely Ford, Tri County Transmission
RVCamp W: Williamsburg Travel Trailer Park
ATM E: Exxon
Parks W: Big South Fork NRRA
Other E: Tourist Info.

GIFT SHOP & MUSEUM
606-539-4100
WILLIAMSBURG, KENTUCKY
800-315-0286
Cumberland Inn
operated by
Marriott Conference Centers
Conference & Banquet Facilities • Indoor Pool
Jacuzzi & Exercise Room • Outdoor Garden Cafe
Full Service Restaurant
Special Rates For Tour Groups
AAA, AARP & Senior Citizens
Guest Laundry Service • Handicap Accessible
1274
KENTUCKY ¥ I-75 ¥ EXIT 11

1288

Open 24 Hours

606-549-0162
Gasoline & High Speed Diesel Pumps
Full Service Restaurant
Truck Accessories • Private Showers
Laundry Facilities • ATM Machines
D.A.T. Load Boards • Sandwich Shop
Certified Scales • Copy & Fax Services
KENTUCKY • I-75 • EXIT 11

EXIT TENNESSEE

(1) KY Welcome Center (RR, HF, Phones, Picnic, Pet Walk; Northbound)

↑KENTUCKY

↓TENNESSEE

(161) TN Welcome Center (RR, HF, Phones, Picnic, Vending, Pet Walk; Southbound)

160 U.S. 25 West, Jellico
Gas E: Amoco(*, K), Citgo (Stuckey's Express), Exxon(*, D), Texaco(*)
W: Shell(*, K), Sommerset (Towing)
Food E: Billy's Restaurant (Billy's Motel), Exxon, Johnny B's Reataurant (Jellico Motel), Subway (Exxon)
W: Arby's (Shell), Best Western, Buddy's Bar-B-Q, Days Inn, Gregory's (Days Inn), Hardee's, Heritage Pizza, Shell, Taco Village
Lodg E: Billy's Motel, Jellico Motel
W: Best Western, Days Inn (see our ad this page)
AServ W: B&B Auto Supply, Jim & Son Towing Service, Sommerset (Towing)
RVCamp W: Indian Mountain State Park (3 Miles), Indian Mountain State Park (3 Miles)
Med W: + Hospital
ATM W: Shell
Parks W: Indian Mountain State Park (3 Miles)
Other W: Flowers Bakery Thrift Store, Jack's Car Wash, Sheriff Dept.

144 Stinking Creek Road

141 TN 63 W, Oneida, Huntsville
FStop W: Texaco Truck/Auto Center(*)
Gas E: BP(*) (Stuckey's)
W: Exxon(*)
Food E: Perkins Family Restaurant
W: Dairy Queen (Texaco), Homemade Mountaintop Fudge (Texaco), Texaco Truck/Auto Center
Lodg W: Comfort Inn
Other W: Big South Fork Recreation Area, Fireworks Superstore

134 N. U.S. 25 West, E. TN 63, Caryville, La Follette, Jacksboro
Gas E: Exxon(*, D, LP), Shell(*)
W: Amoco(*) (Fireworks), BP
Food E: Pizza Palace, Waffle House
W: Scotty's 55 Cent Hamburgers, SHONEY'S Shoney's
Lodg E: Cove Lake Center, Family Inns of America, Hampton Inn, Lakeview Inn, Super 8
W: Budget Host Inn
AServ E: Talley Tires
Med E: + Hospital
ATM E: Exxon, First State Bank, Shell
W: Amoco (Fireworks)
Parks E: Cove Lake State Park (.5 Miles)
Other E: Fireworks Supercenter, Laundromat (Cove Lake Center), Russel's Market & Deli
W: US Post Office

(130) Weigh Station (Southbound)

(130) Weigh Station

129 U.S. 25 W South, Lake City
Gas W: BP, Citgo(*, K), Exxon(*, D, LP), Phillips 66(*), Shell(*), Texaco
Food W: Cottage Restaurant, Cracker Barrel, Domino's Pizza, Home Cooking (Lamb's Inn Motel), KFC, McDonald's(PLAY), The Lamb's Inn Motel
Lodg W: Blue Haven Motel, Days Inn, Lake City

EXIT TENNESSEE

Motel, The Lamb's Inn Motel
AServ W: BP, First American
RVCamp W: Mountain Lake Marina
Other E: Pernell Dist., Inc.(LP)
W: Appalachian Heritage Trail, Uncle Sam's Fireworks

128 U.S. 441, Lake City
Gas E: BP(*, K), Phillips 66(*)
RVCamp E: Mountain Lake Marina & Campground (1.3 Miles)
Parks E: Norris Dam State Park (2.3 Miles)
Other W: Hillbilly Market & Deli

122 TN 61, Norris, Clinton
FStop W: Citgo(*, SCALES), Quik Fuel(*, SCALES)
Gas E: Phillips 66(*), Shell(*, LP)
W: Exxon(*, D, K), Fina(*, LP), Git 'N Go(*, D, PLAY), Texaco(*, D)
Food W: Burger King (Exxon), Exxon, Golden Girls Restaurant, Hardee's(PLAY), Krystal, McDonald's(PLAY), Subway (Exxon), Waffle House, Wendy's
Lodg W: Best Western, Holiday Inn Express, Jameson Inn, Super 8
RVCamp E: Fox Inn Campground(LP), TVA Public Campground
ATM E: Shell
W: Exxon, People's National Bank, Quik Fuel
Other E: Twin Gables Antique Mall

117 Route 170, Raccoon Valley Road
TStop E: Raccoon Valley TS(*)
FStop E: Delta Express(*, K)
Gas E: BP(*, CW), Shell(*)
Lodg W: Valley Inn
TServ E: Raccoon Valley TS
RVCamp W: KOA Kampground (.75 Miles), Racoon Valley RV Park, Yogi Bear Camp Resort(LP) (.1 Miles)
ATM E: Delta Express

112 TN 131, Emory Road, Powell
Gas E: BP(*, D, K, CW), Chevron(*, LP), Pilot(*, LP, K)
W: Phillips 66(*, D, K), Shell(*, D, LP)
Food E: Aubrey's Restaurant, BP, Buddy's Bar-B-Q (BP), Chevron, Dairy Queen (Pilot), McDonald's(PLAY), Pilot, Pizza Inn Express (Chevron), Steak 'N Shake, TCBY (BP), TCBY (Pilot), Taco Bell (Pilot), Wendy's
W: Hardee's, SHONEY'S Shoney's (Comfort Inn), Waffle House

1845

Sponsored by Interatate America and Ramada Inn, Limited and Plaza Hotels of Tennessee
RAMADA
For information on how you can sponsor a child call 800-556-7918
TENNESSEE • I-75

At the Kentucky/Tennessee State Line
DAYS INN
423-784-7281
800-DAYS INN
Jellico, TN
Restaurant on Premises
Deluxe Continental Breakfast
Outdoor Pool • Exterior Corridors
Remote TVw/HBO, ESPN, CNN, TNT
Meeting/Banquet Facilities
Pets Allowed • Handicap Accessible
Truck/Large Vehicle Parking
Electronic Door Locks
In Room Safe • TDD's Available
Discounts for AAA • CAA • CSA • AARP
I-75 Exit 160
1557
TENNESSEE • I-75 • EXIT 160

Bold red print shows RV & Bus parking available or nearby

EXIT TENNESSEE

Lodg E: Budgetel, Holiday Inn Express
W: Comfort Inn
ATM E: Commercial Bank, Pilot
W: Phillips 66', Shell
Other E: Ingles
W: Mayes Aviation Airplane Rides & Charter Flights

110 Callahan Dr
Gas E: Phillips 66[*]
W: Amoco[*, LP]
Food E: Quality Inn, The Courtyard Buffet (Quality Inn), The Pizza Eatery
Lodg E: Quality Inn, Roadway Inn
W: Scottish Inns
TServ W: Volvo GM Truck
ATM W: Amoco
Other E: Glass Doctor
W: United Parcel Service

108 Merchant Dr
Gas E: BP[*, D, LP, CW], Citgo[*, D, LP, K], Pilot[*, D, LP], Texaco[*, D, LP, CW]
W: Conoco[*, K], Exxon[*, D], Pilot[*, LP, K], Shell[*]
Food E: Applebee's, Cracker Barrel, Denny's (Best Western), El Chico Mexican Restaurant, Logan's Roadhouse Steaks & Ribs, Monterrey Mexican, O'Charley's, Pizza Hut, Ryan's Steakhouse, Sagebrush Steakhouse, Shoney's, Sonic, Waffle House
W: Baskin Robbins (Pilot), Bob Evan's Restaurant, Burger King[PLAY], Captain D's Seafood, Darryl's, Exxon, Great American Steak & Buffet Co., IHOP, Mandarin House Chinese Buffet, McDonald's[PLAY], Nixon's Deli, Outback Steakhouse, Pilot, Red Lobster, TCBY (Exxon), Waffle House
Lodg E: Best Western (see our ad this page), Comfort Inn, Days Inn, Hampton Inn, Ramada Suites, Sleep Inn
W: Econolodge, Family Inns of America, LaQuinta, Red Roof Inn, Super 8
AServ E: Instant Oil Change
W: Qwik Oil
RVCamp E: Campers Corner Too Sales & Services
Med E: Prompt Care Medical Center (Walk-In Clinic)
ATM E: Citgo, Pilot
W: Conoco, First American, First Tennessee Bank, Home Federal Bank, SunTrust
Other E: Car Wash, Ingles Supermarket[RX]
W: Baptist Bookstore, Baptist Bookstore, The Clean Machine Car Wash[CW], WalGreens Pharmacy

(108) South I-275, East I-640, Knoxville, Asheville (Unnumbered Exit)

Note: I-75 runs concurrent below with I-640. Numbering follows I-640.

1709

Highway Host
118 Merchant Drive
Knoxville, TN 37912

Truck/Large Vehicle Parking
Restaurant/Lounge on Premises
Kids Under 12 Stay Free
Indoor Pool • In Room Coffee
Meeting/Banquet Facilities
Handicap Accessible • Coin Laundry
Exterior/Interior Corridors
Free Local Calls • Free Newspaper M-F

423-688-3141 • Reservations 1-800-826-4360
TENNESSEE • I-75 • EXIT 108

EXIT TENNESSEE

EXIT TENNESSEE

3 N I-75, S I-275, Knoxville, Lexington

3B US 25 W, North Gap Rd, Clinton (Eastbound)

1 TN 62, Western Ave
Gas N: Racetrac[*], Texaco[*, D]
S: Shell[D] (Wrecker Service)
Food N: Baskin Robbins, Central Park Hamburgers, KFC, Little Caesars Pizza, Long John Silver, McDonald's[PLAY], Nixon's Deli, Panda Chinese Restaurant, SHONEY'S, Shoney's, Subway, Taco Bell, Wendy's
S: Dad's Donuts & Delights, Domino's Pizza, Hardee's, Krystal, Tracy's Family Restaurant
AServ S: Advance Auto Parts, Bradley's Automotive Center, Mighty Muffler, Shell (Wrecker Service), West Haven Muffler Shock Center
ATM N: First Tennesee Bank, Kroger Supermarket[24], Racetrac
S: First Tennessee Bank
Other N: Kroger Supermarket, WalGreens Pharmacy
S: Car Wash, Super Wash House, US Post Office

Note: I-75 runs concurrent above with I-640. Numbering follows I-640.

Note: I-75 runs concurrent below with I-40. Numbering follows I-40.

385 North Junction I-75, I-40, East Junction I-640, Lexington, Knoxville

383 Papermill Dr
FStop S: Pilot[*, LP, K]
Gas S: BP[*, LP, CW], Citgo[*], Spur[*]
Food N: Holiday Inn
S: Smokey Market Deli, Spur, Waffle House
Lodg N: Holiday Inn
S: Super 8

380 U.S. 11, U.S. 70, West Hills
Gas S: BP[*, CW], Conoco[*, LP], Texaco[*, D]
Food S: Backyard Burgers (Conoco), Borders Books, Music & Cafe, Conoco, Cozumels (Mexican Grill), Dunkin Donuts (Conoco), KFC, Kaya Korean Restaurant, Romano's Macaroni Grill, Steak & Shake, Steak-Out Char-Broiled Delivery, Subway, Taco Bell
Lodg S: Comfort Hotel, Howard Johnson
AServ S: BP, Capettas Auto Trim, NTB, Penske
ATM S: Conoco, First American Bank, First Tennessee Bank, First Vantage Bank Of Tennessee, Food Lion, SunTrust, Texaco
Other S: Bi-Lo Grocery, Borders Books, Music & Cafe, Food Lion, K-Mart, Kingston Pike Pet Hospital, Kohl's, PetsMart, State Hwy Patrol, West Town Mall

379 Gallaher View Rd, Walker Springs Road, Bridgewater Road
Gas N: Aztex[*, D, LP] (Texaco), Exxon[*, LP]
S: BP[*, D, LP, CW]
Food N: Subway (Exxon)
S: Can Ton Restaurant (Chinese), Joe Muggs Coffee Shop, Mrs Winner's Chicken, Old Country Buffet, SHONEY'S, Shoney's
AServ N: Sam's Club, Wal-Mart[24, RX]
S: Firestone Tire & Auto, Goodyear Tire & Auto, Jim Codgdil Dodge, Ted Russell Ford, Ted Russell Nissan
Med S: Park Med Ambulatory Care Walk-In Medical Center
ATM N: Exxon
S: Union Planters Bank
Other N: Sam's Club, Wal-Mart[RX]
S: Books-A-Million, CVS Pharmacy[RX], Pet

EXIT	TENNESSEE
	Supply, Walker Springs Plaza Shopping Center, **Winn Dixie Supermarket**(24, RX)
378AB	Cedar Bluff Road
Gas	N: Amoco(*), Pilot(*, LP, K), Texaco(*), Weigel's Farm Store(*, K) (Amoco)
	S: Exxon(*, CW)
Food	N: Arby's, BelAir Grill, Burger King(PLAY), Cedar Grill, Cracker Barrel, Dunkin Donuts, El Mercado (Mexican Market), Holiday Inn Select, Jigger's Restaurant (Ramada Inn), KFC, Long John Silver, McDonald's, Papa John's, Pilot, Pizza Hut, Prince Deli & Sports Bar, Quizno's Subs, Ramada Inn, Stefano's Chicago Style Pizza, Taco Bell (Pilot), The Soup Kitchen, Waffle House, Wendy's
	S: Applebee's, Bob Evan's Restaurant, Corky's Ribs & BBQ, Denny's, Grady's, Hops Restaurant, Outback Steakhouse, Pizza Hut
Lodg	N: Hampton Inn, Holiday Inn Select, Ramada Inn, Scottish Inns
	S: Best Western, Courtyard by Marriott, Extended Stay America, La Quinta Inn, Microtel Inn, Red Roof Inn, Residence Inn, Signature Inn, Wyndham Garden Hotel
AServ	N: Texaco
	S: Harry Lane KIA Chrysler Plymouth
Med	N: **+ Hospital**
	S: **+ Metro Medical (Primary Care)**
ATM	N: Amoco, BankFirst, First American, First Tennessee Bank, **Food City Grocery**(LP), Pilot, SunTrust Bank, Weigel's Farm Store (Amoco)
	S: Tenn. Credit Union, Union Planter's National Bank
Other	N: Coin Laundry, **El Mercado**, **Food City Grocery**
	S: CVS Pharmacy(24), Celebration Station, The Marketplace (Mall)
376A	TN 162 North, Oak Ridge
Med	N: **+ Hospital**
376B	Jct. I-40 & I-140
374	TN 131, Lovell Rd
TStop	N: **TravelCenters of America**(*, SCALES)
	S: **Pilot Travel Center**(*, K, SCALES)
Gas	N: Amoco(*, D, 24), BP(*, CW), Marathon(*, D), Texaco(*, CW)
	S: Citgo (Wrecker Service), Speedway(*)
Food	N: **Country Pride (TravelCenters of America)**, **McDonald's**(PLAY), Prince Deli, **Taco Bell (TravelCenters of America)**, **TravelCenters of America**, Waffle House
	S: Arby's, Krystal(24), **Pilot Travel Center**, SHONEY'S Shoney's, **Wendy's (Pilot Travel Center)**
Lodg	N: **Best Western**, Knight's Inn, **Travelodge (TravelCenters of America)**
	S: DAYS INN **Days Inn**, Motel 6
AServ	S: Citgo (Wrecker Service)
TServ	N: **TravelCenters of America**(SCALES)
ATM	N: BP
	S: **Pilot Travel Center**
373	Campbell Station Road, Farragut
FStop	N: **Texaco**(*, D, K, CW)
Gas	N: Amoco(*)
	S: BP(*, LP, CW), Pilot Travel Center(*, D, LP, K), Speedway(*, K)
Food	S: Applecake Tearoom, Applewood, **Cracker Barrel**, Hardee's
Lodg	N: Comfort Suites Hotel, Super 8
	S: Budgetel Inn, Holiday Inn Express
RVCamp	N: **Buddy Gregg Motor Homes, Inc.**
ATM	N: **Texaco**
	S: Pilot Travel Center
Other	S: Appalachian Antiques, Campbell Station Antiques, **Station West**
(372)	**Weigh Station (Westbound)**
(372)	**Weigh Station (Eastbound)**

EXIT	TENNESSEE
369	Watt Road
TStop	N: **Flying J Travel Plaza**(*, LP, SCALES)
	S: **Petro Travel Plaza**(*, SCALES), **T/A TravelCenters of America**(*)
Gas	S: BP(*)
Food	N: **Flying J Travel Plaza, The Cookery (Flying J Travel Plaza)**
	S: **Burger King (Truckstop of America), Iron Skillet Restaurant**(24) **(Petro TS), Perkins (TA), Petro Travel Plaza, Pizza Hut (TA)**
TServ	S: **Petro Travel Plaza**(SCALES)
TWash	S: **Petro Travel Plaza**
Other	S: **Knoxville Travel Center, 76**
368	Junction I-75 South & I-40, Knoxville, Chattanooga
	Note: I-75 runs concurrent above with I-40. Numbering follows I-40.
84AB	Junction I-40, Nashville, Knoxville (Northbound)
81	U.S. 321, TN 95, Lenoir City, Oak Ridge (Ft Loudon Dam, Great Smoky Mtn. National Park)
FStop	W: **Shell**(*, D, K)
Gas	E: Amoco(*, LP, 24), BP(*, D, CW), Exxon(*, D), Phillips 66(*, K), Shell(*, LP), Texaco(D)
	W: Citgo(*) (Fireworks)
Food	E: Asian Garden, Baskin Robbins (Exxon), Dinner Bell Restaurant, Exxon, KFC, SHONEY'S Shoney's, Subway (Exxon), Terry's (Crossroads Inn), Waffle House(24)
	W: Citgo (Fireworks), Italian Deli
Lodg	E: Crossroads Inn, King's Inn
	W: Comfort Inn, Econolodge, Ramada Limited
AServ	E: Texaco
	W: Rocky Top Chevrolet
ATM	E: Amoco, Exxon
Parks	E: **Great Smoky Mountain National Park**
Other	E: **Tourist Info.**
76	TN 324, Sugar Limb Road
72	TN 72, Loudon
Gas	E: Shell(*, D)
	W: Citgo(*), Phillips 66(*, LP)
Food	E: Shell, Wendy's (Shell)
	W: Bird House Cafe, Citgo, Phillips 66, Roaster Chicken (Citgo)
Lodg	E: Holiday Inn Express
	W: **Knight's Inn (see our ad this page)**
RVCamp	W: **Express Campground (Water, Electric, & Dump Station)**
Med	W: **+ Riverbend Walk In Clinic**
ATM	W: Citgo
Parks	E: **Fort Loudon State Park (20 Miles)**
Other	E: **Sequoya Museum (20 Miles)**

Knights Inn
15100 Highway 72
Loudon, TN 37774
423-458-5855
TRUCK PARKING
• Scenic Mountain View
• Free Breakfast • Free 24 Hour Coffee
• Restaurants Nearby
• Express Campground (water, electric, dump station)
• Senior Citizen Discount/Corporate Rate
• Pool, HBO, Fax Services
1092
TENNESSEE • I-75 • EXIT 72

EXIT	TENNESSEE
68	TN 323, Philadelphia
Gas	E: BP(*, D, K)
Other	W: **Cowboy's Dream Ranch**
62	TN 322, Oakland Road, Sweetwater
Gas	E: **Phillips 66**(*)
Food	E: **Dinner Bell Restaurant (Phillips 66), Phillips 66**
TServ	W: **Miller's Diesel Repair**
RVCamp	W: **KOA Kampground (1 Mile)**
Med	E: **+ Hospital**
60	TN 68, Sweetwater, Spring City
FStop	W: **Exxon**(*, LP, K)
Gas	E: Marathon(*), Raceway(*), Texaco(*, D)
	W: BP(*, D), Phillips 66(*, CW)
Food	E: Huddle House, **McDonald's**(PLAY)
	W: Blanton's Resturant (Ice Cream & Bakery), Blimpie's Subs (Phillips 66), **Cracker Barrel**, Denny's (Best Western), **Flea Market Mall**, Phillips 66, Quality Inn
Lodg	E: **Budget Host Inn**, Comfort Inn, DAYS INN Days Inn, Sweetwater Hotel/Convention Center (Travelodge)
	W: Best Western, Quality Inn
AServ	W: Five Star Muffler
TServ	W: **68 Tire & Service Center**
RVCamp	W: **TN's Largest Flea Market**
Med	E: **+ Hospital**
ATM	E: Texaco
	W: **Exxon**, Phillips 66
Other	W: **Flea Market Mall**
56	TN 309, Niota
TStop	E: **Crazy Ed's Fireworks Supercenter**(*) **(BP)**
Food	E: **Crazy Ed's Fireworks Supercenter (BP)**, **Subway (Crazy Ed's TS)**
AServ	W: Michael's Wheels & Tires
TServ	E: **Crazy Ed's Fireworks Supercenter (BP)**
RVCamp	E: **Country Music Campground**
ATM	E: **Crazy Ed's Fireworks Supercenter (BP)**
52	TN 305, Mount Verd Road, Athens
Gas	E: Phillips 66(*, D, K)
	W: Exxon(*, LP)
Lodg	E: **Heritage Motel & Campground**
	W: Ramada Limited
RVCamp	E: **Heritage Motel & Campground**, **Heritage Motel & Campground**, **Over-Niter RV Park (.75 Miles)**
Other	E: **Crazy Ed's Fireworks**, **McMinn County Living Heritage Museum**
49	TN 30, Athens, Decatur
FStop	E: **Texaco**(*)
Gas	E: BP(*, K, CW), Exxon(*, LP, 24), Raceway(*), Shell(*, D)
	W: Phillips 66(*, D, LP, K)
Food	E: Alcapulco, Applebee's, Burger King(PLAY), Dairy Queen(D, LP) (Shell), Exxon, Hardee's, Shell, SHONEY'S Shoney's, TCBY (Exxon), The Soup Kitchen, Uncle Bud's Catfish & Chicken, **Waffle**

1094
SUPER 8 MOTEL
Super 8 Motel
Athens, TN
423-745-4500
• Outdoor Pool
• Free Continental Breakfast
• Non-Smoking Rooms
• Free Cable TV - ESPN & CNN
• Tour Buses Welcome
• 15% Discount with Coupon
• Soup Kitchen Restaurant
TENNESSEE • I-75 • EXIT 49

Bold red print shows RV & Bus parking available or nearby

EXIT TENNESSEE

House, Wendy's

Lodg **E:** Days Inn, Homestead Inn, **Knight's Inn**[PLAY] **(see our ad this page)**, Super 8
W: Homestead Inn West

AServ **W:** Heritage GMC

TServ **E:** **Roberts Brothers Motors**

RVCamp **E:** **Athens I-75 Campground**[LP], **KOA Kampground**

Med **E:** **Hospital**

ATM **E:** Exxon

(45) **Rest Area (RR, HF, Phones, Picnic, Vending, Pet Walk)**

42 TN 39, Riceville Road

Gas **E:** Exxon[*, D]

Lodg **E:** Relax Inn

RVCamp **E:** **Mouse Creek Campground**

36 TN 163, Calhoun

33 TN 308, Charleston

TStop **W:** **Texaco**[*, K, SCALES]

Gas **E:** Citgo[*, K], Fireworks Food Mart[LP, K] (Citgo)

Food **W:** **Texaco**, The Ponderosa Cafe (Texaco)

AServ **E:** Fireworks Food Mart (Citgo)

RVCamp **E:** **33 Campground**

ATM **W:** **Texaco**

27 Paul Huff Pkwy, Cleveland

Gas **W:** **BP**[*, D], Shell[*, LP]

Food **W:** **BP**, **Denny's**, **Hardee's**, **Mama Bea's Deli**[D, K], Waffle House, Wendy's

Lodg **W:** Best Western, Classic Suites, Comfort Inn, E Q Exclusive Quarters, Hampton Inn, Royal Inn, **Super 8**

Med **E:** **Cleveland Community Hospital**

ATM **W:** **BP**, Shell

Other **E:** Red Clay State Historic Area

25 TN 60, Cleveland, Dayton

2421 Georgetown Road
Cleveland, TN 37311
423-478-1137
800-843-5644

- Free Cable TV & HBO
- Non-Smoking Rooms Available
- Extra-Large Rooms & Kitchenettes Available
- Restaurants Nearby
- Free Coffee • Truck Parking
- All Major Credit Cards Accepted
- Weekly Rates Available

1825

TENNESSEE • I-75 • EXIT 25

Cleveland, Tennessee

423-476-2112

- Continental Breakfast Included with Milk & Cereal
- Kids 12 and under Stay & Eat Free
- Outdoor Pool
- Pets Allowed
- Exterior Corridors

1477

2550 Georgetown • Cleveland, TN 37311

Tennessee • I-75 • Exit 25

EXIT TENNESSEE

Gas **E:** Amoco[D] (Wrecker Service), BP[*, D, LP, CW], Chevron[*, D, K], Racetrac[*], Shell[*, D, LP], **Texaco**[*, D]
W: Amoco[*, LP, K]

Food **E:** Burger King[PLAY], Chalet (Quality), **Cracker Barrel**, Hardee's, Hong Kong Super Buffet, McDonald's[PLAY], Quality Inn, Roblyn's Steak House, Schlotzsky's Deli, Shoney's, Stadfeld's Family Restaurant, Waffle House
W: Amoco, Apple's Restaurant (Holiday Inn), Holiday Inn, Krispy Kreme Doughnuts (Amoco)

Lodg **E:** Colonial Inn, **Days Inn (see our ad this page)**, Econolodge, Heritage Inn, **Knight's Inn (see our ad this page)**, Lincoln Inn Motel, Quality Inn, Red Carpet Inn, Travel Inn
W: **Budgetel Inn**, Holiday Inn

AServ **E:** 25th Street Auto Parts, Amoco (Wrecker Service)

Med **E:** **Cleveland Community Hospital**, **Pine Ridge Emergency Center**

1541

423-899-5151
800-811-6616

Continental Breakfast Included

Kids Under 12 Stay Free
Outdoor Pool
Meeting/Banquet Facilities
Handicap Accessible
Interior Corridors • Coin Laundry
Walking Distance to Restaurants
Minutes to Area Attractions

2341 Shallowford Village Dr. • Chattanooga, TN

Tennessee • I-75 • Exit 5

Econo Lodge

423-499-9550 1050
800-55-ECONO

7421Bonny Oaks Drive
Chattanooga, TN

61 Rooms Well Appointed Room

Free Continental Breakfast

Free Local Calls
In Room Coffee
In Room Refrigerators
Fax, Copying & Coin Laundry

Home Away From Home

Spend A Night Not A Fortune

Tennessee • I-75 • NB Exit 7B • SB Exit 7

1542

423-238-5951
800-800-8000

I-75 • EXIT 11
Ooltewah, TN

$35.99 +tax 1 Person

- Restaurant on Premises
- Kids Under 12 Stay Free
- Indoor Pool • Exterior Corridors
- Pets Allowed (under 20lbs, w/permission)
- Handicap Accessible
- Truck/Large Vehicle Parking
- Close to Restaurants/ManyArea Attractions

Tennessee • I-75 • Exit 11

EXIT TENNESSEE

ATM **E:** Bank of Cleveland, SunTrust
W: Amoco

Other **E:** Car Wash, **Cherokee Pharmacy & Medical Supply**, **Community Animal Hospital**, **The Laundry Basket "Too"**

(23) **Truck Inspection Station, Weigh Station (Northbound)**

(24) **Weigh Station (Northbound)**

20 U.S. 64, Bypass East, Cleveland

Gas **W:** Citgo[*], **Exxon**[*, LP, 24]

Food **W:** **Restaurant**

Lodg **W:** Hospitality Inns Of America

AServ **W:** **Exxon**[24]

TServ **W:** **Gibson's Truck & Auto Repair**, **Mid-Continent Diesel Service**[SCALES]

RVCamp **E:** **KOA Kampground (1 Mile)**

Parks **E:** **Red Clay State Park (16 Miles)**

Other **W:** **Fireworks Supermarket**

(16) **Scenic View, Parking Area (Southbound)**

(13) **Weigh Station, Parking Area (Phones; Southbound)**

11 North U.S. 11, East U.S. 64, Ooltewah

FStop **W:** **Exxon**[*, LP, K, CW]

Gas **E:** Amoco[*], Chevron (Wrecker Service), Citgo[*, LP, K], Racetrac[*]

Food **E:** Arby's, Burger King[PLAY], Hardee's, Kreme House Country Cookin', Little Caesars Pizza, McDonald's[PLAY], PT Noodles, Subway, Taco Bell, The Donut Palace, Wendy's
W: **Exxon**, **TCBY (Exxon)**, **Waffle House**

Lodg **W:** **Super 8 (see our ad this page)**

AServ **E:** Auto Value Parts Store, Chevron (Wrecker Service), Guarantee Muffler Shop, Haven's Service Center, Lew's Import Service, Ooltewah Auto Center, Sunshine Fast Lube[CW], Tommy's Garage

Med **E:** **Columbia Care Medical Center**

ATM **E:** **Bi-Lo Grocery**[24, RX], Chevron (Wrecker Service), Citgo, MCB Ooltewah Bank, Racetrac
W: **Exxon**

Parks **W:** **Harrison Bay State Park (9 Miles)**

Other **E:** **ACE Hardware**[LP], **Bi-Lo Grocery**[RX]

7AB U.S. 7, 11, Lee Hwy.

Gas **W:** Texaco[*, LP]

Food **W:** **Best Western**, **Denny's (Best Western)**, Waffle House

Lodg **W:** **Best Western**, Comfort Inn, Country Hearth Inn, Days Inn, Econolodge (see our ad this page), Motel 6, Quality Inn

ATM **W:** Texaco

5 Shallowford Road

Gas **W:** Amoco[*], Citgo, Exxon[*], Texaco[*]

Food **E:** Acropolis, Alexander's Restaurant, Arby's, Burger King, Central Park Chicken, Country Place Restaurant, El Meson, Krystal, Outback Steakhouse, Schlotzsky's Deli, Taco Bell, The Olive Garden
W: Applebee's, Buckhead Roadhouse, **Cracker Barrel**, Fazoli's, Glen Gene Deli, O'Charley's, Ocean Avenue, Papa John's Pizza, Pizza Hut, Rio Bravo, SHONEY'S Shoney's, Sonic, Subway, Waffle House, Wendy's

Lodg **E:** Comfort Suites Hotel, Courtyard by Marriott, Wingate Inn
W: Country Suites by Carlson, **Days Inn (see our ad this page)**, Fairfield Inn, Hampton Inn, Holiday Inn, Holiday Inn Express, Homewood Suites Hotel, Knight's Inn, La Quinta Inn, Main Stay Suites, Microtel Inn, Ramada Inn, Red Roof Inn, Sleep Inn

AServ **E:** Firestone, Master Care Auto Service

ATM **E:** First Tennessee Bank

Bold red print shows RV & Bus parking available or nearby

EXIT TENNESSEE

1087

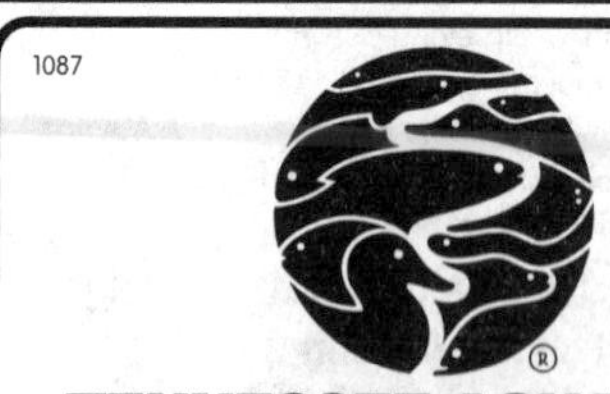

TENNESSEE AQUARIUM & IMAX® 3D THEATER

Explore new depths at the world's largest freshwater aquarium with 9,000 animals. Experience state-of-the-art film technology at the IMAX 3D Theater.

1-800-262-0695
www.tennis.org

CHATTANOOGA • I-24 • EXIT 178

TOUR BUSES WELCOME

1540

I-75 • Exit 7
Chattanooga, TN
423-894-6720
800-THE-ROOF

- Restaurant on Premises • Handicap Accessible
- Continental Breakfast • Kids under 12 Stay Free
- Outdoor Pool • Exterior Corridors
- Truck or Large Vehicle Parking
- Minutes from Downtow & Area Attractions
- Walking Distance to Several Restaurants

TENNESSEE • I-75 • EXIT 1

W: Bi-Lo Grocery(RX), Citgo, Texaco
Other E: Barnes & Noble, Hamilton Place Mall, Joshua's Christian Stores, Pier 1 Imports, Staple's, WalGreens Pharmacy
W: Bi-Lo Grocery(RX), Eye Wear Optical

4A Hamilton Place Blvd (Reaccess Southbound Only)
Food E: Grady's Goodtimes Restaurant, Tia's Tex Mex
Med E: ✚ Physicians Care Walk-In Clinic
ATM E: Tennessee Valley Federal Credit Union
Other E: Hamilton Place Mall, Regal Cinemas

4 Junction Hwy 153, Airport, Chickamauga Dam

3AB TN 320 West, E. Brainerd Road
Gas E: Amoco(*, LP), Exxon(*, LP)
Food E: Baskin Robbins (Ice Cream and Yogurt), Subway, TCBY (Exxon)
ATM E: Exxon
Other W: Brainerd Hills Animal Hospital, Dragon Dreams (Dragon Museum and Shop)

2 Junction I-75, I-24 West Chattanooga, Nashville
Other W: Tennessee Aquarium & IMAX 3D Theater (see our ad this page--take I-24 West)

(1) **TN Welcome Center (RR, HF, Phones, Picnic, Vending, Pet Walk; Northbound)**

1AB U.S. 41, East Ridge (Northbound)
Gas E: BP(*, LP), Exxon(*, K)
W: Amoco, Conoco(*, D, LP, K, CW), Texaco(*, D, CW)
Food E: Canoe's Burgers, Garden Inn, Mr. T's Pizza, Trip's Seafood
W: Arby's, Burger King, Central Park Drive Thru,

EXIT TENNESSEE

EXIT TENNESSEE/GEORGIA

Country Vittles Buffet, Cracker Barrel, Hardee's, Krystal, Long John Silver, McDonald's(PLAY), Oriental Market (Food & Gifts), Porto Fino Italian, SHONEY'S, Shoney's, Subway, Taco Bell, Uncle Bud's Catfish & Chicken, Waffle House, Wally's Family Restaurant
Lodg E: Airport Inn, Best Western, EconoLodge, Holiday Inn, Quality Inn & Suites, Ramada
W: Hospitality Inns of America, Red Roof Inn (see our ad this page), Scottish Inns, Super 8, Waverly Motel, World Inn
AServ W: Amoco
TServ E: Trantham Service Center and Wrecker
RVCamp E: Camp Jordan Park and Arena, Shipp's RV Service Center, Yogi Bear Camp Resort(*, RV DUMP)
W: Holiday Trav-L-Park (.5 Miles)
Med W: ✚ Hospital
ATM E: BP, Bi-Lo Grocery, Exxon
W: Pioneer Bank, Texaco
Other E: Bi-Lo Grocery, Carwash, Supreme Products Factory Outlet Store (Bedspreads & Draperies)
W: Coin Laundry, East Ridge Chiropractic, East Town Antique Mall

↑TENNESSEE

↓GEORGIA

142 **(353)** GA 146, Rossville, Ft. Oglethorpe
Gas E: BP(*, LP), Chevron(*, LP)
W: Exxon(*), Texaco(*, LP)
Food E: Nina's Restaurant (Knights Inn)
W: TCBY (Exxon)
Lodg E: HoJo Inn, Knight's Inn
ATM E: BP, Chevron
W: Exxon, Texaco
Other W: Gateway Antique Mall

(352) **GA Welcome Center (RR, HF, Phones, Picnic, Vending, RV Dump, RV Water, Pet Walk; Westbound)**

141 **(349)** GA 2, Battlefield Pkwy, Ft. Oglethorpe, Ringgold, Chickamauga State Park
FStop E: Save-a-ton(*, LP)
Gas E: Exxon(*)
W: Exxon(D), Racetrac(*, 24), Texaco(*)
Food E: TCBY (Exxon)
W: Bar-B-Q Corral
AServ W: Exxon
TServ E: Covington Detroit Diesel Allison, Freightliner
RVCamp W: KOA Campgrounds(LP) (.25 Miles)
Med W: ✚ Hospital
ATM E: Covington Detroit Diesel Allison, Exxon, Save-a-ton
W: Racetrac, Texaco
Parks W: Chickamauga Nat'l Park

140 **(347)** GA 151, Ringgold, LaFayette, Summerville
FStop E: Golden Gallon(*), Texaco Truck/Auto Stop(*)
Gas E: Amoco(*, CW)
W: Amoco(*, LP), Chevron(*, CW, 24), Exxon(*)
Food E: Aunt Effie's Down Home Cooking, Country Bumpkin, Hardee's, KFC, Krystal, McDonald's(PLAY), Pizza Hut, Subway, Taco Bell, Waffle House
W: Wendy's
Lodg E: DAYS INN Days Inn, Hampton Inn, Holiday Inn Express, Super 8
W: Comfort Inn
AServ E: Advance Auto Parts, Walter Jackson Chevrolet

Bold red print shows RV & Bus parking available or nearby

EXIT GEORGIA

W: Benny Jackson Ford, Guy Yates Towing
TServ W: Peterbilt
RVCamp E: Country Bumpkin (.25 Miles)
ATM E: Amoco, Capital Bank, Gateway Bank and Trust, Golden Gallon, Northwest Georgia Bank, Texaco Truck/Auto Stop
W: Amoco, Exxon
Other E: CVS Pharmacy(RX), Car Wash, Ingles Food Market, Revco

139 **(344)** U.S. 41, U.S. 76, Ringgold
TStop W: AmBest (Truck Wash), Citgo(*, SCALES), Cochran's Travel Center(SCALES)
FStop W: Fuel Mart(*, SCALES)
Gas E: BP(*, LP), Cowboy's(*, LP)
W: Phillips 66(*), Texaco(*)
Food W: Cochran's Travel Center, Waffle House
Lodg W: Friendship Inn
TServ W: Cochran's Travel Center(SCALES), Hammerhead Truck Tire Service & Repair, Southeast
TWash W: Choo Choo Truck Wash Plaza Inc.(D, SCALES)
ATM E: BP
W: Citgo

(343) Weigh Station (Eastbound)

138 **(340)** GA 201, Tunnel Hill, Varnell
Gas W: Chevron(*), Texaco(*)
Food W: Krispy Kreme Doughnuts (Texaco)
ATM W: Texaco
Other W: Self Serve Car Wash

137 **(335)** U.S. 41, U.S. 76, Dalton, Rocky Face
Gas E: BP, Chevron(*, D), Racetrac(*), Texaco(*, LP)
W: Circle M Amoco(*, LP), Phillips 66(*)
Food E: Blimpie's Subs (Chevron), Mr. Biscuit, Tampico Mexican Grill Buffet, Waffle House
W: Atlantis Restaurant (Howard Johnson), Best Western, Howard Johnson(24), Maggic's Pizza & Deli, Ta Gin Chinese, The Deli, The Rib Shack
Lodg E: Country Hearth Inn
W: Best Western, EconoLodge, Howard Johnson, Motel 6, Willow Dale Lodge
AServ E: AAA Tire Store, BP
TServ W: Truck and Trailer Parks, Inc.
Med E: Hospital
ATM E: Texaco
W: Phillips 66
Other E: The Home Depot(LP)
W: West Yellow Knife Trading Post

136 **(333)** GA 52, Walnut Ave, Dalton
Gas E: BP(*), Chevron(*, CW), Exxon(*, CW), Racetrac(*)
W: Texaco(*, LP)
Food E: Applebee's, Bel Air Grill, Bojangles, Burger King(PLAY), Captain D's Seafood, Cellar Restaurant & Lounge, Chick-Fil-A, Ci Ci's Pizza, Cracker Barrel, Dairy Queen, Emperor Garden Restaurant (Chinese), IHOP, Jimmy's Restaurant and Lounge, KFC, Kroger Restaurant, Lizzy's Deli, Long John Silver, McDonald's(PLAY), O'Charley's, Pizza Hut, Prime Sirloin, SHONEY'S Shoney's, Steak N' Shake, TCBY, Taco Bell, Waffle House, Wendy's
W: Red Lobster, Sensations Restaurant & Lounge (Holiday Inn)
Lodg E: Best Inns of America, Days Inn, Hampton Inn, TraveLodge
W: Comfort Suites Hotel, Country Inns & Suites, Holiday Inn, Jameson Inn, Wingate Inn
AServ E: BP, Brooker Ford, Edd Kirby Chevrolet & Geo, Exxon
W: Texaco
ATM E: 1st Union Bank, Dalton Factory Outlet Mall, Hardwick's Bank, Wachovia Bank
Parks E: Ft Mountain State Park
Other E: America's Best Contacts & Eyeglasses, Coin Car Wash, Dalton Factory Outlet Mall, K-Mart(RX), Kroger Supermarket(RX), Tanger Factory Outlet, West Point Pepperell Mill Store

EXIT GEORGIA

W: Chamber of Commerce, NW Georgia Trade & Convention Center

135 **(328)** GA 3, to U.S. 41
TStop E: Pilot Travel Center(*)
W: Fuel City(*)
FStop W: Phillips 66(*, LP)
Food E: Arby's (Pilot), Southside Cafe (Super 8 Motel), TJ Cinnamon's (Pilot), Waffle House
W: Bill's BBQ
Lodg E: Super 8
TServ E: TruckPro(LP)
ATM E: Pilot Travel Center

134 **(325)** Carbondale Road
FStop W: Phillips 66(*, K)
Gas E: Chevron(*, D, LP)
W: Golden Gallon Citgo(*, LP)
Food E: Annette's Cactus Cafe, Doc's BBQ-N-Grill (Knight's Inn)
W: Campsite BBQ
Lodg E: Knight's Inn
TServ W: TCI Truck Tire Center
RVCamp E: Camping (Country Boy Inn), Pa-Paw's Park Campground
ATM W: Golden Gallon Citgo, Phillips 66

133 **(320)** GA 136, Resaca, LaFayette
TStop E: Flying J Travel Plaza(*, RV DUMP)

PRIME OUTLETS
CALHOUN
Nearly 100 Designer Outlet Stores and Food Court
J. Crew • Jones New York • Liz Claibrone
Ask for your FREE COUPON BOOK
1855 706-602-1300
GEORGIA • I-75 • EXIT 129

1584
RAMADA LIMITED
RAMADA LIMITED
1204 Red Bud Road, NE
Calhoun, GA 30701
Calhoun
$36.95 4 Persons
25" Cable TV w/HBO & Showtime
— Bus & RV Parking —
— Outdoor Pool —
— Close to Calhoun Factory Outlets —
— Complimentary Continental Breakfast —
— Across from Shoney's Restaurant —
— Kids Under 12 Stay Free —
— Special Rates for Tour Groups —
706-629-9207
Calhoun, GA
GEORGIA • I-75 • EXIT 130

EXIT GEORGIA

Food E: The Cookery (Flying J)
TServ E: A & J Tire & Repair, Dependable Tire and Repair, TT Calhoun Truck & Trailer
TWash E: Dependable Truck Wash
RVCamp E: TT Calhoun Truck & Trailer

(319) Rest Area (RR, HF, Phones, Picnic, RV Dump; Westbound)

132 **(318)** U.S. 41, Resaca
Gas W: Exxon(*, D, CW), The Right Stuff(*, LP)
Food E: Best Western, Hardee's, Huddle House, Wendy's
W: Chuckwagon Restaurant (Super 8 Motel), Super 8
Lodg E: Best Western
W: Burget Inn, Duffy's Motel, Econolodge, Smith Motel, Super 8

131 **(317)** GA 225, Calhoun, Chatsworth
Lodg W: Express Inn
AServ W: Blackstock's Radiator/Alternator/Starter Repair
Parks E: New Echota Historic Site
Other E: Vann House/New Echota Historic Site

130 **(315)** GA 156, Redbud Road, Calhoun
Gas E: Citgo(*, D, LP), Exxon(*)
W: BP(*, LP, CW), Chevron(*, LP, CW), Shell(*), Texaco(LP)
Food E: TCBY (Exxon), Waffle House
W: Arby's, Harbin's (Howard Johnson), SHONEY'S Shoney's, Subway (BP)
Lodg E: Scottish Inns
W: Howard Johnson, Ramada Limited (see our ad this page)
AServ W: Texaco
RVCamp E: KOA-Calhoun (1.5 Miles)
ATM E: Citgo, Exxon
W: BP, Teller Yourself

129 **(312)** GA 53, Calhoun, Fairmont
Gas E: Amoco(*), Texaco(*, D)
W: BP(*), Chevron(*, D), Exxon(*, LP), Fina(*), Shell(*, CW)
Food E: BJ's (Budget Host), Savannah's (Quality Inn)
W: Arby's, Brangus Cattle Co., Checker's, Golden Corral Family Steakhouse, Hickory House, Huddle House, IHOP (Days Inn), KFC, Krystal, Long John Silver, McDonald's(PLAY), Pizza Hut, Subway (Fina), Taco Bell, Waffle House, Wendy's
Lodg E: Budget Host Inn, Quality Inn
W: Days Inn, Guest Inn, Hampton Inn, The Jameson Inn
AServ W: Mr. Service Chevrolet, Geo
ATM E: Texaco
W: Exxon
Other E: Prime Outlets at Calhoun (see our ad this page), Ga State Patrol
W: Winn Dixie Supermarket(RX)

(308) Rest Area (RR, HF, Phones, RV Dump; Eastbound)

128 **(305)** GA 140, Adairsville, Barnesley Garden
TStop E: Patty's Truckstop
W: Citgo Pit Stop(*, SCALES)
Gas E: Amoco(*, D, 24), Shell(*, LP) (Wrecker Service)
W: BP(*), Exxon(*)
Food W: Burger King(PLAY), Hardee's, Subway (BP), Taco Bell, Waffle House
Lodg E: TraveLodge
W: Comfort Inn, Ramada Limited
AServ E: Shell (Wrecker Service)
W: Bartow County Tires
TServ E: Cobra Truck Repair- Tires
W: Citgo Pit Stop(SCALES)
TWash W: Citgo Pit Stop
RVCamp W: Family Leisure Resort
ATM E: Shell (Wrecker Service)

EXIT		GEORGIA
127		**(296)** Cassville - White Road
	FStop	E: **Speedway**(*, LP)
	Gas	E: Amoco(*), Conoco(*)
		W: BP(*, D, LP), Chevron(*), Shell(*, D)
	Food	E: The Flaming Grill
		W: **JP's Villa Cognito (Howard Johnson Express Inn)**, Village Cafe (Budget Host Inn), Waffle House
	Lodg	W: Budget Host Inn, Econolodge, **Howard Johnson Express Inn**
	RVCamp	W: **KOA Campgrounds**
	ATM	W: BP
126		**(293)** U.S. 411, Chatsworth, White
	TStop	W: **Coastal**(*, D)
	FStop	E: **Exxon**(*, D, LP)
	Gas	E: Conoco(*, LP)
		W: Chevron(*)
	Food	W: First Pitch (Holiday Inn), **Truck Line Cafe (Coastal)**, Waffle House
	Lodg	E: **Courtesy Inn**, **Scottish Inns**
		W: Holiday Inn
	ATM	W: **Coastal**
125		**(290)** GA 20, Rome, Canton
	FStop	E: **Speedway**(*, LP)
	Gas	E: Chevron(*, D) (Subway)
		W: BP(*, LP), Texaco(*)
	Food	E: Arby's, **McDonald's**(PLAY), Morrell's BBQ, Subway (Chevron), Wendy's
		W: **Cracker Barrel**, Pruett's BBQ, SHONEY'S Shoney's, **Waffle House**
	Lodg	E: Comfort Inn, Econolodge, Motel 6, Ramada, **Super 8**
		W: Bartow Lodge, Days Inn, Hampton Inn
	RVCamp	W: **McKaskey Campground (2 Miles)**
124		**(287)** GA 113, Main St, Cartersville
	Gas	W: BP(*, D)
	Food	W: Blimpie Subs & Salads (BP)
123		**(285)** Red Top Mountain Road
	Gas	E: Conoco(*, LP)
	Parks	E: **Red Top Mtn State Park (2 Miles)**
122		**(283)** Emerson - Allatoona Road
	RVCamp	E: **Allatoona Landing Campground Beach Marina (2 Miles)**
121		**(278)** Glade Road, Acworth
	Gas	E: BP(*, D, CW), Exxon(*)
		W: Chevron(*, CW), Citgo(*)
	Food	E: Subway (BP)
		W: Baskin Robbins, Burger King(PLAY), Casa Mia Pizza & Italian, Dunkin Donuts, His & Her Southern Cookin, KFC, Krystal, Pizza Hut, Subway, Taco Bell, Waffle House
	Lodg	W: TraveLodge
	AServ	W: Auto Zone, NAPA Auto Parts
	ATM	W: Premier Bank
	Other	W: **CVS Pharmacy**, Coin Laundromat, **Ingles Supermarket**, **K-Mart**
120		**(276)** GA 92, Woodstock, Acworth
	FStop	W: **Fina**(*)
	Gas	E: Exxon(*, D), Shell(*, D), Texaco(*)
		W: Amoco(*, CW), BP(*, CW)
	Food	E: Hardee's, SHONEY'S Shoney's
		W: Bamboo Garden, Best Western, Dairy Queen (Fina FS), Domino's Pizza, Family Buffet Restaurant (Fina FS), McDonald's(PLAY), Ricardo's Mexican, Waffle House, Wendy's
	Lodg	E: Holiday Inn, Ramada
		W: Best Western, Days Inn, Hometown Lodge, Quality Inn, Super 8
	ATM	E: Shell
	Other	W: **CVS Pharmacy**, **Publix Supermarket**
118		**(272)** Wade Green Road, Kennesaw
	Gas	E: BP(*, CW), Chevron(*), Racetrac(*)
		W: Texaco(*, D)
	Food	E: Arby's, Del Taco, Mrs. Winters, Taco Bell, Waffle House
		W: Blimpie Subs & Salads (Texaco)
	Lodg	E: Rodeway Inn
	AServ	E: Chevron, Goodyear
		W: Q-Lube
	ATM	E: Premier Bank
	Other	E: **Eckerd Drugs**
117		**(270)** Chastain Road
	Gas	E: Chevron(*, CW)
		W: Amoco(*), Exxon(*), Texaco(*)
	Food	E: Cracker Barrel
		W: Arby's, Blimpie's Subs (Exxon), Del Taco, Mrs Winner's Chicken, Subway (Texaco), TCBY (Exxon), Waffle House, Wendy's
	Lodg	E: Best Western, Fairfield Inn, Studio PLUS
		W: Country Inn & Suites, Sun Suites
	Other	E: **Outlets Ltd. Mall**

Kennesaw, GA

Comfort Inn

770-419-1530

- Free Deluxe Continental Breakfast
- Coin Laundry
- Outdoor Pool
- Meeting/Banquet Facilities
- Handicap Accessible

1492

DAYS INN

770-419-1576

- Free Continental Breakfast
- Outdoor Pool
- Meeting/Banquet Facilities
- Handicap Accessible
- Coin Laundry

GEORGIA ▪ I-75 ▪ Exit 116

EXIT		GEORGIA
		W: Ga State Patrol
116		**(269)** Barrett Pkwy, Kennasaw
	Gas	E: Texaco(*, D)
		W: BP(*), Exxon(*, CW)
	Food	E: Applebee's, Baskin Robbins, Fuddruckers, Grady's American Grill, Happy China II, Honey Baked Ham, Ippolito's Italian, Manhattan Bagel, McDonald's(PLAY), Mellow Mushroom Pizza, My Friend's Place, Olive Garden, Red Lobster, Rio Bravo Cantina, Schlotzsky's Deli, SHONEY'S Shoney's, Smoothie King, Starbucks Coffee, Subway, Taco Mac, The Honey Baked Ham Co., Three Dollar Cafe, Waffle House
		W: Blimpie Subs & Salads (BP), Chick-Fil-A, Chili's, Cookers, Golden Corral Family Steakhouse, Outback Steakhouse, Romano's Macaroni Grill, Steak N' Shake, T.G.I. Friday's
	Lodg	E: Econolodge, Holiday Inn, Red Roof Inn, Shelley's Inn
		W: Comfort Inn (see our ad this page), Days Inn (see our ad this page), Hampton Inn
	AServ	E: Big 10 Tires, Firestone, Midas
	RVCamp	W: **KOA-Atlanta North (2 Miles)**
	Med	E: **Physicans Immediate Med**
	ATM	E: Colonial National Bank, NationsBank, SouthTrust Bank, Texaco
	Parks	W: **Kennesaw Mountain Battfield National Park**
	Other	E: Joshua's Book Store, Kinko's, TJ Maxx, **Town Center at Cobb**, Toys R Us
115		**(267)** Junction I-575, GA 5, Canton
114AB		**(268)** GA 5, U.S. 41, Marietta , Canton Rd. (Limited Access)
	Med	W: **Hospital (Take 114B)**
113		**(264)** North Marietta Pkwy
	Med	W: **Hospital**
	Other	E: **White Water/American Adventures Theme Parks**
112		**(262)** GA 120 Loop, Marietta, Roswell
	Gas	E: Chevron(*, 24), Texaco(*)
		W: Fina(*), QuikTrip(*, 24)
	Food	E: Shoney's
		W: All Star Sports Bar & Grill, Applebee's, Chili's, China Kitchen, Hardee's, International Grocery & Deli, Le Buzz Cafe, Longhorn Steakhouse, Pizza Chef, Subway, TJ Applebee's, Tasty China, The Edge
	Lodg	W: Hampton Inn, Ramada, Super 8, Wyndham Garden Hotel
	RVCamp	W: **La Siseta RV Camp**
	ATM	W: Summit National Bank
	Other	W: **International Grocery and Deli**, U-Haul Storage center
111		**(261)** GA 280, Delk Road, Lockheed, Dobbins AFB
	Gas	E: EZ Serve(*) (Subway), Exxon(*, CW), Texaco(*, D)
		W: Amoco(*, CW), BP(*, CW), Chevron(*, CW, 24)
	Food	E: China Wok, Denny's (Howard Johnson), Hardee's, KFC, McDonald's (Texaco), **McTavish's (Scottish Inns)**, Murphy's Deli, Papa John's Pizza, Spaghetti Warehouse, Taco Bell, Texas Bar-B-Q, Waffle House
		W: Cracker Barrel, Waffle House
	Lodg	E: Courtyard by Marriott, Drury Inn, Howard Johnson (see our ad opposite page), **Motel 6**, **Scottish Inns**, Sleep Inn (see our ad opposite page), Traveler's Inn
		W: Best Inns of America, Comfort Inn, Fairfield Inn, Holiday Inn, La Quinta Inn, Wingate Hotel
	AServ	E: Q-Lube
		W: Service Max
	RVCamp	W: **La Siesta RV Resort Park (1.25 Miles)**
	ATM	E: EZ Serve (Subway), NationsBank (Texaco),

Bold red print shows RV & Bus parking available or nearby

EXIT	GEORGIA
	Texaco
Other	**E:** Coin Laundry
	W: Big A Car Wash, Coin Laundry, Fast Trip Convenience Store, KaLors Bookstore
110	**(260)** Windy Hill Road, Smyrna
Gas	**E:** Amoco[*, CW], BP[*]
	W: Chevron[*, CW, 24], Texaco[*, D]
Food	**E:** Blimpie Subs & Salads (BP), Pappadeaux, Pappasito's Cantinia
	W: Arby's, Chick-Fil-A, McDonald's[PLAY], Popeye's Chicken, Three Dollar Cafe, Waffle House, Wendy's
Lodg	**E:** Econo Lodge, Extended Stay America, Home Gate Inn, Marriot Hotel, Park Inn International (see our ad this page)
	W: Best Western Bradbury Suites, Clarion Suites, Country Inns and Suites, Hilton, Master's Inn, Red Roof Inn
AServ	**W:** Chevron[24]
Med	**W:** ✚ Kennestone Hospital, ✚ Windy Hill Hospital
ATM	**W:** NationsBank, Texaco, Wachovia Bank
Other	**W:** Target
109B	I-285 West Birmingham
109A	**(261)** Junction I-285, I-275
108	**(259)** Mt. Paran Road, Northside Pkwy, to U.S. 41
107	**(258)** West Paces Ferry Road, Northside Pkwy
Gas	**E:** BP[*, D, CW], Chevron[*, CW]
	W: Amoco
Food	**E:** Caribou Coffee, Chick-Fil-A, China Moon Restaurant, Florida Fish Co, Freshen's Yogurt, Gorins Ice Cream, Houston's, McDonald's[PLAY], Mrs. Fields Bakery, OK Cafe, Pero's Italian & Pizza Buffet, Starbucks Coffee, Steak & Shake, Taco Bell
AServ	**E:** BP, Chevron
	W: Amoco[24], Amoco
Med	**E:** ✚ Colombia West Paces Medical Center
ATM	**E:** NationsBank, NationsBank, SouthTrust, Suntrust Bank, Wachovia Bank
Other	**E:** A & P Supermarket, CVS[RX], Carriage Cleaners and Laundry, Chapter 11 Discount Books, Kinko's Copies, Treehouse Animal Clinic, Winder and Roberts Drugs[RX], Wolf Camera and Video
106	**(257)** Moores Mill Road
Med	**E:** ✚ Columbia West Paces Medical Center
104	**(255)** Howell Mill Road
Gas	**E:** Texaco[*, LP]
	W: Exxon[*, D, CW]
Food	**E:** Chick-Fil-A, Emerald Isle Pub and Grill, Felini's Pizza, Golden Mt Chinese Restaurant, Hardee's, McDonald's
	W: Arby's, Chinese Buffet, Copper Kettle Restaurant, Einstein Bros Bagels, El Amigo, Green Derby Restaurant & Bar (Holiday Inn), KFC, Mellow Mushroom Pizza, Picadilly Cafeteria, Planet Smoothie, Popeye's Chicken, Sensational Subs, Subway, Taco Bell, Wendy's
Lodg	**E:** Budget Inn
	W: Holiday Inn, Howard Johnson
AServ	**E:** Goodyear Tire & Auto, Xpress Lube
	W: J & R Auto Service, Jiffy Lube, Master Care Auto Service, Precision Tune & Lube, Tune Up Clinic
ATM	**E:** SouthTrust, Texaco
	W: NationsBank
Other	**E:** Coin Laundry, Howell Mill Pharmacy, U.S. Post Office
	W: Kroger Supermarket[RX]
104A	**(255)** Northside Dr, US 41 (Northbound)

HOWARD JOHNSON® Marietta, GA 1619

— Cable TV with Remote —
— Indoor/Outdoor Swimming Pool —
— Extra Large Mini-Suites (40% have Jacuzzis) —
— Alarm Clock/Radio —
— Refrigerator/Microwave/Hairdryer —
— 24 Hour Denny's Restaurant —
— Lounge with Live Music —
— Free In-Room Movies —
— Coffee Shop on Premises —

770-951-1144

GEORGIA ▪ I-75 ▪ EXIT 111

Atlanta NW
770-952-9005
800-753-3746
1175 Powers Ferry Place
Marietta, GA 30067
1684

Deluxe Continental Breakfast
Indoor Pool • Hot Tub • Exercise Room
Handicap Accessible
Coin Laundry • Interior Corridors
Business Center with Free Internet Access

GEORGIA ▪ I-75 ▪ EXIT 111

770-952-3251

Outdoor Pool • Fitness Center
Restaurant • In Room Coffee Makers
25" Remote Control TV w/Free HBO
AARP, AAA, Special Tour & Group Rates
Kids Under 17 Stay Free
Convenient to Downtown Atlanta and Cobb Galeria Mall

1159 2767 Windy Hill • Marietta, GA 30067

GEORGIA ▪ I-75 ▪ EXIT 110

Downtown Atlanta
1545
RAMADA INN®
70 John Wesley Dobbs Ave. NE • Atlanta, GA

Restaurant/Lounge on Premises
Outdoor Pool • Handicap Accessible
Meeting/Banquet Facilities
Pets Allowed • Coin Laundry
Interior Corridors • Gift Shop
In Room Voice Mail • Cable w/HBO
Parking Free (Based on Availability)

404-659-2660• 888-593-6227

GEORGIA▪ I-75 ▪ EXIT 96

EXIT	GEORGIA
Gas	**W:** BP[*, CW] (Wrecker Service)
Food	**W:** Oga's Hickory BBQ, Richards, Waffle House
Lodg	**W:** Days Inn
AServ	**W:** BP (Wrecker Service)
Other	**W:** Buckwood Pet Hotel, E-Z Market[*], Northside Drive Pet Hospital
103	**(252)** Junction I-85 North, Greenville
102	**(251)** Fourteenth St, Tenth St, Techwood Dr (Southbound, Difficult Reaccess)
Gas	**E:** Amoco[*, 24], BP[*, D, CW]
Food	**E:** Central Subs and Gyros, Dunkin Donuts, Einstein Bros Bagels, Philly Connection, Tamarind Thai, Vini Vidi Vici Italian
	W: Blimpie's Subs, Chinese Buddha Restaurant, Kokopelli's Pizza, Silver Skillet Restaurant
Lodg	**E:** Best Western, Hampton Inn, Marriott
Other	**W:** CVS[RX], Office Depot, Wolf Camera & Video
101	**(251)** Fourteenth St, Tenth St, Georgia Institute of Technology (Northbound)
Gas	**E:** Chevron[*, 24]
Food	**E:** Checkers Burgers, Domino's Pizza
Lodg	**E:** Regency Suites Hotel, Residence Inn
ATM	**E:** Chevron
Other	**E:** US Post Office
100	**(250)** U.S. 78, U.S. 278, North Ave, Georgia Institute of Technology (Difficult Reaccess, Crawford Long Hospital)
Gas	**E:** BP[*, D, CW]
Food	**E:** KFC, Subway, The Varsity (An Atlanta landmark)
Lodg	**W:** Holiday Inn Express
Med	**E:** ✚ Crawford Long Hospital
ATM	**E:** BP, NationsBank
Other	**E:** Public Transportation (MARTA)
	W: The Coca Cola Company
99	**(250)** Williams St, World Congress Center, Georgia Dome (Southbound)
Lodg	**W:** Days Inn
98	**(250)** Pine St, Peachtree St, Civic Center (Northbound, Difficult Reaccess)
Food	**E:** Mick's, Pleasant Peasant
	W: All Star Cafe, Corner Bakery, Morton's STeak House
Lodg	**W:** Howard Johnson, Hyatt
ATM	**W:** Wachovia Bank
97	**(249)** Courtland St, Georgia State University (Southbound, Difficult Reaccess)
Food	**W:** Fishermann's Cove
Lodg	**E:** Imperial Hotel
	W: Hilton, Marriott, Radison Hotel, TraveLodge
96	**(249)** Ga. 10, International Blvd., Freedom Pwky., Carter Center
Lodg	**W:** Courtyard, Fairfield Inn, Radisson, Ramada Inn (see our ad this page)
AServ	**W:** Beaudry Ford
Med	**W:** ✚ Georgia Baptist Hospital
95	**(249)** Butler St, JW Dobbs (Southbound)
94	Edgewood Ave., Auburn Ave., J.W. Dobbs
Food	**E:** Church's Chicken
Med	**W:** ✚ Grady Memorial Hospital
Other	**W:** SWeet Auburn Police Station
93	**(248)** Martin Luther King Jr. Blvd,

Bold red print shows RV & Bus parking available or nearby

EXIT GEORGIA

State Capitol, Underground Atlanta ,Turner Field (Southbound, Reaccess Northbound Only)

Food **W:** McDonald's

92 **(248)** Junction I-20, Augusta, Birmingham

Other **E:** **Zoo Atlanta (see our ad this page -- East on I-20)**, **Cyclorama (see our ad this page -- East on I-20)**

91 **(247)** Fulton St. , Central Ave., Georgia Dome, New Atlanta Stadium (Reaccess Southbound Only, Zoo Atlanta)

90 **(247)** Abernathy Blvd., Capital Ave.

Gas **W:** Amoco

Food **E:** Bullpin Bar and Grill, KFC

Lodg **E:** Hampton Inn, Holiday Inn Express

Other **E:** Ryder

89 **(246)** University Ave, Pryor St

Gas **E:** Exxon[*, D]

Food **W:** Brook's Cafeteria

AServ **E:** Anderson's Alignment Service, GPC, NAPA Auto Parts

TServ **E:** **Cummins**

Parks **W:** **Atlanta City Park (Pittman Park)**

88 **(243)** GA 166, Langford Pkwy, East Point, Lakewood Frwy (To Fort McPherson)

87 **(243)** Junction I-85 S. Atlanta Airport, Montgomery (Southbound)

86 **(242)** Cleveland Ave

Gas **E:** Amoco[*], Chevron[*, 24]
W: Citgo[*, D], Shell[*]

Food **E:** Checkers Burgers, Church's Chicken, McDonald's
W: Happy Chinese Cafe, Krystal, Pizza Hut, Walter's Cafe, Yasin's Fish Supreme

Lodg **W:** DAYS INN Days Inn, New American Inn

AServ **E:** Discount Auto Parts

Med **W:** ✚ **Hospital**

Other **E:** **Coin Laundromat**, **K-Mart**, Lakewood Amphitheater, **Piggly Wiggly**
W: **D & J Coin Laundry**, Scoggins Car Wash

82 **(240)** U.S. 19, U.S. 41, Henry Ford II Ave, Aviation Blvd, Central Ave, Hapeville (Services on Central Ave. & Hapeville exit)

Gas **E:** Chevron[*, D]
W: Amoco[*, CW]

Food **E:** Checker's, Waffle House
W: Best Western, IHOP (Best Western), Krystal, McDonald's

Lodg **W:** Best Western

ATM **E:** NationsBank

Other **E:** **U.S. Post Office**
W: Coin Laundry

81AB **(239)** Junction I-285 East - Augusta, Greenville West - Atlanta Airport, Chatanooga

80 **(239)** GA 85 South, Riverdale (Southbound, Difficult Reaccess)

78 **(237)** GA 331, Forest Pkwy

FStop **W:** **BP**[*]

Gas **E:** Chevron[*, CW]

Food **E:** Thomas Market & Restaurant, Waffle House
W: **Waffle House**

Lodg **E:** Rodeway Inn
W: DAYS INN **Days Inn**, Ramada

EXIT GEORGIA

AServ **E:** Chevron
W: Lee Tire Company

TServ **E:** **Atlanta Freightliner**[24]
W: **Cummins South**

RVCamp **E:** **Holiday RV Superstore**[LP] **(see our ad this page -- 1.7 Miles)**

Other **E:** **JC Penney Outlet Store**, Stovell Marine, Tith Equipment Co, Inc. (Cummins)
W: **Georgia State Patrol Station**

77 **(236)** U.S. 19, U.S. 41, Old Dixie Hwy.

FStop **W:** **Fuel Mart**[*]

Gas **E:** Phillips 66[*, D]

Food **E:** Waffle House
W: Benefield's (Days Inn), Checker's, Chuck E Cheese's Pizza, DAYS INN Days Inn, El Meson, KFC, Rice Wok Restaurant, SHONEY'S Shoney's, **Waffle House**, Waffle House

Lodg **E:** Super 8, TraveLodge
W: Comfort Inn (see our ad this page), DAYS INN Days Inn (see our ad this page), EconoLodge, Holiday Inn, SHONEY'S Shoney's

RVCamp **E:** **Sagon Motor Homes (see our ad this page)**

AServ **W:** Landmark Dodge

Med **W:** ✚ **Hospital**

ATM **W:** **Fuel Mart**

Other **W:** Arrowhead Coin Laundry, Coin Laundry, **Cub Foods**, **Old Time Pottery**

1242
1-800-RV-FOR-FUN
Atlanta, GA • I-75 • Exit 78E

CYCLORAMA
Civil War Museum
History happens here!
Located at Grant Park, The Atlanta Cyclorama has long been an historical landmark in The South. Come experience The Battle of Atlanta, enjoy the two story museum and see a real steam engine – The Texas.
Next to Zoo Atlanta
404-624-1071
GRANT PARK
800 Cherokee Ave., SE

The "Texas," one of the steam locomotives used in the Great Locomotive Chase through North Georgia in April, 1862
GEORGIA • I-75 • EXIT 92

GEORGIA • I-75 • EXIT 91

FULL SERVICE & PARTS SHOP
1048

8859 Tara Blvd.
Jonesboro, GA
30236
770-477-2010
Hours:
Mon- Sat
9am-6pm
Holiday Rambler • Monaco • Damon
Specialize in Pre-Owned Gas & Diesel Coaches
1-800-433-6626
See our website: www.SAGONMOTORHOMES.COM
GEORGIA • I-75 • EXIT 77

1491

FREE Hot Breakfast
52 TV Channels
6 Miles South of Airport
Near Southlake Mall
770-968-4700 • Jonesboro, GA
GEORGIA • I-75 • EXIT 77

Comfort Inn
Exit 77 • Jonesboro, GA
770-961-6336
• Free Deluxe Continental Breakfast
• Cable TV with Free HBO
• Free Local Calls
• 6 Miles From Airport
• Brand New Rooms
• Outdoor Pool
1499
GEORGIA • I-75 • EXIT 77

100% Satisfaction Guaranteed
1233

Southlake~Atlanta
6597 Jonesboro Road
Morrow, GA
770-960-1957
Free Deluxe Continental Breakfast, Local Calls, HBO, Showtime & 50 Channels, Walking Distance to Southlake Mall 21 Restaurants & Great Shopping • Easy Access From I-75 Heated Pool • Jacuzzi • In-Room Movie AAA & AARP Discount
GEORGIA • I-75 • Exit 76

Bold red print shows RV & Bus parking available or nearby

EXIT		GEORGIA

76 **(233)** GA 54, Morrow, Lake City

- **Gas** **E:** BP(*, CW), Chevron(*), Hess(*, D)
  W: Exxon(*, CW), Texaco(*, CW)
- **Food** **E:** Bob Evan's Restaurant, Cracker Barrel, Krystal, Tilgreen's, **Waffle House**
  W: KFC, Long John Silver, McDonald's, Pizza Hut, SHONEY'S, Shoney's, Waffle House
- **Lodg** **E:** Best Western, Drury Inn, Fairfield Inn, Red Roof Inn
  W: Quality Inn (see our ad oppositepage)
- **AServ** **E:** Chevron
  W: Willett
- **Med** **E:** ✚ **Primary Medical Care (Minor Emergency Walk-In)**
- **ATM** **E:** First Union Bank
- **Other** **W:** Jonesboro Historic District, **Southlake Mall**, **Toys R Us**

75A **(231)** Mount Zion Blvd

- **Gas** **W:** Exxon(*, CW)
- **Food** **W:** Arby's, Blimpie Subs & Salads, Chili's, Del Taco, Joe's Crab Shack, LongHorn Steakhouse, Los Toribis, McDonald's(PLAY), Mrs Winner's Chicken, Papa John's Pizza, Philly Connection, Rio Bravo, Steak N' Shake, TCBY, The Atlanta Bread Co., Truett's Grill, Waffle House, Wendy's
- **Lodg** **W:** Country Inn & Suites, Extended Stay America, Sleep Inn, Sun Suites
- **AServ** **E:** Auto Nation USA
  W: NTB, Xpress Lube
- **ATM** **W:** Phoenix Federal Credit Union, **Publix Supermarket**(RX)
- **Other** **W:** **AMC 24 Theaters**, **Barnes & Noble**, **Home Depot**, Performing Arts Center, **Petsmart**, **Publix Supermarket**(RX), **Target**

75 **(228)** GA 138, Jonesboro, Stockbridge

- **Gas** **E:** Racetrac(*)
  W: Amoco(*), Chevron(*, 24), Citgo(*)
- **Food** **E:** Baskin Robbins, Best Western, Chick-Fil-A, Cici's Pizza, Damon's Ribs, Emperor's Gourmet Chinese, Folks, Frontera Mexican, Gregory's Bar & Grill, Hickory Hams Cafe, Kenny Roger's Roasters, Krystal, Los Toribis Mexican, Marson's Fresh Cookin', Pasta Matt's (Best Western), Philly Connection, Subway, Waffle House
  W: Waffle House
- **Lodg** **E:** Best Western, DAYS INN **Days Inn (see our ad this page)**
- **AServ** **E:** X-Press Lube
  W: Citgo
- **ATM** **E:** **Kroger Supermarket**, SouthTrust Bank
- **Other** **E:** **Kroger Supermarket**, **Lowe's**, Wolf Camera

74 **(227)** I-675 to east I-285 (Northbound)

73 **(224)** Hudson Bridge Road, Eagle's Landing Pkwy

- **Gas** **E:** BP(*), Texaco(*, CW)
  W: Phillips 66(*, LP)
- **Food** **E:** Baskin Robbins, Dairy Queen, Dunkin Donuts, McDonald's(PLAY), Subway, Waffle House, Wendy's
  W: China Cafe Three, Fifteenth Street Pizza & Calzones, Memories Restaurant
- **Lodg** **E:** AmeriHost Inn
  W: **Super 8 (see our ad this page)**
- **Med** **E:** ✚ **Henry General Hospital**
- **ATM** **E:** BP, First Newton Bank
- **Other** **E:** **CVS**(RX), **Hudson Bridge Pharmacy**(RX)

72 **(222)** Jodeco Road, Flippen

- **Gas** **E:** Amoco(*), Citgo(*, LP, K)
  W: BP(*, LP), Chevron(*, D, LP)
- **Food** **E:** Amoco, Chester's Fried Chicken (Amoco), Hardee's, Waffle House
  W: Cherdan's Seafood Co.
- **RVCamp** **W:** **KOA Campgrounds**
- **Med** **E:** ✚ **Hospital**
- **ATM** **E:** Citgo
  W: Chevron
- **Other** **W:** Shorty's Clean-up Shop

71 **(221)** Jonesboro Road, Lovejoy

- **FStop** **E:** **Mapco Express**(*, LP)
- **ATM** **E:** **Mapco Express**

70 **(219)** GA 20, GA 81, McDonough, Hampton

- **FStop** **W:** **Speedway**(*, LP)
- **Gas** **E:** Amoco(*), BP(*)
  W: Shell(*)
- **Food** **E:** Arby's, Burger King(PLAY), Dairy Queen, KFC, McDonald's, Mrs Winner's Chicken, Pizza Hut, Sizzling Platter Family Steakhouse, Taco Bell, Waffle House, Wendy's
  W: **Dusters**, **Speedway**, **Starvin' Marvin (Speedway)**
- **Lodg** **E:** Budget Inn, Hampton Inn, **Red Carpet Inn**
  W: Comfort Inn, **EconoLodge (see our ad this page)**, Masters Inn
- **AServ** **W:** Shell
- **ATM** **E:** BP

69 **(216)** GA 155, McDonough

- **TStop** **E:** **LJL Truck Center**
- **FStop** **E:** **Texaco**(*, CW)
  W: **Citgo**(*)
- **Gas** **E:** Chevron(*, D)
  W: Amoco, BP(*, CW)
- **Food** **E:** Chevron, McGhin's Southern Pit Barbecue, Subway (Chevron), Waffle House
  W: BP, BP, Holiday Inn, SHONEY'S, Shoney's, Smash Hit Subs (BP), **Waffle House**
- **Lodg** **E:** DAYS INN Days Inn, Sunny Inn, Welcome Inn
  W: Holiday Inn
- **AServ** **E:** Bellamy-Strickland Oldsmobile, Chevrolet, Gmc Trucks, Goodyear, Legacy Ford
  W: Amoco
- **TServ** **E:** **Perimeter Transport Refrigeration & Truck Repair**, **Select Trucks Freight Liner**
  W: **Citgo**
- **RVCamp** **E:** **Joe Geffery RV Sales & Service**
- **ATM** **E:** Chevron

68 **(212)** Locust Grove, Hampton

- **Gas** **E:** Amoco(*, CW), BP(*, D), Chevron(*), Exxon(*, D, CW), Shell(*)
  W: Chevron(*, LP)
- **Food** **E:** BP, Burger King(PLAY) (Chevron), Chevron, Daddy Wayne's Restaurant (No name motel), **Huddle House**, No Name, **Red Carpet Inn**, Subway (BP), **Waffle House**, **Wendy's**
  W: Anne Family Restaurant (Scottish Inns), Our Family House Restaurant (Super 8 Motel), **Scottish Inns**, **Super 8**

1089
Special Group Tour Rates

1279 Hampton Rd • McDonough, GA
770-957-2651
- Non-Smoking Rooms • Free Ice
- Free Remote TV, Cable, HBO
- Children Under 18 Stay Free
- Microwave & Refrigerator (Some Rooms)
- Free Coffee & Donuts (6-9AM)
- Senior Rooms AARP Discount

AAA
GEORGIA • I-75 • EXIT 70

Super 8 Motel
1451 Hudson Bridge Rd.
Stockbridge, GA 30281
770-474-5758
770-474-1297 (Fax)
NEWLY RENOVATED
Outdoor Heated Pool
Super Start Breakfast
Kids Under 12 Stay Free
Remote Control Cable TV
w/HBO/ESPN/CNN

Restaurant Nearby
Coin Laundry
All Queen Beds
In Room Microwave, Refrigerator,
Hairdryer, Clock Radio
Coffee in All Rooms
Golf Nearby
Group Rates
Suites w/VCR, Free Movies
$38.88 +tax 1-2 Persons
1726
GEORGIA • I-75 • EXIT 73

1598

& Suites
7385 Hannover Parkway N.
Stockbridge, GA 30281
Multi-Item Continental Breakfast
Outdoor Pool
Meeting Facility
Handicap Accessible
Exercise Room
Truck/Large Vehicle Parking
Exterior Corridors
In-Room Movies Available
All Rooms have a Microwave,
Refrigerator, & Hair Dryer
Walk to Many Restaurants
www.Javanihotel.com
770-507-4440
GEORGIA • I-75 • EXIT 75

EXIT GEORGIA

Lodg E: No Name, **Red Carpet Inn**
W: **Scottish Inns, Super 8**
ATM E: Chevron
Other E: **Tanger Factory Outlet**

67 **(205)** GA 16, Griffin, Jackson
FStop E: **Citgo**[*]
Gas E: BP[*]
W: Amoco[*], Chevron[*, D, 24] (Hand Dipped Ice Cream), Texaco[*, D]
Food E: Simmon's BBQ
AServ W: Amoco
RVCamp W: **I-75 RV & Mobile Home Park (.25 Miles)**
ATM E: BP
W: Texaco
Parks E: **Indian Springs State Park**
Other E: **Lee Wrangler Outlet (Citgo)**

66 **(201)** GA 36, Jackson, Barnesville
TStop E: **T/A TravelCenters of America**[SCALES]
W: **Flying J Travel Plaza**[*, LP, SCALES] **(Conoco Gas)**
FStop E: **Fuel City**[*] **(SMilesGas)**
W: **BP**[*]
Gas W: Citgo[*]
Food E: **Fuel City (SMilesGas)**, **Hot Stuff Pizza (TA Travel Center)**, Smiley's Grill (Fuel City), Subway (TA TS), **T/A TravelCenters of America**, Taco Bell (TA TS)
W: **Flying J Travel Plaza (Conoco Gas)**, **Hardee's (Flying J Travel Plaza)**
TServ E: **T/A TravelCenters of America**[SCALES]
TWash E: **T/A TravelCenters of America**
W: **Eagle One Truck Wash, Flying J Travel Plaza (Conoco Gas)**
ATM W: **BP**

65 **(198)** High Falls Road
RVCamp W: **High Falls Campground**[LP] **(.2 Miles)**
Parks E: **High Falls State Park (1.8 Miles)**

64 **(193)** Johnstonville Road
Gas E: Amoco[*], BP[*]
AServ E: BP

(190) **Weigh Station (Southbound)**

(190) **Weigh Station (Northbound)**

63 **(187)** GA 42, Forsyth (Northbound)
Gas E: Shell[*, 24]
Food E: Four Fronts Steakhouse (Super 8 Motel), **Super 8**
W: Iron Skillet
Lodg E: Best Western, **Super 8**, **Valu Inn**
AServ W: Steven's Garage Truck Auto Repair
Other E: **Indian Spring State Park (15 Miles)**
W: Antique Mall

62 **(187)** GA 83, Forsyth, Monticello
Gas W: Amoco[*, LP], Citgo[*, D], Conoco[*, D, LP], Exxon[*, CW], Texaco[*]
Food E: EconoLodge, Tejado Mexican (EconoLodge)
W: Burger King, Captain D's Seafood, China Inn, Hardee's, McDonald's, Pizza Hut, Subway, Taco Bell, Waffle House, Wendy's
Lodg E: EconoLodge, New Forsyth Inn, **Passport Inn**
W: DAYS INN Days Inn, **Tradewinds Motel**
AServ W: Citgo, Exxon
RVCamp E: **KOA Campgrounds**
Med W: ✚ **Hospital**
ATM W: Exxon
Other W: **CVS**[RX], **Coin Laundry**, **Piggly Wiggly Supermarket**, **Visitor Information**, **Wal-Mart**[RX]

61 **(186)** Juliette Road, Tift College Dr
Gas W: BP[*], Chevron[*], Shell[*]
Food W: Dairy Queen, Holiday Inn, Hong Kong Palace Chinese, **Lelands Restaurant (Holiday Inn)**, Waffle House
Lodg W: Ambassador Inn, **Hampton Inn**, Holiday Inn
AServ W: BP, Ford Parts & Service, Shell
RVCamp E: **KOA Campgrounds (.5 Miles)**

EXIT GEORGIA

EXIT GEORGIA

Other E: **Jarrell Plantation Historic Site**, Piedmont Wildlife Refuge
W: **Ingle's Supermarket**, Visitor Information

60 **(184)** GA 18, Forsyth
Gas W: Amoco[*, 24], Texaco[*, D]
Food W: SHONEY'S, Shoney's
Lodg W: Comfort Inn
AServ W: Forsyth Ford
ATM W: Amoco
Other E: **Jarrell Plantation Historical Site (18 Miles)**
W: **Forsyth Antique Mall**, **Georgia State Patrol**

59 **(180)** Rumble Road, Smarr
Gas E: BP[*, D, LP], Shell[*]
Food E: BP, Subway (BP)
Other E: Chrome Components

(179) **Rest Area (RR, Phones, Picnic, Vending, RV Dump; Southbound)**

58 **(178)** Junction I-475, Valdosta (Southbound)

57 **(175)** Pate Rd, Bowling Broke (Northbound, No Reaccess)

56 **(172)** Bass Rd
Other E: **Starcadia Entertainment Park**
W: **Macon Museum of Arts & Sciences**

55 **(171)** U.S.23, GA. 87, Riverside Dr

55A **(169)** to U.S. 23, Arkwright Rd, Riverside Dr
Gas E: Shell[*]
W: Chevron[*]
Food E: Carrabba's Italian Grill, Logan's Roadhouse Steaks & Ribs, Outback Steakhouse, Waffle House, Wager's
W: Applebee's, Arby's, Burger King, Chick-Fil-A[PLAY], Chin's Wok, Cracker Barrel, Dunkin Donuts, Fresh Air BBQ, Holiday Inn, Hooters, KFC, LongHorn Steakhouse, McDonald's[PLAY], Papa John's, Papouli's Gyros, Rio Bravo, SHONEY'S, Shoney's, Steak & Ale, Steak 'N Shake, TCBY, Taco Bell, Uncle Chan's Thai Cuisine, Waffle House, Whatta Pizza
Lodg E: Courtyard by Marriott, La Quinta Inn, Red Roof Inn, Residence Inn, Sleep Inn, Super 8
W: Hampton Inn, Holiday Inn, Macon Studio Plus, Wingate Inn
AServ E: Huckabee Buick Cadillac, Mr. Goodwrench Quick Lube, Saturn of Macon
W: Butler Lexus, Fivestar Hyundai, Dodge, Chrysler Plymouth, Jeep, Sutton Acura
Med W: ✚ **Hospital**
ATM W: First Colony Bank, **Kroger Supermarket**[24, RX], **Publix Supermarket**[RX], Wachovia Bank
Other W: Baptist Bookstore, **Barnes & Noble**, **K-Mart**[RX], **Kroger Supermarket**[RX], **Publix**

Bold red print shows RV & Bus parking available or nearby

EXIT GEORGIA

Supermarket[RX], Regal Cinemas

54 **(167)** GA 247, Pierce Ave

Gas W: Amoco[*, LP], Amoco[*], BP[*, D, CW], Chevron[*, 24], Exxon[*], Fina[*, D, LP], Texaco[*]

Food W: Amoco, Applebee's, Bennigan's, Best Western, Blimpie Subs & Salads (Amoco), Captain D's Seafood, Denny's, El Indio, Fina, Macon Music City Restaurant, Mikata Sushi Bar, Oriental Express Wok, Pier 97, Pizza Hut, S&S Cafeteria, Sports Spot Grill & Bar, Steak-Out, Subway (Fina), Texas Cattle Co, Waffle House, Wendy's, White Columns Restaurant (Best Western)

Lodg E: Days Inn
W: Ambassador Inn, Best Western, Comfort Inn, Holiday Inn Express, Howard Johnson (see our ad opposite page)

AServ W: Exxon, Jackson Oldsmobile, Pontiac, GM, Macon Expert Tire, Mercedes Benz, Volvo, Mike Houston's Auto Care

Med W: Hospital

ATM W: Chevron, First Liberty Bank, NationsBank, Security National Bank, Sun Trust Bank

Other W: Eckerd Drugs[RX], National Pride Car Wash

53 **(165)** Jct I-16, Savannah, to U.S. 29, Gray

52 U.S.41, GA19, Hardeman Ave, Forsyth St, Downtown

Gas E: Fina[*]
W: Amoco[CW]

Food E: Church's Chicken, Sid's Soup, Salad, Sandwich

AServ W: Amoco

Med E: Hospital

ATM E: SunTrust

Other E: Animals & Things Animal Hospital[24], BoNo's Car Wash, Tourist Info., U.S. Post Office
W: Fountain Car Wash (Amoco), Macon Museum of Arts & Sciences

51 **(163)** GA. 74 W., Mercer Univ. Dr

Gas W: Citgo[*], Fina[*, D]

AServ W: Metric Motors

Other W: Animal Emergency Care, Tobesofkee Recreation Area

50 **(162)** U.S. 80, GA22, Eisenhower Pkwy

Gas W: Amoco[*], Chevron[*, CW], Shell[*], Speedway[*, LP]

Food W: Captain D's Seafood, K-Mart[RX], Little Caesars Pizza (K-Mart), McDonald's[PLAY], SHONEY'S Shoney's, TCBY, Taco Bell

AServ W: Auto House Mercedes Benz Service & Sales, Goodyear Tire & Auto, Meineke Discount Mufflers, Pep Boys Auto Center

Other W: Food Max, K-Mart[RX]

49 **(160)** U.S.41, GA 247, Pio Nono Ave

1127

Newly Renovated

$32.50*

1-4 Persons

*Show ad at check-in. Based on Availability. Not Valid during special events or holidays Sunday - Thursday

Color TV with Free HBO
Fax & Copy Services
A/C • Phones • Pool • Laundromat
King & Queen Beds • Truck Parking
Free Coffee & Donuts in AM

912-956-5100
800-325-2525

GEORGIA • I-75 • EXIT 46

EXIT GEORGIA

Gas E: Exxon[*, D, LP], Racetrac[*]

Food E: Huddle House, Waffle House (Masters Inn)
W: China Star, Dab's Cafe, Johnny V's, KFC, McDonald's[PLAY], Pizza Hut, Quick Cash Cafe, Regular Meals Home Cooked, Subway, Waffle House

Lodg E: Masters Inn

AServ E: Discount Auto Parts, Five Star New & Used Cars
W: Raffield Tire Master

ATM E: Racetrac
W: First Macon Bank & Trust, Food Max[24], Security National Bank

Other W: Eckerd Drugs[RX], Food Max, National Pride Car Wash

Note: I-75 runs concurrent below with I-475. Numbering follows I-475.

4 **(15)** Bolingbroke, U.S. 41

Gas E: Exxon[*, D, LP], Fina[*, D]

Food E: Sweet Sue's Tea Room

3 **(10)** Zebulon Road, Wesleyan College, Macon

Gas E: BP[*, CW]
W: Citgo[*, LP] (U-Haul Distributors), Exxon

Food E: BP, Buffalo's Cafe, Chick-Fil-A (Kroger), Chin's Wok (BP), Fox's Pizza Den, Hong Kong Restaurant, Kroger Supermarket, Rick Tanner's Rotisserie Grill, Subway, Waffle House, Wendy's
W: Polly's Corner Cafe

Lodg E: Fairfield Inn, Jameson Inn

AServ W: Exxon

Med E: Hospital

ATM E: Kroger Supermarket, Rivoli Bank & Trust, Sun Trust Bank

Other E: Kroger Supermarket

(8) Rest Area (RR, Phones, Picnic, Vending; Northbound)

2 **(5)** GA 74, Macon, Thomaston, Mercer University Dr

Gas W: Phillips 66[*, D, K], Shell[*]

Food E: Waffle House
W: Church's Chicken (Phillips 66), Family Inns of America, Fazoli's Italian Food, Phillips 66

Lodg W: Family Inns of America

AServ E: Car-Tech, Yancey Tire Co.

TServ E: Goodyear Brad Reagan Inc.

Other E: McKinney's[LP], Olympia Family Fun Center

1 **(3)** U.S. 80, Macon, Roberta

FStop E: Fina[*, LP]

Gas E: Citgo, Racetrac[*]
W: Amoco, BP[*, D], Shell[*]

Food E: Citgo, Cracker Barrel, JL's Famous Pit BBQ, Racetrac, SHONEY'S Shoney's, Subway

Over 85 Historic Aircraft & Home of Georgia Aviation Hall of Fame

1183

MUSEUM OF AVIATION

Marvel at the world's fastest aircraft the SR-71 Blackbird! Indoor and outdoor exhibits on 43 acres span a century of flight. See the story of the Flying Tigers, Hump Pilots, Tuskegee Airmen and the saga of WWII B-17's in Europe. Exciting hourly Smithsonian large-screen movies. Gift shop and Victory Cafe. RV parking and picnic grounds. Open daily from 9-5.

Just 7 miles east in Warner Robins • 912-926-6870 • FREE ADMISSION

GEORGIA • I-75 • EXIT 45

EXIT GEORGIA

(Citgo), Waffle House
W: Blimpie Subs & Salads (Shell), Burger King, El Zarape Mexican Restaurant, McDonald's, Shell

Lodg E: Best Western, Comfort Inn, Days Inn, Discovery Inn, Hampton Inn, HoJo Inn, Holiday Inn, Motel 6, Quality Inn, Ramada Inn, Rodeway Inn, Super 8, TraveLodge
W: EconoLodge, Knight's Inn, Passport Inn

AServ W: Amoco, BP

ATM E: Citgo
W: Shell

Note: I-75 runs concurrent above with I-475. Numbering follows I-475.

48 **(156)** Junction I-475 N, Atlanta (Left Exit Northbound)

47 **(155)** Hartley Bridge Road

Gas E: Fina[*, D, LP], Phillips 66[*, D], Shell[*]
W: Citgo[*, LP], Exxon[*]

Food E: Golden Wok, Kroger Supermarket[24], Players Grill, Popeye's Chicken (Kroger), Wendy's
W: Subway, Waffle House

Lodg W: Motel

AServ W: Auto Masters

ATM E: Kroger Supermarket, Phillips 66
W: Citgo

Other E: Kroger Supermarket

46 **(149)** GA 49, Byron, Fort Valley

FStop W: Citgo[*], Fina[*], Speedway[*, LP]

Gas E: Shell[*], Texaco[*]
W: BP[*], Racetrac[*]

Food E: Burger King[PLAY], Hickory Smoked BBQ, McDonald's, Pizza Hut, SHONEY'S Shoney's, Waffle House
W: Blimpie Subs & Salads (Citgo), Citgo, Country Cupboard (Passport Inn), Dairy Queen, Fina, Huddle House, Icecream Churn (Citgo), Passport Inn, Popeye's Chicken, Subway, Waffle House

Lodg E: Best Western, Super 8
W: Comfort Inn, Days Inn (see our ad this page), Econolodge, Passport Inn

AServ W: BP, Brannen Ford, Butler Chevrolet, Oldsmobile

TServ E: Davis Atlantic Truck Sales & Service
W: Fina

RVCamp E: Mid State RV Center[LP] (.5 Miles)
W: Interstate Camping[LP] (.35 Miles)

ATM W: Racetrac

Other E: Antique Mall, Peach Festival Outlet Center

45 **(146)** GA 247, Centerville, Warner Robins

FStop W: Citgo[*]

Gas E: Exxon[*], Shell[*, LP], Speedway[*]

Food E: Subway (Villager Lodge), Villager Lodge, Waffle House
W: Red Carpet Inn, Wally's Weiner World

Lodg E: Villager Lodge
W: Red Carpet Inn

AServ E: Exxon

RVCamp E: RV Sales & Service
W: Robins Travel Park

Med E: Hospital

Other E: Museum of Aviation (see our ad this page)

44 **(142)** GA 96, Housers Mill Road

Gas E: Shell[*]

AServ E: Shell

RVCamp E: Perry Ponderosa Park[LP] (.1 Miles)

Other E: Museum of Aviation

43A **(138)** Thompson Road, Perry - Fort Valley Airport

FStop E: Happy Stores[*, LP, RV DUMP] (Phillips 66)

EXIT		GEORGIA
	Food	E: Chester's Fried Chicken (Happy Stores), Happy Stores (Phillips 66)
	ATM	E: Happy Stores (Phillips 66)
43		(137) U.S. 341, Perry, Fort Valley
	FStop	E: Speedway(*)
	Gas	E: Amoco(*, CW), Shell(*, D) W: BP(*), Chevron(*, D, CW), Conoco(*, D, LP), Racetrac(*)
	Food	E: Arby's, Baskin Robbins (Shell), Burger King(PLAY), Captain D's Seafood, Chick-Fil-A, China Moon Restaurant, Hardee's, KFC, Krystal, McDonald's, My Sister's Cafe, Pearson Farms, Pizza Hut, Quincy's Family Steakhouse, Red Lobster, Shell, SHONEY'S Shoney's, Subway, TCBY, Taco Bell, Waffle House, Wendy's W: Angelina's Italian Cafe (Quality Inn), Green Derby Restaurant & Bar (Holiday Inn), Holiday Inn, Quality Inn
	Lodg	E: Fairfield Inn, Hampton Inn, Jameson Inn, Ramada Inn, Red Gable Inn, Super 8 W: Comfort Inn, DAYS INN Days Inn, Econolodge, Holiday Inn, Knight's Inn, Passport Inn, Quality Inn
	RVCamp	E: Boland's Perry Overnite Park(LP) (.35 Miles) W: Crossroads Travel Park (.1 Miles)
	Med	E: Hospital
	ATM	W: Chevron, Racetrac
	Other	E: Antiques, K-Mart(RX), Kroger Supermarket W: Sports Center Parts & Service
42		(134) U.S. 41, GA 127, Perry, Marshallville, GA 224, Welocme Center
	Gas	E: Exxon(*), Speedway(*, LP), Texaco(*)
	Food	E: Cracker Barrel, Scottish Inns, Waffle House
	Lodg	E: Best Western, Crossroads Motel, Red Carpet Inn, Rodeway Inn, Scottish Inns, TraveLodge
	AServ	E: Hamby Chrysler Plymouth, Jeep Eagle
	ATM	E: Exxon
	Other	E: Georgia National Fairgrounds, Tourist Info. W: Georgia State Patrol
41		(127) GA 26, Montezuma, Hawkinsville
	FStop	W: Chevron(*)
	Food	W: Icecream Churn (Chevron)
	RVCamp	E: Twin Oaks RV Camp (.2 Miles)
40		(122) GA 230, Unadilla, Byromville
	FStop	E: Dixie(*)
	Gas	E: Fina(*, D) W: Phillips 66(*)
	Food	W: BBQ (Phillips 66), Phillips 66
	AServ	E: Brannen Motors Chevrolet, Geo Ford, Fina
39		(121) U.S. 41, Unadilla
	TStop	W: All State Truck Stop(LP) (Citgo gas)
	Gas	E: BP(*), Shell(*), Texaco(*)
	Food	E: Cotton Patch Restaurant (Scottish Inns), Dairy Queen (Texaco), Scottish Inns, Subway, Texaco W: All State Truck Stop (Citgo gas)
	Lodg	E: Economy Inn, Scottish Inns W: Passport Inn
	TServ	E: Bally Berkeley Pumps & CAT W: All State Truck Stop (Citgo gas)
	ATM	W: All State Truck Stop (Citgo gas)
(118)		Rest Area (RR, Phones, Picnic, Vending, RV Dump; Southbound)
38		(117) Pinehurst
	FStop	W: BP(*)
	Food	W: New Colony Inn
	Lodg	W: New Colony Inn
37		(112) GA 27, Vienna, Hawkinsville
	Gas	E: Shell W: Fina(*)
	AServ	E: Shell
36		(109) GA 215, Vienna, Pitts

EXIT		GEORGIA
	Gas	E: BP (Fruit Stand) W: Amoco(*), Chevron(*), Citgo(*, D)
	Food	W: Bryant's BBQ, Huddle House, Knight's Inn, Popeye's Chicken
	Lodg	W: Knight's Inn
	AServ	W: Little Flint Auto Mart
	Med	E: Hospital W: Dooly Medical Center
	Other	W: Antique Mall
(108)		Rest Area (RR, Phones, Picnic, Vending, RV Dump; Northbound)
35		(104) Farmers Market Road
	FStop	W: Phillips 66(*, LP, CW)
	Lodg	E: Super 8
	TServ	W: Hess Garage
	RVCamp	W: Hess Garage
34		(102) GA 257, Hawkinsville, Cordele
	Gas	E: Shell(*) W: Cordele Pecan House
	Med	W: Hospital
33		(101) U.S. 280, GA 90, Cordele, Abbeville, GA 30,
	FStop	E: Mapco Express(*, LP) (see our ad this page)
	Gas	E: Citgo(*), Exxon(*, D), Texaco(*) W: Amoco(*, CW), BP(D), Chevron(CW), Racetrac(*)
	Food	E: Baskin Robbins (Madco), Denny's, Mapco Express, Perkin's Family Restaurant (Madco), Ramada, Waffle House W: Captain D's Seafood, Hardee's, KFC, Krystal(24), McDonald's(PLAY), Pizza Hut, SHONEY'S Shoney's, TCBY, Taco Bell, Wendy's
	Lodg	E: DAYS INN Days Inn (see our ad this page), Ramada W: Athens Motel, Best Western Colonial Inn, Comfort Inn, Economy Inn, Hampton Inn, Holiday Inn, Passport Inn, Rodeway Inn

1401
MAPCO Express
Open 24 Hours
Perkins Family Restaurant
We make it special for you
31 Baskin Robbins. Where Wonders Never Cease.
912-271-5775
Gasoline & High Speed Diesel Pumps
Full Service Restaurant
Truck Accessories • Private Showers
Laundry Facilities • ATM Machines
D.A.T. Load Boards • Sandwich Shop
Certified Scales • Copy & Fax Services
GEORGIA • I-75 • EXIT 33

800-248-1123
912-273-1125
DAYS INN
215 7th Street S
Cordele, GA
Outdoor Pool
Golf Packages
Free Coffee
Cable w/HBO
Free Local Calls & Parking
Restaurant next Door
Near Andersonville Historic Site
Truck/Large Vehicle Parking
GEORGIA • I-75 • EXIT 33

EXIT		GEORGIA
	AServ	E: Sun Belt Mercury, Lincoln, & Ford, Texaco W: BP, Chevron
	ATM	E: Madco Express W: Cordele Banking Company, Racetrac
	Parks	W: Jimmy Carter National Historic Site, Veteran Memorial State Park
	Other	E: Georgia State Patrol W: Ellis, Tourist Info.
32		(99) GA 300, GA - Florida Pkwy,
31		(97) GA 33, Wenona
	TStop	W: AmBest Truck Stop(*, SCALES, 24) (BP)
	Food	W: AmBest Truck Stop (BP), Great American Buffet (Am Best), Hardee's (Am Best), Pizza Hut (Am Best), TCBY (Am Best)
	Lodg	E: Quality Motel
	TServ	W: AmBest Truck Stop(SCALES, 24) (BP)
	RVCamp	E: America's Camping Center RV Sales, Service, & Parts (RV Wash), Cordele RV Park (.5 Miles), RV World W: KOA Campgrounds(LP)
	Other	E: Old House Antiques
30		(92) Arabi
	FStop	W: BP(*)
	Gas	E: Chevron(*), Phillips 66(*)
	Food	E: Budget Inn
	Lodg	E: Budget Inn
	RVCamp	W: Southern Gates RV Park and Campground (.25 Miles)
(85)		Rest Area (RR, Phones, Picnic, Vending, RV Dump; Northbound)
29		(84) GA 159, Ashburn, Amboy
	FStop	W: BP(*, 24)
	Gas	E: Shell(*) W: Phillips 66(*)
	Food	W: BP, Lo Joie's Kitchen (Phillips 66), Phillips 66, Royal Waffle King(24) (BP), Subway (BP)
	Lodg	W: Knight's Inn
	RVCamp	W: Knight's Inn & RV Park (.1 Miles)
28		(82) GA 107, GA 112, Ashburn, Fitzgerald
	Gas	W: BP(*, LP), Chevron(*)
	Food	W: Hardee's, Huddle House, McDonald's(PLAY), Pizza Hut, SHONEY'S Shoney's
	Lodg	W: Comfort Inn, DAYS INN Days Inn, Ramada Limited, Super 8
	AServ	W: Paco Chevrolet
	Parks	W: Sheehaw Park
	Other	W: Rite Aide Pharmacy(RX)
27		(80) Bussey Road, Sycamore
	FStop	E: Exxon(*, LP)
	Gas	E: Shell(*) W: Chevron
	Food	E: Exxon, Subway (Exxon)
	Lodg	E: Budget Inn
	AServ	E: Gene's 24 Hr. Tire & Truck Service(24) W: Chevron
	RVCamp	E: Lakeview Campground
26		(78) GA 32, Sycamore, Ocilla
	Parks	E: Jefferson Davis Park & Museum
(76)		Rest Area (RR, Phones, Picnic, Vending, RV Dump; Southbound)
25		(75) Inaha Road
	Gas	E: BP(*) W: Citgo(*)
	Food	W: Citgo, Dairy Queen (Citgo), Stuckey's (Citgo)
	AServ	E: BP
	ATM	E: BP
24		(72) Willis Stills Road, Sunsweet
	FStop	W: BP(*, D)
	RVCamp	W: Branch Bros. Farm Market RV Camping
23		(69) Chula - Brookfield Road

Bold red print shows RV & Bus parking available or nearby

EXIT GEORGIA

(Camping on West Side)

Gas E: Phillips 66[*, 24]

Food E: Chula Family Restaurant (Red Carpet), Red Carpet Inn

Lodg E: Red Carpet Inn

22 **(66)** Brighton Road

21 **(64)** U.S. 41, Tifton ABAC

Gas E: Chevron[*, D], M & S[*, CW]
W: Citgo[*]

Food W: Citgo

Med E: + Hospital

Other E: Food Lion Supermarket

20 **(63)** Eighth St

Gas E: Exxon[*], Texaco[*, D]

Food E: Hardee's, KFC, Los Compadres, Peking House
W: Split Rail Grill

Lodg E: DAYS INN Days Inn

Med E: + Hospital

ATM E: Winn Dixie Supermarket[24, RX]

Other E: Coin Car Wash, Georgia State Patrol, Winn Dixie Supermarket[RX]
W: Georgia Agrirama

19 **(62)** Second St, Tifton

FStop E: Dixie[*]

Gas E: BP[*, LP], Chevron[*]
W: Citgo[*, D, CW]

Food E: Arby's, Burger King[PLAY], Central Park, Checkers Burgers, Chicago Pizza & Pasta Kitchen, China Garden, El Montezuma, Golden Corral Family Steakhouse, Krystal, Little Caesars Pizza, Long John Silver, McDonald's, O'Neal Country Buffet, Pizza Hut, Red Carpet Inn, Red Lobster, Subway, Taco Bell, Yogurt You'll Love
W: Best Western, Denny's, Waffle House

Lodg E: Howard Johnson (see our ad this page), Red Carpet Inn, Super 8
W: Best Western, Comfort Inn

AServ E: Advance Auto Parts, Dixie, Jeff Fender Pontiac, Buick, Cadillac, Super Lube

Med E: + Hospital

ATM E: Citizen's Bank, First Community Bank, NationsBank

Other E: Cinema 6, Food Max[24], K-Mart, Tifton Mall, Wal-Mart[RX]

18 **(62)** to U.S. 82, U.S. 319, Sylvester, Tifton, GA 520

Gas E: BP[*], Exxon[*, D, CW], Shell[*, D]
W: Amoco[*, LP], Chevron[*, 24], Racetrac[*]

Food E: Charles Seafood Restaurant, Cracker Barrel, Masters Inn, Sonic, Waffle House (Masters Inn), Western Sizzlin'
W: Amoco, Captain D's Seafood, Chick-Fil-A[PLAY], Subway (Amoco), Waffle House, Wendy's

Lodg E: Courtyard by Marriott, Hampton Inn, Masters Inn

1879

1103 King Rd, Tifton, GA

912-386-2100

Outdoor Pool • In Room Coffee
Remote Cable TV w/HBO
Restaurant on Premises
Meeting/Banquet Rooms
Gas Station on Property
Microwave & Refrigerator Avail.
GA Historic Agrirama, Shopping Mall,
Abraham Baldwin College,
E.B. Hamilton Softball Complex Nearby

GEORGIA • I-75 • EXIT 19

EXIT GEORGIA

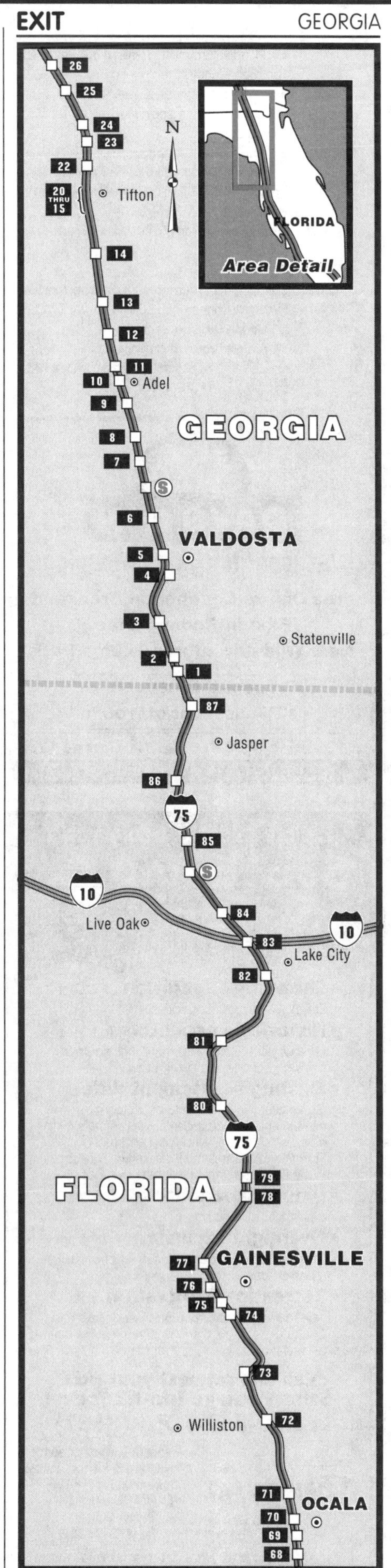

EXIT GEORGIA

W: Holiday Inn, Ramada Limited, Scottish Inns

AServ E: Page Auto & Tire Center
W: Prince Chevrolet, Oldsmobile

TServ W: MacReynold's Truck & Trailer

Med E: + Hospital

ATM E: Exxon, Shell
W: NationsBank, Racetrac

17 **(61)** Omega Road

RVCamp E: Covered Wagon RV Park & Campground

16 **(60)** South Central Ave

TStop W: Tifton Travel Center[*, RV DUMP, SCALES] (Shell gas)

Food W: Krispy Kreme Doughnuts (Tifton TS), Steak 'N Shake (Tifton Travel Center), Tifton Travel Center (Shell gas)

TServ W: Tifton Travel Center[SCALES] (Shell gas)

RVCamp W: Amy's South Georgia RV Park (1 Mile), Express RV Wash

Med E: + Hospital

15 **(59)** Southwell Blvd, Tifton

14 **(55)** Eldorado, Omega

Gas E: Chevron[*]
W: Phillips 66[*], Shell[*]

AServ W: Shell

13 **(49)** Kinard Bridge Road, Lenox

FStop E: Dixie[*]
W: BP[*]

Gas W: Texaco[D]

Food E: Gabi's Cafe & Restaurant (Knight's Inn), Knight's Inn
W: BP, Blimpie Subs & Salads (BP), Ice Cream Churn (BP), Pit BBQ

Lodg E: Knight's Inn

AServ W: Texaco

(48) **Rest Area (RR, Phones, Picnic, Vending; Southbound)**

(47) **Rest Area (RR, Phones, Picnic, Vending; Northbound)**

12 **(45)** Barneyville Road

Lodg E: Red Carpet Inn

11 **(42)** Rountree Bridge Road, Sparks

Food W: Plantation Inn

Lodg W: Plantation Inn

Parks W: Reed-Bingham State Park

10 **(40)** GA 37, Adel, Moultrie, Nashville

TStop W: Citgo Truck & Auto Plaza[*, SCALES, 24]

Gas E: BP, Shell[*, D]
W: BP[*], Citgo[*]

Food E: Champs BBQ & Seafood, Dairy Queen, Hardee's, McDonald's[PLAY] (Shell), Shell, Subway, Waffle House
W: Baskin Robbins (Citgo), Burger King[PLAY], Captain D's Seafood, Citgo, Citgo Truck & Auto Plaza, DAYS INN Days Inn, Huddle House (Citgo), IHOP (Days Inn), Mama's Table (Citgo TS), Popeye's Chicken, Stuckey's (Citgo), Taco Bell, Western Sizzlin'

Lodg E: Howard Johnson, Scottish Inns, Super 8
W: DAYS INN Days Inn, Hampton Inn

AServ E: Shefflit's Auto Parts & Service

TServ W: Sam's Truck & Auto Repair

Med E: + Hospital

ATM W: Bank of Lenox

Other E: Rite Aid Pharmacy[RX], Winn Dixie Supermarket
W: Adell Factory Stores

9 **(37)** Adel

Gas E: BP

Food E: BP, Rick's Chicken & BBQ (BP)

8 **(33)** Old Coffee Road, Cecil

Gas W: Amoco[*]

EXIT GEORGIA

Lodg E: Stagecoach Inn
AServ W: Amoco
RVCamp W: **Eagles Landing Resort**

7 **(29)** U.S. 41N, GA 122, Hahira, Barney, Lakeland, Moody AFB
FStop W: **Sav-a-Ton**(*, 24)
Gas E: Citgo(*)
W: BP(*, D, K)
Food W: Apple Valley Cafe (Sav-a-Ton), **Sav-a-Ton**

(24) **Weigh Station (Southbound)**

(24) **Weigh Station (Northbound)**

6 **(22)** U.S. 41S, North Valdosta Road
Gas E: BP(*), Shell(*)
W: Citgo(*, D), Days Inn
Food E: Baskin Robbins (Shell), Charlie Trappers Diner, Shell
W: **Burger King (Citgo)**, Dairy Queen, Days Inn, **Stuckey's (Citgo)**
Lodg W: Days Inn
RVCamp W: **Shady Oaks Campground (.25 Miles)**
Med E: **Hospital**
ATM E: BP

5 **(18)** GA 133, Valdosta, Moultrie, Valdosta State University
Gas E: Amoco(*, CW), Citgo(*), Shell(*), Texaco(*)
W: BP(*, LP), Exxon Gas n Go(*)
Food E: Applebee's, Arby's, Burger King(PLAY), **Cracker Barrel**, Denny's, Fazoli's Italian Food, KFC, Krystal, Outback Steakhouse, Quincy's Family Steakhouse, Taco Bell, Texas Roadhouse, Waffle House, Wendy's
W: Best Western, Country Buffet (Best Western)
Lodg E: Club House Inn, Fairfield Inn, Holiday Inn, Jolly Inn, Quality Inn, Scottish Inns, TraveLodge
W: Best Western
RVCamp W: **Riverpark Campground**
Med E: **Hospital**
Other E: **Visit Valdosta on a Southern Safari (see our ad this page)**, **Toys R Us**

4 **(16)** U.S. 84, U.S. 221, Ga. 94, Valdosta, Quitman
TStop W: **Texaco**(*, SCALES)
Gas E: BP(*, D), Citgo(*), Phillips 66, Shell(*, D)
Food E: Aligatou Chinese & Japanese (Quality Inn), Baskin Robbins (Shell), Burger King, IHOP, McDonald's(PLAY), Pizza Hut, Quality Inn, Shell, SHONEY'S Shoney's, Waffle House
W: Austin's Steakhouse (Comfort Inn)
Lodg E: Days Inn, Motel 6, Quality Inn, **Ramada Limited**, Rodeway Inn, Shoney's Inn, Super 8
W: Briarwood Motel, Comfort Inn, Knight's Inn
Med E: **Hospital**
W: **Texaco**

3A **(13)** Valdosta, Old Claytville Rd.
Parks W: **Wild Adventures Park**

3 **(11)** GA 31, Valdosta, Madison/ Florida, Valdosta Airport, Claytville
FStop E: **Speedway**(*, SCALES)
Gas W: BP(*, LP), Texaco
Food E: **Speedway**, Subway (Speedway), Waffle House
Lodg E: **Villager Lodge**
Med E: **Hospital**
Other E: **Big Rosie's Georgia Pecan Farmer's Market (Gas)**, Georgia State Patrol

2 **(4)** GA 376, Lakes Blvd., Lake Park
FStop W: **Citgo Travel Center**(*), **Phillips 66**(*)
Gas E: Amoco(*, CW), Chevron(*), Phillips 66(*), Racetrac(*, 24), Shell(*), Texaco(*) (Bill's Florida Fruit Outlet)
Food E: Blimpie Subs & Salads, Chevron, Chick-Fil-A(PLAY), Farm House Restaurant, Fine Chinese Restaurant, Hardee's, J.J. Express Sandwich & Such (Chevron), SHONEY'S Shoney's, Subway, Waffle House
W: Baskin Robbins (Citgo Travel Center), **Burger King (Citgo Travel Center)**, **Citgo Travel Center**, **Cracker Barrel**, **McDonald's**(PLAY), **Phillips 66**, Picadilly Circus Pizza (Phillips 66), Pizza Hut, Taco Bell, Wendy's

EXIT GEORGIA

Lodg E: Holiday Inn Express, Shoney's Inn
W: Days Inn (see our ad this page), TraveLodge
RVCamp E: **Eagle's Roost Campground (.5 Miles)**, **Giant Recreation World**(LP) **(Service & Parts)**, **Lake Park RV World**, **Town & Country RV Center**
W: **America's RV Center**(SCALES)
ATM E: Park Avenue Bank, **Winn Dixie Supermarket**(24, RX)
W: **Phillips 66**
Other E: Francis Lake Laundromat, **Lakepark Mill Store Plaza**, McConne Head's Car Wash, Vision Center USA, **Winn Dixie Supermarket**(RX)
W: **Factory Stores of America- Lake Park**

(3) **GA Welcome Center (RR, Phones, Picnic, Vending, RV Dump;**

1521

Adjacent to Outlet Shopping

Free Deluxe Continental Breakfast
Free In-Room Coffee
Near Wild Adventures Theme Park

Present this coupon for 10% discount off room.

912-559-0229 • Lake Park, GA

GEORGIA • I-75 • EXIT 2

Explore Valdosta, Georgia on a

1409

- **Shopping Expedition** 65 Outlet Stores...Antiques...Boutiques
- **Historical Encounters** Tour "The Crescent"...a "Gone with the Wind" southern mansion...or take the driving tour
- **Exciting Amusement Rides** Go Wild at "Wild Adventures"...Georgia's newest animal theme park...wild animals, wild rides, wild shows, wild food and fun! Special group rates/meal packages. "Christmas in the Park"...spectacular light show, Dec. 1-31.
- **Dining Experience** Casual or fine dining in a historic home
- **Overnight Excursion** Select from 3,000 affordable rooms...most national chains represented
- **Recreation Exploration** From year-round golf to Grand Bay...Valdosta's mini Okefenokee...walk the boardwalk, nature trail, or bird watch...or bring your canoe

Call and request your FREE Safari Package Trip-Tik Today!
1-800-569-TOUR(8687)

Valdosta-Lowndes County Convention & Visitors Bureau
1703 NormanDr., Suite F • P.O. Box 1964
I-75 at Exit 5 • Valdosta, GA 31603-1964
(912) 245-0513
Fax (912) 245-5240

Visit On-Line... http://www.datasys.net/valdtourism

EXIT GEORGIA/FLORIDA

Northbound)

1 **(2)** Bellville (Florida), Lake Park
TStop E: **TA TravelCenters of America**(*, SCALES) **(BP Gas)**
W: **Flying J Travel Plaza**(*, LP, RV DUMP, SCALES)
Gas E: Shell(*) (NAPA Auto Repair), Texaco(*) (Florida Visitor Center)
Food E: **Dairy Queen (Texaco)**, **TA TravelCenters of America (BP Gas)**, Texaco (Florida Visitor Center), Town & Country Restaurant (TA TS)
W: **Flying J Travel Plaza**, Magic Dragon (Flying J), Pepperoni's (Flying J)
Lodg W: Best Western Lake Park Inn
AServ E: Shell (NAPA Auto Repair)
TServ E: **TA TravelCenters of America**(SCALES) **(BP Gas)**
RVCamp W: **Holiday Campground**
ATM E: Shell (NAPA Auto Repair)

↑GEORGIA

↓FLORIDA

(470) **FL Welcome Center (RR, Phones, Picnic, Vending; Southbound)**

87 **(468)** FL 143, Jennings
FStop W: **Exxon**(*)
Gas E: Chevron(*) (Ice Cream Shop), Texaco(*)
W: Amoco(*, LP)
Food W: **Burger King (Exxon FS)**, **Exxon**, **Jennings House Inn**
Lodg E: **Quality Inn**
W: **Jennings House Inn**, North Florida Inn & Suites
AServ E: Chevron (Ice Cream Shop)
RVCamp W: **Jennings Campground**
ATM W: **Exxon**

86 **(462)** FL 6, Jasper, Madison
TStop W: **Sheffield's TS**(*, 24)
FStop E: **Amoco**(*), **Exxon**(*)
Gas E: Lyman Walker Grove (Indian River fruit), RaceWay(*)
W: Shell(*), Texaco(*)
Food E: **Amoco**, **Burger King (Amoco)**, **Exxon**, **Huddle House (Exxon FS)**, RaceWay
W: Grandma's Cookin' (Sheffield's), **Sheffield's TS**
Lodg E: **Days Inn**
W: Motel 8, Scottish Inns, **Scottish Inns**
TServ W: **Sheffield's TS**(24)
Med E: **Hospital**
ATM W: **Sheffield's TS**
Parks W: **Suwannee River State Park**

85 **(453)** U.S.129, Live Oak, Jasper
Gas E: Texaco(*, CW)
W: BP(*, D), Shell(*)
Food E: Dairy Queen (Texaco), Texaco
W: Icecream Churn (Shell)
RVCamp W: **Spirit of the Suwannee Campground**
Med E: **Hospital**

(447) **Weigh Station, Agricultural Inspection (Southbound)**

(447) **Weigh Station, Agricultural Inspection (Northbound)**

(445) **Rest Area (RR, Phones, Picnic, Vending; Southbound)**

(442) **Rest Area (RR, Phones, Picnic, Vending; Northbound)**

84 **(441)** FL 136, White Springs, Live Oak
FStop W: **A-1 Fuel Stop**(*) **(Citgo Gas)**
Gas E: BP(*), Gate(*, D), Texaco(*)
W: Amoco(*)
Food E: 3B's Restaurant, **McDonald's**
W: **A-1 Fuel Stop (Citgo Gas)**
Lodg E: U.S. Inn

EXIT FLORIDA

W: Colonial House Inn, EconoLodge
RVCamp E: Kelly RV Park, Lee's Country Campground (.7 Miles)
ATM W: A-1 Fuel Stop (Citgo Gas)
Parks E: Stephen Foster State Culture Center
Other E: State Farmer's Market

83 **(436)** Junction I-10, Jacksonville, Tallahassee

82 **(429)** U.S. 90, Live Oak, Lake City
Gas E: BP[*], Chevron[*, CW], Exxon, Gas & Go[*], Texaco[*, D]
W: Amoco[*], Citgo[*, D], Shell[*]
Food E: Arby's, Burger King[PLAY], Cracker Barrel, Gas & Go, Howard Johnson, IHOP (Howard Johnson), KFC, McDonald's[PLAY], Mike's Out to Lunch, Pizza Hut, Santilli's Italian Restaurant, Sonny's BBQ, Subway (Gas & Go), TCBY, Texas Roadhouse, Waffle House, Wendy's
W: Amoco, Boarding House (Holiday Inn), Bob Evan's Restaurant, Holiday Inn, Long John Silver (Amoco), Pablo's (Ramada), Ramada, SHONEY'S, Shoney's, Waffle House
Lodg E: A-1 Inn, Days Inn, Executive Inn, Howard Johnson, Knight's Inn (see our ad this page), Microtel Inn, Rodeway Inn, Villager Lodge, Villager Lodge
W: Best Western, Comfort Inn, EconoLodge, Hampton Inn, Holiday Inn, Motel 6, Ramada, Red Carpet Inn, Roadmaster Inn, TraveLodge
AServ E: Exxon
RVCamp E: Inn and Out RV Camp Park (.25 Miles), Martin Campers/Travel Country[LP] (1.5 Miles)
W: Wayne's RV Resort (.25 Miles)
Med E: ✚ Hospital
Other W: Florida Sports Hall of Fame, Tourist Info.

81 **(424)** FL 47, Fort White, Lake City
Gas E: Texaco[*, D]
W: Amoco[*], BP[*, D], Chevron[*], Citgo[*, LP, K], Express[*]
Food W: Anne's Cafe (BP), BP, Chevron, Dana's Steak, Seafood, & Pasta (Super 8), Express, Icecream Churn (Express), Little Caesars Pizza (Chevron), Subway (Express), Super 8
Lodg W: Super 8
TServ E: CAT Ring Power Corporation
RVCamp W: Casey Jones' Campground[LP]
ATM E: Texaco
W: Express

80 **(415)** U.S. 41, U.S.441, Lake City, High Springs
TStop W: L & G Truckstop[*, SCALES, 24] (Spur Gas, ATM)
FStop W: Amoco[*, D], BP[*]
Gas E: B & B Gas 'N Go[*], Chevron[*, D], Texaco
W: Citgo[*], Sunshine Food Store[*]
Food W: Country Cookin' Restaurant (L&G), Huddle House, I Can't Believe It's Yogurt (L&G), L & G Truckstop (Spur Gas, ATM), Sbarro Pizza (L & G), Subway
Lodg E: TraveLodge, Traveler's Inn
W: Diplomat Motel, EconoLodge
AServ W: Citgo, L & G Truckstop[24] (Spur Gas, ATM)
TServ W: L & G Truckstop[SCALES, 24] (Spur Gas, ATM)
RVCamp W: Wagon Wheel Campground[LP]
ATM W: BP
Parks W: O'Leno State Park
Other W: Wed's Antique & Country Store

(413) Rest Area (RR, Phones, Picnic, Vending; Southbound)

(413) Rest Area (RR, Phones, Picnic, Vending; Northbound)

79 **(406)** CR 236, High Springs, Lake Butler
Gas E: Chevron[*], Texaco[*] (Florida Welcome Station)

EXIT FLORIDA

Food E: Icecream Churn (Chevron)
RVCamp W: High Springs Campground

78 **(400)** U.S. 441, Alachua, High Springs
Gas E: BP[*]
W: Amoco[*, CW], Citgo[*, D], Lil' Champ[*, LP], Mobil[*]
Food E: Joey P's (Traveler's Inn), McDonald's[PLAY], Pizza Hut, Sonny's BBQ, Traveler's Inn, Waffle House
W: Dairy Queen (Mobil), Hardee's[PLAY], Huddle House (Mobil), Mobil
Lodg E: Comfort Inn, Traveler's Inn
W: Days Inn, Ramada Limited
RVCamp E: Traveler's Campground
ATM W: Lil' Champ

77 **(391)** FL 222, Gainesville, Welcome Center

1686
Knights Inn
$31.99* 1-4 Persons
904-752-7720
• Free Golf Greens (27 Hole Course)
• Free Health Club • Free Continental Breakfast
• Free Cable HBO, ESPN & CNN on 25" Color TV
• Free Local Calls • Free Ice
• Free Children Under 12 with Parents
• Pool, Shuffle Board, Golf Range, Playground Area • Fax & Copy Service
• Non-Smoking & Connecting Rooms
• Restaurants, Area Attractions & Shopping Nearby
AAA ♦♦
*Show Ad at check-in based on availability. Not valid with other discounts or during holidays or special events.
FLORIDA ▪ I-75 ▪ EXIT 82

VISITORS & CONVENTION BUREAU OF ALACHUA COUNTY
GAINESVILLE, FLORIDA
Stop & Visit Our New Welcome Center! Now Open — I-75, Exit 77
• OUTDOOR ADVENTURES
Paynes Prairie State Preserve
• MUSEUMS AND GALLERIES
Florida Museum of Natural History
Samuel P. Harn Museum of Art
• TOUR FAVORITES
Alachua County Official Welcome Center
Kanapaha Botanical Gardens
Santa Fe Community College Teaching Zoo
A Walk Though Time
• UNIVERSITY OF FLORIDA
FREE SOUVENIR!
Show this coupon at the Alachua County Welcom Center off I-75, exit 77, and receive a free souvenir gift!
1795

EXIT FLORIDA

Gas E: Chevron[*, D], Mobil[*, D, LP]
W: Gas[*, D] (Ice Cream Churn)
Food E: Wendy's
W: Gas (Ice Cream Churn), Hardee's (Gas)
AServ E: Seminata Detailing
W: Sal's Auto Service
ATM W: Gas (Ice Cream Churn)
Other E: Visit Gainesville & New Welcome Center (see our ad this page)
W: Aalatash Animal Hospital

76 **(388)** FL 26, Gainesville, Newberry
Gas E: Chevron[*, 24], Citgo[*], Shell[*, CW], Speedway[*], Texaco[*, D]
W: BP[*, CW], Chevron[*, D], Mobil[*, LP, CW]
Food E: Bono's Pit BBQ, Hun's Restaurant, La Fiesta, Perkins Family Restaurant[24], Quincy's Family Steakhouse, Red Lobster, Subway, Wendy's
W: Banyans Restaurant (Holiday Inn), Hardee's, Holiday Inn, Little Caesars Pizza, Lucky Lee's, Maui Teriyaki, Napolantano's Pizza Pasta, Pizza Hut, Pizza Hut, Rocky's Ribs, SHONEY'S, Shoney's, Subsacional Subs, TCBY, Taco Bell, Waffle House
Lodg E: Budget Lodge, La Quinta Inn
W: Days Inn, EconoLodge, Fairfield Inn, Holiday Inn
AServ E: Texaco
W: Allied Tire & Service, Chevron, Discount Auto Parts, Jiffy Lube, Pep Boys Auto Center
Med E: ✚ Hospital
ATM E: Citgo, Shell
W: Barnett Bank, M&S Bank
Other E: AMC Theaters, Oaks Mall
W: Eye Place Express, Gainesville Animal Hospital, Home Depot, K-Mart[RX], Lil' Champ, Park Place Car Wash, Publix Supermarket, U.S. Post Office, Wash House Coin Laundry, Winn Dixie Supermarket[RX]

75 **(385)** FL. 24, Gainesville, Archer
Gas E: Chevron[*, D, LP]
W: Mobil[*, D]
Food E: Bob Evan's Restaurant, Burger King, Gainesville Ale House, Imperial Garden Chinese, McDonald's[PLAY], SHONEY'S, Shoney's, Steak 'N Shake, Texas Roadhouse Steaks, Waffle House
W: Cracker Barrel
Lodg E: Cabot Lodge, Courtyard by Marriott, Extended Stay America, Hampton Inn, Motel 6, Ramada Limited, Red Roof Inn, Super 8
AServ E: Auto Depot, Master Care Auto Service, Midas Muffler & Brake, Tuffy Auto Center
RVCamp W: Sunshine Mobile Home and Overnight Park
Other E: Albertson's Food Market[24, RX], Barnes & Noble, Museum of Natural History, Target

74 **(384)** FL 121, Gainesville, Williston, to FL 331
FStop W: Chevron[*, D]
Gas E: Amoco[*, 24], Citgo[*, D]
W: Amoco[*, D] (Ice Cream Churn), Lil' Champ[*]
Food W: The Chuckwagon
Lodg E: Howard Johnson
W: Briarcliff Inn
AServ E: Amoco[24]
ATM E: Amoco

(383) Rest Area (RR, Phones, Picnic; Southbound)

(383) Rest Area (RR, Phones, Picnic; Northbound)

73 **(375)** CR 234, Micanopy
FStop W: Citgo[*]
Gas E: Amoco[*] (Ice Cream Churn), Fina[*]
W: Texaco
Food E: Shoney's
W: Scottish Inns
Lodg W: Scottish Inns

EXIT	FLORIDA

ATM E: Amoco (Ice Cream Churn)
Parks W: **Paynes Ferry State Preserve**
Other E: Smiley's Antique Mall
W: **Textile Town Mill Outlets**

72 **(368)** CR 318, Irvine, Orange Lake, McIntosh
TStop E: **Petro Truck Plaza**[*, LP, RV DUMP, SCALES, 24] **(Mobil gas)**
FStop W: **BP**
Gas E: Amoco[*], Citgo[*]
Food E: Citgo, Dairy Twirl (Citgo), **Iron Skillet (Petro)**, Jim's Pit BBQ (Citgo), **Petro Truck Plaza (Mobil gas)**, **Wendy's (Petro)**
AServ E: Amoco
W: **BP**
TServ E: **Petro Truck Plaza**[SCALES, 24] **(Mobil gas)**
RVCamp W: **Calawood RV Resort (.5 Miles)**
Other W: Wayside Antiques & Christmas Center

71 **(358)** Fl. 326
TStop E: **Checkered Flag Truck Plaza**[*] **(BP Gas)**
FStop E: **Speedway**[*, SCALES]
W: **Chevron**[*, D, 24]
Food E: **Hardee's (Speedway)**, Icecream Churn (Speedway), **Speedway**
W: **Chevron, Dairy Queen (Chevron), Gator's Restaurant (Chevron)**
TServ E: **Mid-Fla. Truck Repair**
RVCamp E: **Liberty RV Service**
ATM E: **Speedway**

70 **(354)** U.S. 27, Ocala,Williston
FStop W: **Texaco**[*, D]
Gas E: Amoco, Racetrac[*, 24], Super Test[*, D]
W: BP[*], Chevron[*, D], Shell[*, D]
Food E: Big Rascal BBQ, Krystal[24], **Quality Inn, Raintree Restaurant (Quality Inn)**
W: Big Heads Restaurant (Days Inn), Chester Fried Chicken (Shell), **Days Inn, Howard Johnson**, Pizza Stop, Ramada, Shell, Waffle House
Lodg E: **Quality Inn**
W: Budget Host Inn, **Days Inn, Howard Johnson**, Knight's Inn, Ramada, Red Coach Inn
RVCamp W: **Arrowhead RV Camp, Oak tree Village Campground (.35 Miles)**

69 **(353)** FL 40, Ocala, Silver Springs
FStop E: **BP**[*, D]
Gas E: Citgo[*], Racetrac[*, 24]
W: Texaco[*]
Food E: Citgo, Days Inn, Holiday Inn, **McDonald's**, Mr. Sub (Citgo), Wendy's
W: Comfort Inn, Denny's (Horne's), Golden Coast Restaurant (Super 8), Horne's, Super 8, Waffle House
Lodg E: Days Inn, Economy Inn, Holiday Inn, Motor Inns
W: Comfort Inn, Horne's, Super 8
RVCamp E: **Motor Inns Motel & RV Resort**
W: **Holiday Trav-L-Park**
ATM E: Racetrac

68 **(350)** FL 200, Ocala, Silver Springs
Gas E: Citgo[LP], Racetrac[*], Texaco[*, D]
W: Amoco[*, CW], Chevron[*]
Food E: Bella Luna Cafe, Bob Evan's Restaurant, Chick-Fil-A, Chili's, Lonestar Steakhouse, Perkin's Family Restaurant, Racetrac, Ruby Tuesday, Shell's Seafood, Shoney's, Star Bar & Grill
W: Burger King[PLAY], **Cracker Barrel**, Dunkin Donuts, Steak 'N Shake[24], Waffle House
Lodg E: Hampton Inn, Hilton, La Quinta
W: Budgetel Inn, Courtyard
AServ E: Citgo
W: Don Olson Tire & Auto Center
RVCamp W: **Camper Village, KOA-Ocala/Silver Springs (.5 Miles)**
ATM E: Racetrac

EXIT	FLORIDA

Other E: **Barnes & Noble, Home Depot, Lowe's**
W: **Disney Travel Center**, Pet Care Center, **Sam's Club**

(346) **Rest Area (RR, Phones, Picnic, Vending; Southbound)**

(346) **Rest Area (RR, Phones, Picnic, Vending; Northbound)**

67 **(341)** CR 484, Belleview
TStop W: **Pilot Travel Center**[*, SCALES]
Gas E: Chevron[*, 24], Citgo[*], Exxon[*]
W: Amoco (U-Haul Distributor)
Food E: Sonny's BBQ
W: **McDonald's**[PLAY], **Pilot Travel Center**, Waffle House
AServ W: Amoco (U-Haul Distributor)
RVCamp W: **Water Wheel RV Park (.5 Miles)**
ATM E: Citgo
Other E: **Drag Racing Museum**, Garlits Museum
W: **Ocala Factory Stores**

(338) **Weigh Station (Southbound)**

(338) **Weigh Station (Northbound)**

66 **(329)** FL 44, Wildwood, Inverness
TStop W: **TA TravelCenters of America**[SCALES, 24] **(BP gas, CB shop)**
FStop E: **Gate**[*]
W: **Citgo**[*], **Speedway**[*, D, SCALES]
Gas E: Amoco[*], Shell[*], Texaco[*] (Tourist Info)
Food E: Burger King[PLAY], Dairy Queen, Denny's, **Gate**, McDonald's, Shell, Shoney's, Steak 'N Shake (Gate), Texaco (Tourist Info), Wendy's
W: **Atrium Restaurant (TA TS)**, **Days Inn**, KFC, **Pizza Hut (TA TS), Subway (TA TS), TA TravelCenters of America (BP gas, CB shop), TCBY (TA TS), Waffle House**
Lodg W: **Budget Suites, Days Inn**, Super 8, Wildwood Inn
AServ E: Amoco
TServ W: **TA TravelCenters of America**[SCALES, 24] **(BP gas, CB shop), Tommy's Tire Shop**
TWash W: **TA TravelCenters of America (BP gas, CB shop)**
RVCamp E: **KOA-Wildwood, Three Flags RV Campground (1 Mile)**
ATM W: **Speedway**

65 **(328)** Florida Tnpk., Orlando, Miami (Southbound, Left Exit Southbound, Reaccess Northbound Only)

64 **(321)** CR 470, Sumterville
FStop E: **Sunshine Travel Center**[*]
Gas W: Chevron[*]
Food E: **Sunshine Travel Center**
W: Chevron, Lake Pennasofskee, Picadilly Pizza (Chevron)

1052

Conley Foretravel Southeast

MOTORHOME
SALES • SERVICE • PARTS

Directions: Take route 64 off of I75, West to route 41, South 2.5 Miles on Right.

800 Cortex Road West • Brandenton, FL 34207
800.777.8531

EXIT	FLORIDA

RVCamp W: **Conley Foretravel Southeast (see our ad this page), Countryside RV Park (.75 Miles), Idle Wild Lodge & RV Park, Pan-Vista Lodge & RV Park, Turtleback RV Resort (.25 Miles)**
Other W: **Lake Panasoffkee**

63 **(314)** FL48, Bushnell
FStop E: **BP**[*]
W: **Citgo**[*]
Gas E: Mobil[*], Texaco[*]
W: Shell[*]
Food E: Dairy Queen (Mobil), KFC, Mobil, Stuckey's (Mobil), Taco Bell
W: **McDonald's**[PLAY], Waffle House
Lodg E: Best Western
AServ W: **Citgo**
RVCamp E: **Red Barn Campground (1 Block), The Oaks Campground**[LP] **(.8 Miles)**
Other E: Bushnell Animal Clinic

62 **(309)** CR 476, Webster
RVCamp E: **Safire Campground, Sumter Oaks RV Park (1.5 Miles)**

(307) **Rest Area (RR, Phones, Picnic; Southbound)**

(307) **Rest Area (RR, Phones, Picnic; Northbound)**

61 **(302)** U.S. 98, FL 50, Orlando, Brookville, Ridge Manor, Weekiwachee
FStop W: **Shaw's Service Station/ Highway 41**
Gas E: Amoco (U-Haul Rental), Racetrac[*], Shell[*]
W: Mobil[*, LP]
Food E: Days Inn, Denny's (Days Inn), Five Star Pizza Palace, **McDonald's**[PLAY], River House Pub, Shell, Toni's Italian, Waffle House, Wendy's
W: Holiday Inn, Mobil, Subway (Mobil)
Lodg E: Days Inn
W: Hampton Inn, Holiday Inn
AServ E: Amoco (U-Haul Rental), C & F Auto
W: **Shaw's Service Station/ Highway 41**
RVCamp E: **Florida Campland, Tall Pines RV Park**
W: **Hidden Valley RV Camp**
Med W: **Hospital**
ATM E: Racetrac, SunTrust, **Winn Dixie Supermarket**[24, RX]
Other E: Laundromat, Tourist Info., **Winn Dixie Supermarket**[RX]

60 **(294)** CR 41, Dade City

59 **(287)** FL 52, Dade City, Newport Richey
TStop E: **Flying J Travel Plaza**[*, LP, RV DUMP, SCALES]
FStop W: **Texaco**[*, SCALES]
Food E: **Country Market (Flying J), Flying J Travel Plaza**
W: **Blimpie's Subs (Texaco), Texaco, Waffle House**
Med E: **Hospital**
ATM W: **Texaco**

58 **(280)** FL 54, Land O' Lakes, Zephyrhills
FStop W: **Amoco**[*]
Gas E: Lucky Food Center[*], Racetrac[*, 24], Shell[*], Texaco[*, LP, CW]
W: Circle K[*, D, LP], Citgo[*, D]
Food E: ABC Pizza, Burger King, Holiday Cafe, Hungry Howie's, Sonny's BBQ, Subway, Waffle House, Wendy's, Winter's Sports Grill
W: **Cracker Barrel**, Denny's (Masters Inn), Masters Inn, McDonald's, Peacock's
Lodg W: Comfort Inn, Holiday Inn Express, Masters Inn, Sleep Inn
AServ E: Discount Auto Parts
ATM E: Racetrac, Sun Trust Bank, Texaco, **Winn Dixie**

EXIT FLORIDA

Supermarket
W: Amoco

Other E: Clean & Wash Laundromat, Publix Supermarket(RX), WalGreens Pharmacy(RX), Winn Dixie Supermarket

(278) Rest Area (RR, Phones, Picnic, Vending; Northbound)

(278) Rest Area (RR, Phones, Picnic, Vending; Southbound)

57 **(275)** Junction I-275 South, Tampa (Southbound, Reaccess Northbound Only)

56 **(271)** CR. 581, Bruce B. Downs Blvd.

55 **(267)** CR. 582 A., Fletcher Ave

Lodg W: Courtyard by Marriott, Extended Stay America, Hampton Inn, Sleep Inn

Med W: ✚ Hospital

54 **(266)** FL. 582, Fowler Ave, Temple Terrace

Food W: SHONEY'S, Shoney's

Lodg W: Shoney's Inn

RVCamp E: Happy Traveler RV Park and Campground (.5 Miles), Spanish Main Travel Resort (2 Miles)

Other W: Busch Gardens

53 **(262)** Junction I-4, Orlando, Tampa, Lakeland, Plant City

52AB **(260)** FL. 574 , Mango

Gas W: Rainbow(*)

Food W: Rainbow

Lodg W: Radisson Hotel

AServ E: Auto Nation USA, Transworld Transmission

ATM W: Rainbow

51 **(257)** FL 60, Brandon

Gas W: Shell(*)

Food E: Bennigan's, Chesapeake Bagel, Grady's American Grill, Olive Garden, Red Lobster, Romano's Macaroni Grill

W: Bob Evan's Restaurant, Burger King, Hooters, McDonald's, Sonny's BBQ, Subway, Sweet Tomatoes, Villa Rina Pizza, Wendy's

Lodg E: Holiday Inn Express, Homestead Vllage, La Quinta

PRIME OUTLETS

ELLENTON

Over 100 Outlet Stores and Food Court
Liz Clairborne • Saks Fifth Avenue

Ask for your **FREE COUPON BOOK**

1857 941-723-1150

FLORIDA ▪ I-75 ▪ EXIT 43

1818

10150 Palm River Road • Tampa, FL 33619

107 Bright New Rooms
Free Continental Breakfast
Outdoor Pool & Exercise Room
Hot Coffee & Tea, Free 24 Hours
Ample Free Parking • Guest Laundry
Brandon Town Mall, 1 mile
20 minutes to Beaches/Busch Gardens

813-661-9719

FLORIDA ▪ I-75 ▪ EXIT 51

EXIT FLORIDA

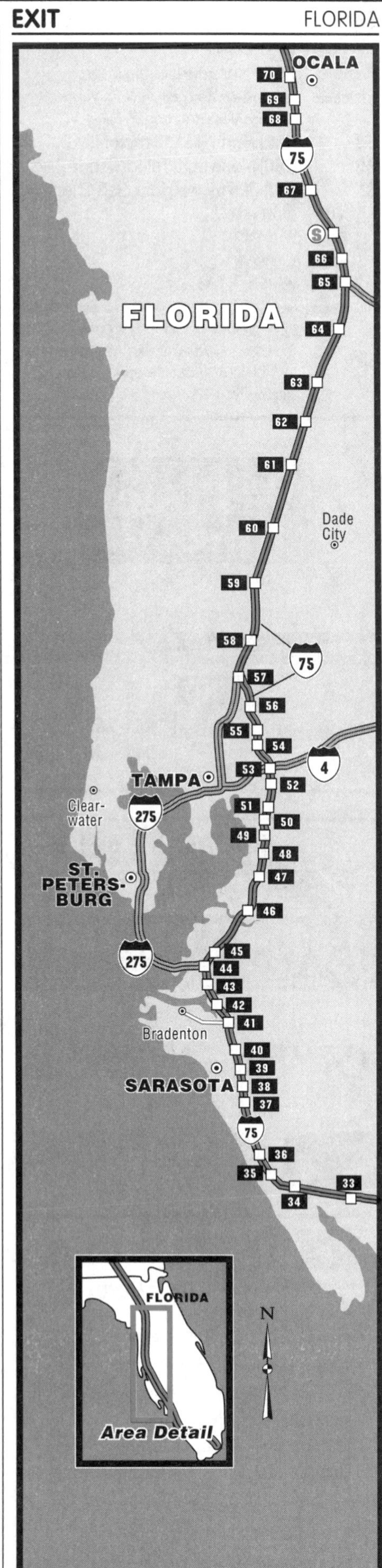

EXIT FLORIDA

W: Budgetel Inn, Comfort Suites Hotel, Courtyard by Marriott, DAYS INN Days Inn, Fairfield Inn (see our ad this page), Hampton Inn, Red Roof Inn

AServ E: 10 Minute Oil Change(CW)

ATM W: Shell

Other E: 4 MC Theaters, Barnes & Noble, Brandon Town Center, Joshua's Christian Bookstore, Lens Crafters

W: Car Wash, Celebration Station, Waccamaw

50 **(256)** Cross Town Expressway, Toll,Tampa (Difficult Reaccess)

49 **(254)** U.S. 301, Riverview (Difficult Reaccess)

ATM E: Nation's Bank

48 **(251)** Gibsonton, Riverview

TServ E: Ringhaver Truck & Engine Service (CAT)

RVCamp E: Alafia River RV Resort (.25 Miles), Hidden River Travel Resort

47 **(247)** CR.672, Apollo Beach, Big Bend Rd

46 **(241)** FL. 674, Ruskin, Sun City Center ,Wimauma

Gas W: Exxon(*)

Food E: Danny Boy's, Hungry Howie's, Scoops & More, SHONEY'S, Shoney's

W: KFC, Maggie's Buffet, McDonald's, Subway

Lodg E: Comfort Inn

W: Holiday Inn Express

RVCamp W: Sun Lake RV Resort

Med E: ✚ Sun City Medical Center

W: ✚ Family Medical Center

ATM E: South Trust Bank

W: Publix Supermarket

Other E: Opti Mart, Wal-Mart(RX)

W: Publix Supermarket

(238) Rest Area (Northbound)

45 **(230)** CR 6, Parrish

RVCamp W: Fiesta Grove RV Camp, Frog Creek Campground, Terra Ceia Village RV Resort

44 **(229)** Junction I-275 North, St. Petersburg

43 **(225)** U.S. 301, Ellenton, Palmetto

FStop W: Speedway(*, D, LP)

Gas E: Chevron(*, CW, 24), Racetrac(*, 24), Shell(*, D, CW)

Food E: McDonald's, Taters Restaurant, Wendy's

W: Lee's Crab Trap, SHONEY'S, Shoney's, Speedway, Subway (Speedway FS), Waffle House

Lodg W: Best Western, SHONEY'S, Shoney's, Shoney's Inn

RVCamp W: Bay Palm RV Park, Ellenton Gardens Travel Resort (1.25 Miles)

ATM E: Racetrac, Shell

W: Speedway

Other E: Prime Outlets at Ellenton (see our ad this page), K-Mart(RX), Optical Eyes Associates, Publix Supermarket, WalGreens Pharmacy(RX)

W: Tourist Info.

42AB **(221)** FL 64 W, Bradenton, FL 64 E, Zolfo Springs, Wauchula

FStop W: Circle K(*) (76 gas)

Gas W: Chevron(*, CW), Citgo(*, D), Racetrac(*), Shell(*)

Food W: Burger King, Cracker Barrel, McDonald's(PLAY), Subway, Waffle House

Lodg W: Comfort Inn, DAYS INN Days Inn, Econolodge, Knight's Inn

TServ W: Circle K (76 gas)

RVCamp W: Winter Quarters RV Resort (1.5 Miles)

Med W: ✚ Hospital

ATM W: Circle K (76 gas), Citgo, Shell

Other E: Little Manetee State Recreational Area

W: Sheriff Dept.

41 **(218)** FL. 70, Bradenton, Arcadia

Gas W: Shell(*, CW)

Bold red print shows RV & Bus parking available or nearby

EXIT FLORIDA

Food W: Bogey's Grill & Pub, China Village, Rainbow Cafe, The Boston Garden, The Orange Dipper
RVCamp W: Horseshoe Cove RV Resort (1.25 Miles), Pleasant Lake RV Resort (.5 Miles), Tropical Gardens RV Park
ATM W: Barnett Bank, Shell
Other W: Publix Supermarket[RX]

40 **(214)** University Pkwy, Sarasota, International Airport
Other W: Sarasota Outlet Center

39 **(210)** FL. 780, Sarasota, St. Armand's, Gulf Beaches, Fruitville Road
Gas W: Mobil[*, CW]
Food W: Blimpie Sub & Salads (Mobil), Don Pablo's Mexican Kitchen, Mobil
Lodg W: Wellesley Inns (see our ad this page)
RVCamp E: Sun-N-Fun RV Resort (1 Mile)

38 **(208)** Fl. 758, Bee Ridge Road, Sarasota
FStop W: Mobil[*]
Gas W: Texaco[*, CW]
Food W: Arby's, Bagel Cafe, Big City Hot Dog & Deli, Blimpie's Subs (Texaco), Checkers Burgers, Chili's, China Wokery, Chinese Cuisine, Domino's Pizza, Krispy Kreme Doughnuts (Mobil), McDonald's[PLAY], Mobil, Pizza Hut, Sarasota Ale House, Shangri-La, Stockyard Steakhouse, Subway (Mobil), Sugar & Spice Family Restaurant, Taco Bell, Texaco, Vincenzo's, Woody's BBQ
Lodg W: Hampton Inn
AServ W: Mobil
Med W: ✚ Hospital
ATM W: Barnett Bank, California Federal Bank, Nation's Bank, Publix Supermarket[RX], South Trust Bank, SunTrust
Other W: Animal Clinic, Cash & Carry United Grocery, Home Depot, K-Mart, Publix Supermarket[RX], The Frame Shop, Waccamaw, WalGreens Pharmacy[RX], WalMart[RX]

37 **(206)** FL 72, Sarasota, Arcadia, Siesta Key
Gas W: Citgo[*, D], Mobil[*, CW]
Food W: Burger King, Citgo, Waffle House, Wendy's, Wings-N'-Weenies
Lodg W: Comfort Inn, Ramada Inn
RVCamp W: Gulf Beach Campground (8.4 Miles), Windward Isle Mobile Home Park (2 blocks)
ATM W: Citgo, First State Bank of Sarasota, Mobil, Mobil, Suntrust
Parks E: Myakka River State Park
Other W: Clark Road Animal Clinic

36 **(200)** FL. 681 South, Venice, Osprey (Southbound, Reaccess Northbound Only)
Lodg W: Ramada Inn (see our ad this page)
Med W: ✚ Hospital
Parks W: Oscar Shera State Recreation Area

35A **(195)** Nokomis, Laurel
RVCamp E: Lake Awesome RV Resort (.5 Miles)
W: Coach Royal
Parks E: Oscar Shera State Park

35 **(194)** Jacaranda, Venice
Gas W: Hess[*, D]
Food W: Blimpie Subs & Salads (Hess), Godfather's Pizza (Hess), Hess, McDonald's
Lodg W: Best Western

EXIT FLORIDA

Med W: ✚ Hospital

34 **(191)** River Road, Englewood
RVCamp W: Ramblers Rest Campground, Venice Campground & RV Park (.75 Miles)

33 **(182)** North Port, Sumpter Blvd

32 **(180)** North Port, Toledo Blade Blvd

31 **(171)** CR 769, Arcadia, Port Charlotte, Kings Hwy
FStop W: Mobil[*]
Gas E: Citgo[*]
W: Hess[*, D], Texaco[*, D]
Food W: Blimpie's Subs (Mobil), Burger King[PLAY], Cafe PJ, Cracker Barrel, Dairy Queen (Texaco), Godfather's Pizza (Hess), Hess, McDonald's[PLAY], Mobil, Peach Garden Chinese Restaurant, Subway, Taco Bell, Texaco, Waffle House,

1315
Wellesley Inns
Look for these Lodging Locations at the exits below
Wellesley | EXIT 39 22 | 941-366-5128 941-278-3949

CAMPING WORLD.
Exit 24
5600 Enterprise Pkwy. • Fort Myers, FL
1-800-553-9730
1424

1708
RAMADA INN®
1660 S. Tamiami Trail • Osprey, FL
Restaurant on Premises
Outdoor Pool • Poolside Tiki Bar
NEWLY RENOVATED
Meeting/Banquet Facilities
25" TV All Rooms • Handicap Accessible
Truck/Large Vehicle Parking
AAA
Coin Laundry • Exterior Corridors
5 minutes to Beaches, Golfing, Shopping
941-966-2121 • Toll Free Reservations: 1-800-2-RAMADA
75S Exit 36 to US 41 Right 2 miles on Left
75N Exit 35A West to US 41 Turn R - 4 miles on Left
FLORIDA ▪ I-75 ▪ EXIT NB35A/SB36

EXIT FLORIDA

Wendy's, Zorba's Pizza
Lodg E: Hampton Inn
AServ W: Discount Auto Parts
RVCamp W: Yogi Bear Camp Resort
Med W: ✚ Hospital
ATM E: Citgo
W: Mobil, Mobil, Publix Supermarket[RX], Texaco
Other E: 7-11 Convenience Store
W: Eckerd Drugs, Optical, Publix Supermarket[RX]

30 **(167)** CR. 776, Charlotte Harbor, Port Charlotte, Harbor View Road, Harbor Heights

29 **(164)** U.S. 17, Punta Gorda, Arcadia
FStop E: Shell[D, 24]
Food E: Shell
RVCamp E: KOA-Punta Gorda/Charlotte Harbor Kampground (1.75 Miles)
W: KOA Campgrounds
Med W: ✚ Hospital
ATM E: Shell
Other E: Brenda's Produce, Punta Gorda Country Club and Golf Course

28 **(163) CR 768, Punta Gorda, Charlotte County Airport, N. Jones Loop Road, Rest Area**
FStop W: Hess[*], Speedway[*, K, SCALES]
Gas W: Amoco[*]
Food W: Amoco, Blimpie's Subs (Speedway), Burger King, Church's Chicken (Speedway), Dairy Queen (Amoco), Hess, McDonald's, Pizza Hut, SHONEY'S, Shoney's, Speedway, Subway (Amoco), Taco Bell, Waffle House, Wendy's
Lodg W: DAYS INN Days Inn, Motel 6
RVCamp E: KOA Campgrounds
W: Alligator Park (1.1 Miles), Gulf View RV Resort
ATM W: Hess
Other W: Tourist Info.

(163) **Rest Area (RR, Phones, Picnic; East Side Of Exit 28)**

(160) **Weigh Station (Southbound)**

(160) **Weigh Station - . (Northbound)**

27 **(158)** CR 762, Cape Coral, North Fort Myers, Tropical Gulf Acres
RVCamp E: Sun & Shade
W: Holiday RV Super Stores (see our ad this page), Punta Gorda RV Resort, Raintree RV Resort

26 **(143)** FL 78, North Fort Myers, Cape Coral, Bay Shore Road, Pine Islands Road
Gas W: Racetrac[*]
RVCamp E: Seminole RV Campground, Up River Campground (1.5 Miles)
W: Holiday RV Camp, Pioneer Village RV Mobile Home Resort (.8 Miles)
ATM W: Racetrac, Racetrac

Bold red print shows RV & Bus parking available or nearby

EXIT FLORIDA

25 **(141)** FL 80, Fort Myers, La Belle
Gas E: Amoco(*), Citgo(*, D)
W: Hess(*, D), Racetrac(*)
Food E: Cracker Barrel, Waffle House
W: Chinese Kitchen, Hardee's, Juicy Lucy's Burgers, Perkins Family Restaurant, Pizza Hut, Subway, Sundae Cafe, Taco Bell
AServ W: Martin's General Repair
RVCamp E: Orange Harbor Mobile Home & RV Park (.25 Miles)
W: North Trail RV Service & Sales
ATM E: Citgo, Citgo
W: Hess
Other E: Eden Winery (15 Miles)
W: Eye Centers of Florida, Laundromat, Publix

24 **(139)** Fort Myers, Luckett Road
TStop W: Pilot Travel Center(*, RV DUMP, SCALES)
Food W: Grandma's Kitchen (Pilot), Pilot Travel Center, Subway (Pilot)
TServ W: Jet Lions Truck Parts, Pilot Travel Center, Pilot Travel Center(SCALES)
RVCamp E: Cypress Woods RV Resort (.5 Miles)
W: Camping World (see our ad this page -- 1/2 Mile), Gulf Coast RV Service, Lazy J Adventures, Orange Grove Mobile Home & RV Park (1.5 Miles), RV Kountry Sky Line
ATM W: Pilot, Pilot Travel Center

23 **(138)** FL. 82, Fort Myers, Immokalee, MLK, Jr. Blvd
Gas W: Racetrac(*), Speedway(*)
ATM W: Speedway, Speedway
Other W: Edison & Ford Estates, Imaginarium

22 **(136)** FL. 884, Fort Myers, Colonial Blvd, Lehigh Acres
Lodg W: Wellesley Inns (see our ad opposite)
Med W: + Hospital
Other W: Nature's Center & Planetarium

21 **(132) Daniels Pkwy, SW. International Airport, Cape Coral, Rest Area**
Gas W: Hess(*), Racetrac(*), Shell(*)
Food W: Arby's, Blimpie Subs & Salads (Hess), Burger King(PLAY), Denny's, Hess, McDonald's, Taco Bell, Waffle House, Wendy's
Lodg W: Comfort Suites Hotel, Hampton Inn, Ramada Inn & Beachfront Resort (see our ad this page), Sleep Inn
Med W: + Hospital
ATM W: NationsBank (Shell), Shell

(132) **Rest Area (RR, Phones, Vending; East Side Of Exit 21)**

1078
Ramada Inn
Beachfront Resort
Directly on the Gulf of Mexico
Private White Sandy Beach
Heated Pool on Gulf
FREE Welcome Cocktail
Newly Remodeled Rooms
Rooms, Efficiencies & Suites
Guest Laundry
Children FREE With Parents
FREE In-Room Coffee
$78 Plus Tax 1-2 Persons 1/5/99-1/29/99 5/1/99 to 12/20/99
$108 1/30/99-4/30/99
Subject to Availability and Black Out Periods
Fort Myers Beach, FL
941-463-6158 • 800-544-4592
FLORIDA • I-75 • EXIT 21

EXIT FLORIDA

20 **(128)** Alico Road, San Carlos Park
RVCamp W: Shady Acres Travel Park (2.5 Miles)

19 **(123)** Estero, CR 850, Corkscrew Road
RVCamp W: Covered Wagon RV Park, Koreshan State Historic Site (2 Miles), Shady Acres Travel Park, Wood Smoke Campground

18 **(116)** Bonita Springs, Gulf Beaches, Bonita Beach Road
FStop W: Hess(*), Hess(*, LP)
Gas W: Amoco(*)
Food W: Amoco, Blimpie Subs & Salads (Hess FS), Hess, McDonald's (Amoco), Waffle House
Lodg W: Days Inn
RVCamp W: Bonita Beach Trailer Park, Bonita Lake RV Resort, Citrus Park RV Resort, Imperial Bonita RV Park
ATM W: Amoco, Hess, Hess FStop, NationsBank (McDonald's)

17 **(112)** CR 846, Naples Park, Immokalee Rd.
RVCamp W: Lake Sand Marino Resort
Parks W: Delnor-Wiggins State Park, Naples Park
Other W: Tourist Info.

16 **(107)** CR 896, Naples, Golden Gate, Pine Ridge Road, Naples Airport
Gas E: Mobil(*, D, 24)
W: Chevron(*, D, CW, 24), Shell(*, D)
Food E: McDonald's (Mobil), Mobil, Patso Cafe
W: Burger King, Cappy's 19th Hole Sports Grill, Shell, Waffle House
Lodg W: Best Western, Knight's Inn
Med E: + Columbia Care Walk-In Medical Unit
ATM E: AM South Bank, Mobil, Publix Supermarket(RX)
W: NationsBank (Shell), Shell
Other E: Crossroads Veterinary Clinic, Publix Supermarket(RX), WalGreens Pharmacy(RX)
W: Naples Airport

15 **(102)** CR. 951, to FL. 84, Naples, Marco Island
Gas W: Amoco(*), Mobil(*, D, 24), Shell(*, D, 24)
Food W: Burger King(PLAY), Checkers Burgers, Cracker Barrel, Dunkin Donuts (Mobil), McDonald's(PLAY), Mobil, Subway (Mobil), Waffle House
Lodg W: Budgetel Inn, Comfort Inn, Holiday Inn Express, Super 8, Wellesley Inns (see our ad this page)
RVCamp W: Club Naples RV Resort (1.2 Miles), Endless Summer RV Camp, Kountree Kampinn, Naples RV Resort, Silver Lake RV Park
ATM W: Amoco, Mobil, Mobil, NationsBank (Shell), Shell
Other W: Prime Outlets at Naples (see our ad this page), Golden Gate Visitor Information Center

14A **(80)** FL. 29, Everglades City, Immokalee
Parks W: Big Cypress National Preserve (17 Miles), Everglades National Park (22 Miles)
Other W: Ted Smallwood's Store (25 Miles)

PRIME OUTLETS
NAPLES
Nearly 70 Deisgner Outlet Stores and Food Court
Anne Klein • OshKosh by Gosh • Izod
Ask for your FREE COUPON BOOK
941-775-8083
1865
FLORIDA • I-75 • EXIT 15

EXIT FLORIDA

(71) Recreational Area (Northbound)
(71) Recreational Area (Southbound)
(63) **Rest Area (RR, Phones, Picnic, Vending; Northbound)**
(63) **Rest Area (RR, Phones, Picnic, Vending; Southbound)**

14 **(50)** Indian Reservation
FStop E: Shell(*, 24)
Food E: Shell

(40) Recreational Area (Southbound)
(38) Recreational Area (Northbound)
((32) Recreational Area (Southbound)
(32) Recreational Area (Northbound)

13AB **(23)** U.S. 27, Miami, South Bay
Parks E: Park

12 **(22)** Arvida Pkwy.

11 **(21)** FL 84 West, Indian Trace
Gas W: Mobil(*, D)
Food W: Antonello Italian Cuisine, Cafe, PaPa John's, Sister's Subs

10 **(17)** Jct I-595, Sawgrass Exprwy, Fort Lauderdale, FL 869, North Coral Springs, West Palm Beach

8 **(15)** Arvida Pkwy West, Westin Bonaventure
ATM W: First Union Bank
Other W: Westin Hills Country Club

7AB **(14)** Griffin Road
Gas E: Amoco(*, CW), Shell(*, D, CW, 24)
Food E: Amoco, Antonio's Pizza-Rant, Burger King(PLAY), China Spring, Dairy Queen, Subway, Waffle House
AServ E: Goodyear
Other E: Animal Clinic, Publix Supermarket(RX)

6AB **(12)** Sheridan St
Med E: + Hospital

5AB **(9)** FL 820, Hollywood Blvd, Pines Blvd
AServ E: Auto Nation USA
Other E: JC Penney's, WalGreen's(RX)

4 **(7)** Miramar Pkwy

3B **(5)** Florida Tnpk. South, Key West, Homestead

3A **(6)** New186th St, Miami Gardens Dr
Gas E: Amoco(*, CW), Chevron(*, CW, 24)
Food E: McDonald's(PLAY), Subway
ATM E: Chevron, Publix Supermarket
Other E: Animal Hospital, Eckerd Drugs(RX), Publix Supermarket

2 Northwest 138th St, Graham Dairy Road
Gas W: Mobil(*, CW)
Food W: Blue Sky Food by the Pound, Dairy Queen, Don Tike, Fruits and Juices, McDonald's, Speedy Ziti Italian, Subway
Med W: + Hospital
ATM W: Mobil, Publix Supermarket
Other W: 20/20 Eye Care Center, Publix Supermarket

1AB FL. 826, Palmetto Exprwy, International Airport

↑FLORIDA

Begin I-75

Bold red print shows RV & Bus parking available or nearby

EXIT	COLORADO
	Begin I-76 COLORADO
	↓COLORADO
1A	NE121, Wadsworth Blvd
1B	NE95, Sheridan Blvd
Food	**S:** Amici's Pizzeria Italian Restaurant, Gooseberries Donuts, Great Panda Chinese Restaurant, Mr B's Roadhouse
Other	**S: The Great American Pet Castle**
3	U.S. 287, Federal Blvd
Gas	**N:** Total
Food	**S:** McDonald's, Panda Express, Subway, Taco House
Lodg	**N:** Alpine Rose Motel, North Valley Federal Motel
	S: Joy Motor Motel, Primrose Motel, White Rock Motel
AServ	**S:** Munoz Auto Service
RVCamp	**S: Deluxe RV Park**
Other	**N:** Car Wash
	S: Old Glory Fireworks
4	Pecos St
5A	I-25 South Denver
5B	North I-25, West U.S. 36, Fort Collins, Boulder
6	Junction I-270 East, Limon
8	CO 224, 74th Ave, Welby, Commerce City
TWash	**S: Austin Co.**
9	CO 2 South, Colorado Blvd, U.S. 6 West, U.S. 85 South, Commerce City
10	88th Ave
Gas	**N:** Conoco(*, D)
Food	**N:** A-Frame Cafe
Lodg	**N: Super 8**
AServ	**N:** Conoco
Other	**S:** Mile High Flea Market
11	96th Ave
TServ	**N: Leonard's Interstate Trailer Sales & Repair, Western Truck & Trailer Sales**
12	U.S. 85 North, Greeley
16	CO2 West, Commerce City
17	CO 51, Brighton
TStop	**N: Tomahawk Auto/Truck Plaza**(*, SCALES)
AServ	**N: Tomahawk Auto/Truck Plaza**
TServ	**N: Tomahawk Auto/Truck Plaza**(SCALES)
TWash	**N: Tomahawk Auto/Truck Plaza**
Med	**N: ✚ Hospital**
19	Barr Lake (Reaccess Westbound Only)
20	136th Ave
RVCamp	**N: Barr Lake RV**(LP) **(Laundry), Laundry Facilities**
21	144th Ave
22	Bromley Lane
Parks	**S: Barr Lake State Park**
23	144th St
25	Lochbuie, CO 7 West, Brighton
FStop	**N: Texaco**(*)
Food	**N: Pearls Restaurant & Lounge (Texaco)**
ATM	**N: Texaco**
31	CO 52, Hudson, Pospect Valley, Boulder
Gas	**S:** Amoco(*, D, CW)
Food	**S:** Longhorn & Co. Restaurant & Lounge, Pepper Pod Restaurant, Pit Stop Picadilly Pizza
AServ	**S: Active Truck Sales Inc.**
TServ	**S: Active Truck Sales Inc.**
RVCamp	**S: KOA Campgrounds**(*) **(Public Laundry)**
Other	**S: Anderson Star Market**, Hudson Mercantile (Antiques & Collectibles), U.S. Post Office
34	Kersey Rd
39	Keenesburg
FStop	**S: Phillips 66**(*)
Food	**S:** C and J Dairy King, Korner Kitchen Cafe, The Last Frontier (Steakhouse)
Lodg	**S:** Keene Motel
AServ	**S:** NAPA, Tim's Car Clinic
Other	**S: Keene Market, Rexall Drugs, U.S. Post Office**
48	Roggen
Gas	**N:** Texaco(*)
	S: Amoco(*)
Lodg	**N: I-76 Motel**
	S: Prairie Motel
AServ	**S:** Amoco
49	Painter Road
57	CR 91
60	To CO 144 East, Orchard
64	Wiggins
66A	CO 39, Goodrich, CO 52, Wiggins
FStop	**N: Amoco**(*)
	S: Sinclair(*, LP)
Food	**N: The Trophy Room (Amoco)**
Parks	**N: Jackson Lake State Park**
66B	U.S. 34 West, Greeley, Estes Park (Westbound, Reaccess Eastbound Only, Difficult Reaccess)
73	Long Bridge Rd
TServ	**N: Temco Truck, Trailer**
(75)	**Weigh Station (Eastbound)**
(75)	**Weigh Station (Westbound)**
75A	Bus Loop I-76 East, US 34, Ft. Morgan
Gas	**S:** Amoco(*)
Food	**S:** Quality Inn
Lodg	**S:** Quality Inn
RVCamp	**S: Wayward Wind Camp**
ATM	**S:** Amoco
79	CO 144, Weldona
80	CO 52, Ft. Morgan, New Raymer
Gas	**S:** Conoco(*, 24), Total(*)
Food	**S:** A & W Restaurant, Arby's, Dairy Queen, **McDonald's**, Subway, Taco John's
Lodg	**S:** DAYS INN Days Inn, Super 8
Med	**S: ✚ Hospital**
ATM	**S:** Conoco
Other	**S: K-Mart, Museum**, Washway Laundromat
82	Barlow Rd, Ft. Morgan
FStop	**N: Texaco**(*)
	S: Coastal(*)
Food	**N: The Fort Restaurant**
	S: Coastal
Lodg	**N: EconoLodge**
RVCamp	**N: Camping**
86	Dodd Bridge Road
89	Hospital Rd
Med	**S: ✚ Hospital**
90B	CO 71 North, Snyder, CO 71 South Brush
TStop	**N: Texaco**(*, LP, SCALES)
Gas	**S:** Conoco(*)
Food	**N:** Pizza Hut, Tex Sahara, Wendy's
	S: McDonald's
Lodg	**N:** Best Western
TServ	**N: Texaco**(SCALES)
TWash	**N: Texaco**
ATM	**N: Texaco**
92B	U.S. 6 East
92A	I-76 to U.S. 34. Brush, to CO 71 South, Limon; to Akron, U.S. 34 Yuma, Wray
95	Hillrose
102	Merino
(108)	**Rest Area (RR, Picnic, Vending, RV Dump, P; Eastbound)**
(108)	**Rest Area (RR, Picnic, Vending, RV Dump; Westbound)**
115	CO 63, Atwood
FStop	**N: Sinclair**(*, LP)
Gas	**S:** Standard(D)
Food	**N: Prairie-Land Cafe (Sinclair)**
	S: The Steak House Fine Dining
AServ	**S:** Standard

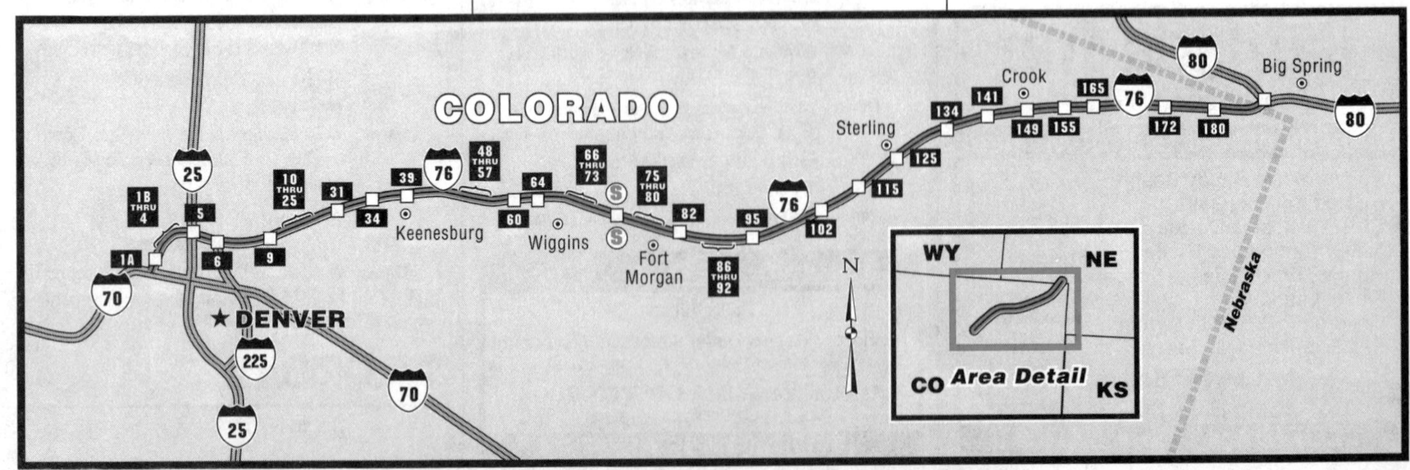

Bold red print shows RV & Bus parking available or nearby

EXIT COLORADO

Med N: Hospital

125 U.S. 6 West, Sterling, to CO 61 South, Otis, to CO 14, to U.S. 138

FStop N: Ampride(*)
S: Total(*)

Food N: RKJ's Family Dining
S: Days Inn, Ramada Inn

Lodg N: Best Western, First Interstate Inn
S: Days Inn, Ramada Inn, Super 8

AServ N: Ampride

RVCamp S: Buffalo Hills Campground(LP)

Med N: Hospital

Other N: Overland Trail Express, Tourist Info.

134 Lliff

141 Proctor

149 CO 55, Crook, Fleming

FStop S: Sinclair(*)

Food S: Sinclair

(151) Welcome Center (RR, Phones, Picnic, Vending, RV Dump; Westbound)

(151) Welcome Center (RR, Phones, Picnic, Vending, RV Dump; Eastbound)

155 Red Lion Rd

165 Sedgwick, Haxtun

FStop N: Conoco(*)

Gas N: Total(*)

Food N: Lucy's Place Cafe, Taco Bell Express (Total)

ATM N: Total

172 Ovid

(180) Rest Area, Welcome Center (RR, HF, Phones, Picnic, Grills, Vending, Pet Walk, P)

180 U.S. 385, Julesburg, Holyoke, COlorado Welcome Center

TStop N: Flying J Travel Plaza(*)

FStop S: Conoco(*)

Gas N: Texaco

Food N: Fast From Scratch, Platte Valley Inn, Sweden Creme
S: Conoco

Lodg N: Platte Valley Inn

AServ N: Texaco

TServ N: Flying J Travel Plaza

Med N: Hospital

ATM N: Flying J Travel Plaza

↑COLORADO

Begin I-76 COLORADO

EXIT OHIO

Begin I-76 OHIO

↓OHIO

2 OH 3, Seville, Medina

RVCamp N: Bob's Maple Lakes Campground (2 Miles)
S: Camping

(6) Weigh Station

7 OH 57, Rittman, Medina

9 OH 94, North Royalton, Wadsworth

11 OH 261, Norton

13AB OH 21, Cleveland, Massillon

14 Cleve - Mass Road

16 Barber Road

Lodg N: Days Inn (see our ad this page)

17A State St (Eastbound, Reaccess Westbound Only)

17 OH 619, Barberton, Wooster Road

18 Jct I-277, U.S. 224 East, Canton, Barberton (Left Exit)

19 Kenmore Blvd

20 Jct I-77 North, Cleveland (Left Exit Eastbound)

21A East Ave (Reaccess Southbound Only)

Gas S: Citgo(*, D)

AServ S: NA Auto Repair

21B Lake Shore, Bowery St (Southbound, Reaccess Southbound Only)

Med N: Hospital

1522
DAYS INN
Restaurant Nearby
Continental Breakfast
Kids 12 and under Stay Free
Outdoor Pool • Golf Nearby
Pets Allowed ($1 per day)
Handicap Accessible
Truck/Large Vehicle Parking
Jacuzzi Suites
330-758-2371
Boardman, OH
OHIO ▪ I-76 ▪ EXIT 16

EXIT OHIO

21C OH 59 E, Acron, Dart Ave. (Reaccess Southbound Only)

Parks S: George Sisler Field/ Summit Lake Park

22A Main Street, Broadway

Other N: Acron Art Museum, Aldi Grocery Store

22B Grant St, Wolf Ledges

Gas S: BP(*)

Food S: McDonald's

23A JCT I-77, Canton

23B OH 8 N, Cuyahoga Falls (Left Exit Eastbound)

24 Arlington St, Kelly Ave

25B Martha Ave, General St, Brittan Rd

26 OH 18, East Market St, Mogadore

FStop N: Shell(*)

Gas S: Speedway(*)

Food N: J.D.'s Restaurant, Tomy's (Shell)
S: East Side Cafe, Lamp Post Restaurant, McDonald's, Pizza, Subway

AServ N: Goodyear Tire & Auto
S: Akron Auto Sales

Other S: Evergreen Mini-Market, Revco Drugs

27 OH 91, Gilchrist Road, Canton Road

29 OH 532, Mogadore, Tallmadge

31 County Road 18, Tallmadge

33 OH 43, Kent, Hartville

RVCamp S: Cherokee Park Campground (2 Miles)

38 OH 5, OH 44, Ravenna

43 OH 14, Alliance

(46) Rest Area (RR, Phones, Picnic)

48 OH 225, Alliance

54 OH 534, Lake Milton, Newton Falls

RVCamp N: Green Acres Lake Park (.5 Miles)

57 To OH 45, Bailey Road, Warren

Note: I-76 runs concurrent below with OHTNPK. Numbering follows OHTNPK.

15 **(60)** Jct I-80 East, to New York City, I-76 West to TNPK (Toll)

16 **(233)** OH 7, Youngstown

TStop S: Penn Ohio Plaza(*, D, SCALES, 24) (Amoco, CB Shop)

FStop S: Speedway(*, D, LP, K)

Food N: Calla-Mar Restaurant & Manor, Dairy Queen, Outer Limits (Knights Inn), Smaldino's Italian (Super 8 Motel)

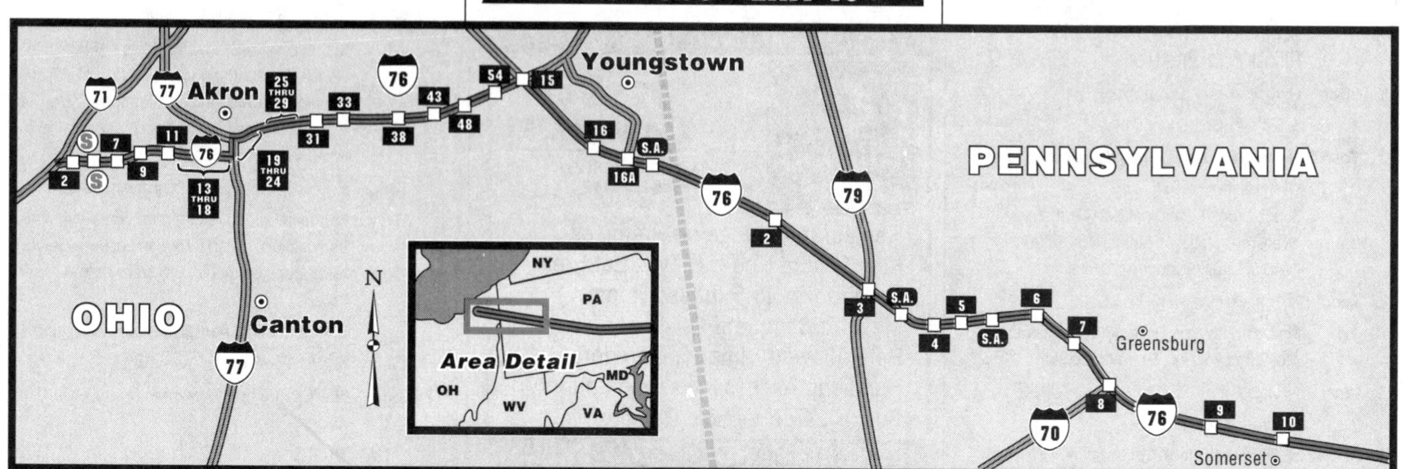

Bold red print shows RV & Bus parking available or nearby

EXIT OHIO/PENNSYLVANIA

S: Giuseppe's (PennOhio TS), Penn Ohio Plaza (Amoco, CB Shop), Roadhouse Restaurant

Lodg N: Budget Inn, Economy Inn, Knight's Inn, Microtel Inn & Suites, Super 8, Days Inn (see our ad this page)

S: Davis Motel, Rodeway Inn

AServ S: North Lima Tire(24)

TServ N: Valley Truck Outfitters

S: Penn Ohio Plaza(SCALES, 24) (Amoco, CB Shop)

ATM S: Penn Ohio Plaza (Amoco, CB Shop)

Other N: Car Wash

16A **(234)** Jct I-680 North, Youngstown (Westbound)

(237) **Glacier Hills Service Plaza**

FStop B: Sunoco(*, D)

Food B: McDonald's

AServ B: Sunoco

(239) Toll Booth (Toll)

↑OHIO

↓PENNSYLVANIA

Note: I-76 runs concurrent above with OHTNPK. Numbering follows OHTNPK.

(1) Toll Plaza (Toll)

1A **(9)** Newcastle, PA 60, Pittsburgh (Toll)

2 **(13)** PA 18, Ellwood City, Beaver Falls (Toll)

Food N: Alpine Inn, Holiday Inn, Sim's Bowl

S: Guiseppe's Italian, Irish Pub (Conley Inn)

Lodg N: Alpine Inn, Beaver Valley Motel, Danny's Motel, Hilltop Motel, Holiday Inn (see our ad this page), Lark Motel

S: Conley Inn, Motel

TServ S: EZ Sleep Bunk Sales Co.

RVCamp S: Camping

Med N: ✚ Hospital

Other N: Sim's Bowl

S: Laser's Roller Rink

(16) **Parking Area (Picnic)**

(22) **Zelienople Service Plaza (Eastbound)**

FStop E: Sunoco(*, D, LP, 24)

Food E: Roy Rogers, TCBY

(24) **Parking Area (Picnic; Eastbound)**

(26) **Parking Area (Picnic; Eastbound)**

(27) **Parking Area (Picnic; Eastbound)**

3 **(28)** Cranberry, I-79, U.S. 19, Pittsburgh, Erie (Toll)

Gas N: Amoco(CW, 24), Exxon(*, D)

S: BP(*, D, LP), Gulf, Sunoco(*, LP)

Food N: Hardee's, Kings Family(24), Long John Silver, Pizza Outlet, Wendy's

S: Bob Evan's Restaurant, Eat N Park, Italian Oven, Lone Star Steakhouse, Max & Erma's, Perkin's Family Restaurant, Sheraton

Lodg N: Fairfield Inn

S: Days Inn, Holiday Inn Express, Oak Leaf Motel, Red Roof Inn, Sheraton, Super 8

AServ N: Exxon

S: Jorden's Service Center

RVCamp N: Pittsburgh North Campground (.75 Miles)

EXIT PENNSYLVANIA

Med N: ✚ Hospital

ATM N: Exxon, Giant Eagle Grocery(RX), National City, Northside Bank, Shop 'N Save Supermarket

S: BP

Other N: Big K-Mart(RX), Eckerd Drugs(RX), Giant Eagle Grocery(RX), Shop 'N Save Supermarket

(31) **Butler Service Plaza (Westbound)**

FStop W: Sunoco(*, D)

Food W: Burger King, Popeye's Chicken

4 **(39)** PA 8, Pittsburgh, Butler, Butler Valley (Toll)

Gas N: BP(*, LP), Exxon(*, D), Sheetz(*, LP, K, 24)

Food N: Eat N Park, Monte Cello's Pizza, Pittsburg North Motor Lodge, Venus Diner

S: Arby's, Baskin Robbins, Donut Connection, McDonald's, Steakhouse (EconoLodge)

Lodg N: Comfort Inn, Pittsburg North Motor Lodge

S: EconoLodge

AServ N: Advanced Auto Parts, BP, Exxon, Gibsonia Auto Parts

S: Goodyear Tire & Auto, Midas Muffler & Brake, Parts America, Premium Plus, Valvoline Oil Change

ATM N: Exxon

S: PNC Bank

Other N: LP Welding Supplies

S: All Pet Animal Hospital, Eckerd Drugs(RX), Rt. 8 Shammy Car Wash

5 **(47)** PA 28, New Kensington, Pittsburgh, Allegheny Valley (Toll)

Gas N: Amoco(CW, 24)

1502

724-846-3700
800-613-1490

Newly Renovated

King Leisure Rooms
Mr. P's Restaurant/Lounge
Indoor Pool, Saunas & Whirlpool
Mini golf, Table Tennis & Game Room
Meeting/Banquet Facilities
Downtown Beaver Falls & Geneva College Nearby

7195 Eastwood Rd • Beaver Falls, PA 15010

PENNSYLVANIA ▪ I-76 ▪ EXIT 2

Pittsburgh/New Kensington

724-335-9171
New Kensington, PA

I-76, Exit #5, PA Rt 28
North Exit #14

Restaurant/Lounge on Premises
Kids 12 and Under Stay & Eat Free
Outdoor Pool • Exercise Room
Meeting/Banquet Facilities
Pets Allowed • Interior Corridors
Handicap Accessible • Coin Laundry
Bus or Large Vehicle Parking

1456

PENNSYLVANIA ▪ I-76 ▪ EXIT 5

EXIT PENNSYLVANIA

Food N: Arabian Knights, Sam Morgan's Clubhouse Inn, Tail Gators

S: Big Time Pizza & Wings, Burger King, Denny's, Jetz Restaurant (Holiday Inn), KFC, Kings Family Restaurant(24), Ladbrokes Racing & Dining, McDonald's, Mother Butler Deserts (Denny's), Periwinkle Bakery, Taco Bell, Wendy's

Lodg N: Clarion Hotel (north on Rt 28 to Exit 14, see our ad this page)

S: Comfort Inn, Days Inn, Holiday Inn, Super 8

AServ N: Cooper Tires

S: Coxon's Ford

Med S: ✚ Medi Center

ATM S: NBOC Bank

Other N: Harmar Full Service Car Wash

(49) **Oakmont Service Plaza (Eastbound)**

FStop E: Sunoco(*, D, 24)

6 **(57)** Junction I-376, U.S. 22, Pittsburgh, Monroeville (Toll)

Gas N: Citgo(*, K), Gulf(D), Sunoco(*, 24)

S: BP(*, CW)

Food N: Bruster's Old Fashion Ice Cream, Taco Bell Express (Citgo)

S: Bageland, Baskin Robbins, Big Boy, Burger King, Daisy's (Palace Inn), Damon's Ribs, Darbar Indian (Sunrise Inn), Dunkin Donuts, Fennigan's (Holiday Inn), Kenny Roger's Roasters, Moio's Italian Pastry Shop, Outback Steakhouse, Ponderosa Steakhouse, Taco Bell

Lodg N: East Exit Motel

S: Days Inn, Hampton Inn, Holiday Inn, King's Motel, Palace Inn, Red Roof Inn, Sunrise Inn, William Penn Motel

AServ N: Advanced Auto Glass, Gulf

S: Cochran Olds/GMC Trucks/Isuzu/Infinity/Suzuki/Saturn, NTB, Valley Buick

Med S: ✚ Hospital

ATM N: Sunoco

S: Dollar Bank, Mellon Bank, PNC Bank

Parks S: Boyce Park

Other N: Giant Eagle Grocery(RX)

S: Eckerd Drugs(RX), Mosside Animal Clinic, Penn Super Pharmacy(RX)

7 **(67)** U.S. 30, Irwin, Greensburg (Toll)

Gas N: BP(*, LP, CW), Sheetz(*, K, 24), Texaco

Food N: Blimpie Subs & Salads (BP), Sheetz

S: Bob Evan's Restaurant, Burger King, China House, Eat N Park, Ilona's Cafe, Lincoln Hills Country Club, McDonald's, Side Show Pizza, Taco Bell, Teddy's, The Italian Oven, Vincent's Pizza & Pasta, Wendy's

Lodg S: Holiday Inn Express, Penn Irwin Motel

AServ N: Import Export Tire Company, Straw Pump Auto Body, Texaco, Truszka Foreign Car Parts/Service, Ultra Sound Car Audio, WD Sales Auto & Truck Parts

S: Advance Auto Parts, Jiffy Lube, Muffler King

TServ N: WD Sales Auto & Truck Parts

RVCamp N: B's RV Center, Turner Airstream, Inc. (1.5 Miles)

ATM N: BP, Sheetz

Bold red print shows RV & Bus parking available or nearby

EXIT	PENNSYLVANIA
	S: Giant Eagle Grocery(24, RX), PNC Bank, Shop 'N Save Supermarket
Other	**N:** Turnpike Laundromat
	S: Eckerd Drugs(RX), Giant Eagle Grocery(RX), Lincoln Hills Country Club, Shop 'N Save Supermarket
(75)	**Hempfield Service Plaza (Eastbound)**
FStop	**E:** Sunoco(*, D)
Food	**E:** Breyer's Ice Cream, McDonald's, Oscar Meyer Hot Dogs
ATM	**E:** Sunoco
8	**(75)** Jct I-70W, U.S. 119, PA 66 N, New Stanton, Greensburg, Wheeling WV (Toll)
RVCamp	**S:** Fox Den Acres Campground (2 Miles)
(78)	**New Stanton Service Plaza (Westbound)**
FStop	**W:** Sunoco(*)
Food	**W:** King's Family, McDonald's
ATM	**W:** Machine
9	**(91)** Donegal, PA 31, PA 711, Legonier, Uniontown (Toll)
FStop	**S:** Citgo(*)
Gas	**S:** Exxon(*, D), Sunoco, Texaco(*)
Food	**N:** Laurel Highlands Lodge, Tall Cedars Inn
	S: Candlelight Family, Dairy Queen
Lodg	**N:** Laurel Highlands Lodge
	S: DAYS INN Days Inn, Donegal Motel
AServ	**S:** Sunoco
RVCamp	**S:** Donegal Campground (.5 Miles), Laurel Highland Campgrounds (.75 Miles), Mountain Pines Campground (3 Miles), Pioneer Park Campground (11 Miles)
ATM	**S:** PNC Bank
Parks	**S:** Kooser State Park, Laurel Hills State Park, Laurel Ridge State Park, Ohiopyle State Park
(94)	**Parking Area (Picnic; Westbound)**
10	**(110)** U.S. 219, Somerset, Johnstown (Toll)
TStop	**S:** Jim's Auto/Truckstop(*)
Gas	**N:** Quick Fill, Sheetz(*), Your Car Wash
	S: Exxon(*)
Food	**N:** Hoss's Steakhouse, Kings Family Restaurant, Pizza Hut, Taco Bell
	S: Arby's, China Garden, Dairy Queen, Dunkin Donuts, Eat N Park, Holiday Inn, Jim's TS, KFC, Little Caesars Pizza, Long John Silver, Maggie Mae's Cafe, McDonald's, Myron's Restaurant, Pine Grill, Ramada Inn, Subway, Summit Diner, Wendy's, Yogurt Ice Cream Classics
Lodg	**N:** Dollar Inn, Economy Inn
	S: Best Western, Budget Host Inn, Budget Inn, DAYS INN Days Inn, Economy Inn, Hampton Inn, Holiday Inn, Knight's Inn, Ramada
AServ	**N:** Dumbaulds Tire, Ford Dealership, Mardis Chrysler Plymouth, Midas Muffler & Brake, Speedy Lube
TServ	**N:** Mulhollen
	S: Jim's Auto/Truckstop
TWash	**N:** Your Car Wash
Med	**S:** ✚ Hospital
ATM	**S:** Jim's TS
Other	**N:** Coin Car Wash, Horizon Outlet Center
	S: Clean Water Car Wash, Coin Laundry, Visitor Information
(112)	**Somerset Service Plaza**
FStop	**B:** Sunoco(*)
Food	**B:** Bob's Big Boy, Hershey's Ice Cream, Roy Rogers, TCBY
	W: Burger King, Hershey's Ice Cream, TCBY
AServ	**B:** Sunoco
ATM	**B:** ATM
11	**(146)** U.S. 220, Bedford, Altoona, Johnstown (Toll)
FStop	**N:** Amoco(*), BP(*)
Gas	**N:** Sunoco(*, D), Texaco(*, D, LP)
Food	**N:** Baskin Robbins, Budget Inn (Sunoco), Burger King, Chester Fried Chicken (BP), China Inn, Clara's Place (Best Western), Denny's, Dunkin Donuts, Ed's Steakhouse, Hardee's, Hoss's Steak & Sea House, Long John Silver, McDonald's (Amoco), Pizza Hut, Sub Express, The Arena (Quality Inn), The Country Apple Restaurant (EconoLodge)
Lodg	**N:** Best Western, Budget Inn, Econolodge, Host Inn, Midway Motel, Quality Inn, Super 8
	S: Motor Town House
TServ	**N:** Mack Truck
RVCamp	**S:** Friendship Village Campground
ATM	**N:** BP
Other	**S:** Visitor Information
(147)	**North Midway Service Plaza**
FStop	**B:** Sunoco(*)
Food	**B:** Hershey's Ice Cream, KFC, Mrs Fields Cookies, Sbarro Italian, TCBY
AServ	**B:** Sunoco
ATM	**B:** PNC Bank
12	**(161)** U.S. 30, Everett, Breezewood, to I-70 East, Hagerstown (Toll)
TStop	**S:** All American 76 Truck Plaza(*, SCALES), T/A TravelCenters of America(*, SCALES)
Gas	**S:** Amoco (TA), BP(*), Citgo(*), Exxon(*, D), Sheetz(*), Sunoco(*), Texaco(*)
Food	**N:** Breeze Manor Restaurant (Quality Inn), McDonald's, Prime Rib Restaurant (Ramada Inn)
	S: Arby's, Arthur Treacher's Fish & Chips, Blimpie's Subs (Am Best), Bob Evan's Restaurant, Bonanza Steakhouse, Burger King, Dairy Queen(*, SCALES) (TA), Deli Cafe (Sunoco), Family House Restaurant (Bus Parking), Gateway Restaurant (TA), Hardee's, Hershey's Ice Cream (Am Best), KFC, Little Caesars Pizza (TA), McDonald's, Oven Fresh Bakery (TA), Perkins Family Restaurant (Am Best), Pizza Hut, Post House Cafeteria (Am Best), Stuckey's Express (Exxon), Subway, Taco Bell, Taco Maker (Am Best), Uncle Bud's Pizza (Am Best), Wendy's
Lodg	**N:** Pan Am Motel, Quality Inn, Ramada Inn
	S: Best Western, Breezewood Motel, Comfort Inn, Econolodge (TA), Penn Aire Motel, Wiltshire Motel
TServ	**S:** AmBest, T/A TravelCenters of America
RVCamp	**N:** Breezewood Campground (.25 Miles)
ATM	**S:** Sunoco, T/A TravelCenters of America
(172)	**Sideling Hill Service Area (RV Dump)**
FStop	**B:** Sunoco(*)
Food	**B:** Bob's Big Boy, Burger King, Pretzel Time, TCBY
AServ	**B:** Sunoco
ATM	**B:** PNC Bank
Other	**B:** RV Dump Station, Tourist Info.
13	**(179)** U.S. 522, McConnelsburg, Mount Union (Toll)
Gas	**N:** Amoco(*), Exxon(*)
Food	**N:** Fort Family Restaurant
Lodg	**N:** Downe's Motel #2

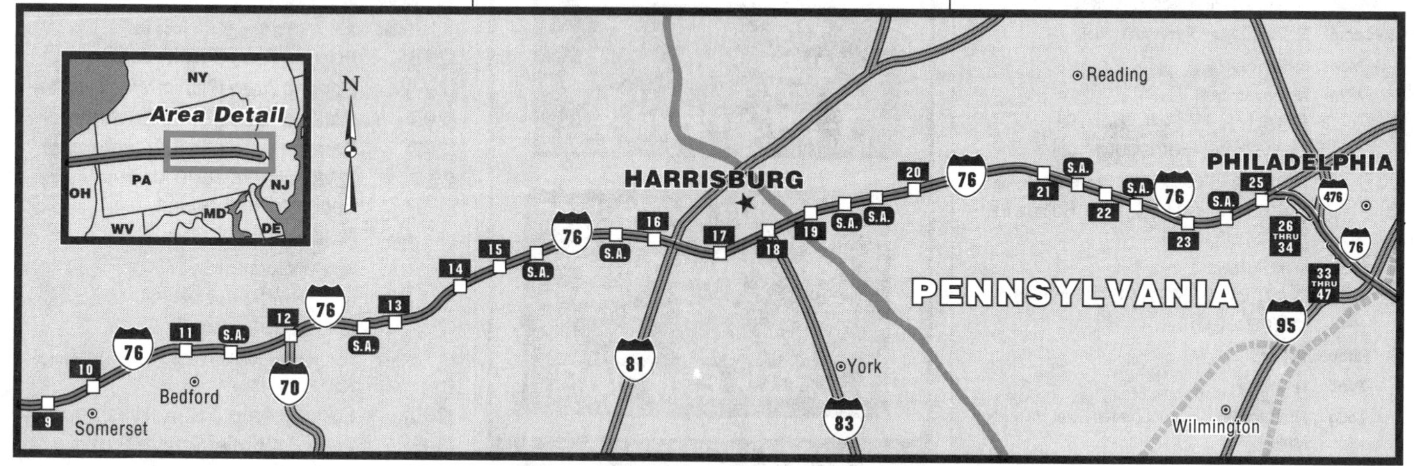

Bold red print shows RV & Bus parking available or nearby

S: Downe's Motel
ASery N: Amoco
Med N: Hospital
Other N: State Police

14 **(189)** PA 75, Fort Loudon, Willow Hill (Toll)
Food S: TJ's Restaurant
Lodg S: Willow Hill Motel

15 **(201)** PA 997, Blue Mountain, Shippensburg, Chambersburg (Toll)
Gas S: Johnnies
Food S: Johnnies
Lodg S: Blue Mountain Brick Motel, Kenmar Motel

(203) Blue Mountain Service Area (Westbound)
FStop W: Sunoco[*]
Food W: Mrs. Field's, Roy Rogers, TCBY
AServ W: Sunoco
ATM W: PNC Bank

(214) Pennsylvania State Police (Westbound)

(215) Parking Area (Picnic; Eastbound)

(219) Plainfield Service Area (Eastbound)
FStop E: Sunoco[*]
Food E: Roy Rogers, TCBY
AServ E: Sunoco

(224) Parking Area (Picnic; Eastbound)

16 **(226)** U.S. 11, to I-81, Carlisle, Harrisburg (Toll)
TStop N: All American Truck Plaza, AmBest Truck Stop[*, SCALES], Flying J Travel Plaza[*, LP, SCALES], Gables of Carlisle[*, SCALES]
Gas N: BP[*], Citgo, Gables[*, LP], Shell, Texaco[*, LP]
Food N: AmBest Truck Stop, Arby's, Best Western, Bob Evan's Restaurant, Budget Host Inn, Carelli's, Dunkin Donuts, Eat N Park, Embers Inn, Flying J Travel Plaza, Hardee's, Holiday Inn, Iron Kettle Restaurant, McDonald's, Middlesex Diner, Subway, Western Sizzlin'
S: Hoss's Steak and Seahouse
Lodg N: Appalachian Motor Inn, Best Western, Budget Host Inn, Econolodge, Embers Inn, Hampton Inn, Holiday Inn, Quality Inn, Rodeway Inn, Super 8, Thrift Lodge
S: Motel 6
AServ N: Citgo
TServ N: AmBest Truck Stop (CB sales & service), Flying J Travel Plaza, Soco All American
TWash N: AmBest Truck Stop, Gables TS
RVCamp S: Carlisle Campground (1 Mile)
Med S: Hospital
ATM N: Farmers Trust

17 **(236)** U.S. 15, Gettysburg Pike, Gettysburg, Harrisburg (Toll)

(237) Parking Area (Picnic; Eastbound)

18 **(242)** Junction I-83, York, Baltimore, Harrisburg (Toll)
Med S: Hospital

19 **(247)** Jct I-283, PA 283, Hershey, Harrisburg (Toll)
FStop N: Citgo[*]
Food N: Wendy's
Lodg N: Days Inn, Doubletree Hotel, Hollywood Motel
S: Holiday Inn (2 locations on I-283 -- see our ad this page)
AServ N: Citgo
Med N: Hospital
Other S: Harrisburg Int'l Airport

(251) Highspire Service Plaza (Eastbound)
FStop E: Sunoco[*, D, 24]
Food E: TCBY
N: Sbarro Italian
ATM E: Sunoco

(252) Parking Area (Both Sides)

(253) Parking Area (Eastbound)

(254) Parking Area (Westbound)

(255) Picnic Area (Picnic; Westbound)

Nationwide Reservations: 1-800-257-3297
1648
DAYS INN®
Restaurant/Lounge on Premises
Kids Under 12 Stay & Eat Free
Outdoor/Indoor Pool
Meeting/Banquet Facilities
Tennis on Premises
Truck/Large Vehicle Parking
Coin Laundry
Exterior/Interior Corridors
U.S. 222S, to 30W, to PA 501S., right at second light.
717-299-5700 • Lancaster, PA
PENNSYLVANIA • I-76 • EXIT 21

1576
Two Locations
Holiday Inn®
Full Service Restaurant
Lounge
Swimming Pool
Health Club Facilities
Spectra vision
Newly Renovated Spacious Guest Rooms
Holiday Inn - Harrisburg
4751 Lindle Road
Harrisburg, PA 17111
717-939-7841
I-283 • Exit 1
Holiday Inn - Lancaster
Host Golf Resort
Conference Center
Golf & Indoor Tennis
717-299-5500
I-283 • Exit 30E
PA • I-283 • 2 LOCATIONS

(259) Lawn Service Plaza (Westbound)
FStop N: Sunoco[*]
Food N: Burger King

(262) Parking Area (Picnic; Westbound)

(263) Parking Area (Picnic; Eastbound)

(264) Picnic Area (Eastbound)

20 **(266)** PA 72, Lebanon, Lancaster (Northbound, Toll)
FStop N: Texaco[D]
Food N: Hull's Stagecoach, Little Corner of Germany Cafe, Mt Hope Family Restaurant
Lodg N: Hull's Stagecoach Motor Inn
S: Friendship Inn, Red Carpet Inn, Roadway Inn
AServ N: Auto Repair
TServ N: Hilltop Truck Service (Texaco)
RVCamp S: Pinch Pond Campground (3.5 to 4.0 Miles)
Med N: Hospital, VA Medical Center
Other S: Renaissance Fair

(268) Parking Area (Picnic; Eastbound)

(269) Parking Area (Picnic; Eastbound)

(270) Parking Area (Picnic; Eastbound)

(274) Picnic Area (Picnic)

21 **(286)** U.S. 222, Reading, Ephrata (Southbound, Toll)
Gas S: Citgo[*, LP]
Food S: Black Horse Restaurant, Country Pride BBQ, Geoffery's (Holiday Inn), Procopio's Pizza, Zinn's Diner
Lodg S: Days Inn (S. on U.S. 222 to PA 501S, right at second light -- see our ad this page), Black Horse Lodge, Comfort Inn, Holiday Inn, Penn Amish Motel, Pennsylvania Dutch Motel, Red Carpet Inn
AServ S: Scubber Auto (Wrecker Service)
TServ S: Dutchman Truck Service
RVCamp N: Dutch Cousins Wooded Campgroung, Shady Grove Campground, Sill's Campground, Sun Valley Campground
S: Hickory Run Campground, KOA Campgrounds (.13 Miles), Red Run Campground
Med N: Hospital
ATM S: BBNB Nat'l Bank, Fulton Bank (Weaver Mkt)
Other S: Antique Malls, Doll Express, Tourist Info., Weaver Mkt Supermarket[RX]

(289) State Police Outpost

(290) Bowmansville Service Plaza, Rest Area (RR, Phones; Eastbound)
FStop S: Sunoco[*, D]
Food S: Bob's Big Boy, TCBY, Taco Bell

(291) Parking Area (Picnic; Eastbound)

(294) Parking Area (Picnic; Westbound)

(295) Parking Area (Picnic; Eastbound)

(297) Parking Area (Picnic; Eastbound)

22 **(298)** Jct I-176, PA10 Morgantown, Reading (Northbound, Toll)
Food N: Heritage
S: Celebrations (Holiday Inn)
Lodg N: The Inn at Morgantown
S: Holiday Inn
Other N: Carr's Recreation Park, Hopewell Furnace Nat'l Historic Site

(300) Parking Area (Picnic; Westbound)

(305) Peter J. Camiel Service Plaza

EXIT PENNSYLVANIA

(Westbound)
- **FStop** W: Sunoco(*)
- **Food** N: Roy Rogers, Sbarro Italian, TCBY

23 **(312)** PA 100, Pottstown, West Chester (Southbound, Toll)
- **Med** S: Hospital

(320) Parking Area

(325) Valley Forge Service Area, Rest Area (Phones, Picnic, RV Dump; Eastbound)
- **FStop** S: Sunoco(*)
- **Food** S: Burger King, Mrs Fields Cookies, Nathan's, TCBY

24 **(326)** Jct I-76 E, to U.S.202, to I-476, Philadelphia, Valley Forge

25 **(326)** Valley Forge, Mall Blvd, Northtown Rd
- **Gas** N: Exxon(*), Mobil(*, CW)
- **Food** N: Bennigan's, Charlie's Place, Chili's, Denny's, Dick Clark's American Bandstand Grill, Doubletree, Dunkin Donuts, Food & Spirits Co, Food Court at The Plaza King Of Prussia Mall, Jade Diner, Lone Star Steakhouse, Ruby Diner, Starbucks Coffee, T.G.I. Friday's, Uno Pizzeria
- **Lodg** N: Best Western, Doubletree, Fairfield Inn, Holiday Inn, MacIntosh Inn
- **AServ** N: Jiffy Lube (The Plaza King Of Prussia Mall), Penske, Sears (The Plaza King Of Prussia Mall)
- **ATM** N: CoreStates Bank
- **Other** N: Pearl Express, The Plaza King Of Prussia Mall

26AB **(327)** U.S. 202, King of Prussia, West Chester (Northside Services Merge With Exit 25,)
- **Gas** N: Exxon(*), Exxon
  S: Sunoco(*)
- **Food** N: Brandywine Grill, Carlucci's Grill, Chili's, Houlihan's, McDonald's, Pizzaria Uno, Rath Bone
- **Lodg** N: Holiday Inn, Howard Johnson, Motel 6
- **AServ** N: Exxon, Jiffy Lube
- **Med** S: Hospital
- **ATM** N: Jefferson, Mellon Bank, Merridian, PCN Bank
  S: Royal Bank of Pennsylvania
- **Other** N: Wa Wa Food Market
  S: Plymouth Mall

(328) King of Prussia Plaza (RR, HF, Phones, Picnic)

27 **(330)** PA 320, Gulph Mills (Eastbound)

28AB **(331)** Jct I-476 Chester, Plymouth Meeting

29 **(332)** PA 23, Conshohocken (Westbound, Reaccess Eastbound Only, Toll)

30 **(336)** Gladwyne (Westbound, Reaccess Eastbound Only)

31 **(337)** Belmont Ave, Green Lane Ave, Manayunk
- **Gas** S: Sunoco(*)
- **AServ** N: Tony's Transmissions
- **Med** N: Hospital

32 **(340)** Lincoln Dr, Kelly Dr (Left Exit Eastbound)

33 **(340)** U.S. 1 South, City Ave

34 **(340)** U.S. 1 North, Roosevelt Blvd

35 **(342)** Montgomery Dr, West River Dr (No Trucks Or Busses)

36 **(343)** U.S. 13, U.S. 30 West, East Fairmount Park, Girard Ave, Philadelphia Zoo

37 **(344)** Spring Garden St, Haverford Ave (Eastbound, Reaccess Westbound Only)

38 **(344)** Junction I-676, U.S. 30 East, Central Philadelphia (Left Exit Eastbound)

39 **(344)** 30th St, Station Market St

40 **(345)** South St (Left Exit Eastbound)

41 **(346)** Gray Ferry Ave, University Ave

42 **(347)** 28th St

43 **(386)** Passyunk Ave, Oregon Ave, to PA291

44 **(387)** PA 291, Chester

45 **(349)** PA 611, Broad St

46AB **(349)** to I-95, Paker Ave
- **Food** S: Holiday Inn
- **Lodg** S: Holiday Inn

(352) Neshaminy Service Plaza (RR, HF, Phones, Picnic, RV Dump)

↑PENNSYLVANIA

Begin I-76 OHIO

Notes:

EXIT	OHIO

Begin I-77

↓OHIO

163 East 9th St., Junction I-90

162B East 22nd, East 14th
- **Med** E: St. Vincent Charity Hospital
- **ATM** E: Ohio Educational Credit Union

162A Woodland Ave, East 30th St
- **Other** E: Bello Foods Wholesale

161B Junction I-490 West, East 55th St, Toledo

161A OH 14, Broadway (Northbound, Reaccess Southbound Only)
- **Food** E: Sin Tavern & Cafe
- **AServ** W: A & E Auto Sales & Repair
- **TWash** E: United Truck Wash

160 Pershing Ave (Northbound, Reaccess Southbound Only)
- **Gas** E: Clark[*, K]
- **Food** E: Donut Factory, Fourty Niner Restaurant
- **Med** E: Hospital
- **ATM** E: Clark

159B Fleet Ave. (Difficult Reaccess)
- **Gas** E: BP[*, D, LP]
- **Food** E: Open Pantry Market (Fried Chicken), Village Pizza
- **AServ** E: Bert's & Son Auto Parts, Kilner's Auto Sales
- **Parks** W: Washington Park Recreation Area

159A Harvard Ave, Newburgh Heights
- **Gas** W: BP[*, D], Marathon[*, K]
- **Food** E: Borderline Cafe, Brown's Tavern
  W: Subway (BP)
- **ATM** W: BP, Marathon
- **Other** E: Brown's Food Market
  W: Zoo

158 Grant Ave, Cuyahoga Heights
- **Other** W: Police Department

157 OH21, OH17, Granger Rd., Rexville Rd. (Southbound)

156 Junction I-480, Toledo, Youngstown

155 Rockside Rd, Independence
- **Gas** E: Sunoco[*]
  W: BP[D]
- **Food** E: Bob Evan's Restaurant, Chester's Fried Chicken, Chi Chi's Mexican Restaurant, Denny's, Holiday Inn, Mountain Jack's, Shula's Steakhouse (Hilton)
- **Lodg** E: Budgetel Inn, Comfort Inn, Hilton, Holiday Inn, Red Roof Inn
  W: Harley Hotel
- **Parks** E: Cayuga Valley National Recreation Area (2 Miles)

153 Pleasant Valley Rd, Seven Hills, Independence

151 Wallings Rd

149 OH 82, Brecksville, Broadview Hts
- **Gas** W: BP[*, LP]
- **Food** W: BP, Country Kitchen, Domino's Pizza, Mr Hero Subs
- **Lodg** W: Days Inn

147 to OH 21, to I-80, Miller Rd (Southbound, Difficult Reaccess)
- **Med** E: Veterans Administration Medical Center
- **Parks** E: Dover Lake Waterpark (5 Miles), Kaiser Valley National Recreation Area

145 OH 21, to I-80, Brecksville Rd, OH Tnpk (Northbound, Reaccess Southbound Only)
- **FStop** E: Speedway[*, D, LP]
- **Gas** E: BP[*]
- **Food** E: Dairy Queen, Holiday Inn, Richfield Family Restaurant
- **Lodg** E: Brushwood Motel, Holiday Inn, Super 8
- **Med** W: Acron General Community Health Center
- **ATM** E: Speedway
- **Parks** W: Earnest Run Metro Park

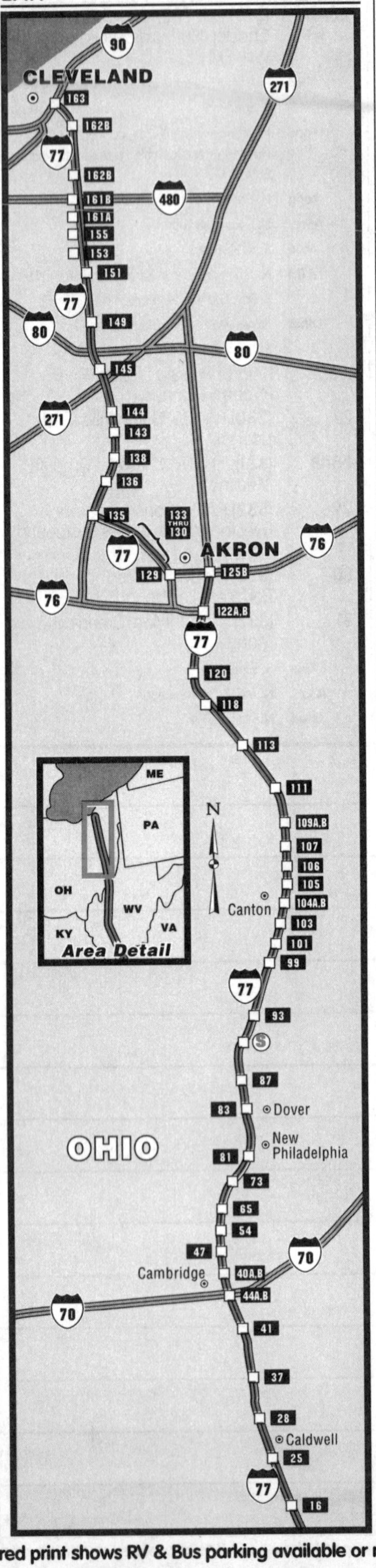

144 Junction I-271 North, Erie (PA)

143 OH 176, to Jct I-271 South, Richfield
- **Gas** W: Sunoco[*]
- **Food** W: McDonald's
- **ATM** W: McDonald's
- **Parks** E: Cuyahoga Valley Nat'l Recreation Area

(141) Rest Area (RR, Phones, Picnic; Southbound)

(141) Rest Area (RR, Phones, Picnic; Northbound)

138 Ghent Rd
- **Gas** W: BP[*]
- **Food** W: Jimbo's Drive-In

137AB OH 18, Fairlawn, Medina
- **Gas** E: Amoco[*, D], BP[*, LP, CW, 24], Marathon[*, LP]
- **Food** E: Applebee's, Bob Evan's Restaurant, Brubaker's Pub, Buck's Westside Bar & Grill (Holiday Inn), Chi Chi's Mexican Restaurant, Chili's, Cracker Barrel, Friendly's, Lone Star Steakhouse, Macaroni Grill, Mustard Seed Market & Cafe, Olive Garden, On Tap Grill & Bar, Red Lobster
  W: Burger King, Damon's Ribs, Don Pablo's Mexican, Eastside Mario's, Fuddruckers, Miss Kitty's Steakhouse, Outback Steakhouse, Shell's Seafood, T.G.I. Friday's
- **Lodg** E: Courtyard by Marriott, Fairfield Inn, Hampton Inn, Holiday Inn, Red Roof Inn, Super 8
  W: Best Western, Comfort Inn (see our ad this page), Extended Stay America, Radisson, Residence Inn, Studio PLUS
- **Med** W: Acron General Health & Wellness Center
- **ATM** E: Amoco, Bank One, Key Bank
  W: NationalCity Bank
- **Other** E: Acme Supermarket, K-Mart Supercenter[RX], Mustard Seed Market & Cafe

136 OH 21 South, Massillon (Left Exit Northbound)

135 Cleve - Mass Rd (Northbound, Reaccess Southbound Only)

133 Ridgewood Rd, Miller Rd (Difficult Reaccess)
- **Gas** E: Citgo[*, D, LP]

132 White Pond Dr, Mull Ave
- **Food** E: Fontano Restaurant, Interstate Kitchen
- **Parks** E: Jed Good Park & Golf Course

1448
Comfort Inn
Akron West
130 Montrose West
Akron, OH 44321
330-666-5050
Toll Free Reservations:
800-221-2222
Comfort Inn
- Bus & RV Parking
- Indoor Pool • Guest Laundry
- Free Continental Breakfast
- 53 Whirlpool Rooms
- Special Rates for Tour Groups

OHIO ▪ I-77 ▪ EXIT 137

Bold red print shows RV & Bus parking available or nearby

EXIT OHIO

131 OH 162, Copley Rd
- **Gas** W: BP[*, D]
- **Food** W: McDonald's
- **Other** E: Coin Car Wash, Coin Laundry, Zoo
  W: Animal Clinic

130 OH 261, Wooster Ave
- **Gas** E: Citgo[*, D], Clark[*, D, LP, K]
- **Food** E: Ann's Place[24], Burger King, Church's Chicken, New Ming Chinese, Rally's Hamburgers, White Castle Restaurant
  W: KFC
- **Other** E: Coin Car Wash
  W: Builder's Square[LP]

129 Junction I-76, Canton

Note: I-77 runs concurrent below with I-76. Numbering follows I-76.

21A East Ave (Reaccess Southbound Only)
- **Gas** S: Citgo[*, D]
- **AServ** S: NA Auto Repair

21B Lake Shore, Bowery St (Southbound, Reaccess Southbound Only)
- **Med** N: ✚ Hospital

21C OH 59 E, Acron, Dart Ave. (Reaccess Southbound Only)
- **Lodg** N: Ramada Plaza (see our ad this page)
- **Parks** S: George Sisler Field/ Summit Lake Park

22A Main Street, Broadway
- **Other** N: Acron Art Museum, Aldi Grocery Store

22B Grant St, Wolf Ledges
- **Gas** S: BP[*]
- **Food** S: McDonald's

23A JCT I-77, Canton

Note: I-77 runs concurrent above with I-76. Numbering follows I-76.

125B Junction I-76 East, Youngstown

125A OH 8 North, Cuyahoga Falls (Left Exit)

124B Lovers Lane, Coal Ave (Southbound)

124A Archwood Ave., Firestone Blvd N (Southbound, Reaccess Northbound Only)

123B OH 764, Wilbeth Rd, Waterloo Rd
- **Food** E: Carl's B & K Drive In, Castle Pizza, Dairy Queen
- **AServ** E: Texas 10 Minute Oil & Lube
  W: Firestone
- **ATM** E: National City Bank

123A Waterloo Rd (Southbound, Reaccess Northbound Only)
- **Gas** W: BP[*, LP]

EXIT OHIO

- **Food** W: Guy's Restaurant, Italo's, Rally's Hamburgers, Scorchers Casual Eatery
- **Other** W: Brown Street Laundry, Car Wash, Giant Eagle Supermarket

122AB Junction I-277, to I-76, U.S. 224, Mogadore, Barberton

120 Arlington Rd
- **Gas** E: Speedway[*, D, LP, K]
  W: BP[*]
- **Food** E: Big Boy, Denny's, Friendly's, Kenny Roger's Roasters, Pizza Hut, Ryan's Steakhouse, White Castle Restaurant
  W: BP, Blimpie Subs & Salads (BP), Bob Evan's Restaurant, Burger King, King Buffet, McDonald's, Taco Bell, Wendy's
- **Lodg** E: Comfort Inn, Holiday Inn, Red Roof Inn
  W: DAYS INN Days Inn
- **RVCamp** W: RV Super Center, Sirpilla RV Super Center[LP]
- **Other** E: Big K-Mart[RX], Full Service Car Wash, Wal-Mart[RX] (Vision Center)

118 OH 241, to OH619, Masillon Rd
- **Gas** E: Speedway[*, LP, K]
  W: Citgo[*, LP], Duke[*]
- **Food** E: Belgrade Garden South Restaurant, Bobby's Bistro, Gionino's Pizzeria, Subway
  W: Arby's, Lucky Star Chinese, McDonald's[PLAY], Menches Brothers
- **Lodg** W: Super 8
- **AServ** W: Green Auto Collision, Mack's Transmission
- **Med** W: ✚ Green Medical Center
- **ATM** E: Second National Bank
  W: Citgo, Giant Eagle Food Store[RX], Key Bank
- **Other** W: Coin Car Wash, Giant Eagle Food Store[RX], Green Animal Medical Center

113 Akron - Canton Airport
- **RVCamp** W: Clays Rv Center
- **Other** W: Airport

111 Portage St, Canal Fulton, North Canton
- **TStop** E: 76 Auto/Truck Plaza[*, D, SCALES]
- **Gas** E: Shell[*, LP, CW], Sunoco[*, D, LP]
  W: BP[*, D, LP]
- **Food** E: 76 Auto/Truck Plaza, Brew House Pub & Grill, Burger King, Chieng's Express, Marian's Donuts, Subway
  W: Borders Books & Music, Chuck E Cheese's Pizza, Cracker Barrel, Don Pablo's Mexican Restaurant, Einstein Bros Bagels, Joe's Crab Shack, Longhorn Steakhouse, McDonald's, McDonald's (Wal-Mart), Pizza Hut, Quizno's Classic Sub, Starbucks Coffee, Wendy's
- **Lodg** W: Best Western, Motel 6
- **RVCamp** E: Winn's RV Center Inc. (1.2 Miles)
- **ATM** E: Bank One, Shell
  W: BP, Giant Eagle Grocery[24, RX], Star Bank
- **Other** W: Borders Books & Music, Giant Eagle Grocery[RX], Home Depot, Wal-Mart[RX] (Vision Center)

109AB Belden Village St, Whipple Ave, Everhard Rd
- **Gas** E: Shell[*, LP, CW], Super America[*, D, LP]
- **Food** E: Blimpie Subs & Salads, Burger King, Colonial Lanes Bowling, Dairy Queen, Denny's, Fazoli's Italian Food, McDonald's, Taco Bell
  W: Damon's Ribs, Mulligan's, Pizza Hut, Ponderosa Steakhouse, Shaheen
- **Lodg** E: Comfort Inn, Fairfield Inn, Hampton Inn, Residence Inn
  W: DAYS INN Days Inn, Super 8
- **AServ** E: Horizon Audio, Mullinax Ford, Saturn of Belden Village
  W: Procare, Sears
- **Other** E: Colonial Lanes Bowling, North Canton Skate Center
  W: Belden Village Mall

EXIT OHIO

107B U.S. 62, Alliance (Eastbound)

107A OH 687, Fulton Rd
- **Gas** W: Citgo[*]
- **Food** E: Italo's Restaurant, Sports Page Bar & Grill, Woody's Root Beer & Sandwiches
  W: Kustard Korner
- **Other** E: Medicap Pharmacy[RX]
  W: Animal Clinic, Football Hall of Fame, Schneider's Pet Hospital

106 13th St
- **Food** W: The Stables Restaurant
- **Med** E: ✚ Hospital
- **Parks** E: Canton City Stadium Park/Monument Park, JFK Memorial Fountain

105 OH 172, Tuscarawas St, Downtown Tuscarawas
- **Gas** W: Gas & Oil One Stop Shop
- **Food** W: Lindsey's Restaurant, McDonald's, Subway, Wendy's
- **Lodg** E: Canton Inn, Towne Manor Motel
- **Med** W: ✚ Hospital
- **Parks** E: Canton City Waterworks Park, Discover World, McKinley's National Memorial Park

104AB 104 A- U.S. 30 E., East Liverpool 104 B- U.S. 30, U.S. 62 W., Massillon

103 OH 800 South, Cleveland Ave (Difficult Reaccess)
- **FStop** W: Ziegler Tire & Oil[D, K]
- **Gas** E: BP[*], Citgo, Shell[*, LP, CW], SuperAmerica[*, LP, K]
- **Food** E: Arby's, Subway (Shell), Taco Bell

101 OH 627, Faircrest St
- **TStop** E: 77 Gulliver's Travel Plaza[*, D, SCALES]
- **Food** E: 77 Gulliver's Travel Plaza, Ice Cream & Yogurt (77 Gulliver's Travel Plaza)
- **ATM** E: 77 Gulliver's Travel Plaza

99 Fohl Rd, Navarre
- **Gas** W: Shell[*, LP, 24]
- **Food** W: Subway (Shell)
- **RVCamp** W: Bear Creek KOA Kampground
- **ATM** W: Shell

93 OH 212, Bolivar, Zoar
- **Gas** E: Dairy Mart[*], Shell[*, LP, K, 24]
  W: BP[*, D], Citgo[*]
- **Food** E: Der Dutchman (Amish), Kickin' Kountry, McDonald's, Pizza Hut, Vaughan's Pub & Grill, Wendy's, Wilkshire's Family Restaurant
  W: Dairy Queen
- **Lodg** E: Historic Springhouse Bed & Breakfast, Sleep Inn
- **RVCamp** W: KOA Kampground
- **Med** W: ✚ Bolivar Clinic
- **ATM** E: Charter One Bank
- **Parks** E: State Memorial Park
  W: Fort Laurens
- **Other** E: Coin Car Wash, Giant Eagle Grocery[RX], Town & Country Vet, Wilkshire Golf Course
  W: Public Golf Course

(92) Weigh Station (Southbound)

(92) Weigh Station (Northbound)

87 U.S. 250, Strasburg, OH 21, Massillon
- **Gas** W: Citgo[*]
- **Food** W: Hardee's, Leonard's Fine Foods & Spirits, McDonald's, McNutt's (Citgo), The Manor
- **Lodg** W: Ramada Limited, Twins Motel
- **AServ** W: J & T Auto Body
- **TServ** E: Hoover Truck & Equipment
  W: Cummins Diesel
- **ATM** W: Citgo

(85) Rest Area (RR, Phones, Picnic; Southbound)

(85) Rest Area (RR, Phones, Picnic;

Bold red print shows RV & Bus parking available or nearby

EXIT OHIO

Northbound)

83 OH 39, OH 211, Sugarcreek, Dover
- **Gas** E: BP[*, D], Shell[*, 24], Speedway[*, K]
  W: Marathon[*]
- **Food** E: Blimpie Subs & Salads (Shell), Bob Evan's Restaurant, Denny's, KFC, McDonald's, SHONEY'S, Shoney's, Wendy's
  W: Dairy Queen (Marathon), Westside Drive Thru
- **Lodg** E: Knight's Inn
  W: Comfort Inn
- **AServ** E: Dan's Transmission, Flynn Tire, Parkway Nissan Licoln Mercury
  W: Rosenberry's Auto Body
- **Med** E: ✚ Hospital
- **ATM** E: Shell
  W: Marathon
- **Other** E: Warther's Museum
  W: Oak Pointe Animal Clinic

81 U.S. 250, OH 39, New Philadelphia
- **TStop** W: Eagle Auto Truck Plaza[D]
- **Gas** E: BP[*], Shell[*, 24]
  W: Marathon[D, LP]
- **Food** E: Big Boy, Bogey's Grill & Pub (Days Inn), Burger King, Denny's, Don Pancho's Tex Mex Cafe, Hong Kong Super Buffet, Little Caesars Pizza (K-Mart), Long John Silver, McDonald's, McDonald's (Wal-Mart), Randall's Family Restaurant (Motel 6), Schoenbrunn Inn, Taco Bell, Texas Roadhouse (Holiday Inn), The Spaghetti Shop, Wal-Mart SuperCenter[24, RX] (Vision Center), Waters Edge Restaurant
  W: Eagle Auto Truck Plaza
- **Lodg** E: DAYS INN Days Inn, Holiday Inn, Motel 6, Schoenbrunn Inn, Super 8, TraveLodge
- **AServ** E: Advanced Auto Parts, BP, K-Mart Supercenter[24, RX], Kaycee's Car Care Inc., Quality Farm & Fleet[LP], Wal-Mart SuperCenter[24] (Vision Center)
  W: Marathon
- **TServ** W: All State Truck Sales, Raven's
- **RVCamp** W: Hobart Propane[LP], Tepee RV Camp (2 Miles)
- **ATM** E: K-Mart Supercenter, Wal-Mart SuperCenter (Vision Center)
- **Other** E: Aldi Food Store, K-Mart Supercenter[RX], Quality Farm & Fleet, Wal-Mart SuperCenter[RX] (Vision Center)
  W: Lincoln Welder's Propane Filling Station[LP]

73 OH 751, CR 21, Stone Creek
- **Gas** W: Marathon[*, K]
- **Food** W: TJ's Restaurant

65 U.S. 36, Newcomerstown, Port Washington
- **TStop** W: Duke[*, LP, K, SCALES] (ATM)
- **Gas** W: BP[*]
- **Food** W: Duke (ATM), McDonald's
- **Lodg** W: Duke (ATM)
- **AServ** W: BP
- **TServ** W: Duke[SCALES] (ATM)

54 OH 541, CR 831, Kimbolton, Plainfield
- **Gas** W: Shell[*, K]
- **Food** W: Happy Jack's
- **RVCamp** E: Campground

47 U.S. 22, Cambridge, Cadiz
- **Gas** W: BP[*]
- **AServ** W: BP
- **RVCamp** E: Campground
- **Med** W: ✚ Hospital
- **Other** W: Degenhart Glass Museum, Tourist Info.

46AB U.S. 40, Old Washington, Cambridge
- **Gas** W: BP[*, CW], Speedway[*, LP, K]
- **Food** W: Burger King, J & K Restaurant, McDonald's, Mr Lee's Family Restaurant
- **Lodg** W: Long's Motel
- **ATM** W: BP, Star Bank

EXIT OHIO

- **Other** W: Coin Laundry, Guernsey Veterinary Clinic, Riesbeck's Grocery, Sav-A-Lot Grocery

44AB Junction I-70, Wheeling, Columbus

41 OH 209, OH 821, CR 35, Byesville
- **Gas** W: BP[*]
- **Food** W: McDonald's
- **AServ** W: BP
- **ATM** W: National City Bank
- **Other** W: Byesville Pharmacy[RX], Byesville Police Dept, IGA Store

(40) Rest Area (RR, Phones, Picnic; Northbound)

37 OH 313, Pleasant City, Senecaville
- **Gas** E: Duke[*, LP], Starfire Express[*, D]
- **Food** E: Buffalo Grill, Subway
- **AServ** E: Clark's Auto Sales, Dave's Complete Car Care, Starfire Express
- **TServ** E: Exit 37 Truck Service
- **ATM** E: Duke
- **Other** E: Weber Grocery

(37) Rest Area (RR, Phones, Picnic; Southbound)

28 OH 821, Belle Valley
- **Gas** E: Smith's Grocery[*], Sunoco[*, D, K]
- **Food** E: Oasis Grill
- **AServ** E: Sunoco
- **RVCamp** E: Camping
- **Parks** E: Wolf Run State Park (2 Miles)

25 OH 78, Caldwell, Woodsfield
- **Gas** E: BP[*], Sunoco[*, D]
- **Food** E: Lori's Family Restaurant, McDonald's
- **Lodg** E: Best Western
- **AServ** E: Clewell Chevrolet, Oldsmobile Dealer
- **ATM** E: Sunoco
- **Other** E: Tourist Info.

16 OH 821, Macksburg, Dexter City
- **Food** E: Restaurant & Mini Mart Grocery

6 OH 821, Marietta, Lower Salem
- **FStop** W: BP[*, D, LP, K]
- **Gas** E: Exxon[*, D, K]
- **Food** E: Sub Express (Exxon)
- **RVCamp** W: Campground
- **Med** W: ✚ Hospital
- **ATM** E: Exxon

(4) Rest Area (RR, Phones, Picnic, Vending; Northbound)

1 OH 7, Marietta
- **FStop** E: Go Mart[*, D]
- **Gas** E: Ashland[*]
  W: BP[*, D], Marathon[*, D]
- **Food** E: Dairy Queen, Damon's Ribs (Comfort Inn), Memories (Holiday Inn), Ryan's Steakhouse
  W: Applebee's, Bob Evan's Restaurant, Hong Kong Chinese American Restaurant, McDonald's, Pizza Hut, SHONEY'S, Shoney's, Subway
- **Lodg** E: Comfort Inn, EconoLodge, Holiday Inn
  W: Knight's Inn, Super 8
- **AServ** E: Ashland, Wal-Mart[24, RX] (Vision Center)
  W: Marathon
- **TServ** W: Marietta Mack
- **RVCamp** E: Camping
  W: Campground
- **Med** E: ✚ Physicians Care Walk-In Clinic
  W: ✚ Hospital, ✚ Quick Care Walk In Center
- **ATM** E: Go Mart
  W: Bank One, Kroger Supermarket[24, RX], Marietta Savings Bank
- **Other** E: Aldi Grocery Store, Car Wash, Pioneer Golf Range, Wal-Mart[RX] (Vision Center)
  W: K-Mart[RX], Kroger Supermarket[RX], Marietta Tourist Info., Revco Drugs[RX]

EXIT OHIO/WEST VIRGINIA

↑OHIO

↓WEST VIRGINIA

185 WV 14, WV 31, Williamstown
- **Gas** W: Go Mart[*]
- **Food** W: Dutch Pantry Family Restaurant
- **Lodg** W: DAYS INN Days Inn

179 WV 2, WV 68, Emerson Ave, Vienna, North Parkersburg
- **Gas** E: Exxon[*]
  W: BP[*, D, LP]
- **Food** W: Cinnamon Street Bakery (BP), Eddie Pepper's Mexican Restaurant (BP), Sub Express (BP)
- **Lodg** W: Expressway Motor Inn
- **Med** W: ✚ Hospital
- **ATM** W: BP

176 U.S. 50, 7th St, Downtown
- **Gas** W: BP[*, D], Chevron[*, D, LP], Exxon[*, K]
- **Food** W: Bob Evan's Restaurant, Burger King, Char House, Long John Silver, McDonald's, Mountaineer Family Restaurant[24], Omelet Shoppe, Paradise Grille (Ramada Inn), SHONEY'S, Shoney's, Subway (Chevron)
- **Lodg** E: Best Western
  W: Holiday Inn, Ramada Inn, Red Roof Inn, The Stables Motor Lodge
- **AServ** W: Interstate Auto Broker
- **ATM** W: Chevron
- **Parks** E: North Bend State Park
- **Other** W: Animal Veterinary Emergency Treatment

174 WV 47, Staunton Ave

173 WV 95, Camden Ave, Downtown
- **Gas** E: Marathon[*, D]
- **Food** E: Corral RV Camping
- **RVCamp** E: Corral RV Camping, Lightner's RV Service & Campground[LP], RV Service (Travel Trailer - Frontage Rd), Trailer Center Campground (1.25 Miles)
  W: Camping
- **Med** W: ✚ Hospital
- **Parks** W: Blennerhaffett Historical Park

170 WV 14, Mineral Wells
- **TStop** E: Liberty Truck Stop[*, D, SCALES] (ATM, Truck Wash), Parkersburg Truck Stop[*, D, SCALES]
- **FStop** E: BP[*, D, LP, K]
- **Gas** E: Chevron[*, K, CW], Exxon[*]
- **Food** E: Exxon, Liberty Truck Stop (ATM, Truck Wash), McDonald's, Piccadilli Pizza (Parkersburg), Subway, Wendy's, Western Steer Family Steakhouse
  W: Cracker Barrel, Napoli's Pizza
- **Lodg** E: Comfort Suites Hotel, Hampton Inn, Liberty Truck Stop (ATM, Truck Wash)
  W: AmeriHost Inn, Microtel Inn
- **AServ** E: BP
- **TServ** E: Benson Truck Bodies, Liberty Truck Stop[SCALES] (ATM, Truck Wash), Parkersburg Truck Stop[SCALES]
- **ATM** E: BP, WesBanco

(169) Weigh Station (Southbound)

(169) Weigh Station (Northbound)

(166) Rest Area (RR, Phones, Vending, RV Dump; Southbound)

(166) Rest Area (RR, Phones, Vending, RV Dump; Northbound)

161 WV 21, Rockport
- **Gas** W: Marathon[*, D, K]

154 WV 1, Medina Rd

146 WV 2 South, Silverton, Ravenswood

Bold red print shows RV & Bus parking available or nearby

EXIT		WEST VIRGINIA
	Gas	W: BP[*], Exxon[*], Marathon[*, D]
	Lodg	W: **Scottish Inns**
138		U.S. 33, Ripley
	Gas	E: Duke[*, D], Exxon[*, LP, CW], Marathon[*, D, K]
		W: Exxon[*, D]
	Food	E: Cozumel, **Gabby's Grill & Bar**, KFC, **Kam Bo Chinese**, Long John Silver, **McCoy's Conference Center (Same As Best Western)**, **McDonald's**, **McDonald's (Wal-Mart)**, **Pizza Hut**, Twister's Sports Grill, Wendy's
		W: Ponderosa Steakhouse, SHONEY'S, Shoney's, Subway
	Lodg	E: **McCoy's Conference Center (Same As Best Western)**, **Super 8**
		W: Holiday Inn Express
	AServ	E: Napa Auto, Quality Farm & Fleet
	RVCamp	E: **Ruby Lake Campground (7 Miles)**
	Med	W: **Hospital**
	ATM	E: **Kroger Supermarket[RX]**, One Valley Bank, United National Bank
	Other	E: **Jackson Animal Clinic**, **Kroger Supermarket[RX]**, Quality Farm & Fleet, **Rite Aid Pharmacy[RX]**, **Sav-A-Lot Grocery**, **Wal-Mart[RX] (Vision Center)**
132		WV 21, Ripley, Fairplain
	FStop	E: **Go Mart[*, D]**
	Gas	E: BP[*, D, LP, CW]
	Food	E: **Burger King**, Cinnamon Street Bakery (BP), Eddie Pepper's Mexican Restaurant (BP), Hot Stuff Pizza (BP)
	Lodg	W: **77 Motor Inn**
	AServ	E: Denbigh-Garrett Ford Lincoln Mercury
		W: Mountain Auto Parts Inc.
	RVCamp	E: **Four Season RV Service[LP]**
	ATM	E: **Go Mart**
	Parks	E: **Cedar Lake**
124		WV 34, Kenna
	Gas	E: Exxon[*]
	Food	E: Patty's Country Cookin
119		WV 21, Goldtown
116		WV 2, Haines Bridge Rd, Sissonville
	RVCamp	E: **Rippling Waters Campground (4.2 Miles)**
114		WV 622, Sissonville, Pocatalico
	Gas	E: Gas[*, D, K]
	Food	E: Linda's Sports Bar & Grill
	AServ	E: Triple A Transmission Service
	ATM	E: **B & B Market**
	Other	E: **B & B Market**
111		WV 29, Tuppers Creek Rd
	Gas	W: BP[*, D]
	Food	W: Subway (BP)
	RVCamp	W: **Shamblin's RV Boat & Camper Store**
106		WV 27, Edens Fork Rd
	Gas	W: Chevron[*, D]
	Lodg	W: Chevron
104		Junction I-79 North (Left Exit)
102		U.S. 119, Westmoreland Rd
101		Junction I-64 & I-72, Huntington
100		Broad St, Capitol St (Difficult Reaccess)
	Gas	W: Chevron
	Food	W: Cagney's, Embassy Suites, Heart O' Town, Outback Steak House, Pavilion Cafe (Heart O' Town), Quarrier Diner, Young's Food House
	Lodg	W: Cagney's, Embassy Suites, Heart O' Town
	AServ	W: Chevron, Firestone Tire & Auto, Ziebart TidyCar
	Med	W: **Charleston Area Medical Center**, **Columbia St Francis Hospital**
	ATM	W: Huntington Banks
	Other	W: **Capitol Market**
99		WV 114, Greenbrier St, State Capitol
	Gas	W: Chevron[*], Exxon[*, D]
	Food	W: Domino's Pizza, Fire House No 4, New China

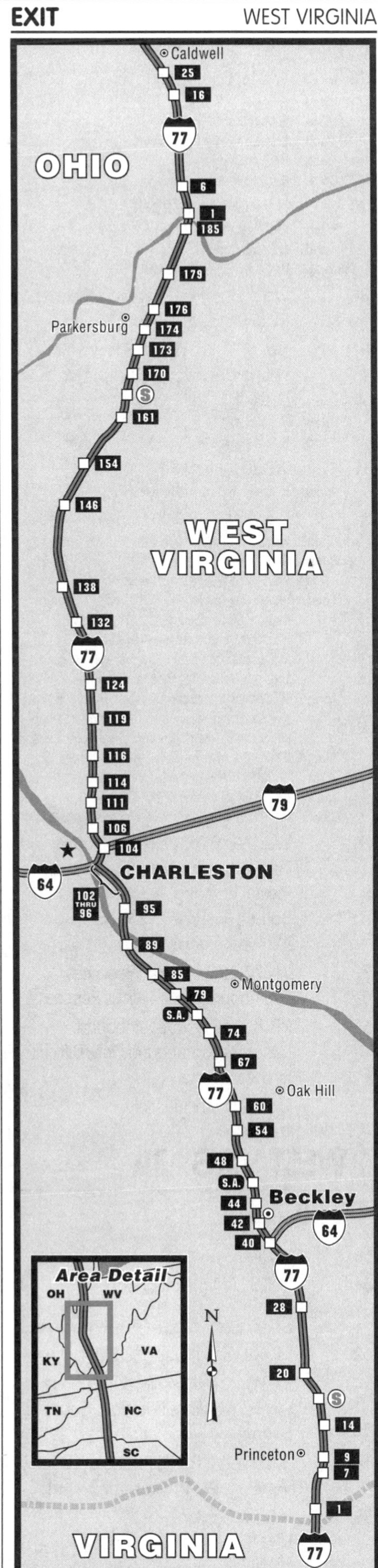

EXIT		WEST VIRGINIA
		Restaurant, Rally's Hamburgers, Subway, Wendy's
	ATM	W: Bank One, Chevron
	Other	W: Airport, **West Virginia State Capitol Building**
98		WV 61, 35th Street Bridge (Southbound, Toll)
	Food	W: Shoney's
97		WV 60, Kanawha Blvd, Midland Trail
96		U.S. 60 East, Belle (Difficult Reaccess)
	Food	E: Gino's Italian, Tudor's Biscuit House
		W: Dano's
	Lodg	W: Budget Host Inn
95		WV 61, MacCorkle Ave
	FStop	E: **Go Mart[*]**
	Gas	W: Exxon[*, D]
	Food	E: Applebee's, Bob Evan's Restaurant, **Go Mart**, Graziano's Italian, Krispy Kreme Doughnuts, Lone Star Steakhouse, McDonald's, Taco Bell, Wendy's
		W: Burger King, Cancun Mexican Restaurant, Captain D's Seafood, Chi Chi's Mexican Restaurant, Hooters, Ponderosa Steak House, Taco Bell
	Lodg	E: DAYS INN **Days Inn**, Knight's Inn, Motel 6, Red Roof Inn
	AServ	E: Advance Auto Parts, **K-Mart[RX]**, W H Service Center
		W: Brake Shop, Danny's Service Center, Subaru Dealer
	ATM	E: Bank One, **Go Mart**
		W: Bank One, **Kroger Supermarket[24, RX]**, One Valley Bank
	Other	E: **K-Mart[RX]**
		W: **Hills Grocery Store**, **Kanawha Mall**, **Kroger Supermarket[RX]**
89		WV 61, WV 94, Marmet, Chesapeake
	FStop	E: **Exxon[*, D, K]**
	Gas	E: Go Mart[*], Sunoco[*, K]
	Food	E: Craddocks 60's Cafe, Gino's Pizza, **Hardees[24]**, Subway (Exxon), Tudor's Biscuit World
	AServ	E: Hudson's Auto Repair, NAPA Auto Parts
	ATM	E: **Exxon**, Go Mart, **Kroger Supermarket[24, RX]**
	Other	E: **Kroger Supermarket[RX]**, **Rite Aid Pharmacy[RX]**
85		US 60, Hwy 61, Chelyan, Cedar Grove (Toll)
	Gas	E: No Name[*, D]
	AServ	E: No Name, Paul White Chevrolet Geo
(83)		Toll Plaza C (Toll)
79		Sharon, Cabin Creek Rd
74		WV 83, Paint Creek Rd
(72)		**Travel Plaza (RV Dump; Northbound)**
	FStop	N: **Exxon[D, RV DUMP]**
	Food	N: Hot Dog City, **Roy Rogers (Travel Plaza)**, **TCBY (Travel Plaza)**
	ATM	N: **Exxon**
(69)		**Rest Area (RR, Phones)**
66		WV 15, Mahan
	FStop	W: **Sunoco[*]**
60		WV 612, Mossy, Oak Hill
	Gas	E: Exxon[*, D]
	Food	E: Miss Ann's Fancy Food
	AServ	E: Exxon
	RVCamp	E: **Camping (Full Hookup)**
	ATM	E: Exxon
	Parks	E: **Plum Orchard Lake Park**
(56)		Toll Plaza (Toll)
54		WV 23, WV 2, Plum Orchard Lake, Pax
	Gas	E: BP[*]
		W: Exxon[*, D, K]
	Food	W: Long Branch[K]
	Parks	E: **Plum Orchard Lake Park (Public Fishing Area)**
48		U.S. 19, Summersville, North Beckley

EXIT VIRGINIA

(Toll)

(45) Travel Plaza (Southbound)
- FStop W: Exxon[RV DUMP] (Tamarack TP)
- Food W: Mrs Fields Cookies (Tamarack TP), Sbarro Italian (Tamarack TP), TCBY (Tamarack TP), Taco Bell (Tamarack TP)
- Other W: Tamarack Huge Craft Center (Tamarack TP)

44 WV 3, Harper Rd, Beckley
- FStop W: Go Mart[*]
- Gas E: Chevron[*, D, LP, K, CW], Exxon[*, D], Shell[*]
  W: BP[*, CW]
- Food E: Applebee's, Beckley Pancake House, Bennett's Smokehouse & Saloon, Bojangles (Shell), Dairy Queen, Morgan's, Omelet Shoppe, Outback Steak House, Pizza Hut, Pizza Inn (Shell), Shell, TCBY (Shell)
  W: BP, Baskin Robbins (BP), Bob Evan's Restaurant, Cracker Barrel, Fox's Pizza, Pasquale Mira (Days Inn), Subway (BP), Texas Steakhouse, Wendy's
- Lodg E: Comfort Inn, Courtyard by Marriott, Fairfield Inn, Holiday Inn, Howard Johnson (see our ad on this page), Motor Lodge, Super 8, The Courtyard By Marriott
  W: Country Inn and Suites, Days Inn, Hampton Inn, Shoney's Inn
- RVCamp W: Lake Stephens
- Med E: ✚ Doctors Immedia Care (7 Days/Week, No Appt), ✚ Hospital
- ATM E: Chevron, Exxon, Shell
  W: Go Mart
- Other E: CVS Drugstore[RX]

42 WV 16, WV 97, Mabscott, Robert C Byrd Dr (Difficult Reaccess)
- Parks E: Twin Falls Resort Park

40 Junction I-64 East, Lewisburg

EXIT VIRGINIA

(29) Toll Plaza A, North Ghent (Toll)

28 WV 48, Ghent, Flat Top
- FStop E: Exxon[*, D, K]
- Gas E: Marathon[*, D, LP, K]
- Food E: Eddie's Restaurant, Exxon
- Lodg W: Econolodge
- Other E: US Post Office

20 U.S. 119, Camp Creek
- FStop E: Exxon[*, LP]
- Food E: Home Cookin'
- RVCamp W: Camp Creek State Park

(18) Weigh Station, Rest Area (Phones, RV Dump; Southbound)

(17) Travel Plaza, Weigh Station (RR, Phones, Picnic, RV Dump; Northbound)
- FStop N: Exxon[D]
- Food N: Roy Rogers[24], TCBY[24]

14 WV 20, Athens Rd
- Parks E: Pipestem Resort State Park

9 U.S. 460, Princeton
- TStop E: I-77 Truck Stop - 24 hr[*]
- FStop W: Marathon[*, LP, K]
- Gas W: Amoco[*, D], Chevron[*, 24], Exxon[*]
- Food W: Amoco, Applebee's, Bob Evan's Restaurant, Captain D's Seafood, Cracker Barrel, Hardee's, Johnston's Inn, King's Palace, McDonald's[PLAY], Omlet Shoppe, SHONEY'S, Shoney's, Texas Steakhouse, Wendy's
- Lodg W: Comfort Inn, Days Inn, Hampton Inn, Johnston's Inn, Princeton Motel, Ramada, Sleep Inn, Super 8, Town & Country Motel, Turnpike Motel
- TServ E: I-77 Truck Stop - 24 hr
- ATM W: Amoco, Marathon
- Parks W: Pipestem Resort St Pk
- Other W: Historical Society Museum, WV State Police

(9) West Virginia Welcome Center, Tourist Information (RR, Phones, Picnic, Vending, Pet Walk; Eastbound, Eastside Exit 9, No Trucks Allowed, Post Office)

7 WV 27, Ingleside Rd. (Reaccess Southbound Only, Difficult Reaccess)

5 RT 112, Ingleside (Southbound, Reaccess Northbound Only, Difficult Reaccess)

1 U.S. 52 North, Bluefield
- Med W: ✚ Hospital

↑ WEST VIRGINIA

↓ VIRGINIA

66 VA 598

64 U.S. 52, VA 61, Rocky Gap
- Gas E: BP[*, K]
- Other E: US Post Office, Woody's Grocery (Buffet Pizza)

62 CR 606, South Gap

(62) VA Welcome Center (RR, Phones, Picnic, Vending, Pet Walk; Southbound)

(57) Rest Area (RR, HF, Phones, Picnic, Vending, Pet Walk; Northbound)

58 U.S. 52, Bastian
- FStop E: BP[*, K]
  W: Citgo[*, LP, K]

EXIT VIRGINIA

- Gas W: Exxon[*, D, K]
- Food E: BP, Buffet Pizza (BP)
- ATM E: BP
- Other W: Indian Village & Museum

(56) Truck Escape Ramp

52 U.S. 52, VA 42, Bland
- FStop W: Shell[*, D, LP, K]
- Food W: Dairy Queen (Shell), Shell, The Log Cabin Rest (Big Walker Motel)
- Lodg W: Big Walker Motel
- AServ W: Tire Outlet
- TServ W: Tire Outlet
- ATM W: Shell
- Other E: Coin Car Wash
  W: Hole In The Wall Antiques

(52) Weigh Station (Southbound)

(52) Weigh Station (Northbound)

47 CR 717, CR 601, Deer Trail Park
- RVCamp W: Deer Trail Park Family Campground, Stony Fork Campground
- Other W: Big Walker Mountain Hwy

41 CR 610, Peppers Ferry Road
- TStop W: Wilderness Road Travel Center[*, SCALES, 24]
- FStop W: Shell[*]
- Food E: Sagebrush Steakhouse
  W: Country Kitchen (Ramada Inn), Family Rest (Wilderness Road TS), Ramada, Subway (Wilderness Road TS), TCBY (Wilderness Road Truck Stop), Taco Bell (Wilderness Road TS), Wilderness Road Travel Center
- Lodg E: Rodeway Inn, Sleep Inn, Super 8
  W: Hampton Inn, Ramada
- Med W: ✚ Hospital
- ATM W: Shell, Wilderness Road Travel Center

40 Junction I-81 South, North US 52, Bristol (Southbound)

Note: I-77 runs concurrent below with I-81. Numbering follows I-81.

73 U.S. 11, South Wytheville
- Gas E: Exxon, Mobil[*, LP], Shell[*, D]
- Food E: Bob Evan's Restaurant, El Puerto Mexican Restaurant, KFC, Mom's Country Store, Peking Restaurant, SHONEY'S, Shoney's, Steak House & Saloon, Waffle House
- Lodg E: Days Inn, Holiday Inn, Interstate Motor Lodge, Motel 6, Red Carpet Inn, Shenandoah Inn, Wythe Inn
- AServ E: Exxon
- Med E: ✚ Hospital

77 Service Road
- TStop E: Flying J Travel Plaza[*, LP, RV DUMP, SCALES]
- FStop E: Citgo[*] (Fuel Stop)
- Gas E: Conoco, Texaco[*, D]
  W: Exxon[*] (RV Diesel)
- Food E: Burger King, Subway (Citgo), Thads Restaurant[SCALES] (Flying J)
- RVCamp E: KOA Campgrounds (.5 Miles)
- Other E: Gale Winds (Go-carts, putt-putt, family games)
  W: State Police

80 U.S. 52 South, VA 121 North, Fort Chiswell, Maxmeadows
- TStop E: Petro[SCALES]
- FStop W: Citgo[*, LP]
- Gas E: BP[*, D], Exxon[*] (Petro TS)
  W: Amoco
- Food E: Buck's Pizza, Iron Skillet Restaurant (Petro TS), Little Caesars Pizza (Petro TS), Wendy's (Petro TS)
  W: McDonald's
- Lodg E: Comfort Inn
  W: Country Inn
- AServ E: Lee's Tire, Brake, & Muffler

Bold red print shows RV & Bus parking available or nearby

EXIT — VIRGINIA/NORTH CAROLINA

RVCamp E: Fort Chiswell RV Campground
ATM E: Petro TS
Other E: Car Wash, Laundromat

Note: I-77 runs concurrent above with I-81. Numbering follows I-81.

32 Junction I-81 North, U.S. 11, Roanoke

24 VA 69, Poplar Camp
FStop W: Citgo[*, K]
AServ E: Poplar Camp Auto Service
Parks E: New River & Shot Tower

19 CR 620, Twin County Airport

14 U.S. 58, U.S. 221, Hillsville, Galax
FStop W: Chevron[*, CW], Exxon[*]
Gas E: Citgo[*]
W: BP[*, LP]
Food E: Peking Palace, Subway (Citgo)
W: Countryside, Dairy Queen (Exxon), McDonald's[PLAY], SHONEY'S Shoney's
Lodg E: EconoLodge
W: Best Western, Comfort Inn, Holiday Inn
AServ W: Chevron
RVCamp E: Carroll Wood Campground
W: Carrollwood Campground (.5 Miles)
Med W: Hospital
ATM W: Exxon
Parks W: Carroll County Recreation Park
Other W: Southwest VA Farmers Market

8 VA 148, CR 755, Fancy Gap
FStop W: Exxon[*]
Gas E: Citgo[*, LP, K]
W: BP[*]
Food W: Mayberry Station
Lodg W: Days Inn
AServ E: Allen's Garage
W: David L. Smith Inc.
RVCamp E: Camping
W: Camping

1 VA 620
Food E: Wallace Bros BBQ
Other W: Stuart's Creek WMA

(1) VA Welcome Center (RR, Phones; Northbound)

↑VIRGINIA

↓NORTH CAROLINA

(106) NC Welcome Center (RR, Phones; Southbound)

(103) Weigh Station (Southbound)

(103) Weigh Station (Northbound)

101 NC 752, Mount Airy
Lodg E: Comfort Inn (see our ad this page)
Med E: Hospital (12 Miles)

100 NC 89, Mount Airy, Galax
TStop E: Brintle's Travel Plaza[*]
Gas E: Exxon[*, D], Marathon[*, D, K], Texaco[*, D, LP, K]
Food E: Brintle's Travel Plaza, Wagon Wheel
Lodg E: Best Western
AServ W: Blue Ridge Towing
RVCamp W: Camping
Med E: Hospital (12 Miles)
ATM E: Exxon

93 Dobson
FStop E: Exxon[*]
Gas E: Citgo[*]
Food E: Dairy Queen (Exxon), Surry Inn
Lodg E: Surry Inn
RVCamp W: Camping

EXIT — NORTH CAROLINA

85 SR 1138, C.C. Camp Rd
FStop W: Chevron[*, LP]
Food W: Chevron
Med W: Hospital

83 U.S. 21 Bypass, Sparta (Left Exit)

82 NC 67, Elkin, Jonesville, Boonville
FStop E: Amoco[*, LP], Chevron[*, LP]
W: Exxon[*]
Gas E: BP[D, K] (Hardware Store)
Food E: Arby's, Cracker Barrel, Jordan's Country Restaurant
W: Baskin Robbins (Exxon), Bojangles, Jim's Seafood & Grill, McDonald's[PLAY], SHONEY'S Shoney's, Waffle House, Wendy's
Lodg E: Holiday Inn
W: Comfort Inn, Days Inn, Hampton Inn
ATM E: Amoco
W: Exxon

79 U.S. 21 South, U.S. 21 Business, Arlington, Jonesville
FStop W: Texaco[*, LP]
Gas E: Shell[*, LP, K]
Food W: Sally Jo's Kitchen
Lodg E: Super 8
W: Country Inn
Med E: Yadkin County Emerg. Med. Service Station 2

73AB U.S. 421, Winston - Salem, Wilkesboro, Yadkinville
TStop W: Coastal
FStop E: Amoco[*, D], Exxon[*]
Food E: Village House Restaurant, Welborn Motel
Lodg E: Welborn Motel, Yadkin Inn

(72) Rest Area (RR, Phones; Northbound)

65 NC 901, Harmony, Union Grove
FStop W: Amoco[*, LP], BP[*], Texaco[*]
Food W: Burger Barn, S&S Cafe[24], Subway (Texaco)
AServ W: Union Grove Tire & Auto
RVCamp E: Vanhoy Farms RV Park (Full Hookup; .4 Miles)
W: Fiddler's Grove Camping (1.5 Miles)
ATM W: Texaco

(63) Rest Area (RR, Phones; Southbound)

59 Tomlin Mill Rd

54 U.S. 21
FStop W: Exxon[*, LP]
Gas E: Citgo[*]
ATM W: Exxon

51AB Junction I-40, Winston, Salem, I-77

50 East Broad St, Downtown
Gas E: Crown[*, CW], Etna[*, D, LP]
Food E: Bojangles, Burger King[PLAY], Cozumel Mexican Restaurant, El Tio's, Golden China, Hardee's, Pizza Hut, SHONEY'S Shoney's, TCBY, Village Inn Pizza Parlor, Wendy's
Lodg E: Fairfield Inn, Red Roof Inn
Med E: Carolina Primary & Urgent Care (No appt. necessary)
W: Hospital
ATM E: Harris Teeter Supermarket, NationsBank
Other E: Car Wash, Eckerd Drugs[RX], Harris Teeter Supermarket, Johnson Cleaners Laundry Mart (Coin Laundry), K-Mart[RX], Signal Hill Mall, Winn Dixie Supermarket[RX]

10% Discount With Ad*

Comfort Inn
Exit 101 • Mt. Airy, NC
336-789-2000
800-672-1667

- Free Deluxe Continental Breakfast
- Evening Cappuccino 6-8pm
- Free Local Calls • Data Port Phones
- Cable TV with Free HBO
- Fax Service • Outdoor Pool
- Restaurant within Walking Distance

*Some Restrictions Apply 1460

I-77 Exit 101 Hwy74E to Exit 11 Hwy 601S

NORTH CAROLINA ▪ I-77 ▪ EXIT 101

EXIT — NORTH CAROLINA

49B Downtown Statesville
Gas E: PDI[*, D]
W: Amoco[*], Chevron, Citgo[*]
Food E: KFC
Lodg W: Best Stay Inn

49A U.S. 70, G Bagnal Blvd
Gas E: BP[*, CW], Circle K[*], Texaco[*, LP, K]
Food E: Waffle House
Lodg E: Best Western, Comfort Inn, Holiday Inn, Super 8
W: Microtel Inn
Other E: Scana Propane Gas[LP]

45 Troutman, Barium Springs
FStop W: Chevron[*]
Food W: Chevron
RVCamp E: KOA Campgrounds (.5 Miles)
ATM W: Chevron

42 U.S. 21, NC 115, Troutman
FStop E: Wilco Citgo[*]
Food E: Subway (Wilco), Taco Bell (Wilco)
RVCamp W: Duke Power State Park & Campground
Parks W: Duke Power State Park & Campground

(38) Rest Area (RR, Phones; Southbound)

(38) Rest Area (RR, Phones; Northbound)

36 NC 150, Mooresville, Lincolnton
Gas E: Exxon[*], Shell[*, LP]
W: BP[*, CW], Texaco[*, D, K, CW]
Food E: Denny's, Fat Boys, Krispy Kreme Doughnuts (Shell), La Pizza Cafe, Peking Palace, Taco Bell, Waffle House, Wendy's
W: Arby's, Cracker Barrel, Hardee's, Monterrey Mexican
Lodg E: Days Inn, Ramada
W: Hampton Inn, Super 8
Med E: Hospital
ATM E: Exxon
W: BP, Texaco
Other E: Auto Bell Car Wash, Harris Teeter Supermarket, K-Mart[RX]
W: CVS[RX], Food Lion Supermarket

33 U.S. 21 North
Gas W: Citgo[*, D]

30 Davidson, Davidson College
Gas E: Exxon[*]
Food W: North Harbour Cafe
ATM E: Exxon

28 U.S. 21, NC 73, Lake Norman, Cornelius
Gas E: Cashion's[*, LP], Citgo[*, LP]
Food E: Bojangles, Carrows, Holiday Inn, Mom's Country Store & Restaurant, SHONEY'S Shoney's, SHONEY'S Shoney's Prime Bakery/Buffet
W: Bruegger's Bagel & Bakery, Burger King[PLAY], Caile Ristras Mexican Steakhouse, Hickory Hams, KFC, Lone Star Steakhouse, Lotus 28 Chinese, McDonald's[PLAY], Pizza Hut, Queen Bee Palace Chinese, Subway, Taco Bell, Uptown Pasta, Wendys
Lodg E: Hampton Inn, Holiday Inn
W: Best Western, Comfort Inn, Microtel Inn, Quality Inn & Suites
ATM E: Cashion's, Citgo
W: First Union, Lincoln Bank

Bold red print shows RV & Bus parking available or nearby

EXIT NORTH CAROLINA

Other W: Harris Teeter Supermarket[24], U.S. Post Office

25 NC 73, Concord, Lake Norman
- Gas E: Shell[*], Texaco[*]
  W: BP[*, CW]
- Food E: Burger King[PLAY], Chick-Fil-A, Chili's, Fuddruckers, Hop's Restaurant & Bar, Longhorn Steakhouse, McDonald's[PLAY], Philly Connection, TCBY, U.S. Subs (Texaco), Wendys
  W: Arby's, Blimpie Subs & Salads (BP), Bob Evan's Restaurant, Bojangles, Dairy Queen, Subway
- Lodg E: Country Inn & Suites
  W: Courtyard by Marriott
- ATM E: Texaco, Wachovia Bank, Winn Dixie Supermarket[RX]
  W: BB&T, BP
- Other E: Airport, Pet Mania, Winn Dixie Supermarket[RX]
  W: Book Nook, Food Lion Supermarket

23 Huntersville
- Gas E: Amoco[*, CW], Texaco[*, LP]
- Food E: Captain's Gallery, Hardee's, Hero Express, The Steak & Hogie Shop, Waffle House, Wendys
- Lodg E: Holiday Inn Express
- Other E: Eckerd Drugs[RX], Food Lion Supermarket

18 Harris Blvd, Reanes Rd
- Gas E: Texaco[*, D]
- Med E: ✚ Hospital

16AB U.S. 21 North, Sunset Rd, NC 115
- TStop E: Jake's Auto Truck Stop[*, 24] (Phillips 66)
  W: Jake's Sunset[*]
- Gas E: Amoco[*, LP]
  W: BP[*, D, CW], Citgo[*, D, CW]
- Food E: Captain D's Seafood, Hardee's, Jake's Auto Truck Stop (Phillips 66), KFC, McDonald's, Subway, Taco Bell, Waffle House, Wendys
  W: Bubba's B.B.Q, Burger King[PLAY], Denny's, Domino's Pizza, Waffle House
- Lodg E: DAYS INN Days Inn, Super 8
  W: Sleep Inn
- RVCamp W: Independence RV Sales & Services[LP]
- Parks W: Latta Plantation Park
- Other E: Winn Dixie Supermarket[RX]

13 Junction I-85, Greensboro

12 LaSalle St
- Gas W: Citgo[*], Texaco[*]

11 Junction I-277, NC 16 , Brookshire Freeway

10CB Trade St West, Fifth St, Downtown Charlotte-10C, Trade St., Fifth St., East-10B
- Gas W: Amoco[*, K], Phillips 66[*]
- Food W: Bojangles, Church's Chicken
- Lodg E: DoubleTree Hotel

10A U.S. 29, NC 27, Morehead St (Difficult Reaccess)
- Food W: Alex's Brown Derby, Coffee House Seven Sedes, Open Kitchen

9A West Blvd.

9 I-277, U.S. 74, to U.S.29, to N.C.27, John Belk Frwy. (Northbound)
- Med E: ✚ Hospital Trauma Unit
- Other E: Charlotte Convention Center

8 NC 160, Remount Rd (Northbound, Reaccess Southbound Only)

7 Clanton Rd, NC 49
- FStop E: Citgo[*]
- Gas W: Amoco[*], Citgo[*, K]
- Food E: EconoLodge[24], Express Family Restaurant (EconoLodge)
- Lodg E: EconoLodge, Motel 6, Ramada, Super 8

EXIT NORTH CAROLINA

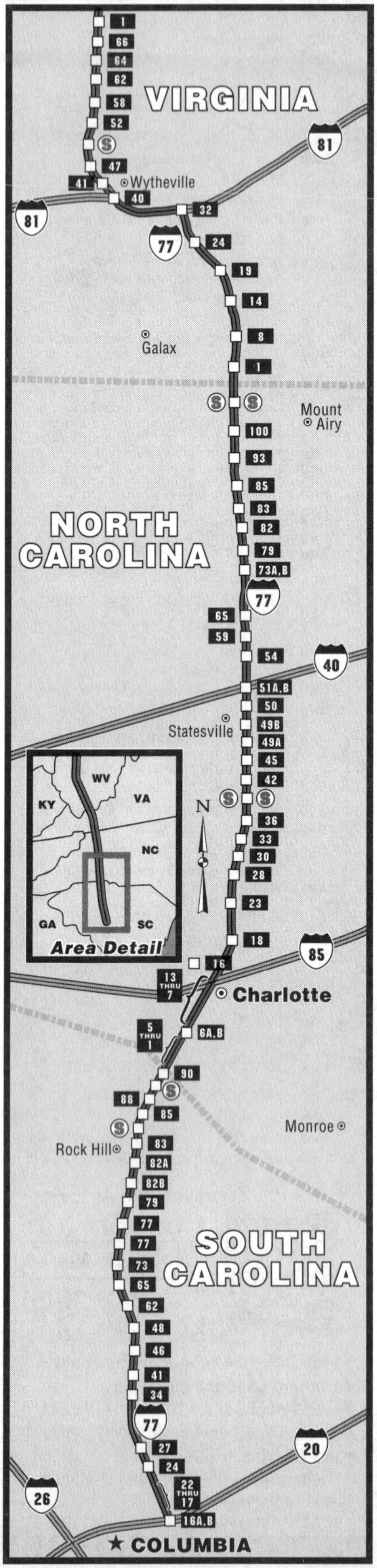

EXIT NORTH CAROLINA

- ATM E: Citgo
- Parks W: Clanton Park
- Other E: Coin Car Wash

6B NC 49 South, U.S. 521, Billy Graham Pwky., South Tryon St., Woodlawn Road (East Side Services Same As 6A)
- Gas W: Phillips 66[*]
- Food W: Clarion Hotel, Classic Sports Restaurant (Clarion Hotel), Embassy Suites, PJ MacKenzie's (Embassy Suites), The Locker Room
- Lodg W: Clarion Hotel, Embassy Suites, La Quinta Inn & Suites, Sleep Inn, Summerfield Suites
- Other W: Carolina Naviation Museum

6A U.S. 521 S., Woodlawn Rd (Difficult Reaccess, Same West side services as 6B)
- Gas E: BP[*, D, CW], Citgo[*, 24], Exxon[*, D, CW], Speedway[*, LP], Texaco[*, D, CW]
- Food E: Azteca Mexican (Days Inn), BW-3 Grill & Pub, Bankers Restaurant, Bojangles, Captain D's Seafood, China House Buffet, DAYS INN Days Inn, Dragon Inn, Harper's Pizza, Steak,Pasta (Woodland Suites), IHOP, Krispy Kreme Doughnuts, Playa Caracol Mexican, Steak & Ale, The Gentleman's Club, Woodland Suites, Zepeddie's Pizzeria
- Lodg E: DAYS INN Days Inn, Holiday Inn, Howard Johnson, Sterling Inn, Woodland Suites
- ATM E: BB&T

5 Tyvola Rd
- Gas E: Citgo[*, CW]
- Food E: Black-Eyed Pea, Chili's, Gordon's Restaurant, Hilton, Kabuto Japanese Steak House and Sushi Bar, McDonald's, Porter House Steak Restaurant (Hilton), Sonny's BBQ, The Men's Club
- Lodg E: Candlewood Studio Hotel, Charlotte Studio Plus, Comfort Inn, Hampton Inn, Hilton, Marriott, Residence Inn
  W: Extended Stay America
- ATM E: Bi-Lo Grocery, Wachovia Bank
- Other E: Bi-Lo Grocery

4 Nations Ford Rd
- Gas E: Amoco[*], Citgo[*]
  W: Shell[*]
- Food E: Hardee's
  W: Burger King (Shell), Shell
- Lodg E: Best Inn Suites, Innkeeper, La Quinta Inn, Red Roof Inn, Villager Lodge

3 Arrowood Rd
- Food E: Wendy's
- Lodg E: AmeriSuites (see our at hispage), Courtyard by Marriott, Fairfield Inn

2 Junction I-485 East, James G. Martin Freeway

(2) **NC Welcome Center (RR, Phones; Northbound)**

1 Westinghouse Blvd
- FStop E: Amoco[*]
- Gas W: Texaco[*, D, CW]
- Food E: Jake's II Restaurant, Subway, Waffle House
  W: Burger King
- Lodg E: Super 8
- AServ W: Texaco
- ATM W: First Union

1317
AMERISUITES
AMERICA'S AFFORDABLE ALL-SUITE HOTEL
North Carolina • Exit 3

Bold red print shows RV & Bus parking available or nearby

EXIT NORTH/SOUTH CAROLINA

↑NORTH CAROLINA
↓SOUTH CAROLINA

90 U.S. 21, Carowinds Blvd
- **Gas** E: Citgo(*, D, CW)
  W: BP(*), Exxon(*, CW)
- **Food** E: Bojangles, Days Inn, Denny's
  W: BP, Blimpie Subs & Salads (BP), El Cancun Mexican, Exxon, Fresh Break Restaurant (Exxon), KFC, Madeline's Lunch Buffett (Ramada), Mom's Restaurant, Ramada, SHONEY'S, Shoney's, Wendy's
- **Lodg** E: Days Inn
  W: Comfort Inn, **Holiday Inn Express (see our ad this page)**, Ramada, Sleep Inn
- **RVCamp** E: **Jerry Lathan's RV World, RV World, Radisson Grand Resort (1.5 Miles)**
  W: **Paramount's Carowinds Campground (1 Mile)**
- **Med** E: **Hospital**
- **ATM** E: **Carrowind Blvd. Mall**, Citgo
  W: Exxon
- **Parks** W: **Paramount's Carowinds Theme Park**
- **Other** E: **Carrowind Blvd. Mall**, James K. Polk Memorial
  W: Farmer's Market Fireworks, **Outlet Marketplace**

(89) **SC Welcome Center (RR, Phones, Picnic, Vending; Southbound)**

(89) **Weigh Station (Northbound)**

88 Gold Hill Rd, Taga Cay
- **Gas** E: Texaco(*, K)
- **AServ** W: Fort Mill Ford
- **RVCamp** W: **Lazy Daze Campground (.5 Miles), Tracy's-RV Inc.**

85 SC 160, Fort Mill
- **Gas** W: BP(*, LP)
- **Food** W: BP, Bojangles (BP), Burger King
- **AServ** W: Bob's Automotive, C&N Tire Inc. Goodyear
- **Med** W: **Fort Hill Medical Park**
- **Other** E: **Winn Dixie Supermarket(24)**

(84) **Weigh Station (Southbound)**

83 Sutton Rd

82A US 21, SC 161, York, Rock Hill (Difficult Reaccess)
- **Gas** W: Phillips 66(*, LP, K), Texaco(*)
- **Food** W: Outback Steakhouse
- **Lodg** W: Regency Inn
- **Med** W: **Riverview Med Center(24)**, **Urgent Care Family Medicine**
- **ATM** W: Phillips 66
- **Other** E: **Home Depot**
  W: **Museum of York County**, Putt-Putt Golf, Skate Center

1075

Convention & Visitors Bureau

800-866-5200

Rock Hill, SC

20 Miles South of Metropolitan Area, Charlotte, NC
30 Minutes Away from Charlotte Douglas International Airport
Paramount's Carowinds Theme Park
The Museum of York County • Glencairn Garden
Historic Brattonsville (Pre-Revolutionary War Plantation)
The Catawba Cultural Preservation Project
Outlet Shopping (Outlet Marketplace, Fort Mill, SC)
Historic Downtown Areas of York, Clover & Rock Hill

SOUTH CAROLINA • I-77 • EXIT 79

EXIT SOUTH CAROLINA

Truck/RV Parking

1503

I-77 • Exit 81

2640 North Cherry Rd.
Rock Hill, CS 29730

803-329-1122

Casey's Restaurant/Lounge on Premises
Outdoor Pool • Exercise Room
Meeting/Banquet Facilities
Handicap Accessible • Golf Packages
Coin Laundry • Interior Corridors
Nearby Attractions: Carowinds, Cherry Park, & Catawba Gambling

South Carolina • I-77 • Exit 82

1196

I-77 • Exit 90W

3560 Lakemont Blvd.
Fort Mill, SC 29715

803-548-0100
800-HOLIDAY

"Newcomer of the Year" Award Winner
Free Award Winning Breakfast
Free Cable TV with HBO
25" Large Screen TVs • Pool
In Room Coffee Makers
Special Rates for Tour Groups

Charlotte, NC • I-77 • Exit 90W

BRAND NEW MOTEL

1718

Special
Sunday-Thursday
$40.00 Sgl

$45.95
2-4 Persons

New 62 Rooms
Continental Breakfast
Kids Under 12 Stay Free
25" Cable TV w/HBO, MAX, ESPN
Handicap Accessible • Coin Laundry
Exercise Room • Interior Corridors

803-980-0400 • 800-800-8000

I-77 Exit 82B Turn L at light

SOUTH CAROLINA • I-77 • EXIT 82B

Rockhill, South Carolina

Inn & Suites

- Pool • New Rooms
- Free Continental Breakfast
- Cable TV with Free HBO
- 24 Hour Restaurant
- Meeting & Banquet Room
- 2 Room Suites
- In-Room Whirlpool

803-329-3121

1526

SOUTH CAROLINA • I-77 • EXIT 82-B

EXIT SOUTH CAROLINA

82B U.S. 21 South, Rockhill
- **FStop** E: **Phillips 66**
- **Gas** E: Exxon(*, CW)
  W: Racetrac(*)
- **Food** E: IHOP, Sonny's BBQ
  W: Bucko's, **Day Break Restaurant (Days Inn)**, **Days Inn**, Denny's (Quality Inn), McDonald's, Quality Inn, Taco Bell, Tienda Mexicana Three Amigos, Waffle House
- **Lodg** E: **Holiday Inn (see our ad this page)**
  W: Best Way Inn, Comfort Inn, Country Inn & Suites, **Days Inn**, **EconoLodge**, Quality Inn & Suites (see our ad this page), Ramada Limited, Regency Inn, Super 8 (see our ad this page)
- **AServ** E: Exxon, **Phillips 66**
  W: B & B Tire & Wheels, Burns Chevrolet GM, Burns Nissan, Muffler Master, PEP Boys Auto Parts & Service Center
- **Med** W: **Hospital**
- **ATM** E: Exxon, Sail River Credit Union
  W: Racetrac
- **Other** E: **Home Depot**

79 SC 122, Dave Lyle Blvd, Downtown
- **Gas** E: BP(*, CW), Mike's Wrecker Service(*)
- **Food** E: Applebee's, **Cracker Barrel**, Hardee's, J & K Cafeteria, O'Charley's
- **Lodg** E: Hampton Inn
- **AServ** E: Honda's Cars of Rock Hill, Meineke Discount Mufflers, Mike's Wrecker Service, Sears
- **Other** E: **Galleria Cinemas, Lowe's, Rock Hill Galleria Mall, Wal-Mart(RX) (1-hr photo, vision center)**
  W: **York County Visitor's Center (see our ad this page)**

77 U.S. 21, SC 5, Rock Hill, Lancaster
- **FStop** W: **Phillips 66(*, LP)**
- **Gas** E: BP(*), Citgo(*, D, CW)
  W: Exxon(*, D)
- **Food** E: BP, Subway (BP)
  W: Blimpie Subs & Salads (Phillips 66), **Phillips 66**, **Waffle House**
- **Med** W: **Hospital**
- **ATM** E: BP
  W: Max Video Games, **Phillips 66**
- **Parks** E: **Andrew Jackson State Park**
- **Other** W: Max Video Games

75 Porter Rd
- **Gas** E: Citgo(*), Shell(*)
- **Food** E: Shell, Shell In
- **Other** E: **Rocket Stop Fireworks (Shell)**

73 SC 901
- **FStop** E: **Citgo(*)**
- **Med** W: **Hospital**

(66) **Rest Area (RR, Phones, Picnic, Vending; Southbound)**

(66) **Rest Area (RR, Phones, Picnic, Vending; Northbound)**

65 Chester, S.C. 9, Fort Lawn
- **FStop** E: **Texaco(*)**
  W: **Citgo(*)**
- **Gas** E: Amoco(*, 24), BP(*)
- **Food** E: Amoco, BP, Chicago Pizza, Krispy Kreme Doughnuts (Amoco), Subway (Amoco), Waffle House
  W: **Country Omelet, Front Porch, KFC, McDonald's**
- **Lodg** E: **Days Inn, EconoLodge, Relax Inn**
  W: **Comfort Inn, Super 8**
- **Med** W: **Hospital**
- **Parks** E: **Landsford Canal State Park**
  W: **Chester State Park**
- **Other** W: Ryder Truck Rental

62 Rd 56, Richburg, Fort Lawn

55 SC 97, Great Falls, Chester
- **FStop** E: **BP(*, LP)**

Bold red print shows RV & Bus parking available or nearby

EXIT	SOUTH CAROLINA
ATM	E: BP
Parks	W: Chester State Park
48	SC 200, Winnsboro
TStop	E: Shell[*, SCALES] (Restaurant) (see our ad this page)
ATM	E: Shell (Restaurant)
46	Rd 20, White Oak
41	Rd 41, Winnsboro
Parks	E: Lake Wateree State Park
34	SC 34, Ridgeway, Camden
Gas	W: Citgo[*, D, K]
Lodg	W: Ramada Limited
AServ	E: Jerry's Wrecker[24]
RVCamp	E: Ridgeway RV Campground (.9 Miles)
Med	W: ✚ Hospital
ATM	W: Citgo
27	Blythewood Rd
FStop	E: Exxon[*]
Gas	E: Citgo[*, CW]
Food	E: Blythewood Pizza & Subs, Bojangles (Exxon), Exxon, McDonald's, Restorante Mexico, W.G.'s Chicken Wings, Waffle House, Wendy's
AServ	E: Jim Hall Auto Service
ATM	E: Exxon

The universal sign for the world's best-selling gasoline.

Open 24 Hours
Easy Access
Truck Wash & ATM
24 Hour Restaurant

Clean Restrooms • Diesel
Fast, Courteous Service
Air & Water • Pay At Pump
Convenience Store with Fresh
Hot Coffee & Fountain Drinks
All Major Credit Cards
803-482-2118
1494

SOUTH CAROLINA ▪ I-77 ▪ EXIT 48

EXIT	SOUTH CAROLINA
Other	E: Blythewood Antiques, Blythewood Pharmacy[RX], Foodliner Supermarket, U.S. Post Office
24	U.S. 21, North Columbia
FStop	E: Texaco[*, LP]
Gas	E: BP[*]
Food	E: Meyer's BBQ, Subway (Texaco), Texaco
AServ	E: Abell's Auto Service, Mosely Tire & Lube
ATM	E: BP
Other	E: Blythewood Animal Hospital
22	Killian Rd
19	SC 555, Farrow Rd
Gas	E: Citgo[*, CW]
Food	W: Waffle House[24]
Lodg	E: Courtyard by Marriott
ATM	E: Wachovia Bank
Parks	W: Carolina Research Park
Other	W: South Carolina Archives & History Center
18	U.S. 277, Columbia, I-20 West, Augusta (Southbound, Reaccess Northbound Only)
17	U.S. 1, Two Notch Rd
Gas	E: Amoco[*, CW, 24], BP[*, CW], Exxon[*]
Food	E: Arby's, Burger King[PLAY], Denny's, Mallard's Restaurant (Ramada Plaza Hotel), Ramada Plaza Hotel, Waffle House W: Chili's, Fazoli's Italian Food, Hop's Restaurant & Bar, IHOP, Lizard's Thicket (Red Roof Inn), Outback Steakhouse, Red Roof Inn
Lodg	E: Fairfield Inn, In Town Suites, Ramada Plaza Hotel, Wyngate Inn W: AmeriSuites (see our ad this page), Comfort Inn, Hampton Inn, Holiday Inn, Microtel Inn, Red Roof Inn
Med	E: ✚ Doctors Care
ATM	E: Exxon, SouthTrust
Parks	E: Sesquicentennial Park
Other	E: Gregg Animal Hospital, U-Haul Center[LP], U.S. Post Office W: Home Depot
16AB	Junction I-20, Augusta, Florence
15	SC 12, Fort Jackson (Southbound, Reaccess Northbound Only)
Gas	E: Shell[*, CW, 24] (see our ad this page)
13	Decker Blvd, Dentsville
12	Forest Drive, Forest Acres, Fort Jackson
10	Fort Jackson Blvd, SC760
9	U.S. 76, U.S. 378, Barners Ferry Rd
6	SC 768
5	SC 48, Bluff Rd

1318

South Carolina • Exit 17 • 803-736-6666

↑SOUTH CAROLINA

Begin I-77

The universal sign for the world's best-selling gasoline.

Open 24 Hours
Easy Access
ATM
Pizza
Hot Dogs

1493
Clean Restrooms
Pay at Pump
Air & Water
Convenience Store
Fresh Hot Coffee
& Fountain Drinks
803-736-7147

SOUTH CAROLINA ▪ I-77 ▪ EXIT 15A

I-78 E →

EXIT	PENNSYLVANIA
	Begin I-78

↓PENNSYLVANIA

EXIT	PENNSYLVANIA
1	**(8)** PA 343, Fredericksburg, Lebanon (Reaccess Eastbound Only)
Gas	S: Redner's[LP]
Food	S: Esther's
RVCamp	S: Camping (5 Miles)
ATM	S: Redner's
Other	S: Redner's Grocery[RX]
2	**(10)** PA 645, Frystown
TStop	S: All American Truckstop[SCALES]
FStop	S: Shell[*]
Food	S: All American Truckstop
Lodg	N: Fairview Motor Court S: All Americn Motel, Motel of Frystown
ATM	S: All American Truckstop, Shell

81
PENNSYLVANIA
NEW JERSEY
Fredericksburg
Bethel
Hamburg
Fogelsville
Allentown
Bethlehem
Bloomsbury
NY
PA
NJ
OH
WV
MD
DE
Area Detail

EXIT		PENNSYLVANIA
3		**(13)** PA 501, Bethel
	FStop	**N:** Texaco[*, D]
	Gas	**S:** Amoco[*], Exxon[K], Pennzoil Oil Change
		S: Amoco
4		**(15)** Grimes
5		**(16)** Midway
	FStop	**N:** Midway[*, CW], Texaco
	Food	**N:** Blue Mountain Country Kitchen, Midway Diner
	Lodg	**N:** Comfort Inn
6		**(17)** PA 419, Rehrersburg
	Gas	**N:** Best[*]
	AServ	**N:** Best
7		**(19)** PA 183, Strausstown
	Gas	**N:** Mobil[*]
		S: Best[*], Texaco[*, K]
	Food	**N:** Dutch Motel, Mobil
	Lodg	**N:** Dutch Motel
8		**(23)** Shartlesville
	Gas	**N:** Citgo[*], Texaco[*, D]
	Food	**N:** Dairy Queen[*], Stuckey's[*]
		S: Blue Mountain Family Restaurant, Haag's Pennsylvania Dutch Cooking, Shartlesville Motel
	Lodg	**N:** Dutch Motel
		S: Fort Motel, Shartlesville Motel
	RVCamp	**N:** Appalachian Campsites (.13 Miles), Mountain Springs Camping Resort (.75 Miles)
		S: Hillcrest Campsites (1.63 Miles), Pennsylvania Dutch Campsite
	Other	**S:** Post Office
9AB		**(29)** PA 61, Pottsville, Reading
	Gas	**N:** Mobil[*, CW]
	Food	**N:** Cracker Barrel, Wendy's
10		**(30)** Hamburg
	Gas	**S:** Getty[*, 24]
11		**(35)** PA 143, Lenhartsville
	Gas	**S:** Sunoco
	Food	**S:** C.J. Hummel, Pennsylvania Dutch Restaurant
	RVCamp	**N:** Blue Rocks Campground (1 Mile)
		S: Robin Hill Camping Resort (2 Miles)
12		**(41)** PA 737, Kutztown, Krumsville
	Gas	**S:** Texaco[*]
	Food	**N:** The Krumsville Inn
		S: Sky View Family Restaurant
	Lodg	**N:** The Krumsville Inn, Top Motel
	RVCamp	**N:** Pine Hill Campground (1.63 Miles), Robin Hill Campground
13		**(45)** PA 863, Lynnport, New Smithville
	TStop	**N:** Texaco[*]
	Gas	**N:** MICO[*, D]
	Food	**N:** Terry's Place Restaurant
		S: Golden Key Hotel
	Lodg	**S:** Golden Key Hotel, Super 8
14AB		**(50)** PA 100, Fogelsville, Trexler Town
	Gas	**S:** Exxon[*]
	Food	**N:** Arby's, Cracker Barrel, Long John Silver, Pizza Hut
		S: Burger King, Subway (Exxon), Yocco's 100
	Lodg	**N:** Comfort Inn
		S: Cloverleaf Inn, Holiday Inn
	Other	**N:** Eckerd Drugs[RX]
15		**(54)** PA 309N, PA Turnpike, Tamaqua
16AB		**(55)** U.S. 222, Hamilton Boulevard
	Gas	**S:** Sunoco[CW]
	Food	**N:** Ambassador Restaurant
		S: Charcoal Drive-in, Tom Sawyer Diner
	Lodg	**N:** Comfort Suites Hotel, Holiday Inn Express
	Other	**N:** Dorney Amusement Park, Wild Water King Theme Park (.5 Miles)
17		**(56)** PA 29, Cedar Crest Boulevard
	Gas	**N:** Texaco[*, D, LP]
	Food	**S:** Spice of Life Restaurant
	Med	**N:** + Cedarcrest EmergiCenter
		S: + Lehigh Valley Hosptital
18A		**(57)** Lehigh St.
	Gas	**N:** Hess[*, D]
		S: Gettys, Mobil[LP], Texaco[D]
	Food	**N:** Willy Jo's

EXIT		PENNSYLVANIA/NEW JERSEY
		S: Dunkin Donuts, Friendly's, McDonald's, The Brass Rail
	Lodg	**N:** Days Inn
	Other	**S:** Food 4 Less Grocery[24]
18B		**(58)** Emaus Avenue (Difficult Reaccess)
	Gas	**N:** Hess[*, D], Texaco[D]
		S: Shell, Sunoco
	Food	**N:** Marsala's Pizzeria & Restaurant
	Other	**N:** South Mountain Pharmacy[RX]
		S: Sharon Coin Laundry
19		**(61)** to PA 145, Summit Lawn (Eastbound)
20AB		**(61)** PA 145 N., PA 309 South, S 4th St., Quakertown
21		**(67)** Hellertown, Bethlehem, PA412
	Gas	**N:** Citgo[*, LP], Texaco
		S: Exxon[*, D]
	Food	**N:** Chris's Restaurant, Wendy's
		S: Vassie's Drive In
	Med	**N:** + Hospital
22		**(75)** Exit to PA 611, Easton, Philadelphia
	Gas	**N:** Citgo[*, LP]
		S: Shell[*]
(78)		**PA Welcome Center (RR, Phones; Westbound)**

↑PENNSYLVANIA

↓NEW JERSEY

EXIT		NEW JERSEY
3		**(5)** U.S. 22, to PA 33, CR 122, Alpha, Phillipsburg
	TStop	**N:** Penn-Jersey Truckstop[*, 24]
	FStop	**N:** US Gas[*, D, 24]
	Gas	**N:** US Gas[*, 24]
	Food	**N:** McDonald's, Perkins Family Restaurant, The Almond Tree, US Gas
	Lodg	**N:** Holiday Inn, Phillipsburg Inn
	Other	**N:** CR Pharmacy[RX], Home Depot, Lanco Supermarket & Drugstore
(4)		**Weigh Station (Eastbound)**
4		Warren Glen, Stewartsville (Westbound, Reaccess Eastbound Only)
6		Warren Glen, Asbury (Eastbound, Reaccess Westbound Only)
7		NJ 173, West Portal, Bloomsbury
	TStop	**S:** Pilot[SCALES, 24], TravelCenter America Truckstop[*, SCALES]
	Food	**S:** Subway (Pilot), TravelCenter America Truckstop
	TServ	**S:** Pilot[SCALES, 24]
(8)		**Rest Area (RR, Picnic, P; Westbound)**
11		**(12)** NJ 173, West Portal, Pattenburg
	Gas	**N:** Coastal[*], Texaco
	Food	**N:** Mountain View Shalet, Villa Pizza
	RVCamp	**N:** Camping
12		**(14)** New Jersey 173, Jutland, Norton
	TStop	**N:** Johnny's Citgo
	Gas	**N:** Exxon[*], Johnny's Citgo
		S: Shell[LP]
	Food	**N:** Johnny's Citgo
		S: Bagelsmith's Deli
	RVCamp	**N:** Spruce Run Recreation Area
13		NJ 173 West, Service Road (Westbound, Reaccess Eastbound Only)
	FStop	**N:** Clinton Truckstop[*]
	Food	**N:** Louise's Diner
15		NJ 173 East, Clinton, Pittstown
	Gas	**N:** Amoco, Citgo[*, LP, CW], Clinton Car Care[CW], Texaco[D]
	Food	**N:** Clinton House
	Lodg	**N:** Holiday Inn Select
	AServ	**N:** Amoco, Texaco
	Other	**N:** Historical Museum & Arts Center

EXIT		NEW JERSEY
		S: Lanco Supermarket, Wal-Mart
16		NJ 31 North, Washington (Eastbound)
	RVCamp	**N:** Spruce Run State Rec. Area (1.5 Miles)
17		**(18)** NJ 31, Clinton, Flemington, Washington DC
	Food	**N:** King Buffet, McDonald's
	Other	**N:** Amerigas[LP], Coin Car Wash
18		**(19)** U.S. 22, Annandale (Westbound, Difficult Reaccess)
	RVCamp	**N:** Campground
	Med	**S:** + Hospital
20		**(21)** Lebanon, Cokesbury
	Gas	**S:** Exxon[*, CW], Shell[D], T & T Repairs
	Food	**S:** Bagelsmith's Deli, Bambino's Pizzeria, Dunkin Donuts (Exxon), Lebanon Plaza Deli
	RVCamp	**S:** Round Valley Recreation Area
	Other	**S:** U.S. Post Office
24		**(25)** NJ523, to NJ517, Oldwick, Whitehouse
26		**(27)** NJ 523 Spur, North Branch, Lamington
29		**(31)** Jct I-287 to US 202, US 206, Morristown
(33)		**Scenic Overlook (Westbound, No Trailers Or Trucks)**
33		**(34)** NJ 525, Bernardsville, Martinsville
	Gas	**S:** Amoco[D]
	Food	**N:** Christine's
	Lodg	**N:** Somerset Hills Hotel
	Med	**N:** + V.A. Medical Center
		S: + Hospital
	Other	**N:** Golf Museum
36		**(37)** CR527, Spur, Basking Ridge, Warrenville
	Gas	**N:** Exxon[24]
40		**(41)** County Road 531, The Plainsfield, Gillette, Watchung (No Vehicles Over 5 Tons)
	Med	**S:** + Hospital
41		Berkeley Heights, Scotch Plains, US22 (Difficult Reaccess)
43		New Providence, Berkeley Heights (Westbound)
44		New Providence, Berkeley Heights (Eastbound)
	Med	**N:** + Overlook Hospital
45		**(46)** Summit, Glenside Avenue (Eastbound)
48		**(49)** NJ 24, to I-287, Springfield, Morristown
49AB		Maplewood, Springfield, Union (Eastbound)
50AB		**(52)** Union, Millburn (Westbound, Reaccess Eastbound Only)
	Gas	**N:** Amoco[24], Exxon, Mobil
		S: Texaco
	Other	**N:** U.S. Post Office
52		**(53)** NJ Garden State Parkway (No Trucks)
54		U.S. 1, U.S. 9, Hillside, Irvington (Eastbound, Reaccess Eastbound Only)
	Med	**S:** + Newark Beth Israel Medical Center
55		Hillside, Irvington (Westbound)
	Med	**S:** + Newark Beth Israel Medical Center
56		Clinton Avenue, Irvington
	Med	**N:** + State Trauma Center
57		U.S. 1, U.S. 9, U.S. 22, Newark Airport
58AB		Junction I-95, U.S. 1, U.S. 9, New Jersey Turnpike, Newark

↑NEW JERSEY

Begin I-78

EXIT	PENNSYLVANIA

Begin I-79

↓PENNSYLVANIA

44AB **(184)** 44A - PA 5, 12th St, East, 44B - PA 5, 12th St, West
- Gas W: BP[*, LP, CW]
- Food W: Bob Evan's Restaurant, Chan An Restaurant, Oscar's Pub & Restaurant, Smooth Jazz Cafe
- AServ W: Conway & O'Malley, Dick Casey Body Works, Erie Tires For Less, Forest City Auto Parts, Monroe Muffler & Brakes, Pro Audio
- Med E: ✚ Hammot Medical Center
  W: ✚ Prompt Care
- ATM W: First Western Bank, Mellon Bank, National City Bank
- Other W: Sav A Lot Food Stores

43 **(182)** U.S. 20, 26th St
- FStop W: Country Fair[*, D, LP]
- Food E: Almost Famous Pizza House
  W: McDonald's, Pizza Fair (Country Fair), Sub Fair (Country Fair)
- AServ E: Auto Body World, Luke's Automotive, Phil's Atlantic Service, Silver Auto Parts
  W: Auto Land, Plaza 79 Body Shop Plus, Ras Auto Service
- Med E: ✚ St. Vincent Medical Center
- ATM W: Country Fair, National City Bank
- Parks W: Presque State Park, Waldemeer Park
- Other W: Revco[RX], Westridge Laundry[24]

41 **(180)** U.S. 19, Kearsarge
- Food E: Arby's, Chi- Chi's, Ponderosa, Red Lobster, The Brown Derby Roadhouse
- AServ E: Sears
- RVCamp E: Ferraro RV Rental Sales & Service
  W: Camping
- Med E: ✚ Hospital
- ATM E: Mellon Bank
- Other E: Mill Creek Mall, Pharmor[RX]

40 **(177)** Jct. I-90, Buffalo, Cleveland

39 **(174)** McKean
- RVCamp W: Erie KOA Kampground

38 **(165)** U.S. 6 N, Albion, Edinboro
- Food E: Highlander Golf Course
- RVCamp W: Lianas Lake Park Campground
- Parks E: Wooden Nickel Buffalo Farm
- Other E: Camboro Animal Hospital, Highlander Golf Course

(163) Rest Area (RR, Phones, Picnic, Vending; Southbound)

37 **(154)** PA 198, Saegertown, Conneautville
- Gas W: Citgo
- AServ W: Citgo
- Parks E: Erie National Wildlife Refuge (17 Miles)

36AB **(147)** 36A - U.S. 6, U.S. 322, Meadville, 36B - Conneaut Lake
- FStop E: Citgo[*, D, LP, K]
- Gas E: Marathon[CW], Sheetz[*, D, LP, K, 24], Sunoco
- Food E: Applebee's, Big Boy, Cracker Barrel, Dairy Queen, Perkin's Family Restaurant, Referee Sports Bar & Grill (Days Inn), Sandalini's, Sub Fair (Citgo)
  W: Ponderosa
- Lodg E: Days Inn (see our ad this page), Holiday Inn, Motel 6
  W: Super 8
- AServ E: Advanced Auto Parts, Kirkpatrick Buick/Pontiac/GM, Robinson's Auto Repair
  W: Auto Zone Discount Auto Parts, Classy Auto Service[CW]
- Med E: ✚ Hospital

EXIT	PENNSYLVANIA

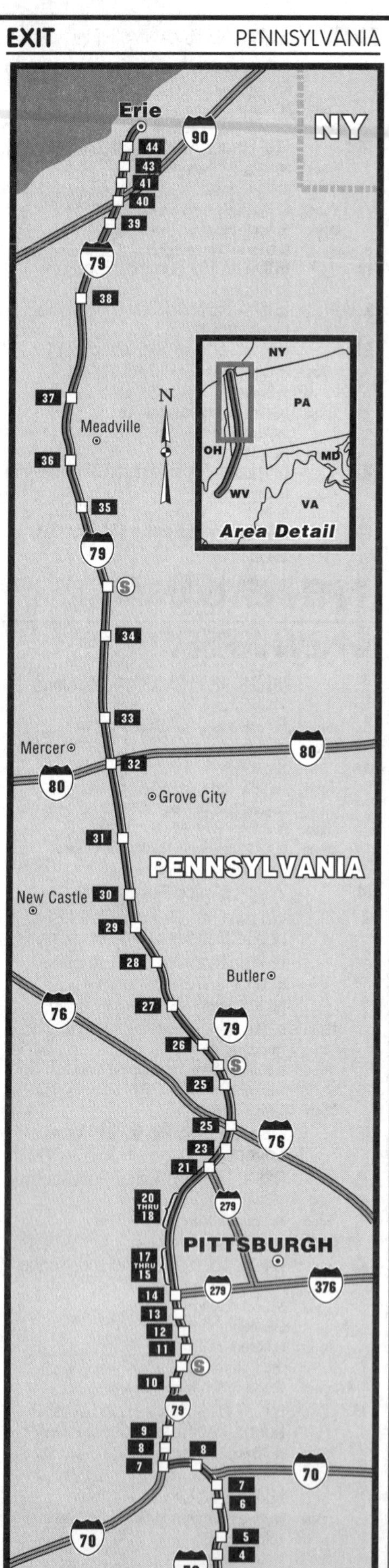

EXIT	PENNSYLVANIA

- ATM E: Citgo, Giant Eagle Supermarket[24, RX], Sheetz
- Parks W: Pymatuning State Park
- Other E: Giant Eagle Supermarket[RX], Langdon & Levito Animal Hospital[24]

35 **(141)** PA 285, Geneva, Cochranton
- TStop W: Geneva Truck Stop Texaco[*, D, SCALES]
- Gas W: Gulf[D, K]
- Food W: Geneva Truck Stop Texaco, Palmer's Restaurant
- AServ W: Detailing by Chas
- TServ E: Geneva Truck and Equipment
  W: Geneva Truck Stop Texaco[SCALES]

(136) Weigh Station/ Rest Area (Southbound)

(136) Weigh Station/ Rest Area (Northbound)

34 **(130)** PA 358, Greenville, Sandy Lake
- TStop E: LakeWay[D, 24]
- Food E: LakeWay
- RVCamp W: Camp Wilhem, Farma Campground, Goddard State Campground, Vacationland Campground
- Med W: ✚ Hospital (13 Miles)
- Parks W: MK Goddard State Park, Pymatuning State Park

33 **(121)** U.S. 62, Mercer, Franklin
- FStop W: Sunoco[*, D, K]
- Gas E: Citgo[*, LP, CW]
- AServ W: Adessa Body Shop, Baun's
- ATM E: Citgo
  W: Mercer County State Bank
- Other W: State Police

32 **(116)** Junction I-80, Clarion, Sharon

31 **(113)** PA 208 & 258, Grove City
- FStop E: Citgo[*, D, LP]

Meadville Days Inn Conference Center

1232

- Indoor Pool and Jacuzzi
- Davenports Full Service Restaurant and Referees Sports Bar
- Cable TV with FREE HBO, ESPN, CNN and Much More
- Centrally located for Grove City Outlets, Erie's Presque Isle Beaches and Millcreek Mall
- Minutes to Conneaut Lake Park and Pymatuning State Park
- Special Motor Coach Rates
- Ask about our **Golf Packages**
- Kids 12 and Under Stay & Eat Free
- Pets Allowed
- Handicap Accessible
- Coin Laundry • Interior Corridors
- Truck or Large Vehicle Parking

814-337-4264

*Subject to Availability. Not applicable with any other discounts. Not valid during holidays and special events.

PENNSYLVANIA ▪ I-79 ▪ EXIT 36A

Bold red print shows RV & Bus parking available or nearby

EXIT PENNSYLVANIA

Gas E: BP[*, LP]
W: Pennzoil Oil Change[*, D, K, CW], Sunoco[*]
Food E: Blimpie Subs & Salads (BP), **Country Fair (Citgo)**
W: Eat 'n Park, **Prime Outlets at Grove City**, **McDonald's**, Subway (Sunoco)
Lodg W: Amerihost, Comfort Inn
AServ W: Pennzoil Oil Change, Sunoco
RVCamp **W: KOA Campgrounds**
Med **E: Hospital**
ATM E: BP, Citgo
Other **W: Prime Outlets at Grove City (see our ad this page), LP Interstate Machine & Fabricating[LP], Tourist Info.**

(109) Rest Area (RR, Phones, Picnic, Vending; Southbound)

(107) Rest Area (RR, Phones, Picnic, Vending; Northbound)

30 **(105)** PA 108, Slippery Rock
RVCamp **E: Camping**
W: Slippery Rock Campground
Parks **E: Moraine State Park**

29 **(99)** U.S. 422, New Castle, Butler
Food **W: Auto Auction**
AServ **W: Auto Auction**
RVCamp **W: Cooper's Lake Campground (1.5 Miles), Rose Point Park Campground (3 Miles)**
Parks **E: Moraine State Park**
W: Living Treasures Animal Park, McConnells Mill State Park (2 Miles)

28 **(96)** PA 488, Portersville, Prospect
AServ W: Bill's Auto Towing & Repair
RVCamp **E: Bear Run Campground (.5 Miles)**
Parks **E: Moraine State Park**
W: McConnells State Park (3 Miles)
Other **E: Porter's Cove Area**

27B **(88)** to U.S. 19, PA 68, Zelienople (Southbound, Reaccess Northbound Only)
RVCamp **W: Indian Brave Camping Resort**

27A **(87)** PA 68, Zelienople (Northbound, Reaccess Southbound Only)
Gas W: Exxon[*]
Food W: Thompson's Family Restaurant
AServ W: Plymouth Dodge, Truck
RVCamp **W: Indian Brave Camping Resort**

26 **(85)** PA 528, Evans City (Reaccess Northbound Only)
Food W: Icecutter Restaurant, Red Pin Restaurant (Bowling Lanes)
AServ E: Merideth Battery, R & R Tire Service/ Jerry Fisher Auto Body
W: Northland Ford, R & K Couriers, Yoder Pontiac, Oldsmobile, GMC

(80) Weigh Station (Phones; Southbound)

(80) Weigh Station (Northbound)

25 **(76)** U.S.19 N, to Jct I-76, PA 228, Mars, Cranberry, PA Tnpk (Southbound, Difficult Reaccess)
Gas W: Amoco[*, CW, 24], Exxon[*, D, LP], Sheetz[*, 24]

PRIME OUTLETS
GROVE CITY
Over 140 Outlet Stores and Food Court
Jos. A. Bank • Liz Claiborne • Donna Karan
Ask for your FREE COUPON BOOK
888-545-7221
1859
PENNSYLVANIA • I-79 • EXIT 31

EXIT PENNSYLVANIA

Food **W: Big Boy**, Boston Market Restaurant, Burger King, **Denny's**, Dunkin Donuts, Einstein Bros Bagels, Hardee's, Hartners Restaurant, Kings Family, Long John Silver, Perkins Family Restaurant, Pizza Outlet, Wendy's
Lodg W: Fairfield Inn, Hampton Inn, Oak Leaf Motel, Red Roof Inn
AServ W: Beacon Auto Parts, Exxon, Goodyear Tire & Auto[*], Grease Monkey, Jiffy Lube, Meineke Muffler, Pennzoil Oil Change, Pep Boys Auto Center
RVCamp **E: Pittsburg North Campground, Pittsburg North Campground[LP]**
Med **W: Hospital**
ATM W: Citizen's National Bank, Exxon, **Giant Eagle Grocery[RX]**, Mars National Bank, National Bank, Northside Bank, PNC Bank, Sheetz
Other **W: Big K-Mart, Cranberry Mall, Eckerd Pharmacy[RX]**, Gentle Touch Laundry, **Giant Eagle Grocery[RX], Phar Mor Drugs[RX], Shop 'N Save Supermarket[24, RX], Wal-Mart[LP, RX]**

25B Cranberry (Northbound, Left Exit , Difficult Reaccess)
Gas W: Sunoco[*]
Food W: Arby's, Bob Evan's Restaurant, Brighton Hot Dog Shoppe, Eat 'N Park, Lone Star Steakhouse, Max & Erma's, McDonald's
Lodg W: Days Inn, Holiday Inn Express, Junction Inn, Sheraton, Super 8
AServ W: Toyota Dealer

23 **(75)** to U.S. 19 South, Warrendale (Northbound, Reaccess Southbound Only)
Gas E: Amoco
AServ E: Best Deal Auto Detail, Kar Plus[CW], Precision Auto Works

22 **(73)** PA 910, Wexford
Gas E: BP[*]
Food E: Bruster's Old Fashion Ice Cream, **King's Family**
W: Carmody's Restaurant
Lodg E: EconoLodge
Med **W: Chilren's Hospital of Pittsburg North**
ATM **E: T-Bones Grocery**
Other E: Car Wash, **T-Bones Grocery**, VIP Do-It-Yourself Car Wash

21 **(71)** Jct I-279 South, Pittsburgh, Washington (Left Exit Southbound)

20 **(68)** Mount Nebo Rd
Gas E: Texaco[*, LP, K]
AServ E: Texaco
Med **W: Hospital**

19 **(67)** PA 65, Emsworth, Sewickley
Med **W: Hospital**

18 **(65)** Neville Island, PA 51
Gas E: Gulf[*, D, K]
Food E: Frank & Mary's Inn, Gulf, Islander Restaurant & Bar
Lodg E: Neville Motel
AServ E: Belloma's, Silversox Limo Service
W: Steel City Tire, Tri State Motors
TServ **E: Penske Truck Rental & Leasing**
Other **W: Neville Island Laundromat**

17 **(64)** PA 51, Coraopolis, McKees Rocks (Northbound)
Med **E: Hospital**
Parks **W: Robinson Township Parks & Recreation**

16AB **(61)** PA 60, Airport, 16A- W. U.S. 22, 30 16B- Crafton
FStop **E: Exxon[*, D, LP, 24]**
Gas W: Sunoco[*, LP]
Food E: King's Family[24]
Lodg E: Days Inn, EconoLodge, Motel 6

EXIT PENNSYLVANIA

AServ W: Altvater's, Auto House, Auto Star Service, J&N Foreign Car Service, Sunoco
Med **E: Hospital**
ATM E: King's Family
W: Sunoco

15 **(58)** U.S. 22, U.S. 30, Airport (Northbound)

14 **(58)** Jct I-279, North to Pittsburgh

13 **(57)** Carnegie
AServ W: Bishop Auto

12 **(54)** Heidelberg, Kirwan Heights
Food E: Dairy Queen, Dunkin Donuts, Eat N Park, Peter's Place
AServ E: Advanced Auto Glass, Meineke Discount Mufflers, Speedee Muffler King, Valvoline Oil Change
Med **E: Hospital**
Other E: Car Wash

11 **(52)** PA 50, Bridgeville
Gas E: BP[*, LP, CW], Exxon[*, D]
W: Texaco[*]
Food E: Blimpie Subs & Salads (BP), Bo Sue's Ice Cream Shop, Burger King, **King's Family[24]**, **McDonald's[PLAY]**, Pop Edward's Famous Roast Beef, Rachel's Doghouse Hot Dogs
Lodg W: Knight's Inn
AServ E: Burgunder Dodge, Colussy Chev., Exxon, Midas Muffler & Brake, Monroe Muffler & Brakes, Napa Auto
W: Formost Auto Body Repair, Texaco
ATM E: BP, Exxon
Other E: Book Sale
W: Car Wash

(50) Weigh Station/Rest Area (RR, Phones, Picnic, Vending; Southbound)

(50) Rest Area/Weigh Station (RR, Phones, Picnic, Vending; Northbound)

10A **(48)** Southpointe, Hendersonville

10 **(45)** to PA 980, Canonsburg (Difficult Reaccess)
Gas W: BP[*, LP, 24], CoGo's[*, LP]
Food W: Hoss's Steak, KFC, Long John Silver, McDonald's[PLAY], Pizza Hut, Taco Bell, Wendy's
Lodg W: Super 8
AServ W: Advance Auto Parts, John's Automotive, Tatano Brothers Auto
Med **W: Hospital**
ATM W: BP, CoGo's
Other W: Skating Rink

9 **(43)** PA 519, Houston, Eighty Four
Gas E: Amoco[*]
W: Sunoco[*]
AServ E: Amoco
W: Sunoco
Med **E: Hospital**
W: Hospital

8 **(21)** PA 136, Beau St.

8B **(41)** Meadow Lands
Gas W: BP[*, D, LP]
Food E: Holiday Inn, Ladbroke The Meadows (Horse Farm & Racing), McDonald's, Triumphs Restaurant (Ladbroke The Meadows)
W: Blimpie Subs & Salads (BP), Meadow Inn, Mr. Hungry
Lodg E: Holiday Inn
AServ E: Racetrac Motors
W: Larry's Auto Service
ATM W: BP, **Convenient Food Mart**

EXIT	PENNSYLVANIA/WEST VIRGINIA
Other	**E:** Ladbroke The Meadows (Horse Farm & Racing)
	W: Convenient Food Mart, Trolley Museum (2.5 Miles), Washington County Fairgrounds
Exit	**(37)** Jct I-70, New Stanton, Washington, West Virginia
7	**(33)** U.S. 40, Laboratory Rd.
RVCamp	**W:** KOA Campgrounds
(31)	Parking Area, Weigh Station (Southbound)
6	**(30)** U.S. 19, Amity, Loan Pine
Gas	**W:** Exxon[*, D, LP, K]
Food	**W:** Subway (Exxon), TCBY (Exxon)
RVCamp	**W:** Lone Pine RV Center[LP]
ATM	**W:** Exxon
5	**(23)** Marianna, Prosperity
Gas	**W:** Texaco[*, D]
4	**(18)** to U.S. 19, PA 221, Ruff Creek, Jefferson
Gas	**W:** Amoco[*, D], Ruff Creek General Store[D] (Grocery Store)
Other	**W:** Ruff Creek General Store (Grocery Store)
3	**(14)** PA 21, Masontown, Waynesburg
Gas	**E:** Amoco[*, D]
	W: BP[*, LP, 24], Citgo[*, D, LP], Exxon[*, D, LP]
Food	**W:** Chester Fried Chicken (Citgo), Dairy Queen, Golden Corral Family Steakhouse, Golden Wok Chinese, KFC, Taco Bell (Exxon), Wendy's
Lodg	**E:** Comfort Inn
	W: EconoLodge, Super 8
AServ	**E:** Amoco
	W: Amerilube, Bortz, Chevrolet, Cadillac, Geo
Med	**E:** ✚ Greene County Medical Plaza/ Washington Hospital
	W: ✚ Hospital
ATM	**W:** Citgo, Community Bank
Other	**E:** Airport
	W: Ames, PA State Police, Revco Drugs[RX], Shop 'N Save Supermarket
2	**(7)** Kirby, Garards Fort
(5)	PA Welcome Center (RR, Phones; Northbound)
1	Mount Morris
TStop	**E:** Citgo[*, D, SCALES, 24]
Gas	**W:** Ashland[*, K], BP[*, D, K]
Food	**E:** Citgo
AServ	**E:** Honda Mazda Dealer
	W: Max's Body Shop
RVCamp	**W:** Mt. Morris Travel Trailer Camp (1.5 Miles)
ATM	**E:** Citgo
	W: BP
Other	**W:** Coin Car Wash

↑PENNSYLVANIA

↓WEST VIRGINIA

(159)	WV Welcome Center (RR, Phones, Picnic, Vending, RV Dump; Southbound)
155	U.S. 19, WV 7, West Virginia University
Gas	**W:** Exxon[*, D]
Med	**E:** ✚ Hospital
152	**(153)** U.S. 19, Westover, Morgantown
Gas	**E:** BP[*, LP, K, CW], Exxon[*]
Food	**E:** Donut Connection, Double Play,

EXIT WEST VIRGINIA

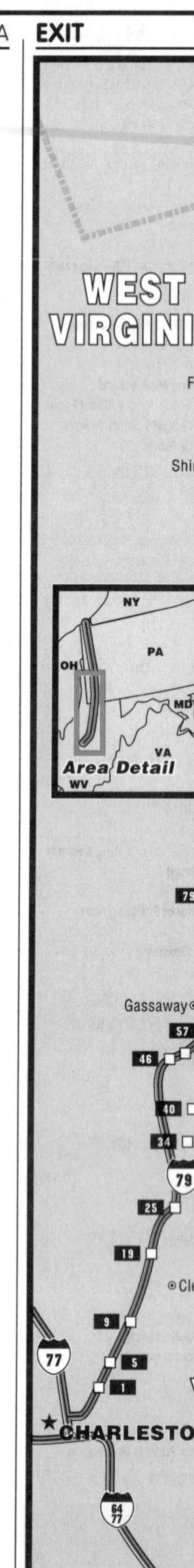

EXIT	WEST VIRGINIA
	McDonald's[PLAY], Pizza Hut, Subway, Western Sizzlin'
	W: Bob Evan's Restaurant, Burger King, Captain D's Seafood, Garfield's
Lodg	**E:** EconoLodge
AServ	**E:** Martin's Auto Ranch, Midas Muffler & Brake
	W: Charles Auto Refinishing Center, Precision Lube Express, Sears
TServ	**E:** Martin's Auto Ranch
Med	**E:** ✚ Wedgewood Family Practice (Walk-in Clinic)
ATM	**E:** BP, Exxon, Shop n Save Supermarket, Wesbanco
Other	**E:** Shop n Save Supermarket
	W: Eckerd Drugs[RX], Morgantown Mall, Pharmor Drugs[RX], Super K-Mart[24, RX] (Grocery)
148	Junction I-68 East, Cumberland
146	WV 77, Goshen Rd
(141)	Weigh Station (Southbound)
(141)	Weigh Station (Northbound)
139	East Fairmont, WV 33, Prickett's Creek Rd
Gas	**E:** Chevron[*]
	W: Exxon[*]
Food	**W:** Country Store and Cafe
TServ	**E:** Ridgerunner
RVCamp	**E:** Prickett's Creek Campground (.8 Miles)
Parks	**E:** Prickett's Fort Park
137	WV 310, Downtown Fairmont
FStop	**E:** Exxon[*, D]
Gas	**W:** Chevron[*, D, LP, K, CW, 24]
Food	**E:** Emporium Restaurant, Simmering Pot (Holiday Inn)
	W: Dairy Creme Corner, KFC, McDonald's, Wendy's
Lodg	**E:** Holiday Inn
AServ	**E:** Exxon
ATM	**W:** One Valley Bank
Other	**E:** Village Pantry Grocery
	W: Warehouse Grocery
135	WV 64, Pleasant Valley Rd
Other	**W:** Middleton Animal Clinic
133	WV 64/1, Kingmont Rd
FStop	**E:** BP[*, D]
Food	**E:** Cracker Barrel
	W: DJ's 50's & 60's Diner
Lodg	**E:** Super 8
	W: Comfort Inn & Suites
ATM	**E:** BP
132	U.S. 250, South Fairmont
Gas	**W:** Exxon[*, D], Go Mart[*], Sunoco[*]
Food	**E:** EconoLodge, Hardee's, Hometown Hot Dogs, Hunan's, Marino's Italian Restaurant (EconoLodge), Subway
Lodg	**E:** EconoLodge, Red Roof Inn
AServ	**E:** NAPA Auto Parts, Pick Up City
	W: Exxon, Penn Toyota
TServ	**E:** Pick Up City
RVCamp	**E:** Cummins Cumberland, Inc. (.5 Miles)
	W: Brand Trailer Sales RV Service and Sales
ATM	**E:** Huntington Bank, OneValley Bank, Shop 'N Save Supermarket
Parks	**E:** Tygart State Park (21 Miles)
Other	**E:** Shop 'N Save Supermarket
125	WV131, Saltwell Rd , Shinnston

Bold red print shows RV & Bus parking available or nearby

EXIT — WEST VIRGINIA

Gas W: Exxon(*, D, LP)
Food W: Subway (Exxon)
ATM W: Exxon

124 WV 707, FBI Center Rd

(123) **Rest Area (RR, Phones, RV Dump; Southbound)**

(123) **Rest Area (RR, Phones, Picnic, RV Dump; Northbound)**

121 WV 24, Meadowbrook Rd
Gas E: Go Mart(*)
W: Exxon(*, D)
Food E: Blimpie Subs & Salads (Go Mart), Bob Evan's Restaurant, Carl's Cafe (Go Mart)
W: Burger King, **Outback Steakhouse**, **Ponderosa Steakhouse**
Lodg E: Hampton Inn
W: EconoLodge
AServ W: Quick Slick Oil Change
ATM E: Bank One, Go Mart
W: Exxon
Other W: **Petland**

119 U.S. 50, Clarksburg, Bridgeport
Gas E: Chevron(*, D, LP, 24), Exxon(*, D)
Food E: Caf Steele's Sports Cafe, **China Buffet**, **Damon's**, **Days Inn**, Eat N Park, **El Rincon Mexican**, **Elby's Big Boyoy**, **Hostetler's Bagels**, **Italian Oven**, KFC, Little Caesars Pizza, Long John Silver, SHONEY'S **Shoney's**, Taco Bell, **Texas Road House**, The Simmering Pot (Holiday Inn), **USA Steak Buffet**, Wendy's, Western Steer Family Steakhouse
Lodg E: **Days Inn**, Holiday Inn, Knight's Inn, **Ramada Limited**, Sleep Inn
AServ E: **Advance Auto Parts**, Exxon, Midas Muffler & Brake, Plaza Service Center
ATM E: Huntington Bank, **Kroger Supermarket**(24, RX), Wes Banco Bank
Other E: **Giant Eagle Supermarket**(RX), **K-Mart**(RX), **Kroger Supermarket**(RX)

117 WV 58, Anmoore
Food W: **GD's Grocery & Deli**
AServ W: Tom's Used Cars(CW)

115 WV 20, Stonewood, Nutter Fort
Gas E: Chevron(*, LP), Texaco(*, D)
Food E: Dee's Diner, **Marty's Italian Bakery**, Mountaineer Family Restaurant (Texaco)

110 WV270, Lost Creek (Reaccess Southbound Only)
Gas E: BP(*, D), Citgo(*, K, CW)
Food E: Chicago Style Pizza (BP), Lost Hawg, Sub Express (BP)
AServ E: **Official West Virginia Inspection Station**
ATM E: Harrison County Bank
Parks W: **Watters Smith Memorial State Park (7 Miles)**
Other E: DC's General Store, **Lost Creek Laundromat**, **Village Pharmacy**(RX)

105 WV 7, Jane Lew
TStop E: **I-79 Truck Stop**(*, D, RV DUMP, SCALES) **(Truck Wash)**
Gas E: Chevron(*, CW)
Food E: **I-79 Truck Stop (Truck Wash)**, **The Wilderness Plantation (Chevron)**
Lodg E: **I-79 Truck Stop (Truck Wash)**, **The Wilderness Plantation**
TServ E: **I-79 Truck Stop**(SCALES) **(Truck Wash)**
ATM E: Chevron
W: Citizens Bank-Jane Lew Branch

EXIT — WEST VIRGINIA

99 U.S. 33, U.S. 119, Weston, Buckhannon
Gas E: Exxon(*, D), **Sheetz**(*, LP, K, 24)
Food E: **Comfort Inn**, **Gino's Pizza & Spaghetti**, **McDonald's**, **SheetzaPizza (Sheetz)**, **Subway**, **Taco Bell (Sheetz Convience Store)**, **Western Sizzlin'**
Lodg E: **Comfort Inn**, **Super 8**
AServ E: **Advance Auto Parts**, Exxon, **Quality Farm & Fleet**(LP) **(Pet Supply)**
RVCamp W: **Twin Lake Camper Sales**
Med W: **Hospital**
ATM E: **Kroger Supermarket**(LP), Progressive Bank, **Sheetz**
Parks E: **Black Water Falls (72 Miles)**, **Canaan Valley Park (72 Miles)**
Other E: **CVS Pharmacy**(RX), **Kroger Supermarket**, **Quality Farm & Fleet (Pet Supply)**, **Wal-Mart**(RX)

96 WV 30, S. Weston
Food W: Stouts Bait Shop & General Store
AServ W: Stouts Bait Shop & General Store
RVCamp E: **Broken Arrow Campground (1.4 Miles)**, **Broken Wheel Campground & Country Store**(*) **(1.75 Miles)**
Parks E: **Stonewall Jackson Lake State Park**
Other W: Stouts Bait Shop & General Store

91 Roanoke
RVCamp E: **Stonewall Jackson Lake State Park (3.1 Miles)**
W: **Whisper Mountain Campground (5 Miles)**
Parks E: **Burnsville Lake Park**

(85) **Rest Area (RR, Phones, Picnic, RV Dump; Southbound)**

(85) **Rest Area (RR, Phones, Picnic, RV Dump; Northbound)**

79 WV 5, Burnsville, Glenville
Gas E: Exxon(*), Texaco(D)
W: Go Mart(*)
Food E: Burnsville Diner, Main Street Cafe, Seventy-Niner Restaurant
W: Giovanni's Pizza
Lodg E: Motel 79
AServ E: NAPA Auto Parts, Texaco
W: Go Mart
ATM W: Bank of Gassaway
Parks E: **Burnsville Dam Riffle Run (3.5 Miles)**
W: **Cedar Creek State Park (24 Miles)**
Other E: **Fominko's General Store**

67 U.S. 19, WV 15, Flatwoods
TStop W: **Ashland Convenience Store**(*, D, 24)
FStop E: **Chevron**(*, D), **Go Mart**(*, D)

INTERSTATE EXIT AUTHORITY

EXIT — WEST VIRGINIA

Gas E: **Ashland Convenience Store**(*, D, LP, CW), Exxon(*)
W: Citgo(*)
Food E: Dairy Queen, KFC, **Lloyd's Family Restaurant**, **McDonald's**, **Stancati's Pizza (Mid-Mountain Lanes)**, Subway, Visions (Days Inn), Waffle Hut(24) (Motel), **Western Steer Family Steakhouse**
W: **Ashland Convenience Store**, SHONEY'S **Shoney's**, Wendy's
Lodg E: **Chevron**, **Days Inn**, Motel
W: **Ashland Convenience Store**
AServ E: Jones Chevrolet, Oldsmobile, Buick Dealer
RVCamp E: **Gerald R Freeman**, **Sutton Lake Campground**
ATM E: Exxon, **Go Mart**, Home National Bank
Parks E: **Sutton Lake Recreation Area**
Other E: **ACE Hardware (Truck Rental)**, **Coin Laundromat**, **Mid -Mountain Bowling Lanes**, Police
W: **Factory Outlet Center**

62 WV 4, Sutton, Gassaway
Gas W: Save Mart(*)
Food W: Long John Silver, Pizza Hut
RVCamp W: **Sutton Lake Campground**
Med W: **Hospital**
Other W: **Kroger Supermarket**(RX), **Revco Pharmacy**

57 U.S. 19 South, Beckley

51 WV 4, Frametown

(49) **Rest Area (RR, Phones, Picnic, RV Dump; Southbound)**

(49) **Rest Area (RR, Phones, Picnic; Northbound)**

46 WV 11, Servia Rd

40 WV 16, Big Otter
FStop E: **Go Mart**(*, D)
Gas W: Exxon(*, D)
Lodg W: **Country Inn (Exxon)**, Exxon
ATM W: Exxon
Other W: **G-Mart Grocery**

34 WV 36, Wallback, Clay

25 WV 29, Amma
Gas E: Exxon(*, D, CW)
Parks E: **Sandy Brae Golf Course**

19 U.S. 119, Clendenin
FStop E: **BP**(*, D)

9 WV 43, Elkview, Frame Rd
Gas W: Exxon(*, D, LP), SuperAmerica(*, LP)
Food W: Arby's (Exxon), McDonald's, **Pizza Hut**, **Ponderosa Steakhouse**, **Subway**
AServ W: **Advance Auto Parts**
ATM W: SuperAmerica
Other W: **K-Mart**(RX), **Revco Drugs**(RX)

5 WV 114, Big Chimney
Gas E: Exxon
Food E: Hardee's(24), Lettie Jane's
AServ E: Exxon
Other E: Rite Aid Pharmacy(RX), **Super Valu Grocery**, Yeager Airport

1 U.S. 119, Mink Shoals
Food E: **Harding's Family Restaurant**
Lodg E: **Sleep Inn**

↑WEST VIRGINIA

Begin I-79

Bold red print shows RV & Bus parking available or nearby

EXIT CALIFORNIA

Begin I-80

↓CALIFORNIA

4 Treasure Island (Left Exit)

(7) Toll Plaza (Westbound, Toll)

8 West Grand Ave.

Exit **(9)** Powell St., Emeryville 9A
- Gas N: Shell[*, D, CW, 24]; S: 76[*]
- Food N: Charlie Brown's Steak & Lobster; S: Bettore's Pizza, Burger King, Denny's, Lyon's, Sundae's Yogurt, Togo's
- Lodg N: Holiday Inn; S: Four Points Hotel Sheraton
- ATM S: Wells Fargo
- Other S: Crown Books, Triple Play Batting Cages, Wells Fargo

Exit **(9)** Ashby Ave., Bay Street - 9B

Exit **(11)** University Ave, Berkeley

Exit **(12)** Gilman St - 12A

Exit **(12)** Albany - 12B

Exit **(13)** Central Ave
- Gas S: Exxon[*], Shell[*, 24]
- Food S: White Knight

Exit **(14)** Carlson Blvd (No Trucks Over 3.5 Tons)
- Gas N: 76[*, 24]
- Lodg N: 40 Flags Motel; S: Super 8
- RVCamp N: **Ralph's RV Service Center**
- Other S: Chuck's Auto Salon

Exit **(14)** Potrero Ave. (Eastbound, Reaccess Westbound Only)
- Gas S: Chevron[*, 24]
- Food S: Carrow's Restaurant, Piggy's Pizza & Ribs
- Lodg S: TraveLodge
- AServ S: Kragen Auto Supply
- Other S: **Foods Co.**, Pet Vet, **Target**

Exit **(15)** MacDonald Ave. 15A (No Reaccess)
- Gas S: Chevron[*, 24]
- Food S: Hacienda's, Kwang Tung Restaurant, Mira Vista Donut & Deli, Taco Bell, Wendy's
- AServ N: Auto Expert, Montgomery Ward, Oil Changers; S: AAMCO Transmission, Ben's Auto Repair, Team Richmond Auto Parts & Service, Winston Tire
- ATM N: Imperial Savings Bank, Mechanics Bank; S: Bank of America, Washington Mutual
- Other S: Home Depot, **Lucky Food Center**[RX], Richmond Animal Hospital, **Safeway Grocery**[RX], Super Car Wash

EXIT CALIFORNIA

15 Cutting Blvd., to I-580, San Rafael Bridge
- Gas N: Alaska[D]; S: 76[D, 24], Just Cheap
- Food S: Church's Chicken, Jack-in-the-Box
- Lodg S: Freeway Motel
- Other S: **Target**

Exit **(16)** San Pablo Ave.
- Gas N: 76[*]
- Food N: Pup Hut, Sunlight Indian Cuisine; S: Baker's Square, Tsing Tao
- AServ N: Rich Products/ Harley Davidson's, Taggart's Auto Clinic; S: Smith Chrysler, Plymouth
- RVCamp N: **Camp Quest RV**
- Other N: Enterprise Rent-a-Car, Mel & Sons Auto Shop; S: Thrifty Car Rental

17A McBryde Ave

Exit **(17)** Solano Ave
- Gas N: BP[*]
- Food N: **Broiler (Casino San Pablo)**, Denny's[24], Mae's Coffee House, Nations, Taco Bell
- RVCamp S: **Dave's Camperland, Windy Flat RV Repair**
- ATM N: Cal Fed
- Other N: **Casino San Pablo, Coin Laundry, Lucky**[RX], **Pay Less Drugs**; S: Grand Prix Car Wash

Exit **(17)** San Pablo Dam Road
- Gas N: BP[*]
- Food N: Denny's[24], Maexican & Italian Restaurant, May's Coffee House, Old Saigon Restaurant, Taco Bell[24], Tong's Chinese Food
- RVCamp S: **Camp-A-Land**
- ATM N: Cal Fed, Lucky Food Center[RX]
- Other N: Coin Op Laundry, Lucky Food Center[RX], Mail Boxes Etc, Rite Aid Pharmacy[RX]; S: Grand Prix Auto Wash

Exit **(18)** El Portal Drive

Exit **(19)** Hilltop Drive
- Food N: Chevy's Mexican
- Lodg N: Courtyard by Marriott
- AServ N: Oil Changers, Sears Auto Center
- ATM N: Bank Of America, Home Savings Of America
- Other N: **Hilltop Mall**, Mechanics Bank

Exit **(20)** Richmond Pkwy., Fitzgerald Dr. 20B
- Food N: IHOP, McDonald's[PLAY], Me N Ed's Pizza, Taquiera Maria; S: Applebee's, Cheese Steak Shop, In-N-Out Burger, Numero Uno Mexican Restaurant, Round Table Pizza, Togo's
- AServ N: Hilltop Ford & Nissan, Michael Steads Chrysler, Plymouth, Jeep; S: Kragen Auto Parts

EXIT CALIFORNIA

- ATM S: Food 4 Less[24], Wells Fargo
- Other N: **Barnes & Noble (Starbucks Coffee)**, Greyhound Bus Station, **Pearl Vision Center, Petsmart (Vet Smart)**; S: Food 4 Less, Frame-N-Lens, Super Crown Bookstore, **Target**

Exit **(20)** Appian Way
- Gas N: Beacon[*]; S: Exxon[*]
- Food N: Bangkok Thai Cuisine, McDonald's[PLAY], Peking Garden, Pizza Hut; S: Baskin Robbins, Burger King, Carl Jr's Hamburgers, Catalano's Deli, Hometown Buffet, Hot Dog Station, KFC, Long John Silver, Noah's Bagels, Rick Shaw Chinese Food, Round Table Pizza, Sizzler Steak House, Starbucks Coffee, Taco Bell, Wendy's
- Lodg S: Days Inn, Motel 6
- AServ N: Beacon, Grand Auto Supply; S: Goodyear
- Med N: **+ Dr. Hospital**
- ATM N: Bank Of America, Cal Fed, **Safeway Grocery**; S: ATM, **Lucky's**[RX], Mechanics Bank
- Other N: Full Service Car Wash, **Long's Drugs**[RX], **Safeway Grocery**; S: **K-Mart, Lucky's**[RX], Mail Boxes Etc, **Theater**

Exit **(21)** Pinole Valley Road
- Gas S: Arco[*, CW], Beacon[*], Chevron[*, 24], Shell[*, 24]
- Food S: A La Mode Donuts & Ice Cream, House of Hunan, Jack-In-The-Box, Pizza Plenty, Yummy Yogurt, Zip's Restaurant
- AServ S: Beacon, Shell[24]
- ATM S: **7-11 Convenience Store, Lucky Food Center**
- Other S: **7-11 Convenience Store, Coin Laundry, Lucky Food Center**

Exit **(23)** Hercules, Stockton, CA 4

Exit **(24)** Willow Ave, Rodeo (No Trucks East)
- Gas S: 76[*, CW]
- Food S: Chicago Pizza & Pasta Kitchen, Willow Food, Willow Garden

Exit **(25)** Cummings, Skyway (Eastbound)

Exit **(26)** Martinez, Concord (Westbound)

Exit **(26)** Crockett

Exit **(27)** Toll Bridge (Eastbound, Toll)

Exit **(27)** Sonoma Blvd. (Eastbound)

Exit **(27)** Sequoia (Eastbound)

Exit **(27)** Maritime Academy Drive (Westbound)
- Gas N: Arco[*, D], Chevron[*, 24]
- Food N: Arco, **Chops Restaurant**, Subway (Arco), TCBY

Bold red print shows RV & Bus parking available or nearby

EXIT — CALIFORNIA

(Arco)
Lodg N: Motel 6, **Rodeway Inn**

Exit **(28)** Magazine St
Gas N: Shell(*, 24)
Food N: Rod's Hickory Pit(24)
S: McDonald's
Lodg N: Best In West Motel 7, Budget Motel, Economy Inn, El Curtola, El Rancho Motel
S: Knight's Inn
RVCamp N: **TradeWinds RV Park**
ATM S: **7-11 Convenience Store**
Other S: **7-11 Convenience Store**, Kentwig Lanes

Exit **(29)** Jct. I-780 & I-680, Benicia, Martinez
Lodg S: Holiday Inn (see our ad this page)

Exit **(30)** Georgia St, Central Vallejo

Exit **(31)** Solano Ave, Spring Road
Gas N: Chevron(*, 24)
Food N: Burger King, Church's Chicken, Nitti Gritti Restaurant, Szechuan Cuisine, Taco Bell
S: Smorga Bob's
Lodg N: E-Z 8 Motel, Gateway Motor Hotel
S: Bell Motel, **The Islander Hotel**
AServ N: Chevron(24), U-Haul Center(LP)
Other N: **Coin Laundry**, **Lucky's Grocery**(RX), Rite Aid Pharmacy(RX), U-Haul Center

Exit **(31)** Tennessee St., Mare Island
FStop S: **Trises (Quality Inn)**
Gas S: 76(*), Exxon(*, D, CW), Quality Inn
Food S: Pacifica Pizza
Lodg S: Quality Inn
AServ S: 76
Other S: Crossroads Car Wash

Exit **(31)** Red Wood Parkway East (No Trucks)
Gas N: 76(*)
S: Cheaper(*), Shell(*, CW, 24)
Food N: Annie's Panda Garden, Denny's
S: Little Caesars Pizza, Papa Murphy's, Royal Jelly Donuts, South Villa Chinese
Lodg N: Days Inn, Motel 6
AServ S: Avery Greene Oldsmobile, GMC, Honda, Chief Auto Parts
Med N: **Hospital**
ATM S: **Safeway Grocery**(RX)
Other S: **Redwood Veterinary Clinic**, **Safeway Grocery**(RX)

Exit **(32)** CA 37, Napa

Exit **(32)** Columbus Pwky.
Food S: Black Angus Steakhouse, Chevy's Mexican, IHOP, Olive Garden, Red Lobster, Ryan's Steakhouse, Subway, Taco Bell, Wendy's
Lodg S: Comfort Inn, Ramada Inn
AServ S: PEP Boys, Vallejo Toyota
ATM S: Union Bank of California
Other S: Applebee's, Cinema, **Costco**, Frame-N-Lens, Home Depot, Long's Pharmacy(RX), Postal Annex, **Save Mart Supermarket**

(33) **Rest Area (RR, Phones, Picnic; Westbound)**

33 San Rafael, CA. 37

Exit **(37)** American Canyon Rd.

Exit **(44)** Red Top Road
Gas N: 76(*, 24)
ATM N: 76

45 County Road 12, Napa, Sonoma

Exit **(46)** Junction I-680, Benicia, Green Valley Road

EXIT — CALIFORNIA

Exit **(46)** Suisun Valley Road
TStop N: **Jimmy's Truck Stop**(*, LP, SCALES)
FStop S: **Chevron**(*)
Gas S: 76(*, D), Arco(*, LP, 24), Shell(*, D, CW)
Food N: **Jason's (Jimmy's TS)**, **Jimmy's Truck Stop**
S: Arby's, Burger King(PLAY), Carl Jr's Hamburgers(PLAY), Cordelia Deli, Denny's, McDonald's(PLAY), Old San Francisco Express Pasta, Subway, Taco Bell, Wendy's
Lodg S: Best Western, Economy Inns of America, Hampton Inn, Overniter Lodge
TServ N: **Jimmy's Truck Stop**(SCALES)
RVCamp S: **Camping World RV Service (see our ad this page)**
ATM N: **Jimmy's Truck Stop**
S: 76, Arco, Shell
Other S: **Scandia Amusement Park/ Shopping Mall**

(37) **Weigh Station (Westbound)**

(47) **Weigh Station (Eastbound)**

Exit **(49)** Rio Vista, CA. 12E., Chadbourne Rd., Suisun City
Lodg S: Motel 6
AServ S: Fairfield Toyota, Steve Hopkins Honda

Exit **(50)** West Texas Road, Fairfield (First Ramp)
Lodg S: Motel 6
AServ S: Fairfield Toyota, Isuzu, Honda Dealer, Steve Hopkins Acura

Exit **(50)** West Texas Road, Fairfield (Second access ramp)
Gas N: Shell(*, D, CW)
Food N: Chuck E Cheese's Pizza, Gordito's Restaurant
S: Cenario's Pizza, Fairfield Donut, Frank & Yuen's Restaurant, Jack-In-The-Box, McDonald's, Nations Burgers, Pelayo's
AServ S: Pep Boys Auto Center
Other S: **Food 4 Less**, Home Depot, Post Masters, **Target**, **WalGreens Pharmacy**(RX)

Exit **(51)** Travis Blvd
Gas N: Arco(*), Chevron(*, CW, 24)
Food N: Burger King(PLAY), Denny's, Denny's(24), In-N-Out Burger, McDonald's, My Cafe, New York Pizza Kitchen, North Bay Coffee Co., Peking Restaurant, Subway, Taco Bell, Teriyaki Kitchen

1461
Holiday Inn
SAN JOSE NORTH
777 Bellew Drive • Milpitas, CA 95035
408-321-9500 • 800-HOLIDAY
• Excellent location in the heart of Silicon Valley
• 305 rooms on 12 floors • Gift shop
• In-room cable TV and pay movies
• In-room coffee makers, irons, ironing boards
• Electronic door locks • Full-service restaurant
• Lounge with piano music on weekday nights
• Dining and night life destinations within 1 mile
Independently owned by Milpitas Joint Venture and operated by Bristol Hotels & Resorts™
I-680 to Hwy. 237W (Exit 45) Exit McCarthy Blvd. Take a right on McCarthy, left on Bellew Dr. Hotel is on the left.

CAMPING WORLD®
Suisun Valley Rd. Exit
4350 Central Place • Cordelia, CA
1-800-448-1253
1423

EXIT — CALIFORNIA

S: Chevy's Mexican Restaurant, Fresh Choice, Marie Callender's Restaurant, Red Lobster
Lodg N: Holiday Inn Select, Motel 6
AServ N: Fairfield Nissan & Hyundai
S: Firestone
ATM N: Arco, Raley's Food Center(RX)
S: Bank of America
Other N: California Highway Patrol Post, Provident Bank, Raley's Food Center(RX)
S: **Solano Mall**

Exit **(52)** Waterman Blvd , Travis Air Force Base
Food N: Coffee World, Dynasty Restaurant, Hungry Hunter, Round Table Pizza, Strings Italian Cafe, TCBY
AServ N: Anthony Buick, Pontiac, GMC Trucks, Woodard Chevrolet Dealership
ATM N: First Bank & Trust Co., **Safeway Grocery**(RX), West America Bank
Other N: Mail Boxes Etc, **Safeway Grocery**(RX)

Exit **(54)** North Texas St
Gas S: Arco(*, 24), BP(*), Shell(*, CW)
Food S: **Lou's Junction**
Lodg S: E-Z 8 Budget Motel

Exit **(56)** Cherry Glen Road, Lagoon Valley Road

Exit **(56)** Pena, Adobe
Lodg S: Ranch Hotel
Parks S: **Lagoon Valley Regional Park**

57 Cherry Glen Road

Exit **(58)** Merchant St, Alamo Drive
Gas N: Arco(*, D, 24) (Jiffy Lube), Chevron(*), Shell(*, D, CW, 24)
Food N: Alberto's Mexican, Bakers Square Restaurant, Baskin Robbins, Cenario's Pizza, Digger's Deli, Donut Queen, Hong Kong Restaurant, KFC, Kel's Diner, Lyon's, Pepperoni's, Pluto's Hot Dog, Round Table Pizza, Solano Baking Co., Taqueria #2 Guadalajara, Wren's Cafe
S: Ho's Donuts & Coffee, Jack-In-The-Box, McDonald's(PLAY), Pizza Hut, Port Of Subs, Stir Fry
Lodg N: Alamo Inn
AServ N: Arco(24) (Jiffy Lube), Jiffy Lube (Arco), Red's Grass & Auto
RVCamp N: **Travel Time RV Center**
ATM N: Bay View Bank, Shell
S: Golden One Credit Union
Other N: **Grocery Outlet**, U Save Speed Wash, Vaca Valley Animal Hospital
S: **Food 4 Less**(24) **(Grocery Store)**, Mail Boxes Etc

Exit **(59)** Davis St
Gas S: Quik Stop Market(*)
Food S: Grandma's Platter House
AServ N: Bernie's City Garage
S: Advanced Muffler, Cecil's Hi-Tech Auto Repair, Christian's Auto Service, GM Specialists, Gemini Auto Repair, Shiloh Auto Service, Vacaville Transmissions
RVCamp S: **Sunrise Trailer Park**
Other S: **Midvalley Veterinarian**

Exit **(59)** Peabody Rd., Elmira (Eastbound)

Exit **(59)** Mason St, Travis AFB (Westbound)
Gas N: Texaco(*, CW, 24)
S: Shell(*), USA Gasoline(*)
Food S: Cable Car Coffee Co., Carl Jr's Hamburgers, Domino's Pizza, Donut Wheel Donuts, El Azteca, Formosa, Hi-Way Sandwiches, Solano Baking Co., Sushi Sen, Wah Shine, Wienerschnitzel
AServ N: NAPA Auto Parts
S: Agean Tire Service, PEP Boys, Petrillo's Tire & Auto Service, Shell, Vacaville Ford
Med S: **Hospital**
ATM N: Texaco

EXIT CALIFORNIA

S: 7-11 Convenience Store(24), West America Bank
Other **S:** 7-11 Convenience Store, Greyhound Bus Station, **Launderland Coin Laundry**, Red Carpet Car Wash, **U.S. Post Office**, **Wonder Hostess Bakery Outlet**

Exit **(60)** Monte Vista Ave, Allison Drive, Nut Tree Parkway
Gas **N:** 76(*), Chevron(*, LP, 24)
Food **N:** Arby's, Burger King(PLAY), Denny's(24), Great Crepe Coffee House, Hisui Japanese Steakhouse, IHOP, McDonald's(PLAY), Murillo's, Nations, Pelayo's Mexican Restaurant, Round Table Pizza, Royal Motel (Murillo's), Taco Bell, Wendy's, Yen King Restaurant
S: Baskin Robbins, Big Apple Bagels, Boston Market Restaurant, Chili's, Chubby's, Fresh Choice, Java City, KFC, Pelayo's Mexican Restaurant, Pizza Hut, Starbucks Coffee, String's Italian Cafe, Togo's
Lodg **N:** Best Western, **Brigadoon Lodge**, **Royal Motel (Murillo's)(see our ad this page)**, Super 8
AServ **N:** Brake Master Auto Service, Firestone Tire & Auto, Frontier Tire, Grand Auto Supply Tires & Service, Jim Dandy Transmissions, Ken's Performance Center, Midas Muffler & Brake
ATM **N:** 76
S: Bank Of America, **Safeway Grocery**, Sierra West Bank
Other **N:** 7 Flags Car Wash, Vacaville Car Wash
S: **Safeway Grocery**, **Target**, **Vaccaville Commons (Mall)**

Exit **(61)** I-505 North, Redding, Winters

Exit **(63)** LeisureTown Road
Gas **S:** Beacon(*, D)
Food **S:** Hickory Pit, Jack-In-The-Box, Quality Inn (Vaca Joe's), Vaca Joe's
Lodg **S:** Quality Inn (Vaca Joe's)
AServ **S:** Beacon
Med **N:** + **Kaiser Permanente**

Exit **(64)** Meridian Road, Weber Road

Exit **(66)** Midway Road, Lewis Road

Exit **(69)** Dixon Ave
Gas **S:** Arco(*), Chevron(*, D) (Arcadia Bay Coffee Co), Shell(*, D, CW) (Dixon Lube & Tune, Piccadilly)
Food **S:** Arcadia Bay Coffee Co, Carl Jr's Hamburgers(PLAY), Chevron (Arcadia Bay Coffee Co), **Los Altos**, **Mr. Taco**, Piccadilly (Shell), Shell (Dixon Lube & Tune, Piccadilly)
AServ **S:** Dixon Lube & Tune (Shell), Shell (Dixon Lube & Tune, Piccadilly)
ATM **S:** Shell (Dixon Lube & Tune, Piccadilly)
Other **S:** Dixon Produce Market

Exit **(70)** Pitt School Road
Gas **S:** Chevron(*, 24), Exxon(*)
Food **S:** Arby's, Asian Garden Chinese, Baskin Robbins, Burger King, Candy Bouquet, Chevy's Mexican, Denny's, IHOP(24), Jalisco Mexican, Java California, LaBella's Pizza, Marcey's Ice Cream & Yogurt, Maria's Mexican Restaurant, Mary's Pizza Shack, McDonald's(PLAY), Peking, Pizza Hut, Solano Baking Co., Subway, Taco Bell
Lodg **S:** Best Western
ATM **S:** Chevron, **Safeway Grocery(RX)**
Other **S:** Mail Boxes Ect., **Safeway Grocery(RX)**

Exit **(71)** Curry Road, First Street
Food **S:** Cattlemens Restaurant, Jack-in-the-Box (Under Construction)

72 Milk Farm Road, Dixon

Exit **(73)** Pedrick Road
Gas **N:** 76(*, LP)
AServ **N:** 76
ATM **N:** 76

Exit **(74)** Kidwell Road

EXIT CALIFORNIA

Exit **(75)** CA 113 North, Woodland

Exit **(76)** UC Davis

Exit **(77)** Richards Blvd, Davis
Gas **N:** Shell(*, 24)
S: Chevron (Under Construction)
Food **N:** Caffe Italia (Davis Inn), Caffino, Davis Inn, In-N-Out Burger, Murder Burger
S: Jack in the Box, Wendy's
Lodg **N:** Davis Inn
S: Holiday Inn Express
AServ **N:** Advanced Auto Repair & Towing, Charlie's Muffler & Transmission Shop, Davis Radiator, G & R Automotives, Johnny's, Ray's Auto with NAPA Auto Parts, Speedy Auto Glass

Exit **(79)** Olive Drive (Westbound)

Exit **(80)** Mace Blvd
Gas **S:** 76(*), Chevron(*, CW, 24), No Name(*, D), Shell(*, CW)
Food **S:** Burger King, Cindy's Restaurant, Denny's, Lamp Post Pizza, McDonald's(PLAY), Mocha Joe's, Subway, Taco Bell(24), The Golden Garden Chinese Restaurant
Lodg **S:** Howard Johnson, Motel 6
AServ **S:** Courtesy Pontiac, Oldsmobile, Buick, GMC Truck, Davis Nissan & Freeway Ford & Mercury, Hanlees Chevrolet, Toyota, Geo Dealership, Swift Jeep, Chrysler, Plymouth, & Dodge, University Honda Dealership
RVCamp **S:** **La Mesa RV**
Other **S:** El Macero Veterinary Clinic, Enterprise Rent-a-Car, Mail Boxes Etc., The Nugget Market

Exit **(81)** EChiles Road (Eastbound)

Exit **(86)** Frontage Road (Westbound)

Exit **(88)** West Capitol Ave, West Sacramento -88A

Special Rates for Tour Groups
RAMADA INN®
2600 Auburn Blvd • Sacramento, CA
Restaurant/Lounge on Premises
Continental Breakfast • Interior Corridors
Outdoor Pool • Exercise Room
Meeting/Banquet Facilities
Pets Allowed • Handicap Accessible
Truck/Large Vehicle Parking
Airport shuttle • Coin laundry
Golf Course, Pro shop & Skeet Range
1792
916-487-7600 • 800-272-6232
I-80 Exit Walt South to Auburn, Rt on Auburn, hotel 1 mi left
California ▪ I-80 ▪ Exit 100

Royal Motel
1/4 Mile to Nuttree
Pool/Spa • Coin Laundry
HBO & ESPN
Conference Rooms
Truck Parking
Complimentary Continental Breakfast
Close to Shopping & Restaurants
1173
707-448-6482
CALIFORNIA ▪ I-80 ▪ NUTTREE EXIT

EXIT CALIFORNIA

FStop **N:** **Exxon(*) (CFN Commercial Fueling)**
Gas **N:** Chevron(*, CW), Shell(*, CW, 24)
S: Arco(*)
Food **N:** **Eppie's Restaurant**
S: Burger King, Denny's
Lodg **N:** Granada Inn
AServ **N:** Gabriel's
RVCamp **S:** **KOA RV Campground**
ATM **N:** Chevron, Shell
S: Arco

Exit **(88)** Jct. U.S. 50, Business 80 Loop, Sacramento -88B

Exit **(89)** Reed Ave
Gas **S:** Arco(*, 24)
Food **N:** Jack in the Box
TServ **N:** **Sacramento Valley Ford**, **Sierra Detroit Diesel-Allison**
RVCamp **N:** **Sacramento Valley Ford**
ATM **S:** Arco

Exit **(91)** West El Camino Ave
TStop **N:** **76 Auto/Truck Plaza(*, LP, SCALES) (Shell Gas)**
Gas **N:** Chevron(*, D)
Food **N:** **76 Auto/Truck Plaza (Shell Gas)**, Burger King(PLAY), Chevron, **I Can't Believe It's Yogurt (76 TStop)**, **Silver Skillet (76 TStop)**, **Subway (Chevron)**
RVCamp **N:** **Mike Daugherty Chevrolet RV Center (1.25 Miles)**, **Safari RV Stores (1 Mile)**
ATM **N:** **76 Auto/Truck Plaza (Shell Gas)**

Exit **(92)** Junction I-5, CA 99, Sacramento (I-5 & CA 99 South), Redding (I-5 & CA 99 North)

93 Truxel Road

94 Northgate Blvd
Gas **S:** Shell(*, CW)
Food **S:** Carl Jr's Hamburgers, Finnegan's, McDonald's, Taco Bell
Lodg **S:** Extended Stay America, **Travelers Inn**

95 Norwood Ave
Gas **N:** Arco(*)
Food **N:** Jack-In-The-Box, McDonald's, New Hong Kong Chinese, Subway
AServ **N:** Chief Auto Parts
Other **N:** **Sav-Max Foods**

97 Raley Blvd, Del Paso Heights, Marysville Blvd
FStop **N:** **Bell Gas 'N Diesel(*, D, LP)**
Gas **N:** Arco(*), Chevron
Food **S:** Connie's Drive-in
AServ **N:** Chevron
S: Hooten Tire Co, North Side Tires, Parrish Tire & Wheel

98 Winters St

99 Longview Drive, Light Rail Station

100 Capital City Freeway, Sacramento, Bus. I-80, To CA99 South
Lodg **S:** **Ramada Inn (see our ad this page)**

101 Madison Ave.
Gas **N:** Beacon(*), Shell(*)
S: Arco(*)
Food **N:** Betos Mexican, Brookfield's Family Restaurant, Cyber Java, Denny's, Latte Express, What a Pizza, Willie's Restaurant (Philippino/American)
S: A & W Drive-In, Boston Market Restaurant, Eppie's(24), IHOP, Jack-In-The-Box
Lodg **N:** Motel 6, Super 8
S: Holiday Inn, La Quinta
AServ **S:** American Auto Repair, Niello Acura, Porsche Dealer, Performance Chevrolet, Geo, Imports, Suburban Ford
RVCamp **S:** **Mark-J Mobile Home & RV Park**

EXIT CALIFORNIA

ATM N: Shell
S: Home Savings Of America

Other N: Bumper Boat Pond Lil' Indy Raceway, Hillsdale Animal Hospital
S: Date Ave. Veterinary, Mardi Gras Lanes Bowling

103 Greenback Lane, Elkhorn Blvd, Orangevalle

Gas N: 76[24]

Food N: McDonald's, Pizza Hut, Subway
S: Baskin Robbins

AServ N: 76[24]

Med N: Immediate Care Medical Clinic

ATM S: Circle K[*]

Other N: Longs Drugs[RX], Safeway Grocery
S: Cinedomes, Circle K

(104) Weigh Station (Eastbound)

(104) Weigh Station (Westbound)

106 Antelope Road, Citrus Heights

Gas N: 76[*, LP]

Food N: Burger King, Carl Jr's Hamburgers[PLAY], Chubby's, Giant Pizza, KFC, McDonald's[PLAY], Subway, Taco Bell, Yogurt Delite

AServ N: 76

ATM N: Home Savings Of America, Raley's Supermarket[RX]

Other N: 7-11 Convenience Store, ACE Hardware, Albertson's Grocery, Mail 4 You, Optometrist, Pets, Postal Express, Raley's Supermarket[RX], Rite Aid Pharmacy[RX], Veterinarian

107 Roseville, Riverside Ave, Citrus Heights

Gas N: Arco[*]
S: Exxon[*, D], Shell[*, CW]

Food N: Susie's Country Oaks Cafe
S: Back 40 Texas BBQ, California Burgers, Espresso Drive-Thru, Golden Donuts, Jack-In-The-Box, Jimboy's Tacos, Moonlight Cafe (Vietnamese)

AServ S: Do-It-Right Transmissions, Economy Garage, K-Mart[RX], Winston Tire

RVCamp S: Village RV Part, Sales, Service

ATM S: World Savings

Other N: 7-11 Convenience Store[*], Car Wash, Coin Laundry, Roseville Telephone Museum
S: Alicia's Dog Grooming, K-Mart[RX]

109 Douglas Blvd, Sunrise Ave.

Gas N: 76[*, LP, CW], Arco[*], Exxon[*]
S: Arco[*], Chevron[24], Shell[*, 24]

Food N: Baker Ben's Donuts[24], Baskin Robbins, Burger King, Chubby's, Jack-In-The-Box, KFC, McDonald's[PLAY], Mountain Mike's Pizza, Primos Restaurant & Pies, Roseville Gourmet, Sam's Sub Shop, Taco Bell, Yogurt Delite
S: Carl Jr's Hamburgers[PLAY], Carrows Restaurant[24], Del Taco, Denny's[24], First Choice Chinese, Lorenzo's Mexican, Parker's Hot Dogs, Round Table Pizza, Teriyaki In & Out, Thai Basil Restaurant, Yama Sushi, Yoshi Chinese

Lodg N: Heritage Inn
S: Oxford Inn

AServ N: Auto Service of Roseville, Big O Tires, Firestone Tire & Auto, Grand Auto Supply, Kragen Auto Parts, Midas Muffler & Brake, Roseville Eye Care
S: Andrews Lincoln, Mercury, Auto Service Truck Stop, Chevron[24], Quality Tune Up, Roseville Toyota, Shell[24]

Med S: Hospital

ATM N: Bank Of America, Placer Savings Bank, U.S. Bank
S: Safe Federal Credit Union, Western Valley Credit Union

Other N: Cover To Cover Books, Michael's Craft Store, Pet Care, Price Less Drug Stores[RX], U.S. Post Office
S: Launderland Coin Laundry, Office Depot, Rite Aid Pharmacy[RX], The Bible House, Ward's Wash & Dry Coin Laundry

110 Atlantic St., Eureka Road

Gas S: Shell[*, CW]

EXIT CALIFORNIA

Food S: Black Angus Steakhouse, Brookfield's Restaurant, Carvers Steaks and Chops, Taco Bell, Wendy's

AServ N: Roseville Auto Parts
S: America's Tire Company, Roseville Auto Mall

Other N: Atlantic Street Veterinary Hospital
S: Sam's Club, Sunsplash Water Park, United Artist Theaters

111A Rocklin, Taylor Road (Eastbound, Reaccess Westbound Only)

Food N: Cattlemen's Restaurant

RVCamp N: Holiday RV Super Stores (see our ad this page)

111B CA 65, Lincoln, Marysville (Limited Access Hwy)

113 Rocklin Road

Gas N: Beacon, Exxon[*]
S: Arco[*]

Food N: Arby's, Baskin Robbins, Burger King, Carl Jr's Hamburgers, China Gourmet, Chinese Cuisine, Coffee Co., Denny's, Hacienda Del Rable, Jack-In-The-Box, Jasper's Giant Hamburgers, KFC, Mountain Mike's Pizza, Papa Murphy's Pizza, Subway, Taco Bell[24]
S: Susanne Restaurant & Bakery (Rockland Park Hotel)

Lodg N: First Choice Inns
S: Rockland Park Hotel

AServ N: Beacon

RVCamp N: Camping World (see our ad this page)

ATM N: Safeway Grocery

Other N: Cathy's Pet Shop, Rite Aid Pharmacy[RX], Safeway Grocery, Sierra Food & Deli[*]

114 Sierra College Blvd

Gas N: 76[D, LP], Chevron[*, CW]

Food N: McDonald's (Chevron)

AServ N: 76

RVCamp N: KOA-Loomis (.5 Miles)

116 Loomis, Horseshoe Bar Rd.

Food N: Burger King[PLAY], Round Table Pizza, Taco Bell

ATM N: Raley's Supermarket

Other N: Raley's Supermarket

117 Penryn

Food N: Cattlebarons Cafe

121A Newcastle

Gas S: Arco[*, 24], Exxon[*, D]

Food N: Newcastle Pizza, Newcastle Restaurant, The Blue Goose
S: Denny's

AServ N: Monroe Transmission, Newcastle Auto Tune & Electric

Other N: Fire Department, Quality Market[*], U.S. Post Office
S: Fire Station, Highway Patrol, Home On The Range Golf Range

CAMPING WORLD®
Rocklin Rd. Exit
4435 Granite Dr. • Rocklin, CA
1-800-437-5332
1432

EXIT CALIFORNIA

121B CA 193, Lincoln, Taylor Rd.

TServ S: Superior Equipment Repair

123 Ophir Rd. (Westbound, Reaccess Eastbound Only)

122 Auburn, Maple St, Nevada St.

Gas S: Shell[*]

Food S: Bootlegger's Old Town Tavern Grill, Cafe Delicias, Mary Belle's, Shanghai Restaurant, Tio Pepe

ATM S: Shanghai Restaurant

Other S: Historic Old Auburn, Tsuda Grocery

124 CA 49, Grass Valley, Placerville

Gas N: 76, Shell[*]

Food N: Foster's Freeze Hamburgers, IN-N-Out Burger, Marie Callender's Restaurant
S: Taco Tree

Lodg N: Holiday Inn

AServ N: 76, Placer Smog and Auto Repair
S: 49er Auto Clinic

ATM N: Shell

Parks N: Empire Mines State Park (2 Miles)

Other N: Kinko's Copies, Rite Aid Pharmacy[RX], Staples Office Superstore
S: City of Auburn City Hall & Civic Center, Placer County Courthouse, Police Department

125A Elm Ave.

Gas S: Rowdy Randy's[*], Sierra Superstop

Food N: Flower Garden Bakery, Round Table Pizza, Taco Bell, The Breakfast Club, Togo's
S: Edelweiss Restaurant

Lodg S: Elmwood Motel

AServ N: J & W Auto Service
S: Sierra Superstop, Toms Sierra Tire

RVCamp S: Show & Ford RV[LP]

ATM N: Lucky Grocery Store, Wells Fargo Bank
S: Bank of America, U.S. Bank

Other N: 7-11 Convenience Store, Long's Drugs, Lucky Grocery Store, Rite Aid Pharmacy[RX], Sharon's Books, Sierra Optometry Center
S: Auburn Area Chamber of Commerce

125B Lincoln Way, Russell Rd. (Difficult Reaccess)

Gas S: Sierra Superstop[CW], Texaco[*, D]

AServ S: Auburn Auto Service (Ken's Towing), Sierra Superstop, Texaco

Other S: Foothill Market[*]

126 Foresthill, Auburn Ravine Road

Gas N: Beacon[*], Flyers[*, D], Thrifty[*]
S: 76[CW], Arco[*, 24], Chevron[*, 24], Shell[*]

Food N: Arby's, Denny's, Sam's Hof Brau, Sushi Bar, Sweetpea's, Taco Bell, Wienerschnitzel, Wimpy's Hamburgers
S: Bagel Junction, Baker's Square Restaurant, Baskin Robbins, Burger King, Burrito Shop, China Express, Country Waffles, Dairy Queen, David's Thai Cuisine, Ikeda's, Izzy's Giant Burgers, Jack-In-The-Box, KFC, Lou La Bonte's, Lyon's Restaurant, McDonald's, Pizza Chalet, Subway, Szechuan Food

Lodg N: Auburn Inn, Foothills Motel, Sleep Inn, Super 8
S: Best Western, TraveLodge

AServ S: 76, Shell

ATM N: Flyers
S: Bank of America, Chevron, Raley's Supermarket[RX], Sierra West Bank

Other N: Foothill Car Wash, Foothills Bowl, Prospector Hill 18 Hole Mini Golf
S: Boards In Motion Sales & Rental, Placer County Visitor's Center, Raley's Supermarket[RX], Thrifty Wash Coin Laundry

127 Bowman

Gas N: Bowman Card Lock[CW] (Private)

Food S: Sizzler

RVCamp N: Bowman Mobile Home & RV Park

Other S: Fire Department

EXIT CALIFORNIA

128 Bell Road
RVCamp N: **KOA Campgrounds (3 Miles)**
Med N: **Hospital (3 Miles)**

129 Dry Creek Road

130 Clipper Gap, Meadow Vista

133 Applegate
Gas N: Beacon(*)
Lodg N: The Original Firehouse Motel
S: Motel
AServ S: Applegate Garage
Other S: Fire Station, **U.S. Post Office**

134 Heather Glen

135 West Paoli Lane
Gas S: Weimar Country Store(*, D)

136 Weimar, Cross Road
Other N: Fire Department
S: **U.S. Post Office, Weimar Village Grocery**

138 Canyon Way, Placer Hills Road
Food N: **Dingus McGee's**
S: Velarde's California Cantina
AServ S: Colfax Garage, Sierra Chevorlet Dealership, Tom's Sierra Tires
RVCamp S: **Sierra Chevrolet, GM**

140 Colfax, Grass Valley, CA 174
Gas N: 76(*), Chevron
S: Chevron(*, D), Sierra Super Stop(*, LP)
Food N: A & W Drive-In, Colfax Kitchen, Colfax Max, Ed's Little Hen Restaurant, Mr. C's Doughnut Depot, Pizza Factory, Rosy's Cafe, Taco Bell
S: **Shang Garden Chinese Restaurant**, Subway
AServ N: Chevron, Denny & Sons Automatic Transmissions, Riebes Auto Parts
Other N: Colfax Vision Center, Fire Station, **Laundromat**, Pet Grooming & Supplies, **Sierra Market**, U Haul(LP)

145 Magra Road, Rollins Lake Road
RVCamp N: **Camping**

146 Secret Town Road, Magra Road

148 Gold Run (Westbound)
Other S: Sierra Animal Wellness Center

(149) **Rest Area (RR, Phones, Picnic, RV Dump, RV Water; Eastbound)**

150 Dutch Flat
Gas S: Araco Gas Mart(*)
Food N: Monte Vista Inn
S: **Cafe**
AServ N: Air Conditioning Service
S: Araco Gas Mart
RVCamp N: **Dutch Flat Campground and RV Resort**

152 Alta

Exit **(153)** Runaway Truck Ramp (Westbound)

153 Crystal Springs

154 Baxter
RVCamp S: **Baxter RV Campground (.25 Miles)**

156 Drum Forebay Road

160 Blue Canyon

Exit **(161)** Break Check Area (Eastbound)

161 Nyack Road
Gas S: **Shell**(*, D, LP)
Food S: **Nyack Coffee Shop and Restaurant (Shell)**
Other S: **U.S. Post Office (Shell)**

(162) Vista Point Observation Point (Westbound, Reaccess Westbound Only)

162 Emigrant Gap

EXIT CALIFORNIA

163 Laing Road (Eastbound)
Food S: Rancho Sierra Inn
Lodg S: Rancho Sierra Inn

166A Yuba Gap
Parks S: **Sno-Park**
Other S: Lake Valley Reservoir

166B CA 20 West, Nevada City

169 Eagle Lakes Road
RVCamp N: **Campground**

170 Cisco Grove
Gas S: Chevron(*)
Food S: Cisco's
Parks N: **Cisco Grove Sno-Park**

172 Big Bend (Eastbound)

173 Rainbow Road, Big Bend
Food S: Rainbow Lodge
Lodg S: Rainbow Lodge
RVCamp S: **Tahoe National Forest**

176 Kingvale
Gas S: Shell(*)
AServ S: **Nyack Towing**(LP)
TServ S: **Nyack Towing**

183 Soda Springs, Norden, Sugar Bowl
Gas S: 76(*)
Food S: **Donner Summit Lodge**
Lodg S: **Donner Summit Lodge**
Other S: Serene Lake, Ski Areas (1-3 Miles)

186 Castle Peak Area, Boreal Ridge Rd.
Lodg S: Boreal Inn
Other S: **Auburn Ski Club Ski Sport Museum**, Boreal Skiing Area, Skier Information

(188) **Rest Area (RR, Phones, Picnic; Westbound)**

(188) **Rest Area (RR, Phones, Picnic; Eastbound)**

Exit **(190)** Vista Point (Eastbound)

190 Donner Lake

(191) Vista View Point (Westbound)

193 Truckee, Donner Pass Rd.
Gas N: Shell(*)
S: 76, Chevron(*)
Food S: Donner House, The Beginning Restaurant
Lodg S: Alpine Village Motel
AServ S: 76
Parks S: **Donner Memorial State Park**
Other N: **Tahoe Truckee Factory Stores**, Truckee Donner Chamber of Commerce

193B Agricultural Inspection Station (Westbound)

194 CA 89 South, Lake Tahoe
Gas S: Shell(*)
Food N: Dairy Queen, Little Caesars Pizza, Nik-N-Willie's Pizza, Pizza Junction, Sizzler Steak House, Wild Cherry's Coffee House
S: Burger King, China Garden, Coffee, KFC, Los Alto's Mexican, McDonald's, Papa Murphy's Pizza, Pizzeria, Subway, Truckee Bagel Company, Wong's Garden
Lodg S: Super 8
AServ S: NAPA Auto Care Center, Stone's Tire, Truckee Automotive
Med N: **Hospital**
ATM N: Bank of America
S: **Lucky Grocery Store**, Placer Savings Bank
Other N: 7-11 Convenience Store, ACE Hardware, **AmeriGas**(LP), CA Highway Patrol, Fire Department, Launderland Coin Laundry, Optometrist, **Rite Aid Pharmacy**(RX), **Safeway Grocery**, Tru Value Hardware, Truckee Mountain Sports
S: **Long's Drugs, Lucky Grocery Store**, Touchless Car Wash, **U.S. Post Office**

EXIT CALIFORNIA/NEVADA

195 Central Truckee
Food S: Jordan's Restaurant
Med N: **Tahoe Forest Hospital**
Other N: **Tahoe Forest Pharmacy**(RX)

196 CA 89 North, CA 267 South, Sierraville, Loyalton
RVCamp N: **Coachland RV Park**

198 Prosser Village Road

(202) **Donner Pass Inspection Facility, Weigh Station (Westbound)**

207 Hirschdale Road
Gas S: **United Trails**(*, LP)
RVCamp S: **United Trails, United Trails**

208 Floriston

210 Farad

↑CALIFORNIA

↓NEVADA

1 Verdi, Gold Ranch Road (Westbound, Reaccess Westbound Only)

2 I-80 Business, Verdi
Gas N: Arco(*)
Food N: The Branding Iron Cafe

3 Verdi (Westbound, Reaccess Eastbound Only)

(4) **Weigh Station (Eastbound)**

4 Garson Road, Boomtown
TStop N: **Boomtown Truckstop**(*, RV DUMP, SCALES)
Gas N: Chevron(*, CW)
Food N: **Boomtown Hotel & Casino**
Lodg N: **Boomtown Hotel & Casino**
TServ N: **Boomtown Truckstop**(SCALES)
RVCamp N: **Boomtown RV Park (.25 Miles)**
Other S: Verdi Fire Station

5 East Verdi, Bus. Loop 80 (Westbound, Reaccess Eastbound Only)

(6) **Truck Parking Area (Westbound)**

(6) **Truck Parking Area (Eastbound)**

7 Mogul

8 West 4th St. (Eastbound, Difficult Reaccess)

9 Robb Dr.

10 McCarran Blvd. West
Gas S: Citgo(*)
Food S: **Little Caesars Pizza (K-Mart)**
Other S: **Super K-Mart**(24, RX)

12 Keystone Ave., Bus. Loop 80
FStop S: **Washoe Keystone Motor Fuel**(K, 24) **(Pacific Pride)**
Gas N: 76(LP), Arco(*), Shell
S: 76(*, D), Chevron(*, 24)
Food N: Domino's Pizza, Le Grande Cafe (Gateway Inn), Pizza Hut, Stardust Pizza, The Purple Bean
S: Baskin Robbins, Burger King, Coffee Grinder Inn, Flavers Espresso & Yogurt, Higgy's Pizza, Jack-In-The-Box, KFC, McDonald's, One Stop Burger Shop, Pizza Baron, Port of Subs, Round Table Pizza, Szechuan Express, Taco Bell, Wendy's
Lodg N: Gateway Inn, Motel 6
AServ N: 76, Q-Lube, Shell
S: Allied Auto Parts, Grand Auto Supply Tires &

Bold red print shows RV & Bus parking available or nearby

EXIT NEVADA

Service, Meineke Discount Mufflers, Midas Muffler & Brake, Precision Automotive
RVCamp S: P & S Hardware, RV Supplies
Med S: Medina Medical Center
ATM N: Norwest Bank
S: Bank of America, Wells Fargo
Other N: 7-11 Convenience Store(*), Raley's Supermarket, Sav-On Drugs(RX), Starlite Bowl
S: Albertson's Grocery(24, RX), Animal Shack, Coin Op Laundromat, Mail Boxes Etc., P & S Hardware, RV Supplies, Sundance Bookstore

13 Downtown Reno, Virginia St
Gas N: Citgo(*), Texaco(*, D)
S: Texaco(*)
Food N: Blimpie Subs & Salads, Giant Burger, The Break Away
S: Art Gecko's Southwest Grill, Dairy Queen
Lodg N: Capri Motel, Coed Lodge, Silver Dollar Motor Lodge, Sundance Motel, University Inn
S: Chalet Motel, Circus Circus Hotel, Coach Inn, Flamingo Motel, Golden West Motor Lodge, Heart of Town Motel, Monte Carlo Motel, Ponderosa Motel, Ramada Plaza Hotel & Casino, Savoy Motor Lodge, Shamrock Inn, Showboat Inn, Silver Legacy Resort & Casino, Uptown Motel
AServ S: Goodyear, Roy Foster's Downtown Service
Med N: Hospital
S: St. Mary's Regional Medical Center
ATM S: Bank of America
Other N: Public Laundromat
S: Rino Historical Museum

14 Wells Ave.
Gas S: Chevron(*, D, 24), Texaco(*, D)
Food S: Carrows Restaurant, Chicago Express(24), Denny's(24)
Lodg N: Motel 6
S: Days Inn, EconoLodge, Holiday Inn (see our ad this page)
AServ S: Rankins Auto Service, Texaco Express Lube
TServ S: Goodyear
RVCamp S: Reno RV Park (1.75 Miles)
Med N: Hospital

15 U.S. 395, Carson City, Susanville (Limited Access Hwy)
RVCamp S: Reno Hilton RV Park (.75 Miles)

16 Victorian Ave, E. 4th St
FStop S: Arco(*, LP) (Pacific Pride)
Gas N: Arco(*)
S: Chevron(*)
Food S: Cinnamon Street Bakery (Arco), Halfway Club Pizza, Hot Stuff Pizza (Arco), Smash Hit Subs (Arco)
Lodg N: Motel 6, Pony Express Lodge
S: Gold Coin Motel, Star Motel
AServ S: All Tires & Wheels, Chevron, D&D Foreign Car
Other N: In & Out Car Wash

EXIT NEVADA

17 Rock Blvd, Nugget Ave.
Gas N: Arco(*), Chevron(*, 24), Exxon(*)
Lodg N: Craig Motel, Safari Motel, Tarry Motel, The Courtyard, Victorian Inn, Wagon Train Motel
AServ N: Johnson Automotive, Sparks Tire
RVCamp S: Rivers Edge RV Park (2 Miles)
ATM N: Exxon
Other N: Fire Department, Mail Boxes & More, Rock N B Laundromat

18 NV 445, Pyramid Way (Eastbound, Reaccess Westbound Only)
Gas N: Citgo(*)
Food N: Silver Club Hotel
S: The Nugget Hotel
Lodg N: Nugget Roof Garden Hotel, Silver Club Hotel
S: The Nugget Hotel
AServ N: Davis Automotive, Scudder's Performance
ATM N: Citgo
Other N: Spark's Chamber of Commerce, Spark's Museum

19 E. McCarran Blvd.
TStop N: 76 Auto/Truck Plaza(*, LP, RV DUMP, SCALES)
Gas N: Beacon(*, D), Chevron(*), Western Mountain(*)
Food N: Burger King, Espresso Plus, IHOP, Jerry's, KFC, Sierra Sid's Restaurant (76), Szechuan Express, Wendy's
S: Black Forest House (German), Denny's(24)
Lodg N: Inn Cal, Western Village, Windsor Inn
S: Best Western
AServ N: 76 Auto/Truck Plaza
TServ N: 76 Auto/Truck Plaza(SCALES)
TWash N: 76 Auto/Truck Plaza
RVCamp N: Victorian RV Park
ATM N: Norwest Bank, Wells Fargo
Other N: Spark's Car Wash

20 Sparks Blvd.

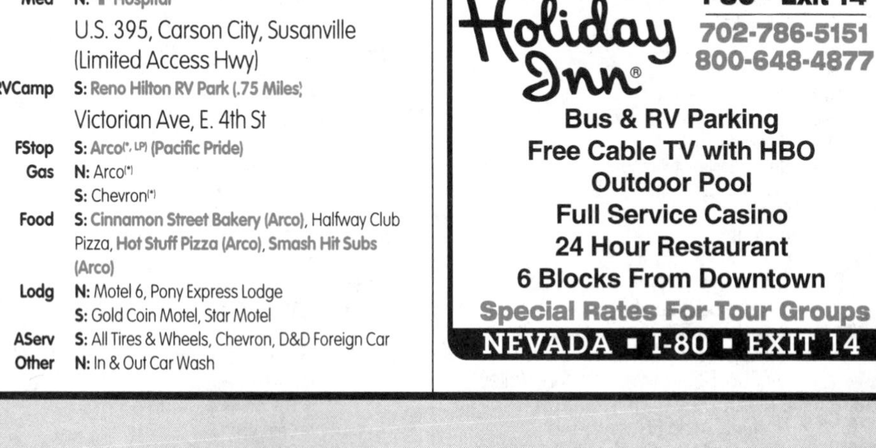

EXIT NEVADA

FStop N: Interstate Oil Co.(LP) (Pacific Pride)
Gas N: Texaco(*, D, CW)
Food N: Outback Steakhouse, The Grand Stand
TServ S: Sierra Freightliner, Tyres International
Parks N: Shadow Mountain Park
Other N: Factory Outlets, King's Skate Country & Lazer Storm, Wild Island Water Park

21 Vista Blvd, Greg St.
Gas N: Chevron(*)
Food N: McDonald's (Chevron)
TServ S: Alamo Truck Center, International
Med N: Hospital

22 Lockwood

23 Mustang
Food N: Mustang Station
AServ N: Mustang Auto Reckers & Garage
RVCamp N: Sage Trailer Park

(25) Weigh Station (Westbound)

(27) Scenic View (Eastbound)

28 NV 655, Patrick, Waltham Way

32 Tracy, Clark Station

36 Derby Dam

38 Orchard

40 Painted Rock

(41) Rest Area (RR, HF, Phones, Picnic, RV Dump, P; Westbound)

(42) Weigh Station (Eastbound, All Trucks Must Exit)

43 Wadsworth, Pyramid Lake
Gas N: 76(*, LP)
RVCamp N: I-80 Campground(LP), Ya-A-Doiaka RV Camp (76)

46 South U.S. 95 Alt, West Fernley
TStop S: Pilot Travel Center(*, SCALES)
Food S: Dairy Queen (Pilot), Wendy's (Pilot)
TWash S: Blue Beacon Truck Wash (Pilot)
RVCamp S: Fernley RV Park (1 Mile)
Parks N: Pyramid Lake

48 U.S. 50 Alt, East Fernley, South Alt. U.S. 95
TStop N: Truck Inn(*, RV DUMP)
FStop N: 76(*)
S: Silverado(*)
Gas S: Chevron(*), Texaco(*, D)
Food N: Annie B's (Truck Inn)
S: McDonald's, Pizza Factory, Silverado, Taco Bell (Texaco)
Lodg N: 7 ZZZ Motel (Truck Inn)
S: Best Western, Super 8
TServ N: Heart of Town Tires, Truck, & Auto Service

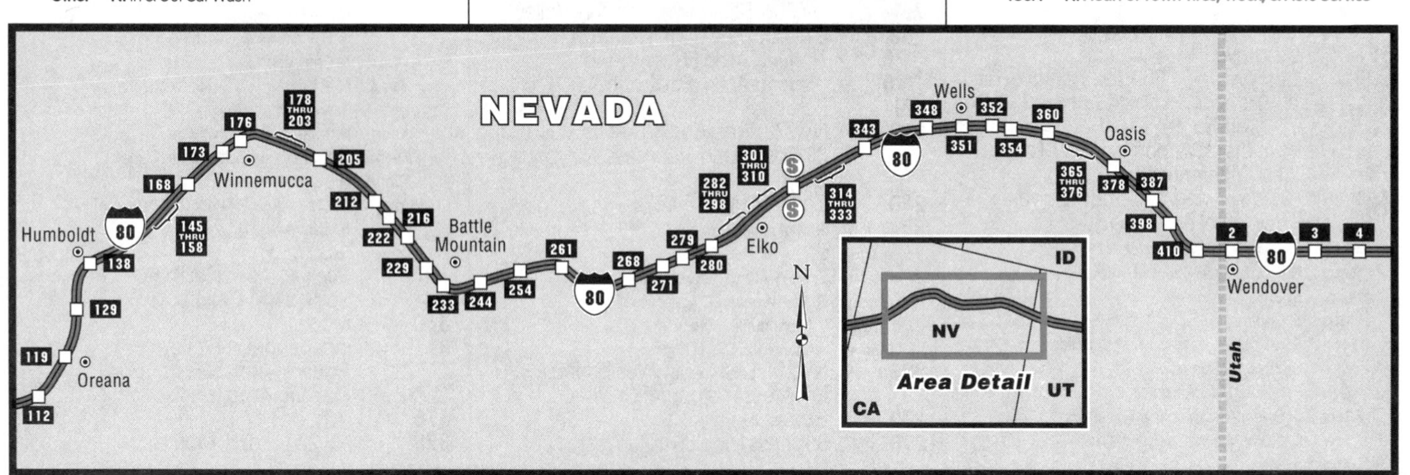

Bold red print shows RV & Bus parking available or nearby

EXIT NEVADA

S: Goodyear Tire & Auto
TWash N: Splash Super Truck Wash(SCALES)
RVCamp S: Best Western Fernley Inn RV Park (.25 Miles), RV Park (Best Western)
ATM S: Norwest Bank, Warehouse Market Grocery Store
Other S: Mrs. O's Wash & Dry Coin Laundry, Warehouse Market Grocery Store

65 Hot Springs, Nightingale
78 Jessup
83 U.S. 95 South, Fallon, Las Vegas, Rest Area (P)
(83) Rest Area (RR, Phones, Picnic, Grills, (P); Located At Exit 83)
93 Toulon
105 Lovelock, Bus. Loop 80 (Eastbound, Reaccess Westbound Only)
Gas N: Beacon, Exxon(*, D)
Food N: LaCasita Mexican Restaurant
Lodg N: Brookwood Motel, Lafon's Motel, Lovelock Inn
AServ N: Beacon, Jim's Tire Shop, Nutter's Tow, Stovall's Auto Clinic, Vonsild's Complete Auto Repair
Med N: ✚ Hospital
Other S: Suburban Propane
106 Downtown Lovelock
Gas N: 76, Mini Mart(*), Two Stiffs(*)
Food N: Davin's Dining, Mama Jean's Grill, McDonald's, Pizza Factory
Lodg N: Covered Wagon Motel, Desert Haven Motel, Sage Motel, Sunset Motel, Windmill Motel
AServ N: 76, 76, California Garage, Complete Auto & Truck Repair
TServ N: Complete Auto & Truck Repair
Other N: ACE Hardware, Coin Car Wash, Coin Laundry, Fire Department, Safeway Grocery
107 East Lovelock (Westbound, Reaccess Eastbound Only)
FStop N: Chevron(*, D)
Food N: Sturgeon's, Wee-B's Subs & Pizza
Lodg N: Best Western, Cadillac Inn, Desert Plaza Inn, Sierra Motel, Super 10 Motel
RVCamp N: Lazy K Campground Park(LP)
112 Coal Canyon
119 Oreana, Rochester
129 Rye Patch Dam
FStop S: Burns Brothers Travel Stop(*, LP) (Arco)
Food S: Burns Brothers Travel Stop (Arco)
RVCamp N: Rye Patch Dam Recreational Area
Parks N: Rye Patch State Recreation Area
138 Humboldt
145 Imlay
149 NV 400, Unionville, Mill City
RVCamp S: Star Point Mobile Home and RV Park
151 Mill City, Dun Glen
TStop N: Burns Brothers Travel Stop(*) (Arco)
Food N: Mrs. B's (Burns Bros. TS), Taco Bell (Burns Bros. TS)
Lodg N: Super 8 (Burns Bros. TS)
TServ N: Burns Brothers Travel Stop (Arco)
158 Cosgrave
(158) Rest Area (RR, Phones, Picnic, Grills, RV Dump, (P); Located At Exit 158 On The South Side)
168 Rose Creek, Airport Industrial Loop
173 West Winnemucca
176 U.S. 95 North, Winnemucca Blvd, Downtown, Bus. Loop 80
TStop S: Flying J Travel Plaza(*, LP, RV DUMP, SCALES)
FStop N: Pacific Pride Commercial Fueling(24)
S: Bi-State Petroleum
Gas S: Chevron(*)
Food S: Arby's, Burger King, Denny's (Holiday Inn Express), McDonald's(PLAY)
Lodg S: Holiday Inn Express, Motel 6, Ramada Limited
AServ S: Owens Ford, Mercury, Wal-Mart(RX)
TServ S: Humboldt Diesel (Freightliner)
RVCamp S: Model T RV Park (.75 Miles)

EXIT NEVADA

Other N: Tippin Gas Co.(LP)
S: Wal-Mart(RX)
178 Winnemucca Blvd., Downtown
Gas S: Pump 'N' Save(*, CW)
Food S: Dave's Dugout
Lodg S: Bull-Head Motel, Cozy Motel, Downtown Motel, Frontier Motel, Scott Shady Court Motel
RVCamp S: Westerner Trailer Lodge, Winnemucca RV Park (1 Mile)
Med S: ✚ Hospital
180 Winnemucca Blvd. East
RVCamp N: Hi-Desert RV Park (.75 Miles), Winnemucca RV Park (1 Mile)
187 Button Point
(187) Rest Area (RR, HF, Picnic, Grills, (P); Located At Exit 187 On The North Side)
194 Golconda, Midas
Gas N: Waterhole #1 Grocery Store
Food N: Z Bar & Grill
Lodg N: Waterhole #1 Grocery Store
Other N: U.S. Post Office (Waterhole #1 Grocery Store)
Exit **(200)** Golconda Summit (Truck Parking)
203 Iron Point
205 Pumpernickel Valley
212 Stonehouse
216 Valmy
FStop N: 76(*, LP)
Food N: Bar & Grill (76)
Lodg N: Golden Motel
RVCamp N: 76
Other N: U.S. Post Office (76), Valmy Volunteer Fire Dept.
(216) Rest Area (RR, Picnic, Grills, RV Dump, (P); Located At Exit 216 On The South Side)
222 Mote
229 Bus. Loop 80 West, Battle Mountain
Gas N: 76(*)
RVCamp N: Colt RV Park
Other N: Emigrant Trail Interpretive Center
231 NV 305, Downtown Battle Mountain, Austin
Gas N: Big R's(*)
Food N: Big R's, McDonald's
Lodg N: Super 8
AServ N: NAPA Auto Parts
Med N: ✚ Hospital
ATM N: Norwest Bank
Other N: Civic Center (Library, Visitor's Info.), Midway Market(*), Mills Pharmacy, U.S. Post Office
233 East Battle Mountain
244 Argenta
254 Dunphy
(258) Rest Area (RR, Picnic, Grills, RV Dump, (P); Westbound)
(258) Rest Area (RR, Picnic, Grills, RV Dump, (P); Eastbound)
261 NV 306, Beowawe, Crescent Valley
268 Emigrant
(270) Parking Area (Westbound)
(270) Parking Area (Eastbound)
271 Palisade
279 NV 278, West Carlin, Eureka, Bus. Loop 80 (Eastbound, Reaccess Westbound Only)
280 Central Carlin , Eureka
TStop S: Pilot Travel Center(*, RV DUMP, SCALES)
Gas S: Texaco(*, D)
Food S: Burger King (Texaco), Subway (Pilot TS)
Lodg S: Best Western, Cavalier Motel
AServ S: Intermountain Tire
TServ N: Anderson Diesel Repair
282 NV 221, East Carlin (Westbound, Reaccess Eastbound Only)
292 Hunter
298 Business Loop 80, Elko West

EXIT NEVADA

301 NV 225, Elko Downtown
Gas N: Maverick(*)
Food N: 9 Beans & A Burrito, Arby's, Denny's, Hogi Yogi, Maverick, McDonald's(PLAY), Papa Murphy's Pizza, Round Table Pizza
S: KFC
Lodg N: Shilo Inn
AServ N: Wal-Mart(RX)
S: Checker Auto Parts
RVCamp S: Cimarron West RV & Trailer Park
ATM N: Elco Federal Credit Union, Raley's Supermarket
Other N: Cinemas 4, Coin Laundry, Dirt Busters Car Wash, K-Mart(RX), Port Of Subs, Raley's Supermarket, Wal-Mart(RX)
S: Smith's Grocery Store(24, RX)
303 Elko East
FStop N: Chevron(*, LP) (CFN Fueling Station)
Gas S: Chevron(*, 24)
Food S: Baskin Robbins, Burger King, High Desert Inn, JR's Bar and Grill(24) (Best Western Gold Country), McDonald's(PLAY), Perfect Subs, Pizza Barn, Pizza Hut, Red Lion Inn, Taco Time
Lodg S: Best Western (Ameritel), Best Western (Gold Country), High Desert Inn, Motel 6, Red Lion Inn
AServ S: Gallagher Ford, Western Auto
RVCamp S: Double Dice RV Park (1 Mile), Gold Country RV Park
Med S: ✚ Hospital
ATM S: Albertson's Grocery, Wells Fargo
Other S: Alan's Optician, Albertson's Grocery, Christian Books & Gifts, Rite Aid Pharmacy, U.S. Post Office
310 Osino
Exit **(312)** Check Station (Westbound, All Vehicles With Livestock Must Stop)
Exit **(312)** Check Station (Eastbound, All Vehicles With Livestock Must Stop)
314 Ryndon, Devil's Gate
RVCamp S: KOA Campgrounds(LP), RV Camp(*) (Laundry), Ryndon RV Park
317 El Burz
321 NV 229, Halleck, Ruby Valley
328 River Ranch
333 Deeth, Starr Valley
343 Welcome, Starr Valley
RVCamp N: Welcome RV Camp
348 Crested Acres
RVCamp N: Welcome Good Neighbor Park
351 Bus. Loop 80, West Wells
Gas N: Amoco(*, D)
Food N: Chinatown Motel & Casino
Lodg N: Chinatown Motel & Casino
AServ N: Well's Auto & Hardware
RVCamp N: Chinatown Motel, Chinatown Motel & Casino, Mountain Shadows RV Park(*, LP)
Parks S: Angel Lake Recreation Area
Other N: Public Library, Stuart's Grocery, U.S. Post Office
S: Chimney Rock Municipal Golf Course
352 Great Basin Hwy, U.S. 93, East Wells
TStop N: Texaco(*, SCALES)
S: Flying J Travel Plaza(*, LP, SCALES)
Gas N: Chevron(LP)
Food N: 4 Way Cafe (Texaco), Burger King
S: The Cookery (Flying J TS)
Lodg N: Motel 6, Rest Inn, Super 8
AServ N: Chevron, Les Schwab Tire Center
TServ N: Texaco(SCALES)
RVCamp N: Crossroads RV Park (1.25 Miles), Moutain Shadows (1 Mile)
Other N: Car Wash
(354) Parking Area (Eastbound, Reaccess Eastbound Only)
360 Moor
365 Independence Valley
(373) Parking Area (Westbound)
(373) Parking Area (Eastbound)
376 Pequop
378 NV 233, Oasis, Montello

Bold red print shows RV & Bus parking available or nearby

EXIT	NEVADA/UTAH
FStop	N: Chevron(*, LP)
Food	N: Chevron
AServ	N: Chevron
Other	N: Post Office
387	Shafter
398	Pilot Peak
410	Bus. Loop 80, U.S. 93 Alt, West Wendover, Ely
Gas	S: Chevron(*, 24)
Food	S: Burger King
Lodg	S: Nevada Crossing Hotel, Peppermill Hotel & Casino, Rainbow Casino, Super 8
RVCamp	S: KOA Kampground, State Line RV Park (1 Mile)
Other	S: Fire Station, Trucker's Lounge(*)
(410)	Nevada Welcome Center (RR; Located At Exit 410 On The South Side)

↑NEVADA

↓UTAH

EXIT	UTAH
2	UT 58, Wendover
3	Port of Entry, Weigh Station (Westbound)
(3)	Port of Entry, Weigh Station (Eastbound)
4	Bonneville Speedway
TStop	N: Amoco(*, LP, SCALES, 24)
(10)	Rest Area (RR, Phones, Picnic, P; Westbound)
(10)	Rest Area (RR, Phones, Picnic, P; Eastbound)
41	Knolls
49	Clive
Exit	(54) View Area (Eastbound)
Exit	(54) View Area (Westbound)
56	Aragonite
62	Military Area, Lakeside
70	Delle
FStop	S: Sinclair(*, 24)
Food	S: Delle Cafe
77	Rowley, Dugway
84	UT 138, Grantsville, Tooele
88	Grantsville
99	UT 36, Tooele, Stansbury
TStop	S: T/A TravelCenters of America(*, SCALES)
Gas	S: Chevron(*, D, 24), Texaco(*)
Food	S: Country Pride Restaurant (TA Travel Centers of America), McDonald's, Subway (Chevron)
Lodg	S: Oquirrh Motor Inn
TServ	S: T/A TravelCenters of America(SCALES)
102	UT 201, 2100 South, Magna, West Valley City (Eastbound, Reaccess Westbound Only)
Med	S: ✚ Hospital
104	Saltair Dr., UT 202
Parks	N: Great Salt Lake State Park
Other	N: Great Salt Lake State Marina, Saltair Beach
111	7200 West
113	5600 West
Food	N: Amelia's Grill (Holiday Inn), Perkin's Family Restaurant, Pizza Hut (Holiday Inn), The Hotel Cafe (Comfort Inn)
Lodg	N: Comfort Inn, Fairfield Inn, Holiday Inn, Ramada Limited, Sheraton, Super 8
ATM	N: Beehive Credit Union, First Security Bank
114	Wright Bros. Dr. (Westbound, Reaccess Eastbound Only)
Food	N: Chez Julien
Lodg	N: Hilton Inn, La Quinta Inn
115	Airport, 40th West, Airport North, Temple (Limited Access Hwy)
117	I-215, Ogden, Provo (Exit under construction)
118	UT 68, Redwood Road (Eastbound, Exit under construction)
RVCamp	N: Camp VIP (.5 Miles)
Parks	N: Utah State Fairpark
120	I-15, North Ogden (Exit under construction)

Note: I-80 runs concurrent below with I-15. Numbering follows I-15.

EXIT	UTAH
311	Junction I-80W, Salt Lake International Airport, Reno
310	6th So. St, City Center (Difficult Reaccess)
Gas	E: Chevron(*, CW), Circle K(*), Phillips 66(*), Sinclair(*)
Food	E: "J" Burger, Albertos Mexican, Best Western, Denny's, Hilton, Iggy's Sports Grill, McDonald's, Quality Inn, Quality Inn
Lodg	E: Best Western, Cavanaugh's Hotel, Crystal Inn, Hampton Inn, Hilton, Motel 6, Quality Inn, Quality Inn, Quality Inn, Super 8, TraveLodge
AServ	E: Brigham Street Service, Mark Miller Toyota
ATM	E: Sinclair
Other	E: Brewvies Cinema & Pub
309	13th So. St, 21st So. St. (Difficult Reaccess)
Gas	E: Citgo(*)
Food	E: Cafe Trang (Vietnamese, Chinese), China Pearl, Main Street Cafe (Holiday Inn), Miquelita's Mexican
Lodg	E: Diamond Inn, Holiday Inn
AServ	E: Atex Automatic Transmission, Classics & More Sales & Service, Ford Superstore, Ken Garff Honda, Lelis Automatic Transmission Service Inc., Meineke Discount Mufflers, Midas, Rick Warner Mazda, Nissan, Saturn of Salt Lake, Steve Harris Motors, Utah Auto Parts W: Japanese Auto Repair
308	21st So. St. (Difficult Reaccess, Limited Access Hwy)
Food	E: McDonald's
Other	E: Home Depot, U-Haul(LP)
307	Junction I-80E, to U.S. 40, Denver, Cheyenne (Exit under construction)

Note: I-80 runs concurrent above with I-15. Numbering follows I-15.

EXIT	UTAH
124	U.S. 89, State St.
Gas	N: Texaco(*, D, LP)
Food	N: Jo Jo's Restaurant, The Bagelry, Zorba's Drive-In S: KFC, Pizza Hut, Salt Lake Doughnut
Lodg	S: Ramada Inn
AServ	N: Discount Tire Company, Hayes Bros. Buick, Hinkley's Dodge Trucks, John Mecham Chrys, Plym, Jeep, State Auto Repair, Texaco S: Auto Machine, Transmission Exchange
Med	S: ✚ Regional Hospital
ATM	S: Bank One
Other	N: Classic Bowling, Honda of Salt Lake (Motorcycles)
125	700 East
126	1300 East, Sugar House, UT 181, 13th St. East
Gas	N: Chevron(*, CW, 24)
Food	N: Hogi Yogi, Olive Garden, Red Lobster, Sizzler Steak House, Taco Bell, Training Table (Gourmet Burgers), Wendy's
ATM	N: Chevron
Other	N: Barnes & Noble, Deseret Book, Mail Boxes Etc., ShopKo(RX) (Optical), The Mad Popper (Popcorn, Candy), Toys R Us
127	2300 East, Holladay (Eastbound, Reaccess Westbound Only)
Food	S: Connie's Pizza
AServ	S: Greg's Texaco
Other	S: Car Wash, Wash Spot Dog Wash
128	South I-215, Belt Route (Eastbound)
129	UT 186 West, Foothill Drive, Parleys Way
Med	N: ✚ Hospital
130	Junction I-215, Belt Route (Westbound)
Parks	N: Cotton Wood Ski Area
Exit	(130) Chain-Up Area (Eastbound)
131	Quarry Exit (Eastbound, Reaccess Westbound Only)
Exit	(132) Unnamed Exit (Westbound)
132	Ranch Exit
133	Utility Exit (Reaccess Westbound Only)
134	UT65, Emigration Canyon, East Canyons
Parks	N: Mountain Dell Recreation Area
Exit	(136) Runaway Truck Ramp (Westbound)
137	Lambs Canyon
140	Parleys Summit
Gas	S: Sinclair(*)
Food	S: Parleys Grill (Sinclair)
Other	S: Park Pantry(*)
Exit	(140) Brake Check Area (Westbound)
Exit	(140) Brake Check Area (Eastbound)
143	Jeremy Ranch
Gas	N: Amoco(*, 24)
Food	N: Blimpie Subs & Salads (Amoco)
ATM	N: Amoco
Exit	(144) View Area (Eastbound)
145	UT224 South, Kimball Junction, Park City
Gas	S: Chevron(*, CW), Texaco(*, D, CW)
Food	S: Arby's, Denny's (Best Western), Kenny Roger's Roasters, McDonald's, Southern Maid Donuts, Subway, Taco Bell
Lodg	S: Best Western, Holiday Inn Express
RVCamp	N: Hidden Haven RV Park (1 Mile)
ATM	S: Texaco
Other	S: K-Mart, Smith's Grocery Store, U.S. Post Office, Utah Winter Sports Park (2 Miles), Wal-Mart
(147)	Rest Area (RR, Phones, Picnic, Vending, P; Westbound)
148	U.S. 40 East, Heber, Denver
FStop	N: Sinclair(*)
Food	N: Blimpie Subs & Salads (Sinclair)
152	Ranch Exit (Eastbound, Reaccess Eastbound Only, Difficult Reaccess, Exit under construction)
156	UT 32 South, Wanship, Kamas (Difficult Reaccess)
Gas	S: Sinclair(*)
Food	N: Spring Chicken Inn S: Rafter-B (Sinclair)
AServ	N: "R" Auto Shop
Parks	N: Rockport State Park
Other	N: Rail Trail
164	Coalville
FStop	N: Amoco(*, LP)
Gas	S: Sinclair(*, D)
Food	S: EJ's Place, Steve's To-Go
Lodg	S: Blonquist Motel, Moore Motel
AServ	S: Moore Motor Chev, Buick
RVCamp	N: Holiday Hills RV Park
ATM	S: Zion's Bank
Other	S: Echo Reservoir, Key Drug, Norge Laundry & Cleaning Village, Rail Trail, U.S. Post Office
Exit	(166) View Area (Eastbound)
Exit	(166) View Area (Westbound)
168	Junction I-84W, Ogden, Henefer, Morgan
169	Echo
(170)	Rest Area (RR, Phones, Picnic, Vending, P; Westbound)
(170)	Rest Area (RR, Phones, Picnic,

EXIT UTAH/WYOMING

Vending, P; Eastbound)
180 Emory (Westbound, No Reaccess)
185 Castle Rock
189 Ranch Exit
193 Wahsatch

↑UTAH

↓WYOMING

(1) **Port of Entry, Weigh Station (Westbound)**
(1) **Port of Entry, Weigh Station (Eastbound)**
3 Bus. Loop 80, Bus. U.S. 189, To WY 89, Harrison Dr.
- TStop N: **Flying J Travel Plaza**[*, SCALES]
- Gas N: Chevron[*, D, 24], Sinclair[*, 24], Texaco[*, D] (Pacific Pride)
  S: Phillips 66[*, D]
- Food N: Burger King, JB's Restaurant
  S: A & W Hot Dogs & More (Phillips 66), KFC
- Lodg N: Days Inn, Weston Plaza, Weston Super Budget Inn
- AServ N: Evanston Motor Co. Chrys, Eagle, Dodge
- Med N: **+ Hospital**
  S: **+ Hospital**

5 North WY89, WY150, Front St.
- Gas N: Amoco[*]
- Food N: Arby's, Dragon Wall Chinese, **McDonald's**, Papa Murphy's Pizza, Shakeys Pizza (Amoco), Subway, Taco John's, Wendy's
- AServ N: Auto Zone, Q Lube
- Med S: **+ Hospital**
- Other N: **IGA Supercenter**[RX], **Wal-Mart**[RX]

6 **Bear River Dr, Bus. Loop 80, U.S. 189, Wyoming Welcome Center (RR, Phones, RV Dump)**
- FStop N: **Texaco**[*]
- Gas N: Amoco[*, D, LP]
- Food N: Blimpie Subs & Salads (Amoco)
- Lodg N: Alexander Motel, Evanston Inn, **Motel 6**, Prairie Inn
- RVCamp N: **Phillips RV Camping & Trailer Park (.5 Miles), Sunset RV**
- Other S: **Bear River State Park**

(6) **Rest Area (RR, Phones, RV Dump; Located At Exit 6 On South Side, No Semi Trucks Allowed)**
10 Painter Rd
13 Divide Rd.
18 U.S. 189 North, Kemmerer
21 Coal Rd
23 Bar Hat Rd.
24 Leroy Rd.

EXIT WYOMING

(28) **Parking Area (Westbound)**
(28) **Parking Area (Eastbound)**
28 French Rd.
30 Bigelow Rd
- TStop N: **Burns Brothers Travel Stop**[*, LP, SCALES] **(Amoco)**
- Food N: **Mrs. B's Restaurant (Burns Bros. TS)**

33 Union Rd.
(33) **Parking Area (Eastbound)**
34 Bus. Loop 80, Fort Bridger
- RVCamp S: **Wagon Wheel**

39 WY412, WY414, Carter Mtn. View
41 **WY413, Lyman, Rest Area (RR, Phones, Picnic)**
- TStop N: **Gas-N-Go**[*]
- Food N: **Cowboy Inn Cafe (Gas-N-Go TS)**
- TServ N: **Terry's Diesel Service (Gas-N-Go TS)**
- RVCamp S: **KOA Kampground (1.2 Miles)**

(41) **Rest Area (RR, Phones, Picnic; Located At Exit 41 On The South Side)**
48 Bridger Valley
53 Church Butte Rd.
(54) **Parking Area (Eastbound)**
(59) **Parking Area (Westbound)**
(59) **Parking Area (Eastbound)**
61 Granger, Cedar Mountain Rd.
66 U.S. 30 West, Kemmerer, Pocatello, Granger
68 Little America
- TStop N: **Little America**[*, SCALES]
- TServ N: **Little America**[SCALES]

(70) **Parking Area (Westbound)**
(70) **Parking Area (Eastbound)**
72 Westvaco Rd.
83 WY372, LaBarge Rd.
85 Covered Wagon Rd.
- RVCamp S: **Adams RV Parts & Service**[LP] **(1.6 Miles)**

89 Bus. Loop 80, Bus. U.S. 30, To WY 530, Green River
- Gas S: Exxon[*], Texaco[*]
- Food S: Penny's Diner[24]
- Lodg S: Oak Tree Inn

91 Green River
- Gas S: Gas-Mat, Mini-Mart[*]
- Food S: Arctic Circle Hamburgers, McDonald's, Pizza Hut, Subway, Taco John's, Wild Horse Cafe
- Lodg S: Coachmen Inn, Mustang Motel
- AServ S: NAPA Auto Parts
- RVCamp S: **Adam's RV**
- Other S: **Tourist Info. (2 Miles)**

99 U.S. 191 South, E. Flaming Gorge Rd.
- TStop S: **Conoco**[*]

EXIT WYOMING

- Food S: **Cruel Jack's (Conoco)**, Log Inn Supper Club, **Ted's Supper Club**
- RVCamp N: **KOA Kampground (1 Mile), RV Dealer**

102 Bus. Loop 80, Bus. U.S. 30, Dewar Dr, Rock Springs
- Gas N: Exxon[*, CW], MiniMart[*], Texaco[*]
  S: Amoco[*, D], Citgo[*], Texaco
- Food N: Denny's[24], Fiesta Guadalajara (The Inn), Pam's BBQ, TacoTime
  S: A & W Hot Dogs & More (Amoco), Arby's, Burger King, McDonald's[PLAY], Mr. C's (Holiday Inn), Pizza Hut, Subway, Sweet Treats & Ice Cream, Taco Bell, Village Inn, Wonderful House (Chinese)
- Lodg N: Motel 6, Ramada Limited, The Inn
  S: **Comfort Inn, Holiday Inn, Motel 8, Super 8**
- AServ S: Big A Auto Parts, Texaco
- ATM N: American National Bank, **Smith's Grocery Store**[RX]
- Other N: **K-Mart**[RX], **Smith's Grocery Store**[RX], Twin Theater, **Wal-Mart (White Mountain Mall), White Mountain Mall**
  S: Coin Laundry, Rock Springs Chamber of Commerce

103 College Dr, Rock Springs
- Gas S: Mini Mart[*, 24]
- Med S: **+ Hospital**

104 North U.S. 191, Elk St.
- TStop N: **Flying J Travel Plaza**[*, LP, SCALES], **Texaco**[*]
- Gas N: Exxon[*, D], Phillips 66[*], Sinclair[*]
  S: Exxon[D]
- Food N: **Burger King (Texaco TS)**, Santa Fe Trail Restaurant (EconoLodge), Taco Time, **Thad's Restaurant (Flying J Travel Plaza), The Renegade Cafe (Texaco TS)**
  S: De Amigos Restaurant, Scoreboard Grill
- Lodg N: **Best Western**, EconoLodge
  S: Days Inn
- AServ S: Exxon
- Med S: **+ Hospital**
- Other N: Wholesum Bakery Thrift Shop
  S: Fine Arts Center, **Old City Hall Museum**

107 Pilot Butte Ave, To WY 430
- FStop S: **Conoco**[D] **(Pacific Pride)**
- Gas N: 7-11 Convenience Store[*], Gas For Less[LP], Phillips 66
  S: Texaco[*, D]
- Food S: Sands Cafe (Chinese/American), Sands Inn
- Lodg N: El Rancho, Springs Motel, Thunderbird Motel
- AServ S: 5 Star Towing & Repair, Metrick Motors, Rizzi's 66 Service

111 Airport Rd, Baxter Rd.
122 WY371, Superior
130 Point of Rocks
- TStop N: **Conoco**[*, LP]
- Food N: **Point Bar-N (Conoco TS)**
- Other N: **Jolly Jac's Fireworks & Laundromat, U.S. Post Office**

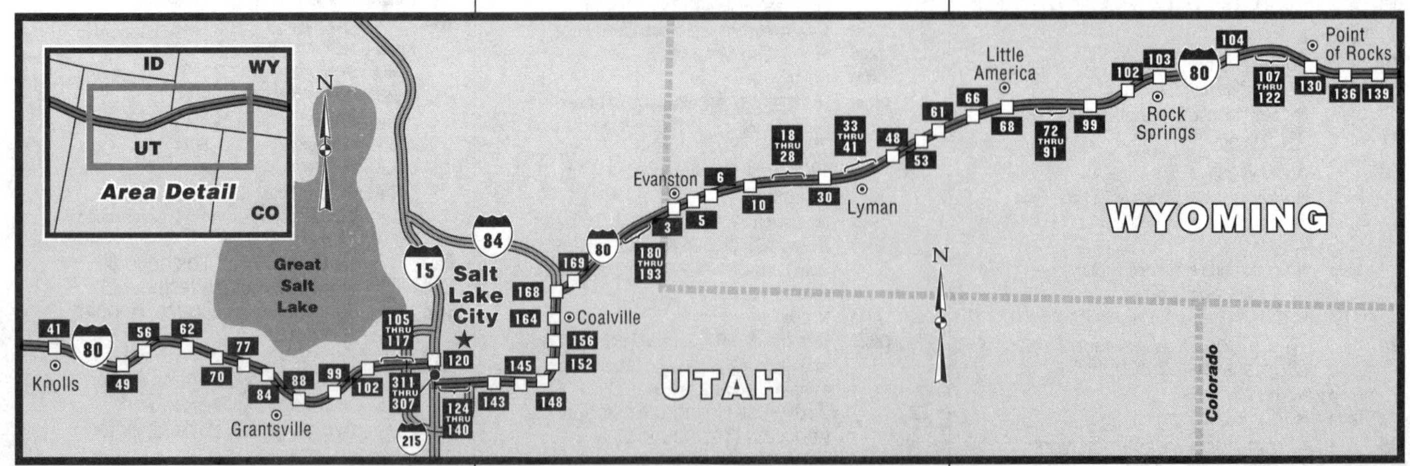

Bold red print shows RV & Bus parking available or nearby

EXIT WYOMING

(136) **Parking Area (Eastbound)**
136 Black Butte Rd.
139 Red Hill Rd.
142 Bitter Creek Rd.
(142) **Parking Area (Westbound)**
(142) **Parking Area (Eastbound)**
(143) **Rest Area (RR, Phones, Picnic; Westbound)**
(144) **Rest Area (RR, Phones, Picnic, RV Dump; Eastbound)**
146 Patrick Draw Rd.
150 Table Rock Rd.
Gas S: **Major Gas**(*)
RVCamp S: **Major Gas**
152 Bar X Rd.
154 B L M Rd
156 G L Road
158 Tipton Rd.
165 Red Desert
Gas S: Save-Way(*) (Towing)
Lodg S: Save-Way (Towing)
AServ S: Save-Way (Towing)
166 Booster Rd.
168 Frewen Rd.
170 Rasmussen Rd.
173 Wamsutter
FStop N: **Texaco**(LP)
S: **JT Service**(*)
Gas S: Conoco(D), **Gas For Less**(*)
Lodg S: **Motel, Sagebrush Motel (Gas For Less)**
AServ N: **Texaco**
S: Conoco, **JT Service**
TServ N: **Texaco**
S: **Gas For Less**
184 Continental Divide Rd.
187 WY789 South, Baggs Rd.
(188) **Parking Area (Eastbound)**
(189) **Parking Area (Westbound)**
196 Riner Rd.
201 Daley Rd.
204 Knobs Rd.
206 Hadsell Rd
209 Johnson Rd.
TStop N: **Flying J Travel Plaza**(*, SCALES)
Food N: **The Cookery (Flying J Travel Plaza)**
TServ N: **Flying J Travel Plaza**(SCALES)
(211) **Weigh Station (Westbound)**
211 Bus. Loop 80, Bus. U.S. 30, To U.S. 287, North WY 781, Rawlins
Gas N: Conoco(CW), One Minit Mart(*, D), Texaco(*)
Food N: Best Western, JB's Restaurant
Lodg N: Best Western, **Super 8**
AServ N: Conoco
RVCamp N: **President's RV Camp, Western Hills Campground, World Campground**
S: **American Presidents Camp (.25 Miles)**
Med N: ✚ **Hospital**
Other N: Self Serve Laundry, **V-1 Propane**(LP)
214 Higley Blvd.
TStop S: **Rip Griffin Truck Stop**(*, SCALES) **(Texaco)**
Food S: **Subway (Rip Griffin TS)**
Lodg S: **Sleep Inn**
TServ S: **Rip Griffin Truck Stop**(SCALES) **(Texaco)**
RVCamp N: **KOA Kampground**
215 Cedar Street, Bus. Loop 80, North U.S. 287, To WY 789, Rawlins
Gas N: Phillips 66(*)
Food N: **Wendy's**
Lodg N: DAYS INN **Days Inn**
219 West Sinclair

EXIT WYOMING

221 East Sinclair
TStop N: **Burns Brothers Travel Stop**(*)
Food N: **Mrs. B's (Burns Bros. TS)**
228 **Fort Steele, Rest Area (RR, Phones, Picnic, RV Dump)**
Other N: **Fort Steele State Historical Site**
(228) **Rest Area (RR, Phones, Picnic, RV Dump; Located At Exit 228 On The North Side)**
235 East U.S. 30, East WY130, Walcott, Saratoga
FStop N: **Mojo Gas**(*)
238 Peterson Rd.
255 WY72, Hanna, Elk Mountain
FStop N: **Conoco**(*)
260 CR402
(262) **Parking Area (Westbound)**
(262) **Parking (Eastbound)**
267 Wagonhound Rd
(267) **Rest Area (RR, Phones, Picnic; Located At Exit 267 On The North Side)**
272 Arlington
FStop N: **Exxon**(*)
RVCamp N: **Arlington Outpost, Exxon**
279 Cooper Cove Rd.
290 Quealy Dome Rd.
FStop S: **Total**(*)
TServ S: **Total**
297 WY12, Herrick Ln.
(307) **Parking Area (Westbound)**
(307) **Parking Area (Eastbound)**
310 **(8)** Bus. Loop 80 East, Curtis St.
TStop N: **Handy Stop**(*), **Pilot Travel Center**(*, SCALES), **Total**(*)
S: **Petro**(*, SCALES)
Food N: **The Outrider Cafe (Total TS), Wendy's (Pilot TS)**
S: **Iron Skillet (Petro)**
Lodg N: **EconoLodge, Super 8**
TServ N: **Total**
S: **Petro**(SCALES)
TWash S: **Blue Beacon Truck Wash (Petro)**
RVCamp N: **Riverside Kampground**
Med N: ✚ **Hospital**
ATM N: **Pilot Travel Center, Total**
Other N: **KOA Kampground**
311 WY130, WY230, Snowy Range Rd, Laramie
FStop S: **76**(*), **Foster's Country Store**(*, LP, 24)
Gas S: Conoco(*, LP)
Food S: Foster's Country Corner (Best Western), McDonald's
Lodg S: Best Western, **Camelot Motel**
AServ S: A-Z Tire Co., Automotive Unlimited
TWash S: **Laramie Car Wash & Truck Wash**
RVCamp S: **Campground, Yeao Marine & RV**
Other S: **Laramie Car Wash & Truck Wash**
313 U.S. 287, 3rd St, Ft. Collins CO, Port of Entry
Gas N: Conoco(*), Exxon(*), Phillips 66(D) (Pacific Pride Commercial Fueling), Texaco
Food N: Cafe Ole, Chuck Wagon Restaurant, Denny's, Great Wall Chinese, Laramie Inn
Lodg N: Laramie Inn, **Motel 8**
S: **Holiday Inn**, Motel 6
AServ N: 24 Hour Towing, Phillips 66 (Pacific Pride Commercial Fueling), Texaco, Walt's Auto Service
Other N: All Creatures Pet Center, Information Center
316 Grand Ave, Bus. Loop 80, U.S. 30 West
Med N: ✚ **Hospital**
323 **WY210, Happy Jack Rd., Rest Area (RR, Phones, Picnic, RV Dump)**
(323) **Rest Area (RR, Phones, Picnic, RV Dump; Located At Exit 323 On The North Side)**

EXIT WYOMING

329 Vedauwoo Rd.
Other S: Ames Monument
Exit **(332)** Points of Interest (Left Exit Both Directions)
335 Buford
FStop S: **Sinclair**(*, LP) **(24 Hr. Towing)**
Other S: **U.S. Post Office (Sinclair)**
339 Remount Rd.
(341) **Parking Area (Westbound)**
342 Harriman Rd.
(344) **Parking Area (Westbound)**
345 Warren Rd.
348 Otto Rd.
358 Bus. Loop 80, U.S. 30 Bus, W. Lincolnway (Reaccess Westbound Only)
TStop N: **Little America**(*, LP)
Lodg N: **Little America**
AServ N: **Little America**
TServ N: **Little America**
(359) **Rest Area (Westbound, Located At Exit 359A)**
359A Jct. South I-25, U.S. 87, Denver
RVCamp S: **A B Campground (2 Miles)**
359C Jct. North I-25, U.S. 87, Casper
362 Junction I-180, U.S. 85, Central Ave, Greeley Colorado
FStop S: **Total**(*)
Gas S: Conoco(*)
Food N: Diamond Horseshoe Cafe
S: **Burger King**, Subway, **Taco John's**
Lodg S: Holiday Inn
AServ N: Big A Auto Parts, Complete Auto Service & Repair(24)
TServ N: **Cheyenne Truck Center, Diesel Service Co. (Cummins), International Dealer**
RVCamp S: **Hideaway RV & Mobile Home Park, RV Service**
Med N: ✚ **Hospital**
ATM S: **Total**
364 WY212, E. Lincolnway
RVCamp N: **RV Camping**
367 Campstool Rd, WY Herford Ranch
RVCamp N: **KOA Kampground**
370 Archer
TStop N: **Sapp Bros.**(*, LP, SCALES)
Food N: **Sapp Bros. "Big C" (Sapp Bros. TS), T-Joe's RV Park**
Lodg N: **Sapp Bros.**
TServ N: **Sapp Bros.**(SCALES)
RVCamp N: **T-Joe's RV Park**
(371) **WY Port of Entry, Weigh Station (Westbound)**
377 WY217, Hillsdale
TStop N: **Burns Brothers Travel Stop**(*, LP, SCALES) **(Amoco)**
Food N: **Mrs. B's (Burns Bros. TS), Taco Bell Express (Burns Bros. TS)**
Lodg N: **Burns Brothers Travel Stop (Amoco)**
TServ N: **Burns Brothers Travel Stop**(SCALES) **(Amoco)**
RVCamp N: **WY Campground (.5 Miles)**
386 WY213, 214, Burns, Carpenter
TStop N: **Cenex**(*)
Food N: **Cenex**
TServ N: **Cenex**
ATM N: **Cenex**
391 Egbert
401 **Pine Bluffs, Rest Area (RR, Phones, Picnic, Vending, RV Dump)**
TStop N: **AmPride**(*, LP)
FStop N: **Total**
Gas N: Redymart(*), Sinclair(D)

Bold red print shows RV & Bus parking available or nearby

EXIT	WYOMING/NEBRASKA
Food	**N:** Subway (AmPride TS), Uncle Fred's Place (Pizza), Wild Horse Restaurant (Total)
Lodg	**N:** Gator's Travelyn
AServ	**N:** AmPride, Sinclair
TServ	**N:** AmPride
RVCamp	**N:** Pine Bluffs RV Park (1.25 Miles)
ATM	**N:** AmPride
(401)	**Rest Area (RR, Phones, Picnic, Vending, RV Dump; Located At Exit 401 On The South Side)**

↑WYOMING

↓NEBRASKA

EXIT	NEBRASKA
1	Link 53B, To U.S. 30
8	Link 53C, Bushnell
(9)	**Rest Area (RR, Picnic; Eastbound)**
(18)	**Weigh Station (Eastbound)**
20	NE71, Kimball, Scottsbluff
Gas	**N:** Phillips 66[*, D]
Food	**N:** Beef & Brunch
	S: Burger King
Lodg	**N:** 1st Interstate Inn, Super 8
RVCamp	**N:** Twin Pines RV Camp
Med	**N:** ✚ Hospital
ATM	**N:** First State Bank
22	Kimball, E. Entrance
Med	**N:** ✚ Hospital
(25)	**Rest Area (RR, Phones, Picnic; Westbound)**
29	Link 53A, Dix
38	Link 17B, Potter
Gas	**N:** Cenex[*, D, LP]
RVCamp	**N:** Camping
48	Unnamed Exit
(51)	**Rest Area (RR, Phones, Picnic; Eastbound)**
55	Sidney, West Entrance, NE19, Bus. Loop 80
59	Link 15J To U.S. 385, Sidney, Bridgeport
FStop	**N:** Texaco[*]
Gas	**N:** Amoco[*]
Food	**N:** Arby's, McDonald's, Runza Restaurant
	S: Country Kitchen (Holiday Inn)
Lodg	**N:** Comfort Inn, Days Inn
	S: Holiday Inn
TServ	**S:** Hoffie's Truck Service
TWash	**S:** Hoffie's Truck Service
RVCamp	**N:** RV Camping
	S: Hoffie's Truck Service
Med	**N:** ✚ Hopsital
Other	**N:** Fort Sidney Museum
(61)	**Rest Area (RR, Phones, Picnic; Westbound)**
69	Link 17E, Sunol
76	Link 17F, Lodgepole
(82)	**Rest Area (RR, Phones, Picnic; Eastbound)**
85	Link 25A, Chappell
Gas	**S:** Texaco
AServ	**S:** Texaco
RVCamp	**N:** Creekside RV Park (.6 Miles)
(87)	**Rest Area (RR, Phones, Picnic; Westbound)**
95	NE27, Julesburg, Oshkosh
(99)	**Scenic View (Eastbound)**
101	U.S. 138, Big Springs, Julesburg
102	Junction I-76 South, Denver
107	25B Link, Big Springs
TStop	**N:** Bosselman Travel Center[*, SCALES]
FStop	**N:** Total[*]
Food	**N:** Char Bar Restaurant
Lodg	**N:** Budget 8 Motel
TServ	**N:** Bosselman Travel Center[SCALES]
TWash	**N:** Bosselman Travel Center
RVCamp	**S:** McGreer's Campground
ATM	**N:** Bosselman Travel Center
Other	**S:** Walker's CB Repair Shop
117	51A Link, Brule
FStop	**N:** Happy Jack's[*]
RVCamp	**N:** Happy Trails Campground (Laundry Facilities), Riverside Campground
(124)	**Rest Area (RR, HF, Phones, Picnic, Grills; Eastbound)**
126	NE 61, Ogallala, Grant
TStop	**S:** 76 Auto/Truck Plaza[*, RV DUMP, SCALES]
FStop	**N:** Amoco[*], Texaco[*]
Gas	**S:** Conoco[*], Phillips 66[*]
Food	**N:** Arby's, Best Western, Country Kitchen, McDonald's, Pioneer Trails Mall, Taco Bell, Valentino's Pizza (Pioneer Trails Mall)
	S: Cassel's Family Restaurant & Pancake House, Dairy Queen, KFC, Subway (Conoco), Wendy's
Lodg	**N:** Best Western, Days Inn, Holiday Inn Express, Ramada Limited
	S: Comfort Inn[*], EconLodge, Super 8
TServ	**N:** Big Mac Truck Repair
	S: 76 Auto/Truck Plaza[SCALES], MCM Truck Repair (Cummins)
RVCamp	**N:** Gold Dust Campground (Holiday Inn Express)
	S: Meyer Camper Court (.75 Miles), Open Corral Camp (.75 Miles)
Med	**N:** ✚ Hospital
ATM	**N:** Amoco, Texaco
	S: 76 Auto/Truck Plaza, Conoco, Phillips 66
Parks	**N:** Ogalalla Nature & Outdoor Classroom
Other	**N:** Howdy Information
	S: Pamida Grocery Store[RX], Truck Permit Station (76 Auto/Truck Stop)
(132)	**Rest Area (RR, Phones, Picnic; Westbound)**
133	51B Link, Roscoe
145	51C Link, Paxton
FStop	**N:** Texaco[*, LP, CW]
Food	**N:** Ole's Lodge (Texaco)
Lodg	**N:** Days Inn (Texaco)
RVCamp	**N:** Texaco
ATM	**N:** Texaco
158	NE 25, Sutherland, Wallace
FStop	**S:** Conoco[*, LP]
RVCamp	**S:** Sutherland Reservoir Park (1 Mile)
ATM	**S:** Conoco
(160)	**Rest Area (RR, HF, Phones, Picnic, Grills, Pet Walk; Eastbound)**
(160)	**Rest Area (RR, HF, Phones, Picnic, Grills, Pet Walk; Westbound)**
164	56C Link, Hershey
TStop	**N:** Texaco[*, LP, RV DUMP, SCALES, 24] (Road Service)
Gas	**N:** Sinclair[*]
AServ	**N:** Texaco[24] (Road Service)
TServ	**N:** Texaco[SCALES, 24] (Road Service)
RVCamp	**N:** KJ's Korner (Sinclair)
ATM	**N:** Sinclair, Texaco (Road Service)
Other	**N:** Truck Permit Station (Texaco)
177	U.S. 83, McCook, North Platte, Maloney, Buffalo Bill Ranch
Gas	**N:** Amoco[*], Conoco[*, D], Phillips 66[*], Total[*, D]
	S: Phillips 66, Total[*, D]
Food	**N:** Applebee's, Branding Iron BBQ, Chinese Restaurant, Perkin's Family Restaurant, Subway (Amoco), Village Inn, Whiskey Creek Saloon Steakhouse Grill
	S: Country Kitchen, Hunan Chinese, Taco Bell (Total)
Lodg	**N:** First Interstate Inn, Hampton Inn, Motel 6, Quality Inn, Sands Motor Inn, Stockman Inn
	S: Comfort Inn, Days Inn, Holiday Inn Express, Ramada Limited, Super 8
AServ	**S:** Bill Summers Nissan, Ford, Audi, Volkswagon, Denny Mogis Mazda, Phillips 66, Ross Perry Jeep & Eagle
TServ	**S:** Bill Summers Nissan, Ford, Audi, Volkswagon
RVCamp	**N:** Holiday Park RV Camp, Larry's RV Sales & Service (2.7 Miles)

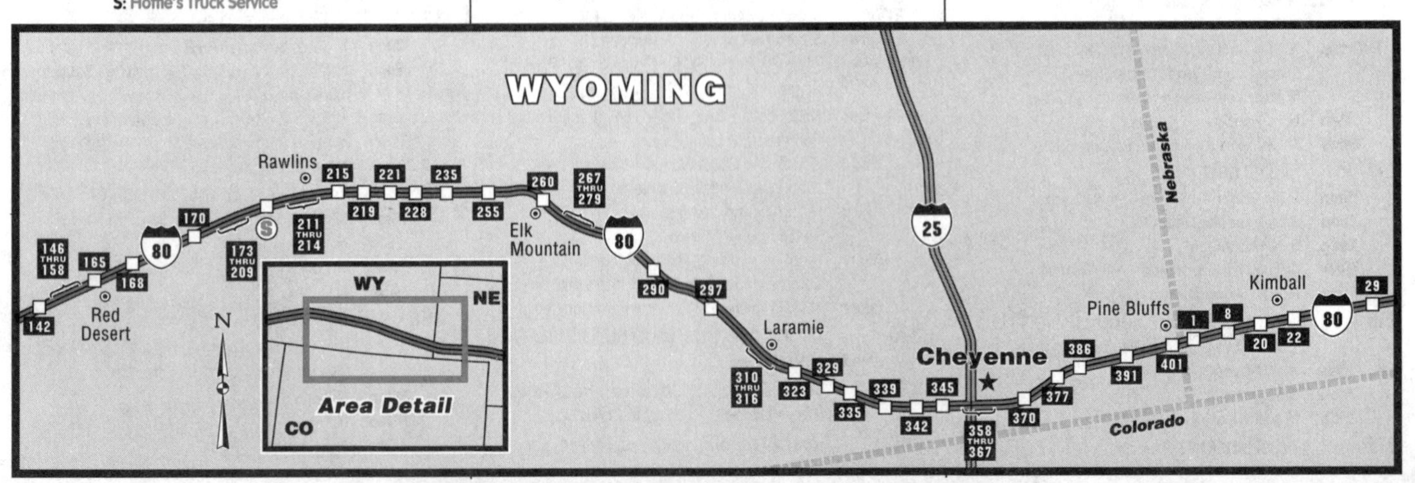

Bold red print shows RV & Bus parking available or nearby

EXIT	NEBRASKA
Med	**N:** ✚ Hospital
ATM	**N:** Amoco, Conoco, Phillips 66, Total, Wal-Mart[RX]
	S: Total
Other	**N:** Buffalo Bill Cody Trading Post, State Police, Wal-Mart[RX]
	S: Tourist Info.
179	56G Link, to U.S. 30, North Platte East Entrance
TStop	**S:** Flying J Travel Center[*, LP, SCALES]
Food	**S:** Country Market Restaurant & Buffet (Flying J Travel Center), Magic Dragon Chinese (Flying J's Travel Center), Pepperoni's (Flying J Travel Center)
(182)	Weigh Station (Eastbound)
(182)	Weigh Station (Westbound)
190	56A Spur, Maxwell, Ft. McPherson
FStop	**N:** Sinclair[*]
AServ	**N:** Sinclair
RVCamp	**S:** Camping
(194)	Rest Area (RR, HF, Phones, Picnic; Eastbound)
(194)	Rest Area (RR, HF, Phones, Picnic; Westbound)
199	Brady
FStop	**N:** No Name[*]
Food	**N:** Dairy Queen (No Name)
211	NE47, Gothenburg
TStop	**N:** Texaco[*]
Gas	**N:** Total[*]
	S: Total[*, LP] (KOA Campground)
Food	**N:** Homestead Cafe (Texaco), McDonald's, Mi Ranchito Mexican, Runza Fine American & Mexican
Lodg	**N:** Travel Inn Motel (Texaco), Western Motor Inn
RVCamp	**S:** KOA Campgrounds
Med	**N:** ✚ Hospital
ATM	**N:** Texaco
Other	**N:** Sod House Museum (Pony Express & Oregon Trail Info.), Truck Permit Station
222	NE 21, Cozad, Eustis
FStop	**N:** Amoco[*], Total[*, 24]
Gas	**N:** Conoco[*, LP]
Food	**N:** Burger King[PLAY], Circle S Restaurant, Dairy Queen, McDonald's, PJ's Restaurant, Pizza Hut, Porky's Pizza, Burgers, & Dogs (Total), Subway
Lodg	**N:** Circle S Motel, Motel 6
AServ	**N:** Platte Valley Auto Mart
Med	**N:** ✚ Hospital
ATM	**N:** Amoco, Total
Other	**N:** Robert Henri Museum (1 Mile)
(227)	Rest Area (RR, HF, Phones, Picnic; Eastbound)

EXIT	NEBRASKA
(228)	Rest Area (RR, HF, Phones, Picnic; Westbound)
231	Darr
TWash	**S:** Truck Wash
237	U.S. 283, Lexington, Arapahoe, Elwood
TStop	**S:** Sinclair[*]
FStop	**N:** Ampride[*]
Gas	**N:** Phillips 66[*, D]
	S: Conoco[*]
Food	**N:** Arby's, Freshway Subs & Salads (Ampride), KFC, McDonald's, Taco Bell, Wendy's
	S: Restaurant (Sinclair)
Lodg	**N:** Comfort Inn, Days Inn, EconoLodge, Gable View Inn
	S: Super 8
TServ	**S:** Nebraska Land Truck Center, Sinclair
Med	**N:** ✚ Hospital
ATM	**N:** Phillips 66
	S: Sinclair
Parks	**S:** Johnson Lake Recreation Area
Other	**N:** Heartland Military Museum
248	Overton
TStop	**N:** Burns Brothers Travel Stop[*]
TServ	**N:** Burns Brothers Travel Stop
ATM	**N:** Burns Brothers Travel Stop
257	U.S. 183, Elm Creek, Holdrege
TStop	**N:** Bosselman's Travel Center[*, SCALES]
Food	**N:** Little Caesars Pizza (Bosselman's), Mary Jo's Restaurant, Subway (Bosselman's), Taco Bell Express (Bosselman's)
Lodg	**N:** 1st Interstate Inn
263	Odessa, 10B Link
TStop	**N:** Sapp Bros. Truck Stop[*]
Food	**N:** Aunt Lu's Cafe (Sapp Bros)
Lodg	**N:** Budget Motel
AServ	**N:** Napa Auto (Sapp Bros)
TServ	**N:** Sapp Bros. Truck Stop
RVCamp	**N:** Budget Motel, Campground
ATM	**N:** Sapp Bros. Truck Stop
Parks	**N:** Union Pacific State Recreation Area
(269)	Rest Area (RR, HF, Phones, Picnic, Pet Walk; Eastbound)
(271)	Rest Area (RR, HF, Phones, Picnic; Westbound)
272	NE44, Kearney, Axtell
Gas	**N:** Phillips 66[*, D], Texaco[*, D]
	S: Amoco[*]
Food	**N:** Carlos O Kelly's Mexican Restaurant, Country Kitchen, Golden Dragon Chinese, Ramada Inn, Red Lobster, U.S.A. Steak Buffet, Whiskey Creek Steakhouse
	S: Fort Kearney Inn, Grandpa's Steakhouse

EXIT	NEBRASKA
Lodg	**N:** AmericInn, Country Inn & Suites, Fairfield Inn by Marriott, Hampton Inn, Ramada Inn, Regency Inn, Western Inn South, Wingate Inn
	S: Fort Kearney Inn
AServ	**N:** Gary's Towing (Texaco), Jeff Spady Chrys, Dodge, Jeep, Texaco
RVCamp	**N:** Clyde & Vi's Campground (.5 Miles)
Med	**N:** ✚ Hospital
ATM	**N:** Fast Cash, First of Nebraska, Phillips 66
Other	**N:** Stage Coach Gifts & Souvenirs, Trails & Rails Museum
279	NE10, Minden, Pioneer Village, Franklin, Ft. Kearny
Gas	**N:** Texaco[*]
Food	**N:** Picadilly Pizza (Texaco)
RVCamp	**S:** Pioneer Village (13 Miles)
Other	**S:** Pioneer Village (13 Miles)
285	10C Link, Gibbon
Gas	**N:** Ampride[*, D]
Food	**N:** Godfather's Pizza (Ampride)
Lodg	**S:** The Country Inn
AServ	**S:** Don's Repair
RVCamp	**N:** Ampride, R&I RV Sales & Service (.2 Miles)
ATM	**N:** Ampride
Parks	**N:** The Windmill Recreation Area
291	10D Link, Shelton
Gas	**S:** K M Gas[D]
Parks	**N:** War Axe State Recreation Area
300	NE11, Wood River
TStop	**S:** Bosselman's[*]
Food	**S:** Subway (Bosselman's)
Lodg	**S:** Motel
RVCamp	**S:** Motel
ATM	**S:** Bosselman's
305	40C Link, Alda, Juniata
TStop	**N:** T/A TravelCenters of America[*, SCALES]
FStop	**N:** Total[*, 24]
TServ	**N:** T/A TravelCenters of America[SCALES]
ATM	**N:** T/A TravelCenters of America
(305)	Rest Area (RR, Phones, Picnic; Westbound)
312	U.S. 34, U.S. 281, Grand Island, Hastings, Doniphan
TStop	**N:** Bosselman's Travel Center[*, SCALES]
Gas	**N:** Conoco[*]
	S: Amoco[*]
Food	**N:** Grandma Max's Restaurant (Bosselman's), Subway (Bosselman's), Taco Bell (Bosselman's), Tommy's Family Restaurant
Lodg	**N:** U.S.A. INNS
	S: Holiday Inn Express
AServ	**N:** Conoco
TServ	**N:** Bosselman's Travel Center[SCALES], Midland's Trailer Repair

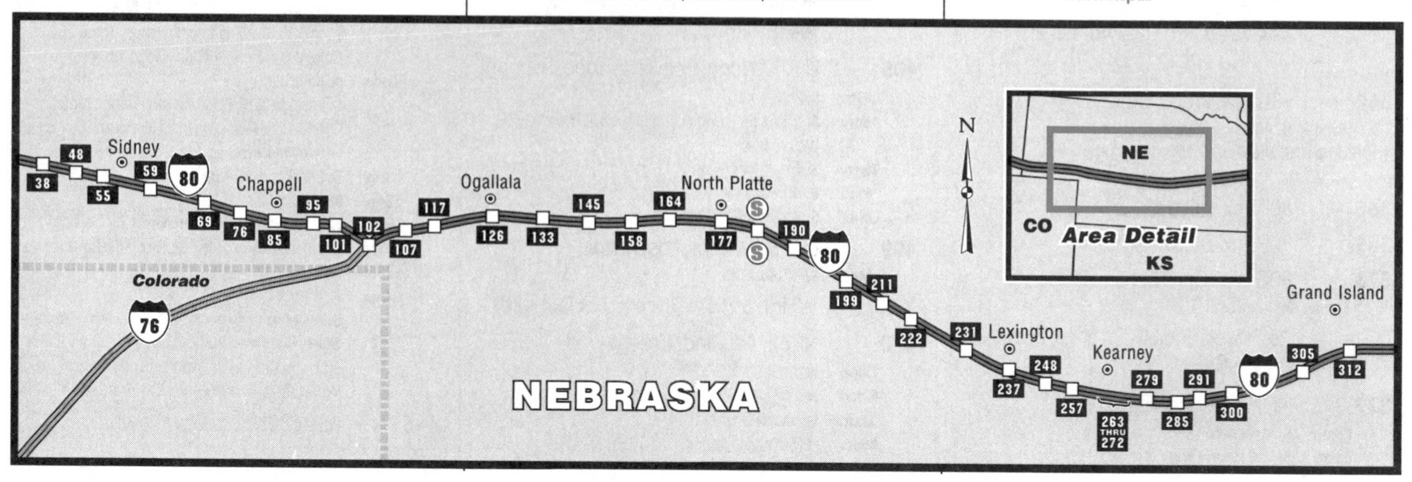

EXIT		NEBRASKA
		S: Ford Trucks, Nebraska Peterbilt, Cummins, Detroit Diesel, Cat
	RVCamp	S: KOA Campgrounds (15 Miles)
	Med	N: Hospital
	ATM	N: Bosselman's Travel Center
	Parks	N: Mormon Island State Rec. Area
	Other	N: Stuhr Museum, Tourist Info.
(315)		Rest Area (RR, HF, Phones, Picnic, Grills, Pet Walk; Eastbound)
(317)		Rest Area (RR, HF, Phones, Picnic; Westbound)
318		NE 2, Grand Island
	RVCamp	S: Grand Island RV Park Good Sam Park
	Other	N: Hospital
324		41B Spur, Giltner
332		NE 14, Aurora, Clay Center
	FStop	N: Texaco(*)
		S: Marlo(*)
	Food	N: Hamilton Motor Inn
	Lodg	N: Hamilton Motor Inn
	Med	N: Hospital
338		41D Link, Hampton
342		93A Spur, Henderson, Sutton
	FStop	S: Fuel Mart(*)
	Food	S: Dell's Restaurant
	Lodg	S: Wayfarer Motel
	TServ	S: Hy-Way Trailer, Inc.
	RVCamp	N: KOA Kampground
		S: Western Campground
	Med	S: Hospital
348		93E Link, Bradshaw
(350)		Rest Area (RR, HF, Phones, Picnic, Grills, Pet Walk; Eastbound)
353		U.S. 81, York, Geneva, McCool Junction
	TStop	S: Petro(*, LP, SCALES)
	FStop	N: Amoco(*), Conoco Sapp Bros.(*, SCALES)
		S: Texaco(*, LP)
	Gas	N: Byco Fuel(*), Texaco(*)
	Food	N: Amigo's Mexican(PLAY), Arby's, Burger King(PLAY), Country Kitchen, Golden Gate Express (Chinese), KFC, McDonald's, Wendy's
		S: Baskin Robbins (Petro), Iron Skillet (Petro), Pizza Hut (Petro), Texaco, U.S.A. Inns
	Lodg	N: Comfort Inn, Comfort Inn, Quality Inn, Super 8, Yorkshire Motel
		S: Holiday Inn, U.S.A. Inns
	AServ	N: John Kohl, Pennzoil Oil Change
	TServ	N: Amoco
		S: Petro(SCALES)
	TWash	S: Petro
	RVCamp	N: Super 8
	ATM	N: Conoco Sapp Bros., Texaco
		S: Texaco
(355)		Rest Area (RR, HF, Phones, Picnic; Westbound)
360		93B Link, Waco, Exeter
	TStop	N: Amoco Burns Bros.(*)
	RVCamp	S: The Double Nickel Campground(*)
	ATM	N: Amoco Burns Bros.
366		80F Link, Utica
369		80E Link, Beaver Crossing
373		80G Link, Goehner
	Gas	N: Texaco(*)
(376)		Rest Area (RR, HF, Phones, Picnic; Westbound)
379		NE 15, Seward, Fairbury
	FStop	S: Phillips 66(*, D, LP, 24)
	TServ	S: The Great Plains Tire Ctr

EXIT		NEBRASKA
	Med	N: Hospital
(381)		Rest Area (RR, HF, Phones, Picnic; Eastbound)
382		U.S. 6, Milford
	Gas	N: Dahle's I-80 Service(*)
	Food	S: Cafe
	Lodg	N: Milford Inn
	AServ	N: Dahle's I-80 Service
	RVCamp	N: Westward Ho Campground
388		NE 103, Crete
	Gas	N: Twin Lakes Gas Station(*, LP)
	RVCamp	N: Campground
395		NW 48th St, U.S. 6, West O Street
	TStop	S: Texaco(*, SCALES)
	Lodg	S: Cobbler Inn
	AServ	S: General Tires
	TServ	S: General Tires, Texaco(SCALES)
	TWash	S: Texaco
	ATM	S: Texaco
	Other	S: State Police, Truck Permit Station
396		US 6, West O St (Eastbound, Reaccess Westbound Only)
	Gas	S: Total(*)
	Lodg	S: Senate Inn Motel, Super 8
	TServ	S: Freightliner Dealer
	Med	S: Hospital
	ATM	S: Total
397		US 77 South, Beatrice (Difficult Reaccess, Limited Access Hwy)
399		Lincoln Municipal Airport, West Adams Street, Northwest 12th Street, Cornhusker Hwy
	Gas	N: Amoco(*, D, CW), Phillips 66(*)
		S: Sinclair(*, D)
	Food	N: Burgers & Breakfast (Great Scott's), Denny's, Great Scott's, Happy Chef, McDonald's(PLAY), New York Pizza (Great Scott's), Quizno's Classic Sub (Great Scott's), Taco Maker (Great Scott's)
		S: The Point After
	Lodg	N: Best Western, Comfort Inn, Hampton Inn, Holiday Inn Express, Motel 6, Sleep Inn, TraveLodge
		S: EconoLodge, Inn 4 Less
	ATM	N: Amoco, Phillips 66
		S: Sinclair
401B		U.S. 34 West
401		Junction I-180 & U.S. 34, 9th St, Downtown Lincoln
	RVCamp	S: Camp-A-Way (.75 Miles)
403		27th St, State Fair Park
	Other	N: Museum, Zoo
(405)		Rest Area (RR, HF, Phones, Picnic; Westbound)
405		U.S. 77 North, 56th St, Wahoo, Fremont
	Gas	S: Phillips 66(*, D, LP)
	AServ	S: Mike's 66 Towing Co. (Phillips 66), Phillips 66, Walker Tire
	TServ	S: Freightliner Dealer
	Med	S: Hospital
	Other	S: Ardvark Antique Mall
409		U.S. 6, Waverly, East Lincoln
	Med	S: Hospital
(420)		Weigh Station (Located at Exit 420)
420		NE 63, Ashland, Greenwood
	TStop	N: Amoco(*, SCALES, 24)
	FStop	N: Phillips 66(*, D)
	Lodg	N: Days Inn
	AServ	N: Tim's Auto Repair

EXIT		NEBRASKA
	TServ	N: Amoco(SCALES, 24)
	RVCamp	N: Campground
	ATM	N: Amoco, Phillips 66
	Other	S: Platte River State Park (12 Miles)
(425)		Rest Area (RR, HF, Phones, Picnic, Pet Walk; Eastbound)
426		Mahoney State Park, Ashland
	Parks	N: Mahoney State Park
	Other	N: SAC Museum
(432)		Rest Area (RR, HF, Phones, Picnic; Westbound)
432		U.S. 6, NE31, Gretna, Ashland
	TStop	N: Flying J Travel Plaza(*, LP, RV DUMP, SCALES)
	Gas	N: Texaco(*, D, LP)
	Food	N: McDonald's
	Lodg	N: Super 8
	RVCamp	N: KOA Campgrounds
	ATM	N: Texaco
	Other	N: Nebraska Crossing Factory Outlets
439		NE370, Gretna, Papaillion, Bellevue
	Gas	N: Sinclair(*, D)
	Lodg	N: Suburban Inn
	Med	S: Hospital
	Other	S: SAC Museum (13 Miles)
440		NE50, Springfield, Louisville
	TStop	N: Sapp Bros(*, LP, SCALES, 24)
	FStop	N: Citgo(*, SCALES), Phillips 66(*)
		S: Amoco(*)
	Food	N: Catfish Charlie's Restaurant, Hardee's, McDonald's(PLAY), Phillips 66, Subway (Sapp Bros), Truckhaven Country Restaurant(24) (Sapp Bros), Wallyburgers (Citgo)
		S: El Bee's Mexican Food
	Lodg	N: Comfort Inn, Park Inn International, Ramada Inn
	AServ	N: Ford, Mazda
	TServ	N: Ford Dealership, Inland Truck Repair, Sapp Bros(SCALES, 24), Volvo Dealer
		S: Fleet Truck Sales, Wick's Trailer Serv, Young Truck Trailers Inc
	TWash	N: Sapp Bros
	Med	S: Hospital (7 Miles)
	ATM	N: Citgo, Phillips 66
		S: Amoco
442		126th St., Harrison St.
444		Q St, L St
445		NE 38, West Center Road, U.S. 275, NE 92, I-L-Q Streets
	Gas	S: 24 Hr(*), Amoco(*, CW), Conoco(D, CW), Phillips 66(*, CW), QuikTrip(*, D)
	Food	N: Abigail's (Sheraton), Austin's Steaks
		S: Arby's, Burger King, Godfather's Pizza, Golden Corral Family Steakhouse, Hardee's, Hong Kong Cafe, Hunan Garden (Chinese), Little King, Long John Silver, McDonald's, SHONEY'S, Shoney's, TCBY, Taco Bell, The Gold Coast Lounge, Three Dollar Cafe, Valentino's (Italian), Village Inn, Wendy's
	Lodg	N: Sheraton
		S: Best Western, Budgetel Inn, Clarion Motel, Comfort Inn, Hampton Inn, Hawthorne Suites Hotel, Holiday Inn Express, Motel 6, Super 8
	AServ	S: Checker Auto Parts
	TServ	N: Int'l Dealer
	RVCamp	N: A. C. Nelson Camper World, RV Service
	ATM	S: Albertson's Grocery, Conoco, First Bank & Trust Co.
	Other	N: Sam's Club
		S: Albertson's Grocery(RX), Bag-n-Save Grocery Store, Cat Clinic, Fed Ex Drop Box, State Police, Suds City Car Wash, Vision Trends Optical, Wash World Coin Laundry
446		Jct I-680North, Downtown

EXIT — NEBRASKA

448 84th St
- **Gas** **N:** Amoco(*, 24)
- **Food** **N:** Denny's, Gata's (Pizza, Chicken, Pasta), McDonald's, Vic's Corn Popper, Winchells Donuts
- **Lodg** **N:** EconoLodge
- **AServ** **N:** Master Tune-Up Specialists, Napa Auto, Westgate Hi-Tech Auto Care
- **ATM** **N:** Amoco, **Baker's Grocery**(RX), First American Savings Bank, First National Bank(24), UBank
- **Parks** **S:** **New City Campground**
- **Other** **N:** **Baker's Grocery**(RX), **Kohl's Drug**, **Pearl Vision Center**

449 La Vista, Ralston, 72nd St
- **FStop** **S:** **Amoco**(*)
- **Gas** **N:** Amoco(*, CW)
- **Food** **N:** Burger King, Grover Street, Holiday Inn, La Strada Cafe Bar Italiano, Perkins Family Restaurant
  S: Anthony's
- **Lodg** **N:** Best Western, Hampton Inn, Holiday Inn, Homewood Suites Hotel, Ramada Inn, Rodeway Inn, Super 8
- **AServ** **N:** Amoco
  S: **Amoco**
- **Med** **N:** ✚ **Hospital**
- **ATM** **N:** Amoco
- **Other** **S:** Federal Express Office

450 60th St
- **FStop** **N:** **Phillips 66**(*)
- **Gas** **N:** Total(*, CW)
- **Lodg** **S:** Satellite Motel
- **AServ** **N:** Alfred Tire, NAPA Auto Parts, **Phillips 66**
  S: Allpro Muffler & Brakes, Burns Body Shop
- **TServ** **N:** **Cummins Great Plains**(D) **(1.3 Miles)**, **Phillips 66**
- **RVCamp** **N:** **Cummins Great Plains (1.3 Miles)**
- **ATM** **N:** Total

451 42nd St
- **Gas** **N:** Conoco(*, D, CW), Phillips 66, Texaco(*, LP, CW)
- **Food** **N:** Grover Inn
  S: Burger King, McDonald's, Taco Bell
- **AServ** **N:** Don's Auto Service (Conoco), Phillips 66
  S: Fast Lube, Pitstop Plus
- **ATM** **N:** Texaco, U.S. Bank

452 South U.S. 75, Bellevue, Jct. North I-480, U.S. 75 Downtown

453 24th St (Eastbound, Reaccess Westbound Only)
- **Food** **N:** Asiana Cafe, Baker's Market Place Cafe, KFC, Shang-Hai Garden Chinese
  S: Taqueiro (Mexican)
- **AServ** **N:** Car Quest Auto Parts, O'Reilly Auto Parts
- **ATM** **N:** First National Bank, UBank
- **Other** **N:** **24th Street Animal Clinic**, **Bakers Grocery**, Vinton Street Car Wash(CW), **WalGreen's**(RX)
  S: **South O Laundry**

EXIT — NEBRASKA/IOWA

454 13th St
- **Gas** **N:** Total(*)
  S: Phillips 66(*, CW)
- **Food** **N:** Goodrich Dairy (Pizza, Ice Cream), McDonald's(PLAY)
  S: Phillips 66
- **ATM** **N:** Total
  S: Phillips 66
- **Other** **S:** **Henry Doorly Zoo**, **Rosenblatt Stadium**

↑NEBRASKA

↓IOWA

1A Junction I-29N, Sioux City (Left Exit)

1B **South 24th St, Council Bluffs, Welcome Center**
- **TStop** **E:** **Pilot**(*, SCALES), **Texaco**(*)
- **Gas** **E:** Amoco(CW), Sinclair(*)
- **Food** **E:** **Arby's (Pilot TS)**, **Burger King (Texaco TS)**, Happy Chef, Happy Chef Restaurant, Leisure Lounge, **TJ Cinnamon's (Pilot TS)**
- **Lodg** **E:** **Best Western**, **Interstate Inn**, **Super 8**
- **AServ** **E:** Amoco, **Goodyear**
- **TServ** **E:** **Boyer's Diesel**, **Goodyear**, **Peterbilt**, **Stoughton Trailers**
- **TWash** **E:** **Texaco**
- **ATM** **E:** **Pilot**, **Texaco**
- **Other** **E:** **Bluff Run Casino**, Hops CB & Stereo
  S: Western Historic Trail Ctr & Welcome Ctr

3 IA 192, Council Bluffs, Lake Manawa
- **TStop** **S:** **Travel Centers of America**(*, D, LP, K, SCALES, 24) **(Country Pride Restaurant)**
- **Gas** **S:** Total(*)
- **Food** **S:** Burger King, Cracker Barrel - Settle Inn, Dairy Queen, Golden Corral Family Steakhouse, Hardee's, Long John Silver, McDonald's(PLAY), Perkin's Family Restaurant, Red Lobster, Sam's Club(*), Subway, Taco Bell, **Travel Centers of America (Country Pride Restaurant)**
- **Lodg** **S:** Cracker Barrel - Settle Inn, Econo Lodge, Fairfield Inn, Motel 6
- **AServ** **S:** Dodge Bluff Dodge, Edwards-O'Neill Hyundai, Edwards-O'Neill Old Cadillac and Subaru, Lake Manawa Nissan, McMullen Ford, Rhoden Pontiac Buick GMC Trucks Suzuki, Sam's Club, Toyota Bluff Lincoln-Mercury, **Wal-Mart**(24, RX)
- **TServ** **S:** **Great Dane Trailers/Jim Hawk Truck Trailers**, **Larry's Diesel Truck and CB Radio**(D), **Travel Centers of America**(SCALES, 24) **(Country Pride Restaurant)**, **V&Y Truck and Trailer Service**(24)
- **TWash** **S:** **Larry's Diesel Truck and CB Radio**
- **ATM** **S:** Total, **Travel Centers of America (Country Pride Restaurant)**, US Bank
- **Other** **S:** Sam's Club, **Wal-Mart**(RX)

4 Jct I-80 East, Des Moines, I-29 South

EXIT — IOWA

Kansas City

5 Madison Ave, Council Bluffs
- **Gas** **N:** Amoco(*, CW, 24)
  S: Phillips 66/Conoco(*, LP, CW), Texaco(*, CW)
- **Food** **N:** Burger King, Great Wall, Kentucky Fried Chicken, McDonald's(PLAY), Pizza Hut, Royal Fort Buffet, Subway, The Garden Cafe
  S: Dairy Queen (In Texaco Gas Station), SHONEY'S, Shoney's, Texaco
- **Lodg** **N:** **Heartland Inn**
  S: Western Inn
- **AServ** **N:** Amoco(24), NTB
- **ATM** **N:** First Bank & Trust Co., First Federal Lincoln, **Hy-Vee Food Store**(RX), Shazaam, US Bank
  S: Phillips 66/Conoco
- **Other** **N:** AAA Service, Drug Town, **Hy-Vee Food Store**(RX), **Mall of the Bluffs**, **Target**, Vision Trends Optical, WalGreens Pharmacy
  S: Scrub & Dub Auto Wash(CW)

8 U.S. 6, Council Bluffs, Oakland (Hospital at this exit)
- **Gas** **N:** Total Convenience Store(*, CW)
- **AServ** **N:** K-Mart
- **Med** **N:** ✚ **Hospital**
- **ATM** **N:** Total Convenience Store
- **Other** **N:** Bomgaars Ace Hardware(LP), **K-Mart**(RX)
  S: **Iowa State Patrol**

17 CR G30, Underwood
- **TStop** **N:** **Phillips 66**(*)
- **Food** **N:** **Restaurant (Phillips 66)**, Subway
- **Lodg** **N:** I-80 Inn
- **Other** **N:** Laundrymat

(20) **Rest Area (RR, Phones, Picnic, RV Dump)**

23 IA244, CR L55, Neola
- **FStop** **S:** **Phillips 66**(*, D)
- **RVCamp** **S:** **Arrowhead Park (.5 Miles)**
- **ATM** **S:** **Phillips 66**

27 Junction I-680W (Left Exit)

29 CR L66, Minden
- **Gas** **S:** **Conoco**(*), Total(*)
- **Food** **S:** A & W Drive-In (Total), **Kopper Kettle (Conoco)**

(32) **Parking Area**

34 CR M16, Shelby
- **FStop** **N:** **Texaco**(*)
- **Food** **N:** Dairy Queen, **The Cornstalk (Texaco)**
- **Lodg** **N:** Sheby Motel Lodge
- **TServ** **S:** **Doug's Truck and Trailer and Towing**
- **ATM** **N:** **Texaco**

40 U.S. 59, Avoca, Harlan
- **TStop** **N:** **Wings America**(*, D, SCALES) **(Conoco Gas)**
- **FStop** **N:** **Phillips 66**(*, D, SCALES)

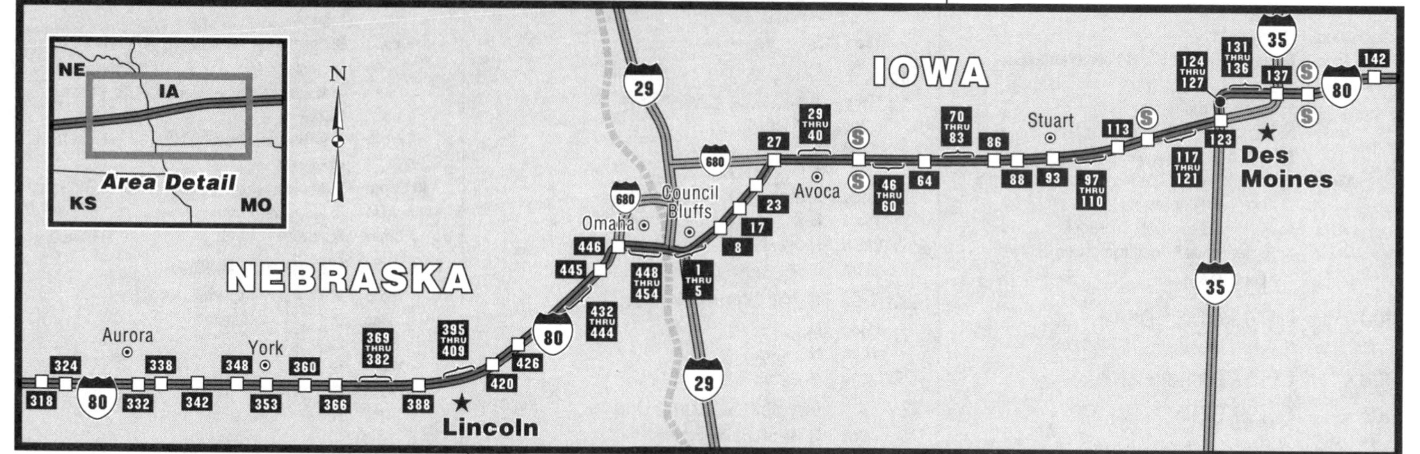

Bold red print shows RV & Bus parking available or nearby

EXIT — IOWA

Food N: Wings America (Conoco Gas)
S: The Embers Cafe
Lodg S: Avoca Motel
TServ N: Phillips 66(SCALES)
RVCamp S: Parkway Campground & Cafe (2 Miles)

(44) Weigh Station

46 CR M47, Walnut Antique City Dr
FStop S: Phillips 66(*)
Gas N: Amoco(*, D, 24)
S: Kum & Go(*)
Food N: Amoco, McDonald's (Located in Amoco), The Villager
S: Kum & Go
Lodg N: Super 8
S: Walnut Creek Inn
AServ S: Towing and Auto Repair
RVCamp S: Walnut Creek Inn & RV Park
ATM N: Amoco
S: Kum & Go

51 CR M56, Marne

54 IA173, Elk Horn, Kimballton

57 CR N16, Atlantic
Med S: Hospital (7 Miles to the South)

60 U.S. 6, U.S. 71, Atlantic, Audubon
FStop S: Phillips 66(*)
Gas S: Texaco(*)
Food S: Phillips 66
Lodg S: EconoLodge
AServ S: Phillips 66

64 CR N28, Wiota

70 IA148, Anita, Exira
Parks S: Lake Anita State Park (5 Miles south of exit)

75 CR G30

76 IA925, CR N54, Adair
FStop N: Phillips 66(*, D)
Gas N: Amoco(*, D, 24)
Food N: Happy Chef, Mikey's Dairy Sweet
Lodg N: Adair Guest Inn, Best Western
AServ N: Amoco(24)
ATM N: Amoco
Other N: Adair Campground / City Park

(80) Rest Area (RR, HF, Phones, Vending, RV Dump)

83 CR N77, Casey
RVCamp N: Casey City Park

86 IA25, Guthrie Center, Greenfield
Gas S: Conoco(*)
Food S: Conoco

88 CR P20, Menlo

93 CR P28, Stuart, Panora
FStop N: Conoco(*)
S: Phillips 66(*, D)
Gas N: Amoco(*)
Food N: Burger King(PLAY), Harris House Restaurant, McDonald's(PLAY), Subway
S: Country Kitchen
Lodg N: Stuart Motor Lodge, Super 8
S: New Edgetowner Motel
AServ N: Amoco, Denny's Tire Service, Ron's Auto Supply, Wallace Auto Supplies
ATM N: McDonald's, Security State Bank
Other N: Jubilee Foods(LP), Laundrymat with Car Wash

97 CR P48, Dexter

100 U.S. 6, Redfield, Dexter
RVCamp N: Dexter City Park (1 Mile)

104 CR P57, Earlham

106 CR F90, CR P58
RVCamp N: KOA Campgrounds (1 Mile)

EXIT — IOWA

Other S: LP Farrel Gas

110 U.S. 169, Desoto, Adel (John Wayne birthplace 14 miles to the south)
Gas S: Amoco(*), Casey's(*)
Lodg S: Desoto Motor Inn, Edgetowner Motel
AServ S: Highway Auto & Tire
Other S: Laundrymat, US Post Office

113 CR R16, Van Meter

(114) Weigh Station (Eastbound)

117 CR R-22, Waukee, Booneville
FStop S: Phillips 66(24)
Gas S: Kum and Go(*)
Food S: Taco Johns
Lodg S: Hi-Ho Hotel
RVCamp N: Timberline Best Holiday Trav-L-Park (1.5 Miles)
ATM S: Phillips 66

(119) Rest Area (RR, HF, Phones, Picnic, Grills, Vending, RV Dump)

121 74th St, West Des Moines
Gas S: Kum & Go(*, LP)
Food S: Arby's, Blimpie's Subs, Burger King(PLAY), McDonald's, Taco Johns
Lodg N: Hampton Inn
S: Candle Wood Suites, Marriott, Motel 6, Wingate Inn
ATM N: Earlham Savings Bank, Hyvee(24, RX)
S: Kum & Go
Other N: Hyvee(RX)

123A I-235 West Des Moines and Des Moines

123B I-35 & I-80 split

124 University Ave, Clive
Gas N: Amoco(*, CW), Kum & Go(*, CW), Quik Trip(*)
S: Phillips 66(*, CW, 24)
Food N: Cracker Barrel, Mustard's Rib Restaurant
S: Applebee's, Baker's Square, Big Apple Bagels, Chatter's Casual Cafe, Chili's, Cucos Mexican Cafe, Damon's (Holiday Inn), McDonald's, Outback Steakhouse, Palmer's Deli, The Tavern
Lodg N: Budgetal Inn, Country Inn Suites
S: Courtyard by Marriott, Fairfield Inn, Heartland Inn, Holiday Inn, Residence Inn, The Inn, Wildwood Lodge
Med S: Urgent Care Clinic
ATM S: Banker's Trust, State Employees Credit Union

125 U.S. 6, Hickman Road, Adel, Welcome Center
TStop N: Flying J(*, LP)
Food N: Flying J
S: Iowa Machine Shed (Comfort Suites)
Lodg S: Comfort Suites Hotel, Four Points Hotel Sheraton, Sleep Inn
AServ S: GMC Trucks, Goodyear Tire & Auto, Oldsmobile, Honda Dealer
TServ S: Goodyear

126 Douglas Ave, Urbandale
TStop N: Pilot Travel Center(SCALES, 24)
Gas S: Phillips 66(*, CW)
Food N: Pilot Travel Center
S: Dragon House
Lodg S: Days Inn, Econolodge
TServ N: Pilot Travel Center(D, SCALES)
TWash N: Pilot Travel Center
ATM N: Pilot Travel Center, Pilot Travel Center

127 IA 141, Grimes, Perry
FStop N: Phillips 66(*, D, LP)
Food N: Subway
RVCamp N: Cutty's RV Park

129 NW 86th St., Camp Dodge
Gas N: Heartland Pantry(*) (Phillips 66)

EXIT — IOWA

Other N: Wynnsong Cinema's

131 IA 28, Merle Hay Road, Urbandale
Gas N: Coastal(*, D), QuikTrip(*)
S: Amoco(*, D, LP, CW, 24), QuikTrip(*), Sinclair(*, LP)
Food N: North Inn Diner (The Inn), Pagiai's Pizza, The Inn
S: Arby's, Bennigan's, Burger King, Denny's, Embers(24), Famous Dave's BBQ, Hostetler's BBQ, McDonald's, Perkins Family Restaurant, The Ground Round, Wendy's
Lodg N: Best Inns of America, The Inn
S: Comfort Inn, Days Inn, Four Points Hotel Sheraton, Holiday Inn, Roadway Inn, Super 8
AServ N: Jordan Motors, Super Lube(CW)
S: All Pro Auto Center, Car Star Collision Repair, Ford, Hummels Nissan, Lincoln, Mercury, Sinclair, Stevens Foreign & Domestic, Toyota
Med S: VA Hospital
ATM S: US Bank
Other N: Animal House, Village Animal Hospital
S: Animal Medical Clinic, Carmike Cinemas, Discovery Zone, Touchless of Merle Hay(CW)

135 IA 415, 2nd Ave, Polk City
Gas S: Coastal(*), QuikTrip(*, K)
TServ N: Interstate Detroit Diesel
S: Freightliner Dealer
Other N: Iowa State Patrol

136 U.S. 69, East 14th St, Ankeny
FStop S: Casey's General Store(*, D), QuikTrip(*, SCALES)
Gas N: Amoco(*, D, CW), Phillips 66(*, CW), Sinclair(*, D)
Food N: Bonanza Steakhouse, Bontels Restaurant, Country Kitchen, Okoboji, Red Baron (Best Western)
S: Broadway Diner, Casey's General Store, Magic Food Restaurant, QuikTrip
Lodg N: Best Western, Motel 6
S: 14th Street Inn
AServ N: Sinclair
S: Farm & Country Tires and More(LP), Ford Truck
TServ N: McKenna Truck Center
S: Housvay Mack Trucks, James W. Bell Cummins, Ruan Truck Sales
RVCamp N: Cummins Great Plains (.4 Miles)
ATM S: Casey's General Store
Other N: K-Mart(RX)

137B Jct. I-35, Minneapolis

137A Jct. I-235

(141) Weigh Station

141 US 6, US 65, Pleasant Hill, Des Moines
Lodg N: Archer Motel, Broadway Motel, Motel 8

142 U.S. 65, Hubbel Ave, Des Moines, Bondurant, Altoona
TStop S: Bosselman Travel Center(*)
Gas S: Cenex(*, D)
Food S: Adventureland Inn, Blimpie Subs & Salads, Burger King, Godfather's Pizza, McDonald's(PLAY), Pizza Hut, Taco Bell, Taco John's, Viking Dining and Lounge
Lodg S: Country Inn Motel, Heartland Inn, Holiday Inn Express
TServ S: Bosselman Travel Center(*, D, CW), Peterbilt Dealer
TWash S: Bosselman Travel Center, Bosselman Travel Center(CW)
RVCamp S: Adventureland Campground (.38 Miles)
ATM S: Bosselman Travel Center
Other S: Adventure Land

143 Bondurant, Altoona
TStop N: 76 Auto/Truck Plaza(SCALES)
Gas S: KC's General Store(*)
Food N: 76
TServ N: 76
TWash N: 76(SCALES)
ATM N: 76

Bold red print shows RV & Bus parking available or nearby

EXIT IOWA

(148) Rest Area (RR, Phones, Picnic, Vending, RV Dump)

149 Mitchellville

(151) Weigh Station (Westbound)

155 IA 117, Colfax, Mingo (Walnut Creek National Wildlife Refuge and Neil Smith Prairie Learning Center)
- **FStop** S: Phillips 66(*, D, LP, CW), Texaco(*, D, 24)
- **AServ** S: Phillips 66
- **ATM** S: Texaco

159 Cnty Road F48, Baxter

164 IA 14, US 6, Newton, Monroe
- **Gas** N: Amoco(*, LP, CW, 24), Conoco(*), Phillips 66(*, D)
- **Food** N: Country Kitchen, Golden Corral Family Steakhouse, KFC, Perkins Family Restaurant, Subway
- **Lodg** N: Days Inn, Holiday Inn Express, Ramada Limited (see our ad this page), Super 8
  S: Best Western
- **AServ** N: Amoco, Conoco
- **Med** N: Hospital
- **ATM** N: Phillips 66

168 Southeast Beltline Drive
- **RVCamp** N: Rolling Acres Family Campground (.75 Miles)

173 IA 224, Kellogg, Sully
- **FStop** N: Citgo(*, D)
- **Food** N: Iowa's Best Burger Cafe
- **RVCamp** N: Kellogg RV Park (.25 Miles)

179 Lynnville, Oakland Acres

(181) Rest Area (RR, Phones, Picnic, Vending, RV Dump)

182 IA 146, Grinnell, New Sharon (Fun Valley Ski Area located at this exit: Hospital 4 miles North of exit)
- **Gas** N: Coastal(*)
- **Food** N: City Limits Restaurant
- **Lodg** N: Best Western, Days Inn, Super 8
- **Med** N: Hospital

191 U.S. 63, Tama, Montezuma
- **TStop** S: Citgo(*, D, LP, 24)
- **FStop** S: Fuelmart(*)
- **Food** S: Citgo, Dinner Bell Restaurant, Fuelmart
- **AServ** S: Citgo(24)
- **TServ** S: Citgo(24)

197 Brooklyn
- **FStop** N: Amoco(*)
- **Food** N: Amoco, Brooklyn - 80(*) (RV Camping located)
- **TServ** N: Amoco
- **RVCamp** N: Brooklyn - 80 (RV Camping located)

201 IA 21, Balle Plaine, What Cheer
- **TStop** S: Kwik Star(*, D, LP, SCALES) (Conoco)
- **FStop** N: Texaco(*)
- **Food** N: Texaco
- **TServ** S: Kwik Star, Kwik Star(SCALES) (Conoco)
- **RVCamp** N: Texaco
- **ATM** S: Kwik Star (Conoco)

205 Victor

(209) Rest Area (RR, Phones, Picnic, Vending)

211 Millersburg, Ladora

216 Marengo, North English
- **FStop** N: Texaco(*)
- **Food** N: Texaco(*)
- **Med** N: Hospital (6 Miles to the north)

220 IA 149, Iowa County Road V 77, Williamsburg, Parnell
- **FStop** N: Phillips 66(*, D) (Landmark Restaurant)
- **Gas** N: Conoco(*) (Has gift shop)
- **Food** N: Arby's, McDonald's, Phillips 66 (Landmark Restaurant), Pizza Hut (Tanger Outlet Center), Rocky Mountain Chocolate Factory (Tanger Outlet Center), Subway (Tanger Outlet Center)
- **Lodg** N: Best Western, "Quiet House", Crest Motel (AAA), Super 8
  S: Ramada Limited
- **ATM** N: Phillips 66 (Landmark Restaurant), Tanger Outlet Center
- **Other** N: Conoco (Has gift shop), Tanger Outlet Center

225 U.S. 151, IA W 21, Cedar Rapids, Amana Colonies, Welcome Center
- **Gas** S: Amoco(*), Phillips 66(*)
- **Food** S: Amoco, Colony Haus Restaurant, Colony Village Restaurant, Holiday Inn (Seven Villages Restaurant)
- **Lodg** N: Comfort Inn
  S: Days Inn, Holiday Inn (Seven Villages Restaurant), My Little Inn Motel, Super 8
- **Other** S: Little Amana Shops, Little Amana General Store, (Amana Wollens Outlet)

230 Johnson Cnty. W38, Oxford, Kalona Village Museum
- **Food** N: Sleepy Hollow Campground(*, LP) (Restaurant, Good Sam's)
- **TServ** N: Located at Blackhawk Ave.
- **RVCamp** N: Sleepy Hollow Campground (Restaurant, Good Sam's)

(237) Rest Area (RR, Phones, Picnic, Vending, RV Dump)

237 Tiffin

239A Jct. U.S. 218 S, Mt. Pleasant, Keokuk

239B Jct. I-380, Cedar Rapids, Waterloo

NEWTON, IOWA

1589

I-80 & Hwy 164

RAMADA LIMITED

515-792-8100
800-272-6232

Free Continental Breakfast
Free Local Calls
King/Queen Beds
Restaurant on-Site
Remote Cable TV/HBO/ESPN/CNN
Children Under 12 Stay Free w/Parents
Bus, Rv & Truck Parking
Outside Outlets
Pets Allowed With Permission $10 Charge
Convenient to 2 Casinos, Horse Racing & Shopping

AT&T HBO

$39.95* +tax — 1-2 Persons/ 1 Bed
$45.95* +tax — 2-4 Persons/ 2 Bed

*with Cuopon at Check In. Based on Availability.
Not alid with other discounts, during holidays or special events.

IOWA • I-80 • Exit 164

240 IA 965, Coralville, North Liberty
- **TStop** N: Heartland Express(D)
- **Gas** N: Texaco(*)
- **Food** N: Best Western(*) (Mexican Lunch Buffett), Express Way Motel (Heartland Express)
- **Lodg** N: Best Western (Mexican Lunch Buffett), Express Way Motel (Heartland Express)
- **AServ** S: Sears
- **TServ** N: Heartland Express
- **TWash** N: Heartland Express
- **Other** N: Target
  S: Mall (Undre Construction)

242 Coralville
- **TStop** S: Hawk-I Texaco(*, D, SCALES)
- **FStop** S: QuikTrip(*, D)
- **Gas** S: Amoco(*, LP, CW), Coastal(*)
- **Food** N: Wheatherbees Food and Sprits (Hampton Inn)
  S: Arby's, Cancun Mexican Restaurant, Country Kitchen, Hawk-I Texaco, KFC, McDonald's, Perkins Family Restaurant
- **Lodg** N: Clarion Hotel, Hampton Inn
  S: Best Western Canteberry Inn and Suites, Big Ten Inn, Comfort Inn, Econolodge, Fairfield Inn, Motel 6, Super 8 (No large trailers or trucks)
- **AServ** S: Amoco, Clear Company Auto Body shop, Duffy's European Auto and Cycle Shop, Georgetown Auto Mechanical Repair Specialist
- **TServ** S: Bryant's Truck Service Center, Bud's Tire and Transmission(24) (Emergency Service), Hawk-I Texaco(SCALES), Midwest Frame and Axel Service, Ruan
- **TWash** S: Hawk-I Texaco
- **RVCamp** S: Coralville Edgewater Park (Picnic area, boat ramp)
- **Med** S: Sports Hospital, VA Hospital
- **ATM** S: Hawk-I Texaco
- **Other** S: UPS

244 Dubuque St, Coralville Lake

246 IA 1, Dodge St, Mount Vernon
- **Gas** N: Phillips 66(*, CW)
  S: Sinclair(*)
- **Food** S: T.G.I. Friday's (Carlton Inn and Suites)
- **Lodg** N: Raddison
  S: Country Inn and Suites
- **Other** S: Creature Comfort Vet. Services

249 Herbert Hoover Highway

254 Cnty. Road X30, West Branch
- **FStop** N: Amoco(*, CW)
- **Gas** N: Amoco(*, CW)
  S: Phillips 66(*)
- **Food** S: McDonald's
- **Lodg** S: Presidential Motor Inn
- **ATM** S: Phillips 66
- **Other** N: Herbert Hoover National Historic Site & Presidential Musuem
  S: Pet Hospital

259 West Liberty, Cty. Road X40
- **FStop** S: Amoco(*, RV DUMP, 24)
- **Food** S: Mom's Kitchen (KOA Campground), Rockitz Diner
- **Lodg** S: Econolodge
- **RVCamp** S: KOA Campgrounds(*, LP) (.25 Miles, Laundry, Deli)

265 Atalissa
- **FStop** S: Phillips 66(*, D, SCALES) (No Auto Fuel. Diesel And Home Heating Fuel Only)
- **Food** S: Birdy's Restaurant (Phillips 66)

267 IA 38, Tipton, Moscow
- **Gas** N: Sinclair(*)
- **Food** S: The Cove Restaurant
- **RVCamp** N: Cedar River Campground (Open April 15-Oct. 15), Minifarm Acres Camping

(268) Weigh Station

Bold red print shows RV & Bus parking available or nearby

EXIT IOWA

(270) **Rest Area (Phones, Picnic, Vending, RV Dump)**

271 U.S. 6, IA 38, Wilton, Muscatine

277 Durant, Bennett

280 Scott Cnty. Y30, New Liberty, Stockton
- **FStop** S: **Burns Brothers Travel Stop**(*)

284 Scott Cnty. Y40, Walcott, Plainview
- **TStop** N: **Iowa 80 Truck Stop**(*, CW, SCALES) **(Amoco, Ambest)**
- **FStop** N: **Phillips 66**(*, D)
  S: **Pilot**(*, 24)
- **Food** N: Dairy Queen (Iowa 80 Truckstop), Daybreak Food (Phillips 66), **Granma's Kitchen (CB Sales and Service)**, **ITC Pizza**, Iowa 80 Kitchen (Iowa 80 Truckstop), Subway (Iowa 80 Truckstop), Wendy's (Iowa 80 Truckstop)
  S: McDonald's, Subway (Pilot)
- **Lodg** N: **Super 8 (Iowa 80 Truckstop)**
  S: Days Inn
- **TServ** N: **Iowa 80 Truck Stop**(SCALES) **(Amoco, Ambest)**
  S: **Freightliner**
- **TWash** N: **Iowa 80 Truck Stop**(CW) **(Amoco, Ambest)**
- **ATM** N: **Iowa 80 Truck Stop (Amoco, Ambest)**
- **Other** N: **Granma's Kitchen (CB Sales and Service)**

290 **Jct. I-280, US 6 Left Exit, Rock Island, Moline, Welcome Center**
- **Med** S: **+ Hospitals**

292 IA 130, Maysville
- **TStop** N: **Flying J Travel Plaza**(*, D, LP, K, RV DUMP, SCALES) **(Conoco)**
- **Gas** S: Amoco(*, 24), Fred's Towing & Gas(24)
- **Food** N: Cookery (Flying J's), **Flying J Travel Plaza (Conoco)**
  S: **Iowa Machine Shed**
- **Lodg** S: Comfort Inn
- **AServ** N: Blane's Farm & Fleet, Eastern Iowa Tire
  S: Fred's Towing & Gas(24)
- **TServ** N: **Interstate Diesel, Truckland Truck Service**
- **TWash** N: **Western Star Trucks**
- **RVCamp** N: **AmeriGas/Interstate RV Park**(LP) **(.7 Miles), Interstate RV Park & Campground (1.25 Miles)**
  S: **Wayne's RV Storage/Repairs**
- **Other** N: Blane's Farm & Fleet, Wacky Water's Adventure Water Park
  S: Leisure Lanes

295AB U.S. 61, Brady St., Elridge, Dewitt
- **Gas** S: Shell
- **Food** S: Best Western, Burger King, Country Kitchen, **Cracker Barrel**, Dancers Inn (Best Western), Hardee's, Thunder Bay Grille, Village Inn
- **Lodg** S: Best Western, Budgetel Inn, Country Inn and Suites, Days Inn, Economy Inn, Exel Inn, Heartland Inn, Holiday Inn, Motel 6, Ramada, Residence Inn, Super 8
- **AServ** S: Auto Check, Dave & Sam's, Mid State RV Center
- **TServ** S: **Avis Truck Repair, Bauler Tire Repair, Mitchell, Fadler Truck Parts, Jim Hock Truck/Trailer, Penske**
- **ATM** S: Norwest Bank
- **Other** S: Cinema, **N. Brady Animal Hospital**, UPS Truck/Trailer, White Haven Animal Clinic

298 I-74E, Peoria, Bendorf, Riverfront, Moline

(300) **Rest Area (RV Dump)**

(300) **Rest Area**

301 Middle Road

306 **U.S. 67, Le Claire, Bettendorf, Iowa Welcome Center**
- **Food** N: Slagles Bakery & Deli, Steventon's
- **Other** N: Buffalo Bill Museum (2 Miles), **Camping**

EXIT IOWA/ILLINOIS

↑IOWA

↓ILLINOIS

1 IL 84, East Moline, Savanna
- **Gas** S: Amoco(*)
- **Food** S: **The Brothers Family Restaurant**
- **AServ** S: McCarty Auto Parts
- **RVCamp** S: **Fishermens Corner Rec. Area (1.5 Miles)**
- **ATM** S: Metro Bank
- **Other** S: Rapid City Car Wash

(1) **Rest Area/Tourist Information (P); Southbound)**

(2) **Weigh Station (Southbound)**

(2) **Weigh Station (Northbound)**

4A IL 5, IL 92 W., Silvis, East Moline

4AB I-88, IL 92E., Silvis, East Moline, IL5, IL92E., Steriling, Rock Falls
- **RVCamp** S: **Luden Landing (April-October, 5 Miles)**

7 Colona
- **Gas** N: Conoco(*)

9 U.S. 6

10 East, I-74 To Peora, Galesburg, West, I-74/ I-280 To Moline, Rock Island

19 IL 82, Geneseo, Cambridge
- **FStop** N: **Phillips 66**(*, D) **(Showers)**
- **Food** N: **Coffee Shop (Deck Plaza)**, Hardee's, Subway
  S: **KFC**
- **Lodg** N: **Deck Plaza**
- **AServ** N: Hutch Craft Auto/RV
- **TServ** N: **Phillips 66 (Showers)**
- **Med** N: **+ Hospital**
- **Other** N: **Wal-Mart**(LP, RX)

27 Galva, Atkinson
- **TStop** N: **Shell**
- **Gas** N: Amoco(*, LP, K)
- **Food** N: **Shell**, Woodshed (Shell TS)
- **TServ** N: **Bikes, C.B. Radios, Wash Out Plus — Tires, Batteries, Brakes**
- **ATM** N: **Shell**

33 IL 78, Kewanee, Prophets Town, Annawan
- **Gas** S: Amoco(*, CW), Fuel 24, Phillips 66(*)
- **Food** S: The Loft
- **AServ** S: Amoco, Jackson Collison Repair, The Backyard Shop
- **Parks** S: **Johnson Salk State Park**
- **Other** S: Car Wash

45 IL 88, Peoria, Sterling
- **Gas** N: Quik Stop K(*, D)
- **Food** N: Crossroad's Family Restaurant (Home Cooking), Days Inn
- **Lodg** N: Days Inn
- **ATM** N: Quik Stop K
- **Other** N: President Reagan's First Home

(51) **Rest Area (RV Dump, (P); North-bound)**

(51) **Rest Area (HF, RV Dump)**

56 IL 26, Dixon, Princeton
- **TStop** N: **Pilot**(*, D)
- **Gas** S: Amoco(*, CW), Phillips 66(*), Shell(*)
- **Food** N: **Pilot**, Restaurant (Pilot TS)
  S: Country Kitchen, Days Inn, **McDonald's**, Prime Quarter Steakhouse (Grill Your Own), Restaurant (Days Inn), Sullivans Food, Taco Bell, The Big Apple Family Restaurant, Wendy's
- **Lodg** N: **Super 8**
  S: Birds Nest Motel, Comfort Inn, Days Inn, Princeton Motor Lodge
- **AServ** S: Auto Zone Auto Parts
- **TServ** N: **Arrow Trailer & Equipment Co., Pilot**
- **Med** N: **+ Hospital**
- **ATM** S: Citizen First National Bank, First of America, Union Bank
- **Other** S: **Animal Clinic**, Burau Vision Care, Eagle Country Market, Super Wash, **Wal-Mart**(LP, RX)

EXIT ILLINOIS

61 Jct. I-180, Hennepin

70 IL 89, Ladd, Spring Valley
- **Gas** N: Casey's Store(*)
- **Lodg** S: **Motel Riviera**
- **ATM** N: Casey's Store

73 Plank Road
- **TStop** N: **Sapp Brothers**(*, LP, SCALES) **(Citgo, Food)**
- **Food** N: Burger King (Sapp), **Great American Buffet (Sapp Brothers)**, Interstate Pancakes, Subway (Sapp)
- **AServ** N: Mid City Sales & Service (Tires)
- **TServ** N: **Goodyear Tire & Auto, JCJ Trucking, Kenworth, Mitchell Truck Wash, Sapp Brothers**(SCALES) **(Citgo, Food), Unitz Truck Service**
- **TWash** N: **Mitchell Truck Wash, Sapp Brothers (Citgo, Food)**
- **RVCamp** N: **Barney's Lake Camping**
- **ATM** N: **Sapp Brothers (Citgo, Food)**

75 IL 251, Peru, Mendota
- **TStop** N: **Marathon**(*, SCALES) **(Food), Tiki Truck Stop**(*, RV DUMP, SCALES)
- **Gas** N: Amoco(*, LP), **Shell**(*)
  S: Amoco(CW)
- **Food** N: Arby's, Hamilton's Restaurant (Marathon), **McDonald's**, Picadilly Circus Pizza (Marathon), **Pine Cone Restaurant (Tiki Inn), Shell, Tiki Inn, Tiki Truck Stop**
  S: Bob Evan's Restaurant, Burger King, Dairy Queen, Dunkin Donuts, Kline's Cafe Specialty Foods, Maid/Rite Diner, Oogie's, Red Lobster, Steak & Shake, **Subway**, Wendy's, Willaby's Sports
- **Lodg** N: Comfort Inn, Days Inn, Motel 6, Quality Inn, **Super 8, Tiki Inn**
  S: Fairfield Inn
- **AServ** N: **Marathon (Food)**
  S: Amoco, Auto Glass Center, Big A's, Goodyear, Hammers General Tires, JP Auto Center, **K-Mart**(RX), Midas Muffler & Brake, Monroe Pontiac, Buick, Montgomery Ward, NAPA Auto Parts, Valvoline Oil Change(CW)
- **TServ** N: **Marathon**(SCALES) **(Food), Tiki Truck Stop**(SCALES)
- **RVCamp** N: **Tiki RV Park (.5 Miles)**
- **Med** S: **+ Hospital**
- **ATM** N: **Marathon (Food), Tiki Truck Stop**
  S: Econo Food Mart, First Federal, First State Bank, LaSal Bank
- **Other** S: Econo Food Mart, **K-Mart**(RX), **Peru Mall**, Progress Park Animal Hospital, Super Car Wash, **Target**(RX), **Wal-Mart**(RX), **WalGreens Pharmacy**(RX)

77 IL 351, La Salle
- **TServ** S: **Mack's**
- **Other** S: Illinois State Police

79AB Jct. I-39, U.S. 51, Bloomington, Norman, Rockford

81 Il 178, Utica
- **Gas** S: Amoco(*)
- **Food** S: Cagin Connection Restaurant/Bait Shop
- **Lodg** S: Starved Rock Gateway Motel
- **AServ** S: Greg's Automotive
- **RVCamp** N: **KOA Campgrounds (2 Miles)**
  S: **Cubby Hole Storage**
- **ATM** S: Amoco

90 IL 23, Ottawa, De Kalb
- **Gas** N: Amoco(*)

Bold red print shows RV & Bus parking available or nearby

EXIT		ILLINOIS
		S: Amoco[*], Shell[*]
	Food	S: Dunkin Donuts, Hardee's, Jimmy John's Gourmet Subs, KFC, Little Caesars Pizza, Ponderosa
	Lodg	N: Holiday Inn Express
		S: Comfort Inn, Ottawa Inn, Super 8, The Surrey Motel
	AServ	N: Amoco, Blane's Farm & Fleet, Honda, Ottawa Ford, Ozer Oldsmobile, Pontiac, Truck
		S: Amoco, Lube Max
	TServ	S: International Truck Service
	Med	N: + Hospital
	ATM	S: First National Bank of Ottawa, Union Bank
	Other	N: Classic[CW]
		S: Car Wash, K-Mart[LP, RX], Kroger Supermarket[RX], One Hour Family Optical, U.S. Post Office, Wal-Mart[RX]
93		IL 71, Ottawa, Oswego
	TStop	N: Shell[*, SCALES]
	FStop	N: J&L Gas
	Food	N: PJ's Family Restaurant (Shell), Shell
		S: New Chiam Chinese/American
	AServ	S: Ottawa Collison
	TServ	N: Shell[SCALES]
	ATM	N: Shell
97		Marseilles
	RVCamp	S: Glen Wood RV Resort
105		Seneca
	RVCamp	S: Whispering Pines RV Park[LP] (Sales & Service)
112AB		IL 47, Morris, Yorkville
	TStop	N: Standard[*, SCALES] (Amoco)
	Gas	N: Citgo
		S: Amoco[*], Clark, Mobil, Shell[*, 24]
	Food	N: Denny's (Day's Inn), Holiday Inn, Piggy's (Holiday Inn), R-Place (Standard), Standard (Amoco)
		S: Bob's Hot Dogs, Burger King[PLAY], Hong Kong (Mandarin), KFC, Mara's Diner & Pancake House, Maria's Ristorante Pizza & Meals (Italian), McDonald's, Pizza Hut, Sherwood Oaks Family Restaurant, Taco Bell, Wendy's
	Lodg	N: Comfort Inn, Days Inn, Days Inn, Holiday Inn
		S: Morris Motel, Park Motel, Super 8
	AServ	S: Fisher's Auto Parts, Olson's Quick Lube Service Center, Shell[24], Tafty Chevrolet Buick, Wal-Mart[RX] (Vision)
	TServ	N: Standard[SCALES] (Amoco)
	RVCamp	S: Gebhard Woods State Trail Access (1 Mile)
	Med	S: + Hospital
	ATM	N: Standard (Amoco)
		S: Clark, Grindy National Bank, Shell
	Parks	N: William G Stratton State Park
	Other	N: Cinema
		S: Aldi, Health Mart Drug & Pharmacy[RX], Softe Car Wash, Wal-Mart[RX] (Vision), WalGreens Pharmacy[RX]
(116)		Rest Area (RR, Phones, Vending, P; Southbound)
(116)		Rest Area (RR, Phones, Vending, P; Northbound)
122		Minooka
	FStop	N: Citgo
	Gas	S: Amoco[*]
	Food	S: McDonald's[PLAY], Rosati's Pizza, Sister's Diner, Subway, Wendy's
	AServ	N: Citgo
		S: Simotes Auto
	ATM	S: Amoco, Citizens First National Bank, Founder's Bank
	Other	S: Animal Hospital, Manuka Pharmacy[RX], SuperValu Foods[RX]
126AB		Jct. I-55, St. Louis, Chicago
	RVCamp	S: Leisure Lake Camping
127		Houbolt Rd
	Gas	N: Amoco[*]
	Food	N: Cracker Barrel, Wendy's
	Lodg	N: Fairfield Inn, Hampton Inn, Ramada Inn
130AB		IL 7, Larkin Ave, Joliet, Rockdale
	Gas	N: Citgo[*, LP], Clark[*, LP], Marathon[*], Shell[*, CW], Speedway[*, LP], Thornton's Food Mart[*, LP]
	Food	N: Bob Evan's Restaurant, Boston Market Restaurant, Bulley's BBQ, Burger King, Checker's, Dunkin Donuts, El Famous Burrito, Family Table Restaurant, McDonald's, Old Fashion Restaurant Pancakes, PJ's Italian Food, Pizza Hut, Silverston Family Restaurant, Steak & Shake, Subway, Taco Bell, Wendy's, White Castle Restaurant
	Lodg	N: Comfort Inn, Holiday Inn, Microtel Inn, Motel 6, Red Roof Inn, Super 8 (No Trailers)
	AServ	N: Adam's Pontiac, Bill Jacob's Chevrolet, Car X Muffler, Goodyear Tire & Auto, Meineke Discount Mufflers, NTB, Oldsmobile, GMC, Trucks, Pep Boys Auto Center, Tuffy Auto Center (Mufflers), Tyson Auto Service (Chrylser, Jeep)
	TServ	N: International Trucks Sales & Service Repair
		S: Spring/Align
	Med	N: + Hospital
	ATM	N: Clark, Cub Food[RX], First American, Marathon, Sam's Club, Speedway
	Other	N: Aldi Grocery Store, Animal Medical Center, Bell Ray Farms Fresh Market, Car Wash, Cub Food[RX], K-Mart, Sam's Club, Wal-Mart[24, RX], Whitehand Pantry
131		Midland Ave, Center St, Wheeler Ave.
	AServ	N: Uniroyal Tire & Auto
132AB		Chicago St, U.S. 52 East, IL 53
	Gas	N: King Gas[*]
	Other	N: Coin Operated Laundry, McDonough Food Store, Milano Baking Co.
133		Richards St.
134		Briggs St
	Gas	N: Speedway[*]
		S: Amoco[*], General Store[*, D]
	RVCamp	S: Martin Camper Park (1 Mile)
	Med	N: + Hospital
	ATM	S: Amoco, Bank of Joliet, General Store
137		U.S. 30, Maple St, New Lenox
	Gas	S: Speedway[*, D]
	Food	N: Les Brothers Restaurant
		S: AJ Hot Dogs & Gyros, Burger King, Domino's Pizza, KFC, McDonald's[PLAY], New Lenox Restaurant, Pizza Hut, Pizzano Pizza & Restaurant, Taco Bell, White Horse Inn
	AServ	S: Goodyear
	ATM	S: First Chicago, Jewel/Osco, NISB Bank
	Other	N: K-Mart[RX]
		S: ACE Hardware, Animal Hospital, Coin Operated Laundry, Eagle Country Market, Jewel/Osco, Super Wash, WalGreens Pharmacy[RX]
(143)		Weigh Station (Eastbound)
145AB		U.S. 45, 96th Ave, Monken A. Frankford, Orchard Park
	RVCamp	S: Timber View RV Center[LP] (.8 Miles)
(148)		Weigh Station (Westbound)
148AB		IL 43, Harlem Ave
	Food	N: Burger King[PLAY], Cracker Barrel, Wendy's
	Lodg	N: Budgetel Inn, Fairfield Inn, Hampton Inn, Wingate Inn
	TServ	N: Transportation Trailer Sales
	RVCamp	N: Windy City Beach & Camping Resort (1.75 Miles)
	Parks	N: Kinley Park
151AB		Junction I-57, Chicago, Memphis
154		Kedzie Ave (Eastbound, No Reaccess)
	Med	N: + Hospital
155		I-294 East To Indiana, West To Chicago, Memphis (Toll)
		Note: I-80 runs concurrent below with I-294. Numbering follows I-294.
3		IL 1, Halsted St (Toll)
	Gas	N: Citgo[*, D], Clark, Truck Maintenance Operation (Shell)
	Food	N: Alf's Pub, Burger King, Hot Spot Drive-In, Wendy's, Yellow Ribbon Restaurant
		S: Arby's, Best Western, Boston Market Restaurant, Dunkin Donuts, IHOP, McDonald's, Shooter's Buffet, Subway, Taco Bell, Washington Square Family Restaurant
	Lodg	N: Budgetel Inn, Comfort Suites Hotel, Hampton Inn, Hilton Garden Inn, Holiday Inn Express,

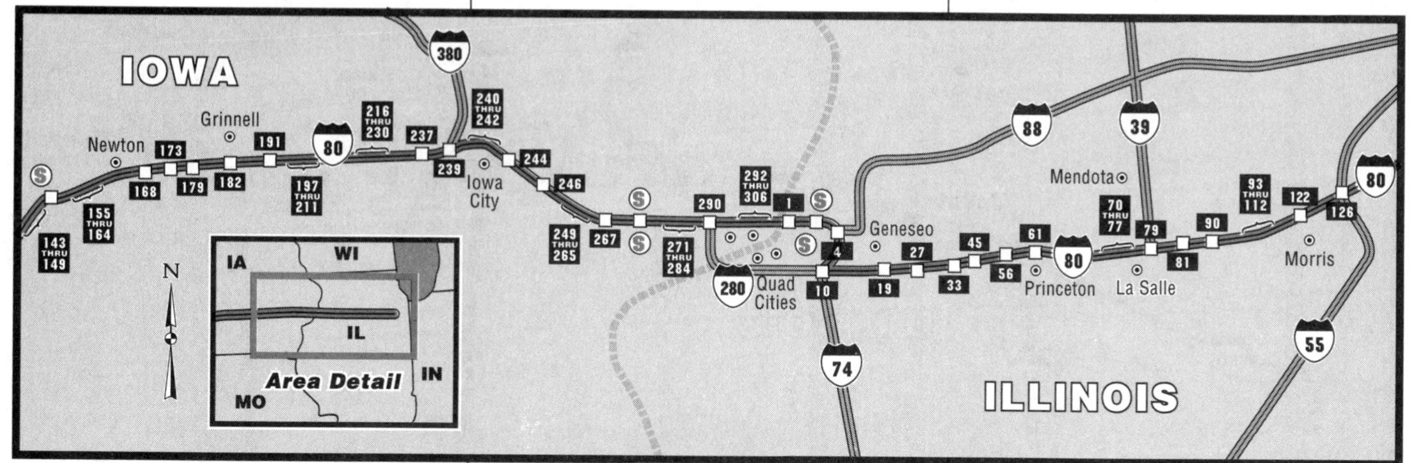

EXIT	ILLINOIS/INDIANA
	Knight's Inn, Ramada, Red Roof Inn, Sleep Inn
	S: Applebee's, Best Western, Days Inn, Motel 6
AServ	**S:** K-Mart(*, 24, RX), Super Trak
TServ	**N:** Road Ready, Ryder, Truck Maintenance Operation (Shell)
RVCamp	**N:** Chicago Heights
ATM	**N:** Clark, Mutual Bank
	S: Beverly Bank
Other	**S:** Builder Square 2(LP), K-Mart(RX)
4	Dixie Highway (Eastbound, No Reaccess)
	Note: I-80 runs concurrent above with I-294. Numbering follows I-294.
(160)	Lincoln Oasis- Rest Area (P)
Gas	**S:** Mobil(*, D)
Food	**S:** Burger King, Mobil, Popeye's Chicken, TCBY (Mobil)
ATM	**S:** Mobil
160A	IL 394, Danville
160B	Junction I-94 West, Chicago
161	U.S. 6, IL 83, Torrence Ave
Gas	**N:** Amoco(*, CW, 24)
	S: Clark(*), Mobil(*, D), Shell(*)
Food	**N:** Arby's, Best Western, Bob Evan's Restaurant, Checkers, Chili's, Hooters, Outrigger's Fish, That Oriental Place (Chinese), Wendy's
	S: Al's Hamburgers, Brown's Chicken, Cafe Borgia (Roman Food), Dairy Queen, Golden Crown Restaurant, McDonald's, Pappy's Gyros
Lodg	**N:** Best Western, Fairfield, Holiday Inn, Red Roof Inn, Super 8
AServ	**N:** Car X Mufflers & Brakes, Firestone Tire & Auto, Goodyear Tire & Auto, Pep Boys, The Big K-Mart(RX)
	S: Jiffy Lube, Mobil, Sam's Club, Shell
Med	**N:** ✚ Ingle's Family Care Center
ATM	**N:** Amoco, US Bank
	S: Advanced Bank
Other	**N:** Convention and Visitors Bureau, Fannie Mae Candies, The Big K-Mart(RX)
	S: Petsmart, Sam's Club

↑ILLINOIS

↓INDIANA

EXIT	INDIANA
1	Calumet Ave, U.S. 41 North
Gas	**N:** Amoco(*, D, CW), Gas City(*)
	S: Marathon(*)
Food	**N:** Rick's Grill, Subway (Amoco)
	S: Boston Market Restaurant, Burger King, Edwardo's Natural Pizza, Taco Bell, Wendy's
Med	**N:** ✚ Hospital
ATM	**N:** Amoco, Gas City, WalGreens Pharmacy(24, RX)
Other	**N:** Calumet Laundromat, WalGreens Pharmacy(RX)
	S: Revco(RX), Sterks Grocery
2AB	U.S. 41 South, IN 152 North, Indianapolis Boulevard
FStop	**S:** Speedway(*, LP, SCALES)
Gas	**N:** Shell(*, CW, 24), Witham's(*)
	S: Amoco(*, 24)
Food	**N:** Arby's, Chop Suey, Dunkin Donuts, Papa John's Pizza, The Wheel, Woodmar Restaurant
	S: Burger King
Lodg	**S:** Ameri-Host Inn
AServ	**N:** Car X Mufflers & Brakes, Midas Muffler & Brake
	S: The Big K-Mart(RX)
Med	**N:** ✚ Hospital
ATM	**N:** Mercantile Nat'l Bank of Indiana, People's Bank
	S: Speedway
Other	**N:** Woodmar Animal Clinic
	S: The Big K-Mart(RX)
3AB	Kennedy Ave
Gas	**S:** Citgo, Clark(LP), Shell, Speedway(*, LP)
Food	**S:** Cracker Barrel, McDonald's, Wendy's
Lodg	**S:** Courtyard, Fairfield Inn, Residence Inn
AServ	**S:** Citgo, One Stop Auto Repair, Shell
ATM	**S:** Clark
5AB	IN 912, Cline Ave
Food	**S:** Bob Evan's Restaurant, Burger King
Lodg	**S:** Holiday Inn, Motel 6, Super 8
AServ	**S:** Michelin Tire Service
TServ	**N:** International Truck Service
	S: Schneider National
Med	**N:** ✚ Hospital
6	Burr St, Gary
TStop	**N:** Pilot(*, D, SCALES, 24)
Gas	**N:** Amoco(*)
	S: Shell(*)
Food	**N:** KFC (Travel Centers of America), Pizza Hut (Travel Centers of America), Ricco's Pizza, Subway (Pilot), Taco Bell (Travel Centers of America), Travel Centers of America(*, D, SCALES)
AServ	**N:** B&G Citgo
TServ	**N:** Speedco Truck Lube, Travel Centers of America(SCALES)
TWash	**N:** Travel Centers of America
RVCamp	**S:** Gerry's RV Park

PRIME OUTLETS
FREMONT
Over 50 Outlet Stores
Polo • Tommy Hilfiger • Nautica
Ask for your FREE COUPON BOOK
219-833-1684
1858
INDIANA • I-80 • EXIT 16

EXIT	INDIANA
ATM	**N:** Amoco, Pilot
	S: Shell
9AB	Grant St
10AB	Broadway
Gas	**N:** Amoco(*, 24)
	S: Amoco(*, 24)
Food	**N:** Broadway BBQ
Med	**N:** ✚ Hospital
11	I-65 South, Indianapolis (Eastbound)
12AB	Junction I-65 North, Gary
13	Central Avenue (Reaccess Westbound Only)
AServ	**S:** Frank's Auto Repair, S & F Tire
Other	**S:** 7 Elephants Deli & Foodmart
15AB	U.S. 6 East, U.S. 20, IN 51, Ripley St
TStop	**N:** Petro(*, SCALES), Travel Port(*, SCALES)
FStop	**N:** Speedway(*, SCALES)
	S: Speedway(*, SCALES)
Gas	**S:** 76(*), Marathon(*, CW)
Food	**N:** Dunkin Donuts (Speedway), McDonald's (Petro)
	S: Arman's Polish Sausage et. al, Long John Silver, Miami Subs, Papa G's Gyros, Ruth & Bud's Grill, Snak Time Family Restaurant
AServ	**N:** Petro
	S: Discount Transmission
TServ	**N:** Travel Port, Weber's
TWash	**N:** Blue Beacon Truck Wash, Murray (Travel Port), Red Baron (Speedway)
ATM	**N:** Machine (Petro)
16	Junction I-90/I-80 (Toll)
Other	**S:** Prime Outlets at Fremont (see our ad this page)
17	Junction I-65, U.S. 12, U.S. 20, Dunes Hwy., Indianapolis
Med	**S:** ✚ Hospital
21	I-80, I-94, U.S. 6, IN. 51 W., Des Moines (Difficult Reaccess)
TStop	**N:** Dunes Plaza(*, 24), Petro(*, SCALES, 24), TravelPort(*, SCALES)
FStop	**N:** Speedway(*, LP, SCALES)
Food	**N:** Buckhorn Family Restaurant (Travelport), Burger King, Iron Skillet Restaurant (Petro), McDonald's(PLAY), Ponderosa, Subway (Travelport), Wing Wah
AServ	**N:** Jiffy Lube
TServ	**N:** Petro, Weber's Truck Repair
TWash	**N:** Blue Beacon Truck Wash (Petro), Murray Truck Wash (Travelport), Red Baron
Other	**N:** Coin Car Wash
(22)	Travel Plaza (Both Directions, RV Parking)

Bold red print shows RV & Bus parking available or nearby

EXIT INDIANA

FStop N: SC(LP, SCALES)
Gas N: BP(*, D)
Food N: Baskin Robbins, Fazoli's Italian Food, Hardee's
Other N: Tourist Info.

23 Portage
Gas S: Amoco, Marathon(*)
Food S: Burger King, Dunkin Donuts, KFC, McDonald's(PLAY), Subway, Wendy's
Lodg N: Lee's Inn
AServ S: Amoco, Marathon, Muffler Shops, Portage Quick Change Oil
ATM N: Pennacle Bank
S: First National, Indiana Federal Bank
Other S: Town & Country Grocery(24), WalGreens Pharmacy(24, RX)

(24) Indiana Toll Plaza (Toll)

31 Indiana 49, Chesterton, Valparaiso
Med S: Hospital
Parks N: Indiana Dunes State Park
Other N: Indiana Dunes National Lakeshore, Tourist Info. (2 Miles)

39 U.S. 421, Michigan City, Westville

49 Indiana 39, La Porte
Lodg S: Cassidy Motel
TServ N: Tomenko Tire & Truck Service
Other S: Kingsbury State Fish & Wildlife Area

(56) Travel Plaza & Service Area
FStop N: SC
Gas N: BP(*, D)
Food N: Baked Goods, Dairy Queen, McDonald's
Other N: Travel Emporium(*)

72 U.S. 31 By - Pass, South Bend, Plymouth, Niles
FStop N: Speedway(*, LP)
Food N: Hardee's (Speedway)

EXIT INDIANA

ATM N: Speedway
Parks S: Potato Creek State Park

77 U.S. 33, Bus. U.S. 31, South Bend, Notre Dame University
Gas S: Amoco(CW, 24), Phillips 66(*, D)
Food N: Burger King, Denny's, Fazoli's Italian Food, J & N Restaurant(24), Marco's Pizza, McDonald's, Pizza Hut, Ponderosa, Steak & Ale, Subway
S: Bennitt's Restaurant, Bill Knapp's Restaurant, Bob Evan's Restaurant, Colonial Pancake House, Donut Delight, King Gyro's, Perkins Family Restaurant, Schlotzsky's Deli, SHONEY'S Shoney's, Wendy's
Lodg N: DAYS INN Days Inn (see our ad this page), Hampton Inn & Suites, Motel 6, Ramada, Super 8
S: Best Inns of America, Holiday Inn, Howard Johnson, Knight's Inn, Signature Inn, St. Mary's Inn
AServ N: Giant Auto Supply
S: Amoco, Q Lube
ATM N: Standard Federal
Other N: All Star Car Wash, Key Bank, North Village Mall, WalGreens Pharmacy(RX)
S: Rose Land Animal Hospital

83 Mishawaka
RVCamp N: KOA Campgrounds

(90) Travel Plaza
FStop N: SC
Gas N: BP(*, D)
Food N: Arby's, Dunkin Donuts, South Bend Chocolate Co.
Other N: Tourist Info.

92 Indiana 19, Elkhart
Gas N: Citgo(*), Phillips 66(*, D)
S: Clark(*), Marathon(*, D)
Food N: Andini Fine Dining, Applebee's, Lee's Famous Recipe Chicken (Phillips 66), Steak 'n Shake
S: Blimpie's Subs, Bob Evan's Restaurant, Burger King, Callahan's(24), DaVincci's Pizza, King Wha Chinese, McDonald's(PLAY), Olive Garden, Perkins Family Restaurant, Red Lobster, Weston Restaurant (Weston Plaza Hotel)
Lodg N: Comfort Inn, Diplomat Motel, Econolodge, Hampton Inn, Holiday Inn Express, Knight's Inn, SHONEY'S Shoney's, Turnpike Motel
S: Budget Inn, Ramada, Red Roof Inn, Signature Inn, Super 8, Weston Plaza Hotel
RVCamp N: American Trailer Supply, Dan's Service Center (Hitches & Trailers), Elkhart Campground (1 Mile), Traveland RV Service, Worldwide RV Sales & Service
ATM N: NBD
S: Key Bank, Marathon
Other N: Aldi Supermarket, K-Mart(RX), Martin's Supermarket, Revco Drugs, Visitor Information
S: Car Wash World

101 IN 15, Bristol, Goshen

EXIT INDIANA/OHIO

RVCamp N: Eby's Pines Camping

107 U.S. 131, Indiana 13, Constantine, Middlebury
FStop N: Mobil(*)
Lodg N: Plaza Motel
AServ N: Dick's Auto Parts
RVCamp S: KOA Campgrounds (1.25 Miles)

121 Indiana 9, Howe, LaGrange
Gas N: J & M Service Center(D)
Food N: Golden Buddha
Lodg N: Green Briar Inn, Travel Inn Motel
S: Super 8
AServ N: J&M Service Center
Med N: Hospital

(126) Service Area
FStop N: SC
Gas N: BP(*, D)
Food N: Baskin Robbins, Fazoli's Italian Food, Hardee's
Other N: Tourist Info.

144 Junction I-69, U.S. 27, Angola, Ft. Wayne, Lansing (Toll)
TStop N: 76 Auto/Truck Plaza(*, SCALES)
FStop S: Pioneer, Speedway(*, SCALES)
Gas S: Marathon(*), Shell(*)
Food N: Baker Street Family Restaurant (76 TS), Subway (76 TS)
S: Deli Mart (Marathon), Hardee's (Speedway), Red Arrow Restaurant(24)
Lodg N: Lake George Inn
S: E&L Motel, Hampton Inn, Holiday Inn Express, Redwood Lodge
TServ N: 76 Auto/Truck Plaza, Gulick Trucks & Parts Service
S: Volvo Dealer
RVCamp S: Yogi Bear Camp Resort
Parks S: Pokagon State Park
Other S: Country Meadows Golf Resort, Horizon Outlet Center

(146) Service Area
FStop N: BP(*, D)
Food N: Baked Goods, Dairy Queen, McDonald's

(153) Indiana Toll Plaza (Toll)

↑INDIANA

↓OHIO

Note: I-80 runs concurrent below with OHTNPK. Numbering follows OHTNPK.

1 Ohio49, Edon, Edgerton, Allen Mi
Gas N: Mobil(*, LP)

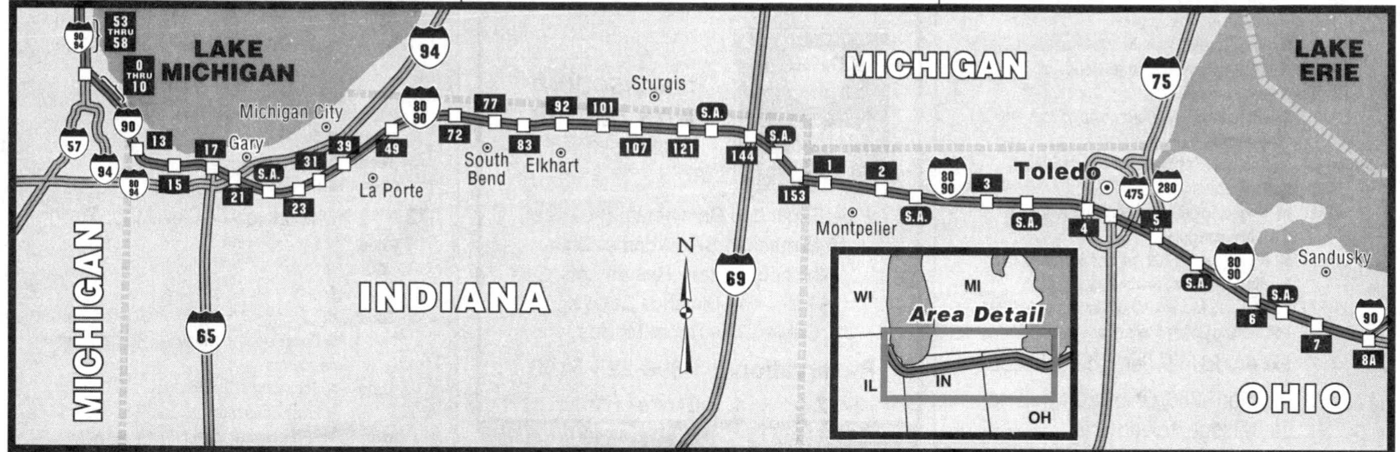

Bold red print shows RV & Bus parking available or nearby

EXIT OHIO

Food N: Burger King
ATM N: Mobil
Other N: Ohio Tourist Center

(2) Ohio Toll Plaza (Toll)

10 Ohio 15, Bryan, Montpelier (Toll)
FStop S: Pennzoil Oil Change[*, D]
Gas S: Marathon[*, D]
Food S: Country Fare, Subway (Marathon)
Lodg S: EconoLodge, Holiday Inn, Rainbow Motel
TServ S: Hutch's Tractor & Trailer Repair
Med S: ✚ Hospital
ATM S: Pennzoil Oil Change

(21) Service Plaza (Eastbound)
FStop B: Sunoco[*]
Food B: Hardee's
AServ B: Sunoco
TServ B: Sunoco
Other N: Tourist Info.

34 Ohio 108, Wauseon (Toll)
FStop S: Hy-Miler[*, D, K, 24] (Shell)
Food S: Hy-Miler (Shell), Smith's
Lodg S: Arrowhead Motor Lodge, Del-Mar Best Western, Super 8
RVCamp S: Executive Travelers Sales & RV Service
ATM S: Hy-Miler (Shell)
Other N: Fulton County Fairgrounds

39 OH. 109, Delta, Lyons (Toll)

(49) Service Area
FStop B: Sunoco[*, D]
Food B: Charlie Brown's Family Restaurant & General Store
AServ B: Sunoco

52 Ohio 2, Toledo Airport, Swanton (Toll)
Lodg S: Toledo Airport[LP]
AServ S: Express Auto, Xpress Auto & Truck Service
TServ S: Xpress Auto & Truck Service
RVCamp S: Storage Rental
Other S: Toledo Airport

59 U.S. 20, to U.S. 23, to I-475, Maumee, Toledo (Toll)
Gas N: Amoco[*], BP[*, D, LP], Speedway[*, D, LP]
S: Amoco[*, D], Speedway[*, LP]
Food N: Arby's, Bentley's (Ramada), Blimpie Subs & Salads, Bob Evan's Restaurant, China Buffet, Connie Mac's Bar and Grill, East of Chicago Pizza Co., Flattop Grill, Little Caesars Pizza, Mark Pi's China Gate Restaurant, Max's Diner, McDonald's, Nick's Cafe, Pizza Hut, Tandoor Indian Restaurant
S: Bavarian Brewing Company, Big Boy, Brandie's Diner, Chi Chi's Mexican Restaurant, Cookie Lady, Fazoli's Italian Food, Fricker's, Friendly's, Popoff's Pizza and Lebanese Food, Ralphie's Burgers, Red Lobster, Schlotzsky's Deli
Lodg N: Budget Inn, Holiday Inn, Motel 6, Ramada
S: Comfort Inn, Cross Country Inn, Days Inn, Hampton Inn, Red Roof Inn
AServ N: Auto Express, Big K-Mart[RX], Kaz's Auto Center, Murry's Discount Auto Store, Napa Auto, Tom's Tire & Auto
S: Bob Schmidt GM, Harmon Auto Glass, Hatfield Oldsmobile
RVCamp S: Maumee Mobile Home Court (.5 Miles)
Med N: ✚ Hospital
ATM N: Amoco, Toledo Area Catholic Credit Union
S: Huntington Bank
Other N: Big K-Mart[RX], Putt Putt Golf & Games, Southwyck Lanes, Southwyck Mall
S: Maumee Market, Maumee Sports Mall (Putt Putt, Batting Cage), Meijer Grocery

72 Exit 4A, Jct I-75, Perrysburg, Toledo

71 Junction I-280, Ohio 420, to I-75, to Stony Ridge, Toledo (Toll)

EXIT OHIO

TStop N: Flying J Travel Plaza[*, D, LP, K, SCALES], Petro[*, D, LP, SCALES, 24], Stoney Ridge Truck Plaza[*, D, SCALES]
S: 76 Auto/Truck Plaza[*, D, SCALES, 24], TravelCenters of America[*, D, SCALES, 24]
FStop N: Johnny's On the Spot Fuel Stop[D]
S: Speedway[*, D, SCALES, 24]
Food N: Crossroad's Family Restaurant (Howard Johnson), Flying J Travel Plaza, Iron Skillet (Petro), Krispy Kreme Doughnuts (Petro), Pizza Hut (Petro), Stoney Ridge Truck Plaza
S: 76 Auto/Truck Plaza, Country Pride (TA), McDonald's, Sbarro Pizza (TA), Wendy's
Lodg N: Budget Inn, Howard Johnson, Knight's Inn, Ramada Limited, Stoney Ridge Motel
TServ N: Speedco[24], Stoney Ridge Truck Plaza[SCALES]
S: 76 Auto/Truck Plaza[SCALES, 24], Fleet Tire Center, TravelCenters of America[SCALES, 24], Williams Detroit Diesel
TWash N: Petro
S: Stony Ridge Truck Wash (TS), TravelCenters of America
ATM N: Flying J Travel Plaza

(77) Service Plaza
FStop B: Sunoco[*, D]
Food B: Fresh Fried Chicken, Hardee's
AServ B: Sunoco
Other B: Tourist Info.

81 OH 51, Elmore, Woodville, Gibsonburg

91 Ohio 53, Fremont, Port Clinton (Toll)
FStop S: Shell[*, D, 24]
Food N: Days Inn, Sneaky Fox Steak House
S: Buffet (Holiday Inn), Shell
Lodg N: Best Budget Inn, Days Inn
S: Fremont Turnpike Motel, Holiday Inn
AServ S: Nickel's Service
Med S: ✚ Hospital

Newly Renovated!
1512

216-324-5411
• Mr. D's Restaurant on Premises
• Adjacent to Midway Mall & Movie Theater
• Meetings & Banquets up to 300 people
We help simplify your life by providing AT&T communications from every room. And be sure to use the Call ATT Calling Card for all your calls and to access a range of timesaving calling features. To order a card, dial:
AT&T
1-800-CALL AT&T
OHIO ▪ I-80 ▪ EXIT 145

1225

10% DISCOUNT WITH THIS AD!
(Code LEXIT)
Free Expanded Continental Breakfast
15 Minutes to Sea World of Ohio
Whirlpool Suites / Restaurants
AT&T Long Distance Service
Cable TV/In Room Movies
Reservations: 1-800-228-5150
330-626-5511 • Streetsboro, OH
OHIO ▪ I-80 ▪ EXIT 187

EXIT OHIO

(100) Commodore Perry Service Plaza
FStop B: Sunoco[*]
Food B: Rax[D]
AServ B: Sunoco
Other B: Travel Information

110 OH 4, Sandusky, Bellevue

118 U.S. 250, Sandusky, Norwalk (Toll)
Gas N: Marathon[*], Speedway[*]
Food N: Dick's Place, Fun Chaser's Ice Cream, Marathon, McDonald's, Subway
S: Colonial Inn South, Homestead Farm
Lodg N: Comfort Inn, Days Inn, Hampton Inn, Homestead Inn, Motel 6, Ramada Limited, Super 8
S: Colonial Inn South, Homestead Farm
AServ S: Dorr Chevrolet/Geo
RVCamp N: Holiday Trav-L-Park[*, LP], Milan Travel Park (.25 Miles)
ATM N: Marathon
Other N: Lake Erie Factory Outlet Center

136 Vermilion, Vaumhart Rd.

(139) Service Plaza
FStop B: Sunoco[*, D, LP, 24]
Food B: Bob's Big Boy, Burger King, TCBY
AServ B: Sunoco[24]
TServ B: Sunoco[24]

143 Jct. I-90, Ohio 2 (Toll)

145 Ohio 57, Lorain, Elyria (Toll)
Gas N: BP[*, CW], BP[*, D], Speedway[*, D]
S: Shell[*, 24]
Food N: Arby's, Bob Evan's Restaurant, Country Kitchen, Delphine Restaurant, Funtime Family Fun Center, McDonald's (BP), McDonald's, Mountain Jack's Restaurant, Pizza Hut, Red Lobster, Tavern On The Mall, Wendy's
S: Mario's Restaurant (Ramada Inn)
Lodg N: Best Western, Camelot Inn, Comfort Inn, Days Inn, EconoLodge, Holiday Inn (see our ad this page)
S: Howard Johnson, Journey Inn, Ramada Inn
AServ N: Conrad's Total Car Care & Tire Center, Firestone Tire & Auto, Grease Monkey, Sears (Midway Mall), Tuffy Auto Center
Med S: ✚ Hospital
ATM N: BP, Lorain National Bank, Lowe's, National City Bank, Northern Savings & Loan Co., Star Bank
Other N: Funtime Family Fun Center, K-Mart, Lazer Clean Car Wash[24], Lowe's, Midway Mall, Ryko Auto Car Wash, White Glove Car Wash
S: Belle Coin Laundry

151 Junction I-80, I-480, North Ridgeville, Cleveland (Toll)

158 Ohio State Penitentiary, To North Olmstead, Cleveland (Difficult Reaccess)
RVCamp S: Crystal Springs (1.5 Miles)

161 Junction I-71, U.S. 42, Strongsville, Cleveland

(170) Towpath Service Plaza
FStop B: Sunoco[*, D]
Food B: McDonald's
AServ B: Sunoco

173 Ohio 21, to I-77, Cleveland, Akron
FStop S: Speedway[*, LP]
Gas N: Clark[*]
S: BP[*]
Food N: Lake Motel[24], My Place (Scottish Inns)
S: Dairy Queen, Holiday Inn, Richfield Family Restaurant
Lodg N: Lake Motel, Scottish Inns
S: Brushwood Motel, Holiday Inn, Super 8
AServ S: BP, Richfield Radiator Repair

Bold red print shows RV & Bus parking available or nearby

EXIT	OHIO
TServ	N: Exit 11 Truck Sales & Tire
180	Ohio 8, to I-90, Akron, Jct. I-271
187	Junction I-480, Ohio 14, Streetsboro (Toll)
Gas	S: Amoco[*, D], Dairy Mart[*]
Food	S: Bob Evan's Restaurant, Burger Central Restaurant, Golden Flames Steakhouse, **McDonald's**[PLAY], Perkin's Family Restaurant
Lodg	S: Comfort Inn (see our ad at opposite page), Fairfield Inn, Microtel Inn & Suites, Palms Motel, **Super 8 (see our ad at this page)**
AServ	S: Clubman Motor Works, Defer Tire, Alignment, & Brakes, Streetsboro Foreign Auto, **Wal-Mart**[RX]
Med	S: **+ Med Center One**
ATM	S: First Merit, Huntington Bank, **McDonald's**
Other	S: **CVS Pharmacy**[RX], **Country Counter Stop N Shop, Streetsboro Market Square, Wal-Mart**[RX]
193	Ravenna Rd., OH 44
Med	S: **+ Hospital**
(197)	**Brady's Service Plaza**
FStop	B: **Sunoco**[*, D]
Food	B: Dunkin Donuts, Popeye's Chicken, TCBY, Taco Bell
AServ	B: **Sunoco**
209	Ohio 5, Warren
TStop	S: **Judy & J's**[*, D, LP]
Food	S: **Judy & J's**
Lodg	N: **Budget Lodge**
	S: **Rodeway Inn**
TServ	S: **Judy & J's**
RVCamp	S: **Camping**
ATM	S: **Judy & J's**
Other	N: Paul Tessler Golf Course
215	Lordstown (Eastbound, Reaccess Westbound Only)

EXIT	OHIO
216	Lordstown (Westbound, Reaccess Eastbound Only)
219	Junction I-76, I-80 East

Note: I-80 runs concurrent above with OHTNPK. Numbering follows OHTNPK.

EXIT	OHIO
223AB	Ohio 46, Niles
TStop	N: **Universal Truck Plaza**[SCALES]
	S: **76 Auto/Truck Plaza**[RV DUMP, SCALES]
FStop	S: **Fuel Mart**[*], **Speedway**[*, LP]
Gas	N: Citgo[*, LP]
	S: BP[*, D], Sunoco[*]
Food	N: Bob Evan's Restaurant, Burger King, **Country Kitchen (Universal Truck Plaza), NT Mugs (Budget Inn)**
	S: Antone's, Arby's, **Cracker Barrel (Bus Parking)**, McDonald's, Perkins Family Restaurant, Subway (Sunoco), Taco Bell, The Ranch Family Restaurant, Wendy's, Winston's Tavern (Best Western)
Lodg	N: **Budget Luxury Inn (Universal Truck Plaza), TraveLodge**
	S: Best Western, Hampton Inn, Knight's Inn, **Super 8**
TServ	N: **CB Repair, Universal Truck Plaza**
	S: **76 Auto/Truck Plaza, Freightliner Dealer**
TWash	N: **Universal Truck Plaza**
	S: **76 Auto/Truck Plaza**
ATM	N: Citgo
Other	N: Coin Car Wash
224	Ohio 11 South, Canfield
224B	I-680, Youngstown
226	Salt Springs Rd, to McDonald
TStop	S: **Petro**[SCALES], **Pilot Travel Center**[SCALES]
FStop	S: **Mr. Fuel**
Gas	N: Shell[*, D, CW]
Food	N: McDonald's, Summit Carry-Out & Deli
	S: **Arby's (Pilot Travel Center)**, Baskin Robbins, **Iron Skillet (Pilot Travel Center)**
TServ	S: **Petro, Pilot Travel Center**
TWash	S: **Eagle One (Pilot Travel Center), Frank's Truck Wash (Petro TStop)**
227	U.S. 422, Girard
Gas	N: Amoco[*], McQuaids[*], Shell[*, D, CW]
Food	N: Burger King, Dairy Queen, Jab Hotdog Shop, Rocco's Pizza
Lodg	N: Days Inn (see our ad this page)
ATM	N: Charter One Bank
228	Ohio 11, Warren, Ashtabula (Left Exit Eastbound)
229	Ohio 193, Belmont Ave
Gas	N: Shell, Speedway[*]
	S: Amoco[*], Rich, Speedway[*]
Food	N: **Days Inn**, Granny's Home Cooking, Handel's Ice Cream, Ramada Inn, Station Square, Tally Ho Tel
	S: Antone's Restaurant, Arby's, Armando's Italian, Arthur Treacher's Fish & Chips, Bob Evan's Restaurant, C.R. Berry's Burgers, Cancun Restaurant, Inner Circle Pizza, Long John Silver, McDonald's, Perkins Family Restaurant, Pizza Hut, Taco Bell, Western Sizzlin'
Lodg	N: Days Inn, Holiday Inn, Motel 6, Ramada Inn, **Super 8 (see our ad this page)**
	S: Comfort Inn, Econolodge
AServ	N: Pennzoil Oil Change
	S: Goodyear Tire & Auto, Monroe Muffler & Brakes, Super Shop Automotive Performance Centers
Med	S: **+ Hospital**
ATM	N: Charter One Bank
	S: Bank One, Home Savings and Loan Company,

330-544-1301
Niles, Ohio
DAYS INN
• Restaurant Nearby
• Continental Breakfast Included
• Kids Under 12 Stay Free
• Tennis/Golf Nearby
• Interior Corridors
• 25" Remote Control TV w/HBO
OHIO • I-80 • EXIT 227

1753
Super 8 Motel
4250 Belmont Ave
Youngstown, OH 44505
330-759-0040
Free Coffee & Breakfast
Restaurant & Bar on Premises
Bus Parking
Free Cable w/HBO/ESPN
Free Local Calls
Near Shopping Mall, Museum, Airport and 30 Golf Courses
OHIO • I-80 • EXIT 229

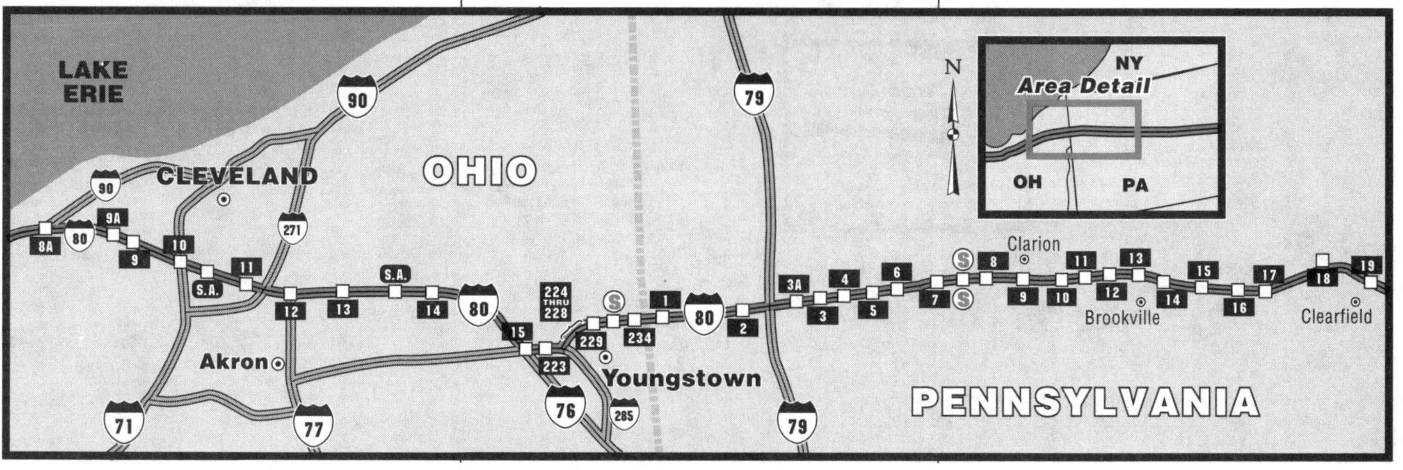

Bold red print shows RV & Bus parking available or nearby

EXIT OHIO/PENNSYLVANIA

Mahoning National Bank, Metropolitan Savings Bank
Other N: Hi Land Foods(*)
S: Big John's Car Wash, Phar Mor Drugs

(232) Weigh Station (Westbound)

234B U.S. 62, Ohio 7, to Hubbard, Sharon
RVCamp N: Homestead Campground (2 Miles)

(236) OH Welcome Center (RR, Phones, Picnic; Westbound)

↑OHIO

↓PENNSYLVANIA

(1) PA Welcome Center (RR, Phones, Picnic; Eastbound)

1 **(5)** PA 18, PA 60, Sharon, Hermitage

2 **(15)** U.S. 19, Mercer
Gas N: Amoco, Citgo
Food N: Howard Johnson, McDonald's
Lodg N: Howard Johnson
AServ N: Amoco, Exit 2 Tire & Service
RVCamp N: Evergreen Trailer Sales, Inc.(LP) (1.5 Miles)
S: KOA Campgrounds, The Junction 19-80 Campground (.25 Miles)
Other N: PA. State Police Patrol Post, Tourist Info.

2A **(119)** Junction I-79, Erie, Pittsburgh

3A **(24)** PA 173, Sandy Lake, Grove City
Med S: ✚ Hospital
Other S: Wendall August Forge

3 **(29)** PA 8, Barkeyville, Franklin
TStop N: Phoenix Auto Truck Plaza(*, LP)
S: Kwick Fill(*, SCALES), TravelCenters of America(*, SCALES)
FStop S: Citgo(*, 24)
Food N: Burger King, Country Kettle (Phoenix TS), Kings Family Restaurant(24)
S: Country Pride (TravelCenters of America), Kimberly's Restaurant, Roadhouse Restaurant (Kwik Fill), Subway (TravelCenters of America)
Lodg N: Days Inn
S: Kwick Fill
TServ N: Diesel Injection, Phoenix Auto Truck Plaza
S: Kwick Fill(SCALES)
TWash S: Kwick Fill
RVCamp N: Dennis Trailer Sales(LP) (2.5 Miles)
ATM N: Phoenix Auto Truck Plaza

(31) Rest Area (RR, Phones, Picnic, Vending; Westbound)

4 **(35)** PA 308, Clintonville
FStop N: Gulf(*, LP)

EXIT PENNSYLVANIA

TServ N: Kenworth Motor Truck Equipment
ATM N: Gulf

5 **(42)** PA 38, Emlenton
TStop N: Emlenton Truck Plaza(*, SCALES)
FStop N: Texaco(*, D, 24)
Food N: Emlenton Truck Plaza
Lodg N: Emlenton Motor Inn (Emlenton TS)
AServ N: Snyder Bros. Auto Service & Towing
TServ N: Emlenton Truck Plaza(SCALES)
RVCamp N: Candlelight Campground, Gaslight Campground (.25 Miles)
ATM N: Emlenton Truck Plaza

6 **(46)** PA 478, Emlenton, St Petersburg (Closed Due to Construction)

7 **(54)** to PA 338, Knox
FStop N: Gulf(*)
Food N: B.J.'s Eatery
Lodg N: Wolf's Den Bed and Breakfast
TServ S: Good Tire Service
RVCamp N: Wolf's Camping Resort (.13 Miles)

(57) Weigh Station

8 **(60)** PA 66 North, Shippenville
Gas N: Citgo(*)
Food N: Citgo
ATM N: Citgo
Other N: Pennsylvania State Patrol Post

9 **(62)** PA 68, Clarion
Gas N: BP(24), Exxon(*), Kwick Fill(*, D)
Food N: Arby's, Burger King, Long John Silver, Perkins Family Restaurant, Pizza Hut, Subway (BP), Taco Bell, Timberlands Restaurant (Holiday Inn)
Lodg N: Comfort Inn, Days Inn, Holiday Inn, Super 8
AServ N: Wal-Mart(RX)
Med N: ✚ Hospital
Other N: Clarion Mall, Wal-Mart(RX)

10 **(65)** PA 66 South, Clarion, New Bethlehem

11 **(71)** U.S. 322, Strattanville
TStop N: Keystone Short Way(*)
FStop N: Exxon(*)
Food N: Keystone Short Way
TServ N: Keystone Short Way
ATM N: Keystone Short Way

12 **(73)** PA 949, Corsica
Parks N: Clear Creek State Park (12 Miles)
Other S: U.S. Post Office

13 **(78)** PA 36, Sigel, Brookville
TStop N: TravelCenters of America(*, RV DUMP, SCALES)
FStop N: Agway(*)
Gas S: BP(*), Citgo(*, D), Exxon(*, LP), Sunoco(*, LP, 24)
Food N: Country Pride (TravelCenters of America), Dairy Queen, KFC, McDonald's(PLAY), Pizza Hut, Taco Bell

EXIT PENNSYLVANIA

(TravelCenters of America)
S: American Hotel Restaurant, Arby's, Burger King, Days Inn, Jerry's Subs & Pizza (BP), Subway, The Gold Eagle (Budget Host)
Lodg N: Howard Johnson, Super 8
S: Budget Host, Days Inn, Holiday Inn Express
AServ N: Napa Auto, Stultz Pontiac, Buick, Cadillac, Oldsmobile
S: Payless Oil Lube, Wasko Chrysler, Plymouth, Dodge, Jeep
TServ N: TravelCenters of America(SCALES)
RVCamp N: Dales Smith's Camper Sales (2 Miles)
Med S: ✚ The Brookville Hospital, ✚ The Charles Medical Center
ATM S: Citgo, S & T Bank
Other N: Barber Shop (TravelCenters Of America), Coin Laundry (TravelCenters of America)
S: Coin Car Wash

14 **(81)** PA 28, Hazen

15 **(87)** PA 830, Reynoldsville
TStop S: Diamond J's Truck & Auto Stop(*, SCALES)
Gas S: Diamond J's(*, CW)
Food S: Diamond J's Truck & Auto Stop
Lodg S: Diamond J's Truck & Auto Stop
AServ S: Diamond J's
TServ S: Diamond J's Truck & Auto Stop(SCALES)
ATM S: Diamond J's
Other N: Airport
S: Coin Laundry (Diamond J's)

(88) Rest Area (RR, Phones, Picnic, Vending; Westbound)

16 **(97)** U.S. 219, Du Bois, Brockway
TStop S: Pilot(*, D, SCALES), Sheetz Truckstop(*)
Gas S: BP(*)
Food S: Arby's (Pilot), Dutch Pantry, Fogarty's (Holiday Inn), Sheetz Truckstop, T.J. Cinnamons (Pilot)
Lodg S: Holiday Inn, Miller's Motel
AServ S: Express Lube
Med S: ✚ Hospital
ATM S: Sheetz Truckstop
Other N: Allagheny National Forest

17 **(101)** PA 255, Du Bois, Penfield
Gas N: Amoco(*)
Food N: Jessie's Super Mart
Lodg S: Ramada
RVCamp N: Campground
Med S: ✚ Hospital
Other S: Pennsylvania State Patrol Post

18 **(111)** PA 153, Pennfield
Med S: ✚ Hospital
Parks N: Parker Dam State Park, S.B. Elliott State Park

19 **(120)** PA 879, Clearfield, Shawville
TStop N: Sapp Brothers(*, SCALES)

Bold red print shows RV & Bus parking available or nearby

EXIT PENNSYLVANIA

Gas S: Amoco(*), BP(*)
Food N: Best Western, Sapp Brothers
S: Arby's(PLAY), Burger King, Dutch Pantry, McDonald's, Subway (Inside BP)
Lodg N: Best Western, Sapp Brothers
S: Comfort Inn, Days Inn, Super 8
AServ S: Fullington Buick, Oldsmobile, GMC Truck, Cadillac, Wal-Mart(RX)
TServ N: Sapp Brothers(SCALES)
Med S: Hospital
Other S: Wal-Mart(RX)

20 **(123)** PA 970, Woodland , Shawville
FStop S: Pacific Pride Commercial Fueling(*)

21 **(133)** PA 53, Kylertown, Philipsburg
TStop N: Kwik Fill TS(*, SCALES)
Gas N: Sunoco(*)
S: Citgo
Food N: Napoli's Pizza (Sunoco), Roadhouse Restaurant (Kwik Fill TS)
Lodg N: Kwik Fill TS
AServ S: Citgo
TServ N: E & E Truck Supply, Kwik Fill TS(SCALES)
Med S: Hospital
ATM N: Midstate Bank
Parks N: Black Moshannon State Park
Other N: Coin Laundry, U.S. Post Office

(146) Rest Area (RR, Phones, Picnic, Vending)

22 **(147)** PA 144, Snow Shoe
FStop N: Citgo Show Shoe Truck Plaza, Exxon(*)
Food N: Mountaintop Restaurant (Citgo), Snow Shoe 22 Restaurant (Exxon), Snow Shoe Sandwich Shop
AServ N: Exxon
TServ N: Citgo Show Shoe Truck Plaza, Exxon
RVCamp N: Snow Shoe Park (.5 Miles)
ATM N: Citgo Show Shoe Truck Plaza, Exxon
Other N: IGA Store

23 **(158)** U.S. 220 South, PA 150, Altoona, Milesburg
TStop N: Citgo Truck & Auto Plaza(*), Travel Port(*, SCALES)
Gas N: Amoco(*, LP), Mobil(*, D)
Food N: Buckhorn's Family Restaurant (Travelport), Citgo Truck & Auto Plaza, Holiday Inn, McDonald's, Subway (Amoco)
Lodg N: Citgo Truck & Auto Plaza, Holiday Inn
TServ N: Citgo Truck & Auto Plaza, Travel Port(SCALES)
RVCamp N: Bald Eagle State Park
ATM N: Amoco, Travel Port
Other S: Pennsylvania State Patrol Post

24 **(161)** PA 26, Bellefonte
FStop S: Pacific Pride Commercial Fueling, Texaco
Gas S: Exxon
Food S: Catherman's
AServ S: Exxon, Texaco
TServ S: Texaco
RVCamp N: Fort Bellefonte Campground (1 Mile), KOA Campgrounds (2 Miles)

(171) Parking Area (Picnic; Eastbound)

25 **(173)** PA 64, Lamar
TStop S: T/A TravelCenters of America(*, SCALES)
FStop N: Texaco(*)
Gas N: Gulf
S: Citgo(*), T/A TravelCenters of America(*)
Food N: McDonald's, The Cottage Family Restaurant
S: Sub Express (Citgo), Subway (Truckstop), T/A TravelCenters of America
Lodg N: Comfort Inn, Traveler's Delite Motel
AServ N: Gulf
S: Citgo
TServ S: T/A TravelCenters of America(SCALES)
ATM N: Texaco

26 **(178)** U.S. 220, Lock Haven
Gas S: Exxon(*, D), Sunoco(*, D)
AServ S: Exxon, Sunoco

27 **(186)** PA 477, Loganton
Gas N: Gulf
S: Citgo
Food N: Homemade Ice Cream
S: Watt's Family Restaurant
AServ N: Gulf
RVCamp N: Holiday Pines Campground (2 Miles)

28 **(193)** PA 880, Jersey Shore
FStop N: Citgo(*)
Gas S: BP(*, D)
Food N: Pit Stop Restaurant(24)
Med S: Hospital

(194) Weigh Station, Rest Area (RR, Phones, Picnic, Vending)

29 **(199)** Mile Run

30AB **(210)** U.S. 15, 30A - Lewisburg, Williamsport
Gas S: Citgo(*, K)
Food S: Bonanza (Comfort Inn)
Lodg S: Comfort Inn, Holiday Inn Express
RVCamp S: Nintony Mountain Campground (5 Miles), Willow Lake Campground
Med S: Hospital (U.S.15 South)
ATM S: Citgo

31AB **(212)** Junction I-180, PA 147, Williamsport, Milton

32 **(215)** PA 254, Limestoneville
TStop N: Milton 32 Truck Plaza(*, RV DUMP, SCALES)
S: Petro TS(*, SCALES)
Food N: Milton 32 Truck Plaza
S: Petro TS
TServ N: Milton 32 Truck Plaza(SCALES)
S: Petro TS(SCALES)
ATM N: Milton 32 Truck Plaza
S: Petro TS

(219) Rest Area (RR, Phones, Picnic, Vending; Eastbound)

(220) Rest Area (Westbound, Closed for Construction)

33 **(224)** PA 54, Danville
FStop N: Amoco(*, D)
S: Texaco(*)
Gas N: Mobil(*)
S: Citgo(*)
Food N: Ming's (Howard Johnson), Subway (Amoco)
S: Days Inn, Dutch Pantry, Friendly's, McDonald's(PLAY)
Lodg N: Howard Johnson
S: Days Inn, Red Roof Inn, TraveLodge
Med S: Hospital

34 **(232)** PA 42, Buckhorn
TStop N: Travel Port(*, SCALES)
Gas N: Texaco(*)
Food N: Buckhorn's (Travelport), Burger King(PLAY), KFC, Perkins Family Restaurant, Subs Now (Texaco), Subway (Travel Port TS), TCBY (Texaco), Wendy's, Western Sizzlin'
Lodg N: Econolodge, Quality Inn
TServ N: Travel Port(SCALES)
ATM N: Texaco
Other N: Columbia Mall

35AB **(236)** PA 487, Lightstreet, Bloomsburg
Gas S: Coastal(*, LP)
Food S: Coastal, Denny's, The Inn at Turkey Hill
Lodg S: The Inn at Turkey Hill
Med S: Hospital
ATM S: Columbia Country Farmers Nat'l Bank

Other S: Tourist Info.

36 **(241)** U.S. 11, Lime Ridge, Berwick

37 **(242)** PA 339, Mifflinville, Mainville
TStop N: Brennan's Auto/Truck Plaza(*)
FStop N: Gulf(*)
Gas N: Brennan's Auto/Truck Plaza(*)
Food N: Brennan's Auto/Truck Plaza, McDonald's, Spur's Steak & Ribs
Lodg N: Super 8
TServ N: Brennan's Auto/Truck Plaza
S: Minuteman Towing(24)

(246) Weigh Station/Rest Area (RR, Phones, Picnic, Vending)

38 **(256)** PA 93, Conyngham, Nescopeck
TStop N: Pilot Travel Center(*, SCALES)
Gas N: Sunoco
S: Texaco(*)
Food N: Subway (Pilot)
Lodg S: Days Inn
AServ N: Sunoco
TServ S: Drumm's Truck Service
RVCamp N: Campground, Council Cup Campground, Moyers Grove Campground
Med S: Hospital
ATM N: Pilot Travel Center

38A **(260)** Junction I-81, Harrisburg, Wilkes - Barre

39 **(263)** PA 309, Mountain Top, Hazleton
FStop N: Mountain View
S: Amoco(*, 24)
Gas N: Texaco(*)
Food N: Kisenwether's Family Restaurant, Mountain View
Lodg N: Econolodge
AServ N: Kisenwether's Truck Service
TServ N: Kisenwether's Truck Service
RVCamp N: KOA Campgrounds (.5 Miles)
Med S: Hospital
ATM N: Mountain View

(270) Rest Area (RR, Phones, Picnic; Eastbound)

40 **(273)** PA 940, PA 437, White Haven, Freeland
Gas N: Amoco(*), Mobil(*)
Food N: Subs Now (Amoco)
AServ S: Schlier's Towing & Auto Service
TServ S: Schlier's Towing & Auto Service
RVCamp S: Sandy Valley Campground

41 **(274)** PA 534, Hickory Run
TStop N: Bandit Truckstop(*), Hickory Run Plaza(*)
Gas N: Bandit Truckstop(*)
Food N: Bandit Truckstop, Hickory Run Plaza
RVCamp S: Lehigh Gorge Campground (.75 Miles)
ATM N: Bandit Truckstop, Hickory Run Plaza
Parks S: Hickory Run State Park

42 **(277)** PA Tnpk, PA 940, Wilkes Barre, Allentown
Gas N: Amoco(*), Exxon, Texaco(*)
Food N: Arby's, Burger King, Famosa Pizza & Subs, McDonald's
Lodg N: Howard Johnson
ATM N: Amoco

43 **(284)** PA 115, Blakeslee
Gas S: Exxon(*)
Food S: Pizz-Nut
AServ S: Exxon
RVCamp N: Fern Ridge Campground (.75 Miles)
ATM S: Exxon
Other N: State Police

45A **(293)** Junction I-380 West, Scranton

Bold red print shows RV & Bus parking available or nearby

EXIT	PENNSYLVANIA
(295)	**Rest Area (RR, Phones, Picnic, Vending; Eastbound)**
44	**(299)** PA611, Scotrun (Westbound, Reaccess Eastbound Only)
Gas	**N:** Sunoco[*, D]
Food	**N:** Scotrun Diner
Lodg	**N:** Scotrun Motel
AServ	**N:** Steve's Auto Service, Sunoco
RVCamp	**N: Campground**
45	**(298)** PA 715, Tannersville (Camelback Ski Area)
Gas	**N:** BP[*], Mobil[*] **S:** Amoco, Exxon[*, CW]
Food	**N:** Billy's Pocono Diner **S:** Tannersville Diner, Train- Coach Restaurant[24]
Lodg	**N:** Pocono Lodge **S:** Best Western
AServ	**S:** Amoco, Schlier's Towing
RVCamp	**N: Maplerock Campground**
ATM	**N:** Mellon Bank, Mobil **S:** Exxon
Parks	**N: Big Pocono State Park (6 Miles)**
Other	**N: The Crossings Factory Outlet**
46B	**(303)** PA 611, Bartonsville
TStop	**N: Pocono Mountain Travel Center[SCALES], Pocono Two-Way CB Shop**
FStop	**N: Texaco[*, SCALES]**
Gas	**N: Pocono Mountain Travel Center**
Food	**N:** Down Under (Holiday Inn), **Pizza Hut (Pocono TS), Subway (Pocono TS), TCBY (Pocono TS), Taco Bell (Pocono TS)**
Lodg	**N: Comfort Inn**, Holiday Inn
AServ	**N: Pat & Red's Tire Service**
TServ	**N: 24 Hr Tire & Towing, Pat & Red's Tire Service**
TWash	**N: Texaco**
46A	**(303)** to South PA 33, to South U.S. 209, Snydersville (Westbound)
47	**(304)** Ninth St, Bushkill (Eastbound, Reaccess Westbound Only)
Food	**N:** Arby's, Beef and Ale Restaurant, Boston Market Restaurant, Burger King, Dunkin Donuts, Fat Cat Pizza 2, McDonald's[PLAY], Pizza Hut, Ponderosa
AServ	**N:** Abeloff Pontiac, GMC Truck, Grey Chevrolet, Oldsmobile, Cadillac, Geo
ATM	**N:** Mellon Bank, Nazareth National Bank, PNC Bank
Other	**N:** CVS Pharmacy[RX], Colonial Bowling Lanes, Sav A Lot Food Stores, **Stroud Mall**
48	**(305)** U.S. 209 Business, Main St
Gas	**N:** Gulf, Mobil[*] **S:** Texaco[*]
Food	**N: Perkins Family Restaurant** **S:** Mommies' Coffee Shop (Texaco)
Lodg	**N:** Four Points Hotel Sheraton
AServ	**N:** Gulf **S:** Bud Warners Auto Garage
TServ	**S: Claude Cypher's Truck Parts**
Other	**S:** Texaco
49	**(306)** Dreher Ave (Westbound, Reaccess Eastbound Only)
50	**(307)** PA 191, Broad St
Gas	**S:** Sunoco[*, 24]
Food	**N:** KFC, McDonald's[24] **S:** Compton's Pancake House, Taco Bell (Sunoco)
Lodg	**N:** Best Western **S:** Days Inn
AServ	**N:** Napa Auto
Med	**N: + Hospital**
ATM	**N:** First Union Bank
51	**(308)** East Stroudsburg
Gas	**N:** Texaco[*]
Food	**N:** Kasa's Pizzeria

EXIT	PENNSYLVANIA/NEW JERSEY
	S: Budget Motel
Lodg	**S:** Budget Motel, Super 8
AServ	**N:** Schlier's Service Center
Med	**N: + Hospital**
ATM	**N:** Texaco, **Wawa Food Market**
Other	**N: Wawa Food Market**
52	**(309)** U.S. 209, PA 447, Marshalls Creek
Gas	**N:** Gulf
Food	**N:** Landmark Family Restaurant, Mosier Dairy & Deli[*, LP], Shannon Inn & Pub
AServ	**N:** Gulf
RVCamp	**N: Happy Campers RV Service**
Med	**N: + Hospital**
53	**(310)** PA 611S, Delaware Water Gap
Gas	**S:** Amoco[*], Gulf
Food	**S:** Gateway in the Gap (Ramada), Water Gap Diner
Lodg	**S:** Ramada
AServ	**S:** Gulf
ATM	**S:** Amoco
Other	**S: Delaware Gap Recreation Area**

↑PENNSYLVANIA

↓NEW JERSEY

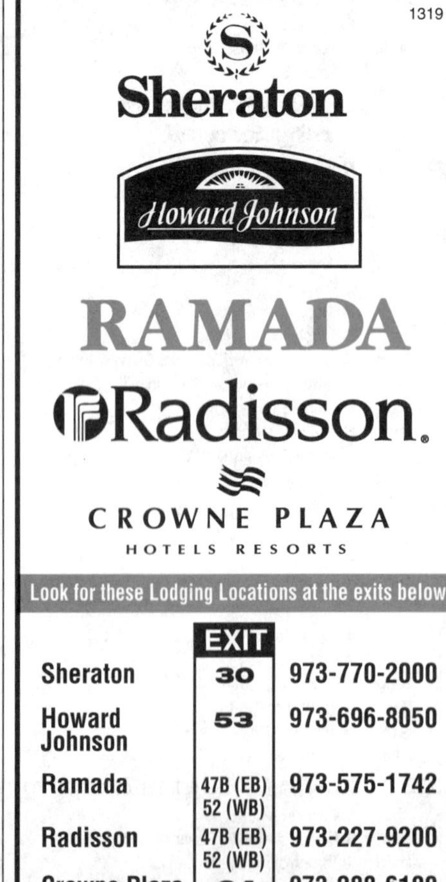

EXIT	NEW JERSEY
(1)	**Rest Area (RR, Picnic, P)**
(2)	**Weigh Station (Eastbound)**
4AB	NJ 94, Columbia, Portland
TStop	**N: T/A TravelCenters of America[*, SCALES]**
Food	**N: Country Pride (TA)**, McDonald's[24], **Taco Bell**
Lodg	**N: T/A TravelCenters of America**
AServ	**S:** Hummel's Garage[24] (Towing)
TServ	**N: T/A TravelCenters of America[SCALES]**
RVCamp	**N: Campground**
Med	**N: + Hospital**
ATM	**N: T/A TravelCenters of America**
4C	NJ 94 North, Columbia, Portland
(7)	**Welcome Center, Rest Area (P; Eastbound)**
(7)	**Scenic Overlook (Westbound, Cars Only)**
12	**(10)** NJ 521, Hope, Blairstown
RVCamp	**S: Triplebrook Campground (see our ad this page)**
Other	**N: State Police** **S: Land of Make Believe**
19	NJ 517, Hackettstown, Andover
RVCamp	**N: Camping**
Med	**N: + Hospital**
(20)	**Scenic Overlook**
(21)	**Rest Area (Phones, P)**
25	U.S. 206, Newton, Stanhope (International Trade Center, Waterloo Village)
26	U.S. 46, Budd Lake, Hackettstown (Westbound, Reaccess Eastbound Only)
Gas	**S:** Texaco[D], Town & Country
AServ	**S:** DC Auto Werks, Goodyear, Texaco, Town & Country
27	U.S. 206, NJ 183 , Netcong, Sommerville
Gas	**N:** Mobil[D] **S:** Texaco[*, D, 24]
Food	**N:** El Coyote Mexican Restaurant, Joseph's Family Reataurant
AServ	**N:** Family Ford, Mobil
RVCamp	**S: Fla-Net Park (1.5 Miles)**
ATM	**S:** Texaco
Parks	**N: State Park**
Other	**S:** NJ State Police Station
28	to NJ 10, Ledgewood, Lake Hopatcong
Gas	**S:** G&N
Food	**S:** Cliff's Dairy, Muldoon's
AServ	**S:** G&N, Meineke Discount Mufflers, Towne Toyota
Other	**S:** Car Wash
30	**(31)** Howard Blvd, Mount Arlington
Gas	**N:** Exxon[D]
Food	**N:** Davy's Hot Dog Deli
Lodg	**N:** Four Points Motel (Formerly Sheraton) (see our ad this page)
AServ	**N:** Exxon
ATM	**N:** Summit Bank
(32)	**Truck Rest Area - No Vehicles Under 5 Tons (P; Westbound)**
34	NJ 15, Wharton, Dover, Jefferson, Sparta
Gas	**N:** Gulf
Food	**S:** Dunkin Donuts, Lorenzo's Pizza, Townsquare Diner

Bold red print shows RV & Bus parking available or nearby

EXIT	NEW JERSEY
ASserv	N: Gulf
Other	N: **Olde Lafayette Village (see our ad this page)**
	S: Car Wash, Costco Discount Store
35AB	Mount Hope, Dover
Med	N: ✚ **Hospital**
Parks	N: **Mount Hope Historical Park**
Other	S: **Rockaway Mall**
37	NJ 513, Hibernia, Rockaway
Gas	N: Exxon[D], Shell[24]
	S: Mobil
Food	N: Hibernia Diner, Howard Johnson
	S: Fresh Start Deli
Lodg	N: Howard Johnson (see our ad this page)
AServ	S: Mobil
Med	S: ✚ **Hospital**
ATM	N: The Bank of New York
38	U.S. 46 East, to NJ 53, Denville (Eastbound)
Gas	N: Sunoco
	S: Texaco
Food	N: Burger King[PLAY], Charlie Brown's Restaurant & Lounge, Wendy's
AServ	N: American Car Care Centers, Sunoco
	S: Denville Body Service, Texaco
Med	N: ✚ **Hospital**
Other	S: **Coin Laundry, Denville Animal Hospital**
39	U.S. 46, NJ 53, Denville (Westbound, Reaccess Eastbound Only, Difficult Reaccess)
Med	N: ✚ **Hospital**
42	**(43)** U.S. 202, U.S. 46, Parsippany, Morris Plains
Med	N: ✚ **Hospital**
ATM	N: PNC Bank
43	**(44)** Jct I-287, Morristown, Mahwah, US 46
45	U.S. 46, Whippany, Lake Hiawatha (Eastbound, Difficult Reaccess)
Gas	N: Amoco[*, 24]
Food	N: Applebee's, Boston Market Restaurant, Dunkin Donuts, Eccola Restaurant, Empire Restaurant, Frank's Pizzeria Italian Cuisine, Friendly's
Lodg	N: Ramada Limited, Red Roof Inn
AServ	N: Master Care Car Service by Fireston
RVCamp	N: **Campground**
ATM	N: First Union Bank, PNC Bank
Other	N: **K-Mart**[RX], Path Mart Supermarket[RX]
47A	Jct I-280, Newark, The Oranges (Eastbound)

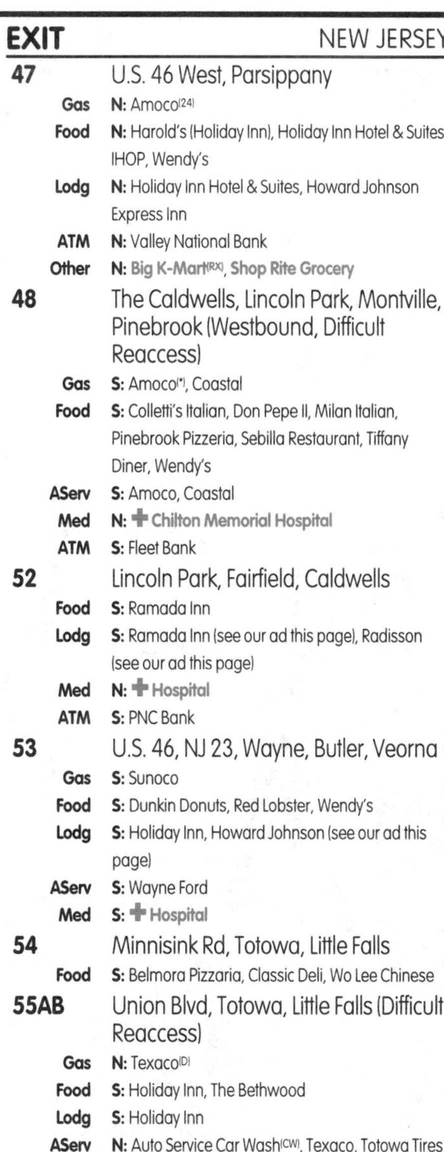

EXIT	NEW JERSEY
47	U.S. 46 West, Parsippany
Gas	N: Amoco[24]
Food	N: Harold's (Holiday Inn), Holiday Inn Hotel & Suites, IHOP, Wendy's
Lodg	N: Holiday Inn Hotel & Suites, Howard Johnson Express Inn
ATM	N: Valley National Bank
Other	N: **Big K-Mart**[RX], **Shop Rite Grocery**
48	The Caldwells, Lincoln Park, Montville, Pinebrook (Westbound, Difficult Reaccess)
Gas	S: Amoco[*], Coastal
Food	S: Colletti's Italian, Don Pepe II, Milan Italian, Pinebrook Pizzeria, Sebilla Restaurant, Tiffany Diner, Wendy's
AServ	S: Amoco, Coastal
Med	N: ✚ **Chilton Memorial Hospital**
ATM	S: Fleet Bank
52	Lincoln Park, Fairfield, Caldwells
Food	S: Ramada Inn
Lodg	S: Ramada Inn (see our ad this page), Radisson (see our ad this page)
Med	N: ✚ **Hospital**
ATM	S: PNC Bank
53	U.S. 46, NJ 23, Wayne, Butler, Veorna
Gas	S: Sunoco
Food	S: Dunkin Donuts, Red Lobster, Wendy's
Lodg	S: Holiday Inn, Howard Johnson (see our ad this page)
AServ	S: Wayne Ford
Med	S: ✚ **Hospital**
54	Minnisink Rd, Totowa, Little Falls
Food	S: Belmora Pizzaria, Classic Deli, Wo Lee Chinese
55AB	Union Blvd, Totowa, Little Falls (Difficult Reaccess)
Gas	N: Texaco[D]
Food	S: Holiday Inn, The Bethwood
Lodg	S: Holiday Inn
AServ	N: Auto Service Car Wash[CW], Texaco, Totowa Tires
56AB	Squirrelwood Rd, West Paterson

1320
RAMADA INN®
New Jersey • Exit 62 • 201-845-3400

EXIT	NEW JERSEY
Gas	S: Mobil[*]
AServ	S: Mobil
ATM	S: PNC Bank
57AB	NJ 19, Downtown Paterson, Clifton
57C	Main St, Paterson
58AB	Madison Ave, Patterson, Clifton
Med	N: ✚ **Trauma Center**
59	Market St, Patterson
Food	N: Bonfire Grill
AServ	N: Cooper Tires, Mercedes Dealership
60	NJ 20, to U.S. 46, Hawthorne, Passaic
Gas	N: Exxon[*], Texaco
Other	N: Blue Cross Animal Hospital
61	NJ 507, Garfield, Elmwood Park
Gas	N: QAC Quality Care
Food	N: Nino's Restaurant
AServ	N: Elmwood Park Auto Body, QAC Quality Care
62A	To Garden State Pkwy, Saddlebrook (No Trucks)
Gas	N: Texaco
Food	N: Allies, Oasis (The Howard Johnson)
Lodg	N: Howard Johnson, Marriott
AServ	N: Texaco
62B	**(63)** to NJ17, to NJ4, Lodi, Fair Lawn
FStop	N: **Hess**[*]
Gas	N: Amoco, Citgo, Gulf
Food	N: Carmella's Italian, The Rusty Nail
Med	N: ✚ **Hackensack Medical Center**
63	**(64)** North NJ17 to NJ 4, Lodi, Fairlawn
FStop	N: **Hess**[*, D]
Gas	N: Amoco[*, 24], Citgo, Gulf[*]
Food	N: Carmella's Pizza, The Rusty Nail
AServ	N: Gulf, P&A Auto Parts
Med	N: ✚ **Hospital**
64	NJ 17 , to NJ4, Hasbrook Heights, Newark, Rochelle Park, Paramus
Gas	N: Sunoco[D]
Food	N: The Crows Nest Restaurant and Pub
Lodg	N: Crowne Plaza (see our ad this page)
AServ	N: Sunoco
Med	N: ✚ **Hospital**
65	Green St, Teterboro,South Hackensack
Food	S: Club 80
66	Hudson St, Hackensack, Little Ferry
Gas	N: Amoco
Food	S: KFC, King Wok
AServ	N: Amoco
Med	N: ✚ **Hospital**
ATM	S: CFS Bank
Other	N: **New Jersey Naval Museum**
	S: **Shop Rite Grocery**[RX]
67	Bogota, Ridgefield Park (Eastbound, Reaccess Westbound Only)
68A	I-95 South, U.S. 46, New Jersey Tnpk South (Toll)
68B	I-95 North, George Washington Bridge, New York
70	U.S. 93, Leonia
70B	Teaneck
71	Broad Ave, Leonia, Inglewood

↑NEW JERSEY

Begin I-80

EXIT NEW YORK

Begin I-81

↓NEW YORK

52 **(183)** De Wolf Point, Island Road
51 **(180)** Island Road, Fineview
Gas **E:** Citgo(*)
W: Fineview(*)
Food **E:** Angel's Diner (Wellesley Plaza), Big Daddy's Ice Cream (Wellesley Plaza), Wellesley Island Plaza(*)
W: Fineview
RVCamp **E:** Seaway Island Resort (1.25 Miles)
W: Campground
Parks **E:** DeWolf State Park
W: Golf Course State Park, Wellsly State Park
Other **E:** U.S. Post Office, Wellesley Island Plaza
(178) NY Welcome Center (RR, Phones; Southbound)
50 **(178)** NY 12, Clayton, Ogdensburg
FStop **E:** Mobil(*, D)
W: Citgo(*)
Gas **W:** Mobil(*) (Bait Store)
Food **E:** Bonnie Castle Downs Restaurant & Resort, Kountry Kottage, Subway
W: Yalvell's Restaurant
Lodg **E:** Bonnie Castle Downs Restaurant & Resort, Green Acres River Motel & Cottages, PineHurst
W: Bridgeview Motel
ATM **W:** Citgo, Mobil (Bait Store)
Parks **W:** Grass Point State Park
Other **W:** Thousand Island Animal Hospital
49 **(169)** NY 411, Theresa , LaFargeville
TStop **W:** Exit 49 Truckstop
FStop **E:** Sunoco(*, D)
Food **W:** Exit 49 Truckstop
(167) Rest Area
48 **(158)** U.S. 11, NY 37, NY 342, Black River , Fort Drum
TStop **E:** Long Ways(*, D)
FStop **E:** Sunoco(*, D)
Gas **E:** Citgo(*, D, LP)
Food **E:** Long Ways
Lodg **E:** Long Ways Motel
TServ **E:** Long Ways
ATM **E:** Long Ways
Other **E:** NY State Police
(156) Parking Area (Southbound)
(156) Parking Area (Northbound)
47 **(155)** NY 12, Bradley St
Gas **E:** Citgo(*, D, LP)
Lodg **W:** Motel 47, The Maples Motel
TServ **E:** Walsh Equipment
Med **E:** ✚ Hospital
46 **(154)** NY 12F, Coffeen St
FStop **E:** Mobil(*, D)
Gas **W:** Citgo(*, LP)
Food **E:** Chappy's 50 Classic Diner, Cracker Barrel
ATM **W:** Watertown Savings Bank
45 **(153)** NY 3, Arsenal St
Gas **E:** BP(*), Citgo(*), Mobil(*), Sunoco(*, CW)
Food **E:** Apollo Restaurant, China Cafe, Denny's, Dunkin Donuts, Friendly's, J Reck Subs (BP), Ponderosa Steakhouse
W: Ann's Restaurant, Bob Evan's Restaurant, Red Lobster
Lodg **E:** Days Inn, Quality Inn
W: Ramada
AServ **E:** Kost Tires
W: Sears
Med **E:** ✚ Hospital
ATM **E:** Marine Midland Bank, Mobil
W: Key Bank
Other **W:** K-Mart, Salmon Run Mall, Sam's Club, Wal-Mart(RX)
44 **(148)** NY 232, Watertown Center
Med **E:** ✚ Hospital
(147) Rest Area (RR, Phones, Picnic; Southbound)
43 **(146)** U.S. 11, Kellogg Hill
42 **(144)** NY 177, Smithville, Adams Center
FStop **E:** Mobil(*, D, LP)
41 **(141)** NY 178, Adams, Henderson
FStop **E:** Citgo(*)
ATM **E:** Citgo
40 **(135)** NY 193, Ellisburg, Pierrepont Manor
Parks **W:** Southwick Beach State Park
(134) Parking Area (Southbound)
(134) Parking Area (Northbound)
39 **(133)** Mannsville
38 **(131)** U.S. 11
37 **(128)** Sandy Creek, Lacona
FStop **W:** Gas Mart(*, D, LP)
Gas **W:** Citgo(*)
Food **W:** Angelo's Bakery, Pizza & Subs, Cathy's Deli, The Snackery
AServ **W:** Northern Repair & Rebuilding, Ontario Tire Service
RVCamp **W:** Angler's Roost Campground, Colonial Campground
ATM **W:** Gas Mart
36 **(122)** NY 13, Pulaski (Northbound, Reaccess Southbound Only, Difficult Reaccess)
FStop **E:** Agway(*, D, LP)
Gas **E:** Citgo(*)
W: Citgo(*), Mobil(*, D)
Food **E:** C & M Diner, Ponderosa
W: Arby's, Burger King, Country Pizza, McDonald's
Lodg **E:** Redwood Motel
W: Country Pizza, Super 8
AServ **W:** NAPA Auto Parts
ATM **W:** Citgo
Other **E:** Fat Nancy's Tackle Shop (Citgo)
W: Kinney Drugs(RX)
35 **(118)** to U.S. 11, Tinker Cavern Road
34 **(115)** NY 104, Mexico
TStop **E:** Ezze Auto and Truckstop(LP, 24)
Food **E:** Ezze Auto and Truckstop
RVCamp **W:** KOA Campgrounds
33 **(111)** NY 69, Parish
Gas **W:** Citgo(*, LP), Mobil(*)
RVCamp **E:** Campground, East Coast Campground, UpCountry Campground
Med **E:** ✚ Parish Health Services Center(*, RX)
ATM **W:** Mobil
32 **(103)** NY 49, Central Square
TStop **E:** Penn-Can Truckstop(*, D)
FStop **E:** Citgo(*, D)
W: BP(*, D)
Food **E:** Wilborn's
W: Arby's, Burger King
AServ **W:** Ford Dealership, NAPA Auto Parts
Other **W:** IGA Store, Rite Aid Pharmacy(RX)
(101) Rest Area (RR, Phones, Picnic, Vending; Southbound)
31 **(99)** Bartell Road, Brewerton
Gas **W:** Citgo(*), Mobil(*), Sunoco(*)
Food **W:** Burger King, Linli's Chinese, Little Caesars Pizza, McDonald's(PLAY), Sam's Lakeside Restaurant, Subway
Lodg **W:** Holiday Inn Express
ATM **W:** Citgo, Fleet Bank, Fulton Savings Bank, Mobil, Smith's Supermarket

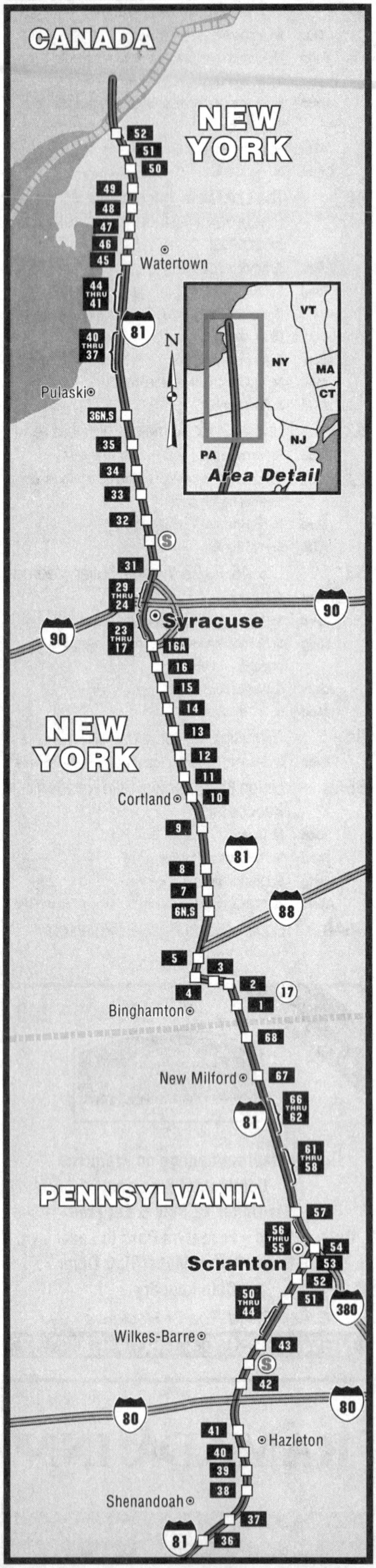

Bold red print shows RV & Bus parking available or nearby

EXIT NEW YORK

Other W: Kinney Drugs[RX], Smith's Supermarket

30 **(95)** NY 31, Cicero, Bridgeport
FStop E: Sunoco[*, D]
Gas E: Hess[*, D], Mobil[*]
W: Kwik-Fill[*]
Food E: Arby's, Dunkin Donuts, Gino & Joe's Pizza, McDonald's[PLAY]
W: Byrne Dairy & Shelby's Donuts, Frank's Cafe, Plainville Farms Restaurant
AServ E: Mobil
W: Meineke Discount Mufflers, Roger Burdick Dodge
RVCamp W: Campers by Ganlen, Gas & Campers RV Sales
ATM W: M & T Bank, Skaneateles Bank
Other W: Airport

29 **(93)** Jct I-481, NY 481, Dewitt, N. Syracuse

28 **(91)** Taft Road, North Syracuse
Gas E: Kwik Fill[*, 24], Sunoco[*, 24]
W: Mobil[*]
Food W: Blimpie Sub & Salads (Mobil)
AServ E: Ballard's Auto Repair, Etolito's Repair, Lonze's Radiator, Walt's Foreign Auto
W: All Pro Auto Parts, Buick Mitsubishi Isuzu Dealer, Cole Muffler, Jiffy Lube
ATM W: Mobil
Other E: Eckerd Drugs
W: U.S. Post Office

27 **(91)** Syracuse Airport

26 **(89)** U.S. 11, Mattydale
Food E: Asian Buffet, Zebb's Grill
W: Burger King, Denny's, Subway, Wendy's
Lodg W: Airflite Motel
AServ E: Goodyear Tire & Auto, K-Mart
ATM W: Fleet Bank
Other E: Eckerd Drugs[RX], K-Mart
W: NTB

25A **(88)** JctI-90, Rochester, Albany

25 **(88)** 7th St, North St, Liverpool
TStop E: Pilot Travel Center[*, SCALES]
Gas W: Mobil[*], Sunoco
Food E: KFC (Pilot), Subway (Pilot)
W: Bob Evan's Restaurant, Burger King, Colorado Mine Steakhouse, Denny's, Friendly's, Italian Carry-Out, J Reck Subs, The Ground Round
Lodg W: (DAYS INN) Days Inn, EconoLodge, Hampton Inn, Quality Inn, Ramada, Super 8
AServ E: Butch's Automotive
W: Sunoco
TServ E: International Truck
ATM W: Chase Bank, Mobil

24 **(87)** Liverpool, NY 370W

23 **(86)** Hiawatha Blvd
ATM E: Key Bank

22 **(86)** NY298, Court St

21 **(86)** Spencer St, Cataba St

20 **(85)** Franklin St, West St

19 **(85)** Clinton St, Salina St

(85) Jct I-690, E Syracuse, Fair Grounds, Baldwinsville

18 **(84)** Harrison St, Adams St
Med E: + Hospital

17 **(82)** South Salina St, Brighton Ave
Gas W: Kwik Fill[*], Mobil[*]
Med W: + Hospital
Other W: Expressway Market C-Store

16A **(81)** Junction I-481N, DeWitt (Left Exit)

16 **(78)** U.S. 11, Onondaga Nation Territory

15 **(73)** U.S. 20, LaFayette
Gas E: Mobil[*]
Food E: Old Tymes Cafe, Quinto's NY Pizza
W: McDonald's
AServ E: NAPA Auto Parts
ATM E: M & T Bank
Other E: IGA Food Store

14 **(66)** NY 80, Tully
FStop E: Mobil[*, D]
Food E: Best Western
W: Burger King
Lodg E: Best Western
ATM E: First National Bank of Courtland

13 **(63)** NY 281, Preble
Gas E: Sunoco[D] (Towing)
AServ E: Sunoco (Towing)

(60) **Rest Area (RR, Phones, Picnic, Vending; Northbound)**

12 **(54)** U.S. 11, NY 281, Homer
Med W: + Hospital

11 **(52)** NY 13, Cortland, Ithaca
Gas W: Mobil[*]
Food E: Denny's
W: Arby's, Bob Evan's Restaurant, China Moon, Friendly's, Little Caesars Pizza, McDonald's, River Junction, Subway, Taco Bell, Wendy's
Lodg E: Comfort Inn, Super 8
W: Holiday Inn
AServ W: Jiffy Lube, Kost Tire, Parts America
Other W: Eckerd Drugs[RX]

10 **(50)** U.S. 11, NY 41, McGraw
FStop W: Agway[LP], Citgo[*], Mobil[*, D], Sunoco[*]
Food W: Burger King (Citgo), J Reck Subs (Citgo), Little Treat Shop, Lori's Diner, Pizza Hut (Citgo), Suburban Skyliner Diner, Subway (Mobil)
Lodg W: EconoLodge, Evergreen Motel
AServ W: Cooper Tires, Tarbell Auto Body Shop

(44) **Parking Area (Picnic; Northbound)**

9 **(40)** U.S. 11, NY 221, Marathon

Super 8 Motel
Rt. 11 Upper Court St

I-81N	I-81S
EXIT 2W	EXIT 3
Rt 17	I-88/81S
Exit 75	Exit 3

• Outdoor Pool • Restaurant & Lounge
• Banquet & Meeting Facilities
• Complimentary AM Coffee
• Free HBO & ESPN & CNN
• Truck & Bus Parking on Property
• Special Bus & Group Rates
1581 607-775-3443
NEW YORK • I-81

Syracuse, New York 1520
RAMADA INN®
1305 Buckley Road • Syracuse, NY
• Easy on/off for Route 81 & NYS Thruway (I-90)
• Complimentary Full American Breakfast with Your Room
• Heated Outdoor Pool
• Very Close to Shops, Restaurants, Gas Stations etc.
• On Premises Restaurant & Lounge
$79* 1-4 Persons
* Show ad at check-in. Based on availability. Not valid during special events or holidays
315-457-8670
www.ramadasyracuse.com
NEW YORK • I-81 • EXIT 25

EXIT NEW YORK/PENNSYLVANIA

(Difficult Reaccess)
Gas W: Citgo[*], Sunoco[*]
Food W: Kathy's Diner, New York Pizzeria, Riley's Cafe, Three Bear Inn
Lodg W: Three Bear Inn
AServ W: Napa Auto
RVCamp W: Country Hill Campground
ATM W: First National Bank of Courtland, Sunoco
Other W: Coin Car Wash

(33) **Rest Area (RR, Phones, Picnic, Vending; Southbound)**

8 **(31)** to U.S. 11, NY 26, to NY 79, NY 206, Whitney Point, Lisle (Reaccess Northbound Only)
Gas E: Kwik Fill[*, LP], Mobil[*, LP]
Food E: Arby's, Subway, The Sundae Shoppe
Lodg E: Point Motel
AServ E: Mike Stolarcyk Chevrolet, Napa Auto, Parts Plus
RVCamp E: Campground
W: Campground
ATM E: First National Bank of Courtland
Other E: Greg's Supermarket

7 **(21)** U.S. 11, Castle Creek
FStop W: Citgo[*]
Gas W: Mobil[*]
AServ E: Sickel's Garage

6B **(17)** U.S. 11, NY 12, Chenango Bridge, to Jct I-88 (Southbound)

6A **(16)** U.S. 11, Norwich, NY12, Chenango Bridge (Northbound)
FStop E: Hess[*]
Gas E: BP[*]
Food E: Bulls Head Restaurant, Burger King, Dunkin Donuts, Grande Pizza, Jones' Humdinger Ice Cream, Kelly's Ice Cream, Papa Beaux, Pizza Hut, Ponderosa, Wendy's
AServ E: Cory North Gate Ford, Mazda, Jiffy Lube, Meineke Discount Mufflers, Midas Muffler & Brake, Sunny Manny's Auto Service, Upfront Auto Clinic[CW]
ATM E: BSB Bank & Trust, Marine Midland Bank
Other E: CVS Pharmacy[24, RX], Coin Laundromat, Giant Supermarket

(15) Jct I-88E (Northbound)

5 **(14)** U.S. 11, Front St
Gas W: Mobil[*, D, LP]
Lodg W: Howard Johnson, Super 8

4 **(12)** NY 7, Binghamton, Hill Crest
TServ E: Cook Brothers Truck Parts

3 **(12)** Industrial Park (Reaccess Northbound Only)
TStop W: Travel Port[*, SCALES]
Gas W: BP[*, D]
Food W: Country Bob's, Subway, Travel Port
Lodg W: Super 8 (see our ad this page)
AServ W: K & C Auto Service
TServ W: Travel Port[SCALES]

2 **(8)** U.S. 11, NY 17E, Industrial Park, New York City

1 **(4)** U.S.11, NY 7, Kirkwood, Conklin
Gas W: Mobil[*, D, LP]
Other W: State Police

(2) **NY Welcome Center (RR, Phones, Picnic; Northbound)**

(0) **Weigh Station (Northbound)**

↑NEW YORK

↓PENNSYLVANIA

68 **(230)** PA 171, Great Bend, Susquehanna

Bold red print shows RV & Bus parking available or nearby

EXIT PENNSYLVANIA

FStop W: Exxon(*)
Gas E: Mobil(*)
W: Sunoco(D)
Food W: Arby's (Exxon), Beaver's Restaurant, Dobb's Country Kitchen, McDonald's, Subway
Lodg W: Colonial Brick Motel
AServ W: B&D Auto Center, Sunoco
RVCamp E: Lakeside Campground
ATM E: Mobil
W: CoreStates Bank, People's Bank
Other W: Bi-Lo Grocery, Coin Car Wash, Coin Laundry, Reddon's Rexall Drugs(RX), Rob's Market

67 **(224)** PA 492, New Milford, Lakeside
Gas W: Amoco(*)
Food W: Amoco
Lodg W: All Season Campground(LP)
RVCamp W: All Season Campground

66 **(219)** PA 848, Gibson
TStop E: Amoco(*, D, SCALES)
Food E: Amoco
TServ E: Gibson Truck & Tire Service
RVCamp E: April Valley Campground
Other E: State Police
W: Old Mill Village Museum

65 **(217)** PA 547, Harford
TStop E: Liberty Auto/Truck Stop(*), Penn-Can Truckstop(*)
Food E: Liberty Auto/Truck Stop, Penn-Can Truckstop
TServ E: Penn-Can Truckstop
RVCamp E: April Valley RV Park
ATM E: Liberty Auto/Truck Stop, Penn-Can Truckstop

64 **(211)** PA 92, Lenox
FStop W: Mobil(*), Texaco(*)
Food W: Bingham's Restaurant, Lenox Dairy Bar, Lenox Restaurant, Mama's Bakery
ATM W: CoreStates Bank
Other W: Lenox Pharmacy(RX)

(208) PA Welcome Center (RR, Phones, Vending; Southbound)

63 **(206)** PA 374, Glenwood, Lenoxville
Med E: + Hospital
Other E: Elk Mountain Ski Resort

(202) Rest Area (RR, Phones, Picnic; Northbound)

62 **(202)** PA 107, Fleetville, Tompkinsville

61 **(200)** PA 438, East Benton
Gas W: Mobil
Food W: The North 40
AServ W: Exxon (Towing), Mobil
ATM W: Exxon (Towing)

60 **(199)** PA 524, Scott
TStop E: Scott 60 Plaza(*)
FStop E: Amoco(*)
Food W: Elaine's Cafe & Deli
Lodg W: Motel 81
ATM E: Amoco

59 **(197)** PA 632, Waverly
Gas W: Sunoco(*, 24)
Food E: Mr. Z's Food Mart
W: Sunoco
ATM W: Sunoco
Other E: Rite Aide Pharmacy(RX)

58 **(194)** U.S. 6, U.S. 11, PA Tnpk, Clarks Summit, Allentown

57 **(192)** U.S. 6 East, U.S. 11 South, Carbondale
Food E: Arby's, Burger King, Denny's, Little Anthony's Pizzeria, Long John Silver, Long Star Steakhouse, Master Grill, McDonald's(PLAY), Perkins Family Restaurant, Rita's Italian Ices, TCBY
AServ E: Firestone Tire & Auto, Sears
Med W: + Hospital

EXIT PENNSYLVANIA

ATM E: First National Community Bank
Other E: Viewmont Mall

56 **(190)** Dickson City, Main Ave
Food E: Giovani's Pizza, Manhattan Bagel

55 **(188)** PA 347, Blakely St, Throop
Gas E: Sunoco(*, 24)
W: Mobil(*)
Food E: Boston Market Restaurant, China World Buffet, Donut Connection, McDonald's, Wendy's
W: Burger King, Friendly's
Lodg E: Days Inn
AServ E: Parts America

54 **(187)** Jct I-84 East
Gas W: Citgo(D)
Food W: Kuzzins Cafe, Tallo's Ristorante
AServ W: Citgo

53 **(184)** Central Scranton Expwy

52 **(184)** PA 307, River St, Moosic
Gas W: Citgo(*, LP), Exxon(*), Shell(*), Texaco(D)
Food W: Chick's Diner, House of China, Profera's Pizza, Ramada Inn, Stampy's Pizza and Hoagies
Lodg W: Ramada
AServ W: Jiffy Lube, Texaco
Med W: + CMC Trauma Service
ATM W: CoreStates Bank, Penn Security Bank
Other W: CVS Pharmacy, Gerrity Supermarket

51 **(182)** Montage Mtn Road, Davis St (Lackawanna Stadium)
FStop W: Sunoco(*, D)
Gas W: Exxon(*)
Food E: Marvelous Muggs Restaurant and Pub
W: Econolodge, Valentino's Restaurant and Lounge
Lodg E: Comfort Inn, Courtyard Inn, Hampton Inn
W: Econolodge
Other E: Lackawanna Coal Mine Tour, PA Anthrosite Heritage Museum
W: U.S. Post Office

50 **(179)** U.S. 11, PA 502, Moosic (Left Exit Northbound, Difficult Reaccess)
Gas E: Mobil(D)
W: Shell(*, D)
Food E: Grande Pizza, Joey's Pizza
Lodg E: Days Inn (see our ad this page), Trotters Motel
AServ E: Domiano Auto Service, Jack Williams Tire and

1844
DAYS INN
Scranton/Wilkes-Barre
4130 Birney Ave.
Moosic, PA
Days Inn
Birney Ave
4th light turn Left
Exit 51
Davis St.
Pa Turnpike
Exit 50
$39.00 1-2 Persons/Queen
$49.00 2-4 Persons/2 Double
Free HBO/Cable • Restaurant
Continental Breakfast
Meeting Facilities
Coin Laundry • Pets Allowed
Handicap Accessible
Bus/Truck/RV Parking
Exterior/Interior Corridors
717-457-6713 • 800-724-3866
Based on availability. Not valid with any other discount.
Pennsylvania • I-81 • Exit 51SB/50NB

"GET OFF AND GOLF INTERSTATE 81"
A Guide Book to 113 daily fee Courses
Near the Highway
$12 + s/h MC-VISA
1496 Call: Adirondack Illustrator 518-962-4977
New York to Tennessee

EXIT PENNSYLVANIA

Auto Service

49AB **(177)** Avoca, Wilkes Barre, 49A - Wilkes Barre Airport, 49B - Avoca
FStop W: Petro
Food E: Damon's Ribs (Holiday Inn Express)
W: Iron Skillet(*, SCALES) (Petro)
Lodg E: Holiday Inn Express
ATM W: Petro(*, D, SCALES) (Sunoco Gas)

48 **(176)** PA Tnpk, PA 9, PA 315, Dupont, Clark Summit, Allentown
TStop W: Skyliner Truck Plaza(*, SCALES)
FStop W: Shell(*)
Gas E: Exxon, Mobil(*), Sunoco
Food E: Bonanza Steakhouse, Howard Johnson
W: Slyliner TS
Lodg E: Howard Johnson, Knight's Inn
W: Skyliner Truck Plaza, Victoria Inn
AServ E: Abraham Geo, Exxon, Sunoco
W: Goodyear Tire & Auto, Vullo Auto Repair
TServ W: Goodyear Tire & Auto, Skyliner, Vullo Truck Repairs
TWash W: Skyliner
ATM E: Core States Bank

47AB **(170)** PA 115, Bear Creek, Wilkes Barre, 47A - 115 S, 47B - 309 N
Gas E: Amoco(*)
Food E: Carriage Stop Inn (Family Restaurant)
Lodg E: Best Western, Melody Motel
W: Holiday Inn
Med E: + Hospital (1 Mile)
W: + VA Medical Center/General Hospital

45 **(165)** PA 309, Mountain Top, Wilks Barre (Left Exit Northbound)
Gas W: Shell(*, CW), Shell(D), Texaco
Food W: Dunkin Donuts, Mark 2 Restaurant, McDonald's, Milazzo's Pizza Subs and Wings, Perkins Family Restaurant, Taco Bell, Tin Tin Exotic Chinese Food
AServ W: Auto Parts America, K-Mart, M.J. Auto Service, Monroe Muffler & Brakes, Texaco
TServ W: M.J. Truck Service
ATM W: PNC Bank
Other W: K-Mart(RX), Thrift Drug

44 **(165)** PA 29, Nanticoke

43 **(159)** Nuangola
Gas W: Shell(*)
Food W: Godfather's Pizza (Shell Gas Station)
RVCamp W: Counsel Cup Campgrounds
ATM W: Shell

(158) Rest Area (RR, Phones, Picnic, Vending; Southbound)
(157) Weigh Station (Southbound)
(156) Rest Area (RR, Phones, Picnic, Vending; Northbound)
(155) Weigh Station (Northbound)

42 **(155)** Dorrance
FStop W: Blue Ridge Plaza(*, D)
Gas E: Sunoco(D)
AServ E: Sunoco(D)
RVCamp E: KOA Campgrounds (2 Miles)
W: Moyer's Grove Campground & Country RV (7.3 Miles)

(151) Junction I-80, Bloomsburg, Stroudsburg

41 **(145)** PA 93, West Hazleton, Conyngham (Penn State University - Hazelton Campus)
Gas E: Mobil, Sunoco(*, D)
Food E: Perkins Family Restaurant, Rossi's
W: Hampton Inn
Lodg E: Comfort Inn, Forest Hill Inn
W: Hampton Inn
AServ E: Mobil
Other E: Airport, State Police

EXIT PENNSYLVANIA

40 **(143)** PA 924, Hazleton (Northbound)
- Gas W: Texaco
- Food E: Carmen's Family Restaurant
- Lodg E: Hazelton Motor Inn

39 **(138)** PA 309, McAdoo, Tamaqua

38 **(134)** Delano

(132) **Parking Area**

37 **(131)** PA 54, Hometown, Mahoney City
- Gas W: Citgo(*), Texaco(*, D)
- AServ W: Texaco
- Parks E: **State Park**

36 **(124)** PA 61, Frackville, St Clair (Must Take Mall Rd To East Services)
- FStop W: **Gulf**(*, LP)
- Gas W: BP(D), Exxon(*, LP), Getty(*, LP), Shell(*, CW)
- Food E: McDonald's
  W: Blimpie's Subs (Getty Gas Station), Cesari's, Dutch Kitchen Restaurant, Hardee's, Subway, The Pizza Place
- Lodg W: Central Hotel (AAA), Econolodge, Granny's Motel
- AServ E: A&A Auto Stores, **K-Mart**, Sears
  W: Goodyear Tire & Auto, Rinaldi's Dodge
- Med W: **✚ Hospital**
- ATM E: First Federal Savings
  W: Core States Bank, Getty, Pennsylvania National Bank
- Other E: **K-Mart, Phar Mor Drugs, Schuylkill Mall, Weiss Markets**
  W: **Ace Hardware, Rite Aide Pharmacy, State Police, Thomas Animal Hospital**

35 **(116)** PA 901, Minersville
- Food E: 901 Pub and Restaurant
- Other E: **Airport (1.5 Miles)**

34 **(112)** PA 25, Hegins
- RVCamp W: **Camp-A-While (1 Mile)**

33 **(107)** U.S. 209, Tremont, Tower City, Pottsville

32 **(104)** PA 125, Ravine
- RVCamp E: **Echo Valley Park (1 Mile)**

31 **(100)** PA 443, Pine Grove
- TStop W: **All American Ambest Truckstop**(*, SCALES)
- FStop W: **Texaco**(*)
- Gas E: Citgo(*)
- Food E: Arby's, **McDonald's**, Pizza-Beer Restaurant, Ulsh's Family Restaurant
  W: **All American Family Restaurant (All American TS), Subway (All American TS)**
- Lodg E: Colony Lodge, **Comfort Inn, Econolodge**
- AServ E: Citgo
  W: Motters Wrecker Service
- TServ W: **All American Truck Plaza**(*)

30 **(91)** PA 72, Lebanon
- Gas E: Exxon(*, D), Shell(*, D, LP)
- AServ E: Exxon
- RVCamp E: **KOA Campgrounds (5 Miles), Lickdale Campground**

(89) Junction I-78E, Allentown

29AB **(85)** PA 934, Annville, Fort Indiantown Gap (29A- PA 934 South Annville 29B- Fort Indiantown Gap)
- Gas W: Texaco(*, D)
- Food E: Harper's Tavern Restaurant, Swatara Creek Inn Bed and Breakfast
  W: Funck's Family Restaurant
- Lodg E: Swatara Creek Inn Bed and Breakfast
- RVCamp E: **Campground**
- Parks W: **Memorial Lake State Park**
- Other W: **Indiantown National Cemetery**

28 **(81)** PA 743, Grantville, Hershey
- Gas E: Mobil(*, D)
  W: Exxon(*), Texaco(*, LP)
- Food W: **Holiday Inn**
- Lodg E: **Econolodge**, Hampton Inn
  W: **Holiday Inn**

(80) **Weigh Station**

(80) **Rest Area (RR, Phones, Picnic, Vending)**

27 **(77)** PA 39, Hershey, Manada Hill
- TStop W: **Sunrise Travel Center**(*, SCALES), **Travel America**(*, SCALES) **(Country Pride)**
- FStop E: **Pilot Travel Center**(*, SCALES)
  W: **Gables Shell**(*, LP, SCALES)
- Gas E: BP(*), Texaco
- Food W: **Subway (Gables), Sunrise Travel Center, Travel America (Country Pride)**
- Lodg E: Sleep Inn
  W: Comfort Inn, **Daystop Inn**
- AServ E: D&K Auto Body Shop, Texaco
- TServ W: **Goodyear Truck Service, Sunrise Travel Center**(SCALES), **Travel America**(SCALES) **(Country Pride)**
- ATM W: **Gables Shell, Sunrise Travel Center**

26AB **(73)** Paxtonia, Linglestown
- Gas E: Citgo(D), Hess(*), Sunoco(D), Texaco(*, D)
- Food E: Burger King, Malley's, McDonald's
  W: Best Western
- Lodg E: Budgetel Inn, Harrisburg Inn
  W: Best Western
- AServ E: C&P Automotive Repair, Citgo, Hartman Chrysler Plymouth Jeep, Hartman Toyota, Sunoco, Texaco
- ATM E: Harris Savings, Mellon Bank, Sunoco

(70) Junction I-83 South, Harrisburg, York

24 **(69)** Progress Ave
- Gas E: Gulf(D)
- Food E: **Cracker Barrel**
  W: Western Sizzlin, Your Place
- Lodg W: Best Western, Red Roof Inn
- AServ E: Gulf
- ATM W: Fulton Bank

23 **(67)** PA 322w, PA 230, Cameron St, Lewistown, U.S. 22

22 **(66)** Front St
- Gas W: Sunoco
- Food W: Chopsticks House, Ponderosa, Taco Bell, Wendy's
- Lodg W: Days Inn, **Super 8**
- AServ W: Sunoco
- Med E: **✚ Hospital**

21 **(65)** U.S. 11, U.S. 15, Enola, Marysville
- Gas E: Sunoco(24)
- Food E: Wendy's
- AServ E: Eddie's Tire, Sunoco(24)

20 **(61)** PA 944, Wertzville Road
- Food E: Pizza Ect.

19 **(60)** PA581 E, to U.S. 11, Camp Hill, Gettysburg (Left Exit Southbound)

18 **(57)** PA 114, Mechanicsburg

17 **(52)** U.S. 11, to I-76, PA Tnpk, Middlesex, New Kingstown
- TStop E: **Flying J Travel Plaza**(*, LP, RV DUMP, SCALES)
  W: **Gables**(*, LP, SCALES), **Soco's All American Truckstop**(*, SCALES)
- Gas E: Citgo(D, 24)
  W: Texaco(*, LP, 24)
- Food E: Bob Evan's Restaurant, Duffy's Restaurant (Holiday Inn), Embers Inn, **Flying J Travel Plaza, Hardee's**, Middlesex Diner, **Trailside (Appalachian Inn)**
  W: Eat 'N Park, **Iron Kettle Restaurant (Soco TS)**, Tavern BBQ
- Lodg E: **Appalachian Trail Inn, Econolodge**, Embers Inn, Holiday Inn (Duffy's), **Super 8**
  W: Best Western, Budget Host Motel, **Quality Inn**, Rodeway Inn
- AServ E: Citgo(24)
- TServ E: **Flying J Travel Plaza**(SCALES)
- ATM E: **Flying J Travel Plaza**

16 **(49)** PA 641, High St (Southbound, Reaccess Northbound Only)
- Gas W: Getty(*, LP)
- Food W: Burger King, Pizza Hut
- Other W: **CVS Pharmacy**(RX), **Carlisle Plaza Mall**

15 **(48)** PA 74, York Road (Northbound)
- Gas W: Gulf(D), Kwik Fill(*)
- Food W: **Farmers Market Restaurant**
- AServ W: Gulf

14 **(47)** PA 34, Hanover St
- FStop E: **Gulf**(D)
- Gas E: Texaco(D)
  W: Exxon(D)
- Food W: Genova Restaurant, Papa John's Pizza, Wendy's
- AServ E: Carlisle Car and Truck, Gulf, Mullen's Towing
  W: Carlisle's Expert Tire, Exxon, Hanover Auto Works
- Other W: **M.J. Carlisle Mall**, Soft Cloth Car Wash, **Tritt's General Store**

13 **(46)** College St
- Gas E: Mobil, Texaco(*, LP, 24)
- Food E: Bonanza Steakhouse, Dunkin Donuts, Great Wall Chinese Restaurant, McDonald's(PLAY), SHONEY'S Shoney's
- Lodg E: **Days Inn, Super 8**
- AServ E: Mobil, Monroe Muffler & Brakes
- RVCamp E: **Western Village Campground (2 Miles)**
  W: **Western Village Campground (1.75 Miles)**
- Med W: **✚ Hospital**
- ATM E: Financial Trust
- Other E: **Eckerd Drugs, Mail Boxes Etc**, Police Department, **Stonehedge Square, Sure Fine Market**

12 **(44)** PA 465, Plainfield
- RVCamp W: **Carlisle Campground (5.5 Miles)**
- Other E: **State Police**

(39) **Rest Area (RR, Phones, Picnic, Vending, Pet Walk; Southbound)**

(38) **Rest Area (RR, Phones, Picnic; Northbound)**

11 **(37)** PA 233, Newville
- Parks E: **Pine Grove Furnace State Park (8 Miles)**
  W: **Colonel Denning State Park (13 Miles)**
- Other E: **Kings Gap EE& TCenter (Five Miles)**

10 **(28)** PA 174, King St
- TStop E: **Pharo's Truck Stop**(*, SCALES)
- Gas E: Sunoco(*, LP, 24)
- Food E: **Pharo's Truck Stop**
- Lodg E: Budget Host Inn
  W: Ameri Host Inn
- AServ W: Interstate Ford
- TServ E: **Pharo's Truck Stop**(SCALES)

9 **(24)** PA 696, Fayette St
- Gas W: Mobil(*, LP)

8 **(20)** PA 997, Scotland
- FStop E: **Shell**(*)
  W: **Amoco**(*)
- Gas W: Sunoco(*, LP, 24)
- Food E: McDonald's
- Lodg E: Comfort Inn, **Super 8**
- ATM E: **Shell**
  W: Financial Trust
- Other E: **Chambersburg Mall**
  W: Wet Wave Coin Car Wash(24)

6 **(16)** U.S. 30, Chambersburg, Gettysburg
- FStop W: **Hess**(*, D)
- Gas E: Sheetz(*, LP, 24)
- Food E: Boston Market Restaurant, Chris's Country Kitchen, KFC, Perkins, SHONEY'S Shoney's, Two Brothers Italian Restaurant
  W: Burger King, Golden China, **Howard**

Bold red print shows RV & Bus parking available or nearby

EXIT	PENNSYLVANIA/MARYLAND
	Johnson, Long John Silver, McDonald's, Pizza Hut, Ponderosa, Roadster Diner, Taco Bell
Lodg	E: Days Inn
	W: Howard Johnson
AServ	E: Meineke Discount Mufflers, Midas Muffler & Brake
	W: Advance Auto Parts
RVCamp	E: Glasgow Rec. Vehicles, Inc.(LP) (1 Mile)
Med	W: ✚ Hospital
ATM	E: Food Lion, Sheetz
Other	E: Chambersburg Animal Hospital, Food Lion, Franklin Center, Tourist Info.
	W: State Police
5	**(14)** PA 316, Wayne Ave
Gas	W: Exxon(*, LP), Quick Fuel(*), Sunoco(*, LP), Texaco(*, D, 24)
Food	E: Bob Evan's Restaurant, Cracker Barrel
	W: Applebee's, Arby's, Denny's, Red Lobster, Wendy's
Lodg	E: Fairfield Inn, Hampton Inn
	W: Econolodge, Holiday Inn
AServ	W: Monroe Muffler & Brakes
TServ	E: A&B Garage
ATM	W: Sunoco, Weiss Market(RX)
Other	W: K-Mart, Wayne Plaza, Weiss Market(RX)
(11)	Weigh Station (Phones; Southbound)
4	**(10)** PA 914, Marion
(7)	Weigh Station (Phones; Northbound)
3	**(5)** PA 16, Greencastle, Waynesboro
TStop	E: Travel Port(*, D, RV DUMP, SCALES)
FStop	E: Texaco(*, D)
Gas	E: Travel Port(*, D, RV DUMP)
	W: Exxon(D)
Food	E: Arby's (Travel Port), Buckhorn Family Restaurant (Travel Port), McDonald's(PLAY), Subway (Travel Port)
	W: Woody's (Green Castle Motel)
Lodg	E: Econolodge, Roadway Inn (Travel Port)
	W: Green Castle Motel
AServ	W: Exxon
TServ	E: Travel Port(SCALES)
Med	E: ✚ Hospital
ATM	E: Texaco, Travel Port
	W: Financial Trust
Other	E: Coin Laundromat
2	**(3)** U.S. 11, Molly Pitcher Hwy
Gas	E: Exxon(*, LP)
	W: Sunoco
Food	E: Brother's Pizza 2, Chef's Kitchen Family Restaurant (Comfort Inn)
Lodg	E: Comfort Inn
AServ	E: Bill Bower's Auto Service
	W: Carbaugh's Garage, Sunoco
TServ	W: Mason Dixon Trucks & Carriers
Other	E: Coin Laundry
(1)	PA Welcome Center (RR, Phones, Vending; Northbound)
1	**(0)** PA 163, State Line
Food	W: Black Steer Steak House
Lodg	W: Econolodge, State Line Motel
TServ	W: Clyde's Truck & Equipment, Mason-Dixon Repair and Service Inc.
RVCamp	W: Keystone RV Campground (1 Mile), Keystone RV Center(LP)

↑ PENNSYLVANIA

↓ MARYLAND

EXIT	MARYLAND
10AB	Showalter Road
Other	E: Airport
9	**(10)** Maugans Ave
FStop	E: Texaco(*)
Gas	E: Amoco, Mobil
Food	E: McDonald's
	W: Burger King, Family Time
AServ	E: Amoco, Battery Warehouse, Christy's Auto, Mobil
	W: Warren Martin Auto Service
TServ	W: Truck Enterprises Kenworth Dealer
ATM	E: Texaco
	W: Hagerstown Trust
Other	E: Coin Car Wash
	W: U Haul Rental(LP)
8	Maugansville Road (Southbound)
7AB	**(8)** Hagerstown , MD58, Cearfoss, Salem Ave.
TServ	W: Grimes Truck Center, Interstate Truck Equipment Inc.
6AB	**(7)** U.S. 40, Hagerstown , Huiett
Gas	E: Amoco(*), Texaco
Food	E: John's Pizza, Richard's Diner
Lodg	E: Days Inn (see our ad this page)
AServ	E: Texaco
Med	E: ✚ Hospital (2 Miles)
Other	E: Coin Laundromat, Visitor Information
5	Halfway Blvd
TStop	W: AC&T(*, SCALES)
Food	E: Crazy Horse Steakhouse, McDonald's, Pizza Hut, Red Lobster, Roy Rogers, SHONEY'S, Shoney's, The Ground Round
Lodg	E: Howard Johnson, Motel 6
AServ	E: Firestone Tire & Auto, Hagerstown Ford, K-Mart
	W: Kiplinger's Auto Center
TServ	W: AC&T(SCALES), C Earl Brown Inc
ATM	E: F & M Bank, First National Bank of Maryland
	W: AC&T
Other	E: K-Mart, Sam's Club, Valley Mall, Wal-Mart(RX)
4	Jct I-70, Hancock, Frederick
3	MD 144, Hancock
TStop	E: Amoco Truck Plaza
FStop	E: Citgo(*, D, LP)
Gas	E: BP(*)
Food	E: Fatboy's Pizza and Subs, Little Sandy's Restaurant, Park N Dine
AServ	E: Kurk Ford
TServ	E: Amoco Truck Plaza
ATM	E: Home Federal Savings Bank
Other	E: C&O Canal Information, Coin Car Wash
2	U.S. 11, Williamsport
FStop	E: ACT(*, 24)
	W: Sunoco(D)
Gas	W: Exxon(D), Shell(*, D)
Food	W: McDonald's
Lodg	W: Days Inn
AServ	W: Exxon, Sunoco
RVCamp	W: KOA Campgrounds (4 Miles)
ATM	E: ACT
	W: American Trust Bank

Bold red print shows RV & Bus parking available or nearby

EXIT MARYLAND/WEST VIRGINIA

Other **W:** Tourist Info.

1 MD 63, MD 68, Williamsport, Boonsboro

AServ **W:** Napa Auto

RVCamp **E:** Campground, Jelly Stone Camp (1 Mile), Safari Campground

Other **E:** Antietam Battlefield, C&O Canal Historical Site

↑MARYLAND

↓WEST VIRGINIA

(25) WV Welcome Center (RR, Phones, Picnic; Southbound)

23 U.S. 11, Marlowe, Falling Waters

Gas **W:** Citgo(*), Texaco(*, D)

Food **W:** Texaco

TServ **W:** Rude's Truck Repair

RVCamp **E:** Falling Waters Campsite(LP) (1 Mile), Recreation Specialists at Falling Waters Campsite(LP)

W: RV Express (Sales & Service)

ATM **W:** Huntington Banks, Texaco

Other **E:** Handy Shopper C-Store

20 WV 901, Spring Mills Road (Southbound)

TStop **E:** 76 Auto/Truck Plaza(*, D, SCALES)

Food **E:** 76 Auto/Truck Plaza, Barney's, Econolodge

Lodg **E:** Econolodge

TServ **E:** 76 Auto/Truck Plaza(SCALES)

ATM **E:** Barney's

(20) Weigh Station (Southbound)

16 WV 9E, North Queen St, Berkeley Springs, Hodgville

Gas **E:** Exxon(*, D), Sheetz(*, 24)

W: Shell(*, D)

Food **E:** Denny's, Golden China Restaurant, Hoss's, KFC, Long John Silver, Taste of Italy

Lodg **E:** Comfort Inn, Knight's Inn, Leisure Inn, Super 8

Med **W:** ✚ Hospital

ATM **E:** Blue Ridge Bank, Exxon, Federal Credit Union, Sheetz

Other **E:** State Police

13 WV 15, King St, Downtown

Gas **E:** Sheetz(*, D, 24), Texaco(*, D)

Food **E:** Burger King, Pizza Hut, SHONEY'S, Shoney's, Subway (Texaco), TCBY (Texaco)

Lodg **E:** DAYS INN Days Inn, Holiday Inn

Med **E:** ✚ Hospital

ATM **E:** Sheetz, Texaco

Other **E:** Tanger Outlet Mall

12 WV 45, Winchester Ave, WV 9 E, Charles Town

FStop **E:** Southern States(*, LP)

Gas **E:** Sheetz(*, 24), Texaco(*, D)

Food **E:** Bob Evan's Restaurant, Hardee's, Little Caesars Pizza, McDonald's, Ponderosa, Ruby Tuesday, Taco Bell

Lodg **E:** Hampton Inn, Krista Lite Motel, Scottish Inns

AServ **E:** American Car Care Centers

RVCamp **E:** Nahkeeta Campground (3 Miles)

ATM **E:** Huntington Banks, Texaco

Other **E:** Food Lion Supermarket (Deli & Bakery), K-Mart(RX), Martin's Grocery(RX), Martinsburg Mall

8 WV 32, Tablers Station Road

Other **E:** Airport

5 WV 51, Inwood, Charles Town

Gas **E:** Citgo(*), Exxon(*), Mobil(D), Texaco(D, LP, CW)

Food **E:** Hardee's, McDonald's, Pizza Hut

AServ **E:** Mobil

W: Haines' Auto

EXIT WEST VIRGINIA/VIRGINIA

RVCamp **W:** Lazy A Campground (9 Miles)

Med **E:** ✚ First Med Walk-In Clinic

ATM **E:** Huntington Banks of WV, OneValley Bank

Parks **E:** Harper Fairy

Other **E:** Berkley Pharmacy(RX), Food Lion Supermarket

(2) WV Welcome Center (RR, Phones, Picnic, Vending; Northbound)

↑WEST VIRGINIA

↓VIRGINIA

323 **(324)** U.S. 11, VA 669, Whitehall

TStop **W:** Flying J Travel Center(*, LP, SCALES)

Gas **E:** Exxon(*, LP)

Food **W:** Flying J Travel Center

321 VA 672, Clearbrook, Brucetown

FStop **E:** Mobil

Food **E:** Old Stone Restaurant(*)

ATM **E:** Mobil

Other **E:** Kingdom Animal Hospital

(320) VA Welcome Center (RR, Phones, Picnic, Vending; Southbound)

317 U.S. 11, to VA 37, Stephenson, to U.S.522N, to U.S.50 W, Winchester

Gas **W:** Amoco(*, D, CW), Exxon(*, D), Mobil(*, D), Quick Stop(*, D), Shell(*)

Food **W:** Blimpie's Subs (Amoco), Burger King, Denny's, Godfather's Pizza (Amoco), McDonald's(PLAY), Quick Stop, Taco Bell

Lodg **W:** Econolodge

AServ **W:** Exxon

Med **W:** ✚ Hospital

ATM **W:** Amoco, First VA Bank, Quick Stop, Shell

315 VA 7, Winchester, Berryville

Gas **E:** Sheetz(*, D, LP, 24)

W: Chevron(D), Citgo(*), Shell(*, D, 24), Texaco(D)

Food **E:** 220 Seafood, Dairy Corner Frozen Custard

W: Arby's, Billy Bow's (Shell), Captain D's Seafood, Citgo, George's Pizza, KFC, Little Caesars Pizza, McDonald's, Shell, SHONEY'S, Shoney's (Shoney's Inn), Wendy's

Lodg **W:** SHONEY'S, Shoney's

AServ **E:** Clark Volvo/Dodge

W: Chevron, Texaco, Winchester Auto Center

Med **W:** ✚ Hospital

ATM **E:** Sheetz

W: Marathon Bank, Wachovia Bank

Other **E:** Winchester Shopping Ctr

W: Food Lion Supermarket, PharmHouse(RX)

313AB U.S. 17, U.S. 50, U.S. 522, Winchester

Gas **E:** Chevron(*, D, LP), Exxon, Shell(*, D), Texaco(*, D)

W: Sheetz(*, D, LP, 24)

Food **E:** Asian Garden, Baskin Robbins (Exxon), Chason's Country Buffet, China Town Buffet,

1485
RAMADA INN®
1130 Motel Drive • Woodstock, VA • 22664
Free Local Calls
50 Channel Cable TV
Full Service Restaurant
Shanley's Lounge
Outdoor Pool
Indoor Corridors with Elevator
AAA & AARP Rates
540-459-5000 • Toll Free Reservations: 1-800-272-6232
VIRGINIA ▪ I-81 ▪ EXIT 283

EXIT VIRGINIA

Cracker Barrel, Dunkin Donuts (Exxon), Hardee's, Hoss' Steakhouse, Jennny's Restaurant (Holiday Inn), Ruberto's Pizza, Texas Steak House, Waffle House

W: Bob Evan's Restaurant, KFC, Lee Jackson Restaurant, McDonald's, Pargo's, Ruby Tuesday

Lodg **E:** Comfort Inn, Holiday Inn, Super 8, TraveLodge

W: Best Western, Budgetel Inn, Hampton Inn, Quality Inn

AServ **E:** Texaco

W: Jiffy Lube

Med **W:** ✚ Hospital, ✚ Urgent Care Clinic

ATM **E:** Exxon, Southern Financial Bank

W: Sheetz

Other **E:** Food Lion Supermarket

W: Apple Blossom Mall

310 VA 37, U.S. 11, CR 642, Kernstown

FStop **W:** Shell

Lodg **W:** Eco Village Budget Motel

AServ **W:** Miller Suzuki

RVCamp **W:** Candy Hill Campground

Med **W:** ✚ Hospital

Other **W:** State Police

307 VA 277, Stephens City , to RT 340

Gas **E:** Citgo(*), Shell(*, D), Texaco(D)

W: Exxon(*), Sheetz(24)

Food **E:** Burger King, Domino's Pizza, KFC, McDonald's, Red Apple Deli (Shell), Roma Restaurant & Pizzeria, Subway (Shell), Taco Bell, Wendy's, Western Steer Family Steakhouse

W: Dunkin Donuts (Exxon), Kaycee Freeze

Lodg **E:** Comfort Inn, Holiday Inn Express

Med **E:** ✚ Urgent Care Clinic

ATM **E:** Texaco, Wachovia Bank

W: Exxon, Sheetz

Other **E:** Coin Car Wash

(304) Weigh Station (Southbound)

(304) Weigh Station (Northbound)

302 VA 627, Middletown, Cedarville

FStop **E:** Exxon(*, LP)

W: Amoco(*, D)

Food **W:** Blimpie's Subs (Amoco), Godfather's Pizza (Amoco)

AServ **E:** Exxon

ATM **W:** Amoco

300 Junction I-66, Washington D.C., Front Royal

298 U.S. 11, Strasburg

Gas **E:** Mobil

Food **E:** Burger King

AServ **E:** Mobil

RVCamp **W:** Battle of Cedar Creek Campground (1 Mile)

Other **E:** Strasburg Museum

W: Belle Grove Plantation

296 VA 55, Strasburg

Other **E:** Hupps Battlefield Museum

291 VA 651, Toms Brook

TStop **W:** The Virginian Truck Center(*), Wilco Travel Plaza(*)

Food **W:** Dairy Queen (Wilco), Milestone(*) (Wilco), The Virginian, Wilco Travel Plaza

Lodg **W:** The Virginian

TServ **W:** The Virginian

TWash **W:** Truck Wash

283 VA 42, Woodstock

Gas **E:** Chevron(*, CW), Texaco(*)

W: Coastal(*), Exxon(D)

Food **E:** Hardee's, KFC, McDonald's(PLAY), Pizza Hut, Ramada, TCBY (Texaco), Taco Bell, Wendy's

Lodg **E:** Ramada

AServ **W:** Exxon (Wrecker Service)

Med **E:** ✚ Hospital

ATM **E:** First Virginia Bank

Other **E:** 7-11 Convenience Store

279 VA 185, VA 675, Edinburg

EXIT VIRGINIA

Gas E: Amoco(*, D), Shell(*)
Food E: Subway (Amoco)
AServ E: Cook's Auto Sales
ATM E: Crestar Bank, Shell
Other E: **Coin Operated Laundry**

277 VA 614, Bowmans Crossing (Northbound, Reaccess Southbound Only)

273 VA 292, VA 703, Mt Jackson, Basye
TStop E: **Sheetz**(*, SCALES), **Shenandoah Truck Center**(*, SCALES)
Gas E: Citgo(*)
Food E: **Baskin Robbins (Sheetz)**, Burger King, **Denny's (Best Western)**, **Pizza (Sheetz)**, **Subs & More (Sheetz)**
Lodg E: **Best Western**
AServ E: Jeff's Auto Body
ATM E: Shenandoah

269 VA 730, Shenandoah Caverns
Gas E: Chevron(*, D, K)
Other W: **Shenandoah Caverns**, **Tuttle & Spice Museum**(*)

264 U.S. 211, New Market, Timberville Luray
Gas E: Chevron(*, D), Exxon, Shell(*, D, LP)
W: Citgo(*)
Food E: Blimpie's Subs, **Johnny Appleseed Restaurant (Quality Inn)**, McDonald's
W: Jane's Cafe
Lodg E: Blue Ridge Inn, Budget Inn, **Quality Inn**, **Ramada Inn (see our ad this page)**
W: DAYS INN Days Inn
AServ E: Exxon
RVCamp E: **Rancho Campground**
ATM E: Crestar Bank, F&M Bank, Shell
Parks E: **Shenandoah Nat'l Park**
Other E: **Applecore Village**, **Fireworks**, **Laundromat**, **Luray Caverns**, **Skyline Drive**
W: **Calvary Museum**, **New Market Civil War Battlesite**, **Tourist Info.**

(262) **Rest Area (RR, Phones, Picnic, Vending)**

257 U.S. 11, VA 259, Mauzy, Broadway.
RVCamp E: **Endless Cavern Campground (5.2 Miles)**, **KOA Campgrounds (3.4 Miles)**

251 U.S. 11, Harrisonburg
Gas W: **Shell**(*, D)
Food W: Bar-B-Q Ranch
Lodg W: Scotish Inn
TServ W: **Highway Motors**, **Ray Car Tires Auto & Truck Tire Center**
Other W: **Fed Ex Drop Box (Shell)**, **Fireworks**, **Huffman Trailer Sales**

247AB U.S. 33, Elkton, Harrisonburg
Gas E: Royal(*)
W: Amoco(*), Chevron(*, D), Etna(*, D, LP), Exxon(*, D) (FedEx Box), Royal(*), Texaco(*)
Food E: Barney's Cafe, Boston Beanery, Captain D's Seafood, Chili's, China Jade, El Charro Mexican, Guiseppe's Pizza, Little Caesars Pizza, Long John Silver, Mr J's Bagels, Pargo's Southern Food, Ponderosa Steakhouse, Red Lobster, Ruby Tuesday, Taco Bell, Texas Steakhouse, Waffle House, Wendy's
W: Arby's, Blimpie's Subs (Amoco), Carasel Frozen Treats, Chang House, China Inn, Golden China, Hardee's, KFC, L'Itilia Restaurant, McDonald's, Mr Gatty's Pizza, Papa John's, Pizza Hut, Sigon Vietnamese, Subway
Lodg E: Comfort Inn, **Econolodge**, **Hampton Inn**, Motel 6, Sheraton Four Points
W: Motel Marvilla, SHONEY'S Shoney's
AServ E: Jiffy Lube, Nisson, Speedee Oil Change

EXIT VIRGINIA

W: Advance Auto Parts, Blue Ridge Heishman's Blue Ridge Tire Co
RVCamp E: **RV Camping**
Med W: **+ Hospital**
ATM E: Central Fidelity, Crestar Bank, F&M Bank, First Union, First Virginia Bank, Jefferson National Bank, NationsBank
W: Amoco, NationsBank
Other E: **Animal House**, **CVS Pharmacy**, **Food Lion Supermarket**, **K-Mart**(RX), **Kroger Supermarket**(RX), **Mail Boxes Etc**, **Rac-N-Sac Groceries**, **Scottswood Valley Shopping Ctr**, **Valley Mall**, **Wal-Mart Supercenter**
W: Car Wash, **CloverLeaf Shopping Center**, **Coin Laundry**, **Fex X Box (Exxon)**, **Rite Aide Pharmacy**, **Rolling Hills Shopping Ctr**, **Save-a-Center Grocery**

245 VA 659, Port Republic Road
Gas E: Chevron(*, D), Exxon(*, D), Texaco(*)
Food E: Blimpie's Subs, Citgo(*, D, K), Dairy Queen, Howard Johnson, J Willowby's Road house (Days Inn), Subway (Exxon)
Lodg E: DAYS INN Days Inn, Howard Johnson
Med W: **+ Hospital**
ATM E: Exxon

243 U.S. 11, Harrisonburg (West Side Services Accessible Pleasant Valley Rd)
TStop W: **Travel Center**(*, D, LP)
Gas W: Amoco(D, CW), Citgo(*), Exxon(*), Mobil(*, D, K)
Food W: **Crab Apple Restaurant (Ramada Inn)**, **Cracker Barrel**, Deli (Exxon), Double Happiness (Chinese), Pano's Seafood, Southside Diner (Travel Center), Waffle House
Lodg W: Ramada, Red Carpet Inn, Super 8 (Tractor Parking Only No Trailers)
AServ E: Big L Tires
W: Amoco, Bob Wade Isuza, Carr's Auto, Exxon, Mobil, Toyota
TServ E: **Big L Tire**, **Freeman Trucking**
W: **ThermoKing**, **Truck Enterprises (Kenworth)**
TWash W: **Travel Truckstop**(*, D, LP, K)
ATM W: F&M Bank, Travel Ctr

240 VA 257, VA 682, Mt Crawford, Bridgewater
Gas W: Exxon(*, D) (FedEx)
Food W: Arby's (Exxon)
Other W: **Fed Ex Drop Box (Exxon)**

235 VA 256, Weyers Cave, Grottoes, Mt Sidney
FStop E: **Mobil**(*, D)
W: **Amoco**(*)
Food W: **Subway (Amoco)**
ATM W: Amoco
Other E: **Grand Caverns**

Ramada Inn
Luray, VA
$49.00 Single/Double
138 Whispering Hill Rd., 211E Bypass
Luray, VA 22835
540-743-4521 • 800-2RAMADA
Restaurant/Lounge on Premises
Complimentary Coffee
Meeting/Banquet Facilities
Handicap Accessible • Exterior Corridors
Miniature Golf on Premises • Outdoor Pool
Truck/Large Vehicle Parking
1654 I-81, Exit 264, Take 211E hotel is 3 1/2 mi on L passed Luray Caverns on 211E Bypass
VIRGINIA ▪ I-81 ▪ EXIT 264

EXIT VIRGINIA

(232) **Rest Area (RR, Phones, Picnic, Vending)**

227 VA 612, Verona
Gas E: Amoco(*, D)
W: Exxon(*)
Food E: Subway (Amoco), Waffle Inn
W: China City (Take-Out), Hardee's, McDonald's
Lodg W: Scottish Inns
AServ E: Verona Car Care Center
RVCamp E: **Waynesboro North Forty Campground (11.6 Miles)**
W: **KOA Campgrounds (2.9 Miles)**
Other W: **Coin Laundry**, **Factory Antique Mall**, **Food Lion Grocery Store**, **Revco Drugs**

225 VA 275, Woodrow Wilson Pkwy, Staunton, Monterey
Food E: **Innkeeper**
W: Holiday Inn, The Host Inn
Lodg E: **Innkeeper**
W: Holiday Inn (Golf Course), **The Host Inn**

222 U.S. 250, Staunton, Fishersville
Gas E: Exxon(*), Texaco(*, D, LP)
W: Augusta(*, LP)
Food E: McDonald's (Exxon), Mrs Rowes Family Restaurant, SHONEY'S **Shoney's**, Texas Steak House
W: Burger King, Shorties Diner, Waffle House
Lodg E: Best Western
W: Comfort Inn, Econolodge, Super 8
AServ W: Augusta(*, LP), McDonnah Truck Service, Tire Mart, Toyota
ATM W: Planters Bank
Other W: **Animal Care**, **Wal-Mart Supercenter**(RX) **(Eye Care, Fireworks)**

221 Junction I-64 East (Southbound)

220 VA 262, U.S. 11, Staunton (Exit To Ltd Access)

217 VA 654, Mint Spring, Stuarts Draft

213 U.S. 11, Greenville

205 VA 606, Raphines, Steeles Tavern

200 VA 710, Fairfield

(199) **Rest Area (RR, Phones; Southbound)**

195 U.S. 11, Lee Hwy
TStop W: **Shell**(*, D)
Gas W: Citgo
Food E: Maple Hall
W: Aunt Sara's Pancake House
Lodg E: Maple Hall
W: Howard Johnson, **Ramada**, Red Oaks Inn

191 Junction I-64 West, Lexington, Charleston
Food W: Shoney's

188AB U.S. 60, Lexington, Buena Vista
Gas W: Exxon(*, D, LP)
AServ W: Exxon
Med W: **+ Hospital (2.5 Miles)**
ATM W: Exxon
Other W: **Stonewall Jackson Museum**

180 U.S. 11, Natural Bridge, Glasgow
Gas E: Fergusons Grocery(*), Shell(*)
W: Chevron(K), Texaco(*, D)
Food E: Fancy Hill
W: **Budget Inn**
Lodg E: Fancy Hill Motel
W: **Budget Inn**
AServ E: Shell
W: Chevron

EXIT VIRGINIA

RVCamp	**E:** Natural Bridge of Virginia (see our ad this page)
Other	**E:** Enchanted Castle Studio Tours
175	U.S. 11, Natural Bridge
Gas	**E:** Exxon(*)
AServ	**E:** Exxon
RVCamp	**E:** Natural Bridge of Virginia (see our ad this page)
168	CR 614, Arcadia
Gas	**E:** Shell(*)
Food	**E:** Spice House Restaurant (Wattstull)
Lodg	**E:** Wattstull Motel
AServ	**E:** Shell
RVCamp	**E:** Yogi Bear Camp Resort (6.1 Miles)
167	U.S. 11, Buchanan (Southbound)
162	U.S. 11, Buchanan
Gas	**W:** BP(D), Texaco(*, LP)
AServ	**W:** BP
ATM	**W:** Texaco
(158)	Rest Area (RR, Phones; Southbound)
156	CR 640, to U.S. 11
150AB	150A - US 220 S to US 460 E, US 11 Troutville, Cloverdale, Lynch, 150B - Clifton Forge, Daleville, Fincastle, US 220N
TStop	**E:** Citgo(*, 24)
FStop	**E:** Pilot Travel Center(*)
Gas	**E:** Dodge's Store(*, K), Exxon
	W: Amoco(*, D, 24), Express(*), Exxon(*, K)

804-845-5975

1827

1500 Main St. Rt 29 Exit 1
Lynchburg, VA

$41
1-3 Persons

Based on availability.
Not valid with other discounts,
during holidays ro special events.

Continental Breakfast • Restaurant on Premises
Outdoor Pool • Coin Laundry Nearby
Kids Under 12 Stay & Eat Free
Meeting/Banquet Facilities
Truck/Large Vehicle Parking
Exterior Corridors • Cable TV w/HBO

I-81 Exit 143, I-581S. to 460E, Exit 501 N 1 mi. Take 29N Exit Main St.
I-64 Take 29 S to Lynchburg, Exit 1 Main St.

VIRGINIA • I-81 • EXIT 143

Natural Bridge

- Inn & Conference Center
- Natural Bridge & Cedar Creek Trail
- Cavern
- Wax Museum
- Restaurant & Lounge
- Driver's Lounge
- Ample Bus Parking

800-533-1410

1490

VIRGINIA • I-81 • EXIT 175 & 180

EXIT VIRGINIA

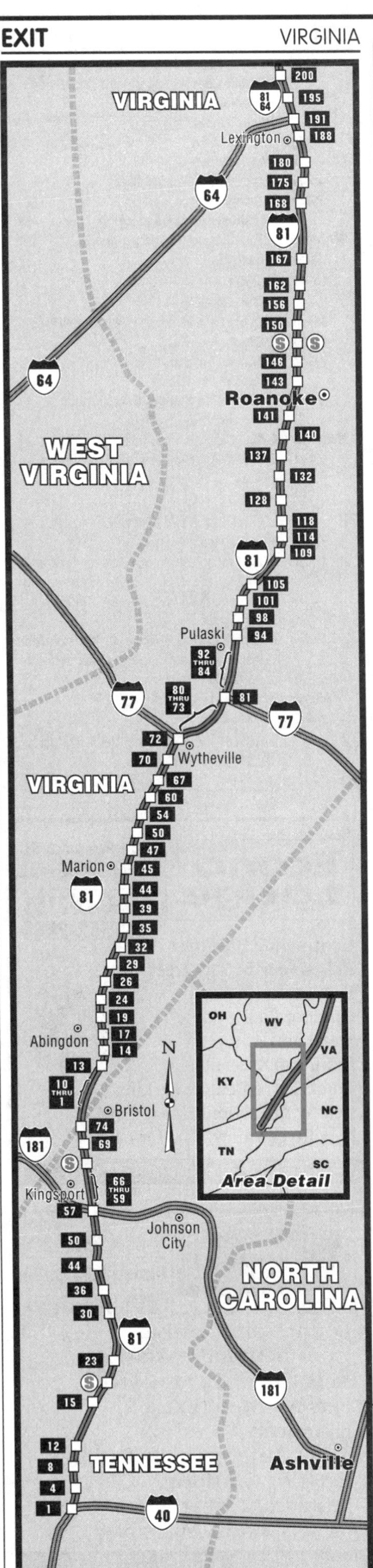

EXIT VIRGINIA

Food	**E:** Burger King, Citgo, Country Pride Restaurant (Citgo), Country-Cookin, Cracker Barrel, Hardee's, Italian Bella, McDonald's, SHONEY'S, Shoney's, Subway (Pilot), Taco Bell, Waffle House
	W: Best Western, Pizza Hut, Western Sizzlin'
Lodg	**E:** Citgo, Comfort Inn, Holiday Inn, TraveLodge
	W: Best Western, EconoLodge
AServ	**E:** Pennzoil Oil Change
	W: Amoco(24)
TWash	**E:** Truck Wash U.S.A(24)
RVCamp	**E:** Berglund Scott Cooper, Butch Mock Motor Sports
ATM	**E:** Wachovia Bank
	W: Bank of Fincastle
Other	**E:** CVS Pharmacy(RX), Winn Dixie Supermarket
	W: Coin Car Wash
(149)	Weigh Station (Southbound)
(149)	Weigh Station (Northbound)
146	VA 115, Hollins, Roanoke
Gas	**E:** Exxon(*), Shell(*, D)
Food	**E:** Country Kitchen (Country Inn & Suites), McDonald's, The Peaks (Days Inn)
Lodg	**E:** Country Inn & Suites, DAYS INN Days Inn, Hampton Inn
143	Junction I-581, U.S. 220, Downtown Roanoke
Lodg	**E:** Ramada Limited (in Lynchburg, see our ad this page)
141	VA 419, Salem, New Castle
Gas	**E:** Texaco(*)
Food	**E:** Burger King (Texaco)
Lodg	**E:** Budgetel Inn, Quality Inn
Med	**E:** + Veterinary Clinic
	W: + Hospital
140	VA 311, Salem, New Castle
137	VA 112, CR 619, Salem
Gas	**E:** Amoco(*, LP), Shell(*, D)
	W: Chevron
Food	**E:** Burger Boy, Denny's, El Rodeo Mexican, Fazoli's, Hardee's, Mama Mia's Italian Restaurant, Omelet Shoppe, SHONEY'S, Shoney's
Lodg	**E:** Comfort Inn, Knight's Inn, Salem Court Motel, Super 8, Windsor Hotel
	W: Holiday Inn
AServ	**E:** Anderson's Auto Repair, Monroe Muffler & Brakes
	W: Chevron
RVCamp	**E:** Snyder's Sales Part & Services
ATM	**E:** Amoco
Other	**E:** Food Lion Supermarket, Wal-Mart(RX)
132	CR 647, Dixie Caverns, Elliston, Shawsville
Food	**E:** Blue Jay Motel
Lodg	**E:** Blue Jay Motel
RVCamp	**E:** Dixie Caverns Campground (.25 Miles)
(129)	Rest Area (RR, Phones; Northbound)
128	U.S. 11, CR 603, Ironto
FStop	**W:** Citgo(*)
Gas	**E:** Mobil(*)

Bold red print shows RV & Bus parking available or nearby

EXIT VIRGINIA

118 U.S. 11, U.S. 460, Christiansburg, Blacksburg
- **FStop** E: Shell[*]
- **Gas** W: Amoco, Chevron, Exxon[*, D], Racetrac[*], Shell[*, LP], Texaco[*]
- **Food** E: Cracker Barrel, Huckleberry Restaurant (Super 8 Motel), Super 8
  W: Bojangles (Shell), Hardee's, McDonald's, Pizza Hut, The Outpost Restaurant, Waffle House, Wendy's, Western Sizzlin'
- **Lodg** E: Days Inn, Hampton Inn, Super 8
  W: EconoLodge (see our ad this page), Howard Johnson (see our ad this page)
- **AServ** W: Amoco, Chevron, Exxon, Toyota Dealer
- **RVCamp** E: Interstate Overnite Park (.5 Miles)
- **Med** W: Hospital
- **ATM** W: Racetrac

114 VA 8, Christiansburg, Floyd
- **Gas** W: Citgo[*], Deli Mart[*, LP]
- **Food** W: Deli Mart
- **AServ** W: A & M Auto Repair, Jack's Garage

109 VA 177, CR 600, Radford
- **TStop** W: BP[*, LP]
- **Gas** W: Marathon[*, K]
- **Med** W: Hospital

(108) Rest Area (Southbound)

(108) Rest Area (RR, Phones; Northbound)

105 VA 232, CR 605, Radford

101 VA 660, Claytor Lake State Park
- **Gas** W: Citgo[*, D, LP]
- **Lodg** E: Claytor Lake Inn
- **AServ** E: Clayton Lake Auto Repair
- **Parks** W: Claytor Lake State Park (2 Miles)

98 VA 100 North, Dublin, Pearisburg
- **FStop** W: Texaco[*]
- **Gas** E: Exxon[*, D], Mobil[*, LP]
  W: Marathon[*]
- **Food** E: Bon Fire Restaurant (Comfort Inn), Subway (Exxon)
  W: Blimpie's Subs (Texaco), Burger King, McDonald's, Waffle House, Wendy's
- **Lodg** E: Comfort Inn, Holiday Inn Express
- **Med** W: Hospital
- **ATM** W: First VA Bank

94 VA 99, Pulaski, Service Road
- **Gas** W: Exxon[*, LP]
- **Lodg** E: Red Carpet Inn
- **AServ** E: Jimmy's Roll Back Service & Auto Repair
- **Parks** W: New River Trail State Park

92 CR 658, Draper
- **Gas** E: BP[*]
- **RVCamp** E: Horseshoe Campground
- **Parks** E: New River Trail State Park

89AB 89A - VA 100S, Hillsville, 89B - US 11N, Pulaski

86 CR 618, Service Road
- **TStop** W: I-81 Auto/Truck Plaza (Chevron)
- **Food** W: The Appletree Restaurant (I-81 Auto/Truck Plaza)
- **Lodg** W: I-81 Auto/Truck Plaza (Chevron)
- **TServ** W: I-81 Auto/Truck Plaza (Chevron)

84 CR 619, Grahams Forge
- **FStop** W: Shell[*]
- **Food** W: Dairy Queen (Texaco FS), Fox Mountain Inn
- **Lodg** W: Fox Mountain Inn
- **Other** W: Grahams Forge Foodette[*]

81 Junction I-77 South, Charlotte

80 U.S. 52 South, VA 121 North, Fort Chiswell, Maxmeadows
- **TStop** E: Petro[SCALES]
- **FStop** W: Citgo[*, LP]
- **Gas** E: BP[*, D], Exxon[*] (Petro TS)
  W: Amoco
- **Food** E: Buck's Pizza, Iron Skillet Restaurant (Petro TS), Little Caesars Pizza (Petro TS), Wendy's (Petro TS)
  W: McDonald's
- **Lodg** E: Comfort Inn
  W: Country Inn
- **AServ** E: Lee's Tire, Brake, & Muffler
- **TServ** E: Petro
  W: Complete Truck Service[24]
- **RVCamp** E: Fort Chiswell RV Campground
- **ATM** E: Petro TS
- **Other** E: Car Wash, Laundromat

77 Service Road
- **TStop** E: Flying J Travel Plaza[*, LP, RV DUMP, SCALES]
- **FStop** E: Citgo[*] (Fuel Stop)
- **Gas** E: Conoco, Texaco[*, D]
  W: Exxon[*] (RV Diesel)
- **Food** E: Burger King, Subway (Citgo), Thads Restaurant[SCALES] (Flying J)
- **RVCamp** E: KOA Campgrounds (.5 Miles)
- **Other** E: Gale Winds (Go-carts, putt-putt, family games)
  W: State Police

73 U.S. 11, South Wytheville
- **Gas** E: Exxon, Mobil[*, LP], Shell[*, D]
- **Food** E: Bob Evan's Restaurant, El Puerto Mexican Restaurant, KFC, Mom's Country Store, Peking Restaurant, Shoney's, Steak House & Saloon, Waffle House
- **Lodg** E: Days Inn, Holiday Inn, Interstate Motor Lodge, Motel 6, Red Carpet Inn, Shenandoah Inn, Wythe Inn
- **AServ** E: Exxon
- **Med** E: Hospital

72 Junction I-77 North, Bluefield, US 52S Charlotte, Roanoke

70 U.S. 21, U.S. 52, Wytheville

Econo Lodge
2430 Roanoke St.
Christianburg, VA
540-382-6161
800-553-2666
Continental Breakfast
Kids Under 12 Stay Free
Restaurant Nearby
Outdoor Pool • Cable TV
Small Pets Allowed
Handicap Accessible
Truck/Large Vehicle Parking
Nearby Attractions: Dixie Cave, New River Valley, Claytor Lake
Group Rates Available
1763
VIRGINIA • I-81 • EXIT 118

Howard Johnson
I-81 • Exit 118
Christianburg, VA
540-381-0150
Lounge on Premises
Continental Breakfast
Kids Under 12 Stay Free
Pets Allowed (Extra $)
Handicap Accessible
Truck/Large vehicle Parking
Exterior Corridors
Restaurant Nearby
Jacuzzi Suites Available
1480
VIRGINIA • I-81 • EXIT 118

- **FStop** E: BP[*, D]
- **Gas** E: Virginia Heights Travel Store[*, D, K] (BP)
  W: Exxon[*, K], Shell[*, CW]
- **Food** E: Arby's, McDonald's[PLAY], Turn One Restaurant, Virginia Heights Restaurant
  W: Scrooge's Restaurant
- **Lodg** W: Comfort Inn
- **AServ** E: BP, Virginia Heights Travel Store (BP)
- **Med** E: Hospital
- **ATM** E: First Virginia Bank
- **Other** E: CVS Pharmacy, Evansham Square, Food Lion Supermarket

67 U.S. 11, Wytheville

(61) Rest Area (RR, Phones, Picnic, Pet Walk; Northbound)

60 VA 90, Rural Retreat
- **FStop** E: Citgo[*, LP]
- **Food** E: Citgo, McDonald's
- **Other** E: Rural Retreat Lake

(54) Rest Area (RR, HF, Phones, Picnic; Southbound)

54 CR 683, Groseclose (Mountain Empire Airport, Settlers Museum Of SW Virginia)
- **FStop** E: Texaco[*, K]
- **Gas** E: Exxon[*, D]
- **Food** E: Cumbow's Restaurant, Dairy Queen (Exxon), Exxon, Village Motel
- **Lodg** E: Village Motel
- **Other** E: Settler's Museum of SW Virginia

50 U.S. 11, Atkins
- **FStop** W: Citgo[*]
- **Food** W: Atkins Diner
- **Lodg** W: Days Inn
- **Other** W: Car Wash, Cullop's Old Stone Tavern

47 U.S. 11, Marion
- **Gas** W: Exxon[*]
- **Lodg** W: Best Western, Econolodge, Virginia House Inn
- **AServ** W: Plymouth Dodge Dealer
- **RVCamp** W: Hungry Mother Family Campground (4.1 Miles)
- **Med** W: Hospital
- **ATM** W: Bank of Marion
- **Parks** W: Hungry Mother State Park

45 VA 16, Marion
- **Gas** E: Shell[*, D, LP]
- **Food** E: Apple Tree Restaurant
- **AServ** W: Grissom Motor Parts (NAPA)
- **Med** W: Hospital
- **Parks** E: Grayson Highlands State Park (33.5 Miles)
- **Other** E: Beemers Market, Mount Rogers Wreck Area Visitors Center

44 U.S. 11, Marion (Difficult Reaccess)
- **AServ** W: Marion Tire Dealer Inc.
- **Other** W: Smyth County Animal Hospital

39 U.S. 11, CR 645, Seven Mile Ford Road
- **Lodg** E: Budget Inn Hotel, Ford Motel
- **RVCamp** W: Interstate Campground (.1 Miles)

35 VA 107, Chilhowie
- **FStop** W: Rouse Fuel Center[*, LP]
- **Gas** E: Gas-Haus, Texaco[*]
  W: Coastal[*], Exxon[*], Gas-N-Go
- **Food** E: Mountainside Restaurant (Knights Inn)
  W: McDonald's[PLAY], Shuler's Pizza Factory, Subway
- **Lodg** E: Knight's Inn
- **AServ** W: Claude Blevins
- **TServ** W: Claude Blevins
- **ATM** W: Wachovia Bank
- **Other** W: Food City, Greever's Drugstore Inc., Laundromat, Our Father's House Bookstore

32 U.S. 11, Chilhowie

29 VA 91, Damascus, Glade Spring,

Bold red print shows RV & Bus parking available or nearby

EXIT — VIRGINIA

Saltville
- **Gas** E: Shell[*, D, LP]
  W: Chevron[*, LP, CW], Exxon[*, D, K, CW]
- **Food** E: Shell, Subway (Shell), Swiss Inn
  W: **Jiff-E-Jack Deli**
- **Lodg** E: Economy Inn & Restaurant, Swiss Inn
- **AServ** E: Apache Towing, **Interstate Auto Parts & Service**, Stage Coach Sales & Service
  W: Hick's Tire & Alignment
- **TServ** E: **Interstate Auto Parts & Service**
- **ATM** E: Shell

26 VA 737, Emory

24 VA 80, Meadowview

22 VA 704, Enterprise Rd

19 U.S. 11, U.S. 58, Abingdon, Damascus
- **FStop** E: **Texaco**[*]
  W: **Citgo**[*]
- **Gas** W: Chevron[*, D, K, CW, 24], Exxon[*, D]
- **Food** E: Cherokee Motel, Cherokee Restaurant (Cherokee Motel), Pizza Plus, **Subway (Texaco FS)**, The Ice Cream Stop, Wildflower Bakery
  W: Bella's Pizza & Subs, Burger King, **Cracker Barrel**, Empire Motor Lodge, Harbor House Seafood, **Omelette Shop**
- **Lodg** E: Cherokee Motel, Holiday Lodge Motel
  W: Alpine Motel, Empire Motor Lodge, Holiday Inn Express
- **RVCamp** E: **Calleb's Cove Campground**
- **ATM** E: Highlands Union Bank
  W: Exxon, First Bank & Trust Co.
- **Other** E: **Highlands Animal Hospital**
  W: **The Arts Depot, Tourist Info.**

17 U.S. 58 Alt, VA 75, Abingdon, South Holston Dam
- **Gas** E: Amoco[*, CW]
  W: Exxon[*], Shell[*, D, LP]
- **Food** E: Domino's Pizza, Long John Silver
  W: Arby's, Hardee's, Hunan Chinese, KFC, Little Caesars Pizza, Los Arcos Authentic Mexican, McDonald's[PLAY], Pappa John's Pizza, Pizza Hut, SHONEY'S, Shoney's, Subway, Sun's Chinese, TCBY, Taco Bell, Wendy's
- **Lodg** E: Hampton Inn
  W: Super 8
- **AServ** E: Mr Transmission, Xpress Lube
  W: Advance Auto Parts, **K-Mart**[RX]

"GET OFF AND GOLF INTERSTATE 81"
A Guide Book to 113 daily fee Courses Near the Highway
$12 + s/h MC-VISA
1497 Call: Adirondack Illustrator 518-962-4977
New York to Tennessee

Comfort Inn
Bristol, VA
AAA ◆◆◆ Approved
"Show Ad at check-in for 10% Discount"
Comfort Inn
FREE Continental Breakfast
Remote Cable TV with HBO
Swimming Pool
Kings • Doubles • Suites
60% Non-Smoking Rooms
Free Local Calls
Several Restaurants Nearby
540-466-3881 • For Reservations 800-228-5150
2368 Lee Highway • Bristol, VA 1069
VIRGINIA • I-81 • EXIT 5

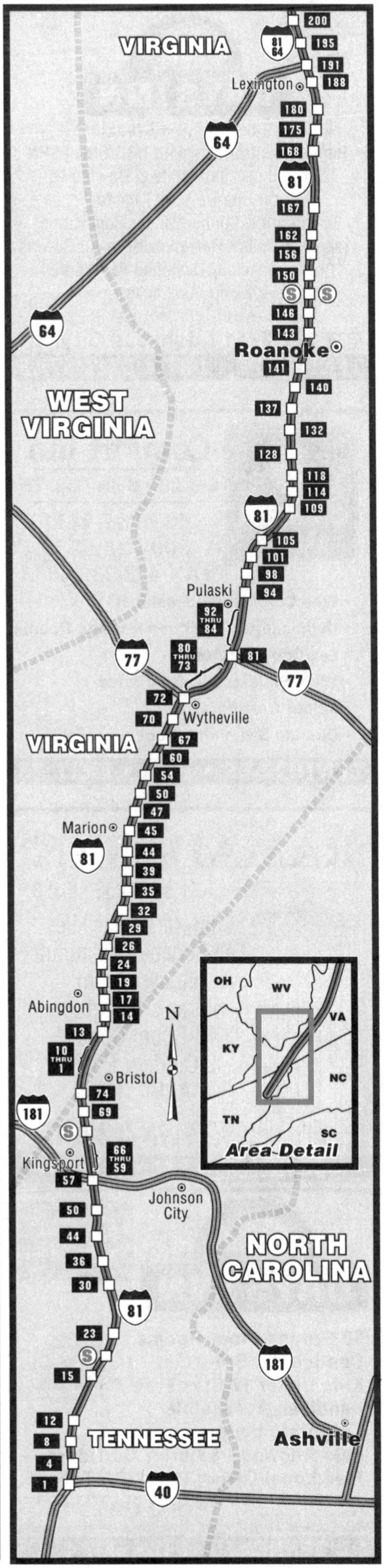

EXIT — C/TENNESSEE

- **ATM** W: First Virginia Bank, **Food City**[RX]
- **Other** E: **Anchor Bookshop**, Mr. Klean Kar Wash, Music Chiropractic Center
  W: Auto Wash, **Food City**[RX], **Food Lion**, **K-Mart**[RX], **Kroger Supermarket**[24, RX], **Revco**[RX]

14 U.S. 19 North, VA 140, Abingdon
- **Gas** W: Chevron[*, D, LP, CW, 24], Exxon[*], Texaco[*, D, K]
- **Lodg** W: Comfort Inn
- **AServ** W: Abington Auto Supply, Empire Ford
- **RVCamp** W: **Riverside Campground**
- **ATM** W: Highlands Union Bank

(13) **Rest Area (RR, HF, Phones, Picnic; Trucks Only)**

13 CR 611, Lee Highway (VA Highland Airport)
- **Gas** W: Texaco[*, D, K]
- **TServ** W: **Blueridge Kenworth**
- **Other** W: **Lee Highway Animal Hospital**

10 U.S. 11, U.S. 19, Lee Highway
- **FStop** W: **Conoco**[*, K, 24]
- **Gas** W: Chevron[*, D, CW, 24]
- **Food** W: Jerry's Steak & Seafood
- **Lodg** W: American Owned, Beacon Motel, Evergreen Motor Court, Red Carpet Inn, Robert E. Lee Motel, Scottish Inns, Skyland Inn, Thrifty Inn Motel
- **Other** W: **Fleenor Mobile Home Park (Overnight Parking)**

7 Old Airport Road, Bonham Road
- **Gas** E: Texaco[*, D]
  W: BP[*, K], Citgo[*], Conoco[*, D, 24]
- **Food** E: Sonic Drive in
  W: Damon's, Fazoli's Italian Food, Holiday Inn, **McDonald's (Wal-Mart)**, Ming Court (Mongolian Buffet), O'Charley's, Perkins Family Restaurant, Prime Sirloin, Subway, Taco Bell, **Wal-Mart Supercenter**[24, RX], Wendy's
- **Lodg** E: La Quinta Inn
  W: Holiday Inn
- **AServ** W: Advance Auto Parts, Exit 7 Muffler Man, GMC, Volvo Dealer, **Wal-Mart Supercenter**[24]
- **RVCamp** W: **Sugar Hollow**
- **Med** W: ✚ **Mountain Spring Family Care (Walk-Ins Welcome)**
- **ATM** E: Highlands Union Bank, Texaco
  W: Citgo, Conoco, First Union, **Wal-Mart Supercenter**
- **Other** W: **Food Country USA**, **Wal-Mart Supercenter**[RX]

5 U.S. 11, U.S. 19, Lee Highway
- **Gas** E: Amoco[*], Shell[*, CW]
  W: Exxon[*, LP]
- **Food** E: Arby's, Burger King[PLAY], Dairy Queen (Amoco), Hardee's, **KFC**, Long John Silver, McDonald's[PLAY], SHONEY'S, Shoney's
- **Lodg** E: Budget Inn, Crest Motel, Siesta Motel, Super 8
  W: Comfort Inn (see our ad this page)
- **AServ** E: Parts Plus
  W: Blevins Tire, Crabtree Buick Pontiac
- **RVCamp** W: **Lee Hwy Campground (1 Mile)**
- **ATM** E: Commonwealth Community Bank
- **Other** E: **Food Lion**[24], **Kroger Supermarket**, **Revco Drugs**

3 Junction I-381 South, Bristol (Bristol Motor Speedway)

1 West U.S. 58, U.S. 421, Bristol, Gate City

(0) **VA Welcome Center (RR, HF, Phones, Picnic; Southbound)**

↑VIRGINIA

↓TENNESSEE

(75) **TN Welcome Center (RR, HF, Phones, Picnic; Northbound)**

Bold red print shows RV & Bus parking available or nearby

EXIT TENNESSEE

74AB U.S. 11W, Kingsport, Bristol
- **Gas** W: Exxon(*)
- **Food** E: Scooter's Restaurant (Quality Inn), Shoney's
  W: Chicago Bar & Grill, Pizzeria Uno
- **Lodg** E: Days Inn, Hampton Inn, Quality Inn
  W: Hamrick Budget Motel, Holiday Inn
- **Med** E: + Bristol Regional Medical Center

69 TN 37, Blountville
- **Gas** E: BP(*, D, K)
- **Food** E: Arby's, BP, Subway(K) (BP)
- **ATM** E: BP

66 TN 126, Kingsport, Blountville
- **Gas** E: Amoco(*, D, K, 24), Exxon(*, D)
  W: Chevron(*, CW, 24)
- **Food** W: McDonald's(PLAY)
- **ATM** W: Chevron
- **Other** W: Factory Stores of America-Tri-Cities

63 TN 357, Tri - City Airport
- **FStop** W: Phillips 66(*, LP)
- **Gas** E: Exxon(*, D, LP)
  W: Amoco(*)
- **Food** E: Baskin Robbins (Exxon), Cracker Barrel, Exxon, Taco Bell (Exxon), Wendy's
- **Lodg** E: La Quinta Inn
  W: Red Carpet Inn
- **AServ** W: Sam's Club
- **RVCamp** W: KOA Kampground (1.25 Miles), Rocky Top Campground (1 Mile)
- **ATM** E: Exxon
- **Other** W: Sam's Club, The Antique Mall

59 TN 36, Kingsport, Johnson City
- **Gas** E: Amoco(*, D, K)
- **Food** E: Shoney's
  W: Arby's, Burger King, Hardee's, Huddle House, La Carreta Authentic Mexican, Little Caesars Pizza, McDonald's(PLAY), Perkins Family Restaurant, Raffael's Pizza, Pasta, etc., Subway
- **Lodg** E: Super 8
  W: Holiday Inn Express
- **AServ** W: Advance Auto Parts, Express Lube
- **ATM** W: First Tennessee Bank, Ingles Supermarket
- **Parks** W: Warrior's Path State Park (2 Miles)
- **Other** W: Food Lion, Ingles Supermarket, Revco Drugs, Southern Classic Car Wash, US Post Office

57AB Junction I-181, South U.S. 23, Johnson City, Kingsport (Limited Access)
- **Lodg** E: Days Inn (see our ad this page)
- **TServ** W: Freightliner

50 TN 93, Jonesborough, Fall Branch
- **AServ** E: NAPA

44 Jearoldstown Road
- **FStop** W: Exit 44 Market & Deli(*)
- **Gas** E: Amoco(*), No Name(*, D)
- **Food** E: No Name

(41) Rest Area (RR, Phones, Picnic, Vending, Pet Walk; Southbound)

(38) Rest Area (RR, HF, Phones, Picnic, Pet Walk; Northbound)

36 TN172, Baileyton Road
- **TStop** W: Davy Crockett Auto/Truck Stop(*, LP, SCALES, 24) (Marathon, Road Service)
- **FStop** E: Speedway(*, K)
  W: Texaco(*, K, CW)
- **Gas** W: BP(*, D, LP, K, 24)
- **Food** E: Blimpie Subs & Salads (Speedway), Speedway

1181

DAYS INN

— Free Continental Breakfast —
Remote Control TV's with HBO/CNN/ESPN
Located near Interstate & Downtown
On-Site Laundry Facility
Restaurant & Lounge(Under Renovation)
Free Local Calls • Refrigerator in All Rooms
Rooms Specially Designed For Women
Electronic Locks
— Outdoor Pool —
423-282-2211 • Johnson City, TN
TENNESSEE • I-81 • EXIT 57AB

Comfort Inn
Exit 23 • Bulls Gap, TN
423-235-9111
800-228-5150
FAX 423-235-0035
- Free Continental Breakfast
- Handicapped Facilities/Meeting Rooms
- Fax/Copy Services
- 100% Satisfaction Guarantee
- Indoor Corridors
- Outside Swimming Pool

1220
TENNESSEE • I-81 • EXIT 23

RAMADA INN®

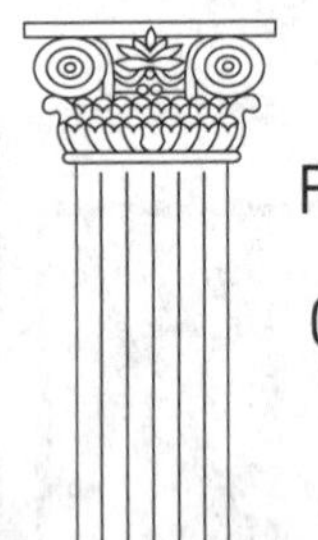

I-81 & US 25E - Exit 8
Conference Facilities
Full Service Restaurant
Fitness Room
Children's Playground
In-Room Coffee
2 Outdoor Pools
AARP Rate
423-587-2400
1165
TENNESSEE • I-81 • EXIT 8

1749

DAYS INN

$39.95* +tax

Truck/ Large Vehicle Parking

50 Ground Floor Rooms
Continental Breakfast
Kids Under 12 Stay Free
Handicap Accessible
Corporate Lodging
Pets Allowed • Exterior Corridors
Free Local Calls • Free USA Today
423-674-2573 • 800 DAYS INN
*Based on Availability. Not valid during special events or holidays.
TENNESSEE • I-81 • EXIT 4

EXIT TENNESSEE

- W: Davy Crockett Auto/Truck Stop (Marathon, Road Service), Subway (Texaco), Texaco
- **Lodg** W: 36 Motel
- **TServ** W: Davy Crockett Auto/Truck Stop(SCALES, 24) (Marathon, Road Service)
- **TWash** E: B&J Truck Wash
- **RVCamp** W: Baileyton Camp Inn-RV Park (1.7 Miles)
- **ATM** E: Speedway
  W: Davy Crockett Auto/Truck Stop (Marathon, Road Service), Texaco
- **Other** E: Car Wash

30 TN 70, Greeneville, Rogersville
- **Gas** E: Exxon(*, D, LP)
- **Food** E: Dairy Queen (Exxon), Exxon, Restaurant
- **ATM** E: Exxon

23 U.S. 11 East, Mosheim, Greeneville, Bulls Gap
- **TStop** E: Texaco Roadrunner Travel Center(*, D)
- **FStop** W: Phillips 66(*, SCALES)
- **Gas** E: Amoco(*, D), BP(*, K)
  W: Citgo(*)
- **Food** E: Pearl's Diner, TCBY (Amoco), Texaco Roadrunner Travel Center, Wendy's (Amoco)
  W: Citgo, McDonald's(PLAY), New York Pizza & Italian Restaurant, Taco Bell (Citgo), Tony's Bar-B-Que
- **Lodg** W: Comfort Inn (see our ad this page), Super 8
- **AServ** W: Tony's Tire Shop(24) (Wrecker Service)
- **Other** E: Home of Andrew Johnson (Visitor Ctr-13 Miles), Jonesborough

(21) Weigh Station (Southbound)

(20) Weigh Station, Parking Area (Northbound)

15 TN 340, Fish Hatchery Road
- **FStop** E: Amoco(*, K)
- **TServ** W: Exit 15 Truck & Trailer Repair

12 TN 160, Morristown, Lowland
- **Gas** E: Citgo(*), Streamline(*, K)
  W: Shell(*, K, 24)
- **ATM** W: Shell

8 U.S. 25 East, Morristown, White Pine (Farmer's Market)
- **Gas** E: Shell(*, D, K)
  W: BP(*, D, CW), Phillips 66(*, D)
- **Food** E: Catawba Restaurant
  W: Hardee's
- **Lodg** W: Parkway Inn, Ramada Inn (see our ad this page), Super 8
- **AServ** E: Shell
- **Parks** W: Cumberland Gap Historic National Park

4 TN 341, White Pine Road
- **TStop** W: Pines Truck Plaza(*)
- **Gas** E: Exxon(*, D)
  W: Amoco(*), Citgo(*), Texaco(*, D, K)
- **Food** W: Huddle House(24)
- **Lodg** E: Crown Inn
  W: Days Inn (see our ad this page), Hillcrest Inn
- **TServ** W: Pines Truck Plaza
- **ATM** W: Texaco
- **Parks** W: Panther Creek State Park (11 Miles)

(3) Rest Area (Southbound)

1AB 1A - I-40 E, Asheville, 1B - I-40 W, Knoxville

↑TENNESSEE

Begin I-81

Bold red print shows RV & Bus parking available or nearby

EXIT	WASHINGTON
	Begin I-82

↓WASHINGTON

EXIT	
(0)	I-90 East Spokane, I-90 West Seattle
3	WA 821S, Thrall Road
(7)	**Parking, View Point**
11	Military Area
(23)	**Rest Area (RR, Phones, RV Dump, P; Westbound)**
(25)	**Rest Area (RR, Phones, Picnic, RV Dump, P; Eastbound)**
26	WA 821N., To WA 823 Canyon Rd, Selah
Gas	N: Shell(*, LP)
Food	N: Nacho East (Shell), Quinto's Classic Subs (Shell), TCBY (Shell)
29	East Selah Road
30AB	Rest Haven Road, Selah
RVCamp	N: **Selah Trailer & Camper Sales(LP) (.5 Miles)**
31	N. 1st Street, N.16th Ave, N. 40th Ave, U.S. 12W, West Naches, White Pass
Gas	S: Arco(*), Exxon(*)
Food	S: Nendel's Inn, Settlers Inn Restaurant, Vineyard Steakhouse
Lodg	S: Allstar Motel, Big Valley Motel, Double Tree Hotel, Nendel's Inn, Pepper Tree Motel, Sun Country Inn
RVCamp	S: **Trailer Inns Good Sam Park, Trailer Village and RV Park**
Med	S: **✚ Hospital**
33	Yakima Ave., Terrace Heights
Gas	S: Citgo(*)
Food	N: Marti's Cafe Bakery and Spirits, **McDonald's (Wal-Mart)**
	S: **Cafe Pavilion (Food Pavilion)**, Dairy Queen, **Oriental Express (Food Pavilion)**, Sub Shop of Yakima, Taco Bell, The Owl's Nest
Lodg	N: Best Western, Oxford Suites
	S: Budget Suites, Cavanaugh's Gateway Hotel
Med	S: **✚ Yakima Family Health Center**
ATM	S: Citgo, **Food Pavilion(RX)**
Other	N: **Vision Center (Wal-Mart), Wal-Mart(RX), Washington's Fruit Place Visitor's Center**
	S: **Food Pavilion(RX)**, Gary's Food Market
34	WA 24E, Moxee, Nob Hill Blvd, Sun Dome Fairgrounds
FStop	S: **Commercial Fueling Network(*)**
Gas	S: Arco(*), Chevron(*, D, CW), Citgo(*), Exxon(D), Shell(*, D)
Food	N: **Little Caesars Pizza (K-Mart)**
	S: TCBY (Chevron)
RVCamp	N: **Yakima KOA (1.25 Miles)**
	S: **Circle H Ranch & Good Sam Park, The White Dove RV Park & Trailer**
Med	S: **✚ Hospital**
Parks	N: **Yakima Sportsman State Park (2 Miles)**
Other	N: **K-Mart(RX)**
	S: **Family Foods, Jackpot Food Market**
36	Union Gap, Valley Mall Blvd
TStop	S: **Texaco(*, LP, SCALES)**
FStop	S: **Arco(*)**
Gas	S: Arco(*)
Food	S: Denny's, **Gear Jammer Restaurant (Texaco TS)**, IHOP, Sea Galley Seafood & Prime Ribs, Settlers Inn Restaurant
Lodg	S: DAYS INN Days Inn, La Casa Motel, Quality Inn, Super 8
TWash	S: **Texaco**
RVCamp	S: **Country Canopy RV**
Med	S: **✚ Valley Medi-Center**
Other	S: Cosco, Rite Aid Pharmacy(RX), **ShopKo Grocery(RX) (Optical)**, Union Gap Police Dept., **Valley Mall**
37	U.S. 97 S., Goldendale; Bend, OR
38	Union Gap (Westbound)
40	Thorp Road, Parker Road
44	Wapato, Donald
Gas	N: Texaco(*, D)
Other	N: **Donald Fruit & Mercantile**
50	To U.S. 97 S., Goldendale, WA 22 E., Toppenish, Buena
Med	S: **✚ Hospital (3 Miles)**
52	Toppenish
Gas	N: Arco(*), BP(*, D) (The Cherry Patch), Chevron(*, 24)
Food	N: El Porton Family Mexican, McDonald's(PLAY), Rocky Mountain Chocolate Factory, Subway
Lodg	N: Comfort Inn
54	Zillah, Yakimah Valley Hwy.
Gas	S: Teapot Dome(D, LP)
Food	N: El Ranchito Tortilla Factory & Restaurant
58	WA 223S, Granger, Vanbelle Rd.
Gas	S: Conoco
Other	S: **Meza's Market & Grocery**
63	Outlook
RVCamp	N: **RV Park (3 Miles)**
67	Sunnyside, City Center, Port of Sunnyside
Med	N: **✚ Hospital**
Other	N: **Bi-Market Grocery**
69	WA 241, Sunnyside, Mapton, Vernita Bridge
FStop	N: **Texaco(*, LP)**
Gas	N: **Arco(*)**
Food	N: Burger King(PLAY), **Taco Maker Express (Texaco)**
Lodg	N: Rodeway Inn
Med	N: **✚ Hospital**
ATM	N: **Texaco**
72	Grandview, Stover Road, Yakima Valley Hwy., Wine Country Rd.
AServ	S: **Chrysler Auto Dealer, Mid-Valley Auto & RV Center**
RVCamp	N: **Camping**
	S: **Chrysler Auto Dealer, Chrysler Auto Dealer, Mid-Valley Auto & RV Center**
75	Grandview, County Line Road
AServ	S: Thomas Auto Parts
RVCamp	S: **Long's Home Center**
Other	S: **Visitor Information**
80	Gap Road, Prosser
TStop	S: **Texaco(*, LP, SCALES)**
Food	S: **Burger King**, Grand Slam Pizza, McDonald's(PLAY), **Northwoods Family Restaurant, The Barn Motor Inn (.25 Miles)**
Lodg	S: **Best Western**
RVCamp	S: **Texaco, Barn RV Park (.25 Miles)**
Med	S: **✚ Hospital**
Other	S: **Visitor Information**
(80)	**Rest Area (RR, Phones, Picnic, P; South Side Exit 80)**
82	WA 22, WA 221, Mabton, Patterson, Prosser
Other	S: **Hospital**
88	Gibbon Road
FStop	S: **Four-P(*, D)**
93	Yakitat Road
96	WA 224E, Benton City, West Richland, WA 225N, Kiona
Gas	N: BP(*, D, LP)
Food	N: Cactus Jack's Cafe (BP)
RVCamp	N: **Beach RV Park**
102	Junction I-182, U.S. 12E, Richland, Pasco, to U.S. 395 Spokane
Med	N: **✚ Hospital**
104	Dallas Rd.
Gas	N: Conoco(*)
Food	N: Hot Stuff Pizza (Conoco), Smash Hit Subs (Conoco)
109	Clear Water Rd., Badger Rd.
RVCamp	N: **Campground**
113	U.S. 395N to I-82, Kennewick, Pasco
Med	N: **✚ Hospital**
Other	N: **State Police**
114	Locust Grove Road
122	Coffin Road
(130)	**Weigh Station (Westbound)**
131	WA 14W, Plymouth, Vancouver
RVCamp	S: **Campground**

↑WASHINGTON

↓OREGON

EXIT	
1	**U.S. 395 S., U.S. 730, Umatilla, Irrigon, McNary Dam, Port of Umatilla, Oregon Welcome Center, Weigh Station (RR, Phones)**
TStop	S: **Crossroads(*, SCALES)**
FStop	S: **Arco(*)**
RVCamp	N: **Hat Rock Campground**
	S: **Umatilla RV Park & Camp & Marina**
Med	N: **✚ Hospital**
	S: **✚ Umatilla Medical Clinic**
Other	S: **US Post Office**
5	Power Line Road
10	Westland Road

↑OREGON

Begin I-82

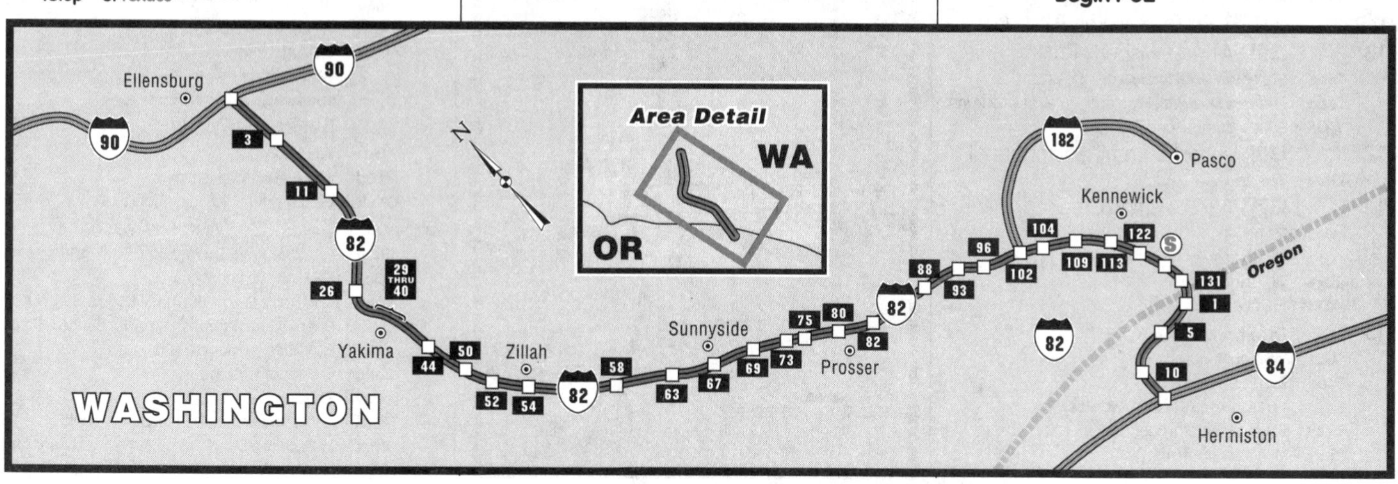

Bold red print shows RV & Bus parking available or nearby

EXIT PENNSYLVANIA

Begin I-83

↓PENNSYLVANIA

(50) Jct I-81, Hazeltown, Allentown, U.S. 322W, Carlisle (Left Exit)

30 **(49)** U.S. 22, Colonial Park, Progress
- Gas **E:** Atlantic[*], Mobil[*], Sunoco, Texaco[*, LP, CW]
  W: Citgo[*], Exxon[*], TLC[*]
- Food **E:** Applebee's, Colonial Park Diner, El Rodeo, Long John Silver, McDonald's, Red Lobster, Taco Bell
  W: Dairy Queen, Dunkin Donuts, Friendly's, KFC, Pasta & Pizza
- AServ **E:** Avellino's Auto Center, BF Goodrich, Goodyear Tire & Auto, Meineke Discount Mufflers, Penbrook Auto Repair, Sears, Sunoco, Tire America, Wimmer Tire
  W: Bob's Auto & Tire Service, Jiffy Lube
- ATM **E:** Commerce Bank, MAC
- Other **E:** **Colonial Park Mall**
  W: **Coin Laundry**

29A **(48)** Union Deposit Rd

29 **(47)** Deery St

28 **(46)** U.S. 322E, to Hershey

(46) Jct I-283S, to I-76, PA Tnpk Airport, Lancaster (Left Exit)

26 Paxtang (Southbound Reaccess Exit 25)

25 **(44)** 19th St

24 **(43)** PA230, 13th St

23 **(43)** Capital, 2nd St

22 **(42)** Lemoyne (Eastside Same As Exit 21)

21 **(42)** Highland Park
- Gas **E:** Exxon[*, CW], Mobil[*], Turkey Hill[*]
  W: Mobil[*], Texaco[*]
- Food **E:** KFC
  W: Rascal's, Royal Sub Shop
- AServ **E:** Mobil
- ATM **W:** Dauphin Deposit Bank
- Other **W:** **Thrift Drug, Weis Market**

20 **(41)** PA581W, Camp Hill

19 **(41)** New Cumberland

18A **(40)** Limekiln Rd
- Gas **E:** BP[*]
  W: Exxon
- Food **E:** Best Western, Bob Evan's Restaurant, Eat N Park, Holiday Inn, Pizza Hut
- Lodg **E:** Best Western, Fairfield Inn, Holiday Inn, MacIntosh Inn
  W: Knight's Inn, Motel 6
- AServ **E:** BP
  W: Exxon
- Other **W:** **West Shore Veterinary Hospital**

(39) Jct I-76, PA Tnpk, to Phil, Pittsburg

18 **(39)** PA114, Lewisberry Rd
- Food **E:** **Captain Wolf Restaurant (Days Inn)**
- Lodg **E:** DAYS INN **Days Inn**, Highland Motel, Keystone Inn
- ATM **E:** New Cumberland Federal Credit Union

17 **(38)** Reesers Summit (Southbound)
- AServ **W:** Ken's Service Ctr

16 **(37)** PA262, Fishing Creek
- Gas **E:** Shell[*, LP]
  W: Texaco[D, LP]
- AServ **W:** Texaco
- ATM **E:** Dauphin Bank

15 **(36)** PA177, Lewisberry
- Gas **W:** Mobil[*, LP]
- Food **E:** Hillside Cafe
  W: Francesco's Itaitian, **Hardees**
- AServ **E:** Gross General Repair
- TServ **W:** **Interstate Truck Park**

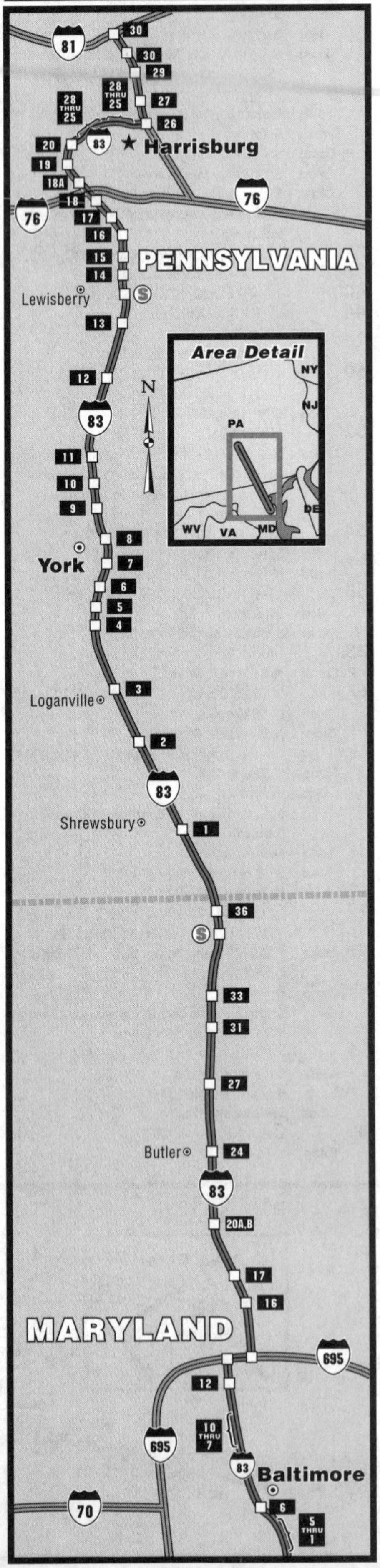

EXIT PENNSYLVANIA

- ATM **W:** Mobil

14A **(35)** PA392, Valley Green
- TStop **E:** **Henry's**[*]
- FStop **E:** **Exxon**[*, LP]
- Gas **E:** Rutters[*]
- Food **E:** 2 Brothers Italian, **Alice's Restaurant (Truckstop)**, Maple Donuts[24], McDonald's[PLAY], Mom's Kitchen, **New China**, **Robin Hoods Diner**
- Lodg **E:** **Super 8**
- TServ **E:** **Henry's**
- ATM **E:** **Exxon**, PNC Bank
- Other **E:** **Eckerd Drugs**[RX], Mail Boxes Etc, **Newberry Common**, **Super Fresh Supermarket**

14 **(35)** PA392, Yocumtown
- RVCamp **E:** **Park Away Park**

(33) **Weigh Station (Northbound)**

13 **(33)** PA382, Newberrytown
- FStop **W:** **Mobil**[*]
- Gas **E:** Exxon[*, LP], Sunoco
- Food **E:** Rutters (Exxon)
- AServ **E:** Sunoco
- TServ **W:** **Penn Detroit Diesel**

12 **(28)** PA295, Strinestown (No Northbound Access Due to Heavy Construction)
- Gas **W:** Exxon[*, LP]
- Food **W:** **I-83 Family Restaurant**, Rutters (Exxon), Wendy's
- ATM **W:** Exxon

11 **(24)** PA238, Emigsville
- Gas **W:** Mobil[*]
- Food **W:** **Sybill's Log Cabin Steak House**, Tom's (Mobil)
- TServ **E:** **C Earl Brown Inc**
- ATM **W:** Drover's Bank
- Other **W:** **Animal Emergency Clinic**

10 **(22)** Bus Rt 83, PA181, to U.S.30W, N George St
- Gas **E:** Exxon[LP], Getty
  W: Sunoco
- Food **E:** Little Caesars Pizza (Exxon), Pizza Romana, Rutter's (Exxon)
- AServ **E:** Getty
  W: Sunoco
- ATM **E:** Exxon

9 **(21)** E & W U.S. 30, Arsenal Rd, Lancaster, Gettysburg (Difficult Reaccess)
- Gas **W:** Exxon, Mobil
- Food **E:** Bob Evan's Restaurant, Round the Clock Diner[24]
  W: Hardees, Long John Silver, McDonald's[PLAY], Taco Bell, Wendy's
- Lodg **E:** DAYS INN Days Inn, Holiday Inn, Red Roof Inn
  W: Motel 6, Super 8
- AServ **W:** Exxon
- Med **W:** ✚ **Hospital**
- ATM **W:** Commerce Bank
- Other **E:** **Tourist Info.**
  W: **CVS Pharmacy**[RX], Car Wash, **Crossroads Shopping Center**, **Weiss Market**

8 **(19)** PA462, Market St
- Gas **W:** Sunoco[*]
- Med **W:** ✚ **Memorial Hospital**
- Other **W:** Bellmont Automated Car Wash

7 **(18)** PA124, Mt Rose Ave
- FStop **E:** **Pacific Pride Commercial Fueling**[*]
- Gas **E:** Exxon[*], Sunoco[*]
- Food **E:** Al Dente Italian, Big Apple Bagels, Burger King, Denny's, Lee Gardens, Pizza Hut (Sunoco), Pizza Hut, Rutter's (Sunoco), Subway
- Lodg **E:** **Budget Host Inn**
- AServ **E:** Exxon
- ATM **E:** Commerce Bank, Sunoco, York Bank
- Other **E:** **Gabriel's Bros Plaza**, **Haynes Acre Shopping**

Bold red print shows RV & Bus parking available or nearby

EXIT PENNSYLVANIA

Center, K-Mart, Weis Market(RX)

6 **(16)** E&W PA74, Queen St
- Gas E: Mobil
- W: Mobil(*), Sunoco
- Food E: Cracker Barrel, Hardees, Maple Donuts, Subs Unlimited, Tail Gators Grill
- W: Donut Delite(24), Subs to Go
- AServ E: Champion Lincoln Mercury, Square Deal Garage
- W: Griffith Honda of York, Shaull Oldsmobile, Cadillac, Hyundai, Sunoco
- TServ E: Snyder's Volvo
- ATM E: Commerce Bank
- W: CoreStates Bank, York Federal
- Other E: South York Plaza
- W: Phar Mor Drugs(RX), Veterinary Clinic

5 **(15)** South George St (Left Exit)
- Med W: Hospital

4 **(14)** PA182, Leader Heights
- Gas E: Mobil
- W: Exxon(*), Sunoco(*, LP, 24)
- Food E: Mr Bill's Quarterdeck Lounge
- W: Famous Express Deli (Exxon), McDonald's, Pizza Hut (Exxon), Rutter's (Exxon)
- Lodg W: Comfort Inn
- AServ E: Maco Auto Service
- RVCamp W: Indian Rock Campground
- ATM W: Exxon, Peoples Bank, Sunoco
- Parks W: Kain Park

3 **(11)** PA214, Loganville
- Food W: Mama's Pizza
- Lodg W: Midway Motel
- AServ W: Loganville Auto Service
- ATM W: The Glen Rock State Bank
- Parks W: Kain, Nixon

2 **(8)** PA216, Glen Rock
- Lodg E: Rocky Ridge Motel
- RVCamp E: Rocky Ridge Motel, Rocky Ridge Motel, Spring Valley Camp

1 **(4)** PA851, Shrewsbury
- FStop E: Citgo(*), Mobil(*)
- Food E: TCBY (Mobil), Tom's (Mobil)
- W: Coach Lite Family Restaurant, Dairy Queen, Hardees, McDonald's(PLAY), Spataro's Pizza & Restaurant
- AServ W: Wal-Mart SuperCenter(RX) (Vision Center)
- ATM E: Citgo, Mobil
- W: Drovers Bank, Mellon Bank, Wal-Mart SuperCenter (Vision Center), York Bank
- Other W: CVS Pharmacy, Giant Food Store(24), K-Mart, Mail Boxes Etc, Shewsbury Veterinary Clinic(LP), Wal-Mart SuperCenter(RX) (Vision Center)

(2) **PA Welcome Center, Rest Area (RR, Phones, Picnic, Vending; Northbound)**

↑PENNSYLVANIA

↓MARYLAND

EXIT MARYLAND

36 MD439, Maryland Line, Bell Air
- Gas W: Maryland Line Service Center(*)
- Food W: Maryland Line Service Center
- AServ W: Maryland Line Service Center
- RVCamp W: Morris Meadows Tra-V-L Park

(35) **Weigh Station (Southbound)**

33 Parkton, MD 45
- Gas E: Exxon(*, D, LP)
- ATM E: Exxon
- Other E: US Post Office

31 Middletown Rd, Parkton

27 MD137, Mt Carmel Rd, Hereford
- Gas E: Exxon(*, D, LP)
- ATM E: First National Bank of MD, Graul's Market Food Store
- Other E: Graul's Market Food Store, Hereford Pharmacy(RX)

Econo Lodge
Baltimore, MD
Cable TV - HBO/ESPN
Kids Under 12 Stay Free
Handicap Accessible
Truck/Large Vehicle Parking
Outdoor Pool
Exterior Corridors
410-622-4900 • 800-424-4777 1472
Maryland ▪ I-83 ▪ Exit 17

24 Bellfast Rd, Butler, Sparks (No Trucks West)

20AB Shawan Rd, Cockeysville
- Lodg E: Courtyard Of Marriott, Embassy Suites, Hunt Valley Inn Marriot
- Parks W: Oregon Ridge State Park
- Other E: Hunt Valley Mall

18 Warren Rd, Cockeysville (Northbound, Reaccess Southbound Only)

17 Padonia Rd
- Food E: Bob Evan's Restaurant, Denny's (Days Inn), Macaroni Grill, Ralphie's Diner, Rothwells Grill
- Lodg E: EconoLodge (see our ad this page), Days Hotel
- AServ E: AAMCO Transmission, Hillen Tire & Auto Service
- ATM E: First National Bank of MD
- Other E: US Post Office

16AB Timonium Rd (Running Concurrent with I-695)
- Gas E: Sunoco(*, D)
- Food E: Chi Chi's Mexican Restaurant, Steak & Ale, TCBY
- Lodg E: Holiday Inn Select, Red Roof Inn
- AServ E: Nationwide Auto World, Sunoco

13 Jct I-695, to Towson

12 Ruxton Rd (Northbound, Reaccess Southbound Only)

10AB Northern Pkwy
- Med W: Hospital

9AB Cold Springs Ln

8 MD25N, Falls Rd

7 28th St, Druid Park, Lake Dr

6 U.S. 1, U.S. 40, North Ave (Downtown)

2 Chase St.

1 Fayette St

↑MARYLAND

Begin I-83

I-84 E →

EXIT OREGON

Begin I-84, Oregon to Utah

↓OREGON

1W Lloyd Boulevard (Westbound, Reaccess Eastbound Only)
- Food S: 1500 Deli East
- Lodg N: Double Tree Hotel
- AServ S: Vic Alfonso Cadillac/Oldsmobile Dealer
- Parks N: Holiday Park
- Other N: LLoyd Cinema, Lloyd's Center

1E 33rd Ave (Eastbound)
- Gas N: BP(*), Texaco(*, D, CW)
- Food S: Poncho's, Shaughnessy's Bar and Grill
- Lodg S: Hollywood Motel
- AServ N: BP, BP
- S: Breslin Pontiac, GMC Trucks, Jiffy Lube, Wallace Buick
- ATM S: Bank of Portland
- Other N: Kienow's Grocery

2 43rd Ave (Westbound, Reaccess Eastbound Only)
- Gas N: Chevron(*)
- Food N: Poor Richard's, The Pagoda, Winchells Donuts
- Lodg N: Rodeway Inn
- Med N: Hospital
- ATM N: Bank of America, Hollywood Bowl
- Other N: Hollywood Bowl

3 58th Ave (Eastbound, Reaccess Westbound Only)
- Gas S: BP(*), Texaco(*)
- Food S: Sandwich Depot Deli
- AServ S: Texaco
- Med S: Hospital
- ATM S: BP

4 68th Ave (Eastbound, No Reaccess)
- AServ N: Danny's Auto Repair
- S: Lee's Automotive Center
- Other N: Coin Laundry, Nickel Wise Market

5 OR 213, 82nd Ave (Eastbound, Difficult Reaccess)
- Food N: Dial a Pizza, Happy Fortune Chinese Restaurant
- S: Elmer's Pancake & Steakhouse
- Lodg N: Motel Cabana
- AServ N: Les Schwab Tires
- S: Auto Repair, Jiffy Lube
- Other N: Animal Hospital, The Plaid Pantry

6 I-205 South, Salem

7 Halsey Street, Gateway District (Eastbound, Difficult Reaccess)
- Gas S: Arco(*, 24)
- Food S: Applebee's, Boston Market Restaurant, Carl Jr's Hamburgers, Izzy's Pizza, McDonald's, Skewers, Subway
- AServ S: Car Toys, Q-Lube
- Med S: Hospital
- ATM S: Key Bank
- Other S: Cub Foods, Fred Meyer Grocery(RX), Great Clips, Tower Books

8 I-205 North, Seattle, Portland Airport (Eastbound)

9A 102 ND Ave, Parkrose (Eastbound, Reaccess Eastbound Only)

9B I-205, Salem, Seattle (Westbound)

10 122 North Ave (Eastbound, Reaccess Eastbound Only)

13 Gresham, 181st Avenue
- Gas S: BP(*, LP, CW)
- Food S: Burger King(PLAY)
- Lodg N: Hampton Inn, Pioneer Motel
- S: Holiday Inn Express, Sleep Inn

EXIT	OREGON
TServ	S: **Firestone**
RVCamp	N: **Rolling Hills Mobile Terrace & RV Park (1 Mile)**
ATM	S: BP
Other	S: Trailblazer Country Store
14	207th Ave., Fairview
RVCamp	N: **American Dream RV Sales and Service, Portland Fairview RV Park (.5 Miles), Rolling Hills**
16A	Wood Village, Gresham (Westbound)
TStop	N: **Krueger's Auto/Truckstop**[SCALES]
Gas	N: Arco[*]
	S: Chevron[*]
Food	N: Good Buddies Restaurant, **Krueger's Auto/Truckstop**, Royal Inn Chinese
Lodg	N: Wood Village Travel Lodge
TWash	N: **Krueger's Auto/Truckstop**
Other	S: Wood Village Market and Deli
16B	Crown Point Hwy (Difficult Reaccess, Exit under construction)
17	Troutdale, Airport
TStop	S: **Burns Brothers Travel Stop**[*, LP, SCALES], **Flying J Travel Plaza**[*, RV DUMP, SCALES]
Gas	S: Chevron[*, LP, CW]
Food	S: Arby's, **Burger King, McDonald's**[PLAY], **Mrs. B's (Burns Bros TStop)**, Shari's Restaurant, **Subway (Burns Bros), Taco Bell**
Lodg	N: Inn America
	S: Phoenix Inn
TServ	S: **Burns Brothers Travel Stop**
TWash	S: **Burns Brothers Travel Stop**
ATM	S: Bank of America, Chevron, **Flying J Travel Plaza**
Other	S: **Columbia Gorge Factory Stores, Visitor Information**
18	Lewis & Clark State Park, Oxbow County Park
22	Corbett
Food	S: Corbett Station
RVCamp	S: **Crown Point RV Park (1.75 Miles)**
(23)	**Scenic View Pointe**
25	Rooster Rock State Park (No Trucks)
28	Bridal Veil
29	Dalton Pointe (Westbound, Reaccess Westbound Only)
30	Benson State Park (Eastbound)
31	Multnomah Falls (Left Exit , Scenic View)
35	Historic Hwy, Ainsworth Park (Ainsworth State Park)
37	Warrendale (Westbound, Reaccess Eastbound Only)
40	Bonneville Dam (Information Center)
41	Fish Hatchery, Eagle Creek Recreation Area (Eastbound, Reaccess Eastbound Only)
44	U.S. 30 West, Cascade Locks
Gas	N: Big D's[D], Chevron[LP], Shell[*, D], Texaco[*]
Food	N: Charburger, Eastwind Drive-In, Solomon Row Pub
Lodg	N: Best Western, Cascade Inn, Cascade Motel, Econo Inn, Scenic Winds Motel
AServ	N: Big D's, Chevron
RVCamp	N: **Bridge Of The Gods Motel & RV Park (1 Mile), Cascade Locks Marine Park (.25 Miles), KOA Campgrounds (.75 Miles)**
Other	N: **Columbia Market**, Port of Cascade Locks Marine Park, Stern Wheeler Cruises, Gift Shop and Museums, **U.S. Post Office**
47	Forest Lane, Herman Creek (Westbound, Reaccess Eastbound Only)
RVCamp	S: **Campground**
51	Wyeth
RVCamp	S: **Camping**
(54)	**Weigh Station (Westbound)**
(55)	**Rest Area, Starvation Creek State Park (RR, Phones, P; Eastbound)**
56	Viento Park
58	Mitchell Point Overlook (Eastbound, Reaccess Eastbound Only)
(60)	Service Road (Westbound, Reaccess Eastbound Only)
62	US 30, West Hood River, Westcliff Drive
Gas	S: Texaco[*, D, LP]
Food	N: Charburger Country
Lodg	N: Columbia Gorge Hotel, Vagabond Lodge
	S: Comfort Suites Hotel, Red Carpet Inn
AServ	S: Cliff Smith Chevrolet, GMC Trucks, Pontiac, Oldsmobile, Les Schwab Tires
Med	S: **+ Hospital**
Other	S: **Wal-Mart**[RX]
63	Hood River City Center
Gas	S: Exxon[*]
Food	S: Golden Rose Chinese, Pietro's Pizza
Lodg	S: Hood River Hotel
ATM	S: Bank Of America
Other	S: **Artifacts Used Books**, Craft Drug Company[RX], The Eye Glass Store, United States Post Office
64	U.S. 30, OR 35, Mt Hood Hwy, White Salmon Gov't Camp
Gas	N: Chevron[*, D]
Food	N: McDonald's, Riverside Grill (Best Western), Taco Time, Tugboat Annie's
	S: China Gorge Restaurant
Lodg	N: Best Western
ATM	N: Chevron
Other	N: Hood River County Museum
(66)	**Rest Area (P; Westbound, No trucks ,Koberg Beach State park)**
69	U.S. 30, Mosier
(73)	**Rest Area (RR, Phones, RV Dump, RV Water, P; Memaloose State Park)**
76	Rowena, Mayer State Park
Parks	N: **Mayer State park**
82	Discovery Center, Waco County Museum
Gas	S: Texaco[*, D]
Lodg	S: Oregon Trail Motel
AServ	S: Doug's Affordable Mufflers, Texaco, Texaco
83	West The Dalles (Eastbound)
FStop	N: **Shell**[*, D]
Gas	S: Chevron[*, D, LP], Exxon[*, LP]
Food	S: A Country Deli, Burger King[PLAY], Circle C, Cousins Restaurant (Quality Inn), Denny's, Lindo's Mexico, McDonald's[PLAY], Papa Murphy's Pizza, Skipper's, Subway, Taco Bell[24]
Lodg	S: Quality Inn
AServ	S: Chevron, Chevron, Schuck's Auto Supply
ATM	S: Wells Fargo
Other	S: **Albertson's Grocery**, Cascade Cinema, **Fred Meyer Grocery**[RX], Rite Aid Pharmacy, Vista Optical, **Wash N Shop Laundry**
84	West The Dalles (Difficult Reaccess)
Food	N: Orient Cafe
	S: Dairy Queen
AServ	N: Ace Automotive and Transmissions, Nelson Tire
Med	S: **+ Hospital**
ATM	S: Columbia River Bank
Other	N: Fun Country Motorcycles and ATVs
	S: **Safeway Drugs**
85	City Center, The Dalles
Gas	S: BP[*]
Food	S: Domino's Pizza, Holesteins Coffee Co.
AServ	S: Precision Auto Repair
Med	S: **+ Hospital**
Parks	N: **Port of the Dalles River Front Park**
Other	S: Dinty's Market
87	U.S. 30, U.S. 197, Dufur Bend
Gas	N: BP[*], Texaco[*, D, LP]
Food	N: BP, Lone Pine Restaurant, McDonald's, O'Calahans (Shilo Inn), Shilo Inn, Taco Bell
Lodg	N: **Lone Pine Motel**, Shilo Inn
RVCamp	N: **Lone Pine Park, Lone Pine RV Center**
ATM	N: BP
Other	N: The Dalles Dam Visitor Center and Tour Train
88	The Dalles Dam
97	OR 206, Celilo Park
Parks	N: **Celilo Park**
Other	N: Celilo Village, Deschutes River
104	U.S. 97, Yakima Bend

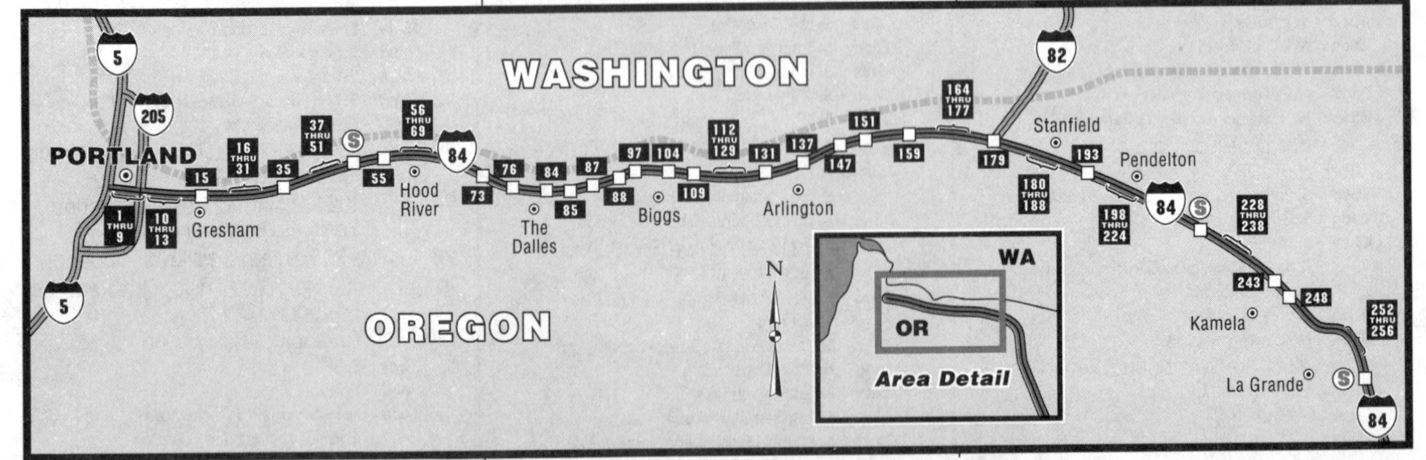

EXIT OREGON

TStop **S:** Biggs Auto/Truckstop[*, D, LP]
Gas **S:** Astro[D, 24], Biggs Auto/Truckstop[*, D], Chevron[*], Grand Central Travel Stop[*, 24] (BP), Texaco[*]
Food **S:** Biggs Auto/Truckstop, Grand Central Travel Stop (BP), Jack's Fine Food, Linda's Restaurant
Lodg **S:** Best Western, Biggs Motel, Dinty Motor Inn[*, 24]
AServ **S:** Chevron, Chevron, Texaco, Texaco
TServ **S:** Biggs Auto/Truckstop, Diesel Repair
RVCamp **S:** Biggs RV Park
ATM **S:** Biggs Auto/Truckstop, Grand Central Travel Stop (BP), Jack's Mini Mart
Parks **N:** Mary Hill State Parks
S: Deschutes Park
Other **S:** Jack's Mini Mart

109 Rufus, John Day Dam
FStop **S:** Pacific Pride Commercial Fueling
Gas **S:** BP[*]
Food **S:** Bob's Texas T-Bone
Lodg **S:** Tyee Motel
RVCamp **S:** Bob's Budget RV Park (.5 Miles)
ATM **S:** BP, BP

(112) **Parking Area (Both Directions, Dam Overlook)**

114 John Day River Recreation Area
123 Philippi Canyon
129 Blalock Canyon
131 Woelpern Road (Eastbound, Reaccess Westbound Only)
136 Viewpoint (Westbound)
137 OR 19, Arlington, Condon
Gas **S:** BP[*, D, LP], Chevron
Food **S:** Happy Canyon, Pheasant Grill Drive-in
Lodg **S:** Village Inn
RVCamp **S:** Columbia River RV Resort (1 Mile), Port of Arlington, Terrace Heights Trailer Park (.75 Miles)
ATM **S:** Bank Of Eastern Oregon, Chevron
Parks **S:** City Parks, Earl Snell Memorial Parks
Other **S:** Post Office, Thrifty Food Store

147 OR 74, Ione, Heppner
151 Threemile Canyon
159 Tower Road
(161) **Rest Area (RR, Phones, Picnic, P)**
164 Boardman
FStop **N:** Texaco[*, D]
S: BP[*, D] (Taco Bell)
Gas **N:** Chevron[*, LP, CW]
Food **N:** C&D Drive-in, Longbranch Room (Dodge City Motel), Lynard's Spud Cellar, Poppy's Pizza
S: Nomad Restaurant, Taco Bell
Lodg **N:** Dodge City Motel, Riverview Motel
S: The Nugget Inn
AServ **N:** Chevron, Chevron
S: Boardman Auto Repair
RVCamp **S:** Driftwood (2 Miles)
ATM **N:** Inland Empire Bank
Parks **N:** Boardman Park (1 Mile)
Other **N:** Post Office
S: Keggler's Century Food Store

165 Port of Morrow
FStop **S:** Pacific Pride Commercial Fueling
TServ **S:** Yeats Trucking Inc

168 U.S. 730, Irrigon
171 Paterson Ferry Road
177 Umatilla Army Depot
179 I-82 West, Umatilla, Kennewick,
180 Westland Road
TServ **S:** Barton Industries-Truck Body & Trailer Repair

182 OR 207, Hermiston, Lexington

EXIT OREGON

FStop **N:** Buffalo Junction[*, D, LP]
Food **N:** Buffalo Junction
RVCamp **N:** Buttercreek RV Park
Med **N:** ✚ Hospital

(186) **Rest Area (RR, Phones, Picnic, Pet Walk, P)**
188 U.S. 395 North, Stanfield, Hermiston
TStop **N:** Pilot[*, LP, SCALES, 24]
Food **N:** Country Cooker (Pilot TS), Pilot, Subway (Pilot TS), Wheatland's Dairy Cafe
RVCamp **N:** Pilot RV Park, Stage Gulch RV Park (1.25 Miles)
S: Fort Henrietta RV Park (1.25 Miles)

193 Echo, Lexington
198 Lorenzen Road, McClintock Rd
TServ **N:** PJ's Truck Repair
199 Yoakum Road , Stage Gulch
202 Stage Gulch, Barnhart Road
TStop **S:** Floyd's Truck Ranch[*]
Food **S:** Ranch Cafe
Lodg **S:** 7 Inn, Floyd's Truck Ranch Motel
TServ **N:** International Dealer, Woodpecker Truck
S: Floyd's Truck Ranch
ATM **S:** Floyd's Truck Ranch

207 Airport, West Pendleton
Gas **N:** Chevron[*, D, LP], Texaco[*, D, LP]
AServ **N:** Chevron, Chevron, Texaco, Texaco
RVCamp **N:** Brooke RV West
Other **N:** Cash & Carry United Grocery

209 U.S. 395, OR 37, John Day Pendleton
Gas **N:** ARCO[*, 24]
S: Texaco[*]
Food **N:** Godfather's Pizza, KFC, Rodeo Cafe and Grill, Taco Bell, The Lunch Box
S: Burger King, Denny's, Klondike Pizza, McDonald's[PLAY], Subway, Wendy's
Lodg **S:** Chaparral Motel
AServ **N:** Twig Zeigler's Transmission and Auto Repair
S: K-Mart, Kube Lube, Sunshine Gas And Wash
TServ **S:** Sunshine Gas And Wash
RVCamp **S:** Thompson RV Service (.75 Miles)
ATM **N:** Pacific One Bank, Safeway Grocery[RX]
S: Texaco
Other **N:** Dean's Market and Deli, Rite Aid Pharmacy, Safeway Grocery[RX], Wal-Mart[RX]
S: K-Mart

210 Pendleton, OR 11, Milton - Freewater (Hospital)
FStop **S:** BP[*, D]
Gas **S:** Texaco[*, D, LP]
Food **S:** Kopper Kitchen
Lodg **S:** Best Western, Double Tree Hotel, Holiday Inn Express, Motel 6, Super 8
RVCamp **S:** Camping (1.25 Miles), Mountain View RV Park
Med **N:** ✚ Hospital
Other **N:** State Police
S: Bi-Mart[RX]

213 U.S. 30, OR 11, Pendleton City Center (Difficult Reaccess)
216 Milton - Freewater, Walla Walla
TStop **N:** Arrowhead Truck Plaza[*, SCALES]
Food **N:** Arrowhead Truck Plaza
TServ **N:** Arrowhead Truck Plaza[SCALES]
RVCamp **N:** Wildhorse Gaming Resort & RV Park (.25 Miles)
ATM **N:** Arrowhead Truck Plaza

(222) View Point (Eastbound)
224 Poverty Flat Road, Old Emigrant Hill Road
(227) **Weigh Station (Westbound)**
228 Deadman's Pass
(228) **Rest Area (RR, Phones, Picnic, P)**

EXIT OREGON

234 Emigrant Park (Westbound, Reaccess Eastbound Only, Difficult Reaccess)
238 Meacham
243 Mt Emily Road, Summit Rd.
248 Kamela, Spring Creek Road (Oregon Trail Visitors Park)
Parks **N:** Oregon Trail Interpretive Park (3 Miles)
252 OR 244, Ukiah (Hilgard State Park)
Parks **S:** Hilgard State Park
256 Perry (Eastbound, Reaccess Westbound Only)
257 Perry (Westbound, Reaccess Eastbound Only)
(259) **Weigh Station (Eastbound)**
259 U.S. 30, La Grande (Eastbound, Reaccess Westbound Only)
261 OR 82, La Grande, Elgin
FStop **N:** BP[*]
S: Exxon[*, CW] (Pacific Pride)
Gas **N:** Chevron[*, D], Texaco[*, D, LP]
S: Conoco[*]
Food **N:** Denny's, Joe's Place, Pizza Hut
S: Dairy Queen, Klondike Pizza, McDonald's[PLAY], Skippers Seafood, Taco Time, Wendy's
Lodg **N:** Howard Johnson
S: Best Western, Mr. Sandman Motel, Super 8
AServ **N:** Chevron, Robert's Ford, Mercury, and Lincoln
S: Napa Auto
TServ **N:** Eagle Truck & Machine Co
S: Truck Service Center
TWash **N:** Truck Wash (Car Wash)
RVCamp **N:** Camping[LP], La Grande Rendezvous RV Resort (.5 Miles)
Med **S:** ✚ Hospital
ATM **S:** Exxon (Pacific Pride), Western Bank
Other **N:** AmeriGas, R & C Family Store
S: Albertson's Grocery, Coast to Coast Hardware, Grand Auto Supply, Rite Aid, Vista Optical

265 OR 203, La Grande Union, US 30
TStop **S:** Flying J Travel Plaza[*, SCALES]
Food **S:** Flying J Travel Plaza, Flying J Travel Plaza, TCBY (Flying J Travel Plaza)
RVCamp **N:** Hot Lake RV Park (5 Miles)
ATM **S:** Flying J Travel Center, Flying J Travel Plaza

268 Foothill Road
(269) **Rest Area (RR, Phones, Picnic, RV Dump, P)**
270 Ladd Creek Road (Eastbound, Reaccess Westbound Only)
273 Ladd Canyon
278 Clover Creek
283 Wolf Creek Ln.
285 U.S. 30, OR 237, North Powder, Union
FStop **N:** Cenex[*, LP]
Lodg **N:** Powder River Motel
RVCamp **N:** RV Park and Storage
Other **N:** Evans Corner Groceries
S: Anthony Lakes (19 Miles), Wildlife Viewing Area

(295) **Rest Area (RR, Phones, Picnic, P)**
298 OR 203, Medical Springs, Haines, Bakers City Airport
302 OR 86 East, Richland, Hells Canyon
RVCamp **S:** Baker RV[LP] (2.2 Miles), Oregon Trails West RV Park[LP]
Med **S:** ✚ Hospital
Other **S:** Miniature Golf

304 OR 7 South, Baker City Center, Geiser Grand Hotel

Bold red print shows RV & Bus parking available or nearby

EXIT OREGON

TStop S: Baker's Truck Corral[*, LP, SCALES]
FStop N: Conoco[*]
S: Texaco[*, LP, CW]
Food N: Burger King, TCBY (Conoco FS)
S: Best Western, Gold Skillet Dinner and Drive-In, McDonald's[PLAY], Pizza Hut, Subway, Sumpter Junction, Taco Time
Lodg N: Super 8
S: Best Western, Eldorado Inn, Quality Inn
AServ S: Nell's Discount Auto Parts & Auto Service
TServ S: Baker Truck Corral, Eastern Oregon Truck Parts and Services
TWash S: Baker Truck Corral, Baker's Truck Corral
RVCamp S: Mountain View RV Park (2 Miles)
ATM N: Conoco
S: Texaco
Other S: Baker City Coin Laundry, Baker City Information Center and Museum

306 U.S. 30 West, Baker City , Haines
Other N: State Police

317 Pleasant Valley (Difficult Reaccess, 8 miles to reaccess ramp, follow I-84 W)

327 Durkee
FStop N: Oregon Trail Travel Plaza[*, LP]
Food N: Oregon Trail Travel Plaza, Wagon Wheel Restaurant
AServ N: Interstate Battery (Oregon Trail Travel Plaza)

330 Plano Road, Cement Plant Rd.

335 **Weatherby, Rest Area (RR, HF, Phones, Picnic, Grills, Vending, RV Dump, RV Water, P)**

(335) **Rest Area (RR, Phones, Picnic, P; Westbound, Access by Exit 335)**

338 Lookout Mountain

340 Rye Valley

342 Lime (Eastbound, Reaccess Westbound Only)

345 Lime

353 Huntington
TStop N: Farewell Bend[*]
Food N: Farewell Bend, Farewell Bend Motel (Farewell Bend TS)
Lodg N: Farewell Bend, Farewell Bend Motel (Farewell Bend TS)
AServ N: Farewell Bend TS
TServ N: Farewell Bend TS
RVCamp N: Farewell Bend State Park
ATM N: Farewell Bend
Parks N: Farewell Bend State Park

(353) **Weigh Station (Westbound)**

(354) **Weigh Station (Eastbound)**

356 Or 201, Weiser
RVCamp N: Oasis RV Camp

362 Moores Hollow Road

371 Stanton Boulevard

374 OR 201, Ontario, Weiser
FStop S: Conoco[*, LP]
Lodg S: Budget Inn, Easy Access Motel
AServ S: Doersch Engine & Machine Repair
TServ N: Royals Truck Diesel Repair
S: Ontario Truck Park
ATM S: Conoco
Parks N: Ontario State Park

376AB U.S. 30, Payette, Ontario
FStop S: Conoco[*, D, CW]
Gas N: Chevron[*, CW, 24]
S: Phillips 66[*, LP]
Food N: Burger King, Dairy Queen, Denny's, McDonald's, Taco Time
S: DJ's Family Restaurant, Domino's Pizza, Far East Chinese Restaurant, Klondike Pizza, Sizzler, Taco Bell, Wendy's

EXIT OREGON/IDAHO

Lodg N: Best Western, Colonial Inn, Holiday Inn, Motel 6, Sleep Inn, Super 8
S: Holiday Motel, V-Hotel
AServ N: Option Chrysler Plymouth Dodge
S: Commercial Tires, Dewey Lube, Les Schwab Tires, NAPA Auto Parts (Red's Automotive Repairs)
TServ S: Ontario Diesel
RVCamp S: Rocking R Campers RV Service (Frontage Rd)
Other N: Akins Supermarket[24], K-Mart, State Farm Insurance Service Center, State Police, Wal-Mart[RX]
S: U-Haul Center

(377) **OR Welcome Center (RR, Phones, Picnic, P; Westbound)**

↑OREGON

↓IDAHO

(1) **ID Welcome Center (RR, Phones, Picnic, P; Eastbound)**

3 U.S. 95, Payette , Fruitland
Food N: Palisades Bar and Grill
RVCamp N: Curtis' Neat Retreat

9 U.S. 30, New Plymouth,

13 Black Canyon Junction
TStop S: Stinker Fuelstop[*, SCALES]
Food S: Black Canyon Restaurant (Stinker TS), Stinker Fuelstop
Lodg S: Stinker Fuelstop, Stinker Motel
ATM S: Stinker Fuelstop, Stinker TS

17 Sand Hollow
Gas N: Sinclair[*, LP]

1450

130 Shannon Drive • Nampa, ID 83687

ID Newest Budget Motel

Family Suites
King Size Beds
Outdoor Heated Pool
Dataport/Modem Hookups
Security Cameras & Card Key Locks
Free Cable TV with HBO
Food Court with Full Vending
Coin-Operated Guest Laundry Facility
75% Smoke Free
Fax & Copy Service
Valet Laundry Service
Free Local Calls
24 Hour Front Desk

208-442-0800
Toll Free Reservations:
800-469-INNS

IDAHO ▪ I-84 ▪ EXIT 35

EXIT IDAHO

1452

INN AMERICA
A BUDGET MOTEL

1000 NW Graham Road • Troutdale, OR 97060

OR Newest Budget Motel

King Size Beds
Family & Executive Suites
Outdoor Heated Spa
Dataport/Modem Hookups
Security Cameras & Card Key Locks
Free Cable TV with HBO
Food Court with Full Vending
Coin-Operated Guest Laundry Facility
75% Smoke Free
Fax & Copy Service
Valet Laundry Service
Free Local Calls
24 Hour Front Desk

503-492-2900
Toll Free Reservations:
800-469-INNS

OREGON ▪ I-84 ▪ EXIT 17

Food N: Sand Hollow Country Cafe, Sinclair
Lodg N: Inn America (see our ad this page)

25 ID 44, Middleton

26 U.S. 20, U.S. 26, Notus, Parma
RVCamp N: Caldwell Campground (.25 Miles)
Other N: Rocky Mountain's Fireworks and Fur Co

27 ID 19, Homedale, Wilder
Other S: Tourist Info.

28 10th Ave., City Center
Gas N: Maverik Country Store[*]
S: Amoco[*], Chevron[*, 24], Citgo[*], Shell[*]
Food S: Dairy Queen, Jack-In-The-Box, Mr V's Restaurant, Pizza Hut, Wendy's
Lodg N: Budget Motel
AServ S: Bruneel Tire & Auto Service
RVCamp N: Stardust Mobile Home Park
Med S: ✚ Hospital
ATM N: Maverik Country Store
S: Citgo, Citgo
Parks N: City Park
Other N: Hands Off Coin Car Wash, Luby Park
S: Paul's Market Grocery Store, Tourist Info.

29 Franklin Road, (Airport)
TStop S: Flying J Truck Stop, Sinclair[*, LP]
Food S: Perkin's Family Restaurant
Lodg S: Best Western Caldwell Inns & Suites, Comfort Inn
ATM S: Sinclair

35 ID 55, Marsing, Nampa Blvd
FStop S: Shell[*, D]
Food S: Denny's[24]
Lodg S: Inn America (see our ad this page), Shilo Inn Motel, Super 8
RVCamp S: AmeriGas[LP], Gem Stop/AmeriGas[LP] (.1 Miles)

Bold red print shows RV & Bus parking available or nearby

EXIT IDAHO

Med **S:** ✚ **Hospital**

36 Franklin Boulevard

FStop **S:** **Chevron**[*, D, LP], **Texaco**[*, D, SCALES] **(Taco Bell Express, A&W)**

Food **N:** Noodles Restaurant (Pizza, Pasta), O'Callahan's Restaurant (Shilo Inn)
S: **Chester Fried Chicken (Chevron FS)**, **Hot N Now (Texaco)**, **Taco Bell (Texaco)**

Lodg **N:** Shilo Inn Suites Motel
S: Sleep Inn

RVCamp **S:** **Mason Creek RV Park**, **Minor's RV Sales & Service**

Other **S:** Tri State Marine (Expresso Cafe)

38 Business 84, Garrity Blvd., Mampa Murphy

Gas **S:** Texaco[*, D] (Taco Ole)

RVCamp **S:** **RV Furniture Center**

ATM **S:** Texaco (Taco Ole)

44 ID 69, Meridian, Kuna

Gas **N:** Chevron[*, D, CW]
S: Husky[*, LP], Texaco[*, D, CW]

Food **N:** **Bolo's Pub & Eatery**, KFC, McDonald's, Pizza Hut, Quizno's Classic Subs, Rock Around The Clock Cafe, Shari's Restaurant, Taco Bell, Taco Time
S: JB's Restaurant

Lodg **N:** Best Western
S: Mr. Sandman Motel

AServ **S:** Meridian Ford

RVCamp **N:** **Regional RV Center Service**
S: **Playground Sports and RV Park**[LP] **(1 Mile)**

Med **N:** ✚ **Mercy Medical Center (Family Doctor)**

ATM **N:** Wells Fargo
S: Texaco

Parks **N:** **City Park**[PLAY]

Other **N:** **Tourist Info.**
S: Boondocks Funpark, Intermountain Animal Hospital

46 ID 55, Eagle, McCall

Gas **N:** Texaco[*, D]

Food **N:** Taco Bell (Texaco)

RVCamp **N:** **Fiesta RV Park (3.5 Miles)**
S: **The Play Ground RV Park (.5 Miles)**

Med **N:** ✚ **St. Luke's Meridian Medical Center**

ATM **N:** Texaco, Texaco

49 Jct. I-184, City Center, Franklin Rd.

50AB Cole Road , Overland Rd.

Gas **N:** Chevron[*, 24]

Food **N:** Cancun Mexican Restaurant, Coby's, Cyber Place, Eddie's Restaurant, Jaba Detour, Maria's Homestyle Mexican Restaurant, **McDonald's**[PLAY], Outback Steakhouse, Pizza Hut, Subway, TCBY, Taco Bell
S: Chuck-A-Rama Buffet, Cracker Barrel, KFC, **McDonald's (Wal-Mart)**, Moxie Java,

EXIT IDAHO

NeGrass Restaurant

Lodg **S:** AmeriTel Inns, **Best Rest Inn**

AServ **N:** Economy Transmission
S: Commercial Tires, Jack's Tire & Oil, **Wal-Mart**

TServ **N:** **Western States Truck Shop**

ATM **N:** Chevron, Wells Fargo

Other **N:** ACE Hardware, **Deseret Bookstore**, Express Cuts, Overland Park Cinemas
S: Edward's 21 Cinemas, Game World, Pony Express Courier, **Wal-Mart**[RX] **(Optical)**

52 Orchard Street

Gas **N:** Texaco[*, D] (Taco Bell Express)

AServ **N:** Alamo Rent-A-Car, Dennis Dillon Mazda and Isuzu, Dennis Dillon Nissan, Dennis Dillon Oldsmobile Dealer, Hertz Auto Service

TServ **N:** **Northwest Leasing and Service (Small Trucks)**

1451

INN AMERICA
A BUDGET MOTEL

2799 Airport Way • Boise, ID 83705

ID Newest Budget Motel

Family Suites
King Size Beds
Outdoor Heated Pool
Dataport/Modem Hookups
Security Cameras & Card Key Locks
Free Cable TV with HBO
Food Court with Full Vending
Coin-Operated Guest Laundry Facility
75% Smoke Free
Fax & Copy Service
Valet Laundry Service
Free Local Calls
24 Hour Front Desk

208-389-9800

Toll Free Reservations:
800-469-INNS

IDAHO • I-84 • EXIT 53

EXIT IDAHO

53 Vista Ave., Air Terminal

Gas **N:** Shell[*, CW]
S: Chevron[*, CW]

Food **S:** Denny's[24], Kopper Kitchen

Lodg **N:** Fairfield Inn, Hampton Inn, Holiday Inn (Simmering Pot Restaurant), **Super 8**
S: Best Western, Best Western Airport Motor Inn, Comfort Inn, **Inn America (see our ad this page)**, Motel 6, Sleep Inn

AServ **N:** Avis Rent-a-car, Hertz Rental Cars, National Car Rental
S: Chevron, Thrifty Car Rental

TServ **S:** **Ryder Truck Rental**

ATM **S:** U.S. Bank

Other **N:** **State Police**
S: **Tourist Info.**

54 Broadway Ave. , US 20, US 26, City Center

TStop **N:** **Flying J Travel Plaza**[*, LP] **(Pepperoni's)**
S: **Burns Brothers Travel Stop**[*, SCALES] **(Mrs. B's Homestyle Restaurant)**

Food **N:** Eddy's Bakery Outlet, **Pepperoni's (Flying J TS)**

Lodg **N:** Skyline Motel
S: **Shilo Inn**

AServ **N:** Dowdy's Automotive, Quick Service USA Lube

TServ **N:** **Flying J Travel Plaza**
S: **Burns Brothers Travel Stop**[*, SCALES], **Burns Brothers Travel Stop**[SCALES] **(Mrs. B's Homestyle Restaurant)**, **Detroit Diesel**, **Don's Truck Wash**, **Kenworth Dealer**, **Lake City International**, **Rollin's**, **Ryder Transportation services**, **Trabar**, **Transport Truck**, **Utility Trailer**

TWash **S:** **Burns Bros TS**, **Rollin's**, **Trabar**

RVCamp **S:** **Mountain View RV Park (.25 Miles)**

Med **N:** ✚ **Hospital**

57 ID 21, Idaho City, Gowen Rd.

Gas **S:** Chevron[*, CW]

Food **N:** Perkins Family Restaurant
S: Burger King[PLAY]

TServ **N:** **Idaho Peterbilt**

Other **S:** **Boise Factory Outlets**

59 South Eisenman Road

(62) **Rest Area (RR, Picnic, P)**

64 Blacks Creek Road, Kuna

(66) **Weigh Station**

71 Mayfield, Orchard

TStop **S:** **Boise Stage Stop**[*, SCALES]

74 Simco Road

90 Mountain Home,

FStop **S:** **Desert Winds**[*, LP] **(Texaco, Burger King)**

Food **S:** Thi-Yo-Thai

RVCamp **N:** **AmeriGas**[LP]
S: **KOA Campgrounds (3 Miles)**, **Westside RV**

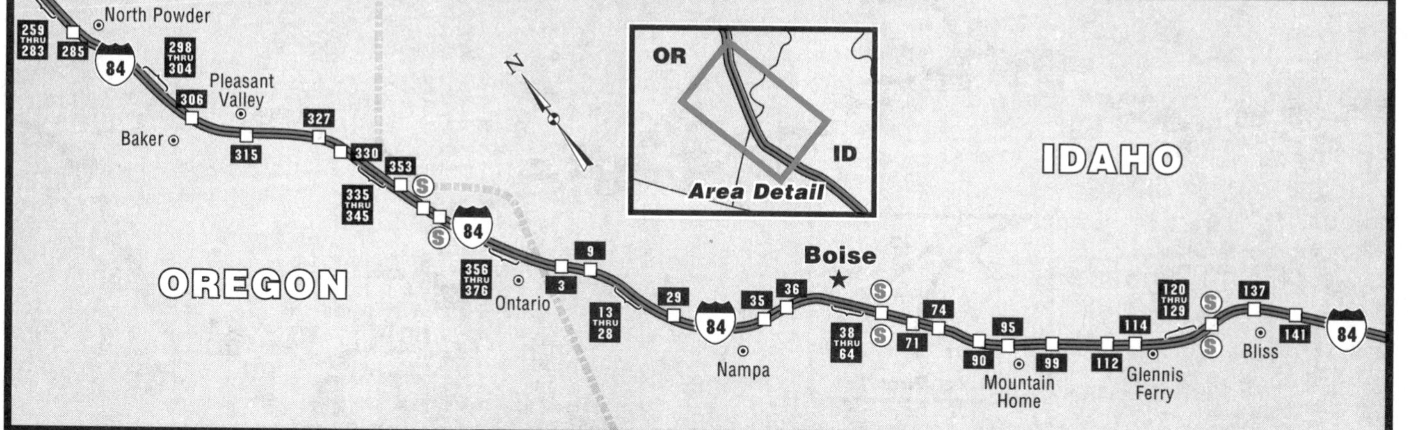

Bold red print shows RV & Bus parking available or nearby

EXIT		IDAHO
		Park
	Med	S: Hospital
95		U.S. 20, Mountain Home, Fairfield
	TStop	N: Pilot Travel Center(*, SCALES) (Subway, Dairy Queen, Great American Family Restaurant)
	Gas	N: Chevron(*, 24)
	Food	N: JB's Restaurant, Jack in the Box
		S: McDonald's
	Lodg	N: Best Western (Foot Hills Motor Inn), Sleep Inn
	RVCamp	S: KOA Campgrounds (2.5 Miles)
	Med	S: Hospital
	ATM	N: Chevron
	Other	S: K-Mart(RX), Tourist Info.
99		Bennett Road, Business loop I-84, Idaho State Hwy 51, ID St Hwy 67 ,Mountain Home
	RVCamp	S: Camping
112		Business I-84, ID 78, Hammett
	Parks	N: Bruno Dunes State Park (15 Miles)
114		Business I-84, ID 78, Cold Springs Road , Hannett (Westbound, Reaccess Eastbound Only)
	RVCamp	S: Cold Springs RV Park
120		Business 84, Glenns Ferry (Eastbound, Reaccess Westbound Only, Difficult Reaccess)
	RVCamp	S: Trails West RV Park
	Parks	S: 3 Islands State Park
121		Business 84, Glenns Ferry, King Hill
	RVCamp	N: Three Island Crossing State Park (1 Mile)
		S: Trails West RV Park (1 Mile)
	Med	S: Medical Care Center
	Parks	S: Three Island State Park
125		Paradise Valley
129		King Hill
(133)		Rest Area (RR, Picnic, P)
137		Bliss, Pioneer Road
	RVCamp	S: Camping
141		U.S. 26, U.S. 30, Hagerman, Gooding
	TStop	S: Texaco(LP) (Raod Runner Cafe)
	FStop	S: Phillips 66(*) (Griffin's Restaurant), Sinclair(*) (Bliss Country Store)
	Food	S: Ox-Bow Cafe(24), Roadrunner Cafe (Texaco)
	Lodg	S: Amber Inn Motel
	RVCamp	S: Hagerman RV Village (8 Miles)
	Med	N: Hospital
	ATM	S: Texaco (Raod Runner Cafe)
147		Tuttle
	RVCamp	S: Float Trips(*)
	Parks	S: Malad Gorge State Park
155		Wendell, ID 46
	RVCamp	N: Intermountain RV Camp
157		ID 46, Wendell , Gooding
	FStop	S: Texaco(*)

EXIT		IDAHO
	Food	N: Cavazo's
		S: Farmhouse Restaurant
	TServ	S: K & D General Truck Repair
	RVCamp	N: Intermountain Motor Homes Inc. RV Sales and Service (Frontage road), Intermountain RV Camp(LP) (7/8 Miles)
	Parks	N: City Park
165		ID 25, Jerome (RV Dump)
	Gas	N: Sinclair(*, D)
	AServ	N: Number One Auto Part Auto Service
	TServ	N: Centennial Truck Repair
	RVCamp	N: Big Trees Mobile Park (1.25 Miles)
	Med	N: Hospital
	Other	N: Sawtooth Veterinary Hospital, Suburban Propane(LP)
168		ID 79, Jerome
	TStop	N: Sinclair(*, LP, 24) (Restaurant)
	FStop	N: Chevron(*, CW)
	Food	N: Burger King
		S: Subway
	Lodg	N: Best Western, Crest Motel
	TServ	N: Kenworth Dealer (Frontage Rd)
	RVCamp	N: Brockman's RV Sales and Service
	ATM	N: Chevron
	Other	N: Quality Trailer sales
(171)		Rest Area (RR, Phones, Picnic, P; Eastbound)
(172)		Weigh Station , Rest Area (P; Eastbound)
173		U.S. 93, Twin Falls, Sun Valley
	TStop	N: Petro(*, LP, SCALES) (Quick Skillet)
	Food	N: Quick Skillet(*) (Petro)
	Lodg	N: Sleep Inn
	AServ	N: Petro (Quick Skillet)
	RVCamp	N: KOA Campgrounds (1 Mile)
	Med	S: Hospital
	ATM	N: Petro (Quick Skillet)
	Other	S: Sho Shone Falls (8 Miles), Tourist Info. (3 Miles)
182		ID 50, Kimberly, Twin Falls
	TStop	S: Texaco(*, SCALES) (Blimpie)
	Gas	N: Sinclair(*, D)
	Food	S: Blimpie's Subs (Texaco TS), Restaurant (Texaco TS)
	Lodg	S: Amber Inn Motel
	RVCamp	N: Anderson's Trav-L-Park, Gary's RV Sales
188		Valley Road, Eden
194		Ridgeway Road , Hazelton
	FStop	S: Amoco(*)
	RVCamp	S: Camping
201		ID 25, Kasota Road, Paul
208		ID 27, Burley, Paul, Bus. I-84
	TStop	N: Phillips 66(*) (Connor's Cafe)
	FStop	S: Sinclair
	Gas	S: Amoco(*), Chevron(*, D, 24) (Subway), Texaco(*)

EXIT		IDAHO/UTAH
	Food	N: Connor's Cafe (Phillips 66)
		S: JB's Restaurant, Joey's Pizzeria, Lee's Chopsticks, Perkins Family Restaurant, Polo's Cafe, RiverHouse Cafe, Subway (Chevron), Taco Bell, The Dinner Store, Wendy's
	Lodg	S: Best Western Burley Inn (Perkins), Budget Motel
	AServ	S: Interstate Auto Repair, Royce and Friends
	TServ	N: International Dealer
	Med	S: Hospital
	ATM	S: Texaco
	Other	S: Snake River Plaza, Wal-Mart(RX)
211		U.S. 30, ID 24, Heyburn, Burley
	FStop	N: Sinclair(*)
	Gas	N: Chevron(*, D) (Restaurant)
	Food	N: Wayside Cafe(24)
	Lodg	N: Tops Motel
	Med	N: Hospital
		S: Hospital
	Parks	N: Lake Walcott State Park (16 Miles)
216		ID 77, ID 25, Declo, Rupert
	FStop	N: Phillips 66(*, LP) (Blimpie)
	Food	N: Blimpie Subs & Salads (Phillips 66)
	RVCamp	N: Snake River Campground, Travel Stop 216 (.25 Miles)
	Parks	N: Lake Wolcott State Park (15 Miles)
222		Jct. I-86, U.S. 30 East, Pocatello
228		ID 81, Yale Road, Malta
(229)		Weigh Station, Rest Area (RR, Phones, Picnic, Vending, P)
(230)		Weigh Station
237		Idahome Road
245		Sublett Road, Malta
	RVCamp	S: Camping
254		Sweetzer Road
263		Juniper Road
(269)		Rest Area (RR, Phones, Picnic, P)

↑IDAHO

↓UTAH

5		UT 30, Park Valley
7		Snowville
	FStop	N: Flying J Travel Plaza(*, D, LP)
	Gas	N: Chevron(*)
	Food	N: Restaurant (Flying J TS), Round-Up Cafe
	Lodg	N: Outsiders Inn
	RVCamp	N: Lottie-Dell Campground (.75 Miles)
12		Ranch Exit
16		Hansel Valley
17		Ranch Exit
20		Blue Creek
24		Valley

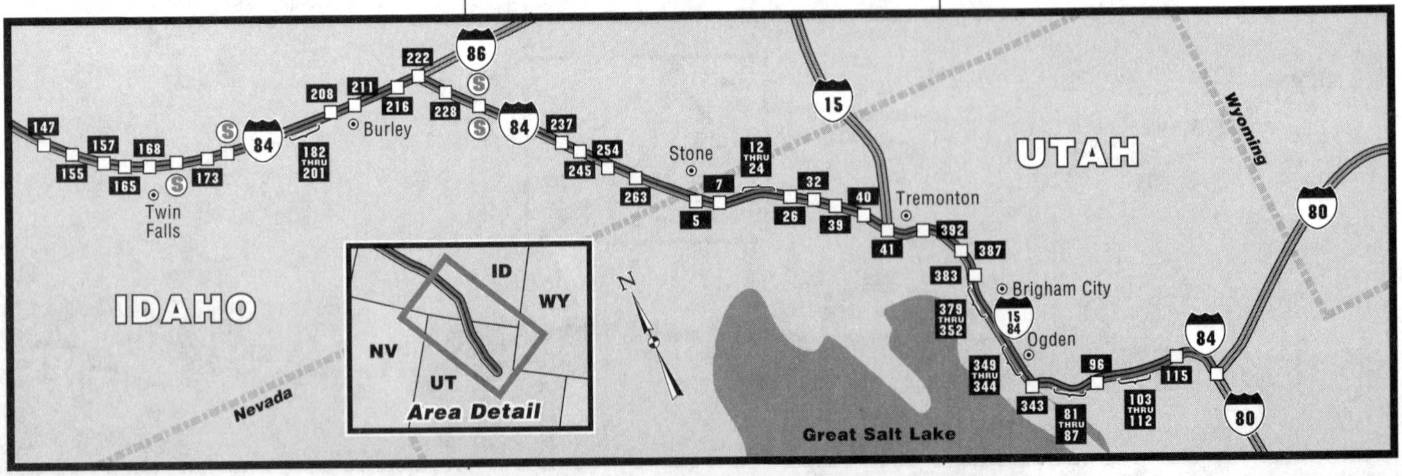

Bold red print shows RV & Bus parking available or nearby

EXIT	UTAH
26	UT 83, Howell, Thiokol
32	Ranch Exit
39	Garland, Bothwell
Med	N: Hospital
40	UT 102, Tremont, Bus. I-84
FStop	N: Chevron(*) (Burger King), Texaco(*, LP)
Food	N: Burger King (Chevron FS), Denny's, McDonald's(PLAY)
Lodg	N: Western Inn
AServ	N: Chevron
TServ	N: Chevron
TWash	N: Semi Wash
Med	N: Hospital
Other	N: Car Wash S: Rocket Display, Golden Spike National Historic Sight
41	I-15, North Pocatello
	Note: I-84 runs concurrent below with I-15. Numbering follows I-15.
392	I-84 West, Tremonton, Boise
387	UT 30 East, Riverside, Logan
383	Business 15, Tremonton, Garland (Hospital)
Med	E: Hospital
382	JUnction I-84 W Boise Junction I-15 N Pocatello
379	UT 13, Business 15, Business 84, Tremonton
375	UT 240 to UT 13, Honeyville, Bear River
Other	E: Crystal Hot Springs
(370)	Rest Area (P; Southbound)
368	UT 13, Brigham City, Corinne , 900 North St.
Parks	W: Bear River Bird Refuge
Other	E: Golden Spike National Historic Site
366	Forest St.
364	U.S. 91, U.S. 89, Brigham City, Logan , 1100 South St.
Med	E: Hospital
(363)	Rest Area (P; Northbound)
361	Port of Entry
360	UT 315, Willard, Perry

EXIT	UTAH
Gas	E: Flying J Travel Plaza(*) (Country Market Buffett)
Food	E: Country Market Buffett (Flying J)
Other	W: Willard Stay State park
354	UT 126, U.S. 89, Willard
352	UT 134, Farr West, Pleasant View
Gas	E: Maverik Country Store and Bakery(*, PLAY) W: Hoagies Petro Mart(D)
Food	E: McDonald's, Subway
ATM	E: Maverik Country Store and Bakery
Other	W: Intermountain Truck Sales
349	Defense Depot, Harrisville
Gas	W: Texaco
Other	E: Mulligan's Golf and Games
347	UT 39, 12th Street
Gas	E: Flying J Travel Plaza, Phillips 66(CW)
Food	E: Jeremiah's Restaurant W: Country Side Grill
Lodg	E: Best Western High Country Inn W: Sleep Inn
AServ	E: Steve's Car Care
TServ	W: General Diesel Truck Repair, Pilot Travel Center(*, SCALES)
ATM	E: Phillips 66
Other	E: Hair Quarters
346	UT 104, 21st Street, Wilson Lane
TStop	E: Flying J Travel Center(*, SCALES)
FStop	E: Arby's
Gas	E: Chevron(*, CW) (Arby's) W: Texaco(*) (Freeway Cafe)
Food	E: Cactus Reds, Pamorac Saloon
Lodg	E: BestRest Inn, Big Z Motel, Comfort Suites Hotel (Cactus Reds Restaurant) W: Super 8
TServ	E: J Care Service Center(D, SCALES), Lake City International, Ogden Diesel Sales and Service
RVCamp	W: Century Mobile Home RV Camp
Med	E: Talbert Medical Group
ATM	E: Flying J Travel Center
Other	E: Holiday Island
345	UT 53, 24th Street (Northbound, Reaccess Southbound Only)
Gas	E: Sinclair(*), Texaco
Food	W: Western sunrise Cafe
Other	E: West Side Laundromat
344	UT 79, Ogden, 31st Street
343	I-84 East, Cheyenne (Southbound)

EXIT	UTAH
	Note: I-84 runs concurrent above with I-15. Numbering follows I-15.
81	UT26, I-15, Riverdale
Gas	N: Conoco(*, D, LP, CW)
Food	N: Applebee's, Boston Market Restaurant, Carl Jr's Hamburgers, Chili's, Einstein Bros Bagels, Frozen yogurt, La Salsa, Super Subs, Salad, and Soups, Zuka Juice
Lodg	S: Motel 6
AServ	N: Nobus, Petersen Nissan, Pontiac, Buick, GMC, Peterson HOnda, MItsubishi, Peterson nissan
Other	N: Media Play, Pearl Vision Center, Super Cuts, Super Target, Wal-Mart
85	Uintah, South Weber
87AB	US89, Ogden, Salt Lake
(91)	Rest Area (RR, Picnic, P; Eastbound)
92	UT 167, Mount Green, Huntsville (Eastbound, Reaccess Westbound Only)
(94)	Rest Area (RR, Picnic, P; Westbound)
96	UT167, Peterson, Mount Green, Stoddard
Gas	S: Phillips 66(*)
AServ	S: Phillips 66
Other	S: Coin Car Wash
103	UT66, Morgan
Food	S: Buzzys Grill, Country Cafe
AServ	S: Heiner Ford Dealership, Mye's Auto, Nelson Auto Repair, Peterson body Repair, Wally's Automotive
Other	S: Morgan City Park, Morgan Drugs, Morgan Food Center, Visitor Information
106	Ranch Exit
108	Taggart
111	Croydon
112	Henefer
115	Henefer, Echo (Westbound)

↑UTAH

Begin I-84, Utah to Oregon

I-84 E

EXIT	PENNSYLVANIA
	Begin I-84, Pennsylvania toMassachusetts

↓PENNSYLVANIA

EXIT	PENNSYLVANIA
(0)	Jct I-81, to Wilks - Bear, PA, Binghamton, NY
1	Tigue St, Dunmore
FStop	S: Texaco(D, K)
Food	N: Holiday Inn
Lodg	N: Holiday Inn
AServ	S: Texaco
2	PA 435, Elmhurst
(4)	Junction I-380, Scranton, Mt Pocono
4	**(8)** PA 247, PA 348, Mount Cobb (PA247 - No Trucks Over 10.5 Tons)
FStop	N: Mobil(*, D)
Gas	N: Citgo(*)
ATM	N: LA Bank
Other	N: Four Star Super Mkt
5	**(14)** PA191, Newfoundland, Hamlin
TStop	N: Howe's Auto/Truck Plaza(D, SCALES) (Exxon Gas)
FStop	N: Exxon(D)
Food	N: Comfort Inn (Howe's Truckstop), Twin Rocks (Howe's Truckstop)
Lodg	N: Comfort Inn (Howe's Truckstop)
TServ	N: Howe's Truckstop
6	**(20)** PA 507, Green Town Lake, Lake Wallenpaupack
FStop	N: Exxon(D)
Gas	N: Mobil(*)
Food	N: John's Italian Restaurant
Other	N: Claws N'Paws Animal Park
(24)	Weigh Station, Rest Area (RR, Phones, Picnic, Vending, Pet Walk)
7	**(27)** PA 390, Tafton, Promised Land State Park
Parks	N: Promised Land State Park
8	**(30)** PA 402, Porter's Lake, Blooming Grove
9	**(35)** PA 739, Dingman's Ferry, Lord's Valley
Gas	S: Sunoco(*)
Food	S: McDonald's
AServ	N: Lord's Valley Towing
10	**(46)** U.S. 6, Milford
Gas	N: Mobil(*, D) S: Citgo(*)
Food	S: Red Carpet Inn Restaurant (Red Carpet Inn)
Lodg	S: Red Carpet Inn
AServ	N: My Place Auto Service (Towing Service)
11	**(54)** U.S. 6, U.S. 209, Matamoras (No Trucks 7PM To 7AM)
Gas	N: 24 Hr Gas & C-Store(*), Citgo(*), Shell(*) S: Mobil(*)
Food	N: Landmark, Polar Bear Ice Cream Cafe S: Best Western, Coffee Bar (Lazy River Books), McDonald's, Peking Garden, Perkins, Pizza

EXIT PENNSYLVANIA/NEW YORK

1145

Seasonal Rates Available

Best Western at Hunt's Landing
— Indoor Pool & Sauna —
— Suites & Jacuzzi Rooms—
— Full Service Restaurant & Lounge —
— Seafood Feast - Fri, Sat., & Sun. —
— In Room Coffee, Movies & Cable TV —
30 Acres on the Scenic Delaware River
717-491-2400 • Reservations 1-800-308-2378
PENNSYLVANIA • I-84 • EXIT 11

Village Inn Diner, Wendy's
- **Lodg** **N:** West Falls Motel
  S: Best Western (see our ad this page), Blue Spruce Motel, Village Inn
- **AServ** **N:** Shell
- **RVCamp** **S:** **Hickory Grove Campground, Tri-State RV Park (1 Mile)**
- **Other** **N:** **Tri-State Canoe**
  S: **Eckerd Drugs, Grand Union Grocery Store, K-Mart[RX], Lazy River Books (Coffee Bar), Wal-Mart[RX], Westfall Ctr**

↑PENNSYLVANIA

↓NEW YORK

1 U.S. 6, NJ 23, Port Jervis, Sussex
- **FStop** **N:** **Mobil[*]**
  S: **Citgo[*], Gulf[*, D, LP], Xtra[*]**
- **Food** **N:** Arlene & Tom's Diner, Dunkin Donuts
  S: Dairy Queen, McDonald's, Village Pizza
- **Lodg** **N:** **Deer Dale Motel, Painted Aprons Motor Lodge**, Shady Brook Motel
  S: Comfort Inn
- **RVCamp** **N:** **Campground (2 Miles)**
- **Med** **N:** **+ Hospital**
- **Other** **N:** **Erie Depot, Ft Decker Historic Site**
  S: **Rite Aide Pharmacy, Shop Lite Grocery Store, Tri- State Mall**

(3) **Scenic Overlook, Parking Area (No Services)**

2 **(5)** Mountain Road

3 **(15)** U.S. 6, NY 17M, Middletown, Goshen
- **FStop** **S:** **Sunoco[*, D, LP]**

EXIT NEW YORK

- **Gas** **N:** Citgo[*, D], Hess[D], Mobil[*, D], Texaco[*], Wally Mart[D]
  S: **84 Quick Stop[*]**
- **Food** **N:** 6-17 Diner, Blimpie's Subs, Boston Market Restaurant, Bradley Corner's Restaurant, Burger King, Cancun Inn (Mexican & Spanish), Carvel Ice Cream Bakery, China Town Restaurant, Dunkin Donuts, Ground Round, McDonald's, Momma Pina Pizza, Peking Restaurant, Perkin's Family Restaurant, Ponderosa Steakhouse, Taco Bell, Wendy's
  S: 84 Quick Stop Deli, Salt & Pepper Deli, Pizza, Tudy's Coffee Shop
- **Lodg** **S:** Days Inn, Global Budget Inn Of America
- **Med** **N:** **+ Hospital**
- **ATM** **N:** M&T Bank, MSB Bank
- **Other** **N:** **Campbell Shopping Ctr**, Crystal Clean Car Wash, **Middletown Commons Shopping Center, Redner's Warehouse Groc, Rite Aide Pharmacy, Shop-Rite Grocery**
  S: **U.S. Post Office**

(17) **Rest Area (RR, Phones, Picnic, Vending, Pet Walk; Eastbound)**

4 **(19)** NY 17, Binghamton, New York
- **Med** **S:** **+ Hospital**
- **Other** **S:** **State Police**

(23) **Rest Area (RR, Phones, Picnic, Vending; Westbound)**

5 **(29)** NY 208, Maybrook, Walden, New Paltz
- **TStop** **S:** **Travel Port[*, SCALES]**
- **Gas** **N:** Exxon, Mobil
  S: **Sunoco (Travel Port)**
- **Food** **N:** Blazing Bagels, Burger King, Gold Chain Chinese Restaurant, Leaning Tower III (Pizza), McDonald's
  S: **Buckhorn Restaurant (Travel Port), Pizza Hut (Travel Port), The Roadside Inn**
- **Lodg** **N:** Super 8
  S: **Super 8**
- **AServ** **N:** Exxon, Mobil (Wrecker Service)
- **TWash** **S:** **Blue Beacon Truck Wash (Travelport)**
- **RVCamp** **N:** **Price Rite Trailer Sales[LP] (1.5 Miles), Winding Hill Campground**
- **ATM** **N:** Orange County Trust Company, Shop Rite Grocery
- **Other** **N:** **Eckerd Drugs, Shop Rite Grocery**
  S: **Variety Farms C-Store**

6 **(34)** NY 17K, Montgomery, Newburgh
- **Gas** **N:** Mobil[*, LP, CW]
  S: Exxon[*]
- **Food** **N:** **Stewart Airport Diner**
  S: Courtyard By Marriott, Deli (Exxon)

EXIT NEW YORK

- **Lodg** **N:** Comfort Inn
  S: Courtyard By Marriott
- **Other** **S:** **Stewart Int'l Airport**

7A **(37)** Junction I-87 Thruway, NY 300, Union Ave

7B **(37)** NY 300, Union Ave
- **Gas** **N:** Exxon[*], Mobil[*, CW]
  S: Getty[*], Sunoco[*]
- **Food** **N:** Ground Round, King Buffet, McDonald's, Roy Rogers, Subway, Taco Bell, Wendy's
  S: Burger King, Cafe International (Ramada Inn), Denny's, Holiday Inn, Neptune Diner, Yobo Oriental
- **Lodg** **S:** Hampton Inn, Holiday Inn, Howard Johnson, Ramada Inn, **Super 8**
- **AServ** **N:** Auto Palace, Exxon (Wrecker Service), Mavis Discount Tire, Midas Muffler & Brake, Pitstop Oil Change, Sears
  S: Getty, Newburgh Nissan
- **RVCamp** **S:** **KOA Camp (8 Miles)**
- **ATM** **N:** All Bank, Fleet Bank
  S: Fleet Bank
- **Other** **N:** **Dairy Mart C-Store, Newburgh Mall, Weis Supermarket**
  S: **Tourist Info.**

8 **(37)** NY 52, Walden
- **Gas** **N:** Citgo[*]
  S: Gulf[*]
- **Food** **S:** The Eatery Den
- **AServ** **S:** Century Auto Services
- **Med** **S:** **+ Hospital**

10 **(39)** U.S. 9 W, NY 32, Newburgh, Highland
- **Gas** **N:** Texaco[*]
  S: Exxon[*, D], Gulf, Sunoco[*, 24]
- **Food** **N:** Burger King, KFC, Lexus Diner, New York Bagel & Bean's Coffee Shop, Perkins Family Restaurant, Roma Imperial Restaurant & Pizza
- **AServ** **N:** Firestone Tire & Auto, Texaco
  S: Gulf
- **Med** **S:** **+ Hospital**
- **ATM** **S:** Exxon
- **Other** **N:** **Medical Arts Pharmacy[RX]**
  S: **Dairy Mart Convenience Store**

11 **(41)** NY 9D, Wappinger Falls, Beacon
- **Med** **N:** **+ Hospital**
- **Other** **N:** **Tourist Info.**

12 **(45)** NY 52, Fishkill
- **Gas** **N:** Coastal[*, LP]
  S: Shell[*], Sunoco
- **Food** **S:** Fishkill Frostee Hot Dog Stand, Home Town Deli, **I-84 Diner**
- **AServ** **S:** Brownell Mercury/Lincoln/Saab, Shell, Sunoco
- **Med** **S:** **+ Fishkill Medical Center**
- **ATM** **N:** Coastal

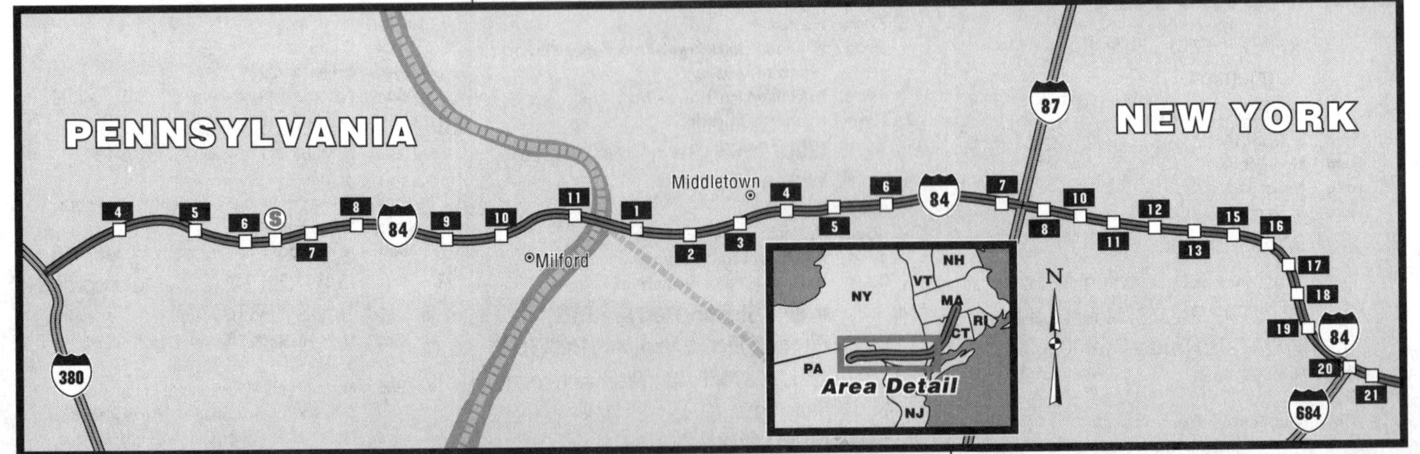

Bold red print shows RV & Bus parking available or nearby

EXIT NEW YORK/CONNECTICUT

1321
Wellesley Inns
Value Never Looked This Good!
New York • Exit 13 • 914-896-4995

13 **(46)** U.S. 9, Poughkeepsie, Peekskill
Gas N: Mobil(*, LP), Mobil(*, CW)
Food N: Boston Market Restaurant, Denny's, New York Deli, Pizza Hut, Stanley's Eatery (Holiday Inn)
S: McDonald's, Moog's Farm
Lodg N: Courtyard by Marriott, Holiday Inn, Main Stay Suites, Residence Inn, **Wellesley Inn (see our ad this page)**
ATM N: Bank of Hudson
S: Hudson Valley Credit Union
Other N: **Sam's Club**, **Wal-Mart**(RX)
S: **Drug World**(RX), **Dutchess Mall Shopping Center**

15 **(51)** Lime Kiln Road

16 **(53)** Taconic State Pkwy, Albany

(55) **Rest Area (RR, Phones, Picnic, Pet Walk; Eastbound)**

(55) **Rest Area (RR, Phones, Picnic; Westbound)**

17 **(59)** Ludingtonville Road
FStop S: **Hess**(*, D)
Gas S: Sunoco
Food S: 17-84 Country Grill, **Blimpie's Subs (Hess)**, Lou's Restaurant & Deli
AServ N: Metric Motors
S: Sunoco
RVCamp S: **Carmel Camper Service**(LP)

18 **(62)** NY 311, Lake Carmel, Patterson

19 **(65)** NY 312, Carmel
Med S: **Hospital**

20 **(68)** Jct I-684, US 6, US 202, US 22, White Plains, Brewster, Pawling

21 **(69)** U.S. 6, U.S. 202, NY 121, North Salem, Brewster (Westbound)

↑NEW YORK

↓CONNECTICUT

1 Saw Mill Road

(2) **Weigh Station, Rest Area (RV Dump; Eastbound)**

2AB **(1)** U.S. 6, U.S. 202, Mill Plain Road, Old Ridgebury Rd
Lodg S: Hilton

3 **(4)** U.S. 7, Norwalk (Left Exit)
AServ S: Sears
Other S: **Danbury Airport**, **Danbury Fair Mall**

4 U.S. 6, U.S. 202, Lake Ave
Gas N: Amoco(*), Gulf, Texaco(*, D, CW)
Food N: Dunkin Donuts, McDonald's
Lodg N: Ethan Allen Inn, Super 8
AServ N: Gulf

5 CT 37, CT 39, CT 53, Downtown Danbury
Gas N: BP, Texaco(*)
S: Mobil(*)
Food S: Deli & Snack Shop, Taco Bell

EXIT CONNECTICUT

Lodg N: Exit 5 Motel
AServ N: BP
S: Avis Lube

6 CT 37, New Fairfield
Gas N: Shell(CW), Texaco
S: Amoco(*)
Food N: Bella Italia Restaurant, Burger King, Carvel Ice Cream Bakery, McDonald's, Mykono's
S: KFC
AServ N: Shell
S: A&S Auto Sales(24) (Wrecker Service), Axel's Foreign Auto Parts, Bob's Auto Supply
ATM N: First Union Bank
Other N: **A & P Supermarket**, **Brooks Pharmacy**
S: **Deep's Market**, **Railway Museum**

7 **(8)** U.S. 7, U.S. 202, New Milford, Brookfield (Left Exit)

8 **(9)** U.S. 6, Newtown Road, Bethel
Gas N: Gulf, Mobil(*, D), Texaco(D, CW)
S: Shell(*, CW), Texaco(*, D)
Food S: Blimpie's Subs, Chili's, Dunkin Donuts, Friendly's, Italian & Pizza, McDonald's, Mike's Pizza, Taco Bell
Lodg N: Ramada (see our ad this page)
S: Holiday Inn
AServ S: Action GMC Trucks, Mohawk Tire & Auto Goodyear, Pound Fair Tire, Roberts Pontiac, Buick, Texaco
Med S: **Hospital**
ATM S: First Union
Other S: **CVS Pharmacy**(RX), Expect Discount Pharmacy(RX), **Super Stop Grocery**(RX)

9 **(12)** CT 25, Brookfield, Bridgeport

10 **(15)** U.S. 6 West, Newtown, Sandy Hook
Gas S: Amoco(*, D), Shell(*, 24)
Food S: Blue Colony Diner, New Town Pizza Palace
ATM S: Chase Manhattan Bank
Other S: **Newton Drug Center**(RX)

11 **(17)** CT 34, Derby, New Haven

13 **(19)** River Road (Eastbound)

14 **(20)** CT 172, South Britain
Gas N: Texaco(*)
Food N: Tartuso Restaurant, Thatcher's Restaurant
Other S: **State Police**

15 **(22)** U.S. 6, Southbury, Seymour
Gas N: Citgo, **International**, Shell
Food N: Citgo, Dunkin Donuts, Jordan's Restaurant, McDonald's, Oriental Gourmet, Subway
AServ N: Shell
TServ N: **International**
ATM N: Fleet Bank, People's Bank, Webster Bank
Parks S: **Kettletown State Park**
Other N: **CVS Pharmacy**(RX), **K-Mart**, NAPA Auto Parts, **Southbarry Plaza Shopping Center**

16 **(25)** CT 188, Middlebury
Gas N: Mobil(*)
Food N: Patty's Pantry & Deli
Lodg N: Hilton

17 **(29)** CT 63, CT 64, Naugatuck, Watertown
Gas S: Mobil(*, D)

1322
RAMADA
Connecticut • Exit 8 • 203-792-3800

EXIT CONNECTICUT

Food N: Maggie Macfly's
S: Dunkin Donuts (At Mobile), Java Coast Fine Coffee, Leo's Deli Buffet
Other S: **Primrose Square**

18 **(32)** West Main St, Highland Ave (Difficult Reaccess)
Gas N: Texaco
Food N: New Moon Chinese, Robinwood Lunchenette
AServ N: Texaco
Med N: **Waterbury Hospital**
Other N: **CVS Pharmacy**(24, RX)

19 **(32)** CT 8 South, Naugatuck

20 **(32)** CT 8 North, Torrington (Left Exit)

21 **(32)** Meadow St, Banks St
Gas S: Exxon(*, D)
Food S: Sun Kee Kitchen

22 **(33)** Union St, Downtown Waterbury
Gas N: Gult
Lodg N: Courtyard by Marriott, Quality Inn
Med N: **St.Mary's Hospital**
ATM N: First Union, Webster Bank
Other N: **Post Office**

23 **(34)** CT 69, Wolcott, Prospect, Hamilton Ave
Med N: **Hospital**

24 **(37)** Harpers Ferry Road (No Reaccess)
Gas S: Texaco(*)

25 **(41)** Harpers Ferry Rd.
Gas N: Exxon(*), Gulf(*, D)
S: Mobil, Texaco(*)
Food N: Bob's Grocery, China Buffet, Dunkin Donuts, Friendly's, Nardelli's
S: Bagel Mania, Burger King, Carvel Ice Cream Bakery, Dunkin Donuts (Texaco), Friendly's, Golden Wok, McDonald's(PLAY), Neno's Restaurant
Lodg S: Super 8
AServ S: Loehman Geo, Chevrolet, Mobil
ATM S: Webster Bank
Other S: **CVS Pharmacy**(RX), **Coin Laundry**, **Super Stop & Shop**

25A Austin Rd.

26 **(38)** CT 70, Cheshire, Prospect

27 **(41)** Jct I-691 East, Meridan

28 **(41)** CT 322, Marion, Mildale
TStop S: **T/A TravelCenters of America**(*, SCALES)
Gas N: Gulf(*), Sunoco(*)
S: Mobil(*)
Food S: Burger King, China Gourmet, Dunkin Donuts, Smokin Gun Grill, **T/A TravelCenters of America**
Lodg S: DAYS INN Days Inn
AServ N: Mantz Auto Sales & Repair
S: Mobil, Quick Call Check
RVCamp S: **Bell Camper Land**(LP)

(42) **Rest Area (RR, Phones, RV Dump; Eastbound)**

29 **(42)** Milldale, CT 10

30 **(43)** West Main St, Marion Ave, Southington
Gas S: Mobil(*)
AServ S: Mobil
TServ S: **Aszklar**
Med S: **Bradley Memorial Hospital**
Other N: **Ski Area**

31 **(44)** CT 229, West St, Bristol
FStop N: **Sunoco**(*, D)
Gas N: Mobil(*)
S: Citgo(*), Gulf(*)

EXIT CONNECTICUT

Food **N:** Dunkin Donuts (Mobil)
S: Vallendino Pizza, Westview Seafood
AServ **S:** Gulf
RVCamp **N:** **Redman's Trailer Sales(LP) (5 Miles)**

32 **(46)** CT 10, Queen St
Gas **N:** Shell(*)
S: Sunoco(*)
Food **N:** Chili's, D'Angelo's, Denny's, Friendly's, McDonald's, Subway, TCBY, Taco Bell
S: Bickford's Family Restaurant, Blimpie's Subs, Friendly's, **Little Caesars Pizza (K-Mart)**
Lodg **N:** Motel 6
S: Holiday Inn Express, Red Carpet Inn, Susse Chalet
AServ **S:** **K-Mart(RX)**, Southington Chevrolet, Speedy
ATM **S:** Webster Bank
Other **N:** **Coin Laundry(RX)**
S: **K-Mart(RX)**

33 **(49)** CT 72, Plainville, Bristol (Left Exit)

34 **(49)** CT 372, Crooked St, Plainville (Left Exit)
FStop **N:** **Gasoline Alley(*)**
Food **N:** Chung's Buffet, **Howard Johnson**, Manhattan Bagel
Lodg **N:** **Howard Johnson**
AServ **N:** Crowley's Vokeswagon
S: Tire Repair
ATM **N:** Peoples Savings and Trust
Other **N:** **Big Y Supermarket, Rite Aide Pharmacy**
S: **Jim's Grocery**

35 **(50)** CT 72, to CT 9, New Britain, Middletown (Left Exit Westbound)
Med **S:** ✚ **Hospital**

36 **(51)** Slater Road

37 **(53)** US 6, Fienemann Road, Farmington
Lodg **N:** Marriott
Med **S:** ✚ **Hospital**

38 **(54)** U.S. 6 West, Bristol

39 **(54)** CT 4, Farmington (Left Exit)
Med **N:** ✚ **Hospital**

39A **(55)** CT9, Newington , New Britain

EXIT CONNECTICUT

40 **(56)** CT 71, New Britain Ave, Corbins Corner (Difficult Reaccess)
Food **S:** Joe's American Bar & Grill, Wendy's
AServ **S:** Sears Auto Center
ATM **S:** Fleet Bank

41 **(57)** South Main St, Elmwood
Food **S:** Charley's Place, China Buffet, IHOP
ATM **S:** Webster Bank
Other **N:** **Noah's Webster's Home Historical Site**

42 **(58)** Trout Brook Dr, Elmwood (Left Exit)

43 **(58)** Park Road, West Parkford Center (Left Exit)
Other **N:** **Police Dept, Science Center of Connecticut**

44 **(59)** Prospect Ave
Gas **N:** Exxon(*, CW), Texaco(*, CW)
Food **N:** Bess Eaton Donuts, Burger King, Carvel Ice Cream Bakery, Chinese Buffet, D'Angelo's, Gold Rock Diner & Restaurant, Hometown Buffet, McDonald's, Wendy's
Other **N:** **Shaw's Food & Drug**

45 **(60)** Park Road, Flatbush Ave (Left Exit Westbound)

46 **(59)** Sisson Ave (Left Exit)

47 **(59)** Sigourney St

48 **(60)** Asylum St, Capital Ave
Med **N:** ✚ **Hospital**

49 **(60)** Civic Center, Ann St, High St

50 **(61)** Main St

51 **(62)** Junction I-91 North, Springfield

52 **(62)** Junction I-91 South, New Haven, U.S. 44, Main St

53 **(63)** U.S. 44, East Hartford

EXIT CONNECTICUT

54 **(64)** CT 2 W, Downtown Hartford (Left Exit Westbound)

55 **(64)** CT 2, Norwich, New London

56 **(64)** Governor St, East Hartford (Left Exit)

57 **(65)** CT 15, to I-91, Charter Oak Bridge

58 **(65)** Roberts St, Silver Lane, Burnside Ave
Food **N:** The Grill
Lodg **N:** Holiday Inn, Wellesley Inn (see our ad this page)
TServ **N:** **Freightliner Dealer**
ATM **N:** BSW

59 **(66)** Junction I-384, Providence

60 **(67)** U.S. 44W, Middle Tnpk W, U.S. 6, Manchester
Food **S:** Chez Ben Diner
AServ **S:** Final Inspection
Med **S:** ✚ **Hospital**

61 **(69)** Jct 291W, Windsor

62 **(70)** U.S. 44, Buckland St
Gas **N:** Exxon(D)
S: Citgo(D), Mobil(*, D)
Food **N:** Between Round Bagel, Boston Market Restaurant, Bug-A-Boo Creek Steakhouse, Chili's, Friendly's, Mandarin Mae Chinese, Olive Garden, Pizza Hut, Starbucks Coffee, Taco Bell
S: Chowder Town Seafood, Chuck E Cheese's Pizza, Dunkin Donuts, Friendly's, Golden Dragon, Ground Round Restaurant, Manhattan Bagel, McDonald's, Papa Gino's, Subway, Wooster Pizza Shop
AServ **N:** Exxon
S: Citgo, Firestone Tire & Auto, Manchester Honda
ATM **S:** SBM, Webster Bank
Other **N:** Borders Books & Music, **Sam's Club**
S: **Mail Boxes Etc, US Post Office**

63 **(72)** CT 30, CT 83, South Windsor
Gas **N:** Texaco(D, LP)
S: Exxon(D), Getty(D), Gulf, Shell(*), Sunoco(*, D)
Food **N:** McDonald's(PLAY), Uno Pizzeria
S: Acadia Restaurant, King Buffet, Palace Restaurant & Lounge, Roy Rogers, Toppers

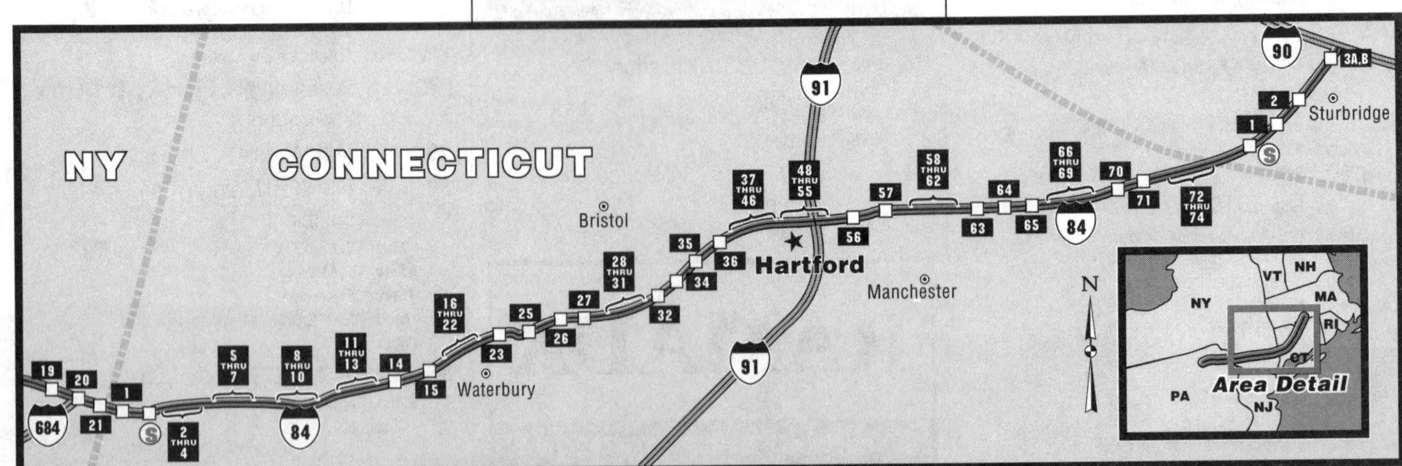

Bold red print shows RV & Bus parking available or nearby

EXIT CONNECTICUT

Lodg **S:** Connecticut Inn Motor Lodge
AServ **S:** Gulf, Marnde Ford, Lincoln, Mazada
Med **S:** + **Hospital**
Other **S:** **Big Y Supermarket**, Rite Aid Pharmacy

64 **(73)** CT 30, CT 83, Vernon Center, Rockville

Gas **N:** Mobil(*), Sunoco
Food **N:** 99 Restaurant, Anthony's Pizza, Damon's, Denny's, Dunkin Donuts, Friendly's, Kim's Oriental, McDonald's(PLAY), Papa Geno's, Taco Bell
Lodg **N:** Holiday Inn Express
AServ **N:** Goodyear Tire & Auto, Jiffy Lube, **K-Mart**, Sunoco
ATM **N:** First Federal Savings, Fleet Bank, People's Bank, Savings Bank of Rockville, **Super Stop N Shop**(RX)
Other **N:** CVS Pharmacy(24, RX), **K-Mart**, **Mail Boxes Etc**, **Super Stop N Shop**(RX)

65 **(73)** CT 30, Vernon Center

Gas **N:** Mobile(*), Shell, Texaco(*, CW)
Food **N:** Bickford's Family Restaurant, Burger King, Joy Wok Chinese, KFC, Lotus Restaurant
AServ **N:** Firestone Tire & Auto, Mobile, Post Road Plaza, Shell(*)
ATM **N:** Holland Bank, SBM Bank
Other **N:** **Vernon Drug**

66 **(75)** Tunnel Road, Vernon, Bolton

67 **(77)** CT 31, Rockville, Coventry

Gas **N:** Mobil(*), Texaco(*, D)
Food **N:** Bess Eatin Donuts, Blimpie's Subs, China Taste, McDonald's, Sue's Kitchen, Theo's Family Restaurant
RVCamp **N:** **Campground**
Med **N:** + **Hospital**
ATM **N:** The Savings Bank of Rockville

68 **(81)** CT 195, Tolland, Mansfield

Gas **N:** Gulf, Mobil
S: Citgo(*), Getty(*, D), Texaco(*)
Food **S:** Bagels & More, Lee's Garden Chinese Restaurant, Rhodo's Pizza

EXIT CONNECTICUT

AServ **N:** Gulf, Mobil, NAPA Auto Parts
S: Texaco
ATM **S:** SBM Bank
Other **S:** **Toland Pharmacy**(RX)

69 **(84)** CT 74 to U.S. 44, Willington

RVCamp **S:** **Campground**
Other **N:** **State Police**

(84) **Rest Area (RR, Phones, Picnic, RV Dump)**

70 **(86)** CT 32, Willington, Stafford Springs

Gas **S:** Mobil(*), Sunoco(*, D)
RVCamp **N:** **Rainbow Acres Campground (1.5 Miles)**
S: **Campground**
Med **N:** + **Hospital**

71 **(88)** CT 320, Ruby Road

TStop **S:** **T/A TravelCenters of America**
Gas **N:** Citgo(D)
Food **S:** **Burger King (TA Truckstop)**, **Country Pride Restaurant (TA Truckstop)**, **Dunkin Donuts (TA Truckstop)**
Lodg **S:** **Sleep Inn (TA Truckstop)**
AServ **N:** **Red-Art's Service Center**
TServ **N:** **Red-Art's Service Center**
RVCamp **S:** **RV Dump Station**

72 **(92)** CT 89, Westford, Ashford

Lodg **N:** Ashford Motel
RVCamp **N:** **Campground**
S: **Campground**

73 **(93)** CT 190, Stafford Springs , Union

RVCamp **S:** **Campground**

(95) **Weigh Station (Westbound)**

74 **(97)** CT 171, Union, Holland MA

Gas **N:** Citgo(*)
Food **N:** Citgo
S: **Traveler Restaurant**
AServ **S:** Goodhall's Garage, Jerry Yost's Chrysler, Plymoth, Jeep

EXIT CONNECTICUT/MASSACHUSETTS

RVCamp **N:** **Rainbow Acres Family Campground (1.6 Miles)**
S: **Campground**

(96) **Rest Area**

↑CONNECTICUT

↓MASSACHUSETTS

1 **(4)** Mashapaug Road, Southbridge

TStop **N:** **Sturbridge Isle**(*)
FStop **S:** **Mobil**(D)
Gas **N:** Texaco(*, D)
Food **N:** **Boston Pizza & Deli (Sturbridge Isle)**, **Country Kitchen Restaurant (Sturbridge Isle)**
S: **Roy Rogers**, **Sbarro Pizza**
RVCamp **N:** **Campground**
Med **S:** + **Hospital**

2 **(5)** to MA 131, Sturbridge, Southbridge

Food **S:** Hebert Candy & Ice Cream
RVCamp **N:** **Yogi Bear Camp Resort**
S: **Campground**
Other **N:** **Olde Sturbridge Village**

3AB **(7)** U.S. 20, Worcester, Palmer

TStop **S:** **New England Truck Stop**(SCALES)
Gas **N:** Citgo(*), Mobil(*, D)
S: Texaco (Express Lube)
Food **N:** **Best Western**, Burger King, Friendly's, McDonald's, Piccadilly Pub & Restaurant, Sturbridge Host Hotel, Sturbridge's Pizza House (Citgo)
S: **Heritage Family Restaurant**, **New England Truck Stop**
Lodg **N:** **Best Western**, Old Sturbridge Village Lodges, Sturbridge Host Hotel, Super 8
S: Quality Inn, Travel Nest
ATM **N:** Fleet Bank
Other **N:** **State Police**

↑MASSACHUSETTS

Begin I-84, Massachusetts to Pennsylvania

Notes:

EXIT VIRGINIA

Begin I-85

↓VIRGINIA

68 Junction I-95S, U.S.460E, Rocky Mt, NC

65 Squirrel Level Road

63AB U.S. 1
- **FStop** E: Chevron(*, CW), Exxon(*, LP), Texaco(*, D)
- **Gas** E: Citgo(*, LP)
  W: Amaco
- **Food** E: Burger King (Citgo), Exxon, Hardee's, Waffle House
  W: Dunkin Donuts, McDonald's
- **AServ** E: Citgo
  W: Greyline
- **Med** W: ✚ State Hospital
- **Parks** E: Pamplin Civil War Park

61 U.S. 460, Blackstone
- **FStop** E: East Coast(*, D)
- **Gas** W: Texaco(D, LP)
- **Food** W: Bullet's, Dunkin Donuts
- **RVCamp** E: Picture Lake Camping (2.1 Miles)
- **ATM** E: East Coast

(55) Rest Area (RR, Phones, Picnic, Vending)

53 VA 703, Dinwiddie
- **FStop** W: Exxon(*, D)
- **Food** W: Thats A Burger
- **AServ** W: Exxon (Towing)
- **Parks** W: Petersburg National Battlefield

48 VA 650, DeWitt

42 VA 40, McKenney
- **Gas** W: Citgo(*, D), Exxon(*, D, LP)
- **Food** W: Dairy-Freeze
- **AServ** W: Lafonna's Auto Service
- **Other** W: Saunder's Gas, Oil, Propane, Wallace's Market

39 VA 712, Rawlings
- **FStop** W: Chevron(*)
- **Gas** W: Citgo(D) (Nottaway Motel)
- **Food** W: Nottaway Restaurant
- **Lodg** W: Nottaway Motel
- **Other** E: VA Battlerama

34 VA 630, Warfield
- **Gas** W: Exxon(*, D)
- **AServ** W: Warfield Service Center

(32) Rest Area (RR, Phones, Picnic, Vending)

28 U.S. 1, VA 46, Alberta, Lawrenceville
- **FStop** E: Amoco(*)
- **Gas** W: Citgo(*)
- **Other** W: Synergy Gas(LP)

27 VA 46, Blackstone, Lawrenceville (Northbound, Reaccess Southbound Only)

24 VA 644, Meredithville

(22) Weigh Station

15 U.S. 1, South Hill, Kenbridge
- **Gas** W: Shell(*, D)
- **Food** W: Kahill's Restaurant, Lake Country BBQ (Shell)
- **Med** W: ✚ Hospital

12 U.S. 58, VA 47, Norfolk, South Hill
- **FStop** W: Exxon(*)
- **Gas** E: Racetrac(*), Shell(*, CW)
  W: Amoco(D, CW), Chevron(*), Petrol(*, LP), Texaco(*, D, CW)
- **Food** E: Bagel's Plus, Bojangles

EXIT VIRGINIA/NORTH CAROLINA

  W: Brian's Steak House & Lounge, Burger King, Denny's, Golden Corral Family Steakhouse, Hardee's, KFC, McDonald's, New China Restaurant, Taco Bell, The Medicine Shoppe, Wendy's
- **Lodg** E: Hampton Inn (see our ad this page)
  W: Best Western, Comfort Inn (see our ad this page), Econolodge, Super 8
- **AServ** E: Amerilube
  W: Chevron (Towing), Colony Tire, Frank Jackson Ford, Lincoln, Mercury
- **Med** W: ✚ Hospital
- **ATM** E: Signet Bank
  W: First Citizens Bank, First Viriginia Bank
- **Other** E: Wal-Mart(RX)
  W: Car Wash, Coin Laundry, Farmer's Foods, Fresh & Friendly Food Store, Revco Drugs, Rite Aide Pharmacy, Winn Dixie Supermarket

4 VA 903, Bracey, Lake Gaston
- **TStop** E: Simmons Auto/Truck Terminal(*, SCALES)
- **Gas** E: Amoco(*, D, LP)
- **Food** E: Bracey's Junction, Dairy Queen, Simmons Truckstop
  W: Countryside Family Restaurant
- **Lodg** W: Days Inn
- **TServ** E: Simmons
- **ATM** E: Signet Bank (Simmons)

(2) Welcome Center (RR, Phones, Picnic, Vending; Northbound)

↑VIRGINIA

↓NORTH CAROLINA

233 U.S. 1, Wise
- **TStop** E: Wise Truck Stop(*)
- **Gas** E: Shell(*, D)
- **Food** E: Wise Truck Stop
- **Lodg** E: Budget Inn
- **AServ** E: Shell(*)

(231) Welcome Center (RR, Phones, Vending; Southbound)

229 Oine Road

226 Ridgeway Road
- **Other** W: State Recreation Area

223 Manson Road
- **RVCamp** E: BP

220 U.S. 1, U.S. 158, Norlina, Fleming Road
- **TStop** W: Chex(*, SCALES)
- **Gas** E: Exxon(*, D)
- **Food** W: Floyd's Grill
- **Lodg** W: Chex
- **AServ** W: Floyd's Auto Repair
- **TWash** W: Chex
- **ATM** W: Chex Truckstop

218 U.S. 1 South, Raleigh (Left Exit Southbound)

217 Satterwhite Point, Nutbush Bridge
- **Gas** W: Exxon(*, D)

215 U.S. 158 East Bypass
- **FStop** E: Winoco(*, D)
- **Gas** E: Shell(*, D)
- **Food** E: 220 Seafood, Burger King, Dockside Seafood Restaurant, Freeze Made Dairy Bar, Golden China, Nunnery-Freeman Barbacue, PD Quix Fast Food, Subway, Taste Freeze, Waffle & Pancake House
- **Lodg** E: Budget Host Inn, Comfort Inn, Howard Johnson, Quality Inn, Scottish Inns
- **AServ** E: A&E Imported Auto Parts, East Carolina Tire

EXIT NORTH CAROLINA

- **ATM** E: NationsBank
- **Other** E: Coin Laundry, Food Lion Grocery Store, Revco Drugs

214 NC 39, Henderson
- **Gas** E: BP(*)
  W: Amoco(*, LP), Shell(*, LP)
- **Food** E: Dabney Road Restaurant, The Sandwich Shop
  W: Hot Stuff Pizza (Amoco)
- **AServ** E: King Tire
  W: Doug's Towing & Recovery
- **Other** E: Little River LP(LP), U.S. Post Office
  W: Kerr Lake Recreation Area

213 Dabney Rd
- **Gas** E: Citgo(*, D), Shell(*, LP)
  W: Exxon(*), Shell, Speed-EZ(*, LP)
- **Food** E: Bamboo Garden Chinese, Birds Deli & Bakery, Dairy Queen, Denny's, Lans Chinese, Little Caesars Pizza, McDonald's, Pino's Italian, Pizza Inn, Subway, Wendy's
  W: Gators, Golden Corral Family Steakhouse, Krispy Kreme Doughnuts
- **Lodg** W: Holiday Inn Express
- **AServ** E: Goodyear Tire & Auto
  W: Boyd's Chevrolet, Buick, Chrysler Auto Dealer, Henderson's Motors, Simmons Parts & Service, Wal-Mart
- **Med** W: ✚ Hospital
- **ATM** E: Centura Bank, Fidelity Bank, First Citizens Bank
  W: Shell
- **Other** E: Eckerd Drugs, Food Lion Grocery Store, Henderson Mall, Opti Eye Care Center, Postal Plus, Revco Drugs, Winn Dixie Supermarket
  W: Henderson Square(RX), Wal-Mart(RX)

212 Ruin Creek Road
- **Gas** E: Shell(*)
  W: Amoco(*)
- **Food** E: Cracker Barrel, Mazatlan Mexican

1816
Comfort Inn
918 E. Atlantic St.
South Hill, VA
804-447-2600
Comfort Inn
Continental Breakfast
Kids Under 12 Stay Free
Pets Allowed • Handicap Accessible
Tennis/Golf/South Fitness Center Nearby
Truck/Large Vehicle Parking
Exterior Corridors
12 mi from Lake Gaston
Boat Hook-Up on Property
Virginia • I-85 • Exit 12

Hampton Inn
Newest Property at Exit
South Hill, VA
804-447-4600 • 800-HAMPTON
• Deluxe Continental Breakfast
• Kids Under 12 Stay Free
• Outdoor Pool • Exercise Room
• Meeting/Banquet Facilities
• Handicap Accessible • Coin Laundry
• Tennis/Golf Nearby • Boat Hook-up
• Truck/Large Vehicle Parking
• Airport Shuttle • Interior Corridors
• Business Center at Hotel
1817
VIRGINIA • I-85 • EXIT 12

Bold red print shows RV & Bus parking available or nearby

EXIT	NORTH CAROLINA
	(Days Inn), The Silo Steaks & Seafood
	W: Baskin Robbins, Burger King, Western Sizzlin'
Lodg	E: Days Inn
Med	W: Maria Parham Hospital
ATM	W: Amoco
209	Poplar Creek Road
206	U.S. 158, Oxford
Gas	E: Citgo(*, D)
	W: Texaco(*, D)
AServ	E: Citgo
204	NC 96, Oxford
FStop	E: Amoco(*, D)
Gas	W: Shell(*)
Food	W: Burger King, China Wok Chinese, KFC, Little Caesars Pizza, McDonald's, Peter's Bakery, Pizza Hut, Ramada, Rena's Family Restaurant, Subway, Taco Bell, Yogurt Depot
Lodg	E: King's Inn Motel
	W: Ramada
AServ	E: Boyd Oldsmobile/GMC Trucks
Med	W: Hospital
ATM	W: Central Carolina Bank
Other	W: Byrd's Supermarket, Coin Laundry, Wal-Mart
202	U.S. 115, Oxford, Clarksville
(199)	Rest Area (RR, Phones, Picnic, Vending)
191	NC 56, Butner, Creedmoor
FStop	E: Amoco(*, CW), Trade Mart(*)
	W: Shell(*)
Gas	E: BP(*)
	W: Exxon(*, LP)
Food	E: Bob's Barbecue, Bojangles, Burger King, China Taste, KFC, McDonald's, Pizza Hut, Subway, Taco Bell, Wendy's
	W: Hardee's, The Depot (Exxon)
Lodg	E: Comfort Inn
	W: Econolodge, Holiday Inn Express, Sunset Inn
AServ	E: M&H Tire
	W: JR Tire & Auto
ATM	E: Carolina Central Bank, Fidelity Bank
Other	E: Car Wash, Coin Laundry, Dutch Eye Center, Eckerd Drugs, Food Lion Supermarket
189	Butner
186	U.S.15, Creedmoor, Butner
183	Redwood Road
Gas	E: Days Inn
Food	E: Toddle House Diner (Days Inn)
Lodg	E: Days Inn
AServ	E: Yarbo Automotive
182	Red Mill Road
FStop	E: Exxon(*, D)
TServ	E: Kenworth
180	Glenn School Road
FStop	W: Mobil(*, D)
AServ	E: Mark's Auto Service
179	East Club Blvd, to U.S. 70 E, Raleigh
Gas	W: BP(D), Exxon(*), Mobil(*)
AServ	W: BP, Kennedy Auto Service
178	Roxboro Road, U.S. 70 (Northbound)
177B	NC 55 E, Avondale Dr. (Difficult Reaccess)
177A	Downtown Durham
176	U.S. 501, Gregson St
175	Guess Road
174	Hillandale Road

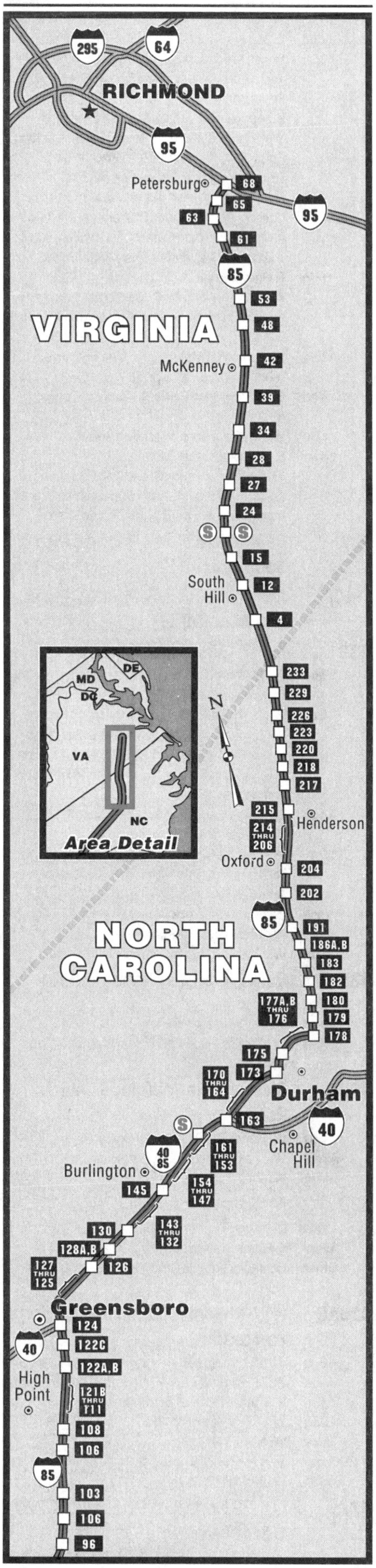

EXIT	NORTH CAROLINA
Food	E: Shoney's
174B	Bypass U.S. 15, U.S. 501 (Southbound)
173	U.S. 15, U.S. 501 South
172	U.S. 70
170	To NC 751, U.S. 70, Duke University
TStop	E: Dixie Truckstop(*)
Food	E: Dixie Truckstop, Harbor Bay Seafood, Skyland (Best Western)
Lodg	E: Best Western (Skyland Inn), Scottish Inns
AServ	W: Bull City Radiator
Parks	W: Eno River State Park
165	NC 86, Chapel Hill, Hillsborough
164	Hillsborough
Gas	E: Exxon(*, LP)
Food	E: McDonald's
Lodg	E: Holiday Inn Express
ATM	E: Exxon
163	Junction I-40, Raleigh
161	To U.S. 70, NC 86
160	Efland
FStop	W: Texaco(*)
Gas	W: BP(*, D)
Food	W: Missy's Grill
AServ	W: BP
ATM	W: Texaco
(159)	Weigh Station (Northbound)
(159)	Weigh Station (Southbound)
157	Buckhorn Road
FStop	E: Amoco(*)
154	Mebane
FStop	E: Pacific Pride Commercial Fueling(*, LP) (Shell gas)
	W: Texaco(*)
Gas	W: Amoco
Food	E: Blimpie Subs & Salads (Pacific Pride), Pacific Pride Commercial Fueling (Shell gas)
	W: McDonald's(PLAY)
Lodg	W: Budget Inn
AServ	W: Amoco
Other	W: Mebane-Oaks Car Wash, Peaches & Cream Children's Outlet, Winn Dixie Supermarket
153	NC 119, Mebane
FStop	E: BP, Citgo
	W: Exxon
Gas	E: BP(*)
	W: Exxon(*)
Food	E: BP, KFC (BP), Pizza Hut (BP), Taco Bell (BP)
	W: Baldwin's Best Too Restaurant, Burger King (Exxon), Domino's Pizza, Exxon, Oyster Bar, Subway, Yum Yum's Chinese Food
Lodg	E: Hampton Inn
ATM	E: BP
	W: Cashpoint, Exxon
Other	W: CVS Pharmacy(RX), Food Lion Grocery Store, Piedmont Veterinary Clinic, The Laundry Basket
152	Trollingwood Road
TStop	E: Speedway(*, LP, SCALES)
FStop	W: Amoco(*), Fuel City(*)
Gas	W: Amoco(*)
Food	E: Country Kitchen Restaurant (Speedway), Speedway
	W: Golden Nugget Restaurant
ATM	E: Speedway
	W: Fuel City
150	Haw River, Green Level
TStop	W: Flying J Travel Center(*, SCALES), Wilco(SCALES) (Travel Plaza)
FStop	W: Flying J, Wilco (Citgo)

EXIT	NORTH CAROLINA
Food	W: Dairy Queen (Wilco), Flying J Travel Center, Krispy Kreme Doughnuts (Wilco), Stuckey's (Wilco), The Cookery (Flying J), Wendy's (Wilco)
TServ	W: Flying J Travel Center(SCALES)
TWash	W: Flying J Travel Center
Other	W: Alamance Community College
148	**NC 54, Chapel Hill, Carrboro, Graham**
FStop	E: BP(*)
Gas	E: Amoco(*, 24), Country Store Gas(*), Quality(LP)
Food	E: Waffle House W: Doug's Cafe (EconoLodge), EconoLodge
Lodg	W: EconoLodge, Embers Motor Lodge
ATM	E: Amoco, BP
Other	W: The Challenge Golf Course
147	**NC 87, Graham, Pittsboro**
FStop	W: Citgo(*)
Gas	E: Servco(*, D) (Coin Laundry) W: Citgo, Exxon(*, D, CW), Texaco(*)
Food	E: Arby's, Bojangles, Burger King, Domino's Pizza, Las Brisas Mexican Restaurant, Pizza Hut, Sagebrush Steakhouse, Subway, TCBY, Wendy's W: Biscuitville, Golden China, Hardee's, McDonald's(PLAY), Taco Bell
AServ	E: County Ford, Edwards Tire, Stearns Chevrolet
ATM	E: Centura Bank, Mid Carolina Bank W: BB&T Bank, Central Carolina Bank, Community Saving Bank, NationsBank, Wachovia Bank
Other	E: CVS Pharmacy(RX), Cobert Vision Center, Coin Laundry, Highway Patrol Post, Snow Camp, Winn Dixie Supermarket W: Flowers Foods, Lowe's Foods, South Court Pharmacy, Tarheel Drugs(RX), Vintage Advantage Antiques
145	**NC 49, Liberty, Burlington, Downtown**
FStop	E: Texaco(*, LP, CW)
Gas	E: Speedway(*, LP), Starvin Marvin W: BP(*, CW)
Food	E: Captain D's Seafood, SHONEY'S Shoney's W: Bojangles, Burger King, China Inn Buffett, Hardee's, Hot Shots Grill & Bar, KFC, Quincy's Family Steakhouse, Ship Ahoy Restaurant, Subway, Waffle House
Lodg	E: DAYS INN Days Inn, Motel 6 W: Comfort Inn, Holiday Inn, Scottish Inn
AServ	E: Texaco W: Nichole's Dodge
ATM	E: Texaco W: CCB Bank
Other	E: NC Highway Patrol W: Antique Mall, Burlington Outlet Center, Eckerd Drugs(RX), Food Lion Grocery Store, Nicholas Dodge, Tanger Outlets
143	**NC 62, Alamance**
Gas	W: Circle K(*), Exxon(*, CW)
Food	E: Hardee's, Waffle House W: Cutting Board Steakhouse, Libby Hill Seafood, Nick's Cuisine, Ramada Inn, The Cutting Board
Lodg	W: Ramada Inn (O'Hara's Restaurant), Ramada Inn
AServ	W: Big Shirley Mitsubishi, Big Shirley Oldsmobile, Cadillac, GM, Dick Shirley Chevrolet, Stearn's Ford
ATM	W: CCB Bank, Cashpoint, Central Carolina Bank, Circle K, Exxon
Other	E: Alamance Historical Museum, Burlington Outlet Mall, JR's Cigars Superstore W: Alamance State Historic Site, Eckerd Drugs(RX), Food Lion Grocery Store, Plaza Veterinary Hospital
141	**Elon College**
Gas	E: Amoco(*), BP(*), Shell(*, LP) W: Phillips 66(D)
Food	E: Bogey's Sports Bar & Grill, IHOP, International House of Pancakes, Mayflower's Seafood Restaurant, Outback Steakhouse, Shea Restaurant W: Applebee's, Arby's, Bedrock Cafe, Best Western of Burlington, Bojangles, Burger King, Chick-Fil-A, Cookout, Cracker Barrel, Errichiello's Pizza, Golden Corral Family Steakhouse, K-Mart Supercenter(24, RX), Little Caesars Pizza (K-Mart), O'Charley's, Rockola Restaurant (Best Western), Sal's Italian, Subway, The Summit Restaurant, The Village Grill
Lodg	E: Hampton Inn W: Best Western, Best Western of Burlington, Country Suites by Carlson, Courtyard by Marriott, Super 8
AServ	W: Burlington Motors Ford, Mercury, Lincoln, Jiffy Lube, Phillips 66, Phillips 66
Med	E: ✚ Alamance Regional Medical Center, ✚ Hospital
ATM	W: First State Bank, Wachovia Bank
Other	E: Lake Mackintosh Marina W: Burlington Animal Hospital, Elon Home for Children, K-Mart, K-Mart Supercenter(RX), Wal-Mart(24, RX) (One hour photo, vision center)
(140)	**Rest Area (RR, HF, Phones, Picnic; Southbound)**
(140)	**Rest Area (RR, HF, Phones, Picnic; Northbound)**
138	**NC 61, Gibsonville, Whitsett**
TStop	W: TA TravelCenters of America(*, SCALES) (ATM, Lodging)
Gas	W: BP (TravelCenters of America)
Food	W: Burger King (TA), Country Pride Restaurant (TravelCenters of America), Popeye's Chicken (TA), TA TravelCenters of America (ATM, Lodging)
Lodg	W: Adesta Lodging (TA), Day Stop (TravelCenters of America)
TServ	W: TA TravelCenters of America(SCALES) (ATM, Lodging), Truck Service (TravelCenters of America)
TWash	W: Piedmont Truck Wash, TA TravelCenters of America (ATM, Lodging)
ATM	W: Machine (TravelCenters of America)
135	**Rock Creek Dairy Road , Sedalia**
Gas	W: Citgo(*)
Food	W: McDonald's(PLAY)
Other	W: Charlotte Hawkin's Brown Memorial, Food Lion
132	**McLeansville, Mtn Hope Church Road**
Gas	W: Handi Pik(*), Shell(*, CW), Texaco(*, D)
AServ	W: Shell, Texaco
ATM	W: Shell
130	**McConnell Road**
Gas	E: Texaco(*)
AServ	E: Harrison's, Texaco
Other	W: Replacements Unlimited Fine China Retail Store
128AB	**NC 6 to North US 29 to US 222 North, East Lee St.**
Gas	W: BP(*), Phillips 66
Food	W: BP, Blimpie Subs & Salads (BP), Krispy Kreme Doughnuts (Phillips 66), Phillips 66
Lodg	W: Holiday Inn Express
TServ	W: Hertz Penske
RVCamp	E: Greensboro Campground (1.5 Miles)
ATM	W: BP, Phillips 66
127	**U.S. 29 North, U.S. 70 East, U.S. 220, U.S. 421, Reidsville, Danville (Northbound, No Reaccess)**
126	**U.S. 421 South, Sanford, MLK Jr. Drive, Siler City**
Gas	E: Exxon(*)
Food	E: Biscuitville, Burger King, Domino's Pizza, Golden Pizza, McDonald's(PLAY), Old Hickory's Barbecue, Pizza Pronto, Subway, Szechuan Chinese Restaurant, Wendy's
AServ	E: Advantage Auto Stores, Exxon, Goodyear Tire & Auto, Hall Tire Company, Tom's Tire & Auto
ATM	E: BB&T Bank, Cashpoint
Other	E: A-1 Convenience Store, Advance Auto Parts, Bi-Lo Grocery, Buchannan's Discount Drugs(RX), CVS Pharmacy(RX), Carolina Pride Car Wash, Food Lion Grocery Store, Post Office, Revco Drugs
125	**South Elm - Eugene Street, Downtown Greensboro**
FStop	E: Amoco(*, K, CW, 24)
Gas	E: Amoco(*, D, CW), Texaco(*, D) W: Citgo(*, LP), Crown(*)
Food	E: Big City Pizza, Howard Johnson, Torero's Mexican Restaurant (Howard Johnson) W: BT's Sandwich Cafe Express, Sonic Drive in, VIP Express Chinese
Lodg	E: Cricket Inn, DAYS INN Days Inn, Howard Johnson, Howard Johnson, Super 8 W: Homestead Lodge, Ramada Inn
AServ	E: Shep's Towing & Recovery W: Auto Zone Auto Parts, Superior Auto Parts Store
TServ	E: Alice - Chalmers Lift Trucks
ATM	E: Amoco W: Cashpoint, Citgo
Other	W: Auto Zone Discount Auto Parts, Coin Op Laundromat, Coint Laundry, Food Lion Grocery Store, Kerr Drugs(RX), Visitor Information
124	**Randleman Road**
Gas	E: BP(*, CW), Exxon, Texaco(*, K, 24) W: Amoco(*, 24), Shell(*, K)
Food	E: BP, Blimpie Subs & Salads (BP), Cafe 212, Cookout, Mayflower's Seafood Restaurant, Quincy's Family Steakhouse, Waffle House, Wendy's W: Arby's, Ben's Diner, Burger King(PLAY), Captain D's Seafood, China Town Express, Dairy Queen, Jed's BBQ, KFC, McDonald's(PLAY), Pizza Hut, Sub Station II, Taco Bell, The Spring Valley Restaurant
Lodg	E: Cavalier Inn W: Budget Motel, Southgate Motor Inn
AServ	E: Exxon, Korman Auto Works BMW, Porsche, Mercedes W: Grease Monkey, Meineke Discount Mufflers, Precision Tune, Reed Tires Inc.
TServ	E: Cummins Diesel
ATM	E: Machine (Texaco) W: Amoco, Wachovia Bank
Other	E: The Optical Place W: Dry Clean America, Eckerd Drugs(RX), Food Mart, New Globe Car Wash
122C	**Rehobeth Church Road, Vandalia Road**
Gas	W: Citgo(*, K)
Food	W: Lackey's Pub, Shannon Hills Cafe
Lodg	E: Motel 6
AServ	W: Complete Auto Service, Creek Ridge Automotive Inc. Sales Service Repair
Other	W: New Beginnings Christian Bookstore
122AB	**U.S. 220 South, Asheboro (Difficult Reaccess)**
121	**Holden Road**
Gas	E: Texaco(*, CW)
Food	E: Arby's, Burger King(PLAY), Denny's, K & W

Bold red print shows RV & Bus parking available or nearby

EXIT NORTH CAROLINA

Cafeteria, Texaco
Lodg W: Americana Hotel, Howard Johnson, Traveler's Express
AServ E: Ron's Auto Repair
ATM E: Texaco
Parks W: Gilford Courthouse National Park
Other E: Camping, Camping[LP], K-Mart[RX], Waterpark, Winn Dixie Supermarket

120 Groometown Road
FStop W: Phillips 66[*, 24]
Food W: Krispy Kreme Doughnuts (Phillips 66), Phillips 66
ATM W: Phillips 66

118 U.S. 29 South, U.S. 70 West, Jct. I-85 Business, Jamestown, High Point (Difficult Reaccess)

113 NC 62, Archdale
Gas W: BP[*, CW]
Lodg W: Best Western

111 U.S. 311, Archdale, High Point
FStop W: Texaco[*, LP, CW]
Gas W: Amoco[*, CW, 24], Exxon[*, CW], Phillips 66[*, D, CW]
Food E: Hardee's, Little Caesars Pizza, Wendy's
W: Exxon, McDonald's (Amoco), Texaco, Waffle House
Lodg E: Inn Keeper
W: Comfort Inn, Hampton Inn
Med W: + Hospital
ATM W: Amoco, Exxon
Other E: Archdale Antique Mall, CVS Pharmacy[RX], Food Lion Grocery Store
W: Theater & Exhibition Center, United States Post Office

108 Hopewell Church Road

106 Finch Farm Road
Gas E: Exxon[*, D, K]
W: Circle J[*, K]
Food W: Circle J, Circle J Grill (Circle J)

103 NC 109, Thomasville, Denton
Gas E: Dell's Place[*, LP], Texaco[*, LP]
W: Amoco[*], BP[*, D], Coastal[*], Phillips 66 (U-Haul)
Food E: Arby's, Little Caesars Pizza, Taco Bell
W: Biscuitville, Burger King, Captain Tom's Seafood, China Garden, Hardee's, Mayberry Ice Cream Parlor, McDonald's[PLAY], Mr. Gatti's, Sunrise Grille, Waffle House, Wendy's, Zeko's Pizza
Lodg W: Ramada Limited
AServ W: Phillips 66 (U-Haul)
Med W: + Med Zone Urgent Care Center
ATM W: Amoco, BB&T, First Citizen's Bank, NationsBank, Winn-Dixie Marketplace[24]
Other E: CVS Pharmacy[RX], Ingle's Supermarket, K-Mart[RX]
W: Coin Laundry, Eckerd Drugs[RX], Oakley's Books & Gifts, Winn-Dixie Marketplace

102 Lake Road
Gas W: Phillips 66[*, K], Texaco[*]
Food W: Krispy Kreme Doughnuts (Texaco), Texaco
Lodg W: Days Inn
Med W: + Hospital

(100) Rest Area (RR, Phones; Southbound)

(99) Rest Area (RR, Phones; Northbound)

96 U.S. 64, Asheboro, Lexington
FStop W: Chevron[*] (U-Haul)
Gas E: Mobil[*]
Food W: Randy's Restaurant
AServ E: Modern Tire & Service
W: Chevron (U-Haul)

EXIT NORTH CAROLINA

ATM E: Mobil

94 Old U.S. 64
Gas E: Texaco[*, K]
RVCamp W: Camping

91 NC 8, Southmont
FStop E: Amoco[*, D], Texaco[*]
Gas E: Citgo[*, LP], Phillips 66[*]
W: Exxon[*, D], Quality Mart[*, LP, K]
Food E: Jimmy's BBQ, KFC, McDonald's, Sonic Drive In, The Pizza Oven, Wendy's
W: Arby's, Burger King[PLAY], Cafe 8 Yogurt, Cracker Barrel, Hardee's, Hunan Chinese, Krispy Kreme Doughnuts (Quality Mart), LaFunete Mexican, Little Caesars Pizza, Quality Mart, Taco Bell
Lodg E: Comfort Suites Hotel, Super 8
W: Holiday Inn Express
RVCamp E: High Rock Lake Campground
Med W: + Hospital
ATM E: Citgo
W: Exxon
Other E: Car Wash
W: Belk's, Hemrick's, Ingles Supermarket, Wal-Mart[24, RX]

88 Linwood
Gas W: BP[*, D, K]
Med W: + Hospital
ATM W: BP

87 U.S. 29, U.S. 52, U.S. 70, Lexington, High Point, Winston-Salem, Business Loop 85 (Northbound, Reaccess Southbound Only, Difficult Reaccess)
Med W: + Hospital

86 Belmont Road, NC 97
TStop W: Phillips 66[*, SCALES]
Food W: Phillips 66
TServ W: Phillips 66[SCALES]

85 Clark Road
Food E: Tracks End Motel
Lodg E: Tracks End Motel

83 NC 150 E (Northbound)
Gas W: Lakeview Oil Company[CW]
AServ W: Lakeview Oil Company
Other W: Old Time's Antiques

82 U.S. 29, U.S. 70, N.C. 150 West, Spencer (Southbound, Left Exit Southbound)

81 Spencer
Gas E: Amoco[*, LP]
W: Texaco[*, K]
AServ W: Mike's Automotive

79 High Rock Lake, Spencer, East Spencer
Lodg E: Chanticleer Motel
Parks E: Stan Nicols Park
Other W: North Carolina Transportation Museum

76AB U.S. 52, Albemarle, Salisbury (76B West to Salisbury, 76A East to Albemarle, U.S. 52)
Gas E: Amoco[*], Racetrac[*, 24], Speedway[*]
W: BP[*, D, CW], Exxon[D], Shell[*]
Food E: Applebee's, IHOP, Italy Cafe, Lighthouse Family Seafood, Lone Star Steakhouse, Philly Connection, Pizza Hut, SHONEY'S, Shoney's
W: Bojangles, Burger King, Captain D's Seafood, China Garden, Dunkin Donuts, El Cancun, Hardee's[PLAY], KFC, McDonald's, Taco Bell, Waffle House, Wendy's
Lodg E: Happy Traveler Inn

EXIT NORTH CAROLINA

W: EconoLodge, Harold's Motel
AServ E: Meineke Discount Mufflers, Yost & Crowe Auto Service
W: Exxon, Firestone Tire & Auto
Med W: + Hospital
ATM E: Amoco, Cashpoint
Other E: Animal Care Center of Salisbury, Food Lion Supermarket, Lowe's, Salisbury Animal Hospital, Tinsel Town Theaters
W: K-Mart[RX], Post Office, Recreation Center, Sam's Full Service Car Wash, Visitor Information

75 U.S. 601, Jake Alexander Blvd, Rowan
Gas W: Amoco[*], Citgo[*, 24], Exxon[*, D]
Food E: Arby's, Grand Fellow's Pizza (Ramada Limited), Ramada Limited
W: Holiday Inn, Ichiban Japanese Steakhouse, Jasmine's (Holiday Inn), Ryan's Steakhouse, Sagebrush Steakhouse, Stadium Club, Subway, Waffle House, Wendy's
Lodg E: Ramada Limited
W: Days Inn, Hampton Inn, Holiday Inn
AServ W: Brad Farrah Pontiac, GMC, Cloninger, Gerry Wood Honda, Chrysler
RVCamp W: Bull Hill Campground
Med W: + VA Medical Center
Other W: Moore's Building Supplies, Rowan County Airport, Wal-Mart[RX]

74 Julian Road

72 Peach Orchard Road

71 Peeler Road
TStop W: Texaco[*, SCALES, 24], Wilco Citgo Truck Stop[*]
Food W: Express Cafe (Wilco), Krispy Kreme Doughnuts (Wilco), Taco Bell (Wilco), Texaco, Wilco Citgo Truck Stop
TServ W: Texaco[SCALES, 24], Wilco Citgo Truck Stop
Other E: Southern Marine Repair Sales & Service

70 Webb Road
Other E: Webb Road Flea Market
W: State Police

68 NC 152, China Grove, Rockwell, US 29, Landis, Cannapolis (Southbound, Reaccess Northbound Only)

63 Kannapolis
FStop E: Speedway[*, LP, K, SCALES]
Food E: Speedway, Subway (Speedway)
Lodg E: Best Western
AServ W: J&L Tire & Diesel Service[24]
TServ W: J&L Tire & Diesel Service[24]
ATM E: Speedway
Other W: Field Crest-Cannon Stadium

60 Earnhardt Road
Gas E: Shell[*]
Food E: Burger King, Cracker Barrel
Lodg E: Hampton Inn, Sleep Inn
Med E: + Hospital

(59) Rest Area (RR, Phones; Southbound)

(59) Rest Area (RR, Phones; Northbound)

58 U.S. 29, U.S. 601, Kannapolis, Concord, Cahrlotte Speedway, Monroe
Gas E: BP[*], Crown[*, CW], Texaco[*]
Food E: Burger King, Chick-Fil-A, China Orchad, Colonial Inn, Golden Corral Family Steakhouse, KFC, Little Caesars Pizza, Mayflower Seafood, McDonald's[PLAY], Pizza Hut, Sonic Drive-In, Subway, Taco Bell, Waffle House, Wendy's
W: Adventures Funpark, Eddie's Pizza (Funpark),

EXIT		NORTH CAROLINA
		IHOP, Ryan's Steakhouse
	Lodg	E: Colonial Inn, Holiday Inn Express, Mayfair Motel, Roadway Inn
		W: Comfort Inn, Fairfield Inn
	AServ	E: Brake Xpert Muffler Shop
	Med	E: + Hospital
	ATM	E: Texaco
	Other	E: Carolina Mall, Carolina Mall Cinemas, Contact Lens & Glasses Shop, Eckerd Drugs(RX)
		W: Adventures Funpark, Caberras Animal Hospital, Drug Emporium(RX), Home Depot, Target(RX)
55		NC 73, Davidson, Huntersville
	FStop	W: Phillips 66(*)
	Gas	E: Exxon(*)
		W: BP(*)
	Food	E: Waffle House
		W: Angelo's Fish House, BP, Huddle House(24)
	Lodg	W: Days Inn
	AServ	W: BP
	ATM	E: Exxon
		W: BP
52		Poplar Tent Road
	FStop	E: Texaco(*, D, LP)
	ATM	E: Texaco
	Other	E: Motor Com Museum
		W: Airport
48		To Speedway Blvd., Charlotte Motor Speedway, Concor Regional Airport
46		Mallard Creek Church Road
45AB		Harris Blvd (45A goes East, 45B goes West)
	Food	E: Applebee's, Chick-Fil-A, Chili's, Golden Bagel, Max & Erma's, T.G.I. Friday's, Taco Bell
	Lodg	E: Courtyard by Marriott, Drury Inn, Hilton, Holiday Inn (see our ad this page), Sleep Inn
	AServ	E: Wal-Mart
	Med	E: + Hospital
	ATM	E: First Union, Home Federal Bank, SouthTrust Bank
		W: First Union
	Other	E: Baptist Bookstore, Cahrlotte Museum of History, Hanaford Supermarket(RX), Police Station, Sam's Club, Vision Works, Wal-Mart
43		To U.S. 29, to NC 49 (Northbound, Reaccess Southbound Only)
41		Sugar Creek Road
	Gas	E: Racetrac(*), Texaco(*, D, CW)
		W: BP(*, CW), Exxon(*, D, LP)
	Food	E: Bojangles, McDonald's(PLAY), Taco Bell, Wendy's
		W: SHONEY'S, Shoney's, Texas Ranch Steakhouse, Waffle House
	Lodg	E: Best Western, Brookwood Inn, Continental Inn, Microtel, Red Roof Inn
		W: Comfort Inn, Days Inn (see our ad this page), Fairfield Inn, Holiday Inn Express, Roadway Inn, Super 8
	TServ	W: Ameri-Truck Goodyear, Freightliner Dealer(24), Goodyear Commercial Tire Center
	RVCamp	E: Elmore Mobile Home Park (2 Miles)
	ATM	W: BP
40		Graham St
	Food	E: Hardees, Hereford Barn Steak House
	Lodg	E: Quality Inn
	TServ	E: Adams International Trucks, Cummins, Great Dane Trailer Service, Peterbilt of Carolina, Tar Hill Ford Truck, Volvo & GMC
		W: Adkinson Truck Service
	Other	E: Thermo King
39		Statesville Ave
	TStop	E: Pilot Travel Center(SCALES)
	Gas	W: Citgo(*, CW)
	Food	E: Pilot Travel Center, Subway (Pilot TS)
		W: Bojangles, Ed's Dairy Bar
	Lodg	W: Knight's Inn (see our ad this page)
	AServ	E: Car Quest Auto Center, Statesville Avenue Garage
		W: J&K Auto Repair
	TServ	E: Custom Hydraulics
		W: Bailey's Truck Service, Guignard, International, Mack Truck Sales, Truck Pro's Parts Warehouse
	Other	E: Coin Car Wash
38		Junction I-77, U.S. 21, Statesville, Columbia
37		Beatties Ford Road
	Gas	E: Petro Express(*, K), Phillips 66(*, D), Texaco(*, D, CW)
		W: Amoco(*), Coastal(*)
	Food	E: Burger King(PLAY), McDonald's, Rudean's

1632

800-843-5644
704-596-8784
2909 N. I-85 Service Rd.
Charlotte, NC 28269

• All Ground Floor Rooms •
• Free Continental Breakfast •
• Swimming Pool •
• Kids Under 12 Stay & Eat Free •
• Free Cable TV with HBO •
• Handicap Accessible •
• Airport Shuttle Service •
I-85 N Exit 39, behind Citgo Gas Station
NORTH CAROLINA • I-85 • EXIT 39

1476

University Executive Park
Charlotte, NC
704-547-0999
800-SMILE2U

Mr. P's Restaurant/Lounge
Cable TV w/Free HBO/CNN/ESPN
Meeting Facilities • Free Local Phone Calls
Copy Service, Fax Machine, Executive Level
Outdoor Heated Lap Pool, Whirlpool, Sauna
University Plaza Shopping Center Across Street
Eastland Mall Close By • Blockbuster Pavilion - 4 mi
Charlotte Motor Speedway - 7 mi
North Carolina • I-85 • EXIT 45A

704-597-8110
Charlotte, NC
DAYS INN
1408 W. Sugar Creek
I-85 • Exit 41
1153

Complimentary Coffee
Non-Smoking Rooms
Outdoor Pool
Bus Parking • Tour Pkg
Free HBO/ESPN/CNN

NORTH CAROLINA • I-85 • EXIT 41

www.cabarruscvb.com

Exits 49 - 63

Pan for Gold and tour a gold mine.
Step inside a historic grist mill.
Shop speciality, antique and outlet stores.
Stroll through our gardens and parks.
Experience auto racing & visit the race shops.
And . . . Rest and Relax in
One of our great hotels.

Exit 55

Days Inn	704.786.9121

Exit 58

Colonial Inn	704.782.2146
Comfort Inn	704.786.3100
Fairfield Inn	704.795.4888
Holiday Inn Express	704.786.5181
Mayfair Motel	704.786.1175
Rodeway Inn	704.788.8550
Studio One	704.788.2151
Wisteria B&B	704.792.1897

Exit 60

Hampton Inn	704.793.9700
Sleep Inn	704.788.2150

Exit 63

Best Western Inn	704.933.5080

Visit our Visitor Information Center at Exit 60
Open April 1999

1-800-848-3740

Call today for a free visitor guide or call us from the road for help planning your visit to Cabarrus County
1454
NORTH CAROLINA • I-85

Bold red print shows RV & Bus parking available or nearby

EXIT NORTH CAROLINA

Restaurant
W: Amoco, McDonald's (TraveLodge), TraveLodge
Lodg **W:** TraveLodge
AServ **W:** Coastal
Med **W:** ✚ **Mecklenburg County Health Dept**
ATM **E:** NationsBank, Wachovia Bank
Parks **E:** **West Charlotte Park & Recreation Area**
W: **Hornets Nest Park**
Other **E:** **Charlotte Coin Laundry**
W: Brush-In-Bubble Car Wash, Simply Sudsy

36 NC16 , Brookshire Blvd. Downtown
Gas **E:** Amoco[*, D]
W: Exxon[*, CW], Speedway[*, LP]
Food **E:** China City
W: Bojangles, Bullets Deli (Exxon), Burger King, Exxon, JJ's Submarine Sandwich Shop, Speedway, Wendy's
Lodg **E:** Hornet's Rest Inn
AServ **E:** Engine World
W: Brake Experts
Med **E:** ✚ **Hospital (Trauma Center)**
ATM **W:** Exxon

35 Glenwood Dr
Gas **E:** Citgo[*, D]
Lodg **E:** **Innkeeper**
AServ **E:** Citgo

34 NC 27, Freedom Drive, Tuckaseegee Road
Gas **E:** Amoco[*, K, CW], Exxon[*]
Food **E:** Chad's Family Buffet, IHOP, Ruby Palace Chinese, Subway, Tung Hoi Chinese, Wendy's
W: Genesis 1
Lodg **W:** Apartment Inn, **Howard Johnson**, Ramada Limited (see our ad this page)
AServ **E:** Amoco, Ashley Road Auto Center, Exxon
W: Jiffy Lube, Polk's Auto Repair
Med **E:** ✚ **Pro-Med Minor Emergency Center**

EXIT NORTH CAROLINA

ATM **E:** **Bi-Lo Grocery**, State Employees Credit Union
Other **E:** **Action Clean Coin Laundry**, **Bi-Lo Grocery**, **Freedom Mall**, **U-Haul Center**[LP]

33 U.S. 521, Billy Graham Pkwy, Charlotte - Douglas Intern. Airpt
Gas **E:** BP[*, CW]
W: Exxon[*, D]
Food **E:** BP, Blimpie Subs & Salads (BP), Days Inn, Journey's Grill (Days Inn)
W: Cracker Barrel, Exxon, Prime Sirloin Steakhouse, Waffle House
Lodg **E:** Days Inn, Sheraton
W: Fairfield Inn, Hampton Inn, La Quinta Inn, Microtel Inn, Pennywise Inn, Red Roof Inn
ATM **E:** BP
W: Exxon
Other **E:** **Post Office**

32 Little Rock Road
Gas **W:** Amoco[*] (Circle K), Exxon[*, D]
Food **E:** Best Western, Waffle House
W: Arby's, **Bradley Motel**, Hardee's, Hickory House Restaurant, Little Caesars Pizza, Little Rock Deli, SHONEY'S, Shoney's, Subway
Lodg **E:** Best Western, Courtyard by Marriott, EconoLodge
W: **Bradley Motel**, Comfort Inn, **Country Inn & Suites**
AServ **W:** Gerrard Tire Company
ATM **W:** Amoco (Circle K)
Other **W:** **Food Lion Supermarket**, Suzuki Motor Sports of Charlotte

29 Sam Wilson Road
Gas **W:** Texaco[*, D, K]
Food **W:** Stingers

(28) **Weigh Station (Southbound)**

(28) **Weigh Station (Eastbound)**

27 NC 273, Mount Holly, Belmont

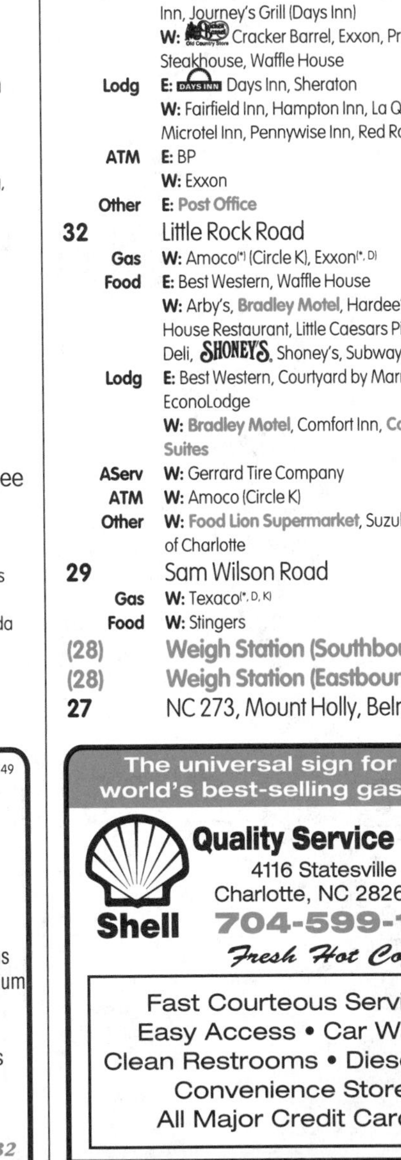

EXIT NORTH CAROLINA

FStop **W:** **Texaco**[*] **(Western Union)**
Gas **E:** Exxon[*]
W: BP[*]
Food **E:** Arby's, Burger King[PLAY], Domino's Pizza, KFC, Pizza Hut, Subway, Taco Bell, The Captain's Cap Restaurant, **Waffle House**, Wendy's
W: BP, Krispy Kreme Doughnuts (BP)
AServ **E:** Exxon, McKinney Chevrolet
ATM **E:** First Union, NationsBank, Wachovia Bank
W: **Texaco (Western Union)**
Other **E:** **College Park Pharmacy**, **Eckerd Drugs**[RX], **Food Lion Supermarket**, Rose's Discount Store

26 Belmont, Mount Holly
Food **E:** Bagels, Bojangles, Happy China, **Hardee's**, McDonald's[PLAY], Papa John's Pizza, Quincy's Family Steakhouse
AServ **E:** Advance Auto Parts, Dixon Ford, McKenney Jeep Eagle, Chrysler
ATM **E:** First Gaston Bank, South Trust Bank
Other **E:** **Bi-Lo Grocery**[RX], **Kerr Drugs**[RX], **Winn Dixie Supermarket**

23 NC 7, McAdenville, Lowell
FStop **W:** **Chevron**[*]
Gas **W:**)Shell[*] (see our ad this page
Food **W:** **Chevron**, **Hardee's**, **Hillbilly's BBQ**
AServ **W:** Shell

22 Cramerton, Lowell
Gas **E:** Amoco[*], World Gas[*, CW]
Food **E:** The Boardwalk
AServ **E:** Haygood Mercury Lincoln Ford, McKenney Salinas Mitsubishi, Sonny Hancock Mazda
Other **E:** Kate's Skating Rink, Ryder Distributor, Scooter's Car Wash & Detail, U-Haul Distributor, **Wilkinson Animal Hospital**

21 Cox Road, Ranlo
Gas **E:** Citgo[*, K]
W: Exxon[*], Phillips 66[*, CW]
Food **E:** China House Restaurant, Don Pablo's Mexican Restaurant, Jackson's Cafeteria, Longhorn Steakhouse, Max Mexican Eatery, Pizza Inn
W: IHOP
Lodg **E:** Caravan Motel, Holiday Motel
W: **Super 8 (see our ad this page)**, **Villager Lodge**
AServ **E:** Craig Dodge, Gastonia Nissan, Speedy Oil Change & Tune-Up, Tire Kingdom
W: Exxon
TServ **E:** **Tire Kingdom**
Med **E:** ✚ **Hospital**
W: ✚ **Hospital**
ATM **E:** Carolina's Telco Federal Credit Union, First Union Bank, **Harris Teeter Supermarket**[24]
W: First Citizen's Bank, State Employees Credit Union
Other **E:** **ANF Gastonia Lanes**, **Batting Cages & Putt-Putt**, **Bi-Lo Grocery**[24], **Gaston Mall**, **Gaston Veterinary Hospital**, **Hanaford Drugstore**[RX], **Harris Teeter Supermarket**, **Home Depot**
W: **Eckerd Drugs**[RX], **Medical Center Pharmacy**

20 NC 279, New Hope Road
Gas **E:** Texaco[CW]
Food **E:** Captain D's Seafood, Red Lobster, The Italian Oven
W: Bojangles, Cracker Barrel, Hickory Hams Cafe, KFC, Outback Steakhouse, Waffle House
Lodg **W:** Comfort Suites Hotel, Fairfield Inn, Hampton Inn, Innkeeper
AServ **E:** Firestone Tire & Auto
W: R & M Auto Center
Med **W:** ✚ **Hospital**
Other **E:** **East Ridge Mall**, **Shiele Museum & Planetarium**
W: United Artist Theaters

19 NC 7, East Gastonia
Gas **E:** Shell[*] (see our ad this page)
W: Servco[K]

Bold red print shows RV & Bus parking available or nearby

EXIT	N CAROLINA/S CAROLINA
AServ	E: Shell
Other	E: **Amtrak**
	W: **Shirley's Fresh Food & Groceries**
17	U.S. 321, Gastonia, Lincolnton
FStop	W: **Shell[*] (see our ad this page)**
Gas	E: Exxon[*, D, CW, 24]
Food	E: **Days Inn, Hardee's, Pancake House**
	W: Waffle House, Wendy's, Western Sizzlin'
Lodg	E: **Days Inn**
	W: Motel 6
AServ	E: Kelly Tires, People's Auto Center
RVCamp	E: **Allen's Mobile Home Parts & Supplies**
ATM	E: Exxon
Parks	W: **Park**
Other	E: **Shiele Museum**
	W: **Gaston Town Museum**
14	NC 274, East Bessemer City, West Gastonia
FStop	W: **Citgo[*, K]**
Gas	E: Phillips 66[*, D]
	W: BP[*]
Food	E: Burger King[PLAY]
	W: BP, **Bojangles**, Subway (BP), Waffle House
Lodg	W: **EconoLodge, Knight's Inn**
ATM	E: BB&T
Other	E: Super Clean Coin Car Wash
13	Bessemer City, Edgewood Rd.
Gas	W: Amoco[*], Shell[*] (see our ad this page)
Food	W: **Master's Inn**
Lodg	W: **Master's Inn**
AServ	W: Shell
Parks	E: **Crowders Mountain State Park**
10B	U.S. 74 West, Kings Mountain, Shelby, Asheville (Difficult Reaccess)
10A	U.S. 29, U.S. 74 East (Difficult Reaccess)
8	NC 161, King's Mountain
Gas	W: Amoco[*, K] (Laundromat)
Food	W: Burger King, McDonald's[PLAY], **Waffle House**
Lodg	W: **Comfort Inn**, Ramada
AServ	W: Fred Caldwell Chevrolet, Sullens
TServ	W: **Jones & Sons Truck Repair, Sterling Equipment Co.**
RVCamp	E: **Camping**
Med	W: **+ Hospital**
(6)	**Rest Area & Weigh Station (RR, Phones; Southbound)**
5	Dixon School Road
TStop	E: **Texaco Travel Center[SCALES]**
Gas	E: BP (24 hour Towing)
Food	E: **Subway (Texaco), Texaco Travel Center, The Diner (Texaco)**
AServ	E: BP (24 hour Towing)
TServ	E: **L & G Diesel Service, Texaco Travel Center[SCALES]**
ATM	E: **Texaco Travel Center**
4	U.S. 29 South (Southbound, Reaccess Northbound Only)
(3)	**NC Welcome Center (RR, Phones; Northbound)**
2	NC 216, Kings Mountain, Military Park
Gas	W: Chevron[*, K]
Parks	E: **Kings Mountain Military Park**

↑NORTH CAROLINA

↓SOUTH CAROLINA

EXIT	SOUTH CAROLINA
106	U.S. 29, Grover, Blacksburg
TStop	W: **Wilco Travel Plaza[SCALES] (BP gas)**
Gas	W: Crown[*], Exxon[*]
Food	W: Crown, **Dairy Queen (Wilco)**, Hot Stuff Pizza (Crown), **Krispy Kreme Doughnuts (Wilco), Stuckey's (Wilco), Wendy's (Wilco), Wilco Travel Plaza (BP gas)**
ATM	W: Crown, Exxon, Stateline Games[24], **Wilco Travel Plaza (BP gas)**
Other	W: **Grover Car Wash & Coin Laundry**, Stateline Games
104	Road 99
TStop	E: **Citgo Truck & Auto Plaza[*, SCALES]**
TServ	E: **Citgo Truck & Auto Plaza[SCALES]**
(103)	**Welcome Center & Rest Area (RR, Phones; Southbound)**
102	SC 198, Blacksburg, Earl
TStop	W: **Flying J Travel Plaza[*, LP, RV DUMP, SCALES] (Conoco gas)**
FStop	E: **Exxon[*, D]**
Gas	E: Phillips 66[*] (Fireworks)
	W: Texaco[*, D]
Food	E: **Hardee's**
	W: **Flying J Travel Plaza (Conoco gas), Krispy Kreme Doughnuts, McDonald's[PLAY], The Cookery (Flying J), Waffle House**
ATM	E: **Exxon**
	W: **Flying J Travel Plaza (Conoco gas)**
100	SC 5, Shelby
FStop	W: **Speedway[*, LP, SCALES]**
Gas	W: Texaco[*]
Food	W: **Speedway, Subway (Speedway)**, Texaco, Wilson's Country Store & Cafe (Texaco)
ATM	W: **Speedway**
98	Frontage Road (Northbound,

The universal sign for the world's best-selling gasoline.

1445

Handy Pantry
3001 North Chester St.
Gastonia, NC 28052
704-865-7791
Fresh Hot Coffee!

Clean Restrooms • Diesel
Fast Food Nearby
Easy Access • 24 Hours
Convenience Store
Fast, Courteous Service
All Major Credit Cards

NORTH CAROLINA ▪ I-85 ▪ EXIT 17

The universal sign for the world's best-selling gasoline.

1446

Edgewood Shell
Rt. 3 Box 122
Bessemer City, NC 28016
704-629-4446
Fresh Hot Coffee!

Easy Access • Clean Restrooms
Diesel Fuel
Fast Courteous Service
Air & Water • Convenience Store
All Major Credit Cards
24 Hour Wrecker Service

NORTH CAROLINA ▪ I-85 ▪ EXIT 13

Bold red print shows RV & Bus parking available or nearby

EXIT — SOUTH CAROLINA

Reaccess Exit 100)
Food — E: Broad River TruckStop Restaurant

96 SC 18
FStop — W: Exxon(*)
TServ — W: Tri State Diesel

95 Road 82 to SC 18, to SC 150, Boiling Springs, Gaffney
FStop — E: Citgo(*), Fuel Stop
Food — E: Aunt M's Good Cookin' (Citgo), Blackbeard's Arsenal & Grill, Citgo, Fatz Cafe, Mr. Waffle, Sherry's Diner
W: Norma's Truck Stop Restaurant
Lodg — E: Gaffney Inn, Shamrock Inn
AServ — E: Wallace White Pontiac, Buick, GMC Truck
Med — E: Hospital, Hospital
Other — E: Lowe's

92 SC 11, Chesnee, Gaffney, Cherokee Foothills Scenic Highway
Gas — E: Amoco(*, D, CW)
W: Chevron(*, LP), Phillips 66(*), Texaco(*, D, K)
Food — E: Amoco, Applebee's, Bojangles, Burger King, Calabash Brothers Chicken & Shrimp (Amoco), McDonald's(PLAY), New China II, Pizza Hut, Quincy's Family Steakhouse, Sagebrush Steakhouse, Sonic Drive-In, Subway, Taco Bell, Wendy's
W: Waffle House
Lodg — E: The Jameson Inn
W: Comfort Inn (see our ad this page), Days Inn
AServ — W: Chevron
ATM — E: NationsBank
Other — E: Eckerd Drugs(RX), Ingles Supermarket, The Tide Car Wash, Wal-Mart(24, RX)
W: Cowpens Battlefield

90 SC 105, Gaffney

1109

Comfort Inn
I-85 • Exit 92, Gaffney
864-487-4200

- Free Deluxe Continental Breakfast
- 25" Cable TV - HBO & ESPN
- Microwave/Refrigerators in all Rooms
- Exercise Room • Pool
- Whirlpool Room Available

SOUTH CAROLINA • I-85 • EXIT 92

1621

RAMADA INN®
1000 Hearon Circle • **Spartanburg, SC** • *29303*

Restaurant/Lounge on Premises
Outdoor Pool
Meeting/Banquet Facilities
Pets Allowed
Handicap Accessible
Truck/Large Vehicle Parking
Exterior/Interior Corridors

864-503-9048 • Toll Free Reservations: 1-800-272-6232

Take **I-85 Business** North to Exit 4, go under the overpass first right
SOUTH CAROLINA • I-85(Bus.) • Exit 72

EXIT — SOUTH CAROLINA

Gas — E: BP(*, CW)
W: Citgo(*), Quick Stop
Food — E: BP, Dairy Queen (BP)
W: Baskin Robbins (Citgo), Burger King (Citgo), Carolina Factory Shops, Citgo, Cracker Barrel, Starlight Diner
ATM — W: Citgo
Other — E: Christmas Shop
W: Carolina Factory Shops, Hemrick's

(89) Rest Area (RR, Phones; Northbound)

(88) Rest Area (Southbound)

87 Road 39
RVCamp — E: Pine Cone Campground (1.4 Miles)
Other — W: Catalog Clothing Outlet, Lemon Farm Peaches & Cream, World of Clothing

83 SC 110, Cowpens
TStop — W: Mr. Waffle(*) (Lodging)
Gas — E: Home Store(*) (Fireworks)
Food — W: Mr. Waffle (Lodging), Mr. Waffle Restaurant (Mr. Waffle TS)
TServ — E: Gibson's Truck & Auto Repair, Horton's Truck Repair
W: Mr. Waffle (Lodging)
TWash — W: Mr. Waffle (Lodging)
Other — E: Abbott Farms Peaches, Red Star Fireworks
W: Red Star Fireworks

82 Frontage Road (Northbound, Reaccess Northbound Only)

80 Road 57, Gossett Rd

78 U.S. 221, Chesnee, Spartanburg
TStop — W: Homer's Auto Truck Plaza(*)
Gas — E: Shell(*, D)
W: BP(*, CW), Exxon(*, D), Racetrac(*)
Food — E: Hardee's, Waffle House
W: Burger King (Exxon), Exxon, Ham House (Homer's TS), Homer's Auto Truck Plaza, McDonald's(PLAY), Racetrac, Southern BBQ (Racetrac), Wendy's
Lodg — E: Motel 6, Sun & Sand Motel
AServ — E: Bojan's Tire & Lube Service
W: Advance Auto Parts
TServ — E: Interstate Truck & Auto
ATM — W: Exxon
Other — E: Abbot Farm Peaches
W: Ingles, Red Star Fireworks

77 I-85 Business Loop South

75A S.C. 9, Spartanburg, Boiling Springs
FStop — W: BP(*, D, LP)
Gas — W: BP(*, D), Phillips 66(*)
Food — W: Burger King (BP), Fatz Cafe, Long John Silver (BP), McDonald's(PLAY), Pizza Hut
Lodg — W: Jameson Inn

DAYS INN *Duncan, South Carolina*
1607

Continental Breakfast
Kids Under 12 Stay Free
Outdoor Pool • Golf Nearby
Restaurant & Lounge Nearby
Meeting/Banquet Facilities • Coin Laundry
Handicap Accessible • Exterior Corridors
Coffee Makers, Hair Dryers, Microfridge
864-433-1122

South Carolina • I-85 • Exit 63

EXIT — SOUTH CAROLINA

AServ — W: Advance Auto Parts, Express Lube Too(CW)
ATM — W: BP
Other — W: CVS Pharmacy(RX), Parr's Car Wash

72 U.S. 176 to I-585, Spartanburg, Inman
Lodg — E: Ramada Inn (see our ad this page)
Med — E: Hospital

70 Jct. I-26, Ashville, Columbia

Note: I-85 runs below as I-85 Business Loop. Numbering follows I-85B.

7 Bryant Road
Gas — E: Amoco(*, LP)

6 Converse & Wofford Colleges, SC 9 Boiling Springs Rd
Food — E: Waffle House
Lodg — E: Comfort Inn, Days Inn
W: Best Western, Travelers Inn
RVCamp — E: Winfield Co Inc Mobile Home and RV Supply

5AB Junction I-585 South, U.S. 176, Pine Street, Downtown (Difficult Reaccess)
Food — W: Fatz Cafe, Steak & Ale
Lodg — W: Ramada, Super 8

4B SC 56, Asheville Hwy
FStop — E: Texaco(*)
Gas — E: Exxon(*, LP), Speedway(*, LP)
W: Shell(*)
Food — E: Arby's, Bojangles, Burger King, Domino's Pizza, Hardee's, KFC, Miami Subs Grills, Pizza Hut, Quincy's Family Steakhouse, Taco Bell, Waffle House
W: Carolina BBQ, Darie Dream, McDonald's, Steak & Ale, Waffle House, Wendy's
Lodg — E: Courtyard by Marriott, Extended Stay America, Fairfield Inn
W: Quality Hotel, Spartanburg Motor Lodge
AServ — E: Exxon
ATM — E: Bi-Lo Grocery, NationsBank
W: Wachovia Bank
Other — E: Bi-Lo Grocery, Eckerd Drugs

4A Viaduct Road

3 SC 295, New Cut Road
Food — E: So Then Diner
AServ — E: Superior Parts

2C **(3)** Fair Forrest Rd (Reaccess Via Frontage Rd)
Gas — E: Phillips 66(*, K)
Food — E: Cracker Barrel, Wilson World
W: J.D. Peaches Rest. (Holiday Inn)
Lodg — E: Budget Inn, Residence Inn, Wilson World
W: Holiday Inn

2B Junction I-26 West, Asheville

2A Junction I-26 East, Columbia

1 Road 41, North Blackstock Rd (Southbound, Reaccess Northbound Only)
Lodg — W: Hampton Inn, Tower Motel

Note: I-85 runs above as I-85 Business Loop. Numbering follows I-85B.

69 I-85N Bus. Loop, Spartanburg (Northbound)

68 SC 29, Greer

66 U.S. 29, Wellford, Lyman

63 SC 290, Duncan, Moore

EXIT SOUTH CAROLINA

TStop **W:** Pilot(SCALES, 24) (Fireworks), TravelCenters of America(*, SCALES) (BP)
Gas **E:** Exxon(*)
W: Amoco(*, LP, K)
Food **E:** Arby's (Exxon), Denny's, Exxon, Pizza Inn, Waffle House
W: Bojangles, Country Pride (TravelCenters of America), Dairy Queen (TravelCenters of America), Demetre's Gourmet Grill & Bar, Hardee's, McDonald's(PLAY), Pilot (Fireworks), TravelCenters of America (BP), Waffle House, Wendy's (Pilot FS)
Lodg **E:** Microtel Inn (see our ad this page)
W: Comfort Inn, Days Inn Days Inn (see our ad this page), TravelCenters of America (BP)
TServ **W:** TravelCenters of America(SCALES) (BP)
TWash **W:** Pilot (Fireworks), USA Truck Wash
RVCamp **W:** Sonny's Camp & Travel
Med **E:** + Hospital
ATM **E:** Exxon, NationsBank

(62) Rest Area (RR, Phones)

60 SC 101, Greer, Woodruff
FStop **E:** Citgo(*, D)
Gas **E:** Amoco(*, K), Coastal(*, LP, K)
W: Exxon(*, K)
Food **E:** Backwoods Bar and Grill
W: Burger King (Exxon), Exxon
Lodg **W:** Super 8 (see our ad this page)
TServ **E:** Fruehauf Trailer Services Inc., Williams Detroit Diesel - Allison
RVCamp **E:** Richard's RV Servicenter
Med **W:** + Hospital
ATM **E:** Citgo, Coastal
W: Exxon
Other **W:** BMW Visitors Center, Greer Hertiage Museum

57 Greenville - Spartanburg International Airport (Airport Traffic Only)

56 SC 14, Pelham, Greer
FStop **W:** Amoco(*, LP)
Gas **E:** Texaco(*, D)
W: Exxon(*, LP)
Food **E:** Rick's Place
W: Waffle House
TServ **E:** Carolina International
W: Goodyear Commercial Tire Center
RVCamp **W:** Greenville Kamper and Boats, Holiday Superstores RV-Marine(LP) (see our ad this page)
Med **W:** + Hospital
ATM **W:** Amoco
Other **E:** Abbot Farm Peaches, Red Star Fireworks

54 Pelham Road
Gas **E:** Amoco(*, LP), BP(*, CW)
W: Amoco(*, LP), Exxon(*, CW)
Food **E:** Amoco, Brady's Biscuits & Burgers, Burger King, Joe's Crab Shack (Amoco)
W: Acropolis, Applebee's, Atlanta Bread Company, Boston Market Restaurant, California Dreaming, Happy China, Hardee's, J & S Cafeteria, Joe's Crab Shack, Logan's Roadhouse Steaks & Ribs, Macaroni Grill, Max & Erma's, Mayflower Seafood, McDonald's, Miami Subs Grills, Old World Bread, On the Border Mexican Cafe, Ruby Tuesday, Schlotzsky's Deli, Tony Roma's
Lodg **E:** Holiday Inn Express
W: Extended Stay America, Fairfield Inn, Hampton Inn, Marriott, Microtel Inn, Residence Inn, Wingate Inn
ATM **W:** Amoco, BB&T, Exxon, First Union, NationsBank, Wachovia Bank
Other **W:** Bi-Lo Grocery(24, RX), CVS Pharmacy(RX), Regal 10 Theaters

51 Junction I-385, SC 146, Columbia, Greenville, Woodruff Road (Splits in three parts)

EXIT SOUTH CAROLINA

Gas **E:** Hess(*), Red Robin(*)
Food **E:** Marcelino's
Lodg **W:** Microtel Inn & Suites (see our ad this page)
ATM **E:** Red Robin, Wachovia Bank

51B SC 146, Woodruff Road
Gas **W:** Racetrac(*)
Food **W:** Burger King, Capris Italian, Cracker Barrel, McDonald's(PLAY), Waffle House
Lodg **W:** La Quinta Inn
AServ **E:** Goodyear Tire & Auto
W: Auto Express Montgomery Ward
ATM **W:** Racetrac
Other **E:** All Creatures Animal Hospital
W: Greenville Mall, The Home Depot

48AB U.S. 276, Mauldin, Greenville (48 B goes to the north, 48A goes to the south)
FStop **E:** Speedway(*, LP)
Gas **W:** BP(*, 24), Exxon(*)
Food **E:** Charlie T's Buffalo Wings & Subs, Shoney's, Waffle House
W: Olive Garden
Lodg **E:** Red Roof Inn
W: Howard Johnson, Value-Lodge
AServ **W:** Brachman Automotive, Century BMW, Sunrise Cadillac Oldsmobile

46C Mauldin Road, SC 291, Augusta Road, Pleasantburg Drive
Gas **W:** Amoco(*), Texaco(*, D)
Food **W:** Amoco, Arby's (Amoco), Steakout, Subway
Lodg **W:** Comfort Inn, Ramada Limited, Suburban Lodge
AServ **W:** AAMCO Transmission, Jiffy Lube, Precision Tune Auto Care
ATM **W:** Amoco, Carolina First, Harris Teeter Supermarket
Other **W:** Bi-Lo Grocery(RX), CVS Pharmacy(RX), Harris Teeter Supermarket, Southern States Antiques

46B SC 291 South
Gas **W:** Texaco(*, D)
Lodg **W:** Ramada Limited
Other **W:** Bi-Lo Grocery(RX)

46A Augusta Road
Gas **E:** Chevron(*), Hess(*), Phillips 66(*, LP)
Food **E:** Bojangles, Dug Out, Waffle House
W: Charlie T's Original Wings & Subs, Dixie Family Restaurant

1-800-RV-FOR-FUN
Greenville, SC • I-85 • Exit 56

MICROTEL
Duncan, South Carolina
1609
• Restaurants Nearby
• Handicap Accessible Rooms Available
• Golf Nearby
• Electronic Lock on All Rooms
• Interior Corridors
864-433-1000
South Carolina • I-85 • Exit 63

EXIT SOUTH CAROLINA

Lodg **E:** Camelot Inn, Holiday Inn
W: Days Inn Days Inn, Motel 6, TraveLodge
AServ **E:** Bargain Tire
Other **E:** Mick's Car Wash

45AB U.S. 25, SC 291, Greenwood, Greenville
Gas **E:** Hess, Li'l Cricket(*)
Food **E:** Bojangles, Holiday Inn Restaurant, Waffle House
W: Dixie Family Restaurant
Lodg **E:** Camelot Inn, Holiday Inn, Motel 6
W: Cricket Inn, Days Inn Days Inn
AServ **E:** Used Tires
Other **E:** Augusta Road Grocery, Nick's Car Washes

44 U.S. 25, Whitehorse Road
FStop **E:** Exxon(*)
Gas **W:** Texaco(*)
Food **E:** El Cactus, Exxon, Subway (Exxon)
W: Famous BBQ Restaurant, McDonald's (Texaco), Quincy's Family Steakhouse, SHONEY'S Shoney's, Texaco, Waffle House
AServ **W:** L & L Discount Muffler
TServ **W:** Christopher Trucks
Med **W:** + Hospital
ATM **E:** Exxon

43 Piedmont, S.C. 20

42 Junction I-185, U.S. 29, Greenville

40 SC 153, Easley
Gas **E:** Exxon(*)
W: Texaco(*, D)
Food **W:** Arby's, Burger King, Hardee's, KFC
Lodg **W:** Executive Inn, Super 8 (see our ad this page)
ATM **E:** Exxon

39 Road 143, Piedmont
Gas **E:** BP(*)
W: Texaco(*, LP, K)

MICROTEL
Inn & Suites
• Opposite Greenville Mall
• Rooms with One or Two Queen Size Beds
• Interior Corridor
• Electronic Locks
• $5.00 Off With This Coupon
• ARP & AAA Discounts
864-297-3811 1608
South Carolina • I-85 • Exit 51

1736

Brand New Property
1515 Hwy 101 S
Greer, SC
864-848-1626
Free Continental Breakfast
Outdoor Pool
Cable TV w/HBO/ESPN/CNN
Large Vehicle Parking
King & Queen Beds
Executive Suites w/ Micro & Frige Available
Next to GSP Int'l Airport
Near BMW Zentrum Museum, Zoo, Greenville & Haywood Mall and Palmetto Convention Center
South Carolina • I-85 • EXIT 60

Bold red print shows RV & Bus parking available or nearby

EXIT SOUTH CAROLINA

AServ E: BP
ATM W: Texaco
Other E: The State Place
W: Antique Mall, Memories Antique Mall, Papa Haven Dolls, Books, & Collectables

35 SC 86, Piedmont, Easley
FStop E: Speedway Truck/Auto Plaza[*, LP, SCALES]
Food E: Country Kitchen (Speedway), Speedway Truck/Auto Plaza
TServ E: K & K Auto & Truck Stop, Southland Transportation Inc., Speedway Truck/Auto Plaza[SCALES]
ATM E: Speedway Truck/Auto Plaza

34 U.S. 29, Williamston, South Anderson (Southbound)

32 SC 8, Pelzer, Belton
Gas E: Citgo[*]
AServ E: Citgo
ATM E: Citgo

27 Anderson, SC 81
TStop W: Anderson Truck Plaza[*, SCALES, 24]
FStop E: Phillips 66[*]
Gas E: Citgo[*], Exxon[*]
Food E: Arby's, McDonald's[PLAY], Waffle House
W: Anderson Truck Plaza, Fireside Restaurant Buffett & Salad Bar (Anderson Truck Plaza)
Lodg E: Holiday Inn Express

BRAND NEW
3104 Earl E. Morris Hwy 153
Piedmont, SC 29673

864-220-1836
SUPER 8 MOTEL
FREE Continental Breakfast
Jacuzzi Suites Available
Remote Control Cable TV w/HBO
Bus Parking
Near Greenville Zoo, Clemson University & Hartwell Lake
1730
SOUTH CAROLINA • I-85 • EXIT 40

1324

South Carolina • Exit 19 • 864-232-3000

EXIT SOUTH CAROLINA

TServ W: Anderson Truck Plaza[SCALES, 24], Pro Stop, Welbourn
Med E: ✚ Hospital
ATM E: Exxon
W: Anderson Truck Plaza
Other E: Big Zack's 10,000 Fireworks, Racing Gear Outlet

(23) Rest Area (RR, Phones; Southbound)

21 U.S. 178, Anderson, Liberty
FStop E: Texaco[*]
Other E: Civic Center

19AB U.S. 76, SC 28, Anderson, Clemson, Pendleton, Seneca, Garrison Area
Gas E: Exxon[*, D]
W: Racetrac[*, 24]
Food E: Charlie T's Original Buffalo Wings, Dot Masters Food & Spirits, Hardee's, Katherine's Kitchen
W: Buffalo's Cafe, Cracker Barrel, Outback Steakhouse, Waffle House, Wendy's
Lodg E: Days Inn (see our ad this page), Park Inn, Royal American Motor Inn, AmeriSuites (see our ad this page)
W: Comfort Inn, Hampton Inn, Jameson Inn
ATM E: Exxon
W: Racetrac
Other W: Fireworks

(18) Rest Area (RR, Phones, Vending; Northbound)

14 SC 187, Clemson, Research Park
FStop E: Fuel Mart[*]
Gas W: Amoco[*, D, LP]
Food E: Huddle House[24]
Lodg W: Economy Lodge
RVCamp E: KOA Kampground (1 Mile)
ATM W: Amoco
Other W: Clemson Research Park

11 SC 24, SC 243, Anderson, Townville, Westminster
FStop E: Speedway[*, K]
W: Pizza Plenty (Texaco)
Gas W: Texaco[*, LP]
Food E: Marvin's Mother's Deli (Speedway), Speedway
W: Texaco, Townville Station Rest.
RVCamp W: Hartwell Four Seasons Campground
ATM E: Speedway
Other E: Fireworks Superstore, South Carolina National Guard, The Racin' Station Conv. Store[*]

(9) Weigh Station (Northbound)

4 SC 243, Road 23, Fair Play
TStop E: Cherokee Run[*, SCALES] (Shell gas)
Food E: Cherokee Run (Shell gas), Glenn's Diner
Lodg E: Days Inn (see our ad this page),
TServ E: Cherokee Run[SCALES] (Shell gas)
RVCamp E: Thousand Trails (.6 Miles)

DAYS INN
Spartanburg, South Carolina
Truck/ Large Vehicle Parking
Across from Panthers Football Camp
Continental Breakfast
Kids Under 12 Stay Free
Outdoor Pool • Golf/Tennis Nearby
Exterior Corridors • Free Cable w/HBO
Closest to Memorial Auditorium, Library, Wofford, SMC, USCS & Converse Colleges & Duncan Park Field
1602
864-585-4311
South Carolina • I-85 • Exit 4

EXIT SOUTH CAROLINA/GEORGIA

ATM E: Cherokee Run (Shell gas)
W: Russel's General Store
Other E: Weldon Island Recreation Area
W: Russel's General Store

2 SC 59, Fair Play
Lodg E: Econolodge
RVCamp E: Lakeshore Campground (.75 Miles)
Other E: Crazy Steve's Fireworks

1 SC 11, Walhalla
FStop W: Amoco[*, D, K]
Food W: Gazebo Restaurant & Deli
RVCamp W: Camping
ATM W: North of the Border Video Game Parlor
Parks W: Lake Hartwell State Park
Other W: I-85 Fireworks Outlet, North of the Border Video Game Parlor

(1) Rest Area (RR, Phones, Vending; Northbound)

↑SOUTH CAROLINA

↓GEORGIA

59 **(177)** GA 77S, Elberton, Hartwell
Gas E: BP[*, LP]
Food E: BP, Dad's (BP)
Parks W: Hartwell State Park

(176) GA Welcome Center, Rest Area (RR, Phones, RV Dump; Southbound)

58 **(173)** GA 17, Lavonia, Toccoa, Royston, Helen
Gas E: BP[*], Racetrac[*, 24], Texaco[*, D, K]
W: Exxon[*, LP], Shell[*]
Food E: Fernside Home Cooking Buffet, KFC, McDonald's, Subway, Waffle House
W: Arby's, Burger King, Hardee's, Pizza Hut, SHONEY'S, Shoney's, Wendy's
Lodg E: Regency Inn & Suites, Sleep Inn
W: Shoney's Inn
RVCamp E: Lake R. B. Russell State Park
Med E: ✚ Hospital
ATM E: Racetrac
W: Exxon
Parks E: Hart State Park
W: Tugaloo State Park
Other W: Lavonia Antique Market

(171) Weigh Station (Northbound)

(169) Weigh Station (Southbound)

57 **(166)** GA 106, GA 145, Carnesville, Toccoa
TStop E: Wilco Travel Plaza[*, SCALES] (Citgo Gas)
W: Echo[*, LP, SCALES, 24]
Gas E: Shell[*]
Food E: Dairy Queen (Wilco), Krispy Kreme Doughnuts (Wilco), Piccadilly Circus Pizza (Shell), Shell, Stuckey's (Wilco), Wendy's (Wilco), Wilco Travel Plaza (Citgo Gas)
W: Echo
TWash W: Echo
Med E: ✚ Hospital
ATM E: Wilco Travel Plaza (Citgo Gas)

56 **(164)** GA 320, Carnesville (Toccoa Falls College)
TStop E: Sunshine Travel Center[*, K, 24]
Food E: Hardees (Sunshine Travel Center), Sunshine Travel Center
AServ E: Harper's Auto Truck Plaza, Truck Tires[24]
Med E: ✚ Hospital
ATM E: Sunshine Travel Center

(160) Rest Area (RR, Phones, RV Dump;

EXIT	GEORGIA
	Northbound)
55	**(160)** GA 51, Homer, Franklin Springs
TStop	**W:** Petro[*, LP, RV DUMP, SCALES, 24]
FStop	**E:** Shell[*, RV DUMP] (Restaurant)
Food	**E:** Subway (Shell)
	W: Iron Skillet (Petro), Petro, Pizza Hut (Petro)
TServ	**W:** Petro[SCALES, 24]
TWash	**W:** Petro
Med	**E:** + Hospital
ATM	**E:** Shell (Restaurant)
Parks	**E:** Victoria Bryant State Park (Camping)
54	**(154)** GA 63, Martin Bridge Road
53	**(149)** U.S. 441, GA 15, Commerce, Homer, Banks Crossing
TStop	**E:** T/A TravelCenters of America[*]
FStop	**E:** Citgo[*]
	W: BP[*, D, K]
Gas	**E:** Amoco[*, 24]
	W: Phillips 66[*, D], Racetrac[*]
Food	**E:** BJ's Grill (The Pottery), Captain D's Seafood, New Bali Restaurant, SHONEY'S, Shoney's, Sonny's Real Pit Barbecue, South Fork Steak House, Stringers Seafood, T/A TravelCenters of America, Taco Bell, Waffle House, Zaxby's
	W: Arby's, Burger King, Checkers Burgers, Cracker Barrel, Dairy Queen, KFC, La Hacienda Mexican, McDonald's[PLAY], Pizza Hut, RJ T-Bones Steakhouse, Ryan's Steakhouse, Subway, Waffle House, Wendy's
Lodg	**E:** DAYS INN Days Inn, Guest House Inn, Hampton Inn, Holiday Inn Express
	W: Comfort Inn, Dollar Wise, Howard Johnson, Ramada Limited (see our ad t his page), The Jameson Inn
AServ	**E:** Amoco[24]
	W: Gordon Pontiac, Buick, GMC
TServ	**E:** T/A TravelCenters of America
RVCamp	**E:** Commerce/Athens KOA (1.75 Miles), The Pottery Campgrounds
	W: Flea Market Campground
Med	**E:** + Hospital
ATM	**E:** Citgo, Regions Bank
	W: Phillips 66, Racetrac, Wachovia Bank
Other	**E:** Antebellum Trails, Commerce Factory Stores, Liz Claiborne Outlet Store, The Pottery
	W: Atlanta Dragway, Showcase Antiques, Tanger Factory Outlet, Trackside Antiques
52	**(147)** GA 98, Commerce, Maysville
FStop	**E:** Fuel Mart[*], Speedway[*, LP]
Gas	**W:** Shell[*]
Food	**E:** Speedway
AServ	**E:** Holman's Tire & Auto
TServ	**E:** Holman's Tire & Auto
Med	**E:** + Hospital
51	**(140)** GA 82, Dry Pond Road, Holly Springs Road
TServ	**W:** Interstate Truck Sales & Service
50	**(136)** U.S. 129, GA 11, Gainesville, Jefferson
FStop	**E:** Phillips 66[*, D, LP]
Gas	**E:** BP[*], Shell[*]
Food	**E:** Arby's, Hardee's, Hog Mountain Cafe, McDonald's, Waffle House
	W: Katherine's Kitchen, Waffle House
Lodg	**E:** Comfort Inn
ATM	**E:** Shell
Other	**E:** Crawford W. Long Museum
	W: Georgia's Largest Flea Market (Has Food Court)
49	**(129)** GA 53, Braselton, Lanier Raceway, Winder
FStop	**W:** BP[*], Speedway[*, LP, SCALES]
Gas	**E:** Shell[*, LP], Texaco[*, D, LP, K]

EXIT	GEORGIA
	W: Fina[D, LP] (Full Service)
Food	**E:** Waffle House
	W: BP, Church's Chicken (Speedway), Speedway, Subway (BP)
AServ	**W:** Fina (Full Service)
ATM	**E:** Texaco
	W: Speedway
48	**(125)** GA 211, Winder
Gas	**W:** BP[*, D, LP, K]
Food	**W:** BP, Way to Go Pizza (BP)
Lodg	**W:** DAYS INN Days Inn
ATM	**W:** BP
Parks	**E:** Fort Yargo State Park (Camping, Picnic)
Other	**W:** Chateau Elan (Winery, Spa, Inn, Conference Center, Golf Club and Villas)
47	**(120)** Hamilton Mill Parkway, Hamilton Mill Road
FStop	**E:** Circle K[*]
Gas	**E:** BP[*]
	W: Shell[*]
Food	**E:** BP, Blimpie Subs & Salads (BP), Buffalo's Cafe, Dos Copas Mexican Grill, McDonald's[PLAY], Mr. Edd's Pizza and Grill, Subway
	W: Huddle House (Shell), Shell
AServ	**W:** Hamilton Mill Auto Repair Center, Northwest Auto Inc.
ATM	**E:** Circle K, First Commerce Bank, Publix Supermarket
Other	**E:** Publix Supermarket
46	**(115)** GA 20, Lawrenceville, Buford
Med	**E:** + Hospital
(113)	Rest Area (RR, HF, Phones, Picnic, RV Dump; Southbound)
45	**(113)** Junction I-985N, Gainesville, Lake Lanier Parkway (Northbound, Left Exit)
(112)	Rest Area (Northbound)
44	**(111)** GA 317N, Suwanee
Gas	**E:** Amoco[*, LP, CW], BP[*, CW], Phillips 66[*, D, K]
	W: Chevron[*, 24], Exxon[*, CW, 24], Exxon[*, K]
Food	**E:** Applebee's, Arby's, Burger King[PLAY], Checkers Burgers, Cracker Barrel, Del Taco, Holiday Inn, Mrs Winner's Chicken, Outback Steakhouse, Taco Bell, The Orient Garden Chinese, Waffle House, Wendy's
	W: McDonald's[PLAY], Taste of China, Waffle House
Lodg	**E:** Comfort Inn, Fairfield Inn, Holiday Inn (see our ad this page), Red Roof Inn & Suites (see our ad this page), Sun Suites
	W: DAYS INN Days Inn (see our ad this page), Falcon Inn (Best Western), Ramada Limited (see our ad this page)

SUWANEE, GA

1487

Holiday Inn®

I-85 • Exit 44

2955 Hwy. 317
Suwanee, GA 30024

770-945-4921
800-Holiday

Full Service 120 Renovated Guest Rooms

Outdoor Swimming Pool

Nickels Lounge • Country Harvest Buffet & Eatery

Special Rates For Tour Groups

Nearby Shopping Mall

Free Bus Parking

GEORGIA ▪ I-85 ▪ EXIT 44

1597

RAMADA LIMITED

RAMADA LIMITED
U.S. Hwy 441
Commerce, GA 30529

706-335-5191

$ 38.95* +tax
2 Adults-2 Kids

35 Restaurants Nearby
Deluxe Continental Breakfast
Outdoor Pool • Golf Nearby
Pets Allowed • Exterior Corridors
130+ Factory Outlet Stores
Truck/Large Vehicle Parking

*Not valid with other discounts, special events or with previous reservations. Based on availability and guide lines.

GEORGIA ▪ I-85 ▪ EXIT 53

1620

DAYS INN®
WAKE UP TO US
Suwanee, Georgia

Easy Access to Truck Parking
120 Clean Comfortable Rooms
62 Channel Cable TV with Free ESPN & HBO
Complimentary 24 Hr Coffee
Special Rates For Tour Groups
Fax Service Available

770-945-8372 • 1-800-325-225

GEORGIA ▪ I-85 ▪ EXIT 44

RAMADA LIMITED

RAMADA LIMITED
317 Sawmill Drive
Suwanee, GA 30024
770-614-6222

Many Restaurants Nearby
Free Continental Breakfast
Kids Under 12 Stay Free
Outdoor Pool • Golf nearby
Pets Allowed (Charge)
Handicap Accessible • Airport Shuttle
Truck/Large Vehicle Parking
Exterior Corridors • Coin Laundry

1588

GEORGIA ▪ I-85 ▪ EXIT 44

red roof inns & Suites

I-85 & Lawrenceville-Suwanee Rd
77 Gwinco Boulevard
Suwanee, GA 20024

770-271-5559

BRAND NEW

1618

Outdoor Pool • In Room Coffee
Continental Breakfast
50 Mini Suites • Refrigerator/Microwave
Meeting Facilities • Data Ports
Interior Corridor25" TV w/Remote
Near Gwinnett Mall, Gwinnett Civic Center,
Lake Lanier, Chateau Elan Winery, Road Atlanta

GEORGIA ▪ I-85 ▪ EXIT 44

Bold red print shows RV & Bus parking available or nearby

EXIT		GEORGIA
	ASErv	W: Exxon
	ATM	E: Amoco, Phillips 66, Premier Bank
	Other	E: **Ski Nautiques (Marine and Boating Supply)**
		W: **Falcons' Training Camp**
43		**(109)** Old Peachtree Road
	Gas	E: QuikTrip[*]
	ATM	E: QuikTrip
	Other	W: **Gwinnett Civic Center**
42		**(107)** GA 120, Duluth, Lawrenceville
	FStop	E: **Speedway**[*, K]
	Gas	W: Amoco[*, CW], BP[*, CW], Chevron[*, CW]
	Food	W: Amoco, Split Second (Amoco)
	ASErv	W: BP
	Med	E: ✚ **Hospital**
	ATM	E: **Speedway**
		W: Amoco, Chevron
41		**(106)** GA 316E, Barnes Rd. (No Reaccess)
40		**(104)** Pleasant Hill Road
	FStop	E: **Shell**[*, D, CW]
		W: **Phillips 66**[*, CW]
	Gas	E: Chevron[*, CW, 24], Circle K[*, LP], Phillips 66[*, LP]
		W: Amoco[*], BP[*, D, CW], QuikTrip[*], Texaco[*, CW]
	Food	E: Baskin Robbins, Blimpie's Subs, Buffalo's Cafe, Burger King, Carrabbas Italian Restaurant, Chesapeake Bagel Bakery, Chick-Fil-A, Combo Express Chinese, Cooker, Corky's Ribs & BBQ, Dunkin Donuts, Georgia Diner[24], Geronimo's Cafe, Grady's, Guacamole's, Hardee's, Hickory Hams, Kinyobee, Krispy Kreme Doughnuts, Los Loros, Mandarin House III, McDonald's, Monterrey Mexican, New York Pizza, O'Charley's, Philly Connection, Poona Indian Gourmet, Popeye's Chicken, Red Garlic, Roadhouse Grill, Romano's Macaroni Grill, Ruby Tuesday, S & S Cafeteria, Schlotzsky's Deli, Shiki, Subway, T.G.I. Friday's, The Original Pancake House, Waffle House, Wendy's
		W: A Fondue Restaurant, Applebee's, BP, Barnacle's Seafood, Baskin Robbins, Black-Eyed Pea, Blimpie Subs & Salads (BP), Bruegger's Bagel & Bakery, Burger King, Chili's, Circus Pizza World, County Seat Cafe, Cripple Creek, Devito's Pizza, El Torero, Golden China Restaurant, Hooters, IHOP, Johnnie's Pizza & Subs, KFC, Longhorn Steakhouse, Manhatten Bagel, Marchello's Italian Rest., Matsuri Restaurant, McDonald's[PLAY], Mick's, Mother India Restaurant, Mrs Winner's Chicken, My Friend's Place, Olive Garden, On The Border, Philly Connection, Pizza Hut, Provino's Iltalian Restaurant, Red Lobster, Rio Bravo Cantina, Roaster Rotisserie, Rugby Sports Bar and Grill, Ryan's Steakhouse, Sho Gun, SHONEY'S Shoney's, Skeeter's, Starbucks Coffee, Steak 'N Shake, Subway, TCBY, Taco Bell, Tung Sing Chinese, Waffle House, Wangs Chinese, Wendy's
	Lodg	E: Comfort Suites Hotel (see our ad this page), Hampton Inn, Holiday Inn Express, Homestead Village, Marriott, Residence Inn
		W: Ameri Suites (see our ad this page), Courtyard by Marriott, DAYS INN Days Inn, Extended Stay America, Fairfield Inn, Ramada Limited, Suburban Lodge, Summer Suites, Wyndham Garden Hotel, Wyngate Inn
	ASErv	E: Eurasain Motor Sports, Goodyear Tire & Auto, **K-Mart**, Tune Up
		W: **Atlanta Toyota Trucks**, Batteries Plus, Brake-O Brake Shop, Econo Lube & Tune, Firestone Tire & Auto, Goodyear Tire & Auto, Midas Muffler & Brake, Precision Tune & Lube, Q-Lube
	TServ	E: **Nalley Motortrucks**
	Med	E: ✚ **Med Plus (Walk-Ins welcome)**
		W: ✚ **Any Lab Test**, ✚ **Physicians Immediate Med (Minor Emerg, 9am-9pm, no appt necessary)**
	ATM	E: Chevron, Circle K, First Union Bank, SunTrust Bank
		W: **Kroger Supermarket**[24], NationsBank, SouthTrust Bank
	Other	E: **Eckerd Drugs**, **K-Mart**[RX], **Kinko's Copies**[24], **Mail Boxes Etc**, **Office Depot**, **Pro Golf Discount**, **Publix Supermarket**, **The Home Depot**, **United Mail Services**, **Wal-Mart**[24], **Winn Dixie Supermarket**
		W: **Ace Checks Cashed**, **Carmike Cinemas**, Cinema 12 Theaters, College Cove Miniature Golf Course, **Drug Emporium**, **General Cinemas**, **Gwinnett Place Mall**, **Island Mania**, **Kids R Us**, **Kroger Supermarket**, **Mail Boxes Etc**, **OfficeMax**, **Pearl Vision Center**, **Pets Etc.**, **PetsMart**, **Pirates Cove Adventure Golf**, **Q-Zar (Lazer Game)**, Southeastern Railway Museum, **Target**, **The Aviarium (A Bird Pet Store)**, **US Post Office**, **Venture Mall**, **Wolf Camera**
39A		**(103)** Steve Reynolds Blvd (Northbound, Reaccess Southbound Only)
	Gas	W: QuikTrip[*], Texaco[*, CW]
	Food	W: Barbecues Galore[LP], Coffee New York, Han Gang, Waffle House
	Lodg	E: Sun Suites Extended Stay Hotel
	ATM	E: SunTrust Bank, Wachovia Bank
	Other	E: Bass Pro Shop
		W: **Boater's World**, **Costco Wholesale Warehouse**, Incredible Universe, One-Hour Photo, **Sam's Club**, **Waccamaw**
39		**(102)** GA 378, Beaver Ruin Road
	FStop	E: **Shell**[*]
		W: **Texaco**[*, D, CW]
	Gas	E: Racetrac[*]
		W: Amoco[*, CW, 24]
	ASErv	E: Timmers Chev-GM
	ATM	E: **Shell**
38		**(101)** Indian Trail - Lilburn Road
	Gas	E: QuikTrip[*, 24], Texaco[*, LP, CW]
		W: BP[*, D, CW], Chevron[*, CW, 24], Conoco[*, LP]
	Food	E: Blimpie Subs & Salads, Burger King[PLAY], Dunkin Donuts, McDonald's[PLAY], SHONEY'S Shoney's, Taco Bell, Waffle House
		W: Arby's, Dairy Queen, El Taco Veloz, La Pantera Rosa, La Sultana, La Tapatia, Lee's Golden Budda, Lupita's Mexican, Mega Tacos, Papa John's Pizza, Taylor's, The Grill Cafe, Waffle House, Wendy's, Yahoo Sushi Bar
	Lodg	E: Shoney's Inn, **Suburban Lodge**, **Super 8 (see our ad this page)**
		W: Red Roof Inn, Villager Lodge
	ASErv	E: Express Lube
		W: Five Star Chrysler Plymouth Jeep, Jiffylube
	RVCamp	E: **Jones Mobile Home Estates and RV Park (.1 Miles)**
	ATM	E: Atlantic States Bank, NationsBank, QuikTrip, Wachovia Bank
		W: Chevron
	Other	W: Carmax Auto Superstore, Greyhound Bus Station, Malibu Grand Prix, **Patient's Pharmacy**[RX], **The Laundry Express (Coin Laundry)**, **Winn Dixie Supermarket**
37		**(99)** GA 140, Jimmy Carter Blvd.

1325

Georgia • Exit 40 • 770-623-6800

Duluth, GA

770-931-9299

Toll Free Reservations: 800-228-5150

Easy Access to Gwinnett Mall

- Continental Breakfast
- Kids Under 12 Stay & Eat Free
- Indoor Pool • Exercise Room
- Meeting/Banquet Facilities
- Handicap Accessible • Interior Corridors
- Microwaves, Refrigerators, Coffee Makers

1687 3700 Shackleford Rd • Duluth, GA

GEORGIA • I-85 • EXIT 40

1586

Super 8 Motel

5150 Willow Oak Trail
Norcross, GA 30093

770-931-5353

- Jacuzzi Suites • Outdoor Pool
- Kids Under 12 Stay Free
- Restaurants Nearby
- Meeting/Banquet Facilities
- Handicap Accessible
- Truck/Large Vehicle Parking
- Exterior Corridors • Mall Nearby

Georgia • I-85 • Exit 38

ATLANTA/NORCROSS

Quality Inn

First exit outside of I-285 on I-85 North

770-449-7322

TRUCKER'S SPECIAL

$39 95* Single | $44 95* Double/King

1682

- New Rooms/AAA ◆◆
- Free Continental Breakfast
- In Room Coffee• Microfridge Available
- Outdoor Pool • Guest Laundry
- Electronic Locks
- 25" TV Remote w/HBO/CNN/ESPN
- Restaurants Nearby
- Dataport & Fax • USA Today
- Free Local Calls • Small Pets
- Within minutes of Gwinnett Mall • Gwinnett Civic & Convention Center • Stone Mountain • Downtown • Lake Lanier

*Subject to Availability

Truck Parking

GEORGIA • I-85 • EXIT 37

EXIT GEORGIA

Gas E: Knight's Import Service, Texaco[*, D, CW], Texaco[*]
W: Chevron[*]
Food E: Atlanta Bread Company, Bennigan's, Checkered Parrot, Chick-Fil-A, Chili's, Cracker Barrel, Denny's, Einstein Bros Bagels, Mandarin Garden Chinese, McDonald's[PLAY], Shoney's, Steak & Ale, Taco Bell, The Varsity, Waffle House
W: Pappa Deaux Seafood, Waffle House
Lodg E: Amberly Suite Hotels, Best Western, Club House Inn, La Quinta Inn, Motel 6, **Quality Inn** **(see our ad previous page)**
W: Drury Inn
AServ E: Auto Extreme, Knight's Import Service
W: Pep Boys Auto Center
TServ W: **Ford Truck Service**
ATM E: First Union Bank, Texaco, Texaco
W: NationsBank
Other E: **Cub Foods**, Georgia Antique Center, **Lens Crafters**, Wolfe Camera
W: Gwinnett Co. Police Dept., Pop Tart Convenience Store, **RW Goodtimes Unforgettable Fun**, Vet Clinic

36A **(97)** Pleasantdale Road
FStop W: **Quick Fuel**, **QuikTrip**[*, 24]
Food E: Burger King, Pleasantdale Chinese Fast Food
W: Cafe 36
Lodg W: Holiday Inn Express
TServ W: **Import Trucks**, **Trucks of Atlanta**
RVCamp E: **Morgan's RV**
ATM W: Wachovia Bank

36B **(96)** Northcrest Road (Accessible Via Pleasantdale Exit)
Gas W: BP[D, CW]
Food W: Waffle House
Lodg E: Econolodge
AServ W: BP
TServ W: **GMC Trucks of Atlanta**
RVCamp E: **Morgan RV's**, **Northcrest RV Storage**
Other E: **E&B Boat Gear**, Northcrest Academy of Golf, **Old Sport Golf**

35AB **(96)** I-285, Chattanooga, Augusta

34 **(94)** Chamblee - Tucker Road
Gas E: Amoco[*, 24], Fina[*, D]
W: QuikTrip[*], Texaco[*, D, LP]
Food E: El Padrino, Masters Inn, Oriental Restaurant (Chinese)
W: Dairy Queen, Selena's Mexican, Waffle House
Lodg E: Masters Inn, TraveLodge
W: Country Heart Inn, Motel 6
AServ E: Chamblee-Tucker Automotive
ATM W: QuikTrip
Other W: Dry Clean Coin Laundry, Ryder Truck Rental

33 **(93)** Shallowford Road, Doraville
Gas E: Shell[*]
W: Circle K[*, LP], Texaco[*, LP, 24]
Food E: Chinese Gourmet, La Playa, New Odessa, Waffle House
W: Anthony's Pizza Express, Chicken Plaza, Quality Inn
Lodg W: Quality Inn, The Lodge
AServ W: Apollon Auto Repair
ATM E: Shell
W: Circle K
Other E: **Big Food Supermarket**, **Coin Laundry**, Dekalb Police Station, U-Haul
W: **Atlanta Veterinary Skin & Allergy Clinic**

32 **(91)** U.S. 23, GA 155, Clairmont Road, Decatur
Gas E: Chevron[CW], Speedway[*, LP]
W: Amoco[*, D, CW]
Food E: Barley's Country Style Subs, IHOP, Madras Indian Cuisine, Mimi's In A Minute, Mo's Pizza & Sandwich Shop, Sidelines Sports Grill, Trymes II, Waffle House
W: Las Brasas Cantina, McDonald's, Waffle House
Lodg W: Days Inn (see our ad this page)
AServ E: Chevron, Japanese Car Specialists/ NAPA, Robert Bosch Parts & Service, Texaco Express Lube, Tune-Up Clinic, Vall Repair II[CW]
W: **K-Mart**
ATM E: SouthTrust Bank, Wachovia Bank
Other E: **Barwick's Pharmacy**[RX], **CVS Pharmacy**[RX], **Coin Laundry**, **IGA Grocery Store**, **U.S. Post Office**
W: **Airport**, **K-Mart**

31 **(90)** GA 42, North Druid Hills Road
Gas E: Amoco[*, 24], Crown[*, CW], QuikTrip[*]
W: BP[*, D, CW], Chevron, Crown[*, D, LP, CW]
Food E: Boston Market Restaurant, Burger King[PLAY], Chick-Fil-A, Dusty's Barbecue, Einstein Bros Bagels, El Torero, Grady's, Le Peep Restaurant, Lettuce Souprise You, McDonald's[PLAY], Morrisons Cafeteria, TCBY
W: Atlanta Diner (Radisson Inn), Cafe Lawrence's, Captain D's Seafood, Chinese Food, Denny's, Dollar Cafe, Dunkin Donuts, Folks, Frutii Valle, Fuzzy's Place, Havana Restaurant, International Cafe, Krystal, Lotus Garden Chinese, Phuket Thai Restaurant, Radisson, Red China, Rusty Nail, The Honey Baked Ham Co., Waffle House
Lodg E: Courtyard by Marriott, Homestead Village
W: Hampton Inn, Radisson, Red Roof Inn
AServ E: Amoco[24]
W: A to Z Auto & Truck Repair, BP, Chevron, Elite Auto Service, Euro Cars USA, Gordy Tire Service, Texaco Express Lube
Med E: **Egleston Chilren's Hospital**
ATM E: Associated Federal Employee's Credit Union, NationsBank, QuikTrip, SunTrust
W: Wachovia Bank
Other E: Baptist Bookstore, **Eckerd Drugs**[RX]
W: **Brito Supermarket**, **Buford Super Laundromat**, **CVS Pharmacy**, Casino 3011 Club Mexicano, High Speed Car Wash, **Lawrence Animal Hospital**, Sun Tan Cleaners & Coin Laundry

30 **(89)** to GA 400 North, Cheshire Bridge Road, Lenox Road
Gas E: BP[*, D, LP, CW], Citgo[*], Exxon[*, D], Fina[*, D, LP], Spur[*]
Food E: Bai Pong Thai, Bamboo Luau Chinese, Dunk'n Dine[24], Happy Herman's Deli, Original Pancake House, Seasiam, South of France, Varsity Jr Drive-In, Waffle House
W: Chicago's Sports Bar & Grill, Pancho's, The Cabin
Lodg E: Budgetel Inn
W: Buckhead Bed & Breakfast
AServ E: Highland Automotive, Precision Tune
ATM E: SouthTrust Bank, Wachovia Bank

ATLANTA
1617
DAYS INN
— CONTINENTAL BREAKFAST —
— Cable TV Showtime-ESPN-CNN-Disney —
— Outdoor Swimming Pool —
— Restaurants Nearby —
— Refrigerator & Laundry —
— Convientent to Buckhead & Downtown Atlanta —
404-633-8411 • Atlanta, GA
GEORGIA • I-85 • EXIT 32

EXIT GEORGIA

Other E: **Patient's Pharmacy**[RX], **Return to Eden Vegetarian Supermarket**, **Tara Antiques**, **Tara Movie Theater**
W: **Dogwood Hospital for Animals**

29 **(87)** GA 400 North, Buckhead, Cumming (Northbound, Toll)

28 **(86)** GA 13S to Peachtree St. (Difficult Reaccess, Services are on exit 27 Monroe Dr., Armour Drive, off of exit 28)
Gas E: BP, Chevron[*, D, CW]
Food E: Del Taco, Denny's, Don Juan's Spanish Restaurant, Franco's Pizza & Grill, Mrs Winner's Chicken, The Other Side Restaurant, Wendy's
Lodg E: Comfort Inn, In Town Suites
AServ E: Baker Imported Car Parts, Brake-O Brake Shop, No Pie Imported Car Parts, Pete Levins, Volvo Auto Repair
W: Meineke Discount Mufflers
ATM E: Chevron, Sun Trust Bank
W: Wachovia Bank
Other E: Buckhead Animal Clinic, Express Lanes Bowling Alley
W: Buckhead Design Center Antiques, Sam's Club

27 Junction I-75 North, Marietta, Chatanooga

Note: I-85 runs concurrent below with I-75. Numbering follows I-75.

103 **(252)** Junction I-85 North, Greenville

102 **(251)** Fourteenth St, Tenth St, Techwood Dr (Southbound, Difficult Reaccess)
Gas E: Amoco[*, 24], BP[*, D, CW]
Food E: Central Subs and Gyros, Dunkin Donuts, Einstein Bros Bagels, Philly Connection, Tamarind Thai, Vini Vidi Vici Italian
W: Blimpie's Subs, Chinese Buddha Restaurant, Kokopelli's Pizza, Silver Skillet Restaurant
Lodg E: Best Western, Hampton Inn, Marriott
Other W: CVS[RX], Office Depot, **Wolf Camera & Video**

101 **(251)** Fourteenth St, Tenth St, Georgia Institute of Technology (Northbound)
Gas E: Chevron[*, 24]
Food E: Checkers Burgers, Domino's Pizza
Lodg E: Regency Suites Hotel, Residence Inn
ATM E: Chevron
Other E: US Post Office

100 **(250)** U.S. 78, U.S. 278, North Ave, Georgia Institute of Technology (Difficult Reaccess, Crawford Long Hospital)
Gas E: BP[*, D, CW]
Food E: KFC, Subway, The Varsity (An Atlanta landmark)
Lodg W: Holiday Inn Express
Med E: **Crawford Long Hospital**
ATM E: BP, NationsBank
Other E: **Public Transportation (MARTA)**
W: **The Coca Cola Company**

99 **(250)** Williams St, World Congress Center, Georgia Dome (Southbound)
Lodg W: Days Inn

98 **(250)** Pine St, Peachtree St, Civic Center (Northbound, Difficult Reaccess)
Food E: Mick's, Pleasant Peasant
W: All Star Cafe, Corner Bakery, Morton's STeak

EXIT	GEORGIA
	House
Lodg	**W:** Howard Johnson, Hyatt
ATM	**W:** Wachovia Bank
97	**(249)** Courtland St, Georgia State University (Southbound, Difficult Reaccess)
Food	**W:** Fishernman's Cove
Lodg	**E:** Imperial Hotel
	W: Hilton, Marriott, Radison Hotel, TraveLodge
96	**(249)** Ga. 10, International Blvd., Freedom Pwky., Carter Center
Lodg	**W:** Courtyard, Fairfield Inn, Radisson
AServ	**W:** Beaudry Ford
Med	**W:** + **Georgia Baptist Hospital**
95	**(249)** Butler St, JW Dobbs (Southbound)
94	Edgewood Ave., Auburn Ave., J.W. Dobbs
Food	**E:** Church's Chicken
Med	**W:** + **Grady Memorial Hospital**
Other	**W:** SWeet Auburn Police Station
93	**(248)** Martin Luther King Jr. Blvd, State Capitol, Underground Atlanta ,Turner Field (Southbound, Reaccess Northbound Only)
Food	**W:** McDonald's
92	**(248)** Junction I-20, Augusta, Birmingham
91	**(247)** Fulton St. , Central Ave., Georgia Dome, New Atlanta Stadium (Reaccess Southbound Only, Zoo Atlanta)

Atlanta, Georgia
Park Plaza INTERNATIONAL®
ATLANTA AIRPORT
1419 Virginia Ave
College Park, GA 30337
$64.00*
1-4 Persons/Double Rooms Based on Availability
1161 404-768-7800
Atlanta Airport
Restaurant/Lounge on Premises
Fitness Center • Outdoor Pool
In-Room Movies • Free Cable TV W/HBO
FREE Airport Shuttle • FREE Parking
In Room Iron/Board & Hairdryers
Food Court
AAA
Present Ad At Check In For Discount
GEORGIA ▪ I-85 ▪ EXIT 19 SB/19B NB

1200 Virginia Avenue
Hapeville, GA 30344
404-209-1800
1613
194 Rooms - 6 Stories
Continental Breakfast
Walk to Many Restaurants
Guest Laundry
Every Room: Iron & Ironing Board,
Alarm Clock, Nintendo, PPV Movies, Hair Dryer
24 Hour Shuttle to Airport
Free Local Calls
GEORGIA ▪ I-85 ▪ EXIT 19A

EXIT	GEORGIA
90	**(247)** Abernathy Blvd., Capital Ave.
Gas	**W:** Amoco
Food	**E:** Bullpin Bar and Grill, KFC
Lodg	**E:** Hampton Inn, Holiday Inn Express
Other	**E:** Ryder
89	**(246)** University Ave, Pryor St
Gas	**E:** Exxon(*, D)
Food	**W:** Brook's Cafeteria
AServ	**E:** Anderson's Alignment Service, GPC, NAPA Auto Parts
TServ	**E:** **Cummins**
Parks	**W:** **Atlanta City Park (Pittman Park)**
88	**(243)** GA 166, Langford Pkwy, East Point, Lakewood Frwy (To Fort McPherson)
87	**(243)** Junction I-85 S. Atlanta Airport, Montgomery (Southbound)

Note: I-85 runs concurrent above with I-75. Numbering follows I-75.

EXIT	GEORGIA
24	**(77)** GA 166, Lakewood Freeway (Northbound)
23	**(76)** U.S.19, U.S. 41, Stewart Ave (Southbound, Difficult Reaccess)
Gas	**E:** Conoco(*, LP) (Blimpie), Hess(D)
Food	**E:** Arby's, Blimpie's Subs, Burger King, Del Taco, Jade Buddha Chinese, Mrs Winner's Chicken
Lodg	**W:** Town & Country Hotel Courts
AServ	**E:** Auto Zone Auto Parts
	W: Nalley Chevrolet, Nalley Honda & Kia
Other	**E:** CVS(RX), **Kroger Supermarket**(RX), Radio Shack
	W: Crystal Clean Coach Carwash
22	**(75)** Cleveland Ave, East Point (Northbound)
Gas	**E:** Conoco(*, LP), Hess(D)
	W: Amoco(*, CW, 24)
Food	**E:** Arby's, Blimpie's Subs (Conoco), Jade Buddha Chinese Restaurant, Mrs Winner's Chicken, Popeye's Chicken (Kroger)
	W: Church's Chicken, KFC
Med	**W:** + **Hospital**
ATM	**E:** Kroger Supermarket
Other	**E:** Auto Zone, **CVS**, **Kroger Supermarket**(RX), Radio Shack

I-85S Ex 18 L on Riverdale Rd, 2nd light R, then R on Sullivan Rd.
I-85N Ex 18 R on Riverdale Rd., 1st Light R then R on Sullivan Road
Follow Georgia International Trade & Convention Center Signs.
GEORGIA ▪ I-85 ▪ EXIT 18

EXIT	GEORGIA
	W: Dekalb Car Wash, Giant Food Store
21	**(74)** Sylvan Road, Central Ave, Hapeville
Gas	**E:** Fina(*, D, LP)
Food	**E:** Chicken and Beef Bowl
Lodg	**E:** In Town Suites
	W: Mark Inn
Other	**E:** **Papa Foodmart**
	W: Sylvan Cleaners
20	**(73)** Loop Rd. (Southbound)
19AB	**(72)** Virginia Ave., College Park
Gas	**W:** Chevron(*, CW, 24), Texaco(D)
Food	**E:** Malone's, McDonald's, Morrison's Cafeteria, Pondivits, Waffle House
	W: BBQ Kitchen, Happy Buddha Chinese, Hardee's, Hartsfield's Bar & Grill, KFC, La Fiesta, Steak & Ale, Waffle House
Lodg	**E:** Drury Inn, Hilton Hotel, Red Roof Inn (see our ad this page), Renaissance Hotel
	W: Country Suites and Inns, Crowne Plaza Hotel, Econolodge, Holiday Inn, Howard Johnson (see our ad this page), Park Plaza (see our ad this page)
AServ	**E:** Uniroyal Boyd Tire Co\plain
Med	**E:** + **Hospital**
18A	**(72)** Camp Creek Pkwy, Atlanta Airport
18B	**(72)** Riverdale Road, GA 139
Food	**E:** Ruby Tuesday
Lodg	**E:** Comfort Suites Hotel, Courtyard Marriot, Hampton Inn, Microtel Inn, Sheraton Gateway, Sleep Inn, Sumner Suites, **Super 8 (see our ad this page)**, Wingate
	W: DAYS INN Days Inn, Embassy Suites, Marriott, Quality Inn, TraveLodge, Westin Hotel
Other	**E:** **Georgia International Convention Center**
17	**(71)** Junction I-285, Macon, Birmingham (Southbound)
16AB	**(70)** GA 279, Old National Hwy, Atlanta Int'l Airport
Gas	**E:** Exxon(*, D), Racetrac(*), Texaco(*)
	W: Amoco(*)
Food	**E:** Burger King(PLAY), Club Cabana, El Nopal, El Ranchero Mexican, Formosa Chinese Buffet, McDonald's(PLAY), Picadilly Cafeteria, Steak & Ale, Waffle House, Zheng's Buffett
	W: Denny's, Dipper Dan Ice Cream, Ike's Buffalo Wings, Jamaica Jamaica, Los Angeles Mexican Food Market, Phoenix Dragon, Taste of Africa, Tropical REstaurant, Waffle House, Zab E Lee
Lodg	**E:** Best American Inn, Budgetel Inn, DAYS INN Days Inn, Double Tree Club Hotel, Fairfield Inn, Red Roof Inn
	W: La Quinta Inn
AServ	**E:** Xpress Lube
	W: Goodyear Tire & Auto
Med	**E:** + **Med-First Physician**
Other	**E:** Atlanta Area Animal Clinic, Coin Laundromat, Dry Cleaning and Laundry, **Kroger Supermarket**(RX), Old National Discount Mall
	W: CVS, Secretarius Books and Themes
16A	**(69)** GA 14, GA 279 (Northbound)
15	**(68)** Junction I-285, Atlanta Bypass
14	**(67)** Flat Shoals Road
FStop	**W:** **Speedway**(*) **(Starvin Marvin)**
Gas	**W:** Amoco(*, 24)
Food	**W:** Hardee's, Waffle House
Lodg	**W:** Union Inn
13	**(66)** GA 138, Union City, Jonesboro
Gas	**E:** BP(*)
	W: Chevron(*, CW, 24), Racetrac(*, 24), Texaco(*, D)

Bold red print shows RV & Bus parking available or nearby

EXIT		GEORGIA
		(Church's Chicken, NationsBank), USA Gasoline[D, 24]
	Food	E: Waffle House
		W: Arby's, Burger King[PLAY], China King Restaurant, Corner Cafe Hot Wings, Cracker Barrel, IHOP, JR Crickets, KFC, Krystal, McDonald's[PLAY], Pizza Hut, Shoney's, Subway, TCBY, Taco Bell, Wendy's
	Lodg	E: Econolodge, Ramada Limited
		W: Days Inn (see our ad this page)
	AServ	E: BP, BP, Gene Evans Ford, Steve Rayman Pontiac, Buick, GMC Truck
		W: Firestone Tire & Auto, Goodyear Tire & Auto, Jiffy Lube, Precision Tune & Lube, Sears Auto Center
	ATM	W: Fairbanco, NationsBank, Racetrac, SunTrust, Texaco (Church's Chicken, NationsBank)
	Other	W: **Eckerd Drugs**, Family Bookstores, **Kroger Supermarket**[24, RX], **Shannon Theatres**, **South Park Mall**, Toys R Us, **United Artist Theaters**, William's Cleaners
12		**(61)** GA 74, Fairburn, Peachtree City, Fayetteville, Tyrone
	Gas	E: Amoco[*], Chevron[*, D, LP, CW] (Subway), Racetrac[*]
		W: BP[*, D, CW]
	Food	E: Subway (Chevron), **Waffle House**
	Lodg	W: **Efficiency Motel**
	ATM	E: Chevron, Racetrac, Racetrac
11		**(56)** Collinsworth Road, Palmetto, Tyrone
	Gas	W: Fina[*, LP]
	Food	W: Frank's Family Restaurant
	RVCamp	W: **South Oaks Mfg. Home Community (.5 Miles)**
	FStop	E: **BP**[*, D], **Phillips 66**[*, D, LP, 24] **(Blimpie)**
		W: **Chevron**[*, LP, CW, 24]
	Gas	W: Shell[*, D] (Krystal)
	Food	E: Blimpie Subs & Salads, **Hardee's**
		W: Krystal
	ATM	W: Shell (Krystal)
9		**(46)** GA 34, Newnan, Peachtree City, Shanondoah (Hospital on West side, tourist info)
	Gas	E: Chevron[*, D, LP], Citgo[*, D, LP] (Dunkin Donuts, Subway), Shell[*, LP]
		W: Amoco[*, LP, CW], Phillips 66[*, LP], Racetrac[*]
	Food	E: Applebee's, Arby's, Atlanta Bread Company, Dunkin Donuts (Citgo), Hooters, McDonald's (Wal-Mart), Philly Connection, Ryan's Steakhouse, Schlotzsky's Deli, Sprayberry's BBQ, Subway (Citgo), Waffle House
		W: Chick-fil-A Dwarf House, Cracker Barrel, Folks, Hardee's, IHOP, Waffle House
	Lodg	E: Hampton Inn
		W: Shenandoah Inn Best Western
	AServ	E: Wal-Mart
		W: Budget Tires, KC Cars Auto Service, Patton Chevrolet, Oldsmobile, Chrysler, Jeep, Southtown Pontiac, Buick, Cadillac, GMC Truck
	Med	W: **Hospital**
	ATM	W: Amoco, First Union Bank, Phillips 66
	Other	E: Lowe's, **Peachtree Factory Outlet Stores**, Upton's, **Wal-Mart Supercenter**[RX]
		W: Fed Ex/ UPS Postal Center, Rainbow Systems[CW], Three Crowns Antiques
8		**(41)** U.S. 27, U.S. 29, Moreland, Greenville, to GA 16, Senoia, Griffin (Roosevelt State Park, The Little White House)
	FStop	W: **Amoco**[*, D, LP, 24]
	Gas	W: BP, Phillips 66[*, 24], Speedway[*, D, LP]
	Food	W: **Denny's (Days Inn)**, **Huddle House**, McDonald's[PLAY], **Waffle House**

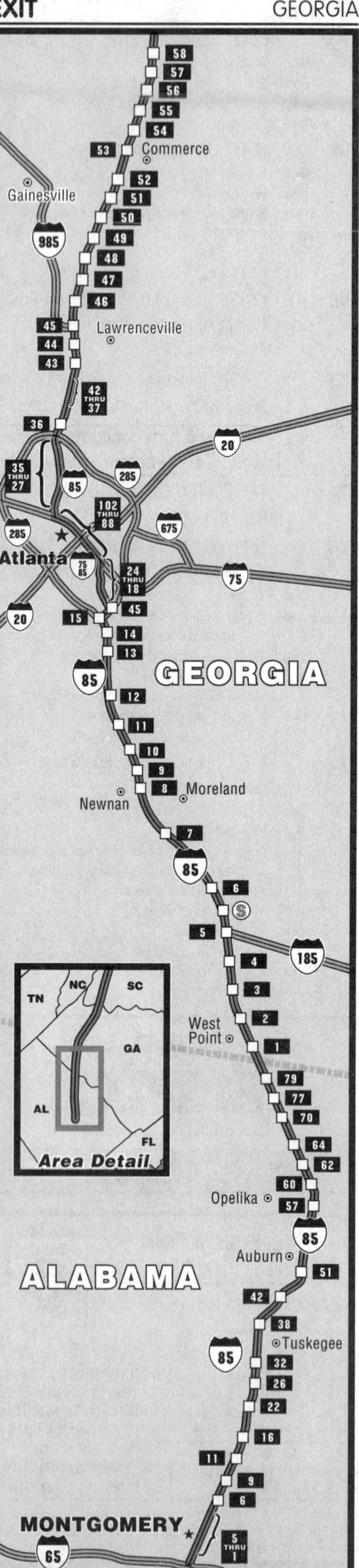

EXIT		GEORGIA
	Lodg	W: **Days Inn (Denny's)(see our ad this page)**, **Ramada Limited**, Super 8
	AServ	W: BP
	ATM	W: Phillips 66
7		**(35)** U.S. 29, Grantville
	FStop	W: **Amoco**[*, D, LP], **Phillips 66**[*]
	AServ	W: East Auto Body (PPG Collision Repair Center)
	ATM	W: **Amoco**, Amoco FS, **Phillips 66**
6		**(28)** GA 54, GA 100, Hogansville, Luthersville (Flat Creek Camp Ground)
	TStop	W: **Nobel Auto Truck Plaza**[*, SCALES] **(BP Gas, Travel Store)**
	FStop	E: **Shell**[*, D, LP]
		W: **Amoco**[*, D, LP]
	Gas	W: Citgo[*, D, CW] (KFC, Taco Bell)
	Food	W: Buford's Hickory Grill, **Janet's Country**

DAYS INN
Tour Buses Welcome!
Kids Under 12 Stay Free
Outdoor Pool
Restaurant/Lounge on Premises
Meeting/Banquet Facilities
Pets Allowed • Coin Laundry
Handicap Accessible
Tennis/Golf Nearby
Truck/Large Vehicle Parking
Close to Callaway Gardens,
Six Flags & The Little White House
770-253-8550
Newman, GA
1600
GEORGIA ▪ I-85 ▪ EXIT 8

DAYS INN SOUTH ATLANTA
1505
Union City, GA
- Free Continental Breakfast
- Cable TV/Showtime
- In Room Coffee
- Close To Shannon Mall, Cracker Barrel,
- Adjacent to Walmart
- 8 Mi. South of Airport
- Outdoor Pool

770-964-3777
800-DAYS-INN
GEORGIA ▪ I-85 ▪ EXIT 13

Bold red print shows RV & Bus parking available or nearby

EXIT		GEORGIA
		Cooking (Nobel TS), KFC (Citgo), McDonald's[PLAY], Subway, Taco Bell, Waffle House, Wendy's
	Lodg	W: Hummingbird Inn, Key West Inn
	TServ	W: Crockett Bros.[*] (Nobel TS)
	RVCamp	W: Flat Creek Campground
	ATM	E: Shell W: Citgo (KFC, Taco Bell), Citiizens Bank
	Other	W: Ingles Supermarket
(23)		Weigh Station (Eastbound)
(23)		Weigh Station (Westbound)
5		**(20)** Junction I-185 South, Columbus (Calloway Gardens, Fort Benning)
4		**(18)** Georgia 109, La Grange (La Grange College, Hospital)
	FStop	W: Amoco[*, D, LP], Spur[*, D, LP]
	Gas	W: Racetrac[*], Shell[*, LP] (Blimpie)
	Food	W: Bonzai Japanese Steakhouse, Burger King[PLAY], Knickers, Ryan's Steakhouse, Subway, Waffle House
	Lodg	E: La Grange Inn (Best Western) W: AmeriHost Inn, Holiday Inn Express, Jameson Inn, Ramada Inn (see our ad this page), Super 8
	ATM	W: Shell (Blimpie)
	Parks	E: F.D.Roosevelt State Park
	Other	W: Carmike Cinemas, West Georgia Commons
3		**(14)** U.S. 27, LaGrange (Ga State Patrol)
	Gas	W: Amoco[*, LP]
	Lodg	W: Hampton Inn
	ATM	W: Amoco
	Other	E: Georgia State Patrol Post
2		**(13)** GA. 219, LaGrange
	TStop	E: La Grange Auto/Truck Plaza[*, LP, SCALES] (Travel Store, Texaco Gas)

1569

RAMADA INN®

1513 Lafayette Pkwy • La Grange, GA • 30240

Restaurant/Lounge on Premises
Comlimentary Deluxe Continental Breakfast
Kids Under 12 Stay & Eat Free
Outdoor Pool • Exercise Room
Meeting/Banquet Facilities
Handicap Accessible • Exterior Corridors
Tennis/Golf Nearby
Truck/Large Vehicle Parking
Outside Electric Outlets for Boat Parking

706-884-6175

GEORGIA • I-85 • EXIT 4

1738

DAYS INN®

— FREE Deluxe Continental Breakfast —
— Renovated Rooms —
— Meeting & Banquet Rooms —
— Guest Laundry • Outdoor Pool —
— Truck & RV Parking —
— Remote Control Cable TV w/HBO —
— Handicap Rooms —

Call Toll Free: 800-325-2525

706-882-8881 • La Grange, GA

GEORGIA • I-85 • EXIT 2

EXIT		GEORGIA
	FStop	W: Amoco[*, D, LP], Speedway[*, D, LP, SCALES] (Starvin Marvin)
	Food	E: Days Inn, Huddle House, LaGrange Truck Plaza Restaurant, Waffle House W: Hardee's, McDonald's[PLAY]
	Lodg	E: Admiral Benbow Inn, Days Inn (Restaurant)(see our ad this page)
	TServ	E: La Grange Auto/Truck Plaza[SCALES] (Travel Store, Texaco Gas)
	ATM	W: Amoco, Speedway (Starvin Marvin)
1		**(2)** GA 18, West Point, Callaway Gardens
	FStop	E: Shell[*, D, LP]
	Gas	E: Amoco[*, 24] (AM South Bank)
	Lodg	E: TraveLodge
	ATM	E: Amoco, Amoco (AM South Bank)
(1)		GA Welcome Center (RR, HF,

EXIT		GEORGIA/ALABAMA
		Phones, Picnic, RV Dump; Northbound)

↑GEORGIA

↓ALABAMA

EXIT		
79		U.S. 29, Lanett, Valley
	Gas	E: Amoco[*, D, LP, CW] (Krispy Kreme), Racetrac[*, 24] W: Exxon[*, LP, 24], Phillips 66[*]
	Food	E: Burger King[PLAY], Captain D's Seafood, KFC, Krispy Kreme Doughnuts (Amoco), Krystal, Magic Wok, McDonald's[PLAY], Subway, Taco Bell (Amoco), Waffle House, Wendy's W: SHONEY'S, Shoney's
	Lodg	W: Days Inn (see our ad this page), Econolodge, Super 8
	AServ	E: Bryan's Transmission Service W: Auto Zone Auto Parts
	Med	E: ✚ Hospital
	Other	E: CVS W: Homestyle Laundry, Riverside Veterinary Clinic
(78)		Rest Area, Welcome Center (RR, HF, Phones, Picnic, RV Dump; Southbound)
77		CR 208, Valley, Huguley
	FStop	E: Amoco[*, D, K], Texaco[*] (Waffle King (24 HRs))
	Food	E: Krispy Kreme Doughnuts (Amoco FS), Waffle King[24] (Texaco)
	Lodg	E: Holiday Inn Express
	AServ	E: King Chevrolet, King Ford, Mercury, Lincoln, Chrysler, Plymouth, Dodge
	Med	E: ✚ Hospital
70		CR. 388, Cusseta, La Fayette
	TStop	E: Perlis[*, SCALES] (Texaco Gas, Subway, Country Pride Restaurant)
	Gas	E: BP[*]
	Food	E: Country Pride (Perlis TS), Subway (Perlis TS)
	AServ	E: Perlis TS
	TServ	E: Perlis
	RVCamp	E: B&B RV Park
	Other	E: Perlis Boot Outlet
64		U.S. 29, Opelika
	Gas	E: Amoco[*, CW] W: Exxon[*]
	AServ	E: Amoco, Amoco
62		U.S. 280, U.S. 431, Opelika, Phenix City
	FStop	E: Texaco[*, D] (Krispy Kreme, Church's Chicken)
	Gas	E: BP[*, D, CW], Chevron[*] W: Exxon[*, LP, 24], Shell[*, LP]
	Food	E: Church's Chicken (Texaco FS), Denny's, Durango Steakhouse (Ramada Limited), Krispy Kreme Doughnuts (Texaco FS), McDonald's[PLAY], Subway W: Cracker Barrel, The Grille Store, Waffle House, Western Sizzlin'

EXIT ALABAMA

Lodg E: Days Inn, Holiday Inn (see our ad this page), Knight's Inn, Motel 6, Ramada Limited (Durango)
W: Best Western (Mariner Inn), Comfort Inn
Other W: Food World Supermarket, USA Factory Stores (see our ad this page)

60 AL. 51, AL. 169, Opelika, Hurtsboro
Gas E: Amoco[*, CW], Leco[*]
W: Chevron[*, 24] (Krystal)
Food E: Hardee's
W: Krystal (Chevron)
Med W: ✚ Hospital
Other E: Swifty Car Wash[24]
W: Coin Car Wash

58 U.S. 280 W., Opelika
Gas W: Chevron[*, D] (Subway, Bread and Buggy)
Food W: Subway (Chevron)
Other W: Bread and Buggy (Chevron)

57 Glenn Ave, Auburn Opelika Airport
Gas W: Phillips 66[*]
Lodg E: Super 8 (see our ad this page)

51 U.S. 29, Auburn (University of Auburn, Chewacla State Park, Leisure Tme Camp Grounds)
Gas E: Amoco[*, D, K, CW, 24]
W: Exxon[*, LP], RaceWay[*], Texaco[*]
Food E: Ford Wok Grill, Hot Stuff Pizzaria (Amoco)
W: Waffle House
Lodg E: Hampton Inn, Super 8 (see our ad this page)
W: Comfort Inn, Econolodge
AServ W: CL Gregory Ford
RVCamp E: Leisure Time Campground
ATM E: Amoco
Parks E: Chewacla State Park
Other E: Pet Vet
W: Village Antiques

(44) Rest Area (RR, HF, Phones, Picnic, RV Dump; Southbound)

(44) Rest Area (RR, HF, Phones, Picnic, RV Dump; Northbound)

42 To U.S. 80, AL. 186, Wire Road
FStop W: Amoco[*, D] (Torch 85 Restaurant)
Food W: Torch 85 (Amoco)
ATM W: Amoco FS

38 AL.81, Tuskegee, Notasulga
Gas E: Texaco[*, D]

ALABAMA • I-85 • EXIT 22

EXIT ALABAMA

Food E: Western Inn Restaurant
Lodg E: Western Inn Hotel

32 AL. 49 North, Tuskegee, Franklin
Gas E: Amoco[*]
Food W: J&S Country Smokehouse

26 AL. 229 N., Tallassee
Med W: ✚ Hospital

22 To U.S. 80, Shorter (Camp Ground, Greyhound Race Track)
TStop E: Petro 2-Chevron[*, SCALES] (Travel Store)
FStop E: Amoco[*] (Krispy Kreme)
Gas E: Exxon[*] (Kold Keg)
Food E: Krispy Kreme Doughnuts (Amoco FS), Petro TS
Lodg E: Days Inn (see our ad this page)
TServ E: Petro 2-Chevron
RVCamp E: Winddrift Travel Park
ATM E: Exxon
Other E: CRazy Bill's Fireworks

16 Cecil, Waugh , Mount Meigs
Gas E: BP[*]
Food E: Fuller's Char House BBQ
AServ E: Interstate Automotive, Waugh Auto Repair
Other E: Crazy Bill's Fireworks

11 U.S. 80, Mitylene, Mt. Meigs
Gas W: Chevron[*, CW, 24]
ATM W: Chevron

9 AL. 271 to AL. 110, Auburn University at Montgomery, Taylor Road
Med W: ✚ Hospital

1523

129 N. College St. • Auburn, AL 36830
334-821-4632
AT&T
Non-Smoking Rooms
AT&T Services
Nearby Attractions:
Auburn Football Stadium,
Golf Course, U.S.Factory
Outlets Mall, Dining Places
& Chewacla State Park
Special Rates for
Military Employees,
Federal & State
Goverments Employees,
Senior Citizens,
Truckers Rates
Group Rates Offered
ALABAMA • I-85 • EXIT 51/57

EXIT ALABAMA

Other W: Southern Christian University

6 U.S. 80 , U.S. 231, AL 21, East Blvd (Air Force Base, MLK Jr., Expressway)
Gas E: Chevron[*, CW, 24], Citgo[*] (Cohen's, Philly Connection), Exxon[*, D]
W: Citgo[*] (Car Wash), Shell[*]
Food E: American Pie (Ramada Inn), Burger King[PLAY], Cracker Barrel, Cuco's Mexican, Fifth Quarter Steak & Seafood, Luigi's Pizzaria, Ming's Garden, Schlotzsky's Deli, Shogun Japanese, Taco Bell, Waffle House
W: Church's Chicken, Denny's, KFC, Lone Star Steakhouse, McDonald's[PLAY], Outback Steakhouse, SHONEY'S, Shoney's, Waffle House
Lodg E: Best Inn, Best Suites, Budgetel Inn, Courtyard by Marriott, Fairfield Inn, Hampton Inn, La Quinta Inn, Montgomery Studio Plus, Quality Inn, Ramada Inn, Residence Inn
W: Best Western, Comfort Suites Hotel, Holiday Inn, Motel 6, Wynfield Inn
AServ E: Exxon, Xpert Tune
W: Capitol Chevrolet, Express Lube, Kia Smart Cars, Lexxus, Reinhardt Toyota, Royal Chrysler/ Plymouth, Jeep/Eagle
ATM E: AmSouth Bank, Chevron
Other E: Antique Galleries, Brunswick Woodmere (Bowling), Carmike Cinemas, Coin Car Wash, Lowe's, Sam's Club, Waccamaw

4 Perry Hill Road
Gas W: Chevron[*, CW, 24], Citgo[*, D, K], Texaco[*, LP]
Food W: Hardee's, New China
ATM E: Whitney Bank
Other E: Bruno's, Hour Glass Optical, Rite Aid[RX]
W: Pick Wick Antiques, Rite Aid[RX]

3 Ann St
Gas E: BP[*, D, LP, CW, 24], Citgo[*, LP]
W: Amoco[*, CW, 24], Exxon[*] (Burger King)
Food E: Arby's, Captain D's Seafood, Country's BBQ, Domino's Pizza, Down The Street Cafe, Great Wall Chinese, Hardee's, McDonald's[PLAY], Taco Bell, Waffle House, Wendy's
W: Burger King (Exxon)
Lodg E: Days Inn
W: Villager Lodge
AServ E: Big 10 Tires
ATM E: AM South, SouthTrust Bank
Other W: Ann St Car Wash

2A Mulberry St.
Med W: ✚ Jackson Hospital

2 Forest Ave. (Northbound)
Med W: ✚ Hospital
Other E: CVS

1 Union St. (Hospital, Alabam St University)
Gas E: Amoco[*, CW], Exxon[*]
AServ W: Mr. Transmission
Med W: ✚ Hospital
ATM W: Colonial Bank

↑ALABAMA

Begin I-85

Bold red print shows RV & Bus parking available or nearby

EXIT	IDAHO
	Begin I-86
	↓IDAHO
1	I-84 East, Ogden, Junction I-84 West (Westbound)
(4)	Weigh Station
15	Raft River Area
FStop	**S:** Sinclair[*]
(19)	Rest Area (RR, Phones, Picnic, P; Eastbound)
21	Coldwater Area
28	Massacre Rocks State Park
RVCamp	**N:** Camping
Parks	**N:** Massacre Rocks State Park
Other	**S:** Register Rock Historical Site
(31)	Rest Area (RR, Phones, Picnic, P; Westbound)
33	Neeley Area
36	Bus. I-86, ID 37, American Falls, Rockland
RVCamp	**S:** Indian Springs RV Resort (2 Miles)
Med	**N:** ✚ Hospital
40	ID 39, American Falls, Aberdeen
TStop	**S:** Amoco[*, LP, SCALES]
Lodg	**S:** Hillview Motel
AServ	**N:** Rick's Cheverolet, Oldmobile
RVCamp	**N:** Willow Bay Recreation Area
Other	**N:** American Falls Recreation Area
44	Seagull Bay
49	Rainbow Road
52	Arbon Valley
FStop	**S:** Bannock Peak
56	Pocatello, Air Terminal
58	U.S. 30, West Pocatello
RVCamp	**S:** Cummins Intermountain, Inc. (1 Mile)
61	U.S. 91, Chubbuck, Yellowstone Ave
FStop	**N:** Amoco
Gas	**S:** Chevron[*], Flying J Travel Plaza[*, D, CW] (Taco Bell)
Food	**N:** Arctic Circle Hamburgers, Burger King, Johnny B. Goode, Lei's Mongolian Barbecue, Pizza Hut, Subway **S:** Denny's, McDonald's, Mongolian Noodles
Lodg	**N:** DAYS INN Days Inn, Motel 6 **S:** Pine Ridge Inn
RVCamp	**N:** Budget RV Park, DAYS INN Days Inn **S:** Herb's RV Service
Other	**N:** Eddy's Bakery Outlet, Hiar Cuts Etc, Warehouse Grocery **S:** Grocery Outlet, Mall, Wal-Mart[RX]
63	Jct. I-15, Idaho Falls, Salt Lake City
	↑IDAHO
	Begin I-86

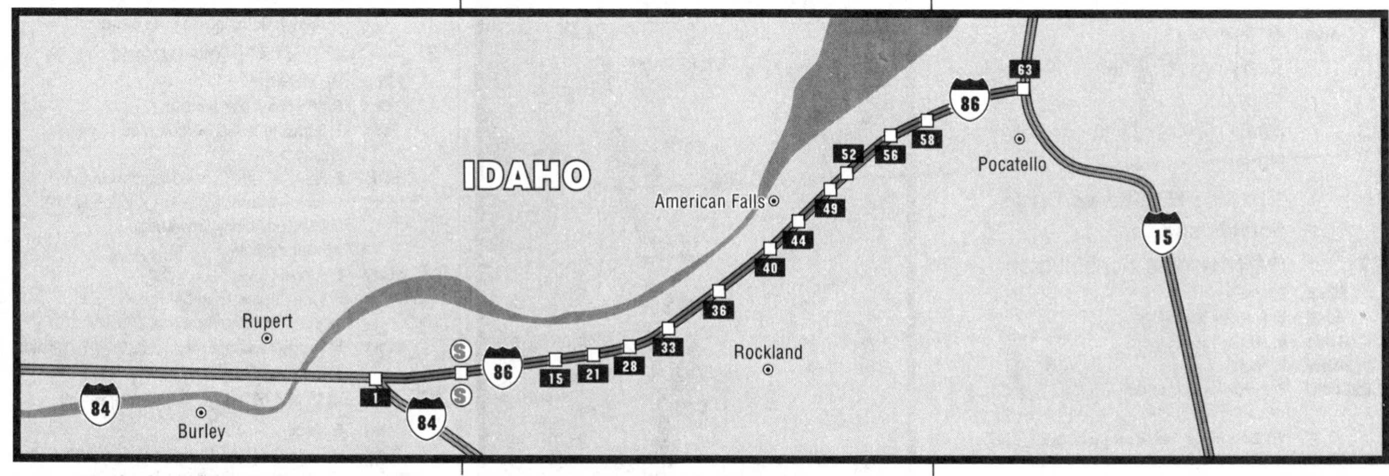

I-87 S →

EXIT	NEW YORK
	Begin I-87
	↓NEW YORK
43	**(175)** U.S. 9, Champlain
TServ	**W:** Champlain Peterbilt Service
42	**(174)** U.S. 11, Moors, Rouses Point
TStop	**W:** 11-87 Truck Plaza[*, SCALES]
FStop	**W:** Mobil[LP], Sunoco[*, 24]
Gas	**E:** Citgo[*, CW], Mobil[*] **W:** Petro Canada
Food	**E:** Art's Place, Choices Chinese, Peppercorn Family Restaurant, Pizza Plus (Mobil) **W:** 11-87 Truck Plaza, Burger King, Dunkin Donuts (Petro), McDonald's
TServ	**W:** 11-87 Truck Plaza[SCALES]
ATM	**E:** AlBank **W:** Mobil
Other	**E:** Grand Union Supermarket, Kenny Drugs[RX], Rite Aide Pharmacy[RX], U.S. Post Office **W:** Miromar Factory Outlet Center
41	**(168)** NY 191, Chazy, Sciota
Other	**E:** State Police
(162)	NY Welcome Center (RR, Phones, Picnic; Northbound)
40	**(160)** NY 456, Beekmantown, Point au Roche
Gas	**E:** Mobil[*]
Lodg	**E:** Stonehelm Motel
39	**(156)** NY 314, Cumberland Head, Plattsburg
Gas	**E:** Mobil[*], Stewart's Shops[*]
Food	**E:** Domenic's, Gus' Red Hots, Oz Subs, Sweeney's Restaurant
Lodg	**E:** Chateau Motel, Landmark Hotel, Rip Van Winkle Hotel, Sundance Motel, Super 8
RVCamp	**E:** Campground, Plattsburg RV Park (.35 Miles)
Parks	**E:** State Park Beach
Other	**E:** Plattsburg Animal Hospital, Plattsburg Beach
38	**(155)** NY 22N, Dennemorre, NY 374W, Plattsburg
Med	**E:** ✚ Hospital
Other	**W:** Sherriff's Department
37	**(153)** NY 3, Plattsburgh, Saranac Lake
Gas	**E:** Short Stop Deli **W:** Exxon[*], Petro Canada, Sunoco
Food	**E:** Comfort Inn, Dairy Queen, Mangia, Pizza Hut, Wendy's **W:** Anthony's Restaurant, Barkin' Dog Restaurant, Butcher Block, Friendly's, Ground Round, Howard Johnson, Lums Restaurant, Ponderosa, Red Lobster, Sunoco
Lodg	**E:** Comfort Inn **W:** Budgetel Inn, DAYS INN Days Inn, EconoLodge, Howard Johnson, Travelers Inn
AServ	**E:** Drew Buick, Firestone, Knight GMC **W:** Jiffy Lube, Midas Muffler, Monroe Muffler & Brakes, Parts America, Sears
Med	**E:** ✚ Hospital **W:** ✚ Urgent Care Clinic, ✚ Urgent Care Clinic
ATM	**E:** Key Bank **W:** Adirondack Bank, Al Bank, Midland Bank, NBT Bank
Other	**E:** Consumer's Square, Grand Union Grocery Store[RX], Sam's Club, Wal-Mart[RX] **W:** Auto Zone, Big K-Mart[RX], Center Mall, Eckerd Drugs
36	**(150)** NY 22, Lake Shore
FStop	**E:** Mobil[*]
TServ	**E:** Charlebois, Cummins International & Mitsubishi
35	**(144)** NY 442, Peru, Valcour
RVCamp	**E:** Ausabale Chasm KOA, Ausabale Pines, Iroquois Campground (1.5 Miles) **W:** Birchwood Campground

EXIT NEW YORK

34 **(138)** NY 9 North, Ausable Forks, Keeseville
- Gas E: Sunoco
- Food E: Pleasant Corners Restaurant, Tastee Freeze
- AServ E: Sunoco
- RVCamp W: Ausable River Campsite (1 Mile)
- Other E: Keeseville Veterinary Clinic

33 **(135)** U.S. 9, NY 22, Keeseville
- Lodg E: Chesterfield Motel
- AServ E: Power Champs
- RVCamp E: Campground

32 **(123)** Lewis, Willsboro
- TStop W: Betty Beaver's Truck Stop & Diner
- FStop W: Pierce's Gas(*)
- RVCamp E: Spruce Mill Campsite

(123) Rest Area (RR, Phones, Picnic; Northbound)

31 **(117)** NY 9 North, Elizabethtown, Westport
- Gas E: Mobil(*)
- Lodg E: Hilltop Motel
- Med W: ✚ Hospital

(112) Rest Area (RR, Phones; Northbound)

30 **(104)** U.S. 9, NY 73, Keene Valley, N Hudson

(99) Rest Area (RR, Phones, Picnic; Southbound)

29 **(94)** Newcomb, North Hudson
- FStop E: Mobil(*, D)
- Food E: Frontier Town Motel
- Lodg E: Frontier Town Motel
- AServ E: Mobil
- RVCamp E: Paradise Pines Camping, Yogi Bear Camp Resort
  W: Blue Ridge Falls Campground
- Other E: North Hudson Grocery

28 **(89)** NY 74, Ticonderoga - Ferry, Crown Point
- Gas E: Sunoco(*, D, LP)
- Lodg E: Schroon Lake Bed & Breakfast, Sweet Dreams Hotel
- AServ E: Sunoco
- Other E: State Police

(83) Rest Area (RR, Phones, Picnic; Southbound)

(83) Scenic Overview, Rest Area (RR, Phones, Picnic; Northbound)

27 **(82)** U.S. 9, Schroon Lake (Northbound, Reaccess Southbound Only)
- RVCamp E: Campground

26 **(79)** U.S. 9, Pottersville, Minerva (Difficult Reaccess)
- FStop W: Mobil(*)
- Food W: Black Bear
- RVCamp W: Ideal Campsite (.25 Miles), Wakonda Family Campground (1.75 Miles)
- Other W: U.S. Post Office

25 **(73)** NY 8, Chestertown, Hague
- FStop W: Sunoco(*)
- Gas W: Mobil
- RVCamp E: Rancho Pines (1 Mile), Riverside Pines Campground

24 **(67)** Bolton Landing
- RVCamp E: Good Sam Campground, Lake George/ Schroon Valley Resort (.75 Miles)

EXIT NEW YORK

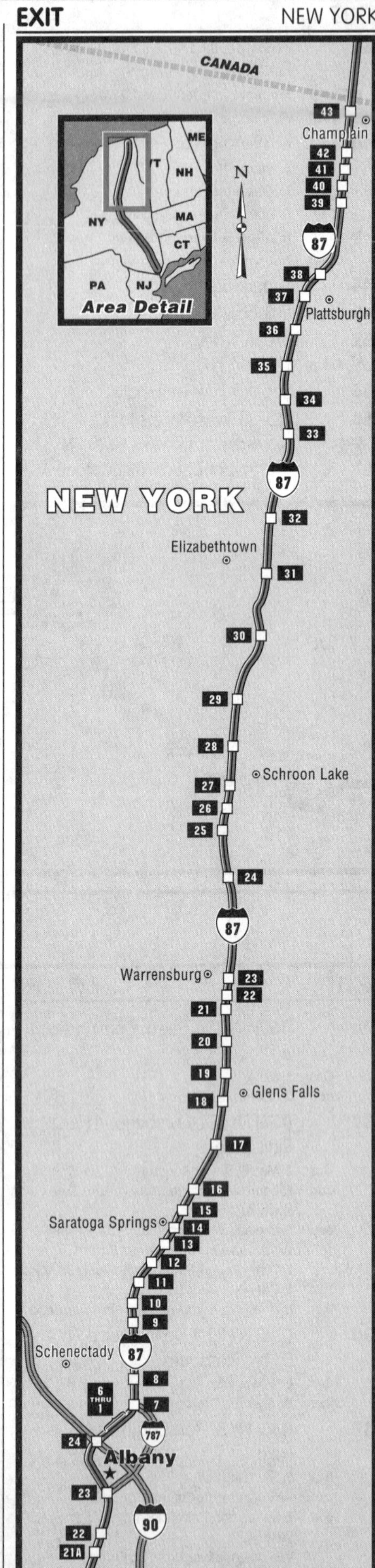

EXIT NEW YORK

(64) Parking Area (Northbound)

23 **(60)** Warrensburg, Diamond Point
- Gas W: Citgo(*), Mobil(*)
- Food W: Brunetto's, McDonald's
- Lodg W: Super 8
- AServ W: Ford Dealership
- RVCamp E: Evergreen Camping Resort (1 Mile)
  W: Rainbow View Family Campground (.25 Miles), Warrensburg Travel Park (1 Mile)

22 **(55) U.S. 9, NY 9 N, Diamond Point, Scenic Overlook**
- Food E: Betty's Place, Giuseppe's, Luigi's Italian, Mario's, New York Pizza, Scillion Spathetti House, Tomarac Inn
- Lodg E: Admiral Motel, Bamoral Motel, Blairhouse Motel & Cottages, Brookside Motel, Cedar Hurst, Dwarfs Motor Inn, EconoLodge, Framcove Motel, Green Acres, Heritage Motel, Hilside, Lake Haven Motel, Mandella Hotel, Mohawk Motel, Motel Montreal, Nortic Motel, Oasis Motel, Sunrise Motel, Tomarac Inn
- RVCamp E: Adirondack Camping Village (1.5 Miles), Mohawk Camping on Lake George (1 Mile)

21 **(53)** NY 9 N, Lake Luzerne
- FStop W: Mobil(*, 24)
- Gas E: BP(*), Stewarts(*), Sunoco
- Food E: Barnsider's BBQ & Steak, Mountaineer Restaurant
- Lodg E: Best Western, Cobble Mountain Manor, Colonial Williams Motor Inn, Kennah's Motel, Lincoln Log Colony, TraveLodge
  W: Kathy's Motel
- AServ E: Sunoco
- RVCamp E: King Phillips, Lake George RV Park, Wippoorwill Campground (1.25 Miles)
- Other E: Tourist Haunted Attraction (Golf), Waterslide World

20 **(49)** NY 149, Fort Ann, Whitehall
- Gas E: Mobil
- Food E: Subway (Mobil), The Log Jam Restaurant, The Meetings Place (Days Inn), Trading Post
- Lodg E: DAYS INN Days Inn, Samoset Cabins
- RVCamp E: Lake George Campsite (1 Mile), Lake George RV Park (1.25 Miles), Lake George Sales(LP)
- Other E: Factory Outlet Center

19 **(47)** U.S. 9, NY 254, Glens Falls, Hudson Falls
- Gas E: Citgo(*), Mobil(*), Sunoco(*, 24)
  W: Mobil(*)
- Food E: Burger King, Friendly's, Seven Steers Western Grill
- Lodg E: Howard Johnson
  W: Ramada
- RVCamp E: Lake George Campsite(LP) (1 Mile), Lake George RV Sales(LP) (1.4 Miles)
- Med E: ✚ Convenient Care Walk-in
- Other E: Aviation Mall
  W: State Police

18 **(45)** Glens Falls, Corinth
- Gas E: Citgo(*, D), Gulf(*), Hess(D), Mobil(*)
- Food E: Carl R's Cafe, Lox of Bagels & Moor, Pizza Hut, Subway (Gulf)
  W: McDonald's
- Lodg E: Susse Chalet
  W: Super 8
- Med E: ✚ Hospital

(43) Rest Area (RR, Phones, Picnic)

17 **(40)** U.S. 9, South Glens Falls
- TStop E: Buddy Beaver's Truck Stop(D)
- FStop E: Mobil(*)
- Gas E: Gulf(*, LP)
- Food E: Buddy Beaver's Truck Stop, Mobil
- Lodg E: Swiss American Motel

Bold red print shows RV & Bus parking available or nearby

EXIT — NEW YORK

W: Terry's Motel
RVCamp E: **American Campgrounds**
Parks W: **Moreau Lake State Park**

16 — **(36)** Ballard Rd, Gansevoorit, Willton
TStop W: **Sunoco**(*)
Gas W: Mobil(*, LP)
Food W: **Sunoco**
RVCamp E: **Cole Brook Campsite (1 Mile)**
W: **Freedom RV Outlet (Sales & Service)**

15 — **(30)** NY 50, Saratoga Springs, Gansevoort, NY29, Schuylerville
Gas E: Hess(*, D), Mobil(*, LP)
Food E: Blimpie Sub & Salads (Mobil), Burger King, McDonald's, Ponderosa Steakhouse
AServ E: Saratoga Auto Park
ATM E: 1st National Bank, Key Bank, Midland Bank, Mobil
Other E: **K-Mart, Saratoga Mall, Wal-Mart**(RX)

14 — **(28)** NY 9P, NY 29, Saratoga Springs, Schuylerville

13 — **(24)** U.S. 9, Saratoga Springs
Gas W: Mobil(*), Sunoco(*, 24)
Food E: Andy's Pizza, Chez Sophie, The Leprechaun
W: Packhorse Restaurant
Lodg E: Locust Grove Motel, Maggiore's Inn, The Post Road Lodge
W: Coronet Motel, Roosevelt Suites, Thorobred Motel

12 — **(21)** Malta, Ballston Spa
FStop E: **Mobil**(*, D, LP, CW)
Gas E: Sunoco(D)
Food E: Briarwood, Malta Diner, McDonald's, McGoo's Bagel Shop, Subway, Tasty's Chinese, Venezia Pizza & Pasta
Lodg E: Riveria Motel
RVCamp E: **Northway Travel Trailers**(LP) **(.75 Miles), RV & Camping Accesories**
Med E: ✚ **Malta Walk-in Clinic**
ATM E: **Grand Union Supermarket**(24), Key Bank, Pioneer Bank, Tructco Bank
Parks E: **Saratoga National Historic Park**
Other E: **CVS Pharmacy**(RX), **Grand Union Supermarket, Stewarts Shops**

11 — **(19)** Burnt Hill, Round Lake
FStop W: **Mobil**(*, LP)
Gas W: Sunoco(*, D, LP, 24)
Food W: Adirondack Restaurant, **Gran-Prix**
Lodg W: **Gran-Prix**
AServ W: Sunoco(24)
Other W: **Stewart's Shops**

10 — **(16)** Ushers Rd, Jonesville

(14) — **Rest Area (RR, Phones, Picnic; Northbound)**

1164

Comfort Inn

Nestled Between Albany & Saratoga

518-373-0222
800-228-5150

- *Complimentary Continental Breakfast*
- *HBO/In-room VCRs/Videos*
- *Jacuzzi Rooms Available*
- *Fitness Center*
- *Heated Outdoor Pool*
- *Free Local Phone Calls*

Exit 9E off Northway (I-87) 41 Fire Rd., Clifton Park, NY

NEW YORK ▪ I-87 ▪ EXIT 9

EXIT — NEW YORK

9 — **(13)** NY 146, Clifton Park, Halfmoon
Gas E: Hess(*, D)
W: Exxon, Mobil(*, CW), Sunoco
Food E: Burger King, Fohan Buffet, Four Star Pizza & Subs, Mr. Sub, Panda Garden
W: Applebee's, Boston Market Restaurant, Bruegger's Bagel & Bakery, Denny's, Domino's Pizza, Dragon Buffet, Dunkin Donuts, East Wok, Friendly's, KFC, Mama Maria's Italian, Mangia Cafe, McDonald's, Persnickety Coffee Bar, Taco Bell, Wendy's
Lodg E: Comfort Inn (see our ad this page)
W: Best Western
AServ E: Goodyear Tire & Auto, Midas Muffler & Brake, Valvoline Oil Change
W: Auto Zone, Exxon, Sunoco
ATM E: Key Bank, Troy Savings Bank
W: Amsterdam Savings Bank, Fleet Bank, Fleet Bank, Marine Midland Bank, Mobil, **Price Chopper Supermarket**, Trustco Bank
Other E: **CVS Pharmacy**(RX)
W: **CVS Pharmacy**, Eckerd Drugs(RX), **K-Mart, Price Chopper Supermarket**

8A — **(12)** Grooms Rd, Waterford

8 — **(10)** Vischer Ferry, Crescent
Gas W: Mobil(*), Sunoco(*, 24)
Food E: **McDonald's**
W: Mr Sub (Mobil)
ATM W: Key Bank
Other E: **U.S. Post Office**
W: **CVS Pharmacy**(RX), Raindancer Car Wash, **Stewart's Shops**

7 — **(6)** U.S. 9, NY 7E, Troy, Cohoes
Gas E: Mobil(*)
Food E: Dunkin Donuts (Mobil), Holiday Inn Express, Kirker's Restaurant, Monte Mario Motel, Mr. Sub, Subway
Lodg E: Century House Inn, Hampton Inn, Holiday Inn Express, Monte Mario Motel, Sicamore Hotel
AServ E: Cotman Transmission, Latham Ford, Midas Muffler & Brake, NAPA Auto Parts, Nemith Volvo, Mercury, Lincoln, Nissan, Northeast Acura, Service Parts Auto Store, Smith Pontiac, GMC
Med E: ✚ **Hospital**
ATM E: Capital Communication Federal Credit Union, Trustco Bank

6 — NY 7 West, NY 2, Schenectady, Watervliet
Gas W: Mobil(*)
Food E: Dakota Steak & Seafood, Ginza Japanese Cuisine, Pizzeria Uno
W: Bennigan's, Friendly's, King's Buffet, Sebastian's
Lodg W: Clarion Inn, Microtel, Super 8
AServ E: Nemer VW/Jeep/Eagle
W: Goodyear Tire & Auto, Jiffy Lube
ATM E: Fleet Bank
Other E: **Latham Circle Shopping Mall (Lathams Farms), Sam's Club, Wal-Mart**(RX)

5 — NY 155, Latham
Other W: **Colony Police Dept.**

4 — NY 155, Wolf Rd, Albany Airport
Gas E: Hess(*), Sunoco(*)
Food E: Arby's, Ben & Jerry's Ice Cream, Burger King, Duck House, Holiday Inn, Macaroni Grill, Maxie's Bar & Grill, Olive Garden, Outback Steakhouse, Pizza Hut, Professor, Real Seafood Company, Subway, Wolf Road Diner
W: Peony Chinese
Lodg E: Best Western, Courtyard by Marriott, Hampton Inn, Holiday Inn, Marriott, Red Roof Inn
W: Wingate Inn
AServ E: Ford Dealership
ATM E: Capital Bank, Fleet Bank, Key Bank

EXIT — NEW YORK

2 — **(1)** NY 5 East, Albany
Gas W: BP(*)
Food E: Bangkok Thai Restaurant
W: Domino's Pizza, Houlihan's, L-Ken's Sandwich, Mr Sub, Northway Inn, Red Lobster
Lodg E: Central Motel, Cocca's Motel, DAYS INN Days Inn, Susse Chalet
W: Northway Inn, Super 8
AServ E: Goodyear Tire & Auto, Sears
W: Monroe Muffler & Brakes
ATM E: Trustco Bank
Other E: Barnes & Noble Booksellers, **Colonie Center Mall, Northway Mall**

1 — **(0)** Junction I-90 , New York , Buffalo , Boston

1B — **(0)** to U.S. 20, Western Ave
Gas W: Exxon(*), Sunoco
Food E: Bountiful Bread, Bruegger's Bagel & Bakery, Burger King, Cafe Londonbury, Coco's, Cowan Lobel Gourmet Food, Denny's, Mangia Mexican, Peach'n Cream Coffee Shop, Star Buck's Coffee, T.G.I. Friday's, TCBY
W: China Buffet, Jade Fountion, KFC, McDonald's, Pizza Hut, Ponderosa, Sidedoor Cafe, Wendy's
Lodg E: Holiday Inn Express
AServ W: Tire Warehouse
TServ W: **H.L.Gage Sales International**
ATM E: All Bank, Fleet Bank, Trustco Bank
W: Key Bank
Other E: **Albany County Veterinary Hospital, Dinapoli Opticians, Post Office, Revco Drugs, Shopping Plaza**
W: **Crossgate Mall, Sam's Club**

Note: I-87 runs concurrent below with NYTHWY. Numbering follows NYTHWY.

24 — **(148)** Junction I-90, Albany
Other N: **Crossgates Mall**

23 — **(142)** Junction I-787, U.S 9W Albany, Rensselaer
TStop E: **Big M Truckstop**(*)
Gas E: Mobil(*)
Food E: Big M Truckstop, Domino's Pizza, Reuters Sports Bar & Grill, TCBY
Lodg E: Howard Johnson
AServ E: Buff O Matic II, Glenmont Family Tire & Auto, Mobil
TServ E: **Roberts Towing & Recovery Center**
Med W: ✚ **Hospital**

(139) — **Truck Inspection, Parking Area (Phones, Picnic; Southbound)**

22 — **(135)** NY 144, NY 396, Selkirk
AServ E: Valley Auto & Tire Service
Other E: **State Police**

21A — **(134)** to I-90 East, MATNPK, Boston (No Vehicles Over 10'6" Wide)

(127) — **New Baltimore Service Area**
FStop B: **Mobil**
Food B: **Bob's Big Boy, Mrs Fields Cookies**, Roy Rogers, **TCBY**
AServ B: Mobil
ATM B: On Bank

21B — **(125)** U.S. 9 W, NY 81, Coxsackie
TStop W: **Fox Run Truckstop**(LP, SCALES)
FStop W: **Sunoco**(*)
Lodg W: **Fox Run (Fox Run Truckstop)**
AServ W: Dr How's Automotive
Other W: **New Baltimore Animal Hospital**

21 — **(114)** NY 23, Catskill, Cairo
Gas W: Mobil(*)

EXIT		NEW YORK
	Food	W: 21 Restaurant, Days Inn, Log Cider Cafe, Rip Van Winkle Motor Lodge
	Lodg	W: Days Inn, Green Lake Resort, Rip Van Winkle Motor Lodge
	AServ	E: 10 Min Quick Lube
	RVCamp	W: Indian Ridge Camp Sites
	Other	E: State Police
		W: Tourist Info.
(104)		Parking Area (Phones; Southbound)
(103)		Mauldin Service Area
	FStop	E: Mobil
	Food	E: Carvel Ice Cream Bakery, McDonald's
	AServ	E: Mobil
20		(101) NY 32, Saugerties, Woodstock
	FStop	E: Getty
		W: Hess
	Gas	E: Mobile, Stewarts Shop[*]
		W: Hess[*, D]
	Food	E: Dairy Queen, McDonald's, Star Pizza, The Stairway Cafe
		W: Casey's, Howard Johnson, LaCucina Family Restaurant
	Lodg	W: Cloverleaf Hotel, Comfort Inn, Howard Johnson
	Other	E: CVS Pharmacy, Grand Union Grocery Store
(99)		Rest Area (Phones; Northbound)
(96)		Ulster Service Area (Southbound)
	FStop	E: Mobil
	Food	E: Nathan's Restaurant, Roy Rogers, Strathmore's Bagel & Deli, TCBY
	AServ	E: Mobil
	ATM	E: Onbank
19		(92) NY 28, Kingston, Rhinecliff Bridge
	Gas	E: BP
	Food	E: B'N Bagels, Blimpie's Subs, Chic's Restaurant, Elaine's Diner, Plaza Pizza
		W: Kingston's Family Restaurant (Travelodge), Ramada, Skycop Steak House
	Lodg	E: Holiday Inn, Super 8
		W: Ramada, Skycop Motel, Super Lodge, TraveLodge
	AServ	E: Auto Plaza & Tire, BF Goodrich, BP, Parts America
		W: Johnson Ford/Nissan, Throughway Nissan
	RVCamp	W: Johnson's RV Camper Barn
	Med	E: + Hospital
	ATM	E: Bank of New York, Fleet Bank, Ulster Savings Bank
	Other	E: Coin Laundry, Grand Union Grocery Store, Kindgston's Plaza Shopping Center, Tourist Info., WalGreens Pharmacy
		W: State Police, Tourist Info.
18		(76) NY 299, Poughkeepsie, New Paltz
	Gas	E: Citgo, Mobil
		W: Sunoco[*]
	Food	E: Austrian Village Restaurant, China Buffet, College Diner, La Bella Pizza & Pasta
		W: Bertone's Deli, Blue Jeans Steak House, Burger King, Dunkin Donuts, Gadaletl's Seafood, Great Wall Kitchen Chinese, McDonald's, Napali Pizza, New Paul's Hot Bagels, Pasquale's Pizza & Italian, Pizza Hut, Plaza Diner, TCBY
	Lodg	E: 87 Motel, Days Inn, Econolodge
		W: Super 8
	AServ	E: Citgo, Mobil
		W: Auto Parts, Midas Muffler & Brake
	RVCamp	W: KOA Campgrounds (9 Miles), Yogi Bear Camp Resort (9 Miles)
	ATM	W: Fleet Bank
	Other	E: Cumberland Farms Convenient Store, Diamond Car Wash

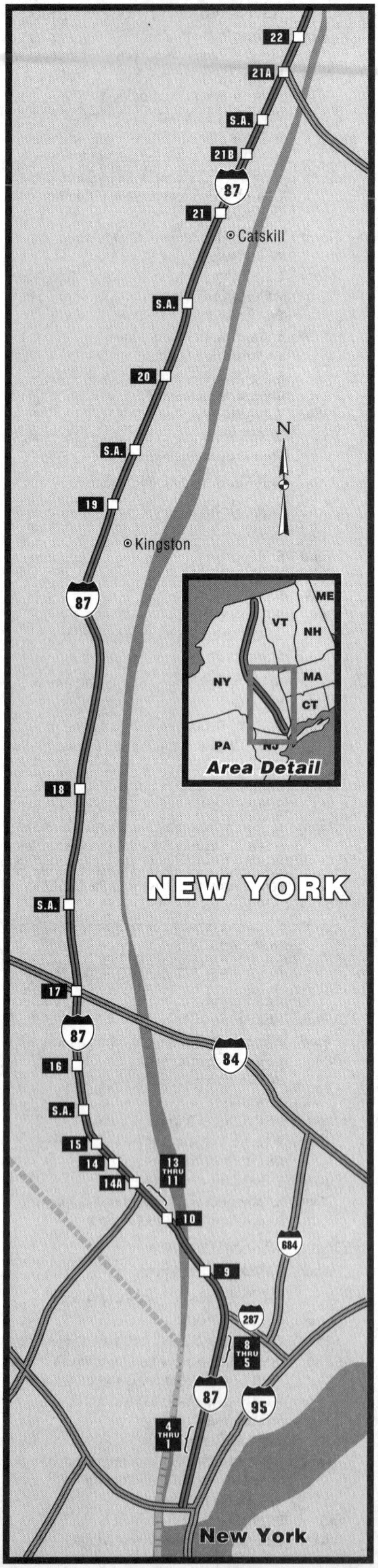

EXIT		NEW YORK
		W: Adair Winery (6 Miles), Baxter's Pharmacy, Coin Laundry, Eckerd Drugs, New Paltz Plaza, Rite Aide Pharmacy, Shoprite Grocery
(66)		Modena Service Area (Southbound)
	FStop	W: Mobil
	Food	W: Arby's, Carvel Ice Cream Bakery, Mama Ilardo's, McDonald's
	AServ	W: Mobil
	ATM	W: Onbank
(65)		Platekill Service Area (Northbound)
	FStop	W: Mobil
	Food	E: Bob's Big Boy, Nathan's Restaurant, Roy Rogers
	AServ	E: Mobil
	ATM	E: Onbank
17		(60) Junction I-84, NY 17K, Newburgh, Stewart Airport
	Gas	E: Getti's[*], Sunoco[*]
	Food	E: Banta's Steak & Stein, Burger King, Denny's, Monroe's Restaurant, Neptune Diner, Ramada Inn, Windmill Cafe, Yobo's Oriental
		W: Cake Bins, Diana's Pizza, Flower of the Orient, Pizza Hut, Plaza Deli, Shop Rite Grocery, Siam Restaurant
	Lodg	E: Days Inn, Hampton Inn, Holiday Inn, Ramada Inn, Super 8
	AServ	E: Meineke Discount Mufflers, Rizzo's
		W: Colandrea Pontiac, Buick, NAPA Auto Parts, Newburg Auto Parts, STS Tire & Auto, Sunshine Ford
	RVCamp	E: KOA Camping
	ATM	E: Hudson Valley Credit Union, Key Bank, Marine Midland Bank
		W: Bank of New York, First Hudson Valley Bank
	Other	E: Flannery's Animal Hospital, Lloyd's Convenience Store, Tourist Info., Wal-Mart

SPECIAL RATES FOR GROUPS
Howard Johnson Inn
1255 Route 17 South
Ramsey, NJ
201-327-4500
• Free Continental Breakfast
• Cable TV with HBO-ESPN
• Meeting & Conference Room
• Microwave & Refrigerator in Rooms
• Cocktail Lounge on Premises
• Restaurant on Premises
• Outdoor Swimming Pool • Free Local Calls
Free USA Today
Discount Rates for AAA, AARP, Senior, Corporate & Military
1218
NEW JERSEY ▪ I-87 ▪ EXIT 15

1327
Sheraton
RAMADA
Wellesley Inns
Look for these Lodging Locations at the exits below
EXIT
Sheraton 15* 201-529-1660
Ramada 15* 201-529-5880
Wellesley 14B 914-368-1900
* I-287 to Exit 66 in NJ

Bold red print shows RV & Bus parking available or nearby

EXIT	NEW YORK
	W: Ames Shopping Center, Rite Aide Pharmacy, Steve's Coin Laundry, Vision City
16	(45) U.S. 6, NY 17, Harriman
Gas	W: Exxon(*, D)
Food	W: Brookside Restaurant, Triangle Deli
Lodg	W: American Budget Inn
AServ	W: Rallye Chev, Buick
Other	W: Coin Laundry, Tourist Info., Woodbury Commons Factory Outlet
(33)	Ramapo Service Area
FStop	E: Sunoco
AServ	E: Sunoco
Other	E: Tourist Info.
15A	(31) NY 17N, NY59, Sloatsburg, Suffern
15	(30) NJ17S, Jct I-287S, New Jersey
Lodg	W: Sheraton (see our ad this page), Ramada (see our ad this page), Wellesley (see our ad this page), Howard Johnson (see our ad this page)
14B	(28) Airmont Rd, Montbello
14A	(23) Garden State Pkwy
14	(22) NY 59, Springvalley, Nanuet
13	(21) Palisades Pkwy, New Jersey, Bear Mountain (Passenger Cars Only)
12	(19) NY 303, W Nyack
11	(18) U.S. 9W, Nyack, S Nyack (Southbound)
Gas	W: Exxon, Texaco(*)
Food	W: KFC, McDonald's
Lodg	W: Super 8
AServ	W: Action Nissan, Exxon, J&L Auto & Tire Center, Jean's Auto Repair & Sales, Jiffy Lube, Midas Muffler & Brake
Med	W: + Hospital
(19)	Tappan Zee Bridge (Toll)
9	(13) U.S. 9, Tarrytown
8	(12) Jct I-287E, Cross Westchester Expressway, White Plains
7A	(11) Saw Mill River Pkwy (Passenger Cars Only)
7	(8) NY9A, Ardsley (Northbound, Reaccess Southbound Only)
(8)	Service Area (Northbound)
FStop	B: Sunoco
Food	B: Burger King, Roy Rogers, TCBY
(5)	Toll Plaza (Toll)
6A	(5) Cooporate Dr
6	(4) Tuckahoe Rd, Yonkers, Bronxville
4	(3) Cross County PKWY, Mile Square Rd
Gas	W: Sunoco, Texaco(*, D)
Food	W: Roy Rogers, Wild Cactus Cafe
AServ	W: Firestone Tire & Auto, Sunoco
ATM	E: Chase Manhattan Bank
Other	E: Mall at Cross Country
3	Mile Square (Northbound)
2	Yonkers Ave, Raceway (Northbound)
1	(0) Hall Place, McLean Ave

↑NEW YORK

Begin I-87

I-88 E →

EXIT	NEW YORK
	Begin I-88

↓NEW YORK

EXIT	NEW YORK
1	(0) NY7W, Binghamton
2	NY12A West, Chenango Bridge
AServ	N: Bridge Auto Care(*), By the Book Car Care(CW)
ATM	N: All Bank, Bridge Auto Care
Other	N: U.S. Post Office
3	(4) NY369, Port Craine
Gas	S: Discount Petroleum, Hess(*, D), Kwik Fill(*, LP)
ATM	S: Hess
Parks	N: Chenango State Park
Other	S: U.S. Post Office
4	(8) NY17E, Sanitaria Springs
FStop	S: Getty(*)
ATM	S: Getty
Parks	S: Nathanial Cole Park
5	(12) Martin Hill Rd, Belden
RVCamp	N: Belden Hill Campground (.75 Miles), Belden Manor
6	(16) NY79, Harpursville, Nineveh
RVCamp	S: Hawkins RV Jayco Dealer
Other	S: U.S. Post Office
7	(23) NY41, Aston
8	(29) NY206, Bainbridge, Masonville
FStop	N: Sunoco(*, CW, 24)
Food	N: Taco Bell (Sunoco FS)
Lodg	N: Riverside Motel
AServ	N: Parts Plus
RVCamp	N: Riverside RV Camping
ATM	N: NBT Bank, Sunoco
Parks	S: Oquaga Creek State Park
Other	N: US Post Office
9	(32) NY8, Sidney
RVCamp	N: Tall Pines Campground
Med	N: + Hospital
Other	S: Visit Otsego & Schoharie Counties - the heart of Leatherstocking Country (see our ad on Pg. 454)
10	(37) NY7, Unadilla
Other	N: State Police
(39)	Rest Area (RR, Phones, Picnic, Vending, Pet Walk; Eastbound)
11	(40) NY357, Unadilla, Franklin
RVCamp	N: KOA Campgrounds
(42)	Rest Area (RR, Phones, Picnic, Vending, Pet Walk; Westbound)
12	(46) NY7, Otego, Wells Bridge
FStop	S: Sunoco(*, D, LP)
Food	S: Sunoco
TServ	S: Sunoco
13	(53) NY205, to NY23W, Oneonta, Morris
Gas	N: Citgo(*)
Food	N: Citgo
AServ	N: Parts Plus

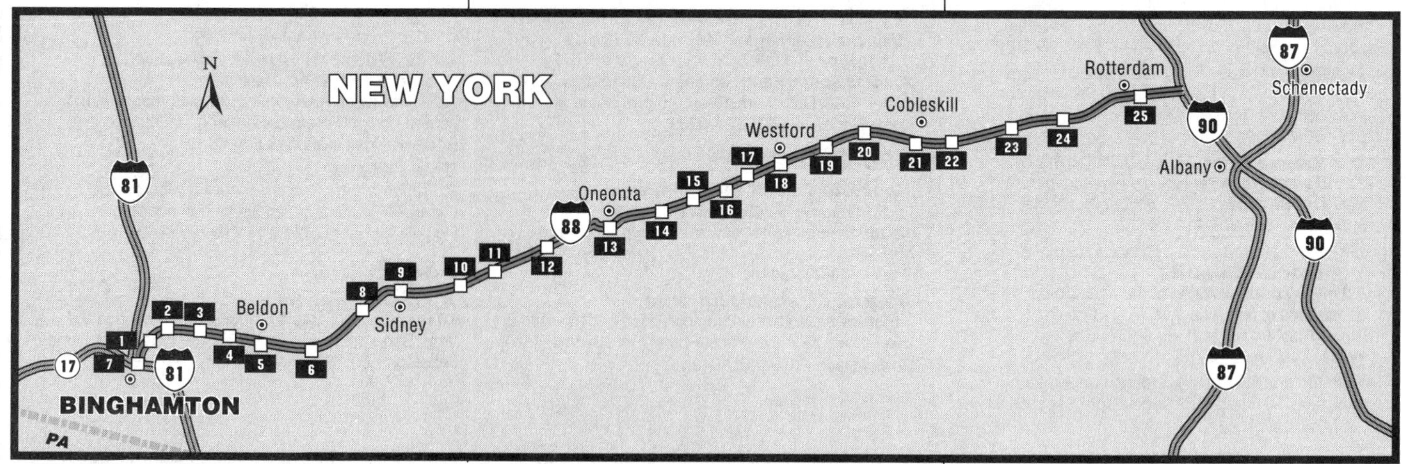

Bold red print shows RV & Bus parking available or nearby

THE TREASURES OF LEATHERSTOCKING COUNTRY

National Baseball Hall of Fame
Open all year
I-88 Exit 17

Fenimore House Museum
Open early spring to late fall
I-88 Exit 17

The Farmers' Museum
Open early spring to late fall
I-88 Exit 17

Here in Otsego & Schoharie Counties – the heart of Leatherstocking Country – we have two halls of fame and two prehistoric caverns. A multitude of museums and landmarks, opera and theater festivals, art galleries and historical reenactments. All in an area of unsurpassed beauty and charm.

Discover antiquing and camping, horseback riding and sailing, soccer and baseball games, Broadway shows and country fairs. Explore our country roads and quaint villages nestled in the rolling hills of Leatherstocking Country.

Our treasures are waiting for you, just minutes off Interstate 88. Come visit!

I ♥ NY®

Howe Caverns
Open all year
I-88 Exit 22

New York Power Authority
Open all year
I-88 Exit 23

OTSEGO & SCHOHARIE COUNTIES, NEW YORK

For information: **Otsego County Chamber** (Exits 12-19 of I-88, including Cooperstown) **800-843-3394**
Schoharie County Chamber (Exits 20-23 of I-88) **800-41-VISIT**

I-88 Exit 23

The Apple Barrel
0.5 miles south. The ultimate country store! Junction Route 30 and 30A, Schoharie • 518-295-7179

Schoharie Valley Farms
1.0 mile south. A farm for all seasons. Valley grown fruits, vegetables, etc. March - December, open daily. Route 30, Schoharie • 518-295-7139

George Mann Tory Tavern
1.5 miles south. A fully restored Colonial tavern. Intersection of Routes 443 and 30, Schoharie • 518-295-7128

Old Stone Fort Museum Complex
2.0 miles south. A century-old museum of rural New York life. Open May - October. North Main Street, Schoharie • 518-295-7192

Dr. Christopher S. Best Home & Medical Exhibit
8.0 miles south. Victorian home and office of two generations of family doctors. May - October. Route 145, Middleburgh • 518-827-4239

Barber's Farm
11 miles south. A family farming tradition for over 140 years. 50 varieties of vegetables in season. Route 30, Middleburgh • 518-827-5452

North Blenheim Covered Bridge
18 miles south. The longest single-span wooden covered bridge in the world. Route 30, North Blenheim.

Lansing Manor Museum
20 miles south. An elegant early-1800s country estate. Free. Memorial Day through Columbus Day. Route 30, North Blenheim • 800-724-0309

Blenheim-Gilboa Power Project Visitors' Center
20 miles south. Hands-on energy tour of the center. Free. Daily from 10 am - 5 pm. Route 30, North Blenheim • 800-724-0309

I-88 Exit 22

Caverns Creek Grist Mill Museum & Country Store
1.5 miles east. Water-powered flour mill built in 1816. May 15 - October 15. Route 7 to Caverns Road, Howes Cave • 518-296-8448

Iroquois Indian Museum
1.5 miles east. Outstanding collection of contemporary Iroquois artwork and crafts. Route 7 to Caverns Road, Howes Cave • 518-296-8949

Howe Caverns
2.5 miles east. Open all year. 80-minute guided tour includes a underground boat ride. Route 7 to Caverns Road, Howes Cave • 518-296-8900

Secret Caverns
4.0 miles east. Go underground to see a thundering 100-foot waterfall. May - October. Route 7 to Caverns Road, Howes Cave • 518-296-8558

Best Western Inn of Cobleskill and B.W. Delaney's
4.5 miles west. AAA-rated. Spacious rooms, indoor heated pool, on-premises bowling, restaurant. Route 7, Cobleskill • 518-234-4321

The Patent
2.5 miles south. Country shopping with old-time charm. Gifts and accessories for home & garden. Route 145, East Cobleskill • 518-296-8000

I-88 Exit 20

Buck Hill Farms
10 miles south. Maple products made right on the farm. Shop open year-round. Route 10 to Fuller Road, Jefferson • 607-652-7980

EXIT		NEW YORK
	RVCamp	N: Campground, Gilbert Lake State Park, Susquehanna Trail Campsites (1 Mile)
	ATM	N: Citgo
	Parks	N: Gilbert Lake State Park
	Other	N: Susquehanna Trail
14		(55) NY28S, Main St (Eastbound, Reaccess Westbound Only)
	Gas	N: Sunoco(*)
	Food	N: Alfresco's Italian, Golden Guernsey Ice Cream
	Med	N: ✚ Hospital
	Other	N: Coin Laundry
		S: Southside Animal Hospital
15		(56) NY23, NY28S, Davenport, Oneonta
	FStop	S: Red Barrel(*, CW)
	Gas	S: Getty(*, CW)
	Food	S: Christopher's Country Lodge, McDonald's, McDonald's (Wal-Mart), Neptune Diner(24), Perkins, Red Barrel, Sabatini's Little Italy, Taco Bell (Red Barrel), Wal-Mart(RX), Wendy's
	Lodg	S: Christopher's Country Lodge, Riverview Motel, Super 8
	AServ	S: Midas Muffler & Brake, Napa Auto, Wal-Mart
	TWash	S: Red Barrel(CW)
	Med	N: ✚ Hospital
	ATM	S: Hannaford Supermarket(RX), NBT Bank, Red Barrel
	Other	S: Aldi Grocery Store, Hannaford Supermarket(RX), Southside Mall, Wal-Mart(RX)
16		(58) Emmons, West Davenport
	Food	N: Farm House Restaurant
	Lodg	N: Master Host Inns
	Other	N: Eckerd Drugs(RX), Price Chopper Supermarket(RX)
17		(61) to NY7, NY28N, Colliersville, Copperstown
18		(70) Schenevus
(74)		Rest Area (RR, Phones, Picnic, Vending; Eastbound)
19		(76) to NY7, Worcester, East Worcester

EXIT		NEW YORK/ILLINOIS
	Gas	N: Stewart's Shop(*), Sunoco(*, D, CW)
	Food	N: Chris' Pizzeria, Stewart's Shop
	AServ	N: NAPA Auto Parts
	ATM	N: Stewart's Shop
(79)		Rest Area (RR, Phones, Picnic, Vending; Westbound)
20		(88) NY7, NY10S, Richmondville
	Gas	S: Mobil(*, D, LP)
	Food	S: Paisano's
	Lodg	S: 88 Motel
	RVCamp	S: Hi-View Campsites
	ATM	N: Bank of Richmond
		S: Mobil
21		(90) NY7, NY10N, Warnerville, Cobbleskill
	FStop	S: Hessmart
	Gas	S: Hessmart
	Food	N: Pee Wee's
		S: Hessmart
	AServ	N: Murray's, Warnerville Garage
	Med	N: ✚ Hospital
	Other	N: Post Office, SUNY Cobleskill P&C Foods
22		(95) NY7, NY145, Cobbleskill, Middleburgh
	FStop	N: Agway, Hessmart
	Gas	N: Hessmart, Mobil
	Food	N: Apollo Diner, Boreall's, Bull's Head Inn, Burger King, Cobleskill Diner, Dunkin Donuts, McDonald's, Pizza Hut, Taco Bell
		S: Best Western
	Lodg	N: Boreall's
		S: Best Western, Holiday Motel
	AServ	N: Roosevelt Towing
	RVCamp	S: Twin Oaks Campground
	Med	N: ✚ Hospital
	ATM	S: Bank of Richmond, Central National Bank, Trustco Bank
	Other	N: Howes Caverns, Iroquois Museum
		S: Police Station, Post Office, Wal-Mart
23		(101) NY7, NY30, NY30A, Schoharie, Central Bridge
	Gas	N: Red Barrel Conv. Store

EXIT		ILLINOIS
	Food	N: Valley Inn
		S: Dunkin Donuts
	RVCamp	N: Country Roads (25 mi), Hideway Campground, Locust Park (1 Mile)
	ATM	N: Bank of Richmond
24		(112) U.S. 20, NY7, Duanesburg
	Gas	N: Mobil(*)
	Food	N: Dunkin Donuts (Mobil)
	RVCamp	S: Frosty Acres Campground
	Other	N: State Police
25		(116) NY7, Rotterdam, Schenectacy (Toll)
(25)		Toll Booth (Toll)

↑NEW YORK

↓ILLINOIS

(1AB)		I-80W, Des Moines, I-80E, 74, Peoria
(2)		Former IL 2
(6)		IL92E, Joslin
	Other	S: Sunset Lake Camping (April-October)
(10)		Hillsdale, Port Byron
	FStop	S: Citgo(*, D, LP, K)
	Food	S: Cafe (Citgo), Citgo
	ATM	S: Citgo
(18)		Erie, Albany
(26)		IL 78, Morrison, Prophetstown
	Parks	N: Morrison State Park & Lyndon
(36)		US 30W, Rock Falls, Sterling
	RVCamp	N: Ruffit Park (.25 Miles)
		S: Crow Valley Campground (1 Mile)
	Med	N: ✚ Hospital
(41)		IL 40 Rock Falls, Sterling
	Gas	N: Blackburn, Casey's General Store, Clark(*, LP), Mobil(*)
	Food	N: Arthur's Deli, Bennigan's (Holiday Inn), Burger King(PLAY), First Wok Chinese, Gi Gi's Pizza, Holiday Inn, KFC, Long John Silver, McDonald's, Subway, The Red Apple Family
	Lodg	N: All Seasons Motel, Holiday Inn, Super 8
	AServ	N: Auto Zone Auto Parts, Blackburn,

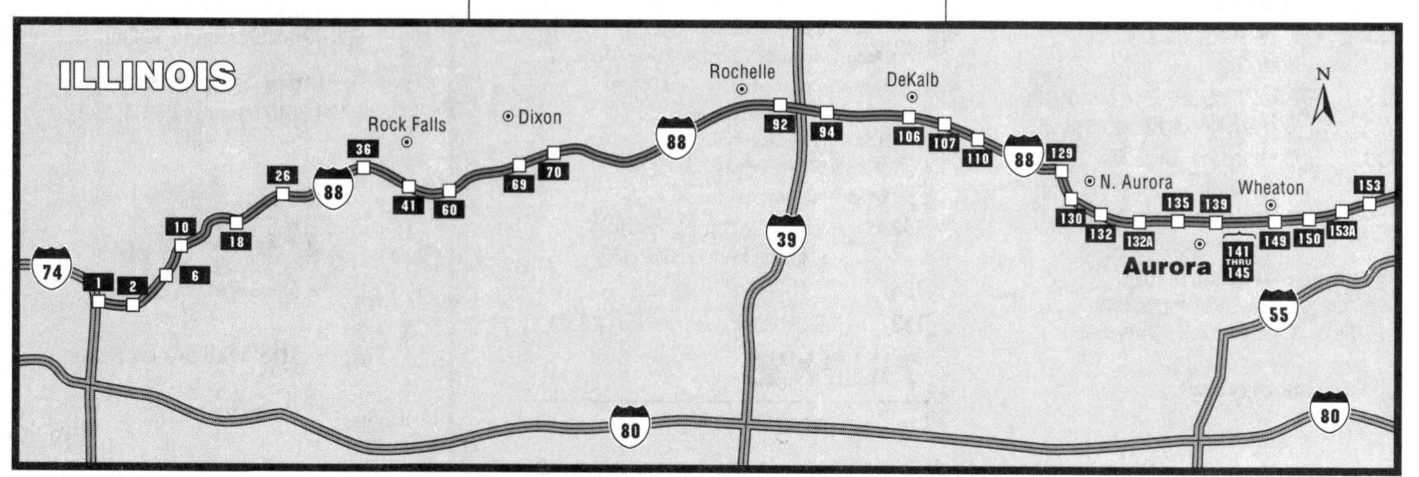

Bold red print shows RV & Bus parking available or nearby

EXIT ILLINOIS

Hall's After Collison, Kurtz Glass, Mark's Auto, Schreiner's Express Lube
TServ N: Brad Ragin Goodyear
Med N: ✚ Hospital
ATM N: Amcore Bank, Clark, Community State Bank, Mobil, Sterling National Bank
Other N: Eagle Country Market, President Reagan Birthplace, Sav A Lot Food Stores, Super Wash, Tru Value Hardware(LP), Wal-Mart(RX), WalGreens Pharmacy(RX)

(60) US 30, Rock Falls
RVCamp N: Camping

(69) IL 88 (Toll)

(70) IL 26, Dixon (Toll)
Lodg N: Comfort Inn, Motel 8
Other N: John Deer Historic Site, President Reagan Boyhood Home

(92) IL 251, Rochelle, Mendota
FStop N: Citgo(*, LP)
Gas N: 76(*, D), Shell(*)
Food N: Blimpie's Subs (Citgo), Citgo, I Can't Believe It's Not Yogurt, Rochelle Restaurant & Pancake House, Taco John (Citgo)
AServ N: Dodge City Of Rochelle, Fast Lube, Rochelle Auto Body, Thornton's Body Shop, Tom McClain Ford Mercury, Zips Auto Body
TServ N: Peter's GMC Truck (Goodyear)
Med N: ✚ Hospital
ATM N: Amcore Bank, Citgo
Other N: Coin Car Wash, Super Wash

(94) Jct I-39, US 51, Rockford, Bloomington/Normal (Difficult Reaccess)

(106) Dekalb Toll Plaza (Toll)

(107) IL38, IL23, Annie Glidden Rd., Dekalb

(108) Rest Area (P)

110 IL 38, Piece Rd. (Difficult Reaccess)

129 IL 56W, US 30, IL 47, Sugar Grove (Difficult Reaccess)

130 Orchard Rd. (Difficult Reaccess)
AServ N: Chrysler Auto Dealer, Fox Valley Ford Dealer, Saturn Dealership

132 IL31 Aurora, Batavia
Gas S: Mobil(*), Thornton Food Mart
Food S: Best Bet Gyro's, Bilias Restaurant, Denny's
Lodg N: Asbury Court

EXIT ILLINOIS

S: Howard Johnson
AServ S: Firestone Tire & Auto
Med S: ✚ Mercy Health Care Center
Other S: Lincoln Way Dental Center

132A Aurora Plaza Station

135 Farnsworth Ave.
Gas N: Amoco(*)
S: Marathon(*), Shell
Food N: Pappa Bear Restaurant
Lodg N: Motel 6
AServ S: Shell
Other S: White Hen Pantry

139 IL59
Gas N: 76(*), Amoco(*, CW)
S: Mobil(*, D)
Food N: Cafe 59
S: Adamo's Pizza,  Cracker Barrel, Danny's Grille, Golden Wok, Steak & Shake, Subway, Wendy's
Lodg S: Red Roof Inn, Sleep Inn
AServ N: Mr. Jim's Auto Care (76)
Other S: White Hen Pantry(*)

141 Winfield Rd.
Gas N: Amoco(*, CW), Mobil(*, CW)
S: Mobil
Food N: McDonald's (Amoco)
Lodg S: AmeriSuites (see our ad this page)

143 Naperville Rd.
Gas S: Mobil(*, CW)
Food N: Rio Bravo
S: Arby's, Bertucci's Brick Oven Pizza, Bob Evan's Restaurant, Buona Beef, Casa Lupita, McDonald's, Old Peking, T.G.I. Friday's, Wendy's
Lodg N: Radisson Hotel
S: Courtyard by Marriott,  Days Inn, Exel Inn, Fairfield Inn, Hampton Inn, Holiday Inn Select, TraveLodge, Wyndham Garden Hotel
Other S: Visit Naperville (see our ad this page)

145 IL 53, Bryant Avenue (Difficult Reaccess)
Gas S: Amoco(*, CW), Shell
Lodg S: Hyatt
AServ S: Amoco, Honda Volvo Dealer, Infiniti Dealer

149 Jct. I-355, Downer's Grove, Joilet

150 IL 56, Highland Ave, Downer's, Lombard, Butterfield Rd. (Difficult Reaccess)
Food N: Bakers Square Restaurant, Diamond Back Char House, Olive Garden
S: Highland Grill
Lodg N: Red Roof Inn
Med S: ✚ Hospital
Other N: Mall

153A IL83S, Oakbrook, Hindale (Difficult Reaccess)

154 Jct I-294

153 Oakbrook, Cermak Rd., IL83N

↑ ILLINOIS

Begin I-88

EXIT ILLINOIS

1276

Wondering where to call it a night?

NAPERVILLE

- Over a dozen hotel choices
- Over 100 dining choices
- Historic Downtown Shopping
- The Scenic Riverwalk
- Historic Naper Settlement

We work hard to make you want to stay awhile with our City Style and Small Town Smiles

Days Inn
630-369-3600 (Naperville Rd. Exit)
Excel Inn
630-357-0022 (Naperville Rd. Exit)
Fairfield Inn
630-577-1820 (Naperville Rd. Exit)
Hampton Inn
630-505-1400 (Naperville Rd. Exit)
Holiday Inn Select
630-505-4900 (Naperville Rd. Exit)
Sleep Inn
630-778-5900 (Route 59 Exit)
Naper Settlement
630-420-6010 (Naperville Rd. Exit)

Naperville Visitors Bureau
800-642-STAY

Illinois

Bold red print shows RV & Bus parking available or nearby

EXIT VERMONT

Begin I-89

↓VERMONT

22 **(130)** U.S. 7 South, Highgate Springs
- **Other** E: Duty Free Shop

21 **(123)** VT 78, to U.S. 7, Swanton
- **FStop** E: Exxon
- **Gas** W: Mobil(D), Sunoco(D), Texaco(*)
- **Food** W: Dunkin Donuts, McDonald's, Pam's Place, Rootie's, The Old My-T-Fine Creamery
- **AServ** W: NAPA Auto Parts
- **ATM** E: Exxon
  W: Mobil
- **Other** W: Grand Union Grocery Store

20 **(118)** U.S. 7, VT 207, St. Albans
- **Gas** W: Mobil(*), Shell(*)
- **Food** W: Burger King, Diamond Jim's Grill, Dunkin Donuts, KFC, McDonald's(PLAY), Pizza Hut, Royal Dynasty, Warner's
- **AServ** W: Ford Dealership, Handy Chevrolet/Olds
- **RVCamp** W: Camper's Plus
- **ATM** W: Franklin Lamoille Bank

19 **(114)** U.S. 7, VT 36, VT 104, St. Albans
- **FStop** W: Gulf(*)
- **Lodg** W: Comfort Inn
- **Med** W: ✚ Hospital

(111) Rest Area (Southbound)

18 **(106)** U.S. 7, VT 104A, Georgia Center, Fairfax
- **FStop** E: Mobil(*, D, 24), Texaco(*, D, CW)
- **Gas** E: Citgo(*)
- **Food** E: Citgo, Georgia Farm House Ice Cream, Michaeleo's Snack Bar
- **RVCamp** E: Homestead Campgrounds (.25 Miles)

17 **(98)** U.S. 2, U.S. 7, Lake Champlain Islands , Milton
- **Gas** E: Mobil, Texaco(*, D)
- **Food** E: Texaco
- **RVCamp** E: Campground
  W: Campground

(96) Weigh Station (Westbound)

(96) Weigh Station (Eastbound)

16 **(92)** U.S. 2, U.S. 7, to VT 15, Coalchester, Winooski
- **Gas** W: Go Go Gas, Texaco(*, D, CW)
- **Food** E: Lighthouse Restaurant, SHONEY'S Shoney's
  W: Junior's Pizza, Libby's Blue Line Diner, McDonald's, Rathskeller Pizza
- **Lodg** E: Hampton Inn
  W: Fairfield Inn, Hi-Way Motel, Motel 6
- **Other** E: Shaw's Supermarket

15 **(90)** VT 15, Winooski, Essex Jct (Northbound, Reaccess Southbound Only)
- **Gas** W: Exxon(*), Mobil(*)
- **Food** E: Bagel Factory
  W: Westside Deli
- **Lodg** E: DAYS INN Days Inn

14 **(89)** U.S. 2, Burlington, S Burlington
- **Gas** E: Citgo, Shell(*, D), Sunoco(CW), Texaco(D)
  W: Mobil
- **Food** E: Al's Burgers, Burger King, Cork & Board Restaurant, Dunkin Donuts, EconoLodge, Friendly's, Holiday Inn, Howard Johnson, KFC, Lee Zachery Pizzaria, McDonald's, Ramada Inn, Silver Palace Chinese, TCBY
- **Lodg** E: Anchorage Bank, Comfort Inn (see our ad this page), EconoLodge, Holiday Inn, Howard Johnson, Ramada Inn
  W: Sheraton

13 **(88)** Junction I-189, U.S. 7, Shelburn , Burlington (Difficult Reaccess)
- **Gas** E: Mobil, Texaco
- **Food** E: Bagel Bakery, Friendly's, Perry's Fish House, Pizza Hut

EXIT VERMONT

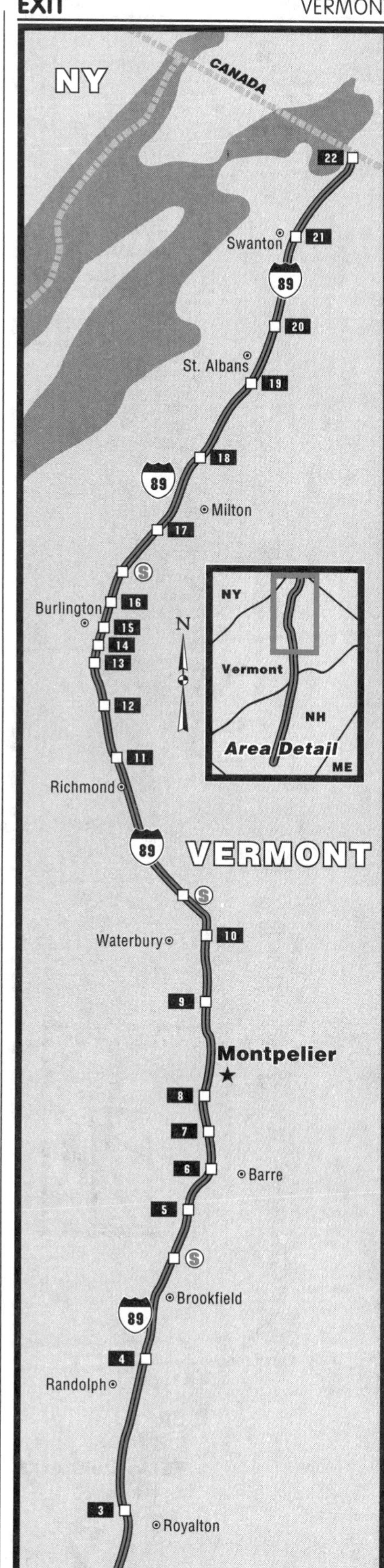

EXIT VERMONT

- W: Burger King, Hannaford Supermarket, McDonald's, Ponderosa Steak House
- **Lodg** E: Hawthorne Suites Hotel
  W: TraveLodge
- **Other** W: KMart

12 **(84)** VT 2A, to U.S. 2, Williston, Essex Jct
- **Gas** E: Mobil(*), Sunoco(LP, CW, 24)
- **Food** E: Better Bagel, Evergreen Eddie's, Friendly's, I Can't Believe It's Yogurt, Koval' Coffee Shop, Men at Wok Chinese, Mexicali Mexican, Pepperoni Pizza & More
- **Lodg** E: Susse Chalet
  W: Residence Inn
- **AServ** E: Sunoco(24)
- **RVCamp** E: Pete's RV Center (2 Miles)
- **Other** E: Mail Boxes Etc, Simons Deli & Grocery, TLC Laundrymat, VT State Police, Wal-Mart(RX)

(82) Rest Area (RR, Phones, Picnic, Vending, Pet Walk)

11 **(78)** U.S. 2 to VT 117, Richmond, Williston
- **Gas** E: Citgo(*, D)
  W: Mobil(*)
- **Food** E: Chequered House Motel
- **Lodg** E: Chequered House Motel
- **Other** E: Blue Flame Corp.(LP)

(67) Rest Area/Weigh Station (Eastbound)

10 **(64)** to U.S. 2, VT 100, Waterbury, Stowe
- **Gas** E: Exxon(*), Mobil(*, D)
  W: Citgo(*, D), Gulf(*)
- **Food** W: Crossroads Beverage & Deli, Great Wall Chinese, Lee Zachary Pizza House
- **Lodg** E: Batchor Brooks, Holiday Inn
  W: Stage Coach Inn
- **Other** E: Ben & Jerry Ice Cream Factory, Lots O'Suds Car Wash(CW)
  W: Car Wash, Ideal Market, Post Office

AWARD WINNING HOTELS!

New Hotel
1998 Gold Hospitality Award Winner
I-89 • Exit 19
St. Albans, VT
Inn & Suites
802-524-3300

- Free Deluxe Continental Breakfast
- Indoor Pool & Fitness Center
- Free Cable Television
- In Room Movies • Free Local Calls
- 100% Satisfaction Guaranteed

Mention this ad and 10% off

8 Gold Hospitality Awards!

I-89 • Exit 14E
S. Burlington, VT
802-865-3400

- Free Deluxe Continental Breakfast
- Free Local Calls • In Room Movies
- Coffee & Tea Served 24 Hours
- Cable with HBO/CNN
- Outdoor Heated Pool & Fitness Room
- 100% Satisfation Guaranteed
- Excludes UVM Graduation Weekend
- Space availability

1121

VERMONT ▪ I-89

EXIT		VERMONT
9		**(59)** U.S. 2 to VT 100B, Middlesex, Moretown
	Gas	**W:** Citgo (Towing)
	Food	**W:** Camp Meade Motor Inn
	Lodg	**W:** Camp Meade Motor Inn
	AServ	**W:** Citgo (Towing)
	Other	**W:** **Vermont State Patrol Post**
8		**(53)** U.S. 2, VT 12, Montpelier
	RVCamp	**E:** **Campground**
7		**(50)** to U.S. 302, VT 62, Barre, Berlin
	FStop	**E:** **Mobil**[*]
	Food	**E:** SHONEY'S, Shoney's
	Lodg	**E:** Comfort Inn
	Med	**E:** **+ Hospital**
	ATM	**E:** **Shaw's Supermarket**
	Other	**E:** **Shaw's Supermarket**
6		**(47)** VT 63, VT 14, South Barre
	RVCamp	**E:** **Campground**
5		**(43)** VT 64, to VT 12, to VT 14, Northfield, Williamstown
	RVCamp	**E:** **Campground**
(33)		**Weigh Station/Rest Area (both dir.)**
4		**(31)** VT 66, Randolph, to VT 12, VT 14
	Gas	**W:** Mobil[*]
	Food	**W:** McDonald's
	RVCamp	**E:** **Lake Champagne Campground (1.1 Miles)**
		W: **Campground**
	ATM	**W:** Mobil
3		**(22)** VT 107, Bethel, Royalton
	Gas	**E:** Texaco[*, CW]
	Food	**E:** Eaton's, Village Pizza
2		**(13)** VT 14, VT 132, Sharon
	Gas	**W:** Citgo[*]
	Food	**W:** Brooksie's Steak & Seafood
	Lodg	**E:** Half-Acre Motel
		W: The Columns Motor Lodge
	ATM	**W:** Citgo
	Other	**W:** **Post Office**
(9)		**Weigh Station/Rest Area (both dir.)**
1		**(4)** U.S. 4, Woodstock, Rutland
	Gas	**W:** Citgo[*], Mobil[*]
	RVCamp	**W:** **Pine Valley RV Resort[LP] (.5 Miles)**
	ATM	**W:** Mobil
(1)		Jct I-91, Brattleboro, White River Jct

↑VERMONT

↓NEW HAMPSHIRE

EXIT		NEW HAMPSHIRE
20		**(60)** NH 12A, West Lebanon, Claremont
	Gas	**E:** Mobil[*, LP], Sunoco[*]
		W: Citgo[D]
	Food	**E:** Boston Market Restaurant, Brick Oven Pizza, Einstein Bros Bagels, KFC, Shorty's Mexican Roadhouse, Subway, Taco Bell
		W: Applebee's, Burger King, China Lite Restaurant, Chinese Buffet, D'Angelo's, Denny's[24], Friendly's, Ice Cream Fore-You, McDonald's, Pizza Hut, Royal India Restaurant, TCBY, Weathervane Seafood, Wendy's
	Lodg	**W:** Economy Inn, Radisson
	Other	**E:** **Brooks Pharmacy, K-Mart[RX], Mail Boxes Etc, Shaw's Grocery**
		W: **CVS Pharmacy[RX]**, Car Wash, **Shaw's Grocery**
19		**(58)** U.S. 4, NH 10, Lebanon, Hanover
	Gas	**E:** Exxon[*, D], Mobil[*]
		W: Sunoco
	Food	**E:** Blimpie's Subs (Mobil), China Station, Little Caesars Pizza
	AServ	**E:** Flander's & Patch Ford, Honda
		W: Dave's Auto Repair, Robert's Auto Service (Towing), Sunoco
	Other	**E:** Coin Car Wash, **Coin Laundry, Grand Union Grocery Store[24]**

VERMONT

Randolph

Royalton

Lebanon

NEW HAMPSHIRE

New London

Concord

Area Detail

NY

Vermont

NH

ME

N

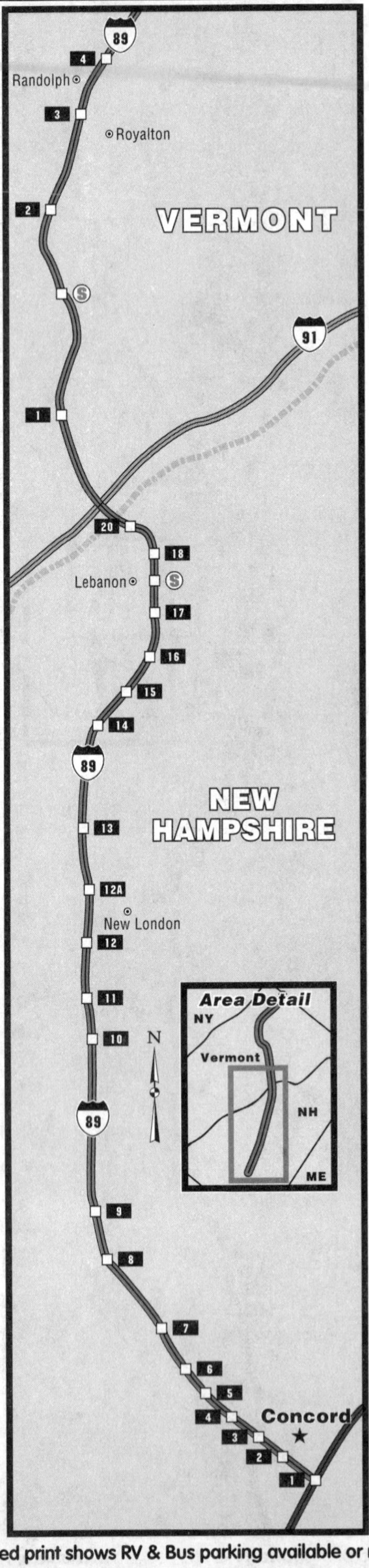

EXIT		VERMONT/NEW HAMPSHIRE
(56)		**Weigh Station (Westbound)**
(56)		**Weigh Station (Eastbound)**
18		**(56)** NH 120, Lebanon, Hanover
	TStop	**E:** **Boise Exit 18 TS**
	Gas	**W:** Citgo[*, D], Exxon[*]
	Food	**E:** **Boise Exit 18 TS**
		W: Bagel Basement, Chester's Fried Chicken (Exxon), Citgo, Peking Tokyo Chinese Restaurant, Village Pizza
	Lodg	**E:** Holiday Inn Express
	Med	**E:** **+ Hospital**
		W: **+ Hospital**
	ATM	**E:** Lake Sunapee Bank
		W: Lake Sunapee Bank
17		**(54)** U.S. 4, NH 4A, Enfield, Canaan
	Food	**E:** Riverside Grill
	AServ	**E:** **Exit 17 Auto & RV Repair, Northern States Tire**
	RVCamp	**E:** **Campground, Exit 17 Auto & RV Repair**
	Other	**E:** **Shaker Museum**
16		**(52)** Eastman Hill Rd, Purmort
	FStop	**E:** **Evans Exit 16 Truck Stop[*] (Exxon)**
	Gas	**W:** Mobil[D]
	Food	**E:** **Dunkin Donuts (Exxon), Pizza (Exxon)**
		W: Burger King (Mobil)
15		**(50)** Montcalm
14		**(48)** North Grantham (Southbound, Reaccess Northbound Only)
13		**(43)** NH 10, Grantham, Croydon
	FStop	**E:** **Gulf[LP]**
	Gas	**W:** Mobil[*] (Towing)
	Food	**E:** Doodels Diner
	AServ	**W:** Mobil (Towing)
	ATM	**W:** Lake Sunapee Bank, Sugar River Savings Bank
(40)		**Rest Area (RR, Phones, Picnic)**
12A		**(37)** Georges Mills, Springfield
	Parks	**E:** **Sunapee State Park**
12		**(35)** NH 11 West, New London, Sunapee
	Lodg	**E:** Maple Hill Farm Bed/Breakfast
	RVCamp	**W:** **Otter Lake Campground (.75 Miles)**
	Med	**E:** **+ Hospital**
11		**(31)** NH 11 East, King Hill Rd, New London
10		**(27)** to NH 114, Sutton
	Parks	**E:** **Winslow State Park**
		W: **Wadleigh State Park**
9		**(20)** NH 103, Warner, Bradford
	FStop	**E:** **Mobil[*, D]**
	Gas	**E:** Citgo[*, D, LP]
	Food	**E:** **McDonald's**, Pizza Hut (Citgo), Subway (Citgo), TCBY (Citgo)
	Other	**E:** **Market Basket**
8		**(17)** NH 103, Warner (Reaccess Southbound Only)
	Other	**W:** **Indian Museum**
7		**(15)** NH 103, Davisville, Contoocook
	RVCamp	**E:** **Campground**
6		**(11)** NH 127, Contoocook, W Hopkinton
5		**(9)** U.S. 202, NH 9, Keen, Henniker (Southbound, Left Exit Southbound, Difficult Reaccess)
4		**(7)** to NH 103, Hopkinton (Northbound)
3		**(4)** Stickney Hill Rd (Northbound, Reaccess Southbound Only)
2		NH 13, Clinton St, Concord
	Med	**E:** **+ Hospital**
	Other	**E:** **Cilly Veterinary Clinic**
1		Junction I-93, Concord, Logging Hill Rd
	Gas	**E:** Mobil[*]
	Food	**E:** The Grist Mill
	Lodg	**E:** Hampton Inn

↑NEW HAMPSHIRE

Begin I-89

Bold red print shows RV & Bus parking available or nearby

EXIT WASHINGTON

Begin I-90

↓WASHINGTON

2BC I-5 North, Vancouver, I-5 South Portland

3AB Rainier Ave. (No Reaccess)
- Gas **N:** Texaco(*)
  S: Citgo(*)
- Food **N:** May Hong, Pho & Banh Mi Saigon (Vietnamese), Stan's Fish & Chips
  S: Baskin Robbins, Burger King, Dong Vinh Co., Number One Ice Cream, Oh Boy Oberto, Toshio's Teryiaki
- AServ **N:** Budd & Co. Complete Auto Service
  S: A-1 Auto Body & Repair, Budd's Muffler City, Budget Batteries, Deere Auto, Valley Gear & Transmission Services
- Med **N:** ✚ **Family Dr. Medical Clinic**, ✚ **Pacific Medical Center**
  S: ✚ **Family Doctor Medical Clinic**, ✚ **Pacific Medical Center**
- ATM **S:** Citgo
- Other **N:** **Rainier Veterinarian Hospital**

6 West Mercer Way

7C To Mercer Island Only (Left Exit Eastbound)

7 Island Crest Way
- Gas **S:** Chevron(*), Texaco(D)
- Food **S:** Baskin Robbins, Chabela's Southwest Style Cuisine, Denny's, Gourmet Delight, McDonald's(PLAY), Natures Pantry, Pizza Man, Roberto's Pizza & Pizza, Seven Star Restaurant, Starbucks Coffee, Subway, Thai On Mercer, Toni Maroni's Pizza, Tully's Coffee, Zi Pani Breads Cafe
- Lodg **S:** TraveLodge
- AServ **S:** Simba's Auto Service, Texaco
- ATM **S:** InterWest Bank, Key Bank, U.S. Bank
- Parks **N:** **Luther Burbank Park**
- Other **S:** **Albertson's Grocery Store**, Auto Spa Car Wash, Looks Pharmacy(RX), Quality Food Center, **WalGreen's**(RX)

8 E. Mercer Way

9 Bellevue Way

10AB South I-405, Renton, Tacoma; North I-405, Bellevue, Everett, Fenton & Richard Rd.

11ABC 161st Ave. S.E., 156th Ave S.E., 150th Ave. S.E., 148th Ave. S.E.
- Gas **N:** Texaco(D, LP)
  S: 76(D, LP)
- Food **N:** Dairy Queen, East India Gate, Greenwood Mandarine Chinese Food, Gulliver's, Lil' Jon's Restaurant, McDonald's
  S: Baskin Robbins, Domino's Pizza, Outback Steakhouse, Pizza Hut
- Lodg **N:** DAYS INN Days Inn, Embassy Suites
- AServ **N:** Bellvue Mazda, Chaplan's Bellevue Subaru, Texaco, Village Quick Oil Change Center
  S: 76
- RVCamp **N:** **Trailer Inns (1 Mile)**
  S: **Trailer Inn**
- Other **N:** 711(*), **Arrowood Animal Hospital**, **Safeway Grocery**
  S: **Albertson's Grocery**(LP, RX), **Bosley's Pet Food**, Rite Aid Pharmacy(RX)

13 Southeast Newport Way, West Lake Sammanish Pkwy. S.E.

15 WA 900 East, Renton
- Gas **N:** Arco(*, 24)
  S: Texaco(*, CW)
- Food **N:** George's Subs, Holiday Inn, IHOP, O'char (Tai Cuisine), Tully's Coffee
  S: Acapulco Fresh Mexican, Baskin Robbins, Burger King, Cascade Garden Chinese, Georgio's Subs, Godfather's Pizza, Issaquah Cafe, McDonald's(PLAY), Toshi's Teryiaki, Tully's Coffee
- Lodg **N:** Holiday Inn, Motel 6
- AServ **S:** Autoworks of Issaquah, Bill's Auto Detail, Evergreen Ford Dealership, Express Tune, Firestone Tire & Auto, I M S Auto Parts, Issaquah Tire Service, Midas Auto Service, Mike's Issaquah Transmission Service, Speedy Auto Glass, United Auto Body
- RVCamp **S:** **Camping (4 Miles)**, **RV Service & Sales**
- Med **S:** ✚ **MedCare Medical Clinic**
- ATM **S:** U.S. Bank
- Parks **N:** **Lake Sammanish State Park**
- Other **N:** **Crown Books Superstore**, **Pickering Place Mall**
  S: **Look's Pharmacy**, **Meadows Cat Hospital**, **Quality Food Center**, Salmon Hatchery & Zoological Park, **The Ark Pet Supplies**, UPS, FedEx, Western Union Service, **Zoo**

17 Front St, E. Lake Sammamish Pkwy.
- FStop **S:** **Cenex**(*, LP)
- Gas **N:** 76(LP)
  S: Arco(*), Chevron(*), Shell(*, D, LP), Texaco(*, D, CW)
- Food **S:** Far Far's, Front Street Deli & Quick Stop, Skippers Seafood & Chowder, The Roost, X X X Root Beer Drive-In
- AServ **N:** 76
  S: Big O Tires, East Mobil Auto Glass, Gilman Auto Body, Issaquah Auto Tech, Issaquah Muffler & Brake, Mo's Automotive Service, Novus Windshield Repair Co., Precision Tune, Rob's Transmission Shop, Ruby's Towing Service (Arco), Shell, Taj Collision Center
- RVCamp **N:** **Issaquah Village RV**
- ATM **S:** Chevron, One Seafirst Bank, Texaco
- Other **S:** Issaquah Veterinarian Hospital, Road Star Car Wash, **Visitor Information**, Zoo

18 East Sunset Way (Westbound, Reaccess Eastbound Only)

20 High Point Way

22 Preston, Fall City
- Gas **N:** Chevron(*, D)
- Food **N:** Coffee Too, Savannah's Burger's
- AServ **N:** Joe Laranger's Automotive Center, Inc.
- RVCamp **N:** **Snoqualmie River (4.5 Miles)**
  S: **Blue Sky RV Park (.5 Miles)**

(23) **Weigh Station (All Trucks Must Exit When Open)**

25 WA 18 West, Auburn, Tacoma

27 Snoqualmie, North Bend (Eastbound, Reaccess Westbound Only)

31 WA 202 West, North Bend, Snoqualmie, Snoqualmie Falls
- Gas **N:** Chevron(*, D, CW), Texaco(*, D)
- Food **N:** Arby's, Blimpie Subs & Salads, Dairy Queen(PLAY), **McDonald's**, Mitzel's American Kitchen, Romio's Pizza & Pasta, Starbucks Coffee, Taco Time (Mexican), Yum Yang Chinese Restaurant
- ATM **N:** Chevron, Texaco, Washington Mutual
- Other **N:** **Factory Stores at North Bend**, **Safeway Grocery**(24, RX), **State Police**, **Visitor Information**

32 436th Ave. Southeast

34 Edgewick Road
- TStop **N:** **Seattle East Auto Truck Plaza**(*, SCALES)
- FStop **N:** **Texaco**(*, LP)
- Gas **N:** BP(*, D)
- Food **N:** **Ken's Restaurant (Seattle East TS)**, Pizza Hut (BP), **Subway (Texaco)**, Taco Bell (BP)
- Lodg **N:** Edgewick Inn, Norwest Inn Motel
- TServ **N:** **Cascade Diesel & Truck Repair-Cummins**, **Seattle East Auto Truck Plaza**(SCALES)
- TWash **N:** **Seattle East Auto Truck Plaza**
- RVCamp **N:** **Norwest Inn RV Park (.5 Miles)**
- ATM **N:** BP, **Seattle East Auto Truck Plaza**, **Texaco**

38 Fire Training Center

42 Tinkham Road

45 Lookout Point Road, USFS Rd 9030

47 Denny Creek, Asahel Curtis, Tinkham Rd.

52 West Summit (Eastbound)

53 Snoqualmie Pass Rec. Area
- Gas **S:** Chevron(*)
- Food **S:** Summit Inn, The Trading Post Deli & Pizza
- Lodg **S:** Summit Inn, The Summit
- Other **S:** **Time Wise Grocery & Deli**

54 Hyak Gold Creek

62 Stampede Pass, Lake Kachess

63 Cabin Creek Road
- RVCamp **S:** **Cabin Creek RV Park**

70 Easton, Sparks Road
- Gas **N:** Texaco(*, D, LP)
- Food **N:** Parkside Cafe (Texaco), Texaco
- AServ **N:** **Cascade Towing & Auto Repair**
- RVCamp **N:** **RV Town**
  S: **Lake Easton Campground (.25 Miles)**
- Parks **S:** **Lake Easton State Park (.5 Miles)**
- Other **S:** Sno-Park

71 Easton, Tree Farm Road
- Food **S:** CB's Motel
- Lodg **S:** CB's Motel
- AServ **S:** Easton Towing
- RVCamp **S:** **Rustic Villa Mobile Home & RV Park**
- Parks **S:** **Iron Horse State Park Trail Head**
- Other **S:** **CB's Grocery**(LP), Country Store, **John Wayne Trail Access**, **U.S. Post Office**

74 West Nelson, Sliding Road

78 Golf Course Rd.
- RVCamp **S:** **Sun Country Golf Resort**

(80) **Weigh Station**

80 Roslyn, Salmon, La Sac

84 South Cle Elum
- FStop **N:** **Pacific Pride Commercial Fueling**
- Gas **N:** Chevron(*, D, CW), Texaco(*, D, LP)
- Food **N:** Buttercup Restaurant, Caboose Tavern, Cavallini's Restaurant, Dairy Queen, El Caporal (Mexican), Fat Daddy's Pizza, Golden Ocean Chinese Restaurant, Jack-In-The-Bean Shop, Longhorn Steakhouse, Mama Vallone's Steakhouse, Stacone's (Pasta & Steaks), **Sunset Cafe**
- Lodg **N:** Ramblin' Rose Bed & Breakfast, Stewart Lodge, **Timber Lodge Inn**
- AServ **N:** Chevron, Kittitas County Glass, NAPA Auto Parts, Texaco
- RVCamp **N:** **Whispering Pines RV Park**(LP)
  S: **Whispering Pines RV Park & Service**(LP)
- ATM **N:** Chevron, Key Bank, Kittitas Valley Bank, Seafirst Bank
- Other **N:** **Cascade East Animal Clinic**, **Cle Elum Drugs**(RX), **Fairway Grocery**, Glondo's Sausage Company, **Information Center**, **Safeway Grocery**, Sundries Drugs & Gifts(RX), **U.S. Post Office**, **Valley Laundromat**

EXIT WASHINGTON

85 WA 970 N., WA 903, Cle Elum Wenatchee
- Food N: Homestead Restaurant BBQ
- Lodg N: Wind Blew Inn
- RVCamp N: RV Park Trailer Corral (1 Mile), Twin Pines RV Park & Drive-In (.5 Miles)
- Other N: Telephone Museum, Visitor Information

(89) Rest Area (RR, Phones, Picnic, RV Dump, P)

93 Elk Heights Road, Tannenum Creek

101 Thorp Hwy., Thorp
- Other N: Thorp Fruit & Antique Mall, Thorp Post Office

106 U.S. 97 N, Wenatchee, Ellensburg
- FStop N: Pilot Travel Center(*, SCALES)
- Gas N: BP(*), Chevron(*, LP, CW), Conoco(*)
- Food N: Blue Grouse Restaurant, Dairy Queen, Perkins Family Restaurant, Subway (Pilot)
- RVCamp S: KOA Campgrounds
- ATM N: Pilot Travel Center
- Other N: Clymer Museum, County Museum Historic District, Visitor Information
  S: Washington State Patrol

109 Canyon Road, Ellensburg
- TStop S: Flying J Travel Plaza(*, SCALES)
- FStop N: Exxon(*)
- Gas N: BP(*), Chevron(*), Shell(*), Texaco(*)
- Food N: Appleseed Inn Restaurant, Arby's, Baskin Robbins, Best Western, Bruchi's Cheesesteaks & Subs, Burger King, Casa de Blanca Restaurant (Mexican), McDonald's(PLAY), Ranch House Restaurant, Subway, Taco Bell
  S: Leaton's Family Restaurant, Sacks Restaurant (Flying J)
- Lodg N: Best Western, Comfort Inn, Super 8, The Inn At Goose Creek
- RVCamp S: Leaton's RV Park, R & R Resort Inn & RV Camp (.25 Miles)
- Med N: Hospital
- ATM N: BP, Shell, Texaco
  S: Flying J Travel Plaza, Leaton's Family Restaurant
- Other N: Big Apple Country Store, Museum & National Historic Resort

110 I-82 East, Yakima, South U.S. 97 (Difficult Reaccess)

115 Kittitas
- FStop N: Texaco(*, LP)
- Gas N: BP(*, LP)
- Food N: RJ's Cafe
- Parks N: Olmstead Place State Park

(126) Rest Area (RR, Phones, Picnic, P)

136 Vantage, Huntzinger Road
- Gas N: Conoco(*), Texaco(*, D)

EXIT WASHINGTON

- Food N: Blustery's, Golden Harvest Dining Lounge, The Wanapum Inn
- AServ N: Dean's Towing & Auto Service(LP)
- RVCamp N: KOA Campgrounds (.5 Miles)
  S: Getty's Cove Campground (4.1 Miles)
- ATM N: Conoco
- Parks S: Wanapum Recreation Area (3 Miles)
- Other N: Ginkgo Petrified Forest, The Store Grocery & Sporting Goods

137 WA 26 East, Othello, Richland, To WA 243

139 Scenic View (Westbound)

143 Silica Road

149 WA 281 North, George, Quincy
- FStop S: Exxon(*)
- Gas S: BP(*, LP)
- Food S: Martha Inn Family Dining, Subway (BP)
- TServ S: Bassetts Truck Repair(SCALES)
- RVCamp S: Post Road Trailor Court
- Med N: Hospital (12 Miles)
- ATM S: BP, Exxon
- Other N: The Gorge Amphitheater
  S: Visitor Information

151 WA 281 N., Quincy, Wenatchee
- FStop N: Texaco(*)
- Food N: Hot Stuffed Pizza (Texaco), Smash Hit Subs (Texaco)
- RVCamp N: Shady Tree RV Park
- Med N: Hospital (12 Miles)
- ATM N: Texaco
- Other N: Grand Coulee Dam

154 Adams Road

(161) Rest Area (P; Eastbound)

(162) Rest Area (RR, Phones, Picnic, RV Dump, P; Westbound)

164 Dodson Road
- RVCamp N: RV Park

169 Hiawatha Road

174 Mae Valley State Patrol
- RVCamp N: Suncrest Resort RV Park
  S: RV Park & Camping
- Other S: Mae Valley State Patrol

175 Moses Lake State Park, Mae Valley (Westbound)
- Parks N: Moses Lake State Park

176 Moses Lake, WA 171 North, Bus. I-90
- Gas N: BP(*), Texaco(*, D)
- Food N: Best Western, Kayoji's Japanese, Perkins Family Restaurant
- Lodg N: Best Western, Interstate Inn, Motel 6, Oasis Budget Inn, Super 8

EXIT WASHINGTON

  S: Lakeshore Motel
- AServ N: Affordable Auto Repair
- RVCamp N: Big Sun Resort (.75 Miles)
- Med N: Hospital

179 WA 17, Othello, Moses Lake, Ephrata
- TStop N: Ernie's Truck Stop(*, SCALES)
- Gas N: Arco(*), Conoco(*, D), Exxon(*, LP), Shell(*)
- Food N: Arby's, Bob's Cafe, Burger King, Denny's (Truck Parking Nearby), Ernie's Truck Stop, McDonald's (Truck Parking Nearby), Shari's Restaurant, Shilo Inn Motel
- Lodg N: Holiday Inn Express, Shilo Inn Motel
- RVCamp S: Burnham's RV Service, Mar Don Campground (15 Miles), Sun Country RV Service, Willows Campground (2 Miles)
- Med N: Hospital
- ATM N: Conoco
- Other N: Car Wash

(180) Rest Area (RR, Phones, Picnic, RV Dump, P)

182 Wheeler, "O" Road, N.E./S.E.

184 "Q" Road N.E./S.E.

188 Warden, "U" Road N.E./S.E.

196 Batum, Schrag, Deal Rd

(198) Rest Area (RR, Phones, Picnic, P)

206 WA 21, To U.S. 395, Lind, Odessa

215 Paha, Pachard

220 U.S. 395 South, Ritzville, Pasco
- FStop N: Cenex(LP), Exxon(*), Vista
- Food N: Jakes for Steaks Cafe(24), Texas John's Southern Style Restaurant
- AServ N: Chuck's Automotive Service & Towing, Les Schwab Tires, NAPA Auto Parts
- ATM N: Vista
- Other N: State Police

221 WA 261 South, Ritzville, Washtucna
- Gas N: Chevron(*), Shell(*), Texaco(*, D, LP)
- Food N: Crab Creek Cook House & Coffee Co., McDonald's (Chevron), Perkins Family Restaurant, Piccadilly's Pizza (Texaco), TCBY (Shell), Taco Bell (Shell), Zip's Drive-In
- Lodg N: Best Western
- RVCamp N: Best Western, Best Western Heritage Inn & RV Park
- Med N: Hospital
- ATM N: Chevron, Shell, Texaco
- Other N: Ritzville Historic Area, Visitor Information

226 Coker Road, Ritzville Access Truck Route
- RVCamp S: Camping

231 Tokio, Weigh Station (All Trucks

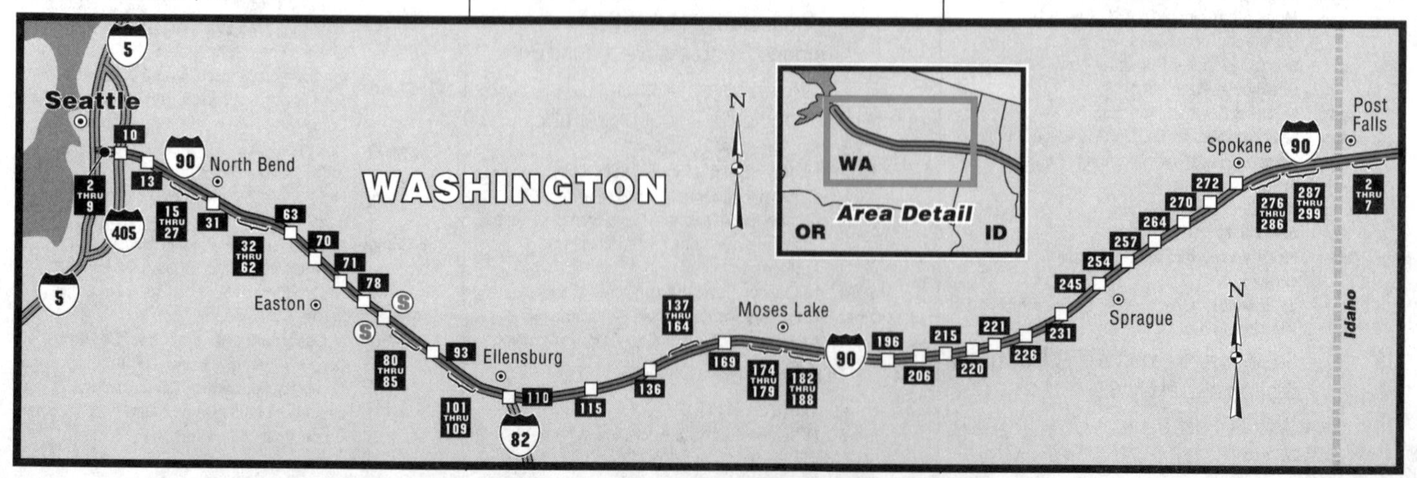

Bold red print shows RV & Bus parking available or nearby

EXIT	WASHINGTON
	Must Exit When Open)
Gas	S: Exxon(*, D, LP)
Food	S: Exxon
(242)	**Rest Area (RR, HF, Phones, Picnic, RV Dump, P)**
245	WA 23, Sprague, Harrington, Steptoe, Edwall, St. John
FStop	S: **Commercian Fueling Network**
Gas	S: Chevron(*, D)
Food	S: Cathy's Food & Gifts, Downtown Cafe, Maggie's Farm Cafe, The Rusty Rail Tavern, The Sprague Tavern, The Viking
Lodg	S: **Last Roundup Motel (.5 Miles)**, Purple Sage Motel
RVCamp	S: **Four Season Campground (1.25 Miles), Last Roundup Motel (.5 Miles), Sprague Lake Resort (2 Miles)**
ATM	S: U.S. Bank
Other	S: **Sprague Grange Supply**(LP), U.S. Post Office, Veterinarian Clinic
254	Fishtrap
RVCamp	S: **Fishtrap RV Camp**
257	WA 904, Tyler, Cheney
264	Cheney, Medical Lake, WA 902, Salnave Rd.
RVCamp	N: **Barber's Resort Campground, Clear Lake Campground, Connie's Cove Campground, Nallard Bay Resort (2 Miles)**
Parks	N: **Clear Lake Recreation Area, Clear Lake Recreation Area**
270	WA 904, Four Lakes, Cheney
Gas	S: Exxon(*)
Lodg	S: Saddle Inn
RVCamp	S: **Peaceful Pines (7 Miles)**
272	WA 902, Medical Lake
Gas	N: Texaco(*, D)
Lodg	S: **Super 8**
TServ	S: **Cummins Diesel & Thermal King, Freightliner**
TWash	S: **All American Truck Wash**
RVCamp	N: **Overland Station Campground**
	S: **Smokey Trails Campground, Yogi Bear Camp Resort (2 Miles)**
276	Geiger Field State Patrol
TStop	N: **Flying J Travel Plaza**(*, LP, SCALES)
Food	N: Denny's, **Lazy J Cafe, Subway (Flying J Travel Plaza)**
Lodg	N: Best Western, **The Starlite Motel**
RVCamp	S: **Hideaway Campground, Sunset Campground**
277	Airport, U.S. 2 W., Davenport (Difficult Reaccess)
Food	N: Sierra Mirage (Days Inn), Spokane House (Rodeway Inn)
Lodg	N: DAYS INN Days Inn, Hampton Inn, Motel 6, Rodeway Inn
279	U.S. 195 South, Colfax, Pullman (Limited Access)
280A	Maple Blvd.
Med	N: **+ Veteran's Hospital**
280B	Lincoln St (Westbound)
Gas	N: Chevron(*, CW), Conoco(*), Exxon(*)
Food	N: Burger King, Burger King, Coyote Cafe, Godfather's Pizza, Hot Stuffed Pizza (Exxon), IHOP, McDonald's, Senor Froggy (Mexican), TCBY (Exxon), Taco Bell, Taco Bell, The Shack Restaurant, Wendy's, Zip's Burgers
Lodg	N: Collins Hotel, Trade Winds Motor Inn
AServ	N: Barton Olds, Cad, GMC, Big O Tires, Car Quest Auto Parts, Downtown Toyota, Honda, Master Mechanics, Mechanic's Pride Auto Service, Napa Auto, Safelite Auto Glass, Saturn of Spokane, Southerland Motors Mercedes Benz, Toyota
Med	N: **+ Hospital**
ATM	N: Chevron, Conoco, Exxon, Washington Trust Bank
Other	N: Minimart
281	U.S. 2, Newport, U.S. 395 Colville
Gas	N: Conoco(*), Shell(CW), Texaco(D)
Food	N: Arby's, Best Western, Dick's Hamburgers, Doodle's Restaurant, Just Like Home Restaurant, Rancho Chico Restaurant, Taco Time, Waffles n More
Lodg	N: Best Western, Howard Johnson Express
AServ	N: America's Home for Car Service, Les Schwab Tires, Shell
Med	S: **+ Fifth & Browne Medical Center, + Sacred Heart Medical Center**
ATM	N: Kwik Mart
Parks	N: **Riverside State Park (10 Miles)**
Other	N: **Arena**, Kwik Mart, **Visitor Information**
282A	Trent Ave, Hamilton St. (Difficult Reaccess)
282B	Second Ave. (Difficult Reaccess)
Gas	S: Shell(*, D, LP)
Food	S: Shogun Japanese Steak & Seafood
Lodg	S: Shilo Inn
AServ	S: Perfection Tire Co.
ATM	S: Shell
Other	S: Antique Mall, Kosco's Wholesale
283A	Altamont St.
Gas	S: Circle K(*)
283B	Freya St., Thor St. (Reaccess Eastbound Only)
FStop	N: **Pacific Pride Commercial Fueling**(LP)
Gas	N: Chevron(*, CW), Conoco(D)
	S: Citgo(*), Texaco(*)
Food	N: Peking Garden (Chinese, American), Ron's World Famous Hamburger, Subway, The Otto
	S: Taco Bell Express (Texaco), Total Health Center
AServ	N: Alternative Auto Center & Accessories, Spokane Transmissions
TWash	N: **Pacific Pride Commercial Fueling**
RVCamp	S: **Park Lane Motel & RV Park**
ATM	N: Chevron, Washington Trust Bank
	S: Citgo
284	Havana St (Reaccess Westbound Only)
Food	N: Baskin Robbins, Grocery Outlet, Little Caesars Pizza (K-mart), McDonald's(PLAY), Southeast Oriental Express & Cafe
Lodg	N: **Park Lane Motel & RV Park**
AServ	N: American Radiator, BJ's Muffler Shop, **K-Mart**(RX), Poor Boy's Custom Wheels & Tires, Schucks Auto Supply
RVCamp	N: **Park Lake RV Park (.25 Miles)**
	S: **Camping (1.5 Miles)**
Other	N: FedEx World Service Center, **K-Mart**(RX), Northern Energy Propane(LP), Wash House Laundromat
285	Sprague Ave (Reaccess Eastbound Only)
FStop	N: **Texaco**(*), **Thunderbird**
Food	N: Denny's
	S: Taco Time, Zip's Hamburger Drive-In
AServ	N: Alton's Tires
	S: Al's Auto Supply, Alton's Tire, Bob's Transmission Service, C & L Tire & Wheel, C & T Body & Frame, J and F Automotive, Jaremko Nissan, River City Auto Glass, Spokane Chrysler Plymouth
TServ	N: **Sound Tire, Titan Truck**
RVCamp	N: **By-Rite RV, Quality RV Service, Ray's RV Service**
	S: **L & L RV Service, Milestone RV Center**
Other	N: East Wind Pet Wellness Clinic, Entenmann's Bakery Outlet, Snyder Bakery
	S: TLC Veterinary Clinic
286	Broadway Ave, Interstate Fair-grounds
TStop	N: **Flying J Travel Plaza**(*, LP, SCALES)
Gas	S: Citgo(*)
Food	N: My Place Bar & Grill, Zip's Family Drive-In
Lodg	N: **Broadway Motel, Comfort Inn**
AServ	S: Kimpson's Collision & Alignment Center
TServ	N: **Allison Transmissions, Flying J Travel Plaza**(SCALES), **Husky International Trucks, Peterbilt Dealer, Transport Equip. Volvo, Cummins, Detroit Diesel, Williams Equipment Co. Kenworth**
ATM	S: Citgo
Other	N: Ferrellgas(LP)
287	Argonne Road, Millwood
Gas	N: Holiday(*, D, LP)
	S: BP(*, D), Chevron(*, LP), Exxon(*)
Food	N: Burger King(PLAY), Denny's, Goodtymes Pub, Jack-In-The-Box, Longhorn BBQ, Marie Callender's Restaurant, Max's Itilian Subs, McDonald's(PLAY), Papa Murphy's, Subway, Taco Bell Express (Holiday), The Farmer's Patio, Wolffy's Rockin' 50's
	S: Casa De Oro (Mexican), Godfather's Pizza, Isaac's Frozen Yogurt, Little Caesars Pizza, Perkins Family Restaurant, Sub Stop Sandwiches (Chevron), Tokyo Teriyaki
Lodg	N: Motel 6, Super 8
	S: Holiday Inn Express, Quality Inn
AServ	N: Shuck's Auto Supply
	S: Precision Tune Auto Care, Quaker State Oil & Lube
ATM	N: F and M Bank, Holiday, Tidyman's Food Market(RX)
	S: **Safeway Grocery**(24, RX)
Parks	N: **State Park**
Other	N: ACE Hardware(LP), Coin Op Laundry, **Super Save Drugs**, The Journal L.D.S. Bookstore, Tidyman's Food Market(RX)
	S: Rite Aid Pharmacy, **Safeway Grocery**(RX), **The Book Exchange**
289	WA 27 South, Pines Road, Indiana Ave.
Gas	N: Citgo(*)
	S: BP(*, CW), Shell(*, D, LP)
Food	N: Derringer's Grog & Grill, Take a Break Restaurant & Lounge
	S: Applebee's, Jack-in-the-Box, Tully's To Go (Shell)
Lodg	S: Best Western
AServ	N: Central 4 Wheel Drive
	S: Shell
TServ	N: **Detroit Diesel, Edward's Engine Rebuilders Inc.**
Med	N: **+ Valley Young People's Clinic**
	S: **+ Natural Medical Clinic, + Valley Hospital & Medical Center**
ATM	N: Citgo
	S: New Century Bank
Other	S: **Hander Eye Clinic**, Spokane Eye Clinic
291	Sullivan Road, Veradale, Indiana Ave.
Gas	S: Chevron(*, CW), Texaco(*, D, LP)
Food	N: Toni Romas
	S: Double Tree Hotel, Espresso Shack, Jack-in the-Box, McDonald's(PLAY), **McDonald's (Wal-Mart)**, Noodle Express Teryaki Bowls, Schlotzsky's Deli
Lodg	S: Comfort Inn, Double Tree Hotel
AServ	S: **Wal-Mart**(RX) **(Vision Center)**

EXIT — WASHINGTON/IDAHO

RVCamp S: Bell RV (.75 Miles)
Med S: ✚ Valley Medical Center
ATM S: Chevron, Spokane Railway Credit Union
Other N: Hanson Center, Spokane Valley Mall
S: Wal-Mart[RX] (Vision Center)

293 Barker Road, Greenacres
TStop N: GTX Truckstop[*]
Lodg N: Alpine Motel
RVCamp N: Alpine RV Park, KOA Campgrounds (1 Mile)
S: Northwest RV Service, Spokane Gun Club & RV Park (1 Mile)
ATM N: GTX Truckstop

294 Sprague Ave, Business Rte. (Westbound, Reaccess Eastbound Only)

296 Liberty Lake, Otis Orchards
Gas N: Shell[*, D, LP]
S: BP[*, LP], Chevron[*, D, LP, CW]
Food N: Restaurant, Sidewok Oriental Cafe Express, Sports World, Subway (Shell)
S: 10th Hole Bar & Grill, Burger King[PLAY], Fitzbillies Bagels, McDonald's[PLAY], Papa Murphy's Pizza
ATM N: Shell
S: Albertson's Food Store[24, RX], Seafirst Bank, United Security Bank
Other S: Albertson's Food Store[RX]

(299) Weigh Station, Port of Entry (RR, Phones, Picnic, P)

299 Rest Area, Port of Entry, Idaho Road, State Line (P)

↑WASHINGTON
↓IDAHO

2 Pleasant View Road, Race Track, Seltice Way
TStop N: Flying J Travel Plaza[*, LP, SCALES]
Gas N: Texaco[*]
S: Exxon[*]
Food N: Burger King[PLAY], McDonald's[PLAY], Subway, Tora Viejo (Mexican)
S: Jack-In-The-Box, Michel's Restaurant, Riverbend Grill Food & Spirits
Lodg N: Howard Johnson's Express Inn, Suntree Inn
S: Riverbend Inn, Sleep Inn
AServ N: All Tune & Lube
TServ N: Larry's Truck Tire Service
TWash N: Splash 'N' Dash Truck/RV Wash
RVCamp N: All Tune & Lube, Splash 'N' Dash Truck/RV Wash, Splash n' Dash RV Wash, Suntree RV Park
ATM N: Flying J Travel Plaza, Texaco
S: Exxon
Other S: Factory Outlets, Prime Outlets at Post Falls (see our ad this page)

5 Spokane Street, Treaty Rock
FStop S: Pacific Pride
Gas N: BP[*, D, CW], Texaco[*, D]
S: Handy Mart[*]
Food N: Andy's Pantry Family Dining[24], Bagel Works, Bobby's Cafe, Down the Street Family Restaurant, Little Rascal's Pizza, McDuff's Restaurant, Rob's Seafood & Burger
S: Waffles n More
Lodg S: Best Western
AServ N: Les Schwab Tire Center, Parts Plus, Perfection Tire Co.
S: Banner Auto Parts & Supply, Performance Specialty Auto Repair
RVCamp S: RV Service
ATM N: BP, Texaco, Wells Fargo

EXIT — IDAHO

Parks S: Falls Park, Treaty Rock Park
Other N: Spencer's Excel Foods, St. Vincent Books & More Store, Sub Shop Laundromat
S: Centennial Trail, Post Falls Police Department, Visitor Information

6 Bus. Loop I-90, Seltice Way, City Center (Reaccess Eastbound Only)
Gas N: Citgo[*, 24], Exxon[*, RV DUMP]
Food N: La Cabana Mexican, Paul Bunyan Famous Hamburgers, Pizza Hut, The Falls
S: Arby's, Godfather's Pizza, Hot Rod Cafe, Little Caesars Pizza, McDonald's[PLAY], Papa Murphy's Pizza, Subway, Taco Bell
AServ N: NAPA Auto Parts
S: Al's Auto Supply, Jiffy Lube
RVCamp N: Camping
S: Traveland RV Service
Med N: ✚ North Idaho Immediate Care Center
ATM N: Citgo, First Security Bank, Mountain West Bank, Super One Foods[24, RX], U.S. Bank
S: Tidyman's Northwest Fresh Market, Washington Trust Bank
Other N: Post Falls Eye Clinic, Super One Foods[RX], Treaty Rock Historic Site
S: Animal House, Little Mo's Optical, Tidyman's Northwest Fresh Market

7 ID 41, Rathdrum, Spirit Lake
Gas N: Exxon[D, LP]
S: Chevron[*, D]
Food S: Casey's Restaurant & Brewery, KFC
TServ N: Astro Starter & Alternator Repairs
S: Truck Parts Full Service Truck & RV Repair
RVCamp N: Camping, Valley RV Repair
S: Ross Point Truck Repair (.2 Miles), Seltice RV Sales (Frontage Rd), Truck Parts, Truck Parts Full Service Truck & RV Repair
ATM N: Exxon

(9) Rest Area, Port of Entry, Weigh Station (P)

11 Northwest Blvd, Apple Way
Gas N: Country Quik Stop[*]
Lodg S: DAYS INN Days Inn(see our ad this page)
RVCamp S: Boulevard Motel & RV Park, Ray's RV Service[LP], Robin Hood Campground & RV Park (1.5 Miles)
ATM N: Country Quik Stop

PRIME OUTLETS
POST FALLS
Over 60 Outlet Stores and Food Court
Mikasa • Levis • Bass
Ask for your **FREE COUPON BOOK**
1867
208-773-4555
IDAHO • I-90 • EXIT 2

Friendliest Staff in Coeur d'Alene
1398

2200 Northwest Blvd • Coeur d'Alene, ID 83814
Free Deluxe Continental Breakfast & Local Calls
Hot Tub and Sauna • Exercise Room
Pets Welcome • Large Vehicle Parking
Interior Corridors
2 Minutes From Downtown
& Lake Coeur d'Alene
208-667-8668 • 800-DaysInn
Idaho • I-90 • Exit 11

EXIT — IDAHO

S: First Bank & Trust Co.

12 U.S. 95, Sandpoint, Moscow
Gas N: Chevron[*], Holiday[*, D], Shell[*, D, LP]
Food N: Arby's, Bagel B's, Burger King, Coeur D'Alene Inn, Dragon House Restaurant, Fitzbillies Bagels, JB's Restaurant, Jungle Juice, Log Cabin Restaurant, McDonald's, Paddy's Chicken To Go, Pastry & More, Pelican's Restaurant, Perkins Family Restaurant, Pizza Hut, Rosauers Family Restaurant, Taco Bell, Thai Palace (Asian Foods), The Back Door Sport Pub & Grill, The Pizza Shoppe, Tomato Street Italian Restaurant
S: Figaro's Italian Restaurant, Jack-In-The-Box, Mr. Steak, Schlotzsky's Deli, Sea Of Subs, Shari's Restaurant, Spokandy Chocolates & Ice Cream, Starbucks Coffee, TCBY, The Bagel Basket
Lodg N: Budget Host, Coeur D'Alene Inn, Comfort Inn, Motel 6, Shilo Inn, Super 8
S: AmeriTel Inn, Inn America (see our ad this page)
AServ N: Big O Tires
TServ S: Kootenai Chiropractic Clinic
RVCamp N: Foretravel (see our ad this page)Shady Acres & Tamarack RV Parks
Med S: ✚ Kootenai Medical Center
ATM N: Bank of America, Holiday, Rosauers Food & Pharmacy[24, RX]
S: Albertson's Grocery[24], First Security Bank, Mountain West Bank
Other N: Antiques, Appleway Car Wash, Northern Lights Mall, Rosauers Food & Pharmacy[RX]
S: Albertson's Grocery, Cour D' Aleane Eye Clinic, Little Mo's Optical, North Idaho Cancer Center, Rite Aid Pharmacy[RX], Shop Ko Supermarket[RX] (Optical), Wild Waters Waterslide Park

13 4th St, City Center

1453

A BUDGET MOTEL
702 21st Street • Lewiston, ID 83501
ID Newest Budget Motel
Family Suites
King Size Beds
Outdoor Heated Pool
Dataport/Modem Hookups
Security Cameras & Card Key Locks
Free Cable TV with HBO
Food Court with Full Vending
Coin-Operated Guest Laundry Facility
75% Smoke Free
Fax & Copy Service
Valet Laundry Service
Free Local Calls
24 Hour Front Desk
Directions: I-90, Exit 12 Highway 95
208-746-4600
Toll Free Reservations:
800-469-INNS
IDAHO • I-90 • EXIT 12

Bold red print shows RV & Bus parking available or nearby

EXIT	IDAHO
FStop	S: Exxon(*, LP)
Gas	N: Citgo(*), Conoco(*, D), Exxon(*, D, LP)
Food	N: Baskin Robbins, Bruchi's Cheesesteaks & Subs, Dairy Queen, Davis Muffins & Donuts, Denny's, Godfather's Pizza, Hot Stuffed Pizza (Conoco), IHOP, Java Hut, KFC, Little Caesars Pizza, Taco John's, Topper Too, Wendy's S: Hunter's Bar & Grill, Subway
Lodg	N: Fairfield Inn
AServ	N: Alton's Tires & Mufflers, Atlas Automotive, Auto Express (Montgomery Ward), Kelly's Tires, Lake City Auto Body Service, Les Schwab Tire Center, Montgomery Ward, NAPA Auto Parts, Schuck's Auto Parts, Silver Lake Auto Body & Paint, The Independent Auto Service & Repair S: Car Quest Auto Center, Coeur D' Alene Lube Center, Knudtsen's Chev, Geo, Ponderosa Motors
RVCamp	N: Erickson's RV Camp & Rental
ATM	N: Well's Fargo
Other	N: Hastings Books, Music, & Video, Montgomery Ward, Wonder Bakery Thrift Shop
14	15th St
15	Bus Loop I-90, City Center, Sherman Ave., Fernan
FStop	S: Exxon(*, LP)
Gas	S: Cenex, Piggie's Gas Mart(*)
Food	S: Cal-Bob's BBQ, Chillers, Chuck Wagon Cafe, Cove Bowl, Eduardo's Mexican Restaurant, Tubs
Lodg	S: Cedar Motel & RV Park, El Rancho Motel, Holiday Inn Express, Holiday Motel, Lake Drive Motel, Monte Vista Motel, Sundowner Motel, The Bates Motel
AServ	S: American Computune
RVCamp	S: Cedar Campground, Cedar Motel & RV Park, Monte Vista RV Park
Other	N: Ranger Station-Idaho Panhandle National Forest, Visitor Information S: Animal Medical Center
17	Mullan Trail Rd.
22	ID 97, Harrison, Wolf Lodge District, St. Maries, Coeur D' Alene Scenic Byway
Lodg	N: Wolf Lodge Creek Bed & Breakfast, Wolf Lodge Inn
RVCamp	N: Wolf Lodge Campground (1.75 Miles) S: KOA Campgrounds (.5 Miles), Squaw Bay Resort (7.5 Miles)
Other	S: Wolf Lodge Bay
(27)	Parking Area (Westbound)
28	4th of July Pass Recreation Area
Other	S: The Mullin Tree Historical Site
(32)	Parking Area (Westbound)

1057

Foretravel Northwest, Inc.

MOTORHOME
SALES • SERVICE • PARTS

Directions: I-90 exit #12 (Hwy 95 N) Go 3½ miles Nouth on Hwy 95 to Canfield Street. Turn Right 1 block to North Government Way. Turn Left 3 blocks.

7416 N Government Way • Coeur d'Alene, ID 83814
800.945.8561

EXIT	IDAHO
34	ID 3, Rose Lake, St. Maries, White Pines Scenic Route
FStop	S: Conoco(*, LP)
Gas	S: Rose Lake General Store(*)
Food	S: Country Chef Cafe
39	Old Mission State Park
Parks	S: Cataldo Mission National Historic Site, Old Mission State Park
40	Cataldo
Lodg	N: Cataldo Inn
RVCamp	S: Coeur D'Alene River RV Park
43	Kingston, Prichard, Coeur D' Laene River Rd., French Gulch
Gas	N: Texaco(*, D)
Parks	N: National Forest Access
45	Pinehurst
Gas	S: Chevron(*, LP), Conoco(*, D), Pat's Carousel
AServ	S: Chevron, Pat's Carousel
RVCamp	S: KOA Campgrounds, Pinehurst RV Sales(LP)
Other	S: Kohal Pharmacy, Laundry XPress (Coin & Dry Clean), Pinehurst Animal Farm & Supply
48	Smelteville
FStop	N: Silver Valley Car & Truck Stop
Food	N: Buffalo Nickel Bar & Grill S: A.J.'s Cafe
RVCamp	N: Buffalo Nickle RV Park, White's Buffalo RV Park
Other	S: Empire Store, U.S. Post Office
49	Bus. Loop 90, Bunker Ave, Silver Mountain
Gas	N: Chevron(*)
Food	N: Chester Fried Chicken To Go (Chevron), McDonald's, Sam's Cafe Deluxe, Silver Horn Motor Inn, Subway
Lodg	N: Silver Horn Motor Inn S: Motel 6, Silver Mountain Motel
Med	N: + Immediate Care Center, + Kellogg Medical Clinic, + Shoshone Medical Care Center
ATM	N: Chevron
Other	S: Museum
51	Bus. Loop 90, Division St, Wardner
Gas	N: Conoco(*, D), Jack's(*)
Food	N: Broken Wheel Restaurant, Humdinger Drive-In S: Inland Lounge, Kopper Keg Pizza, Meister Burgers, Wah Hing Restaurant (Chinese), Zanys Pizza
Lodg	N: Motel 51, Trail Motel S: McKinley Inn
AServ	N: Dave Smith Chev, Pont, Olds, Buick, Cad, GMC Trucks, Les Schwab Tires, NAPA Auto Parts, Stovern Supply Co. S: Reco's Muffler & Repair
TServ	N: Les Schwab's Truck Tire Service
ATM	S: First Security Bank, U.S. Bank
Other	N: Kellog Animal Hospital, Shoshone Glass, Stein's IGA Grocery, Sunnyside Pharmacy
54	Big Creek
Other	N: Historic Site Sunshine Disaster
57	Bus. Loop 90, Osburn
Gas	S: Texaco(*, D)
Food	S: Osburn Club
AServ	S: Garry's Lube & Oil, Silver Auto Collision Repair
RVCamp	S: Blue Anchor Trailer Park(LP)
ATM	S: Texaco
Other	S: U.S. Post Office
60	Bus. Loop 90, Silverton, Osburn
Lodg	S: Silver Leaf Motel
RVCamp	S: Camping
Med	N: + Silver Valley Medical Center

EXIT	IDAHO/MONTANA
Other	N: National Forest Ranger Station, U.S. Post Office
61	Bus. Loop 90, Wallace, S. Frontage Rd, N. Frontage Rd.
Gas	S: Conoco(*, D)
Food	S: Lincoln's Wallace Station J.G.'s Restaurant
Lodg	S: Best Western, Silver Valley Inn
RVCamp	S: Down By The Depot RV Park
Other	S: Wallace Information Center
62	Bus. Loop, ID4, Wallace Burke
Gas	S: Exxon(*, D, LP), Sinclair(*)
Food	S: 13 13 Club Historic Saloon & Grill, E.J.'s Pizza, Eagle's Club, Mrs. Dean's Ice Cream Parlour, Pizza Factory, Silver Corner Cafe, Silver Lantern Drive-In, Suites Cafe & Lounge, The Brooks Hotel, The Jameson Dining Room
Lodg	S: Ryan Hotel, Stardust Motel, The Brooks Hotel
RVCamp	S: Down-by-the-Depot RV Park
Med	S: + Family Practice Doctor
Other	S: Excel Foods Grocery, Tabor's Modern Drug, The Jameson, Veterinarian Clinic, Wallace N. Pac. Depot R.R. Museum
64	Golconda District
65	Compressor District
66	Gold Creek (Eastbound)
(67)	Parking Area
67	Morning District
RVCamp	N: Camping
68	Bus. Loop, Mullan (Eastbound)
69	Bus. Loop 90, Mullan, Shoshone Park, Atlas Rd.
Parks	N: Shoshone Park (3 Miles)
(70)	Runaway Truck Ramp
(72)	Runaway Truck Ramp
(73)	Historical Site (Westbound)

↑IDAHO

↓MONTANA

EXIT	MONTANA
(0)	Parking Area, Truck Break Check Pulloff Area
0	Lookout Pass, Visitor Info, Local Access
(5)	Rest Area (RR, Phones, Picnic, P)
5	Taft Area
10	Saltese
Food	N: Elk Glenn Motel
Lodg	N: Elk Glenn Motel
Other	N: U.S. Post Office
(15)	Weigh Station (Left Exit Both Directions)
16	Haugan, Savenac
FStop	N: $10,000 Silver Dollars(LP)
Food	N: $10,000 Silver Dollars
Lodg	N: $10,000 Silver Dollars Motel
RVCamp	N: $10,000 Silver Dollars
ATM	N: $10,000 Silver Dollars
18	DeBorgia
Gas	N: Cenex(*)
Food	N: Pinecrest Lodge
Lodg	N: Hotel Albert, Pinecrest Lodge
RVCamp	N: Campground (1.5 Miles)
ATM	N: Pinecrest Lodge
Other	N: Bear Trap Grocery (Cenex), U.S. Post Office (Cenex)

EXIT		MONTANA
22		Henderson
	RVCamp	**N:** Camping
25		Drexel
29		Fishing Access (Westbound, Reaccess Westbound Only)
30		Two Mile Road
33		MT 135, St. Regis
	FStop	**N:** Conoco(*)
	Gas	**N:** Conoco(*, D), Exxon(*)
	Food	**N:** Conoco, Frosty, Hot Stuffed Pizza (Exxon), Jaspers Restaurant, O.K. Cafe Casino Family Dining (The Log Cabin Motel), Traveler's Inn Saloon
	Lodg	**N:** St. Regis Motel, Super 8, The Log Cabin Motel
	RVCamp	**N:** Campground St. Regis, KOA Campgrounds (1 Mile), Schober's Truck/RV & Auto Service, St Regis KOA Camp (1 Mile), St. Regis Camp (The Log Cabin Motel)
	ATM	**N:** Jaspers Restaurant
	Other	**N:** Stang's Food Center, U.S. Post Office, Visitor Information
37		Sloway Area
	RVCamp	**S:** Camping
43		Dry Creek Road
	RVCamp	**N:** National Forest Campground
47		Hwy 257, Superior
	FStop	**S:** Exxon(*)
	Gas	**N:** BP(*), Cenex(*, CW), Conoco(*, D)
	Food	**N:** Casino Restaurant Sports Bar, Durango's Restaurant (BP), Warnken's Breadboard
	Lodg	**N:** Budget Host Motel
	AServ	**N:** Fred's Auto Repair, NAPA, Superior Auto Body & Glass
		S: Carl's Auto Repair
	RVCamp	**N:** National Forest Campground (7 Miles)
	Med	**N:** ✚ Hospital
	ATM	**N:** Conoco
		S: Exxon
	Other	**N:** Castle's IGA Store (True Value Market), Corner Car Wash, Mineral County Law Enforcement Center, Mineral Pharmacy, National Forest Ranger Station, Superior Drug Store & Fountain, True Value Market, U.S. Post Office
55		Lozeau Quartz
	Gas	**N:** No Name(LP)
	Food	**N:** No Name
(58)		Rest Area (RR, HF, Phones, Picnic, P)
	RVCamp	**N:** National Forest Campground (Entrance at Rest Area Westbound)
61		Tarkio

EXIT		MONTANA
66		Fish Creek Road
70		Cyr
(72)		Parking Area (P; Eastbound)
(73)		Parking Area (P; Westbound)
75		Alberton
	Gas	**N:** Panther Express
	RVCamp	**S:** River Edge Resort Motel(LP)
77		Hwy 507, Alberton, Petty Creek Road
82		Nine Mile Road
	AServ	**S:** Nine Mile Towing & Auto Repair
85		Huson
	Gas	**S:** Huson Mercantile(D)
	Other	**S:** U.S. Post Office (Huson Mercantile)
89		Frenchtown
	Gas	**S:** Conoco(*, D)
	Food	**S:** Alean Bar & Cafe, Cinnamon Street Bakery, French Connection Sports Bar (Hot Stuffed Pizza, Eddie Peppers Mexican), Frenchtown Club, Smash Hit Subs (Conoco), The Coffee Cup Restaurant
	AServ	**S:** Pete's 4x4 Garage
	ATM	**S:** Conoco
	Parks	**N:** Frenchtown Pond State Park (1.5 Miles)
	Other	**S:** Broncs Grocery, Laundromat, U.S. Post Office
(93)		Inspection Station
96		U.S. 93N, MT 200W, Kalispell, Weigh Station
	TStop	**N:** Muralt's Travel Plaza(*, LP, SCALES)
		S: Cross Road's Travel Center(*, LP, RV DUMP)
	Food	**S:** 4B's Restaurant (Cross Road's), Fred's Lounge Casino, Marvin's Grill
	Lodg	**N:** DAYS INN Days Inn
		S: Redwood Lodge
	TServ	**N:** Freightliner Dealer, Muralt's Travel Plaza(SCALES), Peterbilt Dealer
		S: Cross Road's Travel Center, Kenworth Williams Equip.
	TWash	**N:** Muralt's Travel Plaza, Wash Works
	RVCamp	**N:** Jellystone RV Park (.5 Miles), Jellystone RV Resort, Jim & Mary's RV Park (.75 Miles), The Outpost Family Campground (2 Miles)
		S: Dry Dock RV Repair (2 Miles)
	ATM	**N:** Muralt's Travel Plaza
		S: Cross Road's Travel Center, Marvin's Grill
	Parks	**N:** Glacier National Park
101		U.S. 93S, Reserve St., Hamilton
	TStop	**S:** Vino's Truck Stop(*)
	FStop	**S:** Cenex(*, D, LP, RV DUMP)
	Gas	**N:** Conoco(*, D)
		S: Ole's(*, CW)
	Food	**S:** 4B's Restaurant, Hot Stuffed Pizza (Vino's), Joker's Wild Casino & Restaurant, McDonald's, McKenzie River Pizza Co., Smash Hit Subs (Vino's), Taco Time
	Lodg	**N:** Best Western
		S: 4 B's Inn, Comfort Inn, Hampton Inn, Motel 6, Ruby's Reserve Street Inn, Super 8, Traveler's Inn Motel
	AServ	**S:** Jacobson Bros., Montana Car Care
	TServ	**S:** Detroit Diesel, Onan Cummins
	RVCamp	**N:** Camping
		S: Bretz RV & Marine (2.8 Miles), Missoula/El Mar KOA (1.5 Miles), Onon Truck & RV Service
	ATM	**N:** Conoco
		S: Cenex, Joker's Wild Casino & Restaurant, Vino's Truck Stop

EXIT		MONTANA
104		U.S. 93 South, Orange Street
	Gas	**S:** Conoco(*), Sinclair(D, LP)
	Food	**S:** Pagoda Chinese, Subway
	Lodg	**S:** Budget Motor Inn
	AServ	**S:** Thompson's Auto Service (Sinclair)
	Med	**S:** ✚ Providence Center, St. Patrick's Hosp.
	ATM	**S:** Conoco
	Other	**S:** Ole's Laundromat
105		Business I-90, U.S. 12W, Van Buren Street
	FStop	**S:** Conoco(*), Pacific Pride Commercial Fueling
	Gas	**S:** Cenex(D), Conoco(*, D), Sinclair(*)
	Food	**S:** Burger King, Double Tree Hotel, Eddie Pepper's Mexican Restaurant (Conoco), Finnegan's Family Restaurant, Goldsmith's Premium Ice Cream, Hot Stuffed Pizza (Conoco), Little Caesars Pizza, McDonald's, McKay's on the River, Pizza Hut, Press Box(24), Quizno's Classic Subs, Taco Bell
	Lodg	**S:** Campus Inn, Canyon Motel, Creekside Inn, Double Tree Hotel, Goldsmith's Bed & Breakfast, Grizzly Family Inn, Holiday Inn Express, Hubbards Ponderosa Lodge, Thunder Bird Motel
	AServ	**S:** Champion Auto Stores, Conoco, Jiffy Lube
	ATM	**S:** Buttrey Supermarket(RX), Conoco, Sinclair
	Other	**S:** Broadway Market, Buttrey Supermarket(RX), Coin Car Wash, Eastgate Veterinary Clinic, Visitor Information
107		East Missoula
	TStop	**N:** Conoco(*)
	Gas	**N:** BP(*)
	Food	**N:** Kolbs Cafe
	Lodg	**N:** Aspen Motel, OK Motel
	AServ	**N:** Bill's Transmission, Bill's Transmission, Carl's Auto
	TServ	**N:** Bill's Transmission, Bill's Transmission, Five Valley Diesel, Nick's Diesel Power
	Other	**N:** Coin Laundry (BP)
109		MT 200 East, Bonner, Great Falls
	TStop	**N:** Exxon Travel Plaza(*, LP)
	Gas	**N:** Conoco(*)

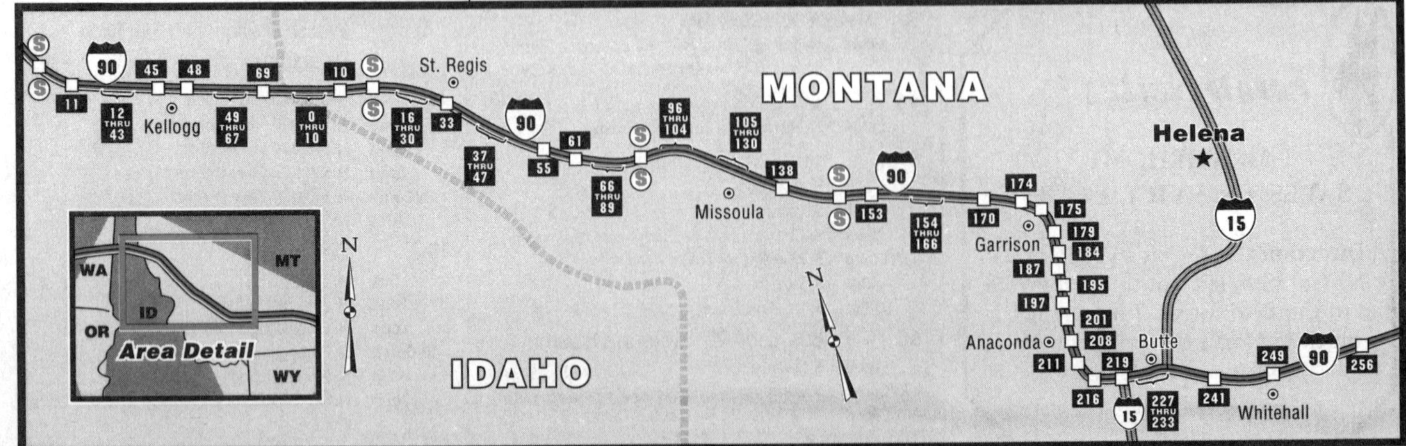

Bold red print shows RV & Bus parking available or nearby

EXIT MONTANA

Food N: Arby's (Exxon), Lucky Lil's Casino (Exxon), River City Grill, Subway (Exxon)
AServ N: Milltown Garage
TServ N: Brian Motors
ATM N: Exxon Travel Plaza, No Name
Other N: Captain John Mullan Trail Historic Site, Two Rivers Market, U.S. Post Office

113 Turah
RVCamp S: Turah Store Campground (1.5 Miles)

120 Clinton
Gas S: Conoco(*, D, LP)
Other S: U.S. Post Office

126 Rock Creek Road
Gas S: Rock Creek Lodge
Food S: Rock Creek Lodge
Lodg S: Rock Creek Lodge
RVCamp S: Elstrom's Stage Station (.5 Miles), Rock Creek Lodge

(128) Parking Area (P)

130 Beavertail Road
RVCamp S: Campground (Beavertail Hill S.P.)
Parks S: Beavertail Hill State Park (.25 Miles)

138 Bearmouth Area
Gas N: Chalet Bearmouth(*)
Food N: Chalet Bearmouth(RV DUMP)
Lodg N: Chalet Bearmouth
RVCamp N: Bearmouth Campground
Other N: Garnet Ghost Town

(143) Rest Area (RR, HF, Phones, Picnic, Pet Walk, P)

(151) Weigh Station

153 MT 1, Drummond, Philipsburg (Eastbound, Reaccess Westbound Only)
Food S: D-M Restaurant, Frosty Freeze, Swede's Place
Lodg S: Drummond Hotel(RX)
RVCamp S: Drummond City Park Camping
Other S: Front Street Market

154 To MT 1, Drummond, Philipsburg (Westbound, Reaccess Eastbound Only)
FStop S: Exxon(*)
Gas S: Cenex(D, LP), Sinclair(*, D, CW)
Food S: Wagon Wheel Cafe & Motel
Lodg S: Sky Motel, Wagon Wheel Cafe & Motel
AServ S: Diesel Key Lot
RVCamp N: The Good Time Camping & RV
ATM S: Exxon
Other N: Pintler Scenic Loop

162 (646) Jens

166 Gold Creek
RVCamp S: Mak-A-Dream Campground

(167) Rest Area (RR, HF, Phones, Picnic, Pet Walk, P; Westbound)

(169) Rest Area (RR, HF, Phones, Picnic, P; Eastbound)

170 Phosphate

174 U.S. 12E., Garrison, Helena (Eastbound, Reaccess Westbound Only)
Gas N: No Name

175 U.S. 12E, Garrison, Helena (Westbound, Reaccess Eastbound Only)
RVCamp N: Bernie & Sharon's Riverfront RV Park

179 Beck Hill Road

184 Business I-90, Deer Lodge
FStop S: Conoco(*, CW, RV DUMP)

EXIT MONTANA

Gas S: BP(*)
Food S: 4 B's Restaurant (Steak & Prime Rib), BP, McDonald's
Lodg S: Super 8
RVCamp S: Indian Creek Campground(LP)
ATM S: BP, Conoco

187 Business I-90, Deer Lodge (Reaccess Eastbound Only)
RVCamp N: KOA Campgrounds (Open May 1st To Oct.15th)
Med N: ✚ Hospital
Other N: Grant-Kohrs Ranch Nat'l Historic Site

195 Racetrack

197 Hwy 273, Galen

201 Warm Springs, Anaconda, Frontage Rd.
Gas S: Sinclair(*)
Med S: ✚ Montana State Hospital
Other S: Coin Laundry (Sinclair)

208 MT 1, Anaconda, Opportunity, Phillipsburg, Pintler Scenic Loop (Reaccess Eastbound Only)
Med S: ✚ Hospital

210 Scenic Loop Information Turnout (Westbound)

211 Hwy 441, Gregson, Fairmont, Hot Springs
RVCamp S: Fairmont RV Camp (2 Miles)

216 Ramsay

219 Jct. I-15N, I-90. Butte (Port Of Montana Trasportation)

Note: I-90 runs concurrent below with I-15. Numbering follows I-15.

121 Jct I-15S, Idaho Falls, I-90W, Missoula
TStop E: Flying J Travel Center(*, LP)
W: Conoco(*, LP)
Food E: Rocker Inn
W: Arby's (Conoco)
Lodg E: Rocker Inn
AServ W: Rocker Repair
TServ W: Rocker Repair
ATM E: Flying J Travel Center

122 Rocker, Weigh Station (All Trucks Must Exit When Weigh Station Is Open)

124 I-115, City Center (Northbound, Left Exit Northbound, Reaccess Southbound Only)

126 Montana Street
Gas E: Cenex(*), Sinclair
W: Conoco(*), Exxon(*, D)
Food E: Joker's Wild Casino
W: Matt's Drive-In Service
Lodg E: Eddy's Motel
AServ E: Les Schwab Tires, Sinclair
TServ E: Interstate Repair
RVCamp W: KOA Campgrounds
Med E: ✚ Community Health Center, ✚ Rocky Mountain Clinic
W: ✚ Hospital
ATM W: Conoco
Other E: Jerry's Fireworks, Museum & Historic District, Safeway Grocery

127 Bus I-15, Bus I-90, Harrison Ave
FStop W: Exxon(*, LP)

EXIT MONTANA

Gas E: Cenex(*, D, CW), Conoco(*), Sinclair
W: Conoco(*, D), Sinclair(*)
Food E: Arctic Circle Hamburgers, Denny's, Hanging 5 Family Restaurant, Hardees, Hot Stuff Pizza (Cenex), John's (Porkchop Sandwich), Oasis Casino, Palomino Club, Smash Hit Subs (Cenex), WarBonnet Inn
W: 4 B's Restaurant(24), Burger King(PLAY), Chicken To Go (Exxon), Godfather's Pizza, Kentucky Fried Chicken, McDonald's, Perkins Family Restaurant & Bakery, Pizza Hut, Plaza Royale Casino, Taco Bell
Lodg E: DAYS INN Days Inn, Holiday Inn Express, WarBonnet Inn
W: Best Western, Comfort Inn, Super 8
AServ E: Leipheimer Nissan Toyota, Lisac's Tires
W: Glen's Automotive Maintenance & Repair, Whalen Tire, Lube, & Oil
ATM E: Conoco
W: Conoco, Exxon, First National Federal Bank, Sinclair
Other E: Animal Hospital, Safeway Grocery(24, RX)
W: Butte Plaza Mall, Suds 'N Fun Laundromat (Exxon), Town Pump Car Wash

Note: I-90 runs concurrent above with I-15. Numbering follows I-15.

227 Jct. I-15N, Helena, Great Falls, I-15S, Butte

228 Hwy 375, Continental Drive

233 Homestake

(235) Rest Area (RR, HF, Phones, Picnic, P; All Trucks Must Stop For Grade Information)

241 Pipestone
RVCamp S: Piipestone Campground(LP)
Other N: Delmoe Lake

249 MT 55, to MT 69, Whitehall, Dillon, Virginia City
TStop S: Exxon(*)
Food S: Lucky Lil's Casino (Exxon), Subway (Exxon)
Lodg S: Super 8
AServ S: Q-Lube, Valvoline Oil Change
ATM S: Exxon
Other N: U.S. Forest Station

256 Hwy 359, Cardwell, Boulder
FStop S: Conoco(*, LP)
RVCamp S: Cardwell Store & RV Park (.25 Miles)
Parks S: Lewis & Clark Caverns State Park, Yellowstone National Park

267 Milligan Canyon Road

274 U.S. 287, Helena, Ennis
FStop S: Exxon(*, LP)
Gas N: Conoco(*)
Food N: Prairie Plaza, Steer In
Lodg N: Fort Three Forks Motel
TServ N: Ron's Diesel Repair
RVCamp N: Fort Three Forks Motel & RV Park (.25 Miles)
S: KOA Campgrounds (1 Mile)
ATM S: Exxon
Parks S: Lewis & Clark Caverns State Park, Yellowstone National Park
Other N: Canyon Ferry Lake, Wheat Montana Bakery & Deli

278 MT 2, Three Forks, Trident, Hwy 205
Parks N: Missouri Headwaters State Park

283 Logan, Trident
Parks S: Madison Buffalo Jump State Monument (7 Miles)

288 Hwy 346, Hwy 288, Manhattan,

EXIT MONTANA

Amsterdam, Churchill
Gas N: Conoco(*, D)
RVCamp N: **Manhattan Camper Court(LP)**

298 Hwy 291, MT 85, Amsterdam, Belgrade, West Yellowstone
TStop S: **Flying J Travel Plaza(*, LP, SCALES)**
FStop S: **Chalet Market(*)**
Gas N: Conoco(*), Exxon(*, D, CW)
Food N: Burger King, Charlie's Deli & Coffee Shop, McDonald's, Rosa's Pizza, Subway (Exxon), Taco Time
S: Country Kitchen, **Flying J Travel Plaza**
Lodg S: Homestead Motel, **Super 8**
AServ N: NAPA Auto Parts, Q-Lube
S: Belgrade Tire
TWash S: **Rabbit Car-Truck Wash**
RVCamp S: **Hidden Campground RV Park, Lexley Acres Campground (.5 Miles)**
ATM N: Albertson's Food Market(RX), Conoco, Exxon, **Lee & Dad's IGA(RX)**
Other N: Albertson's Food Market(RX), **Lee & Dad's IGA(RX)**, Valley Center Coin Operated Laundry

305 Hwy 412, N 19th Ave, Springhill
Gas N: Exxon(*)
Food N: Monkey Don's Rib Joint, Moonbean's Coffee House
Other S: Cosco(RX)

306 Hwy 205 N 7th Ave
Gas N: Conoco(*)
S: Conoco(*, D), Exxon(*)
Food N: Apple Tree Restaurant, Geyser's Park Fun & Food Center, Grums Deli & Gourmet Market, McDonald's(PLAY)
S: Applebee's, Hardee's (Conoco), Santa Fe Red's Cantina
Lodg N: Fairfield Inn, Prime Rate Motel, Ramada Limited, Sleep Inn, Super 8
S: Best Western, Bozeman Inn, Comfort Inn, DAYS INN Days Inn, Hampton Inn, Holiday Inn
AServ N: Big Sky Service & Radiator, **Bridgestone**, D & B Muffler Shop, Gensemer's Auto, Keysers Auto Repair
S: Capital Speedy Auto Glass, **K-Mart(RX), Wal-Mart(RX)**
TServ N: **Bridgestone**
RVCamp N: **C&T Trailor Supply Store, Camping**
ATM S: Conoco, County Market(RX), Exxon
Other N: Bozeman Pet Center
S: Bozeman Information Center, County Market(RX), **K-Mart(RX)**, Scrubby's Car Wash, U.S. Post Office (County Market), **Vision Center (Wal-Mart), Wal-Mart(RX)**

309 Bus. Loop I-90, U.S. 191, Main Street, Frontage Road, Bozeman, West Yellowstone
Gas S: Exxon(*), Sinclair(*)
Food S: Hero Subs (Exxon)
Lodg S: Continental Motel, Ranch House Motel, Western Heritage Inn
AServ N: Courtesy Body Shop, Dick Walters Motors Subaru, Audi, Jeep, Eagle, Isuzu, Volks
S: Auto Stop
RVCamp N: **Sunrise Campground(LP)**
S: **Rocky Mountain RV & Auto Service**
Med S: **✚ Hospital**
ATM S: Exxon, Sinclair
Parks S: **Lindley Park**
Other S: Bozeman Area Chamber of Commerce, Buggy Bath Car Wash

313 Bear Canyon Road
RVCamp S: **Bear Canyon Campground**

316 Trail Creek Road

319 Jackson Creek Road

324 Ranch Access

(325) **Parking Area; Truck Chain-up Area**

(327) **Parking Area; Truck Chain-up Area**

330 Local Access, Cokedale Rd., Livingston
TStop N: **Yellowstone Truck Stop(*)**
Food N: **Restaurant (Yellowstone Truck Stop)**
TServ N: **Yellowstone Truck Stop**

333 U.S. 89S, City Center, Yellowstone National Park, Gardiner
FStop S: **Conoco(*, CW)**
Gas N: Holiday(*)
S: Cenex(*), Exxon(*)
Food N: Crazy Coyote Mexican, Dairy Queen, Domino's Pizza, Homeade Kitchen, Paradise Inn Motel, Pizza Hut
S: A-Dough-B Bakery, Hardee's, **Lucky Lil's Casino (Conoco), McDonald's(PLAY), Subway**
Lodg N: Best Western, Budget Host Parkway Motel, Livingston Inn, Paradise Inn Motel
S: Comfort Inn, **Super 8**
AServ N: Livingston Ford Mercury, Whiting Motors Chevrolet
RVCamp N: **Kimo RV & Auto Service, Livingston Inn Motel & Campground, Paradise Oasis, Windmill RV Park**
S: **KOA Campgrounds (Open April 15th thru October 31st), Osen's Drive Thru (.5 Miles), Rock Canyon Campground (2 Miles)**
Med N: **✚ Hospital**
ATM N: **Pamida Discount Ctr(RX)**
S: Cenex, **Conoco**
Parks S: **Yellowstone National Park**
Other N: Car Wash, **County Market Total Discount Foods**, Launder Clean Coin Laundry, **Pamida Discount Ctr(RX)**, Scrub Tub Laundry, **Western Drug**
S: **Buttrey Food & Drug(RX), Colmey Veterinary Hospital**

337 I-90 Bus Loop, Livingston
RVCamp N: **Camping**

340 U.S. 89 North, White Sulphur Springs

343 Mission Creek Road

350 East End Access

352 Ranch Access

354 Hwy 563, Springdale

362 DeHart

367 Big Timber
Gas N: Conoco(*, LP)
Food N: **Crazy Jane's Family Eatery(24) (Conoco)**
Lodg N: **Super 8**
RVCamp N: **Spring Creek Camp & Trout Ranch**
ATM N: Conoco
Other N: **Big Timber Visitor Information, Historic Point (.5 Miles)**

370 U.S. 191, Business 90, Big Timber, Harlowton
RVCamp N: **Spring Creek Camp & Trout Ranch**

377 Greycliff
Food S: **Four Winds Inn Ranch House Cooking (Truck Stop)**
RVCamp S: **KOA Campgrounds**
Parks S: **Greycliff Prairie Dog Town State Park, Prairie Dog Town State Park & Monument**
Other S: **Big Timber Water Slide Park (KOA Campground)**

(381) **Rest Area (RR, HF, Phones, Picnic, P)**

384 Bridger Creek Road

392 Reed Point
Gas N: Sinclair(*, D)
Food N: Waterhole Saloon (Chester Fried Chicken)
Lodg N: Hotel Montana Bed & Breakfast
RVCamp N: **Cedar Hills Campground(LP)**
Other N: **U.S. Post Office**

396 Ranch Access

400 Springtime Road

408 MT 78, Absarokee, Columbus, Rapelje
FStop S: **Exxon(*, RV DUMP)**
Food S: Apple Village Cafe, **KFC (Exxon), McDonald's**, Sport's Hut, **Taco Bell (Exxon)**
Lodg S: Super 8

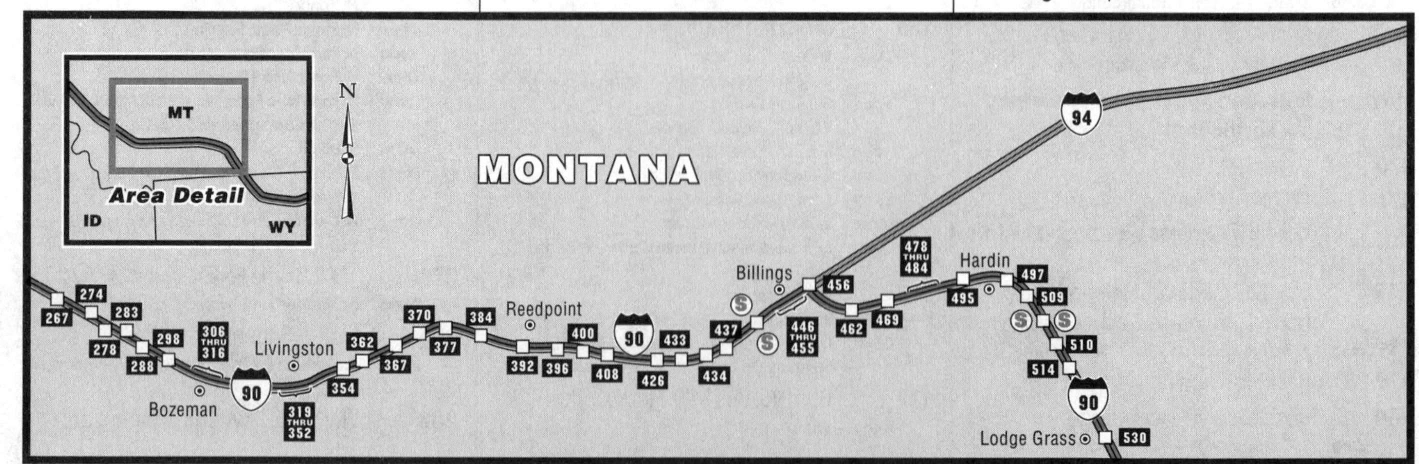

Bold red print shows RV & Bus parking available or nearby

EXIT	MONTANA
AServ	S: J.C. Tire Cooper Tires
RVCamp	S: Mountain Range RV Camp
Med	S: Hospital
ATM	S: Exxon
Parks	S: Granite Peak Park
Other	S: Car Wash, Visitor Information
(419)	Rest Area (RR, HF, Phones, Picnic, P)
426	Park City
TStop	S: Cenex(*)
Gas	S: Kwik Stop(*)
AServ	S: Rich's Repair & Tire Shop
433	Bus Loop I-90, West Laurel (Eastbound, Reaccess Westbound Only)
Gas	N: Conoco(*)
Food	N: Caboose Saloon
Lodg	N: Wagon Wheel, Welcome Travelers Motel
ATM	N: Caboose Saloon
Other	N: Auto Wash, Coin Operated Laundry
434	U.S. 212, U.S. 310, Laurel, Red Lodge
FStop	N: Exxon(*)
Gas	N: Cenex(*, D, LP, CW), Conoco(*)
Food	N: Burger King(PLAY), Hardee's, Little Big Men Pizza, Locomotive Restaurant & Casino, Pizza Hut, Subway, Taco John's
Lodg	N: Best Western
AServ	N: Expert Lube & Wash, Fichtner Chev, Geo, Laurel Ford, Rapid Tire
ATM	N: Conoco, Exxon, Jan's IGA Food Store(24)
Parks	S: Yellowstone National Park
Other	N: Jan's IGA Food Store, Western Drug
437	South Frontage Road, Bus Loop 90, E. Laurel
TStop	S: Sinclair(RV DUMP, SCALES)
RVCamp	S: Camp Western (Sinclair), Pelican RV Park
Other	S: Laurel East Veterinarian Services
(439)	Weigh Station
446	King Ave. W., Mulloney Lane, S. Frontage Rd.
TStop	N: Sinclair
Gas	N: Conoco(*), Holiday(*, D) S: Conoco(*, D)
Food	N: Denny's, Fuddruckers, Gusick Restaurant & Bar, Jade Palace, Perkins Family Restaurant, Taco John's S: Apple Tree Restaurant, Cracker Barrel, Silver Dollar Restaurant & Casino
Lodg	N: C'mon Inn, Comfort Inn, Days Inn, Fairfield Inn, Quality Inn, Super 8 S: 2nd Motel 6, Best Western, Clarion Hotel, Holiday Inn, Kelly Inn, Motel 6, Ramada Limited
AServ	N: Big Sky Auto Mall Mazda, Chrys, Plym, Jeep, Conoco, KIA, NAPA Auto Parts
TServ	N: CAT Trucks & Engines, Sinclair
RVCamp	N: Big Sky Campground, Magic Carpet Recreational Vehicles (.5 Miles) S: Billings Big Sky RV Park
ATM	N: Yellowstone Bank S: Conoco
Other	S: Big Splash Water Park, Billings Plaza Trade Center
447	S Billings Blvd
Gas	N: Conoco(*, D)
Food	N: 4 B's, Burger King(PLAY), McDonald's, Subway (Conoco), Won-800 Casino Sports Lounge
Lodg	N: Sleep Inn
AServ	N: Rocky Mountain Auto Body & Restoration
RVCamp	N: Hanser's RV Towing & Service (.7 Miles)
ATM	N: Conoco
Parks	N: Geyser Park Family Fun Center S: Chief Plenty Coups State Park
Other	N: Geyser Park Family Fun Center

EXIT	MONTANA
450	MT 3, 27th Street, City Center
Gas	N: Conoco(*), Exxon(*), Sinclair(*, LP)
Food	N: Blondy's, Lucky Cuss, Pizza Hut, Subway (Exxon), The Bungalow
Lodg	N: Howard Johnson, War Bonnet Inn
AServ	N: Car Quest Auto Center, Sinclair
TWash	N: Hoogie's
RVCamp	S: KOA Campgrounds (.75 Miles), Yellowstone River (.25 Miles)
Med	N: Hospital
ATM	N: Conoco
Other	N: Billings Chamber of Commerce Visitors Center, U.S. Post Office
452	Bus. Loop I-90, U.S. 87 North, City Center, Roundup
FStop	N: Exxon(*) S: Cenex(*)
Gas	N: Conoco(*, D) S: Texaco(*)
Food	N: Big Dipper Drive In, Little Caesars Pizza (Conoco), Planet Lockwood Restaurant S: V.R. Grill
Parks	S: Chief Plenty Coups State Park, Pictograph Cave State Park
Other	S: Pictograph Cave
455	Johnson Lane
TStop	S: Flying J Travel Plaza(*, LP, RV DUMP, SCALES)
Gas	S: Exxon(*)
Food	S: Burger King, Flying J Travel Plaza, Jackpot Diner Casino
AServ	S: Fly-N-Lube(CW)
TServ	S: Fly-N-Lube
TWash	S: Fly-N-Lube(CW)
RVCamp	S: Tour America RV Service
ATM	S: Exxon, Flying J Travel Plaza, Little Horn State Bank
456A	I-90E, Sheridan; Jct I-94E (Eastbound)
456B	Jct I-94E, Miles City, Bismarck (Westbound)
462	Pryor Creek Road
469	Arrow Creek Road
(476)	Rest Area (RR, HF, Phones, Picnic, P)
478	Fly Creek Road
484	Toluca, Frontage Road
495	Hwy 47, City Center
FStop	N: Texaco(*, K) S: Broadway(LP), Exxon(*), Sinclair(*, RV DUMP)
Gas	S: Cenex(*, D)
Food	N: Purple Cow Family Restaurant (Texaco) S: American Inn, Dairy Queen, Farwest Restaurant Casino, McDonald's, Pizza Hut, Taco Bell, Taco John's
Lodg	S: American Inn, Super 8
RVCamp	N: Hardin-KOA Bighorn Valley (1 Mile) S: Grandview Campground, Sunset Village RV Park (1.5 Miles)
Med	S: Hospital
ATM	S: Broadway, Cenex, Exxon, Sinclair
Parks	S: Bighorn Canyon Recreational Area
Other	S: Big Horn Veterinarian Hospital
497	Bus Loop I-90, MT 313, Third Street, Hardin
Med	S: Hospital
Other	S: Big Horn County Museum Visitors Center
503	Dunmore
509	Crow Agency
Gas	N: Conoco(*)
Parks	S: Big Horn Canyon National Recreation Area
Other	N: Crow Mercantile, Laundromat, U.S. Post Office

EXIT	MONTANA/WYOMING
(510)	Weigh Station (Left Exit Both Directions)
510	U.S. 212 E, Little Big Horn Battlefield, Broadus
Gas	N: Sinclair(*, D)
Food	N: Custer Battlefield Trading Post & Cafe, Little Big Horn Casino, Sinclair
Lodg	S: Little Big Horn Motel
RVCamp	S: Little Big Horn Camping
Med	N: Indian Health Service Hospital
Other	N: Custer Battlefield Monument
514	Garryowen
Gas	N: Conoco(*)
Other	N: Custer Battlefield Museum (Conoco), Reno Battlefield Museum
530	Hwy 463, Lodge Grass, Owl Crossing Rd.
544	Wyola
549	Aberdeen

↑MONTANA

↓WYOMING

EXIT	WYOMING
1	Parkman
9	U.S. 14 W, Ranchester, Dayton, Grey Bull, Lovell, Yellowstone Teton National Parks
RVCamp	S: Lazy R Campground (1 Mile)
Parks	S: Big Horn Canyon National Recreation Area, Teton National Park, Tongue River Creative Playground, Yellowstone National Park
Other	S: Connor Battlefield
14	Acme Road
16	Decker Mount
(16)	Parking Area (Westbound)
20	Main Street (Wyoming Port Of Entry)
TStop	S: Exxon(*)
Gas	S: Cenex(*), Conoco(*)
Food	S: Country Kitchen (Exxon), Little Caesars Pizza (K-Mart), McDonald's(PLAY), Pizza Hut, Subway (Conoco), Trails End Motel
Lodg	S: Bramble Motel, Super 8, Trails End Motel
AServ	S: A Towing & Repair
TServ	S: 10-4 Diesel Truck Repair, Steve's Truck & RV Service
RVCamp	S: KOA Campgrounds (.5 Miles), Sheridan Big Horn Mtn. KOA (1 Mile)
ATM	S: Exxon
Other	S: K-Mart(RX), Wyoming Port Of Entry
23	WY 336, Fifth St
Gas	N: The Rock Stop
Food	N: Subway (The Rock Stop)
Med	S: Hospital
Other	N: Rest Area, Wyoming Wildlife Visitors Center
(23)	WY Welcome Center, Rest Area (RV Dump, Pet Walk)
25	Bus Loop I-90, U.S. 14 East, Sheridan, Big Horn, Ucross
FStop	S: Sinclair(*, D, LP), Texaco(D)
Gas	S: Bison Oil(LP), Holiday(*, D), Quik Sak
Food	S: Arby's, Burger King, Carl's Corner, Golden China Restaurant, Little Caesars Pizza, McDonald's (Wal-Mart), Ole's Pizza & Spaghetti House, Taco Bell
Lodg	N: Comfort Inn S: Days Inn, Holiday Inn, Lariat Motel, Mill

EXIT WYOMING

Inn, Parkway Motel
- **AServ** N: Hi-Tech Transmissions, Top End Auto Machine
- S: ACE Muffler, Cooper Tires, Firestone Tire & Auto, Fremont Toyota, NAPA Auto Parts, Sheridan Motor
- **RVCamp** N: **Sheridan RV Park (8 Blocks From Interstate)**
- S: **Sheridan RV Park (1.1 Miles)**
- **ATM** S: Buttery's Foods[RX], First Interstate Bank, Holiday, Sheridan State Bank[24], **Wal-Mart[RX]**
- **Other** N: Moxey Veterinary Hospital
- S: Buttery's Foods[RX], Car Wash, **Carl's Super**, Coin Laundry, Coin Laundry[24], **Wal-Mart[RX]**, Warehouse Market

(31) **Parking Area (Eastbound)**

33 Meade Creek Road, Big Horn
- **Other** N: Bradford Brinton Memorial

37 Story, Prairie Dog Creek Road

(39) **Parking Area, Scenic Turnout (Westbound)**

44 U.S. 87N, Piney Creek Road, Story, Banner (Difficult Reaccess)
- **Other** N: **Phil Kearny Historical Site**

47 Shell Creek Road

51 Lake De Smet
- **RVCamp** N: **Camping**

53 Rock Creek Road

56A Bus. I-25, Bus. I-90, Buffalo, U.S. 87 (Eastbound, Reaccess Westbound Only)

56B Jct. I-25 South, U.S. 87, Casper (Eastbound, No Reaccess)

58 Bus. Loop I-90, U.S. 16, Buffalo, Ucross
- **FStop** S: **Sinclair[*]**
- **Gas** S: Exxon[*, D]
- **Food** S: **Cowbow Bar & Grill**
- **Lodg** S: **Bunkhouse Motel**
- **RVCamp** N: **Buffalo KOA Kampground (1.25 Miles)**, **Deer Park (.75 Miles)**
- S: **Big Horn Industries[LP]**, **Indian Campground (1 Mile)**
- **Med** S: **Hospital**
- **ATM** S: Exxon
- **Other** S: Big Horn Industries[LP], **National Historic District**

(61) **Parking Area (Eastbound)**

(61) **Parking Area (Westbound)**

65 Red Hills Road, Tiperary Road

(68) **Parking Area (Westbound)**

69 Dry Creek Road

73 Crazy Woman Creek Road

77 Schoonover Road

82 Indian Creek Road

88 **Powder River Road (RR, Phones, Picnic, Pet Walk)**

(88) **Rest Area (RR, Phones, Picnic, Pet Walk; Located at Exit 88)**

91 Dead Horse Creek Road

102 Barber Creek Road

106 Kingsbury Road

113 Wild Horse Creek Road

EXIT WYOMING

116 Force Road

124 Bus. Loop I-90, U.S. 14, U.S. 16 West, Gillette
- **Gas** N: Conoco[*, 24], Texaco[*, D]
- S: Citgo[*, D]
- **Food** N: Fireside Lounge, Granny's Kitchen, **Hong Kong Chinese**, Long John Silver, Pizza Hut
- **Lodg** N: Best Western, Motel 6, **Super 8**
- **AServ** N: Texaco, Todd Service & Supply, Top Notch Auto
- S: Big Horn Tire
- **RVCamp** N: **Green Tree's Crazy Woman Campground (.75 Miles)**
- **Med** N: **Hospital**
- **ATM** N: Conoco
- S: Citgo
- **Other** N: **Dan's Supermarket[RX]**

126 WY 59, Gillette, Douglas
- **TStop** S: **Flying J Travel Plaza[*, LP]**
- **FStop** N: **Co-Op[*, LP]**
- **Gas** S: Exxon[*], Texaco[D] (Credit Card Only)
- **Food** N: McDonald's, Subway, The Prime Rib Restaurant
- S: Blimpie Subs & Salads, Burger King, Dairy Queen, KFC, Las Margaritas Mexican Family Restaurant, Mingles Lounge, Perkins Family Restaurant, Pizza Hut, **Taco Bell (Flying J Travel Plaza)**, Wendy's
- **Lodg** S: Days Inn, Holiday Inn
- **AServ** N: Plains Tire & Battery
- S: Big O Tires, Midas
- **ATM** N: Buttery's Foods
- S: **Albertson's Grocery[RX]**, First Interstate Bank, **Wal-Mart[RX]**
- **Parks** N: **Lasting Legacy Park[PLAY]**
- **Other** N: All God's Creatures Pet Shop, The Eye Glass Factory
- S: **Albertson's Grocery[RX]**, Bride of Christ Bible & Bookstore, E-Z Too Auto Wash, E-Z Too Car Wash 2, FedEx Building, **K-Mart[RX]**, **Wal-Mart[RX]**

128 Gillette, Port Of Entry
- **FStop** N: **Pacific Pride Commercial Fueling[*]**, **Texaco[*]**
- **Gas** N: Citgo[*], Gascard[D] (Credit Card Only)
- **Food** N: Mona's Cafe (American & Mexican)
- **Lodg** N: Econolodge
- **AServ** N: **Texaco**
- **RVCamp** N: **Green Tree's Crazy Woman Campground (2 Miles)**
- S: **High Plains Campground**
- **ATM** N: Citgo
- **Other** S: **Port Of Entry**

129 Garner Lake Road
- **RVCamp** S: **High Plains Campground RV Service & Repair (1 Mile)**, **RV Service & Repair**
- **Other** N: Wyoming State Patrol Station

132 Wyodak Road

(138) **Parking Area (Westbound)**

(138) **Parking Area (Eastbound)**

141 Rozet

153 **Bus Loop I-90, U.S. 14 East, U.S. 16, Moorcroft, Newcastle, Aglett, Upton, Devils Tower, Rest Area (RR, Phones, Picnic)**

(153) **Rest Area (RR, HF, Phones, Picnic)**

154 East Moorcroft
- **FStop** S: **Conoco[*]**
- **Gas** S: Texaco[*, D]
- **Food** S: **Hot Stuff Pizza (Conoco)**, Subway
- **Lodg** S: Moorcourt Motel, Wyoming Motel

160 Wind Creek Road

EXIT WYOMING/SOUTH DAKOTA

(163) **Parking Area (Westbound)**

(163) **Parking Area (Eastbound)**

165 Pine Ridge Road, Pine Haven

(171) **Parking Area (Eastbound)**

172 Inyan Kara Road

(177) **Parking Area (Eastbound)**

178 Coal Divide Road

185 Bus. Loop I-90, West U.S. 14 To WY 116, Sundance
- **Gas** S: Texaco[*, D]
- **AServ** S: Texaco
- **ATM** S: Texaco
- **Other** N: **Devil's Tower National Monument**

187 WY 585, Sundance, New Castle
- **Gas** N: Amoco, Conoco[*]
- **Food** N: Flo's Place
- **Lodg** N: Best Western
- **AServ** N: Amoco
- S: **Pennzoil Oil Change**
- **TServ** S: **Pennzoil Oil Change**
- **ATM** N: Conoco
- **Other** N: **Devil's Tower National Monument**, Hoppy's Car Wash

189 **Sundance, Rest Area**
- **FStop** N: **Amoco[*]**
- **Lodg** N: Best Western
- **RVCamp** N: **Mountain View Campground (.75 Miles)**
- **Med** N: **Hospital**
- **ATM** N: **Amoco**
- **Other** N: **Devil's Tower National Monument**
- S: Port of Entry Station

(189) **Rest Area (RR, HF, Phones, Picnic, RV Dump; Eastbound, Located at Exit 189)**

(190) **Weigh Station**

191 Moskee Road

199 WY 111, Aladdin

205 Beulah
- **FStop** N: **Conoco[*]**, **Wyoming State Line Station[*, LP]**
- **Other** N: **U.S. Post Office (Wyoming State Line Station)**

↑WYOMING

↓SOUTH DAKOTA

(1) **Rest Area (RR, HF, Phones, Picnic, RV Dump; Eastbound)**

2 McNenny State Fish Hatchery
- **Other** N: **McNenny State Fish Hatchery**

10 U.S. 85 North, Bus. Loop I-90, Spearfish, Belle Fourche
- **Gas** S: The Valley Corner Gas Groceries[*]
- **Food** S: Margie's Dinner Club
- **RVCamp** S: **KOA Campgrounds (.25 Miles)**
- **ATM** S: The Valley Corner Gas Groceries

12 Spearfish
- **Gas** S: Amoco[*, CW], Sinclair[*, D]
- **Food** S: The Millstone Family Restaurant
- **Lodg** S: Kelly Inn, Red Apple Inn
- **RVCamp** S: **Spearfish City Campground**
- **Med** S: **Hospital**
- **ATM** S: Amoco

14 U.S. 14 A, Spearfish Canyon, Black Hills National Forest, Spearfish Canyon Byway

Bold red print shows RV & Bus parking available or nearby

EXIT — SOUTH DAKOTA

Gas S: Amoco(*, D)
Food N: Happy Chef, Holiday Inn
S: Best Western, KFC, On the Run Pizza & Subs (Amoco)
Lodg N: Comfort Inn, Fairfield Inn, Holiday Inn
S: All American Inn, Best Western, Super 8
AServ S: Harleys Auto Body, Johnson Ford
RVCamp S: **Chris' Campground (1.25 Miles), Mountain View Campground (1 Mile), Spearfish Mobil Homes**
Med S: **+ Hospital**
ATM S: Amoco
Parks N: **Black Hills National Forest**
Other S: **High Plains Heritage Center, K-Mart(RX)**

17 U.S. 85 South, Deadwood, Lead

RVCamp S: **KOA Campgrounds**
Other S: **Deadwood National Historic Landmark, Winter Recreation Area**

23 SD 34 West, Whitewood

FStop S: **Sinclair(*)**
Gas S: Conoco(*, D)
Food S: Maggie's Diner, On the Run Pizza (Conoco)
Lodg S: Tony's Motel
AServ S: Performance Plus
RVCamp N: **Northern Hills Homes(LP) (.5 Miles)**
ATM S: Conoco
Other S: **Casino Laundromat**

30 Business Loop I-90, U.S. 14 A, East SD 34, Sturgis, Deadwood, Lead

FStop S: **Phillips 66(*), Texaco(*, D) (Casino)**
Gas N: Conoco(*), Sinclair(*, D)
S: Trailside General Store(*)
Food N: Bagel's & More, McDonald's(PLAY), Pizza Hut, Subway, The Five Works Steakhouse
S: Boulder Canyon Restaurant, Burger King(PLAY), **Phillips 66**
Lodg S: Canyon Inn, DAYS INN Days Inn, Super 8
AServ N: Owens Auto Service, Zylstra Body & Framework
RVCamp N: **Days End Campground RV Park**
ATM N: Sinclair
S: **Texaco (Casino)**
Other N: **Pamida Discount Center(RX)**, Park Ave. Car Wash & Laundromat(CW)

32 SD 79 North, Sturgis

FStop N: **Exxon(*)**
Gas N: Conoco(*)
Food N: Country Kitchen, Mom's Restaurant, Sturgis Bar & Grill, Taco John's
Lodg N: Best Western, National 9 Inn, South Pine Motel
AServ N: D And D Motors, Jacobsen Ford, Jacobsen Tire & Exhaust Center
RVCamp N: **Camping**
Med N: **+ Fort Mead VA Hospital, + Sturgis Community Healthcare Center**
Other N: McPherson Propane(LP), **National Motorcycle Museum, Northern Hills Eyecare**, Southside Car Wash(CW), **The Drug Store of Sturgis**

34 Black Hills National Cemetery

Other S: **Black Hills Nat'l Cemetery**

37 Pleasant Valley Road

RVCamp N: **Rush-No-More Campground (1 Mile)**
S: **Bull Dog RV Campground (.3 Miles)**

(38) **Weigh Station (Westbound)**

40 Tilford Road, Bethlehem Road

(42) **Rest Area (RR, HF, Phones, Picnic, RV Dump, RV Water; Westbound)**

(42) **Rest Area (RR, HF, Phones, Picnic, RV Dump, RV Water; Eastbound)**

44 Piedmont

46 Piedmont, Elk Creek Road

Gas S: Conoco(*)
Food N: Elk Creek Steakhouse Lounge
S: Subway (Conoco)
RVCamp N: **Elk Creek Resort & RV Park (1 Mile)**
S: **Covered Wagon Resort (.5 Miles), Valley Campground**
Other N: **Petrified Forest (1 Mile)**

48 Stagebarn, Canyon Road

Gas S: Sinclair(*, D)
Food N: Cattleman's Club Steaks
S: Classics Bar & Grill
TServ N: **Peterbilt**
RVCamp S: **Covered Wagon Resort (1.5 Miles)**
Med S: **+ Piedmont Medical Center**
Other S: **Stage Stop Groceries**, Stagebarn Car Wash(CW), Stagebarn Laundromat

51 Bus Loop I-90, SD 79, Black Hawk Road (Difficult Reaccess)

RVCamp N: **Fort Welikit Family Campground (.5 Miles)**

55 Deadwood Ave

TStop S: **Sinclair(*, LP, RV DUMP, SCALES)**
Food S: **Pizza Hut (Sinclair TS), Subway (Sinclair TS), The Windmill (Sinclair TS)**
TServ S: **International, Sinclair(SCALES)**
TWash S: **Sinclair**

57 I-190, U.S. 16 West, Rapid City, Mt. Rushmore, Black Hills National Forest (Left Exit)

RVCamp S: **Otto's Service Center (1.5 Miles)**
Other S: **Black Hills National Forest, Crazy Horse Monument, Mt. Rushmore**

58 Haines Ave

Gas N: Conoco(*)
S: Gas N' Snax(*, 24), Sinclair(*)
Food N: Applebee's, Hardee's, La Costa Mexican
S: Taco John's
Lodg N: TraveLodge
AServ N: Big O Tires, Tires Plus
S: Country General
Med S: **+ Hospital, + Rapid Care Medical Center**
ATM S: Sinclair
Other N: World of Pets
S: Country General, **Optical (ShopKo), ShopKo Grocery(RX)**

59 LaCrosse Street

Gas N: Amoco(*, CW, 24), Phillips 66(*)
S: Exxon(*), Wal-Mart (Credit Card Only)
Food N: A & W Restaurant (Phillips 66), Denny's, Happy Chef, Howard Johnson
S: Golden Corral Family Steakhouse, **McDonald's (Wal-Mart)**, Millstone Family Dining, Perkins Family Restaurant (Ramada Inn)
Lodg N: Econolodge, Howard Johnson, Super 8
S: AmericInn Inn, Comfort Inn, DAYS INN Days Inn, Fair Value Inn, Foothills Inn, Motel 6, Quality Inn, Ramada Inn, Rushmore Motel, Thrifty Motor Inn
AServ N: Amoco(24)
S: **Wal-Mart(RX)**
ATM N: Amoco, Phillips 66
S: **Wal-Mart**
Other N: **Rushmore Mall**
S: **Vision Center (Wal-Mart), Wal-Mart(RX)**

60 Truck U.S. 16 To SD 79, North Street (Difficult Reaccess, Limited Access Hwy)

AServ S: **Ed's Towing & Repair, Mid-American Motors**
TServ S: **Ed's Towing & Repair, Ed's Towing & Repair, Mid-American Motors**
RVCamp S: **AmeriGas/Rapid City(LP), Berry Patch Campground (.25 Miles), Dee Jay Camper Center (2 Miles), Ed's Towing & Repair, Green Star Camper Center (1.5 Miles)**

61 Elk Vale Road

TStop N: **Conoco(*, LP, RV DUMP, SCALES)**
TServ N: **Black Hills Truck & Trailer, Conoco(SCALES)**
S: **Freuhauf Truck Service, Hill's Brake & Equipment Co.**
TWash N: **Conoco**
RVCamp N: **The Langland Trailer Sales & Service (.1 Miles)**
S: **KOA Campgrounds**
ATM N: **Conoco**
Other N: Visitor Information

63 Ellsworth A.F.B Commercial Entrance, Box Elder (Eastbound, Reaccess Westbound Only)

66 Ellsworth A.F.B. Main Entrance, Box Elder

FStop N: **Conoco(*, CW)**

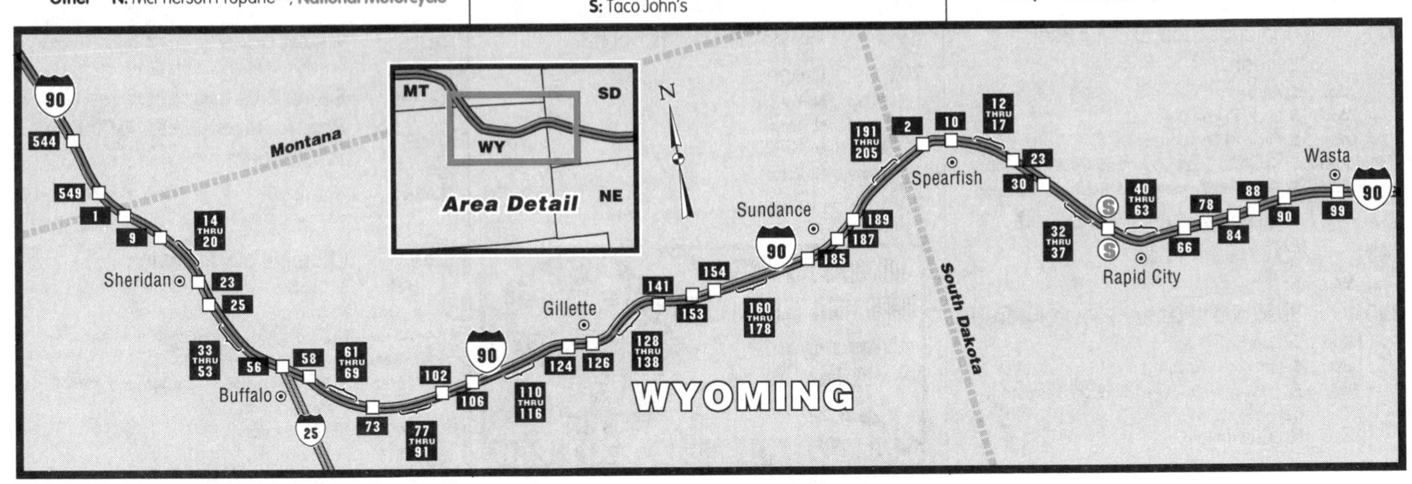

EXIT	SOUTH DAKOTA
Food	N: McDonald's, Pizza Hut, Taco John's
Other	N: South Dakota Air & Space Museum
(69)	**Parking Area (Westbound)**
(69)	**Parking Area (Eastbound)**
78	New Underwood
FStop	S: Frontier[*]
Food	S: Frontier
Lodg	S: Frontier
ATM	S: Frontier
84	CR 497
88	CR 473 (No Reaccess)
90	Unnamed
99	Wasta
Food	N: Packard Cafe
Lodg	N: Redwood Motel
AServ	N: Wasta Service Center
RVCamp	N: Camping (1 Mile)
Other	N: U.S. Post Office
(99)	**Rest Area (RR, HF, Phones, Picnic, RV Dump; Westbound)**
(99)	**Rest Area (RR, HF, Phones, Picnic, RV Dump; Eastbound, Highway Patrol Station)**
101	CR T - 504, Jensen Road
107	Cedar Butte Road
109	Bus Loop I-90, Wall
110	Badlands, SD 240, Badlands Loop, Wall
Gas	N: Amoco[*, D], Conoco[*], Exxon[*, D]
Food	N: Cactus Cafe & Lounge, Dairy Queen, Elkton House Family Dining, Subway, Wall Drug & Cafe
Lodg	N: Best Western, Days Inn, Fountain Motel, Hitching Post Motel, Homestead Motel, Kings Inn, Knight's Inn, Sands Motor Inn, Super 8, Wall Food Center & Grocery Store, Wall Motel, Welsh Motel
AServ	N: Amoco
RVCamp	N: Arrow Campground (.75 Miles), Sleepy Hollow Campground & RV Park (.75 Miles)
ATM	N: Amoco, Conoco, Exxon, First Western Bank
Parks	S: Badlands National Park (7 Miles)
Other	N: Laundromat, National Grasslands Visitor Center, U.S. Post Office, Wild West Wax Museum
112	U.S. 14, Phillip, Pierre State Capitol
116	Unnamed
121	Unnamed
127	Unnamed
(129)	**Parking Area (Eastbound)**
131	Badlands Loop, SD 240, Badlands Interior
Gas	S: Amoco[*]
Food	S: Circle 10 Campground
Lodg	S: Circle 10 Campground
RVCamp	S: Circle 10 Campground (.5 Miles)
Other	S: Badlands Trading Post, Prairie Homestead
(138)	**Scenic Overlook (Westbound)**
143	SD 73 North, Philip
Med	N: + Hospital (15 Miles)
150	Bus. Loop I-90, SD 73 South, Kadoka
FStop	S: Conoco[*]
Gas	S: Amoco[*], Texaco[*]
Food	S: Conoco, Happy Chef, Sidekick's Restaurant (Texaco)
Lodg	N: Dakota Inn
	S: Budget Host Inn, Super 8, Wagon Wheel Motel
RVCamp	S: Kadoka Campground RV Park, Ponderosa Motel & RV Park (.5 Miles)
ATM	S: Amoco, Conoco
Other	S: Kadoka Laundromat
152	Kadoka, South Creek Road
TStop	N: Burns Brothers Travel Stop[*]
TServ	N: Burns Brothers Travel Stop
Other	S: Badlands Petrified Gardens
163	SD 63 South, Belvidere
FStop	S: Amoco[*], Phillips 66[*]
Food	S: Belvidere Chuckwagon Cafe & RV Camp
Lodg	S: Belvidere Motel
RVCamp	S: Belvidere Chuckwagon Cafe & RV Camp
(165)	**Rest Area (RR, HF, Phones, Picnic, RV Dump; Eastbound)**
(166)	**Rest Area (RR, HF, Phones, Picnic, RV Dump; Westbound)**
170	SD 63 North, Midland
FStop	N: Texaco[*]
RVCamp	N: KOA Campgrounds (.5 Miles), South Dakota's Original 1880 Town (Props From "Dances With Wolves")
Other	N: South Dakota's Original 1880 Town (Props From "Dances With Wolves")
172	Unnamed
177	Unnamed
183	**Okaton, White River Scenic Overlook**
Gas	S: West Lakes Ghost Town[*]
Other	S: U.S. Post Office
188	**Parking Area (Westbound)**
191	Bus. Loop I-90, Murdo
192	U.S. 83 South, Murdo, White River, Rose Bud
TStop	N: Texaco[*, LP]
FStop	N: Sinclair[*]
Gas	N: Amoco[*], Kwik Mart[*], Phillips 66[*]
Food	N: Homemade Ice Cream, KFC, Murdo Drive-In, Star Restaurant, Sub Station, Tee Pee Restaurant
Lodg	N: Anchor Inn, Best Western, Chucks Motel, Hospitality Inn, Lee Motel, Sioux Motel, Super 8, Tee Pee Motel
	S: Country Inn
AServ	N: Phillips 66
TServ	N: Texaco
RVCamp	N: Camp McKen-Z, Tee Pee R/V Camp (1 Mile)
ATM	N: Amoco, First National Bank
Other	N: Murdo Veterinarian Clinic, Pioneer Auto Museum, Super Valu Grocery
(194)	**Parking Area (Westbound)**
(194)	**Parking Area (Eastbound)**
201	Draper
FStop	N: Total[*]
Food	N: Total
AServ	N: Total
TServ	N: Total
208	Unnamed
212	U.S. 83 North, SD 53, Fort Pierre, Pierre State Capitol
FStop	N: Phillips 66[*, LP]
Food	N: Vivian Junction Restaurant
Med	N: + Hospital (34 Miles)
ATM	N: Phillips 66
Other	N: Cultural Heritage Ctr (33 Miles), OAHE Dam (40 Miles)
214	Vivian
(218)	**Rest Area (RR, HF, Phones, Picnic, RV Dump, Pet Walk; Eastbound)**
220	Unnamed
(221)	**Rest Area (RR, HF, Phones, Picnic, RV Dump; Westbound)**
225	Bus Loop I-90, Presho
RVCamp	N: Camping
Other	N: Pioneer Museum
226	Bus Loop I-90, U.S. 183, Winner, Presho
235	SD 273, Kennebec
FStop	N: Conoco[*, K]
Gas	N: King's
Lodg	N: Budget Host Inn, Gerry's Motel, King's Motel
AServ	N: Conoco
RVCamp	N: KOA Campgrounds (.25 Miles)
241	Lyman
248	SD 47 North, Reliance, Lower Brule, Big Bend Dam
Food	N: Golden Buffalo
Lodg	N: Golden Buffalo Motel (see our ad this page)
RVCamp	N: Golden Buffalo Casino
Parks	N: Big Bend Dam Recreation Area
251	SD 47 South, Gregory, Winner
260	Bus. Loop I-90, Oacoma, Chamberlain
FStop	N: Amoco[*, LP, CW]
Food	N: Burger King (Amoco), Oasis Restaurant
Lodg	N: Comfort Inn, Days Inn, EconoLodge, Oasis Inn
RVCamp	N: Al's Oasis (.25 Miles), Familyland Campground, Harry K Chevrolet, Olds, Pontiac, Buick (.6 Miles)
Other	N: Wildlife Adventure Museum
263	Chamberlain
FStop	N: Sinclair[*, LP]
Food	N: A & W Drive-In, Casey's Cafe, Pizza Hut, Taco John's
Lodg	N: Super 8
AServ	N: Sinclair
Other	N: Casey's Drugs[RX], Future Home of South Dakota Hall of Fame, St. Joseph's Akta Lakota Museum, Super Valu Foods, The American Creek Recreation Center (2 Miles)
(264)	**Scenic Overlook, Rest Area (RR, HF, Phones, Picnic, Grills, RV Dump; Westbound)**
(264)	**Scenic Overlook, Rest Area (RR, HF, Phones; Eastbound)**
265	Chamberlain, Pukwana
FStop	S: Conoco[*]
Gas	N: Amoco[*]
AServ	N: Amoco, Gary's & Ralph's Body Shop
TServ	S: A&R Truck Service[24]
RVCamp	S: Happy Campers Campground, KOA Campgrounds
Med	N: + Hospital
ATM	N: Amoco

SLOTS -BLACK JACK -POKER
DINING -MOTEL -RV PARK -CAMPING
-Boat Ramp to Missouri River
-Summer Rodeos and POW WOWS
Experience it!
Golden Buffalo Casino
Lower Brule South Dakota
1-605-473-5577
Lower Brule, SD EXIT 248

EXIT SOUTH DAKOTA

- **Other** N: Alco Food Store, Mid River Veterinarian Clinic, Sioux Museum & Cultural Center (1 Mile)

272 SD 50, Pukwana
- **Parks** S: Platte Creek Recreation Area (32 Miles), Snake Creek Recreation Area (38 Miles)

284 SD 45 North, Kimball
- **FStop** N: Phillips 66(*)
- **Gas** N: Amoco(*, CW)
- **Food** N: Frosty King Drive-In, Phillips 66
- **Lodg** N: Super 8, Travelers Motel
  S: Kimball Motel
- **AServ** N: Amoco
- **RVCamp** N: Mini Mart Park, Parkway Campgrounds & Mini Mart (.25 Miles)
- **ATM** N: Phillips 66
- **Other** N: Parkway Mini Mart

289 SD 45 South, Platte

(293) Parking Area (Westbound)

(293) Parking Area (Eastbound)

296 White Lake
- **Gas** N: Texaco(*)
- **Lodg** N: White Lake Motel
  S: Motel & RV Camp
- **RVCamp** S: Camping, Motel & RV Camp

(301) Rest Area (RR, HF, Phones, Picnic, RV Dump; Westbound)

(301) Rest Area (RR, HF, Phones, Picnic, RV Dump; Eastbound)

308 Bus Loop I-90, Plankinton
- **FStop** N: Cenex(LP), Phillips 66(*)
- **Gas** N: AJ's Mini Mart(*)
- **Food** N: Phillips 66
- **Lodg** N: Super 8, The Nobleman Bed & Breakfast
- **AServ** N: AJ's Mini Mart, Cenex, Skip's Auto Service
- **RVCamp** N: Gordy's Campground

310 U.S. 281, Stickney, Aberdeen, Huron, Fort Randall Dam
- **FStop** S: Conoco(*) (CFN Commercial Fueling Network)
- **Food** S: A & W (Conoco)
- **Other** S: Yankton Tribal Sioux Headquarters (59 Miles)

319 Mt. Fernon

325 Betts Road
- **RVCamp** S: Famil-E-Fun Campground

330 Bus Loop I-90, SD 37 North, Mitchell, Corn Palace
- **Food** N: Holiday Inn (see our ad this page)
- **Lodg** N: EconoLodge, Holiday Inn, Motel 6
- **RVCamp** N: Goldies Shady Acres Campground (1 Mile), Jack's Campers Sales, Service(LP), Mallard Cove Camping
  S: Dakota Campground (.5 Miles)

EXIT SOUTH DAKOTA

- **Med** N: Hospital (3 Miles)
- **Other** N: Corn Palace, Friends of Middle Border Museum, Prehistoric Indian Village Museum

(330) Weigh Station (Located at Exit 330)

332 Bus Loop I-90, SD 37 South, Mitchell, Parkston
- **TStop** N: Texaco(*, RV DUMP, SCALES)
- **Gas** N: Amoco(*, LP, 24), Texaco(*)
- **Food** N: Arby's, Bonanza Steakhouse, Burger King (Amoco), Country Kitchen, Happy Chef, Hardee's, McDonald's, Perkins Family Restaurant, Subway (Texaco TS), The Pizza Ranch, Truck Haven Restaurant (Texaco TS), Twin Dragon Chinese
- **Lodg** N: AmericInn Motel, Best Western, Comfort Inn, Days Inn, Super 8, Thunderbird Motel
- **AServ** N: Texaco
- **TServ** N: Texaco(SCALES)
  S: Trail King Truck Service
- **TWash** N: Mega Wash
- **RVCamp** N: R & R Campground & RV Park
- **Med** N: Hospital (2 Miles)
- **ATM** N: Amoco, K-Mart(RX)
- **Other** N: K-Mart(RX), Mega Wash, UPS Parcel Service

335 Riverside Road
- **RVCamp** N: KOA Campgrounds (1 Mile)

(336) Parking Area (Eastbound)

(337) Parking Area (Westbound)

344 SD 262 East, Fulton, Alexandria
- **FStop** S: Texaco(*, CW)
- **Food** S: Texaco
- **AServ** S: Texaco

350 SD 25, Emery, Farmer
- **Other** N: De Smet - Home of Laura Ingalls Wilder (55 Miles)

1/4 mile North of I-90
HO5730
Newly Renovated Hotel in 97
Holiday Inn®
1534
• Only Full Service Hotel in Mitchell
• Large Holidome with Indoor Pool & 2 Whirpools • Exercise Room
• Full Size 18 Hole Minature Golf Course
• Block & Barrel Bar & Grill
• Video Lottery Gambling
• Ample Parking for Large Vehicles
605-996-6501 • 800-888-4702
SOUTH DAKOTA ▪ I-90 ▪ EXIT 330

EXIT SOUTH DAKOTA

353 Spencer, Emery
- **TStop** S: Amoco Burns Bros Travel Stop(*)
- **Food** S: Subway(*) (Amoco Burns Bros TS)

357 Bridgewater, Canova

(362) Rest Area (RR, HF, Phones, Picnic, RV Dump; Westbound)

(362) Rest Area (RR, HF, Phones, Picnic, RV Dump; Eastbound)

364 U.S. 81, Salem, Yankton
- **Food** N: Edith's Cafe
- **RVCamp** N: Camp America Campground (1 Mile)

368 Canistoda

374 Montrose
- **RVCamp** S: Camping (5.5 Miles)
- **Parks** S: Lake Vermillion Recreation Area (5 Miles)
- **Other** N: Montrose Veterinarian Clinic

379 SD 19, Humboldt, Madison

387 Hartford
- **FStop** N: Phillips 66(*, K)
- **AServ** N: Phillips 66
- **TServ** N: Phillips 66

390 SD 38, Buffalo Ridge
- **Gas** S: Buffalo Ridge Ghost Town Gas(*)
- **RVCamp** N: Camp Dakota, Sioux Fall Kamp Dakota Campground (.25 Miles)
- **Other** S: Buffalo Ridge Ghost Town (Buffalo Ridge Gas)

396A Jct. I-29 South

399 Bus Loop I-90, SD 115, Cliff Ave, Airport
- **TStop** N: Sinclair(*, SCALES) (CB Shop, Laundry)
  S: Pilot Travel Center(*, 24)
- **FStop** S: Holiday(*)
- **Gas** N: Total(*, LP)
  S: Cenex(*, D, LP, CW)
- **Food** N: Cody's Restaurant (Sinclair TS), Sinclair (CB Shop, Laundry)
  S: Arby's, Burger King, McDonald's, Perkin's Family Restaurant, Pilot Travel Center, Subway(24) (Pilot Travel Center)
- **Lodg** S: Cloud 9 Motel, Comfort Inn, Days Inn, Super 8
- **AServ** S: Hunter Automotive Brake Service
- **TServ** S: American Rim & Brake, Cummins, Dakota Volvo, Dorsey Trailers, Graham Tire Co., International, Interstate Detroit Diesel, Kenworth Dealer, Peterbilt Dealer, Pilot Travel Center(24), Vander Haag's
- **TWash** S: Pilot Travel Center
- **RVCamp** N: KOA Kampground (.5 Miles), Spader Camper Center
- **Med** N: Hospital

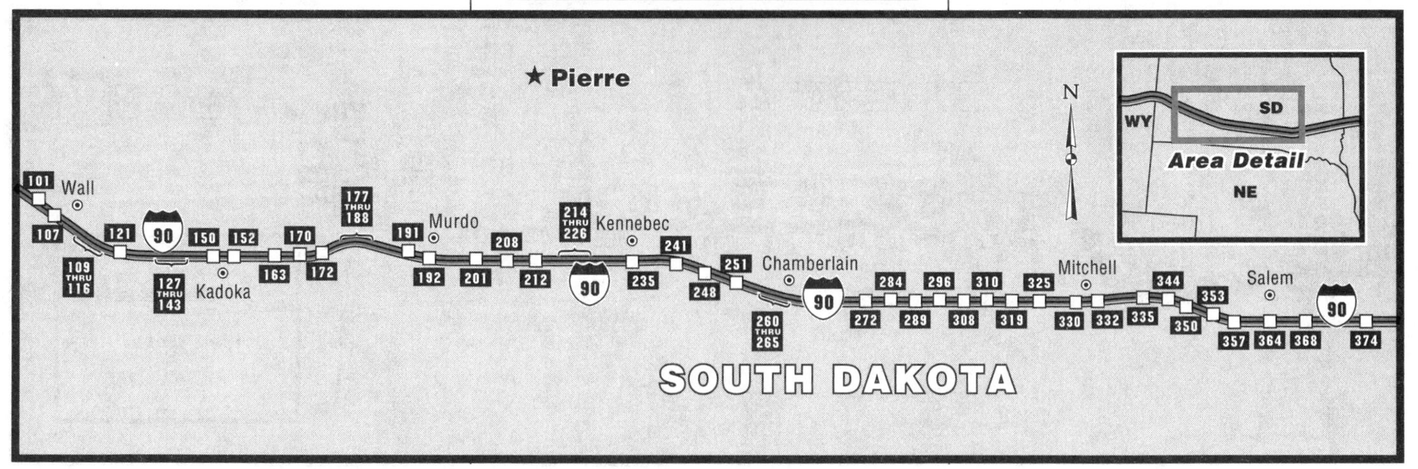

Bold red print shows RV & Bus parking available or nearby

EXIT	SOUTH DAKOTA/MINNESOTA
Other	**S:** The Wash Out[CW]
400	Jct I-229
402	EROS Data Center, U.S. Geological Survey
RVCamp	**N:** Yogi Bear Camp Resort[LP] (1.5 Miles)
406	SD 11, Corsan, Brandon
Gas	**S:** Amoco[*, 24], Ampride[*]
Lodg	**S:** Holiday Inn Express
AServ	**S:** Checkered Flag Auto Repair, Knudtson Collision Repair, Valvoline Oil Change
TServ	**S:** Luverne Truck Equipment
ATM	**S:** Amoco, Ampride
Parks	**S:** Big Sioux Recreation Center (4 Miles), Palisades Park
410	Valley Springs, Garretson
Parks	**S:** Beaver Creek Nature Area (6 Miles South), Palisades State Park (7 Miles)
(412)	Rest Area (RR, Phones, Picnic, RV Dump; Eastbound)
(412)	Rest Area (RR, Phones, Picnic, RV Dump; Westbound)

↑SOUTH DAKOTA

↓MINNESOTA

EXIT	MINNESOTA
(1)	MN Welcome Center (RR, HF, Phones, Picnic; Northbound)
1	MN 23, CR 17, Jasper, Pipestone
Other	**N:** Pipestone National Monument (30 Miles)
3	CR 4, Beaver Creek (Reaccess Westbound Only)
5	CR 6, Beaver Creek, Hills (Westbound)
Gas	**N:** Texaco[D]
12	U.S. 75, Luverne, Rock Rapids
Gas	**N:** Amoco[*], Casey's General Store[*], Cenex[*, D], Co-Op, Ferrell Gas, Phillips 66
Food	**N:** Amoco, Country Kitchen, Homemade Donuts (Casey's General Store), JJ's Tasty Drive In, McDonald's, Pizza Hut, Scotty's Bar & Grill, Subway (Amoco), Taco John's **S:** Magnolia Steak House (Super 8 Motel), Super 8
Lodg	**N:** Comfort Inn, Cozy Rest Motel, Hillcrest Motel **S:** Super 8
AServ	**N:** Align Tech & Tire, Chrysler Auto Dealer, Exhaust Pros
RVCamp	**N:** Camping **S:** Camping
Med	**N:** ✚ Hospital
ATM	**N:** First National Bank
Parks	**N:** Blue Mounds State Park
Other	**N:** Coin Car Wash, Jubilee Foods Grocery, Pipestone Nat'l Monument, Rock County Co-Op Car Wash, Tru Value Hardware **S:** Pharmacy[RX]
18	CR 3, Magnolia, Kanaranzi
(24)	Rest Area (RR, HF, Phones, Picnic, Pet Walk; Eastbound)
(24)	Rest Area (RR, HF, Phones, Picnic, Pet Walk; Westbound)
26	MN 91, Lake Wilson, Adrian
FStop	**S:** Cenex[*, 24]
Gas	**S:** Amoco[*]
Food	**S:** Amoco, Restaurant (Amoco)
AServ	**S:** Cenex, Cenex[24]
TServ	**S:** Cenex, Cenex[24]
RVCamp	**S:** Adrian Campground
Other	**S:** Laundry Facilities (Adrian Campground), Self Service Car Wash
33	CR 13, Wilmont, Rushmore
42	MN 266, CR 25
Lodg	**S:** Budget Host Inn, Super 8
Other	**S:** Camping
43	U.S. 59, Slayton, Worthington, Flayton
FStop	**S:** Cenex[*], Phillips 66[*, CW]
Gas	**S:** Casey's General Store[*], Conoco[*], Texaco[*, D], Total[*]
Food	**S:** Cenex, Dairy Queen, Domino's Pizza, Godfather's Pizza, Hardee's, KFC, Luen Fong Chinese, McDonald's[PLAY], Perkin's Family Restaurant, Pizza Hut, Ruttles 50's Grill, Subway, Taco Bell (Cenex), Taco John's, Wendy's
Lodg	**N:** Ramada Inn **S:** AmericInn, Best Western, Budget Inn, Ramada Inn
AServ	**S:** Car Quest Auto Center, Conoco, Conoco, GM Auto Dealership, Joe's Exhaust Pros, K-Mart, NAPA Auto Parts, RBS Transmission, Spomer Chevrolet Pontiac Oldsmobile Buick Cadillac Mazda
RVCamp	**S:** Camping
Med	**S:** ✚ Hospital
ATM	**S:** Cash Machine, Cenex, Cenex, First State Bank, Phillips 66
Other	**S:** Car Wash, Colonial Coin Laundry, EconoFood, Fleet Family Center[LP], Hi -Vee Food Store, K-Mart, Optical (Shopko), Shopko Grocery (Optical), Sterling Drugs[RX]
45	MN 60, Windom
FStop	**S:** Worthington Travel Plaza[*, SCALES] (Texaco gas)
Food	**S:** Hot Stuff Pizza (Texaco), Smash Hit Subs (Texaco), Worthington Travel Plaza (Texaco gas)
Lodg	**S:** Best Western
RVCamp	**S:** Camping
(46)	Weigh Station (Eastbound)
47	CR 3 (Eastbound, Reaccess Westbound Only)
50	MN 264, CR 1, Brewster, Round Lake
RVCamp	**S:** Camping
57	CR 9, Heron Lake
64	MN 86, Lakefield
RVCamp	**N:** Camping **S:** Camping
Parks	**N:** Kilen Woods State Park (12 Miles)
(69)	Rest Area (RR, HF, Phones, Picnic; Eastbound)
(73)	Rest Area (RR, HF, Phones, Picnic, Pet Walk; Westbound)
73	U.S. 71, Jackson
FStop	**N:** Whoa 'n Go Truck Stop[*] (Conoco gas)
Gas	**S:** Amoco[*]
Food	**N:** Best Western, Best Western, Hardee's **S:** Amoco, Burger King (Amoco), Santa Fe Crossing Motel
Lodg	**N:** Best Western, Super 8 **S:** Budget Host, Earth Inn Motel, Prairie Winds Hotel, Santa Fe Crossing Motel
AServ	**N:** Goodyear Tire & Auto **S:** GM Auto Dealership, Hedenquist, Schultz's I-90 Towing & Repair
TServ	**N:** Goodyear Tire & Auto
RVCamp	**N:** Camping, KOA Kampground
Med	**S:** ✚ Hospital
ATM	**N:** Conoco Fuel Stop (Conoco FS), Whoa 'n Go Truck Stop (Conoco gas) **S:** Amoco
Parks	**N:** Kilen Woods State Park
80	CR 29, Alpha
87	MN 4, St James, Sherburn
Gas	**S:** Texaco[*, LP]
Food	**S:** Homemade Pizza (Texaco), Ma Faber's Home Cookin, Texaco
RVCamp	**N:** Caverns Landing Campground, Everett Campground (5 Miles)
ATM	**S:** Texaco
93	MN 263, CR 27, Welcome, Ceylon
Gas	**S:** Welcome Campground
RVCamp	**S:** Welcome Campground[*] (Laundry, showers, gas)
Other	**S:** Laundry (Welcome Campground)

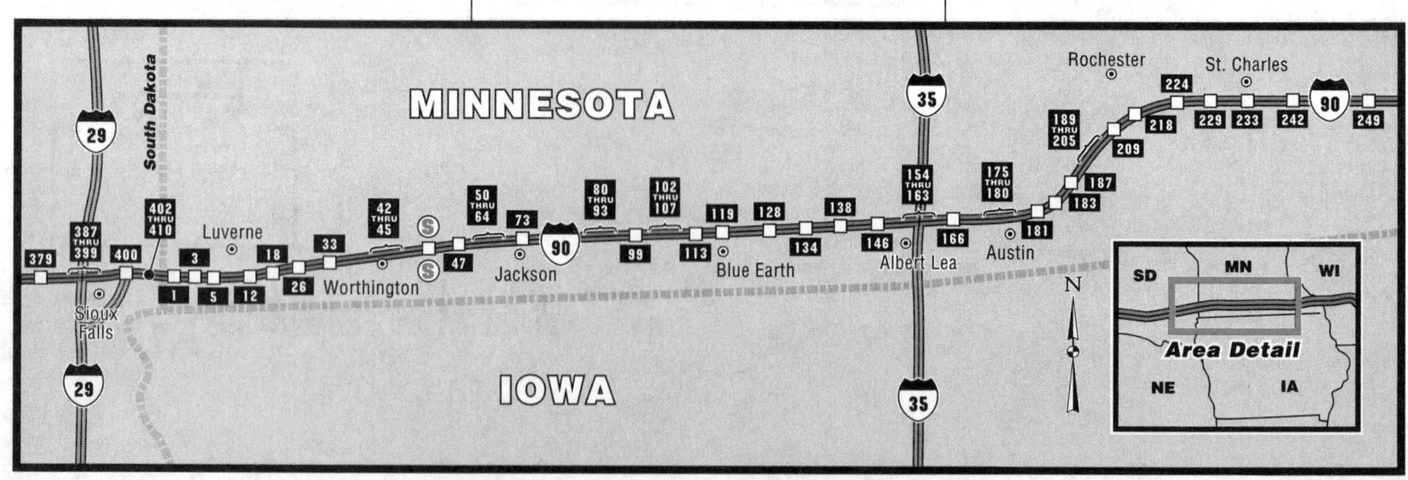

Bold red print shows RV & Bus parking available or nearby

EXIT MINNESOTA

99 CR 39, Fairmont, Bus. Loop I-90

102 MN 15, Madelia, Fairmont
- **FStop** S: Cenex(*), Super America(*)
- **Gas** S: Phillips 66(*, CW)
- **Food** S: China Restaurant, Happy Chef, Holiday Inn, McDonald's(PLAY), Perkin's Family Restaurant(24), Pizza Hut, Taco Bell (Cenex), The Green Mill (Holiday Inn)
- **Lodg** S: Comfort Inn, Holiday Inn, Super 8
- **AServ** S: Car Quest Auto Center, GM Auto Dealership
- **TServ** N: Truck Service
  S: Chesley Freightliner
- **TWash** N: Truck Service, Truck Wash
- **RVCamp** S: Camping
- **Med** S: Hospital
- **ATM** S: Super America
- **Parks** S: Lincoln Park
- **Other** S: K-Mart

107 MN 262, CR 53, Granada, East Chain
- **RVCamp** S: Flying Goose Campground (1 Mile, Open May to Oct)

113 CR 1, Huntley, Guckeen

(119) Rest Area (RR, HF, Phones, Picnic, Pet Walk; Eastbound)

(119) Rest Area (RR, HF, Phones, Picnic, Pet Walk; Westbound)

119 U.S. 169, Blue Earth, Mankato
- **FStop** S: Sinclair(*)
- **Gas** S: Texaco(*)
- **Food** S: Country Kitchen, Dairy Queen, Hardee's, Hot Stuff Pizza (Texaco), McDonald's(PLAY), Pizza Hut, Subway, Taco Bell (Texaco), Texaco
- **Lodg** S: AmericInn Motel, Super 8
- **AServ** S: Sinclair, Sinclair FS
- **TServ** S: Sinclair FS
- **RVCamp** S: Camping
- **Med** S: Hospital
- **ATM** S: Sinclair, Texaco
- **Other** S: Super Wash Automatic & Coin Car Wash, Wal-Mart(RX)

128 MN 254, CR 17, Easton, Frost

134 MN 253, CR 21, Minnesota Lake, Bricelyn

138 MN 22, Wells, Kiester
- **RVCamp** S: Camping (1 Mile)

146 MN 109, CR 6, Alden
- **FStop** S: Amoco(*, LP)
- **Gas** S: Cenex(*, LP)
- **Food** N: Main St Grill
  S: Amoco
- **AServ** S: Alden Truck & Auto Repair, Alden Truck & Auto Repair, Cenex
- **TServ** S: Alden Truck & Auto Repair, Amoco Fuel Stop
- **Parks** N: Moran Park
- **Other** N: Coin Car Wash, U.S. Post Office

154 MN 13, Waseca, Albert Lea
- **FStop** N: SuperAmerica(*)

157 CR 22, Albert Lea
- **FStop** S: Citgo(*, LP, CW)
- **Gas** S: Conoco(*, LP, CW)
- **Food** S: Cafe Don'l, Citgo, Dairy Queen, Deli & Cafe (Hy-Vee Grocery), McDonald's, Northbridge Mall, Subway(*) (Citgo FS)
- **Lodg** S: AmericInn, Holiday Inn Express
- **AServ** S: Indy Lube
- **Med** S: Hospital
- **ATM** S: Citgo, Citgo Fuel Stop (Conoco), Conoco, Conoco, Hy-Vee Grocery(24, RX)
- **Other** S: Bridgeport Car Wash, Coast to Coast Hardware(LP), Coin Operated Car Wash, Hy-Vee Grocery(RX), Mall Theater, Northbridge Mall, Optical (Shopko), Shopko Grocery(RX) (Optical)

159AB 159A Jct I-35 South, Des Moines, 159B Jct. I-35 North to Twin Cities

(162) Rest Area (RR, Phones, Picnic, Vending; Eastbound)

163 CR 26, Hayward
- **FStop** S: Amoco(*, D)
- **Gas** S: Cenex(D) (Have to use credit card, ATM card)
- **Food** S: Netts Diner
- **AServ** S: Amoco, Auto Service (Amoco FS)
- **RVCamp** S: KOA Kampground
- **Parks** S: Myre-Big Island State Park

166 CR 46, Oakland Road
- **RVCamp** N: KOA Kampground (.5 Miles)

(171) Rest Area (RR, Phones, Picnic, Vending; Westbound)

175 MN 105, CR 46, Oakland Road, Bus. Loop I-90
- **FStop** N: Phillips 66(*)
  S: Conoco(*)
- **Gas** S: Amoco(*)
- **Food** N: Hovland Sports, Phillips 66, Restaurant (Phillips 66 FS), Sports Family Dining
  S: Conoco
- **Lodg** N: Rodeway Inn
- **AServ** S: Amoco, Amoco, Austin Ford Mercury, Male Saxtons Austin Ford Lincoln Mercury
- **RVCamp** N: Nelson's Wheel Estates Mobile Home Park (.5 Miles)
- **Med** S: Hospital

177 U.S. 218, 14th St NW
- **FStop** S: Total(*, K)
- **Gas** N: Little Duke's On the Go Gas & Grocery(24, RX)
- **Food** N: Applebee's, Diamond Days Hot Dog Co., KFC, Little Duke's On the Go Gas & Grocery, Oak Park Mall
  S: Hardee's(PLAY)
- **Lodg** S: Super 8
- **AServ** N: Indy Lube, K-Mart(RX), K-Mart(RX)
- **Med** S: Hospital
- **ATM** N: Hy-Vee Food Store
- **Other** N: Hy-Vee Food Store, K-Mart(RX), K-Mart(RX), Oak Park Cinemas, Oak Park Mall, Shopko(RX) (Optical), Target

178A 4th St NW
- **Gas** S: Amoco(*, LP, CW), Conoco(*, D, LP, CW), Severson(*, LP, K, CW), Sinclair(D)
- **Food** N: Holiday Inn, Holiday Inn, Perkin's Family Restaurant, The Green Mill (Holiday Inn), Torge's Grill (Holiday Inn)
  S: Burger King(PLAY), Severson, Subway (Severson)
- **Lodg** N: DAYS INN Days Inn, Holiday Inn
- **AServ** S: Sinclair
- **Other** N: I-Vee Food Store

178B 6th St NE Downtown, Austin
- **Other** S: Hormel Ham Co.

179 11th Dr NE
- **TStop** N: Citgo(*, LP, SCALES)
- **Food** N: Citgo, Citgo Truck Stop
- **TServ** N: Citgo(SCALES), Citgo Truck Stop
- **TWash** N: Citgo

180BA U.S. 218S, 21st St NE, Lyle (180A is Westbound)
- **Gas** S: Texaco(*, LP)
- **Lodg** S: Austin Motel
- **ATM** S: Texaco

181 28th St NE

183 MN 56, Brownsdale, Rose Creek
- **FStop** S: Cenex(*) (Pump 24 (use cards only))
- **AServ** S: Cenex FS

187 CR 20
- **RVCamp** S: Beaver Trails Campground

189 CR13, Elkton

193 MN 16, Dexter, Preston, Grand Meadow, Spring Valley
- **TStop** S: Amoco(*) (Laundry, showers)
- **Food** S: Amoco (Laundry, showers), Holland Lounge (Mill Inn), Mill Inn, Wind Mill Restaurant (Amoco TS)
- **Lodg** S: Mill Inn
- **ATM** S: Amoco (Laundry, showers), Cash Machine (Amoco TS)

(202) Rest Area (RR, Phones, Picnic, Vending; Eastbound)

205 CR 6

209AB 209A South U.S. 63, East MN 30, , Stewartville, 209B North U.S. 63, West MN 30, Rochester
- **TStop** S: Texaco(*)
- **Food** S: Hungry Bear (Texaco TS), Texaco
- **TServ** S: Texaco, Texaco Truck Stop
- **TWash** S: Texaco Truck Stop
- **RVCamp** S: Camping
- **ATM** S: Cash Machine (Texaco TS), Texaco

218 U.S. 52, Chatfield
- **RVCamp** S: KOA Kampground

(222) Rest Area (RR, Phones, Picnic, Vending; Westbound)

224 CR 7, Eyota

229 CR 10, Dover

233 MN 74, St Charles
- **TStop** S: Texaco(*, K, RV DUMP)
- **Food** S: Texaco, The Amish Oven (Texaco)
- **TServ** S: Texaco
- **ATM** S: Texaco
- **Parks** S: Whitewater Park

242 CR 29, Lewiston

(244) Rest Area (RR, Phones, Picnic, Vending; Eastbound)

249 MN 43, Rushford
- **TServ** N: Peterbilt Dealer(LP)

252 MN 43, Winona
- **Med** N: Hospital

257 MN 76, Houston
- **RVCamp** S: Camping

266 CR12, Nodine
- **TStop** S: Amoco(*, 24)
- **Food** S: Amoco, Subway (Amoco TS), Trucker's Inn Restaurant(24)
- **TServ** S: Amoco(24), Amoco Truck Stop
- **TWash** S: Amoco
- **Parks** N: Great River Bluff State Park, O. L. Kipp State Park

269 U.S.14, U.S. 61, Winona (Westbound)

270 U.S. 61N, Dakota (Eastbound, Reaccess Eastbound Only)

272A Dresbach (Reaccess Westbound Only)
- **Gas** S: Mobil(*)
- **AServ** S: Mobil

272B Dresbach (Westbound, Reaccess Eastbound Only)
- **Gas** S: Mobil(*, D)

Bold red print shows RV & Bus parking available or nearby

EXIT		MINNESOTA/WISCONSIN
	Lodg	N: Dresbach Motel
	AServ	S: Mobil, Mobil
275		**U.S. 14, U.S. 61, La Crescent, La Crosse, Minnesota Welcome Center**
	Med	**N: + Hospital**

↑MINNESOTA

↓WISCONSIN

EXIT		WISCONSIN
(1)		**WI Welcome Center (RR, Phones, Picnic, Vending, RV Dump)**
2		CR B, French Island
	FStop	N: **Mobil**[LP]
	Gas	S: Citgo[*, D, LP]
	Food	S: Autumns Rib Restaurant (Days Inn), Days Inn
	Lodg	S: Days Inn
	TServ	N: **Debauche Truck & Diesel (International, Cummins)**
	RVCamp	N: **Jay's RV Sales & Service**
	ATM	S: Citgo, Tyme Machine
	Other	S: Quillin's Island
3AB		U.S. 53, WI 35, La Crosse (3A southbound)
	Gas	N: QuikTrip[*, LP]
		S: Amoco[*, CW], QuikTrip[*, LP], SuperAmerica[*, D, LP]
	Food	N: Dairy Queen[PLAY], Happy Joe's Pizza, Nutbush City Limits Restaurant
		S: Best Western, Burger King, Chee Peng Palace Chinese, Coney Island, Country Kitchen, Eduardo's Pizza Wagon, Embers Restaurant & Bakery, KFC, McDonald's, Moxie's On The River (Best Western), Pizza Hut, Ponderosa Steakhouse, Rocky Ricoco's Pizza
	Lodg	N: Onolaskan Inn
		S: Best Western, Burkestone Inn, Excel Inn, Hampton Inn, Knight Saver Inn, Road Star Inn, Super 8
	AServ	N: Dee's Muffler Shop, Nosske Body Shop
		S: Amoco, Goodyear
	RVCamp	S: **Camping**
	Med	S: **+ Hospital**
	ATM	S: Tyme Machine
	Parks	S: **Great River State Trail**
	Other	N: **Central Animal Hospital**, Snow White Laundromat
		S: Amtrak Terminal, **Shopko**[RX], Sir Speedy Cleaning & Copying
4		U.S. 53N, WI 157, La Crosse, Onalaska
	Gas	N: QuikTrip[*, LP]
		S: QuikTrip[*, LP], QuikTrip[*, LP]

EXIT		WISCONSIN
	Food	N: Tom's Turkey Express
		S: Bakers Square Restaurant, Burger King[PLAY], Famous Days, Grizzly's Grill, Leedo Chinese Food, Red Lobster, Rocky Rococo Pizza, Shakeys Pizza, Taco Bell
	Lodg	S: Comfort Inn
	AServ	S: **Sam's Club**, Tires Plus, Wonder Lube, Zip Lube
	ATM	N: QuikTrip, Trane Federal Credit Union
		S: **Festival Foods**
	Other	S: AAA Office, **Festival Foods**, Pet Co., **Sam's Club**, Ship Shape Car Wash, **Wal-Mart**[LP, 24, RX], Wisconsin Vision
5		WI 16, Onalaska
	Gas	N: Woodman's[*, CW]
		S: Holiday[*, D, LP], Phillips 66[LP], QuikTrip[*, D, LP, 24]
	Food	S: A & W Hot Dogs & More (Holiday), Applebee's, Chi-Chi's Restaurant, China Inn, Chuck E Cheese's Pizza, Ciatti's Italian, Fazoli's Italian Food, Holiday, McDonald's[PLAY], Old Country Buffet, Olive Garden, Perkin's Family Restaurant, Wendy's
	Lodg	N: Budgetel Inn, Hampton Inn, Microtel Inn
		S: Holiday Inn Express
	AServ	N: Woodman's
		S: Blane's Farm & Fleet, Goodyear, Sears
	Med	S: **+ Hospital**
	ATM	S: Coulee State Bank, **Cub Food**[24], M & I Bank, Norwest Bank, QuikTrip
	Other	N: **Woodman's Supermarket**
		S: **Barnes & Noble**, Blane's Farm & Fleet, **Cub Food**, **Shopko**[RX] **(Optical)**, State Trails, **Target**, Valley Square Theaters, **Valley View Shopping Mall**
(10)		**Weigh Station (Eastbound)**
12		CR C, West Salem
	Lodg	S: AmericInn
	RVCamp	N: **Camping**, **Coulee Region RV Service**[LP]
	Other	N: **Veteran Memorial Public Campground (2 Miles)**
15		WI 162, Bangor, Coon Valley
	Gas	S: **Wehrs Used Trucks**
	AServ	S: **Wehrs Used Trucks**
	TServ	S: **Wehrs Used Trucks**
(20)		**Rest Area (RR, Phones, Picnic, Vending; Eastbound)**
(22)		**Rest Area (RR, Phones, Picnic, Vending; Westbound)**
25		WI 27, Sparta, Melvina
	FStop	N: **Citgo**[*]
	Food	N: Amish Cheese House (Citgo), **Citgo**, Happy Chef
	Lodg	N: Country Inn, Super 8
	RVCamp	S: **Camping**
	Med	S: **+ Hospital**

EXIT		WISCONSIN
	Other	S: Lacrosse River Elroy Sparta State Trails
28		WI 16, Sparta, Ft. Mc Coy
41		WI 131, Tomah, Wilton
	Lodg	N: Brentwood Inn
	Med	N: **+ VA Medical Center**
	Other	S: **State Police**
43		U.S. 12, WI 16, Tomah
	Lodg	N: Rest Well Motel
45A		I-90, Junction I-94, to Madison
45B		Jct I-94, St Paul, O'Clair, LaCross
(48)		**Weigh Station (Westbound)**
49		CR PP, Oakdale
	TStop	N: **Citgo Travel Center**[*]
	FStop	N: **Speedway**[*, LP]
	Gas	S: Mobil[*, LP]
	Lodg	S: Oak Dale Motel
	RVCamp	N: **Granger's Campground (.33 Miles)**, **Kamp Dakota (.5 Miles)**
	ATM	S: Mobil
	Parks	S: **Mill Bluff State Park**
(55)		**Rest Area (RR, Phones, Picnic, Grills; North At Exit 55)**
55		CR C, Camp Douglas, Volkfield
	FStop	S: **Amoco**[*]
	Gas	S: Mobil[*, LP]
	Food	S: **German House**, Mobil, Subway (Mobil)
	Lodg	S: Walsh's K&K Motel
	ATM	S: **Amoco**, Mobil
	Parks	S: **Mills Bluff State Park**
	Other	S: Camp William National Guard Museum, Coin Operated Laundry, Omaha Trail
61		WI 80, Necedah, New Lisbon
	TStop	N: **Mobil**[*, D], **New Lisbon 76 Auto/Truck Stop**[*, D, SCALES]
	FStop	N: **Citgo**[*, D]
	Food	N: **76**, **Citgo**, **Grandma's Kitchen (Citgo)**, **New Lisbon 76 Auto/Truck Stop**, Subway (Citgo)
	Lodg	N: Edge of the Wood Motel
	TServ	N: **New Lisbon 76 Auto/Truck Stop**[SCALES]
	RVCamp	N: **Camping**
		S: **Camping**
69		WI 82, Mauston, Necedah
	TStop	S: **Kwik Trip - Amoco**[*, D, LP, 24]
	FStop	N: **Cenex Travel Mart**[*, D, LP], **Phillips 66**[*, D], **Shell**[*, D]
	Gas	S: Citgo[*]
	Food	N: **Cenex Travel Mart**, **Country Kitchen**, **Park Oasis Inn**, Taco Bell (Cenex), The Family Restaurant (Park Oasis Inn)
		S: A & W, Culver's Frozen Custard & Burgers, Garden Valley Restaurant, Hardee's, Hardy Platter[24] (Amoco), **Kwik Trip - Amoco**,

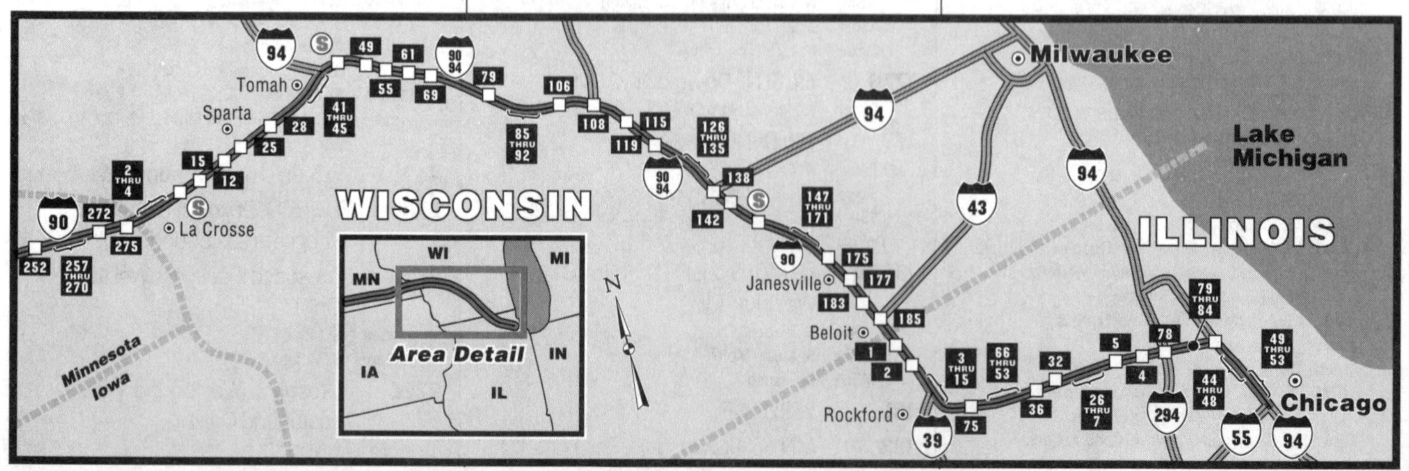

Bold red print shows RV & Bus parking available or nearby

EXIT | WISCONSIN

McDonald's, Roman Castle Italian, The Alaskan Motel
Lodg N: Country Inn & Suites, Park Oasis Inn, Super 8
S: The Alaskan Motel
TServ S: Kwik Trip - Amoco[24]
Med S: + Hospital
ATM S: Bank of Mauston
Parks S: State Park
Other N: Dragons Ben Mini Golf
S: Car Wash, Cheese Mart, Coin Operated Laundry

(76) Rest Area (RR, Phones, Picnic, Vending, RV Dump; Eastbound)

(76) Rest Area (RR, Phones, Picnic, Vending, RV Dump; Westbound)

79 CR, HH, Lyndon Station
FStop S: Shell[*, LP]
RVCamp N: Crocket's RV Campground (2 Miles), Dreamfield RV Sales & Service[LP], Yukon Trails Camping (.5 Miles)

85 U.S. 12, WI 16, Wisconsin Dells
TServ S: G & S Inc
RVCamp N: Arrowhead Campground (.75 Miles), Dells Timberland Campground (2 Miles), Eagle Flats Campground (.25 Miles), Stand Rock Campground (1 Mile)
S: Camping
Parks S: Rocky Arbor State Park

87 WI 13 North, Wisconsin Dells
FStop N: Amoco[*, D, LP, RV DUMP] (Towing), Mobil[*, LP]
Gas N: Shell[*]
Food N: Black Bark Stage Coach Buffet, Burger King[PLAY], Country Kitchen, Denny's, Luigi's Pizzaria, Paul Bunion's Cook Shanty, Perkins Family Restaurant, Taco Bell, Wendy's
Lodg N: Best Western, Comfort Inn, DAYS INN Days Inn, Dells Eagle Motel, Holiday Inn, Super 8, The Polynesian Motel
AServ N: Amoco (Towing)
RVCamp N: KOA Campgrounds (2 Miles), Sherwood Forest Campground (1.5 Miles), Tee Pee Park Campground (1 Mile)
S: Bonanza Campground (2 Miles)
ATM N: Mobil, Shell
Parks N: Beaver Springs Fishing Park
Other N: Timberfalls Water Park/Putt Putt

89 WI 23, Lake Delton, Reedsburg
FStop N: Mobil[*]
Gas N: Terry's Shortstop[*, LP] (Marathon)
Food N: Granny Good Things Bake Shop, Hometown Cafe (Mobil), Mobil
Lodg N: Malibu Inn, Olympia Motel, Roadway Inn, Sahara Motel
RVCamp N: Yogi Bear Camp Resort (1 Mile)
S: Country Roads Motor Home & RV Park (.75 Miles)
Other N: Coin Operated Laundry, Crystal Grand Music Theater

92 U.S. 12, Baraboo, Lake Delton
FStop N: Mobil[*, LP]
Gas N: Amoco[*], Citgo[*, CW]
Food N: Burger King[PLAY], Cheese Factory Restaurant, Cheese Store, Danny's Diner, McDonald's[PLAY], Ponderosa, Subway, Wintergreen Resort, Wintergreen Restaurant (Wintergreen Resort)
Lodg N: Alakai Hotel & Suites, Black Wolf Lodge, Camelot, Country Squire Motel, Del Rancho, Grand Marquis Inn, Lake Motel, Ramada Limited, Wilderness Hotel, Wintergreen Resort
S: Good Nite Inn, Motel 6, Vagabond Motel
TWash N: Car & Truck Wash
RVCamp N: Yogi Bear Camp Resort (1.5 Miles)
S: American RV Sales, Dell Boo Campground

EXIT | WISCONSIN

(2 Miles), Fox Hill RV Park (RV Sales & Service), Pioneer Camping (.75 Miles), Red Oak Campground (2 Miles), Scenic Traveler RV Sales & Service, Yogi Bear Camp Resort (2 Miles)
ATM N: Citgo, Mobil
Other N: Car & Truck Wash

106 WI 33, Portage, Baraboo
FStop S: Mobil[*]
Gas N: Amoco[*]
Food S: Coffee Shop
RVCamp S: Kamp Dakota (.63 Miles)
Med N: + Hospital

108AB WI 78, I 39 To U.S. 51, Wausau, Merrimac, Stevens Point
TStop S: Petro[*, LP, SCALES]
Gas S: Phillips 66[*, LP] (Towing)
Food S: Dairy Queen (Petro), Little Caesars Pizza (Petro), Petro, The Iron Skillet (Petro)
Lodg S: Comfort Suites Hotel, DAYS INN Days Inn
AServ S: Phillips 66 (Towing)
TServ S: Petro[SCALES]
TWash S: Petro

(114) Rest Area (RR, Phones, Picnic, Vending, RV Dump; Eastbound)

(114) Rest Area (RR, Phones, Picnic, Vending, RV Dump; Westbound)

115 CR CS, Poynette, Lake Wisconsin
FStop N: Citgo[*, D, LP]
Food N: McDonald's, Subway
AServ N: Grahams Auto & Truck Clinic[CW]
TServ N: Grahams Auto & Truck Clinic, Truck & Repair[24]
TWash N: Citgo
RVCamp N: Jade RV Park, Smokey Hollow Campground (2 Miles- Open 12 Months)

119 WI 60, Lodi, Arlington
AServ S: Trucks Central

126 CR V, Dane, De Forest
Gas N: Amoco[*, CW, 24]
S: Phillips 66[*, LP]
Food N: Cheese Chalet, Culver's Frozen Custard & Hamburgers, McDonald's, Subway
Lodg N: Holiday Inn Express
RVCamp N: KOA Campgrounds
ATM N: Amoco
Other N: State Police

131 WI 19, Waunakee, Sun Praire
FStop N: QuikTrip[*, D, LP]
Gas N: Mobil, Super America[*, D, LP]
Food N: A & W Drive-In, Columbo Yogurt (SuperAmerica), McDonald's[PLAY], Mouse House Cheese Haus, Super America, Taco Bell (SuperAmerica)
Lodg N: DAYS INN Days Inn, Super 8
TServ N: Wisconsin Kenworth
Other N: Lazer Clean Car Wash, Truck Wash[D]

132 U.S. 51, Madison, De Forest
TStop N: Marathon[*, LP, SCALES], Shell[*, SCALES]
S: 76 Auto/Truck Plaza[*, RV DUMP, SCALES]
FStop S: Pumper Truck Stop[*]
Food N: Marathon, Pine Cone[*, SCALES] (Shell), Shell, The Copper Kitchen (Marathon)
S: 76 Auto/Truck Plaza, Deli (Pumper), Pumper Truck Stop, Subway (Pumper)
TServ N: Diesel Specialists of Madison
S: Brad Ragin Tire Service, Freightliner[24], Peterbilt Dealer, Polk Diesel & Machine, Transport Refridgeration Inc. Thermal King
RVCamp N: Token Creek Park (.5 Miles)
S: WI RV World RV Service
ATM N: Marathon, Shell

EXIT | WISCONSIN

135AB U.S. 151, Madison, Sun Prairie
Gas S: Amoco[*], Shell[*] (Towing), Sinclair[*]
Food S: Applebee's, Bread Smith, Carlos O'Kely, Chili's, Country Kitchen, Dunkin Donuts, Hardee's, IHOP, KFC, McDonald's, Mountain Jack's Prime Rib, Olive Garden, Perkins Family Restaurant, Pizza Hut, Ponderosa, Red Lobster
Lodg S: Comfort Inn, Crown Plaza, Hampton Inn, Select Inn
ATM S: Amoco, Bank One, First Federal, Firststar Bank
Other S: Essex Square, Half Price Books

138A I-94 East Milwaukee (Difficult Reaccess)

138B WI 30, Madison (Difficult Reaccess)

142AB U.S. 12, U.S. 18, Madison, Cambridge
FStop N: Mobil[*, D, LP]
Food N: McDonald's[PLAY], Mobil, Ramada Inn, Subway (Mobil), Suzan's (Ramada Inn)
Lodg N: Motel 6, Ramada Inn, Wingate Inn

(147) Weigh Station (Eastbound)

147 CR N, Stoughton, Cottage Grove
FStop S: Pleasant Springs Travel Center[*, LP] (Mobil)
Gas S: Amoco[*]
Food S: Amoco, Burger King (Amoco), Country-View Restaurant, Cousins' Sub's (Mobil), Pleasant Springs Travel Center (Mobil)
RVCamp S: Camping
Med S: + Hospital
ATM S: Amoco, Pleasant Springs Travel Center (Mobil)
Parks S: State Park
Other N: The Corner C-Store

156 U.S. 51 North, Stoughton (Reaccess Westbound Only)
Food S: Coachman's Inn, Coachman's Inn
Lodg S: Coachman's Inn

160 U.S. 51 South, WI 73, WI 106, Edgertown, Deerfield
TStop S: Edgerton Oasis Shell[*, LP, SCALES]
Food S: Wingate Restaurant (Shell)
AServ S: Edgerton Oasis Shell
TServ S: Edgerton Oasis Shell[SCALES]
RVCamp N: Hickory Hills Campground (2 Miles)
S: Camping (2 Miles), Creekview Campground (1.5 Miles), Wisconsin RV World[LP] (.3 Miles)
Med S: + Hospital
ATM S: Edgerton Oasis Shell

163 WI 59, Milton, Edgerton
Gas N: Mobil[*, LP, CW], Shell[*]
Food N: Burger King (Shell), Cousins' Sub's, McDonald's, Red Apple Restaurant, Shell
Lodg N: Comfort Inn
AServ N: Shell
TServ S: 59/I-90 Trucks & Parts
RVCamp N: Hidden Valley RV Resort & Campground (.75 Miles), Lakeview Campground (1.5 Miles)
Med S: + Urgent Care Clinic (2 Miles)
ATM N: Shell

(169) Rest Area (RR, Phones, Picnic, Vending; Eastbound)

171AB WI 26, Janesville, Milton, U.S. 14W
TStop S: Citgo[*]
FStop N: Coastal[*, D]
Gas S: Amoco[*, CW], Kwik Trip[*], Woodman[*, CW]
Food N: Alfresco Cafe (Best Western), Best Western, Cracker Barrel
S: Applebee's, Arby's, Burger King, Chi Chi's Mexican Restaurant, Citgo, Cornerstone Grill, Country Kitchen, Culver's Frozen Custard, Diamon Dave, Fazoli's Italian Food, Hardee's, Hoffman House (Ramada Inn), K-Mart[RX], KFC,

Bold red print shows RV & Bus parking available or nearby

EXIT WISCONSIN/ILLINOIS

Peking China Restaurant, Perkins Family Restaurant, Prime Quarter Steakhouse, **Ramada Inn**, Rossetta's Pizza, Shakeys Pizza, TCBY, The Ground Round, Wong's Chinese Restaurant
- Lodg N: **Best Western (see our ad this page)**, Hampton Inn, Motel 6
- S: Oasis Motel, **Ramada Inn**, **Select Inn**, Super 8
- AServ S: Bumper to Bumper (Auto Parts), Champion Auto, Everhart O'Leiry Pontiac, Mazda, Jiffy Lube, **K-Mart**, Mieneke, Pernot Classic Collison Auto Repair, Sear's
- TServ S: **International Truck Service**, **Transport America**
- RVCamp N: **Kamp Dakota**
- Med S: **+ Hospital**
- ATM S: Amoco, First Federal, First Financial, FirstStar
- Other S: **Janesville Shopping Mall**, **K-Mart(RX)**, Rock Animal Clinic, **Target**, **Wal-Mart(RX)**, Wonder Car Wash

171C East U.S. 14, Janesville, Milton
- TStop N: **Jamesvill Travel Plaza Mobil(*, LP, SCALES)**
- Food N: Damon's, **Jamesvill Travel Plaza Mobil**, SHONEY'S Shoney's, Wendy's (Mobil TS)
- S: Asia Buffet, Cousins' Sub's, McDonald's, Olive Garden, Taco Bell
- Lodg N: Holiday Inn Express, Microtel
- AServ N: Batteries Plus
- S: Gordie Bouchi Ford, Lincoln, Mercury, S & F Tire
- RVCamp N: **Kamp Dakota**
- ATM N: **Jamesvill Travel Plaza Mobil**
- Other S: Preferred Pets, Shopko(RX) (Optical), Skattin Place

175AB WI 11, Delavan, Janesville
- FStop N: **Shell(*)**
- Food N: **Denny's**, **Shell**, **Subway (Shell)**
- Lodg N: Budgetel Inn
- ATM N: **Shell**

177 WI 351, Avalon, Janesville

183 CR S, Shopiere Road
- FStop S: **Citgo(*, LP)**
- AServ S: L & C Automotive
- RVCamp N: **Turtle Creek Campsite (2 Miles)**
- Med S: **+ Hospital**

185A WI 81, Beloit, Milwaukee
- TStop S: **Pilot Travel Center(*, LP, K, SCALES) (Shell)**
- FStop S: **Citgo(*)**, **Super America(*, LP)**
- Gas S: 76(*, LP), Amoco(*), Phillips 66(*)
- Food S: 76, Arby's, Burger King, Country Kitchen (Econo Lodge), Culver's Frozen Custard, **Dairy Queen (Pilot)**, EconoLodge, Fazoli's Italian Food, **McDonald's(PLAY)**, **Pilot Travel Center (Shell)**, **Shirley's Home Cooking (Super America FS)**, Subway(*, LP) (76), **Super America**, **Taco Bell (Super America FS)**, Tinnon Fish, Meats (76), Wendy's
- Lodg S: Comfort Inn, EconoLodge, Fairfield Inn, Holiday Inn Express, **Super 8**
- AServ S: Bud Weiser, Gene Dencker Buick, Pontiac, GM, **Wal-Mart(RX) (Vision)**
- ATM S: 76, National Home League, Phillips 66, **Super America**
- Other S: Aldi's Market, Luxury 10, **Wal-Mart(RX) (Vision)**

185B Jct I-43N, Milwaukee

(187) **Rest Area (RR, Phones, Picnic, Vending)**

↑WISCONSIN

↓ILLINOIS

(1) U.S. 51N, IL 75, S. Beloit
- Lodg S: Knight's Inn
- AServ S: Beloit Ford Lincoln Mercury, Finley's

EXIT ILLINOIS

(1) **IL Welcome Center (RV Dump, P; Eastbound)**

3 Rockton Road, CR 9

12 IL76, Poplar Grove

15 U.S. 20, Downtown Rockford

(76) I-39, Rockford, Roscoe

Note: I-90 runs concurrent below with NWTLWY. Numbering follows NWTLWY.

(75) Toll Plaza 1 (Toll)

(66) East Riverside Blvd (Toll)
- Gas S: Amoco(*, LP, CW, 24), Mobil(*, D)
- Food S: Culver's Frozen Custard, McDonald's
- AServ S: Blain's Farm & Fleet With Auto Service, Napleton's Auto Works, Precision Alternator & Starter
- TServ S: **Rockford Truck Service (Kenworth, Volvo, GMC)**
- ATM S: Amoco, Riverside Community Bank
- Other N: Country Lane Kennels (Grooming/Boardin)

(63) U.S. 20 Bus., State Street
- Gas N: **Phillips 66(*, D, CW)**
- S: Citgo(*, LP), Mobil(*)
- Food N: Cracker Barrel, **Phillips 66**, Subway (Phillips 66)
- S: Blimpie's Subs (Mobil), Burger King, Country Kitchen, Dairy Queen, Gerry's Pizza, Givanni's, Hoffman House Restaurant (Holiday Inn), Holiday Inn, McDonald's, Mobil, O'Kelly's Mexican Cafe, Steak & Shake, The Machine Shed, Thunder Bay Grill
- Lodg N: Best Western, Excel Inn
- S: Best Suites, Candlewood Your Studio Hotel, Comfort Inn, Courtyard by Marriott, Extended Stay America, Fairfield Inn, **Hampton Inn**, Holiday Inn, Ramada Limited, Red Roof Inn, Residence Inn, Studio PLUS, Super 8
- AServ S: Lube Pro's, **Sam's Club**, Saturn of Rockford
- ATM N: **Phillips 66**
- Other N: The Time Museum
- S: Heavenly Ham, Magic Waters Amusement Park, Mailboxes Etc., **Sam's Club**, **Wal-Mart(RX)**

(61) Jct I-39, U.S. 20, Rockford,

PRIME OUTLETS
HUNTLEY
Over 80 Outlet Stores
Bugle Boy • Nine West • Jones New York
Ask for your FREE COUPON BOOK
1860
847-669-9100
ILLINOIS • I-90 • EXIT 32

1175
Newly Renovated
Best Western
BUS & RV PARKING
Best Western - Janesville
— Large Spacious Rooms—
Indoor Recreation Area w/ Pool & Whirlpool
— Coffee Makers in All Rooms —
— Full Service Restaurant & Lounge —
Special Rates for Motor Coach Groups
608-756-4511
WISCONSIN • I-90 • EXIT 171A

EXIT ILLINOIS

Bloomington, Normal

(55) Toll Plaza 5 (Toll)

(54) **Belvidere Oasis (RR, HF, Phones)**
- FStop N: **Mobil(D)**
- Food N: McDonald's, **Mobil**
- ATM N: **Mobil**

(53) Belvedere-Genoa Rd., Sycamore (Toll)
- RVCamp N: **Camping**
- Other N: Fairgrounds

(41) Toll Plaza 7 (Toll)

(36) U.S. 20, Marengo, Hampshire
- TStop N: **76 Auto/Truck Plaza(*, RV DUMP, SCALES)**, **Elgin Truck Stop(*, SCALES) (Shell)**, **Mobil(*, SCALES)**
- Food N: **76 Auto/Truck Plaza**, **Dairy Queen (Mobil)**, **Mobil**, **Restaurant (Elgin T/S)**, **Restaurant**, Subway (Mobil), **Wendy's**
- TServ N: **76 Auto/Truck Plaza(SCALES)**, **Elgin Truck Stop(SCALES) (Shell)**
- RVCamp N: **Camping**
- ATM N: **Elgin Truck Stop (Shell)**, **Mobil**
- Other N: CB Shop (Mobil), IL Railway Museum, Wild West Town

(32) IL 47, Woodstock (Reaccess Eastbound Only, Difficult Reaccess)
- Other N: Prime Outlets of Huntley (see our ad this page)

(27) Toll Plaza 8

(26) Randall Road, Sleepy Hollow Rd. (8 Ton Per Axle Wt Limit)
- Med S: **+ Hospital**
- Other S: Kane Fairgrounds

(25) Toll Plaza 9 (Toll)

(23) IL 31, Elgin (Toll)
- Gas N: Amoco(*, LP, CW), Thornton's
- Food N: Alexanders Restaurant, **Cracker Barrel**, Wendy's
- Lodg N: Budgetel Inn, Crown Plaza, Hampton Inn, Super 8
- ATM N: Amoco
- Other N: Hostess Thrift Store

(22) IL 25, Elgin
- Gas S: Shell(*), Speedway
- Food S: Arby's, George's Family Restaurant, Roll N Donut, Subway
- Lodg N: DAYS INN Days Inn
- AServ S: Amoco, Midas Muffler & Brake
- Med N: **+ Sherman Hospital**
- S: **+ Hospital**
- ATM S: Shell
- Parks N: **Trouts Park**
- Other N: Coin Operated Laundry

(20) Beverly Rd. (Reaccess Northbound Only)

(14) IL 59, Sutton Road (Toll)

(13) Barrington Road (Reaccess Northbound Only, Difficult Reaccess)
- Gas S: Amoco(*, CW), Shell(*)
- Food S: Chili's, IHOP, Lone Star Steakhouse, Max & Erma's, Romano's Macaroni Grill, Steak & Shake, TGI Friday, The Assembly American Bar & Cafe
- Lodg S: Ameri Suites (see our ad this page), Budgetel Inn, La Quinta Inn, Red Roof Inn
- ATM S: Amoco
- Other N: AMC 30 Theaters, Animal Hospital

(12) Roselle Road (Reaccess Northbound Only, Difficult Reaccess, Toll)
- Other N: Midieval Times Dinner & Tournament

(8) Jct I-290

Bold red print shows RV & Bus parking available or nearby

EXIT		ILLINOIS
7		Arlington Heights Road
	Lodg	S: AmeriSuites (see our ad this page)
5		Elmhurst Road (Reaccess Eastbound Only)
4		Jct IL 72, Lee St
		Note: I-90 runs concurrent above with NWTLWY. Numbering follows NWTLWY.
77		Jct I-294N
78		Jct I-294, I-190, River Road, Mannheim Road
79A		Cumberland Ave South
79B		Cumberland Ave North
80		Canfield Road
81A		IL 43, Harlem Ave
	Gas	S: Amoco(*), Shell(*, CW)
	Food	S: La Scala, Mr. K's, Sally's Restaurant, Skylark Restaurant, Wendy's
	AServ	S: Midas Muffler
81B		Sayre Ave
82A		Nagle Ave.
82B		Bryn Mawr Ave
82C		Austin Ave. (Difficult Reaccess)
83AB		Central Ave, Foster Ave
84		Lawrence Ave
	Gas	N: Amoco
	Food	S: Baskin Robbins, Dunkin Donuts, Gale Street Inn, Hunan Chinese, Jefferson Restaurant, Krakus Polish Deli, Little Spain, Magnolia Restaurant, McDonald's, Rey's Restaurant, Theresa & Magnolia Polish Restaurant, Zona Rosa Mexican Cuisine
	AServ	N: Amoco(*)
		S: Firestone Tire & Auto
	Other	S: **Dental Clinic**
85		I-94, Skokie, Chicago
		Note: I-90 runs concurrent below with I-94. Numbering follows I-94.
44A		Keeler Ave, Irving Park Road, IL 19
	Gas	S: Amoco(*), Mobil(*), Shell(*)
	AServ	S: Amoco
	ATM	S: Midwest Bank
45		Addison Street
	Gas	S: Citgo(*)
	Food	N: Little Caesars Pizza
		S: Subway (Citgo)
	Other	N: **K-Mart**
45B		Kimball Ave
	Gas	N: Marathon(*, D)
		S: Amoco
	Food	S: Dunkin Donuts, Subway, Subway
	Other	S: **Dominick's Grocery, WalGreens Pharmacy**
46A		California Ave
	Gas	N: Cabwerks
		S: Mobil(*)
	Food	N: KFC
		S: IHOP, Popeye's Chicken
	AServ	N: James Auto Repair
		S: Mobil
47A		Fullerton Ave
	Gas	S: 76, Amoco
	Food	N: Chuck E Cheese's Pizza, Dixie Que Restaurant, Dunkin Donuts, Popeye's Chicken, Scoops Ice Cream, Subway
		S: Domino's Pizza
	AServ	S: 76, Amoco(24)
	ATM	N: Midtown Bank
	Other	N: Express Car Wash
		S: **Fullerton Western Pharmacy**
48A		Armitage Ave Ashland Ave
	Gas	S: Amoco(*)
48B		IL 64, North Ave
	Gas	N: Amoco(*, CW)
		S: Amoco(*), Citgo, Shell
	Food	N: Art's Drive In, Hollywood Grill, Tripp's Chicken
	AServ	N: Goodyear Tire & Auto, Nortown Automotive
		S: American Transmission, Shell
	ATM	N: Cash Machine (Amoco)
49A		Division Street
	Gas	S: Amoco(*), Shell(*)
	AServ	S: Amoco(*), Shell
50A		Ogden Ave (Reaccess Eastbound Only)
	AServ	S: Firestone Tire & Auto
	TServ	S: **International Transmission**
50B		Ohio Street (No Reaccess)
	Gas	S: Marathon(*)
51		Jct I-290
51B		West Randolph St (Difficult Reaccess)
	Food	N: Jim Ching's Restaurant, Perez Restaurant, S & S Restaurant
		S: New Star Restaurant (Chinese)
51C		E Washington Blvd (Difficult Reaccess)
51D		Madison Street
51E		Monroe St.
51F		Adams Street
	Food	S: Greek Island, Pegasus Restaurant, San Torini Restaurant
51G		Jackson Blvd
	Food	N: Greek Town Gyros, Sorbes Restaurant
		S: Mitchell's Restaurant
	Lodg	N: New Jackson Hotel
	AServ	S: Toyota Dealer
51H		Jct I-290W, West Suburbs
52A		Taylor Street, Roosevelt Road
	Gas	N: Amoco
	Food	N: Eppel's Restaurant
	AServ	N: Midas Muffler & Brake
52C		18th Street
53		Jct I-55, Chicago
	Gas	N: Shell(*)
	Food	N: Ken Tones (Italian Beef & Sausage)
	AServ	N: Joe's Auto Repair
53B		Junction I-55 South, I-90/94 West
54		31st Street
	Gas	N: Shell(*)
	Food	N: Fat Albert's Italian Food, Maxwell Street Depot
	Med	N: **+ Hospital**
55B		Pershing Road
56A		43rd Street
56B		47th Street
57A		51st Street
	Food	N: McDonald's
57B		Garfield Blvd
	Gas	N: Amoco(CW)
		S: Shell(*), Speedway(*)
	Food	N: Checkers Burgers, KFC, Mr. Pizza King
		S: Wendy's

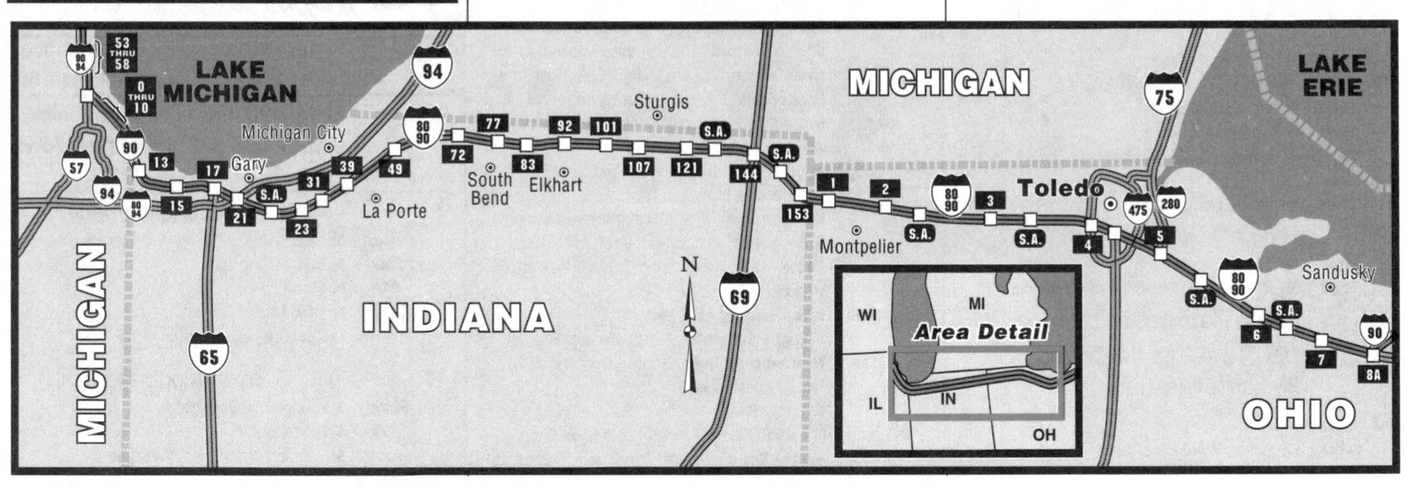

EXIT ILLINOIS/INDIANA

Other **N:** WalGreens Pharmacy

58A 59th Street

Food **N:** Church's Chicken

58B 63rd Street (No Reaccess)

59A Junction I-90, Indiana (Toll)

↑ILLINOIS

↓INDIANA

Note: I-90 runs concurrent above with I-94. Numbering follows I-94.

0 U.S. 12, U.S. 20, U.S. 41, Indianapolis Blvd (Difficult Reaccess)

Gas **S:** 76[*]

Food **S:** Burger King, KFC, McDonald's, Vienna Hot Dogs

3 Cline Ave, Indiana 912 E (Eastbound)

5 U.S. 41, Hammond

10 Indiana 912, Cline Ave

13 Grant St

15 Broadway, Illinois 53

17 Junction I-65, U.S. 12, U.S. 20, Dunes Hwy, Indianapolis (Toll)

Note: I-90 runs concurrent below with I-80. Numbering follows I-80.

21 Junction I-80 (Illinois tollway), Junction I-94, U.S. 6 West, Indiana 51, Des Moines (Toll, Services On IN 51)

(22) Service Area

Gas **N:** BP[D, SCALES]

Food **N:** Baskin Robbins, Fazoli's Italian Food, Hardee's

23 Portage (Toll)

Gas **S:** Amoco, Marathon[*, LP]

Food **S:** Burger King, Dunkin Donuts, KFC, McDonald's, Subway, Wendy's

Lodg **N:** Lee's Inn

AServ **S:** Amoco, Marathon, Portage Quick Change Oil

ATM **S:** First National Bank, NBD, Portage Bank

Other **N:** Woodland Park
S: Town & Country Grocery, WalGreens Pharmacy[RX]

(24) Indiana Toll Plaza (Toll)

31 Indiana 49, Chesterton, Valparaiso (Toll)

Parks **N:** Indiana Dunes State Park

39 U.S. 421, Michigan City, Westville (Toll)

49 Indiana 39, La Porte (Toll)

Food **N:** Briarhill Golf Club

Lodg **N:** The Cassity Motel

TServ **S:** Tomenko Tire & Truck Service

Med **N:** ✚ Hospital

Other **N:** Briarhill Golf Club

(56) Service Area (Westbound)

FStop **N:** BP[*, D]

Food **N:** Baked Goods, Dairy Queen, McDonald's

(56) Service Plaza (Eastbound)

72 U.S. 31 By - Pass, South Bend, Plymouth, Niles (Toll)

73 District 11

Other **N:** Indiana State Police Post

EXIT INDIANA

77 U.S. 33, U.S. 31, South Bend, Notre Dame University (Toll)

Gas **S:** Amoco[*, LP, CW, 24], Phillip 66[*, D, K, CW]

Food **N:** Arby's, Burger King, Damon's Clubhouse (Super 8), Denny's, Dixie Cream Donut Shop, Fazoli's Italian Food, J & N Restaurant[24], Marco's Pizza, McDonald's, Papa John's Pizza, Pizza Hut, Ponderosa Steakhouse, Steak & Ale, Subway
S: Bennitt's Buffet, Bill Knapp's, Bob Evan's Restaurant, Bruno's Pizza, Colonial Pancake House, Donut De-lite, Gipper's (Holiday Inn), Great Wall Chinese, Hot Stuff Pizza (Phillips 66), Kicker's, King Gyro's, Perkin's Family Restaurant, Pizza King, Schlotzsky's Deli, Wendy's

Lodg **N:** DAYS INN Days Inn, Hampton Inn & Suites, Motel 6, Ramada Inn, Super 8
S: Best Inns of America, Holiday Inn, Howard Johnson, Knight's Inn, Signature Inn, The Inn At St. Mary's

AServ **S:** Amoco[24], Carex Muffler Shop, Q Lube[CW], Rino Linings, Tim's Auto Body

RVCamp **N:** Spaulding Lake

Med **S:** ✚ Hospital

ATM **N:** First Source Bank, Key Bank, Norwest Bank, Standard Federal
S: Amoco, Phillip 66

Other **N:** All Star Car Wash, Marty Scharff's Deli & Meat Market, WalGreens Pharmacy[24, RX]
S: Laundry, Notre Dame Golf Course

83 Mishawaka (Toll)

Gas **S:** Amoco[*, D, CW], Citgo[*], Mobil[*, LP]

Food **S:** America's Donuts & Bagels (Mobil), Subway (Mobil)

RVCamp **N:** KOA Kampground (2 Miles)

Med **S:** ✚ South Bend Clinic At Granger

ATM **S:** Amoco, Citgo, Mobil

Other **N:** Morris Animal Hospital
S: Animal Clinic

(90) Service Area (Eastbound)

Gas **B:** BP[*, D]

Food **B:** Arby's, Dunkin Donuts, Pizza Hut, South Bend Chocolate Co.

(90) Service Plaza (Westbound)

92 Indiana 19, Elkhart (Toll)

Gas **N:** Citgo[*, K], Phillips 66[*, D]
S: Clark[*, LP], Marathon[*], Marathon

Food **N:** Applebee's, Cracker Barrel, Cracker Barrel, D'Antini's (Comfort Inn), Lee's Famous Recipe Chicken (Phillips 66), Lin Chinese, Noble Roman Pizza (Phillips 66), One Stop Food Store (Phillips 66), SHONEY'S Shoney's, Steak 'N Shake, Subway (Phillips 66)
S: Big Daddy's Star Dust Cafe, Blimpie Subs & Salads, Bob Evan's Restaurant, Bresler's Ice Cream, Burger King, Callahan's, DaVinci's Pizza, Delissimo Pizza, Subs, & Breakfast (Marathon), King Wha Chinese, McDonald's[PLAY], Olive Garden, Past Time Family Cafe, Past Time Sports Bar & Grill, Perkin's Family Restaurant, Red Lobster, Ruby's Pizza Factory, Weston Plaza, Yuri's Teppan Yaki Japanese

Lodg **N:** Best Western, Comfort Inn, Diplomat Motel, EconoLodge, Hampton Inn, Holiday Inn Express, Ken Pyke Motel, Knight's Inn, The Inn At Elkhart
S: Budget Inn, DAYS INN Days Inn, Ramada Inn, Red Roof Inn, Signature Inn, Super 8, Weston Plaza

AServ **N:** Sult Body Shop & Motors
S: Eclipse Conversion, Northside Auto Service

TServ **N:** Americana Trailer Supply, Dan's Hitch & Truck Accessories
S: Dually Depot

RVCamp **N:** Elkhart Campground[LP], Sult Body Shop & Motors, Travel Wood[LP], Worldwide Recreation

EXIT INDIANA/OHIO

Vehicles (RV Sales & Service)
S: Dually Depot

Med **S:** ✚ Hospital, ✚ Osolo Urgent Care

ATM **N:** Citgo, NBD
S: Key Bank[24], Marathon

Other **N:** Aldi, Big K-Mart, Car Wash, Martin's Supermarket, Revco[RX], Visitor Information
S: Gordan's Food Service, Menard's, Nickles Bakery Thrift Store, Northern Pride Car Wash

96 Elkhart East

RVCamp **N:** Campground

101 IN 15, Bristol, Goshen (Toll)

RVCamp **S:** Phoenix USA Inc.

107 U.S. 131, Indiana 13, Constantine, Middlebury (Toll)

FStop **N:** Mobil[*, D, K]

Lodg **N:** Plaza Motel

AServ **N:** Dick's Auto Parts

RVCamp **S:** Twin Mill RV Camping

ATM **N:** Mobil

(108) Rest Area (Trucks Only)

121 Indiana 9, Howe, LaGrange (Toll)

Food **N:** Golden Buddha

Lodg **N:** Greenbriar Inn, Hampton Inn, Travel Inn
S: Super 8

AServ **N:** J & M Service Center[D]

Med **S:** ✚ Hospital

Other **N:** Stateline Golf Center

(126) Service Area (Eastbound)

Gas **B:** BP[*, D]

Food **B:** Baskin Robbins, Fazoli's Italian Food, Hardee's

144 Jct I-69, U.S. 27, Angola, Ft Wayne, Lansing (Toll)

Gas **N:** Marathon[K]

Food **N:** Deli Mart (Marathon), Marathon, Taco Bell (Marathon)
S: Mulligan's (Country Meadows)

Lodg **N:** Holiday Inn Express
S: E & L Motel, Super 8

TServ **S:** Gulick Trucks & Parts Service

RVCamp **N:** Yogi Bear Camp Resort

Parks **N:** Pokagon State Park

Other **N:** Horizon Outlet
S: Country Meadows Golf Resort

(146) Service Plaza

Gas **B:** BP[*, D]

Food **B:** Baked Goods, Dairy Queen, McDonald's

(153) Indiana Toll Plaza (Toll)

↑INDIANA

↓OHIO

Note: I-90 runs concurrent above with I-80. Numbering follows I-80.

Note: I-90 runs concurrent below with OHTNPK. Numbering follows OHTNPK.

1 Ohio49, Edon, Edgerton, Allen Mi

Gas **N:** Mobil[*, LP]

Food **N:** Burger King

ATM **N:** Mobil

Other **N:** Ohio Tourist Center

(2) Ohio Toll Plaza (Toll)

10 Ohio 15, Bryan, Montpelier (Toll)

FStop **S:** Pennzoil Oil Change[*, D]

Gas **S:** Marathon[*, D]

Food **S:** Country Fare, Subway (Marathon)

Bold red print shows RV & Bus parking available or nearby

EXIT OHIO

Lodg S: EconoLodge, Holiday Inn, Rainbow Motel
TServ S: Hutch's Tractor & Trailer Repair
Med S: Hospital
ATM S: Pennzoil Oil Change

(21) Service Plaza (Eastbound)
FStop B: Sunoco(*)
Food B: Hardee's
AServ B: Sunoco
TServ B: Sunoco
Other N: Tourist Info.

34 Ohio 108, Wauseon (Toll)
FStop S: Hy-Miler(*, D, K, 24) (Shell)
Food S: Hy-Miler (Shell), Smith's
Lodg S: Arrowhead Motor Lodge, Del-Mar Best Western, Super 8
RVCamp S: Executive Travelers Sales & RV Service
ATM S: Hy-Miler (Shell)
Other N: Fulton County Fairgrounds

39 OH. 109, Delta, Lyons (Toll)

(49) Service Area
FStop B: Sunoco(*, D)
Food B: Charlie Brown's Family Restaurant & General Store
AServ B: Sunoco

52 Ohio 2, Toledo Airport, Swanton (Toll)
Lodg S: Toledo Airport(LP)
AServ S: Express Auto, Xpress Auto & Truck Service
TServ S: Xpress Auto & Truck Service
RVCamp S: Storage Rental
Other S: Toledo Airport

59 U.S. 20, to U.S. 23, to I-475, Maumee, Toledo (Toll)
Gas N: Amoco(*), BP(*, D, LP), Speedway(*, D, LP)
S: Amoco(*, D), Speedway(*, LP)
Food N: Arby's, Bentley's (Ramada), Blimpie Subs & Salads, Bob Evan's Restaurant, China Buffet, Connie Mac's Bar and Grill, East of Chicago Pizza Co., Flattop Grill, Little Caesars Pizza, Mark Pi's China Gate Restaurant, Max's Diner, McDonald's, Nick's Cafe, Pizza Hut, Tandoor Indian Restaurant
S: Baverian Brewing Company, Big Boy, Brandie's Diner, Chi Chi's Mexican Restaurant, Cookie Lady, Fazoli's Italian Food, Fricker's, Friendly's, Popoff's Pizza and Lebanese Food, Ralphie's Burgers, Red Lobster, Schlotzsky's Deli
Lodg N: Budget Inn, Holiday Inn, Motel 6, Ramada
S: Comfort Inn, Cross Country Inn, Days Inn, Hampton Inn, Red Roof Inn
AServ N: Auto Express, Big K-Mart(RX), Kaz's Auto Center, Murry's Discount Auto Store, Napa Auto, Tom's Tire & Auto
S: Bob Schmidt GM, Harmon Auto Glass, Hatfield Oldsmobile
RVCamp S: Maumee Mobile Home Court (.5 Miles)
Med N: Hospital
ATM N: Amoco, Toledo Area Catholic Credit Union
S: Huntington Bank
Other N: Big K-Mart(RX), Putt Putt Golf & Games, Southwyck Lanes, Southwyck Mall
S: Maumee Market, Maumee Sports Mall (Putt Putt, Batting Cage), Meijer Grocery

71 Junction I-280, Ohio 420, to I-75, to Stony Ridge, Toledo (Toll)
TStop N: Flying J Travel Plaza(*, D, LP, K, SCALES), Petro(*, D, LP, SCALES, 24), Stoney Ridge Truck Plaza(*, D, SCALES)
S: 76 Auto/Truck Plaza(*, D, SCALES, 24), TravelCenters of America(*, D, SCALES, 24)
FStop N: Johnny's On the Spot Fuel Stop(D)
S: Speedway(*, D, SCALES, 24)
Food N: Crossroad's Family Restaurant (Howard Johnson), Flying J Travel Plaza, Iron Skillet (Petro), Krispy Kreme Doughnuts (Petro), Pizza Hut (Petro), Stoney Ridge Truck Plaza
S: 76 Auto/Truck Plaza, Country Pride (TA), McDonald's, Sbarro Pizza (TA), Wendy's
Lodg N: Budget Inn, Howard Johnson, Knight's Inn, Ramada Limited, Stoney Ridge Motel
TServ N: Speedco(24), Stoney Ridge Truck Plaza(SCALES)
S: 76 Auto/Truck Plaza(SCALES, 24), Fleet Tire Center, TravelCenters of America(SCALES, 24), Williams Detroit Diesel
TWash N: Petro
S: Stony Ridge Truck Wash (TS), TravelCenters of America
ATM N: Flying J Travel Plaza

72 Exit 4A, Jct I-75, Perrysburg, Toledo

(77) Service Plaza
FStop B: Sunoco(*, D)
Food B: Fresh Fried Chicken, Hardee's
AServ B: Sunoco
Other B: Tourist Info.

81 OH 51, Elmore, Woodville, Gibsonburg

91 Ohio 53, Fremont, Port Clinton (Toll)
FStop S: Shell(*, D, 24)
Food N: Days Inn, Sneaky Fox Steak House
S: Buffet (Holiday Inn), Shell
Lodg N: Best Budget Inn, Days Inn
S: Fremont Turnpike Motel, Holiday Inn
AServ S: Nickel's Service
Med S: Hospital

(100) Commodore Perry Service Plaza
FStop B: Sunoco(*)
Food B: Rax(D)
AServ B: Sunoco
Other B: Travel Information

110 OH 4, Sandusky, Bellevue

118 U.S. 250, Sandusky, Norwalk (Toll)
Gas N: Marathon(*), Speedway(*)
Food N: Dick's Place, Fun Chaser's Ice Cream, Marathon, McDonald's, Subway
S: Colonial Inn South, Homestead Farm
Lodg N: Comfort Inn, Days Inn, Hampton Inn, Homestead Inn, Motel 6, Ramada Limited, Super 8
S: Colonial Inn South, Homestead Farm
AServ S: Dorr Chevrolet/Geo
RVCamp N: Holiday Trav-L-Park(*, LP), Milan Travel Park (.25 Miles)
ATM N: Marathon
Other N: Lake Erie Factory Outlet Center

136 Vermilion, Vaumhart Rd.

(139) Service Plaza
FStop B: Sunoco(*, D, LP, 24)
Food B: Bob's Big Boy, Burger King, TCBY
AServ B: Sunoco(24)
TServ B: Sunoco(24)

143 Jct. I-90, Ohio 2 (Toll)

Note: I-90 runs concurrent above with OHTNPK. Numbering follows OHTNPK.

144 OH 2, Sandusky

145A OH 57, To I-80, Elyria, Lorain
FStop S: Speedway(*)
Gas S: BP(*, D)
Food S: Bob Evan's Restaurant, Country Kitchen, Fun Times, Holiday Inn, McDonald's, Mountain Jacks, Pizza Hut, Red Lobster, Rubins Restaurant, Wendy's
Lodg S: Best Western, Camelot Inn, Comfort Inn, Days Inn, Econolodge, Holiday Inn (see our ad on I-80, Exit 445, OH)
AServ S: Sears, Tuffy Auto Center
TServ N: Goodyear Tire & Auto
Med S: Hospital
ATM S: Lorain Nat'l Bank, National City Bank, Star Bank
Other N: U-Haul Center(LP)
S: Automatic Car Wash, Car Wash, K-Mart, Midway Mall, Sams Club, State Police

148 Sheffield, Avon, OH 254
Gas S: Speedway(*, LP, K)
Food S: Abigail's Tea Room, Burger King, China, Cracker Barrel, KFC, Marco's Pizza, McDonald's, Pizza Hut, Sips & Nibbles, Subway, Sugar Creek Restaurant, Taco Bell
AServ N: Goerlich Mufflers, Mike Bass Ford
ATM S: First Merit Bank
Other S: Aldi Grocery Store, CVS Pharmacy(RX), Car Wash, Rini Rego Grocery, Sears Hardware(LP)

151 OH 611, Sheffield, Avon
FStop N: BP(*, D, LP, CW), Speedway(*, D, LP, K, SCALES)
Food N: Church's Chicken (Speedway), McDonald's, Subway (BP)
AServ S: Ray's
TServ S: Ray's
RVCamp N: Avon RV Superstore
ATM N: BP, Speedway

153 OH 83, Avon
AServ S: Avon Auto Care(K)
ATM S: Premier Bank & Trust
Other N: The Range

156 Bassett Rd , Crocker Road
Gas N: BP(*, CW), Shell(*, CW, 24)
Food N: Wallaby's Grill
S: Baskin Robbins, Bob Evan's Restaurant, Bruegger's Bagel & Bakery, Max & Erma's, McDonald's, Subway, T.G.I. Friday's, Tai Pan Japanese, Wendy's
Lodg N: Holiday Inn, Red Roof Inn, Residence Inn, Westlake Studio Plus
S: Hampton Inn
AServ S: Procare
Med S: Gemini Westlake Health Care, Hospital
ATM N: BP
S: Bank One, Fifth Third Bank, Key Bank, Lorain National Bank, Rini Rego Grocery, Star Bank
Other S: CVS Pharmacy(RX), K-Mart, Marc's Grocery, Rini Rego Grocery

159 OH 252, Columbia Road
Gas S: Amoco, BP(*, CW), Shell
Food N: Cooker's Bar & Grill, Outback Steakhouse
S: Houlihan's, KFC, McDonald's, Taco Bell
Lodg N: Courtyard by Marriott, Cross Country Inn
AServ S: Lube Stop, Mueller Tire, Shell
Med N: Lakewood Medical Center
S: Hospital
ATM S: CVS Pharmacy(RX), Charter One Bank, National City Bank, Strongsville Savings Bank
Other S: CVS Pharmacy(RX), Finast Supermarket

160 Clague Rd (Westbound)
Gas S: BP(*, LP)
Food S: Panorama Dining
AServ N: Kane's Auto
S: BP
Med S: Hospital
Parks N: Reese Park
Other N: Bay Animal Clinic, Bay Pharmacy(RX)

161 OH 2, OH 254, Detroit Rd, Rocky River (Reaccess Westbound Only)

162 Hilliard Blvd, Rocky River (Westbound)
Gas S: BP(*), Shell(*)
Food S: Rock Cliff
AServ S: BP
ATM S: Shell

EXIT	OHIO
Other	S: Dairy Mart(*), **Rocky River Animal Hospital**
163	OH 237, Rocky River Drive
164	McKinley Ave
165	Warren Road, Bunts Rd., W. 140th St.
Med	S: ✚ **Hospital**
165B	West 140th St, Bunts Rd
Gas	N: Sunoco(*)
Other	N: **Dairy Mart C-Store**
166	West 117th St
Gas	N: BP(*, D), Shell(*, CW, 24)
	S: Gas USA(*, D, K)
Food	S: **Church's Chicken**, Pizza Pan, Tonio's Cafe, **White Castle Restaurant**, Wong's Place
AServ	N: City Auto Parts
	S: Speedee Muffler
ATM	S: First Merit, Gas USA
167A	West 98th St, West Blvd
Food	S: B & J Family Restaurant, Marco's, West Charlie Family Restaurant
AServ	S: Super Lube & Brake
ATM	S: Star Bank
Other	S: **Vexall Discount Drugs(RX)**
167	Lorrain Ave, OH 10 (Difficult Reaccess)
Gas	S: BP(*)
Parks	S: **Cleveland Zoo**
Other	S: **Rite Aid Pharmacy(RX)**, **Vollick's Bi-Rite**
169	West 41st St.
Med	N: ✚ **Hospital**
Other	S: Rock N Roll Hall of Fame
170A	OH 14, Broadway, US 42, West 25th St. (Reaccess Westbound Only)
Gas	N: Marathon(*, D)
	S: Road Mart
Food	S: Players Grill, Super Restaurant, Tony's Deli
AServ	N: Marathon, Sunshine Car Company
	S: Ramo's Auto Repair & Towing
Med	S: ✚ **Hospital**
Other	N: **Sun Valley Mart**
	S: Cleveland Zoo, Coin Laundromat
170B	Jct I-71 South to Columbus
170C	Jct. I-490, I-77
171AB	E. 22nd St., U.S. 422, OH 14, Broadway, Ontario St.
Other	N: Jacob's Steel Home of Cleveland Indians
171	West 14th St., Abbey Ave.
172A	Jct I-77S, to Akron
172B	Cleveland State College, E. 22nd St.
Med	S: ✚ **St. Vincent Charity Hospital**
172C	Downtown Cleveland
173A	Prospect Ave
AServ	S: Cadillac
Med	N: ✚ **Hospital**
173B	Chester Ave
Gas	S: BP(*)
AServ	S: Midas Muffler & Brake
173C	Superior Ave, St Clair Ave
Gas	N: BP(*, CW)
Food	S: Golden Plaza, Superior Restaurant
AServ	N: Meineke Discount Mufflers
	S: NAPA Auto Parts, Nad Hatter National Mufflers
Parks	N: **City Side Gardens**
174A	Lakeside Ave (Reaccess Westbound Only)
TServ	N: **Midtown Truck Repair**
TWash	S: **Truck Wash**

EXIT	OHIO
174B	OH 2 West, Lakewood
Other	N: **Science Museum**
175	East 55th St, Marginal Road
Parks	N: **Cleveland Lake State Park**
Other	S: Natural Gas Vehicles Public Dispenser
176	East 72nd St
Parks	S: **Gordan Park**
177	University Circle, MLK Jr Dr
Med	S: ✚ **Hospital**
Parks	S: **Rockefeller Park**
178	Eddy Road, Bratenahl
179	OH 283, Lake Shore Blvd, Bratenahal (Reaccess Westbound Only)
Food	N: Tien Luck Chinese
Other	N: Lakeshore Snack Shop
180A	East 140th St
180B	East 152nd St.
Gas	N: Clark(*)
	S: BP(*)
Food	N: Jackie Chan's
AServ	N: All State Auto Sales, Century Tire Service
ATM	S: BP
181	East 156th St (No Trucks)
Gas	N: Clark(*)
AServ	N: Century Tire Service
182A	East 185th St
Gas	N: BP(*, D, LP), Sunoco(*, 24)
	S: Citgo(*, D), Shell(*, 24), Speedway
Food	N: BP, Muldoon's
AServ	N: Euclid Auto Service, Pennzoil Oil Change, Star Muffler
	S: Acdelco Eastside Automotive, Euclid Auto Service, Hask Auto Service, Rainbow Muffler

Cleveland

With spectacular attractions like the Rock & Roll Hall of Fame and Museum, SeaWorld and a wealth of performing arts & cultural institutions - Cleveland has it all!

Cleveland Visitor Centers

* Tower City Center, 50 Public Square
Cleveland Hopkins Intl. Airport, Baggage Claim Level
West Bank of the Flats - *Memorial Day -Mid-October only*
* East Bank of the Flats, Old River Road, beneath the Main Ave. Bridge, 216/621-2218

** Location of Restaurant Reservations Service-Receive a priority reservation when you reserve through the Visitor Information Center*

"Touch Cleveland" Visitor Information Kiosk Locations

Instant information at the touch of your finger, phone connection service to purchase attractions tickets and hotel restaurant reservations
Aurora Premium Outlets
Cleveland Hopkins International Airport, Baggage Claim Level
Cleveland Convention Center
I-X Center
Playhouse Square Center
Powerhouse-West Bank of the Flats
University Circle

Greater Cleveland
The New American City
Convention & Visitors Bureau of Greater Cleveland
1486

Seasonal Cleveland & Attraction Packages
1-800-321-1004
For group information call, 1-800-321-1001
Greater Cleveland Convention and Visitors Bureau
www.travelcleveland.com

EXIT	OHIO
ATM	N: BP, Metropolitan Bank & Trust, Sunoco
	S: Citgo
Other	N: **Finast Grocery Store**, **McBill Grocery Store**
182B	East 200th St
Gas	N: Clark(K), Gas(*)
	S: BP(CW)
Food	S: Shot'z Bar & Grill
AServ	N: Case Honda, Nex Auto Service, PS Tire, Smolic Tire
	S: Bosh Service, Eclift Foreign Motors
Med	N: ✚ **Hospital**
ATM	N: Gas
Other	N: **Discount Drug Mart(RX)**
	S: Aga Welder's Choice
183	East 222nd St
Gas	N: Sunoco(*)
	S: Sunoco(*, D)
Food	N: RJ's Bar & Grill, Tap House, Wajtila's Bakery
AServ	N: Flickinger Goodyear Tire & Auto
	S: Dave's Precision Automotive, Suburban Auto Body
ATM	N: Sunoco
Other	N: Redi Wash
	S: Car Wash(24)
184A	Babbitt Rd
Food	S: **K-Mart Supercenter(RX)**
AServ	N: Clay Matthews Pontiac
	S: A Better Brake & Muffler Service, Euclid Transmission, Tidy Car
ATM	S: **K-Mart Supercenter**
Other	S: **Euclid Square Mall**, **K-Mart Supercenter(RX)**, Midwest Welding(LP)
184B	OH 175, East 260th St
Gas	N: Shell(24)
Food	S: Pacers Restaurant
AServ	N: Shell(24)
	S: Euclid Transmission, Mueller Tire, **Stephen's Auto & Truck Accessories**
TServ	S: **Stephen's Auto & Truck Accessories**
Other	S: Animal Pound, **Euclid Animal Hospital**
185	OH 2 East, Painesville (Left Exit)
186	U.S. 20, Euclid Ave
Gas	N: Sunoco(*, 24)
Food	N: Arthur's Steaks, **Denny's**, Doc's Steak & Seafood, Lily's Restaurant & Bar (Four Points Hotel), McDonald's
	S: American Cafe
Lodg	N: Four Points Sheraton, Hampton Inn
	S: Invoy Motel
AServ	N: Glavic Dodge, Saturn, Mullinex East Ford
	S: The Lube Stop
ATM	S: Huntington Bank
Other	S: **Coin Laundry**, **Convenient Food Mart(*)**
187	Wickliffe, Richmond Heights, Willoughby, OH 84, Bishop Rd.
Gas	S: BP(*, D, CW), Shell(*, CW)
Food	S: Bakers Square Restaurant, Chester's Fried Chicken (Shell), **McDonald's**, Quizno's Classic Sub
Lodg	S: Holiday Inn
AServ	S: Rainbow Muffler, Tony La Riche Chevrolet/ Geo
Med	S: ✚ **Hospital**
Other	S: **Marc Grocery**
188	Jct I-271 S., Acron, Columbus
189	OH 91, Willoughby Hills, Willoughby
Gas	N: BP(*, D, CW), Shell(*, CW)
Food	N: Bob Evan's Restaurant, Bruegger's Bagel & Bakery, Cafe Europa, Harley Hotel, Peking Chef, Pizza and Restaurant
	S: Fazio's
Lodg	N: Fairfield Inn, Harley Hotel, TraveLodge
Med	N: ✚ **Hospital**
ATM	N: BP

Bold red print shows RV & Bus parking available or nearby

EXIT OHIO

Other **N: CVS Pharmacy[RX], Convenient Mart, WalGreens Pharmacy[RX]**

(190) **Weigh Station (Eastbound)**

190 Jct I-271S to Columbus, Express Lanes (Westbound, Left Exit Westbound)

193 OH 306, Kirtland , Mentor

Gas N: BP[*, LP]
S: Marathon[*, CW]

Food N: McDonald's, Subway (BP)
S: Bluey's Cafe, **Burger King**, Roadhouse Steaks

Lodg N: EconoLodge
S: Days Inn (see our ad this page), Red Roof Inn

AServ S: Marathon

ATM N: BP

(198) **Rest Area (RR, Phones, Picnic, Vending; Eastbound)**

(198) **Rest Area (RR, Phones, Picnic, Vending; Westbound)**

200 OH 44, Chardon, Painesville

Gas S: BP[*, LP]

Food S: **McDonald's**, Red Hot Grill (Quail Hollow), Subway (BP)

Lodg S: Quail Hollow Resort

Med N: **Hospital**

ATM S: BP

205 Vrooman Road

Gas S: BP[*, D]

212 OH 528, Madison, Thompson

Gas S: Marathon[*, D]

Food N: McDonald's, Potbelly's Family Restaurant

AServ S: Radiator King

EXIT OHIO

RVCamp **S: Camping**

218 OH 534, Geneva

TStop **S: Kwik Fill Auto Truck Plaza[*, D, 24]**

Gas N: BP[*], Sunoco[K]

Food **N: Geneva Country Kitchen[24]**, Geneva Inn Restaurant, **McDonald's**, Wendy's
S: Applewood Family Restaurant (Kwik Fill Truck Stop), Kwik Fill Auto Truck Plaza

Lodg **N: Howard Johnson (see our ad this page)**

AServ N: Sunoco

TServ **N: Goodyear Tire & Auto[D]**

TWash **N: Goodyear Tire & Auto**

RVCamp **S: Kenisee's Grand River Camp (1.25 Miles)**

Med **N: Hospital**

Parks **N: Geneva Lake Park (9 Miles)**
S: Harper Field Bridge Metro Park

Other S: Bilicic's Busy Mart

223 OH 45, Warren, Ashtabula

FStop **S: Speedway[*, D, LP, 24]**

Gas S: BP[*]

Food N: Mr C's Restaurant
S: **Burger King**, Clay Street Inn, JD's on the Freeway (BP), **McDonald's, Subway (Speedway)**

Lodg N: Comfort Inn, **TraveLodge**
S: Hampton Inn

RVCamp **S: Camping, Indian Creek (10 Miles)**

ATM **S: Speedway**

Parks **S: Kenisee Lake Park**

Other N: Chapel Hills Golf Course
S: Niagara Falls Info Center

228 OH 11, Youngstown, Ashtabula

235 OH 84, OH 193, Kingsville

TStop **S: T/A TravelCenters of America[*, D, SCALES]**

FStop **S: Speedway[*, D, K, SCALES]**

Gas N: Citgo[*, LP]

EXIT OHIO/PENNSYLVANIA

S: Amoco[*]

Food **N: Glad-E-O C-Store[*]**
S: Country Pride (TA), Jonathan's Family Dining, Stills Family Restaurant, **Subway (Speedway), T/A TravelCenters of America**

Lodg N: Dav-Ed Motel
S: Kingsville Motel

AServ S: Amoco, **Kingsville Towing & Repair[LP]**

TServ **S: Kingsville Towing & Repair, T/A TravelCenters of America[SCALES]**

RVCamp **N: Campground**

Other **N: Glad-E-O C-Store**

241 OH 7, Conneaut, Andover

Food **N: Burger King**
S: Beef and Beer Family Restaurant

Lodg **N: Days Inn**

AServ **N: Auto Zone, K-Mart**

RVCamp **N: Evergreen Lake Park[LP]**

Med **N: Hospital**

Other **N: CVS Pharmacy[RX], Giant Eagle Supermarket, K-Mart**

(243) **OH Welcome Center/ Weigh Station (RR, Phones, Picnic, Vending; Westbound)**

↑OHIO

↓PENNSYLVANIA

(1) **PA Welcome Center/ Weigh Station (RR, Phones, Picnic, Vending; Eastbound)**

1 **(3)** U.S. 6 N, Cherry Hill, West Springfield

TStop **S: BP[*, D, LP, 24] (Towing)**

Food **S: Hitchen Post Restaurant[24] (BP)**

AServ **S: BP[24] (Towing)**

TServ **S: BP[24] (Towing)**

ATM **S: BP (Towing)**

2 **(6)** PA 215, Albion, East Springfield

Gas S: Sunoco[*]

Lodg S: Miracle Motel

AServ S: Morley's

3 **(10)** PA 18, Platea, Girard

Gas N: Gulf[D, K]

AServ N: Gulf

TServ **N: Keystone Diesel Engine Co, Sidley Mack Sales & Service**

Other **N: State Police**

4 **(16)** PA 98, Franklin Center, Fairview

AServ N: Weston's Auto Service
S: Hodges, Platz Garage

RVCamp **S: Folly's End Campground**

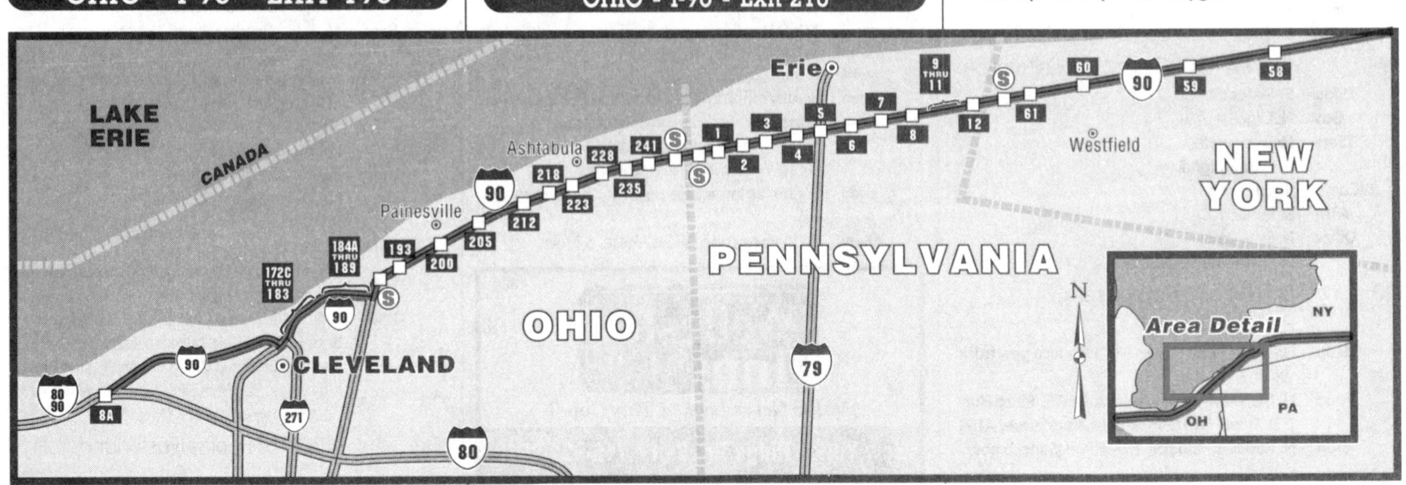

EXIT PENNSYLVANIA

5 **(18)** PA 832, Sterrettania, Presque Isle
- TStop — N: Shell(*, D, 24)
  S: AmBest Truck Stop(*, D, SCALES, 24) (CB Repair)
- FStop — N: Citgo(*, D) (Towing)
  S: Shell(*, D, LP, SCALES)
- Food — N: Burger King, Shell
  S: Green Shingle (Am Best), Peppermill Family Restaurant (Best Western)
- Lodg — S: Best Western
- TServ — S: Erie Truck & Trailer Parts, Poplar Thruway Service Garage (Am Best)
- TWash — S: AmBest Truck Stop (CB Repair)
- RVCamp — N: Hills Family Campground
  S: Erie KOA Kampground (1.5 Miles), RK Campground
- Parks — N: Walameer Park (8 Miles)

Exit **(22)** Junction I-79, Pittsburgh, Erie

6 **(24)** U.S. 19, Waterford, Peach St
- Gas — N: Citgo(*, D), Citgo(*), Kwik Fill(*, D)
  S: Exxon(*, D)
- Food — N: Applebee's, Burger King, Damon's Rib House, Eat N Park, McDonald's (Wal-Mart), McDonald's(PLAY), Old Country Buffet, Wal-Mart(RX) (1-hr photo)
  S: Bob Evan's Restaurant
- Lodg — N: Motel 6
  S: Comfort Inn, EconoLodge, Hampton Inn, Microtel, Residence Inn
- AServ — N: Wal-Mart (1-hr photo)
- Med — N: St. Vincent Health Center
- ATM — N: Citgo, Citgo, Mellon Bank, National City Bank, PNC Bank
  S: Exxon
- Other — N: Builders Square, Giant Eagle Grocery(RX), Home Depot, K-Mart(RX), Sam's Club, The Downs, Wal-Mart(RX) (1-hr photo)

7 **(27)** PA 97, Waterford, State St
- TStop — S: Pilot(LP, K, SCALES, 24) (Travel Center)
- FStop — S: Shell(*)
- Gas — N: BP(*, D, 24), Citgo(*, D, LP), Kwik-Fill
- Food — N: Arby's, Barbato's, Big Boy, McDonald's
  S: Dairy Queen (Pilot), Little Hemlot's House, Pilot (Travel Center)
- Lodg — N: Days Inn, Red Carpet Inn, Red Roof Inn
  S: Quality Inn & Suites, Super 8
- Med — N: Hamot Medical Center
- ATM — S: Shell
- Other — N: Eerie Zoo

8 **(29)** PA 8, Hammett, Parade St
- Gas — N: Citgo(*)
  S: BP(*)
- Food — N: Wendy's
- Lodg — S: Ramada
- AServ — N: Jack Cooney's
- TServ — S: Five Star (Cummins, CAT), Lake Erie Ford Trucks, Lake Peterbilt
- Med — N: Hospital
- ATM — N: Citgo

9 **(32)** PA 430, Wesleyville, Colt Station
- FStop — S: Sunoco(*)
- Gas — N: Citgo(*, K)
- TServ — N: Beckworth
  S: Fyda Freightliner
- RVCamp — S: Camping
- ATM — S: Sunoco
- Other — N: State Police
  S: Dawn's CB Sales & Service

10 **(35)** PA 531, Harborcreek, Phillipsville
- TStop — N: Travel Port(*, RV DUMP, SCALES) (Sunoco gas, truck wash, ATM)
- Food — N: Buckhorn Family Restaurant (TS), Pizza Hut (TS), Travel Port (Sunoco gas, truck wash, ATM)
- Lodg — N: Rodeway Inn (TS), Travel Port (Sunoco gas, truck wash, ATM)
- TServ — N: Robert's Truck Service, Travel Port(SCALES) (Sunoco gas, truck wash, ATM)

EXIT PENNSYLVANIA/NEW YORK

10A **(36)** PA 17 East, Jamestown

11 **(41) PA 89, North East, Welcome Center**
- Gas — N: Shell(*)
- Food — N: Super 8
- Lodg — N: Super 8
- AServ — N: Shell
- RVCamp — S: Family Affair Campground
- Other — N: Information Center

12 **(45)** U.S. 20, State Line
- TStop — N: T/A TravelCenters of America(SCALES, 24)
- FStop — N: BP(*), Kwik Fill(*, LP, SCALES)
- Food — N: BP, Kwik Fill, McDonald's, Pizza Hut (TS), Subway (BP), T/A TravelCenters of America, Taco Bell (TA TS), The Gathering Restaurant
- Lodg — N: Red Carpet Inn
- ATM — N: BP
- Other — N: Mum's, Tourist Info.
  S: Niagra Fireworks

(46) **Weigh Station (Westbound)**

(46) **PA Welcome Center (RR, Phones, Vending; Westbound)**

↑PENNSYLVANIA

↓NEW YORK

Note: I-90 runs concurrent below with NYTHWY. Numbering follows NYTHWY.

61 **(495)** Shortman Road, Ripley
- TStop — N: Shell(SCALES, 24) (Western Union)
- Food — N: Block Bell Family Restaurant (Shell), Shell (Western Union)
  S: Budget Host, Colonial Squire Restaurant (Budget Host Inn)
- Lodg — S: Budget Host
- TServ — N: Shell(SCALES, 24) (Western Union)

(494) Toll Booths (Toll)

60 **(485)** NY 394, Westfield, Mayville
- Gas — N: Keystone(*)
  S: Mobil(*, D, K)
- Lodg — S: Thruway Holiday Motel
- RVCamp — N: KOA Kampground
- Med — S: Hospital
- Parks — N: Lake Erie State Park
- Other — N: Chautaugua Institution, Tourist Info.
  S: Webb's Lake Resort

59 **(468)** NY 60, Dunkirk, Fredonia, Gowanda
- FStop — S: Keystone(*)
- Gas — S: Sunoco
- Food — S: Arby's, Bob Evan's Restaurant, Cracker Barrel, KFC, Perkin's Family Restaurant, Ponderosa Steakhouse, Quality Vineyard Inn, The Sunny Vinyard (Quality Vinyard Inn)
- Lodg — S: Comfort Inn, Days Inn, Quality Vineyard Inn
- AServ — S: Lightning Lube, Midas Muffler & Brake, Monroe Muffler & Brakes, Sunoco
- RVCamp — S: Allegheny & Lake Erie State Park
- Med — S: Hospital
- ATM — S: Fleet Bank, Tops Grocery & Pharmacy
- Other — S: Auto Parts Parts America, Eckerd Drugs(RX), K-Mart(RX), Lucky Lanes Bowling Alley, Movie Plex 59, Tops Grocery & Pharmacy, Wal-Mart(RX) (Optical center)

1329
Wellesley Inns
Value Never Looked This Good!
New York • Ridge Rd. Exit • 716-621-2060

EXIT NEW YORK

58 **(456)** U.S. 20, NY 5, Silver Creek, Irving
- Gas — N: Citgo(*), Kwik Fill(*, LP)
- Food — N: Burger King(PLAY), Pit Stop Family Restaurant
- AServ — N: American Transmission, Jim White's Quality Cars & Trucks
- RVCamp — N: Camping
- Med — N: Hospital
- Other — N: U.S. Post Office

(447) **Angola Service Plaza (Eastbound)**
- FStop — B: Mobil(D)
- Food — B: Denny's
- ATM — B: OnBank

57A **(445)** Eden, Angola

(443) **Parking Area (Phones, Picnic; Eastbound)**

(443) **Parking Area (Phones, Picnic; Westbound)**

57 **(436)** NY 75, Hamburg, East Aurora
- TStop — N: Exit 57 Truck Plaza(*, SCALES) (Atlantic gas, cinema, bowling, lodging)
- FStop — S: The Simmering Pot (Holiday Inn)
- Gas — S: Kwik Fill, Stop & Gas
- Food — N: Exit 57 Truck Plaza (Atlantic gas, cinema, bowling, lodging), Snack Shop (Exit 57 TS)
  S: Arby's, Bob Evan's Restaurant, Camp Road Diner, Holiday Inn, Pizza Hut, Subway, Venti's Pizza
- Lodg — N: Days Inn (Exit 57 TS), Howard Johnson
  S: Holiday Inn, Red Roof Inn
- AServ — N: Continental Transmission, West-Herr Mitsubishi
  S: Goodyear, Mike Basil Chevrolet, Valvoline Oil Change
- TServ — N: Exit 57 Truck Plaza(SCALES) (Atlantic gas, cinema, bowling, lodging)
- TWash — N: Exit 57 Truck Plaza (Atlantic gas, cinema, bowling, lodging)
- ATM — S: Convenient Food Mart, Key Bank, Rochester Community Bank
- Other — N: Erie County Fairgrounds
  S: Camp Road Pharmacy(RX), Convenient Food Mart

56 **(432)** NY 179, Mile Strip Road, Blazedall, Orchard Park
- Gas — N: Sunoco(*, 24), Uni-Mart(*)
- Food — N: Cracker Barrel, Odyssey Family Restaurant(24)
  S: Applebee's, Boston Market Restaurant, Lin Chinese Buffet, Olive Garden, Outback Steakhouse, Pizza Hut, Ruby Tuesday, The Poppyseed Restaurant
- Lodg — N: EconoLodge
- AServ — N: Gregoire's Auto Service
  S: Firestone
- ATM — N: Sunoco
  S: Key Bank, Woodlawn Auto Workers' Federal Credit Union
- Other — S: BJ's Wholesale Club, Books Etc., Builders Square II, Chi-Chi's Mexican Restaurant, General Cinemas (McKinley Mall), Kids R Us, Mail Boxes Etc., McKinley Mall, PetsMart, Toys R Us, Wegmans Grocery Store(RX)

Exit **(430)** Toll Booths (Eastbound, Toll)

Bold red print shows RV & Bus parking available or nearby

EXIT NEW YORK

Exit **(430)** Toll Booths (Westbound)

55 **(430)** U.S. 219, Ridge Road, Lackawanna, West Seneca
- **Gas** S: Coastal(*, CW)
- **Food** S: Arby's, Perkin's Family Restaurant, Ponderosa Steakhouse
- **Lodg** N: Wellesley Inns (see our ad this page)
- **AServ** N: Hooker Automotive Service, Midas Muffler & Brake; S: Monroe Muffler & Brakes
- **Med** N: **Hospital**
- **ATM** S: M&T Bank
- **Other** S: Delta Sauna Coin Car Wash, **Home Depot**

54 **(428)** NY 16, NY 400, West Seneca, East Aurora

53 **(426)** Junction I-190, Downtown Buffalo, Canada

52A **(425)** William St

52EW **(424)** 52E- Depew, Walden Ave East, Cheektowaga, 52W- Galleria Drive, Walden Ave. West, Buffalo (52W only goes to the north)
- **TStop** S: **Sunoco**(*, SCALES)
- **Food** N: Arby's, Bob Evan's Restaurant, T.G.I. Friday's; S: **Jim's Restaurant**(24) **(Sunoco)**, Olive Garden, Sheraton, **Sunoco**
- **Lodg** N: Hampton Inn; S: Sheraton
- **AServ** N: Dunlop Tires, Paul Batt Buick; S: Goodyear Penske Auto Service
- **TServ** S: **Sunoco**(SCALES)
- **Med** N: **St. Joseph's Hospital**
- **ATM** N: Marine Midland Bank, Rochester Community Bank
- **Other** N: **Aldi Grocery Store**, E & B Discount Marine, Four City Auto Parts, **Target**(RX); S: Borders Books & Music, **General Cinemas (Walden Galleria Mall)**, **K-Mart**(RX), Kids R Us, **Walden Gallaria Mall**, **Wegmans Food & Pharmacy**(RX)

51 **(422)** NY 33, Buffalo, Airport
- **Gas** S: Mobil(*)
- **Food** S: Airport Cafe, Burger King
- **Med** N: **Hospital**
- **ATM** S: M & T Bank, Midland Marine Bank
- **Other** N: State Police; S: Delta Sonic Car Wash

50A **(421)** Cleveland Dr (Eastbound, Reaccess Westbound Only)
- **Gas** S: Coastal(*, LP)
- **Food** N: Lunetta's
- **AServ** S: Coastal
- **ATM** S: **Tile Pharmacy**(RX)

EXIT NEW YORK

- **Other** S: **Tile Pharmacy**(RX), Wilson Farm

50 **(420)** Junction I-290, Niagra Falls (Toll, Last Exit before the toll)
- **Lodg** N: Howard Johnson (see our ad this page)

Exit **(419)** Toll Booths (Eastbound)

Exit **(419)** Toll Booths (Westbound)

49 **(417)** NY 78, Depew, Lockport, Lancaster (Buffalo Airport)
- **Food** N: **Cracker Barrel**, Mighty Taco, Picasso Pizza, Protocol Restaurant; S: Bob Evan's Restaurant, Garden Place Hotel
- **Lodg** N: Fairfield Inn, Holiday Inn Express, Lancaster Motor Inn, Microtel, Ramada, Wellesley Inns (see our ad this page; S: Garden Place Hotel, Hospitality Inn, Howard Johnson, Red Roof Inn
- **AServ** N: Mitsubishi Motors, National Tire & Battery
- **Other** N: Media Play, Regal 16 Cinemas; S: Buffalo Airport

(412) **Clarence Service Plaza (Westbound)**
- **FStop** W: **Sunoco**(*)
- **Food** W: Burger King (Sunoco), Nathan's (Sunoco), **Sunoco**
- **ATM** W: OnBank (Sunoco), **Sunoco**

48A **(402)** NY 77, Pembroke, Medina, Akron, Corfu
- **TStop** S: **Flying J Travel Plaza**(LP, SCALES), **T/A TravelCenters of America**(*)
- **Food** S: **Apple Creek Family Restaurant (TA TS)**, **Exit 48A Diner**, **Flying J Travel Plaza**, **T/A TravelCenters of America**
- **Lodg** S: EconoLodge
- **AServ** S: NAPA Auto Parts & Pembroke Automotive

EXIT NEW YORK

- **TServ** S: **T/A TravelCenters of America**
- **RVCamp** S: **Darien Lakes Campground**
- **Other** S: **Darien Lake Theme Park & Camping Resort**, NAPA Auto Parts & Pembroke Automotive, National Wildlife Refuge

(397) **Pembroke Service Plaza (Eastbound)**
- **FStop** E: **Sunoco**(*)
- **Food** E: **Burger King**, **Mrs Fields Cookies**, **Popeye's Chicken**, **TCBY**
- **ATM** E: OnBank

48 **(390)** NY 98, Batavia, Albion, Attica
- **Food** S: **Best Western**, Bob Evan's Restaurant, Holiday Inn
- **Lodg** N: Comfort Inn; S: **Best Western**, Crown Inn, **Days Inn**, Holiday Inn, Microtel, Park-Oak Hotel, Super 8
- **Other** S: Batavia Downs, Geneffa County Fair

47 **(379)** Junction I-490, NY 19, Leroy, Rochester, Brockport
- **RVCamp** N: **Timberline Lake Park (Exit 1 off I-490; 1.2 Miles)**; S: **Frost Ridge Campground (2 Miles)**

(376) **Ontario Service Plaza (Westbound)**
- **Food** W: Ben & Jerry's Ice Cream, **McDonald's**
- **AServ** W: Mobil
- **ATM** W: OnBank

(366) **Scottsville Service Plaza (Eastbound)**
- **FStop** E: **Mobil**
- **Food** E: **Burger King**, **Dunkin Donuts**, **TCBY**
- **AServ** E: Mobil
- **Other** E: **Tourist Info.**

46 **(362)** Jct I-390, Rochester, Corning
- **Lodg** N: Ramada Inn

(353) **Parking Area (Phones, Picnic; Eastbound)**

45 **(351)** Junction I-490, Rochester, Victor
- **Other** S: Fishers & Hanoi Lake, Prime Outlets at Waterloo (see our ad this page)

(350) **Seneca Service Plaza (Westbound)**
- **FStop** W: **Mobil**(*)
- **Food** W: **Burger King (Mobil)**, **Mobil**, **Mrs Fields Cookies (Mobil)**, **Sbarro Pizza (Mobil)**
- **AServ** W: **Mobil**

44 **(347)** NY 332, Canandaguia, Farmington
- **Food** S: Sunrise Field Inn
- **Lodg** S: Sunrise Field Inn
- **RVCamp** S: **KOA Campgrounds**
- **Other** S: **State Police**, Sunnonburg Gardens

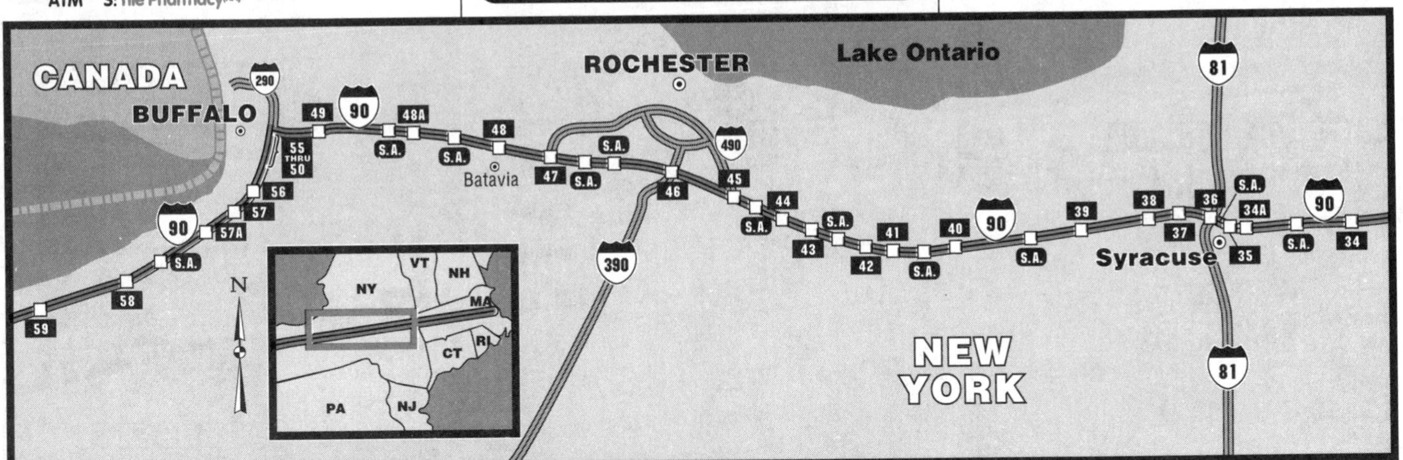

EXIT NEW YORK

43 **(340)** NY 21 Manchester, Palmyra, Newark, Thelps, Shortsville, Clifton Springs

- **FStop** S: Mobil(*)
- **Food** S: McDonald's, Steak-Out Restaurant
- **Lodg** S: Abbott's Motel, Roadside Inn
- **Other** S: Keuka Lake

(337) **Clifton Springs Service Plaza (Eastbound)**

- **FStop** E: Sunoco(*)
- **Food** E: Roy Rogers (Sunoco), Sbarro Italian (Sunoco), Sunoco, TCBY (Sunoco)
- **AServ** E: Sunoco
- **ATM** E: Sunoco

42 **(327)** NY 14, Geneva, Lyons, Seneca Lake, Sodus Bay, Ithaca

- **FStop** S: Mobil(*, SCALES) (Visitor Info)
- **Food** S: Goody's (Mobil), Mobil (Visitor Info)
- **Lodg** S: Mobil (Visitor Info), Relax Inn (Mobil)
- **RVCamp** N: Cheerful Valley Campground (.5 Miles) S: Junius Ponds Cabins & Campgrounds (1 Mile)

(324) **Junius Ponds Service Plaza (Westbound)**

- **FStop** W: Sunoco(*)
- **Food** W: Roy Rogers, TCBY
- **Other** W: State Police

41 **(320)** NY 414, Waterloo, Clyde , Cayuga Lake

- **FStop** S: Mobil(*, LP, K, 24)
- **Food** S: Magee Country Diner
- **ATM** S: Mobil
- **Parks** S: Women's Right National Park
- **Other** S: Finger Lakes Outlet Center, Montezuma Wildlife Refuge, Seneca Falls, Waterloo, Women's Hall of Fame

(318) **Parking Area (Phones, Picnic; Westbound)**

(310) **Port Byron Service Plaza (Eastbound)**

- **FStop** E: Mobil
- **Food** E: Ben & Jerry's Ice Cream, Mama Ilardo's Pizza, McDonald's
- **ATM** E: M & T Bank
- **Other** E: Travel Information

40 **(304)** NY 34 Weedsport, Auburn, Oswego

- **FStop** S: Mobil(*, D), Sunoco(*, LP)
- **Gas** S: Kwik Fill
- **Food** S: Arby's, DB's Drive In, Mais Oriental Food, Sunoco, Village Diner
- **Lodg** S: Best Western, Days Inn
- **AServ** S: Performance Automotive Inc.
- **TServ** S: Pullen's Truck Repair
- **RVCamp** N: Riverforest Park (1 Mile)
- **Med** S: + Hospital
- **ATM** S: Cayuga Bank, Sunoco
- **Other** N: Whitford Airport S: Big M Grocery Store, Coin Laundry, Fairgrounds, U.S. Post Office

(292) **Warners Service Plaza (Westbound)**

- **FStop** W: Mobil
- **Food** W: Ben & Jerry's Ice Cream, Mama Ilardo's Pizza, McDonald's, Mobil
- **AServ** W: Mobil
- **ATM** W: Mobil

39 **(289)** Junction I-690, NY 690, Syracuse, Fulton, Onondaga Lake, Solvay, Baldwinville (Take Jones Road to get to services)

- **Food** N: Denny's
- **Lodg** N: Comfort Inn
- **TServ** N: Pen Truck Detroit Diesel Allison

38 **(286)** CR 57, Liverpool, Syracuse

- **Food** N: Hooligan's, Mazzye's Meats
- **Parks** S: County Park, Onondaga Lake Park, St. Marie Park
- **Other** N: Flamingo Bowl, Liverpool Golf Driving Range & Miniature Golf, Pier 57 S: Courtland 1,000 Islands, Salt Museum, St. Marie Living History Museum

37 **(284)** Electronics Pkwy, Syracuse

- **Gas** S: Hess(*, K)
- **Food** S: Blimpie Subs & Salads (Hess), Buffet Chinese Restaurant, Godfather's Pizza (Hess), Hess, Holiday Inn (Convention Center)
- **Lodg** S: Holiday Inn (Convention Center), Homewood Suites, Knight's Inn, Ramada Inn
- **ATM** S: Hess
- **Parks** N: Electronics Park

36 **(283)** Junction I-81, Watertown, Binghamton, Syracuse, Syracuse Airport

(280) **DeWitt Service Plaza (Eastbound)**

- **FStop** N: Sunoco
- **Food** N: Ben & Jerry's Ice Cream, McDonald's
- **ATM** N: OnBank

35 **(279)** NY 298, Syracuse, East Syracuse

- **Gas** S: Mobil(*), Sunoco(*)
- **Food** S: Denny's, Dunkin Donuts, East Wok, Howard Johnson, Hub Diner, J Reck Subs, Joey's Fine Italian, La Pizzeria, McDonald's, Pronto's Pizza
- **Lodg** S: Comfort Inn, Courtyard by Marriott, Days Inn, Embassy Suites, Fairfield Inn, Hampton Inn, Holiday Inn (see our ad on this page), Howard Johnson, John Milton Inn, Marriott, Ramada Limited (see our ad this page), Red Roof Inn, Residence Inn
- **AServ** S: Instant Oil Change
- **ATM** S: Mobil, Sunoco

34A **(277)** Junction I-481, Syracuse, Oswego

(266) **Chittenango Service Plaza (Westbound)**

- **FStop** N: Sunoco
- **Food** N: Dunkin Donuts, Sbarro Italian, TCBY
- **ATM** N: OnBank

34 **(262)** NY 13, Canastoca, Chittenango

- **Gas** S: Mobil(*, D, CW), Save On(*)

East Syracuse, New York

1208

Carrier Circle

Holiday Inn®

6555 Old Collamer Rd. South

315-437-2761

Toll Free Reservations:

800-HOLIDAY

Exit Carrier Cir. 298 East, hotel on left.

In Room Coffee Maker • Complimentary USA Today Newspaper, Local Phone Calls, Faxes, Data Ports, Voice Mail • Cable TV Room Service • Free Parking • Indoor Pool Sauna • Whirlpool • Fitness Center
• 1/2 Price Appetizers • Kids Activities
• Banquets in Lounge 5pm to 7pm M-Th
• Full Service Restaurant

NEW YORK ▪ I-90 ▪ EXIT 35

1474

RAMADA LIMITED

6590 Thompson Road

Free Continental Breakfast Buffet
Free Cable TV with HBO
Guest Coin Laundry
3 Adjacent Restaurants
RV Parking Adjacent to Motel
Single Rooms From $35.99
Non-Smoking Rooms

315-463-0202 • Syracuse, NY

Take first right from circle 300yds ahead on right.

NEW YORK ▪ I-90 ▪ EXIT 35

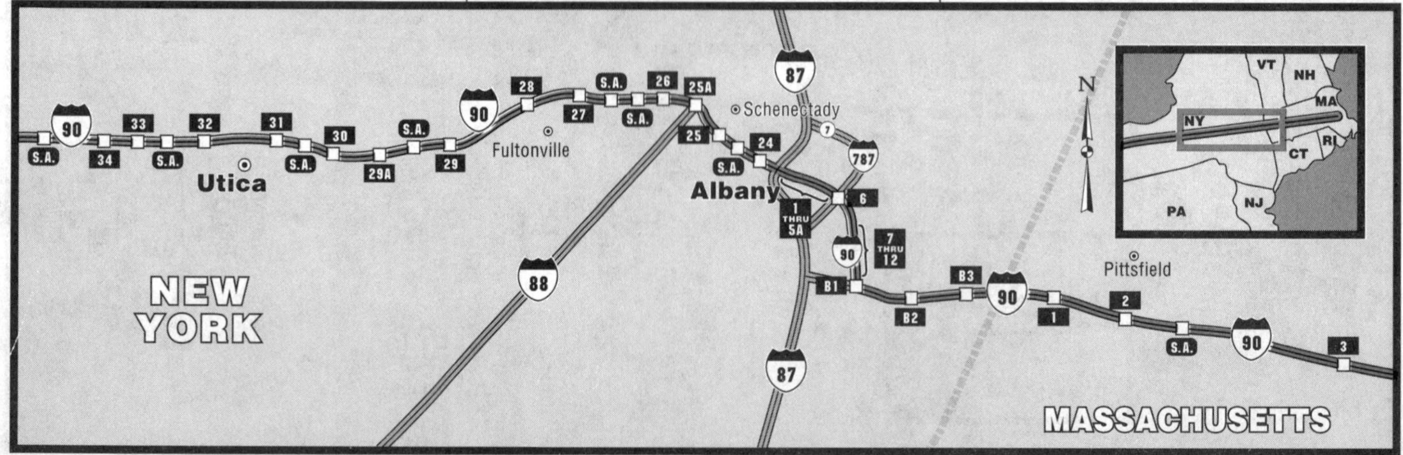

Bold red print shows RV & Bus parking available or nearby

EXIT NEW YORK

Food S: Arby's, McDonald's
Lodg S: Days Inn, Graziano's Motel
RVCamp S: Ta-Ga-Soke Campground (7 Miles), The Landing Campground (7 Miles), Verona Beach State Park/Camping (7 Miles)
Other S: International Boxing Hall of Fame

(256) **Parking Area (Phones, Picnic; Westbound)**

33 **(253)** NY 365, Verona, Oneida
FStop N: Save On[*, D]
Gas N: Citgo[*], Mobil[*]
Food N: Joel's Front Yard Steak House
Lodg N: Super 8, Verona Motor Inn
RVCamp N: Verona Beach State Park
S: The Villages of Turning Stone (1.5 Miles)
Med S: ✚ Hospital
ATM N: Mobil

(250) **Parking Area (Phones, Picnic; Eastbound)**

(244) **Oneida Service Plaza**
FStop N: Sunoco
Food N: Burger King, Sbarro Italian, TCBY
AServ S: Sunoco
ATM N: OnBank

32 **(243)** NY 233, Westmoreland
Gas S: Mobil
Food S: Carriage Motor Inn, Carriage Motor Inn, Westmoreland Diner
Lodg S: Carriage Motor Inn
AServ S: JB Tuttle Auto Sales & Service
ATM S: Mobil
Other N: Delta Lake (10 Miles), Erie Canal Village (10 Miles), Ft Stanwix National Monument (10 Miles), Oriskney Battlefield (10 Miles)
S: Airport, US Post Office

31 **(233)** Junction I-790, NY 8, NY 12, Utica
FStop S: Sunoco[*, D]
Gas N: Citgo[*], Mobil[*]
S: Hess[D], Mobil[*]
Food N: Burger King, Franco's Pizza & Pasta, Good Friend Chinese Restaurant, Johnny's, Lot-A-Burger, Lupino's Pizza, Paesano's Italian Restaurant, Pazzario's Pizzeria
S: McDonald's, Pizza Hut, Reck Subs, Taco Bell, Wendy's
Lodg S: A-1 Motel, Best Western, Happy Journey Motel, Motel 6, Red Roof Inn, Super 8
AServ N: Papandrea's Automotive
S: Monroe Muffler & Brakes
ATM N: Adirondack Bank, Fleet Bank, Marine Midland Bank, SBU Bank
S: Sunoco
Other N: Coin Laundromat, Eckerd Drugs[RX], Price Chopper Supermarket, Rite Aid Pharmacy[RX]

(227) **Schuyler Service Plaza (Westbound)**
FStop N: Sunoco
Food N: Breyer's Ice Cream, McDonald's
ATM N: OnBank
Other N: State Police

30 **(220)** NY 28, Herkimer, Mohawk
Gas N: Citgo[*]
Food N: Chef's Home Cooking, Denny's, Friendly's, Mr Shake Ice Cream, Subway (Citgo), Tony's Pizza
S: Mohawk Station
Lodg N: Budget Inn, Herkimer Motel
AServ N: Skinner Ford
Med S: ✚ Hospital
ATM N: Citgo
Other S: Big M Supermarket

29A **(211)** NY 169, Little Falls, Dolgeville

EXIT NEW YORK

Med N: ✚ Hospital
Other N: General Herkimer Home

(209) **Iroquois Service Plaza**
FStop B: Sunoco
Food B: Burger King, Dunkin Donuts, TCBY
E: Bob's Big Boy, Mrs Fields Cookies, Roy Rogers
AServ B: Sunoco
ATM B: OnBank

29 **(194)** NY 10, Canajoharie, Sharon Springs
Gas N: Gulf[*], Stewart's Convenient Store
S: Sunoco[*]
Food N: Little Buffet Chinese, McDonald's, Pizza Hut
S: Main Street Pub, Pizza Mercato, Tony's Pizzaria, Village Restaurant
AServ N: Roosevelt's Auto Service Towing
ATM N: Central National Bank
S: Central National Bank
Other N: Grand Union Grocery Store, Rite Aide Pharmacy[RX], U.S. Post Office

(184) **Parking Area (Phones, Picnic; Eastbound)**

(184) **Parking Area (Phones, Picnic; Westbound)**

28 **(182)** NY 30A, Fultonville, Fonda
TStop N: Glen Travel Plaza[*, D, LP] (Towing), Travel Port Truckstop[*]
FStop N: Getty
Gas N: Gulf, Sunoco[*, LP]
Food N: Buckhorn Family Restaurant[24] (Travel Port TS), Glen Travel Plaza (Towing), McDonald's, Sugar Shack Bar and Grill, The Poplars Inn, Travel Port Truckstop
Lodg N: Cloverleaf Inn, Glen Travel Plaza (Towing), The Poplars Inn, Travel Port Truckstop
AServ N: Auggie's Auto Parts, Gulf
TWash N: Getty
Med N: ✚ Hospital
ATM N: Glen Travel Plaza (Towing)

27 **(174)** NY 30, Amsterdam
FStop N: Getty[*]
Gas N: Mobil[*]
Food N: Amsterdam Diner[24] (Super 8 Motel), Valley View Motor Inn
Lodg N: Super 8, Valley View Motor Inn
Med N: ✚ Hospital
ATM N: Getty, Mobil
Other N: Coin Laundry (Valley View Inn)

(172) **Mohawk Service Plaza (Eastbound)**
FStop E: Sunoco
Food E: Breyer's Ice Cream, McDonald's
ATM E: ONBank

1826

6505 Niagara Falls Blvd
Niagara Falls, NY
716-283-8791
Lounge on Premises
Kids Under 12 Stay Free
Meeting/Banquet Facilities
Outdoor Pool • Free Coffee
Handicap Accessible
Truck/Large Vehicle Parking
Coin Laundry • Interior Corridors
Tours Available at Hotel Desk
Take I-290W to I-190N Exit 22 East
NEW YORK • I-90 • EXIT 50

EXIT NEW YORK

(168) **Pattersonville Service Plaza (Westbound)**
FStop W: Sunoco
Food W: Bob's Big Boy, Mrs Fields Cookies, Roy Rogers
ATM W: M & T Bank

26 **(162)** Junction I-890, NY 5 S, Schenectady

25A **(159)** I-88, NY 7, Schenectady, Binghamton

25 **(154)** Junction I-890, NY 7, NY 146, Schenectady

(153) **Guilderland Service Plaza (Eastbound)**
FStop E: Sunoco
Food E: Ben & Jerry's Ice Cream, McDonald's, Mr Subb
AServ E: Sunoco
ATM E: OnBank

23 I-87 S NY

24 **(149)** Jct I-87N, Jct I-90 E, Albany, Montreal

Note: I-90 runs concurrent above with NYTHWY. Numbering follows NYTHWY.

1 **(147)** Westbound Junction I-87

2 **(146)** Washington Ave, Fuller Road, State University

3 **(145)** Albany, State Offices

4 **(2)** NY 85, Albany, Slingerlands

5 **(3)** Everett Road

5A **(4)** Cooporate Woods Blvd

6 **(5)** NY9, Loudonville, Arbor Hill, Jct I-787

7 **(139)** Rensselaer, Washington Ave (Eastbound, Reaccess Westbound Only, No Trucks over 5 ton)

8 Defreestville

9 U.S. 4, E Greenbush Road, Rensselaer, Troy
Food S: Cracker Barrel
Lodg S: Susse Chalet

10 **(13)** Miller Road, Schodack Center

11 **(133)** U.S. 9, U.S. 20, Nassau
Gas N: Citgo[*, D], Hess[*, D]
Food S: Burger King, Chuck's Brown Derby
Lodg S: Four Seasons Motel
ATM N: Key Bank
Other N: State Police
S: Coin Laundry, Drumm Veterinary Hospital, Grand Union Grocery Store, Rite Aide Pharmacy[RX]

(18) **Rest Area (RR, Phones; Westbound)**

12 **(19)** U.S. 9, Hudson
Parks S: Martin Van Buren

(19) Toll Booth (Toll)

B1 **(1)** Jct I-87 to New York City, Jct I-90 E, Boston

B2 **(15)** NY 295, Taconic State Pkwy

(B17) Toll Booth

Bold red print shows RV & Bus parking available or nearby

EXIT NEW YORK/MASSACHUSETTS

B3 **(23)** NY 22, Austerlitz, New Lebanon
- **TStop** **N:** AmBest TS Citgo(*, SCALES)
- **FStop** **N:** Mobil(*, SCALES)
- **Gas** **S:** Sunoco(*, D)
- **Food** **N:** AmBest TS Citgo, Racing Cafe
- **Lodg** **S:** Berkshire Spur Motel
- **TServ** **N:** Mobil(SCALES)
- **RVCamp** **S:** Woodlands Hills RV Camp

(3) Toll Booth (Toll)

↑NEW YORK

↓MASSACHUSETTS

1 **(3)** MA 41, West Stockbridge (Westbound)

(8) Lee Service Plaza, Welcome Center
- **FStop** **N:** Mobil(*)
  - **S:** Mobil(*)
- **Food** **S:** Burger King, TCBY

2 **(11)** U.S. 20, Lee, Pittsfield , Adams (Toll)
- **TStop** **S:** Lee Travel Plaza(*)
- **FStop** **S:** Texaco
- **Gas** **N:** Shell(*, D)
- **Food** **N:** Burger King, Friendly's, McDonald's
  - **S:** Lee Travel Plaza
- **Lodg** **N:** Pilgrim Motel, Sunset Motel, Super 8
  - **S:** Lee Travel Plaza
- **AServ** **S:** Bob Denley Auto Service, NAPA Auto Parts, Texaco
- **Other** **N:** Prime Outlets at Lee (see our ad this page)
  - **S:** Berkshire Outlet Village

(29) Blandford Service Plaza (Picnic, Vending, Pet Walk)
- **FStop** **B:** Mobil(*)
- **Food** **N:** Burger King (Mobil)
- **ATM** **B:** Mobil

3 **(40)** U.S. 202, MA 10, Westfield, Northampton (Toll)
- **Gas** **N:** Mobil(*)
  - **S:** Texaco(D)
- **Food** **S:** Bickford's Family Restaurant, Dunkin Donuts, Friendly's
- **Lodg** **S:** Westfield Motor Inn
- **AServ** **S:** Texaco(D), Texaco
- **Med** **N:** ✚ Urgent Care Clinic
  - **S:** ✚ Hospital

EXIT MASSACHUSETTS

- **Other** **S:** Arrow Prescription Center Drugstore(RX)

4 **(45)** Jct I-91, U.S. 5, West Springfield, Holyoke (Toll)
- **Gas** **N:** Shell(*, CW)
  - **S:** Citgo
- **Food** **N:** Dunkin Donuts
  - **S:** B'shara's Restaurant (see our ad at I-91 Exit 13A MA), Bickford's Family Restaurant, Chili's, Donut Dip, Friendly's(*), Kenny Roger's Roasters, Pizza Hut, Subway
- **Lodg** **S:** Econolodge (see our at this page), Corral Motel, Hampton Inn, Knight's Inn, Motel 6, Quality Inn, Ramada Hotel, Red Roof Inn, Super 8
- **AServ** **S:** BMW, Blade Collision Repair, Century Auto Services, Express Lube
- **Med** **N:** ✚ Providence Hospital
- **Other** **S:** Mall

5 **(49)** MA 33, Chicopee, Westoverfield
- **Food** **S:** Admiral DW's, Burger King, Denny's, IHOP, Pizza Hut, Trumpet's (Comfort Inn), Wendy's
- **Lodg** **S:** Best Western, Comfort Inn
- **AServ** **S:** Bob Pion Pontiac, Buick, GMC, Chicopee Cadillac, Olds, Midas Muffler, Monroe Muffler & Brakes, Strauss Discount Auto
- **ATM** **S:** Bank of Boston, Chicopee Savings, Fleet Bank, Super Stop Shop
- **Other** **S:** Big Y Supermarket, CVS Pharmacy, East Coast Market Place, Fairfield Mall, Super Stop Shop

6 **(51)** Jctl-291, Springfield, Hartford (CT)
- **FStop** **S:** Pride(*, D, SCALES)
- **Gas** **S:** Pride(*)
- **Food** **S:** Fifty's Diner, McDonald's, Ramada Inn, Subway
- **Lodg** **S:** Motel 6, Plantation Inn, Ramada Inn
- **TServ** **S:** Dave's Truck Repair

7 **(55)** MA 21, Ludlow , Belchertown
- **Gas** **N:** Cumberland Farms(*), Gulf(*), Mobil, Pride(*, D), Sunoco(*, CW)
- **Food** **N:** Burger King, McDonald's
  - **S:** Dunkin Donuts, Friendly's, Joy's Country Kitchen, Subway
- **AServ** **N:** Express Lube, Ludlow Tire Center, Mobil
- **ATM** **N:** Bank Boston, Bay Bank, Fleet Bank
- **Other** **N:** Big Y Supermarket, CVS Pharmacy, Rocky Bay Hardward, Serv-U Auto
  - **S:** Bat Ring Beach

(56) Service Plaza
- **FStop** **B:** Mobil(*)
- **Food** **B:** Roy Rogers

8 **(63)** MA 32, Palmer, Amaherst
- **Gas** **S:** Mobil(*)
- **Food** **N:** McDonald's
  - **S:** Dunkin Donuts (Mobil)

PRIME OUTLETS
LEE
Over 60 Outlet Stores and Food Court
Calvin Klein • Jones New York • Gap
Ask for your FREE COUPON BOOK
413-243-8186
1863
MASSACHUSETTS ▪ I-90 ▪ EXIT 2

Group Rates Available
Econo Lodge.
I-90 • Exit 4
1533 Elm St.
W Springfield, MA 01089
413-734-8278 • 800-553-2666
FREE Coffee & Continental Breakfast
Some Rooms w/ Jacuzzi & King Size Bed
Remote Color TV, Cable, HBO/ESPN
Lounge Next Door
Meeting/Banquet Facilities
Pets Allowed • Handicap Accessible
Truck/Large Vehicle Parking
1566
Massachusetts ▪ I-90 ▪ Exit 4

FREE CONTINENTAL BREAKFAST
1252
SUPER 8 MOTEL
Super 8
800-800-8000
508-347-9000
• Swimming Pool
• Free Cable TV with HBO
• Rooms with Lakeview Available
• Walk to Old Sturbridge Village
• Adjacent to Many Restaurants
358 Main Street • Sturbridge, MA
Massachusettes ▪ I-90 ▪ Exit 9

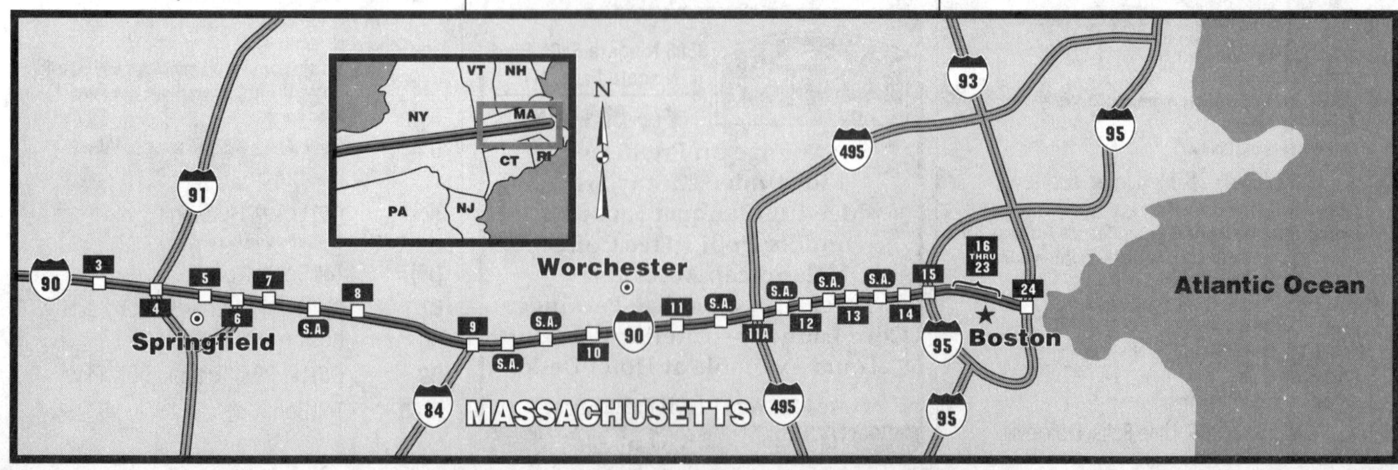

Bold red print shows RV & Bus parking available or nearby

EXIT	MASSACHUSETTS
AServ	N: Auto Gallery, Baldyag's Auto Repair, GM Auto Dealership, Goodyear Tire & Auto, Palmer Auto Mall, The Car Store
	S: A-Plus Transmission Center, Doorman's Garage
RVCamp	S: **Camping**
Other	N: **Big Y Supermarket**, **Brooks Pharmacy**, Car Wash
9	**(78)** Jct I-84, U.S. 20, Sturbridge
Lodg	S: Super 8 (see our ad this page)
(80)	**Service Plaza (Eastbound)**
FStop	E: **Mobil**
Food	E: Mrs. Fields Bakery, Roy Rogers, TCBY
Other	E: **Tourist Info.**
(84)	**Service Plaza (Westbound)**
FStop	W: **Mobil**(*)
Food	W: **Burger King**, Taco Bell
Other	W: **Tourist Info.**
10	**(90)** Jct I-395, I-290, MA 12 , Auburn, Worcester
Gas	N: Texaco(*)
	S: Shell(*)
Food	N: Ramada Inn
	S: D'Angelo's, Dunkin Donuts, Friendly's, Holiday Pizza, Quality Pizza, Wendy's
Lodg	N: Ramada Inn, Days Inn (see our ad this page)
AServ	S: Herb Chamber's Toyota, Shell
ATM	N: First MA Bank
	S: **Honey Farms Mini Mart**
Other	S: **CVS Pharmacy**(24, RX), Coin Laundromat, **Honey Farms Mini Mart**
11	**(96)** MA 122, Millbury, Worcester, Providence, RI

EXIT	MASSACHUSETTS
Gas	N: Getty
AServ	N: Getty, Samara Jeep Eagle
(104)	**Service Plaza (Westbound)**
FStop	N: **Mobil**
Food	N: Sbarro Pizza
11A	**(106)** Jct I-495, NH, to Maine, Cape Cod
12	**(111)** MA 9, Framingham
(115)	**Service Plaza (Westbound)**
Gas	N: **Mobil**
Food	N: Burger King, Popeye's Chicken, TCBY
13	**(117)** MA 30, Natick, Framingham
(118)	**Service Plaza (Eastbound)**
FStop	S: **Mobil**

1643
Chairman's Award
508-832-8300
DAYS INN
426 Southbridge St. • Auburn, MA 01501
Continental Breakfast
Pool/Jacuzzi/Exercise Room
Cable TV HBO/ESPN/DIX
Restaurant Nearby
Meeting/Banquet Facilities
Tennis/Golf Nearby
5 Sunburst Quality Award Winner
Massachusetts • I-90 • Exit 10

EXIT	MASSACHUSETTS
Food	S: Burger King, TCBY
ATM	S: Bank Boston
(120)	State Patrol Headquarters
14	**(123)** Junction I-95, MA 128, MA 30
Med	S: **+ Hospital**
15	**(124)** Junction I-95, MA 30, Weston
16	**(125)** West Newton
17	**(128)** Newton, Watertown
Gas	N: Citgo, Getty, Sunoco
Food	N: Bertucci's Brick Oven Pizza, Corner Deli, Einstein Bros Bagels, Newton Corner House of Pizza, Uno Pizzeria
Lodg	S: Sheraton
AServ	N: Citgo, Clay Chevrolet, Geo, Frost Cadillac, Getty, Honda Village Dealer, Sunoco
ATM	N: Bank Boston
18	**(131)** Allston, Cambridge, Brighton (Eastbound, Left Exit Northbound)
Lodg	N: Days Inn
(131)	Toll Plaza (Toll)
19	**(131)** Allston, Cambridge (Eastbound)
20	**(131)** Allston, Cambridge
21	**(132)** Massachusetts Ave, Boston (Eastbound)
22	**(133)** Prudential Center, Copley Square
23	**(134)** Downtown Boston, South Station
24	**(134)** Junction I-93, Central Artery

↑ MASSACHUSETTS

Begin I-90

Notes:

EXIT — VERMONT

Begin I-91

↓VERMONT

29 **(177)** To U.S. 5, Derby Line

(176) **Welcome Center, Rest Area (Southbound)**

28 **(172)** U.S. 5, VT 105, Newport, Derby
- **Gas** **E:** Exxon[*, D, LP, 24], Petrol King[*]
  W: Gulf[*, D], Texaco[*, D]
- **Food** **W:** Dunkin Donuts (Gulf), McDonald's, Village Pizza
- **Lodg** **W:** Pepin's Motel, Super 8
- **AServ** **W:** Mulkin's Chevrolet, Oldsmobile, Buick, Pontiac, Cadillac
- **RVCamp** **E:** Char-Bo Camping, Fireside RV Camping
- **Med** **E:** ✚ Hospital
- **ATM** **W:** Texaco
- **Other** **E:** Coin Car Wash, State Police
  W: Rite Aid Pharmacy[RX], Shop 'N Save Supermarket

27 **(170)** VT 191, to U.S. 5, VT 105, Newport
- **Gas** **W:** Vermont Gas Systems Inc[LP]
- **Other** **W:** State Police

(169) **Rest Area (RR, Phones; Northbound)**

(167) **Rest Area (Picnic)**

26 **(162)** U.S. 5, VT 58, Orleans, Irasburg
- **Gas** **E:** Irving[D], Sunoco[*, LP]
- **Food** **E:** Village Pizza (Orleans General Store)
- **AServ** **E:** Irving
- **RVCamp** **E:** Campground
- **ATM** **E:** Howard Bank
- **Other** **E:** Austin Rexall Drugs, Cole's Market, Orleans General Store, Wilcox Market

25 **(156)** VT 16, Barton, Hardwick
- **Gas** **E:** Gulf[*, LP]
- **RVCamp** **E:** Belview Campground (2 Miles)

(141) **Rest Area (RR, Phones; Westbound)**

24 **(140)** VT 122, Wheelock, Sheffield

23 **(137)** U.S. 5, Lyndonville, Burke
- **Gas** **E:** Gulf[*, D], Mobil[*]
- **Food** **E:** Dunkin Donuts (Mobil), McDonald's
- **Lodg** **E:** DAYS INN Days Inn
  W: Lyndon Motor Lodge
- **AServ** **E:** NAPA Auto Parts
- **ATM** **E:** Passumpic Bank
- **Other** **E:** Amerigas, Rite Aid Pharmacy[RX], Shop 'N Save Supermarket

22 **(133)** to U.S. 5, St Johnsbury (Exit On Steep Grade)
- **Med** **E:** ✚ Hospital

21 **(131)** U.S. 2 to VT 15, St Johnsbury, Montpelier

20 **(129)** U.S. 5, St Johnsbury, Passumpsic
- **Gas** **E:** Irving[*, D], Mobil[*]
- **Food** **E:** Anthony's Diner, Chunbo Chinese, McDonald's, Subway
- **AServ** **E:** Mobil
- **ATM** **E:** Howard Bank
- **Other** **E:** Car Wash

19 **(128)** Junction I-93 South

18 **(120)** U.S. 5, Barnet, Peacham
- **RVCamp** **E:** Campground
  W: Campground

(115) **Parking Area (Southbound)**

17 **(110)** U.S. 302, Wells River, Woodsville NH
- **TStop** **W:** P & H Truck Stop[SCALES]
- **FStop** **E:** Mobil[*]
- **Food** **E:** Warners Gallery Restaurant
  W: P & H Truck Stop
- **Med** **E:** ✚ Hospital
- **ATM** **W:** P & H Truck Stop

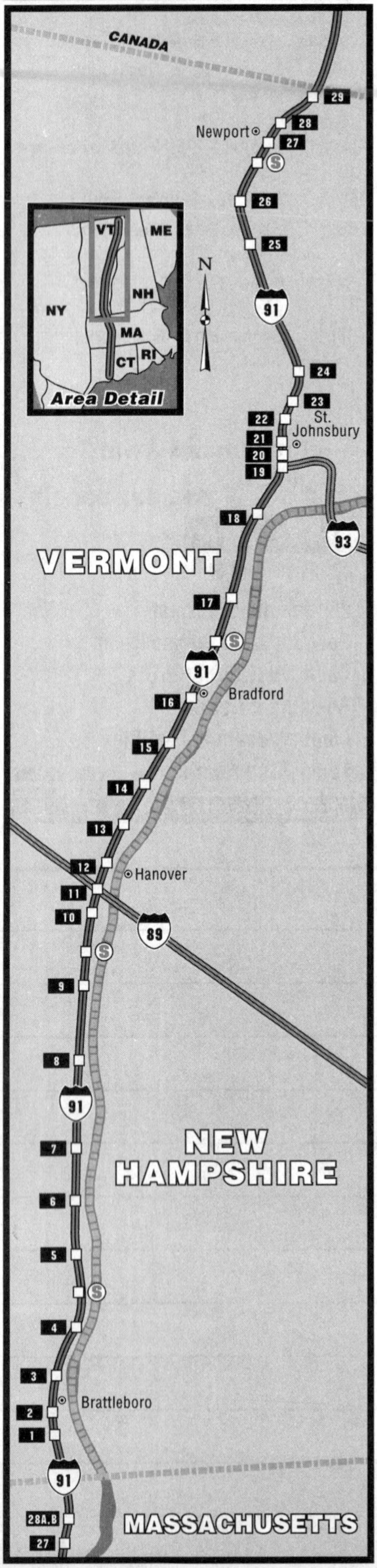

(101) **Rest Area (RR, Phones; Westbound)**

16 **(97)** U.S. 5, to VT 25, Bradford
- **Other** **W:** State Police

15 **(97)** U.S. 5, Fairlee, Orford NH
- **Gas** **E:** Mobil[*], Texaco[*]
- **Food** **E:** Mobil
- **Lodg** **W:** Lake Morey Inn
- **AServ** **E:** Texaco
- **Other** **E:** Fairlee General Store

14 **(84)** VT 113 to U.S. 5, Thetford
- **RVCamp** **E:** Rest N' Nest (.13 Miles)
  W: Campground
- **Parks** **W:** Thetford Hill State Park (2 Miles)

13 **(75)** U.S. 5, VT 10A, Norwich, Hanover NH
- **RVCamp** **E:** Campground
- **Med** **E:** ✚ Hospital

12 **(72)** U.S. 5, Wilder, White River Junction
- **Gas** **E:** Gulf[*], Mobil[*]
- **Food** **E:** Blood's Seafood
- **Other** **E:** Coin Laundry, White River Animal Hospital

11 **(70)** U.S. 5, White River Junction
- **FStop** **W:** Texaco[*, 24]
- **Gas** **E:** Gulf[*], Mobil, Sunoco[*]
  W: Citgo[*], Exxon[LP]
- **Food** **E:** AJ's, Cross Roads Cafe, Gillian's Restaurant, McDonald's, Ramada
  W: Exxon, Howard Johnson (Best Western)
- **Lodg** **E:** Coach An' Four Motel, Comfort Inn, Ramada
  W: Best Western, Hampton Inn, Super 8
- **AServ** **E:** Gateway Motors, Mobil, Sunoco, White River Toyota
  W: Citgo
- **RVCamp** **W:** Campground
- **Med** **W:** ✚ VA Hospital
- **ATM** **E:** Mascoma Savings Bank
- **Other** **E:** U.S. Post Office

10 **(70)** Junction I-89, to New Hampshire

(68) **Rest Area/Weigh Station (RR, Phones, Picnic)**

(68) **Rest Area/ Weigh Station (RR, Phones)**

9 **(61)** U.S. 5, VT12, Hartland, Windsor
- **Med** **E:** ✚ Hospital

8 **(51)** U.S. 5, VT 12, VT 131, Ascutney, Windsor
- **FStop** **E:** Citgo, Texaco[*, D, 24]
- **Gas** **E:** Mobil, Sunoco
- **Food** **E:** Mr. G's Restaurant
- **AServ** **E:** Citgo, Sunoco
- **RVCamp** **E:** Getaway Mountain Campground (2 Miles), Running Bear Camping Area (1.5 Miles)
- **Med** **E:** ✚ Hospital
- **Other** **E:** Max's Country Village Store

7 **(42)** U.S. 5, VT 11, VT 106, Springfield VT, Charlestown NH
- **FStop** **W:** Mobil[LP], Texaco[*]
- **Lodg** **W:** Holiday Inn Express, Howard Johnson
- **AServ** **W:** Mobil
- **RVCamp** **W:** Campground
- **Med** **W:** ✚ Hospital
- **ATM** **W:** Texaco

(39) **Rest Area**

(39) **Rest Area**

6 **(35)** U.S. 5, VT 103, Rockingham, Bellows Falls
- **Gas** **W:** Citgo[*, LP], Sunoco[*, LP]
- **AServ** **W:** Citgo

Bold red print shows RV & Bus parking available or nearby

EXIT — VERMONT/MASSACHUSETTS

- ATM — W: Sunoco

5 — **(29)** U.S. 5, Westminster, Walpole NH

(24) Rest Area (RR, Phones)

(23) Rest Area (RR, Phones)

(22) Weigh Station (Westbound)

(20) Weigh Station (Northbound)

4 — **(18)** U.S. 5, Putney

- FStop — W: Sunoco[*, D, 24]
- Gas — W: Gulf, Mobil
- Food — E: Putney Inn; W: Casa Del Sol, Curtis BBQ
- Lodg — E: Putney Inn
- AServ — W: Gulf, Mobil
- ATM — W: Chittenden Bank, River Valley Credit Union, Sunoco

3 — **(12)** U.S. 5, VT 9 East, Brattleboro, Keene

- FStop — E: Citgo
- Gas — E: Agway, Mobil[*, CW]
- Food — E: Bickford's Family Restaurant, Brattleboro House of Pizza, Chung Yan Chinese, Dunkin Donuts, Friendly's, KFC, McDonald's[PLAY], Pizza Hut, Steak Out Restaurant, Village Pizza
- Lodg — E: Colonial Motel, Days Inn, Lamp Lighter Inn, Motel 6, Quality Inn, Super 8
- AServ — E: Auto Mall Buick, Pontiac, GMC, Dodge, Chrysler, NAPA Auto Parts
- ATM — E: Brattleboro Savings & Loan, First Vermont Bank, Mobil, Rite Aid Pharmacy[RX], River Valley Credit Union
- Other — E: Bucket of Suds Laundromat, Mail Boxes Etc, Rite Aid Pharmacy[RX]

2 — **(9)** VT 9, to VT 30, Brattleboro, Bennington

- Gas — E: Sunoco; W: Mobil[*], Texaco[*]
- Food — W: The Country Deli
- Lodg — E: The Tudor Bed/Breakfast
- AServ — E: Sunoco
- RVCamp — E: Vermont RV Sales & Sevice[LP] (2 Miles)

1 — **(8)** U.S. 5, Brattleboro

- FStop — E: Texaco[*, CW]
- Gas — E: Coastal[*, CW], Mobil[*], Sunoco[*]
- Food — E: Burger King, Dunkin Donuts (Mobil), Exit 1 Village Pizza, Subway (Texaco FS), Vermont Inn Pizza
- Lodg — E: EconoLodge
- AServ — E: Car Quest Auto Parts, Roberts Jeep/Chevrolet/Olds/Cadillac
- RVCamp — E: Campground
- Med — E: ✚ Hospital
- ATM — E: Chittenden Bank, Vermont National Bank
- Parks — E: Fort Dummer State Park (1.6 Miles)
- Other — E: Brooks Pharmacy

(0) VT Welcome Center (RR, Phones, Vending; Westbound)

↑VERMONT

↓MASSACHUSETTS

(54) Parking Area (Westbound)

(54) Parking Area (Eastbound)

28AB — **(50)** MA 10, Bernardston, Northfield

- Gas — W: Citgo[*, D], Sunoco
- Food — E: Andiamo Italian; W: Four Leaf Clover, Pizza Ect., Thunder Lodge Vegetarian (Thunder Lodge)
- Lodg — E: Fox Inn; W: Falls River Inn, Thunder Lodge
- AServ — W: Sunoco
- RVCamp — E: Campground; W: Travelers Woods of New England (.75 Miles)
- Other — W: Marshall's Country Corner

EXIT — MASSACHUSETTS

27 — **(46)** MA 2 East, Greenfield, Boston

- Gas — E: Dairy Mart[*], Mobile[*], Sunoco[*, CW]
- Food — E: Burger King, Denny's, Dunkin Donuts, Friendly's
- AServ — E: Brown Dodge, Chrysler, Jeep, Cherry Rum Auto, Lorez Pontiac, Oldsmobile, GMC, Buick, Meineke Discount Mufflers, Mobile
- Med — E: ✚ Hospital
- ATM — E: Bank Boston
- Other — E: CVS Pharmacy

26 — **(43)** MA 2 W, MA 2A E, Greenfield Center, N Adams

- Gas — E: Citgo[D], Mobil[*], Palmer[*, D]; W: Texaco[*]
- Food — E: China Gourmet, Dunkin Donuts, Howard Johnson; W: Bickford's Family Restaurant, Bricker's, Friendly's, McDonald's, New Fortune Chinese, Turnbull's Family Restaurant
- Lodg — E: Howard Johnson; W: Candlelight Resort Inn, Super 8
- AServ — E: Citgo, Palmer; W: BJ's Tire Center[LP], Country Nissan Dealer
- Med — E: ✚ Hospital
- ATM — E: Mobil; W: United Bank
- Other — W: Waldbaum's Grocery Store

(37) Weigh Station (Westbound)

(37) Weigh Station

25 — **(36)** MA 116, Deerfield, Conway (Difficult Reaccess)

- Food — E: Chandler's
- Lodg — E: Motel 6
- RVCamp — W: White Birch Campground (2 Miles)
- Med — E: ✚ South Deerfield Animal Clinic

SUPER 8 MOTEL

413-536-1980
800-800-8000

1515 Northhampton St.
Holyoke, MA 01040

Restaurant on Premises
Continental Breakfast
Outdoor Pool
Handicap Accessible
Exterior/Interior Corridors

Area Attractions:

Riverside Amusement Park
Basketball Hall of Fame
Ingleside Mall
Eastern States Exposition
Children's Museum
5 Colleges Nearby

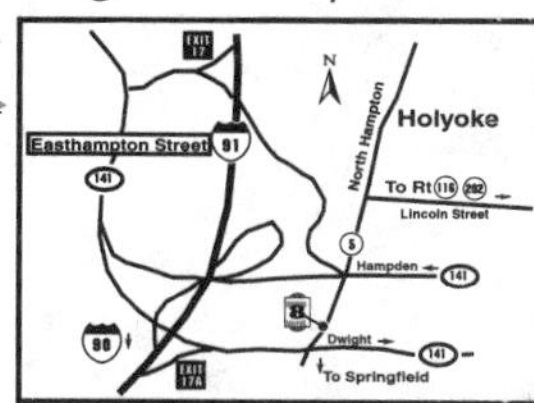

Higher rates on weekends and special events.

I-91N Exit 17A then L at light
I-91S Exit 17 Left at 1st light and Left at 2nd light

Massachusetts ▪ I-91 ▪ Exit 17A

EXIT — MASSACHUSETTS

- ATM — E: United Bank

24 — **(34)** U.S. 5, MA 10, MA 116, Whately (Difficult Reaccess)

- TStop — W: BP Truckstop
- Gas — E: Mobil[*]
- Food — E: New England Country Sampler, Sugarloaf Delif; W: BP Truckstop
- Lodg — E: Motel 6
- ATM — E: BankBoston
- Other — E: Tourist Info.

(33) Parking Area (Westbound)

(33) Parking Area (Eastbound)

23 — **(32)** U.S. 5, Whately, MA10, N Hatfield (Southbound, Reaccess Northbound Only, Difficult Reaccess)

- Food — E: Jimmy's Long Steamed Dogs, Tom's Long HotDog & Burgers
- Lodg — E: Colony Motel, Rainbow Motel
- RVCamp — E: Rainbow Campground

22 — **(30)** U.S. 5, MA 10, N Hatfield, Whately (Northbound, Reaccess Southbound Only)

21 — **(27)** U.S. 5, MA 10, Hatfield

- Gas — W: Sunoco[*]
- Food — W: Sister's Deli
- Lodg — W: Country View Motel
- RVCamp — W: Long View RV Service[LP]
- ATM — W: United Bank

20 — **(26)** U.S. 5, MA 9, MA 10, Northampton, Hadley (Southbound, Difficult Reaccess)

- Gas — W: BP, Mobil[*], Pride[*, D]
- Food — W: Bluebonnet Diner, Burger King, D'Angelo's Sandwich Shop, Pizza Hut (Mobil)
- AServ — W: Brake King, Dana Chevrolet/VW, Firestone Tire & Auto, Monroe Muffler & Brakes, NAPA Auto Parts, Town Fair Tire
- Med — W: ✚ DVA Medical Center
- ATM — W: SIS Bank

19 — **(25)** MA 9, N Hampton, Amhurst (Northbound, Difficult Reaccess)

- Gas — E: Citgo, Getty[*]
- Food — E: Banana-Rama Frozen Yogurt, Webster's Fish Hook
- AServ — E: Citgo

18 — **(23)** U.S. 5, N Hampton, E Hampton

- Gas — E: Mobil; W: Shell[*]
- Food — W: 5-91 Diner
- Lodg — E: The Inn at North Hampton; W: Days Inn
- AServ — E: Mobil
- ATM — W: East Hampton Savings Bank
- Other — W: Pleasant Street Car Wash

(19) Scenic View (Southbound)

17AB — **(16)** MA 141, Holy Oke, E Hampton

- Gas — E: Citgo, Gulf, Mobil[*, D]
- Food — E: Bess Eaten Donuts, Real China, Subway, Taco Bell
- Lodg — E: Super 8 (see our ad this page)
- AServ — E: Citgo, Gulf, Magna Buick, Mobil
- ATM — E: Bank of Western MA, Fleet Bank, Fleet Bank 2
- Other — E: Brooks Pharmacy

16 — **(14)** U.S. 202, Westfield, S Hadley

- Food — E: The Yankee Pedlar Inn
- Lodg — E: The Yankee Pedlar Inn
- Med — E: ✚ Hospital
- ATM — E: United Corporate Bank
- Parks — E: Hertiage State Park

15 — **(12)** Ingleside

- Gas — E: Shell[*]
- Lodg — E: Holiday Inn
- AServ — E: Sears Auto Center
- Med — E: ✚ Hospital

EXIT MASSACHUSETTS/CONNECTICUT

ATM **E:** Fleet Bank
Other **E:** Barnes & Noble Bookstore, **Holyoke Mall**

14 **(11)** Junction I-90, MA Tnpk to Boston, Albany NY (Toll)

13AB **(9)** U.S. 5, Springfield
Gas **E:** Citgo(*)
W: Mobil(*, CW), Sunoco(*, D)
Food **E:** B'Shara's, Bigford's Pancakes & Family Fair, Donut Dip, Piccadilly Pub & Restaurant, Subway, The Galley Restaurant
W: Abdow's Family Restaurant, Berkshire Mountain Grill, Burger King, Chi Chi's Mexican Restaurant, Chili's, D'angelo's, Debbie Wong, Empire Buffet (Quality Inn), Friendly's, Hoops (Ramada), North Garden Chinese, Pizza Hut
Lodg **E:** Arrowhead Motel, **Capri Motel**, Cyril's Motel, Knight's Inn, Red Roof Inn, Super 8
W: Elsie's Motel, Hampton Inn, Quality Inn, Ramada
AServ **E:** Balise Lexus, Honda, Toyota, Red's Auto Repair & Towing
ATM **W:** BankBoston, SIS Bank
Other **W:** **Riverdale Shopping Center**

12 **(8)** Junction I-391 North, Chicopee

11 **(7)** U.S. 20 West, Birnie Ave, W Springfield
Med **E:** ✚ **Bay State Medical Center**

10 **(7)** Main St, Springfield (Northbound)
Gas **E:** Mobil(*, CW)
Food **E:** McDonald's
Med **W:** ✚ **Bay Street Trauma Center**
ATM **E:** BankBoston
Other **E:** **Post Office**

9 **(7)** U.S. 20 West, West Springfield, MA 20 E (Northbound, Reaccess Northbound Only)

8 **(7)** Junction I-291, U.S. 20 East, Boston, Ludlow (Closes due to construction)

7 **(6)** Columbus Ave, Springfield Center (Southbound, Closed due to construction)

6 Springfield Center (Northbound, Closed due to construction)
AServ **E:** **Robbey's Repair**
TServ **E:** **Robbey's Repair**
ATM **E:** Bank of Western MA
Other **E:** Rowley Memorial Animal Hospital

5 Broad St, Springfield
FStop **W:** **Sunoco**(*, CW)
Gas **E:** Mobil(*, D)
AServ **E:** Houser Hyundai, Buick
W: The Body Shop
Other **W:** Basketball Hall of Fame

4 **(5)** Main St, MA83, East Longmeadow
Gas **E:** Sunoco(*, 24), Texaco(*, D)
Food **E:** Antonio's Pizza
AServ **E:** Houser Buick, Saturn of Springfield
W: Balise Chevrolet, Olds
ATM **E:** Bank Boston

3 **(5)** U.S. 5 N, North Columbus Ave. (No Reaccess)

2 **(4)** MA 83, Forest Park, East Longmeadow (No Reaccess)

1 **(4)** U.S. 5 South, Forest Park, Longmeadow (No Reaccess)

↑MASSACHUSETTS
↓CONNECTICUT

49 **(58)** U.S. 5, Enfield St

EXIT CONNECTICUT

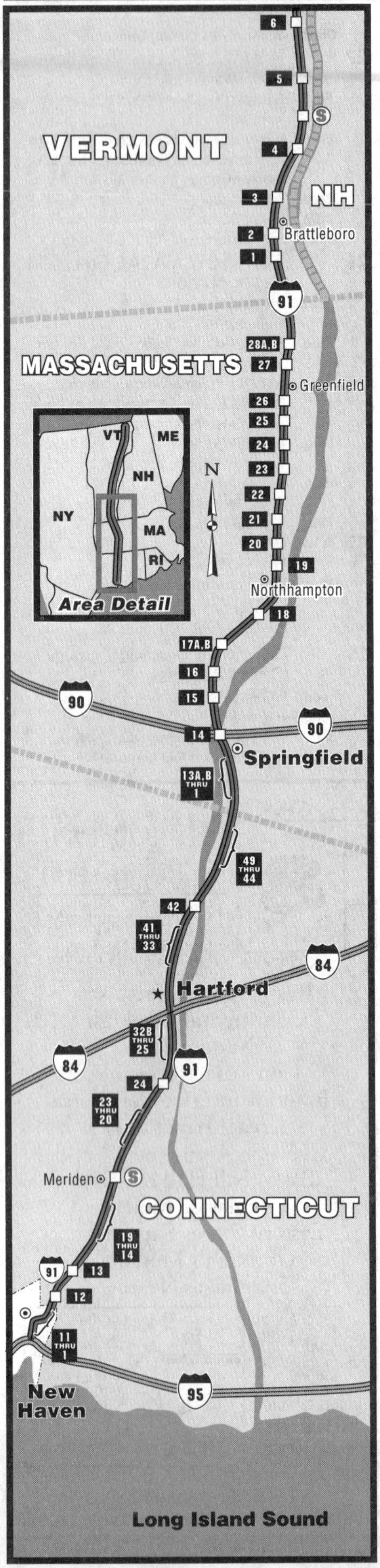

EXIT CONNECTICUT

Gas **E:** Citgo(*), Mobil(*)
Food **E:** Friendly's, McDonald's, Twistie's Ice Cream & Yogurt
W: Cloverleaf Cafe, Cloverleaf Motel, Dairy Queen
Lodg **E:** Harley Hotel
W: Cloverleaf Motel
AServ **E:** Meineke Discount Mufflers, State Line Service
W: Auto Repairs
Other **W:** **Taylor Rentals**(LP)

48 **(56)** CT 220, Elm St, Thompsonville
Gas **E:** Mobil(*)
Food **E:** Bruegger's Bagel & Bakery, Burger King, Chi Chi's Mexican Restaurant, China Buffet, Denny's, Dunkin Donuts (Mobil), Figaro Clam Bar, Friendly's, Kenny Roger's Roasters, McDonald's(PLAY), Pumpernickel Pub & Restaurant, Wendy's
AServ **E:** Sears
Other **E:** **Enfield Square Mall**, **Super Food Mart**(24, RX)

47 **(55)** CT 190, Somers, Fuffield
Gas **E:** Gulf(*, CW)
Food **E:** Abdow's, Chang's Garden, D'Angelo's, Dunkin Donuts, Ground Round, HomeTown Buffet, KFC, McDonald's, Olive Garden, Pizza Hut, Taco Bell
Lodg **E:** Motel 6, Red Roof Inn
AServ **E:** Goodyear Tire & Auto
Med **E:** ✚ **Hospital (10 Miles)**
ATM **E:** Bank Boston, New England Bank, People's Bank, **Shaw's Supermarket**
Other **E:** **Barnes & Noble Bookstore**, RX Place(RX), **Rexall Drugs**, **Shaw's Supermarket**, **WalGreens Pharmacy**

46 **(53)** U.S. 5, King St
Gas **E:** Mobil(*, CW)
Food **E:** Astro's Plaza
W: Christine's Restaurant
Lodg **W:** Super 8
Other **E:** Car Wash
W: **Post Office**

45 **(51)** CT 140, Ellington, Warehouse Point
FStop **W:** **Sunoco**(*)
Gas **E:** Shell(*, CW, 24)
Food **E:** Blimpie Subs & Salads, Burger King, Dunkin Donuts, Friendly's, Kowloon Chinese, Sofia's Seafood/Pasta/Pizza
Lodg **W:** Best Western
AServ **E:** **Cammon Care**, Killam Ford
RVCamp **E:** **Cammon Care**
Med **E:** ✚ **East Windsor Medical Center**
ATM **E:** FBM Bank, New England Bank
Other **E:** **Coin Laundry**

44 **(50)** U.S. 5 South, East Windsor
FStop **E:** **Citgo**(*)
Gas **E:** Citgo(*, D)
Food **E:** Dunkin Donuts, **East Windsor Restaurant**(24), Harp Cafe, Tobacco Valley Grill & Tavern
Lodg **E:** Holiday Inn Express
AServ **E:** East Windsor Auto
Other **E:** **Wal-Mart**(RX)

42 **(49)** CT 159, Windsor Locks
Gas **W:** Gulf(D) (Towing)
Food **W:** Charlie-Ten
AServ **W:** Gulf (Towing)

41 **(49)** Center St (Reaccess Southbound Only)
Food **W:** Ad's Pizzaria
Lodg **W:** Howard Johnson Plaza Hotel

Bold red print shows RV & Bus parking available or nearby

EXIT CONNECTICUT

AServ E: Muscow's Garage
RVCamp E: **Longview RV Super Store**
40 **(48)** Bradley International Airport, CT 20
39 **(48)** Kennedy Rd (Northbound)
Gas W: Shell(*, D, CW)
Other W: **K-Mart(RX), Super Stop & Shop(RX)**
38 **(46)** CT 75, Poquonock, Windsor
Gas E: Mobil(*, D)
Food E: China Sea, Domino's Pizza, McDonald's, Subway, The Beanery Bistro
Lodg W: Courtyard by Marriott
37 **(45)** CT 305, Bloomfield Ave, Windsor Center
Gas E: Mobil(*)
W: Citgo(*, D)
Food E: McDonald's(PLAY)
Other W: Veterinary Center
36 **(44)** CT 178, Park Ave
35B **(45)** Windsor, Bloomfield, Jct I-291
35 **(45)** Junction I-291, Manchester
Med W: **+ Hospital**
34 **(41)** CT 159, North Main St, Hartford
33 **(40)** Jennings Rd
Gas W: Exxon(*, D), Mobil(*, CW)
Food W: Burger King, Dunkin Donuts (Mobil), McDonald's, Subway
Lodg W: Red Roof Inn, Super 8
AServ W: Brothers' Toyota, Chambers Mazda, Mitsubishi, Hyundai, Jiffy Lube, Liberty Honda, Midas Muffler & Brake, Mobil, Thomas Cadallic, Toyota, Infiniti
Other W: U.S. Post Office
32B **(39)** Junction I-84 West, Trumbull St, Waterbury
Gas W: Citgo(D, CW)
Lodg W: Holiday Inn
AServ W: Goodyear Tire & Auto
30 **(38)** Junction I-84 East, CT 2, E Hartford, New London (Northbound)
29A **(37)** Capital Area
Med W: **+ Hospital**
28 **(36)** U.S. 5, CT 15, Berlin TNPK, Wethersfield, Newington
27 **(35)** Airport Rd, Brainard
FStop E: **Texaco(*, D, CW)**
Gas W: Citgo(*)
Food E: McDonald's, US Chowder Pot IV Seafood & Prime Rib
W: Baker's Dozen Donuts, Burger King, Dunkin Donuts, Wendy's
Lodg E: DAYS INN Days Inn, Grand Chalet
AServ W: Citgo, Cross Country Auto, **JAI**, John's Service Center, Madina's Auto Body, Master's Auto, Meineke Discount Mufflers, Midtown Tire & Auto Supply, S & S Precision, Super Lube
TServ E: **Interstate Ford, Nutmeg International**
W: **JAI**
26 **(35)** Marsh St, Old Wethersfield
25 **(34)** CT 3, Wethersfield, Glastonbury
24 **(32)** CT 99, Wethersfield, Rocky Hill

EXIT CONNECTICUT

Gas E: Mobil(*)
W: Mobil(*), Texaco(*)
Food E: Bickford's Family Restaurant, Boston Market Restaurant, On The Border Mexican Cafe
W: D'Angelo's, Denny's, Emperial Palace Chinese, KFC, Luna Mia Restaurant, Old Country Buffet, Red Lobster, The Ground Round
Lodg E: Susse Chalet, Travelers Motor Lodge
W: Motel 6, Ramada
AServ W: Texaco
ATM W: People's Bank
Other W: **Mail Boxes Etc**
23 **(30)** To CT 3, West St, Rocky Hill
Gas W: Citgo
Food W: Bagels Away, D'Angelo's, Elizabeth's Bar & Restaurant, McDonald's, Michelangelo's Pizzeria
Lodg E: Marriott
AServ W: Citgo
Med E: **+ VA Hospital**
ATM W: Citizen's Bank
Parks E: **Dinosaur State Park**
Other W: Amity Bookstore, Coin Car Wash
22 **(28)** CT 9, New Britain, Middletown, Old Saybrook
21 **(27)** CT 372, Cromwell, Berlin
Gas E: Sunoco(D)
W: Citgo(D), Mobil(D)
Food E: Radisson
W: Blimpie's Subs, Burger King, Cromwell's Diner(24), McDonald's, Yes Buffet
Lodg E: Comfort Inn, Radisson
W: Holiday Inn, Super 8
AServ E: Sunoco
W: Citgo, Firestone Tire & Auto
Med W: **+ Walk In Clinic**
Other E: Krauzer's Food Store
W: **Companion Animal Hospital**, N&J Books, **Wal-Mart(RX) (Vision Center)**
20 **(24)** Country Club Rd, Middle St
(23) **Rest Area (RR, Phones, RV Dump)**
(22) **Weigh Station (RV Dump; Northbound)**
19 **(21)** Baldwin Ave, Preston Ave (Southbound, Reaccess Northbound Only)
18 **(20)** Junction I-691W, Meridian, Waterbury
17 **(19)** CT 15 South, West Cross Pkwy , East Main St.
Lodg W: Ramada Plaza Hotel (see our ad this page)
16 **(18)** East Main St, Shelton (Northbound)
FStop E: **Texaco(*)**
Gas E: Gulf, Mobil(*), Smart Stop(D)
W: Amoco(*, 24), Getty(*), Gulf, Sunoco(D)
Food E: American Steak House, Lido's Pizzeria, Olympos Diner
W: Bess Eaton Donuts, Boston Market Restaurant, Burger King, Dunkin Donuts, Friendly's, Great Wall Chinese, KFC, McDonald's, Taco Bell

RAMADA
Plaza Hotel & Conference Center
203-238-2380 1331
Connecticut • Exit 17SB & 16 NB

EXIT CONNECTICUT

Lodg E: Hampton Inn, Meriden Inn
W: East Inn
AServ E: Colony Ford Dealership, Gulf, Smart Stop
W: Gulf
Med W: **+ Hospital**
ATM E: First Bank & Trust Co.
W: Dime Savings Bank, First Union Bank
Other E: Hoyts Cinema
W: **Brooks Pharmacy, Hancock's Pharmacy(RX)**
15 **(16)** CT 68, Yalesville, Durham
Lodg W: Courtyard by Marriott, Susse Chalet
(14) **Rest Area (RR, Phones, Picnic; Southbound)**
14 **(13)** CT 150, East Center St, Wallingford (Southbound, Difficult Reaccess)
Other E: **East Center Market**
13 **(11)** U.S. 5 Wallingford, North Haven
Parks W: **Wharton Brook State Park**
12 **(9)** U.S. 5, Washington Ave
Gas W: Exxon(*, D)
Food E: Angelo's Pizza, Boston Market Restaurant, Burger King, D'angelo's, Dunkin Donuts, Friendly's, McDonald's(PLAY), The Rustic Oak
W: Antonio's Pizza, Athena's Diner, D' Errico's, Danny's Pizza, Roy Rogers
Lodg W: Holiday Inn
AServ W: Northhaven Auto Body Shop, Parese Service Center
Other W: Washington Avenue Car Wash
11 **(8)** CT 22, North Haven (Northbound)
Gas E: Shell, Sunoco(*)
Food E: Bellini's, Hunan Chinese, Subway, Wendy's
AServ E: Shell
ATM E: Chase Bank, Dime Savings Bank, First Union Bank(PLAY), Fleet Bank, Webster Bank
Other E: **CVS Pharmacy(RX), Super Food Mart, Washington Center Mall**
10 **(7)** CT 40, Hamden, Mt Carmel
9 **(5)** Montowese Ave
FStop W: **No Name(*, 24)**
Gas E: Citgo
W: Sunoco(*)
AServ W: Sunoco
Other E: **Dairy Mart**
8 **(3)** CT 17, CT 80, Middletown Ave, N Branford
Gas E: Amoco(*, CW), Exxon(*), Shell(*, CW), Sunoco(*)
W: Mobil(D)
Food E: Dunkin Donuts (Amoco), Dunkin Donuts, McDonald's, Pizza Hut, Taco Bell
Lodg E: Motel 6
AServ E: Instant Oil Change
W: A & A Used Auto Parts, Mobil
Other E: **K-Mart(24, RX)**
7 **(3)** Ferry St, Fair Haven (Southbound, Difficult Reaccess)
6 **(2)** U.S. 5, Willow St, Blatchly Ave
5 **(1)** U.S. 5, State St (Northbound, Difficult Reaccess)
4 **(1)** State St
3 **(1)** Trumbull St
2 **(0)** Hamilton St
1 **(0)** CT 34, Downtown New Haven

↑ CONNECTICUT

Begin I-91

I-93 S →

EXIT VERMONT/NEW HAMPSHIRE

Begin I-93

↓VERMONT

(11) I-91S to Whitewater Jct, I-91N to St Johnsbury

1 **(7)** to U.S. 2, Vermont 18, St. Johnsbury
- Lodg **E:** Aime's Motel
  W: The Moon Struck Inn
- RVCamp **E: Moose River Campground (.33 Miles)**
- Other **E: Pettio Country Store**(*)

(1) **VT Welcome Center (RR, HF, Phones, Picnic)**

↑VERMONT

↓NEW HAMPSHIRE

44 **(130) NH 18, NH 135, Monroe, Waterford VT, Rest Area & Scenic View**

43 **(126)** NH 135, to NH 18, Littleton, Dalton
- RVCamp **W: Crazy Horse Campground**

42 **(124)** U.S. 302, NH 10, Littleton, Woodsville
- Gas **E:** Gulf(*), Sunoco(*, 24)
  W: Mobil(*)
- Food **E: Burger King**, Cafe Munchies, Jing Fong, McDonald's, Pizza Hut, Subway, The Clam Hut, The Clam Shell
  W: Continental Motor Inn
- Lodg **W:** Continental Motor Inn
- AServ **E:** Convenient Lube
  W: Crosstown Motors Chrysler, Dodge, Jeep, Eagle
- RVCamp **W: KOA Campgrounds**
- ATM **W:** Berlin National Bank, Littleton Banking Center
- Other **E:** Brooks Pharmacy(RX), Littleton Laundry, **Rite Aid Pharmacy**(RX)

41 **(123)** U.S. 302, NH 18, NH 116, Littleton, Whitfield
- Gas **E:** Irving(*, D, 24)
- Food **E:** Bishop's Ice Cream, Eastgate Motor Inn
- Lodg **E:** Eastgate Motor Inn, Thayers Inn
- Med **E: + Hospital**
- ATM **E:** Guaranty Bank, Irving

40 **(121)** U.S. 302, NH 10 East, Bethlehem, Twin Mtn
- Gas **E:** Exxon
- Food **E:** Adair Country Inn
- Lodg **E:** Adair Country Inn
- AServ **E:** Exxon
- RVCamp **E: Snowy Mountain Campground (1 Mile)**
- Med **W: + Hospital**

39 **(119)** NH 18, NH 116 , N Franconia, Sugar Hill (Southbound)

38 **(117)** NH 18, NH 116, NH 117, NH 142, Franconia, Sugar Hill, Lisbon (Difficult Reaccess)
- Gas **W:** Mobil
- Food **W:** Cannon Ball Pizza, Dutch Treat Restaurant, Franconia Dairy Bar & Restaurant, Quality Bakery
- Lodg **E:** Red Coach Inn
  W: Gail River Motel
- AServ **W:** Mobil
- RVCamp **W: Fransted Campground (1 Mile)**
- ATM **W:** People's Bank

37 **(114)** NH 142, NH 18, Franconia, Bethlehem
- Food **W:** Hill Winds, The Village House
- Lodg **E:** The Inn At Forest Hills
  W: Hill Winds, Raynor's Motor Lodge
- RVCamp **W: Franstead Family Campground**

36 **(113)** NH 141, South Franconia

EXIT NEW HAMPSHIRE

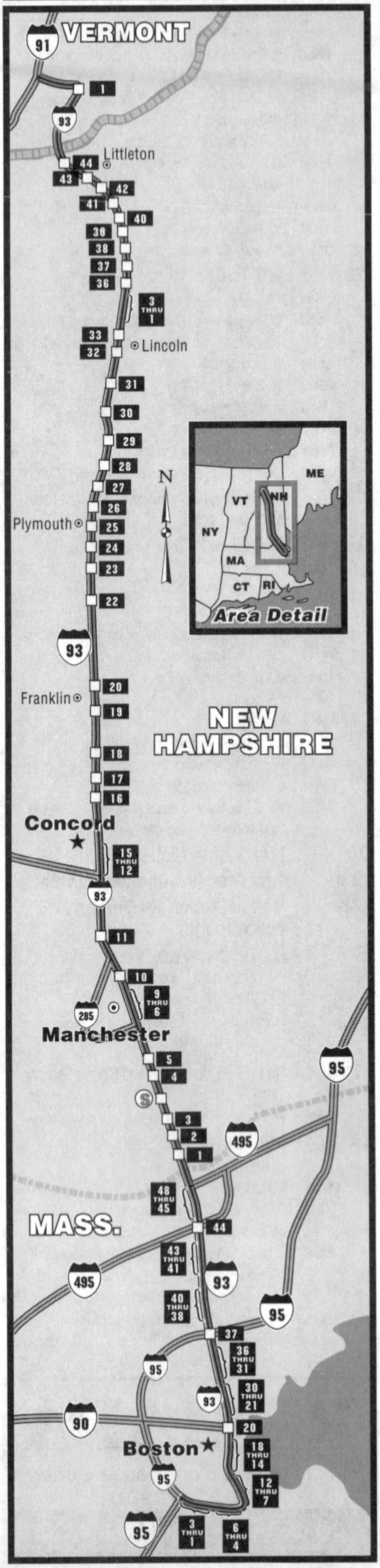

EXIT NEW HAMPSHIRE

35 **(112)** U.S. 3, Twin Mountain, Lancaster
- Other **E: White Mountain National Forest**

Note: I-93 runs concurrent below with FNPKWY. Numbering follows FNPKWY.

3 **(111)** NH 18, Echo Lake Beach, Peabody Lodge
- Other **E: Govenor Gallen Memorial**
  W: Echo Lake Swimming & Parking Area

2 **(110)** Cannon Mountain Tramway, Old Man Viewing
- Other **W: Park Information Center**

(110) **Trail Head Parking Area (Southbound)**

(109) **Boise Rock Parking Area (Northbound, No Trucks)**

1A **(108)** Lafayette Place Campground (No Busses)
- Parks **W: Franconia Notch State Park (Southbound Access Only)**

(108) **Trail Head Parking Area (RR, Phones)**

(107) **Rest Area (RR)**

1 **(105)** U.S. 3, The Flume Visitor Center
- Other **E: Applachian Trail, Flumes Gorge & Visitor Center**

Note: I-93 runs concurrent above with FNPKWY. Numbering follows FNPKWY.

33 **(103)** U.S. 3, North Woodstock, North Lincoln
- Gas **E:** Irving(*, D)
- Food **E:** Longhorn Palace, Mountaineer Motel, Notch View Country Kitchen
- Lodg **E:** Drummer Boy Motor Inn, Green Village by the River, Mount Coolidge Motel, Mountaineer Motel, Pemmi Motor Ct., Profile Motel, Red Doors Motel
  W: Country Bumpkins Campground & Cottages(LP), Cozy Cabins, Mount Liberty Motel
- AServ **W:** Ted's White Mountain Garage
- RVCamp **W: Cold Springs Camp, Country Bumpkins Campground & Cottages, Lost River Gorge**
- Other **E: Whale's Tale Water Park**

32 **(101)** NH 112, North Woodstock, Lincoln
- Gas **E:** Citgo(*), Irving(*), Mobil(*, LP, CW)
- Food **E:** Bill & Bob's Famous Roast Beef, Bishop's Homemade IceCream Outlet, Burger King, Chieng Garden, Dragon Light, Dunkin Donuts (Citgo), Earl of Sandwich, Elvio Pizzeria, GH Pizza & Greek Restaurant, McDonald's, Michael's, Mr W's House of Pancakes, Old Timber Mill, The Country Mile, The Italian Garden, White Mountain Chowder House, White Mtn Bagel Company & Outback BBQ
- Lodg **E:** River Green Restort Hotel, The Lincoln Motel, The Mill House Inn
- AServ **E:** Big A Auto Part Store
- RVCamp **W: KOA Campgrounds, Maple Haven Camping (1 Mile)**
- Med **E: + Winwood Medical Center**
- ATM **E:** Citizen's Bank, Fleet Bank
- Other **E: Rite Aid Pharmacy**(RX)

31 **(98)** To NH 175, Tripoli Rd
- RVCamp **E: Russel Pond Campground**
  W: KOA Campgrounds (2 Miles), Waterest Campground (1 Mile)

30 **(95)** U.S. 3, Woodstock, Thornton
- Food **E:** Frannie's Place, Jack-O-Lantern Resort
- Lodg **E:** Jack-O-Lantern Resort, Pioneer Motel

29 **(89)** U.S. 3, Thornton
- Lodg **W:** Gilcrest Motel
- RVCamp **E: Pemi River Campground**

28 **(88)** NH 49, Campton, Waterville Valley, to NH175

Bold red print shows RV & Bus parking available or nearby

EXIT NEW HAMPSHIRE

Gas E: Citgo[*] (Towing), Mobil[*] (Towing)
Food E: The Lost Sailor Grill
W: Scandanavi Inn
Lodg W: Scandanavi Inn
AServ E: Citgo (Towing), Mobil (Towing)
RVCamp W: **Branch Brook Campground (1 Mile)**
Parks E: **White Mountain National Forest (2 Miles)**
Other E: **Quik Pik Grocery**

27 **(84)** Blair Bridge, W Campton , to U.S. 3
Food E: The Covered Bridge Restaurant
Lodg E: Best Western, Red Sleigh Chalets & Motel

26 **(82)** U.S. 3, NH 25, NH 3A, Plymouth, Rumney
Food W: McDonald's
Lodg W: Pilgrim Inn, Susse Chalet
RVCamp W: **Campground**
Med W: **Hospital**

25 **(81)** NH 175A, Holderness Rd, Plymouth
FStop W: **Irving**[*, D]
Gas W: Mobil
Food W: Bridgeside Diner
AServ W: Mobil
Med W: **Hospital**

24 **(76)** U.S. 3, NH 25, Ashland, Holderness, Squam Lake Region
FStop E: **Irving**[*, D]
Gas E: Mobil[LP, CW]
Food E: Burger King[PLAY], Dunkin Donuts (Mobil), **Subway (Irving)**
Lodg E: Comfort Inn
AServ E: Ashland Auto Parts, Mobil
RVCamp E: **Ames Brook Campground (1.5 Miles)**, **Squam Lakes Resort**
ATM E: **Irving**, Pemigewass National Bank

23 **(70)** NH 132, NH 104, Meredith, New Hampton
FStop E: **Irving**[*, D]
Gas E: Citgo[*]
Food E: Dunkin Donuts, **Irving**, Rossi's Italian & Pizza
RVCamp E: **Ames Brook Campground**, **Clearwater Campground**, **Yogi Bear Camp Resort**
W: **Davidson's Countryside Campground (2 Miles)**
ATM E: Franklin Savings Bank

22 **(62)** NH 127, Sanbornton, W Franklin
Med W: **Hospital**

20 **(57)** U.S. 3, NH 11, NH 140, Tilton, Laconia
FStop E: **Exxon**[*], **Irving**[*]
Gas E: Mobile
Food E: Applebee's, Burger King[PLAY], Dunkin Donuts, Great American Diner, Lee Gardens, McDonald's, Oliver's Restaurant, **Pizza Hut (Irving)**, **Taco Bell (Irving)**, Upper Crust Pizzeria
W: **McDonald's (Wal-Mart)**
AServ E: BJ's Tire Center, VIP Discount Auto Service
W: Tilton,Ford, Chrysler,Plymouth, Dodge, **Wal-Mart[RX] (Tire & Lube)**
ATM E: Concord Savings Bank, **Irving**
W: Concord Savings
Other E: **Shaw's Grocery**
W: **Wal-Mart[RX] (Tire & Lube)**

19 **(55)** NH 132, Northfield, Franklin (Reaccess Southbound Only)
Gas W: Mobil[*]
Med W: **Hospital**
ATM W: Franklins Savings Bank

(52) **Rest Area (RR, Phones, Picnic; Eastbound)**

18 **(49)** NH 132, Canterbury
Gas E: Sunoco[*]

17 **(46)** U.S. 4 to U.S. 3, NH 132, Penacook, Boscawen

16 **(41)** NH 132, East Concord

EXIT NEW HAMPSHIRE

Gas E: Mobil[D]
AServ E: Mobil
Other E: **Mill Stream Market**, Sunflower's Bakery

15 **(39)** Jct I-393, U.S.4, US 202, Main St
FStop W: **Mobile**
Gas W: Citgo, Exxon[*], Getty[*], Gulf[*], Irving, Merritt[*]
Food W: Friendly's
AServ W: Citgo
Med W: **Hospital**
ATM W: Concord Savings Bank, Gulf

14 **(39)** NH 9, Loudon
FStop E: **Texaco**[*, D, CW]
Gas W: Exxon[*], Gulf[*, D], Merritt[*]
Food E: Boston Market Restaurant, Einstein Bros Bagels, Family Buffet, Pizzeria Uno, Week's Family Restaurant
W: Tea Garden Restaurant, The Gas Lighter
Lodg W: Holiday Inn, Sheraton
AServ E: Auto Zone, Midas Muffler & Brake
W: Exxon
Med W: **Hospital**
ATM E: **Shaw's Grocery Store**
W: Gulf
Other E: **Market Basket**, **Osco Drugs[RX]**, **Shaw's Grocery Store**, **Shop 'N Save Supermarket**
W: CVS Pharmacy[RX]

13 **(38)** U.S. 3, Manchester St
Gas E: Gulf[*], Sunoco[*, D]
W: Gibbs[*, D]
Food E: Dunkin Donuts, Egg Shell, Hong Kong Island Kitchen, Landmark Lounge, Skuffy's, Veffide Restaurant
W: Al's Capitol City Diner, Burger King, D'Angelo's Sandwich Shop, Dunkin Donuts, Hawaiian Isle II, KFC, McDonald's, Miami Subs, Papa Gino's
AServ E: Carlson's Chrysler/Plymouth, Excel Transmission Shop, Fiermonti Oldsmobile Saab, Isuzu of Concord, Star Brake Service, Toyo Tires, Volvo of Concord
W: Goodyear Tire & Auto, Meineke Discount Mufflers, **Patsy's GMC Trucks**
TServ W: **Patsy's GMC Trucks**
RVCamp E: **RV Sports Center**
Med W: **Hospital**

12 **(37)** NH 3A, Bow
Gas E: Exxon[*], Irving[*]
Food E: Dunkin Donuts (Exxon), Subway (Irving)
Lodg E: Brick Tower Motor Inn, DAYS INN Days Inn
AServ E: Concord Mazda Volkswagon Saturn, John Grappone Ford Dealership
TServ E: **John Grapone**
RVCamp E: **John Grapone**
Med W: **Hospital**
ATM E: Exxon, Irving

(36) Jct I-89, Dartmouth, Lake Sunapee, White River Junction

(31) **Rest Area (RR, Phones, Picnic, Vending; Westbound)**

(31) **Rest Area (RR, Phones; Eastbound)**

(29) Toll Plaza (Toll)

11 **(29)** NH 3A, Hooksett (Toll)

(27) Junction I-293, Everett Tnpk, Manchester

10 **(26)** NH 3A, Hooksett
FStop E: **Irving**
Gas W: Exxon[*]
Food W: Big Cheese Pizza, Dunkin Donuts (Exxon)
ATM E: Bank Boston
W: Exxon
Other W: **Riverside Park**

9 **(24)** U.S. 3, NH 28, Hooksett, Manchester
Gas E: Exxon[*], Hooksett Mini Market[*]
W: Exxon[*, D], Mobil[*], Sunoco[D]
Food E: Chantilly's, Hooksett Bagel & Deli, Ice Cream Depot

EXIT NEW HAMPSHIRE

W: Boston Market Restaurant, Burger King, Cheung Kee Chinese, D'Angelo's Sandwich Shop, Fired Up BBQ, Happy Garden, KFC, La Carreta, Luisa Pizza & Pasta, Papa Genio's, Pinker's Seafood, Shogun Japanese Steak House, Shorty's Mexican Road House
Lodg E: Firebird Motel
AServ W: Sunoco, VIP Auto Center
ATM E: Exxon, Fleet Bank
W: BankBoston, Exxon, St.Mary's Bank
Other E: Car Wash
W: **Shop 'N Save Supermarket**

8 **(22)** Wellington Bridge, Bridge St (Closed for Construction)
Med W: **Hospital**

7 **(21)** NH 101 East, Portsmith, Seacoast

6 **(21)** Candia Rd, Hanover St (Difficult Reaccess)
Food E: **Candia Rd Convenient Store & Sub Shop**
AServ E: Transmission Man
Med W: **Hospital**

(19) Junction I-293, NH 101, West Manchester, Bedford

5 **(15)** NH 28, North Londonderry
FStop E: **Sunoco**[*]
Gas W: Exxon[*, D]
Food E: **Dunkin Donuts (Sunoco)**, Poor Boy's Family Dining, **Subway (Sunoco)**

4 **(12)** NH 102, Derry, Londonderry
Gas E: Citgo[*, D], Mobil, Mutual, Shell[*, CW], Sunoco
W: Charter, Citgo[*], Exxon, Texaco[*, CW]
Food E: Burger King[PLAY], Derry, Dunkin Donuts (Shell)
W: Coffeeberries, Great American Subs, Honey Dew Donuts (Texaco), **Little Caesars Pizza (K-Mart)**, Maple Garden Chinese, McDonald's, Papa Gino's, Pizza by George, Wendy's, Whipper Snappers
AServ E: Mobil, Sunoco
W: Exxon, Gladstone's Ford/Dodge/Chrysler/ Plymouth, Instant Lube
ATM E: Shell
W: Andover Bank, BankBoston
Other W: **K-Mart**, **Market Basket Supermarket**, Osco Drugs, **Shaw's Grocery**, **WalGreens Pharmacy**

(7) **Weigh Station**

3 **(6)** NH 111, Windham, N Salem
Gas E: Citgo[*]
W: Exxon[*, D, 24], Sunoco[*, 24]
Food E: Capri Pizza, Windham House of Pizza
W: Dunkin Donuts, Subway
ATM E: Southern NH Bank

2 **(3)** To NH 38, NH 97, Salem, Pelham
Gas W: Citgo[*, D]
Food W: Adam's, Dusty's Ice Cream (Citgo), Holiday Inn, Rutabagas Cafe
Lodg E: Red Roof Inn
W: Holiday Inn, Susse Chalet
ATM W: Southern NH Bank
Other W: **Lucy's Country Store**

1 **(2)** NH 28, Rockingham Park Blvd, Salem
FStop E: **Exxon**[*]
Gas E: Citgo[D], **Exxon**[*], Getty
Food E: 99 Restaurant, Bickford's Family Restaurant, Burger King, Denny's, Findeisen's Ice Cream, Friendly's, Grand China, McDonald's
Lodg E: Park View Inn
AServ E: Citgo, Getty, Sears
Other E: Barnes & Noble Bookstore, Delahunty's Coin Car Wash, **K-Mart**, **Lens Crafters (Walgreens)**, **Osco Drugs**, **Rockingham Mall**, **Salem Animal Hospital**, **Shaw's Grocery**, **WalGreens Pharmacy (LensCrafters)**

(1) **Welcome Center (RR, Phones, Picnic, Vending, Pet Walk; Eastbound)**

Bold red print shows RV & Bus parking available or nearby

EXIT	NEW HAMPSHIRE/MASSACHUSETTS

↑NEW HAMPSHIRE
↓MASSACHUSETTS

48 **(47)** MA 213, Methuen, Haverhill

47 MA 213, Pelham St, Pelham, Methuen
- Gas E: Shell, Sunoco[*, 24]
  W: Getty
- Food W: Days Inn (see our ad this page)
  Fireside Restaurant
- AServ E: Shell
  W: Clark Chrysler, Plymouth, Jeep, Eagle, Getty
- Med E: ✚ Hospital

46 **(44)** MA 110, MA 113, Lawrence, Dracut
- Gas E: Getty, Mobil[*], Shell[*, CW]
  W: Coastal
- Food E: Burger King[PLAY], Dunkin Donuts, McDonald's, Papa Gino's, Pizza Hut
  W: Dunkin Donuts, Jackson's, Royal House Of Pizza
- AServ E: Mobil, Shell
- Med E: ✚ Hospital
- ATM E: Andover Bank, Fleet Bank
- Other E: Osco Drugs

45 **(43)** River Rd, South Lawrence
- Gas W: Mobil[*, 24]
- Food W: Dunkin Donuts (Mobil), Grill 93, Tage Inn
- Lodg E: Andover Marriot
  W: Tage Inn
- ATM W: Mobil
- Parks E: Lawrence River Front State Park

44AB **(41)** Junction I-495, Lawrence, Lowell

43 **(39)** MA 133, North Tewksbury, Andover
- Gas E: Mobil[*, 24]
- Food E: Dunkin Donuts (Mobil), Ramada
- Lodg E: Ramada
- ATM E: Mobil

42 **(38)** Dascomb Rd, Tewksbury

41 **(35)** MA 125, Andover, North Andover

40 **(34)** MA 62, North Reading, Wilmington

39 **(33)** Concord St

38 **(32)** MA 129, Reading, Wilmington
- Gas W: Mobil
- Food W: Burger King, Dunkin Donuts, Royal Dynasty
- AServ W: Mobil

37AB **(29)** Junction I-95, Waltham, Peabody

36 **(27)** Montvale Ave, Stoneham, Woburn
- Gas E: Mobil
  W: Citgo[*, D], Exxon[*], Getty, Shell
- Food E: Al La Kitchen Pizza & Subs, Dunkin Donuts, Monty's Restaurant
  W: Bigford's Family Restaurant, Einstein Bros Bagels, Friendly's, McDonald's, Pancakes Family Fair, Primo's Italian, Spud's (Howard Johnson)
- Lodg W: Howard Johnson
- AServ E: Mobil, Rite Way
  W: Getty, Getty, Shell, Shell
- Med W: ✚ Hospital
- ATM W: BankBoston, Einstein Bros Bagels, US Trust
- Other E: Car Wash, Coin Car Wash

EXIT	MASSACHUSETTS

35 Winchester Highlands (Southbound, Reaccess Northbound Only)

34 **(26)** MA 28 North, Stoneham, Melrose (Northbound)
- Gas E: Mobil
- Food E: Friendly's
- Lodg E: Spot Pond Motel
- AServ E: Mobil
- Med E: ✚ Boston Regional Medical Center
- Other E: The Stone Zoo

33 MA 28, Fellsway, Winchester
- Med E: ✚ Hospital
  W: ✚ Hospital

32 **(23)** MA 60, Medford Square, Malden
- Gas W: Exxon
- Food W: Dunkin Donuts
- Lodg E: AmeriSuites (see our ad this page)
- AServ E: Gem Auto Parts, Instant Oil Change, Ulta Tech
  W: Exxon
- Med W: ✚ Hospital
- ATM E: Medford Cooperative Bank

31 MA 16, Mystic Valley Pkwy, Arlington

29 MA 28, MA 38, Somerville, Everett (Reaccess Southbound Only)
- Gas W: Global, Gulf, Merit
- Food E: McDonald's
  W: Dunkin Donuts, Louie's

1874

Restaurant/Lounge on Premise
Continental Breakfast
Kids Under 12 Stay Free
Indoor Pool • Exercise Room
Meeting/Banquet Facilities
Truck/Large Vehicle Parking
Airport Shuttle • Coin Laundry
Rockingham Park Race Track

978-686-2971 • Methuen, MA
Massachusetts ▪ I-93 ▪ EXIT 47

1365

Massachusetts • Exit 032 • 781-395-8500

1642

Continental Breakfast
Restaurants Nearby
Meeting/Banquet Facilities
Tennis/Golf Nearby
Truck Parking
Jacuzzi

4 Sunburst Quality Award Winner

781-932-1000 • 850 Hangham St.
Massachusetts ▪ I-93 ▪ Exit 7

EXIT	MASSACHUSETTS

- AServ W: Gulf
- Med W: ✚ Hospital
- Other E: K-Mart

27 U.S. 1 North, Tobin Bridge

26 Storrow Drive, Cambridge

25 Causeway St, North Station

24 Callahan Tunnel, Logan Airport, Gov. Center

23 High St, Congress St

22 Atlantic Ave, Northern Ave

21 Kneeland St, Chinatown

20 Junction I-90, MA Turnpike, Chinatown, Kneeland

18 Massachusetts Ave, Roxbury (Left Exit Northbound)
- Med S: ✚ University Hospital

17 East Berkeley St, Broadway

16 South Hampton St, Andrew Square
- Gas W: Economy
- Food E: Alex's Roast Beef & Pizza, Dunkin Donuts
  W: Little Caesars Pizza
- AServ W: Boston Tire[24], Economy
- Med W: ✚ Boston Medical Center
- Other W: K-Mart

15 Columbia Rd, Edward Everett Square

14 Morrissey Blvd (Northbound)
- Other W: JFK Library

13 Freeport St, Dorchester
- Gas W: Citgo, Mutual, Shell
- Food W: Carvel Ice Cream Bakery, Linda Mae's, Pizza, Puritans Pizza Restaurant, Susse Chalet, Swiss House Restaurant, The Candy House
- Lodg W: Susse Chalet
- AServ W: Citgo, Shell, Toyota & GM Dealer, Westminister Dodge
- ATM W: Citizens Bank
- Other W: CVS Pharmacy[RX]

12 MA 3A, Neponset, Quincy

11AB To MA203, Granite Ave, Ashmont

10 Squatum St, Milton (Reaccess Northbound Only)

9 Adams St, Milton, N Quincy (Difficult Reaccess)

8 Furnace Brook Pkwy, Quincy (No Reaccess)

7 MA 3 South, Braintree, Cape Cod
- Lodg E: Days Inn (see our ad this page)

6 West Quincy Braintree, MA 37
- Gas E: Sunoco[CW]
  W: Mobil[*]
- Food W: Uno Chicago Bar & Grill
- Lodg W: Sheraton
- AServ E: Dave Dinger Ford, Nisson Dealership
- Other E: Barnes & Noble Bookstore
  W: South Shore Shopping Plaza

5AB MA 28, Randolph, Milton
- Gas E: Citgo[*, CW], Shell[*, 24], Texaco[CW]
- Food E: D'Angelo's, Dunkin Donuts, Holiday Inn
- Lodg E: Holiday Inn
- AServ E: Shell[24]
- ATM E: BankBoston

4 MA 24 South, Brockton, Fall River

3 Houghton's Pond, Ponkapoag Trail

2AB MA 138, Stoughton
- Gas W: Gulf[D], Mobil[*, 24], Sunoco Texaco[*]
- Lodg W: Howard Johnson
- AServ W: Sunoco

1 Junction I-95

↑MASSACHUSETTS

Begin I-93

Bold red print shows RV & Bus parking available or nearby

EXIT — MONTANA

Begin I-94

↓MONTANA

0 Jct West I-90, Billings; I-90 East, Sheridan

6 CR 522, Huntley, Shepherd
- FStop N: **Pryor Creek[*]**
- Food N: **Pryor Creek**
- RVCamp N: **Camping**

14 Ballantine, Worden
- FStop S: **Sinclair[*]**
- Food S: Longbranch Cafe
- RVCamp S: **Longbranch RV Park & Mobile Home Court**
- ATM S: **Sinclair**

23 Pompeys Pillar
- Other N: **Pompeys Pillar Landmark**

36 Waco

(38) **Rest Area (RR, Picnic, P; Eastbound)**

(41) **Rest Area (RR, Picnic, P; Westbound)**

47 Custer
- Gas S: Conoco[*, D]
- Food S: Junction City Saloon, No Name Motel
- Lodg S: No Name Motel
- Other S: Custer Food Market, U.S. Post Office

49 MT 47, Hardin, Little Bighorn Battlefield
- Food S: Cafe
- Parks S: **The Little Bighorn Battlefield**

53 Bighorn

63 Ranch Access

(65) **Rest Area (RR, Phones, Picnic, P; Eastbound)**

(65) **Rest Area (RR, Phones, Picnic, P; Westbound)**

67 Hysham

72 CR 384, Sarpy Creek Road

82 Reservation Creek Road

87 MT 39, Colstrip

93 U.S. 12 West, Forsyth, Roundup
- FStop N: **Conoco**
- Food N: Rails Inn Motel
- Lodg N: Rails Inn Motel, Shade Tree Inn, **Westwind Motor Inn**
- AServ N: Big Sky Service
- Med N: **✚ Hospital**

EXIT — MONTANA

- Other N: Amerigas[LP], Amoco Home Oil Company[LP]

95 Forsyth
- Gas N: Conoco[*], Exxon[*, D, 24]
- Food N: Dairy Queen, M & M Pizza
- Lodg N: Best Western, Hillside Inn
- AServ N: Heberle Ford
- RVCamp N: **Campground Wagon Wheel**
  S: **Wagon Wheel RV Camp**
- Med N: **✚ Hospital**
- Parks N: **Rosebud Recreation Area**
  S: **Rosebud Recreation Area**
- Other N: Yellowstone Valley Veterinarian Clinic

(99) **Weigh Station (Eastbound)**

(99) **Weigh Station (Westbound)**

103 CR 447, CR 446, Rosebud, Rosebud Creek Road

106 Rosebud, Butte Creek Road

(113) **Rest Area (RR, Phones, Picnic, RV Dump, P; Westbound)**

(114) **Rest Area (RR, Phones, Picnic, RV Dump, P; Eastbound)**

117 Hathaway
- Other N: U.S. Post Office

126 Moon Creek Road

128 Local Access

135 Miles City
- RVCamp N: **KOA Campgrounds (2 Miles)**

138 MT 59, Miles City, Broadus
- FStop N: **Cenex[*, RV DUMP], Exxon[*, CW] (Pacific Pride Commercial Fueling)**
- Gas N: Conoco[*]
- Food N: **4B's Family Dining**, Best Western, Boardwalk Restaurant, Dairy Queen (Conoco), Gallagher's Family Restaurant (Ruby's Casino), Hardee's, KFC, McDonald's, Subway, Taco John's, Varsity Sport's Bar & Grill
  S: New Hunan American/Chinese
- Lodg N: Best Western, Budget Host Inn, DAYS INN Days Inn, Motel 6
  S: Comfort Inn, Holiday Inn Express, **Super 8**
- RVCamp N: **KOA Campgrounds (7 Miles), KOA Campgrounds (1 Mile)**
- Med N: **✚ Holy Rosary Health Center, ✚ Hospital**
- ATM N: **Cenex**, Conoco, **Exxon (Pacific Pride Commercial Fueling)**
- Other N: **County Market Grocery, K-Mart[RX]**, **Osco Drug[RX]**

141 East U.S. 12, Bus. Loop I-94, Miles City, Baker
- TStop N: **Flying J Travel Plaza[*]**

EXIT — MONTANA

- Lodg N: Star Motel
- TServ N: **Flying J Travel Plaza**
- RVCamp N: **Big Sky Campground**
- ATM N: **Flying J Travel Plaza**

148 Valley Access

159 Diamond Ring, Frontage Rd

169 Powder River Road

176 CR 253, Terry
- Gas N: Cenex[*]
- Food N: Overland Restaurant
- Lodg N: **Diamond Motel**
- RVCamp N: **Diamond Motel & Trailer Park (.75 Miles), Terry RV Oasis (.75 Miles)**
- Med N: **✚ Hospital**

185 CR 340, Fallon

192 Bad Route Road

(192) **Rest Area, Weigh Station (RR, Phones, Picnic, P; Located at Exit 192)**

198 Cracker Box Road

204 Whoopup Creek Road

206 Pleasant View Road

210 Glendive, Circle
- Parks S: **Makoshika State Park**
- Other S: **Camping**

211 MT 200 South, Circle (Westbound, Reaccess Eastbound Only)

213 MT 16, Sidney
- FStop N: **Exxon[*]**
  S: **Sinclair[*, RV DUMP]**
- Gas S: Cenex[*, D], Sinclair[*]
- Food S: **Sinclair**
- Lodg S: Budget Host Inn
- AServ S: **D & R Repair**, Sinclair
- TServ S: **D & R Repair**
- RVCamp N: **Green Valley Campground**
- ATM S: Cenex
- Other N: **MT Highway Patrol**

215 Bus. Loop I-94, Glendive, City Center
- Gas N: Conoco[*]
  S: Exxon[*], Sinclair[*, D]
- Food N: CC's Family Cafe, Kings Inn
- Lodg N: DAYS INN Days Inn, Kings Inn, Super 8
  S: Glendive's Budget Motel
- AServ S: Bob's Body Shop, Sinclair
- RVCamp N: **Glendive Campground**
- Med S: **✚ Glendive Medical Center**
- Parks S: **Makoshika State Park**
- Other N: **Frontier Gateway Museum**

224 Griffith Creek, Frontage Road

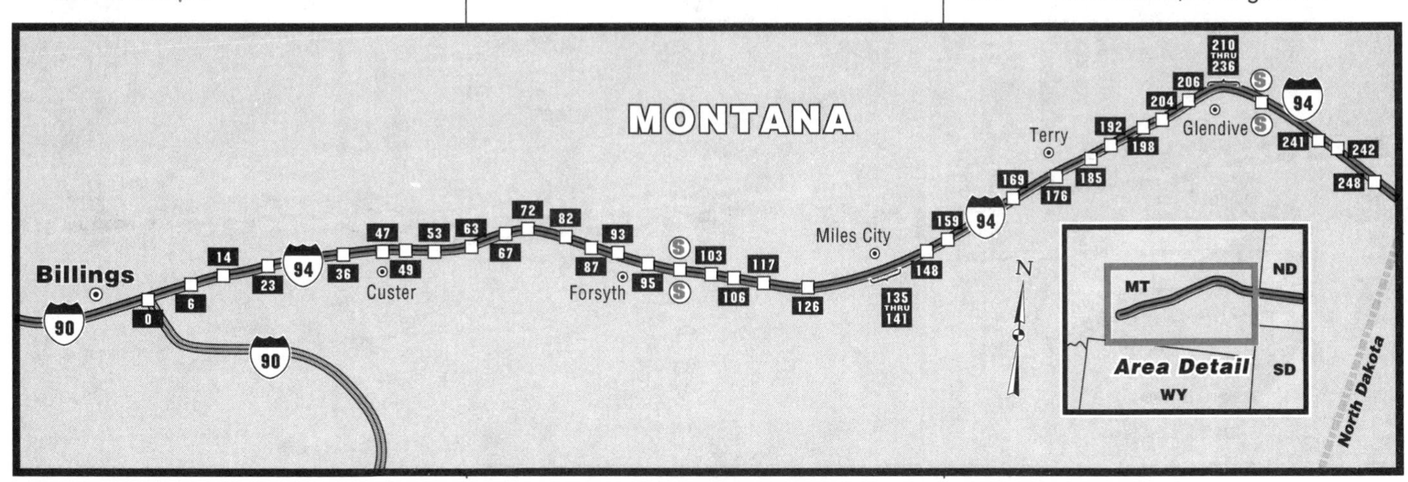

Bold red print shows RV & Bus parking available or nearby

← W I-94 E →

EXIT — MONTANA/NORTHDAKOTA

231 Hodges Road

236 Ranch Access

(240) **Weigh Station (RV Dump; Eastbound)**

(240) **Weigh Station (RV Dump; Westbound)**

241 MT 7, To CR 261, Wibaux, Baker (Eastbound, Reaccess Westbound Only)

- FStop — **S: Co-Op Farmland**[*, CW]
- Gas — S: Conoco[*, D]
- Food — S: Longhorn Cafe, Tastee Hut
- Lodg — S: Super 8, W-V Motel
- AServ — **S: Co-Op Farmland**

(242) **Rest Area (P; Westbound, Reaccess Eastbound Only, Located at Exit 242)**

242 MT 7, To CR 261, Wibaux, Baker (Westbound, Reaccess Eastbound Only)

248 Carlyle Road

↑MONTANA

↓NORTH DAKOTA

(1) **Weigh Station (Eastbound)**

(1) **Weigh Station, Rest Area (Westbound)**

1 ND 16, Beach

- TStop — **S: Flying J Travel Plaza**[*, LP]
- FStop — **S: Cenex**[*]
- Lodg — N: Outpost Motel
  - S: Buckboard Inn
- ATM — **S: Cenex**

7 Home on the Range

10 Sentinel Butte, Camel Hump Lake

(13) **Rest Area (RR, Phones, Picnic; Eastbound)**

(15) **Rest Area (RR, Phones, Picnic; Westbound)**

18 Buffalo Gap

- RVCamp — **N: Camping**

(21) **Scenic View (Eastbound)**

23 W River Road (Westbound, Reaccess Eastbound Only)

EXIT — NORTH DAKOTA

24 Historic Medora, Theodore Roosevelt National Park

- RVCamp — **S: Medora Campground (1.5 Miles)**
- Parks — **S: Theodore Roosevelt National Park**

27 Historic Medora (Eastbound, Reaccess Westbound Only)

- RVCamp — **S: Medora Campground (2 Miles), Red Trail Campground (1.75 Miles)**

(32) **Rest Area (RR, Phones, Vending; Located at Exit 32)**

32 **Painted Canyon, Visitor's Center & Rest Area (RR, Phones, Vending)**

- Other — **N: Painted Canyon Visitor Center**

36 Fryburg

42 U.S. 85, Belfield, Grassy Butte, Williston

- FStop — **S: Amoco**[*, LP]
- Gas — S: Conoco[*, D]
- Food — **S: Amoco**, Dairy Queen, Rendevous, Trapper's Kettle
- Lodg — **S: Trapper's Inn Motel & Camping**
- AServ — S: NAPA
- RVCamp — **S: Campground, Trapper's Inn Motel & Camping**
- ATM — S: Conoco
- Parks — **N: Theodore Roosevelt National Park - North Unit**
- Other — **N: Theodore Roosevelt National Park**

51 South Heart

59 Bus Loop I-94, Dickinson

- RVCamp — **S: Camp On The Heart (1.5 Miles)**
- Parks — **S: Patterson Lake Recreation Area**

61 ND 22, Dickinson, Kill Deer

- FStop — **N: Cenex**[*, LP, CW]
- Gas — N: Sinclair[*, D]
  - S: Amoco[*, LP, CW], Cenex[*, D, LP, CW], Conoco[*], Holiday[*, D]
- Food — N: Applebee's, **Arby's**, Bonanza Steakhouse, Burger King, **Chester Fried Chicken To Go (Dan's Discount Foods)**, Dairy Queen, El Rodeo, **Espresso (Dan's Discount Foods)**, Happy Joe's Pizza & Ice Cream, Hospitality Inn, **Moose Bros. Pizza (Dan's Discount Foods), Pizza To Go (Cenex)**, Sergio's Mexican Restaurant, TCBY, Taco Bell, Taco John's, The Donut Hole, Wendy's
  - S: China Doll Chinese, Country Kitchen, Domino's Pizza, KFC, King Buffet, McDonald's, Perkins Family Restaurant, Pizza Hut, Subway
- Lodg — N: AmericInn & Suites, **Comfort Inn**, Hospitality Inn
  - S: Best Western, Budget Inn, **Select Inn**, Super 8
- AServ — N: Harmon Glass, Midas, NAPA Auto Parts, Pennzoil Oil Change

EXIT — NORTH DAKOTA

- S: Conoco, NAPA (Amoco)
- RVCamp — **S: RV Camping**
- Med — **S: ✚ Hospital**
- ATM — **N: Buttrey Supermarket**[RX], **Cenex**, Dakota Community Bank, **Dan's Discount Foods**[24], Great Plains National Bank, Norwest Bank, **Prairie Hills Mall**, Western Cooperative Credit Union
  - S: American State Bank & Trust, Amoco
- Other — **N: Buttrey Supermarket**[RX], Chiropractic Clinic, **Dan's Discount Foods, Prairie Hills Mall, Prairie Maid Coin Laundry, Wal-Mart**[RX]
  - S: Joachim Regional Museum, Police & Sheriff's Dept., **Tourist Info.**

64 Bus. Loop I-94, Dickinson, City Center

- FStop — **S: Amoco**[*]
- AServ — **S: George's Tire Shop**, Parkway Ford
- TServ — **S: Amoco, George's Tire Shop, Schmidt's Repair Inc.**
- RVCamp — **S: Camping**
- ATM — **S: Amoco**

(69) **Rest Area (RR, Phones, Picnic, RV Dump; Eastbound)**

(69) **Rest Area (RR, Phones, Picnic, RV Dump; Westbound)**

72 Gladstone, Lefor

78 Taylor

84 ND 8, Richardton, Mott

- FStop — **N: Cenex**[*]
- Food — **N: Hot Stuff Pizza (Cenex), Smash Hit Subs (Cenex)**
- Med — **N: ✚ Hospital**
- Parks — **N: Schnell Ranch Recreation Area (3 Miles)**

90 Antelope

(94) **Rest Area (RR, Phones, Picnic, RV Dump; Eastbound)**

(94) **Rest Area (RR, Phones, Picnic, RV Dump; Westbound)**

97 Hebron

102 Glen Ullin, Lake Tschida, Hebron

108 Glen Ullin

- RVCamp — **N: Camping**

110 ND 49, Glen Ullin, Beulah, Lake Tschida

113 Geck Township

117 Dengate

(119) **Rest Area (RR, Phones, Picnic, RV Dump; Eastbound)**

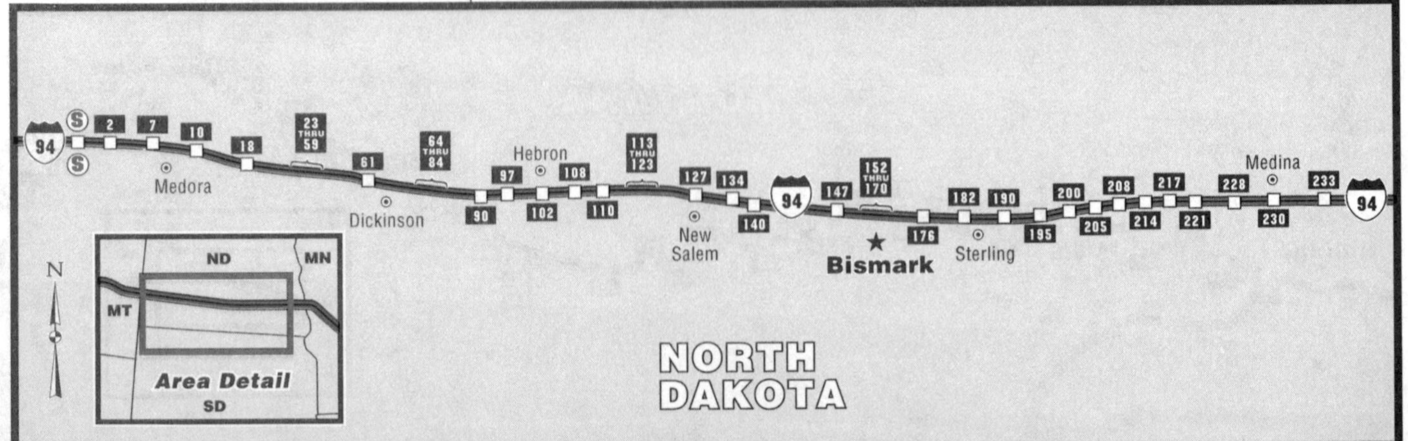

Bold red print shows RV & Bus parking available or nearby

EXIT	NORTH DAKOTA
(119)	**Rest Area (RR, Phones, Picnic, RV Dump; Westbound)**
120	Blue Grass, Ullin
123	Almont
127	ND 31, New Salem, Hannover
FStop	**S:** **Amoco**(*, LP), **Conoco**(*)
Food	**S:** RJ's Restaurant, Sunset Cafe
Lodg	**S:** **Sunset Motel**
AServ	**S:** **Amoco**
Med	**S:** ✚ **New Salem Clinic**
ATM	**S:** **Amoco**
Other	**N:** **Knife River Indian Villages (35 Miles)** **S:** **Gaebe Pharmacy**(RX), **Golden West Grocery Store**, Laundromat, **New Salem Veterinarian Clinic**, **World's Largest Cow**
134	Judson, Sweet Briar Lake
(135)	**Scenic View (Westbound)**
140	Crown Butte
147	ND 25, Center, Crown Butte Dam
TStop	**S:** **Amoco**(*)
TServ	**S:** **Amoco**
TWash	**S:** **Amoco**
ATM	**S:** **Amoco**
(151)	**Scenic View (Eastbound)**
152	**(4)** Sunset Drive
Gas	**N:** Conoco(*, CW) **S:** **Amoco**(*, LP, CW)
Food	**N:** Best Western **S:** Los Amigos Mexican
Lodg	**N:** Best Western, The Ridge Motel
RVCamp	**S:** **Camping**
Med	**S:** ✚ **Medcenter One**, ✚ **SCCI Hospital**
ATM	**S:** **Amoco**
Parks	**S:** **Fort Lincoln State Park (7 Miles)**
153	Mandan Ave
FStop	**N:** **Conoco**(*)
AServ	**N:** **Conoco**
TServ	**N:** **Conoco**
Parks	**S:** **Dakota Park**, **Fort Lincoln State Park**
155	Bus. Loop I-94 To ND 6, Mandan, City Center (Left Exit)
Parks	**S:** **Fort Lincoln State Park**
156	Bus Loop I-94, City Center, Bismarck Express (Left Exit)
Other	**N:** **Bismarck Zoo**
157	Divide Ave
FStop	**N:** **Conoco**(*, D, LP, CW) **S:** **Cenex**(*, LP, CW, RV DUMP)
Food	**N:** **McDonald's**(PLAY) **S:** Piccadilly Pizza & Subs
ATM	**N:** **Conoco** **S:** **Econo Foods**(24, RX), Piccadilly Pizza & Subs
Other	**S:** **Econo Foods**(RX)
159	U.S. 83 N Bismarck, Minot, City Center, Willton
FStop	**N:** **Mini Mart**(*)
Gas	**N:** Sinclair(*, D) **S:** Amoco(*), Conoco(*, D, LP, CW)
Food	**N:** A&B Pizza, Arby's, Burger King, HongKong Chinese American, KFC, Kroll's Kitchen, **McDonald's**(PLAY), O'Brians, Paradiso Mexican Restaurant, Perkins Family Restaurant, Red Lobster, Rock'n 50's Cafe, Royal Fork Buffet, Schlotzsky's Deli, Space Alien's Grill & Bar **S:** Cary's Family Restaurant, Casper's East 40 Food & Drink, Dairy Queen, International Restaurant, Kelly Inn, North American Steak Buffet, Pizza Hut, Subway, Taco Bell, Taco John's, The Donut Hole, The Wood House Restaurant

EXIT	NORTH DAKOTA
	(Hamburgers), Wendy's
Lodg	**N:** AmericInn, Comfort Inn, Comfort Suites Hotel, Country Suites, Fairfield Inn by Marriott, Motel 6 **S:** Best Western, DAYS INN Days Inn, Kelly Inn, Select Inn, Super 8
AServ	**N:** Capital Heights Auto Clinic, Harman Glass, **K-Mart**, Mr. Muffler, Northwest Tire **S:** Conoco
Med	**S:** ✚ **Hospital**
ATM	**N:** Bank Center First, **Dan's Supermarket**(RX), Gate City Federal, Norwest Bank **S:** US Bank
Other	**N:** Country Hearth Bakery Outlet, Country House Deli & Subs, **Dan's Supermarket**(RX), Eye Care, **Gateway Mall**, High Performance Car & Truck Wash, **K-Mart**, **Osco Drugs**
161	Lincoln, Bismarck Expwy, Centennial Road
TStop	**S:** **Amoco**(*, SCALES)
FStop	**N:** **Cenex**(*, LP, RV DUMP)
Food	**N:** **Hot Stuff Pizza (Cenex FS)**, **Smash Hit Subs (Cenex FS)**
Lodg	**S:** Ramada Limited
AServ	**S:** Bismarck Auto Service, **Bismarck Truck Equipment**, Brendel's Collision & Paint Center, C K Frame & Collision Center, Capital Tire Goodyear, **Mid-Dakota Wheel Alignment & Frame Service**, Pat's Auto, Silvernagel Auto Repair, The Oil Wizard
TServ	**S:** **Bismarck Truck Equipment**, **Butler CAT Engine Service**, **International**, **Interstate Detroit Diesel**, **Mid-Dakota Wheel Alignment & Frame Service**, **North Country Trucks & Parts**, **Trucks of Bismarck Freightliner**, **Wallworks Truck Center Kenworth**
TWash	**S:** **Truck Wash**
RVCamp	**N:** **Bismark KOA-Kampground (1 Mile)**, **RV Dump (Cenex FS)** **S:** **Capital R.V. Center Inc.**(LP)
ATM	**N:** **Cenex** **S:** **Amoco**
Other	**S:** Missouri Valley Veterinarian Clinic
(169)	**Rest Area (RR, Phones, Picnic, RV Dump; Eastbound)**
(169)	**Rest Area (RR, Phones, Picnic, RV Dump; Westbound)**
170	Menoken
176	McKenzie
182	U.S. 83 South, ND 14, Sterling, Wing
FStop	**S:** **Cenex**(*, LP, RV DUMP)
Food	**S:** Tops Restaurant
190	Driscoll
195	Long Lake
200	ND 3, Dawson, Steele, Tuttle
FStop	**S:** **Amoco**(*, LP), **Conoco**(*) **(CFN Commercial Fueling Network)**
Food	**S:** **Hot Stuff Pizza (Conoco)**, **Lone Steer Motel & Campground**
Lodg	**S:** **Lone Steer Motel & Campground**, **OK Motel Camper & Lodging**
AServ	**S:** **Amoco**
TServ	**S:** **Conoco (CFN Commercial Fueling Network)**
RVCamp	**S:** **Campground**, **Lone Steer Motel & Campground**, **OK Motel Camper & Lodging**
Med	**S:** ✚ **Q & R Clinic Steele**, **Medcenter 1**
205	Robinson
208	ND 3S, Dawson, Napolean, Camp Grasick
RVCamp	**N:** **LaQua Dakota RV Campground** **S:** **Camping**

EXIT	NORTH DAKOTA
214	Tappen
Gas	**S:** Amoco(*)
AServ	**S:** Amoco
217	Pettibone
(221)	**Rest Area (RR, Phones, Picnic, RV Dump; Eastbound)**
221	Crystal Springs
(224)	**Rest Area (RR, Phones, Picnic, RV Dump; Westbound)**
228	ND 30 South, Streeter
230	Medina
RVCamp	**N:** **Camping**
233	Halfway Lake
238	Cleveland, Gackle
242	Windsor
245	Oswego
248	Lippert Township
251	Eldridge
(254)	**Rest Area (RR, Phones, Picnic, RV Dump; Eastbound)**
(254)	**Rest Area (RR, Phones, Picnic, RV Dump; Westbound)**
256	Woodbury (Exit under construction)
TServ	**S:** **Wiest**
RVCamp	**S:** **KOA Campgrounds (1 Mile)**
257	Bus Loop I-94, Jamestown (Eastbound, Left Exit Eastbound, Reaccess Westbound Only, Difficult Reaccess)
TServ	**N:** **Englandh's Cummins**
258	U.S. 281, Jamestown, Edgly, Ellendale
FStop	**N:** **Sinclair**(*) **S:** **Conoco**(*)
Gas	**N:** Amoco(*, CW)
Food	**N:** Arby's, McDonald's(PLAY), Wagon Masters Restaurant **S:** Bonanza Steakhouse, Burger King(PLAY), King House (Chinese), **Little Caesar's Pizza (K-Mart)**, Perkins Family Restaurant, Sergio's Mexican Restaurant, **Subway (Conoco)**
Lodg	**N:** Comfort Inn, DAYS INN Days Inn, Holiday Inn Express **S:** Best Western
AServ	**N:** Big A Auto Parts, Klein's Collision Center, Lloyd's Motors Toyota, Master Care Car Service, Midwest Auto Glass
TWash	**N:** **South Hill Car Wash & Truck Wash**(CW)
RVCamp	**N:** **Chuckwagon Camping**, **Frontier Fort Campground (1 Mile)**, **Thompson Motor Home Sales, Inc. (1.8 Miles)** **S:** **Snows Appliance & RV Sales**
Med	**N:** ✚ **Hospital**
ATM	**N:** Amoco **S:** First Community Credit Union, **Wal-Mart**(RX)
Other	**N:** Fort Frontier Museum, Frontier Village, **South Hill Car Wash & Truck Wash**, Southwood Veterinarian Clinic **S:** **Buffalo Mall**, **K-Mart**, Master Bakery Outlet, **Wal-Mart**(RX)
260	U.S. 52 West, Bus. I-94, Jamestown
TStop	**N:** **Amoco**(*, LP, SCALES)
Lodg	**N:** Starlite Motel
AServ	**N:** Walt Sanders Dodge, Buick, Chev
TServ	**N:** **Amoco**(SCALES), **Hansen Tire Service**, **Uniroyal Truck Center**

Bold red print shows RV & Bus parking available or nearby

EXIT NORTH DAKOTA

RVCamp N: Jaycee Campsite (1 Mile)
Med N: + Hospital
ATM N: Amoco
Other N: Prairie Veterinarian Hospital

262 Bloom

269 Spiritwood

272 Urbana

276 Eckelson

281 Sanborn, Litchville

283 ND 1 North, Rogers

288 ND 1 South, Oakes

290 Valley City
Food N: Kenny's Family Restaurant
Lodg N: Bel-Air Motel
S: Flickertail Inn
AServ N: 20/20 Auto Center, Miller Motors
Med N: + Hospital
Other N: Barnes Historical Museum

292 Kathryn, Valley City
FStop N: Amoco[*, LP, CW]
Food N: Amoco
Lodg N: Super 8, Wagon Wheel Inn
AServ S: Dietrich's
TServ S: Dietrich's
Med N: + Hospital
ATM N: Amoco
Parks S: Fort Ransom State Park, Fort Ransom State Park

294 Bus. Loop I-94, Valley City
RVCamp N: Camping
Med N: + Hospital

296 Peak

298 Cuba

302 ND 32, Oriska, Fingal

(304) Rest Area (RR, Phones, Picnic; Left Exit Both Directions)

307 Tower City
FStop N: Mobil[*]
Food N: Mobil
TServ N: Mobil
RVCamp N: Tower Motel Camping

310 Hill Township

314 ND 38, Buffalo, Alice

317 Ayr

320 Embden

322 Absaraka

324 Wheatland, Chaffee

(327) Truck Parking (Eastbound)

328 Lynchburg

331 ND 18, Casselton, Leonard, Governor's Drive
FStop N: Phillips 66[*, CW]
Food N: Club 94, Phillips 66, The Rock
Lodg N: Shamrock Motel
AServ N: Gordy's Service Center[CW], Interstate Body Shop
TServ N: Gordy's Service Center
TWash N: Gordy's Service Center[CW]
ATM N: Phillips 66

(337) Parking Area-Truck Parking Only (Westbound)

338 CR 11, Durbin, Mapleton
FStop N: AmPride[*]
AServ N: AmPride

EXIT NORTH DAKOTA/MINNESOTA

TServ N: AmPride

340 Kindred, Davenport

(342) Weigh Station (Eastbound)

(342) Weigh Station (Westbound)

342 Raymond

343 West Fargo, Bonanzaville, U.S.A.
Food N: Smoky's Tavern & Steakhouse
Lodg N: Hi-10 Motel, Highway Host American Family Restaurant
RVCamp N: Red River Valley Fair Campground (.5 Miles)
Other N: Bonanzaville Heritage Museum, Red River and Northern Plains Regional Museum

346A Horace
Gas S: Conoco[*, D, LP]
AServ S: Conoco

346B West Fargo

348 45th Street
TStop N: Petro[*, SCALES]
Gas N: Amoco[*, CW]
Food N: Cinnamon Street Bakery (Amoco), Hot Stuff Pizza (Amoco), Iron Skillet Restaurant (Petro), McDonald's
Lodg N: C'mon Inn, Sleep Inn
TServ N: Petro[SCALES]
TWash N: Petro
ATM N: Petro
Other N: Visitor Information

349B I-29 N, U.S. 81, Grand Forks, Fargo

349A I-29 S, U.S. 81, Sioux Falls

350 25th Street
Gas N: Stop 'N Go[*, LP]
S: Mini Mart[*, 24]
ATM N: Stop 'N Go
S: Mini Mart

351 Bus U.S. 81, Downtown Fargo
Gas N: Mobil[D, CW], Sinclair[*, LP], Stop 'N 'Go[*, LP]
S: 7-11 Convenience Store[*, 24], Amoco[*, CW], Phillips 66[*, D, CW]
Food N: Baskin Robbins, Duane's House Of Pizza, Godfather's Pizza, Great Harvest Bread Co., Great Wall Chinese Food, Grinder's Taco Shop, Hornbacher Express, Luna Coffee, Pizza Hut
S: Burger King[PLAY], Denny's, Domino's Pizza, Expressway Inn, Happy Joe's Pizza, KFC, May Days, McDonald's, Papa Murphy's Pizza, Pepper's Cafe, Subway, Taco Bell
Lodg S: Expressway Inn, Rodeway Inn
AServ N: Mobil
S: Amoco, Gateway Chevrolet, K-Mart
RVCamp N: Lindenwood Park (1 Mile)
Med N: + Heartland Hospital
ATM N: Gate City Federal, Hornbacher Express, U.S. Bank
S: Community First, Phillips 66, State Bank of Fargo
Other N: Animal Health Clinic, Mail Boxes Etc., Sinkler Optical, The Medicine Shoppe[RX], Thrifty Drugs[RX]
S: Fargo Coin Laundry, K-Mart

↑NORTH DAKOTA

↓MINNESOTA

1A U.S. 75, Moorhead
Gas N: Phillips 66[CW], Sinclair[CW], Spur[*]
S: 76[*], Amoco, Orton's
Food N: Burger King, Debbie's Homestyle Kitchen, Domino's Pizza, Fryn' Pan, Little Caesars Pizza
S: Best Western, Courtney's Restaurant, Golden Phoenix Asian Cuisine, Hardee's, Red River Cafe

EXIT MINNESOTA

(Best Western), Speak Easy Restaurant, Village Inn
Lodg S: Best Western, Motel 75, Super 8
AServ N: Champion Auto Service, Phillips 66, Phillips 66, Sinclair
S: Amoco, Amoco, Lott's Repair & Auto Sales, Pontiac Dealer, Selland Pontiac GMC Trucks Olds Cadillac
ATM N: Norwest Bank
S: State Bank of Hawley, Sunmart Grocery[24]
Other N: Family Dentistry, Tourist Info.
S: FM Animal Hospital, Moorehead Marine (Boat Service), Osco Drugs, Sunmart Grocery, Whale Of A Wash

1B 20th Street (Eastbound, Reaccess Westbound Only)
Food S: Dreamers
ATM E: Gate City Federal

(2) Rest Area (RR, HF, Phones, Picnic; Eastbound)

2 Moorhead, CR 52, Bus. Loop 94
RVCamp N: KOA Kampground (1 Mile; frontage road), Larry's RV Service

(4) Weigh Station (Eastbound)

6 MN 336, CR 11
TStop N: Citgo[*, SCALES], Phillips 66[*, LP, SCALES]
Lodg N: Citgo, Trucker's Inn (Citgo)
TServ N: Citgo[SCALES], Phillips 66
TWash N: Citgo, Phillips 66
RVCamp N: Camping

15 CR 10, Downer, Sabin

22 MN 9, Barnesville

24 MN 34, Barnesville
Food N: Tastee Freez
Other N: Butch's Boat's

32 MN 108, CR 30, Lawndale, Pelican Rapids

38 Rothsay
FStop S: Amoco[*, LP]
Food S: Amoco, Rothsay Cafe (Amoco), Tower House
AServ S: Amoco
TServ S: J's Tire & Service
ATM S: Amoco
Other S: Picnic Area (Prarie Chicken Statue)

50 CR 88, U.S. 59N, Pelican Rapids, Detroit Lake
FStop N: Texaco[*, LP, RV DUMP]
Food N: Texaco
RVCamp N: Camping
Med N: + Hospital (6 Miles)
ATM N: Texaco, Texaco

54 MN 210W, Breckenridge, Fergus Falls
FStop N: Cenex[*]
Gas N: Amoco[*, CW], Spur[*, CW]
Food N: Burger King, Cenex, Debbie's Homestyle Kitchen, Freshway Subs & Pizza (Cenex), Godfather's Pizza, KFC, King Buffet, McDonald's, Mr C's Family Dining (BBQ Ribs), Perkin's Family Restaurant[24], Ponderosa, Subway
S: Mabel Murphy's Food & Drinks
Lodg N: Americinn Inn, Best Western, Comfort Inn, DAYS INN Days Inn, Motel 7, Super 8
AServ N: Bridgestone Tri State Tire, Car Quest Auto Parts, Falls Olds, Pontiac, GMC Trucks, Hedahls Auto Mates Auto Parts, Nelson Ford Mercury Lincoln, Pennzoil Oil Change, Preferred Body Shop, Spur, Valvoline Oil Change[CW]
S: Auto Glass Specialist
TServ N: Bridgestone Tri State Tire, International
RVCamp N: Pine Plaza

EXIT MINNESOTA

Med N: Hospital
ATM N: Community First National Bank
Other N: 4 Seasons Coin Car Wash, Companion Animal Hospital, Target, Tourist Info., West Ridge Mall
S: Wal-Mart[RX]

55 CR 1, Fergus Falls
Other N: County Museum, Interstate Inc.[LP]

57 MN 210E, CR25, Fergus Falls
Med N: Hospital (2 Miles)

(60) Rest Area (RR, HF, Phones, Picnic; Eastbound)

61 U.S. 59S, CR 82, Fergus Falls
FStop N: Citgo[*, LP]
Food N: Big Chief Cafe (Citgo), Citgo
RVCamp N: Camping
S: Camping
Med N: Hospital (6 Miles)

67 CR 35, Dalton
RVCamp N: Clearlake Resort & Campground
S: Camping

(69) Rest Area (RR, HF, Phones, Picnic; Westbound)

77 MN 78, CR 10, Barrett, Ashby
RVCamp N: Sundowner RV Park & Campground
S: Camping
Med S: Hospital

82 MN 79, CR 41, Evansville, Elbow Lake
RVCamp S: Camping
Med S: Hospital

90 CR 7, Brandon
RVCamp N: Camping
S: Oak Park Kampground
Other S: Ski Area

97 MN 114, CR 40, Garfield, Lowry
RVCamp N: Oak Park Kampground
S: Camping

(100) Rest Area (RR, Phones, Picnic, Pet Walk; Eastbound)

100 MN27

103 MN 29, Alexandria, Glenwood
FStop N: Texaco[*]
S: Conoco[*, LP, CW]
Gas N: Amoco[*, CW], Citgo[*]
S: B & H[*, D], Mobil
Food N: Amoco, Country Kitchen, Flagship Restaurant (Texaco), Hardee's, McDonald's, Perkin's Family Restaurant, Subway (Amoco), Taco Bell, Texaco
Lodg N: Americinn Motel, Comfort Inn, DAYS INN Days Inn, Super 8

EXIT MINNESOTA

S: Country Inn & Suites, Holiday Inn
AServ N: GM Auto Dealership, Steinbring Cadillac Chevrolet Mazda
S: Lee Buick Pontiac Oldsmobile
TServ S: Alexandria Diesel
RVCamp N: Campground
S: Alexandria RV Service, Camping
Med N: Hospital (2 Miles)
ATM N: Amoco, Amoco
S: B & H, BNH
Other N: Target[RX], Tourist Info., Wal-Mart[RX]

(105) Rest Area (RR, HF, Phones, Picnic; Westbound)

114 MN 127, CR 3, Westport, Osakis
RVCamp N: Camping

119 CR 46, West Union

124 Sinclair Lewis Ave. (Eastbound, Reaccess Westbound Only)

127 U.S. 71, MN 28, Glenwood, Sauk Centre, Rest Area (RR, Phones, Picnic)
TStop S: Texaco[*, LP, SCALES]
FStop N: Amoco[*, CW], Holiday[*, CW]
Gas N: KC's General Store[*], SuperAmerica[*]
Food N: Amoco, Dairy Queen, Hardee's, McDonald's[PLAY], Pizza Hut, Subway, Taco John's (Amoco)
S: Restaurant (Texaco), Texaco
Lodg N: Americinn Motel, Econolodge, Gopher Prairie Motel, Hillcrest Motel, Super 8
S: Super 8
AServ N: Boyer Motors, Boyer Motors, Ford Dealership, John Wiese Ford, Kawy's Auto & Truck Serv, Mertz Auto Sales, S/W Exhaust
S: Dan Welle's South Town, GM Auto Dealership
TServ N: Kawy's Auto & Truck Serv
S: Felling Trailers, Sauk Centre Tire, Texaco[SCALES], Texaco Truck Stop
RVCamp N: Campground (2 Miles), Sinclair Lewis Campground (1.25 Miles)
S: MPG RV Service
Med N: Hospital
ATM N: Amoco FS, Holiday, Super America, SuperAmerica
S: Texaco TS
Parks N: Sauk Center Park (Picnic Area)
Other N: Polipnick's Grocery Store, Sinclair Lewis Interpretive Ctr
S: Sauk Centre Veterinary Clinic

131 MN 4, Meire Grove

135 CR 13, Melrose
FStop N: Mobil[LP]
S: Conoco[*, D]
Gas N: Phillips 66[*, D]

EXIT MINNESOTA

Food N: Burger King, Hardee's
S: Conoco, Countryside Family Restaurant, Dairy Queen, Hot Stuff Pizza (Conoco FS)
Lodg S: Super 8
AServ N: Mobil[LP], Tire One
S: Loren Collison Ctr
TServ N: Ford Truck Service, Mobil, Mobil
S: Truck Service
RVCamp N: Camping
Med N: Hospital (1 Mile)
ATM N: Melrose State Bank, Phillips 66
Other N: Melrose Fire & Ambulance
S: Free-Way Foods, Melrose Veterinary Clinic, Veterinary Clinic

137 MN 237, CR 65, New Munich

140 CR 11, Freeport
Gas N: Conoco[*, D], Mobil[*, D]
Food N: Charlie's Cafe, Conoco
AServ N: Amoco Motor Club[24] (Towing), Cooper Tires
ATM N: Melrose Credit Union
Other N: Corner Store, Jay's Car Wash, U.S. Post Office
S: Freeport Farm Center[LP]

147 MN 238, CR 10, Albany
FStop N: Holiday[*, RV DUMP]
Gas N: Ashland[*], Holiday[*, D], Texaco[*, D, LP], Thellen
Food N: Dairy Queen, Hillcrest Family Restaurant, Sands Restaurant (Sands Motel), Texaco
S: KFC
Lodg N: Country Inn & Suites, Sands Motel
AServ N: Albany Chrysler Center, Auto Value Parts Store, Joel Snyder, Plymouth, Thelen
S: Syl's Ford
TWash N: Albany's
Med N: Hospital
ATM N: Cash Machine (Holiday), Holiday
Other N: Albany Coin Car Wash, Amby's IGA Food Store, Laundromat

(152) Rest Area (RR, HF, Phones, Picnic; Westbound)

153 CR 9, Avon
Gas N: Phillips 66[*, D, LP, K], Texaco[*, CW]
Food N: Burger Treat, Mr. G's Pizza, Phillips 66, Rascals Restaurant, Texaco
Lodg N: Americinn Inn
AServ N: Central Auto Service
S: Martini Auto Parts, Sacks & Tires Repair One[CW]
RVCamp S: Camping
ATM N: Phillips 66, Texaco
Other N: Dahlin's Supermarket, Laundromat, U.S. Post Office
S: National[LP]

156 CR 159, St Johns University

158 CR 75, St Cloud (Eastbound, Left Exit

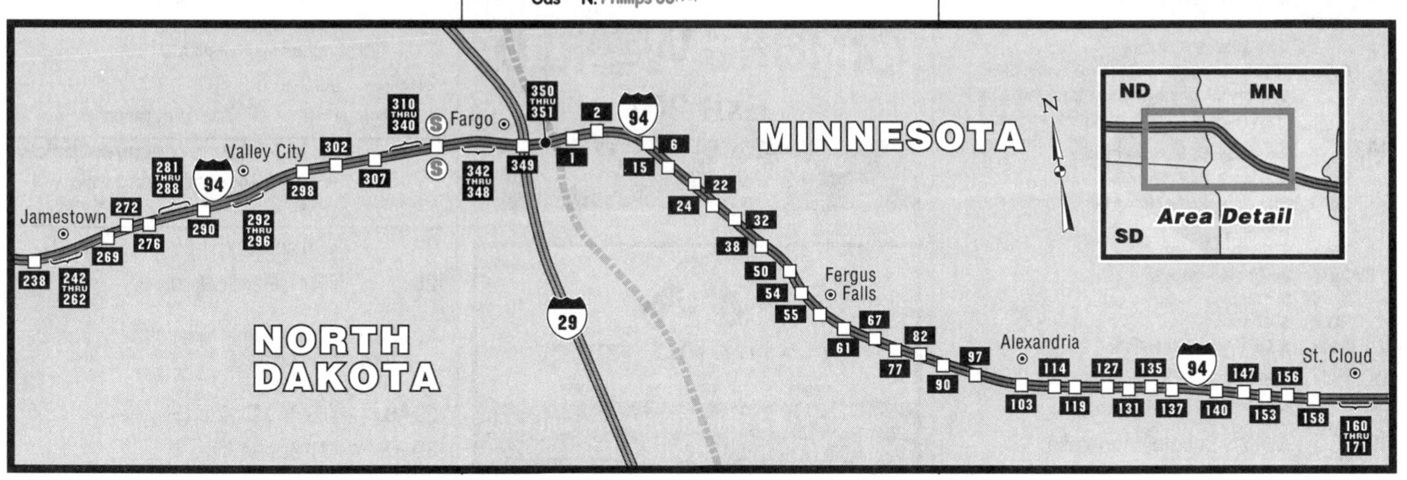

Bold red print shows RV & Bus parking available or nearby

EXIT MINNESOTA

Eastbound, Reaccess Westbound Only)

160 CR 2, St Joseph

164 MN 23, Paynesville, Waite Park, Rockville, Cold Springs

- Food N: Antique Mall, Antique Mall Coffee Shop
- Lodg N: Comfort Inn (5 Miles), Country Inn & Suites (5 Miles), Motel 6 (4 Miles)
- Other N: Antique Mall

167AB MN 15, Kimball, St Cloud, Waite Park (167B North to St. Cloud, 167A South to Kimball)

- Med N: + Hospital

171 CR 7, CR 75, St Augusta, St Cloud

- FStop N: Fuel Stop(*, LP, CW), Holiday(*, CW, RV DUMP)
- Food N: Fresh Way Sub & Salad (FS), Fuel Stop, Holiday, Hot Stuff Pizza (Holiday), McDonald's(PLAY), Smash Hit Subs (Holiday)
- Lodg N: Americinn Motel, Raddison, Travel House Motel
- AServ N: Goodyear, Royal Tire Inc.
- TServ N: Joe's Auto & Truck Repair
  S: Ziegler CAT, Zips Diesel Service
- Med N: + Hospital
- ATM N: Fuel Stop, Holiday
- Other S: County Park

(177) Rest Area (RR, HF, Phones, Picnic; Westbound)

178 MN 24, Annandale, Clearwater

- TStop N: Clearwater Travel Plaza(*, D, LP, CW, SCALES) (Coin Laundry, Citgo gas)
- Gas N: Ashland(*, D, LP), Holiday(*, LP)
  S: Phillips 66(*)
- Food N: Ashland, Clearwater Travel Plaza(24), Clearwater Travel Plaza (Coin Laundry, Citgo gas), Dairy Queen, Hardee's, Holiday, Hot Stuff Pizza (Holiday), Java Brothers Coffee (Clearwater Truck Plaza), Nelson Brothers Restaurant & Bakery (Clearwater Truck Plaza), Pizza Hut (Ashland), Subway, The Ole Kettle Restaurant
  S: Brigitte's Cafe (Phillips 66), Longhorn (Phillips 66), Phillips 66, R & R Plaza Pizza
- Lodg N: Budget Inn
- AServ N: Interstate Automotive & Towing, Mark's Auto Sales, Valvoline Oil Change
  S: Mathison Motors Auto Service
- TServ N: Clearwater Travel Plaza(LP, CW, 24), Clearwater Travel Plaza(SCALES) (Coin Laundry, Citgo gas), Mr Tire, Valvoline Oil Change
- TWash N: Clearwater Travel Plaza(CW) (Coin Laundry, Citgo gas), Clearwater Truck Plaza
- RVCamp N: KOA Kampground (1.75 Miles)
  S: A-J Acres Campground (1.5 Miles)
- ATM N: Ashland, Cash Machine (Holiday), Clearwater Travel Plaza(24), Holiday
- Other N: Centre Drug(RX), Coborn's Grocery, Coin Laundry (Clearwater Truck Plaza), Pet Clinic, The Clearwater Clinic, Tru Value Hardware

183 CR 8, Silver Creek, Hasty

- TStop S: Conoco(*, LP, SCALES)
- Food S: Conoco, Pump House Restaurant(SCALES) (Conoco)
- TServ S: Conoco, Conoco(SCALES)
- RVCamp N: Whole Service RV
  S: Camping
- ATM S: Conoco
- Parks S: Lake Maria State Park

(187) Rest Area (RR, HF, Phones, Picnic, Pet Walk; Eastbound)

193 MN 25, Buffalo, Monticello

- FStop S: Amoco(*, LP)
- Gas N: Ferrell Gas(LP), Holiday(*, D, LP)
  S: SuperAmerica(*, D), Total(*, D, LP, CW)
- Food N: Burger King, Country Grill, Dairy Queen, JP's Annex Food & Drink, KFC, Perkin's Family Restaurant, Skillet Restaurant, Taco Bell
  S: Best Western, Chin Yuen Chinese (Best Western), Comfort Inn, McDonald's, Subway, Super Mom's Deli (SuperAmerica), SuperAmerica, Tree House (Comfort Inn), Wendy's
- Lodg N: Americinn Inn
  S: Best Western, Comfort Inn
- AServ N: Auto Value
  S: Champion Auto Stores, Conoco Ultra Lube, Dave Peterson's Monticello Ford Mercury, Ford Dealership, GM Auto Dealership, Geo ULD Chevrolet Oldsmobile GM, Glass Hut, Goodyear Tire & Auto, Total
- RVCamp N: Campground, Monticello RV Center
- Med N: + Hospital
- ATM N: Cash Machine (Holiday), First Bank & Trust Co., First National Bank, Marquette Bank
  S: Amoco, Amoco, Super America, SuperAmerica, Total
- Parks N: Lake Maria State Park (8 Miles)
- Other N: K-Mart(RX), Maus Foods Grocery(RX), Monticello Mall(RX), Pet Center, Uptown Eye Care
  S: Monticello Big Lake Pet Hospital

195 CR 75, Monticello (Westbound, Reaccess Eastbound Only)

- FStop N: Total(*, D, LP)
- Food N: Jam 'n Joe's Espresso Shop (Total), Total
- Med N: + Monticello Big Lake Hospital
- ATM N: Total
- Other N: Scrub A Dub Car Wash

201 CR 19, Albertville, St Michael (Eastbound, Reaccess Westbound Only)

- Other S: ACE Hardware(LP)

202 CR 37, Albertville

- FStop S: Phillips 66(*)
- Gas N: Conoco(*, D, LP)
  S: Amoco(*, LP)
- Food S: Country Pizza Parlor, Hot Stuff Pizza (Phillips 66), Stephen's Bros (Phillips 66)
- AServ S: Amoco, Amoco, Car Quest Auto Center
- ATM N: Cash Machine (Conoco), Conoco
  S: Amoco, Highland Bank
- Other S: Ellis' Auto Brite Car Wash

205 MN 241, CR 36, St Michael

- Lodg N: Crow River Motel

207 MN 101, Rogers, Elk River

CAMPING WORLD
Exit 207
21200 Rogers Dr. • Rogers, MN
1-800-801-8177
1433

1332
AMERISUITES
AMERICA'S AFFORDABLE ALL-SUITE HOTEL
Minnesota • I-94, Exit 216 to I-494, Exit 11AB
On U.S. 212 • Eden Prairie • 612-944-9700

- TStop N: 76 Auto/Truck Plaza(*, RV DUMP, SCALES)
- Gas N: SuperAmerica(*, LP)
  S: Amoco(*, LP, CW), Holiday(*, LP), Sinclair(*), Super America(*, D)
- Food N: Burger King, McDonald's(PLAY)
  S: Dairy Queen, Domino's Pizza, Happy Chef, Kernel Restaurant, Subway
- Lodg N: Super 8
  S: AmericInn
- AServ S: Auto Body Plus, Miller Chevrolet, Sinclair, Sinclair
- TServ N: 76 Auto/Truck Plaza, 76 Auto/Truck Plaza(SCALES)
  S: Glen's Truck Center
- TWash N: 76 Auto/Truck Plaza, 76 Auto/Truck Wash
- RVCamp N: Camping World (RV Sales) (see our ad this page)
- Med S: + Northwest Family Clinic
- ATM N: 76 Auto/Truck Plaza, 76 Auto/Truck Plaza, SuperAmerica
  S: Holiday, Holiday, State Bank of Rogers, Steven's Market, Super America
- Other S: Rogers Drug(RX), Rogers Pet Clinic, Steven's Market, Super Value Grocery, The Rogers Fire Dept, Tru Value Hardware, U.S. Post Office, Value Rite Drug

213 CR 30, 95th Ave N

- Gas N: Conoco(*, D), Super America(*, D)
- RVCamp S: KOA Camping (2 Miles)
- ATM N: Conoco, Super America, Super America
  S: TCF Bank
- Other S: Rainbow Food Grocery, Target Greatland(RX)

(215) Rest Area, Indian Mound (RR, HF, Phones, Picnic; Eastbound)

215 MN 109, Weaver Lake Road

- Gas N: Super America(*, D), Texaco(*, CW)
- Food N: Arby's, Bagel Bakery, Bakers Square Restaurant, Boston Market Restaurant, Broadway Pizza, Burger King, Caribou Coffee, Champp's, Chin Yong Restaurant, Coffee Shop, Dairy Queen, Domino's Pizza, Famous Dave's BBQ, Frankie's To Go, Hot Wok, J. Cousienau, KFC, Little Caesars Pizza, May Inn (Chinese), McDonald's, Old Country Buffet, Pappa John's Pizza, Pizza Hut, Sbarro, Stewart Anderson's Cattle Co., Subway, Taco Bell, The House of May Nin (Chinese & American), Wendy's
  S: Applebee's, Fuddruckers
- Lodg N: Hampton Inn, Radisson
- AServ N: Auto Glass, Express Lube, Goodyear Tire & Auto, Midas, Texaco, Tires Plus
- ATM N: Cub Foods(24, RX), Cub Foods, Highland Bank, Norwest Bank, Texaco, Texaco, US Bank
- Other N: Cub Foods(RX), Dental Clinic, K-Mart(RX), Kohl's Dept Store, Mail Boxes Etc., Maplegrove Animal Hospital, Maplegrove Eye Clinic, Optical Center, Pearl Vision, Petco, U.S. Post Office, Ultra Auto Cleaning, Vision World, WalGreens Pharmacy(RX)

216 Jct. I-494

- Lodg N: AmeriSuites (see our ad this page)

Note: I-94 runs concurrent below with I-694. Numbering follows I-694.

27 I-94 split from I-694, to St Cloud

28 CR 61, Hemlock Lane

- Gas I: Amoco(*, CW)
- Food I: Perkin's Family Restaurant
- Lodg I: Red Carpet Inn
- ATM I: Amoco

29AB U.S. 169 (Divided Hwy)

30 **(31)** Boone Ave.

Bold red print shows RV & Bus parking available or nearby

EXIT MINNESOTA

Food **O:** Northlind Inn
Lodg **O:** Northlind Inn, Sleep Inn
AServ **I:** NTB
Other **I:** **Home Depot**, **Petsmart**

31 County Road 81
Gas **I:** Amoco(*, CW)
O: 76(*), Texaco
Food **I:** Wings & Ribs
O: Best Western, Best Western, Charlie's (Best Western), Dairy Queen, Wendy's
Lodg **I:** Budget Host Inn
O: Best Western
AServ **I:** Kara Collision & Glass, Kennedy Transmission, Reno Automotive
O: 76, Texaco
TServ **I:** **ABM Truck Service**
ATM **I:** Amoco, Amoco
O: Texaco

33 Brooklyn Blvd.
Gas **O:** Mobil(*, D, CW), Total(*)
AServ **O:** Big Wheel, Car X, Diamond Auto Detailing, Dodge Truck Dealer, GM Auto Dealership, Honda, Oldsmobile, Mazda Dealer
RVCamp **O:** **Truck/RV Service**
ATM **I:** **Rainbow Food Grocery**(24)
O: Mobil
Other **I:** **Rainbow Food Grocery**, WalGreens Pharmacy(RX)

34 MN 252, Shingle Creek Pkwy., East River Rd.
Gas **O:** Mobil(*, LP, CW)
Food **I:** Ground Round, Leeann Chin Chinese (Carry Out), Perkin's Family Restaurant, Subs Ect., The Inn On The Farm (Historic Bed & Breakfast)
O: Barnacle Bill's, Chi Chi's Mexican Restaurant, **Cracker Barrel**, Denny's, Hardee's, Northern Lights (Hilton), Olive Garden, T.G.I. Friday's, The Hilton
Lodg **I:** Country Inn & Suites, The Inn On The Farm (Historic Bed & Breakfast)
O: AmericInn & Suites, Budgetel Inn, Comfort Inn, Holiday Inn, Super 8, The Hilton
AServ **I:** First Federal, Tires Plus
O: Mobil, Mobil
Other **I:** Mail Boxes Etc., **Police Station**, **Target**

35A Minnesota 100

35B I-94 Jct East

Note: I-94 runs concurrent above with I-694. Numbering follows I-694.

225 MN North 252, I-694 East

226 49th Ave., 53rd Ave.
Gas **S:** Texaco
AServ **S:** Texaco
Parks **N:** **Regional Park**

228 Dowling Ave.

229AB CR 81, Washington Ave., West Broadway Ave.
Gas **N:** Old Colony(*, D, CW)
S: Citgo(*)
Food **N:** Broadway Bar & Pizza, Old Colony
S: McDonald's, **Merwin Drug**(RX), Subway, Taco Bell, The Villager, Vietnamese, Hong Kong, Wendy's, White Castle Restaurant
AServ **S:** Auto Max Discount Muffler & Brakes, Tires Plus
Med **S:** **North Urgent Care**
ATM **N:** Old Colony
S: Citgo, **Sullivan's Grocery**, US Bank
Other **S:** **Merwin Drug**(RX), Spin Cycle Coin Laundry, **Sullivan's Grocery**, **Target**, WalGreens Pharmacy(RX)

EXIT MINNESOTA

230 MN55, Olson Hwy., 7th St. North (Westbound)

231A Jct. I-394, U.S. 12W

231B Lyndale Ave., Hennepin Ave. (Reaccess Northbound Only, Difficult Reaccess, Hazmat Vehicles Prohibited Thru Tunnel, Must Exit Here)

233AB Jct. I-35 West, 11th Street (Left Exit Westbound, Difficult Reaccess)
Lodg **N:** Holiday Inn Express

234A MN 55, Hiawatha Ave. (Reaccess Westbound Only, Difficult Reaccess)

234B 5th Street (Reaccess Eastbound Only, Difficult Reaccess)

234C Cedar Ave. (Westbound, Reaccess Eastbound Only)
Med **N:** **Hospital**

235A 25th Ave, Riverside Ave.
Gas **N:** Citgo(*)
S: Amoco
Food **N:** Bruegger's Bagel & Bakery, Davanni's Pizza & Hoagie's, Starbucks Coffee
S: Perkin's Family Restaurant
AServ **S:** Amoco
Med **N:** **Fairview University Medical Center**
ATM **N:** Citgo
Other **S:** Riverside Market

235B Huron Blvd.

236 MN 280, University Ave. (Left Exit Westbound, Difficult Reaccess)

237 Cretin Ave, Vandalia St.

238 MN 51, Snelling Ave.
Gas **S:** 76(CW), Citgo(CW), Phillips 66(*), Total(D)
Food **N:** Applebee's, Blimpie's Subs, Burger King, McDonald's, Perkin's Family Restaurant
S: Pizza Central, The Malt Shop
AServ **N:** Firestone Tire & Auto
S: Citgo, Freeway Auto Body, Phillips 66, Schelen Auto Electric Inc., Tires Plus
ATM **N:** FirstStar
S: Liberty Motor Bank
Other **N:** Fannie Farmer, **Metro Dental**, Pearl Vision, Pet Center, **Rainbow Foods Supermarket**(24), **WalGreens Pharmacy**(RX)
S: Car Wash

239A Hamline Ave. (Reaccess Eastbound Only, Difficult Reaccess)
Gas **N:** Amoco(*, CW)
S: Tracy's One Stop Auto Mart(*, D, LP, CW)
Food **N:** Hardee's, Rio Bravo, Sheraton Inn, Subway
Lodg **N:** Sheraton Inn
AServ **N:** Champion Auto Service, Midway Chevrolet, Midway GM, Chevrolet, Whitaker Buick
ATM **N:** Cub Food(RX)
S: Tracy's One Stop Auto Mart
Other **N:** Cub Food(RX), **K-Mart**(RX), Mail Boxes Etc., PetsMart, Sear's Optical, **Target**(RX)

239B Lexington Pkwy
Gas **N:** Amoco(*), SuperAmerica(*, D)
Food **N:** Dairy Queen, KFC, White Castle Restaurant
AServ **N:** Amoco, NAPA
ATM **N:** SuperAmerica
Other **N:** Car Wash

240 Dale Street
Gas **N:** Clark(*)
Food **N:** Hickory Chips, Popeye's Chicken, Wendy's, Wings & Ribs
AServ **N:** American Auto Radiator & Air Conditioning Service, Meineke Discount Mufflers, Tires Plus
ATM **N:** Food Smart Groceries, Western Bank
Other **N:** **Dental Clinic**, Food Smart Groceries, **Unidale Mall**

EXIT MINNESOTA

241A Marion St, Kellogg Blvd.
Food **N:** Benjamin's (Best Western), Best Western, McDonald's
Lodg **N:** Best Western
AServ **N:** Ford, Sear's
ATM **N:** University National Bank

241B 5th St, 10th St (Difficult Reaccess)

241C Jct I-35E South (Left Exit Westbound)

242B Jct I-35E North, U.S. 10W (Left Exit)

242A 12th St., State Capitol
Food **N:** Embassy Suites, Woolley's Restaurant (Embassy Suites)
Lodg **N:** Embassy Suites, Travel Inn
AServ **N:** Firestone
Med **N:** **Regions Hospital (Emergency)**

242C 7th Ave (Eastbound, Difficult Reaccess)
Gas **N:** SuperAmerica(*, D)

242D U.S. 52, 6th St. (Difficult Reaccess)

243 U.S. 61, Mounds Blvd., Kellog Blvd. (Left Exit Westbound, Difficult Reaccess)

244 U.S. 10, U.S. 61
Food **N:** Peking Restaurant

245 White Bear Ave.
Gas **N:** SuperAmerica(*, D, LP)
S: Amoco(*, CW)
Food **N:** Ambers, Dazanni's Pizza, Hardee's, Ramada Inn, Subway, Summer Field Restaurant (Ramada)
S: Arby's, Baker's Square, Ground Round Restaurant, KFC, McDonald's, My Choice Chinese, Papa John's Pizza
Lodg **N:** Excel Inn, Ramada Inn
AServ **N:** Jiffy Lube(CW)
S: Suburban, Chrysler, Plymouth, Volkswagon
ATM **N:** SuperAmerica
Other **S:** **Lens Crafters**, **Target**(RX)

246A Ruth St. (Reaccess Westbound Only)
Gas **N:** Amoco(CW), Sinclair(*)
S: Conoco(*, CW)
Food **N:** Bruegger's Bagel & Bakery, Domino's Pizza, Fannie Farmer, Ho Ho Gourmet, Peking Way Chinese, Perkin's Family Restaurant
S: Burger King, Dorothy Ann Bakery & Cafe, Godfather's Pizza, Taco Bell
AServ **N:** Amoco, Master Care Auto Service (Firestone), Sinclair
S: Bumper to Bumper
ATM **N:** Amoco, MidAmerica Bank
S: **Byerly's Grocery**, TCF Bank
Other **N:** **Deutsches Haus**, Mail Boxes Etc., **Pet Land**, Snyder Pharmacy(RX), Vision World
S: **Byerly's Grocery**, Coin Laundry, Eye Care, Police Station, **Snyder Pharmacy**(RX)

246BC McKnight Road
Food **S:** Michael's Restaurant
Lodg **S:** Holiday Inn

247 MN 120, Century Ave.
Gas **S:** Ashland, Conoco(*, D, LP), Sinclair, SuperAmerica(*, D)
Food **N:** Blackie's BBQ, Denny's, Toby's On The Lake
S: Country Inn & Suites, The Green Mill (Country Inn)
Lodg **N:** Super 8

Bold red print shows RV & Bus parking available or nearby

EXIT MINNESOTA/WISCONSIN

1333
AMERISUITES
AMERICA'S AFFORDABLE ALL-SUITE HOTEL
Minnesota • Exit 249 • 612-854-0700

PRIME OUTLETS
WOODBURY
Over 50 Outlet Stores and Food Court
Eddie Bauer • Spiegel • Levis
Ask for your FREE COUPON BOOK
612-735-9060
1869
MINNESOTA • I-94 • EXIT 251

S: Country Inn & Suites
ASERV N: Harman Glass, Precision Tune
S: Car Quest, Merit Chevrolet
ATM S: SuperAmerica

249 I-494 South & I-694 North
Lodg S: AmeriSuites (see our ad this page)

250 CR 13, Radio Drive, Inwood Ave
Gas S: Holdiay Gas[*, LP]
Food S: Angeto's Pizza, Blimpie's Subs, Caradelle Chinese & Vietnamese Cuisine, Champps Americana, Domino's Pizza, Don Pablo's Mexican, Einstein Bros Bagels, Jin Ying Chinese, Lav Azza Cafe Expresso (French Bakery), Sunsets, T.G.I. Friday's, The Boston Market, Wendy's, Zapata Mexican Restaurant
ASERV S: Heppner's Auto Center, Rapid Oil Change, Tires Plus, Valvoline Oil Change
ATM S: Cub Food[RX], U.S. Bank
Other S: Cub Food[RX], Lenscrafters, Mailboxes Etc., PetsMart, Tamarack Shopping Center

251 CR 19, Woodbury Drive, Keats Ave
FStop S: SuperAmerica[*, D]
Food S: Burger King[PLAY], Dairy Queen (Horizon Outlet), Sara Lee (Horizon Outlet)
Lodg N: Countryside Motel (Frontage Rd)
S: Holiday Inn Express
RVCamp N: Lake Elmo Park Reserve Campground (1 Mile)
S: KOA Campgrounds (1 Mile)
ATM S: Eastern Heights Bank, SuperAmerica
Other S: Prime Outlets at Woodbury (see our ad this page), The Book Store

253 CR 15, Manning Ave
RVCamp S: KOA Campgrounds (1 Mile)
Parks S: Afton State Park

(256) Rest Area (RR, Phones, Picnic, Vending; Westbound)

(257) Weigh Station (Westbound)

258 MN 95, Hastings, Stillwater
Food N: Bungalow Inn
Lodg N: Bungalow Inn
RVCamp N: River Terrace Park (2 Miles)

↑MINNESOTA

↓WISCONSIN

1 WI 35, Hudson
Gas N: Auto Stop[*], Freedom Value Center[*, LP, CW]
Food N: Dairy Queen, Hickory Chicken & Ribs
ATM N: First Federal

2 CR F, Carmichael Road, Prescott
Gas N: Conoco[*, D, LP], Freedom[*, LP], Standard (Amoco)

EXIT WISCONSIN

S: Amoco[*, LP, CW]
Food N: Coach's Grill & Pizzeria, Domino's Pizza, KFC, Taco John
S: Arby's, Burger King, Country Kitchen (Phillips 66), McDonald's, SHONEY'S, Shoney's, Taco Bell, Wendy's
Lodg N: The Royal Inn
S: Fairfield Inn, Holiday Inn Express
ASERV N: Gilbert Pontiac, Oldsmobile, GMC, Standard (Amoco)
S: Dave Holt Ford, Indian Head Glass, NAPA Auto Parts, Tires Plus
Med N: + Hospital
ATM N: First Federal, S&M Bank
S: Citizen's State Bank, Country Market[RX]
Parks S: Pak & Mail
Other N: Duling Optical, Hudson Bowling, RJ's Grocery, Tru Value Hardware[LP]
S: Country Market[RX], K-Mart[RX], Wal-Mart[RX]

3 WI 35S, River Falls

4 U.S. 12, CR U, Somerset
TStop N: TA TravelCenters of America[*, SCALES, 24] (Mobil)
Gas N: Citgo[*, D, LP, CW]
Food N: Fulton's Riverlanding Restaurant (Travel Center), JR Ranch Motel, JR Ranch Motel, TA TravelCenters of America (Mobil)
Lodg N: JR Ranch Motel
TServ N: TA TravelCenters of America[SCALES, 24] (Mobil)
ATM N: TA TravelCenters of America (Mobil)

(8) Weigh Station (Eastbound)

10 WI 65, New Richmond, Roberts, River Falls

16 CR T, Hammond

19 U.S. 63, Baldwin, Amery, Ellsworth
FStop N: Phillips 66[*, D]
S: Conoco[*, LP]
Gas N: Freedom[*, D, LP]
Food N: A & W Drive-In, Brownwood (Phillips 66), Hardee's[PLAY], Phillips 66
S: Conoco, Ray's 24-Hr. Restaurant (Conoco), The Coachman Supper Club
Lodg N: Colonial Motel
S: Super 8
ATM N: Phillips 66

24 CR B, Woodville, Spring Valley
Gas N: Mobil[*, LP]
Food N: D&M Diner Home Cooking (Woodville Motel), Woodville Motel
Lodg N: Woodville Motel

28 WI 128, Wilson, Glenwood City, Spring Valley, Elmwood
FStop N: Kwik Trip[*, LP]
Food N: Hardy Platter (Kwik Trip), Kwik Trip
ATM N: Kwik Trip

32 CR Q, Knapp

41 WI 25, Menomonie, Barron
Gas N: Cenex[*, CW]
S: Amoco[CW], Citgo[*], Nills Fleet Farm[D, LP, K], Super America[*, D, LP]
Food N: Burger King (Cenex), Cenex
S: Bolo (Bolo Inn), Bolo Country inn, Citgo, Country Kitchen, Dairy Queen, Hardee's, Kernel Restaurant, Little Caesars Pizza, McDonald's[PLAY], Perkins Family Restaurant, Pizza Hut, Taco Bell, Taco John's, Wendy's
Lodg S: Americinn, Best Western, Bolo Country Inn, Super 8
ASERV S: Amoco, Johnson Motors Buick, Pontiac, GMC, Trucks, Keys Chevrolet & Oldsmobile, Menomonie Chrysler Center, Muffler Shop, NAPA, Nills Fleet Farm, Northtown Ford,

EXIT WISCONSIN

Mercury, Sam's Auto Supply, Wonder Lube[CW]
TServ S: Nills Fleet Farm, Northwest International
RVCamp N: KOA Campgrounds[LP] (.25 Miles), RV Sales, Twin Springs Campground & Cabins (2 Miles)
ATM N: Cenex, Mutual Savings Bank, Wisconsin Credit Union
S: Citizen State Bank, First American Bank of Wisconsin, FirstStar, Super America
Other N: Wal-Mart[LP, RX]
S: Amazon Pet Center, Bowling Alley, Coin Laundromat, K-Mart[RX]

(43) Rest Area (RR, Phones, Picnic, Vending; Eastbound)

(43) Rest Area (RR, Phones, Picnic, Vending; Westbound)

45 CR B, Menomonie
TStop S: Amoco[*]
FStop N: Mobil, Phillips 66[*]
Food N: Phillips 66
S: Amoco, Heckel's Family Restaurant (Amoco), Subway (Amoco)
TServ S: Amoco, Kenworth, Truck Scale
TWash S: Amoco
ATM N: Phillips 66

(48) Weigh Station (Westbound)

52 U.S. 12, WI 29, WI 40, Elk Mound, Chippewa Falls, Colfax

59 U.S. 12, WI 124, County EE, Elk Mound, Chippewa Falls
FStop N: Citgo[*, LP], Holiday[*, LP, SCALES]
Food N: B&B Pizzeria, Burger King (Citgo), Charcoal Grill Family Restaurant, Citgo, Holiday, McDonald's, Subway (Holiday)
Lodg N: Americinn, DAYS INN Days Inn, Super 8
ASERV N: Meyer's Auto & Truck Sales[24] (Towing)
TServ N: O'Claire Mac Sales & Service, Riverstates Truck & Trailer Freightliner Cumings[24], Thermal King Refrigeration
Med N: + Hospital
ATM N: FirstStar, Holiday

65 WI 37, WI 85, Eau Claire, Mondovi
Lodg N: Park Inn & Suites
Med N: + Hospital
ATM N: Firststar National Bank

68 WI 93, Eleva, Eau Claire
Gas N: Amoco[*, LP], Kwik Trip[*, LP], Super America[*, LP, CW]
Food N: Burger King[PLAY], Dairy Queen, Great Harvest Bread Co.
Lodg N: The Village North Inn
ASERV S: Carter Ford, Truck, Ken Vance Motors, Northland Windshield
TServ S: Northwest Enterprises
ATM N: RGU, Super America
Other N: Oakwood Hills Animal Hospital, Scrub Hub (Clothes & Carwash)

70 U.S. 53, Eau Claire, Chippewa Falls, Cnty Rd. AA, Golf Rd.
Gas N: Conoco[*, D, LP]
Food N: A & W Drive-In, Applebee's, Baker's Square, Fazoli's Italian Food, Garfield's, Mancino's, McDonald's[PLAY], Olive Garden, SHONEY'S, Shoney's
Lodg N: Country Inn, Heartland Inn
ASERV N: Sam's Club, Sear's
ATM N: First Star
Other N: Cinema, Oak Wood Shopping Mall, Pak Mail, Petco, Sam's Club, Target, Wal-Mart[LP, RX] (Optical)

81 CR HH, CR KK, Foster, Fall Creek
Gas S: Cenex[*]

88 Cnty Rd. R, U.S. 10, To WI 27, Osseo,

Bold red print shows RV & Bus parking available or nearby

EXIT WISCONSIN

Fairchild
- TStop N: Holiday[RV DUMP, SCALES]
- FStop N: Mobil[*, LP]
  S: Super America[*]
- Gas N: Phillips 66[*]
  S: Amoco[*]
- Food N: Dad's Delight Bowling & Restaurant, Dairy Queen (Phillips 66), Hardee's[PLAY], Heckel's Big Steer Restaurant[24], Phillips 66
  S: McDonald's, Roadway Inn, Subway
- Lodg N: Budget Host Inn
  S: Roadway Inn
- AServ N: C&D Automotive Sales & Service, Nelsgunderson Chevrolet, GM, The Loft Service Center[24] (Towing)
  S: Amoco
- TServ N: Holiday[SCALES], The Loft Service Center[24] (Towing)
- RVCamp N: Osseo Camping Resort (.5 Miles)
- Med S: ✚ The Osseo Area Medical Center
- ATM N: Holiday, Mobil
  S: Super America
- Other N: Dad's Delight Bowling & Restaurant, K-N-K Carwash

(91) Rest Area (RR, Phones, Picnic, Vending; Eastbound)

(94) Rest Area (RR, Phones, Picnic, Vending; Westbound)

98 WI 121, Alma Center, Pigeon Falls
- Gas S: Cenex[*, D]
- Food S: Northfield Merchantile
- AServ S: Amunson Service Center, Cenex
- Other S: Northfield Merchantile

105 WI 95, Hixton, Alma Center
- FStop S: Cenex[*, D], Phillips 66[*]
- Food S: Jeffrey's Cafe (Phillips 66), Phillips 66
- Lodg N: Motel 95
- RVCamp N: Camping

115 U.S. 12, WI 27, Black River Falls, Merrillan
- FStop S: Amoco[*, D]
- Gas S: Conoco[*, LP], Holiday[*, LP], Phillips 66
- Food N: Kountry Kettle (The Pines Motor Lodge), The Pines Motor Lodge
  S: Dairy Queen (Phillips 66), Hardee's[PLAY], KFC, Phillips 66, Subway
- Lodg N: The Pines Motor Lodge
- AServ S: Rush Buick
- Med S: ✚ Hospital
- Other S: Coin & Automatic Car Wash

116 WI 54, Black River Falls, Wisconsin Rapids
- TStop S: Far-B Citgo[*, SCALES]
- FStop N: Cenex[*, LP]
  S: Kwik Trip[*, LP] (Amoco)
- Food N: Arrowhead Lodge Best Western, Cenex, Perkins Family Restaurant, Subway (Cenex), Taco Bell (Cenex)
  S: Burger King[PLAY], Far-B Citgo, Kwik Trip (Amoco), McDonald's, Pizza Hut, Taco Time
- Lodg N: Arrowhead Lodge Best Western, Holiday Inn Express, North Country Lodge
  S: American Heritage Inn
- TServ S: Far-B Citgo[SCALES], Power Brake Wisconsin
- RVCamp N: Parkland Village Campground (.25 Miles)
- Med S: ✚ Hospital
- ATM N: Cenex
  S: Jackson County Bank, Kwik Trip (Amoco)
- Other N: Black River Recreational
  S: Wal-Mart[LP, RX]

128 CR O, Millston
- Gas S: Phillips 66[*, D]
- Lodg S: Millston Motel
- RVCamp N: State Forest Campground
- Other N: U.S. Post Office

(132) Rest Area (RR, Phones, Picnic; Eastbound)

(132) Rest Area (RR, Phones, Picnic; Westbound)

135 CR E W, Warrens
- Food S: Kim's Texas Longhorn Grill
- RVCamp N: Yogi Bear Camp Resort[PLAY] (.5 Miles)

143 U.S. 12, WI 21, Tomah, Necedah
- TStop N: Quik Trip[*, LP, SCALES, 24] (Amoco)
- Gas N: Citgo[*], Mobil[*, D]
  S: Citgo[*], Shell[*, D]
- Food N: Bradford Dining (Holiday Inn), Citgo, Country Kitchen, Hardy Platter (Quik Trip), Perkins Family Restaurant (Holiday Inn), Quik Trip (Amoco)
  S: Citgo, Cranberry Cupboard (Citgo), Culver's Frozen Custard & Burgers, Hardee's, KFC, McDonald's, Subway, Taco Bell
- Lodg N: AmeriInn, Holiday Inn, Super 8
  S: Comfort Inn, Cranberry Suites Motel, Econolodge
- AServ N: Denny's Automotive Center, Mobil
- TServ N: Quik Trip[SCALES, 24] (Amoco)
- RVCamp S: Bubnich Motors & RV's (1.75 Miles), Camping
- Med N: ✚ Hospital
- ATM N: Citgo, Mobil
  S: Citgo, Shell
- Other N: Humbird Cheese

144 Jct I-90, La Crosse

Note: I-94 runs concurrent below with I-90. Numbering follows I-90.

45A I-90, Junction I-94, to Madison

45B Jct I-94, St Paul, O'Clair, LaCross

(48) Weigh Station (Westbound)

49 CR PP, Oakdale
- TStop N: Citgo Travel Center[*]
- FStop N: Speedway[*, LP]
- Gas S: Mobil[*, LP]
- Lodg S: Oak Dale Motel
- RVCamp N: Granger's Campground (.33 Miles), Kamp Dakota (.5 Miles)
- ATM S: Mobil
- Parks S: Mill Bluff State Park

(55) Rest Area (RR, Phones, Picnic, Grills; North At Exit 55)

55 CR C, Camp Douglas, Volkfield
- FStop S: Amoco[*]
- Gas S: Mobil[*, LP]
- Food S: German House, Mobil, Subway (Mobil)
- Lodg S: Walsh's K&K Motel
- ATM S: Amoco, Mobil
- Parks S: Mills Bluff State Park
- Other S: Camp William National Guard Museum, Coin Operated Laundry, Omaha Trail

61 WI 80, Necedah, New Lisbon
- TStop N: Mobil[*, D], New Lisbon 76 Auto/Truck Stop[*, D, SCALES]
- FStop N: Citgo[*, D]
- Food N: 76, Citgo, Grandma's Kitchen (Citgo), New Lisbon 76 Auto/Truck Stop, Subway (Citgo)
- Lodg N: Edge of the Wood Motel
- TServ N: New Lisbon 76 Auto/Truck Stop[SCALES]
- RVCamp N: Camping
  S: Camping

69 WI 82, Mauston, Necedah
- TStop S: Kwik Trip - Amoco[*, D, LP, 24]
- FStop N: Cenex Travel Mart[*, D, LP], Phillips 66[*, D], Shell[*, D]
- Gas S: Citgo[*]
- Food N: Cenex Travel Mart, Country Kitchen, Park Oasis Inn, Taco Bell (Cenex), The Family Restaurant (Park Oasis Inn)
  S: A & W, Culver's Frozen Custard & Burgers, Garden Valley Restaurant, Hardee's, Hardy Platter[24] (Amoco), Kwik Trip - Amoco, McDonald's, Roman Castle Italian, The Alaskan Motel
- Lodg N: Country Inn & Suites, Park Oasis Inn, Super 8
  S: The Alaskan Motel
- TServ S: Kwik Trip - Amoco[24]
- Med S: ✚ Hospital
- ATM S: Bank of Mauston
- Parks S: State Park
- Other N: Dragons Ben Mini Golf
  S: Car Wash, Cheese Mart, Coin Operated Laundry

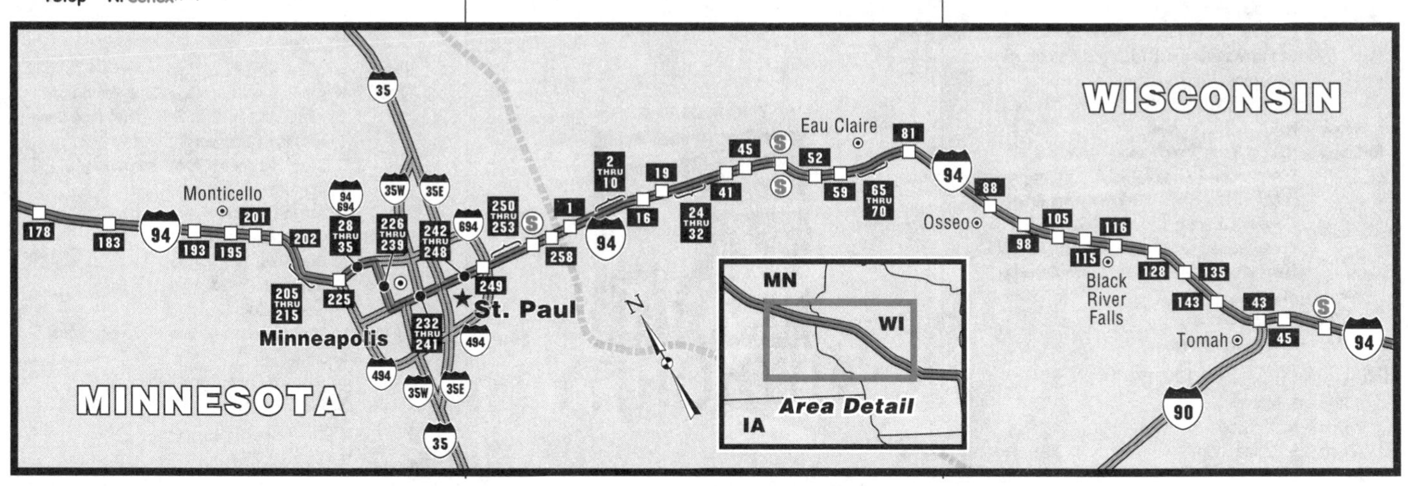

Bold red print shows RV & Bus parking available or nearby

EXIT	WISCONSIN
(76)	Rest Area (RR, Phones, Picnic, Vending, RV Dump; Eastbound)
(76)	Rest Area (RR, Phones, Picnic, Vending, RV Dump; Westbound)
79	CR, HH, Lyndon Station
FStop	S: Shell(*, LP)
RVCamp	N: Crocket's RV Campground (2 Miles), Dreamfield RV Sales & Service(LP), Yukon Trails Camping (.5 Miles)
85	U.S. 12, WI 16, Wisconsin Dells
TServ	S: G & S Inc
RVCamp	N: Arrowhead Campground (.75 Miles), Dells Timberland Campground (2 Miles), Eagle Flats Campground (.25 Miles), Stand Rock Campground (1 Mile)
	S: Camping
Parks	S: Rocky Arbor State Park
87	WI 13 North, Wisconsin Dells
FStop	N: Amoco(*, D, LP, RV DUMP) (Towing), Mobil(*, LP)
Gas	N: Shell(*)
Food	N: Black Bark Stage Coach Buffet, Burger King(PLAY), Country Kitchen, Denny's, Luigi's Pizzaria, Paul Bunion's Cook Shanty, Perkins Family Restaurant, Taco Bell, Wendy's
Lodg	N: Best Western, Comfort Inn, Days Inn, Dells Eagle Motel, Holiday Inn, Super 8, The Polynesian Motel
AServ	N: Amoco (Towing)
RVCamp	N: KOA Campgrounds (2 Miles), Sherwood Forest Campground (1.5 Miles), Tee Pee Park Campground (1 Mile)
	S: Bonanza Campground (2 Miles)
ATM	N: Mobil, Shell
Parks	N: Beaver Springs Fishing Park
Other	N: Timberfalls Water Park/Putt Putt
89	WI 23, Lake Delton, Reedsburg
FStop	N: Mobil(*)
Gas	N: Terry's Shortstop(*, LP) (Marathon)
Food	N: Granny Good Things Bake Shop, Hometown Cafe (Mobil), Mobil
Lodg	N: Malibu Inn, Olympia Motel, Roadway Inn, Sahara Motel
RVCamp	N: Yogi Bear Camp Resort (1 Mile)
	S: Country Roads Motor Home & RV Park (.75 Miles)
Other	N: Coin Operated Laundry, Crystal Grand Music Theater
92	U.S. 12, Baraboo, Lake Delton
FStop	N: Mobil(*, LP)
Gas	N: Amoco(*), Citgo(*, CW)
Food	N: Burger King(PLAY), Cheese Factory Restaurant, Cheese Store, Danny's Diner, McDonald's(PLAY), Ponderosa, Subway, Wintergreen Resort, Wintergreen Restaurant (Wintergreen Resort)
Lodg	N: Alakai Hotel & Suites, Black Wolf Lodge, Camelot, Country Squire Motel, Del Rancho, Grand Marquis Inn, Lake Motel, Ramada Limited, Wilderness Hotel, Wintergreen Resort
	S: Good Nite Inn, Motel 6, Vagabond Motel
TWash	N: Car & Truck Wash
RVCamp	N: Yogi Bear Camp Resort (1.5 Miles)
	S: American RV Sales, Dell Boo Campground (2 Miles), Fox Hill RV Park (RV Sales & Service), Pioneer Camping (.75 Miles), Red Oak Campground (2 Miles), Scenic Traveler RV Sales & Service, Yogi Bear Camp Resort (2 Miles)
ATM	N: Citgo, Mobil
Other	N: Car & Truck Wash
106	WI 33, Portage, Baraboo
FStop	S: Mobil(*)
Gas	N: Amoco(*)
Food	S: Coffee Shop
RVCamp	S: Kamp Dakota (.63 Miles)
Med	N: + Hospital
108AB	WI 78, I 39 To U.S. 51, Wausau, Merrimac, Stevens Point
TStop	S: Petro(*, LP, SCALES)
Gas	S: Phillips 66(*, LP) (Towing)
Food	S: Dairy Queen (Petro), Little Caesars Pizza (Petro), Petro, The Iron Skillet (Petro)
Lodg	S: Comfort Suites Hotel, Days Inn
AServ	S: Phillips 66 (Towing)
TServ	S: Petro(SCALES)
TWash	S: Petro
(114)	Rest Area (RR, Phones, Picnic, Vending, RV Dump; Eastbound)
(114)	Rest Area (RR, Phones, Picnic, Vending, RV Dump; Westbound)
115	CR CS, Poynette, Lake Wisconsin
FStop	N: Citgo(*, D, LP)
Food	N: McDonald's, Subway
AServ	N: Grahams Auto & Truck Clinic(CW)
TServ	N: Grahams Auto & Truck Clinic, Truck & Repair(24)
TWash	N: Citgo
RVCamp	N: Jade RV Park, Smokey Hollow Campground (2 Miles- Open 12 Months)
119	WI 60, Lodi, Arlington
AServ	S: Trucks Central
126	CR V, Dane, De Forest
Gas	N: Amoco(*, CW, 24)
	S: Phillips 66(*, LP)
Food	N: Cheese Chalet, Culver's Frozen Custard & Hamburgers, McDonald's, Subway
Lodg	N: Holiday Inn Express
RVCamp	N: KOA Campgrounds
ATM	N: Amoco
Other	N: State Police
131	WI 19, Waunakee, Sun Praire
FStop	N: QuikTrip(*, D, LP)
Gas	N: Mobil, Super America(*, D, LP)
Food	N: A & W Drive-In, Columbo Yogurt (SuperAmerica), McDonald's(PLAY), Mouse House Cheese Haus, Super America, Taco Bell (SuperAmerica)
Lodg	N: Days Inn, Super 8
TServ	N: Wisconsin Kenworth
Other	N: Lazer Clean Car Wash, Truck Wash(D)
132	U.S. 51, Madison, De Forest
TStop	N: Marathon(*, LP, SCALES), Shell(*, SCALES)
	S: 76 Auto/Truck Plaza(*, RV DUMP, SCALES)
FStop	S: Pumper Truck Stop(*)
Food	N: Marathon, Pine Cone(*, SCALES) (Shell), Shell, The Copper Kitchen (Marathon)
	S: 76 Auto/Truck Plaza, Deli (Pumper), Pumper Truck Stop, Subway (Pumper)
TServ	N: Diesel Specialists of Madison
	S: Brad Ragin Tire Service, Freightliner(24), Peterbilt Dealer, Polk Diesel & Machine, Transport Refridgeration Inc. Thermal King
RVCamp	N: Token Creek Park (.5 Miles)
	S: WI RV World RV Service
ATM	N: Marathon, Shell
135AB	U.S. 151, Madison, Sun Prairie
Gas	S: Amoco(*), Shell(*) (Towing), Sinclair(*)
Food	S: Applebee's, Bread Smith, Carlos O'Kely, Chili's, Country Kitchen, Dunkin Donuts, Hardee's, IHOP, KFC, McDonald's, Mountain Jack's Prime Rib, Olive Garden, Perkins Family Restaurant, Pizza Hut, Ponderosa, Red Lobster
Lodg	S: Comfort Inn, Crown Plaza, Hampton Inn, Select Inn
ATM	S: Amoco, Bank One, First Federal, Firststar Bank
Other	S: Essex Square, Half Price Books
138A	I-94 East Milwaukee (Difficult Reaccess)

Note: I-94 runs concurrent above with I-90. Numbering follows I-90.

EXIT	WISCONSIN
138B	Airport (Left Exit)
244A	I-90W, Blair, Wisconsinville, WI 30, Madison, Jamesville
244B	CR N, Sun Prairie, Cottage Grove
FStop	N: Citgo Super Store(*, LP)
Gas	N: Amoco(*) (Towing)
AServ	N: Amoco (Towing), Citgo Super Store
TServ	N: Citgo Super Store
(245)	Weigh Station (Eastbound)
250	WI 73, Marshall Deerfield
259	WI 89, Lake Mills, Waterloo, Marshall
TStop	N: Phillips 66 Lake Oasis Truck Stop(*, D, SCALES)
FStop	S: Amoco(*), Kwik Trip(*, LP)
Gas	S: 76(*)
Food	S: Amoco, Country Chef Restaurant (Amoco), McDonald's(PLAY), Subway, The Pizza Pit
Lodg	N: Lake Country Inn
	S: Pyramid Motel
AServ	S: 76
TServ	N: Phillips 66 Lake Oasis Truck Stop(SCALES)
RVCamp	S: RV Country Campers RV Center
Med	S: + Lake Mills Medical Art With Urgent Care
ATM	S: Commonwealth Credit Union, Kwik Trip
(261)	Rest Area (RR, Phones, Picnic, Vending; Eastbound)
(264)	Rest Area (RR, Phones, Picnic, Vending; Westbound)
267	WI 26, Watertown, Johnson Creek
TStop	N: Shell Pine Cone Travel Plaza(*, SCALES) (Showers)
FStop	S: Citgo(*, D, LP)
Food	N: Arby's, Cinnabon, Pine Cone Restaurant (Shell), Quick Stop Brat. Shop, Shell Pine Cone Travel Plaza (Showers)
	S: Citgo, Hardees (Citgo), The Gobbler Restaurant
Lodg	N: Days Inn
	S: King Arthur's Inn & Motel
AServ	N: Goodyear Tire & Auto
TServ	N: Goodyear Tire & Auto
Med	N: + Hospital
ATM	N: Shell Pine Cone Travel Plaza (Showers)
	S: Citgo
Other	N: Johnson Creek Outlet Center
	S: Star Cinemas
275	CR F, Sullivan, Ixonia
RVCamp	S: Camping

INTERSTATE
EXIT
AUTHORITY

Bold red print shows RV & Bus parking available or nearby

EXIT	WISCONSIN
277	Willow Glen Road (Eastbound, Reaccess Westbound Only)
282	WI 67, Dousman, Oconomowoc
Food	**N:** Mr Slow's Sandwiches
Other	**N:** Summit Animal Clinic
283	CR P, Sawyer (Reaccess Eastbound Only, Difficult Reaccess)
285	CR C, Delafield (Reaccess Eastbound Only, Difficult Reaccess)
Gas	**N:** Amoco, Mobil(*, LP)
Food	**N:** David's Bakery & Cafe, The Carpenter's Pub
AServ	**N:** Amoco
ATM	**N:** BankOne
Other	**N:** U.S. Post Office
287	WI 83, Hartland, Wales
Gas	**S:** Amoco(*, CW), PDQ(*)
Food	**N:** Cousins' Sub's, Emporer's Kitchen (Chinese), Hardee's, I Can't Believe It's Yogurt, **McDonald's**(PLAY), SHONEY'S, Shoney's, Winchester's Restaurant **S:** Burger King, Dairy Queen, Heidi's Cafe (Gourmet Coffee), Marty's Pizza, Rococo Pizza, Subway
Lodg	**N:** Country Pride, Holiday Inn Express **S:** Budgetel Inn
AServ	**S:** Pennzoil Oil Change
RVCamp	**N:** **Naga-Waukee Park (1 Mile)**
ATM	**N:** M&I Bank, Wakesha State Bank **S:** First Star, PDQ
Other	**N:** Century Foods, Naga-Waukee Park (Ice Arena), Vision Care Center **S:** Gollash Pharmacy(RX), Hillside Cinemas, **Target**, **Wal-Mart**(RX), Warden's Ace Hardware(LP)
290	CR SS North
291	CR G, Pewaukee
Gas	**S:** Amoco(*)
Food	**N:** Country Inn Hotel, Country Inn Hotel
Lodg	**N:** Country Inn Hotel
293AB	CR T, Waukesha, Pewaukee
Gas	**N:** Mobil(*, LP)
Food	**N:** Denny's, Fazoli's, McDonald's(PLAY), Mr Wok, Peking House Chinese, Rococo Pizza, Subway, Taco Amego Mexican Restaurant, Waldo Pepper's Restaurant, Weissagerber's Gasthaus Restaurant, Wendy's
Lodg	**N:** Excel Grand Hotel
AServ	**N:** Batteries Plus, Firestone, Lazer Lube, Mobil
TServ	**N:** **Badger Utility Semi-Trailer Service & Parts**, **Peterbilt**
ATM	**N:** First Star, WalGreens Pharmacy(RX)
Other	**N:** Biebel True Value Market(LP), Osco Drug(RX), Pet Land, WalGreens Pharmacy(RX)
294	CR J, Waukesha
Gas	**N:** Mobil(*)
Food	**N:** Machine Shed Restaurant
Lodg	**N:** Comfort Suites Hotel
Med	**N:** **+ Medical Assoc. Urgent Care**(RX) **(Optical)**
ATM	**N:** M & I Bank
295	WI 164, Waukesha, Sussex
Med	**S:** **+ Hospital**
297AB	U.S. 18, CR Y, Waukesha, Barker, Bluemound Road
Gas	**N:** PDQ(*, D)
Food	**N:** Annie's American Cafe, Applebee's, Arby's, Cousins' Sub's, Heavenly Ham, KFC, McDonald's, Oscar's Frozen Custard & Sandwiches, Perkin's Family Restaurant, Schlotzsky's Deli, Subway, Taco Bell, Zorba's Home Cooking
Lodg	**N:** Budgetel Inn, Extended Stay America, Fairfield Inn, **Hampton Inn**, Holiday Inn, Motel 6, Select Inn, Super 8

EXIT	WISCONSIN
AServ	**N:** Jiffy Lube, Kuettner Olds, GMC, NTB, Team Tire Plus
Med	**N:** **+ Hospital**
ATM	**N:** BankOne, Equitable Bank
Other	**N:** Animal Clinic, Market Cinema, Pet World, Putt Putt, State Police, **Target**, WalGreens Pharmacy(RX), Westown Movie Theaters
301AB	Moorland Road
Gas	**N:** Amoco, Mobil(CW)
Food	**N:** Bakers Square & Bakery, Fuddruckers, McDonald's, Schlotzsky's Deli, Sheraton, Uno Chicago Bar & Grill, Whitney's Fine Dining (Sheraton) **S:** Best Western, Maxwell's Restaurant (Best Western)
Lodg	**N:** Sheraton **S:** Best Western, Embassy Suites, Residence Inn
AServ	**N:** Brookfield Motor Car Co., F&F Michelin Tire Service, Firestone, Goodyear, Sears Auto Center
ATM	**N:** Mutual Savings Bank, North Shore Bank, WalGreens Pharmacy(*, RX)
Other	**N:** **Brookfield Square Mall**, Stein Optical Express, WalGreens Pharmacy(RX)
304AB	WI 100
Gas	**N:** Clark(LP), Shell(*, K, CW) **S:** Phillips 66(*), Super America(*, LP)
Food	**N:** Bagel Tracks, Best Western, Cactus Jack (Best Western), Camelot Inn, Edwardo's Natural Pizza, Giuseppi's Pizza (Italian/American), Hoffman House (Best Western), Java Toast With I Can't Believe Its Yogurt, Pizza Hut, Ramada Inn, Schlotzsky's Deli, Shiva Indian Restaurant (Ramada), Sundome (Ramada), Taco Bell, The Ground Round, The Taste of India (Camelot Inn) **S:** PJ's Subs & Sandwiches
Lodg	**N:** 40 Winks Inn, Best Western, Camelot Inn, Exel Inn, Ramada Inn
AServ	**S:** Quaker State Oil & Lube
TServ	**S:** **Rider Rent A Truck (Big Truck Service)**
RVCamp	**S:** **Hanna Trailers**(LP) **(2 Miles)**
ATM	**N:** Tri City National Bank **S:** Super America
Other	**N:** Milwaukee County Zoo, Posa Market & Deli **S:** Kip's Inn Food Market, **Rider Rent A Truck (Big Truck Service)**
305A	Jct I-895, U.S. 45S, Chicago
305B	U.S. 45 N Split
306	WI 181, 84th Street
RVCamp	**N:** **Wisconsin State Fair RV Park**
Med	**N:** **+ Hospital**
Parks	**N:** **Wisconsin State Fair Park**(LP)
Other	**S:** **Olympic Training Center**, Scrub-A-Dub Car Wash
307A	68th Street, 70th Street
AServ	**N:** Pennzoil Oil Change
Other	**N:** Pennzoil Oil Change
307B	Hawley Road
308C	U.S. 41 North
308B	U.S. 41 South (Left Exit)
308A	VA Center, Milwaukee County Stadium (Left Exit)
309A	35th Street (Difficult Reaccess)
Gas	**N:** Amoco(*, 24), SuperAmerica(*)
Other	**N:** Victory Optical
309B	26th Street, St Paul Ave
310A	Jct I-43N, Green Bay
310B	Jct I-43 South, Chicago, Beloit, Madison
310C	Jct I-794, Downtown Milwaukee

EXIT	WISCONSIN
311	WI 59, National Ave., 6th St. (Southbound, Reaccess Westbound Only)
312A	Lapham Blvd., Mitchell, Beecham
Gas	**S:** Amoco(*), Citgo(*)
AServ	**S:** Amoco
ATM	**S:** Citgo
312B	Beecher St., Lincoln Ave.
Gas	**S:** BP(*, D), Citgo(*, D)
ATM	**S:** Citgo
314A	Holt Ave.
Gas	**N:** Citgo(*, D)
Food	**N:** Dairy Queen (Pik & Save), **Pik & Save**(RX) **(Vision Mart)**, Subway (Pik & Save), Taco Loco (Pik & Save)
Med	**S:** **+ Hospital**
ATM	**N:** **Pik & Save (Vision Mart)**
Other	**N:** Builder Square(LP), **Pik & Save**(RX) **(Vision Mart)**
314B	Howard Ave.
Gas	**N:** Clark(*), Mobil(*), Shell(*, CW)
Food	**N:** Copper Kitchen, George Webb Restaurant, Ho Ho Chinese Food, Peppe's Pizza
AServ	**N:** Mobil
ATM	**N:** Clark, First Star, Mutual Savings Bank
Other	**N:** **Tru Value Hardware**(LP), **WalGreens Pharmacy**(24)
316	Jct I-43, I-894W, Beloit
317	Layton Ave
Gas	**N:** Clark(*)
Food	**N:** Martino's (Hot Dogs & Beef Market) **S:** Big City Pizza, George Webb Restaurant, Howard Johnson, Riccobono Italian/American Food
Lodg	**S:** Howard Johnson
AServ	**N:** Car Wash, Meineke Discount Mufflers, Meyer's Auto Body, Pennzoil Oil Change **S:** Accurate Transmission Service
TServ	**N:** **J.D.'s Truck Service**
Other	**N:** Car Wash **S:** Quick Pantry, Wisconsin Vision
318	General Mitchell Int'l Airport
319	CR ZZ, College Ave
Gas	**N:** Shell(*), Super America(*, D, LP) **S:** Amoco(*), Citgo(*)
Food	**N:** Georgy's Restaurant (Ramada Inn), **McDonald's**, Milwaukee Shrievport Inn, Ramada Inn, SHONEY'S, Shoney's **S:** The Blue Boy Ice Cream Parlor
Lodg	**N:** EconoLodge, Exel Inn, Hampton Inn, Milwaukee Shrievport Inn, Ramada Inn, Red Roof Inn
ATM	**S:** Amoco
Other	**S:** Coin Operated Laundry, Food Mart
320	CR BB, Rawson Ave.
Gas	**N:** **Amoco**(*, 24), Mobil(*, LP, CW)
Food	**N:** Burger King
Lodg	**N:** Budgetel Inn
AServ	**N:** **Amoco**(24)
TServ	**N:** **Amoco**(24)
Other	**N:** South Shore Cinemas
322	WI 100, Ryan Road (Reaccess Westbound Only)
TStop	**S:** **Milwaukee 76 Auto/Truck Stop**(*, SCALES, 24) **(Showers)**, **Speedway**(*, D, SCALES) **(Showers)**
Gas	**S:** Citgo(*)
Food	**N:** **Hardee's**, **McDonald's**(PLAY), **Wendy's** **S:** Apple Creek Family Restaurant (Truck Stop), Arby's, Citgo, Country Kitchen (Speedway), **Milwaukee 76 Auto/Truck Stop (Showers)**, **Perkins Family Restaurant**, **Speedway (Showers)**, Subway (Citgo)

Bold red print shows RV & Bus parking available or nearby

EXIT — WISCONSIN

Lodg S: Knight's Inn
TServ N: Cummins Diesel, Goodyear Commercial Tire Center
S: Freightliner Dealer, Kenworth, Milwaukee 76 Auto/Truck Stop[SCALES, 24] (Showers)
TWash S: Blue Beacon Truck Wash, Speedway (Showers)
ATM S: Speedway (Showers), Tri City National Bank

326 Seven Mile Road
Gas N: Amoco[*, 24]
S: Mobil[*]
Lodg S: Motel
TServ N: Mack & Cummin Engine Repair
RVCamp N: Jellystone Park Campground

327 CR G
Food S: Connie's Country Chalet

(328) Weigh Station (Eastbound)

329 CR K, Racine
FStop N: Pilot Travel Center[*, SCALES]
Gas S: Mobil[*, LP]
Food N: Arby's (Pilot FS), Pilot Travel Center, T.J. Cinnnamons (Pilot FS)
S: A & W Drive-In
AServ N: Michel Auto Service (Towing)
TServ S: Badger Truck Center, Schneider Tire Service, Western Star Trucks
ATM N: Pilot Travel Center

333 WI 20, Racine, Waterford
FStop N: Shell[*, D, CW]
S: Citgo[*, LP], Mobil[*, 24]
Gas N: Kwik Trip
Food N: Burger King, McDonald's
S: Citgo, Culver's Frozen Custard, Juicy Lucy's (Citgo), Mobil
Lodg N: Holiday Inn Express, Paul's Motel, Ramada
S: Rodeway Inn
AServ N: Rosen Hyundai
TServ S: International Service & Sales, Pomps Michellin Market
RVCamp S: Capitol R.V. Center Inc.
ATM S: Citgo, Mobil

335 WI 11, Racine, Burlington
Food S: T-Bird Family Dining
Lodg S: Motel
TServ S: Hood Medics
RVCamp S: Travelers' Inn Motel & Campground (.13 Miles)

337 CR KR, County Line Road
Food S: The Apple Holler Restaurant

339 CR E
FStop N: Speedway[*, LP]

340 WI 142, CR S, Kenosha, Burlington
Gas N: 76[*], Mobil[*, 24] (Wrecker Service)
Food S: Mars Cheese Castle, Star Restaurant
Lodg S: EasterDay Motel
AServ N: Mobil[24] (Wrecker Service)
ATM N: 76
Other S: Kim & Tom Cheese Shop

342 WI 158, Kenosha
TServ S: Lyon's Truck Parts

344 WI 50, Kenosha, Lake Geneva
FStop N: Woodsman[*, CW] (Penzoil)
Gas N: Shell[*, D]
S: Speedway[D], Standard[*, 24] (Amoco)
Food N: Annie's American Cafe, Dunkin Donuts (Shell), Shell, SHONEY'S Shoney's
S: Bratstop Cheese & Restaurant, Burger King, Chefs Table, Cracker Barrel, DAYS INN Days Inn, Denny's (Day's Inn), KFC, Long John Silver, McDonald's[PLAY], Taco Bell, Taste of Wisconsin Family Dining, Wendy's
Lodg N: Budgetel Inn, Super 8

EXIT — WISCONSIN/ILLINOIS

PRIME OUTLETS
KENOSHA
Nearly 70 Outlet Stores
Gap • Nike • Polo
Ask for your FREE COUPON BOOK
414-857-2101
1861
WISCONSIN • I-94 • EXIT 347

1197
DAYS INN
12121 75th Street
Tour Buses Welcome
97 Rooms
Restaurant on Property
Lounge on Property
Indoor/Outdoor Pool & Whirlpool
Free Continental Breakfast
Close to Outlet Malls
15 Minutes to *Six Flags Great America*
414-857-2311 • 800-DAYS-INN
WISCONSIN • I-94 • EXIT 344

S: Best Western, Country Inn & Suites, DAYS INN Days Inn (see our ad this page), Knight's Inn, Quality Suites
ATM N: Shell
S: McDonald's, Standard (Amoco)
Other N: Woodman Market Produce
S: Action Teritory Family Fun Pk., Outlet Mall

345 CR C
AServ N: Nauro Auto Mall
RVCamp S: RV Sales[LP]

(347) Rest Area, Travel Information (RR, HF, Phones, Picnic; Eastbound)

(347) Rest Area (RR, HF, Phones, Picnic; Westbound)

347 WI 165, CR Q, The Lakeview Pkwy, Wisconsin Welcome Center
Gas N: Amoco[*]
Food N: McDonald's, Radisson
Lodg N: Radisson
Other N: Lakeside Market Place Outlet Mall, Prime Outlets at Kenosha (see our ad this page)

↑WISCONSIN

↓ILLINOIS

1A Russell Road (Difficult Reaccess)
TStop S: Travel Authority[*, SCALES] (Mobil)
FStop S: Citgo[*, SCALES], Marathon[*]
Gas S: Mobil
Food S: Citgo, Pizza Hut (Travel Authority), Travel Authority (Mobil)
TServ S: Travel Authority[SCALES] (Mobil), Truck City
TWash S: Travel Authority (Mobil)
RVCamp N: Sky Harbor RV[LP]

1B U.S. 41, Waukegan (Left Exit Eastbound, Difficult Reaccess)

Note: I-94 runs concurrent below with TSTLWY. Numbering follows TSTLWY.

(74) Toll Plaza (Toll)

(70) IL 132, Grand Ave, Waukegan,

EXIT — ILLINOIS

Gurnee
Gas N: Speedway[*, D, LP]
S: Mobil[*, LP]
Food N: Burger King, Cracker Barrel, IHOP, Ichiban Steakhouse, McDonald's[PLAY], Ming's of China Restaurant, Outback Steakhouse, Subway
S: Applebee's, Atrium Cafe (Holiday Inn), Baker's Square, Carraboo's Coffee Shop, Chili's, Denny's, Einstein Bros Bagels, Hayashi Japanese Restaurant, Holiday Inn, Lone Star Steakhouse, Max's and Erma's Restaurant, McDonald's, Pizza Hut, Planet Hollywood, Rainforest Cafe, Red Lobster, Ruby Tuesday, Schlotzsky's Deli, Steak N' Shake, T.G.I. Friday's, Taco Bell, Uno Chicago Bar & Grill (Pizzaria), Wendy's, White Castle Restaurant
Lodg N: Budgetel Inn, Extended Stay America, Hampton Inn
S: Comfort Inn, Fairfield Inn, Holiday Inn (see our ad this page)
AServ S: Fast Lane Lube, Midas Muffler & Brake, Mobil, Sam's Club
Med S: ✚ Acute Care Center
ATM N: Bank
S: First Chicago, Harris Bank
Other N: Piggly Wiggly Supermarket, Six Flags Theme Park
S: Dominic's Grocery[RX], Gurnee Mills Mall, Home Depot[LP], Jewell Osco Drugs[RX], Kinko's, Pearl Vision, Pets Mart, Sam's Club, Spot Not Car Wash, Target[RX], Wal-Mart[RX] (Vision Center)

(69) IL 21, Milwaukee Ave., Libertyville, Graysflack, N. Chicago (Reaccess Westbound Only)
Med S: ✚ Hospital

(65) IL 137, Buckley Rd., IL 120, Belvidere (Reaccess Southbound Only)
Med S: ✚ Hospital

(60) Lake Forest Tollway Oasis (Toll)
Gas E: Mobil
Food E: Baskin Robbins (Mobil), David Berg Hot Dogs (Mobil), Mobil, Wendy's (Mobil)
ATM E: Mobil

(59) IL 60, Town Line Road

(57) IL 22, Half Day Road (Toll)

(54) Toll Plaza 26, Lake-Cook Rd. (Reaccess Eastbound Only, Toll)
Lodg S: Hyatt

(53) Jct I-294 South, O'Hare (Reaccess Eastbound Only, Toll)
Food S: Discovery Bay (Embassy), Embassy Suites
Lodg S: Embassy Suites

51 IL 43, Waukegan Road (Reaccess Eastbound Only)
Gas E: Amoco[*, CW], Shell
Food E: Applebee's, Chili's, Chung Chopsuey, Cooker's Hot Dogs, Full Slab Ribs, Japanese Steakhouse
Lodg E: Red Roof Inn
AServ E: Just Tires
Other E: Borders Books & Music, Jewell Osco Phamacy, Shopping Mall

Note: I-94 runs concurrent above with TSTLWY. Numbering follows TSTLWY.

30A Dundee Rd. (Reaccess Eastbound Only)
Gas S: 76, Amoco[CW]
AServ S: 76

31 Tower Road

Bold red print shows RV & Bus parking available or nearby

EXIT ILLINOIS

33A Willow Rd (Reaccess Eastbound Only)
- **Gas** N: Northfield Auto Clinic

34 U.S. 41S, Lake Avenue (No Reaccess)
- **Gas** N: Amoco
  S: Amoco, Shell
- **Food** N: Akai Hana Japanese, LaMadeleine Cafe, LouMalnati's, Sea Ranch Fresh Fish
  S: Dairy Queen
- **AServ** N: Amoco
  S: Amoco, Shell
- **ATM** N: Amaco, Eden's Bank
- **Other** N: **Borders Books & Music**

35 Old Orchard Road
- **Gas** N: Amoco, Shell
- **Food** N: Boston Market Restaurant, California Pizza Kitchen, EJ's Place
- **AServ** N: Amoco, Shell (Towing)
- **Med** N: **+ Hospital**
- **ATM** N: Citibank, LaSal Bank

37AB IL 58, Dempster Street
- **Gas** N: Amoco, Mobil[*]
  S: Amoco, Hillerich's, Shell[*]
- **Food** N: Hong Kong Chinese, Kaufman's Bakery, Maggie's Hot Dogs & Subs, Mazzini's Pizza, McDonald's, Mr. B's Subs
  S: Baskin Robbins, Golden Chopsticks
- **AServ** N: A Tire & Auto Center, Amoco, Car X Mufflers & Brakes, Firstone, Skokie Auto Parts, Value Transmission Center
  S: Amoco, Midas Muffler & Brake
- **Med** N: **+ Eden's Medical Center**
- **ATM** N: La Salle Bank

39AB Touhy Ave
- **Gas** N: Amoco[*, D], Shell
  S: Amoco, Citgo[*], Mobil, Shell
- **Food** N: Canton Express, Psistaria Greek Tavern
  S: Applebee's, Chicago Style Pizza, Chili's, Chuck E Cheese's Pizza, Dunkin Donuts, Jak's Restaurant, McDonald's, Pete's Fast Food Italian, Sander's Restaurant & Pancake House
- **Lodg** N: Radisson
  S: Holiday Inn (see our ad this page)
- **AServ** N: Uniroyal Tire & Auto
  S: Amoco, Lee Auto Parts, Mobil
- **Other** N: **Dominick's Grocery**
  S: **Book Store, Jewell Osco Drugs**

41B U.S. 14, Peterson Ave
- **Food** N: Campeche Mexican, Sauganash Restaurant
- **Lodg** N: Edens Motel
- **ATM** N: LaSalle Bank
- **Other** N: **Tarpey Drugs**

41C IL 50, Cicero Ave (Reaccess Eastbound Only)

EXIT ILLINOIS

42 Foster Ave
- **Gas** S: Amoco
- **AServ** S: Auto Repair Shop
- **Other** S: **Eden's Foods**

43A Wilson Ave

44A Keeler Ave, Irving Park Road, IL 19
- **Gas** S: Amoco[*], Mobil[*], Shell[*]
- **AServ** S: Amoco
- **ATM** S: Midwest Bank

45 Addison Street
- **Gas** S: Citgo[*]
- **Food** N: Little Caesars Pizza
  S: Subway (Citgo)
- **Other** N: **K-Mart**

45B Kimball Ave
- **Gas** N: Marathon[*, D]
  S: Amoco
- **Food** S: Dunkin Donuts, Subway, Subway
- **Other** S: **Dominick's Grocery, WalGreens Pharmacy**

46A California Ave
- **Gas** N: Cabwerks
  S: Mobil[*]
- **Food** N: KFC
  S: IHOP, Popeye's Chicken
- **AServ** N: James Auto Repair
  S: Mobil

47A Fullerton Ave
- **Gas** S: 76, Amoco
- **Food** N: Chuck E Cheese's Pizza, Dixie Que Restaurant, Dunkin Donuts, Popeye's Chicken, Scoops Ice Cream, Subway
  S: Domino's Pizza
- **AServ** S: 76, Amoco[24]
- **ATM** N: Midtown Bank
- **Other** N: Express Car Wash

1634

Holiday Inn®
HOLIDOME INDOOR RECREATION CENTER
Skokie, IL

- **Holidome - Includes Indoor Swimming Pool, 3 Free Games, Whirlpool, Sauna**
- **AAA & AARP Discounts**
- **E-Space Arcade Entertainment**
- **In Room Coffee Makers**

847-679-8900

ILLINOIS ▪ I-94 ▪ EXIT 39A

EXIT ILLINOIS

- S: **Fullerton Western Pharmacy**

48A Armitage Ave Ashland Ave
- **Gas** S: Amoco[*]

48B IL 64, North Ave
- **Gas** N: Amoco[*, CW]
  S: Amoco[*], Citgo, Shell
- **Food** N: Art's Drive In, Hollywood Grill, Tripp's Chicken
- **AServ** N: Goodyear Tire & Auto, Nortown Automotive
  S: American Transmission, Shell
- **ATM** N: Cash Machine (Amoco)

49A Division Street
- **Gas** S: Amoco[*], Shell[*]
- **AServ** S: Amoco[*], Shell

50A Ogden Ave (Reaccess Eastbound Only)
- **AServ** S: Firestone Tire & Auto
- **TServ** S: **International Transmission**

50B Ohio Street (No Reaccess)
- **Gas** S: Marathon[*]

51 Jct I-290

51B West Randolph St (Difficult Reaccess)
- **Food** N: Jim Ching's Restaurant, Perez Restaurant, S & S Restaurant
  S: New Star Restaurant (Chinese)

51C E Washington Blvd (Difficult Reaccess)

51D Madison Street

51E Monroe St.

51F Adams Street
- **Food** S: Greek Island, Pegasus Restaurant, San Torini Restaurant

51G Jackson Blvd
- **Food** N: Greek Town Gyros, Sorbes Restaurant
  S: Mitchell's Restaurant
- **Lodg** N: New Jackson Hotel
- **AServ** S: Toyota Dealer

51H Jct I-290W, West Suburbs

52A Taylor Street, Roosevelt Road
- **Gas** N: Amoco
- **Food** N: Eppel's Restaurant
- **AServ** N: Midas Muffler & Brake

52C 18th Street

53 Jct I-55, Chicago
- **Gas** N: Shell[*]
- **Food** N: Ken Tones (Italian Beef & Sausage)
- **AServ** N: Joe's Auto Repair

53B Junction I-55 South, I-90/94 West

54 31st Street
- **Gas** N: Shell[*]

Bold red print shows RV & Bus parking available or nearby

GURNEE MILLS

find out why there's
great shopping,
in numbers

With over 200 stores to choose from, Gurnee Mills Outlet Mall offers group tours the following amenities:

- Greeted arrivals/departures
- Convenient motor coach drop-off/pick-up
- Free convenient motorcoach parking
- Motorcoach drivers lounge
- Complimentaries for escort/driver
- Complimentary shopping bag
- Complimentary coupon book (over $750 in savings)
- 20 screen cinema
- 3 Full service restaurants
- 2 Food courts

New Arrivals! — Nautica, Lord & Taylor Clearance Center
Bass Pro Shops Outdoor World • Off 5th — Saks Fifth Avenue Outlet • Bally Shoes
Rainforest Cafe • Levi Outlet by Design • Planet Hollywood • GAP

Conveniently located off I-94 midway between Chicago/Milwaukee.
For more information call
1-800-YES SHOP
(1-800-937-7467)
http://www.gurneemillsmall.com

County, Illinois

CUNEO MUSEUM AND GARDENS

Walk through 500 years of European artistry.
Stroll the heritage gardens.

- 3 miles west of Interstate 94
- 1/2 mile north on Milwaukee Avenue, Vernon Hills, Illinois.

1350 N. Milwaukee Ave. • Vernon Hills, IL
847-362-3042 • Fax 847-362-4130

The Power House/ComEd
A hands-on energy museum
Free Admission
Hours: Monday through Saturday
10:00 AM to 5:00 PM
Directions: I-94 to Rte 173
E. to Sheridan Rd, S. to Shiloh Blvd
E. to the Lake

Visit the Holiday Shoppe for the finest in collectibles, gifts, and everything Christmas!
Open year-round, 7 days a week
Department 56® Gold Key Dealer
Bus and RV parking
EZ on and off - minutes away from six Flags, Gurnee Mills and Great lakes NTC
Liberty, IL • 847-573-1810 • www.holidayshop.net
I-94 • Exit Rt 137 • Buckley Rd. West

Bus & RV Parking • Group Tours Avail • Open Tue-Sun
I-94 • Exit Rt. 60W. • Approx. 7 miles W on Rt. 60/83
1/4 Mile N of Midlethian Rd. • Mundelein, IL
847-566-4520
300 S. Rt 83 • Mundelein, IL 60060

Shopping Made Easy!

35 miles NW of Chicago, convenient to all major expressways

Open All Year
90 Speciality Shops
5 Restaurants
Idyllic Country Setting

For information: 847-634-0888
Website: www.longgroveshops.com

The World's Largest Selection of "Fantasy Sweets" all with HOT TUBS!
• INDOOR POOL • EXERCISE & GAME ROOM
We also offer over 130 clean "Family Style" rooms which all include : Refrig, microwave, 25" Color Cable TV w/Remote & FREE HBO!
www.adventureinninc.com
Just 3 miles east of Gurnee Mills.
3740 Grand Ave. • Gurnee, IL 60031

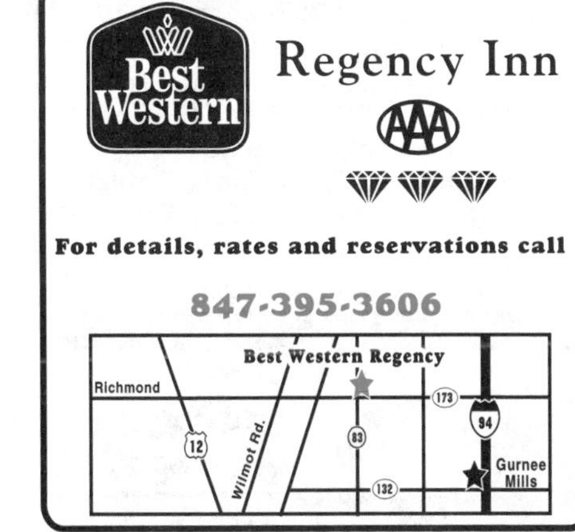

Easy Access!
Adjacent to I-94 & Rt 132 (Grand Ave.)
- Gurnee Mills Across the Street
- Less than a mile to 6 Flags Great America.
- On Site Full Service Restaurant
- Sports Bar • Large Indoor Pool
- Brand New Work Out Facility.
- Special Rates for Groups!

847-336-6300 or 800-HOLIDAY

Lake County, Illinois is located between Chicago and Milwaukee, traversing Interstate 94. It is where one finds incomparable attractions,singular shopping, a host of culinary delights and a wide range of comfortable lodging. For attractions and lodging information, call **800-LAKE-NOW, ext. EXIT**.

Illinois
a million miles from monday

EXIT ILLINOIS

Food N: Fat Albert's Italian Food, Maxwell Street Depot
Med N: ✚ **Hospital**
55B Pershing Road
56A 43rd Street
56B 47th Street
57A 51st Street
Food N: McDonald's
57B Garfield Blvd
Gas N: Amoco[CW]
S: Shell[*], Speedway[*]
Food N: Checkers Burgers, KFC, Mr. Pizza King
S: Wendy's
Other N: **WalGreens Pharmacy**
58A 59th Street
Food N: Church's Chicken
58B 63rd Street (No Reaccess)
59A Junction I-90, Indiana (Toll)
59C 71st Street
60A 75th Street
Gas N: Shell[*]
Food S: KFC
Other N: **WalGreens Pharmacy**
60C 79th Street
Gas N: Shell
S: Amoco[*], Shell[CW]
Food S: Church's Chicken, Dock's Fish, Dunkin Donuts, Subway
Other S: **WalGreens Pharmacy**
61A 83rd Street
Gas N: Shell
Other N: **State Police**
61B 87th Street
Gas N: Amoco[*], Shell
Food N: Burger King, McDonald's
S: 87th Street BBQ, Grand Chinese Kitchen, Reggio's Pizza, Subway
AServ S: Lube Pro's
Other S: **Jewel Grocery, Osco Drugs**
62 U.S. 12, U.S. 20, 95th Street (Difficult Reaccess)
Gas N: Shell[*]
S: Amoco
Food N: Top Dog
S: Expressway 95th Hot Dogs
AServ S: Precision Tune & Lube
63 Junction I-57 South, Memphis
65 95th Street, 103rd Street, Stony Island Ave
66A 111th Street
66B 115th Street
68AB 130th Street
69 Beaubien Woods (Eastbound, Reaccess Westbound Only)
70AB Dolton Ave
71AB Sibley Blvd, IL 83
Gas N: 76[*], Minuteman[*], Mobil[*, D, CW]
S: Amoco[CW], Shell[*, CW]
Food N: Dock's Sea Food, McDonald's, Nicky's Gyros, Popeye's Chicken, Subway
S: Arby's, Dunkin Donuts, Long John Silver, Wendy's, White Castle Restaurant
AServ S: Ultimate Penn
Other N: **Dominick's Grocery & Drugstore**
S: **Fair Play Grocery**, Ultimate Car Wash
73AB U.S. 6, 159th St

EXIT ILLINOIS

Kids Stay Free!
1605
Holiday Inn®
• Indoor Swimming Pool & Gym
• Cable TV with Free HBO & Pay Per View
• Guest Laundry Available
• Full Service Restaurant & Sports Bar
• AAA & AARP & Special Rates for Tour Groups
• Across the Street from Gurney Mills & Six Flags
847-336-6300
ILLINOIS ▪ I-94 ▪ EXIT Grand Ave.W

74A IL 394 South, Danville
Lodg S: **Holiday Inn (see our ad this page)**
74B Junction I-80 West, I-294 (Toll)

Note: I-94 runs concurrent below with I-80. Numbering follows I-80.

161 U.S. 6, IL 83, Torrence Ave
Gas N: Amoco[*, CW, 24]
S: Clark[*], Mobil[*, D], Shell[*]
Food N: Arby's, Best Western, Bob Evan's Restaurant, Checkers, Chili's, Hooters, Outrigger's Fish, That Oriental Place (Chinese), Wendy's
S: Al's Hamburgers, Brown's Chicken, Cafe Borgia (Roman Food), Dairy Queen, Golden Crown Restaurant, McDonald's, Pappy's Gyros
Lodg N: Best Western, Fairfield, Holiday Inn, Red Roof Inn, Super 8
AServ N: Car X Mufflers & Brakes, Firestone Tire & Auto,

1820

I-80/90 at Kennedy Ave • Hammond, IN 46323
94 Bright New Rooms
Free Continental Breakfast
Hot Coffee & Tea, Free 24 Hours
Indoor Pool & Exercise Room
Lake Michigan Casino Boats, 7 Miles
Downtown Chicago 25 Miles
Cracker Barrel, adjacent
219-845-6950
INDIANA ▪ I-94 ▪ EXIT 3

219-762-2136
Portage, IN

Toll Free Reservations: 800-297-3297
1234
• Free Continental Breakfast
• Free Cable, HBO, Pay Per View
• Free Local Calls • Game Room
• Indoor Pool & Hot Tub
• Laundry Facility • In Room Coffee
• Shoney's Adjacent to Property
• Tour Buses Welcome • Truck Parking
3 Sunburst Quality Award Winner
INDIANA ▪ I-94 ▪ EXIT 19

EXIT ILLINOIS/INDIANA

Goodyear Tire & Auto, Pep Boys, **The Big K-Mart[RX]**
S: Jiffy Lube, Mobil, **Sam's Club**, Shell
Med N: ✚ **Ingle's Family Care Center**
ATM N: Amoco, US Bank
S: Advanced Bank
Other N: Convention and Visitors Bureau, **Fannie Mae Candies, The Big K-Mart[RX]**
S: **Petsmart, Sam's Club**

↑ILLINOIS

↓INDIANA

Note: I-94 runs concurrent above with I-80. Numbering follows I-80.

1 Calumet Ave, U.S. 41 North
2AB U.S. 41 South, IN 152 North, Indianapolis Blvd
Gas N: Gas Center[*, CW], Shell, Witham's[*]
S: Speedway[*]
Food N: Arby's, Chop Suey, Dunkin Donuts, Papa John's Pizza, The Wheel, Woodmar Restaurant
S: **Burger King**, Little Caesars Pizza
AServ N: Apex Muffler & Brake, Car X Mufflers & Brakes, Midas Muffler & Brake, Shell
S: K-Mart
Med N: ✚ **Hospital**
ATM N: Mercantile Nat'l Bank of Indiana
Other N: **Woodmar Animal Clinic**
S: **K-Mart**
3 Kennedy Ave
Lodg N: Fairfield Inn (see our ad this page)
5AB IN 912, Cline Ave
Food S: Abigail's (Holiday), Bob Evan's Restaurant, Burger King
Lodg S: Holiday Inn, Motel 6, Super 8
6 Burr St, Gary
9AB Grant St
TStop S: **Flying J Travel Center[*, D, LP, K, 24]**
Gas N: Citgo[*]
Food S: Burger King, **Flying J Travel Center**, McDonald's[PLAY], Subway
TServ S: **American Truck Parts, Flying J Travel Center[24]**
Med S: ✚ **Gary Medical Center**
Other N: Barne's Laundromat, WalGreens Pharmacy[RX]
10AB Broadway , IN53 S
11 I-65 South, Indianapolis
12AB Junction I-65 North, Gary
13 Central Ave
15AB U.S. 6 East, U.S. 20, IN 51, Lake Station
16 IN. 51 N., Ripley St., Jct. I-90 (Toll)
(22) **Service Plaza**
19 Indiana 249, Portage, Port of Indiana
Gas S: Amoco[*, LP, 24], Shell[*, CW, 24]
Food S: **Angel's Garden (Ramada)**, Billy's Hot Dogs, D.D. Crandalls Grill, Drifter's, Lure Hamburgers, McDuffy's, SHONEY'S Shoney's
Lodg S: DAYS INN **Days Inn (see our ad this page), Dollar Inn, Knight's Inn, Ramada, Super 8**
AServ S: Mill's Automotive
TServ N: **Great Lakes Peterbilt**
RVCamp S: **Yogi Bear Camp Resort (1 Mile)**
ATM S: NBD
22AB U.S. 20, Porter, Burn's Harbor
TStop N: **Travel Port[*, D, SCALES]**

EXIT INDIANA

FStop N: Steel City Express(*, D, LP, SCALES)
Gas S: Shell(*)
Food N: Buckhorn Family Restaurant (Travel Port), Subway (Travel Port)
AServ N: Cleveland Tire Co
S: Arnell Chevrolet, GMC, Lakeshore Ford/ Mercury/Toyota, Roger's Repair
TServ N: Ameritech (CB), Travel Port(SCALES)
S: Roger's Repair
TWash N: Travel Port
RVCamp S: Campland RV Service

26AB Indiana 49, Chesterton, Indiana Dunes
Gas S: Amoco(*), Mobil(*, LP, CW), Shell(*, LP, 24)
Food S: Arby's, Bert's Bagels, Blimpie Subs & Salads (Amoco), Bresler's Ice Cream (Amoco), Burger King, Dunkin Donuts, Gelsosomo's Pizzeria, Jade East Chinese, KFC, Little Caesars Pizza, Long John Silver, McDonald's(PLAY), Mulligan's Cafe, Pizza Hut, Subway, Taco Bell, Waterbird Lakeside Dining, Wendy's, Wingfield's Restaurant
Lodg S: EconoLodge, Super 8
AServ S: Oil Works (10 Min. Oil Change)
Med S: ✚ Duneland Health Center of St. Anthony's Hospital
ATM S: First Source Bank, NBD, Shell
Parks N: Indiana Dunes State Park
Other N: Indiana Dunes National Lakeshore
S: Big K-Mart(RX), Coin Car Wash, Coin Laundry, Jewel Osco Supermarket(RX)

(29) Weigh Station (Eastbound)

(29) Weigh Station (Westbound)

34AB U.S. 421, Michigan City, Westville (34B Closed)
Gas N: Clark(*, LP), Meijer Superstore(*, D, LP, K, 24), Mobil(*, D, CW), Speedway(*, D, LP)
Food N: Baskin Robbins, Bob Evan's Restaurant, Chili's, Denny's(24), Dune Land Brew House, Holiday Inn, Jade's Buffet, KFC, Mino's, Noble Roman Pizza (Mobil), Red Lobster, Steak 'N Shake
Lodg N: City Manor, Comfort Inn, Dollar Inn, Holiday Inn, Knight's Inn, Red Roof Inn, Super 8
AServ N: AA Quality, Wal-Mart(24, RX)
RVCamp S: Michigan City Campground (1.5 Miles)
Med N: ✚ Hospital
ATM N: Meijer Superstore, Mobil, NBD, Speedway
Parks N: Creek Ridge County Park
Other N: Aldi, Eyeglass Emporium, Gordan's Food Service, Meijer Superstore, Prime Outlets at Michigan City (see our ad this page), Spot-Not Car Wash, Value Inn Grocery Store(RX), Wal-Mart(RX)

40AB U.S. 20, U.S. 35, Michigan City, La Porte (40B Closed)
Gas S: Amoco(*, D)

EXIT INDIANA

PRIME OUTLETS
MICHIGAN CITY
Over 120 Outlet Stores
Gap Outlet • Eddie Bauer • Polo
Ask for your FREE COUPON BOOK
219-879-6506
1864
INDIANA ▪ I-94 ▪ EXIT 34B

Med N: ✚ Hospital
ATM S: Amoco
Parks N: Dunes National Park
Other N: Museum & Zoo

(43) Rest Area (RR, Phones, Picnic; Westbound)

77 to South Bend , Notre Dame, to U.S.33, U.S. 31 Bus

83 Mishawaka

(90) Service Plaza

92 IN19, to Elkhart
Gas N: Citgo(*)
S: Clark(*), Marathon
Food N: Applebee's, Cracker Barrel, Food Lin Chinese Buffet, SHONEY'S, Shoney's, Steak & Shake
S: Bob Evan's Restaurant, Burger King, Callahan's, Davinti's, King Wha Chinese, McDonald's, Olive Garden, Perkins, Red Lobster
Lodg N: Comfort Inn, Diplomat Motel, Econolodge, Knight's Inn, Shoney's Inn, Turnpike Motel
S: Budget Inn, DAYS INN Days Inn, Ramada Inn, Red Roof Inn, Signature Inn, Super 8, Weston Plaza
RVCamp N: Elkhart Campground, Travel World, Worldwide Recreation
S: RV Sales,Service & Parts
Med S: ✚ Hospital
ATM N: NBD Bank
S: Key Bank
Other N: Coin Car Wash, K-Mart, Martin's Supermarket, Revco Drugs, Visitor Information

101 to IN 15, Bristol, Goshen

107 to U.S. 131, IN13, Middlebury, Constantine

121 IN 9, La Grange, Howe

(126) Service Plaza

144 To I-69, U.S. 27, Angola, Fort Wayne, Lansing

↑INDIANA

EXIT MICHIGAN

↓MICHIGAN

(1) MI Welcome Center (RR, Phones, Vending; Eastbound)

1 MI 239, LaPorte Road
TStop S: New Buffalo Plaza(*, D, SCALES, 24) (Phillips 66 Gas)
Gas N: Marathon(*, D)
Food N: Wheel Inn Restaurant
S: Arby's(24), New Buffalo Plaza (Phillips 66 Gas), Plaza One (New Buffalo Plaza), Wendy's, Zeke's Place
Lodg N: Edgewood Motel
S: Comfort Inn
TServ S: J & A Tire, New Buffalo Plaza(SCALES, 24) (Phillips 66 Gas)
ATM S: New Buffalo Plaza (Phillips 66 Gas)

(2) Weigh Station (Eastbound)

(2) Weigh Station (Westbound)

4AB U.S. 12, New Buffalo, Niles
FStop N: BP(*, D) (Towing)
Gas S: Amoco(*, D)
Food S: Expressway Stop (Amoco)
AServ S: Amoco, Dale's Repair Service, Roger's Wrecker Service
TServ N: BP (Towing)

6 Union Pier
Food N: Red Lake Cafe
RVCamp S: Bob-A-Ron Campground, Lakeside Campground
Parks S: Warren Woods State Park

12 Sawyer
TStop N: Citgo(*, D, K, SCALES, 24)
S: T/A TravelCenters of America(*, SCALES)
Food N: Citgo
S: Country Pride (TA), T/A TravelCenters of America
TServ N: Dunes Truck Service
S: T/A TravelCenters of America(SCALES)
TWash N: Dunes Truck Service
RVCamp N: Camping

16 Bridgman
FStop S: Speedway(*, D, LP, SCALES)
Food S: McDonald's
Lodg S: Bridgman Inn
Parks N: Warren Dunes State Park
Other S: Car Wash

22 John Beers Road
Parks S: Grand Mere State Park

23 Red Arrow Hwy., Stevensville
Gas N: Amoco(*), Shell(*, 24), Speedway(*)
Food N: Big Boy, Burger King, Cracker Barrel,

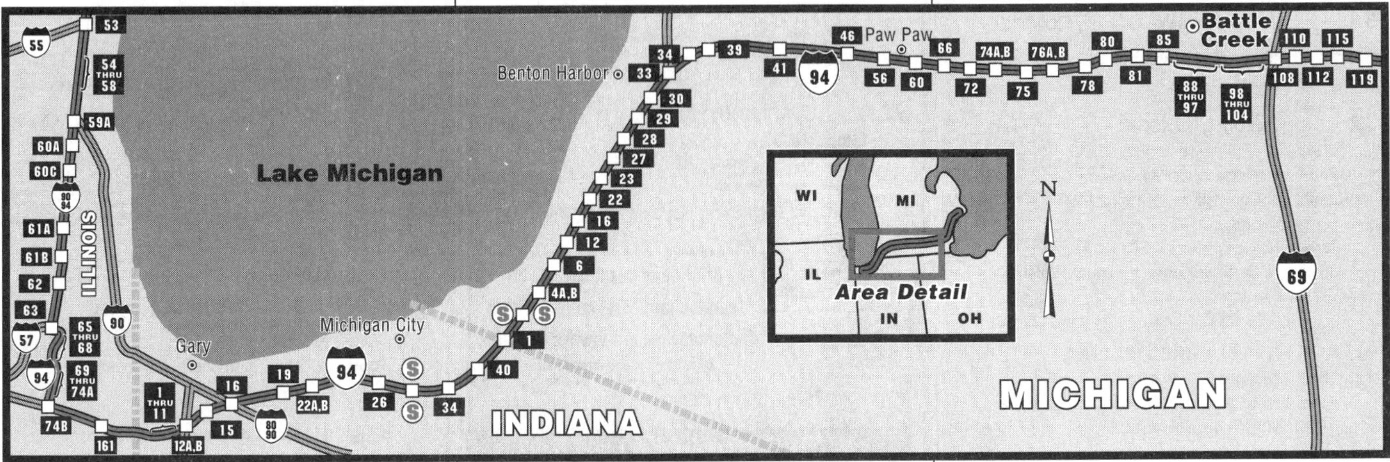

Bold red print shows RV & Bus parking available or nearby

EXIT MICHIGAN

Dunkin Donuts (Amoco), Fireside Inn Restaurant (Park Inn), Long John Silver, McDonald's(PLAY), Popeye's Chicken, Taco Bell (Amoco)
S: New Orleans Cajun Deli, Schuler's
Lodg N: Budgetel Inn, Park Inn, Ray's Hotel
S: Hampton Inn
ATM N: Amoco, Shell

27 MI. 63, Niles Ave.
FStop S: Total(*, D, K)
Gas N: Amoco(*, CW)
Med N: Hospital
ATM N: Amoco

28 U.S. 31, MI 139 N., Niles
FStop N: Total(*, D, K)
Gas N: Citgo(*, D)
S: Marathon(*, D, K)
Food N: Bill Knapp's Restaurant (see our ad this page), Kreamo Breads & Buns, Oven Fresh Bakery, Purple Onion (Days Inn), Red Rose Restaurant (Ramada)
Lodg N: Days Inn, Ramada
S: Quality Inn
AServ N: Kepner Auto Service, Mike's Radiator Service, Nickerson Auto Body & Sales
S: Marathon
RVCamp N: Taylor Rental Center(LP)
ATM N: Shoreline Bank, Total
Other N: Freier Animal Hospital

29 Pipestone Road
FStop S: Citgo(*, D)
Gas N: Meijer Superstore(*, D, LP, K, 24)
Food N: Applebee's, Burger King, Busch Gardens, Hacienda Restaurant, Hardee's, Mancino's Pizza & Grinders, McDonald's, Pizza Hut, SHONEY'S, Shoney's, Steak 'N Shake, Subway
S: Blimpie's Subs (Citgo), Bob Evan's Restaurant, Taco Bell (Citgo FS)
Lodg N: Comfort Inn, Courtyard by Marriott, Motel 6, Red Roof Inn
AServ N: Best Ford/Lincoln/Mercury, Goodyear Tire & Auto, Quick Lube, Wal-Mart(RX) (Optical)
Med N: Orchards Urgent Care Walk-In Clinic
ATM N: Shoreline Bank
Other N: Eyecare Outlet, Gordan's Food Service, K-Mart Supercenter(RX), Meijer Superstore, Orchards Mall, Wal-Mart(RX) (Optical)

30 Napier Ave
TStop N: Petro2(*, D, LP, CW, SCALES, 24) (Mobil Gas)
Gas N: Shell(*, D, 24)
Food N: Piccadilli Pizza (Petro 2)
Lodg N: Super 8
AServ S: Schroeder Pontiac & Buick
Med N: Hospital
ATM N: Petro2 (Mobil Gas), Shell

33 Bus. Loop 94, Downtown, Benton Harbor, St. Joseph

34 Junction I-196, U.S. 31, Holland

(36) Rest Area (RR, Phones, Picnic; Eastbound)

39 Millburg, Coloma
Gas N: Mobil(*, LP, CW)
Food N: McDonald's(PLAY)
RVCamp N: Countryside RV Center (.6 Miles), Krenek RV Center
Parks N: Randall Park & Skating Rink
Other N: Hardings Grocery, Vietnam Veterans Memorial
S: Run 'N Dun Club

41 MI 140, Watervliet, Niles
Gas N: Amoco(*, CW, 24), Citgo(*)
Food N: Burger King, Chicken Coop Restaurant, Waffle House of America

EXIT MICHIGAN

Bill Knapp's Restaurant
Open daily at 11:00 am
Bill Knapp's is a casual, full service family restaurant where Motorcoaches are always welcome.
Over 50 locations throughout: Michigan • Ohio • Indiana
616-925-3212 - Benton Harbor
MICHIGAN • I-94 • EXIT 28
1690

AServ N: Amoco(24)
RVCamp N: Camping
Med N: Community Hospital (W/ Walk-In Clinic)
ATM N: Amoco

(43) Rest Area (RR, Phones, Picnic; Westbound)

46 Hartford
Gas N: Shell(*, D, K)
Food N: Finish Line Grill & Deli, Panel Room Restaurant
AServ N: Betten Family
RVCamp S: American Campgrounds (1 Mile)
Med N: Hartford Medical Center
ATM N: Shell
Other N: Mak's Driving Range, Village Wash Car Wash

52 Lawrence
Food N: Waffle House of America
AServ N: Lawrence Auto Body

56 MI 51, Decatur, Dowagiac
TStop S: Road Hawk Travel Center(*, D, K, SCALES) (Total)
FStop S: Citgo(*, D, K)
Food S: Citgo, Lawson's (Citgo), Nibbles Home Style Food (Road Hawk TS)
ATM S: Road Hawk Travel Center (Total)
Other N: State Police

60 MI 40, Lawton, Paw Paw
Gas N: Amoco(*, CW), Crystal Flash(*, D, LP), Speedway(*, D, K)
Food N: Big Boy, Burger King, Chicken Coop Restaurant, Coyote Creek Restaurant, Hot 'N Now, McDonald's(PLAY), Pizza Hut, Subway, Taco Bell, Wendy's
Lodg N: Mroczek Inn, Quality Inn & Suites
AServ N: Paw Paw Chrysler/ Plymouth/Dodge/Jeep Eagle
Med N: Hospital
Other N: Village Market(24, RX)

66 Mattawan
FStop N: Mobil(*, D, LP)
Gas S: Shell(*, K)
Food N: Main St. Ice Cream, Samuel Mancino's Italian Eatery, Subway (Mobil)
AServ N: Rossman Auto
RVCamp N: R&S RV Service(LP) (.25 Miles)
S: Camping
ATM S: Kalamazoo County State Bank, Shell
Other N: Coin Laundromat, Mattawan Pharmacy(RX), Roger's Foodland
S: Formula K Fun Park

72 Oshtemo, 9th St.
TStop N: Road Hawk(*, D, K)
FStop N: Citgo(*, D) (Pacific Pride)
Gas N: Total(*, D, CW)
Food N: Burger King, Hot Stuff Pizza (Citgo FS),

Bill Knapp's Restaurant
Open daily at 11:00 am
Bill Knapp's is a casual, full service family restaurant where Motorcoaches are always welcome.
Over 50 locations throughout: Michigan • Ohio • Indiana
616-345-8635 - Kalamazoo
616-979-2101 - Battle Creek
MICHIGAN • I-94 • Exit 78/97
1691

EXIT MICHIGAN

McDonald's, Smash Hit Sub (Citgo), The Rock (Road Hawk TS), Total
S: Cracker Barrel
Lodg S: Fairfield Inn
AServ N: Saturn Dealer
Other S: Valley Market

(73) Rest Area (RR, Phones, Picnic; Eastbound)

74AB U.S. 131 North, Three Rivers, Kalamazoo, Grand Rapid

75 Oakland Dr.

76AB Westnedge Ave.
Gas N: Admiral(*, D, K), Clark(*), Meijer Superstore(*, D, LP, 24)
S: Shell(*)
Food N: Arby's, Panda Forest Chinese, Papa John's Pizza, Pappy's Place Mexican, Samuel Mancino's Italian Eatery, Steak 'N Shake
S: Bob Evan's Restaurant, Fanny Mae Candy, Fazoli's Italian Food, KFC, Little Caesars Pizza, Schlotzsky's Deli, Southside Warehouse, Wendy's
Lodg S: Holiday Motel
AServ N: Midas Muffler & Brake
S: Pep Boys Auto Center, Quick Lube
Med S: Westnedge Clinic
Other N: Meijer Superstore, Pet Supplies Plus

78 Portage Road, Kilgore Road
Gas N: Citgo(*, LP, K)
S: Shell(*), Total(D)
Food N: Brewster's Fine Food, Citgo, Dane's Buffet, Hungry Howie's Pizza & Subs, Joe Gourmet Coffee, Subway, Uncle Ernie's Pancake House
S: Bill Knapp's Restaurant (see our ad this page), Gum Ho Chinese, Olympia Family, Pizza King, Propeller Club (Economy Inn), Taco Bell, Theo & Stacy's Family Restaurant
Lodg N: Hampton Inn, Residence Inn
S: Economy Inn, Lee's Inn
AServ N: Allen's Service Center, Pete's B-Line Service, Uncle Ed's Oil Shoppe
S: Total
ATM N: Citgo, Old Kent
Parks N: Milham Park
Other S: Airport, Builder Square, On The Wings Market

80 Sprinkle Road, Cork St.
Gas N: Clark(*), Mobil(*, CW), Wesco(*, D)
S: Amoco(*, D, CW, 24), Speedway(*, D, LP, K)
Food N: Blimpie Subs & Salads (Mobil), Burger King, Cork 'N Cleaver Steak & Seafood, Denny's, Godfather's Pizza, Hot 'N Now Hamburgers, Perkins Family Restaurant, Pizza Hut (Clarion), Taco Bell
S: Country Kitchen, Holly's Landing (Holiday Inn), McDonald's
Lodg N: Clarion, Fairfield Inn, Kelly Inn Best Western, Red Roof Inn
S: Holiday Inn, Motel 6, Quality Inn & Suites
AServ N: D & S Auto Inc., Lentz Mufflers, Pennzoil Oil Change
ATM N: Old Kent
Other N: Car Wash, Sprinkle Road Veterinary Clinic
S: Continental Lanes Bowling

81 Jct. I-94 Bus. Loop 94, Downtown Calamazoo

(84) Rest Area (RR, Phones; Westbound)

85 35th Street
Gas N: Shell(*, CW, 24)
Food N: Burger King (Shell), McDonald's
AServ N: Boyd's Auto Sales
ATM N: Shell
Parks N: River Oaks Park

Bold red print shows RV & Bus parking available or nearby

EXIT MICHIGAN

Other N: Gillmore CCA Museum

88 Climax, Galesburg

92 Business Loop 94, Battle Creek, Springfield

TStop N: **Arlene's Truck Stop(*, D) (Citgo Gas)**
Gas N: Shell(*)
Food N: **Arlene's TS**
RVCamp N: **B & B's Camper Sales & RV Service, Ewing Motorhome & Trailer Sales(LP) (1.3 Miles)**
S: **Timberlake Camping**
ATM N: Shell
Parks N: **Fort Custer Recreation Area**
S: **Coldbrook Park, Scotts Mill Park (11 Miles)**

95 Helmer Road, Springfield

FStop N: **Marathon(*, D, K)**
Food N: Miller's Time-Out

(96) **Rest Area (RR, Phones, Picnic; Eastbound)**

97 Capital Ave

Gas N: Amoco(*, CW), Clark(*)
S: Shell(*, 24)
Food N: Arby's, Gary Field's Comedy Club Dining, Lone Star Steakhouse, McDonald's, Red Lobster, Welcome Inn Family Restaurant
S: Bill Knapp's Restaurant, **Bob Evan's Restaurant**, Burger King, Canton Buffet, **Cracker Barrel**, Denny's, Donut Mill, Fazoli's Italian Food, **Little Caesars Pizza (K-Mart)**, Pizza Hut, Seasoned Skillet Restaurant, Subway, **Taco Bell**, Wendy's
Lodg N: Holiday Inn Express, **Knight's Inn**
S: Battle Creek Inn, Budgetel Inn, Days Inn, Hampton Inn, Motel 6, Super 8
AServ S: Goodyear Tire & Auto, Uncle Ed's Oil Shop
ATM N: Amoco, Clark, First of America
Other S: Coin Car Wash, **K-Mart**, Mission Car Wash, **Van Horn's Market**

98AB MI 66, Sturgis, Downtown Battle Creek

Gas S: Citgo(*, CW)
Food S: Applebee's, Blimpie's Subs (Citgo), Don Pablo's Mexican Kitchen, **McDonald's (Wal-Mart)**, **Old Country Buffet**, Schlotzsky's Deli, Steak 'N Shake, TCBY (Citgo)
AServ S: Firestone Tire & Auto, **Sears**, **Wal-Mart(RX) (Optical)**
ATM S: Citgo, **Felpausch Food Store(24, RX)**
Other S: **Binder Park Zoo**, **Felpausch Food Store(RX)**, **Lakeview Square Mall**, **Sam's Club**, Sears Optical, **TJ Maxx**, **Target**, **Wal-Mart(RX) (Optical)**

100 Beadle Lake Road

Gas S: Jim Hazel's Citgo(D)
Food N: **Moonraker**
AServ S: Jim Hazel's Citgo
RVCamp N: **Camping**, **Murphy's Trailer Rental & Sales, Inc.(LP) (1.3 Miles)**
Parks S: **Binder Park**
Other S: **Binder Park Zoo**, **Warehouse Market**

103 Bus. Loop 94, Battle Creek

104 11 Mile Road, Michigan Ave.

TStop N: **Te-Khi Truck Stop(*, D, SCALES, 24) (Phillips 66)**
FStop N: **Total(*, D, LP)**
S: **Mobil(*, D)**
Food N: **Four Seasons Restaurant (Te-Khi TS)**, **Taco Bell (Total FS)**
S: **Roadrunner Restaurant (Quality Inn)**, **Subway (Mobil)**
Lodg S: **Quality Inn & Suites**
Other N: **C.O. Brown Stadium**
S: **Wheatfield Market**

108 Junction I-69, U.S. 27, Lansing, Ft. Wayne

RVCamp S: **Marshall RV Sales & Service(LP) (2.2 Miles)**

110 Old 27

TStop N: **Shell(*, D, 24)**
Food N: Hillcrest Coffee Shop(24), **Subway (Shell)**
Med S: **+ Hospital**

112 Marshall, Bus. Loop 94

Gas S: Shell(*, 24)
AServ S: Shell(24)

(113) **Rest Area (RR, Phones; Westbound)**

115 22 1/2 Mile Road

TStop N: **115 Truck Stop(*, D, LP) (Total Gas)**
Food N: **115 Truck Stop (Total Gas)**, **115 Truck Stop Restaurant**

119 26 Mile Road

Other N: Tomac Woods Golf Course

121 28 Mile Rd.

Gas N: Mobil(*)
S: Amoco(*, D, LP, CW, 24), Shell(*, K, CW), Speedway(*, D, LP, K)
Food S: A & W Drive-In, **Big Boy**, **Burger King**, Frosty Dan's, KFC, McDonald's, Paradise Inn Chinese, **Pizza Hut**, Ponderosa Steakhouse, Taystee Bakery Outlet
Lodg S: **Adams Arms Best Western**
AServ S: Albion Ford/ Mercury, Albion Tire City, Auto Zone Auto Parts, Bob Frahm GMC, Chevrolet, Buick, Pontiac
RVCamp N: **Camping**
ATM S: Chemical Bank South, Great Lakes Bank Corp
Other S: Car Wash, **Felpausch Pharmacy(RX)**, **Felpausch Supermarket**, **K-Mart**, **Rite Aid Pharmacy(RX)**, **Sears Optical**, **Stadium Plaza**

Bill Knapp's RESTAURANT
Open daily at 11:00 am
Bill Knapp's is a casual, full service family restaurant where Motorcoaches are always welcome.
Over 50 locations throughout: Michigan • Ohio • Indiana
517-783-2701 - Jackson
734-663-8579 - Ann Arbor
1692
MICHIGAN ▪ I-94 ▪ Exit 138/172

124 Michigan 99, Eaton Rapids, Bus. Loop 94, Albion

Other S: Country Bowling Lanes

127 Concord

Other S: **Harley's Antique**

128 Michigan Ave

FStop N: **Sunoco(*, D, LP, SCALES)**
Gas N: Pacific Pride Commercial Fueling(*, D, K) (Amoco)
Food N: **Burger King (Sunoco)**
RVCamp N: **Camping**
Other N: **Cracker Hill Antique**

130 Parma

FStop S: **Citgo(*, D, LP)**
Food S: **Cafe Cracker Hill (76 TS)**, **Citgo**
AServ N: Oil Zone

133 Dearing Road, Spring Arbor

(135) **Rest Area (RR, Phones; Eastbound)**

136 MI. 60, Spring Arbor

137 Airport Road

Gas N: Meijer(*, D, LP, K)
S: Standard(*, CW, 24)
Food N: **Burger King**, **Denny's**, Hot 'n Now Hamburgers, McDonald's, Subway, Wendy's
S: **Cracker Barrel**, **Lone Star Steakhouse**, Olive Garden
AServ N: Lenz Mufflers, Magic Mit Car Wash, **Performance Automotive & Transmission(LP)**
S: **K-Mart(RX)**, **Sam's Club**
RVCamp N: **Lee Truck Service RV Sales & Service**
ATM N: Comerica, Michigan National Bank, Standard Federal
Other N: Coin Laundromat(*), **Meijer Superstore(24)**, Paul's Auto Wash, Union Vision Center Plus
S: **K-Mart(RX)**, **Sam's Club**

138 U.S. 127 North, MI 50, Lansing, Jackson (Difficult Reaccess)

Gas S: Marathon(*, D, K), Shell(*, D, 24)
Food N: **Bill Knapp's (see our ad this page)**, **Gilbert's**, **Red Lobster**, Yen King
S: **Bob Evan's Restaurant**, Davis' Restaurant, **Fazoli's Italian Food**, Ground Round Restaurant, **Old Country Buffet**, **Outback Steakhouse**
Lodg N: Budgetel Inn, Fairfield Inn, Hampton Inn, **Holiday Inn**, Super 8
S: Best Motel, Country Hearth, Motel 6
AServ S: Meineke Discount Mufflers, **Sears**
ATM S: Flag Star Bank, Shell

Bold red print shows RV & Bus parking available or nearby

EXIT		MICHIGAN
	Parks	S: **Cascade Falls Park, Ella Sharp Park**
	Other	N: America's Physique Sports Club, **Clinton Trail Animal Hospital**
		S: **Jackson Crossing Mall, Jackson West Mall, Target**
139		MI 106, Downtown Jackson, Cooper Street
	Gas	S: Citgo[*]
	Food	S: Cherry's Cafe, Dunkin Donuts (Citgo), Mama J's Deli
	Med	S: + **Hospital**
	ATM	S: Citgo
	Other	N: Pacific Pride Commercial Fueling[D]
		S: **Bowlorama**
141		Elm Road
	Lodg	N: **TraveLodge**
	AServ	N: Extreme Dodge
	Med	S: + **Hospital**
142		U.S. 127 South, Hudson
144		Bus. Loop Jackson (Difficult Reaccess)
145		Sargent Rd.
	TStop	S: **Citgo**[*, D, SCALES, 24]
	Gas	S: Sunoco[*, 24]
	Food	S: **145 Restaurant (Citgo TS)**, Anchor Freeze Ice Cream, **Citgo**, Jackson Brewing Co., **McDonald's, Richard's Restaurant**[24], White Castle Restaurant (Sunoco)
	Lodg	S: Colonial Inn
	RVCamp	S: **Camping**
	ATM	S: **Citgo**
147		Race Road (Difficult Reaccess)
	RVCamp	N: **Oaks Camping, Sherwood Forest Camp**
		S: **Greenwood Acres**
	Parks	N: **Waterloo Recreation Area**
	Other	N: **White Tail Deer Museum**
(149)		**Rest Area (RR, Phones; Westbound)**
150		Grass Lake
	RVCamp	S: **Camping**
(151)		**Weigh Station (Eastbound)**
(151)		**Weigh Station (Westbound)**
153		Clear Lake Road
	Gas	N: Total[*, D, LP, K]
156		Kalmbach Road
	Parks	N: **Waterloo Recreation Area**
157		Old U.S.12, Pierce Road
159		MI 52, Chelsea, Manchester
	Gas	N: Amoco[*, D, CW], Mobil[*, LP, CW]
	Food	N: A & W Hot Dogs & More, Big Boy, McDonald's[PLAY], Schumm's Restaurant, **Taco Bell**
	AServ	N: Amoco, Faist Morrow Buick, Chevrolet, Oldsmobile, Palmer Ford
	RVCamp	N: **Lloyd Bridges Sales, Rental, Service & Parts**
	Med	N: + **Hospital**
	ATM	N: Amoco, Key Bank
162		Old US 12, Jackson Road, Fletcher Rd.
	FStop	S: **Clark**[*, D]
	Food	S: Stivers, **Subway (Clark)**
167		Baker Road, Dexter
	TStop	S: **76 Auto/Truck Plaza**[*, SCALES]
	FStop	N: **Speedway**[*]
		S: **Pilot Travel Center**[*, D, K, SCALES]
	Food	S: **76 Auto/Truck Plaza, Wolverine's (76 TS)**
	TServ	S: **76 Auto/Truck Plaza**[SCALES]
	TWash	S: **Blue Beacon Truck Wash**
	ATM	N: **Speedway**
		S: **Pilot Travel Center**
(168)		**Rest Area (RR, Phones; Eastbound)**

EXIT		MICHIGAN
169		Zeeb Road
	Gas	N: Amoco[*, 24]
		S: Mobil[*]
	Food	N: Baxter's Party Store & Deli, **McDonald's**
		S: Arby's, **Banfield's Westside**, Burger King, Domino's Pizza, Pizza Hut, Subway, Taco Bell, Wendy's, Yesterday's Collection Dairy Bar
	AServ	N: Amoco[24]
		S: Mobil
	ATM	S: First of America
	Other	S: Main Stream Car Wash
171		MI 14, Plymouth (Eastbound, Left Exit)
172		Jackson Ave.
	Gas	N: Amoco[*, 24], Marathon[*], Shell[*, CW, 24]
	Food	N: Amoco, Barry Bagels, Bill Knapp's Restaurant, **Golden Chef**, Joanna's Coffee, KFC, **Mountain Jack's Steakhouse**, Schlotzsky's Deli, Shell, **Village Kitchen Restaurant**
		S: City Limits (Clarion), Wall Street
	Lodg	S: Clarion (see our ad this page), Michigan Inn
	AServ	N: Amoco[24], Ann Arbor Muffler, **Big K-Mart**, Midas Muffler & Brake
		S: Muffler Man
	Med	S: + **Hospital**
	ATM	N: First of America, NBD, Standard Federal
	Other	N: **Big K-Mart, Rite Aid Pharmacy**[RX], Veterans Park Sports Complex, **Village Pharmacy**[RX]
		S: **Super Suds Laundry**
175		Ann Arbor, Saline Road
	Gas	N: Shell[*, CW, 24]
		S: **Meijer Superstore**[*, D, LP, K, 24, RX]
	Food	N: Applebee's, Lone Star Steakhouse, Old Country Buffet, Paradise Asain Cuisine
		S: Big Boy, McDonald's, **Outback Steakhouse**, T.G.I. Friday's
	ATM	N: Old Kent
	Other	N: **Colonnade Shopping Center, Cranbrook Village, Parkway Animal Clinic**
		S: **Meijer Superstore**[RX], **Oak Valley Center Mall, Target**
177		State Rd
	Gas	N: Amoco[*, CW], Mobil[*]
		S: Clark[*, D]
	Food	N: Azure Mediterranean Grill, Bennigan's, Bill Knapp's Restaurant (Best Western), Bombay Bicycle Club, Burger King, **Crowne Plaza, Graham's Steakhouse (Crowne Plaza)**, KFC,

1100

Clarion Hotel

Exit 172 • Ann Arbor, MI

734-665-4444

- Restaurant on Premises
- Cocktail Lounge
- Indoor & Outdoor Pool
- Meeting Banquet Facilities
- Sauna, Whirlpool & Exercise Room
- AARP Discounts

AAA ◆◆◆

MICHIGAN • I-94 • EXIT 172

CAMPING WORLD®

Exit 190

43646 I-94 Service Dr. • Belleville, MI
1-800-446-8929

1415

EXIT		MICHIGAN
		Romano's Macaroni's Grill, Seoul Garden, Tim Horton's Coffee & Baked Goods, Wendy's
		S: **Chi-Chi's Mexican Restaurant**, Mark's Midtown Coney Island, McDonald's, Taco Bell
	Lodg	N: Courtyard by Marriott, **Crowne Plaza**, Fairfield Inn, Hampton Inn, Residence Inn, Sheraton Inn, Studio PLUS, Wolverine Inn Best Western
		S: Motel 6
	AServ	N: Amoco, Sears
		S: Clark
	Med	N: + **Hospital**
	ATM	N: Amoco, Comerica Bank
		S: Key Bank
	Other	N: **Briarwood Mall**
180A		U.S. 23 South, Toledo, Flint
180B		Bus. Loop 94, U.S. 24, Ann Arbor
181AB		Michigan Ave, U.S. 12 West, Saline
	Gas	N: Speedway[*], Total[*, D]
	Food	N: **Burger King**, Joe's Pizza, Taco Bell
	AServ	N: Firestone Tire & Auto, Victory Lane Oil Changes
	Med	N: + **Hospital**
	ATM	N: 7-11 Convenience Store, Standard Federal, Total
	Other	N: 7-11 Convenience Store, **Busch's Valu-Land Supermarket, Coin Laundry**, Mr. Goofy's Car Wash, Pearl Vision Center, Rain Station Car Wash, **Rite Aid Pharmacy**[RX], **Wal-Mart**[RX]
183		Business U.S. 12, Huron St, Downtown Ypsilanti
	Gas	N: BP[*, D, K]
	Food	N: Hawkins BBQ, Judges Fish, Chicken, & Ribs
		S: Bentley's (Marriott), **McDonald's**
	Lodg	S: **Marriott**
	Med	N: + **Hospital**
	ATM	N: BP
	Parks	S: **North Bay Park, Rolling Hills County Park (3.5 Miles)**
	Other	N: **Joe's Market**
		S: Eagle Crest Golf Club, **State Police**
185		U.S. 12, Michigan Ave, Willow Run Airport (Eastbound)
186		Willow Run Airport
	Other	N: Willow Run Airport
187		Rawsonville Road
	Gas	S: Mobil[*, D], Speedway[*, D, LP]
	Food	S: Burger King, **Denny's**, KFC, Little Caesars Pizza, **Lone Star Steakhouse**, Maria's Pizzeria, McDonald's[PLAY], Pearl River Restaurant, **Pizza Hut**, Tom Horton's[24], Wendy's
	RVCamp	S: **KOA Camping**
	ATM	S: First of America, NBD
	Other	S: DOC Optical, **K-Mart Supercenter**[RX], Mr. Bubble Car Wash, Petland, **Rite Aid Pharmacy**[RX]
(188)		**Rest Area (RR, Phones, Picnic; Westbound)**
190		Belleville Road, Belleville
	Gas	N: Amoco[*, CW, 24], Marathon[*]
		S: Shell[*, 24]
	Food	N: Bamboo Garden Chinese, **Big Boy, Cracker Barrel**, Hungry Howie's Pizza, **McDonald's**, Taco Bell, **Tin Lizzie Casual Dining**, Wendy's
		S: Burger King, China King, Demetri's Kitchen, Domino's Pizza, Dos Pesos, Subway, Uncle Joe's Coney Island
	Lodg	N: Red Roof Inn
		S: Super 8
	AServ	N: Auto Works, Express Tire, Lube Stop Penzoil 10 Minute Oil Change, Marathon
	RVCamp	N: **Camping World (.85 Miles) (see our ad this page), Hitch 'n Post, Wayne County Fairgrounds (.25 Miles)**

Bold red print shows RV & Bus parking available or nearby

EXIT MICHIGAN

ATM **N:** Amoco
S: Comerica Bank, Shell
Other **N:** Arbor Drugs(RX), Farmer Jack Grocery, Vision Center
S: Belle Coin Laundry, Lodge Lane, Optum Eyes, Seed Rite's Pet Warehouse, U.S. Post Office

192 Haggerty Road
Gas **N:** Mobil(*)
ATM **N:** NBD
Parks **S:** French Landing Historical Park, Lower Huron Metro Park

194AB Junction I-275S., Toledo, Flint

196 Romulus, Wayne
Gas **N:** Shell(*, CW)
S: Mobil(*, D, K), Total(*)
Food **N:** McDonald's
S: Burger King
AServ **N:** Shell
ATM **N:** First of America
Other **S:** Wonder Hostess Bakery & Thrift Shop

197 Vining Rd. (Road Closed to the South)

198B Merriman Rd.
Gas **N:** Total(*)
S: BP(*, D)
Food **N:** Big Boy, Bob Evan's Restaurant, Hilton Suites, Merriman Street Grill, Poms Cafe & Lounge (Clarion Hotel), Subway, Toarmina's Pizza
Lodg **N:** Budgetel Inn, Clarion Hotel, Comfort Inn, Courtyard by Marriott, Crowne Plaza, DoubleTree Hotel, Fairfield Inn, Hampton Inn, Hilton Suites, Marriott, Quality Inn, Ramada Inn, Relax Inn, Shoney's Inn, TraveLodge, Wyndham Garden Hotel
Other **S:** Detroit Airport

198A Metropolitan Airport, Middlebelt
Gas **N:** Citgo(*, D)
S: Amoco(*, D, 24)
Food **N:** Tim Horton's Coffee & Baked Goods(24)
S: Days Inn, Denny's, McDonald's, Rally's Hamburgers, Red Lion (Days Inn), Wendy's
Lodg **N:** Clarioin Hotel (see our ad this page)
S: Days Inn, Howard Johnson, Super 8
Other **S:** Airport

200 Ecorse Road, Inkster
TStop **N:** Marathon(*, D, SCALES, 24)
Gas **S:** BP(*, D, K, 24), Speedway(*)
Food **N:** Granny's Home Cooking (Marathon)
S: Ice Cream Place, Webster's BBQ
AServ **N:** Tommy Tire Co.
S: Forrest Collision, Rainbow Brake
TServ **N:** Tommy Tire Co.
Other **N:** Propane Service(LP)

202AB U.S. 24, Telegraph Road
Gas **N:** Clark(*)
S: Total(*)
Food **N:** Andoni's Family Dining, Burger King, Ruberto's Bakery, Subway
Lodg **S:** Skyline Inn
Other **N:** Aldi, Rite Aid Pharmacy(RX), Rossoni's Animal Hospital

204 Southfield Freeway, MI 39, Pelham Road

206AB Oakwood Blvd, Melvindale
Gas **N:** Marathon(*)
S: BP(*, D)
Food **N:** Oakwood Exit
Lodg **S:** Best Western
AServ **S:** Penske
Parks **N:** Henry Ford Museum & Greenfield Village

208 Schaefer Road
Food **S:** Bill Knapp's Restaurant (see our ad this page)

EXIT MICHIGAN

209 Rotunda Dr
Food **N:** Bill Knapp's Restaurant (see our ad this page)
Parks **N:** Rotunda Field

210A U.S. 12, Michigan Ave
Gas **N:** Marathon(*), Sunoco(*, D, K, 24)
S: Amoco(D, 24), BP(*, D)
Food **N:** Big Boy Elias Brother's, Cafe Chablis, KFC, La-Shish
S: Yum Yum Donuts(24)
Lodg **N:** Days Inn
S: Star Motel
AServ **N:** Danny's Auto Center, Marathon
S: M & K Auto Repair
Med **S:** ✚ Oakwood Health Care Center
ATM **N:** Marathon, Sunoco
S: Amoco
Other **N:** Fairlane Car Wash

210B Addison Ave, MI 153, Ford Rd (Reaccess Eastbound Only, Difficult Reaccess)
Food **S:** Desoto Inn, Lavella Pizza, Paul's Coney Island, Zenith Coney Island Restaurant
AServ **S:** Aoude Car Center, House of Cars, Lee's Brake & Exhaust, Sam's Motors
Other **S:** Di & Di Pet Supplies, Rainbow Laundry Center

211A Lonyo Ave (Reaccess Eastbound Only)
Gas **S:** 76(*, D, 24), Sunoco(*)
Food **S:** Sunflower Pizza
AServ **S:** Carmack's Collision, Ed Collins Motor Sales(CW), Jorgensen Ford, Royal Collision, Sunoco
Other **S:** Power Shower Car Wash

211B Cecil Ave, Central Ave (Reaccess Eastbound Only)
Food **S:** Church's Chicken, Jordan's Family Restaurant, McDonald's, Rally's Hamburgers
AServ **S:** Regal Auto Care
Other **S:** Arbor Drugs(RX)

212A Livernois Ave
Gas **N:** US(*)
S: BP(*, D), Marathon

EXIT MICHIGAN

Food **S:** Pizza & Pita
AServ **S:** B & B Tire & Wheels, Kar-Life Battery Company
ATM **N:** Livernois McGraw Market
Other **N:** Livernois McGraw Market
S: Bi-Rite Auto Parts

212B Warren Ave

213A West Grand Blvd, Warren Ave
Gas **S:** 76
Other **N:** Pay Lo Food Center
S: Yellow Ethel Food Center

213B Junction I-96

214 Grand River Ave, Linwood Ave
Food **S:** Oscar's Coney Island Restaurant
Other **S:** Best Hand Car Wash

214B Trumbull Ave (Hospital)

215AB MI 10, Lodge Freeway

215C MI 1, Woodward Ave, Brush St

216A Junction I-75, Chrysler Fwy, Flint

216B Russell St

217B Mount Elliott Dr

217A Mount Elliot Ave, East Brand Ave, Chene St.
Gas **S:** Mobil(*), Shell(*)
Food **S:** KFC (Taco Bell), Legends Coney Island Restaurant, Taco Bell

218 Van Dyke Ave, MI 53
Gas **N:** Amoco(*), BP(*, D)
S: Shell
Food **N:** Sandwich Shop
AServ **S:** Shell

219 MI 3, Gratiot Ave
Gas **S:** BP(*, K, 24)
Food **N:** Coney Island, Elmo's Fine Food, KFC
S: Burger King
Other **N:** Farmer Jack Grocery

220A French Road
Gas **S:** Shell(*, 24)

220B Conner Ave, City Airport
Gas **N:** BP(*), Marathon(*, CW)
Food **S:** R & G Pizza & Deli
AServ **N:** PAM Towing
Parks **S:** Chandler Park
Other **N:** Airport
S: Wayne County Community College

222A Outer Dr, Chalmers Ave
Gas **N:** Amoco(*), BP(*, D), Shell
Food **N:** Great China, Subway (BP), Universal Restaurant
AServ **N:** Shell
Other **N:** Clark's Car Wash

222B Harper Ave (Eastbound, Difficult Reaccess)
Food **S:** Golden Buddha
AServ **N:** Jiffy Car Wash, Perk's Auto Hand Wash
S: M&S Auto Repair
Other **S:** Hasting's Auto Parts

223 Cadieux Ave
Gas **S:** Amoco(*, 24), Citgo(*, D, K, 24), Mobil(*), Shell(*, 24), Sunoco(*, D)
Food **N:** GD Tubs Food
S: Boston Market Restaurant, McDonald's, Oliver's Pizza, Rally's Hamburgers, Tubby's Submarine, Wendy's
AServ **N:** Collision Custom Painting
S: Express Auto Service, Mobil
Other **S:** Dell Point Grocery, Rite Aide Pharmacy(*)

224A Moross Road

Bold red print shows RV & Bus parking available or nearby

EXIT MICHIGAN

Gas S: Shell[*, 24]
Food S: Dawn Donuts
Other S: **Farmer Jack Grocery**

224B Eastwood Drive, Allard Ave
Food N: Nona's Pizza
Other N: **Police Station**, Salter Memorial Park

225 MI 102, 8 Mile Road, Vernier Road (Difficult Reaccess)
Gas S: Mobil[*]
Food S: Frozen French Custard, KFC, Round Table, Wendy's
Other S: **Kroger Supermarket**, Mr. C's Car Wash

227 9 Mile Road, East Point
Gas N: Speedway[*, D], Sunoco[*, 24]
S: Mobil[*]
Food N: Dolly's Pizza
S: Shore Pointe Motor Lodge
Lodg S: Shore Pointe Motor Lodge
AServ N: Q Lube
S: Maaco, Ziebart
Other N: **Coin Laundry**, Eyeglass Factory, **F & M Drugstore**[24], **Farmer Jack Grocery**, Super Car Wash, **U.S. Post Office (Farmer Jack Grocery)**

228 10 Mile Road
Gas N: Shell[*, CW, 24]
Food N: 3D's Pizza, **East Wind Chinese**, Fairway Sports Bar & Grill, Friendly Family Restaurant, **Jet's Pizza**, **RJ's Vault Grill & Bar**
AServ N: Auto & Marine Parts
Other N: **Fairway Drugs**, **Pet Supply Store**

229 Junction I-696 West, 11 Mile Road, Lansing
Gas S: Total[LP]
AServ S: Moe's Service Center
Other S: 7-11 Convenience Store

230 12 Mile Road
Gas N: Marathon[*, D], Mobil[*, D]
S: Marathon[*]
Food N: **Burger King**, Dunkin Donuts, **Outback Steakhouse**, **Ram's Horn**
AServ N: Arnold Ford/Lincoln/Mercury, Arnold's Mazda
S: Marathon
Med N: ✚ **Elm Animal Hospital**
ATM N: **Farmer Jack Grocery**, Marathon, Mobil
Other N: **Arbor Drugs**, **Embassy Market**, **Farmer Jack Grocery**, Roseville Town Center, Shine Bright Auto Wash, **Super Petz**

231 Mi 3, Gratiot Ave (Eastbound, Left Exit Eastbound, Reaccess Westbound Only)
Gas N: Sunoco[CW]
Food N: **Applebee's**, Arby's, **Boston Market Restaurant**, **Denny's**, Frantone's Pizza, Pizza Hut, The Georgian Inn
AServ N: Consumer Tire, Sunoco

232 Little Mack Ave
Gas N: Speedway[*]
S: Amoco[*, 24], **Meijer Grocery**[*, D, LP, K], Total[*, D, LP]
Food N: Boardwalk (Eastin Hotel), **Chuck E Cheese's Pizza**, **Subway**
S: Chinese & American Cuisine, **Cracker Barrel**, **Bill Knapp's Restaurant (see our ad this page)**, Dunkin Donuts (Amoco), IHOP
Lodg N: **Eastin Hotel**, **Econolodge**, **Red Roof Inn**, Super 8
S: Budgetel Inn
AServ S: **K-Mart**[RX]
Other N: Emerald Green Championship Mini Golf, **Farmer Jack Grocery**, **Macomb Mall**, **Murray's Discount Auto Store**, **Sams Club**
S: **Home Depot**, **K-Mart**[RX], **PetsMart**

234AB Harper Ave
Gas N: Amoco[*], Speedway[*, LP], Speedy Q Mart[*, K], Sunoco[*, LP, K, 24]
Food N: Carmen's Deli & Pizza, McDonald's (Amoco), Mrs. Robinson's Diner, Sorrento Pizza, Teddy's Tavern
S: China Moon, Golden Donuts, Little Caesars Pizza, Sub Company, Subway, Travis Restaurant, **Winner's Sports Cafe**
AServ N: Graphic Auto Care, Jiffy Lube
Med N: ✚ **Hospital**, ✚ **Patterson's Veterinary Hospital**
S: ✚ **Convenient Walk-in Clinic**
ATM S: Old Kent Bank
Other N: Car Wash, **Police Department**, **Sandy's Coin Laundry**, Skateland
S: CK Car Wash[24]

235 Shook Rd. (Westbound, Reaccess Eastbound Only)

236 Metropolitan Parkway
Gas N: Amoco[CW], Marathon, Mobil
Food N: Firehouse Pizza & Ribs, Ram's Horn
S: Fong's Chinese, Little Caesars Pizza, **McDonald's**, Subway
AServ N: Amoco, Marathon, Mr. Muffler, New Car Finish, Oil Change
Med S: ✚ **Hospital**
Other N: **Farmer Jack Grocery**
S: **Arbor Drugs**, **Kroger Supermarket**, **Sear's Hardware**

237 North River Road, Mount Clemens
Gas N: **Amoco**[*, D], **Mobil**[*, D]
Food N: River House, Subway (Mobil)
Med N: ✚ **Car Wash**
Other S: **The Captains Convenience Store**

240 MI 59, Utica, Self Ridge ANG (Eastbound, Reaccess Westbound Only, Exit under construction)

241 21 Mile Road, Selfridge
Gas N: Marathon[*, D], Shell[D]
Food N: Chicago Joe's Pizza, Country Style Bakery & Deli, Hungry Howie's Pizza, Leong's Chinese, Pida Jack's, Pizza N' More, Subway, Travis Restaurant, Vinyard's Galeon Pub
S: **Sugarbush**
AServ N: Chesterfield Auto Wash
Med N: ✚ **Veterinary Hospital**
ATM N: Old Kent Bank

243 MI 3, MI 29, MI 59, Utica, New Baltimore
FStop S: **Speedway**[*, D, LP, K]
Gas N: Citgo[*, D, K], **Meijer Grocery**[D, 24, RX], Shell[D]
S: Mobil[*, D]
Food N: Applebee's, Arby's, Baskin Robbins, **Burger King**, Church's Chicken (White Castle), **Father & Son Pizzeria**, Guss's Coney Island, **Horn of Plenty**[RX], Le Grand Chinese Buffet, Little Caesars Pizza, McDonald's, Papa Ramano's Pizza, **Ponderosa**, **Wendy's**, White Castle Restaurant
S: Big Boy, Buscemis, Hot 'N Now, TCBY (Mobil), Taco Bell
Lodg N: Chesterfield Motor Inn
S: **Lodge Keeper**
AServ N: Auto Quest Collision, Discount Tires, Jiffy Lube, **K-Mart**[RX], Madison Starter, Alternator, & Batteries, Midas Muffler & Brake, **NTB**
S: Mobil
ATM N: Citgo, **Farmer Jack Grocery**, Huntington Bank
Other N: Clearview Car Wash[SCALES], DOC Optical, **Farmer Jack Grocery**, **K-Mart**[RX], **Meijer Grocery**[RX], Murray's Auto Supplies, **Pet Supplies Plus**, **Rite Aide Pharmacy**, Sandbaggers Golf Center, **Sear's Hardware**, **Staples Office Superstore**, **Target**, WalGreens Pharmacy
S: Auto SPA Car Wash

Bill Knapp's RESTAURANT
Open daily at 11:00 am
Bill Knapp's is a casual, full service family restaurant where Motorcoaches are always welcome.
1694
Over 50 locations throughout: Michigan • Ohio • Indiana
810-294-4970 - Roseville
MICHIGAN • I-94 • EXIT 232

(246) **Weigh Station**

247 MI 19, Richmond, New Haven (Eastbound, Reaccess Westbound Only)

248 26 Mile Road, Marine City
Food S: My Place Coffee Donut Shop
Other N: Marsh Oaks Golf Course (Restaurant)
S: Cedar Glen Golf Course (Restaurant)

250 **Rest Area (RR, Phones, Picnic, Vending)**

255 **Rest Area (RR, Phones, Picnic, Vending; Eastbound)**

257 St Clair, Richmond
FStop N: **BP**[D, LP]
AServ N: **Schantz's Repair Services**
ATM N: **BP**
Other N: Golf Course, **State Police**

262 Wadhams Road
FStop S: **Total**[*, D, LP, SCALES]
Food S: Road Hawk (Total)
RVCamp N: **Camping**
ATM S: **Total**
Other N: Riding Stables

266 I-94 Loop, Gratiot Road, Marysville
FStop N: **Amoco**[*, D, SCALES, 24]
Food N: **Burger King**, Mancino's Pizza & Grinders
S: **China Lite**, Hungry Howie's Pizza, Oliver's Pizza (Carter's Grocery)
AServ N: **Amoco**[24], B & H Towing, Venus Body Shop
S: **Marysville Tire & Auto Center**
TServ N: **Marysville Truck Equipment**, **Rush Trucking**
Med S: ✚ **Hospital**, ✚ **Marysville Community Health Center**
ATM N: **Amoco**
S: **Carter's Grocery**[24], Old Kent Bank
Other N: SVS Vision, **Sear's Grocery**
S: Arbor Drugs, **Carter's Grocery**, Classic Pet Supply, Performance Car Wash

269 Range Road
Gas N: **Total**[*, D, CW]
Food N: **Burger King**, **Subway (Total)**
Lodg N: **AmeriHost Inn**
ATM N: **Total**
Other N: **Horizon Outlet Center**

271 Junction I-69

274 **Water St, Welcome Center**
FStop S: **By-Lo Convenience Store**[*, LP]
Gas S: **By-Lo Convenience Store**[*], Total[*, D]
Food N: **Cracker Barrel (On Water St)**
S: **Bob Evan's Restaurant**, Taco Bell (Total)
Lodg S: Comfort Inn, Fairfield Inn, Hampton Inn, Knight's Inn
RVCamp N: **Campground**
ATM S: Total
Parks S: **City of Port Huron Municipile Marina**
Other S: Tom & Jerry's Party Store[*]

↑MICHIGAN

Begin I-94

Bold red print shows RV & Bus parking available or nearby

EXIT | MAINE

Begin I-95

↓MAINE

63 **(298)** U.S. 2, Houlton International Airport, Industrial Park (Northbound Only To Can, Southbound To I-95)
- TServ E: **Shannon's Repair**

62 **(295)** U.S. 1, Houlton, Presque Isle, Rest Area (RR, Phones, Picnic)
- TStop W: **Irving Truckstop**(*, LP, SCALES)
- FStop W: **Citgo**(*, D)
- Gas E: Irving(*, D, 24)
- W: **Exxon**(D, LP)
- Food E: Burger King, Calnan's Mixed Cuisine, KFC, Little Caesars Pizza, **McDonald's**, Pizza Hut, Sing Wah Chinese
- W: Shiretown Motor Inn, York's Dairy Bar
- Lodg W: **Ivey's Motor Lodge**, Shiretown Motor Inn
- AServ E: Brake Service and Parts Inc, VIP Discount Auto Center, Varney's Auto Supply
- W: Northland Motors Nissan, Chrys, Plym, Dodge, Jeep, Eagle, York's Auto Dealership
- TServ W: **Irving Truckstop**(SCALES)
- RVCamp W: **My Brothers Place (2 Miles)**
- Med E: **✚ Hospital**
- W: **✚ Optometrist**
- ATM E: First Citizen's Bank, Irving, Katahdin Trust Company, **Rite-Aid Pharmacy**(RX)
- W: **Citgo, Exxon, Irving Truckstop**
- Other E: Andy's Foodliner, **Rite-Aid Pharmacy**(RX)
- W: **Shop & Save, Wal-Mart**(RX)

61 **(284)** U.S. 2, Smyrna
- Food E: Brookside Motel
- Lodg E: Brookside Motel

60 **(279)** Oakfield, Smyrna Mills, Dyerbrook
- FStop W: **Mobil**(*, D)
- Gas W: Irving(*, D)
- Food W: Country Plasa, Crossroads Cafe, Houlton Farms Dairy Bar
- ATM W: Katahdin Trust Company
- Other W: **Coin Laundry, U.S. Post Office**

59 **(269)** Baxter State Park North Entrance, ME 159, Island Falls, Patten
- FStop E: **Mobil**(*, LP, CW)
- Gas E: Citgo(*)
- Food E: Pipe's Family Restaurant
- TServ E: **Mobil**
- RVCamp E: **Campground**
- Parks W: **Baxter State Park**
- Other E: **Bishop's Market**, Doc Heating Oil(LP)

58 **(257)** ME 11, ME 158, Shermon, Patten
- FStop E: **Mobil**(D, LP, 24)
- W: **Irving**(*)
- Food E: **Mobil**
- W: **Irving**, Shermon Dairy Bar
- Lodg W: Katahdin Valley Motel
- AServ W: Tom's Garage
- Parks W: **Baxter State Park**

57 **(252)** Benedicta (Reaccess Southbound Only)

(245) Scenic View (Picnic; Northbound)

56 **(237)** ME 157, Millinocket, Mattawamkeag
- TStop W: **Irving Truckstop**(*, D, 24)
- Food W: **Irving Truckstop**
- Lodg W: Gateway Inn
- TServ W: **Timberland Truck Brokers**
- RVCamp W: **D & M Trailer Sales, Katahdin Shadows Campground (1.5 Miles), Pine Grove Campground**
- Med W: **✚ Hospital**

(237) Rest Area (RR, Picnic, Grills)

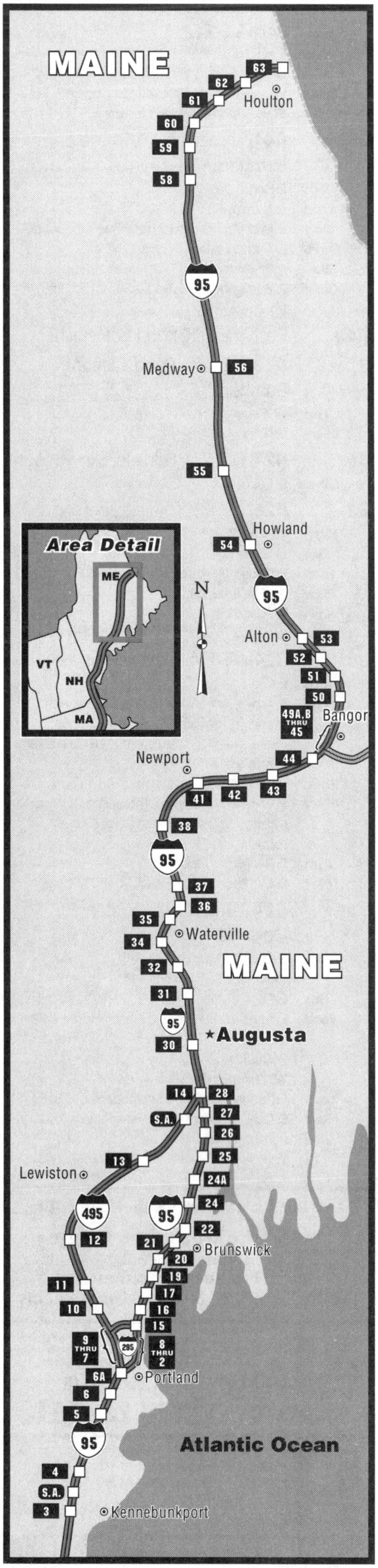

55 **(221)** To U.S. 2, ME 6, ME 116, Lincoln
- RVCamp E: **Campground**
- Med E: **✚ Hospital**

54 **(210)** ME 6, ME 155, Howland, LaGrange, Enfield, Milo
- Gas E: Irving(*)
- Food E: DJ's Ice Cream Parlor, Irving
- AServ E: 95er Towing Service
- RVCamp E: **King's Camping Park**

53 **(193)** ME 16, LaGrange, Milo (Northbound, Reaccess Southbound Only)

(192) Weigh Station (Both Directions, Closed)

52 **(190)** ME 43, Old Town, Hudson

51 **(186)** Stillwater Ave, Orono
- Gas E: Citgo(*, D), Irving(*, D, 24), Texaco(*, D)
- Food E: Burger King, Subway
- Lodg E: Best Western
- Med E: **✚ Dentist, ✚ Optometrist**
- ATM E: Citgo, Irving
- Other W: Dunn's Recreational Center

50 **(184)** Kelly Road, Veazie

49 **(181)** Hogan Road, Korean War Memorial, EM Technical College
- Gas E: Citgo(*)
- W: Citgo(*, D, CW), Exxon(LP, CW)
- Food W: Arby's, Asian Palace, Bonanza Restaurant, Bug-A-Boo Creek Steakhouse, Burger King, China Wall, Colonial House of Pancakes, KFC, **Little Caesars Pizza (K-Mart), McDonald's (Wal-Mart)**, McDonald's(PLAY), Mr. Bagel, Olive Garden, Paul's Speak Easy Restaurant, Pizza Hut, Red Lobster, TCBY, Wendy's
- Lodg W: Bangor Motor Inn, Comfort Inn, Country Inn, Hampton Inn
- AServ E: Bangor Chrys, Plym, Dodge, Bangor Ford & Volkswagon, Bangor Mitsubishi, Saab, Mercedes, Darlings Honda Nissan Dealer, **Sam's Club**, Saturn Dealership, Swetts Service Center (Citgo), Varney Izusu,GMC, Village Subaru, VillageTruck & Auto Center
- W: Goodyear Tire & Auto, **K-Mart**, McQuick's Oil Lube, Parts America, Sears, VIP Discount Auto Center, Van Syckle Ford, Lincoln
- TServ E: **Peterbilt Dealer**
- ATM E: Bangor Federal Credit Union
- W: Bangor Savings Bank, E. Maine Medical Center Credit Union, Fleet Bank, Key Bank, Merrill Merchants Bank, **Shaw's Grocery**
- Other E: **Sam's Club**
- W: Borders Books & Music, Coin Laundry, **K-Mart, Shaw's Grocery**, Super Shop & Save, **Wal-Mart**(RX)

48 **(179)** ME 15, Broadway, Bangor, Brewer
- Gas E: Irving(*)
- W: Exxon, Mobil(*), Texaco
- Food E: Tri-City Pizza
- W: BoBo Chinese, China Lite, Dairy Queen, Friendly's, Governor's Restaurant, KFC, King's Kitchen Chinese, Mama Valdacci's, McDonald's(PLAY), Pizza Hut
- AServ W: Exxon, Kelly Pontaic, Prompto Oil Lube, Texaco, Varney's Auto Supply
- Med E: **✚ St. Joseph Hospital**
- ATM W: Bangor Savings Bank, Christy's Convenience Store
- Other E: Larry Barron's Propane(LP)
- W: Christy's Convenience Store, **Rite Aid Pharmacy**(RX), Rite Aid Pharmacy(RX), **Super Shop &**

Bold red print shows RV & Bus parking available or nearby

EXIT MAINE

Save

47 **(178)** ME 222, Ohio St, Airport, Union St
- Gas: **E:** Citgo(*), Exxon(*); **W:** Exxon(CW), Texaco
- Food: **W:** Burger King, Dunkin Donuts, McDonald's(PLAY), Nicky's Diner, Papa Gino's Pizza, Wendy's
- AServ: **E:** Citgo; **W:** Midas Muffler, **R & M Towing**, Texaco
- TServ: **W: R & M Towing**
- RVCamp: **W: Campground**
- ATM: **E:** Exxon; **W:** Merrill Merchant Bank
- Other: **W:** Bus Station - Concord Trailways, Union Street Laundromat

46 **(177)** U.S. 2, ME 100, Hammond St, Airport
- Food: **E:** Napoli Pizza, Subway
- AServ: **E:** Auto Radiator Service, Gulf, NAPA Auto Parts
- ATM: **W:** Bangor Savings Bank
- Other: **E:** Corner Store

45AB **(176)** To East I-395 & U.S. 1A, to Memorial, to U.S. 2, to ME 100W, Hermon
- FStop: **W: Mobil**(*, CW)
- Gas: **W:** Irving(D, CW)
- Food: **W:** Barnaby's (Ramada Inn), Dunkin Donuts, Holiday Inn, Howard Johnson, Jason's New York Style Pizza, King Sub, Rodeway Inn, The Ground Round
- Lodg: **W:** DAYS INN Days Inn, Econolodge, Fairfield Inn, Holiday Inn, **Motel 6**, Ramada Inn, Rodeway Inn, Super 8
- AServ: **W:** Irving General Automotive, Stratham Tire, Tire Wharehouse
- TServ: **E: Whited Ford**
- RVCamp: **W: Campground**
- ATM: **W:** Fleet Bank, **Mobil**

44 **(173)** Cold Brook Road, Hermon, Hampden
- TStop: **W: Dysart's Truck Stop**(*, SCALES)
- FStop: **E: Citgo**(*)
- Lodg: **W:** Best Western
- TServ: **W: Dysart's, Howard Volvo Truck Center, International, Maine Mack Inc**
- ATM: **E: Citgo**

(172) Rest Area (RR, Phones, Picnic; Southbound)

(169) Rest Area (RR, Phones, Picnic; Northbound)

43 **(167)** ME 69, Carmel, Winterport
- Gas: **E:** Citgo(*, D)
- RVCamp: **W: Campground**

42 **(161)** ME 69, ME 143, Etna, Dixmont
- RVCamp: **W: Campground**

41 **(154)** ME 7, East Newport, Plymouth
- RVCamp: **W: Christie's Campground & Cottages**(LP) **(1.5 Miles)**

40 Ridge Road, Newport, Plymouth (Reaccess Northbound Only)

39 **(151)** ME 7, ME 11, ME 100, Newport, Dexter
- FStop: **W: Irving, Mobil**(*, D)
- Gas: **W:** Citgo(*)
- Food: **W:** China Way, Dunkin Donuts, **Irving**, McDonald's(PLAY), Pat's Pizza, Popeye's Chicken, Sawyer's Dairy Bar, Subway
- Lodg: **W:** Motel
- AServ: **W:** Big A Auto Parts, Car Quest Auto Parts, Hartley's Olds, GMC Trucks, Plym, Eagle, Dodge Trucks, Muffler King
- RVCamp: **W: Campground**
- Med: **E: + Hospital**
- ATM: **W:** Fleet Bank, **Irving**, Key Bank, **Mobil**
- Other: **W:** Mr Car Wash, **Rite Aid Pharmacy**(RX), **Shop 'N Save Supermarket, Wal-Mart**

38 **(144)** Somerset Ave, Pittsfield, Burnham
- Gas: **E:** Exit 38 Gas(*)
- Food: **E:** Subway
- AServ: **E:** Michelin Tire Service, Pine Tree Auto Supply
- RVCamp: **E: Campground**
- Med: **E: + Hospital**
- Other: **E: Bud's Shop 'N Save Supermarket, Rite Aid Pharmacy**(RX)

(141) Rest Area (RR, Phones, Picnic)

37 **(132)** Hinckley Road, Clinton, Burnham
- Gas: **W:** Citgo(*, D)
- AServ: **W:** Citgo

36 **(127)** U.S. 201, Fairfield, Skowhegan
- Other: **E:** Coin Car Wash, Coin Laundry

35 **(126)** ME 139, Fairfield, Benton
- FStop: **W: Citgo**(*, CW, SCALES)
- Gas: **E:** Texaco(*, LP)
- Food: **E:** Gene's Market & Deli (Texaco)
- TServ: **W: Tire & Repair**
- TWash: **W: Citgo**(CW)
- ATM: **W: Citgo**

34 **(124)** ME 104, Waterville, Winslow
- Gas: **E:** Citgo(*), Mobil(*)
- Food: **E:** Arby's, Armory Road Dairy Bar, Bagel Z, Friendly's, **K-Mart**, Killarney's (Holiay Inn), McDonald's(PLAY), The Governor's (Best Western), Wendy's
- Lodg: **E:** Best Western, Holiday Inn, The Atrium Motel
- AServ: **E:** Citgo, Parts America, Thompson VW/Audi/ Mazda, VIP Discount Auto Center, Xpress Lube(CW)
- ATM: **E:** Fleet Bank, Mobil
- Other: **E:** CVS Pharmacy, **K-Mart, Shop "N" Save**

33 **(121)** ME 11, ME 137, Waterville, Oakland
- FStop: **E: Irving**(*, 24); **W: Coastal**(*, LP), **Exxon**(*, D, LP)
- Gas: **E:** Citgo(*), Mobil(*, CW)
- Food: **E:** Angelo's, Burger King (Citgo), Classic Cafe (Budget Host Inn), Pizza Hut, Weathervane Restaurant; **W:** China Express, Pine Acres
- Lodg: **E:** Budget Host Inn, Econolodge, Motor Lodge
- AServ: **E:** Car Quest Auto Parts, Central Main Toyota, Pontiac, Buick, GMC Trucks; **W:** Pullen's Ford/Lincoln/Mercury, R & R Auto Parts
- RVCamp: **W: Mid-Maine Marine RV Repair**
- Med: **E: + Hospital**
- ATM: **E: Irving**
- Other: **E: Wal-Mart**(RX)

2 Locations on I-95 include these Amenities:

Full Service Restaurant & Lounge
Swimming Pool
Health Facilities • Spectra vision
Newly Renovated Spacious Guest Rooms

1572

Holiday Inn

Holiday Inn Civic Center
I-95 • Exit 31A
Augusta, ME
207-622-4751

Comfort Inn

I-95 • Exit 31B
Augusta, ME
207-623-1000

MAINE • I-95 • 2 LOCATIONS

32 **(114)** Lyons Road, Sidney

(110) Rest Area (RR, Phones, Picnic; Southbound)

(107) Rest Area (RR, Phones; Northbound)

31AB **(106)** ME 8, ME 11, ME 27, Augusta, Belgrade
- FStop: **W: Irving**(*, D)
- Gas: **E:** Citgo(*), Getty(*)
- Food: **E:** Captain Cotes Seafood, Olive Garden, TCBY (Getty), The Ground Round (Holiday Inn); **W:** Sally's Steakhouse (Comfort Inn), **Taco Bell (Irving)**
- Lodg: **E:** Holiday Inn (see our ad this page); **W:** Comfort Inn (see our ad this page)
- AServ: **W:** Davis Olds, Cad, Volvo, Mits
- RVCamp: **E: J & M Campers Sales & Service**(LP) **(1.8 Miles)**
- ATM: **E:** Augusta Federal Savings, Fleet Bank; **W: Irving**
- Other: **E:** Barnes & Noble, **Sam's Club, Wal-Mart**

30AB **(106)** U.S. 202, ME 100, ME 17, ME11, Augusta, Winthrop
- Gas: **E:** Citgo(*), Gulf(*), Irving(*), Texaco(*, LP); **W:** Exxon(*), Getty(*)
- Food: **E:** Arby's, Bagel Main & Deli, Best Western, Charlie's Pizza & More, Dairy Queen, Damon's Italian Sandwiches, Hong Kong Isle Chinese, Irving, KFC, McDonald's, Subway; **W:** Bonanza, Margarita's Mexican (Augusta Motel), Tea House Chinese
- Lodg: **E:** Best Western; **W:** Augusta Motel, Super 8, Susse Chalet Guest Lodge
- AServ: **E:** Citgo, Prompto Oil Lube; **W:** Blouin's Chrys, Plym, Dodge, Hyundai, Toyota, Charlie's KIA, Charlie's Motor Mall Mazda, Suz, Jeep, Eagle, Nissan, Exxon, Sears Auto Service
- ATM: **E:** Northeast Bank; **W:** Exxon, Key Bank(24)
- Other: **E:** Car Wash(CW); **W:** Car Quest Auto Parts, Shop "N" Save(24)

Exit **(100)** Jct. I-95 N & I-495N, Maine Tollway (Toll)

28 **(96)** ME 9, ME 126, Litchfield, Gardiner

27 **(94)** U.S. 201, Gardiner
- AServ: **E:** Daniel's Auto Service (Towing)

26 **(88)** ME 197, Richmond, Litchfield

25 **(81)** ME 125, ME 138, Bowdoinham, Bowdoin

24AB **(75)** ME 196, Topsham, Lisbon
- Gas: **E:** Exxon(*), Gibbs(*, D)
- Food: **E:** Arby's, Dunkin Donuts (Exxon), McDonald's, Romeo's Pizza
- AServ: **E:** Meineke Discount Mufflers, Tire Warehouse
- ATM: **E:** Coastal Bank, Five County Credit Union, Gardiner Savings Institution

EXIT MAINE

Other E: Rite Aid Pharmacy[RX], Shop & Save

22 **(72)** U.S. 1, Coastal Route, Brunswick, Bath (Eastbound)

Gas E: Citgo[*, D], Irving[*], Mobil[*, D]

Food E: Dunkin Donuts, Hong Kong Island, MacLean's, McDonald's

Lodg E: Comfort Inn, Econolodge

AServ E: Brunswick Ford, Goodwin's Chevrolet, Texaco Express Lube

RVCamp E: KOA Campgrounds

Med E: ✚ Hospital

21 **(68)** U.S. 1, Freeport (Reaccess Southbound Only, Difficult Reaccess)

20 **(66)** Bradbury Mt., Pownal, ME125, ME 136, Freeport

Gas E: Exxon[*]

Food E: McDonald's

Lodg E: Harraseeket Inn

RVCamp W: Cedar Haven Campground (1.75 Miles)

ATM E: Coastal Bank

Parks W: Bradbury State Park

Other E: Coin Laundry, St John's Federal Credit Union

19 **(65)** U.S. 1, Desert Road, Freeport

Gas E: Citgo[*]

Food E: Blue Onion, Domino's Pizza, Subway, Thai Garden

Lodg E: Coastline Inn, Dutch Village Motel, Super 8

AServ E: R & D Automotive

RVCamp W: Desert Dunes of Maine (2 Miles)

Other E: Freeport Car Wash

17 **(62)** U.S. 1, Yarmouth, Rest Area (RR, Phones, Picnic; Reaccess Northbound Only)

Gas W: Texaco[*, D, CW] (X-press Lube)

Food E: Day's

W: Bill's Pizza & Pasta, Down-East Village, McDonald's, Pat's Pizza, Royal River Natural Foods

Lodg W: Down-East Village, Red Wagon Motel

AServ E: Casco Bay Ford

W: Yarmouth Service Center & Auto

ATM W: Texaco (X-press Lube)

Other E: Tourist Info.

W: Car Quest Auto Center, Peoples Heritage Bank, Super Shop 'n Save, Yarmouth Animal Clinic

16 **(59)** U.S. 1, Cumberland, Yarmouth (Difficult Reaccess)

Gas W: Exxon[*], Mobil[*]

Food W: Birchwood Restaurant, Main Roaster's Coffee Shop, Mr Bagel, Romeo's Pizza, Sharon's Coffee Shop

Lodg W: Brookside Motel

AServ W: Exxon

ATM W: Bath Savings, Mobil

Other W: AAA Office, Bath Savings, Rite Aid Pharmacy[RX]

15 **(55)** U.S. 1, Falmouth

Gas E: Exxon[*, D], Gulf[CW], Mobil

Food E: Blue Island Restaurant & Lounge, Dunkin Donuts, Falmouth House of Pizza, McDonald's, Moose Crossing Fish & Steak, Mr Bagel, Subway

AServ E: Classic Oldsmobile, Cadillac, GMC Truck, Goodyear, Infiniti of Falmouth

ATM E: Key Bank

Other E: Rite Aid[RX], Shaw's Grocery

EXIT MAINE

Note: I-95 runs concurrent below with METNPK. Numbering follows METNPK.

14AB **(99)** Junction I-95 South, ME 9, ME 126

Exit **(98)** Toll Plaza (Toll)

(97) Service Area (Northbound)

FStop E: Citgo

Food E: Burger King, TCBY

(81) Service Area (Southbound)

FStop W: Citgo[*, D]

Food W: Burger King (Citgo)

ATM W: Citgo

13 **(78)** ME 196, Lewiston

Gas W: Mobil[D], Sunoco[*], Texaco[*, D], Unnamed[*, D]

Food E: Fast Breaks

W: Cathay Hut Polenesian, Dunkin Donuts, Fanny's (Ramada Inn), Fast Breaks, Fran's Place, Gendrum's Seafood, KFC (Taco Bell), Korn Haus Keller, McDonald's, Taco Bell (KFC), The Governor's, Wendy's

Lodg E: Super 8

W: Chalet Motel, Motel 6, Ramada Inn, Super 8

AServ E: Double Discount Auto Service, Tire Warehouse, VIP Auto Service

W: Mobil, Modern Speedy Auto Glass, Prompto 10 Min Oil Change, Tire Warehouse Double Discount Auto Parts, Unnamed, VIP Discount Auto Center

TServ W: Maine Commercial Tire

Med W: ✚ Hospital

ATM W: Texaco

12 **(73)** U.S. 202, Auburn, ME 4, ME100

FStop E: Irving[*, D, 24]

W: Bundy's[*, D]

Food E: Blimpie Subs & Salads, Taco Bell (Irving)

W: Auburn Inn, Taco Bell

Lodg E: Sleepy Time Motel, The Auburn Inn

W: Auburn Inn

RVCamp W: Campground

Med E: ✚ Hospital

ATM E: Irving

Parks W: Bradbury Mtn State Park

Other W: Airport

(65) Toll Plaza (Toll)

11 **(61)** U.S. 202, ME 115, ME 4, ME 26, Gray, New Gloucester

Gas E: Exxon, Gulf[*, LP], Mobil[*], Texaco[*]

Food E: Dunkin Donuts, McDonald's, New England Pizzeria, Subway (IGA Supermarket), The Village Kitchen

AServ E: Exxon, Mobile (Towing)

RVCamp E: Campground

W: Campground

ATM E: IGA Supermarket

Other E: IGA Supermarket

(57) Service Area

FStop B: Citgo[D]

Food B: Burger King, TCBY

10 **(50)** ME 26, ME 100,West Falmouth

Med E: ✚ Hospital

EXIT MAINE

9 **(49)** Junction I-95N & I-495 S, U.S. 1, Freeport, Falmouth

8 **(46)** ME 25, US 302, Westbrook, Portland

Gas E: Mobil[*, D], Texaco[*, CW]

W: Exxon[*, D], Fuel Mart[D, 24]

Food E: Buffalo Wings N' Things, Denny's[24], Dunkin Donuts, Governor's Restaurant, KFC, McDonald's[PLAY], Mr Bagel, Pizza Hut, Subway (Texaco)

W: Howard Johnson, Sub Express (Fuel Mart), Verrillo's Restaurant

Lodg E: Motel 6, Susse Chalet

W: Howard Johnson, Super 8

AServ E: Big A Auto Part Store, Rowe Ford, Hyundai, VIP Auto Center

W: Auto Tire Warehouse, Jiffy Lube, Midas, NAPA Auto Parts, Norman David Ford Lincoln Mercury

Med E: ✚ Hospital

ATM E: Mobil, Texaco

W: Infiniti Federal Credit Union

Other E: Super Shop & Save

7 **(43)** to I-295, US 1, ME 114, S Portland, Maine Mall Rd.

Gas E: Mobil[*]

Food E: Chicago Bar & Grill, Chili's, Crickets Restaurant, IHOP, Maine Mall Food Court, Old Country Buffet, Pizza Hut, Pizza Plus, Silver Shell

Lodg E: DAYS INN Days Inn, Fairfield Inn, Sheraton

W: AmeriSuites (see our ad this page)

AServ E: Sears

ATM E: Mobil

6A **(42)** Junction I-295 North, South Portland, Downtown Portland

6 **(40)** U.S. 1, Scarborough

5 **(33)** Junction I-195, Saco, Old Orchard

4 **(30)** ME 111, Biddeford

FStop E: Irving[*]

Food E: Subway (Irving), Wendy's

AServ E: Neil's Motors Inc, VIP Discount Auto Center, Wal-Mart[RX]

W: Tom's Auto Repair

Med E: ✚ Southern Maine Medical Center

ATM E: Shaw's Food & Drugs[RX]

Other E: Shaw's Food & Drugs[RX], Wal-Mart[RX]

3 **(24)** Kennebunk, Service Area (Exit 3 & Service Area are at the same location)

Gas B: Citgo

Food B: Burger King, Sharo's Italian, TCBY

Lodg E: Turnpike Motel

2 **(18)** Wells, Sanford , ME 9, ME109

RVCamp E: Ocean View Cottages & Camping (1.75 Miles), Sea Vu Campground (1.9 Miles)

W: Gregoire's Campground (.25 Miles)

Med W: ✚ Hospital

Note: I-95 runs concurrent above with METNPK. Numbering follows METNPK.

(5) Weigh Station (Northbound)

4 **(6)** to ME 91, to U.S. 1, Yorks, Ogunquit

Gas E: Citgo[*], Dead River[LP], Irving[*], Mobil[*]

Food E: Citgo, Fooder's Pizza, Green Leaves Chinese, Norma's, Sadie's Cafe, Stonewall Kitchen, Vincent Subs & Pizza

Med E: ✚ Hospital

ATM E: Mobil, Sleek Bank

Other E: Mail Boxes Etc, Visitor Information

EXIT MAINE/NEW HAMPSHIRE

PRIME OUTLETS
KITTERY
120 Outlet Stores & Kittery Trading Post
Ask for your FREE COUPON BOOK
888-KITTERY
1862
MAINE • I-95 • EXIT 3

TOUR BUSES WELCOME!
1669

207-439-5555
DAYS INN
Restaurant on Premises
Indoor Heated Pool
Cable TV w/HBO & ESPN
Coin Laundry • Golf/Tennis Nearby
Jacuzzi Suites Available
1/4 mi to Discount Factory
Outlet Shopping Malls
2 Gorges Road • Kittery, ME
Maine • I-95 • Exit 2

(4) Weigh Station (Southbound)

3 **(2)** U.S. 1 North, ME 236 (Northbound)
- Gas E: Getty(*)
- Food E: Sunrise Grill
- Other E: **Prime Outlets at Kittery (see our ad this page)**, **Police Station**

2 **(1)** U.S.1 S, ME 236, Kittery, S Berwick
- TStop E: **Howell's**(SCALES)
- Gas E: Citgo(*, LP), Getty(*); W: Mobil(*, D)
- Food E: Bagel Caboose, Dairy Queen, **Howell's**, Payrin Thai, Sunrise Grill, Taco Bell (Citgo), The Loose Moose Cafe; W: Ben & Jerry's Ice Cream, Bob Clam Hut, Quarterdeck, Subway, The Weathervane
- Lodg E: Blue Roof Motel, **Days Inn (see our ad this page)**, Northeastern Motel, Rex Motel, Super 8
- ATM E: Citgo, **Howell's**; W: Mobil
- Other W: Tanger Factory Outlet

1 ME 103, Dennett Road (Reaccess Southbound Only)

↑MAINE

↓NEW HAMPSHIRE

(20) Rest Area (RR, HF, Phones, Picnic)

7 **(19)** Portsmouth, Newington
- Lodg E: Sheraton; W: Courtyard by Marriott
- Other E: **Tourist Info.**, **USS Albacor Submarine**

6 **(16)** Woodbury Ave, Portsmouth
- Food E: Anchorage Inn, Bickford's Family Restaurant, Meadowbrook Inn
- Lodg E: Anchorage Inn, Holiday Inn, Howard Johnson, Meadowbrook Inn, Portsmouth Inn, The Port Motor Inn

5 **(14)** U.S. 1, Portsmouth, Dover, Spaulding Tnpk, US 4, NH 16
- FStop W: **Exxon**(*), **Texaco**(*)
- Gas W: Gulf
- Food E: Bickford's Family Restaurant
- Lodg E: Holiday Inn, Howard Johnson, Medow Brook Inn, Swiss Chalet, The Port Motor Inn (AAA); W: Hampton Inn, Portsmouth Inn
- AServ E: Pontiac, Oldsmobile, GMC, Cadallic; W: Portsmouth Ford
- Med E: **✚ Hospital**

EXIT NEW HAMPSHIRE/MASSACHUSETTS

4 **(14)** U.S. 4, NH 16, Newington, Dover (Northbound)

3 **(12)** NH 101, Greenland, Stratham
- FStop W: **Sunoco**(*)
- Food W: **Dunkin Donuts (Sunoco)**
- Med E: **✚ Hospital**

2 **(6)** NH 51, to NH 101, Hampton, Manchester (Toll)

1 NH 107, Seabrook, Kingston
- Gas E: AL Prime, Getty, Getty(D), Jack's(*, D), Richdale(*), Sunoco(*); W: Citgo(*)
- Food E: 99 Restaurant & Pub, D'Angelo's Sandwich Shop, Dunkin Donuts, Honey Bee Donuts, McDonald's, Moe's Italian Sandwiches, Papa Gino's, Road Kill Cafe; W: Master MacGrath's
- Lodg E: Hampshire Motor Inn; W: Best Western, Cimarron Suites
- AServ E: Getty, Jiffy Lube, Midas Muffler & Brake, Pronto 10 Min Oil Change
- TServ E: **Seabrook Truck Center**(SCALES)
- ATM E: Fleet Bank
- Other E: **Market Basket**, Pro Wash Car Wash; W: Sam's Club

(0) NH Welcome Center (RR, HF, Phones, Picnic; Northbound)

↑NEW HAMPSHIRE

↓MASSACHUSETTS

(61) MA Welcome Center (RR, Phones; Southbound)

60 MA 286, Beaches, Salisbury (Difficult Reaccess)
- FStop E: **Mobil**(*)
- Food E: Captain Hook's, Chubby's Diner, Hodgie's Ice Cream, Lena's Seafood
- RVCamp E: **Black Bear Campground**

59 Jct I-95, I-495, Boston, Worcester

58AB **(87)** MA 110, to I-495, Salisbury, Amesbury
- Gas E: Sunoco(*, D); W: Mobil(*), Sunoco(*, 24)
- Food E: Crossroads Pizza, Dunkin Donuts (Sunoco), Simon's Roast Beef & Subs, Sylvan Street Grill, The Winners Circle; W: Burger King, Dunkin Donuts, Friendly's, McDonald's(PLAY)
- Lodg W: Susse Chalet
- AServ E: Donna Hue Dodge, Pro Lube Auto Repair; W: Yeo Volkswagen Chevrolet Geo
- ATM E: First Ocean National Bank, Newbury Port Bank; W: Mobil
- Parks E: **Maudslay State Park**
- Other E: Auto Car Wash(24), Crossroads Car Wash

57 MA 113, West Newbury, Newburyport
- Gas E: Mobil(*), Shell(*), Sunoco
- Food E: Cafe Bagel, Dunkin Donuts, Friendly's, McDonald's, Ming Jade Polynesian, Papa Geno's
- AServ E: Midas Muffler & Brake, Shell, Sunoco
- Med E: **✚ Hospital**
- ATM E: Mobil
- Parks E: **Maudslay State Park**
- Other E: **Brook's Pharmacy**, **K-Mart**, **Shaw's Grocery**, White Hen Pantry

EXIT MASSACHUSETTS

56 Scotland Road, Newbury

55 Central St, Byfield , Newbury
- Gas W: Prime
- Food E: Buddy's Restaurant
- Other E: **Byfield General Store**, **Pearson Hardware**; W: **Expo Market Place**, **Tourist Info.**, **U.S. Post Office**

54AB MA 133, Rowley , Georgetown

(54) Weigh Station

(54) Weigh Station

53AB **(75)** MA 97, Topsfield , Georgetown

52 **(73)** Topsfield Road, Topsfield , Boxford

51 Endicott Road, Topsfield, Middleton

50 U.S. 1, Topsfield,Danvers, MA 62
- Gas E: Exxon(*), Mobil(*)
- Food E: Dunkin Donuts (Exxon), Newbury Street Deli & Bakery, Ponpevecchio Restaurant; W: Super 8, Village Green Restaurant
- Lodg W: Super 8
- ATM E: Exxon, Mobil

49 MA 62, Danvers, Middleton (Difficult Reaccess)
- Food W: Putnam Pantry (Candy, Ice Cream), Subway, Supino's Italian
- Med E: **✚ Hospital**
- Other E: **Danvers Animal Hospital**; W: **CVS Pharmacy**, **MA State Police**, **Mail Boxes Etc**, **Stop N Shop Grocery**

48 Centre St, Danvers
- Food W: Calitris Italian
- Lodg W: Comfort Inn, Extended Stay America

47A MA 114, Peabody, Middleton (Difficult Reaccess)
- Gas E: Exxon(*, D), Shell(CW), Sunoco
- Food E: Dunkin Donuts, Jenny's, **McDonald's**, Papa Gino's Pizza; W: Jake's Grill
- Lodg W: Motel 6, Residence Inn
- AServ E: Herb Chambers Dodge, NTB National Tire & Battery, Pace Hyundai/Pontiac, Sunoco

46 US 1, Boston
- FStop W: **Best**(*, D)
- Gas W: Gulf(*, D)
- Food E: Sri Thai Restaurant, Sunrise Pizza & Subs; W: Mama Lucia's, T.G.I. Friday's
- Lodg W: Countryside Motel, Residence Inn
- ATM E: Bank Boston

45 MA 128 North, Gloucester

44 U.S. 1, MA 129, Boston, Everett, Danvers (Difficult Reaccess)
- Gas W: Mobil, Shell, Texaco
- Food W: Bennigan's, Bertucci's Brick Oven Pizza, Bickford's Family Restaurant
- Lodg W: Econo Motor Inn, Holiday Inn
- AServ W: 4-Star Service Center
- Med E: **✚ Hospital**
- Other E: **State Police**

43 Walnut St, Lynnfield Ctr, Saugus (Difficult Reaccess)

Bold red print shows RV & Bus parking available or nearby

EXIT MASSACHUSETTS

Food **W:** Colonial Hilton Resort
Lodg **W:** Colonial Hilton Resort

42 Salem St, Montrose Ave
Gas **E:** Sunoco(*)
Food **E:** Brother Paul's Pizza, Montrose Drive-in Restaurant
W: Hilton
Lodg **W:** Hilton

41 Main St , Lynnfield Ctr, Wakefield

40 **(58)** MA 129, Wakefield Center, North Reading
Gas **E:** Exxon(*)
W: Gulf(*)
Food **E:** Honey Dew Donuts, Lanai Island (Polynesian)
W: Dunkin Donuts, Mandarin Reading
AServ **E:** Exxon
Med **E:** ✚ **Wakefield Medical Center**
Other **E:** **Animal Hospital of Wakefield**

39 North Ave, Reading, Wakefield
Gas **W:** Exxon, Texaco(*, LP)
Food **E:** Best Western
W: Honey Dew Donuts (Texaco)
Lodg **E:** Best Western
AServ **E:** 128 Ford/Volvo/Saab/Mazda/Isuzu/ Oldsmobile
W: 128 Ford, Exxon
Med **E:** ✚ **Hospital**
ATM **E:** Savings Bank

38AB MA 28, Stoneham, Reading
Gas **E:** Gulf, Texaco(*)
W: Exxon(*), Mobil(*), Shell(*)
Food **E:** Boston Market Restaurant, Denny's, Dunkin Donuts, The Ground Round
W: Dunkin Donuts (Exxon), Friendly's, Gregory's Subs & Deli, Harrow's
AServ **E:** Gulf, Texaco
W: Meineke Discount Mufflers, Shell
Med **E:** ✚ **Hospital**
ATM **W:** Mobil
Other **E:** Barry Mart, **CVS Pharmacy(RX)**, **Shaw's Supermarket**

37AB Junction I-93, Boston, Concord

36 Washington St, Woburn, Reading
Gas **E:** Getty
W: Texaco(*, CW)
Food **W:** 99 Restaurant & Pub, Bertucci's Brick Oven Pizza, Chicago Bar & Grill, D'Angelo's Sandwich Shop, J.C. Hillary's Restaurant, Jo's Bar & Grill (Hampton Inn), McDonald's, On The Border Mexican, Papa Genio's, Pizza Hut, T.G.I. Friday's, Uno Pizzeria, Weylu's Thai, Wonder Wok
Lodg **W:** Comfort Inn, Courtyard Inn, Hampton Inn, Red Roof Inn, Susse Chalet
AServ **E:** Crest GMC/ Pontiac/ Buick/ Nissan, Getty
W: NTB National Tire & Battery, Texaco
ATM **W:** Woburn National Bank
Other **W:** **CVS Pharmacy(RX)**, **Market Basket Supermarket**, US Post Office, **Woburn Mall**

35 MA 38, Woburn, Wilmington
Gas **W:** Mobil(*, D), Shell(*)
Food **W:** Baldwin's Restaurant, Dunkin Donuts, Roast Beef Round Up
Lodg **E:** Ramada
W: Sierra Suites
AServ **W:** Mobil, Shell
Med **E:** ✚ **Hospital**
W: ✚ **Hospital**

EXIT MASSACHUSETTS

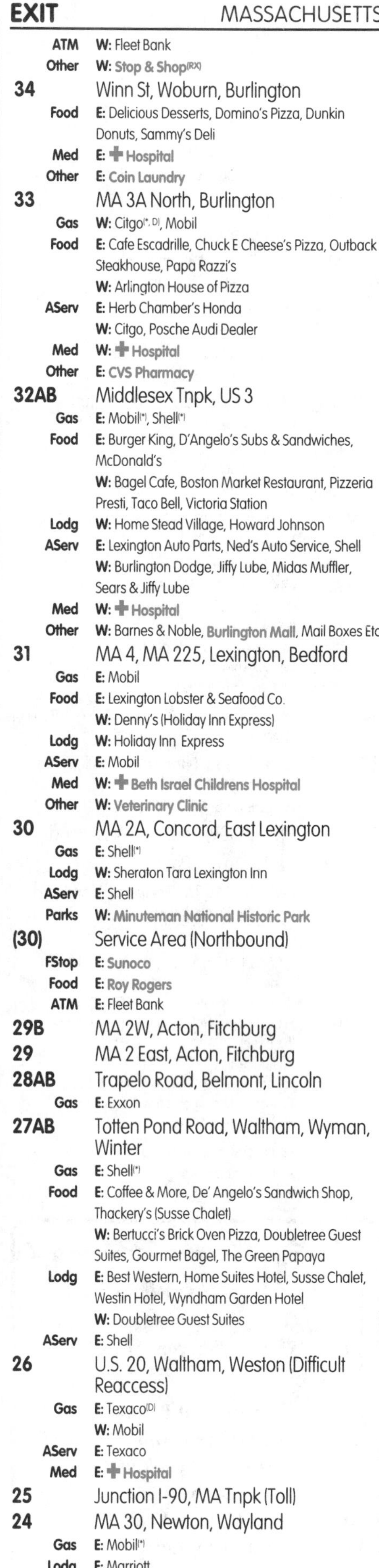

EXIT MASSACHUSETTS

ATM **W:** Fleet Bank
Other **W:** **Stop & Shop(RX)**

34 Winn St, Woburn, Burlington
Food **E:** Delicious Desserts, Domino's Pizza, Dunkin Donuts, Sammy's Deli
Med **E:** ✚ **Hospital**
Other **E:** **Coin Laundry**

33 MA 3A North, Burlington
Gas **W:** Citgo(*, D), Mobil
Food **E:** Cafe Escadrille, Chuck E Cheese's Pizza, Outback Steakhouse, Papa Razzi's
W: Arlington House of Pizza
AServ **E:** Herb Chamber's Honda
W: Citgo, Posche Audi Dealer
Med **W:** ✚ **Hospital**
Other **E:** **CVS Pharmacy**

32AB Middlesex Tnpk, US 3
Gas **E:** Mobil(*), Shell(*)
Food **E:** Burger King, D'Angelo's Subs & Sandwiches, McDonald's
W: Bagel Cafe, Boston Market Restaurant, Pizzeria Presti, Taco Bell, Victoria Station
Lodg **W:** Home Stead Village, Howard Johnson
AServ **E:** Lexington Auto Parts, Ned's Auto Service, Shell
W: Burlington Dodge, Jiffy Lube, Midas Muffler, Sears & Jiffy Lube
Med **W:** ✚ **Hospital**
Other **W:** Barnes & Noble, **Burlington Mall**, Mail Boxes Etc

31 MA 4, MA 225, Lexington, Bedford
Gas **E:** Mobil
Food **E:** Lexington Lobster & Seafood Co.
W: Denny's (Holiday Inn Express)
Lodg **W:** Holiday Inn Express
AServ **E:** Mobil
Med **W:** ✚ **Beth Israel Childrens Hospital**
Other **W:** **Veterinary Clinic**

30 MA 2A, Concord, East Lexington
Gas **E:** Shell(*)
Lodg **W:** Sheraton Tara Lexington Inn
AServ **E:** Shell
Parks **W:** **Minuteman National Historic Park**

(30) Service Area (Northbound)
FStop **E:** **Sunoco**
Food **E:** **Roy Rogers**
ATM **E:** Fleet Bank

29B MA 2W, Acton, Fitchburg

29 MA 2 East, Acton, Fitchburg

28AB Trapelo Road, Belmont, Lincoln
Gas **E:** Exxon

27AB Totten Pond Road, Waltham, Wyman, Winter
Gas **E:** Shell(*)
Food **E:** Coffee & More, De' Angelo's Sandwich Shop, Thackery's (Susse Chalet)
W: Bertucci's Brick Oven Pizza, Doubletree Guest Suites, Gourmet Bagel, The Green Papaya
Lodg **E:** Best Western, Home Suites Hotel, Susse Chalet, Westin Hotel, Wyndham Garden Hotel
W: Doubletree Guest Suites
AServ **E:** Shell

26 U.S. 20, Waltham, Weston (Difficult Reaccess)
Gas **E:** Texaco(D)
W: Mobil
AServ **E:** Texaco
Med **E:** ✚ **Hospital**

25 Junction I-90, MA Tnpk (Toll)

24 MA 30, Newton, Wayland
Gas **E:** Mobil(*)
Lodg **E:** Marriott

Bold red print shows RV & Bus parking available or nearby

EXIT MASSACHUSETTS

- **AServ** E: Mobil
- **Med** E: ✚ Hospital

23 Recreation Road

22 Grove St , MA 16W, Wellesley
- **Gas** E: Gulf
  W: Mobil, Sunoco
- **Food** W: Dunkin Donuts, Papa Razzi's, Riverview Cafe
- **Lodg** E: Holiday Inn (see our ad this page)
- **AServ** E: Gulf
  W: Mobil, Sunoco
- **Med** E: ✚ Newton Wellesley Hospital

(22) Rest Area
- **FStop** W: Sunoco
- **Food** W: Roy Rogers

21 MA 16, Newton, Wellesley
- **Med** E: ✚ Hospital

20 **(36)** MA 9, Boston, Framingham, Worcester
- **Food** W: Wok Chinese
- **AServ** W: Mobile[*, D]
- **Med** W: ✚ Hospital

19AB **(35)** Highland Ave, Newton Highlands, Needham
- **Gas** E: Charter, Gulf
- **Food** E: D'Angelo's Sandwich Shop, Mighty Subs, The Ground Round
- **Lodg** E: Sheraton
- **AServ** E: Berejik Olds, Gulf, Midas Muffler & Brake
  W: Muzi Ford
- **Other** W: Non Stop Car Wash

18 **(33)** Great Plain Ave, West Roxbury
- **Med** W: ✚ Hospital

17 **(32)** MA 135, Needham, Natick
- **Med** W: ✚ Hospital
- **Other** W: Norfolk County Sheriff Office

16 **(31)** MA 109, Dedham, Westwood

(18) Rest Area (RR, Phones)

15 U.S. 1, to MA 1A, Dedham, Norwood (Difficult Reaccess)
- **Gas** W: Shell, Shell
- **Food** E: Chili's, Holiday Inn, J.C. Hillarie's Food & Drink, Vinney Pesta's
  W: Dunkin Donuts, Westwood Jade Chinese
- **Lodg** E: Comfort Inn, Holiday Inn, Ramada Inn (see our ad this page)
  W: Budget Inn
- **AServ** E: Dedham Nissan, Midas Muffler & Brake
  W: Infiniti of Norwood, Shell, Shell
- **Med** E: ✚ Faulkner Hospital

14 **(29)** East St, Canton St
- **Lodg** E: Hilton, Days Inn
- **TServ** E: Cumming's Diesel

Newly Renovated
781-784-1000
395 Old Post Rd., RT 1
Sharon, MA 02067

Deluxe Continental Breakfast
Suites Available • Cable TV w/HBO
Truck Parking • Truckers Discount
Restaurant Nearby
Kids Under 12 Stay Free
Foxboro Stadium 3 mi.
1640
MASSACHUSETTS • I-95 • EXIT 9

EXIT MASSACHUSETTS

- **Med** E: ✚ The Medical Center

(8) Rest Area (Southbound)

13 **(28)** Railway Station, University Ave

12 **(26)** Junction I-93 North, Braintree, Boston, US 1

11AB **(23)** Neponset St, Canton, Norwood
- **Gas** E: Citgo, Sunoco[*]
- **Food** E: TKO Shea's Restaurant
- **Lodg** E: Ramada Inn (see our ad this page)
- **AServ** E: Citgo, Sunoco
- **Med** W: ✚ Hospital

10 **(23)** Coney St, Sharon, Walpole (Southbound, Reaccess Northbound Only)
- **Food** W: 99 Restaurant, Becon's, Dunkin Donuts, Old Country Buffet, Papa Gino's, Taco Bell

RAMADA INN®
& Resort
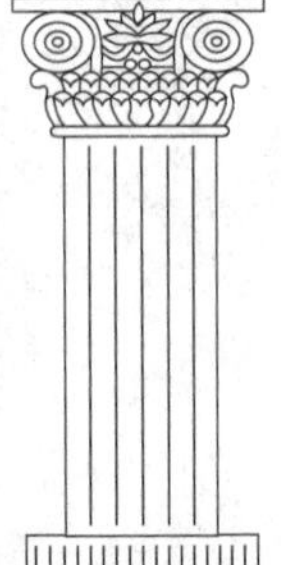
434 Providence Hwy.(Route 1)
Indoor Pool • Whirlpool
Fitness Center
Guest Laundry
Restaurant & Lounge
18 Hole Golf Course
& Driving Range
Business Center
781-769-7000
1630
I-95, Exit 11B to Route 1 North
MASSACHUSETTS • I-95 • EXIT 11B

1573
Two Locations
Holiday Inn®

Golf Course & Indoor Tennis
Full Service Restaurant
Lounge
Swimming Pool
Health Club Facilities
Spectra vision
Newly Renovated Spacious Guest Rooms

Holiday Inn - Mansfield
31 Hampshire Street
Mansfield, MA 02048
508-339-2200
I-95 • Exit 7A

Holiday Inn - Newton
399 Grove Street
Newton, MA 02162
617-969-5300
I-95 • Exit 22

MASS • I-95 • 2 LOCATIONS

EXIT MASSACHUSETTS

- **AServ** W: Acura/Lexus
- **ATM** W: BankBoston

9 **(19)** U.S. 1, to MA 27, Walpole
- **Gas** E: Exxon[*], Mobil[*], US Petroleum
- **Food** E: Clyde's Smokehouse Saloon, Pizza Hut, The Ground Round
  W: Bigford's Family Fair
- **Lodg** E: Boston View Motel
  W: The Sharon Inn, Days Inn (see our ad this page)
- **AServ** E: US Petroleum
- **RVCamp** E: Campers Head Quarters[LP]
- **Other** E: Wal-Mart

8 **(16)** South Main St, Sharon, Foxboro
- **Food** E: Bliss Ice Cream Restaurant & Deli, Tony Lena's Sandwich & Pizza
- **ATM** E: Shaw's Grocery
- **Other** E: Osco Drugs[RX], Shaw's Grocery

7AB **(13)** MA 140, Mansfield, Foxboro
- **Gas** W: Shell
- **Food** E: 99 Restaurant, Piccadilly Pub & Restaurant
  W: Papa Geno's
- **Lodg** E: Courtyard by Marriott, Days Inn (see our ad on this page), Holiday Inn (see our ad this page)Motel 6
- **Other** E: Foxfield Plaza

6AB **(11)** Junction I-495, Worcester, Taunton

(10) MA Welcome Center (RR, Phones, Picnic)

(9) Parking Area (Southbound)

5 **(7)** to MA 152, Attleboro
- **Gas** W: Gulf
- **Food** W: Bill's Pizza & Subs, Bliss Ice Cream Restaurant & Deli, Wendy's
- **AServ** W: Gulf
- **Med** E: ✚ Hospital
  W: ✚ Walk In Clinic
- **ATM** W: Bank of Boston, Fleet Bank, Shaw's Grocery (Citizen's Bank)
- **Other** E: Police Station
  W: Brooks Pharmacy[RX], Shaw's Grocery (Citizen's Bank)

4 **(5)** Junction I-295, Woonsocket

3 **(4)** MA 123, Norton, Attleboro
- **Gas** E: Texaco[*]
- **Med** E: ✚ Hospital
- **Other** E: Capron Zoo

(2) Weigh Station (Northbound)

(2) Weigh Station (Southbound)

2AB **(1)** MA1A, Pawtuket, S Attleboro, Newport Ave.
- **Gas** E: Mobil[*, CW]

508-543-1000
DAYS INN
4 Fisher St.
Foxboro, MA
Continental Breakfast
Tennis/Golf/Skiing Nearby
Restaurant Nearby
Lounge on Premises
Exercise Room • USA Newspaper
Cable TV/HBO/ESPN

5 Sunburst Quality Award Winner
1644
Massachusetts • I-95 • Exit 7A

Bold red print shows RV & Bus parking available or nearby

EXIT MASSACHUSETTS/RHODE ISLAND

Food E: Honey Dew Donuts, McDonald's, Olive Garden
AServ E: Country Pontiac
ATM E: Bank of Boston

1 **(0)** U.S. 1 S, Broadway, Pawtucket (Reaccess Northbound Only, Difficult Reaccess)
Food E: Super Dragon Chinese, Vista Donuts
Lodg E: Days Inn
AServ E: Royal Tire Servcie
Med E: Hospital
Other E: Brook's Pharmacy

↑MASSACHUSETTS

↓RHODE ISLAND

30 **(43)** East St, Central Falls
Food E: Dunkin Donuts
W: D'Angelo's
Other E: Comit Car Wash

29 **(43)** U.S. 1, Broadway, Cottage St (Northbound, Difficult Reaccess)
Food W: De' Angelo's Sandwich Shop
AServ W: Crown Collision, Division Brakes, Firestone Tire & Auto

28 **(42)** RI 114, School St (Northbound, Difficult Reaccess)
Gas E: Sunoco[*, 24]
AServ E: Tire Pro's[24]
W: Apex Auto Service
Med E: Memorial Hospital

27 **(42)** U.S. 1, RI 15, Providence, Pawtucket (Difficult Reaccess)
Gas W: Shell, Sunoco[D]
Food W: Burger King, Dunkin Donuts, The Ground Round (Comfort Inn)
Lodg W: Comfort Inn
AServ W: Shell, Sunoco

26 **(41)** RI 122, Lonsdale Ave, Main St (Northbound, Reaccess Southbound Only)
Med E: Memorial Hospital of RI

25 **(40)** U.S. 1, RI 126, North Main St, Smithfield Ave (Difficult Reaccess)
Gas W: Cumberland Farms[*], DD Mart
Food E: Chili's, D'Angelo's, Papa Gino's, Shang Hai Chinese Restaurant
W: Amanda's Kitchen, Burger King, Chello's, Hunan Garden, Local Hero Deli
AServ W: AAMCO Transmission, Luigi's Auto Repair
Other E: CVS Pharmacy, Shaws Grocery

24 **(39)** Branch Ave
Food E: KFC
AServ E: Action Auto Parts
W: Mobil
Med E: Miriam Hospital
ATM W: Super Stop N Shop[RX]
Other W: Super Stop N Shop[RX]

23 **(38)** RI 146, North Charles St. (Difficult Reaccess)
Gas E: Shell
Food E: Dunkin Donuts (Shell)
W: Dunkin Donuts
Lodg E: Marriott
Med W: Miriam Hospital
Other W: Post Office, Tim's Car Wash

22 **(38)** U.S. 6, RI 10, Downtown, Hartford Ct.

21 **(37)** Broadway, Atwells Ave. (Difficult Reaccess)

EXIT RHODE ISLAND

20 **(37)** Jct. I-195, U.S. 6, Cape Cod (Left Exit)

19 **(36)** Eddy St, Allens Ave
Med W: Hospital

18 **(35)** U.S. 1A, Thurbers Ave (Difficult Reaccess)
Gas E: Extra Mart[*, D]
Food E: Honey Dew Donuts, Stacy's Restaurant
W: Burger King
Med W: Hospital

17 **(34)** U.S. 1, Elmwood Ave (Difficult Reaccess)
Gas W: Sunoco[D]
AServ E: Dick & Sons Auto Repair
W: Sunoco, Tire Warehouse
Med E: Hospital
Parks E: Roger Williams Park & Zoo
Other W: Coin Laundry

16 **(34)** RI 10, to U.S. 1, to RI 2
Med W: St. Joseph's Hospital
Other E: Roger Williams Park & Zoo

15 **(32)** Jefferson Blvd
Gas E: Getty[*], Global[*]
Food E: Bickford's Family Restaurant (Motel 6), Bug A Boo Steak House, Dunkin Donuts
Lodg E: Motel 6, Susse Chalet Inn
AServ E: Getty
TServ W: Colony Ford Trucks
ATM E: Motel 6

14 **(31)** RI 37, to U.S. 1, to RI 2, Cranston, Warwick
Lodg E: Days Inn (see our ad this page)

Western Greenwich Inn
1757

101 Nooseneck Hill Rd.
West Greenwich, RI
401-397-5494
800-528-1234
Lounge on Premises
Indoor Pool & Jacuzzi
Handicap Accessible
Truck/Large Vehicle Parking
Cable TV w/HBO/CNN/TNT/ESPN
Complimentary Continental Breakfast
RHODE ISLAND ▪ I-95 ▪ EXIT 6

EXIT RHODE ISLAND

13 **(30)** T.F. Green Airport
Lodg W: Residence Inn

12B Jct. I-295 N., RI 2 N, 113 W.

12A **(28)** RI 113 East, Warwick
Gas E: Sunoco[*], Texaco[*]
Food E: Holiday Inn
Lodg E: Holiday Inn
AServ E: Sunoco

11 **(28)** Junction I-295, Woonsocket (Northbound)

10AB **(27)** RI 117, Warwick
Med W: Hospital

9 **(25)** RI 4, N Kingstown (Left Exit)

8AB **(24)** RI 2, Quaker Ln. (Difficult Reaccess)
FStop E: Texaco[*, D]
Food E: China Buffet, McDonald's, Outback Steakhouse, Ro-Jack Market Place, Ruby Tuesday
W: Wendy's
Lodg W: Open Gate Motel
AServ W: Ocean Mitsubishi
RVCamp W: Arlington RV Super Center
Med E: Hospital
Other E: Discovery Zone, WalGreens Pharmacy

7 **(21)** Coventry, West Warwick
FStop E: Mobil (Towing)
Food W: Wendy's
AServ E: Mobil (Towing)
W: Chevalier's Auto Service
TServ E: Mobil (Towing)

6A **(20)** Hopkins Hill Road

6 **(18)** RI 3, West Greenwich, Coventry
Gas W: Sunoco[D], Texaco[*]
Food W: Bess Eaton Coffee Shop & Bakery, Dunkin Donuts, Mark's Grille, Yummie's Ice Cream & Yogurt
Lodg W: Best Western (see our ad this page), Congress Inn
AServ W: Sunoco

5AB **(14)** RI 102, W Greenwich, Exeter
TStop W: T/A TravelCenters of America[*, SCALES]
Food W: T/A TravelCenters of America
Lodg W: Classic Motor Lodge
TServ W: T/A TravelCenters of America[SCALES]
ATM W: Centreville Bank, T/A TravelCenters of America

(11) Weigh Station (Northbound)

(11) Weigh Station (Southbound)

4 **(10)** RI 3, to RI 165, Arcadia, Exeter (Northbound, Reaccess Southbound Only)

3AB **(8)** RI 138, Kingston, Newport, Wyoming, Hope Valley
Gas W: Exxon, Gulf[*], Mobil[*, SCALES], Sunoco[*, D]
Food E: Bess Eaton Coffee Shop & Bakery, Dunkin Donuts, McDonald's, Wendy's
W: Bali Village Chinese, Bess Eaton Coffee Shop & Bakery, Bickford's Family Restaurant, Nick's Pizza, Pizza King, Sun Valley Motel, Village Pizza
Lodg W: Sun Valley Motel
AServ E: NAPA Auto Parts
W: Exxon
ATM E: Shop & Stop[RX]
W: Gulf, Washington Trust
Other E: Shop & Stop[RX]
W: Ocean Pharmacy

(9) RI Welcome Center (RR, Phones, Picnic, Vending, Pet Walk, P; Northbound)

2 **(5)** Hope Valley, Alton
RVCamp W: RV Camping

Bold red print shows RV & Bus parking available or nearby

EXIT RHODE ISLAND/CONNECTICUT

1 RI 3, Hopkinton, Westerly
RVCamp **E:** **Frontier Family Camper Park (.75 Miles)**
Med **E:** **Hospital**

↑RHODE ISLAND

↓CONNECTICUT

93 **(111)** CT 216, Clark Falls, Ashaway RI, CT184
TStop **W:** **Republic**(SCALES)
FStop **W:** **Citgo**(*, D, LP)
Gas **E:** Shell(*, 24)
Food **W:** Bess Eaton, **McDonald's**, **Republic**
Lodg **W:** Budget Inn, Stardust Motel
AServ **E:** Shell(24)
TServ **W:** **Republic**(SCALES)
ATM **W:** **Republic**

92 **(108)** CT 2, CT 49, North Stonington, Powcatuck (Difficult Reaccess)
RVCamp **W:** **Highland Orchards Park Inc.**(LP)

(108) Rest Area Welcome Center

91 **(104)** CT 234, North Main St, Stonington, Borough

90 **(101)** CT 27, Mystic Aquarium, Mystic Port
Gas **E:** Mobil
W: Texaco(*, 24)
Food **E:** Bickford's Family Restaurant (The Lodge), Friendly's, Go Fish, Jamm's, McDonald's, Newport Creamery, Steak Loft
W: Ashby's Restaurant, Copperfield's (Best Western), Days Inn, Dunkin Donuts (Texaco), Mystic Bagel, Mystic Ice Cream, Subway (Texaco)
Lodg **E:** Mystic Hilton, Old Mystic Motor Lodge, Seaport Motor Inn, The Lodge
W: Best Western, Comfort Inn, Days Inn, Residence Inn
RVCamp **W:** **Seaport Campground (1.75 Miles)**
Med **W:** **Seaport Walk In Medical Center**
ATM **W:** People's Bank, Texaco

(101) Scenic Overlook (Northbound, No Trucks)

89 **(100)** Allyn St, Noank, Groton Long Point

88 **(98)** CT 117, Noank, Groton Point
Med **E:** **Emergency Medical Treatment**

87 **(96)** CT 349, to U.S. 1, Clarence B Sharp Hwy (Left Exit)

86 **(96)** CT 184, CT 12 (Left Exit Northbound)
Gas **W:** Citgo(*), Cory's(*), Merit(*)
Food **E:** Quality Inn, Rosie's 24 Hr Diner, Skybox Cafe
W: Calzone's Pizza, Chester's Fried Chicken (Cory's), Chinese Kitchen, Domino's Pizza, Dunkin Donuts, Flanagan's (Best Western), IHOP, JB's Fun 'N Food Clam Bar, KFC, Peking Chinese, Russell's Ribs, Taco Bell
Lodg **E:** Clarion, EconoLodge, Grotten Inn & Suites, Morgan Inn, Quality Inn
W: Best Western, Grotten Inn, **Super 8 (RV Hook-Ups)**
AServ **E:** Meineke Discount Mufflers
W: Midas Muffler & Brake
ATM **W:** Liberty Bank, People's Bank
Other **W:** **Super Stop & Shop**

85 **(95)** U.S. 1 North, Thames St, Downtown Groton (Northbound, Difficult Reaccess)
Gas **E:** Citgo

EXIT CONNECTICUT

Food **E:** Norm's Country Lounge Cafe, Norm's Diner
AServ **E:** Citgo, NAPA Auto Parts

84 **(94)** CT 32, Downtown New London, Norwich (Difficult Reaccess)
Gas **W:** Citgo(*), Getty's, Sunoco(*)
Food **W:** Mr. G's Restaurant
Other **E:** **Nathan Hale School House, Shaw Mansion**

83 **(93)** CT 32, New London, U.S. 1, Frontage Rd (Northbound)
Gas **E:** Mobil(CW)
W: Sunoco(*)
Food **E:** Dunkin Donuts (Mobil), Kelly's Coffee & Fudge, Pizza Hut
W: Golden Wok
Lodg **W:** Holiday Inn, Red Roof Inn
AServ **E:** Auto Zone
Med **E:** **Hospital**
W: **Hospital**
ATM **E:** Citizens Bank, Fleet Bank
Other **E:** Brooks Pharmacy(RX)

82A **(92)** New London, Frontage Road, Colchester, Hartford (Northbound)
Food **E:** Pizza Hut
W: Chuck E Cheese's Pizza, Red Lobster
Lodg **W:** Fairfield Inn
AServ **E:** Goodyear Tire & Auto, Town Fair Tire
W: Monroe Muffler & Brakes
ATM **E:** Citizen's Bank

82 **(92)** CT 85, Broad. St, Waterford
Gas **W:** Mobil(*)
Food **W:** Bee Bee's Dairy Restaurant
Other **W:** **Crystal Mall**

81 **(90)** Cross Road
Food **W:** **McDonald's (Wal-Mart)**
Lodg **W:** Lamplighter Motel
Other **W:** **Wal-Mart**(RX)

80 **(89)** Oil Mill Road (Difficult Reaccess)

77 **(2)** CT85, Colchester, Waterford (Northbound)
Gas **E:** Shell
Food **E:** Dunkin Donuts
Lodg **E:** The Oak Del Motel

76 **(88)** Junction I-395 North, Norwich, Plainfield (Northbound)

75 **(88)** U.S. 1, Waterford (Difficult Reaccess)
Gas **W:** Shell(*, CW)
Food **E:** Lou Lou's
W: Bee Bee's Dairy Restaurant, Cappy's Cones Ice Cream, Flander's Donut & Bagel Shop, Flander's Pizza, Flander's Seafood, King's Garden Chinese, McDonald's
AServ **W:** Plaza Ford
RVCamp **W:** **Camping**
ATM **W:** Citizen's Bank
Other **W:** Brooks Pharmacy(RX), **IGA Food Store**

74 **(87)** CT 161, Flanders, Niantic
Gas **E:** Exxon(*), Mobil, Sunoco
Food **E:** Bickford's Family Restaurant (Days Inn), Burger King(PLAY), The Bootlegger Country Steakhouse
W: Flanders Donuts & Bagels, Flanders Pizza
Lodg **E:** Best Western, Connecticut Yankee Inn, Days Inn, Starlight Motor Inn
AServ **E:** Exxon, Mobil, Mobil, Sunoco
RVCamp **W:** **Campground**
Med **W:** **Walk In Clinic**

73 **(86)** Society Road (Northbound, Reaccess Northbound Only)

(85) Rest Area (Southbound)

EXIT CONNECTICUT

72 **(84)** Rocky Neck State Park
RVCamp **W:** **Camp Niantic**(LP)

71 **(84)** Four Mile River Road
RVCamp **E:** **Campground**
Parks **E:** **Rocky Neck State Park**

70 **(79)** U.S. 1, CT 156, Old Lyme (Difficult Reaccess)
Gas **W:** Texaco(D)
Food **W:** Anne's Kitchen, Bess Eaton Donuts, Hide A Way Family Restaurant, Mama Mia Pizza, The Grist Mill
Lodg **W:** Bee & Cecil Inn, The Old Lyme Inn
AServ **W:** Texaco
ATM **W:** Citizens Bank, Fleet Bank, Meritime Bank
Other **W:** **A&P Super Food Mart, Old Lyme Pharmacy, Post Office**

69 **(78)** CT 9 North, Essex, Hartford
Lodg **W:** Comfort Inn

68 **(77)** U.S. 1, Old Saybrook (Reaccess Northbound Only)
FStop **E:** **Citgo**
Gas **E:** Mobil, Texaco(CW)
Lodg **W:** Liberty Inn
AServ **E:** Classic Auto Body, Shoreline Isuzu, Saab, Stanley Motors
Other **E:** Classic Carriage Car Wash

67 **(76)** CT 154, Old Saybrook, Elm St (Northbound, Difficult Reaccess)
Gas **E:** BP(*), Gulf, Mobil, Sunoco(*, 24)
Food **E:** Andriana's Seafood & Steaks, Bagel Bakery, Burger King, Monkey Farm Cafe, Pat's Country Kitchen, Pizza Hut, Pizza Works, Subway, Sully's Seafood, Two Brothers Family Pizza
AServ **E:** Gulf, Mobil, Saybrook Ford
W: Computer Tune & Lube, Grossman Chevrolet, Harver Pontiac, GMC Truck, Lorensen Toyota
ATM **E:** New Haven Savings Bank

66 **(74)** CT 166, Spencer Plain Road
Gas **E:** Citgo(*)
Food **E:** Aleia's, Alforno Brick Oven Pizza, Cookoo's Nest Mexican, Little Thai Restaurant, Mike's Deli, Paesan's Pizza, Sol-E-Mar Cafe, TNT Family Restaurant
Lodg **E:** Days Inn, Heritage Motor Lodge, Sandpiper Motor Inn, Saybrook Motor Inn, Super 8
AServ **E:** Smith Bros Transmission
Other **E:** **DMK Animal Hospital**

(74) Rest Area (RR, Phones, Picnic; Northbound)

65 **(73)** CT 153, Westbrook
Gas **E:** Exxon(*)
Food **E:** Denny's, Dunkin Donuts (Exxon), Westbrook Pizza
AServ **E:** NAPA Auto Parts, Westbrook Honda
Med **W:** **24 Hour Emergency Medical Center (3 Miles)**
ATM **E:** Citizens Bank
Other **E:** Westbrook Pharmacy(RX)

64 **(71)** CT 145, Horse Hill Road

63 **(69)** CT 81, Clinton, Killingworth
Gas **E:** Shell(*)
Other **W:** **Clinton Crossings Premium Outlet (Food Court)**

62 **(66)** Hammonasset State Park
RVCamp **W:** **River Road Campground (1 Mile), Riverdale Farm Campsites (2 Miles)**
Parks **E:** **Hammonasset State Park (1.5 Miles)**

(66) Service Area (RR, Phones, Picnic; Southbound)
FStop **B:** **Mobil**
Food **B:** **McDonald's**

Bold red print shows RV & Bus parking available or nearby

EXIT CONNECTICUT

61 **(65)** CT 79, Madison
- Med — **E:** ✚ **East Shore Medical Center**
- ATM — **E:** Webster Bank
- Other — **E:** **Madison Police**

60 **(64)** CT 79, Madison, North Madison, Mungertown Rd (Southbound)

59 **(61)** Guilford, Goose Lane
- Gas — **E:** Citgo(*), Mobil(*), Texaco(*, D)
- Food — **E:** Boss Pizza & Subs, Dandy Donuts (Mobil), First Garden Chinese, McDonald's, Seabreeze Family Restaurant, Shoreline Diner, Wendy's
- AServ — **E:** Goodyear Tire & Auto, Valvoline Oil Change

58 **(60)** CT 77, Guilford, North Guilford
- Other — **E:** **Tourist Info.**
  W: **Guilford Police Station**

57 **(59)** U.S. 1, North Branford
- AServ — **W:** Saab Dealer

56 CT 146, Leetes Island Road, Stony Creek
- TStop — **W:** **T/A TravelCenters of America**(*, SCALES)
- FStop — **W:** **Berkshire**(*, D, CW)
- Gas — **W:** Mobil(*, CW)
- Food — **W:** Friendly's, **T/A TravelCenters of America**
- Lodg — **E:** Advanced Motel
  W: Ramada Limited
- AServ — **E:** New Age Motor
- TServ — **W:** **Freightliner Sales & Service, T/A TravelCenters of America**(SCALES)
- Other — **W:** **Super Stop & Shop**

55 U.S. 1, North Branford, East Main St
- Gas — **E:** Mobil
  W: Citgo(*, CW), Texaco(*)
- Food — **E:** McDonald's (Motel 6), My Dad's Place
  W: Margarita's Mexican, Su Casa, The Parthenon Diner(24)
- Lodg — **E:** Knight's Inn, Motel 6
  W: Branson Motel, DAYS INN Days Inn
- AServ — **E:** Mobil
- ATM — **W:** Bank Boston
- Other — **E:** **WalGreens Pharmacy**(RX)

54 Branford, Cedar St
- Gas — **E:** Citgo, Mobil(*, CW), Petro Plus
- Food — **E:** Brandford Townhouse, Dunkin Donuts, Fortune Village Chinese
  W: The Lion City Chinese
- AServ — **E:** Citgo, Petro Plus, Shoreline Mitsubishi, Subaru of Branford
  W: Eastshore Auto Body
- Other — **E:** **AAA Office**
  W: **Brandford's Farmers Market, Brushy Hill Shopping Center**

(53) Service Area
- Gas — **B:** Mobil(D)
- Food — **B:** McDonald's
- ATM — **B:** Mobil

53 **(52)** U.S. 1, CT 142, CT 146, Short Beach (Northbound, Difficult Reaccess)
- Gas — **E:** Getty(*)
- Food — **E:** Bagel Connection, Moon Star Chinese

52 **(50)** CT 100, Easthaven , N High St
- Gas — **E:** Citgo
- Food — **E:** Subway
- AServ — **E:** Citgo, Goodyear Tire & Auto

51 **(50)** U.S. 1, Frontage Road , E Haven
- Gas — **E:** Merit, Sunoco(*, 24)
  W: Mobil(*), Sunoco(*)
- Food — **E:** Boston Market Restaurant, Friendly's
  W: Dunkin Donuts, The Bon China Buffet, Wendy's
- Lodg — **E:** Holiday Inn Express
- AServ — **E:** McDermit Chevrolet
  W: Auto Zone

EXIT CONNECTICUT

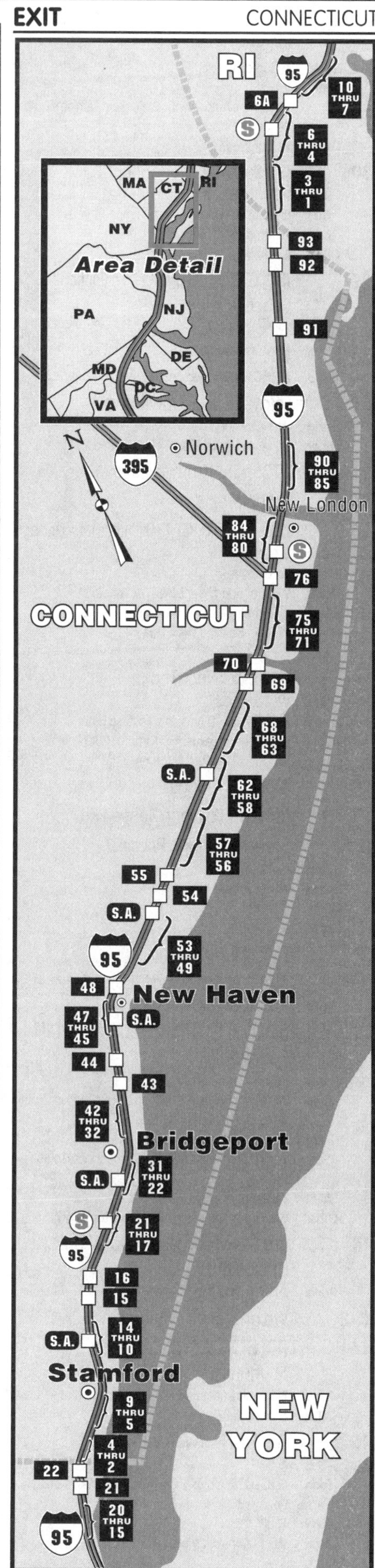

EXIT CONNECTICUT

50 **(49)** Woodward Ave, Lighthouse Point (Northbound, Difficult Reaccess)
- Gas — **E:** Texaco
  W: Forbes, Gulf(*)
- Food — **W:** BJ's Lunch, Dunkin Donuts, Fireside, Planet Mars Cafe
- AServ — **W:** DeNatto & Son Garage, Gulf
- Other — **E:** **Airport**
  W: **Quality Mart**

49 Stiles St (Difficult Reaccess)
- Food — **W:** Lou's Lunch
- AServ — **W:** A&A Towing & Auto Repair, DeMufis Radiator Service, Fountions Garage, Sas-t Service
- TServ — **E:** **PC Truck Repairs**
  W: **Mikes Truck & Trailer Repair**
- Other — **W:** Forbes Car Wash, **Pay Rite Food Market**

48 **(47)** Junction I-91 North, Hartford (Left Exit)

47 CT 34, Downtown New Haven

46 **(49)** Long Wharf Dr, Sargent Dr
- Gas — **W:** Mobil(*, D, LP, CW)
- Food — **W:** Brazi's Pizza & Pasta, Dunkin Donuts (Mobil)
- Lodg — **W:** Grand Chalet, Howard Johnson
- Med — **W:** ✚ **Hospital**
- ATM — **W:** Fleet Bank
- Other — **W:** New Haven Theater

45 **(48)** CT 10 Blvd.
- Gas — **W:** Getty(*)
- Food — **W:** Dairy Queen, Dunkin Donuts, McDonald's(24)
- AServ — **W:** Meineke Discount Mufflers

44 **(46)** CT 10, Kimberley Ave , Downtown New Haven
- Gas — **W:** Getty(*, 24)
- Food — **W:** Dairy Queen, Dunkin Donuts, McDonald's
- AServ — **W:** Catapano Brothers, Meineke Discount Mufflers, Tony Long Warf

43 **(45)** CT 122, First Ave, Downtown
- Gas — **W:** Amaco(*), Mobil(*)
- Food — **W:** China Sea, Dunkin Donuts (Mobil)
- AServ — **E:** Whitey's Garage
  W: Mobil, Walter's Automotive
- Med — **W:** ✚ **Veterns Hospital**

42 **(44)** CT 162, Saw Mill Road
- Gas — **E:** Mobil(*)
  W: Shell(*, 24)
- Food — **E:** Pizza Hut, The Powered Donut, West Haven Pizza Place
  W: American Steak House, D'Angelo's Subs & Salads, Days Hotel, Denny's, Dunkin Donuts, Friendly's
- Lodg — **E:** EconoLodge
  W: Days Hotel
- AServ — **E:** Mobil
- Other — **W:** **7-11 Convenience Store**

41 **(42)** Marsh Hill Road, Orange
- Food — **W:** Outback Steakhouse
- Lodg — **W:** Courtyard by Marriott
- Other — **W:** **Mall**, **Showcase Cinema**

(41) Service Area
- FStop — **B:** **Mobil**
- Food — **B:** **McDonald's**
- ATM — **B:** ATM
- Other — **B:** **Gift Shop**

40 **(41)** Old Gate Lane, Woodmont Road
- TStop — **E:** **Secondi Bros Gulf**(*, LP)
- Gas — **E:** Getty(D), Sunoco(*, 24)
- Food — **E:** Bennigan's, **Cracker Barrel**, D'angelo's, Duchess Burgers (Milford Inn), Dunkin Donuts, Gipper's, **Secondi Bros Gulf**
- Lodg — **E:** Comfort Inn, **Mayflower Motel**, **Milford Inn**
- AServ — **E:** Getty, Mad Hatter Mufflers & Brakes, Sunoco(24)

Bold red print shows RV & Bus parking available or nearby

EXIT — CONNECTICUT

TServ — E: Bethaven Ford Truck, Secondi Bros Gulf
TWash — E: Secondi Bros Gulf
ATM — E: Bank of New Haven, Citizens Bank

39AB — U.S. 1
Gas — E: Gulf (Towing)
W: Mobile[*, CW]
Food — E: Athenian Diner, Mama Teresa Pizza, Pizzeria Uno, The Gathering Steaks, Uno Pizza
W: Burger King, Dunkin Donuts, McDonald's, Miami Subs
Lodg — E: Howard Johnson, Milford Motel, The Connecticut Turnpike Motel
AServ — E: Firestone Tire & Auto, Gulf (Towing), Milford Oldsmobile
W: Town Fair Tire
Med — W: ✚ Hospital
ATM — W: Fleet Bank
Other — W: CT. Post Mall

38 — CT 15, Merritt Pkwy, W Cross PKWY

37 — High St (Northbound, Reaccess Southbound Only)
Gas — E: Gulf, Texaco
Food — E: Kimberly Diner
AServ — E: Colonial Toyota, Gulf, Meineke Discount Mufflers, Texaco
Other — E: 7-11 Convenience Store, Milford City Police, Mobile Vet Clinic

36 — **(37)** Plains Road, Stratford
Gas — E: Exxon[*, D], Sunoco[*, D]
Food — E: Gusto Fine Italian Cuisene, Pasquale's Pizza
Lodg — E: Hampton Inn
Med — E: ✚ Hospital
ATM — E: Fleet Bank

35 — **(36)** School House Road, Bic Dr
Gas — E: Ctigo
Food — E: Armellino's Italian, Wendy's
Lodg — E: The Susse Chalet
W: Red Roof Inn
AServ — E: Courtney Honda, Ctigo, Dan Perkins Chevrolet, Dennis' Auto Parts, Napoli Pontiac, Stephen's Chrysler Plymouth, Stephen's Ford, Steve's Auto Body Shop, Zee Buick GMC Truck
RVCamp — E: Fairchild Trailer Sales
Med — E: ✚ Milford Medical Center

34 — **(35)** U.S. 1, Milford
Gas — E: Gulf[D], Shell
Food — E: Denny's, Dunkin Donuts, Gourmet Buffet International, McDonald's[PLAY], TCBY, Taco Bell
Lodg — E: Devon Motel, Liberty Rock Motel
AServ — E: Action Auto Supply, Brake Masters USA, Brangaccio Bros. Transmission, Gulf, Key Hyundai, Lodus Auto Service
RVCamp — E: Fairchild Sales Inc.[LP] (1 Mile)
Med — E: ✚ Milford Medical Hospital
Other — E: K-Mart, Phil's Pharmacy[RX], Walbaum's Supermarket

33 — **(34)** U.S. 1, CT 110, Ferry Blvd, Devon (Northbound, Difficult Reaccess)
Gas — E: Sunoco
Food — E: Danny's Drive-In, Fagan's Restaurant
W: House of Tung, Mayer's Bagel, Ponderosa
AServ — E: Sunoco
Other — E: Petco Supply Store
W: Petland Pet Supply, Post Office

32 — **(33)** West Broad St, Stratford
Gas — W: Cumberland Farms[*], Gulf[*]
Food — W: Dunkin Donuts, Leonardo's A Pizza, Pepin's Restaurant, Pizza & Italian Restaurant
Med — W: ✚ Hospital
Other — W: Pet Superbowl, Stratford Animal Hospital

31 — **(32)** South Ave.
Gas — E: Gulf[D]
W: Citgo[*]
Lodg — E: Camelot Motel
AServ — E: Gulf
W: Central Auto Supply, Citgo, Sam Lemkie's Auto Repair
Other — W: Car Wash

30 — **(31)** Surf Ave. (Northbound)
FStop — W: Citgo[*]
Gas — E: Shell[*, D]
Lodg — E: Ramada
Other — E: Airport

29 — **(30)** CT 130, Stratford Ave (Difficult Reaccess)
Med — W: ✚ Hospital

28 — **(30)** Main St
Med — E: ✚ Eastport Medical Center

27 — Lafayette Blvd, Downtown
Lodg — W: Holiday Inn
Other — W: State Police, The Barnum Museum

27A — CT25, CT8, Trumball, Waterbury

26 — **(28)** Wordin Ave

25 — **(28)** Fairfield, CT 130 (Difficult Reaccess)
Gas — E: Getty[*]
W: Gulf[*, D]
Food — W: Bridgeport Flyer Diner, McDonald's
AServ — E: Demetri's Auto Service, Getty
W: Don Stevens Tires, Gulf
Other — E: Post Office

24 — **(27)** Black Rock Tnpk
Gas — W: Getty[*], Gulf[*, D]
Food — E: Coffee Isle, D'Angelo's, Fairfield Diner
AServ — E: Bridgeport Lexus, Mark Improt Auto Parts
W: Gulf, Miller Ford & Nisson

23 — **(26)** U.S. 1, Kings Highway

22 — **(25)** CT 132, North Benson Rd.

(25) — Service Area (RR, Phones)
FStop — B: Mobil
Food — B: Hot Subs, McDonald's
AServ — B: Mobil
ATM — B: ATM

21 — **(24)** Mill Plain Road

20 — **(24)** Bronson Road (Difficult Reaccess)
Food — E: Southport Brewing Co.

19 — **(23)** U.S. 1, Center St, Southport (Difficult Reaccess)
Gas — W: Sunoco[*], Texaco[*, D]
Food — W: Athena's Diner, Callahan's Cafe, Dunkin Donuts (Texaco), Friendly's, S&S Dugout
Lodg — W: Piquot Motor Inn
AServ — W: A.D.R. Auto Body, Fetzer Tire, Sunoco, Town Fair Tire
ATM — W: People's Bank
Other — W: Alfred's Car Wash, Southport Car Wash

18 — **(21)** Sherwood Island State Park (Eastbound)
Parks — E: Sherwood Island State Park

(20) — Weigh Station (Southbound)

17 — **(18)** CT 33, CT 136, Westport, Saugatuck
Food — E: Jasmine Restaurant
ATM — E: Lafayette Bank

16 — **(17)** East Norwalk
Gas — E: BP[D]
Food — E: Baskin Robbins, Dunkin Donuts, Mike's Deli, Penny's III Diner
AServ — E: BP
Med — W: ✚ Norwalk Medical Center
Other — E: Rite Aid Pharmacy[RX]

15 — **(16)** U.S. 7, Norwalk, Danbury
Gas — E: Mobil[D], Shell[*], Sunoco[*], Texaco[*]
W: Getty
Food — E: Dunkin Donuts (Texaco)
AServ — E: Maritime Oldsmobile, Chevrolet, Mobil, Shell
Med — W: ✚ Hospital
Other — W: Maritime Aquarium, Police Station

14 — **(15)** U.S. 1, Connecticut Ave, South Norwalk
Gas — W: Amoco[*, 24], Coastal[*], Shell, Texaco
Food — W: Angela-Mia Italian, Cosmos Pizza, Hunan Garden, Pizza Hut, Silver Star Restaurant, Speedy Donuts, Swanky Franky's Seafood, Universal Subs & Salads, Via Roma Italian
AServ — W: Cataling's Auto Body, Coastal, Firestone Tire & Auto, John's Auto Repair, Shell, Texaco, Valvoline Oil Change
Med — W: ✚ Hospital

13 — U.S. 1, Post Road (Difficult Reaccess)
Gas — W: Exxon[CW] (Oil Change), Mobil, Shell[*]
Food — W: Bertucci's Brick Oven Pizza, Carvel Ice Cream Bakery, Carver Dairy Bar, Centro Bistro, Driftwood Diner, Dutchess Restaurant, Friendly's, IHOP, KFC, McDonald's, Pasta Fair, Red Lobster
Lodg — W: Club Hotel
AServ — W: Darien Car Clinic[CW], Mobil
ATM — W: Fairfield County Savings Bank, First Union Bank
Other — W: Exit 13 Car Wash, Stop and Shop Food Mart

(12) — Service Area (Northbound)
FStop — E: Mobil
Food — E: McDonald's
W: Lavava Cafe
AServ — W: Mobil
ATM — W: ATM
Other — W: Postal Service, RV Dump, Tourist Info.

12 — CT 136, Tokeneke Road, Rowayton (Northbound, Reaccess Southbound Only)

11 — U.S. 1, Darien, Rowayton
Gas — E: Amoco[24]
W: Exxon[*]
Food — E: Chuck's Steakhouse
W: Black Foot Goose Grill, Boston Market Restaurant, Dunkin Donuts, Subway, Sugar Bowl Luncheonette, Uncle's Deli, Uppercrust Bagel Co.
Lodg — W: Howard Johnson
AServ — E: H&L Chevrolet & Geo, Miller Automotive
W: BMW of Darion, Exxon
ATM — W: First Union, Fleet Bank
Other — E: Darien Car Wash, Darien Veterinary Hospital
W: CVS Pharmacy[RX], Grieb's Pharmacy[RX]

10 — Noroton
FStop — W: Texaco[*, CW]

Holiday Inn SELECT™ STAMFORD
700 Main St.
Stamford, CT 06901
203-358-8400

Features & Amenities:
★ Newly renovated guest rooms & suites ★
★ Full-service Restaurant ★ Lobby Bar ★ Coffee Bar ★
★ FREE shuttle to downtown attractions ★
★ Fitness center & indoor pool ★
★ Abundant FREE parking ★
★ Located directly off I-95 at exit 8 ★
Independently owned and operated by Bristol Hotels & Resorts™
1467

EXIT CONNECTICUT/NEW YORK

Gas W: Getty, Mobil
Food W: Denny's
AServ W: Bill's Auto Body, Getty, Mobil

(11) Service Area (Southbound)
FStop W: **Mobil**
Food W: McDonald's[PLAY]
ATM W: **Mobil**

9 U.S. 1, CT 106, Glenbrook
Gas W: Gulf[LP]
Food E: Indian Palace, Stamford Motor Inn
W: Blimpie's Subs, Brasita's Restaurant, Chin's Chinese Restaurant, Exit 9 Bagels, McDonald's, Sergio's Pizza, Stamford Restaurant
Lodg E: Stamford Motor Inn
AServ E: Midas Muffler
W: Gulf, Meineke Discount Mufflers
Other W: **Just Cats Veterinary Hospital**

8 Elm St, Atlantic St
Lodg W: Budget Inn, Holiday Inn Select (see our ad this page), Marriott Hotel, Stamford Plaza
Med W: ✚ **Hospital**
Other W: Elm Street Mini Mart[24]

7 CT 137, Atlantic St. (Northbound, Reaccess Northbound Only)
Food E: Sheraton Stanford Hotel
Lodg E: Sheraton Stanford Hotel

6 (7) West Ave., Harvard Ave.
Gas E: BP[CW]
W: Amoco[*], Shell[*]
Food W: Antonio's Italian, Athen's Pizza, Dunkin Donuts, Subway
Lodg E: Grand Chalet
W: Super 8
AServ W: Bee Line Auto & Tire, Expert Auto Service, Marc Service Center
Med W: ✚ **Standford Hospital**
ATM W: Fleet Bank
Other E: **Maxi Discount Pharmacy**[RX]

5 (6) U.S. 1, Riverside, Old Greenwich
Gas W: Getty[*], Mobil[*], Shell[D]
Food W: Hunan Cafe Chinese, McDonald's, Riverside Deli, Starbucks Coffee
Lodg W: Howard Johnson
AServ W: Precision Tune & Lube, Riverside Auto Parts, Shell
ATM W: Chase Bank, People's Bank, Putman Trust
Other W: **CVS Pharmacy**[RX], **Post Office**, U.S. Post Office

4 (5) Indian Field Road, Cos Cob

3 Arch St, Greenwich
Gas W: Mobil, Texaco[*, D]
AServ W: Lexus, Mobil, Saad, Texaco
Med W: ✚ **Greenwich Hospital**

(2) Weigh Station (Northbound)

2 Delavan Ave, Byram

↑CONNECTICUT

↓NEW YORK

22 (14) Midland Ave, Port Chester, Rye

21 (13) Junction I-287, U.S. 1 North, Tappan Zee Bridge (Toll)

20 (14) U.S. 1 South, Rye (Northbound)
Gas E: Shell, Texaco[D]
W: Mobile
Food E: Sunrise Pizzeria
W: Carvel Ice Cream Bakery, Dunkin Donuts, McDonald's[24], Szechuan Empire II
AServ E: Rye Ford Subaru, Shell, Texaco
W: Mobile

EXIT NEW YORK

ATM W: Fleet Bank
Other E: **A&P Supermarket**, US Post Office
W: **Vision World**, **Waldbaum's Supermarket**[24]

19 (12) Playland Pkwy, Rye, Harrison (Difficult Reaccess)

18B (11) Mamaroneck Ave, White Plains
Food E: Hillside Deli, Jenny's Pizza
AServ E: Shell
Other E: **Auto Service Expressway**, **Mavis Discount Tire**

18A (9) Fenimore Road, Mamaroneck (Difficult Reaccess)
Gas E: Hess[*], Shell[24]
AServ E: Expressway Fast Oil Change, Mavis Discount Tire, Shell[24]
Other E: **A&P Supermarket**, Dippin Car Wash

17 (7) Chatsworth Ave, Larchmont (Northbound)

16 (6) North Ave, Cedar St, New Rochelle
Gas E: Getty, Sunoco[*]
Food E: Luke's Hong Kong Garden, Pizza Hut
Lodg E: Ramada
AServ E: Getty, Toyota Dealer
Med W: ✚ **Hospital**

(7) Toll Booth (Northbound, Toll)

15 (5) U.S. 1, New Rochelle, The Pelhams
Gas E: Amoco, BP[D], Citgo[D], Exxon[*], Shorco[*, D, 24]
Food E: D & M Deli, Drakemain Cafe, Subway (Exxon), The Thru Way Diner
AServ E: Citgo

14 (3) Hutchison PKWY S, Whitestone Bridge

13 (2) Conner St, Baychester Ave
FStop E: **Gasateria**[*, D, CW, 24]
Gas E: Citgo[*], Gulf[*, D]
W: Amoco[*, 24], City Gas[D, 24]
Food W: Dunkin Donuts (City Gas), McDonald's[PLAY], Wonder Bakery
Lodg W: Holiday Motel
AServ E: Citgo, Gulf, New England Auto Repair
W: Auto Service Center, Frankie's Auto Service, Jiffy Lube, Lee Myles Auto Service, Meineke Discount Mufflers, Michelin, R & S Service Center
TServ E: **Gabrielli Mack**
Med E: ✚ **Lady of Mercy Medical Hospital**

12 Baychester Ave (Northbound, Left Exit Northbound)

11 Bartow Ave, Co-op City Blvd.
Gas E: Mobil
W: Shell[*, 24]
Food E: Bartow Pizza, Baskin Robbins, Boston Market Restaurant, Chinese Cuisine, Dunkin Donuts, **Little Caesars Pizza (K-Mart)**, Red Lobster, Seven Seas
AServ E: Mobil
W: Shell[24]
ATM E: Amalgamated Bank of NY, Immigrant Savings Bank, Marine Midland Bank
Other E: **Bay Plaza Mall**, **General Vision Eyewear**, **K-Mart**, Rite Aid Pharmacy

10 Gun Hill Road (Left Exit)

9 Hutchinson Pkwy

8C Pelham Pkwy
Med W: ✚ **Hospital**

8B Orchard Beach, City Island

8A Westchester Ave.

7B East Tremont Ave (Difficult Reaccess)

7A to I-295
Food E: Best Bagels in Town, Cross Town Diner

EXIT NEW YORK/NEW JERSEY

AServ E: Mobile

6B I-278 W, Bruckner Express, Triboro Bridge (Left Exit)

6A Junction I-678 South, Bruckner Blvd (Difficult Reaccess)

5B Castle Hill Ave
Food E: Big Market West Indian Grocery, Castle Hill Bake Shop, House of Hero's and Deli
W: Brisas-Delcaribe (Mexican), Castle Hill Grocery
AServ W: R&S Strauss, Senico

5A Westchester

4B Rosedale Ave, Bronx River Pkwy
Parks W: **Bronx Park**
Other W: **Bronx Zoo**

4A Jct I-895 South, Sheridan Expwy, Triboro Bridge
Other E: **Yankee Stadium**

3 Third Ave.
Med W: ✚ **Hospital**

2B Webster Ave
Food E: McDonald's

2A Jerome Ave

1C Junction I-87, Major Deegan Expressway

1B Harlem River Dr, Amsterdam Ave

1A (122) 181 St, NY9A, H Hudson Pkwy

↑NEW YORK

↓NEW JERSEY

73 (122) Palisades Pkwy

72 (122) NJ67, U.S. 9W, Fort Lee
Lodg W: DAYS INN Days Inn, Hilton

71 (122) U.S. 1, U.S. 9, U.S.46

(122) NJ4, NJ17

70 to NJ93, Leonia, Tenack
Lodg W: Marriott
Med W: ✚ **Hospital**

69 (68) Jct I-80, to Patterson

68A (118) U.S. 46, New Jersey Tnpk

68B (118) Junction I-95 North, George Washington Bridge, New York

68 (118) Jct I-80 West, to NJ17

(69) Clara Barton/John Fenwick Service Area

Note: I-95 runs concurrent below with NJTNPK. Numbering follows NJTNPK.

18 (114) U.S. 46, Hackensack

(113) Vince Lombardi Service Area

17 (117) NY 3, Lincoln Tunnel
Food E: Ladelkaribe (At Holiday Inn)
Lodg E: Holiday Inn
W: Radison Suites (see our ad this page)
Other E: **Mall**

16 (113) NY 3, Secaucus, Rutherford
Gas E: Amoco
Food E: Bagels Plus, Chi Chi's Mexican Restaurant, Grettle's Pretzel, Haagen Dazs Ice Cream, Herbert Billard, Hulahan's, McConkey Big City Grill (Holiday Inn), Players Steakhouse (Embassy Suites), Red

EXIT	NEW JERSEY
	Robbin Restaurant (Courtyard By Marriott), Sizzler, Subway
	W: Burger King, Cafe, Pizzeria Uno, TCBY, Tuttaeene Italian
Lodg	**E:** Ameri Suites, Courtyard By Marriott, Embassy Suites, Holiday Inn, Howard Johnson (see our ad this page), Ramada Inn (see our ad this page)
	W: Raddison Suites
ATM	**E:** Summit Bank
Other	**E:** **Meadowland Convention Ctr**
	W: **Hear X (Hearing Aid)**
15	**(109)** Jct I-280, Newark, The Oranges
15E	**(107)** Newark, Jersey City
14C	**(105)** Holland Tunnel
14B	**(105)** Jersey City
14A	**(105)** Bayonne
14	**(105)** Junction I-78, U.S. 1, U.S. 22
(102)	Admiral W.M. Halsey Service Area (Southbound)
13A	**(101)** Newark Airport, Elizabeth Seaport
13	**(100)** Junction I-278, Elizabeth, Goethals Bridge, Verrazano
12	**(96)** Carteret, Rahway
Food	**E:** Blimpie's Subs, Burger Express, Burger King, Carlo's Pizza & Subs, Chopsticks Kitchen Chinese, Hang Hing Chinese, **Holiday Inn**, McDonald's, Riuniti Pizza, The Bus Stop
Lodg	**E:** **Holiday Inn**
AServ	**E:** George Lucas Chevrolet/Geo, Goodyear Tire & Auto
Med	**E:** **✚ Dr's Medi Center (Open 7 Days a Week)**
ATM	**E:** First Union Bank
Other	**E:** **Coin Laundry**, **Revco Drugs**, **Shoprite Grocery**, **Short Stop C-Store**, **WalGreens Pharmacy**
(93)	Thomas A. Edison Service Area
11	**(91)** U.S. 9, Woodbridge, Garden State Pkwy
10	**(88)** Junction I-287, NJ 440, Metuchen
9	**(84)** U.S.11, NJ 18, New Brunswick
Lodg	**W:** **Ramada Inn (see our ad this page)**
(79)	Joyce Kilmer Service Area (Northbound)
8A	**(74)** Jamesburg, Cranbury
(72)	Molly Pitcher Service Area (Southbound)
8	**(68)** NJ 33, Hightstown, Freehold
7A	**(61)** Jct I-195, Trenton, Hamilton

1665

Ramada Inn

732-828-6900

Steakhouse Restaurant on Premises
Lounge w/Entertainment
Kids Under 12 Stay & Eat Free
Outdoor Pool • Exercise Room
Limited Truck Parking
Meeting/Banquet Facilities
Handicap Accessible • Coin Laundry

195 Route 18 South • East Brunswick, NY 08816

NEW JERSEY TRNPK • I-95 • EXIT 9

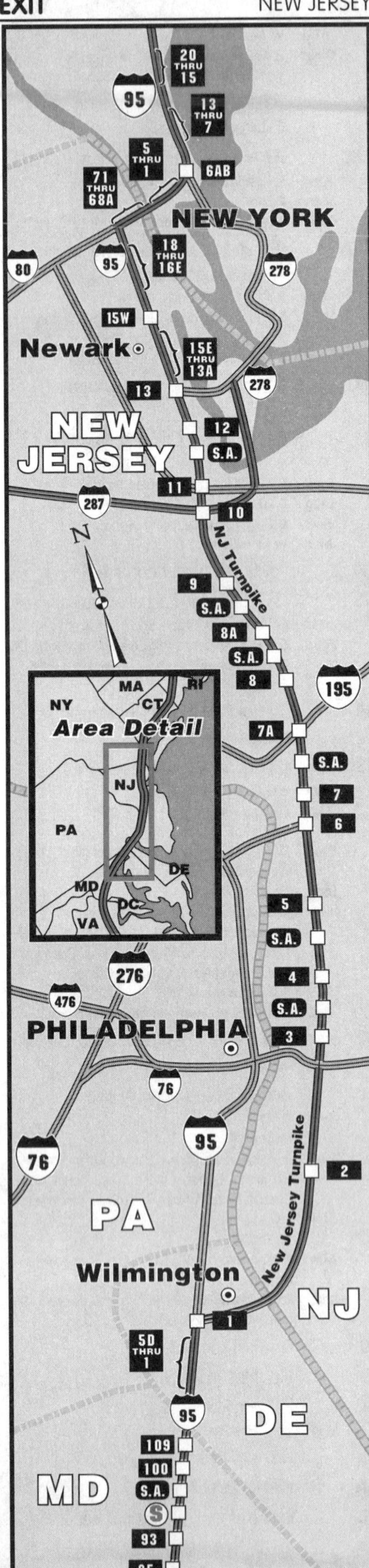

EXIT	NEW JERSEY
(59)	Richard Stockton Service Area (Southbound)
7	**(54)** U.S. 206, Bordentown, Trenton
6	**(51)** Jct PA Tnpk
5	**(44)** Burlington, Mount Holly, Willingboro
(39)	J. Fenimore Cooper Service Area (Northbound)
4	**(34)** NJ 73, Philadelphia, Camden
(29)	Walt Whitman Service Area (Southbound)
FStop	**E:** **Sunoco**
Food	**E:** Nathan's Famous, **Roy Rogers**
AServ	**E:** Sunoco

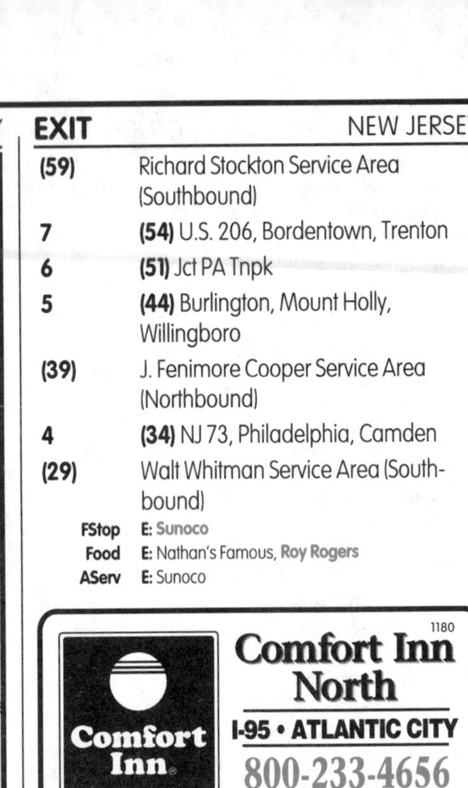

1180

Comfort Inn North

I-95 • ATLANTIC CITY

800-233-4656

Overlooks Atlantic City Skyline

Free Continental Breakfast Daily

I-95 to **Exit 3** (Hwy.76 East) to Atlantic City Expressway (Exit 12). turn left on Hwy. 575, go to 2nd light (Route 30) make a right. Go 7 miles and Comfort Inn is on the right.

I-95 to **Exit 11** (Garden State Pkwy. South) to Exit 40 (30 East). Go 3 miles Comfort Inn is on the right.

NEW JERSEY ▪ I-95 ▪ EXIT 3 & 11

1335

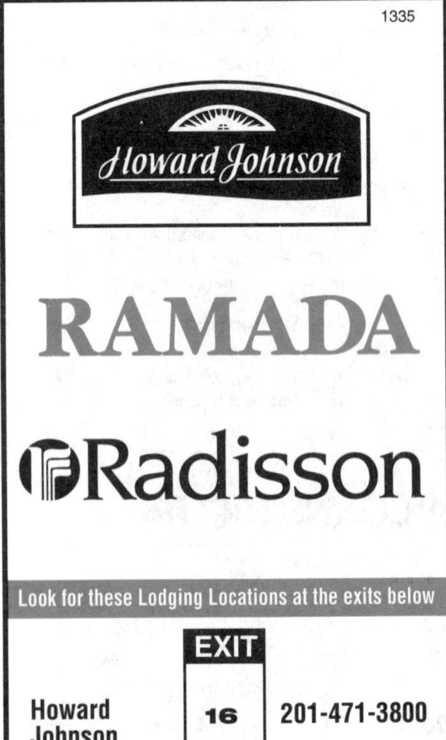

Look for these Lodging Locations at the exits below

	EXIT	
Howard Johnson	16	201-471-3800
Ramada	16	201-778-6500
Radisson	17	201-863-8700

Bold red print shows RV & Bus parking available or nearby

EXIT — NEW JERSEY

3 — **(26)** NJ 168, Camden, Woodbury
- FStop — E: Gulf[*]
- Gas — W: Coastal[D], Texaco[D], Xtra[*]
- Food — W: Bagal Wiches, Club Diner, Dunkin Donuts, Italia Pizza, Pulcinell's, Wendy's
- Lodg — E: Comfort Inn (see our ad this page), Holiday Inn
  W: Bellmawr Motor Inn, Econolodge, Howard Johnson Express (see our ad this page)
- AServ — E: Gulf
  W: Coastal
- ATM — W: Midlantic Bank
- Other — W: NJ State Aquarium

2 — **(13)** U.S. 322, Swedesboro , Chester PA

(5) — Clara Barton Service Area

1A — **(0)** NJ49E, Pennsville, Salem

Note: I-95 runs concurrent above with NJTNPK. Numbering follows NJTNPK.

8AB — CR583S, Princeton Pike

7AB — U.S.206, Lawrenceville, Princeton, Trenton
- Gas — W: Mobil
- Food — W: Lawrenceville Deli
- AServ — W: Mobil
- ATM — W: PNC Bank
- Parks — W: Mercer County Park, Rosedale Park

5AB — **(6)** Federal City Rd (No Trucks Over 10 Tons)

4 — NJ31, Ewing, Pennington
- Parks — W: Washington Crossing Nat'l Park

3 — Scotch Rd
- ATM — E: CoreStates Bank
- Parks — W: Washington Crossing Park
- Other — E: Trenton Mercer Airport

2 — CR 579, Harbourton, W Trenton, Airport
- ATM — W: CoreStates Bank
- Parks — W: South Park At Ewing
- Other — E: Trenton-Mercer Airport (.75 Miles)

1 — NJ29, Trenton, Lambertville

EXIT — NEW JERSEY/PENNSYLVANIA

- Lodg — W: Wellesley Inn (see our ad this page)
- Med — E: ✚ Hospital
- Parks — W: DNR Canal State Park & Scudders Falls

↑ NEW JERSEY

↓ PENNSYLVANIA

31 — **(50)** New Hope, Yardley
- Other — W: Washington Crossing Park (3 Miles)

(50) — Weigh Station, Rest Area (RR, Phones, Picnic, Pet Walk; Southbound)

30 — **(48)** PA332, Newtown, Yardley
- Parks — W: Tyler State Park (4 Miles)

29 — **(45)** U.S. 1, Morrisville, Langhorne (Difficult Reaccess)
- Med — W: ✚ Delaware Hospital

28 — **(43)** PA413, U.S. 1 Bus, Penndel, Levittown
- Gas — E: Texaco[*, LP, CW]
  W: Mobil[*, D]
- Food — E: Chuck E Cheese's Pizza, Dunkin Donuts, Friendly's, Great American Diner
  W: Denny's, McDonald's[PLAY]
- AServ — E: McCafferty Chrysler Jeep, Reedman Chevrolet Oldsmobile
  W: Team Toyota
- Med — E: ✚ Delaware Valley Medical Center
- ATM — E: CoreState
- Other — E: Langhorn Square Mall

26 — **(39)** PA 413, Bristol, Jct I-276, PA Tnpk
- Med — E: ✚ Lower Bucks Hospital

25 — **(36)** PA 132, Street Rd, to US13, Bristol Pike
- Gas — W: Amoco[*, 24], Sunoco[*]
- AServ — W: Cottman Transmissions, Keystone Discount Tire Co
- Parks — E: State Park

1337
Look for this fine Lodging Location at the exit below
Radisson — EXIT 24 — 215-638-8300

PENNSYLVANIA ▪ PA Turnpike ▪ Exit 23

EXIT — PENNSYLVANIA

24 — **(35)** PA 63W, to U.S.13, Woodhaven Rd, Bristol Park
- Gas — W: Texaco[D]
- Food — W: McDonald's
- Lodg — W: Hampton Inn, Radisson (see our ad this page)
- AServ — W: Texaco
- Med — W: ✚ Frankfort Hospital
- ATM — W: Texaco
- Other — W: One Woodhaven Mall

23 — **(32)** Academy Road, Porresdale Ave
- Lodg — W: Best Western (see our ad this page)
- Med — W: ✚ Hospital
- Other — W: Philadelphia NE Airport

22 — **(30)** PA73, Cottman Ave (Northbound, Difficult Reaccess)
- FStop — E: Sunoco[*, D]
- Gas — W: Sunoco[D]
- Food — E: Inna G's
- AServ — E: Rossetti's Collision, Sunoco
  W: Sunoco
- TServ — E: Foster Michelin Big Trucks (Frontage Rd)

21 — **(26)** Bridge St (Difficult Reaccess)
- Gas — E: Citgo[*]
  W: Getty's[*]
- AServ — W: Getty's
- Med — W: ✚ Hospital
- ATM — E: Citgo

20 — **(25)** Pennsauken NJ, Betsy Ross Bridge

19 — **(25)** Allegheny Ave
- Gas — W: Sunoco[*]
- Food — W: Syrenka Restaurant
- Med — W: ✚ Hospital
- Other — W: WaWa Food Market

18 — **(23)** Girard Ave, Lehigh Ave (Northbound, No Reaccess)
- Gas — W: Sunoco[*, D, LP]
- Food — W: Dunkin Donuts
- ATM — W: Sunoco

17 — **(22)** Jct I-676 , Independence Hall, Central Philadelphia, Callowhill St (Left Exit)

16 — **(20)** Columbus Blvd, Washington Ave (Left Exit Southbound, Difficult Reaccess)
- Food — E: The Chart House
- Med — W: ✚ Hospital

15 — **(19)** Jct I-76E, Walt Whitman Bridge, Packer Ave
- Gas — W: Sunoco[*, D], Texaco[*]
- Food — W: Burger King, McDonald's[PLAY], Subway, Wendy's
- AServ — W: R&S

14 — **(17)** PA 611, Broad St, Pattison Ave
- Med — W: ✚ Hospital

13 — Enterprise Ave, Island Ave (Southbound)

12 — Bartram Rd, Essington Ave (Southbound)

11 — **(12)** to I-75 W, PA291W, Central Philadelphia, Island Ave (Northbound)
- Gas — E: Exxon[*, D]
- Lodg — E: Four Points Sheraton, Hilton, Residence Inn, Westin
- Other — E: John Hines National Refuge, Philadelphia International Airport

10 — **(13)** PA291E, Philadelphia International

Bold red print shows RV & Bus parking available or nearby

EXIT		PENNSYLVANIA/DELAWARE
		Airport (Southbound)
	Other	W: Philadelphia International Airport
9		PA420, Essington, Prospect Park
	FStop	E: Coastal[*, 24]
	Gas	E: Mobil[D]
	Food	E: Denny's, Lehman's Restaurant, Philly Cheesesteak, Preston Diner[24], SHONEY'S, Shoney's
	Lodg	E: Comfort Inn, Holiday Inn, Motel 6, Red Roof Inn
	AServ	E: Coastal[24], Mobil
	ATM	E: County Savings Assoc., First Union Bank
	Parks	E: Governor Printz State Park W: Morton Homestead Historic Site, Prospect Park
8		Ridley Park
	Med	W: ✚ Taylor Hospital
7		Junction I-476, Plymouth Meeting
6		PA352, PA320 Edgmont Ave, Providence (Difficult Reaccess)
	Med	W: ✚ Crozer-Chester Hospital
5		Kerlin St, to DE 291 (Northbound, Difficult Reaccess)
4		U.S. 322 ,Comm. Barry Bridge
3		Highland Ave, US 322, Wilmington, W Chester (Difficult Reaccess)
	Gas	E: Sunoco[*, D, 24]
	AServ	E: Murphy Lincoln, Mercury W: Martone's Auto Service
	TServ	E: EPC Truck Service, Goodyear Commercial Tire Center
	Other	W: Garden Food Market C-Store
2		PA 452, Market St
	Gas	E: Getty W: Citgo[*], Exxon[*]
	Food	E: Abe's Place, Dairy King, DiCostanza's W: Linwood Restaurant, Ye Old Meeting House Restaurant
	AServ	E: Getty W: Interstate Auto Electric & Repair
	ATM	W: Citgo, Exxon
1		Chichester Ave
	Gas	E: Sunoco[24] W: Amoco[*, LP, CW]
	AServ	E: Rick's Auto Repair, Sunoco[24]
(1)		Weigh Stations, PA Welcome Center (RR, Phones, Picnic; Northbound)

↑PENNSYLVANIA

↓DELAWARE

EXIT		DELAWARE
11		**(23)** Jct I-495, Port of Wilmington, Baltimore
	Food	E: Calhan's, Crownery, Eatery Family Restaurant (K-Mart), Food Court (Tri-State Mall), Shop & Bag Bakery, Deli W: Evergreen's Restaurant (Hilton), Howard Johnson, Taco Bell
	Lodg	W: Hilton
	AServ	E: Goodyear Tire & Auto W: Gulf, Jiffy Lube
	ATM	E: Wilmington Trust Bank W: PNC Bank
	Other	E: Discount Eye Glasses, K-Mart, Tri-State Mall, US Optical, Wa-Ma C-Store W: Acme Grocery Store, Eckerd Drugs, James Way Shopping
10		**(22)** Harvey Road, to Philadelphia Pike (Northbound, Reaccess Southbound Only)
9		**(19)** DE 3, Marsh Road
	Parks	E: Bellevue State Park
	Other	E: DE State Police, Rockwood Museum
8		**(17)** U.S. 202, Concord Pike, Wilmington, West Chester
	Med	E: ✚ Hospital W: ✚ Alferd I. Dupont Children's Hospital
7AB		**(16)** DE 52, Delaware Ave
	Gas	W: Shell[*]
	Lodg	E: Sheraton Suites
	Med	E: ✚ Hospital W: ✚ Hospital
	ATM	W: Shell
6		**(15)** DE 4, DE 9, Fourth St., MLK Blvd
	Gas	W: Shell
	Food	E: McDonald's
	AServ	W: Shell
	Med	W: ✚ Hospital
5D		U.S. 13, Dover, Baltimore, Norfolk
5C		**(13)** Junction I-295, DE Memorial Bridge, New Castle (Left Exit)
5AB		**(10)** US 202, US 13, DE 141 N, Newport, New Castle
4AB		**(8)** DE 7, Christiana , DE1, DE58, Metroform
	Food	W: Chi-Chi's, Chili's, Michael's Family Restaurant, SHONEY'S, Shoney's
	Lodg	W: Courtyard by Marriott, Fairfield Inn, Hilton, Red Roof Inn, Shoney's Inn
	Med	W: ✚ Hospital
	Other	E: Christina Mall W: Borders Books & Music
3		**(7)** DE 273, Newark, Dover
	Gas	E: Amoco[24], Exxon[D] W: Getty[*], Shell[*]
	Food	E: Authentic Chinese, Bob Evan's Restaurant, Boston Market Restaurant, Wendy's W: Denny's, Donut Connection, Holiday Inn, Pizza Hut
	Lodg	E: Best Western W: Hampton Inn, Holiday Inn, McIntosh Inn
	AServ	E: Exxon
	ATM	E: PNC Bank, WSFS Bank W: 7-11 Convenience Store, Shell
	Other	E: Acme Food Store[24], Happy Harry's Discount Drugs[RX], University Plaza W: 7-11 Convenience Store
(2)		Service Area (RR, Phones, Vending)
	FStop	W: Exxon, Mobil
	Food	W: Bob's Big Boy, Hot Dog City, Mrs Field's Cookies, Roy Rogers, Ruby Moon Coffee, Sbarro Italian, TCBY
	AServ	W: Mobil
	ATM	W: Service Area
1AB		**(3)** DE 896, Newark, Middletown
	FStop	W: Texaco[*]
	Gas	W: Exxon[*, 24], Gulf[*, D], Mobil[*], Shell[*, 24]
	Food	W: Blue Hen Diner, Boston Market Restaurant, Dunkin Donuts, Friendly's, Ground Round, Hand's Kitchen, McDonald's, Pepper's Pizza
	Lodg	W: Comfort Inn, Howard Johnson
	AServ	W: Gulf, Shell[24]
	RVCamp	E: Camping, Southern States RV Service (Approx. 1.75 Miles)
	ATM	W: Exxon, Mobil
	Other	W: White Glove Car Wash

↑DELAWARE

1595

The *difference* between the *ordinary & extraordinary* is the little *extra!*

Invitation Inns

Edgewood

Perryville

Edgewood

At Hess Hotels Group, we take pride in providing our guest the best service and value in the area. All hotels are easy access off I-95, SR40 and minutes from Baltimore atttractions. We offer semi-truck & bus parking at both our Comfort Inn Hotels. Some features include free deluxe continential breakfast, free parking, outdoor pool, fitness rooms and 24 hour restaurants nearby. Discounts for AAA, AARP, Group and Tour Buses.

1-800-408-4748
www.hesshotels.com

Mention this ad and receive a 10% discount off rack rates.

MARYLAND • I-95 • EXIT 77B

Bold red print shows RV & Bus parking available or nearby

EXIT	MARYLAND

↓MARYLAND

109 MD 279, MD 213, Elkton, Newark DE (Toll)

TStop E: Petro[*, LP, SCALES]
W: T/A TravelCenters of America[*, D, RV DUMP, SCALES]
FStop E: Texaco[*, LP]

1221

Where Value Hits a Grand Slam Everyday!
Denny's... good food and friendly service is just down the road!
Look for on I-95 at Exit 77 & 93 in Edgewood & Perryville, Maryland
MARYLAND ▪ I-95 ▪ EXIT 77 & 93

1748

MARYLAND ▪ I-95 ▪ Exit 77A

PRIME OUTLETS
PERRYVILLE
Over 40 Outlet Stores
Mikasa • Nike • Bass
Ask for your FREE COUPON BOOK
410-378-9399
1866
MARYLAND ▪ I-95 ▪ EXIT 93

1780

MARYLAND ▪ I-95 ▪ EXIT 85

EXIT	MARYLAND

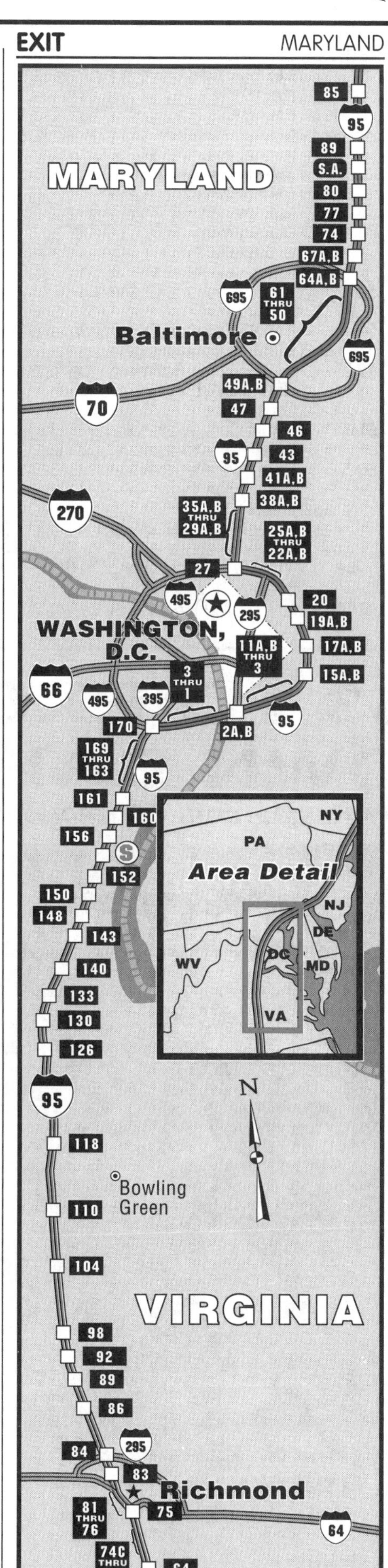

EXIT	MARYLAND

Food E: KFC, McDonald's[PLAY], Petro, Taco Bell
W: Subway (TA Truckstop), T/A TravelCenters of America
Lodg E: Econolodge, Elkton Lodge, Knight's Inn, Motel 6
Med E: ✚ Hospital (3 Miles)
ATM E: Petro, Texaco
W: T/A TravelCenters of America

100 **(101)** MD 272, North East, Rising Sun (Toll)

TStop E: Flying J Travel Plaza[*, LP, RV DUMP]
Food E: Schroeder's Deli, The Cookery (Flying J)
Lodg E: Crystal Inn
Parks E: Elk Neck State Park
Other E: State Police, Upper Bay Museum
W: Plumpton Park Zoo

(97) Chesapeake House Service Area (RR, Phones, Picnic; Left Exit Both Directions)

FStop B: Exxon[*], Sunoco[D]
Food B: Burger King, Mrs Fields Cookies, Pizza Hut, Popeye's Chicken, Starbucks Coffee, TCBY
AServ B: Exxon, Sunoco
ATM B: Exxon, Sunoco

(95) Weigh Station

93 **(94)** MD222, Perryville, Port Deposit

TStop E: Pilot Travel Center[*, SCALES]
Gas E: Exxon[*, D, 24]
Food E: Dairy Queen (Exxon), Denny's, KFC, Subway (Exxon), Taco Bell
Lodg E: Comfort Inn
ATM E: Exxon
Other E: Prime Outlets at Perryville (see our ad this page)

(93) Weigh Station (Southbound, Toll)

89 **(90)** MD155, Churchville, Havre de Grace

Med E: ✚ Hospital
Parks W: Susquehanna State Park
Other E: Decoy Museum
W: Airport

85 MD 22, Aberdeen, Churchville

Food E: Durango's (Sheraton), Golden Corral Family Steakhouse, Grumpy's (EconoLodge), Japan House (Sheraton), McDonald's
Lodg E: Days Inn (see our ad this page), Econolodge, Holiday Inn, Quality Inn & Suites, Red Roof Inn, Sheraton
Other E: Cal Ripken Museum, Ordinance Museum

(82) Service Area, Rest Area (Phones, Vending; Left Exit Both Directions)

FStop B: Exxon[*], Sunoco[*]
Food B: Bob's Big Boy, Cinnabon, Roy Rogers, Ruby Moon Gourmet Coffee[*], Sbarro Italian, TCBY
AServ B: Exxon
ATM B: Exxon, Ruby Moon Gourmet Coffee

80 **(81)** MD 543, Riverside, Churchville

Gas E: Amoco[*], Crown[*, D, LP, CW]
Food E: A & W (Crown), Burger King (Amoco), Cracker Barrel, McDonald's
RVCamp E: Bar Harbor RV Park
ATM E: Amoco, Forest Hill Bank
Other E: Eckerd Drugs[RX], Kline's Supermarket[RX], Mail Call Shipper

77AB MD 24, Edgewood, Bel Air

FStop E: Texaco[*]
Gas E: Exxon[*, D], Shell[*]
Food E: Burger King, Comfort Inn, Denny's (see our ad this page), McDonald's[PLAY], Vitali's (Best Western)
W: King's Chinese, Little Caesars Pizza, Subway
Lodg E: Best Western (see our ad this page), Comfort Inn (see our ad this page), Days Inn (see our ad this page), Sleep Inn (see our ad this page)

Bold red print shows RV & Bus parking available or nearby

EXIT MARYLAND

W: **Rite Aide Pharmacy**

74 MD 152, Joppatowne, Fallston
- **Gas** E: Citgo(*, D)
- **Med** W: **+ Hospital**

67AB MD 43, to U.S. 1, Whitemarsh Blvd, to U.S. 40
- **Gas** W: Exxon
- **Food** E: Cassamea Carry Out
  W: McDonald's, Olive Garden, Ruby Tuesday, T.G.I. Friday's
- **Lodg** W: Hampton Inn
- **Other** E: **7-11 Convenience Store, Byron's Station, Warner Bros. Outlet Store**
  W: **Gunpowder State Park, US Post Office, Whitemarsh Mall**

64AB Junction I-695 Beltway, Towson, Essex

62 Jct I-895 South, Fort McHenry Tunnel, Annapolis, Harbor Tunnel Thruway (Left Exit Southbound)
- **Lodg** E: Holiday Inn (see our ad this page)

61 U.S. 40, Pulaski Highway (Northbound)

60 Moravia Road (Northbound)

59 MD 150, Eastern Ave
- **Gas** W: Amoco(D), Exxon(*, CW)
- **Food** E: Eastwood Inn

58 Dundalk Ave (Northbound)

57 O'Donnell St
- **TStop** E: **Baltimore Travel Plaza(SCALES), Port Travel Plaza(*, SCALES)**
- **FStop** E: **Mobil(*, D)**
- **Food** E: Buckham Family Restaurant, KFC, **McDonald's**, Peter Pan, Sbarro Italian, Subway, Taco Bell, **Tradewinds (Best Western)**, Travel Port Plaza
- **Lodg** E: **Best Western**, Port Travel Plaza

56 Keith Ave

55 Key Highway
- **Med** W: **+ Hospital**
- **Other** W: **Ft McHenry Historic Site**

54 MD 2, Hanover St (Closed Due To Construction)

53 MD395, Baltimore Downtown
- **Lodg** W: Marriott (see our ad this page)

52 MD 295 South, Baltimore, Washington Pkwy, Int'l Airport (Closed Due To Construction)

51 Mount Clare, Washington Blvd (Closed Due To Construction)

50 Caton Ave, West to Wilkens Ave, East Washington Blvd
- **Gas** E: Shell(*)
- **Food** E: Caton House Restaurant, Pargos
- **Lodg** E: Holiday Inn Express

49AB Jct I-695, Pawson, Annapolis, Glen Burnie

47AB Jct I-195, MD 166, Catonsville, Airport

EXIT MARYLAND

1338

Marriott

Baltimore Marriott Inn Harbor

Maryland • Exit 53 • 410-962-0202

1624

Holiday Inn

I-95 • Northbound Exit 60 Southbound Exit 62

6510 Frankford Ave.
Baltimore, Maryland

410-485-7900

Full Service Hotel with Free Parking
Outdoor Pool • Laundry Facilities,
Complimentary Morning Coffee & Newspaper
Kids Under 12 Stay & Eat Free
(when accompanied by paying adult)
Remote Control TV w/Free ESPN/TBS/Disney
Full Service Restaurant and Lounge
w/Room Service Available

Special Rates for Tour Groups

MARYLAND • I-95 • Exit NB 62/SB 60

EXIT 53 TO EXCITING DOWNTOWN BALTIMORE.

Inner Harbor • Little Italy • Restaurants • Attractions • Shopping • Mt.Vernon

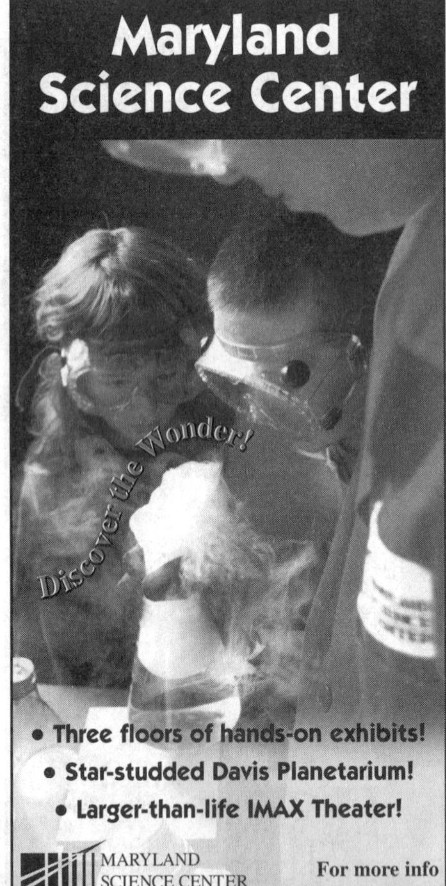

Restaurants & Shops:
- **Hard Rock Cafe**
- **Harborplace and The Gallery**
- **Rusty Scupper**
- **McCormick & Schmicks Restaurant**
- **J. Leonard's Waterside Restaurant**

World-renowned for a collection dating from ancient times through Impressionism, The Walters invites you to experience 5,000 years of cultural richness and variety. Call us at 410-547-9000, ext. 232 for a guided tour of the permanent collection, tailored to your interests.

600 N. Charles Street
Baltimore, MD 21201
www.TheWalters.org

1880.a

Directions to Downtown:
From I-95, Exit 53 Pratt St
Directions to Mt. Vernon:
From I-95, Exit 53 Pratt St to Charles St. N

To advertise here call 800-683-3948

Bold red print shows RV & Bus parking available or nearby

EXIT MARYLAND

PRIME OUTLETS
QUEENSTOWN
Over 55 Outlet Stores
St. John Knits • Brooks Brothers • Lenox
Ask for your **FREE COUPON BOOK**
1868 **410-827-8699**
MARYLAND • Rt 50E/30 In Split

800-801-6449
CHERRY HILL PARK® 1066
A Monumental Experience!
We Accepted: VISA & MasterCard
- 400 RV and Tenting Campsites
- Sites with Water, Sewer & Electric Hookups
- Cabin & Trailer Rentals • 30 or 50 Amp Service
- Cable TV (Showtime) • Playground
- Large RV Parts SuperStore
- Propane Refills • Sparkling Outdoor Heated Pool

Directions: I-495/95, use Exit 25 (US Route One South, College Park.) Make first right onto Cherry Hill Rd. Go one mile to parks entrance. From Baltimore, Southbound I-95, use Exit 29B (Route 212- Calverton). Follow Power Mill Rd. one mile. turn left on Cherry Hill Rd. go one mile.
MARYLAND • I-95 • EXIT 29B

46 Jct I-895 North, Harbor Tunnel (Northbound)
43 MD 100, Glen Burnie, Ellicott City
41AB MD 175, MD 108, Columbia, Jessup, Ellicott City
- **TStop** E: TravelCenters of America[*, SCALES]
- **Gas** E: Exxon[*, D, CW], Shell, TravelCenters of America[*]
- **Food** E: Burger King, Country Pride Restaurant[SCALES] (TC of America), Jerry's Subs & Pizza, McDonald's[PLAY]
- **Lodg** E: Holiday Inn, Knights Inn (TC of America), Red Roof Inn, Susse Chalet
- **Med** W: ✚ Hospital
- **ATM** E: Citizens National Bank, Exxon, NationsBank
- **Other** E: Columbia Eastgate Shopping Center, State Police

38AB MD 32, Fort Meade, Columbia
(37) MD Welcome Center (RR, Phones, Picnic, Vending, RV Dump, Pet Walk)
(36) MD Welcome Center (RR, Phones, Picnic, Vending, RV Dump, Pet Walk)
35AB MD 216, Laurel, Scaggsville
33AB MD 198, Burtonsville, Laurel, Sweitzer Ln
- **Gas** W: Exxon[*, D]
- **Food** W: Blimpie's Subs[*, D] (Exxon), Glass Duck (Best Western)
- **Lodg** W: Best Western

Waldorf, MD 1629

Continental Breakfast
30 Brand New Rooms
Kids Under 12 Stay Free
Handicap Accessible
Truck/Large Vehicle Parking
Pets Allowed • Interior Corridors
Groups Welcome
Jacuzzi & Waterbed Rooms Available
4 Restaurants Within Walking Distance:
Applebee's, Olive Garden, Ground Round, Kenny Rogers
301-932-8957 • 800-800-8000
3550 Crain Hwy • Waldorf, MD 20602
Maryland • I-95 • Exit 7A

EXIT MARYLAND

- **Med** E: ✚ Hospital
- **ATM** W: Exxon

29AB MD 212, Beltsville, Calverton
- **Gas** W: Exxon[D]
- **Food** W: Baskin Robbins, Garden Terrace Cafe (Holiday Inn), McDonald's[PLAY], TJ's of Calverton Restaurant, Wendy's
- **Lodg** W: Holiday Inn, Ramada
- **RVCamp** W: Cherry Hill Park (see our ad this page)
- **ATM** W: Crestar Bank, Equitable Federal Savings Bank
- **Other** W: CVS Pharmacy, County Police, Giant Grocery

27 I-95N, Baltimore

Note: I-95 runs concurrent below with I-495. Numbering follows I-495.

25AB U.S. 1, Baltimore Blvd, Laurel, College Park
- **Gas** I: Amoco[24]; O: Shell[*]
- **Food** O: Moosecreek Steakhouse
- **Lodg** I: Econolodge; O: Holiday Inn
- **RVCamp** I: Campground, Queen Town Motor RV Center
- **Other** I: College Park Animal Hospital, Shoppers Supermarket

24 Greenbelt Station (No Reaccess)
23 MD 201, Kenilworth Ave, Bladensburg, Greenbelt
- **Gas** I: Shell
- **Food** I: McDonald's, Sir Walter Raliegh, TGI Friday
- **Lodg** I: Courtyard; O: Marriott

22AB Baltimore Washington Parkway (No Trucks)
20 MD 450, Annapolis Road, Lanham, Bladensburg

GROUP TOUR PACKAGES
1280

8500 Annapolis Rd • New Carrollton, MD
301-459-6700 • 800-436-0614
239 Guest Rooms
Restaurant/Lounge on Premises
Olympic Size Outdoor Pool
33,000 Sq. Ft. of Meeting/Banquet Facilities
25" Remote Control Cable TV
Pets Allowed
Handicap Accessible
Shuttle to Amtrak/Metro Station
Exterior/Interior Corridors
10 miles to Downtown Washington, DC

Large Bus Parking
I-95/495, Exit 20B (Rte 450 Annapolis Rd.)
Maryland • I-95/495 • Exit 20B

EXIT MARYLAND/VIRGINIA

- **Gas** I: Citgo[*], Shell[*]; O: Mobil[*]
- **Food** I: Chesapeake Bay Seafood, Cuisine China, PaPa John's, SHONEY'S Shoney's, Wendy's; O: Best Western, Burger King, Jerry's Subs & Pizza, McDonald's[PLAY], Pizza Hut, Red Lobster, Red Texas BBQ, Silver Platter (Days Inn)
- **Lodg** I: Ramada Inn (see our ad this page); O: Best Western, DAYS INN Days Inn, Red Roof Inn
- **Med** O: ✚ Hospital
- **ATM** I: Citgo, Maryland Federal Bank, Shell
- **Other** I: CVS Pharmacy, Safeway Grocery, Shoppers Supermarket

19AB U.S. 50, Annapolis, Washington
- **Other** E: Prime Outlets at Queenstown (see our ad this page)

17AB MD 202, Landover Road, Bladensburg, Upper Marlboro
- **Lodg** O: Club Hotel
- **Other** I: County Police, Landover Mall, Sam's Club; O: US Air Arena

15AB MD 214, Central Ave
- **Gas** I: Crown[*, D, 24], Exxon[*, D]
- **Food** I: DAYS INN Days Inn, Jerry's Subs & Pizza, McDonald's[PLAY], Pizza Hut
- **Lodg** I: DAYS INN Days Inn; O: Hampton Inn
- **ATM** I: Exxon

11AB MD 4, Pennsylvania Ave, Washington, Upper Marlboro
- **Gas** I: Exxon[*, CW], Shell[*], Sunoco[D, 24]; O: Texaco
- **AServ** I: Shell, Sunoco[24]; O: Texaco
- **ATM** I: Exxon, Industrial Bank

9 MD 337, Allen Town Road, Andrews AFB (Difficult Reaccess)
- **Gas** I: Mobil[*, CW]

7AB MD 5, Branch Ave, Waldorf, Silver Hill
- **Gas** I: Texaco
- **Lodg** I: DAYS INN Days Inn, Super 8 (see our ad this page)
- **AServ** I: Capital Cadillac, Koons Mazda, Sheehe Ford, Wilson Pal Lincoln, Mercury, Ford
- **Med** O: ✚ Hospital

4AB MD 414, Saint Barnabas Road, Oxen Hill, Marlow Heights
- **Gas** I: Exxon, Shell[*, 24]; O: Exxon[D, CW, 24], Xtra Fuel[*, 24]
- **Food** I: McDonald's; O: Burger King, KFC, McDonald's[PLAY], Wendy's
- **Med** I: ✚ Hospital

3AB MD 210, Indian Head Hwy, Forest Heights
- **Lodg** O: Ramada Inn, Susse Chalet
- **Other** O: Oxen Hill Plaza

2AB Junction I-295, Washington

↑MARYLAND

↓VIRGINIA

1AB U.S. 1, Mt. Vernon
- **Gas** I: Exxon, Merit[D]; O: Amoco[D, 24], Mobil[*, D], Sunoco, Texaco[D]
- **Food** O: Domino's Pizza, Great American Steak & Buffet Co., Howard Johnson
- **Lodg** O: Brookside Motel, Howard Johnson, Red Roof Inn, Statesman Motel, Traveler Motel
- **AServ** O: Heritage Chrysler Jeep Chev, Mobil, Ourisman Dodge/ Suzuki/ Chrysler/ Plymouth, Sunoco, Texaco
- **Med** I: ✚ Hospital
- **ATM** I: Merit; O: Prestar

2AB VA 241, Telegraph Road, Alexandria
- **Gas** O: Amoco, Citgo, Exxon[*, D, LP], Hess[D]
- **Food** O: Pillar's Restaurant

EXIT VIRGINIA

Lodg I: Courtyard by Marriott, Holiday Inn
AServ O: Amoco, Burgundy Auto Repair, Citgo, Exxon, Huntington Car Care, Lee's Auto Repair, Nisson A-1 Auto Honda Toyota
Med I: Hospital
ATM O: 7-11 Convenience Store, Burke & Herbert Bank & Trust, Exxon
Other I: Alexandria Animal Hospital
O: 7-11 Convenience Store

3A Eisenhower Ave., Alexandria
3 VA 613, Vandoran St., Franconia
Lodg O: Comfort Inn
4 Junction I-95 South, Richmond; Junction I-95 North (East Beltway), Alexandria; Junction I-395, Arlington, Washington
4A Junction I-495 North, Rockville
4B I-395 N, Washington, I-95, Richmond

Note: I-95 runs concurrent above with I-495. Numbering follows I-495.

170 Junction I-495, I-395, Rockville
169 VA 644, Old Keen Rd, Springfield, Franconia
Gas E: Mobil
W: Citgo(*, D), Mobil, Shell(*)
Food E: Bennigan's, Bertucci's Brick Oven Pizza, Blackie's Steak, Blue Parrot (Hilton), Chesapeake Bagel Bakery, Daybreak Restaurant (Days Inn), Makati Deli & Donuts, Mozzarella's Cafe, Osaki Japanese Restaurant, Ruby Tuesday, Silver Diner, Starbucks Coffee
W: Baskin Robbins, Chi Chi's Mexican Restaurant, Ding Hou Carry-Out (Chinese), Donut Masters, Dunkin Donuts, Family Restaurant & Pizzeria, Generous George's Pasta & Pizza, Houlihan's, Hunan's Springfield Restaurant, **MaKong Groc & Deli**, Malek's Pizza Palace, McDonald's, Mike's American Grill, Pasta Peddler Restaurant, Payton Place Restaurant, PeKing Garden, Pizza Hut, Popeye's Chicken, Rocco' Italian Restaurant, Roy Rogers, Royal Restaurant, SHONEY'S Shoney's, Subway, T.K. Restaurant (Taiwan), The Bug-A-Boo Creek, Village Chicken
Lodg E: Comfort Inn, DAYS INN Days Inn, Hilton
W: Holiday Inn Express, **Motel 6**
AServ E: Firestone Tire & Auto, Mobil, **Montgomery Ward**, Sheehy Ford
W: Advantage Auto, Citgo, Goodyear Tire & Auto, Jerry's Dodge, K-Mart, Midas Muffler & Brake, Mobil, Shell, Springfield Toyota, Toyota Express, Volkswagen Dealer
Med W: **Inove Urgent Care Ctr**
ATM E: Central Fidelity Bank, NationsBank
W: Crestar Bank, F&M Bank, First Union
Other E: **7-11 Convenience Store**, **Animal Magic Pet Grooming**, **CVS Pharmacy**, **For Eyes Optical (Optical)**, **Petsmart**, **Shopping Mall**
W: **7-11 Convenience Store**, **CVS Pharmacy**, Car Wash, **Concord Centre**, **Fireworks**, **Fisher's Hdwe(LP)**, **Giant Drugs**, **K-Mart**, **Petco Pet Supplies**, **Pro Food Pet Supply**, **South Paws Veterinary Referral**, **Springfield Animal Hospital**, **Springfield Plaza**, **Super Mart C-Store**, **Tower Center**, **Vision Works Opitcal**

167 VA 617, Backlick Road, Fullerton Road (Difficult Reaccess)
166AB VA 790, Ft Belvoir, Newington, Alban Rd, Backlick Rd
FStop E: **Quill's**
Gas E: Exxon(*, D, LP)
Food E: Delly's Deli & Grill, Fun Cafe, Hunter Motel, Ollie's Deli, Terminal Rd Deli (Commerce Ctr)
W: Benjamin's, Tex-Mex
Lodg E: Hunter Motel
163 VA 643, Lorton

EXIT VIRGINIA

Gas E: Citgo(*, LP), Shell
W: Texaco(*, D, CW)
AServ E: Shell (Wrecker Service)
161 U.S. 1, Ft Belvoir, Mt Vernon (Reaccess Exit 160)
160 VA 123 North, Woodbridge to Occoquan
Gas E: Amoco(*, D), Exxon, Shell, Texaco(D)
W: Exxon(*, D), Mobil(*), Shell(*, 24)
Food E: Astorra Pizza, Dixie Bones BBQ, Dunkin Donuts, Hunan Restaurant, Joe's Pizza & Deli, Kowloon Restaurant, **Little Caesars Pizza (K-Mart)**, Lobster Farm Mkt, Lum's, Manni's Italian Restaurant, Market Street Buffet & Bakery, McDonald's, Roy Rogers, SHONEY'S Shoney's (Woodbridge Ctr), Stow Away Restaurant, Sushui Bar & BBQ, Taco Bell, Tex-Mex Chilli Parlor
W: KFC
Lodg E: Comfort Inn, Econolodge, Inns Of Virginia
ATM E: Crestar Bank, Jefferson Nat'l Bank
Other E: **7-11 Convenience Store**, Car Wash, **Fireworks**, **Food Lion Supermarket**, **Food Mart (Woodbridge Ctr)**, **Gordon Plaza**, **Handy Dandy Mkt**, **K-Mart**, **Laundry Salon (Coin Operated Woodbridge Ctr)**, **Patomic Plaza**, **Pets (Gordon Plaza)**, **Tourist Info.**, **Woodbridge Animal Hospital**, **Woodbridge Ctr**
W: **Prince William Marina**

158 VA3000, Prince William Pkwy, Manassas, Woodbridge
Gas W: Mobil(*, CW), Shell(*, CW)
Food W: Red River Crossing BBQ, Wendy's
Lodg W: Fairfield Inn
Other W: **Target(RX)**
156 VA 784, Dale City, Rippon Landing
Gas W: Exxon, Mobil(*), Shell(*), Texaco(*, D)
Food W: Black Eyed Pea, Bob Evan's Restaurant, Carlos O'Kelly's Mexican, Cheaspeake Bay Seafood, Chili's, Domino's Pizza, El Charro Mexican,

1510
540-659-8999
800-228-5150
Stafford, VA
Comfort Inn
Continental Breakfast Included
Kids 12 and under Stay & Eat Free
Outdoor Pool • Exercise Room
Meeting/Banquet Facilities
Handicap Accessible
Truck/Large Vehicle Parking
Coin Laundry • Interior Corridors
Suites w/Jacuzzi, Microwave, Refrigerator
First Left After Exiting I-95
Stafford, VA • I-95 • Exit 143B

Sleep Inn
540-372-6868
800-753-3746
Falmouth, VA
• Continental Breakfast Included
• Kids 12 and Under Stay & eat Free
• Handicap Accessible
• Interior Corridors
• Ponderosa Restaurant Adjacent
Third light make U-turn, hotel will be on right side.
Falmouth, VA • I-95 • Exit 133B

EXIT VIRGINIA

Fu Kien Gourmet Chinese, Jerry's Subs & Pizza, Lone Star Steakhouse, McDonald's, Olive Garden, Palm Tree Chinese, Popeye's Chicken, Red Lobster, Seoul BBQ (Korean), Wendy's
Lodg W: DAYS INN **Days Inn**
Med W: **Hospital**, **Urgent Care Clinic**
Other W: **Ashdale Plaza**, **Dale City Animal Hospital**, **K-Mart**, **Potomic Mills Shopping Center**, **Prince Wiliam Square**

(157) Rest Area (RR, Phones, Picnic, Grills)
(154) Weigh Station, Truckers Rest Area (RR, Phones, Picnic)
152 VA 234, Dumfries, Manassas
Gas E: Amoco(*, D), Sunoco, Texaco(*, D)
W: Citgo(*), Exxon(*, LP), Shell
Food E: Golden Corral Family Steakhouse, Happy Eatery, KFC, McDonald's, Taco Bell
W: **Cracker Barrel**, Don Pepe (Mediterranian), Mont Clair Family Restaurant, Waffle House
Lodg E: Super 8
AServ E: American Car Care Centers, Beatty's Service Ctr, Goodyear Tire & Auto, Grease Monkey, Gumphry's Auto Body, Meineke Discount Mufflers
W: Exxon
Other E: **Coach House Plaza Shopping Center**, **Weens-Botts Museum**

150AB VA 619, Triangle, Quantico
Gas E: Amoco(D), Exxon(*), Shell(*)
Food E: Burger King, Dent's Seafood, McDonald's, Ralph's Ice Cream & BBQ, Tru Grit Restaurant, U.S. Inn (Chinese), Wendy's
Lodg E: Ramada, U.S. Inn
Other E: **Post Office**
W: **Quantico Nat'l Cemetary**
148 Quantico, Marine Base
Other E: **US Marine Airground Museum**
143AB VA 610, Aquia, Garrisonville
FStop W: **BP(*, CW)**
Gas E: Amoco(*), Exxon(*, CW), Shell(*, D)
W: Amoco(*, D, CW), Citgo(*), Crown(*, D, LP, K, CW), Texaco(*, D, CW)
Food E: Carlos O'Kelly's Mexican, Dairy Queen, Davazo's Cafe, Gargoyles Coffee Bar, Hunan's Chef Restaurant, Imperial Garden, KFC, Little Caesars Pizza, Mediterranian Cafe & Market, Pizza Hut, Roy Rogers, Ruby Tuesday, SHONEY'S Shoney's (Days Inn)
W: Baskin Robbins, Botta Bagel & Deli, Buffett King, Burger King, Dad's Deli, Dunkin Donuts, Formosa Chinese Restaurant, Golden Corral Family Steakhouse, **Hardee's (BP)**, Kobe Japanese Restaurant, McDonald's, Popeye's Chicken, Taco Bell, Tony's Pizza & Deli, Wendy's
Lodg E: DAYS INN Days Inn
W: Comfort Inn (see our ad at I-95 Exit 133B VA), Country Inn, Super 8
RVCamp E: **Aquia Pines Camp Resort (.25 Miles)**

1489
Fredericksburg Virginia
Holiday Inn®
• Restaurant & Lounge
• Heated Indoor Pool
• Twirl Spa, Sauna, Game Room
• Exercise Equipment
• Non-Smoking Rooms Available
• Bus Parking
• Civil War & Historical Packages
540-898-1102
Virginia • I-95 • EXIT 126

Bold red print shows RV & Bus parking available or nearby

EXIT — VIRGINIA

W: Aquia Pines Campground
Other — E: Aqua Towne Center, Coin Laundry, Optical, Petmania, Rite Aide Pharmacy
W: Bafferton Center, CVS Pharmacy, Car Wash, Giant Food & Drugs, North Stafford Plaza, Wal-Mart Supercenter[RX]

140 VA 630, Stafford
FStop — W: Texaco[*]
Gas — E: Mobil[*], Texaco
W: Shell[*, D]
Food — E: Chix Subs & Pizza, McDonald's
Other — W: Fireworks

133AB U.S. 17 North, Warrenton, Falmouth
TStop — W: Servicetown Travel Plaza[*, SCALES] (Truck Wash)
FStop — E: Racetrac[*]
W: East Coast[*, D, LP, 24]
Gas — E: Mobil[*, D, CW]
W: Amoco[*, D], Citgo[*], Shell[*], Texaco[*, D]
Food — E: Aliby's Restaurant, Arby's, Family Tie's Pizzeria, Majestic's Restaurant
W: Anthony's Pizza Restaurant, Burger King, Hardee's, Holiday Inn, Johnny Appleseed Restaurant (Best Western), McDonald's, Pizza Hut, Ponderosa, Servicetown Travel Plaza[24], Taco Bell, Waffle House, Wendy's
Lodg — E: Howard Johnson, Motel 6
W: Best Western, Comfort Inn (see our ad opposite page), Days Inn (see our ad this page), Holiday Inn, Ramada Limited, Sleep Inn, TraveLodge
Med — E: + Hospital
Other — E: 7-11 Convenience Store, Coin Laundry
W: Fireworks (Citgo), Fireworks, Food Lion Supermarket, Inglewood Shopping Ctr, Revco Drugs

(131) VA Welcome Center (RR, Phones, Picnic; Southbound)

130AB VA 3, Fredericksburg, Culpepper

Toll Free Reservations:
800-329-7466

DAYS INN — Newly Renovated

1151

Fredericksburg, Virginia
(Fredericksburg South)
I-95 • Exit 126 • 540-898-6800
Continental Breakfast
Outdoor Pool
Cable TV
Bus Parking • Tour Pkgs
Near Historical Attractions
Restaurants Adjacent

Fredericksburg, Virginia
(Fredericksburg North)
I-95 • Exit 133 • 540-373-5340
Bus Parking • Tour Pkgs
Continental Breakfast
Cable TV
Near Historical Attractions

VIRGINIA ▪ 2 LOCATIONS

EXIT — VIRGINIA

Gas — E: Amoco[D, 24], Mobil[CW], Pep Boys Auto Center, Racetrac[*], Shell[*, D, LP, K]
W: Amoco[*], Crown[*, LP, CW], Exxon[*], Shell[*]
Food — E: Arby's, Bagel Station, Bob Evan's Restaurant, Carlos O'Kelly's Mexican, Chesapeake Bay Seafood, DeVancZo Italian Cafe, Dunkin Donuts, Formosa Restaurant, Friendly's, Golden Rail Restaurant, Heavenly Ham, KFC, Lone Star Steakhouse, Long John Silver, Market Street Buffet & Bakery, McDonald's, Popeye's Chicken, SHONEY'S, Shoney's, Top's China Buffet
W: Applebee's, Aunt Sara's Pancake House, Baskin Robbins, Boston Market Restaurant, Burger King, Checkers, Chi-Chi's Restaurant, Denny's, Dragon Inn Chinese & Seafood, Dunkin Donuts, Einstein Bros Bagels, Fuddruckers, Hardee's, IHOP, Italian Oven, Kenny Roger's Roasters, Little Caesars Pizza, McDonald's, Morrison's Cafeteria, Old Country Buffet, Outback Steakhouse, Pancho Mexican Restaurant, Pizza Hut, Red Lobster, Sheraton, Starbucks Cafe, Subway, Taco Bell, Tia's Tex Mex
Lodg — E: Best Western, Hampton Inn
W: Best Western, Econolodge, Ramada, Sheraton, Super 8
Med — E: + Hospital
ATM — E: First VA Bank, Signet Bank of Virginia
W: Crestar Bank, First Union Bank, First Union Bank, Jefferson Nat'l Bank, Virginia First Savings Bank
Other — E: 7-11 Convenience Store, Chancelorsville Battlefield, Fed Ex Drop Box, Fredericksburg Museum, Fredricksburg Area Museum & Cultural Center, Gateway Village Shopping Center, Greenbriar Shopping Ctr, Kenmore Plantation (James Monroe Museum), Maico Hearing Aid Service, Optical, Westwood Shopping Center
W: CVS Pharmacy, Car Wash, Fireworks, Giant Food & Drug Store, K-Mart, Mail House Plus, Petsmart, Spotsylvania Crossing Ctr, Spotsylvania Mall, Target[RX], Village Square, Wal-Mart Supercenter[RX] (Optical)

126 U.S. 1, U.S. 17, Massaponax
FStop — W: Racetrac[*]
Gas — E: BP, Chevron[*, D], Citgo[*, D] (Fireworks), Exxon[*], Fas Mart[*], Mobil, Shell[*, CW], Texaco[*], U-Save
W: Exxon[*, CW]
Food — E: Arby's, China Max, Dairy Queen, Days Inn, Denny's, El Charro Mexican, Hardee's, Holiday Inn, Jimmy's Diner, McDonald's, Pat's Ice Cream, Pizza Connection, Pizza Hut, Rally's Hamburgers, Subway (Exxon), Subway (Lees Hill Center), Taco Bell, Waffle House, Wendy's, Western Sizzlin'
W: Aunt Sara's Pancake House, Blimpie's Subs (Exxon), Burger King, Cousin John's Chicken & Steaks, Cracker Barrel, Damon's Ribs, Edy's Grand Ice Cream, Fantastic Italian Restaurant, Golden China, Hot Stuff Pizza (Exxon), KFC, McDonald's
Lodg — E: Days Inn (see our ad this page), Econolodge, Fairfield Inn, Heritage Inn, Holiday Inn (see our ad this page), Howard Johnson, Royal Inn, Super 8
W: Comfort Inn, WhyteStone's Inn
Other — E: CVS Pharmacy, Car Wash, Country Corner C-Store (Fireworks), Fireworks, Food Lion Supermarket (Deli, Bakery), Lees Hill Center, Maru Pet Shop, Pharmahouse Drugs, Revco Drugs, Safeway Grocery, Visitor Information
W: Dept of Motor Vehicles, Fed Ex Drop Box, Massaponax Outlet Center, South Point Shopping Ctr

118 VA 606, Thornburg
FStop — E: Shell[*, D]
W: Citgo[*, D]
Gas — W: Exxon[*], Shell[*, LP, 24]
Food — W: Burger King, McDonald's
Lodg — W: Holiday Inn Express
AServ — E: Shell (Towing)

EXIT — VIRGINIA

W: Campbell's Wrecker (Citgo), Citgo
RVCamp — W: Campground

110 VA 639, Ladysmith
Gas — E: Shell[D]
W: Exxon[*, K]

(108) Rest Area (RR, Phones, Picnic, Vending)

104 VA 207 to 301, Carmel Church, Bowling Green, Ft. AP Hill
TStop — E: Petro[*, LP, CW, SCALES], Pilot Travel Center[*]
W: Flying J Travel Plaza[*, LP, SCALES]
FStop — E: Mr Fuel[*] (Showers Available), Petro, Texaco[*]
Gas — E: Amoco[*, D, LP, K], Chevron[*, D], Exxon[*, D], Texaco[*, D]
W: Exxon[*, D, K, CW]
Food — E: Dairy Queen (Pilot), Iron Skillet Restaurant (Petro), McDonald's, Perkee's Pizza, Subway (Pilot), Wendy's (Petro)
W: Aunt Sara's Pancake House (Comfort Inn), Country Mkt Restaurant & Buffet, Days Inn, Magic Dragon Chinese, Maria's Cafe Pizza & Subs, Pepperoni's Pizza, Waffle House
Lodg — E: Holiday Inn Express, Howard Johnson
W: Comfort Inn, Days Inn
RVCamp — E: KOA Campgrounds (13.5 Miles)
ATM — E: Exxon, Petro
Other — E: Fireworks
W: Car Wash, Carmel Church Hdwe, Coin Operated Laundry

98 VA 30, Doswell, Westpoint
TStop — E: Doswell All American Travel Plaza[*, RV DUMP, SCALES, 24]
Gas — E: Citgo[*], Texaco[*]
Food — E: All American Truck Plaza (Best Western), Burger King
Lodg — E: Best Western (Kings Dominion), Econolodge (All American Truckstop)
RVCamp — E: All American Truck Plaza[*], Kings Dominion Campground (.5 Miles)
ATM — E: All American Truckstop, Machine (Citgo)
Other — E: Factory Fireworks Outlet, Kings Dominion Theme Park

92AB VA 54, Hanover, Ashland
TStop — W: TravelCenters of America[*, SCALES]
FStop — W: East Coast[*, D, LP, K], Pilot Travel Center[*, D]
Gas — E: Mobil[*]
W: Amoco[*, LP, CW], BP[*], Chevron[*], Exxon[*, D], Shell[*], Texaco[*, LP, CW]
Food — W: Anthony's Italian Pizza, Arby's, Aunt Sara's Pancake House (Ramada), Blimpie's Subs (East Coast), Burger King, Captain D's Seafood, Country Pride Restaurant (TravelCenters of America), Cracker Barrel, Dunkin Donuts (East Coast), Hardee's, KFC, Little Caesars Pizza, McDonald's, McDonald's, Omelet Shoppe, Pizza Hut, Ponderosa Steakhouse, Popeye's Chicken, Season's Restaurant (Holiday Inn), SHONEY'S, Shoney's, Subway (Exxon), Taco Bell, The Smokey Pig Restaurant, TravelCenters of America, Wendy's
Lodg — W: Comfort Inn, Econolodge, HoJo Inn, Holiday Inn, Palm Leaf Motel, Ramada, Super 8, TraveLodge, Twin Oaks Motel
AServ — E: Mobil
W: Advance Auto Parts, Amoco, Chevron, Feild's Auto (Towing), Patrick Pontaic, Buick, GMC, Trak Auto, Tuffy Auto Center
ATM — W: Central Fidelity Bank, First Virginia Savings Bank, Texaco
Other — W: Bumper To Bumper Auto Service, CVS Pharmacy, Coin Operated Laundry, Food Lion Supermarket, Pearl Vision, Rite Aide Pharmacy, Tower Optical, UKrop's Grocery[RX]

89 VA 802, Lewistown Road
TStop — E: Speed & Briscoe 76[RV DUMP, SCALES]
Gas — E: Mobil[*] (Truckstop), Shell[*]
Food — E: I Can't Believe It's Not Yogurt, Pizza Hut, Taco Bell (Truckstop), Truckstop (Truckstop)
AServ — E: Shell
TServ — E: Speed & Briscoe 76

EXIT VIRGINIA

RVCamp E: Americamps Best Holiday Trav-L-Park(LP) (1.1 Miles)
W: Kosmo Village (1.25 Miles)
ATM E: Speed & Briscoe
Other E: County Airport
86 VA 656, Atlee, Elmont
Gas W: Amoco(*, D), Mobil, Texaco(*, CW)
Food W: Best Western, Dairy Queen (Amoco), Sbarro (Amoco, Picnic), Subway (Texaco)
Lodg W: Best Western
AServ W: Mobil
TServ E: Western Branch Diesel(24)
RVCamp E: Duffy's Repair Service (1.9 Miles)
Other E: Hanover Airport
84AB Junction I-295, Williamsburg, Charlottesville (Left Exit Southbound)
83AB VA 73, Parham Road
FStop W: Watch Car Fleet Fuel Management
Gas W: Amoco, East Coast(*, D, LP, K), Exxon, Texaco
Food W: Aunt Sara's Pancake House (Quality Inn), Denny's, El Paso Mexican Restaurant, Hardee's, Little Caesars Pizza, McDonald's, Mings Dynasty (Chinese), Stuffys Subs and Salads, Subway, Theresa'a Italian Village, Wendy's
Lodg W: Broadway Motel, Cavilier, Econolodge, HoJo Inn, Quality Inn
Other W: B. Lewis Genter Botanical Garden, CVS Pharmacy, Food Lion Supermarket(24), Haniford Supermarket, Revco Drugs, Wal-Mart Supercenter
82 U.S. 301, Chamberlayne Ave
FStop E: Exxon(*, D)
Gas E: BP(LP), Mobil(*, D)
Food E: Bojangles, Buger King, Kentucky Fried Chicken, McDonald's, Mello Buttercup and Ice Cream, Red House American and Chinese, Seafood House, Subway, Taco Bell, The Virginia Inn
Lodg E: Chamberlaine Motel, Super 8, The Virginia Inn
81 U.S. 1 (Northbound)
80 VA 161, Lakeside Ave, Hermitage Road (Northbound, Reaccess Southbound Only)
79 Junction I-64, I-195 South, Charlottesville
78 Boulevard
Gas E: Citgo
W: Amoco(*, D), Lucky(*, LP)
Food E: Holiday Inn, Zippy's BBQ
W: Bill's Virginia BBQ, Taylor's Family Restaurant (Days Inn)
Lodg E: Diamond Lodge and Suites, Gadnes Restaurant, Holiday Inn
W: Days Inn
Other W: Tourist Info., US Marine Museum
76B U.S. 1, U.S. 301, Belvidere
Med W: + Belvidere Medical Center
Other W: Maggie Walker Historical Site, VA War Memorial
76A Chamberlayne Ave (Northbound)
Gas E: Citgo
Food E: Burger King, Captain D's Seafood, Dunkin Donuts, Hawks Bar-B-Que And Seafood, McDonald's
Lodg E: Belmont Motel
Other E: 7-11 Convenience Store, Easters Convenience Store
75 Junction I-64 East, Williamsburg Norfolk
74C U.S. 33, U.S. 250, Broad St
Gas E: Exxon(*, CW)
Food E: McDonald's
Med W: + VA Commonwealth Medical Center
Parks E: Richmond Battlefield Park
74B Franklin St (Re-Entry 74A)
74A VA 195, Downtown Expwy, to Jct I-195N (Toll)
73 Maury St, Commerce Road

EXIT VIRGINIA

Food E: Sonny's Grill
Med E: + VA Hospital
69 Bells Road, VA161
FStop W: East Coast, Texaco(*, 24)
Gas W: Exxon(*, D)
Food W: Hardee's, Holiday Inn
Lodg W: Holiday Inn, Red Roof Inn
67 VA 150, Chippenhan Pkwy, to U.S. 60 & U.S. 360 (Divides To VA 613 At Willis Rd)
64 VA 613, Willis Road
FStop W: Texaco(*, D)
Gas E: Exxon(*), Shell(*, CW)
W: Citgo(*), Crown(*, D, LP), Mobil(*)
Food E: Aunt Sara's Pancake House (Ramada), Subway (Exxon), Waffle House
W: Almonds Pit Cooked Bar-B-Que, Dunkin Donuts (Texaco), McDonald's, Pancake House Restaurant (VIP Inn)
Lodg E: Econolodge, Ramada
W: Economy House Motel, Sleep Inn, VIP Inn
62 VA 288, Chesterfield to Powhite Pkwy
Food W: Pietro's Italian Restaurant, Raven Restaurant
Other W: 7-11 Convenience Store
61AB VA 10, Chester, Hopewell
FStop E: Racetrac(*, 24)
W: Exxon(*, LP)
Gas W: Amoco, Citgo(*, D, LP), Crown(*, D, CW), East Coast(*, D)
Food E: Comfort Inn, Hardee's, Imperial Food Buffet
W: Burger King, Captain D's Seafood, Cracker Barrel, Days Inn, Denny's, Friendly's, Hardee's, KFC, McDonald's, Piasano's Italian Restaurant, Pizza Hut, Rosa's Italian Restaurant, SHONEY'S Shoney's, Subway, Taco Bell, Waffle House, Wendy's, Western Sizzlin'
Lodg E: Comfort Inn, Hampton Inn, Holiday Inn (see our ad this page)
W: Days Inn, Fairfield Inn, Howard Johnson, Super 8

Special Rates for Bus and Tour Groups
New Holiday Inn EXPRESS®
Free Deluxe Continental Breakfast
1213
• 95 Rooms (Handicap Rooms Available)
• Free Cable TV with HBO
• Guest Laundry
• Microwave & Refrigerator in All Rooms
• In Room Coffee in All Rooms
• Voice Mail on all Telephones
• Fitness Room with Sauna
• Iron & Ironing Boards in all Rooms
804-751-0123
Reservations: 800-HOLIDAY
VIRGINIA • I-95 • EXIT 61A

EXIT VIRGINIA

Med W: + Med-Care Family Practice
Other E: Surburban Propane(LP)
58 VA 746, VA 620, Walthall
FStop E: Texaco(*, LP)
W: Chevron(*)
Gas W: Amoco(*, D, LP) (Picnic Area)
Food E: TraveLodge
W: Bullet's (Amoco), Dunkin Donuts (Amoco), Interstate Inn
Lodg E: TraveLodge
W: Days Inn (see our ad this page), Interstate Inn
54 VA 144, Temple Ave
FStop W: Texaco(*, D, LP, CW)
Gas E: Chevron(*, LP)
Food E: Applebee's, Arby's, Fuddruckers, Golden Corral Family Steakhouse, Lone Star Steakhouse, McDonald's, Morrison's Cafeteria, Old Country Buffett, Red Lobster, Subway
W: Hardee's
53 Southpark Blvd
Gas E: BP(*, CW), Citgo(*, CW)
Food E: China Man's Buffet, Koreana Korean Food, La Carreta Authentic Mexican, Padow's Hams and Deli, Sagebrush Steakhouse, TCBY (BP), Wendy's
52B Downtown, Washington St, Wythe St
FStop E: Texaco(*, LP)
Gas E: Amoco
W: Crown(*, D)
Food E: Aunt Sara's Pancake House, Pelican Restaurant (Best Western), Ramada Host, Steak & Ale, Subway
W: Church's Chicken, Dairy Queen, Hawks Bar-B-Que, Nick's Pancake and Steakhouse (Howard Johnson)
Lodg E: Best Western, TraveLodge
W: Countryside Inn, Econolodge, Howard Johnson, King Motel, Knight's Inn, Star Motel, Super 8
Med E: + Hospital
Other E: Police Station, Roses Drugstore, S & J Handwash Car Wash, Tourist Info.
52A Wythe St, Washington St (Southbound)
51 Junction I-85 South, U.S.460W, to Durham, to Atlanta
50 U.S. 301, U.S. 460, Crater Rd, County Dr
Med W: + Hospital
50BC U.S. 301, Crater Rd (Northbound)
48AB Wagner Road
Gas W: Chevron(LP), Shell(*), Texaco(*, CW)
Food W: Anabelles' Restaurant and Pub, Arby's, Burger King, Golden Elephant Garden Restaurant (Chinese Buffet), McDonald's, Pizza Hut, Sal's Italian Restaurant, Subway, Taco Bell, The Big Scoop Ice Cream, The Mad Italian Pasta and Steakhouse, Yesterday's Restaurant
Lodg W: Crater Inn
47 VA 629, Rives Road
Gas W: Texaco(*)
Lodg W: Heritage Motor Lodge
AServ W: Texaco(*)

1530
DAYS INN®
Complimentary Coffee
Outdoor Swimming Pool
Near Shopping & Restaurants
Remote Control TV - HBO/ESPN
Truck & Bus Parking
804-520-1010• Petersburg, VA
VIRGINIA • I-95 • EXIT 58

EXIT VIRGINIA

Econo Lodge

16905 Parkdale Rd
Petersburg, VA 23805
804-862-2717

Restaurant/Lounge on Premises
Continental Breakfast
Cable TV w/HBO
All Queen Size Beds
Meeting/Banquet Facilities
Pets Allowed • Handicap Accessible
Outdoor Pool • Golf Nearby
Truck/Large Vehicle Parking
Coin Laundry • Exterior Corridors
Near Many Attractions 1760

VIRGINIA ▪ I-95 ▪ EXIT 41

1262

PETERSBURG
— Easy Access to I-95/I-295 —
— Pool • Playground —
— Pumpkins Restaurant —
— AAA Three Diamond Rating —
— AAA & AARP Discounts —
804-733-4400 • For Reservations 800-329-7466
PETERSBURG, VA ▪ I-95 ▪ EXIT 45

Quality Inn
STEVEN KENT
Petersburg, VA

- Beautiful New Rooms
- Easy Access to I-95 & I-295
- Olympic Pool, Tennis, Playground
- Steven Kent Restaurant
- AAA Three Diamond Rating
- AAA & AARP Discounts

804-733-0600 • For Reservations 800-221-2222
PETERSBURG, VA ▪ I-95 ▪ EXIT 45

804-732-2000

- Pool • Playground
- Free Continental Breakfast
- Tennis • Putting Green
- Great Restaurants within Walking Distance
- Jacuzzi Room
- Free Cable TV with HBO
- Guest Laundry

*Show ad at check-in
Offer not valid with any other discounts during holidays, special events.

1261

VIRGINIA ▪ I-95 ▪ EXIT 45

EXIT VIRGINIA

Area Detail
WV MD DC DE VA NC SC
N
61 · 62 THRU 52 · 51 · 48 THRU 41 · 37 THRU 31 · 24 · 20 THRU 12 · 95 · 11 · 8 Emporia · 4
VIRGINIA · 85
180 · 176 · 173 THRU 169 · 160 · 154 · 150 · 145 · 141 · 138 Rocky Mount · 132 · 127 Wilson · 95
NORTH CAROLINA
121 · 116 · 107 · ★ Raleigh · 106 THRU 98 · 97 · 95 · 40 · 90 THRU 87 · 81 · 79 · 77 · 75 · 73 · 72 · 40
95 · 71 THRU 58 · Fayetteville · 56 THRU 44 · 41 · 40 · 33 THRU 25 · 22 · 20 · 19 THRU 17 · Lumberton · 14 · 10 THRU 2 · 1 · 193
NORTH CAROLINA

EXIT VIRGINIA

Other	W: US SSA Softball Hall of Fame Museum
46	Jct I-295N, to Washington (Left Exit Southbound)
45	U.S. 301
Gas	E: Texaco[D]
	W: Exxon[*, LP]
Food	W: Days Inn, Nanny's Family BBQ, Steven Kent Restaurant (Quality Inn)
Lodg	W: Comfort Inn, Days Inn (see our ad this page), Holiday Express (see our ad this page), Quality Inn (see our ad this page)
41	U.S. 301, VA 35, VA 156, Courtland
FStop	E: Chevron[*, 24]
Food	E: Econolodge, Nino's North Italian Restaurant (KOA Campground)
	W: Rose Garden Inn
Lodg	E: Econolodge (see our ad this page)
	W: Rose Garden Inn, Super 8
RVCamp	E: KOA Campgrounds (.5 Miles)
(40)	Weigh Station
37	U.S. 623, Carson
Gas	W: Amoco[*, D], Texaco[*]
(36)	Rest Area (RR, Phones, Picnic, Vending)
33	VA 602
TStop	W: Davis Truck Plaza[*, RV DUMP]
FStop	W: Chevron
Gas	W: Exxon[*], Shell[D]
Food	W: Burger King, Denny's
Lodg	W: Stony Creek Motel
AServ	W: Brooks Brothers Collison Center, Johnny's 24 Hour Trailer/Truck Repair (Wrecker Service)
31	VA 40, Stony Creek, Waverly
FStop	W: Texaco[*]
Food	W: Stoney Creek Tastee BBQ, Texaco
AServ	W: Carters Car & Truck Repair, JR's Towing, Texaco
24	VA 645
20	VA 631, Jarratt
FStop	W: Citgo[*]
Gas	W: Exxon[*, LP, 24]
Food	W: Blimpie's Subs (Exxon)
17	U.S. 301
Food	E: China Star
Lodg	E: Econolodge, Reste' Motel
RVCamp	E: Jellystone Park Campground[LP, RV DUMP] (1 Mile)
13	VA 614, Emporia
FStop	E: Shell[*, K]
Gas	E: Texaco[*]
Food	E: Pit Cooked BBQ
Lodg	E: Dixie Motel
11AB	U.S. 58, Emporia, South Hill, Norfolk
TStop	W: Sadler Travel Plaza[*]
Gas	E: Amoco[*, LP], Citgo[*, RV DUMP], Phillips 66[*], Shell[*], Texaco[*, D, CW]
	W: Citgo[*, K], Shell[*] (Sadler Travel Plaza), Texaco[*, D]
Food	E: Arby's, Burger King (Citgo), China Dragon Chinese, Dairy Queen, Hardee's, Holiday Inn, KFC, McDonald's, Pizza Hut, Subway, Taco Bell (Amoco), Wendy's, Western Sizzlin'
	W: Days Inn, Johnson Peanut Company, SHONEY'S Shoney's, T.J.'s Family Restaurant
Lodg	E: Holiday Inn (see our ad this page)
	W: Best Western, Days Inn, Hampton Inn
AServ	E: Advance Auto Parts, Auto Mart, Freeman Auto Parts
	W: Exxon[*]
Med	E: ✚ Hospital
Other	E: CVS Pharmacy, Food Lion Grocery Store, Revco Drugs, Winn Dixie Supermarket
8	U.S. 301, Emporia
TStop	E: Amoco[*, D, SCALES]
Gas	E: Citgo, Exxon[*, K]
Food	E: Baskin Robbins, Denny's (Comfort Inn), Homestyle Cooking (Cooking), Marie's Restaurant, Red Carpet Inn
Lodg	E: Comfort Inn, Red Carpet Inn, Quality Hotel (see our ad this page)

Bold red print shows RV & Bus parking available or nearby

EXIT VIRGINIA/NORTH CAROLINA

4 VA 629, Skippers
- **Gas** W: Citgo[*, D]
- **Food** W: Econolodge
- **Lodg** W: Econolodge
- **RVCamp** W: Cattail Creek Campground (2.9 Miles)

(1) VA Welcome Center (RR, Phones, Picnic, Vending)

↑VIRGINIA

↓NORTH CAROLINA

(181) NC Welcome Center (RR, Phones)

180 NC 48, Gaston
- **TStop** W: McElroy Truck Lines, Speedway[*, LP, SCALES]

176 NC 46, Gaston, Garysburg
- **Gas** E: Texaco[*]
  W: Shell[*, 24]
- **Food** E: Stuckey's (Texaco)
  W: Aunt Sara's Pancake House (Comfort Inn), Burger King
- **Lodg** W: Comfort Inn
- **TServ** W: Redwines Parts and Sales Truck Service

173 U.S. 158, Roanoke Rapids, Weldon
- **FStop** E: Speedway[*, LP]
  W: Phillips 66[*, LP, CW]
- **Gas** E: Shell[*], Texaco[*, D, CW] (Picnic Area)
  W: Amoco[*, D, CW] (Picnic Area), Amoco[*, LP], BP[*, CW], Exxon, Racetrac[*], Shell[*, K]
- **Food** E: Blimpie's Subs, Frazier's, Ralph's BBQ, Trigger's Steak House, Waffle House
  W: Blimpie's Subs (Shell), Burger King, China King Chinese Restaurant, Country Porch Restaurant (Roses Dept. Store), Cracker Barrel, Dino's Pizza, Fisherman's Paradise, Hardee's, Holiday Inn, KFC, McDonald's, New China Chinese Restaurant, Piccolowe's, Pizza Hut, Pizza Inn, Ribeye Steakhouse, Ryan's Steakhouse, SHONEY'S, Shoney's, Subway, Taco Bell, Waffle House, Wendy's
- **Lodg** E: DAYS INN Days Inn, Interstate Inns, Orchard Inn
  W: Hampton Inn, Holiday Inn, Motel 6, Sleep Inn/ Comfort Inn
- **AServ** E: Nenc Service Center
  W: Advance Auto Parts, Alan Vester Ford Lincoln, Mercury, Auto Mart, Auto Zone Auto Parts, Draper Wrecker Serv.[24], Exxon, Firestone Tire & Auto, Honda
- **TWash** W: Phillips 66[CW]
- **RVCamp** E: Camping (Interstate Inn)
- **Med** W: ✚ Hospital
- **ATM** E: Speedway
  W: Cashpoint (BP), Centura Bank
- **Other** W: Chockoyotte Park, Coin Car Wash (Phillips 66), Discount Drug Barn, Eckerd Drugs, Food Lion Supermarket, Piggly Wiggly Supermarket, Roses Dept. Store, Wal-Mart[LP, 24, RX]

171 NC 125, Roanoke Rapids
- **Other** W: State Police

169 **(168)** NC 903, Halifax, Littleton
- **TStop** W: Citgo[LP] (Auto Repair, Truck Wash)
- **FStop** E: Exxon[*, D], Speedway[*, LP, K]
- **Food** W: Citgo
- **ATM** E: Speedway

160 NC 161, Louisburg, Roanoke Rapids
- **Gas** E: Exxon
  W: Citgo[*]
- **AServ** E: 561 Auto Repair[*]

154 NC 481, Enfield
- **Gas** E: Mobil[*]
- **RVCamp** W: KOA Campgrounds[LP, RV DUMP] (.8 Miles)

(151) Weigh Station

EXIT NORTH CAROLINA

150 NC 33, Whitakers
- **Gas** W: Texaco[*]
- **Food** W: Dairy Queen, Stuckey's (Texaco)
- **Other** W: Exit 150 Travel Center (No Trucks, No Turn around)

145 to NC4, to NC48, Goldrock
- **FStop** E: Amoco[*], Shell[*, D, LP]
- **Gas** E: BP[*, CW], Texaco[*]
- **Food** E: Denny's, Hardee's, Howard Johnson, Quality Inn, SHONEY'S, Shoney's, Waffle House, Wendy's (Days Inn)
- **Lodg** E: Best Western, Comfort Inn, DAYS INN Days Inn, Deluxe Inn, Howard Johnson, Masters Inn, Motel 6, Quality Inn, Red Carpet Inn, Scottish Inns, Shoney's Inn
- **ATM** E: Cash Point

(142) Rest Area (RR, Phones, Picnic, Vending)

141 NC 43, Red Oak, Dorches
- **FStop** E: I-95 Food Stop[*, D, LP], Texaco[*, D, CW]
- **Gas** W: BP[*]
- **Food** W: River Restaurant (Holiday Inn)
- **Lodg** W: Holiday Inn
- **ATM** E: Texaco

138 U.S. 64, Tarboro, Nashville, Rocky Mount, Winstead Ave
- **Food** E: Double Back's Old World Eatery (Holiday Inn), Outback Steakhouse
- **Lodg** E: Comfort Inn, Hampton Inn, Holiday Inn
- **AServ** E: Davenport Honda, Isuzu, Pontiac, Cadillac
- **ATM** E: Centura Bank, Triangle Bank

132 to NC 58
- **FStop** E: Citgo[*]
- **AServ** E: 24-Hr Towing & Repair

127 NC 97, Airport, Zebulon, Rocky Mount
- **Gas** E: Exxon[*, D]

Newly Renovated

1528

• Cable TV/ESPN
Swimming Pool • Fax Machine • Free Guest Laundry
Free Local Calls • Mr. D's Restaurant & Lounge
Room Service • Meeting & Banquet Facilities
Shopping Center Near Hotel

804-634-4191 For Reservations: 800-HOLIDAY

I-95 SB: First Holiday Inn after I-295 (Richmond) Bypass. Take Exit 11A. Right at light, right on W. Atlantic Street to hotel on left. I-95 NB: Exit 11A. Bare to right off exit. Hotel is on right.

VIRGINIA • I-95 • EXIT 11A

Hotel & Suites

Quality Inn
1190 N. Courthouse Rd.
Arlington, VA
703-524-4000
888-987-2555

1156

• Restaurant/Lounge on Presmises
• Outdoor Pool • Exercise Room
• Meeting/Banquet Facilities
• Pets Allowed • Coin Laundry
• Exterior/Interior Corridors
• Free Parking/Local Calls/In-Room Coffee

Exit 8A, Washington Blvd to Rt. 50E, Courthouse Rd. (Left Exit)

VIRGINIA • I-95 • EXIT 8A

EXIT NORTH CAROLINA

121 U.S. 264, Wilson, Greenville, Zebulon
- **FStop** E: Bullets East Coast[*, LP, K] (UPS Boxes)
- **Gas** E: Amoco[*, LP], Exxon[*, D], Shell[*, LP]
  W: BP[*]
- **Food** E: Aunt Sara's Pancake House, Bullets, Burgers, Chicken And More (East Coast), Hardee's, Subway (Exxon)
  W: Blimpie's Subs (BP), Cracker Barrel, McDonald's
- **Lodg** E: Comfort Inn
- **Med** E: ✚ Hospital (5 Miles)
- **ATM** E: Amoco, Nationsbank
  W: Cashpoint (BP)

116 NC 42, Wilson, Rock Ridge, Clayton
- **FStop** W: Texaco[*, D, LP]
- **Gas** E: Shell[*, D, LP, K]
  W: Mobil[*, D]
- **AServ** W: Bunn's Auto Repair And Sales
- **RVCamp** W: Rock Ridge Campground[LP] (2 Miles)
- **Med** E: ✚ Hospital (6 Miles)
- **ATM** W: Texacp

107 U.S. 301, Kenly, Wilson
- **FStop** E: Citgo[*]
- **Gas** E: Amoco[*], BP[*, LP], Coastal, Exxon[*, D], Texaco[*]
- **Food** E: Burger King, Golden China, McDonald's, Moore's Bar-B-Que, Nik's Pizza, Patrick's Cafeteria, Subway (Coastal), Waffle House
- **Lodg** E: Budget Inn, Deluxe Inn, Econolodge
- **AServ** E: Big A Kenly Service Center[D] (Exxon), Durham's Garage, Kenly Ford Dealer, Texaco, Top Dog Auto Center
- **ATM** E: Citgo
- **Other** E: 1870 Farmstead, Big A Auto Parts, Food Lion Supermarket, Gov. Charles B. Accott, Tabacco Farm Life Museum

106 Truck Stop Road
- **TStop** W: TravelCenters of America[*, SCALES] (Truck Wash), Wilco Travel Plaza[*, SCALES]
- **Gas** W: Texaco[*, D]
- **Food** W: TravelCenters of America (Country Prod), Waffle House, Wilco Travel Plaza
- **Lodg** W: Best Western, DAYS INN Days Inn
- **TServ** W: TravelCenters of America[*, SCALES]
- **ATM** W: TravelCenters of America

105 Bagley Road
- **TStop** E: Citgo Truck & Auto Plaza[*, LP, K, SCALES]
- **Food** E: Stormin Norman
- **TServ** E: Bunns Mobil Truck and Trailer Repair
- **Other** E: Big Boys Travel Store (Citgo)

102 Micro
- **Gas** E: BP
- **AServ** E: BP

101 Pittman Road
- **TStop** E: Truck Stop[D]

(99) Rest Area (RR, Phones, Picnic, Vending)

98 Selma
- **RVCamp** E: KOA Campgrounds[LP] (Dumpsite; .25 Miles; frontage road)

97 U.S. 70, NC39, Selma, Pine Level
- **FStop** E: Citgo[*, LP]
  W: Amoco[*, D], Texaco[*, D, LP]
- **Gas** W: Exxon[*, D]
- **Food** E: Denny's, Kathy's[*]
  W: Bojangles, KFC, McDonald's, Mucho's Mexico (Mexican Restaurant), Oliver's Steakhouse, Pizza Hut, Royal Inn, SHONEY'S, Shoney's, Waffle House
- **Lodg** E: Holiday Inn Express
  W: Comfort Inn, DAYS INN Days Inn, Luxury Inn, Masters Inn, Regency Inn, Royal Inn
- **AServ** W: Exxon
- **TServ** W: I-95 Truck Center

EXIT NORTH CAROLINA

Med W: Hospital
ATM E: Citgo
W: Amoco
Parks E: Cape Lookout National Seashore
Other E: J&R Outlets
W: RV & Truck Parking

95 U.S. 70, Smithfield, Goldsboro
Other E: Visitor Information

93 Smithfield, Brogden Road
Gas W: Shell(*)

90 U.S. 301, U.S. 701, NC 96, Newton Grove
FStop E: Citgo(*, D)
W: Phillips 66(D)
Food E: Roz's Country Buffet
Lodg E: Travelers Inn
AServ E: Rick's Towing
W: Ormond's Auto Sales
RVCamp E: Holiday Travel Park
Other E: Bentonville Civil War Battleground (15 Miles)
W: Highway Patrol

87 Four Oaks (Northbound Reaccess Via Frontage Rd)
Gas W: BP
AServ W: BP

81 Junction I-40, Raleigh, Wilmington

79 NC 50, NC 242, Benson, Newton Grove
FStop E: BP(*)
Gas E: Blackmon's Gas(*), Citgo(*)
W: Coastal(*), Exxon(*), Phillips 66(*, CW)
Food E: Brothers Famous Subs & Pizza, Golden Corral Family Steakhouse, Olde South BBQ, Waffle House
W: Burger King (Exxon), Coastal, Exxon, KFC, McDonald's(PLAY), Pizza Hut, Subway (Coastal)
Lodg E: Dutch Inn
W: Days Inn
AServ E: Wheel Alignment & Balancing, Wood's Muffler & Brake
W: Coastal, Lube Xpress, Phillips 66
ATM W: Exxon
Other E: Food Lion Supermarket
W: Animal Hospital, Flower's Food, Kerr Drugs(RX), Norge Village Coin Laundry

77 Hodges Chapel Road
TStop E: BP Auto Truck Stop(*, SCALES, 24)
FStop E: Speedway(*, K, SCALES)
Food E: BP Auto Truck Stop
TServ E: BP Auto Truck Stop(SCALES, 24), Wetern Star of Dunn Inc.
W: Mid West Transit, Peterbilt of Dunn (Cummins, CAT, Detroit Diesel)
RVCamp E: Speedway Rite Wash RV Wash
ATM E: BP Auto Truck Stop, Speedway

75 Jonesboro Road
TStop W: Sadler Travel Plaza(*, SCALES) (Shell gas)
Gas W: Citgo(*)
Food W: Citgo, Flash Facts Lounge (Citgo), Sadler Travel Plaza (Shell gas), Tart's Diner, The Singing Spur (Citgo)
TServ W: Sadler Travel Plaza(SCALES) (Shell gas)

73 US 421, NC 55, Newton Grove
FStop W: Chevron(*), Exxon(*, K)
Gas W: Exxon(*, D), Texaco(*)
Food E: Wendy's
W: 7 Day Inn, Bojangles, Burger King, Dairy Freeze, Dunn Diner (7 Day Inn), Krispy Kreme Doughnuts (Texaco), Sage Brush Steakhouse, Taco Bell, Texaco, Triangle Waffle
Lodg W: 7 Day Inn, Express Inn of Dunn, Holiday Inn Express, Jameson Inn, Ramada
AServ W: Troy's Auto Sales
Med W: Hospital
ATM W: BB&T, Exxon

72 Pope Road
Gas E: BP(*)
W: Amoco(*, K), Chevron(*, D)
Food E: Best Western
W: Brass Lantern Steakhouse, Gym's Restaurant
Lodg E: Best Western
W: Budget Inn, Super 8
ATM W: Amoco

71 Long Branch Road
Gas E: Shell(*, 24)
Food E: Hardee's(24) (Shell), Shell
TServ E: G&L Truck & Tire Service
ATM E: Shell

70 SR 1811
Lodg E: Relax Inn
AServ E: Interstate Auto
TServ E: Interstate Truck Service

65 NC 82, Godwin, Falcon
FStop W: One Stop Meat Market(K)
Gas W: Sam's(*)
AServ W: One Stop Meat Market

61 Wade
Gas W: BP(*)
Food W: BP
RVCamp E: KOA Campgrounds (.4 Miles)
ATM W: BP

(60) Parking Area

58 US 13, Newton Grove
FStop E: Texaco(*)
Gas E: Citgo(*)
Food E: Days Inn, Tasty World (Days Inn)
Lodg E: Days Inn

56 Bus I-95 S, US 301, Fayetteville, Ft. Bragg, Pope AFB, Eastover (Southbound, Difficult Reaccess)

55 SR 1832, Eastover
Gas W: Texaco(*, LP)
Lodg W: Budget Inn

52 NC 24, Fayetteville, Clinton, Fort Bragg (Difficult Reaccess)
Other W: Botanical Gardens, Military Museum, Museum

49 NC 53, NC 210, Fayetteville
Gas E: Amoco(*, D, K), Exxon(*, D), Texaco(*, LP)
W: Amoco(*, K), Exxon(*, D), Shell(*, D, CW)
Food E: Burger King, Days Inn, Denny's (Days Inn), McDonald's, Pizza Hut, Quality Inn, Waffle House
W: Amoco, Beaver Dam Seafood, Cracker Barrel, Holiday Inn, Jerico's (Plaza Hotel), Plaza Hotel, SHONEY'S Shoney's, Subway (Amoco)
Lodg E: Days Inn, Deluxe Inn, Motel 6, Quality Inn
W: Best Western, Comfort Inn, Econolodge, Fairfield Inn, Hampton Inn, Holiday Inn, Howard Johnson, Innkeeper, Plaza Hotel, Sleep Inn, Super 8
AServ E: Amoco
ATM W: Amoco, Exxon

(48) Rest Area (RR, Phones, Picnic, Vending; Southbound)

(48) Rest Area (RR, Phones, Picnic, Vending; Northbound)

46 NC 87, Elizabethtown, Fayetteville
Med W: Hospital

44 Airport, Snow Hill Road
RVCamp W: Lazy Acres Campground

41 NC 59, Hope Mills, Parkton
Gas E: Texaco(*)
W: BP(*)
RVCamp W: Spring Valley Park Campground (2 Miles)

40 Bus. I-95N, US 301, Fayettville, Fort Brag, Pope Air Force (Northbound, Difficult Reaccess)

33 U.S. 301, N.C. 71, Parkton
Gas E: Amoco
AServ E: Amoco

31 NC 20, St Paul, Raeford
FStop E: Shell(*)
Gas E: Amoco(*, LP, 24), BP(*)
W: Citgo(*, LP, K), Exxon(*, D)
Food E: Burger King, Joe Don Danny's (Shell), Shell
Lodg E: Days Inn
AServ E: Shell
ATM E: Amoco
W: Exxon

25 US 301, Local Traffic

(24) Weigh Station (Southbound)

(24) Weigh Station (Northbound)

22 U.S. 301, Local Traffic
FStop W: BP(*, LP), Subway (Texaco), Texaco(*)
Gas E: Exxon(*, CW)
W: Exxon
Food E: Denny's (Holiday Inn), Hardee's, Holiday Inn, Huddle House, John's Restaurant, Ryan's Steakhouse, Waffle House
W: Texaco, Uncle George's Restaurant
Lodg E: Best Western, Comfort Suites Hotel, Hampton Inn, Holiday Inn, Super 8, Villager Lodge
AServ E: Rise & Shine Towing Service(24)
W: Exxon
Med E: Hospital
ATM E: Exxon

EXIT NORTH/SOUTH CAROLINA

20 NC 211, to NC 41, Lumberton, Red Springs
- **Gas** E: Amoco(*), Citgo(*, 24), Exxon(*, D)
  W: Texaco(*, D)
- **Food** E: Adellio's Restaurant (Quality Inn), Carolina Steak Man Restaurant & Bar, Howard Johnson, **K-Mart(RX)**, Lane's Ice Cream Cafe, **Little Caesars Pizza (K-Mart)**, McDonald's(PLAY), New China Restaurant (Howard Johnson), Quality Inn & Suites, Subway, Village Station Restaurant, Waffle House, Western Sizzlin'
  W: **Cracker Barrel**, Evening Place Seafood, Fuller's Old Fashioned Barbecue, Lung Wah Chinese, Santa Fe Mexican Restaurant
- **Lodg** E: Howard Johnson, Quality Inn & Suites, Ramada Limited
  W: Comfort Inn, Country Inn & Suites, Days Inn, Econolodge, Fairfield Inn
- **Med** E: **Hospital**
- **Other** E: **Food Lion Supermarket**, **K-Mart(RX)**
  W: **Action Zone Family Fun Center**

19 Carthage Road
- **Gas** W: Citgo(*), Exxon(*, CW)
- **Food** E: Travelers Inn
  W: Taqueria Plaza & Restaurant
- **Lodg** E: Travelers Inn
  W: **Knight's Inn**, Motel 6
- **AServ** E: McGrit's Auto

17 NC 72, NC 711, Pembroke
- **Gas** E: BP(*), Citgo(*), Mobil(*, 24), Texaco(*)
- **Food** E: Burger King, **Hardee's**, Little Sparkie's Burgers, **McDonald's**, **Waffle House**
- **Lodg** E: **Southern Inn**
- **AServ** E: BP, Mobil(24), O.K. Auto Service
- **RVCamp** E: **Freeman Motors Truck Center (1.7 Miles)**
- **ATM** E: Citgo

14 US 74, Maxton, Laurinburg, Wilmington, Whiteville, NC beaches
- **FStop** W: **BP(*)**
- **Lodg** W: Exit Inn
- **RVCamp** W: **Sleepy Bear's Family Campground (.8 Miles)**

10 US 301, Fairmont
- **Gas** W: Hunts 301(*)

7 McDonald, Raynham

(5) NC Welcome Center (RR, Phones, Picnic, Vending; Northbound)

2 NC 130, NC 904, Rowland, Fairmont

1AB US 301, US 501, Rowland, Laurinburg
- **FStop** W: **Amoco(*, 24)**, **Texaco(*)**
- **Gas** E: Exxon(*), Shell(*)
  W: Citgo(*)
- **Food** E: Hot Tamale, Peddler Steakhouse, Pedro's Diner
  W: Days Inn (BP gas), Denny's (Days Inn), **Hardee's**, Waffle House
- **Lodg** E: South of the Border Motel
  W: Days Inn (BP gas), **Family Inns of America**, Holiday Inn Express
- **RVCamp** E: **Pedro's Campground**
- **ATM** E: First Citizens Bank
- **Other** E: **Country Antique**, **Rocket City Fireworks**, **Silver Slipper Casino**

↑NORTH CAROLINA

↓SOUTH CAROLINA

EXIT SOUTH CAROLINA

(195) SC Welcome Center (RR, Phones, Picnic, Vending; Southbound)

193 SC 9, SC 57, Dillon, Little Rock
- **FStop** E: **Speedway(*, D, LP)**
- **Gas** E: Amoco(*, CW)
  W: Amoco(*), BP(*, D)
- **Food** E: Burger King, Golden Corral Family Steakhouse, **Huddle House**, SHONEY'S, Shoney's, Wendy's
  W: Hubbard House, **Waffle House**
- **Lodg** E: Budget Inn, Comfort Inn, Days Inn, Hampton Inn, Ramada Limited
  W: Econolodge, **Super 8**
- **TServ** W: **Cottingham Trailor Service**
- **RVCamp** W: **Bass Lake Campground (.5 Miles)**
- **Other** E: **JABS Fireworks**, **Rocket City II Fireworks**
  W: **Fireworks Superstore**

190 SC 34, Dillon
- **Gas** E: Citgo(*)
- **Food** E: Citgo, Dairy Queen (Citgo), Stuckey's (Citgo)
- **AServ** E: Peewee's Auto Service
- **ATM** E: **Dillon's Station**
- **Other** E: **Dillon's Station**

181 S.C.38, Marion, Bennetsville, Lattia.
- **TStop** E: **Flying J Travel Plaza(*, LP, RV DUMP, SCALES) (Conoco Gas)**
- **Gas** E: BP(*), Exxon(*) (Fireworks), Texaco(*)
  W: Exxon(*)
- **Food** E: **Flying J Travel Plaza (Conoco Gas)**, Subway (Texaco), Texaco
  W: Dairy Queen (Wilco), Stuckey's (Wilco), Wendy's (Wilco), **Wilco Travel Plaza(*, SCALES)**
- **AServ** E: BP
  W: Exxon
- **TServ** E: **Flying J Travel Plaza(SCALES) (Conoco Gas)**
  W: **Wilco Travel Plaza(SCALES)**
- **TWash** E: **Flying J Travel Plaza (Conoco Gas)**
- **ATM** E: Exxon (Fireworks), Texaco
  W: Exxon

(172) Rest Area (RR, Phones, Picnic, Vending; Southbound)

(172) Rest Area (RR, Phones, Picnic, Vending; Northbound)

170 SC 327, Marion, Myrtle Beach
- **FStop** E: **Speedway(*)**
  W: **Shell Auto Truck Plaza(*)**
- **Gas** E: Amoco(*)
- **Food** E: **PDQ Waffle and Egg Family Restaurant(24)**
  W: **Shell Auto Truck Plaza**

169 TV Road, Quimby, Florence
- **TStop** W: **Petro(*, CW, RV DUMP, SCALES, 24) (Texaco Gas, Truck Service)**
- **FStop** W: **Advantage(*)**
- **Gas** W: Amoco(*), BP(*)
- **Food** W: **Iron Skillet Restaurant (Petro)**, **Petro (Texaco Gas, Truck Service)**
- **Lodg** W: **Quality Inn**
- **AServ** W: BP
- **TServ** E: **Heavy Duty Truck Repair Inc.**, **Peterbilt Dealer**, **Thummel King of Florence**
  W: **Blanchard Truck Service**
- **TWash** W: **Petro(CW) (Texaco Gas, Truck Service)**
- **RVCamp** E: **KOA Campgrounds(LP) (1.1 Miles)**
- **ATM** W: **Petro (Texaco Gas, Truck Service)**

164 U.S. 52, Florence, Darlington
- **TStop** W: **Pilot Travel Center(*, SCALES)**
- **Gas** E: Exxon(*, D, LP, CW), Racetrac(*), Texaco(*, D)
  W: BP(*), Hess(*, D)
- **Food** E: Baskin Robbins (Exxon), Cracker Barrel, Denny's (Traveler's Lodge), Exxon, Hardee's(24), Holiday Inn, McDonald's(PLAY), Pizza Hut (Exxon), Quincy's Family Steakhouse, Travelers Inn, Waffle House, Wendy's
  W: Arby's, Bojangles, Burger King, Coco Cabana, **Dairy Queen (Pilot)**, **Pilot Travel Center**, Ramada, SHONEY'S, Shoney's, **Subway (Pilot)**, **Thunderbird Inn**
- **Lodg** E: Best Western, Comfort Inn, **Econolodge**, Hampton Inn, Holiday Inn, Motel 6, Super 8, Travelers Inn
  W: Days Inn, Microtel Inn, Radisson Inn, Ramada (see our ad this page), Shoney's Inn, Sleep Inn, **Thunderbird Inn**, Wingate Inn
- **ATM** E: Exxon, Texaco
- **Other** W: Pack Rats Emporium

160AB I-20 Business, Florence, Columbia, Junction I-20 (160A has services, 160B is the junction)
- **FStop** E: **Shell(*) (Pacific Pride Commercial Fueling)**
- **Food** E: Burger King(PLAY), Chick-Fil-A, Huddle House, Outback Steakhouse, Pizza Hut, Red Lobster, SHONEY'S, **Shoney's**, Waffle House, Western Sizzlin'
- **Lodg** E: Courtyard by Marriott, Fairfield Inn, Hampton Inn, Holiday Inn Express, Red Roof Inn
- **ATM** E: NationsBank, **Shell (Pacific Pride Commercial Fueling)**
- **RVCamp** E: **Camping World (see our ad this page)**
- **Other** E: Auto Parts, **Carmike Cinemas**, **Crossroads Center Mall**, **Harrington Vision Center**, **Magnolia Mall**, Toys, **Wal-Mart(RX)**

157 U.S. 76, Florence, Timmonsvile
- **FStop** W: **Shell(*, D, 24)**
- **Gas** E: Amoco(*), BP(D), Exxon(*), Texaco(*, D)
  W: Citgo(*)
- **Food** E: Carolina BBQ, Days Inn, Exxon, McDonald's (Exxon), Miz Ginny's (Days Inn), Waffle House
  W: **Econolodge**, **The Tree Room (EconoLodge)**
- **Lodg** E: Days Inn (see our ad this page), Howard Johnson, Swamp Fox Inn, **Villager Lodge (Extended Stay)**
  W: **Econolodge**, Young's Plantation Inn
- **AServ** E: Amoco
- **RVCamp** E: **Swamp Fox Camping (1.1 Miles)**
- **Med** E: **Hospital**
- **Other** E: **Swamp Fox Fireworks**

153 Honda Way

150 SC 403, Sardis, Timmonsville
- **FStop** W: **Exxon(*, D)**
- **Food** E: **Sardis Auto Truck Plaza(24) (Road Service, BP gas)**, **Steak & Waffle(24)**
  W: **Exxon**, Libby's Country Kitchen (Exxon)
- **Lodg** E: TraveLodge
- **TServ** E: **Sardis Auto Truck Plaza(24) (Road Service, BP**

CAMPING WORLD
Hwy 501 Exit
3632 Hwy. 501 • Myrtle Beach, SC
1-800-845-3571
1430

RAMADA INN
Florence, South Carolina
Restaurant/Lounge on Premises
Free Hot Breakfast Buffet for 2
Remote Control Cable TV w/HBO
Meeting/Banquet Facilities • Room Service
Handicap Accessible • Airport Shuttle Available
Outdoor Pool • Basketball & Volleyball
Exercise Room/Sauna/Whirlpool
Exterior/Interior Corridors • Pets Allowed
$49.95 per night
843-669-4241 • 800-2RAMADA
Same day reservations accepted. w/coupon at check-in. Based on availability. Not valid w/other discounts.
1633
SOUTH CAROLINA • I-95 • EXIT 164

Bold red print shows RV & Bus parking available or nearby

EXIT SOUTH CAROLINA

gas)
RVCamp W: **Lake Honeydew**

146 SC 341, Lynchburg, Olanta
Gas E: Exxon(*)
Lodg E: **Relax Inn**

141 SC 53, SC 58, Shiloh
FStop E: **Exxon**(*, K)
Gas W: Texaco(*, K)
RVCamp E: **Don Mar RV Sales & Service**
ATM E: **Exxon**
Parks E: **Woods Bay State Park**

(139) Rest Area (RR, Phones, Picnic, Vending; Southbound)

(139) Rest Area (RR, Phones, Picnic, Vending; Northbound)

135 U.S. 378, Turbeville, Sumter, Myrtle

Travelodge
1483
843-346-9696
Free Continental Breakfast
• AAA & AARP Commercial Rates
• Truck/Large Vehicle Parking
• Easy Access to I-95
• 25" Remote TV, HBO/CNN/Weather
• Data Port Phones
2200 Cale Yarborough Hwy
Sarids,Timmonsville, SC
South Carolina ▪ I-95 ▪ Exit 150

Florence, SC
1661
DAYS INN
1-4 Persons
$31.95
E-Z On/Off I-95
Restaurant on Premises
New Outdoor Pool Area & Jacuzzi
Kids Stay Free • Free Cable TV • Coin Laundry
Electronic Door Locks/Security Safes
New McDonalds/Exxon Facility
AAA Approved
4 Sunburst Quality Award Winner
843-665-8550 • 800-Days Inn
w/Coupon at Check-in. Based on Availability. Not Validw/Other Discounts or Special Events
South Carolina ▪ I-95 ▪ Exit 157

EXIT SOUTH CAROLINA

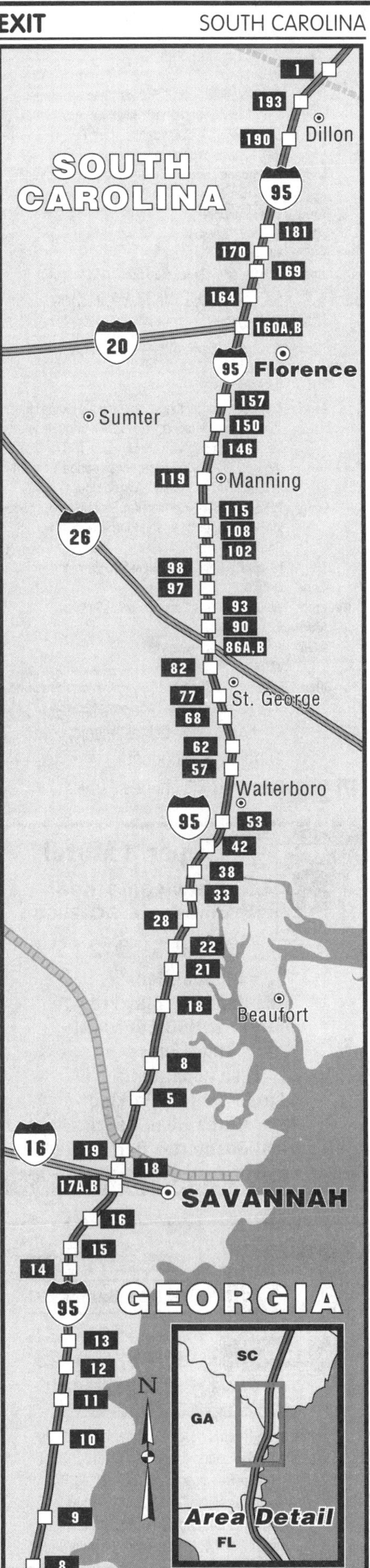

EXIT SOUTH CAROLINA

Beach via Conway
Gas E: BP(*), Citgo(*, 24)
W: Exxon(*, D)
Food E: **Compass Restaurant**
Lodg E: Days Inn, Knight's Inn
ATM W: Exxon

132 SC 527, Sardinia, Bishopville

122 SC 521, Alcolu, Sumter
Gas W: Exxon(*, D, K)
Food W: Shrimper Sea Food
ATM W: Exxon
Other W: Alcolu Car Wash

119 SC 261, Manning, Paxville, Myrtle Beach via Georgetown, Kingstree
TStop E: **TA TravelCenters of America**(*, SCALES, 24) **(Amoco gas)**
Gas E: Shell(*), Texaco(*)
W: BP(*), Exxon(*, 24)
Food E: **Huddle House**, Long John Silver (TA), Sbarro (TA), Shoney's, **TA TravelCenters of America (Amoco gas)**, Taco Bell (TA), The Lodge, Waffle House, Wendy's, **Western Steer Family Steakhouse**
W: BP, Lyle's Subs & More (BP)
Lodg E: **Comfort Inn**, Holiday Inn Express, **Manning Economy Inn**
W: Alpha Inn
AServ E: Stokes-Craven Ford
W: Clarendon Auto Repair & Sales, Exxon(24)
TServ E: **TA TravelCenters of America**(SCALES, 24) **(Amoco gas)**
TWash E: **Mid Eastern**
RVCamp E: **Camper's Paradise (.1 Miles; Propane Filling Station)**
ATM E: **TA TravelCenters of America (Amoco gas)**
W: Exxon
Other E: **Crazy Fireworks**

115 U.S. 301, Manning
FStop W: **Texaco**(*)
Gas E: Exxon(*)
Food E: Shanghai Restaurant (Travelers Inn), Travelers Inn
W: Georgio's Pizza, **Motel Venture**
Lodg E: Carolina Inn, Travelers Inn
W: Days Inn, **Motel Venture**, Sun Set Inn
AServ W: Ram-Bay Auto Repair
ATM E: Exxon
Other W: Car Wash

108 Road 102, Summerton
Gas E: Citgo(*), Shell(*)
Food E: Citgo, Dairy Queen (Citgo), Stuckey's (Citgo)
W: Family Folks Restaurant
Lodg E: TraveLodge
W: EconoLodge
Other E: **Loco Joe's Fireworks**

102 North Santee, Road 400, U.S. 15-301
FStop E: **BP**(*, LP, 24)
Gas E: Texaco(*, LP)
Food E: **BP**, Country Cookin' Restaurant (BP), Jake's II (Santee's Resort), Santee Resort
Lodg E: Santee Resort
RVCamp E: **Cooper's Campground, Santee Lakes Campground (.25 Miles)**
Other W: **Santee National Wildlife Refuge**

(99) Rest Area (RR, Phones, Picnic, Vending; Northbound)

(99) Rest Area (RR, Phones, Picnic, Vending; Southbound)

98 SC 6, Santee, Eutawville
FStop W: **BP**(*, D)
Gas E: Amoco(*), Chevron(*), Citgo(*), Texaco(*, D, LP, K, CW)
W: By-Lo(*) (Fireworks), Citgo(*), Exxon(*), Shell(*, K, 24)
Food E: Antonio's, Citgo, **Days Inn, Georgio's**

EXIT SOUTH CAROLINA

House of Pizza, Huddle House, Jake's Steak & Ribs, KFC, Ramada, SHONEY'S Shoney's, Subway (Texaco), Texaco, The Garden Restaurant (Ramada), Verandah, Western Steer Family Steakhouse
W: Burger King, Cracker Barrel, Denny's, Krispy Kreme Doughnuts (Shell), McDonald's(PLAY), Pizza Hut (Shell), Shell, TCBY (Shell), Waffle House

Lodg E: Ashley Inn, Carolina Lodge, DAYS INN Days Inn, Ramada, Santee Inn, Super 8
W: Budget Motel, Clarks Inn, Comfort Inn (see our ad this page), Economy Inn

AServ W: BP

ATM E: Citgo
W: Exxon, The Bank Of Clarendon

Parks W: Santee State Park

Other E: Lake Marion Golf Course, Santee Factory Stores

97 U.S. 301, Orangeburg (Southbound, Reaccess Northbound Only)

AServ W: Avingers Auto

TServ W: Truck Towing Service

RVCamp W: Camp Pedro (.1 Miles)

93 U.S. 15, Santee, Eloree

90 U.S. 176, Holly Hill, Cameron

Gas W: Exxon(*)

ATM W: Exxon

86AB Junction I-26

82 U.S. 178, Harleyville, Bowman

TStop E: Wilco Travel Center(*, RV DUMP, SCALES) (Exxon)

FStop W: BP(*, LP, K), Texaco(*, D)

Gas E: Amoco(*) (Fireworks)

Food E: Dairy Queen (Exxon TStop), Krispy Kreme Doughnuts (Exxon), Stuckey's (Exxon TStop), Wendy's (Exxon TStop), Wilco Travel Center (Exxon)
W: BP, Ray's Fine Food

Other E: Discount Fireworks, Yesterday's Antiques & Collectibles

77 U.S. 78, St George, Branchville, Reedsville

Gas E: Exxon(*), Shell(*, CW)
W: BP(*), Texaco(*, D, CW)

Food E: Exxon, Georgio's Pizza & Restaurant, Griffin's Family Restaurant, Hardee's(PLAY), Holiday Inn, KFC (Exxon), McDonald's(PLAY), Shell, Subway (Shell), TCBY (Shell), Waffle House, Western Steer Family Steakhouse
W: BP, Eddy's Pepper Mexican Restaurant (BP), Hot Stuff Pizza (BP), Huddle House

Lodg E: Comfort Inn, Economy Inns of America, Holiday Inn, St George Economy Inn
W: Best Western, EconoLodge, Southern Inn, Super 8

ATM E: Exxon, Shell

Other E: CVS(RX), Crazy Bob's Fireworks, Food Lion Supermarket, U.S. Post Office

(74) Parking Area (Southbound)

(74) Parking Area (Northbound)

68 SC 61, Canadys, Bamberg

TStop E: Texaco(*, K, RV DUMP, SCALES)

Gas E: Amoco(*), Citgo(*)

Food E: Chicago Style Pizza (Texaco), Necee's Restaurant(D) (Texaco), Subway (Texaco), Texaco

TServ E: Texaco(SCALES)

ATM E: Texaco

Parks E: Colleton State Park

62 Road 34

Gas W: Exxon(*)

RVCamp E: Lakeside Campground, Lakeside Used RV Parts

57 SC 64, Walterboro, Lodge

FStop E: Texaco(*, CW)

EXIT SOUTH CAROLINA

Gas E: BP(*), Exxon(*, D), Shell(*)
W: Amoco(*)

Food E: BP, Blimpie Subs & Salads (Texaco), Burger King, Dairy Queen (Shell), Huddle House, Shell, Stuckey's (Shell), Subway (BP), TCBY (BP), Taco Maker (BP), Texaco, Waffle House

Lodg E: Carolina Lodge, Howard Johnson, Southern Inn
W: Super 8

Med E: ✚ Hospital

ATM E: Exxon, Texaco
W: Amoco

Other E: Fireworks Outlet, Sad Sam's Fireworks

53 S.C. 63 to U.S. Alt. 17, Walterboro, Varnville

Gas E: Amoco(*), Econo Mart(*, CW), El Cheapo, Exxon(*), Texaco(*)
W: BP(*, K)

Food E: Amoco, Burger King, Comfort Inn, Huddle House, Joint Venture Seafood, Keith's BBQ, Linguettine Restaurant, Longhorn Steakhouse, McDonald's (Amoco), Merrick's Restaurant & Lounge (Comfort Inn), SHONEY'S Shoney's, Waffle House

Lodg E: Best Western, Comfort Inn, EconoLodge, Holiday Inn, Rice Planter's Inn, Thunderbird Inn, Town & Country Inn
W: DAYS INN Days Inn, Deluxe Inn, Hampton Inn

AServ E: Auto

RVCamp W: Green Acres Campground (.7 Miles)

Med E: ✚ Hospital

ATM E: Hobo Joe's Fireworks
W: BP

Other E: Fireworks Supermarket, Hobo Joe's Fireworks, Jolly Joe's Fireworks, Sad Sam's Fireworks

(47) Rest Area (RR, Phones, Picnic, Vending; Southbound)

(47) Rest Area (RR, Phones, Picnic,

1727
Super 8 Motel
Hwy 68 & I-95
Yemassee, SC 29945
803-589-2177
Outdoor Pool
Kids Under 10 Stay Free
Cable TV w/HBO/ESPN/CNN
Kings Beds
Free Local Calls
Large Vehicle Parking
Near Hilton Head Beach,
Historical Beaufort & Parris Island
SOUTH CAROLINA • I-95 • EXIT 38

1206
Comfort Inn
Comfort Inn
Exit 98 • Santee, SC
803-854-3221
800-882-0525
Next to Cracker Barrel
Coffee in All Rooms • Free Continental Breakfast
Hospitality & Meeting Facilities • Outdoor Pool
Jacuzzi Rooms • Handicap & Non-Smoking Rooms
Nearby Attractions: Lake Marion -1/2 Mile
Fishing & Boating • Golf Packages
3 Golf Courses within 1/2 Mile • Factory Outlet Shopping
SOUTH CAROLINA • I-95 • EXIT 98

EXIT SOUTH CAROLINA

Vending; Northbound)

42 U.S. 21, Orangeburg

38 SC 68, Yemassee, Hampton, Beaufort

TStop W: Simon's Truck Stop(*, LP) (Fina, Cable TV, NAPA)

Gas E: Chevron(*, LP)
W: BP(*), Shell(*), Texaco(*)

Food W: BP, China Dragon (Super 8 Motel), Hot Stuff Pizza (Texaco), Simon's Truck Stop (Fina, Cable TV, NAPA), Subway (BP), Super 8, TCBY (BP), Texaco, Village Restaurant

Lodg W: Palmetto Lodge, Super 8 (see our ad this page)

AServ W: Simon's Truck Stop (Fina, Cable TV, NAPA)

TServ W: Simon's Truck Stop (Fina, Cable TV, NAPA)

ATM E: Chevron
W: BP, Shell, Texaco

33 U.S. 17 N., Charleston, Beaufort

Gas E: BP(*, D), Exxon(*), Shell(*, 24), Texaco(*)

Food E: Best Western, DAYS INN Days Inn, Denny's (Best Western), Exxon, Krispy Kreme Doughnuts (Texaco), McDonald's(PLAY) (Exxon), Palmetto Restaurant (Days Inn), Subway (Texaco), TCBY (Texaco), Texaco, Waffle House

Lodg E: Best Western, DAYS INN Days Inn, Holiday Inn Express, Knight's Inn (see our ad this page)

RVCamp E: KOA Campgrounds (.25 Miles), The Oaks at Point South RV Resort (.25 Miles)

ATM E: Exxon, Texaco

Other E: Visitor Information

28 SC 462, Coosawhatchie

TStop W: Texaco Travel Center(*, K, SCALES) (24 hour road service)

Gas W: Amoco(*), BP(*), Chevron(*, D), Citgo(*)

Food W: Citgo, Dairy Queen (Citgo), Stuckey's (Citgo), Texaco Travel Center (24 hour road service)

TServ W: Texaco Travel Center(SCALES) (24 hour road service)

22 U.S. 17 South, Ridgeland

Gas W: Shell(*)

Med W: ✚ Hospital

21 S.C. 336, Hilton Head Island, Ridgeland

Gas W: Chevron(*, D, LP), Exxon(*), Texaco(*)

Food W: Blimpie Subs & Salads (Chevron), Chevron, Depot Restaurant, Hardee's, Hong Kong Chinese Restaurant, Huddle House, Pizza Station 2, Subway, Waffle House

Lodg W: Carolina Lodge, Comfort Inn, EconoLodge, The Station Inn

ATM W: Chevron, Food Lion Supermarket, Texaco

Other W: Eckerd Drugs(RX), Food Lion Supermarket

18 Road 13, Ridgeland

Med W: ✚ Hospital

(17) Parking Area (Southbound)

Outdoor Pool
70 Rooms
Kings Available
Large Vehicle Parking
Restaurant Nearby
843-726-8488
$24.95* +tax Single/1 Person
$28.95* +tax Double/2 Persons
$28.95* +tax King/2 Persons
*Based on Availability. Not valid during special events or holidays
South Carolina • I-95 • Exit 33

Bold red print shows RV & Bus parking available or nearby

EXIT	SOUTH CAROLINA
(17)	Parking Area (Northbound)
8	U.S. 278, Beaufort, Hilton Head, Bluffton, Sun City
TStop	E: **Joker Joe's Truck Stop**(*, SCALES) **(BP, Fireworks)**
Gas	E: Exxon(*) (Welcome Area) W: Chevron(*, D), Shell(*) (Fireworks)
Food	E: **Joker Joe's Truck Stop (BP, Fireworks)** W: Chevron, Pizza Hut (Chevron), Subway (Chevron), TCBY (Chevron)
Lodg	E: Hilton Head Island Beach & Tennis Resort (see our ad this page) W: Ramada Inn
TServ	E: **Joker Joe's Truck Stop**(SCALES) **(BP, Fireworks)**
ATM	E: Exxon (Welcome Area)
Parks	E: **Sgt. Jasper State Park**
5	U.S. 17, U.S. 321, Hardeeville, Estell
TStop	E: **Hardeeville Travel Center**(SCALES) **(NO Fuel)**
FStop	W: **Speedway**(*, LP, K)
Gas	E: El Cheapo(*), Exxon(*, LP) (SC Tourist Information), Shell(*, 24) W: Amoco(*), BP(*, D, CW)
Food	E: Blimpie Subs & Salads (Exxon), DAYS INN Days Inn, Denny's (Days Inn), Exxon (SC Tourist Information), I Can't Believe It's Yogurt (Exxon), **Waffle House** W: Budget Inn, Burger King, Captain Ron's Seafood, Howard Johnson, Jasper's Restaurant (Howard Johnson), Knight's Inn, McDonald's(PLAY), New China Chinese Restaurant (Knight's Inn), SHONEY'S Shoney's, **Wendy's**
Lodg	E: DAYS INN Days Inn (see our ad this page), Economy Inn W: Budget Inn, Carolina Inn Express, Comfort Inn, Holiday Inn Express, Howard Johnson, Knight's Inn, Scottish Inn
TServ	E: **Hardeeville Travel Center**(SCALES) **(NO Fuel)**
Other	E: **Alamo Wholesale Fireworks, Fireworks Papa Joe's**, Fireworks Superstore, **Magic Fireworks**

1147

1-800-475-2631

- Year Round Oceanfront Resort
- 1 & 2 Bedroom Fully Equipped Condos
- Oceanfront Pool & Snack Bar
- Gift Shop, Deli Market & Tennis Center
- Continental Breakfast
- Cocktail Lounge & Light Dining
- Golf, Tennis, Family & Romantic Packages

Come Stay the Night, Week, or Month!

SOUTH CAROLINA • I-95 • EXIT 8

DAYS INN

1162

- 24 Hour Denny's Restaurant
- Free Local Calls • Bus Parking
- 25" Cable TV with Free HBO
- 15 Miles from Savannah
- Outdoor Pool - Guest Laundry
- Special Rates For Tour Groups
- Pets Welcome $5 Pet Charge

803-784-2281 • Hardeeville, SC

SOUTH CAROLINA • I-95 • EXIT 5

EXIT	SOUTH CAROLINA/GEORGIA
	W: **Crazy Joe's Fireworks**
(5)	SC Welcome Center (RR, Phones, Picnic, Vending; Northbound)
(3)	Weigh Station (Northbound)

↑SOUTH CAROLINA

↓GEORGIA

EXIT	
(111)	GA Welcome Center, Weigh Station (RR, Phones, Picnic, Vending, RV Dump; Southbound)
19	**(108)** Georgia 21, Port Wentworth
FStop	E: **Speedway**(*, SCALES) W: **Smile Gas**(*, LP)
Gas	E: Enmark(*) W: BP(*)
Food	E: Enmark, Krispy Kreme Doughnuts (Enmark), Waffle House W: Sunrise Family Restaurant
Lodg	E: Hampton Inn W: Park Inn, Ramada, Sleep Inn
AServ	E: Sleaze Semi-Truck & Auto Repair
TServ	E: **Freightliner Dealer, Peterbilt Dealer, Speedway**(SCALES)
TWash	E: **Savannah Truck Wash, Speedway**
RVCamp	W: **Camping**
ATM	E: **Speedway** W: **Smile Gas**
18A	**(104)** Savannah International Airport
Gas	E: Shell(*)
Food	E: Shell, Taco Maker (Shell)
ATM	E: Shell

Savannah, GA

1681

912-925-6666
888-854-5678

Continental Breakfast
Lounge on Premises
Indoor Pool
Exercise Room
Meeting/Banquet Facilities
Truck/Large Vehicle Parking
Coin Laundry
Exterior Corridors
Handicap Accessible
Airport Shuttle
Cracker Barrel
and Shoney's on Site
Outlet Mall Nearby

6 Gateway Blvd East • Savannah, GA 31419

GEORGIA • I-95 • EXIT 16

EXIT	GEORGIA
18	**(102)** U.S. 80, Pooler, Garden City
Gas	E: Amoco(*, LP), Enmark(*, CW) W: Amoco(*, LP), Gate(*)
Food	E: Amoco, Baldino's Subs (Amoco), Blimpie Subs & Salads (Enmark), **Cracker Barrel**, Enmark, Huddle House, KFC, McDonald's, **Waffle House** W: **Burger King**, Don's Famous BBQ, El Patro, Gate, **Hardee's**, Hong Kong Chinese, Lovezzola's Pizza, Spanky's, Subway (Gate gas), Wendy's, Western Sizzlin'
Lodg	E: Microtel Inn, Ramada Limited W: EconoLodge
AServ	W: Castrol Car Care Center
Other	E: **Air Force Heritage Museum, Carter's Pharmacy, Food Lion Supermarket, Fort Pulaskie National Monument** W: **Coin Laundry**(24)
17AB	**(99)** Junction I-16, Savannah, Macon
16	**(94)** Georgia 204, Savannah, Pembroke
FStop	E: **Shell**(*)
Gas	E: Amoco(*, LP), BP(*, CW), Exxon(*) (Welcome Center) W: Chevron(*, 24)
Food	E: Best Western, **Cracker Barrel**, Denny's (Best Western), **Hardee's**, McDonald's, SHONEY'S Shoney's W: EconoLodge, Giovanni's Italian (Red Carpet Inn), Huddle House, Red Carpet Inn, Subway, The Shell House Seafood, Waffle House
Lodg	E: Best Western, DAYS INN Days Inn, **Hampton Inn, Holiday Inn**, La Quinta Inn, Quality Inn & Suites (see our ad this page), **Shoney's Inn**, Sleep Inn, TraveLodge W: EconoLodge, Red Carpet Inn, **Super 8**
RVCamp	W: **Bellaire Woods Camping**
Med	E: ✚ **Hospital**
ATM	W: Chevron
Parks	E: **Skidaway State Park**
Other	E: **Savannah Festival Outlet Center**
15	**(90)** Georgia 144, Old Clyde Road
FStop	W: **Texaco**(*)
Gas	E: Amoco(*), Exxon(*)
Food	E: Exxon, Millie's BBQ (Exxon)
TServ	W: **Roberts Truck Center, Truck Service**
RVCamp	E: **Waterway RV Camp** W: **Dick Gore's RV World**(LP) **(.3 Miles)**
Parks	E: **Fort McAllister State Park & Historic Site**
14	**(87)** U.S. 17, Coastal Highway, Richmond Hill Georgia Welcome Center
TStop	W: **TA TravelCenters of America**(SCALES, 24) **(Amoco gas)**
FStop	W: **Speedway**(*, LP, RV DUMP), **Texaco**(*)
Gas	E: Amoco(*), Chevron(*, 24), Racetrac(*), Shell(*, D) W: BP(*, CW), Exxon(*)
Food	E: Amoco, Chevron, DAYS INN **Days Inn**, Denny's (Days Inn), Huddle House, Krispy Kreme Doughnuts (Chevron), Mike's Pizza, Sandra Dee's Steaks & Seafood, Subway (Amoco), TraveLodge, Waffle House W: **Arby's**, Burger King(PLAY), Country Pride (TA), Exxon, Harry's Bar & Grill (Ramada Inn), **Holiday Inn, KFC**, Long John Silver (TA), McDonald's (Exxon), Olympus (Ramada Inn), Pizza Hut (TA), **Ramada Inn, TA TravelCenters of America (Amoco gas), Taco Bell**, Waffle House, Wendy's
Lodg	E: DAYS INN **Days Inn**, Motel 6, Royal Inn, Scottish Inns, TraveLodge W: Econolodge, **Holiday Inn, Ramada Inn**
AServ	W: **TA TravelCenters of America**(24) **(Amoco gas)**
TServ	W: **TA TravelCenters of America**(SCALES, 24) **(Amoco gas)**
TWash	W: **Louis' Truck Wash & RV**
RVCamp	W: **KOA Campgrounds (.8 Miles)**

EXIT	GEORGIA
ATM	E: Racetrac
Parks	E: **Fort McAllister State Park & Historic Site**
13	**(76)** U.S. 84, Georgia 38, Midway, Sunbury, Fort Stewart, Hinesville
FStop	W: **El Cheapo(*, SCALES) (BP gas)**
Gas	W: Amoco(*, LP), Shell(*, D)
Food	W: **Holton's Seafood**, Huddle House
RVCamp	W: **Martin's-Glebe Plantation Campground**
Med	W: **+ Hospital**
ATM	W: Amoco, **El Cheapo (BP gas)**
Other	W: **Fort Stewart Museum, Midway Museum**
12	**(67)** U.S. 17, South Newport, Coastal Highway
Gas	E: BP(*), Chevron(*, D), Shell(*), Texaco(*)
Food	E: **McDonald's (Shell)**, Shell
RVCamp	E: **Riverfront RV Park (.2 Miles), South Newport Campground (2 Miles)**
ATM	E: Chevron
11	**(58)** Georgia 57, Georgia 99, Eulonia, Townsend Road
Gas	E: Amoco(*)
	W: Amoco(*), Chevron(*, 24), Shell(*, K), Texaco(24)
Food	W: Amoco, Eulonia Cafe (Days Inn), Huddle House, Krispy Kreme Doughnuts (Shell), Sandy's Pizza (Amoco), Shell
Lodg	W: DAYS INN Days Inn, Ramada Limited
RVCamp	E: **Lake Harmony**
	W: **Lake Harmony RV Park & Campground (.25 Miles), McIntosh Lake Campground (.9 Miles)**
ATM	W: Chevron
Parks	E: **Eulonia Park**
Other	W: Tourist Info.
(55)	Weigh Station (Southbound)
(55)	Weigh Station (Northbound)
10	**(49)** Georgia 251, Darien
FStop	W: **Texaco(*, SCALES)**
Gas	E: BP(*, D), Chevron(*, 24)
	W: Amoco(*), Mobil(*), Shell(*)
Food	E: Dairy Queen, McDonald's(PLAY), Waffle House
	W: Burger King(PLAY), Huddle House, Ice Cream Churn (Mobil), KFC (Texaco), Krispy Kreme Doughnuts (Mobil), Mobil, Shell, Short Stop Subs (Shell), **Texaco**
Lodg	W: Comfort Inn, Hampton Inn, Holiday Inn Express (see our ad this page), Super 8
AServ	W: **Interstate Truck Repair**
TServ	W: **Interstate Truck Repair**
RVCamp	E: **Darien Inland Harbor Campground, Tall Pines Campground**
ATM	E: McDonald's
	W: **Texaco**
Other	W: **Magnolia Bluff Factory Shops, Prime Outlets at Darien (see our ad this page)**
9	**(42)** GA 99, Loop 95
(40)	Rest Area (RR, Phones, Picnic, Vending, RV Dump; Southbound)
8	**(38)** U.S. 17, Georgia 25, Brunswick, North Golden Isles Pkwy
Gas	W: Amoco(*, 24), Shell(*)
Food	W: Krispy Kreme Doughnuts (Shell), Shell
Lodg	E: Fairfield Inn, DAYS INN Days Inn (see our ad this page)
	W: Econolodge, Guest Cottage, Quality Inn
RVCamp	E: **Golden Isles Rest & Rec Campground (1 Mile)**
Med	E: **+ Hospital**
7AB	**(36)** U.S. 25, U.S. 341, Jesup, Brunswick
FStop	E: **Shell(*)**
Gas	E: Amoco(*), Chevron(*, CW, 24), Exxon(*, D), Racetrac(*), Texaco(*)
	W: BP(*, D), Mobil(*, D) (Mr. Pete's Pecans), Phillips 66(*)
Food	E: Burger King, **Cracker Barrel**, DAYS INN Days Inn, International House Of Pancake (Days Inn), KFC, Krystal, McDonald's(PLAY), Pizza Hut, SHONEY'S Shoney's, Taco Bell, Waffle House, Wendy's
	W: Abe's Buffet, Captain Joe's Seafood, Denny's (Comfort Inn), Holiday Inn, Huddle House, Minh-Sun (Chinese), Mulligan's Bar & Grill (Holiday Inn), Quincy's Family Steakhouse, Sonny's BBQ, Waffle House
Lodg	E: Budgetel Inn, DAYS INN Days Inn, Hampton Inn, Knight's Inn, Ramada
	W: **Best Western**, Comfort Inn, Flute Inn, Holiday Inn, Motel 6, Super 8
Med	E: **+ Hospital**
ATM	E: Exxon, Racetrac, Texaco
Other	W: Georgia State Patrol Post, **Winn Dixie Supermarket**
6	**(29)** U.S. 17, U.S. 82, Georgia 520, Brunswick, S. Ga. Pkwy., Waycross
TStop	E: **Pilot Travel Center(*, SCALES) (Amoco gas)**
	W: **Flying J Travel Plaza(*, LP, RV DUMP, SCALES), TravelCenters of America(*, SCALES) (BP)**
FStop	E: **Texaco(*, D)**
	W: **El Cheapo(*, SCALES) (Shell Gas)**

Jekyll Island (Oceanside)
1506
Holiday Inn®
I-95 • Exit 6
200 S. Beachview Dr.
Jekyll Island, GA 31527
912-635-3311
800-HOLIDAY
Beaches • Bike Rentals • Tennis Courts
Pool • Tiki Hut Pool Bar • Kiddie Pool
Full Service Restaurant & Lounge
Live Entertainment • Gift Shop
Championship Golf • Historic District
Trolleys • Guest Laundry • In Room Coffee
Packages Available
GEORGIA • I-95 • EXIT 6

PRIME OUTLETS
DARIEN
75 Outlet Stores and Food Court
Liz Claiborne • Tommy Hilfiger • Nike
Ask for your FREE COUPON BOOK
912-437-2700
1856
GEORGIA • I-95 • EXIT 10

1259
Holiday Inn®
I-95 • Exit 7B
5252 New Jesup Hwy.
Brunswick, GA 31525
912-264-4033
800-HOLIDAY
In Room Coffee Makers
Free Cable TV with HBO
Free American Breakfast
(call for details)
Outdoor Pool/Sundeck
Full Service Lounge & Restaurant
Pets Welcome
JUNCTION OF RT. 341 & I-95
GEORGIA • I-95 • EXIT 7B

Free Continential Breakfast
RAMADA INN®
I-95, Exit 7A & US 341 • Brunswick, GA
213 Rooms
Dining Room/Lounge on Premises
Kids Under 18 Stay Free
In Room Coffee Maker
Free Cable, HBO/ESPN
Outdoor Pool • Handicap Accessible
Meeting/Banquet Facilities
912-264-3621
1546
GEORGIA • I-95 • EXIT 7A

Toll Free Reservations:
800-329-7466
60S. Beachview Drive
1150
Adjacent to Convention Center
Ocean Front • 2 Pools
Continental Breakfast
Bus Parking
Tour Packages
ABA American Bus Association
NTA
GEORGIA • I-95 • EXIT 6

1603
5033 New Jesup Hwy
Brunswick, GA

Restaurant on Premises
Kids Under 12 Stay Free
Outdoor Pool • Tennis & Golf Nearby
Meeting/Banquet Facilities
Handicap Accessible • Exterior Corridors
St. Simons & Jekyll Island Nearby
Cable TV w/HBO & Disney
912-264-4330
GEORGIA • I-95 • Exit 7A

1537
RAMADA INN®
150 Beachview Drive • Jekyll Island, GA • 31527
912-635-2111 • Toll Free Reservations: 1-800-2-RAMADA
Restaurant & Lounge on Premises
Full Breakfast Included
Outdoor Pool • Oceanfront
Meeting & Banquet Facilities
Truck/Large Vehicle Parking
Tennis & Golf Nearby
Interior Corridors
GEORGIA • I-95 • Exit 6

Bold red print shows RV & Bus parking available or nearby

EXIT GEORGIA

Gas E: Exxon[*]
Food E: Huddle House, Oyster Box (Pilot), Pilot Travel Center (Amoco gas), Steak 'N Shake[24] (Pilot), Subway (Pilot), The Georgia Pig BBQ
W: Country Market (Flying J), Country Pride (TA), Dairy Queen (TA), Flying J Travel Plaza, Magic Dragon (Flying J), Pepperoni's Super Slice (Flying J), TravelCenters of America (BP), Waffle House
Lodg W: Daystop Inn (TravelCenters of America), Super 8, TravelCenters of America (BP)
TServ W: Five Star Truck Quick Lube (CB Shop), TravelCenters of America[SCALES] (BP)
TWash E: Pilot Travel Center (Amoco gas)
W: El Cheapo (Shell Gas), Five Star Truck Quick Lube (CB Shop)
RVCamp W: Golden Isles Vacation Park (.75 Miles), Ruscar, Inc. (.7 Miles)
ATM W: Flying J Travel Plaza
Other E: Airport

5 **(26)** Dover Bluff Road
Gas E: Shell[*, D]
Food E: Choo Choo BBQ (Shell), Shell
RVCamp E: Ocean Breeze Camp (2 Miles)

4 **(14)** Georgia 25, Woodbine
FStop W: Sunshine Plaza[*, K, SCALES]
Gas W: BP[*]
Food W: Jack's BBQ, Sunshine Grill, Sunshine Plaza

3 **(7)** Harriett's Bluff Road
FStop E: Texaco[*] (Patton Tire)
Gas E: Shell[*]
Food E: Angelo's Italian, Huddle House, Jack's Famous BBQ (Shell), Shell, Taco Bell (Texaco), Texaco (Patton Tire)
AServ E: Texaco (Patton Tire)
RVCamp E: RV Park Office
W: King George RV Resort (.5 Miles)

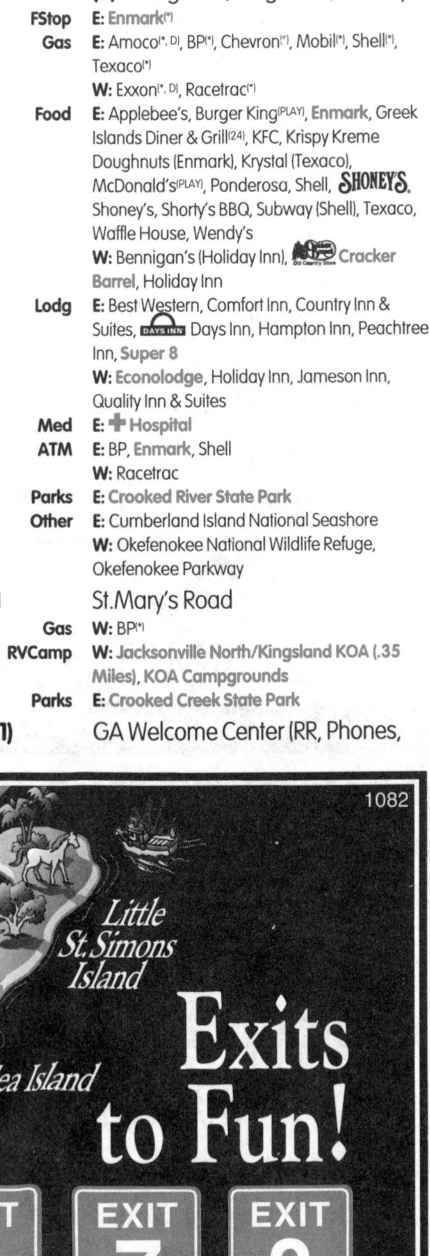

EXIT GEORGIA

2A **(6)** Colerain, St Mary's Road
FStop E: Cone[*]
Food E: Arby's (Cisco), Cisco Travel Plaza[*, SCALES] (BP Gas), Cone, Fresh Way Sub & Salad (Cone)
Other E: Cisco Travel Plaza (BP Gas)

2 **(3)** Georgia 40, Kingsland, St Mary's
FStop E: Enmark[*]
Gas E: Amoco[*, D], BP[*], Chevron[*], Mobil[*], Shell[*], Texaco[*]
W: Exxon[*, D], Racetrac[*]
Food E: Applebee's, Burger King[PLAY], Enmark, Greek Islands Diner & Grill[24], KFC, Krispy Kreme Doughnuts (Enmark), Krystal (Texaco), McDonald's[PLAY], Ponderosa, Shell, SHONEY'S, Shoney's, Shorty's BBQ, Subway (Shell), Texaco, Waffle House, Wendy's
W: Bennigan's (Holiday Inn), Cracker Barrel, Holiday Inn
Lodg E: Best Western, Comfort Inn, Country Inn & Suites, DAYS INN Days Inn, Hampton Inn, Peachtree Inn, Super 8
W: Econolodge, Holiday Inn, Jameson Inn, Quality Inn & Suites
Med E: + Hospital
ATM E: BP, Enmark, Shell
W: Racetrac
Parks E: Crooked River State Park
Other E: Cumberland Island National Seashore
W: Okefenokee National Wildlife Refuge, Okefenokee Parkway

1 St.Mary's Road
Gas W: BP[*]
RVCamp W: Jacksonville North/Kingsland KOA (.35 Miles), KOA Campgrounds
Parks E: Crooked Creek State Park

(1) GA Welcome Center (RR, Phones,

EXIT GEORGIA/FLORIDA

Picnic, Vending, RV Dump; Northbound)

↑ GEORGIA

↓ FLORIDA

(380) Weigh Station, Agricultural Inspection (Southbound)

(380) Weigh Station, Agricultural Inspection (Northbound)

130 **(379)** U.S. 17
Gas W: Amoco[*], Shell[*, 24]
Food W: Country Cafe & Restaurant (Days Inn), DAYS INN Days Inn
Lodg W: DAYS INN Days Inn, Holiday Inn Express
AServ W: Shell[24]
RVCamp E: Hance's RV Park[LP]

(378) FL Welcome Center (RR, Phones, Picnic, Vending; Southbound)

129 **(373)** FL A1A, Callahan, Fl. 200, Yulle, Amilia Island, Fernandina Beach
Gas E: Chevron[*, 24], King's Orange (Florida Citrus Center), Shell[*, 24] (Indian River Fruit Stand)
W: BP[*, D], Citgo[*], Exxon[*, D]
Food E: Burger King[PLAY], Dairy Queen (King's Orange), King's Orange (Florida Citrus Center), McDonald's[PLAY]
W: Citgo, Waffle House
AServ E: Shell[24] (Indian River Fruit Stand)
RVCamp E: Bow & Arrow Campground, Fort Clinch State Park
ATM W: Exxon

128 **(365)** Pecan Park Road
FStop E: Citgo[*]
Gas E: BP[*, D]
Food E: Ice Cream Churn (BP)
ATM E: Citgo
Other E: Jax Raceway
W: Flea Market

127AB **(363)** Duval Road, Jacksonville International Airport
Gas E: Mobil[*, D]
W: Amoco[*], BP[*, D], Chevron[*], Texaco[*, D]
Food W: A & W Restaurant (Chevron), Amoco, Chevron, Denny's, Dunkin Donuts (Amoco), Subway (Amoco), Taco Bell (Chevron), Waffle House
Lodg W: Admiral Benbow Inn, Courtyard by Marriott, DAYS INN Days Inn, Hampton Inn, Holiday Inn, Microtel Inn, Quality Inn, Red Roof Inn
AServ E: Mobil
RVCamp W: Dick Gore's RV World[LP]
ATM W: Amoco, Texaco
Other W: International Airport

126B **(362)** Junction I-295

126A **(362)** FL 9AS, Blount Island

125 **(359)** FL 104, Dunn Ave, Busch Drive
FStop E: Gate[*, D]
Gas W: BP[*, CW], Hess[*], Shell[*, CW, 24], Shell[*, CW], Texaco[*, LP, 24]
Food E: Applebee's, Gate, Hardee's, Krispy Kreme Doughnuts (Gate), Waffle House
W: Arby's, Burger King, Dunkin Donuts, Jaguar Inn, Krystal, McDonald's[PLAY], Quincy's Family Steakhouse, Rally's Hamburgers, SHONEY'S Shoney's
Lodg E: Admiral Benbow Inn
W: Best Western, Jaguar Inn, La Quinta Inn, Motel 6, Super 8
AServ W: Pep Boys Auto Center

EXIT	FLORIDA

Med E: Family Urgent Care
ATM E: First Union, Gate
W: Barnett Bank, Compass Bank, First Union, First Union, Texaco
Other E: Sam's Club
W: Eckerd Drugs[RX], Publix Supermarket, Sears Optical, Winn Dixie Supermarket[24]

124B **(358)** Broward Road
Food W: Days Inn, Red Horse Restaurant
Lodg W: Days Inn

124A **(358)** FL 105, Hecksher Dr, to US 17 (Difficult Reaccess)

123 **(356)** FL 111, Edgewood Ave
Gas W: Amoco[CW, 24], Citgo[*, K]
AServ W: Amoco[24]
Other W: Safeco Grocery

122AB **(356)** FL 115N, Lem Turner Road - goes west (122B), Norwood Ave, FL 117S - goes east (122A)
Gas W: Amoco[*, CW, 24], Hess[K]
Food E: Blue Boy Sandwich Shop, Hardee's
W: Crab Hut, Famous Sandwiches, Golden Eggroll, Krystal
AServ E: Thomas Auto Service
W: Discount Auto Parts, Goodyear Tire & Auto, Jiffy Lube, Meineke Discount Mufflers, Midas Muffler & Brake, One Stop Auto Parts
Other E: Gateway Animal Hospital
W: Star Coin Car Wash

121 **(354)** Golfair Blvd
Gas E: Shell[*, 24], Texaco[*]
W: Amoco[*, K, 24], Exxon[*]
Lodg W: Valu-Lodge
AServ E: Tops Tires
ATM W: Exxon

120AB **(354)** U.S. 1, 20th St (Difficult Reaccess, 120A goes east, 120B goes west)

119 **(353)** FL 114, 8th St
Gas E: Amoco[*, K]
Food E: McDonald's
Med E: University Medical Center

118 **(353)** U.S. 23 North, Kings Road (Southbound)

117 **(352)** Union St , Alternate Hwy 90, Riverfront (Northbound)

116 **(352)** Church St.
Gas E: Amoco[*]

115 **(352)** Monroe St

114A Forsyth St. (Northbound)
Other E: Convention Center

114 **(352)** Myrtle Ave (Northbound)

113 **(352)** Stockton St (Southbound)
Med W: Hospital

112 **(351)** Margaret St (Northbound)

111 **(351)** Junction I-10 West

110 **(351)** College St (Closed For Construction)

109 **(351)** U.S. 17, Riverside Dr. (Under Construction)

108 **(350)** San Marco Blvd
Med E: Wolfson Children Hospital
W: Baptist Outpatient Center

107 FL 13, Hendrick Ave (Difficult Reaccess)
Gas E: BP[*, CW]
Lodg E: Hampton Inn, Hilton Inn

EXIT	FLORIDA

AServ E: BP
Med E: Wolfson Children Hospital
Other E: Museum of Science & History, Southbank River Walks & Museum

106 **(349)** U.S. 90 East, Beach Blvd (Eastbound, Difficult Reaccess)

105 **(349)** U.S. 1 South, Phillips Highway (Difficult Reaccess)
Gas W: Amoco[*, CW]
Lodg W: City Center Motel, Scottish Inns, Super 8
AServ W: Jerry Hamn Chevrolet, O' Steen Volvo, Overbee's Mercedes, Jaguar, Porsche, BMW Sales and Service, Top Notch Automotive

104 **(347)** FL.126, Emerson St
Gas E: Chevron, Shell[*, 24]
W: Amoco[*, CW, 24], BP[*], Exxon[*, CW], Gate[*, D]
Food E: Subway
W: McDonald's, Salton Sandwiches, Taco Bell
Lodg W: Emerson Inn, Howard Johnson
AServ E: Chevron, Chevron, Shell[24]
ATM W: First Union
Other E: Coin Laundromat, Food Lion Supermarket
W: Skate World

103AB **(347)** FL 109, University Blvd., Bowden Road (Southbound, Difficult Reaccess)

JACKSONVILLE, FL
I-95 SB Exit 103B
I-95 NB Exit 102
DAYS INN
SPECIAL TOUR GROUP RATES
904-733-3890
Continental Breakfast
Kids Under 10 Stay Free
Outdoor Pool
Meeting/Banquet Facilities
Handicap Accessible
Exercise Room
Exterior Corridors
25" Cable Ready TV
10 min. from Downtown
5649 Cagle Rd
Jacksonville, FL
Florida • I-95 • Exit 103B

EXIT	FLORIDA

Gas E: Amoco[*, CW], Texaco[*, LP]
W: BP[*, 24], Racetrac[*]
Food E: Captain D's Seafood, Happy Garden Chinese, Krystal, Ying's Chinese
W: BP, Bugsy's Bar and Grill, Burger King, Dunkin Donuts, Garden Grill (BP), IHOP, Ryan's Steakhouse, SHONEY'S Shoney's, Sonny's BBQ, Taco Bell, Waffle House
Lodg W: Comfort Lodge, Econolodge, Ramada, Red Carpet Inn, Vacation Host Apartments and Hotel Service, Days Inn (see our ad this page)
AServ E: Tire Kingdom
W: Big Chief Tire Service, Eurotech Auto Repairs, Frank Griffin Quality Used Cars and Trucks Sales and Service
TServ W: Detroit Diesel
Med W: Specialty Hospital
ATM E: NationsBank (Texaco), SunTrust, Texaco
Other E: Proctor Ace Hardware[LP]
W: University Blvd. Animal Hospital

102 **(345)** FL109, Bowden Road, University Blvd (Northbound)
Gas E: Chevron[*], Gate[*]
Food E: Bono's BBQ, Larry's Giant Subs
AServ E: Edward's Automotive
W: Ernest Air Automotive
Other E: Lil' Champ (Chevron)

101 **(343)** FL.202, Butler Blvd, Jacksonville
Gas W: Shell[*], Texaco[*, D, CW]
Food E: Holiday Inn Express, Quality Inn, Vito's (Quality Inn)
W: Applebee's, Cracker Barrel, Hardee's, Waffle House
Lodg E: Candlewood Studio Hotel, Club Hotel by Doubletree, Hampton Inn, Holiday Inn Express, Main Stay Suites, Marriot, Quality Inn
W: Courtyard by Marriott, Extended Stay America, Jacksonville Studio Plus, Microtel, Quality Inn, Red Roof Inn
Med E: St Luke's Hospital
ATM E: Barnett Bank, Compass Bank
W: Texaco

100 **(341)** FL 152, Baymeadows Road
Gas E: BP[*, CW], Chevron[*, CW, 24], Shell[*, D], Texaco[*, D, CW]
W: Shell[*, CW], Texaco[*, D]
Food E: Arby's, Hardee's, Holiday Inn, T.G.I. Friday's (Holiday Inn), Waffle House
W: Bagoda Chinese Restaurant, Bennigan's, Bombay Bicycle Club, Burger King, Denny's, Golden Dragon, KFC, McAllister's Deli, McDonald's[PLAY], Red Lobster, Steak & Ale, The Atlanta Bread Co, Wendy's
Lodg E: AmeriSuites (see our ad this page), Embassy Suites, Fairfield Inn, Holiday Inn, Homestead Village
W: Best Inns, Comfort Inn, Homewood Suites, La Quinta Inn, Motel 6, Residence Inn, TraveLodge
AServ E: Xpress Lube
ATM E: NationsBank, SunTrust
W: Barnett Bank, Compass Bank, First Union Bank
Other E: Dave Meadows Golf Course
W: Bay Meadows Cinemas, Coastal Vision Center, Office Depot

99 **(339)** Southside Blvd, Fl. 115 (Northbound, Reaccess Southbound Only, Only goes to the east side)

98 **(338)** U.S. 1, Phillips Hwy
Food E: Arby's, Burger King[PLAY], McDonald's[PLAY], Olive Garden, Taco Bell, Waffle House
Other E: The Avenues Mall, Toys R Us

97 **(338)** Jct I-295 N, Orange Park

(331) Rest Area (RR, HF, Phones, Picnic; Southbound)

(331) Rest Area (RR, HF, Phones, Picnic;

Bold red print shows RV & Bus parking available or near

EXIT FLORIDA

Northbound)

96 **(329)** County Road 210, Green Cove Springs

- **TStop** E: **G & M 76 Auto Truck Plaza**(*, SCALES) **(BP)**
- **FStop** E: **Speedway**(*, SCALES)
- **Gas** E: Citgo(*), Exxon(*)
  W: Amoco(*, D), Chevron(D), No Sign(*)
- **Food** E: **G & M 76 Auto Truck Plaza (BP)**, **G & M TS**, Indian Fruit Stand, **Speedway**, Waffle House
- **AServ** W: Chevron, Chevron
- **TServ** E: **G & M 76 Auto Truck Plaza**(SCALES) **(BP)**, **G & M TS**
- **RVCamp** E: **KOA-St. Augustine/ Jacksonville South**
- **ATM** E: **Speedway**
  W: Amoco
- **Other** W: **Phantom Fireworks**

95A **(323)** International Golf Pwky.

- **Gas** E: Shell(*, D)
- **Other** W: World Golf Village

95 **(317)** FL 16, St. Augustine , Green Cove Springs

- **Gas** E: Amoco(*, 24), BP(*), Citgo(*), Shell(*), **Speedway**(*, K)
  W: Exxon(*), Texaco(*, D)
- **Food** E: BP, Burger King(PLAY), Dairy Queen, McDonald's(PLAY), Ocean Palace Chinese Buffet, Pizza Hut (BP), **Speedway**, **Waffle House**
  W: **Cracker Barrel**, Days Inn, **Denny's**, KFC, SHONEY'S, Shoney's, Sonny's BBQ, Wendy's
- **Lodg** E: Guesthouse Inn, Holiday Inn Express, Ramada (see our ad this page)
  W: **Best Western**, Days Inn, Econolodge, Scottish Inns, Super 8
- **AServ** W: Exxon (24 hour towing), Exxon
- **RVCamp** E: **Myers RV Center, Inc. (1 Mile)**
  W: **Stagecoach RV Park (.33 Miles)**
- **ATM** E: Citgo
- **Other** W: **St. Augustine Outlet Center**

94 **(311)** FL.207, St. Augustine, Hastings

- **FStop** W: **Texaco**(*)
- **Gas** E: BP(*), Chevron(*, 24), Gas(*) (Indian Fruit Stand)
  W: Mobil(*)
- **Lodg** W: Comfort Inn
- **AServ** W: Mobil, Texaco, **Texaco**
- **RVCamp** E: **Indian Forest Campground (2 Miles)**, **St. John's RV Park (.25 Miles)**
- **Med** E: **Hospital**
- **Parks** E: **Anastasia State Park**
- **Other** E: St Augustine Beach

93 **(305)** FL.206, Hastings, Crescent Beach

- **Gas** E: Texaco(*)
- **TServ** W: **Continental Truck Service**(24) **(Towing)**
- **RVCamp** E: **Ocean Grove RV Sales and Service**(LP) **(2 Miles)**
  W: **Continental RV Service**(24) **(Towing)**

EXIT FLORIDA

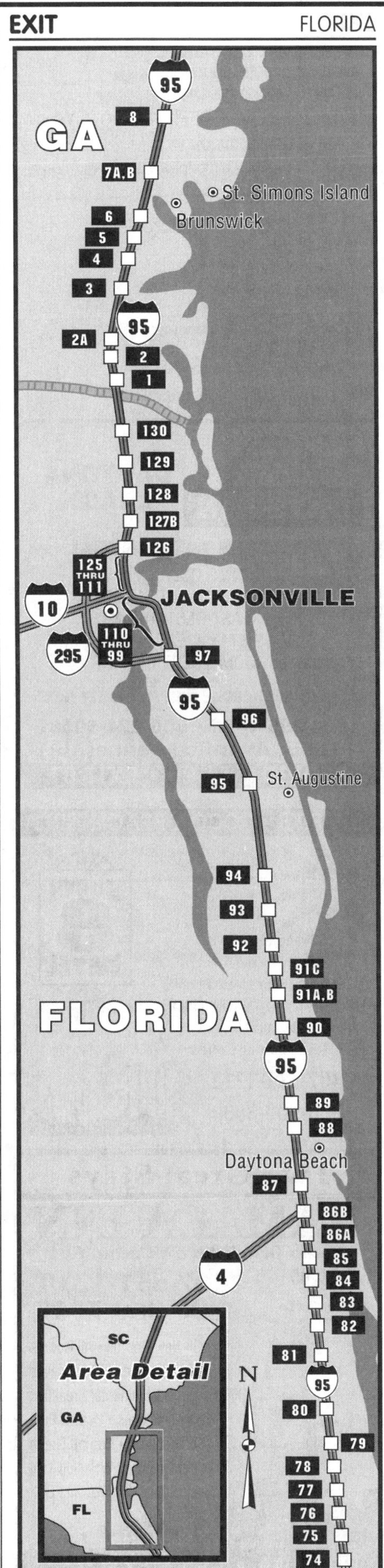

EXIT FLORIDA

- **Other** E: Fort Matnazas, **Marineland of Florida (13 Miles)**

(303) Rest Area (RR, HF, Phones, Picnic; Southbound)

(302) Rest Area (RR, HF, Phones, Picnic; Northbound)

92 **(298)** U.S. 1, St. Augustine, Bunnell

- **TStop** W: **Charlie T's Truck Stop**(*, SCALES) **(76)**
- **FStop** W: **Sunrise**(*)
- **Gas** E: BP(*) (Fruit Stand), Citgo(*) (Fruit Stand), D & L Groves(*) (Fruit Stand), Texaco(*, D)
  W: Shell(*, D)
- **Food** W: Charlie T's Truck Stop, **Charlie T's Truck Stop (76)**, Dairy Queen (Shell), Shell, Stuckey's (Shell), **Sunrise**, Waffle House
- **AServ** E: Texaco, Texaco
- **ATM** W: **Charlie T's Truck Stop (76)**
- **Parks** E: **Favor Dykes State Park**

91C **(289)** Palm Coast to Florida A1 Beaches

- **Gas** E: BP(*), Shell(*, CW)
  W: Chevron(*, LP)
- **Food** E: Caruso's Family Restaurant & Pizzaria, **Cracker Barrel**, Denny's, Dunkin Donuts (Shell), Jasper's Grill, KFC, McDonald's(PLAY), Shell, SHONEY'S, Shoney's, The Sub Base, Wendy's
  W: China One, Hardee's, **K-Mart**, Little Caesars Pizza (K-Mart), Perkins Family Restaurant, Sonny's Pit BBQ, Steak 'N Shake, Subway, Taco Bell
- **Lodg** E: Hampton Inn, Sleep Inn
- **AServ** W: Jiffy Lube, Tire Kingdom, **Wal-Mart Supercenter**(RX)
- **ATM** E: Barnett, Shell
  W: First Union Bank, NationsBank (Winn Dixie), **Winn Dixie Supermarket**(24, RX)
- **Other** E: **Book Rack**, Eye Style Optical
  W: **K-Mart**, **Wal-Mart Supercenter**(RX), **Winn Dixie Supermarket**(RX)

(286) Weigh Station (Eastbound)

(286) Weigh Station (Westbound)

91AB **(284)** FL. 100, Bunnell, Flagler Beach

- **Gas** E: BP(*, LP), Chevron(*, D, CW)
  W: Shell(*)
- **Food** E: Burger King(PLAY), Joe's New York Pizza, McDonald's(PLAY), Oriental Garden, Subway, Vesuvio's Restaurant and Bar
- **AServ** E: Chevron
  W: Flagler Chrysler, Plymouth, Dodge, Jeep, Eagle
- **Med** W: **Hospital**
- **ATM** E: Barnett Bank
- **Other** E: **Animal Hospital**, Gamble Rogers State Recreation Area, **Winn Dixie Supermarket**(RX)

90 **(279)** Old Dixie Highway

- **Gas** W: Texaco(*, D)
- **Lodg** W: Best Western
- **RVCamp** E: **Bulow Resort & Campground**
  W: **Holiday Travel Park**
- **Parks** E: **Tomaka State Park**
- **Other** E: **Bulow Plantation State Historic Site**

89 **(273)** U.S. 1

- **FStop** E: **Amoco**(*), **Mobil**(*), **Texaco**(*, SCALES)
- **Gas** E: BP(*, LP), Citgo(*)
  W: Exxon(*, D)
- **Food** E: Baskin Robbins, Citgo, Denny's (Tourist Info), McDonald's(PLAY), **Mobil**, Waffle House, Wendy's (Mobil FS)
  W: Burger King (Exxon), Dairy Queen, Exxon
- **Lodg** E: Comfort Inn
  W: **Budget Host Motel**, Days Inn, Ramada Inn, **Scottish Inns**, Super 8
- **AServ** E: AJ's Automotive Repair & Service, Citgo, Citgo
- **RVCamp** E: **Giant Recreation World**(LP) **(1 Mile)**, **Sunshine RV Park**

Bold red print shows RV & Bus parking available or nearby

EXIT FLORIDA

W: Sunshine Holiday Camper Resort (.5 Miles)
Med E: Hospital
ATM E: Mobil, Texaco
W: Exxon

88 **(268)** FL 40, Ormond Beach, Ocala, Silver Springs
Gas E: BP[*], Citgo[*]
W: Amoco[*, 24], Chevron[*, CW], Mobil[*, D]
Food E: Applebee's, Boston Market Restaurant, Chili's, Delcato's, Denny's, Don Pablo's Mexican, K-Mart[RX], Little Caesars Pizza (K-Mart), Steak 'N Shake, Subway, Waffle House, Wendy's
W: Amoco, Burger King (Amoco), Cracker Barrel, TCBY (Amoco)
Lodg E: Sleep Inn
Med E: Hospital
ATM E: BP, Barnett Bank, Publix Supermarket[RX], SunTrust Bank
W: Chevron, Mobil
Parks E: Tomoka State Park
Other E: Eye Savers, K-Mart[RX], Publix Supermarket[RX], Regal 12 Cinemas, Wal-Mart Supercenter[RX]

87C LPGA Blvd., Holly Hill

87AB **(262)** U.S. 92 E, Daytona Beach-87A, US 92 W, DeLand -87B
Gas E: Chevron[*, D], Hess[*, D], Racetrac[*, 24]
W: BP[*, CW], Citgo
Food E: Blimpie's Subs (Hess), Daytona Ale House, God Father's Pizza (Hess), Hess, Krystal, Red Lobster, Shoney's, Shoney's, Subway, Waffle House
W: Denny's, IHOP, McDonald's[PLAY]
Lodg E: Holiday Inn, La Quinta Inn
W: Days Inn (see our ad this page), Super 8
RVCamp W: Crazy Horse Campground & Saloon (1 Mile), Town & Country RV Park
ATM E: Chevron, Racetrac
Other W: Mark Martin's Klassix Auto Museum

86AB **(258)** FL. 400 East, South Daytona, - 86A Jct. I-4, West Orlando -86B
Gas E: BP[*, LP]
Other E: International Airport (2 Miles), Museum (4 Miles)

85 **(256)** FL. 421, Port Orange, Daytona Beach Shores
Gas E: Amoco[*, CW]
W: Citgo[*]
Food E: Spruce Creek Pizza
W: Biscuits 'N' Gravy, McDonald's[PLAY], Subway
AServ E: Amoco
W: Xpress Lube
ATM W: Barnett Bank, Caldwell Banker, Commercial National Bank
Other W: 7-11 Convenience Store (Citgo), Publix Supermarket[RX]

(255) Rest Area (RR, Phones, Picnic, Vending; Southbound)

(254) Rest Area (RR, Phones, Picnic, Vending; Northbound)

84AB **(249)** FL. 44, DeLand, New Smyrna Beach
Gas E: Shell[*] (Indian River Fruit)
W: Chevron[*, D]
Food E: Shell (Indian River Fruit)
RVCamp E: KOA Campgrounds
Med E: Hospital

83 **(244)** FL. 442, Edgewater, Oak Hill
Gas E: Chevron[*, D, 24]
TServ E: Florida Shores Truck Center[SCALES]

82 **(231)** CR. 5A, Oak Hill, Scottsmoor
FStop E: BP[*]
Gas W: Citgo[*, D]
Food E: Stuckey's (BP)

EXIT FLORIDA

W: Citgo, Dairy Queen (Citgo)
RVCamp E: Crystal Lake RV Park (1 Block)
Other W: Stuckey's (Citgo)

(227) Rest Area (RR, Phones, Picnic, Vending; Southbound)

(225) Rest Area (RR, Phones, Picnic, Vending; Northbound)

81 **(223)** FL. 46, Sanford, Mims
FStop W: Amoco[*]
Gas W: Shell[*, CW]
Food E: McDonald's
W: Amoco, Shell
RVCamp W: KOA-Cape Kennedy (.5 Miles)
Med E: Hospital
Other W: Amtrak Terminal (30 Miles)

80 **(220)** FL. 406, Titusville

1552

DAYS INN
DAYTONA BEACH
OCEAN FRONT CENTRAL
ALL ROOMS OCEAN VIEW
SWIMMING POOL/KIDDIE POOL
BREAKFAST RESTAURANT
KIDS STAY & EAT FREE
GAMESROOM/GUEST LAUNDRY
Ask for our special Exit Authority rate!
904-255-4492 • 800-224-5056
1909 S. Atlantic Avenue(AIA)
FLORIDA ▪ I-95 ▪ EXIT 87

SUPER 8 - COCOA BEACH AREA

Per Room Plus Tax *Based on Availability
SUPER 8 MOTEL
1062
• 53 Brand New Rooms
• Family Picnic Area
• Large Outdoor Heated Pool
• Remote Cable TV with HBO
• FREE Local Calls
• FREE Morning Coffee
407-631-1212
800-800-8000
I-95 at Exit 76

Two Great Stays
RAMADA INN®
Cocoa Beach Area • Cocoa, FL
$45.00
Per Room Plus Tax *Based on Availability
407-631-1210
800-860-7557
98 New Rooms • All Rooms w/Refrigerators and Microwaves
FREE Deluxe Continental Breakfast
FREE Local Calls • Heated Pool
Shuffleboard • Putting Green
Private Fishing Lake • Walk/Jog Trail
Canfield's Bar and Grill
I-95 at Exit 76 Just 3 Miles South of 528(Beeline)
FLORIDA ▪ I-95 ▪ EXIT 76

EXIT FLORIDA

FStop W: Texaco[*]
Gas E: BP[*, D], Shell[*]
Food E: Shell, Taste of China (Travelodge), TraveLodge
Lodg E: TraveLodge
AServ E: Auto Repair Center
Med E: Hospital
Other E: Marritt Island National Wildlife Refuge, National Seashore Wildlife Refuge

79 **(215)** FL. 50, Titusville, Orlando, Kennedy Space Center
FStop E: Space Shuttle Fuel[*]
Gas E: Amoco[*, LP], Chevron[*], Circle K[*], Shell[*], Texaco[*, D]
Food E: Best Western, Denny's, Durango's (Best Western), McDonald's[PLAY], Ramada, Shoney's, Shoney's, Waffle House, Wendy's
W: Cracker Barrel, Days Inn, Fama's Italian Bistro (Days Inn)
Lodg E: Best Western, Ramada
W: Days Inn, Luck's Way Inn
AServ E: Amoco, Shell, Shell
RVCamp W: High Springs Campground (.5 Miles)
ATM E: Amoco, Circle K, Texaco, Texaco
Other E: Wal-Mart[RX] (Optical Department)

78 **(211)** FL. 407, Orlando, toll hwy 528 W

(210) Parking Area (Picnic; Southbound)

(210) Parking Area (Picnic; Northbound)

77AB **(205)** FL 528, Fl. 528 Toll, Canaveral, Cape - Port A.F.S., Orlando

76 **(202)** FL.524, Coco, Community College
FStop W: Amoco[*, D, 24]
Gas E: Citgo[*, D]
Food W: Super 8
Lodg W: Days Inn, Super 8, Ramada (see our ad this page)

75 **(201)** FL. 520, Cocoa
FStop E: BP[*], Speedway[*, LP, K]
Gas E: Lil' Champs[*]
W: Chevron[*, D, 24]
Food E: IHOP, Waffle House
W: McDonald's[PLAY]
Lodg E: Budget Inn, Cocoa Inn
AServ E: Auto Service
RVCamp W: Teen Missions Christian RV Park (.7 Miles)
Med E: Hospital
ATM E: Bank One[D] (Speedway), Speedway
W: Chevron
Other E: Sky King Fireworks, Thunder Bolts Fireworks
W: Cocoa Stadium

74 **(196)** Fiske Blvd, Rockledge, FL 519,
Gas E: Citgo[*]
RVCamp E: Space Coast RV Resort
Med E: Hospital
Other E: Post Office

RAMADA INN®
1741
Oceanfront Resort
1035 Hwy A1A • Satellite Beach, FL
Restaurant/Lounge Oceanfront on Premises
Kids Under 12 Stay Free
Heated Outdoor Pool • Free Tennis on Premises
Meeting/Banquet Facilities Oceanfront
Private Balconies • Beachfront
Truck/Large Vehicle Parking
Handicap Accessible
Interior Corridors
407-777-7200 • 800-345-1782
FLORIDA ▪ I-95 ▪ EXIT 73

EXIT FLORIDA

73 **(191)** Satellite Beach, Patrick AFB, CR. 509
- **Gas** E: Citgo(*)
  W: Texaco(*)
- **Food** E: Citgo, Denny's, McDonald's(PLAY), Miami Subs, Perkin's Family Restaurant, Wendy's
  W: Burger King, **Cracker Barrel**
- **Lodg** E: Comfort Inn
  W: Budgetel Inn
- **ATM** E: Citgo, Huntington Bank
- **Other** E: **Brevard Zoo**

(189) Parking Area (Picnic; Southbound)

(189) Parkiing Area (Picnic; Northbound)

72 **(183)** FL. 518, Melbourne, Indian Harbor Beach, EauGallie Blvd
- **Gas** E: Amoco(*, D), Citgo(*), Racetrac(*)
- **ATM** E: Citgo, Citgo, Racetrac, Racetrac
- **Other** E: 7-11 Convenience Store (Citgo), Brevard Museum of Art and Science

71 **(180)** U.S.192, West Melbourne, International Airport, Florida Tech
- **FStop** W: **Texaco(*)**
- **Gas** E: Circle K(*), Citgo(*), Mobil(*, D, CW), Speedway(*)
- **Food** E: Denny's, IHOP, Waffle House
- **Lodg** E: Hampton Inn, Holiday Inn, SHONEY'S, Shoney's (Shoney's Inn), TraveLodge, York Inn
- **AServ** E: Space Coast Saturn
- **Med** E: **Hospital**
- **ATM** E: Circle K(*), Circle K, Mobil
- **Other** E: 7-11 Convenience Store (Citgo)

70A **(176)** CR. 516, Palm Bay
- **Gas** E: Lil' Champ(*, D, LP)
- **Food** E: Denny's
- **ATM** E: Huntington Bank (Albertson's)
- **Other** E: **Albertson's Grocery(RX)**

70 **(173)** FL. 514, Palm Bay, Malabar
- **FStop** W: **Speedway(*, LP)**
- **Gas** E: Amoco(*, D), Cumberland Farms(*), Speedway(*, LP)
- **Food** E: First Wok, McDonald's(PLAY), Twisty Cone Ice Cream
  W: Arby's, IHOP, Italy To Go Restaurant, Las Palmas, Lucky Garden Chinese Restaurant, Seven Seas, Starvin' Marvin (Speedway), Subway, Taco Bell, **Waffle House**, Wendy's, Woody's BBQ
- **Lodg** W: Motel 6
- **AServ** E: Firestone Car and Truck Repair, Meineke Discount Mufflers, Mobil 10 Min. Oil Change, Palm Bay Ford
  W: Gatto's Goodyear, Tire Kingdom
- **RVCamp** E: **Enchanted Lakes Estates Mobile Home & RV Resort (1 Mile)**
- **Med** E: **Hospital**
- **ATM** E: Republic Bank
  W: Barnett Bank, Riverside National Bank, **Speedway**
- **Other** W: Books A Plenty, **Eckerd Drugs**, Malabar Pet Hospital, Monnett Eye Center, Optimart, **Publix Supermarket(RX)**, **US Post Office**

(169) Rest Area (RR, Phones, Picnic, Vending; Southbound)

(168) Rest Area (RR, Phones, Picnic, Vending; Northbound)

69 **(156)** Fellsmere Road, CR. 512 , Sebastian
- **Gas** E: Amoco(*), Citgo(*, D)
- **Food** E: Amoco, Citgo, Dairy Queen (Citgo), McDonald's (Amoco), Stuckey's (Citgo)
- **RVCamp** E: **KOA Campgrounds**, **Sunshine RV Park**, **Whispering Palms RV Park**
- **Med** E: **Hospital**
- **ATM** E: Amoco

68 **(146)** FL 60, Vero Beach, Lake Wales
- **TStop** E: **TA TravelCenters of America(SCALES) (Travel Center)**
- **FStop** E: **Citgo(*)**
- **Gas** E: Chevron, Citgo(*), Mobil(*), Shell(*)
- **Food** E: Best Western, **Citgo**, **Courtesy Restaurant**, **Days Inn**, Marotta's Pizza, Poor Man's Castle (Days Inn), **TA TravelCenters of America (Travel Center)**, Waffle House, Wendy's
  W: **Cracker Barrel**, McDonald's
- **Lodg** E: Best Western, **Days Inn**, **Howard Johnson**, **Super 8**
  W: Hampton Inn, Holiday Inn Express
- **AServ** E: Chevron, Mobil
- **Med** E: **Hospital**
- **ATM** E: Citgo
- **Other** E: 7-11 Convenience Store (Citgo)
  W: **Prime Outlets at Vero Beach (see our ad this page)**

67 **(137)** FL. 614, Indrio Road
- **Other** E: Harbor Branch Oceanographic Institution

(133) Rest Area (RR, Phones, Picnic, Vending; Southbound)

(133) Rest Area (RR, Phones, Picnic, Vending; Northbound)

66AB **(131)** FL. 68, Orange Ave.
- **Gas** E: Albritton's(*)
- **RVCamp** W: **Roadrunner Travel Resort RV Park**
- **Parks** E: **Fort Pierce Inlet State Park**

65 **(129)** FL. 70, Okeechobee Road
- **TStop** W: **Citgo(*, SCALES)**, **Pilot (Travel Center)**
- **Gas** W: Chevron(*, CW, 24), Mobil(*, 24), Texaco(*, CW)
- **Food** W: Arby's (Pilot), Burger King, **Citgo**, **Cracker Barrel**, Denny's, Dunkin Donuts (Mobil), KFC, McDonald's, Miami Subs, Mobil, Old Carolina Diner, Perkins Family Restaurant, **Pilot (Travel Center)**, Red Lobster, SHONEY'S, **Shoney's**, Subway (Mobil), Taco Bell, **Waffle House (Citgo)**, Wendy's

Jensen Beach

1578

- Oceanview Restaurant & Lounge
- Beachside Pool & Tiki Bar
- Complimentary Tennis
- Massage Therapy
- Premium Golf Courses Nearby
- Free Parking (Car & Bus)
- Special Rates for Tour Groups

To SR 76 to Stuart. Right on Monterey Rd. Over US1 to East Ocean Blvd, Turn right follow over 2 bridges - continue to hotel.

FLORIDA ▪ I-95 ▪ EXIT 61

PRIME OUTLETS
VERO BEACH

Over 75 Outlet Stores and Food Court
Bugle Boy • Donney & Burke • Polo

Ask for your FREE COUPON BOOK
561-770-6171

1870

FLORIDA ▪ I-95 ▪ EXIT 68

Family owned and operated.

COPLEY'S RV CENTER, INC.

SALES • SERVICE • PARTS • RENTAL

Full Service Dealer • 5 Bays • LP Gas

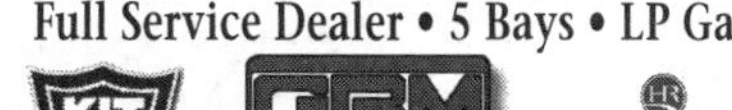

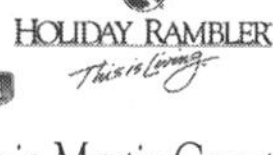

1555

Oldest Dealer in Martin County
Hours: Service Mon-Fri 8-5
Parts Mon-Sat 8-5

561-546-6416 • 561-546-8331

FLORIDA ▪ I-95 ▪ EXIT 60

EXIT FLORIDA

- **Lodg** W: **Days Inn**, **Econolodge**, Hampton Inn, Holiday Inn Express, Motel 6, **Treasure Coast Inn**
- **Med** E: **Hospital**
- **ATM** W: Chevron, **Pilot (Travel Center)**
- **Other** E: Home Depot
  W: Greyhound Bus Station, **R Manufacturers Outlet Center**, Rainforests Amusement, Vision Land Outlet

64 **(125)** County Road 712, Midway Road , Port Saint Lucy

63C **(121)** St. Lucie West Blvd.
- **Gas** E: Chevron(*, CW, 24), Shell(*, D)
- **Food** E: McDonald's, Shell, Subway (Shell), Wendy's
- **Lodg** E: Fairfield Inn by Marriott
- **ATM** E: Chevron
- **Other** E: **St. Lucie Sports Complex (NY Mets Training Camp)**

63AB **(117)** Gatlin Blvd, Port Saint Lucie
- **Gas** E: Amoco(*, D)
- **Med** E: **Hospital**

62 **(110)** CR. 714, Fl. 714, Martin Hwy.

(106) Rest Area (RR, Phones, Vending; Southbound)

(106) Rest Area (RR, Phones, Vending; Northbound)

61C **(102)** CR. 713, Stuart, Palm City,

61 **(100)** FL. 76, Stuart, Indiantown
- **Gas** E: Chevron(*), Mobil(*, D)
- **Food** E: **Cracker Barrel**, McDonald's
- **Lodg** E: Holiday Inn (see our ad this page)
- **Med** E: **Hospital**
- **ATM** E: Chevron

60 **(96)** CR. 708, Hobe Sound
- **RVCamp** E: **Copley's RV Center (see our ad this page)**
- **Parks** E: **Jonathon Dickinson's State Park (11 Miles)**

59AB **(87)** FL. 706, Jupiter, Okeechobee (59 A is east, 59 B is west)
- **Gas** E: Chevron(*), Shell(*, CW), Texaco(*, D, CW)
- **Food** E: Applebee's, Bresler's Ice Cream, Cheeseburgers and More, China Dragon Chinese, IHOP, KFC, McDonald's(PLAY), SHONEY'S, Shoney's
- **Lodg** E: Wellesley Inns(see our ad at I-95 Exit 36 FL)
- **RVCamp** E: **Land Yachts Inc. (Approx. 2.3 Miles)**
- **Med** E: **Hospital**
- **ATM** E: Bank Atlantic, Chevron
- **Other** E: **Historic Museum**, Tourist Info., Veterinarian

58 **(84)** Donald Ross Road

57C **(81)** CR. 809, Military Trail (Southbound, Difficult Reaccess)

57 **(80)** FL. 786, PGA Blvd. , Florida Atlantic
- **Gas** E: Mobil(*)
  W: Shell(*)
- **Food** E: China Wok Garden, Cod and Capers, Durango Steakhouse, PGA Ice Cream and Yogurt, Sakura Japanese, Toojay's Deli
  W: Baskin Robbins, Chianti's, DoubleTree Hotel (Plumbago's), Embassy Suites, Latina's Pizza, Old Boston Pasta House (Embassy Suites), Paddy Mac's Restaurant, The Abbey Road, The Boulevard
- **Lodg** E: Marriott
  W: DoubleTree Hotel (Plumbago's), Embassy Suites
- **AServ** E: Mobil
  W: Shell
- **Med** W: **Hospital**
- **ATM** W: Admiral T Bank, Barnett Bank, Fidelity Federal, First Union Center Bank, **Publix**, South Bank, Sun Trust Bank
- **Other** E: General Cinemas
  W: Eckerd Drugs(RX), One Hour Photo, **Publix**, Robalo's Discount Pharmacy

56 **(77)** North Lake Blvd , CR 809A, Lake Park, North Palm Beach
- **Gas** E: Shell(*), Texaco(*, D)
  W: Chevron(*, CW, 24), Mobil(*, D)
- **Food** E: Arby's, Mario's Pizza, McDonald's, Taco Bell
  W: Hayashi, One Thai Restaurant, Pizza Hut, Pizza King, SHONEY'S, Shoney's, Subway, TCBY
- **Lodg** W: Inns Of America

EXIT		FLORIDA
	AServ	E: Ed Morse Chrysler, Plymouth, Jeep, Eagle, Oldsmobile, Isuzu, Ed Morse Oldsmobile and Isuzu, Schumacher Automotive Service, Wallace Mercury, Lincoln
	RVCamp	E: **Bob Clark's Great Time RV's (1.4 Miles)**
	Med	W: **✚ Northlake Medical Center**
	ATM	E: **Albertson's Grocery Store**
		W: **Publix Supermarket**
	Other	E: **Albertson's Grocery Store**, Home Depot, Pet Emergency Clinic
		W: A one A Foodstores, **Gardens Animal Hospital**, Office Max, Opticians, **Publix Supermarket**
55		**(75)** Blue Heron Blvd.
	FStop	E: **Amoco**[*, CW]
	Gas	E: Shell[*, D, 24]
		W: Mobil[*, CW], Racetrac[*]
	Food	E: Wendy's
		W: Burger King[PLAY], Denny's, McDonald's
	Lodg	E: Villager Lodge
		W: Super 8
	AServ	E: Hetrz, Penske,Aramark
	TServ	E: **Florida Diesel, Freight Liner Trucks of South Florida, JM Tire, Palm Beach Truck**
	Parks	E: **John B McArthur State Park**
	Other	E: Ryder Truck Rental
		W: Camping
54		**(74)** County Road 702, 45th St
	Gas	W: Racetrac
	Food	E: Burger King, Frank's Deli Subs and Salads, Hong Kong Cafe, Palm Cafe and Deli
		W: **Cracker Barrel**, Wendy's
	Lodg	E: DAYS INN Days Inn, Knight's Inn
		W: Courtyard by Marriott, Residence Inn
	AServ	E: Schooley Cadillac
	RVCamp	W: **Palm Beach RV Inc.**[LP] **(1.25 Miles)**
	Med	E: **✚ Hospital**, **✚ Palm Beach Medical Group**
	ATM	E: Republic Security Bank
53		**(71)** Palm Beach Lakes Blvd.
	Food	E: King Chinese Buffet
		W: Bancock House Thai Restaurant, King Solomon's Diner and Restaurant, Margarita Mexican Restaurant, Morrison's Cafeteria, No Anchovies (Comfort Inn), Olive Garden
	Lodg	E: Best Western (Palm Beach Lakes)
		W: Comfort Inn, Wellesley Inn (see our ad at I-95 Exit 36 FL)
	AServ	E: Firestone Tire & Auto, **Target**
	ATM	W: Barnett Bank, Colonial Bank, Hamilton Bank, Union Planter's Bank
	Other	E: **Palm Beach Mall, Target, The Mall Cinema**
		W: **Vision Works**
52AB		**(70)** Fl. 704 , Flagler Museum, Norton Museum, Okechobee
	Gas	W: Chevron[*, D, CW, 24], Shell[*]
	Food	W: Nick's Diner, Shells Seafood, Subs, Thai Paradise
	Lodg	E: Sheraton
	AServ	W: Arrigo Dodge Dealership, Oil Connection Fast Change Oil
	ATM	W: NationsBank (Shell), Shell
	Other	E: **Museum & Fine Arts Center**
		W: Circuit City, Lens Crafters, **United Artist Theaters**
51		**(68)** Belvedere Road, International Airport
	Gas	E: Fina[*, D]
		W: Shell[*]
	Food	W: Denny's, Phillips Seafood, Prego's Subs (Shell), Shell, SHONEY'S, Shoney's
	Lodg	W: Hampton Inn, Holiday Inn, Omni Hotel, Radison Hotel
	AServ	E: Franks Parts and Rebuilder
	Other	W: Palm Beach International Airport, U-Haul Center
50		**(68)** U.S. 98, Southern Blvd, International Airport
	Gas	E: Chevron[*, D, CW]
	Food	E: Capri, Yvette's Ice Cream
	Lodg	W: Hilton
	AServ	E: Chevron, Chevron, Oil Well
		W: Tire Kingdom
	Med	E: **✚ Hospital**
	ATM	E: First Union
	Other	E: **DeSoto Pharmacy, Eckerd Drugs**[RX], **Publix Supermarket, Science Museum, U.S. Post Office, Zoo**
49		**(66)** Forest Hill Blvd
	Other	E: Science Museum Planetarium, Zoo
48		**(65)** 10th Ave North , Lakeworth
	Gas	W: BP[*], Texaco[*, D]
	Food	W: 10th Ave. Cafe, Dunkin Donuts, Lindburgers
	AServ	W: Wayne Akers Ford
	RVCamp	W: **RV Sales**
	Med	W: **✚ Hospital**
	Other	W: Fun Depot Arcade
47		**(63)** 6th Ave. S.
	Med	W: **✚ Hospital**
46		**(64)** Cty Road 812, Lantana Road
	Gas	E: Shell[*, D, 24]
		W: **Costco**
	Food	E: Cuban Restaurant and Cafeteria, Family Rotisserie Chicken, Golden Wok, KFC, McDonald's, Riggin's Crabhouse, Subway
	Lodg	E: Motel 6
	AServ	W: **Costco**
	ATM	E: 7-11 Convenience Store, First Union, Washington Mutual
	Other	E: 7-11 Convenience Store, **Coin Laundry, Eckerd Drugs, Florida Hwy. Patrol Station, Publix Supermarket**, Royal Mart Foodstores
45		**(61)** Hypoluxo Road
	FStop	W: **Shell**[*, D] **(U-Haul Rental)**
	Gas	E: Amoco[*], Mobil[*], Texaco[*, D]
	Food	E: Pizza Hut, SHONEY'S, Shoney's
	Lodg	E: Inns Of America, Super 8
	AServ	E: Don Olson Tire & Auto Center, Long Bottom, Palm Beach Tire Inc., Tire Kingdom
	ATM	E: Texaco
	Other	E: Coin Laundry, Sam's Club
44C		**(59)** Gateway Blvd
44		**(57)** Boynton Beach Blvd
	Gas	E: Texaco[*, LP]
		W: Texaco[*]
	Food	E: Captain Franks Seafood (Take-out)
		W: Checkers Burgers, Mama Jennie's Italian Restaurant, Subway, Waffle House, Wendy's
	Lodg	E: Holiday Inn Express
	AServ	E: Texaco, Texaco
		W: Lloyd Auto Service, Texaco[*], Texaco
	ATM	W: 7-11 Convenience Store
	Other	E: **Coin Laundry**
		W: 7-11 Convenience Store, Lens Crafters, Pet Vet

Bold red print shows RV & Bus parking available or nearby

EXIT		FLORIDA
43		**(56)** Woolbright Road
	Gas	W: Racetrac(*)
	Food	W: Burger King, Cracker Barrel
	Med	E: Hospital
	ATM	W: Fidelity Federal Savings Bank, Racetrac
	Other	W: Home Depot
42AB		**(53)** FL. 806, Atlantic Ave., Delray Beach
	Gas	W: Chevron(*, CW), Shell(*, D)
	Food	W: Silver Wok
	AServ	W: Eastern Auto Care, Foriegn Care Engineering
	Med	W: Hospital, Walk In Clinic
	ATM	W: Chevron, Shell
	Other	W: Atlantic Animal Hospital, Stop 'N 'Go
41		**(51)** Linton Blvd
	Gas	W: Shell(*)
	Food	E: Dairy Queen, McDonald's, Outback Steakhouse, Wolfie's Deli Express W: Blimpie's Subs (Shell), Bono's BBQ, Lucky Chef Chinese Restaurant, Palace Restaurant & Lounge, Shell
	AServ	E: Wallace Chrysler Plymouth, Nisson, Walllace Ford W: Goodman's Auto Service
	ATM	W: First Union Bank, Winn Dixie Supermarket
	Other	E: Circuit City, Office Max, Target W: Disco Laundry, Morikami Museum, Winn Dixie Supermarket
40C		**(50)** Congress Ave , Boca Raton
	Lodg	W: Residence Inn
40		**(48)** FL. 794, Yamato Road , Lynn University
	Lodg	W: DoubleTree, Embassy Suites
39		**(45)** FL. 808, Glades Road
	Gas	W: Amoco(*, 24)
	Food	W: Amoco, Brewzzi, Coffee Roaster Cafe, Domino's Pizza, Hooters, Houston's, Krispy Kreme Doughnuts (Amoco), Macaroni Grill, Monty's Stone Crab, Nick's, Romano's Macaroni Grill, Sheraton Inn
	Lodg	W: Courtyard by Marriott, Holiday Inn, Sheraton Inn
	Med	E: Hospital
	ATM	W: Barnett Bank, NationsBank, Union Planter's Bank
	Other	W: Glades Apothocary, Vision Land
38		**(44)** Palmetto Park Road
	Gas	E: Exxon(*, D)
	Food	E: Bilotti's, Denny's, Red's Backwood BBQ, Subway, Yogurt
	Med	E: Hospital
	ATM	E: Sun Trust Bank
	Other	E: Boca Raton Museum of Art, Children's Museum of Art, International Museum of Cartoon Art, K-Mart, Publix Supermarket(RX), U.S. Post Office
37		**(43)** FL 810, Hillsboro Blvd , Deerfield Beach, Parkland
	Gas	W: Chevron(*, D), Mobil(*, D, CW)
	Food	E: Clock Family Restaurant (La Quinta Inn), La Quinta Inn, Pete's Garden Cafe W: Denny's (Ramada Inn), Ramada Inn
	Lodg	E: Hilton, La Quinta Inn W: Ramada Inn, Village Lodge, Wellesley Inns (see our ad this page))
	ATM	E: Bank Atlantic
	Parks	E: Tivoli Nature Park
	Other	W: Home Depot
36C		**(43)** FL. 869, Southwest 10th St., to I-75 Naples, to Key West by toll Road (Toll)
	Gas	E: Mobil(*, CW)
	Food	E: Cracker Barrel
	Lodg	E: Extended Stay America W: Comfort Suites Hotel, Quality Inn, Wellsley Inn (see our ad this page)

EXIT		FLORIDA
	Other	E: Brands USA
36		**(43)** FL 834, Sample Road , Lighthouse Pointe, TriRail Station
	Gas	E: Shell(*, D) W: Chevron(*), Mobil(*), Texaco(*, D, CW)
	Food	E: Four Corners of Europe Restaurant W: McDonald's(PLAY), Miami Subs
	AServ	E: Shell, Shell W: Chevron, Chevron, Mobil, Mobil, Texaco
	RVCamp	E: Breezy Hill Travel Trailer Park (1.35 Miles), Highland Pines (1.75 Miles), Highland Woods Travel Trailer Park South (1.75 Miles)
	Med	E: Mini Medical Center Walk-In, North Broward Medical Ctr
	ATM	E: Commercial Bank of Florida, Shell W: 7-11 Convenience Store, Mobil
	Other	E: Jeep W: 7-11 Convenience Store, Tom Thumb
35AB		**(39)** Copans Road (35B goes West, 35A goes East)
	Gas	E: Amoco(*, 24) W: Amoco(*, D, CW)
	Food	E: Amoco, Krispy Kreme Doughnuts (Amoco)
	AServ	E: Auto House, Pep Boys Auto Center W: NTB
	Other	E: Wal-Mart(RX) W: Home Depot
34AB		**(36)** FL. 814, Atlantic Blvd (34B goes west, 34 A goes east)
	Food	E: KFC, Miami Subs, Taco Bell W: Pompano Beach Farmers Market
	Med	E: Hospital W: Hospital
	Other	W: Pompano Beach Farmers Market
33		**(34)** CR. 840W., Cypress Creek Road , Stadium,North Lauderdale
	Food	W: Bambino's Deli and Cafe, Barney's Coffee, Bennigan's, Carlucci's Grill, Dunkin Donuts, Longhorn Steakhouse, Moe's Gourmet Bagel, Starlight Diner, Steak & Ale, Sweet Tomatoes, Swensen's Ice Cream
	Lodg	E: Hampton Inn, Westin Hotel W: Marriott, Sheraton Suites
	Med	E: Hospital
	ATM	W: Bank Atlantic, First Union
	Other	W: Fun Scape, Pearl Vision, Regal Cinema's
32		**(36)** FL. 870, Commercial Blvd , Lauderdale by the Sea, Lauderhill
	Gas	W: Amoco(*, CW), Coastal(*), Mobil(*, D), Shell(*, 24)
	Food	E: Subway W: Dunkin Donuts, Holiday Inn, KFC, McDonald's, Miami Subs, Twin Diner, Waffle House
	Lodg	W: Holiday Inn (see our ad this page), Red Roof Inn
	AServ	W: Larry's Tire Inc, Mobil 10 Min. Oil Change, Precision Tune & Lube
	RVCamp	E: Dixie Trailer Supply (1.75 Miles)
	Med	E: Hospital, Walk In Clinic

Newly Renovated

Seasonal Discounted Rates

Holiday Inn®

1158

• US 411 & Commercial Blvd
• Outdoor Heated Swimming Pool
• Two Lighted Tennis Courts
• Coffee Makers in All Rooms
• Restaurant & Lounge
• Nintendo in All Guest Rooms
• Free HBO

954-739-4000 For Reservations: 800-370-1601

FLORIDA ▪ I-95 ▪ Exit 32 ▪ 3 MILES WEST

FLORIDA TURNPIKE ▪ EXIT 62 ▪ 1/2 MILE

EXIT		FLORIDA
	ATM	W: Amoco, Shell
	Parks	W: Easterlin Park (1.25 Miles)
31		FL. 816W., Oakland Park Blvd.
	Gas	E: Chevron(*, CW, 24), Mobil(*) W: BP(*) (U-Haul Rental), Hess(*, D)
	Food	E: Denny's, Miami Subs, Wendy's W: Dunkin Donuts, The Lunch Way Subs and Bakery
	Lodg	W: Days Inn
	AServ	E: Meineke Discount Mufflers, Speedy Transmission W: Lipton Toyota
	ATM	E: Chevron, Chevron, Mobil W: BP (U-Haul Rental)
	Other	E: Swifty Coin Laundry W: Home Depot
30		**(29)** FL. 838W., Sunrise Blvd
	Gas	E: Amoco(*, CW), Texaco(*) W: Fina(*, D)
	Food	E: Burger King, Caribamar W: Captain Crab's, Church's Chicken, McDonald's
	Other	E: Hugh Taylor Birch State Recreation Area
29		**(28)** FL. 842, Broward Blvd, Downtown
	Gas	E: Amoco(*, CW, 24)
	Food	E: Days Inn
	Lodg	E: Days Inn
	AServ	W: Transmission King
	Med	W: Hospital
	Other	E: Arts & Science District W: Amtrak Terminal, Coin Laundry
28		FL. 736, Davie Blvd
	Gas	E: Speedy Food Store(*) W: Amoco(*), Hess(D), Mobil(*, CW)
	Food	W: Cafeteria Santa Barabara, Flannigan's, Miami Subs, Shanghai Gardens, Subway, Wings 'n More
	Other	W: Davie Blvd Pharmacy
27C		**(29)** Junction I-595, Point Everglades (Ft Lauderdale Int'l Airport)
27		**(29)** FL 84W to Fl Turnpike
	Gas	E: Citgo(*, D), Coastal(*, D), Mobil(*, D), Racetrac(*, 24), Texaco(*)
	Food	E: Domino's Pizza (7-11 Convenience Store), Li'l Red's Cookin' W: BJ's American Cafe (Red Carpet Inn), Family Restaurant, Ramada Inn, Tucan's Restaurant (Ramada Inn)
	Lodg	E: Best Western, Budget Inn, Motel 6, Sky Motel W: Cross Roads Motor Park, Ramada Inn, Red Carpet Inn, Villager Lodge
	AServ	E: Texaco, Texaco
	RVCamp	W: Yacht Haven Park Marina
	ATM	E: Racetrac
	Parks	W: Secret Woods County Park
	Other	E: 7-11 Convenience Store (Citgo) W: U-Haul Center
26CD		**(29)** Junction I-595 to Fl. Turnpike I-75 , International Hwy via I-595 , Fort Everglades
26		FL. 818, Griffin Road
	Gas	W: Amoco(*, D), Citgo(*, D, CW)
	Food	E: Moon Dance (Wyndam Hotel), Wyndham Garden Hotel W: Parks Subs and Deli
	Lodg	E: Hilton, Wyndham Garden Hotel
	AServ	W: S&H Auto Service
	Other	W: Thunderbolt Marina
25		**(26)** Stirling Road, FL 848 (Cooper's City & Grand Prix)
	Food	E: Burger King(PLAY), K-Mart(RX), Little Caesars Pizza (K-Mart), McDonald's, Taco Bell W: Balifarence, Chinese Fishing Village, Dunkin Donuts, Juicy Lucy's Restaurant, Miami Subs, Mr M's Sandwich Shop, Subway

EXIT FLORIDA

- **Lodg** **E:** Comfort Inn, Hampton Inn
- **AServ** **W:** Lucy's Auto Clinic
- **RVCamp** **W:** **Oak Grove Trailer Park (.5 Miles)**
- **ATM** **E:** Nat Bank
  - **W:** Barnett Bank, Republic Security Bank
- **Parks** **E:** **John U. Lloyd State Park**
- **Other** **E:** **Barnes & Noble**, **K-Mart(RX)**, **Oakwood Plaza Mall**, Service Merchandise

24 **(25)** FL. 822, Sheridan St
- **Gas** **E:** Mobil(*)
  - **W:** Shell(*, CW)
- **Food** **E:** Denny's
- **Lodg** **W:** DAYS INN Days Inn, Holiday Inn (see our ad this page)
- **Parks** **W:** **Topeekeegee Yugnee Park (.5 Miles)**

23 FL. 820, Hollywood Blvd
- **Gas** **E:** Shell(*)
- **Food** **E:** Dunkin Donuts, IHOP(24), McDonald's, **Mia Casa Mexican**, Miami Subs, Pizza 28
  - **W:** Boston Market Restaurant, McDonald's
- **Lodg** **E:** **HoJo Inn**, Ramada Inn (see our ad this page)
- **AServ** **E:** Goodyear Tire & Auto
- **Med** **W:** ✚ **Hospital**
- **ATM** **E:** Shell
- **Other** **E:** **Eckerd Drugs**
  - **W:** Golf and Country Club, Hollywood Animal Hospital, **Hollywood mall**, TriRail Station

22 FL. 824, Pembroke Road
- **Gas** **E:** Shell(*)
- **Food** **E:** Italian Hoagie Center
- **AServ** **E:** Family Tires, Stephen's Service Center
- **ATM** **E:** Shell

21 FL. 858, Hallandale Beach Blvd
- **Gas** **E:** Amoco(*), Hess(*, D)
  - **W:** Amoco(*, D), Racetrac(*)
- **Food** **E:** Burger King, Denny's, IHOP, Little Caesars Pizza, McDonald's, Smokehouse BBQ
  - **W:** Amoco, Taco Bell (Amoco)
- **Lodg** **E:** Holiday Inn Express
- **RVCamp** **W:** **Holiday Park (.25 Miles)**, **Pembroke RV Service (1 Mile)**
- **ATM** **W:** American Bank
- **Parks** **W:** **Pembroke Park**
- **Other** **E:** Animal Hospital, **Coin Laundry**, WalGreens Pharmacy, **Winn Dixie Supermarket(RX)**

20 **(19)** Ives Dairy Road, Northeast 203rd St., William D Singer Expressway, Aventura
- **Gas** **W:** Amoco(*)
- **Food** **W:** JD's Pizza and Subs, Subway
- **AServ** **W:** Southern Tire and Auto Service Inc
- **Med** **E:** ✚ **Hospital**
- **Other** **W:** 7-11 Convenience Store, **Ives Plaza Animal Clinic**, **Stadium**

19 **(16)** Miami Gardens Dr., FL. 860, North Miami beach
- **Other** **W:** Olita River State Recreation Area

18 **(15)** U.S. 441, FL 826 West Turnpike, FL 9S, FL 826 E, Park and Ride
- **Med** **E:** ✚ **Hospital**

17 , FL 826 E, North Miami Beach, Sunny Isles Beach (Reaccess Northbound Only)
- **Gas** **E:** Amoco(*), Chevron(*), Citgo(*), Shell(*, 24)
- **Food** **E:** Dunkin Donuts, Howard Johnson, KFC, MJ's Lounge
- **Lodg** **E:** Holiday Inn, Howard Johnson, Renaissance Suites
- **AServ** **E:** Chevron, Chevron, LP Evans Mercedes Benz
- **Med** **E:** ✚ **Parkway Medical Plaza**
- **Other** **E:** Citgo, Dade Animal Hospital

16 **(15)** FL. 826 W., Tnpk. N. (Reaccess Northbound Only)
- **Food** **E:** Shoney's

15 **(13)** Northwest 151st St. (Reaccess Northbound Only, Difficult Reaccess)
- **Food** **W:** Jah-Nets Jamaican, May Fu Chinese Restaurant, McDonald's
- **Other** **W:** **Super Saver Discount Drugs**, **Winn Dixie Supermarket**

14 **(12)** Northwest 135th St., Opa -Locka Blvd., FL 916
- **Gas** **W:** Amoco(*, CW), BP(*), Chevron(*, 24), Mobil(*)
- **Food** **W:** China Tea House, Dunkin Donuts, Le Bambou, Pizza Hut, Subway
- **Lodg** **W:** Motel 7
- **AServ** **W:** BP, Goodyear Tire & Auto, Howie's Tires
- **ATM** **W:** Kisslack National Bank
- **Other** **W:** Kwik Stop, Pages of Life Bible Bookstore

13 **(11)** Northwest 125th St, North Miami, Bal Harbor, FL 922, Surfside
- **Gas** **W:** Atlantic(*, D), Shell(*, 24)
- **Food** **W:** Burger King, Chin's Chinese Restaurant, Royal Castle, Wendy's
- **AServ** **W:** C-B Tire Co
- **ATM** **W:** Washington Mutual
- **Other** **W:** Swifty Coin Laundry

12 Northwest 119th St., Fl. 924 (Northbound)
- **Gas** **W:** Amoco(*, CW)
- **Food** **W:** BBQ Barn, Jimmy's Place, KFC, Popeye's Chicken, Sub Center
- **AServ** **W:** A-1 Wheel and Tire, Action Transmission
- **Other** **W:** Car Wash, **Eckerd Drugs(RX)**

11 **(9)** Northwest 103rd St, Miami Shores, FL 932
- **Gas** **E:** Shell(*, CW, 24)
  - **W:** Chevron(*, 24), Mobil(*)
- **Food** **W:** Cesar Discount Cafe, Dunkin Donuts, Esther's Restaurant
- **ATM** **W:** Chevron
- **Other** **E:** 7-11 Convenience Store, Emergency Animal Hospital

10 **(8)** Northwest 95th St
- **Gas** **E:** Amoco(*)
  - **W:** Mobil(*), Shell(*)
- **Food** **W:** McDonald's
- **Med** **W:** ✚ **Hospital**
- **ATM** **W:** First Union Bank
- **Other** **W:** **WalGreens Pharmacy(RX)**

9 **(7)** NW. 79th St., NW. 81st St., FL. 934
- **Gas** **E:** BP(*, D), Chevron(*, D, 24)
  - **W:** Shell(*)
- **Food** **W:** Cafe China, Checkers Burgers
- **Lodg** **W:** DAYS INN Days Inn
- **AServ** **E:** Florida Hydromatic Transmissions, Goodyear, Midas Muffler & Brake
  - **W:** Colonial Chrysler, Jeep, Eagle, Plymouth, Pontiac, Do-It-All Service Center, Miami Lincoln Mercury

9A No Name (Southbound)

8 **(6)** Northwest 62nd St., Northwest 54th St.
- **Food** **W:** McDonald's, Subway
- **ATM** **W:** **Winn Dixie Supermarket**
- **Other** **W:** **Winn Dixie Supermarket**

7 **(5)** Junction I-195, FL.112, Airport

6 **(4)** FL. 836 W, Airport
- **Med** **W:** ✚ **Hospital**

5A **(3)** Northwest 8th St, Orange Bowl, Port of Miami

5 **(3)** I-395, Miami Beach
- **Lodg** **E:** Howard Johnson (see our ad this page)

4 **(2)** Northwest 2nd St (Northbound, Difficult Reaccess)

3A Downtown, Miami Ave. (Southbound)

3 **(2)** U.S. 1, Biscayne Blvd, Downtown, Brickell Ave

2 Southwest 7th St, U.S. 41
- **Gas** **E:** Chevron(*), Exxon(*)
  - **W:** Shell(*, D, 24)
- **Food** **E:** McDonald's, Wendy's
  - **W:** Blimpie Subs & Salads (Shell), PaPa John's, Shell
- **ATM** **E:** First Union Bank
  - **W:** NationsBank (Shell), Shell
- **Other** **E:** Eckerd Drugs(RX)

1 Rickenbacker Causeway, Biscayne Blvd
- **Lodg** **E:** Holiday Inn (see our ad this page)
- **Med** **E:** ✚ **Hospital**

↑ FLORIDA

Begin I-95

1342

Florida • Exit 5 • 305-358-3080

University of Miami

1554

305-667-5611

I-95 • Exit U.S.1

or South on Palmetto Expway(826) Exit on 88st (Kendall Dr.) to US 1North

- Full Service Restaurant • Sports Lounge with Karaoke and "Happy Hour" Specials
- Tropical Landscaped Pool • Free Parking
- Free Personal Fitness Center
- Free Satellite TV with First Run Movies
- Ideal Central Location

FLORIDA • I-95 • EXIT U.S.1

1997 & 1998 Torch Bearer Award-Winner

1568

- Tropical Pool with Waterfall
- Convenient to Airport/Train
- Complimentary Airport Shuttle Service
- 5 Miles to Hollywood Beach
- Restaurant • Lounge • HBO
- Fifteen Minutes to Miami

954-925-9100 For Reservations: 800-480-7623

FLORIDA • I-95 • EXIT 24

RAMADA INN®

1925 Harrison St. • Hollywood, FL • 33020

1734

In the Heart of the Music & Entertainment District.

Walk to Art Galleries, Cafe, Clubs
Minutes from the Beach
Heated Pool • Landscaped Deck
Meeting/Banquet Facilities
Pets Allowed - (Limited Avail.)
Guest Laundry • Covered Parking
13,000' Exercise Facility Next Door
Truck/Large Vehicle Parking

954-927-3341 • 800-230-4206

Exit 23 E along Hollywood Blvd to 20th Ave, Rt 1 Blk to Harrison

FLORIDA • I-95 • EXIT 23

Bold red print shows RV & Bus parking available or nearby

EXIT	MICHIGAN
	Begin I-96
	↓MICHIGAN
1AB	U.S. 31, Ludington, Grand Haven
Gas	**N:** Mobil(*, D)
Lodg	**N:** Alpine Motel, Belaire Motel, Hotel Haven
	S: AmeriHost Inn
AServ	**N:** Action Auto Body, Orrie's Auto Service
Other	**N:** Lakeshore Sports Center
4	Airline Road
Gas	**S:** Speedway(*, LP, K), Wesco(*, D, K)
Food	**S:** Burger Crest, Pizza Reaction, Stafford's Dairy Bar, Subway
Lodg	**S: PJ Hoffmaster State Park**
AServ	**N:** Gary's Auto Service
	S: Braun's Town & Country Auto Service
ATM	**S:** First of America(24)
Parks	**S: PJ Hoffmaster State Park**
Other	**S:** Bowling Alley, **Fruitport Foods Grocery**
5	Fruitport (Westbound, Reaccess Eastbound Only)
8	Rest Area (RR, Phones, Picnic; Westbound)
9	MI 104, Spring Lake, Grand Haven (Eastbound, Reaccess Westbound Only)
Gas	**S:** Mobil(*, K)
Parks	**S: State Park**
10	CR B31, Nunica (Difficult Reaccess)
Food	**N:** Turk's Restaurant
Other	**N: Nunica Grocery**, Post Office
16	CR B35, Eastmanville
FStop	**N: Rinaldi Pizza, Speedway**(*, LP, K)
	S: Pacific Pride Commercial Fueling(LP)
Gas	**N:** Amoco(*, D, CW), Shell(*, D)
Food	**N: Arby's**, Burger King, Little Caesars Pizza, **McDonald's**, Subway, Taco Bell
Lodg	**N:** AmeriHost Inn
RVCamp	**N: Fun N Sun RV Center**
ATM	**N:** Comerica Bank, Shell
Other	**N:** Casemirer's Supermarket, Laundry Mat, **Rite Aide Pharmacy**, West Michigan Veterinary Service
19	Lamont, Coopersville
Gas	**N:** 76(*, D)
Food	**S:** Sam's Joint
AServ	**N:** 76
RVCamp	**N: Prime Time RV**
	S: Vanandel(LP)
23	Marne
Gas	**N:** Shell(*, D, K)
Food	**S:** Inter Urban Cafe, Pit Stop Bar & Grill, Rinaldi Pizza
AServ	**N:** Christ Right Auto, Schneider Tire Service
ATM	**S:** Comerica Bank
Other	**S:** Marne Market, Post Office
25	Eighth Ave, 4 Mile Road (Westbound, Reaccess Eastbound Only)
Gas	**S:** Marathon(*, K)
Lodg	**S:** Wayside Motel
AServ	**S:** Banka's Auto Repair
(25)	Rest Area (RR, Phones, Picnic; Eastbound)
26	Fruit Ridge Avenue
FStop	**S: Amoco**(*, D, LP)
ATM	**S: Amoco**
28	Walker Avenue
Gas	**S:** Meijer(*, D, LP)
Food	**S:** Blimpie's Subs (Meijer), McDonald's
Lodg	**S:** AmeriHost Inn
ATM	**S:** Bank West, Meijer
30AB	MI 37 North, Alpine Avenue, Newaygo
FStop	**S: Hunter's Steakhouse**
Gas	**N:** Amoco(*, LP, CW), Shell(*)
	S: Meijer Grocery(*, D, LP, K, 24), Total(*, D)
Food	**N: Chuck E Cheese's Pizza**, Clock Fine Food, **Cooker**, **Cracker Barrel**, First Wok Chinese, Old Country Buffet, **Olive Garden**, **Outback Steakhouse**, Perkins Family Restaurant, **Russ**, Steak & Shake, Subway, **Taco Bell**, Three Happiness Chinese, Village Inn Pizza Parlor
	S: Arby's, **Burger King**, Fazoli's Italian Food, KFC, Long John Silver, McDonald's (Meijer), McDonald's, Ole Tacos, Pizza Hut (Carry-Out)
Lodg	**S:** Motel 6
AServ	**N: K-Mart**(RX), Keller Ford
	S: Goodyear Tire & Auto, Midas Muffler & Brake, Mr. Bill's, Valvoline Oil Change
Med	**N: ✚ Alpine Health Park**
ATM	**N:** Ameribank
	S: Comerica Bank, Huntington Bank, Old Kent Bank, Total
Other	**N: Grocery Store**, **K-Mart**(RX), Pearl Vision, **Target**
	S: Alpine Coin Laundry, Home Depot, **Meijer Grocery**, SVS Vision
31AB	U.S. 131, Kalamazoo, Cadillac
33	MI 44 Connector, Plainfield Avenue

EXIT	MICHIGAN
Gas	**N:** Total(*, D, LP)
	S: Amoco(*, LP, CW)
Food	**N:** Pizza Hut, Pizza Hut, The Fish Nut, Wendy's
	S: Bill Knapp's Restaurant (see our ad this page), **Denny's**
Lodg	**N:** Lazy T Motel, **Presidents Inn**, Veterinay & Clinic
AServ	**N:** Ace's Transmission, Goodyear Tire & Auto, Meineke Discount Mufflers, Midas Muffler & Brake, NAPA Auto Parts, NTB, Pennzoil Oil Change, Speedy Quik Oil Change, Total, Valvoline Oil Change, West Michigan Transmission
RVCamp	**N: Camps & Cruise**
Med	**N: ✚ Family Physicians Urgent Care**, **✚ Plainfield Medical Center**
ATM	**S:** Bank
Other	**N:** Great Lakes Car Wash, Pockets Billiard Room, SVS Vision, Touch of Class Car Wash
36	Leonard Street
Gas	**N:** Amoco(*, LP, CW)
Food	**N:** Red Hot Inn
Other	**N: Sheriff Dept.**
37	I-196 Junction (left lane exit) Gerald R. Ford Pkwy
38	MI 37 South, MI 44, MI 21, East Belt Line Ave
Food	**S: Duba's Fine Dining**
RVCamp	**N: Camping**
40AB	Cascade Road
Gas	**N:** Marathon(*, D)
	S: Shell, Speedway(*, D, LP)
Food	**N: Forest Hills Grocery**, **Forest Hills Inn**, Hud's Italian
	S: Sigee's Restaurant (Harley)
Lodg	**S: Harley Hotel**
AServ	**N:** BP(*, LP)
	S: Shell
Med	**N: ✚ Forest View Hospital**, **✚ Grand Valley Health Center**
	S: ✚ Hospital
ATM	**N: 7-11 Convenience Store**, **Forest Hills Grocery**, Old Kent Bank, United Bank
	S: Speedway
Other	**N: 7-11 Convenience Store**
43AB	MI 11, 28th Street, Kent County Airport, Cascade
Gas	**N:** Marathon(*, D), **Meijer Superstore**(D, LP, 24)
	S: MSI(*), Mobil(*, CW)
Food	**N:** Big Boy, Brann's Steakhouse (Days Inn), Burger King, Charlevoix Banquet Center, Gipper's Bar & Grill, **Shanghai Garden**
	S: Applebee's, Arby's, **Bob Evan's Restaurant**, Carloso' Kelly's Mexican (Hampton Inn), **McDonald's**, Perkins Family Restaurant, Rio Bravo, Spinnaker's (Hilton)
Lodg	**N:** Budgetel Inn, Country Inn Suites, **Crowne Plaza**

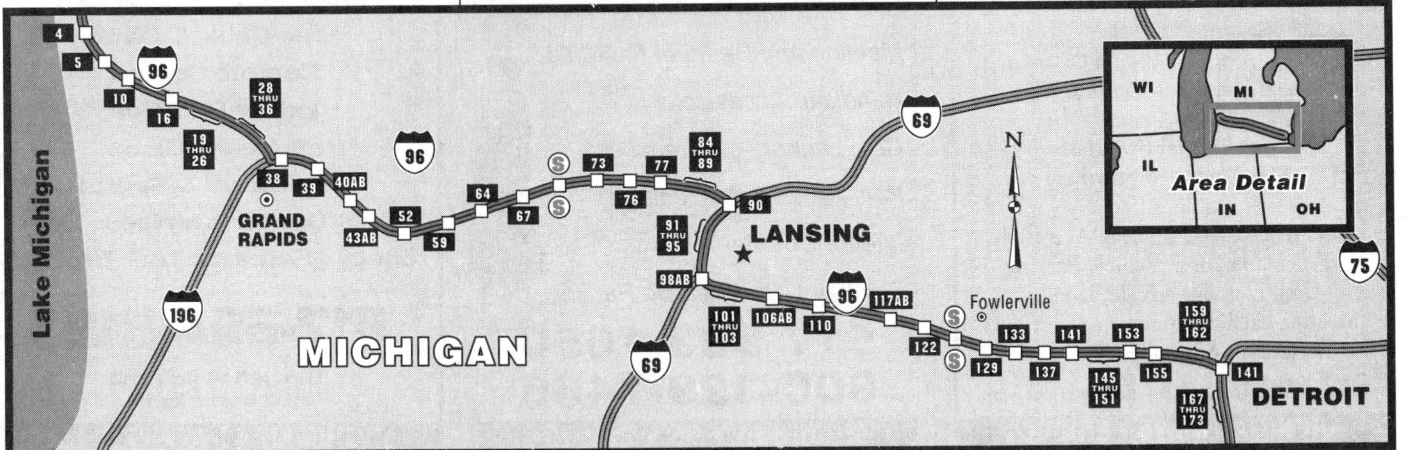

Bold red print shows RV & Bus parking available or nearby

EXIT MICHIGAN

- **Hotel** Days Inn, Hawthorn Suites, Lexington Suites
  - **S:** Econolodge, Excel Inn, Hampton Inn, Hilton, Red Roof Inn
- **AServ** **N:** O'Neill's Body Shop
  - **S:** Car Quest Auto Center
- **ATM** **N:** First of America
- **Other** **N:** **Meijer Superstore**, Scott's Golf Center & Driving Range
  - **S:** Putt Putt Golf & Games

(45) Rest Area (RR, Phones, Picnic, Vending; Westbound)

52 MI 50, Lowell
- **Gas** **N:** Total(*, D, LP, K)
- **Food** **N:** Taco Bell (Total)
- **RVCamp** **S:** **Camping**
- **ATM** **N:** Total
- **Other** **N:** Alto Gas/Propane

59 Clarksville
- **AServ** **N:** J & K Auto Service

(63) Rest Area (RR, Phones, Picnic; Eastbound)

64 Lake Odessa, Saranac
- **Parks** **N:** **Ionia State Park**

67 MI 66, Ionia, Battle Creek, Ionia
- **TStop** **N:** **Scalehouse**(D, SCALES, 24)
- **FStop** **N:** **Total**(*, D, LP, SCALES)
- **Gas** **N:** Amoco(*)
- **Food** **N:** Corner Landing Fine Dining & Cocktails, Scalehouse Restaurant, **Subway (Total)**
- **Lodg** **N:** **Midway Motel**, **Super 8**
- **AServ** **N:** Badder's Auto Parts & Service
- **TServ** **S:** **I-96 Towing & Recovery**
- **TWash** **S:** **I-96 Truck Wash**
- **RVCamp** **N:** **Camping**
- **Med** **N:** **Hospital**
- **ATM** **N:** **Scalehouse**

69 Rest Area

73 Lyons - Muir, Grand River Avenue

76 Kent Street (No Trucks)

77 Grand River Avenue, Junction Business 96, Portland
- **Gas** **N:** Amoco(*, CW), Shell(*, CW), Speedway(*, D, LP), United(*, LP, K)
- **Food** **N:** Arby's, **Burger King**, Diana's Pizza & Subs, McDonald's, Subway (Shell), **Tommie's**
- **Lodg** **N:** Best Western
- **AServ** **N:** Ford & Mercury Dealer, Quicklube
- **Med** **N:** **Portland Veterinary Service**
- **ATM** **N:** Amoco, Independent Bank, Shell, Speedway, **Tom's Grocery**
- **Other** **N:** **Rite Aid Pharmacy**(*), **Tom's Grocery**

1785

6741 South Cedar Street
Lansing, MI

Continental Breakfast
Kids Under 18 Stay Free
Outdoor Pool
Pets Allowed • Handicap Accessible
Truck and Large Vehicle Parking
Coin Laundry • Valet laundry
Meeting Facilities • Interior Corridors
Restaurant & Lounge Next Door
517-694-0454 • Toll Free Reservations: 1-800-2-RAMADA

MICHIGAN • I-96 • EXIT 104

EXIT MICHIGAN

79 Rest Area (RR, Phones, Picnic; Westbound)

84 Westphalia, Eagle
- **Food** **S:** Eagle Inn
- **Other** **S:** **Herm's Meat & Grocery**

86 MI 100, Wright Road
- **FStop** **S:** **Total**(*, D)
- **Gas** **S:** Rural Gas Propane
- **Food** **S:** **Taco Bell (Total)**
- **AServ** **S:** Jerry's Towing Service
- **ATM** **S:** **Total**

(87) Rest Area (RR, Phones, Picnic; Eastbound)

90 Grand River Avenue
- **AServ** **N:** Roger's Auto Parts
  - **S:** Pitchford's Auto Parts
- **Other** **N:** **Airport**, Humane Society Animal Clinic

91 Junction I-69 North, U.S. 27, Flint, Clare

93AB Junction I-69 Business , MI 43, Saginaw Highway
- **Gas** **N:** Shell(*, CW), Total(*, D, LP)
  - **S:** Amoco(*, CW)

1696

Bill Knapp's is a casual, full service family restaurant where Motorcoaches are always welcome.

Over 50 locations throughout: Michigan • Ohio • Indiana

517-321-0931 - Lansing

MICHIGAN • I-96 • EXIT 93B

1115

6501 S. Pennsylvania Ave.
Lansing, Michigan

Restaurant on Premises
Lounge on Premises
Cable TV/HBO
Outdoor Pool
Kitchenettes and Jacuzzi Rooms
Meeting and Banquet Facilities
Handicap Accessible
Coin Laundry on Premises
Pets Allowed ($10 charge)
Interior Corridors
Truck or Large Vehicle Parking

517-393-1650
800-329-7466

Michigan • 96 • Exit 104

EXIT MICHIGAN

- **Food** **N:** Burger King, **Denny's**, **McDonald's**, **Bill Knapp's Restaurant (see our ad this page)**, , North Pine Grill (Best Western), T.G.I. Friday's (Holiday Inn)
  - **S:** **Cracker Barrel**
- **Lodg** **N:** Best Western, Fairfield Inn, Hampton Inn, Motel 6, **Quality Suites**, Red Roof Inn, Residence Inn, T.G.I. Friday's (Holiday Inn)
- **AServ** **S:** Regency Olds/ GMC Trucks/Mazda
- **Med** **N:** **Hospital**, **Westside Medical Center**
- **ATM** **N:** Michigan National Bank, Total
  - **S:** Amoco
- **Other** **N:** **Horrocks Grocery**

95 Junction I-496, Downtown Lansing

97 Junction I-69 South, Charlotte, Ft. Wayne

98AB Lansing Road
- **Food** **N:** Oven Fresh Bakery
  - **S:** Quality Dairy, **Windmill Restaurant**(*, D, LP, K, SCALES) **(Citgo)**
- **Lodg** **S:** **Windmill Motel**, **Windmill Restaurant (Citgo)**
- **AServ** **N:** Goodyear, **Southwest Brakes & Parts**
  - **S:** Cooper Tires
- **TServ** **N:** **Ryder**, **Southwest Brakes & Parts**
  - **S:** **Windmill Restaurant**(SCALES) **(Citgo)**
- **ATM** **S:** Quality Dairy, **Windmill Restaurant (Citgo)**
- **Other** **S:** **State Police**

101 MI 99, Logan Street, Eaton Rapids
- **FStop** **S:** **Sports Bar & Grill**
- **Gas** **N:** QD(*)
- **Food** **S:** McDonald's
- **AServ** **N:** Celebrity Auto Repair, Complete Hitch Auto Service
  - **S:** Shroyer's Auto Service
- **ATM** **N:** QD
- **Parks** **S:** **Grand River Park**
- **Other** **N:** Pleasant Grove Car Wash

LANSING, MICHIGAN

1593

Newly Renovated in 1997!

Holiday Inn®

Free Bus & RV Parking
Easy On-Off Interstate
Complimentary
In Room Coffee
Refrigerators in all Rooms
Free Cable TV with
Remote Control
Indoor Pool Spa
& Health Club
Restaurant & Sports
Bar on Premises
Special Rates for Tour Groups

517-694-8123

Turn left at first and third traffic lights.

MICHIGAN • I-96 • EXIT 104

Bold red print shows RV & Bus parking available or nearby

EXIT MICHIGAN

S: **Rich's Country Store**

104 Business Loop 96, Cedar Street, Holt

Gas N: **Meijer Superstore**(*, LP, K), Speedway(*, K)
S: Total(*, LP)

Food N: Ashley's Restaurant & Lounge, **Bill Knapp's Restaurant (see our ad this page)**, Blimpie's Subs, Bob Evan's Restaurant, Boston Market Restaurant, Butter Nut Bread, Country Skillet, Denny's, **Finley's American Restaurant**, Flapjack, Honeybee's (Best Western), KFC, Kewpee Restaurant, Long John Silver, Mr. Taco, **New China Restaurant**, **Pizza Hut**, Rally's Hamburgers, Wendy's
S: Burger King, Family Style Home Cooking, Frank's Press Box, Ponderosa, Rico's Taco Factory

Lodg N: Best Western, **Days Inn (see our ad opposite page)**, EconoLodge, Super 8
S: **Holiday Inn (see our ad this page)**, **Ramada Limited (see our ad opposite page)**

AServ N: Dodge Truck Dealer, Miller Jeep/Eagle, NTB, University Olds/GMC
S: Eddie's Quick Lube, Muffler Hanger, Muffler Man

RVCamp N: **Lansing Cottonwood Campground (2 Miles)**

Med N: ✚ **Hospital**
S: ✚ **Redi Care Walk-in Urgent Care**

ATM N: Community First Bank, First of America, Michigan National Bank, National Bank of Detroit, Old Kent Bank, Speedway

Other N: 7-11 Convenience Store, **Aldi Supermarket**, **Meijer Superstore**, **Office Max**, Pet Supplies Plus, **Sam's Club**
S: Car Wash, **Kroger Supermarket**(RX)

106AB Junction I-496, U.S. 127, Jackson, Downtown Lansing

110 Okemos, Mason

Gas N: Amoco(*), Marathon(*, CW), Mobil(*, CW)

Food N: Applebee's, **Big Boy**, British Isle Restaurant, Burger King, Cafe Barista, Cafe Oriental, Cookies By Design, Dunkin Donuts (Amoco), Little Caesars Pizza, **McDonald's**, Tubby's Submarine
S: Golden Rose

Lodg N: Comfort Inn, Fairfield Inn, Holiday Inn Express

Other N: **7-11 Convenience Store**

(111) Rest Area (RR, Phones, Picnic, Vending; Westbound)

117AB Dansville, Williamston

Gas N: Pacific Pride

Food N: Rooftop Landing Restaurant

AServ S: Bill's Wrecker & Radiator Service

122 MI 43, MI 52, Webberville, Stockbridge, Perry

FStop N: **Mobil**(*, D, K)

Food N: **McDonald's**, Michigan Brewing Pub, **West Side Deli (Mobil)**

ATM N: **Mobil**

126 Weigh Station

129 Fowlerville

Gas N: Amoco, Shell(*, CW)
S: Mobil(*)

Food N: **Big Boy**, **Fowlerville Farms (Amoco)**, **McDonald's**, Shooters Grill, Taco Bell, Wendy's
S: Dunkin Donuts (South Mobil)

Lodg N: **Best Western**

AServ N: Shell, Waldecker Chevrolet Oldsmobile
S: Plymouth Dodge Jeep Dealer

ATM N: Shell

133 Highland Road, MI 59

Gas N: **Sunoco**(D)

Food N: McDonald's (Sunoco)

RVCamp N: **Camping**

Other N: **Kensington Valley Factory Shops**

(135) Rest Area (RR, Phones, Picnic, Vending; Eastbound)

137 Howell, Pinckney, CR D19

Gas N: Mobil(*), Shell(*, D, LP, K, CW), Speedway(*, LP, K), Total(*)

Food N: Bleu Chameleon (Ramada Inn), Five Star Pizza & Deli, Pastry Shop & Coffee Bar, **Time Out Grill**
S: Country Kitchen (Best Western), The Blind Tiger

Lodg N: Ramada Inn
S: Best Western

AServ S: Howell Auto Repair Center

Med N: ✚ **Hospital**

ATM N: Speedway

Parks S: **Recreation Area**

140 Rest Area (RR, Phones, Picnic, Vending; Westbound)

141 Junction I-96 Business Loop, Howell (Westbound, No Reaccess)

Gas N: Sunoco(*, D, LP, K)

Food N: Log Cabin Restaurant

AServ N: Champion Chevrolet

ATM N: Sunoco

Other N: Tecumseh Golf

145 Grand River Avenue

Gas N: Amoco(*), Shell(*)
S: Clark(*, D, K, 24)

Food N: Arby's, **Cracker Barrel**, KC's Cookery, Outback Steakhouse, Pizza Hut
S: Big Boy, Burger King, **Chili's**, Dunkin Donuts, **KFC**, Lil' Chef, **Lone Star Steakhouse**, Mr. Pita's, **Ponderosa**, Subway (Clark's), Wendy's

Lodg S: **Holiday Inn Express**

AServ N: Brighton Ford/Mercury/Lincoln, Gabe's Auto Glass, Superior Olds Cadillac
S: Midas Muffler & Brake

Med S: ✚ **Hospital**

ATM N: Comerica Bank
S: Standard Federal

Other S: **Farmer Jack Grocery**(RX), **Home Depot**, **K-Mart**(RX), **Meijer Grocery**(24), **Target**, **US Post Office**

147 Brighton

Gas N: Mobil(*, K)

Food N: Cheryl's Place, Coffee Express & More, Tee Bone's Tavern

AServ N: Mechanics Auto Supply, Palarchil's Auto Service, Tire & Muffler Center

Parks N: **Brighton Recreation Area**

Other N: **Spencer Landing Grocery**, **State Police**

148AB U.S. 23, Ann Arbor, Flint

150 Pleasant Valley Road (Westbound)

Food S: EG Nick's

151 Kensington Road

Med S: ✚ **Brighton Hospital**

Parks N: **Island Lake Recreation Area**, **Kensington Metro Park**

153 Kent Lake Road, Kensington

Gas S: Mobil(*)

ATM S: Mobil

Parks N: **Kensington State Park**

155 New Hudson, Milford

Gas S: BP(*, D)

Food S: Poppy's Pizza, Putter's Restaurant

159 Wixom

FStop N: **Marathon**(*, D)

Gas S: Meijer(*, D, LP, K), Mobil(*, CW), Shell(*, CW)

Food S: Arby's, Don's Travelers City, Hennessey's, **McDonald's**, Taco Bell (Shell), Taco Bell

AServ S: Goodyear Tire & Auto, Varsity Ford/Mercury/Lincoln, Zax Auto Wash

Med S: ✚ **Hospital**

ATM N: **Marathon**
S: Meijer, Shell

Parks N: **Proud Lake Recreation Area**

160 Beck Road

AServ S: Ward's Super Service

Med N: ✚ **Hospital**
S: ✚ **Providence Medical Center**(CW, 24)

Parks N: **Mayberry State Park**

162 Novi, Walled Lake

Food N: Denny's, Kerby's Coney Island, New Bangkok Thai Restaurant, Oaks Grill (Double Tree), Pizza Hut, Red Lobster, Starbucks Coffee, Subway
S: **Big Boy**, Bob Evan's Restaurant, Boston Market Restaurant, Grady's, Kims Gardens Chinese, **Olive Garden**, Red Robin, **T.G.I. Friday's**

Lodg N: **Double Tree Hotel**, Hotel Baronette

AServ S: Soft Cloth Auto Wash

Med S: ✚ **Hospital**

ATM N: Comerica Bank, Standard Federal
S: Old Kent Bank

Other N: **12 Oaks Mall**, Eyeglass Factory, **K-Mart**(RX)

165 Junction I-696, I-275 ends

167 8 Mile Road, Novi, Farmington Hills, Maybury State Park

Gas S: **Meijer Grocery**(D, K, 24), Speedway(*, D)

Food S: Big Boy, Chili's, Kirby Coney Island, Kyoto Japanese, **McDonald's**, On The Border, Taco Bell

Lodg S: Hampton Inn, **Hilton**, Office Max, TraveLodge

Med S: ✚ **Center for Specialty Care**, ✚ **Hospital**

Parks S: **State Park**

Other N: **Veterinary Clinic**
S: Best Buy, Costco, **Meijer Grocery**, **Target**

169AB 7 Mile Road

Gas N: Speedway(D, K, 24)

Food N: **Embassy Suites**, **Lone Star Steakhouse**, New York Deli, Pizza Center, **Rijo Bravo**
S: Alexander, Cascade Restaurant (Embassy), Champs Americana, Cooker, Macaroni Grill

Lodg N: **Embassy Suites**

Med N: ✚ **St. Joseph's Urgent Care**

ATM N: Speedway

Other S: **Home Depot**

170 6 Mile Road

Gas S: Amoco(*), Mobil(*, CW)

Food N: **Max & Erma's**, **Seafood Tavern**, The Ground Round, Tremmor's Restaurant (Holiday Inn)
S: **Applebee's**, Charley's Grille, McDonald's, **Papa Vino's**, **Wendy's**

Lodg N: **Best Western**, Courtyard by Marriott, **Holiday Inn**, **Marriott**

Med N: ✚ **Hospital**

ATM N: Comericard, Michigan National Bank, NBD Bank
S: Standard Federal

Other N: **Laural Park Place Mall**
S: **Arbor Drugs**, **Farmer Jack's Supermarket**, **PetsMart**

172 I-275 South, MI 14 West

173A Newburgh Road

Food S: Cake & Bakery

173B Levan Road

Med N: ✚ **Hospital**

Other N: Madonna University

174 Farmington Road

Gas N: Mobil(*, D), Total(*)

Bill Knapp's Restaurant
Open daily at 11:00 am
Bill Knapp's is a casual, full service family restaurant where Motorcoaches are always welcome.
Over 50 locations throughout: Michigan • Ohio • Indiana
517-394-8338 - South Lansing
MICHIGAN • I-96 • Exit 104
1697

← W I-96

EXIT MICHIGAN

S: Amoco[*]
Food S: KFC, Mason's Lounge
Med S: **Lavonia Veterinary Hospital**
ATM S: Amoco

175 Merriman Road
Gas N: Mobil[*], Total[*, D]
S: Sunoco[*, D]
Food N: Tony Balony's Pizzaria
S: Blimpie's Subs, **Mountain Jack's Steakhouse**, Royal Coney Island Restaurant
AServ S: Randy's Collision
ATM N: Total

176 Middlebelt Road
Food N: **Bob Evan's Restaurant, Chi Chi's Mexican Restaurant, IHOP, Olive Garden**
S: Mesquite Junction Steakhouse
Lodg N: **Comfort Inn**
AServ N: Lavonia Brake Clinic & Auto Repair
S: Oil Dispatch
Med N: **Henry Ford Medical Center**
Other S: **Costco, Discount Pharmacy**, Ladbroke Detroit Race Center

177 Inkster Road
Food N: Baskin Robbins, Lavonia Danish Bakery, Murphy's Restaurant, Snookers' Pool & Pub, Subway
ATM S: Comerica Bank
Other N: **7-11 Convenience Store**[24]
S: **Jerusalem Food Market**, John's Mini Storage[LP]

178 Beech Daly Road
Gas N: Sunoco[*]

179 U.S. 24, Telegraph Road
Gas N: Marathon[*, D]
Food N: Church's Chicken, Lucky Lau Chinese, Oliver's Restaurant (Marathon), Taco Bell, White Castle Restaurant

EXIT MICHIGAN

Lodg N: Tel-96 Inn
AServ N: GM Geo Dealer, Goodyear Auto Center
ATM N: Cash Connection, First of America
S: Comericard
Other N: Darts & Billiards, **Express Pharmacy**

180 Outer Dr
Gas N: BP[*, D]
AServ N: BP
Other N: **Coin Laundry**[*, 24]

182 Evergreen Road
Gas N: Sunoco[*, D]
Food N: Sonny's Hamburgers
AServ N: Bill's Tires & Rims, Crafts Tower Auto Service, Earl Scheib Paint & Body

183 MI 39, Southfield Fwy

184 Greenfield Road
Gas N: Amoco[*], BP[*], Sunoco[*]
S: BP[*, D], Shell[*], Sunoco[*, D]
Food N: Greenfield Seli & Soul Food, Rikshaw Chinese, Subway (Amoco)
S: KFC, McDonald's, Rally's Hamburgers, Super Coney Island
AServ N: Greenfield, Midas Muffler & Brake, Sunoco, Tuffy Auto Center
S: Gardner's Auto Service, Greenfield Auto
Other N: **Giant Supermarket**, Mac Full-Service Car Wash
S: **Rite Aide Pharmacy**

187 Grand River Ave. (Eastbound)
Gas N: Amoco[*], Mobil[*], Shell[*, CW]
Food N: Capital Coney Island, China Dragon, McDonald's
S: Coney Island[24]
AServ N: Shell
S: H & R Tires, Joy's Tires, Lee's Tire Market, Parkes Garage, Three Stars Auto Repair & Service
TServ S: **American Motor Coach**

EXIT MICHIGAN

Med S: **Grand River Veterinary**
Other N: **Grand Auto Parts**, Hand Car Wash
S: Detroit Public Library, **Grand Price Food Center, Super Save**

186A Wyoming Ave
Gas N: Marathon[*] (A & W), Shell[*]
Food N: Asian Corned Beef Chinese & American Food, Tubby's Grilled Subs
AServ N: Shell

185 Grand View Ave., Schaefer Hwy.
Gas N: Amoco[*, 24], Mobil[*]
Food N: Capitol Coney Island Family Restaurant, **McDonald's**
AServ N: Grand Auto Repair
S: American Motor Coach, M & E Auto Enterprise
Other N: Good & Clean Hand Car Wash
S: Grand Crise Food Center

186B Davison Ave
Gas N: Marathon[*, D]

188A Livernois Avenue, West Chicago Dr.
Gas N: Mobil[*], Shell[*]
S: BP[*]
Food N: **Burger King**, KFC, McDonald's[PLAY], Wendy's, Young's BBQ
Other S: Full Service Car Wash

188B Joy Road
Food N: Capital One Coney Island, Church's Chicken, Famous Pizza

189 West Grand Blvd, Tireman Ave
Gas N: Amoco, Mobil[*]

190B Warren Ave

↑MICHIGAN

Begin I-96

CA99 S →

EXIT CALIFORNIA

Begin CA99

↓CALIFORNIA

316B Bus.80, Reno
316 US50 South Lake Tahoe; To I-80, I-5, CA 99, San Francisco, Redding
315 12th Ave., Sutterville Rd.
Gas E: Oak Park Market[*]
W: Shell[*]
Food E: Oak Park Market
W: Adalberto's[24], Keith's Patio, Yum Yum Donuts[24]
AServ W: Ellio's German Auto Repair, G & C Tire Service
Other W: **Food King Grocery Store, Launderland Coin Laundry**

313B M.L. King, Jr. Blvd, Fruitridge Rd.
Gas E: Shell[*]
W: Exxon[*]
Food E: Taco Bell[24]
W: El Michoacano, Jimboy's Mexican Fiesta, Kaballo Blanco Restaurante, La Mexicana Bakery, Rick's Hacienda Mexican, Wienerschnitzel
AServ E: Quality Tune Up Shop
W: A&E Auto Parts, L & M Tires, Roble's Muffler & Welding Shop, Shift Right Transmission, Sierra II Transmission, Stoops Auto Repair
Other W: ACE Hardware, Carniceria Lopez[*], **South Sacramento Pet Hospital, South Sacramento Pharmacy**[RX]

312 47th Ave.
Gas W: Arco[*, 24], Ferg's General Store[*], Star[*, D]

EXIT CALIFORNIA

Food E: East West Foods[*]
W: El Arawi Mexican, Pitts Stop Restaurant
Lodg E: South Pointe Inn and Suites
AServ E: Quality Muffler and Brake
W: NAPA Auto Parts, Pitts Stop Restaurant, Star
RVCamp W: **Stillman RV Park**
Other E: East West Foods
W: Fire Department, Jiffy Mart[*]

310 Florin Rd.
FStop W: **Pacific Pride (Credit Only)**
Gas W: 76[*, 24], Chevron[*, 24]
Food E: Denny's, South Villa Restaurant (Chinese/ Philippino)
W: Baskin Robbins, IHOP, Red Runner Pizza, Tahiti Cantonese Buffet
Lodg E: Super 8
AServ E: Jiffy Lube, Lasher VW, Audi, Dodge, Acura, Isuzu, Montgomery Ward, Sears
RVCamp E: **RV Travel World & Repair**
ATM W: Bank of America
Other E: **Florin Mall, Toys R Us**
W: **Home Depot**, Norge Laundry & Cleaning Village, Office Max

308 Mack Rd., Stockton Blvd., Bruceville Rd.
FStop E: **76**[*]
Gas E: Costco Wholesale Warehouse
W: 76, Arco[*], Shell[*, CW]
Food E: Jack-In-The-Box, Laguna, Original Perry's Steak, Taco Loco, Wendy's
W: Angel's Tacos, Burger King, Carl Jr's Hamburgers[PLAY], Chevy's Mexican, Denny's[24], Fat

EXIT CALIFORNIA

Duck's Pizza, I Love Teriyaki, Jim Boy's, KFC, LampPost Pizza, Lucky Donuts, McDonald's[PLAY], Mr. Perry's, Oriental Garden Buffet, Rincon Mexicano, Round Table Pizza, Sari Sari Store, Scuttlebutt Restaurant, Super Taco, Teriyaki Chicken Express
Lodg E: Gold Rush Inn, **Motel 6**, Motel 6
AServ E: **Jo Hill's Transmission & RV's**
TServ E: **Truck Stuff**
RVCamp E: **B & L Trailer Supply, Jo Hill's Transmission & RV's**
Med W: **Kaiser Permanente Hospital**
ATM W: **Food Source Grocery Store**, Wells Fargo
Other E: **Office Depot**, PetsMart
W: Big 5 Cinema, Coin Laundry, Discovery Zone, **Food Source Grocery Store, K-Mart, Long's Drugs**[RX], Optometrist, Rite Discount Market[*], **Target**, Valley Hi Pet Clinic

306 Cosumnes River Blvd, Calvine Rd.
Gas E: Texaco[*]
Food E: Baskin Robbins (Texaco), Blimpie Subs & Salads (Texaco)

305 Sheldon Rd.
RVCamp W: **99 Trailer Park RV (.25 Miles)**
Other W: S.K.M. Market[LP]

304 Laguna Blvd., Bond Rd.
Gas E: Shell[*]
Food E: Applebee's, Burger King[PLAY], IHOP, In-N-Out Hamburgers, Marie Callender's Restaurant, Me N Ed's Pizza, Taco Bell, The Original Mel's
ATM E: Patelco Credit Union
Other E: Mail Boxes Etc., **Raley's Grocery Store**, Staples

Bold red print shows RV & Bus parking available or nearby

EXIT CALIFORNIA

Office Superstore

302 Elk Grove Blvd.
- **Gas** E: Exxon[*], Shell[*, CW]
  W: 76[*, 24], Arco[*]
- **Food** E: Burger King[PLAY], Cassidy's Restaurant, Donut Queen, Hunan Garden, KFC, La Fuente, Mountain Mike's Pizza, Pizza Barn, Pizza Bell, Subway, Szechuan Kitchen
  W: Casa Gomez, Lyon's, **McDonald's (Wal-Mart)**, Pizza Hut, Sunflower, Sushi # Ichi
- **AServ** E: Goodyear Tire & Auto, Maita Chevrolet, Spee Dee Oil Change
- **ATM** E: **Lucky Grocery Store**
  W: The Golden 1
- **Parks** E: **Elk Grove Park**
- **Other** E: ACE Hardware, **Elk Grove Veterinary Hospital**, Golden State Express Car Wash[CW], **Lucky Grocery Store**, Optometry, **Rite Aid Pharmacy**[RX]
  W: **Almost Perfect Books**, **Pak 'N Save Foods**, **Wal-Mart**[RX] **(Vision Center)**

299 Grant Line Rd.
- **Gas** E: Arco[*]
- **Other** E: **Kamp's Propane**[LP]

298 Eschinger

297 Dillard Rd.

295 Arno Rd.

294B Frontage Rd. (Southbound, Reaccess Southbound Only)

294 Mingo Rd. (Northbound, Reaccess Northbound Only)

293 Jackson, CA104
- **Gas** E: Exxon[*, LP]
- **TServ** E: **Royer's Diesel Truck Repair**

292 Walnut Ave. (Northbound, Reaccess Northbound Only)

291 Ayers Ln., Pringle Ave.
- **Gas** W: **Galt**[*, LP, RV DUMP], Phil & Debi's Cheaper[*, D]
- **Lodg** W: Holiday Inn Express
- **AServ** W: Julian's Service Auto Repair
- **Other** E: Anykine Car Wash
  W: **Country Oaks Veterinary Hospital**, **U.S. Post Office**

290 Simmerhorn Rd. (Northbound)
- **Gas** E: Exxon
- **AServ** E: Cain Brothers Auto Service, Exxon

289 Central Galt
- **Gas** W: Exxon[*, D]
- **Food** W: Baskin Robbins (Exxon), Cafe Latte Co., Carl Jr's Hamburgers[PLAY], Chubby's, Denny's, Donuts, Golden Bell Chinese, Hunan House, La Hacienda, **McDonald's**[PLAY], Polar Bear Yogurt, Round Table Pizza, Subway, Taco Bell, Wholey Ravioli
- **AServ** W: Chief Auto Parts, Galt Super Lube
- **ATM** W: Farmers and Merchants Bank, **Save Mart Grocery Store**
- **Other** W: ACE Hardware, Books, Express Laundromat, Police Department, **Rite Aid Pharmacy**[RX], **Save Mart Grocery Store**, Tony's Car Wash

287C Fairfield Dr. (Southbound, Reaccess Southbound Only)

287B Crystal Way, Boessow Rd. (Northbound)
- **Food** E: Golden Acorn
- **Other** E: Dry Creek Ranch Golf Course

287 Liberty Rd.

286 Collier Rd.
- **Gas** W: Chevron[*, 24]
- **Food** W: Lay's (BBQ, Seafood, Steaks)
- **AServ** E: Pacific Auto Center
  W: Ron's Auto Service[LP]
- **Other** W: Collierville Country Store[*, LP]

285 Jahant Rd.
- **FStop** W: **Jahant Food & Fuel**[*, D, LP]
- **Food** W: **Jahant Food & Fuel**
- **Other** W: **Lodi Airport**

EXIT CALIFORNIA

284 Peltier Rd

283 Acampo Rd.

282 Woodbridge Rd.

281B Frontage Rd.
- **RVCamp** E: **Mokelumne Beach Resort & RV Park**

281 Turner Rd.

279 CA12E, Central Lodi, San Andreas
- **FStop** E: **Woolsey Oil Inc.**[D, 24]
- **Gas** E: Shell[*]
  W: 76[*], Beacon[*]
- **Food** E: Habanero Hots Mexican Restaurante
  W: Burger King, Express Doughnuts, Felten's Topaz, Franco's Pizza, The Back Bay, UJ's Family Restaurant
- **Lodg** W: Comfort Inn, Del Rancho Motor Inn, El Rancho Motel
- **AServ** E: Shell
  W: Big O Tires, Cherokee Radiator, Don's Muffler Service, **Lodi Tire**, Performance Automotive (AC Delco)
- **TServ** E: **Truck Accessories**
- **RVCamp** E: **Richard's RV Repairs**
- **Other** E: Fisco (Hardware)
  W: Aldee Market, U Haul[LP]

278 Fairfield, CA12W, Kettleman Ln.
- **Gas** E: 76[*]
  W: Arco[*], Chevron[*, CW]
- **Food** E: **McDonald's**[PLAY]
  W: Carrows Restaurant[24], Denny's, Perko's Cafe, Wendy's
- **Lodg** W: Economy Inn, Holiday Inn Express
- **AServ** E: Geweke Toyota
  W: Geweke Ford Mercury, PEP Boys Auto Parts & Service Center, Q-Lube, Sanborn Chevrolet
- **RVCamp** W: **Geweke RV Service**

277B Lodi, Rt. 99 Bus. (Northbound, Reaccess Southbound Only)
- **Gas** W: Quik Stop[*, 24]
- **Food** W: Omega Restaurant
- **AServ** W: Lodi Honda

277 Harney Ln.

276 Micke Grove Park
- **Parks** W: **Micke Grove Park**

274 Eight Mile Rd.
- **Gas** E: Chevron[*, 24]
- **Food** E: Morada Cafe

273 Morada Ln.

271 Hammer Lane
- **Gas** E: Arco[*]
  W: Shell[LP]
- **Food** E: Denny Boy's Restaurant, Wienerschnitzel
- **Lodg** E: **El Rancho Motel**
  W: Sunshine Inn
- **AServ** W: Shell
- **ATM** E: Wienerschnitzel

270 Frontage Rd.

269C Wilson Way, Central Stockton (Southbound, Reaccess Northbound Only)

269B Cherokee Rd.
- **Food** W: Carl's, **Donut Time**
- **TServ** E: **Goodyear Commercial Tire Center**
  W: **Cherokee Truck Parts**
- **Other** E: CA Highway Patrol
  W: Club Pet

269 Waterloo Rd., Jackson, CA88
- **FStop** W: **Cardlock Fuels**[*]
- **Gas** E: Chevron[*, 24], Ernie's General Store[*], Shell[*]
  W: Waterloo Food & Fuel[*]
- **Food** E: Best Western, Burger King[24], California Inn, Denny's[24] (Comfort Inn), McDonald's, Perko's Cafe, Subway, Taco Bell
- **Lodg** E: Best Western, California Inn, **Comfort Inn**, Guest Inn
- **ATM** E: Chevron, McDonald's
  W: **Cardlock Fuels**

Bold red print shows RV & Bus parking available or nearby

EXIT		CALIFORNIA
268B		Fremont St. East, CA26 , Linden
	TServ	**W:** Mack Diesel Truck Service
	Other	**E:** Dominion Market
268		CA4, West To I-5, Downtown Stockton (Limited Access Hwy)
267B		West Charter Way (Southbound)
267		Main St. (Northbound, Difficult Reaccess)
	Gas	**E:** Exxon(*), Quik Stop(*)
	Food	**E:** T's Drive-In, Wienerschnitzel
	Other	**E:** Buggy Bath Coin Car Wash, Fire Department
266		Farmington Rd, CA4
265		Escalon, Mariposa Rd.
	Lodg	**W:** Mission Motel
	TServ	**W:** Complete Diesel Repair
	Other	**W:** Campora Gas Service Inc.(LP), K-Mart
263B		Clark Dr. (Northbound, Reaccess Northbound Only)
	Other	**E:** Marine Engine
263		Arch Rd.
	FStop	**W:** Gas Card (Credit Only)
	Gas	**E:** Arco(*, 24), Citgo(*)
	Food	**E:** Burger King, Denny's, Jack-In-The-Box, Taco Bell
	ATM	**E:** Citgo
	Other	**W:** U.S. Post Office
262		Frontage Rd. (Northbound, Reaccess Northbound Only)
261		French Camp Rd.
	Food	**W:** French Camp RV Camp
	RVCamp	**W:** French Camp RV Camp
258B		Lathrop Rd.
	Gas	**W:** Exxon(*)
	AServ	**W:** JC Automotive, Rick's Automotive
258		Manteca (Southbound)
	Gas	**W:** Citgo(*)
	Food	**W:** Casper's, Taco Bell(24)
	AServ	**W:** Country Nissan
	Other	**W:** K-Mart, Valley Cinema
256		CA120E, Oakdale, Sonora, Yosemite Ave.
	Gas	**E:** 76(*), Arco(*)
		W: Exxon(*)
	Food	**E:** Brook's Ranch, Burger King, Lyon's(24), Wendy's
		W: Jimmy's Restaurant(24), Lu Lu's Mexican, McDonald's(PLAY), Rick's Donuts, Taqueria Mexican, Three Flames Pizza
	Lodg	**E:** Comfort Inn
		W: Best Western, Manteca Inn
	AServ	**E:** Curt Hughes Dodge, Five Star Muffler Express, Piskel's Auto Air and Radiator, Vern's Towing Inc.
		W: Tradeway Geo, Chevrolet
	RVCamp	**E:** Curt Hughes Dodge, Manteca Trailer & Camper Inc.
	ATM	**W:** McDonald's
	Other	**E:** Honda Power Equipment
		W: Big Boy, Manteca Bowl, Rancho Pharmacy, TG & Y, Wash Time Coin Laundry
255		CA120W, San Francisco, Manteca (Difficult Reaccess, Limited Access Hwy)
254		Austin Rd.
	Parks	**W:** Caswell State Park
252		Jack Tone Rd.
	TStop	**E:** Flying J Travel Plaza(*, LP, SCALES), Jimco Truck Plaza(*, SCALES)
	Food	**E:** Country Market (Flying J)
	TServ	**E:** Jimco Truck Plaza(SCALES)
	ATM	**E:** Flying J Travel Plaza
251B		Milgeo Ave (Northbound, Reaccess Northbound Only)
	FStop	**E:** Pacific Pride
	TServ	**W:** Howard's Truck Tire(24)
251		Ripon
	Gas	**E:** Chevron(*), Shell(*, LP, CW)
		W: Madsen's Sunrise Dairy(*)
	Food	**E:** The Barnwood Restaurant and Deli
		W: Christopaolo's, La Morenita Mexican, Main Street Inn, PaPa Gino's Pizza
	Lodg	**E:** Blue-Light Motel
	AServ	**E:** Chevron
		W: Ripon Auto Center, Ripon Auto Parts, Swier Tire Co. (NAPA Auto Parts)
	Other	**W:** Debbie's Pet Grooming & Supplies, FMC Aquablast Car Wash, Fire Station, King's Laundry, Ripon Veterinary Hospital
249		Hammett Rd.
247B		Riverbank Rd., Salida, CA219
	FStop	**W:** Boyett Petroleum(*) (Pacific Pride)
	Gas	**E:** 76(*, D)
	Food	**E:** Burger King(PLAY)
		W: Bobbie's Country Style Dinner, China Station Restaurant, La Hacienda Mexican, La Isla (Don Pedro Motel), La Salsa Taqueria & Deli, Lamichoacana Taqueria, Pizza Blast, Salida Donuts
	Lodg	**W:** Don Pedro Motel
	AServ	**W:** Bill's Air Cooled Engine Repair, Ocampo's Tires, Paul's Auto Repair, Salida Auto Parts (AC Delco)
	RVCamp	**W:** Valley RV Center
	ATM	**W:** Union Safe Deposit Bank
	Other	**W:** El Rancho Market & Deli, La Michoacana(*), Salida Fire Department, Salida Home Market(*), Salida Public Library, Salida Veterinary Hospital, U.S. Post Office
247		Pelandale Ave.
	Gas	**E:** Chevron(*), Exxon(*)
		W: Arco(*)
	Food	**E:** Carl Jr's Hamburgers, El Rosal Mexican, Foster's Freeze Jr., In-N-Out Hamburgers, Pizza Connection, Subway, Taco Bell, Yakitori Chinese/Japanese
		W: Del Taco(PLAY), McDonald's(PLAY)
	Lodg	**W:** Holiday Inn Express
	RVCamp	**W:** Dan Gamel Modesto RV Center
	ATM	**E:** Save Mart Grocery(RX)
	Other	**E:** Castle Books, One Stop Petcare Veterinarian, Rite Aid Pharmacy(RX), Save Mart Grocery(RX)
245		Beckwith Rd, Standiford Ave.
	Gas	**E:** 76(*, D, 24)
	Food	**E:** Baskin Robbins, Chuck E Cheese's Pizza, Coco's, Garcia's Jo Jo's, Hungry Hunter, KFC, Red Lobster, Wendy's
	AServ	**E:** Firestone Tire & Auto, Pro 10 Minute Oil Change
	ATM	**E:** Save Mart
	Other	**E:** Buddy's Mail Room, Cinemas, Julie's Books, Longs Drugs(RX), Office Max, Save Mart, Village Faire Mall
243		Carpenter Rd., Briggsmore Ave.
	Gas	**E:** Arco(*), Chevron(*, D), Shell(*, CW)
		W: 76(*)
	Food	**E:** Albertos Molcasalsa, Black Angus Steakhouse, Burger King(24), Denny's, Holiday Inn, IHOP, Imperial Garden (Chinese), Jack-In-The-Box, Maria's Taco Shop, Outback Steakhouse
	Lodg	**E:** Best Western, Holiday Inn, Motel 6, Ramada Inn, Super 8
	AServ	**E:** Chevron
		W: Econo Lube & Tune, Kragen Auto Parts
	Med	**E:** ✚ Hospital
	Other	**E:** Food Max, Police Station, Prime Shine Express Car Wash
241		Kansas Ave.
	Gas	**W:** Chevron(*)
	Food	**E:** Cafe Orleans, The Sandwich Shop
		W: Jack-In-The-Box, Pho Viet Chinese, The Bakery, The Early Dawn Cattle, The Pizza Pub
	Lodg	**E:** EconoLodge
		W: TraveLodge
	AServ	**E:** C & S Tire, Northern Tire & Wheel
		W: Kansas Ave. Auto Center
	Other	**E:** D-H Cycles (Suzuki)
		W: Carefree Laundry, Food 'N Save
240		CA108, CA132, San Francisco, Central Modesto, Maze Blvd.
	Gas	**W:** Arco(*)
	Food	**E:** Zavala's Restaurant(24)
	AServ	**W:** D's Tire Service
	Other	**W:** Launderland Coin Laundry, Leo's Market, Roger's Drugstore
239		Tuolumne Blvd., B Street
	Other	**E:** All Star Gas(LP)
		W: 9 Hole Municipal Golf Course
238		Crows Landing Rd.
	AServ	**E:** Mike's Mobile Auto Repair, Parts-R-Us
		W: Economy Tire Co.
237		South 9th St. (Northbound, Difficult Reaccess)
	Gas	**E:** Gas-N-Shop(*, LP)
	Lodg	**E:** Sea Breeze Motel
	AServ	**E:** California Auto Parts, Inc., Complete Auto Repair, Dan's Distributing Co., Quiet Masters Mufflers
	Other	**E:** C & C Marine
236		Hatch Rd.
	Gas	**E:** Chevron(*)
		W: Stop N' Save(*), USA(*)
	Food	**E:** Burger King, Del Hart's Family Dining, La Morenita Mexican, Long John Silver, McDonald's, Rico's Pizza, Scotty's Donuts, Taco Bell, Wendy's
		W: El Tapatio
	Lodg	**E:** Howard Johnson Express
	AServ	**E:** AAA Transmission Service, Big O Tires, Kragen Auto Parts, Quick Lube
		W: Far-Go Auto Parts (Big A), Larry's Tire Mart, Merry Motors
	TServ	**E:** Country Ford Trucks
		W: Larry's Tire Mart
	ATM	**E:** 7-11 Convenience Store
	Other	**E:** 7-11 Convenience Store, K-Mart, Launderland Coin Laundry
235		Whitmore Ave. (Northbound)
	Gas	**E:** Chevron(*)
	Food	**E:** Burrito King Taco Shop, KFC, Los Cazadores
	AServ	**E:** C & M Muffler & Brake
233B		Ceres, Whitmore Ave. (Left Exit Southbound)
	Gas	**E:** Curry's Market(*), Moon Gas(*), Shell(*), Texaco
	Food	**E:** Chivas Crudas (Mexican), Fifth Street Plaza Family Restaurant, Silva's Family Restaurant (Mexican)
	AServ	**E:** Texaco
	ATM	**E:** Curry's Market, Well's Fargo
	Parks	**E:** Whitmore Park
	Other	**E:** Ceres Drug
233		Mitchell Rd.
230		Keyes Rd.
229		Taylor Rd.
	Gas	**E:** Arco(*)
	Food	**E:** Eppie's
	Lodg	**E:** Best Western
	AServ	**E:** Patchetts Ford, Mercury
	TServ	**E:** Bonander Truck(SCALES)
	Other	**E:** Suburban Propane(LP)
228		Monte Vista Ave.
	Med	**E:** ✚ Hospital
227		Fulkerth Rd, Pedretti Park
	Gas	**E:** Shell(*, D, LP, CW)
	Food	**E:** Baskin Robbins, Burrito Villa, Chubby's, Del Taco, Espresso Ave., IHOP, McDonald's (Wal-Mart), Rico's Pizza, Sho Gun, Subway
	AServ	**E:** Balswick's Brake & Front End, Chief Auto Parts
		W: Turlock Auto Mall
	ATM	**E:** Wal-Mart
	Other	**E:** Book Gallery, Food Max(24), Staples Office Superstore, Wal-Mart
226		Patterson, W. Main St.
	Gas	**E:** 76(*)
		W: Arco(*)
	Food	**E:** Burger King(PLAY), Lyon's Family Dining(24)

Bold red print shows RV & Bus parking available or nearby

EXIT	CALIFORNIA
	W: Carl Jr's Hamburgers[PLAY], Dairy Queen, El Sombrero, Golden Dragon, McDonald's[PLAY], Taco Bell
Lodg	E: **Western Budget Motel**
	W: **Motel 6**
AServ	W: Toby's Auto Repair, Turlock Tire Co.
Med	E: **+ Hospital**
ATM	E: 76
224	Central Turlock, Lander Ave, Denair, Oakdale, CA165
Gas	E: Chevron[*, CW, 24], Quick Stop[*, 24]
	W: Arco[*, 24]
Food	E: Denny's[24], Jack-In-The-Box, Round Table Pizza, Subway
	W: **Almond Tree (Comfort Inn)**
Lodg	W: **Comfort Inn**
AServ	E: Kragen Auto Parts
	W: Evi's Tire Shop
Med	E: **+ Hospital**
ATM	E: **Save Mart**
	W: **Almond Tree (Comfort Inn)**
Other	E: Launderland Coin Laundry (Quick Stop), **Longs Drugs**[RX], **Save Mart**
(222)	Rest Area (RR, Phones, Picnic; Southbound)
(222)	Rest Area (RR, Phones, Picnic, Vending; Northbound)
222	Rt. 99 Bus, Golden State Blvd. (Northbound, Reaccess Southbound Only)
220	Merced Ave, Bradbury Rd.
219	Delhi, Shanks Rd.
(218)	Weigh Station (Southbound)
217	2nd Ave. South
216	Collier Rd, Hilmar
RVCamp	W: **Merced River RV Resort (.25 Miles)**
216B	Winton Pkwy.
216C	Hammatt Ave.
Food	W: **Almond Tree Restaurant**[24]
TWash	W: **Rocket Truck Wash**
Other	W: **Livingston Animal Clinic**
212	Hunter Rd.
211	Peach Ave, N. Sultana Ave.
211B	Arena Way
210	Cressey Way
209	Stein Rd.
208	Westside Blvd, Central Ave.
207	Grove Ave, Olive Ave.
206	Atwater (Southbound)
205	Applegate Rd.
Gas	E: Exxon[*], Gas-N-Save[*], Shell[*, D]
Food	E: Almond Tree, Golden Dragon (Chinese), KFC, La Troje (Mexican), Los Panchos (Mexican)
Lodg	E: Super 8, **Valley Motel**
AServ	E: Jack's R Better (Brakes), Lackey's Auto Care (NAPA)
Med	E: **+ Hospital**
Other	E: ACE Hardware, Broadway Laundromat, Carniceria La Mexicana, Olive Market[*], Optometrist, Pacheco's Car Wash, **U.S. Post Office**
	W: CA Highway Patrol
Exit	**(203)** CA 99 Bus, Atwater (Northbound, Difficult Reaccess)
Gas	E: 76[*, LP]
Food	E: Margarita O'Brien's, Tary Boscolo's Italian
Lodg	E: 99 Motel
AServ	E: Murray's Auto Repair
Other	E: **R-N Market**
203	Buhach Rd. (Left Exit Southbound)
AServ	E: Armstrong's Feed
RVCamp	E: **H&H Campers RV Parts and Service**[LP]
Other	E: Armstrong's Feed, **Castle Air Museum**, Castle Airport
201	Franklin Rd. (Northbound)
200	16th Street, Bus. CA99 (Southbound)

EXIT	CALIFORNIA
Food	W: Nagame Japanese
AServ	W: Leo's Garage
199	V Street, West CA140, North CA59, Gustine, Sonora
Gas	E: 76[*, 24], Shell
	W: Arco[*]
Food	E: Carl Jr's Hamburgers, Marie Callender's, Taco El 2 Hermanos
	W: Chester Fried Chicken (Guss & Nick's), Jack-In-The-Box, Pine Cone
Lodg	E: Gateway Motel, Motel 6, San Joaquin Motel, Siesta Motel, Slumber Motel
	W: Best Western
AServ	E: Advance Transmission Co., Banner Transmission Center, Courtesy Olds, Cadillac, Curtis Alignment & Balancing, Del's Auto Parts (CarQuest), Isenberg KIA, VW, Isenberg Motors Inc. (VW, Isuzu), John Roth Chevrolet, Merced Honda, Merced Toyota, Midas Muffler & Brake, Quick Lube 10 Min. Oil Change, Razzari Chrysler, Dodge, Razzari Ford & Mazda, Razzari Nissan
	W: Condell's Radiator & Muffler Service
Other	W: Guss and Nick's[*], Yosemite Harley Davidson
198	R Street
FStop	E: **Pacific Pride Commercial Fueling**
Gas	E: Exxon[*, D, LP], Gas-N-Save[*]
	W: Beacon[*], Shell[*]
Food	E: Apple Annie's Donuts, Betos Mexican, Leny's Italian Cafe, Restaurant Mexicano
	W: Denny's, La Morenta Mexican, McDonald's[PLAY]
Lodg	W: Motel 6
AServ	E: Chief Auto Parts, Costco Wholesale Warehouse, Winston Tires
Other	E: Costco Wholesale Warehouse, Feminine Fitness, **Save Mart, WalGreens Pharmacy**[RX]
	W: Rainbow Bakery Store
197	CA 59S, Los Banos, Martin Luther King Jr. Way
Gas	E: Shell[*, LP]
	W: Beacon[*], World[LP]
Food	E: Fiesta Mexicana, In-N-Out Hamburgers, KFC, Scotty's Donuts, Taco Bell, The Ranch, Wendy's
	W: Paseut Market (Oriental Food Center), Star Garden (Italian/Chinese)
AServ	E: Bob's Radiator, **C & S Motors**, Shell, Yang's Auto Repair
	W: Car Plus, Garza Tire Shop, Merced Auto Diesel & Electric, Performance Auto Repair
TServ	E: **C & S Motors**
Med	W: **+ Hospital**
Other	E: Merced Tower Sports
	W: Food Center, Stop-2-Save[*], U-Haul[LP]
Exit	**(196)** G Street (Northbound, Left Exit Southbound, Reaccess Southbound Only)
FStop	E: **Bartlett Petroleum**[CW, 24] **(Credit Only)**
Food	E: Bar B-Q Restaurant & Bakery, H & W Drive-In, Little Caesars Pizza, Maria's Taco Shop, Panaderia Olmos Bakery, Subway, Taco Bell
AServ	E: AAMCO Transmission
TWash	E: **Bartlett Petroleum**[CW] **(Credit Only)**
Other	E: Car Wash[CW], Fire Department, Lee's Merced Community Food Market, Merced Drug, Merced Power Sports
Exit	**(195)** 16th St. (Northbound, Difficult Reaccess)
Food	E: Maria's Taco Shop, Subway
Lodg	E: California Motel
AServ	E: Kragen Auto Parts
Other	E: Car Wash, Fire Department, Merced Drug
195	Mariposa, Yosemite, East CA 140
Gas	E: 76[*]
Food	E: Best Western, Carrows Restaurant, Domino's Pizza, Victoria's Restaurant
Lodg	E: Best Western, Days Inn, Happy Inn Motel,

EXIT	CALIFORNIA
	Holiday Inn Express, Sandpiper Motel, Sierra Lodge
AServ	E: Bob's Auto Works
Med	W: **+ Hospital**
194	Childs Ave, Motel Dr.
Gas	E: Beacon[*, D], Chevron[*, D, 24]
Food	E: Eagle's Nest (Ramada Inn), McDonald's, Mi Casa Cafe
Lodg	E: Ramada Inn, **Super 8**
AServ	W: Freitas Auto Wreckers & Parts
193	Gerard Ave, Frontage Rd. (Northbound, Reaccess Northbound Only)
Gas	E: Citgo[*]
Exit	**(192)** Mission Ave. (Northbound)
192	Healy Rd, Vassar Ave.
191	Harvard Ave, Yale Ave.
190	McHenry Rd.
189	Mariposa Way
188	Lingard Rd.
187	Pioneer Rd.
186	Worden Ave.
185	Le Grand Rd.
Exit	**(184)** Ranch Rd, Arboleda Dr.
183	Athlone Rd.
182	Buchanan Hollow Rd.
181	Sandy Mush Rd.
180	Yosemite Plainsburg Rd.
179	Harvey Pettit Rd.
TStop	W: **Diesel Country Truckstop**[*] **(Chuckwagon Coffee Shop)**
Food	W: Chuckwagon Coffee Shop
178	Vista Ave.
(178)	Weigh Station (Northbound)
176	Road 15 (Southbound, Reaccess Southbound Only)
177	Le Grand Ave
175	Ave. 26, CA233, Robertson Blvd, Chowchilla
FStop	W: **Shell**[*], **The Way Station**[*] **(Pacific Pride)**
Gas	W: Chevron[*, CW], Texaco[*, D, CW]
Food	E: Taco Bell
	W: Burger King, **Los Tejanos, McDonald's**[PLAY]
Lodg	W: **Days Inn**
AServ	E: Tom DuBose Chev, Olds
RVCamp	W: **Arena RV Park**
173	Ave. 24 1/2
172	Ave. 24
171	CA152, Los Banos, Gilroy (Left Exit Northbound)
170	Avenue 22 1/2, Fairmead
Food	E: Mammoth Orange Hamburgers[*]
169	Ave 19 1/2
168	Road 21 1/2
166	Avenue 20, Avenue 20 1/2
RVCamp	W: **U.S. RV**
164	Avenue 18 1/2
TStop	W: **Pilot Travel Center**[*, SCALES]
Food	W: **Dairy Queen (Pilot TS), Great American (Pilot TS), Subway (Pilot TS), Wendy's**
Lodg	W: Liberty Inn
TServ	W: **G & J Truck Sales, Kenworth, Schoettler Tire**
TWash	W: **G & S Truck Wash**
162	Avenue 17
161	Avenue 16
Gas	W: Shell
Food	W: Farnesi's
Lodg	W: Gateway Inn
AServ	E: Andy's Tire Shop
	W: Donovan Automotive, Shell
RVCamp	W: **RV Park & Mobile Home Park**
Other	E: **Suburban Propane**[LP]
160	Cleveland Ave.
Gas	E: Mobil[*, D, LP], Texaco[*]
	W: Chevron[*, 24]
Food	E: Baskin Robbins, Burger King, Carl Jr's Hamburgers[PLAY], Eppie's Restaurant, Hong Kong

Bold red print shows RV & Bus parking available or nearby

EXIT	CALIFORNIA
	Chinese, Jack-In-The-Box, KFC, Long John Silver, Mandy's Drive-Thru Burritos & Donuts, Mei Wah (Chinese), Subway, Wendy's
	W: Perko's Cafe
Lodg	**W:** Economy Motel
AServ	**E:** Kragen Auto Parts, Madera Toyota, Chev, Olds
ATM	**E:** World Savings
Parks	**E:** Rotary Park
Other	**E:** Longs Drugs, Madera 6, Save Mart, Wash & Dry Coin Laundry
	W: Madera County Fairgrounds, Madera Skate, Wal-Mart(RX) (Vision Center)
159	Central Madera, Fourth St.
Gas	**E:** 76(*, CW), BJ's Gas(*), Chevron(*), Harmin's
Food	**E:** Best Western, Lucca's Restaurant, Maria's Taco Shop, The Village Chinese American, Yum Yum Donuts
Lodg	**E:** Best Western
AServ	**E:** Auto Zone
Parks	**E:** Madera Park
Other	**E:** California AAA, Madera County Museum, Madera Wash Depot Coin Laundry, Police Department Headquarters, Public Library
157	Madera Ave, CA 145, Yosemite, Kerman, Firebaugh
FStop	**E:** Madera Petroleum(D) (Pacific Pride)
Gas	**E:** Stop N Save(*, LP), Texas Gold(*)
	W: Texaco
Food	**E:** El Ranchero Taco Shop, Mejia Taco Shop
	W: Burrito King, Carl Jr's Hamburgers, DiCicco's Italian, The Vineyard
Lodg	**E:** B&Z Motel
AServ	**E:** Madera Cars Unlimited Lube Center, Madera Ford, Mercury, Monterrey Tire Center, Pete's Front End Brake Service
	W: Texaco
Med	**E:** ✚ Hospital
ATM	**W:** 7-11 Convenience Store(*, 24)
Other	**E:** Gateway Car Wash, Gateway Market
	W: 7-11 Convenience Store, Coast to Coast Hardware, Grocery Outlet, Madera Ave. Market, Madera Medical Pharmacy(RX), Madera Veterinary Clinic, Rite Aid Pharmacy
156	Madera, Gateway Dr. (Northbound, Difficult Reaccess)
FStop	**E:** Tesei Petroleum(LP)
Gas	**E:** Beacon(*), Dixie Enterprises
Food	**E:** Rancho Madera Mexican
Lodg	**E:** Dixie Enterprises
AServ	**E:** Madera Automatic Transmissions
Med	**W:** ✚ Madera Community Hospital
154	Ave 12, Rd.29
Med	**W:** ✚ Hospital (2 Miles)
150	Ave 9, Rd 301/2
148	Ave 7, RD 33, Firebaugh
146	Herndon, Grantland Ave, Herndon Ave.
TStop	**E:** Kleins(*, LP, SCALES) (Texaco)
FStop	**E:** Chevron(*, 24)
	W: Shell(*, D, LP)
Food	**E:** Burger King (Kleins TS)
TServ	**E:** Kleins(SCALES) (Texaco), Trucker's Air (Chevron)
ATM	**E:** Chevron
Other	**E:** MP Truck Stop
144	Shaw Ave, Biola
Gas	**E:** Chevron(*, 24), Shell(*), Texaco(*, D, CW)
	W: 76(*), Parkway Mini Mart
Food	**E:** Carl Jr's Hamburgers(PLAY), In-N-Out Hamburgers, McDonald's(PLAY), Subway
Lodg	**E:** Economy Inns of America, Formosa Inn, Holiday Inn Express, Howard Johnson Express
	W: Comfort Inn
AServ	**E:** A & D Auto Parts (CarQuest), Shaw City Engines Auto Parts, Shell
ATM	**E:** Subway
Other	**E:** Harley Davidson of Fresno, Melody Market
	W: Peluso's Grocery, Pet Hospital
142B	Ashlan Ave.
Gas	**W:** Chevron(24), Citgo(*), Mobil(*)
Food	**E:** Foster's Freeze, Harvest Square, Jack-In-The-Box
	W: Brook's Ranch Restaurant (Ramada Inn)
Lodg	**W:** Ramada Inn
AServ	**E:** Johnson's Transmission Service
	W: Chevron(24)
ATM	**W:** Citgo
Other	**W:** Jack's Car Wash Co.(CW)
142	North Golden State Blvd. (Northbound, Difficult Reaccess)
141C	Dakota Ave. (Southbound, Reaccess Southbound Only)
Lodg	**W:** Astro Motel, Star Lite Inn
RVCamp	**W:** Sunset West Mobile Home Park & RV
141B	Shields Ave. (Southbound, Reaccess Southbound Only)
FStop	**W:** Beacon(*, LP)
Gas	**W:** Lupe's Cheaper(*)
Lodg	**W:** Knight's Inn, TraveLodge
RVCamp	**W:** Central Valley RV Outlet
141A	Princeton Ave. (Southbound, Reaccess Southbound Only)
AServ	**W:** John's Motorcycle & Auto Repair, Schoettler Tire
141	Clinton Ave
Gas	**E:** Beacon(*), Exxon(*)
	W: Arco(*, 24), Chevron(*)
Food	**E:** DiCicco's Italian, Pizza Hut, The Berrock Shop
	W: Fresh Doughnuts, Mountain Place Pizza, Romeo's Pizza, The Golden Room (TraveLodge), Trade Winds (Best Western)
Lodg	**W:** Best Western, Fresno Inn, TraveLodge
AServ	**E:** Good Guys Tire Center
	W: Shaw Auto Repair & Mufflers
Other	**E:** Coin Car Wash
	W: Cal Skate, Fresno Wash Station Coin Laundry, Iceoplex
140	McKinley Ave. (Northbound, Reaccess Southbound Only, Difficult Reaccess)
AServ	**E:** AR Transmissions, Ted's Automotive (NAPA)
RVCamp	**W:** Mike Eads RV Sales
139	Olive Ave.
Gas	**E:** Chevron(*, 24)
	W: 76(*, 24)
Food	**E:** Taco Bell(24), Tiny's Olive Branch(24) (Best Western)
	W: Denny's, Donut Queen, KFC, McDonald's, Parkway Inn, Rally's Hamburgers (76), Wendy's
Lodg	**E:** Best Western
	W: DAYS INN Days Inn, Motel 6, Parkway Inn, Plaza Inn, Super 8
AServ	**W:** Bruce's Auto Supply
RVCamp	**W:** Parkview Mobile Home Park
Parks	**E:** Roeding Park
Other	**E:** Chaffee Zoo, Highway Patrol
	W: Veterinary Service
138	Belmont Ave, North Motel Drive
Gas	**W:** Arco(*), Texaco(*, D, LP, 24)
Food	**E:** Judi-Ken's Drive-in
	W: Triangle Drive-In
Lodg	**W:** Best Budget Inn, EconoLodge, Motel 6, Palm Court Inn, Rodeway Inn, Villa Motel, Welcome Inn
AServ	**W:** Texaco(24)
Parks	**E:** Roeding Park
Other	**E:** The Chaffee Zoological Gardens
Exit	**(137)** North To CA41 (Limited Access Hwy)
135B	CA180W, Fresno St., Mendota
Gas	**E:** Citywide Automotive(CW)
	W: 76(*), Shell(*, 24)
Food	**E:** Chihuahua (Mexican), Rally's Hamburgers
	W: Domino's Pizza, Frank & Ed's BBQ, KFC, Sal's Donut House, Triple Burger, Wendy's
Lodg	**E:** Hotel D'Italia
AServ	**E:** Citywide Automotive, Mac's Garage, Regio's Tire Shop
	W: Chief Auto Parts, Liberty Auto Service
ATM	**E:** Bank Of America
Other	**E:** Fire Department, Fresno Metropolitan Museum, Mercado Market, Payless Supermarket
	W: Launderland Coin Laundry
135	CA180E, Ventura St., Kings Canyon
Gas	**E:** Beacon
AServ	**E:** Blue's Auto
134	CA 41, Yosemite, Millerton Lake National Park (Difficult Reaccess, Limited Access Hwy)
133	CA41S, Jensen Ave
FStop	**E:** 76(*, D, SCALES, 24) (Pacific Pride)
	W: Texaco(*)
Gas	**E:** Shell(*, 24)
Food	**E:** Carl Jr's Hamburgers, Denny's, In-N-Out Hamburgers, KFC, McDonald's(PLAY), Taco Bell(24), Wendy's
	W: Subway (Texaco)
Lodg	**E:** Economy Inns of America, Travelers Inn
AServ	**E:** Jensen Pull & Save Recycling
	W: Corvette's Unlimited, Valley Tire Company
TServ	**E:** Central Valley Trailor Repair
	W: Central Valley Truck Center
131	Cedar Ave, North Ave.
FStop	**W:** Bryant Pacific Pride
TServ	**E:** Sierra Nevada Truck Repair
	W: Ry-Den Diesel Inc.
TWash	**E:** Western Truck Wash
129	Chestnut Ave, Malaga (Northbound)
Gas	**E:** Arco(*, 24), Shell(*, 24), Texaco(*)
Food	**E:** Far West Station Restaurant, The Brook's Ranch
TServ	**E:** Fresno Truck Center(24), Golden State Peterbilt, CAT, Cummins, Detroit Diesel, Valley Truck Parts & Equipment
TWash	**E:** Fresno Truck and RV Wash
RVCamp	**W:** Dan Gamel's RV Service, Paul Evert's RV
Other	**E:** Central Car Wash(CW)
128	American Ave, Del Rey (Southbound, Reaccess Northbound Only)
Gas	**W:** Arco(*), Texaco(*)
Food	**E:** Aldo's, El Unico, Judi-Ken's Drive In, Triangle Burger, Will's Texas BBQ
Lodg	**W:** Motel 6
AServ	**W:** Custom Tech, Texaco
126	Clovis Ave.
Gas	**W:** Texaco(*, D, LP)
125B	Adams Ave, Fowler (Southbound)
125	Merced St., Fowler
FStop	**W:** Wright Oil Company(LP)
Gas	**E:** Exxon(*), Zip-N-Go(*)
AServ	**E:** R & R Repair Shop
ATM	**E:** Zip-N-Go
Other	**E:** Fowler Car Wash
123	Manning Ave, Reedley, San Joaquin
FStop	**E:** Texaco(*, SCALES)
Food	**E:** Taqueria El Mexicano
120	Floral Ave, Highland Ave, South CA43, Hanford, Corcoran
FStop	**W:** Pacific Pride(*)
Gas	**E:** 76(*), Chevron(*, CW), Shell(*, D, CW)
	W: Mobil(*, D)
Food	**E:** Ann's Donuts, Brooks Ranch Coffee Shop, Carl Jr's Hamburgers(PLAY), China Garden, El Conquistador (Mexican), McDonald's(PLAY), Me-N-Ed's Pizza, Poppa Murphy's Pizza, Rosa's Pizza, Subway, Taco Bell(24), Wendy's
	W: Andersen's, Baskin Robbins, Burger King(PLAY), McDonald's (Wal-Mart), Pizza Hut
Lodg	**E:** Best Western, Super 8
	W: Holiday Inn
AServ	**E:** Chief Auto Parts, Royal Buick, Pont, Olds, GMC Trucks, Selma Toyota, Swanson-Fahrney Ford

Bold red print shows RV & Bus parking available or nearby

EXIT CALIFORNIA

W: Selma Auto Mall (Chev, Hyundai, Mazda, Honda, Itasca, Vectra, Fleetwood), **Wal-Mart**(RX)
TServ W: **Pacific Pride**
RVCamp E: **RV World Parts & Service**
Other E: **Rite Aid Pharmacy**(RX), **Save Mart**, Selma Cinema
W: **Wal-Mart**(RX)

119 Second St.
Gas E: Beacon(*)
W: Exxon(*), PDQ(*)
Food E: El Campesino, Wilkin's Root Beer Drive-In
AServ E: Auto Zone, Danny's Radiator, Ernie's Chevron Fast Lube, Floyd's Auto Parts (CarQuest), NAPA Auto Parts, Ono's Auto Repair, Tire Shop Tune Up Service(LP)
Med E: ✚ **Hospital**
Parks E: **Berry Park**(PLAY)
Other E: Andy's Car Wash, Family Market, Mr. Lee's Hand Car Wash

117 Mt. View Ave, Caruthers
FStop E: **Darling Oil And Tire**
Gas W: Arco(*, LP)
AServ E: **Darling Oil And Tire**
Other E: Selma Flea Market(SCALES)

116 Bethel Ave, Kamm Ave
RVCamp E: **Viking RV Park**

(114) CA Welcome Center (Located At Exit 114 On the South Side)

114 Conejo, CA 201
Gas E: 76(LP), Chevron(*, LP, CW)
W: Arco(*), Texaco(*, 24)
Food E: Denny's(24), Kady's Kitchen, Pub-N-Sub, The Valley Inn
W: Bobby Salazar's Mexican, Burger King(PLAY), Jack-In-The-Box, **McDonald's**(PLAY), Perko's Cafe, Subway, Swedish Mill (Swedish Inn), Taco Bell
Lodg E: **Jan Lin Motel**
W: Swedish Inn
AServ E: 76
ATM E: 76
Other E: Coin Car Wash, Kingsburg Feed Station (Pet Food), **Kingsburg Veterinary Clinic**
W: **Big K-Mart**, **Kings Market and Deli**

112 Kingsburg, Sanger
Gas W: Shell(*)
Food W: Miranchito Authentic Mexican

(111) Rest Area (RR, Phones, Picnic, Vending; Located At Exit 111 On the East Side)

111 Ave. 384, Rest Area
FStop E: **Exxon**(*, 24)
Food E: **A & W Drive-In**, **Angie's Restaurant (Mexican)**, Restaurante y Taqueria
Lodg E: King's Inn Motel
RVCamp W: **Riverland RV Park**

Exit **(108)** Merritt Dr, Traver
Gas E: Shell(*)

108 Traver (Northbound)
Gas E: Texaco(*)
Food E: Valley Farms
Other E: Valley Farms

106B Betty Drive, Goshen
FStop W: **Texaco**(*, SCALES)
Gas E: Exxon(*)
W: Arco(*)
Lodg W: **Goshen Motel**
TWash W: **Texaco**
RVCamp E: **Visalia RV Sales & Service**(LP)
W: **The Wooden Shoe**
Other E: Friendly Market

Goshen, Ave 304

EXIT CALIFORNIA

Exit **(104)** West CA198, Hanford, Lemoore

104 CA 198E, Visalia, Sequoia Park, Dinuba, Reedley (Divided Hwy)

102 Ave. 280, Exeter, Farmersville

98 Tagus (Northbound)
Lodg E: **Friendship Inn**

97B Tulare, J Street (Southbound)

97A Oaks St. (Northbound, Reaccess Northbound Only)
RVCamp E: **The Magic Touch Rec. Vehicles**

97 Cartmill Ave.

94 Hillman St., Prosperity Ave
Gas E: Chevron(*, CW)
W: 76, Exxon(*)
Food E: Carl Jr's Hamburgers, Haru Japanese Food, Long John Silver, **McDonald's (Wal-Mart)**, Me N Ed's Pizza, Moe's To Go Subs, Taco Bell
W: Apple Annie's, Baskin Robbins, Burger King, Denny's, KFC, McDonald's(PLAY), Pizza Hut, Senor Taco, Subway, Time Out Pizza
Lodg E: Green Gable Inn
W: Best Western, Inns Of America, Motel 6
AServ E: **Wal-Mart**(RX) **(Vision Center)**, Winston Tires
W: Kragen Auto Parts
Med W: ✚ **Tulare Medical Center**
ATM E: Chevron
W: **Lucky's**, Union Bank of California
Other E: **Big K-Mart**(RX), Horizon Outlet Center Tulare, **Longs Drug Store**(RX), **Wal-Mart**(RX) **(Vision Center)**
W: **Lucky's**, Mail Boxes Etc., Rite Aid Pharmacy

93 Lindsay, Central Tulare, CA 137, Visalia
Gas E: Fastrip(*), Texaco(*)
W: Shell(*, LP, 24), Texaco(*, D, 24)
Food E: D'Oliveiras International Cuisine, Donut Factory, Foster's Freeze, Giro's Pizza, Hong Kong Chinese, Morgan's House of Donuts, Wimpy's Hamburgers
W: Ryan's Place, Wendy's
AServ E: Auto Oil Changers, **Bowser & Sons, Auto, Truck, & RV**, Kenny's Tire
W: Auto Zone, Howell's Service Center, Shell(24)
RVCamp E: **Bowser & Sons, Auto, Truck, & RV**
ATM E: Step-Up Market
Other E: K-9 Kuts, Launderland Coin Laundry, Step-Up Market, Touch Free Car Wash(CW)

92 Bardsley Ave.
FStop W: **Exxon**
Gas E: Circle K(*)
AServ W: Auto Parts, **Exxon**
TWash E: **BJ's Car and Truck Wash**(CW)
ATM W: **R-N Market**
Other E: **BJ's Car and Truck Wash**
W: **R-N Market**

90 Paige Ave.
FStop E: **Exxon**(*)
W: **Mobil**(*) **(Pacific Pride)**
RVCamp E: **Tulare RV Park**

89 Tulare, K Street (Northbound, Left Exit Northbound, Difficult Reaccess)
TWash W: **Truck Tub Truck Wash**

85 Ave. 200
Gas W: Chevron(*, 24)
Food W: **Country Cafe**(24), **Lyn's Cafe**
Lodg W: **Agri-Center Motel**
RVCamp W: **Sun N Fun RV Park**

83 Ave. 184

(82) Rest Area (RR, Picnic, Vending; Southbound)

(82) Rest Area (RR, Picnic, Vending; Northbound)

79 Ave. 152
Gas E: Chevron(*, CW)
Food E: My Brothers Place

78 CA190, Tipton, Porterville, Corcoran

75 Ave. 120

Pixley (Southbound)

EXIT CALIFORNIA

Gas W: Exxon(*)
Food W: Coffee Shop, Ritchie Z's
Other W: Coin Car Wash

74 Rd.124 (Northbound, Reaccess Northbound Only)
Food E: 3 Bro's Burgers
AServ E: Barajas Autos
Parks E: **Pixley Park**(PLAY)

73 Unnamed (Northbound)
FStop E: **USA**(*)

72 Court St, Pixley
FStop E: **Bob's Auto Truck Stop**(*, LP), **U.S.A.**(*)
Gas W: Exxon(*)
Food E: **El Sarape**
W: Mary's Donuts
AServ W: Pixley Auto Parts, Soto's Auto Repair
RVCamp E: **Park Drive RV & Mobile Home Park**
Other E: Fire Department
W: Pixley General Store(*), Sparkling Clean Car Wash(CW)

71 Pixley, Terra Bella, Ave. 96
Gas E: Texaco(*)
W: Shell(*, LP)
Food E: Mr. Suds Burger Bunch
Lodg W: Butler Motel
AServ E: C & F Auto Repair, J & W Tire Service

68 Ave. 72 (Southbound)

67B Ave. 72, Ave. 76

67 Ducor, Alpaugh
Gas W: Terrible Herbst
Parks W: **Colonel Allensworth State Historic Park (9 Miles)**

64 Earlimart, Ave. 48
Gas E: Chevron, Fastrip, Fastrip(*)
Food E: La Princesa Bakery, M & B Drive-In, Mendoza's Bakery, Taqueria Jalisco
AServ E: Baeza Service Station, Chevron
W: Discount Auto Parts (CarQuest)
Other E: Earlimart Market(*)

61 Ave. 24 (Difficult Reaccess)

60 Ave. 16 (Southbound, Reaccess Southbound Only)
FStop W: **Shell**(*, SCALES)
Lodg W: **Motel**

58 County Line Rd.
FStop W: **Exxon**(*, D)
Gas E: Arco(*, 24)
Food E: Burger King(PLAY), Fruit Tree Cafe, Jack-In-The-Box, Kong's Dynasty (Chinese/American)
Lodg E: Comfort Inn, Shilo Inn
Other E: **Big K-Mart**

57 Cecil Ave. (Difficult Reaccess)
Gas E: Deli Mart
W: Arco(*), Chevron(*, 24)
Food E: Cuckoo Inn, Taqueria's Das Compadres
W: Antojitos Mexicanos, Nuevo Taco-Mex
Lodg W: Sundance Inn
AServ E: Delano Tire Shop, Transmission Center
W: Texaco Express Lube
ATM W: Chevron
Other E: Floyd's General Store (Hardware)
W: Coin Car Wash(CW)

56 CA 155, Central Delano, Glennville (Difficult Reaccess)
Gas E: Chevron(*), Fast Trip(*)
W: Texaco(*, D, CW)
Food E: El Palenque Mexican, Jenny's Cafe, Maria's Restaurant, Pagoda Restaurant, People's Cafe #2 (Mexican), Rancho Grande Cafe
W: Rosa's Bakery
Lodg E: Motel Rayado
AServ E: Pacific Tires #6, Tino's Auto Repair
Other W: **Jimenez Market**, **Komoto Pharmacy**, Mercado Latino #2

Exit **(55)** Alta Sierra (Southbound, Difficult

EXIT CALIFORNIA

Reaccess)

55B First Ave. (Northbound, Difficult Reaccess)
- **Lodg** E: Hal Mar Inn
- **AServ** E: Sangera Pontiac, Buick, Cad, GMC
- **Other** E: AmeriGas[LP], Delano Propane[LP]

55 Delano Ave, Rt. 99 Bus, Airport, Woollomes Ave.
- **FStop** W: Exxon[*]
- **Food** E: Aldo's
  W: Pioneer Restaurant
- **Lodg** W: Pioneer Motel
- **Med** E: + Hospital
- **Other** E: Delano Municipal Airport

53 Pond Rd., Lake Woollomes

Exit **(50)** Perkins Ave, Elmo Hwy. (Northbound, Difficult Reaccess)

Exit **(50)** Perkins Ave, Elmo Hwy. (Southbound, Difficult Reaccess)
- **Gas** W: Texaco[*, D]
- **Food** W: Callahan's Country Cafe
- **Lodg** W: National 9 Inn
- **AServ** W: LA Tires, Ramirez Moffles Shop
- **TServ** W: Dave's Truck and Tire Repair[SCALES, 24]

49 McFarland, Sherwood Ave. (Difficult Reaccess)
- **Gas** W: Chevron[*]
- **Food** W: El Rey Torito, Golden Oven Bakery, Mariscos Mexican, McDonald's, Sno-White Drive-In
- **AServ** W: NAPA Auto Parts
- **ATM** W: Chevron

47 Whisler Rd.

44 CA 46, Wasco, Paso Robles, Famoso
- **Gas** E: Chevron[*], Mobil[*]
- **Food** E: Famoso Inn (Chevron)
  W: Cafe
- **Lodg** E: Famoso Inn (Chevron)

41 Kimberlina Rd.

39 Merced Ave.
- **TStop** E: Flying J Travel Plaza[*, LP]
- **Food** E: Burger King[PLAY], The Cookery (Flying J TS)

37 Shafter, Lerdo Hwy, Shafter Airport
- **RVCamp** W: Camping

31 7th Standard Rd.
- **AServ** W: 7th Standard Tire Service
- **TServ** W: Bakersfield Truck Center (Freightliner)

30 North CA 65, Porterville, Sequoia Park (Northbound)
- **Gas** E: Arco[*], Texaco[*, D, 24]
- **Food** E: Airport Deli

29 Norris Rd, Oildale (Southbound)

28 Olive Dr.
- **Gas** W: Chevron[*, CW, 24], Citgo[*], Shell[*, 24], Texaco[*, D, CW]
- **Food** E: Los Tacos (Mexican), Sonic Drive-in
  W: Burger King[PLAY], Hodel's, Jack-In-The-Box, Milt's Coffee Shop[24], Mom's Donut Shop, Rusty's Pizza Parlor, Taco Bell, The Old Hacienda (Mexican)
- **Lodg** W: E-Z 8 Motel, Economy Motels of America, Motel 6
- **ATM** W: Bank of America, Vons Grocery[24, RX]
- **Other** E: Airport Veterinary Hospital, Hand Car Wash[CW]
  W: Fire Department, Launderland Coin Laundry, Olive Drive Car Wash[CW], Vons Grocery[RX]

27 Northbound: Oildale, Airport Dr. Southbound: Bakersfield, CA 204, Golden State Ave.
- **FStop** E: Commercial Fueling Network (Credit Only)
- **Gas** E: Exxon[*]
- **Food** E: Parks Place Cafe (Oxford Inn)
- **Lodg** E: Oxford Inn
- **AServ** E: Electric Motor Repair
- **Other** E: Meadows Field Airport (1.5 Miles)

EXIT CALIFORNIA

Exit **(26)** Pierce Rd. (Northbound, Reaccess Northbound Only)
- **FStop** E: Beacon[*]
- **Food** E: Zingo's Cafe
- **AServ** E: Tire Warehouse[24]
- **TWash** E: Beacon
- **Other** E: Home Base

26 WCA58, ECA178, Downtown, Rosedale Hwy.
- **FStop** W: Texaco[*]
- **Gas** E: Arco[*], Shell, Texaco
  W: Shell[*]
- **Food** E: Arby's, Burger King, Denny's[24], IHOP, Tanuki Japanese, The Junction Dinner Lounge (Best Western)
  W: Anderson's Black Angus, Carl Jr's Hamburgers, Cookies By Design, Days Inn, Hungry Hunter, Sushi Kato, Sutter Street (Ramada Inn), Taco Bell[24]
- **Lodg** E: Best Western, E-Z 8 Motel, La Quinta Inn, Road Runner Motel
  W: Courtyard by Marriott, Days Inn, Double Tree Hotel, Ramada Inn
- **AServ** E: Chuck's Automotive, Shell
- **TServ** W: Valley Detroit Diesel, Allison
- **ATM** E: Arco
- **Other** E: Buck Owens' Crystal Palace, Quick N Clean Car Wash
  W: 24 Hr. Fitness, Ice Palace

25 Convention Center, California Ave, Civic Center
- **Gas** E: Arco[*], Chevron[*, 24], Circle K[*]
  W: Shell[*, 24], Texaco[*, D, 24]
- **Food** E: Carrows Restaurant, Herrero Mexican, Jack-In-The-Box, John's Burgers, Taco Bell, Yen Ching (Hampton Inn)
  W: Baskin Robbins (Texaco), Carl Jr's Hamburgers[PLAY], Carrows Restaurant[24], Marie Callender's Restaurant, McDonald's, Regency Lanes (TraveLodge), Roxanne's, Sizzler Steak House, Taco Fresco, Wendy's[SCALES]
- **Lodg** E: Best Western, Extended Stay America, Hampton Inn, Quality Inn
  W: California Inn, Motel 6, Radisson Suites Inn, Residence Inn, Super 8, TraveLodge
- **AServ** E: Jiffy Lube, Oak Lane Automotive, RNZ Imports Inc. Merc, BMW, Volvo, Acura, VW, Honda, Sir Lube
  W: Shell[24], Texaco[24], Three-Way Chevrolet, GM
- **Med** E: + Hospital
- **ATM** W: Home Savings Of America
- **Other** E: Camelot Park Family Fun Center
  W: Barnes & Noble Booksellers

24B Stockdale Hwy, Brundage Lane
- **Gas** E: Mobil[*]
  W: Citgo[*]
- **Food** E: Donna Kaye's Cafe, JB & Marie Chalet Basque Restaurant, KFC, Panda Palace
  W: Foster's Freeze, Shakeys Pizza
- **AServ** E: Carroll's Tire Warehouse, Econo Lube & Tune, Goodyear Certified Auto Service, Midas Muffler & Brake, Specialty Honda Car Repair, Tire Man Bridgestone
  W: Stockdale Auto Electric
- **ATM** W: Citgo
- **Other** E: El Tejon Drugstore[RX], Southwest Veterinary Hospital, Young's Marketplace

HOLIDAY RV SUPER STORES 1244
1-800-RV-FOR-FUN
Bakersfield, CA • Hwy. 99 • Panama La...

EXIT CALIFORNIA

W: Launderland Coin Laundry

24 Jct. 58E, Tehachapi, Mojave (Limited Access Hwy)

23 Ming Ave.
- **Gas** E: Arco[*]
  W: 76[*, D], Texaco[D]
- **Food** E: IHOP, Jack-In-The-Box, Rusty's Pizza, Taco Rey
  W: Brinks Deli, Chuck E Cheese's Pizza, Foster's Donuts, Grand China, Long John Silver, Magoos Pizza, Teriyaki Bowl, The Bagelry, Wendy's
- **Lodg** W: Garden Suites Inn
- **AServ** E: Sears
  W: Kragen Auto Works, Sangera Autohaus Mercedes, Texaco
- **ATM** E: Arco, Bank of America, Home Savings Of America
  W: Bank of America
- **Other** E: Lens Crafters, Michael's (Crafts), Target, Valley Plaza (Mall)
  W: Office Max, Rite Aid Pharmacy[RX], Toys R Us

21 White Ln., Wible Rd.
- **Gas** E: Chevron[*, 24], Mobil[*], Shell[*, CW], Texaco[*, D]
  W: Arco[*], Mobil[CW]
- **Food** E: Burger King, California Pizzeria 'N' Chicken, Denny's, Lee's Chinese, McDonald's[PLAY], Rally's Hamburgers
- **Lodg** E: Comfort Inn, Motel 6, Motel 777
- **AServ** W: Auto Crafters, Discount Tire Center, Southern Auto Supply (CarQuest), Victory Lane Quick Oil Change
- **ATM** W: Arco

20 Panama Ln.
- **Gas** E: Chevron[*, LP], Texaco[*, D]
  W: Arco[*, 24]
- **Food** E: Denny's, In-N-Out Hamburgers, Jack-In-The-Box
- **Lodg** E: Economy Motels of America
- **AServ** E: Kragen Auto Parts
- **ATM** E: Texaco
- **Other** E: Home Base Hardware
  W: Holiday RV Super Store (.5 Miles) (see our ad this page)

18 CA 119W, Taft, Lamont
- **FStop** W: Mikuls Diesel[*, SCALES]
- **Gas** W: Mobil[*, D, LP], Texaco[*, LP, CW]
- **RVCamp** E: Leisure Times RV Repair, Southland RV Park
- **ATM** W: Mobil

16 Houghton Rd., Weed Patch

13 Bear Mountain Blvd., Arvin, CA223
- **FStop** W: Bear Mountain Truck Stop[*, LP, SCALES]
- **Food** E: Beryl's Cafe
  W: Harvest Steak House

10 Union Ave., Greenfield, Rt.99 Bus. (Northbound, Reaccess Southbound Only)

9 Herring Rd.

7 Sandrini Rd.

5 David Rd., Copus Rd.

4 Mettler (Southbound, Reaccess Southbound Only)
- **FStop** W: Pacific Pride[*]
- **Gas** W: Wadkins Market[*]
- **Food** W: Day and Night Market & Restaurant (Mexican/American)
- **Other** W: Farm Fresh Country Store & Fruit Stand

3 CA166, Maricopa, Taft
- **FStop** W: Chevron[*, SCALES, 24], Texaco[*, SCALES]
- **Food** W: Laminita Mexican, Subway (Texaco)
- **AServ** W: Chevron[24]
- **TServ** W: Chevron[SCALES, 24]

0 Jct. I-5

↑CALIFORN...

EXIT	KANSAS
	Begin I-135

↓KANSAS

95AB Junction I-70, US 40E to Topeka, Hays
93 KS 140, State St. Rd.
RVCamp E: Diesel Equipment Specialists, Inc. (1.6 Miles)
92 Crawford Street
TStop W: Phillips 66(*, SCALES)
FStop E: Texaco(*, SCALES)
Gas E: Kwik Shop(*), Texaco(*)
Food E: Anchor Room (Mexican), Beijing Chinese, Blimpie Sub & Salads (Texaco), Braum's Ice Cream & Breakfast, Hickory Hut BBQ, Holiday Inn, Panda's Chinese Restaurant, Russell's Restaurant Family Dining, Spangles, Taco Bell, Western Sizzlin'
W: Red Coach Restaurant & Motel (Phillips 66)
Lodg E: Best Western, Comfort Inn, Fairfield Inn by Marriott, Holiday Inn, Super 8
W: Red Coach Restaurant & Motel (Phillips 66)
TServ W: Phillips 66(SCALES)
Med E: + Hospital
ATM W: Phillips 66
90 Magnolia Road
89 Schilling Road
Gas W: Casey's General Store(*)
Food E: Applebee's, McDonald's (Wal-Mart), Pizza Hut, Red Lobster
Lodg E: Hampton Inn
AServ E: Sam's Club, Wal-Mart(RX)
Med E: + Hospital
ATM E: First Bank Kansas
Other E: Sam's Club, Wal-Mart(RX)
88 9th Street, Schilling Road
86 KS 141, KS 4 East, Herington, Smolen, Gypsum, Mentor
82 KS4 East, Assaria, Salun Road
78 Bus. U.S. 81, KS 4, Lindsborg, Bridgeport
Gas E: Texaco(*)
Food E: Dairy Queen (Texaco)
RVCamp W: Camping
Parks W: Coronado Heights Park
Other W: Old Mills Museum, Sandzen Art Gallery
72 Lindsborg, Roxbury
Other E: Maxwell Wildlife Refuge, McPherson State Fishing Lake
(68) Rest Area (RR, Picnic, RV Dump, P; Left Exit Both Directions)
65 **(61)** Pawnee Road
60 U.S. 56, Bus. U.S. 81, McPherson, Marion
FStop W: Conoco(*)
Gas W: Phillips 66(*, D, CW)
Food W: Arby's, Best Western, Braum's Ice Cream & Dairy Store, Happy Chef Restaurant, Hunan Chinese, KFC, McDonald's(PLAY), McDonald's (Wal-Mart), Perkin's Family Restaurant, Pizza Cafe, Pizza Hut, Sirloin Stockade, Subway, Taco Tico
Lodg W: Red Coach Inn, Super 8
AServ W: Auto Zone Auto Parts, John's Motor Service(CW), Lacy-Regehr Ford, Mercury, and Lincoln, Wal-Mart(RX)
RVCamp E: Kansas Kampers Service
W: Mustang Mobile Park (1.5 Miles)
Med W: + Hospital
ATM W: The Farmer's State Bank
Other W: Wal-Mart(RX)
58 KS 61, Hutchinson
54 Elyria (Difficult Reaccess)
48 KS 260 East, Moundridge
46 KS 260, West Moundridge

EXIT	KANSAS

40 Hesston
FStop W: Phillips 66(*, RV DUMP, SCALES)
Food W: Hesston Heritage Inn, Pizza Hut, Subway
Lodg W: Hesston Heritage Inn
RVCamp E: Cottonwood Grove Campground
ATM W: Phillips 66
Other W: U-Do-It
34 KS 15, North Newton, Abilene
FStop E: Phillips 66(*, LP)
AServ E: Phillips 66
RVCamp E: Mid-Kansas RV Park(LP), Payne Oil Company & RV Camp(LP)
Other E: Coin Operated Laundry (Payne Oil Co.)
W: Kauffman Museum
33 U.S. 50 East, Peabody, Emporia (No Reaccess)
32 Broadway Ave (Difficult Reaccess)
AServ E: Resnik Chrysler, Plymouth, & Dodge
31 First Street
TStop E: Texaco(*, RV DUMP, SCALES) (Lodging)
FStop E: Conoco(*)
Gas E: Ampride(*)
W: Phillips 66(*, D, LP)
Food E: CJ's Pancake House (1st Interstate Inn), KFC
W: Best Western, Braum's Ice Cream & Dairy Store, Sirloin Stockade
Lodg E: 1st Interstate Inn, Days Inn, Super 8
W: Best Western
AServ E: Ampride, Conklin Chevrolet, Olds, Cadillac, GM
W: Phillips 66
30 US 50, KS15, Newton, Hutchinson (Difficult Reaccess, Limited Access Hwy)
28 SE 36th Street
Gas W: Total(*, D, CW)
Food W: Burger King(PLAY)
Other W: Newton Factory Outlet Stores
25 KS 196, Whitewater, El Dorado
(23) Rest Area (Southbound)
(23) Rest Area (RR, Phones, Picnic, Vending, RV Dump, P; Northbound)
22 Sedgwick, 125th Street
19 101st Street
RVCamp W: North Star Mobile Home & RV Park (1 Mile)
17 Kansas Colliseum, Valley Center, 85th Street
Other E: Kansas City Colliseum
16 77th Street
Parks E: Wichita Greyhound Park
14 61st Street, Kechi
TStop W: Coastal(*, SCALES)
Gas E: QuikTrip(*, D)
W: Total(*)
Food E: Casa Grande (Mexican), Wendy's
W: Hen House (Coastal TS), Hot Stuff Pizza (Coastal TS), McDonald's(PLAY), Smash Hit Subs (Coastal TS)
Lodg E: Comfort Inn
W: Super 8
AServ W: Garnett Auto Supply
TServ W: Goodyear Kansasland Tire, Sanders
RVCamp W: Central States Thermo King (.75 Miles)
ATM E: QuikTrip
W: Chisholm Trail State Bank
Other W: Family Vision Care, Park City Antique Mall
13 53rd Street
Gas W: Phillips 66(*, D, CW)
Food W: Best Western
Lodg W: Best Western, Days Inn
ATM W: Phillips 66
11B Junction I-235

EXIT	KANSAS

11A KS 254, El Dorado, Jct. South I-35 (Difficult Reaccess)
10AB KS 96 East. 29th St., Hydraulic (Northbound, Difficult Reaccess)
FStop W: Conoco(*)
RVCamp E: USI Campground (1 Mile)
9 21st Street
Gas E: Amoco(*, D)
Food E: Burger King(PLAY)
8 13th Street
Gas E: Total(*)
Med W: + Hospital
Parks W: Emerson McAdams Park
Other E: 13th St Coin Operated Laundry
7B 8th-9th Streets
Other E: University of Kansas Medical School
7A Central Ave.
6C 2nd-1st Streets
Gas W: Total(D)
Food W: G & G Cafe
AServ W: 1st Street Automotive Service, Autobahn, Bulger Cadillac, Olds, Fisher's Transmissions, Yost
6AB U.S. 54, U.S. 400, Kellogg Ave.
5B U.S. 54, U.S. 400, Kellogg Ave (Northbound, Difficult Reaccess)
5A Lincoln Street
Gas W: QuikTrip(*)
Food E: Dairy Queen
AServ W: Tire Center
ATM E: Commerce Bank
Other W: Dillons Grocery(24)
4 Harry Street
Gas W: Amoco(*)
Food E: Barb's BBQ
W: Sport Burger
AServ E: Economy Tire Service
W: Amoco
Med E: + Hospital
ATM W: Amoco
Other W: Quic 'n Easy Wash-O-Mat
3B Pawnee
Food E: Grandma's Diner
W: Burger King(PLAY), Dog N Shake, KFC, Pizza Hut, Rice & Roll Express (Chinese), Spangles, Winchells Donuts
AServ W: Auto Zone, Jiffy Lube, Mola Auto Repair
RVCamp E: K & R Tratel Mobile Home Park (.25 Miles)
ATM W: Emprise Bank
Other W: Checkers Grocery Store, Richard's Car Wash
3A KS 15 South, Southeast Blvd.
2 Hydraulic Ave
Food W: McDonald's(PLAY)
1C Junction I-235
1AB 47th Street E
Gas E: Coastal(*, CW, 24)
Food E: Potbelly's Family Restaurant
W: Applebee's, Azteca (Mexican), Braum's Ice Cream(PLAY), Dairy Queen, Godfather's Pizza, KFC, Long John Silver, McDonald's, Pizza Hut, Pizza Hut, Spaghetti Jack's Fast Italian, Spangles, Sub & Stuff Sandwich Shop, Subway, Super Wok, Taco Bell, Taco-Tico (Mexican)
Lodg E: Comfort Inn, Holiday Inn Express
W: Red Carpet Inn
AServ W: K-Mart(RX)
RVCamp W: R&D Camperland
ATM E: Coastal
Other W: K-Mart(RX)

↑KANSAS

Begin I-135

Bold red print shows RV & Bus parking available or nearby

EXIT	GEORGIA
	Begin I-185
	↓GEORGIA
16	Junction I-85 S, La Grange, Montgomery
15	**(46)** Big Springs Rd.
14	**(41)** U.S. 27, La Grange (Georgia State patrol)
FStop	**E:** Shell(*, D, LP, K)
Gas	**E:** Amoco(*, LP, 24)
Food	**E:** Waffle House
ATM	**E:** Shell
13	**(34)** Ga. 18, West Point, Pine Mountain (Roosevelt State park, Calloway Gardens)
12	**(30)** Hopewell Church Rd., Whitesville
FStop	**W:** Amoco(*, D, LP, K)
11	**(26)** Ga. 116, Hamilton
Food	**W:** Hunter's Pub & Steakhouse
10	**(19)** GA. 315, Mulberry Grove
FStop	**W:** Chevron(*, D, 24)
ATM	**W:** Chevron
9	**(15)** Smith Rd.
8	GA Welcome Center, Williams Road (RR, Phones, Picnic; West Side Of Exit 8)
Gas	**W:** Amoco(*, LP)
7	**(10)** Ga. 22, U.S. 80, Phenix City Alabama, Macon , to US 27
6	**(9)** Airport Thruway, Columbus Airport
Gas	**W:** Amoco(*, D, LP), Crown(*, LP, CW)
Food	**E:** Blimpie Subs & Salads, China Moon, Shoney's
	W: A Bagel Cafe, Applebee's, Burger King(PLAY), Cafe Di Italia, Captain D's Seafood, Hardee's, IHOP, KFC, Little Caesars Pizza, Los Amigo's, Mandarin House, McDonald's(PLAY), Mediterranean Cafe, Mikata Sushi Bar, Outback Steakhouse, PoFolks, Subway, Taco Bell, Texas Steakhouse & Saloon
Lodg	**W:** Hampton Inn, Sheraton
Med	**W:** ✚ Hospital
ATM	**E:** South Trust Bank
	W: SouthTrust Bank, SunTrust Bank
Other	**E:** Circuit City, HQ Home Quarters Warehouse, Rainbow One Hour Photo, Wal-Mart(RX) (One hour photo, vision center)
	W: Food Max Supermarket(RX), K-Mart(RX), Office Depot, One Hour Photo-one, Wolf Camera and Video
5AB	**(8)** U.S.27, Ga. 85, Columbus, Manchester (5 A goes to the east, 5B goes to the west)
Gas	**W:** BP(*, D, LP), Chevron(*, CW), Conoco(*), Crown(*, LP, CW, 24)
Food	**E:** Krystal, Malone's
	W: Arby's, China Express, Cottage Kitchen, Dolcano's Deli and Grill, Dunkin Donuts, Krystal River Seafood, Logan's Roadhouse Steaks & Ribs, Mama's Pizza, Patrick's, Subway, Waffle House, Wendy's
Lodg	**E:** Budgetel, Super 8
	W: Holiday Inn
AServ	**E:** Montgomery Ward
Med	**W:** ✚ Hospital
ATM	**E:** SouthTrust
Other	**E:** Montgomery Ward
	W: Animal Emergency Center, The Book House
4	**(6)** Macon Rd. (Columbus Museum, hospital)
Gas	**W:** Chevron(*, 24)
Food	**E:** Burger King(PLAY), China Buffet, Choctaw Grill, Daisy's Diner, KFC, Pizza Hut, Taco Bell, Waffle House, Western Sizzlin'

1592

DAYS INN

706-689-6181
Columbus, GA

Continental Breakfast
Lounge on Premises • Restaurant Nearby
Kids Under 12 Stay Free
Outdoor Pool • Tennis/Golf Nearby
Meeting/Banquet Facilities
Truck/Large Vehicle Parking
Exterior Corridors • Cable TV w/HBO & ESPN
Historic District & Confederate Museum Close By
3170 Victory Dr. • Columbus, GA

GEORGIA ▪ I-185 ▪ EXIT 1

EXIT	GEORGIA
	W: Baskin Robbins, Captain D's Seafood, Central Park Hamburgers, China Star Restaurant, Chuck E Cheese's Pizza, Country's BBQ, Denny's, Laredo Mexican, Longhorn Steakhouse, McDonald's(PLAY), Shoney's, Subway
Lodg	**E:** Comfort Inn, Days Inn
	W: La Quinta Inn
AServ	**W:** K-Mart
Med	**W:** ✚ Hospital
ATM	**W:** Columbus Banking & Trust Co., SouthTrust
Other	**E:** Lewis Jones Foodmarket, U-Haul Cneter, United States Post Office
	W: CVS(RX), K-Mart, Office Max, Phar Mor Drugs, Publix Supermarket, Service Merchandise, Toys R Us
3	**(4)** Buena Vista Rd.
Gas	**E:** BP(*, LP), Shell(*)
	W: Chevron, Conoco(*, CW), Speedway(*, D)
Food	**E:** Gus's Drive in, TCBY, Taco Bell, Waffle House
	W: Golden China, Oriental Food and Gift
AServ	**W:** Chevron
Other	**E:** Thomas Drugs
2	**(3)** St. Mary's Rd.
Gas	**E:** Quick Change(*)
	W: Amoco(*, LP, 24) (AM South Bank), BP(*, D)
Food	**E:** Catfish Country, Domino's Pizza
	W: Dairy Queen, Golden Chopsticks Korean Restaurant, Hardee's, Hong Kong Chinese Restaurant, Lula's Diner
ATM	**W:** AM South (Amoco), Amoco (AM South Bank), First Union, South Trust Bank
Other	**W:** Eckerd Drugs(RX), Piggly Wiggly Supermarket
1N	Ga. 520, U.S. 27, U.S. 280, Columbus, Victory Dr.
Gas	**W:** Conoco(*, D, LP, CW), Racetrac(*)
Food	**W:** Country Crossing Buffet, Popeye's Chicken, Smokin Branch BBQ
Lodg	**W:** Econolodge, Days Inn (see our ad this page)
ATM	**W:** Racetrac
1S	Cusetta, Albany, South US 27, US 280E, GA 520 (Southbound, Providence Canyon State Park)
	↑GEORGIA
	Begin I-185

I-195 E →

EXIT	MASSACHUSETTS
	Begin I-195
	↓RHODE ISLAND
1	Downtown Providence
2	U.S. 44W, South Main St (Difficult Reaccess)
Med	**S:** ✚ Hospital
3	Gano St, India Point
Lodg	**S:** Days Inn
6	To RI 103, U.S. 44, E Providence
Gas	**N:** U.S. Petroleum(LP)
Food	**N:** Joseph's Family Reataurant
	S: Armando's Coffee Shop, Santoro's Pizza
	↑RHODE ISLAND
	↓MASSACHUSETTS
1	MA114A, Seekonk, Barrington RI
Gas	**N:** Public
	S: Mobil, Sunoco(*, D)
Food	**N:** 99 Restaurant, Brookway Cafe & Deli, Deleo's, Newport Creamery, Seekonk Creamery
	S: Applebee's, Bigford's Family Restaurant, Bug A Boo Steak House, Burger King, China Wok, Cisco's Pizza, D'Angelo's, Dunkin Donuts, Eastside Mario's, Emerald Inn Chinese Restaurant, Friendly's, McDonald's, Outback Steakhouse, Ramada Inn, Subway, T.G.I. Friday's, Taco Bell
Lodg	**N:** Motel 6
	S: Gateway Motor Inn, Mary's Motor Lodge, Ramada Inn, Susse Chalet, Town & Country
AServ	**N:** Public
	S: Sunoco
ATM	**S:** Bank of Boston, Fleet Bank, Mobil, Ro-Jacks Supermarket
Other	**S:** Ro-Jacks Supermarket, Super Stop & Shop, Wal-Mart(RX)
(3)	Weigh Station (Westbound)
2	**(5)** MA136, Warren RI, Newport RI
Gas	**S:** Mobil(*), Shell(*, CW)
Food	**S:** Cathay Pearl Polonesian, Domino's Pizza, Dunkin Donuts, Rooster's Deli & Eskimo Ice Cream, Subway, The Nut House
ATM	**S:** Slade's Ferry Bank
(6)	Parking Area (Southbound)
(6)	Parking Area (Northbound)
3	**(7)** U.S. 6, MA 118, Swansea, Rehoboth
Gas	**N:** Charter(*)
	S: Cumberland Farms(*)
Food	**N:** Bess Eaton, Burger King, Chinese Food Restaurant, De' Angelo's Sandwich Shop, Dunkin Donuts, Friendly's, Hoy Tin, King Pizza, McDonald's, Mr. Peeper's Ice Cream, Plaza Pizza, Ponderosa, Thai Taste
	S: Anthony's

Bold red print shows RV & Bus parking available or nearby

EXIT MASSACHUSETTS

Lodg	**S:** Swansea Motor Inn
Med	**S:** ✚ Walk In Clinic
ATM	**N:** Compass Bank, Fleet Bank
Other	**N:** RX Place Pharmacy[RX]
4AB	**(10)** MA103, Somerset, Ocean Grove
Gas	**N:** Getty
	S: Shell[*]
Food	**N:** Famous Pizza, Papa's Coney Island Hot Dogs, Roger's
	S: TKO Shea's Restaurant
Other	**N:** Somerset Animal Hospital
5	**(12)** MA79, MA138, Taunton, N Tiverton RI
Gas	**S:** J & P Gas[D], Mutual[*]
Food	**S:** Broadway Pizza, Honey Dew Donuts
AServ	**S:** J & P Gas
Med	**S:** ✚ St. Anne's Hospital
6	**(13)** Pleasant St (Difficult Reaccess)
7	**(13)** MA81, Plymouth Ave
Gas	**N:** Getty
	S: Shell[*]
Food	**N:** 99 Restaurant & Pub, Burger King, Carvel Ice Cream Bakery, De' Angelo's Sandwich Shop, Dunkin Donuts, KFC
	S: Applebee's, Blimpie Sub & Salads, McDonald's[PLAY]
AServ	**N:** Getty
Med	**N:** ✚ Charleton Memorial Hospital
	S: ✚ St. Anne's Hospital, ✚ Walk In Clinic
ATM	**S:** Bank Boston
Other	**S:** Super Stop & Shop, WalGreens Pharmacy
8A	**(14)** MA24S, Tiverton RI, Newport RI
8B	**(15)** MA24N, Taunton, Boston
Food	**S:** The Priscilla Restaurant
Lodg	**S:** Hampton Inn
10	**(16)** MA88, Westport, Horseneck Beach, to U.S.6
11AB	**(19)** Reed Rd, Hixville, Dartmouth
12AB	**(22)** Faunce Corner, N Dartmouth
Gas	**S:** Gibbs, Mobil[*, D]
Food	**S:** 99 Restaurant, McDonald's, Mobil
Lodg	**S:** Comfort Inn
Med	**S:** ✚ Dartmouth Walk-in Clinic
ATM	**S:** Fleet Bank
13AB	**(24)** MA140, Taunton, Dartmouth
15	**(25)** MA18S, Downtown, New Bedford
17	**(26)** Coggeshall
Gas	**N:** Shell[*, CW], Sunoco
Food	**N:** Antonio's, Dunkin Donuts, **McDonald's**[24]
AServ	**N:** Shell, Sunoco
18	**(27)** MA240S, Fairhaven
Gas	**S:** Fast Gas[D]
Food	**S:** Bob's Restaurant & Seafood, Burger King, Great Wall China, Jake's Diner, Pizza Hut, The Pasta House, Wendy's
AServ	**S:** Fast Gas
Med	**S:** ✚ Family Medical Walk-in Clinic
ATM	**S:** Bridgewater Credit Union
Other	**S:** Brooks Pharmacy, Super Stop, Wal-Mart
19AB	**(31)** North Rochester, Mattapoisett
Gas	**S:** Mobil[*]
Food	**S:** Uncle John's Coffee
AServ	**S:** Mobil
20	**(35)** MA105, Marion, Rochester
Food	**S:** The Wave Family Restaurant
21	**(39)** MA28, Wareham
Gas	**S:** Texaco[*]
Food	**N:** Zeadey's
	S: Pizza Hut (Texaco)
Med	**S:** ✚ Hospital
Other	**S:** Wearham Police

↑ MASSACHUSETTS

Begin I-195

I-196

EXIT MICHIGAN

Begin I-196

↓ MICHIGAN

79	Fuller Ave
Gas	**E:** Shell[*, D], Speedway[*, LP]
Food	**E:** Bill's Family Restaurant, Burger King, Checkers Burgers, Dairy Cone, New Beginnings, Russo's Pizza & Sub, Subway, Taco Bell, The Elbow Room Bar & Grill, Wendy's
Med	**W:** ✚ Kent Community Hospital Complex
	W: Sheriff Dept.
78	College Ave
Gas	**E:** Dairy Mart[*, 24]
Food	**E:** Bagel Beanery, McDonald's, Mister Pizza, Pizza Hut, Rite Aid Pharmacy
Med	**E:** ✚ Hospital
77C	Ottawa Ave., Downtown
77AB	Junction U.S. 131, Cadillac, Kalamazoo
Lodg	**E:** **Ramada Limited (see our ad this page)**
76	MI. 45 East, Lane Ave.
75	MI 45, Lake Michigan Dr.
73	Market Ave., Van Andel Arena
72	Bus. Loop 196, Chicago Dr.
70AB	MI 11, 28th St., Wyoming, Walker, Wilson Ave.
Gas	**E:** Amoco[*, D, LP, CW], Shell[*, K, 24]
Food	**E:** **New Beginnings**, Pizza Doro
Lodg	**E:** Land's End Suites
69AB	Jenison, Chicago Dr., Grandville
Gas	**E:** Clark[*]
	W: **Meijer Superstore**[*, D, LP, K, 24, RX], Shell[*], Total[*, LP, K]
Food	**E:** Arby's[24], Brann's Steakhouse, Burger King, Get-Em-N-Go, **Jerry's Country Inn**, Little Caesars Pizza, Ole' Tacos, Pizza Hut, **Russ' Family Restaurant**, Spad's Pizza, **Wendy's**
	W: Big Apple Bagels, Hot n Now, Hungry Howie's Pizza, **McDonald's (Meijer)**, Mr. Fable's, Sara's Pizza
Lodg	**E:** Best Western
Other	**E:** **Fairlanes Bowling**, Loeschner's Village Green Miniature Golf
	W: **Meijer Superstore**[RX], Pearl Vision Center, Strikers Mini Golf, Driving Range, Batting Cage
67	44th St
Gas	**W:** Mobil[*, D, LP]
Food	**W:** **Burger King**, Cracker Barrel
Med	**E:** ✚ Butterworth Health Campus Med + Center, ✚ Spectrum Health
Other	**W:** **Wal-Mart**[RX] **(Optical)**
62	32nd Ave, Hudsonville
Gas	**E:** Mobil[*, D, CW]
	W: Amoco[*, D, CW], BP[*, D, LP, CW]
Food	**E:** Mobil
	W: **Burger King**, **McDonald's**, Subway (Amoco)
Lodg	**E:** Rest All Inn
	W: Amerihost Inn
(58)	Rest Area (RR, Phones, Picnic; Southbound)
55	Byron Rd., Zeeland
Gas	**W:** Citgo[*]
Food	**W:** **McDonald's**[PLAY]
Med	**N:** ✚ Hospital
52	Zeeland, 16th St., Adams St
Gas	**E:** Mobil[*, D]
Food	**E:** **Burger King**, Subway (Mobil)
Med	**E:** ✚ Hospital
	N: ✚ Hospital
49	MI 40, Allegan
TStop	**E:** **Tulip City Truck Stop**[*, D, SCALES] **(Total Gas)**
Food	**E:** **Rock Island Family Restaurant (Tulip TS)**
44	U.S. 31, Holland, Bus. Loop 196, Muskegon

1662

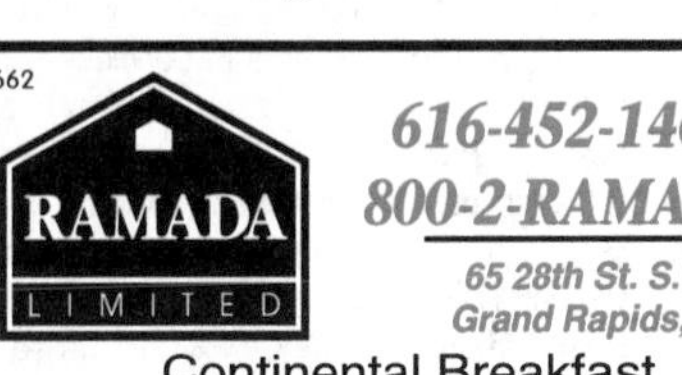

616-452-1461
800-2-RAMADA

65 28th St. S.W.
Grand Rapids, MI

Continental Breakfast
Kids Under 12 Stay & Eat Free
Indoor Pool • Exercise Room
Handicap Accessible
Truck/Large Vehicle Parking
Exterior/Interior Corridors
Cable TV/HBO • In Room Movies
Voice Mail/FAX/Copy Machine
5 miles from Van Andel Arena
I-196W, Exit 77AB, US 131S Exit 81

MICHIGAN • I-196 • EXIT 77AB

(43)	Rest Area (RR, Phones, Picnic; Southbound)
41	County Rd A2, Blue Star Hwy.
Gas	**W:** Marathon[*, D, LP], Shell[*, D, K]
Food	**W:** **Burger King**, Spectator Sports Bar & Grill, Subway (Shell)
Lodg	**E:** Shangrai-La Motel
36	County Rd A2, Douglas, Saugatuck
Lodg	**E:** Hunter's Lodge
34	MI 89, Fennville
Gas	**E:** Shell[*, K]
Food	**E:** What Not
30	Glenn, Ganges, County Rd. A-2
(29)	Rest Area (RR, HF, Phones, Picnic; Northbound)
26	109th Ave., Pullman
Food	**W:** Dutch Farm Market, Southview Bed & Breakfast
Lodg	**W:** Southview Bed & Breakfast
22	North Shore Dr.
Food	**E:** Hawks Head Golf
	W: Cousins Campground[*]
RVCamp	**W:** Cousins Campground
20	Phoenix Rd.
Gas	**W:** Amoco[*, D, CW], Marathon[*, D, K]
Food	**E:** Big Boy, Sherman Dairy Bar
	W: **Arby's**, Hot n Now Hamburgers, Wok Inn Ribs
Lodg	**E:** Guest House Inn
	W: South Haven Motel
Med	**W:** ✚ Hospital
18	MI 140, MI 43, I-196 Loop, Bangor, South Haven
TStop	**W:** **Shell**[*, D, K]
Gas	**W:** Checker[*, K]
Food	**W:** **Ma's Coffee Pot**[24] **(Shell)**
13	Covert
7	MI 63, Hagar Shore Rd.
Food	**W:** DiMaggio's Pizza, Flo & Jerry's Beachside Restaurant, Icecream Vault, Vitale's Market/Deli
4	Coloma, Riverside
Gas	**E:** Marathon[*, D, K, 24]
1	Red Arrow Hwy
(0)	Junction I-94, Chicago, Detroit

↑ MICHIGAN

Begin I-196

I-205

EXIT WASHINGTON/OREGON

Begin I-205

↓WASHINGTON

36 NE 134th St.
- **Gas** **W:** BP[*], Citgo[*], Trail Mart[*, D]
- **Food** **W:** Burger King[PLAY], Burgerville USA[PLAY], J.B's Roadhouse, McDonald's[PLAY], Round Table Pizza, Taco Bell[24]
- **Lodg** **W:** Comfort Inn, Shilo Inn
- **ATM** **W:** BP, Citgo, Citgo, Northwest National Bank, Trail Mart, Trail Mart, Washington Mutual
- **Other** **W:** 7-11 Convenience Store, Hi-School Pharmacy, Salmon Creek Optical, The Book Worm, The Letter Box, Zupan's Market

32 NE 83rd St. Andresen Rd.

30 WA 500 Vancouver Orchards (Reaccess Northbound Only)
- **Gas** **W:** Arco[*], Chevron[*]
- **Lodg** **W:** Comfort Suites Hotel, Holiday Inn Express, Sleep Inn
- **ATM** **W:** Arco, Chevron

28 Mill Plain Rd.
- **Gas** **E:** BP[*], Chevron[*, 24], Texaco[*, D, LP, K, CW]
  W: Arco[*], Texaco[*]
- **Food** **E:** Baskin Robbins, Burger King, Burgerville USA[PLAY], Cascade Lantern, El Charrito, Elmer's, Genghis Khan, Joe's Pasta and Deli House, Outback Restaurant & Lounge, Pizza Hut, Shari's Restaurant, Starbucks Coffee, Taco Bell, Taco King, Yoshi Japanese
  W: Chariots of Fire Pizza, Happy Family Restaurant
- **Lodg** **E:** Extended Stay America, Rodeway Inn, The Guest House Motel, The Travel Lodge
- **Med** **W:** ✚ Hospital
- **ATM** **E:** 1st Independent Bank, Genghis Khan, Northwest National Bank, Seafirst Bank
  W: Arco, Texaco
- **Other** **E:** B&H Safe & Lock, Cascade Park Cinema, Fred Meyer Grocery[RX]

27 Washington 14 W. Vancouver , E Camas

↑WASHINGTON

↓OREGON

24 Airport Way , Portland Airport
- **Food** **E:** Burger King[PLAY], McDonald's[PLAY], Shari's Restaurant[24], Shilo Inn, Subway
- **Lodg** **E:** Comfort Suites Hotel, Courtyard Marriott, Fairfield Inn, Holiday Inn Express, Shilo Inn, Silver Cloud Inn, Super 8
- **Other** **E:** Home Depot, Plaid Pantry

23B U.S 30 Bypass W. Columbia Blvd.

23A **(30)** U.S. 30 Bypass E. Sandy Blvd.
- **FStop** **E:** **Shell**[*]
- **Gas** **E:** Texaco[*, D, CW]
- **Food** **E:** Bill's Steakhouse, Elmer's, Jim Dandy, Mars Chinese
- **Lodg** **E:** Best Western, Econolodge, Travelodge TraveLodge
- **ATM** **E:** Bank Of America, **Shell**

22 The Dalles., Junction E. I-84 & U.S. 30

21B West I-84, US 30, West Portland

21A Stark St., Gilsan St.

20 Washington Street, Stark St. (North-bound, Watch One Ways)
- **Gas** **E:** Chevron[*, LP, CW], Unocal 76[*, 24]
- **Food** **E:** Arby's, Bagel Sphere, Baskin Robbins, Burger King, Coffee's On, Elmers, Fruit Fusion Smoothies & Juices, McMenamins, Motor Moka Cafe, Newport Bay, Tony Roma's, Village Inn Family Restaurant, Wall Street Pizza
  W: Stark Street Pizza Co., Taco Bell[24]
- **Lodg** **E:** Chestnut Tree Motel, Holiday Inn Express, Montavilla
  W: Rodeway Inn
- **AServ** **E:** Unocal 76[24]
- **ATM** **E:** Bank Of America, Portland Teachers' Credit Union, Unocal 76
  W: 7-11 Convenience Store
- **Other** **E:** America's Best Contacts & Eyeglasses
  W: 7-11 Convenience Store, Mart Food Store, Pilgrim Discount Book & Bible

19 U.S. 26, Division St., Powell Blvd. (West side services go off on Powell St, East side services go on Division St)
- **Gas** **E:** Exxon[*]
  W: Texaco[*]
- **Food** **W:** BurgerVille USA, Chuck E Cheese's Pizza, McDonald's[PLAY]
- **AServ** **E:** Exxon
- **Other** **W:** AMF 20th Century Lanes, Q2 Food Stores

17 Foster Rd. (West Side services on one-way streets)
- **Gas** **W:** Chevron[*, 24]
- **Food** **W:** New Copper Penney Restaurant
- **ATM** **E:** 7-11 Convenience Store
- **Other** **E:** 7-11 Convenience Store

16 Johnson Creek Blvd.
- **Gas** **W:** Texaco[*]
- **Food** **W:** McDonald's[PLAY], Ron's Restaurant, Taco Bell[24], Tortilla Flats
- **AServ** **W:** Texaco
- **ATM** **W:** 7-11 Convenience Store, 7-11 Convenience Store, Wells Fargo
- **Other** **W:** 7-11 Convenience Store, 82nd Ave Bowl, 82nd Ave Cinemas, Fred Meyer Grocery, Home Base

14 Sunnyside Rd.
- **Gas** **E:** Unocal 76[*, LP, 24]
- **Food** **E:** CG's Deli, Coffee Bistro, Gustav's Pub & Grill, Izzy's Pizza, KFC, McMenamins, Subway, TCBY, Thai House
  W: Barnes & Noble, Chevy's, Juice Stop, Macheezmo Mouse, Olive Garden, Red Robins, Starbucks Coffee (Barnes & Noble), The Great Harvest Bread Co, ToGo's Eatery
- **Lodg** **E:** Best Western, DAYS INN Days Inn
- **Med** **E:** ✚ Hospital, ✚ Williamette Falls Health Center and Immediate Care
- **ATM** **W:** Bank of America
- **Other** **E:** Mail Boxes Etc, Plaid Pantry
  W: Barnes & Noble, Target

13 OR. 224, W Milwaukee
- **Other** **W:** K-Mart

12AB 12A- E. OR. 212 & OR. 224, Clackamas Estacada, 12B- Webster Rd., Johnson City
- **Gas** **E:** Chevron[*, 24], Texaco[*, CW]
- **Food** **E:** 2 Scoops, Denny's, Elmer's, McDonald's[PLAY], New Cathay Deli, Schnitzel House Deli, Sunshine Pizza Exchange, Taco Bell[24], Wendy's
- **Lodg** **E:** Clackamas Inn, Hampton Inn
- **ATM** **E:** 7-11 Convenience Store, 7-11 Convenience Store, US Bank, Wells Fargo
- **Other** **E:** 7-11 Convenience Store, Cash & Carry United Grocery, Post Office, Vista Optical

11 Gladstone
- **Gas** **W:** Arco[*]
- **ATM** **W:** Arco, Safeway Grocery (Grocery Store)
- **Other** **W:** Safeway Grocery (Grocery Store)

10 Park Place Molalla , OR 213
- **FStop** **E:** **Pacific Pride Commercial Fueling**
- **Med** **E:** ✚ Hospital
- **Other** **E:** Visitor Information

9 OR. 99E. Oregon City Gladstone
- **Gas** **E:** 76[*], Arco
- **Food** **E:** Friendship Chinese, KFC
  W: Hong Kong Express, McDonald's[PLAY], Restaurant (Val-U Inn), Shari's, Subway
- **Lodg** **W:** Val-U Inn
- **AServ** **E:** Arco
- **ATM** **E:** Arco
- **Other** **E:** Town Center Yamaha and Kawasaki
  W: Davi's Locksmith Services, Oregon Book Co, Rite Aid Pharmacy[24]

8 West Linn Lake Oswego , OR 43
- **Gas** **E:** BP
  W: Astro[D, LP], Texaco[D]
- **Food** **W:** Bagel Basket, Pasta's, Starbucks Coffee
- **AServ** **E:** BP
  W: Texaco
- **ATM** **W:** Key Bank, Thriftway
- **Other** **W:** Copy Center, Post Office, Thriftway, West Linn Pharmacy

6 West Linn 10th St
- **Gas** **E:** Chevron[*]
- **Food** **E:** Ixtapa Family Restaurant, McDonald's, McMenamins, Shari's, Williamette's Coffee House
  W: Jack in the Box
- **ATM** **E:** Chevron
  W: US Bank (Albertson's), Washington Mutual
- **Other** **E:** Olson Drugs, Thriftway, Veterinary Clinic
  W: Albertson's Food Market

3 Stafford Rd., Lake Oswego
- **Med** **W:** ✚ Hospital
- **ATM** **W:** Wanker's Country Store
- **Other** **W:** Wanker's Country Store

2 Jct. I-5 , I- 5 N to Tigard, I-5 S to Salem

↑OREGON

Begin I-205

Bold red print shows RV & Bus parking available or nearby

EXIT LOUISIANA

Begin I-220

↓LOUISIANA

17B I-20 West Shreveport, I-20 East Monroe

17A US 79, US 80, Racetrack
- **Gas** **O:** Circle K(*), Racetrac(*)
- **Food** **O:** Waffle House
- **ATM** **O:** Circle K, Racetrac
- **Other** **O:** Kiddie Ima's Entertainment & Pizza

15 Shed Rd

13 Swan Lake Rd

12 LA 3105, Airline Drive, Bossier City
- **Food** **I:** Burger King(PLAY), McDonald's(PLAY), Taco Bell
- **Med** **O:** Bossier Health Center

11 LA 3, Benton, Bossier City
- **Gas** **I:** Chevron(*, CW)
- **Med** **O:** Bossier Health Center
- **ATM** **I:** Chevron

7AB US 71, LA 1, Shreveport, Texarkana
- **Gas** **I:** Chevron(*, CW), Racetrac(*), Texaco(*, D)
  O: Exxon(*, D), Fina(*, D), Mobil(*), Pennzoil Oil Change(*)
- **Food** **I:** McDonald's(PLAY), O'Malley's Deli, Podnuh's BBQ, Taco Bell, Trejo's (Howard Johnson)
  O: Domino's Pizza, Frosty Express, Subway, What A Burger(24), Zince's North Port Restaurant
- **Lodg** **I:** Howard Johnson
- **ATM** **I:** Hibernia, Racetrac
- **Other** **O:** Brookshire's Grocery(RX), Regions Bank
  I: Eckerd Drugs(RX), North Shreveport Animal Hospital
  O: Brookshire's Grocery(RX)

5 LA 173, Blanchard Rd., Cross Lake

2 Lakeshore Drive

1D LA 511, West 70th St. (Westbound)
- **Gas** **O:** Diamond Shamrock(*, CW)
- **Other** **I:** Airport

1C I-20 East, Monroe (Westbound)

1B West I-20, Dallas (Westbound)

1A Jefferson Paige Rd.

↑LOUISIANA

Begin I-220

I-235

EXIT IOWA

Begin I-235

↓IOWA

(0) JCT I-35, I-80

Exit **(1)** Valley West Dr.
- **Gas** **I:** Amoco(*, D, CW, 24)
- **Food** **I:** Bagel Express, Donny Arthur's Sports Bar, Olive Garden, Red Lobster, T.G.I. Friday's, Valley West Inn, Valley West Pub
- **Lodg** **I:** Executive Inn, Valley West Inn
- **ATM** **I:** Amoco, First Star Bank, Hyvee(24, RX), Iowa Savings Bank, NationsBank
- **Other** **I:** Hyvee(RX), Target, Whylie's Eye Care Center

Exit **(2)** 22nd Street
- **Gas** **I:** Amoco(*, CW), Citgo(*)
- **Food** **I:** Burger King, Chi Chi's Mexican Restaurant, Chuck E Cheese's Pizza, Hardee's, Hooter's, Imperial Garden Chinese, Lone Star Steakhouse, McDonald's, Old Country Buffet, Taco Bell
- **Lodg** **I:** Studio PLUS and Extended Stay Hotel
- **ATM** **I:** First Bank & Trust Co., Mercantile Bank, US Bank, West Bank
- **Other** **I:** Half Price Store, Office Depot, One Hour Optical, Osco Drugs

Exit **(3)** 8th Street, West Des Moines, Windsor Heights
- **Gas** **I:** Amoco(*, CW), Coastal(*), Kum & Go(*, 24), QuikTrip(*, 24), Sam's Club
- **Food** **I:** B-Bops Hamburgers, Blimpie's Subs, Burger King, Cabo San Lucas (Best Western), China Star Restaurant, Jimmy's American Cafe, Subway, Toscano Restaurant
- **Lodg** **I:** Best Western
- **AServ** **I:** Amoco, Sam's Club
- **ATM** **I:** Amerius Bank, Banker's Trust, Hyvee Foods and Pharmacy(24, RX), Kum & Go, Kum & Go
- **Other** **I:** Hyvee Foods and Pharmacy(RX), Payless Optical, Sam's Club, Wal-Mart(24, RX)

Exit **(4)** IA 28, 63rd Street (Zoo 9 miles to the outerloop; The Historic Valley Junction is also to the outerloop)

Exit **(4)** 56th Street (Westbound, Reaccess Eastbound Only)

Exit **(5)** 42nd Street
- **Gas** **I:** QuikTrip(*)
- **Food** **I:** Taco John's

Exit **(6)** 31st Street (Westbound, Reaccess Eastbound Only, Difficult Reaccess)

Exit **(7)** Cottage Grove

Exit Martin Luther King Jr. Pkwy, Airport (Left Exit , Reaccess Eastbound Only, Difficult Reaccess)
- **Lodg** **S:** Hampton Inn Airport

Exit **(7)** Keo Way (Left Exit Southbound)
- **Lodg** **I:** Holiday Inn

7 **(8)** 7th Street; 3rd Street, 5th Avenue (Eastbound)
- **Lodg** **O:** Best Western

6 **(9)** East 6th Street

Exit **(9)** Penn Ave. (Eastbound, Reaccess Westbound Only, Difficult Reaccess)

Exit **(10)** US 65 South, US 69 South, East 15th Street, East 14th (Difficult Reaccess)
- **Med** **I:** Des Moines General Hospital

Exit US 65 North, IA 163 West, East University Ave. (Difficult Reaccess, Mile Marker 10.3)
- **ATM** **O:** Community State Bank

Exit **(11)** Guthrie Ave.
- **FStop** **I:** Coastal(*, D)

Exit **(12)** US 6, Euclid
- **Gas** **O:** Coastal(*)
- **Food** **I:** Denny's
  O: Burger King(PLAY), Perkins Family Restaurant
- **ATM** **O:** Firststar Bank, Norwest Bank
- **Other** **O:** Hyvee(24, RX), Vision Center (Leetown Center), WalGreens Pharmacy(24, RX)

↑IOWA

Begin I-235

I-240

EXIT		TENNESSEE
		Begin I-240
		↓TENNESSEE
25AB		25A - I-55 S, Jackson MS, 25B - I-55 N, St Louis MO
24		Millbranch Rd
	Lodg	**O:** Budgetel Inn, Courtyard by Marriott, Hampton Inn
	TServ	**O:** **Kenworth**
23AB		Airways Blvd International Airport
	Gas	**I:** Texaco(*), Total(*)
		O: Mapco Express(LP)
	Food	**I:** B&B Bar-B-Q, Big Dip Dairy Bar, Church's Chicken, Dixie Queen Ice Cream & Hamburgers, Samuel's BBQ & Hot Wings, Subway
		O: Catfish Cabin, Denny's, Fred Gang's Restaurant
	Lodg	**I:** Airways Inn, Economy Inn
		O: DAYS INN Days Inn, Four Points Hotel Sheraton, La Quinta Inn
	ATM	**O:** Union Planter's Bank
	Other	**O:** Airport
21		US 78, Lamar Ave., Birmingham
	Gas	**I:** Citgo(*, D), Citgo, Phillips 66(*)
		O: Amoco(*, CW)
	Lodg	**O:** Econolodge, Ramada Limited, Southeast Motel
	AServ	**I:** Citgo
	Other	**I:** Supervalu Foods
20		Get Well Rd
	Gas	**I:** BP(*, CW)
		O: Amoco(*, CW), Coastal(*, D), Texaco(*, D)
	Food	**I:** McDonald's
		O: Emilio's, Rice Bowl, Subway, Wendy's
	Lodg	**O:** Red Roof Inn
	AServ	**I:** BP

EXIT		TENNESSEE
	Med	**O:** ✚ Family Care
	ATM	**O:** Kroger Supermarket(RX)
	Other	**O:** Kroger Supermarket(RX)
18		Perkins Rd
	Gas	**O:** Circle K(*), Exxon(*, D, LP), Highway, Texaco(*, D, CW), Total(*, D, LP)
	Food	**O:** Applebee's, Arby's, Captain D's Seafood, Danver's Restaurant, IHOP, Pancho's Taco, Pizza Hut, Popeye's Chicken, S & S Cafeterias, Shoney's, Sonic Drive in, Taco Bell, The Olive Garden
	Lodg	**O:** Fairfield Inn, Hampton Inn, Marriot Hotel, Memphis Inn
	AServ	**O:** Exxon
	ATM	**O:** First Tennesee Bank, Union Planter's Bank
	Other	**O:** Expressway Animal Hospital, Kinko's Copies
17		Mt Moriah Rd
	Gas	**I:** BP(*, LP)
		O: Total(*, LP)
	Food	**I:** Crumpy's Hot Wings
		O: Cactus Roses Restaurant & Grill (Holiday Inn), Denny's, El Torero Mexican, Lone Star Steakhouse, Picadilly Cafeteria, Pirtle's Chicken, Wendy's
	Lodg	**O:** Holiday Inn
	ATM	**I:** BP
		O: Union Planter's Bank
16		TN 385 East, Nonconnah Pkwy
15		US 72, Poplar Ave, Germantown
	Food	**I:** Cafe Expresso (The Ridgeway Inn), The Ridgeway Inn
		O: Calla's Italian Restaurant, Cockeyed Camel, Gallina's (Comfort Inn)
	Lodg	**I:** The Ridgeway Inn
		O: Comfort Inn, Holiday Inn, Homewood Suites Motel
	Med	**O:** ✚ Hospital

EXIT		TENNESSEE
13		Walnut Grove Rd
	Med	**O:** ✚ Baptist Memorial Hospital East
12C		I-40 East, Nashville
31B		I-40 West, Little Rock
30		Union Ave, Madison Ave
	Gas	**I:** Exxon(*), Exxon(*, CW)
	Food	**I:** Admiral Benbow Inn, Arby's, Backyard Burgers, Burger King, Burger King, C K's Coffee Shop, Denny's, Krystal, McDonald's, Minh-Chau, Shoney's, Tops Bar-B-Q, Western Steak House & Lounge
	Lodg	**I:** Admiral Benbow Inn, Hampton Inn, Red Roof Inn
		O: La Quinta Inn
	Med	**I:** ✚ Baptist Memorial Hospital, ✚ Methodist Hospitals of Memphis
		O: ✚ Hospital
	ATM	**I:** First Tennessee Bank
		O: First Commercial, Union Planters Bank
29		Lamar Avenue
	Gas	**I:** Total(*)
		O: Citgo(*)
	Food	**I:** China Doll, Rally's Hamburgers
	Lodg	**I:** Coach, Lamplighter Motor Inn
	Med	**I:** ✚ Hospital
	Other	**O:** Kim's Grocery Store
28AB		S Parkway
	Gas	**O:** BP(*), Exxon(*)
	Food	**I:** Coletta's Italian
	Lodg	**I:** Parkway Inn
26		Norris Rd (Difficult Reaccess)
		↑TENNESSEE
		Begin I-240

I-255

EXIT		MISSOURI/ILLINOIS
		Begin I-255
		↓MISSOURI
1		I-55 Jct
(5)		Rest Area (RR, HF, Phones, Picnic, P)
		↑MISSOURI
		↓ILLINOIS
30		JCT I-70, Kansas City
29		**(30)** IL. 162 Glen Carbon, Granite City
	Other	**I:** Pontoon Beach
26		**(28)** Horseshoe Rd
	Other	**O:** Regional Complex & Convention Center, State Police
25B		**(26)** Jct I-55 S I-70 W, Jct 55 N I-70, Indianapolis, Chicago
24		Collinsville Rd.
	Gas	**O:** Amoco(*)
	Food	**O:** Hardee's, Jack in the Box, Winner's Restuarant (Steak, Ribs & Chicken)
	Other	**I:** Fairmont Park RaceTrack
		O: Grandpa's(LP), Shop "N" Save
20		**(23)** I-64 Jct.
19		**(20)** State St. E. St. Louis
	Gas	**O:** Clark(K)
	Lodg	**O:** Western Inn(*)
	Other	**I:** Frank Holten State Park

EXIT		ILLINOIS/MISSOURI
17AB		E. Saint Louis, Belleville, Allrton, Centerville
	Med	**I:** ✚ **Hospital**, ✚ Hospital
15		Mousette Ln.
	Med	**I:** ✚ Hospital
13		**(15)** IL. 157 Cahokia
	Gas	**I:** Amoco(*, CW)
	Food	**I:** Burger King, Captain D's Seafood, China Express, Hardee's, KFC, Pizza Hut, Q Mart Grocery, Rally's Hamburgers
	Other	**I:** Camp Jackson Shopping Ctr, Schnucks Grocery Store, Wal-Mart(RX)
		O: Fisher Pharmacy, Mini Market, Professional Optical
10		**(13)** IL. 3 N Cahokia E. Saint Louis
9		Dupo
6		**(9)** IL. 3 South Columbia
		↑ILLINOIS
		↓MISSOURI
3		Koch Rd
	Med	**I:** ✚ Vetran's Med Ctr
2		**(3)** MO 231, Telegraph Rd
	Gas	**I:** Amoco(*, CW), Shell(*, CW)
		O: CSM(*, D, CW)
	Food	**I:** Boston Market Restaurant, McDonald's(PLAY), Steak & Shake, Wal-Mart(RX) (Eyecare)
	ATM	**I:** Shell

EXIT		MISSOURI
		O: CSM
	Other	**I:** Parts America, Sear's Hardware(LP), Wal-Mart(RX) (Eyecare)
1C		U.S. 61, U.S. 67, MO 267, Lemay Ferry Rd (Reaccess Eastbound Only, Difficult Reaccess)
	Gas	**I:** Amoco, Amoco(*), Phillips 66(*, CW)
		O: Citgo
	Food	**I:** Arby's, Blimpie Subs & Salads, Caddy's, Chinese Buffet, Chuck E Cheese's Pizza, Dairy Queen, Gingham's Homestyle Restaurant, Hooter's, Long John Silver, McDonald's, Old Country Buffet, Ruby Tuesday, Steak 'N Shake, Subway, Taco Bell, Uncle Bill's Pancake & Dinner House, Wendy's
		O: Citgo, Emperior's Garden (Chinese), Jack in the Box, Pappa John's Pizza, Rich Charlie's, Rizzo Italian Dining, White Castle Restaurant, Whittaker's Pizzeria
	AServ	**I:** Amoco
	Med	**O:** ✚ MedFirst
	ATM	**I:** Allegiant Bank, Merchantile Bank
		O: Merchantile Bank, Nation's Bank
	Other	**I:** K-Mart(RX), Mellville Firestation, Pearl Vision, South County Center Plaza, South County Ventura Plaza, South County Vet Office, Sterling Optical, Wehrenberg 8 (Movie Theatre)
		O: Central City South Plaza, National Market(LP, RX), Sam's, WalGreens Pharmacy(RX)
		↑MISSOURI
		Begin I-255

Bold red print shows RV & Bus parking available or nearby

EXIT — STATE

Begin I-264

↓KENTUCKY

0AB I-64, US 150, Lexington, St Louis

1 Bank Street, NW Parkway (Counterclockwise)
- **Gas** I: Loto(*)

2 River Park Dr., Muhammad Ali Blvd.

3 Dumesnil St., Virginia Ave.

4 Bells Lane, Algonquin Pkwy

5 Ralph Ave., Cane Run Rd.
- **FStop** I: **Marathon**(*, D)
- **Gas** I: Speedway
  O: Amoco(*), Dairy Mart(*, K), Thornton's(*, D, LP, K)
- **Food** O: Dunkin Donuts (Thornton's)
- **ATM** O: Dairy Mart, Thornton's

8AB US 31W, US 60, Ft Knox, Shively
- **Gas** I: Amoco(*)
  O: Citgo(*), Speedway(*, K), Sunoco(*, K), Thornton's(*, 24)
- **Food** O: Bojangles, Chi-Chi's Mexican Restaurant, Dunkin Donuts (Thornton's), KFC, McDonald's, O'Charley's, Restaurant (Royal Inn Motel), Taco Bell, The Banquet Table Buffet, The Italian Oven Restaurant
- **Lodg** I: Holiday Inn
  O: Louisville Manor, Royal Inn Motel, Toad Stool Inn
- **Med** O: ✚ Hospital
- **ATM** I: Citizen's Bank, Great Financial Bank
  O: Fifth Third Bank, Thornton's
- **Other** I: Rite Aide Pharmacy

9 Taylor Blvd, Church Hill Downs
- **Gas** O: Ashland(*, K), Dairymart(*)
- **Food** I: Cactus Jack's Bar & Grill
  O: Dairy Queen, Restaurant, Sassy's Subs & Stuff
- **Med** O: ✚ Hospital
- **Other** O: Reasor's Supermarket

10 KY1020, Southern Pkwy, 3rd St.
- **Gas** I: Dairy Mart(*, K)
  O: Thornton's(*, D, LP, K)
- **Food** O: Dunkin Donuts (Thornton's), Long John Silver
- **ATM** I: Dairy Mart
  O: Thornton's

(10) Crittenden Dr., Fair/Expo Ctr. Gates 2, 3, 4

11 Crittenden Dr., Airport, Fair/Expo Ctr

12 I-65, KY 61, Nashville, Indianapolis

14 KY 864, Poplar Level Rd.
- **Gas** I: SuperAmerica(*, D, LP)
- **Food** I: Bamboo House Chinese American Restaurant, Charles Hertzman Bakery, Donut Factory, Frisch's Big Boy, Lolita's Mexican
  O: Arby's
- **TServ** O: **Kenworth, Peterson GMC Trucks**
- **Med** I: ✚ Hospital
- **ATM** I: Bank One
- **Other** I: Abram's Animal Hospital, K-Mart, Kroger Supermarket(RX)

15AB Newburg Rd., KY1703
- **Gas** O: BP(*, LP, CW), SuperAmerica(*, LP)
- **Food** O: Horsefeathers (Ramada), Long John Silver, Oriental Star, Subway, Waffle House
- **Lodg** O: Ramada, Red Roof Inn, Wilson Inn
- **ATM** O: National City Bank, PNC Bank, SuperAmerica
- **Other** O: Animal Emergency Center & Hospital

16 Bardstown Rd, US31E, US150
- **Gas** I: BP(*, CW)
  O: Shell, Thornton's Food Mart(*, LP)
- **Food** I: Buckhead, Darryl's, Krispy Kreme Doughnuts, Thai-Saim Restaurant, The Bakery, The Daily Fare Deli & Market
  O: India Palace (Quality Inn), KFC, McDonald's, Mr. Gatti's, New World Chinese Restaurant, Rally's Hamburgers, Steak 'N Shake, Wendy's
- **Lodg** O: Holiday Inn, Junction Inn, Quality Inn
- **ATM** I: National City Bank
- **Other** I: Markwell's Supermarket, Rite Aide Pharmacy(24)

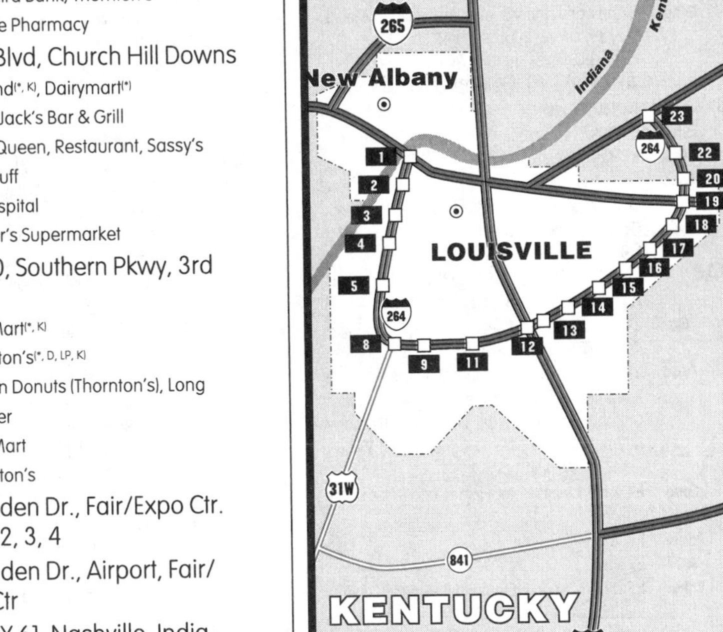

17AB KY155, Taylorsville Rd.
- **Gas** O: Thornton's(*, D)

18 18A - KY1932 S, Breckenridge Ln 18B - KY1932 N, Breckenridge Ln
- **Food** I: China Town, Dooley's Hot Bagels, Mamma Grisanti's Italian, O'Charley's, Rafferty's, Red Lobster, Skyline Chili, Texas Roadhouse, The Italian Oven Restaurant, Wendy's
  O: Rally's Hamburgers
- **Lodg** O: Breckinridge Inn
- **Med** I: ✚ Columbia Suburban Hospital
- **Other** I: Dr. Bizer's Vision World, Korrect Optical, Springer & Lee Optical, Winn Dixie Supermarket(RX)
  O: K-Mart

19AB I-64, Lexington, Louisville

20AB Jct. US 60, Shelbyville Rd., Middle Town, St. Matthews
- **Gas** O: BP(*, LP), Chevron(LP)
- **Food** I: Frisch's Big Boy, Honey Baked Ham Co., Logan's Roadhouse Steaks & Ribs, McDonald's, Moby Dick's, Outback Steakhouse, Remington's, Rollo Pollo Chicken, Taco Bell
  O: Shoney's, Taco Bell
- **Lodg** I: DAYS INN Days Inn
- **Other** I: Drug Emporium

22 Brownsboro Rd., US 42
- **Gas** I: Marathon
  O: BP(CW), Chevron(*, CW), Swifty
- **Food** I: Brewed Awakening Coffee Shop, Gast Haus, Mike Best's Meat Market
  O: Arby's, Baskin Robbins, Bruegger's Bagel & Bakery, Emperor of China, KFC, Kingsley Meat & Seafood, Pizza Hut, Taco Bell, Thai Cafe
- **Lodg** I: Ramada Inn
- **ATM** I: PNC Bank
  O: Bank One, Bank of Louisville, Kroger Supermarket, Republic Bank
- **Other** O: Kroger Supermarket(24), Revco Drugs, Springer & Lee Optical

23AB 23A - I-71N, Cincinatti, 23B - I-71S, Louisville

↑KENTUCKY

Begin I-264

Bold red print shows RV & Bus parking available or nearby

I-265

EXIT		KENTUCKY
	Begin I-265	

↓KENTUCKY

35AB 35A - N. I-71, Cincinatti, 35B - S. I-71, Louisville (Gene Snyder Hwy)
34 KY 22, Brownsboro Rd, Crestwood
- **Gas** O: BP(*, LP)
- **Food** I: 888 Great Wall, Philly Connection, The Italian Oven Restaurant
- **ATM** I: Kroger Supermarket, Stockyards Bank
- **Other** I: Kroger Supermarket(24, RX)

32 KY 1447, Westport Rd, Chamberlain Lane
- **Gas** I: BP(*, CW), Thornton's(*, LP)
  O: SuperAmerica(D, CW)
- **Food** I: Dunkin Donuts (Thornton's)
  O: Burger King, Frisch's Big Boy, HomeTown Buffet, Moby Dick, Subway (SuperAmerica), Waffle House
- **Other** O: Wal-Mart Supercenter(LP, RX) (1-hr photo)

30 KY 146, La Grange Rd, Anchorage, Pewee Valley
27 US 60, Shelbyville Rd, Middletown, Eastwood
- **Gas** I: BP(D, CW), Thornton's Food Mart(*, K)
- **Food** I: Captain D's Seafood, Waffle House, Wendy's
- **ATM** I: Bank of Louisville
- **Other** O: Shelbyville Rd Veterinary Clinic

25AB 25A - I-64 East, Lexington, 25B - I-64 West, Louisville
23 KY 155, Taylorsville, Jeffersontown
19 KY 18, 19; Billtown Rd
17 US 31East, US 150, Bardstown, Louisville, Fern Creek
- **Gas** O: BP(*, LP, CW)
- **Food** I: Double Dragon II, Subway, Taco Bell

EXIT — KENTUCKY/INDIANA

- **Med** I: Immediate Care Center (9am-9pm, 7 days/ week)
- **ATM** I: Bank of Louisville, Kroger Supermarket, Nation City Bank, PNC Bank
- **Other** I: Kroger Supermarket(24, RX)

15 KY 864, Beulah Church Rd
14 Smyrna Rd
- **Gas** I: Citgo(*)
  O: Key Supermarket(*), Marathon(*, D)
- **Food** O: Barrel of Fun
- **ATM** O: Marathon

12 KY 61, Preston Hwy
10AB 10A - N.I-65, Louisville, 10B - S.I-65, Nashville

↑KENTUCKY

↓INDIANA

0 I-64W, St Louis, I-64E Louisville
1 State Street
- **Gas** I: Thornton's Food Market(*)
- **Food** I: Burger King, Chinese Restaurant, Dooley's Bagels & Deli, Dunkin Donuts (Thornton's), Hardee's, Hoosier Pizza, Long John Silver, Subway
- **Med** I: Hospital
- **ATM** I: Community Bank, Kroger Supermarket, National City Bank
- **Other** I: Dahlem Animal Hospital, Hoosier Bowling Lanes, Kroger Supermarket(24, RX), Rite Aide Pharmacy, Target

3 IN 111, Grant Line Rd
- **Gas** I: Dairy Mart(*), Thornton's Food Mart(*, D, K)
  O: Sav-A-Step(*, D, K)
- **Food** I: Burger King, Lee's Famous Recipe Chicken, Little Caesars Pizza, Mancino's Pizza & Grinders, Nifty's, Papa John's Pizza, Pizza Hut, Rich O's BBQ, Sportstime Pizza, Subway, You-A-Carry-Out-A
  O: Frisch's Big Boy, McDonald's
- **ATM** I: NBD, PNC Bank, Regional Bank
  O: Sav-A-Step
- **Other** I: Aldi Grocery Store, K-Mart(RX), Kroger Supermarket

EXIT — INDIANA/TENNESSEE

4 IN 311, Charlestown Rd
- **Gas** I: Convenient Gasoline(*)
  O: Marathon(*, D)
- **Food** I: A Nice Restaurant, Sam's
  O: Big Bubba's Bub-Ba-Q
- **Med** I: S. IN Rehabilitation Hospital
- **Other** O: Especially Pets Small Animal Hospital

7 I-65, Indianapolis, Louisville
10AB 10A - West Jeffersonville, 10B - IN 62E, Charlestown

↑INDIANA

↓TENNESSEE

1 US 41A, 8th Ave, State Capitol, Metro Center Blvd
- **Gas** I: Texaco(*, CW)
  O: Exxon(*)
- **Food** O: Arby's Roast Town, Denny's, Krystal, McDonald's, Shoney's, Subway, Taco Bell
- **Lodg** O: La Quinta Inn, Regal Maxwell House Hotel
- **AServ** O: Exxon

2 W I-24, N I-65 Clarksvle, Louisvle E I-24, S I-65 Nashville

↑TENNESSEE

Begin I-265

I-270 →

EXIT — OHIO

Begin I-270, Columbus

↓OHIO

2 U.S. 62, OH3, Grove City
- **Gas** O: Shell(*, CW, 24), Sunoco(*, LP, 24), SuperAmerica(*, D, LP, CW)
- **Food** O: Frisch's Big Boy, Waffle House
- **Lodg** O: Knight's Inn
- **ATM** O: Sunoco
- **Other** O: Urbancrest

5 Georgesville Rd
- **Gas** I: Amoco(*), Sunoco(*, LP, 24)
- **Food** O: Blocks Bagel & Cafe (Kroger), Lone Star Steakhouse, Ohio Number One Cafe, Wendy's
- **ATM** I: National City Bank
  O: Huntington Bank
- **Other** I: Georgesville Road Animal Hospital
  O: Christian Armory, Kroger Supermarket(24, RX), Lowe's, Regal Cinemas

7 U.S. 40, Broad St
- **Gas** O: SuperAmerica(*, D, LP)
- **Food** I: Bob Evan's Restaurant, Boston Market Restaurant, Honey Baked Ham, Peacock West (Chinese/ American), Subway, Super China Buffet, Wendy's, York Steak House
  O: Arby's, China Inn, Frisch's Big Boy, J Kilin (Ramada), Long John Silver, Pizza Hut, Ramada, Roosters, W G Grinders, **Waffle House**
- **Lodg** O: Holiday Inn Express, Ramada
- **Med** I: Urgent Care Clinic
  O: Hospital
- **ATM** I: Norwest Financial
  O: Big Bear Grocery
- **Other** I: Christian Armory Bookstore, Kids R Us, Media Play, Phar Mor Drugs(RX), Toys R Us
  O: Big Bear Grocery, Kinko's(24)

EXIT — OHIO

8 Junction I-70, Columbus, Indianapolis
10 Roberts Rd
- **FStop** O: **Quick Fuel**
- **Gas** I: BP(*, D, LP, CW)
- **Food** I: Subway
  O: Holiday Inn, **Waffle House**
- **Lodg** O: Holiday Inn, Royal Inn
- **ATM** I: BP

13AB Cemetary Rd, Fishinger Rd , Hilliard, Upper Arlington
- **Gas** I: Citgo(*, LP), Shell(*, CW)
  O: BP(*, LP, CW), Speedway(*, LP)
- **Food** I: Chili's, Damon's Ribs, Home Town Buffet, Spageddie's, T.G.I. Friday's
  O: Bob Evan's Restaurant, Evergreen Chinese, Max & Erma's, **McDonald's**, Roadhouse Grill, **Tim Horton's**, Wendy's
- **Lodg** I: Comfort Suites Hotel, Homewood Suites Hotel
  O: Motel 6
- **AServ** I: K-Mart(RX)
- **ATM** I: Citgo
- **Other** I: Franklin County Fairground, K-Mart(RX), Lowe's

15 Tuttle Crossing Blvd
- **Gas** I: BP(*, LP, CW), United Dairy Farmers(*, D)
  O: Shell(*, CW, 24)
- **Food** I: Bob Evan's Restaurant, Boston Market Restaurant, Cozumel Mexican Restaurant, Grady's American Grill, Longhorn Steakhouse, Macaroni Grill, Malibu Grill, Marriott, River City Grill (Marriott), Wendy's
  O: McDonald's (Wal-Mart), Uno Pizzeria, Wal-Mart(RX) (Vision Center)
- **Lodg** I: Baymont Inn, Marriott, Sumner Suites
- **AServ** O: Wal-Mart (Vision Center)
- **ATM** I: BP, Star Bank, United Dairy Farmers
  O: Shell
- **Other** O: Wal-Mart(RX) (Vision Center)

EXIT — OHIO

17AB U.S. 33, OH 161, Dublin, Marysville (17A inside, 17B outside)
- **Food** I: Baskin Robbins, Bob Evan's Restaurant, Chi-Chi's Mexican Restaurant, China Garden, Hyde Chophouse, Little Caesars Pizza, McDonald's
- **Lodg** I: Courtyard by Marriott, Cross Country Inn, Red Roof Inn
- **Med** I: Dublin Medical Mall
- **ATM** I: Bank One, Heartland, Huntington Bank, National City
- **Other** I: CVS Pharmacy(RX), Kroger Supermarket(RX), Read Mor Bookstore

20 Sawmill Rd
- **Gas** I: BP(*, D, CW), Dairy Mart(*, LP), Shell(*, LP, CW, 24), Sunoco(*)
  O: BP(*, LP, CW), Marathon(*, D, LP)
- **Food** I: Applebee's, Big Sky Red Bakery & Cafe, Bob Evan's Restaurant, Cappuccino Cafe, Damon's, Doubles, Einstein Bros Bagels, Flannigan's, Longhorn Steakhouse, Oriental Cafe, The Italian Oven
  O: BP, Blimpie Subs & Salads (BP), McDonald's, Olive Garden, Taco Bell, Wendy's
- **Lodg** I: Hampton Inn, Hawthorne Suites Ltd., Woodsin Suites
- **AServ** I: BP
  O: Marathon

EXIT		OHIO
	ATM	I: Bank One, The Loan Zone
		O: BP
	Other	I: Borders Books & Music, Christian Armory, Discovery Zone, Phar Mor Drugs(RX), Zany Brainy
22AB		OH 315, Olentangy River Rd. (22A inside, 22B outside)
23		U.S. 23, Delaware, Worthington (Outer Services Take First Right)
	Gas	I: Marathon(*), Sunoco(*)
	Food	I: Chili's, McDonald's, Michael Dominics Steak & Seafood
		O: 55 at Crossroads, Alexander's, Bob Evan's Restaurant, Bravo Italian Kitchen, Casa Fiesta, Champp's, Dick Clark's American Bandstand Grill, Fuddruckers, Holiday Inn, Macaroni Grill, On The Border Mexican, Ruckmoor, Shapin's, Bill Knapp's Restaurant (see our ad this page)
	Lodg	I: Clarion Hotel, EconoLodge
		O: AmeriSuites (see our ad this page), Courtyard by Marriott, Holiday Inn, Homewood Suites, Microtel, Red Roof Inn, Sheraton Suites, Travelodge TraveLodge
	AServ	I: Marathon
	ATM	I: Bank One, Fifth Third Bank, National City Bank
		O: Century Bank
	Other	I: **Kroger Supermarket**, Rite Aide Pharmacy(RX)
		O: 55 Minute Photo
26AB		Jct I-71, Columbus, Cleveland (26A south, 26B north)
27		OH 710, Cleveland Ave
	Gas	O: Citgo(*)
	Food	I: Antolino Pizza, Cheddar's Cafe, Cooker Grill, Fuddruckers, Golden House Chinese Restaurant, McDonald's, Scramblers, Subway, T.G.I. Friday's, Yanni's Greek Grill
		O: Coffee Talk, Grape Vine, KFC, Knight's Ice Cream, Montgomery Inn Ribs, Nicole's Cafe, Nooner's The Eclectic Cafe, Puerto Vallarta Mexican, Schmidt's Restaurant, Wendy's
	Lodg	I: Embassy Suites
		O: Signature Inn
	Med	I: ✚ Grant/Riverside Medical Facility
		O: ✚ Hospital
	ATM	O: Big Bear Grocery(RX)
	Other	I: Home Depot
		O: Big Bear Grocery(RX), CVS Pharmacy(RX), Kinko's, McAllister Camera & Video, The Cat Doctor
29		OH 3, Westerville
	Gas	I: Shell(*, CW), Speedway(*, LP), Sunoco(*, D)
		O: BP(*)
	Food	I: Carsonie's Italian, China House, Domino's Pizza, Larry B's Sports Lounge, Subway
		O: Bob Evan's Restaurant, Denny's, Ponderosa, Tee Jay's Country, Tim Horton's
	Lodg	O: Cross Country Inn, Knight's Inn
	ATM	I: Huntington Bank, Speedway
		O: BP, Bank One, Star Bank
	Other	I: Aldi Grocery Store, CVS Pharmacy(RX), Enniswood Gardens, Fun City Arcade, Super Saver Cinemas 8, U.S. Post Office, Westerville Veterinary Clinic
30AB		OH 161, Minerva Park, New Albany, Blyndon Wood Metro Park
32		Morse Rd (Southbound, Under Construction)
	Gas	I: BP(*), Shell(*, CW)
		O: Citgo(*), Speedway(*, D)
	Food	I: McDonald's (Wal-Mart), Subway
		O: Donato's Pizza
	Other	I: Wal-Mart(RX)
33		Morse Rd., Easton
35AB		I-670, U.S. 62, Airport, Gahanna
37		OH 317, Hamilton Rd, BSCC & DFAS
	Gas	O: Shell(*, CW)
	Food	O: Baskin Robbins, Bob Evan's Restaurant, China Garden, Damon's Ribs, Frisch's Big Boy, Jersey Mike's Subs, Jordan's Mart & Deli, KFC, Lick's Subs, Yogurts, and Muffins, Panda Chinese Express, Taco Bell
	Other	I: Airport
		O: Buckeye Optical, K-Mart(RX)
39		Ohio 16, Broad St
	Med	O: ✚ Mt Carmel East Hospital
41AB		U.S. 40, Main Street, Whitehall, Reynoldsburg
	Gas	O: Shell(*, CW, 24)
	Food	I: Don Pablo's Mexican Kitchen, Spageddie's
		O: Blocks Bagel, Bob Evan's Restaurant, Denny's, Don Parmesan's, Honey Baked Ham, Hooter's, Manhattan Bagel, Outback Steakhouse, Skyline Chili, The Spaghetti Shop
	Med	O: ✚ Hospital
	Other	O: CVS Pharmacy(RX), Schottenstein's, T.J. Maxx, Value City
43AB		Jct I-70, Wheeling, Columbus
46AB		U.S. 33, Bexley, Lancaster (Difficult Reaccess, 46A inside, 46B outside)
49		Alum Creek Dr, Obetz, Groveport, Columbus Motor Speedway
	FStop	O: BP(*, LP)
	Gas	I: Sunoco(*, D, LP)
	Food	I: Donato's Pizza, Subway
		O: J.R. Valentine's, McDonald's, Taco Bell, Wendy's
	Lodg	O: Comfort Inn
52AB		U.S. 23, High St, Circleville (52A inside, 52B outside)
	Gas	I: Speedway(*, LP), Sunoco(*, LP)
		O: BP(*, LP)
	Food	I: Abner's Country, Blimpie Subs & Salads (Sunoco), Bob Evan's Restaurant, Ponderosa, Sunoco
55		Jct I-71, Columbus, Cincinatti

↑OHIO

Begin I-270, Columbus

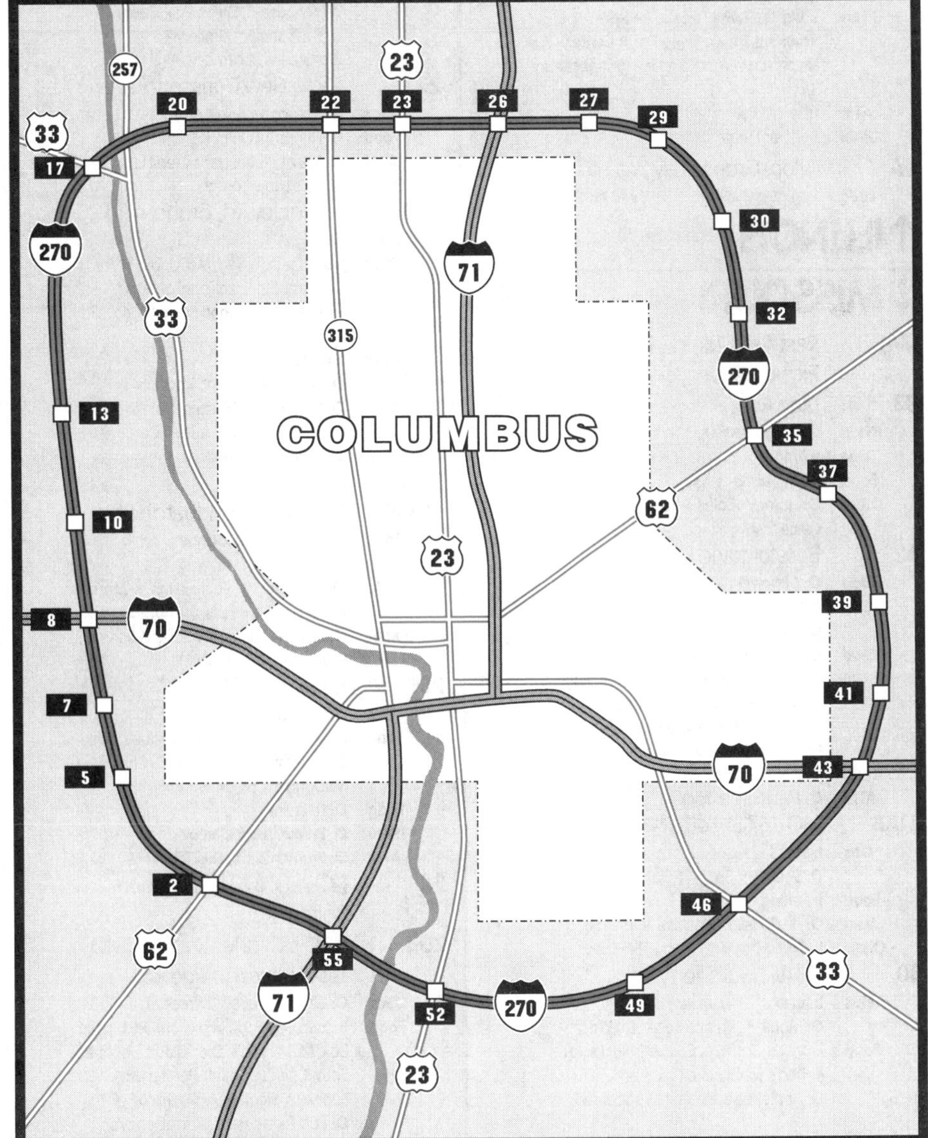

EXIT		ILLINOIS/MISSOURI
	Begin I-270, Illinois	

↓ILLINOIS

12 IL - 159, Collinsville, Edwardsville
9 IL 157, Collinsville, Edwardsville
7 I-255 S Jct I-270 E
6AB IL. 110 Wood River, Pontoon Beach
- **Gas** O: Amoco(*)
- **Food** I: Denny's, McDonald's
  O: Hen House Restaurant
- **Lodg** I: Ramada Limited, Super 8
  O: Best Western
- **Med** I: ✚ Hospital
- **ATM** I: Omni Bank
  O: Amoco

4 **(3)** IL. 203 Granite City
- **Food** O: Charlie's Restaurant
- **TServ** O: Roberts & Dybdahl Truck Services

3B Great River Rd, Alton Il Hwy 3
- **Gas** I: Amoco, Phillips 66(D)
- **Food** I: Hardee's, Waffle House
- **Lodg** I: Canal Motel, Chain Of Rocks Motel, Land Of Lincoln Motel, Sun Motel
- **AServ** I: Amoco
- **TServ** I: Big Jim Public Scales, Hansen Trucking, Prarie Used Truck Center, Riechmann Truck Service (Bridgestone Tire)
- **ATM** I: Sun Motel
- **Other** I: Super 1 Stop

3A Alton, Granite City
- **Lodg** I: Midwest Motel

↑ILLINOIS

↓MISSOURI

(34) Rest Area (RR, HF, Phones, Picnic, P)
33 Lilac Ave
- **FStop** I: Phillips 66(*), QuikT(*, SCALES)
- **Gas** I: Amoco
- **Food** I: Hardee's
- **Other** O: Harney's Sales & Service, US Post Office

32 Bellefontaine Rd.
- **FStop** O: Citgo(*, D)
- **Gas** I: Amoco
  O: Mobil(*), Shell(*, CW)
- **Food** O: Burger King, China King, Denny's, Econolodge, Hunan Restaurant, Jigger's Restaurant (EconoLodge), KFC, McDonald's(PLAY), Pizza Hut, Pappa John's Pizza, Steak & Shake, Subway
- **Lodg** O: Econolodge, Motel 6
- **ATM** O: Merchantile Bank

31AB MO 367 St. Louis
- **Gas** I: Mobil
  O: Shell(*, CW), Shop-N-Gas(*)
- **Food** I: PeKing
- **Med** O: ✚ Christian Hospital Northeast
- **Other** I: Home Depot(LP), Shop "N" Save

30 CR AC, Halls Ferry Rd
- **Gas** I: Amoco(*, CW), Hucks(*), Shell(*, CW)
  O: Mobil(*, D), Phillips 66(*, D), QuikTrip(*)
- **Food** I: Arby's, Church's Chicken, Hucks, KFC, Robert's Steak Buffett
  O: Applebee's, Captain D's Seafood, Casa Gallardo (Mexican), Chuck E Cheese's Pizza, Donut Delight, Easy Street, Popeye's Chicken, Red Lobster, The Olive Garden, Wendy's, White Castle Restaurant
- **Lodg** O: Super 8
- **ATM** I: HMB Bank
  O: Mercantile Bank, QuikTrip
- **Other** I: C Ray Marine Center
  O: Keeton Optician, Kinko's

29 West Florissant Ave
- **Food** I: Burger King(PLAY), Chop Suey, Krispy Kreme Doughnuts, Malone's Grill, McDonald's(PLAY)
  O: Jack in the Box, Old Country Buffet, Pasta House Italian Restaurant
- **AServ** I: Wal-Mart
- **Other** I: Sam's, Wal-Mart
  O: Dierberg Food & Drugs, Mailboxes Etc., Office Depot, Professional Opticle, St Louis Eye Clinic, Venture Center

28 Washington St., Elizabeth Ave.
- **Gas** I: Amoco
  O: Sinclair
- **Food** O: Discovery Zone, Little Caesars Pizza, Mrs O's Cafe & Pie Pantry, Pizza Hut (Discovery Zone), Taco Bell
- **Other** O: Discovery Zone, HQ Home Quarters Warehouse(LP), Office Max, Sears Optical, Snuck's Grocery(LP, RX), WalGreens Pharmacy(*, RX)

27 CR N, New Florissant Rd
- **Gas** O: Amoco(CW), Shell(*, CW)
- **Food** O: Florissant Quick K Shop
- **ATM** O: Spirit Of Saint Louis Credit Union
- **Other** O: RB's Laundromat

26B N. Hanley Rd, Graham Rd.
- **Gas** O: Citgo(*, D)
- **Food** I: Days Inn, McDonald's(PLAY)
  O: Damon's, Fazoli's Italian Food, Hardee's, Long John Silver, Wacovell's Restaurant
- **Lodg** I: Days Inn
  O: Hampton Inn, Red Roof Inn
- **Med** O: ✚ Christian Hospital Northwest
- **ATM** O: Citgo, First Bank & Trust Co.
- **Other** O: Optical Eye Healthcare

26A I-170 S
25AB **(24)** U.S. 67 Lindbergh Blvd
- **Food** O: Jack in the Box, Lindy's Family Restaurant
- **Lodg** O: Budgetel Inn, Fairfield Inn by Marriott, Holiday Inn Express, Surburban Lodge
- **Other** O: Apache Village (RV Sales & Service), WalGreens Pharmacy(RX)

23 McDonnell Blvd.
- **Gas** O: QuikTrip(*)
- **Food** O: Denny's (La Quinta), Hardee's, Jack-In-The-Box, La Quinta, Lion's Choice, McDonald's, Steak 'N Shake
- **Lodg** O: La Quinta
- **TServ** O: Delgel Truck Center
- **ATM** O: Bremen Bank, QuikTrip

22 **(21)** MO. 370 W. Missouri Bottom Rd
20B **(18)** St. Charles Rock Rd, MO 180, Natural Bridge Rd.
- **Gas** O: Citgo(*, D), Mobil(*) (Wrecker)
- **Food** I: Casa Galaroda (Mexican), Jack in the Box, McDonald's, Old St Louis Chopped Souy (Chinese Buffet), Ponderosa, Shoney's, Steak & Shake, Taco Bell
  O: Bob Evan's Restaurant, Denny's, Holiday Inn, O'Malley's (Holiday Inn), Olive Garden, Ryan's Steakhouse, Waffle House
- **Lodg** I: Knight's Inn
  O: Holiday Inn, Motel 6, Red Roof Inn, Super 8
- **Med** I: ✚ DePaul Health
- **Other** I: Animal Emergency Care, Office Depot, WalGreens Pharmacy(RX)

20A **(18)** I-70 Jct. Kansan City & St Louis
17 Dorsett Rd
- **Gas** I: Amoco(CW)
  O: Mobil(D), Phillips 66(*, CW), Shell
- **Food** O: Bruegger's Bagel & Bakery, Budgetel Inn, Choi's Sushi Bar Restaurant, Dairy Queen, Denny's, Dunkin Donuts, Emo's Pizza, Flaco's Taco's, Fuddruckers, Hava Java Coffee, Hunan Chinese, Krieger's Grill, McDonald's, Pappa John's Pizza, Steak & Shake, Subway, Taco Bell, The Pasta House, The Wok Express, Wendy's
- **Lodg** I: Drury Inn
  O: Budgetel Inn
- **AServ** O: Mobil
- **Med** O: ✚ The Med First Physician
- **Other** I: Post Office
  O: Mailboxes Etc., Schnucks 24 Hr Supercenter, WalGreens Pharmacy(RX)

16B D West, Page Ave
16A **(15)** Page Ave, CR D East
- **Lodg** I: Comfort Inn

14 MO. 340 Olive Blvd.
- **Gas** I: Phillips 66(CW), Phillips 66(CW)
- **Food** I: Applebee's, Bristol Bar & Grill (Seafood), China's Olive Cafe, Dairy Queen, Domino's Pizza, Drury Inn, KFC, Lion Choice Roast Beef, Mr Goodcents Subs & Pasta, Padrino's Pizza, Partzei Bakery, Peking Inn Restaurant (Korean), St Louis Smoothie, The Greek Gourmet, Zang Chi
- **Lodg** I: Courtyard by Marriott, Drury Inn
- **Med** O: ✚ Hospital

13 Ladue Rd
12 **(11)** I-64. U.S. 40 U.S. 61 Jct., Wentzille, St Louis (Difficult Reaccess)
- **Med** I: ✚ St John's Hospital

9 MO. 100 Manchester Rd.
- **Gas** I: Phillips 66(D)
  O: Shell(*, CW)
- **Food** I: Houlihan's Restaurant & Bar, Ruby Tuesday
  O: Casa Gallardo (Mexican), Domino's Pizza, Olive Garden, Rick's Cafe, The First Wok (Chinese)

8 Doughtery Ferry Rd
- **Med** I: ✚ St Joseph Hospital (4 Miles)
  O: ✚ Deaconness West Hospital (Emergency Services)

7 Big Bend Rd
5AB **(4)** West, I-44 U.S. 50 Jct.
3 MO. 30, Gravois Rd
2 MO21, Tesson Ferry Rd
- **Gas** O: Mobil, Texaco(CW)
- **Food** O: Calico's Restaurant, Dulany's Grill, Golden Lion Restaurant, Hunan's Royal Oriental Food, Imo's Pizza, Jack in the Box, Leong's Restaurant (Oriental), Little Caesars Pizza, Quiz No's (Subs), St Louis Bread
- **Med** O: ✚ St Anthony's Medical Center
- **Other** O: Bierberg's(RX), Crown Opticle, Discovery Zone, Insty Prints, Mailboxes Etc., WalGreens Pharmacy(RX)

1AB I-55 to St Louis, Memphis
1C 55N St Louis (This Exit is the same as 196/197 & 12A on I-55)

↑MISSOURI

Begin I-270, Missouri

EXIT	MARYLAND

Begin I-270, Maryland

↓MARYLAND

31AB MD 85, Market St., Buckeystown
- **FStop** W: Amoco(CW, 24)
- **Gas** E: AAMCO Transmission, Exxon(*, D, LP, CW), Pennzoil Oil Change, Sheetz(*, LP, 24), Shell(*, LP, CW, 24), Texaco(D, CW)
- **Food** E: Applebee's, Bob Evan's Restaurant, Golden Corral Family Steakhouse, Holiday Inn, Johnny's D's, KFC, Lonestar Steakhouse, McDonald's, Olive Garden, Pargo's, Roy Rogers, Taco Bell
  W: Baskin Robbins, Blimpie Subs & Salads, Cracker Barrel, Hampton Inn
- **Lodg** E: Days Inn, Holiday Inn, Holiday Inn Express
  W: Fairfield Inn, Hampton Inn
- **AServ** E: Pennzoil Oil Change
- **ATM** E: FCNB Bank, First Nat'l Bank of Maryland, Sheetz, Shell
  W: Amoco

(29) Scenic View (Picnic)

26 MD80, Urbana, Buckeystown
- **Gas** E: Exxon(*)
- **ATM** E: Exxon

22 MD109, Barnesville, Hyattstown

(21) Weigh Station (Southbound)

(21) Weigh Station (Northbound)

18 MD121, Boyds, Clarksburg

16 MD27, Father Hurley Blvd, Damascus

15AB MD118, MD355, to Germantown
- **Gas** W: Amoco(24), Exxon(*, CW, 24)
- **Food** E: Grady's II (Hampton Inn)
  W: Pizza Hut
- **Lodg** E: Hampton Inn
- **AServ** W: Amoco(24)
- **Med** E: ✚ Shady Grove Medical Ctr
- **ATM** W: Exxon
- **Other** W: County Police

13AB Middle Brook Rd. (Northbound)
- **Gas** E: Amoco(*, CW), Exxon(*, CW)
- **Food** E: Chinese Pagoda, KFC, Little Caesars Pizza, McDonald's(PLAY), Papa John's, Sakura Japanese, Taco Bell, Wendy's
- **ATM** E: 7-11 Convenience Store, Amoco, Chevy Chase Bank, Exxon, First Virginia Bank, Grand Bank
- **Other** E: 7-11 Convenience Store, Animal Hospital, Discovery Zone, Giant Food Store(RX), Middle Brook Square Shopping Center

11AB MD124, Montgomery Village Ave
- **Gas** E: Exxon(*, D, CW)
  W: Shell(*), Texaco(*, D)
- **Food** E: Boston Market Restaurant, Ichiban Chinese, McDonald's, Roy Rogers, Starbucks Coffee
  W: Denny's, Einstein Bros Bagels, Friendly's, Jerry's Subs & Pizza, Pastry Shop, PeKing Cheers Restaurant, Roy Rogers, Shakeys Pizza, Starbucks Coffee
- **Lodg** E: Courtyard by Marriott, Hilton, Holiday Inn
  W: Red Roof Inn
- **Med** E: ✚ Urgent Care Clinic
- **ATM** E: NationsBank, Sandy Spring Nat'l Bank
  W: Shell, Texaco

Truck or Large Vehicle Parking

1223

Quality Suites Shady Grove

Quality Suites

301-840-0200
800-228-5151

Full Breakfast Included
Managers Reception Mon-Thur
Outdoor Pool • Exercise Room
Meeting/Banquet Facilities
Handicap Accessible
Interior Corridors • Coin Laundry
Coffee Makers • Microwaves • Refrigerators

$59.95 Rate

BASED ON AVAILABILITY

I-495N to I-270N to Exit 8, Shady Grove W to Corporate Blvd. hotel on L
I-270S to Exit 8, Shady Grove First light, L to Corporate Blvd. hotel on L

Maryland ▪ I-270 ▪ Exit 8

- **Other** E: CVS Pharmacy(24, RX), Vision Works
  W: Giant Grocery Store(RX)

10 MD 117, Clomper Rd., MD 124, Quince Orchard Rd. (Northbound, Reaccess Southbound Only)
- **Food** W: Chili's, Il Calstello, Lonestar Steakhouse
- **ATM** W: Chevy Chase Bank
- **Other** W: Giant Supermarket(RX)

9 I-370, Metro Station, Sam Igg Hwy.

8 Shadygrove Rd, Omega Dr. (Difficult Reaccess)
- **Gas** E: Crown(*), Texaco(24)
- **Food** E: Red Lobster
- **Lodg** W: Courtyard by Marriott, Quality Suites (see our ad this page), Sleep Inn
- **AServ** E: Crown, Texaco(24)
- **ATM** W: NationsBank
- **Other** E: 270 Center

6AB MD28, W Montgomery Ave.
- **Gas** W: Shell(*)
- **Food** W: Callaway's (Best Western)
- **Lodg** W: Best Western
- **AServ** W: Shell
- **ATM** W: Citibank, Shell

5 MD 189, Falls Rd
- **Other** W: Police Station

4AB Montrose Rd

1 MD 187, Old Georgetown Rd.
- **Gas** W: Exxon(*)
- **Food** W: Bradley's Ice Cream, Cheasapeak Bay Bagel, Hamburger Hamlet, Ice Cream Cafe, The Beanbag
- **AServ** W: Exxon
- **ATM** W: Crestar Bank, Mellon Financial Center, NationsBank
- **Other** W: CVS Pharmacy, Georgetown Square, Giant Supermarket(24, RX)

↑MARYLAND

Begin I-270, Maryland

I-271 OHIO →

EXIT	OHIO

Begin I-271

↓OHIO

188 Jct. I-90

36 Wilson Mills Rd., Mayfield, Highland Heights
- **Gas** W: BP(*), Marathon(*), Sunoco(*)
- **Food** E: Austin's Steakhouse
  W: Denny's, **Wellington's Restaurant**
- **Lodg** E: Holiday Inn
- **AServ** W: BP, Marathon, Sunoco
- **ATM** W: First Merit Bank, Sunoco
- **Other** E: Village Veternarian Hospital

34 Mayfield Rd., U.S. 322
- **FStop** E: BP(*, D, LP)
- **Gas** E: Sunoco(*)
  W: Shell(*)
- **Food** E: Amy Joy Donuts, Blimpie Subs & Salads (BP), **Cafe 56**, Cork & Bottle Bar & Grill, Davis Bakery & Deli, Domino's Pizza, **Eastside Mario's**, Master Pizza, Mr. Hero, Subway, **Tony Roma's**, Wendy's
  W: **Arrabibta's**, **Bob Evan's Restaurant**, Burger King, **China Express**, **Longhorn Steakhouse**, Longo's Pizza, **McDonald's**, **Moose O' Malley's**, **O Tani Japanese**, Pepperidge Farm, **T.G.I. Friday's**
- **Lodg** W: Budgetel Inn
- **AServ** E: **BP**, Sunoco
  W: Shell
- **Med** E: ✚ Hospital
- **ATM** E: Fifth Third Bank, **Finast Grocery Store**(24), Key Bank, Park View Federal Savings Bank, **Rini Rego Supermarket**, Star Bank, Sunoco
  W: Huntington Bank, **Moose O' Malley's**, Ohio Savings Bank
- **Other** E: **CVS Pharmacy**(24, RX), Dairy Mart(*), **Finast Grocery Store**, **Rini Rego Supermarket**
  W: Best Buy, Doc Eye World, Sears

32 Brainard Rd., Cedar Rd., Pepper Pike, Beachwood, Lyndhurst
- **Food** E: Champp's, J. Alexander's Restaurant
- **ATM** E: National City Bank
- **Other** E: **Brainard Place Pharmacy**(RX), U.S. Post Office

29 US 422 W, OH 87, Chagrin Blvd
- **Gas** E: Gulf(*) (Towing), Marathon(CW), Shell(*, CW, 24)
  W: Amoco(*, D), BP(*, D)
- **Food** E: Coffee & Creations, **Corky & Lenny's**, Domino's Pizza, **McDonald's**, **Pizza Hut**, **Red Lobster**, The Olive Garden, **Uno Pizzeria Restaurant and Bar (Holiday Inn)**, Village Square Pizza, Wendy's
  W: Carver's Steaks and Chops, Charley's Crab, Christino's (Marriott), Moxie Restaurant, **Ristorante Gionvanni's**, Your's Truly
- **Lodg** E: Holiday Inn, The Courtyard Marriott, TraveLodge
  W: Embassy Suites, **Marriott**, Radisson Inn, Residence Inn
- **AServ** E: Gulf (Towing)
- **Med** W: ✚ Parkway Medical Center, ✚ St. Luke's Hospital
- **ATM** E: Fifth Third Bank, Ohio Savings Bank
- **Other** E: CVS Pharmacy(RX), **Gale's Supermarket**

28 OH 175, Richmond Rd., Emery Rd
- **Gas** E: BP(*)
- **Food** E: Astoria Restaurant, Country Kitchen, Honey Girl Bake Shoppe, Master Pizza, Uncle BB's Deli
- **Med** E: ✚ Hospital
- **ATM** E: BP, Star Bank
- **Other** E: Emory Food Mart(*)

27AB JCT I-480, US 422 E

26 Rockside Rd.
- **Gas** E: Speedway(*), Sunoco(*, LP, 24)
- **Food** E: **Burger King**, Corea's Proud Pony Italian American Bistro, Cugino's Pizza, Donut Works, Jenny's Grill (Ramada Inn), Mr. Hero, Perkin's

Bold red print shows RV & Bus parking available or nearby

EXIT OHIO

Family Restaurant
Lodg **E:** Ramada Inn
Med **W:** ✚ Hospital
ATM **E:** America's Cash Express, Parksview Federal
Other **E:** **Indoor Links**, Stop N Go Supermarket

23 OH 14 W, Forbes Rd., Broadway Ave.
Gas **E:** Marathon(*)
W: BP(*, 24)
Food **E:** McDonald's, Pizza Hut, Subway, Taco Bell, Wendy's, Wing Kee Chinese
Lodg **E:** Holiday Inn Express (see our ad this page)
Med **W:** ✚ Hospital
Other **E:** Builder Square, **Sam's Club**

21 OH 14 E, Youngstown

19 OH 82, Macedonia, Twinsburg (Difficult Reaccess)
Gas **E:** Speedway(*)
W: Sunoco(LP)
Food **E:** Blue Willow, Casa D'Angelo's, East of Chicago Pizza Co., Gallery Bake Shoppe, Marco's Pizza, Oriental Dragon, Subway, Zachary's Restaurant
W: Applebee's, Boston Market Restaurant, **Burger King**, Dairy Queen, Frankie's Wok, Fuji Japanese Restaurant, **HomeTown Buffet**, Little Caesars Pizza, **Outback Steakhouse**, Pizza Hut,

Holiday Inn EXPRESS®
Oakwood Village, Ohio
440-786-1998
Free Breakfast Bar
1063
Indoor Pool/Whirlpool/Sauna
Free HBO and Cable TV
In Room Movies
In Room Data Ports
5 miles from Seaworld and Geauga Lake (Seasonal)
2 miles from Shopping and Family Restaurants
I-271 To Exit 23 Broadway Exit going East on Broadway, behind McDonald's on Left side
OHIO ▪ I-271 ▪ EXIT 23

EXIT OHIO

Quizno's Classic Sub, Taco Bell, Wendy's, Winking Lizard
AServ **W:** **K-Mart**(RX), Sunoco, **Wal-Mart**(RX) **(Vision Center)**
ATM **E:** First National Bank
W: **Finast Grocery Store**(RX), Ohio Savings Bank
Other **W:** CVS Pharmacy(RX), **Finast Grocery Store**(RX), **K-Mart**(RX), **Stop N Shop**, **Wal-Mart**(RX) **(Vision Center)**

18 OH 8, Boston Hieghts, Acran, Macedonia, Northfield
Gas **E:** Amoco(*, D), BP(*, D, LP, CW), Speedway(*)
Food **E:** Arizona Steakhouse, BP, Bob Evan's Restaurant, Dolphin Family Restaurant, Donut Tree, Subway (BP)
W: **Applebee's**, **KFC**, McDonald's, **The Ground Round Steakhouse**
Lodg **E:** Budgetel Inn, Knight's Inn, Motel 6, TraveLodge
AServ **E:** Amoco
ATM **E:** BP

12 OH 303, Richfield, Peninsula

10 JCT I-77, Acron, Cleveland

(8) Rest Area (RR, Phones, Picnic; Southbound)

(8) Rest Area (RR, Phones, Picnic; Northbound)

3 OH 94, Wadsworth, North Royalton, I-71 N, Cleveland

1 JCT I-71 S, Columbus

↑OHIO

Begin I-271

I-275 KENTUCKY/OHIO/INDIANA →

EXIT KENTUCKY

Begin I-275

↓KENTUCKY

84 JCT I-71, I-75, Lexington, Louisville going south, Cincinnati going north

83 U.S. 25, U.S. 42, U.S. 127, Dixie Hwy
ATM **I:** People's Bank

82 KY 1303, Turkeyfoot Rd
Food **O:** Applebee's, T.G.I. Friday's
Med **O:** ✚ Hospital
ATM **O:** Caldwell Banker, Star Bank

80 KY 17, Covington, Independence
Gas **I:** SuperAmerica(*, D, LP), United Dairy Farmers(*)
Food **I:** Arby's, Bob Evan's Restaurant, Burger King, Frisch's Big Boy, SuperAmerica, Taco Bell (Super America), Wendy's
TServ **I:** **Freightliner Dealer**
ATM **I:** United Dairy Farmers

79 Taylor, Mill Rd, Covington, KY 16
Gas **O:** BP(*, D, CW)
Food **O:** KFC, McDonald's(PLAY), Oriental Wok, Snappy Tomato Pizza, Subway, Taco Bell
ATM **O:** Fifth Third Bank, Remke's Supermarket
Other **O:** Emergency Veterinary & Specialty Clinic, Remke's Supermarket, Rite Aide Pharmacy(RX)

77 KY 9, Wilder, Maysville, Newport,

EXIT KENTUCKY/OHIO

Alexandria, AA Highway

76 Three Mile Rd, Northern Kentucky University (Eastbound, Reaccess Westbound Only)

74AB to U.S. 27, Alexandria - 74A, Junction I-471, Newport, Cincinnati - 74B (74A goes to the outside, 74B to the inside)
Med **I:** ✚ Hospital
Other **O:** Highland Hikes & Cold Springs

↑KENTUCKY

↓OHIO

72 U.S. 52 West, Kellogg Ave , Coney Island
Food **I:** Lebo's, River Galley Casino
Other **I:** Bill's Carry Out Grocery, Lumpkin Airport, River Galley Casino, Starlight Ballroom
O: River Downs, Riverbend

71 U.S.52 E, New Richmond, Riverbend, River Downs

69 Five Mile Rd
Med **I:** ✚ Hospital

EXIT OHIO

Other **O:** Withrow Nature Preserve

65 OH 125, Amelia, Beechmont Ave
Gas **I:** BP(*, LP), SuperAmerica(*, LP)
Food **I:** Bob Evan's Restaurant, Burger King, Chi Chi's Mexican Restaurant, Days Inn, East Side Inn Restaurant (Days Inn), Frisch's Big Boy, McDonald's, Shell's Great Casual Seafood
O: Arby's, BW-3 Grill, Hooter's, Red Lobster, Szechuan House, Wendy's
Lodg **I:** Cross Country Inn, Days Inn, Red Roof Inn
O: Motel 6
ATM **I:** BP, Guardian Savings Bank
O: Provident Bank
Other **I:** Home Depot

63AB OH 32, Batavia, Newtown (West Services on Eastgate Blvd)
Gas **I:** Ashland(*), Speedway(*, D, LP)
Food **I:** Ashland, Gramma's Pizza (Ashland), Mount Washington Bakery
O: Bob Evan's Restaurant, Frisch's Big Boy, McKenna's Restaurant, O'Charley's, Perkin's Family Restaurant, Wendy's
Lodg **O:** Holiday Inn
ATM **O:** Kroger Supermarket(RX), PNC Bank
Other **O:** Kids R Us, Kroger Supermarket(RX), Son's Super Savings Center, Toys R Us

Bold red print shows RV & Bus parking available or nearby

EXIT		OHIO
59		U.S. 50, Hillsboro
57		OH 28, Milford, Blanchester
	Gas	**I:** BP[*, LP], Shell[*, 24]
	Food	**I:** Ponderosa, R.W. Roosters
		O: Arby's, Burger King, Dunkin Donuts, KFC, Long John Silver, PP Noodles, Taco Bell, White Castle Restaurant
	AServ	**O:** K-Mart[RX]
	Med	**O:** ✚ Walk In Clinic
	ATM	**I:** Star Bank
		O: Key Bank, Thriftway Food & Drug[RX]
	Other	**I:** Milford Animal Hospital
		O: K-Mart[RX], Milford Bowling Lanes, Thriftway Food & Drug[RX]
54		Wards Corner Rd
	Gas	**I:** United Dairy Farmers[*]
		O: BP[*, LP]
	Food	**I:** Bonny Lynn Bakery, Frisch's Big Boy, Gold Star Chili, Subway
	ATM	**O:** BP
	Other	**I:** East Hills Veterinary Clinic
52		Indian Hill, Loveland
	Gas	**O:** Marathon[D]
	AServ	**O:** Marathon
50		U.S. 22, OH 3, Montgomery, Morrow
	Gas	**I:** BP[*, D, LP], Shell[*, CW, 24]
		O: Speedway[*, D, LP]
	Food	**I:** Gold Star Chili, La Rosa's Pizzeria, McDonald's, P.J.'s Restaurant & Lounge, Skyline Chili, Village Wok, Wendy's
		O: Speedway, The Melting Pot (Fondue)
	Med	**I:** ✚ Hospital
	ATM	**I:** Bank One, Fifth Third Bank, Shell, Star Bank
	Other	**I:** Hanson Animal Hospital
		O: Kyle Veterinary Hospital
49		Junction I-71, Columbus, Cincinnati
47		Reed - Hartman Hwy, Blue Ash
	Lodg	**I:** Doubletree Guest Suites, AmeriSuites (see our ad this page)
46		U.S. 42, Sharonville, Mason
	Gas	**I:** Ashland[*], Marathon[*], Shell[*, LP, CW]
		O: BP[*, LP, CW]
	Food	**I:** Arby's, DAYS INN Days Inn, Noodles Restaurant, Szechuan House, Waffle House
		O: Burger King, **Chase Grill (Holiday Inn)**, Damon's Ribs, Dunkin Donuts, Hardee's, **Holiday Inn**, House of Sun Chinese, KFC, McDonald's[PLAY], Mountain Jacks, Perkin's Family Restaurant, Skyline Chili, Taco Bell, Wendy's, White Castle Restaurant
	Lodg	**I:** DAYS INN Days Inn
		O: **Holiday Inn (see our ad this page)**, Motel 6
	AServ	**I:** Marathon

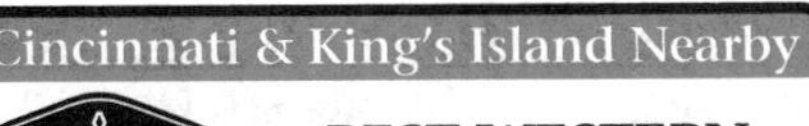

Best Western
BEST WESTERN SPRINGDALE HOTEL AND CONFERENCE CENTRE
1676
Heated Indoor Pool
New Deluxe Guest Rooms
Whirlpool • Exercise Room
Restaurant • Lounge • Gift Shop
Free Newspaper
Group & Tour Bus Packages !
513-671-6600
11911 Sheraton Lane • Springdale, OH
OHIO • I-275 • EXIT 41

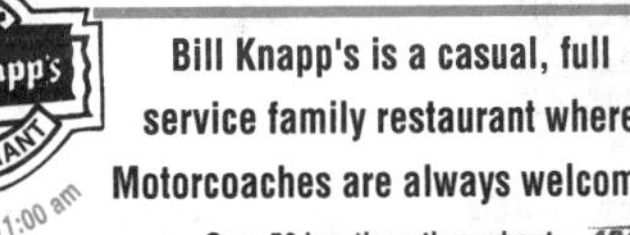

Bill Knapp's is a casual, full service family restaurant where Motorcoaches are always welcome.
1798
Over 50 locations throughout: Michigan • Ohio • Indiana
614-846-4030 Columbus
OHIO • I-270 • EXIT 23

EXIT		OHIO
		O: K-Mart[RX]
	ATM	**I:** Fifth Third Bank
		O: BP, PNC Bank
	Other	**I:** Indian Grocers Food Market, Sharon Woods (1 Mile)
		O: CVS Pharmacy[24, RX], K-Mart[RX]
44		Mosteller Rd
	FStop	**O:** **Quick Fuel**
	Lodg	**I:** Homewood Suites Hotel
	TServ	**O:** **Tri State Ford**
43AB		Jct I-75, Dayton, Cincinnati
42		OH 747, Springdale, Glendale
	FStop	**O:** **Amoco**[*, D, LP]
	Food	**I:** Frisch's Big Boy, KFC, Panda Chinese, Red Squirrel, TCBY, Wendy's
	ATM	**I:** Bank One, Star Bank
	Other	**I:** Borders Books & Music, Kids R Us
41		OH 4, Springfield Pike
	Gas	**I:** BP[*]
		O: Shell[*, CW]
	Food	**I:** Applebee's, Chi Chi's Mexican Restaurant, Dairy Queen, Outback Steakhouse, Pattie Shack Fine Jamaican Cuisine, Penn Station, Perkin's Family Restaurant, Wok & Roll
		O: Bennigan's (Budgetel Inn), Bob Evan's Restaurant, Budgetel Inn, Hooters
	Lodg	**I:** Cross Country Inn, Extended Stay America, Howard Johnson, Best Western (see our ad this page)
		O: Best Western, Budgetel Inn
	Med	**I:** ✚ Doctor's Urgent Care Clinic
	Other	**O:** Showcase Cinemas
39		Forest Park, Winton Rd

Bill Knapp's is a casual, full service family restaurant where Motorcoaches are always welcome.
1797
Over 50 locations throughout: Michigan • Ohio • Indiana
513-385-9240 Cincinnati
513-825-1603 Cincinnati 513-231-5311-Cincinnati
OHIO • I-275 • EXIT 33/39/69

1344
AMERISUITES
AMERICA'S AFFORDABLE ALL-SUITE HOTEL
Look for these Lodging Locations at the exits below

	EXIT	
AmeriSuites	39	513-825-9035
	47	513-489-3666

EXIT		OHIO
	Gas	**I:** Marathon[*, LP]
		O: BP[*, D]
	Food	**I:** Cracker Barrel, **Frisch's Big Boy**, Fuddruckers, Heavenly Ham, Old Country Buffet, **Peking Wok**, Ponderosa, Wendy's
		O: BP, Blimpie Subs & Salads (BP), **K-Mart**[RX], Little Caesars Pizza (K-Mart), McDonald's, See our ad on this page)
	Lodg	**I:** AmeriSuites (see our ad this page), Lee's Inn
	Med	**O:** ✚ Hospital
	ATM	**O:** Meijer Grocery[24] (Grocery)
	Other	**I:** Babies R Us, Discovery Zone, Winton Woods (3 Miles)
		O: **K-Mart**[RX], Meijer Grocery (Grocery), Super Saver Cinema
36		U.S. 127, Mount Healthy, Hamilton, Fairfield
	Gas	**O:** Dairy Mart[*], SuperAmerica[*, K]
	Food	**I:** Arby's, **Burger King**, Frisch's Big Boy, Little Caesars Pizza, McDonald's, Subway, **Taco Bell**
	Other	**I:** County Sheriff's Office, Thriftway Supermarket[RX]
		O: CVS Pharmacy[RX]
33		U.S. 27, Colerain Ave, OH 126
	Gas	**O:** BP[*], SuperAmerica[*, D, LP]
	Food	**I:** Bob Evan's Restaurant, Fazoli's Italian Food, Frisch's Big Boy, Hardee's, KFC, Long John Silver, Outback Steakhouse, Pizza Hut, **Bill Knapp's Restaurant (see our ad this page)**
		O: Burger King, Wendy's
	AServ	**O:** Wal-Mart[RX]
	ATM	**I:** Provident Bank
		O: First National Bank, SuperAmerica, Thriftway Drug[RX]
	Other	**I:** Toys R Us
		O: The Book Rack, Thriftway Drug[RX], Wal-Mart[RX]
31		Blue Rock Rd, Ronald Reagan Cross Cnty Hwy
	Med	**I:** ✚ Hospital
		Note: I-275 runs concurrent below with I-74. Numbering follows I-74.
9		Jct I-275 North , to I-75, Dayton
7		OH 128, Hamilton, Cleves
	Gas	**N:** BP[*, D], Shell[*, D, K]
	Food	**N:** Wendy's
		S: Angelo's Pizza, Bier House & Restaurant
5		Jct I-275 South , to KY
		Note: I-275 runs concurrent above with I-74. Numbering follows I-74.
25		JCT I-74, US 52, Cincinnati, Indianapolis (Left Exit)
21		Kilby Rd

Please request Exit Authority Rate
1842

• Newly Renovated
• Color TV w/HBO, CNN, ESPN
• Movies-On-Demand
• Chase Grill Restaurant
• Pizz Hut Express™
• Indoor Heated Pool, Fitness Center
• Tennis/Sand Volley Ball & Basketball
• Paramount's Kings Island Amusement Park, 8 miles • Discount King's Island Tickets
Award Winning
513-563-8330
1842
OHIO • I-275 • EXIT 46

EXIT OHIO

↑OHIO

↓INDIANA

16 U.S. 50, Lawrenceburg, Greendale, Aurora

- **TStop** O: **Kinnett Truckstop(*, 24) (Marathon Gas)**
- **Gas** O: AmeriStop(*), Shell(*) (Dairy Mart)
- **Food** O: AmeriStop, Cincinnati Doughnuts & Bagels (AmeriStop), **Empress Chili (Kinnett TS)**, **Kinnett Truckstop (Marathon Gas)**
- **Lodg** O: **Argosy Casino (see our ad this page)**, The Wishing Well Motel
- **Med** O: ✚ Hospital
- **Other** O: Riverboat, Taylor Boys Inc. Fireworks

↑INDIANA

EXIT OHIO

$69 ROOMS AND UP
based on availability
Prices vary by season
RESTAURANTS • BUFFET • ENTERTAINMENT
Argosy Casino™ & Hotel
Call 1-888-ARGOSY-7
Must be 21. Photo I.D. required. Guaranteed admission with reservations only.
©1998 by Indiana Gaming Co. L.P. All rights reserved. www.argosycasino.com
I-275 West to Exit 16, Lawrenceburg, IN

EXIT OHIO

↓KENTUCKY

11 to KY 20, Petersburg

7AB KY 237, Hebron

- **Gas** O: Shell(*, D, CW, 24)
- **Food** O: Gold Star Chili, Shell, Subway (Shell)

4AB KY 212, to KY 20, Cincinnati - No. Kentucky Int'l Airport

- **Gas** I: ValAir
- **Lodg** O: Radisson Inn
- **Med** O: ✚ Hospital

2 Mineola Pike

- **Food** I: Holiday Inn, River City Grill (Holiday Inn)
- **Lodg** I: Budgetel Inns & Suites, Holiday Inn
  O: Residence Inn

↑KENTUCKY

Begin I-275

I-275 FLORIDA →

EXIT FLORIDA

Begin I-275, Florida

↓FLORIDA

36 **(52)** Bearss Ave

- **FStop** E: **Citgo(*)**, **Fina(*) (Ryder Truck Rental)**
- **Gas** W: Amoco(*, CW), Chevron(*, D), Shell(*, CW, 24)
- **Food** W: Baby Cakes BBQ, Burger King(PLAY), China Gate Restaurant, Elvis' Cafe & Grill, McDonald's(PLAY), Pizzeria, Subway, Wendy's
- **Lodg** W: **Holiday Inn Express (see our ad this page)**
- **ATM** W: NationsBank, Shell, Tampa Bay Federal Credit Union
- **Other** W: Albertson's Grocery(RX), Eckerd Drugs(RX), Laundromat, Medicine Shoppe(RX), Publix Supermarket, Veterinary Service

35 **(51)** Fletcher Ave

- **Gas** E: Exxon(*, CW), Fina(*, D)
  W: BP(*), Citgo(*, CW)
- **Food** E: Days Inn
- **Lodg** E: Days Inn
  W: Americana Inn
- **AServ** W: BP
- **ATM** W: Barnett Bank
- **Other** E: Academe Animal Hospital
  W: Food Lion Grocery Store, Kash & Karry(RX), WalGreens Pharmacy

34 **(50)** Fowler Ave, FL. 582

- **Gas** E: Shell(*)
  W: Citgo(*, CW)
- **Food** E: Burger King, Jerk Hut Restaurant, Luvy's, McDonald's, Ponderosa Steakhouse, Subway, Waffle House
  W: Boston Grill, Discovery Inn
- **Lodg** E: Howard Johnson, AmeriSuites (see our ad this page)
  W: Discovery Inn, Interchange Motor Inn, Motel 6, Sleep Rite
- **Med** E: ✚ ST. John's Medical Clinic
- **ATM** E: NationsBank
- **Other** E: Eckerd Drugs, Save 'N Pack
  W: U.S. Post Office

33 **(48)** Busch Blvd., FL. 580

- **Gas** E: Amoco, Chevron(*, CW), Exxon(*)
- **Food** E: Best Western, Chevron, Corona's Spanish Food, Hungry Howie's (Amoco), Odoul's Seafood, Saxo's Cafe, Shoney's, Tara's Roti Shop Restaurant & Bar
  W: Burger King(PLAY), Canton Chinese Restaurant, Eddie's Deli, Golden Touch, KFC, Papa John's Pizza, Pine Grove, Waffle House
- **Lodg** E: Best Western, University Motel, **Ramada Limited (see our ad this page)**
  W: Pine Grove
- **Other** E: Action Toys Watercraft
  W: Home Depot

32 **(48)** Bird St (Reaccess Southbound Only)

- **Gas** W: Shell(*)

Off I-275 at Exit 36
TAMPA, FLORIDA
813-961-1000
Take Notice Mr. Bus Driver, "We'll Clean Your Bus!"
Expanded Continental Breakfast
Free Showtime 1 & 2
Free ESPN
Free Local Calls
Handicap Accessible
In Room Coffee Makers
Guest Laundry • Pool
Meeting/Banquet Facilities
Near Bush Gardens
Huge Flat Parking Areas
$39.00 Based on Availability
AAA Approved
400 East Bearss • Tampa, FL 33613
FLORIDA • I-275 • Exit 36

EXIT FLORIDA

- **Food** W: Checker's, Golden Dragon Chinese Restaurant, Havana Village Restaurant, Krispy Kreme Doughnuts, McDonald's, Ponderosa Steakhouse, Subway, Wendy's
- **AServ** W: Shell
- **Other** E: Dog Track, King Trailers Sales & Service
  W: Eckerd Drugs(RX), K-Mart, Kash & Karry United Grocery(RX)

31 **(466)** Sligh Ave

- **FStop** W: **BP(*, K)**
- **Gas** E: Amoco(*, CW, 24), Coastal(*)
- **Food** W: **BP**
- **Lodg** E: El Rancho Motel, Haven Inn, Oasis Motel
- **AServ** E: Amoco(24)
- **ATM** E: Coastal
- **Other** E: U.S. Post Office

30AB U.S. 92, Hillsborough Ave

- **Gas** E: Citgo(*) (Ryder Truck Rental), Mobil(*, CW)
  W: Amoco(*)
- **Food** E: Dairy Queen, High Tide Fish & Chips, Mobil
- **Lodg** E: Columbia Motel
- **AServ** E: Citgo (Ryder Truck Rental)

29 FL. 574, MLK Jr. Blvd

- **Gas** E: Amoco(*), Chevron(*, 24)
  W: Cumberland Farms(*)
- **Food** W: McDonald's
- **Med** W: ✚ Children's Medical Clinic, ✚ Hospital
- **ATM** E: Amoco
- **Other** E: Kash & Karry(RX)
  W: Tampa Stadium

BUSCH GARDENS 1/2 MI
1805

Ramada Limited 2
2106 E. Busch Blvd
Tampa, FL
813-931-3313
DISCOUNT TICKETS AVAILABLE
Continental Breakfast
Double & King Beds
Kids Under 12 Stay Free
Heated Outdoor Pool & Whirlpool
Tennis/Golf Nearby
Exterior Corridors
Jan 15-April 15
$49 Single - 59 Double
2 Adults-Kids Free
April 15-Aug 25
$42 Single-$47 Double
2 Adults-Kids Free
Rates not valid on holidays.
FLORIDA • I-275 • EXIT 33

EXIT		FLORIDA
28		Florbraska St. (Southbound, Reaccess Northbound Only)
27		I-4 E, Orlando
26		Downtown, E. Jefferson St. (Southbound)
	Food	**E:** Expressway Grill
25		Downtown -E/W, Scott St.,Ashley Dr., Tampa St.
	Food	**E:** Domino's Pizza
	Lodg	**E:** Courtyard by Marriott, Holiday Inn Select
	Med	**E:** ✚ Hospital
24		**(41)** Armenia Ave, Howard Ave
	Gas	**E:** Citgo[*]
		W: Amoco[*], Texaco[*]
	Food	**W:** Fourth of July Cafe, Popeye's Chicken
23C		Himes Ave. (Southbound)
	Gas	**W:** Supertest[*, 24]
	Other	**W:** Wal-Mart[RX]
23AB		U.S. 92, Dale Marby
	Gas	**E:** Exxon[*, D, CW], Shell[*, CW, 24]
		W: Amoco[*, D], Citgo[*, CW]
	Food	**E:** Carrabba's Italian Grill, Han Il. Kwan Sushi House, J. Alexander's Restaurant, Jojohni, Louie's Lobster, Pizza Hut, Rio Bravo, Sam Oh Jung
		W: Blimpie's Subs, Checkers, Denny's, Dunkin Donuts, Longhorn Steakhouse, McDonald's, Sweet Tomatoes, Taco Bell, Tia's Mexican, Wendy's
	Lodg	**E:** Courtyard by Marriott
		W: Howard Johnson
	Other	**E:** Borders Books & Music
		W: Home Depot, Wal-Mart[RX]
22		**(29)** Lois Ave.
	Gas	**W:** Radiant[*, D]
	Food	**W:** Charlie's Restaurant
	Lodg	**W:** DoubleTree Hotel, Westin Suites
	Other	**W:** Legends Field, Woolf Animal Hospital
21		West Shore Blvd. , toll FL 589, Veterans Expressway (Southbound, Reaccess Northbound Only)
	Gas	**E:** Citgo[*], Shell[*, CW]
		W: Shell[*]
	Food	**E:** Steak & Ale, Taco Bell, Waffle House
		W: Marriott, Perkin's Family Restaurant (Quality Hotel), Quality Hotel, Shell, Subway (Shell)
	Lodg	**E:** Embassy Suites, Sheraton Grand
		W: Crowne Plaza Hotel, Doubletree Hotel, Marriott, Quality Hotel
	AServ	**E:** Shell

1708

RAMADA INN®

12000 Gulf Blvd. • Treasure Island, FL 33706

Restaurant/Lounge on Premises
Kids Under 12 Stay Free & Eat Dinner Free
Outdoor Pool • Outdoor Spa
Volley Ball • Shuffle Board
Bus/Large Vehicle Parking
Handicap Accessible
Coin Laundry
Interior Corridors
Beachfront

800-228-2828

727-360-7051 • 727-367-6641 (fax)

FLORIDA • I-275 • EXIT 11

EXIT		FLORIDA
		W: Shell
	ATM	**E:** Citgo, City First Bank, NationsBank, Sun Trust Bank
		W: Barnett Bank, NationsBank, Shell
	Other	**E:** WalGreen's[24, RX], West Shore Plaza
20B		West Shore Blvd., FL 60 W, Cypress St., To Fl toll 589, Veterans Expressway , Tampa
	Other	**W:** Tampa International Airport
20AB		**(38)** FL 60E, Kennedy Blvd. (20A) West Shore Blvd., FL 60W, Cypress St., to FL toll 589, Tampa, Veterans Expressway (20B)
	Food	**E:** Ramada Inn, West Shore Cafe (Ramada Inn)
	Lodg	**E:** Ramada Inn, AmeriSuites (see our ad this page)
19		**(32)** S. to FL. 687, to U.S. 92, 4th St. N. (Southbound, Reaccess Northbound Only)
18		FL. 688 W., Largo, Ulmerton Rd. (Southbound, Reaccess Northbound Only)
17		M. L. King St., Nineth St. N. (Southbound, Reaccess Northbound Only)
16		**(30)** FL. 686, Roosevelt Blvd., Largo, Clear Water
15		**(28)** FL.694 W., Pinellas Park, Seminole, Gandy Blvd, Indian Shore
14AB		**(26)** Kenneth City, 54th Ave N (14 AB) (14A - Eastbound, 14B- Westbound)
	Gas	**W:** Citgo[*], Racetrac[*]
	Food	**W:** Days Inn, Nishu's Family Restaurant (Days Inn), Son's Cafe Chinese & Vietnamese
	Lodg	**W:** Days Inn
	ATM	**W:** Racetrac
13		38th Ave N, Reddington Beaches, Maderia Beach
12		**(23)** 22nd Ave. N.
	Other	**W:** Home Depot
11		**(12)** Fl. 595, Fifth Ave. N. (Southbound, Reaccess Northbound Only)
	Lodg	**E: Ramada Inn (see our ad this page)**
	Med	**W:** ✚ Hospital
10		Jct I-375 E., The Pier
9		Jct I-175, Topicana Fields

EXIT		FLORIDA
8		**(21)** 28th St. S. (Southbound, Reaccess Northbound Only)
7		**(21)** 31st St S (Southbound, Reaccess Southbound Only)
6		**(20)** 22nd Ave. S. (Southbound)
	Gas	**W:** Chevron[*], Citgo[*], Shell[*]
	Food	**W:** Church's Chicken, KFC
	AServ	**W:** Shell
5		**(20)** 26th Ave. S., Gulfport (Northbound)
	Food	**W:** Cat Hay Chinese, KFC, King Wah Chinese
	Lodg	**W:** Hosanna Hotel
	Other	**W:** Food Lion
4		FL. 682 W., 54th Ave. S., Pinellas Bay Way, St. Pete Beach, U.S. 19N (Services are on 54th Ave S)
	Gas	**E:** Amoco[*, CW], Mobil[*, D]
		W: Citgo[*], Speedway[*]
	Food	**E:** Popeye's Chicken
		W: Bob Evan's Restaurant, Burger King, Domino's Pizza, Howard Johnson Inn, Hungry Howie's (Howard Johnson Inn), Joffrey's Coffee Co., Long John Silver, Mai Thai Restaurant, McDonald's, Papa John's Pizza, Porto Fino Italian, Taco Bell, Wendy's
	Lodg	**W:** Bay Way Inn, Crystal Inn, Howard Johnson Inn, Pride of St. Petersburg Motor Inn, Days Innd this page)
	ATM	**E:** 7-11 Convenience Store, Barnett Bank, First Union, Republic Bank
		W: Citgo, Publix
	Other	**E:** 7-11 Convenience Store, Albertson's Food Market[RX]
		W: 7-11 Convenience Store (Citgo), Eckerd Drugs[RX], Publix
3		Sky Way Lane, Pinellas Point Dr.
	Food	**E:** Banyon Tree Deli (Days Inn), Days Inn
	Lodg	**E:** Days Inn
	Other	**W:** O'Neill's Marina
2B		**(13)** Sky Way Fishing Pier N, Rest Area
2A		**(7)** Sky Way Fishing Pier S., Rest Area (RR, Phones, Picnic, Vending)
2		U.S. 19 S., Palmetto, Bradenton (Southbound)
1		**(2)** Port Manatee, U.S. 41, Palmetto, Bradenton

↑FLORIDA

Begin I-275, Florida

Bold red print shows RV & Bus parking available or nearby

EXIT — MICHIGAN

Begin I-275, Michigan

↓MICHIGAN

Note: I-275 runs concurrent below with I-96. Numbering follows I-96.

165 Junction I-696, I-275 ends

167 8 Mile Road, Novi, Farmington Hills, Maybury State Park
- **Gas** S: Meijer Grocery(D, K, 24), Speedway(*, D)
- **Food** S: Big Boy, Chili's, Kirby Coney Island, Kyoto Japanese, McDonald's, On The Border, Taco Bell
- **Lodg** S: Hampton Inn, Hilton, Office Max, Travelodge TraveLodge
- **Med** S: ✚ Center for Specialty Care, ✚ Hospital
- **Other** N: Veterinary Clinic
  S: Best Buy, Costco, Meijer Grocery, Target

169AB 7 Mile Road
- **Gas** N: Speedway(D, K, 24)
- **Food** N: Embassy Suites, Lone Star Steakhouse, New York Deli, Pizza Center, RiJo Bravo
  S: Alexander, Cascade Restaurant (Embassy), Champs Americana, Cooker, Macaroni Grill
- **Lodg** N: Embassy Suites
- **Med** N: ✚ St. Joseph's Urgent Care
- **ATM** N: Speedway
- **Other** S: Home Depot

170 6 Mile Road
- **Gas** S: Amoco(*), Mobil(*, CW)
- **Food** N: Bill Knapp's Restaurant, Max & Erma's, Seafood Tavern, The Ground Round, Tremmor's Restaurant (Holiday Inn)
  S: Applebee's, Charley's Grille, McDonald's, Papa Vino's, Wendy's
- **Lodg** N: Best Western, Courtyard by Marriott, Holiday Inn, Marriott
- **Med** N: ✚ Hospital
- **ATM** N: Comericard, Michigan National Bank, NBD Bank
  S: Standard Federal
- **Other** S: Arbor Drugs, Farmer Jack's Supermarket

172 I-275 South, MI 14 West

Note: I-275 runs concurrent above with I-96. Numbering follows I-96.

EXIT — MICHIGAN

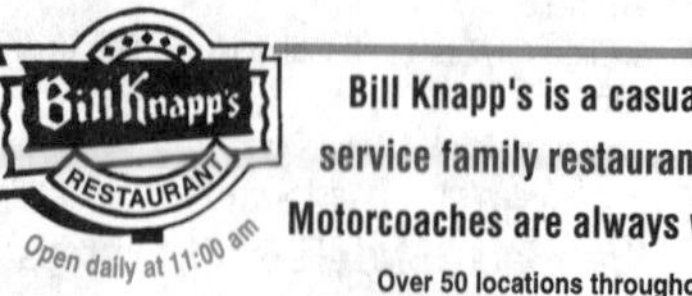

734-459-1616 Plymouth
MICHIGAN • I-275 • EXIT 28

29 I-96 E Junction, Ann Arbor, MI 14

28 Ann Arbor Rd, Plymouth, Livonia
- **Gas** E: Amoco(*, 24), Shell(*)
- **Food** E: Denny's, Dunkin Donuts(24) (Amoco), Water Club Seafood
  W: Bennigan's, Bill Knapp's, Burger King, Steak & Ale
- **Lodg** E: Red Roof Inn
  W: Quality Inn
- **AServ** E: Shell
  W: K-Mart Supercenter(RX)
- **ATM** E: First of America
  W: Michigan National Bank, Standard Federal
- **Other** W: K-Mart Supercenter(RX)

25 MI 153, Ford Rd, Westland, Garden City, Bearborn Heights
- **Gas** W: Amoco(*, D), Shell(*), Sunoco(*, D, K)
- **Food** E: Don Pablo's Mexican
  W: BJ Bowery's, Big K-Mart(24, RX), Bob Evan's Restaurant, Chili's, Church's Chicken, Dunkin Donuts, KFC, Red Oak Steakhouse, Roman Forum, Tim Hortons(24), Twist N' Snake Ice Cream, Wendy's,

Michigan • Exit 028 • 800-833-1516

EXIT — MICHIGAN

White Castle Restaurant
- **Lodg** W: Budgetel Inn, Fairfield Inn, Motel 6
- **Med** W: ✚ Hospital
- **ATM** W: Amoco, First Federal of MI, First of America, Shell
- **Other** E: Home Depot
  W: Big K-Mart(RX)

(24) Rest Area (RR, Phones, Picnic; Northbound)

22 US 12, Michigan Ave, Ypslanti, Dearborn
- **Gas** E: Amoco(*), Shell(*, CW), Speedway(*, D)
- **Food** E: Jonathan's Family Dining, McDonald's, Subway, Wendy's
- **Lodg** E: Country Hearth Inn, Fellows Creek Motel, Super 8, Willo Acres Motel
- **ATM** E: Amoco, Shell

20 Ecorse Rd, Romulus
- **Food** E: Woodland

17 I-275 & I-94 Junction, Detriot, Chicago

15 Eureka Rd
- **Gas** E: Shell(*, D)
- **ATM** E: Shell

13 New Boston, Sibley Rd

11 South Huron Rd
- **FStop** W: Sunoco(*, D)
- **Food** W: Burger King (Sunoco)
- **TServ** W: Jim's Heavy Equip Repair(24)
- **ATM** W: Sunoco

8 Will Carleton, Flat Rock
- **TServ** E: Kaycee Transportation Inc.
- **Other** E: Pacific Pride Commercial Fueling(D)

5 Carleton, South Rockwood

(4) Rest Area (RR, Phones, Picnic; Southbound)

2 U.S. 24, Telegraph Rd
- **Gas** W: Marathon(D, CW)
- **Food** W: Fifth Wheel Truck Stop Restaurant
- **Lodg** E: Glee Motel
- **Other** W: Airport

1 Junction I-75, Detroit, Toledo

↑MICHIGAN

Begin I-275, Michigan

I-276 PENNSYLVANIA

EXIT — PENNSYLVANIA

Begin I-276

↓PENNSYLVANIA

(330) Police Station (Eastbound)

25 **(333)** Norristown, to I-476 (Toll)
- **Med** N: ✚ Hospital

(334) Jct. I-476

26 **(338)** PA 309, Ft Washington, Philadephia, Ambler, Toll Rd (Toll, Highland Ave, To Piketown Rd, West Penn Dr)
- **Gas** N: Exxon(CW), Mobil(*)
- **Food** N: Friendly's, Holiday Inn, Koners Ye Old Beef & Ale, Palace of Asia (Indian Cuisine, Ft Washington Inn), Park Place Deli, Subway
- **Lodg** N: Clarion, Ft Washington Inn, Holiday Inn
- **ATM** N: CoreStates Bank, PSFS Bank
- **Other** N: Post Office

27 **(343)** PA611, Willowgrove, to Doylestown, Jenkinstown (Toll)

EXIT — PENNSYLVANIA

- **Gas** N: Amoco(*, D, K), Hess(*, D), Mobil(*), Mobil(*, D, CW), Texaco(*)
- **Food** N: Bagels Plus, Bennigan's, China Garden, Domino's Pizza, Donut Haven, Nino Pizza-Rama, The Bakers Inn, Williamson Restaurant
  S: Dunkin Donuts, Giulo's Italian
- **Lodg** S: Hampton Inn
- **Med** N: ✚ Hospital
- **Other** S: Thrift Drug

28 **(351)** US1, Philadelphia, Trenton (Toll)
- **FStop** S: Sunoco(*, D)
- **Gas** S: Amoco(CW), Exxon(D), Getty(*, LP), Mobil, Sunoco(*)
- **Food** S: Baskin Robbins, Bumpers (Raddison Inn), Dumino's, Dunkin Donuts, Miami Grill, Steak & Ale, Subs
- **Lodg** S: Howard Johnson, Knight's Inn, Neshaminy Inn, Penn Motel, Raddison Inn, Red Roof Inn, The Lincoln Motel
- **ATM** S: Summit Bank

(352) Neshaminy Service Center
- **FStop** N: Sunoco
  S: Sunoco(*, D)

EXIT — PENNSYLVANIA

- **Food** N: Burger King, Nathan's
  S: Beyers Ice Cream, Hot Dogs Under Construction, McDonald's(PLAY)

29 **(357)** US13, Levittown, Delaware Valley, Bristol, to I-95 (Toll)
- **FStop** S: Bristol Fuel(D), Coastal(LP)
- **Gas** N: Citgo(*, D)
  S: Mobil, Sunoco(*, D)
- **Food** N: Dallas Diner, Divas (EconoLodge), Edgley
  S: Big Apple Grill, Big Daddy's Italian Style Sandwiches, Boston Market Restaurant, Burger King, Dari-Deli, Days Inn, Italian Family Pizza, McDonald's, Pizza Hut, Subway, The Grand Family Diner, The Original Eagle
- **Lodg** N: Comfort Inn, Econolodge
  S: Days Inn, The-Vow Motel
- **Med** S: ✚ Hospital
- **Other** N: Pets Best Friend Veterinary Hospital
  S: Super Fresh Food Market(RX), Thrift Drug

↑PENNSYLVANIA

Begin I-276

EXIT CALIFORNIA

Begin I-280

↓CALIFORNIA

(53) Rest Area (RR, HF, Phones, Picnic)
Exit **(52)** Junction I-280, San Jose
40 McLaughlan Ave.
Exit **(39)** 7th Street, CA 82
Exit **(37)** Guadalupe Pky., CA 87
Exit **(38)** Bird Ave.
Gas **I:** 76[*, D, LP], Chevron[*, D, 24]
AServ **I:** Chevron[24]
Other **I:** Car Spa, Shop & Save
Exit **(37)** Race Street, Southwest Expressway (Northbound, No Reaccess)
Exit **(36)** Meridian Ave. (Southbound)
Food **O:** H Salt Fish N Chips, Mr. Chau's, Taco Bell, Wienerschnitzel
Exit **(35)** Bascom Ave. & Leigh Ave.
Exit **(34)** Junction I-880 , Oakland, CA 17
Exit **(33)** Winchester Blvd. Campbell (Southbound)
Gas **I:** Exxon[*]
O: Arco[*, D], Gas & Shop[*, D, LP]
Food **I:** Burger King, Chevy's Mexican, Chili's, Flames, Lyon's, Mandarian House, Moulin Rouge Coffee Roasting Company, Mr. Chau's, Ocean Harbor, Rock'n Tacos, Sweet Treats Cafe, ToGo's
O: Florentine, Marie Callender's Restaurant, Tho Saigon
ATM **I:** Great Western Bank
Other **I:** Hobbes Restaurant, Playland, Town & Country Village, Winchester Mystery House
Exit **(32)** Saratoga Ave.
Gas **I:** Arco[*], Chevron[*, 24]
O: BP[*], Exxon[*], Shell
Food **I:** Azabu, Bankok Garden, Bijan Bakery & Cafe, Black Angus Steakhouse, Burger Factory, Burger King, Coco's, Coyoacan Cafe Mexican, Family BBQ, Happi House, Harry's Hofbrau, High Thai, Le Papillon, McDonald's, Tasty Doughnuts, U-Bake Pizza
O: Baskin Robbins, Chinese, Denny's, Round Table Pizza, Tony Roma's
Lodg **O:** Howard Johnson (see our ad this page)
AServ **I:** Chevron[24]
O: BP, Exxon
ATM **I:** 7-11 Convenience Store, 7-11 Convenience Store, Arco, Bank Of The West, Lucky Food Center
O: 7-11 Convenience Store, 7-11 Convenience Store
Other **I:** 7-11 Convenience Store, Lucky Food Center, Sara Creek Veterinary Clinic
O: 7-11 Convenience Store
Exit **(31)** Stevens Creek Blvd., Lawrence Expressway (Going Northbound only reads Lawrence Expressway)
Gas **O:** 76[*], Rotten Robbie[*, D]
Food **I:** Boston Market Restaurant, City Espresso, Cookies By Design, House of Bagels, McDonald's, Mountain Mike's Pizza, Mr. Chau's, Pizza Adore, Pollo Rey, Rock 'N Tacos
O: IHOP, Subway
Lodg **O:** Howard Johnson, Woodcrest Hotel
ATM **I:** Bank of America, Safeway Drugs[24, RX]
O: 7-11 Convenience Store
Other **I:** Mail Boxes Etc, Parcel Plus, Payless Drugs, Safeway Drugs[RX]
O: 7-11 Convenience Store
Exit **(30)** Wolfe Rd.
Gas **I:** Arco[*]
O: BP
Food **I:** Cafe Gourmet, China Paradise, Duke Of Edinburgh, Fantasia Coffee & Tea, Kingswood Teppan Steakhouse, Samkee, Southland Taste Restaurant, Sushi Depot, The Wa Wa Bakery, Wolfe Cafe
O: Azuma, El Torito, Erik's Deli Cafe, Fresh Choice, Harry's Hofbrau, McDonald's, Pizza Hut, T.G.I. Friday's, Taco Grill
Lodg **I:** Courtyard by Marriott, Marriott
AServ **O:** BP
ATM **I:** Bank Of The West, East West Bank
O: Great Western Bank
Other **I:** Ranch Market
Exit **(29)** De Anza Blvd.
Gas **I:** Chevron[*, CW]
O: Arco[*]
Food **I:** Carl Jr's Hamburgers, Manley's Donuts
O: Outback Steakhouse, Peppermill, Santa Barbara Grill
Lodg **I:** Cupertino Inn
AServ **O:** Arco
ATM **I:** Bank of America, United National Bank
Other **I:** Jelly Franco's PW Market, Kinko's[24], Rite Aid Pharmacy[RX]
Exit **(28)** CA 85 North to Mountain View, South to Gilroy
Exit **(27)** Grant Rd., Foothill Expwy.
Gas **I:** Chevron[*, 24]
Food **I:** China Shuttle, Hickory Pitt, Jazzy Java Cafe, Pacific Steamer, Pasta Grotto, Red Pepper
AServ **I:** Chevron[24]
Other **I:** Payless Drugs, Rite Aid Pharmacy[RX]
26B Jct. Ca. 85 S., Gilroy
26 Grant Rd., Foothill Expwy.
Exit **(25)** Magdalena Rd.
Exit **(24)** El Monte Rd., Moody Rd.
Exit **(23)** Page Mill Rd., Palo Alto - 23A
Exit **(23)** Alpine Rd., Portola Valley
Med **I:** ✚ Hospital
Exit **(22)** Sand Hill Rd.
Med **E:** ✚ Hospital
Exit **(21)** Woodside Rd., CA 84
Exit **(20)** Farm Hill Blvd. (No Trucks)
Exit **(19)** Edgewood Rd.
Med **E:** ✚ Hospital
Exit **(18)** La Vista Point - 18B
Exit **(18)** San Mateo, E. Ca. 92 to Hayward, CA 92W to Half Moon Bay
Exit **(17)** Bunker Hill
(16) Rest Area (RR, Phones; Northbound)
(16) Rest Area (RR, Phones; Southbound)
Exit **(15)** Black Moutain Rd, Hayne Rd.
Exit **(14)** Trousdale Dr. , Burlingame
Med **I:** ✚ Hospital
Exit **(13)** Millbrae Ave.

Exit **(13)** 13B- CA 35, Skyline Blvd, Pacifica (Reaccess Southbound Only)
Exit **(12)** Crystal Springs Road (Southbound, Reaccess Northbound Only)
Exit **(11)** San Bruno Ave., Sneath Lane
Gas **O:** Chevron[24]
Food **I:** Bakery, Baskin Robbins, Carl Jr's Hamburgers, Gourmet Coffee, King Chopstix, La Petite Boulangerie, Manilla Eatery, OK Corral Burger Saloon, Taco Bell, Vicino Deli, Vietnam Village
ATM **I:** No Name
O: 7-11 Convenience Store, 7-11 Convenience Store, Chevron
Other **I:** Long's Drugs[RX], Molly Stone's
O: 7-11 Convenience Store
Exit **(10)** I-380 to U.S. 101, San Franscisco International Airport (Southbound, I-380 east accessible from the north)
10A Sneath Ln. (Difficult Reaccess)
Gas **W:** BP[*, D], RWA
Food **W:** Bakers Square Restaurant
Exit **(9)** Avalon Dr. , West Borough Blvd
Gas **O:** Arco[*], Exxon[*, D]
Food **O:** Denny's, Kamameshi Japanese Cuisine, McDonald's, West Borough Deli
AServ **O:** Arco
ATM **O:** Arco, Exxon, Sanwa Bank, World Savings Bank
Other **O:** Mail Boxes Etc, WalGreen's[RX]
9A Westborough Blvd.
Gas **W:** Arco, Exxon[D]
Food **W:** McDonald's, Paradise Restaurant, West Borough Deli
ATM **W:** Sanwa Bank
Other **W:** WalGreens Pharmacy
Exit **(8)** Hickey Blvd. , Colma
Gas **I:** Chevron[*, D, CW], Shell[*, CW, 24]
O: Shell[*, CW, 24]
Food **O:** El Torito, Hungry Hunter, Koi Palace, Peppermill, Sizzler
ATM **I:** Chevron
O: Bank of America, Cal Fed
Exit **(7)** Serramonte Blvd. (Southbound)
Gas **I:** Chevron[*]
O: 76[*], Olympic[*]
Food **I:** Beverages & More, Deli, Fresh Choice, Round Table Pizza, Sizzler
O: Boston Market Restaurant, McDonald's, Starbucks Coffee, Toones
ATM **O:** 76, Bank Of The West, Bay View Bank, Washington Mutual, Wells Fargo, World Savings Bank
Other **I:** Complete Eyeglasses, Frame-N-Lens, Target, The Drug Barn[RX]
O: Clean-X-Press
Exit **(6)** Pacifica, Ca. 1 South, Mission Street
Gas **I:** 76[*]
O: Arco[*, 24], Exxon[*, D, LP], Shell
AServ **O:** Arco[24], Exxon
Med **O:** ✚ Seton Medical Center
Other **I:** Lucky's Grocery Store, Serra Bowl
Exit **(5)** Eastmore Ave., Mission Ridge (Southbound)
Gas **E:** BP[*]
W: Arco[*], Exxon[D], Shell
Med **W:** ✚ Hospital
ATM **E:** Bank of America
Exit **(4)** Daly City, West Lake District
Gas **I:** Chevron[*]
Exit **(3)** CA 1 North
Exit **(2)** Ocean Ave. & Geneva Ave.
Exit **(2)** San Jose Ave.
Exit **(1)** Alemany
Exit **(1)** Jct. I-280 & U.S. 101

↑CALIFORNIA

Begin I-280

EXIT		GEORGIA

Begin I-285

↓GEORGIA

1 GA 279, GA 14, Old National Hwy, South Fulton Pkwy
Gas I: Amoco(*), Chevron(*, 24)
O: Exxon(*, D), Racetrac(*, 24), Texaco(*)
Food I: Dapper Dan Ice Cream, Denny's, Ike's Buffalo Wings, Jamaica Jamaica, Phoenix Dragon, Taste of Africa, Waffle House, Zab-E-Lee Thai
O: Arby's, Best American Inn, Burger King(PLAY), Church's Chicken, Club 321 II, Club Hotel by Doubletree, Days Inn, El Ranchero (Best American Inn), Formosa Chinese Buffet, McDonald's, O'Hara's (Days Inn), Piccadilly Cafeteria, Taco Bell, Waffle House, Zheng's Buffett
Lodg I: La Quinta Inn
O: Best American Inn, Budgetel Inn, Club Hotel by Doubletree, Days Inn, Fairfield Inn, Red Roof Inn
Med O: The Med First Physician

2 **(1)** Washington Road
Gas O: Chevron(*, 24), **Mark Inn**
Food O: Hickory Smoked BBQ, Philly Cheesesteak
Lodg O: **Mark Inn**

3 **(2)** Camp Creek Pkwy, Atl. Airport, College Park, Eastpoint
Gas I: BP(*, LP, CW), Citgo(*)
Food I: Checkers, McDonald's(PLAY), Mrs Winner's Chicken
Lodg I: Sheraton

4A GA 166, Lakewood Fwy, GA.154 (Reaccess Northbound Only, Difficult Reaccess)

4B Campbellton Rd., GA 154 South, GA 166 West (More services on Campbellton Rd., Separate exit off of the west side)
Gas O: Amoco(*, CW), Racetrac(*), Shell(*, LP), Texaco(*)
Food O: Church's Chicken, Mrs Winner's Chicken, St. Mark BBQ

5 Cascade Rd
Gas I: Chevron(*), Coastal
O: Amoco(*), BP(*, CW)
Food I: Papa John's Pizza
O: Home Depot, KFC, Mrs Winner's Chicken (Home Depot)
AServ I: Chevron, Coastal
Med O: Southwest Hospital
Other I: Ingle's Supermarket
O: Home Depot

6 GA 139, Martin Luther King Jr. Dr, Adamsville
Gas I: BP(*, CW), Fina(*)
O: Chevron
Food I: Club 321, Mrs Winner's Chicken
AServ O: Chevron
ATM I: E-Z Shopper
Other I: E-Z Shopper

7A Junction I-20 East, Atlanta, Abernathy Hwy.

7B I-20 West, Birmingham, Tom Murphy Freeway (Left Exit Northbound)

8 **(11)** U.S. 78, U.S. 278, Bankhead Hwy
TStop I: **Petro Travel Plaza**(*, SCALES) **(Truck Wash)**
FStop I: **Citgo**(*, LP)
Gas I: Amoco(*, D)
O: Amoco(*, CW), Texaco(*)
Food I: Iron Skillet(24) (Petro Travel Plaza), Mrs Winner's Chicken, **Petro Travel Plaza (Truck Wash)**
ATM I: **Citgo**

9 Bolton Rd. (Northbound, No Reaccess)

10 **(15)** GA 280, South Cobb Dr, Smyrna
Gas O: Amoco(*), BP(*, D), Exxon(D, CW), Racetrac(*)
Food O: Amoco, Arby's, Blimpie Subs & Salads (Racetrac), Checkers Burgers, Church's Chicken, Krystal, McDonald's (Amoco), Mrs Winner's Chicken, Racetrac, Subway, TCBY (Racetrac), Taco Bell, Waffle House, Wendy's
Lodg I: Microtel Inn
O: AmeriHost Inn, Knight's Inn, **Sun Suites**
Med O: Hospital

11 **(16)** South Atlanta Rd
TStop I: **Pilot Travel Center**(*)
Gas I: Exxon(*, D, CW)
Food I: **KFC (Pilot), Pilot Travel Center, Subway**(24) **(Pilot)**
O: Waffle House
Lodg O: Holiday Inn Express

12 **(17)** Paces Ferry Rd, Vinings
Gas I: BP(*, LP), Texaco(*, LP, CW)
Food I: Blimpie Subs & Salads (Texaco), Eckerd Drugs(RX), Einstein Bros Bagels, Home Depot, Mrs Winner's Chicken (Home Depot), Subway, Texaco
Lodg I: Studio PLUS
O: Fairfield Inn, La Quinta Inn
ATM I: Publix Supermarket(RX), Texaco
Other I: Home Depot, Publix Supermarket(RX), Wolf Camera & Video

13 **(19)** U.S. 41, Cobb Pkwy, Dobbins Airforce Base
Gas O: Chevron(*, CW), QT(*)
Food I: Barnes & Noble, Buffalo's Cafe, Cumberland Mall, Deli Planet, Krispy Kreme Doughnuts, Malone's, Renaissance Waverly Hotel
O: Applebee's, Arby's, Black-Eyed Pea, China Buffet, Cozumel Mexican Restaurant, Doc's Food & Spirits, Double Tree Guest Suites, Dunkin Donuts, Haveli Indian Cuisine, Jade Palace, KFC, McDonald's(PLAY), Minato Japanese Restauarant Sushi & Steak, Morrison's Cafeteria, Old Hickory House, Papa John's Pizza, Pizza Hut, Sonny's BBQ, Steak & Ale, Steak 'N Shake, Taco Bell, Waffle House, Wendy's
Lodg I: Courtyard by Marriott, Embassy Suites, Renaissance Waverly Hotel, Sheraton Suites
O: Double Tree Guest Suites, Holiday Inn Express, Homestead Village, Sumner Suites
Other I: Barnes & Noble, Cumberland Mall, Lens Crafters, Waccamaw
O: Pearl Vision Center

14 Junction I-75, Atlanta, Chattanooga, Marietta

15 **(22)** Northside Dr, New Northside Dr, Powers Ferry Rd.
Gas I: Amoco(*, CW), Chevron(*, CW, 24)
O: Texaco(*, CW)
Food I: Blimpie Subs & Salads, McDonald's(PLAY), Rio Bravo

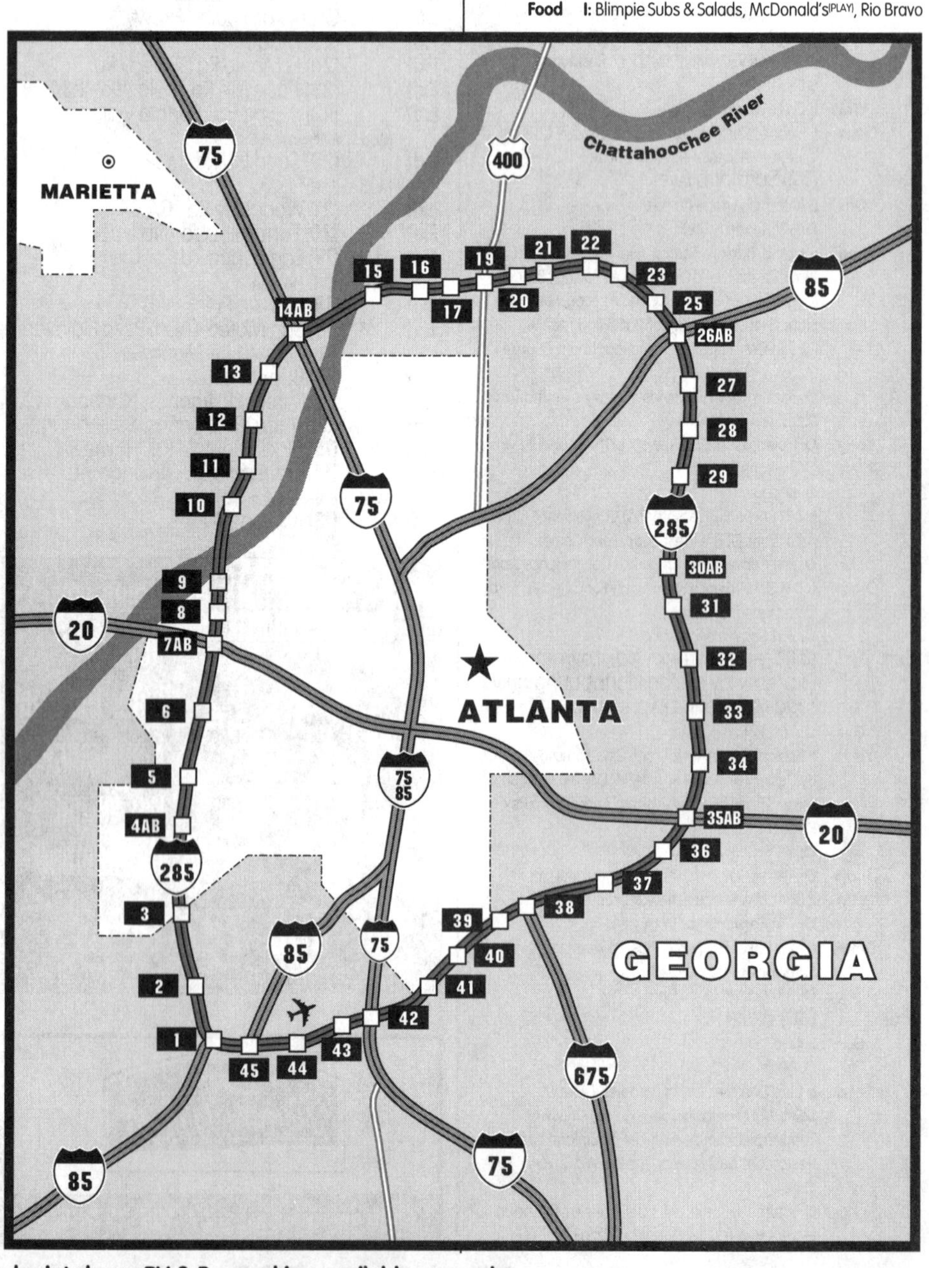

Bold red print shows RV & Bus parking available or nearby

EXIT GEORGIA

Cantina, Sushi Huku, Wendy's
Lodg I: Crown Plaza Hotel
ATM I: Amoco, Chevron, Publix Supermarket, Sun Trust Bank, Wachovia Bank
O: Texaco
Other I: CVS Pharmacy, Powers Ferry Animal Clinic, Publix Supermarket

16 **(23)** Riverside Dr.

17 **(25)** U.S. 19 South, Roswell Rd, Sandy Springs
Gas I: Chevron(24), E-Z Serve(*), Texaco(*, CW)
O: Chevron, Shell(*)
Food I: China Cooks, Days Inn, El Taco Veloz, Frankie's, Il Forno Pizza & Pasta, Jilly's Ribs (Days Inn), Jolie-Kobe Bakery, La Movida Nightclub & Restaurant, Shamshiri Persian Cuisine, Southern Style Cookin', Taqueria Deldado Mexican
O: American Pie, Billy McHale's Restaurant, Boston Market Restaurant, Casablanca Salvadorian & Mexican Restaurant, El Toro, Good Ol' Day's, Hong Kong Cafe, Persian Cuisine, Ruth's Chris Steakhouse, Taco Mac, Three Dollar Cafe
Lodg I: Days Inn
O: Country Hearth Inn
ATM O: SunTrust Bank
Other I: Quik Shot Convenient Store(LP)
O: K-Mart(RX), Mail Boxes Etc.

18 Glenridge Dr., Glenridge Connector (No Reaccess)
Med I: Hospital

19 **(27)** U.S. 19N, GA 400, Atlanta, Cumming (Difficult Reaccess, Toll)
Lodg O: AmeriSuites (see our ad this page)

20 Peachtree - Dunwoody Rd (Westbound, Reaccess Eastbound Only)
Food I: Shoney's
O: Arby's, Carlini's Italian Restaurant (DoubleTree Guest Suites), DoubleTree Guest Suites, Einstein Bros Bagels, Papino's Pizza, Pasta, & Salad, The Derby
Lodg O: Comfort Suites Hotel, DoubleTree Guest Suites, Fairfield Inn, Marriott
Med I: Northside Hospital, Scottish Rite, St. Joseph
Other O: Eckerd Drugs(RX), Publix Supermarket

21 Ashford - Dunwoody Rd (Continued commerce on the outside)
Gas O: Exxon(*)
Food O: Crowne Plaza Hotel, La Grotta (Crowne Plaza Hotel)
Lodg O: Crowne Plaza Hotel
ATM O: Wachovia Bank

22 **(28)** Chamblee - Dunwoody Rd, N. Shallowford Rd, N. Peachtree Rd
Gas I: BP(*), Citgo(*, LP), Phillips 66(*), Texaco(*)
O: Amoco(*, LP), Amoco(*, CW), BP(*, CW), Chevron(*, CW), Phillips 66(*, CW)
Food I: Arby's, Blimpie Subs & Salads, Hanwoori, La Botana Tex-Mex Restaurant, Lynn's China Express, Mad Italian, Malone's Bar & Grill, Taco Bell, Wendy's
O: Burger King, Del Taco, Denny's, Goldberg's Bagel Co. & Deli, Kroger Supermarket, Lucky China, Mrs Winner's Chicken, Popeye's Chicken (Kroger), Starbucks Coffee, Subway, Waffle House, Waffle House
Lodg I: Holiday Inn Select, Residence Inn
O: Four Points Hotel Sheraton
AServ I: BP

EXIT GEORGIA

1359

Georgia • Exit 019 • 770-343-9566

1112
Comfort Inn
Comfort Inn
I-285 Exit 25, North Atlanta
770-455-3700
• FREE Full Hot Breakfast Buffet
• 25" TV with VCR in All Rooms with HBO & ESPN • Cable
• Interior Corridors • Pool
• Complimentary Shuttle Service to MARTA
• 1 Mile West of I-85
GEORGIA ▪ I-285 ▪ EXIT 25

SUPER 8
Exit 29 • Tucker, GA
770-491-8778
800-800-8000
• Kids 12 & Under Stay & Eat Free
• Handicap Accessible
• Tennis Nearby
• Golf Nearby
• Truck/Large Vehicle Parking
• Exterior Corridors
• Cable TV w/HBO
• Malls Nearby
• 10 min. to Stone Mountain Park

GEORGIA ▪ I-285 ▪ EXIT 29

Med O: Chamblee-Dunwoody Medical Center, Peachford Hospital
ATM I: Citgo, Summit National Bank, Texaco
O: Chevron, Kroger Supermarket, NationsBank, SunTrust Bank
Other I: Big H Food Store, Chamblee Lanes
O: CVS Pharmacy(RX), Joshua's Christian Bookstore, Kroger Supermarket, One Hour Moto Photo

EXIT GEORGIA

23AB GA 141 South, Peachtree Industrial Blvd, Chamblee- 23A, 23B GA 141 North, Peachtree Industrial Blvd. (Continued Commerce)
Food I: Waffle House

23B GA 141 North, Peachtree Industrial Blvd
Food I: Oga Restaurant, Piccadilly Cafeteria

24 Tilly Mill Rd, Flowers Rd (Northbound, No Reaccess, Have to exit off of 23B)

25 U.S. 23, Doraville, Buford Hwy.
Gas I: Crown(*, LP, CW), Fina(*, LP, K)
O: Amoco(*, 24)
Food I: Captain D's Seafood, Dollar Express Chinese Restaurant, House of Peking, Mandarin Delight, Monterrey Mexican, Szechuan Gardens, Taco Bell, Waffle House
O: Arby's, Baldinos Subs, Burger King(PLAY), Chick-Fil-A, KFC, Krystal, Mrs Winner's Chicken, Taqueria La Reyna
Lodg I: Comfort Inn (see our ad this page)

26A **(33)** Junction I-85 South, Chamblee - Tucker Rd , Junction I-85 North, Greenville

27 **(34)** Chamblee - Tucker Rd (North-bound)
Gas I: Amoco(*)
O: BP(*, CW), Chevron, Citgo(*, LP), Phillips 66, Texaco(*, CW)
Food I: All Star Sports Bar & Grill, McDonald's, Mexicali Restaurant, Philly Connection, Pizzeria, Round Dragon Chinese Restaurant, TCBY, Waffle House
O: Arby's, Blimpie Subs & Salads, Galaxy Diner, Hot Wings, Hunan Inn Chinese, KFC, Mrs Winner's Chicken, S & S Cafeteria, Sam's Gourmet Chinese Restaurant, Taco Bell
Lodg O: Motel 6
Other I: Buddy's Store(LP), Kroger Supermarket(RX), Post Net (UPS, Fax, Copy), Thirty-Minute Photo
O: Eckerd Drugs(RX), Photo Genie, Post Office, Tracy's Medicine Center, Winn Dixie Supermarket

27A Northlake Parkway
Food O: Old Hickory House
Lodg I: Hampton Inn, Towne Place Suites

28 GA 236, LaVista Rd, Tucker
Gas I: Amoco(*, LP, CW, 24), BP(*, CW), Texaco(*, CW)
O: Chevron(*, CW, 24), Circle K(*)
Food I: Black-Eyed Pea, Fuddruckers, Gorins Ice Cream, Lucky Key Chinese Restaurant, Manderin Palace, Mellow Mushroom, Premier Indian Restaurant, Taco Bell
O: Checkers Burgers, Chili's, Folks, IHOP, La Bonnie (Ramada), O'Charley's, Olive Garden, Piccadilly Cafeteria, Ramada, Schlotzsky's Deli, Steak & Ale, Waffle House
Lodg I: Courtyard by Marriott, Fairfield Inn, Hampton Inn, Raddison, Wyndham Garden Hotel
O: Country Inn & Suites by Carlson, Ramada
AServ I: BP, Texaco
Med I: Northlake Regional Hospital (2-3 Miles)
ATM I: First Union, NationsBank, Wachovia Bank
O: Circle K
Other I: Pearl Vision Center, Toys R Us, Veterinarian (PetSmart)

29 U.S. 29, Lawrenceville Hwy
Gas I: Amoco(*, CW), Racetrac(*, 24)
O: BP(*, CW), Shell(*)
Food I: Waffle House
O: Waffle House
Lodg I: Masters Inn Economy, Red Roof Inn
O: Knight's Inn, Super 8 (see our ad this page)
AServ I: Amoco
Med I: Montreal Medical Center
O: Columbia Lakeside Regional Hospital, Northlake Regional Medical Center
ATM O: Shell

← I-285 GEORGIA

EXIT GEORGIA

30AB U.S. 78 West, Decatur, Atlanta , U.S. 78 East, Snellville, Athens (Difficult Reaccess)
Lodg **O:** Days Inn (see our ad this page)
31 **(39)** East Ponce de Leon, Clarkston
FStop **O:** **Texaco**[*]
Gas **O:** Chevron[*], Citgo[*]
Food **O:** Citgo, Ponce Cafe & Grill
Med **I:** + Dekalb Medical Center
O: + Northlake Regional Medical
ATM **O:** **Texaco**
32 **(41)** GA 10, Memorial Dr, Avondale Estates
Gas **I:** Amoco[*, CW], Fina[*]
O: Texaco[*]
Food **I:** KFC, Waffle King
O: Applebee's, Arby's, Burger King, Church's Chicken, Denny's, Hardee's, Mama's Restaurant & Buffet, Steak 'N Shake, Wendy's
Lodg **O:** Guesthouse Inn
ATM **O:** SouthTrust Bank
32A **(42)** Transit Parking Marta Only (Northbound, Reaccess Southbound Only)
33 U.S. 278, Covington Hwy
FStop **O:** **Crown**[*, D, LP, CW]
Gas **I:** BP[*, 24], Texaco[*, CW]
O: Chevron[*, CW, 24], Citgo[*, LP]
Food **I:** Arby's, Blimpie Subs & Salads, Checkers Burgers, Honey Baked Ham Co., KFC, Taco Bell, Wendy's
O: Waffle House
Other **I:** CVS Pharmacy[RX], Cub Foods, Target
O: U-Haul Center[LP]
34 **(44)** GA 260, Glenwood Rd
Gas **I:** Racetrac[*, 24], Texaco[*]
Food **I:** Glenwood Diner, King's Wings Express, Miss Dossey's, Mrs Winner's Chicken
Lodg **I:** Glenwood Inn
O: Old English Inn, Super 8
ATM **I:** Racetrac
Other **I:** Dekalb Police Station, Deluxe Laundromat, U.S. Post Office
O: Buddy's Food Depot
35 **(46)** Junction I-20, Atlanta, Augusta
36 **(48)** GA 155, Flat Shoals Rd, Candler Rd
Gas **I:** Circle K[*], Conoco[*, CW], Shell[*, D, K]
O: Citgo[*, LP], Dyno Mart[*], Fina[*]
Food **I:** Checkers Burgers, Dairy Queen, Homebox

EXIT GEORGIA

Restaurant, KFC, McDonald's[PLAY], Pizza House, Taco Bell, WK Wings, Waffle King[24] (Shell)
O: Real Pit Bar-B-Q, Wings Submarines
Lodg **I:** Gulf American Inns
AServ **O:** Fina
ATM **I:** Circle K
O: Fina
37 **(51)** Bouldercrest Rd
TStop **I:** **Pilot Travel Center**[*, SCALES, 24]
Gas **I:** Amoco[*, 24]
O: Chevron[*, LP, 24]
Food **I:** **Dairy Queen (Pilot)**, Domino's Pizza, Hardee's, KFC, **Pilot Travel Center**, W.K. Wings, **Wendy's (Pilot)**
Lodg **I:** Dekalb Inn
ATM **I:** **Pilot Travel Center**
Other **I:** CVS Pharmacy[RX]
O: Sugar Creek Golf & Tennis Complex
38 **(52)** Junction I-675 South, Macon
39 **(53)** U.S. 23, Mooreland Ave., Ft. Gillam
TStop **O:** **TA TravelCenters of America**[*, SCALES] **(Lodging)**
FStop **I:** **Conoco**[*]
O: **Amoco**[LP]
Food **O:** **Blimpie Subs & Salads (TA), Charlie's, Country Pride Restaurant (TA), Popeye's Chicken (TA), Rio Vista (Catfish and Hush-puppies), TA TravelCenters of America (Lodging), Waffle House**

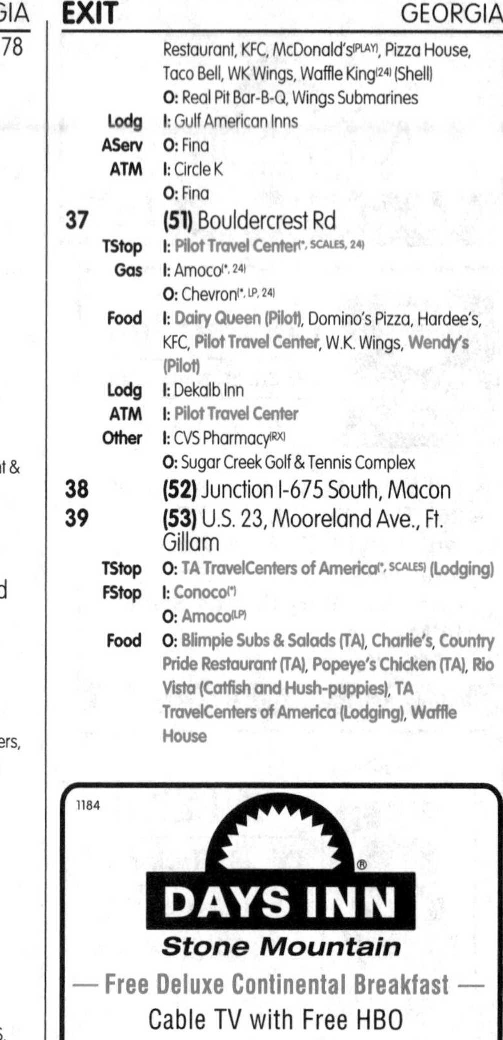

EXIT GEORGIA

AServ **O:** **Amoco**
TServ **I:** **Southern Towing Services, William's Detroit Diesel Allison**
O: **Amar Trailer Parts & Service, Arrow Truck Sales, Charlie's Truck Tires, Fruehauf, Goodyear Truck Service, Southern Truck Parts Repair (Cummins, CAT, Detroit Diesel), Sunbelt Cat Parts & Services, TA TravelCenters of America**[SCALES] **(Lodging), Used Trucks International, Woods Truck Tires**
TWash **O:** **TA TravelCenters of America (Lodging)**
Med **O:** + Mooreland Medical Clinic
40 **(55)** GA 54, Jonesboro Rd, Forest Park
Gas **O:** Amoco[*], Phillips 66[*]
Food **I:** Time After Time Cafe
O: Arby's, McDonald's[PLAY], Shoney's
Lodg **I:** Super 8
TServ **O:** **Trucks of Atlanta**
ATM **O:** Phillips 66
Other **O:** Atlanta Exposition Center, Home Depot
41 **(58)** Junction I-75, Atlanta, Macon, to Old Dixie Highway(turn off) (Services are on Old Dixie Highway, I GPS for junction, O GPS for services)
Gas **I:** Amoco[*, D], Chevron[*, 24]
Food **I:** Waffle House
Lodg **I:** Home Lodge
Other **I:** Frank's Outboard Marine Accessories Parts & Service, Mercury Outboards
42 **(59)** Clark Howell Hwy, Loop Road (Difficult Reaccess, Going westbound use exit 41)
43 GA 139, Riverdale Rd, Ga. International Covention Center
Gas **I:** Hess[*, D], Racetrac[*]
O: BP[*, CW], Speedway[*, LP], Texaco[*, CW]
Food **I:** McDonald's, Wendy's
O: Waffle House
Lodg **O:** Comfort Inn, Days Inn, Ramada Inn
TServ **O:** **Central Truck Part Inc.**
ATM **I:** Racetrac
Other **I:** Airport, Georgia International Convention Center, North Clayton Police
44 **(63)** Junction I-85 South, Atlanta, Montgomery

↑ GEORGIA

Begin I-285

I-287 NEW JERSEY →

EXIT NEW JERSEY

Begin I-287

↓ NEW JERSEY

66 **(67)** NJ17S, to Mahwah
TStop **E:** **Travel Port Express**[*, D, SCALES]
FStop **E:** **International FuelStop**[*], **Mobil**[*]
Gas **E:** Dean[D], Getti[*, D], Gulf, U-Save
Food **E:** Burger King, Mason Jaw Family Restaurant, McDonald's, Ramada Inn, State Line Diner, Subway, Vido's Pizza
Lodg **E:** Comfort Inn, Courtyard by Marriott, Ramada Inn (see our ad opposite page), Sheraton (see our ad opposite page)
ATM **E:** First Union Bank, Summit Bank
59 **(60)** NJ208S, Franklin Lakes
58 **(59)** U.S.202, Oakland

EXIT NEW JERSEY

Gas **W:** Exxon
Food **E:** Baskin Robbins, Blimpie's Subs, Bread Basket Deli, Jr's Pizza & Subs, KFC, Linda's Chicken, Oakland Bagels & Pastry, Oakland Bakery, Sun Yuan, The Pepper Mill, Topps China
W: Cafe L'Amore, Hot Bagels
ATM **E:** Fleet Bank, Hudson City Savings Bank, The Bank of New York, Valley National Bank
Other **E:** CVS Pharmacy, Drug Fair, Grand Union Grocery Store, Oakland Drugs, Oakland Vision Center
57 **(58)** Skyline Dr, Ringwood
53 **(54)** CR694, Alt CR511, Bloomingdale, Pompton Lakes

EXIT NEW JERSEY

Gas **E:** Coastal[*, D], Sunoco
Food **E:** Bella Italia, Blimpie's Subs, Charcoal Grill Cheese Steak, Dough House, Riverdale Lunchenette, Rosemary Lunch Dinner & Sage
Other **E:** Post Office, Riverdale Police
52AB **(53)** NJ23, Riverdale, Wayne, Butler
Gas **E:** Amoco[CW]
Food **E:** Venny's Pizza
Med **E:** + Chilton Hospital
47 U.S. 202, Montville, Lincoln Park
Gas **E:** Exxon[*]
Med **W:** + Hospital
ATM **E:** South Burgeon Savings Bank

Bold red print shows RV & Bus parking available or nearby

EXIT	NEW JERSEY
45	**(46)** Myrtle Ave, Boonton (Southbound, Reaccess Northbound Only)
Gas	**W:** Citgo(*), Exxon(*, D)
Food	**W:** Boonton Pharmacy, McDonald's
Other	**W:** Jack's IGA Supermarket
43	Intervale Rd, Mountain Lakes (Reaccess Northbound Only, Difficult Reaccess)
Gas	**E:** Texaco(*, D)
Food	**E:** Bevac Qua's
42	U.S.46, U.S.202, Dover, Clifton
Gas	**W:** Exxon
Food	**W:** Embassy Suites, Fuddruckers, Lucky's Star Kitchen, McDonald's, The Diner, The Great Wazu, Wendy's
Lodg	**W:** Days Inn, Embassy Suites
Med	**E:** Hospital
ATM	**W:** Summit Bank
Other	**W:** Sav On Pharmacy, US Post Office
41AB	Jct I-80, Delaware Water Gap, New York City
40AB	CR511, Parssipany Rd, Whippany (B - Lake Parssipany, Lake Shore Dr)
Gas	**W:** Mobil
Food	**W:** Frankinstein Pizza, Lake Parssipany Luncheonette, Woks Chinese Kitchen
ATM	**W:** First Union Bank
39AB	NJ10, Dover, Whippany
Gas	**W:** Mobil
Food	**W:** Demiamo, Hilton, Howard Johnson (Chinese)
Lodg	**W:** Hilton, Howard Johnson (see our ad this page)
37	NJ24E, Springfield, Columbia (Difficult Reaccess)
36	CR510, Morris Ave, Lafayette, Ridgedale
Gas	**W:** Amoco
Food	**E:** Governor Morris Hotel
	W: Ridgedale Lunch
Lodg	**E:** Governor Morris Hotel
35	NJ124, Old NJ124, Madison Ave
Food	**W:** Ceede's Restaurant, Hamilton Coffee Shop
Med	**E:** Morristown Memorial Hospital (Trauma Ctr)
ATM	**E:** NationsBank
	W: Chase Bank, TNC Bank
Other	**W:** Kings Grocery
33	**(34)** Harter Rd (Difficult Reaccess, No Trucks Over 5 Tons)
Other	**E:** Morriston Police
(15)	Rest Area (RR, HF, Phones, Picnic, P)
30AB	U.S.202, Bernardsville, Basking Ridge

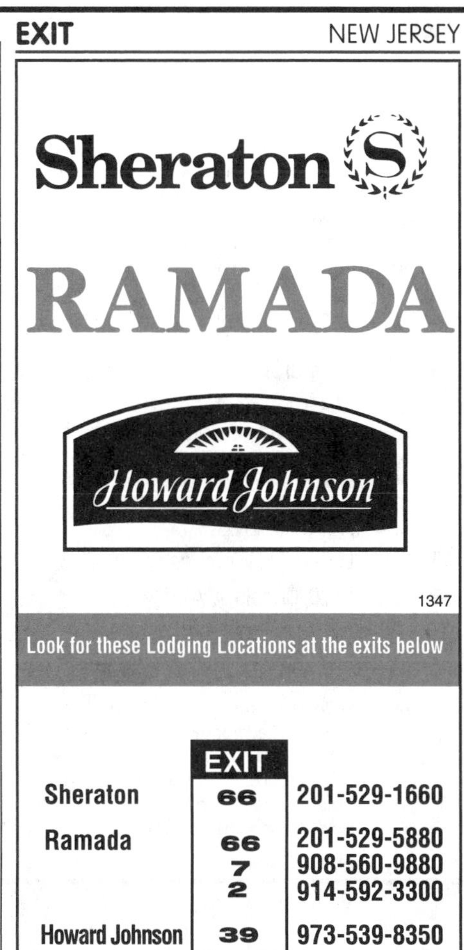

INTERSTATE EXIT AUTHORITY

EXIT	NEW JERSEY
Food	**W:** The Grain House (Old Mill Inn)
Lodg	**W:** Old Mill Inn
26	Mount Airy Rd, Liberty Corner, VA Hospital
Med	**E:** VA Hospital
22	U.S.202, U.S.206, Bedminster, Pluckemin
Gas	**E:** Amoco
Food	**E:** Blimpie's Subs, Golden Palace (Chinese), McDonald's, Nina's Pizza, TCBY
ATM	**E:** Peapack Gladstone Bank, TNC Bank
Other	**E:** Kings Supermarket, Revco Drugs
21AB	Jct I-78, to Clinton, Newark
13	**(18)** U.S.202, U.S.206S, U.S.22W, Summerville, Flemington
12	Weston Canal Rd, Manville, South Bound Brook
Lodg	**E:** Ramada Inn (see our ad this page)
11A	**(15)** U.S.22E, to New York City
(14)	NJ28, Bound Brook, Summerville
Gas	**E:** Amoco(*), Mobil
Food	**E:** Big Daddy's, Carvel Ice Cream Bakery, Costa del Sol, Pompeii Italian, Subway, The Fill In Station Deli
Med	**W:** Hospital
ATM	**E:** Summit Bank
6	**(11)** CR527, New Brunswick
Gas	**W:** Amoco
Food	**E:** Marriot
	W: Cafe Alfredo, Hong Kong Chinese, Quality Inn, Vinny & Sons Pizzaria, Zee Best Bagel
Lodg	**E:** Marriot
	W: Quality Inn
ATM	**W:** Summit Bank
Other	**W:** Cedar Lane Animal Clinic, Drug Fare
5	**(11)** Bound Brook, Highland Park
(11)	Centenial Ave, Highland Park, Middlesex
(10)	Weigh Station (Northbound)
4	Centennial Ave (Reaccess Southbound Only)
3	**(7)** South Randolphville Rd, Piscataway
Gas	**E:** Mobil
2	**(6)** CR529, Eddison, Dunellen
1	CR529, Dunellen, Eddison
1A	**(4)** Durham Ave, South Plainfield (Northbound, Reaccess Southbound Only)
Med	**E:** Hospital
(3)	CR501, Metuchen, New Durham (Southbound, Reaccess Northbound Only)
(2)	NJ27S, to New Brunswick (Northbound, Reaccess Southbound Only)
(1)	U.S.1, CR531
(0)	CR514W, Jct I-95, NJ Tnpk, Woodbridge, Bonhampton

↑NEW JERSEY

Begin I-287

I-290 MASSACHUSETTS

EXIT — MASSACHUSETTS

Begin I-290, Massachusetts

↓MASSACHUSETTS

9 Swanson Rd & Auburn
- **Gas** **S:** Getty(*), Shell(*)
- **Food** **S:** Addow's, Arby's, Auburn Town Pizza, Burger King, McDonald's(PLAY), Yong Shing
- **Lodg** **S:** Auburn Motel, Buget Motel, Days Inn
- **ATM** **S:** Fleet Bank, Webster's Savings

11 Worchester, College Sqaure
- **Gas** **N:** Texaco(*, D, CW)
- **Food** **N:** Culpeppers Bakery & Cafe, Pizzeria Delight, Wendy's
- **ATM** **N:** Commerce Bank

12 Millbury
- **Food** **S:** Dunkin Donuts, Market Deli

13A Vernon Street, Kelly Square
- **Gas** **N:** Exxon(*, CW), Merritt
- **Food** **N:** Kelly's Square Pizza
- **Med** **S:** ✚ Hospital

14 MA 122, Uxbridge, Bar
- **FStop** **S:** **Mobil(*)**
- **Gas** **S:** Citgo(*, D), **Mobil(*)**
- **Food** **N:** Bill's Sandwich Shop
  S: Auntie Dot's Pizza, Campy's Deli, Dunkin Donuts (Citgo), Graften Hill Donuts, Lindy Lue's, Roberts Fish & Chips
- **ATM** **S:** BankBoston
- **Other** **S:** George's Bakery

15 Shrewsbury St., E. Central
- **Gas** **S:** Mobile
- **Food** **N:** Worchester Fashion Outlet Mall
  S: Arthur's, Boulevard Diner, Brew City Grill, Cafe Dolce, Italian Kitchen, Leo's, Wonder Bar Pizza
- **Lodg** **N:** Crowne Plaza, Hampton Inn
- **AServ** **S:** Mobile
- **Med** **N:** ✚ Fallon Medical Center
- **ATM** **N:** Honey Farms Convenience
  S: Family Bank
- **Other** **N:** Honey Farms Convenience, Post Office, Worchester Fashion Outlet Mall

16 Central St.

17 MA 9, Belmont St.
- **Food** **S:** Belmont Grill, Jim's Pizza, Roberts Fish & Chips
- **Lodg** **N:** Crown Plaza Motel
- **Med** **S:** ✚ Memorial Hospital
- **ATM** **S:** 24 Convenience Store
- **Other** **S:** 24 Convenience Store

18 Lincoln St., Worchester Blvd

19 I-190, Lincoln, MA12

20 MA70, Lincoln, Burncoat St.
- **Gas** **N:** Exxon(*), Shell(CW), Sunoco
  S: Getty
- **Food** **N:** Baskin Robbins, Bickford's Family Restaurant, Carvel Ice Cream Bakery, Denny's, Dunkin Donuts, Dunkin Donuts, Friendly's, Little Caesars Pizza, McDonald's(PLAY), Papa Gino's, Subway (Exxon), Taco Bell, Wendy's
  S: Betty's Fish & Chips, Lincoln House of Pizza, Riley's Restaurant
- **Lodg** **N:** Day's Lodge, Holiday Inn
- **AServ** **N:** Sunoco
  S: Getty
- **Med** **N:** ✚ Hahnemann Hospital
  S: ✚ Memorial Health Care
- **ATM** **N:** BankBoston, Fleet Bank
- **Other** **N:** CVS Pharmacy(RX), Shaw's Supermarket, WalGreens Pharmacy(RX)
  S: CVS Pharmacy(RX)

21 Plantation St., Worchester (Reaccess Westbound Only, Difficult Reaccess)
- **Food** **N:** Christie's Pizza, Mick's
- **Lodg** **N:** Days Inn
- **Med** **S:** ✚ Hospital
- **Other** **N:** Premier Optical

22 Main St., Shrewsbury, Worchester

23AB MA140, Shrewsbury, Boyalston
- **Gas** **N:** Citgo(*, D, LP), Mobil(*)
- **Food** **N:** Dragon 88, Dunkin Donuts (Citgo)
- **AServ** **N:** Citgo, Mobil

24 Church St., N Boyalston

25AB Hudson St., Salamon Pond Mall Rd., Northboro
- **Lodg** **N:** Super 8

26 Jct. I-495

↑MASSACHUSETTS

Begin I-290, Massachusetts

I-290 ILLINOIS

EXIT — ILLINOIS

Begin I-290, Illinois

↓ILLINOIS

1A Jct I-90, Tollway To Chicago, Rockford (Left Exit Eastbound)

1B IL72, Higgins Rd. , IL58 Golf Rd., Woodfield Rd.
- **Gas** **W:** Wolf Car Wash(CW)
- **Food** **W:** Bennigan's, California Cafe, Denny's, Denny's Family Style Italian, Garfield, Hooters, Hulahan's, Rainforest Cafe, Red Lobster, Ruby Tuesday, Stir Crazy Cafe, Taco Bell, Wendy's
- **Lodg** **W:** Drury Inn, LaQuinta Inn
- **AServ** **W:** Sear's
- **ATM** **W:** La Salle Bank
- **Other** **W:** Cinaplex Oden, Sear's, Woodfield Theatre

4 IL53, Biesterfield Rd.
- **Food** **W:** Marino's Pizza
- **Med** **E:** ✚ Hospital
- **Other** **W:** Quick Stop

5 Thorndale, Elgin O'Har Expwy.
- **Food** **E:** Wyndham Garden Hotel
  W: **Wendy's**
- **Lodg** **E:** Wyndham Garden Hotel
  W: Extended Stay America

7 Jct I-135, Lake St. I-355 S. Tollway, Juliet

10AB I183, Parkway

12 Lake Rd., York Rd., US20 W
- **Food** **W:** Burger King, Christopher's Pancake, East Wind Chinese, Easter Sundae Ice Cream Creation, Hang Time (Holiday Inn), Holiday Inn, Hunan Palace (Chinese), Leza's European Deli, Little Caesars Pizza, Mimmo's Pizza, Nee Noodle Shop, Steven's Steakhouse
- **Lodg** **W:** Holiday Inn
- **TServ** **W:** **Freight Liner of Chicago(24)**
- **Med** **W:** ✚ Elmhurst Hospital
- **Other** **W:** Animal Health, Convenient Food Mart, Copy Service, Dental Clinic, Little Shopper Food Shop

13B I-20 E., Lake St.

13A U.S. 20, IL64 North Avenue.,
- **Med** **E:** ✚ Hospital

14AB St. Charles Rd.
- **Gas** **E:** Citgo, Union 76(CW)
- **Food** **E:** Dunkin Donuts, LosMarichi's, McDonald's
- **ATM** **E:** National Bank of Commerence

15AB I-290W Rockford, I-294 Tollway, I-88

16 Wolf Rd.
- **Lodg** **N:** Holiday Inn, Renanissance Inn

17B US12, US20, US45, Mannheim

18 25th Ave

19A 17th Ave
- **Gas** **S:** Citgo(*)

20 Herst Ave.
- **Gas** **N:** Amoco(*), Shell(*, CW)
  S: Union 76
- **Food** **N:** Dunkin Donuts, KFC
  S: Burger King, Checker's, Dunkin Donuts, Poor Boy Sandwiches
- **Med** **S:** ✚ Hospital

21B IL43, Harlem Avenue
- **Med** **N:** ✚ Hospital

23A Austin Blvd

23B Central Avenue
- **Med** **N:** ✚ Loretto Hospital

24A Laramie Ave.
- **Food** **N:** Chop Suey
- **Med** **N:** ✚ Hospital

25 Kostner
- **Gas** **N:** Amoco

29B Morgan Street

26A Independance Blvd
- **Gas** **S:** Amoco

26B Homan Avenue
- **Gas** **S:** Minute Man Citgo

27B California Ave (Difficult Reaccess)

28B Ashland Blvd
- **Gas** **N:** Amoco(CW)
- **Lodg** **S:** Hyatt
- **Med** **S:** ✚ St. Lukes Hospital

27C Oakley Blvd, Western Ave

28A Damen Ave.
- **Med** **S:** ✚ Hospital

↑ILLINOIS

Begin I-290, Illinois

Bold red print shows RV & Bus parking available or nearby

EXIT ILLINOIS

Begin I-294

↓ILLINOIS

(52) Lake, Cook Rd., Plaza 26, Riverwood, Deerwood (Reaccess Southbound Only)
- **Food** E: Hyatt
- **Lodg** E: Embassy Suites, Hyatt

(48) Willow Rd.
- **Gas** W: Amoco[*, LP, CW]
- **Lodg** W: AmeriSuites (see our ad this page)
- **Med** E: ✚ Hospital
- **ATM** W: Amoco

(46) Golf Rd. (Southbound, Reaccess Southbound Only)
- **Gas** E: Mobil[*]
- **Food** E: Tiffany's Restaurant
- **Lodg** E: Comfort Inn
- **AServ** E: Mobil
- **ATM** E: Mobil

(44) U.S. 14, Dempster St,

(42) Touhy Ave. Plaza (Toll)

(40) Jct I-90, Kennedy Expwy, NW Chicago, Rockford, I-294S., I-190W. O'Hare, River Rd.

(38) O'hare Oasis, Between Ogden, Fairmack, Roosevelt (RR, HF, Phones; Southbound)
- **Gas** E: Mobil[D]
- **Food** E: Burger King, Cinnabon
- **ATM** E: Mobil

(32) IL19 Irving Park Rd (Southbound, Reaccess Northbound Only, Toll)
- **Gas** E: Clark[*], Marathon[D]
- **Food** W: Mirage Restaurant
- **Lodg** W: Howard Johnson

(31) Jct I-290 W, Roosevelt Pkwy. (Northbound, Reaccess Southbound Only, Difficult Reaccess)
- **Food** E: Country Inn Pizza, Galway Cafe

(31) Jct I-290 E, Eisenhower Expwy.

(30) Cermack Plaza Toll (Southbound, Reaccess Northbound Only, Toll)

(29) I-88 East, Cermack Rd. Plaza

(28) I-88 West, Aurora (Southbound, Reaccess Northbound Only, Toll)

(27) U.S. 34, Ogden (Picnic)
- **Gas** W: Amoco[*], Shell[*]
- **Med** W: ✚ Hospital
- **ATM** W: First Chicago Bank, Shell, Superior Bank

(24) Hensdale Oasis,
- **Gas** E: Mobil
- **Food** E: Baskin Robbins (Hinsdale Oasis), Wendy's (Hinsdale Oasis)

(23) Jct. S. I-55, Stevenson Expwy., St. Louis & Wolf Rd
- **Gas** E: Mobil[D]
- **Food** E: Baskin Robbins, Wendy's

(23) N. I-55 Stevenson Expwy.

(22) 75th St. Willow Springs Rd

(20) Toll Plaza (Southbound, Toll)

(19) 83rd St. Plaza, Number 39 (Northbound, Toll)

(17) US 12, US 20, 95th St., 76 Ave., Hickory Hill, Oaklawn (Toll)
- **Gas** E: Citgo, Clark, Keane, Shell
- W: Shell[*, LP], Super America[*, D]
- **Food** E: Bennigan's, Billy Boy's Restaurant, Bongo Johnny's, Dunkin Donuts, Mi Pueblo, Oak Ridge Restaurant
- W: Arby's, Burger King, Delphians, Less Brothers, Sghoops Hamburgers, Vito & Nicks Pizzeria II, Wendy's
- **Lodg** W: Excel Inn
- **AServ** E: Sear's, Shell
- **Med** E: ✚ Hospital
- **ATM** E: Citgo, Keane, Lasall Bank
- W: Shell, Standard Bank, Super America
- **Other** E: Oak Lawn Medical Center, Sear's, Theatres
- W: 95th Street Produce Market, Minuteman Press, Osco Drugs[RX]

(16) IL 50, Cicero Ave., Alsip, Crestwood
- **FStop** W: **Gas City**[*, D, LP, K]
- **Gas** E: Citgo[*, D], Petro Express
- **Food** E: A-l Subs, Bob Evan's Restaurant, Condesa Bel Bar, Continental Pancake House, Copabana, Dunkin Donuts, Onion Field Restaurant
- W: Applebee's, Boston Market Restaurant, **Gas City**, Hardee's, IHOP, JC's Pub Restaurante, Lone Star Steakhouse, Mango's Pizza, Portillo's Hot Dog, Rosewood West Restaurant, Subway (Gas City), Terragon
- **Lodg** E: D-lux Budget Motel
- W: Bugetel Inn, Hampton Inn
- **TServ** E: **Tolway Truck Park**
- **ATM** E: First Suburban Bank
- W: **Gas City**
- **Other** W: Domonicks' Grocery, Low's Theatre, Pack N Mail, Target[RX]

(12) US 6, 159th St., Harvey, Marcum
- **Food** W: Baskin Robbins, Burger King, McDonald's, Subway, Taco Bell, White Castle Restaurant
- **TServ** E: **Kenworth**
- **ATM** W: Suburban Bank
- **Other** W: WalGreens Pharmacy

11 Jct I-80W

↑ILLINOIS

Begin I-294

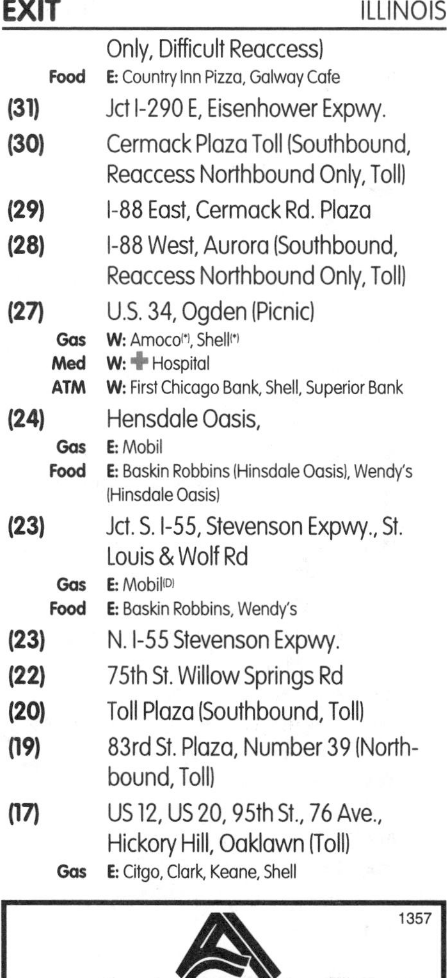

I-295 NEW JERSEY →

EXIT NEW JERSEY

Begin I-295, New Jersey

↓NEW JERSEY

(5) Clara Barton Service Area

(1) Penns Grove

1AB Pennsville, Salem, US 130, Pennsgrove, U.S. 40, Atlantic City (Northbound)
- **Gas** E: Exxon[D]
- W: Coastal[*, D]
- **Food** E: Burger King[PLAY], Cracker Barrel, KFC, McDonald's[PLAY], Taco Bell
- W: Domino's Pizza
- **Lodg** W: Seaview Motel
- **AServ** E: Exxon
- **ATM** E: Burger King
- W: Coastal

1C Hook Rd.
- **Lodg** E: White Oak Inn
- **Med** E: ✚ Hospital

2A US 40W, Dale Memorial Bridge, I-295 S

2B U.S. 40E, NJ Tnpk

2C U.S. 130, Deepwater
- **TStop** E: **Pilot Travel Center**[*, D, SCALES]
- W: **T/A TravelCenters of America**[*, SCALES]
- **Gas** E: Mobil[D]
- **Food** E: **Subway (Truckstop)**, Travaglini's (Wellesley)
- W: Blimpie's Subs (TA), Popeye's Chicken (TA)
- **Lodg** E: **Friendship Inn**[SCALES], **Landmark Inn**, Wellesley Inn & Suites
- **Med** E: ✚ Hospital

(3) Rest Area (RR, Phones, Picnic, Vending, RV Dump, P; Northbound)

CAMPING WORLD®
Exit 10
602 Heron Dr. • Swedesboro, NJ
1-800-889-8923
1418

(4) Weigh Station (Northbound)

4 NJ 48, Pennsgrove, Woodstown
- **Food** W: Roman Pantry Pizza

7 Auburn, Pedricktown
- **TStop** E: **295 Auto/Truck Plaza**[*, SCALES]
- **Food** E: **295 Auto/Truck Plaza**
- **Lodg** E: **295 Auto/Truck Plaza**

10 Center Square Rd, Swedesboro
- **Gas** E: Texaco[*, D]
- **Food** E: McDonald's
- **Lodg** E: Holiday Inn Select
- **AServ** E: Texaco
- **Med** W: ✚ Urgent Care Clinic (Pure Land Ind Complex)
- **ATM** E: Wa Wa Food Market, Woodstown National Bank & Trust
- **RVCamp** W: **Camping World (see our ad this page)**
- **Other** E: Wa Wa Food Market

11 **(12)** U.S. 322E, to NJ Tnpk, Mullica Hill, Bridgeport

13 **(14)** U.S.130 S, U.S. 322W, Bridgeport (Southbound)

EXIT NEW JERSEY

14 CR 684, NJ44, Repaupo Town, Gibbs Town

15 CR 607, Harrisonville, Gibbs Town

16A CR 653, Swedesboro, Paulsboro

16B CR 551 Spur, Gibbstown, Mickleton

17 CR 680, Gibbstown
- **Food** W: Burger King(PLAY), **Dutch Inn**(24), Mr. P's Deli
- **Lodg** W: **Dutch Inn**
- **ATM** W: First Holmes Savings Bank
- **Other** W: Funari's Thriftway Supermarket, Rite Aide Pharmacy(RX)

18 CR 678, CR 667, Paulsboro, Mt Royal, Clarksboro
- **TStop** E: **Travel Port**(*, SCALES)
- **Gas** E: **Amoco**(D)
  W: Texaco(*, D)
- **Food** E: **Brothers Pizza (Travel Port)**, **Buckhorn Family Restaurant (Travel Port)**, Dragon Nest Chinese, KFC, **McDonald's**(PLAY), Taco Bell, The Starting Gate Restaurant
- **AServ** E: **Amoco**
- **TServ** E: **Travel Port**(SCALES)
- **TWash** E: **Travel Port**
- **ATM** E: **Travel Port**

18B CR 667, Clarksboro, CR678, Mt Royal, Paulsboro

19 CR 656, Mantua

20 CR 643, to CR660
- **FStop** E: **Amoco**(*, 24)
- **Food** E: Angelina's (Best Western)
  W: Helen's Greentree Restaurant
- **Lodg** E: Best Western
- **TServ** W: **Flag Service & Maintenance Inc.**

21 CR 640, National Park, Woodbury
- **Food** E: Country House Restaurant
  W: Amazing Wok I, Vinny's Pizza

22 Jct CR 631, 644, 642, Woodbury, Red Bank
- **Gas** E: Mobil
- **Food** E: TC's Pizzeria
- **AServ** E: Mobil
- **TServ** E: **Freedom Int'l**
- **Med** E: ✚ Underwood Memorial Hospital
- **ATM** E: One Stop Shoppe Food Market
- **Other** E: One Stop Shoppe Food Market

23 U.S. 130 N, to Westville, Gloucester
- **Lodg** W: Cundey's Motel

24AB CR551, NJ45, Westville, Woodbury (Southbound, Reaccess Northbound Only)

25AB **(26)** NJ47, Deptford, Glassboro. (Southbound, Reaccess Northbound Only)
- **Gas** E: Amoco(*, D)
- **Food** W: Baby Luna Pizza
- **TServ** E: **TS Auto & Truck Repair (Towing)**
- **ATM** E: Clover Bank

26 Jct I-76, to Jct I-676, Philadelphia (Left Exit Northbound)

28 NJ 168, to NJ Turnpike, Bellmawr, Runnemede, Mt Ephraim
- **Gas** E: Shell
  W: Amoco(CW), Exxon(LP)
- **Food** E: Burger King, Club Diner
  W: Fast Eddie's Steaks, Wings, Good Friend Chinese, McDonald's(PLAY), Pop's Homemade Italian Ice, Seafood Gallery, Taco Bell
- **AServ** E: Shell
  W: Exxon
- **ATM** E: Commerce Bank

29 **(30)** U.S. 30, Berlin, Collingswood, Hadden Heights, Lawnside
- **Gas** E: Amoco(24), Texaco
  W: Shell(*)
- **Food** E: Burger King, Wendy's
- **Lodg** E: Barrington Motel
- **Med** E: ✚ Hospital

30 Warwick Rd, Lawnside, Haddenfield (Southbound)
- **Med** E: ✚ Hospital
- **Other** E: U.S. Post Office

31 Woodcrest Station

32 CR 561, Haddonfield, Voorhees , Gibbsboro
- **Gas** E: Mobil(*, D)
- **Food** E: Bagel Place, Chinese Regency, Herman's Deli, Nopoli Pizza, Vito's Pizza
- **AServ** E: Mobil
- **Med** E: ✚ Hospital
- **ATM** E: Commerce Bank, PNC Bank
- **Other** E: Eckerd Drugs(RX), U.S. Post Office

34 NJ 70, Cherry Hill, Marlton, Camden
- **Gas** E: Amoco(*, 24)

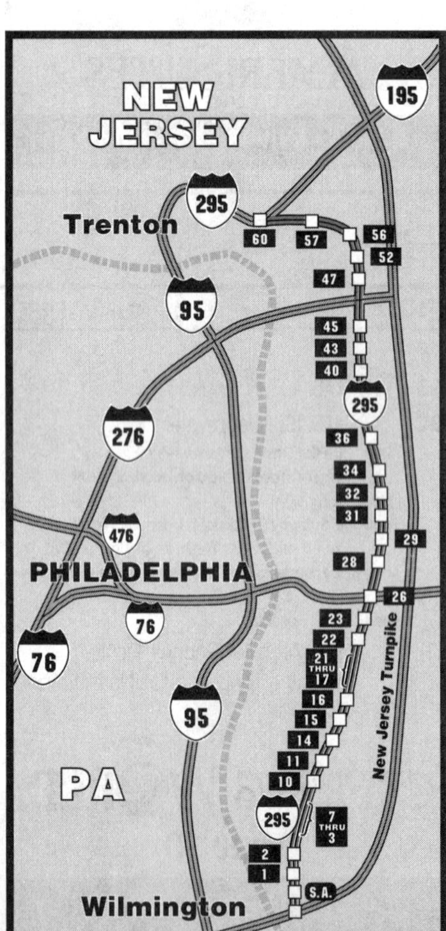
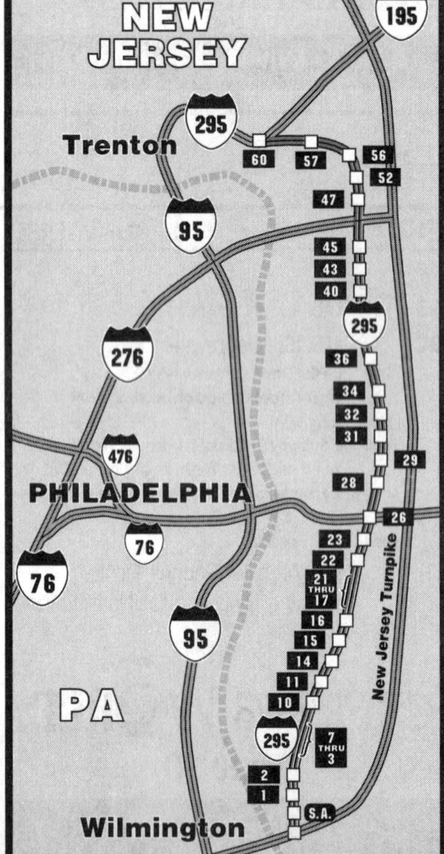

  W: Mobil(24), Texaco(*, D)
- **Food** E: Burger King(PLAY)
  W: Andreotti's Viennese Cafe, Boston Market Restaurant, Einstein Bros Bagels, Manhattan Bagel, Morgan's, Steak N Ale
- **Lodg** W: Four Points Hotel Sheraton
- **AServ** W: Mobil(24), Texaco
- **Med** W: ✚ Hospital
- **ATM** W: Summit Bank
- **Other** W: Cherry Hill Animal Hospital, Magaziner's Covered Bridge Pharmacy(RX)

36 NJ 73, Berlin, Tacony Bridge, to NJ Tnpk
- **FStop** W: **Texaco**(*)
- **Gas** E: Exxon, Gulf(*, D), Mobil(*, D)
  W: Amoco(*, 24), Citgo(*, D, 24), Exxon(D), Shell(24)
- **Food** E: Bob Evan's Restaurant, Kelly's Court (Quality Inn)
  W: Burger King, Dunkin Donuts, Golden Eagle Diner
- **Lodg** E: Courtyard by Marriott, Doubletree, Econolodge, Fairfield Inn, Quality Inn, Raddison, Ramada, Red Roof Inn, Super 8
  W: Bel-Air Motor Lodge, Motel 6, Sharon Motor Inn, Track & Turf Motor Hotel
- **AServ** W: Exxon
- **ATM** E: Mobil

40AB NJ 38, Mount Holly, Moorestown
- **FStop** W: **Texaco**(*)
- **Food** W: **Subway (Texaco)**
- **Med** E: ✚ Hospital

43 Rancocas Woods, Delran
- **Gas** W: Texaco(*)
- **AServ** W: Texaco
- **Med** W: ✚ Hospital

45AB Mount Holly, Willingboro
- **FStop** W: **Exxon**(D)
- **Gas** W: Mobil
- **AServ** W: **Exxon**
- **Med** E: ✚ Hospital
  W: ✚ Hospital

47AB CR 541, Mount Holly, Burlington, NJ Tnpk
- **Gas** E: Exxon(*, D)
  W: Exxon, Gulf(*), Hess(D), Shell(*)
- **Food** W: Checkers Burgers, Shoney's, Wedgewood Farm Family Restaurant
- **AServ** W: Exxon, Gulf, Wal-Mart Supercenter(24, RX) (Optical)
- **Med** W: ✚ Hospital
- **ATM** W: Farmers & Merchants Bank
- **Other** W: Acme Food & Drug(24, RX), Eckerd Drugs(RX), Wal-Mart Supercenter(RX) (Optical)

(50) Rest Area (RR, Phones, Picnic, Vending, RV Dump, P)

52AB Columbus, Florence

56 U.S. 206, to NJ Tnpk, Fort Dix, McGuire AFB (Northbound)
- **TStop** E: **Petro Truck Serv**(*)
- **Food** E: **Iron Skillet Restaurant (Petro)**
- **TServ** E: **Truck Repair**

57 U.S. 130, US206 Burlington, Bordentown
- **Gas** E: Amoco, Exxon, Mobil, Raceway, Shell(*)
- **Food** E: Burger King, Cannie's Restaurant (European Cuisine), Chinese Restaurant, Denny's, Ground Round, McDonald's, Rosario's Pizza, Taco Bell

Bold red print shows RV & Bus parking available or nearby

EXIT		NEW JERSEY

	Lodg	**E:** Econolodge
	ATM	**E:** CoreStates Bank, People's Saving Bank, Summit Bank
	Other	**E:** Acme Grocery
		W: State Police
(58)		Scenic Overlook (Vehicles Over 5 Ton-Prohibited)
60		Jct I-195N, Jct I-95N, NJ29, NJ129, Trenton, Shore Points
61A		Arena Dr E, Whitehorse Ave
61B		**(62)** Olden Ave N (Southbound, Reaccess Northbound Only)
63		**(64)** NJ33, to NJ 535, Trenton, Hamilton Ave, Nottingham
	Gas	**E:** Mobil
	Food	**E:** Pete's Steakhouse, Popeye's Chicken
		W: AJ's Cafe, Joey's Place, Peter Pan Diner
	Med	**W:** + Hospital
64		**(65)** CR 535N, to NJ 33E, Mercerville (Southbound, Reaccess Northbound Only)
65AB		Sloan Ave
	Gas	**E:** Exxon
	Food	**E:** Brookwood Restaurant & Catering, Burger King, China Buffet, Dunkin Donuts, Hoagie Shack, Lenny & Haps Pizza, Taco Bell
	ATM	**E:** Yardsill Nat'l Bank
	Other	**E:** Animal Veterinary Care Center Hospital, Roslidi Thriftway Groc
(35)		Rest Area (RR, HF, Phones, Picnic, RV Dump, P)
67		**(68)** U.S.1, New Brunswick, Trenton
	FStop	**E:** **Amoco**(*, D, LP)
	Food	**E:** Ground Round, Red Lobster
		W: Michael's
	Lodg	**E:** McIntosh Inn, Red Roof Inn
		W: **Howard Johnson**, Motel Mount's, Sleep-E-Hollow Motel, Holiday Inn (see our ad this page)

↑ NEW JERSEY

↓ DELAWARE

EXIT		NEW JERSEY/DELAWARE
9N		DE 9, New Castle Ave, New Castle, Wilmington
	FStop	**W:** **Gulf**(*)
	Gas	**E:** Amoco(*), Conoco
		W: Texaco(*)
	Food	**E:** Dragon Palace Chinese, Giavani's Pizza
		W: Gordan's Seafood, McDonald's
	Lodg	**E:** **Country Inn**
		W: Days Inn, **Motel 6**, Travelodge TraveLodge
	Other	**E:** Food & Fresh Grocery & Pharmacy, Rite Aide Pharmacy

↑ DELAWARE

Begin I-295

Notes:

I-295 VIRGINIA

EXIT — VIRGINIA

Begin I-295, Virginia

↓VIRGINIA

51AB Nuckols Rd
- **Other** S: US Post Office

49AB US 33, to Richmond, Montplier

45AB Woodman Rd

43 Junction I-295, I-95 & US 1 to Richmond

41AB US301, VA2, to Hanover and Richmond (Exit To 64 & 95 To Richmond)
- **FStop** W: **Exxon**[LP]
- **Gas** E: Amoco[*, D], Texaco[*, D, LP]
- **Food** E: Brunetti's Restaurant, Burger King, China Kitchen, Dunkin Donuts (Texaco), McDonald's
- **ATM** E: First Virginia Bank, Signet (Amoco)
- **Other** E: Revco Drug

38 VA 627, Polgreen Rd, Meadowbridge Rd
- **Med** W: ✚ Hanover Medical Mall

37AB US360, Tappahannock, Mechanicsville
- **Gas** E: Texaco[*, LP, CW]
  W: Amoco[*, LP], Citgo[*], Mobil[D]
- **Food** E: Baskin Robbins, Cracker Barrel, Gus' Italian Cafe, Mexico Restaurant, Taco Bell, Ukrop's Cafe'
  I: Shoney's
  W: Mechanicville Seafood, Prairie Schooner, Rendezvous Cafe, Sno-cone Shack
- **ATM** W: Central Fidelity Bank, Creststar Banking, First Virginia Bank, Nationsbank
- **Other** E: Ukrop's Supermarket and Pharmacy, **Wal-Mart**[RX]
  W: Colonial Pharmacy, Mechanicsville Drug Store, Revco Drugs, Winn Dixie Supermarket

34AB VA615, Kreighton Rd

31AB VA156, Highland Springs

28 Jct I-64, U.S. 60, Norfolk, Richmond, Williamsburg

22AB VA5, Charles City, Varina

15AB VA10, Hopewell, Chester
- **Gas** E: Amoco[*, D, LP], Citgo[*, LP]
  W: Chevron[*, LP, CW]
- **Food** W: **McDonald's**
- **Med** E: ✚ Hospital
- **ATM** W: Chevron

9AB VA36, Hopewell, Ft Lee, Colonial Heights
- **Gas** E: Petrol[*, LP, K]
  W: Amoco[*, D, LP], Exxon[*, D], Pilot Travel Center[*, D, LP, K], Texaco[*]
- **Food** E: Honey Bee's, Hong Kong Chinese Restaurant, Mexican Restaurant, Rosa's Italian Food
  W: Bullet's (Exxon), Days Inn, Denny's, Gary's Eatery and Tavern (Comfort Inn), Kanpai Japanese Steakhouse, Leone's Italian Restaurant, McDonald's, Papa John's, Pizza Hut, Shoney's, Splash Seafood, Subway, Taco Bell, Top's Chinese, Waffle House, Wendy's, Western Sizzlin', Zero's Subs
- **Lodg** E: Innkeeper
  W: Comfort Inn, Days Inn, Hampton Inn
- **ATM** W: First Colonial Savings Vank, First VA Bank
- **Other** E: Super Fresh Supermarket
  W: Food Lion Grocery Store, Revco Drugs, Rite Aide Pharmacy, Winn Dixie Supermarket[24]

3AB U.S. 460, Norfolk, Petersburg
- **FStop** E: **East Coast**[*, LP]
- **Gas** E: Texaco[*, K]
  W: **Exxon**[*]
- **Food** E: **Dunkin Donuts**[*] **(East Coast)**, **Subway (East Coast)**
  W: **McDonald's**
- **ATM** W: Exxon

2 Jct I-95S, to Rocky Mount, NC (Left Exit Southbound)

1 **(46)** Jct - 95 to I-85 Petersburg (Southbound)

↑VIRGINIA

Begin I-295, Virginia

I-295 MARYLAND

EXIT — MARYLAND

Begin I-295, Maryland

↓MARYLAND

41A Ellicott City, Glen Burnie

46 JCT I-895N, Harbor Tunnel (Northbound)

47AB JCT I-95, MD166 Catonsville, VWI Airport.

19 JCT695, Glen Burnie, Pawson, Annapolis

18 West Nursery Rd
- **Lodg** E: AmeriSuites (see our ad this page)

17 Jct I-195, Catonsville, Odenton, Lithicum, Aviaton Blvd (Services On Belkridge Landing Rd Frontage Rd)
- **Gas** E: Convenience Store
- **Food** E: Charlie's Cafe (Airport), Holiday Inn (Ridge Rd), Marriott, McDonald's
- **Lodg** E: Empire Airport North, Hampton Inn, Holiday Inn (Ridge Rd), Marriott, Susse Chalet
- **ATM** E: First Nat'l Bank

16 MD100, Glen Burnie, I-95
- **Food** W: 3 Aces Restaurant
- **Lodg** W: Ramada Inn

15 MD175, East Odenton, West Jessup
- **Gas** E: Shell[*, K], Shell
- **Food** E: Parkway Inn
- **Lodg** E: Parkway Inn

14 MD32, East Ft Meade, West Columbia
- **Gas** W: Shell

13 MD198, Ft Meade

12 MD197, Laurel, Bowie
- **Gas** E: Exxon
  W: Getty's[D], Texaco
- **Food** E: China Diner, Little Caesars Pizza
  W: Chintao Chinese Restaurant, Roy Rogers, Subway, TCBY
- **Lodg** W: Red Rood Inn
- **Med** W: ✚ Hospital
- **ATM** W: Citizens National Bank
- **Other** W: US Post Office

11 Powder Mill Rd, Beltsville

10 MD193, Greenbelt, Nassa, Goddard Ctr (No Trucks)
- **Gas** E: Exxon
  W: Citgo[*]
- **Food** E: Chesapeake Bagel Bakery, Chevy's Mexican, Chi Chi's Mexican Restaurant, Denny's, Hunan Treasure, Jasper's, Subway, Wendy's
- **ATM** E: Chevy Chase Bank, First Nat'l Bank of Maryland, Safeway Grocery (Deli Bar), Safeway Grocery
  W: Citgo
- **Other** E: CVS Pharmacy, For Eyes Optical, Safeway Grocery (Deli Bar)
  W: Park Police Station

9 Baltimore Washington Pkwy, Jct 495. (No Trucks)

8 Riverdale Dr
- **Gas** E: Exxon[*, D]
- **Food** E: A Wok Restaurant, Pizza Oven

7 MD450, Bladensburg, Annapolis
- **Gas** E: Amoco, Capitol Plaza Auto Center[*], Econoway, Lowest Price, Mobil, Super Trak
- **Food** E: Bob's Big Boy, Burger King, Dunkin Donuts, Eastern Restaurant (Chinese), Howard Johnson (Italian), Italian Inn, McDonald's, Pizza Hut, Shakeys Pizza, Wendy's
- **Lodg** E: Bladensburg Motel, **Comfort Inn**, Howard Johnson
- **ATM** E: Chevy Chase Bank (Safeway Supermarket), Chevy Chase Bank (The Capital Plaza Mall), Crestar Bank
- **Other** E: Safeway Grocery[RX]
  W: Bladensburg Animal Hospital

6 **(202)** US 1, Bladensburg, Cheverly
- **Gas** W: Exxon
- **Food** W: Fertelli Italian Restaurant
- **Lodg** W: Howard Johnson
- **Other** E: Prince Valley Medical Ctr
  W: Drug Emporium

5 Pennsylvania Ave, & Andrews Airforce Base, Frederick Douglas
- **Gas** E: Amoco, Citgo[*], Mobil[*], Shell[*]
- **Food** W: McDonald's
- **Med** W: ✚ Hospital
- **Other** E: Southeast Animal Hospital

4 Navy Yard, Downtown Washington, I-395

3AB South Capitol St, Downtown, Sutland Pkwy, US Naval Station (Difficult Reaccess)

2 Portland St, Boling Airforce Base

5AB JCT I-95.

6AB US 1, Washington Blvd, to Laurel, Elk Ridge
- **FStop** W: **Quarrels Card Fueling**[24]
- **Gas** W: Extra Fuel[*, D, LP]
- **Lodg** W: **Blvd Motel**

1 US Naval Research Lab
- **Med** W: ✚ Hospital

↑MARYLAND

Begin I-295, Maryland

1349
AMERISUITES
AMERICA'S AFFORDABLE ALL-SUITE HOTEL
Maryland • Exit Nursey Rd. • 410-859-3366

EXIT — IOWA

Begin I-380

↓ IOWA

72 San Marnan
- Gas W: Conoco(*), Holiday(*)
- Food W: Bonanza Steakhouse, Boston Market Restaurant, Burger King, Carlos O Kelly's Mexican Restaurant, Country Kitchen, Godfather's Pizza, Great Dragon Buffet, Long John Silver, McDonald's, Olive Garden, Pizza Hut, Subway, Taco Bell, Taco John's, Wendy's
- Lodg W: Comfort Inn, Fairfield Inn, Heartland Inn, Pine Tree Motel, Super 8
- ATM W: Magna Bank, Tire Plus
- Other W: First Vision Center, Target, The Big K-Mart(RX), Wal-Mart Supercenter(RX)

71 US 218, Waterloo North, Airport

70 River Forrest Rd
- Gas W: Conoco(*, LP), Phillips 66(*, LP)

68 Elkrun Hieghts, Evansdale Dr.
- TStop E: **Elkrun Hieghts Truck Plaza**(*, SCALES), Flying J Travel Center(*, D)
- Food E: Blimpie's Subs, McDonald's(PLAY)
- Lodg E: Ramada Limited
- TServ E: Elkrun Hieghts Truck Plaza

66 IA 297, Raymond, Gilbertville

65 US 20 East, Dubuque

62 Gilbertville, Blackhawk County Road D 38

55 LaPorte City, Jesup, County Road V 65

(54) Weigh Station (Southbound)

(51) Weigh Station (Northbound)

49 IA 283, Brandon

43 IA 150, Independence, Venton

41 IA 363, Urbana
- FStop W: Conoco(*)
- Food W: Dashboard Subs (Conoco)

35 Center Point, County Road W36

28 Toddville, Robins, County Road E 34

25 Boyson Rd.
- Gas E: Phillips 66(*, CW)
- Food E: Blimpie's Subs (Phillips 66), Oscars Restaurant

24B IA 100, Blairs Ferry Rd, Collins Rd, 42nd Street
- Gas E: Quick Shop(*, LP)
  W: QT(*)
- Food E: Hardee's, Papa Juans Mexican Restaurant, Shoney's, Zio Johno's Spaghetti House
  W: Burger King, Egg Roll House Chinese, Godfather's Pizza, Pizza Hut, Royal Fork Buffet Restaurant, Subway, Taj Mahal Restaurant
- Lodg E: Shoney's Inn
- ATM E: Linn Area Credit Union
- Other W: Wal-Mart(LP, 24, RX)

24A Collins Rd, IA 100
- Gas E: Texaco(*)
- Lodg E: Ramada Limited (see our ad this page)
- ATM E: Magna Bank
- Other E: Clarke's Pharmacy(RX)

23 42nd Street
- Food E: Baskin Robbins, Domino's Pizza, Doughnut Land, Hardee's, KFC, Little Caesars Pizza, Tasty Freeze, The Red Lion, The Springhouse Restaurant, Wendy's
- Other E: Clarks Pharmacy

22 Coldstream, 29th Street, Glass Rd, 32nd Street
- Gas E: Texaco(*, LP)

21 H Ave.

20B 7th Street East, Five Season Center

1673

RAMADA LIMITED SUITES

2025 Werner Avenue Cedar Rapids, IA

319-378-8888

- Free Continental Breakfast Bar
- Satellite TV w/HBO & ESPN
- Indoor Pool • Hot Tub • Exercise Room
- Whirlpool Suites • Guest Voice Mail
- In Room Coffee, Hairdryers, Iron & Ironing Board
- Easy In & Out From I-380
- Many Restaurants, Golf, Tennis all Nearby

IOWA ▪ I-380 ▪ EXIT 24A

- Food W: Taco Bell
- Lodg W: Five Season's Crown Plaza
- Other W: **St. Lukes Hospital**

20A (19) IA 94, US 151, Fifth Ave Southwest

19B 1st Ave West, Kingston Stadium (Southbound)
- Gas W: Amoco(*, CW)
- Lodg E: Village Inn Motel

19AC 1st Ave (Northbound)

18 Wilson Ave. Southwest
- TServ W: **Hawkeye International**

17 33rd Ave. S.W., Hawkeye Downs
- Gas W: 66 Handi Mart(*), Amoco(*, CW)
- Food W: Cancun Restaurant, Denny's, Hot Stuff Pizza (66 Handi Mart), McDonald's, Pei's Manderine Restaurant, Perkins Family Restaurant, Subway, Wendy's
- Lodg W: Comfort Inn, Days Inn, Econolodge, Exel Inn, Fairfield Inn, Four Points Hotel Sheraton, Heartland Inn, HoJo Inn, Red Roof Inn, Super 8
- TServ E: **Cummins**
  W: **Brad Regan, Inc.**
- ATM W: Norwest Bank

16AB US 30, US 151, US 218, Mt Vernon, Tama
- Gas E: Phillips 66(*)
- Food E: Blimpie's Subs, Hardee's

13 Cedar Rapids Airport, Ely
- FStop W: **Coastal**(*, D, 24)
- Lodg W: Howard Johnson's
- TServ W: Cedar Rapids Truck Center

(12) Rest Area (RR, Phones, Picnic, Vending, RV Dump)

10 County Road F12, Swisher, Shueyville
- Gas E: Citgo(*, LP)
  W: Sinclair(*, D, LP)

4 County Road F28. North Liberty
- Gas E: Amoco(*)
- Food E: Subway

↑ IOWA

Begin I-380

I-385 SOUTH CAROLINA →

EXIT — SOUTH CAROLINA

Begin I-385

↓ SOUTH CAROLINA

42 U.S. 276, Stone Ave., Traveler's Rest
- Gas W: Amoco(D)
- Food E: Rugby's Sports Grill, The Big Clock Drive-in
  W: Zorba Restaurant & Lounge

40AB SC 291, Pleasantburg Dr.
- Gas E: Exxon, Hess(*), Speedway(*, D, LP), Texaco(*, CW)
- Food E: Bojangles, Hardee's, Pizza Hut, S&S Cafeteria, Steak & Ale, Subway, Taco Casa, Wendy's
- ATM E: Summit National Bank

39 Haywood Rd.
- Gas E: BP(*, LP, CW), Exxon(*, D)
  W: Crown(*, CW)
- Food E: Domino's Pizza, Gourmet Kitchen, Longhorn Steakhouse, Outback Steakhouse, Philly Connection
  W: Arby's, Black-Eyed Pea, Burger King, Carrabba's Italian Grill, Chuck E Cheese's Pizza, Ci Ci's Pizza, Don Pablo's Mexican, El Pollo Loco, Italian Market & Grill, Kanpai Japanese Steakhouse, O' Charley's, Quincy's, Waffle House, Wendy's
- Lodg E: Ameri Suites, Courtyard by Marriott, Hilton, Quality Inn, Residence Inn
  W: Hampton Inn
- Med E: Doctors Care
- ATM E: American Federal, Carolina First, Exxon, NationsBank
  W: BB&T Bank, First Union, Wachovia Bank
- Other W: Phar Mor Drugs

37 Roper Mountain Rd.
- Gas W: BP(*, CW), Exxon(*, LP)
- Food E: Pizza Express (Harris Teeter)
  W: Olympian Greek & Italian Food, Rio Bravo, Waffle House
- Lodg W: Days Inn, Fairfield Inn, Holiday Inn Select
- ATM E: First Citizens Bank (Harris Teeter)
- Other E: Harris Teeter Supermarket(RX)

36AB Junction I-85, Spartanburg, Atlanta (36A goes North, 36B goes South)

35 Woodruff Rd., SC 146
- Gas W: Hess(*, D), Red Robbin(*, LP)
- Food E: Applebee's, Arizona Steakhouse, Bojangles, Boston Pizzaria, Chick-Fil-A, China Wall, Hardee's, Marcelino's
  W: Acropolis, Best BBQ, Cheers Food & Drink, Fuddruckers, Hong Kong Chinese, IHOP, Midori's Steak & Seafood, Monterrey Mexican, Red Robbin, Stock Car Cafe, TCBY
- Lodg W: Hampton Inn
- AServ E: Wal-Mart(24, RX)
- ATM E: Carolina First Bank
  W: Red Robbin, Wachovia Bank
- Other E: Wal-Mart(RX)
  W: Garden Ridge Home Decorations & Crafts, Hemrick's

34 Butler Rd.

33 Bridges Rd.

31 Laurens Rd., SC 417

30 U.S. 276, Standing Springs Rd. Maudlin

29 Georgia Rd., Simpsonville
- FStop W: **Amoco**(*, LP, K)
- Gas W: BP(*, LP)
- Food W: Clancy's Bar & Grill

EXIT	SOUTH CAROLINA
27	Fairview Rd., Simpsonville
Gas	**E:** Exxon(*, D, LP), Sav-Way(*, LP, K), Texaco(*, D) **W:** Amoco(*, LP, CW), BP(*, LP, CW)
Food	**E:** Carolina Fine Foods, Chinese Food, Coach House Restaurant, Hardees, Little Caesars Pizza, Little Pig's, Manzanillo Mexican, McDonald's, Subway **W:** Applebee's, Baskin Robbins, Burger King(PLAY), Dragon Den Restaurant, KFC, Pizza Hut, Ryan's Steakhouse, Taco Bell, Waffle House, Wendy's
Lodg	**E:** Palmetto Inn **W:** Comfort Inn (see our ad this page), Holiday Inn Express, Jameson Inn, Microtel Inn
AServ	**W:** Wal-Mart(24, RX) (One-hour photo, vision center)
Med	**E:** ✚ Hospital
ATM	**E:** BB&T, Winn Dixie Supermarket **W:** Amoco, NationsBank
Other	**E:** Bi-Lo Grocery(24), CVS Pharmacy(RX), Winn Dixie Supermarket **W:** Ingles Supermarket, K-Mart(RX), Wal-Mart(RX) (One-hour photo, vision center)
24	Fairview
Gas	**E:** Exxon(D, LP), Phillip 66(*, LP, K)
Food	**E:** Hardees, Waffle House
AServ	**E:** Exxon
ATM	**E:** Phillip 66
Other	**E:** H & R Mini Mart
23	SC 418, Fountain Inn, Pelzer
Gas	**E:** Exxon(*, D)
Food	**E:** Exxon, Subway

1111

Comfort Inn

Exit 27 • Simpsonville, SC

864-963-2777

• Free Deluxe Continental Breakfast
• Coffee Makers in All Rooms
• Cable T.V./VCR
• All Rooms Microwave/Fridge
• Whirlpool Suites Available
• Pool • Fitness Center • Spa

SOUTH CAROLINA ▪ I-385 ▪ EXIT 27

EXIT	SOUTH CAROLINA
ATM	**E:** Exxon
22	S.C. 14 West, Fountain Inn.
19	SC14 East, Owings
16	SC 101, Woodruff, Gray Court
10	Rd. 23, Barksdale.
9	Enoree, Laurens, U.S. 221
FStop	**E:** Exxon(*)
Food	**E:** Exxon, Krispy Kreme Doughnuts (Exxon), Subway (Exxon)
Lodg	**E:** Southern Economy Inn
ATM	**E:** Exxon
(6)	Rest Area (RR, Phones, Picnic, Vending)
5	SC 49, Laurens
2	SC 308, Clinton, Ora
Med	**W:** ✚ Hospital
1	Junction I-26

↑SOUTH CAROLINA

Begin I-385

I-390 NEW YORK →

EXIT	NEW YORK
	Begin I-390

↓NEW YORK

EXIT	NEW YORK
20AB	**(76)** 20A - Jct I-490 East, to Rochester, 20B - Junction I-490 West to Buffalo
19	**(75)** NY33A, Chili Ave
Gas	**W:** Sunoco
Food	**E:** KFC **W:** Burger King, Pizza Hut, Ramada Inn, Scoop's Restaurant (Ramada Inn)
Lodg	**W:** Motel 6, Ramada Inn
AServ	**W:** Sunoco
Med	**E:** ✚ Hospital
Other	**E:** The Wishing Well **W:** Meyer & Toolan Pharmacy(RX)
18AB	**(74)** Brooks Ave, Airport, NY204 (18B west, 18A east)
Gas	**E:** Mobil(*) **W:** Sunoco(*)
Food	**W:** Blue Horizon Restaurant, Kiese Frozen Custard
Lodg	**E:** Holiday Inn **W:** Comfort Inn, Fairfield Inn
AServ	**E:** Mobil
Other	**W:** Airport, Airport Lane Bowling
17	**(73)** NY383, Scottsville Rd
Gas	**W:** Sunoco(*, D)
Food	**E:** Campi's Sandwich **W:** Subway (Sunoco), Sunoco
Med	**E:** ✚ Hospital
Other	**E:** Rollock's Christian Outlook
16A	**(72)** NY 15, W Henrietta Rd., E. River Rd.
Med	**I:** ✚ Strong Memorial Hospital
16B	NY 15A, E Henrietta Rd, MCC
Food	**W:** Dilly Deli, Fresno's Restaurant, Jack Astor's Bar & Grill, Manhattan Bagel, Phillips European Restaurant & Pastries, T.G.I. Friday's, Tony Roma's
Lodg	**W:** Courtyard by Marriott, Hampton Inn, Wellesley Inn (see our ad this page)
Med	**E:** ✚ Monroe Community Hospital
Other	**W:** Alpha & Omega Books, Eckerd Drugs(RX)
15	**(71)** Jct I-590N (Left Exit Southbound)
14AB	**(69)** NY252, NY15A, E Henrietta Rd
FStop	**W:** Mobil(*, CW)
Food	**W:** Boston Market Restaurant, Burger King, Hooters, Lone Star Steakhouse, Manhattan Bagel, Starbucks Coffee, Subway, Taco Bell
Lodg	**W:** EconoLodge, Holiday Inn
ATM	**W:** Mobil, Top Grocery Store(RX)
Other	**W:** Empire Vision Center, Top Grocery Store(RX)
13	**(68)** Hylan Dr
Gas	**W:** Mobil(*)
AServ	**W:** Sam's Club
ATM	**W:** Mobil
Other	**E:** State Police **W:** Sam's Club, Wal-Mart(RX)
12A	**(66)** 12A - NY253, Lehigh Station Rd
Food	**W:** Wendy's
Lodg	**W:** Fairfield Inn, Highland Motor Inn, Microtel, Red Roof Inn, Super 8
TServ	**W:** Regional International Trucks & Trailers(24)
12B	Junction I-90
11	**(62)** NY15, NY251, Rush, Scottsville
10	**(55)** U.S. 20, NY5, Avon, Lima
9	**(52)** NY15, Lakeville, Conesus Lake, Lavonia
FStop	**E:** Hess(*, CW)
Food	**E:** Dunkin Donuts, Hess, Subway (Hess)

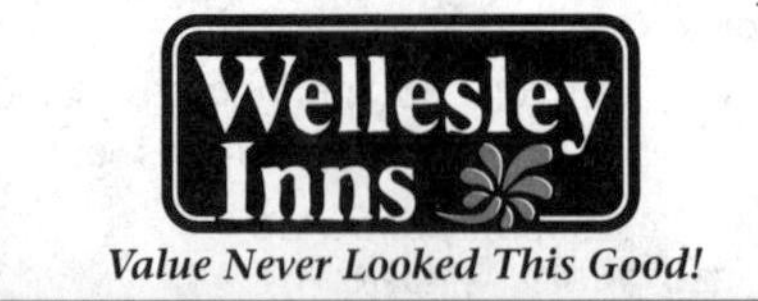

1350

Wellesley Inns

Value Never Looked This Good!

New York • Exit 16 • 716-427-0130

EXIT	NEW YORK
ATM	**E:** Hess
8	**(49)** NY20A, Geneseo
7	**(39)** NY63, NY408, Mt. Morris, Letchworth Park
Gas	**W:** Mobil(*, LP) (U-Haul Distributor)
Food	**W:** Homestead Restaurant
(38)	Rest Area (RR, Phones, Picnic; Southbound)
(38)	Rest Area (RR, Phones, Picnic; Northbound)
6	**(34)** NY36, Sonyea
5	**(24)** Dansville, NY36
TStop	**W:** Travelport(*, RV DUMP, SCALES) (Mobil gas)
Gas	**E:** Kwik Fill(*, LP), Mobil(*, LP, K)
Food	**E:** Arby's, Burger King, Ice Cream Island, McDonald's, Mobil, Pizza Hut, Subway (Mobil) **W:** Buckhorn Restaurant (Travelport), Travelport (Mobil gas)
Lodg	**W:** Daystop (Travelport), Travelport (Mobil gas)
TServ	**W:** Travelport(SCALES) (Mobil gas)
ATM	**E:** Wyoming County Bank
Other	**E:** CVS Pharmacy(RX), Rite Aide Pharmacy(RX), Save A Lot Food Store, Top Grocery Store(24)
4	**(23)** NY36, Dansville, Hornell
Gas	**E:** Citgo(*, D, LP)
Med	**E:** ✚ Hospital
Other	**E:** Burnwell Gas(LP), Dansville Animal Hospital
3	**(17)** NY15, NY21, Wayland
Other	**E:** State Police
2	**(11)** NY415, Cohocton, Naples
(9)	Scenic Area (Northbound)
1	**(2)** NY415, Avoca
Exit	**(0)** Jct NY 17 West, Jamestown, NY 17 East, NY 15, Corning, Elmira (Difficult Reaccess)

↑NEW YORK

Begin I-390

Bold red print shows RV & Bus parking available or nearby

EXIT MASSACHUSETTS/CONNECTICUT

Begin I-395, Massachusetts

↓MASSACHUSETTS

7 (0) Jct I-90 MA TNPK, MA12S, Auburn
Gas W: Shell[*]
Food E: Golden Lion
W: Abdow's, Arby's, Burger King, Papa Gino's
Lodg W: Auburn Motel, Budgetel Inn, Days Inn
ATM E: Bank of Boston
W: Fleet Bank, Webster Five Cents Savings Bank
Other W: Auburn Police, Barnes & Noble Bookstore
6 (12) Jct U.S. 20, Sturbridge, Shrewsbury
Gas E: Gulf[*]
W: Shell
Food E: KFC
W: D'Angelo's, Friendly's, Holiday Pizza, Quality Pizza, Wendy's
AServ W: Shell
Other W: CVS Pharmacy[24, RX], Coin Laundromat
5 (9) Depot Rd, N Oxford
4 (6) Sutton Ave, Oxford, Sutton
Gas W: Mobil[*]
Food W: Dairy Express Pizza, Dunkin Donuts, McDonald's, N & J Donuts, New England Pizza, Subway
ATM W: Fleet Bank
Other W: CVS Pharmacy[RX], Post Office
3 (4) Cudworth Rd, N Webster, S Oxford
Food W: Uncle Tannou's
2 MA16, Webster, Douglas
Gas W: Exxon[*, CW], Getty[*], Hess[*], Shell
Food W: Burger King, Dunkin Donuts (Exxon), Empire Wok, Friendly's, Gil's Seafood Deli, Honey Dew Donuts, Papa Gino's, Webster Donuts, Yum-Yum Chicken
AServ W: Shell
ATM W: Commerce Bank, Fleet Bank
Other W: CVS Pharmacy[RX], Price Chopper Supermarket
1 MA193, Webster
Gas W: Citgo
Food W: Wind Tiki Chinese
AServ W: Citgo
Med E: ✚ Hospital
Other E: Webster Lake Veterinary Hospital

↑MASSACHUSETTS

↓CONNECTICUT

100 (54) Wilsonville, E Thompson
99 (50) CT200, N Grosvenor Dale, Thompson
Lodg E: Lord Thompson Bed & Breakfast
98 (49) Grosvenor Dale, CT12 (Left Exit, Difficult Reaccess)
Gas W: Sunoco[D]
Med W: ✚ Hospital, ✚ Thompson Medical Center
97 (47) U.S.44, Woodstock, E Putnam

EXIT CONNECTICUT

Gas E: BP[*]
W: Shell[LP]
Food E: Dunkin Donuts, KFC, Little Caesars Pizza (K-Mart), McDonald's[PLAY], Subway, Wendy's
W: McDonald's (Wal-Mart)
AServ W: Shell
ATM E: New London Trust, Super Stop & Shop
W: Wal-Mart[RX]
Other E: K-Mart, Super Stop & Shop
W: Wal-Mart[RX]
96 (46) to CT12, Putnam
Food W: Kings Inn
Lodg W: Kings Inn
Med W: ✚ Hospital
95 (45) Kennedy Dr
Med W: ✚ Hospital
Other W: Animal Hospital of Putnam
94 (43) Attawaugan, Ballouville
TServ W: **International Truck Parts & Maintanence**
93 (41) CT101, Dayville, E Killingly
FStop W: **Mobil**[*, D]
Gas E: Extra Fuel, Shell
Food E: Burger King, Carvel Ice Cream Bakery, China Garden, Dunkin Donuts (Extra Fuel), Fitzgerald's Pub & Grill, McDonald's, Subway, Zip's Diner
AServ E: Shell
ATM E: Fleet Bank, Savings Bank of Manchester
W: The Savings Inst.
Other E: A&P Grocery
W: Bell Park Pharmacy[RX]
92 (38) S Killingly
Food W: Giant Pizza
ATM W: Fleet Bank
Other W: Bonneville Pharmacy, State Police
91 (38) U.S. 6W, Danielson, Hartford
90 (35) to U.S. 6E, Providence
(35) **Rest Area (Northbound)**
89 (32) CT14, Central Village, Sterling
FStop W: **Sunoco**[LP]
Gas W: Citgo[*, D, 24]
Food W: Amanda's Restaurant, Subway
Lodg W: Plainfield Motel
AServ W: **Sunoco**
Other W: Vision Care Center
88 (30) CT14A, Plainfield, Oneco
Gas W: Mobil[*]
Lodg W: Renaissance Bed & Breakfast
Med W: ✚ Walk In Clinic
87 (28) Lathrop Rd
Gas E: Texaco[*, D]
W: Citgo[*], Sunoco[*, D, LP]
Food E: Dunkin Donuts, Dunkin Donuts (Texaco), Great Oak Pizza, Hong Kong Star
W: Baker's Donuts, Golden Eagle, Golden Greek, McDonald's
Lodg E: Plainfield Yankee Motor Inn

EXIT CONNECTICUT

ATM E: People's Bank
Other E: CVS Pharmacy, Super Big Y Grocery Store
86 (24) CT201, Hopeville
85 (22) CT164, CT138, Preston City, Pachaug
ATM E: People's Bank
84 (21) CT12, Griswold, Jewett City
FStop W: **Mobil**[*, D]
Gas W: Citgo[*], Shell[*, CW]
Food W: Dandy Donuts (Mobil), McDonald's[PLAY], Pizza Hut (Mobil), Taco Bell (Citgo)
ATM W: Better Value Supermarket[RX]
Other W: Better Value Supermarket[RX]
83A (19) CT169, Lisbon (Northbound, Reaccess Southbound Only)
83 (18) CT97, Occum, Taftville
Gas E: Getty[*]
W: Citgo[*]
82 (14) Yantic, Norwichtown
FStop W: **Mobil**[*, D], **Shell**[*, CW]
Gas W: Texaco[*, D], Tru Value Hardware
Food E: Friendly's Ice Cream
W: Courtyard by Marriott, Rena's Pizza
Lodg W: Courtyard by Marriott
AServ W: Texaco
ATM E: Dime Savings Bank
Other W: Tru Value Hardware
81 (14) CT2, CT32, Norwich, Hartford
Med E: ✚ Hospital
80 (11) CT82, Downtown, Norwich, Salem
Gas E: Mobil[*], Shell
Food E: Bess Eaton, Burger King[PLAY], Dominic's Pizzeria, KFC, McDonald's[PLAY], Subway
W: McDonald's (Wal-Mart)
Lodg W: Ramada Hotel
AServ W: Wal-Mart[RX]
ATM E: Liberty Bank, Shell
W: Dime Savings Bank, Norwich Federal Credit Union
Other W: Wal-Mart[RX]
79A (9) CT2A E, Preston, Ledyard
79 (6) CT163, Uncasville, Montville
78 (5) CT32, New London (Northbound)
(8) Rest Area (RR, Phones, Picnic)
FStop E: **Mobil**[*]
Other E: State Police
77 (2) CT85, Colchester, Waterford
Gas W: Citgo
Food W: Dunkin Donuts
Lodg W: Oakdale Motel
75 (1) U.S.1, Waterford, I-395S (Southbound)

↑CONNECTICUT

Begin I-395, Connecticut

I-395 VIRGINIA ⟶

EXIT VIRGINIA

Begin I-395, Virginia

↓VIRGINIA

9 Pentagon, Crystal City, Richmond, Washington Blvd, Ridge Rd
Food E: California Pizza, Chevy's Mexican Restaurant, Crystal City Mall, Nell's Carry Out, Starbucks Coffee
Lodg E: Doubletree Hotel, Residence Inn

EXIT VIRGINIA

8AB VA 27, Washington Blvd, Ft Myer, & Memorial Bridge
Food W: Marvelous Bagels & Deli, Pizza Movers, Sheraton
Lodg W: Sheraton
7AB VA 120, Glebe Rd.
Gas E: Exxon
Food E: Auggie's Crabbie Pig, Pizza Hut
W: Best Western, Brandy's Restaurant, China

EXIT VIRGINIA

Village Restaurant (EconoLodge)
Lodg W: Best Western, Econolodge
Med E: ✚ Hospital
ATM E: First Virginia Bank
Other E: Rite Aide Pharmacy
6 Shirlington, Quaker Ln
Gas W: Exxon, Texaco
Food W: Best Buns, Bistro-Bistro, California Pizza Kitchen, Caryle Gran, Charlie Chang, Damon's,

EXIT VIRGINIA

Deli Cafe, Honey Baked Ham, St Pepper's, Thai Shirlington
- **Med** E: ✚ Hospital
- **ATM** W: Virginia Bank
- **Other** W: Village Market Grocery

5 King St, Falls Church, Alexandria
- **Gas** W: Exxon[*]
- **Food** E: Atlanta's Pizza, Bagel Bakery, I Can't Believe It's Not Yogurt, Pastry Shop, Roy Rogers, Starbucks Coffee, Subway, The Cafe
  W: Copeland's (Parks Ctr)
- **ATM** E: Chevy Chase Bank, Crestar Bank
- **Other** E: Giant Supermarket, Post Office, Rite Aide Pharmacy, United Optical

4 Seminary Rd
- **Gas** E: Exxon
- **Food** E: Hunan Restaurant, Roma Pizza Deli & Subs, Steak & Ale
  W: Raddison Hotel
- **Lodg** E: Ramada Inn
  W: Raddison Hotel
- **Med** E: ✚ Hospital
- **Other** E: CVS Pharmacy, Safeway Grocery

3AB VA 236, Duke Street, Little River Turnpike, Lincolnia
- **Gas** E: Extra Fuel[*, CW], Exxon[*, D], Texaco[D]
  W: Exxon[*], Mobil[*], Texaco[*]
- **Food** E: Akasaka Japanese Restaurant, Anette's BBQ Haven, Charlie's Chiang Restaurant (Mangolian BBQ), Chesapeake Bagel Bakery, Chi Chi's, Dunkin Donuts, Four Seasons Diner, Friendly's, Good Taste Chinese

6254 Duke Street
Alexandria, VA 22312
703-642-3422
1155
Int'l House of Pancakes
Bus Parking • Tour Pkgs
Meeting Rooms
Free HBO/ESPN/CNN
Near all D.C. Attractions
ABA AMERICAN BUS ASSOCIATION
VIRGINIA • I-395 • EXIT 3B

703-354-4950
Alexandria, VA
DAYS INN
Toll Free Reservations: 800-329-7466
1278
110 S. Bragg Street
Bus Parking ¥ Tour Pkg
Outdoor Pool
Free HBO/ESPN/CNN
Meeting Room
Near D.C. Attractions
Restaurants Adjacent

Newly Renovated

VIRGINIA • I-395 • EXIT 3B

Restaurant, Ho King, Jerry's Subs & Pizza, Lupita's Mexican Restaurant, McDonald's, Mozarella Cafe, Pappa John's, Red Lobster, Ruby Tuesday, Santa Rosa Seafood, Savio's, Scechuan Express, Subway, Thi Hut Restaurant, Ti Lemon Grass Restaurant, Wendy's
  W: Arby's, Bennigan's, Boston Market Restaurant, Casa Fiesta Mexican & Salvadorian Food, Einstein Bros Bagels, Happy Eatery Buffet & Bakery, Hee Been Japanese, IHOP, McDonald's, Pamekay's Donuts, Pizza Hut, Roy Rogers, Subway, Szechuan Delight Chinese Carry-Out
- **Lodg** W: **Comfort Inn (see our ad this page)**, 2 **Days Inn (see our ad this page)**
- **ATM** E: Crestar Bank
- **Other** E: CVS Pharmacy, Giant Supermarket & Pharmacy, Vandorn Safeway Grocery
  W: For Eyes Optical, Latin African Grocery Store (Check Cashing), Rite Aide Pharmacy

2A VA 648, Edsall Rd.
- **Gas** I: Amoco[*], Crown[D, CW], Exxon
  O: Mobil[*]
- **Food** O: **Denny's**
- **Lodg** O: Home-Style Inn
- **ATM** O: NationsBank

1 Jct I-95, Jct I-495

↑VIRGINIA

Begin I-395, Virginia

I-405 CALIFORNIA →

EXIT CALIFORNIA

Begin I-405, California

↓CALIFORNIA

76 Lancaster
75 JCT I-210
74 Rexford St.
73 Jct. I-5
72 Rinaldi Street, Mission Hills
- **Gas** E: Arco[*, 24]
  W: Shell[*]
- **Lodg** W: Grenada Motel
- **Med** E: ✚ Hospital
- **Other** E: Presidente Mexican Restaurant

71A San Fernando Mission Blvd, San Fernando
- **Gas** E: 76[*], Arco[*]
- **Food** E: Good Day Donuts, Subway, Sutters Mill
- **Other** E: Fire Station, Mail-Fax U.S.A.

71B Junction CA 118

70 Devonshire Street, Granada Hills
- **Gas** E: 76[*], Arco[*, 24], Mobil, Shell[D]
- **Food** E: Buon Gusto Ristorante, Holiday Burger, Mandarin Island Chinese, Safari Room, Tasty Thai Food
- **AServ** E: Mobil, Shell
- **ATM** E: Mobil, Vons Grocery
- **Other** E: Vons Grocery

69 Nordhoff Street, Northridge
- **Gas** W: Arco[*]
- **Food** E: ABC Donuts & Chinese Food, El Patio, Mas y Mas (Mexican)
  W: Chips And Salsa (Mexican), Kings Kitchen
- **Lodg** E: Hillcrest Motel
- **ATM** E: 7-11 Convenience Store
- **Other** E: 7-11 Convenience Store

68 Roscoe Blvd, Panorama City
- **Gas** E: Chevron[*]
  W: Shell[*, LP], Texaco[D, CW]
- **Food** E: Burger King, Denny's, Galpin Restaurant, Taco Bell
  W: Coco's, Daily Donuts, Tommy's Hamburgers
- **Lodg** W: Motel 6
- **ATM** E: Chevron
- **Other** E: Roscoe's Grocery

1790
Oak Ridge Inn
A DAYS INN HOTEL
★★★ Rated Hotel
800-350-STAY
1320 Newbury Rd. • Thousand Oaks, CA 01320
Free HBO/Cable
Heated Pool & Spa
In Room Safe
In Room Refrigerator
In Room Coffee Maker
$55
2 to 4 Persons
Great Group Rates and Tour Bus Parking!
I-405, Exit 63 (Hwy 101) Exit at Ventu Park turn Left, turn Left on Newbury Rd. and make 1st Rt.
California • I-405 • Exit 63

W: Wonder Hostess Bakery & Thrift Shop

66 Sherman Way, Reseda
- **Gas** W: 76[D, 24]
- **Food** W: Taco Bell
- **Other** W: U.S. Post Office

65 Victory Blvd, Van Nuys
- **Gas** W: Arco[*, 24]
- **Med** E: ✚ Hospital
- **ATM** W: Arco

64 Burbank Blvd
- **Gas** E: Chevron[*], Shell[*, 24]
- **Food** E: Carriage Inn, Piccola Italia, Zankou Chicken
- **Lodg** E: Cabana Motel, Carriage Inn, El Cortez Motel, Starlight Cottage
- **Other** W: Sepulveda Wildlife Refuge

63 Ventura Blvd
- **Gas** E: Mobil
  W: 76
- **Food** E: Angelena's Soul Food Kitchen, El Pollo Loco, Fred's Deli, Jewell of India, Reubin's Red Hots, Sisley Italian Kitchen, Sumiya Japanese, Take Ten Deli, Vitos Pizza To Go
  W: California Chicken Cafe, China Palace, Racco's Milano Italian Restaurant, Radisson Center, Shihoya Restaurant Chinese (Heritage Motel), Shiraz Restaurant (Middle Eastern), Valley Inn
- **Lodg** W: Heritage Motel, Radisson Center, 2 Days Inn(see our ad this page)
- **AServ** E: Mobil
  W: 76
- **Med** W: ✚ Family Urgent Care
- **ATM** E: Glendale Federal Bank, San Wa Bank,

Bold red print shows RV & Bus parking available or nearby

EXIT CALIFORNIA

Washington Mutual
Other **E:** Rite Aid Pharmacy, Whole Foods Market
W: Little Corner Market, The Post Box

Exit **(63)** Valley Vista Blvd, Sepulveda (Southbound, Reaccess Southbound Only)

61 Mulholland Dr, Skirball Center Dr
Other **E:** Sepulvada Pass Trailhead

60 Getty Center Dr
Other **E:** Getty View Trailhead

58 Moraga Dr (Northbound, Reaccess Northbound Only)
Gas **E:** Chevron[*], Shell
Food **E:** Bel-Air Bar & Grill
AServ **E:** Shell
ATM **E:** Chevron

57 Sunset Blvd
Lodg **W:** Holiday Inn, Summit Hotel

56 Montana Ave (Northbound, Reaccess Southbound Only)

55A Wilshire Blvd West
Med **W:** + VA Medical Center

55B CA 2, Santa Monica Blvd.
Gas **E:** Mobil
W: 76[*], Chevron[D]
Food **E:** Arrosto Coffee, Campos Famous Burritos, Hubba Hubba 50's Cafe, Jin Jiang's Seafood Restaurant, Koo-Koo-Roo California Kitchen, Little Cafe & Restaurant, New York Pizza & Pasta, Toto Caffe Spaghetteria, Winchells Donuts[24], Yoshinoya Beef Bowl
W: Dolores Restaurant, El Mexicano Deli Restaurant, Hearty Burgers, Javan Restaurant (Arabic), La Bottega, Lulu's Alibi, Nanbankan Kabob & Chinese, New Japan, Pink Dot Deli & Bakery, Rex Bakery, Subway, Talay Thai Cuisine, Westside Donuts, Croissants, & Bagels
Lodg **W:** Best Western, Stuart Manor Motel, West End Hotel
AServ **W:** 76, Chevron
ATM **E:** Mobil
Other **E:** California Animal Hospital, Mail Boxes, Box, & Ship, West L.A. Animal Hospital
W: 7-11 Convenience Store, U.S. Post Office

Exit Olimpic Blvd, Pico Blvd.
Food **E:** China Hut, Papa's Pizzeria, Subway
W: Carrillo's Tacos, Japanese Deli, Joyce Cafe, Little Hong Kong Cafe, Noah's Bagels, O-sho Japanese Restaurant, Panda Express, Quizno's Classic Sub, Starbucks Coffee, Teba Saki Chicken, Totoraku BBQ
ATM **E:** 7-11 Convenience Store
W: Sumitomo Bank
Other **E:** 7-11 Convenience Store, K-9 Grooming, Samuel Goldwin Foundation Children's Center, The Loved Dog
W: House of Books, The Olympic Collection Banquet & Conference Center

53A Junction I-10, Santa Monica Freeway

53B National Blvd. (Northbound)
Food **E:** ABC Fast Food (Chinese), El Pollo Loco, Habit Hamburgers, Hollywood Smoothy's, IHOP, Pizza Hut, Subway
ATM **E:** Bank of America, Vons Grocery, Wells Fargo Bank
Other **E:** Sav-On Drugs[24], Vons Grocery

51A Washington Blvd, Venice Blvd
Gas **E:** Chevron, Mobil[*], Shell[D]
W: Super Petrol
Food **E:** Baskin Robbins, Carl Jr's Hamburgers, Donut King, Panda Coin Kitchen, Sushi Bar, Villa Italian Restaurant
W: FatBurger, Spudnuts Donuts, Tacos Aguila
Lodg **E:** Deano's Motel, El Astro Motel, Half Moon Motel, Holiday Inn Express, Sunburst Motel
AServ **E:** Chevron
W: Super Petrol
Other **E:** 7-11 Convenience Store

51B Washington Blvd, Culver Blvd

EXIT CALIFORNIA

Gas **E:** 76[*]
W: 76, Thrifty
Food **E:** Dear John's, Domino's Pizza, Rincon Criollo (Cuban), Taco Bell, Tanner's Coffee Co.
AServ **W:** 76, Thrifty
Other **E:** Allied Model Trains
W: 7-11 Convenience Store

51C CA 90 West, Marina, Del Rey (Limited Access Hwy)

50 Slauson Ave
Gas **E:** Arco[*]
Food **E:** Buffalo Wings, Del Taco, George Petrelli, Royal Chinese, Shakeys Pizza
ATM **E:** Home Savings
Other **E:** Joshua's Book Store, Office Depot

Exit Howard Hughes Parkway, Sepulveda Blvd.

48 La Tijera Blvd.
Gas **W:** 76[*, LP], Arco[*], Chevron[*, 24]
Food **W:** Buggy Whip Restaurant, Marie Callender's Restaurant
AServ **W:** Chevron[24]
Other **W:** U.S. Post Office

47 Florence Ave, Manchester Blvd, CA 42
Gas **E:** 76[*, D, 24]
W: Mobil[*], Shell[D]
Food **E:** Don Amigos (Tacos), Stakey's Deli, Steppin' Up, Tam's Jr. Hamburgers
W: Arby's, Authentic Texas BBQ, Quick-N-Split Burgers, Randy's Donuts, Tottino's Pizza
Lodg **E:** Allright Automotive, Best Western, Cloud 9 Motel, EconoLodge
W: Days Inn, Days Inn, Sand Man Motel
AServ **E:** 76[24]
W: Mobil
Med **E:** + Centinela Hospital
ATM **E:** 76
Other **E:** Wonder Bakery Thrift Shop
W: Inglewood Animal Hospital

46 Century Blvd, L.A. Airport, Imperial Hwy.
Gas **W:** Arco[*], Chevron[*, D, 24]
Food **E:** Casa Gamino Mexican, Flower Drum Chinese, Jim's Taco Fiesta
W: McDonald's, Subway[24], Taco Bell
Lodg **E:** Best Western, Comfort Inn, Marletta's Motel, Motel 6, Tivoli Hotel
W: Hampton Inn, Holiday Inn, Quality Hotel, The Westin Hotel
Med **E:** + Centela Hospital
ATM **W:** Arco

Exit I-105 East Norwalk, I-105 West El Segundo

44 El Segundo Blvd.
Gas **E:** Arco[*]
Food **E:** Christy's, Jack-In-The-Box, Los Chorros, Pizza Hut
W: Chappies Restaurant (Ramada), Denny's
Lodg **E:** El Segundo Inn
W: Ramada
Other **E:** Aloha Drugs[RX]
W: U.S. Air Force Base

43 Rosecrans Ave, Manhatten Beach
Gas **E:** 76[*], Shell[*]
W: Arco
Food **E:** Chaeil Fishing Tackle, El Pollo Loco, Falcon Inn, Subway
W: Carl Jr's Hamburgers, China Chef, Luigi's Restaurant
AServ **E:** Shell
Other **E:** Food 4 Less, Home Depot, Marsh Weldcraft, Staple's, Toys R Us
W: Fire Station, Kinko's[24]

42 Inglewood Ave
Gas **E:** Arco[*]
W: 76[*], Mobil, Shell[D, 24], Texaco[D, 24]
Food **E:** Al-Noor Pakestani Cuisine, Big Fish, Choice's Gourmet, Daphne's Cafe, Domino's Pizza, In-N-Out

EXIT CALIFORNIA

Burger, Mom's Donuts, Terriyaki Magic, Yashinoya Beef Bowl
W: Cafe Manhatten, China Express, Havana Mania Cuban Food, La Salsa (Mexican), Winchells Donuts
AServ **W:** Mobil
Other **E:** Advance Veterinary Care Center
W: Drug Emporium[RX]

41 CA107, Hawthorne Blvd.
Gas **W:** Arco, Thrifty[*]
Food **E:** Diplomat Restaurant (Peruvian, Italian), Golden China, McDens Donuts, McDonald's, Pho Trung Duong, Spires
W: Mario's Mexican, Subway
Lodg **E:** Days Inn, Days Inn

40 CA 91W Hermosa Beach, Prairie Ave, Redondo Beach Blvd, Redondo Beach
Gas **E:** Arco[*], Thrifty[*]
Food **E:** Amigo's Tacos, Chuck E Cheese's Pizza, Little China Cuisine
Other **E:** Servac Pharmacy, Super Hayat Market
W: Alondra Drug[RX], Ralphs Grocery, Sav-On Drugs[RX]

Exit Artesia Blvd, CA 91 E
Gas **W:** 76, Texaco[*, CW]
Food **W:** Burger King (Texaco), China Express, Neno's Pizza, Winchells Donuts
AServ **W:** 76, Texaco
ATM **W:** Texaco

39 Crenshaw Blvd, Torrance
Gas **E:** Arco, Mobil
Food **E:** Denny's[24]
Other **E:** Police Station, U.S. Post Office

38A Western Ave
Gas **W:** Mobil[*]
Food **E:** Del Taco[24], Denny's, Subs R Us, Wok Wok Oriental Restaurant
Lodg **W:** Courtyard by Marriott
Other **E:** Lucky Grocery Store, New Hope Pharmacy, Optometry

38B Normandie Ave, Gardena
Gas **W:** Texaco[*, D, CW, 24]
Lodg **E:** Comfort Inn

Exit Vermont Ave. (Southbound, Reaccess Northbound Only)

37 Junction I-110, San Pedro, Los Angeles

36 Main Street (Northbound, Reaccess Southbound Only)
Other **E:** Goodyear Airship Operations

(35) Weigh Station (Northbound)

(35) Weigh Station

35 Avalon Blvd, Carson
Gas **E:** Arco[24]
W: Arco[*], Shell[24]
Food **E:** Bistro 880, Krazee Grill, Sizzler Steak House, Supreme Donuts, Tony Roma's
Lodg **E:** Ramada Inn
AServ **W:** Shell[24]
Other **W:** County of L.A. Sheriff's Dept., U.S. Post Office

34 Carson Street West
Gas **W:** 76[24]
Food **W:** Delia's (Philippino, Oriental), Pizza Man, Subway, The Roadhouse Cafe, U.S. Donuts, Valerio's City Bakery
Lodg **E:** Comfort Inn
W: Hilton
AServ **W:** 76[24]
Med **W:** + Torrence Memorial Family Medical Center
Other **W:** City of Carson Community Center, Optometry, Postal 'N' More

33A Wilmington Ave.
Gas **E:** Arco[*, 24]
W: Texaco[*, D]
Food **W:** Spires Coffee Shop[24], Subway (Texaco), Taco Bell (Texaco)
AServ **E:** Arco[24]
TServ **W:** **Volvo, Westrux International**
Other **W:** Fire Station

Bold red print shows RV & Bus parking available or nearby

EXIT	CALIFORNIA
33B	Alameda Street
32	Santa Fe Ave
Gas	**W:** 76[*], Shell[*, 24]
Food	**W:** Angel Food Donuts, Fantastic Burger, Tom's Burgers
Lodg	**W:** Arlington Motel
Other	**W:** Weber's Bakery Thrift Store, Western Samoa Taro
31	Junction I-710, Pasadena, Long Beach
Exit	Pacific Ave. (Southbound, Reaccess Northbound Only)
30A	Long Beach Blvd
Food	**E:** La Pizza Loca
Other	**W:** Universal Care Pharmacy
30B	Atlantic Ave
Gas	**E:** Arco[*, D], Chevron[*, CW], Texaco[*, D]
Food	**E:** Black Angus Steakhouse, Denny's[24], El Torito, Granny's Donuts, Mustard's Hot Dogs, Subway (Texaco)
Other	**E:** Target, Uptown Animal Hospital
29A	Orange Ave (Southbound)
29B	Cherry Ave, Spring Hill, Signal Hill
Food	**W:** The Rib
Other	**E:** Yamaha, Honda Motorcycles
29C	Cherry Ave, Signal Hill (Northbound)
Gas	**E:** Mobil
Food	**E:** John's Hamburgers
27	Lakewood Blvd, CA19, Long Beach Municipal Airport
Gas	**W:** Chevron[*, 24], Shell[*, 24]
Food	**W:** Spires[24]
Lodg	**W:** Extended Stay America, Holiday Inn, Residence Inn
Med	**W:** ✚ Hospital
26A	Bellflower Blvd.
Gas	**E:** Chevron[LP]
	W: Shell[*, 24]
Food	**W:** McDonald's
Other	**W:** Target
26B	Woodruff Ave (Northbound)
25	Palo Verde Ave
Gas	**W:** 76[*, 24]
Food	**W:** A. Salt Esquire Fish & Chips, Ave. # 3 Pizza & Subs, Del Taco, Domino's Pizza, Dr. Yi Donuts, Marri's Pizza, Simone's Donuts & Croissants, Subway, Taco Bell
Other	**W:** Super Convenience Food Store
Exit	Studebaker Rd. (Southbound, Difficult Reaccess)
24	Junction I-605, CA 22W, 7th Street, Long Beach
23	7th Street, Longbeach, CA22W (Northbound, Limited Access Hwy)
22	Los Alamitos, Seal Beach Blvd, Seal Beach
Food	**E:** Spaghettini
21	Garden Grove Freeway, CA 22, Valley View St, Bolsachica St. (Limited Access Hwy)
19	Springdale St, Westminster Ave, Westminster
Gas	**E:** 76[*, D], Thrifty[*]
	W: Chevron[*], Shell[24]
Food	**E:** Dino's Italian Restaurant, Don Francisco Mexican, In-N-Out Burger, Kim Duong Restaurant, Rainbow Donuts, Taco Bell Express, Valuetina's Pizza, Westminster Cafe
	W: D-Thai Chinese, Donut Storr[24], Eddie's Spaghetti, H. Salt, esq. Fish & Chips, Hong Kong Express, Jades (Chinese), La Familia (Mexican), Pizza Hut, Subway, Taqueria Mexico
Lodg	**E:** **Motel 6**, Travelodge TraveLodge
	W: Best Western, DAYS INN Days Inn
AServ	**W:** Shell[24]
Other	**E:** 7-11 Convenience Store, Pic 'N' Save, Westminster Lanes
	W: Alfastar Market
18	Goldenwest Street, Bolsa Ave

EXIT	CALIFORNIA
Gas	**W:** Mobil[*]
Food	**W:** Coco's, Don Jose's Mexican Restaurant, El Torito, Golden Donuts, IHOP, Kiku Japanese Restaurant, Togo's Eatery
Other	**E:** U.S. Post Office
	W: Child's View Optical, Dr. Bass Vision Center
16	CA39, Beach Blvd, Huntington Beach
Gas	**E:** Shell[*]
	W: 76[CW], Mobil
Food	**E:** Hong Kong Express Chinese, Little Caesars Pizza (Big K-Mart), Sun's Donuts
	W: Arby's, El Torito, Romano's Macaroni Grill
Lodg	**E:** Super 8, Westminster Beach West Inn
AServ	**W:** Mobil
Med	**W:** ✚ Hospital
Other	**E:** Big K-Mart
	W: AAA Auto Club, Barnes & Noble Booksellers, Huntington Center (Mall), Office Depot, Staples
15	Magnolia Street, Warner Ave
Gas	**W:** Mobil
Food	**E:** Jean's Donuts & Croissants, Pizza Deli, Sagami-Tei Japanese Steakhouse
	W: Bullwinkle's Family Restaurant (Family Fun Center), Carrow's, Ile De France Bakery, Izzy's Bagels, Magnolia Cafe, Tommy's Hamburgers, Tropics Restaurant, Wei's Chinese Restaurant, Winchells Donuts
Lodg	**W:** **Ramada Limited (see our ad this page)**
AServ	**W:** Mobil
Med	**W:** ✚ Emergicare Family Medicine, ✚ Medical Care Center, ✚ Walk In Clinic
Other	**E:** Animal Hospital, Christian Discount Book Center, Optometrist, Plush Puppies
	W: Book Mart, Ralph's Grocery, Sav-On Drugs[RX]
14	Warner Ave. East
Gas	**E:** Texaco[*, D]
Food	**E:** Angelfood Donuts, Del Taco, Little Caesars Pizza, May-yu Restaurant (Shang-hai, Mandarin), Sizzler

RAMADA LIMITED
9125 Recreation Circle
Huntington Beach, CA
714-847-33878
800-826-1964

Bus Parking

Continental Breakfast
Kids Under 12 Stay & Eat Free
Outdoor Pool • Pets Allowed
Handicap Accessible
Truck/Large Vehicle Parking
Exterior Corridors
Beach 4 miles
Disney Land 8 miles
Knotts Berry Farm 9 miles
Medievel Time 9 Miles
Wax Museums 9 Miles
Airport 5 miles
(John Wayne Orange County)
Sea World and Magic Mountain
90 minutes

I-405NB Exit Warner Ave W, Turn R at light (Magnolia) Turn R on Recreation Circle Hotel at end of street
I-405SB Exit R on Magnolia go to 1st light make U-turn. Turn R on Recreation Circle. Hotel at end of street.

CALIFORNIA • I-405 • EXIT 15

EXIT	CALIFORNIA
AServ	**E:** Texaco
13	Brookhurst Street, Fountain Valley
Gas	**E:** Arco[*, 24], Thrifty
	W: Chevron[*, 24], Texaco
Food	**E:** Baskin Robbins, Le Jardin Restaurant, Queen's Kitchen (Chinese), Silky Sullivan's
	W: Big City Bagels, Black Angus Steakhouse, Claim Jumper, Funashin Japanese Restaurant, Juice It Up, Nata'lie Coffee, Ristorante Borrelli, Wendy's
Lodg	**E:** Courtyard by Marriott, Residence Inn
AServ	**W:** Chevron[24], Texaco
Med	**W:** ✚ Orange Coast Memorial Health Center
ATM	**E:** Bank of America, C.U. Service Center, Glendale Federal Bank, Wells Fargo Bank
	W: First Bank & Trust Co.
Other	**E:** Fountain Valley Civic Center, Police Station
	W: Optometrist, U.S. Post Office
12	Euclid Street
Food	**E:** George's Burgers, Souplantation
Other	**E:** Boats/U.S. Marine Center, Staples, The Circuit Skate Center
11A	Harbor Blvd, Costa Mesa
Gas	**W:** Arco, Mobil
Food	**E:** Coco's (La Quinta Inn)
	W: Burger King, Denny's, El Pollo Loco, IHOP, Kaplan's Deli/Bakery, McDonald's[PLAY]
Lodg	**E:** La Quinta Inn
	W: Motel 6, The Inn at Costa Mesa, The Vagabond Inn
AServ	**W:** Arco, Mobil
ATM	**W:** 7-11 Convenience Store[*]
Other	**W:** 7-11 Convenience Store
11B	Fairview Rd
Exit	**(10)** CA 73 S, San Diego, San Joaquin Toll Rd. (Southbound, Toll)
10	Bristol Street
Gas	**W:** 76[D], Chevron[24], Shell[24]
Food	**E:** Scott's Seafood
	W: Max's (Double Tree Hotel), McDonald's
Lodg	**E:** The Westin Southcoast Plaza
	W: Double Tree Hotel, Holiday Inn
AServ	**W:** 76, Chevron[24], Shell[24]
Med	**E:** ✚ Hospital
ATM	**W:** McDonald's
9	CA55, Costa Mesa Fwy, Riverside (Limited Access Hwy)
8	MacArthur Blvd, John Wayne Airport
Gas	**W:** Chevron
Food	**E:** Carl Jr's Hamburgers, Chicago Joe's, Cochi-Vechi, El Torito Grill, Killicks Gourmet Coffee, Kokomo's, McCormick & Schmick's Seafood, McDonald's, Panda Szechwan (Chinese), Schlotzsky's Deli, Sensations, Spires Burgers
	W: El Torito, Gulliver's Prime Rib, IHOP, Java Hut
Lodg	**E:** Embassy Suites
	W: Atrium Hotel, Hilton
7	Jamboree Rd
Food	**E:** Chow Mein (Hyatt Regency)
	W: Houston's, Koo-Koo-Roo, Ruth's Chris Steakhouse
Lodg	**E:** Courtyard by Marriott, Hyatt Regency
	W: Marriott
5	Culver Dr.
Gas	**W:** Chevron[*], Irvine Clean Car Center[CW] (Shell)
Food	**W:** Ameci Pizza, Carl Jr's Hamburgers, Mag's Donut & Bakery, Subway, Wokman Chinese
4	University Dr, Jeffrey Rd.
Med	**E:** ✚ Hospital
3	Sand Canyon Ave
Med	**E:** ✚ Irvine Medical Center
2	CA 133S, Laguna Beach, Laguna Canyon Rd. (Limited Access Hwy)
1	Irvine Center Dr.
0	Jct I-5

↑CALIFORNIA

Begin I-405, California

Bold red print shows RV & Bus parking available or nearby

EXIT	WASHINGTON
	Begin I-405, Washington
↓WASHINGTON	
27	I-5 Jct.
26	WA 527, Bothell, Mill Creek
Gas	**W:** Texaco[*, D], Texaco[*, D]
Food	**E:** Canyon's, McDonald's, Thairama
	W: Baskin Robbins, Denny's, Godfather's Pizza, Mongolian Grill, Papa Murphy's Pizza, Rocker, Sagano Japanese Cuisine, Starbucks Coffee, Sub City, Taco Time, Teriyaki Plus, Tully's Coffee, Zi Pani
Lodg	**W:** Comfort Inn
AServ	**W:** Texaco
Med	**E:** ✚ Evergreen Medical Clinic
ATM	**E:** Seafirst Bank
	W: 7-11 Convenience Store, QFC Grocery[24], Texaco, Washington Mutual, Wells Fargo
Other	**W:** 7-11 Convenience Store, Albertson's Grocery[24, RX], Bartell Drugs, Canyon Park Veterinary Hospital, Cat Clinic, QFC Grocery, Rite Aid Pharmacy, Vision Clinic
24	NE. 195th St., Beardslee Blvd.
Lodg	**E:** Residence Inn, Wyndham Garden Hotel
Other	**E:** Bothel Police
23A	WA 522 E to WA 202, Monroe
23B	WA 522w., Bothel
22	NE 160th St.
Gas	**E:** Chevron[*, 24], Texaco[*, D]
Food	**E:** A & J Grocery & Teriyaki, Denice's Place
ATM	**E:** Chevron
Other	**E:** Victor's Grocery & Deli
20AB	NE 124th St.
Gas	**E:** BP[*, CW], Chevron[*], Texaco[*, D]
	W: Arco[*], BP[*, LP]
Food	**E:** Cafe Veloce, Cowboys Steakhouse & Saloon, Denny's, Evergreen China Restaurant, Pizza Hut
	W: Baskin Robbins, Boston Market Restaurant, Burger King[PLAY], Cucina Presto Pasta Pizza & Salad, Domino's Pizza, Hunan Wok Chinese, Izumi Restaurant, McDonald's[PLAY], Milestones, Mong Thai Restaurant, Olive Garden, Starbucks Coffee, Subway, Taco Del Mar, Taco Time, Wendy's
Lodg	**E:** Clarion Inn, Motel 6, Silver Cloud Inn
AServ	**E:** Chevron
	W: BP
Med	**E:** ✚ **Hospital**
ATM	**E:** Seafirst Bank, Texaco, Washington Mutual, Wells Fargo
	W: Arco, QFC Grocery[24], Totem Lake Food Store
Other	**E:** Larry's Market
	W: Drug Emporium[RX], Mail Boxes Etc, QFC Grocery, Totem Lake Food Store
18	WA 908, Redmond, NE 85th St. ,Kirkland
Gas	**E:** Arco[*], BP[*]
Food	**E:** Burger King, King's Cuisine, McDonald's[PLAY], Outback Steakhouse, Pizza Hut
Med	**E:** ✚ Hospital
ATM	**E:** Arco
17	NE. 70th Place
14	Redmond, WA 520, Seattle
13BA	NE 8th St
Gas	**E:** Arco[*], Chevron[*, CW]
Food	**E:** Burger King, Denny's, Eastside Bar & Grill (Westcoast Bellevue Hotel), Hunan Garden Chinese Food, I Love Sushi, Pumphouse, Sam Ho Restaurant, Taste of Tokyo, Westcoast Bellevue Hotel
	W: 8th Street Sports Bar, Caffe Ello, Dairy Queen, Red Robin, Subway, Taco Time
Lodg	**E:** Westcoast Bellevue Hotel
	W: Doubletree Hotel, Travelodge TraveLodge
Med	**E:** ✚ **Hospital**
	W: ✚ **Hospital**
ATM	**E:** Arco
Other	**W:** Bellevue Vision Clinic, Eyes of Bellevue
12	**(11)** SE 8th St.
11	I-90 Jct., Mercer Island, Seattle- West , Spokane-East
10	Coal Creek Pkwy., Factoria
9	112th Ave. Southeast, Newcastle
7	NE. 44th St.
Food	**E:** Denny's[24], Dino's Beefstro, McDonald's, Subway, Teriyaki Wok
Lodg	**E:** **Traveler's Inn**
ATM	**E:** I-405 Express MiniMart
Other	**E:** I-405 Express MiniMart
6	NE 30th St
Gas	**E:** Arco[*, CW]
	W: Chevron[*, 24], Texaco[*]
ATM	**E:** Arco
	W: 7-11 Convenience Store
Other	**W:** 7-11 Convenience Store
5	WA 900 East, Park Ave. N., Sunset Blvd. Northeast
4	WA 169 S. to WA 900 W, Maple Valley, Enumclaw (Difficult Reaccess)
Gas	**W:** Texaco[*, D]
Food	**E:** Shari's Restaurant
	W: Burger King, Golden Palace, Westernco Donuts, Yoko's Teriyaki
Lodg	**E:** Silver Cloud Inn
	W: **Don-a-Lisa Motel**
TServ	**W:** **International Dealer**
ATM	**W:** 7-11 Convenience Store, Texaco
Other	**W:** 7-11 Convenience Store
2	WA 167, Auburn, Rainier Ave.
Gas	**W:** Chevron[*, 24]
Food	**W:** Boston Market Restaurant, Chinese Restaurant, Holiday Inn Select, Lazy Bee Restaurant, McDonald's, Starbucks Coffee, ToGo's, Yankee Grill (Holiday Inn Select)
Lodg	**W:** Holiday Inn Select
ATM	**W:** Chevron
Other	**W:** General Cinemas, Rite Aid Pharmacy, Thriftway, WalMart
1	WA 181 S Tukwila, West Valley Hwy
Food	**E:** Barnaby's, Embassy Suites, Jack-In-The-Box, Taco Bell, Teriyaki Wok, Tucwilly's Grill (Embassy Suites), Vic's Broiler
Lodg	**E:** Best Western, Embassy Suites, Hampton Inn, Homestead Village, Residence Inn
ATM	**E:** 7-11 Convenience Store
Other	**E:** 7-11 Convenience Store
↑WASHINGTON	
	Begin I-405, Washington

I-410 TEXAS →

EXIT	TEXAS
	Begin I-410
↓TEXAS	
53	I-35, San Antonio, Laredo
51	Somerset Rd., FM 2790, Somerset
49	TX 16S, Spur 422, Palo Alto Rd., Poteet
Food	**I:** Church's Chicken
Med	**I:** ✚ Hospital
48	Zarzamora St.
46	Moursund Blvd.
44	S. US 281, S. Spur 536, Roosevelt Ave., Pleasanton
Gas	**I:** Texaco[*, D]
42	Spur 122, S. Presa St., Southton Rd
FStop	**O:** **Whiteside's Gas & Diesel**
TServ	**I:** **Truck Palace Paint & Body**
41	I-37, N US 281, San Antonio, Corpus Christi, Lucian Adams Fwy
39	Spur 117, W. W. White Rd
37	Southcross Blvd, Sulphur Springs Rd.
FStop	**O:** **Fina**[*]
Med	**I:** ✚ Hospital
35	Rigsby Ave., Victoria , US 87, Sinclair Ave
FStop	**I:** **Datafleet Coastal (Credit Card Sales Only)**
	O: **Diamond Shamrock**[*, D]
Gas	**I:** Chevron[*, D]
	O: Exxon[24]
Food	**I:** Beef & Bourbon Steakhouse, Bill Miller BBQ, El Tipico, Luby's Cafeteria, Taco Cabana[24], Whataburger[24]
	O: Jack-In-The-Box[24], McDonald's[PLAY], Taco Bell
Lodg	**I:** DAYS INN Days Inn
AServ	**O:** Exxon[24]
ATM	**O:** Diamond Shamrock
Other	**I:** Rigsby Veterinary Clinic
34	FM 1346, E. Houston St.
33	US 90, I-10, San Antonio, Houston
32	Dietrich Rd., FM 78, Kirby
32A	FM 78, Kirby
31	I-35, South US 81, San Antonio, Binz - Englemann Rd
31B	Loop 13, W. W. White Rd.
31A	FM 78, Kirby
30	Binz - Englemann Rd, Space Center Dr.
27	South I-35, South I-410 San Antonio
26B	Interchange Pkwy, Perrin Creek Dr
26A	South Loop 368, Alamo Heights
Food	**I:** Ada's Mexican, Wang Goong
25B	FM 2252, Perrin - Beitel Rd.
Gas	**O:** Chevron[*, D, CW, 24], Diamond Shamrock[*, D, CW], Mobil
Food	**I:** Jim's Restaurant[24]
	O: Denny's, Rally's Hamburgers, Schlotzsky's Deli, Taco Bell, Taco Cabana[24], Wendy's
Lodg	**O:** Comfort Inn
AServ	**O:** Mobil
ATM	**I:** NationsBank, San Antonio Federal Credit Union
	O: Diamond Shamrock
Other	**I:** Animal Hospital
	O: **Academy Sports**
25A	Star Crest Dr.

EXIT | TEXAS

Gas I: Conoco[*], Phillips 66
O: Exxon, Texaco[*]
Lodg O: Hawthorn Suites
AServ I: Phillips 66
O: Exxon
Med O: + Northeast Baptist Hospital
ATM O: Texaco

24 Harry Wurzbach Rd, Ft. Sam Houston
Gas I: Texaco[*]
Food I: Don's Taco (Texaco), Texaco, The BBQ Station
ATM I: Texaco
O: Jefferson State Bank
Other I: Northwood Animal Hospital

23 Nacogdoches Rd.
Gas I: Exxon[*, CW], Texaco[D]
O: Circle K[*]
Food I: Jane's Coney Island (Exxon)
O: Au Bon Pain (Club Hotel), Baskin Robbins, Bill Miller BBQ, Caribe Carribean & Mexican, Church's Chicken, Domino's Pizza, Formosa Garden, IHOP, Jack-In-The-Box[24], Luby's Cafeteria, Mama's Cafe, Miami International Cafe & Bakery, Pizza Hut, Schlotzsky's Deli, Sonic, Subway, Taco Cabana, Twin Dragon Chinese, Veladi Ranch Steakhouse, Wendy's
Lodg O: Club Hotel (DoubleTree), Oakview Hotel & Apartment
ATM I: Frost Bank, Guaranty Federal Bank, International Bank of Commerce
O: Broadway National Motor Bank, Circle K
Other O: Forest Oaks Animal Clinic, Sun Harvest Grocery

22 Broadway
Gas I: Diamond Shamrock[*, D], Stop N Go[*]
O: Texaco[*, D, 24]
Food I: 410 Diner, Burger King, Chester's Hamburgers, Hsiu Yu Chinese, Jim's, Magic Time Machine Restaurant, Martha's Mexican Restaurant
O: Capparelli's Pizza, McDonald's[PLAY], Rooty's All American Eatery, Zito's
Lodg I: Best Western, Residence Inn (Marriott)
O: Courtyard by Marriott
ATM I: Chase Bank, Diamond Shamrock, Stop N Go, Wells Fargo
Other O: Emergency Pet Clinic

21B US 281 S, Airport Blvd, Wetmore Rd
Gas I: Texaco[*, D, CW, 24]
Food I: Whataburger[24]
O: Shoney's
Lodg I: Days Inn, Fairfield Inn (see our ad this page)
O: Hampton Inn, La Quinta Inn, Peartree Inn
ATM I: Texaco
Other I: Pearl Vision Center, Target
O: San Antonio International Airport

1821
FAIRFIELD INN
Marriott
San Antonio North Star
88 N.E. Loop 410 • San Antonio, TX
120 Bright, Attractive Guest Rooms
Free Continental Breakfast
Hot Coffee & Tea, Free 24 Hours
Heated Indoor Pool & Exercise Room
Ample Free Parking • Guest Laundry
North Star Mall & Restaurant, 1/4 mile
Downtown Riverwalk/Alamo, 9 miles
210-530-9899
TEXAS • I-410 • EXIT 21A

EXIT | TEXAS

21A Jones Maltsberger Rd.
Food I: **McDonald's (Wal-Mart)**, Pappadeaux Seafood Kitchen, Red Lobster, Shoney's, Texas Land & Cattle Steakhouse
O: Applebee's
Lodg I: Country Inn (Carlson), Courtyard (Marriott), Fairfield Inn (Marriott)
O: Drury Suites, Holiday Inn Express
Other I: Fire Station, **Wal-Mart[24, RX] (Optical, 1-Hr Photo)**

20B McCullough Ave (Counterclockwise)
Food O: Bean Sprout Chinese, Cascabell (DoubleTree Hotel), Holiday Inn Select, Jason's Deli, T.G.I. Friday's
Lodg O: DoubleTree Hotel, Holiday Inn Select

20A US 281N, San Pedro Ave., Johnson City
Food I: Arby's, Bennigan's, Church's Chicken, IHOP[24], Sea Island Shrimphouse, Taco Bell, Taco Cabana, Teaka Molino
O: BBQ's Galore, Souper Salad, Texas Grill & Sports Bar (Hilton)
Lodg O: Hilton
ATM O: Bank of America
Other I: Eyemart Express, San Pedro Bowl
O: Pearl Vision Center, Toys R Us

19B FM 1535, Military Highway, FM 2696 Blanco Rd.
Gas I: Exxon[*]
O: Diamond Shamrock[*]
Food I: Aldino Cucina Italiana (Mall), Burger King (Exxon), Casa de Martha's, Charlotte's, Denny's, Hook Line & Sinker, Jim's[24], Luby's Cafeteria (Mall), Wang's Garden Chinese
O: Baskin Robbins, Bee's Mexican Restaurant, Capparelli's Pizza, Gini's Restaurant, Great Wall Chinese, Jack-In-The-Box, Miami Subs, My Sam Chinese Buffet
ATM I: Compass Bank, Frost Bank
O: Diamond Shamrock
Other O: Sunharvest Farms, Toys R Us

1747
Comfort Inn
San Antonio, TX
210-684-8606
800-228-5150
Continental Breakfast
Kids Under 12 Stay Free
Free Cable TV w/HBO
Restaurants Nearby
Handicap Accessible
Truck/Large Vehicle Parking
Coin Laundry
Exterior Corridors
4 Piano Place
San Antonio, TX 78228
I-410W to ex 13B, U-Turn at Evers, R on Summit Pkwy
I-410E, Ex 13B R on Summit Pkwy to Hotel
TEXAS • I-410 • EXIT 13B

EXIT | TEXAS

19A Honeysuckle Lane, Castle Hills

18 Jackson - Keller Rd, West Ave
Food I: Bill Miller BBQ, Dairy Queen, Little Caesars Pizza, Mei Luck Chinese, Northloop Molino, Subway, The Cookie Lady
Other I: **H-E-B Grocery Store[RX]**, My $39.95 Optical 1-Hr Lab, Wiseman Animal Hospital

17 Vance Jackson Rd.
Gas O: Diamond Shamrock[*, D], Mobil
Food O: Bobbisox (Holiday Inn), Burger King, Jack-In-The-Box[24], KFC, McDonald's[PLAY], Olly's Steaks, Lobster, & Music, Steak & Ale, Taco Bell, Taco Cabana, Teriyaki & More Sushi, Tom's Ribs
Lodg O: Holiday Inn
AServ O: Mobil
ATM I: Fast Stop
O: Compass Bank, Diamond Shamrock
Other I: Fast Stop
O: Target

16B West I-10, N. US 87, El Paso, San Angelo (Left Exit)

16A East I-10, South US 87, San Antonio, Houston (Left Exit)

15 Loop 345, Fredericksburg Rd., Balcones Hts
Gas O: Mobil[*]
Food I: Babe's Old Fashion Food, Bonanza, Jack-In-The-Box, Jim's[24], Kettle Restaurant[24], Luby's Cafeteria, North China Buffet, Ports O' Call, Shoney's, Simi's India Cuisine, Tu Molino, Wendy's, Whataburger[24]
O: La Fonda
Lodg I: Motel Travis, Sumner Suites
AServ O: K-Mart[RX]
ATM O: Frost Bank, Guaranty Federal Bank, Mobil
Other O: K-Mart[RX]

14 Callaghan Rd, Babcock Rd
Gas I: Chevron[*, CW, 24], Diamond Shamrock[*, 24], Exxon[*, CW]
Food I: Zito's Deli
ATM I: Chevron, Diamond Shamrock

14A Summit Parkway
Food O: Burger King[PLAY], Chili's, City Market Cafe & Ice House, Drake's Restaurant, El Chico, Golden Corral Family Steakhouse, HomeTown Buffet, Landry's Seafood House, Shoney's, Souper Salad, U.R. Cooks Steakhouse, Wendy's
AServ O: Wal-Mart[24, RX]
ATM O: Bank United, Instant Cash (Sam's Club Parking

1137

Best Western
Exit 6 • San Antonio
210-675-9690
• Deluxe Continental Breakfast
• Cable TV with Free HBO, ESPN, CNN
• Restaurant with in Walking Distance
• 10 Minutes to Riverwalk & Sea World
• King/Queen Beds • Free Parking
• Coin Operated Laundry
Exit #6 to U.S. Hwy. 90E to Old Hwy. 90 exit
TEXAS • I-410W • EXIT 6

Bold red print shows RV & Bus parking available or nearby

EXIT	TEXAS
	Lot)
Other	O: Movies 16, Wal-Mart(RX)
14B	Callaghan Rd
Gas	O: Diamond Shamrock(*), Phillips 66(*, CW)
Food	O: Ding How Chinese, Pizza Hut, Red Lobster, Whataburger
ATM	O: Diamond Shamrock
14C	Babcock Rd.
Food	O: China Star, Massimo Ristorante Italiano, Nadler's Bakery, Old World, Subway
Med	O: + Hospital
ATM	O: Bank of America, International Bank of Commerce
Other	O: Oak Hills Veterinary Hospital, Postal Center
13	Rolling Ridge Dr., Evers Rd.
Gas	O: Conoco(*, D, 24), Diamond Shamrock(*, 24), Diamond Shamrock(*)
Food	I: Marie Callender's Restaurant O: Capparelli's Pizza, Gin's Chinese Restaurant, Jack-In-The-Box, KFC, Las Palapas, Subway, Thai Taste
Lodg	I: Comfort Inn (see our ad opposite page), Hampton Inn, Travelodge TraveLodge Suites
ATM	O: Conoco, Diamond Shamrock, Diamond Shamrock
Other	O: Animal Hospital, Booketeria, Eckerd Drugs(RX), Glen Oaks Laundromat
13A	Spur 421, Bandera Rd, Evers Rd, TX 16 N, Leon Vly, San Antonio
Gas	I: H-E-B Marketplace O: Diamond Shamrock(*, D), Exxon(D)
Food	I: Cha Cha's, EZ's Pizza & Burgers, Outback Steakhouse, The "M" Grill (H-E-B) O: Bill Miller BBQ, Black-Eyed Pea, IHOP, Jim's Restaurant, McDonald's(PLAY), Schlotzsky's Deli, Taco Cabana
AServ	O: Exxon
ATM	I: Albertson's Grocery(LP, 24, RX) O: Security Service Federal Credit Union
Other	I: Albertson's Grocery(RX), Animal Hospital, Eye Care Eyewear, H-E-B Grocery Store (1 Hr Photo), Target
12	Exchange Parkway (Counterclockwise)
Food	O: Applebee's, Fortune Cookie Chinese Buffet, Jason's Deli, Sea Island Shrimp House, Starbucks Coffee (Barnes & Noble)
Lodg	O: Super 8
ATM	O: Security Service Federal Credit Union
Other	O: Builder Square
11	Ingram Rd.
Gas	I: Texaco(*, D, CW, 24) O: Citgo(*)
Food	O: Burger King, Chinatown Restaurant, Long John Silver, Luby's Cafeteria (Mall), Olive Garden, Subway, Tink-A-Tako, Villa Maria Prado's, Whataburger(24)
Lodg	I: DAYS INN Days Inn, EconoLodge, Red Roof Inn
ATM	O: Guaranty Federal Bank, Lackland Federal Credit Union, NationsBank, San Antonio Federal Credit Union
Other	O: EyeMasters, Ingram Park Animal Hospital Animal Emergency Clinic, My $39.95 Optical, Trinity Vision Center
10	FM 3487, Culebra Rd., St. Mary's Univ.
Gas	O: Exxon(*, D, CW), Phillips 66(*, CW)
Food	I: Barnacle Bill's Seafood, Bill Miller BBQ, Denny's, McDonald's(PLAY), Wendy's O: Blimpie Subs & Salads, Casa Real, Chuck E Cheese's Pizza, Denny's, Fuddruckers, Ming Garden
Lodg	I: Holiday Inn Express, La Quinta Inn O: Best Western
Other	I: Police Department O: Eyemart, Sharp Care Animal Hospital
9	Military Drive, TX 151, Sea World, Stotzer Freeway
Food	O: McDonald's (Wal-Mart)
AServ	O: Wal-Mart(LP, 24, RX) (Optical, 1-Hr Photo)
Other	O: Home Depot, Wal-Mart(RX) (Optical, 1-Hr Photo)
7	Marbach Rd.
Gas	I: Exxon(*, CW), Texaco(*) O: Chevron(*, D, CW, 24), Texaco(*, D, CW, 24)
Food	I: Apetito's, Beijing Express, Church's Chicken, Gilbert's O: Acadiana Cafe, Asia Kitchen & Market, Burger King(PLAY), Chinese Buffet (Mall), Chit Chat Cafe, Golden Wok, Jack-In-The-Box, Jim's, KFC, Lily's Bakery, Little Caesars Pizza, Long John Silver, Luby's Cafeteria, McDonald's(PLAY), Peter Piper Pizza, Pizza Hut, Pizza Inn (K-Mart), Red Lobster, Sirlion Stockade, Sonic, Subway, Taco Bell, Taco Cabana, Whataburger(24)
Lodg	O: Motel 6, Super 8
AServ	O: K-Mart Supercenter(24, RX)
ATM	O: Bank of America
Other	O: Eckerd Drugs(RX) (Mall), H-E-B Grocery Store(24, RX) (1 Hr Photo), K-Mart Supercenter(RX), Target
6	US 90, San Antonio, Del Rio (Limited Access Hwy)
Gas	O: Diamond Shamrock(*)
Food	O: El Pescador(24)
Lodg	I: Best Western
ATM	O: Diamond Shamrock
4	Valley Hi Drive, Lackland A.F.B.
Gas	I: Diamond Shamrock(*), H-E-B, Mobil(*), Phillips 66(*, CW), Stop N Go(24) O: Texaco(*, D, CW)
Food	I: Church's Chicken, McDonald's(PLAY), Medina County Line Cafe, Pizza Hut, Sonic Drive in
ATM	I: Mobil, Norwest Banks, Stop N Go
Other	I: H-E-B Grocery Store(RX) (1 Hr Photo), US Post Office
3B	Ray Ellison Dr., Medina Base Rd. (Counterclockwise)
Gas	O: Diamond Shamrock(*)
ATM	O: Diamond Shamrock
2	FM 2536, Old Pearsall Rd.
1A	Frontage
1	Frontage Rd. (Clockwise, Reaccess Counterclockwise Only)

↑TEXAS

Begin I-410

Notes:

EXIT		MISSOURI
		Begin I-435

↓MISSOURI

67 Gregory Blvd

66 MO 350, Lee's Summit (Left Exit)

65 Eastwood Frwy
- **Gas** I: QuikTrip(*)
- **Food** I: KFC, McDonald's, Pizza Hut, Subway

63C Ray Town Rd., Stadium Dr., Sports Complet (Northbound)

63AB I-70 Jct

61 MO 78, 23rd St.
- **Gas** E: Fisca(*, D)

60 MO 12, 12th St, Truman Rd.
- **Gas** O: Amoco(*, CW), Phillips 66

59 US 24, Winner Rd., Independence Ave
- **Gas** O: QuikTrip(*)
- **ATM** O: QT

57 **(56)** Front St.
- **TStop** O: **Conoco**(*, 24)
- **FStop** O: **QuikTrip**(*, D, 24)
- **Gas** I: Gas Station(*, D, CW), Phillips 66(*, D, CW)
- **Food** I: KFC, **McDonald's**, Pizza Hut, **Shoney's**, Taco Bell, Waffle House, Wendy's; O: **Burger King**
- **Lodg** I: Hampton Inn, Park Place Hotel
- **TServ** O: **Goodyear Tire & Auto**, **International Truck Service**, **Midwest Kenworth**
- **TWash** O: **TNT Truck Wash**
- **Med** I: ✚ Compcare Clinics
- **ATM** I: UMB Bank; O: QuikTrip

55 MO. 210, Richmond N. Kansas City (Difficult Reaccess)
- **Gas** O: King Super Store(*, D, LP)
- **Lodg** O: Red Roof Inn
- **TServ** O: **Midway Truck Center**

54 48th St. Parvin Rd
- **Gas** I: QuikTrip(*)
- **Food** I: Ponderosa
- **Lodg** I: Best Western, Holiday Inn, Super 8

52 I-35 S Jct, U.S. 69, Kansas City Claycomo

51 Shoal Creek Dr.

49AB MO. 152

47 NE 96th St.

46 NE 108th St.

45 **(43)** MO. 291, to I-35 N.

42 N. Woodland Ave

41AB U.S. 169, Riverside, Smithville

40 NW Cookingham Dr

37 MO C, Skyview Ave.

36 **(35)** NW Cookingham Dr.
- **Gas** O: Citgo, Total(*)
- **Lodg** I: Best Western, Club House Inn, Hampton Inn, Holiday Inn

14 I-435 E. Split

15 Mexico City Ave.

31 I-29 Jct U.S. 71 ST. Josephs Kansas City

29 **(25)** CR D NW 120th ST

24 CR N MO 152 NW Barry Rd.

22 **(19)** MO. 45 Weston Parkville

EXIT		MISSOURI/KANSAS

18 **(16)** State Rd 5 Wolcott Dr

15AB KS 5, Leavenworth Rd

14AB Parallel Pkwy
- **Med** I: ✚ **Hospital**

13B US 24, US 40, US 70, State Ave. West

13A U.S 24, U.S. 40 State Ave

12AB I-70 Jct, KS Turnpike

11 Kansas Ave

9 Rt.32 Kansas City, Edwardsville, Bonnersprings

8B Woodend Rd.

8A Holliday Dr.

6C Johnson Dr.

6A Shawney Mission Pkwy (Difficult Reaccess)

5 **(4)** Midland Dr.
- **Gas** I: Circle K, Texaco(*, CW)
- **Food** I: Blimpie's Subs (Texaco), Donuts, Mexicalli Alley, Par T Golf Grill, Pizza Stop, Wendy's

3 87th St
- **Food** I: McDonald's
- **Other** I: K-Mart

2 **(1)** 95th St.

1B KS 10 JCT, Lawrence (Difficult Reaccess)

1A Lackman Rd (Difficult Reaccess)

↑MISSOURI

↓KANSAS

83 I-35 Jct Witichia, DeMoine

82 Quivira Rd
- **Food** O: McDonald's
- **Med** I: ✚ **Overland Park Regional Medical Hospital**

81 **(80)** U.S. 69, Fort Scott
- **Gas** I: Texaco(*)
- **Food** I: McDonald's, Taco Bell

79 US 169, Metcalf Ave.
- **Gas** I: Amoco(CW), Texaco(LP)
- **Food** I: Chi-Chi's Mexican Restaurant, Chuck E Cheese's Pizza, Denny's, Hardee's; O: American Bandstand, Applebee's, McDonald's, St Louis Bread Company, Tippin's
- **Lodg** I: Atrium by Holiday Inn, Club House Inn, Embassy Suites, Holiday Inn Express, Wyndham Garden Hotel, AmeriSuites (see our ad this page); O: Drury Inn, Marriott
- **ATM** I: Amoco, Auto World Tire; O: UMB Bank

77AB Roe Ave, Nall Ave
- **Gas** I: Amoco(LP, CW), Texaco(*)
- **Food** I: A & W Drive-In (Texaco), KFC (Texaco), Mr. Goodcents Subs & Pasta, Winstead's; O: Wendy's
- **Med** O: ✚ Foxhill Medical Building
- **ATM** O: UMB Bank

1351

AMERISUITES
AMERICA'S AFFORDABLE ALL-SUITE HOTEL
Kansas • Exit 79 • 913-451-2553

EXIT		MISSOURI

↑KANSAS

↓MISSOURI

75B State Line Rd
- **Gas** I: Conoco(*); O: Amoco(CW)
- **Food** I: Applebee's, Blimpie's Subs, Chopstix, Fuzzy's, Gates Bar B Que, Guadalajara Cafe, McDonald's(PLAY), Waid's Restaurant, Wendy's; O: EBT Restaurant (UMB Bank)
- **Med** O: ✚ Hospital
- **ATM** I: NationsBank; O: UMB Bank
- **Other** I: Drug Emporium

75A Wornall Rd
- **Gas** I: Amoco(CW), Texaco(*)
- **Food** I: Sub Station, Taco Bell
- **Med** O: ✚ **Hospital**

74 Holmes Rd
- **Gas** I: Gas Station(*)
- **Food** I: Andy's Wok Chinese, Domino's Pizza, Fin and Pete's Grill, Gomer's Chicken, Patnikios Mexican Restaurant, Subway
- **ATM** I: Mercantile Bank; O: Mark Twaine Bank

73 103rd St (Reaccess Eastbound Only)

71 I-470 Jct, US 50, US 71
- **Lodg** O: **Holiday Inn (see our ad this page)**

70 Bannister Rd
- **Gas** O: QuikTrip(*, 24)
- **Food** I: Long John Silver, Old Country Buffet, Taco Bell; O: Bennigan's, Burger King, McDonald's, Red Lobster
- **ATM** O: Commerce Bank, Hillcrest Bank, Midwest United Credit Union
- **Other** O: K-Mart(RX)

69 **(68)** 87th St.
- **Gas** I: Amoco(*, CW); O: Conoco(*), Total
- **Food** O: Benjamin Ranch Cafe, Darryl's, Denny's, Mr. Goodsence Subs and Pasta, Tippin's
- **Lodg** I: Budgetel Inn; O: Benjamin Hotel and Suites, Motel 6
- **Other** O: America's Best Contacts & Eyeglasses, Wal-Mart Supercenter(24)

66B Blue Parkway

66A 63rd St. Raytown (Northbound)

↑MISSOURI

Begin I-435

South on US Hwy 71 to Longview Rd.

Newly Renovated Hotel in 97

Holiday Inn®
SOUTH

1556

• All Rooms Have Interior Entrances
• Pool & Whirlpool • Exercise Room
• Block & Barrel Bar & Grill
• Ample Parking for Large Vehicles
• Special Group Rates Available

816-765-4100 • 888-325-2489
MISSOURI ▪ I-435 ▪ EXIT 71

Bold red print shows RV & Bus parking available or nearby

EXIT TENNESSEE/NORTH CAROLINA

Begin I-440

↓TENNESSEE

1 US 70S East, Westend Ave, Murphy Rd (Eastbound, Reaccess Westbound Only)
- **Gas** **N:** Exxon[*, D], Mapco Express[*]
- **Food** **N:** China King, Dairy Queen, Mr Gatti's Pizza
- **ATM** **N:** Mapco Express, Union Planter's Bank

1A US 70S West, Westend Ave

3 US 431, 21st Ave, Hillsboro Pike

5 Junction I-440 East & I-65, Nashville,Huntsville

6 US 31A, US 41A, Nolensville Pike
- **Gas** **N:** Circle K[*, LP]
  S: Amoco
- **Food** **N:** McDonald's[PLAY]
- **Lodg** **S:** Hickerson's Motel Court
- **AServ** **S:** Amoco
- **ATM** **S:** First American

↑TENNESSEE

↓NORTH CAROLINA

1 Jct. I-24 & I-440

1C Jones Franklin Rd.

3 Hillsboro St., NC54
- **Gas** **W:** Citgo
- **Food** **W:** Waffle House

EXIT NORTH CAROLINA

4 Blue Ridge, US1

5 Lake Boone, Blue Ridge Rd.
- **Gas** **O:** Phillipps 66[*, CW]
- **Food** **O:** Bear Rock, McDonald's, Pizza Inn, Subway
- **ATM** **O:** BB&T Bank, Centura Bank
- **Other** **O:** Eckerd Drugs

7 US70, NC50, Glenwood Ave, Crabtree Valley
- **Gas** **O:** Amoco, BP[*, LP], Exxon
- **Food** **O:** Conners, Pizza Hut, Ruby Tuesday (Mall)
- **Lodg** **O:** Embassy Suites, Fairfield Inn, Four Points Hotel Sheraton, Holiday Inn, Marriott
- **ATM** **O:** First Union, Triangle Bank, Wachovia Bank
- **Other** **O:** Eye Care Center, Post Office

8 Forks Rd., Wakeforest Rd.
- **Gas** **O:** Exxon
- **Food** **O:** Bennigan's, Brubaker's Bakery (Mall)
- **Lodg** **O:** Comfort Inn
- **ATM** **O:** First Citizens Bank, First Union, NationsBank, Wachovia Bank
- **Other** **O:** Kerr Drugs, Post Office, Winn Dixie Supermarket

10 US1, Wake Forest Rd, Sanford
- **Gas** **I:** Amoco[*], BP[*, LP]
- **Food** **I:** Applebee's, Courtney, Jersey Mike's Subs, McDonald's, Sam's Restaurant
  O: Denny's
- **Lodg** **I:** Courtyard by Marriott, Hampton Inn
  O: Cricket Inn, Friendship Inn, Hilton
- **Med** **O:** + Raleigh Comm. Hospital
- **ATM** **I:** Centura Bank

11 US1, US401, Capital Blvd
- **Gas** **O:** BP[*, D], BP, Crown[*, LP, CW], Texaco

EXIT NORTH CAROLINA

- **Food** **O:** Fortune Chinese, Kristin's, Perkins Family Restaurant, Subway, Taco Bell, Waffle House, Wendy's
- **Lodg** **O:** Best Western, Comfort Inn, Country Inn, DAYS INN Days Inn, Fairfield, Raleigh North Motel, Sleep Inn
- **Other** **O:** Davis Mutual Drugs, Med First, Post Office

12 Brentwood Rd., Yonkers Rd. (Difficult Reaccess)

13 US64, New Bern Ave., Greenville
- **Gas** **O:** BP[*], Texaco[*, D, CW]
- **Food** **I:** Swains Charcoal
  O: Arby's, Baskin Robbins, Brian's Steakhouse, Hardee's, K&F Cafeteria, McDonald's, Miami Subs Grills, Pizza Hut, Shoney's, Subway, The Chopstik, Waffle House, Wendy's
- **Lodg** **I:** Howard Johnson
  O: **Red Roof Inn**, Super 8
- **TServ** **I:** **Tri-Point Truck Sales**
- **Med** **I:** + Hospital
- **ATM** **I:** Central Carolina Bank
  O: Cash Point, First Union
- **Other** **I:** Wake Forrest Medical Center
  O: Kerr Drugs

15 Poole Rd., MLKing Blvd
- **Gas** **I:** Citgo[*]
- **Food** **I:** Burger King, McDonald's, Subway, Wang's
- **ATM** **O:** Tarr Hill Credit
- **Other** **I:** Food Lion Supermarket

16 Jct I-40

↑NORTH CAROLINA

Begin I-440

I-459 ALABAMA

EXIT ALABAMA

Begin I-459

↓ALABAMA

33A I-59S, Birmingham

33B I-59N, Gadsden

32 US11, Trussville
- **Gas** **E:** Chevron[*, D, LP, CW], Exxon[*], RacTrac[*], Shell[*], Texaco[*, D]
- **Food** **E:** Jack's, McDonald's[PLAY], Waffle House, Wendy's (Texaco)
- **Lodg** **E:** Hampton Inn
- **ATM** **E:** Exxon, RacTrac

31 Derby Parkway

29 I-20, Birmingham, Atlanta

27 Grants Mill Road

23 Liberty Parkway

19 US280, Mountain Brook, Childersburg
- **Food** **E:** Connie Kanakis' Cafe, McAlisters Gourmet Deli, Morrison Cafeteria, Ralph & Goo's Seafood, Ruby Tuesday, TGI Friday, Tazaki's Greek Fair
  W: Johnny Rocket Hamburger, Macaroni Grill
- **Lodg** **E:** Hampton Inn, Sheraton
- **ATM** **E:** Highland Bank
- **Other** **E:** Schaeffer Eye Care
  W: Animal Clinic, Barnes & Noble Bookstore,

EXIT ALABAMA

Bruno Food & Market, CVS Pharmacy, The Summit

17 Acton Road
- **Gas** **W:** Texaco[*, D, LP, CW]
- **Food** **W:** Krystal, McDonald's[PLAY], NY Bagel Expresso, Pappa Joe's Pizza, Richard's B-B-Q & Grill, Sneaky Peeks (Hot Dogs)
- **ATM** **W:** Texaco
- **Other** **W:** Family Dentist

15 I-65, Montgomery, Birmingham

13 US31, Hoover, Pelham
- **Gas** **E:** Crown[*, LP], Shell[CW]
- **Food** **E:** Baskin Robbins, Bruno's, Chinese Food (Shell), Fuddruckers, Grady's Grill, J Alexander, Logan Farm Honey Hams, Manny's NY Bagels, McDonald's[PLAY], Pizza Hut, Stix Sushi Bar, The Olive Garden, Tia's, Tony Roma's Famous for Ribs, Wendy's
  W: Ali Baba Persian Food, China Buffet, China Saigon Restaurant, Fish Market Restaurant, Guadalajara, Magic Platter
- **Lodg** **E:** Winfrey Hotel
- **AServ** **E:** K-Mart[RX]
- **Med** **W:** + Family Medical Center
- **ATM** **E:** Compass Bank, Trust Bank
  W: Cu Service Ctr
- **Other** **E:** Barnes & Noble, CVS Pharmacy, K-Mart[RX],

EXIT ALABAMA

Kinko's Copies, NTB National Tire & Battery, Pier 1 Imports

W: Center At River Chase, Lenscrafters, Municipal Complex Police Dept Hoover

10 AL150, Hoover, Bessemer
- **Gas** **E:** BP[*, CW], Texaco[D]
- **Other** **E:** Winn Dixie Supermarket

6 Helana, Bessemer
- **Gas** **E:** BP[*, LP, CW], Exxon[*, LP], Shell[*, CW], Texaco[*, CW]
  W: Amoco[*, CW]
- **Food** **E:** Deli Cafe, McDonald's[PLAY], Pizza Hut, TCBY (Shell), Taco Bell (Shell), Waffle House, Wendy's
  W: Morgan Road Diner
- **Lodg** **E:** Sleep Inn
- **Med** **E:** + Parkwest Family Medicine
- **ATM** **E:** Texaco, Winn Dixie Supermarket[RX]
  W: Amoco
- **Other** **E:** CVS Pharmacy[RX], Winn Dixie Supermarket[RX]
  W: Affordable Dentures

1 Bessemer, McCalla
- **FStop** **E:** **Amoco**[*, D]
- **ATM** **E:** **Amoco**
- **Other** **E:** McAdory Animal Clinic

0 Jct. I-59, I-20

↑ALABAMA

Begin I-459

Bold red print shows RV & Bus parking available or nearby

EXIT INDIANA

Begin I-465

↓INDIANA

53BA Junction I-65, Louisville, Indianapolis (53A goes north to Indianapolis, 53B goes south to Louisville)

52 Emerson Ave., Beech Grove
- **Gas** I: Amoco[CW], Marathon[*], Shell[*]
  O: Shell[*, CW, 24], Speedway[*, LP, K] (Fireworks Stand)
- **Food** I: Expo Bowl, KFC
  O: Egg Roll, Fazoli's Italian Food, Fuji Yama Japanese Steakhouse, McDonald's[PLAY], Pizza Hut, **Ramada (Conference Center)**, Steak 'N Shake, Sunshine Cafe[24], White Castle Restaurant
- **Lodg** I: Motel 6
  O: Holiday Inn, **Ramada (Conference Center)**, Red Roof Inn, Super 8
- **AServ** I: Amoco, Marathon
- **Med** I: ✚ Hospital
- **ATM** O: Speedway (Fireworks Stand), Teacher's Credit Union
- **Other** I: Expo Bowl, GreatTimes Amusement

49AB Junction I-74 East, U.S. 421 South

47 U.S. 52, Brookville Rd., New Palestine
- **Gas** O: Shell[*, LP]
- **Food** O: Burger King (Shell), Krispy Kreme Doughnuts (Shell), Shell
- **Med** I: ✚ Hospital
- **ATM** O: Shell

46 U.S. 40, Washington St., Greenfield
- **Gas** I: Thornton's[*, D, LP, K]
  O: Marathon[*], Shell[CW]
- **Food** I: Applebee's, Bob Evan's Restaurant, Chi-Chi's Mexican Restaurant, Dan Pablo's, Fazoli's Italian Food, Hardee's, Mark Pi's Express, McDonald's[PLAY], Pizza Hut
  O: Arby's, China Buffet, Flakey Jake's Burgers, Grindstone Charley's Restaurant, Laughner's Cafeteria, Old Country Buffet, Olive Garden, Shoney's, Skyline Chili, Steak 'N Shake, Subway
- **Lodg** I: Signature Inn
- **AServ** I: K-Mart[RX] (Penske)
  O: Marathon
- **Med** I: ✚ Hospital
- **Other** I: K-Mart[RX] (Penske)
  O: Book World, Osco Drugs[RX]

44AB I-70 Junction, West to Indianapolis, East to Columbus

42 U.S. 36 East, IN 67 North, Pendleton Pike, Lawrence
- **Gas** I: Speedway[*, LP, K]
  O: Amoco[*, CW], Crystal Flash[*, D, K]
- **Food** I: K-Mart[RX], King Ribs BBQ, Little Caesars Pizza (K-Mart), Los Rancheros, McDonald's[PLAY], Subway, Taco Bell
  O: Burger King, Cafe Heidelberg, Pancake House, Pizza Hut
- **Lodg** I: American Inn Motel
  O: Motel East, Ramada
- **Med** I: ✚ **Hospital**
- **ATM** I: Tune Tech, Union Federal Savings Bank

EXIT INDIANA

  O: Amoco
- **Other** I: K-Mart[RX]
  O: Marine Tech

40 Shadeland Ave., 56th St.
- **Gas** O: Marathon[*]
- **AServ** O: Marathon
- **ATM** O: Finance Center Federal Credit Union

37BA IN 37 North, I-69, Fort Wayne, Anderson, Muncie - 37B, 37A - IN 37 South, Indianapolis
- **Med** I: ✚ Hospital

35 Allisonville Rd.
- **Food** I: Bob Evan's Restaurant, Perkin's Family Restaurant, White Castle Restaurant
  O: BW-3 Grill & Pub, Cookies By Design, Hardee's, MCL Cafeteria, Outback Steakhouse, The Melting Pot
- **Lodg** I: Signature Inn
  O: Courtyard by Marriott
- **ATM** O: Cub Foods[24, RX]
- **Other** I: Allisonville Animal Hospital, Kroger Supermarket[RX], Romar Christian Bookstore
  O: Borders Books & Music, Cub Foods[RX], Half Price Books & Magazines, Kids R Us, Mars Grocery[RX], Osco Drug[RX], Waccamaw

33 IN 431, Keystone Ave.
- **Gas** O: Amoco[*], Marathon[*, CW], Shell[*, CW, 24]
- **Food** I: California Pizza Kitchen (Only on 86th street), Keystone Grill
  O: Amoco, Arby's, Bob Evan's Restaurant, Buckets Sportrs Bar & Grill, Burger King, McDonald's (Amoco), Ruth's & Chris Steakhouse, Steak & Ale, Subway, Woodland Bowl
- **Lodg** I: AmeriSuites (On 86th Street)(see our ad this page), Sheraton, Westin Suites
  O: Knight's Inn
- **AServ** O: Marathon
- **ATM** O: Bank One, Marathon, NBD Bank, Shell
- **Other** O: Cat Care Clinic, Tom Wood Subaru, Woodland Bowl

31 U.S. 31, Meridian St.
- **Gas** I: Shell[*, D, CW]
- **Food** I: Deli Jack's, McDonald's
- **Lodg** O: Courtyard by Marriott, Signature Inn, Wyndham Garden Hotel
- **Med** I: ✚ Hospital
  O: ✚ Methodist Medical Plaza
- **Other** I: Kroger Supermarket[24, RX]

27 U.S. 421 North, Michigan Rd.
- **Gas** I: Marathon[*]
  O: 76[*] (Friendly Foods)
- **Food** I: Bob Evan's Restaurant, Chi Chi's Mexican Restaurant, Fortune House Chinese, Holiday Inn Select, Max & Erma's, Ruby Tuesday, San Rino Grill (Holiday Inn Select), Wild Cat Brewing Co., Yen Ching

1352
AMERISUITES
AMERICA'S AFFORDABLE ALL-SUITE HOTEL
Indiana • Exit 33 • 317-843-0064

EXIT INDIANA

  O: Big Apple Bagels, Dairy Queen, Heavenly Ham, McDonald's[PLAY], Planet Pizza
- **Lodg** I: Comfort Inn, Dollar Inn, Drury Inn, Embassy Suites, Fairfield Inn, Hawthorne Suites Ltd., Holiday Inn Select, Quality Inn, Signature Inn, Studio PLUS
  O: Red Roof Inn
- **AServ** I: Marathon
- **Med** I: ✚ Hospital

25 I-65, Chicago, US 52 W (Left Exit)

24 I-465 West

23 86th St.
- **Gas** I: Shell[*, CW], Speedway[*, LP]
- **Food** I: Arby's, Burger King, Dog n Suds, Krispy Kreme Doughnuts (Shell), Shell
- **Lodg** I: Main Stay Suites, Suburban Lodge
- **Med** I: ✚ **Hospital**
- **ATM** I: Bank One, National City Bank
- **Other** I: National FFA

21 71st St.
- **Gas** I: Amoco[*, CW]
- **Food** I: Galahad's Cafe, Hardee's, **McDonald's**, Steak 'N Shake, Subway
- **Lodg** I: Clarion Inn, Courtyard by Marriott, Hampton Inn
- **ATM** I: First of America Bank

20 I-65 North Junction, Chicago (Left Exit)

19 56th St. (Reaccess Southbound Only)
- **Gas** I: Speedway[*, LP, K]
- **Med** I: ✚ Hospital
- **ATM** I: Speedway
- **Other** O: Eagle Creek Golf Course

17 38th St.
- **Gas** I: Amoco[*, CW], Marathon[*, CW], Shell[*, CW, 24]
- **Food** I: Bettie's Seafood, Chi Chi's Mexican Restaurant, China Chef, Dairy Queen, DAYS INN Days Inn, Julian's Caribbe Restaurant, Subway, The Sports Page Bar & Grill (Days Inn), Thoroughbred's Steakhouse
  O: Burger King, Chili's, Cracker Barrel, Don Pablo's Mexican, McDonald's[PLAY], Mountain Jack's Restaurant, Ruby Tuesday, T.G.I. Friday's, Taco Bell
- **Lodg** I: DAYS INN Days Inn
  O: Signature Inn
- **AServ** I: Marathon
- **Med** I: ✚ Hospital
- **ATM** I: Finance Center Federal Credit Union
  O: Bank One, Marsh Supermarket & Pharmacy[24]
- **Other** I: CVS Pharmacy[RX], International Auto Parts, Osco Drugs[RX], Skating Rink, State Fair Grounds
  O: Marsh Supermarket & Pharmacy, Target

16AB U.S. 136, Crawfordsville Road, I-74 West, Peoria
- **Gas** I: Big Foot[*, LP], Shell[*, CW]
- **Food** I: Arby's, BW3's Buffalo Wild Wings Grill & Bar, Buffalo Wild Wings Grill, Burger King, Denny's, Dip n Deli Ice Cream, El Rodeo Authentic Mexican Cuisine (HoJo Inn), Hardee's, Long John Silver, McDonald's, NCL Cafeteria, Taco Bell, Union Jack Family Dining & Pub, Wendy's

Bold red print shows RV & Bus parking available or nearby

EXIT		INDIANA
	Lodg	I: Dollar Inn, HoJo Inn, Motel 6, Red Roof Inn
	ATM	I: Big Foot, NBD Bank
	Other	I: Family Vision Care, Mail Boxes Etc., Marsh Grocery Store(LP, 24, RX), U.S. Post Office, Village Pantry Grocery(LP)
14AB		Tenth St.
	Gas	O: Gas America(*), Shell(*)
	Food	I: Pizza Hut, Wendy's
		O: Gas America, Subway (Gas America)
	Med	I: Hospital
	ATM	I: Cub Foods(24, RX)
		O: First Indiana Bank, Shell
	Other	I: Cub Foods(RX)
13AB		U.S. 36, Danville, Rockville Rd.
	Gas	O: Speedway(*)
	Food	O: Bob Evan's Restaurant
	Lodg	I: Comfort Inn, Sleep Inn
12AB		U.S. 40 East, Washington St., Plainfield
	Gas	I: Amoco(*, 24)
		O: Big Foot(*, LP), Phillips 66(*, D, CW, 24), Shell(*)
	Food	I: Checkered Flag Tavern & Cafeteria, Fazoli's Italian Food, Taco Bell, White Castle Restaurant
		O: Airport Deli, Arby's, Burger King, Dunkin Donuts, Hardee's, KFC, Little Caesars Pizza (K-Mart), Long John Silver, McDonald's, Noble Roman's Pizza, Noble Romans Pizza Express (Philliips 66), Omelet Shoppe, Phillips 66, Pizza Hut, Shoney's, Smiley's Pancake & Steak, Steak 'N Shake, Subway, TCBY (Phillips 66), Wendy's
	Lodg	O: Dollar Inn
	ATM	I: Amoco
		O: Big Foot, National City Bank
	Other	I: Airport Animal Emergency Center, Osco Drugs(RX), WalGreens Pharmacy(24, RX)
		O: Big K-Mart(RX), Patriotic Fireworks, Target, Western Bowl Bowling Alley
11AB		Airport Expressway, International Airport
	Gas	I: Marathon(*, D), Speedway(*, LP)
	Food	I: Adam's Mark Hotel, Days Inn, Denny's(24), JoJo's Restaurant (La Quinta), La Quinta Inn, PK's (Days Inn), Quincy's (Adam's Mark Hotel), Schlotzsky's Deli, The Library Steakhouse & Pub, The Marker (Adam's Mark Hotel), Waffle & Steak
	Lodg	I: Adam's Mark Hotel, Budgetel Inn, Courtyard by Marriott, Days Inn, Extended Stay America, Fairfield Inn, Hampton Inn, La Quinta Inn, Motel 6, Residence Inn
		O: Holiday Inn Select, Ramada Inn
	AServ	I: Marathon
	TServ	I: Speedway International
	ATM	I: NBD Bank, Speedway
	Other	O: Airport
9AB		9A - Junction I-70 East, Indianapolis, 9B - I-70 West, St. Louis, Terra Haute
8		IN 67 South, Kentucky Ave., Mooresville Rd.
	Gas	O: Speedway(*, LP, K), Swifty(K)
	Food	O: KFC
	Med	I: Hospital
7		Mann Rd. (Westbound, Reaccess Eastbound Only)
4		IN 37 South, Harding St., Martinsville, Bloomington
	TStop	I: Pilot Travel Center(*, SCALES, 24)
		O: Flying J Travel Plaza(*, LP) (Conoco gas)
	Gas	O: Citgo(*, CW)
	Food	I: Bender's Restaurant (EconoLodge), EconoLodge, Krispy Kreme Doughnuts (Pilot), Omelet Shoppe, Pilot Travel Center, Wendy's (Pilot)
		O: Flying J Travel Plaza (Conoco gas), Hardee's, McDonald's, Taco Bell, Waffle & Steak, White Castle Restaurant
	Lodg	I: Dollar Inn, EconoLodge, Super 8
		O: Knight's Inn
	TServ	I: Peterbilt Dealer
		O: Flying J Travel Plaza (Conoco gas), Freightliner Dealer, Greent's Truck Service, International Navistar, J & E Tire, Paul's Trailer Service Inc., Speedco Thirty Minute Truck Lube
	TWash	O: Flying J Travel Plaza (Conoco gas)
	Med	I: Hospital
	Other	I: Classy Chassy Go Go
2AB		2A - U.S. 31, IN 37 North, Indianapolis, (outside) 2B - U.S. 31 South East St. (Inside)
	Gas	O: Big Foot(*), Shell(*, CW)
	Food	I: Baskin Robbins, Old Country Buffet, Pizza Hut, Steak & Ale
		O: Bob Evan's Restaurant, Denny's, Heritage Smorgasbord, Red Lobster, Shoney's
	Lodg	O: Comfort Inn, Economy Inn, Holiday Inn Express, Quality Inn, Ramada Limited, Red Roof Inn
	ATM	I: Bank One, First Indiana Bank, Kroger Supermarket(RX)
		O: Shell
	Other	I: CVS Pharmacy(RX), Kroger Supermarket(RX)

↑ INDIANA

Begin I-465

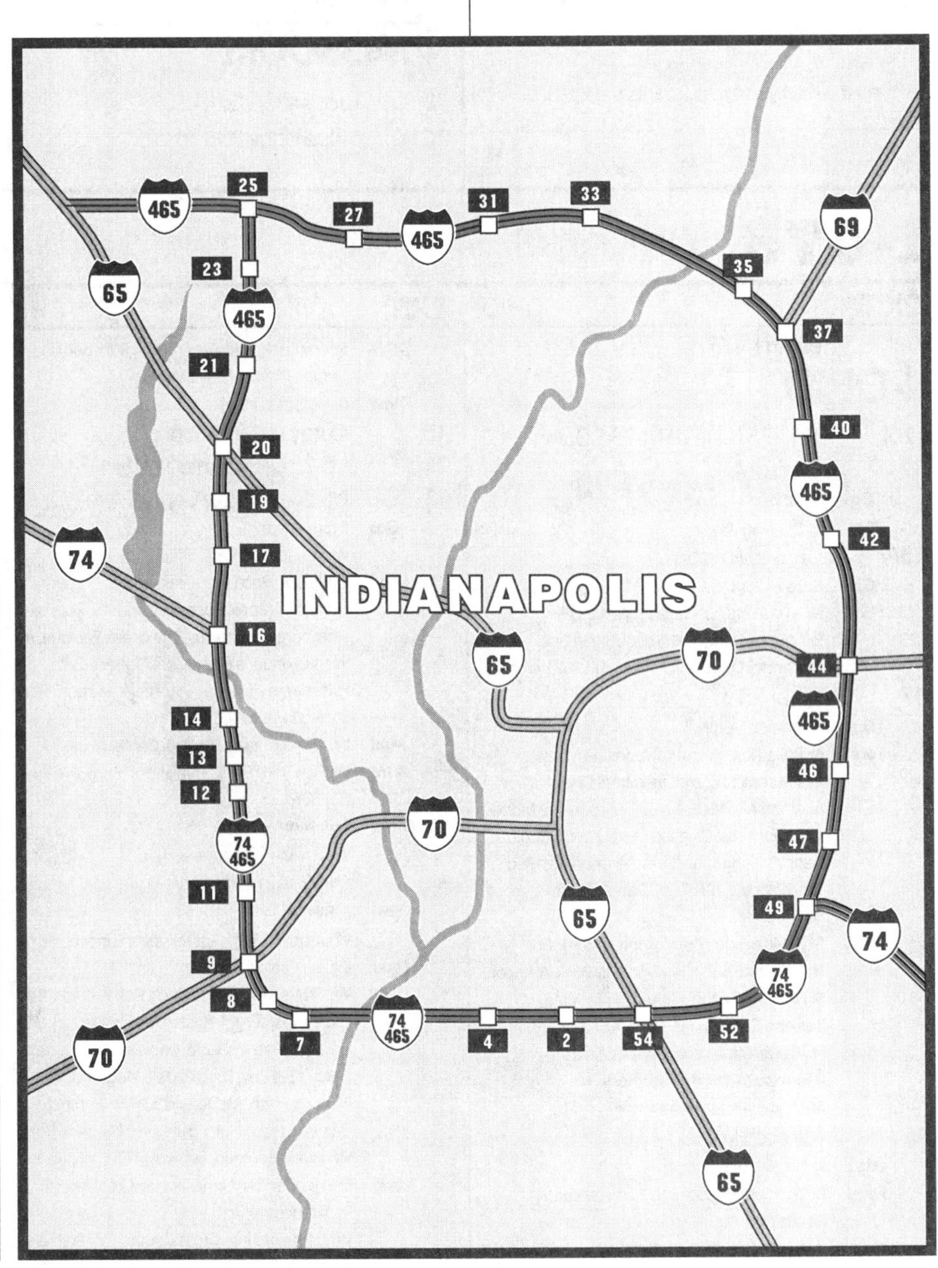

I-470 KANSAS/MISSOURI

EXIT KANSAS

Begin I-470

↓KANSAS

1 JCT I-70

1B Wanamaker Rd., Huntoon St.
- **TStop** **E:** **Topeka Travel Plaza**(*, D)
- **Gas** **W:** Conoco
- **Food** **E:** Cracker Barrel, Sirloin Stockade, Topeka Travel Plaza
  W: Applebee's, Denny's, Golden Corral Family Steakhouse, Luby's Cafeteria, Maggie Moo's Ice Cream, McDonald's, Mr. Goodcents Subs and Pizza, Perkins Family Restaurant, Rudy Tuesday's, Shoney's, Taco Bell, Wendy's
- **Lodg** **E:** Econolodge, Hampton Inn, Motel 6
  W: Comfort Inn, Days Inn, Fairfield Inn
- **TServ** **E:** **Topeka Travel Plaza**
- **Other** **W:** K-Mart, Wal-Mart Supercenter

2 21st St
- **Gas** **E:** Amoco(*, CW), Sinclare(*)
- **Food** **E:** Arby's, I Can't Believe It's Yogurt,

EXIT KANSAS/MISSOURI

McDonald's(PLAY), Pizzetti's Pizza, Subway, The Copper Oven, Wendy's
  W: Chili's, Hardee's, Outback Steakhouse, Sonic Drive-In
- **ATM** **E:** Mercantile Bank, NationsBank
- **Other** **E:** WalGreens Pharmacy
  W: Target

3 Fairlawn Rd., 29th St
- **Gas** **E:** Phillips 66(*, CW)
- **Food** **E:** Clyde Arthurs Restaurant, Courtney's Restaurant, Long John Silver, Pizza Hut
- **Other** **E:** Albert'sons Grocery(RX) (Bank)

4 Gage Blvd
- **Gas** **E:** Amoco(CW)
- **Food** **E:** Hardee's, Taco-Tico
- **ATM** **E:** Fidelity State Bank
- **Other** **E:** WalGreens Pharmacy

5 Burlingame Rd

↑KANSAS

↓MISSOURI

1B Jct. I-435, US71, US50

1C Blue Ridge Blvd

EXIT MISSOURI

4 Raytown Road

5 View High Drive

7 MO350, US 50 Ray Town, Sedalia

9 Douglas St.

10A Colbern Road

10 MS291S, Lees Summit, Harrisonville

12 Woods Chapel Rd.
- **Gas** **W:** Circle K(*)
- **Food** **W:** Bambino's Pizza, Ridgewood Doughnuts

14 Lakewood Blvd, Bowlin Rd.
- **Gas** **W:** QuikTrip(24)
- **Food** **W:** Mr. Goodcents Subs
- **ATM** **W:** QuikTrip

15 JCT I-70

16 US 40
- **Gas** **E:** QuikTrip(*)
  W: Coastal
- **ATM** **E:** UMB Bank
  W: Midwest Bank

↑MISSOURI

Begin I-470

I-475 OHIO

EXIT OHIO

Begin I-475

↓OHIO

(20) JCT I-75 N Detroit, I-75 S Daton

19 Central Ave
- **Gas** **S:** Amoco(*)
- **Med** **S:** ✚ Hospital

18A OH 51, Monroe St.
- **Gas** **S:** 76(*), Clark(*)
- **Food** **N:** Jojo's Original Pizzeria, Wendy's
  S: Chuck's Hungry i, Monroe Street Diner
- **ATM** **N:** Charter One Bank

17 Secor Rd.
- **Gas** **N:** Amoco(*), Clark(*)
- **Food** **N:** Betsy Ross Restaurant, Boston Market Restaurant, KFC, Monroe Street Diner
  S: Al Smith's Place, Big Boy, Breakfast at Marie, China Express, Chinese Restaurant, Claudia's, Denny's, Long John Silver, McDonald's, Meal Time Express, Mr. Philly, Papa's Pizza, Pizza Hut, Wendy's
- **Lodg** **S:** Clarion Hotel, Comfort Inn, Red Roof Inn
- **ATM** **N:** Fifth Third Bank, National City Bank (Amoco)
  S: Huntington Bank, Mid-Am Westgate Banking Center
- **Other** **N:** Kroger Supermarket(24, RX), Shale's Pharmacy, The Firm Pharmacy
  S: **Town Plus Supermarket**(RX)

16 Talmitch Rd.
- **Gas** **S:** BP(*, LP), Speedway(*)
- **Food** **S:** Charcoal House, Chi Chi's Mexican Restaurant

EXIT OHIO

- **ATM** **S:** Key Bank, Mid-Am Franklin Park Banking Center, National City Bank
- **Other** **S:** Orchard Drugs

15 Corey Rd. (Westbound)

14 US 23 N, Sylvania (Left Exit)

13 US 20, OH 120, Central Ave
- **Gas** **E:** Speedway(*)
  W: Amoco(*), BP(*, CW), Speedway(*)
- **Food** **E:** Big Boy, Bob Evan's Restaurant, Burger King, Friendly's, Magic Rock, McDonald's, Rally's Hamburgers, Subway, The Greek Restaurant
  W: Alexander's Pizza, Christopher's Grill, Fortune Inn Chinese, Gourmet Ice Cream Shop, Marco's Pizza, TCBY
- **Med** **W:** ✚ Afterhours Medical Center (Walk-in)
- **ATM** **W:** Fifth Third Bank, Huntington Bank, National City Bank
- **Other** **E:** **K-Mart**
  W: Shales Pharmacy

8 OH 2, Airport Hwy
- **Gas** **E:** BP(*, D)
  W: Amoco(*), BP(*), Speedway(*), Sunoco(*)
- **Food** **E:** Don Pablo's Mexican
  W: Arby's, Arthur Treacher's Fish & Chips, Bob Evan's Restaurant, Boston Market Restaurant, Chili's, Coffee Mill Cafe, Cooker, Dairy Queen, Frisch's Big Boy, Frisco's Deli, Magic Rock, Marco's Pizza, McDonald's, New Empire Chinese, Pizza Hut, Rally's Hamburgers, Ranch Steak and Seafood, Subway, TCBY, Wendy's
- **Lodg** **E:** Extended Stay America, Red Roof Inn, Residence Inn
  W: Courtyard Inn, Cross Country Inn, Fairfield

EXIT OHIO

Inn
- **ATM** **E:** Charter One
  W: Huntington National Bank (Kroger), Key Bank
- **Other** **W:** Kroger Supermarket(RX), Rite Aide Pharmacy

6 Salisbury Rd., I-80/90 Trnpk
- **Gas** **E:** BP(*, CW)
- **Food** **E:** Applebee's, **Bill Knapp's (see our ad this page)**, Marie Cafe, McDonald's, Sam's Diner, Subway, Toledo Big Apple Bagels, Wendy's
  W: Chinese Connection
- **Lodg** **E:** Country Inn & Suites, Studio PLUS, Tharaldson Inn & Suites
- **ATM** **E:** Mid American Bank and Trust Co.

4 US 24, Napoleon, Maumee
- **Med** **E:** ✚ Hospital

2 OH 25, Perrysburg
- **Gas** **N:** 76(*, D), BP(*)
  S: Speedway(*, LP)
- **Food** **N:** Alexanders Pizza, Berry Bagels, Charlie's Restaurant, Hungry Howie's Pizza, La Bella Restaurante, McDonald's, Subway, Wendy's
  S: The China Place
- **Lodg** **S:** Red Carpet Inn
- **TServ** **N:** **Whiteford Kenworth**
  S: **Holt Cat**
- **ATM** **N:** Mid Am Village Square Banking Center, National City Bank (Churchill's Supermarket)
- **Other** **N:** Churchill's Supermarket, Shale's Pharmacy

192 US 23, Maumee (Left Exit)

↑OHIO

Begin I-475

Bold red print shows RV & Bus parking available or nearby

EXIT GEORGIA

Begin I-475, Georgia

↓GEORGIA

4 **(15)** Bolingbroke, U.S. 41
- **Gas** E: Exxon(*, D, LP), Fina(*, D)
- **Food** E: Sweet Sue's Tea Room

3 **(10)** Zebulon Road, Wesleyan College, Macon
- **Gas** E: BP(*, CW)
  W: Citgo(*, LP) (U-Haul Distributors), Exxon
- **Food** E: BP, Buffalo's Cafe, Chick-Fil-A (Kroger), Chin's Wok (BP), Fox's Pizza Den, Hong Kong Restaurant, **Kroger Supermarket**, Rick Tanner's Rotisserie Grill, Subway, Waffle House, Wendy's
  W: Polly's Corner Cafe
- **Lodg** E: Fairfield Inn, Jameson Inn
- **AServ** W: Exxon
- **Med** E: + **Hospital**
- **ATM** E: **Kroger Supermarket**, Rivoli Bank & Trust, Sun Trust Bank
- **Other** E: **Kroger Supermarket**

(8) **Rest Area (RR, Phones, Picnic, Vending; Northbound)**

2 **(5)** GA 74, Macon, Thomaston, Mercer University Dr
- **Gas** W: Phillips 66(*, D, K), Shell(*)

NEWLY RENOVATED

Knights Inn®

$29 50* 1-4 Persons Valid Sun-Thur

4952Romeiser Dr.
912-471-1230
800-843-5644

- Free HBO Cable Color TV
- Microfridge and Kitchenette
- Non Smoking Room Available
- Pool • Fax & Copy Services
- King & 2 Double Beds • All Ground Floor
- Donuts & Coffee in Morning

*W/Coupon at Check-in. Based on Availabilty. Not Valid w/Other Discounts

1128

GEORGIA ▪ I-475 ▪ EXIT 1

MACON, GEORGIA

1228

912-788-0120
I-475 • Exit 1
Toll Free Reservations:
800-HOLIDAY

- Free Cable TV with HBO
- Guest Laundry
- Full Service Restaurant
- Outdoor Pool • Bus & RV Parking
- Fully-Lighted Parking w/ Security

GEORGIA ▪ I-475 ▪ EXIT 1

Bill Knapp's is a casual, full service family restaurant where Motorcoaches are always welcome.

1689

Over 50 locations throughout:
Michigan • Ohio • Indiana

248-689-4010 Troy

MICHIGAN ▪ I-75 ▪ EXIT 69

Perfect Stopover To/From Florida

1683

Quality Inn
4630 Chambers Rd.
Macon, GA 31206
912-781-7000

- Outdoor Heated Pool
- Free Continental Breakfast
- Bus Parking
- In Room Coffee Makers
- Meeting Rooms
- Cable/HBO

GEORGIA ▪ I-475 ▪ Exit 1

EXIT GEORGIA

- **Food** E: Waffle House
  W: Church's Chicken (Phillips 66), Family Inns of America, Fazoli's Italian Food, Phillips 66
- **Lodg** W: Family Inns of America
- **AServ** E: Car-Tech, Yancey Tire Co.
- **TServ** E: **Goodyear Brad Reagan Inc.**
- **Other** E: McKinney's(LP), Olympia Family Fun Center

1 **(3)** U.S. 80, Macon, Roberta
- **FStop** E: **Fina(*, LP)**
- **Gas** E: Citgo, Racetrac(*)
  W: Amoco, BP(*, D), Shell(*)
- **Food** E: Citgo, **Cracker Barrel**, JL's Famous Pit BBQ, Racetrac, SHONEY'S, Shoney's, Subway (Citgo), Waffle House
  W: Blimpie Subs & Salads (Shell), Burger King, El Zarape Mexican Restaurant, McDonald's, Shell
- **Lodg** E: Best Western, Comfort Inn, **Days Inn**, Discovery Inn, Hampton Inn, HoJo Inn, Holiday Inn (see our ad this page), Motel 6, Quality Inn (see our ad this page), Ramada Inn (see our ad this page), Rodeway Inn, **Super 8**, TraveLodge
  W: EconoLodge, Knight's Inn (see our ad this page), **Passport Inn**
- **AServ** W: Amoco, BP
- **ATM** E: Citgo
  W: Shell

↑GEORGIA

Begin I-475, Georgia

SHOW AD FOR 15% OFF DISCOUNT

RAMADA INN®

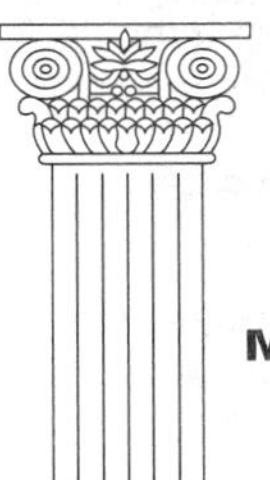

I-475- Exit 1

Cable TV with HBO
Swimming Pool
Disney Channel
Meeting and Banquet Facilities to 400
Lounge

912-474-0871

1114

GEORGIA ▪ I-475 ▪ Exit 1

Notes:

I-476 PENNSYLVANIA

EXIT PENNSYLVANIA

Begin I-476

↓PENNSYLVANIA

39 **(110)** Jct I-81, US 6, US 11, Clark Summit, Scranton (Toll)
38 Keyser Ave., Old Forge, Taylor
37 Wyoming Valley, I-81, PA315, Pittston, Scranton
- **TStop** **W:** Skyliner Truck Plaza Citgo[*, D, SCALES]
- **Gas** **E:** Mobil[*, 24]
  W: Citgo
- **Food** **E:** Howard Johnson
  W: Perkins Family Restaurant, Skyliner Restaurant (Truck Plaza)
- **Lodg** **E:** Howard Johnson
  W: Knight's Inn, Skyliner Truck Plaza Citgo, Victoria Inn
- **Med** **W:** ✚ Hospital

(91) Jct I-81, Toll Plaza (Toll)
(90) Parking Area (Picnic)
36 **(85)** Wilkes - Barre, Bear Creek , PA 115 (Toll)
- **FStop** **E:** Mobil[*, D]
- **Gas** **E:** Amoco[*], Texaco[*, K]
- **Food** **E:** Amoco, JB Pizzeria & Subs (Amoco)
- **Med** **E:** ✚ Hospital

(82) Emergency Parking
(78) Emergency Parking Area
35 **(74)** I-80, PA940, Hazelton, Mt Pokeno (Toll)
- **Gas** **W:** Amoco[*], Exxon, Texaco[*, 24]
- **Food** **E:** Burger King
  W: Arby's, Famosa Restaurant
- **Lodg** **W:** Howard Johnson

(70) Emergency Parking
(66) Hickory Run Service Plaza (RR, Phones, Picnic, Vending)
- **FStop** **B:** Sunoco[*, D]
- **Food** **B:** Aunt Annie's Pretzel, Breyer's Ice Cream, Hot Dog Construction, McDonald's

34 Mahonie Valley, Lehighton, Stroudsburg (Toll)
- **Gas** **W:** Exxon[*]
- **Food** **W:** Platz Restaurant, Subway

33 Leighi Valley, I-78, US22, PA309 (Toll)
(36) Allentown Service Center, Rest Area (RR, Phones, Vending)
- **FStop** **B:** Sunoco[*, D]
- **Food** **B:** Bob's Big Boy, Mrs. Fields Bakery, Pizza Hut, Roy Rogers, TCBY

32 **(24)** PA663, Quakertown, Pottstown (Toll)
- **Gas** **E:** Amoco[*, 24]
- **Food** **E:** Faraco's Pizzeria
- **Lodg** **E:** Econolodge, Rodeway Inn
- **Med** **E:** ✚ Quakerpoint Med Ctr

31 PA63, Lansdale (Toll)
- **Gas** **E:** Citgo[*], Texaco[D]
- **Food** **E:** Kulpsville Kitchen (Days Inn)
- **Lodg** **E:** Days Inn, Holiday Inn
- **AServ** **E:** Citgo, Texaco
- **ATM** **E:** Union Nat'l Bank

25 Jct295, Northtown, Chester, Philadelphia, Allentown (Toll)

↑PENNSYLVANIA

Begin I-476

I-480 OHIO

EXIT OHIO

Begin I-480

↓OHIO

1 Jct. I-80
1A Oberlin, OH 10 W, Norwalk (Left Exit)
1B I-80, OH 10 E, OH Tnpk, Lorain Rd.
- **Gas** **S:** Citgo[*, D, LP], Marathon[*], Shell, Speedway[*, D, K], Sunoco[*, D, LP, K]
- **Food** **S:** Kartels Restaurant, McDonald's (Shell)
- **Lodg** **S:** Super 8, Travelers Inn

3 Stearns Rd.
6BA OH 252, N Olmsted, Great Northern
- **Food** **N:** Chili's, Lone Star Steakhouse, McDonald's (Wal-Mart), Red Robin, Romano's Macaroni Grill, T.G.I. Friday's
- **Lodg** **N:** Courtyard by Marriott, Hampton Inn, Homestead Village Weekly Studios, Radisson Inn
- **Other** **N:** Wal-Mart[RX]

7 Claque Rd., West Lake, Fairview Park
9 OH 237, Grayton Rd., Airport
- **Food** **S:** 100th Group
- **Med** **N:** ✚ Hospital

10 Oh 237, Airport, Berea
11 JCT I-71, Cleveland, Columbus
12 West 150th St., West 130th St.
- **FStop** **S:** Marathon[*, D]
- **Gas** **S:** Shell[*, CW, 24]
- **Food** **S:** American Grille (Budget Inn), Arby's, Bob Evan's Restaurant, Harpo's Sports Club, Hot Rock Concert Club (Parkbrook Inn), Nalley's Ice Cream, Parkbrook Inn, Rusty's Family Restaurant
- **Lodg** **S:** Budget Inn of America (see our ad this page), Parkbrook Inn, Ramada Inn

13 Tiedeman Rd., Brooklyn
- **Gas** **S:** BP[*, D, CW], Speedway[*, D, K]
- **Food** **S:** Blimpie Subs & Salads (BP), Burger King, Ice House Tavern & Grill, Long John Silver, McDonald's, McDonald's (Wal-Mart), Perkin's Family Restaurant, Pizza Hut
- **Other** **S:** Aldi Supermarket, Home Depot, Wal-Mart[RX]

15 US 42, Ridge Rd
- **Gas** **S:** Super America[*, D]
- **Food** **N:** Applebee's, Baskin Robbins, Boston Market Restaurant, Cecil B's Grill, Dunkin Donuts, Golden Corral Family Steakhouse, Manhattan Bagel, McDonald's, Mr. Hero, Skyline Chili
  S: Arby's, BA Sweetie Candy Co., Colonial Eatery Deli Bakery, Denny's[24], K-Mart Supercenter[24, RX], Wendy's
- **Med** **S:** ✚ Hospital
- **Other** **N:** Finast Supermarket[RX], Marc's Pharmay[RX], Sears Optical
  S: Brookpark Fun & Games, Great Northern Superstore, K-Mart Supercenter[RX], Rini Rego Supermarket

Budget Inn
Of America Airport/West
14043 Brookpark Road • Cleveland, OH
Recently Remodeled Rooms
Restaurant • Room Service Available
Full Cable - Showtime, CNN, ESPN
Non-Smoking Rooms Available
Fax & Copier Service • Exercise Room
Guest Laundry Facilities & Game Room
Conference Room up to 135 People
216-267-2350 1674
CLEVELAND • I-480 • EXIT 12

CLEVELAND
216-662-9200
FAX 216-662-8811
1-800-DAYS-INN
1513
DAYS INN
DAYS INN
WARRENSVILLE CENTER RD.
EMERY
NORTHFIELD
480 77 71 8 480 80
Rooms with Phone Jack for Fax Machine
Cable TV with Free HBO
Mall within 2 Blocks
15 Miles from Downtown Cleveland
Close to University
AAA Approved
OHIO • I-480 • EXIT 25C

16 OH 94, State Rd.
- **Gas** **S:** BP[*, CW], Sunoco[*, 24]
- **Food** **S:** BP, Blimpie Subs & Salads (BP), The Goal Post, Victoria's Delight
- **Med** **N:** ✚ Hospital
  S: ✚ Hospital

20AB JCT I-77, Cleveland, Akron
21 Transportation Blvd., East 98th St
- **Food** **N:** Czech Inn
- **Med** **N:** ✚ Hospital

22 OH 17, Granger Rd. (Reaccess Westbound Only)
- **Gas** **S:** Speedway[*], Sunoco[*]
- **Food** **S:** Dairy Whip, Karlon Pastry & Bakery
- **Med** **N:** ✚ Hospital

23 OH 14, Broadway Ave.
- **Gas** **S:** John's Deli[*, D]
- **Food** **N:** Giannetti's, KFC
  S: Wing's Sports Bar & Grill
- **Lodg** **N:** El Dorado Motel
- **Med** **N:** ✚ Hospital

24 Lee Rd., Maple Heights (Westbound)
- **Gas** **S:** Marathon[D], Speedway[*, D]
- **Food** **S:** Geppetto's Pizza & Ribs, Jade Garden Chinese Restaurant
- **Other** **S:** WalGreens Pharmacy[*, RX]

25AB Oh 8, OH 43, Northfield, Warrensville Rd. (Reaccess Westbound Only)
- **Gas** **S:** Marathon[*]

25C OH 8, OH 43, Northfield Rd. (Running Concurrent With I- 271)
- **Gas** **N:** Shell[*]
- **Food** **N:** Baker's Square, Bob Evan's Restaurant, Dunkin Donuts, Golden Hunan, Popeye's Chicken, Subway
  S: Church's Chicken, Hunan, McDonald's, Rally's Hamburgers, White Castle Restaurant
- **Lodg** **N:** Economy Inn, Days Inn (see our ad this page)
  S: Royal Oaks
- **Other** **N:** DOC Optical, Pearl Vision Center, Shop N Go, Super Savings Center

26 I-271 N, Erie PA, US 422, Solon

↑OHIO

Begin I-480

Bold red print shows RV & Bus parking available or nearby

EXIT	NEW YORK
	Begin I-490
	↓NEW YORK
1	**(0)** NY 19, LeRoy, Brockport, Genesee Country Village
FStop	**O:** Coastal[*, K]
Other	**O:** Genesee Country Village
2	**(3)** NY 33, NY 33A Durgeon
FStop	**O:** Sunoco[*]
Food	**O:** Burgeon Family Restaurant, Sunoco
ATM	**O:** Sunoco
3	**(6)** NY 36, Churchville, Mumford
(7)	Parking Area (Eastbound)
(7)	Parking Area (Westbound)
4	**(11)** NY259, N. Chili, W. Chili, Spencerport
Gas	**I:** Mobil[*, LP]
AServ	**I:** Mobil
5	**(14)** NY386, Chili Center
6	**(16)** NY204 East, County Airport
7AB	**(17)** NY 33, NY 531, Gates Center (7A inside, 7B outside)
Gas	**I:** Sunoco[*]
Food	**I:** Denny's, Dunkin Donuts, Perkin's Family Restaurant, The Ground Round, Tomasso's Pizza
	O: Abbott's Frozen Yogurt, Delta House Restaurant
ATM	**I:** Sunoco
Other	**I:** Top Super Food Market[24]
8	**(17)** NY531, Spencerport, Brockport (Westbound)
9AB	**(19)** 9B - I-390 South (inside), 9A - I-390 North (outside) (Left Exit)
10AB	**(20)** Mt. Read Blvd.
Gas	**O:** Gulf[D]
Food	**O:** Combo's Deli
Lodg	**O:** 490 Motel
AServ	**O:** Gulf
11	**(21)** Ames St. South, Child St. North
Med	**I:** ✚ Hospital
Other	**O:** Police Station
12	**(22)** Brown St., Broad St., Frontier Field
13	Inner Loop, St. Paul Ave., Clinton Ave.
14	Broad Street, Plymouth Avenue (Westbound)
15	**(23)** South Ave., NY15, Inner Loop (Eastbound)
16	**(23)** Clinton Ave, Downtown (Westbound)
Lodg	**N:** Hyatt, Sheraton
17	**(24)** Goodman St.
Gas	**I:** Mobil[*]
Food	**I:** Highland Park Diner, Wilson Farm
	W: Imperial Restaurant, USA Pizzeria
AServ	**I:** Mobil
Med	**I:** ✚ Hospital
ATM	**I:** Wilson Farm
Other	**I:** Cinema, Wilson Farm
18	**(24)** Monroe Avenue
Gas	**O:** Hess
Food	**I:** Pizza World
	O: Village Green Cafe
AServ	**O:** Hess
Med	**O:** ✚ Hospital
ATM	**O:** Marine Midland Bank
Other	**I:** Monroe Food Mart
	O: Village Green Bookstore
19	**(25)** Culver Road
20	**(26)** Winton Rd.
Gas	**O:** Hess[*], Mobil, Sunoco
Food	**O:** East Avenue Family Restaurant, McDonald's, Wendy's
AServ	**O:** Mobil, Sunoco
ATM	**O:** M&T Bank
Other	**O:** Wegmans Food & Pharmacy[RX]
21	Jct. 590
22	Pennfield (Eastbound)
23	**(28)** NY441, Lindon Avenue, Pennfield
24	**(29)** East Rochester, W. Commercial Street
25	**(30)** NY31F, Fairport
26	**(32)** Pittsford , NY 31, Palmyra
27	**(34)** NY96, Bushnell Basin (Clockwise)
28	**(35)** NY96 (Reaccess Westbound Only)
29	**(37)** NY 96, Bickter (Last exit before toll)
Gas	**N:** Citgo[*], Mobil[*, LP]
Food	**N:** Brubaker Bagels, Mark's Pizzeria, Oven Door Bakery, Pontillo's Pizza, Sophia's Cafe, Subway, Subway
	O: Uno Pizzeria
Lodg	**N:** Brookwood Inn
	O: Hampton Inn & Suites
ATM	**N:** Marine Midland Bank
Other	**N:** Animal Hospital, Eckerd Drugs
	↑NEW YORK
	Begin I-490

I-494 MINNESOTA →

EXIT	MINNESOTA
	Begin I-494
	↓MINNESOTA
27	Jct I-694, I-94
26	CR10, Bass Lake Rd
Gas	**I:** Conoco[*, LP, CW]
	O: Amoco[*, CW], Sinclair[*, D, LP]
Food	**I:** Garden Cafe, Golden Wok, McDonald's[PLAY], Subway
AServ	**O:** Amoco
ATM	**I:** Norwest Bank
	O: Amoco
Other	**I:** Heritage Animal Hospital, Snyder Pharmacy[RX]
23	CR 9, Rockford Rd.
Gas	**I:** Amoco[*, CW, 24], Holiday[*, LP, CW]
	O: PDQ[*]
Food	**I:** Baker's Square Restaurant, Broadway Station (Pizza), Chili's, Domino's Pizza, Dufner's Soup & Sandwiches, Ming's Garden
	O: Bruegger's Bagel & Bakery, Dairy Queen, Pizza Hut, Subway
ATM	**I:** Amoco, Amoco, Anchor Bank, Holiday, Holiday
	O: PDQ
Other	**I:** Dental Clinic, Mail Boxes Etc., Rainbow Food Grocery[24], Rockford Rd Animal Hospital, Sear's Optical, Target Greatland, WalGreens Pharmacy[RX]
22	MN 55
Gas	**I:** Holiday[*, D, LP]
	O: Holiday[*]
Food	**I:** Best Western, Denny's, Kelly Mill (Best Western), McDonald's
	O: Arby's, Badanni's Pizza, Burger King, Mulligan's, New Dynasty Restaurant, Perkins Family Restaurant
Lodg	**I:** Best Western, Radisson Hotel, Red Roof Inn
	O: Comfort Inn, DAYS INN Days Inn
Med	**I:** ✚ Urgent Care Clinic
ATM	**I:** Franklin National Bank, Riverside Bank
	O: Holiday, Holiday, Norwest Banks
21	CR6
20	Carlton Pkwy
Gas	**I:** Holiday[*, D]
Food	**I:** Einstein Bros Bagels, Red Pepper (Chinese), Subway
	O: Country Inn & Suites, Country Kitchen (Country Inn), Italianni's (Country Inn)
Lodg	**O:** Country Inn & Suites
19B	U.S.12 W. Wayzata
19A	I-394 Jct
17	Minnetonka Blvd
16AB	MN. 7
Gas	**O:** Total[*, LP]
13	MN 62, CR 62
12	CR 39, Valley View Rd. (Reaccess Northbound Only)
Lodg	**I:** Extended Stay America
11C	MN 5 W.
Food	**O:** Bakers Square, Big City Bagels, Chinese Food, TCBY
ATM	**O:** Norwest Bank
Other	**O:** Pak Mail, Rainbow Food Grocery[24], Snyder Pharmacy[RX], The Eyes Have It
11AB	U.S. 212, Prarie Center Drive (Reaccess Eastbound Only, Difficult Reaccess)
Gas	**O:** Amoco, Mobil, Phillips 66[*, CW]
Food	**I:** Don Pablo's Mexican, Subway
	O: Bakers Ribs, Blimpie's Subs, Ciatti's Italian, Dairy Queen, Davanni's Pizza & Hoagie's, Great Mandarin Chinese, KFC, Pappa John's Pizza
Lodg	**I:** AmeriSuites, Courtyard by Marriott, Fairfield Inn, Hampton Inn, Residence Inn, Towne Place Suites
AServ	**O:** Amoco, Mobil
ATM	**I:** Cub Food[24, RX]
	O: First State Bank, US Bank
Other	**I:** Cub Food[RX]
	O: Kinko's[24], Target[RX]
10	U.S. 169 N to CR 18
8	CR 28, Eastbush Lake Rd. (Reaccess Eastbound Only)
7AB	MN 100, CR 34 Normandale Blvd.
Gas	**I:** Phillips 66, Wave[*]
	O: 76[*, D, CW] (1 Mile), 76[*, CW] (11 Miles), Citgo[CW], Citgo[D]
Food	**I:** Burger King, Cheetah Pizza, Chili's, Edington Sandwiches, Embers, La Terrasse (Sofitel), Sofitel, Subway, T.G.I. Friday's
	O: Antonio's (Best Western), Best Western, Gallery Restaurant, Grill, Olive Garden, Tony Roma Rib's
Lodg	**I:** Radisson Motel, Select Inn, Sofitel
	O: Best Western, DAYS INN Days Inn, Holiday Inn
AServ	**I:** Phillips 66
	O: Citgo, Citgo
ATM	**O:** Highland Bank
6B	CR 17, France Ave.
Gas	**I:** Mobil[*, LP]
Food	**I:** Ciao Bella, Fuddruckers, Hawthorn Inn, Hawthorn Inn, Perkins Family Restaurant
	O: Denny's, Grandma's Deli, Joe Senser's Bar & Grill, Lincoln Deli
Lodg	**I:** Best Western, Bradberry Suites Hotel, Hawthorn Inn
	O: Hampton Inn
AServ	**I:** Mobil
Med	**I:** ✚ Hospital
6A	Penn Ave.
Gas	**I:** 76[*], Citgo[*]
Food	**I:** McDonald's

I-494 MINNESOTA

EXIT — MINNESOTA

O: Applebee's, Bruegger's Bagel & Bakery, Chezdanie El Bristo (Doubletree), Doubletree Inn, Dragon Jade Restaurant, Edwardo's, Fannie Mae Candies, KFC, McDonald's, Red Lobster, Starbucks Coffee, Steak & Ale, Subway, Tortilla Ria (Mexican), Wendy's

Lodg O: Doubletree Inn

AServ I: Citgo
O: **Goodyear Tire & Auto**

Med I: ✚ **Hospital**

ATM I: Mobil
O: TCF Bank

Other O: Mail Boxes Etc., Target[RX]

5AB I-35 W, Jct Albert Lea, Minneapolis

4B Lyndale Ave

Gas I: Amoco[*, CW], Super America[*, LP]
O: Phillips 66[D]

Food I: Boston Market Restaurant, Broadway Pizza, Dairy Queen, Don Pablo's Mexican, Einstein Bros Bagels, Hope's Chow Mein (Chinese), Ketsana Ti Restaurant, Pappa John's Pizza, Vietnamese Restaurant

Lodg I: Candlewood Suites, Hampton Inn
O: Extended Stay America

AServ I: Amoco
O: Phillips 66

ATM I: Amoco, Super America, Super America
O: US Bank

Other I: El Jalape Mkt (Latin American, Mexican), Grocery Of The Orient, Veterinary Clinic

4A Nicollet Ave

Gas I: Super America[*, D]
O: Total[*, D, LP]

Food I: Burger King, Chi Chi's Mexican Restaurant, Ember's
O: Chubby Monroe's (79th St Grill), McDonald's

Lodg O: Budgetel Inn, Super 8

ATM I: Super America, Super America
O: Total

Other O: Quik Mart

3 Portland Ave, 12th Ave

Gas I: Phillips 66[*], Sinclair[*, D]
O: Amoco[*, D, CW]

Food I: Arby's, Ground Round Restaurant, Mongolian BBQ Restaurant
O: Denny's (Frontage Rd), First Wok (Chinese), McDonald's (Wal-Mart), Ming Cou Chow Mein (Chinese), Ming Cou Chow Mein, Pizza Gallery, Pizza Gallery, Pizza Hut, Pizza Hut, Scully's Broiler, Subway, Wal-Mart

EXIT — MINNESOTA

Lodg O: Americinn Hotel (Frontage Rd), Comfort Inn (Frontage Rd), Courtyard, Friendly Host Inn, Holiday Inn Express (Frontage Rd), Residence Inn

Other O: Snyder Drugs, Super Value Foods, Wal-Mart, WalGreens Pharmacy[RX]

2BC MN 77

Lodg I: AmericInn Motel, Motel 6

2A 24th Ave

Gas O: Amoco[*, CW], Super America[*, CW]

Food O: American Grill (Marriott), Best Western, Doubletree Grand, Marriott, Marriott, Ninemile (Double Tree Grand), Totem Pole (Best Western)

Lodg O: Best Western, Doubletree Grand, Excel Inn, Fairfield Inn, Marriott, Sheraton Inn, Thunderbird Hotel

1B 34th Ave, HHH Terminal

Food O: Biscane Bay Restaurant (Hilton), Cafe Carabella (Hilton), The Hilton

Lodg O: AmeriSuites, Embassy Suites, Holiday Inn Select, The Hilton

ATM O: Cash Center

Other I: National Cementary
O: National Wildlife Rescue

1A MN 5, Main Terminal, Ft. Snelling

71 CR 31, Pilot Knob Rd

Food O: Holiday Inn Select, Lone Oak Cafe (Holiday Inn Select)

Lodg I: Courtyard Marriott, Heritage Inn
O: Holiday Inn Select

70 I-35 E Jct. Albert Lea, St. Paul

69 MN 149, MN 55 Dodd Rd

67 MN3, Robert St

Gas O: PDQ[*]

Food I: Baker's Square, Bridgeman's Ice Cream & Restaurant, Famous BBQ, Godfather's Pizza, Old Country Buffet, White Castle Restaurant

ATM I: Signal Bank

Other I: Cub Foods[24], Southview Animal Hospital, Southview Animal Hospital

66 U.S. 52, Rochester, St. Paul (Divided Hwy)

Gas O: Super America[*, D, CW]

Food O: Applebee's

Lodg O: Americ Inn, Country Inn

ATM O: Community Bank, Super America

65 7th Ave, 5th Ave

64B MN 156, Concord St.

FStop O: **Super America[*]**

EXIT — MINNESOTA

Gas O: Gas[*, D]

Food I: Best Western, Best Western, Burger King
O: **Blimpie's Subs (Super America)**, Gas, Golden Steer Motor Inn, Golden Steer Motor Inn, **Taco John's (Gas)**

Lodg I: Best Western
O: Golden Steer Motor Inn

ATM I: Breemer's First American Bank, First American Bank

64A Hardman Ave.

TStop I: **Conoco[*, SCALES], Spur Truck Stop[*, SCALES]**

Food I: **Conoco, Metro Restaurant (Spur), Restaurant (Conoco), Spur Truck Stop**

ATM I: **Conoco**, Conoco

63C **(64)** Maxwell Ave.

63AB U.S. 10, U.S. 61, St. Paul, Hastings (Divided Hwy)

Gas O: Amoco

Food O: Subway, Tinucci's

AServ O: Amoco

Other O: U.S. Post Office

60 Lake Rd.

Gas O: Super America[*, D, CW]

ATM O: Super America

59 Valley Creek Rd.

Gas I: PDQ[*]
O: Amoco[*, LP, CW], Super America[*, CW]

Food I: Burger King, China City, Cracker Barrel, Dorothy Ann Bakery & Cafe, Keys Cafe and Bakery, Maggiore Ristorante Italian, McDonald's, Pizza Hut, Subway
O: Applebee's, Broadway Pizza, Cheasapeake Bagel Bakery, Ciatti's Italian, Dairy Queen, Expresso Coffee Shop, Marguerita Murphy's, Old Country Buffet, Perkin's Family Restaurant, Ronnally's Pizza, Starbucks Coffee, The Oriental Restaurant, Yang's Chinese

Lodg I: Hampton Inn
O: Red Roof Inn

ATM I: PBQ
O: Amoco, Mid America Bank, Rainbow Foods Grocery[24], TCF Bank

Other I: Snyder Pharmacy[RX], Valley Creek Lanes
O: Pearl Vision, Rainbow Foods Grocery, Target[RX], WalGreens Pharmacy[RX]

55AB I-94 Junction to Madison, St. Paul

↑MINNESOTA

Begin I-494

I-495 NEW JERSEY/NEW YORK

EXIT — NEW JERSEY

Begin I-495

↓NEW JERSEY

14 to25A, 21st St, Long Island City

15 Van Dam St., South Brooklyn, North Queens Blvd

16 Queensboro Bridge, Green Point Av

Gas I: Ramada Plaza Suite (see our ad this page)

1353
RAMADA®
Plaza Suite Hotel
New Jersey • Exit 16 • 201-617-5600

EXIT — NEW JERSEY/NEW YORK

17 Brooklyn, Queens, Expway278, Stanten Island, LaGuardia Airpt

↑NEW JERSEY

↓NEW YORK

19 Woodhaven Blvd, Rockaway, Queens Blvd, NY25

Gas N: Amoco[*], Getty, Mobil

Food S: Church's Chicken, White Castle Restaurant

Med S: ✚ St John's Queens Hospital

ATM S: Emmigrant Bank

20 Junction Blvd.

21 108th St.

Food S: Main St Bagel Rolls

22 Zanwick Expwy, College Point Blvd

EXIT — NEW YORK

Gas S: Mobil[*]

Med S: ✚ Hospital

23 Main St

Food N: Ill Cimine Italian, Kanwah, Palace Diner, Pioneer Pub Sports Cafe

Med N: ✚ NY Hospital of Queens

24 Kissena Blvd

Gas N: Exxon[*, D]
S: Mobil[*, D]

Food N: Blimpie's Subs, Dunkin Donuts, Kissena Deli, Lum Wok, Wok's Famous Chinese

Med S: ✚ Hospital

Other N: Superior Pharmacy

25 Utopia Pkwy, 188th St

Gas N: Mobil[*], Sunoco[*]
S: Amoco[CW] (Brushless CW), Shell[*], Sunoco

Bold red print shows RV & Bus parking available or nearby

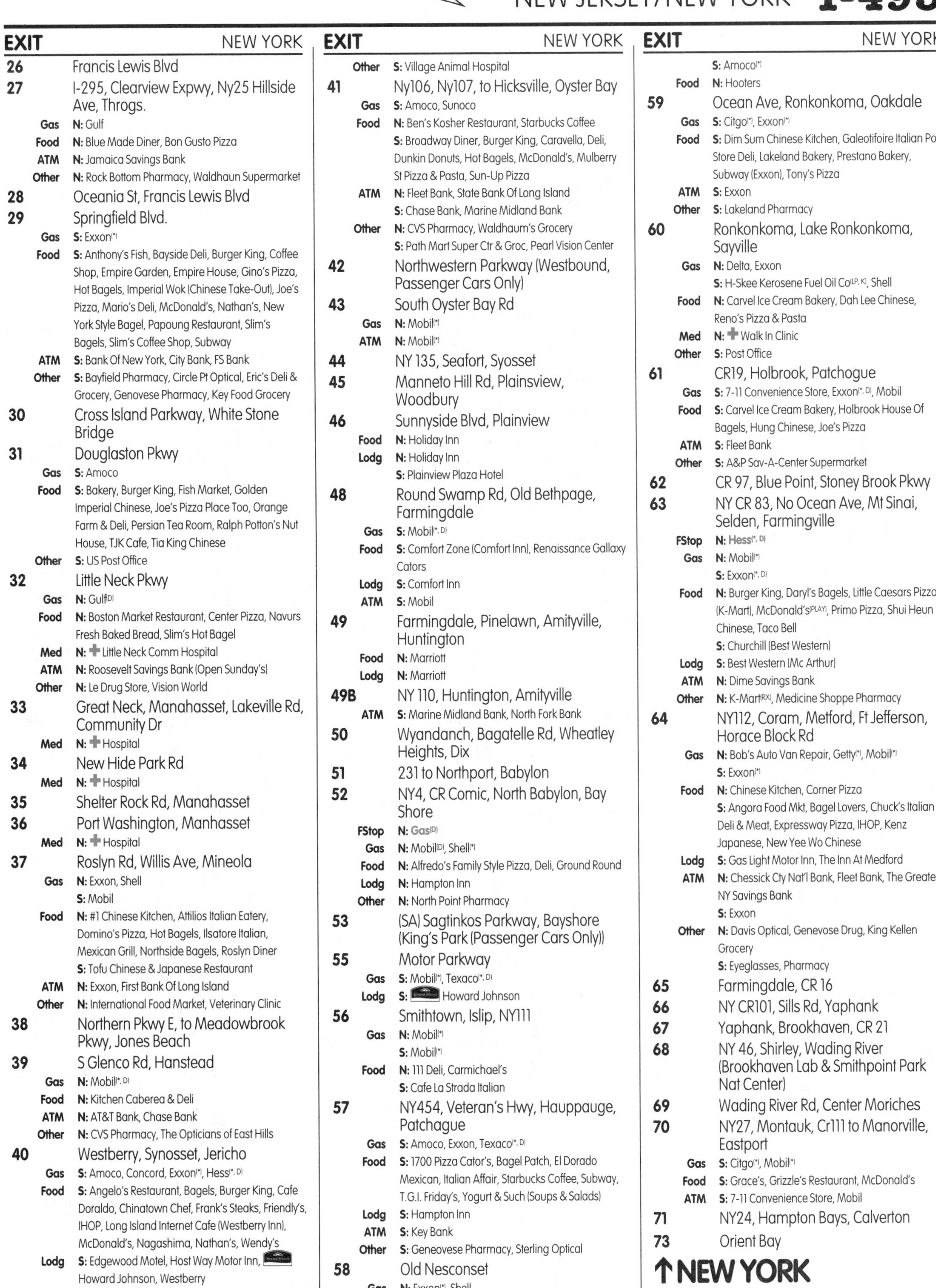

EXIT NEW YORK

26 Francis Lewis Blvd
27 I-295, Clearview Expwy, Ny25 Hillside Ave, Throgs.
Gas **N:** Gulf
Food **N:** Blue Made Diner, Bon Gusto Pizza
ATM **N:** Jamaica Savings Bank
Other **N:** Rock Bottom Pharmacy, Waldhaun Supermarket
28 Oceania St, Francis Lewis Blvd
29 Springfield Blvd.
Gas **S:** Exxon[*]
Food **S:** Anthony's Fish, Bayside Deli, Burger King, Coffee Shop, Empire Garden, Empire House, Gino's Pizza, Hot Bagels, Imperial Wok (Chinese Take-Out), Joe's Pizza, Mario's Deli, McDonald's, Nathan's, New York Style Bagel, Papoung Restaurant, Slim's Bagels, Slim's Coffee Shop, Subway
ATM **S:** Bank Of New York, City Bank, FS Bank
Other **S:** Bayfield Pharmacy, Circle Pt Optical, Eric's Deli & Grocery, Genovese Pharmacy, Key Food Grocery
30 Cross Island Parkway, White Stone Bridge
31 Douglaston Pkwy
Gas **S:** Amoco
Food **S:** Bakery, Burger King, Fish Market, Golden Imperial Chinese, Joe's Pizza Place Too, Orange Farm & Deli, Persian Tea Room, Ralph Potton's Nut House, TJK Cafe, Tia King Chinese
Other **S:** US Post Office
32 Little Neck Pkwy
Gas **N:** Gulf[D]
Food **N:** Boston Market Restaurant, Center Pizza, Navurs Fresh Baked Bread, Slim's Hot Bagel
Med **N:** ✚ Little Neck Comm Hospital
ATM **N:** Roosevelt Savings Bank (Open Sunday's)
Other **N:** Le Drug Store, Vision World
33 Great Neck, Manahasset, Lakeville Rd, Community Dr
Med **N:** ✚ Hospital
34 New Hide Park Rd
Med **N:** ✚ Hospital
35 Shelter Rock Rd, Manahasset
36 Port Washington, Manhasset
Med **N:** ✚ Hospital
37 Roslyn Rd, Willis Ave, Mineola
Gas **N:** Exxon, Shell
S: Mobil
Food **N:** #1 Chinese Kitchen, Attilios Italian Eatery, Domino's Pizza, Hot Bagels, Ilsatore Italian, Mexican Grill, Northside Bagels, Roslyn Diner
S: Tofu Chinese & Japanese Restaurant
ATM **N:** Exxon, First Bank Of Long Island
Other **N:** International Food Market, Veterinary Clinic
38 Northern Pkwy E, to Meadowbrook Pkwy, Jones Beach
39 S Glenco Rd, Hanstead
Gas **N:** Mobil[*, D]
Food **N:** Kitchen Caberea & Deli
ATM **N:** AT&T Bank, Chase Bank
Other **N:** CVS Pharmacy, The Opticians of East Hills
40 Westberry, Synosset, Jericho
Gas **S:** Amoco, Concord, Exxon[*], Hess[*, D]
Food **S:** Angelo's Restaurant, Bagels, Burger King, Cafe Doraldo, Chinatown Chef, Frank's Steaks, Friendly's, IHOP, Long Island Internet Cafe (Westberry Inn), McDonald's, Nagashima, Nathan's, Wendy's
Lodg **S:** Edgewood Motel, Host Way Motor Inn, Howard Johnson, Westberry
ATM **S:** EAB Bank

EXIT NEW YORK

Other **S:** Village Animal Hospital
41 Ny106, Ny107, to Hicksville, Oyster Bay
Gas **S:** Amoco, Sunoco
Food **N:** Ben's Kosher Restaurant, Starbucks Coffee
S: Broadway Diner, Burger King, Caravella, Deli, Dunkin Donuts, Hot Bagels, McDonald's, Mulberry St Pizza & Pasta, Sun-Up Pizza
ATM **N:** Fleet Bank, State Bank Of Long Island
S: Chase Bank, Marine Midland Bank
Other **N:** CVS Pharmacy, Waldhaum's Grocery
S: Path Mart Super Ctr & Groc, Pearl Vision Center
42 Northwestern Parkway (Westbound, Passenger Cars Only)
43 South Oyster Bay Rd
Gas **N:** Mobil[*]
ATM **N:** Mobil[*]
44 NY 135, Seafort, Syosset
45 Manneto Hill Rd, Plainsview, Woodbury
46 Sunnyside Blvd, Plainview
Food **N:** Holiday Inn
Lodg **N:** Holiday Inn
S: Plainview Plaza Hotel
48 Round Swamp Rd, Old Bethpage, Farmingdale
Gas **S:** Mobil[*, D]
Food **S:** Comfort Zone (Comfort Inn), Renaissance Gallaxy Cators
Lodg **S:** Comfort Inn
ATM **S:** Mobil
49 Farmingdale, Pinelawn, Amityville, Huntington
Food **N:** Marriott
Lodg **N:** Marriott
49B NY 110, Huntington, Amityville
ATM **S:** Marine Midland Bank, North Fork Bank
50 Wyandanch, Bagatelle Rd, Wheatley Heights, Dix
51 231 to Northport, Babylon
52 NY4, CR Comic, North Babylon, Bay Shore
FStop **N:** **Gas**[D]
Gas **N:** Mobil[D], Shell[*]
Food **N:** Alfredo's Family Style Pizza, Deli, Ground Round
Lodg **N:** Hampton Inn
Other **N:** North Point Pharmacy
53 (SA) Sagtinkos Parkway, Bayshore (King's Park (Passenger Cars Only))
55 Motor Parkway
Gas **S:** Mobil[*], Texaco[*, D]
Lodg **S:** Howard Johnson
56 Smithtown, Islip, NY111
Gas **N:** Mobil[*]
S: Mobil[*]
Food **N:** 111 Deli, Carmichael's
S: Cafe La Strada Italian
57 NY454, Veteran's Hwy, Hauppauge, Patchague
Gas **S:** Amoco, Exxon, Texaco[*, D]
Food **S:** 1700 Pizza Cator's, Bagel Patch, El Dorado Mexican, Italian Affair, Starbucks Coffee, Subway, T.G.I. Friday's, Yogurt & Such (Soups & Salads)
Lodg **S:** Hampton Inn
ATM **S:** Key Bank
Other **S:** Geneovese Pharmacy, Sterling Optical
58 Old Nesconset
Gas **N:** Exxon[*], Shell

EXIT NEW YORK

S: Amoco[*]
Food **N:** Hooters
59 Ocean Ave, Ronkonkoma, Oakdale
Gas **S:** Citgo[*], Exxon[*]
Food **S:** Dim Sum Chinese Kitchen, Galeotifoire Italian Port Store Deli, Lakeland Bakery, Prestano Bakery, Subway (Exxon), Tony's Pizza
ATM **S:** Exxon
Other **S:** Lakeland Pharmacy
60 Ronkonkoma, Lake Ronkonkoma, Sayville
Gas **N:** Delta, Exxon
S: H-Skee Kerosene Fuel Oil Co[LP, K], Shell
Food **N:** Carvel Ice Cream Bakery, Dah Lee Chinese, Reno's Pizza & Pasta
Med **N:** ✚ Walk In Clinic
Other **S:** Post Office
61 CR19, Holbrook, Patchogue
Gas **S:** 7-11 Convenience Store, Exxon[*, D], Mobil
Food **S:** Carvel Ice Cream Bakery, Holbrook House Of Bagels, Hung Chinese, Joe's Pizza
ATM **S:** Fleet Bank
Other **S:** A&P Sav-A-Center Supermarket
62 CR 97, Blue Point, Stoney Brook Pkwy
63 NY CR 83, No Ocean Ave, Mt Sinai, Selden, Farmingville
FStop **N:** **Hess**[*, D]
Gas **N:** Mobil[*]
S: Exxon[*, D]
Food **N:** Burger King, Daryl's Bagels, Little Caesars Pizza (K-Mart), McDonald's[PLAY], Primo Pizza, Shui Heun Chinese, Taco Bell
S: Churchill (Best Western)
Lodg **S:** Best Western (Mc Arthur)
ATM **N:** Dime Savings Bank
Other **N:** K-Mart[RX], Medicine Shoppe Pharmacy
64 NY112, Coram, Metford, Ft Jefferson, Horace Block Rd
Gas **N:** Bob's Auto Van Repair, Getty[*], Mobil[*]
S: Exxon[*]
Food **N:** Chinese Kitchen, Corner Pizza
S: Angora Food Mkt, Bagel Lovers, Chuck's Italian Deli & Meat, Expressway Pizza, IHOP, Kenz Japanese, New Yee Wo Chinese
Lodg **S:** Gas Light Motor Inn, The Inn At Medford
ATM **N:** Chessick Cty Nat'l Bank, Fleet Bank, The Greater NY Savings Bank
S: Exxon
Other **N:** Davis Optical, Genevose Drug, King Kellen Grocery
S: Eyeglasses, Pharmacy
65 Farmingdale, CR 16
66 NY CR101, Sills Rd, Yaphank
67 Yaphank, Brookhaven, CR 21
68 NY 46, Shirley, Wading River (Brookhaven Lab & Smithpoint Park Nat Center)
69 Wading River Rd, Center Moriches
70 NY27, Montauk, Cr111 to Manorville, Eastport
Gas **S:** Citgo[*], Mobil[*]
Food **S:** Grace's, Grizzle's Restaurant, McDonald's
ATM **S:** 7-11 Convenience Store, Mobil
71 NY24, Hampton Bays, Calverton
73 Orient Bay

↑NEW YORK

Begin I-495

EXIT		MARYLAND
		Begin I-495

↓MARYLAND

27 Jct I-95 N, to Baltimore

25AB U.S. 1, Baltimore Blvd, Laurel, College Park
- Gas I: Amoco[24]
  O: Shell[*]
- Food O: Moosecreek Steakhouse
- Lodg I: Econolodge
  O: Holiday Inn
- AServ O: Shell
- Other I: Shoppers Supermarket

24 Greenbelt Station (No Reaccess)

23 MD 201, Kenilworth Ave, Bladensburg, Greenbelt
- Gas I: Shell
- Food I: McDonald's, Sir Walter Raliegh, TGI Friday
- Lodg I: Courtyard
  O: Marriott
- AServ I: Shell
- ATM I: First Liberty Bank

22AB Baltimore Washington Parkway (No Trucks)

20 MD 450, Annapolis Road, Lanham, Bladensburg
- Gas I: Citgo[*], Shell[*]
  O: Mobil[*]
- Food I: Chesapeake Bay Seafood, Cuisine China, PaPa John's, Shoney's, Wendy's
  O: Best Western, Burger King, Jerry's Subs & Pizza, McDonald's[PLAY], Pizza Hut, Red Lobster, Red Texas BBQ, Silver Platter (Days Inn)
- Lodg I: Ramada Inn
  O: Best Western, Days Inn, Red Roof Inn
- Med O: Hospital
- ATM I: Citgo, Maryland Federal Bank, Shell
- Other I: CVS Pharmacy, Safeway Grocery, Shoppers Supermarket

19AB U.S. 50, Annapolis, Washington

17AB MD 202, Landover Road, Bladensburg, Upper Marlboro
- Lodg O: Club Hotel
- Other I: County Police, Sam's Club

15AB MD 214, Central Ave
- Gas I: Crown[*, D, 24], Exxon[*, D]
- Food I: Days Inn, Jerry's Subs & Pizza, McDonald's[PLAY], Pizza Hut
- Lodg I: Days Inn
  O: Hampton Inn
- ATM I: Exxon

11AB MD 4, Pennsylvania Ave, Washington, Upper Marlboro
- Gas I: Exxon[*, CW], Shell[*], Sunoco[D, 24]
  O: Texaco
- AServ I: Shell, Sunoco[24]
  O: Texaco
- ATM I: Exxon, Industrial Bank

9 MD 337, Allen Town Road, Andrews AFB (Difficult Reaccess)
- Gas I: Mobil[*, CW]

7AB MD 5, Branch Ave, Waldorf, Silver Hill
- Gas I: Texaco
- Lodg I: Days Inn
- Med O: Hospital

4AB MD 414, Saint Barnabas Road, Oxen Hill, Marlow Heights
- Gas I: Exxon, Shell[*, 24]
  O: Exxon[D, CW, 24], Xtra Fuel[*, 24]
- Food I: McDonald's
  O: Burger King, KFC, McDonald's[PLAY], Wendy's
- AServ I: Exxon, Shell[24]
  O: Xtra Fuel[24]
- Med I: Hospital
- ATM O: 7-11 Convenience Store, Industrial Bank, NationsBank

EXIT		MARYLAND/VIRGINIA

- Other I: Coin Laundromat
  O: 7-11 Convenience Store

3AB MD 210, Indian Head Hwy, Forest Heights
- Lodg O: Ramada Inn, Susse Chalet
- Other O: Oxen Hill Plaza

2AB Junction I-295, Washington

↑MARYLAND

↓VIRGINIA

1AB U.S. 1, Mt. Vernon
- Gas I: Exxon, Merit[D]
  O: Amoco[D, 24], Mobil[*, D], Sunoco, Texaco[D]
- Food O: Domino's Pizza, Great American Steak & Buffet Co., Howard Johnson
- Lodg O: Brookside Motel, Howard Johnson, Red Roof Inn, Statesman Motel, Traveler Motel
- AServ O: Mobil, Sunoco, Texaco
- Med I: Hospital
- ATM I: Merit
  O: Prestar

2AB VA 241, Telegraph Road, Alexandria
- Gas O: Amoco, Citgo, Exxon[*, D, LP], Hess[D]
- Food O: Pillar's Restaurant
- Lodg I: Courtyard by Marriott, Holiday Inn
- AServ O: Amoco, Citgo, Exxon
- Med I: Hospital
- ATM O: 7-11 Convenience Store, Burke & Herbert Bank & Trust, Exxon
- Other I: Alexandria Animal Hospital
  O: 7-11 Convenience Store

3A Eisenhower Ave., Alexandria

3 VA 613, Vandoran St., Franconia
- Lodg O: Comfort Inn

4 Junction I-95 South, Richmond; Junction I-95 North (East Beltway), Alexandria; Junction I-395, Arlington, Washington

4A Junction I-495 North, Rockville

4B I-395 N, Washington, I-95, Richmond

5 VA 620, Braddock Rd
- Gas O: Mobil[D]
- Food O: Chesapeake Bagel Bakery, Dairy Queen, Kilroy's
- AServ O: Mobil
- ATM O: Chevy Chase Bank, NationsBank
- Other O: Rite Aide Pharmacy[RX], Safeway Grocery, US Post Office

6 VA 236, Little River Tnpk, Annandale, Fairfax
- Gas I: Citgo[D, CW], Exxon[D], Mobil
- Food I: McDonald's
- AServ I: Citgo, Exxon, Mobil
- ATM I: 7-11 Convenience Store, First Union
- Other I: 7-11 Convenience Store

7 VA 650, Gallows Rd
- Gas O: Exxon[*]
- AServ O: Exxon
- Med O: Inova Fairfax Hospital

8 U.S. 50, Arlington Blvd, Arlington to Lee Hwy
- Gas O: Amoco[CW], Mobil[*, D, CW], Shell[*]
- Food O: Baskin Robbins, Boston Market Restaurant, Chesapeake Bagel, Chevy's Mexican, Dominion Deli, Grevey's Restaurant, McDonald's, Starbucks Coffee, Uno Pizzeria
- Lodg I: Marriott
- AServ O: Shell
- Med O: Hospital
- ATM O: Chevy Chase Bank, NationsBank
- Other O: CVS Pharmacy[24, RX], Giant Food Supermarket, York Towne Center

9 JCT I-66, Vienna, Front Royal (Left Exit, No Trucks Allowed To The East, B Exit Right, C To Ft Royal)

9C I-66 W, Front Royal

EXIT		VIRGINIA/MARYLAND

10AB VA 7, Leesburg Pike, Falls Church, Tysons Corner
- Gas I: Exxon[*]
  O: Crown[*, D], Shell[*]
- Food O: Bertucci's Brick Oven Pizza, Chili's, On The Border Mexican Cafe, Roy Rogers[24]
- Lodg I: Doubletree Hotel
  O: Marriott
- ATM I: United Bank
  O: Crown, NationsBank

11 VA 123, Chain Bridge Rd, McLean, Tysons Corner
- Gas O: Mobil[*], Shell[D]
- Lodg O: Holiday Inn, Marriott, Ritz Carlton
- AServ O: Shell
- ATM O: Shell

12 VA 267, Dulles Airport Exit (Left Exit, Toll)

13 VA 193, Georgetown Pike, Langley, Great Falls

14 George Washington Memorial Pkwy (No Trucks)

↑VIRGINIA

↓MARYLAND

41 Clara Barton Pkwy, Carderock, Glen Echo (No Trucks)

39 MD 190, River Rd, Washington, Potomac

38 Junction I-270, Rockville, Frederick (Left Exit)

36 MD 187, Old Georgetown Rd, Bethesda, Rockville
- Med I: Hospital (2.5 Miles)

34 MD 355, Wisconsin Ave, Bethesda
- Food I: Bellomondo & American Grill (Marriott)
- Lodg I: Marriott

33AB MD 185, Connecticut Ave, Chevy Chase, Kensington (No Thru Trucks Southside)
- Gas I: Amoco, Exxon, Sunoco[*, 24]
- Food I: Einstein Bros Bagels, Starbucks Coffee
- AServ I: Amoco, Exxon, Sunoco[24]
- ATM I: Crestar Bank
- Other I: Chevy Chase Supermarket

31AB MD 97, Georgia Ave, Silver Spring, Wheaton
- Gas I: Amoco[*, D, 24], Exxon[*, D], Shell[*], Texaco[*, D, CW]
- Food I: Domino's Pizza
- AServ I: Amoco[24], Exxon, Shell, Texaco
- Med O: Forest Glenn Hospital
- ATM I: Citibank
- Other I: CVS Pharmacy[RX]

30 U.S. 29, Colesville Rd, Silver Spring, Columbia
- Gas O: Amoco[*, 24], Amoco[24], Shell, Texaco[*]
- Food O: Jerry's Pizza &Subs, PaPa John's, Roy Rogers
- AServ O: Amoco[24], Amoco[24], Shell, Texaco
- ATM O: Amoco, Chevy Chase Bank, Safeway Grocery
- Other O: CVS Pharmacy[RX], Safeway Grocery

29B MD 193 East, University Blvd, Langley Park

28AB MD 650, New Hampshire Ave, Takoma Park, White Oak
- Gas O: Amoco[24], Exxon[*, D], Shell[*]
- Food O: Grand China, KFC, Mike's Cheese Steak & Pizza, Shoney's
- AServ O: Amoco[24], Shell
- ATM O: Chevy Chase Bank, Crestar Bank, Exxon
- Other O: 7-11 Convenience Store, CVS Pharmacy[RX], Hillandale Pharmacy, Safeway Grocery

↑MARYLAND

Begin I-495

Bold red print shows RV & Bus parking available or nearby

EXIT MASSACHUSETTS

Begin I-495

↓ MASSACHUSETTS

54 **(117)** MA150, Amesbury
Gas W: Getty
Food W: Bagel Express
AServ W: Getty
Other W: Osco Drugs[RX]

53 **(115)** Broad St , Merrimac, Merrimacport
Gas W: Texaco
AServ W: Texaco
ATM W: BankBoston

(52) Parking Area (RR, Phones, Picnic)

52 **(111)** MA110, Haverhill, Merrimac
FStop W: Mobil[*, D]
Gas W: Global (Towing)
Food W: Biggart's Ice Cream, Dunkin Donuts
AServ W: Global (Towing)
Med E: ✚ Hospital

51AB **(109)** MA125, Plaistow, NH, Haverhill
Gas E: Mobil (Towing), Richdale[*, 24]
Food E: Brothers Pizza, Dunkin Donuts
AServ E: Mobil (Towing)
Med E: ✚ Hospital
ATM E: First Essex Bank

50 **(108)** MA97, Haverhill, Salem, NH, MA 110, MA 113 (Westbound)
Gas E: Gulf, Sunoco[*, 24]
Food E: 99 Restaurant, Athens Restaurant & Pizza, Bickford's Family Restaurant, Dunkin Donuts, McDonald's, Oriental Garden, Papa Gino's
W: Cafe 97, Dunkin Donuts
Lodg E: Best Western, Comfort Inn
ATM E: Bank Boston, Fleet Bank, Pentucke Bank
Other E: CVS Pharmacy[RX], K-Mart, Market Basket

49 **(107)** MA110, MA113, River St
Gas E: Gulf[*], Sunoco[*]
Food E: 99 Restaurant, Athens Pizza, Bigford's Family Restaurant, Dunkin Donuts, McDonald's, Oriental Garden, Papa Gino's Pizza &More
Lodg E: Best Western, Comfort Inn
Med E: ✚ Hale Hospital
ATM E: BankBoston, Fleet Bank, Pentucke Bank
Other E: CVS Pharmacy, K-Mart

48 **(106)** MA125, Ward Hill, Bradford

47 **(104)** MA213, Methuen, Salem, NH (Difficult Reaccess)
Med W: ✚ Hospital

46 **(103)** MA110, Merrimac St, Pleasant Valley
Gas E: Gulf, Sunoco[*, 24]
Food E: Heavenly Donuts, Lobster Den, Super Swirl Ice Cream
ATM E: First Essex

45 **(102)** Marston St, Lawrence
Food E: Anthony's Pizza & Subs
TServ E: Cody's Garage, Northeast Truck Service
W: B&B Truck & Equipment Repair, Cody's Garage[D]
Med W: ✚ Hospital

44 **(102)** Merrimac St, Sutton St (Difficult Reaccess)
Gas E: Citgo
W: Spague Energy[*]
Food E: Cafe Bakery, Honey Dew Donuts (Richdale Food Store), Sutton Square Grill
W: Italian Deli, J&J Super Sub, Merrimac Restaurant, Paisano's Pizza

EXIT MASSACHUSETTS

AServ E: Citgo

43 **(101)** Massachusetts Ave, N Andover
Gas W: Mobil[*], Shell[*] (Towing)
ATM W: Lawrence Savings Bank

42B **(101)** MA114W. South Lawrence
Gas E: Exxon[*], Gulf[*], Mobil[*, D]
W: Texaco[*, D]
Food E: Boston Market Restaurant, Friendly's, Pasta Palazzi, Pizza Hut
W: Denny's, McDonald's, Pizzeria Bravo, Royal Dragon
Lodg E: Hampton Inn
AServ E: Gulf
W: Texaco
Med W: ✚ Hospital
ATM E: Exxon, Fleet Bank
W: US Trust Bank
Other E: CVS Pharmacy

42A **(100)** MA114E, Middleton

41 **(99)** MA28, Lawrence, Andover
Gas W: Mobil
Food E: Dunkin Donuts
W: Dunkin Donuts (Mobil)
AServ W: Mobil
ATM E: Lawrence Savings Bank

40AB **(97)** Jct I-93 to Concord, NH, Boston

39 **(95)** MA133, Dracut, Andover
Gas E: Charter
Food E: McDonald's
W: Holiday Inn, Wendy's
Lodg W: Holiday Inn, Residence Inn, Susse Chalet, Ramada Inn (see our ad this page)
Med W: ✚ Hospital

38 **(92)** MA38, Lowell, Tewksbury
Gas E: Shell
W: Citgo, Mobil[*], Sunoco, Texaco[D], USA Petroleum[D]
Food E: Applebee's, Burger King, Dunkin Donuts, Jade Buddha Chinese, Pinata's, TD Waffle
W: Dunkin Donuts, Jillie's Roast Beef, Little Caesars Pizza (K-Mart), McDonald's, Milan Pizza, Wendy's
Lodg E: Motel 6, Motel Caswell
AServ E: Shell
W: Citgo, Sunoco, Texaco
Med W: ✚ Hospital
ATM W: Fleet Bank
Other E: Wal-Mart[RX]
W: CVS Pharmacy, K-Mart[RX]

37 **(91)** Woburn St, S Lowell, N Billerica
Gas W: Exxon[*]
Food W: Dunkin Donuts (Exxon), Stefano's Italian
ATM W: Exxon

36 **(90)** Lowell, Connector

2 Locations on I-495 include these Amenities:
Full Service Restaurant & Lounge
Swimming Pool
Health Facilities • Spectra vision
Newly Renovated Spacious Guest Rooms

1574

Holiday Inn Boxborough Adams Place
I-495 • Exit 28
1 Adams Place
Boxborough, Mass
508-263-8701

RAMADA INN
Rolling Green I-495 • Exit 39
Golf Course & Indoor Tennis 508-975-5400
MASS • I-495 • 2 LOCATIONS

EXIT MASSACHUSETTS

35AB **(90)** Lowell Connector, U.S. 3, Nashua, Berlington

34 **(89)** MA4, MA110, Chelmsford
Gas E: Mobil[*], Sunoco[*, 24]
W: Shell
Food E: Dunkin Donuts, Hong Kong Chinese, Radisson Heritage Hotel, Skips, Town Meeting
W: Ground Round
Lodg E: Radisson Heritage Hotel
W: Best Western
AServ W: Shell

(87) Parking Area (Southbound)

(87) Parking Area (Northbound)

32 **(84)** Boston Rd, Westford
Gas E: Exxon[*], Gulf, Mobil[*]
Food E: Applebee's, Beans Coffee, Boston Market Restaurant, Burger King, Colonial Bakery, De' Angelo's Sandwich Shop, Dunkin Donuts, McDonald's[PLAY], Papa Gino's Pizza, Pizza Express
AServ E: Exxon
ATM E: BankBoston, Fleet Bank, Middlesex Bank
Other E: CVS Pharmacy, Osco Drugs, WalGreens Pharmacy[RX]

31 **(80)** MA119, Groton, Acton
Gas E: Mobile[*, D], Shell[*]
Food E: Dunkin Donuts (Shell), Ken's American Cafe, Littleton Sub Shop
Med W: ✚ Hospital
ATM E: Mobile
Other E: CVS Pharmacy[RX], Common Convenience Grocery Store[LP], Post Office

30 **(79)** MA2A, MA110, Littletown, Ayer
Med W: ✚ Hospital

29AB **(78)** MA2, Leominster, Boston

28 **(75)** MA111, Boxboro, Harvard
Gas E: Exxon
Food E: Bravo's Pizza, Jerry's (Holiday Inn)
Lodg E: Holiday Inn (see our ad this page)
AServ E: Exxon

27 **(70)** MA117, Bolton, Stowe
Gas E: Mobil
Food W: Bolten House of Pizza, Herbert's Candy, Ice Cream
AServ E: Mobil
ATM W: Quinton Savings Bank

26 **(67)** MA62, Berlin, Hudson
Gas E: Exxon
W: Texaco[D]
AServ E: Exxon
W: Texaco

25AB **(65)** Jct I-290, MA 85, Marlboro, Worcester
Med W: ✚ Hospital

24AB **(63)** U.S. 20, Northboro, Marlboro
Gas W: Exxon[*], Shell[*, CW, 24]
Food W: Boston Market Restaurant, Bruegger's Bagel & Bakery, China Taste, McDonald's[PLAY], Starbucks Coffee, Subway, Uno Pizzeria, Wendy's
Lodg E: Holiday Inn
W: Best Western, Embassy Suites, Homestead Village, Radisson Inn
Med E: ✚ Hospital
W: ✚ Walk In Clinic
ATM W: Bank Boston, Metro West

23AB **(60)** MA9, Worcester, Framingham
Gas E: Exxon[D], Exxon[*]
Food E: Wendy's
Lodg E: Red Roof Inn
W: Marriot

Bold red print shows RV & Bus parking available or nearby

I-495 MASSACHUSETTS

EXIT	MASSACHUSETTS
AServ	E: Exxon
22	**(58)** Jct I-90, MA Trnpk, Boston, Albany, NY
21AB	West Main St, Upton, Hopkinton
Gas	E: Gulf[*]
Food	E: Dino's Pizza, Subs & More, Dynasty Chinese, Golden Spoon Coffee Shop, Jelly Donuts
Med	E: Hopkinton Walk In Clinic
ATM	E: BankBoston
20	**(50)** MA85, MA16, Milford, Hopkinton
Gas	W: Gulf[D, K], Mobil[*]
Food	W: Wendy's
Lodg	W: Days Inn, Marriot
19	**(49)** MA109, Milford, Medway
Gas	W: Mobil[*, D]
Food	W: Burger King[PLAY], Pizza Hut (Mobil)
Lodg	W: Pagen
ATM	W: BankBoston, Mobil
Other	W: K-Mart
18	MA126, Medway, Bellingham
Gas	W: Charter[*], Mobil[*], Sunoco
Food	E: McDonald's
	W: Dunkin Donuts, Outback Steakhouse, Uno Pizzeria
AServ	W: Sunoco
ATM	E: BankBoston
Other	E: Barnes & Noble Bookstore, Market Basket Supermarket, Wal-Mart[RX]
17	**(43)** MA140, Franklin, Bellingham
Gas	E: Mobil[*]
Food	E: Applebee's, Burger King, D'Angelo's, Dunkin Donuts, Hunan Gourmet II, PaPa Gino's Pizza, Taco Bell, Village Cafe
Med	W: Hospital
ATM	E: Bank of Boston, Mobil, Summit Bank
Other	E: Royal Discount Books
16	**(41)** King St, Franklin, Woonsocket, RI

EXIT	MASSACHUSETTS
Gas	E: Sunoco[*]
Food	E: The Gold Fork
ATM	E: Sunoco
15	**(38)** MA 1A, Wrentham, Plainville
Med	E: Hospital
14AB	**(36)** U.S. 1, N Attleboro, Wrentham
Food	E: Arbor Inn, Luciano's
Lodg	E: Arbor Inn
13AB	**(33)** Jct I-95, Providence, RI, Boston
12	**(30)** MA140N, Mansfield
11	**(30)** MA140S, Norton (Reaccess Northbound Only)
10	**(27)** MA123, Norton, Easton
Food	E: Barnside Grill, Kricket's Corner, Mino's Pizza
Med	W: Hospital
9	**(25)** Bay St, Taunton, Easton
Food	W: Dunkin Donuts, Golden Flower Chinese, Holiday Inn, Pizza Hut
Lodg	W: Holiday Inn
Med	W: Northwood Medical Center
ATM	W: Cresent Credit Union
8	**(22)** MA138, Raynham, Taunton
Gas	E: Mobil[*, CW]
	W: Exxon[*, LP], Texaco[D]
Food	E: Christopher's, Honey Dew Donuts
	W: Brother's Pizza, China Garden, Dunkin Donuts (Exxon), Honey Dew Donuts, McDonald's, Pepperoni's Pizza
AServ	W: Texaco
Med	W: Hospital
ATM	W: Bristol County Savings Bank
7AB	**(19)** MA24, Fall River, Boston
(18)	Weigh Station (Southbound)
6	**(15)** U.S.44, Middleboro, Plymouth
Gas	E: Circle Farm[*, D]
Food	E: Burger King[PLAY], Fireside Grille, Friendly's,

EXIT	MASSACHUSETTS
	Lorenzo's Italian
Lodg	W: Susse Chalet
5	MA18, Lakeville, New Bedford (East Side Services are the same as exit 6)
Gas	E: Circle Farm[*, D]
Food	E: Dunkin Donuts, Fireside Grill, Friendly's, Frosty's Place
4	**(12)** MA105, Middleboro Center, Lakeville
Gas	E: Exxon[*, D], Shell[*, CW, 24], Sunoco[*, 24], Texaco
Food	E: Dairy Queen, Dunkin Donuts, Honey Dew Donuts (Exxon), McDonald's, Papa Timmy's Pizza
Lodg	E: Days Inn
AServ	E: Texaco
ATM	E: Rockland Trust
	W: Bridgewater Savings Bank
Other	E: Brooks Pharmacy[RX], Osco Drugs
(11)	Rest Area (Southbound)
(10)	Rest Area (Southbound)
(10)	Rest Area (Northbound)
3	**(8)** MA28, Rock Village, S Middleboro
FStop	E: **Citgo[*, D]**
Gas	W: Citgo[*, D]
Food	W: Huckleberry's Chicken House
TServ	W: **Exit 3 Truck Center**
2	**(3)** MA58, Carver, W Wareham, Rochester
Gas	W: Citgo[*, LP]
ATM	W: Citgo
1	**(0)** Jct I-195W, Wareham, New Bedford

↑MASSACHUSETTS

Begin I-495

I-526 SOUTH CAROLINA

Begin I-526

↓SOUTH CAROLINA

EXIT	SOUTH CAROLINA
32A	US 17 S., Charleston , Business Spur 526, US 17 N Georgetown
Food	I: Arby's, Louie's Subs, McDonald's[PLAY], Papa John's Pizza
	O: Applebee's, Blimpie Subs & Salads, Krispy Kreme Doughnuts (Piggly Wiggly), McDonald's (Wal-Mart), Piggly Wiggly, Ryan's Steakhouse, Wal-Mart[RX]
Med	I: Hospital
ATM	I: Heritage Trust, Wachovia Bank
	O: Piggly Wiggly
Other	I: Good News The Amazing Christian Store, K-Mart[RX]
	O: Bookland, CVS[RX], Piggly Wiggly, Wal-Mart[RX]
32	Isle of Palms, US 17 N., Georgetown (Eastbound, Reaccess Westbound Only)
Gas	O: Exxon[*], Speedway[*, LP]

EXIT	SOUTH CAROLINA
Food	O: Fazoli's Italian Food, Ice Cream & Sandwich Cafe, Ryan's Steakhouse, Subway
ATM	O: First Union, NBSC
30	Long Point Rd.
Food	O: Waffle House
23AB	Clements Ferry Road
20	Virginia Ave. (Eastbound, Reaccess Westbound Only)
19	North Rhett Ave.
Gas	I: Amoco[*, K]
18AB	US 52, US 78, Rivers Ave.
FStop	O: **Amoco[*, D]**
Gas	O: Phillips 66
Food	I: Marketplace Buffet & Bakery, Mayflower Chinese Restaurant
Lodg	I: Catalina Inn, Economy Inn, North Motel 52
AServ	O: Phillips 66
ATM	O: **Amoco**
Other	I: Outboard Shop
	O: Laundromat, Piggly Wiggly Supermarket
17AB	Jct. 26, Charleston, Columbia

EXIT	SOUTH CAROLINA
Other	I: Visitor Information
	O: Airport
Exit	**(17)** Charleston International Airport, Trident Research Center
17	Montague Ave.
Gas	O: Speedway[*, LP]
ATM	O: Speedway
Other	I: Coliseum
15	Paramont Dr., Dorchester Rd., SC 642
Gas	I: Exxon[*, 24]
Food	I: Burger King[PLAY], Huddle House
Lodg	I: Super 8
ATM	I: Exxon
Other	I: U-Haul Center
13	Leeds Ave
Med	I: Hospital
11AB	SC 61, Ashley River Road, Mark Clark Expressway

↑SOUTH CAROLINA

Begin I-526

EXIT GEORGIA

Begin I-575

↓GEORGIA

13 **(26)** Ga. 5, Howell Branch Rd., Ball Ground
12 Hwy 372 , Airport Dr.
11 Ga. 5, Canton (Reinhart College, Hospital)
FStop **W:** **Exxon**[*, LP]
Gas **E:** Amoco[*]
W: Tim's Auto Buff[CW]
Food **E:** Cafe Cantina, Chick-Fil-A[PLAY], Gondolier, McDonald's (Wal-Mart), Waffle House
W: Applebee's, Blimpie Subs & Salads, Hickory Hams, Houck's, Jitter Beans Sandwich Co, La Cazuela, McDonald's[PLAY], OCharley's, Schlotzsky's Deli, Tanner's, **Waffle House**
Lodg **E:** Comfort Inn, Homestead Inn
ATM **E:** First Market Bank (Wal-Mart), First National Bank, Wal-Mart Supercenter[RX]
W: Bank Of Canton, Etowah
Other **E:** Wal-Mart Supercenter[RX]
W: Belk's, Home Depot, JC Penney's, Pearl Vision Center, Publix
10 **(19)** Ga. 20 E., Canton, Cumming
9 Ga. 140E. Canton, Roswell
Gas **E:** Coastal[*, LP]
8 GA 20, GA 5, GA 120 W, Canton (Lake Alatoona)
7 **(14)** Holly Springs, Canton
Gas **W:** Chevron[*, CW, 24], Racetrac[*, LP, 24]
ATM **W:** Chevron, Kroger Supermarket[RX]
Other **W:** Kroger Supermarket[RX]
6 **(11)** Sixes Rd.
Gas **E:** Chevron[*, D, LP, K, CW, 24]
W: Fina[*, D, LP]
ATM **W:** Fina
5 **(8)** Towne Lake Pkwy., Woodstock
Gas **E:** BP[*, LP, CW], Chevron[*, LP]
Food **E:** Hot Rod Cafe, Waffle House, Waffle King
ATM **E:** BP, Chevron, SunTrust (BP)
4 **(6)** Ga. 92, Wooodstock
Gas **E:** Exxon[*, D, CW], Racetrac[*, 24], Texaco[*, D, LP, CW, 24]
W: Amoco[*, D, CW]
Food **E:** Arby's, Buffalo's Cafe, Canton Donut, Captain D's Seafood, Checkers, Chick-fil-A Dwarf House, China Bay, Dairy Queen, Folks, My Bakery, Ruby Tuesday, Waffle House
W: IHOP, Schlotzsky's Deli, Taco Mac
ATM **E:** Bank of Canton, Exxon, Racetrac
W: Etowah Bank
Other **E:** Pearl Vision Center, Winn Dixie Supermarket[24, RX]
W: Cub Food, Home Depot, Lowe's
3 Bells Fairy Rd.
Gas **W:** Chevron[*, CW], QT[*, 24], Texaco[*, D]
Food **W:** Arby's, Burger King[PLAY], Dunkin Donuts, Ralph's, Subs, Subway, Waffle House
ATM **W:** Chevron, NationsBank, QT
Other **W:** A&P Supermarket[RX], CVS Pharmacy, Eckerd Drugs[RX], Suburban Veterinarian
2 Chastain Rd. , to I-75N (Kennesaw State University)
Gas **E:** BP[*, LP, CW, 24]
1 To I-75, Barrett Pkwy., to US 41
Gas **E:** Chevron[*, LP, CW, 24]
Food **E:** Atlanta Bread Company, Burger King[PLAY], Starbucks Coffee, Waffle House
W: 3 Dollar Cafe, Applebee's, Fuddruckers, Grady's, Happy China II, Honey baked Hams, Ippolito's Italian, McDonald's[PLAY], Mellow Mushroom Pizza, Olive Garden, Red Lobster, Rio Bravo, Schlotzsky's Deli, Shoney's, Starbucks Coffee, Subway, Taco Mac, Waffle House
Lodg **W:** Econolodge, Holiday Inn Express, Red Roof Inn
Med **W:** ✚ Physician's Immediate Med.
ATM **E:** Premier Bank, Sun Trust Bank (Publix)
W: NationsBank, SouthTrust
Other **E:** Drug Emporium, Home Place, Steinmart, Zany Brainy
W: Home Depot, Joshua's Christian Books, Marshall's, TJ Maxx, Toys R Us

↑GEORGIA

Begin I-575

I-580 CALIFORNIA →

EXIT CALIFORNIA

Begin I-580

↓CALIFORNIA

46 Jct. I-580 & I-5 North to Stockton, Sacramento
Exit **(45)** Jct. CA. 132 to Modesto
Exit **(44)** Corral Hollow Rd.
Exit **(43)** Patterson Pass Rd.
Gas **S:** Arco[*]
Exit **(42)** Jct I-205 Tracy & Stockton
Exit **(41)** Grant Line Rd. Byron
Exit **(39)** North Flynn Rd. (Brake Check)
Exit **(38)** North Greenville Rd., Laughlin Rd.
(37) Weigh Station (Westbound)
(37) Weigh Station (Eastbound)
Exit **(36)** Vasco Rd.
FStop **N:** **Shell**[*, CW] **(Gino's)**
Gas **N:** Chevron[*, D, CW]
S: 76[*, D, LP]
Food **N:** **Gino's (Shell FStop)**, **Shell (Gino's)**
S: Blimpie Sub & Salads, Jack-In-The-Box, Virtue's Coffee
ATM **N:** Chevron
Other **S:** C & A Mini Mart & Deli
Exit **(34)** First St., CA 84 ,Springtown Blvd.
Gas **N:** Springtown[*, D]
S: 76[*], 76[*, LP], Chevron[*, 24], Shell[*, CW]
Food **N:** Chinese Buffet, Springtown's Donuts & Bakery
S: Applebee's, Arby's, Baskin Robbins, Big Apple Bagels, Blimpie's Subs, Burger King, Happy Juice, McDonald's, Me N Ed's Pizza, Melo's Pizza & Pasta, Peking Restaurant, Starbucks Coffee, TCBY, Taco Bell, Teriyaki, Togo's
Lodg **N:** Motel 6, **Springtown Motel**
AServ **S:** Chevron[24]
ATM **N:** 7-11 Convenience Store
S: 76, McDonald's, Safeway Grocery, Shell
Other **N:** 7-11 Convenience Store, Palomart, Springtown Express, Springtown Public Golf Course & Coffee Shop
S: Animal Health, Long's Drugs[RX], Mail Boxes Etc, Safeway Grocery, Target
Exit **(33)** N. Livermore Ave., Central Livermore
Exit **(32)** Portola Ave. (Eastbound, Reaccess Westbound Only)
FStop **S:** **Grafco**
Gas **S:** Chevron[*, 24], Shell[*, 24]
Lodg **S:** Palace Motel
AServ **S:** Chevron[24]
Exit **(31)** Collier Canyon Rd. ,Airway Blvd.
Gas **N:** Texaco[*, D, CW, 24]
Food **N:** Baskin Robbins (Texaco), Texaco, Wendy's (Texaco)
S: Beeb's Sports Bar and Grill (Las Positas), Cattlemen's Restaurant
Lodg **N:** Residence Inn
S: Extended Stay America
AServ **N:** Texaco[24]
ATM **N:** Texaco
Other **S:** Airport, Las Positas Public Golf Course
Exit **(30)** El Charro Rd., Fallon Rd.
Exit **(29)** Santa Rita Rd. , Tassajara
Gas **S:** Shell[*, D, CW]
Food **S:** Bagelville, Bakers Square Restaurant, Baskin Robbins, Big Apple Bagels, Blenzers, Boston Market Restaurant, California Burgers, Coffee Company, Cookies By Design, Country Waffles, Doughnuts and Yogurt, El Gallo Taquiera, Erik's Deli Cafe, Kasper's, McDonald's, Nation's Giant Burgers, Pasta Pasta, Pasta Villa, Sassy's Cafe, T.G.I. Friday's, Taco Bell, Wok In
Med **S:** ✚ Hospital
Other **S:** Galaxy Cinemas, Long's Drugs[RX], Mailbox Place, Trader Joe's
Exit **(28)** Hacienda Dr. , Dublin Blvd
Med **S:** ✚ Hospital
Exit **(27)** Hopyard Rd.,Dougherty Rd. (No Trucks Over 3 Tons)
Gas **N:** 76[*, LP, CW], BP[*, D, LP], Shell[*, D, CW, 24]
S: Chevron[*, CW], Shell[*, D, CW]
Food **N:** IHOP, Madame Sun's
S: Arby's, Burger King, Buttercup Pantry Restaurant[24], Denny's, El Molino, Faz Restaurant & Bar (Four Points Hotel), Four Points Hotel Sheraton, Hungery Hunter, In-N-Out Burger, Nation's Giant Burgers, New York Pizza & Deli, Pleasant Asian Cuisine, Taco Bell[24], Yogurt
Lodg **S:** Candlewood, Four Points Hotel Sheraton, Motel 6, Super 8
Other **N:** All Creatures Animal Hospital, Pak N' Save Foods
S: Beverages & More, Home Depot, Kinko's[24]
Exit **(26)** Junction I-680 South to San Jose, North to Sacramento
Exit **(26)** San Ramon Rd. ,Foothill Rd. (No Trucks Over 3 Ton)
Gas **N:** Chevron[*], Shell[*, D]
Food **N:** Burger King[PLAY], Coco's, Country Waffles, Frankie Johnnie & Luigi Too, Starbucks Coffee
S: Black Angus Steakhouse, Masses Sports Cafe
Lodg **N:** Best Western
S: Crown Plaza Hotel, Wyndham Garden Hotel
ATM **N:** Chevron, Shell
S: Bay View Bank, Washington Mutual
Other **N:** Dublin Bowl, Ice Skating Rink
Exit **(25)** Eden Canyon Rd., Palomares Rd.
Exit **(24)** Castro Valley (Westbound,

Bold red print shows RV & Bus parking available or nearby

I-580 CALIFORNIA

EXIT CALIFORNIA

Difficult Reaccess)
Food N: Bodi's Java, Pyzano's Pizzeria, TCBY
Lodg N: EconoLodge
ATM N: TW Market (US Bank), Tracy Federal Bank
Other N: TW Market (US Bank)
Exit **(24)** Crow Canyon Road (Eastbound)
Gas S: 76[*, D, CW], Arco[*], Chevron[*]
Food S: McDonald's
ATM S: Arco
Other S: Quik Stop
Exit **(23)** Strobridge Road
Gas N: 76[*], BP
Food N: Deli & Cafe, Donut Express, McDonald's[PLAY], Wendy's
Lodg N: Holiday Inn Express
AServ N: 76
Med N: ✚Hospital
Other N: Golden Tee
22B Junction I-238 & I-880 (Westbound)
22 CA 238 Hayward
Exit **(21)** 164th Ave. Carolyn St.
Gas N: Beacon[*, D], Chevron[*, 24]
Food N: Uncle Ben's Pizza
Lodg N: Five-Eighty Motel
AServ N: Beacon, Chevron[24]
Exit **(20)** 150th Ave., Fairmont Dr.
Gas S: Arco[*], Shell[*]
Food S: Denny's
AServ S: Shell
Exit **(20)** Benedict Drive
19 Downtown Estudillo Ave. (Difficult Reaccess)
Gas S: Coast
Food S: Bakery, Donuts, Sabino's
Other S: Galvin's Market, Rite Aid Pharmacy[RX]
Exit **(18)** McArthur Blvd., Foothilll Blvd

EXIT CALIFORNIA

(Reaccess Westbound Only)
Exit **(17)** Golf Links Rd., 98th Ave.
Gas N: Shell[*]
S: BP[*]
AServ S: BP
Exit **(16)** Keller Ave.
Exit **(15)** Edwards Ave. (Eastbound)
Exit **(14)** Seminary Ave.
Exit **(14)** Warren Freeway, Berkeley, CA 13
Exit **(13)** McCarther Blvd., High Street (Reaccess Westbound Only)
Gas S: 76[*, 24]
Lodg N: Holiday Motel, Mills Motel, Sage Motel
AServ S: 76[24]
ATM N: 7-11 Convenience Store[*]
Other N: 7-11 Convenience Store
12 High St. (Eastbound, Reaccess Westbound Only)
Gas N: 76[*], Shell[*, 24]
S: BP[*]
Food N: Subway, Yummy Yogurt
S: Dick's Doughnuts
AServ N: 76
S: BP
Other N: High St. Pharmacy[RX], Oakland Veterinary Hospital
S: WalGreens Pharmacy[RX]
Exit **(11)** 35th Ave. (Eastbound, Reaccess Westbound Only)
Gas N: 76[*], Chevron[*], Exxon[*]
S: 76, Quik Stop[*]
Food N: Golden City Restaurant
AServ N: 76
Other N: Farmer Joe's Marketplace
Exit **(9)** Fruitvale Ave., Coolidge Ave.

EXIT CALIFORNIA

(Difficult Reaccess)
8 14th Ave., Park Blvd. (Westbound)
Med S: ✚Hospital
7 Park Blvd.
Gas N: Shell[*]
S: Arco[*]
6 Lake Shore Ave.
Gas N: 76[*], Chevron[*]
S: Chevron[*]
Food N: 4 Star Pizza, Boston Market Restaurant, Ice Creamery, KFC, Kwik Way Dragon, Lakeshore Fountain Restaurant, Starbucks Coffee, Subway, Szechuan, The Burrito Shop, The Lakeside Deli
AServ N: 76, Chevron
Other N: Lucky Grocery Store, Mailbox & General Store, United States Post Office
Exit **(5)** Harrison St. & McArthur Blvd. (Watch one ways)
Gas N: 76[*]
AServ N: 76
4 Broadway & Webster St. (Hwy Patrol, Hospital)
Exit **(3)** Jct. I-980 - I-880 S., Downtown Oakland
Exit **(3)** CA 24E & Berkeley
Exit **(2)** West Street, San Pablo Ave
2 Market St. (Westbound)
1 McCarther Blvd. San Pableo Ave. (Difficult Reaccess)
00 Jct. I-80W San Fransico, I-580 W, & I-80E Sacramento (No Trucks Over 4 Tons)

↑CALIFORNIA

Begin I-580

I-595 FLORIDA

EXIT FLORIDA

Begin I-595

↓FLORIDA

1 SR. 84, SW. 136 Ave. (Westbound)
Gas S: Amoco[*, CW], Chevron[*, LP]
Food S: Antonio's Pizza-Rant, Chevron, China Island Restaurant, Gourmet Bagels, Muffins, and More, McDonald's, Pizza Maniac, Subway, Sushi House Japanese Restaurant
Lodg N: Budgetel Inn, Wellesley Inn
2 Flamingo Rd.
Gas N: Mobil[*, D, CW], Shell[*, D, CW]
S: Cumberland Farms[*]
3 Hiatus Rd. (Long one-way frontage roads)
Gas S: Mobil[*, CW]
Food S: 84 Diner, Deli-Boy Subs, Pizza Hut
4 Nob Hill Rd.
Food S: Burger King[PLAY]
5 Pine Island Rd.
Gas S: Citgo[*], Mobil[*]
Food S: Bellanotte Italian, China Town, Ciro's Deli & Pizzaria, Coffee House, Emerald Restaurant Thai Food, Famous Cafe, Four & Twenty Blackbirds, Garcia's Mexican Food, Indochine, KFC, Kanton-Kanton Chinese Restaurant, Legend's Grill, Little Caesars Pizza, O'live's Ice Cream, P.I. Bagel, Papa Leone's, Pine Yogurt
Lodg S: AmeriSuites (see our ad this page), Wellsley Inn (see our ad this page)
6 University Dr., FL 817
Gas S: Chevron[*, CW, 24]

EXIT FLORIDA

Food N: Bagel Whole, Dominick's Kitchen, IHOP, King China Buffet, McDonald's, Three Guys Italian Cuisine Lounge Pizzeria, Truly Scrumptious
S: Arby's, Burger King[PLAY], Davie Ale House, Dunkin Donuts, I Can't Believe It's Yogurt, Lefty's Wings and Raw Bar, Miami Subs, Papa Roni Pizza, Roadhouse Grill, Subway, Taco Bell, The Shell, Tower Deli, Tower Pizza Restaurant, Vinnie's
Lodg S: Homestead Village
Med N: ✚First Med (Walk-In Med Center)
7 Davie Rd.
Gas S: Racetrac[*]
Food S: Juicy Lucy's, Kenny Roger's Roasters, Shoney's, Subs Miami, Waffle House

EXIT FLORIDA

8 Florida Turnpike, Fl. 91 (Toll)
9AB U.S. 441
10 Fl. 84E.
11AB Junction I-95 N, Ft. Lauderdale, West Palm Beach - 11A, Junction I-95 S, Miami-11B
12A U.S.1, South Dinea
12B International Airport
12C Port Everglades, Fort Lauderdale , U.S. 1 North

↑FLORIDA

Begin I-595

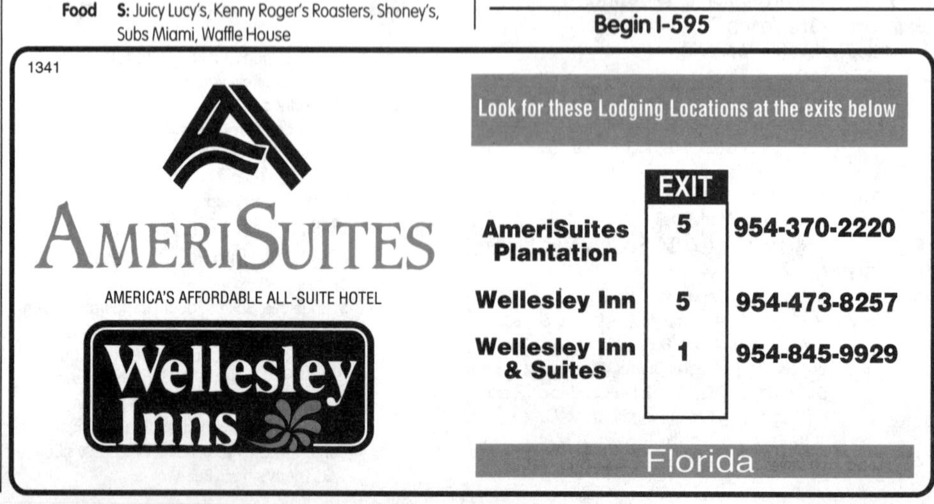

EXIT TEXAS

Begin I-610

↓TEXAS

1A FM 521 Almeda Rd.
FStop I: **Chevron**[*, D, 24]
Gas O: Texaco[*, CW]
1B Fannin St.
Gas I: Conoco
Food O: McDonald's
1C Kirby Dr.
Food I: Restaurant (Sheraton), Shoney's (Shoney's Inn)
O: Joe's Crab Shack, Pappa Sito's Cantina
Lodg I: Days Inn, Sheraton Astrodome, Shoney's Inn
2 US 90 Alt, Buffalo Speedway, S. Main St.
Gas I: Exxon[*], Shell[*]
O: Phillips 66
Food I: Arby's, Bennigan's, Brisket Bar B.Q., Church's Chicken, Denny's, KFC, Main Street Chinese Buffet, Ruchis Taqueria El Rincon De Mexico, Taco Bell, Wendy's
O: Joe's Crab Shack, Steak 'N Egg Kitchen[24], What A Burger[24]
Lodg I: Astro Motor Inn, Howard Johnson
O: 7 Tweety's Diamond Inn, La Quinta Inn, Motel 6, Red Coach Motel, **Super 8**
3 Stella Link Rd.
Gas I: Chevron
O: Conoco[*], Exxon[*, D]
Food I: Domino's Pizza
O: Super Fried Chicken & Taqueria
ATM I: Chevron
Other I: All Cats Veterinary Clinic
O: Stella Link Animal Clinic
4A Braeswood Blvd
Gas I: Chevron[D, CW], Exxon
Food I: Alice's Diner, Boston Market Restaurant, IHOP, McDonald's[PLAY]
O: Austin Coffeehouse, Bandana's Grill, Cafe Express, Doc's Real Italian Ices, Los Tios Mexican Restaurant, Salt Grass Steakhouse, Souper Salad, Starbucks Coffee, Szechuan Empress
ATM I: Bank United, First Prosperity Bank
O: Bank of America, Compass Bank
Other I: Police Station
O: Texas State Optical
4B South Post Oak Rd. (Limited Access Hwy)
5A Beechnut St. (Southbound)
Gas O: Chevron[D, CW]
Food O: Alice's Diner, Bandana's Grill, Boston Market Restaurant, Cafe (Borders), Doc's Real Italian Ices, IHOP, Los Tios Mexican Restaurant, McDonald's, Souper Salad, Starbucks Coffee, Szechuan Empress
ATM O: Bank of America, Compass Bank
Other O: Texas State Optical, The Optical Place
5B Evergreen St., Bellaire Blvd.
6 Bellaire Blvd. (Southbound)
7 Fournace Place, Bissonnet St.
Gas O: Texaco[*, D, CW]
Med O: ✚ Hospital
ATM O: Texas Commerce Bank
8A U.S. 59 South, Victoria; U.S. 59 North, Downtown (Limited Access Hwy)
8B Richmond Ave (Southbound)
Food I: Bayou City's Burger Cafe, Bayou City's Seafood & Pasta, Carmines Big Tomato, Fu's Garden Hunan Cuisine, Luling City Market Bar-B-Que & Bar, Pizza Hut
O: Chinese Cafe, Dimassi's Middle Eastern Cafe, Marie Callender's Restaurant, Smoothie King, Steak & Ale, Subway, The Mason Jar
Lodg I: Courtyard by Marriott, Fairfield Inn by Marriott
ATM O: American Bank, Bank One, Texas Commerce Bank
Other I: Super K Food Store

EXIT TEXAS

O: Sears Optical
8C FM 1093 West Heimer Rd (Northbound)
Gas I: Texaco
O: Shell[*]
Food I: Capt'n Benny's Seafood & Oyster Bar, Le Peep Restaurant, Tokyo Gardens Japanese Restaurant, Westcreek Market & Deli
O: Lunes Uptown Burgers
Lodg I: Red Lion Hotel
9 San Felipe Rd. (Northbound)
Gas I: Exxon[*, D]
Food I: Jack-in-the-Box
Lodg I: Hampton Inn, The Ritz-Carlton
ATM I: Heritage Bank
Other I: Target
9A FM 1093, San Felipe Rd., Westheimer Rd. (Southbound)
Food O: California Pizza Kitchen, Domino's Pizza, Luby's Cafeteria, Rancho Tejas, Subway
Lodg O: Marriott
ATM O: Comerica Bank
9B Post Oak Blvd. (Southbound)
Food O: McDonald's[PLAY], Ninfa's Fine Mexican Food, Willie G's Seafood & Steakhouse
10 Woodway Drive, Memorial Drive
Gas O: Exxon[*, D], Shell[D, CW]
Food O: Swiss Chalet Restaurant
Lodg O: Omni Hotel
Other O: Houston Mounted Police Station
11A I-10 West, San Antonio; I-10 East, Downtown
11B Katy Rd. (Southbound)
12 W. 18th St., Hempstead Rd
Food I: Tea's Bar-B-Q & Broiler, What A Burger
O: Demeris Bar-B-Q
13B U.S. 290 W. Austin (Left Exit Northbound)
13C W. TC Jester Blvd. & E. TC Jester Blvd.
Gas I: Phillips 66[*, D, CW]
O: Chevron[CW], Texaco[*]
Food O: Antone's, Atchafalaya River Cafe, Baskin Robbins, Denny's, Golden Gate, Supreme Sandwiches
Lodg O: Courtyard by Marriott
14 Ella Blvd
Gas I: Shell[*, CW]
O: Exxon[*], Shell[*], Texaco[CW] (Dr. Gleem Car Wash)
Food I: Tecate Mexican Restaurant, Thomas Bar-B-Q
O: Burger King[PLAY], KFC, McDonald's[PLAY], Popeye's Chicken, Taco Bell, Wok Buffet
Med I: ✚ Memorial Hospital Northwest
ATM I: Bank One
Other I: Cunningham Pharmacy
15 Spur 261, North Durham Dr., North Shepherd Dr.
Gas I: Chevron[*, D, CW, 24], Mobil[*], Shell[*], Texaco
O: Texaco
Food I: What A Burger[24]
O: Gabby's Genuine Barbecue, Mi Sombrero, Sonic, Taco Cabana
ATM I: Mobil, Shell
Other O: Sunny's Grocery Store
16 N. Main St., Yale St.
Gas I: Mobil[*], Shell[*, CW], Shop & Save[*]
Food I: Church's Chicken
O: Bar-B-Que Plate Lunch
ATM I: Mobil, Shell
Other I: Sunset Heights Food Market, Wing Fong Food Market
17A Airline Drive (Eastbound)
Gas I: Mobil[*, D], Texaco[*, D]
Food I: Connie's Market Seafood, Golden Seafood House, Jack-in-the-Box
Lodg I: Fiesta Inn Motel, **Western Inn Motel**
Other I: Farmer's Market
17B I-45 North, Dallas (Left Exit Eastbound)

EXIT TEXAS

17C I-45 Downtown (Left Exit Westbound)
18 Irvington Blvd., Fulton Dr.
Gas I: Texaco[*, 24]
O: Chevron[CW, 24]
Food O: Speedy's Burgers
ATM I: Stop N Go, Texaco
O: Chevron
Other O: Lindale Grocery
19A Hardy Street, Elysian Street
19B North Hardy Toll Rd.
20AB 20A - US 59 North, Cleveland 20B - US 59 South, Downtown
20C Hirsch Rd. (Westbound)
21 Lockwood Dr., Hirsch Rd.
Gas I: Conoco[*, D]
O: Chevron[*, CW, 24], Exxon, Gas[*], Hopcus Mini Mart[*]
Food I: Snowflake Donut
O: Burger King, C N Seafood Market & Restaurant, Church's Chicken, Popeye's Chicken, Tasty Fast Foods, Triple J's Smokehouse Bar-B-Q
Other I: B. B. Pharmacy, C & J Supermarkets Co. of Houston
22 Homestead Rd
FStop O: **Texaco**[*, D]
Food O: What A Burger
TServ I: **Goodyear Tire & Auto, Houston Peterbilt Inc., Lone Star GMC Trucks**
O: **Performance Kenworth, Western Star Trucks**
23A Kirkpatrick Blvd
TServ I: **Gulf Coast Truck & Trailor**
O: **Al Tucker Trailors, Inc.**
23B N. Wayside Dr., Liberty Rd.
Gas O: Exxon[*, 24]
24A U.S. 90 E. McCarty Dr., Wallisville Rd.
TStop O: **A-1 Truck Stop (Phillips 66)**
FStop I: **Texaco**[*, D]
Gas O: Chevron[*]
Food O: **Luby's Cafeteria (A-1 Truck Stop)**, Wendy's
TServ I: **Olympic International Trucks Inc.**
ATM I: **Texaco**
O: Texas Commerce Bank
24B Wallisville (Westbound)
FStop O: **Mobil**[*]
Gas O: Texaco[*, D, CW]
Food O: **McDonald's**[PLAY]
ATM O: Pinemont Bank
25 Gellhorn Drive (Eastbound)
TServ I: **CCC Truck Parts Specialists, Houston Freightliner Inc.**
Med I: ✚ Hospital
26A I-10 West, Downtown, I-10 East, Beaumont
26B Market St. (Northbound)
TStop I: **Fu-Kim Restaurant & Truck Stop**[*, 24]
Food I: **Tiger Sports Bar (Fu-Kim TS)**
ATM I: **Fu-Kim TS**
27 Turning Basin Drive (Southbound)
28 Clinton Dr.
Gas O: Mobil[*, D]
29 Port of Houston Main Entrance
30A Manchester St. (Southbound, Reaccess Northbound Only)
Other O: Moonlight Grocery
30B East Tex 225, Pasadena, La Porte, Deer Park (San Jacinto Battlepark)
30C Texas 225 W., Lawndale Ave. (Limited Access Hwy)
30D Lawndale Ave. (Northbound)
31 Broadway Blvd.
Gas I: Conoco[*, D]
O: Diamond Shamrock[*, D, 24], Texaco[*, D]
Food I: Mexico Tipico
O: Ostioneria Villa del Sol, Taqueria Reyes
ATM I: Conoco
O: Diamond Shamrock
32A I-45 South Galveston
32B I-45 North Downtown, TX 35 South,

EXIT	TEXAS
	Alvin
33	S Rd. & Woodridge Dr. (Phones)
Gas	**O:** Phillips 66, Shell[*, CW]
Food	**I:** Piccadilly Cafeteria, Wendy's
	O: Frank's Grill, KFC, Spanky's Pizza, Pasta, Salads, Burgers, What A Burger
ATM	**I:** Savings of America, Texas Commerce Bank
34A	Long Dr., S. Wayside Dr.
Gas	**I:** Chevron, Exxon[*], Texaco[*, 24]
	O: Coastal[*, D], Conoco[*], Diamond Shamrock[*]
Food	**I:** **Wendy's**
ATM	**I:** Texaco
	O: Conoco, Diamond Shamrock
35	Crestmont St., M L King Blvd, Mykawa Rd.
FStop	**I:** **Mobil**[*, D]
Gas	**I:** Conoco[*, D]
Food	**I:** Burger King[PLAY]
	O: Best Seafood Market
36A	Calais Rd., Holmes Rd., FM 865, Cullen Blvd., M L King Blvd
Gas	**O:** 5-11 Convenient Store[*, D]
36B	FM 865, Cullen Blvd (Westbound)
Gas	**O:** Chevron[24], Diamond Shamrock[*, 24], Mobil[*]
Food	**O:** Tri's Bar-B-Que (Diamond Shamrock)
Lodg	**I:** Crystal Inn
	O: Crown Plaza Inn, Cullen Inn
37	Scott Street
Gas	**I:** Shell[*], Texaco[*]
Food	**I:** Bunky's Cafe, Pappa's Bar-B-Q, Seafood King
Lodg	**I:** Motel
Other	**I:** Grocery Save & Save
38A	TX 288 N, Downtown, Zoo TX 288 S. Lake Jackson, Freeport (Limited Access Highway)
38C	S. TX 288 Lake Jackson Freeport
39	Court Of Houston. Main Entrance

↑ TEXAS

Begin I-610

I-635 TEXAS →

EXIT	TEXAS
	Begin I-635

↓ TEXAS

EXIT	TEXAS
35A	TX121S, Dallas - Ft.Worth Airport, TX121N, Bethel Rd.
35	Royal Lane
34	Freeport Pkwy
33	Belt Line Rd.
31	MacArthur Blvd.
30	TX161S, Valley View Ln
29	Luna Rd.
27BC	I-35E West, Dallas - Ft.Worth Airport. I-35E North, Denton
27A	Denton Drive, Harry Hines Blvd.
Lodg	**N:** Holiday Inn Select
	S: Motel 6
Other	**S:** Home Depot
25	Webb Chaple Rd., Josey Lane
Gas	**N:** Shell[*, CW]
	S: Chevron[*], Exxon[*, D], Shell[CW], Texaco[*, D]
Food	**S:** 7-11 & Doughnuts, Alvin Ord's Sandwich Shop, Carribean Grill, Chinese Garden, Ci Ci's Pizza, Dickey's BBQ Pit, El Phoenix, Golden Corral Family Steakhouse, Grandy's, Hall's Chicken, Happy Years, India Oven, International House of Pancakes, Josey's Hamburgers and Subs, Long John Silver, Mrs. Baird's Bakery Outlet, Popeye's Chicken, Surrey Cafe, Taco Cabana, Two Guys From Italy, Whataburger
Lodg	**S:** Courtyard by Marriott
Med	**N:** ✚ RHD Memorial Medical Center
ATM	**N:** Shell
	S: Exxon, Get n Go Food Store, Pulse
Other	**S:** 7-11 & Doughnuts, All Import Auto Parts, Dallas Books Christian Supply, Get n Go Food Store, Pearl Vision Center
24	Marsh Lane
23	Midway Rd, Welch Rd
Gas	**N:** Exxon[*, D, CW]
	S: Mobil[*, D, CW]
Food	**N:** Luby's Cafeteria, Owens, Taco Bell, Vincent's Seafoods, Wal-Mart[RX] (MacDonald's), Wendy's
	S: Cappuccino Restaurant, Denny's, Domino's Pizza, Fu-Fu China, Grandy's, Nelson's Doughnut Shop, Subway
Lodg	**N:** Renaissance Hotel
ATM	**N:** Teachers Federal Credit Unionn
Other	**N:** Wal-Mart[RX] (MacDonald's)
	S: Drug Emporium[RX], Midway Road Animal Clinic
22CD	Toll Way (Toll)
Lodg	**E:** Hilton, The Westin Hotel
22B	Dallas Parkway, Inwood Rd, Welsh Rd.
Other	**E:** Kinko's
22A	Montfort Dr.

1390

Texas • Exit 19A • 972-458-1224

1134

Best Western
Exit 23 • Dallas
972-458-2626
800-524-1038

Newly Remodeled,
Oversized Suites with Full Kitchens
Free Full American Buffet Breakfast
Outdoor Pool/Jacuzzi
Managers Reception Twice Weekly

I-635, exit Preston Rd. Take service road 1 block east.

TEXAS ▪ I-635 ▪ EXIT 23

PLANO
700 East Central Parkway
Plano, Texas 75074
972-881-1881
800-HOLIDAY

• 161 guest rooms • Kids Eat Free
• NEW! Pin & Pockets Electronic Game Room with golf simulator, video games and billards
• Bristol's Restaurant • Outdoor Pool and Spa
• In-room hairdryers • Convenient to SouthFork Ranch, historic Plano and Collin Creek Mall

1462

EXIT	TEXAS
Gas	**E:** Shell[*, CW, 24]
Food	**E:** Brother's Pizza, Burger King[24], China Gate Buffet, Chuck E Cheese's Pizza, McDonald's[PLAY]
Other	**E:** Eagle Postal Center, Pearl Vision Center, Target
21	TX289, Preston Rd.
Gas	**E:** Texaco[*, CW]
	W: Exxon[D], Mobil[*]
Food	**E:** Candella, Denny's, Mona Luna, Popeye's Chicken, Red Peppers Chinese Restaurant
	W: Cafe Greek, Chili's, Hunan Wok, India Palace, Mario & Alberto, Souper Salad
Lodg	**E:** Teracotta Inn, Best Western (see our ad this page)
AServ	**W:** Exxon
ATM	**W:** Guarantee Federal Bank, Mobil, North Dallas Bank
Other	**E:** Boat US Marine Center, Booksale
	W: Fox Photo Lab
20	Hillcrest Rd.
19B	US75S, Coit Rd.
Gas	**E:** Mobil[*, CW]
	W: Fina
Food	**E:** Arby's, Blimpie Subs & Salads, Denny's, El-Pollo-Feliz, Fuji-Ya, Harvey Hotel (Remington's Restaurant), McDonald's[PLAY], Quizno's Classic Subs
	W: Benihana Steak and Seafood, Jack In The Box
Lodg	**E:** Crown Plaza Hotel Suites, Harvey Hotel (Remington's Restaurant), Wyndham Gardens Hotel, AmeriSuites (see our ad this page)
	W: Radisson Hotel, Sheraton Hotel
ATM	**W:** Chase Bank, Fina
19A	Richardson Plano, Sherman, US175
Gas	**E:** Citgo[*] (7-11 Convenience Store)
Food	**E:** Cafe China Super Buffet
Lodg	**E:** Embassy Suites, Holiday Inn Express (see our ad this page), Quality Suites, Wyndham Garden Hotel
ATM	**E:** Dallas Teachers Credit Union
18B	Floyd Rd
18A	Greenville Ave.
Gas	**W:** Exxon[*, CW]
Food	**W:** Cafe Royal Meditteranean Food, Cheddar's, Ci Ci's Pizza, Don Pablo's Mexican, Highpoint Restaurant & Club, JJ's Old Fashioned Hamburgers, Matsu Japanese Restaurant, Olive Garden, Outback Steakhouse, Red Lobster, Sushi Ichiban
Lodg	**W:** Fairfield Inn, Hawthorne Suites Limited, Homegate Studios and Suites, Homewood Suites
Other	**W:** Emergency Animal Clinic, US Post Office
17	Forest Lane, Abrams Rd.

Bold red print shows RV & Bus parking available or nearby

EXIT		TEXAS
	Gas	**E:** Citgo[*], Mobile[*], Texaco[*] **W:** Chevron[*, CW], Texaco[*]
	Food	**E:** Jack In The Box, Pizza Inn, Steak and Ale, Wok Express **W:** Colter's BBQ, Howard Johnson's Inn (Tic Tac Grill), KFC, Kazy's Gourmet, Long John Silver, McDonald's, Royal Inn (Kruathai Kitchen), Subway, Taco Bell, Wendy's, Whataburger, Wok In And Out
	Lodg	**W:** Howard Johnson's Inn (Tic Tac Grill), Royal Inn (Kruathai Kitchen), Suburban Lodge
	AServ	**E:** Texaco
	ATM	**E:** Bank One **W:** Abram's Center National Bank, Bank of America, Chevron, Texaco, Tom Thumb Grocery[RX]
	Other	**W:** Forest Villa Animal Clinic, Tom Thumb Grocery[RX]
16		**Skillman St., Audelia Rd.**
	Gas	**W:** Diamond Shamrock[*, 24] (NationsBank)
	Food	**E:** Arby's, Burger King, Burger Street, Chili's, Dickey's Barbeque Pit, Doughnuts, International House of Pancakes, Le Peep, Long's Garden Chinese Restaurant, Madam Wang's China Buffet, Mother Mesquite's, Mr. Gattis, Seashells and Stuff, Souper Salad, Subway, Texas Chicken, Wok and Go, Yali's Seafood and Grill **W:** Blimpie Subs & Salads, Boston Market Restaurant, Ci Ci's Pizza, Denny's, El Phoenix, Greenhouse Deli, Skillman's Wok, TCBY, Taco Bueno, Tom Thumb Grocery Store[24, RX]
	Lodg	**E:** Homestead Village Efficiencies
	RVCamp	**W:** **Foretravel (see our ad this page)**
	ATM	**W:** Compass Bank, Diamond Shamrock (NationsBank), Tom Thumb Grocery Store
	Other	**W:** Cat Hospital, Mailboxes Etc., Pearl Vision, Tom Thumb Grocery Store[RX]
14		**Plano Rd**
	Gas	**W:** Fina[*], Texaco/U-Haul Distributor[D]
	Food	**E:** Sub Shop **W:** BoBo China, Grill and Deli Stop
	Lodg	**W:** Sleep Inn
	AServ	**W:** Texaco/U-Haul Distributor
13		**Jupiter Rd, Kingsley Rd**
	Gas	**E:** Chevron[*, CW], Texaco[*, D] **W:** Diamond Shamrock[*], Exxon[*, CW], Fina[*]
	Food	**E:** Texaco, Waffle House **W:** Doughnuts, Exxon
	Lodg	**E:** Comfort Inn (see our ad this page) **W:** Holiday Inn
	ATM	**E:** Chevron, Texaco **W:** Diamond Shamrock
11B		**Northwest Hwy, Shiloh Road**
	Gas	**E:** Citgo[*], Racetrac[*, 24] **W:** Chevron[*]
	Food	**E:** Arby's, Braum's, Chili's, Chinese Buffet, Colter's BBQ, Denny's, Ebenezer's Eating and Gathering Establishment, ElChico, Grandy's, KFC, Pepe's and Mito's Mexican Cafe, Steak & Ale, Superstar Restaurant and Buffet **W:** Bennigan's, Taco Cabana[24]
	Lodg	**E:** La Quinta Inn, Ramada Limited **W:** Hampton Inn
	ATM	**E:** Citgo, Racetrac **W:** Chevron
	Other	**E:** Morgan RV's Sales, Service, and Parts, Playzone (for kids), Showplace Lanes Bowling Alley
11A		**Centerville Rd., Ferguson Rd.**
	Gas	**E:** Shell[*, CW], Texaco[*, D] **W:** Citgo[*], Mobil[*, CW]
	Food	**E:** Chuch E. Cheese's, General Pao Chinese Buffet, International House of Pancakes, Jack-In-The-Box, Kroger[RX], McDonald's, Wafle House, Wendy's
	Lodg	**E:** Best Western
	AServ	**E:** Texaco
	ATM	**E:** Bank One, First Federal **W:** Mobil
	Other	**E:** Drug Emporium[RX], Fast Stop Food Store, Kroger[RX], **Target** **W:** McKinney Animal Clinic
9A		**Oates Dr.**
	Gas	**E:** Diamond Shamrock[*, CW, 24] **W:** Citgo[*], Exxon[*, CW], Mobil[*, CW]
	Food	**E:** Albertson's Grocery[LP, 24, RX], Burger King, Pizza Hut **W:** **Cracker Barrel**, Hunan Dragon Chinese, The Doughnut Palace
	ATM	**E:** Diamond Shamrock **W:** Citgo, Exxon, Mobil
	Other	**E:** Albertson's Grocery[RX], Animal Hospital, Eckerd Drugs[RX], Publishers Closeout Books
8AB		**I-30W Dallas, I-30E Texarkana**
7		**Town East Blvd.**
	Gas	**W:** Chevron[*, 24], Shell[*, CW]
	Food	**E:** Chili's, Grady's Bar & Grill, Owens, Saltgrass Steakhouse, Tia's Tex Mex **W:** Arby's, Catdaddy's, China First, Eggroll Mania, El Phoenix, Grandy's, Hooters, Jack In The Box, Miami Subs Grill and Baskin Robbins, Olive Garden, Outback Steakhouse, Razzoo's Cajun Cafe, Red Lobster, Sports City Cafe, Steak and Ale, TGI Fridays, Tony Roma's, Wendy's
	Lodg	**W:** Fairfield Inn
	AServ	**W:** Shell
	ATM	**W:** Chevron
	Other	**E:** General Cinemas, Pearl Vision Center **W:** Celebration Station (for kids), Service Merchandise, Texas Drug Warehouse[RX], Toys R Us
6AB		**US80W Dallas, I-80E Terrell (Difficult Reaccess)**
5		**Gross Rd.**
	Gas	**E:** Diamond Shamrock[*, D, CW], Phillips 66[*], Racetrac[*]
	Food	**E:** Dairy Queen, Denny's, Joe's Crab Shack, Martinez Restaurant **W:** Hoff Brau Steaks
	Lodg	**E:** Comfort Inn, Spanish Trails Inn
	ATM	**E:** Diamond Shamrock, Phillips 66 **W:** Dallas Teachers Credit Union, Town Bank
4		**TX352, Military Parkway, Scyene Rd**
	Gas	**W:** 1 Stop, Chevron[*, CW], Fina[*], Mobile[*], The Working Mans Friend[D]
	Food	**W:** Dairy Queen, Giff's Hamburgers, **International House of Pancakes**, Jack-In-The-Box, McDonald's[PLAY], Pizza Hut, Subway, Taco Bell, Traildust Steakhouse, Waffle House, What A Burger
	Lodg	**W:** **Super 8**
	AServ	**W:** Mobile
	ATM	**W:** Chevron, Mobile
	Other	**W:** Ken's Auto Parts
3		**Bruton Road**
	Gas	**E:** Mobil[*]
	ATM	**E:** Mobil
2		**Lake June Rd.**
	Gas	**E:** Exxon[*, CW] **W:** Citgo[*], Total[*, 24]
	Food	**W:** Arby's, Luby's Cafeteria, Subway
	Other	**E:** Boat Supply and Covers **W:** LBJ Animal Clinic, **Walmart**[RX]
1B		**Elam Road**
	Gas	**E:** Shell[*, CW] **W:** Texaco[*, D, CW]
	Food	**E:** Captain D's Seafood, KFC, Pine Tree Garden Chinese Restaurant, Sonic **W:** Burger King[PLAY], Burger Street, Grandy's, K-Mart[RX] (Little Ceaser's Pizza, Penske Auto Service), McDonald's, Pizza Hut, Pizza Inn, Taco Bell, Taco Bueno
	AServ	**W:** K-Mart (Little Ceaser's Pizza, Penske Auto Service)
	ATM	**E:** Gateway Bank, Shell
	Other	**W:** Chief Auto Parts, Eckerd Pharmacy[RX] (Drive Through Pharmacy), K-Mart[RX] (Little Ceaser's Pizza, Penske Auto Service), Kroger Supermarket[RX]
1A		**Seagoville Rd**

↑TEXAS

Begin I-635

1053

MOTORHOME

SALES • SERVICE • PARTS

Directions: I-635 (LBJ Fwy) exit #16 (Skillman/Audelia). Go 2 miles East on Skillman (becomes Forest Lane) to 4313 Forest Lane.

4213 Forest Lane • Garland, TX 75042

800.666.9977

Comfort Inn

214-340-3501

Indoor Heated Pool & Jacuzzi

Fitness Room & sauna

King Size Beds

HBO, Movies, ESPN Sports, CNN News

Free Continental Breakfast

Complimentary USA Today

Jacuzzi & Kitchenette Suites

Truck/Large Vehicle Parking

Coin Laundry • Meeting Rooms

Special Rates for Tour Groups

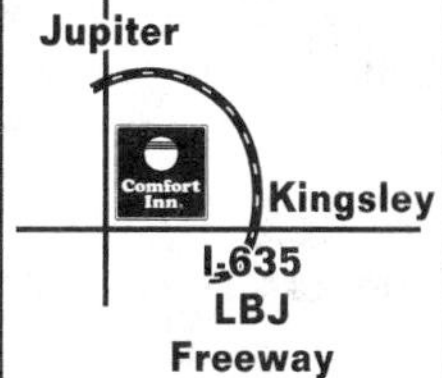

I-635 (LBJ) At Jupiter/ Kingsley Rd.

3536 W. KINGSLEY RD GARLAND TEXAS

1710

TEXAS • I-635 • EXIT 13

I-640 TENNESSEE

EXIT TENNESSEE

Begin I-640

↓TENNESSEE

0 Junction I-40, Nashville, US 25, Asheville

8 Washington Pike, Mall Rd South, Millertown Pike

- **Gas** S: Conoco[*]
- **Food** N: McDonald's
  S: Little Caesars Pizza, Subway
- **AServ** N: Wal-Mart
- **Med** S: ✚St Mary's East Towne, ✚Walk In Clinic
- **ATM** S: First American[24], First Tennessee Bank
- **Other** N: Farmer's Market, Wal-Mart

6 US 441, Broadway

- **Gas** N: Amoco[*], Chevron[*], Conoco[*], Phillips 66[*, CW], Pilot[*, LP]
- **Food** N: Arby's, Cantoon Mexican, Ci Ci's Pizza, Fazoli's Italian Food, Hardee's, Krispy Kreme Doughnuts, Long John Silver, Papa John's Pizza, Quincy's Family Steakhouse, Ruby Tuesday, Shoney's, Subway, Taco Bell
  S: Buddy's Bar-B-Q, Hobo's Family Style Restaurant, Louis' Inn
- **ATM** N: Pilot, SunTrust Bank
  S: Food City
- **Other** S: Food City, K-Mart, Northgate Plaza

3 N I-75, S I-275, Knoxville, Lexington

3B US 25 W, North Gap Rd, Clinton (Eastbound)

1 TN 62, Western Ave

- **Gas** N: Racetrac[*], Texaco[*, D]
  S: Shell[D] (Wrecker Service)
- **Food** N: Baskin Robbins, Central Park Hamburgers, KFC, Little Caesars Pizza, Long John Silver, McDonald's[PLAY], Nixon's Deli, Panda Chinese Restaurant, Shoney's, Subway, Taco Bell, Wendy's
  S: Dad's Donuts & Delights, Domino's Pizza, Hardee's, Krystal, Tracy's Family Restaurant
- **AServ** S: Shell (Wrecker Service)
- **ATM** N: First Tennesse Bank, Kroger Supermarket[24], Racetrac
  S: First Tennessee Bank
- **Other** N: Kroger Supermarket, WalGreens Pharmacy
  S: US Post Office

↑TENNESSEE

Begin I-640

I-675 OHIO

EXIT OHIO

Begin I-675

↓OHIO

26AB I-70

24 OH 444, Fairborn, Wpfab Areas A & C, Enon

22 OH 235, Fairborn, Xenia

- **Other** E: Green County's Career Center

20 Dayton, Yellow Springs Rd.

17 North Fairfield Rd.

- **Gas** E: BP[*, CW]
  W: Speedway[*]
- **Food** E: Bagel Cafe, Boston Market Restaurant, Burger King, Chili's, Cooker's Bar & Grill, Don Pablo's Mexican Restaurant, McDonald's (Wal-Mart), Olive Garden, Red Lobster, Skyline Chili, Steak 'N Shake, T.G.I. Friday's, Wal-Mart[24, RX]
  W: Arby's, Blimpie Subs & Salads, Bob Evan's Restaurant, Chi-Chi's Mexican Restaurant, Cold Beer & Burgers, Greek Isle Deli, Holiday Inn, Kim's Chinese, McDonald's, Taco Bell, The Bagel Shoppe
- **Lodg** W: Fairfield Inn, Hampton Inn, Holiday Inn, Homewood Suites, Red Roof Inn
- **AServ** E: Wal-Mart[24]
- **ATM** E: Star Bank
  W: National City Bank, National City Bank
- **Other** E: Beaver Creek Golf Club, Drug Emporium[RX], Lowe's, Wal-Mart[RX]
  W: Kinko's

16 Grange Hall Road (Southbound, Reaccess Northbound Only)

- **Gas** W: Meijer[*, D, LP], SuperAmerica[*, LP]
- **Food** W: Hardee's, Tuty's Cocktail Lounge, Waffle House
- **ATM** W: National City Bank
- **Other** W: Meijer[24]

15 Wright Patterson Airforce Base Area B, Col. Glenn Hwy

13AB Dayton, Xenia, US 35, Riverside, Beaver Creek

10 Dorothy Ln., Indian Ripple Rd., Kettering

- **Gas** W: BP[*, D, LP]
- **Food** W: Bill Knapp's Restaurant, Burger King, Fulmer Deli & Bakery[24], Pizza Hut
- **Other** W: Christian Rights Bookstore, Fulmer Deli & Bakery, K-Mart[RX]

7 Wilmington Pike, Bellbrook

- **Gas** E: BP[*, CW], Shell[*, CW]
  W: SuperAmerica[*]
- **Food** E: BW-3 Grill & Bar, Beijing Garden Chinese, Burger King, Fazoli's Italian Food, Frisch's Big Boy, McDonald's[PLAY], Mr. Ching's, Pizza Hut, Ponderosa Steakhouse, Subway, Taco Bell, Wendy's
  W: Bob Evan's Restaurant
- **AServ** E: Wal-Mart[24, RX]
- **ATM** E: Bank One, Cub Foods Supermarket[24, RX], National City Bank
  W: SuperAmerica
- **Other** E: Cub Foods Supermarket[RX], Drug Emporium[RX], Mail Boxes Etc., Wal-Mart[RX]

Bill Knapp's RESTAURANT
Open daily at 11:00 am
Bill Knapp's is a casual, full service family restaurant where Motorcoaches are always welcome.
1799
Over 50 locations throughout: Michigan • Ohio • Indiana
937-433-4455 Dayton • 937-429-1020 Dayton
OHIO • I-675 • EXIT 4/10

4AB OH 48, Kettering, Centerville

- **Food** E: Cookies By Design, Double Day's Grill and Tavern, Honey Baked Hams, My Favorite Muffin & Bagel, Outback Steakhouse, Schlotzsky's Deli, Super Subby's, TCBY, Thirsty Dog Brewing Co. & Restaurant, Truffles Cafe
  W: **Bill Knapp's Restaurant (see our ad this page)**
- **ATM** W: Huntington Bank
- **Other** E: Laser Quest, Pearl Vision Center, Showcase Cinemas, Waccamaw

2 Miamisburg, Centerville , OH 725

- **Gas** E: BP[*]
- **Food** E: Camps Americana, Carvers Steaks and Chops, Cooker, J Alexanders Restaurant, Long John Silver, McDonald's, Old Country Buffet, The Chop House
  W: Baskin Robbins, Bravo Italian Kitchen, Buffet King, O'Charley's, T.G.I. Friday's
- **Lodg** E: Hampton Inn
  W: Quality Inn
- **Med** W: ✚Hospital
- **ATM** E: BP, Bank One, Key Bank, National City Bank
  W: Citizens Federal
- **Other** E: Books-A-Million, Kinko's[24]
  W: Books Half Price Records & Magazines, Borders Books & Music, Burlington Coat Factory, K-Mart[RX], Value City

↑OHIO

Begin I-675

Bold red print shows RV & Bus parking available or nearby

EXIT CALIFORNIA

Begin I-680

↓CALIFORNIA

58 Cordelia Rd., GreenValley Rd.
Exit **(57)** Gold Hill Rd.
Gas **W:** Cheaper[*, D]
Exit **(56)** Marshview Rd.
Exit **(55)** Parish Rd.
Exit **(54)** Lake Herman Rd., Vista Point
FStop **W:** **Shell**[*, CW, PLAY]
Food **W:** Carl Jr's Hamburgers (Shell), **Shell**[PLAY], TCBY (Shell)
ATM **W:** **Shell**
Exit **(54)** Industrial Park (Southbound, Reaccess Northbound Only)
53 Bayshore Rd.
Exit **(52)** I-780W, Benicia, Vallejo (Toll)
Exit **(51)** Marina Vista, Martinez
50B Contra Costa Blvd. (Southbound)
Gas **W:** 76, Exxon, Shell[*, D, CW]
Food **W:** Burger King, Carrows, Denny's, KFC, McDonald's, The Velvet Turtle
Other **W:** K-Mart, Target
Exit **(50)** Pacheco Blvd. (Difficult Reaccess)
FStop **W:** **Shell**[*, D, 24]
Gas **W:** 76[*, LP]
Exit **(49)** W. CA 4, Richmond
Exit **(48)** CA 4, Pittsburg, Antioch
Exit **(47)** Concord Ave., Pacheco
Gas **W:** 76[*], Exxon[*], Shell[*, D, CW, 24]
Food **E:** Marie Callender's Restaurant
W: Barnes & Noble, Carrow's Restaurant, Denny's, KFC, Mama Mias Pizzeria, McDonald's[PLAY], Mediterranean City Cafe, Mi Casita, Round Table Pizza, Taco Bell
Lodg **E:** Holiday Inn, Sheraton
AServ **W:** Exxon
Other **E:** United States Post Office
W: Barnes & Noble, K-Mart, Kinko's[24], Target
Exit **(46)** Willow Pass Rd., Taylor Blvd
Food **E:** 360 Gourmet Burritos, Claim Jumper, Denny's, El Torito, Fuddruckers, Grassini (Hilton), Hilton (Grassini), Hungry Hunter, Jungle Cafe, Red Lobster, Sizzler Steak House, Tony Roma's
Lodg **E:** Hilton (Grassini)
ATM **E:** Bank Of The West, Bay View Bank
W: ATM, Bank Of America
Other **E:** Enterprise Rent-a-Car, Water World Fun Park
Exit **(46)** Gregory Lane, Monument Blvd.
Gas **E:** Chevron[*, D, CW]
Food **E:** Peking Blake
W: Baskin Robbins, Boston Market Restaurant, Chinese Restaurant, Lyon's Restaurant, Nations Giant Burger, Starbucks Coffee, The Kabob's House, The Plaza Cafe, Tsing Tao
Lodg **W:** Courtyard by Marriott, Sun Valley Inn Motel
ATM **W:** Bank of America, Cal Fed, Safeway Grocery, Washington Mutual
Other **W:** Fast & Easy Foodstore, Pack N Mail, Payless Drugs[RX], Pearl Vision Center, Safeway Grocery, United States Post Office
45 Concord, Pittsburg, CA 242
44 Contra Costa Blvd.
Gas **E:** Chevron[*, D, LP, CW]
Food **E:** Ming Wah
W: Boston Market Restaurant, Confetti Restaurant, Lyons
Lodg **W:** Marriott, Sunvalley Inn
ATM **W:** Great Western Bank
Other **W:** Payless Drugs
Exit **(43)** Oak Park Blvd., Geary Rd
Gas **W:** Chevron[*, D], Shell[*, D]

EXIT CALIFORNIA

Food **W:** Beverages & More, Burger King, Cafe & Bakery, Golden City Restaurant, Magic Garlic Restaurant, Pasta, Sunnyvale Market & Deli, Wendy's
Lodg **E:** Embassy Suites
AServ **W:** Chevron
ATM **W:** US Bank
Exit **(42)** North Main St., Walnut Creek
Gas **E:** Chevron[*]
W: 76[*, D, 24]
Food **E:** Baja Grill, Black Diamond Restaurant, Chevron, Jack-In-The-Box, Minerva's Cottage, Subway (Chevron), Taco Bell
W: Domino's Pizza
Lodg **E:** Marriott, Motel 6
ATM **W:** 7-11 Convenience Store
Other **E:** Enterprise Rent-a-Car
W: 7-11 Convenience Store
41 Ygnacio Valley Rd. (Reaccess Southbound Only)
Gas **E:** Shell[D, 24]
Med **E:** ✚ Hospital
Exit **(40)** Junction CA 24, Oakland, Lafayette (Difficult Reaccess)
Food **E:** Johnny Love's
40 South Main Street
Food **E:** Moonrise Restaurant, The Original Hick'ry Pit
Med **E:** ✚ Hospital
Exit **(39)** Livorno Rd.
Exit **(38)** Stone Valley Rd.
Gas **W:** Chevron[*, D], Shell[*, D, CW]
Food **W:** Alamo Cafe, Alamo Palace, Bagel St. Cafe, Baskin Robbins, Chinese Restaurant, Don Jose's Mexican Restaurant, Drake Donuts, Espresso To Go, Forli Restaurante & Bar, Hi Tech Burrito, Jitr Thai, Kona Cafe, La Morinda Pizza, Loard's Ice Cream, Pasta Stop, Round Table Pizza, Starbucks Coffee, Taco Bell, The Brass Bear Deli, The Whole Grain Co.
AServ **W:** Chevron
ATM **W:** 7-11 Convenience Store, Bank Of America, Safeway Grocery, Shell, Wells Fargo Bank, World Savings Bank
Other **W:** 7-11 Convenience Store, Alamo Animal Hospital, Alamo Laundromat, Mail Boxes Etc., Post Office, Safeway Grocery, Thrifty Drug & Discounts[RX]
Exit **(37)** El Pintado Rd.
Exit **(37)** El Cerro Blvd.
Exit **(36)** Diablo Rd. , Danville
Gas **E:** 76[*, LP, 24]
Food **E:** Christy's Donuts, Sun's Chinese Cuisine, Taco Bell
W: CoCo's
AServ **E:** 76[24]
ATM **E:** Lucky (Grocery)
W: Bank of the West, US Bank
Other **E:** Lucky (Grocery), Mail Center Plus
Exit **(35)** Sycamore Valley Rd.
Gas **E:** Shell[*, D]
W: 76[*, LP], Arco[*], Exxon[*, D]
Food **E:** Danville Inn, Denny's (Danville Inn)
W: Chef Liang Restaurant, Deli Cafe, El Mido Mexican Restaurant, Emilio's of Danville, Giorgio's Coffee and Backery, High Tech Burrito, Luna Loca Restaurant, Patrick David's Cafe, Piatti, Pizza Machine, Round Table Pizza, Sierra Yogurt Co., Sun Dai Teriyaki, Sunrise Cafe & Bakery, The Gray Impasta, Togo's, Tony Roma's
Lodg **E:** Danville Inn
AServ **W:** 76, Exxon
ATM **W:** Bay View Bank, Lucky Food Center (Bank of America), Union Bank of California, Washington Mutual, Wells Fargo
Other **E:** Danville Veterinary Hospital
W: Danville Bowl, Long's Drugs[RX], Lucky Food Center (Bank of America), Mail Boxes Etc., WalGreens Pharmacy[RX]
Exit **(34)** Crow Canyon Rd., San Ramon (No

EXIT CALIFORNIA

Trucks Over 15 Ton)
Gas **E:** Shell[*]
W: BP[*, D], Chevron[*, 24], Exxon[*, D, LP], Shell[*, CW]
Food **E:** 360 Gourmet Burritos, Baskin Robbins, Blue Tattoo, Burger King, Carl Jr's Hamburgers, Chili's, Hopsing's, IHOP, Jamba Juice, Logan Farms Honey Hams, Max's Diner, Pasta Primavera, Pollo Rey, Round Table Pizza, Ruggi's Restaurant, See's Candy, Starbucks Coffee
W: Bagel Company, Big Horn Grill, Boston Market Restaurant, Dainty Donuts, Diablo Deli, Giuseppe's, In-N-Out Burger, Kasper's, Maestro's, McDonald's, Nation's Giant Burgers, New York Pizza, Pavlo's Pizza & Pasta, Subway, T.G.I. Friday's, TCBY, Taco Bell, The Orient Express
AServ **W:** BP, Chevron[24], Exxon, Shell
Med **E:** ✚ Hospital
ATM **E:** Bank Of America, Glendale Federal Bank, Home Savings Of America, US Bank, Wells Fargo
W: 7-11 Convenience Store, Bay Bank of Commerce, City Bank, Patelco, Safeway Grocery
Other **E:** Book Store, Rite Aid Pharmacy[RX], Super Crown Bookstore
W: 7-11 Convenience Store, Bay Brooks, Enterprise Rent-a-Car, Fast & Easy Mart, Long Drugs[RX], Mail Boxes Etc., Parcel Plus, Safeway Grocery, San Ramon Veterinary Hospital
Exit **(33)** Bollinger Canyon Rd.
Gas **W:** Chevron[*]
Food **W:** Chevron, Chevy's Mexican, Houdini's (Chevron), Marie Callender's Restaurant
Lodg **E:** Marriott
W: Courtyard by Marriott, Homestead Village
ATM **W:** Chevron
Other **E:** Target
Exit **(32)** Alcosta Blvd., Dublin
Gas **E:** BP[*]
W: Chevron[*], Shell[*, D, CW]
Food **W:** Chatillon Restaurant, Hong Kong Delight, Little House Thai Cuisine, McDonald's[PLAY], Mountain Mike's Pizza, New Joe's, PaPa Murphy's Pizza, Royal Gourmet Coffee, SunSun Garden, Taco Bell, Taylor Made Pizza
AServ **E:** BP
W: Chevron
ATM **E:** 7-11 Convenience Store
W: Chevron, Fremont Bank, Lucky Food Center[RX]
Other **E:** 7-11 Convenience Store
W: Lucky Food Center[RX], Mail Boxes Etc., WalGreens Pharmacy[RX]
Exit **(31)** I-580, Oakland to the West, Stockton to the East
Exit **(30)** Stoneridge Dr.
Exit **(29)** Bernal Ave. , Pleasanton
Food **E:** Bernal Cafe & Deli, Mexico Lindo, Rings Super Burgers, Vic's Bakery
ATM **E:** Freemont Bank
Exit **(28)** Sunol Blvd, Castlewood Dr.
Exit **(28)** Sunol (Southbound, Reaccess Northbound Only)
Exit **(27)** CA 84 West , Calaveras
26 Calveras, Sunol, W. CA 84
Exit **(25)** Andrade Rd., Sheraidon Rd
Gas **E:** Sunol-Tree[*]
Other **E:** Country Driving Range
Exit **(23)** Vargas Rd.
Exit **(22)** Mission Blvd, CA 238 , Hayward
Gas **E:** Shell[*]
Food **E:** McDonald's
Exit **(21)** Washington Blvd., Irvington District (No Trucks)
Gas **E:** Quick Stop Markets[*]
Food **E:** Coffee Roasting, Mission Jarrito, Mission Pizza, Yen Ching

← I-680 CALIFORNIA

EXIT	CALIFORNIA
Med	**W:** ✚ Hospital
Other	**E:** Pet Hospital, Royal Food Market
Exit	**(20)** Durham Rd.
Gas	**W:** 76[*, CW, 24] (Subway)
Food	**W:** 76 (Subway), Subway (76)
ATM	**W:** 76 (Subway)
Exit	**(19)** Mission Blvd. to I-880 Warm Springs
Gas	**W:** Exxon[*, D]
Food	**W:** Burger King, Carl Jr's Hamburgers, Domino's Pizza, Doughnut House, Furana, Jack-In-The-Box, KFC, Pacific Deli, Pizza Hut, Round Table Pizza, Taco Bell, The Better Bagel, Wok City Diner, Zorba's Deli Cafe
AServ	**W:** Exxon
ATM	**W:** 7-11 Convenience Store, California Savings, Exxon, Fremont Bank, Lucky Grocery Store
Other	**W:** 7-11 Convenience Store, Book Store, Copies West, Long's Drugs[RX], Lucky Grocery Store
Exit	**(18)** Scott Creek Rd.
Exit	**(17)** Jacklin Rd.
Gas	**W:** Shell[*, CW]
Food	**E:** Caffe Romeo, Chez Christina, Golf Land Pizza & Arcade, Hung Wu, The Pizza Box
Other	**E:** Bonfare Food Market
Exit	**(16)** Calaveras Blvd, Central Milpitas, Jct. CA 237
Gas	**E:** 76[*] (Tire Center), Shell[*, 24]
	W: Shell[*, CW]
Food	**E:** Domino's Pizza, Donuts, Fast Pizza, Java Garden Cafe, Los Reyes, Manilla Rose, Mr. Tung's, Omega Family Restaurant & Lounge, Pizza Hut, Round Table Pizza, Swains, The Hungry Hunter
	W: Chocolate Affaire, Coffee Cafe, Fresh Choice, Georgio's Italian, Hong Kong Gardens, Lyon's[24], Red Lobster
Lodg	**E:** Inn Cal
	W: Embassy Suites, Extended Stay America
AServ	**E:** Shell[24]
Med	**W:** ✚ Kaiser Permanente Office
ATM	**E:** 7-11 Convenience Store
	W: Bank Of America
Other	**E:** 7-11 Convenience Store, Ocean Supermarket
Exit	**(15)** Landess Ave. Montague Expressway
Gas	**E:** 76[*, LP, 24], Arco[*], Chevron[*]
Food	**E:** An's Vietnamese Cuisine, Burger King, China Express, Donut Basket, Jack-in-the-Box, Minh's Vietnamese Restaurant, My Chinese Restaurant, Pho Mai Noodle House, Roadrunner Bagel & Deli, Round Table Pizza, Royal Taco, Savory Chicken & Pizza, Stuft Pizza, Taco Bell, ToGo's
AServ	**E:** Chevron
ATM	**E:** WalGreens Pharmacy
Other	**E:** Home Depot, Jelly Franco's PW Market, Target, WalGreens Pharmacy
Exit	**(14)** Capitol Ave. , Hostetter Rd.
Gas	**E:** Shell[*, CW]
	W: Exxon[*]
Food	**E:** Carl Jr's Hamburgers[PLAY], Chao Chi Chinese Food, Honey Treat Yogurt, Italio's Pizzeria, Phillipino Buffet, Popeye's Chicken
AServ	**W:** Exxon
Other	**E:** Postal Depot, Save Mart[RX]
13	Hostetter Rd.
Gas	**E:** Shell[*, CW]
Food	**E:** Italo's Pizza
Exit	**(12)** Berryessa Rd.
Gas	**E:** Arco[*, 24], Chevron[*], Exxon[*]
Food	**E:** Baskin Robbins, Coffee.com, Denny's, Donuts & Bagels, Jade China Restaurant, McDonald's, New Capital Egg Roll, Round Table Pizza, Sorrento's Pizza, Taco Bell, Valerio's City Bakery
AServ	**E:** Chevron, Exxon
ATM	**E:** Arco, Lucky Grocery Store
Other	**E:** Long's Drugs[RX], Lucky Grocery Store, Mail Boxes Etc, Safeway Grocery
Exit	**(11)** McKee Rd.
Gas	**E:** 76[*, CW], Chevron[*, 24], Shell[*, CW]
	W: World Gas[*, 24]
Food	**E:** Burger King, Country Harvest Buffet, Mountain Mike's Pizza, Starbucks Coffee, ToGo's, Wienerschnitzel
	W: Ambrosia Bakery, Baskin Robbins, Foster's Freeze, Lotus Est., McDonald's[PLAY], Round Table Pizza, Thanh's Sandwiches, Wendy's, Winchells Donuts[24]
AServ	**E:** Chevron[24]
	W: K-Mart
ATM	**E:** Shell, Wells Fargo
	W: Bank Of Santa Clara, World Gas
Other	**E:** Lucky's Grocery Store, Pak N' Save Foods, WalGreens Pharmacy[24, RX]
	W: K-Mart, McKee Landroland
Exit	**(10)** Alum Rock Ave.
Gas	**E:** Shell[*, D, CW, 24]
	W: 76[*], Chevron[*]
Food	**E:** Jack in the Box, The Jewel of India, The Moon Rocks Cafe, The Orient Express, Yogurt Palace
	W: Carl Jr's Hamburgers, El Grullense
AServ	**W:** Chevron
ATM	**E:** Shell
	W: Bank Of America
Other	**E:** Launderland II, M Minute Market & Junior Deli
	W: Jelly Franco's PW Market, United States Post Office
Exit	**(9)** Capitol Expressway
8B	Jackson Ave.
8A	King Rd.
7	U.S. 101, San Francisco
6	McLaughlin Ave.
5B	10th & 11th St.
5	7th St. CA. 82 Virginia St.
Gas	**W:** Shell
	Note: I-680 runs concurrent below with I-280. Numbering follows I-280.
4	Vine St. Almaden Ave.
	Note: I-680 runs concurrent above with I-280. Numbering follows I-280.
3	Guadalupe Pkwy . CA 87
Gas	**E:** 76[*, D], Chevron
2	Median Ave
1	Bascom Ave. Leigh Ave.
0	Jct. 880 CA 17 Oakland

↑ CALIFORNIA

Begin I-680

I-694 MINNESOTA →

EXIT	MINNESOTA
	Begin I-694
	↓ MINNESOTA
27	I-94 split from I-694, to St Cloud
28	CR 61, Hemlock Lane
Gas	**I:** Amoco[*, CW]
Food	**I:** Perkin's Family Restaurant
Lodg	**I:** Red Carpet Inn
ATM	**I:** Amoco
29AB	U.S. 169 (Divided Hwy)
30	**(31)** Boone Ave.
Food	**O:** Northlind Inn
Lodg	**O:** Northlind Inn, Sleep Inn
31	County Road 81
Gas	**I:** Amoco[*, CW]
	O: 76[*], Texaco
Food	**I:** Wings & Ribs
	O: Best Western, Best Western, Charlie's (Best Western), Dairy Queen, Wendy's
Lodg	**I:** Budget Host Inn
	O: Best Western
AServ	**O:** Texaco
TServ	**I: ABM Truck Service**
ATM	**I:** Amoco, Amoco
	O: Texaco
33	Brooklyn Blvd.
Gas	**O:** Mobil[*, D, CW], Total[*]
ATM	**I:** Rainbow Food Grocery[24]
	O: Mobil
Other	**I:** Rainbow Food Grocery, WalGreens Pharmacy[RX]
34	MN 252, Shingle Creek Pkwy., East River Rd.
Gas	**O:** Mobil[*, LP, CW]
Food	**I:** Ground Round, Leeann Chin Chinese (Carry Out), Perkin's Family Restaurant, Subs Ect., The Inn On The Farm (Historic Bed & Breakfast)
	O: Barnacle Bill's, Chi Chi's Mexican Restaurant, Cracker Barrel, Denny's, Hardee's, Northern Lights (Hilton), Olive Garden, T.G.I. Friday's, The Hilton
Lodg	**I:** Country Inn & Suites, The Inn On The Farm (Historic Bed & Breakfast)
	O: AmericInn & Suites, Budgetel Inn, Comfort Inn, Holiday Inn, Super 8, The Hilton
AServ	**O:** Mobil
Other	**I:** Mail Boxes Etc., Police Station, Target
35A	Minnesota 100
35B	I-94 Jct East
35C	MN 252
36	East River Rd.
37	MN 47, University Ave.
Gas	**I:** 76, Amoco[CW]
	O: Super America[*, D]
Food	**O:** Burger King, Cattle Company Steaks & Seafood, Hardee's, Holiday Plus Grocery, McDonald's (Holiday Food), The Cattle Company
AServ	**I:** 76, Amoco
ATM	**O:** Super America, Super America
Other	**O:** Holiday Plus Grocery
38AB	**(39)** Minnesota 65, Central Ave.
Gas	**I:** Ashland[*], Super America[*]
	O: Citgo, Sinclair
Food	**I:** Bascali Brick Oven, Best Western, Boston Market Restaurant, Denny's, Dunkin Donuts, Embers, Hardee's, Jang-Won Korean & Chinese Restaurant, KFC, LaCasita Mexican, Sunshine Restaurant (Best Western), Taco Bell, The Ground Round Restaurant, Tycoon's Tavern & Grill, White Castle Restaurant
	O: Shorwood, Subway
Lodg	**I:** Best Western
ATM	**I:** Ashland, First Bank & Trust Co., Super America, TCF Bank, US Bank

Bold red print shows RV & Bus parking available or nearby

EXIT		MINNESOTA
	Other	I: All Pets Animal Hospital, Dental Clinic, K-Mart, Target(RX)
		O: Brown Berry Bakery Outlet, Dental Clinic
39		Silver Lake Rd.
	Gas	O: Amoco(*, CW), Sinclair
	Food	O: Champ's Americana, McDonald's
	AServ	O: Amoco, Sinclair
	ATM	O: FirstStar, Norwest
	Other	O: Lunds Grocery(24), Snyder Pharmacy
40		Long Lake Rd., Tenth St. NW
41AB		I-35 Junction
42A		Minnesota 51, Hamline, Snelling (Reaccess Eastbound Only)
42B		U.S. 10 W, Anoka Ave (Left Exit Westbound, Reaccess Eastbound Only, Divided Hwy)
43A		Lexington Ave
	Gas	I: Amoco(*, D, CW), Sinclair(*), Total(*)
	Food	I: Blue Fox Bar & Grill, Burger King, Perkin's Family Restaurant
		O: Hampton Inn, The Green Mill
	Lodg	I: Emerald Inn
		O: Hampton Inn
	AServ	I: Amoco
	ATM	I: Amoco, Sinclair
		O: Firststar Bank
	Other	I: Target
43B		Victoria Street
45		Minnesota 49, Rice Street
	Gas	O: Phillips 66(*, CW), Total(*, D, LP)
	Food	I: Burger King(PLAY), Hardee's, Taco John's
		O: Papa John's Pizza, Phillips 66, Taco Bell
	ATM	O: Phillips 66, Total
	Other	O: Dental Clinic
46		I-35 E, U.S. 10 to St. Paul (Left Exit)
47		I-35 East, N to Duluth (Left Exit Eastbound)
	Food	I: Guldens Dining
48		U.S. 61
50		**(49)** White Bear Ave.
	Gas	I: Amoco(*, CW)
		O: Phillips 66(*, CW), Super America(*, D, LP)
	Food	I: Applebee's, Arby's, Bakers Square Restaurant, Chi Chi's Mexican Restaurant, Ciatti's Italian, Cousins' Sub's, Denny's, Godfather's Pizza, Hardee's, Nickelby's Restaurant (Best Western), North China, Old Country Buffet, Perkin's Family Restaurant, Pizza Hut, Pizza Hut, Red Lobster, Taco Bell, The T Bird, Vietnam Restaurant, Wendy's
	Lodg	I: Best Western, Emerald Inn
	AServ	I: Amoco
		O: K-Mart(RX)
	ATM	I: FirstStar, Norwest, TCF Bank
		O: Super America
	Other	O: K-Mart(RX)
51		Minnesota 120
	Gas	I: Conoco(*, LP)
		O: Super America(*, D)
	Food	O: Blimpie's Subs, Bridgeman's Soda House, Jethro's Char-house
52AB		Minnesota 36, Stillwater, St. Paul (Divided Hwy)
	Gas	I: Fleet Farm(*, D, K, CW)
	AServ	I: Fleet Farm
55		Minnesota 5
	Gas	I: Amoco(*, LP, CW, 24), Holiday(*, D, LP, CW)
	Food	I: Amoco, Subway
	AServ	I: Amoco(24)
	ATM	I: Holiday, Holiday
57		County Rd 10, Tenth St. North
	Gas	I: Conoco(*, LP)
		O: Super America(*, D, LP, CW)
	Food	I: Brick Hearth Pizza, Brothers Subs, Burger King, China House Buffet, Hunan Palace, KFC, La Voie Kaffe, Little Caesars Pizza
	ATM	I: Conoco, Conoco, Norwest Bank, Rainbow Food Mkt, Rainbow Foods Market(24), Western Bank
		O: Super America, Super America
	Other	I: K-Mart(RX), Oakdale Optical, Pack N Mail, Rainbow Foods Market
58AB		I-94 Junction, St. Paul, Madison

↑MINNESOTA

Begin I-694

I-695 MARYLAND

Begin I-695

↓MARYLAND

EXIT		MARYLAND
1		MD173, Hawkins Point Rd, Pennington Ave, Ft Smallwood Rd
	FStop	O: **Citgo**(*, CW)
	ATM	O: **Citgo**
23B		**(1)** MD10S, MD 2 S, Glen Burnie, Severna Park (Exit 2 & 3B exit together)
	Food	I: Roy Rogers, Sbarro Pizza
3A		MD 2 N, Brooklyn
	Gas	O: Texaco(*)
	Food	I: Days Inn
		O: China Spring (Chinese), Chuck E Cheese's Pizza, Denny's, Golden Corral Family Steakhouse, Holiday Inn, Hunan Inn, KFC, Old Country Buffet, Pizza Hut, Pizza Hut (Wal-Mart), Taco Bell, Tail Gators
	Lodg	I: Days Inn, Holiday Inn
		O: Hampton Inn, Holiday Inn
	Med	I: + Glen Burnie Medical Clinic
4		Jct I-97S, to Annapolis, Bay Bridge (Left Exit)
5		MD648, Baltimore - Annapolis Blvd, Ferndale
	Gas	I: Shell(*)
		O: Amoco(*, 24)
	Food	O: Little Caesars Pizza, Roy Rogers
	Lodg	I: Comfort Inn
	Other	I: County Police
		O: 7-11 Convenience Store, **Basics Supermarket**, CVS Pharmacy
6		MD170, Camp Meade Rd, Linthicum (Southbound)
	Gas	I: Shell(*)
	Food	I: Bogie's Hoagies, Checkers Burgers, The Rose (Comfort Inn)
	Lodg	I: Comfort Inn
7AB		MD295S, Baltimore Washington Pkwy
8		Hammonds Ferry Rd, MD168, Nursery Rd
	FStop	O: **Citgo**(*, CW)
	Gas	I: Exxon(*), Shell(*, CW)
		O: Amoco(*, 24)
	Food	I: Burger King, KFC, McDonald's(PLAY), Taco Bell, Wendy's
		O: Charlie's Donuts & Subs, G&M
	Lodg	I: Motel 6
	AServ	I: Shell
8A		Jct I-895N Tunnel, Toll Rd
9		Hollins Ferry Rd, Lansdowne
	Gas	I: Exxon(*, D, LP), Mobil(24)
	Food	I: Victor's Place Deli
	AServ	I: Exxon, Mobil(24)
		O: **Goodyear Tire & Auto**
10		U.S. 1 Alt, Washington Blvd
11AB		Jct I-95, Baltimore, Washington
12A		MD 372, Wilkins Ave.
	Food	I: China Kitchen, Pizza 'n Deli, Zipani
	Med	I: + Hospital
12BC		MD372, Wilkens Ave
13		MD144, Frederick Rd, Catonsville
	Gas	O: Amoco(LP, 24), Cisco(*), Crown(LP)
	Food	O: Dunkin Donuts, Roy Rogers
	AServ	O: Amoco(24)
	ATM	O: 7-11 Convenience Store, Amoco, Cisco, First Union
	Other	O: 7-11 Convenience Store
14		Edmonson Ave
	Gas	O: Amoco(*, 24)
	Food	O: Opie's Snoballs, Ice Cream, Soup & Sandwiches, Papa John's Pizza
	AServ	O: Amoco(24)
15AB		U.S. 40, Ellicott City, Baltimore
	Gas	I: Amoco(CW, 24)
		O: Amoco(D), Crown(*, 24), Exxon(*, D), Shell(*, 24)
	Food	I: Burger King, Chi-Chi's Mexican Restaurant, KFC, McDonald's, Ronda's Diner(24)
		O: Dunkin Donuts
	Lodg	I: Days Inn, **Knights Inn (see our ad this page)**
	AServ	I: Amoco(24)
		O: Shell(24)
	ATM	I: First Nat'l Bank of Maryland
		O: Exxon
16		Jct I-70, Frederick
17		Security Blvd, Woodlawn, Rolling Rd
	Gas	I: Amoco(*, 24), Shell(*, CW)
		O: Exxon(*, D)
	Food	I: Boston Market Restaurant, Chih Yuan, China Wong Buffet, Dunkin Donuts, Pargo's (Comfort Inn), Red Lobster (Days Inn), Wendy's
		O: Bennigan's, Burger King, McDonald's(PLAY)
	Lodg	I: Comfort Inn, Days Inn, Motel 6
		O: Holiday Inn (see our ad this page)
	AServ	I: Amoco(24)
	ATM	I: Shell, Susquehanna Bank
		O: Exxon, NationsBank
	Other	I: Food King Grocery Store, Rite Aide Pharmacy
18AB		MD26, Randallstown, Lochearn
	Gas	I: Crown(D, 24)
	Food	I: Domino's Pizza
		O: Burger King, C Pride Two, Dunkin Donuts
	Med	O: + Hospital
	Other	I: CVS Pharmacy(RX)
19		Jct I-795, NW Expressway, Owings Mills, Reisterstown

Baltimore, MD 1470
Knights Inn
Cable TV - HBO/ESPN
Kids Under 12 Stay Free
Handicap Accessible
Truck/Large Vehicle Parking
Exterior Corridors
Outdoor Pool
410-788-3900 • 800-843-5644
Maryland ▪ I-695 ▪ Exit 15B

EXIT		MARYLAND
20		MD140, Reisterstown Rd, Garrison, Pikesville
	Gas	I: Amoco[D, 24], Mobil, Shell[*] O: Exxon[D, 24]
	Food	I: Fuddruckers, McDonald's, Shoney's O: Jasper's
	Lodg	I: Comfort Inn (see our ad this page), Hilton, Ramada Inn, Econolodge (see our ad this page)
	AServ	I: Mobil, Shell
	ATM	I: Crestar Bank, Hopkins Federal Savings Bank O: 7-11 Convenience Store, First Union
	Other	I: Old Court Animal Hospital O: 7-11 Convenience Store
21		Stevenson Rd, to Park Hgts Ave (Difficult Reaccess)
22		Greenspring Ave (No Trucks)
23AB		Jctl-83S, Baltimore, MD25, Falls Rd, Greenspring Ave
	Gas	O: Exxon[D]
	ATM	O: Caldwell Banker, NationsBank
24		Jct I-83 N, Timonium, York PA
25		MD139S, Charles St
	Med	I: ✚ Hospital
26AB		MD45, York Rd, Lutherville, Towson
	Gas	I: Crown[*, D, CW] O: Exxon[*, D]
	Food	I: McDonald's O: Friendly's, The Peppermill
	AServ	O: Exxon
	ATM	I: First Union, Provident Bank of MD O: Columbia Bank, Exxon
	Other	I: Benson Animal Hospital, CVS Pharmacy[24, RX]
27AB		MD146, Dulaney Valley Rd, Towson
	Gas	I: Mobil[*, D]
	Food	I: Boston Market Restaurant, Sheraton
	Lodg	I: Sheraton
	ATM	I: NationsBank
	Other	I: Howard & Morris Pharmacy[RX], Super Fresh Food Market
28		MD 45, Providence Rd.
	Gas	I: Citgo[*, D]
	Food	I: Royal Farm Subs
	AServ	I: Citgo
	ATM	I: Royal Farm Subs
	Other	I: Townson Bowling Lanes
29		MD542, Loch Raven Blvd, Cromwell Bridge Rd
	Gas	O: Crown
	Food	O: Bel Loc Diner, Days Inn, McDonald's
	Lodg	I: Holiday Inn O: Days Inn, Ramada (see our ad this page), Welcome Inn
	Other	O: Beltway Animal Clinic
30AB		MD41, Perring Pkwy
	Gas	O: Texaco[*]
	Food	O: Burger King, Carney Crab House, Denny's, Dunkin Donuts, McDonald's[PLAY], Milanos Restaurant (Italian, American, Greek), Old Country Buffet, Popeye's Chicken, Roy Rogers
	AServ	O: Texaco
	ATM	O: Chesapeake Federal Bank, First Union, Mercantile Bank, NationsBank, Texaco
	Other	O: Giant Supermarket[RX], Perring Animal Hospital, The Mail Stop
31AB		MD147, Harford Rd, Carney, Parkville
	Gas	O: Amoco[*, 24], Mobil[*], Texaco[D]
	AServ	O: Mobil, Texaco
	Other	I: Carney Animal Hospital, Epic Pharmacy[RX] O: CVS Pharmacy
31C		MD 43 East, White Marsh Blvd. (Left Exit, NO Trucks over 5 tons)
32AB		U.S.1, Bel Air, Overlea
	Gas	I: Crown[*] O: Exxon[*, CW]
	Food	I: Carrabba's Italian Grill, Cookies By Design, McDonald's, Mr Crab Seafood, Schonners, Subway, The Canopy BBQ, Vinny's Pizzeria O: Denny's, Dunkin Donuts, IHOP, McDonald's, PeKing House Chinese, Taco Bell, Tully's
	Med	O: ✚ Hospital
	ATM	I: Crown O: 7-11 Convenience Store, Exxon, Harbor Federal
	Other	I: Animal Medical Hospital, Movies 6 Cinema O: 7-11 Convenience Store, Fullerton Animal Hospital, Giant Food & Drug Store[RX], K-Mart[RX], Putty Hill Plaza
33AB		Jct I-95, North to New York, South to Baltimore, Washington (Left Exit Eastbound)
34		MD7, Philadelphia Rd, Rosedale
	FStop	I: **Exxon[*, D]**
	Food	I: Golden Ring Inn O: Baskin Robbins, Gourmet Chinese Restaurant, Wendy's
	Lodg	O: Susse Chalet
	Med	O: ✚ Hospital, ✚ Rossville Group Walk-In Clinic
	ATM	I: **Exxon** O: Heritage Savings Bank, Provident Bank
	Other	O: Eastside Animal Hospital, Giant Food & Drug Store[RX], Golden Ring Plaza
35AB		U.S. 40, Pulaski Hwy, Aberdeen, Baltimore (Services Also Accessible From Exit 34)
	Gas	O: Sunoco[D]
	Food	I: Roy Rogers O: McDonald's
	Lodg	O: Christlen Motel
	TServ	I: **Chesapeak Ford Truck Sales**
	Med	I: ✚ Hospital O: ✚ Franklin Square Hospital
	Other	O: State Police
36		MD702 S, to Essex (Left Exit)
38		MD150 E, Eastern Blvd, Essex, Baltimore
	Gas	O: Enroy[*]
	Food	I: Golden Corral Family Steakhouse, Horn & Horn Smorgasbord, KFC O: Chuck E Cheese's Pizza, Roy Rogers
	Other	I: CVS Pharmacy, East Point Center Shopping Plaza, Metro Supermarket[24], Movies 10
39		Merrit Blvd, Dundalk
40		MD151, North Point Blvd N, MD150 Eastern Blvd
41		Cove Rd, MD20, MD151, Dundalk
	Gas	I: Northpoint Fuel[*, D]
	Food	I: Little Village Pizzeria, McDonald's[PLAY], Northpoint Diner & Donuts, Wendy's
42		MD 151 S, Sparrrows Pt.
	TServ	I: **International Truck**
43		Bethleham Blvd, Sparrows Point (Difficult Reaccess)
44		Broening Hwy, Dundalk (Reaccess Clockwise Only)
(47)		Toll Plaza - Key Bridge (Toll)

↑ MARYLAND

Begin I-695

Econo Lodge
Baltimore, MD
Suites & Jacuzzi Rooms
Cable TV - HBO/ESPN
Kids Under 12 Stay Free
Handicap Accessible
Truck/Large Vehicle Parking
Interior Corridors • Outdoor Pool
1471
410-484-1800 • 800-424-4777
Maryland • I-695 • Exit 20

RAMADA INN®
Towson
8712 Loch Raven Blvd
Baltimore, MD 21286
410-823-8750
800-272-6232
Restaurant/Lounge on Premises
Full Breakfast Daily
Outdoor Pool
Cable TV
Pets Allowed
Truck/Large Vehicle Parking
Meeting/Banquet Facilities
Handicap Accessible
Coin Laundry
Exterior Corridors
Shopping Mall Nearby
1742
MARYLAND • I-695 • EXIT 29B

Baltimore, Maryland
1626

1800 Belmont Ave.
410-265-1400
Toll Free Reservations:
800-HOLIDAY
Outside of I-695 at exit 17
Kids Stay & Eat Free
Tour Bus & RV Parking
Full Service Restaurant & Lounge
Close to Baltimore Inner Harbor
& Baltimore Aquarium
Guest Laundry
Special Rates/Tour Groups AAA & AARP
MARYLAND • I-695 • EXIT 17

Truck or Large Vehicle Parking

COMFORT INN NORTHWEST
410-484-7700
800-732-2548
Full Continental Breakfast
Restaurant on Premises • Outdoor Pool
Kids 18 and Under Stay Free
Handicap Accessible
Meeting Facilities
Pet Allowed • Coin Laundry
Exterior/Interior Coridors
Fully Furnished 2 Bedroom Apts/Suites
$55.95 +tax
10 Wooded Way • Pikesville, MD
1264
MARYLAND • I-695 • EXIT 20

Bold red print shows RV & Bus parking available or nearby

EXIT	MICHIGAN

Begin I-696

↓MICHIGAN

28 Jct. I-94, 11 Mile Rd., Port Heron

27 Roseville, Mi Rt. 3, Gratiot Ave.
- **Gas** **I:** Mobil(*), Total(*, CW)
  O: Amoco(*)
- **Food** **I:** McDonald's (Mobil)
  O: Jo Fruit & Vegtables, USA Grill & Bar
- **Med** **I:** ✚ Roseville Medical Center
- **ATM** **I:** Total
- **Other** **O:** Costco Wholesale Warehouse

26 Groesbeck Hwy., Schoenherr Rd., Mi 97
- **Gas** **I:** Citgo(*, D)
  O: Marathon(D)
- **Food** **O:** Golden Grill

24 Hoober Rd.
- **Gas** **I:** Amoco(24), Mobil(*)
- **Food** **I:** **Chi Chi's Mexican Restaurant**, Doc Family Restaurant, Dunkin Donuts, Pizza Hut (Mobil), Subway, Tim Horton's(24), Xtreme Pizza (Amoco)
  O: Burger King, KFC
- **Lodg** **I:** Holiday Inn Express
- **ATM** **I:** First Federal of Michigan

23 Center Line, MI 53, Van Dyke Ave.
- **Gas** **I:** Amoco(CW, 24)
  O: BP(*)
- **Food** **I:** Burger King
  O: Arby's, Cleme's, Dunkin Donuts, Juliano's, McDonald's, Uncle Sam's Coney Island
- **AServ** **I:** Amoco(24)
- **Med** **O:** ✚ Kaiser Medical Center
- **ATM** **O:** BP, Huntington Bank

22 Mounds Rd.

21 11 Mile Rd.
- **Gas** **O:** Amoco(*, 24), Shell(*, 24), Speedway(*)
- **Food** **O:** Moon Yee Chinese Restaurant, Pizza, Ralph & Myrle's, Subway
- **Med** **O:** ✚ St. John's Hospital
- **ATM** **O:** Michigan National Bank, Shell, Speedway
- **Other** **O:** Parkview Animal Hospital, **Target**, Value Village Grocery

20 Dequindre Rd., John R. Rd.
- **Gas** **O:** Marathon(*, CW)
- **Food** **I:** **Bob Evan's Restaurant**
  O: Coachman Lounge Ribs & Pizza, **Crash Landing**, IHOP, Mak Bakery, Deli, & Pizza, **Ponderosa Steakhouse**
- **Lodg** **I:** Cross Country Inn
  O: Knight's Inn, Red Roof Inn
- **Other** **O:** DOC One Hr. Glasses

18 Jct. I-75, Detroit, Toledo, Flint

17 Bermuda, Mohawk

16 MI 1, Woodward Ave, Main St.
- **Gas** **I:** Mobil(*)
- **Food** **I:** Anna's Coffee Shop
  O: Amici's Pizza, Oxford, Sydney Bogg Chocolate Shop
- **AServ** **I:** Mobil
- **ATM** **I:** Comercia Bank
- **Other** **O:** Holiday Supermarket, Westcott Veterinary Care Center

14 Coolidge Rd., Ten Mile Road
- **Gas** **I:** Total(*, D, CW)
- **Food** **I:** Hungry Howie's, **Jade Palace**, Little Caesars Pizza, Saad's Pastry, **Subway**
  O: **A Taste of the Orient**
- **Med** **I:** ✚ Oak Park Medical Clinic, ✚ **Sinai Family Medical Center**
- **ATM** **O:** Comerica Bank, NBD Bank
- **Other** **I:** Arbor Drugs(RX), **Farmer Jack's Supermarket**
  O: Lincoln Drugs(RX), Rite Aid Pharmacy(RX)

13 Greenfield Rd.
- **Gas** **I:** Mobil(*), Sunoco(*)
- **Food** **I:** Dunkin Donuts, Greek Island Coney Restaurant, New York Bagel, Oriental City, Pita Cafe, Royal Kubo Manila Cousine, Schlotzsky's Deli, Star Bakery, Taste of Israel, Zeman's Bakery
  O: Bagel's Plus, New York Pizza World, Wendy's
- **AServ** **I:** Mobil
- **ATM** **I:** Comerica Bank
  O: 7-11 Convenience Store
- **Other** **I:** Efros Drugs, **Greenfield Animal Hospital**, **Hiller's Food Emporium Grocery**, Optical
  O: 7-11 Convenience Store

12 Southfield Rd., 11 Mile Rd.

Bill Knapp's Restaurant
Open daily at 11:00 am
Bill Knapp's is a casual, full service family restaurant where Motorcoaches are always welcome.
1800
Over 50 locations throughout: Michigan • Ohio • Indiana
248-553-4821 Farmington Hills
MICHIGAN • I-696 • EXIT 5

- **Food** **O:** Panera Bread
- **Med** **O:** ✚ Health Care
- **ATM** **O:** First Federal of Michigan, NBD Bank

11 Evergreen Rd.
- **Food** **I:** BW-3 Grill & Pub, **T.G.I. Friday's**
  O: La Fendi, Papa Romano's Pizza
- **Lodg** **I:** Residence Inn

10 US 24, Telegraph Rd., Mi 10, Northwest Hwy, Lahser Rd.
- **Gas** **I:** Marathon(*)
  O: Mobil(*), Shell(*, CW)
- **Food** **I:** Sunrise Donuts
  O: Gateway Deli, Jewel Grocery
- **Lodg** **I:** **Campbell Wood Studio Hotels**
- **AServ** **I:** Marathon
  O: Mobil, Shell
- **Med** **O:** ✚ Detroit Medical Center, ✚ Henry Ford Medical Center
- **ATM** **O:** Comerica Bank, Mobil, Old Kent
- **Other** **O:** Arbor Drugs(RX), **Farmer Jack's Supermarket**, U.S. Post Office

9 US 24, Telegraph Rd
- **Gas** **I:** Sunoco
- **Food** **O:** Copper Canyon, New Seoul Garden, **Old Country Buffet**, Ruby Tuesday, The Restaurant on Main Street
- **Lodg** **I:** Holiday Inn
  O: Hampton Inn, Marvin's Garden Inn, Red Roof Inn
- **Other** **O:** K-Mart(RX)

5 Orchard Lake Rd.
- **Gas** **O:** Marathon, Mobil(*, D), Shell(*), Sunoco(CW)
- **Food** **O:** Arby's, **Bill Knapp's Restaurant (see our ad this page)**, Einstein Bros Bagels, Jets Pizza, Mrs. Maddox Cake Shoppe, Orchard Grille Restaurant (Best Western), Quizno's Subs, Roosevelts Grill, Ruby Tuesday, Silverman's Deli Restaurant(24), Steak & Ale, Steamers Seafood & Grill, Subway, Sushi Ko, Tribute, Wendy's, Zia's Italian
- **Lodg** **O:** Best Western, **Comfort Inn**, Extended Stay America, Fairfield Inn
- **AServ** **O:** Marathon, Shell
- **ATM** **O:** Comerica Bank

1 Jct. I-96 West & East, I-275 S., Grand River Ave., Toledo

↑MICHIGAN

Begin I-696

I-820 TEXAS →

EXIT	TEXAS

Begin I-820

↓TEXAS

34A Jct I-20E, US287S, Waxahachie, Jct I-20W, Abaline

33C Sun Valley Dr.

32A US287N

32 Wilberger St. (Difficult Reaccess)

31 E. Berry St.

30C Ramey Ave.

30BB TX180, TX303, Rosedale St. (Same Exit As 30B)

30B TX180, TX303, Lancaster Ave.

30A Craig St.

29 Meadowbrook Dr.

28AB I-30W Dallas Ft. Worth

28C Brentwood, Stair Rd.

27 John T. White Bridge St.
- **Gas** **E:** Texaco(*)
  W: Exxon(*, CW), Mobil(*, LP, CW)
- **Food** **W:** Black-Eyed Pea, Braum's Ice Cream, Italy Pasta and Pizza, Luby's Cafeteria, Mr. Jim's Pizza, Sub and Yogurt, Subway
- **ATM** **W:** Albertson's Grocery (NationsBank), Exxon, Kroger Supermarket(RX) (Bank of America), Woodhaven National Bank
- **Other** **E:** Tee One Up Golf Center

EXIT	TEXAS
	W: Albertson's Grocery (NationsBank), Animal Clinic, Kroger Supermarket(RX) (Bank of America), Wal-Mart
26	Randol Mill Rd.
Gas	**E:** Texaco(*, D, LP)
	W: Conoco(*, CW), Fastrac(*)
Food	**W:** Waffle House
ATM	**E:** Texaco
	W: Conoco, Fastrac
25	Trinity Blvd.
24B	TX121S, Downtown Ft.Worth
24A	TX10E, TX183W, Richland Hills
Gas	**E:** Racetrac(*, 24)
	W: Chevron(D)
Food	**E:** Racetrac
	W: Doughnut World, El Chico Mexican Restaurant
Lodg	**W:** Best Western
AServ	**W:** Chevron
Med	**W:** + Hospital
Other	**W:** Coin Operated Laundromat, Pet Clinic, Q Mart Convenience Store
23	Pipeline Rd, Glenview Dr.
Gas	**E:** Chevron(*, CW, 24), Mobil(*, D)
Food	**E:** Burgerstreet, Doughnut Wheel, McDonald's(PLAY), Whataburger
	W: Denny's, Ice Cream Shoppe, Kentucky Fried Chicken, Pulido's Mexican Restaurant
AServ	**E:** K-Mart(RX)
Other	**E:** K-Mart(RX), Toys R Us
	W: Pearl Vision Center, Putt Putt Golf and Games, Quickmart Convenient Store
22B	TX121N, TX183E, Dallas, Ft.Worth Airport, Grapevine
Food	**N:** Shoney's
22A	TX26, Colleyville
Gas	**S:** Texaco(*, D)
Food	**N:** Chuck E Cheese's Pizza, Red Lobster
	S: Arby's, China Cafe, Golden Corral Family Steakhouse, Hooters, IHOP, Luby's Cafeteria, Owens Restaurant, Shoney's, Subway, Waffle House
Lodg	**N:** Motel 6
	S: Budget Inn
Med	**S:** + Hospital
Other	**N:** Eckerd Drugs(RX)
	S: Baptist Bookstore, General Cinemas, Laserquest (entertainment), Movies 8, Pearl Vision

EXIT	TEXAS
21	Holiday Lane
20	Rufe Snow Drive
Gas	**I:** Exxon(*), Mobil(*, D)
	O: Chevron(*, CW), Citgo(*) (Super Big Subs), Diamond Shamrock(*, D)
Food	**O:** Applebee's, Chick-Fil-A(PLAY), Citgo (Super Big Subs), Don Pablo's Mexican, Doughnut Palace, Grandy's, Hunan Wok, McDonald's(PLAY), Ryan's Steakhouse, Taco Bueno, Tony's Italian Restaurant, Wendy's
AServ	**I:** Exxon
	O: Wal-Mart(RX)
ATM	**I:** Northwest Bank
	O: Chevron, Citgo (Super Big Subs), Diamond Shamrock, First National Bank of Texas
Other	**O:** Pro Photo and Studio, Wal-Mart(RX)
19	US377, Denton Hwy (Westbound, Reaccess Eastbound Only)
Gas	**I:** Stop 'N Go(*) (NationsBank)
Food	**O:** Chicken Express Restaurant
Lodg	**I:** Warren Inn
18	Haltom Rd.
Lodg	**I:** Great Western Inn
Other	**I:** Aloha RV and Boat Parking
17A	N. Beach St.
Gas	**I:** Conoco(*, D, CW)
	O: Mobil(*, LP, CW), Shell(*, D, CW, 24) (Jack In The Box)
Food	**I:** Conoco, IHOP, Scotty's Deluxe Dinners
	O: Jack In The Box (Shell), Lubby's Cafeteria, Shell (Jack In The Box), Taco Bueno, Whataburger
Lodg	**I:** Candlewood Suites, Super 8
	O: Courtyard by Marriott, Fairfield Inn
ATM	**I:** Conoco
	O: Shell (Jack In The Box), Summit Community Bank
16A	I-35W North, US 287 Denton
16B	I-35W South, US287 Downtown Ft.Worth
16C	Mark IV Parkway
15	TX156, Blue Mound
Gas	**S:** Citgo(*, D), Texaco(*) (Chella's)
Food	**S:** Arby's, **Buffy's McDonald's** Taco Bell, Texaco (Chella's), Wendy's, What A Burger
Lodg	**S:** **Great Western Inn**
ATM	**S:** Norwest Bank, Texaco (Chella's)
Other	**S:** Autrey's Marine
14	Railhead Rd (Exit under construction)
13	Bus US287, Saginaw Main Street

EXIT	TEXAS
12B	Old Decatur Road
12A	Marine Creek Pkwy,
10AB	TX 199, Jacksboro Hwy, Azle Ave
Gas	**N:** Racetrac(*, 24)
	S: Chevron(*, CW, 24), Texaco(*, D, CW)
Food	**N:** China Gate, Ci Ci's Pizza, Ginger Brown Old Time Restaurant, Jack-In-The-Box, McDonald's(PLAY), Sonic, Subway, Taco Bell, Taco Bueno, Waffle House
	S: Arizola's Mexican Retaurant and Cantina, Long John Silver, What A Burger
Med	**S:** + Family Clinic
ATM	**N:** Alberton's(RX) (NationsBank)
	S: 1st State Bank of Texas, Chevron, Texaco
Other	**N:** Alberton's(RX) (NationsBank), Wal-Mart(RX), WalGreens Pharmacy
9	Quebec Street
Food	**N:** International House of Pancakes
8	Navajo Tr., Cahoba Dr.
Gas	**N:** Texaco(*, D) (Tommy's Hamburgers)
Food	**N:** Texaco (Tommy's Hamburgers)
6	Las Vegas Tr., Heron Dr
5B	Silver Creek Road
5A	Clifford St
4	White Settlement Road
Gas	**E:** Fina(*)
	W: Chevron(*, CW), Diamond Shamrock(*, LP, CW, 24) (Bank One)
Food	**W:** Mancusso's, McDonald's(PLAY), Pengelly's Grill, Waffle House
ATM	**E:** Norwest Bank
	W: Chevron, Diamond Shamrock (Bank One)
3B	I-30E, Downtown Ft. Worth
3C	Westpoint Blvd, Alemeda St
3A	I-30W, Weatherford
2	Route 580, Chapin Rd
Gas	**E:** Citgo(*)
Food	**E:** Burger King(PLAY), Lim's Donut, Subway
Lodg	**W:** La Mirage Inn
ATM	**E:** Citgo, Kroger Supermarket(24, RX) (Bank of America)
Other	**E:** Kroger Supermarket(RX) (Bank of America)
1B	Link Crest Dr
Gas	**E:** Chevron, Fina(D), Mobil(D)
1A	Team Ranch Road

↑TEXAS

Begin I-820

Notes:

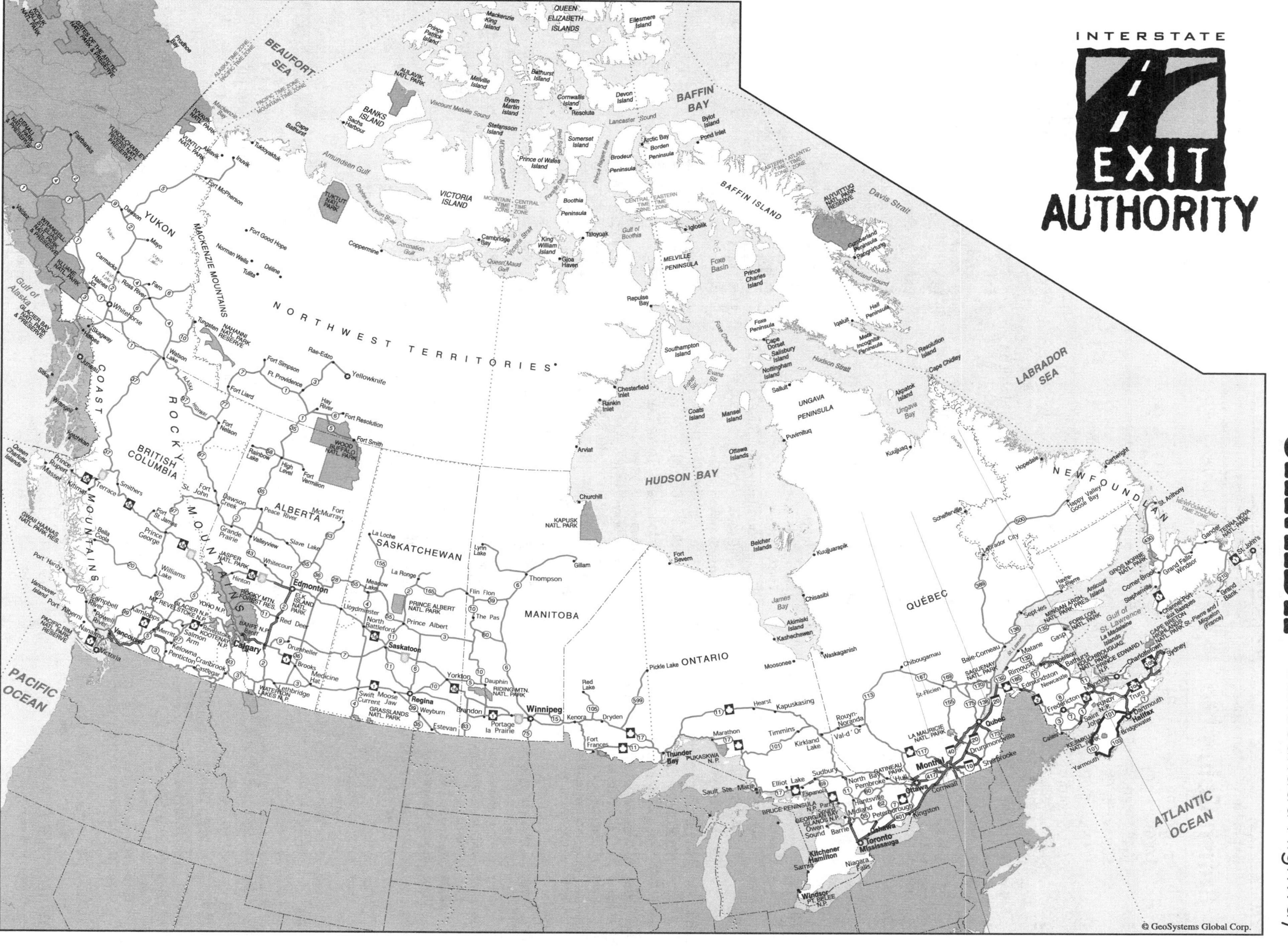
INTERSTATE
EXIT
AUTHORITY
© GeoSystems Global Corp.
BEAUFORT SEA
BAFFIN BAY
Davis Strait
LABRADOR SEA
HUDSON BAY
ATLANTIC OCEAN
PACIFIC OCEAN
Gulf of Alaska
BAFFIN ISLAND
VICTORIA ISLAND
BANKS ISLAND
QUEEN ELIZABETH ISLANDS
MELVILLE PENINSULA
UNGAVA PENINSULA
YUKON
NORTHWEST TERRITORIES
MACKENZIE MOUNTAINS
ROCKY MOUNTAINS
COAST MOUNTAINS
BRITISH COLUMBIA
ALBERTA
SASKATCHEWAN
MANITOBA
ONTARIO
QUÉBEC
NEWFOUNDLAND
Whitehorse
Yellowknife
Vancouver
Victoria
Calgary
Edmonton
Saskatoon
Regina
Winnipeg
Thunder Bay
Toronto
Ottawa
Montréal
Québec
Halifax

EXIT BC

Begin Hwy 1, Vancouver

↓British Columbia

44 Hwy 7, Port Moody, Port Corquitlam

50 104th Avenue, 169th Street, Surrey City Centre (Truck Scales)

53 176 Street, Cloverdale, BC Hwy 15, US Border

58 200 Street, Langley City
- **FStop** **N:** **Shell**(*, D, CW, 24)
- **Gas** **N:** Esso(*, CW)
  S: Chevron(*), Super Save Gas(*)
- **Food** **N:** Chang's Palace, KFC, Mazurati's Pasta Bar, McDonald's(PLAY), Paragon Pizza, Ricky's, Subway, Tim Horton's (Esso)
- **Lodg** **N:** Sand Man Hotel
- **ATM** **N:** Esso, Royal Bank

66 232rd St, Langley, BC10, Ft, Langley,Ferries, Airport
- **Gas** **S:** Chevron(*)
- **Med** **S:** ✚ Hospital
- **ATM** **S:** Chevron

73 264th St, Aldergrove, BC13, USA Boarder
- **Lodg** **N:** Country Meddows Best Western

(82) Rest Area - RR, Phones, Picnic, RV Dump (Westbound)

83 Hwy 1A, Mount Helman, Aldergrove, Surrey

87 Clearbrook Rd, Clearbrook
- **Gas** **N:** Chevron(*), Shell(*, D, LP, CW), Turbo(*)
- **Food** **N:** Chan's Kitchen
- **Lodg** **N:** Econolodge, Holiday Inn Express, Regency Inn Best Western
- **ATM** **N:** Chevron, Turbo

90 Mc Callum Rd
- **Gas** **N:** Chevron(*), Esso(*, CW), Shell(*)
  S: Shell(*)
- **Food** **N:** Tim Horton's (Esso)
  S: McDonald's Express
- **Med** **N:** ✚ Hospital
- **ATM** **N:** Chevron, Esso
- **Other** **S:** Save N' Shop Supermarket

92 Abbotsford, Mission, Sumas USA, BC11
- **Gas** **N:** Shell(*)
- **Food** **N:** Crossroads, Dairy Queen, McDonald's(PLAY), Smitty's
- **Lodg** **N:** Bakerview Inn Best Western, Quality Inn

95 Whatcom Rd
- **Gas** **N:** Petro Canada(*)
- **Food** **N:** Burger King, Subway, Tim Horton's
- **ATM** **N:** Petro Canada

104 #3 Rd, Yarro

109 Yale Rd West

116 Lickman Rd
- **TStop** **N:** **Trans Canada**(*)
- **FStop** **N:** **Esso, Shell**
- **Food** **N:** **Trans Canada**
- **Lodg** **N:** Rainbow Country Best Western, **Trans Canada**
- **TServ** **N:** **AT&T Truck & Trailer Repair, Nielson's Truck Wash, Trans Canada**

119AB Chilliwack, Sardis
- **TStop** **S:** **Husky**(*, LP)
- **FStop** **N:** **Petro Canada**
- **Gas** **S:** Petro Canada(*, 24), Shell(*, 24)
- **Food** **N:** ABC Family Restaurant, Choi Burger Land
  S: Burger King, **Husky**, Taco Time, Tim Horton's, Wendy's
- **Lodg** **N:** Travelodge TraveLodge
  S: Comfort Inn, Sardis Motel
- **Med** **N:** ✚ Hospital

120 Young Rd, Chilliwack
- **Lodg** **N:** Chilliwack Motor Inn

123 Prest Rd

129 Annis Rd

135 Rosedale, Agassiz, Harrison
- **Gas** **N:** Esso(*)
  S: Petro Canada(*)

138 Popkum Rd, Bridal Falls

146 Herriling Island

151 Peters Rd

153 Laid Law, Jones Lake

160 St Elmo Rd, Hunter Creek Rd, Laid Law

Exit Hope
- **FStop** **N:** **Husky**(*)
- **Food** **N:** Husky

168 Flood Hope Rd, Silver Hoper Creek
- **Gas** **S:** Mohawk(*, D)
- **Food** **S:** Silver Creek Pancake House

Exit BC3 E, BC5 N

Exit Wallace St, Town Centre
- **Gas** **S:** Chevron(*), Shell
- **Food** **S:** Dairy Queen
- **Lodg** **S:** Hope Motor Hotel, Slumber Lodge
- **Med** **S:** ✚ Hospital

Exit Commission St
- **Gas** **S:** Esso(D, LP), Ultra Fuels
- **Food** **S:** Subway
- **Lodg** **N:** Skag Motel
  S: Winsdor Motel
- **ATM** **S:** First Heritage
- **Other** **S:** Pharma-Save, Post Office

Exit Hope
- **Gas** **N:** U Save Gas(*)
- **Lodg** **N:** Swiss Chalets Motel
  S: Inn-Town Motel, Red Roof Inns

Exit BC7

Exit Dogwood Valley Rd
- **TStop** **N:** **Husky**(*, LP)
- **Food** **N:** **Husky**
- **TServ** **N:** **Husky**

Exit Albert St
- **Food** **N:** Gold Nugget Pancake House
- **Lodg** **N:** Gold Nugget Motel
- **Other** **S:** Barry's Trading Post, Post Office

Exit Yale, Regents St
- **Gas** **S:** Shell(*, D)
- **Lodg** **N:** Fort Yale Motel, Moffat Motel

Exit Rest Area

Exit North Bend
- **FStop** **N:** **Husky**(*)
- **Gas** **S:** Esso(*, LP)
- **Food** **N:** Charles Hotel Restaurant
  S: Rhodie's Place
- **Lodg** **N:** Charles Hotel
- **TServ** **N:** **Husky**
- **Other** **N:** Fraser Canyon Supermarket
  S: Ambulance Station

Exit Slanzi Rd
- **Food** **N:** Gold Rush
  S: Canyon Cafe
- **Lodg** **N:** Greenwood Inn
  S: Canyon Alpine Motel

Exit Service Rd
- **Gas** **N:** Esso(*, D)
- **Food** **N:** Esso
- **Lodg** **N:** Lytton Pines Motel

Exit Secondary Rd 12, Lytton
- **Med** **N:** ✚ Hospital
- **Other** **N:** Police Station

Exit Jade Springs
- **Food** **N:** Jade Springs Cafe
- **Other** **N:** Shop Easy Supermarket

Exit Skihist Prov Park Rd

Exit Service RD

Exit Side Rd
- **Food** **N:** Shaw Springs Restaurant(24)

Exit Side Rd
- **Gas** **S:** Thrifty(*, D)
- **Food** **S:** Big Horn

Exit BC8, Merritt

Exit North Frontage Rd
- **Gas** **N:** Petro Canada(*, D)
- **Food** **N:** Petro Canada

Exit Business Frontage Rd
- **Food** **S:** Circle J Cafe
- **Lodg** **S:** Circle Motel

Exit BC97C, Ashcroft, Logan Lake, Merritt
- **Food** **S:** The Nag Stop
- **Med** **S:** ✚ Hospital
- **Other** **S:** Police Station

Exit BC97, BC97C
- **FStop** **S:** **Husky**(*, LP)
- **Gas** **N:** Chevron(*), Mohawk(*, D, LP), Shell(*)
  S: Chevron(*), Esso(*), Petro Canada(*, D)
- **Food** **N:** A & W (Chevron), Bill Ma Restaurant, Dairy Queen, Heartland Family Restaurant (Sandman Inn), Herbie's Drive In, Wander Inn
  S: Husky
- **Lodg** **N:** Cash Creek Motel, Oasis Motel, Robbie's Motel, Sage Hills Motel, Sandman Inn
  S: Desert Motel
- **TServ** **N:** **Truck Scale**
- **ATM** **S:** Royal Bank

Exit Quartz Rd
- **Lodg** **N:** Castle Inn Motel, Tumbleweed Motel
  S: Nugett Rd Motel
- **Other** **S:** Great Steak Supermarket

Exit Juniper Beach Park Rd

Exit Savona Access Rd
- **Gas** **N:** Super Save Gas(*, D, LP)
- **Food** **N:** Dey's Cafe

362 BC5, Trans Can 1, Cache Creek, Lytton, Prince George, BC97

366 CopperHead Dr
- **TStop** **S:** **Petro Canada**(*, LP)
- **FStop** **S:** **Chevron, Esso, Shell, Turbo**
- **Lodg** **S:** Petro Canada
- **TServ** **S:** **Freightliner, General Tires, Mack, Peterbilt, Petro Canada**
- **TWash** **S:** **Kozyklean Car, Bus, Truck Wash**

Bold red print shows RV & Bus parking available or nearby

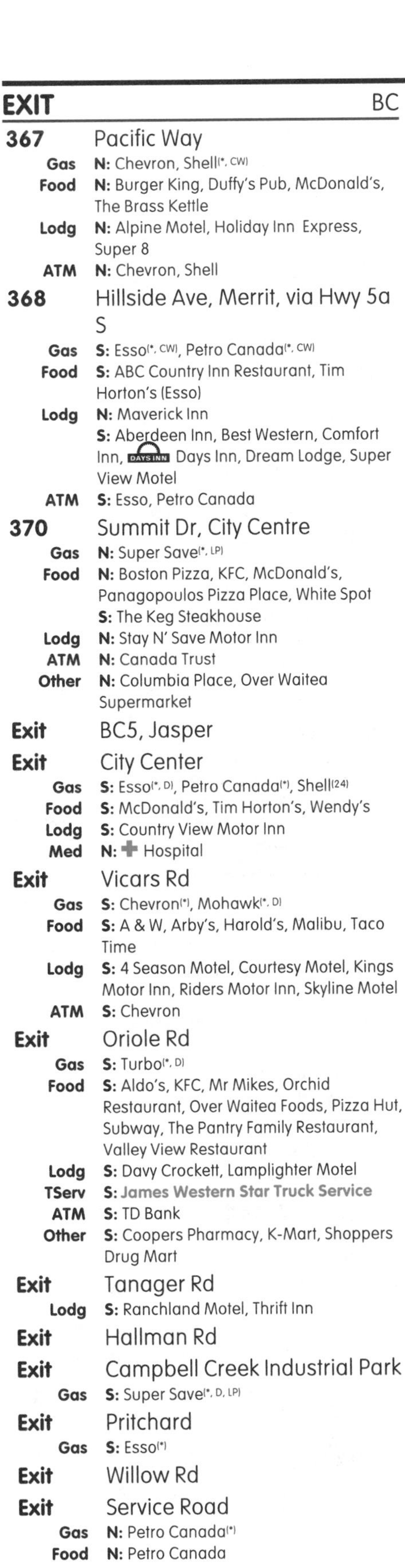

EXIT BC

367 Pacific Way
Gas N: Chevron, Shell[*, CW]
Food N: Burger King, Duffy's Pub, McDonald's, The Brass Kettle
Lodg N: Alpine Motel, Holiday Inn Express, Super 8
ATM N: Chevron, Shell

368 Hillside Ave, Merrit, via Hwy 5a S
Gas S: Esso[*, CW], Petro Canada[*, CW]
Food S: ABC Country Inn Restaurant, Tim Horton's (Esso)
Lodg N: Maverick Inn
S: Aberdeen Inn, Best Western, Comfort Inn, Days Inn, Dream Lodge, Super View Motel
ATM S: Esso, Petro Canada

370 Summit Dr, City Centre
Gas N: Super Save[*, LP]
Food N: Boston Pizza, KFC, McDonald's, Panagopoulos Pizza Place, White Spot
S: The Keg Steakhouse
Lodg N: Stay N' Save Motor Inn
ATM N: Canada Trust
Other N: Columbia Place, Over Waitea Supermarket

Exit BC5, Jasper

Exit City Center
Gas S: Esso[*, D], Petro Canada[*], Shell[24]
Food S: McDonald's, Tim Horton's, Wendy's
Lodg S: Country View Motor Inn
Med N: ✚ Hospital

Exit Vicars Rd
Gas S: Chevron[*], Mohawk[*, D]
Food S: A & W, Arby's, Harold's, Malibu, Taco Time
Lodg S: 4 Season Motel, Courtesy Motel, Kings Motor Inn, Riders Motor Inn, Skyline Motel
ATM S: Chevron

Exit Oriole Rd
Gas S: Turbo[*, D]
Food S: Aldo's, KFC, Mr Mikes, Orchid Restaurant, Over Waitea Foods, Pizza Hut, Subway, The Pantry Family Restaurant, Valley View Restaurant
Lodg S: Davy Crockett, Lamplighter Motel
TServ **S: James Western Star Truck Service**
ATM S: TD Bank
Other S: Coopers Pharmacy, K-Mart, Shoppers Drug Mart

Exit Tanager Rd
Lodg S: Ranchland Motel, Thrift Inn

Exit Hallman Rd

Exit Campbell Creek Industrial Park
Gas S: Super Save[*, D, LP]

Exit Pritchard
Gas S: Esso[*]

Exit Willow Rd

Exit Service Road
Gas N: Petro Canada[*]
Food N: Petro Canada

Exit Chase
Lodg N: Chase Country Inn
Med N: ✚ Hospital

Exit Casino Rd
Gas N: Petro Canada[*, LP]
Food N: Orange Tree Restaurant
ATM S: Salmon Arm Savings & Credit Union
Other N: Post Office
S: Shu Shwap Grocery

EXIT BC

Exit Arnheim Rd
Food N: Sorrento Motel
S: Courtyard Dining Room
Lodg N: Sorrento Motel, Sorrento Motor Inn

Exit Centennial Dr
Food N: Log N' Hearth

Exit Balmoral Rd
Gas N: Tempo[*]
Food S: Restaurant

Exit Sunny Brae Rd
Gas N: Co-Op[*]
Lodg N: Sky Blue Waters Resort Motel & Campground (1 Mile)

Exit Bolton Rd
Gas N: Esso[*, D]
Food N: Esso

Exit Leaving Salmon Arms
Lodg N: Salmon River Motel

Exit (Side Road)
Food N: Joey's Only Seafood
Lodg N: Travelodge TraveLodge

Exit (Side Road)
Gas N: Turbo[*, D]

Exit 10th St SW
Gas S: Shell[*, D, 24]
Food N: Humpty's, McDonald's[PLAY]
Lodg N: Best Western

Exit 3rd St NW
Gas N: Super Save[*, D, LP]
Food N: A & W
S: Smitty's
Lodg S: The Coast Shuswap Lodge

Exit Shuswap St

Exit McLeod

Exit Alexander St
Food N: Dairy Queen
S: Jade Palace
ATM N: CIBC

Exit Ross St
Food N: KFC
S: Subway
Other N: Mail Boxes Etc.

Exit 6th St NE
Gas N: Esso[*], Petro Canada[*]
Food N: Pebbles Restaurant, Tim Horton's
Lodg N: Salmon Arm Motor Hotel
S: Village Motel
ATM N: Esso

Exit in Salmon Arm (service Road)
Lodg S: Orchard Motel
Med N: ✚ Hospital

Exit 30 St NE
Gas N: Co-Op[*, D]
Food N: Carosuel Family Restaurant
S: Rickaby's
Lodg N: Super 8
Other S: Broadview Veterinary Hospital

Exit BC 97B S
Gas S: Fas Gas[*, LP]

Exit Salmon Arm
Lodg S: Cal -Van Motel, Travelers Rest Motel
Other N: Public Golf Course

Exit Silver Sands Rd

Exit BC Hwy 97A
Gas N: Petro Canada[*, D]
S: Shell[*, D]
Food S: Jade Stone Inn, Stern Wheeler, Subway

EXIT BC

Lodg N: Abide With Me Inn, Alpine Motel
S: Paradise Motel
Other S: Buy & Save Supermarket, Police Station

Exit Rauman Rd.
Gas S: Esso[*, LP]
Lodg N: Sicamouse Inn

Exit Bus. Frontage Road
FStop **S: Gasmart[*]**
Gas N: Mohawk[*, D]

Exit Stadnicki Rd.
TStop **N: Husky[*]**
Food **N: Welcome Inn Restaurant**
Lodg S: Monashee Motel
TServ **N: Husky**
TWash **N: High Performance Truck Wash**

Exit Oxbox Frontage Rd., Malakwa Rd

Exit Malakwa Road
Gas N: Thrifty Gas[*, LP]
Food N: Malakwa Cafe
Lodg N: Eagle View Motel

Exit Rest Area, Historic Site

Exit Craigallachie
TStop **N: Ski Line Truck Stop[*, LP] (Restaurant)**
ATM **N: Ski Line Truck Stop (Restaurant)**

Exit 3 Valley Gap
Lodg N: Three Valley Gap Motor Inn (Closed for Winter)

Exit Hwy 23S

Exit LaForme Blvd.
Gas N: Chevron[*], Esso[*]
S: Petro Canada[*], Shell[*, LP]
Food N: Denny's
S: A & W, McDonald's, Scotties Restaurant
Lodg N: Canyon Motor Inn, Sandman Inn, Wayside Inn Best Western
S: Super 8

Exit Hwy 23N
FStop **N: Chevron Commercial Fuel Stop**
Gas N: Super Save[*, D]
Food N: Frontier Family Restaurant
S: Subway
Lodg N: Frontier Motel

Exit Summit Parkway

Exit Revelstoke City Centre, Mt McKenzie Ski Area
Med S: ✚ Hospital

Exit Service Road
Gas N: Petro Canada[*, D, LP]
Lodg N: Glacier Park Lodge Best Western

Exit 12th Street
Gas N: Esso[*, 24]
S: Esso[*], Petro Canada[*, D], Shell[*, D]
Food N: A & W, Humpty's In Golden[24], Sawmill Restaurant, Subway
S: Dairy Queen, Smitty's
Lodg N: Ponderosa Motor Inn
S: Mountain View Inn Best Western, Sportsman Motel, Swiss Village Inn

Exit Service Road
TStop **N: Husky[*] (Restaurant)**
FStop **N: Fas Gas[*, LP]**
Food N: Country Garden Family Restaurant
Lodg S: Prestige Inn, Selkirk Inn Motel, Super 8

Exit Weigh Station (Westbound)

Exit BC 95, Golden Town Centre
Med S: ✚ Hospital

EXIT	BC/AB
Exit	Golden-Donald Road
Food	**S:** Hill Top Restaurant
Lodg	**S:** Golden Gate Motel, Golden Rim Motor Inn
Exit	Lafontaine Rd.
Food	**N:** Golden Mountain Restaurant
Lodg	**N:** Golden Village Inn
Exit	Rest Area
Exit	Field
Exit	AB Hwy 93, Ice Fields Parkway, Jasper
Exit	Lake Louise
Gas	**S:** Esso(*, D), Petro Canada(*, LP)
Food	**S:** Bee Line Chicken & Pizza, Mountain Restaurant
Exit	AB Hwy 93, Banff-Windermere Hwy, Radium Hot Springs, Bow Valley Parkway, AB Hwy 1A, Castle Junction

↑ British Columbia

↓ Alberta

Exit	AB Hwy 1A, Bow Valley Parkway
Exit	Banff
Food	**N:** Big Horn Steakhouse
Lodg	**N:** Timberline Lodge
Med	**S:** ✚ Hospital
Exit	Harvey Heights
Lodg	**N:** Cee-Der Chalets, Gateway Inn Motor, Rundle Ridge Chalets
Exit	Hwy 1A Canmore, Bow Valley Trail
FStop	**S: Petro Canada**(*, LP)
Gas	**S:** Esso(*)
Food	**S:** Craig's Family Restaurant, Tim Horton's, Wendy's
Lodg	**S:** Pocaterran Inn
ATM	**S:** Esso, **Petro Canada**
Exit	Canmore Town Centre
Gas	**S:** Shell(*)
Food	**S:** A & W, Boston Pizza, Dairy Queen, Patrinos Steakhouse
Lodg	**S:** A-1 Motel, Chalet Canmore Resort, Mayfield Motel, Rocky Mountain Ski Lodge
Med	**S:** ✚ Hospital
Exit	AB Hwy 1A, Canmore
Med	**N:** ✚ Hospital
Exit	Service Road
Gas	**N:** Esso(*), Husky(*, D), Payless Gass(*)
Food	**N:** Grizzley Bar Restaurant
Lodg	**N:** Big Horn Motel, Green Acres Motel, Pigon Mountain Motel
Exit	Dead Man's Flats
Exit	Seebe Exshaw
Exit	AB Hwy 40, Kananaskis County, Kananaskis Village
Exit	Morley Rd.
Gas	**S:** Gas Plus(*, D)
Food	**S:** Chief Chiniki
Other	**S:** Chiniki Village Grocery
Exit	Bear Hill Road
Exit	AB 68 S, Sibbald Creek Trail
Exit	Vehicle Inspection Station

EXIT	AB
	(Eastbound)
Exit	Service Road
FStop	**N: Petro Canada**(*, D, LP)
Exit	AB 22 N, Cochran, AB 22S, Bragg Creek Rd.
Exit	Spring Bank Road
Exit	563, Old Banff Road, Coach Road
Exit	Valley Ridge Blvd
Exit	Stoney Trail, 101 Street NW
FStop	**S: Esso**(*)
Lodg	**S:** Econolodge
Exit	Bowfort Rd., Canada Olympic Drive
Gas	**N:** Petro Canada(*, CW, 24), Shell(*)
Food	**N:** McDonald's, Robin's Donuts, Wendy's
TWash	**N: Truck & RV Wash**
ATM	**N:** Petro Canada
Exit	34 Avenue North, AB 2S, Sarcee Trail
Exit	Home Road
Food	**N:** Dairy Queen, KFC, Pizza Hut, The Club House
Other	**N:** Safeway Grocery
Exit	46th Street NW
Gas	**N:** Esso(*, CW), Turbo(*, D, LP, CW) **S:** Shell(*)
Food	**N:** Tim Horton's (Esso) **S:** Smitty's Restaurant, Taco Bell, Taco Bell
Lodg	**S:** Traveler's Inn
ATM	**N:** Esso
Exit	45th Street NW
Gas	**N:** Fast Gas(*, D)
Lodg	**N:** Holiday Motel **S:** Red Carpet Inn
Exit	44th Street NW
Gas	**N:** 7-11 Convenience Store(*) **S:** Husky(*, CW)
Exit	43rd Street NW
Lodg	**N:** Budget Host Inn Motel
Exit	Bownes Road
Exit	Shaganappi Trail
Exit	29th St NW, Uxbridge Dr
Gas	**N:** Shell(*)
Food	**N:** Highball, Luciano's, Mr Sub, Tim Horton's, Wendy's
ATM	**N:** CIBC
Other	**N:** Super Drug Mart **S:** Kenron Pharmacy
Exit	University Dr
Med	**S:** ✚ Hospital
Exit	Banff Trail
Food	**N:** Boston Pizza, McDonald's, Phil's, Red Lobster
Lodg	**N:** Econolodge, Royal Wayne Inn, Travelodge TraveLodge, Village Park Inn Best WEstern
Exit	19th St NW
Food	**N:** White Spot Family Dining
Lodg	**N:** Highlander Hotel **S:** Baniff Trail Motel
Exit	14th St
Exit	12th St
Gas	**N:** Petro Canada(*, CW)
Food	**N:** Loco Lou's Grill, Taco Time

EXIT	AB
Exit	11th St NW
Food	**N:** Arby's, Double Fortune, Subway, The Great Canadian Bagel
Exit	10th St NW
Gas	**S:** Esso(*, CW)
Exit	7th St NW
Food	**N:** Mezzaluna Cafe, North Hill Diner
Exit	6th St NW
ATM	**N:** CIBC
Exit	4th St NW
Gas	**S:** Turbo(*, LP)
Food	**N:** A & W
ATM	**S:** Turbo
Exit	2nd St NW
Food	**N:** Denali's Smoke House Grill **S:** Empress Garden, Woo Fat BBQ House
Med	**S:** ✚ Walk In Clinic
Other	**S:** Star Light Pharmacy
Exit	Center St
Exit	Edmonton Trail
Gas	**N:** Esso(*, CW) **S:** 7-11 Convenience Store(*), Mohawk(*)
Food	**N:** Capri Pizza House, McDonald's (Esso)
ATM	**S:** 7-11 Convenience Store, Mohawk
Exit	4th St
Gas	**S:** Petro Canada
Food	**N:** Juliet's Castle **S:** Aladdin Kitchen, Robin's Donuts
Other	**N:** Trans Canada Veterinary Hospital
Exit	6th St
Gas	**N:** Petro Canada(*, D) **S:** Esso(*, CW)
Food	**S:** Mr Sub
Exit	Russell Rd, AB131, Mocton N
Food	**N:** Ambassador Inn
Lodg	**N:** Ambassodor Motor Inn
Exit	Alberta Hwy 2, Deerfoot Trail
Exit	19 St E
Gas	**N:** Esso(*), Shell(*)
Lodg	**N:** Crossroads Hotel **S:** Holiday Inn
Exit	Barlow Trail
FStop	**S: Mohawk**(*, D)
Gas	**N:** Canpro(*, CW)
Lodg	**N:** Travelodge TraveLodge
TServ	**S: Calgary Peterbilt**
Med	**N:** ✚ Hospital
Exit	36 St E, Sunridge Way
Gas	**N:** Shell(*)
Food	**N:** Reef-N-Beef Restaurant **S:** A & W, McDonald's(PLAY) (Interactive), Taco Time
Lodg	**S:** Coastal Plaza Hotel
Med	**N:** ✚ Hospital
ATM	**N:** Scotia Bank
Other	**N:** Superstore
Exit	Hwy 302, Richer, Ross
Gas	**S:** Mohawk(*)
Lodg	**S: Richer Motor Inn Motor Hotel**
Exit	Unnamed
TStop	**S: Esso**(*, LP), **Shell**(*, CW)
Food	**S: Double S (Esso), Shell**
TServ	**S: Esso, Shell**
Exit	52 St E
Gas	**S:** Esso(*, CW)
Food	**S:** Joey's Only Seafood, KFC, Mr. Schnapp's, Pizza Hut, Subway, Tim Horton's
ATM	**S:** Esso

Bold red print shows RV & Bus parking available or nearby

EXIT AB

Other S: K-Mart, Mail Boxes Etc., Safeway Grocery(RX), Veterinary Clinic

Exit Calgary, 68 St E

Gas N: Petro Canada(*, CW)

Food N: McDonald's, Subway

Med N: + Walk In Clinic

ATM N: Petro Canada(*, CW), Petro Canada, Scotia Bank

Other N: Co-Op Supermarket(RX), Monterey Veterinary Clinic

Exit 84 St. NE

Exit Service Rd

Exit Hwy 1A, West Chestermere, Calgary

Exit Sec Hwy 791

Exit Alberta Hwy 9, Sec Hwy 797

Exit Truck Scale (Westbound), Vehicle Inspection Station (Eastbound)

Exit Alberta Hwy 24

Exit Service Rd

Food N: Restaurant (Wheatland Country Inn)

Lodg N: Best Western, Wheatland Country Inn (Restaurant)

Exit Sec Hwy 817

TStop N: **Husky(*, D, LP) (Restaurant)**

Gas N: Mohawk(D) (Ethonal)

Food N: A & W, Craig's Way Station, **Restaurant(*, D, LP) (Husky)**, Roadhouse Restaurant & Saloon, Smiley's Family Restaurant

Lodg N: Super 8

Med N: + Hospital

ATM N: **Husky(*, D, LP)**, **Husky (Restaurant)**

Exit Strathmore

FStop N: **Petro Canada(*, D)**

Gas N: Esso(*, D), Shell(*)

Food N: Dairy Queen, KFC, Little Village Cafe (Leroy's Motor Inn)

Lodg N: Leroy's Motor Inn (Restaurant)

Exit Frontage Rd

Gas N: Strathmore Highway Camping Company(*, D, LP)

Exit Hwy 21N, Rockyford

Exit Sec. Hwy 561, Standard, Hussar

Exit Sec. Hwy 547, Gleichen

Exit Sec. Rd 842

FStop S: **Petro Canada(*, D, LP) (Restaurant)**

Food S: **Restaurant(*, D, LP) (Petro-Canada)**

AServ S: **Petro Canada (Restaurant)**

Exit RGE 18 Rd 4

Exit Bassano

Exit Sec. Hwy 550, Bassano

Exit Rest Area - RR, Phones, Picnic

Exit Hwy 36

Exit Seconday Hwy 873, Brooks, Duchess

Gas S: Husky(*)

Food S: McDonald's(PLAY), **Restaurant (Heritage Inn)**

Lodg S: **Heritage Inn (Restaurant)**

Med S: + Hospital

Exit Brooks, Sec. Hwy 542

FStop S: **Shell(*, D, 24) (Restaurant)**

Food S: **Smitty's Restaurant(*, D) (Shell)**

Lodg S: **Super 8**

EXIT AB

Med S: + Hospital

ATM S: **Shell(*, D)**, **Shell (Restaurant)**

Exit RGE 14, RD 2

TStop N: **Petro Canada(*, D, LP) (Restaurant)**

Food N: **Humpty's Family Restaurant(*, D, LP) (Petro-Canada)**

Exit TWP 18 Rd 4

Exit Sec. Rd 876, Tilly

Exit Suffield

Gas N: United Fuel(*)

Exit Hwy 524, Hays, Rolling Hills

Exit Service Rd

FStop N: **Shell(*, D)**

Lodg N: Palla's Motel

Exit Redcliff, Service Rd

TStop S: **Transcanada Truck Stop(*, D, LP) (Restaurant)**

Food S: **Trucker's Restaurant(*, D) (Transcanada Truck Stop)**

TServ S: **Ken Huck Truck Repair(*, D, LP) (Transcanada Truck Stop)**, **Transcanada Truck Stop (Restaurant)**

TWash S: **Transcanada Truck Stop(*, D, LP)**, **Transcanada Truck Stop (Restaurant)**

Exit Brier Park Rd

Exit 3 St. NW

Exit 1 St. SW

Gas N: Turbo(*)

Lodg N: Ranch Motel

Exit 6th St. SW, 7th St SW

Gas S: Petro Canada(*, D) (Restaurant), Shell(*, D) (Restaurant)

Food N: Cheedear's Restaurant

S: Black Angus Steakhouse, O'Riley's Restaurant, Restaurant (Shell), Restaurant (Petro-Canada)

Lodg N: Park Lane Motor Hotel

S: Best Western, Callagan Inn

Med N: + Hospital

ATM S: Shell, Shell (Restaurant)

Exit Crows Nest Highway, Lethbridge, Hwy 3, City Centre

Gas N: Mohawk(*) (Ethanol), Petro Canada(*)

Food N: Elieen's Restaurant

S: A & W, ABC Country Restaurant, McDonald's, Subway

Lodg N: Clover Leaf Motor Inn, Searra Motel, Trans Canada Motel

S: Circle T Lodge, Pals Motel, Sun-Dek Motel, Travelodge TraveLodge

Exit 16 St. SW

TStop S: **Husky's(*, D, LP) (Restaurant)**

Gas S: Esso(*), Payless(*)

Food S: Craig's Family Restaurant, **Restaurant(*, LP) (Husky's)**

Lodg S: Belaire Motel

Exit South Ridge Dr., College Ave.

Other S: Tourist Info.

Exit 13 Ave. SE

Gas N: Esso(*), Shell(*)

S: Mohawk(*, LP) (Ethonal)

Food N: Arby's, Country Style, Pizza Hut

Lodg N: Imperial Inn, Motor Inn, Super 8, West Lander Inn

Med N: + Southview Mall Medical Clinic

Exit Medicine Hat, Dunmore Rd SE

Gas N: Petro Canada(*, CW)

Food N: Jim Horton's, McDonald's(PLAY), Perkin's Family Restaurant, Wendy's

EXIT AB/SK

Lodg N: Comfort Inn & Suites, Medicine Hat Lodge

ATM N: Petro Canada, Petro Canada

Other N: The Super Store, Wal-Mart(RX)

Exit Dunmore

Exit Hwy 41N, Oyen, Schuler

Exit Vehicle Inspection Station (Westbound)

Exit Hwy 41, Havre, Elkwater

Exit Irving, Thompson St.

Gas N: Payless(*, LP) (Restaurant)

Food N: Restaurant(*, LP) (Payless)

Exit Walsh

FStop N: **Shell(*, D, LP) (Restaurant)**

Gas N: Canadadian Independent(*, LP)

Food N: Restaurant (Shell)

↑ Alberta

↓ Saskatchewan

Exit Hwy 21, Lester, Cypress Hills

TStop N: **Esso(*, D) (Restaurant, Motel)**

Food N: **Restaurant (Esso)**

Lodg N: **Motel (Esso)**, Prairie Pride Motel

Med S: + Hospital

Exit Paipot

Food S: Restaurant

Exit Tompkins

Gas S: Co-Op(*, D)

Exit Hwy 37, Cabri, Shaunavon

FStop N: **Esso(*, D) (Restaurant)**

Food N: **Restaurant(*, D) (Esso)**

Lodg S: Motel

Exit Hwy 32, West Leader

Exit Truck Scale

Exit Service Road

FStop N: **Esso(*, D) (Restaurant)**

Food N: Restaurant (Esso)

TServ S: **Freightliner**

Exit Lac Pelle Trail

FStop S: **Petro Pass(*, D)**, **Shell Commercial(*, D)**

Food N: K Motel

Lodg N: K Motel (Restaurant)

Exit 11th Ave. NW

TStop S: **Husky(*, LP) (Restaurant)**

Food S: **Restaurant(*) (Husky)**

TServ S: **Mack**

Exit Jackson Drive

Gas N: Shell(*, D, CW)

Food N: Country Kitchen, Dairy Queen, Houston Family Restaurant

Lodg N: Westwin Motel

S: Swift Motel

Exit Central Ave. City Center, Hwy 4

Gas N: Co-Op(*, D, CW), Esso(*, D, CW) (Smittys)

S: 7-11 Convenience Store(*, D), Husky(*, CW), Shell(*, D)

Food N: Broncos Family Diner, Kabos Restaurant, Mom's Korner Restaurant

S: A & W, Carol's Family Restaurant, Dairy King, KFC, McDonald's, Mr Sub, Pizza Hut, Wong's Kitchen

Lodg N: Horseshoe Lodge, Motel Caravel, Travelodge TraveLodge

S: Best Western, City Centre Motel, Rainbow Motel, Safari Motel

Med S: + Hospital

Bold red print shows RV & Bus parking available or nearby

EXIT — SK

ATM N: Esso[*, D, CW], Esso (Smittys), Scotia Bank
S: 7-11 Convenience Store[*], 7-11 Convenience Store
Other N: Wal-Mart[RX]

Exit Hwy 4, Cadillac, Rosetown
Gas N: Petro Canada[*, D] (Humpty's Restaurant)
Food N: Humpty's Restaurant[*, D] (Petro-Canada)
S: Rodeway Motel
Lodg S: Comfort Inn, Imperial 400 Motel, Rodeway Inn (Restaurant)
Other N: Safeway Grocery

Exit Swift Current, Ponderosa Trail

Exit Waldeck

Exit Hebert
Gas N: Can-Op[*, D, LP], Esso[*, D] (Restaurant)
Food N: Restaurant[*, D] (Esso)
Lodg N: Lone Eagle Motel

Exit Morse
Gas N: Esso[*, LP] (Restaurant)
Food N: Esso[*, LP] (Restaurant)
Lodg N: Motel 9

Exit Hwy 19S, Hodgeville

Exit Hwy 58, S-Shamrock, N-Central Butte
TStop N: **Silver Dollar[*] (Restaurant)**
Food N: **Silver Dollar[*]**
TServ N: **Silver Dollar[*], Silver Dollar (Restaurant)**

Exit Access Rd, Caron, Caronbort
FStop N: **Petro Canada[*, D, LP] (Pilgrim Restaurant)**
Lodg N: Pilgrim Inn

Exit 9th Ave., NW
Gas N: Esso[*, D] (Rodos Restaurant)
Food N: Rodos Restaurant[*, D] (Esso)

Exit Hwy 2, S. Main St., N. Prince Albert
TStop N: **Petro Canada[*, D] (Petro-Pass Fuel, Restaurant, TWash)**
Gas N: Shell[*] (Restaurant)
S: Mohawk[*, D, CW]
Food N: **Petro Canada[*, D] (Restaurant)**, Shell[*] (Restaurant)
S: Bonanza, Dairy Queen
Lodg N: **Park Lodge Motor Motel**
S: Humpty's Family Restaurant
TServ S: **Quality Truck Service**
TWash N: **Petro Canada[*, D]**

Exit Hwy 2, Manitoba St. Exp., Canadian Forces Base, Thatcher Dr.
TStop S: **Esso[*, D] (Prairie Oasis Restaurant, Motel)**
Food S: **Prairie Oasis Restaurant[*, D] (Esso TStop)**
Lodg S: **Prairie Oasis Motel[*, D] (Esso)**

Exit Petrolia Road
Gas S: Roadrunner[*, D]
Food S: Roadrunner[*, D] (Restaurant)
Lodg S: Knowles Motel

Exit Hwy 301N, Hwy 31S

Exit Kalium Road

EXIT — SK

Exit Belle Plaine
Gas N: Tempo[*, D]
Lodg N: Chubbys Motel

Exit Weigh Station

Exit Lewvan Dr.

Exit Albert St., Hwy 6N
Gas N: Shell[*, CW]
Food N: Boston Pizza, McDonald's, McDonald's (Wal-Mart), Pizza Hut
ATM N: Bank of Montreal
Other N: Pharmacy (Wal-Mart), Wal-Mart[RX] (McDonald's)

Exit Wascana Pkwy, Univ. Of Regina

Exit Arcola Ave.

Exit Hwy 11N, Saskatoon, Sity Center, Hwy 1W, Moose Jaw
Gas N: Shell[*]
Food N: Burger King, Dairy Queen, Houston Pizza, McDonald's, Smitty's Restaurant
Lodg N: Siesta Motel, Sunrise Motel, Travelodge TraveLodge
ATM N: CIBC
Other N: Shoppers Drug Mart

Exit Fleet St., University Park Drive
Gas N: Esso[*, D], Petro Canada[*, D, CW], Shell[*, D]
S: Petro Canada[D]
Food N: Humpty's Restaurant
S: Pizza Hut, Robin's Donuts
Lodg N: Super 8
ATM S: Scotia Bank, Sherwood Credit Union
Other N: House Animal Hospital, Vick Plaza Animal Clinic
S: Costco, Safeway Grocery, Shoppers Drug Mart

Exit Prince Of Wales Dr
TStop N: **Husky[*, D, SCALES]**
Food N: Country Side Family Restaurant, **Husky[*, D, SCALES] (Restaurant)**
Lodg N: Comfort Inn, Country Inn & Suites, **Husky[*, D, SCALES]**, Travel-Inn

Exit Service Rd
Lodg N: Four Star Motel

Exit Service Rd

Exit Pilot Butte Rd

Exit Great Plains Industrial Drive
TStop S: **Great Plains Truck Stop[*, D, LP] (Esso Gas)**
Food S: **Great Plains Truck Stop[*, D, LP] (Restaurant)**
Lodg S: **Great Plains Truck Stop[*, D, LP]**
TServ S: **Great Plains Truck Stop[*, D, LP]**
TWash S: **Great Plains Truck Stop[*, D, LP]**

Exit Hwy 48E, White City

Exit Hwy 46W, North Regina
Gas N: Tempo[*, D]

Exit Balgonie
Gas N: McIlwaine[*]
Lodg N: Balgonie Motel

Exit McLean

Exit Hwy 35

Exit Hwy 56
Gas N: Esso[*, D] (Restaurant), Value[*]

EXIT — SK/MB

(Restaurant)
Food N: Esso[*, D] (Restaurant), Value (Restaurant)
Lodg N: Shayne Inn Motel

Exit Indian Head
Gas N: Shell[*, D]

Exit Sintaluta

Exit Wolseley
Gas N: Esso[*]

Exit Wolseley, Hwy 617
Gas S: Harvest Fuel[*]
Food S: Harvest Fuel[*] (Restaurant)
Lodg S: Motel
Med N: + Hospital

Exit Grenfell, Hwy 47, Melville
Gas N: Esso[*], Harvest Fuel
Food N: Esso[*]
Lodg N: Homestead Motel

Exit Broadview
Gas S: Esso[*, D]
Lodg S: Edward's Motel

Exit Saskatcatwan, Hwy 201
Food S: Dairy Palace
Lodg N: Moondance Motel

Exit Whitewood, Hwy 9, Carlyle, Yorkton
FStop N: **Petro Canada[*, D] (Restaurant)**
Gas S: Esso[*]
Food N: **Petro Canada[*, D]**
Lodg S: **Whitewood Inn**

Exit Wapella
Gas S: Harvest Fuel (Wendy's)
Food S: Wendy's (Harvest Fuels)
Lodg N: Paton Motel's

Exit Hwy 8N
FStop N: **Esso[*, D] (Crusty's Pizza & Subs)**
Food N: Country Suire Inn, **Crusty's Pizza & Subs (Esso)**, Dairy Queen, Wong's Restaurant
Lodg N: Country Squire Inn
S: Moosimin Motel, Prairie Pride Motel, Twi-light Motel

Exit Moosomin, Hwy 8 S
Gas N: Fast Gas[*]
S: Co-Op[*], Shell[*]
Food N: The Red Barn
S: KFC

Exit Truck Scale

↑ Saskatchewan

↓ Manitoba

Exit Visitor Center - Tourist Info (Closed Winter Months)

Exit MB542S, MB41, Kola

Exit Rest Area - Phones, RR, Picnic

Exit MB256

Exit Elkhorn Jct, Richhill Ave.
Gas S: Esso[*, D]
Food S: Esso[*, D]

Exit MB259
Gas N: Esso[*]

Bold red print shows RV & Bus parking available or nearby

EXIT	MB
	S: Esso(*, D, LP), Petro Canada(*, D), Shell(*, D)
Food	S: Esso(*, D, LP), Shell(*, D)
Lodg	S: **Country Side Inn Motel**, Jays Inn Motel, **Virden Motel**
Med	S: ✚ Hospital
ATM	S: Esso(*, D, LP)
Other	S: Hi-Way Grocery, IGA Supermarket, Police Station
Exit	MB257, Virden Exits
Exit	MB254 S, Oak Lake Beach
Exit	MB254
Exit	Harrison Bridge Rd, North Tower Rd S, Oak Lake
Exit	MB21, Hartney, Shoal Lake
Exit	MB250, Rivers
Exit	MB250S, Souris
Exit	Weigh Station
Exit	Hwy 1A, Kemnay, Brandon
Exit	MB459, Grand Valley
Exit	MB270, Rapid City
Exit	Hwy 10S, Boissevain
TStop	S: **Husky**(*)
Gas	S: Shell(*)
Food	N: Little Chalet Motel S: A & W, **Husky**, Smitty's, Subway(24)
Lodg	N: Little Chalet Motel S: Super 8
TServ	N: **Freightliner** S: **Kelleher Mercury, Lincoln, Mac Arthur Mack**
Exit	Hwy 1A, Hwy 10, Dauphin, Brandon
Gas	N: Esso(*, D) S: Petro Canada(*)
Food	N: Esso, McDonald's S: Beef & Barrell, Harry's Ukrainian Kitchen, Humpty's Family Restaurant
Lodg	N: **Barney's Motel**, Comfort Inn S: Midway Motel
TServ	N: **Mid Canada Truck International**
Exit	MB468, MB110, Charter, Justice
Exit	MB340
Exit	MB464, Brookdale
Exit	Hwy 5, Carberry, Neepawa

EXIT	MB
Food	S: 4 Way Motel
Lodg	S: 4 Way Motel
Exit	Hwy 351, Melbourne
Exit	Tower Line Rd
FStop	N: **Petro Canada**(*)
Food	N: Petro Canada
TServ	N: **Norfolk Transport Truck Repair**
Exit	MB34
Exit	Austin , Springbrook Rd
Exit	Hwy 350, Lavenham, Katrime, Mac Gregor
Gas	S: Mohawk(*, LP)
Food	S: Mohawk
Lodg	S: JK's Motel
Exit	Hwy 242
Exit	Hwy 16, Yellow Head Rt, Hwy 305, St Claude, Neepawa
FStop	S: **Petro Canada**(*)
Exit	Ferris Rd, Munro Rd S
Gas	S: Esso(*, D)
Food	S: Esso
Exit	MB1A City Rt, Portage
Exit	Yellowquill Trail
Lodg	S: Manitobah Inn
Exit	Hwy 240, Southport, Portage
Exit	Hwy 1A, City Rt., Portage
FStop	S: **Shell**(*)
Food	S: Shell
Exit	MB430N, Hwy 13S, Carman, St Amborise, Oakville
Exit	MB331
Exit	Hwy 248, St. Eustache, Elie
FStop	N: **Esso**(*)
Food	N: Esso
Exit	Hwy 332, Dacotah, Starbuck
Exit	Hwy 241, Lido Plage Rd
TServ	N: **Heavy Truck Parts**
Exit	Hwy 26
Gas	S: Arvist(*)
Exit	Gaol Rd

EXIT	MB
Exit	Weigh Station
Exit	MB334
TStop	N: **Husky**(*)
Gas	S: Esso(*, D), Tempo(*)
Food	N: **Husky**
TServ	N: **Husky** S: **Mid City Truck Centre**
ATM	N: Husky
Other	S: Police Station
Exit	Inglenook Rd
Lodg	S: **Alpine Motel**
Exit	Hwy 100, Winnipeg Bypass, Hwy 101N
Exit	Hwy 207, Lorette
FStop	N: **Petro Canada**(*, LP)
Food	N: Salisbury House (Petro Canada)
Lodg	N: Motel 66
Exit	Hwy 206N, Oakbank
Exit	Hwy206S, Landmark
Exit	Hwy 501, Rosewood Rd
Exit	Hwy 207, Dufresne
Exit	Hwy 12, Beausejour, Steinbach
Exit	Hwy 207, Dawson Rd
Exit	Rest Area - RR, Phones, Picnic
Exit	Hwy 503, Old Dawson Trail
Lodg	N: Dawson Trail Inn
Exit	506, Prawda
FStop	N: **Esso**(*), **Shell**(*)
Food	N: Esso, Shell
Exit	Mc Munn Rd
Gas	N: Tempo
Lodg	N: Mc Munn Motor Motel
Exit	Hwy 308, Moose Lake, Sprague
Exit	Township
Lodg	N: Whiteshell Motor Motel
Exit	MB301, Falcon Lake
Exit	MB44, West Hawk Lake

↑ Manitoba

Begin Hwy 1, West Hawk Lake

TCH-2 S →

EXIT	AB
	Begin 2, Edmonton

↓ Alberta

EXIT	AB
Exit	AB14, White Mud Dr, to AB16
Lodg	E: Holiday Inn
Exit	34th Ave
Gas	E: Esso(*, CW) W: Esso(*, CW), Gas Bar(*)
Food	E: Keegan's, McDonald's, Tim Horton's, Wendy's W: Buffett World, Chili's, Denny's, Harvey's, KFC, Taco Bell, Tim Horton's (Esso)
ATM	E: Esso W: Esso
Other	W: Food For Less

EXIT	AB
Exit	23rd Ave
Med	E: ✚ Hospital
Exit	Ellerslie Rd, 9th Ave
Gas	W: Mohawk(*), Shell(*, LP, 24)
Food	W: Mr John's (Mohawk), Shell
Lodg	W: Chateu Motel, Ellerslie Motel
Exit	AB19, Devon, Hwy 625 E, Nisku
Exit	Edmonton Int. Airport, Nisku, 10th Ave
Lodg	E: Executive International Inn, Nisku Inn, Nisku Place Motel
Exit	Leduc North Sector
TStop	E: **Esso**(*)
Food	E: **Esso**
Lodg	E: Airport Motel
TServ	E: **Esso**

EXIT	AB
Exit	Leduc Business Section
Gas	E: Esso(*, CW)
Food	E: A & W, McDonald's(PLAY), Pizza Hut, Subway, Wendy's, Zambelli's
Lodg	E: Leduc Inn, Travelodge TraveLodge
Other	E: Safeway Grocery, Shoppers Drug Mart
Exit	AB39, Drayton Valley, Leduc City Center
Gas	E: Mohawk(*), Petro Canada(*)
Food	E: Boston Pizza, Burger Barron Drive In, Gooseberry's Restaurant, O'Brian's (Best Western), Smitty's
Lodg	E: Denhma Inn Best Western
ATM	E: CIBC
Other	E: Value Drug Mart
Exit	AB2a S

TCH-2 ← N

EXIT AB

Exit Vehicle Inspection (Southbound)
Exit AB616 E, Millet, AB616 W, Mulhurst
Exit AB13
Exit Service Area- Bar Hills
FStop B: **Bar Hills(*, D)**
Exit Rest Area - RR, Phones, Picnic (Northbound)
Exit AB611, Hobbema, Usona District
Exit AB53 E, Ponoka, AB 53 W, Rimbey
Exit Morningside
Exit AB2a N, Ponoka, Wetaskiwin
Exit AB2 S, Lacombe
Exit College Heights
Med E: ✚ Hospital
Exit AB12, Lacombe, Bentley
Med E: ✚ Hospital
Exit 597 E, Joffry, Blackfalds
Exit AB11a
Exit 67th St, East Red Deer
FStop E: **Shell(*)**
Lodg E: Holiday Inn
Exit Rest Area - RR, Phones, Picnic, Heritage Ranch (Westbound)
Exit 32nd St
Exit AB2, Red Deer, City Centre
Food E: Burger King, Kelsey's
Med E: ✚ Hospital
Exit Gasoline Alley, Willow St
Gas E: Esso(*), Petro Canada(*, D, 24), Shell(*)
Food E: A & W, Baskin Robbins, Craig's Way Station, The Westerner, Willy's
Lodg E: Rest E-Z Inn, Southhill Motor Inn, Thunderbird Motel
Exit Mc Kenzie Rd, Gasoline Alley
FStop E: **Fas Gas(*)**

EXIT AB

W: **Esso(*)**
Gas E: Mohawk(*)
W: Husky(*, D), Shell(*, D, LP)
Food W: A & W, Donute Mill, Glen's Family Restaurant, Patty's Family Restaurant, Smitty's
Lodg E: Holiday House Motel
ATM E: Fas Gas
W: Esso, Husky
Exit Alberta Hwy 42, Penhold, Pine Lake
Exit Sec Hwy 590E, Big Valley, Alberta Hwy 54 Innasfial, Caroline
Gas W: Co-Op(*), Esso(*, CW)
Food W: A & W, Dairy Queen, Flames Family Restaurant, McDonald's, White Goose Family Restaurant
Lodg W: Highwayman Motor Inn
Med W: ✚ Hospital
Other W: Co-Op Food Market, Food Town Supermarket
Exit Side Rd Exit
FStop E: **Fas Gas(*, D) (Restaurant)**
Food E: Restaurant (Fasgas)
Exit Sec Rd 587, Vowen
Exit Hwy 27 E Torrington, Trochu, Three Hilds, W Olds College
FStop W: **Husky(*, D) (Restaurant)**
Food W: **Restaurant(*, D) (Husky)**
Exit Sec Rd 582, Didsbury
Med W: ✚ Hospital
Exit Hwy 581, Carstairs
Exit Hwy 2A, Crossfield, Carstaries, Acme
Exit Service Rd
FStop E: **Esso(*, D)**
Food E: Humpty's
Exit Hwy 2A W, Crossfield, Hwy 72E Beiseker, Acme, Drumheller

EXIT AB

Exit 567 West Airdrie Bus Dist, Irricana
Gas W: Esso(*), Petro Canada(*, D), Shell(*), Turbo(*, D, LP)
Food W: A & W, Bagelino's, Dairy Queen, Domino's Pizza, Doubletree Restaurant, KFC, McDonald's(PLAY), Pizza Hut
Lodg W: Horseman Motel, Regency Inn
ATM W: Shell(*), Shell, Turbo, Turbo
Exit E Airdrie, Industrial Area
Gas E: Payless, Petro Canada, **Roadway Diesel(D)**, Turbo(*, D) (Subway)
Food E: Restaurant (Super 8 Motel), Subway(*, D) (Turbo), Wendy's
Lodg E: Super 8 (Restaurant)
TServ E: **Roadway Die Sel Truck Repair**
ATM E: Scotia Bank
Other E: Airdrie Animal Clinic
Exit Airdrie, Bigsprings Rd
Exit Vehicle Inspection (Northbound)
Exit Hwy 566, Kathyrn, Blazac
Gas W: Turbo(*, D, LP) (Restaurant)
Food W: Restaurant (Turbo)
Exit Country Hills Blvd
Exit Beddington Trail
Exit 64 Ave N
Gas W: Petro Canada
Food W: Black Bull Pub, Dairy Queen, Domino's Pizza, Harvey's, KFC, Pizza Hut, Subway, Taco Time
Med W: ✚ Walk In Clinic
ATM W: TD Bank
Other W: Hunter Horn Veterinary Clinic, Super Drug Mart
Exit McKnight Blvd Airport
Exit 32nd Ave N
Gas E: Shell(*)
Food E: Tim Horton's

↑ Alberta

Begin 2, Calgary

TCH-16 E →

EXIT AB

Begin 16, Edmonton

↓ Alberta

Exit 170th, St Hwy 2 S
TStop S: **Shell(*, LP, 24)**
Food S: **Shell**
Lodg S: **Super 8**
TServ S: **Diamond International Trucks, Freightliner, Shell**
Other S: **West Edmonton Truck & Car Wash**
Exit 156th St
Exit 49th St
FStop N: **Husky**
Food N: Yellowhead Motor Hotel(24)
Lodg N: **Yellowhead Motor Hotel**
Exit 142nd St
Gas N: Petro Canada(D)

EXIT AB

Food N: Alvona's Pantry, McDonald's
Exit AB2 N, St Albert Trail
Gas N: Hugh's(D, CW)
Food N: Arby's
Exit 27th St
Gas N: Seven Eleven(*, 24)
Food N: Humpty's
Exit 121st St
Exit 107th St
Exit 97th St, AB28
Gas N: Dawson Motors, Husky(*), Mohawk(*, D), Seven Eleven(*)
S: Esso, Hugh's(CW)
Food N: Boston Pizza, KFC, Keegan's(24), Mr Sub, President Restaurant, Szechuen Paramount
S: Restaurante Portugues
ATM N: Alberta Treasury Bank

EXIT AB

S: Seven Eleven
Other S: Northgate Veterinary Hospital, Seven Eleven
Exit 82nd St
Gas N: Co-Op(D, LP, CW), Esso, Husky(LP, CW)
Food N: Ba Ba's House, Little Caesars Pizza, McDonald's, Mediteranian Bakery, Rice King, Sir Donut, Teresa's Diner
ATM N: CIBC Bank
Other N: Deltan Super Drugs
Exit Capilano Dr, Fort Rd
Gas N: Hugh's(D, CW)
Lodg S: **Sand Motor Hotel**
Exit 66th St
Exit 125th Ave, Bus. Access
TServ N: **Transport Tire**
Exit 50th St, 125th Ave
Gas N: Esso(CW), Hugh's(LP, CW), Husky(D, CW)

Bold red print shows RV & Bus parking available or nearby

EXIT AB

Food N: Applebee's, Arby's, Buffett World, Humpty's, Subway, Tim Horton's, Wendy's

Exit Victoria Trail, 118th Ave
Gas N: Turbo(LP)
S: Domo(*, 24), Esso(CW), Shell(*, CW, 24)
Food S: Albert's, Boston Pizza, Cheers (Travelodge), Dairy Queen, Golden Court, JB's, KFC, McDonald's, Subway, Taco Bell
Lodg S: Jockey Motel, Travelodge TraveLodge
ATM S: Bank of Montreal, Scotia Bank
Other S: Abbotts Field Mall, Garden Market IGA, K Mart, Landry Mat, Police Station, Safeway Grocery

Exit Hayter Rd, 17th St

Exit Meridian St

Exit AB14X S, 101st Ave, Edmonton, Sheerwood Park, Broadmoor Blvd, 17th St NE

Exit AB21 N, Fort Saskatchewan

Exit Ardrossan Access, AB824

Exit Elk Island National Park

Exit AB834

Exit Mundaere Access, AB855, AB15

Exit AB631 E

Exit Hwy 16a E, Vegreville (Services avail. in town)

Exit AB857

Exit Vegreville, Hwy16a W (Westbound, Difficult Reaccess, Services avail. in town)
Med N: ✚ Hospital

Exit Lavoy
Lodg N: Lavoy Motel
Other N: Mike's Grocery

Exit AB36

Exit Innisfree Access, AB870 (More services in town)
FStop N: **Petro Canada(*, LP, 24)**
Food N: Petro Canada

Exit Minburn Access (Services avail. in town)

Exit Mannville Access, Hwy 881
Food N: Gary's Cafe, The Chinese Lantern
Lodg N: Mannville Motel, The Mannville Motel
Med N: ✚ Hospital
Other N: Eastalta Grocery, Mail Post

Exit AB41, Wain Wright, Vermilion, Cold Lake
FStop N: **Husky(*, D, LP)**
Gas N: Shell(*, D)
Food N: KFC, Pizza Hut, Tastee Freeze
Lodg N: Ventura Motel, Vermilion Motor Inn
Med N: ✚ Hospital
Other N: Lakeland College

Exit Weigh Station

Exit Hidden Lake Recreation Area

Exit Hwy 893

Exit Kitscoty Access, AB897 (Services avail. 2KM in town)

Exit 66th Ave, Lloydminster
Gas S: Husky(D, CW)
Food S: Boston Pizza, Lodge Motel, Mc Donalds, Pizza Hut, Taco Time
Lodg S: Lodge Motel

Exit 62nd Ave
FStop S: **Esso(*, D)**
Gas S: Turbo(D, LP)
Food N: Royal Restaurant
S: Bonanza, Jack's Place (Esso)
Lodg S: Ivan hoe Motel
TServ N: **Lakeland Truck & Equip.**
Other S: Mr Sparkle Car Wash

Exit 59th Ave
TStop S: **Husky**
FStop N: **Petro Pass(*)**
Food N: Woo's Kitchen
S: **Husky**
ATM S: **Husky**
Other N: Food Store

Exit 57th Ave
TStop S: **Husky(*, 24)**
Food N: Grainfields Inn (West Harvest Inn)
S: **Dairy Queen (Husky), Domino's Pizza (Husky)**
Lodg N: West Harvest Inn
TServ S: **Husky**

Exit 56th Ave
Food N: Subway, Wendy's
S: Mulberry's Family Rest. (Tropical Inn)
Lodg S: Tropical Inn
ATM S: IGA
Other S: IGA Garden Market, Weir Veterinary Services

Exit 55th Ave
Food S: David's Steakhouse, Wayside Inn
Lodg S: Wayside Inn

Exit 54th Ave
Food S: Red Bull Steak & Grill, Tim Horton's
Other S: Lloyd Mall, Safeway Grocery, Zeller's

Exit 52nd Ave
Gas N: Mohawk(LP)
S: Super Store
Food N: Greek Classic, Pizza 44
ATM S: CIBC Bank
Other S: Lloyd Mall, Safeway Grocery, Super Store, Zeller's

Exit 50th Ave, SK 17
Gas N: Husky
S: Petro Canada(*)
Food N: Centra Suite Hotel, KFC
S: Arby's
Lodg N: Centra Suite Hotel, Lloyd's Motor Inn
ATM N: Scotia Bank

Exit 49th Ave
Gas N: Esso(*)
Food N: Joey's Seafood, Venice House Restaurant
S: Digger's, Humpty's(24)
Other S: Laundry Mat

Exit 48th Ave
Gas N: A&T Gas Bar(D, LP)
S: Co-Op(D, LP)
Food N: Mr Sub
S: Golden Star, Panagopolous Pizza Place
Lodg S: Good Knight Inn
Other N: Laundry Mat

Exit 47th Ave
Gas N: Seven Eleven(*, D)
Food N: Java Adventures
S: Horseshoe Restaurant (Voyager Motel)
Lodg N: Voyager Motel
S: Trailside Inn
ATM N: Seven Eleven

EXIT AB/SK

Exit 46th Ave
Lodg N: Cedar Inn

Exit 45th Ave
Gas N: Shell(*, 24)
Food N: A & W
Med S: ✚ Hospital

Exit 43rd Ave
Gas N: Fas Gas(*, D)
Food N: Imperial 400 Motel
Lodg N: Imperial 400 Motel

Exit 40th Ave
Gas N: Husky(D, LP)
TServ N: **Frontier Peterbilt**

Exit 37th Ave, Lloydminster
TServ N: **Mac Trucks**
S: **Cummins**

↑ Alberta

↓ Saskatchewan

Exit Travel Alberta Information Center (No Trucks)

Exit SK303, Turtleford

Exit Weigh Station

Exit Marshall
Lodg S: Marshall Motel

Exit Main St, Lashburn
Lodg N: Barley's Inn Lashburn
Other N: Mail Post, Pharmacy

Exit Hwy 675, Lashburn
Gas N: Esso(D)

Exit Waseca

Exit Unnamed

Exit SK21, St. Walburg, Maystone
Gas N: Husky(LP, CW), Mother Duck's
Food N: Mother Duck's Restaurant & Bakery, Sonny's
Lodg N: Sandpiper Motel
Med N: ✚ Hospital

Exit N Main St, Maidston
Gas N: A&S Cornerstore(*)
Food N: Cafe' Bouchee', Maidston Cafe (Maidston Hotel)
Lodg N: Maidston Hotel
ATM N: Credit Union
Other N: Co-Op Food Center, Maidston Pharmacy, Mail Post
S: **Truck Pull out Rest Stop**

Exit Unnamed

Exit Unnamed
Lodg N: **Dj's Motel**

Exit Paynton
Gas S: Nes Bi-Lo(*, LP)

Exit Delmas
Lodg S: Delmas Hotel

Exit SK4 S, Swift Current
Gas S: Husky(*, D, LP, CW)
ATM S: Husky

Exit Hwy 16b E, North Battleford Bus. Loop, SK4 N, Meadowlake (Eastbound)
Med N: ✚ Hospital
Other N: City Center (2 Km)

Exit Battleford Service Rd, Hwy 16a

EXIT	BC
	W
FStop	**S: Esso[*, LP]**
Gas	**N: Petro Canada[D, 24]**
Food	**N: Humpty's[24] (Petro Canada)**, Smitty's (Tropical Inn)
	S: Pierre's Place (Esso)
Lodg	N: Roadway Inn, Tropical Inn
	S: Hitching Post Motel, Super 8
Med	N: ✚ Hospital
Other	N: Austin Saddler Western World Boots
Exit	Hwy 16B W, North Battlefords Bus. Loop to SK4 N, Meadowlake, Service Road (Westbound)
FStop	**N: Shell[*, CW]**
Gas	N: Esso, Fas Gas[D]
Food	N: Battleford's Inn, Bonanza, McDonald's, Pizza Hut, Tim Horton's, Variations
Lodg	N: Battleford's Inn
TServ	**N: Murray Tire**
ATM	N: Frontier Mall
Other	N: Frontier Mall, **Golden Eagle Casino**, Met Mart, Pharmacy (Wal-Mart), Shopper's Drug Mart (Open until Midnight), Wal-Mart
Exit	SK40
Other	N: Visitor Information
Exit	Unnamed, Battlefords
Exit	Denholm
Exit	Ruddell
Exit	Maymont, SK376
Gas	S: Payless[*, D, LP]
Food	S: Maymont Hotel, Mom's Cafe
Lodg	S: Maymont Hotel
Exit	Campground
Exit	Radisson, SK340
FStop	**N: Esso[*], Shell[*, LP]**
Gas	S: Co-Op
Food	N: **Esso**, S&M Restaurant
Lodg	N: Motel
Exit	Borden
Gas	N: Tempo
Food	N: Kozy Korner Cafe
Lodg	N: Borden Hotel
Other	N: Co-Op Grocery
Exit	Borden Bridge Campground Access
Exit	Langham
FStop	**N: Shell[CW]**
Food	N: Liu's Restaurant, Pizza Pantry (Open in the Summer)
Lodg	N: Langham Hotel
Other	N: Mail Post
Exit	SK305, Delmany
Exit	Weigh Station
Exit	Dalmeny Access
Exit	71st St
Exit	Marquis Dr
Exit	60th St, SK12, SK11, Blain Lake, Prince Albert (Difficult Reaccess)
TServ	**N: Breadner Trailer Sales & Leasing, Ford Trucks, Mac Trucks, Red Dear Industrial**
Exit	51st St, Service Rd
FStop	**N: Esso[*, LP], Petro Pass[*, LP, SCALES]**
Gas	N: Mohawk[*, CW], Super Save[*, D, LP]
Food	N: Baba's, O'Smile, Tautee Maria's
TServ	**N: Can-Am Rubber Inc, Cummins, Kenworth, Peterbilt, Winacott Spring & Truck Repair, Winacott Western Star**
ATM	N: Mohawk
Other	**N: Car & Truck Wash**
	S: Airport
Exit	Airport Circle Dr W
FStop	**S: Husky[*, LP]**
Gas	S: Co-Op[*, LP, CW]
Food	S: Diner Plus, Husky[24], Riveria Restaurant & Lounge
Lodg	S: Country Inn & Suites, Heritage Inn, **Rivria Inn**, Saskatoon Inn, Travelodge, TraveLodge
TServ	**S: Husky**
ATM	S: Royal Bank, Saskatoon Credit Union
Exit	SK11 S, City Center
Gas	S: Esso[*, CW], Mohawk[*, D], Seven Eleven[*, 24], Shell, Turbo[*, D, LP]
Food	S: A & W, California Subs, Esso, Julians Family Restaurant, KFC, Mano's Restaurant, McDonald's, Mr Submarine, Robin's Donuts & Deli, Sardinia Family Restaurant, Seventy's Family Restaurant, The Kountry Korner, Wendy's
Lodg	S: Best Western, Motel
ATM	S: Shell
Other	S: Landromat
Exit	Northridge Dr N, Alberta Ave S, Saskatoon
Lodg	N: Comfort Inn
Exit	Sightful Ave, Saskatoon
Gas	N: Domo, Fas Gas[*, D]
Food	N: Burger King, Humpty's
ATM	N: CIBC Bank
Other	N: Fire Station
Exit	Quebec Ave, Sasaktoon
Food	S: Arby's, Bun's Master Bakery, Robin's Donuts, Smitty's, Thomas Pizza
Exit	First Ave
Gas	N: Turbo[*, LP]
TServ	**S: International Dealership**
Exit	Your Ave, Venture Circle
Gas	S: Esso[D]
Food	N: Kenny Roger's Roasters, Maurin's Cafe
	S: David's, Domino's Pizza
Exit	Warman Rd, Millar Ave
Exit	Weston Ave
Exit	Attridge Dr, Saskatoon Zoo, Forestry Farm Park
Exit	108th St (Eastbound)
Exit	College Dr, SK5, SK241
Exit	8th St
Gas	N: Esso[CW], Mohawk, Petro Canada, Shell[CW, 24], Turbo[*, D, LP, CW]
	S: Co-Op[*, LP, CW], Esso[*, D, CW], Fas Gas[LP], Shell[*, CW], Super Store
Food	N: Dad's Deli, Debphi, Domino's Pizza, McDonald's, Panarama Pizza, Robin's Donuts, Smiley's Buffet, Smitty's, Tim Horton's Place, Vern's Pizza, Wah Nam
	S: A & W, Ambassador Restaurant, Bonanza, Champs, Fuddruckers, Istanbul Cafe, KFC, Kay's, Kelsey's, Moxey's, Pizza Hut, Red Lobster, Subway
ATM	S: CIBC Bank, Canada Trust, Royal Bank, Saskatoon Credit Union
Other	N: Pharmacy, Safeway Grocery, Wal-Mart, Zellers
	S: Co-Op Grocery & Pharmacy, Super Store
Exit	Taylor St, Saskatoon
Exit	SK11, Regina, 8th St
Gas	N: Esso[*], Shell[LP]
Food	N: Tim Horton's, Vern's Pizza
Other	N: Canarama Pharmacy, Extra Foods
Exit	Boychuck Dr
Exit	SK316
Exit	Clavat
Gas	S: Tempo[*]
Food	**S: Motor Inn Cafe**
Lodg	**S: Motor Inn**
Exit	Weigh Station
Exit	Bradwell
Exit	Picnic Area (Southbound)
Exit	Hwy 397, Allan
Exit	Elstow
Gas	S: Gas Station
Food	S: Restaurant
Exit	Unnamed
Exit	Colonsay
Gas	S: Co-Op
Food	S: Colonsay Restaurant
Lodg	S: Colonsay Hotel
Exit	SK2, Prince Albert, Watros
FStop	**S: Petro Canada[*, LP]**
Food	S: Petro Canada
Exit	Viscount
Lodg	S: Viscount Hotel
Exit	Plunkett, SK365S, Manitoba Beach, Watrous Resort Area
Exit	Guernesey
Food	S: Hotel
Lodg	S: Hotel
Exit	Hwy 20N
Exit	Service Road, Lanegan
Food	N: Mel-O's Family Diner
Exit	Muster St, Lanegan
Food	N: Lam's Wok
Other	N: Highway Confectionary
Exit	Main St, Lanegan
Gas	N: Esso[*, D, LP], Shell
Food	N: Deenee's Coffee & Bakery
Med	N: ✚ Hospital
ATM	N: Credit Union
Other	N: Lannegan Drug Pharmacy, Wuz Cafe
Exit	Hoover St, Lanigan
Food	N: Jan's Steak House
Lodg	N: EZ-Wall Motel
Med	N: ✚ Hospital
Exit	Janson (Service 1 mile south in town)
Exit	SK6, Melfort N
FStop	**N: Esso[*, LP]**
Food	N: Esso
Exit	Hwy 6, Regina S, Melfort
Exit	Main St, Wynyard
FStop	**S: Co-Op[*, D, LP]**
Gas	N: Esso[*, D, LP]
Food	N: Capri Cafe, Main St Meats, Pizza Plus Restaurant, Temper Tree
	S: KFC, **Mom's**, Thoens Pizza
Lodg	N: Southshore Motor Lodge, Wynyard Motel
ATM	N: Bank of Montreal, Wynyard Credit Union
Other	N: Co-Op Grocery, Laundry Mat, Shop

Bold red print shows RV & Bus parking available or nearby

EXIT — SK

Easy Foods, Wynyard Pharmacy

Exit Service Road, Wynyard
- **FStop** S: **Fas Gas**(*), **Shell**(*)
- **Food** S: Fas Gas, MenYuen
- **Lodg** S: **Arrow Head Motor Inn**

Exit Tenth St E, Wynyard
- **Med** N: ✚ Hospital

Exit Mozart

Exit Elfros

Exit SK35, Wadena
- **FStop** N: **Fuel Stop**
- **Food** N: Restaurant

Exit SK310, Foam Lake, Kuroki, Ituna
- **Gas** N: Foam Lake Motors, Hillstop(*, LP)
- **Lodg** S: **La Vista Motel**

Exit Cameron St, Foam Lake

Exit Main St, Foam Lake
- **Gas** N: Co-Op
- **Food** N: Dennis's Cafe, Foam Lake Bakery, Our Place
- **Lodg** N: Western Hotel
- **Med** N: ✚ Hospital
- **ATM** N: Credit Union
- **Other** N: Co-Op Foods, IGA Grocery, McCutcheon Pharmacy

Exit Service Road, Foam Lake
- **Gas** N: Mohawk(*)
- **Food** N: China Place, **Mozart's Family Restaurant**
- **Lodg** N: Foam Lake Motel
- **Med** N: ✚ Hospital

Exit Tuffnell

Exit Sheho
- **Gas** N: Tempo
- **Food** N: Baba's
- **Lodg** N: Queens Hotel
- **Other** N: Lucky Dollar Foods, Parkland Food Store

Exit Insinger

Exit Theodore Service Rd
- **Gas** N: Co-Op(*)
- **Food** N: Friend's Family Restaurant
- **Lodg** S: Motor Motel

Exit SK47, Buchannan N, Melville S
- **Gas** N: Tempo
- **Lodg** N: Hotel California
- **Other** N: Family Foods

Exit Hwy 16a, SK47, Buchannan

Exit Gladstone, Yorktown
- **Med** S: ✚ Hospital

Exit Hwy 16 W, Hwy 9N

Exit Smith Street, Yorktown (Eastbound)
- **Gas** S: Mohawk(LP, CW), Shell(*, CW, 24)
- **Food** S: Family Pizza Cafe, KFC
- **Other** S: Imperial Plaza

Exit SK10E, Dauphin, SK16aW, City Center, SK9N, Yorktown
- **Gas** N: Esso(*), Linden Square(*, D, LP)
  S: Esso, Super Store
- **Food** N: Bonanza, Esso, Giorgio's Restaurant & Deli, Nikki's
  S: Imperial Motel, KFC, Robin's Donuts, Smitty's, Tim Horton's, Wendy's
- **Lodg** S: Holiday Inn, Imperial 400 Motel
- **TServ** N: **Parkland Tire**, **Value Tire & Battery**
- **ATM** N: Canadian Western Bank
  S: Royal Bank, TD Bank & Trust, Yorktown

EXIT — SK/MB

Credit Union
- **Other** N: K Mart, Parkland Mall, Police Station
  S: Super Store

Exit Palliser Way , Yorktown
- **TServ** S: **James Tire**

Exit Tourist Center (No Trucks, Northbound)

Exit SK9, SK10
- **FStop** S: **Petro Canada**(*, LP)
- **Food** S: Humpty's (Petro Canada)

Exit Saltcoats
- **Gas** N: SOS(*)
- **Food** N: Dick Wong, Laketown Hotel
- **Lodg** N: Laketown Hotel

Exit Bredenbury

Exit Hwy 15, Melville

Exit Hwy 80, Church Bridge
- **Gas** N: Co-Op(*)
  S: Tempo(*, D)
- **Food** N: Kings Way
  S: Peters Place, Yellow Rose
- **Other** N: Co-Op Food Store, Mail Post

Exit Unnamed
- **Gas** S: Mohawk

Exit Second St, Langenburg
- **Food** S: Golden Star, Woodland Lanes Restaurant
- **Lodg** S: Hotel
- **Other** N: IGA Grocery Store
  S: Big Way Foods, Pharma Save

Exit Langenburg

Exit SK8, Broad St S
- **Gas** S: Petro Canada(D)
- **Food** S: Chicken Chef

Exit Unnamed
- **Lodg** S: Motel Langenburg Country Inn

Exit Gopherville
- **Gas** S: Harverst Fuel
- **Food** S: Sophia's Restaurant

↑ Saskatchewan

↓ Manitoba

Exit Hwy 83, Roblin

Exit Hwy 83, Russell
- **FStop** N: **Petro Canada**(*, LP)
- **Gas** N: Super Save Gas
- **Food** N: Banner Bakery, Donna's (Petro Canada)
  S: Chicken Chef
- **TServ** N: **Russell Tire**, **Southside Service**
- **Other** N: Police Station, Prairie Mountain Pharmacy, Russell Family Foods

Exit Memorial Ave, Russell
- **Gas** S: Patricia's Restaurant
- **Food** S: Rich Marr
- **Lodg** S: The Jolly Lodger

Exit Hwy 45, Rossburn
- **FStop** N: **Esso**(*)
- **Food** N: Mr Scoop, **The Russell Inn**
- **Lodg** N: **The Russell Inn**
- **Med** N: ✚ Hospital

Exit MB579, Millwood

Exit Russel St
- **Gas** S: Esso(D)
- **Food** S: Esso

Exit MB478, Binscarth

EXIT — MB

Exit MB41S

Exit MB359

Exit Foxwarren, MB475
- **Gas** S: Esso(D)
- **Food** S: Crawford's Restaurant
- **Lodg** S: Kent Hotel

Exit MB83, Bartle

Exit MB476, Angusville

Exit Hwy 472, Solsgirth

Exit MB264N, Rossburn

Exit MB264, Decker

Exit MB42, Bartle
- **Med** S: ✚ Hospital

Exit MB21, Oak Burn, Hamiota, Shoal Lake
- **FStop** S: **Esso**(*)
- **Gas** N: Mohawk(*, D, LP)
  S: Shell(*, CW)
- **Food** N: Rooke's Drive In
  S: Alan Choy's, Esso, Linda's, Omega Pizza
- **Lodg** N: Motel
- **Med** S: ✚ Hospital
- **Other** S: Shaol Lake Pharmacy

Exit MB354, Starth Clair, Oak River
- **Gas** S: Co-Op(*)
- **Lodg** S: Starth Clair Hotel
- **Other** S: Grocery Store

Exit MB354, Elphinstone

Exit MB250, Rivers
- **Food** S: Leisure Inn
- **Lodg** S: Leisure Inn

Exit MB250, Newdale, Sandy Lake

Exit MB270, Rapid City

Exit Rest Area - RR, Phones, Picnic, HF (Northbound)

Exit Hwy 10, Riding Mountain Park, Hwy 16a to Minnadosa, Hwy 16W to Saskatoon

Exit MB355, Minnedosa
- **TServ** N: **Kirk's Truck Service**

Exit Hwy 10, Brandon

Exit Hwy 262, Hwy 16A, Minnedosa
- **FStop** N: **Esso**(D)
- **Food** N: Prairie Pantry Family Restaurant (Esso)

Exit MB466S

Exit MB464, Brookdale - South

Exit Gill Dr N
- **Food** N: Westway Inn
- **Lodg** N: Westway Inn Motel
  S: **Super 8**

Exit Hwy 5 N, Dominion Rd S
- **FStop** S: **Petro Canada**(*, LP), **Petro Canada**(*, D)
- **Gas** N: Harverst Fuel
  S: Esso(*), Shell(D, CW)
- **Food** N: Chalet, **Chicken Corral**, Chicken Delight, **Dairy Queen**, Mr Ribs
  S: Petro Canada
- **Lodg** N: Neepawa Hotel

Exit Fifth Ave, Neepawa

Exit Fourth Ave, Neepawa
- **Gas** S: Turbo(D)

Exit Second Ave, Neepawa
- **Lodg** S: Garden Path Bed & Breakfast

W TCH-16

EXIT MB

Exit First Ave, Neepawa
- **Food** N: Cinnamon Cove, Weston's Bakery Store
- **Lodg** N: Hotel
- **Other** N: Safeway Grocery

Exit Mountain Ave, Neepawa
- **Gas** N: Co-Op[LP]
- **Food** N: Bamboo Restaurant, Beautiful Plain's Bakery, Lee's Restaurant, Plate & Platter, Ziggy's Pizza
- **Lodg** N: Hotel Hamilton
- **Med** N: ✚ Hospital
- **Other** N: Harris Pharmacy, Neepawa Pharmacy, Safeway Grocery, Shop Easy Foods

Exit Five

Exit Broadway Ave

Exit Unnamed
- **Food** S: Breaker Breaker Restaurant[24]

EXIT MB

Exit MB350
- **Gas** S: Harvest Fuel[*]
- **Food** S: Harvest Fuel

Exit Rest Area - Picnic (Northbound)

Exit MB260, Plumas

Exit Dennis St
- **Gas** N: Co-Op
- **Food** N: Fried Chicken & Pizza (Opens at 11:00), Gladston Bakery & Coffee Shop, JB Drive In (Only Open in the Summer)
- **Lodg** N: Gladstone Hotel
- **TServ** N: **Goodyear**
- **Other** N: Gladston Pharmacy, Gladston Supermarket, Spek N' Span Landrymat

Exit MB34, Gladston (Services in town about 1 mile)
- **FStop** S: **Esso**[*]

EXIT MB

- **Food** S: **Esso**
- **Lodg** S: The Motel

Exit MB350, Catrime

Exit MB50, Amaranth

Exit Unnamed
- **Gas** N: Shell
- **Food** N: First Crossing, Yellow Head Restaurant

Exit MB242, Lynch's Point

Exit 227, Warren

Exit Mac Donald

Exit Hwy 1
- **Gas** N: Petro Canada[*, LP]
- **Food** N: Petro Canada

↑ Manitoba

Begin 16, Portage la Prairie

TCH-17 E

EXIT ON

Begin 17

↓ Ontario

Exit Ontario Travel Information Center

Exit Royal Lake Road
- **RVCamp** N: **Royal Lake Resort**

Exit Truck Inspection (Eastbound)

Exit Pye's Road
- **RVCamp** S: **Camping**

Exit Clearwater Bay Town, Rocky Ridge Road
- **FStop** N: **Shell**[*]
- **Food** N: Apple Annies (Shell)

Exit Keewaton Town

Exit Hwy 658 Kenora, Redditt
- **Med** S: ✚ **Hospital**
- **Other** N: Police Station

Exit Ont. Hwy 17, Kenora, Keewatin, Ont. Hwy 17A, Winnipeg
- **Med** S: ✚ **Hospital**

Exit Ont. Hwy 71S, Fort Frances
- **Parks** S: **Rushing River Provincial Park**

Exit Hwy 647
- **Gas** S: **Husky**[*]
- **Food** S: Buster's Restaurant (Husky)
- **ATM** S: **Husky**

Exit Armstrong Street
- **Gas** S: Petro Canada[*, D]

Exit Blue Lake Road
- **Parks** N: **Blue Lake Provincial Park**

Exit Tower Road
- **Food** S: Country Kitchen
- **Lodg** S: Bay View Hotel, Mail Post
- **AServ** N: Hi-Tech Automotive
  S: Auto Value Auto Parts
- **Other** N: Jimmy's Supermarket

Exit Spruce Street Business
- **Lodg** N: Northside Motel

Exit Truck Inspection Station (Eastbound)

EXIT ON

Exit Ont. Hwy 105 N, Ear Falls, Bambertown, Red Lake
- **Gas** N: Esso[*, D]
- **Food** N: Esso
- **Lodg** S: Pine Grove Motel, The Traveler Motel
- **ATM** N: Esso
- **Other** S: Car Wash, Coin Laundry

Exit Vermilion Bay Town

Exit Minnitaki Town, Waldhof Road
- **RVCamp** S: **Birch Dale Campground**

Exit Oxdrift Town

Exit Marguerite Street
- **AServ** N: Auto Value Parts Store
  S: Dingwall Ford Dealer

Exit Third Street
- **Lodg** S: Trans Canada Motel
- **AServ** N: K.K.Pener
- **Other** N: Hillcrest Animal Clinic

Exit First Street
- **Food** S: KFC
- **Lodg** S: Hillcrest Motel

Exit Florence Street
- **Food** N: Dairy Queen
  S: Chalet Inn Restaurant
- **Lodg** S: Chalet Inn Motel
- **AServ** S: GM Dealership

Exit Myrtle Avenue
- **Gas** S: Esso[*], Mohawk[D, CW], Petro Canada
- **TWash** S: **Mohawk**
- **ATM** S: Mohawk

Exit Hwy 594, Downtown Business
- **TStop** N: **Husky**
- **Gas** S: Shell
- **Food** N: Pizza Hut
  S: McDonald's[PLAY], Robin's Donuts, Subway
- **Lodg** N: **Motor Inn - Best Western**, Patricia Hotel
  S: Comfort Inn, Timberland Motel, Town & Country Motel
- **AServ** N: Canadian Tire, Dryden GM Dealer
  S: Auto Pro

EXIT ON

- **TServ** S: **Machine Shop**
- **Other** N: Economy Supermarket

Exit Dryden Town
- **FStop** N: **Can-Op**[*]
- **Lodg** S: Hideway Motel
- **Other** S: **Wal-Mart**[RX]

Exit Truck Inspection (Eastbound)

Exit Hwy 601 North
- **Lodg** N: Evening Star Motel
- **Other** N: Dryden Airport

Exit Barclay Town, Elm Bay Road

Exit Aaron Park Road
- **Parks** N: **Aaron Provincial Park**

Exit King Street
- **Lodg** N: Lang Motel, Pine Grove Motel
- **AServ** N: Lang Motors

Exit Wabigoon Town

Exit Dinorwic Town, QB Hwy 72 N, Sioux Lookout
- **Parks** N: **Ojibway Provincial Park**

Exit James Street
- **Gas** N: Shell[*, D] (Restaurant)
  S: Esso[*, D]
- **Food** N: Westwood Restaurant
  S: Voyager Restaurant
- **AServ** N: Shell
- **ATM** S: Esso

Exit McLeod Street
- **Lodg** N: Majestic Motel
- **Other** N: Harley's Supermarket

Exit East Street
- **Gas** N: Petro Canada[*, D]
- **Food** N: Petro Canada
  S: The New Shanghi
- **AServ** N: Petro Canada
- **ATM** S: CIBIC

Exit Ignace Town
- **Gas** N: Can-Op[*]
- **Lodg** N: Westwood Motel
- **AServ** N: Can-Op
- **Other** N: IGA Supermarket
  S: Police Station

EXIT	ON
Exit	Davey Lake Road
AServ	N: Bumper to Bumper Auto Parts
RVCamp	S: **Davey Lake Road Campground**
Exit	Hwy 599, Savant Lake, Pickle Lake
TStop	S: **Tempo**(*, D, 24)
Gas	S: Tardiff Petroleum(*)
Lodg	S: **Northwoods Motor Inn (Restaurant)**
Parks	N: **Sand Bar Lake Provincial Park (Closed in Winter)**
Exit	Sowden Lake Road
RVCamp	N: **Sowden Lake Campground**
Exit	English River Town
Exit	Blind Bay Road
RVCamp	S: **RV Camping Park**
Exit	Upsala Town
Gas	S: Can-Op(*, D), Shell(*, D, LP)
Other	N: Police Station
Exit	Lac des Mille Lacs
Lodg	S: Black Spruce Motel
Exit	Saw Mill Bay Road
RVCamp	S: **Saw Mill Bay Camp**
Exit	Lac Des Mille Lacs
Gas	N: Esso(*, LP)
Food	N: Gary's Restaurant (Esso)
ATM	N: Esso
Exit	Shabaqua Road
Gas	N: Can-Op(*)
Lodg	N: Timberland Motel
Other	N: Police Station
Exit	Ont. Hwy 11
FStop	S: **Petro Canada**(*, 24)
Exit	Ont. Hwy 590
Lodg	S: Come By Chance Resort
RVCamp	S: **Artesian Wells Resort**
Parks	S: **Kakabeka Falls Provincial Park**
Exit	Florence Street
Gas	N: Trading Post
	S: Esso(*, D)
Food	N: The Pines
	S: The AOK Cafe
Lodg	S: The Cascades Motel
AServ	S: Esso
Other	N: Mail Post
Exit	Kakabeka Falls Town, Oliver Road
Gas	S: Can-Op(*, CW)
Food	N: Sutton's
Lodg	N: Carriage House Motel, Kakabeka Motor Hotel, Tel Star Motel
ATM	S: Can-Op
Other	S: Odena's Supermarket
Exit	C Line Road
Lodg	S: Pine View Motel
Exit	Truck Inspection
Exit	Cooper Road
Other	S: Police Station
Exit	Ont. Hwy 130
TStop	S: **Husky**(*)
FStop	S: **Esso**(*, 24)
TServ	N: **Kenworth, Western Star**
	S: **Husky**
Other	N: Cross Roads Animal Clinic

EXIT	ON
Exit	Fairview Avenue
Gas	N: Suny's(*)
Lodg	N: Over Pass Motel
Exit	Sifton Ave.
AServ	N: Canadian Tire
ATM	N: CIBC
Other	N: A&P Supermarket, **K-Mart**
Exit	Arthur's Street, Ont Hwy 11B, Ont Hwy 17B, Ont Hwy 61
FStop	S: **Shell Commercial Fuel Stop**
Gas	S: Esso(*, CW), Husky(*, D, CW), Shell(*, 24), Spur, Suny's(*)
Food	S: Little Caesars Pizza, Mr Sub, Mr. Chinese, Pizza Hut, Robin's Donuts, Taco Time, Tim Horton's, William's
Lodg	S: Airline Motel, Comfort Inn, Crossroads Motor Inn - Best Western, Valhalla Inn, Victoria's Inn
AServ	S: Mr. Lube, Speedy Brake Center
ATM	S: Esso
Other	S: Meadows Animal Clinic, Pharmasave Pharmacy
Exit	Harbor Expressway
Exit	Oliver Road
Exit	John's Street
Gas	N: Esso(*)
Food	N: Robin's Donuts
Exit	Ont. Hwy 102, Red River Road
Gas	N: Petro Canada(*), Suny's(*, D)
	S: Beaver(*, D, LP), Esso(*, CW), Shell(*, CW)
Food	N: Pagoda Garden's, Rattler's, Robin's Donuts
	S: Domino's Pizza, KFC, Little Caesars Pizza, McDonald's, Mr Sub, Pizza Hut, Port Arthur Brasserie Brew Pub
AServ	N: Bridgestone, Canadian Tire
ATM	N: Bank of Montreal, Suny's, TD Bank
Other	N: Country Fair Plaza, Quality Market Supermarket, **Safeway Grocery**, Zellers
	S: High View Animal Clinic, River Place Mall
Exit	Balsam Street
Gas	N: Petro Canada(*)
AServ	N: Petro Canada
Exit	Hodder Ave., Ont. Hwy 11B, Ont. Hwy 17B Downtown
RVCamp	N: **Trobridge Falls Campground**
Med	S: **✚ Hospital**
Exit	Rest Area - RR, Tourist Info, Phones, Picnic (Westbound)
Exit	Thunder Bay Town, Hwy 527, Spruce River Road
RVCamp	S: **KOA Campgrounds**
Exit	Lake Shore Drive
Lodg	S: Thunder Bay International Hotel
Exit	Crystal Beach Road
Gas	S: Suny's(*, D, LP)
Food	S: Missing Horse Restaurant
Exit	Hwy 587, Pass Lake
TStop	N: **Esso**(*)
Gas	S: Can-Op(*)
Lodg	S: Grann Motel
AServ	S: Can-Op
ATM	N: **Esso**

EXIT	ON
	S: Can-Op
Other	N: Tourist Info.
Exit	Mirrow Lake Road
RVCamp	S: **Mirrow Lake Campground**
Exit	Ouimet Canyon Road
Parks	N: **Quimet Canyon Provincial Park**
Exit	Dorion Town, Dorion Loop Road, Maple Drive
Gas	N: Can-Op(*, D), Shell(*, CW)
	S: Spur(*, D)
Lodg	S: Dorion Inn
Other	N: Coin Laundry
Exit	Wolf River Road
RVCamp	N: **RV Camping**
Exit	Hwy 628, Red Rock
Lodg	S: Red Rock Inn
Exit	Truck Inspection, Weigh Station (Westbound)
Exit	Maatta's Road
TStop	S: **Husky**(*, D, LP)
Lodg	N: Beaver Motel, Birchfield Motel, Town & Country Motel
	S: Vacationland Motel
AServ	N: Brennan's Ford Dealer
	S: Goodyear
TServ	S: **Husky**
Other	N: Police Station
	S: Tourist Info.
Exit	Hwy 585
FStop	N: **Petro Canada**(*, 24)
Gas	S: Esso(*)
Food	S: KFC Express (Esso), Pizza Hut (Esso)
Exit	First Street
Lodg	S: Northland Motel
Exit	Nipigon Town, Railway St., Bus. Section, Hillside Acres Rd.
Lodg	N: Nipigon Hotel
	S: Nipigon Inn
Med	S: **✚ Hospital**
Exit	Ont. Hwy 11E, Cochrane
Exit	Little Gravel River
Gas	N: Can-Op(*)
Lodg	N: Gravel River Motel
Exit	Rainbow Falls Provincial Park Road
Parks	N: **Rainbow Falls Provincial Park**
Exit	White Sand Winston Road
Gas	S: Can-Op(*)
Lodg	S: Fallen Rock Motel
Exit	Simon Street, Walker Lake Road
RVCamp	N: **Travel Rest**
Exit	Peary Street
Gas	N: Can-Op(*), Petro Canada
Food	N: KFC, Pizza Hut
	S: Twin Spot Restaurant
Lodg	N: Cosiana Inn, Norwest Motel, Villa Binca Station Inn
AServ	S: G.Figliomeni & Sons Ford Dealer
Exit	Winnipeg Street
Gas	S: Esso(*)
Food	S: Voyager Restaurant
Lodg	S: Voyager Motel
Exit	Drummond Street

Bold red print shows RV & Bus parking available or nearby

EXIT	ON
Exit	Schreiber Town, Ontario Street Business
Food	**S:** Rosie & Josie's
Lodg	**N:** Sunset Motel
	S: Cliffside Motel
Other	**N:** Police Station
Exit	Aguasabon Gorge Road
RVCamp	**S: Agausabon Falls Campground**
Other	**S:** Aguasabon River Gorge & Aguasabon Falls
Exit	Lake View Drive
Med	**S: + McCausland Hospital**
Exit	Cartier Road, Simco Plaza
Gas	**N:** Esso
Food	**N:** Jade Garden Restaurant, Red Dog Restaurant, Roy Pizzeria
Lodg	**N:** Imperial Motel, Norwood Motel, Red Dog Inn
ATM	**N:** CIBC
Other	**N:** Costa's Food Market, Nugget Food Store, Ronkainen's Pharmacy
Exit	Hudson Drive, Terrace Heights Drive
Gas	**S:** Shell(*)
AServ	**S:** Bumper to Bumper Auto Parts, Shell
Exit	Terrace Bay Town, Mill Road
AServ	**N:** Spadoni GM Dealer
Exit	Neys Provincial Park Road
Gas	**N:** Can-Op(*, D)
Food	**N:** Neys Restaurant
RVCamp	**N: Neys RV Park**
Parks	**S: Neys Provincial Park**
Exit	Hwy 626, Downtown
Gas	**N:** Petro Canada(*, D)
	S: Esso(*)
Food	**N:** Marino's Restaurant, Peninsula Restaurant
	S: Paesamo Italian
Lodg	**N:** Peninsula Inn Motel
	S: Airport Motor Inn Best Western, Heritage Inn
Med	**S: + Hospital**
Other	**S:** Police Station
Exit	Marathon Town
FStop	**N: Esso(*, D)**
Other	**S:** Tourist Info.
Exit	Hwy 627, Heron Bay, Pic River
Exit	Hwy 614
Exit	White Lake Provincial Road
TStop	**N: Esso(*)**
Food	**N:** Esso Restaurant, Gloria's Restaurant
Lodg	**N:** Dunc Lake Resort, Gloria's Motel
ATM	**N: Esso**
Parks	**S: White Lake Provincial Park**
Other	**N:** Coin Laundry (Esso)
Exit	White River Town, Elgin Street Business, Hwy 631N
TStop	**S: Huskey(*)**
Gas	**S:** Esso(*, D), Stewart's(*, D)
Food	**N:** Mini Mart Restaurant
	S: A & W, Continental Restaurant
Lodg	**N:** White River Motel
	S: Continental Motel
AServ	**S:** Stewart's
TServ	**S: Huskey's**
Other	**N:** Police Station
	S: Tourist Info.
Exit	Obatanga Provincial Park
Exit	Paint Lake Road
Gas	**S:** North Country(*, LP)
Lodg	**S:** North Country Lodge
Exit	Township
Food	**S:** Northern Lights Restaurants
Lodg	**S:** Northern Lights Motel
AServ	**S:** Ford Dealership
Exit	Wawa Town, Ont. Hwy 101, Wawa, Chipleau
Med	**N: + Hospital**
Other	**N:** Tourist Info., Wawa Airport
Exit	Pine Wood Drive
Gas	**S:** Chishlom(*, D)
Food	**S:** The Family Kitchen
Lodg	**S:** Superior Courts Motel
AServ	**S:** Langill Chrysler Dealer
Other	**S:** Police Station
Exit	Michipicoten Road
FStop	**S: Can-Op(*)**
Gas	**N:** Esso(*) (Closed for winter season)
Lodg	**N:** Mystic Isle Motel
	S: Kinniwabi Pines Motel
AServ	**S:** Can-Op
Exit	Park Office Road
Other	**N:** Lake Office for Lake Superior Provincial Park
Exit	AgawaBay
Exit	Speckled Trout Creek
Gas	**N:** AgawaBay(*)
Food	**N:** AgawaBay Restaurant
AServ	**N:** AgawaBay
Exit	Crescent Lake Road
RVCamp	**N: Crescent Lake RV Park**
Exit	Lake Superior Provincial Park
Exit	Twilight Road
RVCamp	**S: Twilight Park**
Exit	Trails End Road
Lodg	**S:** Trails End Resort
Exit	Montreal River Harbor Town
Gas	**N:** UPI(*, D) (Restaurant, Mail Post)
Exit	Pancake Bay Provincial Park (Both sides of 17)
Exit	Batchawana Bay
Food	**N:** Blue Water Restaurant, Shore Line Restaurant
Lodg	**N:** Blue Water Motel, **Shore Line Motel**
Exit	Batchawana River
Gas	**N:** UPI(*, LP)
Lodg	**S:** Sunset Inn
RVCamp	**S: Sunset RV Trailer Park**
Exit	Haviland Shores Drive
Gas	**S:** Haviland Trading Post
Lodg	**S:** McCauley Motel
Exit	Mahler Road
Lodg	**N:** Stokely Creek Ski
Exit	Inspection Station (Eastbound)
Exit	Township
Gas	**N:** Can-Op(*, D)
ATM	**N:** Can-Op
Other	**N:** General Store
Exit	Heyden Town, Hwy 556, Serchmont, Ranger Lake
FStop	**N: Esso(*)**
Food	**N:** The Family Restaurant (Esso)
Lodg	**N:** Spruce's Motor Inn (Restaurant)
	S: Haden Motel (Restaurant)
Exit	Troute Lake Road
Food	**N:** Woody's Restaurant
RVCamp	**N: Christie's Camper Sales, Trout Lake Resort**
Exit	Fifth Line Road
Lodg	**S:** KOA Campground Cabins
RVCamp	**S: KOA Campgrounds**
Exit	Fourth Line Road
Gas	**N:** Petro Canada(*, LP)
Food	**N:** Gino's Restaurant, Riuniti Restaurant
Lodg	**S:** Ambassador Motel
AServ	**N:** Maitland Motors, Michelin Tire
TServ	**N: Lakeway Truck Centre - International**
Exit	Third Line Road
AServ	**S:** Bridgestone, Prouse Buick, GM Dealer
TServ	**S: TMS Truck Centre - Kenworth**
Exit	Terrance Avenue
Food	**N:** Alpen Hof Restaurant, Guzzo's Family Restaurant
Lodg	**S:** Adams Motel
AServ	**S:** Great Northern Auto Centre
Exit	Hwy 550, Ont. Hwy 17B
FStop	**N: Husky(*, CW) (Restaurant)**
Gas	**N:** Ultramar(*, D)
	S: Can-Op(*, D) (Restaurant), Shell(*, D)
Food	**N:** Baker's Dozen, Giovanna's Restaurant, Minelli's Restaurant
	S: KFC, Lone Star, McDonald's, Purple Lantern
Lodg	**S:** Comfort Inn, Water Tower Inn
AServ	**N:** Esquire Honda
	S: Riverside Chrysler, Plymouth, Jeep, Eagle Dealer
Exit	Hwy 550, Hwy 565, Hwy 17B
FStop	**S: Petro Pass**
Food	**S:** Country Style, Mr Sub
Lodg	**S:** Holiday Motel, **Super 8**
AServ	**S:** Goodyear, Midas Muffler, Superior Chrysler, Dodge, Jeep Dealer
Exit	Wellington Square Road
Food	**S:** McDonald's
Other	**S:** Basics Supermarket, Wellington Square Mall
Exit	Boundary Road
Gas	**S:** Petro Canada(*)
Lodg	**S:** Truck Road Motel, White Beach Motel
AServ	**S:** Petro Canada
Exit	Dacey Road
Gas	**S:** Esso(*, CW)
Lodg	**S:** Traveler's Motel
Exit	Sault St. Marie Town
TStop	**S: Husky(*) (Restaurant)**
Lodg	**S:** Pine Grove Motel, Shady Pines Motel, Shady Rest Motel
Exit	Garden River Town
Exit	Echo Bay Town, Hwy 638

Bold red print shows RV & Bus parking available or nearby

EXIT	ON
Gas	S: Can-Op[*], Wordlaw Fuels[*]
Food	S: D&J's, Nancy Lee's Subs
AServ	S: Wordlaw Fuels
Other	N: Post Office
Exit	Hwy 548, St. Joseph Island
Gas	S: UPI[*]
Parks	S: **Fort St. Joseph National Historic Park**
Exit	Lake Huron Drive
Gas	N: Esso[*]
AServ	N: Esso
Exit	Center Line Road
RVCamp	N: **Sunrise Valley Camp**
Exit	Crawford Street
Gas	S: Shell[*, D]
Exit	Bruce Mines Town, Cunningham Street
Food	N: Country Cottage Cafe
Lodg	S: Bavarine Inn
Exit	Big Perch Bay Road, Trunk Road
RVCamp	S: **Pudding Stone Harbor Park**
Exit	Lake Saw Drive
Lodg	S: Carolyn Beach Motel
Exit	Thessalon Town, Ont Hwy 17B, Ont. Hwy 129, Chapleau
Gas	N: Can-Op[*]
Other	N: Tourist Info.
	S: Police Station
Exit	Brown Lee Road
RVCamp	N: **Brownlee Lake Campground**
Exit	Sowerby Town
Exit	Eley Road
Lodg	S: Estock Motor Inn (Restaurant)
Exit	Warnock Road
Food	N: Three Aces Restaurant
Lodg	S: Iron Bridge Motel, Parker's Motel
Exit	Clarissa Street
Gas	S: Shell[*]
Food	N: Queen Room Restaurant
Exit	Iron Bridge Town, Chiblow Lake Road
Gas	N: Esso[*, D]
Lodg	N: Van Every's Motel
	S: Village Inn
Exit	MacIver Drive
Lodg	N: MacIvers
Exit	Mississagi Village Road
Gas	S: Willie's Gas Bar[*, D]
Exit	North Street
Food	N: McDonald's
Exit	Woodward Ave., Martin St
Lodg	S: **Old Mill Motel**
ATM	N: Royal Bank
Other	N: IDA Pharmacy
Exit	Lawton Street
Food	N: Tim Horton's
Exit	Cobden Ave.
Food	N: KFC, Mr Sub
ATM	N: Scotia Bank
Other	N: Easy Wash Coin Laundry, Loeb Supermarket
Exit	Queen Avenue
Gas	N: Esso[*, CW]

EXIT	ON
Food	N: Lake View Restaurant
Lodg	N: Lake View Inn
Exit	Laborne Avenue, Blind River
Gas	N: McLeod's[*]
Lodg	N: North Shore Wayside Inn
Exit	King Edward's Street
Gas	N: Esso
AServ	N: Mill Town GM Dealer, North Shore Ford Dealer
Other	N: Coin Laundry, Mic's Coint Laundry
Exit	East Industrial Park
Food	S: Eldo Restaurant
Lodg	S: Eldo Inn
AServ	S: M. S. R. Tire Service
TServ	S: **M. S. R. Tire Service**
Other	N: Timber Village Museum
	S: U-do-it Car Wash
Exit	Leacock Street
Food	S: Country Style Restaurant
AServ	N: Auto Pro
Other	N: Tourist Info.
Exit	Blind River Town, Hospital Road
Med	N: ✚ **St. Joseph's Health Centre**
Exit	Algome Mills Town
Exit	Shepard's Lane
Lodg	N: Roy's Motel
Exit	Spragge Town
Food	N: Rocky's Restaurant
AServ	N: Algoma GM Dealer, Sabourin Auto Center
RVCamp	S: **KOA Campgrounds**
Exit	Ont. Hwy 108, Elliot Lake
Parks	N: **Mississiga Provincial Park**
Other	S: Truck Inspection Station
Exit	Serpent River Town, Handi-Spot Road
Lodg	N: Kennebec Motel
Exit	Cutler Town, Village Road East
Gas	S: Kenabutch[*]
Exit	Hamilton Street
Gas	N: Sonnys[D, LP]
Food	N: The Picnic Basket
AServ	N: Sonnys
Exit	John's Street, Truck Road
Gas	S: BF[*]
Food	N: Vance's Restaurant
Lodg	N: Vance's Motor Inn
ATM	N: Scotia Bank
Exit	Spanish Town, Richards Street
Food	N: Lucky Snack Bar, Shorties Restaurant
Exit	Water Falls Road
Lodg	N: Water Falls Lodge
TServ	S: **Walford Truck & Tractor**
RVCamp	N: **Water Falls Park**
Exit	Wourninen Road , Kring Road
TStop	N: **Roy's Truck Stop**[*]
RVCamp	S: **Blue Heron Resort**
Exit	Aberdeen Street
Lodg	N: Wayside Motel
Exit	Ont. 553 North, Imperial St S
Food	S: Malcom's Country Kitchen, Sauble River Restaurant
Lodg	S: Clifton Hotel

EXIT	ON
AServ	S: Ray's Auto Service
Parks	N: **Chute's Provincial Park**
Exit	Second Street
Lodg	S: Mohawk Motel
AServ	N: John's Auto Repair
Exit	Third Street
Gas	N: BF[*, D]
	S: Shell[*]
Exit	Massey Town, Birch Lake Road
Food	S: Pine Grove Restaurant
Lodg	S: Pine Grove Motel
Exit	Agnew Lake Road
Gas	N: OLCO[*]
Lodg	N: Agnew Lake Lodge, Black Bear Lodge, Webbly Motel
RVCamp	N: **Agnew Lake Lodge Limited, Black Bear Camp**
Exit	Webwood Town, George St.
Food	S: Jennies Restaurant
Exit	Ont. Hwy 6, Espanola
Gas	N: Esso[*, 24] (Restaurant)
Food	S: Goodman's Restaurant
Lodg	N: **Alta Vista Motel**
	S: Goodman's Motel
AServ	S: Rainbow GM Dealer
ATM	N: Esso (Restaurant)
Other	S: Police Station
Exit	MaKerrow, Hardwood Road
Gas	N: BF[*]
Lodg	N: Portage Lodge
RVCamp	N: **Portage Road**
Exit	Sand Bay Road
RVCamp	N: **Sand Bay Camp**
Exit	Birch Street
RVCamp	N: **Riverside Campground**
Exit	Spencer Lane South, Spencer Lane North
TStop	N: **Esso**[*]
Food	N: Rainbow Truck Stop Restaurant
	S: Ga Ga Bo Chinese
TServ	N: **Esso**
Exit	Nairne Centre, Taylor St.
Food	S: The Busy Bee Country Store & Restaurant
Exit	Ronko Road, Worthington Road
Gas	S: New North Fuels[*]
ATM	S: New North Fuels
Exit	Regional Road 4, Worthington
RVCamp	N: **Maple Mountain Trailer Park**
Parks	N: **Fairbank Provincial Park (Open Seasonal)**
Exit	Ont. Hwy 144, Timmins
Exit	Hwy 55, Sudbury, Lively
Exit	Ont. Hwy 69, Hwy 46, Toronto, Sudbury
Exit	Region Hwy 55, Sudbury
Exit	Hwy 93, 2nd Avenue, Coniston
Gas	S: Petro Canada[*, D]
Food	S: Coni's Restaurant
AServ	S: Petro Canada
ATM	S: Caisse Bobulaire, Nickel's Center Credit Union
Other	S: Guardian Drugs, Value Mart Supermarket

Bold red print shows RV & Bus parking available or nearby

EXIT		ON
Exit	Road 90, Garson	
Other	N: Sudbury Airport, Tourist Info.	
Exit	Mountain View Road	
Gas	S: Mr. Gas(*, D)	
AServ	N: Gerry's Automotive	
Exit	Wahnapitae Town, Banks Street	
Gas	N: Pioneer(*, D, LP)	
Food	N: Pioneer Restaurant	
Exit	Beaudry Drive	
RVCamp	N: **Uncle Ed's RV Parking**	
Exit	Sunset Road	
RVCamp	N: **White Birch Camp**	
Exit	Kukagami Road	
Gas	N: UP(*, D, LP) (Ethanol)	
Lodg	N: Sportsman Lodge	
Exit	Hagar Town, Ont. Hwy 535	
Gas	N: Esso(*, D)	
Food	N: Chip's Stand	
Lodg	N: Rainbow Motel	
Exit	Ont. Hwy 539	
Gas	S: Shell(*, LP)	
AServ	N: Bob's Auto Body Shop	
Other	N: Police Station, Post Office	
Exit	Ont. Hwy 575	
FStop	N: **Co-Op**(D, LP)	
Food	N: L'Echo Restaurant (Co-Op)	
Exit	Rue. Belanger Street	
Food	S: TC Restaurant	
Lodg	S: TC Hotel	
Exit	Ont. Hwy 64, Lavigne, Novelle	
Gas	S: Esso(*, D)	
AServ	S: Goodyear	
Other	S: Food Land Supermarket	
Exit	Veuve River Road, Boulay Road	
RVCamp	S: **Camp LaPage, Riverdale Camp**	
Exit	Levac Road	
RVCamp	S: **Cache Bay Trailer Park**	
Exit	Ch. Leblanc Rd.	
Lodg	N: Sunshine Motel	
RVCamp	N: **Sunshines RV Park**	
Exit	Ont. Hwy 64N	
AServ	N: Tremblay GM Dealer	
TServ	N: **Half-Way Trailer Sales**	
Other	S: Tourist Info.	
Exit	Kings Street	
Gas	S: Petro Canada	
Food	S: Mr Sub	
Lodg	N: King Edward's Hotel	
Exit	Parker Street	
Gas	S: Mr. Gas(*, D)	
Food	N: KFC	
	S: Tim Horton's	
Exit	Mipissing	
Gas	N: Canadian Tire Petroleum, Vantage(*, D)	
Exit	Church's Street	
AServ	N: Canadian Tire	
Exit	Michaud Street	
Gas	S: Shell(*, D, 24)	
Lodg	N: Motel Champlain	
AServ	N: Quality Auto Supplies	
	S: Auto Pro, Sturgeon Falls Chrysler	
Exit	Clarks Street	
Food	N: Gervais(24)	
Lodg	N: Lincoln Motel, Moulin Rouge Motel	
Exit	Coursol Rd.	
Gas	N: Esso(*, CW)	
Food	N: McDonald's	
	S: China House Restaurant	
Med	N: ✚ **West Nipissing General Hospital**	

EXIT		ON
Other	N: A&P Supermarket	
Exit	Sturgeon Falls	
Exit	Ch. Michaud Rd., Ch. Golf Course Road	
Lodg	N: Red Rock Motel	
AServ	N: Goodyear	
Exit	Couchie Industrial Road	
RVCamp	N: **Carlson's Sports RV Center**	
Exit	Germanville Road	
Gas	N: Xeon(*)	
AServ	N: John C. Hoper GM Dealer	
Other	N: Police Station	
Exit	Truck Inspection Station (Westbound)	
Exit	Algonquin Ave., Ont. Hwy 11, Timmins, Cochrane	
Gas	N: Mac Ewen(*), Shell(*, D, 24)	
	S: Beaver(*), Candian Tire Petroleum(*, CW), Petro Canada(D)	
Food	N: McDonald's, The Submarine, Zellers	
	S: Burger World, Casey's Grillhouse, KFC, Mr Sub	
Lodg	S: Voyager Inn	
AServ	S: Cabaru Suzuki, Petro Canada	
Med	S: ✚ **Hospital**	
Other	N: Guardian Drugs, IGA Supermarket, North Bay Airport	
	S: Dean's Pharmacy	
Exit	O'Brien Street	
Food	S: Colonel Hogaie	
Lodg	N: Comfort Inn	
Exit	Ont. Hwy 63, Cassells Street, Trout Lake Road	
Gas	S: UPI(*)	
AServ	S: UPI	
Med	S: ✚ **After Hours Medical Walk-in Clinic**	
ATM	S: Bank of Montreal, TD Bank & Trust	
Other	S: A&P Supermarket, Shoppers Drug Mart	
Exit	Ont. Hwy 17B, Fisher Street	
Gas	S: Esso(*), Shell(*)	
Food	N: McDonald's (Wal-Mart)	
	S: Subway (Esso)	
AServ	N: Tire & Lube Express (Wal-Mart)	
TServ	N: **Best Way Truck Center, International Dealer**	
ATM	S: Esso	
Other	N: Independent Supermarket, North Gate Square Mall, **Wal-Mart**(RX)	
Exit	Seymour Street	
FStop	N: **Petro Pass Commercial**	
Gas	N: Pioneer(*, D)	
Food	N: Country Style, Don Cherry's	
	S: Tim Horton's	
Lodg	N: TraveLodge	
AServ	N: Northern Honda	
Exit	Ont. Hwy 11S, Toronto	
Exit	Acme Access Road, Twin Lakes Road	
AServ	S: George Stockfish Ford Dealer	
Exit	Bay View Road	
Gas	N: Mr. Gas(*, D)	
Exit	North Bay City	
Exit	Ont. Hwy 94, Corbeil	
Gas	S: Kwik-Way(*, D)	
Exit	Hwy 531, Bonfield	
Gas	S: Esso(*, D)	
Food	S: Valley View Restaurant	
Lodg	S: Valley View Motel	
Exit	Ch. Gagne Road	
Gas	S: Gagne's Gas(*, D)	

EXIT		ON
ATM	S: Gagne's Gas	
Exit	Rutherglen Town, Talon Lake Road	
Gas	S: Econo(*, D)	
Food	S: Tavern Restaurant	
RVCamp	N: **Ship's Cove Marina & Resort, Talon Lake Trailer Park**	
Exit	Kiosk Road	
Food	S: Fern's Restaurant	
Parks	S: **Algonquin Provincial Park**	
Exit	Samuel de Champlain	
Parks	N: **Samuel de Champlain Provincial Park (Closed in Winter Months)**	
Other	N: Voyageur Museum	
Exit	Ch. Tiger Lake Road	
RVCamp	S: **Tiger Lake Park**	
Exit	Ch. Neault Road	
Lodg	N: Rosco's Holiday Cottages	
Exit	Ch. Earl's Lake Road, Ch. Chant Plein Lake Road	
Food	S: Welcome Inn Restaurant	
Lodg	S: Welcome Inn	
AServ	N: North Tech Auto	
Exit	Mattawab Town	
Food	N: Two Rivers Motel	
Lodg	N: Two Rivers Motel	
AServ	N: Juliens Auto Body	
Exit	Turcotte Park Road	
Gas	N: Gas(*)	
AServ	N: Bangs Brothers Garage	
RVCamp	N: **Sid Turcotte Park**	
Other	N: Police Station	
Exit	Ont Hwy 533	
Gas	N: Petro Canada(*, 24), Shell(*, D)	
Food	N: Mattawa House Restaurant, Subway	
	S: Draper Restaurant	
Lodg	N: Mattawa House Motel	
AServ	N: Petro Canada	
Med	N: ✚ **Hospital**	
ATM	N: Scotia Bank	
Other	N: Mattawa Pharmacy	
	S: Police Station	
Exit	Mattawab	
Gas	S: Esso(*)	
Lodg	N: Valois Motel	
AServ	S: Esso	
Exit	Burrett's Road	
FStop	N: **Breton's**(*)	
Lodg	N: Breton's Motel	
Exit	Brent Road	
RVCamp	S: **Cedar Lake**	
Parks	S: **Algonquin Provincial Park**	
Exit	Dunlop, Crescent	
Gas	N: BB's(*)	
Lodg	S: Aftica Motel	
Exit	Deux Rivieres Town	
Lodg	N: King Fisher's Lodge	
RVCamp	N: **Antlers**	
Exit	Bisset Creek Town	
Exit	Stone Cliff Town, Station Road	
Gas	N: Shell(*)	
Exit	Pine Valley Road	
Lodg	N: Pine Valley Resort (Open May - October)	
RVCamp	N: **Pine Valley Tent & Trailer Park**	
Exit	Kenny Road	
Parks	N: **Driftwood Provincial Park**	
Exit	Mackey Creek Rd.	
RVCamp	N: **Lakeview Trailer Park Campground**	
	S: **Camelot Trailer Park**	

Bold red print shows RV & Bus parking available or nearby

EXIT	ON
Exit	Mackey Town, Boudreau Rd.
Lodg	S: Mackey Motel
Exit	Harvey Creek Rd.
Lodg	N: Hill Top Motel
Exit	Rolphton, Hwy 635
TStop	S: Esso(*)
Lodg	S: Rolphton Motel
Exit	Cutler Lane
TStop	N: Carty's(*)
Food	N: Katie's Kitchen (Carty's)
Exit	Pine Crest Rd.
Lodg	N: Pine Crest Resort
Exit	Moore's Rd.
RVCamp	N: Ryan's Campsites
Exit	Bass Lake Road
FStop	S: Esso(*)
RVCamp	S: Kanukawa Outfitters
Exit	Tooley Rd.
Lodg	N: Pines Motel
	S: Eddy Inn
Exit	McKey Road, McAnulty
Lodg	S: Deep River Motel
Exit	Ridge Road
Gas	S: Petro Canada(*)
AServ	S: Canadian Tire
Other	S: Police Station
Exit	Deep River Rd.
Gas	N: Esso(D)
	S: Carty's Gas(*)
Food	N: Godfather's Pizza
	S: Burger King, Pure & Simple (Bear's Den Motel), Subway
Lodg	N: Imperial Motel
	S: Bear's Den Motel
AServ	N: Esso
	S: Subaru of Deep River
ATM	N: Scotia Bank
Other	N: Guardin Drug Pharmacy, Value-Mart Supermarket
Exit	Deep River Town, Wylie Rd., Townline Rd.
Med	N: ✚ Hospital
Exit	Chalk River Town, Main St., Plant Road
Gas	N: Ultramar(*, D)
	S: Shell(*, D)
Food	N: The Tree Top(24)
	S: The Wood Quarter

EXIT	ON
Lodg	S: Chalk River Motel
ATM	N: Ultramar
Exit	Hwy 17, Paquette Rd, Petawawa
Other	N: Canadian Forces Base, Military Museum
Exit	Hwy 37, Murphy Rd., Petawawa
RVCamp	N: RV Camping
Exit	Cty Rd. 26, Petawawa
RVCamp	N: Achray Grand Lake, Pine Ridge Park
Parks	N: Algonquin Provincial Park
Exit	Hwy 58, Round Lake Road, Barry's Bay, Pembroke
Gas	N: Suny's(*)
ATM	N: Suny's
Parks	S: Bonne Chere Provincial Park
Exit	Ont Hwy 41, Eganville, Pembrook
TStop	N: Ervin Big Truck Stop(*, D)
Food	N: Big Stop
Lodg	N: Pembrook Inn Best Western
AServ	S: Hammel's Auto
TServ	S: Kenworth
Med	N: ✚ Hospital
ATM	N: Ervin Big Truck Stop
Other	N: Police Station, Tourist Info.
Exit	Cty Rd. 24, White Water Rd.
RVCamp	N: River Run, Wilderness Tours
Exit	West Meath, Twp Rd. 31
Gas	S: Stinson(*, D)
Exit	West Meath, Twp Rd. 37
RVCamp	N: Lakeside Cottage & Trailer Park
Exit	Cty Hwy 8, Main Street
Gas	S: Stinson(*)
AServ	S: Stinson
Exit	Cobden
Gas	N: Shell(*) (Restaurant, Motel)
RVCamp	N: Bona Vista Campground
Exit	Cty. Rd. 21, Cedar Haven Park Road, Foresters Falls
RVCamp	N: Cedar Haven Park, Owl Rafting, Inc., River Run Park, Wilderness Tours
Exit	Pinewood Park Rd., Cross Canada Road
AServ	N: Woody's Repair
Exit	Cty Rd 41, Haley Station, Ont Hwy 653, Chanux
Exit	Price Rd., Cty 4, Storyland Rd.
RVCamp	N: KOA Campgrounds, River Run Park
Other	N: Storyland Park (Seasonal)

EXIT	ON
Exit	Cty 20, Bruce Street, Renfrew
Gas	S: Stinson(*)
AServ	S: Stinson
Med	S: ✚ Hospital
Other	S: Police Station
Exit	Ont 60, Ont 132, O'Brien Rd., Renfrew
Food	S: OBrien's (Renfrew Inn)
Lodg	S: Renfrew Inn
Other	S: Tourist Info.
Exit	Ont Hwy 508, Cty 1
Gas	S: McEwing(*, D)
Other	S: Calabogie Tourist Area
Exit	White Lake Rd., County 2, Renford County
FStop	S: Stinson(*, D)
Gas	N: Canadian Tire, Gas(*, D, LP, CW, 24), Petro Canada(*)
Food	N: Bill & Tonia's Restaurant, Luck Sing Restaurant, McDonald's(PLAY), Subway, Tim Horton's, Wendy's
Lodg	N: Arnprior Motor Inn, Country Squire Motel, Twin Maples Motel
AServ	N: Canadian Tire
Med	N: ✚ Hospital
Other	N: A&P Supermarket, Arnprior Animal Hospital, Loeb Supermarket
Exit	Basking Dr.
Other	N: Tourist Info.
Exit	Ont. Hwy 15S, Hwy 59N Herrick Drive
Exit	Madawaska Blvd.
AServ	N: Ford, Lincoln, Mercury Dealer
Other	N: Police Station
Exit	Arnprior
Exit	Hwy 22
Gas	N: Stinson(*, D, LP)
AServ	N: Euro Asian
Parks	N: Fitzory Provincial Park
Other	N: Morris Island Conservation Area
Exit	Hwy 20, Antrim
Other	N: Carleton Bus Lines, Police Station
Exit	Antrim
TStop	E: Antrim(*)
TServ	E: Western Star Sales & Service

↑ Ontario

Begin 17, Ottawa

TCH-20 E →

EXIT	QC
	Begin 20, Near Montreal
	↓ Québec
2	QB325 Riviere-Beaudette
FStop	E: Vosco(*, 24)
Food	W: Restaurant La Borte Du Quebec
Lodg	E: Pan Holidayer Inn
6	Ch. St-Phomas
9	St-Zotique, St-Polycarype, St-Telesphore
FStop	E: Produits Petroliers Real
12	Les Coteaux

EXIT	QC
TServ	E: Centre Du Camion Potvin Et Fils
17	QB 201S Point Mgr Langlois, Salberri-de-Valleyfield
Med	E: ✚ Hospital
Other	E: Police Station (10 Km)
18	QB201N Coteau-du-Lac, Saint-Clet
Gas	W: Essex(D), Esso(*, D)
Food	W: Ultra Restaurant
Lodg	W: Des Erables, Hotel Marcel Lebenc
19	Ch. St-Emmanuel
Other	W: BEM
22	Ch. St-Dominque

EXIT	QC
25	Weigh Station
26	Les Credes, Saint-Lazarde
FStop	W: Astro(*)
Food	W: Astro Restaurant
ATM	W: Astro
29	Hwy 540, Hwy 40, Hwy 417
35A	Pincourt, Terrasse Vaudreuilarsse-Vauderuil
Gas	E: Petro Canada(*)
ATM	E: LeFaubourd De'lle Mall
Other	E: LeFaubourd De'lle Mall, Maxi Supermarket, Pharmaprix Pharmacy
35	N-d-L-Ile-Perrot

EXIT QC

Gas E: Petro Canada(*)
Food E: Domino's Pizza, Dunkin Donuts, Le Four
Other E: Animal Clinic, Mail Boxes Etc., Metro Supermarket

37 Grand Blvd
Gas E: Shell(*), Ultramar(*, D, CW)
Food E: Billy's K's, Dairy Queen, Del-ile Grecque
Lodg E: Montrel Motel

39 Ste-Anne-de-Bellevue
Gas E: Esso(*, CW)

48 Boul. St. Charles
Gas E: Esso(*, CW)
W: Petro Canada(*, D)
Food E: McDonald's

49 Ave Cartier

50 Boul. St.Gean
Gas W: Petro Canada
Food W: Topaze
ATM W: Banque & Trust, Banque Royale
Other W: Metro Supermarket

53 Boul. des Sources
Gas N: Uldramar(*, CW)

90 Hwy 15, QB132, Ponds, Jacque Cartier-Victoria Champlain, La Prairie-U.S.A. Varennes
Lodg N: Days Inn

91 Boul Industrial, Rue Metrobole

92 Boul Mortagne
FStop S: Shell(*, 24)
Gas N: Shell(*, D, CW), Ultramar(*, D, CW)
Food N: Giorgio, Harvey's, Le Biftheque Steak House
S: Burger King, Casey's, Chili's, Maison de Jade, Mario's, Mike's, Valentine, Wyoming
Lodg N: Comfort Inn, Hotel Welcominns
ATM N: Banque Royale
Other N: Cache- A-Leau
S: Postnet

95 Boul Montarville, Rue de Touraine
FStop S: Ultramar(*, D)
Food S: Le Boygeur(24)
TServ S: Ressorts Rive-Sud

(96) Weigh Station

98 Hwy 30, Brossard, Sorel

102 St Julie, St Bruno, St Amabale
FStop S: Petro Canada(*, D)
Gas N: Shell(*, D, LP, CW), Ultramar(*, D, LP)
S: Esso(*, D, CW), Sergaz(*, D, CW)
Food N: Alexandera, Mike's, Tim Horton's
S: Bacini, Burger King(PLAY), Dunkin Donuts, La Tour Steaks, McDonald's(PLAY), Perle D' Asie, Pizza Hut, St Hubert, Subway
Med S: + Clinique Medicale Des Haut-bois
ATM N: CIBC
Other N: Metro Supermarket

105 QB239, St Basile-Le-Grand, McMasterville
Gas S: Continental(D), Petro Canada(*, D)
Food N: Le Rossignol
S: Resto 105
Lodg S: Motel Veloeil

109 Veioelle, Rue St Gane-Baptiste, St Mathleu-De-Veloeil

112 QB233, Beloeli, St Marc-sur-Richelieu
Lodg S: Hotel Rive Gauche

113 QB133, Mont-St-Hilaire, St Jean-sur-Hichelieu, St Charles-sur Richelieu
FStop S: Shell(*, D, LP, 24)
Food S: Le Buzz, Shell
Lodg S: Motel Le Transit

115 La Grande-Allee

(117) Rest Area - RR, Phones, Picnic, Concession

120 QB227, St Madeleine, St Jean Baptiste
Gas S: OLCO(*, D)

123 St Hyacinthe, La Presentation
TServ N: Kenworth

130 QB137, QB235, St Hyacinthe, St Denis
FStop N: Esso(*, D)
Gas N: Crevier, Scrgas(*, D), Ultramar(*, D)
S: Shell(*, D, CW, 24)
Food N: Collibri, Harvey's, McDonald's (Wal-Mart), Valentine(LP)
S: Brasserie Steak House, Burger King(PLAY), Dunkin Donuts, L'Empereur De Chine Buffet, Maire Antointte, McDonald's(PLAY), PFK, Pizza Hut, St Hubert
Lodg N: Motel Le Copian
S: Hotel Hebergerment, Hotel Le Eauphin
TServ N: Esso
S: Beaudoin International(24)
ATM N: Banque of Scotia
S: Banque Nationale
Other N: Pharmacy (Wal-Mart), Wal-Mart

133 St Hyacinthe, Rue Girouard

134 St Hyacinthe, Rue Yamaska

138 QB224, St Simon, St Rosalie
FStop N: Astro(*, D)

141 Granby, Via 132 S (Left Exit)

143 St Valerien-de-Milton
Food N: Lextra Terrasse

145 St Liboire, St Simon
TStop S: Irving(*, D, 24)
Gas S: Le Petrolier(D), OLCO(*, D)
Food S: Irving, La Boutine d'Or, OLCO
Lodg S: OLCO
TServ S: Irving

147 Quebec 116E, Upton, Acton Vale
Gas S: Esso(D, 24)
Food S: Hotel la Liberte
Lodg S: Hotel la Liberte

150 St-Hugues

152 St-Helene
TStop N: Esso(*, D, CW)
FStop S: Shell(*, D, LP), Ultramar Cipeline Commercial
Gas N: Petro Canada(*, D)
S: Ultramar(*, D)
Food N: Esso, Harvey's, Le Quebecois
S: Bar-L'Heleniose, McDonald's, Tim Horton's
Lodg S: Days Inn
TServ N: Esso

(157) Rest Area - RR, Phones, Picnic, Concessions (Westbound)

157 St-Nazaire, Wickham

160 Quebec 239, St-Eugene, St-Guillaume

166 10 e rang de St- Germain

170 Quebec 122, St- Germaine, Yamaska Sorel

173 Hwy 55 S, Drummondville, Sherbrooke

175 QB143 N, Boul. Lemire, St. Bonaventure, St-Fracios du Lac
TServ N: Freightliner of Drummondville, International of Drummondville

177 QB143 S, Drummondville, St Majorique
Gas N: Petro T(*, D, LP)
S: Esso(*, D), Petro Canada(*, D), Shell(*)
Food N: Motel Blanchet
S: Burger King, Dunkin Donuts, McDonald's (Wal-Mart), Pizza Hut, St Hubert, Subway, Tim Horton's, Wendy's
Lodg N: Motel Blanchet, Motel Drummond
S: Comfort Inn
Med S: + Hospital
ATM S: Provigo Supermarket
Other S: Galeries Drimmond, Les Promenades Drummondville, Maxi's Supermarket, Provigo Supermarket, Wal-Mart

179 Chemin du Golf

181 St Charles de Drummond, Drummondville, St joachim-de-Courval
Other N: Musee de la Cuisine

185 QB255, St Cyrille, Bale-du-Febvre
TStop N: Irving(*, D, 24)
Food N: Irving

191 St Brigitte
Gas N: Crevier(D, 24)
S: Crevier(*, D)
Food N: Licencie
Lodg S: The 4 Saisons Motel

196 QB259, St Perpetue, Nicolet, N.-G-Du-Bon-Conseil

200 QB155, St Leonard-d' Aston
FStop N: Esso(*)
Food N: Esso

202 Chemin, Haut-de-La-Riviere
Gas N: Esso(*, D)
Food N: Restaurant Madrid
Lodg N: Hotel Madrid

204 Rang des Cedres, Rang des Plaines
Gas N: Viagas(D)
Food S: Captain Fred's(24)
Lodg S: Captain Fred's

210 Hwy 55 N, Hwy 955, QB161, St Valere, St Albert, St Eulalie, Trois-Rivieres
FStop S: Sonerco(*)

Bold red print shows RV & Bus parking available or nearby

EXIT QC

Gas **N:** Shell(*)
S: Petro T(D, CW)
Food **N:** Kastel, Relais 210(24)
S: Le Lys
Lodg **S:** Motel Marie Dan
215 Rang des Epinettes
220 QB261, Defoy, Decancour, Daveluyville
Gas **N:** Esso(*, D), Petro Canada(*, D, LP)
S: Senerco(*, D)
Food **N:** La Belle Quebecoise
(225) Rest Area - RR, Phones, Picnic, Concession
228 QB165, 2e Rang de St-Louis-de-Blandford
Gas **S:** Gas Station(D, 24)
Food **S:** Restaurant 228(24)
235 QB162, QB263, Lemieux, Princeville, Victoriaville, St-Louis-de-Blandford
Gas **N:** Viagaz(*, D)
S: Petro T(D)
Food **N:** Viagaz
243 QB218, Manseau, Les Becquets
FStop **N:** Esso(*, D, 24)
Gas **S:** Shell(*, D)
Food **N:** Esso
Lodg **N:** Le Toit Rouge
TServ **N:** Esso
253 QB265, Villeroy, Plessisville, Thetford Fines, Dschaillons
FStop **S:** Esso(*, D, 24)
Food **S:** Bouf, tonne
(255) Rest Area - RR, Phones, Picnic, Concessions
256 15e et 16e Rangs de Villeroy
FStop **N:** Crebier(*, 24)
Gas **S:** Sonerco(*, D)
Food **N:** Crebier
S: L'Ultra
Lodg **N:** Crebier
S: Sonerico
261 Val-Alain
Gas **N:** Petro -T(D), Ultramar(D)
S: Sonerco
Food **N:** Le Lysee
266 4e et 5e Rangs de Val-Alain
271 Joly
Gas **S:** Eko(*)
278 QB271, Laurier-Station, St Flavien, St Croix
FStop **N:** Ultramar(*, 24)
Gas **S:** Esso(*)
Food **N:** Marie-Jo, Rayalco
S: Subway
Lodg **N:** Motel Rayalco
285 Issoudun
291 QB273, St. Agapit, St. Apollinaire, St. Antoine de Tilly
Gas **N:** Esso(*, D, LP, 24)
S: Ultramar(D)
Food **N:** 4 As, Le Saint Apo (Esso)
S: Lizzon

EXIT QC

Lodg **N:** Motel, Motel 4 As
TServ **N:** Masse Trucks
Other **S:** Brunet Pharmacy, IGA Supermarket
296 Route du Cap
TStop **N:** Petro Canada(*, D, 24)
Food **N:** Bivac (Petro Canada)
TServ **N:** Petro Canada
TWash **N:** Petro Canada
(307) Rest Area - RR, Phones, Picnic, Concession
305 St Nicholas, St Etienne
FStop **N:** Shell(*, D, CW)
Gas **N:** Irving, Petro Canada(*, D, LP)
Food **N:** Harvey's, Le Berneville Restaurant, Restaurant L' Eravliere
TServ **N:** Kenworth Quebec (2 Km east)
ATM **N:** Petro Canada
311 QB116, St Nicholas, St Redempteur
FStop **N:** Ultramar(*, D)
Gas **N:** Shell(*, LP)
S: Esso(*, D, CW), Petro Canada(*, CW)
Food **N:** Ashton(24), Tim Horton's, Ultramar
S: Dunkin Donuts, McDonald's(PLAY), Mike's, Subway
Lodg **S:** Motel Berneres
Other **N:** Metro Supermarket, Provigo Supermarket
S: Clinique Veterinare St Nicholas, IGA Supermarket
314 Hwy 73, QB175, Quebec, St. Georges, Charny
318 Ste. Jeane-Chrysostome, Ste. Romuald North
FStop **N:** Sonic(*, D, LP, CW)
S: Irving(*, D, LP, 24)
Gas **N:** Eko(*, D, LP)
Food **N:** McDonald's(24)
321 Chemin des Lles
Food **N:** Le Kanadien(24)
Med **N:** ✚ Hospital
325 QB173, QB277, Levis Down-town, Pintendre, Lac-Etchemin
FStop **S:** OLCO(*, D), Shell(*, D)
Gas **N:** OLCO(*, D)
Food **N:** McDonald's (Wal-Mart), Pizza Royale
S: Normandine(24), Shell
Lodg **S:** Comfort Inn, Motel Valon
TServ **S:** Ford Trucks, Volvo
Med **N:** ✚ Hospital
Other **N:** Wal-Mart
327 Rte Mgr-Bourget
Med **N:** ✚ Hospital
330 Rt Lallemand
Lodg **S:** Manoir de Beaumont (7 Km)
337 Beaumont, QB279, St. Charles, St Damien
Gas **N:** Shell(*) (2 Km)
341 Beaumont, St. Charles
Gas **S:** Petro Canada(*, D)
Food **S:** L'Edate (Petro Canada)
Lodg **S:** Motel 341
(344) Rest Area - RR, Coffee
348 St Michel, La Durantaye, QB281

EXIT QC

356 St Vallier, St Raphael
Lodg **N:** Motel sur Mer (5 Km)
364 Berthier-sur-Mer, St Francois
FStop **S:** Ultramar(*, D)
Food **S:** La Pause (Ultramar)
369 St Pierre
Gas **S:** Astro
Food **S:** Bar chez Diane (Astro)
Med **N:** ✚ Hospital
376 QB228, Montmagny, Ch. des Poirier
FStop **S:** Esso(*, D, CW)
Gas **S:** Shell
Food **S:** Cafe Internet, Dunkin Donuts (6 Km), La Plaza (Esso), McDonald's
Lodg **S:** Hotel L'Oiseliere (5 Km), Motel 232
TServ **S:** Chabot Ford
Med **S:** ✚ Hospital
378 QB283, Montmagny, St.-Fabien-de-Panet
Gas **N:** Ultramar(*)
388 Cap-St.Ignace
Gas **S:** Petro Canada(*, D)
Food **S:** Au Rocher
Lodg **S:** Motel
(395) Rest Area - RR, Phones, Picnic, Snacks
400 QB285, L'Islet, St Eugene
Gas **N:** Petro Canada(*)
S: Eko(*, D, CW)
Food **N:** L'Eveil
414 St-Jean-Port-Joli, St Aubert, St-Pamphile, QB204
FStop **N:** Fuel Stop(*, D)
S: Petro Canada(*, D)
Gas **S:** Esso(*, D), Petro Canada (2)(*, D)
Food **S:** Dunkin Donuts, Petro Canada
Lodg **S:** Motel La Seigneurie
430 St- Roch-des-Aulnaies, St Louise, QB132
436 QB230, La Pocatiere, Av.Industrielle
Gas **S:** Esso(*, D, CW, 24), OLCO(*, D, LP), Sonic(D)
Food **S:** Cap Martin(24), Motel Martinet
Lodg **S:** Hotel & Motel Cap Martin, Motel Martinet
439 La Pocatiere, St-Onesime
FStop **S:** Ultramar(*, D, RV DUMP)
Food **S:** McDonald's(24), Mike's
Lodg **S:** DAYS INN Days Inn
Med **S:** ✚ Hospital
Other **S:** Police Station
444 QB132, La Pocatiere, Av. de la Grande-Anse , Riviere-ouelle
TStop **S:** Petro Canada(*), Sergas(*, D)
Food **S:** Le Martinet (Petro Canada), Pat Arret Routier (Sergas)
TServ **S:** Sergas
450 Riviere-Ouelle, St-Pacome, St-Gabriel
TStop **N:** Ultramar(*)
Food **N:** L'Escale(24) (Ultramar)
Lodg **N:** Ultramar
456 QB287, St-Denis, St-Philippe-

EXIT		QC
	de-Neri, Mont-Carmel	
Gas	S: Eko(*, D), Petro Canada(*, D)	
(459)	Rest Area - RR, Phones, Concession, Picnic	
465	Kamouraska, St Pascal, St Bruno	
Food	S: Le Bec Fin, Montagne	
Lodg	S: Motel L' Amite, **Motel de la Montagne**	
TServ	N: **RMS Garage**(24)	
Other	S: Police Station	
474	St. Germain, St. Helene	
Gas	N: **Petro Canada**(*, D)	
	S: Benco(*, D)	
Food	N: **Petro Canada**	
488	QB289. St. Alexandre, Pohenegamook, Nouveau-Brunswick	
Gas	N: Gas Station(*)	
480	St. Andre, St Joseph	
Lodg	N: Manoir St. Andre	
496	Notre Dame- du Portage	
507	QB132, Boul. Cartier	
Gas	S: Esso(*, D), Petro Canada(*, D, CW)	
Food	N: Sablonnet Chinese	
	S: Normandine, Restaurant au Faubourg, St Hubert (Motel Boulevard)	
Lodg	N: Motel Damour, Motel Loupi	
	S: Comfort Inn, Motel Boulevard Cartier	
Other	N: Le Chateau De Reve	
499	QB185, Edmundston, N-B., Cabano, Deglis	
503	QB132, Rue Fraser	
Gas	S: Esso(*, D), Petro Canada(*, D, LP)	
Food	S: Burger King (2 Km), Dunkin Donuts (2 Km), Hotel Universel, McDonald's (2 Km)	
Lodg	S: Hotel Levesque, Hotel Universel	
514	Cacouna, St. Arsene	
TServ	N: **Service de Pneus Cacouna**	

↑ Québec

Begin 20, Near Montreal

Hwy 40 E →

EXIT		QC
	Begin 40	

↓ Québec

EXIT		QC
1	QB342, Pointe- Fortune	
2	Montee, Wilson,Ponte-Fortune	
6	Montee, Baie St Thomas	
9	QB342, Rigaud	
Gas	S: Ultramar(*)	
Lodg	S: Hotel Vinti	
12	QB342, Rigaud	
Gas	S: Petro Canada(*)	
Food	N: Pierre de Rigaud	
Other	S: Metro Supermarket	
17	QB201, Montee, Lavigne, Salaberry-de-Valleyfield	
FStop	N: **Petro Canada**(*, D)	
Gas	S: Shell(*, 24)	
Food	N: Burger King, Dunkin Donuts, Pizza Hut, Resto Express (Petro Canada)	
	S: **McDonald's**(24)	
Lodg	N: **Hudson Inn**	
22	St Lazare, Hudson	
26	QB342, Hudson, St. Lazare (Difficult Reaccess)	
60	Mirabel, Hwy 13 Lacine Laval	
62	Coute Vertu, Boul. Hymus, Boul. H. Bourassa	
Food	S: **Le Seville Restaurant (Days Inn)**	
Lodg	S: **Days Inn**	
TServ	S: **Kenworth**(24)	
65	Hwy 520, auto Route, Cote-de-Liesse, Boul Chavindish	
TServ	S: **Freightliner**	
66	Hwy 15, Hwy 10, Aut. Decarie, Sherbrooke, Pont Champlin (Left Exit)	
67	QB 117 N, Boul. M.-Laurin	
70	Hwy 15 Laval, St. Jerome, Rue Deslauriers, Ch. Rocklend	
71	Boul. St. Laurent, Boul d l'Acaie	
73	QB 335, Av. C.-Colomb, Rue St. Hubert	
75	Hwy 19, St Michel, St. Papinsau	
Gas	N: Crevier(*, D)	
	S: Shell(*, 24)	
Food	N: Robins Donut & Deli, Valentine	
	S: Dunkin Donuts	
76	Hwy 25N, QB125, Boul Lacordarie	
Gas	N: Ultramar(*, D)	
	S: Esso(*, D, CW)	
Food	S: Dunkin Donuts	
ATM	S: Esso	
78	Boul Langelier	
81	Boul H.-Bourassa	
80	Hwy 25, Hwy 20, Tunnel L.-H.-Lafontaine (Left Exit)	
82	Boul Ray-Lawson, Boul Roi-Rene, Boul Les-Galeries d' Anjou	
Gas	S: Castrol(D), Petro Canada(*, D, LP), Sunoco(*, D), Ultramar(*, D, CW), Ultramar(*, D, LP)	
Food	S: Dunkin Donuts(24), Mario's(24)	
TServ	N: **Freightliner**	
85	Avenue Marien, Boul St Jean Baptiste	
FStop	S: **Ultramar**(*)	
87	QB138, Boul Tricentenair, Rue Sherbooke, Boul Henri-Bourassa	
Other	S: Police Station	
94	QB344, Lachenaie	
96	Hwy 640, Laval, Charlemagne, St Eustache	
Gas	S: Ultramar(*, D, CW)	
Food	S: Poulet Frit, St Hubert	
Lodg	S: Hotel Travelodge	
Other	S: Lave-Auto 640	
97	Le Gardeur, Charlemagne, Boul Pierre-Le-Gardeur (Eastbound, Reaccess Westbound Only)	
98	Repentigny, Le Gardeur	
Gas	S: Petro Canada(*, D, CW), Ultramar(*, D, 24)	
Food	S: Dunkin Donuts, McDonald's (Wal-Mart), Pacine, Pizza Hut, Poulet Frilot Kentucky, Tim Horton's	
Med	N: + Clinique Medical Brien	
ATM	S: Banque de Montreal	
Other	N: A.Lauriault, IGA Supermarket(24), Pharmacy	
	S: Les Galeries Rive Nord, Les Galeries de Repentigny, Provigo Supermarket, Wal-Mart(RX)	
100	Rue Industriel, Rue Valmont	
Gas	S: Esso(*, D, LP, CW), Shell(*, D, LP, CW, 24)	
Food	S: Rlafleur, Tim Horton's, Valentine	
Other	N: Quilles G	
108	QB343, QB341, St Sulpice, L'Assomption, L' Epiphanie	
118	Service Area (Left Exit)	
FStop	B: **Esso**(*, D, 24)	
Food	B: **Benny Express**(24)	
122	Hwy 31, QB 131, Joilette, La Valitrie	
130	Lanoraie	
Gas	N: Sonic(*, D, LP)	
141	Rang St-Philome (Eastbound, Reaccess Westbound Only)	
144	QB 158, Berthierville, St-Gabriel	
FStop	S: **Ultramar**(*, D, LP)	
Gas	N: Shell(*, D, 24)	
	S: Esso(*, D, CW), Petro Canada(*, D, 24), Sonic(D)	
Food	S: **McDonald's**, St. Huberte, Tim Horton's	
Lodg	S: Days Inn	
Other	S: Police Station	
151	St. Cuthbert, St. Viateur	
Gas	N: Sonic(*, D)	
155	St-Bartheleny, Maskinonge	
159	Rest Area - RR, Phones, Picnic, Tourist Information (Eastbound)	
160	Rang De La Riviere Sud-Est	
166	Louiseville	
Med	N: + Hospital	
174	QB138, Yamachiche	
Gas	N: Esso(*, D, LP)	
Food	N: La Porte De La Manu	
Lodg	N: **Motel La Porte De La Manuricie**	
TServ	N: **R. Theriault Inc**	
Med	N: + Hospital (6 Km)	

Bold red print shows RV & Bus parking available or nearby

EXIT	QC
180	QB 153, Yamacheiche
Lodg	**N:** Motel La Bonne Etoile
187	QB 138, Point du Lac
Lodg	**S:** Auberge de Lac St Pierre
189	Rang St Chartles, Pointe du Lac
FStop	**N: Astro**
Food	**N:** La Plasse 189
192	Chemin des Petites-Terres
193	Weigh Station
196	Hwy 55, Shawinigan Trois-Rivieres, Quebec
198	Boul. des Recolletes
199	Boul des Forges, Downtown
Gas	**N:** Ultramar(*, D)
	S: Petro Canada(*, D, 24)
Food	**N:** Pizza Royale
	S: Ti-coq
Med	**S:** ✚ Hospital
201	Boul. des Chenaux
202	Boul. des Estacades
Gas	**N:** Shell(*, D, 24)
Food	**N:** McDonald's (Wal-Mart), Mike's Restaurant, Tim Horton's
	S: Sir Huberts
ATM	**N:** Bank Royale
Other	**N:** Jean Couto Drug Store (Post Office), Maxi Supermarket, Smales Galeries du Cap, Wal-Mart
203	Hwy 157, Rue Thibeau N., St-Louis de France, Shawinigan Sud, Sud Centre Ville, Rue Thibeau, Sud
Gas	**N:** Irving(*, D, CW)
Food	**N:** Normandine
	S: Thibeauo
ATM	**N:** Banque Nationale
205	Ste Martag du Cap, Boul des Praires

EXIT	QC
Gas	**N:** OLCO(*, D, 24)
	S: Shell(*, LP)
Food	**S:** Arrent 205
Lodg	**S:** Penn-mass Hotel
Med	**S:** ✚ Hospital
ATM	**S:** Shell
210	QB 532, Saint Maurice
220	QB 359, St Luc de Vincennes, Grand Mere, Champlain
229	QB 361, St. Genevieve de Batiscan, St. Narcisse/Batiscan
236	QB 159, St. Anne de la Peride, St. Prosper, St. Tite
Other	**N:** Police Station
254	QB363, St. Marc des Carrieres, Grondines, Deschambauld
FStop	**N: Ultramar**(*, D)
	S: Petro(*, D, CW)
Food	**N: Normandine**
Lodg	**S:** Auberge Chemin du Roy, **Motel Le Chavigny**
257	St. Gilbert, Des Chambault
261	Notre Dame De Proteus, Portenus
Gas	**S:** Irving(*, LP, 24)
Lodg	**S:** Hotel Sieur Leneus
Other	**S:** Police Station
269	St. Basile, Pont Rue QB 358, Che-Sante
Lodg	**S:** Motel Chalet Morin
274	Donnacona
Gas	**S:** Esso(*), Petro Canada(*, D), Ultramar(*)
Food	**S:** KFC, McDonald's, Normandine, Pizza Hut, Tim Horton's
ATM	**S:** Banque Nationale
281	QB 365, Pont Rouge, St. Raymond, Neuville
285	Neuville

EXIT	QC
286	Rest Area - RR, Phones, Picnic, Concessions
(286)	Weigh Station
295	QB367, Rte de Fossambault, St Catherine de la J Cartier, St Augustin de Desmaures
FStop	**N: Esso**(*, D)
298	QB138, Ancinne-Lorette, Boul W-Hamel, St Augustini de des Maures
Gas	**S:** OLCO, Shell(D, LP)
Food	**N:** Le Relais
Lodg	**N:** Motel Colibri
300	Chemin du Lac
302	Rt Jean-Gauvin, Cap-Rouge
Gas	**N:** Shell(*, D, LP, CW, 24)
	S: Ultramar(*, D, LP)
Food	**N:** Le Coq Roti
	S: Dunkin Donuts
Other	**S:** IGA Supermarket
304	Av. Le Gendre
Gas	**N:** Esso(*, D, LP, CW)
Food	**N:** Gab's
Med	**N:** ✚ Clinique Medical
Other	**N:** M. Craig
305	Hwy 540 S, Hwy 20, Aut. Duplessis, Riviere-du-Loup, Rt de l'Aeroport
Food	**N:** McDonald's (Wal-Mart)
Lodg	**N:** Comfort Inn
Other	**N:** Wal-Mart
306	Av Blaise-Pascal
307	Hwy 73, Hwy 40 E, Aut. Henri IV, Pont Pierre la Porte, Chicoutimi, St Anne-de-Beaupri

↑ Québec

Begin 40

Hwy 401 E →

EXIT	ON
	Begin 401, Windsor

↓ Ontario

EXIT	ON
13	ON3, ON3B, Bridge To USA, Tunnel To USA
14	Essex Rd 46, Windsor
TStop	**S: Husky**(*, LP)
FStop	**S: Ultramar**(*)
Food	**S: Husky T Stop**
TServ	**S: 401 Mac, Expressway Truck Center, Husky T Stop, Mike Gale's International, Toromot CAT**
Med	**N:** ✚ Hospital
(20)	Truck Inspection
21	Hwy 19, Manning Rd, Tecumseh
Other	**S:** Police Station
(27)	Truck Scales
28	Hwy 25, Puse Rd, Essex, Puse
34	Hwy 27, Belle River Rd, Woodslee, Belle River
40	Essex County Hwy 31, St Joachim Rd, St Joachim
48	Hwy 35, Comber Rd, Stoney Point, ON77, Leamington
56	ON2, Tilbury
FStop	**N: Esso**(*)
Food	**N:** Cedar Hill Inn
Lodg	**N: Cedar Inn Motel**
(62)	Service Center
FStop	**B: Petro Canada**(*), **Shell**(*)
Food	**B:** KFC, Mr Sub, Tim Horton's
63	ON2, Tilbury
81	Bloomfied Rd, Hwy 27, Chatham
TStop	**S: Bloomfield TStop**(*)
Food	**S: Bloomfield TStop**
Lodg	**N:** Best Western Wheels Inn (5 Km)
TServ	**S: Bloomfield TStop**
90	ON40, Blenheim, Chatham
Other	**N:** Police Station
101	Hwy 15, Kent Bridge Rd, Dresden
109	ON21, Ridgetown, Thamesville
TStop	**S: Esso**(*)
Food	**S:** Esso, Oasis (EconoLodge), Stop 21
Lodg	**S: Econolodge**
117	Hwy 20, Orford Rd, Highgate
129	Hwy 3, Furnival Rd, Rodney, Wardsville
137	ON76, West Lorne
(146)	Service Area
FStop	**B: Petro Canada, Shell**
Food	**B:** McDonald's, Mr Sub, Tim Horton's, Wendy's
149	Hwy 8, Currie Rd, Dutton
Other	**S:** Police Station
157	Elgin County Hwy 14, Iona Rd, Iona, Melbourne
164	Hwy 20, Union Rd, Shedden
177	B&A ON4 London, St Thomas
FStop	**S: Ultramar**
Gas	**S:** Pioneer(*)
Lodg	**S:** Stone Ridge INN
183	ON402, Sarnia

EXIT	ON
186A	Wellington Rd S
186B	Wellington Rd N., ON135, Exeter Rd
Gas	**N:** Esso(*, CW), Petro Canada(*), Petro Canada(*, 24), Shell(*), Sunoco(*, CW), Ultramar(*) **S:** Amoco(*), Sunoco(*)
Food	**N:** Country Style, Country Style (Shell), Lester's Diner, Manhattan Road House, Outback Steakhouse, Pizza Hut, Sub Zone, Tim Horton's, Tim Horton's (Esso), Wendy's **S:** Arby's, Burger King, Hide A Way Family Restaurant, McDonald's(PLAY), Tim Horton's
Lodg	**N:** Days Inn, Econolodge, Hampton Court Hotel, Holiday Inn Express, Howard Johnson, Ramada Inn
Med	**N:** Hospital
ATM	**N:** Esso
Other	**N:** Police Station **S:** Costco, Super Store Mall
189	Highbury Ave
Other	**N:** Fanshawe Pioneer Village (16 Km)
194	Airport Rd
195	ON74, Belmont, Nilestown
TStop	**S:** Husky(*, LP)
Food	**S:** Husky T Stop
199	Hwy 32, Dorchester Rd, Dorchester
TStop	**S:** Fifth Wheel Travel Center(*, LP, CW, SCALES)
Food	**S:** Fifth Wheel TStop
Lodg	**S:** Fifth Wheel TStop
203	ON73, Aylmer
(207)	Truck Inspection Station
208	Hwy 30, Butnam Rd, Avon, Putnam
216	Hwy 10, Culloden Rd, Ingersoll
Lodg	**N:** TraveLodge
218	ON19, Ingersoll, Tillsonburg
Food	**N:** Ram's Horn
Lodg	**N:** Elmhurst Inn **S:** Jet Set Motel
Med	**N:** Hospital
222	Oxford Rd 6, Embro, Stratford
(229)	Service Area
FStop	**B:** Esso
Food	**B:** Burger King, Tim Horton's, Wendy's
230	Oxford County Hwy 12, Sweatburg Rd, Sweatburg, Woodstock
Lodg	**N:** Woodstock Motor Inn
232	ON59, Delhi, Woodstock
Gas	**N:** Maple Leaf(*, CW)
Food	**N:** Kelsey's, Tim Horton's, Wendy's
Lodg	**N:** Quality Inn
TServ	**S:** Woodstock Tire Service
Med	**N:** Hospital
236	Oxford County Hwy 15, Towerline Rd, Woodstock
238	B&A, ON2, Woodstock, Paris
TStop	**S:** Nick's Truck Stop(*, D)
Food	**S:** Nick's Truck Stop
TServ	**S:** Nick's Truck Stop
Other	**N:** Police Station
250	Drumbo Rd, Drumbo, Innerkip
268	Waterloo Rd 97, Plattsville, Ayr
TStop	**S:** Esso(*, CW)
Food	**S:** Esso

EXIT	ON
275	Fountain St, Homer Watson Blvd., Hwy 28, Cambridge, Kitchner
Lodg	**N:** Rodeway Inn (Closed During the winter)
278	ON8, Cambridge, Kitchner, Waterloo
Gas	**N:** Shell(*, D, CW, 24)
Other	**N:** Pets Mart Pet Hospital
282	ON24, Cambridge
Gas	**S:** Double Gas(*), Esso(*, CW), Petro Canada(*, 24), Petro Canada(*, 24)
Food	**S:** Jade Garden, Taco Bell, Tim Horton's, Tim Horton's
Lodg	**N:** Comfort Inn, Holiday Inn **S:** Days Inn, Super 8
TServ	**S:** Cambridge Mac
ATM	**S:** Esso
Other	**N:** Shoppers Drug Mart, Tri City Centre **S:** Knob Hill Farms Supermarket
286	Hwy 33, Townline Rd, Cambridge
(66)	Service Center
FStop	**B:** Petro Canada
Food	**B:** McDonald's
295	ON6 N, Guelph (Reaccess Eastbound Only)
299	ON6 S, Hamilton, Hwy 46, Brock Rd, Guelph
TStop	**N:** My Little Margie's(*, D)
Gas	**N:** Cango(*, D), Pioneer(*, D, CW)
Food	**N:** My Little Margie's, Tim Horton's, Timmy's Donut & Deli (Cango)
TServ	**N:** My Little Margie's
312	Hwy 1 Guelph Line, Campbellville, Burlington
Gas	**N:** Sunoco(*, D)
Food	**N:** Mohawk Inn
Lodg	**N:** Mohawk Inn
320	ON25, Milton, Halton Hills, Acton
TStop	**S:** Fifth Wheel Auto & Truck Plaza(*)
Gas	**S:** Esso(*, 24)
Food	**S:** Country Style Donuts, Fifth Wheel, Harvey's, Kelsey's, McDonald's
Lodg	**S:** Fifth Wheel, Quality Inn
Med	**S:** Hospital
Other	**S:** Police Station
324	Hwy 4, James Snow Pkwy
(326)	Weigh Station, Truck Inspection
328	Hwy Trafalgar Rd, Halton Hills, Georgetown, Oakville
TStop	**S:** Trafalgar Truck Stop(*)
FStop	**S:** Pioneer(*, LP)
Gas	**N:** Esso(*, D), Shell(*)
Food	**N:** Coffee Time **S:** Tim Horton's, Trafalgar Truck Stop
ATM	**N:** Esso **S:** Pioneer
333	Winston Churchill Blvd
336	Hwy 1, Mississauga Rd, Erin Mills Pkwy
Lodg	**S:** Delta Hotels
342	ON10, Brampton, Mississauga
Gas	**S:** Esso(*), Petro Canada(*, D)
Food	**S:** Coffee Time, Tim Horton's, Tim Horton's (Esso), Wendy's
Lodg	**S:** Holiday Inn

EXIT	ON
344	QUE Hamilton Via 403 , ON410, Brampton
346	Dixie Rd
Gas	**N:** Petro Canada(*, CW), Sunoco(*)
Food	**N:** Angie's, Master Steaks(24), Subway, Tommy K Donuts
Lodg	**N:** Best Western **S:** Four Points Hotel Sheraton, Super 8, TraveLodge
TServ	**N:** Toronto Truck Centre **S:** Kenworth
351	Carling View Dr
Lodg	**N:** Hotel Novotel
352	QEW Hwy Via 427 S
354	Martin Grove Rd, Dixon Rd
Gas	**N:** Petro Canada(D), Petro Canada(*, D, CW), Shell(*, 24)
Food	**N:** Country Style, Grisantai's, Harvey's, Kelsey's, Perkin's Family Restaurant, Pizza Hut, Stripes, Subway, Swiss Chalet, Tim Horton's
Lodg	**N:** Howard Johnson, International Plaza, Radisson Suites
Other	**N:** Animal Airport Hospital
355	ON409, ON427N, Belfield Rd
356	Islington Ave
357	Weston Rd
Food	**S:** McDonald's, Mr Sub, Subway, Tim Horton's
Med	**S:** Hospital
Other	**S:** Crossroads Centre
359	ON400, Barrie, Black Creek Dr
362	Keele St
Gas	**N:** Canadian Tire(*, LP), Esso(*), Petro Canada(*, 24)
Food	**N:** Coffee Time, Marta's Cafe, Pizza Hut
Lodg	**N:** Howard Johnson
ATM	**N:** Bank of Montreal, CIBC
Other	**N:** McMullan Pharmacy, Sav-A-Centre, Shoppers Drug Mart
365	Allen Rd
366	Bathurst St
367	Hwy 11A, Avenue Rd
369	Yonge St, Hwy 11
Gas	**N:** Esso(*), Petro Canada(*)
Food	**N:** Coffee Time, Country Style (Esso), Tim Horton's (Petro Canada)
ATM	**N:** Esso, Petro Canada
371	Bayview Ave
Gas	**N:** Esso(*), Shell(LP)
373	Leslie St
Med	**N:** North York General Hospital
375	ON404, Don Valley PKWY
Lodg	**N:** Ramada Hotel
376	Victoria Park Ave
Gas	**S:** Petro Canada(*, D, 24)
Food	**N:** Church's Chicken, Country Style, Harvey's, Pizza Hut, Subway, Tim Horton's, Wendy's
378	Warden Ave
Gas	**S:** Petro Canada(D), Shell(*, D, CW, 24)
Food	**S:** China Buffet King
Lodg	**S:** Quality Inn & Suites
379	Kennedy Rd
Lodg	**N:** Sheraton
Other	**S:** Kennedy Rd Pharmacy

Bold red print shows RV & Bus parking available or nearby

EXIT		ON
381	McCowan Rd	
	Med	S: + Hospital
	Other	S: Scarborough Town Centre
383	Markham Rd, ON 48	
	Gas	N: Petro Canada(*, 24)
		S: Petro Canada(*, D, CW)
	Food	N: Coffee Time, Golden Griddle, Shoeless Joe's (Travelodge)
		S: McDonald's(PLAY), The Keg Steakhouse
	Lodg	N: TraveLodge
		S: Holiday Inn Express, Howard Johnson
385	Neilson Rd	
	Med	S: + Hospital
387	Morningside Av	
	Gas	N: Esso(*)
	Food	N: Donut Town
	Med	S: + Hospital
	Other	N: IGA Supermarket
389	Meadowvale Rd	
	Food	N: Chou's Garden, Dip N Dunk, Maple Garden
	Other	N: Pan Drugs Pharmacy
392	Hwy 2, Sheppard Ave, Kingston Rd	
	Gas	N: Beaver(*), Esso(*)
	Food	N: Casa Mia Italian, Eddie's Cafe, Joey's Only Seafood, McDonald's(PLAY), Mr Sub, Tex Grill
	Med	N: + Family Doctor's Medical, Dental
	ATM	N: Bank of Montreal, Royal Bank
	Other	N: IDA Pharmacy, Sav-A-Centre
394	Hwy 38, Whites Rd	
	Gas	N: Esso(*, D), Shell(*, D, LP)
		S: Petro Canada(*, CW)
	Food	N: Lone Star Cafe, Subway, Tim Horton's
	ATM	N: Scotia Bank
	Other	N: Payless Pharmacy
397	Liverpool Rd	
	Gas	N: Esso(*, D, CW), Petro Canada(*, D, CW)
		S: Shell
	Food	N: Burger King, Gallantry 's, Golden Griddle, KFC, Mario's Eastside, Mary Brown's, McDonald's, Pizza Hut, Tim Horton's, Walt's Grill
		S: Austrian Deli & Bakery, Bayly's, Coffee Time, Fish & Chips, Sunwin Chinese
	Med	N: + Pickering Medical Centre
	ATM	N: Esso, Scotia Bank
		S: CIBC
	Other	N: K-Mart, Pickering Town Centre
		S: Bayridge Pharmacy, Price Chopper
399	Brock Rd, Hwy 1	
	Gas	N: Sunoco(*, D)
		S: Petro Canada(*, D, 24)
	Food	N: Tim Horton's
		S: Country Style, Mr Sub, Subway
	TServ	S: **East End Trucks Center Limited**
401	Westney Rd, Hwy 31	
	Food	S: Kesley's
403	Hwy 44, Harwood Ave	
	Gas	S: Esso, Shell(*, D, CW)
	Food	N: Macks
		S: Bakers Dozen, Double Double, KFC, The Ranch, Wimpy's Diner
	Med	S: + Hospital
410	ON 12, Brock St	
	Gas	N: Sunoco(*, D)
	Food	N: McDonald's(PLAY), Mr Sub, Pizza Hut, Tim Horton's, Wendy's
	ATM	N: Sunoco
	Other	N: Police Station
412	Hwy 26, Thickson Rd	
	Gas	N: Pioneer(*, D), Sunoco(*, D, LP, CW)
	Food	N: Coffee Time, Country Style, Oh Canada Eatery, Tim Horton's, Wendy's
	Lodg	N: Quality Suites
	ATM	N: Sunoco
416	Hwy 54, Park Rd	
	Food	S: Go Go Pizza & Subs, Mr Burger, Oasis Restaurant
	Med	N: + Hospital
418	Hwy 16, Ritson Rd, Hwy 2, Simcoe St	
	Gas	N: Sunoco(*)
	Lodg	N: Cloverleaf Motel
419	Hwy 33, Harmony Rd, Hwy 22, Bloar St	
	Lodg	N: Holiday Inn
	Med	N: + Hospital
425	Hwy 34, Courtice Rd, Courtice	
	Food	S: **Stippy's(24)**
431	Waverley Rd, Hwy 57, Bowmanville	
	TStop	S: **Fifth Wheel Truck Stop(*, SCALES)**
	FStop	N: **Shell(*, D, LP, 24)**
	Gas	N: Sunoco(*, D)
	Food	N: Shell, Tim Horton's, Wendy's
		S: **Fifth Wheel TStop**
	Lodg	S: **Fifth Wheel TStop**
	ATM	S: Fifth Wheel TStop
432	Liberty St, Bowmanville, Port Darlington	
	Gas	N: Pioneer(*, CW)
	Food	N: Baskin Robbins, Coffee Time, Golden Griddle, Harvey's, Subway, Taco Time
	Lodg	N: The Flying Dutchman
	Med	N: + Hospital
(430)	Weigh Station	
435	Bennett Rd	
436	QB35, QB115, Orono, Lindsay	
440	Hwy 17, Mill St, Newcastle, Bond Head	
(444)	Service Center	
	FStop	B: **Esso(D)**
	Food	B: Tim Horton's
448	Hwy 18, Newtonville Rd, Newtonville	
(454)	Service Center	
	Gas	B: Esso(*)
	Food	B: Mr Sub, Tim Horton's, Wendy's
456	Wesleyville Rd	
461	ON2, Welcome, Port Hope	
	Food	N: The Welcome Inn
	Lodg	N: **The Welcome Inn**
464	QB28, Port Hope, Peterborough	
	TStop	N: **Esso(*, D)**
	Gas	S: Petro Canada(*, 24), Shell(*, D, 24)
	Food	N: Church's Chicken, **Harvey's (Esso)**
		S: Arby's, Tim Horton's (Shell)
	Lodg	N: **Comfort Inn**, **Swiss Chalet (Esso)**
	Med	S: + Hospital
474	QB45, Cobourg, Baltimore	
	Gas	N: Shell(*, D)
	Lodg	N: Hillside Motel
487	Hwy 23, Aird St, Centreton, Grafton	
497	Hwy 25, Percy St., Big Apple Dr., Colborne, Castleton	
	Gas	S: Petro Canada(*, D, CW)
	Food	S: Apple Barrel Restaurant
509	Quebec 30, Brighton, Campbellford	
	Gas	S: Shell(*, D, LP)
	Food	S: **Coffee Time(24)**
521	Service Center	
	FStop	N: **Shell**
		S: **Petro Canada**
	Food	N: Mr Sub, Tim Horton's, Wendy's
		S: McDonald's
522	Hwy 40, Woller Rd.	
525	Ont 33, Trenton, Frankford, Batawa	
	Med	S: + Hospital
526	Hwy 4, Glen Miller Rd., Trenton, CFB Trenton	
	Gas	N: Sunoco(D)
	Food	S: Tim Horton's
	Lodg	S: **Comfort Inn**, Holiday Inn
	Other	N: Trenton Pet Hospital
538	Hwy 1, Wallbridge-Loyalist Rd., Stirling	
	TStop	S: **10 Acre Truck Stop(*, D, SCALES)**
	FStop	N: **Ultramar**
	Food	N: Mo's Country Restaurant
		S: 10 Acre Restaurant
	Lodg	N: **Voyager Motel**
	TServ	N: **International**
		S: **Wheeler's Garage**
	TWash	S: **10 Acre Truck Wash**
	ATM	S: **10 Acre Truck Stop**
543AB	Ont Hwy 14, Ont Hwy 62, Madoc, Marmora, Belleville	
	Gas	N: Petro Canada(*, D, 24)
		S: Canadian Tire(*, D, LP), Pioneer(*, D, 24), UPI(*, D)
	Food	N: McDonald's (Wal-Mart), Tim Horton's (Petro)
		S: Burger King, KFC, Little Caesars Pizza, Market House Grille, Moviole Cafe, Pizza Hut, Subway, Swiss Chalet, Taco Bell, The Garden Restaurant, Wendy's
	Lodg	S: Bellview Motel, Best Western, **Comfort Inn**, **Quality Inn**
	ATM	S: CIBC
	Other	N: Wal-Mart
		S: K-Mart, Shoppers Drug Mart
544	Ont 37, Belleville, Tweed	
	Med	W: + Hospital
556	Hwy 7, Shannonville Rd., Shannonville	
566	Ont. 49, Hwy 15 Marysville Rd., Tyendinaga M. T., Picton	
	FStop	S: **Sunoco(*, D, 24)**
	Food	S: Mike's (Sunoco)
570	Hwy 10, Deseronto Rd., Deseronto	
578	Quebec Hwy 41, Napanee, Kaladar	
	Gas	N: Star(*, D)
		S: Canadian Tire(*, D), Petro Canada(*, D, 24)
	Food	N: Mo's Pizza & Subs, Napanee Fish & Chips

Hwy 401

EXIT		AB
	S: Mary Brown's, **McDonald's**, Pizza Hut, Tim Horton's	
Lodg	N: **Royal Napanee Inn**	
ATM	S: CIBC	
Other	S: A&P Supermarket	
579	Hwy 5, Palace Rd., Newburgh, Napanee	
592	Service Area (Westbound)	
Gas	S: Petro Canada(*, D)	
Food	S: McDonald's(PLAY, 24)	
593	Quebec Hwy 133, Hwy 4, Camden East Rd., Mill Haven, Camden E	
599	Hwy 4, Wilton Rd., Amherstville, Odessa, Yarker	
Gas	S: Mr. Gas(*, D)	
Lodg	S: Wilton Road Motel	
610	**(604)** Service Center (Eastbound)	
FStop	S: **Esso**	
Food	S: KFC, Tim Horton's	
611	Harrow Smith, Ont 38, Sharbot Lake	
613	Hwy 9, Sydenham Rd., Kingston, Sydenham	
615	St. John McDonald Boul., Kingston	
Med	S: + Hospital	
617	Division St., Kingston, West Port	
Gas	S: Esso(*, D, CW), Petro Canada(*, D), Shell(*, D, 24)	
Food	S: Arby's, Denny's, KFC, Mag's, Mario's, McDonald's(PLAY), Mr Sub, Pizza Hut, Taco Bell, Tim Horton's, Wendy's	
Lodg	S: Comfort Inn, Days Inn, First Canada Inn	
TServ	S: **Kenworth**	
ATM	S: Esso, Petro Canada	
Other	S: Drug Mart, IGA Supermarket	
619	Montreal St., Kingston, Batterseab	
623	Ont 15, Hwy 15, Kingston, Smiths Falls, C. F. B. Kingston	
Gas	S: Mr. Gas(*, D)	
Lodg	S: Lord Nelson Motel	
632	Cty 16, Joyceville Rd., Joyceville	
TStop	S: **Husky(*, D, LP)**	
645	Ont Hwy 32, Gananoque, Crosby	
Gas	S: Cango(*, D, CW), Mr. Gas	

EXIT		AB
Lodg	S: Thunderbird Motor Inn	
Other	N: Police Station	
	S: 1,000 Island Animal Clinic	
648	Ont Hwy 2, Cty 2, Gananoque	
659A	**(652)** Weigh Station	
659	Hwy 3, Reynolds Rd., Lansdowne, Ivy League	
661	Hill Island, Bridge to USA	
675	Mallory Town Rd., Mallory Town, Rockport, Athens	
684A	Service Center (Westbound)	
FStop	W: **Esso, Esso**	
Food	W: Tim Horton's, Wendy's	
684	Service Center (Eastbound)	
FStop	E: **Esso**	
Food	E: Tim Horton's, Wendy's	
685	1,000 Island Pkwy., Rockport	
687	Hwy 2	
Gas	S: Petro Canada(*)	
Lodg	S: Long Beach Inn	
696	Ont. 29, Smith's Falls, Brockville	
Gas	N: Esso(*, D, CW), OKO(*), Petro Canada(*, D, 24), Petro Canada(*, D, CW)	
Food	N: Burger King, Harvey's, Juke Box Cafe, KFC, McDonald's, Pizza Hut, Taco Bell	
	S: Dairy Queen	
Lodg	N: Comfort Inn, Queen's Inn, Super 8	
	S: Days Inn, Royal Brock Motel	
ATM	N: Esso	
Other	N: Drug Mart, Wal-Mart	
	S: Brockville Centre, Pharma Plus	
698	N. Augusta Rd., Brockville	
Med	S: + Hospital	
Other	N: Police Station	
705	Matiland Rd., Merrickville	
716	Edwards St., Prescott, Domville	
Gas	S: Econo(*), Esso(*) (Subway), Petro Canada(*), Ultramar(*)	
Food	S: Burger King, Mick's Restaurant, Tim Horton's, Tony's Fish & Chips (Econo)	
Other	S: Police Station	
728	Ont 16, Bridge to USA, Ottawa, Kemptville	
TStop	N: **Esso(*, D)**	
730	RD 22, Shantley Rd., Cardinal	
TStop	S: **730 Truck Stop(*)**	
Food	S: 730 Truck Stop	
TServ	S: **730 Truck Stop**	

EXIT		AB
738	Rd 1, Carmin Rd., Iroquois	
TServ	N: **Polar Reefer Service(24)**	
750	Ont 31, Morrisburg, Winchester, Ottawa	
TStop	N: **750 Truck Stop(*, D, 24)**	
Food	N: Trucker's Delight (750 Truck Stop)	
757	Service Center	
FStop	E: **Shell(D)**	
Food	E: KFC	
758	Upper Canada Rd.	
762	Service Center	
FStop	N: **Esso(*)**	
Food	N: KFC, Tim Horton's	
770	Dickenson Dr., Ingleside, Rd 14	
778	Moulinette Rd., Long Sault	
789	Ont. 138, Brookdale Ave., Cornwall, Ottawa	
FStop	N: **Irving Commerical(*, 24)**	
Food	N: Subway (Irving)	
792	Ave McConnell, Cornwall	
TStop	N: **Fifth Wheel(*, D, SCALES, 24)**	
FStop	N: **W. O. Stinson(*, D, LP)**	
Lodg	N: Fifth Wheel (Restaurant)	
TServ	N: **Cornwall Truck Maintenance**	
TWash	N: **Blue Beacon (Fifth Wheel)**	
796	Ch. Boundary Rd., Corwall	
Gas	S: BX(D), Warden(*, D)	
804	Summers Town Rd., Summers Town Rd 27	
FStop	S: **Petro Pass(*)**	
814	Road 2, Ontario 34, Lancaster, Alexandria, Hawkesberry	
Gas	N: Esso(*, D), Mac Ewen(*, 24)	
Food	N: Boureau Chips, Dairy Queen, Restaurant	
824A	Weigh Station	
824	Tourist Information	
825	Ontario 23, 4th Line Road	
TStop	N: **Currey Hill(*) (Esso)**	
	S: **Real's Truck Stop(*, SCALES) (Shell, Restaurant)**	
Food	N: Curry Hill Restaurant	
ATM	S: **Real's Truck Stop (Shell, Restaurant)**	
829	Service Center	
FStop	W: **Shell(*)**	
Food	W: Wendy's	

↑ Alberta

Begin 401, Lancaster

Hwy 417

E →

EXIT		ON
	Begin 417	

↓ Ontario

EXIT		ON
155	Hwy 49, Almonte, Ch. March Rd., Carp	
FStop	N: **Shell(*)**	
145	Ont Hwy 7W Toronto, Carlton Place	
144	Hwy 5, Ch. Carp Road, Stittsville, Carp	
Gas	S: Petro Canada(*, CW)	
142	Promenade Plannadius Dr., Hwy 88	
140	Prom. Terry Fox Dr.	
Food	N: Denny's, Harvey's, Joey's Only Seafood, Kelsey's, McDonald's	
	(Wal-Mart), Subway	
Med	N: + Medical Center	
ATM	N: Scotia Bank, TD Bank & Truck	
Other	N: Loblaws Supermarket(RX), Mail Boxes Etc., Wal-Mart(RX)	
138	Hwy 49, Ch. March Rd., Ch. Eagleston Rd., Kanata	
Gas	S: Shell(*, D)	

Bold red print shows RV & Bus parking available or nearby

EXIT	ON
Other	N: Police Station
134	Prom Moodie Dr
131	ON416 S
130	Ch Richmond Rd, Prom. Bayshore Dr
129	Ch Pincrest Rd, Ch Greenbank RD
Gas	S: Shell(*, 24)
Food	S: Le Biftheque
Other	S: Pincrest Shopping Center
127AB	Woodroffe Ave
126	Av Maitland Ave., Nepean
124	Av Carling Ave, AV Kirkwood Ave.
Lodg	S: Embassy West Hotel, Talisman Hotel
Other	N: Food Basic Supermarket, Mail Boxes Etc., Pharma Plus Pharmacy
123	Prom. Island Park Dr
Med	S: ✚ Hospital Royal Ottawa Hospital
122	Ave Parkdale,
Med	S: ✚ Hospital
121A	ON16, ON31, Ave Bronson Ave , Airport (Difficult Reaccess)
Gas	S: Drummonds(*, D), Esso(*)
Food	N: Baskin Robbins, Dunkin Donuts, Harvey's
	S: McDonald's
119	Rue Metcalf, Rue Catherine St
Lodg	S: Super 8
ATM	S: Canada Trust
Other	N: Police Station
118	Rue Nicholas St, Ave Mann Ave. (Difficult Reaccess)
Med	S: ✚ Hospital
117	Prom. Riverside Dr, Prom. Vanier Pkwy
Med	S: ✚ Hospital
Other	N: From Parc
115	St Laurent Blvd
Food	N: Pizza Pizza, Zuma's Rodeo
Lodg	N: Chimo Hotel, Comfort Inn, Welcome Inns
113AB	ON17E, Rockland, Parkway Prom.
112	Chemin, Innes Rd
Gas	N: Esso(*)
Food	N: Chuck & Harlod's (Travelodge)
Lodg	N: Travelodge TraveLodge
Med	S: ✚ Hospital
110	Chemin, Walkley Rd
104	Chemin, Hwy 27, Anderson Rd
96	Ch. Boundrary Rd, Hwy 41, Metcalfe, Marionville, Carlsbad Springs
Gas	S: Sunoco(*, D, LP)
88	Ch. Rockdale Rd, Hwy 33, Vars & Russell
Gas	N: Sunnys(*, D)
	S: Mac Ewen(*, LP), Sunnys(*, D)
Food	S: Subway
79	Hwy 4, Ch. Limoges Rd, Limoges, Embrun
FStop	N: **Ultramar**(*, D)
Food	N: Chez Nardo
66	Ch. St. Albert Rd, Hwy 7, Casselman, Crysler
FStop	S: **Petro Canada**(*, LP, 24)
Gas	N: Esso(*, CW), Mac Ewen(*, LP)
Food	N: Bus Station, Chez Rich, McDonald's(PLAY), Subway, Tim Horton's
	S: **Restauparc - Pizza Hut, Dunkin Donuts, Burger King**(24)
Lodg	S: **Restauparc Motel**
Other	N: Jean Coutu Pharmacy, Police Station
(60)	Truck Inspection Station
58	ON138, Monkland, Cornwall
FStop	N: **Esso**(D)
51	Ch. Highland Rd, St Isidore, Maxville
FStop	N: **Petro Canada**(*, 24), **Shell**(*, 24)
	S: **Mac Ewen**(*)
Food	N: Burger King, Mike's Diner, Pizza Hut, Shell
35	Ch. Mc Crimmon Rd, Hwy 23, St Bernadine
27	ON34, Alexandria
FStop	S: **Herb's**(*)
Food	S: Herb's
TServ	S: **Herb's Truck & Auto Repair**
17	Hwy 10, Ch. Barb Rd, Bankleek Hill
9	ON17, Hawksbury, Rockland (Reaccess Eastbound Only)
5	Church Prescott & Russell Rd, Hwy 4, Chute a Blondeau, Hwy 14, St Eugene

↑ Alberta

Begin 417

Hwy 640

EXIT	QC
	Begin 640
	↓ Québec
2	St. Joseph-du-Lac, Pointe-Calmed
Gas	N: Petroles Belisle(*, D)
	S: Crevier(*, LP, 24)
8	Deaux-Mondagnes, Boul. des Promeandes, Ste-Nardhe-sur-le-Laz
Gas	N: Uldramar(*)
Food	N: Dunkin Donuts, Valentine
Other	N: Metro Supermarket
11	QB143, Lachute Blvd., Arthur-Sauve
Gas	N: Shell(*)
	S: Ultramar(*, CW)
Food	N: Pizza Le Four
Med	N: ✚ Hospital
Other	N: Police Station
14	25th Ave.
Gas	S: Uldramar(*)
ATM	S: Uldramar
Other	S: Metro Supermarket
16	Hwy 13 S., Dovall Airport, Laval Montreal
20	Hwy 15, Mirabel Airport, St-Gaerome, Boiseriand
22	QB117, St-Therese RoseMere, Blainville
Gas	S: Altramar(*)
Other	S: Provigo Supermarket, Wal-Mart
24	Monte Lesge, Chemin, Bas Ste-Therese
26	Lorraine
Food	N: LaRomanella Italian
Other	N: Animal Hospital, Provigo Supermarket
28	QB335, Bois-des Filion, St-Anne des Blaines
35	QB337N.,Boul. Entreprise, Boul. des Seigneurs
38	QB337, Ch. des Anglais, Ch. Gascon, La Plaine
Gas	S: Shell(*, 24)

↑ Québec

Begin 640

TRAVEL NOTES

Date

Notes

TRAVEL NOTES

Date	Notes

TRAVEL NOTES

Date

Notes

TRAVEL NOTES

Date

Notes

TELEPHONE DIRECTORY

Name	Phone	Name	Phone

TELEPHONE DIRECTORY

Name	Phone	Name	Phone

INDEX

Florida's First Theme Park • Est. 1936

www.cypressgardens.com

FAMILY OF FOUR SAVES $49[40]*

Each single day adult ticket purchaser may bring in one youth (ages 6-17) FREE. Kids five and under always FREE.

*Based on 2 kids free and two adults receiving $3.75 discount each.

Not valid with other discounts or on the purchase of multi-visit passes or special ticket events. Expires 12/31/99

PLU#1083

PRIME OUTLETS

FREE COUPON BOOK
SAVE ON FAMOUS BRANDS

Present this coupon at any Prime Outlet listed on our color ad on page 23* for a FREE Coupon Book

*see color section in front of book

888-901-SHOP

Offer expires 12/31/99

PRIME OUTLETS – *This is shopping.*™

$10 OFF*

*Valid for one night only. Discount is off rack card rate. Subject to availability. Expires 12/30/99.

FREE*
Pay-Per-View Movie

*Valid for one pay-per-view movie. Subject to availability. Expires 12/30/99.

AMERICA'S AFFORDABLE ALL-SUITE HOTELS

1-800-833-1516

www.amerisuites.com

PRIME OUTLETS

FREE COUPON BOOK
SAVE ON FAMOUS BRANDS

Present this coupon at any Prime Outlet listed on our color ad on page 23* for a FREE Coupon Book

*see color section in front of book

888-901-SHOP

Offer expires 12/31/99

PRIME OUTLETS – *This is shopping.*™

$10 OFF*
Sunday - Thursday

*Valid for one night only. Discount is off rack card rate. Subject to availability. Expires 12/30/99.

$15 OFF*
Friday & Saturday

*Valid for one night only. Discount is off rack card rate. Subject to availability. Expires 12/30/99.

1-800-444-8888

www.wellesleyinns.com

PRIME OUTLETS

FREE COUPON BOOK
SAVE ON FAMOUS BRANDS

Present this coupon at any Prime Outlet listed on our color ad on page 23* for a FREE Coupon Book

*see color section in front of book

888-901-SHOP

Offer expires 12/31/99

PRIME OUTLETS – *This is shopping.*™

EXIT AUTHORITY

This coupon good for
$1.00 OFF
the year 2000 edition
of Exit Authority.

Send with your order for Exit Authority, year 2000, and save an additional $1.00 off the purchase price.

Offer good through January 31, 2000

PRIME OUTLETS

FREE COUPON BOOK
SAVE ON FAMOUS BRANDS

Present this coupon at any Prime Outlet listed on our color ad on page 23* for a FREE Coupon Book

*see color section in front of book

888-901-SHOP

Offer expires 12/31/99

PRIME OUTLETS – *This is shopping.*™

Attention Merchants!

For more information on how you can participate in the Exit Authority Travel Coupon Program . . .

Call today, 1-800-494-5566

PRIME OUTLETS

FREE COUPON BOOK
SAVE ON FAMOUS BRANDS

Present this coupon at any Prime Outlet listed on our color ad on page 23* for a FREE Coupon Book

*see color section in front of book

888-901-SHOP

Offer expires 12/31/99

PRIME OUTLETS – *This is shopping.*™

KNOW THE EXIT BEFORE YOU EXIT

KNOW THE EXIT BEFORE YOU EXIT

KNOW THE EXIT BEFORE YOU EXIT

KNOW THE EXIT BEFORE YOU EXIT

KNOW THE EXIT BEFORE YOU EXIT

KNOW THE EXIT BEFORE YOU EXIT

KNOW THE EXIT BEFORE YOU EXIT

KNOW THE EXIT BEFORE YOU EXIT

KNOW THE EXIT BEFORE YOU EXIT

KNOW THE EXIT BEFORE YOU EXIT